BAKER'S
BIOGRAPHICAL DICTIONARY OF
MUSICIANS

CREDITS

Laura Kuhn
Classical Editor

Dennis McIntire
Associate Classical Editor

Lewis Porter
Jazz Editor

William Ruhlmann
Pop Editor

Key to Contributors

AB	Andrew Barlett	ETA	E. Taylor Atkins	NAL	Nancy Ann Lee
AG	Andrew Gilbert	GB	Greg Baise	NC	Norene Cashen
BH	Brock Helander	GBr	Gig Brown	NS	Nicolas Slonimsky
BJH	B. J. Huchtemann	GJ	Gregg Juke	PK	Peter Keepnews
BM	Bill Moody	GK	Gregory Kiewiet	PM	Patricia Myers
BP	Bret Primack	GM	Garaud MacTaggart	PMac	Paul MacArthur
BR	Bryan Reesman	HB	Hank Bordowitz	RB	Ralph Burnett
BW	Bill Wahl	JB	Joshua Berrett	RC	Richard Carlin
CH	Chris Hovan	JC	John Chilton,	RI	Robert Iannapolto
DB	Dan Bindert		*Who's Who of Jazz*	SC	Safford Chamberlain
DCG	David C. Gross	JC-B	John Chilton,	SH	Steve Holtje
DD	David Demsey		*Who's Who of British Jazz*	SKB	Susan K. Berlowitz
DDD	Dean D. Dauphinais	JE	James Eason	SP	Sam Prestianni
DK	Dan Keener	JM	Jeff McMillan	TP	Ted Panken
DM	Dennis McIntire	JO	Jim O'Rourke	TS	Tom Smith
DO	David Okamoto	JTB	John T. Bitter	WB	Will Bickart
DPe	Damon Percy	LK	Laura Kuhn	WF	Walter Faber
DPr	David Prince	LP	Lewis Porter	WKH	W. Kim Heron
DR	Dennis Rea	MF	Michael Fitzgerald	WR	William Ruhlmann
ED	Eric Deggans	MM	*Music Master Jazz*		
EH	Ed Hazell		*and Blues Catalogue*		
EJL	Eric J. Lawrence	MS	Matthew Snyder		

BAKER'S
BIOGRAPHICAL DICTIONARY OF
MUSICIANS

VOLUME 1
AALT - CONE

Centennial Edition

NICOLAS SLONIMSKY
Editor Emeritus

LAURA KUHN
Baker's Series Advisory Editor

Schirmer Books
an imprint of the Gale Group
New York • Detroit • San Francisco • London • Boston • Woodbridge, CT

Copyright © 1900, 1905, 1919, 1940, 1958, 1971 by G. Schirmer, Inc.
Copyright © 1978, 1984, 1992 by Schirmer Books
Copyright © 2001 by Schirmer Books, An Imprint of the Gale Group

Schirmer Books
1633 Broadway
New York, New York 10019

Gale Group
27500 Drake Road
Farmington Hills, Michigan 48331-3535

The title *Baker's Biographical Dictionary of Musicians* is a registered trademark.

Silhouette of Nicolas Slonimsky used with the permission of Electra Yourke.

Library of Congress Catalog Card Number: 00-046375

Printed in the United States of America

Printing number
1 2 3 4 5 6 7 8 9 10

Library of Congress Cataloging-in-Publication Data

Baker's biographical dictionary of musicians.—Centennial ed. / Nicolas Slonimsky, editor emeritus.
      p. cm.
    Includes bibliographical references and discographies.
    Enl. ed. of: Baker's biographical dictionary of musicians. 8th ed. / rev. by Nicolas Slonimsky.
    ISBN 0-02-865525-7 (set : alk. paper) — ISBN 0-02- 865526-5 (vol. 1) — ISBN 0-02-865527-3 (vol. 2) — ISBN 0-02-865528-1 (vol. 3) — ISBN 0-02-865529-X (vol. 4) — ISBN 0-02-865530-3 (vol. 5) — ISBN 0-02-865571-0 (vol. 6)
    1. Music—Bio-bibliography—Dictionaries. I. Slonimsky, Nicolas, 1894-
II. Slonimsky, Nicolas, 1894- Baker's biographical dictionary of musicians.

    ML105.B16 2000
    780'.92'2—dc21
    [B]

                                              00-046375

CONTENTS

Note from the
PUBLISHER

On December 25, 1995, Nicolas Slonimsky, the renowned, witty, and much-loved musical lexicographer who edited the fifth through the eighth editions of *Baker's Biographical Dictionary of Musicians,* died. He was 101 years old and had been the helmsman of *Baker's* since 1958.

This ninth, centennial edition is the first since that time not to include new material compiled or written by the incomparable Nicolas. It is an ending, but also a beginning. Following Slonimsky's custom of (albeit sometimes reluctantly) expanding the boundaries of traditional music, this new edition includes a massive influx of nearly 2,000 completely new entries on popular and jazz musicians, written or edited by William Ruhlmann and Lewis Porter. Laura Kuhn and Dennis McIntire have updated and expanded many thousands of the entries on classical musicians.

No longer the voice of a single, singular man, *Baker's* continues to evolve, and its caretakers continue to strive toward that elusive goal of comprehensiveness.

NEW YORK, OCTOBER 2000

Preface to the
CENTENNIAL EDITION

Classical Entries

Welcome to the ninth, centennial edition of *Baker's Biographical Dictionary of Musicians*, celebrating both 100 years of *Baker's* publications and the close of the tumultuous twentieth century. Since the last edition of *Baker's* (1992), much has transpired in music, and the present edition pays especially close attention to the most noteworthy individuals, activities, and events of our century's final decade. In many ways, the 1990s were not kind to the arts, and particularly not to serious music. The diminishing levels of both government and corporate support, the increasing indifference of general audiences, the virtual death of independent recording labels, the lack of adequate performance spaces, especially in our larger cities—these are just a few of the unhappy developments of the past decade that have affected, and continue to affect, classical music and musicians. One could easily assert that never before has the musician's life been more challenging and troubled, and that never before should the parent's admonition to the child *not* to pursue a career in music be louder!

But, in other ways, the 1990s have been very kind to the arts and, paradoxically, especially to serious music. Technology and the Internet are influencing far more than the stock market, affording musicians greater options as to how their music might be made and disseminated. Self-sufficiency is the overriding catchword, with the widespread availability of MIDI technology, high-speed, multimedia computers, sophisticated electronic instruments, and fiber-optic technology/broadband transmission contributing to a situation wherein composers are better able to self-produce, self-promote, and self-publish. These new means to creativity have enlivened the field tremendously, and for many musicians, the very real spirit of adventure and discovery made possible by such media offset the tedium and anxiety that go hand in hand with the learning of the endlessly new. Lexicography, too, has not gone unaffected. Questions of reliability and accuracy aside, the Internet affords us easier, faster, and certainly more democratic access to information about individuals and institutions the world over. Not to worry that with this democratization of information via so extraordinarily public means comes a very real threat to the life expectancy of the book. Change is inevitable, one might glibly say, but John Cage, our century's most beloved musical anarchist, would surely have been proud.

But I have to wonder what Nicolas Slonimsky, the inimitable editor of past editions of *Baker's Biographical Dictionary of Musicians* and surely the father of us all, would have thought. His processes of information collection and manuscript preparation were far different from ours! I can't help but remember, not so long ago, his weekly trips to the local university library, where he'd rummage through recent periodicals and other publications for the latest tidbit of musical information. I also remember him dictating his entries with meticulous precision, composing as he spoke, to a succession of secretaries seated at a remarkably noisy (and not terribly reliable) Remington electric typewriter. All the while, the four-foot stacks of paper surrounding them on every available surface threatened to collapse in the tiny bedroom that doubled as an office in his West Los Angeles bungalow home. Word of a new symphony, a new premiere, or a new appointment that might arrive in person or through the mail was a mixed blessing, for while it could be happily added to the information being endlessly collected, it would also likely necessitate a complete retyping job. The idea of revision without retyping was completely unfathomable to us back then, and such news more often than not sent everyone to the dining-room table for tea and momentary commiseration.

But I like to think that we've made good use of what technology provides, without *too* much complaint, and that Nicolas would be both proud and amazed at the relative ease with which we now do our work. And that through our continuing commitment to comprehensive coverage of music and musicians across ages and genres, *Baker's Biographical Dictionary of Musicians* maintains its viability as a serious music reference work well into the new millennium. While virtually every entry carried forward from previous editions has been rewritten or revised to reflect life changes of living individuals and current research into the lives of the deceased, with works lists and bibliographies simultaneously updated and expanded to accommodate the endless flow of new information, the ninth edition of *Baker's* also includes more than 1,000 *new* classical entries. These new entries give collective voice to the latest generation of composers, scholars, performers, conductors, and countless other categories of individuals involved in this murky business of music. And for those of you already familiar with previous editions of *Baker's Biographical Dictionary of Musicians*, you're sure to notice a few other significant changes as well. Most obvious, of course, is our new, multivolume format, which has been made necessary by the sheer magnitude of materials collected for its pages. This expanded edition, happily and for the first time, incorporates a far greater proportion of musicians variously active in the fields of popular music, rock music, and jazz.

In addition to its listed contributors, this book is made possible through the efforts of a great many people, most of whom are thanked, inadequately, in our list of acknowledgments. However, special note, as ever, must be made of the incomparable Dennis McIntire, without whom the classical entries in this present volume would surely be lacking. Nicolas would find a stream of impossibly perfect adjectives to describe Dennis's efforts, but let me just say that Dennis, like Nicolas before him, accomplishes his extraordinary lexicographical feats the old-fashioned way—through genuine curiosity, painstaking research, and dogged pursuit of the tiniest desired detail, all with good humor and style, and that he brings his work to print with nothing but pencil, paper, and, of course, the faithful assistance of *his* electric typewriter.

LAURA KUHN
NEW YORK, OCTOBER 2000

Popular Entries

Unlike many other kinds of books, a dictionary is a living document; successive editions follow the bends of history. Opinions change, new facts are unearthed, usages are coined, and the dictionary reflects the altered landscape. It must also be, however, to some extent a slave of the (dare one say it) *popular* will. *Baker's* has changed greatly from its first edition when, as Nicolas Slonimsky notes in the preface to the sixth edition, "Theodore Baker … collected biographical data from his friends who played in the Boston Symphony Orchestra." Still, through the years the book retained its focus on classical music, and it was not until the fifth edition in 1958 that *Baker's* began tentatively to include what Slonimsky calls "the glamorized purveyors of popular subculture of whatever degree of vulgarity," i.e., writers and performers of popular music, and as that description, also from the sixth edition's preface, implies, even by 1978 these barbarians were hardly being admitted on an equal footing. In the eighth edition in 1992, Irving Berlin, the most successful songwriter of the twentieth century, was accorded only three paragraphs; Duke Ellington and Bob Dylan had to settle for one each. Some Slonimsky favorites might draw favorable mention (borrowing a term from tennis, he referred to both Bruce Springsteen and Frank Zappa as "seeded," presumably a compliment), but no popular musician was thought to merit extended attention.

It is perhaps no wonder, then, that in my lifelong appreciation of popular music and my two decades of professional attention to it, I never had much use for *Baker's*, picking up a copy of the portable edition, only once, in 1995, but after brief perusal, replacing it on a bookstore shelf as unworthy of addition to my personal library. I couldn't know, of course, that the following year I would be asked to become a contributor! It was then that the powers that were at Schirmer Books, looking forward to the next edition of *Baker's*, and without the guiding hand of the late Slonimsky, determined upon a more deliberate course for incorporating non-classical music into the book. In fact, the initial decision was to create two separate satellite books, a popular-music *Baker's* and a jazz *Baker's*, after which some of their entries would be absorbed into the main *Baker's*. Lewis Porter was contracted to provide the jazz book, and I undertook the popular-music tome, writing the pre-rock entries, with the rock entries adapted from Brock Helander's Schirmer work *The Rock Who's Who* and augmented by recent additions from Hank Bordowitz.

In the end Schirmer Books decided to insert the amassed non-classical entries into this edition of *Baker's*. There is some worthwhile reflection to be made on the jazz and pop entries themselves, as well as on the approach taken in writing them, which necessarily differs from that of the classical entries.

A challenge in including popular musicians in a book long devoted to classical musicians is that there are great differences in nomenclature. How well I remember the day when Lewis Porter and I sat in a conference room at Schirmer with Laura Kuhn, who had thoughtfully prepared "Instructions for Editors and Contributors." Porter and I eagerly perused Kuhn's proffered eleven single-spaced, typed pages (actually, I was somewhat apprehensive, while Porter seemed bemused), noting the peculiarities of style bequeathed to us by our esteemed predecessor. ("Death by suicide should be noted, in parenthesis, at the onset of the entry.") We were drawn up short by the discussion, on page 6, of "Works Lists." What exactly, we both wanted to know, was meant by "works"? We noted that relatively few of the musicians about whom we would be writing composed symphonies or operas, though many of them wrote songs. No entirely satisfactory resolution of such stylistic conflicts was made or, I would suggest, was really possible, and the reader will see that "Disc." rather than "Works" introduces a partial discography for popular musicians known for their record albums.

It remains to be noted that, no doubt, this first attempt at describing the lives of popular and jazz musicians is not perfect. Nicolas Slonimsky has chronicled the many difficulties in obtaining accurate information, and I have found them to be only compounded in the world of pop with its layer of press agents striving to promote their clients at the expense of accuracy. The vast proliferation of information in recent years has, to an extent, served only to increase the spread of inaccuracies, and websites have now outdistanced the hastily written obituary as the top source for distortions. As Dave Brubeck has said, "I've found out that once something is in print it is quoted over and over again." The intrepid lexicographer can attempt to reduce, but not eliminate, inaccuracy.

This centennial edition of *Baker's* is a living document, chronicling the past, observing the present, and looking forward to its next incarnation.

WILLIAM J. RUHLMANN
NEW YORK, OCTOBER 2000

Classic Baker's
Prefaces by
NICOLAS SLONIMSKY

PREFACE TO THE FIFTH EDITION

The present edition is virtually a new book, with most of the entries rewritten, radically edited, and greatly expanded. Some 2,300 biographies have been added, including not only contemporary figures but also many neglected musicians of the past.

A maximum emphasis has been laid on the abundance of factual data. In entries on composers, the titles of major compositions—operas, ballets, symphonic works—are given as completely as is practical, with exact dates of first performances. In entries on musicologists, most of their published books in various languages, and some of their significant articles in the musical press, are listed. As to performers, their most signal accomplishments are brought out, with dates of their European and American débuts. A similar service is done for outstanding music teachers, with a list of their educational positions.

The design of the present edition is a self-contained biographical dictionary of musicians. Bibliography is given in ample measure, but the reader is not directed to other reference works for essential information.

I have received invaluable assistance from scholars and librarians in America and in Europe during the preparation of this edition, but the actual writing has been done by myself, and I must therefore accept full responsibility for the resulting product.

A biographical dictionary ought to be a democratic assembly of factual information. Great men of music are naturally given preponderance, but the "little masters" are also treated with consideration. Bibl, Kittl, Lickl, and Titl, and their ilk, are tendered lexicographical hospitality, if not lavish accommodations.

Authorities have been consulted, but not trusted. In fact, many persistent errors find their origin in authoritative works of reference, compiled by illustrious lexicographers whose great reputations have for years discouraged independent scrutiny.

Unfortunately, prime sources of musical biography, the memoirs of the subjects themselves, are rarely reliable. Berlioz embellished his life by romantic exaggeration, and often abused credulity. Wagner gave a fairly accurate account of his life, but he deliberately omitted episodes that are of legitimate interest, for instance the fact that he was incarcerated for debt in the Clichy jail in Paris from October 28 to

November 17, 1840. These dates I have secured from the Palais de Justice, Paris.

Reminiscences by members of the family and intimate friends of famous musicians must also be treated with circumspection. In some cases, the censoring of certain aspects of a musician's life is unavoidable. The standard biography of Tchaikovsky by his brother Modest understandably leaves out the true reasons for the failure of his unfortunate marriage.

Some biographical materials that have been widely circulated are plain forgeries. Such are the notorious Chopin-Potocka correspondence (in which Chopin appears as a gay Lothario) and the unspeakable edition of *Mémoires d'une chanteuse allemande,* ascribed—most foully—to the famous singer Wilhelmine Schröder-Devrient; it still figures in most bibliographies as a source book instead of the pornographic fabrication that it is.

Many cherished legends of musical biography have been removed by recent investigations, and I have tried to keep up with the corrective discoveries. Sweelinck never went to Venice. Corelli never went to Paris as Lully's rival. Stravinsky's *Pulcinella* contains virtually no themes by Pergolesi (though they are attributed to Pergolesi in Stravinsky's sources). Friedrich Witt wrote the "Jena" symphony, not Beethoven. Purcell's trumpet voluntary was composed by Jeremiah Clarke. Wagner did not invent the term "Leitmotif;" neither did Hans von Wolzogen; it was originated by Friedrich Wilhelm Jähns, in the preface to his book on Weber, published in 1871. And, of course, Bizet never composed the famous *Habanera* from *Carmen;* he transplanted it from a collection of Spanish songs by Sebastian Yradier.

The commonly accepted story of Haydn's *Farewell Symphony* tells us that Haydn staged his musical act in order to induce Prince Esterházy to grant his orchestra a vacation. But a much more plausible explanation is contained in a little-known book by an Italian friend of Haydn, Giacomo Gotifredo Ferrari, published at London in 1830. According to Ferrari's version, Esterházy intended to disband the orchestra and Haydn's *Farewell Symphony* was a stratagem to move the patron's heart, and to save the orchestra. Obviously, it succeeded.

It is usually stated that 20,000 persons attended Beethoven's funeral, and the figure is supported by contemporary accounts. But the population of Vienna at the time of Beethoven's death was about 320,000, and it is hardly likely that one person out of every sixteen, including children, gathered to pay tribute to the dead master. I have therefore replaced 20,000 by the non-committal "hundreds." On the other hand, the famous account of Beethoven's dying during a violent storm has been triumphantly confirmed. I have obtained from the Vienna Bureau of Meteorology an official extract from the weather report for March 26, 1827, stating that a thunderstorm, accompanied by strong winds, raged over the city at 4:00 in the afternoon.

A certain element of informed guesswork is inevitable in any biography, and is justified as long as it is clearly presented as conjecture. Jean Marie Leclair, the 18th-century French violinist, was murdered in his own house (by stabbing); his estranged wife was a professional engraver who owned sharp tools; there was no sign of a struggle at the scene of the assassination; ergo ...

****

The pursuit of accurate information has been long and arduous. To begin at the beginning, i.e., at birth: musicians, through the centuries, have altered their birth dates, invariably in the direction of rejuvenation. The chronicle of falsification begins with Johann Jakob Froberger, who gave his date of birth to his physician, Nicolaus Binninger, as May 18, 1620. When his baptism certificate was discovered, it revealed that he was baptized on May 19, 1616. A plausible surmise is that he gave the correct day and month, falsifying only the year; it is therefore fairly certain that the day of his birth was May 18, and that he was baptized on the following day.

In his handwritten autobiographical notice for Mattheson's *Grundlage einer Ehrenpforte,* Telemann stated that he was born in 1682, whereas he was actually born a year earlier; again, the day and the month of his birth, March 14, were given correctly.

I have obtained hundreds of birth certificates from all over the world to establish correct dates. The differences between the professed and actual ages have ranged from one to nineteen years. A few exceptions should be noted. Mozart's librettist, Emanuel Schikaneder, gave his birth year as 1748, but he was actually born in 1751. It is said that he married a woman some years his senior and wished to bring their ages closer together.

Ethel Leginska, pianist and conductor, wrote me to correct her date of birth from 1883 to 1886. Her birth certificate confirmed the latter date.

The famous Brazilian composer Villa-Lobos apparently did not know when he was born, for when I told him during a meeting in Paris that he was born in 1887, and not in 1881, 1890, or some other year, as variously given in reference works, he seemed genuinely surprised. I obtained the 1887 date from the registries of the school he attended as a child in Rio de Janeiro. Since then, his birth certificate has been discovered, confirming this date.

In some cases it is possible to arrive at a complete birth date synthetically. It is known, for instance, that Jacob Obrecht was born on Saint Cecilia's day, November 22, and that he entered the University of Louvain on August 17, 1470. The normal age of entrants being between 17 and 18, the year of Obrecht's birth can be deduced as 1452, thus providing the full date of birth, November 22, 1452. But a similar attempt to establish the birth date of the famous Belgian theorist Johannes Tinctoris from the presence of a person of that name among the entrants at the University of Louvain in 1471, fails because of false identification: Tinctoris was definitely known to be a native of Brabant, whereas his Louvain namesake was from Flanders; also, the real Tinctoris was already a figure in scholarly circles at the time his namesake entered the University.

Vivaldi's year of birth seems to be hidden forever from the inquiring eye; only an approximate date between 1675 and 1678 is offered in his biographies. But in an article published in 'Nueva Antologia' of August 1, 1942, Fausto Torrefranca, makes this tantalizingly cryptic statement: "Se è vera la data che ho ripescato in un vecchio repertorio del quale nessuno si è servito, Vivaldi sarebbe nato nel 1669, I'll giugno." *Nessuno?* I have decided to accept this date, even without palpable certification, in the hope that further findings will confirm it, for exact dates are rarely fabricated whole, and the year 1669 is quite compatible with the precisely known dates of Vivaldi's tonsure and ordination to the priesthood.

Cases of mistaken identity complicate the search for birth certificates. The bicentennial of Giovanni Battista Viotti was widely celebrated in 1953, but as it turned out, the celebration honored Viotti's infant brother. A Giovanni Battista Viotti was indeed born in Fontanetto, Italy, on May 23, 1753, but he died on July 10, 1754. On May 12, 1755, another child was born to the Viottis, and in memory of their first-born, he was given the same Christian names (a common practice in Catholic families) plus two additional names, Guglielmo Domenico. This was Giovanni Battista Viotti, the composer.

Biographical notices for Giacomo Insanguine list his year of birth variously between 1712 and 1742. I applied for a copy of his birth certificate at the registries in his native town of Monopoli, and received a document stating that Giacomo Insanguine was born there in 1712. However, this date did not fit into the known chronology of his education and career. I pressed further; the registries were searched again, and a death certificate was found showing that a Giacomo Insanguine died in 1726 at the age of 14. On March 22, 1728, a boy was born to the bereaved parents, and was named Giacomo Antonio Francesco Paolo Michele. This was the composer Insanguine.

The Italian composer and conductor Angelo Mariani, who was born on October 11, 1821, insisted in his communications to Francesco Regli, editor of a biographical dictionary, that he was born on October 11, 1824, and that he had an elder brother of the same name born exactly three years earlier, which led to mistaken identification. Mariani's birth certificate proves, however, that he was born in 1821.

A famous case of claimed mistaken identity is that of Beethoven, who was eager to prove that he was born in 1772 rather than 1770, and that it was another Ludwig van Beethoven who was born at an earlier date. True, a Ludwig Maria van Beethoven was born on April 1, 1769, but he died a few days later. Beethoven was born in the following year.

The true date of birth of Caruso will never be known with certainty; upon inquiry, I have received from the Demographic Office in Naples 13 birth certificates for 13 Enrico Carusos, all born about the time that Caruso was born, but none matching the known names of his parents. The chances are that the birth of Caruso, who was one of 18 children, was never registered.

Discrepancies of a few days in dates of birth are very common, owing to the substitution of the date of baptism for that of birth. Oddly enough, such errors occur even when the actual date of birth is included specifically in the baptism certificate. For over three centuries the date of birth of Lully was readily ascertainable, since his registry of baptism, indicating his birth on the day before, was preserved in the state archives in Florence. Yet it is the date of Lully's baptism, and not that of his birth, that is given in most reference works. Unless a prior claim is made, I was the first to obtain the text of the baptism certificate of Lully, and to establish his correct birth date, November 28, 1632.

It has been repeatedly stated in various writings on Mahler that he was not sure of his exact date of birth, and that his birth certificate was lost. Yet a simple request addressed to the archivist of the municipality of Kalischt, where Mahler was born, brought me a copy of his birth certificate confirming the generally accepted date, July 7, 1860. His centennial will thus be celebrated with the perfect assurance that the date is right.

Several reference works state that the birth of Sigismond Thalberg was never registered, and that a search in the archives of Geneva, where he was born, proved unavailing. Yet I have obtained the supposedly lost birth certificate without any difficulty, establishing his birth date as January 8, 1812. Inquiring still further, I learned to my disappointment that I was not the first to discover the supposedly lost document; its text was published in a musical magazine early in the 20th century, with the purpose of refuting the claim of loss. But there was more to the Thalberg case than the mere matter of his birth date. He openly asserted that he was the natural son of Count Moritz Dietrichstein and Baroness von Wetzlar. Yet the birth certificate states unambiguously that his parents were Joseph Thalberg and Fortunée Stein, both of Frankfurt. The certificate also indicates that both parents were married, but it does not state clearly whether they were married to each other. At this point, my investigation had to stop.

There is a fair percentage of illegitimate births among musicians. One famous Italian singer, Lucrezia Agujari, was known as La Bastardella; unless the name under which she was registered at birth is ascertained, there is no hope of obtaining her birth certificate. Delicacy compels me not to mark the established illegitimacy of musicians of more recent date.

When birth certificates cannot be secured, the next best sources of information are registries of birth in family Bibles, marriage certificates, school reports, and the like. The date of birth of Kaspar Othmayr, March 12, 1515, is verified by his astrological chart, and one may be sure that he gave the right date to his astrologer.

Death dates are often listed a day late, owing to the delay in announcement, or to a difference in time zones. Arnold Schoenberg's death is given as July 14, 1951 in most European sources, whereas he died on July 13, in Los Angeles. The date is particularly significant since Schoenberg (who was born on the 13th of the month) held a superstitious belief that 13 was his unlucky number. He was genuinely perturbed when he was told by a friend that the sum of the digits of his age (76) during the last year of his life was 13. According to an intimate account, he died 13 minutes before midnight, Los Angeles time, which of course was early morning July

14, in the Eastern states and in Europe.

Conversely, European deaths are occasionally reported in America as having occurred on the preceding date according to local American time. For some reason, the date of Prokofiev's death was generally reported in the West as having taken place on March 4, 1953, although he died on March 5, 1953, at 6:00 in the afternoon, Moscow time, which was also March 5 in Western Europe and America.

Melba died in Sydney in the early morning, on February 23, 1931, Australian time, but her death was announced in New York papers that were on the streets on February 22. This was, of course, due to the day's advance of Australian time over American time.

* * * * * * *

A number of musicians, including celebrities, have disappeared without leaving a trace. It was only in the 20th century that Vivaldi's place of death was finally traced to Vienna. Bononcini, the rival of Handel, also went to Vienna to die, but this was not discovered until very recently. I believe that the present edition is the first musical dictionary to contain this information and the exact date of Bononcini's death.

In order to ascertain the fate of musicians who were lost during the cataclysm of World War II and the European revolutions preceding and following it, I resorted to advertising in the German press and in the Russian émigré newspapers. I received a number of replies from relatives and friends of the subjects, and was able to establish the death dates of several former luminaries on the musical scene, among them Count Sheremetiev, a musical Maecenas in old St. Petersburg, who died in a poorhouse near Paris, and the once famous German tenor Paul Kalisch, husband of Lilli Lehmann, who died at the age of 90 in an Austrian castle. Then there were the deaths in German concentration camps, and in air raids. Several well-known musicians could not be accounted for, and probably never will be.

One of the most fantastic episodes in my hunt for missing persons was the search for Heinrich Hammer, conductor and composer, born in Germany in 1862, and active in Washington, D.C., about the turn of the century. He was last reported in Pasadena in the 1920's, but inquiries there failed to provide any information. I appealed for help to my favorite librarian at the Music Division of the Library of Congress, and he, always a man of instantaneous action, placed transcontinental telephone calls (at his own expense!) to various contacts in Pasadena, until he reached Hammer's son. This gentleman, an employee of the telephone company, happened to be working atop a telephone pole at the time, but a connection was established on the road line. The climax of the story was spectacular: a clipping from the Los Angeles 'Times' of October 25, 1953, was produced, carrying on its society page a picture of Heinrich Hammer, 91, and his young bride Arlene, 22, whom he had married the year before. Their address was given in the story, but when I wrote to him for further information on his musical activities, the letter came back marked: "Deceased: address unknown." It was relatively easy to find out that he had moved to Phoenix, Arizona, where he died on October 28, 1954.

* * * * * * *

Some technical aspects of the present edition are enumerated hereunder:

INCLUSION AND EXCLUSION. Although this is technically a dictionary of musicians, many other individuals connected with music are included, so that the proper title of the book ought to be *Baker's Biographical Dictionary of Musicians, Librettists, Publishers, Impresarios, and Sundry Other Men, Women, and Children Who Have to Do with Music.* Diaghilev was not a professional musician, but his influence on the course of 20th-century composition was so powerful that his name cannot be left out. The same consideration applies to patrons of music, some of whom could not read notes, but who have promoted music by generous donations. Whenever there was a question about inclusion or exclusion, the benefit of the doubt was given to the candidate.

PROPORTIONATE REPRESENTATION. Theoretically, in a book of reference, the amount of space should be proportionate to the importance of the subject. But this is not practical. Biographical information is very scant on important musicians of the Middle Ages and Renaissance, and it would be pointless to try to fill the space by unwarranted speculation in lieu of factual material. A prolific composer of ephemeral works may command more space than his less prolific but more inspired colleagues. Abundance of factual material being the paramount aim, the ideal of proportionate representation cannot be sustained.

MARRIAGES AND DIVORCES. When a musician marries a musician, it is of some enlightenment to the reader to be apprised of this fact. The same holds true for musical divorces. When there is a multiplicity of marriages (as in the case of Eugène d'Albert), only musical marriages deserve a listing. The unique marriage of the male soprano Tenducci (he was a triorchis) must be mentioned, if for no other reason than its bibliographical consequences, for his wife wrote a book on the affair.

BODILY AND MENTAL ILLS. Dictionary entries on the Wagnerian tenor Schnorr von Carolsfeld inform us that he died of a chill contracted when he sang at the world première of *Tristan und Isolde*, but the fact is that he sang three more performances within the next ten days, and died several weeks later of a heart condition aggravated by overweight. The melodramatic elaboration of the 29-year-old singer's death is typical of the old-fashioned art of biography. The new-fashioned biography is apt to emphasize unpleasant ailments, particularly the *morbus gallicus*. But is it necessary in a musical dictionary to say, e.g., that Paganini suffered from this affliction? One thinks not. On the other hand, a mention of Chopin's tuberculosis, which affected his entire career, cannot be omitted from his biographical entry; besides, consumption is a poetical illness. Similarly essential is the mention of the paralysis and blindness of Frederick Delius, and, of course, the deafness of Beethoven and Smetana.

Speculation as to psychological causes of physical decline and death, rampant in old-fashioned biography, has no place in a factual work of reference. Accordingly, I have excluded from this edition such psychological diagnoses as the statement that the 18th-century composer Isouard was so deeply "mortified" by his failure to be elected to the French Academy that ("although a married man," thoughtfully remarks a 19th-century reference work) he "abandoned work, plunged into dissipation, and died."

As a tribe, musicians, and particularly composers, are apt to be mentally unbalanced to a greater degree than members of other professions. The insanity of Schumann, Smetana, Hugo Wolf, and MacDowell is a tragic concluding chapter in the biography of each of these composers. But temporary mental derangements need not be reported.

BIBLIOGRAPHY. Particular attention has been paid to the listing of little-known publications containing factual material not available elsewhere. As a rule, other reference books are not listed as bibliography; exceptions have been made for autobiographical entries in *Die Musik in Geschichte und Gegenwart* and Loewenberg's compendium, *Annals of Opera*, but these are cited mostly for an extension in detail rather than as essential supplement.

Titles of books, when inordinately long, are abbreviated, but without cutting off the limiting clauses. It is quite improper to list Karl Grunsky's *Die Technik des Klavierauszuges, entwickelt am dritten Akt von Wagners Tristan* simply as *Die Technik des Klavierauszuges*, even though the author offers valuable suggestions as to general techniques of piano reduction while analyzing the specific problem of the third act of *Tristan und Isolde*.

Old spelling in various languages is often preserved, when a book is particularly famous. For instance, Martin Agricola's work *Ein kurtz deudsche Musica* is not made into *Eine kurze deutsche Musik*, which would be an unwarranted modernization. Varieties of spelling in different editions of some old books are also given occasionally. For instance, the editions of a work by Christopher Simpson are differentiated as *The Principles of Practicle Musick* and *Practicall Musick*.

Practical sense rather than bibliothecarian pedantry is applied in borderline cases. It would not serve the student or the scholar to spell David as Dauid, just to bow to some old usages. Arbeau's *Orchésographie* is listed with the subtitle in modern French rather than in the form in which it appears in the first edition of 1589: *Et Traicté an Forme de Dialogue, par lequel toutes Personnes peuuent facilement apprendre & practiquer l'honneste exercice des dances.*

To list or not to list? That is the question that befuddles the lexicographer. One cannot guide oneself entirely by library card catalogues, for they list impartially dissertations of great documentary value and worthless popular booklets. Besides, the title-page does not always correspond to the content. For instance, A. A. Elwart published a booklet on Louis-Gilbert Duprez, subtitled "avec une biographie authentique de son maître A. Choron." The subtitle is hardly justified, for there are but a couple of pages on Choron, containing little information. On the other hand, there are books whose titles, sometimes overly modest, gave no hint about the wealth of material contained in them.

TITLES OF COMPOSITIONS. Composers are notoriously inconsiderate of biographers and bibliographers. With malice aforethought, they change the titles of their works, produce their operas abroad under translated titles, or convert original subtitles into titles. Under such circumstances, compilers of musical dictionaries cannot be blamed for duplicating works. Don Emilio Arrieta y Corera wrote an opera, *La Conquista de Granada,* which was produced in Madrid in 1850, and revived under the title *Isabel la Católica* in 1855. The opera got a double listing in the *Crónica de la Opera Italiana en Madrid,* published in 1878; the index to this book listed the two titles as interchangeable, but this precaution did not deter several biographers from listing two operas in place of one. Charles Martin Loeffler's *Poem* for orchestra, inspired by Verlaine's *La bonne chanson,* was first performed and published simply as *Poem;* Loeffler reorchestrated it, and had it performed under the title *La bonne chanson.* As a result, the work twinned in several dictionaries.

FIRST AND LAST NAMES. Variants of spellings of celebrated musical names (Des Prez, Després, etc.) are indicated in parentheses, and the selection of the main entry is made according to the weight of scholarly opinion, frequency of usage, etc. In this edition Piccinni is preferred to Piccini, Janequin to Jannequin. Alternative spellings are indicated by cross reference. One of the most vexing problems has been the decision to modernize the German name Carl to Karl. The tendency towards modernization has been strong in the last decades, and has found its reflection in the successive editions of the present dictionary. A special problem is presented by the changes of spelling effected by emigrant musicians themselves. Arnold Schönberg changed his name legally to Schoenberg when he became an American citizen. Carlos Salzedo dropped the acute accent that originally marked the antepenultimate letter of his last name. Carlos Surinach dropped the tilde over the n. Other composers changed the form of their names in order to insure correct pronunciation in the adoptive country. Preferred listing must be decided according to the number and relative importance of works published under the old name or the new. Thus, the original name of Aladár Szendrei has been retained, even though he changed it in America to Alfred Sendrey. Edgar Varèse began using the form Edgard about 1942, but all his works are published without the terminal d in the first name.

The French music scholar Lionel de La Laurencie used the capital letter in La in the bibliographical sections of his books, but small l in the footnotes in the same books. The listing under La Laurencie is preferred here to conform to library catalogues. Another scholarly Frenchman, Gedalge, did not use the acute accent in most of his signed prefaces, but the accent is present in many title pages of his publications. The accentless form appears to be more authentic.

NOBILIARY PARTICLES. When a nobiliary particle (de, van, von) is intimately associated with the customary form of a name, then the corresponding entry is given under such a particle. Alternatives are given for reference. Victoria De Los Angeles is listed under De Los Angeles, with references under Angeles and Los. Although Beethoven took pride in the supposed nobility represented by the particle van, it would be preposterous to have such a listing under the letter V, even for reference purposes. The numerous other *vans* are distributed either under V or under the main body of the name. Usage, rather than consistency, is accepted as a guide.

The English composer Gustav Holst was of remote Swedish ancestry, and his original name was Von Holst. At the outbreak of World War I, he followed the suggestion of Percy A. Scholes and dropped the Germanic-sounding particle. There seems to be no point in giving a cross reference under Von Holst.

PSEUDONYMS. Real names of composers or writers on music better known by their pseudonyms are given in parentheses. In some cases the choice has been difficult. In the last edition of this dictionary, the main entry on Edmund Rubbra was under Duncan-Rubbra, the name under which he published some of his early works. Duncan was the name of his first wife, which he adopted, but his subsequent works were all performed and published under his real name and there seems to be no reason for perpetuating the Duncan-Rubbra form. The primary entry for the Russian composer and musicologist Boris Asafiev is placed under that name, with a cross reference under his pseudonym Igor Glebov. Philip Heseltine published most of his music under the name Peter Warlock, but Heseltine is preferred for the main entry.

TRANSLITERATION FROM THE RUSSIAN. Adequate transliteration of Russian names into the Latin alphabet is as impossible as squaring a circle. Russians who have made their careers abroad have adopted their own transliterations, which have become familiar, and which resist the logic of phonetics. There is no reason for the compulsion to do violence to such well-established forms as Rachmaninoff or Koussevitzky. On the other hand, there is no reason to follow the German spellings Strawinsky and Tschaikowsky. Since Stravinsky has become an American citizen, the spelling of his name in the Latin alphabet has become established. As to Tchaikovsky, his name can be rendered with phonetic fidelity in English as Chikovsky (chi as in China), but so drastic a departure from the familiar appearance of a famous name can only lead to confusion. The *Encyclopædia Britannica* compromises on the half-German, half-English form Tschaikovsky.

The s in Russian names is often doubled to avoid being vocalized into z. There is only one s in the Russian spelling of Mussorgsky, but the deletion of the supernumerary s would run counter to established usage. On the other hand, Russian names that have not established themselves in a unique form have been transliterated letter by letter, as Asafiev and Stasov.

The first name and patronymic are given in the entries on most Russian musicians who have made their careers in Russia, but not for emigrants. Russian forms of the first name are used in conjunction with the patronymic—Sergey Sergeyevitch Prokofiev, Nikolai Yakovlevitch Miaskovsky. For Russian-born musicians active abroad, first names usually are assimilated with the corresponding names in the language of the country of residence. But there are inevitable exceptions. My own name Nicolas is an anomaly in this respect, being the French form of the Russian Nikolai; there should be every reason for me to anglicize it into Nicholas, but since I began publishing my compositions and my books under an aitchless first name, I might as well keep it so.

GEOGRAPHICAL NAMES. Changes of place names are annoying to lexicographers and mapmakers alike. If the metamorphosis of St. Petersburg to Petrograd and then to Leningrad leaves no doubt in the minds of informed readers that all three represent the same city on the banks of the Neva, elsewhere on the European map the befuddlement is considerable. One can travel from Pressburg to Bratislava to Pozsony without budging an inch. A person born in Klausenburg finds himself nominally transported to Kolozsvár and then to Cluj, while living in the same house all his life.

Sometimes a town resumes its former name. Perm was renamed Molotov after the Soviet Revolution, but when Molotov fell into disgrace in 1957, the name Perm was restored. In Poland, Katowice was renamed Stalinogorod in 1953, but resumed its old name in 1956.

Then there is the case of Liège. For over a century, it bore an unnatural acute accent on the middle letter. In 1946 the Municipal Council resolved that the accent be changed. Should we cling pedantically to the chronology of Lièges orthography, we would find a Belgian musician born in a place with an acute accent, and dying there with a grave.

ABBREVIATIONS. All abbreviations have been removed from this edition, except those in common usage, e.g., vol., ed., prof., Jan., Feb., Aug., etc.; and also the obvious ones, such as symph., orch., publ., etc. No more the impenetrable consonant jungle of Ztschr., Vschr., vcs., Kchm., mvt., or Kgl.

APPARENT ERRORS. Among tens of thousands of names, titles, and dates errors seem inevitable. Yet some apparent errors are not errors at all. The words of *Die Forelle* of Schubert are by Schubart; Roselius edited works by Raselius; H. Reimann is not a misprint for H. Riemann. Two Czech-born conductors, both named Adler but unrelated, are stated in the present edition to have been respectively in charge of the Kiev State Opera and of the Kiev State Orchestra during the same period in the 1930's. This looks like flagrant confusion of identities, but it is not. How many real errors, typographical or otherwise, have escaped notice? I can only hope that the percentage is low.

* * * * * * *

My heart overflows with gratitude to many wonderful people who have helped me in putting together this edition, and have saved me from blunders that I might otherwise have committed, to my everlasting horror and shame. There are first of all the anonymous (for their names are illegible on various documents received by me) registrars, clerks, and keepers of archives, thanks to whom I have been able to establish correct dates of birth and death, first performances of important works, and other details. Among music scholars who have been of assistance, I should mention Karl H. Wörner in Germany, Victor De Rubertis in Argentina, Vasco Mariz in Brazil, Klaus Pringsheim in Japan, Josip Andreis in Yugoslavia, the Society of Polish Composers in Warsaw, Pierre Debièvre in Paris, and Ulisse Prota-Giurleo in Naples. I owe especial gratitude to Mme. W.-L. Landowski of Paris, who provided accurate and important information on French music, not accessible by ordinary means. Théodore d'Erlanger, of Paris, secured for me some valuable documentation.

Nathan Broder, Associate Editor of *The Musical Quarterly*, has assumed the overwhelming task of going over the entire manuscript, questioning every suspicious item, scrutinizing factual discrepancies, providing missing information, and also rewriting some entries. He has kept his vigil faithfully, from Aaron to Zwyssig.

I have reserved for the end my testimonial for William Lichtenwanger, Assistant Reference Librarian in the Music Division of the Library of Congress, a man of fierce determination, who gets his historical, biographical, or bibliographical quarry in the face of the most disheartening failures by others. Because he treats no subject as trivial, and no musician as unworthy of the most tender bibliographical attention, he has been able to furnish unique and precious data (working on his own time, too!). His familiarity with a dozen or so languages (including Turkish and Japanese) has increased enormously the scope of his inquiry.

As for myself, I should like to quote from a letter that Alfred Einstein wrote me shortly before his death, wondering "... ob wir—und natürlich vor allem Sie—im Himmel einmal dafür belohnt werden, dass wir einige Ungenauigkeiten aus der Welt geschafft haben..." To which I would add my favorite Latin phrase, so conveniently self-exonerating: *Feci quod potui—faciant meliora potentes.*

Nicolas Slonimsky

PREFACE TO THE SIXTH EDITION

If I were to write an autobiography (which God forbid!) I would call it *I am a footnote*, or *I am a parenthesis*. I am a footnote in the entry on Carl Maria von Weber in the Fifth Edition of *Grove's Dictionary* and a parenthesis in the article on Lully in *Die Musik in Geschichte und Gegenwart*. And I am a paragraph in the Fifteenth Edition of the *Encyclopaedia Britannica* under Pandiatonicism, which is my polysyllabic brainchild.

Dr. Samuel Johnson defines a lexicographer in his famous dictionary as "a harmless drudge." Harmless? Not necessarily. In fact, lexicography, when practiced in excess, may well be harmful to the lexicographer's psyche. Consider the melancholy case of John Wall Callcott (1766–1821) as related in *Baker's Biographical Dictionary of Musicians:* "His mind gave way from overwork on a projected biographical dictionary of musicians, ... He recovered, but not sufficiently to continue his work." Callcott reached the letter Q, associated with such disturbing images as queer, quaquaversal, and quagmire, and then quit.

One of my predecessors in editing *Baker's* jotted down these words in the margin of the galley proofs: "I will go mad if I have to continue this for a long time." Another music editor, working on another dictionary, deliberately rented a room on the ground floor lest he should be tempted to jump out the window in despair over the contents of the book.

Although most of my friends regard me as an eccentric, I am not given to suicidal impulses while working on a dictionary. But I am rather paranoiac in my suspicions about melodrama, except in opera librettos. I never believed that Salieri poisoned Mozart, even though I memorized, as part of my school assignment in St. Petersburg, Salieri's monologue in Pushkin's play *Mozart and Salieri,* in which Salieri explains his reason for poisoning Mozart lest his blazing genius should eclipse the work of such humble votaries in the divine art of harmony as himself. In another tale of Mozart, I became suspicious of the reports in practically every reference work and every biography that a fierce snowstorm was raging in Vienna on the day of his funeral in December 1791, which made it impossible for his friends to follow his body to the cemetery (the snowballs were as large as tennis balls, the top Vienna Mozartologist Erich Schenk asserts). Why wasn't this meteorological phenomenon as much as mentioned in early Mozart biographies? It would have at least explained why Mozart's widow did not attend the funeral, if not her failure to pay dues for keeping Mozart's grave in perpetuity, which was the reason why he was eventually moved to the place of common burial. The snowstorm episode appears for the first time in Otto Jahn's monumental biography of Mozart, and the only source to substantiate it was an anonymous article published in a Vienna newspaper on the occasion of Mozart's centennial in 1856. Some Mozartologists identified the writer (who signed his report as "a man of the people") as the bartender of Mozart's favorite Vienna tavern, although by the time of Mozart's centennial he himself, if still living, would have been about a hundred years old. To resolve my puzzlement, I wrote to the Vienna Weather Bureau for a report on the climatic conditions on that December day in 1791. Great was my malicious sense of gratification when I received a report that the temperature on that day was well above freezing and that a gentle Zephyr wind blew from the West. No snowballs. No frigid weather which frightened away Mozart's friends. No melodrama, except the tragedy of Mozart's death so young. Encouraged by the prompt response of the Vienna Weather Bureau (which had kept records for more than two centuries), I inquired about another melodramatic episode: an electric storm on the afternoon of Beethoven's death. Yes, there was an electric storm, even though it was hardly likely that Beethoven in his debilitated physical condition could have lifted his clenched fist toward heaven in a gesture of defiance of *Jupiter tonans.*

Not every melodramatic report is necessarily a pabulum for the gullible. I became incredulous of the tale told in *Baker's* about the French singer Alexandre

Taskin who reportedly displayed an untenorlike bravery during a conflagration at the Opéra-Comique in Paris on the night of May 25, 1887, when he sang in *Mignon*. The lives of hundreds of panic-stricken opera-goers were supposedly saved thanks to his *sang-froid*. Well, it turns out that there was a rather horrendous fire at the Opéra-Comique on that night, and that "le beau Taskin," as he was known to his admirers, did display courage in calming down the audience, and was commended for it by the French government.

I was smugly confident of the accuracy of the report that the Italian conductor Gino Marinuzzi was assassinated by the anti-Fascist partisans in Milan on August 17, 1945, as duly noted in *Baker's*, and also in *Grove,* in *Riernann's Musik-Lexikon* ("ermordet") and in the Italian encyclopedia *La Musica* ("morì assassinato"). But why did the anti-Fascist partisans wait so long after the end of the Mussolini regime to shoot him? True, he was the author of a triumphal ode on the occasion of the historic meeting between Hitler and Mussolini in an Alpine tunnel, but many other Italian composers expressed a similar lack of precognition in glorifying the Fascist regime. I received many letters from Italian composers during the Fascist years, dated E.F. XV, E.F. XVIII, etc., i.e., Era Fascista followed by the year, in Roman numerals, since Mussolini's march on Rome ("tough on Jesus Christ," a witty Bostonian remarked when I showed him these letters), and they remained unscathed. However that might be, the publishers of *Baker's* received an irate letter from a Milan lawyer, acting on behalf of the Marinuzzi family, protesting that the account of the assassination was false and demanding an immediate rectification. Gino Marinuzzi, the letter said, died peacefully in a Milan hospital on the date correctly given in *Baker's,* succumbing not to a bullet wound but to hepatic anemia. Fortunately, *Baker's* VI was still in a fluid state, and the publishers were able to pacify the Marinuzzi family lawyer, promising to make a correction. But why did the Marinuzzis wait all these years for firing their salvo, and why zero in on *Baker's* rather than on their own Italian dictionaries? And where did the original report of assassination come from? The *Corriere della Sera,* Milan's major newspaper, carried an *R.I.P.* notice of Marinuzzi's death, with no mention of the cause. The case was clinched eventually by the Servizio Mortuario of the city of Milan, stating that Marinuzzi had indeed died of acute atrophy of the liver. No bullets, no assassination, no melodrama.

Beware of false suspicions! Could Raselius have written a book on Roselius? He could, and he did. Could Gabriel Faure (no accent) have written a monograph on Gabriel Fauré (accent)? He could and he did. Was Schubart really the author of the words of *Die Forelle* by Schubert? Yes, he was. Could two composers, each named Victor Young, have been active in the movies in Hollywood during the same period? They were. Could I myself have had a classmate, in a St. Petersburg high school, called Nicolas Slonimsky? I had, and since I joined the class after him, my name was registered as Nicolas II, which was the official name of the then reigning Czar of all the Russians.

Among the many persistent errors plaguing musical biography is the belief that Wagner originated the term *Leitmotiv.* He did not; it was first proposed by Friedrich Wilhelm Jähns in the preface to his book on Weber published in 1871. Bizet did not write the famous *Habanera* in *Carmen.* He took it from a collection of Spanish songs by Sebastián Yradier, without any alteration of key, harmonization, tempo, rhythm, and dynamics.

The Russians have a marvelously expressive word for a story unsupported by evidence—"nyebylitsa," an "un-was-ity." Famous last words by historic personages are almost all such un-was-ities. Madame Roland's exclamation on her way to the guillotine, "Liberty, how many crimes are committed in thy name!" first appeared in print in Lamartine's *Histoire de la Revolution française,* or so it is cited in *Bartlett's Familiar Quotations.* But browsing through the 1793 volume of *The Annual Register* of London I came upon a Paris dispatch quoting the famous phrase. Is one to suppose then that the British Paris correspondent actually followed the tumbril taking Madame Roland to the place of execution and actually heard her utter the famous apostrophe? Not bloody likely.

"Lexicographis secundus post Herculem labor" was the judgment pronounced by Joseph Justus Scaliger (1540–1609), himself a lexicographer of stature. The mythological reference is, of course, to the labor performed by Hercules in cleaning up the manure-filled stables of King Augeus, son of the sun god Helius. Hercules did the job in twenty-four hours; to clean up a clogged music dictionary takes a little longer. But sanitation must be done with circumspection; one never knows what shining gems, what bits of fascinating tektite, are embedded in rejected debris. Take the story of the Italian singer Giulio Rossi as related by *Baker's*. He started out as a tenor, but unintentionally plunged into the Tiber on a cold day and as a consequence became a *basso profondo*. Incredible? Yes, incredible, but what lexicographer would have the heart to throw it into the pile of refuse? I couldn't. So—*stet!*

There should be no such spirit of acceptance for the purple prose that some editors indulged in while describing the life and works of admired persons. I had to deflate somewhat the verbal effusions in the original *Baker's* entry on A. W. Thayer, biographer of Beethoven. Here is a sample: "Unhappily, his wonderful capacity for work was overtaxed, and volume IV of his nobly conceived Beethoven biography, executed with a painstaking thoroughness and scrupulous fidelity beyond praise, was left unfinished. Though he lived for years in straitened circumstances, he resolutely refused offers from firms like Novello & Co. and G. Schirmer, Inc., hoping to recast entirely the English version of his *Beethoven*." Suffocating! Give us air to breathe!

A biographical dictionary ought to be a democratic assembly of factual information. Great masters are by right to be given preferential treatment, but opaque luminaries, e.g., Bibl, Kittl, Lickl, or Titl, ought to be tendered hospitality, if not lavish accommodations. Ay, there's the rub! Proportionate representation is the ideal desideratum, but availability of information and productivity of work determine the space allowance. One would fain wish that there were more biographical information on Shakespeare than on Pepys, on Josquin Desprez than on a whole gallery of later madrigalists, on Bach than on Reger. As it is an unhappy editor must gather every bit of information on the great masters of the past and make a judicious selection of biographical data and a list of works of *dii minores* in the arts.

One must also beware of lexicographical zombies, typographical clones and monsters. The great Eitner, who spent a lifetime in tabulating manuscripts in European libraries, was also progenitor of such teratological creatures. Working on a pile of anonymous French songs, he apparently mistook the nouns in their titles for names of composers. Thus we learn from Eitner that "La Chanson d'un gai Berger" was a song by Ungay Berger, and that "La Chanson de l'Auberge Isolée" was composed by Mlle. Isolée L'Auberge. There must be a number of desperate music researchers trying to find out who Mr. Gay Shepherd and Miss Isolated Tavern were in life. *Cobbett's Cyclopedia of Chamber Music* is responsible for spawning D. Michaud (a misprint for D. Milhaud), Marcel Babey (for Marcel Labey), and, most intriguing, a famous violinist, Heinrich Wehtan, generated through the transliteration of the Russian spelling in Cyrillic letters of the name of Henri Vieuxtemps via a German translation of an article originally written in Russian by a contributor to *Cobbett*.

To exorcise such vampires and to drive a stake through their hideous hearts I myself decided to create a monster as the last entry of the 1958 edition of *Baker's*. Never fear: I killed it in page proofs. But here it is *à titre documentaire*:

Zyžík, Krsto, Czech composer; b. Pressburg, Feb. 29, 1900. [1900 was not a leap-year in the West.] He traveled widely to Pozsony and Bratislava [Pozsony and Bratislava are respectively the Hungarian and Slovak names of Pressburg], and back to Pressburg. He attracted attention with his oratorio *Dieta Wormsová* written for the quadricentennial of the Diet of Worms in a vermicular counterpoint. [Diet of Worms was an actual historic assembly, held in the city of Worms in 1521; it condemned Luther as a heretic]; then brought out a bel canto work *Strč prst skrz* *krk* (a Czech tongue-twister, meaning *put your finger on your throat*), using only consonants in consonant harmony. His works include *Pinč mj šuga* (*Pinch me, Sugar*, or *Pinch Meshuga* in phonetical transcription) for chorus and pinched strings; *Smyccový Kvartet* (string quartet) for woodwind quintet; *Sappho LXIX* for 2 female participants (Lesbos Festival, 1955); *Macho* for large secular organ (male player), etc. In 1979, after many years of aggravated floccillation and severe dyscrasia, he was committed to a dissident asylum. See Sol Mysnik [rather obvious anagram of Slonimsky], *A Czech Checkmate: The Story of Krsto Zyžík* (Los Angeles, 1979).

The most authentic sources of information ought to be diaries and autobiographies, correspondence and reminiscences of friends and relatives. But much too frequently, at least in musical biography, accounts by musicians themselves are tainted by a desire for self-glorification hidden behind a mask of assumed modesty. "Look at me," they seem to tell the reader, "and marvel at my accomplishments; starting out in poverty, privations and need, and by dint of faith in my destiny and hard work, rising to the top of the pyramid of fame, recognition and even wealth." Wagner's autobiography abounds in trivia, including some tedious pages about his pet dogs, but he never mentions the episode of his incarceration at the Clichy prison in Paris from October 28 to November 17, 1840, for non-payment of debt. True, it was one of those permissive jailings, with easy family furloughs, but still the episode is a legitimate part of Wagner's biography. Naturally, Wagner never gave an account in his autobiography of his cavalier treatment of the women in his life, nor did he make clear the circumstances of the birth of his natural daughter Isolde born to Cosima on April 10, 1865, while she was still married to Hans von Bülow. In 1914 Isolde petitioned the Bavarian Civil Court to grant her a share in Wagner's royalties; her claim was rejected on the grounds that there was no evidence that Cosima had ceased all communication with her legitimate husband Hans von Bülow within the period of ten months before Isolde's birth, a legal maximum for the length of gestation. The court also overruled the evidence submitted by Isolde's lawyer husband, based on the phrenological and hemological similarities between Wagner and Isolde.

It was fashionable among artists of the nineteenth century to claim paternity from celebrated or titled persons. Was the French cellist François Servais actually a bastard child of Liszt, as was claimed for him in various sources, including *Baker's?* He was born in St. Petersburg, or so the dictionaries said, in 1846, a date that fits the chronology of Liszt's liaison with Princess Sayn-Wittgenstein. But nothing in the voluminous correspondence between her and Liszt during that period indicated that she was a prospective mother. My earnest inquiries in Russia brought no results. The verdict in this case, therefore, must remain unproven.

A more involved claim of desirable paternity concerns the once famous pianist Sigismond Thalberg who apparently authorized the report that he was the son of a Prince Dietrichstein and a baroness. Further inquiries were discouraged by a footnote in the 1954 edition of *Grove's Dictionary* stating that Thalberg's birth certificate (he was born in Geneva) was unobtainable. Distrustful of this notice, I wrote to Geneva and obtained a copy of the certificate by airmail within a matter of days. I discovered later that the document had been previously published in a Belgian magazine on the occasion of Thalberg's centenary in 1912. The certificate stated that Thalberg was a legitimate son of Joseph Thalberg and Fortunee Stein, both of Frankfurt-am-Main, and that he was born in Geneva on January 8, 1812. The case was further complicated by the publication in various sources of a letter allegedly written by Thalberg's natural mother to Prince Dietrichstein at the time of Thalberg's birth, suggesting that he should be given the name Thalberg, so that he would grow as peacefully as a Thal (valley) and would tower over humanity as high as a Berg (mountain). Just who fabricated this letter and for what purpose remains unclear. The Supplement to *Riemann's Musik-Lexikon*, published in 1975, adds an intriguing bit of information that Thalberg was indeed adopted by Prince Dietrichstein later in life.

The strange lure of aristocratic birth seems to be undiminished even in our own century. An English singer who was active in recital and on the light opera stage in the early 1900's under the name Louis Graveure declared in an interview published in *The New York Times* in 1947 that he was of royal or possibly imperial birth, and that it would be worth a fortune to him to find out who he really was. Well, for the modest sum of two shillings and sixpence I obtained from London a copy of his birth certificate which dispelled the mystery. His real name was Wilfrid Douthitt, and he used it in his early appearances in England as a baritone; later he changed to tenor and gave concerts as Louis Graveure, which was his mother's maiden name.

Much more honest was the search for true paternity undertaken by the American folk songster and poet Rod McKuen. He knew he was illegitimate, and his mother never told him who his father was. He undertook a long quest, almost epic in its simple grandeur, and in the end established the identity of his father, a backwoods lumberjack.

The desire to recreate one's life according to one's fancy is universal, and artists are particularly apt to imagine, and at times consciously to contrive, the tales of might-have-been. Was Liszt actually kissed on the brow by Beethoven at the concert he played in Vienna as a child? There is a charming lithograph of the supposed event, which is reproduced in several Liszt biographies. But the evidence of Beethoven's archives suggests that Beethoven was annoyed by Liszt's father's bringing the child Liszt to Beethoven's quarters, and that he never went to the concert despite Schindler's efforts to persuade him to attend. Liszt did play for Beethoven in private, but whether he was kissed on the brow or not remains uncertain.

Working on a biographical dictionary of musicians, I have found myself in the uncomfortable position of private detective. Some years back I received a letter from a Russian woman living in Rome, Italy. She asked my help to find out whether her father, the Russian violinist Bezekirsky who emigrated to America when she was a child, was still alive. Since Bezekirsky was in *Baker's,* I had to search for him anyway to bring him up to date, dead or alive. Tracking him down through several music schools where he taught violin, I finally reached him in a small locality in upstate New York. Delighted that I could restore a missing father to an anxious daughter, I wrote to both giving their mutual addresses. Frankly, I expected letters full of emotional gratitude for my humanitarian endeavor, but I got none from either father or daughter. I do not relish unfinished human symphonies, so I wrote to Bezekirsky again asking him to let me know whether he established contact with his long-lost offspring. Great was my shock when I received from him a postcard scribbled in English in a senile hand, saying as follows: "Your mission was successful, if you call several unpleasant and demanding letters from my daughter a success. I am in no position to help her in any way." I never heard from the daughter.

One of the sharpest rebukes I ever received for trying to obtain information was administered by the remarkable English composer Kaikhosru Sorabji. I made the terrible *faux pas* of describing him as an Indian composer. "Do not dare to call me an Indian," he thundered in reply. "We are Parsi, followers of Zarathustra." He flatly refused to supply biographical data about himself, but he sent me a signed copy of his formidable *Opus Clavicembalisticum,* and pointed out for my information that it is the greatest polyphonic work since Bach's *Kunst der Fuge.* For all I know, it may be exactly that, at least in the grandeur of conception and extraordinary skill of its structure. But his rebuke to me was mild in comparison with the eruption of invective he poured on Percy Scholes for what he deemed to be an undignified and inadequate entry on him in the *Oxford Companion to Music.* Scholes sent the letter to me with the inscription "For your delectation." It is worth reproducing *in toto:*

My Good Sir:

A valued friend draws my attention to a lucubration of yours under the entry of my name in a recently published book of reference. One is hard put to it at which to marvel the more, the exiguity of your sense of proportion or the poverty of your taste in devoting double the amount of space to cheap impertinences regarding the place and date of my birth (which is as little business of yours as of any other prying nosey busybody) to that which is devoted to my work, which is all that concerns anyone and which carefully conveys inaccurate and false information by leaving out material facts. Formerly I used to consider it enough when dealing with these stupid and impudent enquiries from lexicographical persons, deliberately to mislead them as to dates and places. This is a mistake: their enquiries should either be ignored or refused. And the sooner folk of their kidney grasp the fact that one is under no moral obligation to provide them with accurate, or indeed any information at all just because they choose to ask for it, the very much better for all concerned.

I have the honour to be, Sir, Yours very faithfully,

Kaikhosru Shapurji Sorabji

Sorabji is a unique figure in music, and his full biography would be fascinating. Erik Chisholm, who knew him personally, told me that the gate of Sorabji's castle in Dorset bears this legend: "Visitors Unwelcome. Roman Catholic Nuns in Full Habit May Enter Without An Appointment." In reckless disregard of Sorabji's demurrer at biographical information about him, I wrote to the London registry of birth to find out at least when and where he was born. To my surprise the document stated that his real name was Leon Dudley Sorabji; Kaikhosru was apparently his Parsi name assumed later in life. I informed Eric Blom, who was then working on the Fifth Edition of *Grove,* of my findings. His response was prompt. "I knew right along," he wrote, "that Sorabji's name was Leon Dudley, but if you value your life I would not advise you to put it in print, for I fear that if you do he would take the next plane to America and assassinate you personally." And Samuel Johnson said that a lexicographer is a "harmless drudge!"

Once in a while in a beleaguered lexicographer's life the subject of an entry in a biographical dictionary voices his gratitude for the honor. A letter I received from Walter Stockhoff, an American composer whose music was praised by Busoni as "a fresh voice from the New World that could revitalize the tired art of Europe," certainly warmed the cockles of my heart. "As pure, cool, crystal-clear water," he wrote me, "revives one thirsting in the desert, so intelligence, understanding, sympathy and sense of values come to brighten one's pathway. There is a noble generosity in your giving thought to my work. Through the greatness of your nature you strengthen others."

* * * * * * *

Chronological memory is treacherous. Casals owned the manuscript of the B- flat major string quartet, op. 67, of Brahms, given to him by a Vienna collector. It was, he told me, mysteriously connected with his life, for he was conceived when Brahms began the composition of the quartet, and was born when Brahms completed it. Leaving aside the problem of knowing the date of one's conception, the chronology does not support this fancy. Brahms wrote the work during the summer and fall of 1875, and it was first performed in Berlin on October 30, 1876. Casals was born two months after its performance and could not have been conceived fourteen or fifteen months previously.

Lexicographical cross-pollination of inaccurate information in similar wording is a hazard. Philip Hale used to say that when several mutually independent reference works vouchsafe identical data, he deems the information reliable. Not necessarily so. If we consider the case of Mascagni, one comes upon a curious iteration of idiom that arouses suspicion. The 1906 edition of *Grove's* states that Mascagni was compelled to study music "by stealth" because his father, a baker, wanted him to be a lawyer. The *Oxford Companion to Music* paraphrases *Grove's:* "Mascagni was the son of a baker who took music lessons by stealth." The 1940 edition of *Baker's* echoes: "Mascagni's father (a baker) wished him to study jurisprudence, but he learned piano-playing by stealth." What is this obsession with the quaint locution "by stealth" in all these reference works? In point of fact, Mascagni's father was quite proud of his achievement as a musician and eagerly supported his studies at the Conservatory of Milan, as attested by their published correspondence.

If autobiographies are inevitably images of one's life as refracted through a prism resulting in an attractive and colorful spectrum, it is nevertheless strange that a composer would alter the history of the creation of a particular work. Berlioz did so paraleptically in his most famous score *Symphonie fantastique* by leaving out of its program the fact that one of the movements was taken from his early school work and that he implanted the unifying *idée fixe* surgically in a vacant measure containing a fermata, in order to justify its inclusion. And yet this manipulation creates the false impression of coherence. Of course, composers need not apologize to their biographers and analysts for revising their works in the light of later wisdom. Mahler denied the programmatic intent of several of his symphonies even though the descriptive titles appeared in the manuscripts. Beethoven carefully disavowed the pictorial nature of his *Pastoral Symphony* by stating that the music represented an impression rather than a description of a day in the country, and this despite the birdcalls and the electric storm in the score. Schoenberg, who was opposed to representational music, nevertheless yielded to the importunities of his publishers in authorising romantic titles for the individual movements of his *Five Orchestral Pieces*.

On the other hand, Stravinsky's latter-day denial that his early *Scherzo fantastique* was inspired by his reading of Maeterlinck's *La Vie des Abeilles* is puzzling. In Robert Craft's *Conversations with Igor Stravinsky,* in reply to the question about the subject matter of the work, Stravinsky replies unequivocally: "I wrote the *Scherzo* as a piece of pure symphonic music. The bees were a choreographer's idea … Some bad literature about bees was published on the fly-leaf of the score to satisfy my publisher who thought a 'story' would help to sell the music." This declaration was most unfair to the publisher and to the choreographer. In his own letters to Rimsky-Korsakov at the time of composition of the score (1907), published in Moscow in 1973, Stravinsky writes: "I intended to write a scherzo already in St. Petersburg, but I lacked subject matter. It so happens that I have been reading *La Vie des Abeilles* by Maeterlinck, a half-philosophical, half-poetic work, which captivated me completely. At first, I intended to use direct quotations so as to make the program of my piece quite clear, but then I realized that it would not do because in the book the scientific and poetic elements are closely interwoven. I decided therefore to guide myself by a definite programmatic design without actual quotations, and to entitle the work simply *The Bees,* after Maeterlinck, a fantastic scherzo."

In the nineteenth century America was, to all practical purposes, a German colony in instrumental music and an Italian colony in opera. Lillian Norton would have never made a singing career had she not changed her name to Nordica. Conductors had to be German or Austrian (Damrosch, Muck, Henschel, Nikisch, Mahler). Pianists prospered when their last names ended with "sky" or "ski." Paderewski was a shining example of grandeur and glory. (I myself profited peripherally when I entered the United States in 1923 exempt from the rigid quota imposed by the Immigration Office on Slavs and such, exception being made for "artists," particularly those whose names looked and sounded artistic.) Ethel Liggins, an Englishwoman, intent on making an American career was advised to change her name to Leginska ("ska" being the feminine counterpart of "ski"). She told me interesting stories about herself; among her many memories, she said that as a child she was bounced by Winston Churchill on his knee after his return as a hero from the Boer War. She volunteered her own date of birth, April 13, 1886, and I checked on it by securing her birth certificate; it was correct. Now, Churchill came home in glory in 1899, and since it is unlikely that he proceeded right away to bounce Liggins (not yet Leginska) on his knee, she must have reached a nubile adolescence at the time, and the whole episode assumed a totally different complexion. "Botheration!" she exclaimed when I pointed out the embarrassing chronology to her. "How do you know when Churchill returned to England from South Africa? You are not British!"

No greater splendor among contemporary orchestral conductors surrounded the career of Leopold Stokowski, who lived to be 95, working in music to the last days of his life. And his name ended in "ski"! Invidious rumors had it that his real name was Stokes, and that he polonized it as many other artists did. False! He was born in London, the son of a Polish cabinet maker named Kopernik Joseph Boleslaw Stokowski and an Irish woman Annie Marion Moore-Stokowski, on April 18, 1882. Not satisfied with his true half-Polish origin, he for some reason chose to maintain that he was totally Polish, born in Cracow in 1887 (rather than 1882), and that his name was Leopold Boleslawowicz Stokowski. This bit of fantasy appears in the main volume of *Riemann's Musik- Lexikon*. When I sounded the alarm, pointing out that the patronymic ending on "which" or "wicz" or "witch" is possible in Russian, but not in Polish, the *Riemann's* editors sent me a photostat copy of the original questionnaire in Stokowski's own hand embodying all this fanciful information. By way of rebuttal, I forwarded to the *Riemann's* people a copy of Stokowski's birth certificate which I had obtained from London. The 1975 supplement to *Riemann's* carries a corresponding correction.

Among many fantastic tales that accompany musical biographies there is one concerning Werner Egk. The name sounded like a manufactured logogriph, or an acronym for "ein guter Künstler," and even more self-anointed "ein genialer Künstler." I wrote to the director of the archives of the City of Augsburg where Egk was born, and elicited information that his real name was Mayer. If so, whence Egk? The composer himself came forward with an explanation that was more puzzling than the original riddle: he changed his name from Mayer to Egk after his marriage to Elisabeth Karl; the initials of her first and last name formed the outer letters of Egk, and the middle "g" was added "for euphony." Guttural euphony?

No experience in my "harmless drudgery" equaled the Case of Walter Dahms, an obscure German author of musical biographies. According to musical lexika that listed his name, including *Baker's*, he went to Rome in 1922, and promptly vanished. I did not care to leave him dangling like an unshriven ghost, an elusive zombie. I used to mention Dahms to every musicologist I met as a disappearing act, and one of them told me that there was nothing mysterious about Dahms, that he went to Lisbon, Portugal, adopted a Portuguese-sounding pseudonym and continued publishing books on music. I inserted this seemingly innocuous bit of information in my 1965 Supplement to *Baker's*, but unbeknownst to myself it unleashed a fantastic chain of events. The editors of the Supplement to *Riemann's Musik-Lexikon* who were also interested to bring Dahms up to date seized upon my addendum and inquired through Santiago Kastner, London-born German-educated music scholar resident in Lisbon, to find out facts about Dahms. But no one in the rather flourishing German colony in Lisbon, not even anyone at the German Embassy, knew anything about Dahms. The *Riemann* editors would not be pacified. "Baker (really Slonimsky)," they wrote Kastner again, "is greatly valued here because of its reliability. Behind the bland statement that Dahms was still in Lisbon in 1960 must lie a lot of painstaking research." Kastner volunteered a guess that Dahms may be a German-speaking Portuguese citizen named Gualterio Armando, Gualterio being a Portuguese form of Walter, and Armando containing three letters of the name Dahms. He addressed the question directly to Dahms, whether he was or was not Dahms. All hell broke loose thereafter. "I am not identical with anyone but myself," replied Gualterio Armando. "I have absolutely nothing to say about Herr W. D. mentioned in your letter because I know nothing about him. I hope that this will put an end to this whole business once and for all." Kastner reported his failure to the *Riemann's* editors, and announced that he was through with his investigation, but voiced his conviction that Dahms "must be identical with that ass

Gualterio Armando after all." Why was he so vehement in denying his real identity? He died on October 5, 1973, carrying the secret to his grave.

Among the unburied musical ghosts that haunted me through the years was Alois Minkus, an Austrian composer of operas and ballets who spent most of his career in Russia. For a hundred years, first under the Czars, then under the Soviets, his ballets never ceased to be the favorite numbers in the Russian ballet repertory. Not a year passed without my receiving an insistent inquiry from Russia and abroad as to the fate of Minkus after he left Russia in 1891. Some reference works have him dead in that year; others prolong his life until 1907, with the date accompanied by a parenthetical question mark. I must have written a dozen letters to various registries of vital statistics in Vienna on the supposition that Minkus returned to Vienna where he was born and died there. I did obtain his birth certificate ascertaining that he was born on March 23, 1826, rather than 1827 as most Russian and other music reference sources have it, but the Vienna archivists could tell me nothing as to his date of death. Then in the summer of 1976 I made one more half-hearted inquiry in Vienna. To my astonishment I got a clue that all death notices before 1939 were moved from the Stadtarchive, the Landesarchiv, and from the Vienna Rathaus and its numerous subdivisions to the corresponding parochial registries. Hot on the scent, I wrote to the proper Lutheran parish, and to my absolute joy of discovery I received a document certifying that Alois Minkus died at Gentzgasse 92 in Vienna, on December 7, 1917, in the 92nd year of his life, from pneumonia, and that his mortal remains were deposed at the cemetery of Döbling. I immediately rushed this information and the pertinent documentation to the editors of the big Russian musical encyclopedia which had just reached the letter M, and the date got in at the last moment before going to press, with an appropriate proud parenthetical clause testifying to its authenticity.

One of the most fantastic episodes in my hunt for missing musical persons was the search for Heinrich Hammer, German conductor and composer who emigrated to the United States about the turn of the century, and then vanished from the musical scene. I appealed for help to William Lichtenwanger, who combines profound erudition with a detective flair that would have made him a rich man had he dedicated himself to the search for missing heirs and holders of unused bank accounts. Quick as a panther, he produced a clipping from *The Los Angeles Times* of October 25, 1953, which carried on its society page a photograph of Heinrich Hammer, 91, and his young bride Arlene, 22. Their address was given in the story, but when I wrote to him my letter came back with the notation "Deceased." But when and where? Lichtenwanger got on the telephone, and after a few inquiries got hold of Hammer's son, a repair worker of the California telephone company. Unbelievably, contact was established with him atop a telephone pole, and he gave Lichtenwanger the needed information. Hammer had moved to Phoenix, Arizona, where he died on October 28, 1954, just a year after his marriage.

* * * * * * *

How much of personal life ought to be reported in a dignified biographical dictionary? Volumes have been written speculating about the identity of Beethoven's "Immortal Beloved," even though the famous letter addressed to her was never sent off. Should a biographer be so bold as to doubt a great man's own confession of love? A conscientious biographer took exception to Goethe's declaration that he had never loved anyone as much as Lili Schönemann. "Here the great Goethe errs," he commented: "His greatest love was Frederike Drion." From the sublime to contemporary love lore. The formidable Hungarian pianist Nyiregyhazi was married nine times, and admitted to 65 extra-marital liaisons. Is this proper information in a biographical dictionary? The marriages, perhaps; the liaisons, only famous ones, like Liszt's and Chopin's.

It was only recently that the known homosexuality of Tchaikovsky became a matter of open discussion in his biographies; first inkling of it appeared in the preface to the 1934 edition of Tchaikovsky's correspondence with his benefactress Madame von Meck. In 1940 a collection of his letters to the family, including those to his brother and biographer Modest who was also a homosexual, was published in Russia, but it was soon withdrawn from publication and became a sort of bibliographical phantom; an expurgated edition was published later. In subsequent books on Tchaikovsky published in Russia the matter is unmentioned. But a strange mass of unfounded rumors began circulating both in Russia and abroad shortly after Tchaikovsky's death that he committed a "suicide by cholera," that he deliberately drank unboiled water during a raging cholera epidemic in St. Petersburg, and this despite his fear of cholera which had been the cause of his mother's death. The stories that I heard during my visit to Russia in 1962 were right out of Gothic horror tales. It seems that Tchaikovsky became involved in a homosexual affair with a young member of the Russian Imperial family, and that when Czar Alexander III got wind of it, he served the Tchaikovsky family an ultimatum: either have Tchaikovsky take poison, or have him tried for sodomy and sent to Siberia. Tchaikovsky accepted the verdict, and with the connivance of his personal physician Dr. Bertenson, was given a poison that produced symptoms similar to those of cholera. As additional evidence that Tchaikovsky did not die of cholera, the proponents of this theory argue, was the fact that his body was allowed to lie in state and that several of his intimates kissed him on the mouth, as the Russian death ritual allows, whereas cholera victims were buried in zinc-lined sealed coffins to prevent contagion.

Dramatic deaths should rightly be noted in biographies, but grisly details had better be left out. It is not advisable to follow the type of reporting exemplified in an obituary of Sir Armine Woodhouse in *The Annual Register of London* for the year 1777, noting that his death "was occasioned by a fishbone in his throat."

Percy A. Scholes took credit for sending the British writer on music, Arthur Eaglefield Hull, to his death under the wheels of a train. He wrote me: "Hull's suicide was the result of my exposure of his thefts in his book *Music, Classical, Romantic and Modern*. He threw himself under a train."

A suicide directly connected with a musical composition was that of Rezsö Seress, Hungarian author of the sad, sad song "Gloomy Sunday." At one time the playing of the tune was forbidden in Central Europe because it drove several impressionable people to suicide. Seress himself jumped out the window, on a Monday, not gloomy Sunday.

Musical murders are surprisingly few; singers are occasionally murdered out of jealousy, but not famous singers. The most spectacular murder, never conclusively solved, was that of the French eighteenth-century musician Jean Marie Leclair, stabbed to death in his own house. Since nothing was taken, it could not have been a burglary. I proposed a theory that he was done to death by his estranged wife who was a professional engraver and publisher of some of Leclair's music, and had sharp tools at her disposal, but my painstaking argumentation in favor of this theory was pooh-poohed by the foremost French music historian Marc Pincherle and others.

* * * * * * *

Dementia, insanity and bodily disintegration are scourges that hit many composers, and in most cases they were caused by syphilis. Undoubtedly, the tragic illnesses of Schumann, Smetana, Hugo Wolf and MacDowell were all caused by the lues, the *morbus gallicus* as it was usually described in the past centuries. In his book on Delius, Sir Thomas Beecham remarks ruefully that the goddess Aphrodite Pandemos repaid Delius cruelly for his lifelong worship at her altar. Delius died blind and paralyzed.

In light of recent disclosures, free from displaced piety for a great man, it appears that Beethoven, too, was the victim of syphilis. His deafness was only a symptom (as in the case of Smetana) which does not necessarily indicate a venereal infection. But there are too many other circumstances that lead to this sad conclusion, recounted in the recent study by Dieter Kerner, *Krankheiten grosser Musiker*.

Even the worshipful speculation as to psychological causes of physical decline and death, so cherished in old-fashioned biography, has no place in a book of reference. I brushed aside such probings into a person's psyche as found in an old entry on the eighteenth-century French composer Isouard, to the effect that he was so deeply "mortified" by his failure to be elected to the French Academy that "although a married man," he abandoned work, "plunged into dissipation, and died."

Triskaidecaphobia, an irrational fear of number 13, demonstrably affected the state of mind of two great composers, Rossini and Schoenberg. In addition to his superstition about the malevolent character of 13, Rossini was also fearful of Friday. He died on November 13, 1868, which was a Friday. Numerologists could cite his case to prove predestination. Schoenberg's case is remarkable because there is so much recent evidence that his triskaidecaphobia was not a whimsical pose. He was born on the 13th of the month of September in 1874, and he regarded it ominous in his personal destiny. He sometimes avoided using 13 in numbering the bars of his works. When he realized that the title of his work *Moses und Aaron* contained 13 letters, he crossed out the second "a" in Aaron, even though the spelling Aron can not be substantiated either in German or in English. When someone thoughtlessly remarked to him on his 76th birthday that $7 + 6 = 13$, he seemed genuinely upset; he died at that age. On his last day of life, July 13, 1951, he remarked to his wife that he would be all right if he would survive the ominous day, but he did not, and died.

* * * * * * *

Going over my list of *morituri,* centenarians or near-centenarians, I came upon the name of Victor Küzdö, a Hungarian-American violinist born, or so the old edition of *Baker's* said, in 1869. I wrote to Küzdö at his last known address which I found in an old musical directory, in effect asking him whether he was living or dead. A few days later I received from him a dictated postcard saying that, although practically blind, he was still alive and well in Glendale, California. Furthermore, he took the opportunity to correct his date of birth: he was born in 1863, not in 1869, and had shortly before celebrated his 100th anniversary! But this was not the end of the story; soon afterwards I got a letter from a real-estate man in Glendale notifying me that Küzdö was in the habit of diminishing his age, and that he was actually 103, not 100! How could he be sure? Simple: he was a numerologist. When the inevitable end came to Küzdö on February 24, 1966, his death certificate gave his age as 106. He was born in 1859, not in 1860, not in 1869.

The most remarkable woman centenarian on my list was Margaret Ruthven Lang, of the Boston musical dynasty of Lang, who died at the age of 104 in 1972. She was a regular symphony goer since the early days of the Boston Symphony. On her 100th birthday the orchestra played the hymn *Old Hundred* in her honor. The Russian-French singer Marie Olénine d'Alheim lived to be 100. Among other recent centenarians was the French conductor and composer Henri-Paul Busser who died in 1973 at the age of 101.

It would be most interesting to compile actuarial tables of life expectancy of musicians according to their specialties. One thing appears certain: great musicians die young; consider Mozart, Schubert, Chopin, Mendelssohn, Scriabin. It is a fascinating speculation to project Mozart's life from 1756 into 1840, and Schubert's life to an even later date! One may indulge in a revery that very great musicians are summoned to Heaven because they would be more at home there.

Statistically speaking, organists live the longest lives, perhaps because their sedentary occupation keeps them from wasting their energy on idle pastimes. Scholars and pedagogues come next in longevity; conductors are fairly durable, too; among instrumentalists, those handling big instruments, like the double bass or trombone, live longer than violinists who in turn live longer than flutists and oboe players who are apt to be frail in physique. Among singers, tenors dissipate their vitality faster than bass singers. In all musical categories mediocrities outlive great artists by a large margin.

* * * * * * *

In addition to all the troubles involved in the compilation of a biographical dictionary, there are people who concoct sinister plots to further bamboozle the proverbial "harmless drudge." Mikhail Goldstein, a respectable Russian violinist, annoyed by his unfair treatment by the Soviet Music Publishing House in systematically rejecting his compositions, decided to take revenge on them. He invented a Russian composer named Ovsianiko-Kulikovsky, furnished him with a plausible biography, obtained a quantity of old manuscript paper and composed a symphony in his name, pretending that he found the score in the archives of the Odessa Conservatory where he was librarian at the time. The Soviets swallowed the bait and published the score, proclaiming it to be a major discovery; it was also recorded, and greeted with enthusiastic reviews, not only in Russia but elsewhere. (Shall I confess, blushingly? I reviewed the recording for *The Musical Quarterly*, and announced with some reservations that if the work were genuine it would be the first Russian symphony ever written.) A doctoral dissertation was published on the work. When Goldstein admitted the hoax, he was accused of trying to appropriate an important piece of national legacy. The situation degenerated into a farce, and Goldstein got out of Russia as soon as he could get an exit visa. But, as in Prokofiev's *Lieutenant Kije*, it was too late to kill off Ovsianiko-Kulikovsky, and his symphony is still listed in some record catalogues and is kept on the shelves of music libraries.

An even more dangerous mystification was perpetrated by the eminent Italian music scholar Alberto Cametti who claimed discovery of an important biographical notebook of Palestrina, which established the elusive exact date of Palestrina's birth. He said he purchased the document from one Telemaco Bratti, and even went to the trouble of reproducing, or rather forging, part of the manuscript in an article he wrote on the subject. Another Italian music scholar Raffaele Casimiri embraced the "discovery" as a gift of God to all true Palestrinologists. Then Alberto Cametti let it pass through various channels that the name of the alleged discoverer of the document, Telemaco Bratti, was an anagram of Alberto Cametti. A great inner storm ensued in the confined company of Italian music scholars, but in the meantime the hoax found its way into reputable bibliographies. (It was thanks to a knowledgeable friend that I myself did not fall into the trap in giving the exact date of Palestrina's birth in my edition of *Baker's*; this date remains unknown to this day.)

* * * * * * *

It is amazing that grown men and women would deliberately falsify their vital statistics, particularly their dates of birth, in order to appear younger in a reference work. The gambit is understandable among actresses and prima donnas; and it has been said that a woman has the privilege of improvising her age. It would also be understandable for men in their dotage who marry girls in their nonage, but both men and women of music rejuvenate themselves lexicographically even when they are not stage performers.

The Spanish composer Oscar Esplá produced his passport to prove to me that he was born in 1888 and not in 1886 as I had it in *Baker's*. But I had obtained a copy of his birth certificate which confirmed the accuracy of the earlier date.

Mabel Daniels, the Boston composer, once included in a piece a C-sharp against C, explaining that she "had to use a dissonance," since she was living in the same town with me. She petulantly accused me of being "no gentleman" in putting her down as born in 1878 rather than 1879, her own chosen year. She was born in November 1878, just a few weeks away from 1879, so why should I not accept the later year, she pleaded. Poor Mabel! She lived a full life until well into her tenth decade, dying in 1971.

A desire to appear young, if only on paper, is not a modern phenomenon. Since time immemorial, musicians, poets, painters, actors, even politicians, exercised their unquestionable prerogative to fib about their age. Johann Jakob Froberger gave the date of May 18, 1620 as that of his birth to his physician, but his certificate of baptism reveals that he was baptized on May 19, 1616. It is a reasonable assumption that the day and the month of his birth, as given by himself, were correct, and that he was baptized on the next day, in 1616, not 1620.

In his handwritten autobiographical note for Mattheson's *Grundlage einer Ehrenpforte*, Telemann stated that he was born in 1682, whereas he was born a year earlier; as in many such cases, the day and the month of his birth, March 14, were given correctly.

The Italian composer and conductor Angelo Mariani, who was born on October 11, 1821, insisted in his communications to Francesco Regli, editor of an Italian biographical dictionary, that he was born on October 11, 1824. Mariani's birth certificate proves that he was born in 1821.

It was common practice in Catholic families to give identical Christian names to infants born after the death of a previous son, or a daughter, so as to perpetuate the memory of the lost child. This has led to a number of mistaken identities. The bicentennial of Giovanni Battista Viotti was widely celebrated in 1953, commemorating the birth in Fontanetto, Italy, of an infant of that name born on May 23, 1753, who died in the following year, on July 10, 1754. On May 12, 1755, another child was born to the Viottis and was given the names Giovanni Battista Guglielmo Domenico, retaining the first two names from those of their deceased son. This second similarly-named child was the composer whose bicentennial was celebrated two years early.

Biographical notices for Giacomo Insanguine found in old music dictionaries list his year of birth variously between 1712 and 1742. I applied for a copy of his birth certificate from the registries of his native town of Monopoli, and received a document purporting to show that he was born in 1712, a date that did not seem to agree with the known facts of his education and career. I pressed for further search, which revealed that a Giacomo Insanguine who was born in 1712 died in 1726 at the age of 14. On March 22, 1728, a boy was born to the bereaved parents, and was given the names Giacomo Antonio Francesco Paolo Michele. This was the composer Insanguine.

Beethoven was eager to prove that he was born in 1772, not in 1770, and that he had an older brother who was born in 1770. It was discovered that a Ludwig Maria van Beethoven was born on April 1, 1769, but he died a few days later. The great Beethoven was born in the following year.

Next to birth certificates, the best sources of information are family bibles, marriage certificates and school registries. The date of birth of Kaspar Othmayr, March 12, 1515, is verified by his astrological chart, and one can be sure that in those remote times no one would hoodwink one's own astrologer. Even in modern times there are practicing astrologers among composers; of these, Dane Rudhyar is professionally the most successful.

In one famous event the correct age of the protagonist became a matter of life or death. On June 28, 1914, Gavrilo Princip, a young Serbian patriot, assassinated Crown Prince Franz Ferdinand of Austria. His act precipitated World War I, which precipitated the Russian Revolution, which precipitated the rise of Hitler, which precipitated World War II, etc., etc., etc. According to the Austrian law of the time no person less than twenty years of age could be executed for a capital crime. Gavrilo Princip was born on July 25, 1894, according to the Gregorian calendar, and was not quite twenty when he turned the world upside down. This saved him from execution, and he died in prison of tuberculosis of the bone marrow on April 28, 1918.

Oscar Wilde was not so lucky in his own chronology. He had whittled two years off his true age, claiming that he was born in 1856, whereas his real year of birth was 1854. Owing to a peculiar twist of English law, persons under forty indicted for immorality were granted leniency. Oscar Wilde was arrested for sodomy in 1895, and would have benefited by the law had it not been for the prying investigation of the court clerk who secured Wilde's birth certificate proving that he was over forty at the time of his offense. This precluded leniency, and Wilde got a severe sentence. Despite the availability of the correct date, the *Encyclopaedia Britannica* carried the 1856 date in its article on Oscar Wilde right through its thirteenth edition. The

Century Cyclopedia still gives the wrong date.

Much confusion is created in musical biography by the discrepancy in dating past events according to the Russian and Western calendars. The Greek Orthodox Church refused to accept the Gregorian calendar, and continued to use the Julian calendar until 1918. The Julian calendar was also in force in Bulgaria and Rumania during the same period. As a result, the dating of Russian births and deaths lagged behind the Western calendar, by 11 days in the 18th century, 12 days in the 19th century and 13 days in the 20th century. (The increase in discrepancy was caused by the fact that the years 1800 and 1900 were leap-years in Russia but not in the West.) Stravinsky was born on June 5, 1882, according to the Julian calendar, which corresponded to June 17 of the Western calendar. But after 1900, when the difference between the two calendars increased by a day, he began celebrating his birthday on June 18. As his 80th anniversary approached in June 1962, he let it be known that he was going to celebrate it on June 18, which gave occasion to *The New York Times* to say that the faces of some lexicographers would be red on June 18, Stravinsky's preferred date for his birth, seeing that most dictionaries, including two edited by me, gave this date as June 17. I sent a rebuttal explaining my reasons for sticking to the June 17 date, and *The New York Times* published it under the caption, "It Is All Clear Now." This aroused Stravinsky's anger, and he shot off a wire to the paper reasserting his prerogative to celebrate his birthday on any date he wished. He declared his intention to mark the date in the twenty-first century on June 19, assuming that the difference between the two calendars would continue to increase a day each century, but he overlooked the fact that the year 2000 will be a leap year according to both Gregorian and Julian calendars, because Pope Gregory ruled on the advice of learned astronomers that the year divisible by 400 must be reckoned as a leap year.

* * * * * * *

Are trivia worth mentioning in a biographical dictionary? It all depends. If such trivia have significant bearing on the subject's life and career, they should be given consideration. The unique case of the male castrato Tenducci who eloped with a young girl and subsequently married her, deserves comment to dispel incredulity. He was a triorchis, and was therefore capable of marriage even after he was two-thirds castrated. His wife wrote a book of memoirs on the affair.

There remain a few categories that ought to be dealt with in separate rubrics.

INCLUSION AND EXCLUSION. *Baker's Biographical Dictionary of Musicians* must necessarily include men and women active in music who were not professional musicians, such as aristocratic patrons and patronesses, wealthy promoters of musical events, impresarios, music publishers, ballet masters who played important roles in commissioning and performing works from composers, and of course music critics. A practical criterion for including names of little-known composers, performers and pedagogues should be the degree of likelihood that a music student, or a concert goer, or a person who wants to know who is who in music would look it up in a dictionary. Thousands of names hover in the perifery of the music world and many more populate the index pages of biographies of famous composers. Still more are modest members of world orchestras who have distinguished themselves in various ways. Hugo Leichtentritt told me that Riemann, with whom he studied, used to play chamber music with amateurs and professionals at his home in Leipzig, and after each session, would ask them to fill out questionnaires for inclusion in his *Musik-Lexikon*. Theodore Baker, the compiler of the original edition of the present dictionary, collected biographical data from his friends who played in the Boston Symphony Orchestra. As a result, the early editions of both lexica became over-populated with individuals who were perfectly honorable practitioners of their art, but who failed to leave an indelible, or even delible, mark on the sands of music. Most of these long-dead servants of music, whether borrowed by Baker from Riemann and other collectors of musical flesh, or installed anew by Baker and his successors out of personal friendship, have been allowed in the present edition to remain under their individual lexicographical tombstones for humanitarian reasons, rather than relegated to the common graves of crumbling newspaper clippings in public libraries; still, the paragraphs devoted to them originally have been mercifully cut down to commensurate size. No more will the impatient user of the dictionary be offered long lines of printed matter dealing with this or that obscure orchestral player, church organist or provincial music teacher, relating in stultifying detail the advancement of their dull careers. But musical, or even unmusical, figures that multidentally smile on us from huge posters or gold-rimmed record albums, the glamorized purveyors of popular subculture of whatever degree of vulgarity, the Beatles and other singing coleoptera, are welcomed to this edition of *Baker's* even more liberally than they were to the 1958 edition and to the 1965 and 1971 supplements. When, overcoming a natural revulsion, I dictated to my California secretary a paragraph on Humperdinck, the pop singer whose manager had the supreme *chutzpah* to appropriate the honored name of the composer of *Hänsel und Gretel* because it sounded "funny" and would attract attention, she was genuinely surprised at my liberality, but revealed her complete ignorance as to the existence of an earlier musician of the same name as the glorified rock singer.

DATES OF PERFORMANCE. A determined effort has been made in the present edition to list as many exact dates as possible of first performances of major works, especially operas and symphonies, not only by celebrated masters but also by modern composers. Care had to be taken to avoid duplication, for many composers are, and have been, in the habit of changing the titles of their works and then presenting them as new compositions. For instance, Don Emilio Arrieta y Corera wrote an opera, *La Conquista de Granada,* which was produced in Madrid in 1850 and revived under the title *Isabel la Católica* in 1855. The opera got a double billing in the valuable compilation *Cronica de la Opera italiana en Madrid* published in 1878, the index of which correctly lists the two titles interchangeably, but this precaution has failed to deter other publications from duplicating the work. Quite often, composers append an optional descriptive title to an earlier work, which is apt to be duplicated in the catalogue.

SPELLING OF NAMES. Variants of spelling of celebrated musical names cause uncertainty, and choice had to be made in the present edition of *Baker's* guided by common usage; alternative spellings are then cross-referenced. Spanish, Portuguese and Latin American names commonly include both the paternal and maternal surname; a selection has to be made according to preferred usage. Thus, Alejandro García Caturla is listed under Caturla, the name he used in his published works; Oscar Lorenzo Fernandez is listed under Fernandez. In some instances, a musician changes the form of his name in the middle of his career. In the earlier editions of this dictionary the main entry on Edmund Rubbra appeared under Duncan-Rubbra; Duncan was the name of his first wife, which he adopted in some of his works; later he reverted to the legal name Rubbra, which is therefore used in the present edition of *Baker's.* Philip Heseltine published most of his music under the witching surname Peter Warlock, but Heseltine would seem preferable for a biographical dictionary. Americanization has produced several changes in the spelling of names; Arnold Schoenberg changed the spelling of his last name from Schönberg to Schoenberg when he emigrated to the United States. Carlos Salzedo dropped the acute accent that marked the antepenultimate letter of his original name. Eugen Zádor dropped the accent and changed his first name to Eugene when he came to America. Aladár Szendrei made his career in Europe under his original Hungarian name and surname, but changed it phonetically to Sendrey when he emigrated to the United States; a cross-reference has been made in the present edition under Sendrey to his original name. Edgar Varèse was baptized as Edgard Varèse, but most of his works were published with the first name spelled Edgar; in 1940 or thereabouts he changed it back to his legal name Edgard. However, the present edition of *Baker's* keeps the familiar form Edgar. The existence of alternate spellings Carl and Karl in many German names creates considerable confusion. The 1958 edition of *Baker's* modernized virtually all Carls to Karls, with some curious results, such as the spelling Karl Philipp Emanuel Bach instead of the standard Carl; the traditional spelling has been restored in the present edition. A curious case is that of Carl Ruggles, the American composer, whose real first name was Charles. He changed it to Carl as a youth when he decided to devote himself to music; he hoped that the Germanic form of the name would give him a better chance to succeed in the highly German-minded musical world of early twentieth-century America.

NOBILIARY PARTICLES. Early in this century it was common in American and British usage to put the nobiliary particle "von" in front of German names, such as "Von Bülow" and the like. In the wake of World War I the "von" became unpopular among the Allied nations. The original full name of the English composer Gustav Holst, who was of Swedish ancestry, was Von Holst. During the war, at the suggestion of Percy A. Scholes, he dropped the objectionable "von" from his name. Anton von Webern eliminated the "von" after the fall of the Austro-Hungarian Empire in 1918; the present edition lists his name under Webern, Anton von, in appreciation of the fact that he used the full name in titles of many of his early works. A more difficult problem is encountered in the Dutch and Flemish nobiliary particle Van. Beethoven was very proprietary about his own "van" and regarded it as a proof of his noble origin, an important claim at the time when he tried to assure the guardianship of his nephew. The French and Spanish "de" and the Italian "di" often become coalesced with the last name. Debussy was Bussy to friends in his youth; Madame von Meck, the patroness of Tchaikovsky, who employed Debussy as a house musician and teacher in Moscow, referred to him as Bussy. No book of reference would list Bussy as an alternative for Debussy, but in some other names, not necessarily French, this nobiliary particle retains its independent existence. De Koven is an example. But De Falla is improper; his name should be listed under Falla, Manuel de.

RUSSIAN NAMES. The Russian alphabet has two untractable letters: one is represented by the Cyrillic symbol "ЬΙ," the other by a fence of three sticks with a line underneath it, and a wriggle, or a cedilla, on the right of the protracted horizontal line. Only Turkish has the phonetic equivalent of "ЬΙ," represented by an undotted "i" in the new Turkish alphabet. As for the second Cyrillic symbol aforementioned, it can be very adequately represented by the coalescence of the sounds "sh" and "ch" in a compound word such as fish-chips. The Russian sound for "e" is palatalized into "yeh" as in the now accepted English spelling of Dostoyevsky. English and American music dictionaries have inherited the spelling of Russian names of composers and performers from German, which has no "ch" sound, and in which the Russian (and English) "v" sound is represented by "w." As a result, we had Tschaikowsky for at least half a century. British and American librarians, realizing that Tsch=Ch, began spelling Tchaikovsky as Chaikovsky. But if we follow phonetics, then why do we need the diphthong "ai"? Why not plain "i" as in China? Here we come to the antinomy of sound, sight and audio-visual association: Chikovsky has an impossible look. A compromise is necessary: hence, Tchaikovsky in *Baker's*. "Ch" in Rachmaninoff has a guttural German sound that English does not possess. The spelling Rachmaninoff is part-German ("ch") and part-French ("ff"), but this is the way he signed his name, familiar from printed music and concert programs. Most British sources prefer Rakhmaninov.

Once we start on the road to phonetics we will be bound for disaster. The name of the poet Evtushenko is pronounced Yevtushenko, but the eye rebels against its aspect. Besides, an unpalatalized "e" in such an initial sound is not necessarily un-Russian; some people from the northern provinces or from Siberia would say Evtushenko, just as if it were written in English. Another thing: the final diphthong "iy," as it is often represented phonetically in names like Tchaikovsky (or for that matter in Slonimsky), is nearest to the French "ille" in "volaille," but it is not as emphatically articulated. There is no reason to add ugliness to a name like Tchaikovsky by spelling it Tchaikovskiy. Then there is the vexing problem of transliterating Russian names of French or German origin back into their original languages. Some music dictionaries transliterate Cui as Kyue, a visual monstrosity.

Cui was the son of a Napoleonic soldier who remained in Russia after the campaign of 1812 and married a Russian woman. His French name Cui ought to stay. The Soviet composer Shnitke (spelled phonetically in English) was of German origin, and his father signed his name in German as Schnittke; this spelling ought to remain even in an English reference work. The same consideration holds for names like Schneerson (Jewish-German) or Steinpress (pronounced Shteinpress in Russian) and Steinberg (for Shteinberg). If we try to transliterate foreign names in Russian back and forth, we will arrive at mutations such as Betkhoven and (yes, unbelievable but true) Poochcheenee, used for a time in the bibliography of *Notes*. I am proud to say that I opened such a vigorous letter-writing campaign against this practice that it was stopped. To conclude, the transliteration of Russian names and Russian titles of works should be guided by ear and by sight. There are seasonal changes and fashions for some Russian names. It used to be Sergey, Bolshoy Theater, etc. Now it is Sergei, Bolshoi, etc. Both visually and phonetically, these altered spellings are fine. In this edition of *Baker's* the paternal names have been omitted in listings of Russian composers, except in that of Piotr Ilyich Tchaikovsky which has become traditional. The pronunciation of Russian names has been indicated only when mispronunciation is common, as for instance in Balakirev (stress on the second syllable, not the third), Borodin (stress on the last syllable). The pronunciation of Khachaturian's name, with the accent on the third syllable, has become so common that it would be idle to try to change it to the proper pronunciation with the accent on the last syllable; equally futile would it be to persuade people to compress the last two vowels into one: "yan." The doubling of "s" between vowels in Russian names such as Mussorgsky is admittedly Germanic in origin; but in seeking to avoid the vocalization of the middle "s" in Mussorgsky the doubling of "s" becomes essential. Thus it is Mussorgsky rather than Musorgsky, Vassily rather than Vasily; but in less familiar names like Stasov, a single "s" is postulated. Illogical? So is the language itself.

GEOGRAPHIC NAMES. Place names have been playing musical chairs during the wars and revolutions of the first half of the present century. I was born in St. Petersburg, left Petrograd in 1918, and revisited Leningrad in 1962. One can travel from Pressburg to Bratislava to Pozsony without budging an inch. A person born in Klausenburg finds himself nominally transferred to Kolozsvár and then to Cluj without moving from one's house. Sometimes a town renamed to honor a current revolutionary figure resumes its original name when the eponymous hero falls into disfavor. Perm was renamed Molotov after the Soviet Revolution, but became Perm once more when Molotov faded out in 1956. In Poland, Katowice was named Stalinogorod in 1953 but became Katowice once more in 1956 when Stalin was posthumously disfranchised. In all such cases, common sense is the only guide in tracing the movements of a biographical subject. Then there is Liège. For over a century it bore an unnatural acute accent over its middle letter. In 1946 its Municipal Council resolved that the accent should be changed to the grave one. A Belgian musician born in a town with an acute accent may die there with a grave.

ABBREVIATIONS. All abbreviations except the obvious ones, like vol., prof., symph. orch., etc., and the names of the months (except March and April, which remain unabbreviated) have been eliminated from this edition. No more the impenetrable jungle of Ztsch. Vsch., vcs., mvt. or Kgl.

BIBLIOGRAPHY. In listing sources of information pertaining to the subject of an entry, a conscientious bibliographer ought to use common sense. It would serve no rational purpose to cite general histories of music for references to Bach, Mozart or Beethoven in the bibliographical section; obviously each of such books will have extended chapters on great masters of music. But in bibliographies on modern composers, it is worthwhile to mention collections of articles containing informative material relating to such composers. The same consideration would apply to books on great conductors, great instrumentalists, or great singers; they ought to be listed if they contain useful biographical information. Magazine articles of extensive length are also proper bibliographical material. Title pages are sometimes deceptive.

A brochure on Louis-Gilbert Duprez by A. A. Elwart bears the claim on its title page "avec une biographie authentique de son maître A. Choron." Upon examination, it turns out that it contains only a couple of pages on Choron. On the other hand, there are books modestly titled that provide a wealth of biographical information not available in special monographs on the subject. Since it is patently impractical to append an evaluation of each bibliographical item in a book of general reference, a reader's attention can be called to a particularly valuable publication by a word or two, such as "important," "of fundamental value," etc. Conversely, a warning should be given against worthless publications of a biographical nature that for some reason have become widely read. A famous, or infamous, example is a purported book of memoirs attributed to the nineteenth-century German prima donna Wilhelmina Schröder-Devrient and duly listed under her name in the bibliography of a number of respectable music dictionaries. It is a mildly pornographic (as pornography went at the time of its publication a hundred years ago) volume recounting her amours with famous people. It was made available in German and French; there is even a French edition in existence illustrated with erotic drawings. Less obvious in intent, but much more harmful in its effect, is the notorious correspondence between Chopin and Potocka manufactured by a Polish woman in 1945 and broadcast over the Warsaw Radio during the first months after the liberation of Poland from Nazi occupation. Respectable music scholars and Chopinologists eagerly accepted these letters, which portrayed Chopin as a sex maniac given to verbal obscenities, as genuine. In one of Chopin's alleged letters he is made to use a sexual pun on a vulgar Polish word that was not in use until 1900; and there were other indecencies. The poor woman who concocted these letters committed suicide, but even then some people refused to give up their faith in the authenticity of this clumsy forgery.

Archaic spelling of the titles of old books is preserved in the present edition of *Baker's*. Martin Agricola's work, *Ein deudsche Musica*, retains its ancient title. Varieties of spelling in different editions of old English books are indicated, as in Christopher Simpson's *Practicall Musick*. Inordinately long book titles are abbreviated unless they contain some specific limiting clauses. For instance, Karl Grunsky's volume, *Die Technik des Klavierauszuges entwickelt am dritten Akt von Wagners Tristan und Isolde,* treats the problem of piano reduction only of the third act of *Tristan,* and it would be misleading to list it as *Die Technik des Klavierauszuges* plain and simple. In all such cases, practical sense rather than pedantic considerations should guide the compiler.

POLTERGEIST. Typographical errors are not just human failures of perception. They are acts of a malevolent mischievous spirit that lays its eggs in the linotype ribbon. Or else how are we to account for alterations that are obviously intended as mockery? Such fanciful conceits as "scared music," "pubic rectal," or "anals of music" cannot be accidents endemic to the typesetter. Avaunt! Avaunt! (Memo to proofreader: typos intentional to illustrate the dreadful dangers in writing books; do not change to "sacred music," "public recital" and "annals of music.")

I have a recurrent dream: I am in the dock facing a trio of stern judges vaguely resembling my school teachers of long ago, about to hear a sentence pronounced upon me for incompetence, negligence, dereliction of duty, fraudulent pretense at lexicographical expertise. The judges exhibit grotesquely enlarged entries from my edition of *Baker's*, engraved on huge slabs of granite, as evidence against me. In my anguish I plead extenuating circumstances. Yes, I was guilty of procrastination, sloth, accidie, pigritude (a lovely old word for laziness), stupidity perhaps, but did I not try? Did I not get from Naples the birth certificates of 13 Enrico Carusos before giving up? Did I not locate Edward Maryon in England after his publisher told me he had been dead for years? Maryon bequeathed to me his manuscripts and other memorabilia, going back to the seventeenth century (he was of nobility; his full name was Maryon d'Aulby), which were sent to me in a huge trunk by his executors after his death. I donated the materials to the Boston Public Library.

At least one living composer showed kindness to me in appreciation of my efforts to get his biography right (and failing), Ezra Sims of Massachusetts. I got his string quartets all mixed up in my 1971 Supplement to *Baker's,* and created a non-existent String Quartet No. 2, composed according to my mistaken impression in 1962. In an unparalleled act of forgiveness, Sims composed a piece scored for a quintet for winds and strings, called it String Quartet No. 2, dated it 1962, although he wrote it in 1974, and dedicated it to me so that I "may be now less in error."

De minimis non curat lex, says an old legal maxim. But still there are minutiae that ought to be attended to in a reference work. The title of Leoncavallo's most famous opera is *Pagliacci,* without the definite article, not *I Pagliacci.* The original manuscript score is in the Library of Congress in Washington, D.C., and the title page can be examined by any doubting person. But the bronze plaque underneath the precious relic bears the wrong title *I Pagliacci!* Aaron Copland's best known work *Lincoln Portrait* was listed in *Baker's* 1958 as *A Lincoln Portrait,* and Copland specifically pointed out to me that the score has no such indefinite article in its title. And yet the program of its very first performance carried an intrusive "A," and many symphony programs repeated the error.

* * * * * * *

My medulla oblongata, or whatever part of the brain controls lexicographical reflexes, overflows with gratitude to many unselfish people who have helped me in putting together the 1958 edition of *Baker's,* its two supplements, of 1965 and 1971, and, most importantly, the present swollen edition. First to be thanked are the multitudinous registrars, clerks and keepers of city or state archives all over the habitable world who have provided me with copies of birth and death certificates that have made it possible to establish correct chronology in the lives of thousands of musicians represented in *Baker's.* The editors of the *Riemann Musik-Lexikon* have most generously let me have hundreds of documents pertaining to musical biography and copies of a number of birth and death certificates which I had not had in my possession—a most extraordinary example of scholarly cooperation. Boris Steinpress, editor of the Soviet musical encyclopedia, patiently collected for me dates of first performances of Russian operas and symphonies and corrected numerous errors encountered in the articles on Russian composers in the previous editions of *Baker's.* Grigori Schneerson of Moscow was a great lexicographical and personal friend during many years of our correspondence. And there were many others in Russia and in other countries in Europe.

How can I thank William Lichtenwanger, that magus of musical, and not only musical, encyclopedias, the polynomial scholar who possesses in his head a cross-reference to all subjects biographical, historical and lexicographical? A polymath, a polyglot at home in all European languages, an enlightened opsimath in Russian and a philological connoisseur of Turkish and Japanese, he was willing to read and to critically annotate the galley proofs of the entire bulk of the present edition of *Baker's;* he got for me precious biographical data on *Baker* inmates who dwelt in the lexicographical nirvana for decades. To quote from James Joyce's "work in progress," written in bird language, "Have you *aviar* seen any*wing* to *eagle* it?" Lichtenwanger is unique.

Much as I welcome people volunteering corrections in *Baker's* and other lexicographical publications of which I have been in charge, I admit that I was somewhat startled when in August 1972 I received a letter from Stephen W. Ellis of Glenview, Illinois, in which he tore to pieces my 1971 Supplement to *Baker's,* sideswiping also at the basic 1958 volume. "Grossly incomplete," "flagrantly inaccurate," "absurd," "shockingly out of date," "sadly inadequate," "ridiculous," "disgraceful," and even "criminal," were some of his expletives. The 1971 Supplement must have been a "one-man job," he correctly surmised. But who *was* Stephen W. Ellis? I had never heard of him, and I could not find his name in any index of articles on music. Yet the man exhibited such precise knowledge of so many obscure items of music history and musical biography that he could not have been just an amateur. My first impulse was to respond with lofty indignation: "Sirrah! Do you realize that you are addressing one whom the *Penguin Dictionary of Music* called 'a modern prince of

xxxviii

musical lexicography,' and for whom Percy A. Scholes invoked, in a personal letter *(rubesco referens),* the famous lines of Goldsmith, 'and still the wonder grew that one small head could carry all he knew?' One, who ..." But I quickly cooled down, realizing how valuable Ellis could be for the completely new edition of *Baker's.* I wrote him with genuine curiosity, asking how on earth he could have collected such a mountain of information on music and musicians, which he dispensed with such certainty of his sources. I was sure he was not an academic person, I wrote him, but I guessed that he was a record collector, that he was about 42 years old, married, and had two children. I was right, as it turned out, that he was not a professional musicologist (no professional musicologist would possess such a variety of knowledge), that he was an ardent collector of records, and subscribed to bulletins issued by unions of composers all over the world. He was not 42, but only 30 years old at the time; yes, he was married, but had only one child (a second child came along soon). By profession, he was a copy reader for a small publishing house. A fortunate publishing house it was indeed! It did not take me long to persuade Ellis to help me in putting together the present edition of *Baker's;* in fact he was eager to help. His proofreading ability, I soon found out, was prodigious, but what was most remarkable, and what still astounds me, is his uncanny knack for digging up information about contemporary composers, in precise detail, and his perseverance in getting these data for *Baker's* from reluctant, recalcitrant and unwilling musicians. The wealth of information about modern Finns, Swedes, Norwegians and Danes which he was able to gather for me was truly comprehensive; he was comparably "teeming with the news," to borrow a phrase from Gilbert and Sullivan, about composers of Iceland, Japan, Belgium, Holland, Spain and Portugal; he seemed to be able to get more information about the musicians of Rumania than I could after my trip to Rumania in 1963; he was equally successful with Poles, Yugoslavs, Czechs and Bulgarians, not to mention Americans. His special contribution was information on hard-to-get Australians. All told, he sent me about 1250 biographies, each having a very complete list of works. I could not use all this material, and I had to cut down drastically on some catalogues of works. Inevitably, I had to use my own verbiage for the introductory paragraphs of each entry, but the hard core of information on hundreds of these contemporary composers from all lands under the lexicographical sun was furnished by Ellis.

My effusive thanks are owed to Samuel Sprince of Boston, Massachusetts. Like the Canadian Royal Mounties, he never failed to get his man; in this context, the man (or the woman) was some obscure musician whose opaque name made an insignificant blur on a page in an old edition of *Baker's* and who somehow remained unnoticed by subsequent editors. Still, such unfortunates had to be taken care of, dead or alive, to preserve the continuity of *Baker's* heritage. Sprince tracked down for me quite a number of such personages, most of them in a nursing home hovering between uncertain life and certain death. Several of them met their Maker without the benefit of an obituary, and were lost until some relative could be found to supply the missing obit. It is unfortunate that so many musicians die out of alphabetical order, so that when a dictionary is already half-printed, a *revenant* from the early part of the alphabet is apt to make a belated appearance. The entries under the early letters of the alphabet in the present edition of *Baker's* already constitute a sizable mortuary.

The following individuals and institutions have lent their most valuable assistance in preparing the present edition of *Baker's:*

Patsy Felch, Head Reference Librarian, and Don Roberts, Head Music Librarian, Northwestern University Music Library, Evanston, Illinois
Centre Belge de Documentation Musicale, Brussels
Per Olof Lundahl, Executive Secretary, Swedish Music Information Center, Stockholm
Bálint András Varga, Head of Promotion, Editio Musica Budapest, Budapest
Jarmo Sermilä, former Executive Secretary, Finnish Music Information Centre, Helsinki

Kimiko Shimbo, Secretary General, The Japan Federation of Composers, Tokyo

Rina Smits-Westhof, Librarian, Foundation Donemus, Amsterdam

Canadian Music Centre, Toronto

Timothy Rice, faculty of music, University of Toronto

Czechoslovak Music Information Centre, Prague

Magnhild Stoveland, Society of Norwegian Composers, Oslo

Secretaria de Estado da Comunicação Social, Lisbon

Union of Rumanian Composers, Bucharest

Iceland Music Information Centre, Reykjavik

Dimiter Christoff, Secretary General of the UNESCO International Music Council in Sofia, Bulgaria

Teresa Mochtak, Head of the Music Department, Polskie Wydawnictwo Muzyczne Edition, Warsaw

James Murdoch, National Director, Australia Music Centre, Ltd., Sydney

Wilhelm Hansen Edition, Copenhagen

Esperanza Pulido, editor, *Heterofonía*, Mexico City

Hellenic Association for Contemporary Music, Athens

Instituto de Cultura Puertorriqueña, San Juan

Benjamin Bar-Am, Secretary, League of Composers in Israel, Tel Aviv

I conclude this rather inflated preface, as I did my 1971 Supplement to *Baker's*, with a cherished quotation from a letter I received from Alfred Einstein shortly before his death. In his characteristic mood of gentle humor, he wondered "ob wir, und natürlich vor allem Sie, im Himmel einmal dafür belohnt werden, dass wir einige Ungenauigkeiten aus der Welt geschafft haben...." Onward to a heavenly reward!

Nicolas Slonimsky
Los Angeles, California
September 1978

Preface to the Seventh Edition

This is the third time I preside over the changing fates of *Baker's Biographical Dictionary of Musicians:* the number would be five if I were to count the 1965 and 1971 Supplements between the regular 1958 and 1978 editions. Every time I approach my task I make a solemn vow to myself that this time over there will be no avoidable errors generated by a mysterious amblyopia, the cause of which may be hysteria, poisoning with ethyl or methyl alcohol, lead, arsenic, thallium, quinine, ergot, male fern, carbon disulfide, or *Cannabis indica* (the plant from which marijuana and hashish are derived). Green cucumbers! The cow jumped over the moon! I swore to myself in the paragraph on the Poltergeist in the preface to the 1978 edition of *Baker's* that I would exercise strict control over common dyslexia leading to the transposition of adjacent letters, such as occurs when "sacred music" is converted into "scared music." But lo and behold, there was "scared music" again on page 1866 in the 1978 edition on which I worked with such desperate dedication. Dyslexia is treacherous and elusive. I asked a couple of professional writers to read the sentence containing "scared music" and they sailed right through it, asking irrelevantly, "What's wrong? He did not compose any sacred music?"

In this edition I have determined to include a number of rock-'n'-roll musicians, crooners, songstresses, movie stars who occasionally sang, in fact, everyone with an operative larynx short of singing whales.

The most delicate part of my lexicographical pursuits is to determine who is alive and who has crossed the bar, to use Tennyson's poetic euphemism. I have in my possession a list of all the inmates of *Baker's Biographical Dictionary of Musicians* who were born in the nineteenth century (myself included) and who, according to actuarial tables, ought to be among the "stiffs," as I inelegantly call them. More than two hundred of them have already died on me since the 1978 publication of *Baker's*. The champion among the living as of the summer of 1984 is Paul Le Flem, who celebrated his 103rd anniversary on March 18, 1984. (Alas, Paul Le Flem died at his summer estate in Trégastel, Côtes-du-Nord, on July 31, 1984.) I hold my breath for his continued health out of grateful remembrance for his front page write-ups in the Paris journal *Comoedia* of the concerts of American music I conducted in Paris in the summer of 1931. The trouble about the unknown dead is that not all of them rate an obituary in the public press. The only way the newspapers can be apprised of the demise of a notable musician (or artist, or writer, or actor) is for a relative or friend of the departed to inform a newspaper. The death of Hugo Leichtentritt, an estimable German-American scholar, is a case in point. He lectured at Harvard, and after his mandatory retirement lived in Cambridge with his nonagenarian mother. She kept a vigilant eye on his whereabouts. Once he ventured forth with a middle-aged woman student, who induced him to have dinner with her. His mother anxiously waited for him to return, and reprimanded him severely for going out unescorted. She soon died. One day Leichtentritt's sister, who also lived in Cambridge, phoned me and asked what to do with his manuscripts; I could not understand what she meant. "But Hugo is dead," she said. "I buried him on Tuesday. I have to get his belongings out of the apartment to avoid paying his rent next month." I said I would come right over. When I arrived at his place, his sister had already piled up his pitiful music manuscripts for further disposition. I noticed the score of his cello concerto, in which he had written, in German, "Herr Piatigorsky said he might perform it upon occasion." This *Gelegenheit* never came. Leichtentritt's sister grumbled something to the effect that he was not a composer but only a writer about other composers, and that his own compositions were of no importance. I said all manuscripts by scholarly musicians were of value, and volunteered to send them to the Library of Congress for safekeeping in perpetuity. They were gratefully accepted by Harold Spivacke, chairman of the Library's Music Division, who had studied with Leichtentritt in Berlin, and were deposited in a special collection in the Music Division, to be kept until the unlikely eventuality that some music historian would "discover" them. I notified the *Boston Herald* of Leichtentritt's death, and a belated obituary appeared under the caption "Noted Music Scholar Dies in Obscurity." I also sent a telegram to Olin Downes, the music editor of the *New York Times*, who knew and admired Leichtentritt. According to the rules of the obituary department of the *New York Times*, I had to submit some kind of official certification of his death or a statement from a member of the family, to avoid a possible error. (It had happened once that the *New York Times* published an obit of a living person.) In due time a compassionate notice appeared on the obituary page.

It is annoying to miss a ghost, but it is terrifying to bury someone who is still alive. The strangest case of such a premature burial is found in the 1928 edition of a memoir by Amy Fay, entitled *Music Study in Germany*. In his preface to this edition, the eminent Oscar Sonneck remarked that almost all the people mentioned therein were dead, including the author herself. But Amy Fay was not dead at the time; she had only moved to a small town in Massachusetts, a locality that seemed to be the equivalent of a cemetery to people living in larger communities. She died on Feb. 28, 1928, and Sonneck himself died later that year, on Oct. 30, 1928. I inquired at the publisher whether she had collected any royalties in her incorporeal state, but was told that the information was restricted.

Shall I confess? In rushing into print my 1971 Supplement to *Baker's*, and eager to bring up to date the latest entombments, I caught sight of an obit in the *New York Times* of William John Mitchell, an American music pedagogue; he died in Binghamton, N.Y., on Aug. 17, 1971. I received the last page proofs of the 1971 Supplement in September of that year, and in haste jotted down the date under the entry on Donald Mitchell, a British musicologist who was just then transacting business with G. Schirmer, the publisher of *Baker's Dictionary*, and was commuting between London and New York. I could not believe my eyes when I received the published copy of the Supplement and saw that the date of death of W. J. Mitchell had got into the entry on Donald Mitchell. Trembling in fear, I tried to calm myself with the thought that it would be unlikely that Donald Mitchell himself would come across this item and discover himself dead. No balm in Gilead! Only days after the publication of the tainted little book, I received an anguished letter from Hans Heinsheimer, director of publications at G. Schirmer, bristling with despairing question marks and exclamation points, addressed, "Not so dear Nicolas," and telling me that Donald Mitchell had just stormed into his office brandishing the dreadful book. He had never even been to Binghamton, he protested, so how could he have died there? This is one of those situations in which the more you try to explain the reasons for your predicament the deeper you sink into the ill-smelling mud of inconsistency. In desperation I wrote to the managing director of the firm telling him of what I had wrought, and begging him to eliminate the entire entry containing the hideous death notice, or else to blacken and cover utterly the single horripilating line. If the printer could not do it, would he hire a couple of menial helpers to ink out the mortuary reference manually? Only a couple of thousand copies of the 1971 Supplement were printed, and I volunteered to cover the expenses of the reparations. No, it could not be done; the books had already been sent out to retailers and music stores and could no longer be retrieved. Just as I was slowly recovering from my distress, a letter came from Donald Mitchell containing some up-to-date information about his newest publications, and mentioning ever so casually that he did not die in Binghamton, or any other place. A sense of gnawing guilt was instantly washed off the atrium and ventriculum of my heart, and I wrote Mitchell an impassioned letter hailing his spirit of Christian forgiveness. He replied that it was well worth it to endure a temporary (and, as it proved, a harmless) burial to have received such a "charming" letter from me.

The avenging Eumenides willed it that I myself became, retroactively, a victim of a premature entombment. Early in the 1960s the Philadelphia Orchestra program book quoted something I wrote on Shostakovich, prefixing my name with the adjective "late." Several of my friends were greatly alarmed and called me up to find out under what circumstances I had died. I immediately shot off a wire to the management of the Philadelphia Orchestra, protesting that I was late only in delivering my manuscripts to the publisher. In reply, I received a penitential letter from the orchestra's program book annotator, apologizing for his "stupid" mistake, but trying to deflect my discomfiture by saying that he was definitely under the impression that he had read about my demise in the papers. I wrote back, saying that he must have read about the actual decease of Lazare Saminsky, with whom I was often confused.

During recent years, a tendency has developed to add demeaning details to the lives of the great. To judge by some recently published scholia, it is essential for a composer of stature to have had syphilis. Of course, some of them did, but why should a respected music dictionary inject spirochetes and vibrions into Schubert's arteries? Even more fascinating for biographers is the discovery that a great composer was a victim of poison. The alleged murder of Mozart by Salieri still agitates playwrights and would-be Mozartologists. A variant of the Mozartocidal theories is that he was killed by the estranged husband of his alleged mistress. The tale is calculated to stir the blood of idle readers much more than a prosaic finding that Mozart had died of nephritis.

Suicides by famous musicians make equally attractive reading. In my preface to the 6th edition I covered the case of Tchaikovsky's Choleric Suicide, but now more is to be added. Rumors of Tchaikovsky's suicide sprouted in British and American journals almost immediately upon his death. Tchaikovsky was a notoriously melancholy genius, and once he really tried to end his difficult existence by walking into the cold waters of the Moskva River, but the chill was so unpleasant that he walked right back to shore. When he died of cholera in November of 1893, it was widely believed that he had deliberately drunk unboiled water in a restaurant during a raging cholera epidemic. Why would Tchaikovsky commit suicide? Imagination ran wild. Tchaikovsky had had a homosexual liaison with a member of the Romanov dynasty, it was said; Czar Alexander III found out about it and in his righteous wrath served notice on Tchaikovsky either to do away with himself or else stand trial, be disgraced, and undergo exile for life in Siberia. It is true that homosexuality was a statutory offense in old Russia, and it continued to be such under the Soviet regime. When subterranean gossip began to spread around the Moscow Conservatory, where Tchaikovsky was teaching, about some exotic sexual ways among faculty members, Tchaikovsky decided to end the nasty talk by marrying a rather stupid spinster. But on the wedding night she sat on his lap, and Tchaikovsky, repelled by such an unnatural (to him) contact, ran out of his apartment and walked the streets of Moscow in utter despair. He never faced his uncomprehending bride again, but he paid her substantial alimony from funds generously provided by his adoring but not very bright benefactress, Madame von Meck, whom Tchaikovsky was careful never to meet face to face. The first Russian mention of Tchaikovsky's pederasty appeared in the preface to the correspondence between Tchaikovsky and Madame von Meck, published in 1934; but Tchaikovsky was an idol of Russian musicians, and Soviet officials gave orders not to mention in print that he was what he was. A serial biography of Tchaikovsky that began publication in East Germany was quickly suppressed. But this Victorian prejudice did not apply to articles and books published outside Russia, and if anything, it whetted the appetite of writers in the West for more sensational stories. The most outrageous of them all, because it totally lacked any documentary evidence, was the one published in a small Russian periodical in America, authored by a Madame Orlova, who before emigration had worked in a music publishing house in Moscow. In her story, it was not a member of the Romanov dynasty who was involved with Tchaikovsky, but the nephew of a certain Russian nobleman. Outraged by the victimization of his young relative, the uncle threatened to report it to the Czar unless Tchaikovsky committed suicide. A court of honor was then set up by alumni of the law school which Tchaikovsky had attended as a youth, and he was sentenced to death by a unanimous decision of this incredible "court." A Czarist official gave Tchaikovsky some arsenic tablets, with instructions for use. Tchaikovsky's family doctor, Lev Bertenson, a highly esteemed physician, was also drawn into the conspiracy, according to the story. This was in striking contradiction to the known correspondence between Dr. Bertenson and Modest Tchaikovsky, Tchaikovsky's brother and biographer, detailing the course of Tchaikovsky's illness. But the crucial letter in which Dr. Bertenson offered his condolences to Modest Tchaikovsky had mysteriously disappeared from the archives at the Klin Museum, or so asserted one of the champions of Madame Orlova's theories. This was a surprise to me, for I had copied the letter in question during my visit at Klin in 1935, and published it, in an English translation, in Herbert Weinstock's biography of Tchaikovsky. Cholera epidemics in St. Petersburg were frequent and deadly. Tchaikovsky's mother had died of cholera. Tchaikovsky's body was allowed to lie in state, and friends reverentially kissed him on the mouth, as was the common Slavic custom. Had Tchaikovsky died of cholera, would they not have risked contamination? Not so; cholera could be transmitted only by the ingestion of contaminated food or water, not by contact with the body of one of the victims. Chekhov, the famous Russian writer who served as a medical inspector during the cholera epidemic that carried off Tchaikovsky, makes no mention in his reports of such a danger. The sources of Madame Orlova's story would hardly stand in court. A certain person told her in 1966 that he had heard it in 1913 from a woman who heard it in turn from her husband, who died in 1902. This is certainly an extraordinary way of building up the chain of evidence, without a single piece of paper to substantiate it.

****

Dealing with people and their inevitable frailties is often a problem of morality, compassion, and decent respect for personal privacy. But in retelling a person's life one cannot omit essential facts. So when Liberace's chauffeur and constant companion sued him for $379,000,000 for abandonment, and the story made the front page of that scrupulously informative publication, *The National Enquirer,* one could not ignore it simply because of its scabrous connotations. And what a strange sum to ask in payment for dissolution of employment! Why not a round sum, like $400,000,000? Anyway, the plaintiff lost his suit and was left to make do with just a house, a car, and some petty cash in five figures granted oh, so liberally by Liberace before the break.

A delicate problem confronted me in putting together a biographical sketch on the electronic composer Walter Carlos, who on St. Valentine's Day of 1971 had surgery performed in which his natural male organ was everted to form a respectable receptive vagina, and thereby became Wendy Carlos. He recounted his transformation in full anatomical detail in an interview with *Playboy* magazine. I listed him/her as Carlos, Wendy (née Walter). In my preface to the 6th edition of *Baker's* I had already cited other curious biological phenomena, such as the elopement of the castrato Tenducci with a young English girl who bore him a child (he was a triorchis).

Such human stories are always welcome to the prurient palate, but the fundamental duty of any self-doubting lexicographer is to make sure that hard facts are accurately reported, and this requirement applies especially to the dates of birth and death. Copying data from other dictionaries would be a case of *petitio principii,* considering that editors and publishers of supposedly immaculate lexica must know deep in their heart's ventricula and their brain's sulci, or wherever conscience resides in their mortal frames, that when these facts come ostensibly from the horse's mouth, they may in reality originate at the other end of the horse. For years, Riemann's *Musik-Lexikon* was my "freeman's music-lexicon"; I put total faith in its Supplements. When it said "nicht," canceling a date as it appeared in the basic volume, I accepted the negation absolutely. Thus, when the Riemann Supplement said "nicht" to Cherubini's date of death, March 15, 1842, and replaced it with March 13, I corrected my correct date as it appeared in *Baker 5,* and replaced it with the incorrect correction in *Baker 6,* only to be assailed by a chorus of private correctors telling me that the Riemann correction was all wet. Unbelieving, I wrote to the registry of deaths in Paris, asking for Cherubini's death certificate. Blessed be the Catholic countries and their public servants, who since Napoleonic times discharge their services free to anyone! By return airmail (they did not even charge me for the *timbres-poste*!) I got a photocopy of Cherubini's death certificate, stating that he expired on March 15, not March 13, 1842, thus confirming my *Baker 5* date, confounding my *Baker 6* date, and enabling me to restore the correct *Baker 5* date in the present *Baker 7.* Now that my faith in Riemann's Supplement has been so rudely shaken, I have begun questioning every "nichting" in it, which means more work. But, normal, intelligent people may ask, who the hell cares? Well, nobody except a small band of benighted chronologists who are determined to put things straight.

* * * * * * *

Some facts, reports, or accepted interpretations of musical events that took place, or did not take place, according to the fancy of a particular historian, are obviously impossible to verify. What was the origin of the British custom of standing up when the strains of the Hallelujah Chorus ring out at the close of Part II of Handel's *Messiah*? Seems that George II was so moved when he heard it at the first London performance in Covent Garden Theatre on March 23, 1743, that he stood up; the audience followed suit, and by so doing established a British custom. Another interpretation, amounting to a *lèse majesté,* is that George II was seized with an irrepressible itch in his buttocks, and had to get up to put his hand inside his breeches to scratch.

Beethoven specifically denied having said "Thus fate knocks at my door" with reference to the opening notes of the Fifth Symphony, but the quotation lingers in the corridors of music history. One of my favorite stories about Rossini deals with the project of his *concitoyens* of Pesaro to erect a statue for him while he was still living. They had raised enough money to build the pedestal but they needed 10,000 francs for the statue itself, so they put it up to Rossini. "Ten thousand francs!" Rossini was supposed to have exclaimed. "For 10,000 francs I will stand on the pedestal myself." *Se non è vero è ben trovato.*

Historic facts are by necessity historians' facts, for we know about them from reports by historians. Did Caesar really exclaim "Et tu Brute" when he was stabbed by his friend? Shakespeare was right in his use of ungrammatical double superlatives, saying that it was "the most unkindest cut of all." Great men often quote themselves in their memoirs for self-aggrandizement. Did Napoleon really deliver that famous phrase, on seeing the Egyptian pyramids, that forty centuries looked down upon his soldiers? Goethe did say "mehr Licht" before he died, a phrase that has been elevated to a philosophical profundity, but some of those present thought he merely asked that the window blinds be raised to let more light into the room. The most famous words of recorded history may have never been uttered, or if they were, their meaning might have been unremarkable.

Titles of famous musical compositions are often nicknames generated by popular usage or created by publishers for the sake of promotion. *Moonlight Sonata* was merely *Sonata quasi una fantasia*. God only knows who gave the name *Emperor Concerto* to Beethoven's Piano Concerto in E-flat. *Appassionata Sonata* fits the music but Beethoven never called it so. Chopin had a batch of unwarranted sobriquets for many of his works. The *Raindrop Prelude* may have been written while rain was falling rhythmically on the roof of the monastery of Valldemosa, but Chopin denied this connection. Then there is the *Minute Waltz*, which can be played in sixty seconds only by omitting repeats. Handel never heard any blacksmith whistle the tune he incorporated in one of his harpsichord suites, but the title *The Harmonious Blacksmith,* spontaneously generated more than a hundred years after its composition, can no longer be removed from hundreds of published editions of the piece. Haydn holds the record of nicknamed compositions. The most notorious is the *Farewell Symphony,* in which one player after another departs from the scene, leaving the conductor to wield his baton before a nonexistent orchestra. According to the common accounts in music dictionaries, Haydn's intention was to indicate to his employer, Prince Esterházy, that his musicians needed a vacation, but the more plausible explanation is that the Prince planned to disband the orchestra and that Haydn tried to move his heart by his clever stage play. At least a dozen of Haydn's string quartets have acquired a nickname. Of Mendelssohn's *Songs without Words*, only a couple or so have authentic titles. And whoever thought of calling Mozart's great C major Symphony the *Jupiter Symphony* ? The name apparently first emerged in England. Spurious as many of these titles may be, it is the duty of a conscientious lexicographer to list them, in quotation marks or in italics, according to typographical preference.

* * * * * * *

In my preface to the 6th edition I sang paeans, dithyrambs, hosannahs, and hallelujahs to Steve Ellis, who corrected oodles of stupid errors that infested the previous edition of my ailing dictionary. And I paid tribute to the dogged determination of Samuel Sprince in tracking down solitary deaths of *Baker's* musicians who never made it into the public press. After the publication of the 6th edition of *Baker's,* Ellis continued to supply me with up-to-date lists of works by composers of so-called third-world countries, and whenever the sad occasion required it, their dates of death. I joyfully added all this information to the present edition.

A few months after the publication of the 6th edition of *Baker's* in 1978, I received a letter from one Dennis McIntire of Indianapolis, asking my forbearance for his intrusion upon my busy time. His justification for addressing me frontally was his concern about the omission in my tome of a number of reputable contemporary singers, conductors, violinists, and pianists. Would I have time to answer his queries? I jumped from my seat at the very thought that I might not be interested, and replied in an exclamatory affirmative. During one of my transcontinental travels I stopped over in Indianapolis to meet McIntire. Age: 35; glasses. Profession: college instructor in cultural history and literature. Avocation: voracious, ferocious reading. Passion: listening to recordings from his own immense collection of phonograph albums. Knowledge about composers and performers, dead and living: unbounded. We cemented a firm intellectual and personal friendship. I invited him to visit me in Los Angeles; he stayed with me for a week, and spent most of his time examining my card file that I had collected in anticipation of the birth of the 7th edition of *Baker's,* yet in limbo, picking up errors and pointing out inadequacies, right out of his head. Ever since, we maintained a voluminous correspondence, if that is the term to describe the constant flow of information arriving from him in a steady stream on neatly typed single-spaced sheets, while I could reciprocate only by acknowledging receipt in florid terms of wonderment at his erudition and his investigative skill in finding out things. Altogether he sent me 1,425 new articles, including many rewrites of the old entries.

It has ever been my notion that people who know most about composers and performers are not professional musicians, while venerable academics whose names stand for musicological greatness know their Mozart and Beethoven, their Handel and Haydn, their Brahms and Bruckner, their Schubert and Schumann, but are utterly ignorant of the lesser breed who populate biographical dictionaries of musicians. As if to confirm my contention, I found, to my absolute astonishment and delight, that Dennis McIntire did not compose music, could not even read music, and did not play an instrument. Yet he possessed a fine discrimination as to the absolute value of musical compositions and the relative artistry of performers, and is the author of numerous articles in music journals.

I must be lucky. On top of the galactic immensities of McIntire's contribution, I received a communication from Mike Keyton, a mathematician (a specialist in advanced calculus) from Dallas, Texas, who was also a reader of *Baker's.* He, too, scrutinized it carefully, weeding out discrepancies, logical hiatuses, vacuities, and various puzzlements. He, too, was a rabid record collector, and he had access to obscure newsletters and dealers' catalogues containing information not obtainable in general reference works. He was writing a doctoral dissertation on Euler, the famous mathematician who also was a musician of sorts, and whose name I had in *Baker's.* Sure enough, he found that the date of Euler's death in *Baker's* was a month off, which was a shame, since Euler had spent many years in Russia and died in the capital city of St. Petersburg where I was born 111 years later. Knowing my interest in mathematical puzzles, Mike sent me some good ones. We exchanged comments on such abstruse subjects as the sieve of Eratosthenes, the Greek who devised an early trick of fishing out prime numbers. Mike arranged for me to give a series of lectures, some of them on nonmusical subjects, in schools where he taught. Unafraid of tackling enormous tasks, he proceeded to systematically check *Baker's* dates vs. the dates in the formidable multivolume *New Grove.* The *New Grove* had me down on some British biographies, but I had some winning points too, which filled me with justifiable pride. Some time later Mike came to visit me in Los Angeles, and we had a wonderful time together. Contrary to all expectations, he not only could read music but could actually compose some, not without a measure of modernistic fioriture.

The number of people who seemed to take a masochistic pleasure in scanning the thousands of entries in *Baker 6* in search of inconsistencies, self-contradictions, imbecilities, inanities, and plain idiocies, was augmented by an accession from England, in the person of a schoolteacher named David Cummings. True to form among musicographical volunteers, he could not read music, but by God, he knew more about musicians than most editors of special dictionaries, myself included. The wonderful thing about him was that he was willing and able to collect detailed information on contemporary British composers, including the exact dates of first performance of their major works. He seemed to be surprised that I was so glad to receive his addenda atque corrigenda, and said that most music editors regarded him as a nuisance. I assured him that such was not the case with me. So herewith I extend to David Cummings my hand in lexicographical friendship across the sea.

In handling the materials which I received first from Ellis and then in an even greater abundance from McIntire, I faced a case of conscience: to what extent should I acknowledge their contributions? There was no problem about the lists of works that I received from them; there can be no individual authorship attached to such compilations. But what about the biographical sections? Well, in practically all cases, I revised them radically, imparting to the text, for better or for worse, my inimitable touch; whether I ruined their original by such wholesale substitution is beside the point. *Le style c'est l'homme,* and I surely injected my verbiage into the text without stint. No one, I hope, can dissect the final product so as to discover stylistic, grammatical, or syntactic elements existing before my intervention. *Dixi et animam levavi.*

The help I received from these friends and correspondents is not all. In addition, Ellis, McIntire, and myself were the recipients of priceless information from countless librarians, curators, orchestral managers, opera directors, and individual musicologists from all parts of the world. Russian musicians have been amazingly cooperative. I recall with sadness and gratitude the various bits of information I received from my dear late friend Gregory Schneerson; Boris Steinpress, the author of an invaluable book on operatic premieres, helped me enormously to establish exact dates of performances of works by Soviet composers. And the Union of Soviet Composers itself sent me all kinds of informative material. In Russia they publish monographs about their composers; my nephew Sergei Slonimsky already had a rather solid book on him published in Moscow long before he reached the status of bona fide celebrity (if he has reached it now).

All those wonderful contributions from far and wide would amount to naught if they were messed up by copyists and proofreaders. During the last year of my travail I had the extraordinary luck of securing the services of the sweetest 28-year-old lady who ever belied the common belief that good-looking girls are necessarily dumb. And to add to my lucky find, she is bilingual in English and German, unafraid of Umlauts, and attacking sesquipedalian compound Teutonic nouns with hardly a blink of the eye. She claims that she actually enjoys doing lexicographical work. But she has one serious defect: unwarranted shyness. So her name will have to be noted here in the form of a Krebsgang: M.M. Elk Anid. Here M.M. may stand for Music Major, which in fact she is.

Effusive credit is to be given to the splendiferous Laura Kuhn, who lent me spiritual succor in the lamentable state of my mental exhaustion by illuminating scholiums to adorn my rather sciolistic pages. Thanks, Laura.

Last but not least. I am perilously short of laudatory participles or exalting gerunds to describe the editorial assistance I received from Sylvia Juran, charged by my publishers to exercise vigilance over the factual contents of the multitudinous entries in the present volume, to watch over grammatical and syntactical propriety, and to weed out insidious solecisms. For these tasks she is admirably equipped. She is a linguist, with expertise not only in the "usual" Roman and Teutonic languages but also in Russian and Polish, and fully versed in the bewildering variety of diacritical signs occurring in the titles of musical works and bibliographic items in such exotic idioms. She sent me hundreds of queries, couched with a compassionate regard for my sensitivity, never correcting my recurring inanities and gross incongruities with blunt remonstrances but invariably using gentle question marks even in the most obvious cases of my embarrassing delinquencies. As Shakespeare said, and Schubert sang, "Who is Sylvia? what is she … that she might admired be."

The following individuals and institutions have lent their most valuable assistance in preparing the present edition of *Baker's:*

Steven Aechternacht, Artistic Director, Houston Symphony Orchestra
Dr. William W. Austin, Professor of Music, Cornell University, Ithaca, New York
Australia Music Centre, Sydney
Antony Beaumont, Cologne

Christopher Bishop, Managing Director, Philharmonic Orchestra, London

Stanislaw Bromilski, Head of the Music Department, Polska Agencja Artystyczna, Warsaw

Robert L. Brubaker, Curator of Special Collections, Chicago Historical Society

Canadian Music Centre, Toronto

Charles Collett, formerly of the British Broadcasting Corporation, London

Columbia Artists Management, Inc., New York

Christopher Dyment, London

John S. Edwards, General Manager, Chicago Symphony Orchestra

Richard D. Freed, Baltimore

Dr. Robert Freeman, Director, Eastman School of Music, Rochester, New York

Prof. Raymond Gallois-Montbrun, Director, Conservatoire National Supérieur de Musique, Paris

Dr. Karl Geiringer, Santa Barbara, California

Dr. Peter Girth, Intendant, Berlin Philharmonic Orchestra

Dr. phil. habil. Dieter Härtwig, Deputy Artistic Director, Dresden Philharmonic Orchestra

Vigdis Hauge, Norsk Musikkinformasjon, Oslo

Gisela Huwe, Press Office, Berlin Philharmonic Orchestra

Indianapolis-Marion County Public Library, Central Library Arts Division Staff: Dan Gann, Head; Virginia Andis, Sue Chapman, Claire Connor, Eileen Dolan-Heitlinger; Madge Engle, Nancy Norcross Gootee, Gwen Harden, Kathy Read, and Ophelia Georgiev Roop

Gunnar Arne Jensen, Artist and Concert Manager, Sveriges Riksradio, Stockholm

Arthur Kaplan, Public Relations Department, San Francisco Opera

Dr. János Kárpáti, Chief Librarian, Franz Liszt Academy of Music, Budapest

Koninklijke Nederlandse Toonkunstenaars-Vereniging, Amsterdam

Steven Ledbetter, Director of Publications, Boston Symphony Orchestra

Sir Anthony Lewis, formerly Principal, Royal Academy of Music, London

Per Olof Lundahl, STIMs Informationscentral för Svensk Musik, Stockholm

Dr. Hugh Macdonald, Gardiner Professor of Music, University of Glasgow

Dr. Vasco Mariz, Rio de Janeiro

Erich Mauermann, Bayerischer Rundfunk, Munich

Archives Office, Metropolitan Opera, New York

Inge Müller, Danmarks Radio, Copenhagen

Jack Murphy, Archives Office, New York Philharmonic Orchestra

Kären Nagy, Head Reference Librarian at Northwestern University and compiler of the "Index to Music Necrology" for *Notes*

Archie Newman, Head of Press and Public Relations, Royal Philharmonic Orchestra, London

Danny Newman, Lyric Opera of Chicago

Mimi O'Malley, Office of the Executive Director, Philadelphia Orchestra

Donald E. Osborne, Mariedi Anders Artists Management, Inc., San Francisco

Dr. Jiří Pauer, Head, Prague National Theater Opera

Prof. Samuel F. Pogue, College-Conservatory of Music, University of Cincinnati

Dr. Jack W. Porter, Executive Director, The Jussi Bjoerling Memorial Archive, Indianapolis

Ida Poulsen, Librarian, Det Kongelige Teater, Copenhagen

Harold Rosenthal, Editor, *Opera,* London

Klaus G. Roy, Director of Publications, Cleveland Orchestra

Royal Opera House, Covent Garden, London

Hans-Hubert Schönzeler, London

Desmond Shawe-Taylor, Music Critic, *Sunday Times,* London

Wayne D. Shirley, Reference Librarian, The Library of Congress, Washington, D.C.

Jeanne Siegel, Office of the President, The Juilliard School of Music, New York

Maynard Solomon, New York

Dr. Hella Somogyi, Hochschule für Musik und Darstellende Kunst, Vienna

Eberhard Steindorf, Konzertdramaturg, Dresden State Opera and Orchestra

Dr. H.H. Stuckenschmidt, Berlin

Dr. Benjamin Suchoff, New York Bartók Archive

Teatro alla Scala, Milan

Dr. Hans Tischler, Professor of Musicology, School of Music, Indiana University, Bloomington

Peter Tracton, Publicity Director, ICM Artists, Ltd., New York

Yvonne K. Unrath, Alumni Liaison Officer, The Curtis Institute of Music, Philadelphia

Sjoerd G.A.M. van den Berg, Public Relations Officer, Concertgebouw Orchestra, Amsterdam

Leon Van Dyke, Maxim Gershunoff, Inc., New York

Anna Van Steenbergen, Secretary General, Centre Belge de Documentation Musicale, Brussels

Prof. Bálint Vázsonyi, School of Music, Indiana University, Bloomington

Paul Vetricek, Vienna State Opera

Willem Vos, Artistic Advisor, Rotterdam Philharmonic Orchestra

Dr. Charles H. Webb, Dean, School of Music, Indiana University, Bloomington

Dr. Joachim E. Wenzel, formerly Archivist, Hamburg State Opera

Special acknowledgment must be accorded the following individuals:

Dr. Stanley Sadie, editor in chief of *The New Grove Dictionary of Music and Musicians* and editor of the *Musical Times*. Dr. Sadie, as well as Susan Feder, editorial coordinator of the forthcoming *New Grove Dictionary of Music in the United States,* was most unselfish in allowing updated material in their files to be utilized in *Baker 7.* In return, corrections and revisions were duly sent to *The New Grove* editors in London and New York for their future use.

Dr. Kurt Oehl, professor of the Johannes Gutenberg University in Mainz and one of the editors of the Riemann *Musik-Lexikon.* Throughout the period *Baker 7* was in preparation, Dr. Oehl shared a vast amount of material in his files for use in the new edition.

Brigitta Grabner, secretary, Vienna Philharmonic Orchestra. Thanks to her, dates of tenure for the various conductors of the Vienna Philharmonic Orchestra have been verified, world premieres confirmed, etc. Her willingness to provide all the program lists of the subscription series from the founding of the orchestra in 1842 was extraordinary.

R. Michael Fling, reference librarian, The Music Library, Indiana University, Bloomington. A great debt is owed to Fling for his patience and perseverance in answering every query sent to him.

Nicolas Slonimsky
El Pueblo de Nuestra Señora la Reina de Los Angeles
September 1984

PREFACE TO THE EIGHTH EDITION

My life as a diaskeuast is connected by an invisible but substantial thread with the illustrious German-educated American lexicographer Theodore Baker. He was the one who published the first edition of this eternally famous (in musicological circles) *Baker's Biographical Dictionary of Musicians.* He published it first in 1900 as a modest, slim compilation that paid tribute to a number of his contemporaries in the field that only then evolved as musicology, a science of music. Whether the biography of musicians can be called a science is a moot question. What is scientific about discovering that Beethoven jotted down an instruction to his charwoman to purchase for him in the store—among sundry daily articles—a piece of soap? But what kind of soap? Of what color? Beethoven's handwriting was well-nigh indecipherable. (His copyist said he would rather transcribe ten pages of Rossini's original manuscripts than a single page of Beethoven's.) But, after years of meticulous chirography, a German-born English music scholar ascertained that Beethoven's indecipherable word was *gelb,* yellow. Problem solved: the soap Beethoven preferred for his toilette was *gelb.* (He left the dishwashing to his well-informed menial.) Is this musicology?

But, from the ridiculous to the sublime. Is the contemplation of Beethoven's famous, but probably mythical, "immortal beloved" musicology? A prosaic lexicographer like my spectral Theodore Baker would not have philosophized about Beethoven's absent (alas!) sex life. He attended to facts. But mere facts are so jejune, so unappealing, so paltry. How much more exciting to speculate about the identity of Beethoven's imaginary flame! Accordingly, a number of musicographers squandered their expendable energies in endless conjecture. And what about Beethoven's possessive affection for his fatherless nephew? Some otherwise normal and serious Germans wasted their time worrying about the nature of Beethoven's desire to replace the missing parent. The adoption plan had to be submitted to the Austrian court, which was an extremely severe legal institution. Beethoven himself had a peculiar sense of legality, naively believing that he could overcome the strictures of the established state law. He tried to prove that he was a fit guardian by claiming noble social descent evidenced by the nobiliary particle, "van", attached to his name. But the court disagreed, rendering the judgment that "van" was a common Dutch particle not to be confused with the truly noble "von".

So much stuff has been written and so much paper wasted on the controversy connected with Beethoven's abortive dedication of his so-called Eroica Symphony that it may not be irrelevant to point out that Napoleon and Beethoven were nearly the same age; Napoleon was older by a year and four months. And thereby hangs a tale. When Napoleon was safely put away in the inaccessible island of St. Helena, his English custodians were well aware of his continuous hold on the imagination of Europeans, who had been at different times conquered by him. Indeed, the responsibility that the English felt over the care, feeding, and psychological welfare of their famous prisoner went so far as to compel them to commission the composition of an oratorio for a special performance at St. Helena. The name of a little-known Austrian composer was suggested, but a music publisher proposed in a conversation with Beethoven, recorded in Beethoven's famous conversation books (Beethoven's deafness was a positive factor in the preservation of such discussions), that the commission should be made to Beethoven himself. Beethoven reacted with interest, even expressing the view that had he elected to study military science, he would have been as great on the field of battle as he was on the pages of a symphony. Nothing came of this project and Napoleon died without benefit of a musical consecration.

Incidentally, and perhaps irrelevantly, I am against capital punishment, but I would gladly pull the switch on a member of a publishing management who was introduced to me as a specialist in German, on the strength, I understand, of his having taken a quickie course at a respectable New York university. Going over the page proofs of the 6th edition of *Baker's Biographical Dictionary of Musicians,* he

1

found an obvious error, the famous nobiliary particle spelled "van." He crossed it out and in dark red pencil wrote on the margin in very large letters, "V-O-N." The referent was Beethoven. I restrained my murderous feelings towards the aforesaid expert in German, but asked my publisher not to let him near my final page proofs.

Artists are perpetually in need of money. Mozart was woefully short of funds sufficient to provide for his family, and periodically wrote pathetic begging letters to a friendly banker for loans that he never bothered to repay. Many such letters are extant and, as manuscripts, are worth much more than the original donation so humbly entreated. Thus, a recipe for a musical genius to raise money is rather simple: write a begging letter to a rich friend, wait a century or so, and sell the letter for an imposing sum of money. Mozart's fame, however, was such that extravagant capital gains are not needed to sustain his immortality. Many immortals of music have streets and theaters named in their honor, but who has a whole town named for him? Mozart has, in the Canadian province of Saskatchewan.

Contemplating the laws of probability in the lives of great composers, we could let our imaginations run. Mozart died at a tragically young age, but what if he had lived as long as Verdi? He could have been a drinking companion of Berlioz, and, who knows, even a mentor to Wagner and Liszt. Continuing in this vein, we could imagine Schubert playing four-hand piano with Chopin. We could visualize Tchaikovsky at the age of 73, attending a performance of Stravinsky's *Rite of Spring.* He would have thought that music had become the handmaiden of hell. Yet Rachmaninoff, whose concept of music was so close to Tchaikovsky's, actually studied Stravinsky's score with interest. Shall we go on in this chronological phantasmagory? All we have to do is to read what great composers said about each other when they were contemporaries. Or, worse still, read reviews by supposedly enlightened journalists about composers of their own time. Can it be believed that an intelligent English music critic would have written the following review of Chopin's recital in London: "The entire works of Chopin present a motley surface of ranting hyperbole and excruciating cacophony." But avaunt the stormy clouds of artistic incomprehension! Let us return to the clear weather of today's music. Or is it cloudless? No, this is a book of biographical events and we must try not to confuse facts with opinion. In his essay "What is art?," Tolstoy tried to solve esthetic problems, but even he, the titan of universal comprehension, failed.

Now I must recollect myself and reaffirm the formal and prosaic *raison d'être* of the present 8th edition of *Baker's,* which represents a gathering of information that has come since the publication of the previous edition. Any new edition of a biographical dictionary of musicians aims to augment, refine, and update the contents of the previous edition, and the present work is no exception. For the first time since the 5th edition, substantial rewrites of entries on several major figures have been undertaken, incorporating the latest in research.

The 8th edition is also chock-full of new entries. A significant constituency is reflected in the number of non-European musicians who have risen to fame on the world scene during the second half of the 20th century. One has to abandon patronizing condescension to so called Third World artists. Indeed, the classification "Third World," traditionally used to represent the vast territories of Asia and Africa, may have to be redefined. Who would have imagined that one of the greatest contemporary cellists would be a Chinese called Yo-Yo Ma? Or that the youthful Korean conductor Myung-Whun Chung would be selected to head the newly formed Bastille Opera in Paris? *Tempora mutantur et nos mutamur in illis.* It would have been unimaginable a scant half century ago that two of the most important American symphony orchestras—the Boston Symphony Orchestra and the New York Philharmonic—would be led by Asian musicians: Seiji Ozawa of Japan and Zubin Mehta of India! The art of symphonic conducting had been for many years preponderantly Germanic. Henry Lee Higginson, founder of the Boston Symphony Orchestra, specified in his contracts of financial support that the conductor must be a German. It was a great shock to him when Karl Muck was interned as an enemy alien toward the end of the First World War. Distressed, Higginson withdrew all financial support from the Boston Symphony Orchestra.

But *revenons à nos moutons,* as the French say, lest the aforesaid muttons get stranded in the columns of our dictionary. Indeed, new lambs arrive from all over the world and a significant number of them have wandered in from Japan. Their biographies were supplied by the Japanese Union of Composers, an organization that issues periodical catalogues remarkable in their completeness and in some respects excelling music dictionaries and catalogues by music publishers in Europe and America. Another national group of musicians well represented in *Baker's* for the first time is the Koreans, who were individually and personally responsive to requests for biographical information.

Music history knows many women who adorned the opera stage and became celebrated under the colorful Italian definition of *diva,* "the divine one." Popular books on opera tell stories, not always verifiable, about worshipful admirers who unharnessed the carriage horses of the current diva to pay homage by pulling the carriage to the house, palace, hotel, or wherever the object of their adoration was making her temporary habitation. Envious rivals to such *prime donne* suggested that these adulatory excesses were remunerated. Anyway, the custom went into desuetude with the advent of the automobile.

From its inception, *Baker's* listed biographies of great female singers dating from the beginning of opera, but what was missing in previous editions was a rightful place for women composers. And yet there were such, worthy of note, long before *Baker's* saw its first light of day. In the 18th century, ladies with a compositional bent confined their efforts to songs and occasional harp pieces, but in the 19th century women were writing orchestral music and even operas. The names of most of them have been duly tabulated in previous editions of *Baker's,* but many more musical suffragettes, if such a borrowing from the world of politics can be allowed, have since made their appearance on symphony programs. One such modern musical woman, Ellen Zwilich, was awarded the Pulitzer Prize in Music, the first to be received by a woman composer. Thea Musgrave has emerged as an important composer of symphonies and operas. The Soviet composer Sofia Gubaidulina has acquired fame on par with any of her male colleagues.

The new *Baker's* has increased not only its coverage of women, but also of ethnomusicologists, a term of relatively recent origin which has now acquired its proper place in new dictionaries of musical terminology. But though we can catch up with the sedentary academic ethnomusicologists, the more elusive ethnic musicians sometimes escape our net. Multi-media composers and performance artists have also attained a legitimate place among practicing musicians. They freely combine the arts of speech, dance, and even gymnastics with lighting effects, all of which are written into the score. Many of these novel effects have been anticipated by earlier composers. In his *Poem of Fire,* Scriabin introduced an instrument listed as "*luce,*" using the Italian word for light, but technical problems still frustrate the realization of the effect that Scriabin visualized in his futuristic dream.

Modern technology enables the artisans of new sonorities to perform scales and harmonies independent of the established division of the octave into 12 chromatic intervals. The Russian electrical engineer Theremin constructed an instrument that produced any fractional interval by the wave of the hand, but the results were rarely accurate. It was not until the invention of electronic keyboard instruments that accurate fractional intervals could be achieved and that an octave could be divided into any number of equal intervals, causing Bach's "equal temperament" to be no longer a *conditio sine qua non* of intervallic equality. The Mexican composer Julián Carrillo claimed to have constructed instruments that produced sounds divisible into any number of equal intervals down to 1/64 of an octave, but the accurate division of the octave could never be achieved. With the accession of musical electronics, any desired effect of fractional tonality can be achieved. But is this extension of musical means welcome? Is a new Bach even now creating an electronic masterpiece? The availability of new means of sonic production has not yet occasioned the appearance of a creator of surpassing genius.

When we speak of forward leaps, we invariably encounter the phenomenon of John Cage, the primary experimenter with chance. When he first met his audience in the 1940s, he was an object of derision as an intruder into the sacred temple of the Muses. But, as has happened to visionaries from Pythagoras to Schoenberg, he eventually proved the validity of his innovations. The *Encyclopaedia Britannica* unreservedly states that he is the single greatest influence on composers of the second half of the 20th century. He even began collecting the world's most prestigious appointments and most opulent prizes, from Harvard to Kyoto. His mind-boggling, syllable-tossing stage work entitled *Europeras 1 & 2* garnered sensational headlines all over the world.

One of the most laborious aspects in the preparation of the present edition has been the compiling of a world necrology of musicians, which I have inelegantly tabulated in a list entitled "Stiffs." As the present edition went to press, the number of stiffs exceeded 600. *Morituri te salutant.* Such spirits cannot be gathered merely by scanning obituary notices in major newspapers or music magazines, but demand luck and persistence equal to that of Hamlet's gravedigger who produced the skull of "poor Yorick." A properly compiled biography of a stiff must include place and date of death, but it ought also to contain a sort of mournful coda about a musician's life and career as well as reference to the cause of death. Unfortunately, published death notices rarely mention the specific cause of a person's demise. Difficulties abound in chasing down those extravagant spirits, to quote Hamlet addressing his father's ghost. ("Extravagant" meaning, of course, walking beyond the proper limits for the dead, not being careless about money. One American production of *Hamlet*, not trusting the verbal expertise of its audience, replaced the Shakespearean word with the common adjective "restless.")

Specific causes of death are occasionally suppressed in obituary notices because of purely social considerations. Unesthetic illnesses such as gout, which was a frequent affliction of large, fat men of power in 18th-century England, were considered unfit for print. The proverbial illness of 19th-century artistic poverty was tuberculosis, which took many young lives; it was euphemistically replaced in print with "consumption." Cancer as a cause of death was also unmentionable. In Tolstoy's short novel *The Death of Ivan Ilych*, the progressive symptoms of the protagonist's disease plainly point to a cancerous condition, but the ominous word itself is nowhere to be found in the text. And then came AIDS, a cruel and ironic acronym for Acquired Immune Deficiency Syndrome.

In simpler days there were simpler answers for disease. Scrofula, common from the Middle Ages well into the 19th century, affected the sufferer with painful glandular swellings that came to be known as the King's Evil. The cure was simplicity itself. All you had to do was to petition an anointed sovereign to touch the diseased area. Belief in the healing power of crowned royalty was so widely accepted that the kings of England and France set aside certain days of the year when those afflicted could come for a cure. Charles II of England lent his healing touch to some 90,000 of his subjects. In 1712 Queen Anne freely administered the cure for the King's Evil to hundreds of Englishmen; among them was Samuel Johnson who was touched as a small child. In France, on Easter Sunday, 1686, Louis XIV touched 1,600 persons while giving credit to God, saying: "Le Roi te touche; le Dieu te guérisse."

Nothing in the history of musical biography can compare in sheer ferocity to the witch's sabbath that descended upon the world of music at the death of Tchaikovsky in 1893. Despite unequivocal and unimpeachable testimony to the reality of Tchaikovsky's fatal illness of cholera, the apparently irresistible rumor of suicide splashed the world's newspapers with sensational headlines. The glamour attached to the name Tchaikovsky caused other deviations from truth about his life and death.

Tchaikovsky is an icon in Russia, second only to Lenin. The primacy of Tchaikovsky's genius and of his name led to the elimination of all mention of his homosexuality from all biographical material published in Russia. Censorship extended also to Russian translations of books in foreign languages. Tchaikovsky himself tried to cover up his preference for the inverted mode of love by contracting a nominal marriage to a young conservatory student, but this desperate ploy collapsed when Tchaikovsky explained the situation to her on their wedding night. They were never divorced, and Tchaikovsky arranged to pay her annual stipends as long as their marriage was in force. It ought to be mentioned that homosexuality was a criminal offense in the Czarist Russian legal code and remained so even after the revolution.

Mental disease was long taboo in musical biographies, since it was often connected with paresis, a final stage of syphilis. Schumann contracted syphilis as a young man, and, as his condition worsened, tried to commit suicide by jumping into the Rhine. (He was rescued.) He also suffered an auricular nightmare, tinnitus, which caused him to hear the tone of middle A ringing constantly in his ears. His distraction was such that he began to lose his grip on reality; he no longer wished to see his cherished Clara, the "Chiara" as he tenderly called her in his *Carnaval,* nor did he ask about his seven children. (Apparently two of his three daughters died insane.) Seems that old Professor Wieck, Clara's father, who opposed their marriage so bitterly that the young couple had to go to court to overcome his objections, might have been right after all in suspecting Schumann of pathological instability.

Another syphilitic composer was Hugo Wolf, who eventually had to be confined to an insane asylum. Mahler suffered from an extreme case of neurasthenia; at one time he consulted Freud for help. On the margin of his unfinished 10th Symphony he scrawled: "Devil take me away with you!" Edward MacDowell, American nationalist composer, succumbed totally to the insanity of paresis, falling into a state of childhood, unable to take care of his physiological functions. A charitable subscription in his behalf had to be circulated in New York City to enable him to end his life in peace.

What has all this to do with the factual preoccupation of a musical biographer? Nothing, except a warning, *cave canem,* which may mean either "careful of the dog" or "caution, I may sing!" There is a clan of musical biographers who believe that to qualify as a genius, a musician has to possess a countervailing sin leading to either murder or self-destruction. A most attractive example of such a violent life is that of Don Carlo Gesualdo, who wrote elegant madrigals, but also (so the story goes) hired assassins to do away with his erring spouse and her lover. Some modern musicologists positively salivate over Gesualdo's supposed darksome deed, but, unfortunately, trustworthy documentation of the event is lacking.

But why was Schubert, the modest, inoffensive Schubert, classified a perennial misfit? In one frothy little movie he was depicted as the hopeless suitor of a worldly aristocratic lady to whom he played the first movement of his *Unfinished Symphony.* She liked the tunes, but their disparity of social rank made it impossible for her to consider his as yet unspoken offer of marriage. "If so," Schubert said in this silly movie, "I will let my symphony remain incomplete, just as my love for you must be." More recently, one speculative writer proposed an alternate solution for Schubert's celibacy: he preferred men. Proof? Schubert addressed a classmate using the second person singular, *du.* But what about Brahms and other unmarried men of music? Brahms liked women but he never went beyond kissing their hands in a fine Viennese manner. Musical biographers who should have known better claimed that he proposed marriage to Clara Schumann, but there is not one scintilla of evidence that he did. Why can't biographers admit that there are some men who simply never get around to contracting a marriage?

One of the values of *Baker's* to music scholars is the inclusion of luminary obscurities (can such oxymorons be allowed in a supposedly scholarly volume?). Let us consider the case of Joseph Paul Johannes Hoch, the wealthy businessman who founded the famous conservatory in Frankfurt, Germany, which counted among its graduates such famous musicians as Pfitzner, Hindemith, and MacDowell, and had among its distinguished faculty the likes of Raff and Humperdinck. The biographies of these illustrious persons dutifully cite their connection with Hoch's conservatory, but who was Hoch? Unexpectedly, his biography turned up in the business section of a 19th-century almanac, complete with dates.

In my stubborn search for facts, particularly funerary facts, I conducted a special hunt for the once-famous Spanish wunderkind Pepito Arriola. He was of my own generation, and I remember attending his concert in St. Petersburg early in the century. He played Schumann and Chopin and he wore blue velvet pants. And then he disappeared into the Lethe of musical oblivion. There was a long article with illustrations of Pepito in a Spanish dictionary published in the 1920s, but no mention of what happened to him after he ceased to be a wunderkind. I finally located him in an obscure German volume dealing with child prodigies. He had died unknown, unnoticed, unwept.

Dramatic circumstances surrounding the demise of celebrated musicians have been given due note in the present edition. Herbert von Karajan, who believed that he could attain physical immortality by cryogenics, succumbed to a heart attack when the helicopter that he owned and operated arrived too late to take him to the hospital. The former concertmaster of the Boston Symphony Orchestra, Richard Burgin, suddenly interrupted a bridge game, of which he was an enthusiast, and said in great distress, "What color are hearts?" He ceased to distinguish colors and died a few weeks later.

Different geographical locations and dates for the birth of identical twins surely deserve attention. The Bulgarian composer Pantcho Vladigerov was born in Switzerland but his twin brother Luben had emerged on the previous day in Bulgaria. It seems their mother was distrustful of Bulgarian obstetrics and, after giving birth to the first twin, decided to take the train to Switzerland to bear the second, hours later, in improved medical circumstances.

One adventure in musical sleuthing that I cannot forbear to relate occurred when I came upon the name of João Gomes de Araújo, a Brazilian opera composer, who, according to biographical notes available in my sources, was born in 1846 and served as inspector of the Conservatory of São Paulo. That was reason enough for me to write, in 1940, to the administration of the aforesaid conservatory for information about his life and death. To my delighted astonishment, I received in reply a message from the ancient man himself, which said, in quaint but clear English: "It is a fact that I was born on the fifth of August, 1846, but in spite of this being quite a long existence, I should say that I am still healthy and fit for anything." São Paulo was the second stop after Rio de Janeiro on my Latin American trip of musical discovery, and I notified Gomes of my traveling plans. Sure enough, he met me at the railroad station. He wore no glasses and walked briskly without the aid of a cane. He accompanied me to his humble house where he introduced me to an old man, confined to a wheelchair. "This is my son," he said. Alas, Gomes did not live to be 100; he died in 1942.

Another fantastic search for a potential spirit was that for an English composer and music theorist, Edward Maryon, the author of an unusual book entitled *Marcotone*. I wrote to the American publisher of that book and inquired whether the author was still alive (the opus in question having been published in 1919). I received a reply that Maryon must have died long ago, but when and where, his publisher did not know. I persevered, writing to various bibliographers and music editors in London, but none was even aware of Edward Maryon's existence. Then I wrote to the owner of the house where Maryon was known to have lived, only to learn that the house itself had been destroyed during the London blitz early in World War II. I finally wrote to Scotland Yard, the ultimate in matters of natural and unnatural deaths. I received a courteous reply, which explained that the famous police institution kept track only of deaths due to criminal activity, and that there was no record of Maryon having been a victim of crime. And then, quite unexpectedly, I got a letter from an English music scholar who knew Maryon personally. Maryon was apparently very much alive, and I was given his address. Losing no time, I wrote to Maryon, who expressed astonishment that anyone in the United States would be interested in his productions. He complained that no one in

England took the slightest note of his music. We had a lively correspondence until he died in 1954.

Shortly after his death, I received notice that a trunk had arrived for me care of the Boston Public Library. A letter from the executors of Maryon's estate accompanied the package, which explained that they had acted at the deceased's explicit instruction to send all his musical manuscripts and personal documents to me since I was the only person who had taken any interest in his work. The trunk contained not only music manuscripts but also the original patents of nobility conferred upon Maryon's forebears by British monarchs going back to Henry V. What was I to do with this extraordinary bequest? Eventually the whole collection went to the Library of Congress, where it presumably still resides.

Several Russian musicians who left Europe after the revolution simply disappeared. Seeking clues as to their whereabouts, I addressed a letter to the editor of a Russian newspaper published in New York in the hope of finding their relatives. To my great satisfaction I received a reply from a relative of Vasili Sapelnikov, informing me that his last known residence was in San Remo, Italy. I wrote at once to the municipal authorities of San Remo and obtained the exact date of the composer's death, which I duly communicated to my Russian lexicographical colleagues (and also added to Sapelnikov's entry in the 6th edition of *Baker's*). Yet, try as I might, I could not find out what happened to multiconsonantal Nikolai Shcherbachev, a composer anointed by Mussorgsky as a "young genius," who was associated with the nationalist group of St. Petersburg musicians in the second half of the 19th century. According to a brief notice which appeared in the last issue of a Russian music magazine published in Petrograd in 1918, Shcherbachev had left Russia after the revolution and was employed in Europe in various capacities including that of a croupier in the casino of Monaco. I lost no time writing to the directorate of that famous gambling house and in due time received a polite reply: after thorough investigation, no Russian employee could be found with a name even remotely resembling that of Shcherbachev. Subsequently, I came upon an obituary notice of a man of the same name who died in Paris. I immediately wrote to the family asking whether there was any connection. There was none. Nor was there any connection between Mussorgsky's "young genius" and one Vladimir Shcherbachev, a composer active in Leningrad. And, although several of Nikolai Shcherbachev's songs and instrumental pieces had been published by Belaiev, its Paris office had no information about him. However, a tantalizing notice had appeared in a little bulletin of composers published in France, listing the name of Nikolai S., who, according to this bulletin, died in Cannes in 1920. Oh, yes, I wrote there. Wrong town, wrong number, wrong name. I decided not to draw the saga of inquiry out any longer and left him out of *Baker's* altogether.

Among biomusical curiosa, the case of two Russian cellists, Gregor Piatigorsky, who emigrated and earned world fame, and his younger brother Alexander, who remained in Moscow, deserves telling. To avoid confusion, Alexander Piatigorsky changed his name to Stogorsky. Now, *piat* in Russian means five, and *sto* means one hundred. The story goes that the younger brother claimed that he was 20 times more important than his sibling. The second part of their names, *gorsky,* means "of the mountain." So, the lesser known cellist was worth one hundred mountains against five for his celebrated brother.

Serge Koussevitzky is a magical name. Famous first as a double bass player, he later achieved renown as a conductor. Koussevitzky had a nephew who also played the double bass and then became a conductor. They both began their careers in Russia. Such coincidence of name and career could not be tolerated, and the uncle ordered his nephew to amputate the first syllable of his surname. The younger Koussevitzky became Sevitzky. Both wound up in the United States, and, as fate would have it, both received positions as conductors in Boston, the uncle with the great Boston Symphony Orchestra and the nephew, much later, with a minor local orchestra. Rather than keep a low profile, Sevitzky had the temerity to announce a performance of Beethoven's Ninth Symphony at an Easter concert during the same week that Koussevitzky had scheduled it with the Boston Symphony Orchestra. The uncle summoned his ambitious nephew to his apartment and ordered him to cancel his performance. "How dare you lift your stick over Beethoven!" he thundered. But his irrepressible nephew dared to invoke American freedom as the right to conduct anything he chose. Koussevitzky threw him out of the house. Then Koussevitzky died, and Sevitzky decided to claim part of his estate, perhaps as compensation for a life spent under the shadow cast by his famous uncle. He had no chance to win and blackened his name forever with millions of Koussevitzky worshippers. Eventually, he obtained a post with another provincial American orchestra, but failed to retain it. Stubborn to the end, he decided to go on a European tour as conductor, paying his own way. He died during a rehearsal in Greece.

The sempiternal begetter of the original edition of the present dictionary, Theodore Baker, was an American-born scholar who went to Germany early in his twenties to acquire knowledge of the science and history of music. He settled in Leipzig, where he published a worthwhile investigation of the music of American Indians. So totally engrossed did he become in German culture and in the German language itself that his first American edition of *Baker's* was full of German idioms. Thus, in describing Berlioz (whose music he did not particularly appreciate) Baker conceded that Berlioz was undoubtedly "genial," which did not refer to his easy-going nature, but, in the German sense, to his "possessing genius."

Baker's method of selecting entrants for his dictionary was sometimes idiosyncratic; many he included were musicians with whom he had been personally and professionally connected. In this way, Baker followed the example of that great man of musical information, Hugo Riemann, who was himself an amateur performer on the violin and liked to assemble and play in string quartets at his residence. As a result, early editions of Riemann's famous *Musiklexikon* are filled to the brim with obscure German string players. It took the efforts of several editors of both Riemann's and Baker's volumes to cleanse the originals of perfectly deserving but utterly unknown practicing musicians.

It is awkward for me to describe my own labors on the biographies contained in Theodore Baker's monumental compilation. But since nobody applied himself to the task of selecting proper entrants, I have to take the honor and the blame for the contents of Baker's tome beginning with the 5th edition. Moreover, I had the gall (if not the more colloquial *chutzpah*) to find errors even in the sublime lexicographical edifice of Hugo Riemann's *Musiklexikon.* And it is with some measure of pride that I quote the acknowledgement of my contributions in Riemann's 12th edition, thanking me for my "numerous valuable biographical dates and materials." In his preface to the 1940 edition of *Baker's*, Carl Engel called me "that lexicographic beagle of keen scent and sight." Eric Blom in his 5th edition of *Grove's Dictionary of Music and Musicians* said, "To none do I owe a greater debt than to Nicolas Slonimsky, who never ceases to undertake arduous detective work all over Europe and America in order to rectify mistakes made by his colleagues." Catherine Drinker Bowen, author of several biographies of musicians, remarked that my "hawk-like, lie-detecting eye brings terror to all writers on musical subjects." In his *Oxford Companion to Music,* Percy A. Scholes referred to me as "the world's most ingenious and pertinacious musicological detective."

I cannot deny that I was peculiarly amused and delighted by more recent responses of two music critics. Martin Bernheimer of the *Los Angeles Times* greeted the appearance of the 6th edition of *Baker's* with a shout (how else can I describe this?): "Do not walk, run to the nearest bookstore and get the latest edition of *Baker's Biographical Dictionary of Musicians* edited by Nicolas Slonimsky!" Robert Commanday of the *San Francisco Chronicle* offered the elegant commendation: "I appreciate Slonimsky's verbal acuity."

It now behooves me to sing the praises of my helpers in the present and previous editions of *Baker's.* The first to catch me on errors and inadequacies was Steve Ellis who castigated me for various sins of omission and commission. I was woefully remiss in covering the list of works of the Rumanian composer Mihalovici. Was I ignorant of the supplement to the Rumanian dictionary that listed all anyone could wish to know about Mihalovici? I was. But by far the greatest debt of gratitude I owe is to the formidable historiographer of Indianapolis, Dennis McIntire. He deserves a special medal for bravery beyond the call of duty for compiling a mass of information gathered from all points of the globe, amounting to more than two thousand typewritten pages, unimpeachable in accuracy. A further word for Bakerology is due to Michael Keyton of Dallas, a professor of mathematics who contributed information about musicians who were also mathematicians. Unstinted praise goes to Samuel Sprince of Massachusetts whose determination in establishing facts calls for a maximum of musicological savoir-faire. Am I running out of words of praise? The crowning contribution to the present edition came from Laura Kuhn, a lady of exquisite learning, a seeded (to use a tennis term for top-notch quality) musicologist, who has already commended herself by numerous contributions of enlightened musical criticism to musicological publications; she also possesses the precious gift of communicating this knowledge in clear language to classes of college students and to participants in public conferences on music. She has the all-important ability to collate and to edit the immensity of materials that has come to hand from various sources during the process of preparing this 8th edition.

To conclude, I offer a Latin sentence that appeared in some early published books of the 16th century: "Igitur eme, lege, fruere." Therefore buy, read, enjoy.

Nicolas Slonimsky
St. Petersburg–Paris–Boston–Los Angeles
8 August 1990

ACKNOWLEDGMENTS

Michael Alchin, State Library of New South Wales, Sydney

Charles Amirkhanian, Artistic Director, Other Minds, San Francisco

Prof. Dr. Irmgard Bontinck, Director, Institut für Muziksoziologie, Hochschule für Musik und darstellende Kunst, Vienna

John Chilton, for use of data leased from *Who's Who of Jazz: Storyville to Swing Street* (Philadelphia: Chilton Book Company, 1972) and *Who's Who of British Jazz* (London: Cassell, 1997)

John Clem, Edinburg, Virginia

Daisy Coll, Sociedades de Autores y Compositores de Venezuela, Caracas

Richard Corrado, Vice President, ICM Artists, Ltd., New York

Prof. Dr. Octavian Lazăr Cosma, Vice President, Union of Composers and Musicologists of Romania, Bucharest

David Cummings, Editor, *International Who's Who in Music and Musicians' Directory*, London

Bill Daugherty, New York

Deborah G. Davis, Director, Scherman Library, Mannes College of Music, New York

Joanna Demopoulos, Deputy Director, National Library of Greece, Athens

DONEMUS, Amsterdam

Roger Dooner

Agnes Eisenberger, President, Colbert Artists Management, Inc., New York

Stephen W. Ellis, Glenview, Illinois

Colin Escott, Toronto

Angela Fabry, Director, Performing Artists International, Fort Worth

Finnish Music Information Centre, Helsinki

R. Michael Fling, Collection Development and Acquisitions Librarian, William and Gayle Cook Music Library, School of Music, Indiana University, Bloomington

Jim Fox, Venice, California

Will Friedwald, New York

Stephen M. Fry, Music Reference Librarian, University of California at Los Angeles

Gary Giddins, New York

Don Gillespie, Edition Peters, New York

Linda S. Golding, President, Boosey & Hawkes, Inc., New York

Olga Golsinky, Director, Music Information Center, Ukraine Composer's Union, Kiev

Alan A. Green, Assistant Head, Music/Dance Library, Ohio State University, Columbus

Helga Sif Guðmundsdóttir, Iceland Music Information Centre, Reykjavík

David Hoffman, Karen McFarlane Artists, Inc., Cleveland

Anna J. Horton, Manager, Art and Music Department, Public Library, Cincinnati

Sven Lars Imfeld, Stadttheaer, Bern

Indianapolis-Marion County Public Library, Central Library, Arts Division, Newspapers and Periodicals Division, and Social Sciences Division

Helmut Kallmann, Co-Editor, *Encyclopedia of Music in Canada,* Toronto

Annette Kehrs, Concert-Opera-Media Division, Schott Musik International GmbH & Co., Mainz

Bill Kirchner, New Jersey

Sheila Knutsen, Librarian, Public Library, Seattle

Edward Komara, Music Librarian-Blues Archivist and Associate Professor, University of Mississippi, University, Mississippi

Georgia (Mrs. Kay) Kyser, Chapel Hill

Richard Kostelanetz, New York

Richard de La Rosa, President, ProPiano, New York

Frank Liberman

Tomas Löndahl, Swedish Broadcasting Corp., Stockholm

Anders Lönn, Statens Musikbibliothek, Stockholm

Marjorie Lund, Norwegian State Academy of Music, Oslo

Lars Mahinske, Editorial Division, *Encyclopaedia Britannica,* Chicago

Wayne Martin, Kirkwood, Missouri

Alec McLane, Music Librarian and Director of the World Music Archives, Wesleyan University Library, Middletown, Connecticut

Gregg M. Medley, Indianapolis

Doug Mitchell

Corinne Monceau, Centre de Documentation de la Musique Contemporaine, Paris

Dan Morgenstern, Director, Institute of Jazz Studies at Rutgers University–Newark

Bendt Viinholt Nielsen, Danish Music Information Center, Copenhagen

Alain Pâris, Editor, *Dictionnaire des interprètes et de l'interprétation musicale au XXe siècle,* Paris

Anthea Parker, Information Resources Manager, Australian Music Centre, Sydney

John Pennino, Assistant Archivist, Metropolitan Opera, New York

Erdmuthe Pirlich, Konzertdirektion Hans Ulrich Schmid GmbH & Co., Hannover

Katie Plybon, Promotions Assistant, G. Schirmer, Inc., New York

Mare Põldmäe, Estonian Music Information Centre, Tallinn

Peter Pullman, New York

Dr. Frank Reinisch, Breitkopf & Härtel, Wiesbaden

Charles Reynolds, Associate Librarian, University Library, University of Michigan, Ann Arbor

John H. Richardson, Katonah, New York

Rosie Ridenour, Indianapolis

Sabine Rosenberg, Hamburg State Opera

Ric Ross, Thousand Oaks, California

Mikel Rouse, New York

Klaus G. Roy, Cleveland Heights, Ohio

Jan Olof Rudén, Swedish Music Information Center, Stockholm

Dr. Stanley Sadie, O.B.E., Editor Emeritus, *The New Grove Dictionary of Music and Musicians,* London

Christiane Schafferhans, Deutsches Rundfunkarchiv, Frankfurt am Main

Dr. Dietmar Schenk, Archivist, Hochschularchiv, Hochschule der Künste, Berlin

Wilhelm Schlüter, Internationales Musikinstitut, Darmstadt

Dr. Elliott Schwartz, South Freeport, Maine

Mojmir Sobotka, Librarian, Czech Music Information Centre, Prague

Sociedad Argentina de Autores y Compositores de Música, Buenos Aires

George Sturm, Executive Director, Music Associates of America, Englewood, New Jersey

Prof. John Szwed, Yale University

Randy Talmadge

Joel Thomas, Askonas Holt, Ltd., London

Manfred Thönicke

David Torres, San Angelo, Texas

Union of Composers of Russia, Moscow

Frank Villella, Archives, Chicago Symphony Orchestra
Alena Volná, Executive Manager, Music Information Centre of Slovakia, Bratislava
F. B. Wiggins, Arlington, Virginia
William N. Williams, San Francisco
Izabela Zymer, Librarian, Library of the Polish Composers' Union, Warsaw

ABBREVIATIONS

A.B.	Bachelor of Arts
ABC	American Broadcasting Company
A.M.	Master of Arts
ASCAP	American Society of Composers, Authors, and Publishers
assn./Assn.	association/Association
assoc.	associate
aug.	augmented
b.	born
B.A.	Bachelor of Arts
bar.	baritone
BBC	British Broadcasting Corporation
bjo.	banjo
B.M.	Bachelor of Music
brs.	brass
bs.	bass
CBC	Canadian Broadcasting Corporation
CBS	Columbia Broadcasting System
Coll.	College
cons./Cons.	conservatory/Conservatory
d.	died
dept./Dept.	department/Department
diss.	dissertation
D.M.A.	Doctor of Musical Arts
drm.	drums
ed(s).	edit(ed), editor(s), edition(s)
enl.	enlarged
f.	formed
flt.	flute
gtr.	guitar
har.	harmonica
H.S.	High School
IRCAM	Institut de Recherche et de Coordination Acoustique/Musique
ISCM	International Society for Contemporary Music
inst./Inst.	institute/Institute

kybd.	keyboards
M.A.	Master of Arts
mdln.	mandolin
M.M.	Master of Music
MS(S)	manuscript(s)
Mus.B.	Bachelor of Music
Mus.D.	Doctor of Music
Mus.M.	Master of Music
NAACP	National Association for the Advancement of Colored People
NBC	National Broadcasting Company
n.d.	no date
NEA	National Endowment for the Arts
NHK	Japan Broadcasting Company
no(s).	number(s)
N.Y.	New York
org.	organ
op(p).	opus
orch./Orch.	orchestra/Orchestra
p(p).	page(s)
PBS	Public Broadcasting Service
perc.	percussion
perf.	performance
Ph.D.	Doctor of Philosophy
phil./Phil.	philharmonic/Philharmonic
pno.	piano
posth.	posthumously
prof.	professor
publ.	publish(ed)
RAI	Radiotelevisione Italiana
rds.	reeds
rec.	recorded
rel.	released
rev.	revised
RIAS	Radio in the American Sector
S.	San, Santo, Santa
sax.	saxophone
sop.	soprano
Ss.	Santi, Sante
St(e).	Saint(e)
sym(s).	symphony (-ies)
synth.	synthesizer
tamb.	tamborine
ten.	tenor
tr.	translate(d), translation
trmb.	trombone
trpt.	trumpet
univ./Univ.	university/University
vln.	violin
voc.	vocals
vol(s).	volume(s)
WDR	Westdeutscher Rundfunk (West German Radio)
wdwnd.	woodwinds

A

Aaltonen, Erkki (Erik Verner), Finnish violinist, violist, conductor, and composer; b. Hämeenlinna, Aug. 17, 1910; d. Helsinki, March 8, 1990. He studied violin at the Helsinki Cons., composition privately with Raitio and Palmgren, and conducting at the Sibelius Academy in Helsinki (diploma, 1947). He played in the Helsinki Phil. (1936–66) and was director of the Kullervo Choir (1956–63). From 1966 to 1973 he was music director in Kemi, where he also was director of the Music Coll. (1967–73).

WORKS: DRAMATIC: Ballet music; film scores. **ORCH.:** *Hämeenlinna*, rhapsody (1945); 5 syms. (1947; *Hiroshima*, 1949; *Popular*, 1952; 1959; 1964); 2 piano concertos (1948, 1954); *Folk Music* (1953–60); Violin Concerto (1966). **CHAMBER:** 5 string quartets; piano pieces. **VOCAL:** Choral pieces; songs.—**NS/LK/DM**

Aaltonen, Juhani "Junnu," tenor and alto saxophonist, flutist; b. Kouvola, Finland, Dec. 12, 1935. Aaltonen began as a baritone saxophonist in the late 1950s, working, for example, in Heikki Rosendahl's group in Inkeroinen. Since moving to Helsinki in 1961 he has become known for his versatility as a studio and jazz musician, appearing in numerous radio broadcasts of dance and jazz bands from at least 1966. He studied flute at the Sibelius Academy and uses piccolo, alto, and bass flute. His work with Heikki Sarmanto and Edward Vesala won him the jazz musician of the year award from the Finnish Jazz Federation in 1968. After studying at the Berkelee Coll. of Music in the early 1970s he continued to work with Vesala, as well as with Arild Andersen in Norway (late 1970s) and The New Music Orchestra in Helsinki (from 1975).

DISC.: *Prana Live at Groovy* (1981); *Springbird* (with Senegalese drummers; 1978); *Etiquette* (1974). **E. VESALA:** *Nana* (1970).—**LP**

Aarne, Els, Estonian composer and teacher; b. Makeyevka, Ukraine, March 30, 1917; d. Tallin, June 14,

1995. She studied piano with Lemba at the Tallinn Cons. in Estonia and composition with A. Kapp. From 1944 to 1974 she taught at the Tallinn Cons.

WORKS: ORCH.: Piano Concerto (1945); 2 syms. (1961, 1966); Double Bass Concerto (1968); 3 cello concertos (1974, 1980, 1987). **CHAMBER:** Wind Quintet (1965); Nocturne for Cello and Piano (1970); 2 cello sonatas (1979, 1985). **VOCAL:** *Fatherland*, cantata for Chorus and Orch. (1939); *Sing, Free People*, cantata (1949); numerous songs.—**NS/LK/DM**

Aaron, churchman and music theorist who was known as **Aaron Scotus** after the belief that he was born in Scotland; date of birth unknown; d. Cologne, Nov. 18, 1052. He was Benedictine abbot at St. Martin and at St. Pantaleon in Cologne from 1042. His three treatises, *De utilitate cantus vocalis, De modo cantandi et psallendi*, and *De regulis tonorum et symphoniarum*, are not extant. —**NS/LK/DM**

Aaron or **Aron, Pietro,** Italian music theorist and composer; b. Florence, c. 1480; d. probably in Bergamo, c. 1550. He became cantor at Imola Cathedral about 1515. About 1522 he went to Venice and entered the household of Sebastiano Michiel, the Grand Prior of the Order of St. John of Jerusalem. In 1525 he became his maestro di casa. In 1536 he took the habit of the Cross Bearers and entered the S. Leonardo monastery in Bergamo. His treatises are highly valuable for their treatment of theory as well as aspects of music history.

WRITINGS: *Libri tres de institutione harmonica* (Bologna, 1516); *Thoscanello de la musica* (Venice, 1523; rev. eds. 1529, 1539, and 1562 as *Toscanello in musica*; Eng. tr., 1970); *Trattato della natura et cognitione di tutti gli tuoni di canto figurato...* (Venice, 1525; Eng. tr., 1950, in O. Strunk, *Source Readings in Music History*; 2nd ed., rev. 1998, by L. Treitler); *Lucidario in musica di alcune oppenioni antiche e moderne* (Venice, 1545); *Compendiolo di molti dubbi, segreti et sentenze intorno al canto fermo, et figurato...* (Milan, n.d.).

BIBL.: J. Link Jr., *Theory and Tuning: A.'s Meantone Temperament and Marpurg's Temperament "I"* (Boston, 1963); B. Blackburn, E. Lowinsky, and C. Miller, eds. and trs., *A Correspondence of Renaissance Musicians* (Oxford, 1991).—**NS/LK/DM**

Aav, Evald, Estonian composer; b. Reval, Feb. 22, 1900; d. there (Tallinn), March 21, 1939. He was a student of A. Kapp at the Tallinn Cons. (1926). His works include the first national Estonian opera, *The Vikings* (Tallinn, Sept. 8, 1928), a symphony (1939), and a tone poem, *Life*.—**NS/LK/DM**

Aavik, Juhan, Estonian conductor, pedagogue, and composer; b. Holstre, near Reval, Jan. 29, 1884; d. Stockholm, Nov. 26, 1982. He studied at the St. Petersburg Cons. After conducting in Tartu (1911–23), he was a professor and director of the Reval (Tallinn) Cons. (1925–44) before settling in Sweden. He publ. a history of Estonian music (4 vols., Stockholm, 1965–69).

WORKS: DRAMATIC: Opera: *Autumn Dream* (1939). ORCH.: Violin Concerto (1945); 2 cello concertos (1945, 1949); 2 syms. (1946, 1948); Double Bass Concerto (1950). VOCAL: *Requiem* (1959); choruses; songs. OTHER: Chamber music.—**NS/LK/DM**

Abaco, Evaristo Felice dall'
See **Dall'Abaco, Evaristo Felice**

Abaco, Joseph-Marie-Clément
See **Dall'Abaco, Joseph-Marie-Clément**

Abate, Greg, jazz saxophonist, flutist; b. Fall River, Mass., May 31, 1947. Abate grew up in Woonsocket, R.I. (he now lives in Cranston, R.I.), and attended the Berklee Coll. of Music from 1966 to 1970. In 1973–74, he toured with Ray Charles. He has worked with other big bands, including Artie Shaw (dir. by Dick Johnson) for two years beginning in 1985. Abate is a Selmer clinician who has also taught privately at the Univ. of R.I. (1983 and 1988) and, since 1990, at the Music School in Providence.

DISC.: *Bop City: Live at Birdland* (1991); *Straight Ahead* (1992); *Dr. Jekyll and Mr. Hyde* (1995); *Bop Lives* (1996); *Happy Samba* (1997).—**LP**

ABBA, Swedish pop band, formed 1970. **MEMBERSHIP:** Benny Andersson, kybd., gtr., voc. (b. Stockholm, Sweden, Dec. 16, 1946); Bjorn Ulvaeus, gtr., voc. (b. Gothenburg, Sweden, April 25, 1945); Agnetha "Anna" Faltskog, voc. (b. Jonkping, Swedent, April 5, 1950); Anna-Frid "Frida" Lyngstad, voc. (b. Narvik, Norway, Nov. 15, 1945).

One of the few non-British European groups to achieve consistent success stateside, ABBA issued a series of international hits beginning in 1974 that established them as the world's #1 pop group by 1977.

Formed in 1970 in Stockholm, Sweden, ABBA first gained international recognition as the winner of the Eurovision network song contest in 1974. Their winning song, "Waterloo," became an American hit from their debut album of the same name. Major hits through 1980 included "SOS," "Fernando," "Dancing Queen," "Take a Chance on Me," and, perhaps their finest offering, "The Winner Takes All." Following *Super Trouper* and their final major hit, "When All Is Said and Done," ABBA disbanded. Faltskog and Lyngstad each recorded solo albums in the early 1980s, while Andersson and Ulvaeus achieved their greatest subsequent success as composers for the musical *Chess*. In the mid-1990s ABBA experienced a revival of interest in their music, when it was used in the Australian movies *Muriel's Wedding* and *Priscilla, Queen of the Desert*.

DISC.: ABBA: *Waterloo* (1974); *ABBA* (1975); *Greatest Hits* (1976); *Arrival* (1976); *The Album* (1978); *Voulez-Vous* (1979); *Greatest Hits, Vol. 2* (1979); *Super Trouper* (1980); *The Visitors* (1980); *The Singles* (1982); *I Love ABBA* (1984); *ABBA Live* (1986); *Gold—Greatest Hits* (1993); *Thank You for the Music* (1995). **FRIDA LYNGSTAD:** *Something's Going On* (1982). **AGNETHA FALTSKOG:** *Wrap Your Arms Around Me* (1983); *I Stand Alone* (1988). **BENNY ANDERSSON, BJORN ULVAEUS, AND TIM RICE:** *Chess* (Broadway original cast) (1988).

BIBL.: Marianne Lindvall, *ABBA: The Ultimate Pop Group* (Edmonton, 1977); Harry Edington and Peter Himmelstrand, *ABBA* (Magnum, 1978); John Tobler, *ABBA for the Record: The Authorized Story in Words and Pictures* (Stafford, England, 1980); Rosemary York, *ABBA in Their Own Words* (London, 1981).

Abbà-Cornaglia, Pietro, Italian pianist, organist, teacher, and composer; b. Alessandria, March 20, 1851; d. there, May 2, 1894. He studied with Antonio Angeleri (piano) and Lauro Rossi and Mazzucato (composition) at the Milan Cons. He was organist at Alessandri Cathedral (1880–94) and director of his own music school. His works included the operas *Isabella Spinola* (Milan, 1877), *Maria di Warden* (Venice, 1884), and *Una partita a scacchi* (Pavia, 1892), a Requiem and other sacred pieces, chamber music, organ pieces, and songs. —**NS/LK/DM**

Abbadia, Natale, Italian composer; b. Genoa, March 11, 1792; d. Milan, Dec. 25, 1861. He composed the opera *Giannina di Pontieu* (1812), the farce *L'Imbroglione ed il castigmatti*, masses, and motets. —**NS/LK/DM**

Abbado, Claudio, eminent Italian conductor, brother of **Marcello Abbado** and uncle of **Roberto Abbado;** b. Milan, June 26, 1933. He began violin lessons at age eight with his father, the violinist, conductor, and pedagogue Michelangelo Abbado. After piano lessons from his mother and brother, he entered the Milan Cons. and studied with Enzo Calace (piano), Bettinelli and Paribeni (composition), and Votto (conducting). In 1955 he attended Gulda's piano classes at the Salzburg Mozarteum. He pursued training in conducting with C. Zecchi and Galliera at the Accademia Musicale Chigiana in Siena (summers, 1956–57), and with Swarowsky at the Vienna Academy of Music (1956–58). In 1958 he made his formal conducting debut in Trieste with *The Love for 3 Oranges*, and completed his training in conducting at the Berkshire Music Center in Tanglewood, where he won the Koussevitzky Prize. In 1963 he was one of the three co-winners in the Mitropoulos Competition in N.Y., which led to his appointment as an asst. conductor of the N.Y. Phil. in 1963–64. In 1965 he made his first appearance at Milan's La Scala as a sym. conductor, was a conductor with the Vienna Phil., and made his British debut with the Hallé Orch. in Manchester. Abbado became closely associated with the Vienna Phil. in subsequent years, appearing frequently with it in Vienna, on tours, and on recordings from 1972. In 1967 he made his first appearance as an opera conductor at La Scala, and in 1968 he became its principal conductor and music director, later serving as its artistic director from 1976 to 1986. During his tenure, Abbado raised artistic standards to great heights. In 1968 he conducted *Il Barbiere di Siviglia* at the Salzburg Festival, and also made his debut at London's Covent Garden. On Oct. 7, 1968, he made his Metropolitan Opera debut in N.Y. conducting *Don Carlos*. In 1972 Abbado became principal guest conductor of the London Sym. Orch. In 1979 he assumed the position of its principal conductor, and then was its music director from 1983 to 1988. He founded the European Community Youth Orch. in 1978 and conducted it until organizing the Chamber Orch. of Europe in 1981, which he subsequently served as artistic advisor. In 1982 he founded La Filarmonica della Scala in Milan for the purpose of giving concerts at La Scala. From 1982 to 1986 he was principal guest conductor of the Chicago Sym. Orch. In 1984 he conducted *Simon Boccanegra* at the Vienna State Opera. He was chief conductor of the Vienna State Opera from 1986 to 1991. In 1987 he was honored with the title of Generalmusikdirektor of Vienna. In 1988 he founded and became artistic director of the Gustav Mahler Youth Orch. in Vienna. From 1989 to 2000 Abbado was artistic director of the Berlin Phil., where his tenure was particularly noteworthy for his efforts to broaden its repertoire. He also toured and recorded with it. In 1994 he was artistic director of the Salzburg Easter Festival.

Abbado has demonstrated a capacity for drawing forth fine performances from his musicians in both the symphonic and operatic repertory. His command of the repertory extends from the Classical masters to the latest representatives of the avant-garde. Among his many honors are the Mozart Medal of the Mozart-Gemeinde of Vienna (1973), the Golden Nicolai Medal of the Vienna Phil. (1980), the Gran Croce of Italy (1984), the Gold Medal of the International Gustav Mahler Soc. of Vienna (1985), the Cross of the Légion d'honneur of France (1986), honorary doctorates from the univs. of Aberdeen (1986), Ferrara (1990), and Cambridge (1994), the Bundesverdienstkreuz of Germany (1992), and the Ring of Honor of the City of Vienna (1994).

BIBL.: H. Grünewald, H.-J. von Jena, and U. Meyer-Schoellkopf, *Das Berliner Philharmonische Orchester mit C. A.* (Berlin, 1994).—NS/LK/DM

Abbado, Marcello, Italian music educator, pianist, conductor, and composer, brother of **Claudio Abbado** and uncle of **Roberto Abbado;** b. Milan, Oct. 7, 1926. He studied with Gavazzeni and Lorenzoni (piano

diploma, 1944) and Ghedini and Paribeni (composition diploma, 1947) at the Milan Cons. After teaching piano at several conservatories, he was successively appointed director of the Piacenza Liceo Musicale (1958), the Rossini Cons. in Pesaro (1966), and the Milan Cons. (1972). He also toured as a pianist and conductor. Among his works were stage music, *Costruzioni* for 5 Small Orchs. (1964), a Double Concerto for Violin, Piano, and Two Chamber Orchs. (1967), a Quadruple Concerto for Piano, Violin, Viola, Cello, and Orch. (1969), a Double Concerto for Flute, Guitar, and Orch. (1995), chamber music, piano pieces, and vocal scores. —NS/LK/DM

Abbado, Roberto, Italian conductor, nephew of **Claudio Abbado** and **Marcello Abbado;** b. Milan, Dec. 30, 1954. He was a student of Ferrara in Venice and at the Accademia Nazionale di Santa Cecilia in Rome (1976–77). While still a student, he appeared as a guest conductor with the Orch. di Santa Cecilia in 1977. In 1978 he made his debut as an opera conductor with *Simon Boccanegra* at the Macerata Festival. After conducting in Verona (1979) and Venice and Palermo (1980), he made his debut at the Vienna State Opera conducting *Il Barbiere di Siviglia* at the Zürich Opera and *Don Carlo* at the Deutsche Oper in Berlin. He made his debut at Milan's La Scala with *Il Barbiere di Siviglia* in 1983, and at the Teatro Comunale in Florence with *L'Italiana in Algeri* in 1986. In 1990 he conducted *Adriana Lecouvreur* at his first appearance at the Bavarian State Opera in Munich. In 1991 he made his North American debut as a guest conductor with the Orch. of St. Luke's in N.Y. From 1991 to 1998 he was chief conductor of the Munich Radio Orch. In 1992 he conducted *La forza del destino* at his first appearance at the San Francisco Opera. He made his Metropolitan Opera debut in N.Y. on March 3, 1994, conducting *Adriana Lecouvreur*, and that year made his first appearance at the Hamburg State Opera with *Aida*. In 1995 he conducted *Lucia di Lammermoor* at the Opéra de la Bastille in Paris, and in 1996 *Norma* at the Houston Grand Opera. He also appeared as a guest conductor with many orchs. on both sides of the Atlantic. —NS/LK/DM

Abbatini, Antonio Maria, distinguished Italian composer and teacher; b. Tiferno, 1609 or 1610; d. there, c. 1677. He received his musical training from the Nanino brothers in Rome, where he spent the greater portion of his life. From 1626 to 1628 he was maestro di cappella at St. John Lateran. After serving in that capacity at Orvieto Cathedral (1633), he returned to Rome to hold that position at S. Maria Maggiore (c. 1640–46), S. Lorenzo a Damaso (1646–49), S. Maria Maggiore (1649–57), S. Luigi dei Francesi (1657–67), Santa Casa in Loreto (1667), and once more at S. Maria Maggiore (1672–77). With M. Marazzoli, he composed the opera *Dal male il bene* (Rome, Feb. 12, 1653), historically significant as one of the earliest examples of the inclusion of the ensemble finale. He also wrote the operas *Ione* (Vienna, 1664 or Rome, 1665) and *La comica del ciclo, overo La Baltasara* (Rome, 1668), and the dramatic cantata *Il pianto di Rodomonte* (publ. in Orvieto, 1633). Among his sacred works are a *Missa* for 16 Voices

(Rome, 1634), *Il terzo libro di sacre canzoni* for 2 to 6 Voices (Orvieto, 1634), *Il quinto libro di sacre canzoni* for 2 to 5 Voices (Rome, 1638), *Il sesto libro di sacre canzoni* for 2 to 5 Voices (Rome, 1653), and various motets.

BIBL.: F. Coradini, *A. M. A. e Lorenzo Abbatino: Notizie biografiche* (Arezzo, 1922); K. Andrae, *Ein römischer Kapellmeister im 17. Jahrhundert: A.M. A. (ca. 1600–79). Studien zu Leben und Werk* (diss., Univ. of Hamburg, 1985).—**NS/LK/DM**

Abbey, John (York), English organ builder; b. Whilton, Northamptonshire, Dec. 22, 1785; d. Versailles, Feb. 19, 1859. He settled in France in 1826. After building an organ for the Paris Exposition, he built organs for many French cathedrals. In 1831 he installed an organ at the Paris Opéra. His innovations in the English type of bellows were adopted by many French organ builders.—**NS/LK/DM**

Abbott, Emma, American soprano; b. Chicago, Dec. 9, 1850; d. Salt Lake City, Jan. 5, 1891. She was a pupil of her father, a singer and music teacher. After vocal training from Achille Errani in N.Y., she sang with Chapin's choir there (1870–72). She then pursued vocal studies in Milan with Sangiovanni and in Paris with Marchesi, Wartel, and Delle Sedie. On May 2, 1876, she made her professional debut as Maria in *La Fille du régiment* at London's Covent Garden. On Feb. 8, 1877, she made her U.S. debut in the same role in N.Y. From 1878 she toured with her own company in the U.S. giving performances of operas and operettas in English. She made a habit of interpolating hymns into her performances of operas by Bellini and Donizetti as a specialty.

BIBL.: S. Martin, *The Life and Professional Career of E. A.* (Minneapolis, 1891).—**NS/LK/DM**

Abdullah, Ahmed, trumpeter, composer, leader; b. Harlem, May 10, 1947 (some authorities give his birth year as 1946). He started playing at age 13, and when he was 16 his parents moved to the Lower East Side of Manhattan. He attended Brooklyn Tech. H.S., Queens Coll., and Kingsboro Coll., and privately studied composing and arranging with Cal Massey and trumpet with Carmine Caruso, Chris Capers, and James Stubbs. Abdullah's first professional experience was with a band called The Master Brotherhood. During the early 1970s he backed Solomon Burke, Little Johnny Taylor, and Wilson Pickett as part of Cliff Driver and the Ram Rods, and worked with Joe Simon and Lonnie Young-blood. He also played with Massey, King Rubin and the Counts, Earl Coleman, Lynn Oliver, and The Brotherhood of Sound. Abdullah's work in the Melodic Art-Tet (with Charles Brackeen, Ronnie Boykins, and Roger Blank) led to an association with Sun Ra from May 1975 through 1997. In 1986 he founded The Group with Marion Brown, Billy Bang, Andrew Cyrille, and Sirone, and together they toured Europe.

In 1972 he formed his own group, Abdullah, which recorded one track in 1976. He worked and recorded with Ed Blackwell in 1979 and toured in The Ed Blackwell Project in 1991. Abdullah has also recorded with Arthur Blythe and Billy Bang, and he worked from 1973 to 1983 with choreographer and dancer Dianne McIntyre and was a soloist with New York Dancemobile. In 1987 he formed The Solomonic Unit (later Sextet) around the talents of Charles Moffett. In October 1991 they toured Bulgaria, Yugoslavia, Greece, and Turkey under the auspices of the U.S. Information Agency; they toured Germany a year later. In 1995 through June 1996, Abdullah and his wife, Monique Ngozi Nri, produced concerts in Manhattan by The Sun Ra Arkestra and his own group. With the death of Moffett in 1997, the name of the group was changed to Diaspora. Abdullah has also taught in programs offered by Young Audiences, Orch. of St. Luke, and Carnegie Hall, and with dancer/choreographer Mickey Davidson. His performances at the Skopje (1971) and Leverkreusen (Germany, 1972) jazz festivals were televised.

DISC.: *Live at Ali's Alley* (1978); *Life's Force* (1978/79); *Liquid Magic* (1987); *Solomonic Quintet featuring Charles Moffett* (1987); *Dedication* (1997).—**LP**

Abdul-Malik, Ahmed (born Jonathan Timms), jazz bassist, oud (Middle Eastern lute) player; b. Brooklyn, N.Y., Jan. 30, 1927; d. Long Branch, N.J., Oct. 2, 1993. An early world music pioneer whose father was from Sudan, Abdul-Malik also played modern jazz with Art Blakey, Randy Weston, and, during 1957–58, with Thelonious Monk. He began violin at age seven, and also played cello, tuba, and piano. He performed in a band for Greek, Syrian, and gypsy weddings during junior high school. He later attended N.Y.'s H.S. of Music and Performing Arts and played in the All City Orch.—he may have been on bass by then. Abdul-Malik became an established jazz bassist with Art Blakey (1945, 1948), Randy Weston (1957), Monk (1957–58), Earl Hines (1964), Ken McIntyre (1971), and others. He also remained active in Middle Eastern music, playing the oud on a State Department tour of South America (prob. 1960) and presenting many programs at schools and colleges, mostly around N.Y. In 1961 he visited Africa. Four years later he began working toward a doctorate in music at the N.Y. Coll. of Music; later he taught at Brooklyn Coll. and, from 1970, at N.Y.U. Abdul-Malik was given the Pioneer in Jazz Award by BMI in 1984. A stroke impaired his speech and movement for several years before his death in 1993.

DISC.: *Jazz Sahara* (1958); *East Meets West* (1959); *Museum of Ahmed Abdul-Malik* (1961); *Sounds of Africa* (1962); *Eastern Moods of A. A.-M.* (1963); *Spellbound* (1964).—**LP**

Abe, Kaoru, jazz alto and soprano sax player, also various other reeds; b. Kawasaki, Japan, May 3, 1949; d. Japan, Sept. 9, 1978. Since his early death, Abe has attained cult status among fans of avant-garde music. Performing with established artists such as Masayuki Takayanagi, Yosuke Yamashita, Derek Bailey, and Milford Graves, he established himself as a unique and aggressive voice in improvised music. His solo performances (many of which were recorded for DIW) are legendary.

DISC.: *Partitas* (1973).—**ETA**

Abe, Kōmei, Japanese composer and teacher; b. Hiroshima, Sept. 1, 1911. He studied cello at the Tokyo Academy of Music (graduated in 1933), where he also took postgraduate courses with Pringsheim (composition, 1933–36) and Rosenstock (conducting, 1935–39). He then was a prof. at the Elizabeth Music Coll. in Hiroshima, and subsequently at the Kyoto Municipal Univ. of Arts (1953–77). In his compositions, he demonstrated an assured command of traditional forms.

WORKS: ORCH.: *Theme and Variations* (1935; Tokyo, Feb. 8, 1936); *Kleine Suite* (1936; Tokyo, Feb. 27, 1937); Cello Concerto (Tokyo, March 31, 1942); Piano Concerto (1945; Tokyo, March 27, 1947); 2 syms.: No. 1 (Tokyo, May 9, 1957) and No. 2 (Tokyo, Oct. 10, 1960); *Serenade* (Tokyo, Oct. 7, 1963); *Sinfonietta* (1964; Tokyo, Jan. 14, 1965); *Piccola Sinfonia* for Strings (1984). **CHAMBER:** 16 string quartets (1934, 1937, 1939, 1941, 1946, 1948, 1950, 1952, 1955, 1978, 1982, 1987, 1989, 1990, 1992, 1994); 2 flute sonatas (1942, 1949); Clarinet Quintet (1942); *Divertimento* for Saxophone and Piano (1951; also for Orch., 1953); *Divertimento* for 9 Instruments (1954); Sextet for Flute, Clarinet, Violin, Viola, Cello, and Piano (1964). **Piano:** 3 sonatinas for children (1972); *Dreamland*, 22 short pieces for children (1986). **OTHER:** Choral music; songs; film music.—NS/LK/DM

Abeille, (Johann Christian) Ludwig, German pianist, organist, and composer; b. Bayreuth, Feb. 20, 1761; d. Stuttgart, March 2, 1838. He studied in Stuttgart, where he settled. In 1782 he joined the private band of the Duke of Württemberg, and in 1802 he became Konzertmeister. By 1815 he was court organist and director of music. He retired in 1832. He wrote the Singspiels *Amor und Psyche* (Stuttgart, 1800) and *Peter und Ännchen* (Stuttgart, 1809), a Piano Concerto, chamber music, piano pieces, and songs.—NS/LK/DM

Abejo, Rosalina, Filipino-born American pianist and composer; b. Tagoloan, July 13, 1922; d. Fremont, Calif., June 5, 1991. She studied at the Philippine Women's Univ. (M.M., 1957), with F. Labunski in Cincinnati, and with Barlow at the Eastman School of Music in Rochester, N.Y. She joined the Order of the Virgin Mary, and was the first nun to conduct a sym. orch. Among her works were various orch. pieces, including *Thanatopsis* (1956), *The Trilogy of Man* (1971), the symphonic poem *Guerrilla* (1971), a Guitar Concerto, and a Marimba Concerto, chamber music, piano pieces, and songs.—NS/LK/DM

Abel, Carl Friedrich, German viola da gambist and composer; b. Cöthen, Dec. 22, 1723; d. London, June 20, 1787. He was the son of the viola da gambist and violinist Christian Ferdinand Abel (b. Hannover, c. 1683; d. Cöthen, 1737), with whom he most likely studied. By 1743 he was a viola da gambist in the Dresden court orch., and remained with it until about 1757. After traveling on the Continent, he settled in London and made his debut as a keyboard artist and composer on April 5, 1759. From 1764 until his death he was a court musician to Queen Charlotte. With J. C. Bach, he also was active in the notable Bach-Abel Concerts from 1765 to 1782. After another sojourn on the Continent, he returned to London and was active in the Grand Pro-

fessional Concerts from 1785 to 1787. Abel composed 23 syms., 2 works designated as Sinfonia Concertante, 6 concertos for Harpsichord or Piano, 7 flute concertos, 2 cello concertos, much chamber music, and various viola da gamba pieces. He also wrote overtures to T. A. Arne's opera *Love in a Village* and S. Arnold's opera *The Summer's Tale*. W. Knape edited his works (Cuxhaven, 1958–74) and a *Bibliographische-thematisches Verzeichnis der Kompositioen von K.F. A.* (Cuxhaven, 1971).

BIBL.: W. Knape, *Die Sinfonien von K. F. A.* (diss., Univ. of Leipzig, 1934); S. Helm, *C. F. A., Symphonist: A Biographical, Stylistic and Bibliographical Study* (diss., Univ. of Mich., 1953); W. Knape, *K.F. A.: Leben und Werk eines frühklassischen Komponisten* (Bremen, 1973); M. Charters, *The Bach-A. Concerts* (diss., Univ. of London, 1978).—NS/LK/DM

Abell, John, Scottish countertenor, lutenist, and composer; b. Aberdeenshire, 1652; d. probably in Cambridge, after 1716. He was a chorister in the Chapel Royal in London, and about 1679 he also became a musician in the King's Private Music. In 1684 he took his Mus.B. at Cambridge. A Catholic sympathizer, he left England after the 1688 revolution and traveled throughout Europe. In 1699 he returned to England, where he was successful mainly as a singer until 1716. He publ. the uninspired vols. *A Collection of Songs, in Several Languages* (1701), *A Collection of Songs, in English* (1701), and *A Choice Collection of Italian Ayres* (1703). —NS/LK/DM

Abendroth, Hermann, prominent German conductor and pedagogue; b. Frankfurt am Main, Jan. 19, 1883; d. Jena, May 29, 1956. He studied in Munich with Wirzel-Langenham (piano), Mottl (conducting), and Thuille (composition). In 1903–04 he conducted the Munich Orchestral Soc. In 1905 he went to Lübeck as a sym. conductor (until 1911), and also conducted the City Theater (1907–11). After serving as music director in Essen (1911–15), he was appointed music director of the Gürzenich Orch. and director of the Cons. in Cologne in 1915. In 1918 he was made Cologne's Generalmusikdirektor. In 1933 the Nazi government removed him from his positions, but in 1934 he was appointed music director of the Leipzig Gewandhaus Orch., succeeding Bruno Walter, who had been removed as a Jew. Abendroth also served as a prof. at the Leipzig Cons. With the collapse of the Nazi regime in 1945, he remained in the Eastern sector of Germany as music director of the Weimar National Theater. In 1946 he was made Generalmusikdirektor there. In 1949 he became chief conductor of the Leipzig Radio Sym. Orch., and then of the (East) Berlin Radio Sym. Orch. in 1953. Abendroth's willingness to serve the Nazi and East German Communist regimes made him suspect in some circles but there was no denying his distinction as an interpreter of the Austro-German masters.—NS/LK/DM

Aber, Adolf, German musicologist; b. Apolda, Jan. 28, 1893; d. London, May 21, 1960. He studied with Kretzschmar, Stumpf, Wolf, and Friedlaender. From 1919 to 1933 he served as chief music critic for the

Leipziger Neueste Nachrichten. He then left Germany and settled in London, where he became an editorial adviser with the Novello publishing firm.

WRITINGS: *Handbuch der Musikliteratur* (1922); *Die Musikinstrumente und ihre Sprache* (1924); *Die Musik im Schauspiel, Geschichtliches und Ästhetisches* (1926); *Verzeichnis der Werke von Brahms* (1928).—**NS/LK/DM**

Abert, Anna Amalie, distinguished German musicologist, daughter of **Hermann Abert;** b. Halle, Sept. 19, 1906; d. Kiel, Jan. 4, 1996. She studied with her father, with Blume, and with Sachs at the Univ. of Berlin (Ph.D., 1934, with the diss. *Die stilistischen Voraussetzungen der "Cantiones sacrae" von Heinrich Schütz*). She then joined the faculty of the Univ. of Kiel, where she completed her Habilitation in 1943 with her *Claudio Monteverdi und das musikalische Drama* (publ. in Lippstadt, 1954), and later was a prof. there from 1950 to 1971. In addition to valuable contributions to learned journals, she also publ. *Christoph Willibald Gluck* (Munich, 1959), *Die Opern Mozarts* (Wolfenbüttel, 1970; Eng. tr., 1973, in *The New Oxford History of Music*), *Richard Strauss: Die Opern* (Velber, 1972), and *Geschichte der Oper* (Kassel, 1994).

BIBL.: K. Hotschansky, ed., *Opernstudien: A. A. A. zum 65. Geburtstag* (Tutzing, 1975); idem, ed., *Traditionen-Neuansätze: Für A. A. A. (1906–96)* (Tutzing, 1997).—**NS/LK/DM**

Abert, Hermann, eminent German musicologist, son of **Johann Joseph Abert** and father of **Anna Amalie Abert;** b. Stuttgart, March 25, 1871; d. there, Aug. 13, 1927. He studied with his father, and then with Bellermann, Fleischer, and Friedlaender at the Univ. of Berlin (Ph.D., 1897, with the diss. *Die Lehre vom Ethos in der griechischen Musik*; publ. in Leipzig, 1899). He completed his Habilitation in 1902 at the Univ. of Halle with his *Die ästhetischen Grundsätze der mittelalterlichen Melodiebildung* (publ. in Halle, 1902), where he was made an honorary prof. in 1909 and a lecturer in 1911. In 1920 he became a prof. at the Univ. of Leipzig. From 1923 he was a prof. at the Univ. of Berlin. Abert's most important work was his exhaustively rewritten and revised ed. of Jahn's biography of Mozart, which he publ. as *Wolfgang Amadeus Mozart: Neu bearbeitete und erweitert Ausgabe von Otto Jahns "Mozart"* (2 vols., Leipzig, 1919, 1921; rev. by his daughter, 1955–56). Among his other books were *Robert Schumann* (Berlin, 1903; 4th ed., 1920), *Die Musikanschauung des Mittelalters und ihre Grundlagen* (Halle, 1905), *Niccolò Jommelli als Opernkomponist* (Halle, 1908), *Johann Joseph Abert, 1832–1915: Sein Leben und seine Werke* (Leipzig, 1916), and *Goethe und die Musik* (Engelhorn, 1922). F. Blume ed. his *Gesammelte Schriften und Vorträge* (Halle, 1929).

BIBL.: F. Blume, ed., *Gedenkschrift für H. A. von seinen Schülern* (Halle, 1928); K. Funk, *H. A.: Musiker, Musikwissenschaftler, Musikpädagoge* (Stuttgart, 1994).—**NS/LK/DM**

Abert, Johann Joseph, German conductor and composer, father of **Hermann Abert;** b. Kochowitz, Sept. 20, 1832; d. Stuttgart, April 1, 1915. He studied double bass and composition at the Prague Cons. (1846–53). In 1853 he settled in Stuttgart as a double bass player in the Court Orch., where he subsequently served as its conductor from 1857 to 1888. Abert became best known as a composer of operas, his most successful being *Astorga* (Stuttgart, May 20, 1866). Others were *Anna von Landscron* (Stuttgart, Dec. 19, 1858), *König Enzio* (Stuttgart, May 4, 1862; rev. as *Enzio von Hohenstaufen*, Stuttgart, April 11, 1875), *Ekkehard* (Berlin, Oct. 11, 1878), and *Die Almohaden* (Leipzig, April 13, 1890). Among his other works were syms., including the programmatic *Columbus* (Stuttgart, Jan. 26, 1864), overtures, chamber music, and sacred and secular vocal scores.

BIBL.: H. Abert, *J. J. A., 1832–1915: Sein Leben und seine Werke* (Leipzig, 1916).—**NS/LK/DM**

Abos, Girolamo, Maltese composer and teacher of Spanish descent; b. La Valetta, Nov. 16, 1715; d. Naples, Oct. 1760. He settled in Naples, where he most likely received his training at the Cons. Poveri di Gesù Cristo. In 1742–43 he was on its faculty, and he also taught at the Cons. S. Onofrio a Capuana from 1742, where he was maestro from 1748 to 1760. He likewise taught at the Cons. della Pietà dei Turchini, where he was secondo maestro from 1754 to 1759. Abos became best known as a composer of both opera buffa and opera serie.

WORKS: DRAMATIC: *Le due zingare simili*, opera buffa (Naples, 1742); *Il gelosa*, commedia (Naples, 1743); *Le furberie di Spilletto*, commedia (Florence, 1744); *La serva padrona*, opera buffa (Naples, 1744); *La moglie gelosa*, commedia (Naples, 1745); *Artaserse*, opere serie (Venice, Carnival 1746); *Pelopida*, opera serie (Rome, 1747); *Alessandro nelle Indie*, opera serie (Ancona, 1747); *Arianna e Teseo*, opera serie (Rome, Dec. 26, 1748); *Adriano in Siria*, opera serie (Rome, 1750?); *Tito Manlio*, opera serie (Naples, May 30, 1751); *Erifile*, opere serie (Rome, 1752); *Lucio Vero o sia Il vologeso*, opera serie (Naples, Dec. 18, 1752); *Il Medo*, opera serie (Turin, Carnival 1753). **OTHER:** Masses and other sacred vocal music.—**NS/LK/DM**

Abraham, Gerald (Ernest Heal), eminent English musicologist; b. Newport, Isle of Wight, March 9, 1904; d. Midhurst, March 18, 1988. A man of many and varied interests, he studied philology and mastered the Russian language. He was active with the BBC (1935–47) and served as ed. of the *Monthly Musical Record* (1945–60); after being the first prof. of music at the Univ. of Liverpool (1947–62), he returned to the BBC as asst. controller of music (1962–74). In 1974 he was made a Commander of the Order of the British Empire. He publ. *Borodin: The Composer and His Music* (1927; 2nd ed., 1935); *This Modern Stuff* (1933; 2nd ed., rev., 1952, as *This Modern Music*; 3rd ed., 1955); *Studies in Russian Music* (1935; 2nd ed., 1969); *Masters of Russian Music* (with M. Calvocoressi, 1936; 2nd ed., rev., 1958); *A Hundred Years of Music* (1938; 4th ed., rev., 1974); *Chopin's Musical Style* (1939); *On Russian Music* (1939); *Beethoven's Second-period Quartets* (1942); *Eight Soviet Composers* (1943); *Tchaikovsky* (1944); *Rimsky-Korsakov: A Short Biography* (1945); *Design in Music* (1949); *Slavonic and Romantic Music* (1968); *The Tradition of Western Music* (1974); *The Concise Oxford History of Music* (1979); *Essays on Russian and East European Music* (1985). He also ed. Calvocoressi's *Mussorgsky* (1946; 2nd ed., rev., 1974) and symposiums on Tchaikovsky (1945), Schubert (1946; 2nd ed., 1952), Sibelius (1947; 2nd ed., 1952), Grieg (1948; 2nd ed., 1952), Schumann (1952), and Handel (1954). For *The New Oxford History of Music*, he ed. vol. III, *Ars Nova and the Renaissance 1300–1540* (with A. Hughes, 1960), vol. IV, *The Age of Humanism 1540–1630* (1968), vol. VIII, *The Age of Beethoven* (1982), and vol. IX, *Romanticism 1830–1890* (1990).—NS/LK/DM

Abraham, Max, German music publisher; b. Danzig, July 3, 1831; d. Leipzig, Dec. 8, 1900. He became a partner of the Bureau de Musique von C. F. Peters in Leipzig in 1863, and in 1867 he inaugurated the famous Edition Peters.—NS/LK/DM

Abraham, Paul (originally, **Pál Ábrahám**), Hungarian composer; b. Apatin, Nov. 2, 1892; d. Hamburg, May 6, 1960. He studied in Budapest, and began his career as a composer of serious scores. Turning his attention to lighter music, he became conductor and composer at the Fváriosi Operettszinház in 1927. He scored his greatest success with the operetta *Viktória* (Budapest, Feb. 21, 1930), which subsequently was performed widely abroad. Other works of merit included the operettas *Die Blume von Hawaii* (Leipzig, July 24, 1931) and *Ball im Savoy* (Berlin, Dec. 23, 1932), and his film score for *Die Privatsekretärin* (1931). With the rise of the Nazi regime, Abraham left Europe and settled in the U.S. in 1938, where he made ends meet as a pianist. He eventually settled in Hamburg, ill and largely forgotten. All the same, several of his works continued to be revived long after his death.

WORKS: DRAMATIC: Music Theater: *Zenebona* (Budapest, March 2, 1928); *Az utolsó Verebély lány* (Budapest, Oct. 13, 1928); *Szeretem a feleségem* (Budapest, June 15, 1929); *Viktória* (Budapest, Feb. 21, 1930; also known as *Viktoria und ihr Husar*); *Die Blume von Hawaii* (Leipzig, July 24, 1931); *Ball im Savoy* (Berlin, Dec. 23, 1932); *Märchen im Grand- Hotel* (Vienna, March 29, 1934); *Viki* (Budapest, Jan. 26, 1935); *Történnek még csodák* (Budapest, April 20, 1935); *Dschainah, das Mädchen aus dem Tanzhaus* (Vienna, Dec. 20, 1935); *3: 1 a szerelem javára* (Budapest, Dec. 18, 1936); *Roxy und ihr Wunderteam* (Vienna, March 25, 1937); *Júlia* (Budapest, Dec. 23, 1937); *Fehér hattyú* (Budapest, Dec. 23, 1938).

BIBL.: G. Sebestyén, *P. A.: Aus dem Leben eines Operettenkomponisten* (Vienna, 1987).—NS/LK/DM

Abrahamsen, Hans, Danish composer; b. Copenhagen, Dec. 23, 1952. He studied horn, theory, and music history at the Royal Danish Cons. of Music in Copenhagen (1969–71), then composition at the Jutland Academy of Music in Århus with Gudmundsen-Holmgreen and Nørgård. His music presents an effective blend of folkloric Scandinavian elements and modernistic devices often veering off into atonal melos, viralized by polyrhythmic dynamic contrasts.

WORKS: ORCH.: *Skum* (Foam; 1970); *Sym. in C* (1972); 2 numbered syms. (1974, 1982); *Stratifications* (1973–75); *Nacht und Trompeten* (1981; Berlin, March 25, 1982); *Märchenbilder* for 14 Players (1984; London, Feb. 7, 1985); *Cello Concerto* (1987). **CHAMBER:** *Fantasy Pieces after Hans-Jørgen Nielsen* for Flute, Horn, Cello, and Piano (1969; rev. 1976); *October* for Piano, Left Hand (1969; rev. 1976); *Herbst* for Tenor, Flute, Guitar, and Cello (1970–72; rev. 1977); *Round and In Between* for Brass Quintet (1972); 2 woodwind quintets: No. 1, *Landscapes* (1972) and No. 2, *Walden* (1978); *Nocturnes*, 4 pieces for Flute and Piano (1972); *Flowersongs* for 3 Flutes (1973); *Scraps* for Cello and Piano (1973); 2 string quartets: No. 1, *10 Preludes* (1973) and No. 2 (1981); *Flush* for Saxophone (1974; rev. 1979); *Songs of Denmark* for Soprano and 5 Instruments (1974; rev. 1976); *Double* for Flute and Guitar (1975); *Winternacht* for 7 Instruments (1976–79); *Canzone* for Accordion (1978); *Aria* for Soprano and 4 Instruments (1979); *Geduldspiel* for 10 Instruments (1980); *6 Pieces* for Violin, Horn, and Piano (1984); *10 Studies* for Piano (1983–87); *Storm and Still* for Cello (1988); *Hymn* for Cello or Viola (1990); *Capriccio Bagatels* for Violin (1990). **VOCAL:** *Herbst* for Tenor or Soprano, Flute, Guitar, and Cello (1972–77); *Universe Birds* for 10 or 5 Sopranos (1973); *Denmark Song* for Soprano, Flute, Clarinet, Percussion, Piano, and Viola (1974); *Aria* for Soprano, Flute, Percussion, Harp, and Cello (1979); *2 Grundtvig-Motets* for Chorus (1983–84); *Herbstlied* for Soprano, Harpsichord or Piano, Clarinet, Violin, and Cello (1992).—NS/LK/DM

Abrams (Abramovitch), Max, drummer, percussionist; b. Glasgow, Aug. 11, 1907; d. Eastbourne, East Sussex, England, Nov. 5, 1995. Abrams played in the local Boys' Brigade Band as a teenager. He worked in a juvenile group (Archie Pitt's Busby Band) in the mid-1920s and with Chalmers Wood at Glasgow Locarno in 1928. He went to South Africa with saxophonist Vic Davis in 1930 and returned to Britain the following year, working with Joe Gibson before joining saxophonist Tommy Kinsman at Ciro's Club, London, in autumn 1931. Abrams worked with briefly with Teddy Sinclair (1932) and Jack Hylton (1932–33), then joined the house band at the Gargoyle Club, London, in the summer of 1933. With Sydney Lipton from 1934 until 1935, and with Carroll Gibbons from 1935 until 1939, Abrams established his reputation as a highly successful drum teacher during this period. He also led his own recording bands and made drum tuition records. After stints in various groups, including Sid Phillips's, Abrams toured variety halls with George Scott-Wood in 1942 and 1943, then, as a Sub Lieutenant in the Royal Navy Volunteer Reserves, coached cadet bands. Abrams worked with Jack Payne from the summer of 1944 until late 1945, then worked briefly with Stephane Grappelli before rejoining Sid Phillips from December 1945 until the early 1950s. A freelancer beginning in the 1950s, Abrams and ran his own prestigious drum school in London. He continued to teach full time until 1977, then moved to Eastbourne, Sussex, where he occasionally took on new pupils until the early 1990s.

DISC.: M.A. AND HIS RHYTHM MAKERS: Two titles in 1936, two in 1937.—JC-B

Abrams, Muhal Richard, pianist, composer, leader (also clarinet, saxophones); b. Chicago, Sep. 19, 1930. Abrams studied piano at Chicago Musical Coll. for four years beginning at age 17, but says he was essentially self- taught. He first worked professionally in 1948 and wrote arrangements for saxophonist King Fleming from 1950. Abrams frequently sat in with local and visiting musicians, including Miles Davis, Sonny Rollins, Gene Ammons, Johnny Griffin, Dexter Gordon, Art Farmer, Max Roach, Sonny Stitt, and Johnny Griffin.

Beginning in 1955, he played in Walter Perkins's group MJT + 3, for which he also wrote. In 1961 Abrams formed The Experimental Band with Donald Rafael Garrett and the band was to include many of the new Chicago musicians. This led to Abrams becoming the Association for the Advancement of Creative Musicians' first president on May 8, 1965. He emphasized grounding in tradition and experimentation with new forms; his many protégés included Lester Bowie, Anthony Braxton, and trombonist George Lewis. Abrams played with Woody Herman, Ruth Brown, and Lambert, Hendricks & Ross, the went to Europe with his own group in 1973. He moved to N.Y. around 1977 and performed and recorded there in various contexts: solo; in duos with Lewis, Braxton, Leroy Jenkins, and Amina Claudine Myers; in small groups; and with a big band. Beginning in 1967, Abrams recorded his innovative compositions. In the mid-1980s he wrote a piece on commission for the Kronos String Quartet. In the late 1980s he led a quintet that included John Purcell and Stanton Davis. Also in the late 1980s, Abrams was associated with classical pianist Ursula Oppens. Several of Abrams's albums from the 1980s and 1990s feature a band of about 12 people performing music that mixes free improvisation and dissonant writing with swing traditions. His daughter Richarda Abrams sings on "Song For All."

DISC: *Levels and Degrees of Light* (1967); *Young at Heart, Wise in Time* (1969); *Things to Come from Those Now Gone* (1972); *Afrisong* (1975); *Sightsong* (with Malachi Favors; 1975); *Lifelong Ambitions* (1977); *Spiral: Live at Montreux* (1978); *Duet* (with Amina Claudine Myers; 1981); *Blues Forever* (1981); *Rejoicing with the Light* (1983); *View from Within* (1984); *Roots of Blue* (1986); *Colours in Thirty-Third* (1986); *Hearing a Suite* (1989); *Family Talk* (1993). **ART ENSEMBLE OF CHICAGO:** *Fanfare for the Warriors* (1973). **MJT + 3:** *Branching Out.*—LP

Abramsky, Alexander, Russian composer; b. Lutsk, Jan. 22, 1898; d. Moscow, Aug. 29, 1985. He studied at the Moscow Cons. (graduated, 1926). Among his works were the opera *Laylikhon and Anarkhon* (1943), a Piano Concerto (1941), and choral pieces, including the cantata *Land of the Silent Lake* (1971).—NS/LK/DM

Ábrányi, Emil, Hungarian conductor and composer, grandson of **Kornél Ábrányi;** b. Budapest, Sept. 22, 1882; d. there, Feb. 11, 1970. He studied composition with Koessler at the Academy of Music in Budapest and conducting with Nikisch in Leipzig. After conducting in Cologne (1904–07) and Hannover (1907–11), he returned to Budapest as conductor at the Royal Opera. He also was director of the municipal theater (1921–26).

WORKS: DRAMATIC: Opera: *A ködkirály* (The King of the Mist; Budapest, 1902); *Monna Vanna* (Budapest, March 2, 1907); *Paolo e Francesca* (Budapest, Jan. 13, 1912); *Don Quijote* (Budapest, Nov. 30, 1917); *Ave Maria* (Budapest, 1922); *Az énekl dervis* (Singing Dervishes; 1935); *Liliomos herceg* (The Prince with the Lillies; 1938); *Bizánc* (Byzantium; 1942); *Éva boszorkány* (Sorceress Eve; 1944); *Balatoni rege* (The Tale of Balaton; 1945); *A Tamás templom karnagya* (The Cantor of St. Thomas Church; 1947).—NS/LK/DM

Ábrányi, Kornél, Hungarian pianist, pedagogue, writer on music, and composer, grandfather of **Emil**

Ábrányi; b. Szengyörgyábrány, Oct. 15, 1822; d. Budapest, Dec. 20, 1903. He came from a wealthy family originally named Eördögh, which means "devil." His father changed the name to Ábrányi, the name of his estate. He toured as a pianist throughout Hungary. After studying piano with Fischhof in Vienna (1846–47), he went to Pest and studied composition with Mosonyi. In 1860 he helped to found the first Hungarian music journal, the *Zenészeti lapok,* which he edited until 1876. He also was founder-director of the National Assn. of Choral Societies (1867–88) and an asst. prof. at the Budapest Academy of Music (1875–88). Ábrányi took a major part in the formation and encouragement of the Hungarian national school of composition. His own works include much piano music, choral pieces, and songs. His most important writings include biographies of Mosonyi (1872) and Erkel (1895), *Képek a múlt és jelenbl* (Pictures from Past and Present; 1899), and *A magyar zene a 19. században* (Hungarian Music in the 19th Century; 1900). He also wrote an autobiography, *Életembl és emlékeimbl* (From My Life and Memories; 1897).—NS/LK/DM

Abravanel, Maurice, distinguished Greek-born American conductor of Spanish-Portuguese Sephardic descent; b. Saloniki, Jan. 6, 1903; d. Salt Lake City, Sept. 22, 1993. He attended the univs. of Lausanne (1919–21) and Zürich (1921–22) before studying composition in Berlin with Kurt Weill. In 1924 he made his conducting debut in Berlin, and then conducted widely in Germany until he was compelled to go to Paris by the advent of the Nazis in 1933. After touring Australia (1934–36), he made his Metropolitan Opera debut in N.Y. conducting *Samson et Dalila* on Dec. 26, 1936, remaining on its roster until 1938; then conducted on Broadway. In 1940–41 he was a conductor at the Chicago Opera. In 1947 he became music director of the Utah Sym. Orch. in Salt Lake City, which, by the time of his retirement in 1979, he had molded into one of the finest U.S. orchs. He also served as artistic director of the Music Academy of the West in Santa Barbara from 1954 to 1980. From 1982 he was active at the Tanglewood Music Center. On his 90th birthday on Jan. 6, 1993, the Utah Sym. Orch.'s concert hall was renamed in his honor.

BIBL.: L. Durham, *A.!* (Salt Lake City, 1989).—NS/LK/DM

Abreu (Rebello), Sergio (b. Rio de Janeiro, June 5, 1948) and **Abreu, Eduardo** (b. Rio de Janeiro, Sept. 19, 1949), sibling Brazilian guitarists. They first studied with their grandfather, Antonio Rebello, and then with Adolfina Raitzin Tavora; they began their career in 1963 with concerts throughout South America, making their European debut in London in 1968, and their U.S. debut in N.Y. in 1970; they later toured extensively all over the world.—NS/LK/DM

Absil, Jean, eminent Belgian composer and pedagogue; b. Bon-Secours, Oct. 23, 1893; d. Brussels, Feb. 2, 1974. After studying organ, piano, and composition with Alphonse Oeyen in Bon-Secours, he pursued training at the Brussels Cons. with Desmet (1st prize in organ, 1916), Moulaert (piano), Lunssens (1st prize in harmony, 1916), and DuBois (1st prize in counterpoint and fugue, 1917). He completed his studies in composition with Gilson (1920–22). In 1921 he won the Prix Agniez for his 1st Sym., in 1922 the 2nd Prix de Rome for his cantata *La guerre,* and in 1934 the Prix Rubens. In 1938 he garnered wide recognition for his Piano Concerto, which was commissioned by the Ysaÿe Competition. From 1922 to 1964 Absil was director of the Etterbeek Music School. He also taught at the Brussels Cons. (1930–39) and the Chapelle Musical Reine Elisabeth (1939–59). In 1955 he became a member and in 1968 president of the Académie Royale Belgique. He received the Belgian government's Prix Quinquennial in 1964.

WORKS: DRAMATIC: *Peau d'âne,* lyrical poem (1937); *Ulysse et les sirènes,* radio play (1939); *Fansou ou Le Chapeau chinois,* musical comedy (1944); *Le Miracle de Pan,* ballet (1949); *Pierre Breughel l'Ancien,* radio play (1950); *Épouvantail,* ballet (1950); *Les Voix de la mer,* opera (1951; Brussels, March 26, 1954); *Les Météores,* ballet (1951). **ORCH.:** 5 syms. (1920, 1936, 1943, 1969, 1970); *La Mort de Tintagiles,* symphonic poem (1923–26); *Rapsodie flamande* (1928; also for Wind Ensemble); *Berceuse* for Small Orch. and Cello or Saxophone (1932); 2 violin concertos (1933, 1964); *Petite suite* for Small Orch. (1935; also for Wind Ensemble); 3 piano concertos (1937, 1967, 1973); *Rapsodie No. 2* (1938); *Hommage à Lekeu* (1939); Cello Concertino (1940); *Sérénade* (1940); *Variations symphoniques* (1942); Viola Concerto (1942); *Rapsodie roumaine* for Violin and Orch. (1943); *Concerto grosso* for Wind Quintet and Orch. (1944); *Jeanne d'Arc,* symphonic poem (1945); *Rites,* triptych for Wind Ensemble (1952); *Rapsodie brésilienne* (1953); *Mythologie,* suite (1954); *Croquis sportifs* for Wind Ensemble (1954); *Divertimento* for Saxophone Quartet and Chamber Orch. (1955); *Introduction et Valses* (1955); *Legend* for Wind Ensemble (1956); *Suite,* after Romanian folklore (1956); *Suite bucolique* for Strings (1957); *Fantaisie concertante* for Violin and Orch. or Piano (1959); *Danses bulgares* (1959; also for Wind Quintet or Piano); *Rapsodie bulgare* (1960); *2 Danses rituelles* for Small Orch. (1960); *Triptyque* for Small Orch. (1960); *Fantaisie-humoresque* for Clarinet and Strings or Piano (1962); *Rapsodie No. 6* for Horn and Orch. or Piano (1963); Viola Concertino (1964); *Nymphes et faunes* for Wind Orch. (1966); *Allegro brillante* for Piano and Orch. (1967); *Fantaisie-caprice* for Saxophone and Strings (1971); Guitar Concerto (1971); *Ballade* for Saxophone, Piano, and Small Orch. (1971); *Déités,* suite (1973). **CHAMBER:** 4 string quartets (1929, 1934, 1935, 1941); 2 piano trios (1931, 1972); 2 string trios (1935, 1939); *Fantaisie rapsodique* for 4 Cellos (1936); Cello Quartet (1937); Quartet for Saxophones (1937); Piano Quartet (1938); *Fantaisie* for Piano Quartet (1939); *Concert à cinq* for Flute, Violin, Viola, Cello, and Harp (1939); 2 suites for Cello and Piano (1942, 1968); *Chaconne* for Violin (1949); *3 Contes* for Trumpet and Piano (1951); Suite for Trombone and Piano (1952); *Sonatine en duo* for Violin and Viola (1962); Saxophone Sonata (1963); *3 Pièces* for Organ (1965); Quartet for Clarinets (1967); Sonata for Solo Violin (1967); *Croquis pour un carnaval* for 4 Clarinets and Harp (1968); *Suite mystique* for 4 Flutes (1969); Violin Sonata (1970); *Esquisses* for Wind Quartet (1971); *Images stellaires* for Violin and Cello (1973); also numerous guitar pieces. **PIANO:** *3 Impromptus* (1932); 3 sonatinas (1937, 1939, 1965); *3 Marines* (1939); *Bagatelles* (1944); *2 Grand Suites* (1944, 1962); *Sketches on the 7 Capital Sins* (1954); *Variations* (1956); *Chess Game,* suite (1957); *Passacaglia* (1959); *Rapsodie No. 5* for 2 Pianos (1959); *Humoresques* (1965); *Ballade*

(1966); *Asymétries* for 2 Pianos (1968); *Alternances* (1968); *Féeries* (1971); *Poésie et vélocité,* 20 pieces (1972). **VOCAL:** *La Guerre,* cantata (1922); *Philatélie,* chamber cantata (1940); *Les Bénédictions,* cantata (1941); *Les Chants du mort,* cantata for Vocal Quartet and Small Orch. (1941); *Le Zodiaque* for Chorus, Piano, and Orch. (1949); *Phantasmes* for Contralto, Saxophone, Piano, and Percussion (1950); *Le Cirque volant,* cantata (1953); *Petites polyphonies* for 2 Voices and Orch. (1966); *À cloche-pied* for Children's Chorus and Orch. (1968).

BIBL.: R. de Guide, *J. A.: Vie et oeuvre* (Tournai, 1965). —NS/LK/DM

Abt, Franz (Wilhelm), German conductor and composer; b. Eilenburg, Dec. 22, 1819; d. Wiesbaden, March 31, 1885. He was educated in Leipzig at the Thomasschule and the Univ. In 1841 he went to Zürich as conductor of the Allgemeinen Musikgesellschaft. He became 2nd conductor at the Braunschweig court in 1852, and subsequently was its 1st conductor from 1855 to 1882. Abt wrote over 600 works, becoming best known for his songs and choral pieces. In his day, his songs became so well known that some were mistaken for genuine folk songs.

BIBL.: B. Rost, *Vom Meister des volkstümlichten deutschen Liedes F. A.* (Chemnitz, 1924).—NS/LK/DM

Accardo, Salvatore, outstanding Italian violinist and conductor; b. Turin, Sept. 26, 1941. He studied with Luigi d'Ambrosio at the Cons. S. Pietro a Majella in Naples and with Yvonne Astruc at the Accademia Musicale Chigiana in Siena. He won the Vercelli (1955), Geneva (1956), and Paganini (Genoa, 1958) competitions, then pursued a remarkable career, appearing both as soloist with major orchs. of the world and as recitalist. He was also active in later years as a conductor. In 1993 he was appointed music director of the Teatro San Carlo in Naples. He publ. *L'arte del violino* (ed. by M. Delogu; Milan, 1987). As a violin virtuoso, Accardo excels in a vast repertoire; in addition to the standard literature, he performs many rarely heard works, including those by Paganini. His playing is marked by a fidelity to the classical school of violin playing, in which virtuosity is subordinated to stylistic propriety. —NS/LK/DM

Accorimboni, Agostino, Italian composer; b. Rome, Aug. 29, 1739; d. there, Aug. 13, 1818. He was a pupil of Rinaldo di Capua. He composed 13 stage works (1768–85), the most notable being his comic opera *Il regno delle Amazzoni* (Parma, Dec. 27, 1783). Among his other works were a Sym. and sacred music, including an oratorio.—NS/LK/DM

AC/DC, American heavy metal band, formed 1974. **MEMBERSHIP:** Ronald Belford "Bon" Scott, voc. (b. Kirriemuir, Scotland, July 9, 1946; d. there, Feb. 20, 1980); Angus Young, lead gtr. (b. Glasgow, Scotland, March 31, 1959); Malcolm Young, rhythm gtr. (b. Glasgow, Scotland, Jan. 6, 1953); Mark Evans, bs.; Phil Rudd, drm. Ron Scott was replaced by Brian Johnson (b. Newcastle, England, Oct. 5, 1947).

A prototypical heavy-metal band formed in Sydney, Australia, in 1974, AC/DC established themselves in Great Britain and then the United States on the basis of tireless touring, and eventually broke through with 1979's *Highway to Hell.*

Recording songs that focused on sex, violence, and the occult packaged in live-action album covers, AC/DC achieved notoriety in 1985 when Los Angeles mass murderer Richard Ramirez, known as the Night Stalker, cited recordings by the band as the source of his satanic inspiration. Fundamentalist Christians and others in the United States were outraged, and the band was accused of planting messages in their music that were detectable only when their albums were played backward. The controversy spurred Tipper Gore of the Washington-based Parents' Music Resource Center to call for warning labels on albums, which in turn ignited the issue of censorship in mass media.

Persevering with vocalist Brian Johnson after the alcohol-related death of Bon Scott in 1980, AC/DC garnered tremendous popularity with *Back in Black*—ostensibly the best-selling (more than nine million copies) heavy-metal album in history—and *For Those About to Rock, We Salute You.* Projecting a blue-collar charm to their young, mostly male fans, and eschewing synthesizers, AC/DC again sparked public hostility when several fans were crushed to death in a rush to the stage at a 1991 show in Salt Lake City.

DISC.: *Dirty Deeds Done Cheap* (1976); *High Voltage* (1976); *Let There Be Rock* (1977); *Powerage* (1978); *If You Want Blood, You've Got It* (1978); *Highway to Hell* (1979); *Back in Black* (1980); *For Those About to Rock, We Salute You* (1981); *Flick of the Switch* (1983); *'74 Jailbreak* (1984); *Fly on the Wall* (1985); *Who Made Who* (soundtrack to film *Maximum Overdrive*; 1986); *Blow Up Your Video* (1988); *The Razor's Edge* (1990); *Live* (special collector's edition; 1992); *Live* (1992); *Ballbreaker* (1995); *Bonfire* (1997).

BIBL.: Richard Bunton, *AC/DC: Hell Ain't No Bad Place to Be* (London, 1982); Malcolm Dome, *AC/DC* (London, 1982); Paul Ezra, *The AC/DC Story* (London, 1982); Mark Putterford, *AC/DC Illustrated Biography* (London, 1992).

Achron, Isidor, Lithuan-born American pianist, teacher, and composer, brother of **Joseph Achron;** b. Warsaw, Nov. 24, 1892; d. N.Y., May 12, 1948. He studied with Essipova (piano), Liadov (composition), and Steinberg (orchestration) at the St. Petersburg Cons. In 1922 he settled in the U.S., becoming a naturalized citizen in 1928. After serving as accompanist to Heifetz (1922–33), he pursued a career as a soloist with orchs. and as a recitalist. His compositions, all in the moderate Romantic manner prevalent of his time, included 2 piano concertos (No. 1, N.Y., Dec. 9, 1937, composer soloist, and No. 2, 1942), a *Suite Grotesque* for Orch. (St. Louis, Jan. 30, 1942), and numerous works for Piano and Violin.—NS/LK/DM

Achron, Joseph, Lithuanian-born American violinist and composer, brother of **Isidor Achron;** b. Lozdzieje, Russian Poland, May 13, 1886; d. Los Angeles, April 29, 1943. He studied violin in Warsaw and made his debut there at age 7, then was a pupil of Auer (violin) and Liadov (composition) at the St. Petersburg

Cons. (1898–1904), where he also later studied theory and composition (1907). After a sojourn in Palestine (1924–25), he settled in the U.S. and became a naturalized citizen in 1928. In 1934 he went to Hollywood, where he was active as a violinist and composer. His early works are marked by characteristic Russian harmonies with a distinctly Romantic aura; later he developed an idiom based on structural principles employing atonal and polytonal devices. In his *Golem Suite* for Chamber Orch. (1932), the last section is the exact retrograde movement of the first sections, which symbolizes the undoing of the monster Golem.

WORKS: ORCH.: *Hazan* for Cello and Orch. (1912); 3 violin concertos: No. 1 (Boston, Jan. 24, 1927, composer soloist), No. 2 (Los Angeles, Dec. 19, 1936, composer soloist), and No. 3 (Los Angeles, March 31, 1939, composer soloist); *Golem Suite* for Chamber Orch. (1932); Piano Concerto (1941). **CHAMBER:** 4 *tableaux fantastiques* for Violin and Piano (1907); *Chromatic String Quartet* (1907); 2 violin sonatas (1910, 1918); *Hebrew Melody* for Violin and Piano (1911); *2 Hebrew Pieces* for Violin and Piano (1912); *Suite bizarre* for Violin and Piano (1916); *Elegy* for String Quartet (1927); Sextet for Flute, Oboe, Clarinet, Bassoon, Horn, and Trumpet (1938). **OTHER:** Piano pieces; choral works; film music.

BIBL.: P. Moddel, *J. A.* (Tel Aviv, 1966).—NS/LK/DM

Achúcarro, Joaquín, le;2.375qSpanish pianist and teacher; b. Bilbao, Nov. 1, 1936. He revealed a talent for music as a child but first studied physics. After determining upon a career in music, he studied at the Accademia Musicale Chigiana in Siena. He won 1st prize in both the Geneva and Viotti competitions, and then pursued further training in Germany and Switzerland. After completing his studies in Vienna and Salzburg, he captured 1st prize in the Liverpool Competition in 1959, which led to his engagement as a soloist with the London Sym. Orch. In subsequent years, he appeared as a soloist with all of the leading British orchs. He also appeared with major orchs. on the Continent, and in the U.S., South America, Japan, and Australia. Upon occasion, he also appeared in the dual capacity of soloist- conductor with orchs. in England, Germany, Italy, and Spain. In 1989 he was appointed to the Joel Estes Tate Endowed Chair in Piano at Southern Methodist Univ. in Dallas, but he continued to pursue an active concert career. In 1992 he received the Premio Nacional de Musica from the Spanish government, in 1996 King Juan Carlos awarded him with the Gold Medal of Fine Arts of Spain, and in 1999 UNESCO honored him with the title of Artist for Peace. In addition to his admired performances of Beethoven, Schubert, Schumann, Chopin, and other masters of the Romantic era, he has displayed a remarkable grasp of the Spanish idiom of such composers as Granados, Falla, and Rodrígo.—NS/LK/DM

Acker, Dieter, German composer and pedagogue; b. Sibiu, Romania (of German parents), Nov. 3, 1940. He studied piano, organ, and theory with Franz Dressler in Sibiu (1950–58), and composition with Toduţ at the Cluj Cons. (1959–64), where he then was on faculty (1964–69). From 1969 to 1972 he taught at the Robert Schumann Cons. in Düsseldorf. In 1972 he joined the faculty of the Munich Hochschule für Musik, where he was a prof. of composition from 1976.

WORKS: ORCH.: *Texturae I* (1970); *Quodlibet II* for Chamber Orch. (1975); 4 syms., including No. 1, *Lebensläufe* (1977–78), No. 3 (1992), and No. 4 (1998); Bassoon Concerto (1979–80); 2 violin concertos (1981; 1994–95); Concerto for Strings (1984); 2 piano concertos (1984, 1998); *Musik* for Strings and Harp (1987); *Ballad* for Violin and Orch. (1989); *Musik* for Oboe and Strings (1989); *Musik* for 2 Horns and Strings (1989); 2 sinfonia concertantes (1991, 1991); *Musik* for Viola, Harp, and Strings (1992); *Fresko* (1999). **CHAMBER:** 3 string trios (1963, 1983, 1987); 5 string quartets (1964; 1965–66; 1966–68; 1971–75; 1990); Clarinet Quintet (1973); *Nachstücke* for 2 Flutes (1978); *Mörike Sonata* for Cello and Piano (1978); *Serenata Notturna* for Wind Quintet (1983); String Sextet (1983); *Rilke Sonata* for Violin and Piano (1983); *Eichendorff Sonata* for Clarinet and Piano (1983); *Quibbles* for Brass Quintet (1983); 3 piano trios, including No. 2 (1984) and No. 3 (1992); *Kammerspiel* for 12 Solo Instruments (1985); Viola Sonata (1985); Harp Quartet (1986); 2 piano quartets (1986, 1986); Quartet for Violin, Clarinet, Cello, and Piano (1987); Quartet for Oboe, Violin, Viola, and Cello (1988); Trio for 2 Flutes and Piano (1988); Octet for Clarinet, Horn, Bassoon, 2 Violins, Viola, Cello, and Double Bass (1989); Trio for Trumpet, Trombone, and Piano (1990); *Sinfonia brevis* for 10 Brass Instruments (1993); Septet for Oboe, Clarinet, Bassoon, Violin, Cello, Piano, and Percussion (1994); Trio for Horn, Violin, and Piano (1995); Quintet No. 1 for Strings (1996); Bassoon Sonata (1996); Saxophone Quartet (1997); *Egnale III* for 4 Bassoons (1997); Oboe Sonata (1997); Trombone Sonata (1997); *Scene spezzate* for 8 Instruments (1998). **KEYBOARD:** Piano pieces; organ music. **VOCAL:** Motets a cappella; songs.**—NS/LK/DM**

Ackerman, William, successful American composer, guitarist, and entrepreneur; b. Germany, Nov. 16, 1949. Ackerman was orphaned and subsequently adopted at the age of nine by a Stanford Univ. (Palo Alto, Calif.) professor. He soon began playing guitar, eventually mastering the folk, classical, and rock styles. He studied at Stanford Univ., dropping out just before graduation to become a carpenter; as an avocation, he composed guitar pieces for theater productions. Ackerman eventually invested $300 to make a record, initiating a business that grew in 13 years to become the $3,000,000 Windham Hill Records Corp. In 1992 he resigned from his position as CEO of Windham Hill and later sold his remaining interest in the company. He then established a spoken word label, Gang of Seven, and built a state-of-the-art digital recording studio across the front yard of his house in Vt. Ackerman is among the most important and best composers in the "New Age" style, which was created and popularized by his record company, and which generally involves folk and modal elements performed by guitar, piano, or electronics.

DISC.: *Passage* (1981); *Past Light* (1983); *Conferring with the Moon* (1986); *Imaginary Roads* (1988); *The Opening of Doors* (1992); *Sound of Wind Driven Rain* (1998); *In Search of the Turtle's Navel* (1998).**—NS/LK/DM**

Ackermann, Otto, admired Romanian-born Swiss conductor; b. Bucharest, Oct. 18, 1909; d. Wabern, near Bern, March 9, 1960. After attending the Bucharest Cons. (1920–25), he studied with Prüwer, Szell, and Valeska

Burgstaller at the Berlin Hochschule für Musik (1926–28). He was active at the Royal Opera in Bucharest (1925–26) and at the Düsseldorf Opera (1928–32) before becoming chief conductor of the Brno Opera in 1932, and then of the Bern Opera in 1935. After conducting at the Theater an der Wien in Vienna (1947–53), he served as Generalmusikdirektor of the Cologne Opera (1953–58); subsequently conducted at the Zürich Opera. Ackermann distinguished himself as an interpreter of the standard operatic and symphonic repertory. He also had a special affinity for the operettas of the Viennese Strauss family and of Lehár.**—NS/LK/DM**

Ackley, Alfred H(enry), American minister and composer; b. Spring Hill, Pa., Jan. 21, 1887; d. Whittier, Calif., July 3, 1960. He studied harmony and composition in N.Y. and London. Following his ordination in the Presbyterian Church in 1914, he held pastorates in Pa. and Calif. Ackley wrote some 1,500 hymns, of which the most famous was *He Lives* (1933). He also wrote gospel songs, secular songs, and children's songs. His brother, Bentley DeForest Ackley (b. Spring Hill, Pa., Sept. 27, 1872; d. Winona Lake, Ind., Sept. 3, 1958), was a composer and ed. of gospel songs. He served as pianist and private secretary to Billy Sunday (1908–15). In 1910, with Homer Rodeheaver, he founded the Rodeheaver-Ackley publ. firm in Chicago. He wrote more than 2,000 gospel songs.**—LK/DM**

Ackté (real name, **Achté**), **Aino,** Finnish soprano; b. Helsinki, April 23, 1876; d. Nummela, Aug. 8, 1944. She studied first with her mother, the soprano Emmy Strömer-Achté (1850–1924), and then with Duvernoy, Girodet, and P. Vidal at the Paris Cons. On Oct. 8, 1897, she made her operatic debut as Marguerite at the Paris Opéra, which role she also chose for her Metropolitan Opera debut in N.Y. on Feb. 20, 1904; sang there until 1905. On Jan. 16, 1907, she made her first appearance at London's Covent Garden as Elsa; on Dec. 8, 1910, she sang Salome in the first British perf. of Strauss's opera there, which led the satisfied composer to invite her to repeat her success in Dresden and Paris. In later years, Ackté pursued her career in Finland. In 1938–39 she was director of the Finnish National Opera in Helsinki. Her other notable roles included Elisabeth, Senta, Juliette, Ophélie, Gilda, and Nedda.

WRITINGS: *Minnen och fantasier* (Stockholm, 1916); *Muistojeni kirja* (The Book of My Recollections; Helsinki, 1925); *Taiteeni taipaleelta* (My Life As an Artist; Helsinki, 1935). **—NS/LK/DM**

Acuff, Roy (Clayton), American country singer and fiddler; b. Maynardville, Tenn., Sept. 15, 1903; d. Nashville, Nov. 23, 1992. Acuff codified the old-time approach to country music from his position as host of the Grand Ole Opry, but he also effected a transition from the dominance of string bands to that of vocalists and introduced such innovations as the use of the dobro. His vocal style was broadly influential and can be heard in the music of Hank Williams, Lefty Frizzell, and others. He was among the most successful country music recording artists of the late 1930s and 1940s; his hits include "The Great Speckled Bird" and "Wabash Cannonball."

Acuff was the son of Neill and Ida Florence Carr Acuff. His father, who played the fiddle, had various occupations when he was a child, later becoming a minister, a lawyer, and a judge. The family moved to the Knoxville suburb of Fountain City in November 1919. After graduating from high school, Acuff worked at menial jobs while hoping to become a professional baseball player, but he suffered attacks of sunstroke in 1929 that left him bedridden and triggered a nervous breakdown. During his recovery he taught himself to play the fiddle and sing, and in the summer of 1932 he performed in a medicine show, then played in bands around Knoxville.

By 1934 Acuff and his band, at first called the Tennessee Crackerjacks and then the Crazy Tennesseans, were performing on local radio stations. Their most popular song, a Gospel tune called "The Great Speckled Bird" (music from a traditional English melody, lyrics by the Reverend Guy Smith, based on Jeremiah 12:9, with verses added by Acuff), earned them a contract with the American Record Company (later acquired by Columbia Records). Their initial recording session, in Chicago in October 1936, produced 20 tracks, among them "Wabash Cannonball" (music and lyrics by William Kindt), a 1905 composition given its most popular previous recording by The Carter Family. The song was sung by harmonica player Sam "Dynamite" Hatcher, with Acuff imitating a train whistle. There was a second session in March 1937, but none of the recordings were issued at first.

Acuff made a first, unheralded appearance on the Nashville-based Grand Ole Opry radio program in October 1937. Returning in February 1938, he earned a regular spot on the show, plus a weekday morning show on WSM and a series of personal appearances. Released on the Columbia-distributed Vocalion label, "The Great Speckled Bird" and "Wabash Cannonball" became hits by the end of the year, the latter selling a million copies. At the behest of radio officials, the name of Acuff's band was changed to the Smoky Mountain Boys. All but one of the band members quit at the start of 1939 in a dispute over musical direction: they wanted a more modern approach, whereas Acuff favored a more traditional one. He replaced them.

The Grand Ole Opry rose in popularity, and when it was picked up for national broadcast in October 1939, Acuff was its host. By the spring of 1940 he and the show had gained sufficient recognition to be the subject of a low-budget feature film, *Grand Ole Opry*, released by Republic Pictures in June. (Acuff appeared in seven more B movies before the decade was over.)

At the end of 1942, Acuff entered into a partnership with songwriter Fred Rose to form the Acuff-Rose Publishing Company, the first music publisher based in Nashville and devoted to country music. Acuff contributed his name, his songs, and the seed money to found the company, which was run by Rose, and later by Rose's son Wesley. It became enormously successful, fostering the rise of country music and of Nashville as the center of the country music industry.

Acuff scored three Top Ten country hits in 1944: "The Prodigal Son" (music and lyrics by Fred Rose), "I'll Forgive You but I Can't Forget" (music and lyrics by J. L. Frank and Pee Wee King), and "Write Me Sweetheart" (music and lyrics by Acuff). In April 1946 he left the Grand Ole Opry because of the show's low pay, and because having to be in Nashville every Saturday night made touring difficult. He returned a year later with a pay raise and greater flexibility in scheduling. His next Top Ten country hit came in 1947 with "(Our Own) Jole Blon," one of the biggest country hits of the year. But his 1948 hit "The Waltz of the Wind" (music and lyrics by Fred Rose) was his last to reach the Top Ten of the country charts for a decade.

Acuff was touted as a Tenn. gubernatorial candidate in 1944 and 1946, but he declined each time. In 1948 he finally allowed his name to appear on the Republican primary ballot. He did not campaign, but he won the nomination easily. Still, the state's long tradition of Democratic party dominance made his election impossible. Nevertheless, he received more votes than any statewide Republican candidate before him.

Acuff's next hit came as a writer; his song "As Long as I Live" became a Top Ten country hit for Kitty Wells and Red Foley in 1955. After short stints on several labels, Acuff signed to Hickory Records, a subsidiary of Acuff-Rose, in 1957 and reached the country Top Ten with "Once More" in 1958. This was his last major hit, although he placed records in the country charts in the 1960s, 1970s, and 1980s. In November 1962 he became the first living person elected to the Country Music Hall of Fame.

A political and musical conservative, Acuff helped to close the gap between country and rock by participating in the Nitty Gritty Dirt Band's three-record set *Will the Circle Be Unbroken* in 1972; the album went gold, and Acuff and the band earned a Grammy nomination for Best Country Vocal Performance by a Duo or Group.

After the opening of Opryland in 1972, Acuff cut down on touring and concentrated on performing at the Grand Ole Opry. He continued to appear until shortly before his death from congestive heart failure at the age of 89 in 1992.

DISC.: *Songs of the Smokey Mountains* (1955); *Favorite Hymns* (1958); *Great Speckled Bird* (1958); *Country Music Hall of Fame* (1963); *R. A. Sings American Folk Songs* (1963); *The Voice of Country Music* (1965); *R. A. Sings Hank Williams* (1966); *Famous Opry Favorites* (1967); *Treasury of Country Hits* (1969); *The Best of R. A.* (1970); *Greatest Hits* (1970); *Steamboat Whistle Blues* (1985); *Columbia Historic Edition* (1985); *The Essential R. A.: 1936–1949* (1992); *The King of Country Music* (1994); *The RC Cola Shows, Vol. 1 & 2* (1999); *The RC Cola Shows, Vol. 3 & 4* (2000).

WRITINGS: With W. Neely, *R. A.'s Nashville: The Life and Good Times of Country Music* (N.Y., 1983).

BIBL.: A. Dunkleberger, *King of Country Music: The Life of R. A.* (Nashville, 1971); E. Schlappi, *R. A., The Smoky Mountain Boy* (Gretna, La., 1978).—WR

Adam, Adolphe (Charles), noted French composer, son of **Jean (Louis) Adam;** b. Paris, July 24, 1803; d. there, May 3, 1856. He was encouraged by his friend Hérold to pursue a career as a composer. After studying piano with Lemoine, he entered the Paris Cons. at 17 and received training from Benoist (organ), Reicha (counterpoint), and Boieldieu (composition). In 1825 he won a 2ⁿᵈ prize in the Prix de Rome with his cantata *Ariane a Naxos.* His first successful stage score was the opéra-comique *Pierre et Catherine* (Paris Opéra-Comique, Feb. 9, 1829). Adam achieved his first great success with his opéra- comique *Le chalet* (Opéra-Comique, Sept. 25, 1834). It was followed by the even more successful opéra-comique *Le postillon de Lonjumeau* (Opéra-Comique, Oct. 13, 1836). His most celebrated score, the ballet *Giselle, ou Les Wilis* (Paris Opéra, June 28, 1841), has remained a repertory staple for over 150 years. In 1844 he was made a member of the Institut de France. He founded the Opéra-National in Paris in 1847, which was forced to close as a result of the revolutionary events of 1848. Adam was left bankrupt and was forced to take up music journalism to eke out a living. In 1849 he obtained the post of prof. of composition at the Paris Cons., which he held until his death. The opéra-comique *Si j'étais roi* (Paris Théâtre-Lyrique, Sept. 4, 1852) proved one of his finest late works. His operetta *Les pantins de Violette* was premiered at the Paris Bouffes-Parisiens on April 29, 1856, just 4 days before his death. In addition to his *Giselle,* Adam is still fondly remembered for his *Cantique de Noël,* known in Eng. as *O Holy Night.*

WORKS (all 1ˢᵗ perf. in Paris unless otherwise given): **DRAMATIC: O p é r a - c o m i q u e :** *Pierre et Catherine* (Feb. 9, 1829); *Danilowa* (April 23, 1830); *Trois jours en une heure* (Aug. 21, 1830; in collaboration with Romagnesi); *Joséphine, ou Le retour de Wagram* (Dec. 2, 1830); *Le morceau d'ensemble* (March 7, 1831); *Le grand prix, ou Le voyage à frais communs* (July 9, 1831); *Le proscrit, ou Le tribunal invisible* (Sept. 18, 1833); *Une bonne fortune* (Jan. 28, 1834); *Le chalet* (Sept. 25, 1834); *La marquise* (Feb. 28, 1835); *Micheline, ou L'heure d'esprit* (June 29, 1835); *Le postillon de Lonjumeau* (Oct. 13, 1836); *Le fidèle berger* (Jan. 6, 1838); *Le brasseur de Preston* (Oct. 31, 1838); *Régine, ou Les deux nuits* (Jan. 17, 1839); *Le reine d'un jour* (Sept. 19, 1839); *La rose de Péronne* (Dec. 12, 1840); *La main de fer, ou Le mariage secret* (Oct. 26, 1841); *Le roi d'Yvetot* (Oct. 13, 1842); *Lambert Simnel* (Sept. 14, 1843; completion of a work by H. Monpou); *Cagliostro* (Feb. 10, 1844); *Le toréador, ou l'accord parfait* (May 18, 1849); *Giralda, ou La nouvelle Psyché* (July 20, 1850); *La poupée de Nuremberg* (Feb. 21, 1852); *Le farfadet* (March 19, 1852); *Si j'étais roi* (Sept. 4, 1852); *Le sourd, ou L'auberge pleine* (Feb. 2, 1853); *Le roi des halles* (April 11, 1853); *Le bijou perdu* (Oct. 6, 1853); *Le muletier de Tolède* (Dec. 16, 1854); *À Clichy* (Dec. 24, 1854); *Le houzard de Berchini* (Oct. 17, 1855); *Falstaff* (Jan. 18, 1856); *Mam'zelle Geneviève* (March 24, 1856). **O p e r e t t a :** *Les pantins de Violette* (April 29, 1856). **O p e r a :** *Richard en Palestine* (Oct. 7, 1844); *La bouquetière* (May 31, 1847); *Le Fanal* (Dec. 24, 1849). Also various vaudevilles and other stage pieces. **B a l l e t :** *La chatte blanche* (July 26, 1830; in collaboration with C. Gide); *Faust* (London, Feb. 16, 1833); *La fille du Danube* (Sept. 21, 1836); *Les mohicans* (July 5, 1837); *L'écumeur de mer* (Feb. 21, 1840); *Die Hamadryaden* (Berlin, April 28, 1840); *Giselle, ou Les Wilis* (June 28, 1841); *La jolie fille de Gand* (June 22, 1842); *Le diable à quatre* (Aug. 11, 1843); *The Marble Maiden* (London, Sept. 27, 1845); *Griselidis, ou Les cinq sens* (Feb. 16, 1848); *La filleule des fées* (Oct. 8, 1840; in collaboration with C. de Saint- Julien); *Orfa* (Dec. 29, 1852); *Le corsaire* (Jan. 23, 1856). He also wrote sacred and secular choral works, numerous songs, romances, ballads, many piano pieces, etc.

WRITINGS: *Souvenirs d'un musicien...précédés de notes biographiques* (Paris, 1857); *Derniers souvenirs d'un musicien* (Paris, 1859).

BIBL.: J. Halévy, *Notice sur la vie et les ouvrages d'A. A.* (Paris, 1859); A. Pougin, *A. A.* (Paris, 1877); W. Studwell, ed., *A. A. and Léo Delibes: A Guide to Research* (Westport, Conn., 1987).—NS/LK/DM

Adam, Claus, Austrian-born American cellist, pedagogue, and composer; b. Sumatra, Dutch East Indies (of Austrian parents), Nov. 5, 1917; d. N.Y., July 4, 1983. His father was an ethnologist. After studies at the Salzburg Mozarteum, he went to N.Y. in 1929 and became a naturalized citizen in 1935. He studied cello with Stoffnegen, Dounis, and Feuermann, conducting with Barzin, and composition with Blatt. After playing in the National Orchestral Assn. in N.Y. (1935–40), he was first cellist in the Minneapolis Sym. Orch. (1940–43). Following composition lessons with Wolpe, he was a cellist with WOR Radio in N.Y. (1946–48) and the New Music Quartet (1948–55). From 1955 to 1974 he was a member of the Juilliard String Quartet. He also taught at the Juilliard School of Music (1955–83) and the Mannes Coll. of Music (1974–83) in N.Y., numbering among his students Stephen Kates, who premiered his Cello Concerto, and Joel Krosnick, who eventually replaced him in the Juilliard String Quartet. In 1976 he was composer-in-residence at the American Academy in Rome. Adam's career as a composer was overshadowed by his success as a cellist and pedagogue. His works, which were marked by pragmatic modernism free from doctrinaire adherence to any particular technique, included a Cello Concerto (1972–73; Cincinnati, Oct. 26, 1973), *Concerto Variations* for Orch. (1976; N.Y., April 5, 1977), 2 string quartets (1948, 1975), Piano Sonata (N.Y., May 2, 1948), String Trio (1967), *Herbstgesang* for Soprano and Piano, after Trakl (1969), *Fantasy* for Cello (1980), and *Toccato and Elegie* for String Quartet (1983; from an unfinished 3ʳᵈ string quartet).—NS/LK/DM

Adam, (Jean) Louis, Alsatian pianist, teacher, and composer, father of **Adolphe (Charles) Adam;** b. Müttersholz, Dec. 3, 1758; d. Paris, April 8, 1848. He settled in Paris in 1775, where he was a prof. at the Cons. (1797–1842). His pupils included Kalkbrenner and Hérold. He wrote virtuoso piano pieces, of which his variations on *Le Roi Dagobert* were once popular. He also authored the manuals *Méthode, ou Principe général du doigte pour le forte- piano* and *Méthode nouvelle pour le piano* (1802; 5ᵗʰ ed., 1832).—NS/LK/DM

Ádám, Jeno, Hungarian conductor, pedagogue, and composer; b. Szigetszentmiklós, Dec. 12, 1896; d. Budapest, May 15, 1982. He studied organ and theory at the Budapest Teacher Training Coll. (1911–15), composition with Kodály at the Budapest Academy of Music (1920–25), and conducting with Weingartner in Basel (1933–35). He was conductor of the orch. (1929–39) and the choir (1929–54) at the Budapest Academy of Music, where he also was a teacher (1939–59). In 1955 he was made a Merited Artist by the Hungarian government and in 1957 was awarded the Kossuth Prize. Among his writings were textbooks on singing (with Kodály) and *A muzsikáról* (On Music; Budapest, 1954). His compositions, written in a Romantic style, are notable for their utilization of Hungarian folk tunes, particularly in his operas, i.e. his *Magyar karácsony* (Hungarian Christmas; 1930; Budapest, Dec. 22, 1931) and *Mária Veronika* (1934–35; Budapest, Oct. 27, 1938). He also composed *Dominica*, orch. suite (1926), 2 string quartets (1925, 1931), Cello Sonata (1926), many vocal pieces with orch., choral works, and folksong arrangements.—NS/LK/DM

Adam, Theo, distinguished German bass-baritone; b. Dresden, Aug. 1, 1926. As a boy, he sang in the Dresdner Kreuzchor and studied voice in his native city with Rudolf Dittrich (1946–49). On Dec. 25, 1949, he made his operatic debut as the Hermit in *Der Freischütz* at the Dresden State Opera, and in 1952 made his first appearance at the Bayreuth Festival, quickly rising to prominence as one of the leading Wagnerian heroic bass-baritones of his time. He was a principal member of the Berlin State Opera from 1953, and made guest appearances at London's Covent Garden, the Vienna State Opera, the Paris Opéra, the Salzburg Festivals, the San Francisco Opera, and the Chicago Lyric Opera. On Feb. 7, 1969, he made his debut at the Metropolitan Opera in N.Y. as Hans Sachs. In addition to his Wagnerian roles, he also sang in operas by Mozart, Verdi, and R. Strauss with notable success; he appeared in various contemporary works as well, creating the leading roles in Cerha's *Baal* (1981) and Berio's *Un Re in ascolto* (1984). In 1979 he was made an Austrian Kammersänger.

WRITINGS: *Seht, hier ist Tinte, Feder, Papier...* (1980); *Die hundertste Rolle, oder, Ich mache einen neuen Adam* (1987).
—NS/LK/DM

Adam de la Halle (also **Adan le Bossu** ["the hunchback," although he was not a hunchback], **Adan le Boscu d'Arras, Adan de la Hale, Adan d'Arras,** etc.), French trouvère poet and composer; b. Arras, c. 1247; d. probably in Naples, c. 1287. He was educated in Paris. He was active as a member of the Arras pui before entering the service of Robert II, count of Artois; he later was in Italy in the service of the count's uncle, Charles of Anjou. His extensive output includes monophonic jeux-partis and chansons, and polyphonic rondeaux and motets. See E. de Coussemaker, ed., *Oeuvres complètes du trouvère Adam de la Halle: Poésies et musique* (Paris, 1872), N. Wilkins, ed., *The Lyric Works of Adam de la Hale*, Corpus Mensurabilis Musicae, XLIV (1967), and J. Marshall, ed., *The Chansons of Adam de la Halle* (Manchester, 1971). He also wrote *Le jeu du Robin et de Marion* (ed. by F. Gennrich in Musikwissenschaftliche Studienbibliothek, XX, Langen, 1962), a dramatic work with music that is akin to the narrative pastourelle.

BIBL.: H. Guy, *Essai sur la vie et les oeuvres littéraires du trouvère A. d. l. H.* (Paris, 1898); R. Barth- Wehrenalp, *Studien zu A. d. l. H.* (Tutzing, 1982).—NS/LK/DM

Adam de St. Victor, celebrated French churchman and poet who flourished in the first half of the 12th century. By 1107 he was precentor at Notre Dame Cathedral in Paris, where he served as a high official for more than two decades. In 1133 he donated his prebend to the Abbey of St. Victor in Paris, where he subsequently lived and later served as a canon until his death (c. 1148). He played a major role in the development of the late sequence. It is possible that he was also a composer. For eds. of texts attributed to Adam de St. Victor, see L. Gautier, *OEuvres poétiques d'Adam de St.-Victor, précédées d'un essai sur sa vie et ses ouvrages* (Paris, 1858–59; 3rd ed., 1894), M. Legrain, ed., *Proses d'Adam de Saint-Victor* (Rome, 1899), E. Misset and P. Aubry, eds., *Les Proses d'Adam de Saint-Victor: Texte et musique* (Paris, 1901), H. Prevost, ed., *Recueil complet des célèbres séquences du maître Adam le breton, chanoine régulier de l'abbaye royale de Saint-Victor de Paris (XIIe siècle) d'après les manuscrits de la même abbaye* (Ligugé, 1901), C. Blume, G. Dreves, and H. Bannister, eds., *Analecta hymnica medii aevi*, LIV-LV (Leipzig, 1915, 1922), D. Wrangham, ed., *The Liturgical Poetry of Adam of St. Victor from the Text of Gautier, with Translations into English in the Original Metres and Short Explanatory Notes* (London, 1939), G. Vecchi, ed., *Adam de S. Victor: Liriche sacre* (Bologna, 1953), and F. Wellner, ed. and tr., *Adam de Saint-Viktor: Sämtliche Sequenzen, lateinisch und deutsch* (Munich, 1955).

BIBL.: E. Hegener, *Studien zur "zweiten Sprache" in der religiösen Lyrik des zwölften Jahrhunderts: A. v. S. V., Walter von Châtillon* (Ratingen, 1971); M. Fassler, *Musical Exegesis in the Sequences of A. and the Canons of St. Victor* (diss., Cornell Univ., 1983).—NS/LK/DM

Adam von Fulda, German music theorist and composer; b. Fulda, c. 1442; d. Wittenberg, 1505. He was at the Benedictine monastery in Vormbach until about 1490 when he was compelled to leave upon his marriage. He then entered the service of Friedrich the Wise of Saxony as a singer, later becoming his historiographer in 1492 and his Kapellmeister in 1498. In 1502 he became prof. of music at the Univ. of Wittenberg. He was the author of the valuable treatise *De musica* (1490; publ. in M. Gerbert, *Scriptores ecclesiastici de musica sacra potissimum*, 3 vols., 1784). He also wrote a history of Saxony (1504), which was left unfinished at his death from the plague. It was completed by Johannes Trithemius, Abbot of Würzburg. He also wrote religious verse that appeared posthumously as *Ein sehr andechtig christenlich Buchlein* (1512). Among his compositions were a Mass, a Magnificat, 7 hymns, 2 antiphons, a respond, and songs.

BIBL.: W. Ehmann, *A. v. F. als Vertreter der ersten deutschen Komponistengeneration* (Berlin, 1936).—NS/LK/DM

Adamberger, (Josef) Valentin, notable German tenor and teacher; b. Munich, July 6, 1743; d. Vienna, Aug. 24, 1804. He studied at the Jesuit Domus Gregoriana in Munich, where he received vocal instruction from J. E. Walleshauser. In 1760 he became a member of the Kapelle of Duke Clemens, and then of the Elector's Hofkapelle in 1770. In 1777 he went to Italy, where he appeared in major opera serie roles in Modena, Venice, Florence, Pisa, and Rome. After singing at the King's Theatre in London from 1777 to 1779, he again sang in Italy. He then settled in Vienna, where he made his debut at the National Singspiel on Aug. 21, 1780. On July 16, 1782, he created the role of Belmonte in Mozart's *Die Entführung aus dem Serail*. After the company disbanded in 1783, he became a member of the Italian company at the Burgtheater. In 1785 he joined the new German company under imperial auspices at the Kärnthnertortheater. He created the role of Herr Vogelsang in Mozart's *Der Schauspieldirektor* on Feb. 7, 1786. After the German company disbanded in 1789, he rejoined the Italian company at the Burgtheater. In 1793 he retired from the stage but remained active at the imperial Hofkapelle and as a teacher. Mozart wrote the arias K.420 and K.431, as well as the cantata *Die Maurerfreude*, K.417 for him. Adamberger was also known for his roles in operas by J. C. Bach, Sarti, Sacchini, Bertoni, Umlauf, and Dittersdorf.—NS/LK/DM

Adami da Bolsena, Andrea, Italian castrato soprano and composer; b. Bolsena, Nov. 30, 1663; d. Rome, July 22, 1742. He studied in Montefiascone and Rome, where he entered the Sistine Chapel in 1678. After serving Cardinal Pietro Ottoboni (1689–99), he returned to the Sistine Chapel as maestro di cappella in 1700, a position he held until 1714. He publ. the valuable treatise *Osservazioni per ben regolare il coro dei cantori della Cappella pontificia* (Rome, 1711).—LK/DM

Adamis, Michael, Greek composer; b. Piraeus, May 19, 1929. He studied at the Athens Cons. (1947–51), the Piraeus Cons. (1951–56), with Papaioannou (composition) at the Hellikon Cons. in Athens (1956–59), and electronic music at Brandeis Univ. in Waltham, Mass. (1962–65). He wrote incidental music for plays, *Liturgikon Concerto* for Oboe, Clarinet, Bassoon, and String Orch. (1955), *Variations* for String Orch. (1958), *Sinfonia da camera* for Flute, Clarinet, Horn, Trumpet, Percussion, Piano, and String Orch. (1960–61), chamber music, vocal pieces, and numerous works for tape. —NS/LK/DM

Adamowski, Joseph (actually, **Josef**), PolishAmerican cellist, brother of **Timothée Adamowski;** b. Warsaw, July 4, 1862; d. Cambridge, Mass., May 8, 1930. He studied with Goebelt at the Warsaw Cons. (1873–77) and with Fitzenhagen and Tchaikovsky at the Moscow Cons. From 1889 to 1907 he played in the Boston Sym. Orch. In 1896 he married the pianist **Antoinette Szumowska,** with whom he and his brother formed the Adamowski Trio.—NS/LK/DM

Adamowski, Timothée, Polish-American violinist, conductor, teacher, and composer, brother of **Joseph Adamowski;** b. Warsaw, March 24, 1857; d. Boston, April 18, 1943. He was a pupil of Katski and Roguski at the Warsaw Cons. (graduated, 1874) before completing his studies at the Paris Cons. In 1879 he made his first tour of the U.S., and then was a violinist in the Boston Sym. Orch. (1884–86; 1889–1907) and conductor of its summer pops concerts (1890–94; 1900–1907). In 1888 he founded the Adamowski String Quartet. With his brother Joseph and his sister-in-law **Antoinette Szumowska,** he organized the Adamowski Trio in 1896. From 1908 to 1933 he taught violin at the New England Cons. of Music in Boston. He composed works for violin and piano, and songs.—NS/LK/DM

Adams, Bryan, hard-rocking Canuck who quit school at 16 to chase his rock and roll dreams, and 20 years later was singing duets with Barbra Streisand; b. Nov. 5, 1959, Kingston, Canada. The son of a Canadian diplomat, Bryan Adams went to boarding schools around the world. This only convinced him that he probably could do better without school. He spent the money put aside for college on a piano and started working with rock bands and writing songs. He hooked up with Jim Vallance, who worked with the dance rock band Prism. Together they wrote tunes for Kiss, Bachman-Turner Overdrive, and Loverboy. This earned them a publishing contract with Almo Music and a recording contract with A&M, a scant three years after Adams quit school.

Adams's eponymous debut tanked. His second album, *You Want It You Got It,* fell about 20 spots shy of the Top 200 albums, while the single "Lonely Nights" didn't break the Top 80. He hit the road, supporting acts such as the Kinks and Loverboy. Two years later, in 1983, he released *Cuts Like a Knife,* with the breakthrough single "Straight from the Heart." The single went Top Ten. On the strength of that hit, "This Time," and the Top 20 title track, the album reached #8 and sold a million copies in the U.S. Five months later, he followed that up with *Reckless.* That album topped the charts and sold five million copies, with the Top Ten tunes "Run to You" and "Summer of 69" as well as the Top 20 "Somebody" and his duet with Tina Turner, "It's Only Love." All of these established a larger-than-life video presence for the diminutive Adams. "It's Only Love" earned him and Turner an MTV Award for Best Stage Performance. Another track from the album, the ballad "Heaven," was included in the film *A Night in Heaven.* That song topped the charts. Suddenly Adams became the poster boy for the power ballad. His next album, *Into the Fire,* included the Top Ten lead single "Heat of the Night," but "Hearts on Fire" barely broke the Top 30.

Adams took his video presence to Hollywood, doing a cameo in Clint Eastwood's *Pink Cadillac* and spending considerable time on the road. In 1990 he was awarded the Order of Canada. He also went Hollywood musically, with his biggest hits of the 1990s coming in films. This started with "(Everything I Do) I Do It for You," the #1 song that ran under the credits for the 1991 film *Robin Hood, Prince of Thieves* and holds the Guiness record for most weeks atop the British charts (16). The song was nominated for an Oscar and won an American Music Award (Pop/Rock Single), *Billboard* Music Award (Top World Single), Grammy (Best Song Specifically Written for a Motion Picture or Television show), and an MTV Movie Award (Best Song). It helped propel Adams's *Waking Up the Neighbours* to #6 on the charts and quadruple platinum status in America. The album topped the U.K. charts and kicked off a tour that lasted the better part of three years. Adams teamed up with Rod Stewart and Sting to form a triumvirate of former rockers for the chart-topping theme "All for Love" from the 1993 remake of *The Three Musketeers.* His song "Have You Ever Really Loved a Woman," for the film *Don Juan de Marco* also topped the charts and was nominated for an Oscar, as was his duet with Barbra Streisand, "I Finally Found Somebody," for her film *The Mirror Has Two Faces.*

Adams took a 1993 greatest hits collection to the Top Ten, but his 1995 live album didn't chart. The *18 'til I Die* album attempted to regain some of his rock and roll credibility, despite including "Have You Ever Really Loved a Woman." Tracks like "The Only Thing That Looks Good on You Is Me" and "Let's Make a Night to Remember" sent the record to platinum in the U.S. Adams released an album recorded for the MTV *Unplugged* series that didn't even go gold. Nor did the follow-up, *On a Day Like Today,* despite including a duet with Mel "Sporty Spice" C. of the teen sensation group The Spice Girls.

DISC.: *Bryan Adams* (1980); *You Want It You Got It* (1981); *Cuts like a Knife* (1983); *Reckless* (1984); *Into the Fire* (1987); *Live! Live! Live!* (1988); *Waking Up the Neighbors* (1991); *The Live Volume* (1992); *So Far So Good* (1993); *18 'Til I Die* (1996); *Unplugged* (1997); *On a Day Like Today* (1998).—**HB**

Adams, Charles,

American tenor and pedagogue; b. Charlestown, Mass., Feb. 9, 1834; d. West Harwich, Mass., July 4, 1900. He studied in Boston, where he appeared as a soloist in the Handel and Haydn Society's performance of *The Creation* in 1856. He appeared in opera and concert in the West Indies and Holland in 1861. After further training with Barbieri in Vienna, he sang with the Berlin Royal Opera (1864–67) and the Vienna Court Opera (1867–76). He also appeared at Milan's La Scala, at London's Covent Garden, and in the U.S. In 1879 he settled in Boston as a voice teacher. Among his students were Melba and Eames. Adams was best known for his Wagnerian roles, especially Lohengrin and Tannhäuser.—**NS/LK/DM**

Adams, John (Coolidge),

prominent American composer and conductor; b. Worcester, Mass., Feb. 15, 1947. He studied clarinet with his father, and then with Felix Viscuglia of the Boston Sym. Orch. He pursued training in conducting with Mario di Bonaventura at Dartmouth Coll. (summer, 1965) and in composition with Leon Kirchner at Harvard Univ. (B.A., 1969; M.A., 1971). In 1970 Adams was composer-in-residence at the Marlboro (Vt.) Festival. From 1972 to 1982 he taught at the San Francisco Cons. of Music, where he also was director of its New Music Ensemble. In 1978 he became new music advisor of the San Francisco Sym., and then served as its composer-in-residence from 1982 to 1985. In 1982 he was awarded a Guggenheim fellowship. From 1988 to 1990 he held the position of creative advisor of the St. Paul (Minn.) Chamber Orch. His Violin Concerto (1993) won the Grawemeyer Award of the Univ. of Louisville in 1995. In 1997 he was elected a member of the American Academy of Arts and Letters. Adams's interest in the music of John Cage, Morton Feldman, and other American composers of an experimental persuasion, as well as his interest in electronic music, most notably the synthesizer, effectually determined his course as a composer. His transformation of minimalist procedures by combining formalized structures with stylistic diversity led him to create works that won considerable popular appeal in both the concert hall and the opera house.

WORKS: DRAMATIC: *Nixon in China,* opera (Houston, Oct. 22, 1987); *The Death of Klinghoffer,* opera (1990; Brussels, March 19, 1991); *I Was Looking at the Ceiling and Then I Saw the Sky,* song play (Berkeley, May 11, 1995). **ORCH.:** *Christian Zeal and Activity* (San Francisco, March 23, 1973, composer conducting); *Common Tones in Simple Time* (1979); *Shaker Loops* for Strings (1983; also for String Septet); *Harmonielehre* (1984–85; San Francisco, March 21, 1985); *The Chairman Dances* (1985); *Short Ride in a Fast Machine* (Mansfield, Mass., June 13, 1986); *Tromba Lontana,* fanfare (Houston, April 4, 1986); *Fearful Symmetries* for Orch. or Chamber Orch. (N.Y., Oct. 29, 1988, composer conducting); *Eros Piano* for Piano and Orch. or Chamber Orch. (London, Nov. 24, 1989, composer conducting); *El Dorado* (San Francisco, Nov. 11, 1991, composer conducting); *Chamber Sym.* (1992; The Hague, Jan. 17, 1993, composer conducting); *Violin Concerto* (1993; Minneapolis, Jan. 19, 1994); *Gnarly Buttons* for Clarinet and Orch. (1996); Piano Concerto, *Century Rolls* (Cleveland, Sept. 25, 1997); *Naive and Sentimental Music* (1998; Los Angeles, Feb. 19, 1999). **CHAMBER:** Piano Quintet (1970); *Shaker Loops* for String Septet (1978; also for String Orch.); *John's Book of Alleged Dances* for String Quartet and Foot-controlled Sampler (Escondido, Calif., Nov. 19, 1994); *Road Movies* for Violin and Piano (Washington, D.C., Oct. 23, 1995). **Piano:** *China Gates* (1977); *Phyrgian Gates* (1977). **VOCAL:** *Harmonium* for Chorus and Orch., after John Donne and Emily Dickinson (1980; San Francisco, April 15, 1981); *Grand Pianola Music* for Voices and Orch. (1981–82; San Francisco, Feb. 20, 1982); *The Wound-Dresser* for Baritone and Orch. or Chamber Orch., after Walt Whitman (1988–89; St. Paul, Minn., Feb. 24, 1989, composer conducting); *Choruses from "The Death of Klinghoffer"* for Chorus and Orch. (1990; Cleveland, April 25, 1991, composer conducting). **OTHER:** *Hoodoo Zephyr* for MIDI Keyboard (1993). **ARRANGEMENTS:** *Berceuse élégiaque* for Chamber Orch., after Busoni's *Berceuse No. 7* of his *Elegies* (St. Paul, Minn., June 9, 1989, composer conducting); *The Black Gondola* for Orch. or Chamber Orch., after Liszt's *La Lugubre gondola II* (St. Paul, Minn., Oct. 27, 1989, composer conducting); *Wiegenlied* for Orch. or Chamber Orch., after Liszt's *Wiegenlied* (London, Nov. 24, 1989, composer conducting); *Le Livre de Baudelaire,* 4 songs for Soprano and Orch., after Debussy's *Cinq Poèmes de Baudelaire* (Amsterdam, March 10, 1994, composer conducting).—**NS/LK/DM**

Adams, John Luther,

gifted American composer; b. Meridian, Miss., Jan. 23, 1953. He was influenced in his youth by the experimental practices of Frank Zappa, Edgar Varèse, Morton Feldman, and Henry Cowell. After studies with Leonard Stein and James Tenney at the Calif. Inst. for the Arts in Valencia, he moved to Alaska (1975), where he played timpani in the Fairbanks Sym. Orch. (1982–92). He joined the faculty of the Oberlin (Ohio) Cons. of Music in 1998, and in 1999 became president of the American Music Center. With Michael Gordon, Mikel Rouse, David First, Ben Neill, et al., Adams is an apt representative of the 1990s compositional school called totalism. He is also a devoted environmentalist and outdoorsman, and many of his works evoke the placid beauty of the Alaskan terrain.

WORKS: *Clouds of Forgetting, Clouds of Unknowing* for Orch. (1990–95); *Strange and Sacred Noise* for Percussion Ensemble (1991–97); *Dream in White on White* for String Quartet, Harp, and String Orch., in "white note" tonality (1992); *Earth and the Great Weather* (1993), a plotless opera tonally evoking Alaska, including recorded sounds from nature and a recitation of Eskimo place names; *The Time of Drumming* for Orch. (1995; Long Beach, Calif., Oct. 16, 1999; also 2 Pianos, 4 Percussion, and Timpani, 1997); *In the White Silence* for Celesta, Harp, 2 Vibraphones, String Quartet, and String Orch. (Oberlin, Nov. 11, 1998); *In A Treeless Place, Only Snow* for Harp, Celesta, 2 Vibraphones, and String Quartet (Portland, Ore., Nov. 19, 1999); *The Light That Fills the World* for Chamber Ensemble (San Francisco, Nov. 20, 1999); *Time Undisturbed* for 3 Kotos and Sho (1999; also for Western Ensemble of Piccolo, Alto Flute, Bass Flute, 3 Harps, and Sustaining Keyboard).—**LK/DM**

Adams, Pepper (Park III), jazz baritone saxophonist; b. Highland Park, Mich., Oct. 8, 1930; d. N.Y., Sept. 10, 1986. Although Adams was second in popularity to Gerry Mulligan, many musicians preferred him as an improviser. Adams was raised in Rochester, N.Y., where he first worked on tenor saxophone and clarinet. He moved to Detroit, where he made some unissued recordings in 1949 and became part of the circle of local talent including Tommy Flanagan and Thad Jones. He switched to the baritone sax and, after two years in the army, returned to Detroit, where he became a member of the house band at the Bluebird Club, accompanying Miles Davis and others, and spent a long period with Kenny Burrell's group. He was nicknamed "The Knife" for his bold, slashing attack. He recorded with John Coltrane, Paul Chambers, and Curtis Fuller in 1956, and later that year moved to N.Y., where he became much in demand among big bands, including those of Stan Kenton, Maynard Ferguson, Benny Goodman, Lionel Hampton, Thelonious Monk, and The Thad Jones–Mel Lewis Orch., which performed Monday nights and occasionally toured from 1965–76. He worked with Charles Mingus around 1958 and co-led quintets with Donald Byrd (ca. 1959 to the end of 1961) and Thad Jones (mid-1960s). Adams became ill in 1985 and was diagnosed with lung cancer, which spread throughout his body. He played the 1986 Fourth of July weekend in Montreal, but returned home with pneumonia, according to his wife, Claudette. He died at home a few months later. Nick Brignola and Jerry Sawicki are among his protégées. Adams also played bassoon on a couple of Enja albums in the 1970s.

DISC.: *Various artists, Jazzmen: Detroit* (1956); *Cool Sound of Pepper Adams* (1957); *Critics Choice* (1957); *P. A. Quintet* (1957); *10 to 4 at the 5-Spot* (1958); *Plays Compositions of Charles Mingus* (1963); *Encounter!* (1968); *Reflectory* (1978); *Conjuration: Fat Tuesday's Sessions* (1983); *Live—Jazz by the Sea* (1998).—**LP**

Adams, Suzanne, American soprano; b. Cambridge, Mass., Nov. 28, 1872; d. London, Feb. 5, 1953. She studied with Bouhy and Mathilde Marchesi in Paris, where she made her operatic debut as Gounod's Juliette at the Opéra on Jan. 9, 1895; remained on its roster until 1898. On May 10, 1898, she made her first appearance at London's Covent Garden as Juliette and sang there until 1904; on Nov. 8, 1898, she sang Juliette

again in her Metropolitan Opera debut during the company's visit to Chicago, and then again for her formal debut with the company in N.Y. on Jan. 4, 1899. She remained on its roster until 1903, but also was active as an oratorio singer in the U.S. and Europe. After the death of her husband, the cellist Leo Stein, in 1904, she retired from the operatic stage but appeared in vaudeville in London before settling there as a voice teacher. Her best roles, in addition to the ubiquitous Juliette, were Donna Elvira, Marguerite de Valois, and Micaëla. —**NS/LK/DM**

Adams, Thomas, English organist and composer; b. London, Sept. 5, 1785; d. there, Sept. 15, 1858. At age 11, he became a student of Thomas Busby. He pursued his career in London, where he became organist at Carlisle Chapel, Lambeth, in 1802, and at St. Paul's, Deptford, in 1814. In 1824 he was made organist at St. George's, Camberwell, and in 1833 at St. Dunstan-in-the-West, Fleet Street, positions he held until his death. Adams acquired a notable reputation as an organ virtuoso. In addition to various fugues, voluntaries, interludes, and other organ pieces, he also wrote some piano and vocal music.—**NS/LK/DM**

Adaskin, Murray, Canadian composer and teacher; b. Toronto, March 28, 1906. He studied violin in Toronto with his brother Harry Adaskin and with Luigi von Kunits, in N.Y. with Kathleen Parlow, and in Paris with Marcel Chailley. Returning to Toronto, he was a violinist in the Sym. Orch. there (1923–36). He then pursued training in composition with Weinzweig (1944–48), with Milhaud at the Aspen (Colo.) Music School (summers, 1949–50; 1953), and with Charles Jones in Calif. (1949–51). In 1952 he became head of the music dept. at the Univ. of Saskatchewan, where he also was composer-in-residence from 1966 until his retirement in 1972. From 1957 to 1960 he was conductor of the Saskatoon Sym. Orch. In 1973 he settled in Victoria, where he continued to be active as a teacher and composer. In 1931 he married **(Mary) Frances James**. In 1981 he was made a member of the Order of Canada. Adaskin's output followed along neo-Classical lines with occasional infusions of folk elements; in some of his works, he utilized serial techniques. He composed the operas *Grant, Warden of the Plains* (1966; Winnipeg, July 18, 1967) and *The Travelling Musicians* (1983).

BIBL.: G. Lazarevich, *The Musical World of Frances James and M. A.* (Toronto, 1987).—**NS/LK/DM**

Adderley, Cannonball (Julian Edwin), jazz alto saxophonist, one of the masters on his instrument; brother of **Nat Adderley;** b. Tampa, Fla., Sept. 15, 1928; d. Gary, Ind., Aug. 8, 1975. Nicknamed "Cannonball" (originally "Cannibal" due to his large appetite), Julian began playing saxophone in 1942. He was a precocious student and graduated from Fla. A & M. Coll. in 1946. The following year he began working as music teacher and band director at Dillard H.S. in Fort Lauderdale, performing locally. Drafted in 1952, Adderley conducted and played lead alto in an army dance band at Fort Knox in Ky. He declined a commission to become a sergeant because officers could not be performers. He then studied at the naval music school in Washington, D.C., and performed around town. In 1955 he and his brother, cornetist Nat, visited N.Y. On his second night there, "Cannonball" created a sensation when he sat in with Oscar Pettiford's group at Cafe Bohemia. He began recording on June 26 and led his own band for a while, then joined Miles Davis from October 1957 until September 1959, when he and Nat reformed their quintet, this time for good. The group became one of jazz's most popular, thanks in part to Nat's hit "Work Song." It experienced an even wider success with its early fusion gospel hit "Mercy, Mercy, Mercy" (written by Joe Zawinul) in 1966. Adderley is seen briefly on screen during the first film Clint Eastwood directed, *Play Misty for Me* (1971). He also appeared on *BBC-TV Theatre* (May 12, 1964). In later years he infrequently played soprano saxophone. In July 1975, Adderley suffered a stroke while on tour, and died thereafter. His legacy deeply affected Kenny Garrett, Richie Cole, Mike Smith, and many others.

DISC.: *Presenting C. A.* (1955); *Spontaneous Combustion* (1955); *Alabama Concerto* (1958); *Somethin' Else* (1958, with Miles Davis); *Cannonball and Coltrane* (1959); *Know What I Mean?* (1961, with Bill Evans); *Live in Japan* (1963); *Fiddler on the Roof* (1964); *Mercy, Mercy, Mercy! Live at the It Club* (1966); *74 Miles Away/Walk Tall* (1967); *Accent on Africa* (1968); *In Person* (1970); *Black Messiah* (1972).—**GBr**

Adderley, Nat(haniel Sr.),

jazz cornetist; brother of **Cannonball Adderley;** b. Tampa, Fla., Nov. 25, 1931; d. Lakeland, Fla., Jan. 3, 2000. Under his father's and brother's influence, Nat took up trumpet in 1946, switched to cornet in 1950, and played in an army band from 1951–53. After touring with Lionel Hampton (1954–55), he joined his brother's first quintet until late 1957, then worked with J. J. Johnson and a Woody Herman small group before rejoining his brother from September 1959 through Cannonball's death in July 1975. Nat's "Work Song" and "Jive Samba" were among the group's most popular compositions. He led his own quintets beginning in 1975, and sometimes played mellophone and French horn. In 1997, Adderley had his right leg amputated in Lakeland, Fla., due to diabetes. He retired from playing music, and died from complications of his disease in early 2000. His son, Nat Adderley Jr., is an accomplished pianist and longtime musical director for popular singer Luther Vandross.

DISC.: *Introducing N. A.* (1955); *Work Songs* (1960); *In the Bag* (1962); *Little Big Horn* (1964); *Sayin' Somethin'* (1966); *Scavenger* (1968); *Little New York Midtown Music* (1978); *On the Move* (1983); *Talkin' About You* (1990); *We Remember* (1995).

BIBL.: Orrin Keepnews, "N. A., in the View from Within." *Jazz Writing 1948–1987* (N.Y., 1988).—**LP/GBr**

Addinsell, Richard (Stewart),

English composer; b. London, Jan. 13, 1904; d. there, Nov. 14, 1977. He studied law at Hertford Coll., Oxford, and music at the Royal Coll. of Music in London, in Berlin, and in Vienna. He wrote various scores for the theater, films, and radio; among his best film scores were *Fire Over England* (1937), *Goodbye Mr. Chips* (1939), *Dangerous*

Moonlight (1941; contains a movement for piano and orch. that became immensely popular as the *Warsaw Concerto*), *Blithe Spirit* (1945), and *A Tale of Two Cities* (1958).—**NS/LK/DM**

Addison, Adele,

black American soprano; b. N.Y., July 24, 1925. She studied at Westminster Choir Coll., Princeton, and the Berkshire Music Center at Tanglewood, and also took lessons with Povla Frijsh. She made her N.Y. debut at Town Hall in 1952, then sang with the New England Opera and the N.Y.C. Opera; she made numerous appearances with major American orchs. Her extensive repertoire included works extending from the Baroque era to the 20th century.—**NS/LK/DM**

Addison, Bernard (S.; Bunky),

jazz guitarist, banjoist; b. Annapolis, Md., April 15, 1905; d. Rockville Centre, N.Y., Dec. 18, 1990. Addison played violin and mandolin as a child, and moved to Washington, D.C. in 1920. He was soon co-leading a band with Claude Hopkins, worked for a while in Oliver Blackwell's Clowns, then went to N.Y. with Sonny Thompson's Band and also worked in the Seminole Syncopators in 1925. From 1925 until 1929, Addison worked mainly for Ed Small, first as a sideman, then leading his own band. From 1928 he concentrated on guitar, working with, among others, Louis Armstrong at the Cocoanut Grove in N.Y., Art Tatum in Toledo, Ohio (1931–32), and Fletcher Henderson (from early 1933 until the summer of 1934). Addison toured America and Europe with The Mills Brothers from 1936 until 1938, worked with Stuff Smith in 1939, then mostly led his own groups until army service in World War II. He toured with The Ink Spots in the late 1950s and continued freelancing in the 1960s, when he worked mainly as a teacher.—**JC/LP**

Addison, John (Mervyn),

English composer; b. Chobham, Surrey, March 16, 1920; d. Bennington, Vt., Dec. 7, 1998. He studied at the Royal Coll. of Music in London. Although he wrote several orch. and chamber works, he composed mainly for the theater, films, and television. Among his many film scores, particularly effective in films with epic subjects and with understated humor, were *Tom Jones* (1963; Academy Award), *Torn Curtain* (1966), *The Charge of the Light Brigade* (1968), *Sleuth* (1972), *The Seven Per Cent Solution* (1976), and *Strange Invaders* (1983).—**NS/LK/DM**

Ade, Sunny (Prince Sunday Adeniyi Adegeye),

major star of the urban Yoruba juju style and one of the few African musicians to gain a following overseas; b. Ondo, Nigeria, Sept. 1946 (exact date unknown). His father, Prince Samuel Adeniyi Adegeye, was a Methodist trader and amateur church musician. His mother, Princess Marian Adeniyi Adegeye, sang in chapel choirs. Ade dropped out of school at about age 14 and worked as a drummer with a local highlife group, Moses Olaiya and his Federal Rhythm Dandies, while picking up acoustic guitar, which he began playing in public in 1965. In 1966, Ade formed a shortlived group called The High Society Band. The following year he launched his first major band, The Green Spots. The group's debut record, made in 1967, sank almost without a trace (Ade once estimated selling a total of 23 copies). But the second record, "Challenge Cup '67," a song in praise of a popular football team released in 1968, sold a reputed 23,000 copies. The band's first LP, *Alanu Loluwa*, appeared the same year on the Nigeria-Africa Song label.

For any juju group aiming at permanent stardom, an instantly recognizable sound, preferably with a memorable name, was crucial. Ade first increased his frontline from the standard two guitars to four or five. In 1974, Ade launched his own record label, Sunny Alade Records, whose first release, "Synchro System," introduced and was named after a new, catchy dance style that reflected his increasing commitment to electronics. In 1975, Ade made his first tour outside Africa, performing in Washington, D.C., Boston, N.Y., and Detroit as part of a U.S. government-sponsored cultural exchange program. It was on his return home from this trip that Ade, a prince by birthright, was dubbed "king" by Nigeria's musical press. By this time, his band was the creative leader in the field of juju, with a sound built on his own high, clear vocal tone, the use of synthesizers and other innovations, and the now-standard Nigerian recording procedure of segueing from one song to another without a break in the rhythm. Ade also introduced the pedal steel guitar, the vibraphone, and the remixing of multitrack recordings, and electrified the talking drum (already a lead instrument in its own right).

Ade's definitive move into the international scene came in 1982, when he signed a contract with the British company Island Records, which had introduced Jamaican reggae to the world. By this time Ade's albums on his own label were selling more than 200,000 copies apiece, and Island counted on similar sales for their own first release. In hope of turning Ade into a international star, the company hired as producer a Frenchman with experience in working with African musicians, Martin Meissonnier, and launched a major media campaign in both the U.S. and Britain. Ade's first Island LP, *Juju Music*, was a remix of a previous Alade label release that simplified the complex juju rhythms to a light funk beat and inserted Meissonnier's own synthesizer part. On both sides of the Atlantic, press coverage of both the recording and an early 1983 concert tour was largely enthusiastic, and the album made it into the *Billboard* charts in February 1983, just as Ade began a 22-city U.S. tour. But it did not break into the Top 100 album charts, and U.S. sales of around 60,000, though phenomenal for an African artist, fell far short of Island's target. The second release, *Synchro System* (not a re-mix of Ade's 1974 album but a new studio recording) sold about the same quantity amid tepid press reviews. The third Island release, *Aura*, featured U.S. star Stevie Wonder on one track in an attempt to increase sales. But the critics were again cool, Wonder did nothing for sales, and Island cancelled the rest of Ade's contract.

However, in Nigeria, Ade was still a major star, and a wealthy man. Along with his band and record label, he owned a successful Lagos nightspot, the Ariwa Club. But perhaps as a result of the Island experience, his lyrics increasingly turned to themes of jealousy, rumor, authority, and destiny. In 1984, Ade disbanded his group during a tour of Japan, and the following year he dissolved the Sunny Alade record label. In 1986, he formed a new group, the Golden Mercury (which included most members of his old one), launched a new label, Atom Park, and resumed his previous level of recording and performance. In 1987 he also returned to the international music scene with a tour in support of a Mercury-label compilation drawn from his recent Nigerian releases. Unlike the Island releases, *Return of the Juju King* was Ade straight, as was the 17-piece band that he brought to Europe and the U.S. for the 1987 tour. Ade's return to the international scene continued with a pair of successful concerts in Britain in 1988; the release the same year on the U.S. RykoDisc label of *Live Live Juju*, a recording of a Seattle concert; and another U.S. tour in 1989.

Also in 1989, Ade recorded an album, *Wait for Me*, containing two cuts advocating birth-control made with the young, American-educated female pop-star Onyeka. The following year, it was revealed that the recording had been funded by the USAID's Office of Population. Ade and Onyeka were criticized by some African-Americans as "accomplices to an attack on African cultural traditions and religious beliefs" (though the production of political and social praise songs to order is itself a well-established cultural tradition). Nigerian critics focused on his cooperation with a pop star, and commented that his 12 children hardly enhanced his credibility as a spokesman for birth-control.

Meanwhile, Ade's health was causing concern. In February 1991, he became ill during a performance in Lagos and went to London to recuperate from what was officially stated to be exhaustion. By May the same year he was back on stage, and in 1992 he launched yet another record label, Sigma, which—unlike his previous ones—handled its own distribution. Meanwhile he continued to play regularly at home and made annual overseas tours. And in early 1994 he set up the King Sunny Ade Foundation, whose principal aim is to help both young musicians and struggling older artists. The foundation is currently building a headquarters, including recording and production studios, performance venues, recreational facilities, housing for use by visiting artists, and residences for elderly and retired musicians with no other means of support. The foundation is also planning an education program.

DISC.: *Juju Music* (1982); *Synchro System* (1983); *Aura* (1985); *Live Live Juju* (1988); *Live at Hollywood Palace* (1992); *E Dide* (1995).—**LP**

Adelburg, August, Ritter von,

Austrian violinist and composer; b. Pera, Turkey, Nov. 1, 1830; d. Vienna, Oct. 20, 1873. He studied with Mayseder (violin) in Vienna (1850–54) and with Hoffmann (composition), then toured Europe as a violinist. He wrote the operas *Zrinyi* (Pest, June 23, 1868) and *Martinuzzi* (Buda, 1870), an overture, violin concerto, choral pieces, 5 string quartets (1863–64), sonatas, *L'école de la vélocité* for Violin, and songs.—**NS/LK/DM**

Adès, Thomas (Joseph Edmund), remarkable English composer and pianist; b. London, March 1, 1971. He studied piano with Paul Berkowitz and composition with Robert Saxton at the Guildhall School of Music and Drama in London, and then pursued his training with Hugh Wood, Alexander Goehr, and Robin Holloway at King's Coll., Cambridge (M.A., 1992) before taking his M.Phil. at St. John's Coll., Cambridge. He also took courses in Dartington (1991) and Aldeburgh (1992). In 1993 he attracted notice as a pianist and composer when he gave a London recital featuring the premiere of his *Still Sorrowing*. His *Living Toys* for Chamber Ensemble (1993) secured his reputation as a composer of promise. In 1993–94 he was a lecturer at the Univ. of Manchester, and also served as composer-in-association with the Hallé Orch. in Manchester from 1993 to 1995. His chamber opera, *Powder Her Face* (Cheltenham Festival, July 1, 1995), established him as a dramatic composer of marked talent. From 1995 to 1997 he was fellow commoner in creative arts at Trinity Coll., Cambridge. He was the Benjamin Britten Prof. of Music at the Royal Academy of Music in London (from 1997), musical director of the Birmingham Contemporary Music Group (from 1998), and artistic director of the Aldeburgh Festival (from 1999). In 1998 he was awarded the Elise L. Stroeger Prize of the Chamber Music Society of Lincoln Center in N.Y. He is currently composing a commissioned 2nd opera for Covent Garden, to a libretto by James Fenton, to premiere in 2001.

WORKS: DRAMATIC: *Powder Her Face*, chamber opera (Cheltenham Festival, July 1, 1995). ORCH.: Chamber Sym. (1990); *...but all shall be well* (1993); *These Premises Are Alarmed* (1996); *Asyla* (1997); *Concerto Conciso* for Piano and Orch. (1997–98). CHAMBER: *Catch* for Clarinet, Piano, Cello, and Violin (1991); *Living Toys* for Chamber Ensemble (1993); *Sonata da Caccia* for Ensemble (1993); *The Origin of the Harp* for Chamber Ensemble (1994); *Arcadiana* for String Quartet (1994). KEYBOARD: P i a n o : *Darkness Visible* (1992); *Still Sorrowing* (1992); *Traced Overhead* (1996). O r g a n : *Under Hamelin Hill* for Chamber Organ (1992). VOCAL: *Aubade* for Soprano and Piano (1990); *5 Eliot Landscapes* for Soprano and Piano (1990); *Fool's Rhymes* for Chorus and Ensemble (1992); *Life Story* for Soprano and Ensemble (1993).—NS/LK/DM

Adgate, Andrew, American singing teacher, conductor, and tunebook compiler; b. Norwich, Conn., March 22, 1762; d. Philadelphia, Sept. 30, 1793. He settled in Philadelphia, where he assisted Andrew Law in a singing school. In 1784 he organized the Institution for the Encouragement of Church Music. He founded a "Free School..." for the diffusion of the knowledge of vocal music in 1785, which became the Uranian Soc. and in 1787 the Uranian Academy. It was supported by subscription and charged its students no fees. From 1785 to 1790 Adgate conducted concerts, including a "Grand Concert" on May 4, 1786, of works by Handel, Lyon, Billings, and Tuckey with a chorus of 230 voices and an orch. of 50 players. Among his compilations were *Select Psalms and Hymns for the Use of Mr. Adgate's Pupils* (1787), *The Rudiments of Music* (1788), and *The Philadelphia Harmony* (1789).

BIBL.: H. Cummings, *A. A.: Philadelphia Psalmodist and Music Educator* (diss., Univ. of Rochester, 1975).—NS/LK/DM

Adkins, Cecil (Dale), American musicologist, organologist, and bibliographer; b. Red Oak, Iowa, Jan. 30, 1932. He was educated at the Univ. of Omaha (B.F.A., 1953), the Univ. of S.Dak. (M.M., 1959), and the Univ. of Iowa (Ph.D., 1963, with the diss. *The Theory and Practice of the Monochord*). In 1963 he became director of the early music program at N. Tex. State Univ. (later renamed the Univ. of N. Tex.) in Denton, where he was made prof. of musicology in 1969 and a Regents Prof. in 1988. From 1987 to 1991 he was president of the American Musical Instrument Soc., which awarded him its Curt Sachs Medal in 1999 for his manifold contributions to the study, history, and preservation of musical instruments. He published *A Topical Index to Edmond de Coussemaker's Scriptores de musica medii aevi, nova series* (Denton, 1968) and *The "ab Yberg" Positive Organ: Basle, Historical Museum 1927–58* (Boston, 1979). With A. Dickinson, he published the volumes *Acta musicologica: An Index Fall 1928–Spring 1967* (Basel, 1970), *Doctoral Dissertations in Musicology* (Philadelphia, 1972, 1984, 1990, 1996), *International Index of Dissertations and Musicological Works in Progress* (Basel and Philadelphia, 1977), and *A Trumpet by Any Other Name: A History of the Trumpet Marine* (Buren, 1991).—NS/LK/DM

Adler, Clarence, American pianist, teacher, and composer, father of **Richard Adler;** b. Cincinnati, March 10, 1886; d. N.Y., Dec. 24, 1969. He studied with R. Gorno at the Cincinnati Coll. of Music (1898–1904), with R. Joseffy in N.Y., and with Godowsky in Berlin (1905–09). After touring Europe with the Hekking Trio, he made his U.S. debut as soloist with the N.Y. Sym. Orch. on Feb. 8, 1914. He subsequently appeared with other U.S. orchs., gave recitals, and played in chamber music settings. In later years he was active as a teacher. He wrote several piano pieces and arrangements. —NS/LK/DM

Adler, F. Charles, American conductor; b. London (of an American father and a German mother), July 2, 1889; d. Vienna, Feb. 16, 1959. He studied with Halm (piano), Beer-Walbrunn (theory), and Mahler (conducting). After serving as Mottl's assistant at the Munich Court Opera (1908–11), he held the post of 1st conductor at the Düsseldorf Opera (from 1913). From 1919 to 1933 he was active as a sym. conductor in Europe, and he also was owner of the Edition Adler in Berlin. In 1937 he founded the Saratoga Springs (N.Y.) Music Festival. —NS/LK/DM

Adler, Guido, eminent Austrian musicologist; b. Eibenschütz, Moravia, Nov. 1, 1855; d. Vienna, Feb. 15, 1941. He was a student of Bruckner and Dessoff at the Vienna Cons., and then studied at the Univ. of Vienna (Dr.Jur., 1878; Ph.D., 1880, with the diss. *Die historischen Grundklassen der christlichen abendländischen Musik bis 1600*; completed his Habilitation, 1882, with his *Studie zur Geschichte der Harmonie*, which had been publ. in Vienna, 1881). With Chrysander and Spitta, he founded the *Vierteljahrsschrift für Musikwissenschaft* in 1885, the same year he became prof. of music history at the German Univ. in Prague. From 1895 to 1927 he was prof.

of music history at the Univ. of Vienna. He also was ed. of the monumental Denkmaler der Tonkunst in Österreich series (84 vols., 1894–1938). In 1937 he was made a corresponding member of the American Musicological Soc.

WRITINGS: *Richard Wagner: Vorlesungen* (Leipzig, 1904); *Joseph Haydn* (Vienna and Leipzig, 1909); *Der Stil in der Musik* (Leipzig, 1911; 2nd ed., 1929); *Gustav Mahler* (Vienna, 1916); *Methode der Musikgeschichte* (Frankfurt am Main, 1919); ed. *Handbuch der Musikgeshichte* (Frankfurt am Main, 1924; 2nd ed., rev., 1930); *Wollen und Wirken: Aus dem Leben eines Musikhistorikers* (Vienna, 1935).

BIBL.: *Studien zur Musikgeschichte: Festschrift für G. A.* (Vienna, 1930); E. Reilly, *Gustav Mahler und G. A.* (Vienna, 1978). —NS/LK/DM

Adler, Kurt, Czech-American conductor; b. Neuhaus, Bohemia, March 1, 1907; d. Butler, N.J., Sept. 21, 1977. He studied musicology with Guido Adler and Robert Lach at the Univ. of Vienna. After serving as asst. conductor of the Berlin State Opera (1927–29) and the German Theater in Prague (1929–32), he was conductor of the Kiev Opera (1933–35) and the Stalingrad Phil. (1935–37). In 1938 he settled in the U.S. He was asst. conductor (1943–45), chorus master (1945–73), and a conductor (1951–68) at the Metropolitan Opera in N.Y.

WRITINGS: *The Art of Accompanying and Coaching* (Minneapolis, 1965); *Phonetics and Diction in Singing* (Minneapolis, 1967).—NS/LK/DM

Adler, Kurt Herbert, notable Austrian-American conductor and operatic administrator; b. Vienna, April 2, 1905; d. Ross, Calif., Feb. 9, 1988. He studied at the Vienna Academy of Music and the Univ. of Vienna. He made his debut as a conductor at the Max Reinhardt Theater in Vienna in 1925, and subsequently conducted at the Volksoper there, as well as in Germany, Italy, and Czechoslovakia. He served as assistant to Toscanini at the Salzburg Festival in 1936. As Hitler moved upon central Europe, Adler moved to the U.S., and from 1938 to 1943 was on the staff of the Chicago Opera; he subsequently was appointed choirmaster (1943), artistic director (1953), and general director (1956) of the San Francisco Opera. After his retirement in 1981, he was made general director emeritus. Under his direction, the San Francisco Opera prospered greatly, advancing to the foremost ranks of American opera theaters. In 1980 he was awarded an honorary knighthood by Queen Elizabeth II of England.

BIBL.: K. Lockhart, ed., *The A. Years* (San Francisco, 1981). —NS/LK/DM

Adler, Peter Herman, Czech-American conductor; b. Gablonz, Bohemia, Dec. 2, 1899; d. Ridgefield, Conn., Oct. 2, 1990. He studied with Fidelio Finke, Vitslav Novák, and Alexander von Zemlinsky at the Prague Cons. After conducting opera in Bremen (1929–32) and sym. concerts in Kiev (1933–36), he settled in the U.S. and appeared as a guest conductor. From 1949 to 1959 he was music director of the NBC-TV Opera in N.Y., and then of the Baltimore Sym. Orch. (1959–68). In 1969 he helped found the NET (National Educational Television) Opera in N.Y., with which he appeared as a conductor. On Sept. 22, 1972, he made his Metropolitan Opera debut in N.Y. conducting *Un ballo in maschera.* He was director of the American Opera Center at the Juilliard School in N.Y. (1973–81). —NS/LK/DM

Adler, Richard, American songwriter; b. N.Y., Aug. 3, 1921. With Jerry Ross, Adler wrote music and lyrics to several hit songs in the early 1950s, among them "Rags to Riches." The two then wrote the songs for two successful Broadway musicals, *The Pajama Game* (featuring "Hey There" and "Hernando's Hideaway") and *Damn Yankees* (featuring "Heart" and "Whatever Lola Wants"). Following Ross's early death, Adler continued to write for the musical theater, although he also worked in government and advertising.

Adler's parents were Clarence and Elsa Adrienne Richard Adler. His father was a concert pianist and music teacher. Adler attended the Univ. of N.C. at Chapel Hill, where he studied playwrighting with Paul Green. Graduating with a B.A. in 1943, he joined the navy and spent the rest of World War II serving in Central America. In 1946 he returned to N.Y. and found a job as a writer in the public relations department of the Celanese Corporation of America. During the next few years he increasingly turned his attention to songwriting.

Adler had his first chart record in November 1950, with a novelty answer-song to the recent hit "Goodnight Irene" (music and lyrics by Lead Belly) called "Please Say Goodnight to the Guy, Irene" (music and lyrics also by John Jacob Loeb), recorded by Ziggy Talent. He formed a partnership that year with Jerry Ross (Jerold Rosenberg); they collaborated on both music and lyrics. They enjoyed their first success when Eddy Howard and His Orch. took "The Strange Little Girl" into the charts in June 1951. On Sept. 4, 1951, Adler married Marion Hart Rogier. They had two sons, one of whom, Christopher Adler, became a lyricist. They divorced on Jan. 3, 1958.

Adler and Ross wrote special material for various performers and for the television series *Stop the Music.* They earned their first Top Ten hit in January 1953 with "Even Now" (music and lyrics also by Dave Kapp), recorded by Eddie Fisher. "Rags to Riches" gave them their first million-selling #1 hit in November, in a recording by Tony Bennett. The following month they were the primary songwriters for the Broadway revue *John Murray Anderson's Almanac,* which ran 229 performances. They wrote all the songs for the book musical *The Pajama Game,* which opened in May 1955 and became a giant hit, running 1,063 performances and winning the Tony Award for Best Musical. The cast album reached the Top Ten, and the score generated three hits: "Hey There," which topped the charts and sold a million copies in a recording by Rosemary Clooney; "Hernando's Hideaway," a #1 for Archie Bleyer; and "Steam Heat," which Patti Page took into the Top Ten. Adler and Ross returned to Broadway in May 1955 with *Damn Yankees,* which repeated the success of *The Pajama Game:* it ran 1,019 performances and won the Tony Award for Best Musical; the cast album reached the Top Ten; and the score spawned three hits, "Heart" for Eddie Fisher and "Whatever Lola Wants" for Sarah Vaughan, each of which made the Top Ten, and "Two Lost Souls" for Perry Como and Jaye P. Morgan, which reached the Top 40. Unfortunately, Ross died of chronic bronchiectasis at age 29 on Nov. 11, 1955.

Adler's first work as a sole songwriter came with the Broadway play *The Sin of Pat Muldoon* (N.Y., March 13, 1957), which he coproduced and for which he wrote the title song. In August 1957 a faithful film adaptation of *The Pajama Game,* starring Doris Day, opened; the soundtrack album reached the Top Ten. Adler married British actress and singer Sally Ann Howes on Jan. 3, 1958; they divorced in 1966. He returned to writing independent songs, penning the lyrics to Robert Allen's music for "Everybody Loves a Lover," which became a Top Ten hit for Doris Day in July 1958. In September a faithful film adaptation of *Damn Yankees* opened; the soundtrack album reached the charts. Adler coproduced and wrote music and lyrics for two television musicals broadcast in the fall, *Little Women* and *The Gift of the Magi* (his wife appeared in the latter). He and Robert Allen had another chart success in January 1959, when the Four Lads took "The Girl on Page 44" into the Top 40.

Adler next turned to writing a new Broadway musical. *Kwamina,* starring Sally Ann Howes, opened in October 1961; it was a failure, running only 32 performances, but the cast album reached the charts. After this, Adler wrote commercial jingles and produced and staged special shows for the Kennedy and Johnson administrations. In 1964 he became a trustee of the John F. Kennedy Center for the Performing Arts in Washington, D.C., retaining the post until 1977. He was a consultant on the arts for the White House from 1965 to 1969. During this period his older songs were revived for hits. In December 1962 the Shirelles reached the Top 40 with a new recording of "Everybody Loves a Lover"; "Rags to Riches" was revived for a chart entry by Sunny & the Sunliners in November 1963; and Decca Records reissued Burl Ives's 1953 recording of "True Love Goes On and On" (music and lyrics by Richard Adler and Jerry Ross) for a chart entry in December 1963.

Adler's next significant musical project was a television musical, *Olympus 7-0000,* broadcast in September 1966, which he coproduced and for which he wrote the songs. His next stage musical, *A Mother's Kisses* (New Haven, Sept. 23, 1968), got as far as out-of-town tryouts but closed before reaching Broadway. On Dec. 27, 1968, he married Ritchey Farrell Banker; they divorced in 1976. (In the early 1980s he married Mary St. George.) Elvis Presley revived "Rags to Riches" for a Top 40 hit in March 1971. Adler coproduced a revival of *The Pajama Game* (N.Y., Dec. 9, 1973) that ran 65 performances on Broadway and coproduced the unsuccessful Richard Rodgers–Sheldon Harnick musical *Rex* (N.Y., April 25, 1976). With lyricist Will Holt, he wrote the songs for *Music Is,* a musical version of Shakespeare's *Twelfth Night,* but it ran only eight performances on Broadway after opening in December 1976.

In the second half of the 1970s Adler turned to composing symphonic works, notably *Memory of Childhood,* premiered by the Detroit Sym. on Oct. 6, 1978; *Retrospectrum,* premiered by the Soviet Emigré Orch. at Carnegie Hall on July 10, 1979; *Yellowstone,* introduced by the Metropolitan Brass Quartet in N.Y., then rewritten for sym. orch. as *Yellowstone Overture* and premiered by the American Philharmonic Orch. in N.Y. on Nov. 2, 1980; *Wilderness Suite,* premiered by the Utah Sym. on Feb. 5, 1983; *Eight by Adler,* an adaptation of eight of his popular songs, performed by the Chicago City Ballet in 1984; *The Lady Remembers (The Statue of Liberty Suite),* premiered by the Detroit Sym. in Washington, D.C., on Oct. 28, 1985; and *Fanfare and Overture for the U.S. Olympics Festival* (1987).

A Broadway revival of *Damn Yankees* opened on March 3, 1994, and ran 510 performances, during which Jerry Lewis joined the cast. Lewis starred in a touring production of the show that played internationally for years. Returning to the musical theater, Adler wrote the music and cowrote the lyrics with librettist Bill C. Davis for the musical *Off-Key,* which was produced at the George Street Theatre in New Brunswick, N.J., starting April 7, 1995.

WORKS (only works for which Adler was a primary, credited songwriter are listed): **MUSICALS/REVUES** (dates refer to N.Y. openings): *John Murray Anderson's Almanac* (Dec. 10, 1953); *The Pajama Game* (May 13, 1954); *Damn Yankees* (May 5, 1955); *Kwamina* (Oct. 23, 1961); *Music Is* (Dec. 20, 1976). **FILMS:** *The Pajama Game* (1957); *Damn Yankees* (1958). **TELEVISION:** *Little Women* (Oct. 16, 1958); *The Gift of the Magi* (Dec. 9, 1958); *Olympus 7-0000* (Sept. 28, 1966).

WRITINGS: With L. Davis, *"You Gotta Have Heart": An Autobiography* (N.Y., 1990).—**WR**

Adler, Samuel (Hans),

esteemed German-born American composer, conductor, and pedagogue; b. Mannheim, March 4, 1928. His father was a cantor and composer, and his mother an amateur pianist. Adler began violin study as a child with Albert Levy. In 1939 the family emigrated to the U.S. After composition lessons with Fromm in Boston (1941–46), he studied with Hugo Norden (composition) and Geiringer (musicology) at Boston Univ. (B.M., 1948) before pursuing composition training with Piston, Thompson, and Fine at Harvard Univ. (M.A., 1950). He also attended the classes of Copland (composition) and Koussevitzky (conducting) at the Berkshire Music Center in Tanglewood (summers, 1949–50). In 1950 he joined the U.S. Army, and was founder-conductor of the 7th Army Sym. Orch., for which he received the Army Medal of Honor. Upon his discharge, he went to Dallas as music director of Temple Emanu-El (1953–56) and of the Lyric Theater (1954–58). From 1957 to 1966 he was prof. of composition at N. Tex. State Univ. in Denton. He was prof. of composition (1966–94) and chairman of the music dept. (1973–94) at the Eastman School of Music in Rochester, N.Y. In 1997 he became prof. of composition at the Juilliard School in N.Y. Adler has received many honors and awards, including the ASCAP-Deems Taylor Award (1983) for his book *The Study of Orchestration.* In 1984–85 he held a Guggenheim fellowship. In 1990 he received an award from the American Academy and Inst. of Arts and Letters. In his compositions, he has followed a path of midstream modernism, in which densely interwoven contrapuntal lines support the basically tonal harmonic complex, with a frequent incidence of tangential atonal episodes. Much of his music is inspired by the liturgical cantilena of traditional Jewish music while oriental inflections also occur.

WORKS: DRAMATIC: *The Outcasts of Poker Flat*, opera (1959; Denton, Tex., June 8, 1962); *The Wrestler*, sacred opera (1971; Dallas, May 1972); *The Lodge of Shadows*, music drama for Baritone, Dancers, and Orch. (1973; Fort Worth, Tex., May 3, 1988); *The Disappointment*, reconstruction of an early American ballad opera of 1767 (1974; Washington, D.C., Nov. 1976); *The Waking*, celebration for Dancers, Chorus, and Orch. (1978; Louisville, April 1979). **ORCH.:** 6 syms: No. 1 (Dallas, Dec. 7, 1953), No. 2 (1957; Dallas, Feb. 12, 1958), No. 3, *Diptych* (1960; rev. 1980–81), No. 4, *Geometrics* (1967; Dallas, May 1970), No. 5, *We Are the Echoes*, for Mezzo-soprano and Orch. (Fort Worth, Tex., Nov. 10, 1975), and No. 6 (1985); 3 concertinos (1954, 1976, 1993); *Toccata* (1954); *Summer Stock*, overture (1955); *The Feast of Lights* (1955); *Jubilee* (1958) *Rhapsody* for Violin and Orch. (1961); *Song and Dance* for Viola and Orch. (1961); *4 Early American Folk Songs* for Strings (1962); *Elegy* for Strings (1962); *Requiescat in Pace*, in memory of President John F. Kennedy (1963); *City by the Lake* (1968); Organ Concerto (1970); *Concerto for Orchestra* (1971); *Sinfonietta* (1971); *A Little Bit...* for Strings (1976); Flute Concerto (1977); *Joi, Amor, Cortezia* for Chamber Orch. (1982); 2 piano concertos: No. 1 (1983; Washington, D.C., Jan. 3, 1985) and No. 2 (1996; San Francisco, July 6, 1997); *In Just Spring*, overture (1984); Saxophone Quartet Concerto (1985; Leeuwarden, June 25, 1986); *The Fixed Desire of the Human Heart* (Geneva, July 5, 1988); *Beyond the Land* (1988; Oklahoma City, March 10, 1990); *Shadow Dances* (1990); *To Celebrate a Miracle* (1991); Wind Quintet Concerto (1991; Mannheim, June 1, 1992); *Celebration*, for the 100th anniversary of the Cincinnati Sym. Orch. (1993; Cincinnati, Oct. 1995); Guitar Concerto (1994); Cello Concerto (1995; Cleveland, Oct. 6, 1998); *Art Creates Artists* (1996); *Lux Perpetua* for Organ and Orch. (1997; Dallas, Feb. 11, 1999); Viola Concerto (1999). **Band:** *Southwestern Sketches* (1961); *Festive Prelude* (1965); Concerto (1968); *A Little Night and Day Music* (1976); *An American Duo* (1981); *Merrymakers* (1982); *American Airs and Dances* (1998). **Wind Ensemble:** *Double Visions* (1987); *Ultralight* (fanfare; 1990); *We Live* (fanfare, 1995); *Serenata Concertante* (1996); *Dawn to Glory* (1998). **Brass:** *Concert Piece* for Brass Choir (1946); *Praeludium* for Brass Choir (1947); *Divertimento* for Brass Choir (1948); *5 Vignettes* for Trombone Choir (1968); *Brass Fragments* for Brass Choir (1970); *Histrionics* for Brass Choir and Percussion (1971); *Trumpet Triptych* for 7 Trumpets (1979). **CHAMBER:** 8 string quartets (1945; 1950; 1953, rev. 1964; 1963; 1969; 1975; 1981; 1990); Horn Sonata (1948); 4 violin sonatas (1948, 1956, 1965, 1989); 2 piano trios (1964, 1978); Sonata for Solo Cello (1966); *7 Epigrams* for Wind Sextet (1966); *Quintalogues* for Flute, Oboe, Clarinet, Bassoon, and Percussion (1968); *Canto I* for Trumpet (1970), *II* for Bass Trombone (1970), *III* for Violin (1976), *IV* for Saxophone (1975), *V* for Soprano, Flute, Cello, and 3 Percussionists (1968), *VI* for Double Bass (1971), *VII* for Tuba (1972), *VIII* for Piano (1973), *IX* for Timpani and Roto Toms (1976), *X* for Cello (1979), *XI* for Horn (1984), *XII* for Bassoon (1989), *XIII* for Piccolo (1994), *XIV* for Clarinet (1996), and *XV* for English Horn (1996); *Xenia* for Organ and Percussion (1971); *4 Dialogues* for Euphonium and Percussion (1974); *Aeolus, King of the Winds* for Clarinet and Piano Trio (1978); *Line Drawings* for Saxophone Quartet (1979); Sonata for Solo Flute (1981); *Gottschalkiana* for Brass Quintet (1982); Viola Sonata (1984); Oboe Sonata (1985); *Double Portrait* for Violin and Piano (1985); Sonata for Solo Guitar (1985); *Acrostics* for Flute, Oboe, Clarinet, Violin, Cello, and Harpsichord (1986); *Herinnering* for String Quartet (1987); *Pasiphae* for Piano and Percussion (1987); Clarinet Sonata (1989); *Close Encounters* for Violin and Cello (1989); *Sounding* for Alto Saxophone and Piano (1989); *Triolet* for Flute, Viola, and Harp (1989); *Ports of Call* for 2 Violins and Guitar (1992); *Into the Radiant Boundries of Light* for Viola and Guitar (1993); *Clarion Calls*, suite for Trumpet and Organ (1995); *Diary of a Journey: 4 Snapshots* for Flute, Bassoon, and Cello (1995); *Contrasting Inventions* for Alto and Tenor Saxophone (1998); *"Be Not Afraid, the Isle Is Full of Noises"* for Brass Quintet (1999). **KEYBOARD: Piano:** *Sonata breve* (1963); *Gradus* (3 books, 1979); *Sonatina* (1979); *Duo Sonata* for 2 Pianos (1983); *Eine Enge Berg Fugue* for Piano, 8-Hands (1996). **Organ:** 2 meditations (1955, 1964); *Toccata, Recitation, and Postlude* (1959); *Epistrophe*, sonata (1990); *Festive Proclamation* (1995). **VOCAL:** *Miscellany* for Mezzo-soprano, English Horn, and String Quartet (1956); *The Vision of Isaiah* for Bass, Chorus, and Orch. (1962); *B'shaaray tefilah*, sabbath service for Bass, Chorus, and Organ or Orch. (1963); *Behold Your God*, Christmas cantata for Soloists, Chorus, Winds, and Percussion (1966); *The Binding*, oratorio for Chorus and Orch. (1967); *From Out of Bondage* for Soloists, Chorus, Brass Quintet, Percussion, and Organ (1968); *Lament* for Baritone and Chamber Orch. (1968); *A Whole Bunch of Fun*, secular cantata for Mezzo-soprano or Baritone, 3 Choruses, and Orch. (1969); *Begin My Muse* for Men's Chorus and Percussion Ensemble (1969); *We Believe*, ecumenical mass for Mixed Voices and 8 Instruments (1974); *A Falling of Saints* for Tenor, Baritone, Chorus, and Orch. (1977); *Snow Tracks* for High Voice and Wind Ensemble (1981); *The Flames of Freedom* for Chorus and Piano (1982); *Choose Life*, oratorio for Mezzo-soprano, Tenor, Chorus, and Orch. (1986); *High Flight* for Chorus and Chamber Orch. (1986); *'Round the Globe*, folk song suite for Treble Voices and Piano or Orch. (1986); *Stars in the Dust*, cantata for Soloists, Chorus, and Orch. (1988); *Any Human to Another*, cantata for Chorus, Piano, and Orch. (1989); *Ever Since Babylon*, cantata for Soloists, Chorus, and Orch. (1991; Chicago, March 8, 1992); *Reconciliation* for Soprano, Flute, Clarinet, Violin, Cello, and Piano (1992); *Time in Tempest Everywhere* for Soprano, Oboe, Piano, and Chamber Orch. (1994; Cleveland, May 1, 1995); *A Prolific Source of Sorrow: 5 Chinese Songs* for Flute and Chorus (1994; Washington, D.C., May 1, 1995); *Family Portraits* for Chorus and Band (1995); *Rogues and Lovers* for Chorus and Band (1995; Tampa, Jan. 12, 1996); *Psalm Trilogy* for Chorus (1997); *My Beloved Is Mine* for Chorus (1998; N.Y., May 1, 1999).

WRITINGS: *Anthology for the Teaching of Choral Conducting* (N.Y., 1971; 2nd ed., 1985, as *Choral Conducting: An Anthology*); *Singing and Hearing* (N.Y., 1979); *The Study of Orchestration* (N.Y., 1982; 2nd ed., 1989).—**NS/LK/DM**

Adlgasser, Anton Cajetan, German organist and composer; b. Inzell, Upper Bavaria, Oct. 1, 1729; d. of a stroke while playing the organ, Salzburg, Dec. 22, 1777. He received training in organ and violin. He may have also studied composition with Eberlin in Salzburg, whom he succeeded as court and cathedral organist in 1750. From 1760 he also was organist at the Trinity Church there. Mozart praised him as a master of counterpoint. He wrote an opera, *La Nitteti* (Salzburg, 1766), school dramas, 7 syms., keyboard concertos, oratorios, liturgical works, and keyboard sonatas.

BIBL.: W. Rainer, *Das Instrumentalwerke A.C. A.s* (diss., Univ. of Innsbruck, 1963).—NS/LK/DM

Adlung, Jakob, distinguished German music scholar and organist; b. Bindersleben, near Erfurt, Jan. 14, 1699; d. Erfurt, July 5, 1762. He began his music studies with his father, the teacher and organist David Adlung. While matriculating at the Erfurt Gymnasium (1713), he stayed with Christian Reichardt, who taught him organ. He then studied theology, philosophy, philology, and other subjects at the Univ. of Jena (graduated, 1726), and concurrently received further training in organ from Johann Nikolaus Bach. From 1727 until his death he was organist of Erfurt's Prediger church. He also was a prof. of languages at the Erfurt Gymnasium, a teacher of organ, and builder of keyboard instruments. Adlung was an important writer on music theory and aesthetics. His valuable books are *Anleitung zu der musikalischen Gelahrtheit* (Erfurt, 1758; 2nd ed., rev., 1783, by J. Hiller), *Musica mechanica organoedi* (ed. by J. Albrecht; Berlin, 1768), and *Musikalisches Siebengestirn. Das ist: Sieben zu der edlen Tonkunst gehörige Fragen* (ed. by J. Albrecht; Berlin, 1768).—NS/LK/DM

Adni, Daniel, Israeli pianist; b. Haifa, Dec. 6, 1951. He began his training in Haifa, where he made his debut when he was 12. He pursued training in piano with Perlemuter and studied solfège and sight reading at the Paris Cons. (1968–69), winning premiers prix in all three. In 1970 he completed his training with Anda in Zürich and made his London recital debut at Wigmore Hall. His debut as a soloist followed in 1971 when he appeared with Klemperer and the New Philharmonia Orch. at the Royal Festival Hall in London. He gave recitals for the first time in Scotland in Edinburgh in 1971, and in Spain in San Sebastián and in Canada in Toronto in 1972. His German debut followed in 1973 when he was a soloist with Lawrence Foster and the Berlin Radio Sym. Orch., the same year that he made his Norwegian debut in a recital in Oslo. In 1974 he made his first appearance in Switzerland in a recital at the Tonhalle in Zürich. He appeared as a recitalist in Japan for the first time in Tokyo in 1975, and also was a soloist that same year with the Tokyo Phil. and the Jersulaem Sym. Orch. He made his U.S. debut in 1976 in a recital at the 92nd Street Y in N.Y. His first appearance in the Netherlands came in 1978 as a soloist with Leitner and the Rotterdam Phil. In 1979 he made his debut as a soloist in the U.S. with Maazel and the Cleveland Orch. He made his debut with the Israel Phil. in Tel Aviv with Myung-Whun Chung conducting. In addition to appearances as a soloist and recitalist, Adni has been active as a chamber music player. While he has been closely associated with the Classical and Romantic masters from Beethoven to Brahms, he has also exhibited a flair for the music of Debussy, Grainger, Ravel, and Prokofiev.—NS/LK/DM

Adolfati, Andrea, Italian composer; b. Venice, c. 1721; d. Genoa, Oct. 28, 1760. He was a student of Galuppi. After serving as maestro di cappella at S. Maria della Salute in Venice, he was in the service of the Modena court (1745–48). Subsequently he was director of music at the Annunziata church in Genoa (1748–60) and maestro di cappella in Padua (1760). He wrote 10 operas (1746–55), a Sinfonia, an overture, chamber music, and sacred works.—NS/LK/DM

Adolphus, Milton, American composer; b. N.Y., Jan. 27, 1913; d. Hyannis, Mass., Aug. 16, 1988. He studied composition with Scalero in Philadelphia. Among his works were 13 syms., a Percussion Concerto (1980), and chamber music, including 31 string quartets.—NS/LK/DM

Adomián, Lan, Russian-born Mexican composer; b. near Mogilev, April 29, 1905; d. Mexico City, May 9, 1979. He emigrated to the U.S. in 1923, and studied at the Peabody Cons. of Music in Baltimore (1924–26) and at the Curtis Inst. of Music in Philadelphia (1926–28), where his teachers were Bailly (viola) and R. O. Morris (composition). He moved to N.Y. in 1928, where he conducted working-class choruses and bands. In 1936 he joined the Abraham Lincoln Brigade and went to Spain to fight on the Republican side during the Spanish Civil War. Upon his return to America, he wrote music for documentary films. In 1952 his radical politics made it prudent for him to leave the U.S. He moved to Mexico and became a naturalized citizen. Adomián was uncommonly prolific as a composer. Among his voluminous works are an opera, *La Macherata* (1969–72), a dramatic scene, *Auschwitz*, for Baritone and Instruments (1970), 8 syms., choruses, and songs.

BIBL.: *La voluntad de crear* (2 vols., Mexico City, 1980–81).—NS/LK/DM

Adorno (real name, **Wiesengrund**), **Theodor,** significant German social philosopher, music sociologist, and composer; b. Frankfurt am Main, Sept. 11, 1903; d. Visp, Switzerland, Aug. 6, 1969. He studied with Sekles (composition) and Eduard Jung (piano) at the Hoch Cons. in Frankfurt am Main. He also took courses in philosophy, sociology, psychology, and musicology at the Univ. of Frankfurt am Main (Ph.D., 1925). Following further training with Berg (composition) and Steuermann (piano) in Vienna, he completed his Habilitation at the Univ. of Frankfurt am Main (1931). From 1928 to 1931 he ed. the journal *Anbruch*, and also was Privatdozent at the Univ. of Frankfurt am Main until being dismissed by the Nazis in 1933. In 1934 he went to Oxford, and in 1938 to N.Y., where he joined the Institut für Sozialforschung. He also was music director of the Princeton Radio Research Project (until 1940). After living in Los Angeles (from 1941), he returned to Frankfurt am Main (1949). In 1950 he became an honorary prof. and in 1956 a prof. of philosophy and sociology at the Univ. there. Adorno exercised a deep influence on the trends in musical philosophy and general aesthetics, applying the sociological tenets of Karl Marx and the psychoanalytic techniques of Sigmund Freud. In his speculative writings, he introduced the concept of "cultural industry," embracing all types of music, from dodecaphonic to jazz. His compositions, mainly vocal, were reflective of modern trends.

WORKS: 6 Short Pieces for Orch. (1925–29); *Kinderjahr*, 6 pieces for Small Orch., after Schumann's op.68 (1941); 6 Studies for String Quartet (1920); String Quartet (1921); String Trio (1921–22); 2 Pieces for String Quartet (1925–26); *Variations* for Violin (1946); String Trio (1946); also piano music, including *Die böhmischen Terzen* (1945); 2 Songs for Voice and Orch. (1932–33); many songs with piano; choral pieces.

WRITINGS (all publ. in Frankfurt am Main unless otherwise given): *Philosophie der neuen Musik* (Tübingen, 1949; 3rd ed., 1967; Eng. tr., 1973); *Versuch über Wagner* (Berlin, 1952; 2nd ed., 1964; Eng. tr., 1991); *Prismen: Kulturkritik und Gesellschaft* (1955; Eng. tr., 1967; 3rd Ger. ed., 1969); *Dissonanzen: Musik in der verwalteten Welt* (Göttingen, 1956; 3rd ed., Aug., 1963); *Klangfiguren: Musikalische Schriften I* (Berlin, 1959); *Mahler: Eine musikalische Physiognomik* (1960; 2nd ed., 1963; Eng. tr., 1992); *Einleitung in die Musiksoziologie: Zwölf theoretische Vorlesungen* (1962; 2nd ed., 1968; Eng. tr., 1976); *Der getreue Korrepetitor: Lehrschriften zur Musikalischen Praxis* (1963); *Quasi una fantasia: Musikalische Schriften II* (1963; Eng. tr., 1992); *Moments musicaux: Neu gedruckte Aufsätze 1928 bis 1962* (1964); *Ohne Leitbild: Parva aesthetica* (1967; 2nd ed., 1968); *Berg: Der Meister des kleinsten Übergangs* (Vienna, 1968; Eng. tr., 1991); *Impromptus: Zeite Folge neu gedruckter musikalischer Aufsätze* (1968). A complete ed. of his writings in 20 vols. commenced publication in Frankfurt am Main in 1970.

BIBL.: M. Horkheimer, ed., *T.W. A. zum 60. Geburtstag* (Frankfurt am Main, 1963); H. Schweppenhäuser, ed., *T.W. A. zum Gedächtnis* (Frankfurt am Main, 1971); K. Oppens et al., *Über T.W. A.* (Frankfurt am Main, 1971); W. Gramer, *Musik und Verstehen: Eine Studie zur Musikästhetik T.W. A.* (Mainz, 1976); O. Kolleritsche, ed., *A. und die Musik* (Graz, 1979); B. Lindner and W. Ludke, eds., *Materialien zur ästhetischen Theorie T.W. A.s: Konstruktion der Moderne* (Frankfurt am Main, 1980); M. Jay, *A.* (London, 1984); S. Schibli, *Der Komponist T.W. A.: Vorläufige Anmerkungen zu einem noch nicht überschaubaren Thema* (Frankfurt am Main, 1988); T. Müller, *Die Musiksoziologie T.W. A.s: Ein Model ihrer Interpretation am Beispiel Alban Bergs* (Frankfurt am Main, 1990); R. Klein, *Solidarität mit Metaphysik?: Ein Versuch über die musikphilosophische Problematik der Wagner-Kritik T.W. A.s* (Würzburg, 1991); M. Paddison, *A.'s Aesthetics of Music* (Cambridge, 1993); L. Sziborsky, *Rettung des Hoffnungslosen: Untersuchungen zur Ästhetik und Musikphilosophie T.W. A.s* (Würzburg, 1994); M. Paddison, *A., Modernism and Mass Culture: Essays on Critical Theory and Music* (London, 1996); C. Dennis, *A.'s Philosophy of Modern Music* (Lewiston, N.Y., 1998); R. Klein and C.-S. Mahnkopf, eds., *Mit den Ohren denken: A.s Philosophie der Musik* (Frankfurt am Main, 1998); R. Witkin, *A. on Music* (London, 1998).—**NS/LK/DM**

Adriaenssen, Emanuel, South Netherlands lutenist, teacher, and composer; b. Antwerp, c. 1554; d. there (buried), Feb. 27, 1604. He studied in Rome. Upon his return to Antwerp in 1574, he founded a school for lutenists. He gained a notable reputation as a lute virtuoso and distinguished teacher. Adriaenssen publ. *Pratum musicum...* (Antwerp, 1584; 2nd ed., rev., 1600) and *Novum pratum musicum...* (Antwerp, 1592), lute music containing fantasias, dances, and arrangements of vocal works.

BIBL.: G. Spiessens, *Leven en werk van de Antwerpse luitcomponist E. A. (ca.1554–1604)* (Brussels, 1974–76).—**NS/LK/DM**

Adrio, Adam, distinguished German musicologist; b. Essen, April 4, 1901; d. Ritten, Bozen, Sept. 18, 1973. He studied with Abert, Schering, and Blume at the Univ. of Berlin (Ph.D., 1934, with the diss. *Die Anfänge des geistlichen Konzerts*; publ. in Berlin, 1935), where he also taught (1932–45). After completing his Habilitation at the Free Univ. in Berlin (1949), he was a reader (1951–53) and a prof. (1953–67) of musicology there. Adrio was an authority on Protestant church music, contributing many articles to *Die Musik in Geschichte und Gegenwart* and to music journals; also ed. the works of Johann Hermann Schein.—**NS/LK/DM**

Adson, John, English composer; place and date of birth unknown; d. London, 1640. He was in the service of the Duke of Lorraine (1604–08). In 1614 he was made a London wait. In 1625 he entered the English court band. By 1633 he was musician in ordinary for the King's wind instruments, and in 1634 he was named music teacher to Charles I. He publ. *Courtly Masquing Ayres* (London, 1611; 2nd ed., 1622).—**LK/DM**

Aebersold, Jamey, jazz educator, saxophonist; b. New Albany, Ind., July 21, 1939. Aebersold has been best known since the 1970s as the producer and marketer of over 80 play-along albums that have become the most widely used of such recordings for jazz. He sometimes demonstrates jazz techniques on these albums, primarily on alto saxophone, but he also plays piano and bass. Aebersold earned a Masters in Saxophone at Ind. Univ. in 1962 and was awarded an honorary doctorate there in 1992. Since 1971 he has directed a series of week long Summer Jazz Workshops at various locations in the United States, Canada, and overseas. Aebersold has been active with the International Association of Jazz Educators and entered their Jazz Hall of Fame in 1989. He has been generous in donating materials to isolated jazz programs, such as the one led by Darius Brubeck in Natal, South Africa. Aebersold teaches jazz improvisation at the Univ. of Louisville.

DISC.: *J.A. Sextet at the Notre Dame Collegiate Festival* (1964).—**LP**

Aerosmith, one of America's most tenacious, iconic rock groups, originally formed in 1970, in Sunapee, N.H. **MEMBERSHIP:** Steve Tyler, lead voc. (b. Steve Tallarico, Yonkers, N.Y., March 26, 1948); Joe Perry, lead gtr. (b. Lawrence, Mass., Sept. 10, 1950); Brad Whitford, rhythm gtr. (b. Winchester, Mass., Feb. 23, 1952); Tom Hamilton, bs. (b. Colorado Springs, Colo., Dec. 31, 1951); Joey Kramer, drms. (b. June 21, 1950, N.Y.).

By the age of 19, Steve Tallarico had already worked with various bands and recorded for Verve Records with his own band, Chain Reaction. The group had toured as an opening act for The Byrds, The Beach Boys, and the Jimmy Page Yardbirds. He met guitarist Joe Perry in the summer of 1970 while working at the Tallarico family resort in Sunapee, N.H. Together with the bassist in Perry's Jam Band, Tom Hamilton, they formed the nucleus of the band that would become Aerosmith. They recruited drummer Joey Kramer and guitarist Brad Whitford and started playing anywhere they could, including high schools and in front of the student union at Boston Univ. They all shared an apartment in Boston, practiced at the Fenway Theater, and played when they could, where they could, up and down the East Coast. About this time, Tallarico changed his last name to Tyler.

Columbia Records president Clive Davis caught their act at N.Y.'s Max's Kansas City and gave them a $125,000 deal. They recorded their debut album in just two weeks. It came out early in 1973, and did very well in Boston, but the rest of the country didn't know Aerosmith yet. The group set out to change that, hitting the road, opening for bands ranging from The Kinks to The Mahavishnu Orch. The single "Dream On" topped Mass. radio, but only rose as high as #59 on the national charts.

Aerosmith went into the Record Plant in N.Y. with producer Jack Douglas to make *Get Your Wings*. The album garnered them some attention, especially from *Circus* magazine. A cover of "Train Kept A-Rollin'" got enough play on rock radio to merit release as a single. Because of this and non- stop touring, by 1975 the album went gold.

The combination of rock radio play and incessant touring powered the band's next record, *Toys in the Attic*, to #11. The single "Sweet Emotion" rose as high as #36. "Walk This Way," "Big Ten Inch Record" and "You See Me Cryin'" also got significant play on rock radio. The venues and press coverage started to grow, and the band became headliners playing for 80,000 at Pontiac Stadium outside of Detroit in 1976.

When the group released *Rocks* in 1976 it quickly went platinum and rose to #3. It eventually sold more than 3,000,000 copies. *Creem* readers voted it the #1 album and Aerosmith the #1 band. While *Rocks* didn't generate any pop hits, Columbia re-released some earlier singles that they felt had not received a fair shake. The double-A-sided single of "Dream On"/"Sweet Emotion" hit #3, while "Walk This Way" reached #10. Once again, the band hit the road in a big way, touring 58 cities through America, then moving on to the Far East.

Aerosmith's next album, *Draw the Line*, went platinum even faster, though it peaked at #11. The group did a cameo performance in the unsuccessful film version of *Sergeant Pepper's Lonely Hearts Club Band*; their version of "Come Together" nonetheless hit #23. The band undertook another two-year tour, recording dates for the *Live! Bootleg* album, released in 1978. That hit #13 just before Christmas.

The endless togetherness and the grind of the road took its toll on the band. Tyler and Perry's propensity to party earned them the nickname the Toxic Twins. Heroin, cocaine, alcohol, and whatever else might be circulating backstage also circulated through their bloodstream. "I was a garbage head," Tyler once commented.

Joe Perry left the band to form his Joe Perry Project shortly after *Night in the Ruts* was released. The album did relatively poorly, though it went gold and hit #14. Columbia, sensing that this might mark the end of the

Aerosmith era, released a greatest hits record. This impression was further exacerbated when Brad Whitford left the band to record with Ted Nugent guitarist Derek St. Holmes. Then, Tyler had to take a year off to recover from a motorcycle accident.

Aerosmith's next album, *Rock in a Hard Place*, with replacement guitarists Rick Dufay and Jimmy Crespo, faired poorly on the charts, topping out at #32. Joe Perry's two follow-up records and the Whitford/St. Holmes record also turned out to be commercial failures. On Valentine's Day 1984, Aerosmith reunited backstage at a gig in Boston. Within two months, they signed with newly formed Geffen Records and hit the road. In the interim, however, their substance-abuse problems only got worse. At one show in Springfield, Tyler passed out and fell off the stage about 30 minutes into the set. Their Geffen debut, *Done with Mirrors*, continued their losing streak, topping out at #36. Pop music seemed to have left them behind.

But it wouldn't be long before Aerosmith was back with a vengeance. After the tour, the entire band went into rehab. As they collectively kicked their abuse problems, a remarkable thing happened. One of the new sounds of pop, rap music, which had used hard-rock riffs since its beginning, would now fuel a full- fledged Aersosmith comeback. One of the most successful rap groups, Run-DMC, asked Perry and Tyler to record a rap version of "Walk This Way" with them. The single burned up the charts, going gold and rising to #4. Capitalizing on this success, Aerosmith put out *Permanent Vacation*, which went triple-platinum and topped out at #11, spawning three hit singles: "Rag Doll," which rose to #17; "Dude Looks Like a Lady," which won two MTV Music Awards and charted to #14; and the #3 single "Angel." Aerosmith was back with a vengeance.

Their next album was even more successful. *Pump* rose to #5 and eventually sold seven million copies with the hits "Love in an Elevator" (#5), "Janie's Got a Gun" (#4, a Grammy and two MTV Awards), "The Other Side" (#22 and an MTV Award), and "What It Takes" (#9).

Get a Grip solidified their standing. The album topped the charts and produced the singles "Livin' on the Edge" (#18, an MTV Award and a Grammy for Best Performance by a Duo or Group), "Cryin'" (#12, voted the all-time favorite video on MTV, and the following year's Grammy winner for Best Performance by a Duo or Group), "Amazing" (#24), and "Crazy" (#17).

In the meantime, their old label, Columbia, actively pursued the group and signed them to a massive contract. They immediately released a three-record, best-of compilation called *Pandora's Box*, and packaged all 12 of the group's releases for Columbia as *Box of Fire*. Their first new album for Columbia, *Nine Lives*, entered the charts at #1, and won the 1998 Grammy for Best Rock Album. Trying to cash-in on the band's resurgence, Geffen put out *A Little South of Sanity*, a two-disc live retrospective of the band's years of resurrection on that label.

Taking advantage of Aerosmith's popularity, the makers of the film *Armageddon* (which starred Tyler's daughter, Liv) got them off the road just long enough to record the Dianne Warren–penned lead track for the film, "I Don't Want to Miss a Thing." The song topped the charts, as did the soundtrack album, which featured three other Aerosmith tunes. Once again they hit the road, taking time off to return a favor by recording a tune for Run-DMC's comeback album.

DISC.: AEROSMITH: *Aerosmith* (1973); *Get Your Wings* (1974); *Toys in the Attic* (1975); *Rocks* (1976); *Draw the Line* (1977); *Live Bootleg* (1978); *Night in the Ruts* (1979); *Greatest Hits* (1980); *Rock in a Hard Place* (1982); *Done with Mirrors* (1985); *Classics Live* (1986); *Permanent Vacation* (1987); *Classics Live 2* (1988); *Gems* (1988); *Pump* (1989); *Pandora's Box* (1991); *Get a Grip* (1993); *Big Ones* (1994); *Nine Lives* (1997); *A Little South of Sanity* (1998). **JOE PERRY PROJECT:** *Let the Music Do the Talking* (1980); *I've Got the Rock 'n' Rolls Again* (1981); *Once a Rocker, Always a Rocker* (1984). **WHITFORD/ST. HOLMES:** *Whitford/St. Holmes* (1981).

WRITINGS: *Walk This Way: The Autobiography of Aerosmith* (1997).

BIBL.: M. Putterford, *Aerosmith: The Fall and Rise of Aerosmith* (1991); *The Complete Guide to the Music of Aerosmith* (1997); M. Dome, *Aerosmith: Life in the Fast Lane*; D. Bowler and B. Dray, *Aerosmith: What It Takes*.—HB

Afanasiev, Nikolai (Yakovlevich), Russian composer; b. Tobolsk, Jan. 12, 1821; d. St. Petersburg, June 3, 1898. He studied violin with his father. In 1836 he made his debut as a violinist in Moscow, where he was concertmaster of the orch. at the Bolshoi Theater from 1838 to 1841. In the latter year he became conductor of a landowner's serf orch. outside St. Petersburg. After touring as a violinist from 1846 to 1851, he settled in St. Petersburg, where he was concertmaster and sometimes conductor at the Italian Opera. He then became a piano teacher at the Smolny Inst. in 1853. He composed 9 operas, among them *Taras Bulba, Vakula-kuznets* (Vakula the Smith), *Ammalet-bek* (St. Petersburg, Nov. 23, 1870), and *Stenka Razin*. His other works include 6 syms., 9 violin concertos, a Cello Concerto, and chamber works.—NS/LK/DM

Affré, Agustarello, French tenor; b. St. Chinian, Oct. 23, 1858; d. Cagnes-sur-Mer, Dec. 27, 1931. He studied at the Toulouse Cons. and with Duvernoy at the Paris Cons. In 1890 he made his operatic debut as Edgardo at the Paris Opéra, singing there until 1911. On May 18, 1909, he made his first appearance at London's Covent Garden as Samson. He later sang in San Francisco (1911) and New Orleans (1912). He was esteemed for his lyric-heroic roles, being equally successful in operas by his countrymen, as well as those by Mozart and Wagner.—NS/LK/DM

Afranio de Pavia (family name, **Albonese**), Italian theologian, reputed inventor of the bassoon; b. Pavia, c. 1465; d. Ferrara, c. 1540, as canon of Ferrara. His claim to the invention of the bassoon is based on the attribution to him of the instrument Phagotus, in the book by his nephew *Teseo Albonese Introductio in chaldaicam linguam* (Pavia, 1539).—NS/LK/DM

Agazzari, Agostino, Italian organist, music theorist, and composer; b. Siena, Dec. 2, 1578; d. there, April 10(?), 1640. He went to Rome, where he was maestro di cappella at the Collegio Germanico (1602–03) and the Seminario Romano (1606–07). About 1606 he was made a member of the Accademia degli Intronati in Siena, where he was given the name Armonico Intronato. He then returned to Siena, where he was organist at the Cathedral and later may have served as its maestro di cappella. Agazzari was the author of the influential treatise *Del sonare sopra 'l basso con tutti li stromenti e dell'uso loro nel conserto* (Siena, 1607), one of the earliest works on thoroughbass. He also publ. *La musica ecclesiastica dove si contiene la vera diffinitione della musica come scienza, non piu veduta, e sua nobiltà* (Siena, 1638), an endeavor to bring the practice of church music into accord with the Resolution of the Council of Trent. He composed a dramma pastorale, *Eumelio* (Rome, 1606). He also publ. 17 vols. of sacred vocal works (1602–40), including masses, Psalms, litanies, and motets, which are notable for their continuo accompaniment, and 5 vols. of madrigals (1596–1607).

BIBL.: C. Reardon, *A. A. and Music at Siena Cathedral, 1597–1641* (Oxford, 1994).—NS/LK/DM

Agghazy, Karoly, Hungarian pianist, teacher, and composer; b. Pest, Oct. 30, 1855; d. Budapest, Oct. 8, 1918. He studied at the Pest Cons. (1867–70), the Vienna Cons. (1870–73), with Liszt (piano), and at the Budapest Academy of Music with Volkmann (composition, 1875–78). After touring with Hubay (1878–81), he was a prof. of piano at the Budapest Cons. (1881–83; from 1889). He also taught at the Stern and Kullak conservatories in Berlin (1883–89). He wrote 2 operas, many piano pieces, choral works, and songs.—NS/LK/DM

Agnelli, Salvatore, Italian composer; b. Palermo, 1817; d. Marseilles, 1874. He was a student of Furno, Zingarelli, and Donizetti at the Palermo Cons. After composing 10 comic operas for Naples and Palermo (1837–42), he settled in Marseilles and brought out serious operas, ballets, and sacred works.—NS/LK/DM

Agnesi, Luigi (real name, **Louis Ferdinand Léopold Agniez**), Belgian bass; b. Erpent, Namur, July 17, 1833; d. London, Feb. 2, 1875. He studied at the Brussels Cons. and with Duprez in Paris. After touring Germany and the Netherlands with Eugenio Merelli's opera company, he sang at the Théâtre-Italien in Paris (1864) and at Her Majesty's Theatre in London (1865). He later appeared in concerts in England (1871–74). He was admired for his portrayals of roles in Rossini's operas.—NS/LK/DM

Agnesi-Pinottini, Maria Teresa, Italian harpsichordist, singer, and composer; b. Milan, Oct. 17, 1720; d. there, Jan. 19, 1795. She won success as a composer with her first theater piece, the cantata pastorale *Il ristoro d'Arcadia*, which was given at the Regio Ducal Teatro in Milan in 1747. She wrote her own libretto for the opera *Ciro in Armenia*, which was premiered at the same theater on Dec. 26, 1753. Among her other stage works were *Il rè pastore* (c. 1756), *Sofonisba* (Naples, 1765), and *Nitrocri* (Venice, 1771). She also wrote some instrumental music.—NS/LK/DM

Agnew, Roy (Ewing), Australian pianist, teacher, and composer; b. Sydney, Aug. 23, 1893; d. there, Nov. 12, 1944. He studied with Gerrard Williams in London (1923–28). He was director of the Australian Radio (1938–43), and also taught at the New South Wales State Conservatorium of Music in Sydney. Among his works were orch. pieces, chamber music, many piano pieces, including sonatas, and songs. —NS/LK/DM

Agosti, Guido, Italian pianist, pedagogue, and composer; b. Forlì, Aug. 11, 1901; d. Milan, June 2, 1989. He began his training at an early age and made his first public appearance when he was only 8. He then studied piano with Mugellini, Ivaldi, and Busoni at the Bologna Cons., where he was awarded his diploma at age 13. He also obtained a degree in literature at the Univ. of Bologna and received training in composition from Benvenuti. From 1921 he toured as a soloist with orchs., as a recitalist, and as a chamber music player. He taught at the Venice Cons. (1934–40), the Rome Cons. (1941–45), the Accademia Musicale Chigiana in Siena (1947–63), the Franz Liszt Hochschule für Musik in Weimar (1963–69), and at the Sibelius Academy in Helsinki (1972). Agosti publ. *Osservazioni intorno alla tecnica pianistica* (Siena, 1943) and composed mainly solo piano pieces.—NS/LK/DM

Agostini, Lodovico, Italian singer and composer; b. Ferrara, 1534; d. there, Sept. 20, 1590. He centered his activities on Ferrara. After early training in music, he entered the priesthood. From 1572 he was at the cappella at Ferrara Cathedral. In 1578 he became maestro di cappella to Duke Alfonso II of Este, a post he held until his death. A number of his sacred and secular vocal works were publ. in Milan, Ferrara, and Venice (1567–86).—NS/LK/DM

Agostini, Mezio, Italian composer, pianist, conductor, and pedagogue; b. Fano, Aug. 12, 1875; d. there, April 22, 1944. He studied with Carlo Pedrotti at the Liceo Rossini in Pesaro (1885–92), where he subsequently was a prof. of harmony (1900–09); was then director of the Liceo Benedetto Marcello in Venice (1909–40). He was active as an opera conductor in Venice and other Italian cities, and gave chamber music concerts as a pianist. His *Trio* won 1st prize at the international competition in Paris in 1904. He wrote the operas *Iovo e Maria* (1896), *Il Cavaliere del Sogno* (Fano, Feb. 24, 1897), *La penna d'Airone* (1896), *Alcibiade* (1902), *America* (also entitled *Hail Columbia*, 1904), *L'ombra* (1907), *L'agnello del sogno* (1928), and *La Figlio del navarca* (Fano, Sept. 3, 1938). Other works include a Sym., 4 orch. suites, a Piano Concerto, 2 string quartets, 2 piano trios, a Cello Sonata, a Violin Sonata, the cantata *A Rossini*, numerous piano pieces, and songs.—NS/LK/DM

Agostini, Paolo, Italian organist and composer; b. Vallerano, 1583; d. Rome, Oct. 3, 1629. He was a member of the choir school of S. Luigi dei Francesi in Rome, where he studied with G. B. Nanino. After serving as organist and maestro di cappella at S. Maria del Rus-

cello in Vallerano, he returned to Rome as organist at S. Maria in Trastevere; later was vice-maestro di cappella there and concurrently maestro di cappella at Ss. Trinita dei Pellegrini. He was also vice-maestro at S. Lorenzo in Damaso (1619–26) and maestro di cappella at the Cappella Giulia at St. Peter's (from 1626). His music displays great ingenuity of contrapuntal structure; some of his choral works are written for 48 independent parts.

WORKS (all publ. in Rome): *Salmi della madonna, Magnificat, Ave maris stella, antifone, motetti, lib. 1* for 1 to 3 Voices and Basso Continuo (1619); *Liber secundus missarum* for 4 Voices (1626); *Spartitura delle messe del primo libro* for 4 to 5 Voices (1627); *Spartitura del secondo libro delle messe e motetti* for 4 Voices (1627); *Partitura del terzo libro della messa sine nomine, con 2 Resurrexit* for 4 Voices (1627); *Libro quarto delle messe in spartitura* (1627); *Spartitura della messa et motetto Benedicam Dominum ad canones* for 4 Voices (1627); *Partitura delle messe et motetti con 40 esempi di contrapunti* for 4 to 5 Voices (1627); *Missarum liber posthumus* (1630).—NS/LK/DM

Agostini, Pietro Simone, Italian composer; b. Forlì, c. 1635; d. (murdered) Parma, Oct. 1, 1680. He led an adventurous life. After being expelled from Forlì due to his complicity in a murder, he studied music with Mazzaferrata in Ferrara. He saw military service in Crete and was made a Knight of the Golden Spur. In 1658 he commenced his career as a composer in Venice. In 1664 he went to Genoa and composed for the theater until his intimate association with a nun led to his banishment. He then went to Rome, where he became director of music at S. Agnese. Although Agostini excelled as a composer of secular cantatas, his opera *Gl'inganni innocenti, ovvero L'Adalina* was a notable success at its premiere in Ariccia, near Rome, in 1673. In 1679 he was called to the ducal court in Parma as maestro di cappella, but was murdered the next year. —NS/LK/DM

Agrell, Johan Joachim, Swedish violinist, harpsichordist, and composer; b. Löth, Feb. 1, 1701; d. Nuremberg, Jan. 19, 1765. After studies at the Univ. of Uppsala, he was a violinist in Kassel (1723–46) and Kapellmeister in Nuremberg (from 1746). He wrote syms., cantatas, 5 harpsichord concertos, 2 sonatas for Violin and Harpsichord, 6 sonatas for Solo Harpsichord, and solo harpsichord pieces.—NS/LK/DM

Agricola, Alexander, Franco-Netherlands composer; b. Flanders, c. 1446; d. Valladolid, late Aug. 1506. He entered the service of the Duke of Milan in 1471. In 1474 he went to Cambrai, where he is mentioned as petit vicaire at the Cathedral in 1476. After serving the French royal chapel, he was a singer at the Florence Cathedral in 1491–92 before serving again at the French royal chapel in 1492–93. In 1500 he entered the service of Philip I the Handsome in Burgundy, and followed his patron to Spain in 1501, where he remained until 1503. In 1506 he returned to Spain. His extensive output includes masses and mass movements, hymns, Lamentations, Magnificat settings, motets, and many secular vocal works. See E. Lerner, ed., *A. A.: Opera omnia,* Corpus Mensurabilis Musicae, XXII/1–5 (1961–70).

BIBL.: E. Lerner, *The Sacred Music of A. A.* (diss., Yale Univ., 1958).—NS/LK/DM

Agricola, Benedetta Emilia (née Molteni), Italian soprano; b. Modena, 1722; d. Berlin, 1780. She was a student of Porpora, Hasse, and Salimbeni. In 1743 she made her debut in Berlin in C.H. Graun's *Cesare e Cleopatra*, and was the principal soprano at the court until Giovanna Astrua's arrival in 1748. In 1751 she married **Johann Friedrich Agricola**, and continued in the service of the court until his death in 1774, upon which she was dismissed.—NS/LK/DM

Agricola, Johann Friedrich, German organist, teacher, and composer; b. Dobitschen, Jan. 4, 1720; d. Berlin, Dec. 2, 1774. He went to Leipzig, where he studied law at the Univ. (1738–41), and was a student of Bach. In 1741 he settled in Berlin and completed his training with Quantz. He was made a court composer in 1751, the same year that he married **Benedetta Emilia Agricola** (née **Molteni**). In 1759 he became music director of the Opera. He was a proponent of Italian musical taste and publ. pseudonymous pamphlets of a polemical nature (1749). He also translated and edited Tosi's singing treatise of 1723 as *Anleitung zur Singkunst* (Berlin, 1757; Eng. tr. and commentary, 1995, by J. Baird).

WORKS: DRAMATIC: O p e r a : *Il filosofo convinto in amore* (Potsdam, 1750); *La ricamatrice divenuta dama* (Berlin, Nov. 1, 1751); *Cleofide* (Berlin, Carnival 1754); *La nobiltà delusa* (1754); *Achille in Sciro* (Sept. 16, 1765); *Amor e Psiche* (Oct. 1767); *Il re pastore* (1770); *Oreste e Pilade* (1772; rev. as *I greci in Tauride*, Potsdam, March 1772). OTHER: Oratorios, sacred cantatas, songs, odes, and keyboard music.

BIBL.: H. Wucherpfennig, *J. F. A.* (diss., Univ. of Berlin, 1922).—NS/LK/DM

Agricola (real name, Sore), Martin, German music theorist, teacher, and composer; b. Schwiebus, Jan. 6, 1486; d. Magdeburg, June 10, 1556. He settled in Magdeburg in 1519–20, where he taught music privately and at a parish school. About 1525 he became choirmaster at the Protestant Latinschule. He embraced the Lutheran faith and became one of the earliest Protestant school musicians in his homeland. His *Ein Sangbüchlein aller Sontags Evangelien* (Wittenberg, 1541), a fine setting of German Protestant songs for 2 and 3 Voices arranged in accordance with the church calendar, is the earliest such collection of its kind. His posthumous collection of 54 3- and 4-part instrumental works publ. as the *Instrumentisch Gesenge* (Wittenberg, 1561) is a valuable source on early German instrumentalists. Among his other works were a Magnificat tertii toni, motets, hymns, and sacred songs. His theoretical writings include *Ein kurtz deudsche Musica* (Wittenberg, 1528; 3rd ed., 1533, as *Musica choralis deudsch*; abr. Latin version, 1539, as *Rudimenta musices*), *Musica instrumentalis deudsch* (Wittenberg, 1529; 5th ed., enl., 1545; Eng. tr., 1994), *Musica figuralis deudsch* (Wittenberg, 1532; includes the suppl. *Büchlein von den Proportionibus*), *Scholia in musicam planam Venceslai Philomatic* (n.p., 1538; includes the suppl. *Libellus do octo tonorum regularium compositione*), *Quaestiones vulgatiores in musicum* (Magdeburg, 1543),

and *Musicae ex prioribus editis musicis excerpta* (Magdeburg, 1547).

BIBL.: H. Funck, *M. A.: Ein frühprotestantischer Schulmusiker* (Wolfenbüttel, 1933).—NS/LK/DM

Aguado (y García), Dioniso, Spanish guitarist, teacher, and composer; b. Madrid, April 8, 1784; d. there, Dec. 29, 1849. He received training in Madrid. In 1825 he went to Paris, where he was active as a performer, often in concerts with Sor, and as a teacher. In 1838 he returned to Madrid. He publ. *Estudio para la guitarra* (Madrid, 1820) and *Escuela o método de guitarra* (Madrid, 1825). He wrote many guitar pieces.—NS/LK/DM

Aguiari or **Agujari, Lucrezia,** brilliant Italian soprano, known as La Bastardina and La Bastardella on account of her being the illegitimate daughter of a nobleman; b. Ferrara, 1743; d. Parma, May 18, 1783. She received vocal training from the Abbot Lambertini. In 1764 she made her debut with notable success in Florence. In 1768 she was made a court singer in Parma, where Mozart heard her in 1770 and was greatly impressed by the beauty of her voice and its phenomenal compass, which embraced 3 octaves (C^1- C^4). In 1775–76 she sang at the Pantheon in London. She created leading roles in several operas by the Italian composer **Giuseppe Colla**, whom she married in 1780.

BIBL.: G. Vetro, *L. A., la "Bastardella"* (Parma, 1993). —NS/LK/DM

Aguilera de Heredia, Sebastián, Spanish organist and composer; b. Saragossa (baptized), Aug. 15, 1561; d. there, Dec. 16, 1627. He was organist of Huesca Cathedral (1585–1603), and then at the cathedral of La Seo in Saragossa. Among his extant works are 23 organ pieces, which are particularly notable for their use of medio registro in which each half of the keyboard allows for independent registration. He also publ. the vol. *Canticum Beatissimae Virginia deiparae Mariae octo modis seu tonis compositum, quaternisque vocibus, quinis, senis et octonis concionandum* (Saragossa, 1618), which contains 36 settings of the Magnificat.—NS/LK/DM

Aguirre, Julían, Argentine composer; b. Buenos Aires, Jan. 28, 1868; d. there, Aug. 13, 1924. He was taken to Spain as a child, and studied at the Madrid Cons. In 1887 he returned to Buenos Aires. His best known works are piano miniatures in the form of stylized Argentine dances and songs. His *Huella, Canción argentiana* (1917) and *Gato* (1918) were orchestrated by Ansermet, who conducted them in Buenos Aires (April 6, 1930). The *Huella* was also arranged for violin and piano by Jascha Heifetz. Other compositions include *Atahualpa*, incidental music (Buenos Aires, Nov. 5, 1897); *Preambulo, Triste y Gato* for Orch. (Buenos Aires, Nov. 5, 1910); *Belkiss*, orch. suite (1910); *De mi pais*, orch. suite (Buenos Airea, Oct. 27, 1916); chamber music; numerous piano pieces; choral works; songs.

BIBL.: J. Giacobbe, *J. A.* (Buenos Aires, 1945); C. García Muñoz, *J. A.* (Buenos Aires, 1970).—NS/LK/DM

AGUS

Agus, Giuseppe, Italian composer; b. c. 1725; d. c. 1800. He went to England about 1750 and was active as a ballet composer at the Italian Opera in London. He also wrote dances, trios, sonatas, and vocal pieces. **Joseph Agus** may have been his son.—**LK/DM**

Agus, Joseph, Italian violinist and composer; b. 1749; d. Paris, 1798. He may have been the son of **Giuseppe Agus.** He studied violin with Nardini in Italy. In 1773 he made his debut in London. After being convicted of attempted rape of his godchild **Elisabeth (Weichsel) Billington** in 1778, he went to France. From 1795 he was maître de solfège at the Paris Cons. Among his works were trios, violin duets, catches, and glees. —**LK/DM**

Ahern, David (Anthony), Australian composer; b. Sydney, Nov. 2, 1947; d. there, Jan. 30, 1988. After training with Butterley and Meale, he took courses with Stockhausen in Cologne and with Cardew in London, exploring the outer regions of the art of hypermusical speculations. Returning to Sydney, he became active in avant-garde circles; introduced scores by contemporary Australian, American, and other composers with his own ensemble AZ Music during the 1960s and 1970s. Thereafter, he was estranged from the Australian music scene. His early works are rigidly serial, but after 1965 he began employing random theatrical effects. Among his compositions were orch. pieces, chamber music, and electronic scores.—**NS/LK/DM**

Ahle, Johann Georg, German organist, writer on music, and composer, son of **Johann Rudolf Ahle;** b. Mühlhausen (baptized), June 12, 1651; d. there, Dec. 2, 1706. He succeeded his father as organist in Mühlhausen in 1673, and was made poet laureate by Emperor Leopold I in 1680. He composed sacred and secular music.

WRITINGS (all publ. in Mühlhausen): *Johan Georg Ahlens musikalisches Frühlings-Gespräche, darinnen fürnehmlich vom grund-und kunstmässigen Komponiren gehandelt wird* (1695); *Johan Georg Ahlens musikalisches Sommer-Gespräche* (1697); *Johan Georg Ahlens musikalisches Herbst-Gespräche* (1699); *Johan Georg Ahlens musikalisches Winter-Gespräche* (1701).

BIBL.: Z. Sevier, *The Theoretical Works and Music of J.G. A.* (diss., Univ. of N.C., 1974).—**NS/LK/DM**

Ahle, Johann Rudolf, German organist, writer on music, and composer, father of **Johann Georg Ahle;** b. Mühlhausen, Dec. 24, 1625; d. there, July 9, 1673. He studied theology at the Univ. of Erfurt, where he also served as a cantor and organist. From 1654 to 1673 he was organist at St. Blasius in Mühlhausen, and then was elected burgomaster shortly before his death. He publ. the theoretical vol. *Compendium musices pro tenellis* (Mühlhausen, 1648; later eds. by his son). Ahle was best known as a composer of sacred vocal music. Some of his songs were sung in Protestant churches in Germany for several centuries. J. Wolf ed. a selection of his works in the Denkmäler Deutscher Tonkunst, V (1901).

BIBL.: J. Johnson, *An Analysis and Edition of Selected Sacred Choral Works of J.R. A.* (diss., Southern Baptist Theological Seminary, 1969).—**NS/LK/DM**

Ahlersmeyer, Mathieu, German baritone; b. Cologne, June 29, 1896; d. Garmisch-Partenkirchen, July 23, 1979. He studied in Cologne. In 1929 he made his operatic debut as Wolfram in Mönchengladbach, and then sang at the Berlin Kroll Opera (1930–31) and the Hamburg Opera (1931–33). From 1934 to 1945 he was a member of the Dresden State Opera, where he created the Barber in Strauss's *Die schweigsame Frau* (June 14, 1935). In 1938 he created the role of Egk's Peer Gynt at the Berlin State Opera. From 1946 to 1961 he sang at the Hamburg State Opera, and again from 1962 to 1973. His prominent roles included Don Giovanni, Hans Sachs, Rigoletto, Scarpia, and Hindemith's Matthias Grünewald.—**NS/LK/DM**

Ahlgrimm, Isolde, eminent Austrian fortepianist, harpsichordist, and pedagogue; b. Vienna, July 31, 1914. In 1921 she entered the Vienna Academy of Music, graduating in 1932 in the piano class of Viktor Ebenstein; completed her studies in the master classes there of Emil von Sauer and Franz Schmidt (1932–34). In 1935 she attracted notice at the Hamburg International Music Festival. After making her recital debut as a fortepianist in 1937, she taught herself to play the harpsichord and subsequently concentrated on both instruments. From 1937 to 1956 she was active with the Concerte für Kenner und Liebhaber in Vienna; was also first prof. of harpsichord at the Vienna Academy of Music (1945–49). After teaching at the Salzburg Mozarteum (1958–62), she made her first visit to the U.S. in 1962 at the Oberlin (Ohio) Coll. Cons. of Music; then was a prof. at the Vienna Hochschule für Musik (1964–84). Ahlgrimm did much to further the cause of period instrument performances of music from the Baroque and Classical eras. —**NS/LK/DM**

Ahlin, Cvetka, Yugoslav mezzo-soprano; b. Ljubljana, Sept. 28, 1928; d. Hamburg, June 30, 1985. She studied at the Ljubljana Academy of Music. In 1952 she made her operatic debut at the Ljubljana Opera; after winning 1st prize at the Munich Competition (1954), she was a member of the Hamburg State Opera (1955–74); also was a guest artist in various European opera centers. From 1974 she taught at the Lübeck Hochschule für Musik. Among her best roles were Orpheus, Amneris, Azucena, and Marina.—**NS/LK/DM**

Ahlstrom, David, American composer; b. Lancaster, N.Y., Feb. 22, 1927; d. San Francisco, Aug. 23, 1992. He studied with Cowell, Bernard Rogers, and Haridas Chaudhuri, and at the Eastman School of Music in Rochester, N.Y. (Ph.D. in composition, 1961). After teaching at Northwestern Univ. (1961–62), Southern Methodist Univ. (1962–67), and Eastern Ill. Univ. (1967–76), he settled in San Francisco. He wrote the operas *3 Sisters Who Are Not Sisters,* after Gertrude Stein (San Francisco, Sept. 17, 1982), *Doctor Faustus Lights the Lights,* after Stein (San Francisco, Oct. 29, 1982), and *America, I Love You,* after e.e. cummings (San Francisco, June 25, 1983, composer conducting), a number of theater pieces employing dance and electronics, syms., and chamber music.—**NS/LK/DM**

Åhlström, Olof, Swedish organist, music publisher, and composer; b. Åletorp, Aug. 14, 1756; d. Stockholm, Aug. 11, 1835. He studied organ in Åletorp and was a pupil of Zellbell at the Stockholm Academy of Music. He served as organist at Stockholm's Marian church (1777–86) and Jacobskyrka (from 1786), and also held a royal privilege as a music publisher (1780–1824). Åhlström wrote an opera, *Frigga* (Stockholm, May 31, 1787), incidental music, chamber works, and 2 cantatas, but is best known for his more than 200 songs.

BIBL.: A. Afzelius, *Tonsiaren O. Å.s minne* (Stockholm, 1867).—NS/LK/DM

Ahna, Heinrich Karl Herman de
See **De Ahna, Heinrich Karl Herman**

Ahna, Pauline de, German soprano; b. Ingolstadt, Feb. 4, 1863; d. Garmisch-Partenkirchen, May 13, 1950. She received her musical training in Munich. In 1890 she made her operatic debut as Pamina in Weimar, where she subsequently appeared as Eva, Elsa, and Donna Elvira, and also created the role of Freihild in Strauss's *Guntram* (May 10, 1894). She likewise sang Agathe, Leonore, and Donna Anna in Karlsruhe (1890–91) and Elisabeth at the Bayreuth Festival (1891). On Sept. 10, 1894, she married Strauss, who dedicated several sets of lieder to her. He also depicted her in his *Ein Heldenleben, Symphonia domestica,* and *Intermezzo.*—NS/LK/DM

Ahnsjö, Claes-H(åkan), Swedish tenor and opera administrator; b. Stockholm Aug. 1, 1942. He studied with Erik Saeden, Askel Schiøtz, and Max Lorenz in Stockholm. In 1969 he made his operatic debut as Tamino at the Royal Theater in Stockholm. From 1969 he also sang at the Drottningholm Court Theater. In 1973 he became a member of the Bavarian State Opera in Munich, where he was made a Kammersänger in 1977. His guest engagements took him to the major operatic and concert centers of Europe, the U.S., and Japan. His operatic repertoire included roles by Haydn, Mozart, Rossini, Verdi, and Wagner. He also appeared as a soloist with orchs. and as a recitalist. In 2000 he became artistic director of the Royal Theater in Stockholm. —NS/LK/DM

Aho, Kalevi, prominent Finnish composer, pedagogue, and writer on music; b. Forssa, March 9, 1949. He was a student of Rautavaara at the Sibelius Academy in Helsinki (composition diploma, 1971) and of Blacher at the Staatliche Hochschule für Musik und Darstellende Kunst in Berlin (1971–72). From 1974 to 1988 he lectured on musicology at the Univ. of Helsinki, and then was acting prof. of composition at the Sibelius Academy (1988–93). He has written numerous articles on music for various publications, as well as the vol. *Suomen musiikki* (Helsingissä, 1995). Among his honors are the Leonie Sonning Prize of Denmark (1974) and the Henrik Steffens Prize of Germany (1990). After composing in a neo-Classical vein, he embraced a more modern idiom. In his later works, his style became refreshingly varied, ranging from the traditional to the postmodern.

WORKS: DRAMATIC: *Avain* (The Key), dramatic monologue for Singer and Chamber Orch. (1978–79; Helsinki, Sept. 4, 1979); *Hyönteiselämää* (Insect Life), opera (1985–87; Helsinki, Sept. 27, 1996). **ORCH.:** 10 syms.: No. 1 (1969; Helsinki, Feb. 18, 1971), No. 2 (1970; Helsinki, April 17, 1973), No. 3, *Sinfonia concertante No. 1,* for Violin and Orch. (1971–73; Helsinki, Feb. 20, 1975), No. 4 (1972–73; Helsinki, March 12, 1974), No. 5 (1975–76; Helsinki, April 19, 1977), No. 6 (1979–80; Helsinki, Feb. 13, 1980), No. 7, *Hyönteissinfonia* (Insect Symphony; Helsinki, Oct. 26, 1988), No. 8 for Organ and Orch. (1993; Lahti, Aug. 4, 1994), No. 9, *Sinfonia concertante No. 2,* for Trombone and Orch. (1993–94; Helsinki, Sept. 2, 1994), and No. 10 (1996; Lahti, Feb. 6, 1997); 2 chamber syms. for Strings: No. 1 (Helsinki, Aug. 22, 1976) and No. 2 (1991–92; Kokkola, Feb. 9, 1992); Violin Concerto (1981; Helsinki, Sept. 29, 1982); *Hiljaisuus* (Silence; Finnish Radio, Dec. 23, 1982; first public perf., Helsinki, Oct. 9, 1985); Cello Concerto (1983–84; Helsinki, Sept. 1, 1984); *Fanfare for YS* for Brass Ensemble (Helsinki, April 18, 1986); Piano Concerto (1988–89; Helsinki, Aug. 29, 1990); *Paloheimo Fanfare* (Lahti, Aug. 31, 1989); *Pergamon* for 4 Instrumental Groups, 4 Reciters, and Electric Organ for the 350th anniversary of the Univ. of Helsinki (Helsinki, Sept. 9, 1990). **CHAMBER:** 3 string quartets: No. 1 (suppressed), No. 2 (Helsinki, Nov. 18, 1970), and No. 3 (Helsinki, Oct. 6, 1971); Quintet for Oboe and String Quartet (1973; Jyväskylä, July 2, 1974); Sonata for Solo Violin (1973; Helsinki, April 17, 1978); *Prelude, Toccata, and Postlude* for Cello and Piano (1974; Helsinki, Feb. 14, 1977); *Solo I* for Violin (1975; Kaustinen, Jan. 26, 1986) and *III* for Flute (1990–91; Helsinki, April 14, 1991); Quintet for Flute, Oboe, Violin, Viola, and Cello (1977; Helinki, March 24, 1983); Quintet Bassoon and String Quartet (1977; Helsinki, Jan. 16, 1978); Quartet for Flute, Alto Saxophone, Guitar, and Percussion (Amsterdam, Oct. 1, 1982); Oboe Sonata (1984–85; Helsinki, March 26, 1985); 2 sonatas for Solo Accordion: No. 1 (1984; Kuhmo, July 29, 1989) and No. 2 (1990; Ikaalinen, June 8, 1991); *3 Melodies* for 1 to 4 Kanteles (1984; Kaustinen, June 1985); *Inventions* for Oboe and Cello (1986); *Quartetto piccolo* for 3 Violins and Cello or String Quartet (1989); *Nuppu* for Flute and Piano (Helsinki, Dec. 8, 1991); *Halla* for Violin and Piano (1992; Kuhmo, July 27, 1994); *Epilogue* for Trombone and Organ (1994); Quintet for Alto Saxophone, Bassoon, Viola, Cello, and Double Bass (Lahti, Dec. 7, 1994). **KEYBOARD: Piano:** Sonata (Helsinki, Sept. 6, 1980); *2 Easy Pieces for Children* (1983); *Solo II* (1985; Helsinki, Feb. 27, 1986); Sonatine (1993). **Organ:** *Ludus Solemnis* (1978); *In memoriam* (1980); *3 Interludes* (1993; arr. from the Sym. No. 8; Copenhagen, March 1994). **VOCAL:** *Jäähyväiset Arkadialle* for Voice and Piano (1971); *Lasimaalaus* (Stained Glass) for Women's Chorus (Forssa, May 16, 1975); *Kolme laulua elämästä* (3 Songs about Life) for Tenor and Piano (1977); *Hiljaisuus* (Silence) for Chorus (1978; Helsinki, April 23, 1986); *Sheherazade* for Chorus (1978; Tampere, June 2, 1979); *Kyynikon paratiisi* (A Cynic's Paradise) for Tenor and Chamber Ensemble (Tampere, April 30, 1991; also for Tenor and Piano); *Hyvät ystävät* (Dear Friends) for Baritone and Orch. (Helsinki, Oct. 17, 1992); *Veet välkkyy taas* (The Waters Shimmer Once More) for Men's Chorus (Espoo, May 17, 1992); *Mysteerio* for Women's Chorus (Forssa, Nov. 20, 1994). **OTHER:** Various orchestrations and arrangements.—NS/LK/DM

Ahrens, Joseph (Johannes Clemens), German organist, pedagogue, and composer; b. Sommersell, April 17, 1904; d. Berlin, Dec. 21, 1997. He was a student of Volbach in Münster and of Sittard and Seiffert in Berlin, where he then pursued his career. In

1928 he became a teacher and in 1936 a prof. at the Akademie für Kirchen-und Schulmusik, and also a teacher of church music at the Hochschule für Musik in 1945. In 1934 he became organist at St. Hedwig Cathedral, and in 1945 organist and choirmaster at the Salvatorkirche. He retired from his various positions in 1972. He publ. the vol. *Die Formprinzipien des Gregorianischen Chorals und mein Orgelstil* (Heidelberg, 1978). In 1955 he won the Arts Prize of Berlin, in 1963 he became a member of the Akademie der Künste in Berlin, in 1965 he was made a Knight of the Gregorian Order of Rome, and in 1968 he received the Pontifical Medal of Rome. Ahrens was a notable composer of organ and choral music, his output demonstrating an imaginative handling of traditional forms with contemporary usages, including dodecaphony. He composed a Concerto for Organ, 2 Horns, 2 Trumpets, and 4 Percussion (1958), as well as numerous solo organ works, including *Verwandlungen I-III* (1958–62), *Trilogia contrapunctica* (1972–76), *Trilogia dodekaphonica* (1978), *Passacaglia dodekaphonica* (1980), and several organ masses. Among his choral works were a *St. Matthew Passion* (1955), a *St. John Passion* (1963), and many masses, including the *Missa dodekaphonica* for Chorus and 8 Instruments (1966). —NS/LK/DM

Ahronovich, Yuri (Mikhailovich), Russian-born Israeli conductor; b. Leningrad, May 13, 1932. He studied with Sanderling and Rachlin at the Leningrad Cons. (graduated, 1954). After serving as music director of the Saratov Phil. (1956–57) and the Yaroslavl Sym. Orch. (1957–64), he was chief conductor of the Moscow Radio Sym. Orch. (1964–72). He then emigrated to Israel and became a naturalized citizen. He was music director of the Gürzenich Orch. in Cologne (1975–86) and chief conductor of the Stockholm Phil. (1982–87). —NS/LK/DM

Aiblinger, Johann Kaspar, German conductor and composer; b. Wasserburg, Feb. 23, 1779; d. Munich, May 6, 1867. He was a student of Joseph Schlett in Munich and of Simon Mayr in Bergamo (1802). After further training in Vicenza (1803–11), Venice, and Milan, he served as 2nd maestro di cappella to the viceroy of Milan. Upon his return to Munich, he was made maestro al cembalo of the Italian Opera in 1819. In 1823 he became asst. Kapellmeister at the Royal National Theater, and in 1826 Bavarian court Kapellmeister. He wrote 2 operas, including *Rodrigo und Chimene* (Munich, 1821), 3 ballets, masses, Requiems, liturgies, and Psalms.

BIBL.: P. Hötzl, *Zum Gedächtnis A.s* (Munich, 1867). —NS/LK/DM

Aichinger, Gregor, important German composer; b. Regensburg, 1564 or 1565; d. Augsburg, Jan. 20 or 21, 1628. He entered the Univ. of Ingolstadt in 1578. In 1584 he became household organist to the Frugger family in Augsburg, and also served as organist at St. Ulrich there until his death. He visited Italy in 1584, and then studied with Giovanni Gabrieli in Venice, attended the Univ. of Siena (1586), and journeyed to Rome. In 1588 he resumed his studies at the Univ. of Ingolstadt. He then

revisited Rome, and subsequently attended the Univ. of Perugia in 1599. In 1600 he was once more in Rome, and he also visited Venice. About 1601 he settled in Augsburg. Having taken holy orders while in Italy, he received the benefice of S. Maria Magdalena in Augsburg, where he also was vicarius chori. His works reflect the influence of Lassus and Giovanni Gabrieli, and are particularly noteworthy for their polyphonic mastery. His *Cantiones ecclesiasticae* (Dillingen, 1607) was the first major German publication with thoroughbass, and is also significant for the inclusion of a valuable treatise on thoroughbass notation and performance.

WORKS: *Sacrae cantiones* for 4 to 6, 8, and 10 Voices (Venice, 1590); *Divinae laudes* for 3 Voices (Augsburg, 1602); *Fasciculus sacrarum harmoniarum* for 4 Voices, *3 ricercares a 4* (Dillingen, 1606); *Cantiones ecclesiasticae* for 3 to 4 Voices and Basso Continuo, *1 canzona a 2* and Basso Continuo (Dillingen, 1607); *Sacra Dei laudes sub officio divino concinendae* for 5 to 8 Voices (Dillingen, 1609); *Teutsche Gesenglein: Auss dem Psalter dess H. Propheten Davids* for 3 Voices (Dillingen, 1609); *Triplex liturgiarum fasciculus* for 4 to 6 Voices and Basso Continuo (Augsburg, 1616); *Encomium verbo incarnato* for 4 Voices and Basso Continuo (Ingolstadt, 1617); *Quercus dodonaea* for 3 to 4 Voices and Basso Continuo (Augsburg, 1619); *Corolla eucharistica* for 2 to 3 Voices and Basso Continuo (Augsburg, 1621); *Flores musici ad mensam Ss. convivii* for 5 to 6 Voices and Basso Continuo (Augsburg, 1626).

BIBL.: W. Hettrick, *The Thorough-bass in the Works of G. S. (1564–1628)* (diss., Univ. of Mich., 1968).—NS/LK/DM

Aimon, (Pamphile Léopold) François, French cellist, conductor, and composer; b. L'Isle, near Avignon, Oct. 4, 1799; d. Paris, Feb. 2, 1866. He was only 17 when he became conductor of the theater in Marseilles. From 1821 he conducted at various theaters in Paris. He composed the opera *Les jeux floraux* (Paris, Nov. 16, 1818), 2 bassoon concertos, and 21 string quartets.—LK/DM

Ainsley, John Mark, English tenor; b. Crewe, July 9, 1963. He studied at Magdalen Coll., Oxford, and with Anthony Rolfe Johnson. After making his professional debut as a soloist in Stravinsky's Mass at London's Royal Festival Hall in 1984, he appeared frequently as a soloist with many early music groups from 1985. He made his first appearance with the English National Opera in London as Eurillo in Scarlatti's *Gli equivoci nel sembiante* in 1989. In 1990 he made his U.S. debut as a soloist in Bach's Mass in B Minor in N.Y. under Hogwood's direction. In 1991 he appeared as Mozart's Ferrando with the Glyndebourne Touring Opera, and also sang that composer's Idamante with the Welsh National Opera in Cardiff. His first appearance at the Glyndebourne Festival followed in 1992 as Ferrando, the same year in which he made his debut as a soloist with the Berlin Phil. In 1993 he sang Mozart's Don Ottavio at the Aix-en-Provence Festival, a role he sang again at the San Francisco Opera in 1995. In 1997 he sang in concert at London's Royal Festival Hall. He portrayed Jupiter in *Semele* at the English National Opera in 1999.—NS/LK/DM

Aitken, Hugh, American composer and teacher; b. N.Y., Sept. 7, 1924. He received his primary training at home; his father was an accomplished violinist, and his paternal grandmother was a pianist. He took clarinet lessons and also enrolled in a chemistry class at N.Y.U. From 1943 to 1945 he served as a navigator in the U.S. Army Air Corps. Returning from World War II, he entered the Juilliard School of Music in N.Y. as a student in composition of Wagenaar, Persichetti, and Ward (M.S., 1950); in 1960 he joined the faculty there, and in 1970 became a prof. of music at William Paterson Coll. of N.J. in Wayne. In his music he professes moral dedication to Classical ideals, regarding deviation from the natural melodic flow and harmonic euphony as unjustifiable tonicide.

WORKS: DRAMATIC: *Fables,* chamber opera (1975); *Felipe,* opera (1981). **ORCH.:** Chamber Concerto for Piano, Winds, Brass, and String Quintet (1947; rev. 1977); *Toccata* (1950); Piano Concerto (1953); *Short Suite* for Strings (1954); *Partita I* (1957), *II* (1959); *III* (1964), and *IV* (1964); *7 Pieces* for Chamber Orch. (1957); *Serenade* for Chamber Orch. (1958); *Partita* for Strings and Piano (1960); *Partita* for String Quartet and Orch. (1964); *Rameau Remembered* for Flute, 2 Oboes, Bassoon, and Strings (1980); *In Praise of Ockeghem* for Strings (1981); 3 violin concertos (1984, 1988, 1992); *Happy Birthday* for the 40th anniversary of the Aspen (Colo.) Music Festival (1988); *Songdance* (1992); band music. **CHAMBER:** *Short Suite* for Wind Quintet and Piano (1948); String Trio (1951); Suite for Clarinet (1955); *Partita* for 6 Instruments (1956); Quintet for Oboe and Strings (1957); *8 Studies* for Wind Quintet (1958); *Partita* for Violin (1958); Quartet for Clarinet and Strings (1959); *Trombone Music* (1961); Suite for Bass (1961); *Montages* for Bassoon (1962); *Serenade* for Oboe and String Trio (1965); Trios for 11 Players (1970); *Trumpet!* (1974); *Oboe Music* (1975); *Tromba* for Trumpet and String Quartet (1976); *Johannes* for 5 Renaissance Instruments (1977); *For the Violin* (1978); *For the Cello* (1980); *Op. 95 Revisited* for String Quartet (1980); *Flute Music* (1981); *5 Short Pieces* for 3 Clarinets (1982); Trio for Flute, Clarinet, and Cello (1984); Concertino for Contrabass and String Trio (1984); *Music for the Horn* (1985); Duo for Cello and Piano (1989); *Études and Interludes* for 3 Percussionists (1993); piano pieces; organ music. **VOCAL:** *The Revelation of St. John the Divine* for Soloists, Chorus, and Orch. (1953–90); 10 cantatas (1958–94); *2 Tales from Grimm* for Narrator, Flute, Oboe, String Trio, and Piano (1991); choruses.—**NS/LK/DM**

Aitken, Robert (Morris), Canadian flutist, pedagogue, and composer; b. Kentville, Nova Scotia, Aug. 28, 1939. He studied flute with Nicholas Fiore at the Royal Cons. of Music of Toronto (1955–59); concurrently received lessons in composition from Pentland at the Univ. of British Columbia; then studied electronic music with Schaeffer and composition with Weinzweig at the Univ. of Toronto (B.Mus., 1961; M.Mus., 1964); also flute with Marcel Moyse in Europe and in Marlboro, Vt., Rampal in Paris and Nice, Gazzelloni in Rome, André Jaunet in Zürich, and Hubert Barwahser in Amsterdam. In 1958–59 he was principal flutist in the Vancouver Sym. Orch.; then was 2nd flutist in the CBC Sym. Orch. (1960–64). After serving as co- principal flutist in the Toronto Sym. (1965–70), Aitken devoted himself to a concert career. He also was artistic director of the New Music Concerts in Toronto (from 1971) and of the advanced studies in music program at the Banff Centre School of Fine Arts (1985–89). He taught at the Royal Cons. of Music of Toronto (1957–64; 1965–68), the

Univ. of Toronto (1960–64; 1965–78), the Banff Centre School of Fine Arts (1977–89), and the Staatliche Hochschule für Musik in Freiburg im Breisgau (from 1988).

WORKS: *Rhapsody* for Orch. (1961); Quartet for Flute, Oboe, Viola, and Double Bass (1961); *Music* for Flute and Electronic Tape (1963); *Nosis* for Electronic Tape (1963); Concerto for 12 Solo Instruments (1964); *Spectra* for 4 Chamber Groups (1969); *Kebyar* for Flute, Clarinet, 2 Double Basses, Percussion, and Tape (1971); *Shadows I: Nekuia* for Orch. (1971), *II: Lalitá* for Flute, 3 Cellos, 2 Percussionists, and 2 Harps (1972), and *III: Nira* for Violin, Flute, Oboe, Viola, Double Bass, Piano, and Harpsichord (1974–88); *Spiral* for Orch., with Amplified Flute, Oboe, Clarinet, and Bassoon (1975); *Icicle* for Flute (1977); *Plainsong* for Flute (1977); *Folia* for Woodwind Quintet (1980); *Monody* for Chorus (1983).—**NS/LK/DM**

Aitkin, Webster, American pianist and teacher; b. Los Angeles, June 17, 1908; d. Santa Fe, N.Mex., May 11, 1981. He was a piano pupil of A. Schnabel and E. von Sauer. In 1929 he made his professional debut in Vienna. In 1938 he gave a series of N.Y. recitals featuring all of Schubert's piano works. He later was active as a teacher. —**NS/LK/DM**

Ajmone-Marsan, Guido, Italian-born American conductor; b. Turin, March 24, 1947. He was taken to the U.S. as a child and became a naturalized American citizen in 1962. He studied clarinet and conducting at the Eastman School of Music in Rochester, N.Y. (B.A., 1968); continued his studies in Salzburg, Venice, and Siena. He took a course in conducting with Ferrara at the Accademia di Santa Cecilia in Rome (1968–71). His conducting career received its decisive impetus in 1973, when he won 1st prize in the Solti Competition in Chicago; subsequently he appeared as a guest conductor with the Chicago, Philadelphia, and Cleveland orchs., and with various orchs. abroad. He was music director of Arnhem's Het Gelders Orch. (1982–86), music advisor and principal conductor of the Orch. of Ill. in Chicago (1982–87), and Generalmusikdirektor of the Essen City Theater (1986–90).—**NS/LK/DM**

Akagi, Kei, extremely versatile Japanese keyboard player with a highly individual style and lengthy resume; b. Japan, March 16, 1953. Akagi maintains his own sound no matter what the context. In the last two decades his credits include significant stints with Miles Davis, Stanley Turrentine, Art Pepper, Slide Hampton, Joe Farrell, Airto Moreira, James Newton, Sadao Watanabe, and fusion stalwarts Al DiMeola, Jean-Luc Ponty, and Allan Holdsworth. First influenced by Bud Powell, Akagi came of age listening to everyone from Oscar Peterson, Bill Evans, and Sonny Rollins to late Coltrane and Miles's seminal fusion. His family moved to the U.S. when he was four and he spent his late teens back in Japan, playing guitar and studying composition at the International Christian Univ. in Tokyo. Returning to the States, he became a philosophy grad student at the Univ. of Calif., Santa Barbara, but after two years decided to play music full-time. After early gigs with Blue Mitchell, Art Pepper, and Eddie Harris, Akagi hooked up with Airto and Flora Purim in 1979 and stayed with them until 1985. He spent two years with Miles (1990–91) and much of the rest of the decade with Turrentine. Based in Los Angeles, Akagi is a fine composer who writes angular, dramatic tunes. Akagi's first album was *Symphonic Fusion—The Earth*, a five-part funk-jazz concerto recorded in the early 1980s for a Japanese label.

DISC.: *Symphonic Fusion—The Earth* (1980); *Mirror Puzzle* (1994); *Sound Circle* (1995).—**AG**

A Kempis, Nicolaus, Flemish organist and composer; b. c. 1600; d. Brussels (buried), Aug. 11, 1676. He became organist at Ste. Gudule in Brussels in 1626, which position he formally assumed in 1627. He composed 4 vols. of *Symphoniae* that rank among the earliest sonatas in the Low Countries. His son Thomas (actually, Petrus) a Kempis (b. Brussels [baptized], April 2, 1628; d. Sept. 21, 1688), was also an organist and composer who joined the Premonstratensian order. Another son, Joannes Florentis a Kempis (b. Brussels [baptized], Aug. 1, 1635; d. after 1711), likewise was an organist and composer. After serving as organist at the Eglise de la Chapelle in Brussels from 1657, he succeeded his father at Ste. Gudule about 1671.—**LK/DM**

Akeroyde, Samuel, English composer; b. Yorkshire, c. 1650; d. London, after 1706. He was a musician in ordinary to King James II (1687–90). Several of his songs were included in London plays and in collections of the day.—**NS/LK/DM**

Akimenko (real name, **Yakimenko**), **Fyodor (Stepanovich),** Russian composer; b. Kharkov, Feb. 20, 1876; d. Paris, Jan. 3, 1945. He studied with Balakirev at the Court Chapel in St. Petersburg (1886–90), then with Liadov and Rimsky-Korsakov at the St. Petersburg Cons. (1895–1900). He was the first composition teacher of Stravinsky, whom he taught privately. After the Russian Revolution, he emigrated to Paris. He wrote mostly for piano in the manner of the Russian lyric school. Other works include an opera, *The Fairy of the Snows* (1914), a concert overture (St. Petersburg, Nov. 20, 1899), an orch. fantasy (St. Petersburg, Oct. 28, 1900), *Petite ballade* for Clarinet and Piano, *Pastorale* for Oboe and Piano, Piano Trio, Violin sonata, Cello Sonata, 2 Sonata-Fantasias for Piano, numerous character pieces for piano, and songs.—**NS/LK/DM**

Akiyama, Kazuyoshi, Japanese conductor; b. Tokyo, Jan. 2, 1941. He was a student of Saito at the Toho School of Music in Tokyo. In 1964 he made his conducting debut with the Tokyo Sym. Orch. and that same year he was made its music director, a post he retained for 35 years. From 1972 to 1985 he was resident conductor and music director of the Vancouver (British Columbia) Sym. Orch., and concurrently served as music director of the American Sym. Orch. from 1973 to 1978. From 1985 to 1993 he was music director of the Syracuse (N.Y.) Sym. Orch. He also was music advisor and principal conductor of the Sapporo Sym. Orch. from 1988 to 1998. He was music director of the Hiroshima Sym. Orch. from 1998.—**NS/LK/DM**

Akiyoshi, Toshiko, outstanding Chinese jazz artist; b. Darien, Manchuria, China, Dec. 12, 1929. Toshiko Akiyoshi is living proof that jazz is a world-wide phenomenon. Born in China and raised in Japan, Akiyoshi was introduced to jazz when she was still in her teens through the recordings of Teddy Wilson. While in her twenties and performing around Tokyo, she was heard by Oscar Peterson, who then told impresario Norman Granz that Akiyoshi was "the greatest female jazz pianist." This in turn led to her receiving a scholarship for the Berklee School of Music. She later formed a quartet with her husband at the time, alto saxophonist Charlie Mariano, recording for the Candid label prior to hooking up briefly with Charles Mingus in 1962. Shortly after the Mingus stint, Akiyoshi went back to Japan before returning to America where, in 1965, she was a piano teacher at jazz clinics in Reno, Nev. and Salt Lake City, Utah. Since that time she has founded her big band, now known as the Toshiko Akiyoshi Jazz Orch. (featuring saxophonist Lew Tabackin, her current husband), and recorded with it for RCA, Jam, and Ascent. The orchestra is now considered her main musical voice and her writing and arranging for them are widely considered to be among the best in the world.

DISC.: *Toshiko Mariano Quartet* (1961); *Finesse* (1978); *Interlude* (1987); *Desert Lady–Fantasy* (1995).—**GM**

Akses, Necil Kâzim, Turkish composer and teacher; b. Constantinople, May 6, 1908. He studied at the Constantinople Cons. A stipend from the Turkish government enabled him to enter the Vienna Academy of Music as a cello student in 1926, where he also studied counterpoint and composition with J. Marx (composition diploma, 1931). He then studied with A. Hába and Suk in Prague (until 1934). Upon his return to Turkey, he taught at the Ankara Cons., where he served as its director in 1948–49. He was director of the Ankara State Opera (1958–60; 1971–72). In 1981 he was made a National Artist by the Turkish government and in 1992 he was awarded the Atatürk Arts Prize. His music often incorporated Turkish elements, but the influence of Western art music predominated in his scores.

WORKS: DRAMATIC: O p e r a : *Mete* (1933); *Bayönder* (The Leader; Ankara, Dec. 27, 1934); *Timur* (1954). **ORCH.:** *Çiftetelli* (1934); *Ankara Castle* (1938–42; Ankara, Oct. 22, 1942); *Poem* for Cello and Orch. (Ankara, June 29, 1946); *Ballade* (Ankara, April 14, 1948); 5 syms. (1966–88); Violin Concerto (1969); *Concerto for Orchestra* (1976–77); Viola Concerto (1977). **CHAMBER:** *Allegro feroce* for Saxophone and Piano (1931); Flute Sonata (1939); 4 string quartets; piano pieces. —**NS/LK/DM**

Akutagawa, Yasushi, noted Japanese composer and conductor; b. Tokyo, July 12, 1925; d. there, Jan. 31, 1989. He received training in piano, conducting, and composition (from Hashimoto and Ifukube) at the Tokyo Academy of Music (1943–49). In subsequent years, he devoted himself mainly to composition while making occasional appearances as a conductor. He was president of the Japanese Federation of Composers (1980–89) and the Japanese Performing Rights Soc. (1981–89). His orch. music was widely disseminated outside his homeland. His father was the famous Japanese author of *Rashomon*.

WORKS: DRAMATIC: O p e r a : *Kurai Kagami* (Dark Mirror; Tokyo, March 27, 1960; rev. ver. as *Orpheus in Hiroshima*, NHK-TV, Aug. 27, 1967). **B a l l e t** *The Dream of the Lake* (Tokyo, Nov. 6, 1950); *Paradise Lost* (Tokyo, March 17, 1951); *Kappa* (July 21, 1957); *Spider's Web* (Tokyo, March 17, 1969); also film scores. **ORCH.:** *Prelude* (1947); *3 Symphonic Movements* (Tokyo, Sept. 26, 1948); *Music* (1950); *Triptyque* for Strings (1953); Sinfonia (1953); *Divertimento* (1955); *Symphony for Children: Twin Stars* for Narrator and Orch. (1957); *Ellora Symphony* (1958); *Negative Picture* for Strings (1966); *Ostinato Sinfonica* (Tokyo, May 25, 1967); *Concerto Ostinato* for Cello and Orch. (Tokyo, Dec. 16, 1969); *Ballata Ostinata* (1970); *Rhapsody* (Tokyo, Oct. 4, 1971); *River of Poipa and Tree of Poipa* for Narrator and Orch. (1979); *La Princesse de la Lune* (1982); *Sounds* for Organ and Orch. (1986). **CHAMBER:** *Music for the Strings* for Double String Quartet and Double Bass (1962). **VOCAL:** *Hymn for the 21ˢᵗ Century* for Chorus, Brass, and Orch. (1983); *Inochi* for Chorus and Orch. (1988).—**NS/LK/DM**

Alagna, Roberto, prominent Italian tenor; b. Clichy-sur-Bois, France, June 7, 1963. He received vocal training from Raphael Ruiz. In 1988 he won the Pavarotti Competition in Philadelphia and then made his operatic debut with the Glyndebourne Touring Opera in Plymouth as Alfredo. His first appearance at London's Covent Garden followed in 1990 as Rodolfo. In 1991 he made his debut at Milan's La Scala as Alfredo. Following an engagement as Roberto Devereux in Monte Carlo in 1992, he returned to Covent Garden as Gounod's Roméo in 1994. He sang the Duke of Mantua at his debut at the Vienna State Opera in 1995, the same year he sang Edgardo at the Opéra de la Bastille in Paris. He returned to Paris in 1996 as Don Carlos at the Théâtre du Châtelet. On April 10, 1996, he made his debut at the Metropolitan Opera in N.Y. as Rodolfo. Shortly afterward he married **Angela Gheorghiu**, and then returned to the Metropolitan Opera that year as Nemorino and the Duke of Mantua and to Covent Garden as Don Carlos and Alfredo. In 1997 he was engaged as Macduff at La Scala. He sang Roméo to Gheorghiu's Juliette at the Metropolitan Opera in 1998 to notable acclaim, roles they reprised at the Lyric Opera in Chicago in 1999.—**NS/LK/DM**

Alain, Jehan (Ariste), gifted French organist and composer, brother of **Marie-Claire** and **Olivier Alain;** b. St. Germain-en-Laye, Feb. 3, 1911; d. Petits-Puis, near Saumur, June 20, 1940. He studied organ with his father and piano with Augustin Pierson; then entered the Paris Cons. (1927), where he studied composition with Dukas and Roger-Ducasse (premier prix for harmony and fugue, 1934) and organ with Dupré (premier prix, 1939). He was organist at St. Nicolas Cathedral in Maisons-Lafitte, near Paris (1935–39). His death at 29, while leading a motorcycle patrol in the early months of World War II, was a great loss to French music. In addition to many works for organ and piano, he wrote choral pieces, chamber music, and songs. His works for organ have proved to be the most enduring; among the most frequently performed are *Fantaisies* Nos. 1 and 2 (1934, 1936) and *Litanies* (1937).

BIBL.: B. Gavoty, *J. A., musicien francais (1911–1940)* (Paris, 1945).—**NS/LK/DM**

Alain, Marie-Claire, renowned French organist and pedagogue, sister of **Jehan (Ariste)** and **Olivier Alain;** b. St. Germain-en-Laye, Aug. 10, 1926. She was a pupil of Duruflé (harmony), Plé-Caussade (counterpoint and fugue), and Dupré (organ) at the Paris Cons. At age 11 she made her debut in St. Germain-en-Laye; in 1950, made her formal debut in Paris, the same year she won the Geneva International Competition. In subsequent years, she made frequent tours of Europe; in 1961, made her first tour of the U.S. She lectured at the Haarlem Summer Academy of Organists in the Netherlands (1956–72); also gave master classes around the world. Her exhaustive repertory includes works by the Baroque masters as well as contemporary scores.—**NS/LK/DM**

Alain, Olivier, French pianist, musicologist, and composer, brother of **Jehan (Ariste)** and **Marie-Claire Alain;** b. St. Germain-en-Laye, Aug. 3, 1918; d. Paris, Feb. 28, 1994. He studied organ and piano in his youth; then took courses in composition with Aubin and Messiaen at the Paris Cons. From 1950 to 1964 he served as director of the Cons. in St. Germain-en-Laye; in 1961 he was appointed to the faculty of the École César Franck in Paris. He composed an oratorio, *Chant funèbre sur les morts en montagne* (1950); also motets and pieces for organ and piano.

WRITINGS: *L'Harmonie* (Paris, 1965); *Bach* (Paris, 1970).—**NS/LK/DM**

Alaleona, Domenico, Italian musicologist and composer; b. Montegiorgio, Nov. 16, 1881; d. there, Dec. 28, 1928. He studied organ and clarinet in Montegiorgio, and then was a student of Sgambati (piano), Renzi (organ), and De Sanctis (theory) at the Liceo di Santa Cecilia in Rome. He was active as a choral conductor in Leghorn and Rome before becoming a prof. at the Liceo di Santa Cecilia in 1916. Alaleona made an important contribution to the study of the Italian oratorio in his *Studi sulla storia dell'oratorio musicale in Italia* (Turin, 1908). He also wrote the interesting article "L'armonia modernissima" in the *Rivista Musicale Italiana*, XVIII (1911). As a theorist, he proposed splitting the octave into unorthodox equal divisions and combining the 12 notes of the chromatic scale into single chords. Among his compositions were the opera *Mirra* (1912; Rome, March 31, 1920), the *Sinfonia italiana*, a Requiem, and songs.

BIBL.: G. Cardi, *D. A.: Musicista e musicologo* (Ascoli Piceno, 1957).—**NS/LK/DM**

Alard, (Jean-) Delphin, distinguished French violinist, pedagogue, and composer; b. Bayonne, March 8, 1815; d. Paris, Feb. 22, 1888. He studied with Habeneck (premier prix in violin, 1830) and Fétis at the Paris Cons. In 1831 he made his debut with the Société des Concerts du Conservatoire in Paris. After pursuing a career as a soloist, he joined the royal orch. in 1840, becoming its solo violin in 1842. He held that same position with the imperial orch. from 1853. He was a prof. of violin at the Paris Cons. (1843–75). Among his pupils was Sarasate. In 1884 he gave his farewell concert. He publ. the valuable *École du violin: Méthode complete et progressive* (Paris, 1844), as well as *Maîtres classiques du violin* (Mainz, 1863), an anthology of 18th and 19th century music. Alard composed many brilliant works for violin, including concertos, études, and fantasias.—NS/LK/DM

Alarie, Pierrette (Marguerite),

Canadian soprano and teacher; b. Montreal, Nov. 9, 1921. She studied voice and acting with Jeanne Maubourg and Albert Roberval. After appearing on radio as an actress and singer of popular music, she continued vocal training with Salvator Issaurel (1938–43) and as a scholarship student with Elisabeth Schumann at the Curtis Inst. of Music in Philadelphia (1943–46). In 1943 she made her debut as Mozart's Barbarina in Montreal. She won the Metropolitan Opera Auditions of the Air in 1945, and on Dec. 8 of that year made her debut with the company in N.Y. as Verdi's Oscar; remained on its roster until 1947. In subsequent years, she appeared frequently in opera and in concert with her husband, **Léopold Simoneau**, whom she married in 1946. In addition to her festival appearances in Aix-en-Provence, Edinburgh, Glyndebourne, Vienna, and Munich, she sang opera in Montreal, Toronto, Vancouver, San Francisco, Philadelphia, N.Y., and New Orleans, becoming particularly well known for her performances of works by Mozart and of works from the French repertoire. In 1966 she retired from the operatic stage and in 1970 made her farewell appearance as a concert singer. After teaching and staging opera in Calif. (1972–82), she went to Victoria, British Columbia, where she was founder-director with her husband of the Canada Opera Piccola. In 1967 she was made an Officer of the Order of Canada. In 1990 the French government made her a Chevalière of the Ordre des arts et des lettres de France.

BIBL.: R. Maheu, *P. A., Léopold Simoneau: Deux voix, un art* (Montreal, 1988).—NS/LK/DM

Alary, Jules (Eugène Abraham),

Italian-born French composer; b. Mantua, March 16, 1814; d. Paris, April 17, 1891. After studying at the Milan Cons., he settled in Paris as a voice teacher and composer. He wrote numerous operas, among the most popular being *Le tre nozze* (Paris, March 29, 1851). His opera *La Voix humaine* had the curious distinction of being staged at the Paris Opéra (Dec. 30, 1861) for the sole purpose of making use of the scenery left over after the fiasco of Wagner's *Tannhäuser*. Alary also wrote a mystery play, *Redemption* (Paris, April 14, 1850), much sacred music, and some chamber pieces.—NS/LK/DM

Albanese, Licia,

noted Italian-born American soprano; b. Bari, July 22, 1909. She studied with Emanuel de Rosa in Bari and Giuseppina Baldassare-Tedeschi in Milan. In 1934 she made an unexpected operatic debut at Milan's Teatro Lirico when she was called in to substitute as Cio-Cio-San for the 2nd act of *Madama Butterfly*. In 1935 she made her first appearance at Milan's La Scala as Puccini's Lauretta, and subsequently sang there with distinction in such roles as Mimi and Micaëla. In 1937 she made her debut at London's Covent Garden as Liù. On Feb. 9, 1940, she made her first appearance at the Metropolitan Opera in N.Y. as Cio-Cio-San, and remained on its roster as one of its most admired artists until 1963. In 1964 she rejoined its roster and sang with it until her farewell appearance as Mimi in a concert performance at the Newport (R.I.) Opera Festival on July 12, 1966. During her years at the Metropolitan Opera, she was greatly admired for her portrayals in operas by Puccini. She also excelled as Mozart's Countess, Susanna, Adriana Lecouvreur, Desdemona, Massenet's Manon, and Violetta. In 1945 she became a naturalized American citizen. In 1995 she was awarded the Medal of Arts by President Clinton. —NS/LK/DM

Albani (real name, Lajeunesse), Dame (Marie Louise Cécile) Emma,

famous Canadian soprano; b. Chambly, near Montreal, Nov. 1, 1847; d. London, April 3, 1930. In childhood she studied piano with her mother, and then piano, harp, and singing with her father. In 1856 she made her first public appearance in Montreal as a pianist and singer. In 1860 she sang for the visiting Prince of Wales there. In 1865 her family went to Albany, N.Y., where she sang at St. Joseph's Catholic Church until 1868. She then went to Paris to study voice with Duprez and organ and harmony with Benoist, completing her vocal training with Lamperti in Milan. In 1870 she made her operatic debut as Amina in Messina, taking the professional name of Albani. On April 2, 1872, she made a notable debut at London's Covent Garden as Amina. In succeeding years her career was closely associated with Covent Garden, where she was greatly admired. On Oct. 21, 1874, she made her U.S. operatic debut as Amina with the Max Strakosch company at N.Y.'s Academy of Music. On Dec. 23, 1891, she made her Metropolitan Opera debut in N.Y. as Gilda, but sang there for only one season. Her last great triumph at Covent Garden came on July 24, 1896, when she appeared as Valentine. Thereafter she devoted herself to a concert career, giving her farewell recital at London's Royal Albert Hall on Oct. 14, 1911. After retirement, she fell upon hard times and gave voice lessons and even appeared in English music halls. In 1920 the British government granted her a pension. She was awarded the Gold Medal of the Phil. Soc. of London in 1897. In 1925 she was made a Dame Commander of the Order of the British Empire. Albani was a remarkable artist, excelling in coloratura, spinto, and dramatic roles. She was also a distinguished concert artist.

WRITINGS: *Forty Years of Song* (London, 1911).

BIBL.: C. Macdonald, *E. A.: Victorian Diva* (Toronto, 1984). —NS/LK/DM

Albani, Mattia (real name, Mathias Alban),

violin maker; b. S. Niccolo di Kaltern (Alto Adige), March (baptized, March 28) 1621; d. Bolzano, Feb. 7, 1712. He was a pupil of Jakob Stainer. Violins of

Albani's are extant dating from as early as the end of 1644. His best examples date from 1680 onward. The great vogue his violins enjoyed spawned many forgeries; false Albani labels have been discovered on violins dating from as early as 1640; the original labels appeared from 1690. A son, Giuseppe, his pupil, worked from 1680 to 1722 at Bolzano, and another son, Michele (1677–1730), at Graz. Other violin makers named Albani, or at least using the name on their instruments (perhaps for its commercial value), are the following, none appearing to have been connected with the family of the original Mattia: Mattia (Rome, c. 1650–1715); Nicola (worked at Mantua, c. 1763); Filippo (active c. 1773); Francesco (active at Graz, c. 1724); Michele (at Palermo, 18th century); and Paolo (at Palermo and Cremona, 1630–70).—NS/LK/DM

Albany, Joe (Joseph; possibly Albani),

bebop pianist; b. Atlantic City, N.J., Jan. 24, 1924; d. N.Y., Jan. 12, 1988. After playing accordion as a child, Albany switched to piano in high school and in 1942 joined Leo Watson's group. He worked briefly with Benny Carter, Max Kaminsky, and Rod Cless (at the Pied Piper in N.Y.), as well as Georgie Auld, Boyd Raeburn, and Charlie Parker. His Los Angeles radio broadcasts with Parker and studio work with Lester Young are both preserved on recordings from 1946. Serious problems with drugs and alcohol almost destroyed Albany's career; in addition, his second wife committed suicide while his third almost died from a drug overdose. A home tape recording from 1957 was the only one issued from 1947 until 1971, when his career picked up again. During those years Albany was in the Los Angeles area, although in 1959 he lived in San Francisco and wrote a few songs that Anita O'Day recorded. In 1963 he worked briefly in N.Y. with Charles Mingus and Jay Cameron. Albany made several recordings after 1971 and was the subject of a 1980 documentary, *J. A.—A Jazz Life*. He was a distinctive bebop artist with a light touch, but personal problems—not only drug addiction but also a reported history of quitting gigs (even one with Charlie Parker) over musical and other differences—kept him from success.

DISC.: *The Right Combination* (1957); *At Home Alone* (1971); *Birdtown Birds* (1973); *Bird Lives* (1979); *Portrait of an Artist* (1982).—**LP**

Albéniz, Isaac (Manuel Francisco),

eminent Spanish composer and pianist; b. Camprodón, May 29, 1860; d. Cambo-les- Bains, May 18, 1909. He began piano lessons at a very early age with Narciso Oliveros in Barcelona. He was only 4 when he made his first public appearance as a pianist there with his sister Clementina. In 1867 the family went to Paris, where he had some instruction from A.-F. Marmontel. The family returned to Spain in 1868, and in 1869 Albéniz enrolled in the Madrid Cons. to study with Ajero and Mendizábal. He quit the Cons. by the time he was 10 and set out to roam his homeland, supporting himself by playing in various venues. After an adventuresome sojourn in South America in 1872–73, he returned to Spain to give concerts. In 1875 he played in Puerto Rico, and then visited Cuba and the U.S. before pursuing his studies at the Leipzig Cons. with Jadassohn and Reinecke. In 1877 Count Guillermo Morphy provided Albéniz with a scholarship to study at the Brussels Cons. with Brassin (piano) and Gevaert and Dupont (composition), where he graduated with a 1st prize in 1879. In 1880 he met Liszt who gave him valuable advice. Albéniz subsequently pursued a concert career in Spain and abroad. After settling in Paris in 1894, he devoted himself principally to composing but also taught at the Schola Cantorum (1897–98). In 1900 he returned to Spain but was again in Paris in 1902 before settling in Nice in 1903. Albéniz helped to forge the Spanish national idiom of composition, one reflecting indigenous rhythms and melodic patterns. A gifted pianist, he composed a remarkable body of music for his instrument. His suite *Iberia* (1905–09) is an outstanding example.

WORKS: DRAMATIC: *The Magic Opal*, operetta (London, Jan. 19, 1893); *San Antonio de la Florida*, zarzuela (Madrid, Oct. 26, 1894); *Henry Clifford*, opera (Barcelona, May 8, 1895); *Merlín*, opera (c. 1895; unfinished); *Pepita Jiménez*, comic opera (Barcelona, Jan. 5, 1896). **ORCH.:** *Rapsodia española* for Piano and Orch. (Madrid, March 20, 1887, composer soloist); Piano Concerto (Madrid, Dec. 30, 1887, composer soloist); *Escenas sinfónicas catalanas* (Paris, April 25, 1889); *Catalonia* (1889). **Piano:** *Suite española*, 8 pieces (1886); *Suite antigua* (1887); *Seis danzas españolas* (1887); *12 piezas características* (1888); *España* (1890); *Serenata española* (1891); *Cantos de España* (n.d.); *Iberia*, 12 pieces (1905–09); *Navarra* (n.d.; ed. by D. de Séverac); also 4 sonatas and many other pieces. **VOCAL:** *El Cristo*, oratorio (n.d.); songs.

BIBL.: H. Collet, *A. et Granados* (Paris, 1926; 2nd ed., 1948); A. de las Heras, *Vida de A.* (Barcelona and Madrid, 1940); V. Ruiz Albéniz, *I. A.* (Madrid, 1948); M. Raux Deledicque, *A.: Su vida inquieta y ardorosa* (Buenos Aires, 1950); A Sagardia, *I. A.* (Madrid, 1951); G. Laplane, *A.: Sa vie, son oeuvre* (Paris, 1956); P. Baytelman, *I. A.: Chronological List and Thematic Catalog of His Piano Works* (Warren, Mich., 1993); W. Clark, *I. A.: A Guide to Research* (Levittown, Pa., 1998); idem, *I. A.: Portrait of a Romantic* (Oxford, 1999).—**NS/LK/DM**

Albéniz, Mateo (Antonio Pérez de),

Spanish composer, father of **Pedro Albéniz y Basanta;** b. Basque region, c. 1755; d. San Sebastián, June 23, 1831. He was maestro de capilla in San Sebastián, then at the collegiate church in Logroño (1795–1800), and finally at S. Maria la Redonda in San Sebastián (1800–29). He publ. *Instrucción melódica, especulativa, y practica, para enseñar a cantar y a tañer la música moderna y antigua* (San Sebastián, 1802) and composed much church music. —**NS/LK/DM**

Albéniz y Basanta, Pedro,

Spanish organist, pianist, teacher, and composer, son of **Mateo (Antonio Pérez de) Albéniz;** b. Logroño, April 14, 1795; d. Madrid, April 12, 1855. He studied with his father and was active as an organist in various Spanish towns while still a youth. He later studied piano with Kalkbrenner and Herz in Paris. After settling in Madrid, he became prof. of piano at the Cons. in 1830 and court organist in 1834. He publ. a piano manual (1840) and some 70 piano pieces in a highly developed technical style.—**NS/LK/DM**

Albergati (Capacelli), Pirro, Italian nobleman, music patron, and composer; b. Bologna, Sept. 20, 1663; d. there, June 22, 1735. He held public offices in Bologna, where he also presented many of his works at his palace. His oratorios were given during the annual Lenten music performances (1686–1732). He also publ. 15 vols. of instrumental works, sacred music, and cantatas (1682–1721). His operas and serenatas are not extant.—NS/LK/DM

Alberghi, Paolo Tommaso, Italian violinist, teacher, and composer; b. Faenza (baptized), Dec. 31, 1716; d. there, Oct. 11, 1785. He centered his career on Faenza. After training from Tartini, he was a violinist at the Cathedral, where his brother, Don Francesco Alberghi, was maestro di cappella. In 1755 he became 1st violinist there. Upon the death of his brother in 1760, he succeeded him as its maestro di cappella. He was highly esteemed as a violinist and teacher. Among his works were some 20 violin concertos, which are notable for their late Baroque virtuosity. He also wrote sonatas, trios, and sacred music. His son, Ignazio Alberghi (b. 1758; d. after 1835), was a tenor and composer of sacred music. After serving as maestro di cappella at Faenza Cathedral (1787–96), he was active at the Dresden court. —NS/LK/DM

Albert, Prince, German musician, music patron, and Prince Consort of Queen Victoria; b. Schloss Rosenau, near Coburg, Aug. 26, 1819; d. Windsor, Dec. 14, 1861. He learned to sing, play the piano and organ, and compose. In 1840 he married his 1st cousin, Queen Victoria, and in 1857 was made Prince Consort. He was a devoted supporter of the arts. Among his own compositions are sacred works and some 40 German songs in the manner of Mendelssohn. London's Royal Albert Hall (1871) stands in tribute to him.—NS/LK/DM

Albert, Don (Dominique, Albert Don), jazz trumpeter, bandleader; b. New Orleans, Aug. 5, 1908; d. San Antonio, Tex., March 4, 1980. Albert was a nephew of Natty Dominique and a relative of Barney Bigard. After some parade work in New Orleans, he toured in 1925 with Trent's Number Two Band, and joined Troy Floyd in San Antonio (1926–29), where he also recorded with blues singers. He then returned to New Orleans to recruit musicians for his own band, which subsequently made its debut at the Dallas State Fair, and recorded in 1936. The band was based in Tex., but worked as far afield as N.Y.C. (1937), Buffalo, Mexico, and Canada, before breaking up in Houston in 1939. Beginning in 1932, Albert primarily directed bands rather than playing trumpet. In the 1940s he organized bands for specific engagements, while maintaining a residence in San Antonio. He recorded on trumpet during a 1962 visit to New Orleans, and in Tex. with The Alamo City Jazz Band. During a 1966 visit to N.Y. he sat in with Buddy Tate's band, and he played at a New Orleans festival in June 1969. In the mid-1970s, he retired to San Antonio, Tex.—JC/LP

d'Albert, Eugen (actually, **Eugène Francis Charles**), prominent Scottish-born German pianist, conductor, and composer of English-French descent; b. Glasgow, April 10, 1864; d. Riga, March 3, 1932. He began training with his father, Charles Louis Napoléon d'Albert (b. Nienstetten, near Hamburg, Feb. 25, 1809; d. London, May 26, 1886), and at the age of 10 entered London's National Training School and studied piano with Pauer and theory with Stainer, Prout, and Sullivan. After appearances at London's Popular Concerts, he made his debut as soloist in the Schumann Concerto in London on Feb. 5, 1881. On Oct. 24, 1881, he was soloist in his own Piano Concerto under Richter in London and won extraordinary acclaim. After further training in Vienna and with Liszt, who hailed him as the young Tausig, he pursued a highly successful career as a pianist. In addition to his brilliant performances of Liszt, he was greatly admired for his Bach, Beethoven, and Brahms. In 1895 he became conductor of the Weimar Opera. From 1907 he served as director of the Berlin Hochschule für Musik. During World War I, he repudiated his English heritage, became a naturalized German citizen, and changed his first name to Eugen. His first wife (1892–95) was **(Maria) Teresa Carreño**; he subsequently married five more times. As a composer, d'Albert's output reflects German and Italian influences. Of his major works, he found some success with the operas *Die Abreise* (Frankfurt am Main, Oct. 20, 1898), *Tiefland* (Prague, Nov. 15, 1903), and *Flauto solo* (Prague, Nov. 12, 1905). His character pieces for piano also were in vogue for a time.

WORKS: DRAMATIC: Opera: *Der Rubin* (Karlsruhe, Oct. 12, 1893); *Ghismonda* (Dresden, Nov. 28, 1895); *Gernot* (Mannheim, April 11, 1897); *Die Arbreise* (Frankfurt am Main, Oct. 20, 1898); *Kain* (Berlin, Feb. 17, 1900); *Der Improvisator* (Berlin, Feb. 20, 1902); *Tiefland* (Prague, Nov. 15, 1903); *Flauto solo* (Prague, Nov. 12, 1905); *Tragaldabas* or *Der geborgte Ehemann* (Hamburg, Dec. 3, 1907); *Izeÿl* (Hamburg, Nov. 6, 1909); *Die verschenkte Frau* (Vienna, Feb. 6, 1912); *Liebesketten* (Vienna, Nov. 12, 1912); *Die toten Augen* (Dresden, March 5, 1916); *Der Stier von Olivera* (Leipzig, March 10, 1918); *Revolutionshochzeit* (Leipzig, Oct. 26, 1919); *Scirocco* (Darmstadt, May 18, 1921); *Mareike von Nymwegen* (Hamburg, Oct. 31, 1923); *Der Golem* (Frankfurt am Main, Nov. 14, 1926); *Die schwarze Orchidee* (Leipzig, Dec. 1, 1928); *Mister Wu* (unfinished; completed by L. Blech; Dresden, Sept. 29, 1932). **ORCH.:** 2 piano concertos (1884, 1893); Sym. (1886); *Overture to Grillparzer: Esther* (1888); Cello Concerto (1899); *Aschenputtel*, suite (1924); Symphonic Prelude to *Tiefland* (1924). **CHAMBER:** 2 string quartets (1887, 1893); numerous piano pieces, including a Suite (1883) and a Sonata (1893). **VOCAL:** *Der Mensch und das Leben* for Chorus (1893); *Seejungfräulein* for Voice and Orch. (1897); *Wie wir die Natur erleben* for Soprano or Tenor and Orch. (1903); 2 Lieder for Soprano or Tenor and Orch. (1904); *Mittelalterliche Venushymne* for Tenor, Men's Chorus, and Orch. (1904); *An den Genius von Deutschland* for Solo Voices and Chorus (1904); 58 lieder for Voice and Piano.

BIBL.: W. Raupp, *D. d'A.: Ein Künstler-und Menschenschicksal* (Leipzig, 1930); H. Heisig, "D.'A.s Opernschaffen" (diss., Univ. of Leipzig, 1942).—NS/LK/DM

Albert, Heinrich, German organist and composer; b. Lobenstein, Saxony, July 8, 1604; d. Königsberg, Oct. 6, 1651. He went to Dresden in 1622, where he worked with his cousin Heinrich Schütz. He then went to Leipzig to study law at the Univ. (1623–26), and also came into contact with Schein. In 1627 he went to

Warsaw with a peace delegation, but was seized as a prisoner of war by the Swedes. Upon his release in 1628, he settled in Königsberg. After a period as an authority on fortifications, he took up a career in music in 1630. In 1631 he became the Cathedral organist. His most important works are the 8 vols. of *Arien* (Königsberg, 1638–50), which contain some 170 brief sacred and secular songs, some of them to Albert's own texts. About 25 of them became well known as chorales. His prefaces contain valuable guidance on performance practice, including continuo playing. He also publ. the cantata *Musikalische Kürbs-Hütte* (1645), a cycle of 12 terzets to his own texts.

BIBL.: G. Kraft, ed., *Festschrift zur Ehrung von H. A. (1604–1651)* (Weimar, 1954).—**NS/LK/DM**

Albert, Karel, Belgian composer; b. Antwerp, April 16, 1901; d. Liedekerke, May 23, 1987. He was a student of Jong at the Royal Flemish Cons. in Antwerp. From 1933 to 1961 he was active with the Belgian Radio. He publ. *De evolutie van de muziek van de Oudheid tot aan Beethoven aan de hand van fonoplaten* (Brussels, 1947).

WORKS: DRAMATIC: O p e r a B u ff a : *Europa ontvoerd* (1950). **B a l l e t :** *De toverlantaarn* (1942); *Tornooi* (1953). **ORCH.:** Chamber Sym. (1932); *Pietà* (1933); *Wilde jacht* (1933); *Ananke,* overture (1934); *Lentewandeling* (1935); *Humoresque* (1936); *Het Land* (1937); *Impulsions* (1939); 4 syms. (1941, 1943, 1945, 1966); *Suite flamande* (1947); *De Nacht* (1956); Suite (1958); *Dansende beeldekens* (1959); *3 Constructions* for Strings (1959); Sinfonietta (1968). **CHAMBER:** 2 string quartets (1929, 1941); Trio for Oboe, Clarinet, and Bassoon (1930); Quintet for Flute, Oboe, Violin, Viola, and Cello (1954); *Étude* for Alto and Wind Quintet (1958); Quartet for 4 Saxophones (1960); Brass Quartet (1964). **VOCAL:** *In the Beginning Was the Word* for Baritone and Orch. (1962).—**NS/LK/DM**

Albert, Stephen (Joel), distinguished American composer and teacher; b. N.Y., Feb. 6, 1941; d. in an automobile accident in Truro, Mass., Dec. 27, 1992. He studied piano, horn, and trumpet in his youth. He received training in composition from Siegmeister in Great Neck, N.Y. (1956–58), from Milhaud at the Aspen (Colo.) School of Music (summer, 1958), and from Rogers at the Eastman School of Music in Rochester, N.Y. (1958–60). After studies with Blomdahl in Stockholm, he pursued training with Castaldo at the Philadelphia Musical Academy (B.M., 1962) and with Rochberg at the Univ. of Pa. (1963). He received 2 Rome Prizes (1965, 1966) and 2 Guggenheim fellowships (1967–68; 1978–79). In 1967–68 he held a Ford Foundation grant as composer-in-residence of the Lima, Ohio, public schools and community orch. He taught at the Philadelphia Musical Academy (1968–70), Stanford Univ. (1970–71), Smith Coll. (1974–76), Boston Univ. (1981–84), and the Juilliard School in N.Y. (1988–92). In 1985 he was awarded the Pulitzer Prize in Music for his 1st sym., *RiverRun.* From 1985 to 1988 he was composer-in-residence of the Seattle Sym. Orch., and later of the Bowdoin (Maine) Summer Music Festival (1991–92). As a composer, Albert breathed life into traditional forms; his works are marked by expert craftsmanship, intensity, passion, and lyricism.

WORKS: ORCH.: *Bacchae Prologue* (1967); *Leaves from the Golden Notebook* (1970; Chicago, Dec. 2, 1971); *Voices Within* (Tanglewood, Aug. 14, 1975); 2 syms.: No. 1, *RiverRun* (1983–84; Washington, D.C., Jan. 17, 1985) and No. 2 (1992; N.Y., Nov. 10, 1994); *In Concordiam* for Violin and Orch. (Pittsburgh, Dec. 19, 1986; rev. 1988); *Anthem and Processionals* (Seattle, March 7, 1988); Cello Concerto (Baltimore, May 31, 1990); *Tapioca Pudding* (Baltimore, April 18, 1991); *Wind Canticle* for Clarinet and Orch. (Philadelphia, Oct. 17, 1991). **CHAMBER:** *Illuminations* for 2 Pianos, Brass, Harps, and Percussion (1962); *Imitations (after Bartók)* for String Quartet (1963); *Cathedral Music/Concerto for 4 Quartets* for 2 Amplified Flutes and 2 Amplified Cellos, of 2 Horns, Trumpet, and Trombone, of 2 Percussion, Amplified Harp, and Amplified Guitar, and of Electric Organ, Electric Piano, and 2 Pianos (1971–72); *Tribute* for Violin and Piano (Washington, D.C., Oct. 28, 1988). **VOCAL:** *Supernatural Songs* for Soprano and Orch. (1964); *Wedding Songs* for Soprano and Piano (1964); *Bacchae Canticles* for Narrator, Chorus, and Orch. (Lima, Ohio, May 1968); *Wolf Time* for Soprano, Orch., and Amplified Instruments (1968–69; Seattle, Dec. 3, 1970); *To Wake the Dead* for Soprano, Flute, Clarinet, Harmonium, Piano, Violin, and Cello (Geneseo, N.Y., Nov. 28, 1978); *Into Eclipse* for Tenor and 13 Instrumentalists (1981; Washington, D.C., March 7, 1982; also for Tenor and Orch., Seattle, Sept. 8, 1986); *TreeStone* for Soprano, Tenor, and 12 Instrumentalists (1983–84; N.Y., Jan. 16, 1985; also for Soprano, Tenor, and Orch., N.Y., May 13, 1989); *Flower of the Mountain* for Soprano and Orch. (1985; N.Y., May 17, 1986); *The Stone Harp* for Tenor, Timpani, and Harp (N.Y., Feb. 18, 1988; withdrawn; rev. for Soprano or Tenor, Percussion, Harp, 2 Violas, and 2 Cellos, N.Y., March 7, 1989); *Distant Hills* for Soprano, Tenor, and 11 Instrumentalists (1989; N.Y., April 27, 1990; also for Soprano, Tenor, and Orch., N.Y., Feb. 8, 1992); *Sun's Heat* for Tenor and 11 Instrumentalists (1989; N.Y., April 27, 1990; also for Tenor and Orch., N.Y., Feb. 8, 1992); *Rilke Song* for Soprano, Flute, Clarinet, Violin, Cello, and Piano (N.Y., March 7, 1991); *Ecce Puer* for Soprano, Oboe, Horn, and Piano (Philadelphia, April 11, 1992).

BIBL.: M. Humphrey, *S. A.* (N.Y., 1993).—**NS/LK/DM**

Alberti, Domenico, Italian singer, harpsichordist, and composer; b. Venice, c. 1710; d. Rome, Oct. 14, 1746. He was a student of Biffi and Lotti. In 1736 he went as a page to Spain in the retinue of the Venetian ambassador, and won the approbation of Farinelli for his vocal artistry. He settled in Rome in the service of Marquis Molinari. Alberti is the reputed originator of the arpeggio style of keyboard accompaniment known as the "Alberti Bass." His vol. of 8 sonatas, publ. as op.1 (London, 1748), gives many illustrations of this device. A total of 14 complete sonatas and 10 movements from other sonatas are extant, which demonstrate his adept handling of the gallant style. He also wrote at least three operas.—**NS/LK/DM**

Alberti, Gasparo, Italian composer; b. Padua, c. 1480; d. Bergamo, c. 1560. He was active mainly in Bergamo, where he became a singer at S. Maria Maggiore in 1508 and later served as its maestro di cappella until 1554. He composed sacred music, including 5 masses, 2 Magnificats for Double Choir, 3 dramatic Passions, Psalms, Lamentations, and canticles. —**NS/LK/DM**

Alberti, Giuseppe Matteo, Italian violinist and composer; b. Bologna, Sept. 20, 1685; d. there, Feb. 18, 1751. He studied violin with C. Manzolini and P. M. Minelli, and took lessons in counterpoint with F. Arresti; then played violin in the orch. of S. Petronio in Bologna; he was also a member of the Accademia Filarmonica there, and was its president from 1721. He composed violin concertos, sonatas, sinfonias, and vocal works, several of which were publ. in his lifetime.—**NS/LK/DM**

Alberti, Johann Friedrich, German organist and composer; b. Tonning, Schleswig, Jan. 11, 1642; d. Merseburg, June 14, 1710. He studied theology in Rostock, and jurisprudence at the Univ. of Leipzig; also took courses in music with Werner Fabricius and Vincenzo Albrici. He spent most of his life as cathedral organist in Merseburg. Some of his chorales, publ. in modern eds., testify to his aptitude.—**NS/LK/DM**

Albertini, Joachim (actually, **Gioacchino**), Italian-born Polish composer; b. Pesaro, 1749; d. Warsaw, March 27, 1812. He was a conductor to Prince Karol Radziwill in Neiswiez, later serving as maitre de chapelle to King Stanislaw August Poniatowski in Warsaw (from 1782). In 1795 he received Poland's life pension.

WORKS: DRAMATIC: *La Cacciatrice brillante*, intermezzo (Rome, Feb. 1772); *Don Juan albo Ukarany libertyn* (Don Juan or The Rake Punished), opera (Warsaw, Feb. 23, 1783); *Virginia*, opera seria (Rome, Jan. 7, 1786); *Circe und Ulisses*, opera seria (Hamburg, Jan. 30, 1786); *Scipione Africano*, opera seria (Rome, 1789); *La Virgine vestale*, opera seria (Rome, Carnival, 1803); *Kapelmajster polski* (Polish Kapellmeister), intermezzo (Warsaw, Oct. 28, 1808). OTHER: Sym. (c. 1797); masses and other sacred works.—**NS/LK/DM**

Albertsen, Per Hjort, Norwegian organist and composer; b. Trondheim, July 27, 1919. He studied organ at the Oslo Cons., graduating in 1946; took lessons in composition with Sven Erik Tarp in Copenhagen, Ralph Downes in London, and Hanns Jelinek in Vienna. He was an organist in Trondheim (1947–68); then lectured in the music dept. of the univ. there (1968–72). Much of his music has been written for student performance.

WORKS: DRAMATIC: S c h o o l O p e r a : *Russicola* (1956). ORCH.: Flute Concertino (1948); *Symphonic Prelude* (1951); *Gunnerus Suite* for Strings (1952); *Little Suite* for Strings (1955); *Presentation*, overture (1958); *Notturno e Danza* (1960); *Concerto piccolo* for Violin or Clarinet and Amateur Strings (1961); Concerto for Piano and School Orch. (1969); *Tordenskioldiana* (1972). CHAMBER: Clarinet Sonatina (1950); *4 Religious Folksongs* for Violin, Cello, and Organ (1974); Suite for String Quartet (1984); Violin Sonatine (1985); piano pieces; organ music. VOCAL: 2 folk ballads: *Villemann og Magnill* for Soprano, Baritone, Men's Chorus, and Orch. (1951); *Bendik og Årolilja* for Tenor, Chorus, and Piano (1943; orch. 1979). —**NS/LK/DM**

Albicastro, Henricus (real name, **Heinrich Weissenburg**), Swiss violinist and composer; b. c. 1670; d. Netherlands, c. 1738. He was a cavalry captain in the War of the Spanish Succession, and then settled in the Netherlands. He publ. 9 vols. of chamber music (Amsterdam, from c. 1700), including several fine duo, trio, and quartet sonatas for Strings and Basso Continuo.—**NS/LK/DM**

Albinoni, Tomaso Giovanni, esteemed Italian composer; b. Venice, June 8, 1671; d. there, Jan. 17, 1751. He was the son of a wealthy paper merchant. Although apprenticed to his father, he also received training in violin, singing, and composition. The lure of music led him to pursue the career of a dilettante (in the best sense of the word) composer. He first attracted attention with the premiere of his first opera, *Zenobia, Regina de' Palmireni*, in Venice in 1694. It was also in that year that his 12 trio sonatas, op.1, were publ. in Venice. In succeeding years, he produced an extensive output of secular vocal works and instrumental music. In 1705 he married the soprano Margherita Raimondi, known as "La Salarina," who pursued an intermittent operatic career until her death in 1721. In 1722 Albinoni was called to Munich to oversee the premiere of his opera *I veri amici*, composed for the marriage of the Prince-elector Karl Albert to Maria Amalia, the daughter of the late Emperor Joseph I. Thereafter his operas were performed widely abroad, complementing the extensive dissemination of his instrumental music. Although a lesser master than such contemporaries as Bach, Handel, and Vivaldi, Albinoni developed an individual style marked by fine craftsmanship in which his melodic talent served him exceedingly well. Bach admired his music and composed 4 keyboard fugues on the Italian's op.1. For his instrumental output, see W. Kolneder, ed., *T. G. A.: Gesamtausgabe der Instrumentalmusik* (Berg, 1974 et seq.)

WORKS: DRAMATIC: O p e r a : Albinoni claimed to have written 80 operas, but his count may have included rev. versions and pasticcios. Of the 50 operas generally attributed to him, only three are extant in full: *Zenobia, Regina de' Palmireni* (Venice, 1694), *Engelberta* (Venice, 1709; in collaboration with Gasparini), and *La Statira* (Rome, 1726); arias from some of his other operas are also extant. He also wrote 3 comic intermezzos, of which *Vespetta e Pimpinone* (Venice, 1708) is extant, and 3 serenatas, of which *Il nascimento dell'aurora* (c. 1710) and *Il nome glorioso in terra, santificato in cielo* (Venice, Nov. 4, 1724) are extant. ORCH.: (6) *Sinfonie e* [6] *concerti a cinque* for 2 to 3 Violins, 2 Violas, Cello, and Basso Continuo, op.2 (Venice, 1700); (12) *Concerti a cinque* for 3 Violins, 2 Violas, Cello, and Basso Continuo, op.5 (Venice, 1707); (12) *Concerti a cinque* for 1 to 2 Oboes, 2 Violins, Viola, Cello, and Basso Continuo, op.7 (Amsterdam, 1715); (12) *Concerti a cinque* for 1 to 2 Oboes, 2 to 3 Violins, Viola, Cello, and Basso Continuo, op.9 (Amsterdam, 1722); (12) *Concerti a cinque* for 3 Violins, Viola, Cello, and Basso Continuo, op.10 (Amsterdam, c. 1735–36); several sinfonias and violin concertos. CHAMBER: (12) *Suonate a tre* for 2 Violins, Cello, and Harpsichord, op.1 (Venice, 1694); (12) *Balleti a tre* for 2 Violins, Cello, and Harpsichord, op.3 (Venice, 1701); (6) *Sonate da chiesa* for Violin and Cello or Basso Continuo (Amsterdam, c. 1709; later publ. as op.4); (12) *Trattenimenti armonici per camera* for Violin, Violone, and Harpsichord, op.6 (Amsterdam, c. 1712); (5) *Sonate* for Violin and Basso Continuo *...e uno suario o capriccio...del sig. Tibaldi* (Amsterdam, c. 1717); (6) *Balleti e* (6) *sonate a tre* for 2 Violins, Cello, and Harpsichord, *con le sue fughe tirate à canone*, op.8 (Amsterdam, 1722); *6 sonates da camera* for Violin and Harpsichord, op. posthumous (Paris, c. 1740); also

(6) *Sonate a tre* for 2 Violins, Cello, and Harpsichord (n.d.) and a Violin Sonata (n.d.). **VOCAL: Oratorios:** *Trionfi di Giosuè* (pasticcio; Florence, 1703); *Maria annunziata* (Florence, 1712). **Sacred:** *Messa a tre voci* (n.d.). **Solo Cantatas:** 48, including (12) *Cantate* for Voice and Basso Continuo, op.4 (Amsterdam, 1702).

BIBL.: R. Giazotto, *T. A.: "musico di violini dilettante vento" (1671–1750)* (Milan, 1945); idem, *T. A.* (Brescia, 1953); M. Talbot, *The Instrumental Music of T. A.* (diss., Univ. of Cambridge, 1968); idem, *A: Leben und Werk* (Adliswil, 1980); C. Guaita, *Le cantate di T. A. (1671–1751): Studio storico-critico e bibliografico* (diss., Univ. of Milan, 1986); M. Talbot, *T. A.: The Venetian Composer and His World* (Oxford, 1990).—**NS/LK/DM**

Alboni, Marietta (actually, **Maria Anna Marzia**), famous Italian contralto; b. Città de Castello, March 6, 1823; d. Ville d'Avray, France, June 23, 1894. She studied with Mombelli, Bertinotti, and Rossini. On Oct. 3, 1842, she made her operatic debut as Climene in Pacini's *Saffo* in Bologna. On Dec. 30, 1842, she made her first appearance at Milan's La Scala in Rossini's *Assedio de Corinto*. In 1843 she sang to acclaim in Vienna, and in 1844–45 with great success in St. Petersburg. After highly successful engagements in other cities on the Continent, she went to London to open the first season of the Royal Italian Opera at Covent Garden as Arsace in *Semiramide* on April 6, 1847. In Oct. 1847 she gave 4 "concerts-spectacles" in Paris, returning there on Dec. 2 to make her debut as Arsace at the Théâtre-Italien. In 1848 she returned to London, where she became a rival to Jenny Lind. She continued to make appearances in London until 1858. From June 1852 to May 1853 she toured the U.S. in concert and opera. Due to obesity, she gradually withdrew from operatic appearances after 1863. In 1872 she sang for the last time in opera at the Théâtre-Italien. She subsequently gave occasional concerts seated in a large chair. Her exceptional vocal range extended from contralto G to high soprano C.

BIBL.: A Pougin, *M. A.* (Paris, 1912).—**NS/LK/DM**

Albrecht, family of German-Russian musicians:

(1) Karl (Franz) Albrecht, conductor and composer; b. Posen, Aug. 27, 1807; d. Gatchina, near St. Petersburg, March 8, 1863. He studied harmony and counterpoint with Josef Schnabel in Breslau, and also learned to play string and wind instruments. In 1825 he became 1st violinist in the Breslau Theater orch. He went to Düsseldorf as répétiteur at the Opera in 1835. After conducting his own traveling opera troupe, he went to St. Petersburg in 1838 as conductor of the theater orch. He conducted the German Opera until serving as conductor of the Russian Opera from 1840 to 1850. On Dec. 9, 1842, Albrecht conducted the premiere of Glinka's *Ruslan and Ludmila* there. In 1850 he became a teacher at the orphanage in Gatchina. Among his compositions were the ballet *Der Berggeist* (1825), 3 string quartets, a Mass, and some vocal pieces. His 3 sons were musicians:

(2) Konstantin (Karl) Albrecht, cellist and teacher; b. Elberfeld, Oct. 4, 1835; d. Moscow, June 26, 1893. He studied with his father. After settling in Moscow, he became cellist in the orch. of the Bolshoi Theater. In 1860

he helped his close friend N. Rubinstein organize the Russian Musical Soc. and the Moscow Cons., where he was on the faculty from 1866 to 1889. In 1878 he founded the Moscow Choral Soc. He also was a close friend of Tchaikovsky, whose *Serenade* for Strings was dedicated to Albrecht. He publ. a guide to choral singing (Moscow, 1866; 2nd ed., rev., 1885) and a thematic catalogue of Glinka's ballads, songs, and operas (Moscow, 1891).

(3) Eugen (Maria) Albrecht, violinist and teacher; b. St. Petersburg, July 16, 1842; d. there, Feb. 9, 1894. He was a student of David (violin), Hauptmann (composition), and Karl Brendel (music history) at the Leipzig Cons. (1857–60). Upon his return to St. Petersburg, he was a violinist in the orch. of the Italian Opera from 1860 to 1877. He also was 2nd violin in the quartet of the St. Petersburg branch of the Russian Musical Soc. from 1862 to 1887. In 1877 he became inspector of music of the St. Petersburg theaters and in 1892 librarian of the city's Central Music Library.

(4) Ludwig (Karl) Albrecht, cellist and composer; b. St. Petersburg, May 27, 1844; d. Saratov, 1899. He was a student of Karl Davidov at the St. Petersburg Cons. (graduated, 1865). After teaching at the Moscow Cons. (1878–89), he settled in Saratov. He wrote a cello tutor (2 vols., Moscow, n.d.) and some cello pieces.—**NS/LK/DM**

Albrecht, Alexander, Slovak composer, conductor, and pedagogue; b. Arad, Hungary, Aug. 12, 1885; d. Bratislava, July 30, 1958. He was a student at the Budapest Academy of Music (1904–08) of Koessler (composition), Thomán and Bartók (piano), Szandtner (conducting), and Popper (chamber music), and then in Vienna of Dittrich (organ). After settling in Bratislava, he was active as a conductor and served as director of the church music soc. (1921–52); also was director of the music school. His early works were composed in a late Romantic vein but he later pursued more adventuresome paths.

WORKS: ORCH.: *Scherzo: Humoreske* (1907); *Dornröschen,* symphonic poem (1921); *Symphony in 1 Movement* (1929); *Tobias Wunderlich: Túžby a spomienky* (Desires and Memories), symphonic poem (1935); *Variations* for Trumpet and Orch. (1946; also for Trumpet and Piano); *Scherzo* for Strings (1949; also for String Quartet). **CHAMBER:** Piano Trio (1907); String Quintet (1908); Piano Quintet (1913); String Quartet (1918); Sonatine for 11 Instruments (1925); *Quintetto frammento* for Winds and Piano (1929); Trio for 2 Violins and Viola (1943); *Präludium und Fuge* for Viola and Cello (1950); *Die Nacht* for Cello and Piano (1950); Suite Concertante for Viola and Piano (1952); *Weihnachten* for String Quartet (1956); 6 Pieces for String Trio (1957); piano pieces, including a Sonata (1905) and a Suite (1924); organ music. **VOCAL:** *Mass* (1902); *Drei Gedichte aus dem Marienleben* for Soprano, Chorus, and Orch. (1928); *Cantate Domino* for Chorus and Orch. (1938); *Šuhajko,* cantata on Slovakian Folk Songs for Chorus and Orch. (1950); choruses; songs.

BIBL.: F. Klinda, *A. A.* (Bratislava, 1959).—**NS/LK/DM**

Albrecht, George Alexander, German conductor; b. Bremen, Feb. 15, 1935. He received his training from Hermann Grevesmühl (1942–54), Paul van Kempen at the Accademia Musicale Chigiana in Siena and in Hilversum (1954–55), and Rudolf Hindemith (1956–58). In 1961 he was named to the position of 1st conductor of the Hannover State Opera, where he subsequently was its Generalmusikdirektor from 1964 to 1993. He also was a prof. at the Hannover Hochschule für Musik from 1980 to 1993. In 1993 he became chief conductor of the Philharmonia Hungarica in Marl kreis Recklinghausen and a guest conductor at the Dresden State Opera. He then became Generalmusikdirektor of the National Theater and the State Orch. in Weimar in 1996. In 1997 he also was made a prof. at the Franz Liszt Hochschule für Musik in Weimar. In 1989 he was awarded the Gustav Mahler Gold Medal and in 1996 the Bundesverdienstkreuz of the Federal Republic of Germany. As a guest conductor, he appeared with opera houses in Vienna, Barcelona, Bologna, Trieste, Rome, Turin, Venice, and Madrid. He also was a guest conductor of the Berlin Phil., the Munich Phil., the Dresden State Orch., the Gewandhaus Orch. in Leipzig, the Czech Phil. in Prague, the NHK Sym. Orch. in Tokyo, and all of the German radio orchs.—**LK/DM**

Albrecht, Gerd, German conductor, son of **Hans Albrecht;** b. Essen, July 19, 1935. He studied conducting with Brückner-Rüggeberg at the Hamburg Hochschule für Musik and musicology at the univs. of Kiel and Hamburg. After winning the Besançon (1957) and Hilversum (1958) conducting competitions, he conducted at the Württemberg State Theater in Stuttgart (1958–61). He was 1st conductor in Mainz (1961–63), and then Generalmusikdirektor in Lübeck (1963–66) and Kassel (1966–72). From 1972 to 1979 he was chief conductor of the Deutsche Oper in West Berlin and of the Tonhalle Orch. in Zürich from 1975 to 1980. From 1976 he was a guest conductor at the Vienna State Opera. In 1981 he made his U.S. debut conducting the U.S. premiere of Reimann's *Lear* at the San Francisco Opera. In 1986 he made his first appearance as a sym. conductor in the U.S. when he led a guest engagement with the Houston Sym. Orch. He served as chief conductor of the Hamburg State Opera and the Phil. State Orch. from 1988 to 1997. From 1994 to 1996 he was chief conductor of the Czech Phil. in Prague. He was chief conductor of the Yomiuri Nippon Sym. Orch. in Tokyo from 1998 and of the Danish National Radio Sym. Orch. in Copenhagen from 2000.

WRITINGS: *Wie eine Opernaufführung zustande kommt* (Zürich, 1988).—**NS/LK/DM**

Albrecht, Hans, German musicologist, father of **Gerd Albrecht;** b. Magdeburg, March 31, 1902; d. Kiel, Jan. 20, 1961. He studied at the Essen Cons., the Univ. of Münster, and with Wolf, Abert, Sachs, and Hornbostel at the Univ. of Berlin (Ph.D., 1925, with the diss. *Die Aufführungspraxis der italienischen Musik des 14. Jahrhunderts;* completed his Habilitation there, 1942, with his *Caspar Othmayr: Leben und Werk;* publ. in Kassel, 1950). He taught at the Essen Cons. (1925–37). In 1939 he joined the Staatliche Inst. für Deutsche Musikforschung in Berlin, where he was a prof. (from 1940) and its director (from 1941). In 1947 he became director of the Landesinstitut für Musikforschung in Kiel; also taught at the Univ. of Kiel, where he became a prof. in 1955. He was ed. of *Die Musikforschung* (1948–60) and *Acta Musicologica* (1957–60).

BIBL.: W. Brennecke and H. Haase, eds., *H. A. in Memoriam* (Kassel, 1962).—**NS/LK/DM**

Albrecht, Johann Lorenz, German writer on music and composer; b. Görmar, near Mühlhausen, Jan. 8, 1732; d. Mühlhausen, Nov. 29, 1768. He was educated in Leipzig, then pursued his career in Mühlhausen, where he served as Kantor and music director of the Marienkirche. Among his compositions were a Passion, various cantatas, and keyboard and vocal pieces for students. His writings included *Gründliche Einleitung in die Anfangslehren der Tonkust: Zum Gebrauche musikalischer Lehrstunden...nebst...einem kurzen Abrisse einer musikalischen Bibliothek* (Langensalza, 1761), *Gedanken eines thüringischen Tonkünstler über die Streitigkeit welche der Herr...Sorge wider den Herrn...Marpurg...erreget hat* (n.p., 1761), *Abhandlung über die Frage, ob die Musik bey dem Gottesdienst zu dulden oder nicht* (Berlin, 1764), and *Versuch einer Abhandlung von der Ursachen des Hasses, welche einige Menschen gegen die Musik von sich Blicken* (Frankenhausen, 1765).—**NS/LK/DM**

Albrecht, Otto Edwin, eminent American musicologist; b. Philadelphia, July 8, 1899; d. there, July 6, 1984. He studied at the Univ. of Pa. (A.B., 1921; M.A., 1925; Ph.D., 1931, with the diss. *Four Latin Plays of St. Nicholas from the 12th Century Fleury Play-book;* publ. in Philadelphia and London, 1935), where he was an instructor in French (1923–38) and curator of its Music Library (from 1937); from 1938 he was also a lecturer in its music dept. He retired in 1970 and was made emeritus prof. of music.

WRITINGS: *A Census of Autograph Music Manuscripts of European Composers in American Libraries* (Philadelphia, 1953); *The Mary Flagler Cary Music Collection* (N.Y., 1970).

BIBL.: J. Hill, ed., *Studies in Musicology in Honor of O. E. A.* (Kassel, 1977; Clifton, N.J., 1980).—**NS/LK/DM**

Albrechtsberger, Johann Georg, famous Austrian organist, music theorist, pedagogue, and composer; b. Klosterneuburg, near Vienna, Feb. 3, 1736; d. Vienna, March 7, 1809. He studied organ and figured bass with Leopold Pittner, the dean of the Augustinians in Klosterneuburg, then was a choirboy at the Melk Abbey (1749–54), where he received instruction in organ and composition from Marian Gurtler, its regens chori, and from Joseph Weiss, its organist; he subsequently spent a year in Vienna at the Jesuit seminary before commencing his career as an organist in small towns. He was organist in Melk (1759–65), during which period his outstanding playing brought him to the attention of Emperor Joseph. In 1772 he was called to Vienna to serve as regens chori to the Carmelites; in 1791 he became asst. Kapellmeister at St. Stephen's Cathedral, and in 1793, Kapellmeister, holding the position with great distinction. In addition to his renown as an organist, he was widely esteemed as a teacher of composition. Haydn sent Beethoven to him for study in 1794–95. His important theoretical writings include

Gründliche Anweisung zur Composition... (Leipzig, 1790; 3rd ed., aug., 1821; Eng. tr., 1844), *Kurzgefaste Methode, den Generalbass zu erlernen* (Vienna, c. 1791; 2nd ed., aug., 1792; Eng. tr., 1815), and *Clavierschule für Anfänger* (Vienna, c. 1800). For his complete writings, see I. von Seyfried, ed., *Johann Georg Albrechtsbergers sämmtliche Schriften über Generalbass, Harmonie- Lehre, und Tonsetzkunst* (Vienna, 1826; 2nd ed., 1837; Eng. tr., 1834). He was a prolific composer; his sacred music includes 35 masses, 48 graduals, 42 offertories, and 6 oratorios; his secular works include numerous quintets, quartets, and trios. For his instrumental works, see F. Brodsky and O. Biba, eds., *Johann Georg Albrechtsberger: Instrumentalwerke in Documenta Musicologica* (1968–75).

BIBL.: O. Kappelmacher, *J.G. A.: Sein Leben und seine Instrumentalwerke* (diss., Univ. of Vienna, 1907); G. Uebele, *J.G. A., der Theoretiker* (diss., Univ. of Vienna, 1932); A. Schramek-Kirchner, *J.G. A.s Fugenkompositionen in seinen Werken für Tasteninstrumente* (diss., Univ. of Vienna, 1954); U. Thomson, *Voraussetzungen und Artung der österreichischen Generalbasslehre zwischen A. und Sechter* (diss., Univ. of Vienna, 1960); R. Harpster, *The String Quartets of J.G. A.* (diss., Univ. of Southern Calif., 1975); E. Paul, *J.G. A.: Ein Klosterneuburger Meister der Musik und seine Schule* (Klosterneuburg, 1976); D. Schröder, *Die geistlichen Vokalkompositionen J.G. A.s* (2 vols., Hamburg, 1987); A. Weinmann, *J.G. A.: Thematischer Katalog seiner weltlichen Kompositionen* (Vienna, 1987).—NS/LK/DM

Albrici, Vincenzo, Italian organist, harpsichordist, and composer; b. Rome, June 26, 1631; d. Prague, Aug. 8, 1696. He was the son of Domenico Albrici, an alto singer. He began his career in Rome as a boy soprano at the Collegio Germania under his mentor Carissimi (1641–46), and then was organist and maestro di cappella at the Chiesa Nuovo. In 1652–53 he was at the Swedish court of Queen Christina. He became joint vice-Kapellmeister with Bontempi under Schütz at the Dresden electoral court in 1654. In 1658 he was again in the service of Queen Christina, this time in Rome. In 1662 he returned to Dresden, but in 1664 he went to London and was active at the court of King Charles II. In 1668 he returned to Dresden, where he was made director of Italian music at the electoral court in 1676. Following the dismissal of the Italian musicians in 1680, he became a Protestant and obtained the position of organist at the Thomaskirche in Leipzig in 1681. However, he went to Prague in 1682 to serve as director of music at St. Augustin. Among his works were Latin motets for voices and instruments, Italian solo cantatas, and some other vocal pieces. His brother, Bartolomeo Albrici (b. c. 1640; d. 1687), was an organist, teacher, and composer. He was active at the Swedish court of Queen Christina in 1652–53, and then was organist at the Dresden electoral court from 1654 to 1666, when he settled in London. He publ. a vol. of harpsichord music (1679).—NS/LK/DM

Albright, William (Hugh), American pianist, organist, teacher, and composer; b. Gary, Ind., Oct. 20, 1944; d. Ann Arbor, Sept. 17, 1998. He studied with Rosetta Goodkind (piano) and Hugh Aitken (theory) at the Juilliard Preparatory Dept. in N.Y. (1959–62), and then was a student in composition of Finney and Bassett and in organ of Marilyn Mason at the Univ. of Mich. (1963–70). He also received training from Rochberg, and in Paris with Messiaen at the Cons. (1968) and privately with Max Deutsch. Albright taught at the Univ. of Mich. from 1970, where he was a prof. of music from 1982. He also served as assoc. director of its electronic music studio. In 1979 he was composer-in-residence at the American Academy in Rome, in 1993 he received the Composer of the Year Award from the American Guild of Organists, and in 1995 he won the Richard Wagner Center for Choral Studies Competition. He pursued an active career as a pianist and organist, excelling in ragtime, jazz, and contemporary works. In his compositions, he pursued quaquaversal methods of experimental music, using varied techniques according to need.

WORKS: MULTIMEDIA AND DRAMATIC: *Tic* for Soloist, 2 Jazz-rock Improvisation Ensembles, Tape, and Film (1967); *Beulahland Rag* for Narrator, Jazz Quartet, Improvisation Ensemble, Tape, Film, and Slides (1967–69); *Cross of Gold*, music theater for Actors, Chorus, Saxophone, Trombone, Double Bass, Percussion, and Electric Organ (1975); *Full Moon in March*, 5 songs and incidental music to a play by Yeats (1978; Ann Arbor, Jan. 13, 1979). **ORCH.:** *Alliance*, suite (1967–70); *Night Procession* for Chamber Orch. (1972); *Gothic Suite* for Organ, Strings, and Percussion (1973); *Heater* for Saxophone and Symphonic Band (1977); *Bacchanal* for Organ and Orch. (Lincoln, Nebr., Nov. 16, 1981); *Chasm: Symphonic Fragment* (1988); Concerto for Harpsichord and Strings (1991). **CHAMBER:** *Foils* for Winds and Percussion (1963); *Frescoes* for Wind Quartet (1964); *Salvos* for 7 Instruments (1964); *Caroms* for 8 Instruments (1966); *Amerithon* for Variable Ensemble (1966–67); *Marginal Worlds* for Ensemble (1969); *Danse Macabre* for Violin, Cello, Flute, Clarinet, and Piano (1971); *Take That* for 4 Drummers (1972); *Stipendium Peccati* for Organ, Piano, and Percussion (1973); *7 Deadly Sins* for Optional Narrator, Flute, Clarinet, String Quartet, and Piano (1974); *Introduction, Passacaglia, and Rondo Capriccioso* for Tack Piano and Winds (1974); *Dream and Dance* for Organ and Percussion (1974); *Doo-Dah* for 3 Alto Saxophones (1975); *Peace Pipe* for 2 Bassoons (1976); *Saints Preserve Us* for Clarinet (1976); *Jericho, Battle Music* for Trumpet and Organ (1976); *Shadows* for Guitar (1977); *Halo* for Organ and Metal Percussion Instruments (1978); *4 Fancies* for Harpsichord (1979); *Romance* for Horn and Organ (1981); *Enigma Syncopations* for Flute, Organ, Double Bass, and Percussion (1982); *Brass Tacks*, rag march for Brass Quintet (1983); Saxophone Sonata (1984); *Canon in D (Berimbau!)* for Contrabass and Harpsichord (1984); *3 New Chestnuts* for 2 Harpsichords or Harpsichord and Tape (1986); Clarinet Quintet (1987); *Abiding Passions* for Woodwind Quintet (1988); *The Great Amen* for Flute and Piano (1992); *Pit Band* for Alto Saxophone, Bass Clarinet, and Piano (1993); *Fantasy- Études* for Saxophone Quartet (1993–94); *Rustles of Spring, 1994* for Flute, Alto Saxophone, Violin, Cello, and Piano (1994); *Fantasy Etudes* for Saxophone Quartet (1995). **KEYBOARD: P i a n o :** *9 Pieces* (1962); *Pianoagogo* (1965–66); *3 Orginal Rags* (1967–68); *Grand Sonata in Rag* (1968); *3 Novelty Rags* (1969); *Dream Rags* (1970); *Sweet Sixteenths* (1975); *5 Chromatic Dances* (1976); *Sphaera* (1985); *Stoptime for George* for George Rochberg's 70th birthday (1987); *4 Dance Tributes* (1987–96); *The Machine Age: A Set of Short Piano Pieces for our Time* (1988); *New Leaves* (1991); *Ragtime Lullabye* (1991). **O r g a n :** *Juba* (1965); *3 Organbooks: I* (1967), *II*, with Tape (1971), and *III*, subtitled *12 Études* (1977–78); *King of Instruments*, "Parade of Music and Verse" with Narrator (1978); *De spiritum* (1980–81); *That Sinking Feeling*

(1982); *In Memoriam* (1983); *1732: Im Memoriam Johannes Albrecht*, "program sonata" (1984); *Carillon- Bombarde* (1985); *Chasm*, with optional "echo" instrument or tape (1985); Sym. with Percussion or Tape (1986); *Whistler Nocturnes* (1989); *Flights of Fancy* (1992); *Chorale Prelude for Advent on Nun Komm her Heiden Heiland* (1997); *Cod Piece* (1998). **VOCAL:** *Mass in D* for Chorus, Organ, Percussion, and Congregation (1974); *Chichester Mass* for Chorus (1974); *Pax in Terra* for Soprano, Tenor, and Chorus (1981); *David's Songs* for Chorus (1982); *A Song to David*, oratorio (Minneapolis, Nov. 1, 1983); *Take Up the Song* for Soprano, Chorus, and Piano (1986); *Antigone's Reply* for Chorus and Piano (1987); *Deum de Deo* for Chorus and Organ (1989); *Dona Nobis Pacem* for Chorus and Piano (1992); *Missa Brevis* for Soprano and Organ (1996).—**NS/LK/DM**

Alcaide, Tomáz (de Aquino Carmelo), Portuguese tenor; b. Estremoz, Feb. 16, 1901; d. Lisbon, Nov. 9, 1967. He studied at the Univ. of Coimbra; took voice lessons in Lisbon, and later in Milan. In 1925 he made his operatic debut at the Teatro Carcano in Milan as Wilhelm Meister in *Mignon*. He subsequently sang principal roles in Italian and French operas at La Scala in Milan, the Paris Opéra, the Vienna State Opera, the Salzburg Festival, and the Rome Opera; also made concert tours of Europe and the U.S. After his retirement from the stage in 1948, he settled in Lisbon. He wrote an autobiography, *Um cantor no palco e na vida* (Lisbon, 1961).—**NS/LK/DM**

Alcántara, Theo, Spanish-born American conductor; b. Cuenca, April 16, 1941. He obtained diplomas in piano and composition at the Madrid Cons., and in conducting at the Salzburg Mozarteum. After conducting at the Frankfurt am Main Opera (1964–66), he was director of the opera workshop and sym. orch. at the Univ. of Mich. (1967–74). From 1973 to 1978 he was music director of the Grand Rapids Sym. Orch., a position he also held with the Western Mich. Opera Assn. (1973–79). On May 27, 1978, he made his Metropolitan Opera debut in N.Y. conducting *Don Giovanni*. He was music director of the Phoenix Sym. Orch. from 1978 to 1989, and then served as its laureate conductor from 1989 to 1993. From 1981 to 1984 he also was artistic director of the Music Academy of the West in Santa Barbara. In 1987 he became principal conductor of the Pittsburgh Opera, and concurrently served as artistic director of the Caracas International Opera Festival (1990–93) and artistic director and principal conductor of the Bilbao Sym. Orch. (from 1993). He appeared as a guest conductor with various orchs. and opera companies in the U.S. and abroad.—**NS/LK/DM**

Alcock, John, English organist and composer; b. London, April 11, 1715; d. Lichfield, Feb. 23, 1806. He was a chorister at St. Paul's Cathedral in London and studied with John Stanley. He served as organist at St. Andrew's Church, Plymouth (1737–42), St. Laurence's Church, Reading (1742–50), and Lichfield Cathedral (1750–65), where he also was vicar-choral (1750–1806), Sutton Coldfield parish church, Warwickshire (1761–86), and Tamworth parish church (1766–90). In 1755 he took his B.Mus. and in 1766 his D.Mus. at Oxford. He wrote an opera, 6 concertos (1750), 6 harpsichord suites (1741), organ voluntaries (1774), liturgical works, anthems, catches, and canons. He also wrote a semi-autobiographical novel. His son, also named John Alcock (b. Plymouth [baptized], Jan. 28, 1740; d. Walsall [buried], March 27, 1791), was likewise an organist and composer. He wrote several anthems.—**NS/LK/DM**

Alcorn, Alvin (Elmore), jazz trumpeter; b. New Orleans, Sept. 7, 1912; d. there, 1981. Alcorn was taught musical theory by his sax-playing brother Oliver (born in 1910), then studied trumpet with George McCullum Jr. From around 1928 he played with violinist Clarence Desdune, led his own band, and worked with Armand Piron and with The Sunny South Syncopators (1931). He toured with Don Albert from 1932 until 1937, then returned to New Orleans to rejoin Armand Piron and others. Alcorn served in the army during World War II, after which he worked briefly with Tab Smith, Sidney Desvigne, Alphonse Picou, and others. In 1954 he went to Calif. with Octave Crosby, where he briefly performed with Kid Ory, and about a year later he rejoined Ory there, appeared with him in the film *The Benny Goodman Story*, and toured Europe with him in 1956. From 1958 on he resumed playing around New Orleans, while also working as an official of the local Musicians Union. He toured Europe on several occasions as a soloist in the 1970s, as well as with The New Orleans All Stars in 1966 and with Chris Barber in 1978.—**JC/LP**

Alda (real name, **Davies**), **Frances (Jeanne),** admired New Zealand-born American soprano; b. Christchurch, May 31, 1883; d. Venice, Sept. 18, 1952. She studied with Marchesi in Paris, where she made her operatic debut as Manon at the Opéra-Comique (April 15, 1904). She then appeared at the Théâtre Royal de la Monnaie in Brussels (1905–08), London's Covent Garden (debut as Louise, 1906), Milan's La Scala (1908), and Buenos Aires's Teatro Colón (from 1908). On Dec. 7, 1908, she made her Metropolitan Opera debut in N.Y. as Gilda, continuing on its roster until her farewell appearance as Manon Lescaut on Dec. 28, 1929. She also made appearances in Boston (1909–13) and Chicago (1914–15). From 1910 to 1928 she was married to **Giulio Gatti-Casazza**. In 1939 she became a naturalized American citizen. Among her other notable roles were Gounod's and Boito's Marguerite, Mimi, Nannetta, Desdemona, Violetta, and Aida.

WRITINGS: *Men, Women and Tenors* (autobiography; Boston, 1937).—**NS/LK/DM**

Aldenhoff, Bernd, German tenor; b. Duisburg, June 14, 1908; d. Munich, Oct. 8, 1959. He studied in Cologne, where he began his operatic career; then sang at the Düsseldorf Opera (1938–44), the Dresden State Opera (1944–52), the Bayreuth Festivals (1951–52; 1957), and the Bavarian State Opera in Munich (1952–59). On Feb. 25, 1955, he made his Metropolitan Opera debut in N.Y. as Tannhäuser. He was best known as a Wagnerian.—**NS/LK/DM**

Aldrich, Henry, English music scholar; b. Westminster, Jan. 1648; d. Oxford, Dec. 14, 1710. A man of versatile talents, excelling in music, he was also distinguished as an architect, theologian, linguist, and logician. He was educated at Christ Church, Oxford, receiving the degree of M.A. in 1669. In 1681 he became a canon, and in 1689, dean of Christ Church, and exercised decisive influence on the teaching of music and other arts. He wrote the learned works *On the Commencement of Greek Music, Theory of Organ- building*, and *Theory of Modern Instruments*. He composed several services (one of which, in G, is still sung); in a lighter vein, glees and catches (among them the popular *Catches on Tobacco*). The collections of Boyce, Arnold, and Page contain numerous pieces by Aldrich.

BIBL.: W. G. Hiscock, *H. A. of Christ Church* (Oxford, 1960). —NS/LK/DM

Aldrich, Putnam (Calder), American harpsichordist and pedagogue; b. South Swansea, Mass., July 14, 1904; d. Cannes, France, April 18, 1975. He studied at Yale Univ. (B.A., 1926), then took piano lessons with Matthay in London (1926–27) and harpsichord lessons with Landowska in Paris (1929–33). He then completed his education at Harvard Univ. (M.A., 1936; Ph.D., 1942). He toured as a harpsichordist, and also taught at the Univ. of Tex. (1942–44), Western Reserve Univ. (1946–48), Mills Coll. (1948–50), and Stanford Univ (1950–69). He publ. an important treatise, *Ornamentation in J. S. Bach's Organ Works* (N.Y., 1950), as part of a much larger and very valuable work on Baroque ornamentation, originally submitted as his doctoral diss. at Harvard; the work still awaits publication.

WRITINGS: *Ornamentation in J. S. Bach's Organ Works* (N.Y., 1950); *Rhythm in Seventeenth-century Italian Monody* (London, 1965).—NS/LK/DM

Aldrich, Richard, American music critic; b. Providence, July 31, 1863; d. Rome, June 2, 1937. He studied with Paine at Harvard Univ. (graduated, 1885), then was music critic of the *Providence Journal* (1885–89) and the *Evening Star* (1889–91). From 1891 to 1901 he was assistant to H. E. Krehbiel on the *N.Y. Tribune*, then was music ed. of the *N.Y. Times* (1902–23). A selection of his articles from the *Times* was publ. in *Musical Discourse* (1928) and in *Concert Life in New York, 1902–1923* (1941). He also wrote *Guide to Parsifal* (1904) and *Guide to the Ring of the Nibelung* (1905). His critical writings were urbane and witty; while liberal-minded in regard to milder types of modern music, he vehemently opposed extreme trends.—NS/LK/DM

Aldrovandini, Giuseppe (Antonio Vincenzo), Italian composer; b. Bologna, June 8, 1671; d. there (drowned), Feb. 9, 1707. He most likely was a pupil of Giacomo Perti. In 1695 he became a member of Bologna's Accademia Filarmonica, serving as its principe from 1702. While inebriated, he fell into a canal and drowned. He wrote 15 operas. For Bologna, he composed *Gl'inganni amorosi scoperti in villa* (Jan. 28, 1696), *Dafne* (Aug. 10, 1696), and *Amor torna in s'al so'...* (Carnival 1698), all significant works in the history of the opera buffa in that city. He also wrote instrumental music and a great many sacred works, among them six oratorios, cantatas, motets, etc., some of which were publ. during his lifetime.—NS/LK/DM

Alemán, Oscar (Marcelo), guitarist; b. Resistencia, Argentina, Feb. 20, 1909; d. Buenos Aires, Oct. 10, 1980. Alemán was one of the first guitarists to solo in melodic lines, like his contemporary Django Reinhardt. He made many fine recordings from March 1935 on, but is little known outside his homeland despite a residency in Paris between 1931 and 1940.—LP

d'Alembert, Jean-le-Rond, French philosopher and encyclopedist; b. Paris, Nov. 16, 1717; d. there, Oct. 29, 1783. He was the illegitimate child of one Mme. de Tencin and an artillery officer named Destouches; his mother abandoned him on the steps of the church of St. Jean-le-Rond, which name was subsequently attached to him. Later his father acknowledged him and enabled him to study. He was sent to the Mazarin Coll., and progressed rapidly in mathematics. He also was interested in theoretical musical subjects and published several treatises on acoustics and on the theory of music: *Recherches sur la courbe, que forme une corde tendue mise en vibration* (1749), *Recherches sur les vibrations des cordes sonores* and *Recherches sur la vitesse du son* (both in *Opuscules mathématiques*, Paris, 1761–80), *Reflexions sur la musique en général et sur la musique française en particulier* (1754), and *Reflexions sur la theorie de la musique* (1777). His best- known work on music was *Éléments de musique, théorique et pratique, suivant les principes de M. Rameau* (1752), which went into 6 eds. He contributed several articles on music to the famous *Encyclopédie*, which he ed. with Diderot.

BIBL.: J. Bertrand, *d'A.* (Paris, 1889).—NS/LK/DM

Alemshah, Kourkene, Armenian composer; b. Yerevan, May 22, 1907; d. Detroit, Dec. 14, 1947. He studied in Milan with Pizzetti (1924–30). In 1931 he settled in Paris. His music was strongly permeated with Armenian melos, and the settings were impressionistic. A memorial festival of his music was presented in Paris on Feb. 19, 1950. Among his compositions were the symphonic poems *Légende* (Paris, June 19, 1932) and *La Bataille d'Avarayr* (Paris, June 2, 1934); also *Danses populaires armeniennes* for Orch. (Paris, June 2, 1934). Alemshah died during an American tour, which he undertook as a choral conductor.—NS/LK/DM

Aleotti, Raffaella, Italian composer; b. Ferrara, c. 1570; d. after 1646. Her father was architect to Alfonso II d'Este, Duke of Ferrara. She received lessons in harpsichord and composition from Alessandro Milleville and Ercole Pasquini, and then entered the Augustinian convent of S. Vito in Ferrara, where she took her vows about 1590 and became director of its "concerto grande" about 1593. She publ. *Sacrae cantiones* for 5, 7 to 8, and 10 Voices (Venice, 1593). Her sister, Vittoria Aleotti (b. Ferrara, c. 1573; d. after 1620), was also a composer. After studies with Milleville and Pasquini, she took her vows at S. Vito, where she was closely associated with her sister. She publ. *Ghirlanda de madrigali* for 4 Voices (Venice, 1591).—LK/DM

Aler, John, American tenor; b. Baltimore, Oct. 4, 1949. He studied with Rilla Mervine and Raymond

McGuire at the Catholic Univ. of America in Washington, D.C. (M.M., 1972), with Oren Brown at the American Opera Center at the Juilliard School in N.Y. (1972–76), with Marlene Malas, and at the Berkshire Music Center at Tanglewood. In 1977 he made his operatic debut as Ernesto at the American Opera Center, the same year he won 1st prizes for men and for the interpretation of French art song at the Concours International de Chant in Paris. In 1979 he made his European operatic debut as Belmonte at the Théâtre Royal de la Monnaie in Brussels. He made his first appearance at London's Covent Garden as Ferrando in 1986. In 1988 he made his debut at the Salzburg Festival as Don Ottavio. In 1993 he sang at the London Promenade Concerts. He also sang in many other operatic centers and pursued a career as a concert and oratorio singer. —NS/LK/DM

Alessandrescu, Alfred, Romanian pianist, conductor, and composer; b. Bucharest, Aug. 14, 1893; d. there, Feb. 18, 1959. He studied piano and theory with Kiriac-Georgescu and Castaldi at the Bucharest Cons. (1903–11) and composition in Paris with d'Indy at the Schola Cantorum and with Vidal at the Cons. (1913–14). He was a conductor at the Opera (1921–59) and artistic director of the Radio Sym. Orch. (1933–59) in Bucharest. He also was active as a piano accompanist.

WORKS: *Amurg de toamn* (The Twilight of Autumn) for String Orch. (1910); symphonic poems: *Didona* (1911; Bucharest, March 10, 1913) and *Acteon* (Bucharest, Dec. 20, 1915); *Fantezie român* for Orch. (1913; Bacu, Sept. 22, 1978); Violin Sonata (1914); *Pièce pour quatuor à cordes* (1921); songs.

BIBL.: V. Tomescu, *A. A.* (Bucharest, 1962).—NS/LK/DM

Alessandri, Felice, Italian composer; b. probably in Rome, Nov. 24, 1747; d. Casinalbo, near Modena, Aug. 15, 1798. He received his training in Naples, and then began his career as a harpsichordist and conductor in Turin and Paris. About 1767 he married the singer Maria Lavinia Guadagni (b. Lodi, Nov. 21, 1735; d. Padua, c. 1790), the sister of **Gaetano Guadagni.** The couple found employment at the King's Theatre in London, where Alessandri's operas *La moglie fedele* (Feb. 27, 1768) and *Il re alla caccia* (March 1, 1769) were premiered. His opera *L'argentino* was first performed at the Burg Theatre in Vienna in 1768. He then composed several operas for Italian theaters, including *Calliroe* for the new Teatro alla Scala in Milan (Dec. 26, 1778). From 1784 to 1789 he was active in Russia as a singing teacher, and then was called to Berlin as asst. director of the court opera. However, the operas he wrote for Berlin were failures, and in 1792 he was dismissed by the king and he returned to Italy. His operas *Zemira* (Padua, June 12, 1794) and *Armida* (Padua, July 1, 1794) proved highly successful and led to his being made an honorary member of the Accademia dei Filarmonici of Modena.

WORKS: DRAMATIC: Opera: *Ezio* (Verona, Carnival 1767); *Il matrimonio per concorso* (Venice, Carnival 1767); *La moglie fedele* (London, Feb. 27, 1768); *L'argentino* (Vienna, 1768); *Arianna e Teseo* (London, Oct. 11, 1768); *Il re alla caccia* (London, March 1, 1769); *Argea* (Turin, Carnival 1773); *Creso* (Pavia, 1774); *La cameriera per amore* (Turin, 1774); *Medonte re d'Epiro* (Milan,

Dec. 26, 1774); *Alcina e Ruggero* (Turin, Carnival 1775); *La novità* (Venice, 1775); *La sposa persiana* (Venice, 1775); *Sandrina, ossia La contadina di corte* (Lucca, 1775); *Calliroe* (Milan, Dec. 26, 1778); *Adriano in Siria* (Venice, Dec. 26, 1779); *Erifile* (Padua, June 12, 1780); *Attalo re di Bitinia* (Florence, Sept. 1780); *Il vecchio geloso* (Milan, Oct. 1, 1781); *Arbace* (Rome, Dec. 29, 1781); *La finta principessa, ossia Li due fratelli Pappamosca* (Venice, 1782); *I puntigli gelosi* (Venice, Carnival 1783); *Demofoonte* (Padua, June 12, 1783); *Artaserse* (Naples, Nov. 4, 1783); *L'imbroglio delle tre spose* (Florence, 1784); *La villanella rapita* (Bologna, 1784); *Il ritorno di Ulysse a Penelope* (Potsdam, Jan. 25, 1790); *L'ouverture du grand opéra italien a Nankin* or *La compagnia d'opera a Nanchino* (Berlin, Oct. 16, 1790); *Dario* (Berlin, Jan. 1791); *Vasco di Gama* (Berlin, Jan. 20, 1792); *Virginia* (Venice, Dec. 26, 1793); *Zemira* (Padua, June 12, 1794); *Armida* (Padua, July 1, 1794); *I sposi burlati* (Mantua, Dec. 26, 1798). **OTHER:** 2 oratorios: *Il tobia* (Rome, 1767) and *Bethulia liberata* (Padua, 1781); 6 sinfonie; 6 trio sonatas for 2 Violins and Basso Continuo.

BIBL.: L. Valdrighi, *F. A. maestro di cappella di Federico Guglielmo II re di Prussie (1790–92)* (Modena, 1896). —NS/LK/DM

d'Alessandro, Raffaele, Swiss pianist, organist, and composer; b. St. Gallen, March 17, 1911; d. Lausanne, March 17, 1959. He studied music with Victor Schlatter and Willi Schuh in Zurich; then went to Paris, where he studied composition with Boulanger and organ with Dupré. In 1940 he returned to Switzerland and settled in Lausanne, where he became active as a pianist, organist, and composer.

WORKS: DRAMATIC: Ballet: *Isla persa* (1952). **ORCH.:** 3 piano concertos (1939, 1945, 1951); *Rumba sinfonica* (1940); *Conga contrapuntique* (1941) Violin Concerto (1941); Flute Concerto (1943); 2 syms. (1948, 1953); Bassoon Concerto (1955); Oboe Concerto (1958). **CHAMBER:** 2 violin sonatas (1936, 1953); Cello Sonata (1937); Piano Trio (1940); Flute Sonata (1943); 2 string quartets (1947, 1952); Oboe Sonata (1949); Sonatina for Solo Oboe (1953); Sonatina for Clarinet and Piano (1953); Bassoon Sonata (1957); Sonata for Flute, Viola, and Piano (1958). **Piano:** Sonatina for left hand alone (1939); 24 Preludes (1940); Sonatina for 2 Pianos (1943); 12 études (1952); *Contes drolatiques* (1952); 6 *Klavierstücke* for left hand alone (1958). **OTHER:** Many pieces for organ; choruses; several songs with orch., organ, or piano.—NS/LK/DM

Alessandro, Victor (Nicholas), American conductor; b. Waco, Tex., Nov. 27, 1915; d. San Antonio, Nov. 27, 1976. He received training in horn with his father. After studying composition with Hanson and Rogers at the Eastman School of Music in Rochester, N.Y. (Mus. B., 1937), he pursued training at the Salzburg Mozarteum (1937) and with Pizzetti at the Accademia di Santa Cecilia in Rome (1938). From 1938 to 1951 he was conductor of the Okla. Sym. Orch. He was conductor of the San Antonio Sym. Orch. from 1951 until his death. —NS/LK/DM

Alexander, Haim, German-born Israeli composer and teacher; b. Berlin, Aug. 9, 1915. He studied piano at the Stern Cons. in Berlin. In 1936 he emigrated to Palestine and took courses in piano and composition with Irma and Stefan Wolpe at the Palestine Cons.

(graduated, 1945). He completed his training in Freiburg im Breisgau. From 1945 he was active as a teacher, and later served on the faculties of the Rubin Academy of Music in Jerusalem (1972–82) and the Univ. of Tel Aviv (1972–82). In 1996 he received the Israeli Soc. of Authors, Composers, and Music Publishers (ACUM) Prize in the field of art music for his life's work. Alexander's output encompasses both traditional and avant-garde idioms.

WORKS: ORCH.: *6 Israeli Dances* (1956; also for Piano, 1950); *Morasha* (Heritage), suite for Chamber Orch. (1980); Concerto for Piano and Chamber Orch. (1982); *Late Love* for Chamber Orch. (1997). **CHAMBER:** *Metamorphoses* for Violin (1968); *See My Love* for Trombone (1969); *Nabut* for 9 Players (1971); *Yemenite Dance* for Oboe and Piano (1974); *Hassidic Tunes* for 2 Oboes (1975); *Variations on a Hassidic Niggun* for Oboe (1975); *A Tunisian Wedding Song* for 2 Flutes (1977); *Two Ballades Recollected* for String Quartet (1998). **P i a n o :** *6 Israeli Dances* (1950; also for Orch., 1956); *Sonata brevis* for 2 Pianos (1959); *Soundfigures* (1965); *Patterns* (1973); *3 Pieces in Black and White* (1974); *Metamorphoses on a Theme by Mozart* (1990); Sonata (1994). **VOCAL:** *Journey into the Present* for Narrator and Orch. (1971); *Ba'olam*, 7 songs for Mezzo-soprano or Baritone and 7 Instruments (1976); *Song of Faith* for Chorus and Orch. (1977–78); *Mein Blaues Klavier* for 8 Singers and Percussion (1990); *Questions and Answers* for Soprano, Flute, and Piano (1993–94); *3 Ballads* for Women's Voices (1997); choruses; other songs.—**NS/LK/DM**

Alexander, John, prominent American tenor; b. Meridian, Miss., Oct. 21, 1923; d. there, Dec. 8, 1990. He studied at the Cincinnati Cons. of Music and with Robert Weede. In 1952 he made his operatic debut as Faust with the Cincinnati Opera. On Oct. 11, 1957, he appeared for the first time at the N.Y.C. Opera as Alfredo, where he sang regularly until 1977. On Dec. 19, 1961, he made his Metropolitan Opera debut in N.Y. as Ferrando, remaining on its roster for more than 25 years. In 1968 he sang Rodolfo at his Vienna State Opera debut and in 1970 Pollione at his Covent Garden debut in London. In 1973 he appeared as Don Carlos in the U.S. premiere of the French version of Verdi's opera in Boston. He also toured widely as a concert artist. He taught at the Univ. of Cincinnati-Coll. Cons. of Music from 1974. Alexander maintained an extensive repertory that embraced works from the bel canto era to the 20th century.—**NS/LK/DM**

Alexander, Josef, American composer; b. Boston, May 15, 1907; d. N.Y., Feb. 28, 1992. He studied piano at the New England Cons. of Music in Boston (graduated, 1925; postgraduate diploma, 1926), with Piston (composition) and E.B. Hill (orchestration) at Harvard Univ. (B.A., 1938; M.A., 1941), with Boulanger in Paris (1939), and with Copland (composition) and Koussevitzky (conducting) at the Berkshire Music Center in Tanglewood (1940). He taught at Brooklyn Coll. of the City Univ. of N.Y. (1943–77). In his works, Alexander adopted a facile laisséz-faire idiom marked by a pleasurable admixture of euphonious dissonances.

WORKS: ORCH.: Piano Concerto (1938; Boston, June 8, 1940); *The Ancient Mariner*, symphonic poem (1938; Boston, June 8, 1940); *Doina* (1940); *A New England Overture* (St. Louis, Feb.

12, 1943); *Williamsburg Suite* (N.Y., Aug. 19, 1944); *Dithyrambe* (1947); *Epitaphs* (1947; N.Y., March 8, 1951); 4 syms.: No. 1, *Clockwork* (1948; N.Y., Nov. 28, 1949), No. 2 (1954), No. 3 (1961; N.Y., April 27, 1970), and No. 4 (1968); *Andante and Allegro* for Strings (1952; St. Louis, Feb. 20, 1953); Duo Concertante for Trombone, Percussion, and Strings (1959); *Quiet Music* for Strings (1965); *Trinity* for Brass and Percussion (1976). **CHAMBER:** String Quartet (1940); Piano Quintet (1942); Piano Trio (1944); Wind Quintet (1949); Piano Quartet (1952); Violin Sonata (1953); Cello Sonata (1953); Flute Sonata (1954); Clarinet Sonata (1957); Trombone Sonata (1959); Brass Trio (1971); Horn Sonata (1979); *Of Masks and Mirrors* for Cello, Soprano Saxophone, Piano, and Percussion (1981); *Escapades* for Marimba (1988); also hundreds of solo piano pieces. **VOCAL:** *Canticle of Night* for Mezzo-soprano or Baritone and Orch. (1959); *Gitanjali* for Soprano, Harpsichord, and Percussion (1973); *Symphonic Odes* for Men's Chorus and Orch. (1975); song cycles.—**NS/LK/DM**

Alexander, Meister, German Minnesinger and composer who flourished in the 2nd half of the 13th century, known as Der wilde Alexander. He was a significant composer of Sprüche. See R. Taylor, ed., *The Art of the Minnesinger* (Cardiff, 1968).

BIBL.: R. Haller, *Der wilde A.* (Wurzburg, 1935); J. Biehl, *Der wilde A.: Untersuchungen zur literarischen Technik eines Autors im 13. Jarhhundert* (diss., Univ. of Hamburg, 1970).—**NS/LK/DM**

Alexander, Monty (Montgomery Bernard), jazz pianist; b. Kingston, Jamaica, June 6, 1944. A fresh, delightful,and hard-swinging improvisor, Alexander began playing piano and accordion at age six. He enjoyed local styles such as the calypso, and listened to North American popular music on radio, in movies, and at concerts by Fats Domino, Ray Charles, Louis Armstrong, Professor Longhair, and Nat King Cole. Alexander sat in with mento (traditional Jamaican dance music) and ska (a newer style) musicians and by his mid-teens was fronting his own ska group, Monty and The Cyclones, which issued a number of hit records from 1958 to 1960. He first played in the U.S. in 1961 with Art Mooney in Las Vegas, then settled there in 1963 and played clubs from N.Y. to Clearwater, Fla. His performance in Clearwater got him a job from 1963–67 as house pianist in N.Y. at Jilly's, where he accompanied Sammy Davis Jr., Judy Garland, and, for one set, Frank Sinatra. His work with Milt Jackson and Ray Brown led to further work as a jazz soloist with Dizzy Gillespie, Clark Terry, Herb Ellis, Ray Brown, and Miles Davis. He also worked in 1987 with Sonny Rollins and has led his own groups, occasionally incorporating some Jamaican influence such as steel drums on three "Ivory and Steel" recordings and the use of melodica. He made an album with Jamaican guitarist Ernest Ranglin in 1978. He played on film soundtracks produced by Quincy Jones, served as a consultant to Clint Eastwood during the making of the film *Bird*, and still works with singers including Natalie Cole (on her 1991 Grammy-winning *Unforgettable*) and Mary Stallings.

DISC.: *Alexander the Great* (1965); *This Is M. A.* (1969); *Reunion In Europe* (1976); *Facets* (1979); *Ivory and Steel* (1980); *Triple Treat 1, 2, and 3* (1982, 1987, and 1987); *M. A.'s Ivory and Steel* (1994); *M. A. at Maybeck* (1995).—**LP**

Alexander, Roberta, admired black American soprano; b. Lynchburg, Va., March 3, 1949. She was reared in a musical family; studied at the Univ. of Mich. in Ann Arbor (1969–71; M.Mus., 1971) and with Herman Woltman at the Royal Cons. of Music at The Hague. She appeared as Pamina at the Houston Grand Opera in 1980, as Daphne in Santa Fe (1981), and as Elettra in *Idomeneo* in Zürich (1982). Following a tour of Europe, she made a successful debut at the Metropolitan Opera in N.Y. as Zerlina on Nov. 3, 1983; later sang Bess in *Porgy and Bess* and the title role in Janáček's *Jenůfa*, a role she repeated at her Glyndebourne Festival debut in 1989. In 1984 she made her first appearance at the Aix-en-Provence Festival in Mozart's *La finta giardiniera*. She made her debut in Vienna as Cleopatra in Handel's *Giulio Cesare* at the Theater an der Wien in 1985. In 1986 she was a soloist with the Vienna Phil. at the Salzburg Festival and in 1988 she appeared with the English Chamber Orch. at the London Promenade Concerts. In 1995 she appeared as Vitellia at the Glyndebourne Festival. Among her other operatic roles are Mozart's Fiordiligi, Donna Elvira, Ilia, and the Countess, Offenbach's Antonia, Verdi's Luisa Miller, and Massenet's Manon and Thaïs.—**NS/LK/DM**

Alexandra, Liana, Romanian composer, pianist, and teacher; b. Bucharest, May 27, 1947. She studied composition at the Ciprian Porumbescu Academy of Music in Bucharest (1965–71), and later attended the summer courses in new music in Darmstadt (1974, 1978, 1980, 1984) and visited the U.S. (1983). In 1971 she joined the faculty of the Bucharest Academy (later Univ.) of Music, where she taught composition, orchestration, and analysis. She also played in a duo with the cellist Serban Nichifor. Her compositions have won many prizes, among them the Union of Romanian Composers prizes (1975, 1979, 1981, 1982, 1984, 1987, 1988), Gaudeamus Foundation prizes (1979, 1980), the Romanian Academy Prize (1980), the ISCM Prize (1993), and the ACMEOR Prize of Israel (1998).

WORKS: DRAMATIC: *The Snow Queen*, children's opera (1979); *The Mermaid*, ballet (1982); *Chant d'amour de la dame à la licorne*, chamber opera (1996). ORCH.: 7 syms. (1971; *Hymns*, 1978; 1980–81; 1983–84; 1985–86; 1988–89; 1995–96); *Valences* (1973); Clarinet Concerto (1974); *Resonances* for Piano and Orch. (1974); *Music* for Clarinet, Violin, Viola, Cello, Piano, and Orch. (1975); Concerto for Flute, Viola, and Chamber Orch. (1980); *Jerusalem*, symphonic poem (1990); Concerto for Strings (1991); Concerto for Piano, 4-Hands and Orch. (1993); Concerto for Saxophone and Strings (1997); *Pastorale* for Wind Orch. (1999). CHAMBER: Sonata for Solo Flute (1973); *Lyric Sequence* for Clarinet, Trumpet, and Piano (1974); *Collages* for Brass Quintet (1977); *Incantations II* for Flute, Viola, Cello, Clarinet, and Piano (1978); *Consonances I* for 4 Trombones (1978), *II* for Clarinet and Piano (1979), *III* for Organ (1979), *IV* for Clarinet and Tape (1980), *V* for Organ (1980), and *VI* for Harp (1998); Sonata for 6 Horns (1986); *Intersections*, horn sonata (1989); Cello Sonata (1994); *Ancestrale* for Flute (1996); *5 Movements* for Cello and Piano (1997). VOCAL: *Cantata I* for Women's Chorus and Orch. (1971), *II* for Soprano, Baritone, Chorus, and Orch. (1977), *III* for Chorus and Orch. (1977), and *IV* for Children's Chorus

and Orch. (1978); *2 Sequences* for Soprano and Chamber Orch. (1976); *Incantations I* for Mezzo-soprano, Flute, Percussion, and Harpsichord (1978); *Poem for Romania* for Soprano and Piano (1994).—**NS/LK/DM**

Alexandre, Charles-Guillaume, French violinist, teacher, and composer; b. c. 1735; d. Paris, c. 1787. He held posts as a violinist in Paris before devoting himself to teaching the violin and to composing. He wrote stage works, violin concertos, chamber music, and arrangements of popular opera arias.—**LK/DM**

Alexandrov, Alexander, Russian composer; b. Plakhino, April 13, 1883; d. Berlin, July 8, 1946. He studied with Rimsky-Korsakov and Glazunov at the St. Petersburg Cons. (1899–1901) and later at the Moscow Cons. with Vasilenko (1909–13). In 1928 he organized the Red Army Ensemble, which he conducted on numerous tours in Russia and abroad. His song *Hymn of the Bolshevik Party*, with a new set of words, was proclaimed the Soviet national anthem on March 15, 1944. He died while on a concert tour.—**NS/LK/DM**

Alexandrov, Anatoli, eminent Russian pianist, teacher, and composer; b. Moscow, May 25, 1888; d. there, April 16, 1982. He studied with Taneyev at the Moscow Cons. (1907–10); also studied composition there with Vasilenko and piano with Igumnov, graduating in 1916; subsequently was a prof. there (from 1923). He composed mainly for piano, including 14 sonatas (1914–71), but he also composed 2 operas, *Bela* (Moscow, Dec. 10, 1946) and *Wild Bara* (Moscow, March 2, 1957), as well as incidental music for plays. Other works include 4 string quartets (1914–53), *Classical Suite* for Orch. (1926), *Dithyramb* for Double Bass and Piano (1959), Sym. No. 1 (1965), and several song cycles. In his style of composition, he followed the main lines of Rachmaninoff and Scriabin.—**NS/LK/DM**

Alexanian, Diran, noted Armenian cellist and pedagogue; b. Constantinople, 1881; d. Chamonix, July 27, 1954. While studying with Grützmacher, he had the honor of playing chamber music with Brahms and Joachim, and commenced his career as a virtuoso at age 17. In 1901 he went to Paris, where he later taught at the École Normale de Musique (1921–37). He then settled in the U.S. Among his outstanding students were Maurice Eisenberg and Antonio Janigro. With Casals, he wrote the treatise *Traité théorique et pratique du violoncelle* (1922); also prepared a critical ed. of the Bach solo cello suites (1929).—**NS/LK/DM**

Alexeev, Dmitri, talented Russian pianist; b. Moscow, Aug. 10, 1947. He entered Moscow's Central Music School at the age of 6, and then studied with Bashkirov in Moscow, winning 2nd prize at the Long-Thibaud Competition in Paris (1969) and becoming the first Russian pianist to win 1st prize at the Leeds Competition (1975). He subsequently gave recitals in Europe, Japan, and Australia. He made his American debut as a soloist with the Chicago Sym. Orch. in 1976, and in 1978 appeared at Carnegie Hall in N.Y. He further played duo-piano recitals with his wife, Tatiana Sarkissova. As a soloist, he is notable in the Romantic piano repertoire. —NS/LK/DM

Alfano, Franco, eminent Italian composer and teacher; b. Posilippo, March 8, 1875; d. San Remo, Oct. 27, 1954. He studied composition with Serrao in Naples, and with Jadassohn and Sitt in Leipzig. From the beginning of his musical career, Alfano was interested in opera. His first stage work, *Miranda*, was written when he was barely 20; another opera, *La fonte di Enchir*, followed (Breslau, Nov. 8, 1898). In 1899 he went to Paris and became fascinated by light theater music. While in Paris he wrote *Napoli*, a ballet in the folk manner, which was staged at the Folies-Bérgères (Jan. 28, 1901), proving so successful that it ran for 160 successive performances. Returning to Italy, he began work on an opera based on Tolstoy's novel *Resurrection*. It was premiered as *Risurrezione* in Turin (Nov. 4, 1904) with sensational acclaim; the American premiere (Chicago, Dec. 31, 1925) was equally successful; there were also numerous performances in Germany and France. The opera was widely praised for its dramatic power and melodic richness in the best tradition of realistic Italian opera. Alfano continued to compose industriously for another half-century, but his later operas failed to equal his earlier successes. Among these later works are *Il Principe Zilah* (Genoa, Feb. 3, 1909), *L'ombra di Don Giovanni* (Milan, April 3, 1914), *La leggenda di Sakuntala* (Bologna, Dec. 10, 1921; score destroyed during World War II; recomposed as *Sakuntala*, 1952), *Madonna Imperia*, lyric comedy (Turin, May 5, 1927), *L'Ultimo Lord* (Naples, April 19, 1930), *Cyrano de Bergerac* (Rome, Jan. 22, 1936), and *Il Dottor Antonio* (Rome, April 30, 1949). He completed Puccini's last opera, *Turandot*, adding the last scene. His *Hymn to Bolivar* for Chorus and Orch., written for the centennial of Bolivar's death, was performed in Caracas, Venezuela, on Dec. 22, 1930. Among his other works were 3 syms. (1909, 1932, 1934), 3 string quartets, a Violin Sonata, a Cello Sonata, and a ballet, *Vesuvius* (1938; a symphonic poem was drawn from it in 1946). He was director of the Liceo Musicale in Bologna (1918–23) and of the Turin Cons. (1923–39), superintendent of the Teatro Massimo in Palermo (1940–42), and acting director of the Rossini Cons. in Pesaro (1947–50).

BIBL.: A. della Corte, *Ritratto di F. A.* (Turin, 1935). —NS/LK/DM

Al-Farabi, Abu Nasr, Arabian music theorist and scholar of Turkish descent; b. Farab, c. 870; d. Damascus, c. 950. He was renowned for his writings on philosophy, political science, and the arts. He wrote *Kitab al-Musiqi al-Kabir* (Greater Book About Music), dealing with acoustics, intervals, scales, instruments, and rhythm.

BIBL.: E. Beichert, *Die Wissenschaft der Musik bei A.-F.* (Regensburg, 1931); H. Farmer, *A.-F.'s Arabic-Latin Writings on Music* (Glasgow, 1934); A. Madian, *Language-Music Relationships in A.-F.'s Grand Book of Music* (diss., Cornell Univ., 1992). —NS/LK/DM

Alferaki, Achilles, Russian composer of Greek descent; b. Kharkov, July 3, 1846; d. Petrograd, Dec. 27,

1919. He studied philology at the Univ. of Moscow and received training in piano and music theory. He wrote the opera *St. John's Eve*, as well as numerous piano pieces and songs.—NS/LK/DM

Alfieri, Pietro, Italian music scholar and composer; b. Rome, June 29, 1801; d. there, June 12, 1863. He became a priest and taught Gregorian chant at the Collegio Inglese in Rome. Alfieri was an authority on Gregorian chant, and was the author of the important books *Saggio storico pratico del canto gregoriano o romano per istruzione degli ecclesiastici* (Rome, 1835), *Accompagnamento coll'organo de' toni ecclesiatici* (Rome, 1840), and *Précis historique et critique sur la restauration des livres du chant grégorien* (Rennes 1856; rev. Italian tr., 1857). He also ed. a collection of the music of Palestrina in his *Raccolta di musica sacra* (7 vols., Rome, 1841–46), and completed an edition of the Roman Gradual, Antiphonal, and Hymnal. Alfieri died insane.—NS/LK/DM

Alford, Kenneth J.
See **Ricketts, Frederick J.**

Alfvén, Hugo (Emil), eminent Swedish composer and choral conductor; b. Stockholm, May 1, 1872; d. Falun, May 8, 1960. He was a student of Johan Lindberg (violin) and Aron Bergenson (harmony) at the Stockholm Cons. (1887–90); during this period, he also pursued training in painting with Otto Hesselbom and Oscar Törnå. From 1890 to 1897 he was a violinist in the Royal Opera Orch. in Stockholm. He also studied violin with Lars Zetterquist and composition with Johan Lindegren (1891–97). In 1896, 1897, and 1899 he held the composer's scholarship of the Royal Academy of Music, which allowed him to travel abroad, including a sojourn in Brussels to study violin with César Thomson (1897–98). From 1900 to 1903 he was a Jenny Lind scholar, which enabled him to study in various European cities, including Dresden with Hermann Kutzschbach, where he also received training in conducting (1901–02). From 1910 to 1939 he served as Director Musices of the Univ. of Uppsala. He also was conductor of the Orphei Drängar (1910–47), the Uppsala studentkars allmänna sangförening (1919–31; 1934–38), and the Svenska sangarförbundet (1921–43). In 1908 he was made a member of the Royal Academy of Music. He was awarded an honorary doctorate by the Univ. of Uppsala in 1917. His vivid autobiography was publ. in 4 vols. in Stockholm as *Första satsen: Ungdomsminnen* (1946), *Tempo furioso: Vandringsår* (1948), *I dur och moll: Från Uppsalaåren* (1949), and *Final* (1952). Alfvén's early training in painting is reflected in his adoption as a composer of a carefully crafted but colorful late Romantic idiom. He won distinction as a composer of orch. music and choral works. His folksong settings for chorus were particularly successful in Sweden. Outside his homeland, he remains best known for his popular first Swedish rhapsody for orch., *Midsommarvaka* (Midsummer Vigil; 1903).

WORKS: DRAMATIC: *Bergakungen* (The Mountain King), pantomime drama (1916–23; Stockholm, Feb. 7, 1923);

Gustav II Adolf, incidental music (Stockholm, Nov. 6, 1932); *Den förlorade sonen* (The Prodigal Son), ballet (Stockholm, April 27, 1957). **ORCH.:** 5 syms.: No. 1 (1896–97; Stockholm, Feb. 9, 1897; rev. 1903–04; Stockholm, May 10, 1904), No. 2 (1897–98; Stockholm, May 2, 1899), No. 3 (1905; Göteborg, Dec. 3, 1906), No. 4, *Från havsbandet* (From the Outermost Skerries; 1918–19; Stockholm, Nov. 4, 1919), and No. 5 (1942–52; 1st complete perf., Stockholm, April 30, 1952); 3 Swedish rhapsodies: No. 1, *Midsommarvaka* (Midsummer Vigil; 1903; Stockholm, May 10, 1904), No. 2, *Uppsala-rhapsodi: Akademisk festouverture* (Uppsala, May 23, 1907), and No. 3, *Dala-rhapsodien* (1931; Stockholm, April 27, 1932); *En skärgårdssägen* (A Legend of the Skerries), symphonic poem (1904; Stockholm, March 31, 1905); *Festpel* (1907; Stockholm, Feb. 18, 1908); *Drapa*, in memory of King Oscar II (Stockholm, May 16, 1908); *Bröllopsmarsch* (Wedding March; 1909); *Fest-ouverture* for Military Band (1909); *Elégie (Vid Emil Sjögrens bår* [Elegie: At Emil Sjögren's Funeral], tone poem (Stockholm, Oct. 18, 1918); *Hjalmar Brantings sorgmarsch* (Hjalmar Branting's Funeral March) for Wind Orch. (1924; Stockholm, March 1, 1925); *Synnöve Solbakken*, suite (Stockholm, Oct. 22, 1934); *Festmarsch för orkester till Stockholmsutställningengs öppnande 1930* (1930); *Fest-ouverture* (Malmö, Sept. 24, 1944); *En bygdesaga* (A District Fairy Tale), suite (1944). **CHAMBER:** Violin Sonata (Stockholm, March 20, 1896); *Elegi* for Horn or Cello and Organ (1897); *Serenade* for Violin and Piano (c. 1902); *Serenade på Mammas födelsedag* (Serenade on Mother's Birthday) for Flute, Clarinet, Violin, and Piano (1902); *Andante religioso* for Celesta, Harp, and String Quartet (1913; also for String Orch.); *Roslagspolketta* for Violin and Piano (1956); piano pieces, including 3 *Skärgårdsbilder* (Pictures from the Skerries; 1901–02). **VOCAL: C a n t a t a s :** *Vid sekelskiftet: Nyårskantaten* for Soloist, Chorus, and Orch. (1899; Stockholm, Jan. 1, 1900); *Uppenbarelsekantat* for Bass or Baritone, Chorus, and Orch. (Saltsjöbaden, May 18, 1913); *Kantat vid Baltiska utställningens i Malmö öppnande* for Baritone, Chorus, and Orch. (Malmö, May 15, 1914); *Kantat vid Uppsala läns Kungl. Hushållningssallskaps 100-årsjubileum 1915* for Chorus and Orch. (Uppsala, Dec. 1, 1915); *Kantat vid Reformationsfesten i Uppsala 1917* for Baritone, Chorus, and Orch. (Uppsala, Oct. 31, 1917); *Kantat vid Vårldspostunionens halvesekelsjubileum 1924* for Baritone, Chorus, and Orch. (Stockholm, Aug. 16, 1924); *Kantat vid Uppsala universitets 450-årsjubileum* for Alto, Baritone, Chorus, and Orch. (Uppsala, Sept. 15, 1927); *Kantat vid Svenska Röda korsets högtidssammankomst 2 maj 1930* for Alto, Chorus, and Orch. (Stockholm, May 2, 1930); *Kantat vid Sveriges Riksdags 500-års minnesfest 1935* for Baritone, Chorus, and Orch. (Stockholm, May 28, 1935). **OTHER:** *Herrens bön* for Soprano, Alto, Baritone, Chorus, and Orch. (1899–1901; Stockholm, Dec. 2, 1902); many men's choruses, including *Frihetssång* (1900), *Gustaf Frödings jordafärd* (1911), *Sverges flagga* (1916), and *Gryning vid havet* (1933); numerous folk song arrangements.

BIBL.: S. Svensson, *H. A., Som människa och konstnär* (Uppsala, 1946); P. Lindfors, *H. A. berättar* (Stockholm, 1966); J. Rudén, *H. A.: Kompositioner/Musical Works: Käll-och Verkförteckning/Thematic Index* (Stockholm, 1972); special issue of *Musikrevy*, XXVI/2 (1972); L. Hedwall, *H. A.: En svensk tonsättares liv och verk* (Stockholm, 1973); idem, *H. A.: Ein bildbiografi* (Tierp, 1990).—**NS/LK/DM**

Algarotti, Francesco, Italian scholar; b. Venice, Dec. 11, 1712; d. Pisa, May 3, 1764. He was educated in Rome, Bologna, and Florence, and acquired a notable reputation as a scholar of the arts and sciences. In 1740 Friedrich II the Great of Prussia called him to Berlin and made him a Count, and, in 1747, a Chevalier de l'ordre pour le mérite. He also was an advisor to Augustus III, Elector of Saxony and King of Poland, from 1742 to 1747. Algarotti was involved in operatic productions in Berlin and Dresden, where he arranged and versified Italian librettos to suit the requirements of his patrons. Ill health compelled him to return to Italy in 1753. In addition to numerous writings on classical subjects, architecture, and painting, he wrote the important *Saggio sopra l'opera in musica* (1755). In this influential work, Algarotti proposed that all of the elements in opera be subordinated to a unifying poetic idea. He also included a French libretto for *Iphigénie en Aulide*, which served as a model for others, including Gluck's librettist.

BIBL.: D. Michelessi, *Memorie intorno alla vita ed agli scritti del F. A.* (Venice, 1770); R. Northcott, *F. A., A Reprint of His "Saggio..." and a Sketch of His Life* (London, 1917); G. Schmitt, *F. A. (1712–64) und Frankreich* (diss., Univ. of Heidelberg, 1945). —**NS/LK/DM**

Alghisi, Paris Francesco, Italian organist and composer; b. Brescia, June 19, 1666; d. there, c. March 29, 1733. He was a pupil of Orazio Polaroli, organist of Brescia Cathedral. After service at the Polish court (c. 1681–83), he returned to Brescia and became a member of the order of S. Filippo Neri. He later served as maestro di cappella of the Congregazione dell'Oratorio di S. Filippo Neri and as organist at the Cathedral. He wrote the operas *L'amor di Curzio per la patria* (Venice, 1690) and *Il trionfo della continenza* (Venice, 1691), 9 oratorios, and instrumental pieces.—**LK/DM**

Ali, Rashied (originally **Patterson, Robert),** jazz drummer; b. Philadelphia, July 1, 1935. Ali is best known for his freestyle work with John Coltrane. He came from a musical family; his mother sang with Jimmie Lunceford (perhaps as part of a vocal group). Ali did some studying at the Granoff School, played in the army, and on return started gigging with rhythm and blues and rock groups, such as Dick Hart and The Heartaches, Big Maybelle, and Lin Holt, and saxophonist Len Bailey. He first did jazz gigs with his own group, but he also worked with Jimmy Oliver, Tommy Coles, Orrin Marshall, Lee Morgan, Don Patterson, and Jimmy Smith. Ali drove a cab for two years in the early 1960s and moved to N.Y. in 1963. There he met Pharaoh Sanders, and immediately started working with Sanders and Don Cherry. Ali also worked with Archie Shepp, Earl Hines, Marion Brown, Sun Ra, and Albert Ayler. After sitting in with Coltrane a few times at the Half Note, Ali was hired in November 1965 to form a two-drum team alongside Elvin Jones. After Jones left for good in late March 1966, Ali stayed on. He worked with Alice Coltrane after her husband John's death in 1967, and played gigs in Copenhagen, Germany, and Sweden with Sonny Rollins (c. 1968) and others, before studying with Philly Joe Jones in England. Returning to N.Y., Ali worked with Jackie McLean, Alice Coltrane, Shepp, Gary Bartz, Dewey Redman, and others; ran a jazz loft, Ali's Alley/Studio 77 (1973–79); and formed Survival Records (1972). In the 1990s, his band Prima Materia began revisiting Coltrane's late works. Interviews with Ali appear in the video *The World According to John Coltrane* and the book *John Coltrane: His Life and Music* (Ann Arbor, 1998).

DISC.: *Meditations* (1965); *Concert In Japan* (1966); *Expression* (1967); *J. Coltrane, Interstellar Space* (1967); *A. Coltrane, A Monastic Trio* Exchange (1973); *R. A. Quintet* (1973); *Peace on Earth* (1994); *Prima Materia: Meditations* (1995).—**LP**

Aliabiev, Alexander (Nikolaievich), Russian composer; b. Tobolsk, Siberia, Aug. 15, 1787; d. Moscow, March 6, 1851. His father was the governor of Tobolsk, and Aliabiev spent his childhood there. The family went to St. Petersburg in 1796, and in 1804 settled in Moscow. He studied music in Moscow and had his first songs publ. in 1810. During the War of 1812, he served in the Russian army, and participated in the entry of the Russian army into Dresden and Paris. Returning to Russia, he lived in St. Petersburg, in Voronezh, and in Moscow. In 1825 he was arrested on suspicion of murder after a card game, was sentenced to prison, and in 1828 was deported to his birthplace in Siberia. There he organized concerts of popular music and also composed. In 1831 he was allowed to return to European Russia and lived in the Caucasus and in Orenburg. In 1843 he returned to Moscow, but was still under police surveillance. He wrote more than 100 songs, of which *The Nightingale* became extremely popular; it is often used in the music-lesson scene in Russian productions of Rossini's opera *Il Barbiere di Siviglia*. Among his works for the theater are scores of incidental music to *The Prisoner of the Caucasus* and to Shakespeare's plays, as well as the stage ballads *The Village Philosopher, The Moon Night,* and *Theatrical Combat* (with Verstovsky and Mauer). Other works include a Sym., 3 string quartets, 2 piano trios, a Piano Quintet, a Violin Sonata, a Quartet for 4 Flutes, a Quintet for Wind Instruments, a Piano Sonata, and choruses.

BIBL.: B. Dobrohotov, *A. A.* (Moscow, 1966).—**NS/LK/DM**

Aliprandi, Bernardo, Italian cellist and composer; b. probably in Milan, c. 1710; d. Frankfurt am Main, c. 1792. He went to Munich, where he was made a cellist in 1731, composer of chamber music in 1737, and Konzertmeister in 1744 at the Bavarian court. He retired in 1778. For the Bavarian court opera, he wrote the operas *Mitridate* (1738) and *Semiramide riconosciuta* (1740). He also wrote the festa teatrale *Apollo trà le muse in Parnasso* (Nymphenburg, 1740). Among his other works were a *Stabat mater* (1749) and some instrumental pieces.—**NS/LK/DM**

Ali-Sade, Frangis, Azerbaijani composer; b. Baku, May 28, 1947. She studied piano in Baku as a child. Later she studied composition with Kara Karayev at the state cons. in Baku (1965–72), conducted postgraduate work there (1974–76), and was an assistant to Karayev (1970–76). Since 1976 she has taught composition at the Azerbaijan State Cons., and from 1979 to 1985 she was secretary of the Azerbaijan Composers' Union. She was a co-composer-in-residence (with Kancheli) for the 1999 Lucerne International Festival of Music. Her music

involves a personal, *sui generis* method of organization that combines the timbres and melodies of indigenous Azerbaijan music with the more advanced techniques of Western music.

WORKS: DRAMATIC: O p e r a : *A Legend of the White Horseman,* after a Turkish epic tale (1983–85). **ORCH.:** Piano Concerto (1972); Sym. (1976); Concerto for Chamber Orch. (1986); *Silk Road,* concerto for Percussion and Chamber Orch. (1999–2000). **CHAMBER:** 4 string quartets: No. 1 (1974), No. 1, *Dilogie I* (1988), No. 3, *Mugam-Sajahy,* with percussion and synthesized sound (1993), and No. 4, *Oasis* (1998); *Zu den Kindertotenliedern,* in memory of Mahler, for Clarinet, Violin, and Percussion (1977); *Habil- Sajahy* for Cello and Prepared Piano (1979); *Dilogie II* for 9 Players (1989; rev. 1994); *Crossing I* for Clarinet and Vibraphone/Celesta (1991) and *II* for 11 Instruments (1992–93); *Mirage* for Ud and Chamber Ensemble (1998); *Sturm und Drang* for Chamber Ensemble (1998); *Ask Havasi* for Cello (1998). **KEYBOARD: P i a n o :** 2 sonatas: No. 1, *In memory of Alban Berg* (1969–70) and No. 2 (1990); *Music* (1987; rev. 1997). **O r g a n :** *Fantasy* (1982); *Partita* (1985). **VOCAL:** *Songs About Motherland,* oratorio (1978); *Three Watercolors* for Soprano, Flute, and Prepared Piano (1987); *From Japanese Poetry* for Soprano, Flute, and Prepared Piano (1990).—**LK/DM**

Alison (or Allison, Allysonn, etc.**), Richard,** English composer who flourished in the late 16th and early 17th centuries. He publ. *The Psalms of David in Meter* (London, 1599) and *An Howres Recreation in Musicke* (London, 1606; ed. by E. Fellowes in *The English Madrigalists,* XXXIII, 1924; 2nd ed., rev., 1961). Some of his instrumental music is found in *The First Book of Consort Lessons collected by Thomas Morley* (London, 1599; 2nd ed., rev., 1611; ed. by S. Beck, N.Y., 1959).—**LK/DM**

Alkan (real name, **Morhange**), **Charles-Valentin,** remarkable and eccentric French pianist and composer; b. Paris, Nov. 30, 1813; d. there, March 29, 1888. His father, Alkan Morhange (1780–1855), operated a music school in Paris; his brothers, Ernest (1816–76), Maxime (1818–91), Napoleon (1826–1906), and Gustave (1827–86), all became well-known musicians; all 5 adopted their father's first name as their surname. Charles-Valentin entered the Paris Cons. in 1819 where he studied harmony with Dourlen and piano with Zimmerman, taking premiers prix in solfège (1820), piano (1824), harmony (1827), and organ (1834). He made his public debut as pianist and composer in Paris on April 2, 1826. By 1831 Alkan had established a reputation as a talented pianist in the salons of Paris, and had also begun to demonstrate his unique compositional skills. He played in a trio with A. Franchomme and J. Alard, for whom he wrote 3 chamber works. He visited London in 1833 and 1835, the only times he left Paris. In Paris, he developed friendships with leading musicians, artists, and literati, including Alexandre Dumas, Victor Hugo, George Sand, Eugène Delacroix, and his neighbor, Chopin. On March 3, 1838, he appeared in a concert with Chopin; then, despite the favorable reception, inexplicably he did not appear again until 1844. Following several concerts in 1845, he again enigmatically interrupted his solo piano career for 28 years. Several laudatory articles by Schumann, Fétis, and Léon Kreutzer appeared during the interim concerning his compositions. One article by Kreutzer is significant as it also discusses a Sym. for Orch., which has subsequently disappeared. His piano work *Le Chemin de fer*, op.27 (1844), is the earliest work descriptive of the railroad. In 1848 Zimmerman retired as prof. of piano at the Paris Cons. and suggested Alkan as his successor. Despite intercessions on his part by Sand, the position was given to A. Marmontel; this event propelled Alkan even further into seclusion. After Chopin's death, he moved away from his contingent of artistic companions and became a virtual recluse. In 1857 a deluge of compositions were publ., including the remarkable *12 études dans les tons mineurs*, op.39; *Études 4–7* constitute a sym. for solo piano, *Études 8–10* a concerto for solo piano. In 1859 one of his rare nonpianistic works, the grotesque *Marche funèbre sulla morte d'un papagallo* for Voices, 3 Oboes, and Bassoon, appeared. About this time he also became interested in the pédalier, a pedal board that attaches to a piano, on which he played organ works of Bach and for which he wrote many compositions, including the unique *Bombardo-carillon* for 4 feet alone. In 1873 he returned to the concert stage with a series of 6 recitals at the Salle Érard in Paris. This series was repeated yearly until 1882, 1876 excepted. He also appeared there on Monday and Thursday for 1 hour in a private studio, where he entertained anyone who happened to be present. The remainder of his activities remain shrouded in mystery.

Evidence is strong that his student Elie Delaborde was his natural son, although there is no formal documentation to substantiate the claim. Other students included I. Cervantes, F. Stockhausen Jr., and J. Wieniawski. During his lifetime, Alkan was an enigma; his pianistic skills were highly praised, even compared to those of Chopin and Liszt, and yet his aberrant behavior and misanthropy caused his name not to remain in the foreground. Judging from the scores of his difficult works, his skills must have been formidable. Since his death several pianists, notably Busoni, Petri, Lewenthal, Smith, and Hamelin have kept his works alive. Creating an accurate catalog of his voluminous works would be extremely difficult, since several works were publ. with as many as three different opus numbers in eds. by different publishers; some works were printed using different names, some opus numbers are missing (or possibly were never assigned), and some works were never publ.

WORKS: KEYBOARD: P i a n o S o l o : *Alleleuia*, op.25: *3 Andantes romantiques*, op.13; *Capriccio alla soldatesca*, op.50a; *Caprice, Quasi-caccia*, op.53; *30 Chants, 5 Recueils*, opp.37, 38, 65, 67, and 70; *Danse ibérienne, Zorcico; Esquisse, Le tambour bat aux champs*, op.50b; *48 Esquisses, motifs divises en 4 suites*, op.63; *Étude: Bourée d'Auvergne*, op.29; *Étude, Le chemin de fer*, op.27; *Étude de concert, Le preux*, op.17; *12 Études dans les tons majeures*, op.35; *12 Études dans les tons mineures*, op.39; *Fantaisie, Désir* (1844); *Fantasticheria* (c. 1850); *Fantasticheria; Chapeau bas* (c. 1872); *2 Fughe da cameria, Jean qui pleure et Jean quit rit* (c. 1840); *Gigue et air de ballet dans le style ancien*, op.24; *Grande sonata, Les 4 âges*, op.33; *3 Grandes études*, op.76; *Impromptu* in F major (c. 1845); *Impromptus, 2 Receuils*, op.32 (part publ. earlier as op.26); *3 Improvisations dans le style brillant*, op.12; *Introduction et impromptu, Une fusée*, op.55; *Marche funèbre*, op.26a; *Marche triomphale*, op.27a; *3 Marches da cavalleria*, op.37; *3 Menuets*, op.51; *Minuetto alla tedesca*, op.46; *3 Morceaux dans le genre pathétique*, op.15; *6 Morceaux caractéristiques*, op.8 (republ. as op.16 and as part of op.74); *12 Morceaux caracteristiques, Les Mois*, op.74 (includes op.16); *Nocturne No. 1*, op.22; *Nocturnes Nos. 2 and 3*, op.57; *Nocturne No. 4, Le grillon*, op.60b; *Paraphrase, Super flumina Babylonis*, op.52; *Paraphrase, Salut, cendre du pauvre!*, op.45; *Petite caprice en forme de Zorcico, Réconciliation*, op.42; *Petit conte* (1859); *3 Petites fantaisies*, op.41; *2 Petites pièces*, op.60; *3 Pièces poétiques*, op.18; *25 Préludes*, op.31 (also for Organ); *Rondo brillant*, op.4 (with string quartet ad libitum); *Rondo chromatique*, op.12; *Rondo sur un thème de "Il Barbiere di Siviglia" de Rossini*, op.5; *Rondoletto: Il était un p'tit homme*, op.3; *Saltarelle* in E minor, op.23; *Scherzo focoso*, op.34; *3 Scherzi*, op.16; *Sonatine* in A minor, op.61; *Toccatina* in C minor, op.75; *3 Variations*, op.16; *Variations, Les omnibus*, op.2; *Variations sur le thème de "l'Orage' de Steibelt*, op.1; several other variations; many transcriptions. **P i a n o 4 - h a n d s :** *Finale*, op.17; *3 Marches*, op.40; *Variations-fantasie sur les motifs de "Don Juan"*, after Mozart, op.26. **K e y b o a r d P é d a l i e r o r P i a n o 3 - h a n d s :** *Benedictus*, op.54; *Bombardo-carillon* (4 feet only; c. 1872); *12 Études* (pedals only; c. 1871); *12 Fugues* (n.d.); *11 Grandes préludes et une transcription du "Messie" de Handel*, op.66; *13 Prières*, op.64. **O r g a n :** *Impromptu sur le choral de Luther, "Un fort rampart est notre Dieu"*, op.69; *Petits préludes sur les 8 gammes du plain-chant* (1859); *11 Piéces dans le style religieux et une transcriptions du "Messie" de Handel*, op.72; *7 Prières: Pro organo* (1850). **ORCH.:** *Concerto da Camera* in A minor for Piano and Orch., No. 1, op.10; *Concerto da Camera* in C-sharp minor for Piano and Strings, No. 2. **CHAMBER:** *Grande duo concertant* in F-sharp minor for Violin and Piano, op.21; *Piano Trio* in G minor, op.30; *Sonate de concert* in E minor for Cello or Viola and Piano, op.47. **WIND BAND:** *Pas redoublè.* **VOCAL:** *Hermann et Ketty*, cantata (1832); *L'entrée en loge*, cantata (1834); *Romance du phare d'Eddystone* (1845; not extant); *Etz chajim hi* (1847); *Halelouyoh* (1857); *Marchia funèbre sulla morte d'un papagallo* (1859); *Stances de Millevoye* (1859).

BIBL.: J. Bloch, *C.-V. A.* (Indianapolis, 1941); R. Lewenthal, *The Piano Music of A.* (N.Y., 1964); D. Henning, *C.-V. A.* (diss., Univ. of Oxford, 1975); R. Smith, *A., Vol. I: The Enigma* (London, 1976) and *A., Vol. II: The Music* (N.Y., 1987); B. Schilling, *Virtuose Klaviermusik des 19. Jahrhunderts am Beispiel von C.V. A., 1813–1888* (Regensburg, 1986); B. François-Sappey, ed., *C.V. A.* (Paris, 1991).—NS/LK/DM

Allanbrook, Douglas (Phillips), American composer and teacher; b. Melrose, Mass., April 1, 1921. He studied with Boulanger at the Longy School of Music in Cambridge, Mass. (1941–42). Following military service in Italy during World War II, for which he was awarded the Bronze Star for valor, he studied with Piston at Harvard Coll. (B.A., 1948), with Boulanger on a Paine Traveling Fellowship in Paris (1948–50), and with Ruggero Gerlin (harpsichord) on a Fulbright fellowship at the Cons. di San Pietro a Majella in Naples (1950–52). From 1952 to 1986 he was on the faculty of St. John's Coll. in Annapolis. In 1982 he received an award from the American Academy and Inst. of Arts and Letters. In his works, Allanbrook follows an eclectic course, eschewing only serial techniques and the use of electronic instruments.

WORKS: DRAMATIC: O p e r a : *Ethan Frome*, after Edith Wharton (1950–52); *Nightmare Abbey*, after Thomas Love Peacock (1960–62). **ORCH.:** *Trionfo d'Amore*, overture (1949–50); Harpsichord Concerto (1950); *Concert Music* for Cello and

Strings (1951–53); *Triumph of Reason*, overture (1955); Violin Concerto (1958); 7 syms. (1960, 1962, 1967, 1970, 1976, 1977, 1980); *Serenade* for Piano and Orch. (1982). **CHAMBER:** *Partita* for Cello (1955); 4 string quartets (1955; 1956–57; 1958; 1972); *Fantasy* for Violin and Piano (1956); *Set of Passions* for Violin and Harpsichord (1959); *Game for Two* for Piano and Percussion (1973); *Night and Morning Music* for Brass Quintet (1977); *Invitation to the Sideshow* for Brass Quintet (1980); *Marches for the Quick and the Dead* for Brass Quintet (1982); Quintet for Oboe, Clarinet, Violin, Viola, and Cello (1984); *Commencement Exercises* for Brass Quintet (1985); *25 Building Blocks* for Horn and Piano (1985); *Seven for Seven* for Brass Quintet, Piano, and Percussion (1987); String Quintet (1989). **KEYBOARD: P i a n o :** 2 sonatas (1947, 1949); *Songs Without Words* (1951); *Bagatelles* (1964); *Forty Changes* (1965); *Preludes for All Seasons* (1970); *Venice Music* (1974); *Naples Music* (1975); *Transcendental Studies* (1978); *Night Pieces* (1983–85); *New American Preludes* (1990). **H a r p s i - c h o r d :** *Little Sonatas* (1949); *Fantasy* for 2 Harpsichords (1963); *Studies in Black and White* (1971). **O r g a n :** *Ricercare* (1963). **VOCAL:** *Te Deum* for Chorus, Flute, Brass, Harp, 2 Pianos, and Percussion (1942); Mass for Chorus (1946); *Ash Wednesday* for Soprano, Chorus, and Orch. (1947); *Psalms 130 and 131* for Chorus and Organ (1955); *Seven Last Words* for Mezzo-soprano, Baritone, Chorus, and Orch. (1970); *American Miscellany* for Chorus (1973); *English Mass* for Chorus and Organ (1975); *Tennyson Settings* for Chorus and Brass Quintet (1984); *Moon Songs* for Children's Chorus and Orch. (1986); several songs.

WRITINGS: *See Naples* (memoir; 1995).—**NS/LK/DM**

Allard, Joe (Joseph A.), saxophone teacher; b. Lowell, Mass., Dec. 31, 1910; d. 1991. Allard enjoyed legendary status as an educator. He studied clarinet at the New England Cons., took saxophone lessons from Rudy Wiedoeft, and played alto saxophone with Red Nichols before settling in N.Y. in the late 1930s. He was bass clarinetist with Arturo Toscanini and The NBC Sym. and played first clarinet on Bell Telephone and Dupont radio shows. A saxophonist with the N.Y. Philharmonic in the 1940s, Allard also worked for many years in the Radio City Music Hall Orch. He taught for many years at Juilliard, the Manhattan School of Music, and the New England Cons. And specialized in teaching how to hear the sounds before one plays them—well into the altissimo registers, which he was able to demonstrate awesomely and without warming up—and how to develop a personal tone. His students included Dave Liebman, Michael Brecker, Bob Berg, Pepper Adams, Eddie Daniels, Paul Winter, Dave Tofani, Kenneth Radnofsky, Harvey Pittel, Roger Greenburg, Paul Cohen, and David Demsey. His students, led by Radnofsky, commissioned Gunther Schuller's saxophone Concerto (premiered January 1984), which is dedicated to Allard in honor of his 75th birthday.—**LP/DD**

Alldahl, Per-Gunnar, Swedish composer and teacher; b. Solna, Oct. 11, 1943. He studied organ and composition at the Stockholm Musikhogskölan (1968–71). He later joined its staff as an instructor.

WORKS: *Nulla ars...* for String Orch. (1966; Helsinki, Feb. 24, 1967); *Biceps* for Chamber Orch. and Tape (1968–69; Swedish Radio, Dec. 7, 1969); *Music* for Cello (1968); *Light Music* for 5 Flutes, Hammond Organ, and Vibraphone (1968); *Play* for Orch.

(Bollnäs, April 4, 1970); *Ad lib* for Any Instruments (1971; originally for Bass Clarinet, Trombone, and Cello); *Bruspolska* for Nyckelharps (1972); *Stämma blod* for Chorus and Percussion (1972); *Unisona* for Alto Voice, Flute, Trombone, Double Bass, and Vibraphone (1972); *Från när och fjärran* for Jazz Quartet (1973); *Mot värk* for Chorus and Percussion (1973; sequel to *Stämma blod*); *Knaver-lik* for Nyckelharp and String Orch. (1974); *...ljudens dikt sjunger i venden...* for Narrator, Chorus, and Small Orch. (1974); *Till flöjten, ordern och kärleken* for Chorus and Chamber Ensemble (1980); *Var och en av oss* for Chorus and Organ (1986); *Elva-lek* for 1 or 2 Pianos (1989); *Gamle man* for Men's Chorus and 4 Trombones (1994); *Vinterhat* for Women's Chorus and 1 or 2 Pianos (1996–97).—**NS/LK/DM**

Alldis, John, English conductor; b. London, Aug. 10, 1929. He was a choral scholar under Boris Ord at King's Coll., Cambridge (1949–52; M.A., 1957). In 1962 he founded the John Alldis Choir, which soon achieved distinction under his discerning guidance. He also founded the London Sym. Orch. Chorus in 1966, and served as its director until 1969. From 1966 to 1979 he was a prof. and in 1976 a Fellow at the Guildhall School of Music and Drama in London. He was conductor of the London Phil. Choir from 1969 to 1982, and he also served as joint chief conductor of Radio Denmark in Copenhagen (1971–77) and as conductor of the Groupe Vocal de France (1979–83). From 1989 to 1991 he was music consultant of the Israel Chamber Choir. In 1992 he became chorus master of the Hallé Choir in Manchester. He was named a Chevalier de l'Ordre des Arts et des Lettres of France in 1984. Alldis's repertoire is enormous, ranging from early music to contemporary scores.—**NS/LK/DM**

Allegranti, (Teresa) Maddalena, Italian soprano; b. Venice, 1754; d. probably in Ireland, c. 1802. She made her debut in Venice in 1770. After going to Mannheim to study with Holzbauer, she sang at the court opera there (from 1772). She appeared in Venice and Florence (from 1778). On Dec. 11, 1781, she made her London debut in Anfossi's *I viaggiatori felici*. After serving as prima donna buffa at the Dresden court opera (1783–98), she again sang in London (1799–1801). —**NS/LK/DM**

Allegri, Domenico, Italian composer; b. Rome, 1585; d. there, Sept. 5, 1629. He was maestro di cappella at S. Maria Maggiore from 1610 to 1629, and was one of the first to provide vocal music with an independent instrumental accompaniment. A few of his motets are extant (a soprano solo, a tenor duet, and a bass solo, each accompanied by 2 violins).—**NS/LK/DM**

Allegri, Gregorio, Italian singer and composer; b. Rome, 1582; d. there, Feb. 7, 1652. He was a choirboy at S. Luigi de Francesi in Rome (1591–96), and then a tenor there until 1604. He also received instruction from G. M. Nanino (1600–07). After serving as a chorister at Fermo Cathedral (1607–21), he was maestro di cappella at S. Spirito in Sassia (1628–30) and then a member of the papal choir in Rome. Allegri remains best known for his *Miserere* for 2 Choirs in 4 and 5 parts, a Psalm setting sung each Holy Week at the Sistine Chapel in Rome. It was this work that the youthful Mozart is reported to have heard twice during his visit to the Sistine Chapel, and then wrote it down from memory in spite of the ban on its publication on pain of excommunication. The work was finally publ. via the efforts of Charles Burney by Novello in London. Allegri also composed Masses, Lamentations, and a Te Deum, and likewise publ. *Concertini* for 2 to 5 Voices (2 vols., Rome, 1618–19), *Motecta* for 2 to 6 Voices (Rome, 1621), and *Sinfonia a 4* (ed. by A. Kirchner in *Musurgia universalis*, Rome, 1650).

BIBL.: J. Amann, *A.s Miserere und die Aufführungspraxis in der Sixtina* (Regensburg, 1935).—**NS/LK/DM**

Allegri, Lorenzo, Italian lutenist and composer; b. c. 1573; d. Florence, July 15, 1648. He became a lutenist at the Medici court in Florence in 1604, where he remained until his death. He publ. *Primo libro delle musiche* (Venice, 1618), a collection that contains mostly instrumental music.—**NS/LK/DM**

Allen, Betty, black American mezzo-soprano, teacher, and administrator; b. Campbell, Ohio, March 17, 1930. She attended Wilberforce Univ. (1944–46), the Hartford School of Music (1950–53), and the Berkshire Music Center in Tanglewood; among her mentors were Sarah Peck More, Zinka Milanov, and Paul Ulanowsky. She made her N.Y.C. Opera debut as Queenie in *Showboat* (1954). She made her N.Y. recital debut in 1958. After making her U.S. operatic debut in San Francisco in 1966, she sang with other U.S. opera companies, including the Metropolitan Opera in N.Y. (debut as Commère in *Four Saints in Three Acts* during the company's visit to the Manhattan Forum, Feb. 20, 1973) and the N.Y.C. Opera (1973–75); also toured as a concert singer. She taught at the N.C. School of the Arts in Winston-Salem (1978–87), was executive director (1979–92) and president (1992) of the Harlem School of the Arts, and gave master classes at the Curtis Inst. of Music in Philadelphia (from 1987).—**LK/DM**

Allen, Carl, jazz drummer and band leader; b. Milwaukee, April 25, 1961. Allen is a hard-swinging drummer and congenial leader. He began studies at William Paterson Coll. (N.J.) in 1981 and worked with Freddie Hubbard from 1982–90. Allen's own former bands were starting points for Roy Hargrove, Nicholas Payton, Ed Simon, Teodross Avery, and others. He has also worked with Jackie McLean, George Coleman, Billy Taylor, and Benny Golson. Allen co-produces albums with his partner on the Big Apple label, Vincent Herring, and started a new group in July 1997, which was launched at the Regattabar in Boston with Tim Warfield, Mark Whitfield, Mulgrew Miller, and bassist Rodney Whitaker.

DISC.: *Piccadilly Square* (1989); *The Pursuer* (1993); *Testimonial* (1995); *Manhattan Project* (records for Japan, these released in U.S. too): *We Remember Cannonball*; *Echoes of Our Heroes*; *Dark Side of Dewey*.—**LP**

Allen, Geri, jazz pianist and composer; b. Pontiac, Mich., June 12, 1957. Allen is an acclaimed soloist and composer who began attracting attention in the early 1980s in non-traditional contexts. Raised in Detroit, she was classically trained and later became immersed in jazz, at which point Marcus Belgrave became a mentor at Cass Technical H.S. After graduating with a degree in jazz studies from Howard Univ. in 1979, she studied with Kenny Barron in N.Y., then attended the Univ. of Pittsburgh where she earned a Masters in ethnomusicology, writing her thesis on Eric Dolphy. She returned to N.Y.C. in 1982 and became part of Steve Coleman's M-Base movement in Brooklyn. She has worked with Paul Motian, Charlie Haden, Wallace Roney (a friend from Howard Univ. days), and has led her own groups. She worked with Betty Carter and appeared on her live recording *Feed the Fire* and on Carter's appearance as part of a Kurt Weill public television tribute. She has the distinction of being one of the only pianists ever to work with Ornette Coleman. Allen has taught as an assistant professor of music at Howard and was given that university's Distinguished Alumni Award, the SESAE Special Achievement Award, the Eubie Blake Award from Cultural Crossroads, and the Jazzpar award from Denmark, and was voted a Talent Deserving Wider Recognition in *Down Beat* magazine's 1993 and 1994 Critics Polls. She has also written for the theater.

DISC.: *Printmakers* (1984); *Open on All Sides in the Middle* (1987); *In the Year of the Dragon* (1989); *Twylight* (1989); *Segments* (1989); *Nurturer* (1990); *Maroons* (1992); *Twenty One* (1994).—**LP**

Allen, Henry Robinson, Irish baritone, teacher, and composer; b. Cork, 1809; d. London, Nov. 27, 1876. He received training at the Royal Academy of Music in London. In 1842 he scored a notable success as Damon in *Acis and Galatea* at London's Drury Lane. He later devoted his energies to teaching and composing ballads. His song "When we Two Parted" was particularly successful.—**NS/LK/DM**

Allen, Paul Hastings, American composer; b. Hyde Park, Mass., Nov. 28, 1883; d. Boston, Sept. 28, 1952. He studied at Harvard Univ. (B.A., 1903). After serving in the U.S. diplomatic corps in Italy during World War I, he settled in Boston and composed prolifically. He wrote 12 operas, including *Il filtro* (Genoa, Oct. 26, 1912), *Milda* (Venice, June 14, 1913), *L'ultimo dei Moicani* (Florence, Feb. 24, 1916), *Cleopatra* (1921), and *La piccola Figaro* (1931), 8 syms., including the *Pilgrim Symphony* (1910; won the Paderewski prize), a vast amount of chamber music, choral works, and songs. —**NS/LK/DM**

Allen, Sir Hugh (Percy), eminent English organist and music educator; b. Reading, Dec. 23, 1869; d. Oxford, Feb. 20, 1946. He studied with F. Read in Reading, and at Christ's Coll., Cambridge, as an organ scholar, and at the Univ. of Oxford (Mus.Doc., 1898). At the age of 11, he acted as church organist in Reading. Thereafter he was an organist at various churches and cathedrals until the turn of the century. He was organist at New Coll., Oxford (1901–18), and later (1908–18) director of music at Univ. Coll. in Reading. In 1918 he became prof. of music at Oxford, and, in the same year, director of the Royal Coll. of Music in London, from which he resigned in 1937. He was knighted in 1920. In 1935 he was made a Knight of the Grand Cross of the Royal Victorian Order. For many years, he conducted the London and the Oxford Bach choirs. Allen was an ardent promoter of British music.

BIBL.: C. Bailey, *H.P. A.* (London, 1948).—**NS/LK/DM**

Allen, Sir Thomas (Boaz), notable English baritone; b. Seaham, Sept. 10, 1944. He studied organ and voice at the Royal Coll. of Music in London (1964–68). After singing in the Glyndebourne Festival Chorus (1968–69), he made his operatic debut as Rossini's Figaro at the Welsh National Opera in Cardiff in 1969, where he sang until 1972. In 1971 he made his first appearance at London's Covent Garden as Donald in *Billy Budd*, and quickly established himself there as a leading member of the company. He also sang at the Glyndebourne (from 1973) and Aldeburgh (from 1974) festivals. On Nov. 5, 1981, he made his Metropolitan Opera debut in N.Y. as Papageno. In 1986 he sang the title role in Busoni's *Doktor Faust* in its first stage mounting in England with the English National Opera in London. He made his debut at Milan's La Scala as Don Giovanni in 1987. In 1990 he sang for the first time at the Chicago Lyric Opera as Rossini's Figaro. In 1993 he sang Count Almaviva at the Salzburg Festival. From 1994 he was the Prince Consort Prof. at the Royal Coll. of Music. In 1997 he sang in Beckmesser at Covent Garden, and in 1999 he sang in Sondheim's *A Little Night Music* in Houston. On Jan. 26, 2000, he made his N.Y. recital debut at the 92nd Street Y. In 1989 Allen was made a Commander of the Order of the British Empire. In 1999 he was knighted.

WRITINGS: *Foreign Parts: A Singer's Journal* (North Pomfret, 1994).—**NS/LK/DM**

Allen, Steve (originally **Stephen Valentine Patrick William**), popular pianist, songwriter, comedian; b. N.Y., Dec. 16, 1921; d. Oct. 30, 2000. Allen is a capable musician and a very witty man. He was responsible for showcasing many important jazz artists on his NBC programs. These performers included Art Tatum (with whom he played a duet) twice, and the first appearances of Thelonious Monk and Miles Davis (with John Coltrane). These 1955 programs only survive as audio. Allen always treated the musicians respectfully and made a point to try and educate the viewing audience about jazz and improvisation. He also produced the television series *Jazz Scene* between 1960 and 1962 (some of which are available on home video). Allen produced an instructional video on playing jazz piano and also appeared in the *Benny Goodman Story* film.

DISC.: *The Discovery of Buck Hammer* (1957); *The Wild Piano of Mary Anne Jackson* (1959); *S.A. Plays Jazz Tonight* (1982).—**LP**

Allende (-Saron), (Pedro) Humberto, eminent Chilean composer and pedagogue; b. Santiago, June 29, 1885; d. there, Aug. 16, 1959. He studied violin and theory at the National Cons. in Santiago (1889–1908); then taught in public schools there. In 1918 he visited France and Spain; in 1928 he served as Chilean delegate to the Congress of Popular Arts in Prague, under the auspices of the League of Nations; in 1929 he took part in the Festival of Ibero-American Music in Barcelona. Returning to Santiago, he taught composition at the National Cons. (1930–50). He received the National Arts Prize in appreciation of his work in musical ethnology. His music is marked with an exquisite sense of authentic Chilean folk song, while the purely formal structure follows the impressionistic manner akin to that of Debussy, Ravel, and Granados. His symphonic poem, *La voz de las calles* (1921), incorporates street cries of Chilean cities.

WORKS: ORCH.: Sym. (1910); *Escenas campesinas chilenas* (1913); Cello Concerto (1915); *La voz de las calles*, symphonic poem (Santiago, May 20, 1921); *La despedida* for 2 Sopranos, Contralto, and Orch. (Santiago, May 7, 1934); Violin Concerto (Santiago, Dec. 4, 1942); Piano Concerto (1945). **CHAMBER:** String Quartet (1945). **P i a n o :** 3 sonatas (1906–15); *12 tonadas de carácter popular chileno* (1918–22; also for Orch.). **VOCAL:** Songs.—**NS/LK/DM**

Allers, Franz, Czech-born American conductor; b. Karlsbad, Aug. 6, 1905; d. Las Vegas, Jan. 26, 1995. He studied violin at the Prague Cons., violin, piano, conducting, and composition at the Berlin Hochschule für Musik (diploma, 1926), and musicology at the Univ. of Berlin (1926). After playing in the Berlin Phil. (1924–26), he conducted at the Wuppertal Theater (1926–33), in Ústí nad Labem (1933–38), and with the Ballet Russe de Monte Carlo. He then settled in the U.S. and became a naturalized American citizen. He was active as a guest conductor with various orchs. and on Broadway. On Oct. 13, 1957, he made his N.Y.C. Opera debut conducting *Die Fledermaus*, which score he also chose for his Metropolitan Opera debut in N.Y. on Nov. 30, 1963. He conducted at the Metropolitan until 1969; returned for the 1970–72 seasons and again in 1975–76. He was chief conductor of the Gärtnerplatz State Theater in Munich (1973–76).—**NS/LK/DM**

Allgén, Claude Loyola (actually, **Klas Thure**), Swedish composer; b. Calcutta (of Swedish parents), April 16, 1920; d. in a fire in his home in Täby, near Stockholm, Sept. 18, 1990. He was a pupil of Melchers at the Stockholm Musikhögskolan (1936–41). After training in composition in Denmark, the Netherlands, France, Switzerland, and Italy, he became a Roman Catholic, adopted the given names of Claude Loyola, and pursued training in theology. A prolific composer, he wrote in an exceedingly complex personal style. His output included 2 syms., a Violin Concerto, a Fantasy for Orch., 7 string quartets, a Trio for Violin, Viola, and Cello, sacred and secular choral music, songs, piano pieces, and organ works.—**LK/DM**

Allin, Norman, English bass and teacher; b. Ashton-under-Lyne, Nov. 19, 1884; d. Hereford, Oct. 27, 1973. He studied at the Royal Manchester Coll. of Music (1906–10). He made his operatic debut with the Beecham Opera Co. in London in 1916. In 1922 he became a director and leading bass of the British National Opera Co. in London, remaining with it until 1929; from 1942 to 1949 he was a member of the Carl Rosa Opera Co. He led vocal classes at the Royal Academy of Music in London (1935–60) and the Royal Manchester Coll. of Music (1938–42). In 1958 he was made a Commander of the Order of the British Empire.—NS/LK/DM

Allison, Ben, jazz bassist/composer; b. New Haven, Conn., Nov. 17, 1966. Allison is artistic director and one of five composers-in-residence of the Jazz Composers Collective, a group that presents new music according to the vision of the composers. The Collective presents a concert series and publishes a newsletter, which is distributed at no charge. Allison is also co-leader of The Herbie Nichols Project (with pianist Frank Kimbrough), and has written over 100 works for ensembles of varying size and instrumentation. In 1995 he was awarded a commissioning grant from the Mary Flagler Cary Charitable Trust for a suite entitled *Medicine Wheel*. He has also received grants from Meet the Composer, the Mid Atlantic Arts Foundation, American Composers Forum, and the Aaron Copland Fund. He has taught jazz performance, improvisation, and/or composition at N.Y.U., the Mannes Coll. of Music (N.Y.C.), the New School for Social Research, the Univ. of N.C. (Greensboro), and Appalachian State Univ. (N.C.). Allison has been on the faculty of the Third Street Music School in N.Y.C., a guest lecturer for the New School's Contemporary Music Program, and a composer-in-residence at the Fieldston School in Riverdale, N.Y. He has performed with Lee Konitz, Isaac Hayes, Gregory Hines, Dave Liebman, Clifford Jordan, Jackie Terrason, Billy Hart, Arthur Blythe, Vic Juris, Kenny Werner, The American Tap Dance Orch., The Village Vanguard Orch., The Maria Schneider Jazz Orch., and many others.

DISC.: *Seven Arrows* (1995); *Herbie Nichols Project: Love Is Proximity* (1995).—LP

Allison, Mose (John Jr.), jazz-pop pianist, singer, writer; b. Tippo, Miss., Nov. 11, 1927. Allison is a distinctive jazz pianist, a sly and charming singer primarily in a smooth blues idiom, and a witty and perceptive poet writing such lyrics as, "Ever since the world ended/I don't go out as much." His father was a cotton farmer and storekeeper and amateur stride pianist. Mose heard blues on the jukebox in a gas station. He took piano lessons from the age of five until his early teens, when he taught himself trumpet, which he played in the high school band of nearby Charleston, Miss. He also played piano on weekends in a band at a honky-tonk near Greenwood.

In 1945 Allison enrolled at the Univ. of Miss. in Oxford to study chemical engineering, but soon began playing and writing for the band. During 1946–47 he spent 18 months in army bands, then returned to college in 1950, when he decided to pursue music full time, at first in Lake Charles and then in other towns in La. On a summer job in St. Louis he met Audre Schwartz, whom he married in 1951. (That summer he also visited N.Y.C. for the first time.) They moved to Baton Rouge where he completed his B.A. in English at La. State Univ. in 1952, while continuing to perform locally. After

several more years freelancing in the Southeast and in Tex. and Colo., often with bassist Taylor La Fargue, the Allisons moved to N.Y. in 1956; by 1959 they had four children. Allison worked with Al Cohn, Zoot Sims, Stan Getz (1957), and Gerry Mulligan. During 1957 he also formed his own trio and soon achieved success in this format, performing in N.Y., Paris, Stockholm, and Copenhagen, sometimes with the addition of local musicians.

Allison reached the height of his popularity in the late 1960s and early 1970s, when his clever blues-influenced-but-very-contemporary songs caught on with a college-age audience. For a while, he was a popular touring act, and his songs were covered by artists such as Bonnie Raitt. He has continued to record and tour sporadically into the 1990s. Allison's daughter Amy is an acclaimed singer and songwriter with the country-influenced band Parlor James, whose first release was in 1996.

DISC.: *Back Country Suite* (1957); *The Transfiguration of Hiram Brown* (1959); *I Love the Life I Live* (1960); *Don't Worry About a Thing* (1962); *The Word from Mose* (1964); *Western Man* (1971); *Your Mind Is on Vacation* (1976); *Middle Class White Boy* (1982); *Ever Since the World Ended* (1987); *Earth Wants You* (1993). —LP

Allman Brothers Band, The, southern rock band, formed 1969. **MEMBERSHIP:** Duane Allman, 1st lead and slide gtr., voc. (b. Nashville, Nov. 20, 1946; d. Macon, Ga., Oct. 29, 1971); Gregg Allman, kybd., gtr., voc. (b. Nashville, Dec. 8, 1947); Richard "Dickey" Betts, 2nd lead and slide gtr., dobro, voc. (b. West Palm Beach, Fla., Dec. 12, 1943); Berry Oakley, bs. (b. Jacksonville, Fla., April 4, 1948; d. Macon, Ga., Nov. 11, 1972); Butch Trucks, drm. (b. Jacksonville, Fla.); Jai Johanny "Jaimoe" Johanson, drm. perc. (b. Ocean Springs, Miss., July 8, 1944).

The first—and probably the best—of the many blues- and country-oriented bands to emerge from the South in the 1970s, The Allman Brothers Band established themselves as one of the finest performing groups in the country through touring and the release of the live double-record set *At Fillmore East*. Propelled by the twin lead guitars of Dickey Betts and Duane Allman, a revered session man and perhaps rock's greatest slide guitarist, The Allman Brothers Band helped open up rock to music created outside the recording centers of N.Y. and Los Angeles, and provided the impetus for the rise of other southern bands such as Lynyrd Skynyrd and the Charlie Daniels and Marshall Tucker bands. They persevered despite the deaths of Duane Allman in 1971 and Berry Oakley in 1972, only to disband for separate projects in 1974. The Allman Brothers Band regrouped from 1978 to 1982 and again in 1989 for touring and recording.

In 1958 Duane and Gregg Allman moved to Fla., where they formed their first band while still in high school. In 1965 the brothers assembled the regional band The Allman Joys, which lasted two years. They subsequently formed Hourglass for two albums on Liberty, only to split up in spring 1968 as Duane pursued session work in Muscle Shoals, Ala., backing

Wilson Pickett, Aretha Franklin, and many others. After Duane's death this session work was compiled on two double-record sets entitled *An Anthology*.

The Allman Brothers Band was formed in the spring of 1969 after a jam session between Duane Allman and the members of the groups The 31st of February (which included Butch Trucks) and The Second Coming (which included Dickey Betts and Berry Oakley). Signed by Phil Walden, who subsequently formed Capricorn Records in the band's adopted hometown of Macon, Ga., The Allman Brothers Band recorded their debut album for Atco in 1969. It included the rock classics "It's Not My Cross to Bear," "Trouble No More," and "Whipping Post."

Duane continued his session work with Boz Scaggs (on his overlooked first album), Delaney and Bonnie (*To Delaney from Bonnie*), and, most notable, Eric Clapton (Derek and the Dominos' *Layla and Other Assorted Love Songs*). Duane declined Clapton's invitation to join his group, and The Allman Brothers soon recorded *Idlewild South*, which contained Betts's "In Memory of Elizabeth Reed" and Gregg's "Midnight Rider." Having established themselves as thrilling and dynamic performers, the band switched to Walden's Capricorn label for their breakthrough live double-record set *At Fillmore East*, which included an outstanding 13-minute version of "Elizabeth Reed" and an extended version of Gregg's "Whipping Post."

On Oct. 29, 1971, Duane was killed in a motorcycle accident in Macon. The band subsequently abandoned their twin lead guitar configuration for 1972's *Eat a Peach*, which contained the minor hits "One Way Out" and "Melissa." Pianist Chuck Leavell was added in October 1972, but on Nov. 11, 1972, Berry Oakley was fatally injured in a motorcycle accident, again in Macon. Despite the double loss, The Allman Brothers Band persevered, recruiting bassist Lamar Williams. *Brothers and Sisters*, from 1973, featured the instrumental "Jessica" and the band's only Top Ten hit, Betts's "Ramblin' Man."

Band members then pursued solo projects. Gregg Allman retained Trucks, Johanson, and Leavell for *Laid Back*, which produced a major hit single, "Midnight Rider," and a tour in 1974, the year Betts recorded and toured in support of his first solo album, *Highway Call.* Reunited for 1975's *Win, Lose or Draw*, The Allman Brothers Band fragmented in 1976 following Gregg's testimony against former road manager John "Scooter" Herring, who faced drug charges.

Subsequently Betts formed Great Southern with guitarist Dan Toler; Leavell formed Sea Level with Johanson, Williams, and guitarist Jimmy Nalls; Butch Trucks assembled Trucks; and Gregg formed his own band for 1977's *Playin' Up a Storm*. In June 1975 Gregg married Cher (of Sonny and Cher fame) and endured a stormy marriage; the poorly received 1977 duet album *Allman and Woman—Two the Hard Way*; and a dismal European tour.

In October 1978 The Allman Brothers Band reassembled, with Gregg Allman, Dickey Betts, Johanny Johanson, Butch Trucks, and Dan Toler, plus David Goldflies from Betts's Great Southern. Having resumed the double-lead-guitar format, the reconstituted Allman Brothers scored a major hit with "Crazy Love" from *Enlightened Rogues*. The group then switched to Arista Records for two albums before another breakup. Gregg Allman recorded two albums in the late '80s and reconstituted The Allman Brothers Band once again in 1989, with Betts, Trucks, Johanson, Toler, Goldflies, and others, for touring and recordings on Epic Records. Also in 1989, Chuck Leavell toured as one of the two keyboardists on The Rolling Stones' Steel Wheels tour.

DISC.: THE ALLMAN JOYS: *Early Allman* (1973); *Allman Joys* (1993). HOURGLASS: *Hourglass* (1967); *Power of Love* (1968); *Hourglass* (1973). DUANE AND GREGG ALLMAN: *Duane and Gregg Allman* (1972). 31ST OF FEBRUARY: *31st of February* (1968). DUANE ALLMAN: *An Anthology, Vol. 1* (1972); *An Anthology, Vol. 2* (1974); *Best* (1981). THE ALLMAN BROTHERS BAND: *The Allman Brothers Band* (1969); *Idlewild South* (1970); *At Fillmore East* (1971); *Eat a Peach* (1972); *Brothers and Sisters* (1973); *Beginnings* (1973); *Win, Lose or Draw* (1975); *Wipe the Window, Check the Oil, Dollar Gas* (1976); *Enlightened Rogues* (1979); *Reach for the Sky* (1980); *Brothers of the Road* (1981); *Best* (1981); *Dreams* (1989); *Live at Ludlow Garage, 1970* (1990); *Seven Turns* (1990); *A Decade of Hits, 1969–1979* (1991); *Shades of Two Worlds* (1991); *An Evening with The Allman Brothers Band* (1992); *The Fillmore Concerts* (1992); *Where It All Begins* (1994); *Hell and High Water: The Best of the Arista Years* (1994); *2nd Set* (1995). (THE) GREGG ALLMAN (BAND): *Laid Back* (1973); *Gregg Allman Tour* (1974); *Playin' Up a Storm* (1977); *I'm No Angel* (1987); *Just Before the Bullets Fly* (1988). ALLMAN AND WOMAN (GREGG ALLMAN AND CHER): *Two the Hard Way* (1977). DICKEY BETTS: *Highway Call* (1974). DICKEY BETTS AND GREAT SOUTHERN: *Dickey Betts and Great Southern* (1977); *Atlanta's Burning Down* (1978). DICKEY BETTS BAND: *Pattern Disruptive* (1988). SEA LEVEL: *Sea Level* (1977); *Cats of the Coast* (1978); *On the Edge* (1978); *Ball Room* (1980); *Best of Sea Level* (1990).

BIBL.: Tom Nolan, *The Allman Brothers Band: A Biography in Words and Music* (N.Y., 1976); Scott Freeman, *Midnight Riders: The Story of the Allman Brothers Band* (Boston, 1995).

Almanac Singers, The,

political American folk-singing group. Although they existed only from 1941 to 1943, The Almanac Singers profoundly influenced the development of topical songwriting. Their impact was felt especially in the folk revival of the late 1950s and early 1960s.

The Almanac Singers was more a musical collective than a set group; a large number of full- and part-time members participated during its brief existence. The genesis occurred in December 1940 when Pete Seeger met Lee Hays (b. Little Rock, Ark., March 14, 1914; d. North Tarrytown [now Sleepy Hollow], N.Y., Aug. 26, 1981) through his friend Pete (John Peter) Hawes (b. 1917; d. 1973); Seeger and Hays were each working on songbooks of labor union songs. They began to sing together, their first appearance coming at the Jade Mountain Restaurant in N.Y. Soon they were joined by Hays's roommate, aspiring writer Millard Lampell (b. 1919; d. Oct. 3, 1997). Their songs reflected the current Communist party position supporting the 1939 nonaggression pact between Nazi Germany and the Soviet Union. They consisted for the most part of new lyrics written to familiar folk and country tunes. The trio gave their first major performance at the national meeting of the American Youth Congress held in Washington, D.C., Feb. 7–9, 1941. Soon after, they adopted the group name and began living communally.

The Almanac Singers recorded their debut album, *Songs for John Doe* (a six-song set of three 78-rpm records), probably in March 1941. For the recordings, singer/guitarist Josh (Joshua Daniel) White (b. Greenville, S.C., Feb. 11, 1915; d. Manhasset, N.Y., Sept. 5, 1969) and bass singer Sam Gary joined Seeger, Hays, and Lampell. The songs contained scathing attacks on war in general and Roosevelt and the draft in particular. The album was released in May by the independent Keynote Records label, which, due to the controversial content, issued it on the newly created Almanac Records imprint. Probably the same month, The Almanacs, now including Bess (Elizabeth) Lomax (b. 1921) and White's wife, Carol, recorded a second album of union songs, *Talking Union*, that included "Which Side Are You On?" (music and lyrics by Florence Reece) and "Union Maid" (music and lyrics by Woody Guthrie, additional lyrics by Millard Lampell). The album was released by Keynote in June.

A late-May appearance before the striking Transport Workers' Union at Madison Square Garden led to The Almanac Singers being booked for a tour of union gatherings across the country by the Congress of Industrial Organizations (CIO). On June 22, Germany attacked the Soviet Union, causing Keynote to withdraw *Songs for John Doe* from record stores. Within days, Guthrie, who had been on the West Coast writing songs for a documentary film, returned to N.Y. and was invited to join the group on tour. To finance the trip, they contracted to General Records and held a recording session on July 7 to cut a series of nonpolitical folk songs. At the session, The Almanacs consisted of Seeger, Hays, Lampell, Pete Hawes, and Guthrie. They then bought a car and set out, but Hawes, suffering from pneumonia, dropped out within days. General issued the recordings as two albums, *Deep Sea Chanteys and Whaling Ballads* and *Sod Buster Ballads*, over the summer. The Almanac Singers performed before union gatherings across the upper Midwest, reaching San Francisco by early August. Hays dropped out due to illness, and the remaining trio moved on to Los Angeles. Lampell stayed there (later returning to N.Y.), but Seeger and Guthrie continued to tour as The Almanac Singers, going to the Pacific Northwest and then heading east through Mont. and Minn. They reached N.Y. in October, joined the other Almanacs, and rented a townhouse, dubbed Almanac House, in Greenwich Village, where they held weekly rent parties. They also performed, in varying lineups, around the N.Y. area. Their repertoire began to de-emphasize union songs and emphasize songs reflecting more sympathetic sentiments about the war, such as Guthrie's "Reuben James," which commemorated the sinking of an Allied ship. After Pearl Harbor was attacked by the Japanese on Dec. 7, their songs, notably "Round and Round Hitler's Grave," became as militant as earlier ones had been pacifistic.

In the charged atmosphere of the times, The Almanac Singers attracted mainstream attention. Their appearance on the nationally broadcast radio series *We the People* in January 1942 led to interest from the William Morris booking agency and the major label Decca Records. On Feb. 14 they appeared on the radio series *This Is War*, which was broadcast simultaneously on all four networks. Three days later N.Y. newspapers published stories recalling their antiwar songs of the year before and their ties to the Communist party, effectively destroying their hope of broad popular acceptance. They recorded their fifth and final album, *Dear Mr. President*, for Keynote, at which time the group consisted of Seeger, Lampell, Lomax, bass singer Arthur Stern, Pete Hawes's brother Butch (Baldwin) Hawes (b. 1919; d. 1971), and singer/accordion player Sis (Agnes) Cunningham; it was released in May.

In April the group had traveled to Detroit and performed for the United Auto Workers. Their reception, and the promise of defense work, led several members to move to Detroit in June, and Lomax, Stern, Butch Hawes, and Charlie Polacheck set up a satellite edition of The Almanac Singers that performed extensively for union gatherings throughout the Midwest. Meanwhile, the N.Y. group, now sometimes featuring such performers as Cisco (Gilbert Vandine) Houston (b. Wilmington, Del., Aug. 18, 1918; d. San Bernadino, Calif., April 29, 1961), Brownie McGhee (Walter Brown) (b. Knoxville, Tenn., Nov. 30, 1915; d. Feb. 16, 1996), and Sonny Terry (Saunders Terrell; b. Greensboro, N.C., Oct. 24, 1911; d. N.Y., March 11, 1986), continued a fitful existence. Seeger joined the military service in July, and other members soon followed. More press attacks in January 1943 effectively ended the group; a final Almanac Singers performance, featuring Stern, Cunningham, and Polacheck, took place at Wayne State Univ. on Feb. 17.

Following World War II, many former members of The Almanac Singers met on Dec. 30, 1945, and set up People's Songs, Inc., an organization that fostered the writing and performing of left-wing folk songs and published the *People's Songs Bulletin* starting in February 1946. Subsequently, People's Artists, Inc., the Weavers, and *Sing Out!* and *Broadside* magazines, all featuring former Almanacs, carried on the group's work into succeeding decades. *Talking Union* was reissued on LP by Folkways in 1955 and remains in print. In 1996 three reissues brought all of the group's recordings into print on CD: *That's Why We're Marching: World War II and the American Folk Song Movement* on Smithsonian Folkways; *The Almanac Singers: Their Complete General Recordings* on MCA; and *Songs for Political Action: Folk Music, Topical Songs and the American Left, 1926–1953* on the German Bear Family label.—**WR**

Almeida, Antonio (Jacques) de, French conductor of Portuguese-American descent; b. Paris, Jan. 20, 1928; d. Pittsburgh, Feb. 18, 1997. He studied with Alberto Ginastera in Buenos Aires, attended the Mass. Inst. of Technology, received training in theory from Paul Hindemith at Yale Univ. (B.Mus., 1949), and took courses in conducting with Koussevitzky and Bernstein at the Berkshire Music Center in Tanglewood. After serving as a conductor with the Portuguese Radio in Lisbon (1957–60), he was principal conductor of the Stuttgart Phil. (1960–64). He was the principal guest conductor of the Houston Sym. Orch. (1969–71), and then music director of the Nice Phil. (1976–78). In 1993 he became music director of the Moscow Sym. Orch. As a guest conductor, Almeida appeared with many of the world's major orchs. and opera houses; he also was active in researching and ed. the works of Offenbach. —**LK/DM**

d'Almeida, Fernando, Portuguese composer; b. Lisbon, c. 1600; d. Tomar, March 21, 1660. He was a pupil of Duarte Lobo in Lisbon. In 1638 he entered the Order of Christ at Tomar, where he served as a friar and mestre de capela. He wrote much sacred music, all of which is lost.—**NS/LK/DM**

Almeida, Francisco António de, Portuguese composer; b. c. 1702; d. probably in Lisbon, 1755. He studied in Rome on a royal stipend (c. 1720–26), and then settled in Lisbon and wrote the operas *La pazienza di Socrate* (Carnival 1733) and *La spinalba ovvero Il vecchio matta* (Carnival 1739). Among his other works were various sacred pieces, including the oratorios *Il pentimento di Davidde* (Rome, 1722) and *Giuditta* (Rome, 1726).—**NS/LK/DM**

Almeida, Laurindo, lyrical Brazilian-born American guitarist and composer; b. São Paulo, Sept. 2, 1917; d. Van Nuys, Calif., July 26, 1995. Almeida studied at the Escola Nacional de Música in Rio de Janeiro. After appearing on the radio and leading his own orch., he settled in the U.S. in 1947 and became a naturalized citizen in 1961. He was soloist with Stan Kenton's orch. (1947–50); then appeared as a soloist with sym. orchs. and as a recitalist; also composed for films. In 1971 he married the soprano Deltra Eamon, with whom he appeared in recitals.

DISC.: *Brazilliance* Vol.1 (1953); *Brazilliance Vol.2* (1958); *Bossa Nova All-Stars* (1962); *Brazilian Soul* (1980); *Latin Odyssey* (1982); *Tango* (1985); *Almeida/Carlos Barbosa-Lima/Charlie Byrd Music of the Brazilian Masters* (1989); *Outra Vez* (1991). —**NS/LK/DM**

Almenräder, Carl, German bassoonist, inventor, and composer; b. Ronsdorf, Oct. 3, 1786; d. Biebrich, Sept. 14, 1843. He studied with his father, but was autodidact as a bassoonist. After training in theory from Bernhard Klein, he turned his attention to his career as a bassoonist. In 1810 he became a teacher of bassoon at the new Cologne School. After playing bassoon in the orch. of the Frankfurt am Main Theater (1812–14), he returned to Cologne to serve as a military bandmaster, during which time he served in France. In 1817 he became bassoonist in the orch. of the Mainz Theater. He became closely associated with Gottfried Weber, who encouraged him to pursue research on the bassoon at the B. Schotts Söhne instrument factory in 1817. Almenräder publ. his improvement of the 15-key bassoon in his *Traité sur le perfectionnement du basson avec deux*

tableaux (Mainz, c. 1819). He then ran his own workshop in Cologne (1820–22), where he made flutes and clarinets. In 1822 he became 1st bassonist in the Duke of Nassau's court orch. in Biebrich and Wiesbaden. He also pursued his research at Schott's factory. In 1831 he was joined in a partnership by J. A. Heckel, who subsequently became the leading German manufacturer of German bassoons. Almenräder also publ. a tutor for his 15-key bassoon in his *Fagottschule* (Mainz, 1843). Most of his compositions remain unpubl., but he did publ. a Bassoon Concerto, a Pot-pourri for Bassoon and Orch., Variations for Violin, Viola, and Cello, Introduction and Variations for Bassoon and String Quartet, and Duettinos for 2 Bassoons.—**NS/LK/DM**

Almqvist, Carl Jonas Love, Swedish novelist, short-story writer, dramatist, poet, and composer; b. Stockholm, Nov. 28, 1793; d. Bremen, Nov. 26, 1866. He was educated at the Univ. of Uppsala. After being employed in the dept. of ecclesiastical affairs in Stockholm, he joined friends in western Sweden in setting up an experimental community à la Rousseau in 1823. Following his return to Stockholm, he served as rector of an experimental secondary school from 1829 to 1841. In 1837 he was ordained in the Lutheran church, but his radical views on moral and social reform were not welcome. After being accused of fraud and attempted murder of a moneylender, he fled to the U.S. in 1851. In 1865 he returned to Europe. In addition to his large literary output, Almqvist publ. a collection of songs to his own texts (c. 1830) and a collection of piano pieces as *Fria Fantasier* (1847–49).—**NS/LK/DM**

Alnaes, Eyvind, Norwegian organist and composer; b. Fredriksstad, April 29, 1872; d. Oslo, Dec. 24, 1932. He studied with Holter in Christiania (1889–92) and Reinecke in Leipzig (1892–95), and then was a church organist in Norway. His works included *Variations symphoniques* for Orch. (1898), 2 syms. (1898, 1923), *Marche symphonique* for 2 Pianos, choruses, and songs. —**NS/LK/DM**

Alnar, Hasan Ferid, Turkish conductor, teacher, and composer; b. Constantinople, March 11, 1906; d. Ankara, July 27, 1978. He received training in traditional Turkish music, and then studied harmony with Hüseyin Sadettin Arel and counterpoint with Edgar Manas. He completed his studies in Vienna with J. Marx (composition) and Kabasta (conducting). In 1932 he settled in Ankara, where he taught piano (until 1937) and composition (1937–46) at the State Cons. From 1946 to 1952 he was chief conductor of the State President's Sym. Orch. Alnar's music reflects his interest in both traditional Turkish music and Western art music.

WORKS: DRAMATIC: *Sari Zeybek* (1932–33). ORCH.: *Turkish Suite* (1930); *Prelude and 2 Dances* (1935); *Istanbul Suite* (1937–38); Cello Concerto (1943); Kanun (Turkish psaltery) Concerto (1944). CHAMBER: String Quartet (1933); Piano Trio (1967).—**NS/LK/DM**

Alpaerts, Flor, Belgian composer, conductor, and music educator, father of **Jef Alpaerts;** b. Antwerp, Sept.

12, 1876; d. there, Oct. 5, 1954. He studied composition with Benoit and Blockx and violin at the Royal Flemish Cons. in Antwerp. In 1903 he joined its staff, serving as its director from 1934 to 1941. He conducted the orch. at the Zoological Gardens (1919–51) and was director of the Royal Flemish Opera (1922–23) in Antwerp. His music is marked by an intense feeling for the modalities of Flemish folk songs. His 5-vol. treatise *Muzieklezen en Zingen* was for many years the official textbook in all Flemish music institutions.

WORKS: DRAMATIC: O p e r a : *Shylock* (Antwerp, Nov. 22, 1913). OTHER: Incidental music. ORCH.: 7 symphonic poems: *Psyche* (1900); *Herleving* (1903); *Cyrus* (1905); *Pallieter* (1921); *Thijl Uilenspiegel* (1927); *Avondindruk* (1928); *Zomeridyll* (1928); *Poème symphonique* for Flute and Orch. (1903); *Karakterstuk* for Trumpet and Strings (1904); *Bosspeling* (1904); *Salomé danse* (1907); *Vlaamse Idylle* (1920); *Romanza* for Violin and Small Orch. (1928); *James Ensor Suite* (1929); 2 suites for Small Orch. (1932); *Humor* (1936); *Serenade* for Cello and Orch. (1936); *Small Suite* for Strings (1947); Violin Concerto (1948); *Capriccio* (1953). CHAMBER: *2 Pieces* for Piano Trio (1906); *Avondmuziek* for 8 Woodwinds (1915); 4 string quartets (1943, 1944, 1945, 1950); *3 petites pièces* for Violin and Piano (1944); *4 Bagatelles* for String Quartet (1953). VOCAL: Choral works and songs.—NS/LK/DM

Alpaerts, Jef,

Belgian conductor and teacher, son of **Flor Alpaerts;** b. Antwerp, July 17, 1904; d. there, Jan. 15, 1973. He studied at the Royal Flemish Cons. in Antwerp, and in Paris with Philipp and Cortot (piano) and d'Indy (composition). From 1936 to 1969 he was a teacher at the Royal Flemish Cons. In 1938 he founded the Collegium Musicum Antverpiense, which he led in performances of early music.—NS/LK/DM

Alpenheim, Ilse von,

Austrian pianist; b. Innsbruck, Feb. 11, 1927. She studied with Franz Ledwinka and Winfried Wolf at the Salzburg Mozarteum. She made tours of Europe, Japan, Australia, and the U.S. as a soloist with orchs., as a recitalist, and as a chamber music player. In 1969 she married **Antal Doráti**. She was particularly well known for her sensitive performances of Haydn, Mozart, and Schubert.—NS/LK/DM

Alpert, Herb,

the trumpet player who translated mariachi music into a half-billion dollars; b. Los Angeles, Calif., March 31, 1935. Herb Alpert's father, Louis Goldberg, was a tailor, an immigrant from Kiev who settled in the Fairfax area of Los Angeles. His mother, Tillie, encouraged his classical trumpet studies, which he started in elementary school. He started exploring other avenues after seeing Louis Armstrong perform.

After spending some time at the Univ. of Southern Calif., Alpert took a job as an A&R representative for Keen Records. He produced Jan and Dean's first record, "Baby Talk," and the hit "Alley Oop" for Dante and the Evergreens. He also co-wrote Sam Cooke's 1960 #12 single, "Wonderful World."

After attending a bullfight, Alpert wrote a tune on his trumpet to capture the feeling of the event. The song took on a mariachi flavor. Called "The Lonely Bull," it was released by Alpert and his business partner Jerry

Moss as the first record by The Tijuana Brass (Alpert and studio musicians) on their own A&M Records label. The company operated out of Alpert's garage and the two partners distributed records out of the trunks of their cars. Nevertheless, the record sold more than 700,000 copies.

However, Alpert really didn't catch fire until the release of his 1965 masterpiece *Whipped Cream and Other Delights*. The album featured cover art out of *Playboy*—an undressed woman in a pile of whipped cream—and produced a string of hits, including "A Taste of Honey." From the fall of 1965 through the fall of 1967, Alpert was one of the few artists giving The Beatles a run for their money. He earned a dozen Top 40 hits, ten gold albums, and five Grammy Awards: three for "A Taste of Honey," including Record of the Year in 1965, and two for "What Now My Love" the following year. Singles like "The Spanish Flea," "Casino Royale," and "Tijuana Taxi" hit the charts. Alpert earned a spot in the *Guinness Book of World Records* for simultaneously having five records in *Billboard*'s Top 20 (in 1966), a feat not even The Beatles could manage.

By 1967, Alpert was feeling burned-out from the combination of running A&M Records and touring and recording with his band. A&M started releasing artists other than Alpert, starting with Sergio Mendez, Chris Montez, George McCurn, and The Kenjolairs in the mid-1960s. The label's roster in the late 1960s and early 1970s included Joe Cocker, Carole King, The Baja Marimba Band, Cheech and Chong, and The Carpenters. A&M had become big business, an independent record company to contend with.

Alpert, in the meantime, cut a vocal version of Burt Bachrach's "This Guy's in Love with You" that went to #1, proving he wasn't just a trumpet sensation. He disbanded The Tijuana Brass and put away his horn for close to two years, going without his daily practice for the first time in over a quarter of a century. Alpert's career as a pop star sagged in the 1970s; he recorded several albums with South African jazz star Hugh Masakela, even touring for a while. In 1979, he returned to the charts with a vengeance, catching disco lightning in a bottle with the instrumental "Rise." It was his second #1 single in a row, albeit they were 11 years apart! The song won the Best Pop Instrumental Grammy (his third). The follow-up, "Rotation," also got good dance floor play and hit the pop Top 40.

Alpert recorded sporadically through the 1980s. He scored a minor hit in 1982 with "Route 101," and a pair of hits in 1987 with "Diamonds" and "Making Love in the Rain," both of which featured vocals from A&M artist Janet Jackson. The following year, he mined a gold single with "Keep Your Eye on Me."

Meanwhile, A&M continued to sign and break new artists. They had huge hits with artists as diverse as The Police, Cat Stevens, Peter Frampton, Supertramp, Styx, The Go-Go's, Bryan Adams, and many others. They built one of the finest studios on the West Coast, taking over a two-block-long stretch of Sunset Boulevard that included Charlie Chaplin's old studio for their offices.

In 1989, Alpert and Moss sold A&M records for half a billion dollars to PolyGram Records, retaining only their publishing company. They stayed on as figureheads for a few years, but then left the company they'd started in Alpert's garage 25 years earlier and launched Almo Sounds. Starting from the ground up, they signed the band Garbage and developed it into a platinum act.

Alpert continued to record for the new company. He put out an album of jazz called *Second Wind*. He also invested in Broadway plays, including *Angels in America* and *Jelly's Last Jam*. With some of the millions he now had, he created a foundation to give grants to artists via the Calif. Inst. of the Arts. Into his 60s, he continued to play and record with anyone who suited his fancy. *Passion Dance* hooked him up with some hot Latin artists. The "Colors" in the name of his 1999 album referred to the rhythm section of the funk-rock group Living Colour. Neither sold especially well, but having sold over 72 million records and grown a half-billion dollar record company, Alpert had nothing left to prove.

DISC.: *Lonely Bull* (1962); *Whipped Cream & Other Delights* (1965); *Greatest Hits* (1970); *Four Sider* (1973); *Greatest Hits No. 2* (1973); *Rise* (1979); *Classics* (1987); *North on South St.* (1991); *Midnight Sun* (1992); *Second Wind* (1996); *Passion Dance* (1997); *Herb Alpert and Colors* (1999).—**HB**

Alsina, Carlos Roqué, Argentine composer; b. Buenos Aires, Feb. 19, 1941. He received training in theory in Buenos Aires and then held a Ford Foundation grant in Berlin (1964–66), where he studied with Berio. He taught at the State Univ. of N.Y. at Buffalo (1966–68), and then toured Europe with the New Phonic Art group. His music presents a colorful synthesis of quaquaversal idioms, ranging from stark, cloistered dissonance to overt, triadic formalism. Aleatory techniques are in evidence in his improvisatory performances.

WORKS: DRAMATIC: *Texts 1967*, theater piece for Soprano, Flute, Trombone, Violin, Cello, Double Bass, Percussion, and Piano (1967); *Fusion*, choreographic music for Dancer, 2 Pianos, and 2 Percussionists (1974); *Encore*, musical spectacle (1976); *La Muraille*, opera (Avignon, July 28, 1981); *Del Tango*, azione scenica (1982). **ORCH.:** *3 Pieces* for Strings (1964); *Symptom* (1969); *Dispersion 1969* for Chamber Orch. (1969); *Überwindung* for 4 Instrumental Soloists and Orch. (Donaueschingen, Oct. 18, 1970); *Omnipotenz* for Chamber Orch. (1971); *Schichten I* for Chamber Orch. (1971) and *II* for Chamber Ensemble (1972); *Approach* for Piano, Percussion, and Orch. (1972; West Berlin, March 14, 1973); *Themen II* for Percussion and Strings (1974–75; Royan, March 26, 1975); *Stücke* (Royan, April 4, 1977); *Señales* for Piano and Chamber Orch. (La Rochelle, July 3, 1977); *Decisions* for Chamber Orch. (1977); *Études* for Orch. and Tape (Metz, Nov. 17, 1979); 2 syms.: No. 1, *Prima sinfonia*, for Flute, Soprano, Cello, and Orch. (1983) and No. 2 (1992); Piano Concerto (Paris, Nov. 16, 1985); *Suite indirecte* (1989); *Fantasie* for Clarinet and Orch. (1991); Concerto for Wind Quintet and Orch. (1999–2000). **CHAMBER:** *Quinteto de Maderas* for Wind Quintet (1961); *Funktionen* for Flute, Clarinet, Bassoon, Trumpet, Violin, Cello, Piano, and 2 Percussionists (1965); *Consecuenza* for Trombone (1966); *Auftrag* for 9 Players (1966); *Trio 1967* for Cello, Trombone, and Percussion (1967); *Rendez-vous* for 4 Players (1970); *Unity* for Clarinet and Cello (1973); *A Letter* for Wind Quintet (1973); *Étude* for Zarb (1973); *Themen* for Percussion (1974); *Hinterland* for Piano, Percussion, and Tape (1982); *Voie avec voix* for String Quartet

(1984); *Deux Phases* for 7 Instruments (1987); *Éloignements* for 6 Percussionists (1990); *Passages* for Flute, Clarinet, Violin, Cello, and Piano (1990); *Liens* for Percussion and 9 Instruments (1993). **VOCAL:** *Requiem y aleluya* for Soprano, 5 Instruments, and Percussion (1960); *Oratorio* for 3 Soloists, 4 Actors, and 3 Small Instrumental Ensembles (1964); *Text* for Chorus, Trombone, and 3 Percussion Instruments (1966); *Consecuenza II* for Voice (1971); Cantata for Tenor, Chorus, and Orch. (Radio France, April 22, 1977); *Harmonies* for Children's Chorus, 2 Lectors, Narrator, 4 Soloists, Tape, and Orch. (Paris Radio, Dec. 22, 1979); *Pénomenbres* for Chorus, Children's Chorus, and Orch. (1994). —**NS/LK/DM**

Alsop, Marin, American conductor; b. N.Y., Oct. 16, 1956. She pursued music training at the Juilliard School in N.Y. (B.M., 1977; M.M., 1978). During the summers of 1988 and 1989, she held the Leonard Bernstein Conducting Fellowship at the Tanglewood Music Center, where she was a student of Bernstein, Ozawa, and Gustav Meier. In 1989 she became the first woman to receive the Koussevitzky conducting prize there, and that same year she was a prizewinner in the Stokowski conducting competition in N.Y. In 1984 she became founder–artistic director of her own N.Y.-based orch., Concordia, with which she presented a varied repertoire of not only standard and contemporary works, but also jazz. She was also active as a jazz violinist, and was founder-director of her own swing band, String Fever. She served as music director of the Eugene (Oreg.) Sym. Orch. (1989–96), the Long Island Phil. (1990–96), the Cabrillo Music Festival (from 1992), and the Ore. Festival of American Music (from 1992), as well as principal conductor of the Colo. Sym. Orch. in Denver (from 1993). She also held the first Creative Conductor's Chair with the St. Louis Sym. Orch. from 1996, and was principal guest conductor of the Royal Scottish National Orch. in Glasgow and of the City of London Sinfonietta from 1999.—**NS/LK/DM**

Altani, Ippolit (Karlovich), Russian conductor; b. Ukraine, May 27, 1846; d. Moscow, Feb. 17, 1919. He was a pupil of Zaremba and A. Rubinstein in St. Petersburg. After conducting in Kiev (1867–82), he was chief conductor of Moscow's Bolshoi Theater (1882–1906), where he conducted the premieres of Tchaikovsky's *Mazeppa* (1884) and Rachmaninoff's *Aleko* (1893). He also conducted the Moscow premieres of many other notable works, including Mussorgsky's *Boris Godunov* (1888), and Tchaikovsky's *The Queen of Spades* (1891).—**NS/LK/DM**

Altenburg, Detlef, German musicologist; b. Bad Hersfeld, Jan. 9, 1947. He was educated at the Univ. of Cologne (Ph.D., 1973, with the diss. *Untersuchungen zur Geschichte der Trompete im Zeitalter der Clarinblaskunst (1500–1800)*; publ. in Regensburg, 1973; Habilitationsschrift, 1980, *Studien zum Musikdenken und zu den Reformplänen von Franz Liszt*). From 1983 he was a prof. at the Univ.- Gesamthochschule-Paderborn in Detmold. From 1986 to 1989 he was an ed. for *Die Musikforschung*. An authority on Liszt, he served as ed. of the new critical edition of Liszt's writings (9 vols., Wiesbaden, 1989 et seq.). In 1990 he became president of the Franz-Liszt-

Gesellschaft in Weimar, and was ed. of its *Liszt-Jahrbuch* from 1992. Among his other writings are *Zum Repertoire der Hoftrompeter im 17. und 18. Jahrhundert* (Tutzing, 1976), *Eine Theorie der Musik der Zukunft: Zur Funktion des Programms im symphonischen Werk Franz Liszts* (Graz, 1977), *Die Projekte der Liszt- Forschung* (with G. Winkler; Eisenstadt, 1991), and *Liszt und die Weimarer Klassik* (Laaber, 1997).—NS/LK/DM

Altenburg, Johann Ernst, German trumpeter, organist, and composer; b. Wiessenfels, June 15, 1734; d. Bitterfeld, May 14, 1801. He studied trumpet with his father, and then organ and composition with Römhild in Merseburg. He also studied with Altnikol in Naumburg. From 1757 to 1766 he was a field trumpeter in the French Army, and then was organist in Landsberg. In 1769 he settled in Bitterfeld as organist. He wrote the valuable treatise *Versuch einer Anleitung zur heroisch-musikalischen Trompeter-und Paukerkunst* (Halle, 1795; Eng. tr., 1974). He composed a Concerto for 7 Trumpets and Kettledrums and pieces for 2, 4, 6, and 8 trumpets. —NS/LK/DM

Altenburg, Michael, German composer; b. Alach, May 27, 1584; d. Erfurt, Feb. 12, 1640. He studied theology in Erfurt (1598–1603), and then was active as a clergyman and schoolmaster. In 1609 he went to Torchtelborn, then to Gross-Sommerda in 1621, and finally to Erfurt in 1637. He publ. 16 instrumental *Intraden* (Erfurt, 1620), a collection of sacred and secular songs for 5, 6, and 8 Voices (3 vols., Erfurt, 1620–21), and numerous church anthems.—NS/LK/DM

Altenburger, Christian, German violinist; b. Heidelberg, Sept. 7, 1957. He began violin studies with his father and made his first public appearance when he was only 7. He pursued training with Ernst Morawec at the Vienna Academy of Music, graduating at age 16. In 1976 he made his professional debut in a recital at the Musikverein in Vienna. He completed his studies with DeLay at the Juilliard School in N.Y., graduating in 1978. Thereafter he appeared as a soloist with leading orchs. on both sides of the Atlantic, gave recitals, and played in chamber music settings.—NS/LK/DM

Altès, Ernest-Eugène, French violinist, conductor, and composer, brother of **Joseph-Henri Altès;** b. Paris, March 28, 1830; d. St.-Dyé, near Blois, July 8, 1899. He studied with Habeneck at the Paris Cons., where he won the premier prix for violin in 1848. In 1871 he joined the staff of the Paris Opéra as conductor, retiring in 1887. He composed a Sym., chamber music, and an orch. *Divertissement* on ballet airs by Auber on the occasion of Auber's centennial (1882).—NS/LK/DM

Altès, Joseph-Henri, French flutist, teacher, and composer, brother of **Ernest-Eugène Altès;** b. Rouen, Jan. 18, 1826; d. Paris, July 24, 1895. He studied at the Paris Cons., then became a flutist in the orch. of the Paris Opéra. He was appointed prof. of flute at the Paris Cons. in 1868, holding this post to the end of his life. He publ. a number of flute pieces.—NS/LK/DM

Althouse, Paul (Shearer), American tenor; b. Reading, Pa., Dec. 2, 1889; d. N.Y., Feb. 6, 1954. He studied at Bucknell Univ. and with Perley Aldrich in Philadelphia and Percy Stevens and Oscar Saenger in N.Y. In 1911 he made his operatic debut as Faust with the Chicago-Philadelphia Grand Opera Co. in N.Y. On March 19, 1913, he made his Metropolitan Opera debut in N.Y. as Dimitri in the U.S. premiere of *Boris Godunov*, remaining on its roster until 1920. After further vocal studies in Europe, he returned to the Metropolitan Opera in 1934 as a Heldentenor, singing there until 1940. He also appeared in opera in San Francisco, Chicago, Berlin, Bayreuth, and Salzburg and sang with many U.S. orchs. He spent his last years in N.Y. as a teacher, numbering among his students Eleanor Steber and Richard Tucker.—NS/LK/DM

Altman, Ludwig, German-American organist and composer; b. Breslau, Sept. 2, 1910; d. San Francisco, Nov. 27, 1990. He studied with Arthur Schmitz and Peter Epstein at the Univ. of Breslau, with H. J. Moser, Schering, Wolf, and Blume at the Berlin-Spandau School for Church Music (1929–33), and organ with Arthur Zubke. After serving as organist of Berlin's Neue Synagoge (1933–36), he emigrated to the U.S. and concentrated his career in San Francisco, where he was organist and choral director at Temple Emanu-El (from 1937), organist of the San Francisco Sym. (1940–73), and municipal organist of city (from 1952); also toured widely as a recitalist. His extensive repertory ranged from the Baroque masters to scores by contemporary composers. He wrote much sacred music and solo organ pieces.

BIBL.: E. Glaser and C. Crawford, *L. A.: A Well-Tempered Musician's Unfinished Journey Through Life* (Berkeley, 1990). —NS/LK/DM

Altmann, Wilhelm, German music librarian and scholar; b. Adelnau, near Posen, April 4, 1862; d. Hildesheim, March 25, 1951. He studied with Otto Lustner (violin and theory) in Breslau, took courses in medieval history and classical philology in Marburg and Berlin (1882–85), and received training in library science at the Royal Univ. Library in Breslau. He was a librarian (1889–1900) and a lecturer in medieval history and library science (1893–1900) at the Univ. of Greifswald. In 1900 he became a librarian at the Royal (later State) Library in Berlin, where he was director of its music dept. (1915–27). In 1906 he helped to found the Deutsche Musiksammlung in Berlin. Among his useful books were *Kammermusik Katalog* (1910; 6th ed., 1945); *Orchester-Literatur-Katalog* (vol. I, 1919; 2nd ed., aug., 1926; vol. II, 1919; 3rd ed., 1936; rev. eds. of Frank's *Kleines Tonkünstlerlexicon* as *Kurzegefasstes Tonkünstlerlexikon* (12th ed., 1926; 15th ed., 1948–49); *Handbuch für Streichquartettspieler* (1928–31); *Handbuch für Klaviertriospieler* (1934); *Handbuch für Klavierquartettspieler* (1937); with V. Borissowsky, *Literaturverzeichnis für Bratsche und Viola d'Amore* (1937); *Verzeichnis von Werken für Klavier vier- und sechs-händig sowie für zwei und mehr Klaviere* (1943).—NS/LK/DM

Altmeyer, Jeannine (Theresa), American soprano; b. La Habra, Calif., May 2, 1948. She received instruction from Martial Singher and Lotte Lehmann in Santa Barbara, Calif.; later took courses at the Salzburg Mozarteum. She made her operatic debut as the Heavenly Voice in *Don Carlos* at the Metropolitan Opera (N.Y., Sept. 25, 1971); then sang Freia in *Das Rheingold* at the Chicago Lyric Opera (1972), in Salzburg (1973), and at London's Covent Garden (1975). From 1975 to 1979 she was a member of the Württemberg State Theater in Stuttgart; subsequently appeared in Bayreuth (1979), Paris (1987), Zürich (1989), and Milan (1990). After appearing as Wagner's Venus at the Metropolitan Opera in 1997, she was engaged as Brünnhilde in the *Ring* cycle in Amsterdam in 1998–99. She is notably successful in Wagnerian roles, including Elisabeth, Gutrune, Eva, Brünnhilde, Elsa, and Sieglinde.—**NS/LK/DM**

Altmeyer, Theo(dor David), German tenor; b. Eschweiler, March 16, 1931. He was educated in Cologne. In 1956 he joined the Berlin Städtische Oper, remaining on its roster until 1960; then became a member of the Hannover Opera; later appeared at the Stuttgart Opera and the Vienna State Opera; also toured North America. In 1974 he joined the faculty of the Hochschule für Musik in Hannover; continued to appear in opera and concerts.—**NS/LK/DM**

Altnikol, Johann Christoph, German organist and composer; b. Berma bei Seidenberg (baptized), Jan. 1, 1720; d. Naumburg (buried), July 25, 1759. He was a singer and asst. organist at S. Maria Magdalena in Breslau from about 1740. In 1744 he went to Leipzig to study theology at the Univ. He also sang under J. S. Bach from 1745, and received instruction in keyboard playing and composition from him and acted as his copyist. In 1748 he was organist and schoolteacher in Niederwiesa, and later that year settled in Naumburg as organist at St. Wenceslaus. In 1749 he married Bach's daughter Elisabeth. After Bach's death in 1750, Altnikol took in Bach's mentally handicapped son Gottfried Heinrich Bach. His works include a Magnificat, cantatas, and keyboard pieces, but most are not extant.—**NS/LK/DM**

Altschul, Barry, jazz and pop drummer; b. N.Y., Jan. 6, 1943. Altschul is an innovative artist associated with free jazz, but he has also worked with the mainstream. He began playing drums when he was 11, and later studied with Charlie Persip. By the mid-1960s he was a member of the Jazz Composer's Guild and was working with Paul Bley and others. He worked with Carmell Jones, Leo Wright, and Johnny Griffin in Europe during 1968. From 1970 to 1972 he toured with Circle, along with Chick Corea, Dave Holland, and Anthony Braxton, then continued to freelance with Braxton as well as other avant-garde musicians, including Sam Rivers and the more mainstream Art Pepper. Altschul has also led his own groups and has an interest in world percussion.

DISC.: *Closer* (1965); *Ramblin'* (1966); *Virtuosi* (1967); *Revenge* (1969); *Song of Singing* (1970); *You Can't Name Your Own Tune* (1977); *Another Time, Another Place* (1978); *For Stu* (1979); *That's Nice* (1985).—**LP**

Altschuler, Modest, Russian-American conductor; b. Mogilev, Feb. 15, 1873; d. Los Angeles, Sept. 12, 1963. He studied cello at the Warsaw Cons., and then was a student of Arensky and Taneyev (composition) and Safonov (piano and conducting) at the Moscow Cons. (graduated, 1890). In 1903 he went to N.Y., where he was founder-conductor of the Russian Sym. Soc. (1904–16). Altschuler conducted the premiere of Scriabin's *Le poème de l'extase* (N.Y., Dec. 10, 1908), and the U.S. premiere of his *Prométhée, le poème du feu* (N.Y., March 20, 1915). He also conducted the U.S. premieres of works by Rachmaninoff, Liadov, Ippolitov-Ivanov, and Vasilenko.—**NS/LK/DM**

Alva, Luigi (real name, Luis Ernesto Alva Talledo), noted Peruvian tenor; b. Lima, April 10, 1927. He was a pupil of Rosa Morales in Lima, where he made his operatic debut as Beppe in 1950. He then completed his training at the La Scala opera school in Milan. In 1954 he made his European operatic debut as Alfredo at Milan's Teatro Nuovo, and then sang Paolino in *Il matrimonio segreto* at the opening of Milan's La Piccola Scala in 1955; his La Scala debut followed as Count Almaviva in 1956. In 1957 he sang at the Salzburg Festival, in 1960 at London's Covent Garden (debut as Count Almaviva), and in 1961 at the Chicago Lyric Opera. On March 6, 1964, he made his Metropolitan Opera debut in N.Y. as Fenton; remained on its roster until 1966, and again for the 1967–69, 1971–72, and 1973–75 seasons. In subsequent years, he continued to make appearances in Europe until his retirement in 1989. He served as artistic director of the Fundación Pro Arte Lírica in Lima from 1982. Alva was particularly esteemed for his roles in Mozart's operas, but he also won success for his Italian roles from the early 19th century repertory.—**NS/LK/DM**

Alvarez (real name, Gourron), Albert (Raymond), French tenor; b. Cenon, near Bordeaux, May 16, 1861; d. Nice, Feb. 1, 1933. After studying with Martini in Paris, he made his operatic debut as Faust in Ghent in 1887. He then sang in Lyons and Marseilles before returning to Paris to make his debut at the Opéra as Faust in 1892. In 1894 he created the role of Nicias in *Thaïs* there. He made his first appearance at London's Covent Garden in 1893 as Leicester in de Lara's *Amy Robsart*. In 1894 he created the role of Aragui in *La Navarraise* there. On Dec. 12, 1899, he made his debut with the Metropolitan Opera as Roméo during the company's visit to Boston, and then made his formal debut with it in N.Y. in the same role on Dec. 18, 1899. He remained on its roster until 1903, finding success as Radames, Otello, and Canio. Thereafter he taught voice in Paris.—**NS/LK/DM**

Álvarez, Javier, Mexican composer; b. Mexico City, May 8, 1956. He studied clarinet and composition with Mario Lavista at the National Cons. of Music in Mexico City, and later composition with John Downey at the Univ. of Wisc.–Milwaukee (1980–82). Álvarez then studied composition and electronic music at the Royal Coll. of Music in London (1982), where he settled. In the 1980s, he divided his time between London and Mexico City, teaching composition and computer music technology; later he was a visiting prof. of composition at the Malmö Music Academy in Sweden and a Reader in Composition at the Univ. of Hertfordshire. He received the Austrian Prix Ars Electronica for computer art in 1992. Álvarez is most noted for his electronic and computer music, but writes also for acoustic instruments. His short but infectiously melodic and rhythmic *Metro Chabacano*, in versions for String Orch. or String Quartet, has achieved wide popularity.

WORKS: DRAMATIC: Opera: *Mambo* (1993). **ORCH.:** *Études* for Winds and Strings (1981); *Trireme* for Horn and Orch. (1983); *Yaotl* for Orch., with 2 Guitars, Synthesizer, and Computer Tape (1987); *Metro Chabacano* for Strings (1987; also for String Quartet, 1991); *Gramática de dos* for Orch. and Synthesizer (1991); *Música para piel y palangana* for Percussion and Orch. (1993); *Metro Taxqueña* for Strings (1994); Cello Concerto (1995). **CHAMBER:** *Ayara* for Bassoon and String Quartet (1981); *Lustral* for Harp (1981); *White Mirrors* for Flute, Clarinet, Violin, and Harpsichord (1982); *Característica* for Flute, Oboe, Cello, and Piano (1982); *Ki bone gaku* for Trombone and Marimba (1984); *Trientos* for Flute, Clarinet, Violin, Cello, and Piano (1985); *Quemar de naves* for Chamber Ensemble (1991); *Acordeón de roto Corazón* for Saxophone Quartet (1994); *Serpiente y escalera* for Cello and Piano (1995). **VOCAL:** *Amor es más laberinto* for 5 Soloists, Chorus, and Orch. (1978); *Tres ranas contra reloj* for Vocalise, Violin, Cello, and Piano (1981); *Animal Crackers* for 2 Sopranos, Baritone, Viola, and Piano (1990); *Calacas imaginarias* for Chorus and Tape (1994). **ELECTROACOUSTIC:** *Temazcal* for Amplified Maracas and Tape (1984); *Papaloti* for Piano and Computer (1987); *On Going On* for Baritone Saxophone and Tape (1987); *Acuerdos por diferencia* for Harp and Computer (1989); *Mambo a la Bracque* for Tape (1990); *Mannan* for Kayagum and Electroacoustic Sounds (1992); *Mambo vinko* for Trombone and Tape (1993); *Overture* for Tape (1995).—**LK/DM**

Alvarez (de Rocafuerte), Marguerite d',

English contralto of Peruvian descent; b. Liverpool, c. 1886; d. Alassio, Oct. 18, 1953. She made her first public appearance at a London diplomatic reception when she was 16. After training in Brussels, she made her operatic debut in 1904 as Dalila in Rouen; in 1909 she made her U.S. debut with Hammerstein's company in N.Y. as Fidès; in 1911 she appeared at the London Opera House as the Queen in *Hérodiade* and later sang at London's Covent Garden, in Chicago, and in Boston. In her later years, she devoted herself mainly to a concert career, retiring in 1939.

WRITINGS: *Forsaken Altars* (autobiography; London, 1954; U.S. ed. as *All the Bright Dreams*, N.Y., 1956).—**NS/LK/DM**

Alvary, Lorenzo,

Hungarian-born American bass; b. Debrecen, Feb. 20, 1909; d. N.Y., Dec. 13, 1996. He studied law at the univs. of Geneva (B.L., 1930) and Budapest (LL.M., 1932) and voice in Milan and Berlin. In 1934 he made his operatic debut at the Budapest Opera, and then sang at the Vienna State Opera in 1937. In 1938 he emigrated to the U.S., becoming a naturalized American citizen in 1944. In 1939 he made his U.S. debut as the Police Commissioner in *Der Rosenkavalier* at the San Francisco Opera, where he returned regularly until 1977. On Nov. 26, 1942, he made his Metropolitan Opera debut in N.Y. as Zuñiga, remaining on its roster until 1961; was on its roster there again (1962–72, 1977–78). —**NS/LK/DM**

Alvary (real name, Achenbach), Max(imilian),

German tenor; b. Düsseldorf, May 3, 1856; d. near Gross-Tabarz, Thuringia, Nov. 7, 1898. He studied with Stockhausen in Frankfurt am Main and Lamperti in Milan. In 1879 he made his operatic debut as Max Anders in *Alessandro Stradella* in Weimar. On Nov. 25, 1885, he made his Metropolitan Opera debut in N.Y. as Don José, remaining on its roster until 1889. In 1891 he sang Tristan and Tannhäuser at the Bayreuth Festival, and in 1892 he made his debut at London's Covent Garden as the young Siegfried. He was compelled to retire from the operatic stage due to poor health in 1897. Alvary was especially successful as a Wagnerian. —**NS/LK/DM**

Alvin, Danny (originally Viniello, Daniel Alvin),

jazz drummer; b. N.Y., Nov. 29, 1902; d. Chicago, Dec. 6, 1958. The father of the late Teddy Walters (vocals/guitar), Alvin's first professional work was accompanying "Aunt Jemima" at the Central Opera House, N.Y. in 1918. During the following year he began a three-year spell accompanying vocalist Sophie Tucker. Alvin moved to Chicago in 1922 and joined Jules Buffano's band at Midnite Frolics and worked with Frankie Quartell and Charley Straight before joining The Midway Gardens Orchestra. He spent a brief period with Joe Kayser's band, then worked in Florida with Arnold Johnson's Orchestra during 1926 and 1927. Returning to Chicago, Alvin joined Al Morey's Orchestra, then worked with Wayne King's band until 1930. He also worked with Ted Fio Rite before joining Amos Ostot and His Crimson Serenaders. Alvin led his own band in Chicago at the 100 Club until 1933, then spent three years working mostly with pianist Art Hodes, usually at the Vanity Fair Cafe. Alvin moved to N.Y. in 1936 and did extensive gigging before spending two years with Wingy Manone. After spending time with various groups in the 1940s, Alvin organized his own band for residency at Rupneck's in late 1949. During the 1950s, he led his own Kings of Dixieland and ran his own club.

DISC.: *D. A. and His Kings of Dixieland Play Basin Street* (1958).—**JC/LP**

Alvis, Hayes (Julian),

jazz tuba player, string bassist; b. Chicago, May 1, 1907; d. N.Y., Dec. 29, 1972. Originally a drummer, Alvis played in The Chicago Defender Boys' Band. He played drums and tuba with Jelly Roll Morton on tour dates from 1927 to early 1928, then concentrated mainly on tuba, gigging with many bands in Chicago, then with Earl Hines from late 1928 to 1930. Switching to string bass, Alvis went to N.Y. with Jimmie Noone in the spring of 1931. He worked with The Mills Blue Rhythm Band from 1931 until early 1935 when he joined Duke Ellington (sharing bass duties with Billy Taylor). Alvis left Ellington's band in spring 1938 and formed a short-lived band with Freddy Jenkins. From October 1938 until March 1939 he worked in N.Y. with the "Blackbirds Show." He joined Benny Carter's Big Band at the Savoy in March 1939 and worked with Joe Sullivan from November 1940. During the following spring, Alvis played with Bobby Burnet's band in N.Y. He then joined The Louis Armstrong Orchestra until February 1942,, when he joined The N.B.C. Orchestra. After army service from 1943 until 1945, he worked with The Gene Fields Trio and LeRoy Tibbs. During 1946–47 he played with The Dave Martin Trio and in Harry Dial's Combo; he then spent a long spell as house musician at Cafe Society, N.Y. (From 1940 he was also active in running his own millinery business in New York.) During the 1950s, Alvis was active as a freelancer in N.Y., worked for a spell in Boston with Joe Thomas (1952), and took part in Fletcher Henderson reunion sessions in the summer of 1957. Alvis continued regular playing in the 1960s, including regular work with singer Dionne Warwick.—JC/LP

Alwin, Karl (real name, **Alwin Oskar Pinkus**), German conductor; b. Königsberg, April 15, 1891; d. Mexico City, Oct. 15, 1945. He studied composition with Humperdinck and Hugo Kaun in Berlin. He conducted in Halle (1913), Posen (1914), Düsseldorf (1915–17), and Hamburg (1917–20). From 1920 to 1938 he conducted at the Vienna State Opera. In 1941 he settled in Mexico City. He was married to **Elisabeth Schumann** from 1920 to 1936.—NS/LK/DM

Alwyn, Kenneth (in full, **Kenneth Alwyn Wetherall**), English conductor and composer; b. Croydon, July 28, 1925. He received his training in London. In 1958 he began a long association with the BBC, conducting various radio and television broadcasts. In addition to composing many scores for films and television, he wrote *Echoes* for Narrator, Band, Chorus, and Orch. to commemorate D-Day (1995) and several marches.—NS/LK/DM

Alwyn, William, English composer and teacher; b. Northampton, Nov. 7, 1905; d. Southwold, Sept. 11, 1985. He studied with McEwen at the Royal Academy of Music in London (1920–23), where he subsequently taught (1926–56), although he had failed to graduate. He was also active as a poet, translator, and painter. In 1978 he was made a Commander of the Order of the British Empire. Although Alwyn wrote a significant number of concert and stage works, he was particularly facile when writing for films.

WORKS: DRAMATIC: O p e r a : *Juan, or The Libertine* (1965–71); *Miss Julie* (1970–73; BBC, July 16, 1977). F i l m : Over 60 film scores. ORCH.: 5 syms. (1949, 1953, 1956, 1959, 1973); 3 concerti grossi (1942, 1950, 1964); Oboe Concerto (1951); *The Magic Island* (1952); *Lyra Angelica*, concerto for Harp and Strings (1954); *Autumn Legend* for English Horn and Strings (1955); *6 Elizabeth Dances* (1957); *Derby Day* (1960); 2 sinfoniettas (1970, 1976). CHAMBER: 2 string quartets (1955, 1976); String Trio (1962); Clarinet Sonata (1963); *Naiades*, sonata for Flute and Harp (1971); piano pieces. VOCAL: Song cycles.
—NS/LK/DM

Alypius, Greek music theorist who flourished in the mid 4th century. He wrote the invaluable *Introduction to Music* (critical ed. by K. von Jan in *Musici scriptores graeci*, 1895), the chief source of specific information on ancient Greek notation. It contains a summary of Greek scales in all their transpositions, for both voices and instruments.—NS/LK/DM

Åm, Magnar, Norwegian composer; b. Trondheim, April 9, 1952. He studied organ at the Bergen Cons. and received lessons in composition from Lidholm at the Stockholm Musikhögskolan (1971–72). He was awarded a State Guaranteed Income for Artists and devoted himself to composition. In his output, Åm has generally pursued a freely tonal style. While preferring traditional forms, his experimental bent has led him to explore the realm of electroacoustics.

WORKS: ORCH.: *Song* for Brass and Percussion (1974); *Study on a Norwegian Hymn* for Strings (1977); *ajar* for Double Bass and Orch. (1981); *my planet, my soul*, sym. (1982); *right through all this* (1985); *The Oblique One*, march for Symphonic Band (1985); *can tell you a mile off* for Symphonic Band (1988); *if we lift as one* (1988); *timeless energy* (1991); *Naked Tones* for Symphonic Band (1993); *The Wondering and the Wond: For Orchestra—and the Odd Passing Dolphin* (1996). CHAMBER: 2 *Movements* for String Quartet (1970); *Lyrikk* for 2 Horns and Hardanger Fiddle (1971); *Intermezzo* for 3 Woodwinds (1976); Sonata for Flute, Guitar, and Cello (1976); *Dance* for Harp, Guitar, and Harpsichord (1977); *in nude*, octet for Clarinet, Bassoon, Horn, 2 Violins, Viola, Cello, and Double Bass (1977); *Du, bli her* (You Stay Here!) for Viola and Cello (1979); *sing, pain* for Viola, 2 Cellos, Percussion, and Piano (1979); *like a leaf on the river* for Guitar (1983); *pas de deux* for Violin and Cello (1984); *still* for Flute and Harp (1985); *Freetonal Conversation* for Violin, Cello, and Piano (1986); *hovering depths* for Double Bass (1986); *air...of breath have you come, to breath shall you be* for Double Bass and Tape (1987); *summen...*, canon for 4 Trumpets (1990); *Unio mystica* for Organ (1998). VOCAL: *Prayer* for Soprano, Chorus, and String Orch. (1972); *Mot dag* (Dawn Is Breaking), oratorio for Chorus and Orch. (1972); *point zero*, version A for Soprano, Chorus, Children's Chorus, and Orch. (1978–83), version B for Soprano, Chorus, Congregation, Organ, and Orch. (1978–83), and version C for Soprano, Chorus, Congregation, and Organ (1982); *trollsenga* for Narrator and Saxophone or Flute or Percussion (1980); *Agamemnon*, choral drama for Soprano, Women's Chorus, and 2 Clarinets (1981); *wings* for 3 Choruses and 5 Instruments (1981); *A Cage-Bird's Dream (Music for Closed Eyes)* for Chorus, Violin, 2 Percussion, Piano, and Slides (1982); *Omen* for Reciter, Violin, Horn, and Upright Piano (1983–89); *till we grow out of ourselves* for Soprano, Chorus, Children's Chorus, Narrator, and Organ (1983); *congilia* for Narrator, Violin, Horn, and Piano (1984); *a miracle and a tear* for Chorus (1987); *fritt fram* for Soprano, Flute, Clarinet, Violin, Cello, Percussion, and Piano (1987); *grain of sand seeks oyster* for Soprano, Flute, Clarinet, Guitar, Violin, and Double Bass (1987); *a new-born child* for Chorus, Flute, Percussion, Marimba, and Harp (1988); *and let the boat slip quietly out* for Voice and Orch. (1989); *Pilgrimsmusikk* for Nidaros Cathedral for Boy Soprano, Tenor, Children's Chorus, Mixed Chorus, and Chamber Orch. (1990); *...og livet*, oratorio for 2 Narrators, Soprano and Tenor Voices, Children's Chorus, Mixed Chorus, and Chamber Orch. (1990); *effata* for Soprano, Men's Voices, and Organ (1991); *quiet ruby* for Chorus (1992); *Is it Like this Among Humans, Too?* for Alto, Chorus, Flute, Synthesizer, Piano, and Percussion (1992); *On the Wings of the Ka-Bird*, 7 motets for Chorus (1996); *You Are Loved* for Soprano, Women's Voices, 2 Horns, and Harp (1997);

Wandering Heaven for Alto, 2 Violins, 2 Violas, and 2 Cellos (1998). **OTHER:** *water music*, electro-acoustic piece (1984); *pa en stol*, visual concert for Clarinet, Trumpet, Percussion, Piano, Mime, and Audience (1989); *Tonebath*, music experience (1989); *Voyage*, music experience (1993).—**NS/LK/DM**

Amacher, Maryanne, ingenious American composer and sound installation artist; b. Kates, Pa., Feb. 25, 1943. After piano studies at the Philadelphia Cons. of Music, she studied music in Salzburg and England as an Inst. for International Education Fellow; she also studied with Stockhausen. She trained in both music and computer science at the Univ. of Pa. (B.F.A., 1964), where she received the Hugh Clark Fine Arts Prize and the Laisse Fine Arts Award, and at the Univ. of Ill. at Champaign—Urbana, where she studied acoustics and began composing her first electroacoustic works. She then was a fellow at the Center for Advanced Visual Studies at the Mass. Inst. of Technology (1972–76), where she created projects for solo and group shows in collaboration with the visual artists Scott Fisher and Luis Frangella and with the architect Juan Navarro Baldweg. From 1973 to 1984 she was active in the creation of works with John Cage and his lifetime choreographer partner, Merce Cunningham. In 1975 she composed the storm environment for Cage's multimedia work, *Lecture on the Weather*, and in 1978 the sonic environment *Close Up* that accompanied his 10-hour solo voice composition, *Empty Words*. She and Cage presented both works together in performances in Canada, Germany, and the U.S. (1976–84). In 1976 she received a commission from the Cunningham Dance Foundation to compose the repertoire sound work for the choreographer's *Torse*. This was followed by several other evening-length sound works for the Cunningham Dance Company's "events" in N.Y. (1974–80).

Amacher's work is best represented in three series of multimedia installations: the sonic telepresence series CITY-LINKS #1–22 (from 1967), the architecturally staged MUSIC FOR SOUND-JOINED ROOMS (from 1980), and the MINI-SOUND SERIES (from 1985), a new multimedia form unique in its use of architecture and serialized narrative. In these major works she has adopted the television mini-series format in order to develop a more involving narrative context, a serialized narrative to be continued in consecutive episodes. Evolving scenarios build upon each other over a period of several days or weeks: the 6-part *Sound House*, for example, her first in the series, was produced during a 3-month residency at the Capp Street Project in San Francisco (1985), while *The Music Rooms* was produced by Berlin's DAAD Gallery over a 4-work period (1987). Other works in the series are *Stolen Souls* (1988), commissioned by INKA Digital Arts in Amsterdam, *2021 The Life People* (1989), commissioned by the Ars Electronic Festival and first presented in Beurs van Berlage in Amsterdam, and the *Biaurals* (1990), commissioned by The Electrical Matter and first presented at the Samuel Fleisher Art Memorial in Philadelphia. Installations of MUSIC FOR SOUND-JOINED ROOMS include works created for the Galerie Nachst St. Stephan, Vienna, the Kunsthalle, Basel, the Oggi Music Festival, Lugano, the Cultural Commune di Roma, and the Walker Arts Center in Minneapolis, among many others, while installations of CITY LINKS #1–22 include works created for both solo and group shows at the Museum of Contemporary Art in Chicago (1974), the Walker Arts Center (1974), the Hayden Gallery at the Mass. Inst. of Technology (1975), the Inst. of Contemporary Art in Boston (1975), and at Mills Coll. (1980, 1994). Among her recent endeavors are inclusion in "The American Century, Art and Culture 1950–2000" Sound Art Group Show at N.Y.'s Whitney Museum of American Art (2000) and a 90-minute profile on the composer produced by Frankfurt am Main's Hessischer Rundfunk (2000). She has also been commissioned by the Kronos String Quartet, through funding by the Lila Wallace-Reader's Digest Fund, for a String Quartet with Electroacoustic Installation.

Amacher's work is formidably original, ever pressing on the available edge of available technology. In addition to grants and fellowships from such sources as the NEA, NYSCA, the Pew Memorial Trust, and the N.Y. Artist Fellowship Program (1976–98), she was a Bunting Inst. Fellow at Radcliffe Coll. (1978–79), resident artist at the Capp Street project in San Francisco (1985), recipient of Berlin's Deutscher Akademischer Austauschdienst (DAAD) grant (1986–87), a visiting artist at the Banff Center for the Arts (1991–92), and the first Rosenkrans Artist-in-Residence in Music at Mills Coll. (1993). In 1997 she received both the Prix Ars Electronic Golden Nica Distinction in Computer Music award from the Ars Electronica International Competition for Cyber Arts in Linz, Austria, and a Guggenheim fellowship. In 1999 she received a grant from N.Y.'s Foundation for Contemporary Performance Arts.—**NS/LK/DM**

Amadei, Filippo, Italian composer; b. Reggio, c. 1670; d. probably in Rome, c. 1730. He was a cellist in the service of Cardinal Pietro Ottoboni in Rome (1690–96). His opera *Teodosio il giovane* was performed at the cardinal's palace in 1711. He was in London by 1719, where he gave concerts under the name Sigr Pippo. In 1720 he joined the orch. of the new Royal Academy of Music under Handel's directorship, with which he became active as a composer. He wrote the 1st act of the opera *Muzio Scevola*, for which Bononcini wrote the 2nd act and Handel the 3rd, and which was premiered on April 21, 1721. About 1724 Amadei returned to Rome, and was again in the service of Cardinal Ottoboni until 1729. Among his other works were oratorios and cantatas.—**NS/LK/DM**

Amadie, Jimmy (James), jazz pianist, educator; b. Philadelphia, Jan. 5, 1937. Beginning in the late 1950s, Amadie jammed regularly around Philadelphia, and worked with Mel Torme (recording with him in 1963), Woody Herman, Red Rodney, and Charlie Ventura. He was, for a time, house pianist at the Red Hill Inn in Pennsauken, N.J., where leading names played, and in 1960 he led the house trio at N.Y.'s Copacabana. But having begun the piano relatively late in life, Amadie engaged in a practice regimen so intense—he claims up to 80 hours a week—that he seriously injured his hands with tendinitis, eventually undergoing four operations for reconstructive surgery. He couldn't touch the instrument between 1967 and 1995, and even today can only play for a few minutes at a time, every few weeks. Only by making first takes less than once a month over the course of 18 months was he able to complete his first solo recording, which was released in 1995. Steve Allen has written a lyric to the title track, "Always with Me." Amadie has also composed and conducted music for National Football League Films. He composes and writes his self-published books by dictating them. For his books he developed a harmonic approach based on his system for creating chord voices, and a melodic approach based on tension and release, which he uses to integrate modal, tonal, and bi-tonal playing. A short film about Amadie was shown on *CBS News Sunday Morning* on April 13, 1997.

WRITINGS: *Harmonic Foundation for Jazz and Popular Music; Jazz Improv: How to Play It and Teach It* (Bala Cynwyd, Pa.).

DISC.: *Always with Me* (1995); *Savoring Every Note* (1998). —LP

Amaducci, Bruno, Swiss conductor; b. Lugano, Jan. 5, 1925. He studied at the École Normale de Musique in Paris and at the Milan Cons.; then toured widely as an opera and sym. conductor in Europe, and also appeared in North America. On Oct. 5, 1967, he made his Metropolitan Opera debut in N.Y. conducting *Falstaff*. He became closely associated with the Orch. della Radiotelevisione della Svizzera Italiana in Lugano, where he was active as a conductor and later as chief of music programming.

WRITINGS: *Music of the Five Composers of the Puccini Dynasty* (1973).—NS/LK/DM

Amalia, Catharina, Countess of Erbach, German composer; b. Arolsen, Aug. 8, 1640; d. Cuylenburg, the Netherlands, Jan. 4, 1697. She was the daughter ofCount von Waldeck. In 1664 she married Count Georg Ludwig von Erbach. Among her works were several sacred anthems.—NS/LK/DM

Amalia, Friederike, Princess of Saxony, German composer; b. Dresden, Aug. 10, 1794; d. there, Sept. 18, 1870. She composed several light operas under the name Amalie Heiter, and also wrote sacred music. —NS/LK/DM

Amani, Nikolai, Russian composer; b. St. Petersburg, April 4, 1872; d. Yalta, Oct. 17, 1904. He was a pupil in piano of Essipova and in composition of Rimsky-Korsakov and Liadov at the St. Petersburg Cons. (1890–1900). His life was cut short by tuberculosis. Among his works were a String Trio (1900), piano pieces, and songs.

BIBL.: S. Gentile, *Breve ricordo della vita e opere di N. A., musicista russo* (Palermo, 1911).—NS/LK/DM

Amar, Licco (actually, **Liko**), Hungarian violinist and teacher of Greek descent; b. Budapest, Dec. 4, 1891; d. Freiburg im Breisgau, July 19, 1959. He studied with Emil Bare at the Budapest Academy of Music and with Henry Marteau at the Berlin Hochschule für Musik. He was 2nd violinist in the Marteau String

Quartet (1912–15) and concertmaster of the Berlin Phil. (1915–20) and of the Mannheim National Theater orch. (1920–23). In 1921 he founded the Amar String Quartet, which championed contemporary music until it disbanded in 1929. With the rise of the Nazis to power in Germany in 1933, Amar was compelled to leave the country and in 1935 he became a prof. at the Ankara Cons. From 1957 he taught at the Freiburg im Breisgau Hochschule für Musik.—NS/LK/DM

Amara (real name, **Armaganian**), **Lucine,** American soprano; b. Hartford, Conn., March 1, 1925. She studied with Stella Eisner-Eyn in San Francisco, and attended the Music Academy of the West in Santa Barbara (1947) and the Univ. of Southern Calif. in Los Angeles (1949–50). She also studied with Bobbi Tillander. In 1945 she became a member of the San Francisco Opera chorus. She made her concert debut in San Francisco in 1946, and then sang the title role in *Ariadne auf Naxos* and appeared as Lady Billows in *Albert Herring* in 1949. On Nov. 6, 1950, she made her Metropolitan Opera debut in N.Y. as the Celestial Voice in *Don Carlos*. She continued to sing there until 1991, appearing in 56 lyric or dramatic roles in 882 stage performances. Her other operatic engagements took her to the Edinburgh (1954) and Glyndebourne (1954–55; 1957–58) festivals, the Vienna State Opera (1960), Russia (1965), and China (1983). She also appeared as a soloist with many U.S. orchs. In later years, she served as artistic director of the N.J. Assn. of Verismo Opera and gave master classes in the U.S., Canada, and Mexico. Among her finest roles were Gluck's Eurydice, Donna Elvira, Elsa, Verdi's Leonora and Aida, Nedda, Musetta, Mimi, and Ariadne.—NS/LK/DM

Amat, Juan Carlos (real name, **Joan Carles y Amat**), Spanish physician and writer on guitar playing; b. Monistrol de Montserrat, c. 1572; d. there, Feb. 10, 1652. He publ. the historically valuable book *Guitarra española en cinco ordenes* (Barcelona, 1596). —NS/LK/DM

Amati, renowned family of Italian violin makers working at Cremona. **Andrea Amati** (b. between 1500 and 1505; d. before 1580) was the first violin maker of the family. He established the prototype of Italian instruments, with characteristics found in modern violins. His sons were **Antonio Amati** (b. c. 1538; d. c. 1595), who built violins of varying sizes, and **Girolamo Amati** (b. c. 1561; d. Nov. 2, 1630), who continued the tradition established by his father, and worked together with his brother, Antonio. Nicola, or **Niccolo Amati** (b. Dec. 3, 1596; d. April 12, 1684), was the most illustrious of the Amati family. He was the son of Girolamo Amati, and signed his labels "Nicolaus Amati Cremonens, Hieronimi filius Antonii nepos." He built some of the "grand Amatis," large violins of powerful tone surpassing in clarity and purity those made by his father and his grandfather, Andrea. In Nicola's workshop both Andrea Guarneri and Antonio Stradivari received their training. **Girolamo Amati** (b. Feb. 26, 1649; d. Feb. 21, 1740), son of Nicola and the last of the family, produced violins inferior to those of his father, his grandfather, and his great-grandfather. In his work, he departed from the family tradition in many respects and seemed to be influenced by Stradivari's method without equaling his superb workmanship.

BIBL.: C. Bonetti, *La genealogia degli A., luitai, e il primato della scuola liutistica cremonese* (Cremona, 1938; Eng. tr., 1989, as *A Genealogy of the A. Family Violin Makers, 1500–1740*). —NS/LK/DM

Amato, Pasquale, remarkable Italian baritone; b. Naples, March 21, 1878; d. N.Y., Aug. 12, 1942. He studied at the Naples Cons. (1896–99). In 1900 he made his operatic debut as Germont at the Teatro Bellini in Naples, and then sang in other Italian music centers. In 1904 he sang Amonasro at his debut at London's Covent Garden. In 1907–08 he appeared at Milan's La Scala. On Nov. 20, 1908, he made his Metropolitan Opera debut in N.Y. as Germont, and quickly established himself as one of its principal members, remaining on its roster until 1918 and returning there from 1919 to 1921, excelling in all the major Italian roles as well as several French and German. On Dec. 10, 1910, he created the role of Jack Rance in *La Fanciulla del West* there. After his retirement, he taught voice in N.Y. In 1933 he came out of retirement to celebrate the 25th anniversary of his Metropolitan Opera debut with a gala appearance at N.Y.'s Hippodrome. Amato's extraordinary vocal prowess was equaled by his dramatic versatility, which ran the gamut from serious to comic roles.—NS/LK/DM

Ambros, August Wilhelm, eminent Austrian music historian, nephew of **Raphael Georg Kiesewetter**; b. Mauth, near Prague, Nov. 17, 1816; d. Vienna, June 28, 1876. He studied music before pursuing training in the law at the Univ. of Prague (Jur.D., 1839). He then entered the Austrian civil service and, in 1850, he became public prosecutor in Prague. In 1869 he became prof. of music at the Univ. of Prague, and also gave lectures at the Prague Cons. In 1872 he went to Vienna to serve in the Ministry of Justice, and also taught at the Vienna Cons. His most important work was the monumental *Geschichte der Musik*, which was left unfinished at his death but completed by others. He also wrote an opera, *Břetislav a Jitka*, 2 syms., overtures, keyboard pieces, sacred music, and numerous songs.

WRITINGS: *Die Grenzen der Musik und Poesi: Eine Studie zur Aesthetik der Tonkunst* (Prague, 1856; Eng. tr., 1893); *Culturhistorische Bilder aus dem Musikleben der Gegenwart* (Leipzig, 1860; 2nd ed., 1865); *Geschichte der Musik* (vols. I-III, Breslau, 1862–68; vol. IV ed. by E. Schelle, Breslau, 1878; vol. V ed. by O. Kade, Leipzig, 1882); *Bunte Blätter: Skizzen und Studien für Freunde der Musik der bilden Kunst* (Leipzig, 1872).

BIBL.: P. Naegele, *A.W. A.: His Historical and Critical Thought* (diss., Princeton Univ., 1954); W. Beyer, *Zu einigen Grundproblemen der formalistischen Ästhetik E. Hanslicks und A.W. A.* (diss., Univ. of Prague, 1957).—NS/LK/DM

Ambros, Vladimír, Czech composer; b. Prostjov, Moravia, Sept. 18, 1890; d. there, May 12, 1956. He studied at the Brünn Organ School (1908–10) and at the Frankfurt am Main Cons., later becoming active as a conductor with the Carl Rosa Opera Co. in England.

After World War I, he returned to Prostjov. His works include the operas *Ukradené štstí* (Stolen Happiness; 1924) and *Maryla* (1951), 3 syms. (1941; 1944; 1946–51), *Symphonietta* (1938), a cantata, *Veliký navrat* (Grand Return; 1951), chamber music, and songs.

BIBL.: V. Gregor, *V. A.* (Prostjov, 1969).—NS/LK/DM

Ambrosch, Joseph Karl, Bohemian-born German tenor and composer; b. Krumau, May 6, 1759; d. Berlin, Sept. 8, 1822. He was a pupil of J.A. Koželuh in Prague. In 1784 he made his debut in Bayreuth. From 1791 to 1811 he was the principal tenor at the Berlin Royal Opera. He wrote a number of fine lieder.—LK/DM

Ambrose (Ambrosius), Saint, Italian churchman; b. Tier, c.339; d. Milan, April 4, 374. His father was the Roman prefect in Gaul. Ambrose began his career as a political figure, becoming governor of Liguria and Aemilia about 370. On Dec. 7, 374, he was elected Bishop of Milan. As one of the 4 Doctors of the Roman Catholic church, he was canonized. Ambrose has long been credited with developing Ambrosian or Milanese chant, the introduction of hymns and antiphonal singing in the Roman Catholic Church, the authorship of the *Te Deum*, and the composition of hymns. However, only his composition of hymns can be verified, and he may have written only the words to the hymns attributed to him.

BIBL.: F. Dudden, *The Life and Times of St A.* (Oxford, 1935); H. Leeb, *Die Psalmodie bei A.* (Vienna, 1967).—NS/LK/DM

d'Ambrosio, Alfredo, Italian teacher and composer; b. Naples, June 13, 1871; d. Nice, Dec. 29, 1914. He was a pupil of Bossi (composition) at the Naples Cons., of Sarasate (violin) in Madrid, and of Wilhelmj (violin) in London. He settled in Nice as a violin teacher. Among his works were an opera, *Pia de Tolomei*, a ballet, *Ersilia*, 2 violin concertos (1904, 1913), a String Quintet, a String Quartet, and many violin pieces.—NS/LK/DM

Ambrosius, Hermann, German composer, teacher, and choral conductor; b. Hamburg, July 24, 1897; d. Engen am Hegau, Oct. 25, 1983. He studied in Pfitzner's master classes at the Berlin Academy of Arts (1921–24). In 1926 he joined the faculty at the Leipzig Cons. He settled in Engen am Hegau in 1945 as a teacher and choral conductor. He composed 2 operas, much orch. music, including 12 syms. (1920–63), 3 piano concertos (1926–52), 2 cello concertos (1928–38), 2 guitar concertos (1953–62), and *Der Berg* (1965), and numerous accordion pieces.—NS/LK/DM

Ameling, Elly (actually, **Elisabeth Sara),** outstanding Dutch soprano; b. Rotterdam, Feb. 8, 1934. After studies in Rotterdam and The Hague, she completed her training with Bernac in Paris; won the 's-Hertogenbosch (1956) and Geneva (1958) competitions, then made her formal recital debut in Amsterdam (1961). Subsequent appearances with the Concertgebouw Orch. in Amsterdam and the Rotterdam Phil. secured her reputation. In 1966 she made her London debut and in 1968 her N.Y. debut; her first appearance in opera was as Ilia in *Idomeneo* with the Netherlands Opera in Amsterdam in 1973, but she chose to concentrate upon a career as a concert artist. She gained renown for her appearances with major European orchs. and for her lieder recitals. In 1971 she was made a Knight of the Order of Oranje Nassau by the Dutch government. She established the Elly Ameling Lied Prize to be awarded at the 's-Hertogenbosch competition. Her remarkable career came to a close with a series of farewell recitals in 1995.—NS/LK/DM

Ameller, André (Charles Gabriel), French composer; b. Arnaville, Jan. 2, 1912; d. La Garenne-Colombes, May 15, 1990. He studied at the Paris Cons., where he took courses in composition and conducting with Roger-Ducasse, Aubin, and Gaubert, studied violin and double bass (premier prix, 1934), and later completed his training in composition (premier prix, 1947). From 1953 to 1981 he was director of the Dijon Cons.

WORKS: DRAMATIC: O p e r a : *La Lance de Fingal* (1947); *Sampiero Corso, Monsieur Personne* (1957); *Cyrnos* (Nancy, April 6, 1962). B a l l e t : *La Coupe de sang* (1950); *Oiseaux du vieux Paris* (1967). ORCH.: Cello Concerto (1946); Sym. (1947); *Hétérodoxes* for 2 Flutes, 2 Trumpets, String Quartet, and String Orch. (1969). CHAMBER: String Quartet (1944); Quintet for Piano and Strings (1947); String Trio (1951); *Jeux de table* for Saxophone and Piano (1955); *Airs hétérogènes* for Wind Ensemble (1966); *Suite florentine* for Cello (1986); *Uranie* for Flute and Piano (1986); *Duo concertant* for Double Basses (1987). VOCAL: *Terre secrète*, 6 songs for Voice and Orch. (1956).
—NS/LK/DM

Ameln, Konrad, German musicologist and choral conductor; b. Neuss am Rhein, July 6, 1899; d. Lüdenscheid, Sept. 1, 1994. He studied at the Univ. of Göttingen (1919–21) and with Gutlitt at the Univ. of Freiburg im Breisgau (Ph.D., 1924, with the diss. *Beiträge zur Geschichte der Melodien "Innsbruck, ich muss dich lassen" und "Ach Gott, von Himmel sieh darein"*). After serving as a music consultant to the Central Office for General Librarianship in Leipzig (1926–28), he taught Protestant church music at the Univ. of Münster (1930–39). He also was founder-director of the Lüdenscheider Musikvereinigung (1935–73). He taught at the Landeskirchenmusikschulen in Hannover (1947–48) and the Rhineland (1949–57). With C. Mahrenholz and W. Thomas, he was ed. of the valuable *Handbuch der deutschen evangelische Kirchenmusik* (Göttingen, 1932 et seq.). Ameln was the author of the studies *Leonhard Lechner* (Lüdenscheid, 1957) and *The Roots of German Hymnody of the Reformation Era* (St. Louis, 1964).

BIBL.: G. Schuhmacher, ed., *Traditionen und Reformen in der Kirchenmusik: Festschrift für K. A. zum 75. Geburtstag* (Kassel, 1974).—NS/LK/DM

Amendola, Giuseppe, Italian composer; b. probably in Palermo, c. 1750; d. probably there, 1808. He composed the highly successful comic opera *Il Begliar-Bey di Caramania* (1776), which was performed throughout Europe. He also composed cantatas.—LK/DM

Amengual (-Astaburuaga), René, Chilean composer and teacher; b. Santiago, Sept. 2, 1911; d.

there, Aug. 2, 1954. He studied with Allende at Santiago's National Cons. (1923–35), where he subsequently taught (from 1935) and was its director (from 1945). His early works followed along French lines but he later developed an expressionist idiom

WORKS: ORCH.: *Preludio sinfónico* (1939); Piano Concerto (1941–42); Harp Concerto (1950). CHAMBER: 2 string quartets (1941, 1950); Violin Sonata (1944); Wind Sextet (1953). P i a n o : *Burlesca* (1932–38); Sonatina (1938); *Introduction and Allegro* for 2 Pianos (1939). VOCAL: *El Vaso* for Soprano and Chamber Orch. (1942); choral works; songs.—NS/LK/DM

American Quartet, The, second only to The Peerless Quartet as the most popular vocal quartet of the second decade of the 20th century, its specialties were ragtime and comic numbers; formed 1910. MEMBERSHIP: Billy Murray (the group's leader, who sometimes was billed before its name), John Bieling, Steve Porter, and William F. Hooley. Bieling and Hooley were also members of the Haydn Quartet. The quartet recorded primarily for Victor; when they appeared on Edison Records, they were called the Premier Quartet or the Premier Four.

The American Quartet's first major hit was the gold-selling "Casey Jones" (1910); other early hits were "Call Me Up Some Rainy Afternoon" (1910) (with Ada Jones), "Come, Josephine, in My Flying Machine" (1911) (with Jones), "Oh, You Beautiful Doll" (1912), "Moonlight Bay" (1912), and "Everybody Two-Step" (1912). With the addition of Will Oakland, they also recorded as the Heidelberg Quintet, their hits including "Waiting for the Robert E. Lee" (1912) and "By the Beautiful Sea" (1914). Bieling left the group in 1914 and was replaced by John Young. Subsequent hits included "Rebecca of Sunny- brook Farm" (1914) and "Oh Johnny, Oh Johnny, Oh!" (1917). They had particular success singing topical songs of World War I, recording the British standard "It's a Long, Long Way to Tipperary" at the start of the war in 1914 and, after the U.S. entry in 1917, "Good-Bye Broadway, Hello France" and George M. Cohan's "Over There."

Hooley died in 1918 and was replaced by Donald Chalmers. Murray introduced a new quartet in 1920 that featured Albert Campbell, John Meyer, and Frank Croxton, but this lineup was not as successful as the earlier ones. The American Quartet broke up in 1925.

Amfitheatrof, Daniele (Alexandrovich), Russian-born American composer and conductor; b. St. Petersburg, Oct. 29, 1901; d. Rome, June 7, 1983. He was a son of a famous Russian journalist. He studied composition with Wihtol and Shcherbachov at the St. Petersburg Cons., with Křička in Prague, and with Respighi at the Cons. di Santa Cecilia in Rome (diploma, 1924); also organ at Rome's Pontifical Academy of Sacred Music. After conducting in Italy and Europe, he went to the U.S. in 1937 and became a naturalized citizen in 1944. Amfitheatrof was assoc. conductor of the Minneapolis Sym. Orch. (1937–38), and then went to Hollywood in 1939, where he wrote over 50 film scores until 1965; then settled in Italy. His works followed in the exuberant Romantic tradition espoused by Respighi.

Among his orchestral compositions are *Poema del mare* (1925), *Miracolo della rosa* (1927), *Panorama americano* (1933), and a Piano Concerto (1937–46). He also composed a Requiem (1960) and much chamber music.—NS/LK/DM

Amicis, Anna Lucia de, Italian soprano; b. Naples, 1733; d. there, 1816. She went to London in 1763, where she appeared in concert with Johann Christian Bach. Returning to Naples, she married the physician Francesco Buonsollazzi (1768) and thenceforth appeared under the name De Amicis Buonsollazzi; she continued her active career as an opera singer until 1786. Her talent was appreciated by Mozart, who often mentioned her name in his correspondence.—NS/LK/DM

Amiot, Jean Joseph Marie, French missionary and scholar; b. Toulon, Feb. 8, 1718; d. Beijing, Oct. 9, 1793. He received a classical education. After ordination, he went to Beijing as a Jesuit missionary in 1751. His most important writings on Chinese music remain in MS. His *Mémoire sur la musique des Chinois, tant anciens que modernes* was ed. by P. Roussier (Paris, 1779; reprint, 1973) and was publ. as Vol. VI of Amiot's *Mémoires concernat l'histoire, les sciences, les arts, les moeurs, les usages des Chinois* (Paris, 1780).—NS/LK/DM

Amirkhanian, Charles (Benjamin), American avant-garde composer, influential radio producer, and arts administrator of Armenian descent; b. Fresno, Calif., Jan. 19, 1945. He studied English literature at Calif. State Univ. at Fresno (B.A., 1967), interdisciplinary creative arts at San Francisco State Coll. (M.A., 1969), and electronic music and sound recording at Mills Coll. (M.F.A., 1980). In his early percussion compositions, he experimented with the potentialities of sound phenomena independent of traditional musical content; his *Composition No. 1* is a solo for an amplified orchestral Ratchet (1965), and his *Symphony I* (1965) is scored for 12 Players and 200-odd nonmusical objects, ranging from pitchpipes to pitchforks. In collaboration with the painter Ted Greer, he developed a radical system of notation in which visual images are transduced by performers into sound events. Representative of this intermedia genre are *Micah, the Prophet,* cantata for 4 Intoning Males, 2 Accordions, 2 Drummers, and 2 Painters (1965), and, particularly, *Mooga Pook,* a tetraphallic action for Dancers, realistically notated on graph paper (San Francisco, Dec. 12, 1967). An ongoing series of compositions for a neglected instrument was extended in 1998 when he premiered his Octet for Ratchets, each instrument being amplified. He also evolved the art of "text-sound composition," in which the voice, percussively intoning and articulating decontextualized words and phrases, is featured, either live or recorded, and sometimes both; to this category belong *Words* (1969), *Oratora konkurso rezulto: Auturo de la Jaro,* a quadrophonic tape work in Esperanto featuring the voice of composer Lou Harrison (1970), *If In Is* (1971), *Just* (1972), *Heavy Aspirations,* with the voice of Nicolas Slonimsky (1973), *Seatbelt Seatbelt* (1973), *MUGIC* (1973), *Muchrooms* (1974), *Mahogany Ballpark* (1976), *Dutiful*

Ducks (1977), *Dreams Freud Dreamed* (1979), *Church Car* (1980), *Hypothetical Moments* [in the Intellectual Life of Southern California] (1981), *Andas* (1982), *Dog of Stravinsky* (1982), *Dumbek Bookache* (1986), *Ka Himeni Hehena* (The Raving Mad Hymn) for 4 Speaking Voices and Tape (1997), and *Marathon* (1997). Amirkhanian also spent a number of years touring and performing with the Mugicians Union (with Carol Law, Betsy Davids, and Jim Petrillo) or separately with Carol Law, presenting life text-sound pieces accompanied by painterly light environments produced by mutiple slide projectors.

Most of Amirkhanian's compositions since the early 1980s, many produced for radio broadcast, make extensive use of sampled ambient sounds sampled and manipulated by a Synclavier or Kurzweil digital synthesizer. These exploit tensions between the abstract (musical sounds) and the representational (recognizable sound effects). Among these are *Gold and Spirit* (for the Los Angeles Summer Olympics; 1984), *The Real Perpetuum Mobile* (on the occasion of N. Slonimsky's 90th birthday; Los Angeles, April 27, 1984), *Metropolis San Francisco* (for WDR/Köln Studio 3 Hörspiel; 1985–86), *Walking Tune* ("Portrait of Percy Grainger"; 1986–87), *Pas de voix* ("Portrait of Samuel Beckett"; 1987), *Politics as Usual* (incorporating sounds of gongs in the collections of Lou Harrison and Toni Marcus, mixed with sounds of talking parrots, crunching apples, and revolving ice cubes; 1988), *Im Frühling* (a reverse tone poem in which sounds from nature imitate late 20th century orchestral music; 1990), *Loudspeakers* (comprised of voice recordings of the late Morton Feldman; 1990), *Chu Lu Lu* (1992), and *Son of Metropolitan San Francisco* (1997). An August 1994 trip to the Republic of Armenia resulted in the composition of *Miatsoom* (Reunion, 1994–97), a Hörspiel documenting the sounds of music, voices, and ambiences recorded in that country and in the Republic of Mountainous Karabakh. Amirkhanian served as music director at the radio station KPFA in Berkeley, Calif. (1969–92), for which he was awarded the American Music Center's annual Letter of Distinction (1984) and ASCAP's Deems Taylor Award (1989). He was also producer and host of the "Speaking of Music" interview series at San Francisco's Exploratorium Science Museum (1983–92) and co-founding director (with John Lifton) of the "Composer-to-Composer" Festival in Telluride, Colo. (1988–91). From 1993 to 1997 he was executive director of the Djerassi Resident Artists Program in Woodside, Calif. Since 1992 he has been artistic director of the "Other Minds Festival" in San Francisco. In 1999–2000, along with Carol Law, he was awarded the first-ever Ella Holbrook Walker Fellowship for an extended residency at the Rockefeller Foundation's Bellagio Study & Conference Center in Italy.—NS/LK/DM

Amirov, Fikret (Meshadi Jamil), Azerbaijani composer; b. Gyandzha, Nov. 22, 1922; d. Baku, Feb. 20, 1984. He studied with his father, a tar player and singer, and pursued training in the tar at the Gyandzha Music Coll. After composition study at the Baku Coll., he studied composition with Zeydman at the Azerbaijan State Cons., where he was awarded his diploma for his opera *Ulduz* in 1948. He was artistic director of the

Kirovabad Phil. (1942–43) and the Baku Phil. (1947), director of the Azerbaijan Theater of Opera and Ballet (1956–59), and secretary of the Azerbaijan Composers' Union (from 1956). In 1949 he was awarded a State Prize and in 1965 he was made a National Artist of the USSR. Amirov's dedication to the native music of Azerbaijan is revealed in his use of the mugam, a song-dance form, in his 2 symphonic poems of 1948. His opera *Sevil* (Baku, Dec. 25, 1953) is one of the most important works of its kind in the Azerbaijani theater repertoire. On the whole, his music represents a deft use of Azerbaijani folk elements and Western art music.

WORKS: DRAMATIC: *Ulduz*, opera (1948); *Sevil*, opera (Baku, Dec. 25, 1953; rev. 1955 and 1959); *Arabian Nights*, ballet (1979); musical comedies; incidental music; film scores. **ORCH.:** *Poem* (1941); *To the Memory of the Heroes of the Great National War* (1943); *To the Memory of Nizam*, sym. for Strings (1947); *Shchur and Kyurd Ovsharï*, symphonic mugam (1948); Double Concerto for Violin, Piano, and Orch. (1948); *Azerbaijan Suite* (1950); Piano Concerto (1958; in collaboration with Nazirova); *Azerbaijan Capriccio* (1961); *Symphonic Dances* (1963); *Symphonic Portraits* (1970); *Gyulistan-Bayatï shirazï*, symphonic mugam for Mezzo-soprano, Timpani, and Chamber Orch. (1970). **OTHER:** Chamber music, piano pieces, songs, and folk song arrangements.

BIBL.: D. Danilov, *F. A.* (Baku, 1965).—**NS/LK/DM**

Ammann, Benno, Swiss composer; b. Gersau, June 14, 1904; d. Rome, March 14, 1986. He studied with Karg-Elert, Grabner, and Reuter at the Leipzig Cons. (1925) and with Honegger, Milhaud, and Rousseau in Paris (1934–35); later he attended courses in electronic music conducted by Eimert and Meyer-Eppler in Darmstadt (from 1952). He was active at the Studio R7 in Rome (1969–71), the Inst. of Sonology at the Univ. of Ghent (1971–73), and the Columbia-Princeton Electronic Music Center in N.Y. (1977–78). In his works, Ammann embraced a variety of contemporary means of expression.

WORKS: DRAMATIC: Ballet: *Zweimal Besuch* (1960); *Waterplants* (1974). **ORCH.:** *Vision pastorale* (1954); *Tre Modi* for 2 String Orchs. or Strings and Tape (1962); *Triodon*, 3 pieces for Strings (1963); *Gradations* for Chamber Orch. (1973). **CHAMBER:** *Successions* for Flute (1963); *Syntexte* for Flute, Harp, and Percussion (1966); *IV Phonemata* for Cello (1967); *12 Phases* for Guitar and Tape (1970); *Spatial Forms* for 2 String Quartets (1972); *Mouvements* for Harp and Tape (1976); *The Gnome's Memory* for Tuba and Tape (1979); *Riflessi per quattro* for 4 Clarinets (1981); *Lieto per liuto* for Lute (1983); *Incontri* for 24 Trumpets in 4 Groups (1984). **VOCAL:** *Flucht aus der Tiefe*, cantata for Baritone, 3 Choruses, and Percussion Orch. (1960); *Sumerian Song* for Soprano, 6 Percussion, and Orch. (1971); *Ti Porteranno* for Soprano, Flute, Cello, Trombone, and Percussion (1974); *Tre Canti* for Baritone, 2 Clarinets, and Harp (1983); choral pieces; other songs. **ELECTRONIC:** *Breath of the Desert* (1974); *Splendeurs Nocturnes* (1974–79); *Poemetto* (1977); *Mutazione* (1978); *Wandering strophe* (1979).—**NS/LK/DM**

Ammerbach, Elias Nicolaus, German organist; b. Naumburg, c. 1530; d. Leipzig (buried), Jan. 29, 1597. He attended the Univ. of Leipzig in 1548–49. From 1561 to 1595 he was organist of the Thomaskirche in Leipzig. He brought out the first printed German organ

tablature in his *Orgel oder Instrument Tabulatur* (Leipzig, 1571; 2nd ed., 1583; ed. by C. Jacobs, 1985), in which he introduced a new German notation in which pitches were expressed by letters with rhythm indications above. The vol. contains his arrangements of dances and vocal pieces for organ or other keyboard instrument. He also publ. another vol. of arrangements in his *Ein new kvnstlich Tabulaturbuch* (Leipzig, 1575).

BIBL.: B. Freudenberger, *Studien zu den Orgeltabulaturen 1571 und 1583 des Leipziger Thomasorganisten E.N. A.: Zugleich ein Beitrag zur Intavolierunstechnik im ausgehenden 16. Jahrhundert* (diss., Univ. of Kiel, 1990).—**NS/LK/DM**

Ammon, Blasius, Austrian composer; b. Imst, c. 1560; d. Vienna, between June 1 and 21, 1590. He was a choirboy in the Innsbruck Hofkapelle, where he most likely began his musical training. Following studies in Venice, he returned to Innsbruck and was a member of the Franciscan order until 1580. After serving as Kantor of the Cistercian monastery in Heiligkreuz (1585–87), he settled in Vienna as a priest in the Franciscan monastery. He was a fine composer of sacred vocal music, including introits for 5 Voices (Vienna, 1584) and for 4 Voices (Vienna, 1601), masses for 4 Voices (Vienna, 1588), and motets for 4 to 8 Voices (Munich, 1590) and for 4 to 6 Voices (Munich, 1593).—**NS/LK/DM**

Ammons, Albert (C.), boogie-woogie pianist, father of **Gene Ammons**; b. Chicago, Sept. 23, 1907; d. Chicago, Dec. 2, 1949. Ammons was a leader of the boogie-woogie movement for solo piano from the late 1930s on, often paired in concert and on recordings with Pete Johnson. He began playing piano at age ten, and later worked as a soloist before touring with territory bands, including François Moseley's Louisiana Stompers (summer 1929), William Barbee and His Headquarters (parts of 1930 and 1931), and drummer Louis Banks and His Chesterfield Orch. (1930–34). Ammons headed his own group at several Chicago clubs from 1934 to 1938, making his first records with a sextet in 1936. He moved to N.Y. initially to appear at the "From Spirituals to Swing" concert at Carnegie Hall on Dec. 23, 1938, along with Johnson and Meade Lux Lewis. He then began appearing regularly at Cafe Society and elsewhere in duet with Johnson, sometimes with Lewis added. In the early 1940s, Johnson and Ammons did some touring, with residencies in Hollywood and Chicago, except for a brief period in the spring of 1941, when Ammons accidentally cut off the tip of his finger while preparing a sandwich. During the mid-1940s he suffered temporary paralysis in both hands, but recovered and played mainly in Chicago during the last few years of his life. Due to illness he was inactive in 1949, but played at Mama Yancey's Parlour a few days before his death.

DISC.: *Boogie Woogie Stomp* (1936); *Bass Gone Crazy* (1939). —**JC/LP**

Ammons, Gene (Eugene; "Jug"), jazz tenor saxophonist, son of Albert Ammons; b. Chicago, April 14, 1925; d. of cancer, Chicago, Aug. 6, 1974. Ammons was popular and widely admired for his powerful sound, Lester Young–inspired flow, and deep approach to ballads. Some of his blues-based recordings had an R&B appeal as well. Ammons appeared with King Kolax around 1943 and Billy Eckstine from 1944 to 1946. He is featured in the Eckstine film *Rhythm in a Riff* (1946). From 1947 on, Ammons primarily led his own groups except for a tour with Woody Herman in 1949 and a co-led group with Sonny Stitt from 1950 through 1952. An early hit was the ballad "My Foolish Heart." He suffered compound fractures in both legs when hit by a car in the Midwest in 1954, but soon resumed touring. However, he was arrested in late 1962, and between 1963 and 1969 his career was interrupted by a prison sentence for narcotics violations.

DISC.: *My Foolish Heart* (1950); *Blues up and Down* (1950); *Jammin' in Hi Fi with G. A.* (1957); *Groove Blues* (1958); *Gene Ammons All Stars* (1958); *Big Sound of G. A.* (1958); *We'll Be Together Again* (1961); *Up Tight* (1961); *Prime Cuts* (1961); *Boss Tenors: Straight Ahead* (1961); *Soulful Moods of G. A.* (1962); *Brother Jack Meets the Boss* (1962); *Boss Tenors in Orbit* (1962); *Boss Is Back* (1969); *Chicago Concert* (1971) *G. A. and Friends at Montreux* (1973); *Goodbye* (1974).—**LP**

Amner, John, English organist and composer; b. Ely (baptized), Aug. 24, 1579; d. there (buried), July 28, 1641. He studied at Oxford (B.Mus., 1613) and Cambridge (Mus.B., 1640). From 1610 he served as informator choristarum at Ely Cathedral. He later was ordained to the diaconate and was made vicarius (minor canon), and thus received remuneration as both organist and prebendary. Amner composed English service music and anthems, and publ. the vol. *Sacred Hymnes of 3. 4. 5. and 6. parts for Voyces and Vyols* (London, 1615). He also wrote a Pavan and Galliard for Viols and keyboard variations.—**NS/LK/DM**

Amon, Johannes Andreas, German composer; b. Bamberg, 1763; d. Wallerstein, Bavaria, March 29, 1825. He studied voice with Fracasini and violin with Bauerle in Bamberg, and also received horn lessons from Punto, with whom he toured Germany, France, and Austria. After composition lessons from Sacchini in Paris (1781–82), he again toured with Punto until ill health compelled him to abandon the horn in 1789. He then was active as a violinist, violist, and pianist until becoming Kapellmeister to the Prince of Oettingen-Wallerstein in 1817. Among his works were 2 Singspiels, syms., chamber music, sacred works, songs, and piano pieces.—**LK/DM**

Amorevoli, Angelo (Maria), Italian tenor; b. Venice, Sept. 16, 1716; d. Dresden, Nov. 15, 1798. He first made a name for himself in 1730 when he appeared in Porpora's *Mitridate* and *Siface* in Rome, and in Hasse's *Dalisca* in Venice. After singing in Milan (1731–35), Naples (1736–40), and Florence (1741), he appeared at the King's Theatre in London (1741–43). In 1744–45 he sang in Milan, and then was engaged to sing in Hasse's works in Dresden from 1745. He also appeared in Vienna in 1748 and again in Milan in 1748–49 and 1760–61. He retired in 1764.—**NS/LK/DM**

Amoyal, Pierre, distinguished French violinist and teacher; b. Paris, June 22, 1949. He entered the Paris

Cons. at the age of 10 and took the premier prix when he was only 12. In 1963 he won the Ginette Neveu Prize, in 1964 the Paganini Prize, and in 1970 the Enesco Prize. From 1966 to 1971 he pursued intensive studies with Heifetz in Los Angeles. In 1971 he made his debut as soloist in the Berg Concerto with Solti and the Orchestre de Paris, and thereafter was engaged as a soloist with major orchs. on both sides of the Atlantic. In 1985 he made his auspicious Carnegie Hall recital debut in N.Y. From 1977 to 1987 he taught at the Paris Cons., and then was on the faculty of the Lausanne Cons. In 1991 he founded, with Alexis Weissenberg, the Lausanne Summer Music Academy, which he subsequently served as artistic director. In addition to his appearances with orchs., he has given many recitals and has played much chamber music. His repertoire ranges from Bach to the contemporary era. His concerto repertoire embraces not only the standard works, but also scores by Schoenberg, Respighi, and Dutilleux.—**NS/LK/DM**

Amram, David (Werner III), versatile American instrumentalist, conductor, and composer; b. Philadelphia, Nov. 17, 1930. He studied horn at the Oberlin (Ohio) Coll. Cons. of Music (1948) and pursued his education at the George Washington Univ. (B.A. in history, 1952). After playing horn in the National Sym. Orch. in Washington, D.C. (1951–52) and the 7th Army Sym. Orch. in Europe, he completed his training with Mitropoulos, Giannini, and Schuller at the Manhattan School of Music (1955) and privately with Charles Mills. In addition to the horn, he learned to play the piano, guitar, various flutes and whistles, percussion, and many folk instruments. He first gained wide recognition as a composer with his scores for the theater, films, and television. In 1966–67 he served as the first composer-in-residence of the N.Y. Phil. At 27, he publ. the autobiographical vol. *Vibrations: The Adventures and Musical Times of David Amram* (N.Y., 1968). In 1971 he became music director of the young people's, family, and parks concerts of the Brooklyn Phil., where he introduced an innovative series of programs of a multicultural nature. He also became music director of the International Jewish Arts Festival Orch. in 1987 and director of the Aaron Copland Music of the Americas Festival in 1998. As an instrumentalist and conductor, Amram has taken his multicultural program to cities around the world. The award-winning documentary *Amram Jam* appeared in 1998.

WORKS: DRAMATIC: O p e r a : *The Final Ingredient* (ABC-TV, April 11, 1965); *Twelfth Night* (1965–68; Lake George, N.Y., Aug. 1, 1968); incidental music; film scores. **ORCH.:** *Autobiography* for Strings (1959); *Shakespearean Concerto* for Oboe, 2 Horns, and Strings (N.Y., May 8, 1960); *King Lear Variations* for Woodwinds, Brass, Percussion, and Piano (1965; N.Y. Phil., March 23, 1967); Horn Concerto (1966); Triple Concerto for Woodwinds, Brass, Jazz Quintets, and Orch. (1970; N.Y., Jan. 10, 1971); Bassoon Concerto (1971; Washington, D.C., March 21, 1972); *Elegy* for Violin and Orch. (1971); *The Trail of Beauty* for Mezzo-soprano, Oboe, and Orch. (Philadelphia, March 3, 1977); Violin Concerto (1980; St. Louis, May 2, 1981); *Ode to Lord Buckley*, saxophone concerto (Portland, Maine, March 17, 1981); *Overture: Honor Song* for Cello and Orch. (N.Y., July 3, 1983); *Across the Wide Missouri: A Musical Tribute to Harry*

S. Truman (Kansas City, Mo., May 10, 1984); *Travels* for Trumpet and Orch. (N.Y., March 26, 1985); *American Dance Suite* (Omaha, Oct. 18, 1986); *A Little Rebellion: A Portrait of Thomas Jefferson* for Narrator and Orch. (Washington, D.C., Oct. 21, 1995, E.G. Marshall narrator, composer conducting); *Kokopelli*, sym. (1996; Nashville, Jan. 17, 1997); *Giants of the Night*, flute concerto (1999). **CHAMBER:** Trio for Saxophone, Horn, and Bassoon (1958); Violin Sonata (1960); String Quartet (1961); Sonata for Solo Violin (1964); Wind Quintet (1968); *Native American Portraits* for Violin, Piano, and Percussion (1976); *Landscapes* for Percussion Quartet (1980). **VOCAL:** *Sacred Service for Sabbath Eve* for Tenor, Chorus, and Organ (1961); *The American Bell*, cantata (Philadelphia, July 4, 1962); *A Year in Our Land*, cantata (1964); *Let Us Remember*, cantata (1965); *3 Songs for America* for Baritone and String Quintet (1969).—NS/LK/DM

Amsallem, Franck, jazz pianist; b. Oran, Algeria, Oct. 25, 1961. Amsallem was raised in Nice. He had early music lessons from an old woman who was a friend of the family, but at 14 he wanted to play an instrument seriously. The Nice Cons. thought he had started too late to play classical piano, so they suggested the saxophone, which he played while he continued to play piano on his own, working with dance bands. Amsallem attended a jazz class at the conservatory and won the saxophone prize. Around 1980, he led a trio at the Hyatt Hotel in Nice where he accompanied musicians from the festival in jam sessions, among them Richie Cole and Jerry Bergonzi, who convinced him to attend the Berklee Coll. in Boston. Upon his graduation in 1981, he began studies at Berklee, supported for three years by a French scholarship. He studied writing with Herb Pomeroy, and worked on some classical piano music. Leaving Berklee at age 22, he settled in N.Y., where he earned a Masters in composition at the Manhattan School of Music and developed associations with Bob Brookmeyer (studying under him in a year-long BMI composers workshop), Tim Ries (in a touring quartet since around 1985), Gary Peacock, and Charles Lloyd. Amsallem worked at the Village Vanguard and and at La Villa in Paris, and toured Brazil with Gerry Mulligan. He won second prize at the 1992 jazz piano competition in Jacksonville, Fla., and has won awards from ASCAP, the NEA, and France's Foundation de la Vocation. He receives commissions to write for a variety of groups in the U.S., France, and Canada. Amsallem wrote a suite called "Nuit" for the Flandres-Wallonie Orch., which is a chamber music orchestra, with a rhythm section and Bireli Lagrène as the soloist. He has given master classes in Albi, Nice (both 1997), and elsewhere.

DISC.: *Is That So?* (with Tim Ries; 1990); *Out a Day* (with Gary Peacock; 1992); *Years Gone By* (1997); *Live at the Blue Note* (working title; rec. April 1997; unreleased).—LP

Amy, Gilbert, French composer, music educator, and conductor; b. Paris, Aug. 29, 1936. He studied with Plé-Caussade, Puig- Roget, Milhaud, and Messiaen at the Paris Cons. From 1967 to 1974 he was director of the Domaine Musical concerts in Paris. In 1976 he founded the Nouvel Orchestre Philharmonique de Radio France in Paris, which he served as its first conductor and artistic director until 1981. In 1982 he taught at Yale Univ. From 1984 Amy was director of the Lyons Cons. As a conductor, he appeared with many orchs. in Europe. His compositions have been featured at many contemporary music concerts. In 1979 he was awarded the Grand Prix National de la Musique, in 1983 the Grand Prix de la Sacem, in 1986 the Grand Prix Musical de la Ville de Paris, and in 1988 the Prix de la Critique Musicale. After experimenting with doctrinaire serial procedures, Amy opted for greater freedom in compositional expression.

WORKS: DRAMATIC: O p e r a : *Le premier cercle* (1998). **ORCH.:** *Mouvements* (1958); *Diaphonies* (1962); *Antiphonies* for 2 Orchs. (1963); *Triade* (1965); *Trajectoires* for Violin and Orch. (1966); *Chant* (1968–69; rev. 1980); *Jeux et formes* for Oboe and Chamber Orch. (1971); *Refrains* (1972); *7 Sites* for 14 Instruments (1975); *Écho XIII* for 13 Instruments (1976); *Adagio et stretto* (1977–78); *D'après:Écrits sur toiles* for Chamber Orch. (1984); *Orchestrahl* (1986–89); *Trois scènes* (1994–95). **CHAMBER:** *Variations* for Flute, Clarinet, Cello, and Piano (1956); *Inventions* for Flute, Vibraphone or Marimbaphone, Harp, and Piano or Celesta (1959–61); *Alpha-beth* for Wind Sextet (1963–64); *Cycle* for Percussion Sextet (1964–66); *Relais* for Brass Quintet (1969); *Quasi scherzando* for Cello (1981); *3 Interludes* for Violin and Percussion (1984); *En trio* for Clarinet, Violin, and Piano (1985); *5/16* for Flute and Optional Percussion (1986); *Posaunen* for 4 Trombones (1987); *Mèmoire* for Cello and Piano (1989); *2 string quartets* (1992, 1995); *Le temps du souffle I* for 2 Clarinets and Basset Horn (1993) and *II* for Violin, Saxophone, and Trombone (1994); *Symphonies* for Brass (1994); *En harmonies* for Harp (1995). **KEYBOARD: P i a n o :** Sonata (1957–60); *Épigrammes* (1961; rev. 1967); *Cahiers d'Épigrammes* (1964); *Obliques I-III* (1985–90). **O r g a n :** *7 Bagatelles* (1975); *Quasi una toccata* (1981); *3 Inventions* (1993–95). **VOCAL:** *Oeil de fumée* for Soprano and Piano (1955; orchestrated, 1957); *Cette étoile enseigne à s'incliner* for Men's Chorus and Instruments (1970); *...d'un désastre obscur* for Mezzo-soprano and Clarinet (1970); *D'un espace déployé* for Soprano, 2 Pianos, and 2 Orch. Groups (1972–76); *Sonata pian'e forte* for Soprano, Mezzo-soprano, and 12 Instruments (1974); *Apres "...d'un désastre obscur"* for Mezzo-soprano and Small Ensemble (1976); *Messe* for Soprano, Alto, Tenor, Bass, Children's Chorus ad libitum, Chorus, and Orch. (1982–83); *Écrits sur toiles* for Reciter and Small Ensemble (1983); *Choros* for Countertenor, Tenor, Bass-baritone, Chorus, and Orch. (1989).—NS/LK/DM

Ana, Francesco d', Italian organist and composer; b. probably in Venice, c. 1460; d. there, 1502 or 1503. He was organist at S. Leonardo in Venice before assuming the post of 2nd organist at San Marco there in 1490. His 28 frottolas are notable.—LK/DM

Anacker, August Ferdinand, German composer; b. Freiberg, Saxony, Oct. 17, 1790; d. there, Aug. 21, 1854. He was educated at the Univ. of Leipzig. In 1821 he became cantor in Freiberg, and also founded that city's Singakademie in 1823. His oratorio, *Bergmannsgruss* (1831–32), was widely performed in his lifetime.—NS/LK/DM

Ančerl, Karel, eminent Czech conductor; b. Tučapy, April 11, 1908; d. Toronto, July 3, 1973. He studied at the Prague Cons. (1925–29) with Šourek (percussion) and with Křička and A. Hába (composition); under

Hába's tutelage, he composed a *Suite for Quarter Tone Piano* (1928) and *Music* for String Orch. in quarter tones (1928–29); he also studied conducting with Scherchen in Strasbourg, serving as his assistant in Königsberg (1929–31), and with Talich in Prague (1933–34). In 1933 he became music director of the Prague Radio Orch. As a Jew, he was removed from his post after the Nazi occupation of his homeland in 1939, and in 1942 was deported to the Jewish ghetto camp in Theresienstadt, where he played chamber music as a violist and conducted a camp orch. On Sept. 13, 1944, he conducted the premiere of Pavel Haas's Theresienstadt-composed *Study* for String Orch. In late 1944, Ančerl was transported to the Auschwitz concentration camp, where his entire family was put to death. After his liberation in 1945, he resumed his post with the Prague Radio Orch., and was co- founder of the 5ᵗʰ of May Opera in Prague. In 1950 Ančerl became chief conductor of the Czech Phil. in Prague. In spite of political constraints under the Communist regime, he restored the orch. to world renown, leading it in distinguished tours of Europe, North America, Australia, and Japan. In 1966 he was made a People's Artist by the Czech government. In mid-Aug. 1968 Ančerl was unexpectedly called to Tanglewood, Mass., to conduct the Boston Sym. Orch. as a last-minute replacement for an ailing Charles Munch, and thus was abroad when Soviet bloc troops invaded his homeland on Aug. 20–21. Ančerl refused to return to Czechoslovakia and gave up his post as chief conductor of the Czech Phil. In 1969 he became music director of the Toronto Sym., a post he retained until his death. During much of his Toronto tenure, he was plagued by ill health, due largely to lingering conditions resulting from his Nazi internment. He died at the age of 65. After the Czech Communist regime was swept from power by the Velvet Revolution in 1989, plans were made to return Ančerl's remains to a free Czech Republic. On May 12, 1993, his remains were interred with appropriate ceremony at Prague's Vyšehrad cemetery and a bust of the conductor by the sculptor Jan Kodet was dedicated in his memory. Ančerl was held in great esteem for his idiomatic interpretations of the music of his homeland. He also demonstrated remarkable insight into masterworks of the 20ᵗʰ century.

BIBL.: K. Šrom, *K. A.* (Prague and Bratislava, 1968); J. Karas, *Music in Terezín, 1941–1945* (N.Y., 1985).—**NS/LK/DM**

Anchieta, Juan de, Spanish composer; b. probably in Urrestilla, near Azpeitia, 1462; d. Azpeitia, July 30, 1523. He was related to Ignatius Loyola. In 1489 he entered the service of Queen Isabella as a singer in the court chapel. Upon her death in 1504, he entered the service of her daughter, Joanna, consort of Philip the Fair, serving as chaplain and singer. He also held a benefice at Villarino (from 1499), was rector of the parish church of S. Sebastian de Soreasu in Azpeitia (from 1500), and was Abbot of Arbos (from 1518). In 1519 he was pensioned by the court of Charles V. Among his works were masses, Magnificats, and motets for large choral forces, as well as 4 secular songs, including *Dos ánades*.

BIBL.: A. Cohen, *The Vocal Polyphonic Style of J.d. A.* (diss., N.Y.U., 1953).—**NS/LK/DM**

Ancina, (Giovanni) Giovenale, Italian composer; b. Fossano, Oct. 19, 1545; d. Saluzzo, Aug. 31, 1604. He studied medicine, philosophy, and rhetoric at the Univ. of Turin, graduating in 1567. He also studied medicine in Pavia. In 1574 he went to Rome to study theology and came under the influence of Filippo Neri, whose Congregazione dei Preti dell'Oratorio he joined in 1580. After being ordained in 1582, he served at the Naples oratory (1586–96) until being recalled to Rome. In 1602 he became bishop of Saluzzo. In 1890 he was beatified by Pope Leo XIII. Ancina publ. a valuable anthology of 3-part laudi as *Tempio armonico della beatissima vergine* (Rome, 1599), which includes 5 of his own laudi. He also wrote texts for various laudi.

BIBL.: C. Lombaro, *Della vita di G. A. da Fossano* (Naples, 1656); P. Bacci, *Vita del servo di Dio G. A.* (Rome, 1671); P. Damilano, *G. A.,musicista filippino (1545–1604)* (Florence, 1956). —**NS/LK/DM**

Ancona, Mario, notable Italian baritone; b. Livorno, Feb. 28, 1860; d. Florence, Feb. 22, 1931. He studied with Giuseppe Cima in Milan. After making his operatic debut as Scindia in *Le Roi de Lahore* in Trieste in 1889, he made his first appearances at Milan's La Scala as the King in *Le Cid* in 1890. On May 22, 1892, he created the role of Silvio in *Pagliacci* at Milan's Teatro dal Verme. He made his London debut in 1892 as Alphonse in *La Favorite* at the New Olympic Theater, returning to London in 1893 to sing Tonio in the first mounting there of *Pagliacci* at Covent Garden. On Dec. 11, 1893, he made his Metropolitan Opera debut in N.Y. as Tonio, remaining on its roster until 1897. He sang with the Manhattan Opera (1906–08), in Boston (1913–14), and in Chicago (1915–16) before retiring to Florence as a voice teacher. Ancona was one of the leading baritones of his day. Among his many outstanding roles were Mozart's Figaro and Don Giovanni, Germont, Hans Sachs, Escamillo, Telramund, Amonasro, and Iago.—**NS/LK/DM**

Ancot, family of South Netherlands musicians:

(1) Jean Ancot, *père*, pedagogue and composer; b. Bruges, Oct. 22, 1779; d. there, July 12, 1848. After studying in Paris (1799–1804) with Baillot, Kreutzer (violin), and Catel (harmony), he returned to Bruges as a teacher of violin and piano. Among his extant works are 4 violin concertos, overtures, marches, and sacred music. His 2 sons were also musicians:

(2) Jean Ancot, *fils*, violinist, pianist, and composer; b. Bruges, July 6, 1799; d. Boulogne, June 5, 1829. He studied with his father, and then with Pradher and Henri Berton at the Paris Cons. He was an accomplished pianist, winning success in London (1823–25). Among his large output are piano concertos, violin concertos, and much chamber music.

(3) Louis Ancot, *fils*, pianist, teacher, and composer; b. Bruges, June 3, 1803; d. there, Sept. 1836. He studied with his father. After serving as pianist to the Duke of Sussex in London, he toured widely in Europe. He wrote piano pieces in a salon style.—**NS/LK/DM**

Anda, Géza, eminent Hungarian-born Swiss pianist, conductor, and pedagogue; b. Budapest, Nov. 19, 1921; d. Zürich, June 13, 1976. He studied with Dohnányi at the Franz Liszt Academy of Music in Budapest. In 1938 he made his debut in Budapest. After receiving the Liszt Prize in 1940, he attracted notice as a soloist with Furtwängler and the Berlin Phil. in 1941. In 1942 he settled in Zürich, and in 1955 became a naturalized Swiss citizen. Following the close of World War II in 1945, he pursued a notable career as a soloist with the world's leading orchs. and as a recitalist. In later years, he took up conducting and became active as a pedagogue. Anda was one of the finest interpreters of Mozart, appearing on occasion as both soloist and conductor in Mozart's piano concertos. He also was esteemed for his performances of Beethoven, Liszt, Brahms, and Bartók.—NS/LK/DM

Anday, Rosette, Hungarian mezzo-soprano; b. Budapest, Dec. 22, 1903; d. Vienna, Sept. 28, 1977. She studied violin with Jen Hubay and voice with Mme. Cahier, Georg Anthes, and Gino Tessari. In 1920 she made her operatic debut at the Budapest Opera, then was a member of the Vienna State Opera (1921–61). She also made guest appearances throughout Europe and North and South America. Among her finest roles were Carmen, Clytemnestra, Dorabella, and Orfeo.
—NS/LK/DM

Anderberg, Carl-Olof, Swedish pianist, conductor, and composer; b. Stockholm, March 13, 1914; d. Malmö, Jan. 4, 1972. He studied piano with Olof Wibergh in Stockholm, and took courses in composition there and in Copenhagen, Paris, and London (1936–38), as well as in Vienna and Salzburg; he also studied conducting in Salzburg at the Mozarteum with Paumgartner, Walter, and Weingartner. In 1934 he made his debut as a pianist in Malmö as soloist in his own, youthful Concertino for Piano and Chamber Orch. He was active as a theater conductor, and also served as founder-conductor of the Malmö Chamber Orch. (1946–50). From 1956 he was active in his own music studio in Malmö. He publ. the vol. *Hän mot en ljudkonst* (Towards a New Sound Art; Malmö, 1961). Anderberg was a leading figure in Swedish avant-garde music circles. He developed an individual serial style that incorporated both aleatory techniques and improvisation.

WORKS: DRAMATIC: Opera: *Episode*, chamber opera (1952). **ORCH.:** *Music I* (1947) and *II* (1948) for Chamber Orch.; Sym. (1948); *Cyclus Stellarum I* (1949) and *II* (1957) for Strings; *Teater*, suite (1958); *Transfers* (1960); *Acroama I* and *II* (1965–66); Piano Concerto (Malmö, March 18, 1969); *Concero for a Ballet* for Piano, Winds, Percussion, and Double Basses (1969–70; Swedish Radio, March 4, 1972); *Orkesterspel I* and *II* (Orchestral Game; 1969–70). **CHAMBER:** *3 estampies* for Piano, Percussion, and Violins (1953); 2 string quartets (1955, 1957); Cello Sonata (1956); *4 Serious Caprices* for Clarinet and Piano (1956); *Duo I* for Flute and Piano (1958), and *II* and *III* for Violin and Piano (1968); *Triad* for Violin (1959); *Variationer över Variationer* for Clarinet, Bassoon, Violin, Cello, and Harp (1959); *Hexafoni* for 6 Instruments (1963); *Execution I* for Clarinet, Piano, and Percussion (1963); *Music* for Piano, Winds, and Tape (1970).

Piano: 3 sonatas (1950, 1952, 1956); *Klangskap I* (Soundscape) (1968). **VOCAL:** *Fyra legeringar* (4 Alloys) for Soprano and 5 Instruments (1958); *Höstens Hökar* for Narrator and 5 Instruments (1959); *Di Mi Se Mai* for Soprano, Narrator, and Orch. (1963); *Ströndernas svall* (The Surge of the Seaside), cantata for Soprano, Baritone, Narrator, and Instrumental Ensemble (1963–64); *Dubbelspel* (Double Play) for Soprano, Baritone, Clarinet, Cello, Piano, and Tape (1971); songs.
—NS/LK/DM

Anders, Peter, distinguished German tenor; b. Essen, July 1, 1908; d. in an automobile accident in Hamburg, Sept. 10, 1954. He was a pupil of Grenzebach and Mysz-Gemeiner in Berlin, making his debut there in *La belle Hélène* (1931). After singing in Heidelberg (1932), Darmstadt (1933–35), Cologne (1935–36), Hannover (1937–38), and Munich (1938–40), he was a principal member of the Berlin State Opera (1940–48) and the Hamburg State Opera (1948–54). In 1950 he made his British debut as Bacchus at the Edinburgh Festival; in 1951, appeared as Walther von Stolzing at London's Covent Garden. Anders was one of the finest German tenors of his generation. He excelled in operas by Mozart, Wagner, and Verdi; he also was a noted lieder artist.

BIBL.: F. Pauli, *P. A.* (Berlin, 1963); F. Kösters, *P. A.: Biographie eines Tenors* (Stuttgart, 1995).—NS/LK/DM

Andersen, (Carl) Joachim, Danish flutist, conductor, and composer; b. Copenhagen, April 29, 1847; d. there, May 7, 1909. He studied with his father, the flutist Christian Joachim Andersen. From 1869 to 1877 he played in the Royal Orch. in Copenhagen. In 1882 he became 1st flutist in the Berlin Phil., and also served as an asst. conductor with it. From 1893 he was conductor of the Palace Orch. in Copenhagen. He wrote various works for flute, some with orch. His brother, Vigo Andersen (b. Copenhagen, April 21, 1852; d. [suicide] Chicago, Jan. 28, 1895), was a flutist. He served as 1st flutist in the Theodore Thomas Orch. in Chicago.
—NS/LK/DM

Andersen, Karl August, Norwegian cellist and composer; b. Christiania, Sept. 29, 1903; d. there (Oslo), Aug. 15, 1970. He studied cello and composition in Christiania, then completed his training with Hugo Becker (cello) and Hermann Grabner (composition) in Berlin (1921–22). From 1924 he was a cellist in the Christiania (later Oslo) Phil. He composed in a neo-Classical style.

WORKS: ORCH.: Sym. for Chamber Orch. (1936); Suite (1937); *Allegro festivo e solenne Norwegese* (1950). **CHAMBER:** 3 string quartets (1934; n.d.; 1961–67); Trio for Flute, Clarinet, and Cello (1939); *Variations Over Theme and Rhythm* for Wind Quintet (1966). **VOCAL:** Choral pieces.—NS/LK/DM

Andersen, Karsten, Norwegian conductor; b. Christiana, Feb. 16, 1920; d. there (Oslo), Dec. 15, 1997. He received his training in Norway and Italy. In 1945 he became music director of the Stavanger Sym. Orch., a position he held concurrently with the Stavanger Radio Ensemble. From 1965 to 1985 he was music director of the Bergen Sym. Orch. He also was chief conductor of the Iceland Sym. Orch. in Reykjavík from 1973 to 1980. From 1985 to 1988 he was a prof. of conducting at the Norwegian Musikkhøgskole in Oslo.—NS/LK/DM

Anderson, Beth (actually, Barbara Elizabeth), inventive American composer and performance artist; b. Lexington, Ky., Jan. 3, 1950. After piano studies at the Univ. of Ky. (1966–68), she continued piano training at the Univ. of Calif. at Davis, where she also had courses in composition with Larry Austin, Cage, and Richard Swift (B.A., 1971). Following further training in piano (M.F.A., 1973) and in composition (M.A., 1974) with Robert Ashley and Terry Riley at Mills Coll. in Oakland, Calif., she attended N.Y.U. (1977–78). She was co-ed. and publisher of Ear Magazine (1973–79); also taught at the Coll. of New Rochelle in N.Y. (1978–86). As a composer, she has pursued a diagonal tangent upon her own highly original path. Her resources are manifold, passing through a wide spectrum of sound, sight, and motion in specially designed multimedia productions. She espouses text-sound composition, and also applies collage techniques.

WORKS: DRAMATIC: Queen Christina, opera (Oakland, Calif., Dec. 1, 1973); Soap Tuning, theater piece (1976); Zen Piece, theater piece (1976); Nirvana Manor, musical (1981); Elizabeth Rex, musical (1983); The Fat Opera, musical comedy (N.Y., April 22, 1991). MULTIMEDIA: Morning View and Maiden Spring for Tape, Speaker, Slides, and Light (1978). ORCH.: Revelation (1981); Revel (1985); Minnesota Swale (1994); Piano Concerto (1997). CHAMBER: Music for Charlemagne Palestine for String Quartet (1973); The Praying Mantis and the Bluebird for Flute and Piano (1979); Dream or Trio: Dream for Piano, Flute, and Cello (1980); Little Trio for Flute, Viola, and Guitar (1984); Pennyroyal Swale for String Quartet (1985); Rosemary Swale for String Quartet (1986); Brass Swale for Brass Quintet (1993); Ghent Swale for Violin and Piano (1999); Tales Nos. 1, 2, and 3 for Violin and Piano (1999); piano pieces. VOCAL: Joan, oratorio (Aptos, Calif., Aug. 22, 1974); Precious Memories for Chorus (1997); Magnificat for Chorus (1999); song cycles; solo songs; chants. OTHER: Tape pieces; text-sound compositions, including the opera Riot Rot (1984).—NS/LK/DM

Anderson, "Buddy" (Bernard Hartwell), swing band trumpeter, pianist; b. Oklahoma City, Oct. 14, 1919; Kansas City, Mo., May 9, 1997. Anderson began playing violin at age seven, played trumpet in a military band in junior high school, and then worked in a high school band known as "Dud" McCauley's Syncopators. Late in 1934 he joined a band led by bassist Louis "Ted" Armstrong in Clinton, Okla. He studied music in Quindario, Kans., and gigged in and around Kansas City with Gene Ramey's big band. In the summer of 1938, Anderson went to Xavier Univ., New Orleans, and played in the college orchestra and dance bands. During the summer of 1939 he joined Leslie Sheffield's Band in Oklahoma City, then resumed studies before joining Jay McShann from early 1940 into 1943. After working with other bands around Kansas City, Anderson came to N.Y. with Benny Carter, then during 1944 worked briefly with the big bands of Sabby Lewis, Roy Eldridge, and

Billy Eckstine. Health problems ended his career as a trumpeter, so he took up piano, and gigged for many years in Oklahoma City, where he was also president of the musicians' union.—JC/LP

Anderson, "Cat" (William Alonzo), jazz trumpeter associated with the later career of Duke Ellington; b. Greenville, S.C., Sept. 12, 1916; d. Norwalk, Calif., April 29, 1981. Anderson was the spectacular high note specialist of Duke Ellington's band for most of the period from 1944 through 1971. After being orphaned at the age of four, Anderson was raised in the Jenkins Orphanage of S.C., where he acquired his nickname after beating up a bully. He played various instruments in the school band from the age of seven before concentrating on trumpet, and toured with the band in 1929. Three years later he and several other band members formed The Carolina Cotton Pickers. He left in late 1935 to join guitarist Hartley Toots in Fla., then left Toots in 1936 to play with various bands before joining the Sunset Royals Orch. in the spring of 1942. Anderson next toured with a Special Services Orch., then was briefly with Lucky Millinder before joining Lionel Hampton in 1942. Anderson also played with Erskine Hawkins, then with Sabby Lewis from March 1943, before rejoining Lionel Hampton in 1944. He joined Ellington from September 1944 until January 1947, then formed his own band until 1949. He worked again with Sabby Lewis and gigged with Jimmy Tyler in Boston early in 1950, before rejoining Ellington. In late 1959 Anderson again left to lead his own band, and he freelanced in Philadelphia in 1961. He was with Ellington on and off from the summer of 1961 through early 1971, and for special occasions after that. During the 1970s he was extremely active in studio work and nightclubs around Los Angeles, and toured Europe several times.

DISC.: Carolina Cotton Pickers (1935); Cat on a Hot Tin Horn (1958); C. A. Plays at 4 A.M. (1958); C.A. and The Ellington All Stars (1958); Plays W.C. Handy (1977); Molde Concert (1981).

WRITINGS: The C.A. Trumpet Method: Dealing with Playing in the Upper Register (Los Angeles, 1973).

BIBL.: S. Dance, C. A., The World of Duke Ellington (N.Y. 1967); D. Ellington, C. A., Music Is My Mistress (Garden City, N.Y. 1973).—JC/LP

Anderson, Chris, jazz pianist, composer, singer; b. Chicago, Feb. 16, 1926. Anderson's offbeat style is little known, but had a major impact on Herbie Hancock, who is said to have studied with him in 1960. A fan of film music as a child, Anderson began to play the family piano at age 10. A few years later, after school, he played the blues in South Side bars. He worked in a record store, where he became excited about Nat Cole, Art Tatum, Duke Ellington, Gil Evans, Nelson Riddle, Claude Debussy, and Maurice Ravel. Due to double cataracts he became progressively blind. At 18 Anderson played with guitarist Leo Blevin, who recommended him to Sonny Stitt. Two years later, around 1946, he played with Charlie Parker and Howard McGhee. By this time he was totally blind. During the 1950s Anderson accompanied Sonny Rollins, Clifford

Brown, Max Roach, Gene Ammons, Stan Getz, Johnny Griffin, and Roland Kirk; worked with Wilbur Ware, Clifford Jordan, Von Freeman, George Coleman, and Wilbur Campbell; and mentored pianists Billy Wallace, Harold Mabern, and Hancock. In June 1961 he recorded in N.Y.; probably just after that, he toured for six weeks as accompanist for Dinah Washington. Another health problem, causing fragile bones that often fracture, has kept Anderson from performing on a regular basis. But he has taught privately, and has performed (often on a one night a week basis) as a soloist or in a duo with Larry Ridley, David Williams, Victor Sproles, or Jamil Nasser, among others. During the 1990s, he co-led a quartet with Roni Ben-Hur and, in 1997, appeared at Carnegie Hall with Charlie Haden.

DISC.: *My Romance* (Chicago, 1960); *Inverted Image* (1961); *Love Locked Out* (1990); *Old Friend* (1995); *Solo Ballads* (1997); —LP

Anderson, Ed(ward) ("Andy"), jazz trumpeter; b. Jacksonville, Fla., July 1, 1910. Anderson is best known for his work on Clarence Williams's recordings. He began playing trumpet at age ten, taking his first lessons with the bandmaster at Fla. State Coll. At 15 he went to St. Emma Coll. in Belmead, Va., and was principal trumpet in the college band. He played with Luckey Roberts at the Everglades Club in Palm Beach, Fla., and traveled to N.Y. with him in the spring of 1926. Roberts introduced Anderson to Clarence Williams, who began using him on recordings. During the period 1927–28, Anderson worked with drummer George Howe and Luis Russell at the Nest Club, and with Jelly Roll Morton at the Rose Danceland. In 1929 Anderson subbed for Louis Armstrong at Connie's Inn while Armstrong was in the revue "Hot Chocolates." He played with Benny Carter (at the Arcadia Ballroom), Charlie Johnson, and Bingie Madison, then joined The Mills Blue Rhythm Band from 1930 until the summer of 1934. Anderson later played in Charlie Turner's Arcadians, then joined Hazel Scott's big band early in 1939. After a stint with Frankie Newton's band at the Mime Club, N.Y., in the autumn of 1941, Anderson left full-time music. Eventually he gave up the trumpet, but maintained residency in N.Y.—JC/LP

Anderson, Emily, Irish musicologist; b. Galway, March 17, 1891; d. London, Oct. 26, 1962. She went to Germany for her education, and attended the univs. of Berlin and Marburg. Returning to England, she was employed in the British Foreign Office while pursuing her interest in music history and biography as an avocation. Of value are her translations of the correspondence of Mozart and Beethoven as publ. in *Letters of Mozart and His Family* (3 vols., London, 1938; 2nd ed., rev., 1966 by A. Hyatt King and M. Carolan; 3rd ed., rev., 1985 by S. Sadie and F. Smart) and *The Letters of Beethoven* (3 vols., London, 1961).—NS/LK/DM

Anderson, (Evelyn) Ruth, American composer, orchestrator, flutist, and teacher; b. Kalispell, Mont., March 21, 1928. She received a B.A. in flute (1949) and an M.A. in composition (1951) from the Univ. of Wash.,

and then pursued postgraduate work in the Columbia-Princeton Electronic Music Studio and at Princeton Univ. She received private training in composition from Darius Milhaud and Nadia Boulanger, and in flute from John Wummer and Jean-Pierre Rampal. After serving as solo flutist of the Totenberg Instrumental Ensemble (1951–58) and as principal flutist of the Boston Pops Orch. (1958), she was an orchestrator for NBC-TV (1960–66) and Lincoln Center (1966) in N.Y. In 1968 she became founding director of the Electronic Music Studio at Hunter Coll. of the City Univ. of N.Y., where she also taught composition and theory until her retirement in 1989. Her compositions and installations since the 1970s are increasingly grounded in a holistic concept of music, exploring its potential for stress reduction, enhanced self-awareness, and unity with others. *Points* (1974) is a sonic meditation using sine tones, the basis of all sound, at the threshold of hearing. In *Centering* (1979) the involuntary responses of four observers to a dancer are translated into sound through GSRs (galvanic skin resistance oscillators) attached to their fingers, forming an interdependent loop with the dancer who, in turn, responds spontaneously to the resulting rising and falling pitches. In *Time and Tempo* (1984) the same device controls the motor of a large clock, the viewer's state accelerating time or slowing it to a standstill. Interactive games form the basis of other works, such as *Sonic Solitaire* (1999–).

WORKS: ELECTROACOUSTIC: *The Pregnant Dream* (1968); *ESII* (1969); *DUMP* (1970); *SUM* (State of the Union Message; 1973); *Conversations* (1974); *Points* (1974); *Tuneable Hopscotch, Signatures* (1975); *Dress Rehearsal* (1976); *I come out of your sleep* (1979); *Resolutions* (1984); *Time and Tempo* (1984). **TEXT PIECES:** *Naming* (1975); *A Long Sound* (1976); *Sound Portraits I-II* (1977); *Silent Sound* (1978); *Greetings from the Right Hemisphere* (1979); *Communications* (1980); *Hearing as if...I-VI* (1990–91). **MIXED MEDIA PERFORMANCE AND INSTALLATIONS:** *Triangular Ping-Pong* (1973); *Tuneable Hopscotch* (1975); *Centering* for Dancer, 4 Observers, and Interactive Biofeedback Electronics (1979); *Time and Tempo* (1984); *Home Improvements: Windows; Faucets; Doors* (1999–); *Sonic Solitaire* (1999–). **OTHER:** *Fugue* for Piano or Strings (1948); *The Merchant's Song* for Voice and Piano (1951); *2 Pieces* for Strings (1957); *2 Movements* for Strings (1958).—NS/LK/DM

Anderson, Ivie (Marie; "Ivy"), jazz vocalist associated with Duke Ellington; b. Gilroy, Calif., July 10, 1905; d. Los Angeles, Dec. 28, 1949. Anderson's lively, bubbling sound was a key part of Duke Ellington's sound between 1931 and 1942. From ages 9 to 13 she received vocal training at the local St. Mary's Convent, then studied for two years in Washington, D.C., with Sara Rilt. Anderson began professional work at Tait's Club in Los Angeles, and later worked at Mike Lyman's Tent Cafe. She toured as a dancer in a Fanchon and Marco revue starring Mamie Smith, where she soon became featured as a singer. In 1925 Anderson worked at the Cotton Club in N.Y., then toured with the "Shuffle Along" revue before returning to Los Angeles, where she was featured with Curtis Mosby's Blue Blowers, Paul Howard's Quality Serenaders, Sonny Clay's Band, and briefly with Anson Weeks at the Mark Hopkins Hotel. Anderson was in residency at Frank Sebastian's

Cotton Club, Culver City, then, beginning in January 1928, toured Australia with Sonny Clay in another Fanchon and Marco revue. Returning to the U.S., she toured with her own show, was featured with Earl Hines in the Grand Terrace Revue in 1930, then joined Ellington from February 1931 until August 1942. Anderson also appeared in the 1937 Marx Brothers film *A Day at the Races*. After working with Ellington, she opened Ivie's Chicken Shack restaurant in Los Angeles and continued to sing regularly at West Coast night spots. Chronic asthma prevented Anderson from undertaking extensive tours, but she did work in Mexico City (1944) and in Chicago (1945).—JC/LP

Anderson, June, admired American soprano; b. Boston, Dec. 30, 1952. She received singing lessons as a child and at age 14 made her first appearance in opera in a production of Toch's *Die Prinzessin auf der Erbse*. In 1970 she was the youngest finalist in the Metropolitan Opera National Auditions. After taking her B.A. in French literature at Yale Univ. in 1974, she pursued vocal training in N.Y. with Robert Leonard. In 1976 she attracted favorable notice as soloist in Mozart's Mass in C minor, K.427, with the N.Y. Choral Soc., and then sang at the Chicago Lyric Opera in 1977. On Oct. 26, 1978, she made her debut at the N.Y.C. Opera as the Queen of the Night, and continued to appear there until 1982 when she made her European debut as Semiramide in Rome. In 1983 she scored a major success in N.Y. when she sang Semiramide in a concert performance at Carnegie Hall. In 1984 she was tapped to sing the soundtrack for the Queen of the Night for the film version of *Amadeus*. She made her first appearance at the Paris Opéra as Isabelle in *Robert le diable* in 1985; in 1986 she won accolades at her debut at Milan's La Scala as Amina, and later that year sang for the first time at London's Covent Garden as Lucia. In 1988 she appeared with the Opera Orch. of N.Y. as Beatrice di Tenda with fine success. On Nov. 30, 1989, she made her Metropolitan Opera debut in N.Y. as Gilda to critical acclaim. Her debut at N.Y.'s Carnegie Hall followed on Dec. 12, 1991. In 1992 she sang Lucia at the Metropolitan Opera. In 1993 she was heard as Bellini's Elvira at the San Francisco Opera. In 1996 she appeared as Giovanna d'Arco at Covent Garden, and in 1997 as Norma in Chicago. She also was active as a concert singer.—NS/LK/DM

Anderson, Laurie, imaginative American performance artist and composer; b. Chicago, June 5, 1947. Anderson received violin lessons before studying art history at Barnard Coll. (B.A., 1969) and sculpture at Columbia Univ. (M.F.A., 1972), and then had training from the painter Sol Lewitt. From 1973 to 1975 she taught art history at City Coll. of the City Univ. of N.Y. In 1983 she held a Guggenheim fellowship. Renouncing the tradition of conventional modernism, she set for herself a goal of uniting all arts as they once existed in ancient theatrical practice; in doing so, she made use of all available modern techniques, from topical pop to electronics, even making her own body a part of the instrumental combination, playbacking with herself on magnetic tape and projecting images on a screen. In her performances, she combines speech, song, and bodily

exertions; she also uses a variety of instrumentations, including a homemade violin activated by a luminous bow made of electronic tape. She has become particularly famous for her multimedia cyber-punk projections, extending the principles of cybernetics to deliberately commonplace movements, behavior, and lan- guage. Her programmed compositions are mostly improvisations in which she alters her natural voice electronically, making use of vocal glissando, crooning, panting, and heavy aspiration. Her satirical piece *New York Social Life* uses oriental drum effects; another piece, *Time to Go*, scored for guitar, violin, and organ, portrays the repeated exhortation of a museum guard to visitors to leave at closing time. In 1976 she gave a successful exhibition of psychomusicurgy at the Berlin Akademie der Kunst. In 1981 her song *O Superman (for Massenet)* became a genuine hit. In 1983 she produced her grandiose collage epic entitled simply *United States*, on themes of travel, politics, money, and love. Her book *United States* was publ. in N.Y. in 1984. On Oct. 3, 1989, she presented a large-scale solo work, *Empty Places*, at the Brooklyn Academy of Music. Among her subsequent works, the multimedia pieces *Stories From the Nerve Bible* (1995) and *Songs and Stories from "Moby Dick"* (1999) were notable.

DISC.: *Big Science* (1982); *Mister Heartbreak* (1984); *United States Live* (1984); *Home of the Brave* (1986); *Strange Angels* (1989); *Bright Red* (1994); *The Ugly One with the Jewels and Other Stories* (1995); *Talk Normal: The L. A. Anthology* (2000).

WRITINGS: *United States* (N.Y., 1984).

BIBL.: J. Kardon, ed., *L. A.: Works from 1969 to 1983* (Philadelphia, 1983).—NS/LK/DM

Anderson, Leroy, American composer, arranger, and conductor; b. Cambridge, Mass., June 29, 1908; d. Woodbury, Conn., May 18, 1975. He entered the New England Cons. of Music in Boston when he was 11, and later was a student of Spalding (harmony), Ballantine (counterpoint), Heilman (canon and fugue), and Hill and Piston (orchestration) at Harvard Univ. (B.A., 1929; M.A., 1930), where he then studied German and Scandinavian languages (1930–34) and was director of the univ. band (1931–35). From 1946 to 1950 he was an orchestrator and arranger for the Boston Pops Orch. Between 1954 and 1974 he appeared as a guest conductor of his own works with various North American orchs. In 1988 he was elected a posthumous member of the Songwriters Hall of Fame. Anderson became notably successful as a composer and arranger of light music for orch. His output reveals an inventive melodic and rhythmic bent, which proved immediately appealing.

WORKS: DRAMATIC: *Goldilocks*, musical (N.Y., Oct. 11, 1958); *Lady in Waiting*, ballet music (1958). **ORCH.** (many arranged by the composer or others for strings, band, and piano or for other solo instruments): *Harvard Fantasy* (Boston, June 16, 1936, composer conducting; rev. as *A Harvard Festival*, N.Y., April 1, 1969); *Jazz Pizzicato* for Strings (Boston, May 23, 1938, composer conducting; also for Orch., 1949); *Jazz Legato* for Strings (1938; also for Orch., 1949); *Harvard Sketches* (Boston, May 15, 1939, composer conducting; rev. as *Alma Mater*, Boston, June 14, 1954); *Ticonderoga*, march for Band (1939); *Promenade* (Boston, May 28, 1945, composer conducting); *The Syncopated Clock* (1945); *Chicken Reel* (Boston, May 12, 1946); *Fiddle-Faddle* for Strings (Boston, March 30, 1947; also for Orch., 1948); *Serenata* (Boston, May 10, 1947); *Eire Suite*, renamed *Irish Suite* (Boston, June 6, 1947; rev. 1949); *Sleigh Ride* (Boston, May 4, 1948); *Saraband* (Boston, May 27, 1948); *Governor Bradford March* (Boston, June 3, 1948); *A Trumpeter's Lullaby* (1949; Boston, May 9, 1950); *The Waltzing Cat* (1950); *A Christmas Festival* (Boston, June 12, 1950); *The Typewriter* (1950); *Blue Tango* (1951); *China Doll* (1951); *Belle of the Ball* (1951); *The Phantom Regiment* (1951); *The Penny-Whistle Song* (1951); *Horse and Buggy* (1951); *Plink, Plank, Plunk!* for Strings (1951); Piano Concerto (Chicago, July 18, 1953); *Song of the Bells* (1953); *Summer Skies* (1953); *The Girl in Satin* (1953); *Bugler's Holiday* (1954); *Forgotten Dreams* (1954); *Turn Ye to Me* (1954); *The First Day of Spring* (1954); *The Bluebells of Scotland* (1954); *Sandpaper Ballet* (1954); *Suite of Carols* for Brass Choir (1955); *Suite of Carols* for Strings (1955); *Suite of Carols* for Woodwind Ensemble (1955); *Arietta* (1962); *Balladette* (1962); *The Golden Years* (1962); *Clarinet Candy* (1962); *The Captains and the Kings* (1962); *Home Stretch* (1962).—**NS/LK/DM**

Anderson, Lucy (nèe **Philpot**), English pianist and teacher; b. Bath, Dec. 12, 1797; d. London, Dec. 24, 1878. Her father, John Philpot, was a prof. of music. She settled in London and in 1820 married the violinist George Frederick Anderson (b. London, 1793; d. there, 1876), who served as Master of the Queen's Musick from 1848 to 1870. She became the first woman to be engaged as a soloist by the Phil. Soc. in 1822. She was the piano teacher of Queen Victoria and her children.—**NS/LK/DM**

Anderson, Marian, celebrated black American contralto; b. Philadelphia, Feb. 27, 1897; d. Portland, Oreg., April 8, 1993. She was the aunt of the greatly talented black American conductor James (Anderson) DePreist (b. Philadelphia, Nov. 21, 1936). She gained experience as a member of the Union Baptist Church choir in Philadelphia. After studies with Giuseppe Boghetti, she pursued vocal training with Frank La Forge in N.Y. In 1925 she won 1st prize in the N.Y. Phil. competition, which led to her appearance as soloist with it at the Lewisohn Stadium on Aug. 27 of that same year. In 1929 she sang at N.Y.'s Carnegie Hall, and then made her European debut at London's Wigmore Hall in 1930. She subsequently toured Europe, with increasing success. Her first appearance at N.Y.'s Town Hall on Nov. 30, 1935, proved a notable turning point in her U.S. career, and she thereafter toured throughout the country. In spite of her success, she became the center of national attention in 1939 when the Daughters of the American Revolution denied her the right to give a concert at Constitution Hall in Washington, D.C., citing the organization's long-standing rules of racial segregation. The ensuing controversy led to widespread support for Anderson, who subsequently appeared in concert at the Lincoln Memorial in Washington, D.C. (April 9, 1939). Her success was enormous and secured her reputation as one of America's outstanding musicians. In later years, she toured not only in the U.S. and Europe, but worldwide. On Jan. 7, 1955, she became the first black singer to appear at the Metropolitan Opera in N.Y. when she made her debut as Ulrica. She then continued her concert career until retiring in 1965. Her autobiography appeared as *My Lord, What a Morning*

(N.Y., 1956). Anderson received numerous honors from governments and institutions of higher learning, among them the U.S. Medal of Freedom (1963), a gold medal from the U.S. Congress (1977), and the National Medal of Arts (1986).

BIBL.: K. Vehanen, *M. A.* (N.Y., 1941); J. Sims, *M. A.: An Annotated Bibliography and Discography* (Westport, Conn., 1981); C. Patterson, *M. A.* (N.Y., 1988); A. Tedards, *M. A.* (N.Y., 1988).—**NS/LK/DM**

Anderson, Ray (Robert), jazz trombonist; b. Chicago, Oct. 16, 1952. A wild and rambunctious soloist, Anderson is also a witty performer who sometimes sings in a raspy style. He started music as a youth and began attending AACM concerts and blues shows in Chicago as a teenager. Anderson played in funk bands during the early 1970s, was briefly seen in San Francisco in 1973, and came to N.Y. later that year. Early stints with Mingus led to gigs with Barry Altschul and Anthony Braxton, and many sessions in Latin jazz bands. Anderson has led his own groups since the late 1970s and won the 1981 *Down Beat* Critic's Poll in the category of Talent Deserving Wider Recognition/ Trombone. Since 1987, he has been working with pianist/bandleader George Gruntz. Anderson began to have a larger following around 1989.

DISC.: *Harrisburg Half Life* (1980); *Old Bottles, New Wine* (1987); *What Because* (1989); *Blues Bred in the Bone* (1989); *Every One of Us* (1992); *Big Band Record* (1994).—**LP**

Anderson, T(homas) J(efferson Jr.), black American composer and teacher; b. Coatesville, Pa., Aug. 17, 1928. He studied at W.Va. State Coll. (B.Mus., 1950) and at Pa. State Univ. (M.Ed., 1951) before pursuing training in composition with Huston at the Univ. of Cincinnati Coll.-Cons. of Music (1954), Bezanson and Hervig at the Univ. of Iowa (Ph.D., 1958), and Milhaud at the Aspen (Colo.) School of Music (summer, 1964). He was prof. of music and chairman of the dept. at Langston (Okla.) Univ. (1958–63), and prof. of music at Tenn. State Univ. (1963–69). From 1969 to 1971 he was composer-in-residence of the Atlanta Sym. Orch. From 1972 to 1990 he was prof. of music at Tufts Univ., and also chairman of the dept. (1972–80). In 1988–89 he held a Guggenheim fellowship. Anderson played a major role in the revival of Scott Joplin's music. He arranged Joplin's opera *Treemonisha* for its first complete performance (Atlanta, Jan. 28, 1972). Anderson's own works are audaciously modern, while preserving a deeply felt lyricism. His harmonies are taut and intense without abandoning the basic tonal frame. His contrapuntal usages suggest folklike ensembles, but he freely varies his techniques according to the character of each particular piece.

WORKS: DRAMATIC: *The Shell Fairy*, operetta (1976–77); *Re-Creation* for 3 Readers, Dancer, and Instrumentalists (1978); *Soldier Boy, Soldier*, opera (Bloomington, Ind., Oct. 23, 1982); *Thomas Jefferson's Orbiting Minstrels and Contraband*, a "21st Century celebration of 19th Century form" for Dancer, Soprano, String Quartet, Woodwind Quintet, Jazz Sextet, Computer, Visuals, and Keyboard Synthesizer (1984; DeKalb, Ill., Feb. 12, 1986); *Walker*, chamber opera (1992; Boston, Dec. 9,

1993). **ORCH.**: *Pyknon Overture* (1958); *Introduction and Allegro* (1959); *New Dances* (1960); *Classical Symphony* (1961); *6 Pieces* for Clarinet and Chamber Orch. (1962); *Symphony in 3 Movements*, in memory of President John F. Kennedy (Oklahoma City, April 10, 1964); *Squares: An Essay for Orchestra* (1965); Chamber Sym. (1968; Nashville, Tenn., Nov. 24, 1969); *Intervals* (1970–71); *Messages: A Creole Fantasy* (1979; Atlanta, May 3, 1980); Concerto for 2 Violins and Chamber Orch. (Chicago, May 29, 1988); *Remembrances*, chamber concerto (Cleveland, Oct. 30, 1988); *Bahia, Bahia* for Chamber Orch. (1990). **Band**: *Trio Concertante* for Clarinet, Trumpet, Trombone, and Band (1960); *Rotations* (1967); *In Memoriam Zach Walker* (1968); *Fanfare* for Trumpet and 4 Mini-bands (1976). **CHAMBER**: String Quartet (1958); *5 Bagatelles* for Oboe, Violin, and Harpsichord (1963); *5 Etudes and a Fancy* for Woodwind Quintet (1964); *Connections, a Fantasy* for String Quintet (1966); *Transitions* for Chamber Ensemble (1971); *Swing Set* for Clarinet and Piano (1972); *5 Easy Pieces* for Violin, Piano, and Jew's Harp (1974); *Variations on a Theme by Alban Berg* for Viola and Piano (1977); *Minstrel Man* for Bass Trombone and Percussionist (1978); *Vocalise* for Violin and Harp (1980); *Inaugural Piece* for 3 Trumpets and 3 Trombones (1982); *Intermezzi* for Clarinet, Alto Saxophone, and Piano (1983; also as solo pieces for each of these instruments); *Sunstar* for Trumpet and Cassette Recorder (1984); *Bridging and Branching* for Flute and Double Bass (1986); *Ivesiana* for Violin, Cello, and Piano (1988); *What Ever Happened to the Big Bands?* for Alto Saxophone, Trumpet, and Trombone (1991); *Spirit Songs* for Cello and Piano (1993). **KEYBOARD**: **Piano**: *5 Portraitures of 2 People* for Piano, 4-Hands (1965); *Watermelon* (1971); *Street Song* (1977); *Play Me Something* (1979); *Call and Response* (1982); *Passacaglia and Blues* (1990). **Organ**: *In memoriam: Graham Wootton* (1985). **VOCAL**: *Personals*, cantata for Chorus, Narrator, and Brass Septet (1966); *Variations on a Theme by M. B. Tolson*, cantata for Soprano and 6 Instruments (1969); *This House* for Men's Glee Club and 4 Chromatic Pitch Pipes (1971); *Block Songs* for Soprano, Children's Toys, Chromatic Pitch Pipe, and Jack-in-the-Box (1972); *Beyond Silence* for Tenor and 5 Instruments (1973); *Im Memoriam Malcolm X* for Voice and Orch. (N.Y., April 7, 1974); *Horizons '76* for Soprano and Orch. (1975; Chicago, June 11, 1978); *Spirituals* for Tenor, Narrator, Chorus, Children's Chorus, Jazz Quartet, and Orch. (1979; Atlanta, Jan. 19, 1982); *Jonestown* for Chorus and Piano (1982; Boston, May 6, 1984); *Thomas Jefferson's Minstrels* for Baritone, Men's Glee Club, and Jazz Band (1982; Medford, Mass., April 15, 1983); *What Time is It?* for Boy's Chorus and Jazz Orch. (N.Y., Dec. 1, 1986); *Songs of Illumination* for Soprano, Tenor, and Piano (Medford, Mass., April 27, 1990); *Ancestral Voices* for Bass and Piano (Strasbourg, Sept. 21, 1990); *Dear John, Dear Coltrane* for Chorus and Piano (Minneapolis, Dec. 4, 1990); *Egyptian Diary* for Soprano and 2 Percussionists (1991; Chicago, April 26, 1992); *Here in the Flesh*, hymn for Congregation and Piano (Charlotte, N.C., June 28, 1993).—**NS/LK/DM**

Anderson, Wessell ("Warmdaddy"),

jazz alto saxophonist associated with Wynton Marsalis; b. Brooklyn, N.Y., Nov. 27, 1964. Anderson, whose father was a drummer who toured with bebop saxophonist Cecil Payne, took lessons from Frank Foster through the N.Y.C. Jazzmobile project. Through Jazzmobile, he met Branford Marsalis, who recommended that he study with Alvin Batiste in New Orleans. In 1988, Anderson was hired by vocalist Betty Carter to accompany her, but left after a few months to join Wynton Marsalis's septet. He has played and recorded with Marsalis since, both in small-group settings and as part of the Lincoln Center jazz band. Marsalis bestowed the nickname "Warmdaddy" on Anderson.

DISC.: *Warmdaddy in the Garden of Swing* (1994); *The Ways of Warmdaddy* (1996).—**LP**

d'Andrade, Francesco,

Portuguese baritone; b. Lisbon, Jan. 11, 1859; d. Berlin, Feb. 8, 1921. He studied with Miraglia and Ronconi. In 1882 he made his operatic debut as Amonasro in San Remo, then sang throughout Italy, Portugal, and Spain. In 1886 he made his debut at London's Covent Garden as Rigoletto, singing there until 1890. He then was a member of the Berlin Royal Opera (1906–19). He gained fame for his portrayal of Don Giovanni. His brother, Antonio d'Andrade, was a tenor.—**NS/LK/DM**

Andrašovan, Tibor,

Slovak composer and conductor; b. Slovenská L'upča, April 3, 1917. He studied at the Comenius Univ. (1937–41) and with Suchoň (composition) and Vincourek and Schimpl (conducting) at the Cons. (1940–45) in Bratislava. He completed his training in Prague (1945), where he studied with Ddeček and Doležil (conducting) and took courses at the Charles Univ. From 1950 to 1957, and again from 1968 to 1972, he was artistic director of the SL'U.K. Folk Music and Dance Ensemble. In 1971 he received the title of Artist of Merit and in 1997 the Order of Milan Rastislav Štefánik.

WORKS: **DRAMATIC**: *Orpheus and Euridice*, ballet (1948); *Song of Peace*, ballet (1949); *Fifliar Gel'o*, comic opera (1957); *Gentlemen's Choice*, operetta (1960); *Icar*, ballet (1965); *Solstice Festivities*, ballet (1965); *White Disease*, music drama (1967); *Forester's Wife*, opera (1974); *King of Fools*, musical (1982); *Homecoming*, television opera (1984); *The Shah and Sheherazade*, opera-musical tale (1991); *The Rings of a Tree*, ballet (1994); *Vrabček Mojček*, children's opera (1997); incidental music to plays; film scores. **ORCH.**: *Little Gorali Overture* (1961); *Rebel Overture* (1963); *Dukla: The Gate of Freedom*, overture (1975); *Dances from Slavakia* (1989); *Our Majorettes* for Brass Band or Orch. (1993); *Around Tatra Mountains* (1996); Concerto for Harpsichord and Chamber Orch. (1997). **CHAMBER**: String Quartet, *Folklorica* (1976); *Souvenir* for Violin and Piano (1986); piano pieces. **VOCAL**: *Tokajík*, cantata for Soprano, Chorus, and Orch. (1975); *Constantine and Methodius*, oratorio for Soloists, Chorus, and Orch. (1987); choruses; song cycles. **OTHER**: Pieces for folk music ensembles.—**NS/LK/DM**

André,

family of German musicians of French descent:

(1) Johann André, composer and music publisher; b. Offenbach, March 28, 1741; d. there, June 18, 1799. He was born into a family of silk manufacturers, and was only 10 when he inherited the business. He received some thorough bass training from an itinerant musician, but was basically autodidact. In 1771–72 he worked as a tr. of French comic operas into German for the Theobald Marchand troupe. He then wrote the libretto and music to his first stage work, the comic opera *Der Töpfer* (Hanu, Jan. 22, 1773). In 1774 he founded his own music publishing firm in Offenbach. His collaboration with Goethe on the Schauspiel mit Gesang *Erwin und Elmire*

(Frankfurt am Main, May 1775) established André's reputation as a composer for the theater. His lieder setting of G. A. Bürger's *Lenore* (1775) brought him further notice. From 1777 to 1784 André was music director of Theophil Döbbelin's theater in Berlin, where he brought out the successful works *Claudine von Villa Bella* (1778), *Belmont und Constanze, oder Die Entführung aus dem Serail* (May 25, 1781), and *Der Barbier von Bagdad* (Feb. 19, 1783). In 1784 he returned to Offenbach to take control of his music publishing business.

(2) Johann Anton André, composer, music publisher, teacher, and music theorist, son of the preceding; b. Offenbach, Oct. 6, 1775; d. there, April 6, 1842. He received training in piano, violin, and singing at an early age. In 1787 he became a violin pupil of his brother-in-law, Ferdinand Fränzl, and composed his first Violin Sonata. In 1789 he became a student of Ignaz Fränzl in Mannheim, where he then took composition lessons with G. J. Vollweiler in 1792–93. After studying fine arts at the Univ. of Jena (1796), he took full control of the family music publishing business upon his father's death in 1799. That same year, he acquired the rights to Senefelder's and Gleissner's lithographic process in Munich and purchased the so-called "Mozart-Nachlass" from Mozart's widow in Vienna. From 1800 he publ. many editions of Mozart's works. His edition of Mozart's autograph catalog (1784–91) was publ. as *Thematisches Verzeichnis sämtlicher Kompositionen von W. A. Mozart* (Offenbach, 1805; 2nd ed., 1828, as *W.A. Mozarts thematischer Catalog*). H. Henkel ed. André's *Thematisches Verzeichnis derjenigen Original-Handschriften von W.A. Mozart, welche Hofrath André in Offenbach besitzt* (Offenbach, 1841). André planned a grand *Lehrbuch der Tonsetzkunst* in 6 vols., but only 2 vols. were completed (Vol. I, 1832; Vol. II ed. by H. Henkel, 1842). Among his numerous works were the operas *Rinaldo und Alcina* and *Die Weiber von Weinsberg*, 9 syms., 3 overtures, concertos, chamber music, piano pieces, including didactic works, organ music, choral pieces, and songs. His large family included 15 children, of whom the following should be noted:

(3) Carl August André, music dealer and piano manufacturer; b. Offenbach, June 15, 1806; d. Frankfurt am Main, Feb. 15, 1887. He was director of the music shop established by his father in Frankfurt am Main, where he manufactured pianos from 1839, including the Mozartflügel series from 1853. He was the author of *Der Klavierbau und seine Geschichte* (1855).

(4) (Peter Friedrich) Julius André, pianist, organist, and composer; b. Offenbach, June 4, 1808; d. Frankfurt am Main, April 17, 1880. He was employed in his brother's music shop in Frankfurt am Main from 1864. He wrote an organ method and composed piano, organ, and vocal music.

(5) Jean Baptiste (Andreas) André, pianist and composer; b. Offenbach, March 7, 1823; d. Frankfurt am Main, Dec. 9, 1882. After several tours of Europe as a pianist, he went to Berlin as teacher to Count Bolko von Hochberg. He later was court Kapellmeister to the Prince of Bernburg. His works included choral pieces, many songs, and piano pieces in salon style. For some of his works he used the pseudonym "de St. Gilles."

BIBL.: A. André, *Zur Geschichte der Familie A.—Offenbach am Main* (Offenbach, 1962); idem, *Zur Geschichte der Familie A.* (Garmisch, 1963); W. Matthäus, *J. A. Musikverlag zu Offenbach am Main: Verlagsgeschichte und Bibliographie 1772–1800* (Tutzing, 1974); K. Hortschansky, U. Unverricht et al. *J. A. Musikverlag* (Offenbach, 1974); B. Constapel, *Der Musikverlag J. A. in Offenbach am Main Studien zur Verlagstätigkeit von J.A. A. und Verzeichnis der Musikalien von 1800 bis 1840* (Tutzing, 1998). —NS/LK/DM

André, Franz, Belgian conductor, pedagogue, and composer; b. Brussels, June 10, 1893; d. there, Jan. 20, 1975. He studied with C. Thomson (violin) at the Brussels Cons. and with Weingartner (conducting) in Berlin. He taught at the Brussels Cons. (1920–44). In 1923 he became a violinist in the Belgian Radio Orch. in Brussels, and soon was appointed its conductor; in 1935 he founded its Grand Orchestre Symphonique de l'Institut National de Radiodiffusion, which he served as chief conductor until 1958.—NS/LK/DM

André, Maurice, famous French trumpeter and pedagogue; b. Alès, May 21, 1933. After working as a coal miner as a youth (1947–51), during which time he took up the trumpet, he pursued formal studies with Barthélémy at the Paris Cons., receiving the Prix d'Honneur. He was first trumpeter in the Lamoureux Orch. (1953–60), the Orchestre Philharmonique de l'ORTF (1953–62), and the orch. of the Opéra-Comique (1962–67) in Paris. In 1954 he made his formal debut as a soloist in Paris; then won the Geneva (1955) and Munich (1963) international competitions. From 1967 he pursued an international career as a trumpet virtuoso. He also taught at the Paris Cons. (1967–78) and gave master classes at home and abroad. His exhaustive repertory ranged from works from the Baroque era to contemporary scores. Among composers who wrote works especially for him were Blacher, Jolivet, and Landowski.—NS/LK/DM

Andreae, Marc (Edouard), Swiss conductor, grandson of **Volkmar Andreae;** b. Zürich, Nov. 8, 1939. He studied piano and conducting at the Zürich Cons. (graduated, 1962), composition with Boulanger in Paris (1962–63), and conducting with Ferrara at the Accademia di Santa Cecilia in Rome and at the Accademia Musicale Chigiana in Siena (1964–68). He was conductor of the Orchestre Pro Arte in Zürich (1960–62). After winning 1st prize in the national Swiss competition there in 1966, he was assistant to Peter Maag (1967–68). From 1969 to 1990 he was chief conductor of the Orch. della Radiotelevisione della Svizzera Italiana in Lugano. —NS/LK/DM

Andreae, Volkmar, distinguished Swiss conductor, pedagogue, and composer, grandfather of **Marc (Edouard) Andreae;** b. Bern, July 5, 1879; d. Zürich, June 18, 1962. He studied with Munzinger in Bern and with Wüllner at the Cologne Cons. (1897–1900). After serving as répétiteur at the Munich Court Opera (1900–02), he settled in Zürich and was conductor of its mixed chorus (1902–49) and men's chorus (1904–19); was chief conductor of the Tonhalle Orch. (1906–49) and director of the Zürich Cons. (1914–41). He championed the works of Bruckner, Strauss, Reger, Mahler, and Debussy. In his own compositions, he reflected post-Romantic tendencies.

WORKS: DRAMATIC: Opera: *Ratcliff* (Duisburg, May 25, 1914); *Abenteuer des Casanova* (Dresden, June 17, 1924). **ORCH.:** 2 syms. (n.d.; Zürich, Nov. 3, 1919); *Rhapsody* for Violin and Orch. (1920); *Musik* (Zürich, Nov. 12, 1929); Violin Concerto (1940); Oboe Concertino (1942). **CHAMBER:** 2 piano trios (1901, 1908); Violin Sonata (1903); 2 string quartets (1905, 1922); String Trio (1919); *Divertimento* for Flute and String Trio (1945); piano pieces. **VOCAL:** Various works for Soloists, Chorus, and Orch., choruses, and songs.

BIBL.: F. Seiler, *Dr. V. A....zum Jubiläum seiner 25- jährigen Tätigkeit* (Zürich, 1931); M. Engeler and E. Lichtenhahn, eds., *Briefe an V. A.: Ein halbes Jahrhundert Züricher Musikleben, 1902–1959* (Zürich, 1986).—**NS/LK/DM**

Andreas de Florentia,

Italian organist and composer; place and date of birth unknown; d. c. 1415. In 1375 he became a member of the Order of the Servi di Maria. He was active at the monastery of the Ss. Annunziata in Florence (1380–97) and was prior in Pistoia (1393), and later was leader of the Tuscan Servites (1407–10). He was a leading composer of ballate. See J. Wolf, ed., *Der Squarcialupi-Codex Pal.87 der Biblioteca Medicea Laurenziana zu Florenz* (Lippstadt, 1955), N. Pirrotta, ed., *The Music of Fourteenth-Century Italy*, Corpus Mensurabilis Musicae, VIII/5 (1964), and W. Marrocco, ed., *Italian Secular Music*, Polyphonic Music of the Fourteenth Century, X (Monaco, 1974). —**LK/DM**

Andrée, Elfrida,

Swedish organist, teacher, and composer; b. Visby, Feb. 19, 1841; d. Göteborg, Jan. 11, 1929. She began her training with her father and with Wilhelm Söhrling in Visby. At 14, she entered the Stockholm Cons., where she graduated as an organist at 16. She then pursued training in composition with Ludvig Norman and Hermann Berens. With the assistance of her father, she secured legislation that allowed women to hold positions as organist in 1861. That same year, she became organist of the Finnish Congregation in Stockholm, and in 1862 of the French Reformed Church there. Also through her efforts, women were allowed to become telegraph operators in Sweden and Andrée was the first to attain that distinction in 1865. From 1867 until her death she was organist of the Göteborg Cathedral. She also was director of a series of 800 "popular" concerts and was active as a teacher. In 1879 she was elected a member of the Royal Swedish Academy of Music.

WORKS: DRAMATIC: Opera: *Fritiofs Saga* (n.d.). **ORCH.:** Overture (1873); 2 syms. (1889, 1893). **CHAMBER:** Piano Quintet (1865); Piano Quartet (1865); 2 string quartets (1865, 1895); 2 violin sonatas (n.d., 1872); Piano Trio (1877). **KEYBOARD:** Piano pieces; organ music, including 2 organ syms. **VOCAL:** Choral works; songs.

BIBL.: E. Stuart, *E. A.* (Stockholm, 1925); E. Öhrström, *E. A.: Ett levnadsöde* (Stockholm, 1999).—**NS/LK/DM**

Andreini, Virginia (née Ramponi),

Italian actress and soprano, known as **La Florinda**; b. Milan, Jan. 1, 1583; d. Bologna, 1630. She was active as an actress in the theatrical enterprise of her husband, Giovanni Battista Andreini. Monteverdi wrote the title role of his opera *L'Arianna* for her, which she created in Mantua on May 28, 1608.—**LK/DM**

Andreis, Josip,

eminent Croatian music historian; b. Split, March 19, 1909; d. Zagreb, Jan. 16, 1982. He received training in Romance languages at the univs. of Zagreb and Rome (graduated, 1931); also had private instruction in composition and attended the Zagreb Academy of Music, where he subsequently served on its faculty as prof. of music history and head of the musicology dept. (1945–72). He was ed. of the journal *Muzičke novine* (1950–51). His *Historija muzike* (3 vols., Zagreb, 1951–54; 2nd ed., rev., 1966) is the standard history of music in Serbo-Croat. He was general ed. of the *Muzička enciklopedija* (2 vols., Zagreb, 1958, 1963), the pioneering publ. of its kind in Yugoslavia. He was founder-ed. of the musicological annual *Arti musices* (1969–70). Andreis's contribution to the study of Croatian music history remains of great value.

WRITINGS: *Povijest glazbe* (History of Music; Zagreb, 1942); *Uvod u glazbenu estetiku* (Introduction to the Aesthetics of Music; Zagreb, 1944); *Hector Berlioz* (Zagreb, 1946); *Historija muzike* (3 vols., Zagreb, 1951–54; 2nd ed., rev., 1966); with S. Zlatić, *Yugoslav Music* (Belgrade, 1959); *Vječni Orfej* (Eternal Orpheus; Zagreb, 1968); *Music in Croatia* (Zagreb, 1974). —**NS/LK/DM**

Andreoli, Carlo,

Italian pianist, conductor, and composer, brother of **Guglielmo Andreoli**; b. Mirandola, Jan. 8, 1840; d. Reggio Emilia, Jan. 22, 1908. He studied with his father, Evangelista Andreoli, then with Antonio Angeleri at the Milan Cons. (1852–58). He made his debut as a pianist in Milan in 1858; subsequently appeared as a virtuoso throughout Italy and Europe. With his brother, he organized the Società dei Concerti Sinfonica Popolari of Milan, serving as its conductor from 1877 to 1887. He became insane in 1891, and lingered in this condition for many years until his death.

BIBL.: G. Tebaldini, *In memoria di C. A.* (Milan and Mirandola, 1910).—**LK/DM**

Andreoli, Guglielmo,

Italian pianist, conductor, teacher, and composer, brother of **Carlo Andreoli**; b. Mirandola, Jan. 9, 1862; d. Modena, April 26, 1932. He studied with his father, Evangelista Andreoli, then with Fumagalli (organ), Rampazzini (violin), and Bazzini (composition) at the Milan Cons., where he later taught. With his brother, he was also a conductor with the Società dei Concerti Sinfonici Popolari in Milan (1877–87). He wrote orch. music, piano pieces, and songs.—**NS/LK/DM**

Andreozzi, Gaetano,

Italian composer; b. Aversa, May 22, 1755; d. Paris, Dec. 21?, 1826. He was a pupil of Fenaroli and P. A. Gallo at the Cons. di S. Maria di Loreto in Naples. He also studied with Jomelli, and hence was nicknamed Jommelino. He pursued a successful career as a theater composer, producing some 45 operas.—**NS/LK/DM**

Andrésen, Ivar, Norwegian bass; b. Christiania, July 27, 1896; d. Stockholm, Nov. 25, 1940. He studied at the Royal Opera School in Stockholm. He made his operatic debut in Stockholm in 1919 as the King in *Aida*. From 1925 to 1934 he was a member of the Dresden State Opera, and also appeared at the Bayreuth Festivals (1927–36) and at London's Covent Garden (1928–31). On Nov. 1, 1930, he made his Metropolitan Opera debut in N.Y. as Daland, continuing on its roster until 1932. From 1934 to 1936 he sang at the Berlin State Opera, and in 1935 appeared at the Glyndebourne Festival. His success in Germany led to his being made a Kammersänger. Although principally known as a Wagnerian, he also sang such roles as Sarastro and Osmin to great effect.—NS/LK/DM

Andreví y Castellar, Francisco, prominent Spanish choirmaster and composer; b. Sanahuja, Nov. 7, 1786; d. Barcelona, Nov. 23, 1853. He was a choirboy at Urgel Cathedral, where he commenced his musical training, and then went to Barcelona to study with Juan Quintana (organ) and Francisco Queralt (composition). He was choirmaster at Segorbe Cathedral (1808–14), at S. María del Mar in Barcelona (1814–19), at Valencia Cathedral (1819–30), and at Seville Cathedral (1830–31). In 1831 he became choirmaster of the royal chapel in Madrid, but was removed for political reasons in 1836. He then went to France, where he was maître de chapelle at Bordeaux Cathedral (1839–45). Returning to Barcelona, he was choirmaster of the parish church of La Merced from 1850 until his death. He publ. *Tratado teórico practico de armonia y composición* (Barcelona, 1848; French tr., 1848). His works include the oratorios *La dulzura de la virtud* (Barcelona, c. 1818) and *El juicio universal* (Valencia, 1822), many masses, 3 Stabat mater, a Te Deum, Lamentations, and Psalms.—NS/LK/DM

Andrews, Julie (originally **Julia Elizabeth Wells**), b. Walton-on-Thames, England, Oct. 1, 1935. Whether playing a novice in *The Sound of Music* or the ultimate nanny in *Mary Poppins,* Andrews's innocent image always fit her crystalline soprano voice, which could scale four and a half octaves. A child star on the British music-hall stage, Andrews became a Broadway phenom at age 19, and conquered the silver screen several years later. Musicals were her forte, and her career dipped in the 1970s as the form became less popular, and she was unable to convert her stage and screen success into a solo recording career. She made a comeback after her marriage to director Blake Edwards, though, playing against type in his films *10, S.O.B.* (where she bared her breasts), and *Victor/Victoria,* where she played the challenging gender-bending role of a woman playing a man playing a woman. Through it all, Andrews's voice has remained magnificent; it is one of the definitive instruments of the Broadway stage and movie musicals.

DISC: *My Fair Lady* (Broadway cast recording; 1956); *Julie and Carol at Carnegie Hall* (with Carol Burnett; 1962); *Mary Poppins* (soundtrack; 1964); *The Sound of Music* (soundtrack; 1965); *Thoroughly Modern Millie* (soundtrack; 1967); *A Christmas Treasure* (with Andre Previn; 1968); *A Little Bit of Broadway*

(1977); *Christmas with Julie Andrews* (1982); *Love, Julie* (1989); *Broadway: The Music of Richard Rodgers* (1994); *Thoroughly Modern Julie: The Best of Julie Andrews* (1996); *Broadway: Here I'll Stay—The Words of Alan Jay Lerner* (1996); *Greatest Christmas Songs* (2000).

Andrews Sisters, The, American singing group. **MEMBERSHIP:** LaVerne Sophie Andrews (b. Mound, Minn., July 6, 1911; d. Los Angeles, May 8, 1967); Maxene Angelyn Andrews (b. Mound, Minn., Jan. 3, 1916; d. Hyannis, Mass., Oct. 21, 1995); Patricia Marie (Patty or Patti) Andrews (b. Mound, Minn., Feb. 16, 1918). The Andrews Sisters were the most popular female vocal group of the first half of the 20th century. A lively act combining humor with eclectic novelty songs featuring intricate, rhythmic arrangements, they scored 20 Top Ten hits between 1938 and 1950, the most popular being "Shoo-Shoo Baby," "Rum and Coca-Cola," and "I Can Dream, Can't I?" They also made a series of recordings with Bing Crosby, hitting the Top Ten another 12 times between 1943 and 1951, notably with "Pistol Packin' Mama," "(There'll Be A) Hot Time in the Town of Berlin (When the Yanks Go Marching In)," and "Don't Fence Me In." They also became stars of radio and film, and Patty and Maxene enjoyed renewed success on Broadway in the 1970s.

The Andrews Sisters were the children of Peter and Olga Sollie Andrews, who ran a café in Minneapolis. The four began performing at local talent contests and made their first professional appearance at the Orpheum Theatre in Minneapolis in December 1932. In November 1933 they were hired by bandleader Larry Rich to join his vaudeville troupe. They toured the Midwest RKO circuit with Rich until mid-1934, then found jobs singing with bands. In March 1937 they made their recording debut as part of the orchestra of Leon Belasco. Belasco disbanded his troupe soon after, and the sisters spent the summer in N.Y. While appearing with Billy Swanson's Orch. at the Hotel Edison, they were heard on a local radio broadcast by the A&R director of Decca Records, who signed them. Their second Decca single, "Bei Mir Bist Du Schön" (music by Sholom Secunda, English lyrics by Sammy Cahn and Saul Chaplin), derived from the Yiddish theater, and its novelty appeal made it a success: it topped the hit parade in January 1938.

The Andrews Sisters began to make personal appearances in the Northeast, proving to be effective dancers and comediennes as well as singers. (They also began studying singing with Helen Fouts Cahoon.) They joined the cast of the radio series *Honolulu Bound* in January 1939, and by the end of the year were being featured on Glenn Miller's *Chesterfield Time* show. They reentered the hit parade in April 1939 with the rhythmic novelty song "Hold Tight" (music and lyrics by Leonard Kent, Edward Robinson, Leonard Ware, Jerry Brandow, and Willie Spotswood).

In 1940 the Andrews Sisters were signed to Universal Pictures and moved to the West Coast, where they made a series of films over the next five years. The first was *Argentine Nights,* which opened in October 1940. In December they scored a Top Ten hit with "Ferryboat

Serenade (La Piccinina)" (music by Eldo di Lazzaro, English lyrics by Mario Panzeri). Their second film, *Buck Privates*, in which they appeared with the comedy team Abbott and Costello, was released in February. In it they sang "Boogie Woogie Bugle Boy" (music by Hughie Prince, lyrics by Don Raye), which became a chart record for them, and the 1920 song "(I'll Be with You) In Apple Blossom Time" (music by Albert Von Tilzer, lyrics by Neville Fleeson), which they revived for a Top Ten hit.

Maxene Andrews married Lou Levy, a music publisher and the Andrews Sisters' personal manager, in March 1941; they adopted two children, then divorced in 1951. The sisters quickly followed up the success of *Buck Privates* with two more films in which they were featured with Abbott and Costello, *In the Navy*, released in June 1941, and *Hold That Ghost*, released in August. The U.S. entry into World War II in December 1941 and the beginning of the musicians union recording ban in August 1942 focused the sisters' activities on entertaining at military bases and making films. They appeared in three pictures released in 1942: *What's Cookin'* in Feb.; *Private Buckaroo* in June; and *Give Out, Sisters* in Aug. They scored their next Top Ten hit with "Strip Polka" (music and lyrics by Johnny Mercer) in November.

The Andrews Sisters appeared in another four films released in 1943—*How's About It?*, *Always a Bridesmaid*, *Swingtime Johnny*, and *Moonlight and Cactus*—but these were low-budget B-pictures. Their career took a considerable upturn in the fall of that year, when Decca Records settled with the musicians' union more than a year ahead of the other major labels, allowing its artists to dominate the charts. The sisters began recording extensively on their own and in partnership with Bing Crosby, resulting in a string of hits, many of which had patriotic themes. "Pistol Packin' Mama" (music and lyrics by Al Dexter), with Crosby, was in the Top Ten in December 1943 and sold a million copies. In January 1944 they topped the charts with "Shoo-Shoo Baby" (music and lyrics by Phil Moore) and reached the Top Ten with Crosby with "Vict'ry Polka" (music by Jule Styne, lyrics by Sammy Cahn). "Straighten Up and Fly Right" (music and lyrics by Nat "King" Cole and Irving Mills) was a Top Ten hit in August 1944. Both sides of the Crosby-Andrews single "(There'll Be A) Hot Time in the Town of Berlin (When the Yanks Go Marching In)" (music by Joe Bushkin, lyrics by John De Vries) and "Is You Is or Is You Ain't (Ma Baby)" (music and lyrics by Billy Austin and Louis Jordan) reached the charts in September, with the former hitting #1 and the latter #2.

Their next record with Crosby, "Don't Fence Me In" (music and lyrics by Cole Porter)/"The Three Caballeros" (music by Manuel Esperon, English lyrics by Ray Gilbert), was a million-seller, with "Don't Fence Me In" going to #1 in December and "The Three Caballeros" reaching the Top Ten. Crosby and the Andrews Sisters were the top two recording artists of 1944. The sisters also appeared in two all-star films during the year, *Follow the Boys* in April and *Hollywood Canteen* in December. At the end of the year they began their own weekly radio series, *The Andrews Sisters' Eight-to-the-Bar Ranch*, broadcast on Sunday afternoons.

The Andrews Sisters began 1945 with the biggest hit of the year, the million-selling "Rum and Coca-Cola" (music and lyrics by Morey Amsterdam, Paul Baron, and Jeri Sullivan, based on a song with music and lyrics by Massie Patterson and Lionel Belasco), which went to #1 in Feb. Their next two Top Ten hits came in partnership with Bing Crosby, "Ac-Cent-Tchu-Ate the Positive" (music by Harold Arlen, lyrics by Johnny Mercer) in March and "Along the Navajo Trail" (music and lyrics by Dick Charles, Eddie DeLange, and Larry Markes) in October. They also returned to the Top Ten on their own in October with "The Blond Sailor" (music by Jacob Pfeil, English lyrics by Mitchell Parish and Bell Leib). They concluded their Universal Pictures contract with the release of *Her Lucky Night*, and in October their radio series was refashioned as *The N-K* [for the sponsor, Nash-Kelvinator automobiles] *Musical Showroom*, running on Wednesday evenings through the end of March 1946.

The Andrews Sisters' next Top Ten hit, in February 1946, was "Money Is the Root of All Evil (Take It Away, Take It Away, Take It Away)" (music and lyrics by Joan Whitney and Alex Kramer); on it they were co-billed with Guy Lombardo and his Royal Canadians. In April their voices were heard in the animated Disney feature *Make Mine Music!* In September they reached the Top Ten of the album charts with *The Andrews Sisters*. They returned to the Top Ten of the singles chart with Crosby in November singing the million-seller "South America, Take It Away" (music and lyrics by Harold Rome); with Les Paul in Dec. with "Rumors Are Flying" (music and lyrics by Bennie Benjamin and George David Weiss); and with Lombardo at the end of the year with the million-selling "Christmas Island" (music and lyrics by Lyle L. Moraine).

In 1947 the Andrews Sisters began appearing on the *Your Hit Parade* and *Club Fifteen* radio series. Expanding their touring activities internationally, they performed in London in June and July. They again partnered with Bing Crosby for "Tallahassee" (music and lyrics by Frank Loesser), which reached the Top Ten in July, then returned to the Top Ten on their own with "Near You" (music by Francis Craig, lyrics by Kermit Goell) in October and "The Lady from 29 Palms" (music and lyrics by Allie Wrubel) in November. Patty Andrews married Martin Melcher on Oct. 19, 1947; they divorced on March 30, 1950. In December the Andrews Sisters finally appeared onscreen with Bing Crosby, singing "You Don't Have to Know the Language" in *Road to Rio*. They reached the Top Ten that same month with comedian Danny Kaye singing "Civilization (Bongo, Bongo, Bongo)" (music and lyrics by Bob Hilliard and Carl Sigman).

The Andrews Sisters were the top recording artists of 1948, scoring ten chart entries during the year, including the Top Ten hits "Toolie Oolie Doolie (The Yodel Polka)" (music by Arthur Beul, English lyrics by Vaughn Horton) in May, "You Call Everybody Darling" (music and lyrics by Sam Martin, Ben Trace, and Clem Watts) in October, and "Underneath the Arches" (music and lyrics by Reg Connelly and Bud Flanagan, additional lyrics in the U.S. by Joseph McCarthy) in November. In

May they lent their voices to the animated Disney feature *Melody Time*. LaVerne Andrews married Louis Rogers later that year.

The Andrews Sisters' biggest success of 1949 came at the end of the year with the release of "I Can Dream, Can't I?" (music by Sammy Fain, lyrics by Irving Kahal), which featured a solo lead performance by Patty, in contrast to the group harmonies that usually characterized the sisters' recordings; it topped the charts in January 1950 and sold a million copies. They also scored a Top Ten hit with Bing Crosby, "Quicksilver" (music and lyrics by Irving Taylor, George Wyle, and Edward Pola), in March 1950 and returned to #1 with "I Wanna Be Loved" (music by John Green, lyrics by Edward Heyman and Billy Rose) in June.

The Andrews Sisters' popularity declined after 1950. They scored a final Top Ten hit with Crosby in "Sparrow in the Tree Top" (music and lyrics by Bob Merrill). Patty Andrews married the group's accompanist, Walter Weschler, on Christmas Day 1951. Decca had begun to record Patty as a solo artist after the success of "I Can Dream, Can't I?" After the sisters' contract lapsed at the end of 1953, she launched a solo career and signed to Capitol Records, while LaVerne and Maxene performed as a duo for a time, then separately. By June 1956, however, the group was reunited, and by September they were recording for Capitol. In 1961 they moved to Dot Records, remaining with the label until 1965. LaVerne Andrews became ill with cancer in 1966, and Maxene and Patty continued to perform with a replacement. LaVerne died at 55 in 1967. Maxene and Patty split up in 1968, with Patty returning to solo work and Maxene retiring from music to teach at Lake Tahoe Paradise Coll. of Fine Arts in Nev.

Patty Andrews appeared in *Victory Canteen* (Los Angeles, Jan. 27, 1971), a musical set during World War II. Bette Midler scored a Top Ten hit in July 1973, and two Andrews Sisters compilation albums, *The Best of the Andrews Sisters* and *Boogie Woogie Bugle Girls*, later reached the charts, while the producers of *Victory Canteen* refashioned it into *Over Here!*, starring both surviving Andrews sisters, which opened on Broadway on March 6, 1974; it ran for 341 performances, and the cast album charted. Afterward, Patty and Maxene worked as solo performers. Maxene was on vacation from her role in the Off-Broadway musical *Showtime Canteen* (N.Y., March 14, 1995) when she died of a heart attack in 1995 at 79.

DISC.: *Merry Christmas* (1950); *Berlin Songs* (1951); *Tropical Songs* (1951); *Christmas Cheer* (1951); *The Andrews Sisters in Hi-Fi* (1957); *Boogie Woogie Bugle Girls* (1973); *Over Here!* (1974); *The Best of the Andrews Sisters* (1977); *The Andrews Sisters 50th Anniversary Collection, Vol. 1 & 2* (1987); *Greatest Hits* (1990); *The Andrews Sisters: Capitol Collectors Series* (1991); *Their All-Time Greatest Hits* (1994); *Greatest Hits: The 60th Anniversary Collection* (1998); *V-Disc Recordings* (1999); *20th Century Masters—The Millennium Collection: The Best of the Andrews Sisters* (2000); *Cocktail Hour: The Andrews Sisters* (2000).

BIBL.: M. Andrews and B. Gilbert, *Over Here, Over There: The A. S. and the USO Stars in World War II* (N.Y., 1993).—**WR**

Andricu, Mihail (Gheorghe),

Romanian pianist, teacher, and composer; b. Bucharest, Jan. 3, 1895; d. there, Feb. 4, 1974. He studied at the Bucharest Cons. (1903–09), later serving on its faculty (1926–59). He was also active as piano accompanist to Georges Enesco.

WORKS: DRAMATIC: B a l l e t : *Cenureasa* (Cinderella; 1929); *Taina* (The Secret; 1932; Bucharest, Feb. 8, 1936); *Lucefarul* (The Morning Star; Bucharest, Sept. 24, 1951). **ORCH.:** *Poem* for Piano and Orch. (1923); 8 suites (1924–67); *3 Symphonic Pictures* (1925); 3 chamber syms. (1927, 1961, 1965); *Serenade* (1928); 2 sets of *3 Symphonic Sketches* (1936, 1951); *Fantezie* for Piano and Orch. (1940); 11 syms. (1944; 1947; 1950; 1954; 1955; 1957; 1958; 1960; 1962; 1968; *In Memoriam*, 1970); 13 sinfoniettas (1945–72); *3 Symphonic Pieces* (1950); *Rapsodie* (1952); Violin Concerto (1960); Cello Concerto (1961); *6 Portraits* (1969); *Evocation* (1971); *Miniatures and Images* (1971). **CHAMBER:** *4 Novelettes* for Piano Quartet (1925); Octet (1928); String Quartet (1931); Sextet (1932); 2 quintets (1938, 1956); Violin Sonata (1941); *3 Pieces* for Piano and Winds (1964). **OTHER:** Piano pieces; choral works; songs.—**NS/LK/DM**

Andriessen, Hendrik (Franciscus),

eminent Dutch organist, pedagogue, and composer, brother of **Willem (Christiaan Nicolaas) Andriessen** and father of **Jurriaan Andriessen** and **Louis (Joseph) Andriessen;** b. Haarlem, Sept. 17, 1892; d. Heemstede, April 12, 1981. He studied music with his brother; then took piano and organ lessons with Louis Robert and J. B. de Pauw; studied composition with Zweers at the Amsterdam Cons. (1914–16); subsequently taught harmony there (1926–34). He succeeded his father as organist at St. Joseph's Church in Haarlem (1913–34); was then organist at Utrecht Cathedral (1934–49). He was director of the Royal Cons. of Music in The Hague (1949–57) and special prof. at the Catholic Univ. in Nijmegen (1952–63). His music is Romantically inspired; some of his instrumental works make use of modern devices, including melodic atonality and triadic polytonality. He was particularly esteemed for his revival of the authentic modalities of Gregorian chant; his choral works present a remarkable confluence of old usages with modern technical procedures.

WORKS: DRAMATIC: O p e r a : *Philomela* (Holland Festival, June 23, 1950; *De Spiegel uit Venetië* (The Mirror from Venice; 1964; Dutch TV, Oct. 5, 1967). **ORCH.:** 4 syms. (1930, 1937, 1946, 1954); *Variations and Fugue on a Theme of Kuhnau* for Strings (1935); *Capriccio* (1941); *Variations on a Theme of Couperin* for Flute, Harp, and Strings (1944); *Ballet Suite* (1947); *Ricercare* (1949); *Wilhemus van Nassouwe*, rhapsody (1950); Organ Concerto (1950); *Symphonic Étude* (The Hague, Oct. 15, 1952); *Libertas venit*, rhapsody (1954); *Mascherata*, fantasy (1962); *Symphonie concertante* (1962); Violin Concerto (1968–69); *Concertino* for Oboe and Strings (1969–70); *Concertino* for Cello and Orch. (1970); *Chromatic Variations* for Flute, Oboe, Violin, Cello, and Strings (1970); *Canzone* (1971); *Chantecler*, overture (1972). **CHAMBER:** Cello Sonata (1926); Violin Sonata (1932); *3 Inventions* for Violin and Cello (1937); Piano Trio (1939); Suite for Violin and Piano (1950); Sonata for Solo Cello (1951); Suite for Brass Quintet (1951); Wind Quintet (1951); *Ballade* for Oboe and Piano (1952); *Theme and Variations* for Flute, Oboe, and Piano (1953); 3 string quartets (1957, 1961, 1969); *Pezzo festoso* for Organ, 2 Trumpets, and 2 Trombones (1962); *Canzonetta* for Harpsichord (1963); *Canzone*, Trio No. 2 for Flute, Oboe, and Piano (1965); Viola Sonata (1967); *Concert spirituel* for Flute, Oboe, Violin, and Cello (1967); *Haydn Variations* for English Horn and Piano (1968); Clarinet Sonata (1971); *Choral varié* for 3

Trumpets and 3 Trombones (1973). **KEYBOARD: P i a n o :** 2 sonatas (1934, 1966); *Pavane* (1937); *Serenade* (1950). **O r g a n :** 4 chorales (1913, c. 1918, 1920, 1952); Toccata (1917); *Fête-Dieu* (1918); *Sonata de Chiesa* (1927); Passacaglia (1929); *Sinfonia* (1940); *Intermezzi* (1943); *Theme and Variations* (1949); 4 Studies (1953). **VOCAL:** *Missa Simplex* for Chorus (1927); *Missa Sponsa Christi* for Men's Chorus and Organ (1933); *Missa Christus Rex* for Double Chorus and Organ (1938); 2 Madrigals for Chorus and Strings (1940); *Te Deum Laudamus I* for Chorus and Organ or Orch. (1943–46), and *II* for Chorus and Orch. (1968); *De Zee en het land* (Declamatorium) for Chorus, Speaker, and Orch. (1953); *Veni Creator* for Chorus and Orch. (1960); *Psalm IX* for Chorus, Tenor, and Orch. (1968); *Lux Jocunda* for Chorus, Tenor, and Orch. (1968); *Carmen Saeculare (Horatius)* for Chorus, Soprano, Tenor, Winds, Harpsichord, and Double Bass (1968). **S o l o S o n g C y c l e s** (most with Organ or Orch.): *L'Aube spirituelle* (1916); *L'Invitation au voyage* (1918); *Magna res est amor* (1919); *L'Attente mystique* (1920); *Miroir de peine* (1923); *Cantique spirituel* (1924); *La Vièrge à midi* (1966).

BIBL.: A. de Jager, P. Op de Coul, and L. Samama, eds., *Duizend kleuren van muziek: Leven en werk van H. A.* (Zutphen, 1992).—NS/LK/DM

Andriessen, Jurriaan,

Dutch composer, son of **Hendrik (Franciscus) Andriessen**, brother of **Louis (Joseph) Andriessen**, and nephew of **Willem (Christiaan Nicolaas) Andriessen;** b. Haarlem, Nov. 15, 1925; d. The Hague, Aug. 23, 1996. After training in theory from his father, he studied conducting with Otterloo at the Utrecht Cons. (graduated, 1947). Following studies in Paris, he was a composition student of Copland at the Berkshire Music Center in Tanglewood (summers, 1949–50). His television opera *Kalchas* (Dutch TV, June 28, 1959) was the first such score to be produced in the Netherlands.

WORKS: DRAMATIC: *Kalchas*, television opera (Dutch TV, June 28, 1959); *Het Zwarte Blondje* (The Black Blonde), opera buffa (1964); incidental music to many plays. **ORCH.:** Piano Concertino (1943); *Symphonietta concertante* for 4 Trumpets and Orch. (1947); Piano Concerto (1948); 5 syms.: No. 1, *Berkshire Symphonies* (1949; perf. as the ballet *Jones Beach*, N.Y., March 12, 1950), No. 2 for Wind Orch. (1962), No. 3, *Symphonyen fan Fryslàn* (1963), No. 4, *Aves* (The Birds), for Chorus and Orch. (1963), and No. 5, *Time Spirit*, for Clarinet, Pop Group, 6 Dancers, and Orch. (1970); Flute Concerto (1951); *Cymbeline*, overture (1954); *Inno della Tecnica* (1957); *Ritratto di una citta (Ouverture Den Haag)* (1957); *Thai*, symphonic rhapsody on jazz tunes by King Bhumibol Adulyadej of Thailand (1960); *Concerto Rotterdam* for Jazz Combo and Orch. (1966); *Contra-bande* for Sousaphone and Orch. (1967); *Omaggio a Sweelinck* for Harpsichord and 24 Strings (1968); *Trelleborg Concerto* for Harpsichord and 3 Orch. Groups (1969); *Antifona dell'Aja* (1969); *Pasticcio-Finale* for Orch., Dixieland Band, and Tape (1974); *Monomania e policromia* (1984); *Serenade* for Chamber Orch. (1988); Violin Concerto (1991–92); *Antifoon* for Organ and Wind Band (1992); *Het rozenprieel* for Strings (1996); *La Napoule* for Amateur Orch. (1996). **CHAMBER:** *Hommage à Milhaud* for 11 Instruments (1945; also for Flute and String Quartet, 1948); Violin Sonata (1946); *Octet Divertissement* for Winds (1948); *Rouw past Electra* (Mourning Becomes Electra), suite for 11 Winds and Percussion (1954); 5 trios: 1 for Flute, Oboe, and Piano (1955), 2 for Flute, Viola, and Piano (1955), 3 for 3 Recorders (1957), 4 for Flute, Oboe, and Bassoon (1957), and 5, *Sonata da camera*, for Flute, Viola, and Guitar (1959); *L'incontro di Cesare e Cleopatra*, sextet

for Winds and Piano (1956); Concertino for Bassoon and Winds (1962); *Respiration*, suite for Double Wind Quintet (1962); *Movimenti I* for Trumpet, Horn, Trombone, Strings, and Timpani (1965), *II* for Oboe, Clarinet, Bassoon, Strings, and Percussion (1972), *III* for Violin, Viola, Cello, Winds, and Percussion (1974), and *IV* for Violin and Piano (1992); Trio for Clarinet, Cello, and Piano (1965); *Antifono e Fusione* for Wind Quintet, Brass Quartet, and Timpani (1966); *In pompa magna* for Brass and Percussion (1966); *Quartetto buffo* for Clarinet and String Trio (1974); *The Cave* for Cello, 12 Winds, 4 Keyboard Instruments, and Electronics (1976); Clarinet Quartet (1984); String Trio (1988); Bassoon Sonata (1990); *Divertimento* for 2 Oboes and English Horn (1990); Quartet for Flute, Violin, Viola, and Cello (1992); *6 Moods* for 12 Saxophones (1993); Trumpet Sonata (1994); *Wind Music* for 4 Trombones and Organ (1995); *Scorpius* for Violin, Clarinet, and Piano (1995); *Les jeux des vents* for Wind Quintet (1996). **OTHER:** Piano pieces and vocal music.—NS/LK/DM

Andriessen, Louis (Joseph),

significant Dutch composer and teacher, son of **Hendrik (Franciscus) Andriessen**, brother of **Jurriaan Andriessen**, and nephew of **Willem (Christian Nicolaas) Andriessen;** b. Utrecht, June 6, 1939. He began studies with his father in 1953, and then pursued training with Kees van Baaren at the Royal Cons. of Music at The Hague (1957–62). After winning its composition prize, he completed his studies with Berio in Milan and Berlin (1962–65). Returning to his homeland, he made a name for himself in avant-garde music circles. In 1972 he founded De Volharding (Perseverance), an unconventional wind band devoted to taking music to people in the streets. Andriessen became a teacher of instrumentation at the Royal Cons. of Music at The Hague in 1974, and then taught composition there from 1978. In 1976 he founded the experimental music group Hoketus, with which he remained active until it was disbanded in 1987. With the premiere of his *De Staat* (The Republic) for 4 Women's Voices and Large Ensemble in Amsterdam on Nov. 28, 1976, Andriessen established himself as one of the principal figures in Dutch musical life. In 1977 it won him the Matthijs Vermeulen Prize and the first prize of Unesco's International Rostrum of Composers. He was a lecturer at Yale Univ. in 1987. On June 1, 1989, three parts of his music theater piece *De Materie* (Matter) inaugurated the new Muziektheater in Amsterdam. In 1992 he was awarded the Matthijs Vermeulen Prize for a second time. He served as artistic director of the Meltdown Festival at the South Bank Centre in London in 1994. In 1996 he was a lecturer at Princeton Univ. With E. Schönberger, he publ. the study *Het Apollinische Uurwerk* (Amsterdam, 1983; Eng. tr., 1989, as *The Apollonian Clockwork: On Stravinsky*). While Andriessen's output reflects the influence of such diverse figures as Bach, Ives, Stravinsky, and Charlie Parker, he has found his own unmistakable compositional voice.

WORKS: Flute Sonata (1956); *Elegy* for Cello or Double Bass and Piano (1957); *Nuit d'été* for Piano, 4-Hands (1957); *Séries* for 2 Pianos (1958); *Percosse* for Flute, Trumpet, Bassoon, and Percussion (1959); *Nocturnen* for Soprano and Chamber Orch. (The Hague, Dec. 14, 1959); *Ittrospezione I* for Piano, 4-Hands (1961), *II* for Orch. (1963), and *III (Concept I)* for 2 Pianos and Ensemble (1964), (fragment) for 2 Pianos and Tenor Saxophone ad libitum (1965), and *Concept II* for 2 Pianos and

Ensemble (1965); *Trois pièces* for Piano, Left-Hand (1961); *Aanloop en sprongen* for Flute, Oboe, and Clarinet (1961); *Joli commentaire* for Piano, 4-Hands (1961); *Paintings* for Flute and Piano (1961); *Triplum per chitarra* for Guitar (1962); *Canzone 3.Utinam* for Soprano and Piano (1962); *Registers* for Piano (1963); *A flower song II* for Oboe (1964) and *III* for Cello (1964); *Sweet* for Alto Recorder (1964); *Double* for Clarinet and Piano (1965); *Souvenirs d'enfance* for Piano (1966); *The Garden of Ryoan-gi* for 3 Electric Organs (1967); *Anachronie I* for Orch. (1967; Rotterdam, Jan. 18, 1968) and *II* for Oboe and Orch. (1969); *Contra tempus* for Wind Ensemble, Percussion, and Improvising Ensemble (1968); *Reconstructie*, opera (Holland Festival, June 29, 1969; in collaboration with R. de Leeuw, M. Mengelberg, P. Schat, and J. van Vlijmen); *Choralvorspiele* for Barrel Organ (1969); *Hoe het is* (How it is) for Live Electronics and 52 Strings (1969; Rotterdam, Sept. 14, 1970); *Spektakel* for Wind Ensemble, Percussion, and Improvising Ensemble (1970); *Vergeet mij niet* (Forget me not) for an Oboe/Piano Player (1970); *The 9 Symphonies of Beethoven* for Orch. and Ice-Cream Seller's Bell (1970); *In Memoriam*, electronic piece (1971); *Volkslied* for an Unlimited Number of Any Instruments (1971); *La Voile du Bonheur* for Violin or Voice and Piano (1971); *De Volharding* (Perseverance) for Wind Ensemble (1972); *Thanh Hoa* for Voice and Piano (1972); *De Staat* (The Republic) for 4 Women's Voices and Large Ensemble (1972–76; Amsterdam, Nov. 28, 1976); *Il Duce*, electronic piece (1973); *The Family*, film music for Ensemble (1973); *On Jimmy Yancey* for Wind Ensemble (1973); *Il Principe* for 2 Choruses and Wind Ensemble (1974); *Symfonieën der Nederlanden* (Symphonies of the Netherlands) for 2 or More Wind Bands (1974); *Melodie* for Treble Recorder and Piano (1974); *Hymne to the Memory of Darius Milhaud* for Orch. (1974); *Wals* for Piano (1974); *Workers Union* for Any Loud Group of Instruments (1975); *Nederland, let op uw schoonheyt* (Monuments of the Netherlands) for Brass Band and/or Wind Band (1975); *Hoketus* for 2 Groups of 5 Instruments (The Hague, May 31, 1976); *Mattheus passie* (Matthew Passion), music theater (1976); *Orpheus*, music theater (1977); *Symphony for Open Strings* for 12 Solo String Players (1978); *Laat toch vrij die straat* for Voice and Piano (1978); *Mausoleum* for 2 High Baritones and Large Ensemble (Amsterdam, June 17, 1979); *Ende* for Recorder Player Playing 2 Alto Recorders (1980); *George Sand*, music theater (1980); *Erik Satie: Messe des Pauvres*, arrangement for Chorus and Ensemble (1980); *Un beau baiser* for Chorus (1980); *De Tijd* (The Time) for Women's Chorus and Large Ensemble (1980–81; The Hague, June 1, 1981); *La voce* for Cello (1981); *Commentaar* for Voice and Piano (1981); *Overture to Orpheus* for Harpsichord (1982); *Disco* for Violin and Piano (1982); *Trepidus* for Piano (1983); *Menuet voor Marianne* for Piano (1983); *Y despues* for Voice and Piano (1983); *De Snelheid* (Velocity) for Large Ensemble (1983; San Francisco, Jan. 11, 1984); *De Materie* (Matter; 1984–88; Part I for Tenor, 8 Voices, and Large Ensemble, 1987; Amsterdam, June 1, 1989; Part II, *Hadewijch* for Soprano, 8 Voices, and Large Ensemble, 1988; Amsterdam, June 1, 1989; Part III, *De Stijl* [The Style] for 4 Women's Voices, Woman Speaker, 8 Voices, and Large Ensemble, 1984–85; Amsterdam, June 9, 1985; Part IV for Woman Speaker, 8 Voices, and Large Ensemble, 1988; Amsterdam, June 1, 1989); *Berceuse voor Annie van Os* for Piano (1985); *Dubbelspoor* (Double Track) for Piano, Harpsichord, Glockenspiel, and Celesta (1988); *De Lijn* (The Line) for 3 Flutes (1986); *De Toren* (The Tower) for Carillon (1988); *Nietzsche redet* for Reciter and Ensemble (1989); *Flora Tristan* for Chorus (1990); *Facing Death* for 4 Amplified Strings or String Quartet (1990; Milwaukee, April 5, 1991); *Dances* for Soprano and Chamber Orch. (Amsterdam, April 24, 1991); *M is*

for Man, Music, Mozart for Jazz Singer and Ensemble (Utrecht, Sept. 22, 1991); *Hout* (Wood) for Tenor Saxophone, Marimba, Guitar, and Piano (Amsterdam, Nov. 3, 1991); *Lacrimosa* for 2 Bassoons (1991); *Romance voor Caecilia* for Piano (1991); *The Memory of Roses* for Piano and Toy Piano (1992); *Chorale* for Piano (1992); *Deuxième chorale* for Hand-operated Music Box (1992); *...not being sundered* for Soprano, Flute, and Cello (1992); *Lied* for Piano (1993); *Rosa* (a horse drama), music theater (1993–94; Amsterdam, Nov. 2, 1994); *Zilver* for Mixed Ensemble (1994; Los Angeles, Jan. 11, 1995); *Base* for Piano, Left Hand (N.Y., Oct. 13, 1994); *Een lied van de Zee* (A song of the sea) for Voice (1994; Amsterdam, Jan. 20, 1995); *De Komst van Willibrord* (Willibrord's Arrival) for Carillon (Utrecht, Aug. 29, 1995); *To Pauline O* for Oboe (Rotterdam, Nov. 8, 1995); *Odysseus' Women* for 4 Women's Voices and Chamber Orch. (1995; rev. 1998; Amsterdam, Jan. 29, 1999); *Trilogy of the Last Day* (1996–97; Part I, *The Last Day* for 4 Men's Voices, Child's Voice, and Large Ensemble, Holland Festival, June 7, 1996; rev. 1997; Part II, *TAO* for Piano, 4 Women's Voices, and Ensemble, Donaueschingen, Oct. 18, 1996; Part III, *Dancing on the bones* for Children's Voices and Ensemble, Cologne, June 12, 1997); *De Herauten* (The Heralds) for Brass and Timpani (The Hague, May 28, 1997); *Writing to Vermeer*, opera (1997–99; Amsterdam, Dec. 1, 1999); *De Eerste Minnaar* (The First Lover) for Boy Soprano and Organ (The Hague, June 12, 1998).

BIBL.: E. Restagno, ed., *L. A.* (Turin, 1996).—**NS/LK/DM**

Andriessen, Willem (Christiaan Nicolaas),

Dutch pianist, teacher, and composer, brother of **Hendrik (Franciscus) Andriessen** and uncle of **Jurriaan Andriessen** and **Louis (Joseph) Andriessen;** b. Haarlem, Oct. 25, 1887; d. Amsterdam, March 29, 1964. He studied piano and composition at the Amsterdam Cons. (1903–08). After teaching piano at The Hague Cons. (1910–17) and the Rotterdam Cons., he served as director of the Amsterdam Cons. (1937–53). He also was active as a pianist. Among his works were a Piano Concerto (1908), *Hei, 't was de Mei* for Orch. (1912), a Mass for Soloist, Chorus, and Orch., songs, and piano pieces.—**NS/LK/DM**

Andsnes, Leif Ove,

outstanding Norwegian pianist; b. Stavanger, April 7, 1970. He took up the piano when he was only 5, and at age 16 he entered the Bergen Cons. of Music, where he pursued training with Jiří Hlinka. At 17, he made his formal debut in Oslo and was awarded the Hindemith Prize of Frankfurt am Main. In 1988 he won the Levin Prize of Bergen and the Norwegian Music Critics Prize of Oslo. He made his British debut as soloist with Jansons and the Oslo Phil. at the Edinburgh Festival in 1989, and subsequently was engaged by leading European orchs. In 1990 he won the Grief Prize of Bergen and made his U.S. debut as soloist with Järvi and the Cleveland Orch. at the Blossom Music Festival. He subsequently appeared as a soloist with major North American orchs., including those of Los Angeles, Detroit, San Francisco, St. Louis, Chicago, Toronto, Montreal, and Baltimore. In 1992 he made his first appearance at the London Promenade Concerts as soloist with the BBC Phil. of Manchester. His recital engagements have taken him to London, Munich, Paris, Amsterdam, Berlin, N.Y., and Washington, D.C. In 1998 he received the Gilmore Award. In his performances, Andsnes has demonstrated a musicianship of the highest attainment in a repertoire extending from Haydn to contemporary composers.—NS/LK/DM

Anerio, Felice, significant Italian composer, brother of **Giovanni Francesco Anerio;** b. Rome, c. 1560; d. there, Sept. 26 or 27, 1614. He pursued his career in Rome. He was a choirboy at S. Maria Maggiore from 1568 to 1574, and then sang at the Cappella Giulia from 1575 and at S. Luigi dei Francesi from 1579 to 1584. In 1584 he received the tonsure and was made maestro di cappella at the Collegio degli Inglesi, where he served until 1585. In 1594 he was named composer to the papal choir. He became a deacon in 1607 and soon thereafter was made a priest. With Soriano, he was entrusted with reforming the Roman Gradual in 1611, a task completed in 1612. Anerio composed in a conservative style that was greatly admired for its expressive power.

WORKS: SACRED: *Madrigali spirituali* for 5 Voices (2 vols., Rome, 1585); *Sacri hymni, et cantica* for 8 Voices (Venice, 1595) and for 5, 6, and 8 Voices (Rome, 1602); *Responsoria ad lectiones divini officii feriae quartae, quintae, et sextae sanctae hebdomadae* for 4 Voices (Rome, 1606); also masses, Psalms, spiritual canzonettas, laudi, motets, etc. SECULAR: *Canzonette* for 4 Voices (Venice, 1586); Madrigals for 5 and 8 Voices (Venice, 1587), 6 Voices (Venice, 1509 and Rome, 1602), 3 Voices (Venice, 1598), and 5 Voices (not extant).—NS/LK/DM

Anerio, Giovanni Francesco, important Italian composer and organist, brother of **Felice Anerio;** b. Rome, c. 1567; d. Graz (buried), June 12, 1630. He was associated with the Oratory of Filippo Neri in Rome from about 1583, the year he received the tonsure. In 1584 he became ostiary and in 1586 he was made lector. From about 1605 he was maestro di cappella at S. Spirito in Sassia, and then at Verona Cathedral in 1609. Upon his return to Rome, he was music prefect at the Collegio Romano in 1611–12 and maestro di cappella at S. Maria dei Monti from 1613 to 1620. In 1616 he became a deacon and a priest. From 1624 to 1628 he was choirmaster at the Polish court of King Sigismund III in Warsaw. He died on his way home to Rome. Anerio was a composer of progressive tendencies. He was especially significant for introducing the vernacular oratorio in his *Teatro armonico spirituale di madrigali* (Rome, 1619).

WORKS: SACRED: Motets for 1 to 3 Voices and Basso Continuo (organ; Rome, 1609) and for 1 to 6 Voices and Basso Continuo (organ; 2 vols., Rome, 1611, 1613); *Sacri concentus* for 4 to 6 Voices and Basso Continuo (organ; Rome, 1613) and for 1 to 6 Voices and Basso Continuo (organ; Rome, 1617); Masses for 4 to 6 Voices and Basso Continuo (organ; Rome, 1614); *Selva armonica, dove si contengono motetti...arie* for 1 to 4 Voices and Basso Continuo (organ; Rome, 1617); *Teatro armonico spirituale di madrigali* for 5 to 8 Voices and Basso Continuo (organ; Rome, 1619). SECULAR: Madrigals for 5 Voices (Venice, 1599), for 5, 6, and 8 Voices (Venice, 1608), for 1 to 2 Voices (Venice, 1611), and for 1 to 4 Voices (Venice, 1617); canzonettas, villanellas, etc.

BIBL.: W. Hobbs, *G.F. A.'s "Teatro armonico spirituale di madrigali": A Contribution to the Early History of the Oratorio* (diss., Tulane Univ., 1971); N. Williams, *The Masses of G.F. A.: A Historical and Analytical Study with a Supplementary Critical Edition* (diss., Univ. of N.C., 1971).—NS/LK/DM

Anet, Jean-Baptiste, French violinist, father of **(Jean-Jacques-) Baptiste Anet;** b. Paris, June 20, 1650; d. there, April 26 or 28, 1710. He was a student of Lully. From about 1673 he was in the service of the Duke of Orléans, and from 1699 he was also a member of the 24 Violons du Roy.—NS/LK/DM

Anet, (Jean-Jacques-) Baptiste, noted French violinist and composer, son of **Jean-Baptiste Anet;** b. Paris, Jan. 2, 1676; d. Lunéville, Aug. 14, 1755. He was a pupil of Corelli in Rome (c. 1695–96). Upon his return to Paris, he was in the service of the Duke of Orléans in 1700–01. In 1701 he made his first appearance at the French court. After serving the exiled Elector Maximilian Emanuel of Bavaria (1701–15), he entered the service of King Louis XIV. In 1725 he made his first appearance at the Concert Spirituel in Paris. About 1735 he left the service of the court and in 1737 he went to the Lorraine court in Lunéville, where he was a member of the orch. of Stanislaus Leszczynski, the ex-king of Poland. Anet's last days were marred by illness and poverty. During his years in Paris, he was regarded as the leading French violinist of the era, and was especially admired as a master of improvisation. He publ. 2 vols. of sonatas for Violin and Basso Continuo (Paris, 1724, 1729) and 3 vols. of musettes (Paris, 1726, 1730, 1734).—NS/LK/DM

Anfossi, Pasquale, Italian composer; b. Taggia, near Naples, April 5, 1727; d. Rome, Feb.(?) 1797. He received training in violin at the Loreto Cons. in Naples, and later studied composition with Sacchini and Piccinni. His first opera, *La serva spiritosa*, was first given at the Teatro Capranica in Rome in Carnival 1763. More than a dozen operas followed before Anfossi scored his first great success with *L'incognita perseguitata* at the Teatro delle Dame in Rome in Carnival 1773. Many more operas followed, including *Il trionfo della costanza*, which was premiered at the King's Theatre in London on Dec. 19, 1782. At different times between 1782 and 1786, he acted as music director at the King's Theatre. He then was active in his homeland, where he won notable success with his opera *Le pazzie de' gelosi*, which was first heard at the Teatro Valle in Rome in Carnival 1787. After having composed over 60 operas, Anfossi gave up writing for the stage in 1790. In 1792 he became maestro di cappella at St. John Lateran in Rome, a position he retained until his death. In addition to operas, he also composed about 20 oratorios, masses, Psalms, sinfonie, and chamber music.—NS/LK/DM

Angel, Marie, Australian soprano; b. Pinnaroo, June 3, 1953. Following training in Australia, she joined the Opera Factory Zürich and made her London debut with the company as Handel's Galatea in 1980. From 1982 to 1992 she was a member of the Opera Factory London, with which she appeared in such roles as Monteverdi's Poppea and Euridice, both of Gluck's Iphigenias, Mozart's Countess, Donna Anna, and Fiordiligi, Denise in Tippett's *The Knot Garden*, and Pretty Polly in Birtwistle's *Punch and Judy*. In 1986 she created the role of the Oracle of the Dead in Birtwistle's *The Mask of Orpheus* at the English National Opera in

London and in 1991 Morgana Le Fay in his *Gawain* at London's Covent Garden. In 1994 she created the role of Esmerelda in *Rosa* by Louis Andriessen in Amsterdam. She married **David Freeman** in 1985.—NS/LK/DM

Angelis, Nazzareno de
See **De Angelis, Nazzareno**

Angeloni, Carlo, Italian composer; b. Lucca, July 16, 1834; d. there, Jan. 13, 1901. He was a student of Michele Puccini. Among his works were a number of operas, including *Carlo di Viana* (1855), *Asraele degli Abenceragi* (1871), and *Dramma in montagna* (n.d.).

BIBL.: L. Landucci, *C. A.* (Lucca, 1905).—NS/LK/DM

Angerer, Paul, Austrian conductor, teacher, and composer; b. Vienna, May 16, 1927. He received violin and piano lessons as a child; later he studied violin, piano, and composition at the Vienna Academy of Music. He was made a violist in the Vienna Sym. Orch. (1947), Zürich's Tonhalle Orch. (1948), and Geneva's l'Orchestre de la Suisse Romande (1949); then was 1st violist of the Vienna Sym. Orch. (1953–57). After serving as director and chief conductor of the Vienna Chamber Orch. (1956–63), he was first conductor at the Bonn Stadttheater (1964–66); then was music director of the Ulm Theater (1966–68), chief conductor of the Salzburg Landestheater (1967–72), and director of the South West German Chamber Orch. in Pforzheim (1971–82). In 1982 he founded the Concilium Musicum of Vienna for the performance of 17th and 18th century music on original instruments. From 1982 to 1992 he taught at the Vienna Hochschule für Musik. In 1977 he was made an Austrian Prof. Among his other honors were the Austrian State Prize (1956), the Theodor Körner Prize (1958), and the culture prizes of the city of Vienna (1983) and the State of Niederösterreich (1987).

WORKS: DRAMATIC: *Das verräterische Herz*, pantomime and ballet (1956); *Die Passkontrolle*, television opera (1958); *Hotel Comedie*, musical (1970). **ORCH.:** *Musica ad pulsum et impulsum* for Strings and Percussion (1955); *Musica fera* (1956); *Concerto pour la jeunesse* (1956); *Étude* for Violin and Chamber Orch. (1956); *Gloriatio* for Double Bass and Chamber Orch. (1957); Concerto for Piano and Strings (1962); Viola Concerto (1962); *Ire in orbem* for Strings (1975); *Luctus et gaudium* for Trumpet and Strings (1977). **CHAMBER:** *Musik für Viola* (1948); Quartet for Oboe, Horn, Viola, and Cello (1951); Trio for Recorder, Viola d'Amore, and Lute (1953); *Musica exanimata* for Cello and Piano (1954); Quintet for Flute, Oboe, Clarinet, Horn, and Bassoon (1956); *Chanson gaillarde* for Oboe, Cello, and Harpsichord (1963); *Cogitatio* for 9 Instruments (1964); *Musica articolata* for 13 Winds (1970); *Oblectatio vespertina* for Flute and Harp (1970); Quartet for Recorder, Viola da Gamba, Guitar, and Percussion (1971); *Syngrapha* for Violin, Viola, and Cello (1975); *Exercitium canonicum*, 4 pieces for 2 Violins (1980); *Obolus* for 6 Oboes (1983–84); *Hilasatio* for Viola d'Amore, Flute, Violin, and Double Bass (1987); organ and harpsichord pieces. **VOCAL:** *Missa Seitenstettensis* (1987–88).—NS/LK/DM

Angermüller, Rudolph (Kurt), German musicologist, editor, and music librarian; b. Bielefeld, Sept. 2, 1940. He studied at the Försterling Cons. in Bielefeld and pursued training in musicology in Mainz, Münster, and at the Univ. of Salzburg (Ph.D., 1970, with the diss. *Antonio Salieri: Sein Leben und seine weltlichen Werke unter besonderer Berücksichtigung seiner "grossen" Opern*; publ. in 3 vols., Munich, 1971–74), where he joined its musicological inst. in 1968. He served as chief ed. of the Neue Mozart-Ausgabe (from 1972), and was librarian (from 1972), chief of the research dept. (from 1981), and general secretary (from 1988) of the International Mozarteum Foundation in Salzburg.

WRITINGS: *Untersuchungen zur Geschichte des Carmen-Stoffes* (1967); *W.A. Mozarts Musikalische Umwelt in Paris (1777–78): Eine Dokumentation* (1982); *"Auf Ehre und Credit": Die Finanzen des W.A. Mozart* (1983); with O. Schneider, *Mozart-Bibliographie, 1981–1985: Mit Nachträgen zur Mozart-Bibliographie bis 1980* (1987); *Vom Keiser zum Sklaven: Personen in Mozarts Opern: Mit bibliographischen Notizen über die Mozart-Sänger der Uraufführungen und Mozarts Librettisten* (1989); with J. Senigl, *Mozart-Bibliographie, 1986–1991: Mit Nachträgen zur Mozart-Bibliographie bis 1985* (1992); *Der Salzburger Mozart-Denkmal: Eine Dokumentation (bis 1845) zut 150-Jahre-Enthüllungsgeier* (Salzburg, 1992); *Delitiae Italiae: Mozarts Reisen in Italien* (Bad Honnef, 1994); *Mozart auf der Reise nach Prag, Dresden, Leipzig und Berlin* (Bad Honnef, 1995).—NS/LK/DM

Anglebert, Jean-Henri d'
See **D'Anglebert, Jean-Henri**

Anglés, Higini, eminent Catalonian musicologist; b. Maspujols, Jan. 1, 1888; d. Rome, Dec. 8, 1969. He studied theology and philosophy at the Seminario de Tarràgona (ordained, 1912), then pursued music training with José Cogul (harmony), Vicente de Gilbert (harmony, counterpoint, fugue, and organ), Barberá (composition and folk song), and Pedrell (musicology and music history) in Barcelona (1913–19). In 1917 he became head of the music dept. of the Biblioteca de Catalunya in Barcelona. In 1923–24 he completed his studies with W. Gurlitt at the Univ. of Freiburg im Breisgau and F. Ludwig at the Univ. of Göttingen. From 1927 to 1936 he was prof. of music history at the Barcelona Cons. In 1943 he became director of the Instituto Español de Musicologia. In 1947 he was made director of the Pontifical Inst. of Sacred Music in Rome. He was an authority on Spanish music of the Middles Ages and the Renaissance. He publ. *Cantigas del Rei N'Anfos el Savi* (Barcelona, 1927), *Historia de la música española* (Barcelona, 1935), *La música a Catalunya fins al segle XIII* (Barcelona, 1935), *La música española desde la edad media hasta nuestros dias* (Barcelona, 1941), *L'opera di Morales e lo sviluppo della polifonia sacra spangola nel 1500* (Rome, 1954), and *Studio musicologia* (Rome, 1959). He ed. *El Códex Musical de Las Huelgas* (1927–31) and the works of J. Pujol (1927–32) and J. Cabanilles (1927–56). In 1941 he initiated the series Monuentos de la música española, which publ. *La música en la corte de los Reyes Católicos* (1941–51) and the works of Morales (1952–69), Victoria (1965–69), and Cabezón (1966).—NS/LK/DM

Anglés, Rafael, Spanish organist and composer; b. Rafales, 1731; d. Valencia, Feb. 19, 1816. He was maestro de capilla at the collegiate church of Alcañiz, near Saragossa. In 1762 he became organist at Valencia Cathedral. He composed liturgical music and keyboard pieces.—NS/LK/DM

Anglesi, Domenico, Italian composer; b. c. 1613; d. after Aug. 28, 1669. He was an instrumentalist and composer in the service of the Grand Duke of Tuscany in Florence from 1638. He also was aiutante de camera to Cardinal Giovan Carlo de' Medici. Anglesi wrote stage works and publ. a vol. of *Arie* for Voice and Continuo (Florence, 1635).—LK/DM

Anhalt, István, Hungarian-born Canadian composer, teacher, and writer; b. Budapest, April 12, 1919. He studied composition with Kodály at the Budapest Academy of Music (1937–41), and pursued training in Paris at the Cons. with Fourestier (conducting; 1946–48) and privately with Boulanger (composition) and S. Stravinsky (piano). In 1949 he joined the faculty of McGill Univ. in Montreal, where he was founder-director of its electronic music studio (1964–71). In 1969 he also was the Visiting Slee Prof. at the State Univ. of N.Y. in Buffalo. From 1971 to 1981 he was head of the music dept. at Queen's Univ. in Kingston, Ontario, where he was made prof. emeritus in 1984. In 1967 he was awarded Canada's Centennial Medal, in 1982 an honorary D.M. from McGill Univ., in 1991 an honorary LL.D. from Queen's Univ., and in 1993 the Commemorative Medal for the 125th Anniversary of Canadian Confederation. Among his writings are *Alternative Voices: Essays on Contemporary Vocal and Choral Composition* (1984), *Oppenheimer* (1990), and *A Weave of Life Lines* (1992). In a number of his works, he utilizes synthetic sounds.

WORKS: DRAMATIC: Music Theater and Multimedia: *Arc en ciel*, ballet for 2 Pianos (1951); *Foci* for Amplified Soprano, Instrumental Ensemble, and Electronics (1969); *La Tourangelle* for 3 Sopranos, Tenor, Bass, Instrumental Ensemble, and Tapes (1972–74; Toronto, July 17, 1975); *Thisness*, duodrama for Mezzo-soprano and Piano (1985; Vancouver, Jan. 19, 1986); *Winthrop* for Solo Voices, Chorus, Boy's Chorus, and Orch. (Kitchener, Sept. 6, 1986); *Traces (Tikkun)*, pluri-drama for Baritone and Orch. (1994); *Millennial Mall (Lady Diotima's Walk)*, opera for Soprano, Chamber Chorus, Chorus, and Orch. (1999). ORCH.: *Interludium* for Strings, Piano, and Timpani (1950); *Funeral Music* (1951); Sym. (1954–58); *Symphony of Modules* (1967); *Simulacrum* (Ottawa, Oct. 1987); *Sparkskraps* (1988); *Sonance-Resonance: Welche Töne?* (Toronto, Sept. 13, 1989). CHAMBER: Piano Trio (1953); Violin Sonata (1954); *Doors...Shadows (Glenn Gould in Memory)* for String Quartet (Toronto, Sept. 24, 1992). Piano: Sonata (1951); *Fantasia* (1954). VOCAL: *The Bell Man* for Chorus, Bell, and Organ (1954; rev. 1980); *Cento: Cantata Urbana* for 12 Speakers and Tape (1968); *Foci* for Soprano, Chamber Ensemble, and Tape (1969); choruses; songs. ELECTROACOUSTIC: *Sine Nomine I* (1959) and *II* (1959); *Birds and Bells* (1960); *On the Beach* (1961). —NS/LK/DM

Anievas, Agustin, American pianist and teacher; b. N.Y., June 11, 1934. He commenced piano lessons at age 4 with his mother; following appearances as a child pianist, he pursued formal training with Steuermann, Samaroff, and Marcus at N.Y.'s Juilliard School of Music. In 1952 he made his formal debut as soloist with the Little Orch. Soc. of N.Y.; after winning the Concert Artists Guild Award in 1959 and capturing 1st prize in the Mitropoulos Competition in 1961, he toured widely; served as prof. of piano at Brooklyn Coll. of the City Univ. of N.Y. (from 1974).—NS/LK/DM

Anikulapo-Kuti, Fela
See **Kuti, Fela**

Animals, The, British blues-rock group; formed 1958. MEMBERSHIP: Alan Price, org., pno. (b. Fairfield, County Durham, U.K., April 19, 1942); Eric Burdon, voc. (b. Newcastle upon Tyne, U.K., May 11, 1941); Bryan "Chas" Chandler, bs. (born Dec. 18, 1938, in Newcastle upon Tyne; d. London, July 17, 1996); Hilton Valentine, lead gtr. (b. North Shields, U.K., May 22, 1943); John Steel, drm. (b. Gateshead, County Durham, U.K., Feb. 4, 1941). Later members included Dave Rowberry, kybd. (b. Newcastle upon Tyne, U.K., Dec. 27, 1943); Barry Jenkins, drm. (b. Leicester, U.K., Dec. 22, 1944).

The Animals were one of the most important rhythm-and-blues-based bands to emerge from England in the mid-1960s, second in stature to only The Rolling Stones. Originally formed in 1958 in Newcastle by Alan Price as The Alan Price Combo, the group became known as The Animals sometime after Eric Burdon joined in 1962. Rivaling for a time both The Beatles and The Rolling Stones in popularity, The Animals first gained recognition on the basis of Eric Burdon's raw vocals and Alan Price's subtle arrangements and inspired organ playing. However, The Animals faded within two years of Price's 1965 departure, and Burdon, after moving to Calif. and recording second-rate psychedelic music, eventually reemerged in 1970 backed by War, an American soul ensemble that soon went on to success on their own. In the meantime, Animals' bassist "Chas" Chandler "discovered" and managed Jimi Hendrix, while Price pursued a solo career that established him in England. The original Animals reunited briefly in 1977 and 1983, and Burdon toured in the early 1990s with Robby Krieger and Brian Auger. The Animals were inducted into the Rock and Roll Hall of Fame in 1994.

Gaining local popularity, the band recorded with bluesman Sonny Boy Williamson at Newcastle's Club A-Go-Go in late 1963. Moving to London in January 1964, The Animals signed with manager-producer Mickie Most, who secured them a recording contract with Columbia Records (with American releases on MGM). They scored a top British and American hit with the blues classic "House of the Rising Sun" (note Price's outstanding arrangement and organ work). They followed up with Price and Burdon's "I'm Crying" and four subsequent major American and smash British hits from *Animal Tracks*, including "Don't Let Me Be Misunderstood" (previously recorded by Nina Simone), "We Gotta Get Out of This Place" (by Brill Building songwriters Barry Mann and Cynthia Weil), and "It's My Life." The Animals also managed moderate hit versions of John Lee Hooker's "Boom Boom" and Sam Cooke's "Bring It on Home to Me."

Alan Price departed for a solo career in May 1965, to be replaced by Dave Rowberry. The Animals hit with Carole King and Gerry Goffin's "Don't Bring Me Down" and Ma Rainey's "See See Rider." John Steel was replaced by Barry Jenkins in early 1966 and the rest of the group left Burdon in September 1966. Retaining The Animals' name, Eric Burdon moved to Calif. at the beginning of 1967 and reconstituted the band's lineup. They appeared at the Monterey International Pop Festival in June and recorded a number of second-rate psychedelic hits such as "When I Was Young," "San Franciscan Nights," "Monterey" and "Sky Pilot." Andy Summers, later with The Police, was a member of The New Animals beginning in September 1968, but the group disbanded in December.

In the meantime, Alan Price formed The Alan Price Set, hitting with a remake of Screamin' Jay Hawkins' "I Put a Spell on You" in 1966. Their one album, *The Price Is Right*, contained one of the first Randy Newman songs ever recorded, "Simon Smith and His Amazing Dancing Bear." Disbanding the group in 1968, Price teamed with Georgie Fame from 1969 to 1971 for tours and television. Fame had had a major hit with "Yeh Yeh" in 1965. Chas Chandler "discovered" Jimi Hendrix at N.Y.'s Cafe Wha in 1966 and became his first manager, producing The Jimi Hendrix Experience's first two albums. In the 1970s Chandler managed the English rock band Slade.

Eric Burdon helped form the backup group War with members of Los Angeles' Night Shift and Danish harmonicist Lee Oskar. Recording two albums and the smash hit single "Spill the Wine" with Burdon for MGM, War later became a popular act in its own right. After recording an album with blues singer Jimmy Witherspoon, Burdon formed yet another band, cutting two albums for Capitol.

Alan Price reemerged in 1973 for the soundtrack recording of (and appearance in) the Lindsay Anderson film *O Lucky Man.* He recorded one other album for Warner Bros. before concentrating his activities in England. By the 1980s, Price was well established in England as a performer and composer, writing scores for movies, television, and a stage musical.

The original Animals reunited for tours and the recording of *Before We Were So Rudely Interrupted* and *Ark* in 1977 and 1983, respectively. Eric Burdon performed the lead role of a downfallen rock star in the 1982 film *Comeback*, wrote an autobiography, and recorded the solo album *Wicked Man* in 1988. He toured with guitarist Robby Krieger in 1990 and keyboardist Brian Auger in 1991. The Animals were inducted into the Rock and Roll Hall of Fame in 1994. Chas Chandler died in London on July 17, 1996, while undergoing tests for an aortic aneurysm. Eric Burdon toured once again in 1997, with his new band The Flying I Band.

DISC.: THE ANIMALS: *Live at the Club A Go Go* (recorded 1963 in Newcastle); *With Sonny Boy Williamson* (recorded 1963); *The Animals* (with Eric Burdon; 1964); *On Tour* (1965); *Animal Tracks* (1965); *Best* (1966); *Animalization* (1966); *Animalism* (1966); *Best, Vol. 2* (1967); *Before We Were So Rudely Interrupted* (1977); *Ark* (1983); *Rip It to Shreds: Their Greatest Hits Live* (1984). **ERIC BURDON AND THE ANIMALS:** *Eric Is Here*

(1967); *Winds of Change* (1967); *Twain Shall Meet* (1968); *Every One of Us* (1968); *Love Is* (1968); *Best* (1969). **ERIC BURDON AND WAR:** *Eric Burdon Declares War* (1970); *Black Man's Burdon* (1970); *Love Is All Around* (1976). *Eric Burdon and Jimmy Witherspoon: Guilty!* (1971). **ERIC BURDON BAND:** *Sun Secrets* (1974); *Stop!* (1975); *That's Live* (1988). **ERIC BURDON:** *Wicked Man* (1988); *The Unreleased Eric Burdon* (1992). **ALAN PRICE:** *The Price Is Right* (1968); *O Lucky Man!* (soundtrack) (1973); *Between Today and Yesterday* (1974); *Alan Price* (1977); *Lucky Day* (1979); *Rising Sun* (1980); *House of the Rising Sun* (1981). **HILTON VALENTINE:** *All in Your Head* (1970).

WRITINGS: Eric Burdon, *I Used to Be an Animal, but I'm All Right Now* (Boston, 1986).—**BH**

Animuccia, Giovanni, notable Italian composer; b. Florence, c. 1500; d. Rome, March 20(?), 1571. He was probably the brother of **Paolo Animuccia.** After training in Florence, he settled in Rome. By 1550 he was in the service of Cardinal Guido Ascanio Sforza. In 1555 he succeeded Palestrina as magister cantorum at the Cappella Giulia. He composed his *Laudi spirituali* (2 vols., 1563, 1570) for the Oratory of Filippo Neri, which are noteworthy for their simple chordal style for the encouragement of lay participation. He also publ. 4 vols. of madrigals (1547, 1551, 1554, 1565), a vol. of masses (1567), and a vol. of Magnificats (1568). His works mark a gradual emancipation from the involved formalism of the Flemish school in the direction of a more practical style à la Palestrina. He was a master of polyphony who excelled in canonic writing.—**NS/LK/DM**

Animuccia, Paolo, Italian composer; b. probably in Florence, c. 1500; d. probably in Urbino, c. 1570. He most likely was the brother of **Giovanni Animuccia.** He served as maestro di cappella at St. John Lateran in Rome (1550–52) and at the court of the Duke of Urbino. He composed motets and madrigals.—**LK/DM**

Anitúa, Fanny, Mexican mezzo-soprano; b. Durango, Jan. 22, 1887; d. Mexico City, April 4, 1968. She studied in Rome, where she made her operatic debut as Gluck's Orfeo (1909). She then sang at Milan's La Scala (from 1910), and also throughout South (1911–27) and North (1913) America. Her other roles included Rosina, Cenerentola, Azucena, and Mistress Quickly. —**NS/LK/DM**

Anka, Paul, late 1950s teen star who later made it big as a pop singer/composer; b. Ottawa, Can., July 30, 1941. One of the more sophisticated performers and songwriters to come out of the 1950s, Paul Anka scored a number of hits with his own compositions while still a teenager, beginning with 1957's "Diana." He ultimately sold more than 100 million records and, like a number of teen idols, quickly switched his attention to the nightclub and cabaret circuit. He subsequently pursued a career as a songwriter, composing over 400 songs, including the English lyrics to "My Way," adopted by Frank Sinatra as his theme song, and "The Tonight Show Theme." During the mid 1970s, Anka relocated to Las Vegas and enjoyed renewed popularity with several huge pop and easy-listening hits.

Raised in Canada, Paul Anka first performed in public at the age of 12. Traveling to Hollywood in 1956, he recorded his first—albeit unsuccessful—single, "I Confess," for Modern/RPM Records. In the spring of 1957, at the age of 15, Anka auditioned a song for Don Costa of ABC- Paramount Records in N.Y. that would become one of the biggest selling singles of the 1950s: "Diana." Signed to the label, Anka hit the pop charts consistently over the next three years with compositions that often reflected the simple, even naive, but nonetheless poignant concerns of teenagers. His best-remembered smash hits of the period include "You Are My Destiny," "Lonely Boy" (also a smash R&B hit), "Put Your Head on My Shoulder," "Puppy Love," and "My Home Town."

Paul Anka first performed in Las Vegas in 1959 and became the youngest performer to star at N.Y.'s Copacabana nightclub in 1960. He also appeared in several movies, most notably 1962's *The Longest Day* (for which he also wrote the theme song), and switched to RCA Records by the beginning of 1962. No longer making the charts after 1963, Anka continued to perform on the nightclub circuit, including lucrative engagements in Las Vegas. Having written songs for others beginning in 1958 with "It Doesn't Matter Anymore" for Buddy Holly, Anka concentrated on his songwriting. Subsequently, his "Tonight Show Theme" became one of his most profitable compositions; yet his English lyrics to the French ballad "Comme d'Habitude"—under the new name, "My Way"—in 1969 became perhaps his best-known song and Frank Sinatra's theme song. Anka's "She's a Lady" became a smash hit for Tom Jones in 1971.

Paul Anka re-established himself as a recording artist in 1974–75 on United Artists Records beginning with the top hit "(You're) Having My Baby," recorded with Odia Coates, with whom he toured for several years. Other near-smash hits of the era included "One Man Woman/One Woman Man" (with Coates), "I Don't Like to Sleep Alone," and "Times of Your Life," a top easy-listening hit. Following this brief flourish, Anka continued to write, record, tour, and appear in an occasional television show or movie.

Disc.: *Paul Anka* (1958); *My Heart Sings* (1959); *Swings for Young Lovers* (1960); *At the Copa* (1960); *It's Christmas Everywhere* (1960); *Instrumental Hits* (1961); *Diana* (1962); *Young, Alive and in Love* (1962); *Let's Sit this One Out* (1962); *Our Man around the World* (1963); *Italiano* (1963); *Songs I Wish I'd Written* (1963); *Excitement on Park Avenue* (1964); *Strictly Nashville* (1965); *Live* (1967); *Goodnight My Love* (1969); *Sincerely* (1969); *Life Goes On* (1969); *Paul Anka in the '70s* (1970); *Paul Anka* (1971); *Jubilation* (1972); *Anka* (1974); *Feelings* (1975); *Times of Your Lives* (1975); *Live* (1975); *The Painter* (1976); *The Music Man* (1977); *Listen to Your Heart* (1978); *Headlines* (1979); *Both Sides of Love* (1981); *Walk a Fine Line* (1983); *Live* (1984).—**BH**

Anna Amalia, Princess of Prussia, German keyboard player, music patroness, and composer, sister of Friedrich II the Great; b. Berlin, Nov. 9, 1723; d. there, Sept. 30, 1787. She studied with her brother, the cathedral organist Gottlieb Hayne, and Kirnberger. She was a fine keyboard player. Among her works are music to Ramler's *Der Tod Jesu*, which was also set by C. H. Graun, a Trio Sonata, a Flute Sonata, many chorales, and military marches. She assembled a valuable library of about 600 MSS, which included many by Bach; this Bibliothek-Amalien is housed in Berlin.—**NS/LK/DM**

Anna Amalia, Duchess of Saxe-Weimar, German music patroness and composer; b. Wolfenbüttel, Oct. 24, 1739; d. Weimar, April 10, 1807. She studied with F. G. Fleischer and E. W. Wolf, and was a prominent figure at the Weimar court of her son, the Grand Duke Karl August. She wrote the Singspiel, *Erwin und Elmire*, after Goethe (Weimar, May 24, 1736; ed. by M. Friedlaender, Leipzig, 1921), a Sym., and a *Divertimento* for Piano, Clarinet, Viola, and Cello.

Bibl.: W. Bode, *A., Herzogin von Weimar* (3 vols., Berlin, 1908); O. Heuschele, *Herzogin A. A.* (Munich, 1947). —**NS/LK/DM**

Annibale, Domenico, Italian castrato soprano; b. Macerata, c. 1705; d. probably in Rome, 1779. He sang in Rome in 1725. After appearances in Venice (1727, 1729), he was called to Dresden in the service of the Saxon court, where he won distinction in the operas of Hasse. He was retained there until being pensioned in 1764 and named Kammermusikus. He also sang in Rome (1730, 1732, 1739), Vienna (1731), and London (1736–37). While in London he sang in the premieres of Handel's *Arminio, Giustino,* and *Berenice.*—**NS/LK/DM**

Annibale Il Padovano, Italian organist and composer; b. Padua, c. 1527; d. Graz, March 15, 1575. He was organist at San Marco in Venice (1552–64). In 1566 he was called to Graz as organist to Archduke Carl II, becoming "Obrister Musicus" in 1567 and Kapellmeister in 1570.

Works: (all publ. in Venice): *Il primo libro de ricercari a 4* (1556; ed. by N Pierront and J. Hennebains in *13 Ricercari for Organ, 1556,* Paris, 1934); *Di Cipriano et Annibale madrigali* for 4 Voices (1561); *Il primo libro di madrigali* for 5 Voices (1564; 2 ed. in Denkmäler der Tonkunst Österreich, LXXVII, 1934); *Liber motectorum* for 5 to 6 Voices (1567); *Il primo libro delle messe* for 5 Voices (1573); *Toccate et ricercari d'organo* (1604; ed. in Corpus of Early Keyboard Music, XXXIV, 1969).

Bibl.: G. del Valle de Paz, *A. I. P.: Nella storia della musica del cinquecento* (Turin, 1933).—**NS/LK/DM**

Anosov, Nikolai, Russian conductor, pedagogue, and composer, father of **Gennadi Rozhdestvensky;** b. Borisoglebsk, Feb. 18, 1900; d. Moscow, Dec. 2, 1962. He studied piano and composition at the Moscow Cons. (graduated, 1943), where he later taught. He also was a conductor with the Moscow Sym. Orch., and appeared as a guest conductor throughout Russia and abroad. Anosov wrote a textbook on reading orch. scores, and also composed a Piano Concertino and a Woodwind Quartet. He was married to the soprano Natalia Rozhdestvenskaya, and their son assumed his mother's maiden name.—**NS/LK/DM**

Anrooy (actually, **Anrooij**), **Peter van,** Dutch conductor and composer; b. Zalt-Bommel, Oct. 13, 1879; d. The Hague, Dec. 31, 1954. He studied with Wagenaar in Utrecht, and with Kes and Taneyev in Moscow. After conducting in Groningen (1905) and Arnhem (1910), he was music director of the Residentie Orch. in The Hague from 1917 to 1935. Among his works were *Piet Hein* for Orch. (1901), a *Ballade* for Violin and Orch. (1902), and chamber music.—**NS/LK/DM**

Ansani, Giovanni, remarkable Italian tenor; b. Rome, Feb. 20(?), 1744; d. Florence, July 5, 1826. He began his career with appearances in Bologna and Venice in 1768, and then sang in Udine in 1770. After singing in Copenhagen (1771) and Germany, he appeared in all of the principal Italian opera houses from 1773 until his retirement in 1795. He also sang in London at the King's Theatre in 1780. In later years, he was active as a singing teacher. His most celebrated pupils were Manuel García and Lablache. Ansani's outstanding vocal and histrionic gifts in opera seria demonstrated the role a tenor could play in that genre and hastened the demise of the castrato.—**NS/LK/DM**

Anschütz, Karl, German conductor and composer; b. Koblenz, Feb. 1815; d. N.Y., Dec. 30, 1870. He studied with Friedrich Schneider. In 1848 he went to London, where he conducted the Wednesday Concerts for a time. In 1857 he settled in N.Y. as an opera conductor. He publ. several piano pieces.—**NS/LK/DM**

Anselmi, Giuseppe, noted Italian tenor; b. Nicolosi, near Catania, Oct. 6, 1876; d. Zoagli, near Rapallo, May 27, 1929. He learned to play the violin and appeared in public as a violinist in Nicolosi when he was 13. He sang in operettas before making his operatic debut in Patras, Greece, about 1896. Following vocal training from Mancinelli, he sang in Genoa and Naples in 1900. In 1901 he made his first appearance at London's Covent Garden, and returned there in 1904 and 1909. His engagements also took him to Buenos Aires, Warsaw, Moscow, St. Petersburg, and Spain. In 1918 he retired from the operatic stage, and in 1926 he made his last public appearance as a violinist in Rapallo. Anselmi was a remarkable bel canto stylist, winning special acclaim for his Verdi and Puccini roles. He was also a composer, numbering among his works a *Poema sinfonico* for Orch., chamber music, and songs. His love for Spain, where he had enormous success as a singer, prompted him to bequeath his heart to Madrid; the rest of his body was deposed in Catania Cathedral. —**NS/LK/DM**

Ansermet, Ernest (Alexandre), celebrated Swiss conductor; b. Vevey, Nov. 11, 1883; d. Geneva, Feb. 20, 1969. He studied mathematics at the Univ. of Lausanne and at the Paris Sorbonne, and received music training from Gédalge in Paris and from Denéréaz, Barblan, and Ernest Bloch in Geneva. In 1910 he made his conducting debut in Montreux, where he subsequently conducted sym. concerts. In 1915 he settled in Geneva as a conductor. From 1915 to 1923 he also conducted Diaghilev's Ballets Russes, which he took on tours on Europe and North and South America. During this period, Ansermet attracted favorable notice as the conductor of the premieres of several works by Stravinsky, Ravel, Falla, and Prokofiev. In 1918 he founded l'Orchestre de la Suisse Romande in Geneva, which he led as chief conductor for nearly 50 years. He added luster to his reputation through appearances as a guest conductor with the world's leading orchs. In 1946 he made his debut at the Glyndebourne Festival conducting the premiere of Britten's *The Rape of Lucretia*; subsequently appeared with various major U.S. orchs., and made his belated Metropolitan Opera debut in N.Y. conducting *Pelléas et Mélisande* on Nov. 30, 1952. Ansermet acquired a distinguished reputation as an interpreter of Debussy, Stravinsky, Ravel, Prokofiev, and Bartók. While he conducted the works of various other 20th-century composers, his sympathies did not extend to Schoenberg or his disciples; indeed, Ansermet disdained the 12-tone system and other avant-garde techniques. Among his writings were *Le Geste du chef d'orchestre* (1943), *Les Fondements de la musique dans la conscience humaine* (2 vols., 1961), *Entretiens sur la musique* (with J.-C. Piguet; 1963), and *Les compositeurs et leurs oeuvres* (ed. by J.-C. Piguet; 1989).

BIBL.: F. Hundry, *E. A.: Pionnier de la Musique* (1983). —**NS/LK/DM**

Ansorge, Conrad (Eduard Reinhold), German pianist, pedagogue, and composer; b. Buchwald, Silesia, Oct. 15, 1862; d. Berlin, Feb. 13, 1930. He studied at the Leipzig Cons. (1880–82) and with Liszt in Weimar and Rome (1885–86). In 1898 he became a teacher at the Klindworth-Schwarwenka Cons. in Berlin. In 1920 he gave a piano master class at the German Academy of Music in Prague. As a pianist, Ansorge was known for his insightful interpretations of works from Beethoven to Liszt. He wrote a Piano Concerto, a String Sextet, 2 string quartets, a Cello Sonata, piano pieces, including 3 sonatas, and vocal music.

BIBL.: A. Seidl, *C. A.* (Regensburg, 1926).—**NS/LK/DM**

Ansseau, Fernand, Belgian tenor; b. Boussu-Bois, near Mons, March 6, 1890; d. Brussels, May 1, 1972. He was a pupil of Demest in Brussels. In 1913 he made his operatic debut as Jean in *Hérodiade* in Dijon. He made his first appearance at the Théâtre de la Monnaie in Brussels in 1918. From 1919 to 1928 he sang at London's Covent Garden, where his roles included Faust, Romeo, Massenet's Des Grieux, Canio, Don José, and Cavaradossi. He also sang in Paris at the Opéra-Comique (1920–21), where he appeared as Orfeo, and at the Opéra (1922–34), where his roles included Samson, Tannhäuser, and Lohengrin. From 1923 to 1928 he likewise appeared at the Chicago Civic Opera. He sang regularly at the Théâtre de la Monnaie from 1930 until his retirement in 1939. In later years, he was active as a voice teacher in Brussels. Ansseau was especially admired for his lyric roles, but in later years he also won success in heavier roles.—**NS/LK/DM**

Antegnati, Costanzo, Italian organist, organ builder, and composer; b. Brescia (baptized), Dec. 9,

1549; d. there, Nov. 14, 1624. He was born into a family of organ builders. In 1584 he became organist at Brescia Cathedral. He supervised the building of more than 140 organs and publ. the valuable treatise *L'arte organica* (Brescia, 1608; ed. in the Corpus of Early Keyboard Music, IX, 1965), which contains information on tuning and registration. He publ. masses, motets, Psalms, canzoni, and madrigals in Venice (1571–1608).—**NS/LK/DM**

Antes, John, American Moravian minister and composer; b. Frederick, near Bethlehem, Pa., March 24, 1740; d. Bristol, England, Dec. 17, 1811. He was educated at the Moravian boys's school in Bethlehem. After working as a musical instrument maker in Bethlehem, he went to Herrnhut, Germany, in 1764 to pursue his training. In 1765 he went to Neuwied to learn the watchmaker's trade. He was ordained a Moravian minister in 1769 and in 1770 he went to Egypt as a missionary. In 1779 he was captured by the underlings of Osman Bey, who beat and crippled him in an attempt to extort money from him. In 1781 he returned to Germany. He settled in the Fulneck Moravian community in England in 1785 as warder (business manager). His extant works—3 trios for 2 Violins and Cello, c. 1790, the earliest known chamber pieces by a native American, 31 concerted anthems and solo songs, and 59 hymn tunes—reveal his gifts as a composer. He publ. a description of his efforts to improve the violin tuning mechanism, violin bows, and keyboard hammers in the *Allgemeine musikalische Zeitung*, VIII (1806). He also invented a music stand with which the performer could automatically turn the pages of a score. His interesting autobiography was publ. as "Lebenslauf des Bruders John Antes" in *Nachrichten aus der Brüder-Gemeine*, No. 2 (1845).—**NS/LK/DM**

Antheil, George (actually, **Georg Carl Johann**), remarkable American composer; b. Trenton, N.J., July 8, 1900; d. N.Y., Feb. 12, 1959. He began piano lessons at age 6. After studying theory and composition with Constantin Sternberg in Philadelphia (1916–19), he pursued composition lessons with Bloch in N.Y. (1919–21). Defying the dictates of flickering musical conservatism, Antheil wrote piano pieces under such provocative titles as *Airplane Sonata, Sonata Sauvage, Jazz Sonata,* and *Mechanisms*. In 1922 he went to Europe and toured successfully as a pianist, giving a number of concerts featuring his own compositions. While living in Berlin (1922–23), he met Stravinsky, who had already greatly influenced him. There he also met Elizabeth (Böski) Markus (1902–78), a niece of the Austrian dramatist and novelist Arthur Schnitzler, and the daughter of a wealthy Jewish stockbroker in Budapest, to whom he was married from 1925 until his death. In June 1923 he went to Paris and entered the circle of Joyce, Pound, Yeats, Satie, and the violinist Olga Rudge, with whom he performed his 3 violin sonatas. Antheil was the subject of a monograph by Ezra Pound entitled *Antheil and the Treatise on Harmony with Supplementary Notes* (Paris, 1924; 2nd ed., Chicago, 1927), which, however, had little bearing on Antheil and even less on harmony. He also assisted Pound in the composition of his operas

Le Testament and *Cavalcanti*. Hailed as a genius, Antheil soon became the self-styled *enfant terrible* of modern music and the first U.S.-born composer to be known outside his country to develop a modernist style. He organized a series of important private concerts in Paris with his friend Virgil Thomson, and won extraordinary success with his *Ballet mécanique* for Pianola, Multiple Pianos, and Percussion, including electric bells, airplane propellers, and siren (Paris, June 19, 1926). Originally conceived as music to accompany a film by Dudley Murphy and Fernand Léger, the lack of ability in that era to synchronize the film and music resulted in their becoming independent pieces. A concert featuring this work was given at an all-Antheil event at Carnegie Hall in N.Y. on April 10, 1927, with Aaron Copland and Colin McPhee performing as 2 of the 8 live pianists. Also on the program was the premiere of the raw and impulsive *Jazz Symphony* (1925), performed by the W. C. Handy Orch. under Allie Ross, with the composer at the piano. The work is filled with style quotations from other music and disjunct non-sequiturs, used notably in Antheil's *Violin Sonata No. 2 with Drums* (1923), and presaging the compositions of Charles Ives before the elder composer's earlier scores were circulated or played. The circus-like press reports preceding the N.Y. concert led the audience to ridicule the event as a whole, and this collective memory haunted the composer's career in America until the 1950s when the *Ballet mécanique* was revived to positive acclaim in a trimmed-down version by Antheil (N.Y., Feb. 21, 1954) for 4 Pianos and Percussion. Paul Lehrman reconstructed and arranged the score's early version as originally conceived for 16 Pianolas, 2 Live Pianos, and Percussion (Lowell, Mass., Nov. 18, 1999). In the 1924–25 version and the 1999 revision, the obsessive repetition, lengthy measured silences within a single movement, the use of siren, doorbells, airplane propellers, and mechanistic modular construction within a piece of concert music were all unprecedented. Not until the repetitive music of Riley, Reich, and Glass, some 40 years later, did composers exceed Antheil's own dramatic focus on single repeated phrases to direct microscopic attention to small units of musical detail.

Antheil composed several works in the neo-classical style of Stravinsky—his Piano Concerto No. 2 (Paris, March 12, 1927), *Symphonie en fa* (Paris, June 19, 1926), and *Suite for Orchestra* (Paris, March 12, 1927)—but then returned to his collage and modular construction techniques for the opera *Transatlantic* (Frankfurt am Main, May 25, 1930). The work, produced experimentally on a revolving multi-scene stage with film projections, was based on his own libretto concerning an American presidential election rocked by a sex scandal in which the liberal candidate overcomes the conservative party's attempt to lure him into an untimely sexual affair as the election nears. In a denouement eerily presaging the Bill Clinton scandal by more than 60 years, the candidate survives in spite of his public humiliation to win the election, as voters cast their ballots in his favor based on his political agenda rather than against him for reasons of personal fallibility. From 1927 to 1933 Antheil lived variously in Vienna, Tunis, and Cagnes-sur-Mer, writing opera and stage works for productions in Vienna and

Frankfurt am Main. He also wrote a mystery story, *Death in the Dark* (published by Faber under the pseudonym Stacey Bishop), while living in Rapallo in 1929. The manuscript, surely a collector's item, was edited by friends who were living there temporarily: Ezra Pound, T. S. Eliot, W. B. Yeats, Gerhart Hauptmann, and Franz Werfel. For a Yeats play, *Fighting the Waves*, Antheil wrote stirring incidental music for Chorus and Chamber Orch., which was premiered at the Abbey Theatre (Dublin, Aug. 13, 1929). In 1932–33 he synthesized many elements of his early "mechanistic period" solo piano writing in the lengthy and formally radical suite *La femme 100 têtes* (posth. premiere, Berkeley, Calif., Nov. 20, 1970), after the "novel" of collages by Max Ernst.

In 1933, with the rise of Hitler, Antheil found himself *persona non grata* and returned via Paris to N.Y., where his opera *Helen Retires* (1930–31; N.Y., Feb. 28, 1934), to an overlong libretto by John Erskine, met with failure. Until this time, Antheil was supported in part by patronage from the founder of the Curtis Inst., Mary Louise Curtis Bok, who subsequently dropped him on advice from Josef Hofmann. Antheil composed several scores for George Balanchine's American Ballet. Having begun in 1934 to write film music for the Ben Hecht–Charles MacArthur film studio in Astoria, N.Y., Antheil continued to work in movie scoring for the remainder of his life, dividing his time between composing as necessary for survival and writing serious concert music. With the migration to Southern Calif. of the entire film industry, Antheil relocated there and found himself once again in the midst of a larger-than-life scene: Stravinsky, Schoenberg, Weisler, Weill, Toch, Zeisl, and Adolph Weiss all had immigrated there. Antheil generously attempted to help numerous fellow classical composers obtain film work but few were able to find acceptance. In N.Y. and then in Hollywood, he also undertook numerous unusual occupations, including writing lovelorn columns for *Esquire Magazine*, running the short-lived Siegel-Antheil Gallery (which could not sell the work of Man Ray, Joan Miró, Salvador Dalí, and other prominent European painters who were yet to be accepted in Southern Calif.), producing a book on glandular criminology, and writing predictions on the progress of World War II for the *Los Angeles Daily News* and for an anonymously published book, *The Shape of the War to Come*. He also wrote a regular column, "On the Hollywood Front," for the periodical *Modern Music*. In 1940 he met Hedy Lamarr, formerly married to the Austrian weapons manufacturer Fritz Mandel, with whom he patented a radio-guided torpedo intended to combat the German Luftwaffe by directing the missile with a variety of changing frequencies in order to avoid jamming by the enemy (Patent No. 2,292,387, June 10, 1941). While this invention, which was offered without charge to the U.S. Navy Dept., was deemed by government officials to be impractical, it is now recognized as the forerunner of spread spectrum technology—the basis for all current satellite communications. It would have been realized in the torpedo by means of a tape with pre-punched holes (like a pianola roll) to switch control frequencies during the trajectory of the weapon. Neither Lamarr nor Antheil ever received income from their work on this pioneering invention. Among An-

theil's most important later scores are the 4th (1942; NBC Radio, Feb. 13, 1944), 5th, *Joyous* (1947–48; Philadelphia, Dec. 21, 1948), and 6th (1947–48; San Francisco, Feb. 10, 1949) syms., Violin Concerto (Dallas, Feb. 9, 1947), the ballet *Capital of the World* (1952; telecast, Dec. 6, 1953), the operas *Volpone* (1949–52; Los Angeles, Jan. 9, 1953), *The Brothers* (Denver, July 28, 1954), *The Wish* (1954; Louisville, April 2, 1955), and *Venus in Africa* (Denver, May 24, 1957), the 4th Piano Sonata (N.Y., Nov. 21, 1948), *Valentine Waltzes* for Piano (1949), *Songs of Experience* for Soprano and Piano (1948), and *Eight Fragments from Shelley* for Chorus and Piano (1951), five movements of which were orchestrated and performed at the coronation of Queen Elizabeth II in 1953.

In contrast to his radical work of the 1920s, Antheil's works from the early 1940s were stylistically related to those of Prokofiev, Shostakovich, and Britten, all the while retaining harmonically the occasional "iron ring of modern civilization" from his more youthful music, in the service of a now neo-Romantic style. His abstract music of this period is characterized by explosive fast movements with biting harmonies and melodic patterns often reaching into extremely high instrumental registers, contrasted with poignant and lyrical andantes, all cast in conventional symphonic form. As a composer for films, Antheil was uncompromising in using his best symphonic writing. His important film scores include music for *The Plainsman* (1936), *Angels over Broadway* (1940), *The Fighting Kentuckian* (1949), *Knock on Any Door* (1949), *In a Lonely Place* (1950), *Dementia* (1950), *Not as a Stranger* (1955), and *The Pride and the Passion* (1957), most of which were orchestrated by his pupil Ernest Gold. Antheil also taught privately, numbering Henry Brant, Tom Scott, Benjamin Lees, and Ruth White among his students. He wrote scores for the weekly CBS Television series, "The Twentieth Century," narrated by Walter Cronkite (1957–58) and was in N.Y. working on this project when he succumbed to a heart attack on Feb. 12, 1959. His cantata, *Cabeza de Vaca* (1955–56), orchestrated by Gold, was premiered on a telecast of the CBS program "Omnibus" (June 10, 1962) as a memorial tribute.

WORKS: DRAMATIC: Opera: *Transatlantic* (1927–28; Frankfurt am Main, May 25, 1930); *Helen Retires* (1930–31; N.Y., Feb. 28, 1934); *Volpone* (1949–52; Los Angeles, Jan. 9, 1953); *The Brothers* (Denver, July 28, 1954); *Venus in Africa* (1954; Denver, May 24, 1957); *The Wish* (1954; Louisville, April 2, 1955). **Opera-ballet:** *Flight (Ivan the Terrible)* (1927–30; arr. as *Crucifixion Juan Miro* for String Orch., 1927; not extant). **Ballet:** *Dance in Four Parts* (c. 1933–34; N.Y., Nov. 11, 1934; not extant; based on *La femme 100 têtes*); *Eyes of Gutne* (c. 1934; not extant); *The Seasons* (c. 1934; not extant); *Dreams* (1934–35; N.Y., March 5, 1935); *Serenade* (N.Y., June 9, 1934; not extant; orchestrated from Tchaikovsky); *Transcendance* (Bryn Mawr, Pa., Feb. 7, 1935; not extant; orchestrated from Liszt); *Course* (1935; not extant); *The Cave Within* (c. 1948; not extant); *Capital of the World* (1952; telecast, Dec. 6, 1953). **Incidental Music:** *Fighting the Waves*, to Yeats's play (Dublin, Aug. 13, 1929). **Film:** *The Plainsman* (1936); *Angels Over Broadway* (1940); *Specter of the Rose* (1946); *The Fighting Kentuckian* (1949); *Knock on Any Door* (1949); *In a Lonely Place* (1950); *Dementia* (1950); *The Juggler* (1952); *Not as a Stranger* (1955); *The Pride and the Passion* (1957)

(1957). Also music for plays, radio, and television. **ORCH.**: 2 piano concertos: No. 1 (1922) and No. 2 (1926; Paris, March 12, 1927); *Symphonie No. 1, Zingareska* (1920–22; Berlin, Nov. 21, 1922; rev. 1923); *Ballet mécanique* (1923–25; Paris, June 19, 1926; rev. 1952–53); *A Jazz Symphony* (1925; rev. 1955); *Symphony en fa* (1925–26; Paris, June 19, 1926); *Suite* (1926); *Capriccio* (1930); *Sym. No. 2* (1931–38; rev. 1943); *Morceau (The Creole)* (1932); *Sym. No. 3, American* (1936–39; rev. 1946); *Sym. No. 4, 1942* (1942; N.Y., Feb. 13, 1944); *Water-Music for 4th-of-July-Evening* for Strings (1942–43); *Decatur et Algiers* (1943); *Over the Plains* (1945); *Sym. No. 5, Tragic* (1945–46); *Violin Concerto* (1946); *Autumn Song* (1947); another *Sym. No. 5, Joyous* (1947–48; Philadelphia, Dec. 21, 1948); *Sym. No. 6* (1947–48; San Francisco, Feb. 10, 1949; rev. 1949–50); *American Dance Suite No. 1* (1948); *McKonkeys Ferry Overture* (1948); *Serenade* for Strings (1948) and for Chamber Orch. (1949); *Tom Sawyer* (1949); *Accordion Dance* (1951); *Nocturne in Skyrockets* (1951). **CHAMBER**: *Lithuanian Night* for String Quartet (c. 1919); Sym. for 5 Instruments (1922–23; 2nd ver., 1923); 4 violin sonatas (1923; 1923; 1924; 1947–48); 3 string quartets (1924, 2nd ver., 1925; 1927, rev. 1943; 1948); Concertino for Flute, Bassoon, and Piano (1930); *6 Little Pieces* for String Quartet (1931); *Concert* for Chamber Ensemble (1932); Sonatina for Violin and Cello or Piano (1932); Violin Sonatina (1945); Flute Sonata (1951); Trumpet Sonata (1951); *Bohemian Grove at Night* for 5 Instruments (1952). **P i a n o**: *Airplane Sonata*, Sonata No. 2 (1921); *Sonata Sauvage*, Sonata No. 1 (c. 1922); *Death of Machines*, Sonata No. 3 (1923); *Jazz Sonata*, Sonata No. 4 (c. 1922); Sonata No. 5 (1923); Sonata (1923); *Woman Sonata*, Sonata No. 6 (c. 1923; not extant); *The Perfect Modernist* (c. 1923; not extant); *Mechanisms* (c. 1923); *Habañera, Tarantelle, Serenata* for 2 Pianos (1924); *Sonatina für Radio* (1929); *La femme 100 têtes* (1933); *La vie Parisienne* (1939); *The Ben Hecht Valses* (1943); Sonatas Nos. 3 (1947), 4 (1948), and 5 (1950). **VOCAL**: *Nightpiece* for Soprano and Piano, after James Joyce (1930); *Songs of Experience* for Soprano and Piano, after William Blake (1948); *Two Odes of John Keats* for Narrator and Piano (1950); *Eight Fragments from Shelley* for Chorus and Piano (1951; 3 mvts. orch., 1951); *Cabeza de vaca*, cantata for Chorus (1955–56; orch. by E. Gold, 1959; CBS-TV, June 10, 1962); songs.

WRITINGS: *Bad Boy of Music* (autobiography; N.Y., 1945).

BIBL.: E. Pound, *A. and the Treatise on Harmony with Supplementary Notes* (Paris, 1924; 2nd ed., 1927); D. Friede, *The Mechanical Angel: His Adventures and Enterprises in the Glittering 1920's* (N.Y., 1948); L. Whitesitt, *The Life and Music of G. A., 1900–1959* (Ann Arbor, 1983).—**NS/LK/DM**

Anthonello de Caserta, Italian composer who flourished in the late 14th and early 15th centuries. His output includes a madrigal, 6 ballate, 5 ballades, 2 rondeaux, and a virelai. See W. Apel, ed., *French Secular Music of the Late Fourteenth Century* (Cambridge, Mass., 1950) and *French Secular Compositions of the Fourteenth Century*, Corpus Mensurabilis Musicae, LIII/1 (1970). —**LK/DM**

Anthony, Charles (real name, **Carlogero Antonio Caruso**), American tenor; b. New Orleans, July 15, 1929. He was a student of Dorothy Hulse at Loyola Univ. In 1952 he won the Metropolitan Opera Auditions of the Air, and then completed his training in Rome with Picozzi and Ruisi. On March 6, 1954, he made his Metropolitan Opera debut in N.Y. as the Simpleton in *Boris Godunov*, and subsequently remained on its roster for 40 seasons. Among the more important roles he sang there were Count Almaviva (1954), Rodolfo (1959), Don Ottavio (1960), Nemorino (1961), Alfredo (1962), and Ferrando (1962). He also made guest appearances with other U.S. opera companies.—**LK/DM**

Anthony, James R(aymond), American musicologist; b. Providence, R.I., Feb. 18, 1922. He was educated at Columbia Univ. (B.S., 1946; M.A., 1948), the Univ. of Paris (diploma, 1951), and the Univ. of Southern Calif. in Los Angeles (Ph.D., 1964, with the diss. *The Opéra-Ballets of André Campra: A Study of the First Period French Opéra-Ballet*). After teaching at the Univ. of Mont. (1948–50), he was on the faculty of the Univ. of Ariz. from 1952 until he was made prof. emeritus in 1992. In 1995 he was named a Chevalier de l'Ordre des Arts et des Lettres of France. He publ. the study *French Baroque Music from Beaujoyeulx to Rameau* (London, 1973; 3rd ed., rev. and extended, 1997; French tr., 1981, as *La musique en France à l'époque baroque*). He also contributed articles to many scholarly journals, as well as to *The New Grove Dictionary of Music and Musicians* (1980), *The New Grove Dictionary of Opera* (1992), and the *Dictionnaire de la musique en France aux XVIIe et XVIIIe siècles* (1992).

BIBL.: J. Heyer, ed., *Jean-Baptiste Lully and the Music of the French Baroque: Essays in Honour of J. A.* (Cambridge, 1988). —**NS/LK/DM**

Anthony (Antonini), Ray(mond), jazz trumpeter, bandleader; b. Bentleyville, Pa., Jan. 20, 1922. Anthony played with Glenn Miller for two years and with Jimmy Dorsey for ten years before forming his own band with only his trumpet and a French horn for brass. After navy service (1942–46), including leading a band in the Pacific, Anthony's more conventional dance band was the most successful Miller imitator in the early 1950s. Anthony had several hit singles during 1950–54, including "Dragnet." He co-wrote the novelty tune "The Bunny Hop," and the hit single "Dancing in the Dark," which won an award as the best dance band record of 1953. Anthony was married to actress Mamie Van Doren. He bought The Billy May Band in 1954, hiring Sam Donahue to front it. Anthony also had plenty of film and television work in the 1950s, including an appearance in the film "Daddy Long Legs." He later led smaller combos, had a band in Las Vegas in 1980, and formed bands in the 1980s.

DISC.: *Jam Session at the Tower* (1956); *Swing Back to the 40s* (1991).—**MM**

Antico, Andrea, Italian music publisher and composer; b. Montona, c. 1480; d. probably in Venice, after 1539. He was active as an engraver and publisher in Rome (1510–18), where he was the first to print music in that city. He went to Venice, where he pursued his career in 1520–21. From 1533 to 1539 he was active again in Venice, where he was associated with the Scotto firm. In his editions, Antico engraved blocks that printed music and text together. Among them were sacred works, madrigals, and frottolas, as well as the first printed vol. of Italian keyboard music. He also wrote several frottolas of his own.—**NS/LK/DM**

Antill, John (Henry), Australian composer; b. Sydney, April 8, 1904; d. there, Dec. 29, 1986. He studied with Alfred Hill at the New South Wales State Conservatorium of Music in Sydney; from 1934 to 1971 he worked for the Australian Broadcasting Commission (later Corp.). In 1971 he received the Order of the British Empire, and in 1981 was made a Companion of the Order of St. Michael and St. George.

WORKS: DRAMATIC: O p e r a : *Endymion* (1922; Sydney, July 22, 1953); *The Music Critic* (1953); *The First Christmas* (ABC, Dec. 25, 1969). B a l l e t : *Corroboree* (c. 1935–46; Sydney, July 3, 1950; rev. 1960); *Wakooka* (1957); *Black Opal* (1961); *Snowy* (1961); *Paean to the Spirit of Man* (1968). ORCH.: *Variations* (1953); *Symphony of a City* (1959); *Music for a Royal Pageant* (1962); Harmonica Concerto (1964); *The Unknown Land* (1968). VOCAL: *The Song of Hagar*, oratorio (1958); songs.
—NS/LK/DM

Antoine, Georges, Belgian composer; b. Liège, April 28, 1892; d. Bruges, Nov. 15, 1918. He was a student of Dupuis at the Liège Cons. (1902–13). In 1914 he joined the Belgian army. He died at an extremely young age of an ailment acquired during his military service in World War I. Among his few works are a Violin Sonata (1912–15), Piano Concerto (1914), *Vendanges* for Voice and Orch. (1914), Piano Quartet (1916), *Veillée d'armes*, symphonic poem (1918), and songs.

BIBL.: M. Paquet, *G. A.* (Brussels, 1935).—NS/LK/DM

Antokoletz, Elliott (Maxim), American musicologist; b. Jersey City, N.J., Aug. 3, 1942. He was educated in N.Y., where he studied at the H.S. of Music and Art (1956–60), received training in violin from DeLay and Galamian at the Juilliard School of Music (1960–65), and pursued his academic studies at Hunter Coll. (B.A., 1968, M.A., 1970, in music history) and at the Graduate Center (Ph.D., 1975, with the diss. *Principles of Pitch Organization in Bartók's Fourth String Quartet*) at the City Univ. of N.Y. After teaching at Queens Coll. of the City Univ. of N.Y. (1973–76), he was prof. of musicology at the Univ. of Tex. at Austin from 1976, where he was head of the musicology division from 1992 to 1994. With Michael von Albrecht, he was ed. of the *International Journal of Musicology* in 1992. He is a contributor to many books and journals.

WRITINGS: *The Music of Béla Bartók: A Study of Tonality and Progression in Twentieth-Century Music* (Berkeley and Los Angeles, 1984); *Béla Bartók: A Guide to Research* (N.Y., 1988; 2nd ed., rev. and enl., 1997); *Twentieth Century Music* (Englewood Cliffs, N.J., 1992); ed. with V. Fischer and B. Suchoff, *Bartók Perspectives* (Oxford, 1999).—LK/DM

Antonacci, Anna Caterina, Italian soprano; b. Ferrara, April 5, 1961. She received her vocal training in Bologna. Following her operatic debut in Arezzo as Rossini's Rosina in 1986, she was engaged to sing in such operatic centers as Bari, Rome, Venice, and Bergamo. In 1991 she appeared as Rossini's Anais in Bologna. In 1992 she sang the title role in Rossini's *Ermione* in the first British performance of that opera in concert in London. That same year she appeared as that composer's Elisabetta in Naples. In 1994 she made her debut at London's Covent Garden as Rossini's Elcia. After singing Ermione at the Glyndebourne Festival in 1995, she appeared as Gluck's Armide at Milan's La Scala in 1996. In 1998 she returned to Glyndebourne to sing Rodelinda. Among her other roles of distinction are Fiordiligi, Semiramide, Dorliska, and Adalgisa.
—NS/LK/DM

Antonelli, Abundio, Italian composer; b. Fabrica, near Viterbo, date unknown; d. probably in Rome, c. 1629. He was maestro di cappella at St. John Lateran in Rome (1611–13) and at Benevento Cathedral (1614–15). In his *Gaue virgo gloriosa*, a concerted dialogue, and *Abraham, tolle filium tuum*, a kind of cantata, he anticipated the oratorio. His sacred and secular vocal works were publ. in Rome (1614–29).—LK/DM

Antoni, Antonio d', Italian conductor and composer; b. Palermo, June 25, 1801; d. (suicide) Trieste, Aug. 18, 1859. He studied with his grandfather and with his father, both of whom were musicians, and appeared as conductor of his own Mass for St. Cecilia's Day when he was 12. He also conducted the premiere of his first opera, *Un duello*, in Palermo at the age of 16, and, after touring as a conductor in Italy, France, and England, scored notable success with his opera *Amina ossia L'Orfanella di Ginevra* (Trieste, Carnival 1825). He settled in Trieste and became conductor of the Società Filarmonico-Dramatica (1829).—NS/LK/DM

Antonicelli, Giuseppe, Italian conductor; b. Castrovillari, Dec. 29, 1897; d. Trieste, March 10, 1980. He studied in Turin, where he began his career as a répétiteur at the Teatro Regio. After conducting at Milan's La Scala (1934–37), he served as artistic director of the Teatro Giuseppe Verdi in Trieste (1937–45). On Nov. 10, 1947, he made his Metropolitan Opera debut in N.Y. conducting *Un ballo in maschera*, remaining on its roster until 1950; then served once more as artistic director of the Teatro Giuseppe Verdi in Trieste (1951–68). His wife was **Franca Somigli**.—NS/LK/DM

Antonini, Alfredo, Italian-American conductor and composer; b. Milan, May 31, 1901; d. Clearwater, Fla., Nov. 3, 1983. After studying at the Milan Cons., he emigrated to the U.S. in 1929. From 1941 he was active as a conductor and composer with CBS in N.Y. He also was conductor of the Tampa Phil. (1957–68).—NS/LK/DM

Antoniou, Theodore, Greek-American composer, conductor, and teacher; b. Athens, Feb. 10, 1935. He studied in Athens at the National Cons. (violin and voice, 1947–58), with Manolis Kalomiris (composition), and at the Hellenic Cons. (composition and orchestration with Yannis Papaioannou, 1958–61). He then went to Munich and was a student of Günter Bialas and Adolph Mennerich (composition and conducting) at the Hochschule für Musik (1961–65), and also of Anton Riedl at the Siemens Studio for Electronic Music. He also attended the summer courses in new music in

Darmstadt (1963–66). In 1967 he became music director of the Municipality of Athens Sym. Orch. and of the Hellenic Group of Contemporary Music. In 1968 he was in Berlin under the auspices of the Deutscher Akademischer Austauschdienst. He was composer-in-residence at the Berkshire Music Center at Tanglewood (summer, 1969), Stanford Univ. (1969–70), and the Univ. of Utah (1970–72). From 1970 to 1978 he was prof. of composition and director of the New Music Group of the Philadelphia Coll. of the Performing Arts. He also was conductor of the Philadelphia Musical Academy Sym. Orch. (1971–75) and asst. director of contemporary activities at Tanglewood (summers, 1974–85). In 1978 he became prof. of composition and founder–music director of its contemporary music ensemble Alea III, with which he has programmed over 800 scores by some 500 composers. He was the recipient of the Greek Academy of Arts and Letters Music Award in 1997 for his manifold contributions to contemporary music. Antoniou's early music is remarkably compendious in its integration of quaquaversal layers of sound. Folk elements in Greek modalities are also in evidence, and many of his titles have Greek philosophic or literary connotations. His later style developed to embrace a modified serialism and, in addition, a personal use of free tonality and free atonality. His music is highly dramatic and often virtuosic.

WORKS: DRAMATIC: *Clytemnestra*, sound action for Actress, Dancers, Orch., and Tape (1967; Kassel, June 4, 1968); *Cassandra*, sound action for Dancers, Actors, Chorus, Orch., Tapes, Lights, and Projections (1969; Barcelona, Nov. 14, 1970); *Chorochronos I*, mixed media piece for Baritone, Narrator, Instruments, Tape, Films, Slides, and Light Effects (Philadelphia, May 11, 1973); *Periander*, mixed-media opera (1977–79; Munich, Feb. 6, 1983); *Bacchae*, ballet (1980; Athens, June 25, 1982); *The Imaginary Cosmos*, ballet (1984); *Bacchae*, opera (1991–92; Athens, Aug. 17, 1995); *Monodrama* for Actor and Chamber Ensemble (1992; Athens, April 9, 1994); *Oedipus at Colonus*, opera (1997; Athens, May 9, 1998). **ORCH.:** *Antithesis* (1962; Hannover, Jan. 20, 1966); *Jeux* for Cello and Strings (1963; Hannover, Jan. 23, 1965); *Micrographies* (1964; Kassel, March 4, 1968); Violin Concerto (Athens, Aug. 16, 1965); *Kinesis A B C D* for 2 String Groups (Athens, July 13, 1966); *Op Overture* for Orch. and Tape (1966); *Events I* for Violin, Piano, and Orch. (1967–68; Hagen, June 10, 1968), *II* (Tanglewood, Aug. 30, 1969), and *III* (Barcelona, Oct. 8, 1969); *Katharsis* for Flute and Orch. (Athens, Dec. 22, 1968); *Threnos* for Wind Orch. (1972; Tanglewood, Aug. 7, 1974); *Chorochronos II* (Reutlichen, Oct. 19, 1973); *Fluxus I* (1974–75) and *II* for Piano and Chamber Orch. (1975; Philadelphia, April 4, 1976); Double Concerto for Percussion and Orch. (1977; Philadelphia, April 26, 1978); *The GBYSO Music* (1982; Boston, April 17, 1983); *Skolion* (Athens, July 7, 1986); Concerto for Tambura and Chamber Orch. (Iraklion, Aug. 27, 1988); *Paean* (Boston, Oct. 26, 1989); Concerto/Fantasia for Violin and Chamber Orch. (1989; Boston, April 19, 1990); *North/South* for Piano and Chamber Orch. (N.Y., April 4, 1990); *Celebration* (Boston, Dec. 13, 1994); Concerto for Violin and Strings (1995; Athens, June 1, 1997); Concerto for Marimba, Harp, and Orch. (1995; Athens, Jan. 17, 1997); *Moto Perpetuo* (1995); *Kommos B* (N.Y., July 11, 1996); Guitar Concerto (Corfu, July 13, 1997); Piano Concerto (1998; also for 2 Pianos and Orch., 1999). **CHAMBER:** 2 string quartets (1960, 1998); *Quartetto giocoso* for Oboe, Violin, Cello, and Piano (1965; Berlin, June 8, 1968); *Lyrics* for

Violin and Piano (1967; Washington, D.C., Jan. 9, 1968); *Five Likes* for Oboe (1969; Rothenburg, Jan. 14, 1971); *Synthesis* for Oboe, Hammond Organ, Percussion, Double Bass, and 4 Synthesizers (1971); *Four Likes* for Violin (1972; Berlin, Jan. 31, 1975); *Three Likes* for Clarinet (1973; Vienna, Aug. 18, 1974); *Stichomythia I* for Flute and Guitar (1976; Philadelphia, Nov. 17, 1978) and *II* for Guitar (1977; Athens, March 13, 1979); *Two Likes* for Contrabass (1976; Boston, Nov. 12, 1989); *Parastasis* for Percussion and Tape (1977; Philadelphia, Dec. 10, 1978); *The Do Quintet* for 2 Trumpets, Horn, Trombone, and Tuba (Philadelphia, April 12, 1978); *Aphierosis* for Flute, Clarinet, Piano, Violin, and Cello (1984; N.Y., Jan. 18, 1985); Octet for Flute, Oboe, Clarinet, Bassoon, 2 Violins, Viola, and Cello (Athens, Dec. 4, 1986); *Ertnos* for 9 Players (1987); *Lament* for Flute (Boston, April 1, 1988); *Commos* for Cello and Piano (1989; Athens, April 3, 1990); *Dexiotechniká Idiómela* for 9 Players (1989); *Palermo Maggio 23, 1992* for Flute and Chamber Ensemble (1992); *Epigrams II* for Violin and Harp (1993); Suite for Brass Quintet and Optional Organ and Percussion (Boston, May 16, 1993); Suite for Guitar (1994–95; N.Y., May 30, 1995); Brass Quintet (1995); *Ten Epigrams* for Mandolin (1995; Boston, Dec. 2, 1998); *Frülingswerwachen* for Saxophone, Percussion, and Piano (Athens, Feb. 1996); *Zøn* for 8 Players (Boston, May 5, 1996); *6X12* for 12 Guitars (1996; Athens, Feb. 18, 1997); *Decem Inventiones* for Woodwind Quintet (1996); *Eros II* for Clarinet, Violin, and Piano (1997); Trio Concertante for 2 Violins and Piano (London, May 1998); *Romantic Duo* for Violin and Harp (1998); *Trios SLS* for Bassoon, Piano, and Cello (1999); *Double Reed and Strings* for Oboe, Violin, Viola, and Cello (1999). **VOCAL:** *Melos*, cantata for Medium Voice and Orch., after Sappho (1962; Athens, April 2, 1967); *Kontakion* for Soloists, Chorus, and String Orch. (Berlin, May 7, 1965); *Climate of Absence* for Medium Voice and Orch. (Munich, Nov. 12, 1968); *Moirologhia for Jani Christou* for Medium Voice and Piano (1970; Athens, Oct. 1, 1971); *Nenikikamen*, cantata for Baritone, Mezzo-soprano, Narrator, Chorus, and Orch. (1971; Munich, Feb. 25, 1972); *Verleih uns frieden* for 3 Choruses (1971–72; Kassel, Sept. 30, 1972); *Die weisse Rose*, cantata for Boys' Chorus, Mixed Chorus, Narrators, Baritone, and Orch. (1974–75; Philadelphia, April 25, 1976); *Chorochronos III* for Medium Voice, Piano or Percussion, and Tape (1975; Berlin, Jan. 26, 1977); *Circle of Thanatos and Genesis*, cantata for Tenor, Narrator, Chorus, and Orch. (1977–78); *Revolution der Toten*, cantata for Soprano, Alto, Tenor, Bass, Chorus, and Orch. (1981); *Epigrams* for Soprano and Chamber Orch. (1981; Chicago, April 16, 1982); *Prometheus*, cantata for Baritone, Narrator, Chorus, and Orch. (1983; Athens, July 2, 1984); *11 Aphighisis* for Medium Voice and Piano (1983; also for Medium Voice and Chamber Orch., 1984, Athens, June 17, 1985, and for Medium Voice and Orch., 1996, Athens, March 9, 1998); *Kriti: Oneiro Mega* for Soprano, Tenor, Narrator, and 7 Players (Iraklion, Sept. 18, 1984); *Paravasis I* (Boston, Dec. 4, 1987) and *II* (1992) for Voice and Tape or Any Solo Instrument; *Oraseis Opsonde* for Chorus, 15 Instruments, and Optional Narrator (Boston, July 4, 1988); *Eros I* for Chorus and Orch. (1990) and *II* for Mezzo-soprano, Clarinet, Violin, and Piano (Athens, Sept. 12, 1997); *Agape* for Chorus, Flute, Brass, and Percussion (Boston, July 26, 1990); *Westwinds* for Soprano and Chamber Ensemble (Boston, May 4, 1991); *Ode* for Soprano and Chamber Ensemble (Athens, Dec. 16, 1992); *Celebration III* for Chorus and Orch. (N.Y., May 20, 1995); *Music of the Myth* for Chorus, Cello, Double Bass, and Percussion (Delphi, Aug. 12, 1996); *Cantata Concertante* for Mezzo-soprano, Violin, Piano, Chorus, and Orch. (1998). —NS/LK/DM

Antunes, Jorge, Brazilian composer and teacher; b. Rio de Janeiro, April 23, 1942. He enrolled at the National School of Music at the Univ. of Brazil in Rio de Janeiro in 1960 to study violin; then pursued training in composition and conducting there (from 1964) with Henrique Morelembaum, José Siqueira, and Eleazar de Carvalho; also took courses in physics at the Univ. and studied composition with Guerra Peixe at Rio de Janeiro's Pró-Arte. In 1969–70 he held a postgraduate scholarship at the Torcuato Di Tella Inst. in Buenos Aires and studied with Ginastera, Luis de Pablo, Eric Salzman, Francisco Kröpfl, and Gerardo Gandini. Following research under König and Greta Vermeulen at the Inst. of Sonology at the Univ. of Utrecht (1970), he went to Paris to work with the Groupe de Recherches Musicales de l'ORTFF (1971–73) and to study with Daniel Charles at the Sorbonne (Ph.D. in music aesthetics, 1977, with the diss. *Son Nouveau, Nouvelle Notation*). Antune's avant-garde convictions prompted him to pursue experimental byways while he was still a student at the Univ. of Brazil when he founded the Chromo-Music Research Studio. In 1967 he organized the music research center and became a prof. of electro-acoustic music at the Villa-Lobos Inst. in Rio de Janeiro. In 1973 he became a teacher of composition at the Univ. of Brasilia, where he later served as prof. of composition and acoustics. He also oversaw its electronic music studio and founded the experimental music group GeMUnB. In 1972 he won Rio de Janeiro's National Composition Competition, and in 1983 its Funarte Prize. In 1991 he was awarded the Vitae Prize of São Paulo.

WORKS: DRAMATIC: *Vivaldia MCMLXXV,* chamber opera buffa (1975); *Qorpo Santo,* opera (1983); *Olga,* opera (1987–93); *The Single-tone King,* children's mini chamber opera (1991). **ORCH.:** *Seresta pra Juvenil* for Strings (1966); *Acusmorfose* (1968); *Tartinia MCMLXX* for Violin and Orch. (1970); *Isomerism* for Chamber Orch. (1970); *Poetica* (1971); *Idiosynchronie* for Chamber Orch. and Electronics (1972); *Scryabinia MCMLXXII* for Piano, Lights, and Chamber Orch. (1972); *Concerto para um Mês de Sol* for Amplified Cello and Orch. (1974); *Concerto para um Mês de Neblina* for Violin and Orch. (1992–93). **CHAMBER:** *Insubstituivel Segunda* for Cello and Tape (1967); *Invocation en Defense de la Machine* for 4 Percussionists and Tape (1968); *Tres Comportamentos* for Violin, Cello, and Piano (1969); *Bartokollagia MCMLXX* for String Quartet (1970); *Tartinia MCMLXX* for Violin and Piano (1970); *Music for 8 Persons Playing Things* (1970–71); *Colluwiguia MXMLXXI* for String Quartet (1971); *Flautatualf* for Flute (1972); *Intervertige* for String Quartet, Wind Quartet, 2 Percussionists, and Electronics (1974); *Vortices* for Wind Quintet (1975); *Tres Impressões Cancioneirigenas* for Flute, Viola, and Cello (1976); *Sighs* for Guitar (1976): *Canto Esthereofonico* for 7 Instruments and Tape (1978); *Microformobiles III: Re-tornos* for Violin and Piano (1982); *Dramatic Polimaniquexixe* for Clarinet, Cello, and Piano (1984); *Modinha pour Mindinha* for 7 Violas (1985); *Serie Enfants* for Violin and Tape (1987); *Lecture* for Bass Clarinet (1990); *Amerika 500* for Flute, Bass Clarinet, Percussion, Piano, Viola, and Cello (1992). **VOCAL:** *Missa Populorum Progressio* for Chorus and Tape (1967); *Acusmorfose 1970* for 2 Narrators, 2 Choruses, and 2 Orchs. (1969); *Concertatio I* for Vocal Trio, Orch., and Tape (1969); *Proudhonia* for Chorus and Tape (1972); *Catastrophe Ultra-violette* for Chorus, Orch., and Tapes (1974); *Elegie Violette pour Monseigneur Romero* for 2 Child Soloists, Children's Chorus, Piano, and

Chamber Orch. (1980); *Arbres de Lasar* for Chorus (1988); *Quatre Petites Pièces de Peuple* for Chorus (1991). **OTHER:** *Microformobiles II* for Flute, Clarinet, Viola, Cello, Percussion, Baritone, and the Public (1972); *Source* for Mezzo-soprano, Flute, Viola, Cello, Piano, Synthesizer, and Tape (1974); *Coreto* for Flute, Clarinet, Horn, Viola, Cello, Piano, and 3 Amateur Actors (1975); *Source vers SP* for Dancer, Synthesizer, Flute, Oboe, Mezzo-soprano, Piano, Horn, Viola, Cello, Tape, Amplification, and Lights (1975); *Sinfonia das Diretas* for Orch., Declamation, Choruses, and Tape (1984).—**NS/LK/DM**

Anzaghi, Davide, Italian composer; b. Milan, Nov. 29, 1936. He studied piano, conducting, and composition (with Maggioni) at the Milan Cons., graduating in 1957, and then took courses in composition with Ghedini and Donatoni in Venice. He subsequently taught at the Milan Cons.

WORKS: ORCH.: *Riturgia* (Venice, Sept. 15, 1972); *Limbale* (Bologna, Nov. 10, 1973); *Ausa* (1973; La Rochelle, France, July 5, 1974); *Egophonie* (1974; Milan, Feb. 3, 1975); *Aur'ore* for Chorus and Orch. (1975–76; Milan, Feb. 4, 1977); *Ermosonio* (1978; Milan, Nov. 30, 1979); *Anco* (1984; Milan, March 30, 1985); 3 piano concertos: No. 1 (1987–88; Milan, March 30, 1989), No. 2 (1990–91); No. 3 (1993), and *Concerto breve* for Clarinet and Orch. (1990–91); Violin Concerto (1992). **CHAMBER:** *Limine* for String Trio (1971); *Aulografia* for Flute (1975); *In-Chiostro* for 2 Violins and Viola (1975; rev. 1982); *Alena* for 10 Wind Instruments (1976); *Remota* for 7 Players (1977); *Alia* for Bass Clarinet and Piano (1980); *Oiseau triste* for Piccolo and Piano (1980); *Soavodia* for Clarinet and Piano (1980); *Làbia* for String Quartet (1982); *Ricrío,* brass octet (1982); *Soliludio* for Flute, Clarinet, Violin, Cello, and Piano (1982); *Mitofania* for Flute, Clarinet, Violin, Cello, Piano, and Percussion (1983); *For Four* for String Quartet (1983); *Elan* for 9 Instruments (1984); *Pri-ter* for String Quartet (1985); *Apogèo* for 5 Instruments (1987); *Tremes* for Viola (1988); *Viol-Once-All* for Cello (1988); *Settimino* for Clarinet, Horn, Bassoon, Piano, Violin, Viola, and Cello (1992); *Invenzione* for Piano and 5 Percussionists (1992). **Piano:** *Segni* (1968); *Ritografia* (1971); *Revenants,* 8 prelude-variations (1981).—**NS/LK/DM**

Apel, Willi, eminent German-American musicologist; b. Konitz, Oct. 10, 1893; d. Bloomington, Ind., March 14, 1988. He studied mathematics at the univs. of Bonn and Munich (1912–14), and then of Berlin (1918–21), where he returned in 1936 to take his Ph.D. with the diss. *Accidentien und Tonalität in den Musikdenkmälern des 15. und 16. Jahrhunderts* (publ. in Berlin, 1936; 2nd ed., Aug., 1972). After emigrating to the U.S., he taught at Harvard Univ. (1938–42). From 1950 to 1964 he was a prof. of music at Ind. Univ. in Bloomington, where he continued to lecture as prof. emeritus until 1970. In 1971 he was made an honorary member of the American Musicological Soc. He was founding ed. of the Corpus of Early Keyboard Music and contributed 10 vols. to the series. Apel was an authority on 14th-century music, the history of early instrumental music, and Latin chant. He acknowledged his lack of interest in either opera or modern developments in music; he was a musical purist who regarded the developments of musical composition after the era of Bach as of passing significance to music history.

WRITINGS: *Die Fuge* (Berlin, 1932); ed. *Musik aus früher Zeit für Klavier* (2 vols., Mainz, 1934); *The Notation of Polyphonic*

Music, 900–1600 (Cambridge, Mass., 1942; 5th ed., rev., 1961; Ger. tr., rev., 1970); ed. *The Harvard Dictionary of Music* (Cambridge, Mass, 1944; 2nd ed., rev. and enl., 1969); ed. with A. Davison, *Historical Anthology of Music* (Cambridge, Mass.; Vol. I, 1946; 2nd ed., rev., 1950; Vol. II, 1950); *Masters of the Keyboard* (Cambridge, Mass., 1947); *Gregorian Chant* (Bloomington, Ind., 1958); *Geschichte der Orgel- und Klaviermusik bis 1700* (Kassel, 1967; Eng. tr., rev., 1972); *Die italienische Violinmusik im 17. Jahrhundert* (Wiesbaden, 1983; Eng. tr., 1990); *Medieval Music: Collected Articles and Reviews* (Stuttgart, 1986); with R. Schechner, *By Means of Performance: Intercultural Studies of Theatre and Ritual* (Cambridge, 1990).

BIBL.: H. Tischler, ed., *Essays in Musicology: A Birthday Offering for W. A.* (Bloomington, Ind., 1968).—**NS/LK/DM**

Aperghis, Georges, innovative Greek composer; b. Athens, Dec. 23, 1945. After studies with Papaioannou in Athens, he settled in Paris in 1963 and completed his training with Xenakis, who initiated him into the mysteries of ultramodern techniques involving such arcana as musical indeterminacy and audiovisual coordinates in spatial projection. He was founder-director of the Atelier Théâter et Musique (1976–91), an experimental workshop for theater, music, and language. From 1992 he pursued his career in Nanterre. Aperghis has followed an avant-garde path as a composer, and has produced numerous theater pieces.

WORKS: DRAMATIC: Opera: *Pandaemonium* (1973); *Jacques le Gataliste* (1974); *Histoires de loup* (1976); *Je vous dis que je suis mort* (1978); *Liebestod* (1981); *L'écharpe rouge* (1984); *Tristes Tropiques* (Strasbourg, Oct. 5, 1996); numerous music theater pieces. **ORCH.:** *Contrepoint* (1967); *Libretto* (1968); *Symplexis* for 22 Jazz Soloists and Orch. (1970); *Die Wände haben Ohren* (1972); Overture (1973); *Declamations* (1990). **CHAMBER:** *Antistixis A* for 3 String Quartets (1964–65); *Contrepoint* for 3 String Quartets, Piano, Trombone, and Percussion (1968); Quartet for 4 Double Basses (1970); Quartet for 4 Percussionists (1970); *Parenthèses* for Chamber Ensemble (1977); *Ilios* for 10 Instruments (1978); *Triangle carré* for String Quartet and Percussion Trio (1989). **VOCAL:** *Vesper*, oratorio (1970); *Les lauriers sont coupés* for Voice and Chamber Ensemble (1975); *Un musée de l'homme*, oratorio (1980); *Tingel- Tangel* for Voice, Accordion, and Percussion (1990); *Ritournelles* for 2 Baritones and 9 Instruments (1992).—**NS/LK/DM**

ApIvor, Denis, Irish-born English composer of Welsh descent; b. Collinstown, April 14, 1916. He studied at the Univ. of Wales (1933–34) and Univ. Coll., London (1934–39), and received training in composition from Patrick Hadley and Alan Rawsthorne in London (1937–39). He contributed articles to several books and music journals, ed. works by and wrote articles on Bernard van Dieren, and was active as a translator. ApIvor's works can be divided into three periods: An early melodically based, chromatically inflected period, much influenced by Van Dieren and Peter Warlock through the 1950s; a second, serialist, abstract, and intellectual period until the early 1980s; and a third, recent phase of renewed simplicity. The associations he delineates via extra-musical elements, painting, etc., in various works are most ingenious.

WORKS: DRAMATIC: Opera: *She Stoops to Conquer*, after Goldsmith (1943–47; rev. 1976–77); *Yerma*, after García

Lorca (1955–58); *Ubu roi*, after Jarry (1965–66); *Bouvard and Pecuchet*, after Flaubert (1970). **Ballet:** *The Goodman of Paris* (1951); *A Mirror for Witches* (1951); *Blood Wedding* (1953); *Veneziana* (1953); *Saudades* (1954); *Corporal Jan* (1967); *Glide the Dark Door Wide* (1977). **ORCH.:** *Nocturne* for Strings (1938); Piano Concerto (1948; rev. 1954); 2 violin concertos (1950, 1975); 5 syms. (1952; 1963; 1978–79; 1985; 1991); Guitar Concertino (1953); *Overtones*, after Paul Klee's paintings (1961–62); Triple Concerto for String Trio and String Orch. (1967); *Tarot* for Chamber Orch. (1968); *Neumes*, variations (1969); *El Silencio Ondulado* for Guitar and Chamber Orch. (1972); Cello Concerto (1976–77); *Fantasy Concertante* for Horn and Orch. (1980). **CHAMBER:** Violin Sonata (1944–45); *Concertante* for Clarinet, Piano, and Percussion (1944–45); Wind Quintet (1960); *Mutations* for Cello and Piano (1962); 3 string quartets (1964; 1976; 1989–90); *Crystals* for Percussion, Hammond Organ, Guitar, and Double Bass (1964–65); *Harp, Piano, Piano-Harp* (1966); *Ten-String Design* for Violin and Guitar (1968); *Exotics Theatre* for Chamber Ensemble (1972); *Psycho-pieces* for Clarinet and Piano (1973); Clarinet Quintet (1975); *Chant Eolien* for Oboe and Piano (1977); *Duo Concertante* for Horn and Piano (1981); *Vista* for Double Wind Quintet (1983); *Cinquefoil*, trio for Violin, Flute, and Guitar (1984); *Pieces of 5* for Saxophone (1992); Saxophone Sonatina (1992); Violin Sonatina (1992); *In the Landscape of Spring*, septet (1993); also solo piano, organ, and guitar pieces. **VOCAL:** *The Hollow Men*, cantata after T. S. Eliot (1939; BBC, London, Feb. 21, 1950); *Six Songs of García Lorca* for Voice and Piano or Guitar (1945–46); *Estella Marina* for Chorus and Strings or Organ (1946); *Thamar and Amnon* for Soloists, Chorus, and Orch., after García Lorca (1953–54); Cantata, after Dylan Thomas (1960); *Chorales* for Chorus and Orch., after Hugh Manning (1964–65); *Resonance of the Southern Flora* for Chorus, Organ, and Orch., after Paul Klee (1972); *Fern Hill* for Tenor and 11 Instruments, after Dylan Thomas (1973); *Bats* for Tenor, Piccolo, Violin, and Percussion (1979); *Seven Songs* for Chorus and Small Orch. (1983); *Love's Season* for Voice and String Quintet or Piano (1983); *Majestatas Dei Ultra Stellas* for Chorus and Small Orch. or Piano (1986); *T. S. Eliot Songs* for Voice and Piano (1994); *Lady of Silences* for Small Chorus and Chamber Orch., after T. S. Eliot (1994); *Canzona Delle Lettere Amorose* for Soprano, Baritone, Alto Saxophone, and Bass Guitar (1994); *Give me your flowers, O Spring* for Tenor and 2 Guitars (1996); *Lamentaciones* for Voice and Piano, after García Lorca (1996). **OTHER:** Arrangement of Busoni's *Fantasia contrappuntistica* for Orch. (1940; rev. 1946, 1977), other arrangements, and editions.—**NS/LK/DM**

Aponte-Ledée, Rafael, Puerto Rican composer and teacher; b. Guayama, Oct. 15, 1938. He studied composition at the Madrid Cons. (1957–63), where he completed his training with C. Halffter (1963–64); then took courses with Ginastera at the Latin American Center of Advanced Musical Studies at the Di Tella Inst. in Buenos Aires (1965–66). Returning to Puerto Rico, he founded in San Juan, with the collaboration of Francis Schwartz, the Fluxus group for the promotion of new music (1967); taught composition and theory at the Univ. of Puerto Rico (1968–74) and at the Puerto Rico Cons. (from 1968). His music is highly advanced, employing nearly every conceivable technique of the cosmopolitan avant-garde.

WORKS: *Tema y 6 Diferencias* for Piano (1963; rev. 1986); *Dialogantes 1* for Flute and Violin (1965) and *2* for 3 Flutes, 3 Trombones, and 3 Clarinets (1968); *Elejía* for 13 Strings (1965; also for 50 Strings, 1967); *Presagio de Pájaros muertos* for Narrator and Tape (1966); *Impulsos: In memoriam Julia de Burgos* for Orch. (1967); *Epíthasis* for 3 Oboes, 2 Trombones, Double Bass, and 3 Percussionists (1967); *La ventana abierta* for 3 Mezzo-sopranos, 3 Flutes, Clarinet, Trumpet, 2 Percussionists, Celesta, Piano, Violin, Cello, and Double Bass (1968; also for 3 Mezzo-sopranos, Flutes, Clarinet, 2 Trumpets, Horn, 2 Percussionists, Guitar, Piano, and 2 String Quartets, 1969); *Streptomicyne* for Soprano, Flute, Clarinet, Trumpet, and Piano (1970); *SSSSSS²* for Double Bass, 3 Flutes, Trumpet, and Percussion (1971); *Volúmenes* for Piano (1971); *Elvira en sombras* for Piano and Orch. (1973); *Estravagario, In memoriam Salvador Allende* for Orch. and Tape (1973); *Cuídese de los angeles que caen*, musique concrète (1974); *Los huevos de Pandora* for Clarinet and Tape (1974); *El palacio en sombras* for Orch. without Violins and Cellos (1977); *Estas sombras* for Prepared Piano (1978); *A flor de piel* for 2 Sopranos and Orch. (1980); *Asiento en el Paraíso* for Clarinet, Violin, Cello, and Piano (1984); *Dos cuentos* for Orch. (1986); Cantata for Soli and Orch. (1986); *3 Bagatelles* for Guitar (1987); *Azaleas* for Clarinet (1988); *La muchacha de la bragas de oro* for Orch. (1989); *Canción de albada y Epitafio* for Orch. (1991). —NS/LK/DM

Apostel, Hans Erich (Heinrich), German-born Austrian composer and teacher; b. Karlsruhe, Jan. 22, 1901; d. Vienna, Nov. 30, 1972. He studied in Karlsruhe before settling in Vienna in 1921, where he completed his training with Schoenberg and Berg. He was an ed. at Universal Edition and in that capacity prepared for publication the posthumous works of Berg. He was also active as a teacher. Among his honors were the grand prizes of Vienna (1948) and the Republic of Austria (1957). His works were written in an atonal expressionist style until 1957 when he embraced strict serialism. He also experimented in Klangfarben effects, and applied audible overtones in his piano pieces by holding down the keys without actually striking them.

WORKS: ORCH.: Adagio for Strings, 2 Harps, Celesta, and Piano (1937); *Variationen über ein Thema von Joseph Haydn* (1949; Zurich, May 10, 1951); *Ballade* (1955); *Variations on 3 Folk Songs* for Small Orch. (1956); *Rondo ritmico* (1957); Piano Concerto (1958; Venice, Sept. 24, 1959); *5 Austrian Miniatures* (1959); Kammersymphonie (1965–67; Vienna, June 4, 1968); *Epitaph* for Strings (1969); *Haydn-Variationen, Teil II: Paralipomena dodekaphonica* (1969–70; Donawitz, Oct. 29, 1970); *Passacaglia* (2nd mvt. of an unfinished *Concerto for Orchestra*, 1972; London, July 10, 1974). **CHAMBER:** 2 string quartets (1935, 1956); Quartet for Flute, Clarinet, Horn, and Bassoon (1947–49); sonatinas for Solo Flute (1951), Clarinet (1951), Bassoon (1951), Oboe (1964), and Horn (1964); *5 Bagatelles* for Flute, Clarinet, and Bassoon (1952); *Intrada* for Brass and Percussion (1954); *Studie* for Flute, Violin, and Guitar (1958; rev. 1964); *6 épigrammes* for String Quartet (1962); Cello Sonata (1962); *Kleine Kammerkonzert* for Flute, Viola, and Guitar (1964); *Fischerhaus- Serenade* for 4 Woodwinds, 3 Brasses, and String Quartet (1971); *12 Stücke für 12 Musici* for 4 Winds, 3 Brasses, and 5 Strings (1972). **Piano:** Sonata (1929); *Sonatina ritmica* (1934); *Kubiniana*, 10 pieces (1945–50); *Suite concise*, 7 pieces (1955); *Fantasie* (1959). **VOCAL:** Requiem for Chorus and Orch., after Rilke (1933; Vienna Radio, May 3, 1958); *5 Lieder*, after Hölderlin, for Low Voice and Orch. (1939–40); *3 Lieder*, after Trakl, for Low Woman's Voice, 4 Violins, 2 Cellos, and Double Bass (1951); *5 Lieder* for Medium Voice, Flute, Clarinet, and Bassoon (1953); *Ode* for Alto and Chorus (1962).—NS/LK/DM

Appeldoorn, Dina, Dutch composer; b. Rotterdam, Feb. 26, 1884; d. The Hague, Dec. 4, 1938. She was the composer of several works in the Romantic style, including 2 symphonic poems, *Noordzee* and *Volkfeest*. She also wrote chamber music and songs.—NS/LK/DM

Appledorn, Mary Jeanne van
See van Appledorn, Mary Jeanne

Appenzeller, Benedictus, Netherlands composer and singer; b. c. 1484; d. after 1558. He served as maître de chapelle to Mary of Hungary, the regent of the Netherlands, in Brussels from 1537 until about 1552. Among his extant works are 23 chansons (1542) and several motets. MSS attributions have often confused him with Benedictus Ducis.

BIBL.: D. Bartha, *Benedictus Ducis und A.* (Wolfenbüttel, 1930); G. Thompson, *B. A.: Composer for Mary of Hungary* (diss., Univ. of N.C., 1975).—NS/LK/DM

Appia, Edmond, Swiss conductor and pedagogue; b. Turin, May 7, 1894; d. Geneva, Feb. 12, 1961. He studied violin with Marteau at the Geneva Cons., with Capet in Paris, and at the Brussels Cons. (premier prix, 1920). He was a prof. at the Lausanne Cons. (1924–43) and at the Geneva Cons. (1934–61). After touring widely as a violinist (1932–35), he was appointed to the position of 2nd conductor of the Lausanne Radio Orch. in 1935. From 1938 he served as chief conductor of the Geneva Radio Orch. Appia maintained an exhaustive repertoire, but was especially known for his championship of contemporary Swiss composers.

BIBL.: *Hommage à E. A. (1894–1961): Temoignages de ses amis* (Geneva, 1961).—NS/LK/DM

Applebaum, Edward, American composer; b. Los Angeles, Sept. 28, 1937. He had piano lessons in his youth, and later studied composition with Lazarof and Foss at the Univ. of Calif. at Los Angeles (Ph.D., 1966). In 1969 he was composer-in-residence of the Oakland Sym. Orch. In 1971, became a prof. of theory and composition at the Univ. of Calif. at Santa Barbara. From 1985 to 1987 he was composer-in-residence of the Santa Barbara Sym. Orch., and then of the Music Academy of the West in Santa Barbara (1988). In 1989 he became prof. of composition and director of the new-music ensemble at Fla. State Univ. in Tallahassee. He served as dean (1991–92) and as prof. of music (1991–94) at Edith Cowan Univ. in Perth, Australia.

WORKS: Piano Sonata (1965); String Trio (1966); Concerto for Viola and Chamber Orch. (1967); *Montages* for Clarinet, Cello, and Piano (1968); *Shantih* for Cello and Piano (1969); 4 syms.: No. 1 (1970), No. 2 (St. Louis, Oct. 6, 1983), No. 3 (1989), and No. 4 (1995); *Foci* for Viola and Piano (1971); *The Face in the Cameo* for Clarinet and Piano (1973); *The Frieze of Life*, chamber opera (1974); *To Remember*, trio for Clarinet, Cello, and Piano (1976); *The Garden* for Soprano, Chamber Ensemble, and Tape (1979); *Prelude* for String Quartet (1984); *And with, and to* for Men's Chorus (1984); *The Princess in the Garden* for String Orch. (1985); *Dreams and Voyage*, piano concerto (1986); *Night Waltz*, guitar concerto (1987); *The Waltz in 2* for Narrator and Orch. (1988); *Whispers of Yesterday* for Woodwind Quintet (1988); *Song of the Sparrows*, oratorio for Soloists, Narrator, Choruses, and Orch. (1988).—NS/LK/DM

Applebaum, Louis, Canadian composer, administrator, and conductor; b. Toronto, April 3, 1918; d. April 20, 2000. He studied in Toronto at the Cons. of Music and at the Univ., his principal mentors being Boris Berlin in piano and Willan, Leo Smith, and Mac-Millan in theory; he then pursued training in composition in N.Y. as a scholarship student of Harris and Wagenaar (1940–41). Returning to Canada, he served as music director of the National Film Board (1942–48), for which he composed scores for some 250 films (1942–60). He also served as music director of World Today films in N.Y. (1946–49). From 1955 to 1960 he oversaw the musical activities at the Stratford (Ontario) Festival, for which he composed much incidental music. He served as president of Group Four productions, makers of television documentaries and programs, from 1960 to 1966. From 1971 to 1980 he was executive director of the Ontario Arts Council. From 1980 to 1982 he was chairman of the Federal Cultural Policy Review Committee. He was interim artistic director of the Guelph Spring Festival in 1988–89, and also president of the Composers, Authors, and Publishers Assn. of Canada from 1988 to 1990, and its successor, the Soc. of Composers, Authors, and Music Publishers of Canada, from 1990 to 1992. In 1977 he was made an Officer of the Order of Canada. Applebaum's long association with films and stage productions resulted in a particularly assured command in the composing of dramatic scores.

WORKS: DRAMATIC: *Suite of Miniature Dances*, ballet (1953); *Legend of the North*, ballet (1957); *Ride a Pink Horse*, musical comedy (1959); *Homage*, ballet (1969); *The Legend of Sleepy Hollow*, ballet (1991); *So You Think You're Mozart?*, musical play (1991); incidental music for over 50 plays; film scores; innumerable scores for radio and television. **ORCH.:** *East by North* (1947); *Revival Meeting and Finale* from *Barbara Allen* (1964); *Dialogue with Footnotes* for Big Jazz and Orch. (1984); *Celebration York* for Band (1985); *High Spirits* for Band (1986). **CHAMBER:** *Touch Wood* for Piano (1969); *Essay* for Flute (1973); *Keep Moving* for Piano (1973); *4 Dances in a Nineteenth Century Style* for Brass Quintet (1987). **VOCAL:** *Cry of the Prophet* for Baritone and Piano (1951; rev. 1952); *A Folio of Shakespearean Songs* for Medium Voice and Piano (1954–87); *Inunit*, 5 episodes for Voice and Orch. (1977); *Of Love and High Times* for Soprano, Chorus, Flute, Horn, and Percussion (1981); *The Harper of the Stones* for Narrator and Chamber Ensemble (1987). **OTHER:** Many fanfares and ceremonial pieces. **—NS/LK/DM**

Appleby, Thomas, English organist and composer; b. probably in Lincoln, 1488; d. there, c. 1562. He was organist at Lincoln Cathedral (1538–39). After serving as organist at Magdalen Coll., Oxford (1539–41), he resumed his post at Lincoln Cathedral. He composed sacred works.**—LK/DM**

Appleman, Rich, jazz bassist; b. Altoona, Pa., March 12, 1946. Appleman is chair of bass at the Berklee Coll. of Music, where he earned his bachelors degree in music. He has performed with Lionel Hampton, Gregory Hines, The Fringe, and The Boston Pops Orch., and has worked in the pit bands for theater productions of *The Secret Garden*, *Ain't Misbehavin'*, *A Chorus Line*, *Cats*, *Les Miserables*, *Grease*, and *West Side Story*. The electric bass editor for the International Society of Bassists, Appleman is also a columnist for *Bass Player* magazine. He has made numerous recordings with The Fringe and others, and has played on many radio and television jingles.

WRITINGS: With Joseph Viola, *Contemporary Rhythm for Electric Bass; Chord Studies for Electric Bass.*—**LP**

Appleton, Jon (Howard), American composer and teacher; b. Los Angeles, Jan. 4, 1939. He studied at Reed Coll. (B.A., 1961), with Imbrie in Berkeley, Calif. (1961–62), with Keller at the Univ. of Ore. (M.A., 1965), and with Ussachevsky at the Columbia-Princeton Electronic Music Center (1965–66). In 1966–67 he taught at Oakland Univ. in Rochester, Mich. In 1967 he joined the faculty of Dartmouth Coll., where he founded its Bregman Electronic Music Studio and, in 1979, received an endowed chair. With the engineer Sydney Alonso and the software designer Cameron Jones, Appleton developed the Dartmouth Digital Synthesizer (1972–74) and the Synclavier, a polyphonic digital synthesizer. He received Guggenheim and Fulbright fellowships (1970) and 2 NEA awards (1976). Appleton has written on the technology, theory, aesthetics, and social role of music. With R. Perera, he ed. the anthology *The Development and Practice of Electronic Music* (1975). He publ. *21st-Century Musical Instruments: Hardware and Software* (1989). In addition to his many electronic scores, he has also composed tonal works for acoustic instruments.

WORKS: DRAMATIC: Theater Music: *The Ghost Sonata* (1969); *Subject to Fits* (1978); *Death Takes a Holiday* (1987); *Aunt Dan and Lemon* (1988). **Dance Music:** *Pilobolus* (1971); *Spyrogyra* (1972); *Cameo* (1972); *Anaendrom* (1972); *Aubade* (1973); *Ciona* (1974); *Otahiti* (1978); *The Sydsing Camklang* (1978); *Prelude* (1979); *Nukuoro* (1980); *Beginnings* (1980); *The Tale of William Mariner* (1980). **Film:** *Nobody Knows Everything* (1965); *Anuszkiewicz* (1968); *Scene Unobserved* (1969; in collaboration with W. Wadham, P. Payne, and J. Mellquist); *Computer Graphics at 100 Baud* (1969); *Charlie Item and Double X* (1970); *Glory!, Glory!* (1971); *Arriflex 16SR* (1978); *Hay Fever* (1988); *Rassias in China* (1991). **ORCH.:** *After "Nude Descending a Staircase"* (1965). **CHAMBER:** *2 Movements* for Woodwind Quintet (1963); *6 Movements* for Woodwind Quintet (1964); *4 Explorations* for Violin and Piano (1964); *4 Inventions* for 2 Flutes (1965); *Winesburg, Ohio* for Flute, Clarinet, Violin, Cello, and Piano (1972); *String Quartet* (1976); *Soviet-American Dances* for Flute, Clarinet, Violin, Viola, Cello, Percussion, and Synclavier (1984); *Duo for Oscar* for Piano and Synclavier (1985); *The Endless Melody* for Clarinet and Synclavier (1986); *...to the Islands* for Violin, Saxophone, Accordion, and Contrabass (1989); *Nihon No Omide* for Violin (1996). **Piano:** *3 Lyrics* (1963); Sonata No. 2 (1968); *Duobatoni* for 2 Pianos (1994); *The Turkina Suite* (1995); *Quatre regards sur le Parc du Roy d'Espagne* for Piano, 4-Hands (1995); *Eight Hands* for 2 Pianos, 8-Hands (1996). **VOCAL:** *The American Songs* for Tenor and Piano or Orch. (1966); *Ballad of the Soldier* for Men's Voices, after Brecht (1974); *Sonaria* for 4 Voices and Synclavier (1978); *Le Dernier Voyage* for Children's Chorus, Narrator, and Synclavier (1989); *HOPI: La Naissance du désert* for Children's Chorus and Orch. (1993). **OTHER:** *Double Structure*, mixed media piece (1971; in collaboration with C. Wolff); *The Lament of Kamuela* for Chorus, Tape, Hawaiian Singer, Japanese Classical Singer, Rock Band, Film, and Video (1983); over 50 electronic pieces (1966–97). **—NS/LK/DM**

Aprile, Giuseppe, Italian castrato soprano, known as **Sciroletto** and **Scirolino** after his teacher; b. Martina Franca, Apulia, Oct. 28, 1731; d. there, Jan. 11, 1813. He studied voice with his father, then studied in Naples with Girolamo Abos and Gregorio Sciroli. After singing at the Naples royal chapel in 1752, he made his operatic debut at Naples's Teatro San Carlo in 1753. He then sang regularly at the Württemberg court in Stuttgart from 1765 to 1769, and also toured widely. He subsequently sang in Italy, being named 1st soprano at the Naples royal chapel in 1783. After making his final public appearance in 1785, he devoted himself to teaching voice, numbering among his students Cimarosa.

WRITINGS: *The Modern Italian Method of Singing, with a Variety of Progressive Examples and Thirty-six Solfeggi* (London, 1791).—**NS/LK/DM**

Apthorp, William Foster, American music critic; b. Boston, Mass., Oct. 24, 1848; d. Vevey, Switzerland, Feb. 19, 1913. A graduate of Harvard Univ. (1869), he studied music with Paine. He taught music at the New England Cons. of Music in Boston and lectured on music history at Boston Univ. He wrote music criticism for the *Atlantic Monthly* (1872–77) and was music and drama critic on the *Boston Evening Transcript* (1881–1903). In his criticisms Apthorp violently opposed new Russian, French, and German music (his intemperate attacks on Tchaikovsky elicited protests from his readers). Apthorp was also the annotator of the Boston Sym. Orch. programs (1892–1901).

WRITINGS: *Musicians and Music Lovers* (N.Y., 1894); *By the Way* (essay collection in 2 vols.: "About Music" and "About Musicians"; Boston, 1898); *The Opera, Past and Present* (N.Y., 1901); co-ed. *Scribner's Cyclopedia of Music and Musicians* (N.Y., 1888–90).—**NS/LK/DM**

Aragall (y Garriga), Giacomo (actually, **Jaime**), Spanish tenor; b. Barcelona, June 6, 1939. He was a pupil of Francesco Puig in Barcelona and of Vladimiro Badiali in Milan. In 1963 he won the Verdi Competition in Busseto, sang Gastone in *Jérusalem* in Venice, and appeared as Mascagni's Fritz at Milan's La Scala. In 1966 he made his London debut at Covent Garden as the Duke of Mantua and his Vienna State Opera debut as Rodolfo. On Sept. 19, 1968, he made his Metropolitan Opera debut in N.Y. as the Duke of Mantua. He also sang in Rome, Berlin, Hamburg, Chicago, San Francisco, and other opera centers. In 1992 he sang in the gala ceremonies for the Olympic Games in Barcelona. He appeared as Cavaradossi at the Opéra de la Bastille in Paris in 1994. Among his other roles were Edgardo and Alfredo.—**NS/LK/DM**

Araia or **Araja, Francesco,** Italian composer; b. Naples, June 25, 1709; d. c. 1770. He devoted himself mainly to writing serious operas. In 1735 he was called to the Russian court in St. Petersburg as maestro di cappella, where he produced his most celebrated opera, *Cephalus and Procris* (March 9, 1755), the first such score sung in the Russian language. After an Italian sojourn (1740–42), he resumed his duties in St. Petersburg. In 1759 he retired to Italy, but visited Russia again in 1762 before settling in Bologna.

WORKS: DRAMATIC: O p e r a : *Berenice* (Florence, 1730); *Ciro riconosciuto* (Rome, Carnival 1731); *Il Cleomene* (Rome, 1731); *La forza dell'amore e dell'odio* (Milan, Jan. 1734); *Lucio Vero* (Venice, Carnival 1735); *Il finto Nino, overo La Semiramide riconosciuta* (St. Petersburg, Feb. 9, 1737); *Artaserse* (St. Petersburg, Feb. 9, 1738); *Seleuco* (Moscow, May 7, 1744); *Scipione* (St. Petersburg, Sept. 4 or 5, 1745); *Mitridate* (St. Petersburgs, May 7, 1747); *L'asilo della pace* (St. Petersburg, May 7, 1748); *Bellerofonte* (St. Petersburg, Dec. 9, 1750); *Eudossa incoronata, o sia Teodosio II* (St. Petersburg, May 9, 1751); *Cephalus and Procris* (St. Petersburg, March 9, 1755); *Amor prigioniero* (Oranienbaum, 1755); *Alessandro nell'Indie* (St. Petersburg, Dec. 29, 1755). **OTHER:** Various other stage pieces; *S. Andrea Corsini*, oratorio (Rome, 1731); cantatas; keyboard pieces. —**NS/LK/DM**

Araiza, (José) Francisco, Mexican tenor; b. Mexico City, Oct. 4, 1950. He was a student of Irma Gonzales at the Univ. of Mexico City, where he sang in its choir. He made his concert debut in Mexico City in 1969, where he subsequently appeared for the first time in opera in 1970 as Jaquino. Following additional training with Richard Holm and Erik Werba in Munich, he was a member of the Karlsruhe (1974–77) and Zürich (from 1977) operas. He appeared as a guest artist in Munich, Paris, Vienna, Salzburg, Bayreuth, San Francisco, Chicago, and other opera centers. On March 12, 1984, he made his Metropolitan Opera debut in N.Y. as Belmonte. He scored remarkable success as Lohengrin in Venice in 1990 and as Walther von Stolzing at the Metropolitan Opera in 1993. In 1997 he portrayed Faust at the Zürich Opera. He also had fine success as a concert and lieder artist. Among his other distinguished operatic roles were Tamino, Ferrando, Gounod's Faust, Massenet's Des Grieux, Alfredo, and Rodolfo. —**NS/LK/DM**

Araki, James (Jimmy), bebop alto saxophonist and trumpeter; b. Nov. 6, 1927; d. Honolulu, Hawaii, Dec. 13, 1994. Araki is a Japanese-American credited with introducing bebop to Japanese musicians. After spending the war years at the Gila River Detention Center and performing in camp bands, Araki was drafted out of college to serve in the U.S. Army as a translator at the Tokyo War Crimes tribunal. In his spare time Araki studied bebop theory and performance techniques, which he went on to share with native musicians. His compositions and arrangements ("A.P.O. 500," "Rock Romondo," "Boogie in C," "Tokyo Riff," and "A Night in Pakistan") formed the basis for the first "modern jazz" recording session in Japan in August 1947—performed, ironically, by an all-star band of traditional and swing musicians known as The Victor Hot Club. The following year Araki and jazz critic Nogawa Kobun organized a bebop study group and rehearsal band to perform Araki's original compositions and arrangements in Tokyo. Araki returned to the U.S. in October 1949; after a brief stint performing with Lionel Hampton, Araki embarked on a successful career as a scholar of Japanese literature at the Univ. of Hawaii at Manoa. He returned to Japan often throughout his career, occasionally jamming with his old friends (and arranging a recording session in 1959). In 1991, he was awarded the Order of the Rising Sun, Fourth Class, for his contributions to the study of Japanese literature and the promotion of jazz in Japan.

Disc.: *Jazz Beat: Midnight Jazz Session* (1959); *Kogane jidai no Victor Hot Club* (1973).—ETA

Arakishvili, Dmitri (Ignatievich),
Russian composer, teacher, and conductor; b. Vladikavkaz, Feb. 23, 1873; d. Tbilisi, Aug. 13, 1953. He studied composition in Moscow with Ilyinsky at the Phil. Inst. and privately with Gretchaninov. In 1918 he settled in Tiflis. He composed one of the earliest national Georgian operas, *The Legend of Shota Rustaveli* (Tiflis, Feb. 5, 1919). He also wrote a comic opera, *Dinara* (1926), film music, 3 syms. (1934, 1942, 1951), and some 80 songs. In 1929 he was made a People's Artist of the Georgian SSR, and in 1950 he was awarded the USSR State Prize.—**NS/LK/DM**

Arámbarri (y Garate), Jesús,
Spanish conductor, pedagogue, and composer; b. Bilbao, April 13, 1902; d. Madrid, July 11, 1960. After graduating from the Cons. Vizcaino de Música in Bilbao (1928), he went to Paris and studied composition with Le Flem and Dukas, and conducting with Golschmann. He completed his training in conducting with Weingartner in Basel (1932). In 1933 he returned to Bilbao as conductor of the municipal orch. In 1953 he went to Madrid as conductor of the concert orch. and as a prof. at the Cons. Among his works were vocal pieces, chamber music, and piano works.—**LK/DM**

Aranaz y Vides, Pedro,
Spanish composer and priest; b. Tudela, Navarre (baptized), May 2, 1740; d. Cuenca, Sept. 24, 1820. He studied with Luis Serra at El Pilar Cathedral in Saragossa. From 1769 to 1797 he was maestro de capilla at Cuenca Cathedral. In 1773 he became a priest. He wrote numerous sacred works and some fine tonadillas.—**LK/DM**

Arangi-Lombardi, Giannina,
Italian soprano; b. Marigliano, near Naples, June 20, 1891; d. Milan, July 9, 1951. She studied with Beniamino Carelli at the Cons. di S. Pietro a Majella in Naples. She made her operatic debut as a mezzo-soprano in 1920 at the Teatro Costanzi in Rome as Lola in *Cavalleria rusticana*. After further training from Adelina Sthele in Milan, she sang soprano roles from 1923; appeared at La Scala in Milan (1924–30). In 1928 she accompanied Melba on an Australian tour; also sang in South America. After retiring from the stage, she taught voice at the Milan Cons. (1937–47) and, later, in Ankara. She was at her best in the lyrico- dramatic roles of the Italian repertoire. —**NS/LK/DM**

d'Arányi (de Hunyadvar), Jelly (Eva),
Hungarian-born English violinist, grandniece of **Joseph Joachim** and sister of **Adila Fachiri**; b. Budapest, May 30, 1893; d. Florence, March 30, 1966. She studied with Hubay in Budapest and Grunfeld in Vienna. In 1908 she made her debut in Vienna with her sister. In 1909 she

played for the first time in England. After settling there in 1913, she became a naturalized British subject. She was the soloist in the premiere of Ravel's *Tzigane* for Violin and Orch. (Paris, Dec. 7, 1924) and Vaughan Williams's *Concerto accademico* for Violin and String Orch. (London, Nov. 6, 1925). On Nov. 26, 1927, she made her U.S. debut in recital in N.Y. In addition to her solo appearances, she also played in a trio with Guilhermina Suggia and Fanny Davies, and performed with Felix Salmond and Myra Hess. In 1946 she was made a Commander of the Order of the British Empire.

BIBL.: J. Macleod, *The Sister's d'A.* (London, 1969). —**NS/LK/DM**

Arapov, Boris (Alexandrovich),
eminent Russian composer and pedagogue; b. St. Petersburg, Sept. 12, 1905; d. there, Jan. 27, 1992. He was a scion of an intellectual family; his grandfather was a lawyer; his father was a naturalist. He spent his childhood in Poltava, where he received his early musical training. In 1921 the family returned to St. Petersburg (later renamed Petrograd) and he studied composition with Shcherbachev at the Cons. there, graduating in 1930. He was appointed to its faculty as an instructor (1930) and later prof. (1940). Among his pupils were many Soviet composers of stature, including Dmitri Tolstoy, Falik, Uspensky, Banshchikov, Knaifel, and Sergei Slonimsky. The years 1941–44 Arapov spent in Tashkent, in Uzbekistan, where the entire faculty of the Leningrad Cons. was evacuated during the siege of Leningrad. There he studied indigenous folklore, and wrote an Uzbeki opera, *Khodja Nasreddin*. After the siege was lifted, Arapov returned to Leningrad, resumed his pedagogical duties, and continued to compose. In 1955–56 he was in China, where he wrote several works on Chinese themes. In 1959 he visited Korea, and composed a sym. using the pentatonic Korean modes. Arapov's compositions represent to perfection the evolutionary character of Soviet music, taking their source in the Russian traditions of the previous centuries, making ample use of ethnic materials of the constituent regions of the immense territory of the U.S.S.R., and integrating the native homophonic melorhythms in an increasingly complex tapestry of colorful fabrics, richly ornamented with occasional application of such modern devices as dodecaphonic melodic structures. However, Arapov was also able to produce a virtuoso display of instrumental techniques for piano and other instruments.

Works: DRAMATIC: Opera: *Khodja Nasreddin* (Tashkent, April 1944); *Frigate Victory*, after Pushkin (radio premiere, Leningrad, Oct. 12, 1959); *Rain*, after Somerset Maugham (concert perf., Leningrad, April 25, 1968). **Ballet:** *The Picture of Dorian Gray* (1971; concert perf., Leningrad, April 20, 1973). **Other:** Film scores. **ORCH.:** *Fugato* (Leningrad, Feb. 2, 1928); *Tadzhikistan Suite* (1938; Leningrad, Feb. 13, 1939); 6 syms.: No. 1 (1947), No. 2 (1959; Leningrad, Oct. 2, 1960), No. 3 (1962; Leningrad, March 20, 1963), No. 4 for Narrator, 2 Soloists, 2 Mixed Choruses, and Orch. (1975; Leningrad, June 29, 1977), No. 5 (1981; Leningrad, Nov. 1, 1982), and No. 6 for Soloists, Chorus, and Orch. (1983; Leningrad, Sept. 14, 1985); *Russian Suite* (Leningrad, March 11, 1950); Violin Concerto (1964; Leningrad, April 18, 1965); *Concerto for Orchestra* (Leningrad, April 1969); Concerto for Violin, Piano, Percussion, and

Chamber Orch., in memory of Stravinsky (1973; Copenhagen, Feb. 21, 1974); *4 Preludes and Fugues by J.S. Bach* for Chamber Orch. (1986); symphonic poem (1987). **CHAMBER:** Sonata for Solo Violin (1930); *3 Pieces on Mongolian Themes* for Clarinet, Violin, and Piano (1943); Violin Sonata (1978); Quintet for Oboe, Horn, Harp, Viola, and Cello (1979); Horn Sonata (1981); Cello Sonata (1985); *Decimet* for 10 Instruments (1986). **Piano:** *Variations* (1929); *Humoresque* (1938); 6 Pieces on Chinese themes (1955); *Étude-Scherzo* (1969); 4 sonatas (1970, 1976, 1988, 1990); 3 Pieces (1976). **VOCAL:** Vocal symphonic cycle for Tenor, Baritone, and Orch. (1937; Leningrad, Dec. 27, 1940); *Dzhelal Eddin*, oratorio (Tashkent, Dec. 26, 1944); *Songs of Protest*, suite for Bass and Jazz Orch. (radio premiere, Feb. 12, 1940); *4 Songs* to texts by Alexander Blok (1948); *Monologue* for Baritone, Trumpet, Percussion, and Piano (1969); *Sonnets of Petrarca*, song cycle for Mezzo-soprano and Piano (1975); *4 Seasons of a Year* for Soprano, Tenor, and Instruments (1977); *2 Monologues* for Voice and Piano, to texts by Boris Pasternak (1979); Vocal Cycle for Mezzo-soprano and Instruments, after Russian poets (1988).

BIBL.: A. Kenigsberg, *B. A. A.* (Moscow and Leningrad, 1965); L. Danke, *B. A.* (Leningrad, 1980).—**NS/LK/DM**

Araujo, Francisco.
See **Correa de Araujo, Francisco.**

Araujo, Juan de, Spanish composer; b. Villafranca de los Barros, Extremadura, 1646; d. La Plata, Bolivia, 1712. He was taken to Lima at an early age by his father, where he studied at the Univ. of S. Marcos. After participating in student disruption, he was banished and was active as a choirmaster in Panama. In 1672 he returned to Lima and entered the priesthood. He served as choirmaster at the Cathedral until 1676. From 1680 until his death he was choirmaster at La Plata Cathedral. He was a distinguished composer of villancicos of which he wrote about 200.—**LK/DM**

Arban, (Joseph) Jean-Baptiste (Laurent), French cornetist, conductor, and pedagogue; b. Lyons, Feb. 28, 1825; d. Paris, April 9, 1889. He settled in Paris, where he studied trumpet with Dauverné at the Cons. (1841–45). He was active as a conductor in salon orchs. and at the Opéra. In 1857 he became prof. of saxhorn at the École Militaire. In 1869 he established the cornet class at the Cons., which he taught until 1874 and again from 1880 until his death. From 1873 he made annual visits to St. Petersburg as a conductor. Arban founded the modern school of cornet and trumpet playing in France, and was the author of the standard treatise *Grande méthode complète pour cornet à pistons et de saxhorn* (Paris, 1864). He also made a brilliant arrangement of the *Carnival of Venice* for cornet. Among his other works are a *Fantasie brillante* and variations on themes from Bellini's *Norma* and Verdi's *La traviata.*

BIBL.: J.-P. Mathez, *J.J.-B.L. A. (1825–1889)* (Moudon, 1977). —**NS/LK/DM**

Arbeau, Thoinot (real name, **Jean Tabourot**), French ecclesiastic and writer; b. Dijon, March 17, 1520; d. Langres, July 23, 1595. He was educated in Dijon and Poitiers. He served in ecclesiastical positions in Langres, where he later became vicar-general. Arbeau publ. the invaluable treatise *Orchésographie, et traité en forme de dialogue par lequel toutes personnes peuvent facilement apprendre et practiquer l'honnête exercice des danses* (Langres, 1588; 2nd ed., 1589; Eng. tr., 1948), which treats of social dances of his day with a new tablature to correlate steps and music. It also includes many dance tunes. Its historical value is further enhanced by the information it gives on how dance music of the 16th century was performed.—**NS/LK/DM**

Arbello, Fernando, jazz trombonist; b. Ponce, P.R., May 30, 1907; d. San Juan, P.R., July 26, 1970. Arbello began playing trombone at age 12 and later played in his high school band and a local orchestra. He moved to N.Y. in the mid-1920s, where he worked with Earle Howard (1927), Wilbur De Paris (1928), and June Clark (1929 and 1930). He also worked briefly with Claude Hopkins and Bingie Madison, then regularly with Hopkins from 1931–34. Arbello spent several months with Chick Webb in 1934–35, and was with Fletcher Henderson for most of 1936–37, playing briefly with Lucky Millinder late in 1936. During the late 1930s he played with Billy Hicks, Millinder, Edgar Hayes, Fats Waller, Hopkins, and Benny Carter. Arbello was with The Zutty Singleton Sextet from January to March 1940, led his own band, then rejoined Henderson early in 1941. Arbello later joined Marty Marsala and played with Jimmie Lunceford from 1942 until 1946 (except for a brief stint with Bernie Mann in N.Y. in early 1945). He led his own band throughout the 1950s, worked with Rex Stewart in Boston in 1953, and took part in the Fletcher Henderson reunion in 1957. Arbello was with Machito beginning in 1960 and moved back to P.R. in the late 1960s. He led another band of his own at the Hotel San Juan in 1969 and died a year later.—**JC/LP**

Arbós, Enrique Fernández, notable Spanish violinist, conductor, pedagogue, and composer; b. Madrid, Dec. 24, 1863; d. San Sebastián, June 2, 1939. He received training in violin from Monasterio in Madrid, Vieuxtemps in Brussels, and Joachim in Berlin. In 1886–87 he was concertmaster of the Berlin Phil. He also made successful concert tours of Europe. Returning to Madrid in 1888, he taught at the Cons. In 1889 he was concertmaster of the Glasgow Sym. Orch. From 1894 to 1916 he was a prof. at the Royal Coll. of Music in London. In 1903–04 he was concertmaster of the Boston Sym. Orch. From 1904 to 1936 he was conductor of the Madrid Sym. Orch. He also appeared as a guest conductor in the U.S. (1928–31), and then in Europe. He composed the comic opera *El centro de la tierra* (Madrid, Dec. 22, 1895) and several chamber music pieces. Arbós was a brilliant orchestrator. His arrangement of music from Albéniz's *Iberia* (1927) became very popular.

BIBL.: V. Espinós Moltó, *El Maestro A.* (Madrid, 1942). —**NS/LK/DM**

Arbuckle, Matthew, Scottish-American cornetist and bandmaster; b. Lochside, 1828; d. N.Y., May 23, 1883. At 13, he joined the 26th Regiment of the British Army and served in India and China. After playing in a military band in Canada, he deserted his regiment and went to Troy, N.Y., as a bandmaster in 1857. Shortly afterward, he became a bandmaster in Worcester, Mass. In 1860 he joined the Gilmore Band, which was attached to the 24th Mass. Infantry Regiment in 1861 and saw service in the Civil War. In later years, he continued to perform with Gilmore and other bandmasters. In 1880 he was made bandmaster of the 9th Regiment of N.Y. In 1883 he founded his own band. Arbuckle won considerable distinction as a master of the cornet, and wrote a method for his instrument.—NS/LK/DM

Arcadelt, Jacob or Jacques,
significant Flemish or French composer; b. probably in Liège, c. 1505; d. Paris, Oct. 14, 1568. He was in the papal service from 1540 to 1551, and also was in the service of the Duc de Guise in France until about 1562. Many of his works were publ. in his lifetime, bringing him wide recognition in Italy and France. He was especially known for his secular vocal music, his 200 madrigals being particularly important in the development of that genre. He also wrote 126 chansons, 3 masses, 24 motets, and Lamentations. A. Seay ed. his complete works in Corpus Mensurabilis Musicae, XXXI/1–10 (1965–71).

BIBL.: W. Klefisch, *A. als Madrigalist* (diss., Univ. of Cologne, 1938); E. Helm, *The Beginnings of the Italian Madrigal and the Works of A.* (diss., Harvard Univ., 1939).—NS/LK/DM

Archangelsky, Alexander (Andreievich),
Russian choral conductor and composer; b. near Penza, Oct. 23, 1846; d. Prague, Nov. 16, 1924. He studied at the St. Petersburg Court Chapel. In 1880 he organized a chorus there, with which he toured Russia (1899–1900) and Europe (1907, 1912). He was the first choral conductor in Russia to include women in performances of sacred works. In 1923 he went to Prague as conductor of a students' choir. Among his works were choral pieces and transcriptions.—NS/LK/DM

Archer, Frederick,
English-American organist, conductor, and composer; b. Oxford, June 16, 1838; d. Pittsburgh, Oct. 22, 1901. He studied organ in Leipzig. After serving as organist at London's Alexandra Palace (1873–80), where he also appeared as a conductor, he became organist at Brooklyn's Henry Ward Beecher church and then of N.Y.'s Church of the Incarnation in 1881. He was founder-ed. of *The Keynote* (1883–84). In 1887 he became conductor of the Boston Oratorio Soc. After serving as organist at Chicago's St. James's Church, he became organist of the Carnegie Inst. in Pittsburgh in 1895. From 1896 to 1898 he also was conductor of the Pittsburgh Orch. He wrote a cantata, *King Witlaf's Drinking-Horn*, much organ music, piano pieces, songs, and instruction manuals.—NS/LK/DM

Archer (originally, Balestreri), Violet,
Canadian composer and teacher; b. Montreal, April 24, 1913; d. Ottawa, Feb. 21, 2000. She studied with Shearwood-Stubington (piano; Teacher's Licentiate, 1934) and Weatherseed (organ) at the McGill Cons., and composition with Champagne and Douglas Clarke at McGill Univ. (B.Mus., 1936). After receiving her assoc. diploma

from the Royal Canadian Coll. of Organists (1938), she studied composition with Bartók in N.Y. (1942) and with Donovan and Hindemith at Yale Univ. (B.Mus., 1948; M.Mus., 1949). Later she pursued studies in electronic music at the Royal Cons. of Music of Toronto (1968) and at Goldsmith's Coll., Univ. of London (1973). From 1940 to 1947 she was percussionist in the Montreal Women's Sym. Orch.; from 1943 to 1947 she taught at the McGill Cons. After serving as percussionist of the New Haven (Conn.) Sym. Orch. (1947–49), she was composer-in-residence at N. Tex. State Coll. in Denton (1950–53). From 1953 to 1961 she taught at the Univ. of Okla. She was assoc. prof. (1962–70) and then prof. (1970–78) at the Univ. of Alberta, where she also served as head of the theory and composition dept. (1962–78). In 1983 she was made a Member of the Order of Canada. In 1993 her 80th birthday was celebrated with a festival of her music under the auspices of the Univ. of Alberta and the CBC. Hindemith's influence is paramount in many of her works; also prevalent is the use of folk elements. Overall, her music is structurally strong, polyphonically disciplined, and generally kept within organized tonality, with occasional dodecaphonic episodes.

WORKS: DRAMATIC: O p e r a : *Sganarelle* (1973; Edmonton, Feb. 5, 1974); *The Meal* (1983; Edmonton, Oct. 19, 1985). ORCH.: *Poem* (1940); *Scherzo Sinfonico* (1940); *Fantasia Concertante* for Flute, Oboe, Clarinet, and Strings (1941); *Britannia—A Joyful Overture* (1941); *Fantasy* for Clarinet and Strings (1942); *Fantasy on a Ground* (1946; rev. 1956); Sym. (1946); Clarinet Concertino (1946; rev. 1956); *Fanfare and Passacaglia* (1949); Piano Concerto (1956); *Divertimento* (1957); Violin Concerto (1959); *3 Sketches* (1961); *Prelude-Incantation* (1964); Sinfonietta (1968); Sinfonia (1969); *Little Suite* for Strings (1970); *Divertimento* for Piano and Strings (1985); *Evocations* for 2 Pianos and Orch. (1987); *Improvisation on a Name* for Chamber Orch. (1987); *4 Dialogues* for Classical Guitar and Chamber Orch. (1990). CHAMBER: 3 string quartets (1940, 1949, 1981); Sonata for Flute, Clarinet, and Piano (1944); Quartet for Flute, Oboe, Clarinet, and Bassoon (1944); *Fantasy* for Violin and Piano (1946); *Divertimento No. 1* for Oboe, Clarinet, and Bassoon (1949) and *No. 2* for Oboe, Violin, and Cello (1957); *Fantasy in the Form of a Passacaglia* for Chamber Ensemble (1951); 2 string trios (1953, 1961); 2 piano trios (1954, 1957); *Prelude and Allegro* for Violin and Piano (1954); Cello Sonata (1956); Violin Sonata (1956); *Divertimento* for Brass Quintet (1963); *Introduction, Dance, and Finale* for Trumpet, Horn, Trombone, Tuba, Harp or Piano, and Percussion (1963); Horn Sonata (1965); Clarinet Sonata (1970); Suite for 4 Violins (1971); Alto Saxophone Sonata (1972); Oboe Sonata (1973); *Little Suite* for Trumpet and Piano (1975); Sonata for Viola, Cello, and Piano (1976); Suite for Flute (1976); Oboe Sonatina (1977); Bassoon Sonatina (1978); Clarinet Sonatina (1978); *Divertimento* for Saxophone Quartet (1979); Bassoon Sonata (1980); Sonata for Solo Cello (1981); *12 Miniatures* for Violin and Piano (1982); *Celebration* for Brass Quintet (1983); *Ikpakhuag* for Violin, Cello, and Piano (1984); *I va vari* for Brass Quintet (1985); *Moods* for Clarinet and Alto Saxophone (1985); *6 Miniatures* for String Bass and Piano (1986); *4 Miniatures* for Classical Accordion (1988); *3 Essays* for Saxophone (1988); *Improvisation* for Snare Drum (1990); *Prelude and Dance* for Timpani (1990); *One Fifth on Four* for Xylophone, Celesta, Piano, Clarinet, and Piano (1991). KEYBOARD: P i a n o : 3 *Scenes* (1945); 2 sonatas (1945, rev. 1957; 1979); 3 sonatinas (1945, 1946, 1973); *6 Preludes* (1947); *3 Sketches* for 2 Pianos (1947); Suite

(1947); *Theme and Variations on Là'Haut* (1952); *10 Folk Songs* for Piano, 4-Hands (1953); *Rondo* (1955); *11 Short Pieces* (1960); *Theme and Variations* (1963); *Improvisations* (1968); *Lydian Mood and a Quiet Chat* (1971); *4 Bagatelles* (1977); *4 Contrapuntal Moods* (1978); *Here and Now* (1980); *4 Vignettes* for Piano, 4- Hands (1984); *Dancing on the Seashore* (1991). **O r g a n :** Sonatina (1944); *2 Chorale Preludes* (1948); *Chorale Improvisation on O Worship the King* (1967); *Prelude and Fantasy on Winchester New* (1978); *Festive Fantasy* (1979); *Improvisation on Veni Creator* (1984); *Variations on Aberystwyth* (1984). **VOCAL:** Liturgical pieces for Chorus and Organ; secular choruses and songs. **ELECTRONIC:** *Episodes* (1973).

BIBL.: L. Hartig, *V. A.: A Bio-Bibliography* (N.Y., 1991). **—NS/LK/DM**

Archilei, Vittoria (née Concarini), admired Italian soprano, lutenist, and dancer who was known as **La Romanina**; b. Rome, 1550; d. after 1620. She was married to the singer and lutenist Antonio Archilei (c. 1550–1612), with whom she may have studied. She became a protégée of Cavalieri and was in the service of the court of Ferdinando de' Medici in Florence from 1587, where she was held in great esteem. Caccini, Peri, and d'India were among her admirers. She was the subject of Marino's poem *La morte di Vittoria cantatrice famosa* (1629).**—LK/DM**

Ardévol, José, Spanish-born Cuban composer, conductor, and administrator; b. Barcelona, March 13, 1911; d. Havana, Jan. 7, 1981. He studied with his father in Barcelona, and then settled in Havana in 1931. After Castro's seizure of power in 1959, Ardévol became a leading figure in the reorganization of musical life in Cuba. He served as national director of music until 1965. His orch. and chamber works followed along neo-Classical lines, but he pursued more advanced writing in his vocal scores.

WORKS: O R C H .: Concerto for 3 Pianos and Orch. (1938); 3 syms. (1943, 1945, 1946); *Triptico de Santiago* (Cologne, May 25, 1953); *Música para pequeña orquestra* (Washington, D.C., April 19, 1958). **OTHER:** Several string quartets, numerous piano pieces, and various vocal works, some on revolutionary themes.**—NS/LK/DM**

Arditi, Luigi, Italian conductor and composer; b. Crescentino, Piedmont, July 22, 1822; d. Hove, Sussex, May 1, 1903. He studied violin and composition at the Milan Cons., where his principal mentor was Vaccai and where his first opera, *I briganti*, was premiered in 1841. He began his career in Vercelli and Milan (1842–46), and then went to Havana, where he was active at the Teatro Imperial. His opera *Il Corsaro* was premiered at Havana's Teatro Tacon in 1847, followed by his *Gulnara* there on Feb. 4, 1848. He was a conductor in Canada (1853) and the U.S. (1854–56), where his opera *Le spia* was premiered in N.Y. on March 24, 1856. Thereafter Arditi concentrated on a conducting career. Following tours of Europe, he went to London and conducted at Her Majesty's Theatre from 1858 to 1869. He also took the company on tours. In 1869–70 he conducted at Covent Garden. From 1870 he conducted in Vienna, and he also appeared in St. Petersburg in 1871 and 1873.

After conducting the Covent Garden promenade concerts (1874–77), he was a conductor of Mapleson's touring opera company in the U.S. from 1878 to 1894. He also continued to conduct opera in London. In addition to his operas, Arditi also composed some orch. pieces and songs, being best remembered for his popular vocal waltz *Il bacio*. As a conductor he led the London premieres of works by several important composers, among them Verdi, Gounod, Wagner, Thomas, Boito, and Mascagni.

WRITINGS: *My Reminiscences* (London, 1896). **—NS/LK/DM**

Arel, Bülent, Turkish-born American composer; b. Constantinople, April 23, 1918; d. Stony Brook, N.Y., Nov. 24, 1990. He studied composition with Akses, piano with Ferhunde Erkin, conducting with Ernst Praetorius, and 20th-century music with Edward Zuckmayer at the Ankara State Cons. (1940–47); then took courses in sound engineering in Paris (1951). He taught in Ankara at the State Cons. and at the Teachers Coll. (1947–59); was also a sound engineer and director of Western music programming at the Ankara Radio (1951–59). In 1959 he went to the U.S. on a Rockefeller research grant and worked at the Columbia-Princeton Electronic Music Center until 1963; was also an instructor in electronic music at Yale Univ. (1961–62). After again working at the Ankara Radio (1963–65), he returned to teach at Yale Univ. (1965–70) and Columbia Univ. (1970–71). He was prof. of music and director of the electronic music studio at the State Univ. of N.Y. at Stony Brook from 1971 to 1989. In 1973 he became a naturalized American citizen. In his early works, Arel explored Turkish folk songs; he then wrote pieces alternatively in a neo-Classical and impressionistic manner while experimenting with serial techniques, eventually turning to electronic composition.

WORKS: Piano Concerto (1946); *Suite intime* for Orch. (1949); *Masques* for Winds and Strings (1949); 2 syms. (1951, 1952); *6 Bagatelles* for Strings (1958); *Short Piece* for Orch. (1967); electronic pieces: *Short Study* (1960); *Fragment* (1960); *Electronic Music No. 1* (1960); *Stereo Electronic Music I* (1960) and *II* (1970); *Impressions of Wall Street* (1961); *Music for a Sacred Service* (1961); *Capriccio for T.V.* (1969); dance scores: *Mimiana I* (1968), *II* (1969), and *III* (1973).**—NS/LK/DM**

Arensky, Anton (Stepanovich), Russian pianist, conductor, teacher, and composer; b. Novgorod, July 12, 1861; d. near Terioki, Finland, Feb. 25, 1906. He was a student of Johanssen and Rimsky-Korsakov at the St. Petersburg Cons. (1879–82). From 1882 to 1895 he taught theory and composition at the Moscow Cons. He also conducted concerts of the Russian Choral Soc. in Moscow. He was conductor of the Imperial Court Chapel Choir in St. Petersburg from 1895 to 1901, and then was a prof. at the St. Petersburg Cons. He also made tours as a pianist and conductor. His last days were made difficult by tuberculosis and alcoholism, and he eventually died in a Finnish sanatorium. His best known scores were his *Variations on a Theme of Tchaikovsky* for Strings, his 1st Piano Trio, piano pieces, and songs.

WORKS: DRAMATIC: Opera: *Son na Volge* (A Dream on the Volga; Moscow, Jan. 2, 1891); *Rafael'* (Moscow, May 6, 1894); *Nal' i Damayanti* (Nal and Damayanti; Moscow, Jan. 22, 1904). **Ballet:** *Egyptian Nights* (1900; St. Petersburg, March 21, 1908). **Incidental Music:** To Shakespeare's *The Tempest* for Soloists, Chorus, and Orch. (1905). **ORCH.:** Piano Concerto (1882); *Intermezzo* for Strings (1882); 2 syms.: No. 1 (Moscow, Nov. 24, 1883, composer conducting) and No. 2 (Moscow, Dec. 21, 1889); Suite (1885); Violin Concerto (1891); *Variations on a Theme of Tchaikovsky* for Strings (1894); *Fantasia on a Russian Folksong* for Piano and Orch. (1899); marches. **CHAMBER:** 2 string quartets (1888, 1894); 2 piano trios (1895, 1905); Piano Quintet (1900); many piano pieces. **VOCAL:** Choral music and songs.

BIBL.: G. Tzypin, *A. S. A.* (Moscow, 1966).—NS/LK/DM

Aretino, Paolo, Italian composer; b. Arezzo (baptized), March 1, 1508; d. there, July 19, 1584. He spent his entire career in Arezzo, where he became a priest. After service at S. Maria della Pieve (1530–33), he became a canon at the Cathedral in 1533, where he also was maestro di cappella from 1538 to 1544. He then returned to S. Maria della Pieve as a canon. He publ. much sacred music (Venice, 1544–69) and a vol. of madrigals (Venice, 1558).—LK/DM

Aretz (de Ramón y Rivera), Isabel, Argentine-born Venezuelan folklorist and composer; b. Buenos Aires, April 13, 1909. She studied piano and composition at the National Cons. of Music in Buenos Aires. She subsequently dedicated herself to research in Argentine folklore at the Museo de Ciencias Naturales de Buenos Aires (1938–44). She received her Ph.D. in musicology in 1967 at the Argentine Catholic Univ. in Buenos Aires with the diss. *Música tradicional argentina: La Rioja.* She served as an assoc. member of the Instituto Argentino de Musicología (1938–50), and then was the first prof. of ethnomusicology at the Escuela Nacional de Danzas de Argentina (1950–52). In 1953 she settled in Caracas, Venezuela, as a research fellow in ethnomusicology and folklore at the Instituto Nacional de Folklore de Venezuela. In 1965 she became director of the folklore dept. of the Instituto Nacional de Cultura y Bellas Artes, and, in 1970, of the Instituto Interamericano de Etnomusicología y Folklore. She was married to **Luis Felipe Ramón y Rivera.** As a composer, Aretz's music reflects interest in folk music and contemporary European trends.

WRITINGS: *Música tradicional argentina: Tucumán, historia y folklore* (Buenos Aires, 1946); *El folklore musical argentino* (Buenos Aires, 1953); *Manual de folklore venezolano* (Caracas, 1957; 3rd ed., 1972); *Cantos navideños en el folklore venezolano* (Caracas, 1962); *Instrumentos musicales de Venezuela* (Cumaná, 1967); *La artesania en Venezuela* (Caracas, 1967); *El traje en Venezuela* (Caracas, 1972); *El tamunangue* (Barquisimeto, 1976).—NS/LK/DM

Argenta (Maza), Atáulfo, esteemed Spanish conductor; b. Castro Urdiales, Nov. 19, 1913; d. (of accidental carbon monoxide poisoning), Los Molinos, near Madrid, Jan. 21, 1958. He pursued training in piano at the Madrid Cons., where he took 1st prize at the age of 17. After further studies in Belgium, he went to Germany in 1941 and continued his training at the Kassel Cons. He also found a conducting mentor in Carl Schuricht. In 1943 he returned to Spain and centered his career in Madrid. In 1945 he became a member of the Orquesta Nacional de España, and soon thereafter made his first appearance with it as a conductor. In 1946 he founded the Madrid Chamber Orch. He became chief conductor of the Orquesta Nacional de España in 1947. As a guest conductor, he appeared in Vienna, Glasgow, and London but became especially associated with the Paris Cons. Orch. and l'Orchestre de la Suisse Romande of Geneva. In addition to his idiomatic interpretation of Spanish works, he displayed a remarkable command of a broad repertoire ranging from Vivaldi to Stravinsky.

BIBL.: A. Fernandez-Cid, *A. A.* (Madrid, 1958). —NS/LK/DM

Argenta (real name, **Herbison**), **Nancy,** Canadian soprano; b. Nelson, British Columbia, Jan. 17, 1957. She spent her early years in the settlement of Argenta, from which she later took her professional name. She was a student of Jacob Hamm in Vancouver and of Martin Chambers at the Univ. of Western Ontario. In 1980 she won 1st prize in the S. C. Eckhardt-Gramatté Competition. After further training with Jacqueline Richard in Düsseldorf (1980–81), she settled in London and completed her studies with Vera Rosza. In 1983 she attracted critical attention as La Chasseuresse in Rameau's *Hippolyte et Aricie* at the Aix-en-Provence Festival. As a gifted exponent of the early music repertoire, she was engaged by many of the leading early music groups and by the principal music festivals; in 1989 she appeared as soloist with the English Concert in N.Y. and also made her Wigmore Hall recital debut in London. In 1990 she sang Rossane in the North American premiere of Handel's *Floridante* in Toronto. She made her debut at the Salzburg Festival as Gluck's Euridice in 1996. Among her other esteemed roles are Monteverdi's Poppea and Orfeo, Purcell's Dido and King Arthur, Handel's Astreia, and Mozart's Barbarina and Susanna. Her concert repertoire is expansive, ranging from the Baroque era to contemporary scores. —NS/LK/DM

Argento, Dominick, outstanding American composer and teacher; b. York, Pa., Oct. 27, 1927. He received training in piano from the age of 15, and soon began teaching himself theory and orchestration. After serving as a cryptographer in the U.S. Army in East Africa (1945–47), he pursued studies in piano with Alexander Sklarewski and in composition with Nabokov at the Peabody Cons. of Music in Baltimore (B.M., 1951). He also received private composition instruction from Weisgall. In 1951–52 he held a Fulbright fellowship and studied with Dallapiccola in Florence. From 1952 to 1955 he taught at the Hampton (Va.) Inst. During this period, he also served as music director of the Hilltop Opera in Baltimore. He concurrently pursued training in composition with Cowell at the Peabody Cons. of Music (M.M., 1954), and then completed his composition studies with Rogers, Hovhaness, and Hanson at the

Eastman School of Music in Rochester, N.Y. (Ph.D., 1957). In 1957–58 and in 1964–65 he held Guggenheim fellowships. In 1958 he joined the faculty of the Univ. of Minn., where he was named Regents' Prof. in 1980. In 1963 he co-founded the Center Opera Co. (later the Minn. Opera) in Minneapolis, which was inaugurated with his opera *The Masque of Angels* on Jan. 9, 1964. His remarkable opera *Postcard from Morocco* was premiered there on Oct. 14, 1971. In 1975 he won the Pulitzer Prize in Music for his notable song cycle *From the Diary of Virginia Woolf*. A U.S. Bicentennial commission resulted in his outstanding opera *The Voyage of Edgar Allan Poe*, which was first performed in St. Paul on April 24, 1976. He received an award from the American Academy of Arts and Letters in 1979. His compelling opera *Casanova's Homecoming* opened the Ordway Music Theater in St. Paul on April 12, 1985. It won the National Music Theater Award in 1986. His highly rewarding opera *The Aspern Papers*, after Henry James, was premiered at the Dallas Opera on Nov. 19, 1988, and won wide recognition via its telecast by PBS. His finely crafted opera *The Dream of Valentino* was first performed at the Kennedy Center in Washington, D.C., on Jan. 15, 1994. In 1997 he was named composer laureate of the Minn. Orch. in Minneapolis.

In his distinguished oeuvre, Argento has displayed a remarkable capacity for composing compelling vocal and orch. scores. His operas, choral works, and songs constitute major contributions to the vocal art in the U.S. Early on Argento eschewed the precepts of stark modernism to embrace an imaginative and well crafted style marked by melodic invention, a sure handling of orchestral color, and a heartfelt lyricism. An artful command of text setting is a hallmark of his vocal writing.

WORKS: DRAMATIC: *Sicilian Limes*, opera (1953; N.Y., Oct. 1, 1954); *The Resurrection of Don Juan*, ballet (1955; Karlsruhe, May 24, 1959; orch. suite, Rochester, N.Y., May 5, 1956); *The Boor*, opera buffa after Chekhov (Rochester, N.Y., May 6, 1957); *Colonel Jonathan the Saint*, opera (1958–61; Denver, Dec. 31, 1971); *Christopher Sly*, comic opera after Shakespeare (1962; Minneapolis, May 31, 1963); *The Masque of Angels*, opera (1963; Minneapolis, Jan. 9, 1964); *The Shoemakers' Holiday*, ballad-opera after Dekker (Minneapolis, June 1, 1967); *Postcard from Morocco*, opera (Minneapolis, Oct. 14, 1971); *A Water Bird Talk*, opera after Chekhov and Audubon (1974; N.Y., May 19, 1977); *The Voyage of Edgar Allan Poe*, opera (1975–76; St. Paul, April 24, 1976); *Miss Havisham's Fire*, opera after Dickens (1977–78; N.Y., March 22, 1979; rev. 1995–96); *Miss Havisham's Wedding Night*, opera monodrama (1980; Minneapolis, May 1, 1981); *Casanova's Homecoming*, opera after Casanova (1980–84; St. Paul, April 12, 1985); *The Aspern Papers*, opera after Henry James (1987; Dallas, Nov. 19, 1988); *The Dream of Valentino*, opera (1993; Washington, D.C., Jan. 15, 1994); also incidental music to plays. **ORCH.:** *Divertimento* for Piano and Strings (1954; Rochester, N.Y., July 11, 1956); *Overture to "The Boor"* (1957); *Royal Invitation (Homage to the Queen of Tonga)* for Chamber Orch. (St. Paul, March 20, 1964); *Variations for Orchestra (The Mask of Night)* (1965; Minneapolis, Jan. 26, 1966); *Bravo Mozart!* (Minneapolis, July 3, 1969); *A Ring of Time* (Minneapolis, Oct. 5, 1972); *In Praise of Music* (Minneapolis, Sept. 23, 1977); *Fire Variations* (1981; Moorhead, Minn., April 24, 1982); *Le Tombeau d'Edgar Poe*, suite from the opera *The Voyage of Edgar Allan Poe* (1985; Baltimore, Feb. 27, 1986); *Capriccio* for Clarinet

and Orch., *Rossini in Paris* (1985; St. Louis, May 16, 1986); *Valentino Dances* (Minneapolis, July 13, 1994); *Valse Triste* for Strings and Harp (Minneapolis, July 10, 1996); *Reverie (Reflections on a Hymn Tune)* (Minneapolis, Nov. 26, 1997); *The Town Musicians of Bremen* for Narrator and Orch. (1998; Washington, D.C., April 11, 1999). **CHAMBER:** String Quartet (1956); *The Angel Israfil* for 2 Harps (San Antonio, June 1989). **Organ:** *Prelude for Easter Dawning* (1982). **VOCAL:** *Songs about Spring* for Soprano and Piano, after e.e. cummings (1950; Baltimore, May 22, 1951; aug. version for High Voice and Chamber Orch., Rochester, N.Y., July 14, 1960); *Ode to the West Wind*, concerto for Soprano and Orch., after Shelley (1956; Rochester, N.Y., April 29, 1957); *Six Elizabethan Songs* for High Voice and Piano (1957; Rochester, N.Y., May 6, 1958; also for High Voice and Baroque Ensemble, 1962; Minneapolis, March 8, 1963); *The Revelation of St. John the Divine* for Tenor, Men's Chorus, Brass, and Percussion (Minneapolis, May 16, 1966); *A Nation of Cowslips* for Chorus, after Keats (Minneapolis, April 13, 1969); *Letters from Composers*, 7 songs for High Voice and Guitar (St. Paul, Oct. 23, 1968); *Trio Carmina Paschalla* for Women's Voices, Harp, and Guitar or Harpsichord (St. Paul, Sept. 1970); *To Be Sung Upon The Water* for High Voice, Clarinet, and Piano, after Wordsworth (1973; Minneapolis, Oct. 20, 1974); *Jonah and the Whale*, oratorio for Tenor, Bass, Narrator, Chorus, and Instrumental Ensemble (1973; Minneapolis, March 9, 1974); *From the Diary of Virginia Woolf*, song cycle for Medium Voice and Piano (1974; Minneapolis, Jan. 5, 1975); *A Thanksgiving to God, for His House* for Chorus (Minneapolis, May 6, 1979); *Let All the World in Every Corner Sing* for Chorus, Brass Quartet, Timpani, and Organ (Minneapolis, June 1980); *Peter Quince at the Clavier*, sonatina for Chorus and Piano Concertante, after Wallace Stevens (Pa. State Univ., April 11, 1981); *I Hate and I Love*, song cycle for Chorus and Percussion, after Catullus (Minneapolis, March 14, 1982); *The Andrée Expedition*, song cycle for Baritone and Piano (1982; St. Paul, Feb. 15, 1983); *Casa Guidi*, 5 songs for Mezzo-soprano and Orch., after Elizabeth Barrett Browning (Minneapolis, Sept. 28, 1983; reduced arrangement, London, Nov. 23, 1989; also for Mezzo-soprano and Piano, Los Angeles, Jan. 6, 1984); *Te Deum* for Chorus and Orch. (1987; Buffalo, March 4, 1988); *Easter Day* for Chorus (1988; Minneapolis, March 26, 1989); *A Toccata of Galuppi's* for Chamber Chorus, Harpsichord, and String Quartet, after Robert Browning (1989; Santa Fe, June 24, 1990); *Everyone Sang* for Double Chorus (Pittsburgh, April 20, 1991); *Spirituals and Swedish Chorales* for Chorus (St. Paul, Sept. 25, 1994); *To God ("In Memoriam M.B., 1994")* for Chorus and Offstage Trumpet (Minneapolis, Sept. 25, 1994); *A Few Words About Chekhov* for Mezzo-soprano, Baritone, and Piano (St. Paul, Oct. 12, 1996); *Walden Pond* for Chorus, 3 Cellos, and Harp, after Thoreau (Minneapolis, Oct. 26, 1996); *Miss Manners on Music*, 7 songs for Mezzo-soprano and Piano, after Judith Martin (1997; Washington, D.C., Sept. 12, 1998); *The Vision*, motet for Chorus and String Quartet, after Dante (1999). —NS/LK/DM

Argerich, Martha, outstanding Argentine pianist; b. Buenos Aires, June 5, 1941. She made her first public appearance at the age of 5; after studies with Vincenzo Scaramuzza, she made her debut in Buenos Aires at age 8; later, pursued training with Gulda in Vienna and with Magaloff and Madeleine Lipatti in Geneva; also received lessons from Michelangeli. At the age of 16, she captured 1st prizes in both the Geneva and Busoni competitions; then won the Chopin Competition in Warsaw (1965). She pursued a notable career as a virtuoso, appearing with the leading orchs. of the world, as a recitalist, and as a chamber music artist. Her formidable repertoire ranges from Liszt and Chopin to Ravel and Prokofiev. She was married to **Charles Dutoit** and, later, to **Stephen Kovacevich.**—**NS/LK/DM**

Argiris, Spiros, Greek conductor; b. Athens, Aug. 24, 1948; d. Nice, May 19, 1996. He studied piano with Alfons Kontarsky and received training in conducting in Vienna from Swarowsky and in Fontainebleau from Boulanger. Thereafter he appeared widely as a guest conductor in major opera houses in such locales as Berlin, Hamburg, Munich, Rome, Monte Carlo, Paris, Miami, Baltimore, and Montreal. He also was engaged as a conductor with leading orchs. in Europe and North America. In 1986 he became music director of the Festival of Two Worlds in Charleston, S.C., and Spoleto, Italy. He resigned his post in 1992 in the wake of the dispute between the festival's founder, Gian Carlo Menotti, and its board. In 1987 he was made music director of the Trieste Opera and in 1988 of the Nice Opera. From 1991 to 1994 he also served as music director of the Teatro Bellini in Catania. In 1993 he resumed his association with the Festival of Two Worlds in Charleston.—**NS/LK/DM**

Aribo, writer on music who flourished in the 11th century. He wrote the important treatise *De musica* (c. 1068–78), in which he devised a diagram with the modal tetrachords superimposed on the gamut. The diagram is known as the caprea (goat) due to the speed by which music can be measured by it on the monochord. The diagram superseded those by earlier writers on music.
—**NS/LK/DM**

d'Arienzo, Nicola, Italian composer, pedagogue, and writer on music; b. Naples, Dec. 24, 1842; d. there, April 25, 1915. His entire career was centered on Naples. His parents initially opposed his interest in music, so he studied secretly with Vincenzo Fiore Vanti (counterpoint) and Giovanni Moretti (instrumentation). After his parents relented, he pursued training with Mercadante. He composed all but one of his operas for Naples, winning his most notable success with *Il cuoco e il segretario* (June 11, 1873). His *La figlia del diavolo* (Nov. 16, 1879) stirred controversy for its verismo leanings. He taught harmony and counterpoint (1872–74) and was director (1874–75) of the music school at the Real Albergo dei Poveri. In 1875 he became a teacher of harmony at the Cons., where he taught counterpoint and composition from 1877 to 1912, and also was its director from 1909 to 1911. He publ. *Introduzione del sistema tetracordiale nella musica moderna* (Milan, 1878), *Dell'opera comica dalle origini a G.B. Pergolesi* (1887), and *La musica in Napoli* (Naples, 1900).

WORKS: DRAMATIC: O p e r a (all 1st perf. in Naples unless otherwise given): *Monzù Gnazio, o La fidanzata del parrucchiere* (1860); *I due mariti* (Feb. 1, 1866; rev. version, Milan, 1871); *Le rose* (Feb. 1868); *Il cacciatore delle Alpi* (June 23, 1870); *Il cuoco e il segretario* (June 11, 1873); *I viaggi* (Milan, June 28, 1875); *La figlia del diavolo* (Nov. 16, 1879); *I tre coscritti* (Feb. 10, 1880); *La fiera* (Feb. 1887); not perf.: *Rita di Lister, Lesbo di Rodio,* and

Capitan Fracassa. **ORCH.:** *A Roma,* concerto sinfonico (1871); *Orlando,* sym. (c. 1871); *Pensiero sinfonico* (1871); Violin Concerto (1880); *Piccolo Concerto* for Cello and Orch. (1881); Violin Concerto-fantasia (1912). **CHAMBER:** Piano Trio (1863); Cello Sonata (1884); String Quartet (1888); Nonet (1889); harp pieces; piano music. **VOCAL:** *Cristo sulla croce,* oratorio for Solo Voices, Chorus, and Orch.; *Miserere* for 5 Voices; *Stabat mater* for 6 Solo Voices, Chorus, and Orch.; numerous songs.
—**NS/LK/DM**

Ariosti, Attilio (Malachia), Italian composer, singer, and instrumentalist; b. Bologna, Nov. 5, 1666; d. England, c. 1729. He joined the order of S. Maria de' Servi at the Bologna monastery in 1688, took minor orders in 1689, and received his diaconate in 1692. Abandoning the order, he was in the service of the Duke of Mantua in 1696. With Lotti and Caldara, he collaborated on the opera *Tirsi* (Venice, 1696). In 1697 he went to Berlin as a court composer and staged the first Italian operas there. From 1703 to 1711 he was in the service of the Vienna court. In 1716 he went to London, where he was a composer with the Royal Academy of Music. Among the operas he brought out there were *Coriolano* (Feb. 19, 1723), *Artaserse* (Dec. 1, 1724), *Dario* (April 5, 1725), and *Lucio Vero, imperator di Roma* (Jan. 7, 1727). He also publ. a vol. of six cantatas and six lessons for the viola d'amore (1724), on which he was an accomplished performer. In all, he composed at least 22 operas, instrumental music, five oratorios, and many cantatas.
—**NS/LK/DM**

Aristides Quintilianus, Greek writer on music who flourished about 200 A.D. He wrote a treatise in 3 vols. on music (annotated Eng. tr. by T. Mathiesen as *On Music, in Three Books,* New Haven, 1983). In spite of its flaws, his treatise remains a valuable source on ancient Greek music.—**NS/LK/DM**

Aristotle, great Greek philosopher, logician, and scientist; b. Stagira, 384 B.C.; d. Chalcis, 322 B.C. His writings on music are included in K. von Jan, *Musici scriptores Graeci* (1895).—**NS/LK/DM**

Aristoxenus, important Greek philosopher who flourished in the late 4th century B.C. He was a student in Athens of Aristotle and Theophrastus. Although he wrote on ethics and prepared biographies, it is as a music theorist that his work is invaluable. His writings on harmonic elements (Eng. tr. by O. Strunk in *Source Readings in Music History,* N.Y., 1950; 2nd ed., rev., 1998 by L. Treitler) and on rhythmical elements (introduction and commentary by L. Pearson, Oxford, 1990) are among the most important treatises on ancient Greek music theory.—**NS/LK/DM**

Arizaga, Rodolfo (Bernardo), Argentine composer; b. Buenos Aires, July 11, 1926; d. there, May 12, 1985. He studied philosophy at the Univ. of Buenos Aires and composition with Luis Gianneo; then went to Paris, where he took lessons with Boulanger and Messiaen. Beginning with folkloric composition of the traditional Latin American type, he traversed the entire gamut of modern techniques, including 12-tone structures and aleatory composition, and applied these diverse methods liberally according to need and intention.

WORKS: *Prometeo 45*, opera (1958); *Sonata breve* for Ondes Martenot and Piano (1958); Piano Concerto (1963); *Tientos para Santa Maria* for Orch. (1965); *Música para Christóbal Colón* for Orch. (1966); *Diferenzas del tercer tiento* for Organ (1966); 2 string quartets (1968, 1969); various vocal works and piano pieces.

WRITINGS: *Manuel de Falla* (Buenos Aires, 1961); *Juan José Castro* (Buenos Aires, 1963); ed. *Enciclopedia de la música argentina* (Buenos Aires, 1971); with P. Camps, *Historia de la música en la Argentina* (Buenos Aires, 1990).—**NS/LK/DM**

Arkas, Nikolai (Nikolaievich), Ukrainian composer and writer on music; b. Nikolayev, Jan. 7, 1853; d. there, March 26, 1909. He was active as a collector and compiler of Ukrainian folk songs. His opera *Katerina* (1891; Moscow, Feb. 12, 1899) was one of the earliest Ukrainian works in the genre.

WRITINGS: *Istoriya Ukraini-Rusi* (St. Petersburg, 1908).

BIBL.: L. Kaufman, *N. A.* (Kiev, 1958).—**NS/LK/DM**

Arkhipova, Irina (Konstantinovna), outstanding Russian mezzo-soprano; b. Moscow, Dec. 2, 1925. She attended vocal classes at the Moscow Architectural Inst., graduating in 1948; then continued vocal training with Leonid Savransky at the Moscow Cons., graduating in 1953. She sang with the Sverdlovsk Opera (1954–56); then made her debut as Carmen at Moscow's Bolshoi Theater (1956), where she quickly rose to prominence; traveled with it outside Russia, garnering praise for her appearances at Milan's La Scala (1965) and at the Montreal EXPO (1967). She appeared as Amneris at the San Francisco Opera in 1972 and as Azucena at London's Covent Garden in 1975. In 1992 she sang the Countess in *The Queen of Spades* with the Kirov Opera of St. Petersburg during its visit to the Metropolitan Opera in N.Y. She made her belated Metropolitan Opera debut in N.Y. in a minor role in *Eugene Onegin* in 1997. In 1966 she was made a People's Artist of the U.S.S.R. She excelled particularly in the Russian repertoire, but also distinguished herself in French and Italian music. —**NS/LK/DM**

Arkor, André d', Belgian tenor; b. Tilleur, near Liège, Feb. 23, 1901; d. Brussels, Dec. 19, 1971. He studied with Malherbe and Seguin at the Liège Cons. He made his operatic debut in 1925 as Gérard in *Lakmé* at the Liège Théâtre Royal; then sang in Ghent and Lyons; in 1930 he joined the Théâtre de la Monnaie in Brussels, where he remained as a leading tenor until 1945; from 1945 to 1965 he was director of the Liège Théâtre Royal. He was particularly esteemed as a Mozartean.—**NS/LK/DM**

Arlen, Harold (originally, **Hyman Arluck**), American composer, pianist, and singer; b. Buffalo, N.Y., Feb. 15, 1905; d. N.Y., April 23, 1986. Among the major song composers of the 1930s and 1940s, Arlen was the most overtly influenced by blues and jazz music. Dividing his time between N.Y. and Hollywood, he contrib-

uted to 15 Broadway stage shows and 33 feature films between 1930 and 1963. Among his best-remembered film scores are those for *The Wizard of Oz, Cabin in the Sky,* and *A Star Is Born.* He was nominated for the Academy Award for Best Song nine times, winning for "Over the Rainbow." Among his other major hits drawn from films are "Blues in the Night," "That Old Black Magic," and "Ac-Cent-Tchu-Ate the Positive." Many of his most popular songs originated in the five nightclub revues he wrote for the Cotton Club from 1930 to 1934 with Ted Koehler, including "Between the Devil and the Deep Blue Sea," "I've Got the World on a String," and "Stormy Weather." His other major collaborators were E. Y. Harburg, Ira Gershwin, and Johnny Mercer, and he also worked with Dorothy Fields, Ralph Blane, and Leo Robin, among others. The nature of his music made it popular with African-American performers such as Duke Ellington, Ethel Waters, Cab Calloway, and Lena Horne, and many of his works were composed specifically with black performers in mind. But he also became a particular favorite of Judy Garland, who frequently sang his songs in her films and concerts, and Barbra Streisand, with whom he recorded an album late in his career.

Arlen was the son of Samuel S. and Celia Orlin Arluck. His father was a cantor, and Harold had his first experience in music at the age of seven, singing in a synagogue choir conducted by his father. He began private study on the piano at nine, including instruction from Arnold Cornelissen and Simon Bucharoff. These studies pointed him toward classical music, but he developed an affinity for ragtime. He formed his first band, Hyman Arluck's Snappy Trio, in 1919, and dropped out of high school in 1921. The Snappy Trio expanded into the six-piece Southbound Shufflers and played in clubs and on excursion boats cruising Lake Erie.

In 1924, Arlen wrote his first song, "My Gal, Won't You Come Back to Me?" (aka "My Gal, My Pal"; lyrics by Hyman Cheiffetz). He disbanded The Southbound Shufflers in 1925 and joined The Yankee Six, which grew to 11 pieces and became The Buffalodians. They moved to N.Y. in 1926, and when they broke up he joined the orchestra of Arnold Johnson as pianist, singer, and arranger. Arlen stayed with Johnson until July 1928, then tried to make his way as a solo performer in vaudeville.

Vincent Youmans hired Arlen in 1929 to appear in his musical *Great Day* (N.Y., Oct. 17, 1929) and to serve as his musical secretary. At a rehearsal, Arlen improvised a tune that led Harry Warren to introduce him to Ted Koehler, who set a lyric to it, creating the song "Get Happy." Koehler placed it and other songs written with Arlen in the *9:15 Revue* (N.Y., Feb. 11, 1930), and though the show was short-lived, "Get Happy" became a hit in July 1930 in a recording by Nat Shilkret and The Victor Orch.

By this time Arlen and Koehler had been hired to write half the score of the *Earl Carroll Vanities,* which ran 215 performances and featured "Hittin' the Bottle," successfully recorded by The Colonial Club Orch. Next the songwriters turned to nightclub work and replaced

Jimmy McHugh and Dorothy Fields at the Cotton Club, contributing their first score, for the revue *Brown Sugar*, probably in December. Arlen also teamed with lyricist/librettist/producer Jack Yellen, a family friend from Buffalo, on his first book musical, *You Said It*, which ran for 192 performances starting in early 1931.

That spring, Arlen and Koehler mounted another Cotton Club revue, *Rhythmania*, starring Cab Calloway. The hits that emerged from it were "Kickin' the Gong Around," recorded by Calloway; "Between the Devil and the Deep Blue Sea," recorded by Louis Armstrong; and "I Love a Parade," recorded by The Arden-Ohman Orch. Arlen had not abandoned his ambition to be a performer, and he made occasional recordings. In July 1931 he scored a hit as vocalist with Joe Venuti's Blue Four on "Little Girl" (music and lyrics by Madeline Hyde and Francis Henry). In December "I Love a Parade" and "Temporarily Blue" were featured in the Warner Bros. film *Manhattan Parade*, giving Arlen and Koehler their first screen credits.

Arlen and Koehler wrote some songs for the 1932 edition of the *Earl Carroll Vanities* (N.Y., Sept. 27, 1932), and Cab Calloway had a hit with "I Gotta Right to Sing the Blues" from the show. Calloway also scored hits with "Minnie the Moocher's Wedding Day" and "I've Got the World on a String" from the next edition of the *Cotton Club Parade* (Oct. 23, 1932).

Arlen's last song to be used in a show in 1932 took a convoluted route to becoming a standard. Featured in the play *The Great Magoo* (N.Y., Dec. 2, 1932) under the title "If You Believed in Me" (lyrics by E. Y. Harburg and Billy Rose), it wasn't given much exposure during the show's 11 performances. Under its more familiar title, "It's Only a Paper Moon," it was added to the post-Broadway tour of the revue *Crazy Quilt of 1933* (Albany, July 28, 1933) and published. This led to its being recorded by Paul Whiteman and His Orch. for a hit in October. And in November it turned up in the motion picture *Take a Chance*.

Meanwhile, Arlen was scoring another hit during 1933, which he recorded himself. "Stormy Weather" (lyrics by Koehler) was written for Cab Calloway to sing in the next edition of the *Cotton Club Parade* (April 6, 1933). When Calloway proved unavailable, the song was given to Ethel Waters. In the interim, The Leo Reisman Orch. cut it with Arlen singing, and the record became a best-seller, as did Waters's recording, making "Stormy Weather" the biggest hit of 1933.

Arlen and Koehler signed a one-film deal with Columbia Pictures and went to Hollywood in the fall of 1933 to write songs for *Let's Fall in Love*, released in January 1934. The title song became a best-seller for Eddy Duchin and His Orch. in February; Arlen also had a minor hit with his own recording. The songwriters returned to N.Y. to write their last edition of the *Cotton Club Parade* (March 23, 1934). Among its memorable songs were "Ill Wind," which became a hit for Eddy Duchin with Arlen on vocals, and "As Long as I Live." Thereafter, Arlen and Koehler ceased to collaborate on a regular basis, though they worked together occasionally. Arlen accepted an offer from E. Y. Harburg and Ira Gershwin to write music to their lyrics for the revue *Life

Begins at 8:40, which opened in August 1934. It ran 237 performances and launched two hits, "You're a Builder Upper" by Leo Reisman with Arlen on vocals, and "Fun to Be Fooled" by Henry King and His Orch.

Arlen signed another one-picture deal in 1935 with filmmaker Samuel Goldwyn and returned to Hollywood, where he collaborated with Lew Brown on *Strike Me Pink*, starring Eddie Cantor and Ethel Merman, which was released in January 1936. By that time Arlen had signed a three-picture contract with Warner Bros. *The Singing Kid*, released in April, featured Al Jolson and Cab Calloway, while *Stage Struck* in September and *Gold Diggers of 1937* in December both starred Dick Powell. All three had lyrics by E. Y. Harburg. Thereafter, Arlen worked for the studios only on a freelance basis.

On Jan. 8, 1937, Arlen married former model and chorus girl Anya Taranda, to whom he remained married until her death in 1970. He and Harburg next wrote a Broadway musical, *Hooray for What!* It starred Ed Wynn and ran 200 performances, a modest success for the middle of the Depression. In 1938, Arlen and Harburg returned to Hollywood, where they were hired to write the songs for the children's fantasy *The Wizard of Oz*. Though not a financial success upon initial theatrical release in August 1939, the film generated a #1 song in the Oscar-winning "Over the Rainbow," the most popular recordings of which were by Glenn Miller and His Orch. and the film's star, Judy Garland. The score also featured such charming songs as "Ding Dong! The Witch Is Dead" and "If I Only Had a Brain." (*The Wizard of Oz* finally turned a profit and was recognized as a classic film after it began a series of television broadcasts in the late 1950s.)

Arlen and Harburg contributed songs to the Marx Brothers film *At the Circus*, released in November 1939, including the novelty "Lydia, the Tattooed Lady" for Groucho Marx. Two years passed before Arlen's next film credit, *Blues in the Night*, on which he collaborated with Johnny Mercer. Released in December 1941, the film is best remembered for its Oscar-nominated title song, which earned half a dozen chart recordings, the most popular of which was the #1 version by Woody Herman and His Orch. Arlen and Mercer next teamed up for the all-star wartime film *Star-Spangled Rhythm*, released at the end of 1942. Glenn Miller took "That Old Black Magic" from its score to #1, and the song earned a 1943 Academy Award nomination.

Arlen reunited with E. Y. Harburg to write new songs for the film adaptation of the all-black Vernon Duke–John Latouche musical *Cabin in the Sky*. Released in May, it brought Arlen a second 1943 Oscar nomination with "Happiness Is a Thing Called Joe." He earned his third nomination in a single year for "My Shining Hour," taken from his and Mercer's score for the Fred Astaire film *The Sky's the Limit*, released in September. The song became a Top Ten hit for Glen Gray and The Casa Loma Orch. Also in the film was the torch song "One for My Baby (and One More for the Road)."

Arlen reunited with Ted Koehler for the March 1944 film *Up in Arms*, starring Danny Kaye and Dinah Shore, and the songwriters enjoyed a chart record with "Tess's Torch Song (I Had a Man)," recorded by Ella Mae

Morse, as well as an Academy Award nomination for "Now I Know." Arlen then wrote his first Broadway musical in seven years with Harburg, *Bloomer Girl*, which became the most successful stage work of his career with a run of 654 performances. Bing Crosby scored a Top Ten hit with "Evelina" from the score. Crosby also starred in the next Arlen/Mercer film, *Here Come the Waves*, released at the end of 1944; the war-themed movie musical gave him a major hit with the Oscar-nominated "Ac-Cent-Tchu-Ate the Positive," which he recorded with The Andrews Sisters, though it was Mercer himself who took the song to the top of the charts. Jo Stafford also found a minor hit from the film with "Let's Take the Long Way Home."

Stafford went into the Top Ten with "Out of This World," the Arlen/Mercer title song for the June 1945 comedy in which Eddie Bracken sang with Crosby's voice. Arlen's other hit of 1945 came in September with a Top Ten revival of "It's Only a Paper Moon," by Ella Fitzgerald and The Delta Rhythm Boys. Arlen and Mercer also wrote the songs for the 1946 all-black Broadway musical *St. Louis Woman*, which ran only 113 performances but featured "Come Rain or Come Shine," a chart record for Margaret Whiting. Back in Hollywood, Arlen teamed with Leo Robin for the May 1948 film *Casbah*, which featured the Academy Award nominee "For Every Man There's a Woman." Tony Martin, who starred in the film, recorded the song for a chart entry.

Arlen worked steadily in film in the early 1950s, writing with Mercer (*The Petty Girl*, August 1950), Ralph Blane (*My Blue Heaven*, September 1950; *Down Among the Sheltering Palms*, June 1953), and Dorothy Fields (*Mr. Imperium*, October 1951; *The Farmer Takes a Wife*, June 1953). But the only hits he enjoyed during these years were minor revivals of "Blues in the Night" by Rosemary Clooney in September 1952 and "I've Got the World on a String" by Frank Sinatra in July 1953.

In the last quarter of 1954, Arlen had two film scores and a new Broadway show. For the remake of *A Star Is Born*, starring Judy Garland and released in October, he wrote songs with Ira Gershwin, including the Oscar-nominated "The Man that Got Away." Arlen and Gershwin also wrote the songs for the backstage drama *The Country Girl*, starring Bing Crosby and released in December. For Broadway, Arlen teamed up with novelist Truman Capote on *House of Flowers*, which ran only 137 performances despite a critically acclaimed score including "A Sleepin' Bee."

Arlen's most popular songs continued to enjoy revivals in the mid-1950s. Sammy Davis Jr. took "That Old Black Magic" into the Top 40 in August 1955; Tony Bennett had a chart entry with "One for My Baby (and One More for the Road)" in May 1957, and Louis Prima and Keely Smith returned "That Old Black Magic" to the Top 40 yet again in December 1958. Meanwhile, Arlen wrote two Broadway musicals, 1957's *Jamaica* (with Harburg), starring Lena Horne, which was a hit, running 557 performances; and 1959's *Saratoga* (with Mercer), which failed.

In the 1960s, Arlen's Top 40 song revivals included "Over the Rainbow" by The Demensions in September

1960; "That Old Black Magic" by Bobby Rydell in May 1961; "Let's Fall in Love" by Peaches and Herb in March 1967; and "Ding Dong! The Witch Is Dead" by The Fifth Estate, in July 1967. The composer wrote a final film score with E. Y. Harburg for the animated film *Gay Purr-ee*, featuring the voices of Judy Garland and Robert Goulet and released in December 1962, and he wrote the title song for Garland's final film, *I Could Go on Singing*, released in May 1963. In 1966 he released an album, *Harold Sings Arlen (With Friend)*,accompanied by Barbra Streisand, who had recorded many of his songs on her early albums. He wrote songs for two unproduced musicals, *Softly* (intended for Broadway), in 1966, and *Clippity Clop and Clementine* (for television), in 1973, and contributed some new songs to an Off-Broadway revival of *House of Flowers* that opened in January 1968. He suffered from Parkinson's disease and was largely inactive during the last decade of his life. He died in 1986 at age 81.

Disc.: (only works for which Arlen was a primary credited composer are listed): **MUSICALS/REVUES** (dates refer to N.Y. openings): *Earl Carroll Vanities* (July 1, 1930); *You Said It* (Jan. 19, 1931); *Life Begins at 8:40* (Aug. 27, 1934); *Hooray for What!* (Dec. 1, 1937); *Bloomer Girl* (Oct. 5, 1944); *St. Louis Woman* (March 30, 1946); *House of Flowers* (Dec. 30, 1954); *Jamaica* (Oct. 31, 1957); *Saratoga* (Dec. 7, 1959). **FILMS:** *Let's Fall in Love* (1934); *Strike Me Pink* (1936); *The Singing Kid* (1936); *Stage Struck* (1936); *Gold Diggers of 1937* (1936); *The Wizard of Oz* (1939); *At the Circus* (1939); *Blues in the Night* (1941); *Rio Rita* (1942); *Star Spangled Rhythm* (1942); *Cabin in the Sky* (1943); *The Sky's the Limit* (1943); *Up in Arms* (1944); *Kismet* (1944); *Here Come the Waves* (1944); *Casbah* (1948); *The Petty Girl* (1950); *My Blue Heaven* (1950); *Mr. Imperium* (1951); *Down among the Sheltering Palms* (1953); *The Farmer Takes a Wife* (1953); *A Star Is Born* (1954); *The Country Girl* (1954); *Gay Purr-ee* (1962).

Bibl.: E. Jablonski, *H. A.: Happy with the Blues* (Garden City, N.Y., 1961); Jablonski, *H. A.: Rhythm, Rainbows, and Blues* (Boston, 1996).—**WR**

Arlt, Wulf (Friedrich), German musicologist; b. Breslau, March 5, 1938. He studied musicology at the Univ. of Cologne; then received his Ph.D. in 1966 from the Univ. of Basel with the diss. *Ein Festoffizium des Mittelalters aus Beauvais in seiner liturgischen Bedeutung* (publ. in Cologne, 1970); subsequently completed his Habilitation there in 1970 with his *Praxis und Lehre der "Ars subtilior": Studien zur Geschichte der Notation im Spätmittelalter*. He joined the faculty of the Univ. of Basel as a lecturer in 1965; became a prof. there in 1972. In 1971 he also became director of the Schola Cantorum Basiliensis. Arlt devoted his critical capacities to elucidating the problems of music in the Middle Ages, and contributed important articles on the subject to music journals. He also publ. *Italien als produktive Erfahrung franko-flamischer Musiker im 15. Jahrhundert* (1993) and *Lo Bozolari: Ein Klerikerfest des MA aus Le Puy* (1995). —**NS/LK/DM**

Arma, Paul (real name, **Imre Weisshaus**), Hungarian-born French composer; b. Budapest, Oct. 22, 1904; d. Paris, Nov. 28, 1987. From 1921 to 1924 he attended classes of Bartók at the Budapest Academy of

Music, then went to N.Y., where he became associated with radical political and musical groups and contributed highly complex pieces to Cowell's publication *New Music Quarterly*. A composer of empiric persuasion, he explored quaquaversal paths of modern techniques in contrasting sonorities. In 1930 he went to Paris and worked under the pseudonym Paul Arma. In 1947 he publ. in Paris a modernistically planned *Nouveau dictionnaire de musique*. Typical of his modernistic techniques, reflected in the titles of some of his works, are Concerto for String Quartet and Orch. (1947); Violin Sonata (1949); *31 instantanés* for Woodwind, Percussion, Celesta, Xylophone, and Piano (1951); *Polydiaphonie* for Orch. (1962); *Structures variées* for Orch. (1964); *Prismes sonores* for Orch. (1966); *6 transparences* for Oboe and String Orch. (1968); *Résonances* for Orch. (1971); *6 Convergences* for Orch. (1978); *Silences and Emergences* for String Quartet (1979); *Deux Regards* for Violin and Piano (1982); *Deux Images* for Cello and Piano (1982); numerous experimental pieces for various instrumental combinations.—NS/LK/DM

Armstrong, Karan, American soprano; b. Horne, Mont., Dec. 14, 1941. She was educated at Concordia Coll. in Moorhead, Minn. (B.A., 1963) and received private vocal instruction from various teachers, including Lotte Lehmann in Santa Barbara. In 1966 she made her operatic debut as Elvira in *L'italiana in Algeri* at the San Francisco Opera. After singing minor roles at the Metropolitan Opera in N.Y. (1966–69), she sang with several other U.S. opera companies, including the N.Y.C. Opera (1975–78). In 1976 she made her European debut as Salome at the Strasbourg Opera. She made her Bayreuth Festival debut as Elsa in 1979 and her Covent Garden debut in London as Lulu in 1981. She also sang in Vienna, Munich, Paris, Hamburg, and other European music centers. Among her finest roles are Violetta, Tosca, Mimi, Alice Ford, Countess Almaviva, Eva, Mélisande, and the Marschallin. She also sang contemporary roles, creating the role of Death in Gottfried von Einem's *Jesu Hochzeit* (1980) and the title role in Giuseppe Sinopoli's *Lou Salome* (1981). She married **Götz Friedrich**.—NS/LK/DM

Armstrong (born Hardin), Lil(ian), jazz pianist, singer, composer; b. Memphis, Tenn., Feb. 3, 1898; d. Chicago, Aug. 27, 1971. Though best known as **Louis Armstrong's** second wife, Lil Armstrong was hired by cornetist Joe "King" Oliver and led her own bands, proof of her solid musicianship. She studied music for three years at Fisk Univ., and claimed to have published six songs. In 1917 Armstrong vacationed in Chicago, where she began working as a song demonstrator in Ben Jones' Music Store. She decided to stay in the Windy City and played with Curtis Mosby, trumpeter "Sugar Johnny" Smith, and Freddie Keppard before leading a band at Dreamland in 1920. (She was briefly married during this period, it seems.) Armstrong worked on and off with King Oliver from 1921 until 1924. She married Louis Armstrong on Feb. 5, 1924. Later that year she led a band at the Dreamland in Chicago while Louis Armstrong was in N.Y. with Fletcher Henderson. After that she lived briefly in N.Y.,

then again went to Chicago to lead a band, which Louis Armstrong joined in late 1925. She was the regular pianist on her her husband's famous Hot Five and Hot Seven recordings (1925–27) and composed many of the pieces. She hated to fly, which was one factor that limited her career. (Louis Armstrong turned down several appearances because of her fear.) She also worked in Hugh Swift's Band (1926) and toured with Freddie Keppard (1928). After studying with Louis Victor Saar, she earned a Teachers' Diploma at the Chicago Coll. of Music in 1928, then studied at the N.Y. Coll. of Music with August Fraemcke, earning a postgraduate degree in 1929. She and Louis Armstrong separated in 1931 and were divorced in 1938. Now going by her maiden name, Hardin won a lawsuit against Armstrong for unpaid royalties on songs they co-wrote, and at one point she billed his replacement in her band, Jonah Jones, as "Louis Armstrong the Second."

During the early–1930s Hardin led her own "all-girl" band and guested with Ralph Cooper's Orch. at the Harlem Opera House in 1931. She next formed an all-male band that broadcast regularly on the NBC, WMCA, and WOR networks. She appeared as a soloist in the "Hot Chocolate" and "Shuffle Along" revues, led an all-girl band at Chicago's Regal Theatre in 1934, and in 1935 and 1936 led an all-male band that played residencies in Detroit, Buffalo, and elsewhere. During the late 1930s Hardin lived in N.Y., mainly to be house pianist at the Decca recording studios. In late 1940, she returned to Chicago to play solo at the Tin Pan Alley Club, a stint that was followed by long solo residencies at the Garrick Stage Bar, the Mark Twain Lounge, the Nob Hill Club, and the East Town Bar in Milwaukee. Her songs "Brown Gal" and "Just for a Thrill" were recorded by The Ink Spots. While appearing in Milwaukee Hardin met a visiting Frenchman, Michel Grasje, who convinced her to move to Europe in early 1952. She subsequently worked mainly in Paris, including a billing with Sidney Bechet that was attended by 15,000 people. Hardin made occasional visits to London and a return trip to Chicago in mid-1954. During the late 1950s and 1960s, she was active again around Chicago, and at one point had her own restaurant. She also toured, including dates in Canada. Hardin suffered a fatal heart attack while taking part in a Louis Armstrong Memorial Concert, suggesting that her former husband remained a highly emotional connection for her. She was also a clothing designer and seamstress whose customers included Armstrong, Count Basie, Lucky Millinder, and Fletcher Henderson.

DISC.: *Louis and Me* (1953); *Chicago: The Living Legends* (1961).—JC/LP

Armstrong, Louis, seminal American jazz trumpeter and singer; b. New Orleans, Aug. 4, 1901; d. N.Y., July 6, 1971. As the first prominent jazz soloist, Armstrong is the most influential musician in the history of the genre. His virtuosic playing, notably in the Hot Five and Hot Seven recordings of the mid-1920s, helped to define jazz as a music of improvisatory complexity. His gravelly voice and exuberant personality led him to a broader fame as a popular singer and motion picture performer that his jazz fans sometimes viewed with dismay. Nevertheless, he did more to popularize jazz than any other individual, and his major pop hits, including "All of Me" (1932), "Hello, Dolly!" (1964), and "What a Wonderful World" (1968), were just as much expressions of his musical talent as his astounding trumpet playing.

Armstrong was born into poverty. His father, William Armstrong, was a factory worker who left the family shortly after Louis was born. Louis was raised by his mother, Mary Albert Armstrong, and by his maternal grandmother. While attending grade school, he worked for a junk dealer who encouraged his interest in music and helped him buy a cornet, which he taught himself to play. At 11 he dropped out of school in the fifth grade and joined a street-corner quartet. Convicted of firing a gun in a public place on New Year's Eve, 1912, he was sentenced to a reform school; there he studied with music teacher Peter Davis, joining the school band in which he played the bugle and the cornet and of which he was appointed leader.

Armstrong was released on June 16, 1914. He became a manual laborer over the next few years while gradually finding work as a musician. He became the protégé of cornetist Joe "King" Oliver, from whom he took lessons. When Oliver left New Orleans for Chicago in June 1918, Armstrong took his place in Kid Ory's band. Around this time he married Daisy Parker, a prostitute. (They were divorced on Dec. 23, 1923.) In the spring of 1919 he joined the orchestra of Fate Marable, which played on a Miss. riverboat. He stayed with Marable until the fall of 1921.

Armstrong left New Orleans in August 1922 to join King Oliver's Creole Jazz Band at the Lincoln Gardens Café in Chicago. He made his first recordings with Oliver in the spring of 1923. On Feb. 5, 1924, he married the band's pianist, Lillian Harden, and his wife encouraged him to leave Oliver. He moved to N.Y. in the fall to join the orchestra of Fletcher Henderson; at this time he began to play the trumpet as well as the cornet. He was with Henderson for more than a year, returning to Chicago in November 1925 to play in his wife's band, the Dreamland Syncopators.

Armstrong made his first recording as a leader, "My Heart," on Nov. 12, 1925. From then through December 1928 he recorded frequently in small studio ensembles dubbed the Hot Five or the Hot Seven, and these recordings established him as a star. Meanwhile, in 1926 he played with Erskine Tate's orchestra at the Vendome Theatre and with Carroll Dickerson's orchestra at the Sunset Café.

Armstrong scored his first record hit in July 1926 with the Hot Five recording of "Muskrat Ramble" (music credited to Kid Ory, though it was based on a tune by New Orleans jazz legend Buddy Bolden). In February 1927 he began fronting the group at the Sunset Café, which was called Louis Armstrong and His Stompers. (As a star soloist, Armstrong fronted bands rather than leading them in the conventional sense.) His first vocal hit came in April with "Big Butter and Egg Man" (music and lyrics by Percy Venable and Armstrong), on which he duetted with May Alix. He continued to score hits during 1927 and 1928, notably "West

End Blues" in September 1928; the recording became one of the first to be admitted into the NARAS Hall of Fame in 1974. Meanwhile, he again played in an orchestra nominally under the leadership of Carroll Dickerson at the Savoy Ballroom starting in March 1928.

Armstrong took the band to N.Y. in May 1929, where they appeared at Connie's Inn, a nightclub in Harlem, while he also played in the orchestra of the Broadway revue *Hot Chocolates* (N.Y., June 20, 1929), performing "Ain't Misbehavin'" (music by Fats Waller, lyrics by Andy Razaf), which he recorded for a hit in September. This marked the beginning of his transition from a jazz instrumentalist to a popular entertainer.

Starting in February 1930, Armstrong fronted Luis Russell's band on a tour of the South. In May he went to Los Angeles, where he took over the band at Sebastian's Cotton Club until March 1931. He also found time to make his first film appearance in *Ex-Flame*, released at the end of the year.

Returning to Chicago, Armstrong fronted an orchestra led by Zilner Randolph, with which he toured nationally. Now recording more pop-oriented material for Columbia Records, a major label, he began to have bigger record hits in 1932, including "Chinatown, My Chinatown" (music by William Jerome and Jean Schwartz, lyrics by Jerome), "You Can Depend on Me" (music and lyrics by Charles Carpenter, Louis Dunlap, and Earl Hines), "All of Me" (music by Gerald Marks, lyrics by Seymour Simons; a best-seller in March), "Love, You Funny Thing" (music by Fred Ahlert, lyrics by Roy Turk), "Sweethearts on Parade" (music by Carmen Lombardo, lyrics by Charles Newman), and "Body and Soul" (music and lyrics by Edward Heyman, Robert Sour, Frank Eyton, and John Green).

Armstrong arrived in England for a tour in July 1932, and he spent much of the next several years in Europe. Returning to the U.S. in 1935, he took several important steps in his career. He hired Joe Glaser as his manager (they would stay together until Glaser's death 34 years later); he organized a new band, which he premiered in Indianapolis on July 1; and he signed a contract with Decca Records. During the late 1930s he toured the U.S. regularly, made a diverse set of recordings, and appeared in small roles in a series of films starting with the Bing Crosby vehicle *Pennies from Heaven* in December 1936.

Armstrong divorced his second wife on Sept. 30, 1938; on Oct. 11 he married his long-time companion Alpha Smith. They, in turn, divorced on Oct. 2, 1942. Five days later he married chorus girl Lucille Wilson, to whom he remained married for the rest of his life.

Armstrong briefly returned to Broadway in *Swingin' the Dream* (N.Y., Nov. 29, 1939), a musical version of Shakespeare's *Midsummer Night's Dream* that ran only 13 performances. During the early 1940s he continued to tour, record, and make the occasional film appearance, notably in the all-black musical *Cabin in the Sky* in May 1943. He scored an R&B Top Ten hit with "I Wonder" (music and lyrics by Cecil Grant and Raymond Leveen) in March 1945 and reached the Top Ten of the pop charts with "You Won't Be Satisfied (Until You Break My Heart)" (music and lyrics by Freddy James and Larry

Stork) and the Top Ten of the R&B charts with "The Frim Fram Sauce" (music and lyrics by Joe Ricardel and Redd Evans), both duets with Ella Fitzgerald, in April 1946.

Armstrong disbanded in the summer of 1947, reorganizing a smaller unit he called the All Stars, which made its debut Aug. 13, 1947, at Billy Berg's Club in Los Angeles. With the end of World War II and the recovery of Europe, he embarked on his first European tour in 13 years in February 1948; from then until his death, much of his time would be taken up by international touring.

Armstrong's first Top Ten LP came with *Satchmo at Symphony Hall* in June 1951 ("Satchmo," a corruption of "Satchelmouth," was a nickname he had acquired in 1932); in September he reached the Top Ten on the singles chart with "(When We Are Dancing) I Get Ideas" (music by Julio Sanders, English lyrics by Dorcas Cochran). Another notable recording of this period was "A Kiss to Build a Dream On" (music by Harry Ruby, lyrics by Bert Kalmar and Oscar Hammerstein II), which Armstrong sang in the movie *The Strip* and which he recorded for a hit in early 1952. Forty-one years later the recording was used prominently in the hit film *Sleepless in Seattle* and featured on its chart-topping, triple-platinum soundtrack album.

Leaving Decca Records in 1954, Armstrong freelanced for various labels instead of signing an exclusive deal. This allowed him to record his Top Ten tribute to Fats Waller, *Satch Plays Fats*, for Columbia in 1955, as well as a treatment of "Mack the Knife" (music by Kurt Weill, English lyrics by Marc Blitzstein) that made the Top 40 in February 1956, while moving to Verve Records for a popular duet album with Ella Fitzgerald, *Ella and Louis*, on the charts in December 1956. Meanwhile, "Now You Has Jazz" (music and lyrics by Cole Porter), a duet with Bing Crosby that charted in October 1956 and was drawn from Armstrong's appearance in the film *High Society*, was released on Capitol Records, and Decca, capitalizing on his popularity on records (and on the revival of the song by Fats Domino), scored a Top 40 hit with Armstrong's 1949 recording of "Blueberry Hill" in November.

Armstrong spent most of his time touring, barely slowed down by a heart attack in June 1959. His hit recording of the title song from the musical *Hello, Dolly!* (music and lyrics by Jerry Herman), was a surprise; it topped the charts in May 1964, followed by an LP of the same name that also went to #1 in June and was gold by August. Nominated for two Grammy Awards, Armstrong won one for Best Vocal Performance, Male.

During the last four years of his life, Armstrong was plagued by heart and kidney troubles that put him in the hospital frequently. He scored an international hit in the spring of 1968 with "What a Wonderful World" (music and lyrics by George David Weiss and Robert Thiele), which topped the charts in the U.K. It did not hit in the U.S. at the time, but 20 years later made the Top 40 after being featured in the film *Good Morning, Vietnam*. Armstrong made a triumphant appearance in the film version of *Hello, Dolly!* in 1969. He died two years later at the age of 69.

DISC.: *Satchmo at Symphony Hall* (1951); *L. A. Plays W.C. Handy* (1954); *Satchmo Serenades* (1954); *Satch Plays Fats* (1955); *Satchmo the Great* (1955); *Ambassador Satch* (1955); *Ella and Louis* (with Ella Fitzgerald; 1956); *Ella and Louis Again* (with Ella Fitzgerald; 1957); *L. A. Meets Oscar Peterson* (with Oscar Peterson; 1957); *Let's Do It: Best of the Verve Years* (1957); *The Great Chicago Concert* (1957); *I Love Jazz* (1962); *Hello Dolly!* (1964); *L. A.'s Greatest Hits* (1967); *What a Wonderful World* (1968); *L. A. and King Oliver* (1992); *All Time Greatest Hits* (1994); *16 Most Requested Songs* (1994); *The Complete Ella Fitzgerald and L. A.* (1997); *The Best of Ella Fitzgerald and L. A.* (with Ella Fitzgerald; 1997); *The Complete RCA Victor Recordings* (1997); *Our Love Is Here to Stay: Ella and Louis Sing Gershwin* (1998); *Cocktail Hour: L. A.* (1999); *The Ultimate Collection* (2000); *The Great Summit: The Complete Sessions* (with Duke Ellington; 2000); *20th Century Masters—The Millennium Collection: The Best of L. A.* (2000); *A 100th Birthday Celebration* (2000); *Love Songs* (2000); *The Complete Hot Five and Hot Seven Recordings* (2000).

WRITINGS: *Swing That Music* (N.Y., 1936); *Satchmo: My Life in New Orleans* (N.Y., 1954).

BIBL.: R. Goffin, *Horn of Plenty: The Story of L. A.* (N.Y., 1947); H. Panassié, *L. A.* (Paris, 1947); J. Eaton, *Trumpeter's Tale: The Story of Young L. A.* (N.Y., 1955); A. McCarthy, *L. A.* (London, 1960); M. Jones, J. Chilton, and L. Feather, *Salute to Satchmo* (London, 1970); M. Jones and J. Chilton, *L.: The L. A. Story, 1900–1971* (London, 1971); R. Merryman, *L. A.: A Self-Portrait* (N.Y., 1971); R. Hoskins, *L. A.: Biography of a Musician* (Los Angeles, 1979); H. Westerburg, *Boy from New Orleans: A Discography of L. "Satchmo" A.* (Copenhagen, 1981); J. Collier, *L. A.: An American Genius* (N.Y., 1983); M. Pinfold, *L. A.: His Life and Times* (N.Y., 1987); G. Giddins, *Satchmo* (N.Y., 1988); S. Tanenhaus, *L. A.: Musician* (N.Y., 1988); M. Miller, ed., *L. A.: A Cultural Legacy* (Seattle, 1994); L. Bergreen, *L. A.: An Extravagant Life* (N.Y., 1997); M. Boujut, *L. A.* (N.Y., 1998).—**WR**

Armstrong, Richard, English conductor; b. Leicester, Jan. 7, 1943. He studied at Corpus Christi Coll., Cambridge. In 1966 he joined the staff of the Royal Opera House, Covent Garden, London; in 1968 he became asst. conductor of the Welsh National Opera, Cardiff; from 1973 to 1986 he was its music director; also appeared as a guest conductor. In 1993 he became music director of Glasgow's Scottish Opera and chief conductor of the new National Orch. of Scotland. That same year he was made a Commander of the Order of the British Empire.—**NS/LK/DM**

Armstrong, Sheila (Ann), English soprano; b. Ashington, Northumberland, Aug. 13, 1942. She studied at the Royal Academy of Music in London, winning the Kathleen Ferrier Memorial Scholarship in 1965. Following her operatic debut as Despina at the Sadler's Wells Theatre in London in 1965, she made her debut at the Glyndebourne Festival as Belinda in *Dido and Aeneas* in 1966. In 1971 she made her first appearance in N.Y. as a soloist with the N.Y. Phil. In 1973 she made her debut at London's Covent Garden as Marzelline in *Fidelio*. She toured extensively in England, Europe, North America, and the Far East as a concert singer. In her operatic appearances, she has had particular success in works by Mozart, Rossini, and Donizetti.—**NS/LK/DM**

Arndt, Günther, German choral conductor; b. Berlin-Charlottenburg, April 1, 1907; d. Berlin, Dec. 25,

1976. He was educated at the Akademie für Schul- und Kirchenmusik in Berlin, and also studied musicology at the Univ. of Berlin. He then was engaged as lecturer at the Volkshochschule in Berlin (1932–40). After the end of World War II in 1945, he headed the chamber music dept. of the Berlin Radio RIAS; also conducted the Berlin Motet Choir (1950–60) and the RIAS Chamber Choir (1955–72). He served as deputy head of music for the RIAS (1964–72). He gained distinction as a conductor of an extensive choral repertoire.—NS/LK/DM

Arndt-Ober, Margarethe, German mezzo-soprano; b. Berlin, April 15, 1885; d. Bad Sachsa, March 24, 1971. She studied in Berlin with Benno Stolzenberg and later with Arthur Arndt, who became her husband. In 1906 she made her operatic debut as Azucena in Frankfurt an der Oder; in 1907, joined the Berlin Royal Opera. On Nov. 21, 1913, she made her Metropolitan Opera debut in N.Y. as Ortrud, remaining on its roster until 1917; then was interned until the end of World War I. In 1919 she became a member of the Berlin State Opera, where she sang until the end of World War II. —NS/LK/DM

Arne, Michael, English composer and keyboard player, illegitimate son of **Thomas Augustine Arne;** b. London, c. 1740; d. there, Jan. 14, 1786. He was reared by his aunt, **Susanne Maria Cibber.** His musical talent manifested itself at an early age and, while still young, he publ. *The Floweret* (1750), the first of seven song collections, which included the highly popular song *The Highland Laddie.* Arne became active as a keyboard player and composer at various London theaters and pleasure gardens. In addition to his operas, he contributed numbers to many dramatic scores. His song *The Lass with the delicate air* (1762) became his most successful work. In 1766 he married the singer Elizabeth Wright, a principal member of London's Drury Lane Theatre. On Jan. 2, 1767, she sang in the premiere of Arne's opera *Cymon* there, which scored a notable success. About this time he became engrossed in alchemy, but his experiments proved costly and landed him in debtor's prison. In 1771–72 he toured Germany, during which time he conducted the first public performance of Handel's *Messiah* in that country on May 21, 1772. While in Dublin for a production if his *Cymon* in 1777, he once more was ensnared by his interest in alchemy and once again landed in debtor's prison. Upon his release, he returned to London and was a composer for Covent Garden from 1778 to 1783. His fortunes were variable and he died destitute.

Works: DRAMATIC (all 1st perf. in London unless otherwise given): *The Humorous Lieutenant* (Dec. 10, 1756); *Harlequin's Invasion, or A Christmas Gambol* (Dec. 31, 1759; in collaboration with T. Ayleward and W. Boyce); *The Heiress, or The Antigallican* (May 21, 1759); *Edgar and Emmiline* (Jan. 31, 1761); *Hymen* (Jan. 23, 1764); *Almena* (Nov. 2, 1764; in collaboration with J. Battishill); *Cymon* (Jan. 2, 1767; rev. version Jan. 17, 1778); *Linco's Travels* (April 6, 1767; in collaboration with J. Vernon); *The Maid of the Vale* (Dublin, Feb. 15, 1775); *Emperor of the Moon* (March 22, 1777); *The Fathers, or The Good-natured Man* (Nov. 30, 1778); *The Belle's Strategem* (Feb. 22, 1780); *The Artifice* (April 14, 1780); *The Choice of Harlequin, or The Indian Chief* (Dec.

26, 1781); *Vertumnus and Pomona* (Feb. 21, 1782); *The Positive Man* (March 16, 1782; in collaboration with S. Arnold); *The Capricious Lady* (Jan. 17, 1783); *Tristram Shandy* (April 26, 1783). OTHER: 7 song collections (London, 1750–80).

BIBL.: J. Parkinson, *An Index to the Vocal Works of Thomas Augustine Arne and M. A.* (Detroit, 1972).—NS/LK/DM

Arne, Thomas Augustine, famous English composer, natural father of **Michael Arne** and brother of **Susanna Maria Cibber;** b. London, March 12, 1710; d. there, March 5, 1778. His father, an upholsterer and undertaker, sent him to Eton to study law, but also permitted him to take violin lessons from Michael Festing. Arne's love for music eventually prevailed. With Henry Carey and J. F. Lampe, he organized a theater company in London in 1732 to present in English operas "after the Italian manner." Their company broke up later that same year, and Arne then founded his own enterprise at Lincoln's Inn Fields. On March 7, 1733, his company staged the premiere there of his opera *Rosamond* with his sister in the title role. His company soon merged with Theophilus Cibber's company at the New Theatre, Haymarket, where Arne scored a notable success with the premiere of *The Opera of Operas, or Tom Thumb the Great* on Oct. 29, 1733. In 1737 Arne married the singer **Cecilia Young.** On March 4, 1738, his music for Milton's masque *Comus* was first performed at Drury Lane and secured his reputation as one of the leading English composers of his time. A commission from Frederick, Prince of Wales, led to the composition of music for James Thomson's patriotic masque *Alfred,* which received its premiere in an open-air theater at the Prince's home in Cliveden on Aug. 1, 1740. The final chorus, *Rule Britannia,* became Arne's most celebrated work. In 1742 Arne and his wife visited Dublin, where she sang in the premiere of his oratorio *The Death of Abel* on Feb. 18, 1744. From 1744 to 1749 Arne composed several works for Drury Lane, and thereafter for Covent Garden. In 1755 Arne, his wife, and his gifted pupil, Charlotte Brent, visited Dublin. Arne's marriage had become tempestuous, and in 1756 he and Brent returned to London alone. In 1759 Arne was admitted to the degree of Doctor of Music at Oxford. On Oct. 10, 1759, his setting of *The Beggar's Opera,* with Brent as a leading singer, scored a great success at its first performance at Covent Garden. Success continued there with the premiere of his comic opera *Thomas and Sally, or The Sailor's Return* on Nov. 28, 1760. His greatest triumph followed there on Feb. 2, 1762, with the first performance of his opera *Artaxerxes.* His pasticcio, *Love in a Village,* also proved highly popular at its premiere there on Dec. 8, 1762. However, his subsequent works were failures. Ill health and the loss of Brent in marriage to the violinist Thomas Pinto in 1766 added to his woes. However, his fortunes rebounded when Garrick asked him to compose an ode for the Shakespeare Jubilee in Stratford in 1769. On Nov. 21, 1772, his opera *Elfrida* was premiered at Covent Garden with much success. Shortly before he died, Arne and his wife were reconciled.

Arne composed some 90 works for the stage, including operas, masques, pantomimes, and incidental music. Although his output is uneven, he was without question one of the major English dramatic composers of his time. He also wrote a number of fine instrumental pieces.

WORKS: DRAMATIC (all 1st perf. in London unless otherwise given): *Rosamund* (March 7, 1733); *The Opera of Operas, or Tom Thumb the Great* (Oct. 29, 1733); *Dido and Aeneas* (Jan. 12, 1734); *Love and Glory* (March 21, 1734); *Harlequin Orpheus, or The Magical Pipe* (March 3, 1735); *Harlequin Restor'd, or The Country Revels* (Oct. 18, 1735); *Zara* (Jan. 12, 1736); *The Fall of Phaeton* (Feb. 28, 1736); *Comus* (March 4, 1738); *An Hospital for Fools* (Nov. 15, 1739); *Don John, or The Libertine Destroy'd* (Feb. 13, 1740); *Alfred* (Cliveden, Aug. 1, 1740; expanded version, London, March 20, 1745); *The Judgment of Paris* (Cliveden, Aug. 1, 1740; rev. version, London, April 3, 1759); *Oedipus, King of Thebes* (Nov. 19, 1740); *The Blind Beggar of Bethnal Green* (April 3, 1741); *Miss Lucy in Town* (May 6, 1742); *The Temple of Dullness* (Jan. 17, 1745); *The Picture, or The Cuckold in Conceit* (Feb. 11, 1745); *King Pepin's Campaign* (April 15, 1745); *Harlequin Incendiary, or Columbine Cameron* (March 3, 1746); *Lethe, or Aesop in the Shades* (Jan. 18, 1749); *The Triumph of Peace* (Feb. 21, 1749); *The Muses' Looking Glass* (March 9, 1749); *Henry and Emma, or The Nut-brown Maid* (March 31, 1749); *Don Saverio* (Feb. 15, 1750); *Harlequin Sorcerer* (Feb. 11, 1752); *The Drummer, or The Haunted House* (Dec. 8, 1752); *The Sheep-shearing, or Florizel and Perdita* (March 25, 1754); *Eliza* (May 29, 1754); *Britannia* (May 9, 1755); *Injured Honour, or The Earl of Westmoreland* (Dublin, March 8, 1756); *The Pincushion* (Dublin, March 20, 1756); *Mercury Harlequin* (Dec. 27, 1756); *The Sultan, or Solyman and Zayde* (Nov. 23, 1758); *The Beggar's Opera* (Oct. 10, 1759); *The Jovial Crew* (Feb. 14, 1760); *Thomas and Sally, or The Sailor's Return* (Nov. 28, 1760); *Artaxerxes* (Feb. 2, 1762); *Love in a Village* (Dec. 8, 1762); *The Arcadian Nuptials* (Jan. 19, 1764); *The Guardian Outwitted* (Dec. 12, 1764); *L'Olimpiade* (April 27, 1765); *King Arthur, or The British Worthy* (Dec. 13, 1770); *The Fairy Prince* (Nov. 12, 1771); *Squire Badger* (March 16, 1772); *The Cooper* (June 10, 1772); *Elfrida* (Nov. 21, 1772); *The Rose* (Dec. 2, 1772); *Alzuma* (Feb. 23, 1773); *Achilles in Petticoats* (Dec. 16, 1773); *May-day, or The Little Gipsy* (Oct. 28, 1775); *Phoebe at Court* (Feb. 22, 1776); *Caractacus* (Dec. 6, 1776). Also contributions to various other works. **ORCH.:** 8 overtures (1751); *Four New Overtures or Symphonies* (1767); *Six Favourite Concertos* (c. 1787). **CHAMBER:** *VIII Sonatas or Lessons* for Harpsichord (1756); *VII Sonatas* for 2 Violins and Basso Continuo (1757). **VOCAL:** 2 oratorios: *The Death of Abel* (Dublin, Feb. 18, 1744) and *Judith* (London, Feb. 27, 1761); 2 masses; *Six English Cantatas* (1755); odes, including *An Ode upon dedicating a Building to Shakespeare* (1769); various song collections (1745–77); catches, canons, and glees.

BIBL.: B. Horner, *Life and Works of Dr. A.* (London, 1893); W. Cummings, *Dr. A. and Rule Britannia* (London, 1912); J. Parkinson, *An Index to the Vocal Works of T. A. A. and Michael Arne* (Detroit, 1972).—**NS/LK/DM**

d'Arneiro, (José Augusto) Ferreira Veiga, Viscount, Portuguese composer; b. Macao, China, Nov. 22, 1838; d. San Remo, July 7, 1903. He studied with Botelho, Schira, and Soares in Lisbon. He wrote a ballet, *Gina* (Lisbon, 1866), a *Te Deum* (Lisbon, 1871), and the operas *L'Elisire di Giovinezza* (Lisbon, March 31, 1876) and *La Derelitta* (Lisbon, 1885).—**NS/LK/DM**

Arnell, Richard (Anthony Sayer), English composer, conductor, teacher, and poet; b. London, Sept. 15, 1917. He studied with John Ireland at the Royal Coll.

of Music in London (1935–39). He taught composition at London's Trinity Coll. of Music from 1949 to 1981, then was principal lecturer there from 1981 to 1987. Arnell was ed. of *The Composer* from 1961 to 1964, and again from 1991 to 1993. In 1964 and in 1974–75 he was chairman of the Composers Guild of Great Britain. In 1967–68 he was a visiting lecturer at Bowdoin (Maine) Coll., and then was a visiting prof. at Hofstra (N.Y.) Univ. from 1968 to 1970. From 1975 to 1989 he was music director of the London International Film School, and also of Ram Filming, Ltd., from 1980 to 1991. Arnell's prolific output includes the operas *Love in Transit* (London, Feb. 27, 1958) and *Moonflowers* (Kent, July 23, 1959), the puppet operetta *The Petrified Princess* (London, May 5, 1959), the ballets *Punch and the Child* (1947), *Harlequin in April* (1951), *The Great Detective* (1953), *The Angels* (1957), and a reorchestration of Adam's *Giselle* (1965), many film scores, 7 syms., the symphonic portrait *Lord Byron*, 2 piano concertos, 2 violin concertos, a Harpsichord Concerto, 6 string quartets, 2 quintets, a Piano Trio, piano pieces, organ music, song cycles and solo songs, and electronic music.
—**NS/LK/DM**

Arnestad, Finn (Oluf Bjerke), Norwegian composer and music critic; b. Christiania, Sept. 23, 1915; d. Oslo, Jan. 30, 1998. He studied violin and piano in Oslo and, briefly, composition with Brustad; in 1952 he studied African and oriental folk music in Paris; after returning to Oslo, he was active as a music critic. His music is influenced by French Impressionism, with tangential use of dodecaphony.

WORKS: ORCH.: *Constellation*, intermezzo (1948); *Conversation*, concert intermezzo for Piano and Orch. (1950); *Meditation*, intermezzo (1952); *I.N.R.I.*, 2 concert suites from a symphonic mystery play (1952–55); Violin Concerto (1957); *Aria appassionata* (1962); *Cavatina cambiata* (1965; orig. titled *Dopplersonance*); *Overture* (1970); *Væesletjennet* for Norwegian Recorder and Orch. (1970; based on a 1938 piano piece); *Toccata* (1972); *Arabesque* (1975); Piano Concerto (1976); *Mouvement concertant*, concert piece for Double Bass and Orch. (1978). **CHAMBER:** String Quartet (1947); Sextet for Flute, Clarinet, Bassoon, Violin, Cello, and Piano (1959); Quintet for Flute and Strings (1962); *Suite in Old Dance Rhythms* for Flute, Oboe, Harpsichord, and Strings (1966); Trombone Sonata (1971); Sonata for Solo Violin (1980); Sonata for Solo Double Bass (1980). **Piano:** 2 sonatas (1967; *Ritagliata*, 1967); *Tango*, 3-part canon (1981). **VOCAL:** *Missa Brevis* for Chorus and 6 Instruments (1951); *Amen* for Chorus (1959); *Smeden og Bageren* (The Blacksmith and the Baker) for Baritone, Flute, Oboe, Harpsichord, and Strings (1966).—**NS/LK/DM**

Arnič, Blaž, Slovenian composer and teacher; b. Luče, Jan. 31, 1901; d. Ljubljana, Feb. 1, 1970. He studied organ and theory at the Ljubljana Cons. (1925–29) and at the New Vienna Cons. (1929–32). In 1945 he was appointed prof. at the Ljubljana Academy of Music. Most of his music is of programmatic content; all of his syms. bear descriptive titles, and much of the melodic and rhythmic material of his music reflects the folk motifs of Slovenia.

WORKS: ORCH.: Organ Concerto (1931); *Symphonic Rhapsody* (1933); 2 symphonic poems: *Memento mori* (1934) and

Witch Dance (1951); 6 syms.: *Resurrection* (1935); *Reverie* (1940); *The Whirlwind of War* (1941); *Pioneer* (1948); *Symphony of Labor* (1950); *In the Fatherland's Soul* (1951); *War and Peace* (1960); 3 violin concertos (1953, 1953, 1966); Cello Concerto (1960); Clarinet Concerto (1963); Viola Concerto (1967). **OTHER:** Chamber music; piano pieces; songs.—**NS/LK/DM**

Arnold, Byron, American composer and teacher; b. Vancouver, Wash., Aug. 15, 1901; d. Oscoda, Mich., Dec. 25, 1971. He studied with Rogers and Hanson at the Eastman School of Music in Rochester, N.Y., and then was mainly active as a teacher. He wrote a witty symphonic suite, *5 Incapacitated Preludes* (Rochester, N.Y., April 19, 1937), portraying a serious neurological ailment affecting sight, hearing, and muscular structures.—**NS/LK/DM**

Arnold, Carl, German organist, conductor, and composer, son of **Johann Gottfried Arnold;** b. Neukirchen, May 6, 1794; d. Christiania, Nov. 11, 1877. He studied piano with C. A. Hoffmann and Aloys Schmitt in Frankfurt am Main, and with J. A. André and J. G. Vollweiler in Offenbach. Following tours in Germany, Poland, and Russia as a concert artist, he went to Berlin in 1824. His opera *Irene* was premiered there in 1832, but it was not a success. In 1835 he became music director in Münster. In 1847 he went to Christiania as director of the Phil. Soc., and also became organist at Holy Trinity Church in 1857. His son, Karl Arnold (b. Berlin, June 8, 1824; d. Oslo, Aug. 9, 1867), was also a cellist who was a member of the royal chapel in Stockholm.

BIBL.: H. Herresthal, *C. A. (1794–1877): Ein europäischer Musiker des. 19. Jahrhunderts: Eine Dokumente biographie mit thematischem Werkverzeichnis* (Wilhelmshaven, 1993). —**NS/LK/DM**

Arnold, Denis (Midgley), distinguished English musicologist; b. Sheffield, Dec. 15, 1926; d. Budapest, April 28, 1986. He was educated at the Univ. of Sheffield (B.A., 1947; B.Mus., 1948; M.A., 1950). From 1951 to 1960 he was a lecturer and from 1960 to 1964 a reader in music at Queen's Univ., Belfast; in 1964 he was made senior lecturer at the Univ. of Hull; in 1969 he became prof. of music at the Univ. of Nottingham; from 1975 he was Heather Prof. of Music at the Univ. of Oxford. From 1976 to 1980 he was joint ed. of *Music & Letters.* From 1979 to 1983 he was president of the Royal Musical Assn. In 1983 he was made a Commander of the Order of the British Empire. He was regarded as one of the foremost authorities on Italian music of the Renaissance and the early Baroque period.

WRITINGS: *Monteverdi* (London, 1963; 3rd ed., rev., 1990 by T. Carter); *Marenzio* (London, 1965); *Monteverdi Madrigals* (London, 1967); ed. with N. Fortune, *The Monteverdi Companion* (London, 1968; 2nd ed., rev., 1985, as *The New Monteverdi Companion*); ed. with N. Fortune, *The Beethoven Companion* (London, 1971); *Giovanni Gabrieli* (London, 1974); *Giovanni Gabrieli and the Music of the Venetian High Renaissance* (Oxford, 1979); *Monteverdi Church Music* (London, 1982); ed. *The New Oxford Companion to Music* (2 vols., Oxford, 1983); *Bach* (Oxford, 1984); with E. Arnold, *The Oratorio in Venice* (London, 1986). —**NS/LK/DM**

Arnold, Eddy (originally **Richard Edward**), American country singer, guitarist, and songwriter; b. near Henderson, Tenn., May 15, 1918. Arnold adapted Bing Crosby's relaxed pop singing style to country music and achieved comparable success within his genre, reaching the country singles charts 145 times between 1945 and 1983, including 28 #1 hits. Thirty-two of his singles reached the pop charts. He was especially popular in the late 1940s and early 1950s, and again in the second half of the 1960s, when he became the chief performer of the string-filled, country-crossover style called the Nashville Sound. In his early days his biggest hits were "I'll Hold You in My Heart (Till I Can Hold You in My Arms)" and "Bouquet of Roses." The most successful recording of his latter-day career was "Make the World Go Away."

Arnold was born on his parents' farm, the son of William and Georgia Wright Arnold. Both his parents played musical instruments, his father the fiddle and his mother the guitar. He took up the guitar as a child and had a few lessons. When he was 16 he quit school to work on the farm. He got his professional start in music at 18, playing with a string band over a radio station in Jackson, Tenn. Starting in January 1938 he worked on the radio in St. Louis; there he took voice lessons. In January 1940 he joined Pee Wee King and His Golden West Cowboys, who toured extensively and appeared on the radio in Louisville and on *The Grand Ole Opry* on WSM in Nashville. He married Sally K. Gayhart on Nov. 28, 1941. They had two children.

Arnold left King in the spring of 1943 and got his own radio show on WSM; by 1944 he had a segment on *The Grand Ole Opry* by himself. He signed to RCA Victor Records in November 1943 but was unable to record until December 1944 due to the musicians' union recording ban. In January 1945, RCA released his debut single, "Mommie Please Stay Home with Me" (music and lyrics by Eddy Arnold, Wallace Fowler, and J. Graydon Hall), on its Bluebird subsidiary. His second single, "Each Minute Seems a Million Years" (music and lyrics by Cook Watson), was his first to reach the country charts, in June 1945.

Arnold scored three more country hits in 1946, the most successful of which was "That's How Much I Love You" (music and lyrics by Eddy Arnold, Wallace Fowler, and J. Graydon Hall); it was covered for a Top Ten pop hit for Frank Sinatra. Also in 1946, Arnold began hosting a half-hour weekly network radio show, *Checkerboard Matinee.* In January 1947 he added the *Checkerboard Jamboree* for 15 minutes a day, five days a week. The program ran until September 1950. Among his five country hits in 1947 were three chart-toppers: "What Is Life without Love" (music and lyrics by Eddy Arnold, Owen Bradley, and Vernice McAlpin); "It's a Sin" (music and lyrics by Zeb Turner and Fred Rose); and the biggest hit of the year, "I'll Hold You in My Heart (Till I Can Hold You in My Arms)" (music and lyrics by Eddy Arnold, Hal Harton, and Tommy Dilbeck).

Arnold's album *All Time Hits from the Hills* reached the pop-chart Top Ten in January 1948. Of his nine Top Ten country songs released in 1948, five hit #1: a revival of the 1921 song "Anytime" (music and lyrics by

Herbert Happy Lawson); the million-selling "Bouquet of Roses" (music and lyrics by Steve Nelson and Bob Hilliard); "Texarkana Baby" (music and lyrics by Cottonseed Clark and Fred Rose); "Just a Little Lovin' (Will Go a Long, Long Way)" (music and lyrics by Zeke Clements and Eddy Arnold); and "A Heart Full of Love (For a Handful of Kisses)" (music and lyrics by Eddy Arnold, Steve Nelson, and Ray Soehnel).

In September 1948 Arnold left *The Grand Ole Opry* and later in the year launched the *Hoedown Reunion* radio show as competition. The show ran for a year. He released another 11 Top Ten country hits in 1949, four of which hit #1: "Don't Rob Another Man's Castle" (music and lyrics by Jenny Lou Carson); "One Kiss Too Many" (music and lyrics by Steve Nelson, Ed Nelson Jr., and Eddy Arnold); "I'm Throwing Rice (at the Girl I Love)" (music and lyrics by Steve Nelson, Ed Nelson Jr., and Eddy Arnold); and "Take Me in Your Arms and Hold Me" (music and lyrics by Cindy Walker). During 1949 he also reached the Top Ten of the pop album charts with the three-disc set *To Mother*; made his network television debut on Milton Berle's *Texaco Star Theater*; and acted in his first film, *Feudin' Rhythm* (1950).

Arnold again reached the Top Ten of the pop album charts in early 1950 with *Eddy Arnold Sings*, and he made his second and final film appearance in June in *Hoedown*. He placed seven songs in the country Top Ten during the year, and another seven in 1951, among them the #1 hits "There's Been a Change in Me" (music and lyrics by Cy Coben), a revival of the 1946 song "Kentucky Waltz" (music and lyrics by Bill Monroe), and "I Wanna Play House with You" (music and lyrics by Cy Coben). There were six Top Ten country hits in 1952, among them the chart-toppers "Easy on the Eyes" (music and lyrics by Cy Coben and Eddy Arnold) and "A Full Time Job" (music and lyrics by Gerry Teifer).

In July and August 1952, Arnold hosted a 15-minute, three-times-a-week network television program, *The Eddy Arnold Show,* as a summer replacement for Perry Como. The show returned from July to October 1953, this time as a twice-a-week replacement for Dinah Shore. From January 1955 to the end of 1957, Arnold did a show for syndication under the title *Eddy Arnold Time,* also returning to a national network on a weekly half-hour basis from April to September 1956. He hosted a documentary network television series, *Out on the Farm*, on Sunday afternoons from July to November 1954, and returned to doing a radio series from 1952 to 1953 and from July to September 1956.

While his radio and television activities, along with his personal appearances, did not prevent him from recording a handful of Top Ten country hits each year during the middle 1950s, Arnold began to hit #1 less frequently. His chart-toppers included "Eddy's Song" (music and lyrics by Charles R. Grean and Cy Coben) in January 1953; "I Really Don't Want to Know" (music by Don Robertson, lyrics by Howard Barnes) in May 1954; and a revival of the 1934 song "The Cattle Call" (music and lyrics by Tex Owens) and "That Do Make It Nice" (music and lyrics by Eddy Arnold, Fred Ebb, and Paul Klein), both in October 1955. "You Don't Know Me" (music and lyrics by Cindy Walker and Eddy Arnold),

which he recorded for a Top Ten country hit in September 1956, turned out to be an unusually valuable copyright for him; it was covered and revived by many artists, reaching the pop Top Ten for Ray Charles in 1962 and the top of the country charts for Mickey Gilley in 1981. Arnold's next Top Ten country hit was "Tennessee Stud" (music and lyrics by Jimmy Driftwood) in June 1959. It earned him his first Grammy nomination for Best Country & Western Performance.

Arnold hosted another farming series, *Today on the Farm*, on network television Saturday mornings during the 1960–61 season. He released four Top Ten country hits in 1962 and three in 1964. Then in 1965 he scored a major comeback on records employing a more pop-oriented, middle-of-the-road style dubbed "country-politan" or the Nashville Sound. His breakthrough hit was "What's He Doing in My World" (music and lyrics by Carl Belew, Eddie Bush, Barry Moore, W. S. Stevenson, and Betty J. Robinson), which reached #1 on the country charts in June 1965, followed by the first of nine consecutive #1 country LPs, *The Easy Way,* in August.

In September 1965 he released the album *My World*, containing both "What's He Doing in My World" and a new single, "Make the World Go Away" (music and lyrics by Hank Cochran). It brought him unprecedented success: the LP went gold, becoming the biggest-selling country album of the year and a Top Ten pop album, and earning Grammy nominations for Album of the Year and Best Country & Western Album; "Make the World Go Away" topped the country and easy-listening charts and became his only Top Ten single on the pop charts, earning Grammy nominations for Best Country & Western Single and Best Country & Western Vocal Performance, Male.

In 1966, Arnold released four Top Ten country singles, two of which topped the charts, and three #1 country albums. "I Want to Go with You" (music and lyrics by Hank Cochran) hit the top of the country and easy-listening charts in April, as did an album of the same name. The LP *The Last Word in Lonesome,* named for a Top Ten country single, hit #1 in September. And "Somebody Like Me" (music and lyrics by Wayne Carson) topped the country charts in November, followed by a *Somebody Like Me* album. Arnold enjoyed the same success in 1967: four Top Ten country singles, two at #1, and another three #1 country albums. "Lonely Again" (music and lyrics by Jean Chapel) topped the charts in April, along with an identically titled album. A hits collection, *The Best of Eddy Arnold*, hit #1 in May and went gold. And "Turn the World Around" (music and lyrics by Ben Peters) reached the top of the country charts in October followed by a *Turn the World Around* LP in November.

These recordings also crossed over to the pop charts, and Arnold moved to expand his following beyond the country market. In October 1967 he made his Los Angeles nightclub debut at the Cocoanut Grove in the Ambassador Hotel, and in February 1970 he first appeared in the Empire Room of the Waldorf-Astoria Hotel in N.Y. He became a frequent host on the network television variety series *Kraft Music Hall*, acting as master of ceremonies 17 times between 1968 and 1971 as well as introducing its "Country Fair" series from April to June 1968 and its 1970 Christmas special.

Arnold topped the country charts twice more in 1968: the LP *The Everlovin' World of Eddy Arnold* hit #1 in April, and the single "Then You Can Tell Me Goodbye" (music and lyrics by John D. Loudermilk) in October. But his record sales fell off after the 1960s. He joined MGM Records in 1972, returning to RCA in 1976. He continued to reach the charts until 1983, then gave up recording for the rest of the decade while continuing to make personal appearances. In 1990 his work on a new album was interrupted by heart surgery, but he recovered and released *Hand-Holdin' Songs* in March 1990, followed in January 1991 by *You Don't Miss a Thing*. In April 1993 came *Then and Now: Last of the Love Song Singers*, a double-CD set containing one disc of vintage recordings and one of new performances.

DISC.: *Anytime/E. A. and His Guitar* (1952); *Have Guitar, Will Travel* (1959); *One More Time* (1961); *Christmas with E. A.* (1961); *Cattle Call* (1963); *My World* (1965); *The Last Word in Lonesome* (1966); *The Best of E. A.* (1967); *The Romantic World of E. A.* (1968); *Love and Guitars* (1970); *The Best of E. A., Vol. 2* (1970); *Many Tears Ago* (1985); *Then and Now: Last of the Love Song Singers* (1993); *Memories Are Made of This* (1995); *The Essential E. A.* (1996); *The Tennessee Plowboy and His Guitar* (1998); *Seven Decades of Hits* (2000).

WRITINGS: *It's a Long Way from Chester County* (Old Tappan, N.J., 1969).

BIBL.: D. Cusic, *E. A.: I'll Hold You in My Heart* (Nashville, 1997); M. Freda, *E. A. Discography, 1944–1996* (Westport, Conn., 1997); M. Streissguth, *E. A.: Pioneer of the Nashville Sound* (N.Y., 1997).—**WR**

Arnold, Johann Gottfried, German cellist and composer, father of **Carl Arnold;** b. Niedernhall, Feb. 1, 1773; d. Frankfurt am Main, July 26, 1806. He received early music instruction from his father, a schoolmaster, and made his first public appearance as a cellist at the age of 8. After further training in Kunzelsau and with his uncle in Wertheim, he studied cello with Willmann in Regensburg and with Romberg in Hamburg. In 1797 he became solo cellist in the orch. of the Frankfurt am Main Opera. He composed a Symphonie concertante for 2 Flutes and Orch., 5 cello concertos (1802–08), chamber music, and solo pieces for cello.—**NS/LK/DM**

Arnold, Samuel, celebrated English composer, organist, conductor, teacher, and music scholar; b. London, Aug. 10, 1740; d. there, Oct. 22, 1802. He was a chorister at the Chapel Royal (c. 1750–58), where he studied with Gates and Nares. Arnold subsequently became closely associated with various London theaters. He began his career as harpsichordist and composer at Covent Garden in 1764, where his first dramatic score, the pasticcio *The Maid of the Mill*, was premiered on Jan. 31, 1765. His pantomime *Harlequin Dr. Faustus* was first given there on Nov. 18, 1766, as was his pasticcio *Tom Jones* on Jan. 14, 1769. In 1769 Arnold purchased Marylebone Gardens, where he brought out his reworking of Pergolesi's *La serva padrona* as *The Servant Mistress* on June 16, 1770. His afterpiece *The Portrait* was first performed at Covent Garden on Nov.

22, 1770. In 1773 his oratorio *The Prodigal Son* was given at the Univ. of Oxford, where he took his Doctor of Music degree that same year. In 1774 the dishonest actions of one of his employees at Marylebone Gardens forced Arnold into financial difficulties and he was forced to sell his theater. In 1777 he became music director and composer at the Little Theatre in the Haymarket, for which he wrote numerous scores over the next quarter century. Among the most notable were *Lilliput* (May 15, 1777), *The Spanish Barber* (Aug. 30, 1777), *The Agreeable Surprise, or The Secret Enlarged* (Sept. 4, 1781), *Gretna Green* (Aug. 28, 1783), *Two to One* (June 19, 1784), *Peeping Tom* (Sept. 6, 1784), *Turk and No Turk* (July 9, 1785), *The Siege of Curzola* (Aug. 12, 1786), *Inkle and Yarico* (Aug. 4, 1787), *The Battle of Hexham* (Aug. 11, 1789), *The Surrender of Calais* (July 30, 1791), *The Mountaineers* (Aug. 3, 1793), *The Children in the Wood* (Oct. 1, 1793), *Zorinski* (June 20, 1795), and *Obi, or Three-Fingered Jack* (July 2, 1800). Among his other works, *The Shipwreck* was given at Drury Lane on Dec. 10, 1796, as was *The Veteran Tar* on Jan. 29, 1801. In all, Arnold composed or contributed to over 70 stage works. In 1783 he became organist and composer to the Chapel Royal, and in 1793 he was made organist at Westminster Abbey. He oversaw the unfinished complete edition of Handel's works (180 parts, 1787–97) and ed. the collection *Cathedral Music* (4 vols., 1790). In addition to other oratorios and church music, he wrote harpsichord pieces, choruses, and songs. Arnold was buried in Westminster Abbey.

BIBL.: R. Hoskins, *Dr. S. A. (1740–1802): An Historical Assessment* (diss., Univ. of Auckland, 1984).—**NS/LK/DM**

Arnold, Sir Malcolm (Henry), prolific and versatile English composer; b. Northampton, Oct. 21, 1921. He studied trumpet with Ernest Hall and composition with Gordon Jacob at the Royal Coll. of Music in London (1938–41). He played trumpet in the London Phil. (1941–42), serving as its 1st trumpeter (1946–48), and also played trumpet in the BBC Sym. Orch. in London (1945). He then devoted himself chiefly to composition, developing a melodious and harmonious style of writing that possessed the quality of immediate appeal to the general public while avoiding obvious banality; many of his works reveal modalities common to English folk songs, often invested in acridly pleasing harmonies. His experience as a trumpeter and conductor of popular concerts provided a secure feeling for propulsive rhythms and brilliant sonorities. He had a particular knack for composing effective film music. In his sound track for *The Bridge on the River Kwai* (1957), he popularized the rollicking march *Colonel Bogey*, originally composed by Kenneth Alford in 1914. In 1970 Arnold was made a Commander of the Order of the British Empire, and in 1993 he was knighted. He also received several honorary doctorates, was made a Fellow of the Royal Coll. of Music in 1983, and was named an Honorary Fellow of the Royal N. Coll. of Music in Manchester in 1997.

WORKS: DRAMATIC: O p e r a : *The Dancing Master* (1951); *The Open Window* (London, Dec. 14, 1956). **B a l l e t :** *Homage to the Queen* (London, June 2, 1953); *Rinaldo and Armida* (1954); *Solitaire* (1956); *Sweeney Todd* (1958); *Electra* (1963). **O t h e r S t a g e w o r k s :** *Song of Simeon,* nativity play

(1958); *The Turtle Drum*, children's spectacle (1967). **F i l m :** Over 80 scores, including: *The Captain's Paradise* (1953); *I Am a Camera* (1955); *Trapeze* (1956); *Island in the Sun* (1957); *The Bridge on the River Kwai* (1957); *Inn of the Sixth Happiness* (1958); *Roots of Heaven* (1958); *Nine Hours to Rama* (1962); *The Chalk Garden* (1963); *David Copperfield* (1969). **ORCH.:** Sym. for Strings (1946); 9 numbered syms.: No. 1 (Cheltenham, July 6, 1951), No. 2 (Bournemouth, May 25, 1953), No. 3 (1954–57; London, Dec. 2, 1957), No. 4 (London, Nov. 2, 1960), No. 5 (Cheltenham, 1961), No. 6 (1967; Sheffield, June 28, 1968), No. 7 (1973; London, May 1974), No. 8 (N.Y., May 5, 1979), and No. 9 (1987); solo concertos: 2 for Horn (1945, 1956); 2 for Clarinet (1948, 1974); 1 for Piano Duet (1951); 1 for Oboe (1952); 2 for Flute (1954, 1972); 1 for Harmonica (London, Aug. 14, 1954); 1 for Organ (1954); 1 for Guitar (1958); 1 for 2 Violins (1962); 1 for 2 Pianos, 3-Hands (1969); 1 for Viola (1970); 1 for Trumpet (1981); 1 for Recorder (1988); 1 for Cello (London, March 9, 1989); 1 for Saxophone (1996); 10 overtures: *Beckus the Dandipratt* (1943); *Festival Overture* (1946); *The Smoke* (1948); *A Sussex Overture* (1951); *Tam O'Shanter* (1955); *A Grand, Grand Overture* for 3 Vacuum Cleaners, 1 Floor Polisher, 4 Rifles, and Orch. (London, Nov. 13, 1956); *Commonwealth Christmas Overture* (1957); *Peterloo* (1968); *Anniversary Overture* (1968); *The Fair Field* (1972); *Larch Trees*, tone poem (1943); *Serenade* for Small Orch. (1950); *8 English Dances* in 2 sets (1950–51); *The Sound Barrier*, rhapsody (1952); 3 sinfoniettas (1954, 1958, 1964); *2 Little Suites* (1955, 1962); *Serenade* for Guitar and Strings (1955); *4 Scottish Dances* (1957); *4 Cornish Dances* (1966); Concerto for 28 Players (1970); *Fantasy for Audience and Orch.* (1970); *A Flourish* (1973); *Fantasy for Brass Band* (1974); *Philharmonic Concerto* (1977); Sym. for Brass Instruments (1979); *Irish Dances* (1986); *Welsh Dances* (1988); *Theme and Variations: Fantasy* for Recorder and Strings (1990; also for Recorder and String Quartet). **C H A M B E R :** Trio for Flute, Viola, and Bassoon (1943); *3 Shanties* for Wind Quintet (1944); Duo for Flute and Viola (1945); 2 violin sonatas (1947, 1953); Viola Sonata (1947); Flute Sonatina (1948); 2 string quartets (1949, 1976); Oboe Sonatina (1951); Clarinet Sonatina (1951); Recorder Sonatina (1953); Piano Trio (1955); Oboe Quartet (1957); *Toy Symphony* for 12 Toy Instruments, Piano, and String Quartet (1957); 2 brass quintets (1961, 1988); 5 pieces for Violin and Piano (1965); *Trevelyan Suite* for Wind Instruments (1968); Wind Octet (1988); piano pieces. **VOCAL:** Choral pieces; songs.

BIBL.: A. Poulton, *M. A.: A Catalogue of His Music* (London, 1986); H. Cole, *M. A.: An Introduction to His Music* (London and Boston, 1989); P. Burton-Page, *Philharmonic Concerto: The Life and Music of Sir M. A.* (London, 1994); S. Craggs, *M. A.: A Bio-Bibliography* (Westport, Conn., 1998).—**NS/LK/DM**

Arnold, Yuri (Karlovich), Russian writer on music and composer of German descent; b. St. Petersburg, Nov. 13, 1811; d. Karakash, Crimea, July 20, 1898. He studied at the German Univ. in Dorpat, and then was mainly active as a contributor to Russian journals. From 1863 to 1870 he also was the ed. of the *Neue Zeitschrift für Musik* in Leipzig. He wrote a comic opera, *Treasure Trove* (St. Petersburg, Feb. 1, 1853), and the opera *St. John's Eve*, but the MSS were lost in a fire at the St. Petersburg Opera. His memoirs (3 vols., Moscow, 1893) are an invaluable portrait of 60 years of Russian musical life. —**NS/LK/DM**

Arnoldson, Sigrid, Swedish soprano; b. Stockholm, March 20, 1861; d. there, Feb. 7, 1943. She began her training with her father, the tenor Oscar Arnoldson (1830–81). After further training from Maurice Strakosch and Désirée Artôt, she made her operatic debut as Rosina in Prague in 1885. In 1886 she sang in Moscow, and in 1887 at London's Drury Lane Theatre. In 1888 she returned to London to make her Covent Garden debut, where she sang again from 1892 to 1894. On Nov. 29, 1893, she made her Metropolitan Opera debut in N.Y. as Baucis, where she sang for a season. She then pursued her career in Europe, retiring in 1916. From 1922 to 1938 she taught in Vienna, and then in Stockholm. She was noted for her command of coloratura and lyric roles, but she also was a fine Carmen.—**NS/LK/DM**

Arnould, (Madeleine) Sophie, notable French soprano; b. Paris, Feb. 13, 1740; d. there, Oct. 22, 1802. She studied with Marie Fel and Hippolyte Clairon. In 1757 she joined the Paris Opéra, where she was one of its principal members until her retirement on a state pension of 2,000 livres in 1788. She created the title role in Gluck's *Iphigénie en Aulide* there on April 19, 1774, and also had fine success in operas by Rameau, Monsigny, and Fancoeur. She also became a favorite in Parisian society. Pierné chose her as the subject of his opera *Sophie Arnould* (1927).

BIBL.: A. Deville, *A.iana* (Paris, 1813); E. and J. de Goncourt, *S. A. d'après sa correspondance et ses mémoires* (Paris, 1857); R. Douglas, *S. A., Actress and Wit* (Paris, 1898); B. Dussanc, *S. A.: La plus spirituelle des bacchantes* (Paris, 1938).—**NS/LK/DM**

Arodin (Arnondrin), Sidney (J.), jazz clarinetist/writer; b. Westwego, La., March 29, 1901; d. New Orleans, Feb. 6, 1948. Arodin took up clarinet at the age of 15 and was working regularly within a year. He played on riverboats with drummer Johnny Stein and others, and worked with Freddie Newman at the Ringside in the early 1920s. He went to N.Y. in 1922 with The Original New Orleans Jazz Band, and left them in the summer of 1925. (During this period it seems that Arodin worked for several months in Jimmy Durante's band.) Arodin worked with The New Orleans Rhythm Masters (1926) in San Antonio, Tex.; with The New Orleans Harmony Kings (1927); and recorded with Wingy Manone in N.Y. (December 1927). Returning to New Orleans in 1928, Arodin played with The Halfway House Orch., Sharkey Bonano, Monk Hazel, Johnny Miller, and others. Arodin toured with trombonist Sunny Clapp and His Band of Sunshine (1929), and with Chink Martin in The New Orleans Swing Kings (1930). He recorded with the Jones-Collins Astoria Hot Eight, although he didn't perform regularly with Jones or Collins. Arodin gigged in Kansas City, Mo., in the summer of 1933, then moved to N.Y. with Louis Prima's band in August 1934. He worked with Wingy Manone in 1935, then returned to New Orleans, where he led his own band, including a residency at the Puppy House in 1939–40. Seriously ill in 1941, he never fully recovered and for the rest of his life suffered long periods of illness in New Orleans and Westwego, and made only occasional public appearances. Arodin recovered sufficiently to play for a while on the riverboats, but was taken ill again in St. Louis, returned to New Orleans, and died shortly afterwards. Arodin composed the melody of the popular song "Lazy River."—JC/LP

Aronowitz, Cecil (Solomon), South African-born English violist and teacher of Russian-Lithuanian descent; b. King William's Town, March 4, 1916; d. Ipswich, Sept. 7, 1978. He studied at the Royal Coll. of Music in London, where his principal teachers were Vaughan Williams and Jacob (composition) and Rivarde (violin). He turned to the viola later in life, and served as first violist in the Boyd Neel Orch., the Goldsborough (later English) Chamber Orch., and the London Mozart Players; also was a member of the Melos Ensemble and the Pro Arte Piano Quartet. He was a prof. of viola at the Royal Coll. of Music (1948–75), head of the string school at the Royal Northern Coll. of Music in Manchester (1975–77), and director of string studies at the Snape Maltings School (1977–78).—NS/LK/DM

Arrau, Claudio, celebrated Chilean-born American pianist; b. Chillán, Feb. 6, 1903; d. Mürzzuschlag, Austria, June 9, 1991. He received early training from his mother, and made his first public appearance in Chillán when he was only 5; at age 6, he played in Santiago. After instruction from Bindo Paoli, he received a scholarship from the Chilean government in 1910 to pursue studies in Berlin, where he was a pupil of Martin Krause at the Stern Cons. (1913–18). On Dec. 10, 1914, he made his Berlin debut in a recital, and then attracted considerable attention through tours of Germany and Scandinavia. In 1918 he made his first tour of Europe. In 1921 he performed in South America and in 1922 in London. In the 1923–24 season, he played in the U.S. but, failing to elicit much of a response from audiences and critics, he pursued his career in Europe; also taught at the Stern Cons. (1924–40). In 1927 he won the Grand Prix International des Pianistes in Geneva, and from 1935 he consolidated his European reputation by giving a series of acclaimed cycles of the keyboard works of Bach, Mozart, Beethoven, and others. In 1940 he left war-ravaged Europe for Santiago, where he opened a piano school. In 1941 he made a highly successful tour of the U.S., where he settled. In subsequent years, he appeared with all the major U.S. orchs. and gave countless recitals. Following the end of World War II in 1945, he pursued an eminent international career and established himself as one of the premiere masters of the piano. In 1978 he gave up his Chilean citizenship in protest against the military regime in his homeland; in 1979, he became a naturalized American citizen. All the same, he remained a revered figure in Chile and in 1983 was awarded the Chilean National Arts Prize. In 1984 he toured the land of his birth to enormous acclaim after an absence of 17 years. He died in Austria while preparing for a recital at the new Brahms museum in Mürzzuschlag. Arrau was a dedicated master of the keyboard and an authoritative interpreter of Beethoven; he also gave distinguished performances of Mozart, Chopin, Schumann, Liszt, and Brahms, among others. In his playing, he combined a Classical purity and precision of style with a rhapsodic éclat.

BIBL.: J. Horowitz, *Conversations with A.* (N.Y., 1982); I. Harden, C. A.: *Ein Interpretenportrait* (Frankfurt am Main, 1983); S. Dorantes Guzmán, A.: *El gran artista latinoamericano* (Xalapa, 1991).—NS/LK/DM

Arregui Garay, Vicente, Spanish composer and music critic; b. Madrid, July 3, 1871; d. there, Dec. 2, 1925. He studied at the Madrid Cons., and took 1st prizes in both piano and composition. In 1899 he won the Rome Prize. His orch. score *Historia de una madre* won the National Music Prize in 1910. In addition to composing, he wrote music criticism for the Madrid daily *El debate*. Except for his *Sinfonia vasca*, his music did not follow along Spanish nationalist lines but pursued a determined individual course. Among his other works were the operas *La maja* and *Yolanda*, operettas, zarzuclas, a String Quartet, a Piano Sonata, the oratorio *San Francisco*, a Mass, a cantata, and motets.—NS/LK/DM

Arresti, Giulio Cesare, Italian organist and composer; b. Bologna, c. 1617; d. there, c. 1704. He pursued his career in Bologna, where he was 2nd organist (1649–59) and 1st organist (1659–61; 1671–99) at the church of S. Petronio. He also served as maestro di cappella at S. Salvatore, and later at S. Domenico (1674–1704). In 1666 he helped to found the Accademia Filarmonica, where he was its principe in 1671, 1686, and 1694. His blistering attack on Maurizio Cazzati, the maestro di cappella of S. Petronio, publ. as *Dialogo fatto tra un maestro ed un discepolo desideroso d'approfittare nel contrappunto* (1659), engendered bitter contention between the two men until Cazzati resigned his post in 1671. Arresti was a notable composer of organ music. He also wrote oratorios, masses, and sonatas. His son, Floriano Arresti (b. Bologna, c. 1660; d. there, 1719), was also an organist and composer. After training with Bernardo Pasquini in Rome, he succeeded his father as 2nd organist at the church of S. Petronio in 1692. He also was a member of the Accademia Filarmonica from 1694, and served as its principe in 1714. Among his works were operas and oratorios.

BIBL.: U. Brett, *Music and Ideas in Seventeenth-Century Italy: The Cazzati-A. Polemic* (N.Y. and London, 1989).—LK/DM

Arriaga (y Balzola), Juan Crisóstomo (Jacobo Antonio), greatly gifted Spanish composer; b. Bilbao, Jan. 27, 1806; d. Paris, Jan. 17, 1826. He began to compose at a very early age, producing an Octet for Horn, Strings, Guitar, and Piano at 11, and the opera *Los esclavos felices* at 13. In 1821 he went to Paris and studied violin with Baillot and harmony and counterpoint with Fétis at the Cons. His death just 10 days before his 20th birthday was a tragic loss to Spanish music. He managed, however, to complete a well-crafted Sym. and 3 fine string quartets, as well as the biblical scene *Agar*, fugues, piano pieces, and songs. A memorial was unveiled in his honor in Bilbao in 1933.

BIBL.: J. de Eresalde, *Resurgimiento de las obras de A.* (Bilbao, 1953); B. Rosen, A.: *The Forgotten Genius: The Short Life of a Basque Composer* (Reno, 1988).—NS/LK/DM

Arrieta y Corera, Pascual Juan Emilio,
Spanish composer; b. Puente la Reina, Oct. 21, 1823; d.
Madrid, Feb. 11, 1894. He studied at the Milan Cons.
(1839–45) with Vaccai. He returned to Spain in 1846, and
was a prof. at the Madrid Cons. in 1857; became its
director in 1868. He wrote more than 50 zarzuelas and
several grand operas in Italian. Of these the most
important is *La conquista de Granada*, produced in
Madrid (Oct. 10, 1850), Arrieta conducting, and revived
5 years later under the title *Isabel la Católica* (Madrid,
Dec. 18, 1855). Other successful zarzuelas and operas
are *Ildegonda* (Milan, Feb. 28, 1845), *El Domino Azul*
(Madrid, Feb. 19, 1853), *El Grumete* (Madrid, June 17,
1853; its sequel, *La Vuelta del Corsario*, perf. in Madrid,
Feb. 18, 1863), *Marina* (Madrid, Sept. 21, 1855; rev. and
produced as a grand opera, Madrid, Oct. 4, 1871), and *S.
Francesco da Siena* (Madrid, Oct. 27, 1883).—**NS/LK/DM**

Arrieu, Claude, French composer; b. Paris, Nov.
30, 1903; d. there, March 7, 1990. She studied piano with
Marguerite Long and took courses in composition at the
Paris Cons. with Dukas, G. Caussade, Roger-Ducasse,
and N. Gallon, graduating with a premier prix in 1932.
In 1949 she received the Prix Italia. She was notably
successful as a composer for the theater.

WORKS: DRAMATIC: *Noë*, musical (1934; Strasbourg,
Jan. 29, 1950); *Cadet Roussel*, comic opera (1938–39; Marseilles,
Oct. 2, 1953); *Les Amours de Don Perlimplin et Belisa dans son
jardin*, opera (1947; Tours, March 1, 1980); *Fête galante*, ballet
(1947); *Les Deux Rendez-vouz*, comic opera (1948; Radio France,
June 22, 1951); *La Princesse de Babylone*, comic opera (1953–55;
Rheims, March 4, 1960); *La Cabine téléphonique*, radiophonic
sketch (1958; Paris, March 15, 1959); *Cymbeline*, opera (1958–63);
La Statue, ballet (1968); *Un clavier pour un autre*, comic opera
(1969–70; Avignon, April 3, 1971). ORCH.: Piano Concerto
(1932); Concerto for 2 Pianos and Orch. (1934); *Partita* (1934); 2
violin concertos (1938, 1949); *Petite suite* (1945); Flute Concerto
(1946); Suite for Strings (1959); *Suite funambulesque* (1961);
Concerto for Wind Quintet and Strings (1962); Concerto for
Trumpet and Strings (1965); *Variations classiques* for Strings
(1970). CHAMBER: String Trio (1936); Sonatine for 2 Violins
(1937); Sonatine for Flute and Piano (1943); Violin Sonata (1948);
Wind Quintet (1955); Trio for Piano, Violin, and Cello (1957).
VOCAL: *Cantate sur sept poèmes d'amour en guerre* for Soprano,
Baritone, and Orch. 1946); *Mystère de noël*, oratorio for Soloists,
Chorus, and Orch. (1951); choruses.—**NS/LK/DM**

Arrigo, Girolamo, Italian composer; b. Palermo,
April 2, 1930. He studied at the Palermo Cons., and later
in Rome and Paris. His works are mostly in small forms,
and virtually all with programmatic connotations. The
most important among them are *3 occasioni* for Soprano
and 32 Instruments (1958), *Quarta occasione* for 7 Voices,
Horn, Viola, Mandolin, Guitar, and Celesta (1959),
Fluxus for 9 Instruments (1959), *Episodi* for Soprano and
Flute, to texts by ancient Greek poets (1963), *Shadows* for
Orch. (1965), and *Infrarosso* for 16 Instruments (1967). He
also wrote a "collage opera," *Orden* (1969), consisting of
several not necessarily related numbers, to texts in
French, Italian, and Spanish, and an "epopée musicale,"
Addio Garibaldi (Paris, Oct. 10, 1972).—**NS/LK/DM**

Arrigoni, Carlo, Italian composer; b. Florence,
Dec. 5, 1697; d. there, Aug. 19, 1744. He left Italy as a
young man. In 1732 he was invited to London by a
group favorable to Italian composers in opposition to
Handel, where his opera *Fernando* was premiered on
Feb. 5, 1734. His oratorio *Esther* was first performed in
Vienna in 1738, and then his operas *Sirbace* and *Scipione
nelle Spagne* in Florence in 1739. He also publ. 10 *Cantate
da camera* (London, 1732).—**NS/LK/DM**

Arro, Elmar, Estonian musicologist; b. Riga, July 2,
1899; d. Vienna, Dec. 14, 1985. He studied musicology at
the Univ. of Vienna, where he received his Ph.D. in 1928
with the diss. *Über das Musikleben in Estland im 19.
Jahrhundert*. In 1933 he joined the faculty of the German
Luther Academy in Dorpat; in 1939 he went to Germany
and taught at the Univ. of Heidelberg (from 1955) and
the Univ. of Kiel (from 1968). He was instrumental in
helping to found the Ost-Europa Institut (later the J. G.
Herder Forschungsstelle für Musikgeschichte). After
settling in Vienna, he founded the journal *Musica slavica*.
Arro was an authority on the music of Russia and the
Baltic nations. In addition to his important articles in
journals, he publ. *Geschichte der estnischen Musik* (Dorpat, 1933), ed. with others *Muzïka sovetskoy Estonii*
(Tallinn, 1956), and was founder-ed. of *Musik des Ostens*
(1962 et seq.).—**NS/LK/DM**

Arroyo, João Marcellino, Portuguese statesman
and composer; b. Oporto, Oct. 4, 1861; d,. Colares, near
Lisbon, May 18, 1930. He studied music with his father.
After training in the law, he served in the Portuguese
parliament (1884–1904), and also was minister of foreign affairs and of public education (1900–01). He later
was prof. of law at the Univ. of Coimbra. He wrote 2
operas, *Amor de Perdição* (Lisbon, March 2, 1907) and
Leonor Teles (1910), 2 symphonic poems, choral music,
and songs.

BIBL.: C. Dos Santos, *J. A.* (Lisbon, 1941).—**NS/LK/DM**

Arroyo, Martina, esteemed American soprano of
Hispanic and black descent; b. N.Y., Feb. 2, 1936. Her
principal teacher was Marinka Gurewich, but she also
studied with Turnau at Hunter Coll. of the City Univ. of
N.Y. (B.A., 1956). In 1958 she won the Metropolitan
Opera Auditions of the Air and made her professional
operatic debut in N.Y. in the U.S. premiere of Pizzetti's
Assassinio nella cattedrale. On March 14, 1959, she made
her debut with the Metropolitan Opera as the Celestial
Voice in *Don Carlos*; she subsequently sang minor roles
there until 1963 when she went to Europe, where she
appeared in major roles in Vienna, Düsseldorf, Berlin,
and Frankfurt am Main. From 1963 to 1968 she sang in
Zürich. On Feb. 6, 1965, she scored a remarkable success
at the Metropolitan Opera when she substituted for
Birgit Nilsson as Aida. In subsequent years, she sang
major roles there, and also appeared at London's Covent Garden (from 1968) and the Paris Opéra (from 1973).
In 1989 she retired from the operatic stage. She taught at
the Ind. Univ. School of Music in Bloomington from
1993. Arroyo was especially admired in Verdi spinto
roles, but she also acquitted herself well as Donna Anna,
Liù, Santuzza, and Cio-Cio San. She also proved herself
technically equal to the complex soprano parts in the
works of such avant-garde composers as Varèse, Dallapiccola, and Stockhausen.—**NS/LK/DM**

Artaria, family of Austrian music publishers of Italian descent. Giovanni Artaria and his nephews Carlo and Francesco established a music shop in Mainz in 1765 as Giov. Artaria et Comp. The shop was removed to Vienna in 1766. The first music was publ. in 1778. The firm brought out works by Haydn (more than 300 from 1780), Mozart (83 first and 36 early editions from 1781), making it his most important publisher during his lifetime, and Beethoven (more than 100 editions, including arrangements and reprints). The firm also publ. works by Boccherini, Clementi, Gluck, Salieri, Hummel, Schubert, and many others. It ceased publishing music in 1858 and went out of business altogether in 1932.

BIBL.: F. Artaria and H. Botstiber, *Joseph Haydn und das Verlagshaus A.* (Vienna, 1909); A. Weinmann, *Vollständiges Verlagsverzeichnis, A. & Comp.* (Vienna, 1952).—**NS/LK/DM**

Arteaga, Esteban (Stefano) de, Spanish writer on music; b. Moraleja de Coca, Dec. 26, 1747; d. Paris, Oct. 30, 1799. He became a Jesuit at age 16, but was banished to Corsica when the order was proscribed in Spain. He left it in 1769. He went to Bologna, where he studied philosophy at the Univ. (1773–78), and was befriended by Padre Martini. At Martini's behest, he wrote the important study on opera *Le rivoluzioni del teatro musicale italiano dalla sua origine fine al presente* (Bologne, 1783–88; 2nd ed., Venice, 1785; German tr., 1789, by J. Forkel). Arteaga's work antagonized many Italian writers who resented a foreigner's intrusion into their field, and an acrimonious polemical exchange ensued. Among his other writings were *Investigaciones filosóficas sobre la belleza ideal..* (Madrid, 1789) and *Del ritmo sonoro e del ritmo muto nella musica degli antichi* (ed. by M. Batllori, Madrid, 1944).

BIBL.: E. Rudat, *The Aesthetic Ideas of E.d. A.: Origin, Meaning and Current Value* (diss., Univ. of Calif., Los Angeles, 1969).—**NS/LK/DM**

Artôt (real name, **Montagney**), family of Belgian musicians:

(1) Maurice Artôt, bandmaster, horn player, guitarist, and teacher; b. Gray, Haute-Saône, France, Feb. 3, 1772; d. Brussels, Jan. 8, 1829. After serving as a bandmaster in the French Army, he settled in Brussels as 1st horn player in the orch. of the Théâtre de la Monnaie. He also was active as a guitarist and singing teacher. He had 2 sons who became musicians:

(2) Jean-Désiré Artôt, horn player, teacher, and composer; b. Paris, Sept. 23, 1803; d. Brussels, March 25, 1887. He studied with his father, whom he succeeded as 1st horn player in the orch. of the Théâtre Royal de la Monnaie in Brussels. He also played in the court orch. and taught at the Brussels Cons. from 1843. He composed horn pieces and quartets for cornets à pistons.

(3) Alexandre-Joseph Artôt, violinist and composer; b. Brussels, Jan. 25, 1815; d. Ville d'Avray, France, July 20, 1845. He was a pupil of his father. At age 7, he made his first public appearance at the Théâtre Royal de la Monnaie in Brussels playing a Viotti concerto. After lessons from Snel, he completed his training with Rodolphe and Auguste Kreutzer at the Paris Cons., winning

a premier mix in 1828. Following appearances on the Continent, he made his London debut at a Phil. concert playing his own *Fantaisie* for Violin and Orch. on June 3, 1839. In 1843 he made a successful tour of the U.S. and Cuba with Cinti-Damoreau. He also wrote a Violin Concerto, a Quintet for Strings and Piano, string quartets, and solo violin pieces.

(4) (Marguerite-Joséphine) Désirée (actually, **Désiré**) **Artôt,** distinguished mezzo-soprano, later soprano, daughter of Jean-Désiré Artôt; b. Paris, July 21, 1835; d. Berlin, April 3, 1907. She studied with M. Audran and P. Viardot-García. In 1857 she appeared as a concert artist in Brussels and sang for Queen Victoria in England. On Feb. 5, 1858, she made her debut at the Paris Opéra as Fidès, winning the admiration of Berlioz and other critics. However, intrigues against her soon compelled her to leave the Opéra. In 1859 she sang in Italy and then appeared with Lorini's Italian company at the inauguration of the Victoria-Theater in Berlin. She subsequently pursued her career mainly in Germany, where she excelled in both German and Italian roles. In 1859–60 she appeared with notable success as a concert artist in London, returning there to sing with the Royal Italian Opera at Her Majesty's Theatre (1863) and at Covent Garden (1864, 1866). In 1869 she went to Russia, where she was briefly engaged to Tchaikovsky until her marriage to **Mariano Padilla y Ramos** on Sept. 15, 1869. They subsequently sang together in Germany, Austria, and Russia. She taught singing in Berlin until settling with her husband in Paris in 1889. Their daughter was **Lola Artôt de Padilla.**—**NS/LK/DM**

Artusi, Giovanni Maria, Italian music theorist and composer; b. Bologna, c. 1540; d. there, Aug. 18, 1613. He was a student of Zarlino in Venice. In 1562 he entered the order of the Congregation of S. Salvatore in Bologna, where he was professed in 1563 and spent his life as a canon regular. After Vincenzo Galilei criticized the traditional stance of Zarlino, Artusi felt compelled to defend his teacher in a series of pamphlets that are no longer extant. Artusi then was himself the subject of a dispute with Ercole Bottrigari, who accused him of plagiarism. The accusation was without foundation and may have been prompted by professional jealousy on Bottrigari's part. After publishing *L'arte del contraponto ridotta in tavole* (Venice, 1586), Artusi publ. his first major theoretical vol. In his *Seconda parte dell'arte del contraponto, nella quale si tratta dell'utile et uso delle dissonanze* (Venice, 1589), a thorough examination of the use of dissonance in counterpoint and in the setting of texts. Following Bottrigari's condemnation of Artusi's views on the tuning of instrumental ensemble in his *El Desiderio* (1594), Artusi defended himself in his *L'Artusi, overo Delle imperfettioni della moderna musica ragionamenti dui* (Venice, 1600). It was followed by his *Seconda parte dell'Artusi overo Delle imperfettioni della moderna musica* (Venice, 1603), in which he criticized the use of dissonance and modes in the madrigals of an unnamed composer who later was identified as Monteverdi. As a master of the seconda prattica, Monteverdi was moved to defend himself in his preface to his 2nd book of madrigals (1605). Artusi's reply, publ. under the pseudonym of Antonio Brassino da Todi in 1605, is no longer extant. Monteverdi's brother, Giulio Cesare, came to his brother's defense in his *Dichiaratione*, the preface to his *Scherzi musicali* (1607). Artusi's final reply was publ. as *Discorso secondo musicale di Antonio Braccino da Todi per la dichiaratione della lettera posta ne' Scherzi musicali del sig. Claudio Monteverdi* (Venice, 1608), in which he contended that rhythm should always be the master of harmony and the text. Artusi's major concern in this vol., however, was his view that one of the major problems in modern music was the inability to find the proper tuning of instruments so that musicians could all play together and that any melody could be transposed to any key. Even his detractors could not deny the primacy of Aristoxenus's view that equal tones and equal semitones were the solution to the problem facing the practical musician as well as the theorist of Artusi's day.—NS/LK/DM

Artyomov, Viacheslav (Petrovich),

Russian composer; b. Moscow, June 29, 1940. He studied composition with Pirumov at the Moscow Music School (1958–62) and then at the Moscow Cons. with Sidelnikov, graduating in 1968. Together with Gubaidulina and Suslin, he formed the folk-instrument improvisatory group Astrea in 1975. In his compositions, he applies euphonious dissonances over the basic lines of simulated Russian folk modalities, with asymmetrical rhythms in spasmodically lyric melos.

WORKS: String Quartet (1960); 3 pieces for String Quartet (1960); Piano Concerto (1961); *Chamber Suite* for Wind Quintet (1966); 2 clarinet sonatas (1966, 1971); *Northern Songs* for Mezzo-soprano, Percussion, and Piano (1966); *Jubilee Overture* (1967); *Concerto 13* for Instrumental and Vocal Ensemble (1967); Violin Concerto (1968); *Tempo constante* for Orch. (1970); Accordion Concerto (1971); *Variations* for Flute and Piano (1974); *Capriccio for 1975* for Soprano Saxophone, Baritone Saxophone, and Vibraphone (1975); *Totem* for Percussion Ensemble (1976); *Recitations* for Various Solo Instruments (1976–80); *Elegiac Symphony* for 2 Violins, Percussion, and Strings (1977); *Awakening* for 2 Violins (1978); *The Road to Olympus* for Orch. (1978; Moscow, Oct. 11, 1979); *Invocations* for Soprano and Percussion (1979–80); *Sola Fide*, ballet (1985–87); *Requiem* for Soloists, Chorus, and Orch. (1985–88); *Ave Maria* for Soprano, Chorus, and Orch. (1989).—NS/LK/DM

Artzibushev, Nikolai,

Russian composer; b. Tsarskoe- Selo, March 7, 1858; d. Paris, April 15, 1937. He was a student of Rimsky-Korsakov and Soloviev. After the Russian Revolution of 1917, he went to Paris. He wrote a *Valse fantasia* for Orch., piano pieces, and songs, and also contributed variations to the collaborative *Variations on a Russian Theme* for String Quartet.—NS/LK/DM

Artzt, Alice (Josephine),

American guitarist; b. Philadelphia, March 16, 1943. She studied piano and flute before taking up the classical guitar when she was 13. She pursued training with Ida Presti and Alexandre Lagoya in France and with Julian Bream in England, and also was a student of Otto Luening (composition) and Paul Henry Lang (musicology) at Columbia Univ. (B.A., 1967), and of Darius Milhaud (composition).

From 1966 to 1969 she taught at the Mannes Coll. of Music in N.Y., and then at Trenton (N.J.) State Coll. from 1977 to 1980. In 1969 she made her formal debut in a recital at Wigmore Hall in London, and thereafter pursued a global career as a recitalist and as a soloist with orchs. In later years, she also toured extensively with her own Alice Artzt Guitar Trio. In addition to articles and reviews in journals, she publ. the books *The Art of Practicing* (1978) and *Rhythmic Mastery* (1997). Her repertoire includes not only the standard guitar literature and various works written for her, but also transcriptions of works for guitar solo, duo, and trio, ranging from Handel, Vivaldi, and Haydn to Gershwin, Charlie Chaplin, and Bernstein.—NS/LK/DM

Arundell, Dennis (Drew),

English actor, singer, opera producer, writer on music, and composer; b. London, July 22, 1898; d. there, Dec. 10, 1988. He studied at Tonbridge and with Rootham, Henry Moule, and Stanford at St. John's Coll., Cambridge. Although he made appearances as an actor and singer, he was particularly noted as an opera producer in Cambridge (from 1922) and at the Sadler's Wells Theatre in London (from 1946). In 1974 he became a teacher at the Royal Northern Coll. of Music in Manchester. In 1978 he was made a Member of the Order of the British Empire. Among his compositions were the operas *Ghost of Abel* and *A Midsummer Night's Dream* (1927).

WRITINGS: *Henry Purcell* (London, 1927); *The Critic at the Opera* (London, 1957); *The Story of Sadler's Wells* (London, 1965; 2nd ed., 1977).—NS/LK/DM

Arutiunian, Alexander,

Armenian composer; b. Yerevan, Sept. 23, 1920. He studied at the Yerevan Cons. and with Litinsky in Moscow. In some of his works, he utilized elements of popular genres of his native Armenia.

WORKS: DRAMATIC: O p e r a : *Sayat-Nova* (1963–68). **ORCH.:** Piano Concerto (1941); Trumpet Concerto (1950); Piano Concertino (1951); Sym. (1957); *Chronicle of the Armenian People*, symphonic poem (1961); Horn Concerto (1962); Concerto for 5 Winds and Orch. (1964); *Sinfonietta* (1966); Cello Concertino (1971); *Theme and 6 Variations* for Trumpet and Orch. (1972); *Our Old Songs*, rhapsody for Piano and Orch. (1975); Oboe Concerto (1977); *Armenia–88*, violin concerto (1988); Trombone Concerto (1991); Tuba Concerto (1992). **CHAMBER:** *Armenian Scenes* for Brass Quintet (1984); *Sonata- Retro* for Viola (1984); *Dance for the Young Trombonist* for Trombone Quartet (1989). **VOCAL:** *Cantata of the Fatherland* (1948); *Ode to Lenin*, cantata (1967); *Hymn to Brotherhood*, cantata (1970).—NS/LK/DM

Asafiev, Boris (Vladimirovich),

prominent Russian musicologist and composer; b. St. Petersburg, July 29, 1884; d. Moscow, Jan. 27, 1949. He took courses in history and philology at the Univ. of St. Petersburg (graduated, 1908), and in orchestration with Rimsky-Korsakov and in composition with Liadov at the St. Petersburg Cons. (graduated, 1910). In 1914 he began writing music criticism under the pseudonym Igor Glebov. In 1917 he helped to found the music dept. of the Petrograd Inst. of the History of the Arts, becoming director of its music history dept. in 1920. From 1924 to 1928 he was ed. of the journal *Novaya Muzyka*. From 1925 to 1943 he was prof. of history, theory, and composition at the Leningrad Cons. In 1943 he went to Moscow as a prof. and director of the research section of the Cons., and as a senior research fellow at the Inst. for the History of the Arts. In 1948 he was made chairman of the Union of Soviet Composers. Asafiev was an influential writer on music. Among his works are *Russkaya poeziya v russkoy muzïke* (Russian Poetry in Russian Music; Petrograd, 1921; 2nd ed., rev., 1922); *Instrumental'noye tvorchestvo Chaykovskovo* (Tchaikovsky's Instrumental Works; Petrograd, 1922); *Pyotr Il'ich Chaykovsky: Evo zhizn' i tvorchestvo* (Piotr Ilyich Tchaikovsky: Life and Works; Petrograd, 1922); *Simfonicheskiye etyudï* (Symphonic Studies; Petrograd, 1922; 2nd ed., 1968); *Kniga o Stravinskom* (A Book About Stravinsky; Leningrad, 1929); *Muzïkal'naya forma kak protsess* (Music Form as a Process; 2 vols., Moscow, 1930, 1947; 3rd ed., 1971); *Russkaya muzïka ot nachala XIX stoletiya* (Russian Music from the Beginning of the XIX Century; Moscow, 1930; 2nd ed., 1968, by E. Orlova as *Russkaya muzïka: XIX i nachala XX veka* [Russian Music: The XIX and Early XX Centuries]); *Kompozitorï pervoy polovinï XIX veka: Russkaya klassicheskaya muzïka* (Composers of the First Half of the XIX Century: Russian Classical Music; Moscow, 1945); *Glinka* (Moscow, 1947; 2nd ed., 1950); *Kriticheskiye stat'i, ocherki i retsenzii* (Critical Articles, Essays and Reviews; Moscow, 1967); *Ob opere: Izbranniye stat'i* (Collected Opera Criticism; Leningrad, 1976). As a composer, Asafiev was much less significant. Among his numerous compositions were 11 operas; 28 ballets; 5 syms.: No. 1, *Pamyati Lermontova* (In Memory of Lermontov; 1938), No. 2, *Iz epokh krestyanskikh vosstaniy* (From the Age of the Peasant Uprisings; 1938), No. 3, *Rodina* (Homeland; 1938–42), No. 4, *Privetstvennaya* (Welcome; 1938–42), and No. 5, *Vremena goda* (The Seasons; 1942; unfinished); chamber music; piano pieces; songs.

BIBL.: A. Ossovsky, *B. V. A.: Sovetskaya muzïka* (Moscow, 1945); D. Kabalevsky, *B. V. A.—Igor Glebov* (Moscow, 1954); E. Orlova, *B. V. A.: Put' issledovatel'ya i publitsista* (B.V. A.'s Development as a Researcher and Writer; Leningrad, 1964); J. Jiránek, *Asafajevova teorie intonance: Jeji geneze a vyznam* (A.'s Intonation Theory: Its Origins and Significance; Prague, 1967).—NS/LK/DM

Asawa, Brian, admirable American countertenor; b. Fullerton, Calif., Oct. 1, 1966. He received vocal training in N.Y. In 1991 he became the first countertenor to win the Metropolitan Opera Auditions. In 1991–92 he honed his craft at the San Francisco Opera, and then was awarded a Richard Tucker Music Foundation grant in 1993. He won the countertenor prize in the Plácido Domingo "Operalia" Competition in 1994, and on Feb. 18th of that year he made his Metropolitan Opera debut in N.Y. as the Voice of Apollo in *Death in Venice*. During the next three seasons, he appeared on both sides of the Atlantic, including engagements in Brussels, Cologne, London, Berlin, Amsterdam, Lyons, San Francisco, Seattle, and Göttingen. In 1997 he made an auspicious debut at London's Covent Garden as Tolomeo, a role he also sang at the Opéra de la Bastille in Paris. His portrayal of Arsamene at the Geneva Opera in 1998 won outstanding critical accolades. That same year, he made debut appearances at the Australian Opera in Sydney as Monteverdi's Nero and at the Dallas Opera in *Admeto*. Among his other roles are Farnace in *Mitridate*, Athamas in *Semele*, Xenia in *Boris Godunov*, and Baba the Turk in *The Rake's Progress*. In addition to his operatic roles, he has also won approbation for his remarkable performances of the song repertoire, ranging from Elizabethan lute songs to Ned Rorem and Jake Heggie.—LK/DM

Aschaffenburg, Walter, German-born American composer and teacher; b. Essen, May 20, 1927. He went to the U.S. at the age of 11 and in 1944 became a naturalized citizen. He studied composition with Robert Doellner at the Hartford School of Music (diploma, 1945), Elwell at the Oberlin (Ohio) Coll. Cons. of Music (B.A., 1951), Rogers at the Eastman School of Music in Rochester, N.Y. (M.A., 1952), and Dallapiccola in Florence (1956). In 1952 he joined the faculty of the Oberlin Coll. Cons. of Music, serving as chairman of its theory dept. (1968–73). In 1971 he was made a prof. of composition and theory, and in 1983 chairman of the composition dept., positions he held until his retirement in 1987. In 1955–56 and 1973–74 he held Guggenheim fellowships. In 1966 he received an award from the National Inst. of Arts and Letters. He received the Cleveland Arts Prize in 1980. While Aschaffenburg has employed the 12-tone system in some of his works, his scores are often embued with a meticulous expressivity.

WORKS: DRAMATIC: *The Flies*, incidental music to Sartre's play (1953); *Bartleby*, opera (1956–62; Oberlin, Nov. 12, 1964). **ORCH.:** *Oedipus Rex*, overture (1951); *Ozymandias* (Rochester, N.Y., April 22, 1952); *Elegy* for Strings (1961); *3 Dances* (1966–67); Oboe Concerto (1985; Oberlin, Jan. 25, 1987). **CHAMBER:** Trio for Piano, Violin, and Cello (1950–51); *Divertimento* for Trumpet, Horn, and Trombone (1951); *Chaconne* for Brass Ensemble (1952); Cello Sonata (1953); Sonata for Solo Violin (1954); String Quartet (1955); *Festive Music* for Winds (1963); Wind Quintet (1967); *Proem* for Brass and Percussion (1968–69); *Fan-fare for Herman Melville* for 2 Trumpets and Trombone (1969); *Blossom Music Center Fanfare* for 2 Trumpets and 2 Horns (1970); Duo for Violin and Cello (1971); *A Slight Music* for Clarinet, Bassoon, and Tuba (1975); Concertino for Violin, 10 Winds, and Contrabass (1979–81); *Festive Fanfare and Hymn* for Brass and Percussion (1983); *...from South Mountain* for Brass Quintet (1987); *Coalescence* for Oboe and Cello (1989); *Parings*, 4 pieces for Clarinet and Piano (1992–93). **Piano:** Sonatina (1953–54); *Conversations*, 6 pieces (1973); *Carousel*, 24 little pieces (1980); Sonata for Fortepiano or Piano (1990). **VOCAL:** *The 23rd Psalm* for Tenor, Chorus, Oboe, and Organ (1963); *3 Shakespeare Sonnets* for Tenor and Piano (1966–67); *Libertatem Appellant* for Tenor, Baritone, and Orch. (1974–76); *Laughing Time* for Chorus and Clown (1983).—NS/LK/DM

Aschenbrenner, Christian Heinrich, German violinist and composer; b. Altstettin, Dec. 29, 1654; d. Jena, Dec. 13, 1732. He studied violin with his father, a town musician. After composition lessons with Johann Theile (1668), he completed his training in composition with J. H. Schmeltzer in Vienna (1676–77). He was a violinist in the Zeitz Hofkapelle (1677–82). After serving as Konzertmeister of the Merseburg Hofkapelle (1683–

95), he returned to Zeitz and was director of music until 1713. He then returned to Merseburg as Hofkapellmeister, retiring in 1719 to Jena. Only two of his sacred vocal works are extant.—**NS/LK/DM**

Ascher, Leo, Austrian composer; b. Vienna, Aug. 17, 1880; d. N.Y., Feb. 25, 1942. He received training in law and music. The success of his first operetta, *Vergeltsgott* or *Der Bettlerklub* (Vienna, Oct. 14, 1905), encouraged him to devote himself to composing for the theater. His first major work, *Die arme Lori* (Vienna, March 12, 1909), was followed by his first notable success, *Hoheit tanzt Walzer* (Vienna, Feb. 24, 1912); then followed the highly successful scores *Was tut man nicht alles aus Liebe* (Vienna, Dec. 17, 1914), *Botschafterin Leni* (Vienna, Feb. 19, 1915), *Der Soldat der Marie* (Berlin, Sept. 2, 1916), *Egon und seine Frauen* (Berlin, Aug. 25, 1917), and *Bruder Leichtsinn* (Vienna, Dec. 28, 1917). Among his later works were *Der Künstlerpreis* (Vienna, Oct. 1, 1919), *Was Mädchen träumen* (Vienna, Dec. 6, 1919), *Princessin Friedl* (Berlin, May 14, 1920), *Zwölf Uhr Nachts!* (Vienna, Nov. 12, 1920), *Baronesschen Sarah* (Berlin, Dec. 25, 1920), *Ein Jahr ohne Liebe* (Berlin, Jan. 12, 1923), *Sonja* (Vienna, March 6, 1925), *Das Amorettenhaus* (Hamburg, Jan. 1926), *Ich hab' dich Lieb...* (Vienna, April 16, 1926), *Ninon am Scheideweg* (Berlin, Dec. 27, 1926), *Frühling in Wienerwald* (Vienna, April 17, 1930), and *Bravo Peggy!* (Leipzig, March 27, 1932). He also composed film scores for *Purpur und Waschblau* (1931) and *Mein Leopold* (1932). His last stage work was *Um ein bisschen Liebe* (Vienna, June 5, 1936). With the Anschluss in 1938, Ascher emigrated to the U.S.—**NS/LK/DM**

Ascone, Vicente, Italian-born Uruguayan composer; b. Siderno, Aug. 16, 1897; d. Montevideo, March 5, 1979. He was taken to Uruguay as a child, where he studied trumpet and composition. In his works, he was influenced by Uruguayan folk modalities. He composed 5 operas, including *Paraná Gauzú* (Montevideo, July 25, 1931), 3 syms. (1945, 1955, 1959), the symphonic poem *Sobre el Río Uruguay* (1946), *Politonal* for Piano and Orch. (1967), a Trumpet Concerto (1969), a Violin Concerto (1970), and numerous songs.—**NS/LK/DM**

Ashforth, Alden (Banning), American composer, teacher, and writer on music; b. N.Y., May 13, 1933. He attended Oberlin (Ohio) Coll. (A.B., 1958) and studied composition with Joseph Wood and Richard Hoffmann at its Cons. (Mus.B., 1958); subsequently took courses with Sessions, Babbitt, and Kim at Princeton Univ. (M.F.A., 1960; Ph.D., 1971). He taught at Princeton Univ. (1961), Oberlin Coll. (1961–65), N.Y.U. (1965–66), the City Coll. of the City Univ. of N.Y. (1966–67), and the Univ. of Calif. at Los Angeles (from 1967). He was active as a jazz researcher and as a recorder/producer of many jazz recordings; also contributed articles to the *Annual Review of Jazz Studies* and to *The New Grove Dictionary of Jazz.*

WORKS: DRAMATIC: *The Quintessential Zymurgistic Waffle,* musical comedy (1975; in collaboration with P. Reale). **ORCH.:** *Variations* (1958). **CHAMBER:** Piano Sonata (1955); Sonata for Flute and Harpsichord (1956); *Fantasy-Variations* for

Violin and Piano (1959); *Episodes,* chamber concerto for 8 Instruments (1962–68); *Pas seul* for Flute (1974); *The Flowers of Orcus (Intavolatura)* for Guitar (1976); *St. Bride's Suite* for Harpsichord (1983); other piano pieces. **VOCAL:** *The Unquiet Heart* for Soprano and Chamber Orch. or Piano (1959–68); choral pieces; songs. **ELECTRONIC:** *Cycles* (1965); *Mixed Brew* (1968); *Byzantia: 2 Journeys after Yeats* for Organ and Tape (1971–73).—**NS/LK/DM**

Ashkenazy, Vladimir (Davidovich), greatly gifted Russian pianist and conductor; b. Gorki, July 6, 1937. He became a student of Anaida Sumbatian at the Central Music School in Moscow in 1945, and in 1955 of Lev Oborin at the Moscow Cons., from which he graduated in 1963. In 1955 he won 2nd prize in the Chopin Competition in Warsaw. After capturing 1st prize in the Queen Elisabeth of Belgium Competition in Brussels in 1956, he began to pursue a career as a virtuoso. In 1958 he made his first tour of the U.S., which elicited critical accolades. In 1962 he and John Ogdon were both awarded 1st prize in the Tchaikovsky Competition in Moscow. In 1963 Ashkenazy made his London debut. After leaving the Soviet Union, he went to Iceland in 1968 and in 1972 he became a naturalized Icelandic citizen. He later made his home in Switzerland. In 1969 Ashkenazy made his conducting debut with the Iceland Sym. Orch. in Reykjavík. In 1977 he made his British conducting debut with the Philharmonia Orch. of London, becoming its principal guest conductor in 1981. From 1987 to 1994 he was music director of the Royal Phil. of London, with which he toured Russia in 1989. He also served as principal guest conductor of the Cleveland Orch. from 1987 to 1994. In 1989 he became chief conductor of the (West) Berlin Radio Sym. Orch., continuing in that position when it became the Deutsches Symphonie Orchester Berlin in 1994, and remaining with it until 1999. In 1998 he became music director of the Czech Phil. in Prague. Ashkenazy has appeared as a guest conductor with major orchs. on both sides of the Atlantic. With J. Parrott, he brought out the book *Ashkenazy: Beyond Frontiers* (London, 1984). As a master of the keyboard, he has deftly balanced his superlative technique with a penetrating interpretive insight in a broad repertoire. Among the composers he has revealed a remarkable affinity for are Mozart, Beethoven, Schubert, Chopin, Schumann, Liszt, and Brahms, as well as many Russian composers, notably Scriabin, Rachmaninoff, Prokofiev, and Shostakovich. As a conductor, he has demonstrated an assured command of scores from the 19th and 20th century orch. literature. He has prepared (1981–82) and conducted his own effective orchestration of Mussorgsky's *Pictures at an Exhibition.*—**NS/LK/DM**

Ashley, Robert (Reynolds), pioneering American composer, performer, director, and writer; b. Ann Arbor, Mich., March 28, 1930. He studied theory at the Univ. of Mich. (B.Mus., 1952) and piano and composition with Riegger at the Manhattan School of Music in N.Y. (M.Mus., 1954); then returned to the Univ. of Mich. for further composition study with Finney, Bassett, and Gerhard (1957–60), where he also took courses in psychoacoustics and cultural speech patterns at its Speech

Research Laboratories and was employed as a research assistant (1960–61) in acoustics at its Architectural Research Laboratory. He was active with Milton Cohen's Space Theater (1957–64), the ONCE Festival and ONCE Group (1958–69), and the Sonic Arts Union (1966–76), touring widely with them in the U.S. and Europe; also served as director of the Center for Contemporary Music at Mills Coll. in Oakland, Calif. (1970–81). As the first opera composer of the post-proscenium age, Ashley is one of the most influential and highly acclaimed artists in the 20th-century avant-garde music and experimental performance tradition. He has produced several hundred music and music-theater compositions for live performance as well as audio and video recordings and broadcast television series, which have been performed throughout the world. In his compositions from the mid-1970s, often experimental, technologically driven, and collaborative, he has developed a complex, episodic treatment of his materials, marked by striking imagery, textual multiplicity, and a graceful and highly individualized integration of speech and song. Ashley has also provided music for the dance companies of Douglas Dunn (*Idea from the Church*, 1978), Steve Paxton (*The Park* and *The Backyard*, 1978), Trisha Brown (*Son of Gone Fishin'*, 1983), and Merce Cunningham (*Problems in the Flying Saucer*, 1988). He was married first to the artist Mary Ashley, with whom he collaborated; then to Mimi Johnson, director of Performing Artservices in N.Y. Ashley is one of four featured composers (with Cage, Glass, and Anderson) in Peter Greenaway's video series, *Four American Composers*. His *Perfect Lives* was published, in book form, in 1991.

WORKS: DRAMATIC: O p e r a : *The Wolfman* for Amplified Voice and *The Wolfman Tape* (1964); *That Morning Thing* for 5 Principal Voices, 8 Dancers, Women's Chorus, and Tape, in 4 parts: *Four Ways, Frogs, Purposeful Lady Slow Afternoon,* and *She Was A Visitor* (1967; Ann Arbor, Feb. 8, 1968); *Music with Roots in the Aether,* television opera for Voices and Electronics (Paris, 1976); *Title Withdrawn,* television opera for Voices and Electronics (Paris, 1976; from *Music with Roots in the Aether*); *What She Thinks,* television opera for Voices and Electronics (1976; from *Music with Roots in the Aether*); *Perfect Lives (Private Parts),* television opera for Voices, Piano, and Electronic Orch. (1978–80), in 7 parts: *The Backyard, The Bank, The Bar, The Church, The Living Room, The Park,* and *The Supermarket*); *Music Word Fire And I Would Do It Again Coo Coo: The Lessons,* television opera for Voices, Piano, and Electronic Orch. (1981); *Atalanta (Acts of God),* television opera for Voice, Chorus, and Instruments (Paris, 1982; concert version as *Atalanta (Acts of God), aka Songs from Atalanta* for Voice, Chorus, and Instruments, 1982); *Tap Dancing in the Sand* for Voice (1982); *Atalanta Strategy,* television opera (N.Y., 1984); *Now Eleanor's Idea,* tetralogy: *I: Improvement (Don Leaves Linda)* (1984–85), *II: Foreign Experiences* (1994), *III: eL/Aficionado* (1987), and *Now Eleanor's Idea* (1993); *Yellow Man with Heart with Wings* for Voice and Tape (1990); *Love Is a Good Example* for Voice (1994); *When Famous Last Words Fail You* for Voice (1994); *Yes, But Is It Edible?* for Voice (1994); *Dust* (Yokohama, Nov. 15, 1998). **E l e c t r o n i c   M u s i c   T h e a t e r :** *# + Heat* (1961); *Public Opinion Descends Upon the Demonstrators* (1961; Ann Arbor, Feb. 18, 1962); *Boxing* (1963; Detroit, April 9, 1964); *Combination Wedding and Funeral* (1964; N.Y., May 9, 1965); *Interludes for the Space Theater* (1964; Cleveland, May 4, 1965); *Kitty Hawk (An Antigravity Piece)* (1964; St.

Louis, March 21, 1965); *The Lecture Series* (1964; N.Y., May 9, 1965; in collaboration with M. Ashley); *The Wolfman Motorcity Revue* (1964; Newport Beach, Calif., Jan. 11, 1969); *Morton Feldman Says* (1965); *Orange Dessert* (1965; Ann Arbor, April 9, 1966); *Night Train* (1966; Waltham, Mass., Jan. 7, 1967; in collaboration with M. Ashley); *Unmarked Interchange* (Ann Arbor, Sept. 17, 1965); *The Trial of Anne Opie Wehrer and Unknown Accomplices for Crimes Against Humanity* (Shegboyan, Wisc., April 30, 1968); *Fancy Free or It's There* (1970; Ann Arbor, April 1971); *Illusion Models* (1970); *It's There* (Brussels, April 1970); *Night Sport* (L'Aquila, Italy, April 1973); *Over the Telephone* (N.Y., March 1975). **INSTRUMENTAL:** *Piano Sonata (Christopher Columbus Crosses to the New World in the Niña, the Pinta and the Santa Maria Using Only Dead Reckoning and a Crude Astrolabe)* (1959; rev. 1979); *Maneuvres for Small Hands* for Piano (1961); *Fives* for 2 Pianos, 2 Percussion, and String Quartet (1962); *Details* for 2 Pianos (1962); *In Memoriam...Crazy Horse* for 20 or More Wind, String, or Sustaining Instruments (1963); *In Memoriam...Esteban Gomez* for 4 Instrumentalists (1963); *In Memoriam...John Smith* for 3 Instrumentalists (1963); *In Memoriam...Kit Carson* for 8-part Ensemble (1963); *Trios (White on White)* for Any Sustaining Instruments, Gongs, and Voice (1963); *The Entrance* for Electric Organ (1965); *Waiting Room* for Wind or String Quartet (1965; rev. 1978); *Revised, Finally, for Gordon Mumma* for Pairs of Bell-like Instruments (1973); *Odalisque* for Voice, Chorus, and 24 Instruments (1973); *Basic 10* for Snare Drum (1988); *Superior Seven* for Flute, Chorus, and Instruments (1988); *Outcome Inevitable* for Chamber Orch. of 8 or More (1991); *Van Cao's Meditation* for Piano (1991); *Tract* for Voice and String Trio or 2 Keyboards (1992); *When Famous Last Words Fail You* for Voice and Orch. (N.Y., Dec. 7, 1997). **W i t h   E l e c t r o n i c s :** *Something* for Clarinet, Pianos and Tape (1961); *Complete with Heat* for Instruments and Tape (1962); *In Sara, Mencken, Christ and Beethoven There Were Men and Women* for Voice and Electronics (1972); *String Quartet Describing the Motions of Large Real Bodies* (1972); *How Can I Tell The Difference?* for Violin or Viola, Electronics, and Tape (1974); *Automatic Writing* for Voices, Keyboards, and Electronics (1979); *String Quartet Describing the Motions of Large Real Bodies* for String Quartet and Electronics (1972); *In Sara, Mencken, Christ and Beethoven There Were Men and Women* for Violin and Electronics (1972); *Automatic Writing* for Violin and Electronics (1979). **T a p e :** *The Fourth of July* (1960); *Big Danger in Five Parts* (1962); *Detroit Divided* (1962); *Heat* (1962); *The Wolfman Tape* (1964); *Untitled Mixes* for Jazz Trio and Tape (1965); *Interiors without Flash* (1979); *Factory Preset* (1993). **F i l m** (in collaboration with G. Manupelli unless otherwise given): *The Image in Time* (1957); *Bottleman* (1960); *The House* (1961); *Jenny and the Poet* (1964); *My May* (1965); *Overdrive* (1967); *Dr. Chicago* (in 4 parts: *Dr. Chicago, Dr. Chicago Goes to Sweden, Ride, Dr. Chicago, Ride,* and *Cry Dr. Chicago*; 1968–70); *Portraits, Self-Portraits and Still Lifes* (1969); *Battery Davis* (1970; in collaboration with P. Makanna). **V i d e o :** *The Great Northern Automobile Presence* (1975); *What She Thinks* (1976). **T e l e v i s i o n :** *Music Word Fire* (N.Y., Channel 13/WNET, 1981). **R a d i o :** *Your Money My Life Goodbye* (1999).

BIBL.: T. DeLio, *Circumscribing the Open Universe: Essays on Cage, Feldman, Wolff, A. and Lucier* (Washington, D.C., 1984). —NS/LK/DM

Ashman, Howard (b. Baltimore, Md., May 17, 1950; d. N.Y., March 14,1990) and **Menkin, Allan** (b. 1949, New Rochelle, N.Y.), the songwriters who "gave a mermaid her voice and a beast his soul."

Howard Ashman's father made ice cream cones, and, in a way, Ashman followed in his father's footsteps, creating musical confections that delighted both children and adults.

In his early twenties, Howard Ashman came to N.Y. and found a job editing books, but his heart was in the theater. In his off-time, he wrote plays, getting 'Cause Maggie's Afraid of the Dark produced in 1976. Within a year, he became the artistic director of the Off-Off-Broadway WPA Theater. In 1979, WPA took on the challenge of creating a musical out of Kurt Vonnegut's novel God Bless You Mr. Rosewater. Ashman cowrote the book and created all the lyrics for the compositions of Allan Menkin, beginning one of the most fruitful songwriting relationships of the late 20th century.

Menkin had grown up in New Rochelle, and studied piano and violin. After graduating from N.Y.U., he focused on music. He mostly wrote jingles, occasionally performing his own songs at local clubs. Attending a theater workshop at BMI helped him develop a deep affection for musicals. He met Ashman through the workshop.

Ashman next brought Roger Corman's 1960 B-movie Little Shop of Horrors to Menkin's attention. Together, they turned it into a musical for which Ashman wrote the lyrics and libretto. He also directed the play. It ran for over a decade at the Off-Broadway Orpheum Theater. Ashman also wrote the lyrics and book, and directed Smile, which opened on Broadway on the strength of a score by composer Marvin Hamlish, but it ran for only 40 performances.

Ashman didn't have time to be disappointed, however. Soon after Smile closed, the film version of Little Shop of Horrors opened. Disney soon came calling. They asked Ashman to pen some lyrics for their all-star animation Oliver and Company. While the film wasn't one of the studio's instant classics, Disney asked Ashman and Menkin to collaborate on a new animation. The result was The Little Mermaid, which Ashman coproduced in addition to writing the lyrics. The duo won an Oscar, a Golden Globe, and a Grammy for "Under the Sea," and another Grammy for the soundtrack album as Best Recording for Children. Menkin also wrote outside of the partnership, crafting a song for Home Alone 2 and tunes for the less-successful Disney musical Newsies. He collaborated with David Spencer on a musical version of The Apprenticeship of Duddy Kravitz. They also wrote the Off-Broadway WPA production of Weird Romance.

Menkin and Ashman's work together was so successful that they were asked to collaborate again on another Disney feature, Beauty and the Beast. Again, the duo won a pair of Grammy's, a Golden Globe, and an Oscar for the music. The film also won a Best Picture Oscar for Ashman, who was the executive producer. Unfortunately, Ashman had succumbed to AIDS a year earlier and had not even seen the finished film.

Ashman had been able, however, to write several lyrics for the movie Aladdin; Tim Rice helped Menkin finish the job. This started a frequent collaboration between Rice and the composer.

Menkin teamed up with another theatrical legend, Steven Schwartz, for two more Disney films. With Pocahontas, they won a Best Song Oscar for "Colors of the Wind" and another for Menkin's score. They also wrote the songs for The Hunchback of Notre Dame. Menkin's music was also integral to the film Hercules, written with lyricist David Zippel. He wrote the score for the ABC miniseries Lincoln and the theme for Rocky V, "Measure of a Man," recorded by Elton John.

Menkin went back to the stage, creating a musical version of Dickens's Christmas Carol with lyricist Lynn Ahrens and librettists Michael Ockrent. The show has become an annual fixture at the theater at Madison Square Garden. He as also worked with Tim Rice on the musical King David and with Tom Eyen on Kicks: The Showgirl Musical.—HB

Ashrafi, Mukhtar, Russian composer and teacher; b. Bukhara, June 11, 1912; d. Tashkent, Dec. 15, 1975. He studied composition in Samarkand, with S. Vasilenko at the Moscow Cons. (1934–37), and at the Leningrad Cons. (1941–43). In 1944 he settled in Tashkent, where he was a teacher at the Cons. In many of his works, he glorified themes from Central Asian history.

WORKS: DRAMATIC: O p e r a : Buran (Tashkent, June 12, 1939; in collaboration with S. Vasilenko); Velikiy Kanal (The Great Canal; Tashkent, Jan. 19, 1941; in collaboration with S. Vasilenko); Dilorom (Tashkent, Feb. 5, 1958); Dusha Poeta (A Poet's Soul; Tashkent, July 13, 1960); 2 ballets; many film scores. **OTHER:** 2 syms.; 5 symphonic suites; songs.—NS/LK/DM

Ashton, Algernon (Bennet Langton), English composer; b. Durham, Dec. 9, 1859; d. London, April 10, 1937. He studied with Reinecke and Jadassohn at the Leipzig Cons. (1875–79) and Raff in Frankfurt am Main (1880), and then taught piano at the Royal Coll. of Music in London (1885–1910). His works followed mainly along conventional German lines and included 5 syms., a Piano Concerto, a Violin Concerto, much chamber music, many piano pieces, organ works, choral music, and numerous songs. Although he failed to receive much recognition as a composer, he acquired a certain notoriety by his curious letters in the English press, many of which were publ. in his vols. Truth, Wit and Wisdom (London, 1904) and More Truth, Wit and Wisdom (London, 1905).—NS/LK/DM

Ashwell (also **Ashewell, Hashewell**), **Thomas,** English composer; b. c. 1478; d. after 1513. He was a chorister at St. George's Chapel, Windsor (1491–93) and a singing clerk at Tattershall Coll., Lincolnshire (1502–03). After serving as Informator choristarum at Lincoln Cathedral (1508), he was canon at Durham Cathedral (1513). His works include the Missa "Ave Maria" and the Missa Jesu Christe (ed. in Early English Church Music, I, 1963, XVI, 1976).—LK/DM

Asia, Daniel, American composer and teacher; b. Seattle, June 27, 1953. He was a student of Stephen Albert at Smith Coll. and of Druckman, Weisberg, and

Penderecki at the Yale School of Music (M.M., 1977). He taught at the Oberlin (Ohio) Coll. Cons. of Music (1981–86) and lectured at London's City Univ. In 1988 he became head of the composition dept. at the Univ. of Ariz. in Tucson. He also served as composer-in-residence of the Phoenix Sym. Orch. from 1991. His music belies a variety of American influences, ranging from Copland and Bernstein to John Adams and Druckman.

WORKS: ORCH.: 4 syms.: No. 1 (1987; Seattle, Feb. 19, 1990), No. 2, *Celebration Symphony, In Memory of Leonard Bernstein* (1989–90; Tucson, April 30, 1992), No. 3 (1991–92; Phoenix, May 6, 1992), and No. 4 (1993–94); *Black Light* (1990; N.Y., Oct. 13, 1991); *At the Far Edge* (1991); *Gateways* (1993; Cincinnati, Oct. 7, 1994); Piano Concerto (1994; Grand Rapids, Feb. 10, 1995); Cello Concerto (1997; Greensboro, N.C., Jan. 1998). **CHAMBER:** *Piano Set I* (1976) and *II* (1977); *Dream Sequence I* for Amplified Trombone (1976); and *II* for Flute (1989); String Quartet No. 1 (1976–77); *Sand I* for Flute, Horn, and Double Bass (1977); *Live Images* for 4 Woodwinds (1978); *Rivalries* for Chamber Ensemble (1980); *Scherzo Sonata* for Piano (1978); Piano Quartet (1989); Piano Trio (1996). **VOCAL:** *Sand II* for Mezzo-soprano and Chamber Orch. (1978); *Ossabaw Island Dream* for Mezzo-soprano and Chamber Orch. (1982); *Celebration* for Baritone, Chorus, Brass Quintet, and Organ (1988); *Breath in a Ram's Horn* for High Voice and Piano (1995); *Purer Than Purest Pure* for Chorus (1996).—**NS/LK/DM**

Asioli, Bonifazio, Italian composer and pedagogue; b. Correggio, Aug. 30, 1769; d. there, May 18, 1832. He was born into a musical family, and began to compose and play the harpsichord at an early age. After studies with Angelo Morigi in Parma (1780–82), he returned to Correggio and brought out his first opera, *La volubile*, when he was 15. He also taught at the Collegio Civico there, becoming maestro di cappella in 1786. In 1787 he entered the service of the Marchese Gherardini in Turin, who he continued to serve in Venice (1796–99) and then in Milan. In 1805 he became maestro di cappella and music director at the court of the viceroy Eugène Beauharnis of Milan. He became the first director of the new Milan Cons. in 1808. In 1814 he returned to Correggio, where he ran a music school in his home. Asioli's other operas included *La contadina vivace* (Parma, 1785), *La gabbia de' pazzi* (Venice, 1785), *La discordia teatrale* (Milan, 1786), *Le nozze in ville* (Correggio, 1786), *Cinna* (Milan, Dec. 26, 1792), *Pigmalione* (1796), and *Gustava al Malabar* (Turin, 1802). Among his other scores were many cantatas and some instrumental pieces. He also publ. various theoretical works.

BIBL.: A. Coli, *Vita di B. A. da Correggio* (Milan, 1834); R. Finzi, *Celebrazione del musicista B. A. (1769–1832) nel secondo centenario della nascita* (Reggio Emilia, 1969).—**NS/LK/DM**

Askenase, Stefan, Polish-born Belgian pianist and pedagogue; b. Lemberg, July 10, 1896; d. Bonn, Oct. 18, 1985. He studied with Theodor Pollak in Lemberg and Emil von Sauer at the Vienna Academy of Music. In 1919 he made his debut in Vienna, and subsequently toured throughout the world. He also taught at the Rotterdam Cons. (1937–40) and the Brussels Cons. (1954–61). In 1950 he became a naturalized Belgian citizen. Askenase distinguished himself as an interpreter of Chopin.

WRITINGS: *Wie Meister üben I* (Zürich, 1966). —**NS/LK/DM**

Asola or **Asula, Giammateo** or **Giovanni Matteo,** Italian composer; b. Verona, c. 1532; d. Venice, Oct. 1, 1609. He entered the congregation of secular canons at S. Giorgio in Alga in 1546. From 1566 he held benefices at S. Stefano in Verona, and then was a secular priest in the parish of S. Maria in Organo there from 1571. In 1577 he became maestro di cappella at Treviso Cathedral, and then at Vicenza Cathedral in 1578. About 1582 he settled in Venice, where he became one of the chaplains at S. Severo. His extensive output included 12 vols. of masses and over 30 vols. of sacred music, as well as 2 vols. of madrigals (Venice, 1584, 2nd ed., 1587; 1605). Asola's sacred music reveals the influence of Palestrina. His writing for multiple choirs demonstrates the influence of the Venetian school.

BIBL.: F. Caffi, *Della vita e delle opere di G. A.* (Padua, 1862); D. Fouse, *The Sacred Music of G. A.* (diss., Univ. of N.C., 1960). —**NS/LK/DM**

Asow, Erich Hermann Müller von
See **Mueller von Asow, Erich Hermann**

Aspa, Mario, Italian composer; b. Messina, Oct. 17, 1797; d. there, Dec. 14, 1868. He was a student of Zingarelli in Naples. He composed over 40 operas, the most successful being *Paolo e Virginia* (Rome, April 29, 1843) and *Il Muratore di Napoli* (Naples, Oct. 16, 1850). —**NS/LK/DM**

Aspestrand, Sigwart, Norwegian composer; b. Fredrikshald, Nov. 13, 1856; d. Oslo, Dec. 31, 1941. He studied in Leipzig and Berlin. He composed 7 operas, the most successful of which was *Die Seemansbraut* (Gotha, March 29, 1894).—**NS/LK/DM**

Asplmayr, Franz, Austrian composer and violinist; b. Linz (baptized), April 2, 1728; d. Vienna, July 29, 1786. Following training from his father, he settled in Vienna and joined the Hofkapelle. He served as secretary to Count Morzin (1759–61), and then was a court composer from 1761. Asplmayr became particularly known for his ballet pantomimes, including *Agamemno vengé* (1771), *Ifigenie* (1772), *Acis et Galathée* (1773), and *L'espiègle du village* (1774). He composed the first German-language melodrama, *Pygmalion*, after Rousseau (Vienna, Feb. 19, 1772). Among his other works were the Singspiel *Der Kinder der Natur* (Vienna, July 15, 1778), incidental music, orch. pieces, and chamber works.

BIBL.: H. Riessberger, *F. A.* (diss., Univ. of Innsbruck, 1954). —**NS/LK/DM**

Aspull, George, precocious English pianist and composer; b. Manchester, June 1813; d. Leamington, Aug. 19, 1832. He first gained notice as a youthful pianist in Paris (1825), then toured in England with notable success before his promising career was cruelly cut short by tuberculosis at the age of 19. His father, Thomas Aspull, ed. and publ. the vol. *George Aspull's Posthumous Works for the Pianoforte* (London, 1837). —NS/LK/DM

Asriel, André, Austrian composer and teacher; b. Vienna, Feb. 22, 1922. He was a pupil of Stohr in Vienna, Ernst Meyer in London, and Eisler in Berlin. He was a teacher of theory (1951–67) and a prof. of theory and composition (1967–84) at the Hanns Eisler Hochschule für Musik in East Berlin. Among his works were music for the stage, films, and radio, chamber music, many choral pieces on socialist themes, and other vocal pieces. He publ. *Jazz Analysen und Aspekte* (Berlin, 1966; 4th ed., 1984).—NS/LK/DM

Assmayer, Ignaz, Austrian composer; b. Salzburg, Feb. 11, 1790; d. Vienna, Aug. 31, 1862. He studied piano, organ, and theory with A. Brunmayrs in Salzburg and later with T. Gerls. In 1815 he moved to Vienna, where he took lessons with Salieri. In 1846 he was appointed 1st Kapellmeister in Vienna, succeeding Eybler. He wrote several oratorios, among them *Saul und David, Sauls Tod,* and *Das Gelübde,* which he performed with the Vienna Tonkünstler Soc. He further wrote 21 masses, 2 Requiems, and other sacred works, as well as some 60 instrumental compositions, many of which were publ.—NS/LK/DM

Association, The, pop band, formed 1965. **MEMBERSHIP:** Gary "Jules" Alexander, lead gtr., voc. (b. Chattanooga, Tenn., Sept. 25, 1943); Terry Kirkman, brs., rds., perc., voc. (b. Salinas, Kans., Dec. 12, 1941); Jim Yester, rhythm gtr., kybd., voc. (b. Birmingham, Ala., Nov. 24, 1939); Russ Giguere, gtr., voc. (b. Portsmouth, N.H., Oct. 18, 1943); Brian Cole, bs., voc. (b. Tacoma, Wash., Sept. 8, 1942; d. Los Angeles, Aug. 2, 1972); Ted Bluechel Jr., drm. (b. San Pedro, Calif., Dec. 2, 1942); Russ Giguere was replaced by Richard Thompson (b. San Diego, Calif.) in 1971.

Hitting in 1966 with the psychedelic classic "Along Comes Mary," The Association is best remembered for the softer and more urbane sound of pop hits such as "Cherish," "Windy," and "Never My Love" through 1968. Like the Byrds, the Association grew out of the vibrant folk-rock scene in Los Angeles. Kirkman and Alexander had the original idea to put a group together; both had been active on the scene (Kirkman playing briefly as a duo with Frank Zappa on the local coffeehouse circuit). They brought Cole and Yester into the group to form a quartet, and then Giguere and Bluechel joined while the band was rehearsing in mid-1965. They made their first public performance in Pasadena, Calif.

The group signed with a small local label, Valiant, which issued their first single, "Along Comes Mary," in 1965. (Some conservative critics thought the song was drug-inspired, "Mary" being one of the names for marijuana; to modern ears the song sounds like a harmless pop love ballad.) This was followed by the group's biggest hits, all pop-flavored ballads. Warner

Bros. absorbed the Valiant label to purchase the group's contract, and issued their single "Windy" in 1967 to much hype and fanfare. The group supplied the title song for the 1969 film *Goodbye Columbus,* but soon after their work fell off the charts. They took a more psychedelic-rock turn, but listeners were uninterested in hearing this sunny harmony group take on a more groovy persona.

Giguere left in 1971 and made a solo album issued also by Warner Bros. The Association suffered a crippling blow with the death of group mentor Brian Cole in 1972. The group pretty much disbanded in 1973. Ramos, Bluechel, and Yester released a single together in 1975, and the surviving members of the original group came back together in 1981. Giguere and Ramos have managed to keep the "Association" name alive with various touring groups to the present.

DISC.: THE ASSOCIATION: *And Then … Along Comes the Association* (1966); *Renaissance* (1967); *Insight Out* (1967); *Birthday* (1968); *Greatest Hits* (1968); *Goodbye Columbus* (soundtrack; 1969); *The Association* (1969); *"Live"* (1970); *Stop Your Motor* (1971); *Waterbeds in Trinidad* (1972); *Songs That Made Them Famous* (1984). **RUSS GIGUERE:** *Hexagram 16* (1971).

Astaire, Fred (originally **Frederick E. Austerlitz Jr.**), debonair American dancer, actor, and singer; b. Omaha, May 10, 1899; d. Los Angeles, June 22, 1987. Though Astaire's talent as a dancer—displayed in vaudeville, on Broadway, and in films—overshadowed his other abilities, he was a favorite of such songwriters as Jerome Kern, Irving Berlin, Cole Porter, and George Gershwin, and introduced many of their best- known songs. His phrasing, intonation, and timing matched the sophisticated work they did, especially for the movie musicals in which Astaire starred. At the height of his popularity in the mid-1930s, he scored a series of best-selling records with such songs, among them "Night and Day" (Porter), "Cheek to Cheek" (Berlin), and "The Way You Look Tonight" (music by Kern, lyrics by Dorothy Fields).

Astaire was the second child of Austrian immigrant Frederic E. Austerlitz and Johanna Gelius Austerlitz; his older sister, Adele (b. Sept. 10, 1897; d. Jan. 25, 1981), would become his dancing partner for the stage half of his career. Adele took dancing lessons as a child in Omaha, and her parents recognized her potential for a professional career. The children and their mother moved to N.Y. in 1905, where Astaire and his sister were enrolled in Claude Alvienne's dancing school. They made their professional debut in 1907, and toured as a child act until 1909, when they attended grade school in N.J. for two years. They studied at Ned Wayburn's dancing school, then returned to the stage in 1911 and eventually became vaudeville stars. They crossed over to the legitimate theater with the Broadway revue *Over the Top* (N.Y., Nov. 28, 1917), subsequently appearing in another revue, *The Passing Show of 1918* (N.Y., July 25, 1918), then in the operettas *Apple Blossoms* (N.Y., Oct. 7, 1919) and *The Love Letter* (N.Y., Oct. 4, 1921).

Neither of the 1922 shows in which the Astaires appeared was a hit on Broadway, but they began to be noticed, first in *For Goodness Sake* (N.Y., Feb. 20, 1922)

and then in Kern's *The Bunch and Judy* (N.Y., Nov. 28, 1922). In 1923 they took *For Goodness Sake* to England, retitled *Stop Flirting* (London, May 30, 1923). It was a much bigger hit there, running for 418 performances, and they made their recording debut, cutting the songs "The Whichness of the Whatness" (music by William Daly and Paul Lannin, lyrics by Arthur Jackson) and "Oh Gee! Oh Gosh!" (music by Daly, lyrics by Ira Gershwin) from the show.

By 1924 the Astaires had become sufficiently well known to be the stars of Gershwin's *Lady, Be Good!* (N.Y., Dec. 1, 1924), which ran for 330 performances in N.Y., then went to London in April 1926, where the team again made recordings, this time with Gershwin at the piano. This pattern was repeated with Gershwin's *Funny Face* (N.Y., Nov. 22, 1927), which ran for 250 performances in N.Y. and then moved to London in November 1928. Among the songs from the show that Astaire recorded was "My One and Only" (lyrics by Ira Gershwin), which became his first popular record in April 1929.

The Astaires next appeared in the Florenz Ziegfeld–produced flop *Smiles* (N.Y., Nov. 18, 1930), followed by the successful revue *The Band Wagon* (N.Y., June 3, 1931), which had songs by composer Arthur Schwartz and lyricist Howard Dietz. During its 262-performance run, Astaire, as the featured vocalist for Leo Reisman and His Orch., had a two-sided hit record with its songs "I Love Louisa" and "New Sun in the Sky."

Despite his success onstage and on records, Astaire was considered the less- talented member of the dancing team, since Adele was also a gifted comedienne. When she retired to marry Lord Charles Cavendish, the son of the Duke of Devonshire, in 1932, her brother's future seemed doubtful. But he found success with the Cole Porter show *Gay Divorce* (N.Y., Nov. 29, 1932), which ran 248 performances on Broadway and featured "Night and Day." Astaire's recording of the song (again with Reisman) became a massive hit in December 1932. On July 12, 1933, he married divorced socialite Phyllis Livingston Baker Potter. They had two children and remained married until Mrs. Astaire's death from cancer on Sept. 13, 1954.

Astaire signed a film contract with RKO, which immediately loaned him out to MGM for a cameo in *Dancing Lady* (1933), his movie debut. Within weeks of that movie's opening in December, Astaire's first RKO film, *Flying Down to Rio,* appeared. He was second-billed, but he and Ginger Rogers stole the picture with their dancing. Astaire also had a double-sided record hit in April 1934 with two songs from the film, the title tune and "Music Makes Me" (both music by Vincent Youmans, lyrics by Edward Eliscu and Gus Kahn). After appearing in the London production of *Gay Divorce*, Astaire returned to Hollywood permanently.

Astaire and Rogers repeated their success with 1934's *The Gay Divorcée*, based on the similarly titled Porter show though retaining only "Night and Day" from the original score. Their third movie outing was Kern's *Roberta* (1935), followed by Berlin's *Top Hat* (1935), which featured "Cheek to Cheek"; Astaire's recording topped the hit parade in September and October, and he also reached the hit parade with the title song, "Isn't This a Lovely Day," "No Strings," and "Piccolino," all from the film, which became the biggest financial success of any of the Astaire-Rogers pictures.

Astaire's next entry on the hit parade came with his own composition, "I'm Building Up to an Awful Letdown" (lyrics by Johnny Mercer), in February 1936. The following month, "Let Yourself Go," "Let's Face the Music and Dance," and "I'm Putting All My Eggs in One Basket"—all from *Follow the Fleet* (1936), all written by Irving Berlin—reached the hit parade. Kern and Fields wrote the songs for the sixth Astaire-Rogers film, *Swing Time* (1936). From it, Astaire's reading of "The Way You Look Tonight" topped the hit parade in October and November, and "A Fine Romance" also made the list.

Astaire hosted his own radio program, *The Fred Astaire Show,* over NBC during the 1936–37 season. The Gershwins handled the songs for the next Astaire-Rogers film, *Shall We Dance* (1937), from which Astaire's recordings of "Let's Call the Whole Thing Off" and "They Can't Take That Away from Me" were hit parade entries in May. But after seven straight screen pairings with Rogers, Astaire was costarred with nondancer Joan Fontaine for his next picture, *A Damsel in Distress* (1937). The Gershwin score featured "Nice Work If You Can Get It," which entered the hit parade for Astaire in November, though the film was a disappointment at the box office. RKO reteamed Astaire and Rogers for *Carefree* (1938), with songs by Berlin including "Change Partners," which topped the hit parade for Astaire in October and November 1938, but the film failed to return its relatively high production cost. The ninth Astaire-Rogers film, *The Story of Vernon and Irene Castle* (1939), was billed as their last; a screen biography rather than their usual formula, it was another box office failure, and Astaire left RKO.

Astaire freelanced for different studios in the early 1940s, continuing to sing the songs of the great songwriters. *Broadway Melody of 1940* (1940) and *You'll Never Get Rich* (1941) had scores by Cole Porter; *Holiday Inn* (1942) and *Blue Skies* (1946), in which Astaire costarred with Bing Crosby, were Irving Berlin films; *You Were Never Lovelier* (1942) was by Kern; *The Sky's the Limit* (1943) by Harold Arlen; and *Yolanda and the Thief* (1945) was by Harry Warren.

Astaire announced his retirement in 1946, and the following year he launched a successful string of dance schools. But he stepped in for Gene Kelly in *Easter Parade* (1948) after Kelly was injured; the film also starred Judy Garland and had songs by Berlin. Set to appear opposite Garland again in *The Barkleys of Broadway,* which had songs by Harry Warren and Ira Gershwin, Astaire instead was teamed for a final time with Ginger Rogers when Garland became ill.

Astaire worked steadily in film in the early 1950s, always with top-flight songwriters. *Three Little Words* (1950) was a screen biography of songwriters Harry Ruby and Bert Kalmar; *Let's Dance* (1950) had a score by Frank Loesser; the songs for *Royal Wedding* (1951) were by Burton Lane and Alan Jay Lerner, among them the popular novelty tune "How Could You Believe Me

When I Said I Loved You When You Know I've Been a Liar All My Life," which Astaire recorded with his costar, Jane Powell; *The Belle of New York* (1951) was by Warren; and *The Band Wagon* (1953) retained the Schwartz-Dietz songs, if little else, from Astaire's 1931 stage triumph.

In December 1952, Astaire rerecorded four LPs' worth of the popular songs from his film career backed by a jazz ensemble for the box set *The Astaire Story*. In 1954 he decided on another retirement that proved no more final than the first one. After *Daddy Long Legs* (1955), which had songs by Johnny Mercer, he made film versions of his stage success *Funny Face* and the Cole Porter show *Silk Stockings*, both released in 1957, but these essentially marked the close of his three-decade career in movie musicals. In 1959 he published his autobiography, *Steps in Time*.

Astaire turned to television in the late 1950s, making a straight acting debut on *General Electric Theater* with "Imp on a Cobweb Leash" in December 1957, and starring in three award-winning specials: *An Evening with Fred Astaire* (1958), *Another Evening with Fred Astaire* (1959), and *Astaire Time* (1960). (He did a fourth special, *The Fred Astaire Show,* in 1968.) From 1961 to 1963 he was the host and an occasional actor in the dramatic anthology series *Alcoa Premiere*. His only significant film role during this period was in the post-apocalyptic drama *On the Beach* (1959).

Astaire returned to film musicals with *Finian's Rainbow* (1968), based on the 1947 stage production by Burton Lane and E. Y. Harburg. It was not a success, but the soundtrack album spent six months in the charts.

Astaire continued to appear occasionally on television and in unmemorable films in the early 1970s. In 1974 he was one of the hosts of the MGM anthology film *That's Entertainment!*, reprising his role with *That's Entertainment, Part 2,* two years later. Also in 1974, he had a supporting role in the disaster film *The Towering Inferno* that surprisingly earned him his only Academy Award nomination. (He had been presented with a special Oscar in 1949 for his contributions to film musicals.) He won an Emmy Award as Best Actor in a Drama Special for the 1978 TV movie *A Family Upside Down*.

A fan of horse racing, Astaire married one of the sport's few female jockeys, Robyn Smith, who was in her mid-thirties, on June 24, 1980. He made his final acting appearance in a film with *Ghost Story* in 1981, though he also appeared in the documentary *George Stevens: A Filmmaker's Journey* in 1985. Astaire died of pneumonia in 1987 at age 88.

DISC.: *The F. A. Story, Vol. 1–4* (1952); *The Irving Berlin Songbook* (1952); *Crazy Feet!* (1986); *The Cream of F. A.: 1926–1940* (1993); *Steppin' Out: Astaire Sings* (1994); *F. A. at MGM: Motion Picture Soundtrack Anthology* (1997); *The Complete London Sessions* (1999); *Cocktail Hour: F. A.* (2000). **BIBL.:** A. Hackl, *F. A. and His Work* (Vienna, 1970); H. Thompson, *F. A.* (N.Y., 1970); A. Croce, *The F. A. and Ginger Rogers Book* (N.Y., 1972; rev. ed. 1987); S. Green and B. Goldblatt, *Starring F. A.* (N.Y., 1973); S. Harvey, *F. A.* (N.Y., 1975); M. Freedland, *F. A.* (London, 1976); S. Topper, *A. and Rogers* (N.Y., 1976); B. Green, *F. A.* (N.Y., 1979); P. Carrick, *A Tribute to F. A.*

(Salem, N.H., 1984); J. Mueller, *A. Dancing: The Musical Films* (N.Y., 1985); B. Thomas, *A: The Man, the Dancer* (N.Y., 1984); R. Pickard, *F. A.* (N.Y., 1985); B. Adler, *F. A.: A Wonderful Life* (N.Y., 1987); S. Giles, *F.A.: His Friends Talk* (N.Y., 1988).—**WR**

Astarita, Gennaro, Italian composer; b. probably in Naples, c. 1747; d. after 1803. After composing operas for several Italian cities, he went to Moscow in 1784 as music director of the Petrovsky Theater. In 1795 he was named maestro compositore in St. Petersburg. He wrote over 40 comic operas and sacred music.—**LK/DM**

Aston, Hugh, English composer; b. 1485; d. Nov. 1558. He was educated at the Univ. of Oxford (B.Mus., 1510) and served as magister choristarum at St. Mary Newarke Hospital and Coll. in Leicester (c. 1525–48). His output includes 2 Masses (*Te Deum* for 4 Voices and *Videte manus meas* for 6 Voices), *Gaude mater matris Christe* and *Te Deum landamus*, both for 5 Voices, 4 incomplete works (publ. in Tudor Church Music, X, 1929), and a *Hornepype* for Keyboard.—**LK/DM**

Aston, Peter (George), English conductor, musicologist, and composer; b. Birmingham, Oct. 5, 1938. He studied composition and conducting at the Birmingham School of Music (1956–60), and then musicology at the Univ. of York (1964–69; Ph.D., 1970, with the diss. *George Jeffreys and the English Baroque*). He was a lecturer in music (1964–72) and senior lecturer (1972–74) at the Univ. of York. From 1974 to 1988 he was prof. and head of music at the Univ. of East Anglia, where he served as a professorial fellow from 1998. As a conductor, he was musical director of the Tudor Consort (1959–65) and the English Baroque Ensemble (1967–70). From 1975 to 1988 he was conductor of the Aldeburgh Festival Singers. In 1981 he co-founded and thereafter was artistic director of the Norwich Festival of Contemporary Church Music. He was composer-in-residence and principal guest conductor of the Zephyr Point Choral Festival in Nev. in 1991, 1993, 1995, and 1999. In 1993 he became principal guest conductor of the Sacramento (Calif.) International Bach Festival. Aston was elected a fellow of the Royal Soc. of Arts in 1980. He was made an honorary fellow of the Guild of Church Musicians in 1995 and of the Royal School of Church Music in 1999. As a conductor, he has led performances of works ranging from the 15th century to the present day. He is especially known for his dedication to vocal ensemble music of the 16th and 17th centuries, and of the 20th century British repertoire. He ed. the complete works of George Jeffreys. As a composer, he has written many sacred and secular vocal pieces.

WRITINGS: With J. Paynter, *Sound and Silence* (London, 1970); *The Music of York Minster* (London, 1972); with J. Webb, *Music Theory in Practice* (3 vols., London, 1992–93).

WORKS: DRAMATIC: *Sacrapant the Sorcercer*, children's opera (1967). **CHAMBER:** *Nocturne* for Flute and Percussion (1965); *3 Pieces* for Oboe (1968). **VOCAL:** *Five Songs of Crazy Jane* for Soprano (1963); *Three Shakespeare Songs* for Soprano and Chorus (1964); *My Dancing Day*, chamber cantata for Soprano, Tenor, Flute, Clarinet, and String Quartet (1966); *Haec Dies*, Resurrection cantata for Chorus and Organ (1972); *Carmen*

Luminis, cantata for Chamber Choir and Wind Quintet (1975); *The True Glory* for Chorus and Orch. or Organ (1976); *A Song of the Lord, thy Keeper* for Chorus, String Orch., Piano, and Percussion (1983); *From the Book of Thel*, threnody for 5 Solo Voices or Small Chorus, after William Blake (1983); *A Mass for All Saints* for Chorus and Organ (1987); *Where shall wisdom be found?* for Chorus (1991); *The King of Love* for Soprano, Chorus, and Organ (1992); *Psalm 150* for Chorus and Organ (1995); *How lovely is your dwelling-place* for 2 Choruses (1996); *O be joyful in the Lord* for Chorus and Organ (1999).—**NS/LK/DM**

d'Astorga, Baron Emanuele (Gioacchino Cesare Rincón), Italian composer of Spanish descent; b. Augusta, Sicily, March 20, 1680; d. probably in Madrid, c. 1757. He was of noble Spanish descent and was a baron in his own right. During the revolution of 1708, he was an officer in the Palermo municipal guard. After a sojourn in Vienna (1712–14), he served as a senator in Palermo. In 1744 he settled in Spain in the service of the king. Among his works were the operas *La moglie nemica* (Palermo, 1698), *Dafni* (Genoa, April 21, 1709), and *Amor tirannico* (Venice, 1710), a *Stabat Mater* (Oxford, 1752), his best-known work, and more than 150 cantatas. Johann Joseph Abert wrote an opera on his life, *Astorga* (1866).

BIBL.: H. Volkmann, *E. d'A.* (2 vols., Leipzig, 1911, 1919). —**NS/LK/DM**

Åstrand, (Karl) Hans (Vilhelm), Swedish music historian and lexicographer; b. Bredaryd, Feb. 5, 1925. He studied organ, double bass, and cello; also took courses in Romance languages at the Univ. of Lund (Licentiate, 1958). He was music critic of the Malmö newspaper *Kvällsposten* (from 1950), founder-director of the Chamber Choir '53 (1953–62), and founder (1960) and director (1965–71) of the Ars Nova Soc. for New Music. From 1963 to 1971 he taught music history at the Malmö National School of Drama, and then was music critic of Stockholm's *Veckojournalen* (from 1976). He served as ed. in chief of the fundamental Swedish musical encyclopedia, *Sohlmans musik-lexikon* (5 vols., Stockholm, 1975–79). He was a board member (from 1966) and perpetual secretary (from 1973) of the Royal Swedish Academy of Music in Stockholm. In 1983 he was made a prof. and in 1985 received an honorary doctorate at the Univ. of Lund. Åstrand also contributed various articles on musicological and general music subjects to many books and journals.

BIBL.: B. van Boer Jr., ed., *Gustav III and the Swedish Stage: Opera, Theatre and Other Foibles: Essays in Honor of H. A.* (Lewston, Queenston, and Lampeter, 1993).—**NS/LK/DM**

Astrua, Giovanna, Italian soprano; b. Graglia, near Vercelli, c. 1720; d. Turin, Oct. 28, 1757. She was a pupil of Bravio in Milan. In 1739 she made her operatic debut in Leo's *Il Ciro riconosciuto* at the Teatro Regio in Turin, and then was a member of the Teatro S. Samuele in Venice. In 1745–46 she sang at the Teatro S. Carlo in Naples. From 1746 until she lost her voice in 1756, she was a member of the Berlin Court Opera, where she appeared in operas by Graun and Benda.—**LK/DM**

Atanasov, Georgi, Bulgarian composer and bandmaster; b. Plovdiv, May 18, 1881; d. Fasano, Italy, Nov. 17, 1931. He went to Italy in 1901 and took lessons in composition with Mascagni at the Pesaro Cons. Returning to Bulgaria, he became active as a military bandmaster, as well as a composer. He wrote 2 of the earliest operas on national Bulgarian subjects, *Borislav* (Sofia, March 4, 1911) and *Gergana* (Sofia, June 19, 1917); other operas were *Zapustialata vodenitza* (The Abandoned Mill; Sofia, March 31, 1923), *Altzek*, and *Tzveta*; he also wrote 2 children's operas, *The Sick Teacher* and *About Birds*.

BIBL.: I. Sagaev, *Maestro G. A.* (Sofia, 1961).—**NS/LK/DM**

Atanasov, Nikola, Bulgarian conductor, teacher, and composer; b. Kyustendil, Oct. 25, 1886; d. Sofia, Sept. 30, 1969. He studied with F. Dugan at the Croatian Cons. in Zagreb; after teaching music in Stara-Zagora (1913–22), he was active in Sofia as a conductor (1923–48), and also as a prof. (from 1929) and director (1934–37) of the Cons. In 1912 he wrote the first Bulgarian sym.; composed two more syms. (1922, 1950), as well as 2 overtures, *Christo Botev* (1928) and *Forest Murmurs* (1931); also chamber music; piano pieces; songs.

BIBL.: P. Londev, *N. A.* (Sofia, 1963).—**NS/LK/DM**

Atchley, Kenneth, American composer; b. Lebanon, Tenn., Oct. 7, 1954. He studied composition with Robert Ashley and David Behrman and performance practice with Gordon Mumma at Mills Coll. in Oakland, Calif. (M.F.A., 1982). Atchley's works, built on forms derived from classical music and visual art, are characterized by abstract, electronic sounds and their use of musique concrète; from 1997 he began working with "array fountains," two or more smaller fountains that together form a single, logical fountain to which microphones are attached and the audio signal processed and amplified.

WORKS: *Lolly*, opera for Spoken Word and Inflected Speech, Analog Electronics, and Tape (1978); *Light of Hand (Lumière de Main)* for Women's Chorus, Video, Hanging Chair Sculpture, and Electronics (1982); *American Percussion Music* for Arms Fire and Ensemble Electronics (1983); *Wasserglocken* for Electronics and Bell Sculpture (1984); *Edison's Last Project(ION)*, opera for Spoken Word, Digital Electronics, and Chamber Ensemble (1985); *The Last Seven Words* for Soloist or Ensemble performing Spoken Word, Inflected Speech, and Digital Electronics (1986); *Long Hunter* for Electronics and Water Bells (1987); *Aesclepius* for Electronics, Chamber Ensemble, Percussion, and Dance (1988); *The Rabbit's Song* for Vocals and Digital Electronics (1989); *Swan Lake*, opera for Solo or Ensemble Electronics and Spoken Word (1990); *Don Giovanni*, opera for Solo or Ensemble Electronics and Spoken Word (1990); *Smoke*, opera with Ballet for Ensemble Electronics and Spoken Word (1992); *flowers & ghosts*, solo works for Electric Guitar, Acoustic Guitar, Digital Electronics, and Recorded Media (1993–97); *fountain_1998.11* for Digital Electronics and Recorded Media (1998); *fountain_1999.3* for Digital Electronics and Recorded Media (1999); *fountain_1999.20* for Array Fountain, Digital Electronics, and Recorded Media (1999–2000); *icepond* for Array Fountain and Digital Electronics (2000); *recast* for Array Fountain, Digital Electronics, and Recorded Media (2000).—**LK/DM**

Atherton, David, English conductor; b. Blackpool, Jan. 3, 1944. He was educated at the Univ. of Cambridge,

and in London at the Royal Academy of Music and the Guildhall School of Music and Drama. In 1967 he founded the London Sinfonietta, serving as its music director until 1973. From 1968 to 1980 he was resident conductor at London's Covent Garden. He was principal conductor and artistic advisor of the Royal Liverpool Phil. (1980–83), and then was its principal guest conductor (1983–85). From 1981 to 1987 he served as music director of the San Diego Sym. Orch. He was principal guest conductor of the BBC Sym. Orch. in London (1985–90). He served again as music director of the London Sinfonietta from 1989 to 1991, a position he also held with the Hong Kong Phil. from 1989 to 2000.
—NS/LK/DM

Atkins, Chet (originally **Chester Burton**), American guitarist, producer, and record company executive; b. near Luttrell, Tenn., June 20, 1924. As a performer, Atkins developed a finger-picking style that influenced other guitarists in all areas of music; during a 50-year recording career, he made at least 84 albums, reaching the pop or country charts with 47 releases between 1957 and 1996 and winning 13 Grammys. As a session musician, A&R man, record producer, and company executive for RCA Victor Records, he guided the recording careers of dozens of performers and developed the pop-oriented Nashville Sound to compete with rock 'n' roll and cross over to the pop charts in the late 1950s and 1960s.

Atkins, the son of James Arley Atkins, a music teacher, and Ida Sharp Atkins, was raised on a farm. He first began playing the ukulele at three or four; then turned to the guitar, acquiring one at the age of nine; then, the fiddle. He suffered from asthma, which later made him ineligible for military service, and spent much of his childhood convalescing and practicing the guitar. His parents had divorced when he was six; in 1935 he went to live with his father and stepmother near Columbus, Ga., for health reasons. He was particularly influenced by the finger-picking guitar style of Merle Travis, which he first heard on the radio when he was 14. At 17 he dropped out of high school to work in music full-time.

Atkins was hired as a fiddler by radio station WNOX in Knoxville, Tenn., in 1942; he later played guitar on the station and in concerts with other radio performers. His first recording session was as a sideman in 1944. In 1945 he moved to WLW in Cincinnati. There he met singer Leona Johnson, whom he married on July 3, 1946; they had one child.

Leaving WLW in December 1945, Atkins worked at a succession of radio stations: first WPTF in Raleigh, N.C.; then WSM in Nashville, where in 1946 he cut "Brown Eyes Crying in the Rain" and "Guitar Blues," his first recordings as a leader, for Bullet Records, and first performed on *Grand Ole Opry* with Red Foley; then WRVA in Richmond, Va.; KWTO in Springfield, Mo.; and KOA in Denver.

Steve Sholes, an executive at RCA, heard a radio transcription of Atkins in 1947 and offered him a recording contract; Atkins did his first session for the label in Chicago on Aug. 11, 1947. He didn't score any

hits and returned to working at WNOX in Knoxville. He began playing with the comic musical team of Homer and Jethro and later worked with the Carter Family spin-off group the Carter Sisters and Mother Maybelle. The group went to KWTO in Springfield, then in 1950 was invited to join the Grand Ole Opry, and Atkins moved with them to Nashville.

In Nashville, Atkins worked as a session musician for RCA and other labels and helped set up recording sessions. Eventually he was formally hired by RCA as an A&R assistant. Meanwhile, he collaborated with Boudleaux Bryant on two song hits: "Midnight," which topped the country charts for Red Foley in January 1953, and "How's the World Treating You?" which hit the country Top Ten for Eddy Arnold in July 1953. He also continued to make instrumental guitar records for RCA, scoring his first country chart entry with a version of "Mister Sandman" (music and lyrics by Pat Ballard) in January 1955. In February 1956 he first made the pop charts with "The Poor People of Paris (Jean's Song)" (music by Marguerite Monnot, English lyrics by Jack Lawrence).

Atkins was promoted to RCA's manager of operations for Nashville in the spring of 1957 and put in charge of the new recording studio the label was building in the city. In the wake of the rise of rock 'n' roll, traditional country was losing its audience, and Atkins turned to a more cosmopolitan style for his artists, de-emphasizing the fiddles and steel guitars and adding strings and vocal choruses. The resulting Nashville Sound rejuvenated country's popularity and led to many hits that crossed over to the pop charts.

The 12-inch long-playing record had become an industry standard by the second half of the 1950s, and as a recording artist Atkins usually cut two or three per year, first reaching the pop album charts with *Chet Atkins at Home* in June 1958. His 1961 album *Chet Atkins' Workshop* hit the pop Top Ten. In 1963 he earned his first Grammy nomination for Best Rock & Roll Recording for "Teen Scene," the title track from an album that had placed in both the pop and country charts. He topped the country charts in May 1964 with his LP *Guitar Country*, which earned him a second Grammy nomination for Best Country & Western Album. He scored his biggest country single hit with "Yakety Axe" (music by Boots Randolph and James Rich), his guitar treatment of "Yakety Sax," which peaked in the Top Ten in September 1965 and earned him a Grammy nomination for Best Instrumental Performance (Other than Jazz). He also earned a 1965 Grammy nomination for Best Country & Western Album for *More of That Guitar Country*.

Atkins's next entry in the pop album charts came in March 1966 with *Chet Atkins Picks on the Beatles*, which brought him another Grammy nomination for Best Instrumental Performance (Other than Jazz). His last album to earn substantial pop sales was a collaboration with the Boston Pops Orch. conducted by Arthur Fiedler, *The "Pops" Goes Country*, which charted in June 1966. *Chet Atkins Picks the Best*, released in June 1967, won him his first Grammy for Best Instrumental Performance.

RCA promoted Atkins in March 1968 to division vice president in charge of popular artists and repertoire in Nashville. Despite his corporate responsibilities, he was still able to find time to record. NARAS added a Grammy category in 1969 for Best Country Instrumental Performance, and Atkins competed for the award for the next nine years: in 1969 he was nominated for the album *Solid Gold '69*; in 1970 he was nominated for the track "Yestergroovin'" from the album of the same name and won for *Me and Jerry*, a duet album with Jerry Reed; in 1971 he won again for the single "Snowbird" (music and lyrics by Gene Maclellan); in 1972 he was nominated for *Chet Atkins Picks on the Hits* and for *Me and Chet*, another duet album with Jerry Reed; in 1973 he was nominated for the single "Fiddlin' Around" and for the album *Superpickers*; in 1974 he won for *The Atkins-Travis Traveling Show*, a duet album with Merle Travis; in 1975 he was nominated for the track "Colonel Bogey" with Jerry Reed and won for the single "The Entertainer" (music by Scott Joplin); in 1976 he won for *Chester and Lester*, a duet album with Les Paul; and in 1977 he was nominated on his own for *Me and My Guitar* and with Floyd Cramer and Danny Davis for *Chet, Floyd and Danny*. For a change, in 1978 his second album with Les Paul, *Guitar Monsters*, was nominated for the Grammy for Best Pop Instrumental Performance.

Atkins cut back on his corporate and recording activities in 1979, though he continued to earn Grammy nominations for Best Country Instrumental Performance (for the single "Dance with Me" in 1980 and the album *Reflections*, a duet LP with Doc Watson in 1981), winning his seventh Grammy in the category in 1981 for the album *Country, After All These Years*. He resigned that year from RCA, and in 1982 he left the label as an artist, signing to Columbia Records instead.

Atkins's work for Columbia was more varied, starting with the May 1983 release of an exercise album, *Work It Out with Chet Atkins, C.G.P.* (the initials referring to his self-conferred degree of certified guitar player), which earned him his 25th Grammy nomination for Best Country Instrumental Performance for its track "Tara Theme." His 26th nomination and eighth award in the same category came in 1985 for "Cosmic Square Dance," a jazz-fusion track from *Stay Tuned* that found him duetting with such guitarists as George Benson, Larry Carlton, Earl Klugh, Mark Knopfler of Dire Straits, and Steve Lukather of Toto.

Atkins toured occasionally and recorded an album every year and a half or two years into the mid-1990s, continuing to pile up Grammy nominations and awards. He and Mark Knopfler won two 1990 Grammys, for Best Country Vocal Collaboration for "Poor Boy Blues" and for Best Country Instrumental Performance for "So Soft Your Goodbye." Their duet album, *Neck and Neck*, released in October 1990, earned a 1991 Grammy nomination for Best Country Instrumental Performance. Atkins and Jerry Reed won that award the following year for their duet album *Sneakin' Around*. Atkins won it again in 1994 for the track "Young Thing" from his album *Read My Licks*. He shared another country vocal collaboration nomination the next year for the track "All My Loving" (music and lyrics by John

Lennon and Paul McCartney) from the various artists album *Together—American Salutes the Beatles*. He won his 13th Grammy for Best Country Instrumental Performance of 1996 for the track "Jam Man" (music by Chet Atkins) from his album *Almost Alone*; he earned his 34th nomination in the same category in 1997 for the track "Smokey Mountain Lullaby" from the album *The Day the Finger Pickers Took Over the World* a duet with the Australian guitarist Tommy Emmanuel.

DISC.: *Stringin' Along with C. A.* (1955); *C. A. in Three Dimensions* (1955); *Finger Style Guitar* (1956); *C. A. at Home* (1957); *Mister Guitar* (1959); *C. A.'s Workshop* (1961); *Christmas with C. A.* (1961); *Down Home Guitar* (1961); *Teen Scene* (1963); *The Guitar Genius* (1963); *The Best of C. A.* (1963); *Guitar Country* (1964); *More of That Guitar Country* (1965); *C. A. Picks on the Beatles* (1965); *The Best of C. A., Vol. 2* (1966); *C. A. Picks the Best* (1967); *Solid Gold '69* (1969); *Relaxin' with Chet* (1969); *Me and Jerry* (with Jerry Reed; 1970); *Superpickers* (1973); *The Atkins-Travis Traveling Show* (with Merle Travis; 1974); *Chester and Lester* (with Les Paul; 1975); *Me and My Guitar* (1977); *Chet, Floyd and Danny* (with Floyd Cramer and Danny Davis; 1977); *Guitar Monsters* (with Les Paul; 1978); *Reflections* (with Doc Watson; 1980); *Country, After All These Years* (1981); *Work It out with C. A., C. G. P.* (1983); *Stay Tuned* (1985); *Neck and Neck* (with Mark Knopfler; 1990); *Sneakin' Around* (with Jerry Reed; 1991); *The RCA Years: 1947–1981* (1992); *Galloping Guitar: The Early Years* (1993); *Read My Licks* (1994); *Almost Alone* (1996); *The Essential C. A.* (1996); *The Day the Finger Pickers Took Over the World* (with Tommy Emmanuel; 1997); *Guitar Legend: The RCA Years* (2000). **JERRY REED:** *Me and Chet* (1972).

WRITINGS: With Bill Neely, *Country Gentleman* (Chicago, 1974).

BIBL.: R. O'Donnell, *C. A.* (Nashville, 1967).—**WR**

Atkins, Sir Ivor (Algernon), English organist, conductor, and composer; b. Llandaff, Nov. 29, 1869; d. Worcester, Nov. 26, 1953. He studied in Truro and Hereford. From 1897 to 1950 he served as organist at Worcester Cathedral, and also was conductor of the Three Choirs Festivals for more than 50 years. He was knighted in 1921. Atkins championed the music of Elgar and was active as an ed. of the music of Bach. His own output consisted of choral music.—**NS/LK/DM**

Atlantov, Vladimir (Andreievich), distinguished Russian tenor and baritone; b. Leningrad, Feb. 19, 1939. He studied with Bolotina at the Leningrad Cons., taking the Glinka Prize in 1962 and graduating in 1963. After making his formal operatic debut at Leningrad's Kirov Theater in 1963, he was a student artist at Milan's La Scala (1963–65). He was a medalist at the Tchaikovsky Competition in Moscow in 1966, and in competitions in Montreal and Sofia in 1967. In 1967 he became a member of the Bolshoi Theater in Moscow, with which he later toured with notable success to Milan, N.Y., Paris, and Vienna. From 1977 he also sang baritone roles. In 1987 he made his debut at London's Covent Garden as Otello, one of his most famous roles. In 1990 he sang for the first time with an American opera company when he appeared as Canio with the San Francisco Opera. He returned to the San Francisco Opera as Tchaikovsky's Hermann in 1993. In 1997 he appeared as Otello with Opera Pacific in Costa Mesa,

Calif. He also toured extensively as a concert artist. In addition to the Russian repertoire, Atlantov is esteemed for his portrayals of Don José, Cavardossi, Alfredo, Radames, Posa, and Siegmund.—NS/LK/DM

Atlas, Allan W(arren), American musicologist; b. N.Y., Feb. 19, 1943. He was educated at Hunter Coll. of the City Univ. of N.Y. (B.A., 1964) and N.Y.U. (M.A., 1966; Ph.D., 1971, with the diss. *The Cappella Giulia Chansonnier and the Dissemination of the Franco-Netherlandish Chanson in Italy, c. 1460-c. 1520*). In 1971 he joined the faculty of Brooklyn Coll. of the City Univ. of N.Y., where his service at the Univ.'s Graduate School included appointments as executive officer of the Ph.D.-D.M.A. Programs in Music (from 1989), director of the Center for the Study of Free-Reed Instruments (from 1998), and Distinguished Prof. (from 1998). From 1999 he also was ed. of *The Free-Reed Journal*. In addition to articles in scholarly books and journals, he has publ. important studies on Renaissance music. His varied musicological interests include Puccini, Pergolesi, and the concertina, which he also plays.

WRITINGS: *The Cappella Giulia Chansonnier: Rome, Biblioteca Apostolica Vaticana, G.C.XIII.27* (2 vols., N.Y., 1975–76); ed. *Papers Read at the Dufay Quincentenary Conference, Brooklyn Coll., Dec. 6–7, 1974* (Brooklyn, 1976); ed. *Music in the Classic Period: Essays in Honor of Barry S. Brook* (N.Y., 1985); *Music at the Aragonese Court of Naples* (Cambridge, 1985); *The Wheatstone English Concertina in Victorian England* (Oxford, 1996); *Anthology of Renaissance Music* (N.Y., 1998); *Renaissance Music: Musical Style and Musical Life, 1400–1600* (N.Y., 1998).—NS/LK/DM

Atlas, Dalia (née **Sternberg**), Israeli conductor; b. Haifa, Nov. 14, 1933. After piano training at the Rubin Academy of Music in Jerusalem (graduated, 1952), she studied conducting with various mentors abroad, including Ferrara, Celibidache, Swarowsky, and Boulez. She was the first woman to obtain prizes in the Cantelli (Novara, 1963), Mitropoulos (N.Y., 1964), and Royal Liverpool Phil. (1964) conducting competitions; she later received the Eugene Ormandy Award (Philadelphia, 1980). In the meantime, she launched her career in her homeland by founding the Israel Pro-Musica Orch.; after joining the faculty of the Technion Inst. of Technology in Haifa, she founded its sym. orch. and choir; later founded the Atlas Camerata, a chamber orch., which she conducted on a world tour in 1991. As a guest conductor, she appeared with major orchs. in Europe, the U.S., and Australia.—NS/LK/DM

Attaignant, Pierre, important French music publisher; b. probably near Couai, c. 1494; d. Paris, 1551 or 1552. He settled in Paris by 1514. In 1525 he began to publish music, and from 1537 to 1547 he served as the music printer to the king. Attaignant invented a new method of publishing music whereby staff segments and notes were combined and printed in a single impression. He was thus the first music publisher to succeed at mass production. He publ. numerous chansons, Masses, motets, Psalms, and instrumental pieces.

BIBL.: D. Heartz, *P. A., Royal Printer of Music* (Berkeley, 1969).—NS/LK/DM

Attenhofer, Karl, Swiss conductor and composer; b. Wettingen, May 5, 1837; d. Zürich, May 22, 1914. He studied with Elster, and then at the Leipzig Cons. (1857–58) with Richter and Dreyschock. After serving as director of music in Rapperswil (1863–66), he settled in Zürich and became director of music at the Univ. in 1870 and was named to the position of 2nd director of the Cons. in 1896. Although he composed church and chamber music, he became best known for his choral works and pieces for men's voices.

BIBL.: E. Isler, *K. A.* (Zürich, 1915).—NS/LK/DM

Atterberg, Kurt (Magnus), eminent Swedish composer; b. Göteborg, Dec. 12, 1887; d. Stockholm, Feb. 15, 1974. He studied composition at the Stockholm Cons. with Hallen, and in Berlin with Schillings (1910–12). In 1913 he was appointed conductor at the Drama Theater in Stockholm, holding this post until 1922. In 1919 he began writing music criticism and continued to contribute to Stockholm newspapers until 1957. Concurrently he was also employed at the Swedish patent office (1912–68) and served as secretary of the Royal Swedish Academy of Music in Stockholm (1940–53). He was one of the founders of the Soc. of Swedish Composers in 1924, and was on its board until 1947. During all this time, he composed with inexhaustible energy, producing works in all genres in scores marked by precision of form and technique. Atterberg's name ·attracted unexpected attention when he was declared winner of the ill-conceived Schubert Centennial Contest organized in 1928 by the Columbia Phonograph Co., with the declared intention to finish Schubert's *Unfinished Symphony*. The entire venture was severely criticized in musical circles as an attempt to derive commercial advantage under the guise of an homage to a great composer. Rumors spread that Atterberg had deliberately imitated the style of composition of some members of the jury (Glazunov, Alfano, Nielsen) in order to ingratiate himself with them so as to secure the prize, but Atterberg denied any such suggestion, pointing out that he knew the names only of those in the jury from the Nordic zone, whereas the international membership comprised 10 national zones. Furthermore, the sym. he had submitted was written in a far more advanced style than Atterberg's previous symphonic works and was certainly much more modern than any music by the jury members, using as it did such procedures as polytonality. There can be no doubt, however, that Atterberg was a master technician of his craft, and that his music had a powerful appeal. That it never gained a wider audience can be ascribed only to an unfathomable accident of world culture.

WORKS: D R A M A T I C : O p e r a (all first perf. in Stockholm): *Harvard Harpolekare* (Harvard the Potter; 1915–17; Sept. 29, 1919; rev. as *Harvard der Harfner* and perf. in German at Chemnitz, 1936; a later ver. with new 3rd act perf. in Linz, June 14, 1952); *Bäckahästen* (1923–24; Jan. 23, 1925); *Fanal* (1929–32; Jan. 27, 1934); *Aladdin* (1936–41; March 18, 1941); *Stormen*, after Shakespeare's *Tempest* (1946–47; Sept. 19, 1948). B a l l e t : *Per Svinaherde* (Peter the Swineherd; 1914–15); *De fåvitska jungfrurna*, ballet-pantomime (The Wise and Foolish Virgins; Paris, Nov. 18, 1920). O R C H . : 9 numbered syms.: No. 1 (1909–11; Stockholm, Jan. 10, 1912), No. 2 (1911–13; Stockholm, Feb. 11,

1912), No. 3 (1914–16; Stockholm, Nov. 28, 1916), No. 4, *Sinfonia piccola* (1918; Stockholm, March 27, 1919), No. 5, *Sinfonia funèbre* (1919–22; Stockholm, Jan. 6, 1923), No. 6 (1927–28; Stockholm, Oct. 15, 1928), No. 7, *Sinfonia romantica* (1942; Frankfurt am Main, Feb. 14, 1943), No. 8 (1944; Helsinki, Feb. 9, 1945), and No. 9, *Sinfonia visionaria*, for Mezzo-soprano, Baritone, Chorus, and Orch. (1955–56; Helsinki, Feb. 26, 1957); also a Sinfonia for Strings (1952–53); 9 suites, among them No. 3, for Violin, Viola, and Strings (1917), No. 4, *Turandot* (1921), No. 5, *Suite barocco* (1922), and No. 8, *Suite pastorale* (1931); *Rhapsody* for Piano and Orch. (1909); Violin Concerto (1913; Göteborg, Feb. 11, 1914); Cello Concerto (1917–22; Berlin, Jan. 6, 1923); 2 Suites for the play *Stormen*, after Shakespeare's *Tempest*: No. 1 (1921; rev. 1962–63) and No. 2 (1964–65); *Rondeau retrospectif* (1926); Horn Concerto (1926; Stockholm, March 20, 1927); Piano Concerto (1927–35; Stockholm, Jan. 12, 1936); *Alven* (The River), symphonic poem (1929–30); *Varmlandsrhapsodie* for Selma Langerlöf's 75th birthday (Swedish Radio, Nov. 20, 1933); *Ballad and Passacaglia* (1936); *Rondeau caractéristique* (1939–40); *Indian Tunes* (1950); *Ballad utan ord* (Ballad without Words; 1957–58); Concerto for Violin, Cello or Viola, and Orch. (1959–60; ver. with String Orch., 1963); *Vittorioso* (1962); *Adagio amoroso* for Flute and Strings (1967). **CHAMBER:** 2 string quartets (1915, 1937); Cello Sonata (1925); Piano Quintet (1927); *Variations and Fugue* for String Quartet (1943); *Trio concertante* for Violin, Cello, and Harp (1959–60; rev. 1965). **VOCAL:** *Requiem* (1913); *Järnbäraland*, cantata (1919).—NS/LK/DM

Attwood, Thomas, English organist and composer; b. London (baptized), Nov. 23, 1765; d. there, March 24, 1838. At 9, he became a chorister at the Chapel Royal. In 1781 he was made one of the Pages of the Presence to the Prince of Wales, who made it possible for him to study in Naples with Felipe Cinque and Gaetano Latilla (1783–85). He then went to Vienna, where he received composition lessons from Mozart. In 1787 he returned to England and resumed his court position. He was made music teacher to the Duchess of York in 1791 and to the Princess of Wales in 1795. In 1796 he became organist at St. Paul's Cathedral and composer at the Chapel Royal. In 1813 he helped to organize the Phil. Soc. of London, with which he appeared as a conductor. When the Royal Academy of Music in London was organized in 1823, he was made a prof. In 1825 he became musician-in-ordinary to the king. He was named organist of the Chapel Royal in 1836. Mendelssohn became his close friend, and among his students were his godson, Thomas Attwood Walmisley, George Bridgetower, and Cipriani Potter. As a composer, he was profoundly influenced by his association with Mozart. His output includes music for some 30 stage works, several instrumental pieces, much vocal music, including the fine coronation anthems *I was glad* (1821) and *O Lord, grant the king a long life* (1831), a Service in F major, songs, and glees. Walmisley ed. *Services and Anthems Composed by T. A.* (London, 1852). —NS/LK/DM

Atzmon (real name, **Groszberger**), **Moshe,** Hungarian-born Israeli conductor; b. Budapest, July 30, 1931. He was taken to Palestine in 1944, where he attended the Tel Aviv Academy of Music (1958–62), and then pursued conducting studies at the Guildhall School of Music and Drama in London. In 1964 he won 1st prize in the Liverpool conducting competition, and then appeared as a guest conductor with various British orchs. He was chief conductor of the Sydney (Australia) Sym. Orch. (1969–71), the North German Radio Sym. Orch. in Hamburg (1972–76), the Basel Sym. Orch. (1972–77), and the Tokyo Metropolitan Sym. Orch. (1978–82). With Giuseppe Patanè, he served as co-principal conductor of the American Sym. Orch. in N.Y. (1982–84), and then was chief conductor of the Nagoya Phil. in Japan (1986–92). From 1991 to 1995 he was Generalmusikdirektor of the Dortmund Opera. —NS/LK/DM

Auber, Daniel-François-Esprit, notable French composer; b. Caen, Jan. 29, 1782; d. Paris, May 12, 1871. He was a pupil of Ignaz Anton Ladurner. His first work for the stage, *L'erreur d'un moment* (1805; rev. as *Julie*, 1811), attracted the notice of Cherubini, who became his mentor. Auber first gained success as a composer with his opéra-comique, *La bergère châtelaine* (Paris, Jan. 27, 1820). Shortly after, he met the librettist Scribe, with whom he collaborated on many works for the stage until Scribe's death in 1861. Following the success of Auber's *Le maçon* (Paris, May 3, 1825), a significant work in the development of the opéra-comique genre, he scored an enormous success with his *La muette de Portici* (Paris, Feb. 29, 1828), a work that launched a new era in French grand opera. The latter's vivid portrayal of popular fury stirred French and Belgian audiences, leading to revolutionary disturbances following its premiere in Brussels (Aug. 25, 1830). Another fine success followed with his opéra-comique *Fra Diavolo* (Paris, Jan. 28, 1830), the only score by Auber which remains in the standard repertory. Among his later stage works, the opéras-comiques *La part du diable* (Paris, Jan. 16, 1843), *Haydée* (Paris, Dec. 28, 1847), and *Manon Lescaut* (Paris, Feb. 23, 1856) were influential in the development of the opéra-lyrique genre. From 1842 to 1870 he served as director of the Paris Cons. In 1825 he was named a member of the Légion d'honneur. He was elected to the Inst. of the Académie in 1829. In 1852 Napoleon III appointed him music director of the imperial chapel.

WORKS: DRAMATIC (all 1st perf. in Paris): *L'erreur d'un moment* (amateur perf., 1805; rev. as *Julie*, 1811); *Jean de Couvin* (Sept. 1812); *Le séjour militaire* (Feb. 27, 1813); *Le testament et les billets-doux* (Sept. 18, 1819); *Le bergère châtelaine* (Jan. 27, 1820); *Emma, ou La promesse imprudente* (July 7, 1821); *Leicester, ou Le château de Kenilworth* (Jan. 25, 1823); *La neige, ou Le nouvel Éginard* (Oct. 8, 1823); *Vendôme en Espagne* (Dec. 5, 1823; in collaboration with Hérold); *Les trois genres* (April 27, 1824; in collaboration with Boieldieu); *Le concert à la cour, ou La débutante* (June 3, 1824); *Léocadie* (Nov. 4, 1824); *Le maçon* (May 3, 1825); *Le timide, ou Le nouveau séducteur* (May 30, 1826); *Fiorella* (Nov. 28, 1826); *La muette de Portici* (Feb. 29, 1828); *La fiancée* (Jan. 10, 1829); *Fra Diavolo, ou L'hôtellerie de Terracine* (Jan. 28, 1830); *Le dieu et la bayadère, ou La courtisane amourese* (Oct. 13, 1830); *Le philtre* (June 20, 1831); *La Marquise de Brinvilliers* (Oct. 31, 1831; in collaboration with Batton, Berton, Blangini, Boieldieu, Carafa, Cherubini, Hérold, and Paër); *Le serment, ou Les faux-monnayeurs* (Oct. 1, 1832); *Gustave III, ou Le bal masqué* (Feb. 27, 1833); *Lestocq, ou L'intrigue et l'amour* (May 24, 1834); *Le cheval de* *bronze* (March 23, 1835; rev. version, Sept. 21, 1857); *Actéon* (Jan. 23, 1836); *Les chaperons blancs* (April 9, 1836); *L'ambassadrice* (Dec. 21, 1836); *Le domino noir* (Dec. 2, 1837); *Le lac des fées* (April 1, 1839); *Zanetta, ou Jouer avec le feu* (May 18, 1840); *Les diamants de la couronne* (March 6, 1841); *Le Duc d'Olonne* (Feb. 4, 1842); *La part du diable* (Jan. 16, 1843); *La sirène* (March 26, 1844); *La barcarolle, ou L'amour et la musique* (April 22, 1845); *Les premiers pas* (Nov. 15, 1847; in collaboration with Adam, Carafa, and Halévy); *Haydée, ou Le secret* (Dec. 28, 1847); *L'enfant prodigue* (Dec. 6, 1850); *Zerline, ou La corbeille d'oranges* (May 16, 1851); *Marco Spada* (Dec. 21, 1852); *Jenny Bell* (June 2, 1855); *Manon Lescaut* (Feb. 23, 1856); *La circassienne* (Feb. 2, 1861); *La fiancée du Roi de Garbe* (Jan. 11, 1864); *Le premier jour de bonheur* (Feb. 15, 1868); *Rêve d'amour* (Dec. 20, 1869). **OTHER:** 4 cellos concertos (1 not extant); Violin Concerto; other orch. pieces; chamber music; numerous sacred and secular vocal pieces.

BIBL.: E. de Mirécourt, *A.* (Paris, 1857); B. Jouvin, *A.* (Paris, 1868); A. Pougin, *A.: Ses commencements, les origines de sa carrière* (Paris, 1873); J. Carlez, *A.* (Caen, 1875); A. Kohut, *A.* (Leipzig, 1895); C. Malherbe, *A.* (Paris, 1911); R. Longyear, *D.F.E. A.: A Chapter in French Opéra Comique 1800–1870* (diss., Cornell Univ., 1957); W. Börner, *Die Opern von D.F.E. A.* (diss., Univ. of Leipzig, 1962);H. Schneider, *Chronologische-thematisches Verzeichnis sämtlicher Werke von D.F.E. A. (AWV), Band 1.1–2* (Frankfurt am Main, 1994).—NS/LK/DM

Aubert, family of French musicians:

(1) Jacques Aubert, violinist and composer, known as **le vieux** and **le père**; b. Paris, Sept. 30, 1689; d. Belleville, near Paris, May 17 or 18, 1753. He was a pupil of Senaillé. After working as a dancing-master and violinist, he entered the service of Louis-Henri, Duke of Bourbon and Prince of Condé, in 1719, and wrote music for the stage. He was a member of the 24 Violons du Roi (1727–46), 1st violinist in the Opéra orch. (1728–52), and a performer at the Concert Spirituel (1729–40). In his instrumental works, the Italian influence is revealed but he retains French-style dance forms. His violin concertos were the first to be printed in France, although they may not have been the first composed in that country. Among his works are 12 stage pieces, 5 books of [10] sonatas for Violin and Basso Continuo (1719, 1721, 1723, 1731, c. 1738), 12 suites entitled *Concert de simphonies* (1730, 1731, 1733, 1735–37), 6 concertos for 4 Violins, Cello, and Basso Continuo (1734), 4 concertos for 4 Violins, Cello, and Basso Continuo (1739), sonatas for 2 Violins (1738), and other instrumental pieces. He had 2 sons:

(2) Louis Aubert, violinist and composer, known as **le jeune** and **le fils**; b. Paris, May 15, 1720; d. after 1783. He received training from his father and played in the Opéra orch. while still a child. At age 12, he was nominated a member of the 24 Violons du Roi, a position he officially assumed in 1746. By 1756 he also was 1st violinist in the Opéra orch., where he also was active as a conductor. He was pensioned in 1774. He publ. 6 sonatas for Violin and Basso Continuo (1750), *6 simphonies a quatre* for 3 Violins and Basso Continuo (1755), and 6 trios for 2 Violins and Cello (n.d.).

(3) Jean-Louis Aubert, writer on music, dramatist, and abbé; b. Paris, Dec. 15, 1732; d. c. 1810. He is known for his celebrated reply to Rousseau's *Lettre sur la*

musique françoise during the Querelle des Bouffons which he publ. as *Refutation suivie et détaillée des principes de M. Rousseau de Geneve touchant la musique françoise* (1754).—NS/LK/DM

Aubert, Louis (François Marie), French composer and writer on music; b. Paramé, Ille-et-Vilaine, Feb. 19, 1877; d. Paris, Jan. 9, 1968. He entered the Paris Cons. when he was still a child and studied with Diémer (piano), Lavignac (theory), and Fauré (composition). Diémer was the soloist in the premiere of Aubert's *Fantaisie* for Piano and Orch. in Paris on Nov. 17, 1901. His opera *La Forêt bleue* was first performed in Geneva on Jan. 7, 1913. Aubert's symphonic poem *Habanera* (Paris, March 22, 1919) proved highly successful. While he composed many subsequent scores, he also devoted much time to music criticism. In 1956 he was made a member of the Institut de France. He publ. the vols. *L'Orchestre* (Paris, 1951) and *Notice sur la vie et les travaux de Gustave Charpentier* (Paris, 1956). Aubert's compositions reveal the general influence of Debussy and Ravel.

WORKS: DRAMATIC: Opera: *La Forêt bleue* (1912; Geneva, Jan. 7, 1913). **Ballet:** *La Momie* (1903); *Chrysothémis* (1904); *La Nuit ensorcelée* (1922); *Cinéma* (1953); *La Belle Hélène* (1953). **ORCH.:** *Suite brève* (1900; Paris, April 27, 1916; also for 2 Pianos); *Fantaisie* for Piano and Orch. (Paris, Nov. 17, 1901); *Habanera* (1918; Paris, March 22, 1919); *Dryade* (1921); *Caprice* for Violin and Orch. (1925); *Feuilles d'images* (Paris, March 7, 1931); *Offrand aux victimes de la guerre* (1947); *Le Tombeau de Châteaubriand* (1948). **CHAMBER:** *Suite brève* for 2 Pianos (1900; also for Orch.); *Sillages* for Piano (1913); Piano Quintet (n.d.); *Improvisation* for 2 Guitars (1960). **VOCAL:** *La Légende du sang* for Narrator, Chorus, and Orch. (1902); *6 Poèmes arabes* for Voice and Orch. (1907); *Crépuscules d'automne*, song cycle (1908; Paris, Feb. 20, 1909); *Nuit mauresque* for Voice and Orch. (1911); *Les Saisons* for Soloist, Chorus, and Orch. (1937).

BIBL.: L. Vuillemin, *L. A. et son oeuvre* (Paris, 1921); M. Landowski and G. Morançon, *L. A.* (Paris, 1967).—NS/LK/DM

Aubéry du Boulley, Prudent-Louis, French composer and teacher; b. Verneuil, Eure, Dec. 9, 1796; d. there, Jan. 28, 1869. He studied at the Paris Cons. with Momigy, Méhul, and Cherubini, and then was active as a teacher in Verneuil. He wrote many military band pieces and much chamber music, some of the latter utilizing guitar. He publ. a guitar method and the textbook *Grammaire musicale* (Paris, 1830).

BIBL.: J. de L'Avre, *A. d. B.* (Paris, 1896).—NS/LK/DM

Aubin, Tony (Louis Alexandre), French composer, conductor, and pedagogue; b. Paris, Dec. 8, 1907; d. there, Sept. 21, 1981. He studied harmony with Samuel-Rousseau, counterpoint with N. Galon, and composition with Dukas at the Paris Cons. (1925–30), winning the Prix de Rome with his cantata *Actéon* in 1930. In 1934–35 he studied conducting with Gaubert. In 1937 he became artistic director of the RTF station Paris Mondial. He became a conductor with the French radio in 1945, where he remained until 1960. He also taught composition at the Paris Cons. from 1945 to 1977. In 1970 he became a member of the Academie des Beaux-

Arts. Aubin was a pragmatic composer who cultivated an eclectic idiom.

WORKS: DRAMATIC: Opera: *La jeunese de Goya* (1968–70). **Ballet:** *Fourberies* (1950); *Variations* (1953); *Grand pas* (1953); *Périls* (1958); *Au fil de l'eau* (1970). **OTHER:** Incidental music and film scores. **ORCH.:** 2 syms. (*Symphonie romantique*, 1934–36; 1944); *Le chevalier Pécopin* (1942); *Cantilène variée* (1944; also for Cello and Piano, 1937); *Suite danoise* (1945); *Suite éolienne* for Flute, Clarinet, and Strings (1958); *Divertimento dell'incertezza* for Clarinet and Strings (1967; also for Clarinet and Piano); *Concertino delle scoiattolo* for Oboe, Piano, and Strings (1970). **CHAMBER:** String Quartet (1930); Piano Sonata (1933); *Concertinetto dell'amicizia* for Flute and Piano (1964); *Concertinetto* for Violin and Piano (1964); *Brughiera* for Bassoon and Piano (1966); *Toccatrotta* for Harpsichord (1972); *Divertimento dell'incertezza* for Clarinet and Piano (1973); *Hidalgoyas* for Guitar (1972); *Concertino della brughiera* for Bassoon and Piano (1975). **VOCAL:** *Actéon*, cantata for Soprano, Tenor, Bass, and Orch. (1930); *6 poèmes de Verlaine* for Voice and Piano (1932); *Cressida* for Speaker, Soprano, Tenor, Chorus, and Orch. (1934–37); *Jeanne d'Arc à Orléans*, oratorio (1942).—**NS/LK/DM**

Aubry, Pierre, French musicologist and philologist; b. Paris, Feb. 14, 1874; d. Dieppe, Aug. 31, 1910. He received training in philology (graduated, 1892) and law (graduated, 1894) in Paris, which remained the center of his activities. In 1898 he was named archiviste paléographe at the École des Chartes, and subsequently held teaching positions at the Institut Catholique, the École des hautes Études Sociales, and the Schola Cantorum. Aubry was an authority on French music of the 13th century.

WRITINGS: (all publ. in Paris): *Huit chants héroïques de l'anciennce France, XIIe-XVIIIe siècle: Poèmes et musique* (1896); *L'idée religieuse dans la poésie lyrique et la musique française au moyen âge* (1897); *L'inspiration religieuse dans la poésie musicale en France* (1899); with E. Misset, A. Jeanroy, and L. Brandini, *Mélanges de musicologie critique* (4 vols., 1900–05); *Souvenir d'une mission d'études musicales en Arménie* (1902); *Essais de musicologie comparée* (2 vols., 1903, 1905); with R. Meyer and J. Bédier, *La chanson de Bele Aelis par le trouvère Baude de la Quarière* (1904); *La musique de danse au moyen âge* (1904); with A. Jeanroy and Dr. Dejeanne, *Quatre poésies de Marcabru, troubadour gascon du XIIe siècle* (1904); *Un coin pittoresque de la vie artistique au XIIIe siècle* (1904); *Une "estampida" de Rambaut de Vaqueiras* (1904); *La chanson populaire dans les textes musicaux du moyen âge* (1905); *Au Turkestan: Note sur quelques habitudes musicales chez les Tadjiks et les Sartes* (1905); *Cent motets du XIIIe siècle, publiés d'après le manuscrit Ed.IV.6 de Bamberg* (1905); *Esquisse d'une bibliographie de la chanson populaire hors de France* (1905); with E. Dacier, *Les caractères de la danse: Histoire d'un divertissement pendant la première moitié du XVIIIe siècle* (1905); *La musique et les musiciens d'église en Normandie au XIIIe siècle d'après le "Journal des visites pastorales" d'Odon Rigaud* (1906); *Un "explicit" en musique du roman de Fauvel* (1906); *Estampies et danses royales: Les plus anciens texts de musique instrumentale au moyen-âge* (1907); *La rhythmique musicale des troubadours et des trouvères* (1907); *Le roman de Fauvel: Reproduction photographique du manuscrit français 146 de la Bibliothèque Nationale de Paris, avec un index des interpolations lyriques* (1907); *Recherches sur les "tenors" français dans les motets du XIIIe siècles* (1907); with A. Gastoué, *Recherches sur les "tenors" latins dans les motets du XIIIe siècle d'après le manuscrit de Montpellier* (1907); *Iter hispanicum: Notices et extraits de manuscrits de musique*

ancienne conservés dans les bibliothèques d'Espagne (1908); with A. Jeanroy, *Le chansonnier de l'Arsenal* (1909); with J. Bédier, *Les chansons de croisade* (1909); *Trouvères et troubadours* (1909; Eng. tr., 1914).—**NS/LK/DM**

Auda, Antoine, French musicologist; b. St. Julien-en-Loiret, Oct. 28, 1879; d. Brussels, Aug. 19, 1964. He was a chorister in the Maîtrise de St. Joseph in Marseilles, and later became a lay brother of the Salesian order. From 1905 to 1925 he taught in Liège, and then settled in Brussels, where he pursued musicological research.

WRITINGS: *Manuel de chant à l'usage des paroisses et des maisons d'éducation* (Liège, 1924); *L'école musicale liégeoise au Xe siècle: Etienne de Liège* (Brussels, 1926); *La musique et les musiciens de l'ancien pays de Liège...jusqu'à...1800* (Brussels, 1930); *Les modes et les tons de la musique et spécialement de la musique médiévale* (Brussels, 1930); *Contribution à l'histoire de l'origine des modes et des tons grégoriens* (Grenoble, 1932); *Les gammes musicales: Essai historique sur les modes et sur les tons* (Brussels, 1947); *Les "Motets Wallons" du manuscript de Turin: Vari 42* (Brussels, 1953); *Bathélemy Beaulaigue, poète et musicien prodige* (Brussels, 1957); *Théorie et pratique du Tactus: Transcription et exécution de la musique antérieure aux environs de 1650* (Brussels, 1965).—**NS/LK/DM**

Audran, (Achille) Edmond, notable French composer, son of **Marius-Pierre Audran;** b. Lyons, April 12, 1840; d. Tierceville, Aug. 17, 1901. He was a student of Jules Duprato at the École Niedermeyer in Paris, graduating in 1859. In 1861 he became maître de chapelle of the church of St. Joseph in Marseilles, where he composed sacred music and attracted notice with his operetta *Le Grand Mogol* (Feb. 24, 1877). Settling in Paris, he scored a major success with his comic opera *Les Noces d'Olivette* (Nov. 13, 1879). Even more successful was his next score, *La Moscotte* (Dec. 29, 1880), one of the finest operettas of the day. No less successful was his next score, *Gillette de Narbonne* (Nov. 11, 1882). The revised version of *Le Grand Mogol* (Sept. 19, 1884) made it a repertoire staple. Among his later successful works were *La Cigale et la fourmi* (Oct. 30, 1886), *Miss Helyett* (Nov. 12, 1890), *L'Oncle Célestin* (March 24, 1891), *L'Enlèvement de la Toledad* (Nov. 17, 1894), and *La Poupée* (Oct. 21, 1896).

WORKS: DRAMATIC: Musical Theater (all 1st perf. in Paris unless otherwise given): *L'Ours et le pacha* (Marseilles, 1862); *La Chercheuse d'esprit* (Marseilles, 1864); *La Nivernaise* (Marseilles, Dec. 1862); *Le Petit Poucet* (Marseilles, April 1868); *Le Grand Mogol* (Marseilles, Feb. 24, 1877; rev. version, Paris, Sept. 19, 1884); *Les Noces d'Olivette* (Nov. 13, 1879); *La Mascotte* (Dec. 29, 1880); *Gillette de Narbonne* (Nov. 11, 1882); *Les Pommes d'or* (Feb. 12, 1883); *La Dormeuse éveillée* (Dec. 27, 1883); *Pervenche* (March 31, 1885); *Serment d'amour* (Feb. 19, 1886); *Indiana* (London, Oct. 11, 1886); *La Cigale et la fourmi* (Oct. 30, 1886); *La Fiancée des verts-poteaux* (Nov. 8, 1887); *Le Puits qui parle* (March 15, 1888); *Miette* (Sept. 24, 1888); *La Petite Fronde* (Nov. 16, 1888); *La Fille à Cacolet* (July 10, 1889); *L'Oeuf rouge* (March 14, 1890); *Miss Helyett* (Nov. 12, 1890); *L'Oncle Célestin* (March 24, 1891); *Article de Paris* (March 17, 1892); *Sainte-Freya* (Nov. 4, 1892); *Madame Suzette* (March 29,1893); *Mon Prince!* (Nov. 18, 1893); *L'Enlèvement de la Toledad* (Nov. 17, 1894); *La*

Duchesse de Ferrare (Jan. 25, 1895); La Reine des reines (Oct. 14, 1896); La Poupée (Oct. 21, 1896); Monsieur Lohengrin (Nov. 30, 1896); Les Petites (Oct. 11, 1897); Les Soeurs Graudichard (April 21, 1899); Le Curé Vincent (Oct. 25, 1901).—NS/LK/DM

Audran, Marius-Pierre, French tenor, pedagogue, and composer, father of **(Achille) Edmond Audran;** b. Aix, Provence, Sept. 26, 1816; d. Marseilles, Jan. 9, 1887. After singing in Marseilles, Bordeaux, and Lyons, he was first tenor at the Paris Opéra-Comique. In 1863 he became a prof. of voice and director of the Marseilles Cons.—NS/LK/DM

Auer, Edward, American pianist and teacher; b. N.Y., Dec. 7, 1941. He was a student of Aube Tzerko in Los Angeles (1952–60) before pursuing training at the Juilliard School of Music in N.Y. (1961–62; 1963–66), where he studied with Rosina Lhévinne. He completed his studies in Paris on a Fulbright grant (1966–68). In 1965 he took 2nd prize in the Beethoven Competition and 5th prize in the Chopin Competition, and in 1966 5th prize in the Tchaikovsky Competition. He captured 1st prize in the Long-Thibaud Competition in 1967, and 7th prize in the Queen Elisabeth of Belgium Competition in 1968. Auer appeared as a soloist with various U.S. orchs., among them the Los Angeles Phil., the Atlanta Sym. Orch., the Baltimore Sym. Orch., and the Detroit Sym. Orch., as well as with orchs. in Europe and Japan. In addition to his recital engagements at home and abroad, he played in the Seraphim Trio with Sidney Harth and Yehuda Hanani. From 1976 to 1980 he taught at the Univ. of Calif. at Los Angeles. In 1983 he joined the faculty of the Ind. Univ. School of Music in Bloomington. Auer has won admiration for his performances of Beethoven, Schubert, and Chopin.—LK/DM

Auer, Leopold, celebrated Hungarian violinist and pedagogue, great-uncle of **György (Sándor) Ligeti;** b. Veszprém, June 7, 1845; d. Loschwitz, near Dresden, July 15, 1930. He studied with Ridley-Kohne at the Budapest Cons. After making his debut in the Mendelssohn Concerto in Budapest, he continued his training with Jacob Dont in Vienna and then with Joachim in Hannover (1861–63). He was concertmaster in Düsseldorf (1864–66) and Hamburg (1866–68). In 1868 he was called to St. Petersburg as soloist in the Imperial Orch., and prof. of violin at the newly founded Cons. He became one of the most famous violin teachers in Russia. Among his pupils were Elman, Zimbalist, and Heifetz. Tchaikovsky originally dedicated his Violin Concerto to him, but was offended when Auer suggested some revisions and changed the dedication to Brodsky. Nevertheless, the Concerto became Auer's favorite work, and he made it a pièce de résistance for all his pupils. He was active as a teacher in London (1906–11), Dresden (1912–14), and Norway (1915–17). In the summer of 1917 he left Russia, never to return. On March 23, 1918, he played a concert in N.Y. Settling in the U.S., he devoted himself mainly to teaching, first at the Inst. of Musical Art in N.Y. (from 1926) and then at the Curtis Inst. of Music in Philadelphia (from 1928). He publ. the manuals Violin Playing as I Teach It (N.Y., 1921)

and Violin Master Works and Their Interpretation (1925), and an autobiography, My Long Life in Music (1923). Auer's performances were marked by an assured technique, exemplary taste, and nobility of expression. —NS/LK/DM

Auer, Max, Austrian writer on music; b. Vöcklabruck, May 6, 1880; d. Vienna, Sept. 24, 1962. He studied in Vienna, and later taught in provincial public schools in Austria. He was one of the foremost authorities on Bruckner. He publ. Anton Bruckner: Sein Leben und Werk (Vienna, 1923) and Anton Bruckner als Kirchenmusiker (Regensburg, 1927). He also completed vols. 2–4 (1928, 1932, 1937) of Göllerich's monumental biography, Anton Bruckner: Ein Lebens- und Schaffensbild.—NS/LK/DM

Aufschnaiter, Benedict Anton, Austrian composer; b. Kitzbühel (baptized), Feb. 21, 1665; d. Passau (buried), Jan. 24, 1742. He went to Vienna, where he received his education. In 1705 he was named cathedral and court Kapellmeister in Passau by the prince archbishop, where he served for the rest of his life. Aufschnaiter composed a large body of music, much of it for the church. He also publ. a fine vol. of 6 orch. serenades or suites as Concors discordia (Nuremberg, 1695), which reveal his mastery of the French and Italian styles of instrumental writing.

BIBL.: F. Lehrndorfer, B.A. A.: Domkomponist in Passau (diss., Univ. of Munich, 1920).—LK/DM

Auger, Arleen (Joyce), esteemed American soprano; b. Los Angeles, Sept. 13, 1939; d. Amsterdam, June 10, 1993. She majored in education at Calif. State Univ. in Long Beach (B.A., 1963); then studied voice with Ralph Errolle in Chicago. She made her European operatic debut as the Queen of the Night in Die Zauberflöte at the Vienna State Opera (1967), remaining on its roster until 1974; also chose that role for her N.Y.C. Opera debut (March 16, 1969). She appeared with the conductor Helmuth Rilling on a tour of Japan in 1974, and subsequently gained prominence through a major series of recordings of the music of Bach under his direction; also devoted increasing attention to a concert career. On Oct. 2, 1978, she made her Metropolitan Opera debut in N.Y. as Marzelline in Fidelio, and, in 1984, made a notably successful N.Y. recital debut. Her appearance in the title role of Handel's Alcina in London (1985) and Los Angeles (1986) elicited further critical accolades. In 1986 she was chosen to sing at the royal wedding of Prince Andrew and Sarah Ferguson in London. During the 1986–87 season, she made an extensive concert tour of the U.S. and Europe. In 1992 her career was tragically ended when she was stricken with a fatal brain tumor.—NS/LK/DM

Auger, Brian, British jazz organist, pianist, and composer; b. London, July 18, 1939. Auger was known as an early jazz-rock exponent. He was voted Best New Jazz Artist by Melody Maker in 1964, and created an R&B group, Trinity, that same year with John McLaughlin. The group later included Rick Brown on bass and Mickey Waller on drums. It became known as Steampacket after adding vocalists Long John Baldry and Rod Stewart from Baldy's Hoochie Coochie Men, as well as Vic Briggs on guitar and vocalist Julie Driscoll (who later married jazz pianist Keith Tippetts). Steampacket's vocalists were showcased separately on stage, as was Auger with instrumentals. His distinctive, distorted organ sound was produced by playing the Hammond through a guitar valve amplifier. Ego problems split the group and Auger re-formed Trinity until 1970, at which time the group included Dave Ambrose, bass; Gary Boyle, guitar; and Clive Thacker, drums. He then joined the American jazz-rock group Oblivion Express, with various personnel, followed by reunions of the earlier groups. Auger divided his time between working in the U.S. and Europe, enjoying considerable success. In 1985 he joined up temporarily with a re-formed Spencer Davis Group, then led his own group, Blues Revival. For the next decade, he worked mainly out of Los Angeles. In April 1996, he returned to London and played dates with a new version of Oblivion Express. —LP

Augustine of Hippo, St. (actually, **Aurelius Augustinus**), great Christian church father; b. Tagaste, Numidia, Nov. 13, 354; d. Hippo, Aug. 28, 430. He was educated in Carthage. In 387 he was baptized a Christian by St. Ambrose in Milan, and then returned to Tagaste as a proselyte of his new faith. In 391 he settled in Hippo as assistant to the bishop, Valerius, whom he succeeded in 395. Augustine had a great love for music, which is reflected in his valuable treatise *De musica* (387–91). It is notable for its discussion of rhythm and the theological and philosophical import of the study of music. For a modern ed. of his treatise, see R. Taliaferro, ed. and tr., "On Music: De musica," *The Fathers of the Church, a New Translation: Writings of St. A.* (Vol. II, N.Y., 1947).

BIBL.: A. Vincent, *Analyse du traité de métrique et de rhythmique de S. A. intitulé "De musica"* (Paris, 1849); J. Huré, *S. A. musicien* (Paris, 1924); F. Amerio, *Il "De musica" di S. A.* (Turin, 1929); G. Borhezio, *La musica in S. A.* (Rome, 1931); H. Davenson, *Traité de la musique selon l'esprit de S. A.* (Neuchâtel, 1944); F. van der Meer, *A.us de zielzorger: Een studie over de praktijk van een kerkvader* (Utrecht, 1947; Eng. tr., 1961); G. Bonner, *S. A. of Hippo: Life and Controversies* (Philadelphia, 1963); J. O'Donnell, *A.* (Boston, 1985).—NS/LK/DM

Augustus, Janice G., African-American composer, violinist, and organist; b. Cleveland, Oct. 31, 1945. At an early age, she studied piano extensively with Rose Widder and violin with Gino Antal. She later attended Howard Univ. in Washington, D.C. (1964–69), becoming proficient on several other instruments. From 1976 to 1996 she served as a teacher for the Archdiocese of Los Angeles at Guardian Angel Catholic School in Pacoima, where, from 1971 to 1997, she also was organist and choir director at the Guardian Angel Catholic Church. While she composed and conducted many original works in her capacity as choir director, since 1998 she has devoted herself to composition, rapidly producing small works for and with violin. These include (all 1998) *City Images*, op.4, for Violin and Piano, *Images of Zoria* for

Violin, op.3, *Miniatures* for Two Violins, opp. 7–10, *Miniature* in Two Movements for Violin and Piano, op.6, *Miniature Sonata* for Violin, op.2, and *Six Miniatures* for Violin, op.1, nos. 1–6.—LK/DM

Aula, Giacomo, Italian jazz pianist, composer; b. Lagonegro, March 28, 1967. Aula studied classical music with Maria Martino, African-American music in Torino (where he has lived since 1986), and jazz peformance, jazz orchestra playing, and musicology at Siena Jazz (studying with Enrico Rava, Franco D'Andrea, Bruno Tommaso, Marcello Piras, and Stefano Zenni). In 1994 he earned a degree in electronic engineering from Politecnico di Torino, studying especially electroacoustics and human hearing. Two years later, Aula toured Germany and appeared on Italian television, and he regularly appears at Italian festivals. He performed from 1995–98 in The Orch. Nazionale Giovanile (youth jazz orchestra) with Gianluigi Trovesi (cl.), Bruno Tommaso (dir., arr.), Rudy Migliardi (trmb.), and guests Palle Danielsson (bs.), Peter Erskine (drm.) and James Newton (flt., dir.). An organist and electric bassist, Aula also tours and records with Larry Schneider and teaches piano at the Musicae Fabri School in Montiglio founded by Luciano Bertolotti.

DISC.: L. Bertolotti: *Brain Cigarette* (1996); *Jazz Inside* (1997); *Just Beginning* (1997).—LP

Auld, Georgie (born **John Altwerger**), Canadian-born American jazz tenor saxophonist, bandleader; b. Toronto, May 19, 1919; d. Palm Springs, Calif., Jan. 8, 1990. As a child Auld began on alto saxophone, studying with Michael Angelo in Toronto. In 1929 his family moved to N.Y., where, in 1931, he won a scholarship to study with Rudy Weidoeft for nine months. In 1936, after hearing Coleman Hawkins's recording of "Meditation," he switched to tenor sax. Auld led a small band at Nick's, worked with Bunny Berigan in 1937 and 1938, and joined Artie Shaw's band early in 1939; he played with the group until Shaw disbanded it later that year. Auld briefly led a Shaw alumni group before joining Jan Savitt (spring 1940) and Benny Goodman (November 1940 to June 1941). Following a brief stint with another Artie Shaw group, Auld led his own band beginning in February 1942. The following year he served briefly in the army. Afterwards, he led a quartet at the Three Deuces, N.Y., then formed his big band in September 1943. The band continued through mid-1946, except for a break due to illness in 1945. Auld was open to the new bop style and at one time or another his band included such players as Dizzy Gillespie, Erroll Garner, Serge Chaloff, Joe Albany, Stan Levey, and Al Porcino, with arrangements from Al Cohn, Neal Hefti, and Tadd Dameron. Due to illness, Auld moved to Ariz., then Calif., but soon returned to regular playing, leading a group at the Three Deuces, then in Calif., and playing in Billy Eckstine's band in 1948. He led a band at the Tin Pan Alley Club, N.Y. (spring 1949; a ten-piece group that played in a more bebop-influenced style), then for almost a year acted in the Broadway play *The Rat Race*. Auld worked briefly with Count Basie in the spring of

1950, then led a quintet until August 1951. After another break due to illness, he moved to Calif., opened his own Melody Room Club, and began freelance studio work for MGM and others. He did studio work in N.Y. in the late 1950s, then moved to Las Vegas. During the 1960s he continued to lead bands, one of which toured Japan, and freelanced for various leaders, including a spell in Las Vegas with Benny Goodman (1966). Auld was active in Los Angeles in 1971, occasionally leading a band. He acted in the film, *New York, New York* (1977) and dubbed Robert DeNiro's saxophone parts as well.

DISC.: *G. A. Quintet* (1951); *In the Land of Hi Fi* (1955); *Good Enough to Keep* (1959); *G. A. Plays to the Winners* (1963); *Here's to the Losers* (1964).—**JC/LP**

Auletta, Pietro, Italian composer; b. S. Angelo, Avellino, c. 1698; d. Naples, Sept. 1771. He studied at the Cons. of S. Onofrio in Naples; gained renown with his comic opera *Orazio* (Naples, Carnival 1737). Only a few of his stage works are extant, but *La Locandiera* (Naples, July 10, 1738) survives as a testimony to his abilities as a dramatic composer.—**NS/LK/DM**

Aulin, Tor (Bernhard Vilhelm), noted Swedish violinist, conductor, and composer; b. Stockholm, Sept. 10, 1866; d. Saltsjöbaden, March 1, 1914. He studied with C. J. Lindberg in Stockholm (1877–83) and with Sauret and P. Scharwenka in Berlin (1884–86). In 1887 he established the Aulin String Quartet, and traveled with it in Germany and Russia. He was concertmaster of the orch. of the Royal Opera in Stockholm from 1889 to 1902, but continued his concert career, and was considered the greatest Scandinavian violinist since Ole Bull. Aulin was conductor of the orch. of the Stockholm Concert Soc. from 1902 until it disbanded in 1910. He was concertmaster of the Göteborg Orch. from 1909 to 1912. As a conductor and violinist, he made determined propaganda for Swedish composers. He wrote incidental music to Strindberg's *Mäster Olof*, 3 violin concertos, several suites of Swedish dances for Orch., a Violin Sonata, a violin method, and songs. His sister, Laura Valborg Aulin (b. Gävle, Jan. 9, 1860; d. Örebro, Jan. 11, 1928), was a well-known pianist. She also composed chamber and piano music.—**NS/LK/DM**

Aurelianus Reomensis, French monk and scholar who flourished in Réomé in the 9th century. His treatise, *Musica disciplina* (ed. by L. Gushee in Corpus scriptorum de musica, XXI, 1975; Eng. tr. by J. Ponte in the Colo. Coll. Music Press Translations, III, 1968), contains the earliest information on the melodic character of the church modes.—**NS/LK/DM**

Auriacombe, Louis, French conductor; b. Pau, Feb. 22, 1917; d. Toulouse, March 12, 1982. He studied in Pau, took courses in violin, singing, and harmony at the Toulouse Cons., and received training in conducting from Markevitch in Salzburg. He was founder-conductor of the Toulouse Chamber Orch. (1953–71), which he led in performances of early and 20th-century scores.—**NS/LK/DM**

Auric, Georges, notable French composer; b. Lodève, Hérault, Feb. 15, 1899; d. Paris, July 23, 1983. He first studied music at the Montpellier Cons., then went to Paris, where he was a student of Caussade at the Cons. and of d'Indy and Roussel at the Schola Cantorum. While still in his early youth (1911–15), he wrote something like 300 songs and piano pieces. At 18, he composed a ballet, *Les Noces de Gamache*. At 20, he completed a comic opera, *La Reine de coeur*; however, he was dissatisfied with this early effort and destroyed the MS. In the aftermath of continental disillusion following World War I, he became a proponent of the anti-Romantic movement in France, with the apostles of this age of disenchantment, Erik Satie and Jean Cocteau, preaching the new values of urban culture, with modern America as a model. Satie urged young composers to produce "auditory pleasure without demanding disproportionate attention from the listener," while Cocteau elevated artistic ugliness to an aesthetic ideal. Under Satie's aegis, Auric joined several French composers of his generation in a group described as *Les Nouveaux Jeunes*, which later became known as *Les Six* (the other 5 were Milhaud, Honegger, Poulenc, Durey, and Tailleferre). Auric soon established an important connection with the impresario Serge Diaghilev, who commissioned him to write a number of ballets for his Paris company. Auric's facile yet felicitous manner of composing, with mock-Romantic connotations, fit perfectly into Diaghilev's scheme; particularly successful were Auric's early ballets, *Les Fâcheux* (1924) and *Les Matelots* (1925). He also wrote music for films, of which *Á nous la liberté* (1932) achieved popular success as a symphonic suite. From 1954 to 1977 he served as president of the French Union of Composers and Authors. He served as general administrator of both the Opéra and the Opéra-Comique in Paris from 1962 to 1968. In 1962 he was elected to membership of the Académie des Beaux-Arts.

WRITINGS: *Quand j'etais là* (memoirs; Paris, 1979).

WORKS: DRAMATIC: Ballet: *Les Mariés de la Tour Eiffel* (Paris, June 15, 1921; in collaboration with Milhaus and 4 other members of *Les Six*); *Les Fâcheux* (Monte Carlo, Jan. 19, 1924); *Les Matelots* (Paris, June 17, 1925); *La Pastorale* (Paris, May 26, 1926); *Les Enchantements d'Alcine* (Paris, May 21, 1929); *Les Imaginaires* (Paris, May 31, 1934); *Le Peintre et son modèle* (Paris, Nov. 16, 1949); *Phèdre* (Paris, May 23, 1950); *La Pierre enchantée* (Paris, June 23, 1950); *Chemin de lumière* (Munich, March 27, 1952); *Coup de feu* (Paris, May 7, 1952); *La Chambre* (1955); *Le Bal des voleurs* (1960); *Eurydice* (1963). **Film:** *Le Sang d'un poète* (1930); *A nous la liberté* (1931); *Les Mystères de Paris* (1936); *L'Éternal Retour* (1943); *Le Bossu* (1944); *Torrents* (1946; in collaboration with G. Tailleferre); *La Belle et la bête* (1946); *Symphonie pastorale* (1946); *L'Aigle à deux têtes* (1947); *Les Parents terribles* (1949); *Orphée* (1950); *Moulin Rouge* (1952); *Le Salaire de la peur* (1953); *Notre-Dame de Paris* (1956); *Gervaise* (1956); *Bonjour, tristesse* (1957); *Les Sorcières de Salem* (1957); *Christine* (1958); *Aimez-vous Brahms?* (1960); *La Grande Vadrouille* (1966). **ORCH.:** *Ouverture* (1938); *La Seine au matin* (1938); *L'Hommage à Marguerite Long* (1956); *Suite symphonique* (1960). **CHAMBER:** Violin Sonata (1936); Trio for Winds (1938); Flute Sonata (1963–64); *Imaginées I* for Flute and Piano (1968), *II* for Cello and Piano (1970), *III* for Clarinet and Piano (1973), and *IV* for

Chamber Group (1976). **P i a n o** : Sonatine (1922); *5 Bagatelles for Piano, 4-Hands* (1925–26); *Petite Suite* (1927); *Sonata* (1932); *Partita* for 2 Pianos (1958); *Imaginées V* (1976). **V O C A L:** Many songs.

BIBL.: A. Goléa, *G. A.* (Paris, 1958); J. Roy, *Le groupe des six: Poulenc, Milhaud, Honegger, A., Tailleferre, Durey* (Paris, 1994). —NS/LK/DM

Aurisicchio, Antonio, Italian organist, teacher, and composer; b. Naples, c. 1710; d. Rome, Sept. 3 or 4, 1781. He settled in Rome, where he studied and was active as an organist in various churches. He was at the church of S. Giacomo degli Spagnuoli from 1751 to 1756, and then was its maestro di cappella from 1756 until about 1766. He wrote several stage works but became best known for his sacred music.—LK/DM

Aus der Ohe, Adele, German pianist; b. Hannover, Dec. 11, 1864; d. Berlin, Dec. 7, 1937. She studied with Kullak in Berlin and then with Liszt (1877–84). She played throughout Europe; made her U.S. debut as soloist in Liszt's 1st Piano Concerto (N.Y., Dec. 23, 1886), and continued to appear in the U.S. until 1906. She was soloist in Tchaikovsky's 1st Piano Concerto under the composer's direction at his last concert (St. Petersburg, Oct. 28, 1893).—NS/LK/DM

Austin, Ernest, English composer, brother of **Frederic Austin;** b. London, Dec. 31, 1874; d. Wallington, Surrey, July 24, 1947. He was autodidact in composition. He was the author of *The Fairland of Music* (1922). Among his works were *The Vicar of Bray* for String Orch. (1910), *Hymn of Apollo* for Chorus and Orch. (1918), chamber music, organ pieces, and songs.—NS/LK/DM

Austin, Frederic, English baritone and composer, brother of **Ernest Austin;** b. London, March 30, 1872; d. there, April 10, 1952. He studied with Charles Lunn. After working as an organist and music teacher in Liverpool, he appeared as a singer in London in 1902. In 1908 he made his debut at London's Covent Garden as Gunther in the English-language mounting of the *Ring* cycle. He subsequently was principal baritone of the Beecham Opera Co. In 1920 he prepared a new version of *The Beggar's Opera* for London, in which he scored notable success in the role of Peachum. He then brought out a new edition of its sequel, *Polly* (London, Dec. 30, 1922). After serving as artistic director of the British National Opera Co. in London (1924–29), he devoted himself to teaching voice. Among his other compositions were a Sym., a symphonic poem, and choral music.—NS/LK/DM

Austin, Gene (real name **Eugene Lucas**), easygoing American singer, songwriter, and pianist; b. Gainesville, Tex., June 24, 1900; d. Palm Springs, Calif., Jan. 24, 1972. Austin was second only to Al Jolson as the most successful singer on records in the U.S. in the 1920s, and his calm tenor, in striking contrast to Jolson's sound, marked him as one of the earliest crooners to make use of the new electronic recording equipment of the mid-1920s to create a more intimate vocal style. Austin's recording of "My Blue Heaven" was one of the best-selling records of the first half of the 20th century, and total sales of his hundreds of discs are estimated at 86 million copies.

Austin was the son of Nona and Belle Harrell Lucas. His father died when he was a child, and his mother remarried Jim Austin; when Austin turned to singing, he adopted his stepfather's name to avoid confusion with singer Nick Lucas. Growing up in the northwest La. towns of Yellow Pine and Linden, Austin had no formal musical training, though he learned to sing blues songs and play the piano from local residents. At age 15 he ran away from home to join the circus, where he learned to play the calliope. He joined the U.S. Army and participated in the U.S. action against Pancho Villa in Mexico in March 1916. He was discharged when it was discovered that he was underage, but he reenlisted in April 1917 after the U.S. entered World War I and served in France as a bugler.

After leaving the army in 1919, Austin enrolled at the Univ. of Md. at Baltimore, initially as a pre-dentistry student, later switching to pre-law. But he also led a dance band, and by 1923 he had left college to become part of a vaudeville duo with Roy Bergere. Austin and Bergere made their recording debut with "A Thousand Miles from Home" on Vocalion in 1924. They also wrote songs together, and their "How Come You Do Me Like You Do?" became a hit for Marion Harris in August.

The team split, and Austin began to work as a single. With music publisher Irving Mills and Jimmy McHugh, he wrote "When My Sugar Walks Down the Street," which singer Aileen Stanley agreed to record for Victor if Austin would join her for a duet. The recording, made Jan. 30, 1925, became a hit in May, and Victor signed Austin to a recording contract. His first solo success came quickly, as "Yearning (Just for You)" (music by Joseph Burke, lyrics by Benny Davis) became a hit in June. But his most popular record for the year was "Yes Sir! That's My Baby" (music by Walter Donaldson, lyrics by Gus Kahn), which became a best-seller in September.

Austin scored two more best-sellers in 1926, with "Five Foot Two, Eyes of Blue (Has Anybody Seen My Girl)" (music by Ray Henderson, lyrics by Sam M. Lewis and Joe Young) in May and "Bye, Bye, Blackbird" (music by Henderson, lyrics by Mort Dixon) in September. His peak year, however, was 1927. "To-night You Belong to Me" (music by Lee David, lyrics by Billy Rose) became a best-seller in April, followed by "Forgive Me" (music by Milton Ager, lyrics by Jack Yellen) in August, and on Sept. 14 he recorded "My Blue Heaven" (music by Donaldson, lyrics by George Whiting), which became the biggest hit on records since Ben Selvin's "Dardanella" in 1920; it is estimated to have sold near five million copies.

Two days after the recording of "My Blue Heaven," Austin recorded "The Lonesome Road," for which he had written the lyrics, with music by Nat Shilkret, who conducted the Victor Orch. that backed Austin on most of his recordings. The song became a hit for Austin in March 1928, after which it was interpolated into the first film version of *Show Boat*, released in April 1929.

Shilkret then recorded it for a hit in August 1929, and it was given a third hit recording by Ted Lewis and His Band in May 1930.

Austin's first best-seller of 1928, and the second biggest hit of his career, was the movie theme "Ramona" (music by Mabel Wayne, lyrics by L. Wolfe Gilbert), which he recorded on April 2 and which attained massive popularity in May, selling an estimated three million copies. Austin also scored a best-seller in September with another movie theme, "Jeannine (I Dream of Lilac Time)" (music by Shilkret, lyrics by Gilbert).

Austin's most popular record of 1929 was "Carolina Moon" (music by Joe Burke, lyrics by Davis), which became a best-seller in February. Though he continued to score hits through the end of the year (including "I've Got a Feeling I'm Falling" [lyrics by Rose, music also by Harry Link] and "Ain't Misbehavin'" [lyrics by Andy Razaf], on which he was accompanied by their composer, Fats Waller), Austin went into rapid decline as a recording artist with the onset of the Depression. He had no hits in 1930 and only one, "Please Don't Talk About Me When I'm Gone" (music by Sam H. Stept, lyrics by Sidney Clare)/"When Your Lover Has Gone" (music and lyrics by E. A. Swan), in 1931, after which he left RCA Victor and signed to ARC (its catalog now controlled by Sony Music).

Austin was the vocalist on the *California Melodies* radio series from 1932 to 1934, accompanied by bassist Candy Candido and guitarist Otto "Coco" Heimel, who were billed as Candy and Coco and with whom he worked extensively in the 1930s. He appeared with them in the Joan Crawford film *Sadie McKee*, released in May 1934, singing "After You've Gone" (music by Turner Layton, lyrics by Henry Creamer), his movie debut.

Austin collaborated with Carmen Lombardo on "Ridin' Around in the Rain," which produced equally popular hit records for his crooning successor, Bing Crosby and Earl Burtnett and His Drake Hotel Orch. in May 1934. Austin himself also had a hit with it back on RCA Victor in July, his last popular record for 23 years.

Austin next appeared in the Mae West film *Belle of the Nineties* in September, and West sang his song "When a St. Louis Woman Comes Down to New Orleans" (music by Arthur Johnston, lyrics by Austin and Sam Coslow). In October he and Candy and Coco were in the film *Gift of Gab*.

Austin wrote five songs for and appeared in Mae West's film *Klondike Annie* in March 1936. He was the featured vocalist on the radio series *The Joe Penner Show* on CBS from early 1937 to late 1938. He sang and appeared in the Western film *Songs and Saddles* in 1938 and appeared with Candy and Coco in the Mae West/W. C. Fields film *My Little Chickadee* in February 1940. Austin's final feature film appearances were in *Moon Over Las Vegas* and *Follow the Leader*, both in 1944; he also made many musical shorts and soundies.

Austin recorded and toured in the 1930s and 1940s, and owned and operated a series of clubs and gambling casinos called My Blue Heaven in various states. He re-signed to RCA Victor in 1954 and cut an LP, *Blue Heaven*. On April 20, 1957, NBC-TV aired *The Gene Austin Story*, a biography starring George Grizzard, with Austin dubbing the songs, including his newly written "Too Late," which became a chart record for him in May, leading to a career resurgence.

Austin unsuccessfully sought the Democratic nomination for governor of Nev. in 1962, after which he lived in Fla., where he ran another My Blue Heaven club. He later settled in Calif., where he continued to write songs and perform. He died of cancer at the age of 71, survived by his fifth wife, Maxine; two daughters from earlier marriages; and three grandchildren.

DISC.: *A Time to Relax: 1925–36* (1996); *The Voice of the Southland* (1997).—**WR**

Austin, John Turnell, English-American organ builder; b. Podington, Bedfordshire, May 16, 1869; d. Hartford, Conn., Sept. 17, 1948. He emigrated to the U.S. in 1889 and entered the employ of Ferrand & Votey in Detroit, where he experimented with his "universal wind-chest" system; in 1893 he joined Clough & Warren there, where he utilized his new system. In 1899 he settled in Hartford and founded his own firm, which he headed until his retirement in 1937 when it was reorganized as Austin Organs, Inc. Austin organs have been installed in many U.S. churches and concert halls. —**NS/LK/DM**

Austin, Larry (Don), American composer and teacher; b. Duncan, Okla., Sept. 12, 1930. He was a student of Archer at the Univ. of N. Tex. in Denton (B.M.E., 1951; M.M., 1952). After studies with Milhaud at Mills Coll. in Oakland, Calif. (summer, 1955), he pursued graduate training with Imbrie at the Univ. of Calif. at Berkeley (1955–58). He later studied electronic music at the San Francisco Tape Music Center (1965–66), and computer music at Stanford Univ. (summer, 1969) and the Mass. Inst. of Technology (summer, 1978). In 1958 he joined the faculty of the Univ. of Calif. at Davis, where he was a prof. and director of its bands (1958–72), and founder and co-director of its New Music Ensemble (1963–68). In 1966 he also helped to found the unique and invaluable avant-garde music journal *Source*, which he ed. until it suspended publication in 1972. From 1972 to 1978 Austin was a prof. at the Univ. of S. Fla. in Tampa, where he was chairman of the music dept. (1972–73) and founder-director of the Systems Complex for the Studio and Performing Arts (1972–78). In 1978 he became a prof. at the Univ. of N. Tex., where he was director of the electronic music center (1981–82) and founder-director of the Center for Experimental Music and Intermedia (1982–91; 1993–96). In 1996 he retired from his professorship. He was co-founder and president of the Consortium to Distribute Computer Music (from 1986) and president of the International Computer Music Assn. (1990–94). With T. Clark, he publ. the textbook *Learning to Compose: Modes, Materials, and Models of Musical Invention* (Dubuque, 1989). He has received many commissions, grants, and awards. His compositions have been widely performed and recorded, including his complete realization of Ives's *Universe Sym-*

phony in 1994. In 1996 he became the first American composer to receive the Magistère prize at the International Electroacoustic Music Competition in Bourges for his *BluesAx*. Austin's music ranges widely with utilization of traditional ensembles and diverse combinations of instruments, voices, audio and/or video tape, film, computer sounds, and live electronics.

WORKS: *Piano Variations* (1960); *Fantasy on a Theme by Berg* for Jazz Band (1960); *Suite for Massed Bands* (1961); *Triptych* for Chorus and String Quartet (1961); *Improvisations* for Jazz Soloists and Orch. (1961); *A Broken Consort* for Flute, Clarinet, Trumpet, Horn, Piano, Bass, and Drum Set (1962); *Collage* for Several Instruments (1963); *Music for Richard II* for Shakespeare's play (1963); *In Memoriam JFK* for Concert Band (1964); *Agape*, celebration for Priests, Musicians, Actors, Dancers, Celebrants, Films, Ritual, Sculpture, and Tapes (1970); *Walter* for Viola, Viola d'amore, Tape, and Films (1970–71); *Agape Set*, suite for Jazz Band (1971); *Quartet 3*, electronic music on tape (1971); *Prelude and Postlude to Plastic Surgery* for Keyboards, Film, and Tape (1971); *Quartet 4*, electronic music on tape (1971); *Primal Hybrid*, electronic music on tape (1972); *Quadrants: Event/Complex No. 1* for Symphonic Wind Ensemble (1972), *No. 2* for Chorus and Tape (1972), *Nos. 3-7* for Violin, Piano, Cello, Clarinet, Flute, and Tape (1973), *No. 8* for Viola and Tape (1973), *No. 9* for Percussion and Tape (1974), *No. 10* for Trombone and Tape (1976), and *No. 11* for Contrabass and Tape (1977); *Tableaux Vivants* for 4 to 6 Musicians, Tape, and Slides (1973; rev. 1981); *1976*, text-sound piece on tape (1973); *Phoenix*, computer music on tape (1974); *Universe Symphony*, realization and completion of Ives's work for Multiple Orchs. (1974–93); *Maroon Bells* for Voice, Piano, and Tape (1976); *Organ Mass* (1977); *Catalogo Sonoro—Narcisso* for Viola and Tape (1978); *Catalogo Gesto—Timbro* for Percussionist and Dancer (1978); *Catalogo Voce*, mini-opera for Bass-baritone, Tape, and Slides (1979); *Protoforms: Hybrid Musics* for 3 Sopranos and Real-time Computer Music System (1980); *Ceremony* for Organ and Voice (1980); *Protoforms*, fractals for Computer Band (1980); *Protoforms*, fractals for Cello Choir and Computer Band (1981); *Canadian Coastlines*, canonic fractals for Musicians and Computer Band (1981); *Euphonia: A Tale of the Future*, opera for Soloists, Chorus, Chamber Orch., Digital Synthesizer, and Tape (1981–82); *art is self-alteration is Cage is...*, uni-word omniostic for String Bass Quartet (1982); *Beachcombers* for 4 Musicians and Tape (1983); *Sonata Concertante* for Piano and Computer Music on Tape (1983–84); *Ludus Fractalis*, video piece (1984); *Clarini!* for 20 Trumpets (1985); *Montage: Theme and Variations* for Violin and Computer Music on Tape (1985); *Sinfonia Concertante: A Mozartean Episode* for Chamber Orch. and Computer Music Narrative (1986); *Concertante Cibernetica*, interactions for Performer and Synclavier (1987); *Euphonia 2344*, intermezzo for Voices and Computer Music on Tape (1988); *Snare Drum Cycles* for Snare Dum (1989); *Transmission 2: The Great Excursion* for Chorus, Computer Music Ensemble, and Recorded Dialogue (1989–90); *SoundPoemSet: Pauline Oliveros/Jerry Hunt/Morton Subotnick/David Tudor*, computer music on tape (1991); *La Barbara: The Name/The Sounds/The Music* for Voice and Computer Music (1991); *Accidents 2*, sound projections for Piano and Computer Music (1992); *Rompido!—Music for Dance and Sculpture* for Percussionist and Computer Music on Tape (1993); *Variations-...beyond Pierrot*, sound-play for Soprano, Flute, Clarinet, Violin, Cello, Piano, Hypermedia System, and Computer Music on Tape (1993–95); *Shin-Edo: CityscapeSet* for Computer Music on Tape (1994–96); *BluesAx* for Saxophone and Computer Music on Tape (1995); *Singing!...the music of my own time*, sound-portrait

for Voice and Octophonic Computer Music (1996–99); *Djuro's Tree*, octophonic computer music (1997); *Tarogato!* for Tarogato, Dancer(s), and Octophonic Computer Music on Tape (1998). **—NS/LK/DM**

Austin, Lovie (born **Cora Calhoun**), jazz/ blues pianist, songwriter; b. Chattanooga, Tenn., Sept. 19, 1887; d. Chicago, July 10, 1972. Austin is remembered as the leader of a number of significant recording sessions in the early 1920s. She studied music at Roger Williams Univ. in Nashville and at Knoxville Coll. She married very young to a Detroit movie-house owner, then later married a variety artist and accompanied him and his partner in their act, "Austin and Delaney." Austin toured with Irving Miller's Blue Babies, then went to N.Y. to play for a Club Alabam show. She toured extensively on the T.O.B.A. circuit, with The Sunflower Girls and leading her Blues Serenaders. As musical director and pianist for the Paramount label, Austin accompanied many of the early blues singers, including Ma Rainey and Alberta Hunter. She settled in Chicago, and for 20 years was musical director for the Monogram Theatre, and later the Gem and Joyland Theatres. During World War II Austin was a security inspector at a defense plant, then later resumed theatre work. She played at Jimmy Payne's Dancing School at Penthouse Studios, Chicago, for many years, beginning in the late 1940s. Austin' compositions include "Graveyard Blues," which was popularized by Bessie Smith in the 1920s. **—JC/LP**

Austin, William W(eaver), American musicologist; b. Lawton, Okla., Jan. 18, 1920; d. Ithaca, N.Y., March 15, 2000. He was educated at Harvard Univ. (B.A., 1939; M.A., 1940; Ph.D., 1951, with the diss. *Harmonic Rhythm in Twentieth-Century Music*). In 1947 he joined the faculty of Cornell Univ., where he was a prof. from 1960 until his retirement as a prof. emeritus in 1990. In 1961–62 he held a Guggenheim fellowship. He was made an honorary member of the American Musicological Soc. in 1996.

WRITINGS: *Music in the 20th Century from Debussy Through Stravinsky* (N.Y., 1966); ed. *New Looks at Italian Opera: Essays in Honor of Donald J. Grout* (Ithaca, N.Y., 1968); *"Susanna," "Jeanie" and "The Old Folks at Home": Meanings and Contexts of the Songs of Stephen C. Foster from His Time to Ours* (N.Y., 1975; 2nd ed., 1987); tr. C. Dahlhaus's *Musikästhetik* as *Esthetics of Music* (Cambridge, 1982).**—NS/LK/DM**

Austral, Florence (real name, **Mary Wilson**), Australian soprano; b. Richmond, near Melbourne, April 26, 1892; d. Newcastle, New South Wales, May 15, 1968. She studied on a scholarship at the Melbourne Cons. (1914–18), and then completed her training with Sibella in N.Y. In 1921 she made her London concert debut, followed by her operatic debut there as Brünnhilde with the British National Opera Co. on May 16, 1922. She subsequently appeared as Aida and Isolde with the company. In 1924, 1929, and 1933 she again sang Brünnhilde in London, and returned there to sing at Sadler's Wells (1937–39). She also sang in Australia and the U.S. For a time, she was married to the flutist John Amadio. Austral was admired as a Wagnerian.**—NS/LK/DM**

Auteri Manzocchi, Salvatore, Italian composer; b. Palermo, Dec. 26, 1845; d. Parma, Feb. 21, 1924. He studied in Palermo with Platania and in Florence with Mabellini. He composed several operas, the most successful being *Dolores* (Florence, Feb. 23, 1875) and *Stella* (Piacenza, May 22, 1880).—NS/LK/DM

Autori, Franco, Italian-born American conductor; b. Naples, Nov. 29, 1903; d. Tulsa, Oct. 16, 1990. After study in Italy, he emigrated to the U.S. in 1928 and became a naturalized citizen in 1936. He conducted at the Chicago Civic Opera (1928–32) and the Dallas Sym. Orch. summer series (1932–34). After serving as a staff conductor with the Federal Music Project in N.Y. (1934–37), he was conductor of the Buffalo Phil. (1936–45), assoc. conductor of the N.Y. Phil. (1949–59), and conductor of the Tulsa Phil. (1961–71).—NS/LK/DM

Autry, Gene (originally **Orvin Gene Autry**), the first and most famous singing cowboy; b. Tioga Springs, Tex., Sept. 29, 1907; d. Los Angeles, Calif., Oct. 2, 1998. Autry transformed the image of the country singer with his introduction of western garb and mannerisms into his stage persona. In the 1930s, he was a star of radio, records, and films; from the end of World War II on, he was primarily a canny businessman who invested in diverse activities from real estate to baseball to oil. Besides performing many venerable cowboy hits, he wrote or co-wrote songs in a sentimental ("That Silver Haired Daddy of Mine"), cowboy ("Tumbling Tumbleweeds," "South of the Border"), and blues style ("I Hang My Head and Cry"), as well as his famous Christmas/children's songs ("Frosty the Snowman," "Rudolph, the Red-Nosed Reindeer," "Here Comes Santa Claus," and "Peter Cottontail").

Autry was the son of a Tex. dirt farmer. He began his musical career as a member of the church choir, where his grandfather was the preacher. Like many other rural musicians, he got his first mail-order guitar from Sears in his early teens and began playing at local events. The family moved to Okla. when he was a late teenager, and he found a job with a local railroad line as a telegraph operator. There, he befriended an elder part-time musician, who encouraged him to pursue his career.

Autry began his career as a Jimmie Rodgers imitator; like so many country performers of the late 1920s and early 1930s, he was enamored with Rodgers's sound, which he shamelessly copied. In 1928, supposedly on the advice of famous radio comedian Will Rogers, he traveled to N.Y. in search of radio work. After making the rounds among the music industry bigwigs, he quickly returned to Okla. and radio work on the local station KVOO, in Tulsa, billed as "Oklahoma's Yodeling Cowboy."

In October 1929, he returned to N.Y. and finally broke into the recording world, albeit for the many budget "dimestore" labels that then existed. By the early 1930s, many of these labels had failed due to the Depression, and were consolidated together into the American Recording Company or ARC label. There, talent scout and producer Art Satherley recorded the young singer. Their first hit collaboration was on a sentimental number called "That Silver Haired Daddy of Mine," released in 1931. This led to a radio contract with the influential and powerful WLS station out of Chicago, where he would remain through mid-1934.

At WLS, Autry began downplaying his rural-farm upbringing, while emphasizing his (nonexistent) roots as a cowboy, perhaps influenced by the increasing popularity of movie cowboys such as Ken Maynard. In 1934, Autry gained his first movie role in support of Maynard in *In Old Santa Fe*; in the next year, he starred in his first serial, the unusual *Phantom Empire*, which featured a bizarre mix of science fiction and cowboy antics! He would go on to appear in almost a hundred horse operas, usually accompanied by his favorite horse, Champion. From 1939–56, he starred on radio in "Gene Autry's Melody Ranch," further underscoring his cowboy image.

Autry recorded dozens of western-flavored songs during this period, which became major hits and have entered American folklore as "standards" in the cowboy repertoire. These include the evergreen "Tumblin' Tumbleweeds," "Back in the Saddle Again," and "The Last Roundup." Autry sang them straight—no matter how clichéd the sentiments or lyrics, he sang 'em like he meant 'em—and his audience loved 'em.

After serving in the Army Air Corps in World War II, Autry returned to civilian life to find himself supplanted in the public imagination by another civilian-turned-cowpoke, Roy Rogers, of recent burger-broiling fame. His last successes came with kid-oriented records, including several winter-time perennials like "Rudolph, the Red-Nosed Reindeer," "Frosty the Snow Man," and "Here Comes Santa Claus." Branching out to more moderate-weather holidays, he also cut "(Here Comes) Peter Cottontail." Besides continuing to make films, Autry became an early TV star, appearing in his popular program for six years beginning in 1950.

Autry pretty much retired from music-making in the mid-1950s to focus on his lucrative business ventures. In 1960, he purchased Los Angeles's major league baseball team, adding to his real-estate holdings. In 1969, he was inducted into the Country Music Hall of Fame.

Autry's main importance was not his style, which was a typical mix of country mannerisms with the crooning popularized by Bing Crosby. Rather, it was his image, with the complete Western garb that helped spread the myth of the cowboy as the last American pioneer. Country stars, who had previously appeared in overalls to emphasize their rural background, suddenly began appearing in cowboy hats and chaps. The romance of the West combined with the sentimentality of heart-tugging songs made for an unbeatable companion. It's no surprise that 50 years later country superstar Garth Brooks always appears in a ten-gallon hat.

DISC.: *G. A. at the Rodeo* (1958); *G. A.'s Greatest Hits* (1961); *Back in the Saddle Again* (1968); *Country Music Hall of Fame* (1970); *Columbia Historic Edition* (1982); *The Essential G. A.: 1933–1946* (1992); *A G. A. Christmas* (1994); *G. A.: Blues Singer, 1929–1931* (1996); *Sing Cowboy Sing: The G. A. Collection* (1997);

The Last Round-Up: 25 Cowboy Classics, 1933–1947 (1998); *Always Your Pal, G. A.* (1998); *Here Comes Santa Claus* (1999); *Love Songs* (1999); *20 Greatest Movie Hits* (1999); *20 Golden Cowboy Hits* (2000).—**RC**

Auxcousteaux (also Aux-Cousteaux, Hautcousteaux), Artus, French singer and composer;
b. probably in Amiens, c. 1590; d. Paris, c. 1654. He studied at the St. Quentin Cathedral choir school. After singing haute-contre at Louis XIII's chapel (1613–27), he became maître de musique at St. Quentin in 1631, and also served in that capacity in Amiens (c. 1632–34). He then was a clerk haute-contre at the Paris St. Chapelle, where he was named maître de musique about 1643. About 1651 he received a canonry at the church of St. Jacques de l'Hôpital. His output includes sacred works and chansons.—**LK/DM**

Avdeyeva, Larissa (Ivanovna), prominent
Russian mezzo-soprano; b. Moscow, June 21, 1925. She studied at the Stanislavsky Opera Studio in Moscow. In 1947 she joined the Stanislavsky Music Theater there; in 1952 she became a member of Moscow's Bolshoi Theater, where she distinguished herself as an outstanding interpreter in operas by Tchaikovsky, Borodin, Mussorgsky, and Rimsky-Korsakov; she also made tours of Europe, the U.S., and Japan. She was made a People's Artist of the R.S.F.S.R. in 1964. She married **Evgeny Svetlanov.**—**NS/LK/DM**

Avenary, Hanoch (real name, Herbert Loewenstein),
Israeli musicologist; b. Danzig, May 25, 1908. He studied musicology and other subjects at the univs. of Leipzig, Munich, and Frankfurt am Main; then received his Ph.D. in 1931 from the Univ. of Königsberg with the diss. *Wort und Ton bei Oswald von Wolkenstein* (publ. in Königsberg, 1932). He went to Palestine in 1936 and was active as a publisher of Jewish art books. He also served in the Israeli air force. In 1965 he joined the faculty of Hebrew Univ. in Jerusalem, where he remained until 1972; from 1966 he was also a lecturer at the Univ. of Tel Aviv. His books include *Studies in the Hebrew, Syrian and Greek Liturgical Recitative* (Tel Aviv, 1963); *Hebrew Hymn Tunes: Rise and Development of a Musical Tradition* (Tel Aviv, 1971); *The Ashkenazi Tradition of Biblical Chant between 1500 and 1900* (Tel Aviv, 1978); *Encounters of East and West in Music* (Tel Aviv, 1979); *Kantor Salamon Sulzer und seine Zeit: Eine Dokumentation* (Sigmaringen, 1985).

BIBL.: *Essays in Honor of H. A.* (vol. 10 of *Orbis Musicae*, Tel Aviv, 1991).—**NS/LK/DM**

Aventinus (real name, Turmair), Johannes,
German historian and music theorist; b. Abensberg, July 4, 1477; d. Regensburg, Jan. 9, 1534. He was educated at the univs. of Ingolstadt, Kraków, and Paris. In 1517 he was made Bavarian court historiographer. His treatise *Annales ducum boiariae* (1554) contains considerable but not always trustworthy information about music. The *Musicae rudimenta* (Augsburg, 1516), which is also attributed to Nicolaus Faber, has been ed. by T. Keahey (N.Y., 1971).—**NS/LK/DM**

Averkamp, Anton, Dutch choral conductor and
composer; b. Willige Langerak, Feb. 18, 1861; d. Bussum, June 1, 1934. He studied with Daniel de Lange in Amsterdam, with Friedrich Kiel in Berlin, and with Rheinberger in Munich. In 1890 he founded the famous chorus Amsterdam A Cappella Coor, with which he traveled in Europe, presenting programs of early polyphonic music. He wrote an opera, *De Heidebloem,* which was not produced. He contributed numerous historical articles to music periodicals, and also publ. a manual for singers, *Uit mijn practijk* (Groningen, 1916), and the book *De Koordirigent* (1933).—**NS/LK/DM**

Avidom (real name, Kalkstein), Menahem,
prominent Polish-born Israeli composer and administrator; b. Stanislawow, Jan. 6, 1908; d. Herzliya, Aug. 5, 1995. He emigrated to Palestine in 1925. After taking courses in art and science at the American Univ. in Beirut (B.A., 1928), he went to Paris to study with Rabaud at the Cons. (1928–31). Following a sojourn in Alexandria, Egypt (1931–35), he settled in Tel Aviv as a teacher. From 1945 to 1952 he was secretary-general of the Israel Phil. He was director-general of ACUM (Soc. of Authors, Composers, and Music Publishers) of Israel from 1955 to 1980. From 1958 to 1972 he also was chairman of the Israel Composers League, of which he was elected honorary chairman for life in 1982. In 1961 he received the Israel State Prize for his opera *Alexandra.* In 1982 ACUM awarded him its prize for his life's work. In his extensive output, Avidom ranged widely stylistically. While he utilized folk modalities of the Middle East, he also embraced dodecaphony.

WORKS: DRAMATIC: *Alexandra,* opera (1952; Tel Aviv, Aug. 15, 1959); *In Every Generation,* opera (1955); *The Crook,* comic opera (1966–67; Tel Aviv, April 22, 1967); *The Farewell,* radiophonic opera (1969; broadcast Nov. 1971); *The Pearl and the Coral,* ballet (1972); *The Emperor's New Clothes,* comic opera (1976); *Yodfat's Cave,* musical drama (1977); *The Cave of Jotapata,* dramatic scene (1977); *The End of King Og,* children's opera (1979); *The First Sin,* satirical opera (1980). **ORCH.:** *Polyphonic Suite* for Strings (1938); 10 syms.: No. 1, *A Folk Symphony* (1946), No. 2, *David* (1948; Tel Aviv, Dec. 1, 1949), No. 3, *Mediterranean Sinfonietta* (1951), No. 4 (1955), No. 5, *The Song of Eilät,* for Voice and Orch. (1956–57), No. 6 (1960), No. 7, *Philharmonic* (1961), No. 8, *Festival Sinfonietta* (Jerusalem, July 27, 1966), No. 9, *Symphonie variée,* for Chamber Orch. (1968), and No. 10, *Sinfonia brevis* (1980); Concerto for Flute and Strings (1946); *Music for Strings* (1949); Violin Concertino (1953); *Jubilee Suite* (1959); *Triptyque symphonique* (1966); *Spring,* overture (1972); *Movements for Strings* (1979; also for String Quartet); *Ballet Suite for Youth* for Chamber Orch. (1985); *Prelude* for Youth Orch. (1989). **CHAMBER:** 2 woodwind quartets (1937, 1984); 3 string quartets (1953, 1960, 1991); *Enigma* for 5 Winds, Piano, and Percussion (1962); Brass Quartet (1963); *Monothema,* sonatina for String Quartet (1982); Woodwind Quintet (1983); Sonata for Solo Viola (1984); *Bachiana (B.A.C.H.)* for Brass Quintet (1985); *Trialaogue,* trio-passacaglia for Piano, Viola, and Cello (1985); Trio for Oboe, Piano, and Cello (1986); *Triptyque* for Flute, Horn, and Piano (1988); Clarinet Sonata (1988); *A Tre* for Piano, Viola, and Clarinet (1990); *Pour la Clarinette* (1994). **Piano:** 2 sonatinas (1939, 1945); *12 Changing Preludes* (1965); *6 Inventions on the Name of Artur Rubinstein* (1973); *Piece on the Name of SCHOEnBerG* (1974); *Once Upon a Time...,* 5 tales (1977); Duo Sonatina for

Piano, 4- Hands (1982); *Triptique* (1984); *6 epigrams* (1985–87).
VOCAL: *5 Psalms* for Mezzo-soprano or Alto, 2 Clarinets, and Percussion ad libitum (1976); *12 Hills*, cantata (1976); *Beyond*, cantata for Voice and Instruments (1977); *Peace Upon All*, cantata for Baritone and Chamber Orch. (1994); choruses; songs.
—NS/LK/DM

Avison, Charles, English organist, writer on music, and composer; b. Newcastle upon Tyne (baptized), Feb. 16, 1709; d. there, May 9, 1770. His father, a town wait, was active as a musician. It is likely, therefore, that he received initial training at home. He later studied with Geminiani in London. In 1735 he was made organist at St. John's Church in Newcastle, which post he assumed in 1736. Later that year he became organist at St. Nicholas there, a post he retained until his death. In 1736 he founded a series of subscription concerts in Newcastle, serving as their musical director from 1738 until his death. With John Garth, he also was active with a series of subscription concerts in Durham. Avison sparked a controversy when he publ. *An Essay on Musical Expression* (London, 1752), in which he contended that Geminiani and Marcello were greater composers than Handel. Williams Hayes was prompted to respond in an anonymous critical review entitled *Remarks on Mr Avison's Essay* (Jan. 1753). In return, Avison publ. *A Reply to the Author of Remarks on the Essay on Musical Expression* on Feb. 22, 1753, and later that year publ. the 2nd edition of his *Essay*, which incorporated his *Reply* and included John Jortin's *A Letter to the Author, concerning the Music of the Ancients*. A 3rd edition of Avison's *Essay* appeared in 1775. Avison acquitted himself admirably as a composer of instrumental and chamber music. His 60 concerti grossi for Strings (1740–69), which reveal the influence of Geminiani, are the most notable works of their kind by an English composer of the 18th century.

WORKS (all publ. in London unless otherwise given): **ORCH.:** *Six Concertos in 7 parts* for 4 Violins, Viola, Cello, and Harpsichord, op.2 (Newcastle and London, 1740; rev. with 2 new concertos as 8 concertos for Organ or Harpsichord, 1747); *Two Concertos*: No. 1 in 8 parts for Organ or Harpsichord and Strings (?) and No. 2 for Violins in 7 Parts (No. 1: keyboard part only extant; No. 2: not extant; Newcastle, 1742); *Six Concertos in 7 parts with General Rules for playing Instrumental Compositions* for 4 Violins, Viola, Cello, and Harpsichord, op.3 (1751; also included in *Twenty Six Concertos...in Score for the Use of Performers on the Harpsichord*, London, Edinburgh, and Newcastle, 1758); *Eight Concertos in 7 parts* for 4 Violins, Viola, Cello, and Harpsichord, op.6 (London and Newcastle, 1758; includes rev. of 8 concertos of 1747 with 4 new concertos); *Twelve Concertos in 4 parts* for 2 Violins, Viola, and Cello, op.9 (1766; also for Organ or Harpsichord, or 2 Violins, Viola, Cello, and Organ or Harpsichord, 1766); *Six Concertos in 7 parts* for 4 Violins, Viola, Cello, and Harpsichord, op.10 (1769). **CHAMBER:** *VI Sonatas* for 2 Violins and Bass, op.1 (c. 1737); *Six Sonatas* for Harpsichord, 2 Violins, and Cello, op.5 (1756); *Six Sonatas* for Harpsichord, 2 Violins, and Cello, op.7 (London, Edinburgh, and Newcastle, 1760); *Six Sonatas* for Harpsichord, 2 Violins, and Cello, op.8 (London and Edinburgh, 1764). **OTHER:** *Ruth*, oratorio (Feb. 13, 1765; in collaboration with Giardini); editions and arrangements.

BIBL.: J. Brocklehurst, *C. A. and his Essay on Musical Expression* (diss., Univ. of Sheffield, 1959); N. Stephens, *C. A.: An Eighteenth-century English Composer, Musician and Writer* (diss., Univ. of Pittsburgh, 1968).—NS/LK/DM

Avni, Tzvi (Jacob), German-born Israeli composer, teacher, and writer on music; b. Saarbrücken, Sept. 2, 1927. He emigrated to Palestine in 1935; studied with Abel Ehrlich and Seter at the Tel Aviv Academy of Music (diploma, 1958), and also received private instruction in orchestration from Ben-Haim. He was a student of Copland and Foss at the Berkshire Music Center in Tanglewood (summer, 1963), later pursuing studies in electronic music with Ussachevsky and in music librarianship at Columbia Univ. (1963–64). He also studied with Schaeffer at the Univ. of Toronto (1964). He was director of the AMLI Central Music Library in Tel Aviv (1961–75), served as ed. of the journal *Gitit* (1966–80), was director of the electronic music studio (from 1971) and a prof. (from 1976) at the Rubin Academy of Music in Jerusalem, and was chairman of the Israel League of Composers (1978–80) and of the music committee of the National Council for Culture and Art (1983–87). He received the ACUM Prize in 1966 for his *Meditations on a Drama* and in 1986 for his life's work. In 1973 he won the Engel Prize for his *Holiday Metaphors*. In 1990 he received the Kuestermeier Prize of the Germany-Israel Friendship Assn., and in 1998 the Israel Prime Minister's Prize for his life's work as well as the Culture Prize of the Saarland State of Germany. After utilizing advanced compositional techniques, Avni pursued neo-tonal writing.

WORKS: DRAMATIC: Ballets; incidental music. **ORCH.:** *Prayer* for Strings (1961; rev. 1969); *Meditations on a Drama* for Chamber Orch. (1965); *Holiday Metaphors* (1970); *By the Rivers of Babylon* for Chamber Orch. (1971; also for Full Orch., 1972); *In This Cape of Death* for Chamber Orch. (1974); *2 Psalms* for Oboe and Strings (1975; also for Oboe and String Quartet); *Michtam of David* for Harp and Strings (1975–78; also for Harp and String Quartet); *2 Movements from Sinfonia Sacra* (1977); *Programme Music* (1980); *Mizmor* for Santur or Xylophone and Orch. (1982); *Metamorphoses on a Bach Chorale* (1985); *Kaddish* for Cello and Strings (1987); *Mashav*, concertino for Xylophone, Strings or Winds, and Percussion (1988); *Desert Scenes*, sym. (1990); *The Three Legged Monster*, musical legend for Orch., Piano, and Narrator, after H. Yaddor-Avni (1995); *Pray for the Peace of Jerusalem*, fantasy (1997); *The Ship of Hours*, 4 symphonic sketches after paintings by Mordechai Ardon (Saarbrücken, Oct. 1, 1999). **CHAMBER:** Wind Quintet (1959); *Summer Strings* for String Quartet (1962); *2 Pieces* for 4 Clarinets (1965); *Elegy* for Cello (1967); *5 Pantomimes* for 8 Players (1968); *De Profundis*, 2nd string quartet (1969); *Lyric Episodes* for Oboe and Tape (1972); *Beyond the Curtain* for Piano Quartet (1979); *Tandu* for 2 Flutes (1982); Saxophone Quartet (1990); *Vitrage* for Harp (1990); *Fagotti Fugati* for 2 Bassoons (1991); *Variations on a Sephardic Tune* for Recorder Ensemble (1992); *Anthropomorphic Landscape No. 1* for Flute (1996), *No. 2* for Oboe (1996), and *No. 3* for Clarinet (1997). **P i a n o :** *Capriccio* (1955; rev. 1975); *3 sonatas* (1961; *Epitaph*, 1979; *On the Verge of Time*, 1983); *Triptych* (1994). **VOCAL:** *Collage* for Voice, Flute, Percussion, and Tape (1967); *Jerusalem of the Heavens* for Baritone, Chorus, and Orch. (1968); *The Destruction of the Temple* for Chorus and Orch. (1968); *Synchromotrask* for Woman's Voice, Tape, and a Door (1976); *A Monk Observes a Skull* for Mezzo-soprano, Cello, and Tape

(1981); *Deep Calleth Unto Deep*, Psalm- cantata for Soprano, Chorus, and Orch. or Organ (1988–89); *Three Lyric Songs on Paul Celan's Poems* for Mezzo-soprano, English Horn, and Harp (1991); *Makhelorka*, 3 songs for Women's or Children's Chorus, after García Lorca (1992); *Songs and Melodies: In memoriam Yitzhak Rabin* for Chorus, after N. Zach (1995); *Kol Nazman* (The Entire Time) for Women's Chorus and Piano, after A. Gilboa (1997); *Hodaya* (Thanksgiving) for Chorus, after A. Shlonsky (1997); *Se questo è un uomo*, song cycle for Soprano and Orch., after P. Levi (1998). ELECTRONIC: *Vocalise* (1964). —NS/LK/DM

Avoglio, Christina Maria, Italian soprano who flourished in the 1st half of the 16th century. She became a favorite of Handel, who engaged her as his principal soprano for the 1741–42 Dublin season. On April 13, 1742, she sang in the premiere of his *Messiah* in Dublin. In 1743–44 she appeared at London's Covent Garden. On Feb. 18, 1743, she sang in the premiere of *Samson*, and on Feb. 10, 1744, in the premiere of *Semele* there. She also created the role of Hecate in Samuel Howard's pantomime *The Amorous Goddess* at London's Drury Lane on Feb. 1, 1744. Her last appearance in London was at her benefit concert in 1746.—LK/DM

Avondano, Pedro Antonio, Portuguese composer of Italian descent; b. Lisbon (baptized) April 16, 1714; d. there, 1782. He became a court violinist in Lisbon in 1763. He wrote the opera buffa, *Il mondo della luna* (Lisbon, Carnival 1765), 2 syms., 3 cello concertos, and various sacred works.—LK/DM

d'Avossa, Giuseppe, Italian composer; b. Paola, Calabria, 1708; d. Naples, Jan. 9, 1796. He studied with Gaetano Greco and Francesco Durante in Naples, and later held the position of maestro di cappella at S. Maria Verticelli, Naples, and at Pesaro, where he also conducted the orch. of the municipal theater. He wrote 4 operas, the most popular being *La Pupilla* (Naples, Carnival 1763), and much sacred music.—NS/LK/DM

Avshalomov, Aaron, Russian-born American composer, father of **Jacob (David) Avshalomov;** b. Nikolayevsk, Siberia, Nov. 11, 1894; d. N.Y., April 26, 1965. He studied at the Zürich Cons. In 1914 he went to China, where he wrote a number of works on Chinese subjects, making use of authentic Chinese themes. On April 24, 1925, he conducted the first performance in Beijing of his first opera, on a Chinese subject, *Kuan Yin*; his 2nd opera, also on a Chinese subject, *The Great Wall*, was staged in Shanghai on Nov. 26, 1945, as were *The Soul of the Ch'in*, ballet (May 21, 1933); *Incense Shadows*, pantomime (March 13, 1935); Piano Concerto (Jan. 19, 1936); Violin Concerto (Jan. 16, 1938); 1st Sym. (March 17, 1940, composer conducting); and *Buddha and the 5 Planetary Deities*, choreographic tableau (April 18, 1942). In 1947 Avshalomov went to America, where he continued to compose works in large forms, among them his 2nd (Cincinnati, Dec. 30, 1949), 3rd (1950), and 4th (1951) Syms.—NS/LK/DM

Avshalomov, Jacob (David), Russian-American conductor, teacher, and composer, son of **Aaron Avshalomov;** b. Tsingtao, China, March 28, 1919. His father was Russian and his mother American. He studied with his father before emigrating to the U.S. with his mother in 1937. After studies with Toch in Los Angeles, he went to Portland, Oreg., in 1938 and pursued his training with Lucia and Jacques Gershkovitch. He also played percussion and cello under the latter's direction in the Portland Junior Sym. After attending Reed Coll. (1939–41), he completed his studies with Rogers at the Eastman School of Music in Rochester, N.Y. (1941–43; B.M., M.A.). During World War II, he served in the U.S. Army and in 1944 became a naturalized American citizen. From 1946 to 1954 he taught at Columbia Univ. In 1952 he held a Guggenheim fellowship. In 1953 he was awarded the N.Y. Music Critics Circle Award for his choral work *Tom o' Bedlam*. In 1954 he became conductor of the Portland (Oreg.) Junior Sym., which was renamed the Portland Youth Phil. in 1978. Avshalomov conducted it for 40 years, retiring in 1994. During his tenure, he trained numerous students in the rigors of orchestral playing and led them on 6 international tours. On March 28, 1999, his 80th birthday was celebrated in Portland with a special concert with an orch. of his alumni from the Portland Junior Sym. and Youth Phil. His music reflects the many cultures to which he was exposed; while his forms are cohesive, his materials are multifarious, with tense chromatic harmonies and quasi-oriental inflections.

WORKS: ORCH.: *The Taking of T'ung Kuan* (1943; rev. ver., Detroit, Nov. 20, 1953); *Slow Dance* (1945); Sinfonietta (1946; N.Y., Nov. 29, 1949); *Evocations* for Clarinet and Chamber Orch. (1947; Saratoga Springs, N.Y., Aug. 17, 1950); *The Plywood Age* (Portland, Oreg., June 20, 1955); *Phases of the Great Land* (1959); 3 syms.: No. 1, *The Oregon* (1959–61), No. 2, *Glorious the Assembled Fires*, for Chorus and Orch. (1985), and No. 3, *Symphony of Songs*, for the 70th anniversary of the Portland Youth Phil. (1993; Portland, Oreg., Feb. 26, 1994); *Raptures* (1975); *Open Sesame!* (1985); *Up at Timberline* for Winds and Brasses (1986). CHAMBER: Viola Sonatina (1947); *Quodlibet Montagna* for Brass Sextet (1975). VOCAL: *Prophecy* for Cantor, Chorus, and Organ (1948); *How Long, O Lord*, cantata (1948–49); *Tom o' Bedlam* for Chorus (N.Y., Dec. 15, 1953); *Proverbs of Hell* for Men's Chorus (1954; also for Chorus and Light Percussion, 1988); *Psalm 100* for Chorus and Winds (1956); *Inscriptions for the City of Brass* for Narrator, Chorus, and Orch., to a text from the Arabian Nights (1956); *Now Welcom Somer* for Chorus and Flute (1957); *City Upon the Hill* for Narrator, Chorus, Orch., and "liberty bell" (1965); *I Saw a Stranger Yestere'en* for Chorus and Violin (1968); *The 13 Clocks* for 2 Storytellers and Orch. (1973); *Praises from the Corners of the Earth* for Chorus and Orch. (1976); *The Most Triumphant Bird* for Chorus, Piano, and Viola Concertante (1985); *Songs from the Goliards* for Chorus and Cello Concertante (1992); *Songs in Season* for Chorus, Piano, and Contrabass Concertante (1993).

WRITINGS: *Music Is Where You Make It* (2 vols., 1959, 1979); *The Concerts Reviewed: 65 Years of the Portland Youth Philharmonic* (1991).

BIBL.: E. Encell, *J. A.'s Works for Chorus and Orchestra: Aspects of Style* (diss., Univ. of Wash., 1983).—NS/LK/DM

Ax, Emanuel, outstanding Polish-born American pianist; b. Lwów, June 8, 1949. He began to play the violin at age 6, but soon turned to the piano and studied with his father, a coach at the Lwów Opera. The family settled in N.Y. in 1961 and he pursued piano training with Mieczysław Munz at the Juilliard School of Music. In 1969 he made a concert tour of South America. He received his B.A. in French from Columbia Univ. in 1970, the same year that he became a naturalized American citizen. After placing 7th in the Chopin Competition in Warsaw in 1970 and the Queen Elisabeth of Belgium Competition in Brussels in 1972, he took 3rd place in the Vianna da Motta Competition in Lisbon in 1971. On March 12, 1973, he made his N.Y. debut at Alice Tully Hall. He captured 1st place in the first Artur Rubinstein Competition in Tel Aviv in 1974, and then made his first extensive tour of the U.S. In 1977 he made his London debut. He was awarded the Avery Fisher Prize in 1979. In subsequent years, he was engaged as a soloist with most of the world's leading orchs., and he also toured widely as a recitalist. He likewise pursued an active career as a chamber music artist, often appearing with Yo-Yo Ma. In addition to Ax's remarkable performances of the Classical and Romantic masterworks, he has demonstrated a searching insight into works of the modern era, including those by Schoenberg, Copland, Tippett, Henze, and Lieberson. He also was the soloist in the premieres of John Adams's Piano Concerto, *Century Rolls* (Cleveland, Sept. 25, 1997) and Christopher Rouse's *Seeing* for Piano and Orch. (N.Y., May 6, 1999).—NS/LK/DM

Axman, Emil, Czech composer; b. Rataje, June 3, 1887; d. Prague, Jan. 25, 1949. He studied musicology with Nejedlý and Hostinský at the Univ. of Prague (Ph.D., 1912, with the diss. *Moravské opery ve století 18.* [18th Century Moravian Operas]; publ. in *Časopis moravského musea*, 1912), and received private training in composition with Novák (1908–10) and Ostrčil (1920). In 1913 he became keeper of the music archives at the National Museum in Prague. He was the author of *Morava v české hudb 19. století* (Moravian and Czech Music of the 19th Century; Prague, 1920). His music was of a highly lyrical nature.

WORKS: ORCH.: 2 symphonic poems: *Sorrows and Hopes* (1919–20) and *A Bright Sky* (1921–22); 6 syms.: No. 1, *Tragic* (1925–26), No. 2, *Giocosa* (1926–27; Frankfurt am Main, July 3, 1927), No. 3, *Spring* (1928), No. 4, *Eroica* (1932), No. 5, *Dithyrambic* (1936), and No. 6, *Patriotic* (1942); *From the Beskids* for Chamber Orch. (1934); Violin Concerto (1936); Piano Concerto (1939); Cello Concerto (1940); Double Concerto for Violin, Cello, and Orch. (1944); *Suite in the Form of Variations* (1948). **CHAMBER:** Violin Sonata (1923); 4 string quartets (1924, 1925, 1929, 1946); Cello Sonata (1924); Piano Trio (1924–25); Wind Quintet (1938); Suite for String Quartet (1940); *Divertimento* for Nonet (1944); *3 Moravian Dances* for Nonet (1944); *Variations* for String Quartet (1944). **Piano:** 3 sonatas (*Appassionata*, 1922; *To the Memory of a Great Man*, 1922; 1924); *Sonatina charakeristicka* (1922); *Moravia Sings* (1925; also for Orch., 1935). **VOCAL:** Cantatas, including *My Mother* (1926) and *The Cemetery of Sobotka* (1933); choruses; song cycles.

BIBL.: L. Hovorka, *Sborová tvorba A.ova* (Prague, 1940); F. Pala, *E. A.* (Prague, 1951).—NS/LK/DM

Ayala Pérez, Daniel, Mexican conductor and composer; b. Abalá, Yucatán, July 21, 1906; d. Veracruz,

June 20, 1975. He went to Mérida, Yucatán, to study music, and then entered the National Cons. in Mexico City in 1927, where he studied violin with Ezequiel Sierra and Revueltas, and composition with Ponce, Huízar, and Carrillo. He played in nightclubs in Mexico City. In 1931 he became a violinist with the Orquesta Sinfónica de México. In 1934, together with Moncayo, Contreras, and Galindo, formed the Grupo de los Cuatro. He became conductor of the Banda de Policía in Mérida in 1940 and in 1942 founded the Mérida Sym. Orch. He was director of the Yucatán Cons. (from 1944) and the Veracruz School of Music (from 1955). His music, inspired by ancestral melos of the Mayan civilization and legends, is cast in pentatonic modes and possesses a vigorous rhythmic pulse.

WORKS: DRAMATIC: Ballet: *El Hombré Maya* (symphonic suite, Mexico City, Nov. 21, 1940); *La gruta diabolicá* (1940). **ORCH.:** *Tribú* (Mexico City, Oct. 18, 1935); *Paisaje* (Landscape; 1935; Mexico City, June 2, 1936); *Panoramas de México* (1936; Dallas, Dec. 1, 1940); *Sinfonía de las Américas* (1946); *Mi viaje a Norte America* (1947); *Acuarela nocturna* (1949); *Yaax u ha (Leyanda Mayá)* (1954); *Suite veracruzana* (1957); Concertino for Piano and Chamber Orch. (1970). **Piano:** *Radiograma* (1931). **VOCAL:** *4 Canciones* for Voice and Piano (1932); *Uchben X'Coholte* (Ancient Cemetery) for Soprano and Chamber Orch. (Mexico City, Oct. 13, 1933; ballet ver., 1936; Mexico City, March 6, 1936); *El grillo* (Cricket) for Soprano, Clarinet, Violin, Timbrel, and Piano (1933); *U Kayil Chaac*, an incantation for rain, for Soprano, Mexican Percussion Instruments, and Chamber Orch. (1934); *Brigadier de Choque* for Chorus and Percussion (1935); *Suite infantil* for Soprano and Chamber Orch. (1937); *Los Yaquis y los Seris*, 2 suites for Voice, Chamber Ensemble, and Mexican Percussion Instruments (1938; Mérida, July 31, 1942); *Música instrumental para espectácula de luz y sonido de Uxmal* for 2 Choruses and Orch. (1971). —NS/LK/DM

Ayler, Albert, free-jazz tenor saxophonist; b. Cleveland, Ohio, July 13, 1936; d. Nov. 25, 1970. Ayler's unique approach generally began with a simple theme played with a wide vibrato, followed by a free improvisation based on a total exploration of the speech-like screaming sounds possible on the saxophone. Highly controversial, he was greatly admired by John Coltrane, who would listen and learn from his recordings and once performed with him. On some of his later albums, Ayler astonished his following by incorporating his early blues influences with the current rock styles. Ayler began playing the alto saxophone in his father's band, then took up the tenor sax and, as a teenager in high school, played around Cleveland with R&B bands and toured with blues artist Little Walter. He spent some time in Calif., married, then entered the army in 1958 as a musician. After band and military training at Fort Knox, Ky., in March 1959 he was sent with a band to Europe, then in April 1961 was transferred to a band at Fort Ord, Calif. Discharged from the army in 1961, Ayler worked first in Scandinavia (playing standard songs on his first recordings), then in N.Y. He formed his first compatible band in 1964 with Don Cherry, Gary Peacock, and Sunny Murray, recording and playing infrequently. Ayler appeared at the Newport Jazz Festival in early July 1966. Coltrane brought Ayler to play with him at Lincoln Center in N.Y. on Feb. 19, 1966, and it was almost certainly Coltrane who encouraged Impulse Records to record Ayler beginning in December 1966. Ayler toured Europe in 1964, 1966, and 1970. On his last records he took to singing, playing bagpipes, and adding rock musicians and soul singers to his band. One of these vocalists was his companion, Mary Parks (aka Mary Maria), who seemed to dominate his last few efforts. After missing for 20 days, Ayler's body was found in the East River off of Manhattan on Nov. 25, 1970; the research of Peter Wilson shows that his death was almost certainly a suicide. Ayler's brother, Donald (b. Cleveland, Ohio, Oct. 5, 1942), was a trumpeter in the Cleveland area, but has been mostly inactive since his brother's death.

DISC.: *A. A.: The First Recordings* (1962); *My Name Is A. A.* (1963); *Witches and Devils* (1964); *Vibrations* (1964); *Spiritual Unity* (1964); *Spirits* (1964); *N.Y. Eye and Ear Control* (1964); *Hilversum Session* (1964); *Ghosts* (1964); *Spirits Rejoice* (1965); *Bells* (1965); *Quintet Live at Slug's Saloon* (1966); *Live at Lorrach* (1966); *Village Concerts* (1967); *Love Cry* (1967); *In Greenwich Village* (1967); *New Grass* (1968); *Vol. 1, 2* (1970); *Nuits De La Fondation Maeght* (1970).—**LP**

Ayleward, Richard, English organist and composer; b. Winchester, 1626; d. Norwich, Oct. 15, 1669. He was a chorister under C. Gibbons at Winchester Cathedral (1638–39). He was organist and master of the choristers at Norwich Cathedral (1661–64; 1666–69). His works include a full Service in D, 2 verse settings of the Magnificat and Nunc dimittis, 20 verse anthems, and virginal, lute, and harpsichord pieces.—**LK/DM**

Aylward, Theodore, English organist and composer; b. c. 1730; d. London, Feb. 27, 1801. He served as organist at Oxford Chapel, London (c. 1760–62), St. Lawrence, Jewry (1762–68), St. Michael's, Cornhill (1768–88), and St. George's Chapel, Windsor (from 1788). He also was Gresham Prof. of Music (from 1771). In 1791 he obtained his D.Mus. from Oxford. He composed sacred vocal music, songs, glees, and instrumental pieces.—**LK/DM**

Ayo, Félix, Spanish-born Italian violinist; b. Sestao, July 1, 1933. He studied at the Bilbao Cons., in Paris, and in Rome. After settling in Italy, he became a naturalized Italian citizen. In 1952 he became a founding member of the ensemble I Musici, with which he served as violinist and director until 1967. He toured extensively with it in Europe and the U.S. In 1968 he founded the Quartetto Beethoven, and subsequently toured widely with it.—**LK/DM**

Ayres, Frederic (real name, **Frederick Ayres Johnson**), American composer; b. Binghamton, N.Y., March 17, 1876; d. Colorado Springs, Nov. 23, 1926. He studied with Edgar S. Kelley (1897–1901) and Arthur Foote (1899). His works include an overture, *From the Plains,* 2 string quartets, 2 piano trios, 2 violin sonatas, a Cello Sonata, and numerous songs. In his later music, he showed a tendency toward Impressionism and used moderately complex harmonic combinations.—**NS/LK/DM**

Ayrton, Edmund, English organist and composer, father of **William Ayrton;** b. Ripon (baptized), Nov. 19, 1734; d. London, May 22, 1808. He became organist, rector chori, and "singing-man" at Southwell Collegiate Church or Minister in 1755. In 1756 he pursued training with James Nares. In 1764 he settled in London as a Gentleman of the Chapel Royal. He also served as a vicar-choral at St. Paul's Cathedral (from 1764), as lay vicar at Westminster Abbey (from 1780), and as Master of the Children of the Chapel Royal (1780–1805). In 1784 he obtained his Mus.D. from Cambridge. He composed 2 services, anthems, and secular vocal pieces. His best known work was the anthem *Begin unto my God* for 4 Soloists, Chorus, 2 Oboes, 2 Bassoons, 2 Trumpets, Timpani, and Strings, which was first heard at the thanksgiving service for the end of the War of American Independence at St. Paul's Cathedral on June 29, 1784. Samuel Wesley described Ayrton as "one of the most egregious blockheads under the sun," but this judgment seems unduly severe.—**NS/LK/DM**

Ayrton, William, English writer, editor, and composer, son of **Edmund Ayrton;** b. London, Feb. 24, 1777; d. there, March 8, 1858. He pursued his career in London, where he helped to found the Phil. Soc. in 1813. He was both a music and literary critic for the *Morning Chronicle* (1813–26) and the *Examiner* (1837–51). In 1817 and 1821 he was impresario of the Italian opera at the King's Theatre in Haymarket. In 1823 he founded the *Harmonicon,* a monthly music journal he ed. until 1833. He also ed. *The Sacred Minstrelsy* (London, 1834), *The Musical Library* (London, 1834–37), and *The Madrigalian Feast* (London, 1838). Ayrton married Samuel Arnold's daughter Marianne in 1803. In 1807 he was elected a Fellow of the Soc. of Antiquaries and in 1837 he became a Fellow of the Royal Soc.—**NS/LK/DM**

Azaïs, Hyacinthe, French composer; b. Ladern-sur- Lauquet, near Carcassonne, April 4, 1741; d. Toulouse, c. 1795. He was a choirboy at Carcassonne Cathedral, where he received his training in music. In 1756 he was made sous-maître de musique at the Auch church. In 1765 he became maître de musique at the Sorèze college. After holding a similar post with the Concert de Marseilles (1771–72), he resumed his duties in Sorèze at the renamed École Royale Militaire. About 1782 he settled in Toulouse. He composed 6 syms., chamber music, and vocal pieces. He also wrote a *Méthode de musique sur un nouveau plan* (1776).—**LK/DM**

Azanchevsky, Mikhail, Russian music educator and composer; b. Moscow, April 5, 1839; d. there, Jan. 24, 1881. He studied composition with Richter and Hauptmann at the Leipzig Cons. (1861–64), and piano with Liszt in Rome. After a sojourn in Paris (1866–70) he returned to Russia, where he became executive director of the St. Petersburg Cons. (1871–76). A disciplinarian by nature, he raised the minimal requirements for acceptance of new pupils and engaged important teachers, among them Rimsky- Korsakov. In Paris he purchased the important music library of Anders, which he later presented, together with other acquisitions, to the

St. Petersburg Cons. He composed a concert overture, 2 string quartets, 2 piano trios, a Cello Sonata, a *Festival polonais* for 2 Pianos, and numerous piano solo pieces and songs.—NS/LK/DM

Azkué (Aberasturi), Resurrección María de, Spanish composer and musicologist; b. Lequeitio, Aug. 5, 1864; d. Bilbao, Nov. 9, 1951. He studied theology in Spain, then went to Paris and studied music at the Schola Cantorum. He wrote two operas to Basque texts: *Ortzuri* (Bilbao, 1911) and *Urlo* (Bilbao, 1913), and several zarzuelas. He publ. a valuable collection, *Cancionero popular Vasco* (11 vols.), and *Literatura popular del País Vasco* (4 vols., the last containing musical examples).—NS/LK/DM

Aznavour, Charles (originally **Varenagh Aznavourian**), b. Paris, May 22, 1924. Armenian by decent, Parisian by birth, Aznavour typifies the European lounge singer, the guy whose hard drinking and chain smoking conceals a tender underbelly. Azvanour began to forge his tough-but-tender persona as a singer in the 1950s, drawing on French vocalists and American stars like Frank Sinatra, and he cemented the corresponding visuals—the cigarette, the melancholy visage—in such films as Truffaut's *Shoot the Piano Player*. His suave sentimentality has influenced a wide range of American performers, ranging from Tom Waits to Leonard Cohen; Aznavour was even mentioned in "11 Outlined Epitaphs," the liner notes to Bob Dylan's 1964 *Times They Are A-Changin'* LP. In addition to writing two books, Aznavour has continued to record and act regularly—one of his most winning performances came in the 1985 television show *Children's Songs & Stories with the Muppets,* which found the veteran performer playing alongside Jim Henson's popular felt creatures.

DISC: *Toi et Moi* (1994); *Il Faut Savior* (1995); *Je M'Voyais Deja* (1995); *You and Me* (1995); *65* (1995); *Greatest Golden Hits* (1996); *Hier Encore* (1996); *Idiote Je T'Aaime* (1996); *Exitos Inolvidables* (1997); *The Best of Charles Aznavour: 20 Great Songs in English* (1998); *Aznavour Live: Palais des Congres, 1997/98* (2000).

WRITINGS: *Aznavour by Aznavour* (Chicago, 1972); *Yesterday When I Was Young* (London, 1979).

Azzolina, Jay, jazz guitarist; b. Meriden, Conn., Dec. 23, 1952. Azzolina studied classical guitar at Hartt Coll. of Music in Hartford, Conn. (1971–72), then studied with Pat Metheny and Mick Goodrick at Berklee (1972–76). A thoughtful and creative soloist, he has worked with Spyro Gyra (1989–91, including two LPs), Michael Franks (since 1993), and various others, including Herbie Mann, Jaco Pastorius, and Paul Motian. He has also made recordings with Jeff Beal, David Mann, and Harvie Swartz. Azzolina has taught at the West End Sym. outreach program since 1981, and at various N.Y. colleges since 1986, including S.U.N.Y. in Purchase (since 1992) and Manhattanville Coll. (since 1996). He earned an M.F.A. from Purchase in 1995.

DISC.: Never Too Late (1988).—LP

B

Baaren, Kees van, important Dutch composer and pedagogue; b. Enschede, Oct. 22, 1906; d. Oegstgeest, Sept. 2, 1970. He studied with F.E. Koch at the Berlin Hochschule für Musik and with Pijper in Rotterdam. He was the director of the Amsterdam Academy of Music (1948–53), the Utrecht Cons. (1953–57), and the Royal Cons. of Music in The Hague (1958–70). Baaren was a major influence on many of the leading Dutch composers of the post–World War II avant-garde. After composing along traditional lines, he embraced a serial path à la Pijper and Webern in 1947.

WORKS: ORCH.: Piano Concertino (1934); Suite for School Orch. (1951); *Sinfonia* (1956–57); *Variations* (1959); Piano Concerto (1964); *Musica* (Rotterdam, May 18, 1966; rev. 1968). **CHAMBER:** 2 string quartets (1932–33; *Sovraposizioni I*, 1962); Trio for Flute, Clarinet, and Bassoon (1936); Septet for Flute, Oboe, Clarinet, Bassoon, Horn, Violin, and Double Bass (1952); *Sovraposizioni II*, wind quintet (1963); *Musica* for Flute (1965). **KEYBOARD: P i a n o :** Sonatina (1948). **O r g a n :** *Musica* (1968–69). **C a r i l l o n :** *Musica* for 72 Carillons (1964); *Musica* for 47 Carillons (1964; rev. 1969). **VOCAL:** *The Hollow Men* for Chorus and Orch. (1948); choruses.

BIBL.: J. Hill, *The Music of K. v.B.* (diss., Univ. of N.C., 1970). **—NS/LK/DM**

Babadzhanian, Arno, Armenian pianist and composer; b. Yerevan, Jan. 22, 1921; d. Moscow, Nov. 15, 1983. He studied at the Yerevan Cons., and after graduation in 1947 went to Moscow, where he took courses in piano with Igumnov at the Cons. and in composition with Litinsky at the Armenian Culture Center; he graduated from both in 1948. In 1950 he joined the piano faculty at the Yerevan Cons. His music is derived from the folk-song patterns of Armenia, continuing the line cultivated by Khachaturian, with emphasis on rhythmic coloration in a characteristic quasi-oriental manner. His most ambitious works are a Violin Concerto (1949) and a Cello Concerto (1962), but he also wrote *Heroic Ballad*

for Piano and Orch. (1950), two string quartets (1942, 1947), Piano Trio (1952), Violin Sonata (1959), and a number of popular ballads under such appealing titles as *The Song of First Love* and *Make a Wish.*—**NS/LK/DM**

Babayev, Andrei, Russian composer; b. Azerbaijan, Dec. 27, 1923; d. Moscow, Oct. 21, 1964. He studied in Baku and played native instruments, and then entered the Baku Cons., where he was a student in composition of Gadzhibekov and Karayev, graduating in 1950. He later took advanced courses with Shaporin at the Moscow Cons. His music is inspired mainly by Armenian folk melodies, and he also arranged songs of Central Asia and India. Some of his original songs (*I Met a Girl, Lovely Eyes*, etc.) acquired popularity. Other compositions include *Eagles' Bastion*, opera (1957), *October*, cantata (1947), Sym. (1950), *Indian Fantasy* for Orch. (1958), and pieces for native instruments.—**NS/LK/DM**

Babbi, Gregorio (Lorenzo), famous Italian tenor, father of **(Pietro Giovanni) Cristoforo (Bartolomeo Gasparre) Babbi;** b. Cesena, Nov. 16, 1708; d. there, Jan. 2, 1768. He made his operatic debut in Florence in 1730. In 1741 he entered the service of Charles III, King of Naples, and in 1748 he was engaged by the Teatro San Carlo of Naples, where his wife, Giovanna Guaetta, was also a singer. He was pensioned in 1759.—**NS/LK/DM**

Babbi, (Pietro Giovanni) Cristoforo (Bartolomeo Gasparre), Italian violinist and composer, son of **Gregorio (Lorenzo) Babbi;** b. Cesena, May 6, 1745; d. Dresden, Nov. 19, 1814. He studied violin, counterpoint, and composition with Paolo Alberghi in Faenza; subsequently was primo violino at the festas there (1766, 1769, 1770, 1772) and also played in the orch. of the Rimini Opera (1773). In 1774 he was elected a member of the Accademia Filarmonica of Bologna, then was maestro di cappella at the Teatro Comunale there (1775–78). In 1779 he became primo violino and direttore d'orchestra in Forli. He was called to Dresden in 1781 as provisional Konzertmeister, receiving a permanent appointment in 1782, and proceeded to reorganize the Kapelle. He held an equal place with J.G. Naumann, the Dresden Kapellmeister. He composed operas.—NS/LK/DM

Babbitt, Milton (Byron),

prominent American composer, teacher, and theorist; b. Philadelphia, May 10, 1916. He received early music training in Jackson, Miss., at the same time revealing an acute flair for mathematical reasoning; this double faculty was to determine the formulation of his musical theories. He pursued training in music with Marion Bauer and Philip James at N.Y. Univ. (B.A., 1935). After private lessons with Sessions, he pursued studies with that mentor at Princeton Univ. (M.F.A., 1942). In 1938 he joined the faculty of Princeton Univ. as a music teacher. After teaching mathematics there (1942–45), he again taught music there from 1948. In 1966 he became William Schubael Conant Prof. there, and also served as director of the Columbia-Princeton Electronic Music Center (from 1959). In 1984 he retired as prof. emeritus at Princeton Univ. He also taught at N.Y.'s Juilliard School (from 1973) and at various other venues in the U.S. and Europe. In 1949 and 1964 he received the N.Y. Music Critics' Circle awards. In 1960–61 he held a Guggenheim fellowship. He was elected a member of the National Inst. of Arts and Letters in 1965, and of the American Academy of Arts and Letters in 1986, receiving its Gold Medal in Music in 1988. In 1974 he became a fellow of the American Academy of Arts and Sciences. In 1982 he was awarded a Pulitzer Prize Special Citation for "his life's work as a distinguished and seminal American composer." From 1986 to 1991 he was a MacArthur fellow. In 1992 Princeton Univ. awarded him his Ph.D. for a diss. he had written as a student there but which had been rejected. A new review of his diss. prompted Princeton to award him his Ph.D., noting that the diss. had been so advanced for its time that it could not be properly evaluated. Taking as the point of departure Schoenberg's advanced compositional methods, Babbitt extended the serial principle to embrace 12 different note values, 12 different time intervals between instrumental entities, 12 different dynamic levels, and 12 different instrumental timbres. In order to describe the potential combinations of the basic four aspects of the tone row, he introduced the term "combinatoriality," with symmetric parts of a tone row designated as "derivations." Babbitt's scientific theories have profoundly influenced the musical thinking of young American composers. His "Twelve- Tone Invariants as Compositional Determinants" (Musical Quarterly, April 1960) gives a resume of his system of total serialism. The serial application of rhythmic values is expounded in his "Twelve-Tone Rhythmic Structure and the Electronic Medium" (Perspectives of New Music, Fall 1962). For a general exposition of his views on music, see S. Dembski and J. Straus, eds., Milton Babbitt: Words about Music (The Madison Lectures) (Madison, Wisc., 1987).

WORKS: DRAMATIC: Music Theater: Fabulous Voyage (1946). **ORCH.:** Relata I (1965; Cleveland,

March 3, 1966) and II (1968; N.Y., Jan. 16, 1969); Ars combinatoria for Small Orch. (Bloomington, Ind., July 16, 1981); 2 piano concertos: No. 1 (1985; N.Y., Jan. 19, 1986) and No. 2 (1998); Transfigured Notes for Strings (1986). **CHAMBER:** Composition for 4 Instruments (1948); Composition for 12 Instruments (1948; rev. 1954); 6 string quartets (1948, withdrawn; 1954; 1969–70; 1970; 1982; 1993); Wind Quartet (1953); All Set for 8 Instruments (1957); Sextets for Violin and Piano (1966); Arie de capo for 6 Instruments (1973–74); Paraphrases for 11 Instruments (1979); Groupwise for 7 Instruments (1983); 4 Play for Clarinet, Violin, Cello, and Piano (1984); Whirled Series for Saxophone and Piano (1987); The Crowded Air for 11 Instruments (1988); Consortini for 5 Instruments (1989); Play It Again, Sam for Viola (1989); Soli e Duettini for 2 Guitars (1989); None But the Lonely Flute for Flute (1991); Septet, But Equal for 3 Clarinets, String Trio, and Piano (1992); Counterparts for Brass Quintet (1992); Around the Horn for Horn (1993); Fanfare for All for Brass Quintet (1993); Triad for Clarinet, Viola, and Piano (1994); Arrivals and Departures for 2 Violins (1994); Accompanied Recitative for Soprano Saxophone and Piano (1994); Bicenquinquagenary Fanfare for Brass Quintet (1995); Quartet for Piano and String Trio (1995); Quintet for Clarinet and String Quartet (1996); When Shall We Three Meet Again? for Flute, Clarinet, and Vibraphone (1996); Concerto Piccolino for Vibraphone (1999). **Piano:** 3 Compositions (1947); Partitions (1957); Postpartitions (1966); Tableaux (1972); My Complements to Roger (1978); Canonical Form (1983); Lagniappe (1985); Emblems (Ars Emblemantica) (1989); Envoi for Piano, 4–Hands (1990); Preludes, Interludes, Postlude (1991); Tutte Le Corde (1994); The Old Order Changeth (1998); Allegro Penseroso (1999). **VOCAL:** Du, song cycle for Soprano and Piano (1951); Composition for Tenor and 6 Instruments (1960); 4 Canons for Women's Chorus (1968); A Solo Requiem for Soprano and 2 Pianos (1976–77); More Phonemena for 12 Voices (1978); An Elizabethan Sextette for 6 Women's Voices (1979); The Head of the Bed for Soprano and 4 Instruments (1982); 4 Cavalier Settings for Tenor and Guitar (1991); Mehr "Du" for Soprano, Viola, and Piano (1991); Quatrains for Soprano and 2 Clarinets (1993); No Longer Very Clear for Soprano and 4 Instruments (1994). **OTHER:** Composition for Synthesizer (1961); Vision and Prayer for Soprano and Tape (1961); Ensembles for Synthesizer and Tape (1962–64); Philomel for Soprano and Tape (1964); Correspondences for String Orch. and Tape (1967); Occasional Variations for Tape (1971); Concerti for Violin, Small Orch., and Tape (1974–76); Phonemena for Soprano and Tape (1975); Reflections for Piano and Tape (1975); Images for Saxophone and Tape (1979).

BIBL.: A. Mead, An Introduction to the Music of M. B. (Princeton, N.J., 1993).—NS/LK/DM

Babell, William,

English harpsichordist, violinist, organist, and composer; b. probably in London, c. 1690; d. there, Sept. 23, 1723. He studied music with his father and with Pepusch. He was active in London concert life as an instrumentalist, and also organist of All Hallows. He composed a number of works for the harpsichord, as well as concertos for violin and for flute.—NS/LK/DM

Babin, Victor,

Russian-born American pianist, teacher, and composer; b. Moscow, Dec. 13, 1908; d. Cleveland, March 1, 1972. He studied at the Riga Cons. (graduated, 1927) and with Schnabel (piano) and Schreker (composition) at the Berlin Hochschule für Musik. In 1933 he married **Vitya Vronsky**, with whom he toured extensively as a duo pianist. In 1937 they emigrated to the U.S. and Babin became a naturalized American citizen in 1944. He continued to tour widely with his wife from 1945, and also served as pianist of the Festival Quartet (1954–62). He taught at the Aspen (Colo.) Music School, where he was its director (1951–54), at the Berkshire Music Center in Tanglewood, at the Cleveland Inst. of Music, where he was its director (1961–72), and at Case Western Reserve Univ. His output, in a post-Romantic style, includes two concertos for two Pianos and Orch., orch. pieces, chamber music, songs, and pieces for Piano and Duo Piano. **—NS/LK/DM**

Babini, Matteo, famous Italian tenor; b. Bologna, Feb. 19, 1754; d. there, Sept. 22, 1816. He studied with Cortoni, making his debut in 1780. He then toured England, Russia, Germany, and Austria with great acclaim. He settled in Paris as a court favorite until the Revolution forced him to leave France; he was in Berlin in 1792 and in Trieste in 1796. Brighenti publ. an "Elogio" in his memory (Bologna, 1821).**—NS/LK/DM**

Babitz, Sol, American violinist and writer on music; b. N.Y., Oct. 11, 1911; d. Los Angeles, Feb. 18, 1982. In 1932 he went to Berlin, where he studied violin with Flesch and composition with Juon; also took a course in musicology with Sachs. In 1933 he proceeded to Paris and continued violin instruction with Chailley. Shortly afterward he returned to the U.S., and was a violinist in the Los Angeles Phil. (1933–37). From 1942 to 1961 he played violin in studio orchs. in Hollywood. He publ. *Principles of Extensions in Violin Fingering* (N.Y., 1947), *The Violin: Views and Reviews* (Urbana, Ill., 1959), *The Great Baroque Hoax: A Guide to Baroque Performance for Musicians and Connoisseurs* (Los Angeles, 1970), and *Vocal De-Wagnerization and Other Matters* (with G. Pont; Los Angeles, 1973).**—NS/LK/DM**

Bacarisse, Salvador, Spanish composer; b. Madrid, Sept. 12, 1898; d. Paris, Aug. 5, 1963. He studied at the Madrid Cons. with Conrado del Campo; received the Premio Nacional de Música in 1923, 1930, and 1934. During the Spanish Civil War, he was active in the music section of the loyalist army; after its defeat in 1939, he settled in Paris. He wrote the operas *Charlot* (1933), *El Tesoro de Boabdil* (1958), and *Fuenteovejuna* (1962).

BIBL.: C. Heine, *S. B. (1898–1963): Die Kriterien seines Stils während der Schaffenszeit in Spanien (bis 1939)* (Frankfurt am Main, 1993).**—NS/LK/DM**

Baccaloni, Salvatore, noted Italian bass; b. Rome, April 14, 1900; d. N.Y., Dec. 31, 1969. He began his training at the Sistine Chapel choir school at the Vatican, and then studied with Giuseppe Kaschmann. In 1922 he made his operatic debut as Rossini's Bartolo at the Teatro Adriano in Rome; from 1926 to 1940 he sang at Milan's La Scala, where he was esteemed in buffo roles. In 1928 he made his debut at London's Covent Garden as Puccini's Timur, and in 1930 his U.S. debut at the Chicago Civic Opera as Verdi's Melitone. From 1931 to

1941 he appeared at the Teatro Colón in Buenos Aires, and from 1936 to 1939 at the Glyndebourne Festivals. On Dec. 3, 1940, he made his first appearance with the Metropolitan Opera as Mozart's Bartolo during the company's visit to Philadelphia; then sang for the first time on the Metropolitan stage in N.Y. in the same role on Dec. 7, 1940, and subsequently was its leading buffo artist until 1962; his farewell appearance with the company was as Rossini's Bartolo in Brookville, N.Y., on Aug. 8, 1965. Baccaloni was the foremost comic bass of his generation. Among his memorable roles were Don Pasquale, Osmin, Leporello, Dulcamara, Varlaam, and Gianni Schicchi.**—NS/LK/DM**

Baccusi, Ippolito, Italian composer; b. Mantua, c. 1550; d. Verona, Sept. 2, 1608. He served as asst. maestro di cappella at San Marco in Venice. By 1568 he was in Ravenna, where he pursued his training. By 1572 he was in Verona and served as maestro di cappella at S. Eufemia. After holding that position at Mantua (1583–92), he returned to Verona as choirmaster of the Cathedral. He publ. six vols. of masses (1570–96), seven vols. of madrigals (1570–1605), and other vocal works. His output reveals the influence of the Venetian masters. **—NS/LK/DM**

Bacewicz, Grażyna, notable Polish composer and violinist; b. Łódź, Feb. 5, 1909; d. Warsaw, Jan. 17, 1969. She learned to play the violin in her youth and began to compose at age 13. She then was a student of Józef Jarzębski (violin), Józef Turczyński (piano), and Sikorski (composition) at the Warsaw Cons., graduating in 1932. She also studied philosophy at the Univ. of Warsaw. A scholarship from Paderewski enabled her to study violin with André Touret and composition with Boulanger at the École Normale de Musique in Paris (1932–33). After teaching at the Łódź Cons. (1933–34), she returned to Paris to study violin with Flesch. In 1935 she received honorable mention at the first Wieniawski violin competition in Warsaw, and then played in the Polish Radio Sym. Orch. there (1936–38). From 1945 to 1955 she was active as a concert violinist. From 1966 until her death, she taught at the Warsaw State Coll. of Music. In 1949 she won the Warsaw Prize, and in 1950 and 1952 the National Prize for composition. Bacewicz's large catalog of works generally adhered to neo-Classical principles. After the rise of the new Polish school of composition, she pursued more adventuresome paths.

WORKS: DRAMATIC: *Z chopa król* (The Peasant King), ballet (1953); *Przygody króla Artura* (The Adventures of King Arthur), radio comic opera (1959); *Esik w Ostendzie* (Esik in Ostend), ballet (1964); *Pożądanie* (Desire), ballet (1968); incidental music. **ORCH.:** Suite for Strings (1931); *Sinfonietta* (1932); *3 Caricatures* (1932); *Convoi de Joie* (1933); 7 violin concertos (1937, 1945, 1948, 1951, 1954, 1957, 1965); 2 unnumbered syms. (1938; Sym. for Strings, 1946); 4 numbered syms. (1942–45; 1951; 1952; 1953); Overture (1943); *Introduction and Caprice* (1947); Concerto for Strings (1948); Piano Concerto (1949); *Polish Rhapsody* for Violin and Orch. (1949); 2 cello concertos (1951, 1963); *Polish Overture* (1954); *Partita* (1955); *Symphonic Variations* (1957); *Music* for Strings, Trumpets, and Percussion (1958); *Pensieri Notturni* for Chamber Orch. (1961); *Concerto for Orchestra* (1962);

Musica Sinfonica in Tre Movimenti (1965); *Divertimento* for Strings (1965); Concerto for 2 Pianos and Orch. (1966); *Contradizione* for Chamber Orch. (1966); *In una Parte* (1967); Viola Concerto (1968). **CHAMBER:** Double Fugue for String Quartet (1928); 2 unnumbered sonatas for Solo Violin (1929, 1932); 2 numbered sonatas for Solo Violin (1941, 1958); 1 unnumbered violin sonata (1929); 5 numbered violin sonatas (*Sonata da camera*, 1945; 1946; 1947; 1949; 1951); 2 unnumbered string quartets (1930, 1931); 7 numbered string quartets (1938, 1943, 1947, 1951, 1955, 1960, 1965); Wind Quintet (1932); Trio for Oboe, Violin, and Cello (1935); Suite for 2 Violins (1949); Trio for Oboe, Clarinet, and Bassoon (1948); Quartet for 4 Violins (1949); 2 piano quintets (1952, 1965); Quartet for 4 Cellos (1964); *Incrustations* for Horn and Chamber Ensemble (1965); Trio for Oboe, Harp, and Percussion (1965); etc. **KEYBOARD: P i a n o :** 6 sonatas (1930, 1935, 1938, 1942, 1949, 1953); 2 sonatinas (1933, 1955); *10 Études* (1956); many other pieces. **O r g a n :** *Esquisse* (1966). **VOCAL:** *De Profundis*, cantata for Soloists, Chorus, and Orch. (1932); *3 Songs* for Tenor and Orch. (1938); *Olympic Cantata* for Chorus and Orch. (1948); *Acropolis*, cantata for Chorus and Orch. (1964); other songs.

BIBL.: S. Kisielewski, *G. B. i jej czasy* (G. B. and Her Times; Kraków, 1963); J. Rosen, *G. B.: Her Life and Works* (Los Angeles, 1984); S. Shafer, *The Contribution of G. B. (1909–1969) to Polish Music* (Lewston, N.Y., 1992).—NS/LK/DM

Bach, illustrious family of German musicians. History possesses few records of such remarkable examples of hereditary art, which culminated in the genius of Johann Sebastian Bach. In the Bach genealogy, the primal member was Johannes or Hans Bach, who is mentioned in 1561 as a guardian of the municipality of Wechmar, a town near Gotha. Also residing in Wechmar was his relative Veit Bach; a baker by trade, he was also skillful in playing on a small cittern. Another relative, Caspar Bach, who lived from 1570 to 1640, was a Stadtpfeifer in Gotha who later served as a town musician in Arnstadt. His five sons, Caspar, Johannes, Melchior, Nicolaus, and Heinrich, were all town musicians. Another Bach, Johann(es Hans) Bach (1550–1626), was known as "der Spielmann," that is, "minstrel," and thus was definitely described as primarily a musician by vocation. His three sons, Johann(es Hans), Christoph, and Heinrich, were also musicians. J.S. Bach took great interest in his family history, and in 1735 prepared a genealogy under the title *Ursprung der musicalisch-Bachischen Familie*. *The Bach Reader*, compiled by H. David and A. Mendel (N.Y., 1945; 2nd ed., rev. 1966; rev. and enl. ed., 1998, by C. Wolff as *The New Bach Reader*), contains extensive quotations from this compendium. Karl Geiringer's books *The Bach Family: Seven Generations of Creative Genius* (N.Y., 1954) and *Music of the Bach Family: An Anthology* (Cambridge, Mass., 1955) give useful genealogical tables of Bach's family. Bach's father, Johann Ambrosius, was a twin brother of Bach's uncle; the twins bore such an extraordinary physical resemblance that, according to the testimony of Carl Philipp Emanuel Bach, their own wives had difficulty telling them apart after dark. To avoid confusion, they had them wear vests of different colors. A vulgar suggestion that because of this similarity Bach may have been begotten by his uncle is too gross to require a refutation.

When the family became numerous and widely dispersed, its members agreed to assemble on a fixed date each year. Erfurt, Eisenach, and Arnstadt were the places chosen for these meetings, which are said to have continued until the middle of the 18th century, as many as 120 persons of the name of Bach then assembling. At these meetings, a cherished pastime was the singing of "quodlibets," comic polyphonic potpourris of popular songs. An amusing example attributed to J.S. Bach is publ. in *Veröffentlichungen der Neuen Bach-Gesellschaft* (vol. XXXII, 2).

Entries for Bach family members follow immediately. Entries for other musicians named Bach follow thereafter. —NS/LK/DM

Bach, Carl Philipp Emanuel (the "Berlin" or "Hamburg" Bach), third (and second surviving) son of **Johann Sebastian;** b. Weimar, March 8, 1714; d. Hamburg, Dec. 14, 1788. He was educated under his father's tuition at the Thomasschule in Leipzig, then studied jurisprudence at the Univ. of Leipzig and at the Univ. of Frankfurt-an- der-Oder. Turning to music as his chief vocation, he went to Berlin in 1738, and in 1740 he was confirmed as chamber musician to Frederick the Great of Prussia. In that capacity he arranged his father's visit to Potsdam. In March 1768 he assumed the post of cantor at the Johanneum (the Lateinschule) in Hamburg, and also served as music director for the five major churches. He held these posts until his death. Abandoning the strict polyphonic style of composition of his great father, he became an adept of the new school of piano writing, a master of "Empfindsamkeit" ("intimate expressiveness"), the North German counterpart of the French Rococo. His *Versuch über die wahre Art das Clavier zu spielen...* (two parts, 1753–62; re-ed. by Schelling, 1857; new, but incomplete, ed. by W. Niemann, 1906) became a very influential work which yielded much authentic information about musical practices of the second half of the 18th century. An Eng. tr. of the *Versuch...*, entitled *Essay on the True Art of Playing Keyboard Instruments*, was publ. by W. Mitchell (N.Y., 1949). His autobiography was reprinted by W. Kahl in *Selbstbiographien deutscher Musiker des XVIII. Jahrhunderts* (Cologne, 1948); an Eng. tr. was made by W. Newman, "Emanuel Bach's Autobiography," *Musical Quarterly* (April 1965). His compositions are voluminous (see E. Helm, *Thematic Catalogue of the Works of C.P.E. B.*, New Haven, 1989). E. Suchalla ed. *C.P.E. B.: Briefe und Dokumente: Kritische Gesamtausgabe* (two vols., Göttingen, 1994), and S. Clark tr. and ed. *The Letters of C.P.E. B.* (Oxford, 1997).

WORKS: ORCH.: 20 syms.; about 50 harpsichord concertos; 12 harpsichord sonatinas; concertos arranged from the harpsichord concertos. **CHAMBER:** 3 keyboard quartets; about 20 trio sonatas; more then 30 duo sonatas; 18 solo sonatas; wind music, etc. **KEYBOARD:** About 150 sonatas; fantasias; variations; rondos; fugues; minuets. **VOCAL:** *Magnificat* (1749); the oratorios *Die Israeliten in der Wüste* (1769) and *Die Auferstehung und Himmelfahrt Jesu* (1780); *Morgengesang am Schopfungsfeste*, ode (1783); Passions; sacred cantatas and motets; chamber cantatas; arias; about 300 sacred and secular 300 songs.

Editions of his various works include the following: C. Krebs, ed., *Die Sechs Sammlungen von Sonaten, freien Fantasien und Rondos für Kenner und Liebhaber* (Leipzig, 1895; rev. ed. by L. Hoffmann, Erbrecht, 1953); O. Vrieslander, *Kleine Stücke für Klavier* (Hannover, 1930); O. Vrieslander, *Vier leichte Sonaten* (Hannover, 1932); K. Herrman, ed., *Sonaten und Stücke* (Leipzig, 1938); V. Luithlen and H. Kraus, eds., *Klavierstücke* (Vienna, 1938); K. Herrman, ed., *Leichte Tänze und Stücke für Klavier* (Hamburg, 1949); P. Friedheim, ed., *Six Sonatas for Keyboard* (N.Y., 1967); H. Ferguson, ed., *Keyboard Works of C.P.E. B.* (4 vols., London, 1983).

BIBL.: C. Bitter, *C.P.E. B. und Wilhelm Friedemann Bach und deren Brüder* (2 vols., Berlin, 1868); M. Fleuler, *Die norddeutsche Symphonie zur Zeit Friedrichs des Grossen, und besonders die Werke P.E. B.s* (Berlin, 1908); H. Schenker, *Ein Beitrag zur Ornamentik: Als Einführung zu P.E. B.s Klavierwerke* (Vienna, 1908); O. Vrieslander, *C.P.E. B.* (Munich, 1923); H. Wien-Claudi, *Zum Liedschaffen C.P.E. B.s* (Reichenberg, 1928); H. Miesner, *P.E. B. in Hamburg* (Leipzig, 1929); E. Schmid, *C.P.E. B. und seine Kammermusik* (Kassel, 1931); A.-E. Cherbuliez, *C.P.E. B. 1714–1788* (Zürich and Leipzig, 1940); E. Beurmann, *Die Klaviersonaten C.P.E. B.s* (diss., Univ. of Göttingen, 1952); K. Geiringer, *The Bach Family: Seven Generations of Creative Genius* (N.Y., 1954); C. Haag, *The Keyboard Concertos of K.P.E. B.* (diss., Univ. of Calif., Los Angeles, 1956); G. Busch, *C.P.E. B. und seine Lieder* (Regensburg, 1957); P. Barford, *The Keyboard Music of C.P.E. B.* (London, 1965); E. Suchalla, *Die Orchestersinfonien C.P.E. B.s nebst einem thematischen Verzeichnis seiner Orchesterwerke* (Augsburg, 1968); R. Wade, *The Keyboard Concertos of C.P.E. B.* (Ann Arbor, 1981); H.-G. Ottenberg, *C.P.E. B.* (Leipzig, 1982; Eng. tr., 1988); D. Schulenberg, *The Instrumental Music of C.P.E. B.* (Ann Arbor, 1984); S. Clark, ed., *C.P.E. B. Studies* (Oxford, 1988); W. Horn, *C.P.E. B.: Frühe Klaviersonaten* (Hamburg, 1988); E. Thom, ed., *Die Entwicklung des Doppel- und Gruppenkonzertes im 18. Jahrhundert bis zur "Sinfonia concertante": Fragen der Aufführungspraxis und Interpretation von Werken C.P.E. B.s—ein Beitrag zum 200. Todestag* (Michaelstein/Blankenburg, 1989); H. Marx, ed., *C.P.E. B. und die europäische Musikkultur des mittleren 18. Jahrhunderts: Bericht über das Internationale Symposium der Joachim Jungius Gesellschaft der Wissenschaften Hamburg 29. September-2. Oktober 1988* (Göttingen, 1990); H. Poos, ed., *C.P.E. B.: Beiträge zu Leben und Werk* (Mainz, 1993); G. Wagner, *Die Sinfonien C.P.E. B.s: Werdende Gattung und Originalgenie* (Stuttgart, 1994); A. Nagel, *Studien zur Passionskantate von C.P.E. B.* (Frankfurt am Main, 1995).—NS/LK/DM

Bach, Christoph, second son of **Johann(es Hans)** "der Spielmann" and grandfather of **Johann Sebastian;** b. Wechmar, April 19, 1613; d. Arnstadt, Sept. 12, 1661. He was a court musician in Weimar. From 1642 he was a town musician in Erfurt, and, from 1654, court and town musician in Arnstadt. The only known musical item by him is publ. in the *Bach-Jahrbuch* (1928).—NS/LK/DM

Bach, Georg Christoph, eldest son of **Christoph;** b. Erfurt, Sept. 6, 1642; d. Schweinfurt, April 24, 1697. He was cantor in Themar from 1668, and in Schweinfurt from 1684. A cantata of his is publ. in *Das Erbe deutscher Musik* (vol. II, Leipzig, 1935).—NS/LK/DM

Bach, Heinrich, third son of **Johann(es Hans)** "der Spielmann"; b. Wechmar, Sept. 16, 1615; d. Arnstadt,

July 10, 1692. He was a town musician in Schweinfurt from 1629, in Erfurt from 1635, and in Arnstadt from 1641. From 1641 he was also organist at the Liebfrauenkirche in Arnstadt, a post he held for 51 years, until his death. M. Schneider publ. a thematic index of his works in the *Bach-Jahrbuch* (1907, pp. 105–9). A cantata of his is found in *Das Erbe deutscher Musik* (vol. II, Leipzig, 1935); also three organ chorales in D. Hellmann, ed., *Orgelwerke der Familie Bach* (Leipzig, 1967).—NS/LK/DM

Bach, Johann Aegidius, second son of **Johann(es Hans);** b. Erfurt, Feb. 9, 1645; d. there (buried), Nov. 22, 1716. He succeeded his father as municipal music director in Erfurt in 1682. From 1690 he was also organist at the Michaeliskirche there, succeeding Pachelbel.—NS/LK/DM

Bach, Johann Ambrosius, second son of **Christoph,** twin brother of **Johann Christoph,** and father of **Johann Sebastian;** b. Erfurt, Feb. 22, 1645; d. Eisenach, Feb. 20, 1695. As a boy, he went to Arnstadt, where he was trained as a Stadtpfeifer. In 1667 he became a member of the town band in Erfurt, and from 1671 he was court trumpeter and director of the town band in Eisenach. He was married twice: on April 8, 1668, to Maria Elisabeth Lammerhirt (b. Erfurt, Feb. 24, 1644; d. Eisenach, May 3, 1694), the mother of Johann Sebastian, and on Nov. 27, 1694, to the widow of his cousin Johann Gunther Bach.—NS/LK/DM

Bach, Johann Bernhard, son of **Johann Aegidius,** one of the best organists and composers of his generation; b. Erfurt, Nov. 23, 1676; d. Eisenach, June 11, 1749. He was an organist at Erfurt and Magdeburg, and the successor to **Johann Christoph** as organist at Eisenach (1703); also served the Duke of Saxe-Eisenach. He wrote harpsichord pieces and a number of organ chorales, two of which were publ. in *Das Erbe deutscher Musik* (vol. IX, Leipzig, 1937) and two more in D. Hellmann, ed., *Orgelwerke der Familie Bach* (Leipzig, 1967). He also wrote four orch. suites, one of which was publ. by A. Fareanu (Leipzig, 1920) and another by K. Geiringer, *Music of the Bach Family: An Anthology* (Cambridge, Mass., 1955).—NS/LK/DM

Bach, Johann Christoph, eldest son of **Heinrich,** organist and composer of the highest distinction among the earlier Bachs; b. Arnstadt, Dec. 3, 1642; d. Eisenach, March 31, 1703. From 1663 to 1665 he was an organist in Arnstadt, and from 1665 in Eisenach, where, from 1700, he was court musician. A thematic catalogue of his compositions was publ. by M. Schneider in the *Bach-Jahrbuch* (1907, pp. 132-77). C.P.E. Bach described him as a "great and expressive composer". His works are printed in *Das Erbe deutscher Musik* (vols. I and II, Leipzig, 1935); several of his motets were publ. by V. Junk (Leipzig, 1922); 44 chorales with preludes for organ were ed. by M. Fischer (Kassel, 1936); 3 additional such works attributed to him were ed. by C. Wolff in *The Neumeister Collection of Chorale Preludes from the Bach Circle (Yale University Manuscript LM 4708)* (facsimile ed., New Haven, 1986); his *Praeludium und Fuge* for Organ is in D. Hellmann, ed., *Orgelwerke der Familie Bach* (Leipzig, 1967).—NS/LK/DM

Bach, Johann Christoph, twin brother of **Johann Ambrosius**; b. Erfurt, Feb. 22, 1645; d. Arnstadt, Aug. 25, 1693. He was a Stadtpfeifer in Erfurt from 1666, and, from 1671, in Arnstadt. The physical resemblance between him and his twin brother (father of **Johann Sebastian**) was such that, according to the testimony of C.P.E. Bach, even their wives had difficulty distinguishing between them.—**NS/LK/DM**

Bach, Johann Christoph, brother of **Johann Sebastian** and eldest son of **Johann Ambrosius;** b. Erfurt, June 16, 1671; d. Ohrdruf, Feb. 22, 1721. He was a pupil of Pachelbel. He served as organist at the Thomaskirche in Erfurt and for a short time at Arnstadt. From 1690 he was organist at the Michaeliskirche in Ohrdruf, where Johann Sebastian stayed with him for almost five years.

BIBL.: C. Freyse, *Die Ohrdrufer Bache in der Silhouette: J.S. Bachs ältester Bruder J.C. und seine Nachkommen* (Eisenach, 1957). —**NS/LK/DM**

Bach, Johann Christoph Friedrich (the "Bückeburg" Bach), ninth son of **Johann Sebastian;** b. Leipzig, June 21, 1732; d. Bückeburg, Jan. 26, 1795. He studied music with his father, then attended the Univ. of Leipzig, where he took courses in jurisprudence. Adopting music as his principal vocation, he became a chamber musician in Bückeburg, a post he held until his death. Although less known as a composer than his brothers, he was a fine musician. A selected edition of his works was ed. by G. Schünemann and sponsored by the Fürstliches Institut für Musikwissenschaftliche Forschung (1920–22). Schünemann also ed. several oratorios in Denkmäler Deutscher Tonkunst (vol. 56, 1917). G. Walter ed. the cantata *Die Amerikanerin* (Berlin, 1919), and L. Duttenhofer, a set of six quartets (Paris, 1922); several other chamber works may be found in K. Geiringer, *Music of the Bach Family: An Anthology* (Cambridge, Mass., 1955); three syms. have been ed. in facsimile by H. Wohlfarth (Bückeburg, 1966).

BIBL.: H. Wohlfarth, *J.C.F. B.* (Bern, 1971; includes a catalogue of works); U. Leisinger, ed., *J.C. F. B. (1732–1795): Ein Komponist zwischen Barock und Klassik* (Bückeberg, 1995). —**NS/LK/DM**

Bach, Johann Ernst, only son of **Johann Bernhard;** b. Eisenach, Jan. 28, 1722; d. there, Sept. 1, 1777. He was a pupil of his uncle **Johann Sebastian**. After studying law at the Univ. of Leipzig, he returned to Eisenach and practiced as an advocate. In 1748 he became asst. organist to his father at the Georgenkirche, succeeding him as organist in 1749. In 1756 he became Court Kapellmeister to the fused courts of Weimar, Gotha, and Eisenach. When this arrangement was dissolved in 1758, he retained his position and worked in the administration of the ducal finances in Eisenach. He publ. *Sammlung auserlesener Fabeln mit Melodeyen* (ed. by H. Kretzschmar in Denkmäler Deutscher Tonkunst, vol. 42, 1910) and other works. Only a small portion of his works has been publ.; his Passion oratorio, *O Seele, deren Sehen,* is in Denkmäler Deutscher Tonkunst, vol. 48, 1914. A sonata is in K. Geiringer, *Music of the Bach*

Family: An Anthology (Cambridge, Mass., 1955). Two fantasies and fugues for organ are found in D. Hellmann, ed., *Orgelwerke der Familie Bach* (Leipzig, 1967). —**NS/LK/DM**

Bach, Johann(es Hans), eldest son of **Johann(es Hans)** "der Spielmann"; b. Wechmar, Nov. 26, 1604; d. Erfurt, May 13, 1673. He was apprenticed to Christoph Hoffmann, Stadtpfeifer in Suhl. He was a town musician in Erfurt, and, from 1636, organist at the Predigerkirche there. Several of his compositions are extant. —**NS/LK/DM**

Bach [I], Johann Jacob, father of **Johann Ludwig;** b. Wolfsbehringen, Sept. 12, 1655; d. Ruhla, Dec. 11, 1718. He was organist in Thal before serving as cantor in Steinbach, Wasungen, and Ruhla.—**NS/LK/DM**

Bach [II], Johann Jacob, son of **Johann Ambrosius** and brother of **Johann Sebastian;** b. Eisenach (baptized), Feb. 11, 1682; d. Stockholm, April 16, 1722. He studied to be a Stadtpfeifer with J.H. Halle in Eisenach. In 1704 he became an oboist in the Swedish Guard. While serving in the Swedish Army, he was in Constantinople and received instruction in flute from P.G. Buffardin. From 1713 he was a royal chamber musician at the Stockholm court. Johann Sebastian composed his keyboard work, the *Capriccio sopra la lontananza del suo fratello dilettissimo* (Capriccio on the Departure of His Most Beloved Brother), BWV 992, for Johann Jacob's farewell to his native country. —**NS/LK/DM**

Bach, Johann (John) Christian (the "London" Bach), 11th and youngest surviving son of **Johann Sebastian;** b. Leipzig, Sept. 5, 1735; d. London, Jan. 1, 1782. He received early instruction in music from his father, after whose death in 1750 he went to Berlin to study with his brother **Carl Philipp Emanuel**. In 1754 he went to Italy, where he continued his studies with Padre Martini and also found a patron in Count Agostino Litta of Milan. He converted to the Roman Catholic faith in order to be able to obtain work, and became one of the organists at the Cathedral in Milan (1760–62). He also traveled throughout the country and composed several successful operas during his stay in Italy. In 1762 he went to England, where his highly acclaimed opera *Orione* was given its premiere in London on Feb. 19, 1763. In 1764 he was appointed music master to the Queen. From 1764 to 1781 he gave, together with C.F. Abel, a series of London concerts. When child Mozart was taken to London in 1764, Bach took great interest in him and improvised with him at the keyboard. Mozart retained a lifelong affection for him, and used three of Bach's piano sonatas as thematic material for his piano concertos. Bach was a highly prolific composer, numbering among his works some 90 syms., several piano concertos, six quintets, a Piano Sextet, violin sonatas, and numerous piano sonatas. In his music he adopted the *style galant* of the second half of the 18th century, with an emphasis on expressive "affects" and brilliance of instrumental display. He thus totally departed from the ideals of his father, and became historically a precursor of the Classical era as exemplified by the works of Mozart. Although he was known mainly as an instrumental composer, Bach also wrote successful operas, most of them to Italian librettos; among them were *Artaserse* (Turin, Dec. 26, 1760), *Catone in Utica* (Naples, Nov. 4, 1761), *Alessandro nell' Indie* (Naples, Jan. 20, 1762), *Orione, ossia Diana vendicata* (London, Feb. 19, 1763), *Zanaida* (London, May 7, 1763), *Adriano in Siria* (London, Jan. 26, 1765), *Carattaco* (London, Feb. 14, 1767), *Temistocle* (Mannheim, Nov. 4, 1772), *Lucio Silla* (Mannheim, Nov. 5, 1776), *La clemenza di Scipione* (London, April 4, 1778), and *Amadis de Gaule* (Paris, Dec. 14, 1779). See E. Warburton, general ed., *J.C. B., 1735–1782: The Collected Works* (48 vols., N.Y., 1988–95).

BIBL.: M. Schwarz, *J.C. B.: Sein Leben und seine Werke* (Leipzig, 1901); H. Schökel, *J.C. B. und die Instrumentalmusik seiner Zeit* (Wolfenbüttel, 1926); F. Tutenberg, *Die Sinfonik J.C. B.* (Wolfenbüttel, 1928); C. Terry, *John C. B.* (London, 1929; 2nd ed. by H.C. Robbins Landon, 1967); A. Wenk, *Beiträge zur Kenntnis des Opernschaffens von J.C. B.* (diss., Univ. of Frankfurt am Main, 1932); E. Reeser, *De zonen van Bach* (Amsterdam, 1941; Eng. tr., 1949); K. Geiringer, *The Bach Family: Seven Generations of Creative Genius* (N.Y., 1954); R. Seebandt, *Arientypen J.C. B.s* (diss., Humboldt Univ., Berlin, 1956); E. Downes, *The Operas of J.C. B. as a Reflection of the Dominant Trends in Opera Seria 1750–1780* (diss., Harvard Univ., 1958); J. White Jr., *The Concerted Symphonies of J.C. B.* (diss., Univ. of Mich., 1958); W. Haacke, *Die Söhne Bachs* (Königstein im Taunus, 1962); B. Mekota, *The Solo and Ensemble Keyboard Works of J.C. B.* (diss., Univ. of Mich., 1969); M. Vos, *The Liturgical Choral Works of J.C. B.* (diss., Washington Univ., St. Louis, 1969); E. Warburton, *A Study of J.C. B.'s Operas* (diss., Oxford Univ., 1969); I. Baierle, *Die Klavierwerke von J.C. B.* (diss., Univ. of Graz, 1974); H. Gärtner, *J.C. B.: Mozarts Freund und Lehrmeister* (Munich, 1989); S. Roe, *The Keyboard Music of J.C. B.: Source Problems and Stylistic Development in the Solo and Ensemble Works* (N.Y., 1989); R. Allorto, *Gli anni milanesi di G.C. B. e le sue composizioni sacre* (Milan, 1992).—NS/LK/DM

Bach, Johann Ludwig, son of **Johann Jacob [I];** b. Thal (baptized), Feb. 6, 1677; d. Meiningen (buried), March 1, 1731. He was a great-grandson of Lips Bach (d. Oct. 10, 1620) In 1699 he became a court musician in Meiningen, where he was appointed cantor in 1703, and Court Kapellmeister in 1711. He wrote numerous vocal compositions as well as orch. works, but few have been preserved.

BIBL.: A. Jaffé, *The Cantatas of J.L. B.* (diss., Boston Univ., 1957).—NS/LK/DM

Bach, Johann Michael, brother of **Johann Christoph;** b. Arnstadt, Aug. 9, 1648; d. Gehren, May 17, 1694. He was the father of Maria Barbara, first wife of **Johann Sebastian.** From 1673 he was organist and town clerk of Gehren, where he also worked as a maker of instruments. His works are listed in the *Bach-Jahrbuch* (1907, pp. 109–32); many of them are included in *Das Erbe deutscher Musik* (vol. I, Leipzig, 1935); motets of his are publ. in Denkmäler Deutscher Tonkunst (vols. 49 and 50, 1915). Some of his organ compositions are found in *Das Erbe deutscher Musik* (vol. IX, Leipzig, 1937); 72 organ chorales are included in D. Hellmann, ed., *Orgelwerke der Familie Bach* (Leipzig, 1967); 25 such works,

including 13 recently discovered pieces, are included in C. Wolff, ed., *The Neumeister Collection of Chorale Preludes from the Bach Circle (Yale Univ. Manuscript LM 4708)* (facsimile ed., New Haven, 1986).—NS/LK/DM

Bach, Johann Nicolaus, eldest son of **Johann Christoph;** b. Eisenach, Oct. 10, 1669; d. Jena, Nov. 4, 1753. He was educated at the Univ. of Jena. In 1694 he became organist at Jena, and in 1719 was also at the Univ. He was an expert on organ building and also made keyboard instruments. He wrote a fine *Missa* (Kyrie and Gloria; ed. by A. Fareanu and V. Junk, Leipzig, 1920), a comic cantata, *Der Jenaische Wein- und Bierrufer*, a scene from life at Jena Univ. (ed. by F. Stein, Leipzig, 1921), suites for keyboard, which are not preserved, and organ chorales, of which only one is known. —NS/LK/DM

Bach, Johann Sebastian, the most revered member of the family, whose stature as a composer has led him to be acclaimed as the supreme arbiter and lawgiver of music, a master comparable in greatness of stature with Aristotle in philosophy and Leonardo da Vinci in art; b. Eisenach, March 21 (baptized, March 23), 1685; d. Leipzig, July 28, 1750. He was a member of an illustrious family of musicians who were active in various capacities as performing artists, composers, and teachers. That so many Bachs were musicians lends support to the notion that music is a hereditary faculty, that some subliminal cellular unit may be the nucleus of musicality. The word "Bach" itself means "stream" in the German language; the rhetorical phrase that Johann Sebastian Bach was not a mere stream but a whole ocean of music ("Nicht Bach aber Meer haben wir hier") epitomizes Bach's encompassing magnitude. Yet despite the grandeur of the phenomenon of Bach, he was not an isolated figure dwelling in the splendor of his genius apart from the zeitgeist, the spirit of his time. Just as Aristotle was not only an abstract philosopher but also an educator (Alexander the Great was his pupil), just as Leonardo da Vinci was not only a painter of portraits but also a practical man of useful inventions, so Bach was a mentor to young students, a master organist and instructor who spent his life within the confines of his native Thuringia as a teacher and composer of works designed for immediate performance in church and in the schoolroom. Indeed, the text of the dedication of his epoch-making work *Das wohltemperierte Clavier oder Praeludia und Fugen* emphasizes its pedagogical aspect: "The Well-tempered Clavier, or Preludes and Fugues in all tones and semitones, both with the major third of Ut Re Mi, and the minor third of Re Mi Fa, composed and notated for the benefit and exercise of musical young people eager to learn, as well as for a special practice for those who have already achieved proficiency and skill in this study." The MS is dated 1722. Bach's system of "equal temperament" (which is the meaning of "well-tempered" in the title *Well-tempered Clavier*) postulated the division of the octave into 12 equal semitones, making it possible to transpose and to effect a modulation into any key, a process unworkable in the chaotic tuning of keyboard instruments before Bach's time. Bach was not the first to attempt the tempered division, however. J.C.F. Fischer anticipated him in his collection *Ariadne musica* (with the allusion to the thread of Ariadne that allowed Theseus to find his way out of the Cretan labyrinth); publ. in 1700, it contained 20 preludes and fugues in 19 different keys. Undoubtedly Bach was aware of this ed.; actually, the subjects of several of Bach's preludes and fugues are similar to the point of identity to the themes of Fischer's work. These coincidences do not detract from the significance of Bach's accomplishment, for it is the beauty and totality of development that makes Bach's work vastly superior to those of any of his putative predecessors.

The advent of Bach marked the greatest flowering of Baroque music. Although he wrote most of his contrapuntal works as a didactic exercise, there are in his music extraordinary visions into the remote future; consider, for instance, the A-minor Fugue of the first book of the *Well-tempered Clavier*, in which the inversion of the subject seems to violate all the rules of proper voice-leading in its bold leap from the tonic upward to the seventh of the scale and then up a third. The answer to the subject of the F minor Fugue of the first book suggests the chromatic usages of later centuries. In the art of variations, Bach was supreme. A superb example is his set of keyboard pieces known as the *Goldberg Variations*, so named because it was commissioned by the Russian diplomat Kayserling through the mediation of Bach's pupil Johann Gottlieb Goldberg, who was in Kayserling's service as a harpsichord player. These variations are listed by Bach as the fourth part of the *Clavier-Übung*; the didactic title of this division is characteristic of Bach's intention to write music for utilitarian purposes, be it for keyboard exercises, for church services, or for chamber music. A different type of Bach's great musical projections is exemplified by his *Concerts à plusieurs instruments*, known popularly as the *Brandenburg Concertos*, for they were dedicated to Christian Ludwig, margrave of Brandenburg. They represent the crowning achievement of the Baroque. Numbers 2, 4, and 5 of the *Brandenburg Concertos* are essentially concerti grossi, in which a group of solo instruments—the concertino—is contrasted with the accompanying string orch. Finally, *Die Kunst der Fuge*, Bach's last composition, which he wrote in 1749, represents an encyclopedia of fugues, canons, and various counterpoints based on the same theme. Here Bach's art of purely technical devices, such as inversion, canon, augmentation, diminution, double fugue, triple fugue, at times appearing in fantastic optical symmetry so that the written music itself forms a balanced design, is calculated to instruct the musical mind as well as delight the aural sense. Of these constructions, the most extraordinary is represented by *Das musikalische Opfer*, composed by Bach for Frederick the Great of Prussia. Bach's second son, **Carl Philipp Emanuel**, who served as chamber musician to the court of Prussia, arranged for Bach to visit Frederick's palace in Potsdam; Bach arrived there, accompanied by his son **Wilhelm Friedemann**, on May 7, 1747. The ostensible purpose of Bach's visit was to test the Silbermann pianos installed in the palace. The King, who liked to flaunt his love for the arts and sciences, gave Bach a musical theme of his own

invention and asked him to compose a fugue upon it. Bach also presented an organ recital at the Heiliggeistkirche in Potsdam and attended a chamber music concert held by the King; on that occasion he improvised a fugue in six parts on a theme of his own. Upon his return to Leipzig, Bach set to work on the King's theme. Gallantly, elegantly, he inscribed the work, in scholastic Latin, "Regis Iussu Cantio et Reliqua Canonica Arte Resoluta" ("At the King's command, the cantus and supplements are in a canonic manner resolved"). The initials of the Latin words form the acronym RICERCAR, a technical term etymologically related to the word "research" and applied to any study that is instructive in nature. The work is subdivided into 13 sections; it includes a puzzle canon in two parts, marked "quaerendo invenietis" ("you will find it by seeking"). Bach had the score engraved, and sent it to the King on July 7, 1747. Intellectually independent as Bach was, he never questioned the immanent rights of established authority. He was proud of the title Royal Polish and Electoral Saxon Court Composer to the King of Poland and Elector of Saxony, bestowed upon him in 1736 while he was in the service of Duke Christian of Weissenfels, and he even regarded the position of cantor of the Thomasschule in Leipzig as inferior to it. In his dedications to royal personages he adhered to the customary humble style, which was extended even to the typography of his dedicatory prefaces. In such dedications the name of the exalted commissioner was usually printed in large letters, with conspicuous indentation, while Bach's own signature, preceded by elaborate verbal genuflection, appeared in the smallest type of the typographer's box.

Bach's biography is singularly lacking in dramatic events. He attended the Latin school in Eisenach, and apparently was a good student, as demonstrated by his skill in the Latin language. His mother died in 1694; his father remarried and died soon afterward. Bach's school years were passed at the Lyceum in the town of Ohrdruf; his older brother **Johann Christoph** lived there; he helped Bach in his musical studies; stories that he treated Bach cruelly must be dismissed as melodramatic inventions. Through the good offices of Elias Herda, cantor of the Ohrdruf school, Bach received an opportunity to move, for further education, to Lüneburg; there he was admitted to the Mettenchor of the Michaeliskirche. In March of 1703 he obtained employment as an attendant to Johann Ernst, Duke of Weimar; he was commissioned to make tests on the new organ of the Neukirche in Arnstadt; on Aug. 9, 1703, he was appointed organist there. In Oct. 1705 he obtained a leave of absence to travel to Lübeck to hear the famous organist Dietrich Buxtehude. The impetus of Bach's trip was presumably the hope of obtaining Buxtehude's position as organist upon his retirement, but there was a peculiar clause attached to the contract for such a candidate: Buxtehude had five unmarried daughters; his successor was expected to marry the eldest of them. Buxtehude himself obtained his post through such an expedient, but Bach apparently was not prepared for matrimony under such circumstances.

On June 15, 1707, Bach became organist at the Blasiuskirche in Mühlhausen. On Oct. 17, 1707, he married his cousin Maria Barbara Bach, who was the daughter of **Johann Michael Bach**. On Feb. 4, 1708, Bach composed his cantata *Gott ist mein König* for the occasion of the installation of a new Mühlhausen town council. This was the first work of Bach's that was publ. Although the circumstances of his employment in Mühlhausen were seemingly favorable, Bach resigned his position on June 25, 1708, and accepted the post of court organist to Duke Wilhelm Ernst of Weimar. In Dec. 1713 Bach visited Halle, the birthplace of Handel; despite its proximity to Bach's own place of birth in Eisenach, the two great composers never met. On March 2, 1714, Duke Wilhelm Ernst offered Bach the position of Konzertmeister. In Sept. 1717 Bach went to Dresden to hear the famous French organist Louis Marchand, who resided there at the time. It was arranged that Bach and Marchand would hold a contest as virtuosos, but Marchand left Dresden before the scheduled event. This anecdote should not be interpreted frivolously as Marchand's fear of competing; other factors may have intervened to prevent the meeting. Johann Samuel Drese, the Weimar music director, died on Dec. 1, 1716; Bach expected to succeed him in that prestigious position, but the Duke gave the post to Drese's son. Again, this episode should not be interpreted as the Duke's lack of appreciation for Bach's superior abilities; the appointment may have merely followed the custom of letting such administrative posts remain in the family. In 1717 Bach accepted the position of Kapellmeister and music director to Prince Leopold of Anhalt in Cöthen, but a curious contretemps developed when the Duke of Weimar refused to release Bach from his obligation, and even had him held under arrest from Nov. 6 to Dec. 2, 1717, before Bach was finally allowed to proceed to Cöthen. The Cöthen period was one of the most productive in Bach's life; there he wrote his great set of *Brandenburg Concertos*, the *Clavierbüchlein für Wilhelm Friedemann Bach*, and the first book of *Das Wohltemperierte Clavier*. In Oct. 1719 Bach was in Halle once more, but again missed meeting Handel, who had already gone to England. In 1720 Bach accompanied Prince Leopold to Karlsbad. A tragedy supervened when Bach's devoted wife was taken ill and died before Bach could be called to her side; she was buried on July 7, 1720, leaving Bach to take care of their seven children. In 1720 Bach made a long journey to Hamburg, where he met the aged Reinken, who was then 97 years old. It is a part of the Bach legend that Reinken was greatly impressed with Bach's virtuosity and exclaimed, "I believed that the art of organ playing was dead, but it lives in you!" Bach remained a widower for nearly a year and a half before he married his second wife, Anna Magdalena Wilcken, a daughter of a court trumpeter at Weissenfels, on Dec. 3, 1721. They had 13 children during their happy marital life. New avenues were opened to Bach when Johann Kuhnau, the cantor of Leipzig, died, on June 5, 1722. Although Bach applied for his post, the Leipzig authorities offered it first to Telemann of Hamburg, and when he declined, to Christoph Graupner of Darmstadt; only when Graupner was unable to obtain a release from his current position was Bach given the post. He traveled to Leipzig on Feb. 7, 1723, for a trial performance, earning a favorable recep-

tion. On April 22, 1723, Bach was elected to the post of cantor of the city of Leipzig and was officially installed on May 31, 1723. As director of church music, Bach's duties included the care of musicians for the Thomaskirche, Nicolaikirche, Matthaeikirche, and Petrikirche, and he was also responsible for the provision of the music to be performed at the Thomaskirche and Nicolaikirche. There were more mundane obligations that Bach was expected to discharge, such as gathering firewood for the Thomasschule, about which Bach had recurrent disputes with the rector; eventually he sought the intervention of the Elector of Saxony in the affair. It was in Leipzig that Bach created his greatest sacred works: the *St. John Passion*, the Mass in B minor, and the *Christmas Oratorio*. In 1729 he organized at the Thomasschule the famous Collegium Musicum, composed of professional musicians and univ. students with whom he gave regular weekly concerts; he led this group until 1737, and again from 1739 to 1741. He made several visits to Dresden, where his eldest son, Wilhelm Friedemann, served as organist at the Sophienkirche. In June 1747 Bach joined the Societät der Musikalischen Wissenschaften, a scholarly organization founded by a former member of the Collegium Musicum, Lorenz C. Mizler, a learned musician, Latinist, and mathematician who spent his life confounding his contemporaries and denouncing them as charlatans and ignorant pretenders to knowledge. The rules of the society required an applicant to submit a sample of his works; Bach contributed a triple canon in 6 parts and presented it, along with the canonic variations *Vom Himmel hoch da komm ich her*. This was one of Bach's last works. He suffered from a cataract that was gradually darkening his vision. A British optician named John Taylor, who plied his trade in Saxony, operated on Bach's eyes in the spring of 1749; the operation, performed with the crude instruments of the time, left Bach almost totally blind. The same specialist operated also on Handel, with no better results. The etiology of Bach's last illness is unclear. It is said that on July 18, 1750, his vision suddenly returned (possibly when the cataract receded spontaneously), but a cerebral hemorrhage supervened, and a few days later Bach was dead. Bach's great contrapuntal work, *Die Kunst der Fuge*, remained unfinished. The final page bears this inscription by C.P.E. Bach: "Upon this Fugue, in which the name B-A-C-H is applied as a countersubject, the author died." Bach's widow, Anna Magdalena, survived him by nearly 10 years; she died on Feb. 27, 1760. In 1895 Wilhelm His, an anatomy prof. at the Univ. of Leipzig, performed an exhumation of Bach's body, made necessary because of the deterioration of the wooden coffin, and took remarkable photographs of Bach's skeleton, which he publ. under the title *J.S. Bach, Forschungen über dessen Grabstätte, Gebeine und Antlitz* (Leipzig, 1895). On July 28, 1949, on the 199th anniversary of Bach's death, his coffin was transferred to the choir room of the Thomaskirche.

Of Bach's 20 children, ten reached maturity. His sons Wilhelm Friedemann, Carl Philipp Emanuel, **Johann Christoph Friedrich**, and **Johann (John) Christian** (the "London" Bach) made their mark as independent composers. Among Bach's notable pupils were Johann Friedrich Agricola, Johann Christoph Altnikol, Heinrich

Nicolaus Gerber, Johann Gottlieb Goldberg, Gottfried August Homilius, Johann Philipp Kirnberger, Johann Christian Kittel, Johann Tobias Krebs, and Johann Ludwig Krebs. It is historically incorrect to maintain that Bach was not appreciated by his contemporaries; Bach's sons Carl Philipp Emanuel and the "London" Bach kept his legacy alive for a generation after Bach's death. True, they parted from Bach's art of contrapuntal writing; Carl Philipp Emanuel turned to the fashionable *style galant*, and wrote keyboard works of purely harmonic content. The first important biography of Bach was publ. in 1802, by J.N. Forkel.

Dramatic accounts of music history are often inflated. It is conventional to say that Bach's music was rescued from oblivion by Mendelssohn, who conducted the *St. Matthew Passion* in Berlin in 1829, but Mozart and Beethoven had practiced Bach's preludes and fugues. Bach's genius was never dimmed; he was never a prophet without a world. In 1850 the centennial of Bach's death was observed by the inception of the Leipzig Bach- Gesellschaft, a society founded by Carl Becker, Moritz Hauptmann, Otto Jahn, and Robert Schumann. Concurrently, the publishing firm of Breitkopf & Härtel inaugurated the publication of the complete ed. of Bach's works. A Neue Bach-Gesellschaft was founded in 1900; it supervised the publication of the important *Bach-Jahrbuch*, a scholarly journal begun in 1904. The bicentennial of Bach's death, in 1950, brought about a new series of memorials and celebrations. With the development of recordings, Bach's works were made available to large masses of the public. Modern composers, even those who champion the total abandonment of all conventional methods of composition and the abolition of musical notation, are irresistibly drawn to Bach as a precursor; suffice it to mention Alban Berg's use of Bach's chorale *Es ist genug* in the concluding section of his Violin Concerto dedicated to the memory of Alma Mahler's young daughter. It is interesting to note also that Bach's famous acronym B-A-C-H consists of four different notes in a chromatic alternation, thus making it possible to use it as an element of a 12-tone row. The slogan "Back to Bach," adopted by composers of the early 20th century, seems to hold true for every musical era. The 250th anniversary of Bach's death was commemorated in 2000 with special observances and concerts around the world.

In the list of Bach's works given below, each composition is identified by the BWV (Bach-Werke-Verzeichnis) number established by W. Schmieder in his *Thematisch-systematisches Verzeichnis der musikalischen Werke von J.S. B. Bach-Werke-Verzeichnis* (Leipzig, 1950; 2nd ed., rev., 1990).

WORKS: CHURCH CANTATAS: About 200 are extant. The following list gives the BWV number, title, and date of first perf.: 1, *Wie schön leuchtet der Morgenstern* (March 25, 1725); 2, *Ach Gott, vom Himmel sieh darein* (June 18, 1724); 3, *Ach Gott, wie manches Herzeleid* (Jan. 14, 1725); 4, *Christ lag in Todesbanden* (c. 1707–8); 5, *Wo soll ich fliehen hin* (Oct. 15, 1724); 6, *Bleib bei uns, denn es will Abend werden* (April 2, 1725); 7, *Christ unser Herr zum Jordan kam* (June 24, 1724); 8, *Liebster Gott, wann werd ich sterben?* (Sept. 24, 1724); 9, *Es ist das Heil uns kommen her* (c. 1732–35); 10, *Meine Seel erhebt den Herren* (July 2, 1724); 11, *Lobet Gott in seinen Reichen* (Ascension oratorio; May 19, 1735); 12, *Weinen, Klagen,*

Sorgen, Zagen (April 22, 1714); 13, *Meine Seufzer, meine Tränen* (Jan. 20, 1726); 14, *Wär' Gott nicht mit uns diese Zeit* (Jan. 30, 1735); 16, *Herr Gott, dich Loben wir* (Jan. 1, 1726); 17, *Wer Dank opfert, der preiset mich* (Sept. 22, 1726); 18, *Gleichwie der Regen und Schnee vom Himmel fällt* (c. 1714); 19, *Es erhub sich ein Streit* (Sept. 29, 1726); 20, *O Ewigkeit, du Donnerwort* (June 11, 1724); 21, *Ich hatte viel Bekummernis* (c. 1714); 22, *Jesus nahm zu sich die Zwölfe* (Feb. 7, 1723); 23, *Du wahrer Gott und Davids Sohn* (Feb. 7, 1723); 24, *Ein ungefärbt Gemüte* (June 20, 1723); 25, *Es ist nicht Gesundes an meinem Leibe* (Aug. 29, 1723); 26, *Ach wie flüchtig, ach wie nichtig* (Nov. 19, 1724); 27, *Wer weiss, wie nahe mir mein Ende!* (Oct. 6, 1726); 28, *Gottlob! nun geht das Jahr zu Ende* (Dec. 30, 1725); 29, *Wir danken dir, Gott, wir danken dir* (Aug. 27, 1731); 30, *Freue dich, erlöste Schar* (c. 1738); 31, *Der Himmel lacht! die Erde jubilieret* (April 21, 1715); 32, *Liebster Jesu, mein Verlangen* (Jan. 13, 1726); 33, *Allein zu dir, Herr Jesu Christ* (Sept. 3, 1724); 34, *O ewiges Feuer, O Ursprung der Liebe* (based upon 34a; early 1740s); 34a, *O ewiges Feuer, O Ursprung der Liebe* (part of score not extant; 1726); 35, *Geist und Seele wird verwirret* (Sept. 8, 1726); 36c, *Schwingt freudig euch empor* (based upon secular cantata 36c; Dec. 2, 1731); 37, *Wer da gläubet und getauft wird* (May 18, 1724); 38, *Aus tiefer Not schrei ich zu dir* (Oct. 29, 1724); 39, *Brich dem Hungrigen dein Brot* (June 23, 1726); 40, *Dazu ist erschienen der Sohn Gottes* (Dec. 26, 1723); 41, *Jesu, nun sei gepreiset* (Jan. 1, 1725); 42, *Am Abend aber desselbigen Sabbats* (April 8, 1725); 43, *Gott fähret auf mit Jauchzen* (May 30, 1726); 44, *Sie werden euch in den Bann tun* (May 21, 1724); 45, *Es ist dir gesagt, Mensch, was gut ist* (Aug. 11, 1726); 46, *Schauet doch und sehet* (Aug. 1, 1723); 47, *Wer sich selbst erhöhet* (Oct. 13, 1726); 48, *Ich elender Mensch, wer wird mich erlösen* (Oct. 3, 1723); 49, *Ich geh und suche mit Verlangen* (Nov. 3, 1726); 50, *Nun ist das Heil und die Kraft* (date unknown); 51, *Jauchzet Gott in allen Landen!* (Sept. 17, 1730); 52, *Falsche Welt, dir trau' ich nicht* (Nov. 24, 1726); 54, *Widerstehe doch der Sünde* (July 15, 1714); 55, *Ich armer Mensch, ich Sündenknecht* (Nov. 17, 1726); 56, *Ich will den Kreuzstab gerne tragen* (Oct. 27, 1726); 57, *Selig ist der Mann* (Dec. 26, 1725); 58, *Ach Gott, wie manches Herzeleid* (Jan. 5, 1727); 59, *Wer mich liebet, der wird mein Wort halten* (c. 1723–24); 60, *O Ewigkeit, du Donnerwort* (Nov. 7, 1723); 61, *Nun komm, der Heiden Heiland* (1714); 62, *Nun komm, der Heiden Heiland* (Dec. 3, 1724); 63, *Christen, ätzet diesen Tag* (c. 1716); 64, *Sehet, welch eine Liebe* (Dec. 27, 1723); 65, *Sie werden aus Saba alle kommen* (Jan. 6, 1724); 66, *Erfreut euch, ihr Herzen* (based upon lost secular cantata 66a; April 10, 1724); 67, *Halt' im Gedächtnis Jesum Christ* (April 16, 1724); 68, *Also hat Gott die Welt geliebt* (May 21, 1725); 69, *Lobe den Herrn, meine Seele* (based upon 69a; 1740s); 69a, *Lobe den Herrn, meine Seele* (Aug. 15, 1723); 70, *Wachet! betet! betet! wachet!* (based upon 70a; Nov. 21, 1723); 70a, *Wachet! betet! betet! wachet!* (music not extant; Dec. 6, 1716); 71, *Gott ist mein König* (Feb. 4, 1708); 72, *Alles nur nach Gottes Willen* (Jan. 27, 1726); 73, *Herr, wie du willst, so schick's mit mir* (Jan. 23, 1724); 74, *Wer mich liebet, der wird mein Wort halten* (based partly upon 59; May 20, 1725); 75, *Die Elenden sollen essen* (May 30, 1723); 76, *Die Himmel erzählen die Ehre Gottes* (June 6, 1723); 77, *Du sollst Gott, deinen Herren, lieben* (Aug. 22, 1723); 78, *Jesu, der du meine Seele* (Sept. 10, 1724); 79, *Gott der Herr ist Sonn und Schild* (Oct. 31, 1725); 80, *Ein' feste Burg ist unser Gott* (based upon 80a; Oct. 31, 1724); 80a, *Alles, was von Gott geboren* (music not extant; 1715); 80b, *Ein' feste Burg ist unser Gott* (Oct. 31, 1723); 81, *Jesus schläft, was soll ich hoffen?* (Jan. 30, 1724); 82, *Ich habe genug* (Feb. 2, 1727); 83, *Erfreute Zeit im neuen Bunde* (Feb. 2, 1724); 84, *Ich bin vergnügt mit meinem Glücke* (Feb. 9, 1727); 85, *Ich bin ein guter Hirt* (April 15, 1725); 86, *Wahrlich, wahrlich, ich sage euch* (May 14, 1724); 87, *Bisher habt ihr nichts gebeten* (May 6, 1725); 88, *Siehe, ich will viel Fischer aussenden* (July 21, 1726); 89,

Was soll ich aus dir machen, Ephraim? (Oct. 24, 1723); 90, *Es reisset euch ein schrecklich Ende* (Nov. 14, 1723); 91, *Gelobet seist du, Jesu Christ* (Dec. 25, 1724); 92, *Ich hab in Gottes Herz und Sinn* (Jan. 28, 1725); 93, *Wer nur den lieben Gott lässt walten* (July 9, 1724); 94, *Was frag ich nach der Welt* (Aug. 6, 1724); 95, *Christus, der ist mein Leben* (Sept. 12, 1723); 96, *Herr Christ, der ein'ge Gottessohn* (Oct. 8, 1724); 97, *In allen meinen Taten* (1734); 98, *Was Gott tut, das ist wohlgetan* (Nov. 10, 1726); 99, *Was Gott tut, das ist wohlgetan* (Sept. 17, 1724); 100, *Was Gott tut, das ist wohlgetan* (c. 1732–35); 101, *Nimm von uns, Herr, du treuer Gott* (Aug. 13, 1724); 102, *Herr, deine Augen sehen nach dem Glauben* (Aug. 25, 1726); 103, *Ihr werdet weinen und heulen* (April 22, 1725); 104, *Du Hirte Israel* (April 23, 1724); 105, *Herr, gehe nicht ins Gericht* (July 25, 1723); 106, *Gottes Zeit ist die allerbeste Zeit* (c. 1707); 107, *Was willst du dich betrüben* (July 23, 1724); 108, *Es ist euch gut, dass ich hingehe* (April 29, 1725); 109, *Ich glaube, lieber Herr, hilf meinem Unglauben!* (Oct. 17, 1723); 110, *Unser Mund sei voll Lachens* (Dec. 25, 1725); 111, *Was mein Gott will, das g'scheh allzeit* (Jan. 21, 1725); 112, *Der Herr ist mein getreuer Hirt* (April 8, 1731); 113, *Herr Jesu Christ, du höchstes Gut* (Aug. 20, 1724); 114, *Ach, lieben Christen, seid getrost* (Oct. 1, 1724); 115, *Mache dich, mein Geist, bereit* (Nov. 5, 1724); 116, *Du Friedefürst, Herr Jesu Christ* (Nov. 26, 1724); 117, *Sei Lob und Ehr dem höchsten Gut* (c. 1728–31); 119, *Preise, Jerusalem, den Herrn* (Aug. 30, 1723); 120, *Gott, man lobet dich in der Stille* (c. 1728–29); 120a, *Herr Gott, Beherrscher aller Dinge* (based upon 120; part of score not extant; c. 1729); 120b, *Gott, man lobet dich in der Stille* (based upon 120; music not extant; 1730); 121, *Christum wir sollen loben schon* (Dec. 26, 1724); 122, *Das neugebor'ne Kindelein* (Dec. 31, 1724); 123, *Liebster Immanuel, Herzog der Frommen* (Jan. 6, 1725); 124, *Meinen Jesum lass ich nicht* (Jan. 7, 1725); 125, *Mit Fried' und Freud' ich fahr dahin* (Feb. 2, 1725); 126, *Erhalt' uns, Herr, bei deinem Wort* (Feb. 4, 1725); 127, *Herr Jesu Christ, wahr'r Mensch und Gott* (Feb. 11, 1725); 128, *Auf Christi Himmelfahrt allein* (May 10, 1725); 129, *Gelobet sei der Herr, mein Gott* (c. 1726–27); 130, *Herr Gott, dich loben alle wir* (Sept. 29, 1724); 131, *Aus der Tiefen rufe ich, Herr, zu dir* (1707); 132, *Bereitet die Wege, bereitet die Bahn!* (1715); 133, *Ich freue mich in dir* (Dec. 27, 1724); 134, *Ein Herz, das seinen Jesum lebend weiss* (based upon secular cantata 134a; April 11, 1724); 135, *Ach Herr, mich armen Sünder* (June 25, 1724); 136, *Erforsche mich, Gott, und erfahre mein Herz* (July 18, 1723); 137, *Lobe den Herren, den mächtigen König der Ehren* (Aug. 19, 1725); 138, *Warum betrübst du dich, mein Herz?* (Sept. 5, 1723); 139, *Wohl dem, der sich auf seinen Gott* (Nov. 12, 1724); 140, *Wachet auf, ruft uns die Stimme* (Nov. 25, 1731); 144, *Nimm, was dein ist, und gehe hin* (Feb. 6, 1724); 145, *Ich lebe, mein Herze, zu deinem Ergötzen* (c. 1729); 146, *Wir müssen durch viel Trübsal* (c. 1726–28); 147, *Herz und Mund und Tat und Leben* (based upon 147a; July 2, 1723); 147a, *Herz und Mund und Tat und Leben* (not extant; Dec. 20, 1716); 148, *Bringet dem Herrn Ehre seines Namens* (Sept. 19, 1723); 149, *Man singet mit Freuden vom Sieg* (c. 1728–29); 150, *Nach dir, Herr, verlanget mich* (c. 1708–9); 151, *Süsser Trost, mein Jesus kommt* (Dec. 27, 1725); 152, *Tritt auf die Glaubensbahn* (Dec. 30, 1714); 153, *Schau, lieber Gott, wie meine Feind'* (Jan. 2, 1724); 154, *Mein liebster Jesus ist verloren* (Jan. 9, 1724); 155, *Mein Gott, wie lang, ach lange* (Jan. 19, 1716); 156, *Ich steh' mit einem Fuss im Grabe* (Jan. 23, 1729); 157, *Ich lasse dich nicht, du segnest mich denn* (Feb. 6, 1727); 158, *Der Friede sei mit dir* (date unknown); 159, *Sehet, wir geh'n hinauf gen Jerusalem* (Feb. 27, 1729); 161, *Komm, du süsse Todesstunde* (Oct. 6, 1715); 162, *Ach! ich sehe, jetzt, da ich zur Hochzeit gehe* (Nov. 3, 1715); 163, *Nur jedem das Seine* (Nov. 24, 1715); 164, *Ihr, die ihr euch von Christo nennet* (Aug. 26, 1725); 165, *O heil'ges Geist- und Wasserbad* (June 16, 1715); 166, *Wo gehest du hin?* (May 7, 1724); 167, *Ihr Menschen, rühmet Gottes Liebe* (June 24, 1723); 168, *Tue Rechnung!*

Donnerwort (July 29, 1725); 169, *Gott soll allein mein Herze haben* (Oct. 20, 1726); 170, *Vergnügte Ruh', beliebte Seelenlust* (July 28, 1726); 171, *Gott, wie dein Name, so ist auch dein Ruhm* (c. 1729); 172, *Erschallet, ihr Lieder* (May 20, 1714); 173, *Erhöhtes Fleisch und Blut* (based upon secular cantata 173a; May 29, 1724); 174, *Ich liebe den Höchsten von ganzem Gemüte* (June 6, 1729); 175, *Er rufet seinen Schafen mit Namen* (May 22, 1725); 176, *Es ist ein trotzig, und versagt Ding* (May 27, 1725); 177, *Ich ruf zu dir, Herr Jesu Christ* (July 6, 1732); 178, *Wo Gott der Herr nicht bei uns hält* (July 30, 1724); 179, *Siehe zu, dass deine Gottesfurcht* (Aug. 8, 1723); 180, *Schmücke dich, o liebe Seele* (Oct. 22, 1724); 181, *Leichtgesinnte Flattergeister* (Feb. 13, 1724); 182, *Himmelskönig, sei willkommen* (1714); 183, *Sie werden euch in den Bann tun* (May 13, 1725); 184, *Erwünschtes Freudenlicht* (based upon lost secular cantata 184a; May 30, 1724); 185, *Barmherziges Herze der ewigen Liebe* (July 14, 1715); 186, *Ärg're dich, o Seele, nicht* (based upon 186a; July 11, 1723); 186a, *Ärg're dich o Seele, nicht* (not extant; Dec. 13, 1716); 187, *Es wartet alles auf dich* (Aug. 4, 1726); 188, *Ich habe meine Zuversicht* (c. 1728); 190, *Singet dem Herrn ein neues Lied!* (part of score not extant; Jan. 1, 1724); 190a, *Singet dem Herrn ein neues Lied!* (based upon 190; not extant; 1730); 191, *Gloria in excelsis Deo* (based upon 232, Mass in B minor; c. 1740); 192, *Nun danket alle Gott* (part of score not extant; 1730); 193, *Ihr Tore zu Zion* (c. 1727); 194, *Höchsterwünschtes Freudenfest* (based upon lost secular cantata 194a; Nov. 2, 1723); 195, *Dem Gerechten muss das Licht* (c. 1737); 196, *Der Herr denket an uns* (c. 1708); 197, *Gott ist uns're Zuversicht* (c. 1742); 197a, *Ehre sie Gott in der Höhe* (part of score not extant, c. 1728); 199, *Mein Herze schwimmt im Blut* (Aug. 12, 1714); 200, *Bekennen will ich seinen Namen* (fragment only extant; c. 1742). BWV numbers have been assigned to the following lost or incomplete cantatas: 223, *Meine Seele soll Gott loben* (not extant; date unknown); 224a, *Klagt, Kinder, klagt es aller Welt* (music not extant; March 24, 1729); Anh. 1, *Gesegnet ist die Zuversicht* (not extant; date unknown); Anh. 2, fragment only; Anh. 3, *Gott, gib dein Gerichte dem Könige* (music not extant; 1730); Anh. 4, *Wünschet Jerusalem Glück* (music not extant; c. 1727); Anh. 4a, *Wünschet Jerusalem Glück* (music not extant; 1730); Anh. 5, *Lobet den Herrn, alle seine Heerscharen* (music not extant; Dec. 10, 1718); Anh. 14, *Sein Segen fliesst daher wie ein Strom* (music not extant; Feb. 12, 1725); Anh. 15, *Siehe, der Hüter Israel* (not extant; April 27, 1724); Anh. 17, *Mein Gott, nimm die gerechte Seele* (not extant; date unknown); 1,045, title unknown (autograph fragment only extant; c. 1742); also the following without BWV numbers: *Herrscher des Himmels, König der Ehren* (final chorus only, based upon secular cantata 208, extant; Aug. 29, 1740); *Ich bin ein Pilgrim auf der Welt* (fragment of 4th movement only extant; April 18, 1729); *Ihr wallenden Wolken* (not extant; date unknown); *Leb' ich oder leb' ich nicht* (music not extant; May 19, 1715); *Sie werden euch in den Bann tun* (6-bar sketch only); etc. BWV numbers have been assigned to the following doubtful and spurious cantatas: 15, *Denn du wirst meine Seele* (by J.L. Bach); 53, *Schlage doch, gewünschte Stunde* (by G.M. Hoffmann); 141, *Das ist je gewisslich wahr* (by Telemann); 142, *Uns ist ein Kind geboren* (doubtful); 143, *Lobe den Herrn, meine Seele* (doubtful); 160, *Ich weiss, dass mein Erlöser lebt* (by Telemann); 189, *Meine Seele rühmt und preist* (doubtful); 217, *Gedenke, Herr, wie es uns gehet* (spurious); 218, *Gott der Hoffnung erfülle euch* (by Telemann); 219, *Siehe, es hat überwunden der Löwe* (by Telemann); 220, *Lobt ihn mit Herz und Munde* (spurious); 221, *Wer sucht die Pracht, wer wünscht den Glanz* (spurious); 222, *Mein Odem ist schwach* (by J.E. Bach); Anh. 16, *Schliesset die Gruft! ihr Trauerglocken* (not extant; doubtful); also without BWV number,

Siehe, eine Jungfrau ist schwanger (doubtful). **SECULAR CAN-TATAS:** 22 are extant in full: 30a, *Angenehmes Wiederau, freue dich* (Sept. 28, 1737); 36b, *Die Freude reget sich* (c. 1735); 36c, *Schwingt freudig euch empor* (1725); 134a, *Die Zeit, die Tag und Jahre macht* (Jan. 1, 1719); 173a, *Durchlaucht'ster Leopold* (c. 1722); 198, *Trauer Ode: Lass, Fürstin, lass noch einen Strahl* (Oct. 17, 1727); 201, *Der Streit zwischen Phoebus und Pan: Geschwinde, ihr wirbeln die Winde* (c. 1729); 202, *Weichet nur, betrübte Schatten* (c. 1718–23); 203, *Amore traditore* (date unknown); 204, *Ich bin in mir vergnügt* (c. 1726–27); 205, *Der zufriedengestellte Äolus: Zerreisset, zersprenget, zertrümmert die Gruft* (Aug. 3, 1725); 206, *Schleicht, spielende Wellen* (Oct. 7, 1736); 207, *Vereinigte Zwietracht der wechselnden Saiten* (Dec. 11, 1726); 207a, *Auf, schmetternde Töne* (Aug. 3, 1735); 208, *Was mir behagt, ist nur die muntre Jagd!* (c. 1713); 209, *Non sa che sia dolore* (c. 1734); 210, *O holder Tag, erwünschte Zeit* (c. 1740); 211, *Schweigt stille, plaudert nicht* (Coffee Cantata; c. 1734–35); 212, *Mer hahn en neue Oberkeet* (Peasant Cantata; Aug. 30, 1742); 213, *Hercules auf dem Scheidewege: Lasst uns sorgen, lasst uns wachen* (Sept. 5, 1733); 214, *Tönet, ihr Pauken! Erschallet, Trompeten!* (Dec. 8, 1733); 215, *Preise dein Glucke, gesegnetes Sachsen* (Oct. 5, 1734). BWV numbers have been assigned to the following lost or incomplete cantatas: 36a, *Steigt freudig in die Luft* (music not extant; Nov. 30, 1726); 66a, *Der Himmel dacht auf Anhalts Ruhm und Glück* (music not extant; Dec. 10, 1718); 184a, title unknown (not extant); 193a, *Ihr Häuser des Himmels, ihr scheinenden Lichter* (music not extant; Aug. 3, 1727); 194a, title unknown (not extant); 205a, *Blast Lärmen, ihr Feinde!* (based upon 205; music not extant; Feb. 19, 1734); 208a, *Was mir behagt, ist nur die muntre Jagd!* (music not extant; c. 1740–42); 210a, *O angenehme Melodei!* (music not extant; c. 1738–40); 216, *Vergnügte Pleissenstadt* (only partially extant; Feb. 5, 1728); 216a, *Erwählte Pleissenstadt* (music not extant; c. 1728); 249a, *Entfliehet, verschwindet, entweichet, ihr Sorgen* (music not extant; Feb. 23, 1725); 249b, *Die Feier des Genius: Verjaget, zerstreuet, zerrüttet, ihr Sterne* (music not extant; Aug. 25, 1726); Anh. 6, *Dich loben die lieblichen Strahlen* (music not extant; Jan. 1, 1720); Anh. 7, *Heut ist gewiss ein guter Tag* (music not extant; Dec. 10, 1720); Anh. 8, title unknown (not extant); Anh. 9, *Entfernet euch, ihr heitern Sterne* (music not extant; May 12, 1727); Anh. 10, *So kämpfet nur, ihr muntern Töne* (music not extant; Aug. 25, 1731); Anh. 11, *Es lebe der König, der Vater im Lande* (music not extant; Aug. 3, 1732); Anh. 12, *Frohes Volk, vergnügte Sachsen* (based upon Anh. 18; music not extant; Aug. 3, 1733); Anh. 13, *Willkommen! Ihr herrschenden Götter* (music not extant; April 28, 1738); Anh. 18, *Froher Tag, verlangte Stunden* (music not extant; June 5, 1732); Anh. 19, *Thomana sass annoch betrübt* (music not extant; Nov. 21, 1734); Anh. 20, title unknown (not extant); also, without BWV number, *Auf! süss entzückende Gewalt* (music not extant; Nov. 27, 1725). **OTHER CHURCH MUSIC:** 232, Mass in B minor (assembled c. 1747–49 from music previously composed by Bach); 233, 233a, 234–36, 4 *missae breves*: F major (Kyrie in F major), A major, G minor, G major (late 1730s); 237–41, 5 settings of the Sanctus: C major, D major, D minor, G major, D major (although preserved in Bach's own hand, these appear to be arrangements of works by other composers, 238 excepted); 243a, Magnificat in E-flat major (including 4 Christmas texts: *Vom Himmel hoch, Freut euch und jubiliert, Gloria in excelsis, Virga Jesse floruit*; Dec. 25, 1723); 243, a revision of the preceding, without Christmas texts, as Magnificat in D major (c. 1728–31); 244, *Matthäuspassion* (St. Matthew Passion; first perf. April 11, 1727, or April 15, 1729); 245, *Johannespassion* (St. John Passion; April 7, 1724; later rev.); 248, *Weihnachtsoratorium* (Christmas Oratorio), 6 cantatas for Christmas to Epiphany: *Jauchzet, frohlocket, auf preiset die Tage* (Dec. 25,

1734), *Und es waren Hirten in derselben Gegend* (Dec. 26, 1734), *Herrscher des Himmels, erhöre das Lallen* (Dec. 27, 1734), *Fallt mit Danken, fallt mit Loben* (Jan. 1, 1735), *Ehre sei dir, Gott, gesungen* (Jan. 2, 1735), *Herr, wenn die stolzen Feinde schnauben* (Jan. 6, 1735); 249, Easter Oratorio (first perf. as a cantata, April 1, 1725; rev. as an oratorio 1732–35); motets, including 225, *Singet dem Herrn ein neues Lied* (May 12, 1727), 226, *Der Geist hilft unsrer Schwachheit auf* (Oct. 24, 1729), 227, *Jesu, meine Freude* (July 18, 1723), 228, *Fürchte dich nicht* (Feb. 4, 1726), 229, *Komm, Jesu, komm!* (March 26, 1730), 230, *Lobet den Herrn alle Heiden* (date unknown). Also 247, *St. Mark Passion* (score and parts not extant; March 23, 1731; partial reconstruction from other works made by D. Hellmann, Stuttgart, 1964); 246, *St. Luke Passion* (spurious). **CHORALES:** 3 wedding chorales for 4 Voices: 250, *Was Gott tut das ist wohlgetan*; 251, *Sei Lob und Ehr' dem höchsten Gut*; 252, *Nun danket alle Gott*. Also, 186 arrangements for 4 Voices: 253, *Ach bleib bei uns, Herr Jesu Christ*; 254, *Ach Gott, erhör' mein Seufzen*; 255, *Ach Gott und Herr*; 256, *Ach lieben Christen, seid getrost*; 259, *Ach, was soll ich Sünder machen*; 260, *Allein Gott in der Höh' sei Ehr'*; 261, *Allein zu dir, Herr Jesu Christ*; 262, *Alle Menschen müssen sterben*; 263, *Alles ist an Gottes Segen*; 264, *Als der gütige Gott*; 265, *Als Jesus Christus in der Nacht*; 266, *Als vierzig Tag nach Ostern*; 267, *An Wasserflüssen Babylon*; 268, *Auf, auf, mein Herz, und du mein ganzer Sinn*; 269, *Aus meines Herzens Grunde*; 270, *Befiehl du deine Wege*; 271, *Befiehl du deine Wege*; 272, *Befiehl du deine Wege*; 273, *Christ, der du bist der helle Tag*; 274, *Christe, der du bist Tag und Licht*; 275, *Christe, du Beistand deiner Kreuzgemeinde*; 276, *Christ ist erstanden*; 277, *Christ lag in Todesbanden*; 278, *Christ lag in Todesbanden*; 279, *Christ lag in Todesbanden*; 280, *Christ, unser Herr, zum Jordan kam*; 281, *Christus, der ist mein Leben*; 282, *Christus, der ist mein Leben*; 283, *Christus, der uns selig macht*; 284, *Christus ist erstanden, hat überwunden*; 285, *Da der Herr Christ zu Tische sass*; 286, *Danket dem Herren*; 287, *Dank sei Gott in der Höhe*; 288, *Das alte Jahr vergangen ist*; 289, *Das alte Jahr vergangen ist*; 290, *Das walt' Gott Vater und Gott Sohn*; 291, *Das walt' mein Gott, Vater, Sohn und heiliger Geist*; 292, *Den Vater dort oben*; 293, *Der du bist drei in Einigkeit*; 294, *Der Tag, der ist so freudenreich*; 295, *Des heil'gen Geistes reiche Gnad'*; 296, *Die Nacht ist kommen*; 297, *Die Sonn' hat sich mit ihrem Glanz*; 298, *Dies sind die heil'gen zehn Gebot'*; 299, *Dir, dir, Jehova, will ich singen*; 300, *Du grosser Schmerzensmann*; 301, *Du, o schönes Weltgebaude*; 302, *Ein' feste Burg ist unser Gott*; 303, *Ein' feste Burg ist unser Gott*; 304, *Eins ist Not! ach Herr, dies Eine*; 305, *Erbarm' dich mein, o, Herre Gott*; 306, *Erstanden ist der heil'ge Christ*; 307, *Es ist gewisslich an der Zeit*; 308, *Es spricht der Unweisen Mund wohl*; 309, *Es stehn vor Gottes Throne*; 310, *Es wird schier der letzte Tag herkommen*; 311, *Es woll' uns Gott genädig sein*; 312, *Es woll' uns Gott genädig sein*; 327, *Für deinen Thron tret' ich hiermit*; 313, *Für Freuden lasst uns springen*; 314, *Gelobet seist du, Jesu Christ*; 315, *Gib dich zufrieden und sei stille*; 316, *Gott, der du selber bist das Licht*; 317, *Gott, der Vater, wohn' uns bei*; 318, *Gottes Sohn ist kommen*; 319, *Gott hat das Evangelium*; 320, *Gott lebet noch*; 321, *Gottlob, es geht nunmehr zu Ende*; 322, *Gott sei gelobet und gebenedeiet*; 323, *Gott sei uns gnädig*; 325, *Heilig, heilig*; 326, *Herr Gott, dich loben alle wir*; 328, *Herr, Gott, dich loben wir*; 329, *Herr, ich denk' an jene Zeit*; 330, *Herr, ich habe missgehandelt*; 331, *Herr, ich habe missgehandelt*; 332, *Herr Jesu Christ, dich zu uns wend'*; 333, *Herr Jesu Christ, du hast bereit't*; 334, *Herr Jesu Christ, du höchstes Gut*; 335, *Herr Jesu Christ, mein's Lebens Licht*; 336, *Herr Jesu Christ, wahr'r Mensch und Gott*; 337, *Herr, nun lass in Frieden*; 338, *Herr, straf mich nicht in deinem Zorn*; 339, *Herr, wie du willst, so schick's mit mir*; 340, *Herzlich lieb hab ich dich, o Herr*; 341, *Heut' ist, o Mensch, ein grosser Trauertag*; 342, *Heut' triumphieret Gottes Sohn*; 343, *Hilf, Gott, dass mir's gelinge*; 344, *Hilf,*

Herr Jesu, lass gelingen; 345, Ich bin ja, Herr, in deiner Macht; 346, Ich dank' dir, Gott, für all' Wohltat; 347, Ich dank' dir, lieber Herre; 348, Ich dank' dir, lieber Herre; 349, Ich dank' dir schon durch deinen Sohn; 350, Ich danke dir, o Gott, in deinem Throne; 351, Ich hab' mein' Sach' Gott heimgestellt; 352, Jesu, der du meine Seele; 353, Jesu, der du meine Seele; 354, Jesu, der du meine Seele; 355, Jesu, der du selbsten wohl; 356, Jesu, du mein liebstes Leben; 357, Jesu, Jesu, du bist mein; 358, Jesu, meine Freude; 359, Jesu meiner Seelen Wonne; 360, Jesu meiner Seelen Wonne; 361, Jesu, meines Herzens Freud'; 362, Jesu, nun sei gepreiset; 363, Jesus Christus, unser Heiland; 364, Jesus Christus, unser Heiland; 365, Jesus, meine Zuversicht; 366, Ihr Gestirn', ihr hohlen Lüfte; 367, In allen meinen Taten; 368, In dulci jubilo; 369, Keinen hat Gott verlassen; 370, Komm, Gott Schöpfer, heiliger Geist; 371, Kyrie, Gott Vater in Ewigkeit; 372, Lass, o Herr, dein Ohr sich neigen; 373, Liebster Jesu, wir sind hier; 374, Lobet den Herren, denn er ist freundlich; 375, Lobt Gott, ihr Christen, allzugleich; 376, Lobt Gott, ihr Christen, allzugleich; 377, Mach's mit mir, Gott, nach deiner Gut'; 378, Meine Augen schliess' ich jetzt; 379, Meinen Jesum lass' ich nicht, Jesus; 380, Meinen Jesum lass' ich nicht, weil; 322, Meine Seele erhebet den Herrn; 381, Meines Lebens letzte Zeit; 382, Mit Fried' und Freud' ich fahr' dahin; 383, Mitten wir im Leben sind; 384, Nicht so traurig, nicht so sehr; 385, Nun bitten wir den heiligen Geist; 386, Nun danket alle Gott; 387, Nun freut euch, Gottes Kinder all'; 388, Nun freut euch, lieben Christen, g'mein; 389, Nun lob', mein' Seel', den Herren; 390, Nun lob', mein' Seel', den Herren; 391, Nun preiset alle Gottes Barmherzigkeit; 392, Nun ruhen alle Wälder; 393, O Welt, sieh hier dein Leben; 394, O Welt, sieh dein Leben; 395, O Welt, sieh hier dein Leben; 396, Nun sich der Tag geendet hat; 397, O Ewigkeit, du Donnerwort; 398, O Gott, du frommer Gott; 399, O Gott, du frommer Gott; 400, O Herzensangst, o Bangigkeit; 401, O Lamm Gottes, unschuldig; 402, O Mensch, bewein' dein' Sünde gross; 403, O Mensch, schau Jesum Christum an; 404, O Traurigkeit, o Herzeleid; 405, O wie selig seid ihr doch, ihr Frommen; 406, O wie selig seid ihr doch, ihr Frommen; 407, O wir armen Sünder; 408, Schaut, ihr Sünder; 409, Seelen-Bräutigam; 410, Sei gegrüsset, Jesu gütig; 411, Singet dem Herrn ein neues Lied; 412, So gibst du nun, mein Jesu, gute Nacht; 413, Sollt' ich meinem Gott nicht singen; 414, Uns ist ein Kindlein heut' gebor'n; 415, Valet will ich dir geben; 416, Vater unser im Himmelreich; 417, Von Gott will ich nicht lassen; 418, Von Gott will ich nicht lassen; 419, Von Gott will ich nicht lassen; 257, Wär' Gott nicht mit uns diese Zeit; 420, Warum betrübst du dich, mein Herz; 421, Warum betrübst du dich, mein Herz; 422, Warum sollt' ich mich denn grämen; 423, Was betrübst du dich, mein Herze; 424, Was bist du doch, o Seele, so betrübet; 425, Was willst du dich, o meine Seele; 426, Weltlich Ehr' und zeitlich Gut; 427, Wenn ich in Angst und Not; 428, Wenn mein Stündlein vorhanden ist; 429, Wenn mein Stündlein vorhanden ist; 430, Wenn mein Stündlein vorhanden ist; 431, Wenn wir in höchsten Nöten sein; 432, Wenn wir in höchsten Nöten sein; 433, Wer Gott vertraut, hat wohl gebaut; 434, Wer nur den lieben Gott lässt walten; 435, Wie bist du, Seele, in mir so gar betrübt; 436, Wie schön leuchtet der Morgenstern; 437, Wir glauben all' an einen Gott; 258, Wo Gott der Herr nicht bei uns hält; 438, Wo Gott zum Haus nicht gibt sein' Gunst. **SACRED SONGS:** 69 for Voice with Basso Continuo only: 439, Ach, dass nicht die letzte Stunde; 440, Auf, auf! die rechte Zeit ist hier; 441, Auf, auf! mein Herz, mit Freuden; 422, Beglückter Stand getreuer Seelen; 443, Beschränkt, ihr Weisen dieser Welt; 444, Brich entzwei, mein armes Herze; 445, Brunnquell aller Güter; 446, Der lieben Sonnen Licht und Pracht; 447, Der Tag ist hin, die Sonne gehet nieder; 448, Der Tag mit seinem Lichte; 449, Dich bet' ich an, mein höchster Gott; 450, Die bittre Leidenszeit beginnet abermal; 451, Die goldne Sonne, voll Freud' und Wonne; 452, Dir, dir Jehovah, will ich singen (melody by Bach); 453, Eins ist Not! ach Herr, dies Eine; 454, Ermuntre dich, mein

schwacher Geist; 455, Erwürgtes Lamm, das die verwahrten Siegel; 456, Es glänzet der Christen; 457, Es ist nun aus mit meinem Leben; 458, Es ist vollbracht! vergiss ja nicht; 459, Es kostet viel, ein Christ zu sein; 460, Gieb dich zufrieden und sei stille; 461, Gott lebet noch; Seele, was verzagst du doch?; 462, Gott, wie gross ist deine Güte; 463, Herr, nicht schicke deine Rache; 464, Ich bin ja, Herr, in deiner Macht; 465, Ich freue mich in dir; 466, Ich halte treulich still und liebe; 467, Ich lass' dich nicht; 468, Ich liebe Jesum alle Stund'; 469, Ich steh' an deiner Krippen hier; 476, Ihr Gestirn', ihr hohen Lüfte; 471, Jesu, deine Liebeswunden; 470, Jesu, Jesu, du bist mein; 472, Jesu, meines Glaubens Zier; 473, Jesu, meines Herzens Freud'; 474, Jesus ist das schönste Licht; 475, Jesus, unser Trost und Leben; 477, Kein Stündlein geht dahin; 478, Komm, süsser Tod, komm, sel'ge Ruh'! (melody by Bach); 479, Kommt, Seelen, dieser Tag; 480, Kommt wieder aus der finstern Gruft; 481, Lasset uns mit Jesu ziehen; 482, Liebes Herz, bedenke doch; 483, Liebster Gott, wann werd' ich sterben?; 484, Liebster Herr Jesu! wo bleibest du so lange?; 485, Liebster Immanuel, Herzog der Frommen; 488, Meines Lebens letzte Zeit; 486, Mein Jesu, dem die Seraphinen; 487, Mein Jesu! was für Seelenweh; 489, Nicht so traurig, nicht so sehr; 490, Nur mein Jesus ist mein Leben; 491, O du Liebe meine Liebe; 492, O finstre Nacht; 493, O Jesulein süss, o Jesulein mild; 494, O liebe Seele, zieh' die Sinnen; 495, O wie selig seid ihr doch, ihr Frommen; 496, Seelen-Bräutigam, Jesu, Gottes Lamm!; 497, Seelenweide, meine Freude; 499, Sei gegrüsset, Jesu gütig; 498, Selig, wer an Jesum denkt; 500, So gehst du nun, mein Jesu, hin; 501, So giebst du nun, mein Jesu, gute Nacht; 502, So wünsch' ich mir zu guter Letzt; 503, Steh' ich bei meinem Gott; 504, Vergiss mein nicht, dass ich dein nicht; 505, Vergiss mein nicht, vergiss mein nicht (melody by Bach); 506, Was bist du doch, o Seele, so betrübet; 507, Wo ist mein Schäflein, das ich liebe. BWV numbers have been assigned to the following sacred songs, which are most likely spurious: 519, Hier lieg' ich nun; 520, Das walt' mein Gott; 521, Gott mein Herz dir Dank; 522, Meine Seele, lass es gehen; 523, Ich gnüge mich an meinem Stande. **O r g a n :** 525–30, 6 trio sonatas: E-flat major, C minor, D minor, E minor, C major, G major; 531, Prelude and Fugue in C major; 532, Prelude and Fugue in D major; 533, Prelude and Fugue in E minor; 534, Prelude and Fugue in F minor; 535, Prelude and Fugue in G minor; 536, Prelude and Fugue in A major; 537, Fantasia and Fugue in C minor; 538, Toccata and Fugue in D minor, "Dorian"; 539, Prelude and Fugue in D minor; 540, Toccata and Fugue in F major; 541, Prelude and Fugue in G major; 542, Fantasia and Fugue in G minor; 543, Prelude and Fugue in A minor; 544, Prelude and Fugue in B minor; 545, Prelude and Fugue in C major; 546, Prelude and Fugue in C minor; 547, Prelude and Fugue in C major; 548, Prelude and Fugue in E minor; 549, Prelude and Fugue in C minor; 550, Prelude and Fugue in G major; 551, Prelude and Fugue in A minor; 552, Prelude and Fugue in E-flat major, "St. Anne"; 562, Fantasia and Fugue in C minor; 563, Fantasia in B minor; 564, Toccata, Adagio, and Fugue in C major; 565, Toccata and Fugue in D minor; 566, Prelude and Fugue in E major; 568, Prelude in G major; 569, Prelude in A minor; 570, Fantasia in C major; 572, Fantasia in G major; 573, Fantasia in C major; 574, Fugue in C minor (on a theme by Legrenzi); 575, Fugue in C minor; 578, Fugue in G minor; 579, Fugue in B minor (on a theme by Corelli); 582, Passacaglia in C minor; 583, Trio in D minor; 586, Trio in G major (Bach's organ transcription of a work by Telemann); 587, Aria in F major (transcription from Couperin); 588, Canzona in D minor; 590, Pastorale in F major; 592–97, 6 concertos: G major (arrangement of a concerto by Duke Johann Ernst of Saxe-Weimar), A minor (arrangement of Vivaldi's op.3, no. 8), C major (arrangement of Vivaldi's op.7, no. 5), C major (arrangement of a concerto by Duke Johann

Ernst of Saxe-Weimar), D minor (arrangement of Vivaldi's op.3, no. 11), E-flat major (arrangement of a concerto by an unknown composer); 598, Pedal-Exercitium; 802–5, 4 duettos: E minor, F major, G major, A minor; 1,027a, Trio in G major (transcription from final movement of sonata 1,027). Also the following organ chorales that were discovered in the Neumeister Collection at Yale Univ.: 1090, *Wir Christenleut*; 1091; *Das alte Jahr vergangen ist*; 1092, *Herr Gott, nun schleuss den Himmel auf*; 1093, *Herzliebster Jesu, was hast du verbrochen*; 1094, *O Jesu, wie ist dein Gestalt*; 1095, *O Lamm Gottes unschuldig*; 1096, *Christe, der du bist Tag und Licht, oder: Wir danken dir, Herr Jesu Christ*; 1097, *Ehre sei dir, Christe, der du leidest Not*; 1098, *Wir glauben all an einen Gott*; 1099, *Aus tiefer Not schrei ich zu dir*; 1100, *Allein zu dir, Herr Jesu Christ*; 1101, *Durch Adams Fall ist ganz verderbt*; 1102, *Du Friedefürst, Herr Jesu Christ*; 1103, *Erhalt uns, Herr, bei deinem Wort*; 1104, *Wenn dich Unglück tut greifen an*; 1105, *Jesu, meine Freude*; 1106, *Gott ist mein Heil, mein Hilf und Trost*; 1107, *Jesu, meines Lebens Leben*; 1108, *Als Jesus Christus in der Nacht*; 1109, *Ach Gott, tu dich erbarmen*; 1110, *O Herre Gott, dein göttlich Wort*; 1111, *Nun lasset uns den Leib begrab'n*; 1112, *Christus, der ist mein Leben*; 1113, *Ich hab mein Sach Gott heimgestellt*; 1114, *Herr Jesu Christ, du höchstes Gut*; 1115, *Herzlich lieb hab ich dich, o Herr*; 1116, *Was Gott tut, das ist wohlgetan*; 1117, *Alle Menschen müssen sterben*; 1118, *Werde munter, mein Gemüte*; 1119, *Wie nach einer Wasserquelle*; 1120, *Christ, der du bist der helle Tag*. BWV numbers have been assigned to the following doubtful and spurious works: 131a, Fugue in G minor (spurious); 561, Fantasia and Fugue in A minor (spurious); 567, Prelude in C major (spurious); 571, Fantasia in G major (spurious); 576, Fugue in G major (spurious); 577, Fugue in G major (spurious); 580, Fugue in D major (spurious); 581, Fugue in G major (spurious); 584, Trio in G minor (doubtful); 585, Trio in C minor (by J.F. Fasch); 589, Allabreve in D major (doubtful); 591, Kleines harmonisches Labyrinth (doubtful); also 8 brief preludes and fugues: C major, D minor, E minor, F major, G major, G minor, A minor, B-flat major (doubtful). **O t h e r O r g a n M u s i c :** 45 Chorales in Das Orgel-Büchlein: 599, *Nun komm, der Heiden Heiland*; 600, *Gott, durch deine Güte*; 601, *Herr Christ, der ein'ge Gottes-Sohn*; 602, *Lob sei dem allmächtigen Gott*; 603, *Puer natus in Bethlehem*; 604, *Gelobet seist du, Jesu Christ*; 605, *Der Tag, der ist so freudenreich*; 606, *Vom Himmel hoch, da komm' ich her*; 607, *Vom Himmel kam der Engel Schar*; 608, *In dulci jubilo*; 609, *Lobt Gott, ihr Christen, allzugleich*; 610, *Jesu, meine Freude*; 611, *Christum wir sollen loben schon*; 612, *Wir Christenleut'*; 613, *Helft mir Gottes Güte preisen*; 614, *Das alte Jahr vergangen ist*; 615, *In dir ist Freude*; 616, *Mit Fried' und Freud' ich fahr dahin*; 617, *Herr Gott, nun schleuss den Himmel auf*; 618, *O Lamm Gottes unschuldig*; 619, *Christe, du Lamm Gottes*; 620, *Christus, der uns selig macht*; 621, *Da Jesus an dem Kreuze stund'*; 622, *O Mensch, bewein' dein' Sünde gross*; 623, *Wir danken dir, Herr Jesu Christ*; 624, *Hilf Gott, dass mir's gelinge*; 625, *Christ lag in Todesbanden*; 626, *Jesus Christus, unser Heiland*; 627, *Christ ist erstanden*; 628, *Erstanden ist der heil'ge Christ*; 629, *Erschienen ist der herrliche Tag*; 630, *Heut' triumphieret Gottes Sohn*; 631, *Komm, Gott Schöpfer, heiliger Geist*; 632, *Herr Jesu Christ, dich zu uns wend'*; 633, *Liebster Jesu, wir sind hier*; 635, *Dies sind die heil'gen zehn Gebot'*; 636, *Vater unser im Himmelreich*; 637, *Durch Adams Fall ist ganz verderbt*; 638, *Es ist das Heil uns Kommen her*; 639, *Ich ruf' zu dir, Herr Jesu Christ*; 640, *In dich hab' ich gehoffet, Herr*; 641, *Wenn wir in höchsten Nöten sein*; 642, *Wer nur den lieben Gott lässt walten*; 643, *Alle Menschen müssen sterben*; 644, *Ach wie nichtig, ach wie flüchtig*; 6 chorales publ. by J.G. Schübler, hence the name Schübler-Chorales: 645, *Wachet auf, ruft uns die Stimme* (based upon Cantata 140, 4th movement), 646, *Wo soll ich fliehen hin* (source unknown), 647, *Wer nur den lieben Gott lässt walten*

(based upon Cantata 93, 4th movement), 648, *Meine Seele erhebet den Herren* (based upon Cantata 10, 5th movement), 649, *Ach bleib' bei uns, Herr Jesu Christ* (based upon Cantata 6, 3rd movement), 650, *Kommst du nun, Jesu, vom Himmel herunter* (based upon Cantata 137, 2nd movement); 651, *Fantasia super Komm, Heiliger Geist*; 652, *Komm, Heiliger Geist*; 653, *An Wasserflüssen Babylon*; 654, *Schmücke dich, o liebe Seele*; 655, *Trio super Herr Jesu Christ, dich zu uns wend*; 656, *O Lamm Gottes, unschuldig*; 657, *Nun danket alle Gott*; 658, *Von Gott will ich nicht lassen*; 659, *Nun komm, der Heiden Heiland*; 660, *Trio super Nun komm, der Heiden Heiland*; 661, *Nun komm, der Heiden Heiland*; 662, *Allein Gott in der Höh' sei Ehr*; 663, *Allein Gott in der Höh' sei Ehr*; 664, *Trio super Allein Gott in der Hoh' sei Ehr*; 665, *Jesus Christus, unser Heiland*; 666, *Jesus Christus, unser Heiland*; 667, *Komm, Gott Schöpfer, Heiliger Geist*; 668, *Wenn wir in höchsten Nöten sein (Vor deinen Thron tret ich)*. Chorale preludes in the 3rd part of the *Clavier-Übung*: 669, *Kyrie, Gott Vater in Ewigkeit*; 670, *Christe, aller Welt Trost*; 671, *Kyrie, Gott heiliger Geist*; 672, *Kyrie, Gott Vater in Ewigkeit*; 673, *Christe, aller Welt Trost*; 674, *Kyrie, Gott heiliger Geist*; 675, *Allein Gott in der Höh' sei Ehr*; 676, *Allein Gott in der Höh' sei Ehr*; 677, *Fughetta super Allein Gott in der Höh' sei Ehr*; 678, *Dies sind die heil'gen zehn Gebot'*; 679, *Fughetta super Dies sind die heil'gen zehn Gebot'*; 680, *Wir glauben all an einen Gott*; 681, *Fughetta super Wir glauben all' an einen Gott*; 682, *Vater unser im Himmelreich*; 683, *Vater unser im Himmelreich*; 684, *Christ, unser Herr, zum Jordan kam*; 685, *Christ, unser Herr, zum Jordan kam*; 686, *Aus tiefer Not schrei ich zu dir*; 687, *Aus tiefer Not schrei ich zu dir*; 688, *Jesus Christus, unser Heiland, der von uns den Zorn Gottes wandt*; 689, *Fuga super Jesus Christus unser Heiland*. Further chorales: 690, *Wer nur den lieben Gott lässt walten*; 691, *Wer nur den lieben Gott lässt walten*; 694, *Wo soll ich fliehen hin*; 695, *Fantasia super Christ lag in Todesbanden*; 696, *Christum wir sollen loben schon*; 697, *Gelobet seist du, Jesu Christ*; 698, *Herr Christ, der ein'ge Gottes-Sohn*; 699, *Nun komm, der Heiden Heiland*; 700, *Vom Himmel hoch, da komm ich her*; 701, *Vom Himmel hoch, da komm ich her*; 703, *Gottes Sohn ist kommen*; 704, *Lob sei dem allmächtigen Gott*; 706, *Liebster Jesu, wir sind hier*; 709, *Herr Jesu Christ, dich zu uns wend*; 710, *Wir Christenleut' haben jetzt Freud*; 711, *Allein Gott in der Höh' sei Ehr*; 712, *In dich hab ich gehoffet, Herr*; 713, *Fantasia super Jesu, meine Freude*; 714, *Ach Gott und Herr*; 715, *Allein Gott in der Höh' sei Ehr*; 717, *Allein Gott in der Höh' sei Ehr*; 718, *Christ lag in Todesbanden*; 720, *Ein' feste Burg ist unser Gott*; 721, *Erbarm' dich mein, o Herre Gott*; 722, *Gelobet seist du, Jesu Christ*; 724, *Gott, durch deine Güte (Gottes Sohn ist kommen)*; 725, *Herr Gott, dich loben wir*; 726, *Herr Jesu Christ, dich zu uns wend*; 727, *Herzlich tut mich verlangen*; 728, *Jesus, meine Zuversicht*; 729, *In dulci jubilo*; 730, *Liebster Jesu, wir sind hier*; 731, *Liebster Jesu, wir sind hier*; 732, *Lobt Gott, ihr Christen, allzugleich*; 733, *Meine Seele erhebet den Herren (Fuge über das Magnificat)*; 734a, *Nun freut euch, lieben Christen g'mein*; *O Lamm Gottes, unschuldig*; 735, *Fantasia super Valet will ich dir geben*; 736, *Valet will ich dir geben*; 737, *Vater unser im Himmelreich*; 738, *Vom Himmel hoch, da komm ich her*; 739, *Wie schön leucht't uns der Morgenstern*; 741, *Ach Gott vom Himmel sieh darein*; 753, *Jesu, meine Freude*; 764, *Wie schön leuchtet uns der Morgenstern*; 766, *Christ, der du bist der helle Tag*; 767, *O Gott, du frommer Gott*; 768, *Sei gegrüsset, Jesu gütig*. BWV numbers have been assigned to the following doubtful and spurious works: 691a, *Wer nur den lieben Gott lässt walten* (doubtful); 692, *Ach Gott und Herr* (by J.G. Walther); 693, *Ach Gott und Herr* (by J.G. Walther); 695a, *Fantasia super Christ lag in Todesbanden* (doubtful); 702, *Das Jesulein soll doch mein Trost* (doubtful); 705, *Durch Adam's Fall ist ganz verderbt* (doubtful); 707, *Ich hab' mein' Sach' Gott heimgestellt* (doubtful); 708, *Ich hab' mein' Sach' Gott heimgestellt* (doubtful);

713a, *Fantasia super Jesu, meine Freude* (doubtful); 716, *Fuga super Allein Gott in der Höh' sei Ehr* (doubtful); 719, *Der Tag, der ist so freudenreich* (doubtful); 723, *Gelobet seist du, Jesu Christ* (doubtful); 734, *Nun freut euch, lieben Christen g'mein* (doubtful); 740, *Wir glauben all' an einen Gott, Vater* (doubtful); 742, *Ach Herr, mich armen Sunder* (spurious); 743, *Ach, was ist doch unser Leben* (spurious); 744, *Auf meinen lieben Gott* (doubtful); 745, *Aus der Tiefe rufe ich* (doubtful); 746, *Christ ist erstanden* (doubtful); 747, *Christus, der uns selig macht* (spurious); 748, *Gott der Vater wohn' uns bei* (doubtful); 749, *Herr Jesu Christ, dich zu uns wend'* (spurious); 750, *Herr Jesu Christ, mein's Lebens Licht* (spurious); 751, *In dulci jubilo* (spurious); 752, *Jesu, der du meine Seele* (spurious); 754, *Liebster Jesu, wir sind hier* (spurious); 755, *Nun freut euch, lieben Christen* (spurious); 756, *Nun ruhen alle Walder* (spurious); 757, *O Herre Gott, dein göttlich's Wort* (spurious); 758, *O Vater, allmächtiger Gott* (doubtful); 759, *Schmücke dich, o liebe Seele* (by G.A. Homilius); 760, *Vater unser im Himmelreich* (doubtful); 761, *Vater unser im Himmelreich* (doubtful); 762, *Vater unser im Himmelreich* (spurious); 763, *Wie schön leuchtet der Morgenstern* (spurious); 765, *Wir glauben all' an einen Gott* (spurious); 770, *Ach, was soll ich Sünder machen?* (doubtful); 771, *Allein Gott in der Höh sei Ehr'* (nos. 3 and 8 by A.N. Vetter). **Other Keyboard Music:** 772–86, 15 2-part inventions in the *Clavier- Büchlein für Wilhelm Friedemann Bach*: C major, C minor, D major, D minor, E-flat major, E major, E minor, F major, F minor, G major, G minor, A major, A minor, B-flat major, B minor; 787–801, 15 3-part inventions, called sinfonias, in the *Clavier-Büchlein für Wilhelm Friedemann Bach*: C major, C minor, D major, D minor, E-flat major, E major, E minor, F major, F minor, G major, G minor, A major, A minor, B-flat major, B minor; 806–11, 6 English suites: A major, A minor, G minor, F major, E minor, D minor; 812–17, 6 French suites: D minor, C minor, B minor, E-flat major, G major, E major; 825–30, 6 partitas in part 1 of the *Clavier-Übung*: B-flat major, C minor, A minor, D major, G major, E minor; 831, *Ouvertüre nach französischer Art*, a partita in B minor in part 2 of the *Clavier-Übung*; 846–93, *Das wohltemperierte Clavier* (The Well-Tempered Clavier), in 2 parts: 24 preludes and fugues in each part in all the major and minor keys; 971, *Concerto nach italianischem Gusto* (Concerto in the Italian Style) in part 2 of the *Clavier-Übung*; 988, *Aria mit verschiedenen Veränderungen* (the so-called *Goldberg Variations*), part 4 of the *Clavier-Übung*. Further keyboard works: 818, Suite in A minor; 819, Suite in E-flat major; 820, Ouvertüre in F major; 821, Suite in B-flat major; 822, Suite in G minor; 823, Suite in F minor; 832, Partie in A major; 833, Prelude and Partita in F major; 836 and 837, 2 allemandes in G minor (1 unfinished); 841–43, 3 minuets: G major, G minor, G major; 894, Prelude and Fugue in A minor; 896, Prelude and Fugue in A major; 900, Prelude and Fughetta in E minor; 901, Prelude and Fughetta in F major; 902, Prelude and Fughetta in G major; 903, Chromatic Fantasia and Fugue in D minor; 904, Fantasia and Fugue in A minor; 906, Fantasia and Fugue in C minor; 910, Toccata in F- sharp minor; 911, Toccata in C minor; 912, Toccata in D major; 913, Toccata in D minor; 914, Toccata in E minor; 915, Toccata in G minor; 916, Toccata in G major; 944, Fugue in A minor; 946, Fugue in C major; 950, Fugue in A major (on a theme by Albinoni); 951, Fugue in B minor (on a theme by Albinoni); 953, Fugue in C major; 954, Fugue in B-flat major; 955, Fugue in B-flat major; 958, Fugue in A minor; 959, Fugue in A minor; 963, Sonata in D major; 965, Sonata in A minor (based upon a sonata by J.A. Reinken); 966, Sonata in C major (based upon part of a sonata by J.A. Reinken); 967, Sonata in A minor (based upon the 1st movement of a sonata by an unknown source); 989, Aria variata in A minor; 991, Air with variations in

C minor (fragment); 992, *Capriccio sopra la lontananza del suo fratello dilettissimo* (Capriccio on the Departure of His Most Beloved Brother), in B-flat major; 993, Capriccio in E major; also 924–29, 6 works from the *Clavier-Büchlein für Wilhelm Friedemann Bach*: Praeambulum in C major, Prelude in D minor, Praeambulum in F major, Prelude in F major, Trio in G minor, Praeambulum in G minor; 933–38, 6 preludes: C major, C minor, D minor, D major, E major, E minor; 939–43, 5 preludes: C major, D minor, E minor, A minor, C major; 994, Applicatio in C major, the first piece in the *Clavier-Büchlein für Wilhelm Friedemann Bach*; several pieces in the 2 parts of the *Clavier- Büchlein für Anna Magdalena Bach*; and 972–87, 16 concertos: D major (arrangement of Vivaldi's op.3, no. 9), G major (arrangement of Vivaldi's op.8/II, no. 2), D minor (arrangement of Oboe Concerto by A. Marcello), G minor (arrangement of Vivaldi's op.4, no. 6), C major (arrangement of Vivaldi's op.3, no. 12), C major (source unknown), F major (arrangement of Vivaldi's op.3, no. 3), B minor (source unknown), G major (arrangement of Vivaldi's op.4, no. 1), C minor (source unknown), B-flat major (arrangement of a concerto by Duke Johann Ernst of Saxe-Weimar), G minor (source unknown), C major (arrangement of a concerto by Duke Johann Ernst of Saxe-Weimar), G minor (arrangement of Violin Concerto by Telemann), G major (source unknown), D minor (arrangement of a concerto by Duke Johann Ernst of Saxe-Weimar). BWV numbers have been assigned to the following doubtful and spurious works: 824, Suite in A major (fragment; by Telemann); Allemande in C minor (spurious); 835, Allemande in A minor (by Kirnberger); 838, Allemande and Courante in A major (by C. Graupner); 839, Sarabande in G minor (spurious); 840, Courante in G major (by Telemann); 844, Scherzo in D minor (by W.F. Bach); 845, Gigue in F minor (spurious); 895, Prelude and Fugue in A minor (doubtful); 897, Prelude and Fugue in A minor (partly doubtful; prelude by C.H. Dretzel); 898, Prelude and Fugue in B-flat major (doubtful); 899, Prelude and Fughetta in D minor (doubtful); 905, Fantasia and Fugue in D minor (doubtful); 907, Fantasia and Fughetta in B-flat major (doubtful); 908, Fantasia and Fughetta in D major (doubtful); 909, Concerto and Fugue in C minor (doubtful); 917, Fantasia in G minor (doubtful); 918, Fantasia on a rondo in C minor (doubtful); 919, Fantasia in C minor (doubtful); 920, Fantasia in G minor (doubtful); 921, Prelude in C minor (doubtful); 922, Prelude in A minor (doubtful); 923, Prelude in B minor (doubtful); 945, Fugue in E minor (spurious); 947, Fugue in A minor (doubtful); 948, Fugue in D minor (doubtful); 949, Fugue in A major (doubtful); 952, Fugue in C major (doubtful); 956, Fugue in E minor (doubtful); 957, Fugue in G major (doubtful); 960, Fugue in E minor (unfinished; spurious); 961, Fughetta in C minor (doubtful); 962, Fugato in E minor (by Albrechtsberger); 964, Sonata in D minor (doubtful; arrangement of Violin Sonata 1,003); 968, Adagio in G major (doubtful; arrangement of 1st movement of Violin Sonata 1,005); 969, Andante in G minor (spurious); 970, Presto in D minor (by W.F. Bach); 990, Sarabande con partite in C major (spurious); etc. **Lute:** 995, Suite in G minor; 996, Suite in E minor; 997, Partita in C minor; 998, Prelude, Fugue, and Allegro in E-flat major; 999, Prelude in C minor; 1,000, Fugue in G minor; 1,006a, Partita in E major (arrangement of 1,006). **CHAMBER:** 1,001–6, sonatas and partitas for Solo Violin: Sonata No. 1 in G minor, Partita No. 1 in B minor, Sonata No. 2 in A minor, Partita No. 2 in D minor, Sonata No. 3 in C major, Partita No. 3 in E major; 1,007–12, 6 suites for Solo Cello: G major, D minor, C major, E-flat major, C minor, D major; 1,013, Partita in A minor for Flute; 1,014–19, 6 sonatas for Violin and Harpsichord: No. 1 in B minor, No. 2 in A major, No. 3 in E major, No. 4 in C minor, No. 5 in F minor, No. 6 in G major; 1,021, Sonata in G major for Violin and Basso Continuo; 1,023, Sonata in E minor for Violin and Basso Continuo; 1,027–29, 3 sonatas for Harpsichord and Viola da Gamba: G major, D major, G minor; 1,030, Sonata in B minor for Flute and Harpsichord; 1,032, Sonata in A major for Flute and Harpsichord; 1,034, Sonata in E minor for Flute and Basso Continuo; 1,035, Sonata in E major for Flute and Basso Continuo; 1,039, Sonata in G major for 2 Flutes and Basso Continuo; 1,040, Trio in F major for Violin, Oboe, and Basso Continuo. BWV numbers have been assigned to the following doubtful and spurious works: 1,020, Sonata in G minor for Violin and Harpsichord (doubtful); 1,022, Sonata in F major for Violin and Harpsichord (most likely spurious); 1,024, Sonata in C minor for Violin and Basso Continuo (doubtful); 1,025, Suite in A major for Violin and Harpsichord (doubtful); 1,026, Fugue in G minor for Violin and Harpsichord (doubtful); 1,037, Sonata in C major for 2 Violins and Harpsichord (most likely spurious); 1,031, Sonata in E-flat major for Flute and Harpsichord (doubtful); 1,033, Sonata in C major for Flute and Basso Continuo (doubtful); 1,036, Sonata in D minor for 2 Violins and Harpsichord (most likely spurious); 1,038, Sonata in G major for Flute, Violin, and Basso Continuo (most likely spurious). **ORCH.:** 1,041, Concerto in A minor for Violin; 1,042, Concerto in E major for Violin; 1,043, Concerto in D minor for 2 Violins; 1,044, Concerto in A minor for Flute, Violin, and Harpsichord; 1,046–51, 6 *Brandenburg Concertos*: No. 1 in F major, No. 2 in F major, No. 3 in G major, No. 4 in G major, No. 5 in D major, No. 6 in B-flat major; 1,052, Concerto in D minor for Harpsichord; 1053, Concerto in E major for Harpsichord; 1,054, Concerto in D major for Harpsichord; 1,055, Concerto in A major for Harpsichord; 1,056, Concerto in F minor for Harpsichord; 1,057, Concerto in F major for Harpsichord; 1,058, Concerto in G minor for Harpsichord; 1,059, Concerto in D minor for Harpsichord; 1,060, Concerto in C minor for 2 Harpsichords; 1,061, Concerto in C major for 2 Harpsichords; 1,062, Concerto in C minor for 2 Harpsichords; 1,063, Concerto in D minor for 3 Harpsichords; 1,064, Concerto in C major for 3 Harpsichords; 1,065, Concerto in A minor for 4 Harpsichords (arrangement of Vivaldi's op.3, no. 10); 1,066–69, 4 suites or *ouvertures*: No. 1 in C major, No. 2 in B minor, No. 3 in D major, No. 4 in D major. Also 1,045, concerto movement in D major for Violin (fragment); 1,046a, Sinfonia in F major (early version of 1,046); 1,070, Overture in G minor (most likely spurious). **OTHER WORKS:** 769, *Einige canonische Veränderungen über das Weynacht Lied, Vom Himmel hoch da komm' ich her* for Organ (composed for his membership in the Societät der Musikalischen Wissenschaften); 1,079, *Musikalisches Opfer* (Musical Offering); 1,080, *Die Kunst der Fuge* (The Art of the Fugue).

BIBL.: COLLECTED EDITIONS, SOURCE MATERIAL: *J.S. B.'s Werke*, the first major edition of his collected works, was publ. by the Bach-Gesellschaft (46 vols., Leipzig, 1851–99; vol. 47, suppl., 1932). The Johann-Sebastian-Bach-Inst. of Göttingen and the Bach-Archiv of Leipzig are now preparing a completely new edition, the *Neue Ausgabe sämtlicher Werke* (the *Neue B.-Ausgabe*, or NBA). It began publication in 1954; a Kritischer Bericht accompanies each vol.; in addition, facsimile reproductions of Bach's original MSS and documents may be found in the *Faksimile-Reihe B.scher Werke und Schriftstücke*. There are also innumerable reprints of many of Bach's compositions. The standard thematic catalogue of Bach's works is to be found in W. Schmieder, *Thematisch-systematisches Verzeichnis der musikalischen Werke von J.S. B. Bach-Werke-Verzeichnis* (Leipzig, 1950; 2nd ed., rev., 1990); it includes bibliographical information on each composition. See also M. McAll, ed., *Melodic Index to the Works of J.S. B.* (N.Y., 1962); U. Balestrini, ed., *Catalogo Tematico (Incipit) delle Opere di J.S. B. (BWV 1–1080)* (Milan, 1988); A. Dürr and Y. Kobayashi, eds., *Kleine Ausgabe* (Wiesbaden, 1998). Other important sources are as follows: J. Schreyer, *Beiträge zur B.-Kritik* (vol. 1, Dresden, 1910; vol. 2, Leipzig, 1912); E. Müller von Asow, ed., *J.S. B.: Gesammelte Briefe* (Regensburg, 1938; 2nd ed., with H. Muller von Asow, as *J.S. B.: Briefe, Gesamtausgabe* (Regensburg, 1950); H. David and A. Mendel, eds., *The B. Reader* (N.Y., 1945; 2nd ed., rev., 1966; rev. and enl. ed., 1998, by C. Wolff as *The New B. Reader*, 1998); K. Matthaei, ed., *B.-Gedenkschrift* (Zürich, 1950); P. Kast, *Die B.-Handschriften der Berliner Staatsbibliothek*, Tübinger B-Studien, II-III (Trossingen, 1958); W. Neumann and H.-J. Schulze, eds., *Schriftstücke von der Hand J.S. B.s*, Bach-Dokumente, I (Leipzig, 1963); P. Krause, ed., *Handschriften der Werke J.S. B.s in der Musikbibliothek der Stadt Leipzig* (Leipzig, 1964); M. Geck, ed., *B.-Interpretationen* (Göttingen, 1969); H.-J. Schulze, ed., *Fremdschriftliche und gedruckte Dokumente zur Lebensgeschichte J.S. B.s 1685–1750*, Bach-Dokumente, II (Leipzig, 1969); P. Krause, ed., *Originalausgaben und ältere Drucke der Werke J.S. B.s in der Musikbibliothek der Stadt Leipzig* (Leipzig, 1970); H.-J. Schulze, ed., *Dokumente zum Nachwirken J.S. B.s 1750–1800*, Bach-Dokumente, III (Leipzig, 1972); W. Neumann, ed., *Bilddokumente zur Lebensgeschichte J.S. B.s*, Bach-Dokumente, IV (Leipzig, 1978); R. Leaver, *B.s theologische Bibliothek: Eine kritische Bibliographie—B.'s Theological Library: A Critical Bibliography* (Neuhausen-Stuttgart, 1983); H. Raupach, *Das wahre Bildnis des J.S. B.: Bericht und Dokumente* (Munich, 1983); G. Herz, ed., *B.-Quellen in Amerika—B. Sources in America* (Kassel, 1984); D. Franklin, ed., *B. Studies* (Cambridge, 1989); H.-J. Schulze and C. Wolff, eds., *B. Compendium: Analytisch-bibliographisches Repertorium des Werke J.S. B.s* (7 vols., Leipzig and Dresden, 1986–89); H. Kock and R. Siegel, *Genealogisches Lexikon der Familie B.* (Wechmar, 1995); J. Butt, ed., *Cambridge Companion to B.* (Cambridge, 1997); D. Melamed and M. Marissen, *An Introduction to B. Studies* (N.Y., 1998); M. Boyd, ed., *The Oxford Companion to B.* (Oxford, 1999). **BIOGRAPHICAL:** C.P.E. Bach and J. Agricola publ. an obituary (Nekrolog) in L. Mizler's *Neu eröffnete musikalische Bibliothek* (Leipzig, 1754; reprint ed. by B. Richter in the *B.-Jahrbuch*, 1920; Eng. tr. in H. David and A. Mendel, eds., *The B. Reader* (N.Y., 1945; 2nd ed., rev., 1966; rev. and enl. ed., 1998, by C. Wolff as *The New B. Reader*); Bach's first biographer was J. Forkel, *Über J.S. B.s Leben, Kunst und Kunstwerke* (Leipzig, 1802; Eng. tr., London, 1820; new Eng. tr. with notes by C. Terry, London, 1920); C. Hilgenfeldt, *J.S. B.'s Leben, Wirken und Werke: Ein Beitrag zur Kunstgeschichte des achtzehnten Jahrhunderts* (Leipzig, 1850); C. Bitter, *J.S. B.* (2 vols., Berlin, 1865; 2nd ed., 4 vols., Dresden, 1880; P. Spitta, *J.S. B.* (2 vols., Leipzig, 1873–80; Eng. tr. by C. Bell and J. Fuller Maitland, with many additions, 3 vols., London, 1884–85; 2nd ed., 1899; reprint, 2 vols., N.Y., 1951); A. Schweitzer, *J.S. B.: Le Musicien-poète* (Paris, 1905; aug. German eds., 1908, 1915; Eng. tr. by E. Newman, 2 vols., London, 1911); C. Abdy Williams, *B.* (London, 1900; rev. ed., 1934); A. Pirro, *J.-S. B.* (Paris, 1906; Eng. tr., N.Y., 1957); P. Wolfrum, *J.S. B.* (vol. 1, Berlin, 1906; 2nd ed., 1910; vol. 2, Leipzig, 1910); C. Parry, *J.S. B.: The Story of the Development of a Great Personality* (N.Y. and London, 1909; rev. ed., 1934); J. Tiersot, *J.-S. B.* (Paris, 1912; 2nd ed., 1934); T. Gérold, *J.-S. B.* (Paris, 1925); C. Terry, *B.: A Biography* (London, 1928; rev. ed., 1933); R. Boughton, *B., the Master: A New Interpretation of His Genius* (N.Y. and London, 1930); H. Besseler, *J.S. B.* (Berlin, 1935; new ed., 1956); T. Scott Buhrmann, *B.'s Life Chronologically as He Lived It* (N.Y. 1935); H. Moser, *J.S. B.* (Berlin, 1935; 2nd ed., 1943);

J. Müller-Blattau, *J.S. B.* (Leipzig, 1935; 2nd ed., Stuttgart, 1950); H. Preuss, *B., der Lutheraner* (Erlangen, 1935); R. Steglich, *J.S. B.* (Potsdam, 1935); P. Collaer, *J.S. B.* (Brussels, 1936); W. Gurlitt, *J.S. B.: Der Meister und sein Werk* (Berlin, 1936; 3rd ed., 1949; Eng. tr., St. Louis, 1957); W. Vetter, *J.S. B.* (Leipzig, 1938; 2nd ed., 1943); K. Hasse, *J.S. B.* (Cologne and Krefeld, 1941; 2nd ed., 1948); R. Pitrou, *J.-S. B.* (Paris, 1941; 2nd ed., 1949); A.-E. Cherbuliez, *J.S. B.: Sein Leben und sein Werk* (Olten, 1946; 2nd ed., 1947); H. Gadamer, *B. und Weimar* (Weimar, 1946); H. Keller, *J.S. B.* (Lorch, 1947); E. Fischer, *J.S. B.* (Bern, 1948); H. Engel, *J.S. B.* (Berlin, 1950); G. Fock, *Der junge B. in Lüneburg* (Hamburg, 1950); B. Paumgartner, *J.S. B.: Leben und Werk* (vol. I, Zürich, 1950); R. Petzoldt, *J.S. B.:Sein Leben in Bildern* (Leipzig, 1950); F. Wiegand, *J.S. B. und seine Verwandten in Arnstadt* (Arnstadt, 1950); F. Smend, *B. in Köthen* (Berlin, 1951); W. Neumann, *Auf den Lebenswegen J.S. B.s* (Berlin, 1953; 4th ed., 1962); K. Geiringer, *The B. Family: Seven Generations of Creative Genius* (N.Y., 1954); H. Franck, *J.S. B.: Die Geschichte seines Lebens* (Berlin, 1960); W. Neumann, *B.: Eine Bildbiographie* (Munich, 1960; Eng. tr. as *B.: A Pictorial Biography*, N.Y., 1961; rev. ed. as *B. and His World*, N.Y., 1970); R. Miles, *J.S. B.* (Englewood Cliffs, N.J., 1962); E. Buchet, ed., *J.-S. B.: L'OEuvre et la vie* (Paris, 1963); I. Holst, *B.* (London, 1965); K. Geiringer, *J.S. B.: The Culmination of an Era* (N.Y., 1966); F. Blume, *Der junge B.* (Wolfenbüttel, 1967; Eng. tr. as "J.S. B.'s Youth," *Musical Quarterly* [Jan. 1968]); E. Buchet, *J.-S. B.: Après deux siècles d'études et de témoignages* (Paris, 1968); B. Schwendowius and W. Dömling, eds., *J.S. B.: Zeit, Leben, Wirken* (Kassel, 1976; tr. as *J.S. B.: Life, Times, Influence*, London, 1978); M. Boyd, *B.* (London, 1983); D. Arnold, *B.* (Oxford, 1984); R. de Candé, *J.-S. B.* (Paris, 1984); G. Stiller, *J.S. B. and Liturgical Life in Leipzig* (St. Louis, 1984); H. Wohlfarth, *J.S. B.* (Freiburg im Briegau, 1984; Eng. tr., Philadelphia and Cambridge, 1985); P. Buscaroli, *B.* (Milan, 1985); W. Felix, *J.S. B.* (London, 1985); W. Kolneder, *J.S. B. (1685–1750): Leben, Werk, und Nachwirken in zeitgenössischen Dokumenten* (Wilhelmshaven, 1991); M. Geck, *J.S. B.: Mit Selbstzeugnissen und Bilddokumenten* (Reinbek bei Hamburg, 1993); O. Bettmann, *J.S. B. as His World Knew Him* (Secaucus, N.J., 1995); K. Eidam, *Das wahre Leben des J.S. B.* (Munich, 1999).
CRITICAL, ANALYTICAL: In addition to the following writings, numerous articles of importance may be found in the *B.-Jahrbuch* (1904 et seq.). F. Rochlitz, *Wege zu B.* (extracted from *Für Freunde der Tonkunst*, Leipzig, 1824–37, by J. Müller-Blattau, Augsburg, 1926); M. Hauptmann, *Erläuterungen zu J.S. B.s Kunst der Fuge* (Leipzig, 1841; 2nd ed., 1861); H. Riemann, *Handbuch der Fugenkomposition* (vols. I and II [analysis of *Das Wohltemperierte Klavier*; Berlin 1890–91; 3rd ed., 1914; Eng. tr. by J. Shedlock, 2 vols., London, 1893]; vol. III [analysis of the *Kunst der Fuge*; Berlin, 1894; 3rd ed., 1921]); A. Pirro, *L'Orgue de J.-S. B.* (Paris, 1895; Eng. tr., London, 1902); F. Iliff, *The 48 Preludes and Fugues of J.S. B.* (London, 1897); A. Pirro, *L'Esthétique de J.-S. B.* (Paris, 1907); A. Heuss, *J.S. B.s Matthäuspassion* (Leipzig, 1909); R. Wustmann, *J.S. B.s Kantatentexte* (Leipzig, 1913; 2nd ed., 1967); C. Terry, *B.'s Chorals* (3 vols., Cambridge, 1915, 1917, 1921); idem, *B.'s Mass in B Minor: A Study* (Glasgow, 1915); E. Kurth, *Grundlagen des linearen Kontrapunkts: Einführung in Stil und Technik von B.s melodischer Polyphonie* (Bern, 1917; 5th ed., 1956); H. Grace, *The Organ Works of B.* (London, 1922); C. Terry, *J.S. B.'s Original Hymn-Tunes for Congregational Use* (London, 1922); W. Werker, *Studien über die Symmetrie im Bau der Fugen und die motivische Zusammengehörigkeit der Präludien und Fugen des Wohltemperierten Klaviers von J.S. B.* (Leipzig, 1922); W. Werker, *Die Matthäus- Passion* (Leipzig, 1923); C. Terry, *B.: The Mass in B Minor* (London, 1924; rev. ed., 1931); W. Whittaker, *Fugitive Notes on Certain Cantatas and the Motets of J.S. B.* (London, 1924);

F. Franke, *B.s Kirchen-Kantaten* (Leipzig, 1925); J. Fuller Maitland, *The "48": B.'s Wohltemperiertes Clavier* (London, 1925); idem, *The Keyboard Suites of J.S. B.* (London, 1925); C. Terry, *B.: The Cantatas and Oratorios* (2 vols., London, 1925); idem, *J.S. B.: Cantata Texts, Sacred and Secular, with a Reconstruction of the Leipzig Liturgy of His Period* (London, 1926); M. Zulauf, *Die Harmonik J.S. B.s* (Bern, 1927; 2nd ed., 1937); C. Terry, *B.: The Passions* (London, 1926; 2nd ed., 1935); P. Wackernagel, *B.s Brandenburgische Konzerte* (Berlin, 1928); H. Abert, *B.s Matthäuspassion* (Halle, 1929); F. Atkins, *B.'s Passions* (London,1929); J. Fuller Maitland, *B.'s "Brandenburg" Concertos* (London, 1929; 2nd ed., 1945); A. Hull, *B.'s Organ Works* (London, 1929); C. Terry, *The Four-Part Chorales of J.S. B.* (5 vols., London, 1929); idem, *The Magnificat, Lutheran Masses and Motets* (London, 1929); idem, *B.: The Historical Approach* (London, 1930); K. Ziebler, *Das Symbol in der Kirchenmusik J.S. B.s* (Kassel, 1930); E. Schwebsch, *J.S. B. und die Kunst der Fuge* (Stuttgart, 1931; 2nd ed., 1955); D. Tovey, *A Companion to the Art of Fugue* (London, 1931); C. Terry, *B.'s Orchestra* (London, 1932; 2nd ed., 1958); C. Freyse, *Eisenacher Dokumente um J.S. B.* (Leipzig, 1933); L. Landshoff, *Revisionsbericht zur Urtextausgabe von J.S. B.s Inventionen und Sinfonien* (Leipzig, 1933); C. Terry, *The Music of B.: An Introduction* (London, 1933); H. Huggler, *J.S. B.s Orgelbüchlein* (Bern, 1935); A. Dickinson, *The Art of J.S. B.* (London, 1936; rev. ed., 1950); G. Herz, *J.S. B. im Zeitalter des Rationalismus und der Frühromantik* (Bern, 1936); L. Landshoff, *Musikalisches Opfer* (Leipzig, 1936); A. Schering, *J.S. B.s Leipziger Kirchenmusik* (Leipzig, 1936; 2nd ed., 1954); E. Thiele, *Die Chorfugen J.S. B.s* (Bern and Leipzig, 1936); H. Besch, *J.S. B.: Frömmigkeit und Glaube* (Gütersloh, 1938; 2nd ed., Kassel, 1950); C. Gray, *The 48 Preludes and Fugues of J.S. B.* (London, 1938); W. Neumann, *J.S. B.'s Chorfuge* (Leipzig, 1938); G. Frotscher, *J.S. B. und die Musik des 17. Jahrhunderts* (Wadenswil, 1939); A. Schering, *Das Zeitalter J.S. B.s und Johann Adam Hillers* (Leipzig, 1940); B. Martin, *Untersuchungen zur Struktur der Kunst der Fuge* (Regensburg, 1941); H. Drinker, *Texts of the Choral Works of J.S. B. in English Translation* (4 vols., N.Y., 1942–43); A. Schering, *Über Kantaten J.S. B.s* (Leipzig, 1942; 3rd ed., 1950); S. Taylor, *The Chorale Preludes of J.S. B.* (London, 1942); H. David, *J.S. B.'s Musical Offering: History, Interpretation and Analysis* (N.Y., 1945); F. Blume, *J.S. B. im Wandel der Geschichte* (Kassel, 1947; Eng. tr., 1950); F. Florand, *J.S. B.: L'OEuvre d'orgue* (Paris, 1947); W. Neumann, *Handbuch der Kantaten J.S. B.s* (Leipzig, 1947; 4th ed., 1971); F. Smend, *J.S. B.: Kirchen-Kantaten* (6 vols., Berlin, 1947–49; 3rd ed., 1966); idem, *Luther und B.* (Berlin, 1947); M. Dehnert, *Das Weltbild J.S. B.s* (Leipzig, 1948; 2nd ed., 1949); N. Dufourcq, *J.S. B.: Le Maître de l'orgue* (Paris, 1948); H. Keller, *Die Orgelwerke B.s: Ein Beitrag zu ihrer Geschichte, Form, Deutung und Wiedergabe* (Leipzig, 1948; Eng. tr., 1967); R. Steglich, *Wege zu B.* (Regensburg, 1949); H. Besseler and G. Kraft, *J.S. B. in Thüringen* (Weimar, 1950); W. Blankenburg, *Einführung in B.s h- moll Messe* (Kassel and Basel, 1950; 3rd ed., 1973); H. Dräger and K. Laux, eds., *B.-Probleme* (Leipzig, 1950); H. Keller, *Die Klavierwerke B.s* (Leipzig, 1950); C. Mahrenholz, *J.S. B. und der Gottesdienst seiner Zeit* (Kassel and Basel, 1950); R. Petzoldt and L. Weinhold, eds., *J.S. B.: Das Schaffen des Meisters im Spiegel einer Stadt* (Leipzig, 1950); A. Schmitz, *Die Bildlichkeit der wortgebundenen Musik J.S. B.s* (Mainz, 1950); W. Vetter, *Der Kapellmeister B.: Versuch einer Deutung* (Potsdam, 1950); P. Aldrich, *Ornamentation in J.S. B.'s Organ Works* (N.Y., 1951); W. David, *J.S. B.s Orgeln* (Berlin, 1951); A. Davison, *B. and Handel:The Consummation of the Baroque in Music* (Cambridge, Mass., 1951); A. Dürr, *Studien über die frühen Kantaten J.S. B.s* (Leipzig, 1951; rev. ed., Wiesbaden, 1977); R. Gerber, *B.s Brandenburgische Konzerte* (Kassel and Basel, 1951); F.

Hamel, *J.S. B.: Geistige Welt* (Göttingen, 1951); W. Scheide, *J.S. B. as a Biblical Interpreter* (Princeton, 1952); W. Emery, *B.'s Ornaments* (London, 1953; 2nd ed., 1961); idem, *Notes on B.'s Organ Works: A Companion to the Revised Edition* (London, 1953–57); K. Geiringer, *Symbolism in the Music of B.* (Washington, D.C., 1955); L. Czaczkes, *Analyse des Wohltemperierten Klaviers* (Vienna, 1956–65); A. Dickinson, *B.'s Fugal Works* (London, 1956); H. Engel, *J.S. B.s Violinkonzerte* (Leipzig, 1956); W. Neumann, ed., *J.S. B.: Sämtliche Kantatentexte* (Leipzig, 1956; 2nd ed., 1967); L. Tagliavini, *Studi sui testi delle cantate sacre di J.S. B.* (Padua, 1956); G. von Dadelsen, *Bemerkungen zur Handschrift J.S. B.s, seiner Familie und seines Kreises* (Trossingen, 1957); J. David, *Die zweistimmigen Inventionen von J.S. B.* (Göttingen, 1957); W. Reich, ed., *J.S. B., Leben und Schaffen* (Zürich, 1957); G. von Dadelsen, *Beiträge zur Chronologie der Werke J.S. B.s*, Tübinger B.-Studien, IV–V (Trossingen, 1958); J. David, *Die dreistimmigen Inventionen von J.S. B.* (Göttingen, 1959); W. Whittaker, *The Cantatas of J.S. B., Sacred and Secular* (2 vols., London, 1959; 2nd ed., 1964); E. Bodky, *The Interpretation of B.'s Keyboard Works* (Cambridge, Mass., 1960); R. Donington, *Tempo and Rhythm in B.'s Organ Music* (London, 1960); J. Day, *The Literary Background to B.'s Cantatas* (London, 1961); J. David, *Das wohltemperierte Klavier* (Göttingen, 1962); R. Steglich, *Tanzrhythmen in der Musik J.S. B.s* (Wolfenbüttel, 1962); N. Carrell, *B.'s Brandenburg Concertos* (London, 1963); J. Chailley, *Les Passions de J.-S. B.* (Paris, 1963; 2nd ed., rev., 1984); H. Keller, *Das Wohltemperierte Klavier von J.S. B.: Werk und Wiedergabe* (Kassel, 1965); J. Westrup, *B. Cantatas* (London, 1966); N. Carrell, *B. the Borrower* (London, 1967); M. Geck, *Die Wiederentdeckung der Matthäuspassion im 19. Jahrhundert* (Regensburg, 1967); G. Kraft, *B. in Eisenach* (Jena, 1967); C. Wolff, *Der stile antico in der Musik J.S. B.s* (Wiesbaden, 1968); A. Dürr, *Die Kantaten von J.S. B.* (Kassel and Munich, 1971; 5th ed., rev., 1985); J. Chailley, *L'Art de la fugue de J.-S. B.* (Paris, 1971–72); R. Marshall, *The Compositional Process of J.S. B.: A Study of the Autograph Scores of the Vocal Works* (Princeton, 1972); A. Robertson, *The Church Cantatas of J.S. B.* (London, 1972); W. Kolneder, *Die Kunst der Fuge: Mythen des 20. Jahrhunderts* (Wilhelmshaven, 1977); P. Williams, *The Organ Music of J.S. B.* (3 vols., Cambridge, 1980–84); S. Daw, *The Music of J.S. B.: The Choral Works* (East Brunswick, N.J., 1981); H. Klotz, *Streifzüge durch die Bachsche Orgelwelt* (Wiesbaden, 1981); R. Azekus, *J.S. B. und die Aufklärung* (Leipzig, 1982); A. Heinich, *B.'s Die Kunst der Fuge: A Living Compendium of Fugal Procedures* (Washington, D.C., 1983); P. Williams, ed., *B., Handel and Scarlatti:Tercentenary Essays* (Cambridge, 1985); G. Stauffer and E. May, eds., *J.S. B. as Organist: His Instruments, Music and Performance Practices* (Bloomington, Ind., 1986); H. Vogt, *J.S. B.'s Chamber Music* (1988); R. Marshall, *The Music of J.S. B.: The Sources, the Style, the Significance* (N.Y., 1989); W. Young, *The Cantatas of J.S. B.: An Analytical Guide* (Jefferson, N.C., 1989); J. Butt, *B. Interpretation: Articulation Marks in Primary Sources of J.S. B.* (Cambridge, 1990); R. Tatlow, *B. and the Riddle of the Number Alphabet* (Cambridge, 1990); J. Butt, *B.: Mass in B Minor* (Cambridge, 1991); E. Chafe, *Tonal Allegory in the Vocal Music of J.S. B.* (Berkeley, 1991); C. Wolff, *B.:Essays on His Life and Music* (Cambridge, Mass., 1991); D. Schulenberg, *The Keyboard Music of J.S. B.* (N.Y., 1992); M. Boyd, *B.: The Brandenburg Concertos* (Cambridge, 1993); G. and J. Csiba, *Die Blechblasinstrumente in J.S. B.s Werken* (Kassel, 1994); P. Dirksen, *Studien zur Kunst der Fuge von J.S. B.: Untersuchungen zur Entstehungsgeschichte, Struktur und Aufführungspraxis* (Wilhelmshaven, 1994); L. Burns, *B.'s Modal Chorales* (Stuyvesant, N.Y., 1995); E. Kooiman, G. Weinberger, and H. Busch, *Zur Interpretation der Orgelmusik J.S. B.s* (Kassel, 1995); M. Marissen, *The Social and Religious Designs of J.S. B.'s Brandenburg Concertos* (Princeton, 1995); D. Melamed, *J.S. B. and the German Motet* (Cambridge, 1995); L. Dreyfus, *B. and the Patterns of Invention* (Cambridge, 1996); G. Hartmann, *Die Tonfolge B-A-C-H: Zur Emblematik des Kreuzes im Werk J.S. B.s* (Bonn, 1996); R. Stinson, *B.:The Orgelbüchlein* (N.Y., 1996); J. Butt, ed., *The Sacred Choral Music of J.S. B.: A Handbook* (Brewster, Mass., 1997); M. Geck, ed., *B.s Orchesterwerke: Bericht über das 1. Dortmunder B.-Symposion 1996* (Witten, 1997); M. Heinemann and H.-J. Hinrichsen, eds., *B. und die Nachwelt* (Laaber, 1997 et seq.); C. Wolff, ed., *Wereld van de B.- cantates/The World of the B. Cantatas* (N.Y., 1997 et seq.); M. Marissen, *Lutheranism, Anti-Judaism, and B.'s St. John Passion* (N.Y., 1998). **ICONOGRAPHY:** W. His., *J.S. B.: Forschungen über dessen Grabstätte, Gebeine und Antlitz* (Leipzig, 1895); K. Geiringer, *The Lost Portrait of J.S. B.* (N.Y., 1950); H. Raupach, *Das wahre Bildnis J.S. B.s* (Wolfenbüttel, 1950); F. Smend, *J.S. B. bei seinem Namen gerufen* (Kassel, 1950); H. Besseler, *Fünf echte Bildnisse J.S. B.s* (Kassel, 1956); H. van Tuyll van Serooskerken, *Probleme des Bachporträts* (Bilthoven, 1956); C. Freyse, *B.s Antlitz: Betrachtungen und Erkenntnisse zur B.-Ikonographie* (Eisenach, 1964).—**NS/LK/DM**

Bach, Wilhelm Friedemann (the "Halle" Bach), eldest son of **Johann Sebastian**; b. Weimar, Nov. 22, 1710; d. Berlin, July 1, 1784. He was a pupil of his father. He studied at the Thomasschule in Leipzig (1723–29), and also studied violin with J.G. Graun in Merseburg (1726). In 1729 he enrolled at the Univ. of Leipzig, where he took courses in mathematics, philosophy, and law. In 1733 he became organist of the Sophienkirche in Dresden. In 1746 he was appointed organist of the Liebfrauenkirche in Halle, a post he held until 1764. In 1774 he went to Berlin. As a composer, he was highly gifted. His music reflects the influences of the Baroque and Rococo styles. An ed. of selected works was begun by the Abteilung für Musik der Preussischen Akademie der Künste; vol. I contains four trios (Leipzig, 1935). His Sinfonias opp. 64 and 65 have been ed. by W. Lebermann (Mainz, 1971), opp. 67–71 by M. Schneider (Leipzig, 1914). His piano compositions have been ed. by W. Rehberg in *Die Söhne Bachs* (1933); three excerpts are in K. Geiringer, *Music of the Bach Family: An Anthology* (Cambridge, Mass., 1955). His organ works are printed in E. Power Biggs and G. Weston, eds., *W.F. Bach: Complete Works for Organ* (N.Y., 1947).

BIBL.: C. Bitter, *Carl Philip Emanuel und W.F. B. und deren Brüder* (2 vols., Berlin, 1868); M. Falck, *W.F. B.: Sein Leben und seine Werke* (Leipzig, 1913); K. Stabenow, *J.S. Bachs Sohn* (Leipzig, 1935); K. Geiringer, *The Bach Family: Seven Generations of Creative Genius* (N.Y., 1954); H. Franck, *F., der Sohn J.S. Bachs* (Berlin, 1963).—**NS/LK/DM**

Bach, Wilhelm Friedrich Ernst, son of **Johann Christoph Friedrich**, and grandson and last male descendant of **Johann Sebastian**; b. Bückeburg, May 23, 1759; d. Berlin, Dec. 25, 1845. He studied with his father and with his uncle **Johann Christoph** in London. In 1787 he became music director at Minden, and in 1788 he was named Kapellmeister and harpsichordist to Queen Friedrike of Prussia. In 1797 he was appointed to a similar position to Queen Luise. He also served as music master to the royal princes. He attended the dedication of the J.S. Bach monument in Leipzig on April 23, 1843. See K. Geiringer, *Music of the Bach Family: An Anthology* (Cambridge, Mass., 1955).—**NS/LK/DM**

Bach, August Wilhelm, German organist; b. Berlin, Oct. 4, 1796; d. there, April 15, 1869. After a period of organ playing in churches and in concert, he became a teacher at and later director (1832) of the Royal Inst. for Church Music in Berlin. Mendelssohn was his pupil in organ playing.—NS/LK/DM

Bach, Jan (Morris), American composer and teacher; b. Forrest, Ill., Dec. 11, 1937. He pursued composition studies with Gaburo and Kelly at the Univ. of Ill. (B.M., 1959; D.M.A., 1971); also took courses with Copland (becoming co-winner of the Koussevitzky prize at the Berkshire Music Center in Tanglewood, 1961), Gerhard, and Musgrave. From 1966 he taught theory and composition at Northern Ill. Univ. in De Kalb. In his compositions, Bach effectively combines traditional and contemporary elements in an accessible style.

WORKS: DRAMATIC: *The System*, opera (1973; N.Y., March 5, 1974); *The Student from Salamanca*, opera (1979; N.Y., Oct. 9, 1980); *Romeo and Juliet*, incidental music (1984). ORCH.: *Toccata* (1959); *Burgundy Variations* (1968); Piano Concerto (1975; Chicago, July 8, 1981); *Gala Fanfare* (1979); *Sprint* (1982; Greenwich, Conn., March 26, 1983); Horn Concerto (Chicago, June 4, 1983); *Escapade* (1984); *Alla Breve*, fanfare-overture (1984); *Dompes and Jompes* for Strings (London, April 17, 1986); Harp Concerto (1986; Indianapolis, Feb. 6, 1987); Concerto for Trumpet and Wind Ensemble (1987); *Estampie* (1988); Euphonium Concerto (1990); Steel Drum Concerto (1994). B a n d : *Dionysia* for Symphonic Band (1964); *Recitative and March* for Viola and Wind Ensemble (1966); *The Eve of St. Agnes* for Wind Ensemble (1976); *Praetorius Suite* for Concert Band (1977). CHAMBER: String Trio (1956); *Divertimento* for Oboe and Bassoon (1956); Quartet for Strings (1957); Clarinet Sonata (1957); Quintet for Oboe and Strings (1958); *Partita* for Flute, Harpsichord, and Cello (1958); *Rondelle* for Alto Flute, Violin, Horn or Bassoon, and Piano (1961); *4 2–Bit Contraptions* for Flute and Horn (1964); *Skizzen* for Woodwind Quintet (1967); *Turkish Music* for Multipercussion Solo (1967); *Woodwork* for Percussion Quartet (1970); *Laudes* for Brass Quintet (1971); *Eisteddfod* for Flute, Viola, and Harp (1972); *My Very 1st Solo* for Alto Saxophone and Electric Piano (1974); *Canon and Caccia* for 5 Horns (1977); *Concert Variations* for Euphonium and Piano (1977); Quintet for Tuba and Strings (1978); *Lowlands* for Contrabass and Piano (1981); *French Suite* for Horn (1982); *Helix* for Alto Saxophone, Flute, Clarinet, Bassoon, Horn, Trumpet, Trombone, and 2 Percussionists (1983); *New Egyptian Fanfare* for 3 Trumpets and 3 Percussionists (1983); *8 Duetudes* for Flute and Bassoon (1983) *Gypsy Rock* for String Quartet (1984); *Little Suite* for Harp (1984); *Lazy Blues* for 5 Bassoons (1985); *Triptych* for Brass Quintet (1989); *Anachronisms* for String Quartet (1991). P i a n o : *3 Bagatelles* (1963; rev. 1971). VOCAL: *3 Shakespearean Songs* for Chorus (1960: *Exhotation* for Chorus and Piano (1961; rev. 1964); *A Lyke-wake Dirge* for Chorus or Quartet (1962); *Dirge for a Minstrel* for Chorus (1969); *3 Choral Dances* for Women's Chorus (1969); *Spectra* for Soprano, Baritone, Chorus, and Orch. (1971); *3 Sonnets on Woman* for Tenor and Harpsichord (1972); *My Wilderness* for Chorus (1974); *The Oregon Trail* for Tenor, Baritone, Chorus, and Orch. (1975); *Hair Today* for Chorus (1977); *The Happy Prince* for Narrator, Violin, and Chamber Orch. (1978); *Laudate Dominum* for Chorus, Children's Chorus, and Organ (1981); *5 Sylvan Songs* for Baritone and String Quartet (1981); *A Solemn Music* for Chorus (1987); *We Have But Faith* for Chorus and Organ (1988); *With Trumpet and Drum* for 16 Solo Voices and Piano (1991); *People of Note* for Voices and Instruments (1993).—NS/LK/DM

Bach, Michael, German cellist, composer, and visual artist, also known as **Bach Michael Bachtischa**; b. Worms, April 17, 1958. He studied cello with Pierre Fournier and Janos Starker, then embarked on a career of international concert activity as well as performances on radio, recordings, and television. He made numerous significant contributions to the art of contemporary cello performance; his publication *Fingerboards & Overtones* proposes new ideas concerning overtones and harmonics and is considered a pioneering work in the literature on contemporary technique. In 1990 he developed the Curved Bow (*BACH.Bogen*) for the cello, violin, and viola, which, in polyphonic playing, permits the simultaneous sounding of multiple strings, with the high arch of the bow allowing for full, sustained chords. Rostropovich has been intimately involved in its development, and several contemporary composers, among them Cage, Schnebel, and Walter Zimmermann, have composed works especially for it. Bach is also a composer, often in collaboration with the visual artist Renate Hoffleit, with whom he has created strikingly original string and sound installations. His purely musical compositions are idiosyncratic and highly personal, described by him as "free from compositional conventions." His visual works include *Fingerboards I, II* (both 1990), and *III-VII* (1994–98), which capture the hand's choreography on the cello fingerboard as color impressions, *Fieldwork* (1994), *Mit diesen beiden Händen* (1994), *Lagauche* (1995), and *Olévano* (1995).

WORKS: STRING AND SOUND INSTALLATIONS: With R. Hoffleit: *One⁸ and 15 Strings* (1994; a simultaneous presentation of two works, one by Bach Bachtischa [*Notation 2 for 15 Strings and Five Players*] and one by Cage [*One⁸*], originally conceived for solo cello but performed in this version by 5 cellos together with the string installation *15 Strings* by R. Hoffleit); *Lake Corryntawy String* (1995), in which contact microphones record the sounds of a 100–meter string stretched across Lake Corryntawy; *Notrepos* (1995), incorporating the sounds of tubes and Baroque stone lions (Hoffleit's sculptures) simultaneous with the playing of Baroque cello music (Bach's *Fingerboards*); *Strings of Kaukab Spring* (1996), making use of the resonant potential of trees; *Achill Strings* (1996), in which the ruins of 13 houses in a deserted village are linked and made to sound via strings of up to 120 meters in length; *Achill/Ruit* (1996–97), in which sound recordings and photographs of sound installations collected on Achill Island, Ireland, are transplanted into a multi-level house; *Traffic, Tubes and Soloists* (1997), in which live electronics allow for the intoning of sounds of a busy traffic intersection crossing into the interior of a building, simultaneous with the performance of solo compositions by Bach Bachtischa; *Efeu-Klänge* (1997), performed in the courtyard of a building wherein sounds are made by artist's hand movements on plants and by artist's performance on specially constructed utensils; *...die Leere zwischen den Steinen klingt...* (1999), an installation of 15 strings that develops the idea initially presented in *15 Strings* (1992); *The Black Dog* (2000), exploring the sonic potentials of the exterior court of the partially preserved Romantic Abbey church of Murbach (France); *The castle Schloss Kapfenburg as a musical instrument*

(2000), in which the entire castle is made to sound by the spanning of long strings, performed by some 50 performers. **MUSICAL WORKS:** *C-A-G-E* for Cello (1992); *Ohne Titel* for Cello and 3 Tapes (1992; a reconstruction of an unfinished work for Solo Cello, *Ryoanji*, by Cage); *One-to-Three* for Cello and 3 Tapes (1992); *Röhrenstücke* for Live Electronics (1993); *Notation 1* (1993), *2* (1993–94), and *3* (2000) for Cello (1993–2000); *Notation 1 and 2* for Voice (1993–94); *Notation* for Saxophone (1993–94); *Notation* for Contrabass (1994); *50 Sounds* for Accordion (1995); *52 Sounds* for Violin (1995; rev. 1998); *1, 2, 3* for Cello and 3 Loudspeakers (2000); *+Murbach* for Cello (2000); *A-E-G-C* for Microtonal Piano (2000); *57 Sounds* for Organ (2000); *Notation* for Chamber Orch. (2000).—**LK/DM**

Bacharach, Burt, 1960s tunesmith of frothy pop ballads, b. May 12, 1928, in Kansas City, Mo. Burt Bacharach grew up in N.Y. and studied music theory and composition at McGill Univ. in Montreal in the early 1950s. He later worked as a pianist and arranger and served as Marlene Dietrich's music director from 1956 to 1958. He subsequently teamed with lyricist Hal David (b. N.Y., May 25, 1921), who had been writing song lyrics since 1943. Early successful collaborations included "The Story of My Life" for Marty Robbins and "Magic Moments" for Perry Como. Initially, the two often worked separately. They were associated with a number of hits, such as Sarah Vaughan's "Broken-Hearted Melody" (by David and Sherman Edwards), Gene McDaniels' "Tower of Strength" (by Bacharach and Bob Hilliard), and The Shirelles' "Baby, It's You" (by Bacharach, Mack David and Barney Williams).

In the early 1960s, Bacharach arranged and scored sessions for The Drifters, meeting Dionne Warwick. He wrote The Drifters' "Mexican Divorce" (with Bob Hilliard) and Chuck Jackson's smash R&B and major pop hit "Any Day Now." Bacharach and David began working together regularly in 1962, collaborating on many smash hits. These included Gene Pitney's "Only Love Can Break a Heart" and "Twenty Four Hours from Tulsa," Dusty Springfield's "Wishin' and Hopin'," and Jackie DeShannon's "What the World Needs Now Is Love." Into the 1970s, the duo provided Dionne Warwick with more than 30 chart records, among them being "Anyone Who Had a Heart," "Walk on By," "Message to Michael," "Do You Know the Way to San Jose?" and "I Say a Little Prayer."

Throughout the 1960s, Bacharach and David composed for films, providing the title songs to *What's New Pussycat?* (performed by Tom Jones, 1965) and *Alfie* (performed by Dionne Warwick, 1967), as well as "The Look of Love" (by Dusty Springfield, 1967) from *Casino Royale*, and the top hit "Raindrops Keep Falling on My Head" (by B. J. Thomas, 1969) from *Butch Cassidy and the Sundance Kid*. In the late 1960s, the two collaborated on the successful Broadway musical *Promises, Promises*, from which Dionne Warwick scored two hits, the title song and "I'll Never Fall in Love Again."

Bacharach and David provided smash hits for The Carpenters ("Close to You") and The Fifth Dimension ("One Less Bell to Answer") in 1970, after which they ended their partnership. Bacharach and Dionne Warwick also ended their professional relationship in the

early 1970s. During the 1970s, he performed in public to enthusiastic audiences, both live and on television. Having embarked on his own recording career in 1966, Bacharach recorded the symphonic suite, *Woman*, with the Houston Symphony in 1979.

In 1981, Bacharach began collaborating with lyricist Carole Bayer Sager, (b. N.Y.C., March 8, 1946). She had provided the lyrics for a number of smash hit songs, including "Groovy Kind of Love" (The Mindbenders, 1966), "Midnight Blue" and "Don't Cry Out Loud" (Melissa Manchester, 1975 and 1978, respectively), "When I Need You" (Leo Sayer, 1977), and "Nobody Does It Better" (Carly Simon, 1977). Their first collaboration, with Peter Allen and Christopher Cross, yielded the top hit "Best That You Can Do" as the theme to the film *Arthur* for Cross in 1981.

The couple married in 1982 and soon composed the hits "Making Love" for Roberta Flack and "Heartlight," with and for Neil Diamond. In 1986, they supplied the top hits "On My Own" to Patti Labelle and Michael McDonald, and "That's What Friends Are For" to Dionne Warwick with Stevie Wonder and others. The profits to "That's What Friends Are For," over $1.5 million were donated to the American Foundation for AIDS Research. The following year, Bacharach toured with Warwick, and he and Sager provided Warwick and Jeffrey Osborne with the major hit "Love Power." The couple divorced in 1991. In 1995, he collaborated with British musician Elvis Costello on "God Give Me Strength" from the *Grace of My Heart* soundtrack. Later, the two worked together on 1998's *Painted from Memory*.

With Hal David, Bacharach formed one of the most successful professional songwriting teams in popular music history, writing literally dozens of hit songs. Their compositions featured David's Tin Pan Alley–style lyrics and Bacharach's uncommon rhythms and distinctive melodies, bridges and modulations. In arranging horn and string parts for The Drifters in the early 1960s and for Dionne Warwick throughout the 1960s, Bacharach helped change the sound of contemporary rhythm-and-blues and soul music. After a fallow period during the 1970s, Bacharach reemerged in the 1980s with a number of huge hit compositions in collaboration with lyricist, and ex-wife, Carole Bayer Sager, including Dionne Warwick's "That's What Friends Are For."

DISC.: *Man! His Songs* (1966); *Casino Royale* (soundtrack) (1967); *Reach Out* (1967); *Make It Easy on Yourself* (1969); *Plays His Hits* (1969); *Butch Cassidy and the Sundance Kid* (soundtrack) (1969); *Burt Bacharach* (1971); *Living Together* (1974); *Greatest Hits* (1974); *Futures* (1977); *Burt Bacharach* (1987). Houston Symphony: *Woman* (1979). Elvis Costello: *Painted from Memory* (1998).—**BH**

Bachauer, Gina, eminent Greek-born English pianist of Austrian descent; b. Athens, May 21, 1913; d. there, Aug. 22, 1976. She showed her aptitude as a pianist at age five; entered the Athens Cons., where her teacher was Waldemar Freeman. She then went to Paris, where she took lessons with Cortot at the École Normale de Musique. In 1933 she won the Medal of Honor at the Vienna International Competition; between 1933 and 1935 she received occasional instructions from Rachmaninoff in France and Switzerland; in 1935 she made her professional debut with the Athens Sym. Orch. under the direction of Mitropoulos; she was also piano soloist in Paris in 1937 with Monteux. During World War II she lived in Alexandria, Egypt, and played several hundred concerts for the Allied Forces in the Middle East. On Jan. 21, 1946, she made her London debut with the New London Orch. under the direction of Alec Sherman, who became her second husband. Her first American appearance took place in N.Y. on Oct. 15, 1950. Only 35 people attended this concert, but she received unanimous acclaim from the critics, and her career was assured. The uncommon vigor of her technique suggested comparisons with Teresa Carreño; her repertoire ranged from Mozart to Stravinsky; in both standard and modern works, she displayed impeccable taste. She died of a heart attack in Athens on the day she was to appear as soloist with the National Sym. Orch. of Washington, D.C., at the Athens Festival. In 1976 the Gina Bachauer International Piano Competition was founded in Salt Lake City.—NS/LK/DM

Bachelet, Alfred, French composer; b. Paris, Feb. 26, 1864; d. Nancy, Feb. 10, 1944. He studied at the Paris Cons., receiving the Grand Prix de Rome for his cantata, *Cléopâtre* (1890). From his earliest works, Bachelet devoted himself mainly to opera. In his youth, he was influenced by Wagnerian ideas, but later adopted a more national French style. During World War I, he conducted at the Paris Opéra, in 1919 he became director of the Nancy Cons., and in 1939 he was elected a member of the Académie des Beaux Arts.

WORKS: DRAMATIC: Lyric Dramas: *Scémo* (Paris, May 6, 1914); *Un Jardin sur l'Oronte* (Paris, Nov. 3, 1932). Music Drama: *Quand la cloche sonnera* (Paris, Nov. 6, 1922). Ballet: *La Fete chez la Poupliniere* and *Castor et Pollux* by Rameau (adapted and rewritten). OTHER: Orch. works with voices: *L'Amour des Ondines, Joie, Le Songe de la Sulamith, Noel; Surya* for Tenor, Chorus, and Orch. (1940); *Ballade* for Violin and Orch.; songs.—NS/LK/DM

Bachmann, Sixt (actually, **Joseph Siegmund Eugen**), German keyboard player and composer; b. Kettershausen, July 18, 1754; d. Reutlingendorf, Oct. 18, 1825. He was a gifted child, and on Nov. 5 or 6, 1766, he engaged in an organ competition with the youthful Mozart in Markt Biberbach. In 1771 he entered the Premonstratensian monastery in Ober Marchthal, where he took his vows (1773) and was ordained a priest (1778). After serving as a music teacher and choirmaster there, he settled in Reutlingendorf in 1803. He composed church music, piano sonatas, and organ pieces.—LK/DM

Bachofen, Johann Caspar, Swiss composer; b. Zürich, Dec. 26, 1695; d. there, June 23, 1755. He studied in Zürich at the Cathedral school, receiving the title of V.D.M. (verbi divini minister) in 1720. In 1742 he was named cantor at the Grossmünster Cathedral there, and he concurrently served as Kapellmeister at the German School there (from 1739). He is best known for his popular collection of sacred songs for home use, publ. as *Musicalisches Hallelujah* (1727; many subsequent reprints).

BIBL.: B. Arnold, *The Life and Works of J.C. B.* (diss., Univ. of Southern Calif., 1956).—NS/LK/DM

Bachrich, Sigmund (real name, **Sigismund**), Hungarian violist and composer; b. Zsambokreth, Jan. 23, 1841; d. Vienna, July 16, 1913. He studied violin in Vienna; spent several years in Paris, where he was viola player with the Hellmesberger and Rosé quartets. From 1869 to 1899 he was a member of the viola section in the Vienna Phil. He wrote several operas, among them *Muzzedin* (1883), *Heini von Steier* (1884), and *Der Fuchs-Major* (1889), as well as a ballet, *Sakuntala*. His memoirs were publ. posthumously under the title *Aus verklungenen Zeiten* (Vienna, 1914). In his professional activities he adopted Sigmund as his first name.—NS/LK/DM

Bacilly, Bénigne de, French composer and teacher; b. c. 1625; d. Paris, Sept. 27, 1690. He composed a number of sacred and secular vocal works, but he is best known for an important vocal treatise, *Remarques curieuses sur l'art de bien chanter* (Paris, 1668; Eng. tr., 1968).—NS/LK/DM

Bäck, Sven-Erik, significant Swedish composer; b. Stockholm, Sept. 16, 1919; d. there, Jan. 10, 1994. He studied violin at the Stockholm Musikhögskolan (1938–43); also had training in composition from Rosenberg in Stockholm (1940–45) before pursuing studies in early music with Ina Lohr and Wenzinger at the Basel Schola Cantorum (1948–50); later had advanced composition studies with Petrassi in Rome (1951–52). He played violin in the Kyndel (1940–44) and Barkel (1944–53) string quartets, as well as in the Lilla Chamber Orch. (1943–48). After conducting the "Chamber Orch. '53" (1953–57), he was director of the Swedish Radio music school at Edsberg Castle outside Stockholm (from 1959). In 1961 he was elected to membership in the Royal Academy of Music in Stockholm. In his compositions, Bäck experimented with serialism and, later, electronic sound. His liturgical works are particularly notable.

WORKS: DRAMATIC: Opera: *Tranfjädrarna* (The Twilight Crane), a symbolist subject from Japanese Noh drama (1956; Swedish Radio, Feb. 28, 1957; first stage perf., Stockholm, Feb. 19, 1958); *Ett spel om Maria, Jesu Moder* (A Play about Mary, Mother of Jesus; Swedish Radio, April 4, 1958); *Gastabudet* (The Feast; Stockholm, Nov. 12, 1958); *Fageln* (The Birds; 1960; Swedish Radio, Feb. 14, 1961). Ballet: *Ikaros* (Stockholm, May 1963); *Movements* (Swedish TV, Feb. 27, 1966); *Kattresan* (Cat's Journey; 1969); *Mur och Port* (Wall and Gate; 1970; Stockholm, Jan. 17, 1971); *Genom Jorden, Genom Havet* (Through the Earth, Through the Sea; 1971–72; Stockholm, June 17, 1972). ORCH.: *Sinfonia per archi* (1951); *Sinfonia da camera* (1954); *Fantasy on Dies sind die Heiligen Zehn Gebot* (1954; rev. 1957); Violin Concerto (1957); *A Game around a Game* for Piano, Celesta, Percussion, and Strings (Donaueschingen, Oct. 17, 1959); *Arkitektur 60* for 2 Wind Orchs., Piano, Double Bass, and Percussion (1960); *Intrada* for Small Orch. (Stockholm, April 26, 1964);

175

Arkitektur 65 for 2 Wind Orchs., Piano, Double Bass, and Percussion (1965); Cello Concerto (1965); *O Altitudo II* (1966; also for Organ as *Altitudo I*); *Ruoli per orchestra* (1968); *Aperio* for 3 Orch. Groups and Tape (1973); *Ciklos*, concerto for Piano, Strings, and Percussion (1975); *Sumerki*, serenade for Strings (1976–77); *4 Motets* (1978; also for Strings); *3 Dialogue Motets* for Cello and Strings (1984); *Ekvator* for Orch. and Tape (1988); *Pro Musica Vitae*, concerto for Strings (1989). **CHAMBER:** 4 string quartets (1945, 1947, 1962, 1981); String Quintet (1948); *Préambule pour Pierre* for String Quartet (1949); Sonata for Solo Flute (1949); *Nocturne* for 3 Recorders, Percussion, Lute, Viola da Gamba, and Violin (1953); Trio for Violin, Cello, and Double Bass (1954); *Nature morte* for Viola, Bassoon, and Percussion (1955); Sonata for 2 Cellos (1957); *Favola* for Clarinet, Percussion, and Piano (1962); *Postludium* for Flute, Piano, and Percussion (1967); *Sentire* for Flute, Cello, and Piano (1969); Trio for Violin, Viola, and Cello (1970); *Decet* for Wind Quintet, String Quartet, and Double Bass (1973); *Fa-Ce* for Bassoon and Harpsichord or Piano (1975); *Signos* for 6 Percussion (1979); *Trio in 1 Movement* for Piano, Violin, and Cello (1984); *3 consorts* for 2 Trumpets and 3 Trombones (1993). **P i a n o :** *Expansive Preludes* (1949); *Sonata alla ricercare* (1950); *Danssuit* for 2 Pianos (1951); *Impromptu* (1957); *Tollo I* for Piano Duet (1974) and *II* for 2 Pianos and Microphones (1975); *Sonata in 2 Movements and Epilogue* (1980). **VOCAL:** *Ur Johannes* for 3 Voices and Organ ad libitum (1944); *Ur Johannes 9* for Voices and Organ (1947); *Svanesang* for Chamber Chorus, Flute, Viola, and Timpani (1947); *Gladje i Gud*, cantata for Soloist, Voices, and Organ (1948); *Dithyramb* for Woman's Voice, Unison Chorus, and Chamber Orch. (1949); *Sinfonia sacra* for Voices and Orch. (1953); *Uppbrottets massa* for Soloist, Unison Voices, Organ, and Percussion (1967); *Neither Nor* for Soprano, Piano, and Percussion (1971); *Där fanns en brunn* for Chorus, Flute, Clarinet, Cello, Percussion, and Piano or Organ (1973); *Just da de langsta skuggorna...* for 4 Singers and 10 Instruments (1974); *Naktergalen och Hoken* for Chorus, String Orch., Piano, and Percussion (1975); *Te Deum* for Chorus, Brass, and Organ (1980); *Annus Solaris* for 2 Soprano and Tape (1980); various choral pieces. **—NS/LK/DM**

Backer-Grøndahl, Agathe (Ursula),

Norwegian composer and pianist; b. Holmestrand, Dec. 1, 1847; d. Ormöen, near Christiania, June 16, 1907. She studied in Norway with Kjerulf and Lindeman, in Florence with Hans von Bülow, and in Weimar with Liszt. She married the singing teacher Grøndahl (1875). Among her piano works, *Études de concert, Romantische Stücke*, and *Trois morceaux* became well known and have been frequently reprinted. She also wrote a song cycle, *Des Kindes Frühlingstag*.

BIBL.: I. Hoegsbro, *Biography of the Late A. B.-G.* (N.Y., 1913); O. Sandvik, *A. B.-G.* (Oslo, 1948); C. Dahm, *A. B. G.: Komponisten og pianisten* (Oslo, 1998).**—NS/LK/DM**

Backers, Cor,

Dutch pianist, conductor, music historian, and composer; b. Rotterdam, June 5, 1910. He studied piano with Dirk Schafer and composition at the Rotterdam Cons. He gave piano recitals in the Netherlands; also traveled through Europe and East Africa; conducted the chamber choir Haags Kamerkoor (1950–60), specializing in forgotten masterpieces of the past. He publ. a valuable compendium, *Nederlandse componisten van 1400 tot op onze tijd* (The Hague, 1941;

2nd ed., enl., 1948), which details the evolution of music in the Netherlands, with particular emphasis on modern Dutch music; he also publ. monographs on Handel, Puccini, Gershwin, and others. He composed mostly for voices and organ, numbering among his works a "declamatorio," *Joost de Decker*, for Narrator and Piano; a Piano Sonata (1935); *Six Goethe-Lieder* for Chorus (1969); *Missa Sancta* for Soloists, Chorus, and Organ (1973–74); and *Te Deum Laudamus* for Chorus and Organ or Orch. (1973–75).**—NS/LK/DM**

Backhaus, Wilhelm,

eminent German-born Swiss pianist and pedagogue; b. Leipzig, March 26, 1884; d. Villach, Austria, July 5, 1969. He studied with Reckendorf in Leipzig (1891–99), making his debut there at the age of eight. After studying briefly with d'Albert in Frankfurt am Main (1899), he began his career with a major tour in 1900, aquiring a fine reputation in Europe as both a pianist and a teacher. He made his U.S. debut on Jan. 5, 1912, as soloist in Beethoven's Fifth Piano Concerto with Walter Damrosch and the N.Y. Sym. Orch. In 1930 he settled in Lugano, where he continued to teach, and became a naturalized Swiss citizen. Following World War II, he resumed his concert tours; made his last appearance in the U.S. at a recital in N.Y. in 1962, at the age of 78, displaying undiminished vigor as a virtuoso. He died while visiting Austria for a concert engagement. He was particularly distinguished in his interpretations of Beethoven and Brahms.

BIBL.: F. Herzog, *W. B.* (Berlin, 1935); A. Eichmann, *W. B.* (Ghent, 1957; Eng. tr., 1958).**—NS/LK/DM**

Bacon, Ernst,

remarkable American composer; b. Chicago, May 26, 1898; d. Orinda, Calif., March 16, 1990. He studied theory at Northwestern Univ. with Lutkin (1915–18), and later at the Univ. of Chicago with Oldberg and T. Otterstroem (1919–20); also took private piano lessons in Chicago with Alexander Raab (1916–21). In 1924 he went to Vienna, where he took private composition lessons with Weigl and Schmidt. Returning to America, he studied composition with Bloch in San Francisco, and conducting with Goossens in Rochester, N.Y.; completed his education at the Univ. of Calif. (M.A., 1935). From 1934 to 1937 he was supervisor of the Federal Music Project in San Francisco; simultaneously deployed numerous related activities, as a conductor and a music critic. He was on the faculty of Converse Coll. in S.C. (1938–45) and Syracuse Univ. (1945–63). In 1939 and 1942 he held Guggenheim fellowships. He also engaged in literary pursuits—wrote poetry and publ. a book of aphorisms—and espoused radical politics. A musician of exceptional inventive powers, he publ. a brochure, *Our Musical Idiom* (Chicago, 1917), when he was 19; in it he outlines the new resources of musical composition. He later publ. *Words on Music* (1960) and *Notes on the Piano* (1963). In some of his piano works, he evolved a beguiling technique of mirror reflection between right and left hands, exact as to the intervals, with white and black keys in one hand reflected respectively by white and black keys in the other. However, Bacon is generally regarded as primarily a composer of lyric songs.

WORKS: DRAMATIC: *Take Your Choice* (San Francisco, 1936; in collaboration with P. Mathias and R. Stoll); *A Tree on the Plains*, musical play (Spartanburg, S.C., May 2, 1942); *A Drumlin Legend*, folk opera (N.Y., May 4, 1949); *Dr. Franklin*, musical play (1976). **Ballet:** *Jehovah and the Ark* (1968–70); *The Parliament of Fowls* (1975). **ORCH.:** *Fantasy and Fugue* (1926); *Symphonic Fugue* for Piano and Strings (1932); 4 syms.: No. 1 for Piano and Orch. (1932; San Francisco, Jan. 5, 1934), No. 2 (1937; Chicago, Feb. 5, 1940), No. 3, *Great River*, for Narrator and Orch. (1956), and No. 4 (1963); *Bearwall* for Piano and Strings (1936); *Country Roads, Unpaved* (1936); *Ford's Theater* (1946); *From these States* (1951); *Fables* for Narrator and Orch. (1953); Concerto grosso (1957); *Elegy* for Oboe and Strings (1957); *Erie Waters* (1961); 2 piano concertos: No. 1, *Riolama* (1963) and No. 2 (1982); *Over the Waters*, overture (1976). **CHAMBER:** Piano Quintet (1946); Cello Sonata (1946); Quintet for String Quartet and Double Bass (1950); *Peterborough*, suite for Viola and Piano (1961–82); *A Life*, suite for Cello and Piano (1966–81); *Tumbleweeds* for Violin and Piano (1979); Piano Trio (1981); Violin Sonata (1982); Viola Sonata (1987); piano pieces. **VOCAL:** Cantatas: *On Ecclesiastes* (1936); *The Lord Star* (1950); *By Blue Ontario* (1958); *Nature* (1968–70); *The Last Invocation*, Requiem after Whitman, Dickson, and others, for Bass, Chorus, and Orch. (1968–71); numerous songs; arrangements.—**NS/LK/DM**

Bacquier, Gabriel (-Augustin-Raymond-Théodore-Louis), noted French baritone; b. Béziers, May 17, 1924. He studied at the Paris Cons., winning three premiers prix. In 1950 he made his debut in Landowski's *Le Fou* in Nice with José Beckman's Compagnie Lyrique, and remained with the company until 1952; then sang at the Théâtre Royal de la Monnaie in Brussels (1953–56). He was a member of the Opéra-Comique (1956–58) and the Opéra (from 1958) in Paris. In 1962 he made his U.S. debut as the High Priest in *Samson et Dalila* in Chicago; in 1964 he first appeared at London's Covent Garden; on Oct. 17, 1964, he made his Metropolitan Opera debut in N.Y. as the aforementioned High Priest, and continued to sing there until 1982. In 1987 he became a teacher at the Paris Cons. He was made a Chevalier of the Légion d'honneur in 1975. He was equally at home in both dramatic and comic roles, numbering among his most esteemed portrayals Leporello, Dr. Bartolo, Dulcamara, Boccanegra, Falstaff, Golaud, and Scarpia.—**NS/LK/DM**

Badarzewska, Thekla, Polish composer of salon music; b. Warsaw, 1834; d. there, Sept. 29, 1861. At the age of 17 she publ. in Warsaw a piano piece, *Molitwa dziewicy* (A Maiden's Prayer), which was republ. as a supplement to the Paris *Revue et Gazette Musicale* in 1859, and unaccountably seized the imagination not only of inhibited virgins, but of sentimental amateur pianists all over the world. More than 100 eds. of this unique piece of salon pianism, dripping maudlin arpeggios, were publ. in the 19th century, and the thing was still widely sold even in the 20th century. Badarzewska wrote 34 more piano pieces in the salon style, but none of them matched *A Maiden's Prayer*. An ungentlemanly German critic opined in an obituary that "Badarzewska's early death saved the musical world from a veritable inundation of intolerable lachrymosity."—**NS/LK/DM**

Badea, Christian, Romanian-born American conductor; b. Bucharest, Dec. 10, 1947. He studied violin and composition at the Bucharest Cons.; subsequently took courses in Brussels, in Salzburg, and at the Juilliard School in N.Y. He conducted at the Spoleto Festival of Two Worlds in Charleston, S.C., and Spoleto, Italy; served as music director of the Savannah (Ga.) Sym. Orch. (1977–84) and the Columbus (Ohio) Sym. Orch. (1983–91).—**NS/LK/DM**

Baden, (Peter) Conrad (Krohn), Norwegian organist, teacher, and composer; b. Drammen, Aug. 31, 1908; d. Oslo, June 11, 1989. He began his training with the Drammen organist Daniel Hanssen in 1926; after pursuing organ studies at the Oslo Cons. (graduated, 1931), he received composition instruction in Leipzig (1931–32), with Honegger and Rivier in Paris (1951–52), and in Vienna (1965). He served as a church organist in Drammen (1928–61) and Oslo (1961–75); taught at the Oslo Cons. (1948–73) and the Oslo Academy of Music (1973–78). His neo-Romanticism eventually gave way to a more modern style of composition.

WORKS: ORCH.: 6 syms. (1952; 1957; *Sinfonia Piccola*, 1959; 1970; *Sinfonia Voluntatis*, 1976; *Sinfonia Espressiva*, 1980); *Divertimento* (1951); *Gioia*, overture (1951); Concertino for Clarinet and Strings (1953); *Pastorale and Fugue* for Chamber Orch. (1957); *Eventyr-Suite* (Fairy Tale Suite; 1960); *Variazioni* (1963); *Fantasia Breve* (1965); *Concerto for Orchestra* (1968); *Intrada Sinfonica* (1969); Viola Concerto (1973); Piano Concerto (1979); Concerto for Bassoon and Strings (1981); *Rondo* (1983); *Pastorale* for Chamber Orch. (1983). **CHAMBER:** Violin Sonata (c. 1942); 3 string quartets (1944, 1946, 1961); 2 trios for Flute, Oboe, and Clarinet (1957, 1964); 2 woodwind quintets (1963, 1982); Sonata for Solo Flute (1958); *Divertimento* for Flute, Oboe, and Clarinet (1964); *Hymnus* for Alto Voice, Flute, Oboe, and Viola (1966); *Mini-Trio* for Flute, Clarinet, and Bassoon (1977); Flute Sonata (1984); piano pieces; organ music. **CHORAL:** Mass for Soloists, Chorus, and Orch. (1949); cantatas for Skien's 600th (1958), Strömsö Church's 300th (1966–67), and Dröbak Church's 200th (1973) anniversaries; *Mennesket* (The Human Being), cantata (1971).—**NS/LK/DM**

Badescu, Dinu (Constantin), Romanian tenor; b. Craiova, Oct. 17, 1904. He studied in Bucharest. He made his operatic debut as a baritone in 1931 in Cluj as Germont, returning later that year to make his tenor debut as Lionel in *Martha*. He was a leading member of the Bucharest Opera (1936–61); also sang at the Vienna Volksoper (1941–44) and at the Vienna State Opera (from 1948); he was highly successful as a guest artist with the Bolshoi Theater in Moscow, in Leningrad, Budapest, Prague, et al., making a specialty of lyrico-dramatic roles in Verdi's operas.—**NS/LK/DM**

Badia, Carlo Agostino, Italian composer; b. probably in Venice, 1672; d. Vienna, Sept. 23, 1738. His first known work was his oratorio *La sete di Cristo in croce* (Innsbruck, 1691); soon thereafter he was made a court composer at Innsbruck. In 1694 he was called to Vienna, where he became Musik-Compositeur of the Imperial Court, a post he held for the rest of his life. His first wife was Anna Maria Elisabetta Nonetti, a prominent singer at the Viennese court (d. 1726). Badia was an important composer in his day, producing some 25 works for the stage and about 40 oratorios.

WORKS: DRAMATIC: *La Ninfa Apollo* (1692); *Amor che vince lo sdegno, ovvero Olimpia placata* (Rome, Carnival 1692); *La Rosaura ovvero Amore figlio della gratitudine* (Innsbruck, 1692); *L'Amazone corsara, ovvero L'Alvilda, regina de' Goti* (Innsbruck, 1692); *Bacco, vincitore dell'India* (Vienna, Carnival 1697); *La pace tra i numi discordi nella rovina di Troia* (Vienna, May 21, 1697); *L'idea del felice governo* (Vienna, June 9, 1698); *Lo squittinio dell'eroe* (Vienna, July 26, 1698); *Imeneo trionfante* (Vienna, Feb. 28, 1699); *Il Narciso* (Vienna, June 9, 1699); *Il commun giubilo del mondo* (Vienna, July 26, 1699); *Cupido fuggitivo da Venere e ritrovato a' piedi della Sacra Reale Maestà d'Amalia* (Vienna, Carnival 1700); *Le gare dei beni* (Vienna, Feb. 21, 1700); *Diana rappacificata con Venere e con Amore* (Vienna, April 21, 1700); *La costanza d'Ulisse* (Vienna, June 9, 1700); *L'amore vuol somiglianza* (Vienna, Jan. 7, 1702); *L'Arianna* (Vienna, Feb. 21, 1702); *Il Telemacco, ovvero Il valore coronato* (Vienna, March 19, 1702); *La concordia della Virtù e della Fortuna* (Vienna, April 21, 1702); *Enea negli Elisi* (Vienna, July 26, 1702); *La Psiche* (Vienna, Feb. 21, 1703); *Napoli ritornata ai Romani* (Vienna, Oct. 1, 1707); *Ercole, vincitore di Gerione* (Vienna, Nov. 4, 1708); *Gli amori di Circe con Ulisse* (Dresden, June 20, 1709); *Il bel genio dell'Austria ed il Fato* (Vienna, Nov. 1723).—**NS/LK/DM**

Badia, Conchita (Conxita)

Badia, Conchita (Conxita), noted Spanish soprano; b. Barcelona, Nov. 14, 1897; d. there, May 2, 1975. She studied piano and voice with Granados, and also had lessons with Casals and Manuel de Falla. She made her debut in Barcelona as a concert singer in 1913 in the first performance of *Canciónes amatorias* by Granados, with the composer as piano accompanist. She subsequently devoted herself to concert appearances, excelling as an interpreter of Spanish and Latin American music; often appeared in performances with Casals and his orch. in Barcelona. In later years she taught voice in Barcelona, where her most famous pupil was Montserrat Caballé.

BIBL.: J. Alavedra, *Conxita B.: Una vida d'artista* (Barcelona, 1975).—**NS/LK/DM**

Badings, Henk

Badings, Henk (actually, **Hendrik Herman**), eminent Dutch composer and pedagogue; b. Bandung, Dutch East Indies, Jan. 17, 1907; d. Maarheeze, June 26, 1987. He was orphaned at an early age and taken to the Netherlands; studied mining engineering at the Delft Polytechnic Univ. before taking up composition without formal training; an early sym. was premiered by Mengelberg and the Concertgebouw Orch. in Amsterdam (July 6, 1930). After composition lessons with Pijper (1930–31), he taught at the Rotterdam Cons. (1934–37), the Amsterdam Lyceum (1937–41), and the Royal Cons. of Music at The Hague (1941–45). In 1945 he was barred from professional activities as a cultural collaborator during the Nazi occupation of his homeland, but in 1947 was permitted to resume his career. From 1961 to 1977 he taught at the Univ. of Utrecht musicological inst.; also was a prof. of composition at the Stuttgart Hochschule für Musik (1966–72). Badings began his career as a composer in the Romantic vein. In his melodic foundation, he often employed the scale of alternating major and minor

seconds. From 1950 he experimented with electronic sound and also adapted some of his works to the scale of 31 melodic divisions devised by the Dutch physicist Adriaan Fokker.

WORKS: DRAMATIC: Opera: *De Nachtwacht* (The Night Watch; 1942; Antwerp, May 13, 1950); *Liebesränke* (Love's Ruses; 1944–45; Hilversum, Jan. 6, 1948); *Orestes*, radio opera (Florence, Sept. 24, 1954); *Asterion*, radio opera (Johannesburg, April 11, 1958); *Salto mortale*, television chamber opera (Dutch TV, Eindhoven, June 19, 1959; first opera to be accompanied solely by electronic sound); *Martin Korda, D.P.* (Amsterdam, June 15, 1960). **Ballet For Instruments:** *Balletto Grottesco* for 2 Pianos (1939); *Orpheus und Eurydike* for Soloists, Chorus, and Orch. (Amsterdam, April 17, 1941); *Balletto Serioso* for Orch. or 2 Pianos (1955); *Balletto Notturno* for 2 Pianos (1975). **Ballet For Electronic Sound:** *Kain und Abel* (The Hague, June 21, 1958; first all-electronic sound ballet); *Evolutions* (Hannover, Sept. 28, 1958); *Der sechste Tag* (Innsbruck, Nov. 7, 1959); *Jungle* (Amsterdam, 1959); *The Woman of Andras* (Hannover, April 14, 1960); *Marionetten* (Salzburg, 1961). **ORCH.:** 4 violin concertos (1928; 1933–35; 1944; 1947); 1 unnumbered sym. (Amsterdam, July 6, 1930); 14 numbered syms.: No. 1 for 16 Solo Instruments (1932; Hilversum, March 19, 1959), No. 2 (Amsterdam, Oct. 5, 1932), No. 3 (1934; Amsterdam, May 2, 1935), No. 4 (1943; Rotterdam, Oct. 13, 1947), No. 5 (Amsterdam, Dec. 7, 1949), No. 6, *Psalm*, for Chorus and Orch. (Haarlem, June 25, 1953), No. 7, *Louisville* (1954; Louisville, Ky., Feb. 26, 1955), No. 8, *Hannover* (1956; Vancouver, Jan. 11, 1957), No. 9 for Strings (1959; Amsterdam, Dec. 17, 1960), No. 10 (1961; Rotterdam, Jan. 29, 1962), No. 11, *Sinfonia Giocosa* (Eindhoven, Oct. 26, 1964), No. 12, *Symphonische klangfiguren* (The Hague, Nov. 20, 1964), No. 13 for Wind Orch. (Pittsburgh, June 29, 1967), and No. 14, *Symphonische Triptiek* (Ghent, Sept. 4, 1968); 2 cello concertos (1930, 1939); 2 piano concertos (1939; *Atlantic Dances*, 1955); Saxophone Concerto (1951–52); 2 organ concertos (1952, 1966); 2 concertos for 2 Violins and Orch. (1954, 1969); 2 flute concertos (1956, 1963); Concerto for Bassoon, Double Bassoon, and Wind Orch. (1964); Concerto for 2 Pianos and Orch. (1964); Concerto for Viola and Strings (1965); *Pittsburgh Concerto* for Clarinet, Brass, Percussion, and Tape (1965); Concerto for Violin, Viola, and Orch. (1965); Concerto for 3 Horns, Wind Orch., and Tape (1970); *American Folk Song Suite*, concerto for English Horn and Wind Orch. (1975); *Azioni musicali* (1980); Triple Concerto No. 3 for Flute, Oboe, Clarinet, and Orch. (1981); Concerto for Orch. (1982); Quadruple Concerto for 4 Saxophones and Orchestra (1984); *Serenade* for Strings (1985). **CHAMBER:** 6 quintets: No. 1 for Flute, Piano, and String Trio (1928), No. 2 for Wind Quintet (1929), No. 3 for Harp, Flute, and String Trio (1936), No. 4 for Wind Quintet (1948), No. 5 for Piano Quintet (1952), and No. 6 for Clarinet, Violin, Cello, Guitar, and Harp (1986); 2 cello sonatas (1929, 1934); 6 string quartets (1931, 1936, 1944, 1966, 1980, 1984); 5 violin sonatas (1933; 1939; 1952; 1931, rescored 1966; 1984); 9 trios for Various Instrumental Combinations (1934–62); 3 sonatas for Solo Violin (1940, 1951, 1951); 2 sonatas for Solo Cello (1941, 1951); Sonata for Solo Harp (1944); Viola Sonata (1951); much piano music, including 6 sonatas (1934, 1941, 1944, 1945, 1945, 1947); organ pieces. **VOCAL:** Oratorios: *Apocalypse* (1948; Rotterdam, Nov. 25, 1959) and *Jonah* (Adelaide, Sept. 30, 1963); *St. Mark Passion* (1971; Rotterdam, May 18, 1992); *Missa antiphonica* (1985); cantatas; choral pieces.

BIBL.: P. Klemme, *Catalog of the Works of H. B., 1907–87* (Warren, Mich., 1993).—**NS/LK/DM**

Badini, Ernesto, Italian baritone; b. San Colombano al Lambro, Sept. 14, 1876; d. Milan, July 6, 1937. He studied at the Milan Cons. and with Cesari. In 1895 he made his operatic debut as Rossini's Figaro in San Colombano al Lambro; sang in many regional opera houses of Italy. In 1913 Toscanini chose him for the Verdi centennial celebrations in Parma, then invited him to Milan's La Scala, where he created Puccini's Gianni Schicchi (1922); remained on its roster until 1931. He also appeared at Rome's Teatro Costanzi (1921) and London's Covent Garden (debut as Gianni Schicchi, 1924). In addition to buffo roles, Badini also sang a number of contemporary roles.—NS/LK/DM

Badinski, Nicolai, Bulgarian-born German composer, violinist, and teacher; b. Sofia, Dec. 19, 1937. He studied mathematics at the Univ. (1955) and pursued music training at the Bulgarian State Cons. (diploma, 1961) in Sofia, and then attended the master classes in composition of Wagner-Régeny at the Academy of Arts in East Berlin (1967–70), worked with Ligeti, Stockhausen, Xenakis, and C. Halffter in Darmstadt (summers, 1974–78), and studied with Dallapiccola and Donatoni at the Accademia Musicale Chigiana in Siena (summers, 1975–76). In 1971 he was a visiting prof. at the univs. of Stockholm and Copenhagen. In 1976 he settled in West Berlin, and in 1979 he became a naturalized German citizen. In 1977 he won first prize in the Viotti composition competition in Vercelli, in 1978 the Stockhausen composition competition in Bergamo-Brescia, in 1979 the Trieste Prize for symphonic music, in 1980–81 the Prix de Rome, and in 1982 the Prix de Paris. He served as composer-in-residence of the Djerassi Foundation in Calif. in 1987. Badinski is a member of the European Academy of Arts, Sciences, and Humanities in Paris.

WORKS: ORCH.: 3 syms. (1967, 1978, 1981); 3 violin concertos (1970–71; 1971–72; 1971–72); Viola Concerto (1975); *Homage to Stravinsky* for 12 Solo Strings or String Orch. (1978–79); *Drang zum Ausdruck* (1981–82); *Connections* for Violin, Piano, and Orch. (1982–83); *Scherzo électroacoustique* (1984–85); *Die "trunkene" Fledermaus* (1991–92); *Erleuchtung* for Violin and Orch. (1992–93); *Signals* for 8 Trumpets and Orch. (1993–94); *Seven Memorial Stones: In Memoriam of the Holocaust Victims* (Requiem) for String Orch. (1993–94). CHAMBER: 3 string quartets (1965, 1973, 1978); Octet (1972); *Pitture* for Violin, Viola, and Cello (1975); *Decipio,* 7 Pieces for Various Instruments (1976 et seq.); *Disegni* for Flute and Instrumental Ensemble (1984); *Jesus Christ* for Violin, Viola, and Double Bass (1996). VOCAL: *Widerspiegelungen der Weisheit* for Soloists, Chorus, and Orch. (1983–84).—NS/LK/DM

Badura-Skoda, Eva (née Halfar), German musicologist; b. Munich, Jan. 15, 1929. She studied at the Vienna Cons. and took courses in musicology, philosophy, and art history at the univs. of Heidelberg, Vienna, and Innsbruck (Ph.D., 1953, with the diss. *Studien zur Geschichte des Musikunterrichtes in Österreich im 16., 17. und 18. Jahrhundert*). In 1962 and 1963 she led summer seminars at the Salzburg Mozarteum. In 1964 she was the Brittingham Visiting Prof. at the Univ. of Wisc. at Madison, where she served as prof. of musicology from 1966 to 1974. She was a visiting prof. at Boston Univ.

(1976), Queen's Univ. in Kingston, Ontario (1979), McGill Univ. in Montreal (1981–82), and the Univ. of Göttingen (1982–83). In 1986 she was awarded the Ehrenkreuz for arts and letters by the Austrian government. She contributed many articles to books, reference works, and journals, and also ed. scores by Haydn, Dittersdorf, Mozart, and Schubert. In 1951 she married **Paul Badura-Skoda,** with whom she collaborated on the vols. *Mozart-Interpretation* (Vienna, 1957; Eng. tr., 1961; 2nd ed., rev., 1996) and *Bach-Interpretation* (Laaber, 1990; Eng. tr., 1992). With P. Branscombe, she ed. the vol. *Schubert Studies:Problems of Style and Chronology* (Cambridge, 1982). She also ed. the report of the international Haydn congress held in Vienna in 1982 (Munich, 1986) and was an ed. of a vol. on Schubert and his friends (Cologne and Vienna, 1999).—LK/DM

Badura-Skoda (real name, **Badura**), **Paul,** Austrian pianist, music scholar, and composer; b. Vienna, Oct. 6, 1927. He was reared by his stepfather, whose surname he adopted professionally. He studied piano and conducting at the Vienna Cons. (1945–48), and attended the piano master classes of Edwin Fischer in Lucerne. In 1948 he made his debut in Vienna. After winning third prize in the Long-Thibaud Competition in Paris in 1949, he performed throughout Europe. On Jan. 10, 1953, he made his U.S. debut in N.Y. He played for the first time in Tokyo in 1959, and in 1964 he made his first appearance in Moscow. From 1966 to 1971 he served as artist-in-residence at the Univ. of Wisc. at Madison. In addition to his solo career, he also gave duo piano recitals with Jörg Demus. In 1977 he was awarded the Cross of Honor by the Austrian government and in 1992 he was made a Chevalier of the Légion d'honneur of France. While he became particularly known for his performances of the Viennese classics, he also programmed contemporary works. He ed. scores by Mozart, Beethoven, Schubert, and Chopin. Among his own works were several instrumental and vocal pieces. In 1951 he married **Eva Badura-Skoda** (née Halfar), with whom he collaborated on the books *Mozart-Interpretation* (Vienna, 1957; Eng. tr., 1961; 2nd ed., rev., 1996) and *Bach-Interpretation* (Laaber, 1990; Eng. tr., 1992). With Demus, he publ. the study *Die Klaviersonaten von Ludwig van Beethoven* (Wiesbaden, 1970). —NS/LK/DM

Baermann, Carl (actually, **Karl Bärmann**), German-American pianist, pedagogue, and composer, son of **Karl Bärmann;** b. Munich, July 9, 1839; d. Newton, Mass., Jan. 17, 1913. He studied piano with Wanner and Wahlmuth, and composition with F. Lachner and Cornelius in Munich. He completed his training with Liszt, who befriended him. He taught at the Munich Königliche Musikschule, and was made a prof. there in 1876. On Dec. 22, 1881, he made his U.S. debut as a pianist in Boston, where he remained active as a pianist and teacher. Among his students of note were Frederick Converse and Amy Beach. He composed a *Festival March* for Orch. and various piano pieces; among the latter, *12 Étuden* (1877) and the *Polonaise pathétique* (1914) were publ.—NS/LK/DM

Baervoets, Raymond, Belgian composer; b. Brussels, Nov. 6, 1930; d. Rome, Aug. 19, 1989. He studied with Absil, Bourguignon, and Barbier at the Brussels Cons., and then with Defossez at the Accademia di Santa Cecilia in Rome (1961–62). His music followed along classical lines, with contents evolving in an ultra-chromatic coloristic idiom with occasional use of quarter tones.

WORKS: DRAMATIC: B a l l e t : *Métamorphose* (1963); *La Chasse fantastique* (Antwerp, Sept. 28, 1968). ORCH.: *Mouvement symphonique* (1955); *Elégie et Passacaille* (1956); Concerto for Guitar and Chamber Orch. (1958); Violin Concerto (1961); *Composizione* (1962); *Notturno* for Chamber Orch. (1971); *Immagini* for Chamber Orch. (1976); *Memoria* (1975–76); Piano Concerto (1981); *Douze épisodes pour "La Métamorphose" de Kafka* (1986). CHAMBER: *Impromptu* for Trombone and Piano (1958); *Étude* for String Quartet (1961); *Musica Notturna* for Harpsichord, Violin, Cello, and Flute (1969); Quartet for Flute, Clarinet, Violin, and Piano (1974); piano pieces. OTHER: Vocal works, including *Les Dents de la terre* for Narrator, Soloists, Chorus, and 2 Orchs. (1968).—NS/LK/DM

Baeyens, August, Belgian composer; b. Antwerp, June 5, 1895; d. there, July 17, 1966. He studied at the Royal Flemish Cons. in Antwerp. From 1911 he was a violist in Belgian orchs., and later served as director of the Royal Flemish Opera in Antwerp (1944–48; 1953–58). Despite his intimate assn. with the Flemish currents in the music of Belgium, he turned away from the dominant national direction and wrote music in a distinctly expressionistic style, rooted in a quasi-atonal chromaticism.

WORKS: DRAMATIC: *De Dode Dichter,* ballet (1920); *De Liefde en de Kakatoes,* a "grotesque" (1928); *Coriolanus,* radio opera (1941); *De Ring van Gyges,* opera (1943); *De Triomferende Min,* opera (1948). ORCH.: *Entrata* (1917); *Niobé* (1918); 8 syms. (1923, 1939, 1949, 1952, 1954, 1955, 1958, 1961); *4 Small Pieces* (1923); *Arlequin* (1924); *Cyclops* (1925); *Sinfonia Breve* (1928); *Arkadia,* chamber sym. (1951); *Notturno* (1953); Viola Concerto (1956); Trumpet Concerto (1959); Horn Concerto (1960); *Rhapsodie* for Clarinet and Orch. (1966). CHAMBER: 6 string quartets (1922, 1925, 1927, 1949, 1951, 1962); Wind Quintet (1950); Concertino for Oboe, Clarinet, and Bassoon (1951); *Piranesi Suite* for Flute and Cello (1951); Violin Sonata (1952). P i a n o : Sonata (1930). VOCAL: *Lofzang aan de haven,* cantata (1929); *Barabbas* for Narrator and Orch. (1949); songs.—NS/LK/DM

Baez, Joan, sweet-voiced folksinger of the 1960s; b. Staten Island, N.Y., Jan. 9, 1941. Joan Baez started performing in public, accompanying herself on guitar, at small clubs around Cambridge and Boston in the late 1950s and soon graduated to N.Y.'s Greenwich Village. Successful appearances at the 1959 and 1960 Newport Folk Festivals followed, with Baez moving to Calif. in 1961. She met Bob Dylan in April 1961 at Gerde's Folk City in Greenwich Village and spent considerable time with him between 1963 and 1965. Her first three albums consisted of standard folk fare, primarily traditional English and American ballads, and her second, *Volume 2,* proved her commercial breakthrough. Her fourth album, *In Concert, Part 2,* featured "We Shall Overcome," the song that became the protest anthem of the 1960s. That and subsequent albums contained her versions of songs by then-unrecognized folk artists such as Dylan ("Don't Think Twice," "It's All over Now, Baby Blue," and others) and Phil Ochs ("There but for Fortune"). In June 1965, she established the Inst. for the Study of Nonviolence in Carmel, Calif., beginning a lifelong commitment to nonviolence and protest.

With 1967's *Joan,* Joan Baez began recording songs by contemporary songwriters such as Tim Hardin ("If I Were a Carpenter"), Simon and Garfunkel, and Lennon and McCartney. Between 1968 and 1973, she recorded six albums in Nashville. *Any Day Now,* released in 1969, was a double-record set comprised entirely of songs by Bob Dylan. *One Day at a Time* included the labor anthem "Joe Hill," Jagger and Richards' "No Expectations," and Steve Young's "Seven Bridges Road." She also covered material by songwriters such as Willie Nelson, Hoyt Axton, and John Prine, achieving her only major hit in 1971 with Robbie Robertson's "The Night They Drove Old Dixie Down."

Baez began writing her own songs in the early 1970s and signed with A&M Records in May 1972. She placed six of her songs on *Come from the Shadows,* including the undisguised "To Bobby," as well as sister Mimi Farina's "In the Quiet Morning." Her 1975 *Diamonds and Rust* album contained her own compositions "Winds of the Old Days" and the hit title song, plus John Prine's "Hello in There" and Janis Ian's "Jesse." During 1975 and 1976, she toured with Bob Dylan's curious Rolling Thunder Revue. After two final albums for A&M, she switched to Portrait Records (reissued on Epic) for *Blowin' Away* and *Honest Lullaby.*

Joan Baez confirmed her commitment to humanitarian causes with the 1979 formation of the human rights organization, Humanitas International. During the 1980s, she toured internationally in support of human rights organizations, including Poland's Solidarity movement and Palestinian civil disobedience groups. In 1985, she sang on the Amnesty International tour and appeared at Live Aid. Her second autobiography, *And a Voice to Sing With,* was published in 1987. That same year she began recording for the small Gold Castle label. In 1992, in order to reinvigorate her musical career, Baez ceased operation of Humanitas International. She recorded her first major label release in 13 years, *Play Me Backwards,* for Virgin and later recorded *Ring Them Bells* for Guardian Records.

One of the finest female vocalists to emerge from the early 1960s folk scene, Joan Baez was the first folk singer of the era to achieve massive international success. One of the first solo folk singers to record best-selling albums of traditional folk material, she subsequently helped introduce Bob Dylan to a wider audience as she became one of the first folk singers to become involved with protest movements. Associated with the protest classic, "We Shall Overcome," Baez later enjoyed popularity as a song interpreter before emerging as a singer-songwriter, particularly with 1975's *Diamonds and Rust* album. Although accorded star status in Europe, she was reduced to mere celebrity status in the U.S. and remained without an American record label for much of the 1980s. While continuing to involve herself with international protest and freedom movements in the 1990s, Baez recorded only sporadically.

WRITINGS: *Daybreak* (N.Y., Dial Press, 1968); *And a Voice to Sing With: A Memoir* (N.Y., Summit Books, 1987).

DISC.: *Joan Baez* (1960); *Volume 2* (1961); *In Concert* (1962); *In Concert, Part 2* (1963); *Five* (1964); *Farewell Angelina* (1965); *Noel* (1966); *Joan* (1967); *Baptism* (1968); *Any Day Now* (1968); *David's Album* (1969); *One Day at a Time* (1970); *Blessed Are ...* (1971); *Carry It On* (soundtrack) (1971); *Come from the Shadows* (1972); *Where Are You Now, My Son* (1973); *Gracias a la Vida—Here's to Life* (1974); *Diamonds and Rust* (1975); *From Every Stage* (1976); *Gulf Winds* (1976); *Blowin' Away* (1977); *Honest Lullaby* (1979); *Recently* (1987); *Diamonds and Rust in the Bullring* (1989); *Speaking of Dreams* (1989); *Brothers in Arms* (1991); *Play Me Backwards* (1992); *Ring Them Bells* (1995).

BIBL.: H. Garza, *Joan Baez* (N.Y., 1991).—**BH**

Baggiani, Guido, Italian composer; b. Naples, March 4, 1932. He studied composition at the Accademia di Santa Cecilia in Rome; then attended courses given by Stockhausen in Cologne, which were crucial for his further development. In Rome he organized a group for propagandizing contemporary music with the meaningful name of Nuova Consonanza. In 1970 he was appointed prof. of composition at the Pesaro Cons. In 1972 he formed a group with the curious Italian-American name Gruppo Team Roma for performances of electronic music. His principal works are *Mimesi* for Strings and Woodwinds (1967); *Metafora* for Solo Strings (1968); *UBU-ng* for Soprano, Piano, Vibraphone, Electric Guitar, and six Chinese Gongs (1970); *Twins* for Piano and Magnetic Tape (1971); *Memoria* for Chamber Orch. and Two Magnetic Tapes (1972); *Accordo Presunto* for Two Instrumental Groups and Electronic Media (1973); *ContriAzione* for Two Orchs. (1975); *Double* for Chamber Ensemble (1977); *Il crudo e il cotto* for Four Female Voices, Two Flutes, Two Clarinets, and Electronic Media (1982).—**NS/LK/DM**

Bahner, Gert, German conductor; b. Neuwiese, March 26, 1930. He was educated at the Leipzig Hochschule für Musik. In 1957 he made his debut at the Berlin Komische Oper. From 1958 to 1962 he was music director in Potsdam, and then Generalmusikdirektor of Karl-Marx-Stadt (1962–65). In 1965 he became first conductor of the Berlin Komische Oper, and in 1969 its music director. In 1973 he became music director of the Leipzig Opera. In 1983 he settled in (East) Berlin as an opera conductor; also taught at the Hochschule für Musik.—**NS/LK/DM**

Bähr, (Franz) Josef, noted Austrian clarinetist; b. Feb. 19, 1770; d. Vienna, Aug. 7, 1819. He was in the service of Prince Kraft Ernst of Oettingen-Wallerstein (1787–94). He settled in Vienna in 1797, and then became a court musician in the service of Count Johann Joseph Liechtenstein. Beethoven was impressed by his talent, and during the period 1796–1802 wrote his major solo clarinet parts with Bahr in mind.—**NS/LK/DM**

Bai (also **Baj**), **Tommaso,** Italian singer and composer; b. Crevalcuore, near Bologna, c. 1650; d. Rome, Dec. 22, 1714. He was a tenor at the Vatican, where he became maestro di cappella on Nov. 19, 1713. The best-known composition by Bai, follower of Palestrina, is a five-part *Miserere* sung during Holy Week in the Papal Chapel alternately with those by Allegri and Baini. It is reprinted in various collections (Choron, Burney, Peters). Other works of Bai are included in C. Proske's *Musica Divina* (1853–63).—**NS/LK/DM**

Baif, Jean-Antoine de, French poet; b. Venice, Feb. 19, 1532; d. Paris, Sept. 19, 1589. He was taken to Paris as a child, and formed a friendship with Ronsard and other eminent poets. In 1570, with the musician Joachim Thibault de Courville, he founded the Académie de Poésie et de Musique, which met in Baif's home (1571–74) and which pursued the aim of reviving the music and poetry of ancient Greece. He developed a system of "musique mesurée," which he believed would possess a moral force similar to the Greek ideas of "ethos." Settings of his early sonnets and chansons were composed by Arcadelt, F. Roussel, and Cereau, and of his chansonnettes mesurées and Psalms by Lassus, Le Jeune, Mauduit, and others.

BIBL.: M. Auge-Chiquet, *La Vie, les idées et l'oeuvre de J.-A. d.B.* (Paris, 1909).—**NS/LK/DM**

Bailey, Buster (William C.), jazz clarinetist; b. Memphis, Tenn., July 19, 1902; d. Brooklyn, April 12, 1967. He took up clarinet at 13 while attending the Clay Street School in Memphis. He joined W. C. Handy's Orch. in 1917, and toured with Handy until settling in Chicago in 1919. Bailey came to N.Y. in October 1924 to join Fletcher Henderson's band. He would remain associated with Henderson through 1937, with a few breaks to take other jobs, most notably making a European tour in May 1929 with Noble Sissle, and two years back home working with Sissle's band from 1931–33. He also played a year-long stint with Mills Blue Rhythm Band from late 1934–late 1935. After leaving Henderson, he briefly worked with other bands before joining John Kirby in May 1937. He played regularly with Kirby until summer of 1944 (except for a brief absence because of an injured hand in summer 1941), and again in 1945–46. After the war, he primarily worked worked with trumpeter Henry "Red" Allen's band, besides occasional pitband and session work. He was regularly featured at leading jazz festivals during the late 1950s and early 1960s. Bailey's last major position was as a member of Louis Armstrong All Stars. He joined the group in July 1965, and remained with it until the time of his death. He died in his sleep at his home in Brooklyn.

DISC.: *All About Memphis* (1958). F. Henderson: *Hocus Pocus* (1934). M.B.: *Serenade* (1950); *M.B. Sings* (1951).—**JC/LP**

Bailey, Lillian
See **Henschel, Lillian June (née Bailey)**

Bailey, Mildred (Eleanor Rinker), pop-jazz singer; b. Tekoa, Wash., Feb. 9, 1903; d. Poughkeepsie, N.Y., Dec. 12, 1951. Eleanor Rinker was the daughter of Charles and Josephine Rinker; she received her first musical instruction from her mother. The family moved to Spokane in 1912. When she was 14 her mother died of tuberculosis and she was placed in a boarding school. She later lived in Seattle. In 1920 she worked in a music store as a demonstration singer, and began to perform in clubs. During this period she married and divorced the man who gave her the name Bailey. She left Washington to tour West Coast theaters in a vaudeville revue, then settled in Los Angeles, where she performed on radio and in clubs. There she married Benny Stafford; they later divorced.

Mildred Bailey's brother, Al Rinker, was part of a duo with Bing Crosby in Spokane, and when the two came to Los Angeles, she put them up and helped them get work in vaudeville. They were then hired by Whiteman and later helped her get a job with him. Whiteman used her on his radio program but at first did not record her with his band. Her first recording, "What Kind o' Man Is You?," on Oct. 5, 1929, was made with a satellite group drawn from Whiteman's orchestra under the leadership of guitarist Eddie Lang. After she made several recordings with Glen Gray and the Casa Loma Orch. in September 1931, including "When It's Sleepy Time Down South" (music and lyrics by Leon René, Otis René, and Clarence Muse), Whiteman finally decided to have her sing with him on records. The Whiteman recording of "When It's Sleepy Time Down South" with Bailey on vocals became a hit in November 1931. "All of Me" (music and lyrics by Seymour Simons and Gerald Marks) did even better, becoming a best-seller in February 1932.

Meanwhile, Bailey was also recording under her own name, and her rendition of "Georgia on My Mind" (music by Hoagy Carmichael, lyrics by Stuart Gorrell) had become a minor hit in January 1932. Although the Mills Brothers had the most successful recording of "Rockin' Chair" (music and lyrics by Hoagy Carmichael) in the spring of 1932, the song became so closely associated with Bailey that she was billed as the "Rockin' Chair Lady." Whiteman had a double-sided hit in September on which both songs were sung by Bailey: "We Just Couldn't Say Goodbye" (music and lyrics by Harry Woods) and "I'll Never Be the Same" (music by Matty Melneck and Frank Signorelli, lyrics by Gus Kahn).

Bailey left Whiteman in 1933, and married xylophonist Red Norvo. Her next hit, in August, was "Lazy Bones" (music and lyrics by Johnny Mercer and Hoagy Carmichael), on which she was backed by the Dorsey Brothers Orch. In November she was the vocalist on Glen Gray and the Casa Loma Orch.'s hit recording of "Heat Wave" (music and lyrics by Irving Berlin). Benny Goodman and His Orch. used her as the singer on "Ol' Pappy" (music by Jerry Livingston, lyrics by Marty Symes and Al J. Neiburg), which became a hit in February 1934.

In addition to performing solo, Bailey also sang with Ben Bernie's band and appeared on radio shows in 1934–35. She retired, but her husband persuaded her to become the vocalist in the big band he organized in the fall of 1936. She recorded both with Norvo and on her own, and her next solo hit, "Trust in Me" (music by

Milton Ager and Jean Schwartz, lyrics by Ned Wever) spent six weeks in the hit parade starting in February 1937. Another solo, "Where Are You?" (music by Jimmy McHugh, lyrics by Harold Adamson), was in the hit parade for eight weeks starting in April.

Bailey and Norvo topped the hit parade in May 1938 with "Please Be Kind" (music by Saul Chaplin, lyrics by Sammy Cahn) and again in June with "Says My Heart" (music by Burton Lane, lyrics by Frank Loesser)—two of the biggest hits of the year. Her solo recording of "So Help Me" (music by James Van Heusen, lyrics by Eddie DeLange) was in the hit parade for 12 weeks starting in September, and "Have You Forgotten So Soon?" (music by Abner Silver, lyrics by Sam Coslow and Edward Heyman) with Norvo, made the list for four weeks starting in December.

Norvo disbanded in 1939; later, he and Bailey divorced. Bailey became a featured singer on Benny Goodman's *Camel Caravan* radio show and made several records with him, including "Darn That Dream" (music by James Van Heusen, lyrics by Eddie DeLange), which topped the hit parade in March 1940.

Bailey continued to perform in clubs and record during the 1940s, though her career was slowed by health problems—especially diabetes, due to her obesity. She had her own radio series during the 1944–45 season but was less active in the late 1940s and died at age 48 in 1951.

Bailey was among the earliest white singers to be influenced by black-based blues and jazz music and to gain acceptance as a jazz singer; drawing on the examples of Bessie Smith and Ethel Waters, she in turn influenced Billie Holiday and Ella Fitzgerald. When hired by Paul Whiteman in 1929, she became the first woman to be a featured vocalist in an important dance orchestra. Under her own name, and as a band singer, she scored a number of hits, notably "All of Me," "Please Be Kind," "Says My Heart," and "Darn That Dream."

DISC.: *Mildred Bailey, Volume 1* (1929); *Her Greatest Performances* (1929); *The Rockin' Chair Lady* (1931); *The Paul Whiteman Years* (1931); *Mildred Bailey, Volume 2* (1931); *Squeeze Me* (1935); *The Legendary V-Disc Series* (1940); *Mildred Bailey Radio Show* (1944); *The Uncollected Mildred Bailey* (1944); *All of Me* (1945); *M. B.* (1946); *Majestic Mildred Bailey* (1946); *Me and the Blues* (1946); *Mildred Bailey Serenade* (1950); *Mildred Bailey Sings* (1951); *Mildred Bailey* (1952); *Mildred Bailey Memorial Album* (1952); *Mildred Bailey Songs* (1952); *Mildred Bailey* (1954); *Mildred Bailey* (1974); *Harlem Lullaby* (1992); *The Rockin' Chair Lady (1931–1950)* (1994); *Sweet Beginnings* (1995); *Band Vocalist, Vol. 2* (1995); *A Forgotten Lady* (1996); *American Legends No. 4: Mildred Bailey* (1996); *L'Art Vocal, Vol. 9: 1931–1939* (1997); *All of Me* (1998); *Mildred Bailey 1935–1944: Thanks for the Memory* (1998); *Mildred Bailey, 1929–1932* (1999); *Mildred Bailey, 1932–1936* (2000); *The Blue Angel Years* (2000); *Smoke Dreams* (2000); *Mildred Bailey, 1937–1938* (2000).—**WR**

Bailey, Norman (Stanley),

English baritone; b. Birmingham, March 23, 1933. He received a B.Mus. degree from Rhodes Univ. in South Africa; then studied at the Vienna Academy of Music, his principal teachers there being Julius Patzak, Adolf Vogel, and Josef Witt.

He made his operatic debut with the Vienna Chamber Opera in 1959 in *Cambiale di matrimonio*; was then a member of the Linz Landestheater (1960–63), the Wuppertal Opera (1963–64), the Deutsche Oper am Rhein in Düsseldorf (1964–67), and the Sadler's Wells Opera in London (1967–71). In 1969 he made his first appearance at London's Covent Garden, and that same year his debut at Bayreuth at Hans Sachs. On Oct. 23, 1976, he made his Metropolitan Opera debut in N.Y. as Hans Sachs. In 1985 he sang in the premiere of Goehr's *Behold the Sun* in Duisburg. He appeared as Stromminger in *La Wally* at the Bregenz Festival in 1990. In 1996 he made his Glyndebourne Festival debut as Schigolch in *Lulu*. In 1977 he was made a Commander of the Order of the British Empire. He was particularly noted for his performances in Wagner's operas. In 1985 he married **Kristine Ciesinski.—NS/LK/DM**

Baillie, Dame Isobel (Isabella), esteemed Scottish soprano; b. Hawick, Roxburghshire, March 9, 1895; d. Manchester, Sept. 24, 1983. She was a pupil of Sadler Fogg in Manchester and of Guglielmo Somma in Milan. In 1921 she made her concert debut in Manchester, and thereafter made numerous appearances as an oratorio and lieder artist in England. In 1933 she sang for the first time in the U.S. She taught at the Royal Coll. of Music in London (1955–57), Cornell Univ. in Ithaca, N.Y. (1960–61), and the Manchester School of Music (from 1970). In 1951 she was made a Commander of the Order of the British Empire; in 1978 she was made a Dame Commander of the Order of the British Empire. She sang in hundreds of performances of *Messiah*, and was also noted for her championship of works by Elgar, Vaughan Williams, and Howells. Her autobiography was aptly titled *Never Sing Louder Than Lovely* (London, 1982).—**NS/LK/DM**

Baillot, Pierre (-Marie-François de Sales), celebrated French violinist and composer; b. Passy, near Paris, Oct. 1, 1771; d. Paris, Sept. 15, 1842. At the age of nine, he became a violin pupil of Sainte-Marie. Following studies with Pollani in Rome, he returned to Paris in 1791 and became a member of the orch. of the Théâtre Feydeau. In 1795 he became a teacher of violin at the newly opened Paris Cons. During this time, he also pursued training in composition with Cherubini, Reicha, and Catel. In 1802 he became a member of Napoleon's private instrumental ensemble. From 1805 to 1808 he toured in Russia with the cellist Lamarre. In 1814 he organized a series of chamber music concerts in Paris, but also continued to make tours. In 1821 he became first violinist in the orch. of the Paris Opéra. He also was solo violinist in the Royal Orch. from 1825. Baillot's repertoire was quite extensive for a violinist of his day. In addition to the great composers of the period, he included the works of early masters at his concerts. On March 23, 1828, he was soloist in the first Paris performance of Beethoven's Violin Concerto at a concert of the Société des Concerts du Cons. Among his works were a Sym. Concertante for Two Violins and Orch., nine violin concertos, three string quartets, 15 trios, and six violin duos. He wrote the manual *L'Art du violon* (1834; Eng. tr., 1991, as *The Art of the Violin*).—**NS/LK/DM**

Bain, Wilfred, American music educator and administrator; b. Shawville, Quebec, Jan. 20, 1908; d. Bloomington, Ind., March 7, 1997. He was educated at Houghton Coll. (A.B., 1929) and York Univ. (M.A., 1936; Ed.D., 1938). He was head of the music dept. at Central Coll., S.C. (1929–30), then of voice and choral music at Houghton Coll. (1931–38). He was dean of music at North Tex. State Univ. (1938–47). In 1947 he was appointed dean of the Ind. Univ. School of Music in Bloomington. By the time he retired in 1973, it had become one of the foremost music schools in the world. —**NS/LK/DM**

Bainbridge, Simon (Jeremy), English composer; b. London, Aug. 30, 1952. He was a student at the Royal Coll. of Music in London (1969–72), where he received training in composition from John Lambert. He then attended the Berkshire Music Center at Tanglewood (summers, 1973–74). From 1983 to 1985 he was composer-in-residence for Southern Arts, and then was mainly active as a composer and teacher in London. His *Ad Ora Incerta* for Mezzo-soprano, Bassoon, and Orch. (London, March 29, 1995) won the Grawemeyer Award of the Univ. of Louisville in 1997.

WORKS: DRAMATIC: *Trace*, dance piece (1987). **ORCH.:** *Heterophony* (1970); *3 Pieces* for Chamber Ensembles (1970–82; also for Orch., 1997; Bristol, Feb. 7, 1998); Viola Concerto (1976); *Fantasia* for Double Orch. (1983–84); *The Devil's Punchbowl* for Chamber Orch., Children, and Instrumental Ensemble (1987); *Cantus contra cantum* (1989; rev. 1990); Double Concerto for Oboe, Clarinet, and Chamber Orch. (1990); *Toccata* (Birmingham, June 26, 1992); *Landscape and Memory* for Horn and Orch. (London, Nov. 5, 1995); Guitar Concerto (Birmingham, Nov. 15, 1998); *Towards the Bridge* for Chamber Orch. (London, May 1, 1999). **CHAMBER:** Wind Quintet (1970–71; rev. 1974); String Quartet (1972); *Music for Mel and Nora* for Oboe and Piano (1979; rev. as *Concertante in Moto Perpetuo* for Oboe and 9 Players, 1983); *Metamorphosis* for Chamber Ensemble (Amsterdam, June 6, 1988); String Sextet (1988); *Marimolin Inventions* for Violin and Marimba (1990); *Mobile* for English Horn and Piano (London, Nov. 7, 1991; also for Viola and 4 Players, London, March 25, 1994); *Kinneret Pulses* for Viol Consort (N.Y., Nov. 8, 1992); Clarinet Quintet (Cheltenham, July 5, 1993); *For Miles* for Trumpet and 6 Players (London, June 29, 1994); *Henry's Mobile* for Viol Consort (London, May 2, 1995); *Henry's Rondeau* for 5 Players (London, Oct. 18, 1995); *60 Seconds for Elliott* (Schwarz) for Clarinet (1996). **VOCAL:** *Landscapes and Magic Words* for Soprano and Ensemble (1982); *A Song from Michelangelo* for Soprano and Ensemble (1989); *Caliban Fragments and Aria* for Mezzo-soprano and Ensemble (1991); *A Song from Tagore* for Children's Voices and Ensemble (1991); *From an English Folk Song* for Soprano and 4 Players (London, June 7, 1992); *Herbsttag* for 2 Antiphonal Choruses (1993; London, April 16, 1994); *Ad Ora Incerta* for Mezzo-soprano, Bassoon, and Orch., after Primo Levi (1994; London, March 29, 1995); *4 Primo Levi Settings* for Mezzo-soprano, Clarinet, Viola, and Piano (Cheltenham, July 7, 1996); *'Tis Time I Think* for Soprano and String Quartet, after A.E. Housman (1996); *Éicha* for Mezzo-soprano, Chorus, and 10 Players (Oxford, April 19, 1997). —**NS/LK/DM**

Baines, Anthony, English organologist; b. London, Oct. 6, 1912; d. Farnhem, Surrey, Feb. 2, 1997. He

183

studied at the Royal Coll. of Music in London. After playing bassoon in the London Phil. (1935–39; 1946–48) and working as a conductor, he concentrated on organology. In 1946 he helped to found the Galpin Soc., serving as ed. of its journal (1955–63; 1971–83). In 1970 he joined the faculty of the Univ. of Oxford as a lecturer on music and as curator of the Bate Collection of Historical Instruments. He retired in 1981.

WRITINGS: *Woodwind Instruments and Their History* (London, 1957; 3rd ed., rev., 1967); *Bagpipes* (Oxford, 1960; 3rd ed., 1995); ed. *Musical Instruments Through the Ages* (Baltimore, 1961; 2nd ed., rev., 1976); *European and American Musical Instruments* (London, 1966); *Brass Instruments: Their History and Development* (London, 1976); ed. *The Oxford Companion to Musical Instruments* (Oxford, 1992).—NS/LK/DM

Baini, Giuseppe (also known as Abbate Baini),

Italian writer on music and composer; b. Rome, Oct. 21, 1775; d. there, May 21, 1844. He received rudimentary training from his uncle, Lorenzo Baini, then entered the Seminario Romano, where his instructor, Stefano Silveyra, indoctrinated him with the spirit of Palestrina's music. In 1795 he became a member of the papal choir at St. Peter's. He continued his studies there with Bianchini, and in 1802 took courses with Jannaconi, whom he succeeded as maestro di cappella at St. Peter's (1818). In 1821 he wrote his masterpiece, a ten-part *Miserere*, which was accepted for singing at the Sistine Chapel during Holy Week, in alternation with the *Misereres* of Allegri and Bai. He also wrote many Psalms, hymns, masses, and motets. His great ambition was to publ. a complete ed. of Palestrina's works, but he was able to prepare only two vols. for publication. The monument of his devotion to Palestrina was his exhaustive biography, *Memorie storico-critiche della vita e delle opere di Giovanni Pierluigi da Palestrina* (Rome, 1828; Ger. tr. by Kandler, with notes by Kiesewetter, 1834), which remains extremely valuable despite its occasional inaccuracies. He also wrote a *Saggio sopra l'identità de' ritmi musicali e poetici* (1820). Haberl publ. an essay on Baini in the *Kirchenmusikalisches Jahrbuch* (1894).—NS/LK/DM

Bainton, Edgar Leslie,

English composer and pedagogue; b. London, Feb. 14, 1880; d. Sydney, Australia, Dec. 8, 1956. He studied piano and composition at the Royal Coll. of Music in London with Davies and Stanford. He taught piano and composition at the Cons. of Newcastle upon Tyne from 1901 until 1914, and also was its director (1912–14). The outbreak of World War I found him in Berlin, and he was interned as an enemy alien. After the end of the War, he resumed his pedagogical activities as director of the Newcastle Cons. In 1934 he went to Australia and was director of the State Cons. at Sydney until 1947. As a composer, he followed the tenets of the English national school, writing in broad diatonic expanses with a Romantic élan. His works include the operas *Oithona* (Glastonbury, Aug. 11, 1915) and *The Pearl Tree* (Sydney, May 20, 1944), 3 syms. (1903–56), *Before Sunrise* for Voice, Chorus, and Orch. (1917), *Paracelsus*, symphonic poem (1921), *Concerto-Fantasia* for Piano and Orch. (Carnegie Award, 1917; London, Jan. 26, 1922), chamber music, and songs.

BIBL.: H. Bainton, *Remembered on Waking: E.L. B.* (Sydney, 1960).—NS/LK/DM

Baird, Julianne,

American soprano and teacher; b. Statesville, N.C., Dec. 10, 1952. She studied at the Eastman School of Music in Rochester, N.Y. (B.A. in music history, 1973, M.A. in musicology, 1976), with Harnoncourt at the Salzburg Mozarteum (diploma in performance practice, 1977), and with George Houle at Stanford Univ. (Ph.D., 1991, with the diss. *Johann Friedrich Agricola's Anleitung zur Singkunst (1757): A Translation and Commentary*; publ. 1995). She commenced her vocal career as a member of the Waverly Consort and Concert Royal in N.Y., where she made her operatic debut in Gluck's *Orfeo*. Following her solo debut with the N.Y. Phil. under Mehta's direction in 1983, she sang with many orchs. in the U.S. After singing in *The Fairy Queen* in Toronto in 1989, she appeared in the U.S. premiere of Handel's *Siroe* in N.Y. in 1991. She also was a soloist in Bach's *St. John Passion* in London and sang in Handel's *Acis and Galatea* in Ottawa in the latter year. After singing in *Dido and Aeneas* in London in 1992, she toured France, Switzerland, and Poland in 1993 and Mexico in 1994. In 1995 she sang in recital at N.Y.'s Merkin Hall. She portrayed Handel's Galatea at N.Y.'s Lincoln Center in 1996. In 1998 she was engaged to sing in that composer's *Apollo and Dafne* in Portland, Ore. As a teacher, Baird gave master classes in various locales and served on the faculty of Rutgers Univ. in Camden. Her fine vocal gifts are complemented by her expert knowledge of the early music repertoire in which she has excelled. She is especially admired for her performances of works by Monteverdi, Charpentier, Bach, Handel, Purcell, and Telemann.—NS/LK/DM

Baird, Martha,

American pianist and music patroness; b. Madera, Calif., March 15, 1895; d. N.Y., Jan. 24, 1971. She studied at the New England Cons. of Music in Boston and with Artur Schnabel in Berlin; appeared as soloist with Beecham in London and Koussevitzky in Boston. In 1957 she married John D. Rockefeller Jr., and became a benefactress of opera and concert music.—NS/LK/DM

Baird, Tadeusz,

prominent Polish composer; b. Grodzisk Mazowiecki, July 26, 1928; d. Warsaw, Sept. 2, 1981. He studied music privately in Łódź with Sikorski and Woytowicz (1943–44); then at the Warsaw Cons. with Rytel and Perkowski (1947–51); had piano lessons with Wituski (1948–51); also studied musicology with Lissa at the Univ. of Warsaw (1948–52). In 1949, together with Krenz and Serocki, he founded a progressive society of composers under the name Group 49. In 1956 he became active in initiating the first International Festival of Contemporary Music, during the "Warsaw Autumn." In 1977 he was appointed prof. of composition at the Chopin Academy of Music in Warsaw. As a composer, Baird won numerous awards, among them the Fitelberg Competition of 1958, three prizes of the Tribune Internationale des Compositeurs in Paris (1959, 1963, 1966), and the Polish State Awards for his three syms. (1951, 1964, 1969). He also was awarded the Commander's Cross of the Order of Poland's Revival (1964) and the Order of the Banner of Labor, second and first Class (1974, 1981). His early music followed the neo-Romantic modalities characteristic of Polish music; further evolution was marked by complex structures in the manner of dynamic expressionism, with occasional applications of serialism.

WORKS: DRAMATIC: Opera: *Jutro* (Tomorrow; 1964–66). **ORCH.:** Sinfonietta (1949); 3 syms. (1950; *Sinfonia quasi una fantasia*, 1952; 1969); *Overture in Old Style* (1950); *Colas Breugnon*, suite for Flute and Strings (1951); *Overture giocosa* (1952); *Concerto for Orch.* (1953); *Cassazione* (1956); *4 Essays* (1958); *Espressioni varianti* for Violin and Orch. (1958–59); *Variations without a Theme* (1961–62); *Epiphany Music* (1963); *4 Dialogues* for Oboe and Chamber Orch. (1966); *4 Novelettes* for Chamber Orch. (Hanover, N.H., July 16, 1967); *Sinfonia breve* (1968); *Psychodrama* (1971–72); Oboe Concerto (Warsaw, Sept. 23, 1973); *Elegy* (1973); *Concerto lugubre* for Viola and Orch. (1974–75; Nuremberg, May 21, 1976); Double Concerto for Cello, Harp, and Orch. (1976); *Scenes* for Cello, Harp, and Orch. (1976); *Canzona* (1980). **CHAMBER:** *4 Preludes* for Bassoon and Piano (1954); *Divertimento* for Flute, Oboe, Clarinet, and Bassoon (1956); String Quartet (1957); *Play* for String Quartet (1971); *Variations in Rondo Form* for String Quartet (1978). **VOCAL:** *Lyrical Suite*, 4 songs for Soprano and Orch. (1953); *4 Love Sonnets*, after Shakespeare, for Baritone and Chamber Ensemble (1956; also for Baritone, Strings, and Harpsichord, 1969); *Exhortations* on old Hebrew texts for Narrator, Chorus, and Orch. (1959–60); *Erotyki* (Love Songs), cycle of 6 songs for Soprano and Orch. (1961); *Study* for 28 Mixed Voices, 6 Percussion Players, and Piano (1967); *4 songs* for Mezzo-soprano and Chamber Orch. (1966); *5 Songs* for Mezzo-soprano and Chamber Orch. (1968); *Goethe- Briefe*, cantata (1970; Dresden, June 6, 1971); *Voices from Afar*, 3 songs for Baritone and Orch. (1981).

BIBL.: T. Zielinski, *T. B.* (Kraków, 1966); K. Tarnawska-Kaczorowska, *T. B.: Glosy do biografii* (Kraków, 1997). **—NS/LK/DM**

Bairstow, Sir Edward (Cuthbert),
English organist, pedagogue, and composer; b. Huddersfield, Aug. 22, 1874; d. York, May 1, 1946. He studied organ and theory at the Univ. of Durham (Mus.B., 1894; Mus.D., 1901); was organist at Wigan (1899–1906), at Leeds (1906–13), and at York Minster (1913–46); also was prof. of music at the Univ. of Durham (from 1929). In 1932 he was knighted. He composed church music, anthems, part-songs, and an organ sonata (1937). He publ. *Counterpoint and Harmony* (1937) and *The Evolution of Musical Form* (1943).

BIBL.: E. Bradbury, "Sir E. B.: A Birthday Tribute," *Musical Times* (Aug. 1944).**—NS/LK/DM**

Bajoras, Feliksas,
Lithuanian composer; b. Alytus, Oct. 7, 1934. He studied violin and composition at the Lithuanian Cons. in Vilnius (1957–63). In his compositions, he employs the melorhythmic features of Lithuanian folklore in a modern harmonic dressing.

WORKS: ORCH.: 3 syms.: No. 1 (1964; rev. 1968–70), No. 2, *Stalactites*, for Strings (1970), and No. 3 (1972; rev. 1976); *Intermezzo and Postlude* for Chamber Orch. (1964); *Suite of Verbs* for Chamber Orch. (1966); *Prelude and Toccata* for Strings (1966); *Legends*, symphonic poem (1969); *Mourning Music* for Wind Orch. (1972); *Rondo* (1976). **CHAMBER:** Violin Sonatina (1961); *Variations* for Double Bass and String Quartet (1968); *4 Pieces* for String Quartet (1968); *Cycle of 15 Pieces* for Violin and Piano (1973); 2 string quartets (1974, 1975); Suite for Septet (1975); Violin Sonata (1979). **Piano:** *3 Pieces* (1958); *Variations* (1959); *Variations on a Folk Theme* (1971).**—NS/LK/DM**

Bakala, Břetislav,
Czech conductor and composer; b. Fryšták, Feb. 12, 1897; d. Brno, April 1, 1958. He studied with Kurz (piano), Neumann (conducting), and Janáček (composition) at the Brno Cons. He was chief conductor of the Opera (1929–31), the Radio Sym. Orch. (1937–56), and the State Phil. (1956–58) in Brno, where he also taught conducting at the Janáček Academy of Music (1951–58). Bakala championed the music of Janáček. His own works include a *Scherzo* for Orch. (1923), a *Fantasie* for String Quartet, choruses, and songs. **—NS/LK/DM**

Bakaleinikov, Vladimir,
Russian-American violinist, conductor, pedagogue, and composer; b. Moscow, Oct. 12, 1885; d. Pittsburgh, Nov. 5, 1953. He studied violin with Michael Press. After graduating from the Moscow Cons. (1907), he was the violist in the Grand Duke of Mecklenburg String Quartet (1910–20), a teacher at the St. Petersburg Cons. (1913–20), and an opera conductor at the Musicalnaya Drama in St. Petersburg (1914–16). He taught at the Moscow Cons. (1920–24) and was head of the opera branch of the Moscow Art Theater (1920–27). From 1927 to 1937 he was asst. conductor of the Cincinnati Sym. Orch. In 1940–41 he was assoc. conductor of the Pittsburgh Sym. Orch. His most brilliant student was Lorin Maazel. He wrote a Viola Concerto (1937) and a suite of oriental dances for orch., and publ. arrangements of works by Bach and Beethoven. He was the author of *Elementary Rules of Conducting* (1937) and *The Instruments of the Band and Orchestra* (1940).**—NS/LK/DM**

Bake, Arnold Adriaan,
Dutch music scholar; b. Hilversum, May 19, 1899; d. London, Oct. 8, 1963. He studied oriental languages at the Univ. of Leiden; received his Ph.D. in 1930 from the Univ. of Utrecht with the diss. *Bytrage tot de Kennis der Voor-Indische musiek* (publ. in Paris, 1930). He subsequently went to India, where he studied Indian music and languages at Tagore's school in Santiniketan; he also served as music adviser to the All India Radio in Delhi and as director of European music of the Calcutta Radio. In 1948 he went to London, where he became a lecturer on Sanskrit and Indian music at the School of Oriental and African Studies. His interests also included Indian philosophy, tribal music, and dance. In 1937 he was made a corresponding member of the American Musicological Soc. **—NS/LK/DM**

Baker, Anita,
tiny powerhouse who helped unleash a new generation of female soul singers; b. Toledo, Ohio, Jan. 26, 1958. Abandoned by her mother at the age of two, Anita Baker was raised by family members and parishoners from their Baptist Church in Detroit. She heard recordings of Sara Vaughn and Aretha Franklin at

home, and sang solo in church. By the time she was 16, she worked in her aunt's beauty parlor by day, and sang in clubs by night. At age 20 she cut an album with the Detroit soul band, Chapter 8. Although they had a minor hit, "I Just Want to Be Your Girl," the album didn't sell and they were dropped by their label and broke up.

Baker took the band's failure personally and stopped singing. She did odd jobs around Detroit, finally landing a receptionist position at a law firm, ironically because they loved how her voice sounded over the telephone. Happy with a job that gave her a decent salary, vacation, and benefits, she stopped singing, until a former employee from her old record company lured her to Los Angeles with the promise of a similar job, a car, and a recording contract for his new label. While the car never materialized, the job and the recording contract did. She recorded *The Songstress*, an album of ballads going against the grain of the dance music that dominated pop at the time. The album sold nearly 200,000 copies, largely thanks to the rise of "quiet storm" radio, which offered an alternative to dance music and a home for ballads like the single, "Angel."

After a contract dispute with the record company, Baker signed to Elektra. The company offered her creative control, which she maintains. She went into the studio with her colleague from Chapter 8, Michael Powell, to cut a batch of what she liked to refer to as "fireside love songs." The album went over budget, so she dipped into her personal funds. The results were her 1986 album *Rapture*. The album's big hit, "Sweet Love," was part of the soundtrack to an episode of the hit television series *Moonlighting*, and rose to #8. The second single, "Caught Up in the Rapture," just broke the Top 40. The album rose to #11 and eventually sold in excess of five million copies. Baker came home from the 1986 Grammy Awards with awards for Best R&B Vocal Performance and Best R&B Song. She took a 14–piece band on the road, expanding her jazz influences even more in concert. Although Baker didn't make an album of her own in 1987, her tune "Ain't No Need to Worry" with the Winans earned them a Best Soul Gospel Performance Grammy.

Baker's next album, *Giving You the Best That I Got*, took off on release, and within three weeks, it had sold two million copies. It stayed on top of the charts for four weeks, spawning the #3 title track, and the #14 "Just Because" (which went #1 R&B). Again, she took home a Best R&B Song and best R&B Vocal Performance for the title track. A year later, the song won her Best R&B Vocal Performance, Female. The album sold three million copies.

Baker also became one of the most in-demand live artists on the road. At one point she claimed to be the fourth-highest paid singer, not setting foot on stage for less than five figures. In 1989, while on the road with Luther Vandross, Baker miscarried and took time off from the stage.

Baker had also heard complaints about *Giving You the Best That I Got* sounding too much like *Rapture*. To inject a little freshness into the mix of her next album, she called on a group of all-star jazz musicians including Kenny Kirkland, Earl Klugh, and others. Recording much of the album live in the studio over the course of 11 days, *Compositions* was by far the fastest album Baker ever made. Hailed as a stylistic breakthrough, it was far more challenging than either of her previous records, yet it still climbed to #5 on the charts, sold a million copies, and won her yet another Best Vocal Performance, Female, Grammy.

Baker survived a second miscarriage, and desperately wanted to have a baby. She took time off and had two sons within two years. For the next four years, she spent most of her time with her new family, taking time only to record "Witchcraft" for the Frank Sinatra *Duets* album.

Baker's "comeback" record *Rhythm of Love* sold a million records within six days of release. Fusing all of her previous influences, the album had a bit of jazz, a bunch of ballads, a bit of R&B, a taste of gospel, and even some new jack swing. The single, "Body and Soul," only hit #36, but the album sold two million copies. After its release, Baker got involved in a lawsuit with her record company, and suspended release of new recordings.

DISC.: *Songstress* (1983); *Rapture* (1986); *Giving You the Best That I Got* (1988); *Compositions* (1990); *Rhythm of Love* (1994).
—HB

Baker, Benjamin Franklin, American singer, teacher, and composer; b. Wenham, Mass., July 10, 1811; d. Boston, March 11, 1889. He was a singer, choir director, and music teacher in Salem, Mass. In 1833 he made a tour as a singer. In 1837 he settled in Boston, where he studied with John Paddon. He was active as a church music director and in 1841 he was made superintendent of music in the public schools. He made many appearances as a soloist with the Handel and Haydn Soc. In 1851 he founded the Boston Music School, which he led as principal and head of singing until it closed in 1868. He also was ed. of the *Boston Musical Journal*. He publ. 2 harmony textbooks (1847, 1870) and collaborated on more than 25 vols. of hymns, anthems, songs, and glees. He also wrote various vocal works.
—NS/LK/DM

Baker, Chet (actually, **Chesney Henry**), jazz trumpeter, singer; b. Yale, Okla., Dec. 23, 1929; d. Amsterdam, May 13, 1988, in a fall from a second floor hotel room window. When Baker was 13, he was given a trumpet (initially a trombone, but he was too small to handle it). Soon he began sitting in with jazz groups in Calif., including one session that was recorded with Charlie Parker, who reportedly was impressed. Baker achieved national fame working with the Gerry Mulligan quartet in 1952, then led his own group with Russ Freeman (1953–4). He began using marijuana in the late 1940s and eventually became a serious heroin addict with several run-ins with the law; he spent time in the stockade and in jails in N.Y., Italy (1960–1), and England. He was beaten by hoodlums in San Francisco in 1968, chipping one tooth. His teeth were already in such bad shape that they eventually had to be replaced, yet he was able to recover and play superbly on some later dates. His death was thought to be a drug related accident. He left behind several broken marriages. At the time of his death, he was scheduled for a tour of the Netherlands.

Baker is widely admired for his sunny lyrical sense and sensitive expressivity. During the 1950s, he had many imitators, especially among white players; though compared with Miles Davis and clearly influenced by him, Baker's style would never be mistaken for the much darker one of Davis. Though he played mostly by ear and was not a good reader, Baker negotiated changes accurately. He reached a wider audience by adding light, casual, "cool" vocals to his repertory. He was the subject of photographer Bruce Weber's stylish documentary film, *Let's Get Lost*. Besides his jazz work, he also worked with minimalist composer Terry Riley during the early 1960s.

DISC.: *Complete Pacific Jazz Studio Recordings of the Chet Baker Quartet with Ross Freeman* (1953–1956); *Complete Pacific Jazz Live Recordings of the C. B. Quartet* (1954); *Chet Baker Sextet* (1954); *Chet Baker Big Band* (1954); *Boston* (1954); *Complete Barclay Recordings* (1955); *Chet in Paris, Vol. 1, 2, 3, 4* (1955); *The Route* (1956); *Playboys* (1956); *Live in Europe* (1956); *Chet Baker and Crew* (1956); *Gerry Mulligan Reunion with Chet Baker* (1957); *In N.Y.* (1958); *In Milan* (1959); *Italian Sessions* (1962); *Live in Paris* (1963); *Smokin'* (1965); *Groovin'* (1965); *Cool Burnin'* (1965); *Comin' on with the C. B. Quintet* (1965); *Boppin' with the C. B. Quintet* (1965); *Baker's Holiday: Plays and Sings* (1965); *She Was Too Good to Me* (1974); *Best Thing for You* (1977); *Touch of Your Lips* (1979); *Day Break* (1979); *C. B. with Wolfgang Lacker* (1979); *Studio Trieste* (1982); *In Concert* (1982). *Live in Sweden with the Ake Johansson Trio* (1983); *Blues for a Reason* (1984); *Chet's Choice* (1985); *Candy* (1985); *Diane: C. B. and Paul Bley* (1985); *Strollin'* (1985); *My Favourite Songs, Vols. 1 and 2* (1988); *Silence* (1990); *Newport Years, Vol. 1* (1992).

BIBL.: I. Wulff, *C. B. in Concert* (Germany, 1990); C. Baker, *As Though I Had Wings: The Lost Memoir* (c. 1997).—**LP/MM**

Baker, Claude, American composer and teacher; b. Lenoir, N.C., April 12, 1948. He received training in theory and composition at East Carolina Univ. in Greenville, N.C. (B.M., 1970), and then pursued studies in composition principally with Adler and Benson at the Eastman School of Music in Rochester, N.Y. (M.M., 1973; D.M.A., 1975). He was an instructor in theory and composition at the Univ. of Ga. (1974–76), and then a prof. of those subjects at the Univ. of Louisville (1976–88); in 1985, was also a visiting prof. of composition at the Eastman School of Music. In 1988 he became a prof. at the Ind. Univ. School of Music in Bloomington. He also served as composer-in-residence of the St. Louis Sym. Orch. from 1991 to 1999. In 1976 he won the Manuel de Falla Prize of Madrid. He held Yaddo fellowships in 1978 and 1980. In 1979 and 1984 he won Kennedy Center Friedheim awards. He held Rockefeller Foundation fellowships to the Bellagio Study and Conference Center in Italy in 1982 and 1995. He held a fellowship (1990–91) and composer-in-residence grants (1993–94; 1994–95) of the NEA. Baker composed a number of eclectic instrumental scores in which he mixed both tonal and atonal elements. With his *Awaking the Winds* for Orch. (1991–93), he turned to a more freely chromatic style of expression.

WORKS: ORCH.: Concertino for 3 Quintets, Piano, and Percussion (1969–70; Greensboro, N.C., July 20, 1970); *Strophes* for Strings (1971–72); *Capriccio* for Concert Band or Wind Ensemble (1974; Rochester, N.Y., Feb. 6, 1976); *Speculum Musicae, Pars II* (Greensboro, N.C., July 22, 1976); *Caractères* for Bass Trombone and Wind Ensemble (1975–76; Athens, Ga., March 12, 1976; rev. 1977; Louisville, Feb. 19, 1978); *The Glass Bead Game* (1982; Louisville, Feb. 11, 1983); *3 Pieces* for 5 Timpani, 5 Roto-toms, and Orch. (1989; Rochester, N.Y., Dec. 8, 1990; also for 5 Timpani, 5 Roto-toms, and Wind Ensemble, 1990; Kansas City, Mo., Feb. 21, 1991); *Shadows: 4 Dirge-Nocturnes* (1989–90; St. Louis, May 18, 1990); *Awaking the Winds* (1991–93; St. Louis, May 14, 1993; also for Chamber Orch., Cleveland, Jan. 23, 1994); *Blow Out...* (St. Louis, Oct. 1, 1994); *Whispers and Echoes* (1994–95; St. Louis, Sept. 22, 1995); *Yet Another Set of Variations...* (1995–96; St. Louis, May 19, 1996); *The Mystic Trumpeter* (1998–99; St. Louis, April 16, 1999). **CHAMBER:** *Invention* for Flute and Clarinet (1968); String Quartet No. 1 (1968–69); *3 Bagatelles* for 2 Horns and 2 Trombones (1969); *2 Pieces* for Violin and Cello (1970); *Canzonet* for Tuba (1972); *Jeu de cartes* for Wind Quartet, 4 Tape Recorders, and Card Dealer (1974; Athens, Ga., Jan. 23, 1975); *Speculum Musicae* for String Quartet, Wind Quartet, Brass Trio, Piano, and Percussion (1974–75; Rochester, N.Y., Feb. 23, 1975); *Banchetto Musicale* for Clarinet, Violin, Piano, and Percussion (1977–78; Manchester, Vt., July 29, 1978); *Elegy* for Violin (1978–79; N.Y., Dec. 17, 1979); *Divertissement* for Clarinet, Violin, Cello, and Piano (1979–80; Louisville, April 12, 1981); *Omaggi e Fantasie* for Tuba and Piano (1980–81; rev. 1987; Athens, Ga., Feb. 8, 1988; also for Double Bass and Piano, 1984; Rochester, N.Y., Nov. 20, 1985); *4 Nachtszenen* for Harp (1985; Bowling Green, Ohio, Oct. 24, 1987; rev. version, Paris, July 11, 1990); *Fantasy Variations* for String Quartet (Troy, N.Y., Aug. 15, 1986); *Tableaux Funèbres* for Piano and String Quartet (1987–88; Louisville, March 20, 1988); *Flights of Passage: From Silent Sun to Starry Night* for Piano (1997–98; N.Y., Feb. 19, 1998). **VOCAL:** *3 Songs on Poems by Kenneth Patchen* for Soprano and Chamber Ensemble (Rochester, N.Y., April 14, 1971); *How Tyll Got His Name Ulenspiegel* for Narrator and Horn (Rochester, N.Y., April 28, 1971); *Rest, Heart of the Tired World* for Soprano and Orch. (1972–73; Rochester, N.Y., April 24, 1973); *4 Songs on Poems by Kenneth Patchen* for Soprano and Orch. (1973; rev. 1975; Granada, July 3, 1976); *Into the Sun* for High Voice and Orch. (1995–96; Washington, D.C., Sept. 12, 1996); *Sleepers Awake* for Mezzo-soprano, Percussion, and Strings (St. Louis, Nov. 11, 1998).—**NS/LK/DM**

Baker, Dame Janet (Abbott), celebrated English mezzo-soprano; b. Hatfield, Yorkshire, Aug. 21, 1933. Her parents were music-lovers and she grew up in an artistic atmosphere. She was a student of Hélène Isepp and Meriel St. Clair in London. She began her career singing in the Leeds Phil. Choir, with which she made her debut as a soloist in Haydn's *Lord Nelson Mass* in 1953. In 1955 she became a member of the Ambrosian Singers. In 1956 she won second prize in the Kathleen Ferrier Competition, making her operatic debut as Roza in Smetana's *The Secret* with the Univ. of Oxford Opera Club. In 1959 she was awarded the Queen's Prize and began to sing major roles with the Handel Opera Soc. From 1962 she also appeared at the Aldeburgh Festival. In 1964 she toured Russia as Lucretia with the English Opera Group. In 1966 she made her debut at London's Covet Garden as Hermia in Britten's *A Midsummer Night's Dream*, her U.S. debut as soloist in Mahler's *Das*

Lied von der Erde with the San Francisco Sym., and her N.Y. recital debut. In 1967 she appeared as Dorabella with Glasgow's Scottish Opera, returning there as Berlioz's Dido in 1969, Strauss's Octavian in 1971 and Composer in 1975, and Gluck's Orfeo in 1979. In 1970 she sang Diana in *La Calisto* at Glyndebourne, returning there as Penelope in *Il ritorno d'Ulisse in patria* in 1972. On May 16, 1971, she created the role of Kate in Britten's *Owen Wingrave* on BBC-TV, a role she sang again at the work's premiere staging at Covent Garden in 1973. In 1971 she appeared as Monteverdi's Poppea with the Sadler's Wells Opera in London, returning there as Donizetti's Mary Stuart in 1973 and with its successor, the English National Opera, as Massenet's Charlotte in 1977. She sang in concert with Abbado and the London Sym. Orch. at the Salzburg Festival in 1973. In 1982 she retired from the operatic stage singing Gluck's Orfeo at Glyndebourne, although as late as 1989 she appeared in a concert performance of the role in N.Y. From 1983 to 1991 she was president of the Scottish Academy of Music and Drama in Glasgow. She was chancellor of the Univ. of York from 1991. She publ. the autobiographical vol. *Full Circle* (London, 1982). In 1970 she was made a Commander of the Order of the British Empire. She was made a Dame Commander of the Order of the British Empire in 1976. In 1990 she was awarded the Gold Medal of the Royal Phil. Soc. of London, and in 1994 she was made a Companion of Honour. Baker was one of the outstanding singers of her era. In addition to her expansive operatic repertoire, she won great renown as a concert artist in a repertoire of Lieder, English and French songs, and oratorio. She was especially distinguished in her performances of Schubert, Schumann, and Mahler.

BIBL.: A. Blyth, *J. B.* (London, 1973).—NS/LK/DM

Baker, David (Nathaniel), black American jazz instrumentalist, teacher, and composer; b. Indianapolis, Dec. 21, 1931. He was educated at Ind. Univ. (B.M.Ed., 1953; M.M.Ed., 1954), and also studied theory privately with Heiden, Schuller, Orrego-Salas, William Russo, and George Russell. He subsequently taught music in small colleges and public schools. In 1966 he became chairman of the dept. of jazz studies at Ind. Univ. As a jazz performer, he played the trombone with Stan Kenton, Lionel Hampton, and Quincy Jones. His own compositions fuse jazz improvisation with ultramodern devices, including serial procedures. In 2000 he was honored with the American Jazz Master Award and also received an NEA fellowship. He has written many articles on jazz; among his books are *Jazz Improvisation: A Comprehensive Method of Study for All Players* (1969) and *Techniques of Improvisation* (1971); with L. Belt and H. Hudson, he ed. *The Black Composer Speaks* (1978), and he also ed. *New Perspectives on Jazz* (Washington, D.C., 1991).

WORKS: ORCH.: *Reflections* for Orch. and Jazz Ensemble (1969); Concerto for Violin and Jazz Band (1969; Bloomington, Ind., April 5, 1970); Concerto for Flute, Jazz Ensemble, and String Quartet (1971); Concerto for Double Bass, Jazz Ensemble, String Quartet, and Solo Violin (1972); Concerto for Trombone, Jazz Band, and Chamber Orch. (1972); *Kosbro* (1973; rev. 1975); *Levels,* concerto for Double Bass, Jazz Band, Flute Quartet, Horn

Quartet, and String Quartet (1973); *Le Chat qui pêche* for Orch., Jazz Quartet, and Soprano (1974); *2 Improvisations* for Orch. and Jazz Combo (1974); Concerto for Tuba, Jazz Band, Percussion, Chorus, Dancers, Slide Projections, and Tape Recorders (1975); Concerto for Cello and Chamber Orch. (1975–76); Concerto for 2 Pianos, Jazz Band, Chamber Orch., and Percussion (1976); Clarinet Concerto (1985); *Concert Piece* for Trombone and Strings (Bloomington, Ind., Nov. 3, 1991); *Images of Childhood* (1998; Indianapolis, Feb. 25, 1999). CHAMBER: String Quartet No. 1 (1962); Viola Sonata (1966); *Ballade* for Horn, Saxophone, and Cello (1967); Violin Sonata (1967); *Salute to Beethoven* for Piccolo, Wind Quintet, Flute Choir, Jazz Ensemble, and Tape (1970); Sonata for Brass Quintet and Piano (1970); Sonata for Piano and String Quintet (1971); Sonata for Tuba and String Quartet (1971); Sonata for Viola, Guitar, and Double Bass (1973); Cello Sonata (1973); Sonata for Violin and Cello (1974); Suite for Violin (1975); *Contrasts* for Piano Trio (1976); *Ethnic Variations on a Theme of Paganini* for Violin and Piano (1976); *Roots* for Piano Trio (1976); *Fantasy* for Alto Saxophone, 4 Cellos, and Percussion (1977); *Shapes* for Percussion Ensemble (1977); *Concerto for Fours* for Flute, Cello, Tuba, Double Bass, 4 Tubas, 4 Double Basses, and 4 Percussion (1980); *Singers of Songs, Weavers of Dreams* for Cello and Percussion (1980); Sonata for Violin, Cello, and 4 Flutes (1980); *Dedication* for Soprano Saxophone, Double Bass, and String Quartet (1981); *Blues* for Violin Ensemble and Piano (1985); *Calypso* for Violin Ensemble and Piano (1985); *En rouge et noir* for Flute, Piano, Double Bass, and Drums (1985); Suite for Horn, Trumpet, Saxophone, and Rhythm Section (1985); Quintet for Jazz Violin and String Quartet (1987; Washington, D.C., March 13, 1988); Duo for Clarinet and Cello (Indianapolis, Oct. 25, 1988); *Impressions* for 2 Cellos (Bloomington, Ind., Sept. 8, 1989); piano pieces; numerous other works for jazz ensembles of various instruments. VOCAL: *Lutheran Mass* for Chorus and Jazz Septet (1967); *The Beatitudes* for Chorus, Soloists, Narrator, Jazz Ensemble, String Orch., and Dancers (1968); *Black America:To the Memory of Martin Luther King,* jazz cantata (1968); *Catholic Mass for Peace* for Chorus and Jazz Ensemble (1969); *A Song of Mankind* for Chorus, Orch., Jazz Ensemble, Rock Band, Lights, and Sound Effects (1970); *Songs of the Night* for Soprano, String Quartet, and Piano (1972); *Give and Take* for Soprano and Chamber Ensemble (1975).—LP/NS

Baker, Julius, American flutist and teacher; b. Cleveland, Sept. 23, 1915. He studied at the Eastman School of Music in Rochester, N.Y., and with William Kincaid at the Curtis Inst. of Music in Philadelphia. He played in the Cleveland Orch. (1937–41). He then was first flutist of the Pittsburgh Sym. Orch. (1941–43), the CBS Sym. Orch. in N.Y. (1943–51), the Chicago Sym. Orch. (1951–53), and the N.Y. Phil. (1965–83). He also taught at the Juilliard School of Music in N.Y. (from 1954), the Curtis Inst. of Music (from 1980), and at Carnegie-Mellon Univ. in Pittsburgh (from 1991). —NS/LK/DM

Baker, Lavern (Dolores Williams), big-lunged R&B star of the 1950s; b. Chicago, Nov. 11, 1929; d. N.Y.C., March 10, 1997. Dolores Williams began singing in church at the age of 12, and started performing professionally at Chicago's Club DeLisa in 1946, billed as "Little Miss Sharecropper." Spotted by bandleader Fletcher Henderson, she initially recorded for the OKeh subsidiary of Columbia Records in 1948, subsequently recording for RCA-Victor in 1949. Adopting the name Lavern Baker, she performed and recorded for King Records with Todd Rhodes's band in 1952–53, and signed with Atlantic Records in 1953 upon her return from a solo European tour. Her third release, Winfield Scott's novelty song "Tweedle Dee," became a smash R&B and major pop hit in early 1955. However, white artist Georgia Gibbs quickly covered the song for Mercury and scored an even bigger pop hit. Through 1956 Baker scored smash R&B hits with "Bop-Ting-A-Ling"/"That's All I Need" and the ballads "Play It Fair" and "Still" (covered by The Commodores in 1979), backed with "I Can't Love You Enough," a major pop hit. In 1957 "Jim Dandy" became a top R&B and major pop hit and was followed by the inevitable followup, "Jim Dandy Got Married." She toured with deejay/promoter Alan Freed's rock 'n' roll stage shows, and performed in two of his movies, *Rock, Rock, Rock* and *Mister Rock and Roll*, both from 1957.

In 1958 Lavern Baker achieved her biggest hit with the soulful ballad "I Cried a Tear," featuring saxophonist King Curtis. She also recorded her acclaimed *Sings Bessie Smith* album, on which she paid homage to the famous blues queen—an unusual move for a pop songstress. Subsequent hits included "I Waited Too Long" (written by Neil Sedaka), the rave-up "Saved" (written and produced by Jerry Leiber and Mike Stoller), and blues legend Ma Rainey's "See See Rider." By 1964 Baker had left Atlantic, managing her final, albeit minor, hit with "Think Twice," recorded with Jackie Wilson, on Brunswick Records in 1966. While touring Asia in 1969 she became seriously ill and moved to the Philippines, where she managed and occasionally performed at a Marine NCO club on Subic Bay for over 20 years. She briefly returned to the United States for Atlantic's 40th anniversary celebration at Madison Square Garden in 1988, and later came back to take Ruth Brown's place in the musical *Black and Blue* during the second half of 1990. Baker was awarded the Rhythm and Blues Foundation's Career Achievement Award in 1990 and inducted into the Rock 'n' Roll Hall of Fame in 1991. She resumed touring and recording, including "Slow Rollin' Mama" for the soundtrack to the popular film *Dick Tracy*, but suffered two strokes, as well as diabetes. She died at a N.Y. hospital on March 10, 1997.

A major R&B artist of the 1950s, Lavern Baker scored some of the earliest crossover hits onto the pop charts, including "Tweedle Dee" and "Jim Dandy." However, cover versions of several of her hits, primarily by white artist Georgia Gibbs, kept her from achieving as large a sales success as she might otherwise have accomplished. Performing in early rock 'n' roll movies and tours, Baker's career went into eclipse in the mid-1960s with the rise of soul music. She eventually re-emerged in the 1990s, performing on the cabaret and nightclub circuit, as well as in blues and rock-revival festivals, until her death in 1997.

DISC.: *Lavern* (1956); *Lavern Baker* (1957); *Sings Bessie Smith* (1958); *Blues Ballads* (1959); *Precious Memories* (1959); *Saved* (1961); *See See Rider* (1963); *Best* (1963); *Let Me Belong to You, Brunswick* (1970); *Live in Hollywood '91* (1991); *Woke Up This Morning* (1992).—BH

Baker, Michael Conway, American-born Canadian composer; b. West Palm Beach, Fla., March 13, 1937. He moved to Canada in 1958 and became a naturalized Canadian citizen in 1972. He studied at the London (Ontario) Coll. of Music (assoc. degree, 1959), with Jean Coulthard and Elliot Weisgarber at the Univ. of British Columbia (B.M., 1966), at Western Washington Univ. (M.A., 1971), and with Sir Lennox Berkeley in London (1974–75). From 1980 to 1995 he was a part-time teacher of film music at the Univ. of British Columbia. In 1998 he was awarded the Order of British Columbia. In addition to his many concert works, he has composed over 180 film, television, and music video scores.

WORKS: DRAMATIC: B a l l e t : *The Letter* (1974). M u s i c T h e a t e r : *Washington Square* (1978). ORCH.: *Counterplay* for Viola and Strings (1971; also for Viola and Piano); *Okanagan Landscapes* for Piano and Orch. (1972); *Contours* for Double Bass, Harpsichord, and Strings (1973); *A Gabriel Fauré: In Memoriam* (1973); Concerto for Flute and Strings (1974); *Point No Point* for Viola and String Orch. (1975); Concerto for Piano and Chamber Orch. (1976); *Duo Concertante* for Violin, Viola, and Strings (1976); *A Struggle for Dominion* for Piano and Orch. (1976); 2 syms. (1977, 1993); *Baroque Diversions* for Chamber Orch. (1981); *Evocations* for Flute, String Trio, and Orch. (1981); *Rita Joe*, tone poem (1983); *Chanson joyeuse* (1987); *Through the Lion's Gate* (1989); *The Colours of Space* for Horn and Orch. (1991); *A Theme for Dennis* for Piano and Strings (1992); *The Flight of Aphrodite* for Violin and Orch. (1993); *Celebration Canada* (1993); *Cinderella: Frozen in Time* (1993); *Summit Concerto* for Trumpet and Orch. (1994); *Vancouver Variations* for Oboe and Chamber Orch. (1995); *Horizons: The Orca Bay Theme* (1995); *Farewell, Diana* for Chamber Orch. (1997); Harp Concerto (2000). CHAMBER: *Ballade* for Cello and Piano (1961); Flute Sonata (1963); *5 Epigrams* for Woodwind Trio (1965); Wind Quintet (1965); Piano Quartet (1966); *Scherzo* for Trumpet and Organ (1967); String Quartet (1969); *Concert Piece* for Organ, Piano, and Timpani (1969–70); Piano Trio (1972); *Elegy* for Flute and Organ (1972); *Music for 6 Players* for Flute, Oboe, Harpsichord, and String Trio (1973); *Combinations* for Double Bass and Harpsichord (1974); *En rapport* for 2 Guitars (1974); *4 Views from a Nursery Tune* for Violin, Horn, and Piano (1975); *Dance Sequences* for Cello (1975); *Mirage* for Trumpet, Horn, and Organ (1981); *Red on White* for Flute and String Trio (1981); Duo for Flute and Bassoon (1981); *Intermezzo* for Flute and Harp (1988); *Generations* for Flute and Piano (1990); *Eridanus: A Tribute to Malcolm Lowry* for 9 Players and Narrator (1993); *To Play With Angels* for Violin and Cello (1995); *Passacaglia* for Violin, Viola, and Piano (1996). KEYBOARD: P i a n o : *Capriccio* for 2 Pianos (1964); 4 pieces (1973); Sonata (1975); *Theme for Jane* (1981); *Rainforest Suite* (1987). O r g a n : Numerous pieces. VOCAL: *Dialogues* for Baritone, Chorus, and Orch. (1971); *7 Wonders*, song cycle for Voice and Piano (1983); *Street Scenes* for Men's Chorus and Piano (1985); *Capriccio* for Solo Voices, Instruments, and Orch. (1986); *Take Each Day Anew* for Soprano, Trumpet, and Organ (1992); *A Psalm for Our Time* for Chorus and Orch. (1996). OTHER: Film, television, and music video scores.—NS/LK/DM

Baker, Theodore, American writer on music, and the compiler of the original edition of the present dictionary bearing his name; b. N.Y., June 3, 1851; d. Dresden, Oct. 13, 1934. As a young man, he was trained for business pursuits, but in 1874 he decided to devote himself to musical studies. He went to Leipzig, where he took courses with Oskar Paul. He received his Ph.D. there in 1882 for his diss. *Über die Musik der nordamerikanischen Wilden*, the first serious study of American Indian music. He lived in Germany until 1890, then returned to the U.S., and became literary ed. and translator for the publishing house of G. Schirmer, Inc. (1892); he retired in 1926 and went back to Germany. In 1895 he publ. *A Dictionary of Musical Terms*, which went through more than 25 printings and sold over a million copies; another valuable work was *A Pronouncing Pocket Manual of Musical Terms* (1905). He also issued *The Musician's Calendar and Birthday Book* (1915–17). In 1900 G. Schirmer, Inc., publ. *Baker's Biographical Dictionary of Musicians*, which became Baker's imperishable monument. The first ed. included the names of many American musicians not represented in musical reference works at the time; a second ed. was publ. in 1905; the third ed., rev. and enl. by Alfred Remy, was issued in 1919; the fourth ed. appeared in 1940 under the general editorship of Carl Engel. A Supplement in 1949 was compiled by Nicolas Slonimsky, who undertook in 1958 a completely rev. fifth ed. of the Dictionary and compiled the Supplements of 1965 and 1971. In 1978 Slonimsky edited the sixth ed., in 1984 the seventh ed., and in 1991 the eighth ed.—**NS/LK/DM**

Bakfark, Valentin (or Bálint),

celebrated Hungarian lutenist; b. Kronstadt, 1507; d. Padua, Aug. 15, 1576. He was brought up by the family of his brother's wife, Greff (or Graew), and used that name in conjunction with his own; the spelling **Bacfarc** or **Bekwark** is also encountered. As a youth he was in the service of the King of Hungary (1526–40) in Buda, where he studied lute. He was later attached to the court of Sigismund II Augustus of Poland in Wilno (1549–66). He subsequently traveled in Germany, France, and Italy, eventually settling in Padua, where he died of the plague. He publ. works for the lute in tablature: *Intabulatura* (Lyons, 1552; reprinted as *Premier Livre de Tablature de Luth*, Paris, 1564). A second book, *Pannonii Harmonicarum Musicarum...tomus primus*, appeared in Kraków in 1564, and was reprinted in Antwerp in 1569. Some of his works are included in Denkmäler der Tonkunst in Österreich (vol. XVIII, 2).—**NS/LK/DM**

Baklanov (real name, Bakkis), Georgy (Andreievich),

esteemed Latvian baritone; b. Riga, Jan. 17, 1881; d. Basel, Dec. 6, 1938. He studied at the Kiev Cons. and with Vanya in Milan. In 1903 he made his operatic debut in Kiev as A. Rubinstein's Demon; after singing at Moscow's Bolshoi Theater and in St. Petersburg (1905–09), he appeared throughout Europe. On Nov. 8, 1909, he made his U.S. debut as Barnaba in *La Gioconda* in the first performance at the Boston Opera House, where he sang with notable success until 1911 and again from 1915 to 1917. On Feb. 16, 1910, he made his only appearance with the Metropolitan Opera as Rigoletto during the company's visit to Baltimore. From 1917 to 1926 he was a member of the Chicago Opera. He later was a principal artist of the Russian Opera Co. of N.Y. In addition to Rigoletto, Baklanov was also highly praised for his portrayals of Prince Igor, Boris Godunov, Méphistophélès, and Scarpia.—**NS/LK/DM**

Balada, Leonardo,

Spanish-American composer and teacher; b. Barcelona, Sept. 22, 1933. He studied piano at the Barcelona Cons., and went to N.Y. and pursued studies at the N.Y. Coll. of Music (1956–57), the Juilliard School of Music (1958–60), and the Mannes Coll. of Music (1961–62). His principal mentors in composition were Copland, Tansman, and Persichetti. He also studied conducting with Markevitch. He taught at the United Nations International School (1963–70), and then joined the faculty of Carnegie-Mellon Univ. in Pittsburgh in 1970, where he served as a prof. from 1975. In his works, Balada has utilized both constructionist and expressionist elements. Since 1968 he has blended ethnic and traditional elements with avant-garde procedures.

WORKS: DRAMATIC: O p e r a : *Hangman, Hangman!*, chamber opera (Barcelona, Oct. 10, 1982); *Zapata!* (1982); *Cristóbal Colón* (1987; Barcelona, Sept. 24, 1989); *Death of Columbus* (1994); *The Town of Greed*, chamber opera (1999). **ORCH.:** *Musica tranquila* for Strings (1960); 3 piano concertos: No. 1 (1964), No. 2 (Pittsburgh, April 15, 1974), and No. 3 (1999; Berlin, Feb. 12, 2000); Guitar Concerto (1965; Madrid, Oct. 21, 1967); *Guernica* (1966; New Orleans, April 25, 1967); 4 syms: No. 1, *Sinfonia en negro*, homage to Martin Luther King Jr. (1968; Madrid, June 21, 1969), No. 2, *Cumbres*, for Band (Pittsburgh, April 18, 1971), No. 3, *Steel Symphony* (1972; Pittsburgh, Jan. 12, 1973), and No. 4, *Lausanne*, for Chamber Orch. (Lausanne, Dec. 7, 1992); Bandoneon Concerto (1970); *Persistences*, sinfonia concertante for Guitar and Orch. (1972; Madrid, Jan. 9, 1987); *Auroris* (1973; Madrid, Jan. 25, 1974); *Ponce de Leon* for Narrator and Orch. (New Orleans, Oct. 9, 1973); *Homage to Casals* (1975; Pittsburgh, May 7, 1976); *Homage to Sarasate* (1975; Pittsburgh, May 7, 1976); Concerto for 4 Guitars and Orch. (1976; Barcelona, Dec. 17, 1977); *3 Anecdotes*, concertino for Castanets or Wood Percussion and Chamber Orch. (1977; first perf. with wood percussion, Pittsburgh, Nov. 8, 1978, and with castanets, Santander, Aug. 28, 1980); *Sardana* (1979; Pittsburgh, Oct. 21, 1982); *Quasi un pasodoble* (1981; N.Y., Nov. 24, 1982); Violin Concerto (N.Y., Nov. 11, 1982); *Fantasias sonoras* (Pittsburgh, Oct. 4, 1987); *Zapata: Images* (1987; Madrid, March 18, 1988); *Alegrias* for Flute and Strings (1988; N.Y., Feb. 16, 1989); *Music for Flute and Strings* (1988; also for Flute and String Quartet); *Divertimento* for Strings (Girona, Spain, Aug. 14, 1991); *Columbus: Images* (1991; Madrid, Jan. 10, 1992); *Celebration* (Barcelona, Nov. 19, 1992); *Music (Lament from the Cradle of the Earth)* for Oboe and Orch. (Pittsburgh, Nov. 5, 1993); *Shadows* (1994; Cincinnati, March 31, 1995); *Morning Music* for Flute and Chamber Orch. (1994; Pittsburgh, March 12, 1995); *Echoes* (Dublin, May 14, 1999); *Concierto Magico* (1997; Cincinnati, March 13, 1998); *Line and Thunder* (Pittsburgh, Feb. 20, 1998); *Folk Dreams* (1998; Dublin, May 14, 1999). **B a n d :** *Quasi Adelita* for Symphonic Wind Ensemble (1981; Washington, Pa., May 14, 1982); *Song and Dance* for Wind Ensemble (1992; Pittsburgh, Feb. 18, 1994); *Union of the Oceans* (Aviles, Spain, Sept. 29, 1993). **CHAMBER:** Violin Sonata (1960); Concerto for Cello and 9 Players (1962); *Geometrias No. 1* for Flute, Oboe, Clarinet, Bassoon, Trumpet, and Percussion (1966) and *No. 2* for String Quartet (1967); *Cuatris* for Instrumental Ensemble (1969); *Mosaico* for Brass Quintet (1970); *Tresis* for Flute, Guitar, and Cello (1973); *Apuntes* for Guitar Quartet (1974); Sonata for 10 Winds (1980); *Music for Flute and String Quintet* (1988; also for Flute and String Orch.); *Diary of Dreams* for Piano, Violin, and Cello (1995); guitar music; piano pieces. **VOCAL:** *Maria Sabina* for Narrators, Chorus, and Orch. (1969; N.Y., April 17,

1970); *Las moradas* for Chorus and Instrumental Ensemble (1970); *No-Res*, cantata (1974; Barcelona, Oct. 18, 1997); *Torquemada*, cantata (1980); *En la era* for Voice and Piano (1989); *Thunderous Scenes*, cantata for Soloists, Chorus, and Orch. (Alicante, Spain, Sept. 24, 1992); Oratorio (1997).—**NS/LK/DM**

Balakauskas, Osvaldus, Lithuanian composer and teacher; b. Ukmerge, Dec. 19, 1937. He studied at the Vilnius State Pedagogical Inst. (graduated, 1961) and with Boris Liatoshinsky (composition) at the Kiev Cons. (1964–69). From 1972 to 1985 he was advisor to the Union of Lithuanian Composers. Since 1985 he has taught at the Lithuanian Academy of Music, with the exception of a period from 1992 to 1994 when he served as the Lithuanian ambassador in France, Spain, and Portugal. In 1996 he was awarded the Lithuanian National Prize for his music.

WORKS: DRAMATIC: *We, the Sparrows*, puppet opera (1983); *Macbeth*, ballet (1988). **ORCH.:** Piano Concertino (1966); *Ludus modorum*, cello concerto (1972; also for Amplified Cello, Flute, Violin, Piano, and Tape, 1982); 2 syms. (1973, 1979); *The Mountain Sonata* for Piano and Orch. (1975); *Ad astra* (1976); *Passio strumentale* for String Quartet and Orch. (1980); Concerto for Oboe, Harpsichord, and Strings (1981); *Sinfonia concertante* for Violin, Piano, and Orch. (1982); *Spengla Ula* for Strings (1984); *Bachjahr* for Flute and Chamber Orch. (1985); *Opera strumentale*, 5 fragments (1987); *Ostrobothnian Symphony* for 20 Strings (1989); *Polilogas* for Saxophone and 20 Strings (1992); *Meridionale (Hommage à Witold Lutosławski)* for Chamber Orch. (1994). **CHAMBER:** *Dance Suite* for Violin and Piano (1964); *Variations* for Flute, Oboe, and Bassoon (1965); Suite for Cello and Piano (1965); *Auletika* for Flute and Oboe (1966); *Extrema* for 7 Instruments (1966); *Aerophonia* for Wind Quintet (1968); Violin Sonata (1969); *Quartetto concertante* for Flute, Violin, Cello, and Piano (1970); 2 string quartets (1971, 1971); *Les musiques*, chamber sym. for Cello and Wind Quintet (1972; also for Flute, Violin, Amplified Cello, Piano, and Tape, 1982); Violin Sonatina (1972); *9 Sources* for Oboe and Harpsichord (1974); *Retrospective I* (1974) and *II* (1994) for Cello and Piano; *Like a Touch of a Sea Wave* for Violin and Piano (1975); *A Tree and a Bird*, viola sonata (1976); *Orgy-Catharsis* for Electric Cello and Tape (1979); *Heterophony* for Electric Cello and Tape (1980); *Tracery*, chamber sym. for Flute, Violin, Cello, Piano, and Tape (1981); *Veda-Seka-Budi* for 5 Percussionists (1990); *Rain for Kraków* for Violin and Piano (1991); *Maggiore-minore* for Viola, Saxophone, and Piano (1994); *Bop-Art* for Trombone and Piano (1995); *Betsatta* for Cello, Piano, and String Quartet (1995); *Erasmus* for Trumpet, Trombone, and Tape (1996). **KEYBOARD: P i a n o :** *3 Caprices* (1964); *Cascades*, sonata (1967); *Studi sonori* for 2 Pianos (1971); *Cascades 2* (1986); *Once More* for 2 Pianos (1987). **O r g a n :** Sonata (1973); *Enneatonic* (1980). **VOCAL:** *Dada Concerto* for 4 Voices and Instrumental Ensemble (1982); *Tyla-Le Silence* for 4 Voices and Chamber Orch. (1986); *Chopin-Hauer* for Soprano, Tenor, 2 Pianos, Viola, Actors, and Tape (1990); *Requiem* for Mezzo-soprano, Chamber Chorus, and String Orch. (1995). —**NS/LK/DM**

Balakirev, Mily (Alexeievich), greatly significant Russian composer; b. Nizhny-Novgorod, Jan. 2, 1837; d. St. Petersburg, May 29, 1910. Following early piano lessons with his mother, he had several piano lessons with Alexander Dubuque in Moscow. After his mother's death, he lived at the Alexandrovsky Inst., where he studied music theory with Karl Eisrich, who introduced him to Oulibicheff. He often played the piano and conducted in private musical evenings at Oulibicheff's estate, and was given access to the large library there for private study. In 1853 he went to the Univ. of Kazan to study mathematics. In 1855 Oulibishev took him to St. Petersburg, where he met Glinka, who encouraged him to continue his music training. On Feb. 24, 1856, he made his St. Petersburg debut in the dual capacity of pianist and composer, playing his one-movement Piano Concerto. During that year, he became acquainted with Cui and Stasov. In Feb. 1858 he played Beethoven's 5th Piano Concerto before the Czar and the imperial family, but in spite of his success he seemed unwilling to pursue a career as a pianist. After Oulibicheff's death in 1858, he received sufficient funds to pursue the luxury of composition. Several of his works, including the overture to *King Lear* and 16 songs, were well received. In 1863 he appeared for the first time in public as a conductor and, with Gavriil Lomakin, founded the Free Music School in St. Petersburg. The purpose of the school was to provide free music education to needy students, while providing them with the training suitable for overseeing parish choirs or for becoming soloists. During the summers from 1860 to 1863, he went to the Caucasus Mountains, to Yaroslavl, along the Volga, to Rostov on the Don, and to Tiflis, during which period he collected, notated, and harmonized many Russian songs, including the universally popular *Song of the Volga Boatmen*. In 1858 he began assembling a group of talented young composers known as the Balakirev Circle—Borodin, Cui, Gussakovsky, Mussorgsky, and Rimsky-Korsakov—with the intention of developing a national Russian music in opposition to a passive imitation of existing Classical Germanic music. In 1866 he went to Prague to arrange for the production of Glinka's operas, but the outbreak of the Austro-Prussian War forced his return to St. Petersburg. He revisited Prague in 1867 and conducted *Ruslan and Ludmila* (Feb. 16, 17, and 19) and *A Life for the Czar* (Feb. 22), but fear of hostilities towards the Russian works and conductor ended his stay. In honor of Slav visitors following the Pan-Russian Ethnographical Exhibition in Moscow, a Free School concert was given on May 24, 1867, during which music of the Balakirev Circle was performed. The critic Vladimir Stasov memorialized the concert with an article in which he proudly declared that Russia also had its "moguchaya kuchka" ("mighty little group" or "handful") of fine musicians, which incorrectly became known as "The Mighty Five."

In the summer of 1867, Balakirev succeeded Anton Rubinstein as conductor of the Russian Musical Soc. During his first year, he invited Berlioz to visit and share the podium in a series of ten concerts. On Feb. 9, 1868, Balakirev was appointed director of the Free School, giving him control over the two most important concert organizations in St. Petersburg at the time. However, in the spring of 1869, he was forced to resign from the Russian Music Soc. because of his "radical programs." The previous summer he had written his oriental fantasy for piano, *Islamey*, using a Kabardian theme he had found on a trip to the Caucasus in 1863 and a Tartar melody from the Crimea he had heard sung in Moscow. When Nikolai Rubinstein played it in St. Petersburg, it served only to polarize further the tensions created by Balakirev's dismissal. *Islamey* was subsequently performed throughout the world by many notable pianists, including Liszt.

In an attempt to fund the concerts, Balakirev scheduled a piano recital in Nizhy-Novgorod in 1870, but managed a profit of only 11 rubles, far short of his 426 ruble debt. Following four more concerts, Balakirev lost interest in music, withdrew completely from public life, became a religious convert, began visiting a soothsayer, and took a job as a clerk with the Warsaw division of the Central Railway Co. in 1872 for a menial salary. He was offered a professorship at the Moscow Cons. by N. Rubinstein but refused, pleading the lack of necessary technical knowledge. In 1873 he became music inspector for two St. Petersburg schools, the Maryinsky Inst. and the Coll. of St. Helen. He returned to composition about 1878 with *Tamara*, which was completed in 1882. Following N. Rubinstein's death in 1881, he was offered the directorship and conductorship at the Moscow Cons., but declined the positions. In 1881 Rimsky-Korsakov resigned the directorship of the Free School of Music and Balakirev succeeded his successor. On Feb. 27, 1882, he made his return conducting Berlioz's *Te Deum*, and on March 29 of the same year he conducted the premiere of Glazunov's 1st Sym. In 1883 he became music director of the Imperial Chapel. Because of the copyright laws in Russia and the lack of participation with other countries, Balakirev rescored, edited, or rewrote many of his earlier works in order to protect his interests. This resulted in the multitude of versions culminating in *Russia*, *In Bohemia*, and *Spanish Overture*. He was instrumental in editing the works of Glinka and conducted concerts to raise money for a memorial in Smolensk, which was unveiled on June 6, 1885. In 1891 he visited Chopin's birthplace and assisted in raising money for a memorial unveiled at Zelazowa Wola on Oct. 17, 1894, the last time he appeared publicly as a pianist. After the funeral of Czar Alexander III in 1894, he resigned his position with the Imperial Chapel. On April 23, 1898, he conducted the premiere of his 2nd Sym. at a Free Music Concert. In retirement he returned to composing and to editing former works. In 1904 he wrote a cantata using quotations from Glinka's music for the centennial of Glinka's birth. The cantata was performed at the unveiling of the Glinka memorial in St. Petersburg on Feb. 16, 1906, which was Balakirev's last public appearance. His autobiography was publ. in *Russkakya Ruzykalnaya Gazeta* (1910).

Balakirev's significance in music was due to his ability to motivate and encourage others to compose music along lines advocated by his philosophy to develop a Russian school of composition. His impact upon Russian music was mostly felt in the advocation of nationalistic works incorporating materials that rivaled developments elsewhere. In his own music, he could not seem to find the same commitment that he obtained from others, leaving only a few works of significance. His musical concepts did not change significantly during the course of his life. Similarly, his compositions, which extended over decades, do not reflect any advancements.

WORKS: DRAMATIC: Incidental music to Shakespeare's *King Lear* (1858–61; rev. 1902–05). **ORCH.:** *Grande Fantaisie on Russian Folksongs* for Piano and Orch. (1852); 2 piano concertos: No. 1, in F sharp minor, in 1 movement (1855–56; St. Petersburg, Feb. 24, 1856) and No 2, in E-flat major (1861–62; 1906–09; completed by S. Liapunov); *Overture on a Theme of a Spanish March* (1857; rev. as *Spanish Overture*, 1886); *Overture on Themes of 3 Russian Songs* (1858; Moscow, Jan. 2, 1859; rev. 1881); *Second Overture on Russian Themes* (1863–64; St. Petersburg, April 18, 1864; publ. as the musical picture *1000 Years*, 1860; rev. as the symphonic poem *Russia*, 1884); *Overture on Czech Themes* (St. Petersburg, March 24, 1867; rev. as *In Bohemia*, 1905); *Tamara*, symphonic poem (1867–82; St. Petersburg, March 19, 1883); Suite (1901–08); *Suite on Pieces by Chopin* (1909). **CHAMBER:** Septet for Flute, Clarinet, 2 Violins, Viola, Cello, and Piano (1852); Octet for Flute, Oboe, Horn, 2 Violins, Viola, Cello, and Piano (1855–56); Romance for Cello and Piano (1856). **Piano:** 3 nocturnes (1856, rev. 1898; 1901; 1902); 3 scherzos (1856, 1900, 1901); 7 mazurkas (1861, rev. c. 1884; 1861, rev. c. 1884; 1886; 1886; 1900; 1902; 1906); *Islamey* (St. Petersburg, Dec. 12, 1869; rev. 1902; orchestrated by A. Casella, 1908; Chicago, Nov. 19, 1909); 7 waltzes (1900; 1900; 1901; 1902; 1903; 1903–04; 1906); Sonata in B-flat minor (1900–05); Suite for Piano, 4–Hands (1909). **VOCAL:** 45 songs for Voice and Piano; choral music; transcriptions. **OTHER:** *Sbornik russkikh narodnïkh pesen* (Collection of Russian Folksongs; St. Petersburg, 1866); *30 russkiikh narodnïkh pesen* (30 Russian Folksongs; Leipzig, 1898).

BIBL.: V. Muzalevsky, *M.A. B.: Kritiko-biograficheskiy ocherk* (M.A. B.: Critical-biographical Essay; Leningrad, 1938); A. Kandinsky, *Simfonicheskiye proizvedeniya M. B.a* (Symphonic Works of M. B.; Moscow and Leningrad, 1950); V. Kiselyov, *Avtografi ï M.A. B.a i materialï, svyazannïye s evo deyatel'nost'yu v fondakh gosudarstvennovo tsentral'novo muzeya muzïkal'noy kul'turï imeni M.I. Glinka* (M.A. B.'s Autographs and Other Materials Connected with his Activities, Contained in the Archives of the M.I. Glinka Central Museum of Culture, Moscow; Moscow, 1959); Y. Kemlyov et al., eds., *M.A. B.: Issledovaniya i stat'i* (M.A. B.: Research and Articles; Leningrad, 1961); idem, *M.A. B.: Vospominaniya i pis'ma* (M.A. B.: Reminiscences and Letters; Leningrad, 1962); E. Garden, *B.: A Critical Study of his Life and Music* (London, 1967); I. Kunin, *M.A. B.: Zhizn' i tvorchestvo v pis'makh i dokumentakh* (M.A. B.: Life and Works in Letters and Documents; Moscow, 1967); A. Liapunova and E. Yazovitskaya, *M.A. B.: Letopis' zhizni i tvorchestva* (M.A. B.: Chronicle of his Life and Works; Leningrad, 1967); S. Neef, *Die Russischen Fünf: B., Borodin, Cui, Mussorgski, Rimski-Korsakow: Monographien, Dokumente, Briefe, Programme, Werke* (Berlin, 1992).—**NS/LK/DM**

Balanchine, George (real name, **Georgi Melitonovich Balanchivadze**), celebrated Russian-American choreographer, son of **Meliton (Antonovich)** and brother of **Andrei (Melitonovich) Balanchivadze**; b. St. Petersburg, Jan. 22, 1904; d. N.Y., April 30, 1983. He attended the Imperial Theater School in St. Petersburg, where he learned the rudiments of classical dance. He also took piano lessons at the Petrograd Cons., and acquired a certain ability to read scores. In 1924 he undertook a tour through Germany and England; then joined Diaghilev's Ballets Russes in Paris, for which he created a number of works. In 1933, at the invitation of Lincoln Kirstein, he went to N.Y.; together they formed the School of American Ballet, which opened on Jan. 2, 1934. In 1935 it was incorporated as the American Ballet, with Balanchine as its chief choreographer. The group was renamed the Ballet Soc. in 1946, and in 1948 it was reorganized as the N.Y. City Ballet, and became part of the City Center. In 1962 Balanchine made a tour of Russia with this company. He was distinguished for his modern productions, with music by Stravinsky, Ives, and other contemporary composers. In 1983 he received the Presidential Medal of Freedom. Early in that year he was hospitalized with an ailment diagnosed as "progressive cerebral disintegration." As a gesture of devotion, he was named director emeritus of the N.Y. City Ballet, but had to abandon all active work, and soon died of pneumonia. Balanchine adored women; he used to say, "Ballet is woman." He was married five times, each time to a dancer: the first was Tamara Geva, whom he married in Russia when he was 18 and she was 15; his second wife was Alexandra Danilova, whom he married in 1927; his third and most famous wife was Vera Zorina, whom he married in 1938; then followed Maria Tallchief, and, finally, Tanaquil LeClercq, from whom he was divorced in 1969. In his long life as a choreographer, Balanchine created nearly 200 ballets to musical scores ranging from the Baroque to the avant-garde; he once said, "Music must be seen, and dance must be heard."

BIBL.: G. and F. Mason, *B.'s Complete Stories of the Great Ballets* (Garden City, N.Y., 1954); B. Taper, *B.* (N.Y. 1963); H. Koegler, *B. und das moderne Ballet* (Hannover, 1964); L. Kirstein, *The New York City Ballet* (N.Y., 1973); *Choreography by G. B.: A Catalogue of Works* (N.Y., 1983).—**NS/LK/DM**

Balanchivadze, Andrei (Melitonovich), Russian composer, son of **Meliton (Antonovich) Balanchivadze** and brother of **George Balanchine;** b. St. Petersburg, June 1, 1906. He studied with his father; then entered the Tiflis Cons., where he took courses in piano, and in composition with Ippolitov-Ivanov. In 1935 he joined its staff, and in 1962 became chairman of the composition dept.; numerous Georgian composers studied under him. In his music, he makes use of Georgian folk motifs in a tasteful harmonic framework characteristic of the Russian national school. Among his works is the first Georgian ballet, *The Heart of the Mountains* (1936). He also composed another ballet, *Mtsyri* (Tbilisi, 1964), three syms. (1944, 1959, 1984), a symphonic poem, *The Ocean* (1952), four piano concertos (1944, 1946, 1952, 1968), choruses, and songs.

BIBL.: G. Ordzhonikidze, *A. B.* (Tbilisi, 1967). —**NS/LK/DM**

Balanchivadze, Meliton (Antonovich), noted Russian composer, father of **George Balanchine** and **Andrei (Melitonovich) Balanchivadze;** b. Banodzha, Dec. 24, 1862; d. Kutaisi, Nov. 21, 1937. He was educated in the ecclesiastical seminary in Tiflis, where he sang in a chorus. In 1880 he became a member of the local opera theater; in 1882 he organized a chorus and arranged Georgian folk songs. In 1889 he went to St. Petersburg, where he took voice lessons, and in 1891 entered Rimsky-Korsakov's class in composition. In 1895 he organized a series of choral concerts of Georgian music. After the Revolution he returned to Ga., where he

continued his work of ethnic research. He composed a national Georgian opera, *Tamara the Treacherous* (1897), and a number of songs in the manner of Georgian folk music.

BIBL.: P. Khuchua, *M. B.* (Tbilisi, 1964).—**NS/LK/DM**

Balart, Gabriel, Spanish composer; b. Barcelona, June 8, 1824; d. there, July 5, 1893. He studied at the Paris Cons. He composed various pieces of salon music, which enjoyed some success. In 1849 he went to Milan as a theater conductor, and in 1853 he was appointed music director of the Teatro del Liceo in Barcelona. For a time his light opera *Amor y Arte* enjoyed considerable success.—**NS/LK/DM**

Balasanian, Sergei, Tadzhik composer; b. Ashkhabad, Aug. 26, 1902; d. Moscow, June 3, 1982. He studied at the Moscow Cons., graduating with a degree in music history in 1935. From 1936 to 1943 he was mainly active in Tadzhikistan, then was in charge of radio programming there. In 1948 he joined the faculty of the Moscow Cons., serving as chairman of the composition dept. from 1962 to 1971. He was one of the founders of the national school of composition in Tadzhikistan. In his works, he made use of native folk motifs, in ingenious harmonic coloration.

WORKS: DRAMATIC: O p e r a : *The Revolt of Vose* (1939; rev. 1959); *The Blacksmith Kova* (1941); *Bakhtyor and Nisso* (1954). **B a l l e t :** *Leyly and Medzhnun* (1947); *Shakuntala* (1963). **ORCH.:** 4 symphonic suites on Central Asian folk motifs; *Armenian Rhapsody* (1944); *The Islands of Indonesia* (1960). **OTHER:** Numerous choruses, songs, and instrumental pieces. —**NS/LK/DM**

Balassa, Sándor, distinguished Hungarian composer and teacher; b. Budapest, Jan. 20, 1935. He studied choral conducting at the Béla Bartók Music Secondary School (1952–56) and composition with Szervánszky at the Franz Liszt Academy of Music (graduated, 1965) in Budapest. From 1964 to 1980 he was a music producer for the Hungarian Radio, and then was a prof. at the Franz Liszt Academy of Music until his retirement in 1996. In 1972 he was awarded the Erkel Prize, in 1983 the Kossuth Prize, and in 1988 and 1999 the Bartók-Pásztory Prize. He was made a Merited Artist in 1983 and an Outstanding Artist in 1989 by the Hungarian government.

WORKS : O p e r a : *Az ajtón kívül* (The Man Outside; 1973–76); *A harmadik bolygó* (The Third Planet; 1986–87); *Karl and Anna* (1987–92). **ORCH.:** Violin Concerto (1964); *Iris* (1971); *Lupercalia,* concerto in memory of Stravinsky for Woodwinds and Brass (1972); *Tabulae* for Chamber Orch. (1972); *Glarusi ének* (Chant of Glarus; 1978); *Az örök ifjúság szigete* (The Island of Everlasting Youth), overture (1979); *Hivások és kiáltások* (Calls and Cries; 1981; Boston, Oct. 21, 1982); *Egy álmodozó naplója* (A Daydreamer's Diary; 1983); *Három fantázia* (3 Fantasies; 1984); *Szőlőcske és halacska* (Little Grape and Little Fish; 1987); *Tünder Ilona* (Fairy Ilona; 1992); *Csaba királyfi* (Prince Csaba) for Strings (1993); *Bölcskei Concerto* for Strings (1993); *Mucsai táncok* (Dances from Mucsa; 1994); *A Nap fiai* (Sons of the Sun; 1995); *Négy arckép* (4 Portraits; 1996); *301–es parcella* (301

Parcel; 1997); *Pécsi Concerto* for 5 Soloists and String Orch. (1998); *Magyar koronázási zene* (Hungarian Coronation Music; 1998); *Hunok völgye* (Val d'Anniviers; 1999). **CHAMBER:** *Divertimento* for 2 Dulcimers (1961–93); *Dimensioni* for Flute and Viola (1966); Wind Quintet (1966); Percussion Quartet (1969); Trio for Violin, Viola, and Harp (1970); *Xenia* for Chamber Ensemble (1970); *Intermezzo* for Flute and Piano (1971); *The Last Shepherd* for Cello (1978); *Quintetto d'ottoni* (1979); Harp Sonatina (1993); *Fűzérke* for Flute, Viola, and Harp (1994); *Jánosnapi muzsika* (John's Day Music) for Violin (1994); String Quartet (1995); *Nyirbátori harangok* (Bells of Nyirbátor) for 12 Brass Instruments (1996); Duet for Flute and Harp (1998); *Pastoral and Rondo* for Violin and Horn (1998). **VOCAL:** *8 Songs from Rottenbiller Street* for Soprano and Piano (1954; rev. 1997); 2 Songs for Mezzo-soprano and Piano, after Attila József (1954; rev. 1994); 2 Songs for Soprano and Piano, after Dezső Kosztolányi (1957); *Antinomia* for Soprano, Clarinet, and Cello (1968); *Requiem Kassák Lajosért* (Requiem for Lajos Kassák) for Soprano, Tenor, Baritone, Chorus, and Orch. (1969); *Cantata Y* for Soprano and Orch. (1970); *Kyrie* for Women's Chorus (1982); *Bnatomtól szabadulnék* for Women's Chorus (1988); *Oldott kéve* (Untied Sheaf) for Chorus (1991); *Damjanich imája* (Damjanich's Prayer) for Chorus (1993); *Árvák éneke* (Orphan's Chant) for Chorus (1995); *Favágó* (Woodcutter) for Chorus (1998); *Holdének, Naphimnusz* (Chant of the Moon, Anthem of the Sun) for Men's Chorus (1998); *Winter Cantata* for Children's Chorus and String Orch. (1999); *Christmas Legend* for Women's Chorus (1999).—**NS/LK/DM**

Balatka, Hans, Czech-American conductor, music educator, music journalist, and composer; b. Hoffnungsthal, near Olmütz, Feb. 26, 1825; d. Chicago, April 17, 1899. He began his music studies in Hoffnungsthal, and then attended the Univ. of Olmütz. In 1845 he went to Vienna to study music with Sechter and Proch, and also studied law at the Univ. In 1849 he went to Milwaukee and founded a men's chorus, followed by a string quartet in 1850. He was founder-music director of the Milwaukee Musical Soc. (1850–60), music director of the German theater (1855–60), and founder-director of his own singing-school. In 1860 he went to Chicago, where he was music director of the Phil. Soc. until 1869 and was active as conductor of various singing organizations. After again conducting the Milwaukee Musical Soc. (1871–72), he settled in Chicago and in 1879 he organized the Balatka Academy of Music. He also was active as a music journalist. Balatka composed some orch. music, a Piano Quartet, piano pieces, choral works, and songs, but his importance rests upon his work as a conductor and music educator.—**NS/LK/DM**

Balbastre (or **Balbâtre**), **Claude** (**-Bénigne**), French organist and composer; b. Dijon, Jan. 22, 1727; d. Paris, May 9, 1799. In about 1750 he began studying with Jean-Philippe Rameau. Between 1755 and 1782 he served as organist in concerts held by the Concert Spirituel. In 1756 he was named organist at St. Roch in Paris; in 1760 he was organist at Notre-Dame de Paris, serving there three months a year. He wrote 14 piano suites based on the motifs of French Christmas songs, as well as numerous organ pieces.—**NS/LK/DM**

Balbi, Lodovico or **Ludivico,** Italian composer; b. Venice, c. 1545; d. there, before Dec. 15, 1604. He was

a pupil of Costanzo Porta in Padua (1565–67). He sang in the choir at San Marco in Venice (from 1570), and then was maestro di cappella at S. Maria Gloriosa dei Frari in Venice (1578–82?), at the Cappella Antoniana in Padua (1585–91), at Feltre Cathedral (1593–97), and at Treviso Cathedral (1597–98). He wrote masses, motets, Psalms, madrigals, etc.

BIBL.: H. Wing, *The Polychoral Motets of L. B. and Leone Leoni* (diss., Boston Univ., 1961); G. Borelli, *I concerti ecclesiastici di L. B.* (diss., Univ. of Parma, 1963).—**NS/LK/DM**

Balbi, Melchiore, Italian theorist and composer; b. Venice, June 4, 1796; d. Padua, June 21, 1879. He was a pupil of Nini, Valeri, and Calegari in Padua. From 1818 to 1853 he was theater conductor in Padua, and from 1854 maestro di cappella at the Basilica San Antonio. He wrote three operas, all produced in Padua: *La notte perigliosa* (1820), *L'abitator del bosco* (1821), and *L'alloggio militare* (1825).—**NS/LK/DM**

Baldi, João José, Portuguese composer; b. Lisbon, 1770; d. there, May 18, 1816. He studied at the Seminário Patriarcal in Lisbon, and in 1789 he became mestre de capela at Guarda Cathedral. In 1794 he went to Faro Cathedral in a similar capacity, and then returned to Lisbon in 1800 to become second mestre de capela at the Royal Chapel of Bemposta; he was made first mestre de capela there and at the Lisbon Cathedral in 1806, holding these posts until his death. He composed mostly sacred works, as well as some piano music. —**NS/LK/DM**

Baldwin, American firm of instrument makers. The firm was founded by Dwight Hamilton Baldwin (b. North East, Pa., Sept. 15, 1821; d. Cincinnati, Aug. 23, 1899), a minister and school singing teacher, in Cincinnati in 1862. In 1866 Lucien Wulsin (b. 1845; d. Aug. 4, 1912) joined the firm as a clerk. In 1873 he became a partner and the firm became D.H. Baldwin & Co. The company established its reputation as a dealer in keyboard instruments. In 1889 its subsidiary, the Hamilton Organ Co. of Chicago, began to make reed organs. Another subsidiary, the Baldwin Piano Co. of Cincinnati, began making a line of affordable upright pianos in 1891. Wulsin purchased control of the company with another partner, George W. Armstrong Jr. (b. Cincinnati, Aug. 18, 1857; d. there, June 27, 1932), in 1903. Wulsin headed the company until his death, and then Armstrong led it from 1912 to 1926. Lucien Wulsin Jr. (b. Cincinnati, March 17, 1889; d. there, Jan. 13, 1964), was head of the company from 1926 until his death. In 1947 the Baldwin electronic organ was introduced for church and home use. The company took control of the Bechstein piano firm of Berlin in 1963. In 1965 the company introduced the Baldwin SD-10 concert grand piano. The company became one of the largest of its kind through its production of a broad range of instruments.—**LK/DM**

Baldwin, John, English tenor, anthologist, and composer; b. c. 1559; d. London, Aug. 28, 1615. He was a tenor lay clerk at St. George's Chapel, Windsor, in 1575, and later was a Gentleman without pay (1594–98) and a full member (from 1598) of the Chapel Royal. His Commonplace-book (1581–1606) preserves valuable works of the era, and also includes some of his own compositions. He also completed the Sextus partbook of Tudor Masses in the Forrest-Heyther collection and prepared a copy of Byrd's anthology of keyboard music as *My Ladye Nevells Booke* (1591).—**LK/DM**

Bales, Richard (Henry Horner), American conductor and composer; b. Alexandria, Va., Feb. 3, 1915; d. Lake Ridge, Va., June 25, 1998. He studied at the Eastman School of Music in Rochester, N.Y. (Mus.B., 1936), at the Juilliard Graduate School in N.Y. (1938–41), and with Koussevitzky at the Berkshire Music Center in Tanglewood (summer, 1940). In 1935 he made his conducting debut with the National Sym. Orch. in Washington, D.C.; then was conductor of the Va.-N.C. Sym. Orch. (1936–38). In 1942 he became the first music director of the National Gallery of Art in Washington, D.C., and in 1943 founded the National Gallery Orch., which he conducted until his retirement in 1985. He also was music director of the Washington, D.C., Cathedral Choral Soc. (1945–46). In 1960 he received the Alice M. Ditson Award. During his long tenure at the National Gallery of Art, he introduced numerous works by American composers, both old and new.

WORKS: ORCH.: *Music* for Strings (1940); *From Washington's Time* for Strings (1941); *National Gallery Suites: I* (1943), *II* (1944), *III* (1957), and *IV* (1965); *Theme and Variations* for Strings (1944); *Music of the American Revolution*, Suite No. 2 for Strings (1952); *Stony Brook Suite* for Strings (1968); *Fitzwilliam Suite* for Strings (1972); *The Spirit of Engineering*, suite (1984). **CHAMBER:** *Sarcasms* for Violin, Viola, and Cello (1937); String Quartet (1944); *Reverie and Virginia Reels* for Violin and Piano (1989). **OTHER:** Piano pieces, including the suite *To Elmira with Love* (1972; orchestrated, 1983), *Diary Pages* for 2 Pianos (1978), and *Aaronesque* (for Aaron Copland's 80th birthday; 1980); various vocal scores, choral pieces, and songs; also film scores and many transcriptions and arrangements.—**NS/LK/DM**

Balfe, Michael William, notable Irish composer; b. Dublin, May 15, 1808; d. Rowney Abbey, Hertfordshire, Oct. 20, 1870. He was the son of a dancing master, and as a small child played the violin for his father's dancing classes. He subsequently took violin lessons with O'Rourke. After his father's death on Jan. 6, 1823, Balfe went to London, where he studied violin with Charles Edward Horn and composition with Carl Friedrich Horn. In 1824 he was engaged as a violinist at the Drury Lane Theatre; also sang in London and in the provinces. His patron, Count Mazzara, took him to Italy in 1825, where he took composition lessons with Federici in Milan and voice lessons with Filippo Galli and also produced his first ballet, *La Perouse* (1826). He met Rossini, who advised him to continue singing lessons with Bordogni; in 1828 he was engaged as principal baritone at the Italian Opera in Paris. In Italy he married the Hungarian vocalist Lina Rosa (b. 1808; d. London, June 8, 1888). Returning to England in 1833, he devoted himself to the management of opera houses and to composition. He was manager of the Lyceum Theatre during the 1841–42 season. He made London his principal residence, with occasional visits to Vienna (1846),

Berlin (1848), St. Petersburg, and Trieste (1852–56). Apart from his administrative duties, he displayed great energy in composing operas, most of them to English librettos; of these, *The Bohemian Girl*, produced at the Drury Lane Theatre in London on Nov. 27, 1843, obtained an extraordinary success and became a perennial favorite on the English stage; it was also tr. into French, German, and Italian. In 1864 he retired to his country seat at Rowney Abbey. His daughter, Victoire, made her debut as a singer at the Lyceum Theatre in London in 1857.

WORKS: DRAMATIC: Opera: 3 early operas in Italian, *I rivali di se stessi* (Palermo, 1829), *Un avvertimento ai gelosi* (Pavia, 1830), and *Enrico IV al Passo della Marna* (Milan, Feb. 19, 1833); in French, *L'Étoile de Séville* (Paris Opéra, Dec. 17, 1845). The following operas were produced in English at Drury Lane and Covent Garden in London and other theaters: *The Siege of Rochelle* (Drury Lane, London, Oct. 29, 1835); *The Maid of Artois* (May 27, 1836); *Catherine Grey* (May 27, 1837); *Joan of Arc* (Nov. 30, 1837); *Diadeste, or The Veiled Lady* (May 17, 1838); *Falstaff* (in Italian, July 19, 1838); *Këolanthe, or The Unearthly Bride* (March 9, 1841); *Le Puits d'amour* (Opéra-Comique, Paris, April 20, 1843; in Eng. as *Geraldine*, Princess's Theatre, London, Aug. 14, 1843); *The Bohemian Girl* (Drury Lane Theatre, London, Nov. 27, 1843); *Les Quatre Fils Aymon* (Opéra-Comique, Paris, July 9, 1844; in Eng. as *The Castle of Aymon*, Princess's Theatre, London, Nov. 20, 1844); *The Daughter of St. Mark* (Nov. 27, 1844); *The Enchantress* (May 14, 1845); *The Bondman* (Dec. 11, 1846); *The Maid of Honour* (Dec. 20, 1847); *The Sicilian Bride* (March 6, 1852); *The Devil's in It* (July 26, 1852); *Moro, the Painter of Antwerp* (Jan. 28, 1882; orig. produced as *Pittore e duca*, Trieste, Nov. 21, 1854); *The Rose of Castille* (Oct. 29, 1857); *Satanella, or The Power of Love* (Dec. 20, 1858); *Bianca, or The Bravo's Bride* (Dec. 6, 1860); *The Puritan's Daughter* (Nov. 30, 1861); *Blanche de Nevers* (Nov. 21, 1863); *The Armourer of Nantes* (Feb. 12, 1863); *The Sleeping Queen*, operetta (Aug. 31, 1864); *The Knight of the Leopard* (Liverpool, Jan. 15, 1891; orig. produced in London as *Il talismano*, June 11, 1874). **VOCAL:** *Mazeppa*, a cantata, and 2 other cantatas; ballads; glees; songs.

BIBL.: W.A. Barrett, *B.: His Life and Work* (London, 1882); G. Biddlecombe, *English Opera From 1834 to 1864 With Particular Reference to the Works of M. B.* (N.Y., 1994).—**NS/LK/DM**

Balfoort, Dirk Jacobus, Dutch violinist, teacher, and writer on music; b. Utrecht, July 19, 1886; d. The Hague, Nov. 11, 1964. He studied violin with Evert Cornelis. He publ. *De Hollandsche vioolmakers* (Amsterdam, 1931), *Het Musiekleven in Nederland in de 17e en 18e eeuw* (Amsterdam, 1938), and *Antonio Stradivari* (Amsterdam, 1945).—**NS/LK/DM**

Balkwill, Bryan (Havell), English conductor; b. London, July 2, 1922. He was educated at the Royal Academy of Music in London. He was an asst. conductor of the New London Opera Co. (1947–48) and assoc. conductor of the International Ballet Co. (1948–49); then was music director of the London Festival Ballet (1950–52) and of Opera for All (1953–63); also conducted at the Glyndebourne Festivals (1950–58), and in London at Covent Garden (from 1953) and at the Sadler's Wells Opera (from 1957). From 1959 to 1965 he was resident conductor at the Royal Opera, Covent Garden; then was music director of the Welsh National Opera in Cardiff (1963–67) and of the Sadler's Wells Opera (1966–69). He served as a prof. of music at the Ind. Univ. School of Music in Bloomington from 1978 to 1992.—NS/LK/DM

Ball, Michael, English composer; b. Manchester, Nov. 10, 1946. He began composing at an early age, writing a children's opera when he was 11. In 1964 he entered the Royal Coll. of Music in London, where he studied with Howells, Searle, and Lambert, and was awarded all of its major composition prizes. He then completed his training with Donatoni in Siena (summers, 1972–73), where he also attended the master classes of Berio and Ligeti.

WORKS: DRAMATIC: O p e r a : *The Belly Bag* (1992). ORCH.: *Resurrection Symphonies* (1982; Manchester, May 23, 1984); *Frontier!* for Brass Band (1984); *Omaggio* for Wind Band (1986); Concerto for Organ, Brass, Percussion, and Strings (1987); *Danses vitales: Danses macabres* (1987); *Farnesong* for Chamber Orch. (1990); *Midsummer Music* for Brass Band (1991); *Chaucer's Tunes* for Wind Band (1993); Concerto for Saxophone and Wind Band (1994). CHAMBER: *The Piper at the Gates of Dawn* for Recorder and Tape (1983); *Music for an Island* for 2 Guitars (1989); *Serenade for Seikilos* for Saxophone Quartet (1991). P i a n o : *Miriam's Music* (1991). VOCAL: *Sainte Marye Virgine*, motet for Chorus (1977–79); *A Hymn to God My God* for 16 Solo Voices (1983–84); *Pageant* for Chorus, Winds, and Brass (1984–85); *Lindisfarne Fragments*, song cycle for Baritone and Piano (1988); *The Pentecost Castle* for Chorus (1988); *Nocturnes* for Chorus, 2 Pianos, and 2 Percussion (1990). —NS/LK/DM

Ballantine, Edward, American composer and teacher; b. Oberlin, Ohio, Aug. 6, 1886; d. Oak Bluffs, Mass., July 2, 1971. He studied with Walter Spalding at Harvard Univ., graduating with highest honors in 1907; took piano courses with Schnabel and Ganz in Berlin (1907–09). In 1912 he was appointed instructor at Harvard, becoming asst. prof. in 1926, and assoc. prof. in 1932; he retired in 1947. His first publ. work was a musical play, *The Lotos Eaters* (1907); three of his orch. pieces were performed by the Boston Sym. Orch.: *Prelude to The Delectable Forest* (Dec. 10, 1914), *The Eve of St. Agnes* (Jan. 19, 1917), and *From the Garden of Hellas* (Feb. 9, 1923); and one, *By a Lake in Russia*, by the Boston Pops (June 27, 1922). He also wrote a Violin Sonata and songs. His most striking work is a set of piano variations on *Mary Had a Little Lamb* (1924) in the styles of 10 composers; a second series of variations on the same tune (1943) includes stylizations of Stravinsky, Gershwin, and others.—NS/LK/DM

Ballard, prominent family of French music printers and composers:

(1) Robert Ballard, music printer; b. Montreuil-sur-Mer, c. 1527; d. Paris (buried), July 8, 1588. With his cousin, **Adrien Le Roy**, he founded the printing establishment of Le Roy & Ballard. King Henri II granted them a privilege to print music on Aug. 14, 1551. They were named music printers to the king on Feb. 16, 1553, a distinction the firm retained until the middle of the 18th century. Following Ballard's death, printing ceased

until Le Roy was joined by Ballard's widow, Lucrèce, a partner in 1591. At his death in 1598, the childless widower Le Roy bequeathed his share of the firm to Lucrèce and the Ballard heirs. Lucrèce was then joined by her son, **(2) Pierre Ballard**. During the second half of the 16th century, the firm maintained almost total monopoly of music printing in France. The firm printed some 3,000 works, many in elegant editions.

(2) Pierre Ballard, music printer, son of **(1) Robert Ballard**; b. Paris, c. 1577; d. there, Oct. 4, 1639. King Henri IV named him music printer to the king on March 25, 1607, and thereafter his mother ceased to have an interest in the firm and his editions were issued under his own name.

(3) Robert Ballard, lutenist, teacher, and composer, son of **(1) Robert Ballard**; b. probably in Paris, c. 1575; d. c. 1650. He seems to have played no role in the family music printing firm. Instead, he devoted himself to performing, teaching, and composing. In 1612 he entered the service of the regent, Maria de' Medici, as maître de luth; that same year, he was made tutor to the young King Louis XIII. In 1618 he was made a musicien ordinaire du roi. He wrote music for the court ballets, much of which was transcribed for the lute. His works were ed. by A. Souris and S. Spycket as *Robert Ballard: Oeuvres* (Paris, 1963–64).

(4) Robert Ballard, music printer, son of **(2) Pierre Ballard**; b. Paris, c. 1610; d. there, before May 1673. He was a bookseller until inheriting the family music printing establishment upon his father's death in 1639. King Louis XIII named him sole printer to the king for music on Oct. 24, 1639. Under his direction, the firm publ. orch. scores for the first time, and also initiated a song collection series.

(5) Christophe Ballard, music printer, son of **(4) Robert Ballard**; b. Paris, April 12, 1641; d. there, before May 28, 1715. He was a bookseller until joining his father in 1666. He was named sole printer to the king for music on May 11, 1673. The firm to continued to hold its own until its hegemony was seriously threatened by the new method of printing from engraved plates as opposed to its old movable type method. His son, Jean-Baptiste-Christophe Ballard (b. Paris, c. 1663; d. there, May 1750), succeeded to the business in 1715, but its fortunes waned. He was succeeded in turn by his son, Christophe-Jean-François Ballard (b. Paris, c. 1701; d. there, Sept. 3, 1765), but the firm soon became only a shadow of its former self, having lost both its eminence and success.—NS/LK/DM

Ballard, Hank, singer–songwriter best-known for writing "The Twist"; b. Detroit, Nov. 18, 1936. Ballard was born in Detroit but raised from age seven in Besemer, Ala., by relatives after his father died. He ran away from home at age 15, returning to Detroit and finding work on an assembly line. In his off-hours, he began to sing, and was heard by Sonny Woods of the vocal group, The Royals.

The Detroit-based Royals originally formed in 1950, with members Jackie Wilson and Levi Stubbs (later of The Four Tops). The group's membership eventually stabilized with Henry Booth and Charles Sutton (leads and tenors), Lawson Smith (baritone) and Sonny Woods (bass), with Alonzo Tucker on guitar. Spotted by R&B talent scout Johnny Otis in early 1952 at the Paradise Club in Detroit, The Royals signed with Cincinnati's Federal label upon Otis's recommendation and achieved early success with the Otis ballad, "Every Beat of My Heart."

Hank Ballard joined in 1953 when Lawson Smith was drafted into the army, and The Royals soon registered a R&B smash with "Get It." Changing their name to The Midnighters in April 1954, the group scored a top R&B hit with Ballard's blatantly sexual "Work with Me Annie." Although banned from radio station airplay, the song sold over a million copies. Through 1955, The Midnighters achieved major R&B hits with "Sexy Ways," the inevitable followups: "Annie Had a Baby," and "Annie's Aunt Fannie," and "It's Love Baby (24 Hours a Day)." Etta James recorded the "answer" to the Annie songs entitled "The Wallflower" (subtitled "Roll with Me Henry"), with songwriting credit going to James, Ballard, and Otis. White cover artist Georgia Gibbs quickly co-opted the song for a major pop hit.

In the second half of the 1950s, The Midnighters endured a number of personnel changes, including the departures of Charles Sutton and Sonny Woods, the return of Lawson Smith, and the addition of guitarist Cal Green and vocalist Norman Thrasher. They switched to King Records for singles releases, and became Hank Ballard and The Midnighters in 1959. Their 1959 smash R&B hit "Teardrops on Your Letter" was backed by Ballard's song "The Twist," which initially drew little attention. Rereleased after another dance-novelty number, "Finger Poppin' Time," became a smash pop and R&B hit for the group in 1960, "Teardrops" became an R&B smash. However, it took Chubby Checker's cover version—a blatant copy of Ballard's record—to capitalize on the song, scoring top pop hits with it in both 1960 and 1961, and thus launching the international dance craze.

Despite losing out on the Twist craze, Hank Ballard and the Midnighters continued to enjoy popularity on the R&B and pop charts. They scored their biggest popular success with the late 1960s "Let's Go, Let's Go, Let's Go," a smash pop and top R&B hit. Other major pop hits through 1961 included "The Hoochi Coochi Coo" and "The Switcheroo," but after 1962, neither The Midnighters, nor Ballard's solo, achieved another major hit. The group disbanded in the mid 1960s, and Ballard left the King label in 1969. He subsequently joined the James Brown Revue in the late 1960s and early 1970s, dropping out of the music scene from 1974 to 1982. Hank Ballard resumed touring in the 1980s, eventually recording for After Hours Records in the 1990s.

DISC.: *You Can't Keep a Good Man Down* (1969); *Naked in the Rain* (1992). The Midnighters: *Sing Their Greatest Juke Box Hits* (1956); *Hank Ballard and The Midnighters* (1956); *Singin' and Swingin'* (1959); *The One and Only, King* (1960); *Mr. Rhythm and Blues* (1960); *Spotlight on Hank Ballard* (1961); *Let's Go Again* (1961); *Dance Along* (1961); *The Twistin' Fools* (1962); *Jumpin' Hank Ballard* (1963); *The 1963 Sound* (1963); *Greatest Hits* (1964); *A Star in Your Eyes* (1964); *Those Lazy, Lazy Days* (1965); *Glad Songs, Sad Songs* (1966); *24 Hit Tunes* (1966); *Hank Ballard Sings 24 Great Songs* (1968); *20 Hits, 1953–1962* (1977); *Work with Me Annie: The Best of* (1993). "King All Stars": *The King All Stars* (1991).—**BH**

Ballard, Louis W(ayne), preeminent native American composer and music educator; b. Devil's Promenade, Quapaw Indian Reservation, Okla., July 8, 1931. He was of distinguished Quapaw-Cherokee descent and was given the name Honganózhe (Grand Eagle). In his youth, he was immersed in native American music but also received piano lessons at the local Baptist mission school. He later pursued an intensive study of the musics of various native American tribes. He studied at the Univ. of Okla., and then at the Univ. of Tulsa, where he took B.M., B.M.E., and M.M. degrees. He also studied with Milhaud and Castelnuovo-Tedesco. From 1962 to 1969 he was an administrator with the Inst. of American Indian Arts in Santa Fe. From 1969 to 1979 he was in charge of the music curriculum of the U.S. Bureau of Indian Affairs school system. He also was chairman of minority concerns in music education for the state of N.Mex. from 1976 to 1982. He publ. *My Music Reaches to the Sky* (1973) and *Music of North American Indians* (1975). In some of his compositions, he has used the name Joe Miami. In his music, Ballard combines native American elements with advanced Western compositional techniques.

WORKS: DRAMATIC: *Jijogweh, the Witch-water Gull*, ballet (1962); *Koshare*, ballet (1965; Barcelona, May 16, 1966); *The 4 Moons*, ballet commemorating the 60th anniversary of the statehood of Okla. (Tulsa, Oct. 28, 1967); *Sacred Ground*, film score (1975); *The Maid of the Mist and the Thunderbeings*, dance piece (Buffalo, Oct. 18, 1991; symphonic suite, Aptos, Calif., Aug. 8, 1993); *Moontide*, opera (1994). **ORCH.:** *Fantasy Aborigine No. 1: Sipapu* (1963; Santa Fe, April 12, 1964), *No. 2: Tsiyako* (Seattle, Oct. 10, 1976), *No. 3: Kokopelli* (Flagstaff, April 5, 1977), *No. 4: Xactce'oyan-Companion of Talking God* (N.Y., Nov. 15, 1982), and *No. 5: Naniwaya* (1988; Tulsa, Sept. 21, 1989); *Scenes from Indian Life* (1964; Rochester, N.Y., May 2, 1968); *Why the Duck Has a Short Tail* for Narrator and Orch. (Tempe, Ariz., May 8, 1969); *Devil's Promenade* (Tulsa, May 22, 1973); *Incident at Wounded Knee* for Chamber Orch., dramatizing the rebellion of the Sioux Indians at the locality known as Wounded Knee in S.Dak. (Warsaw, Oct. 24, 1974); *Siouxiana* for Wind Ensemble (Grand Forks, N.Dak., Jan. 28, 1974); *Ishi: America's Last Civilized Man* (Aptos, Calif., Aug. 24, 1975); *Wamus-77* for Band (Washington, D.C., Nov. 24, 1977); *Nighthawk Keetowah Dances*, suite for Concert Band (Chicago, April 5, 1978); *Ocotillo Festival Overture* for Concert Band (Tempe, Ariz., March 11, 1979); *The Maid of the Mist and the Thunderbeings*, suite (Aptos, Calif., Aug. 8, 1993; also as a dance piece, Buffalo, Oct. 18, 1991); *The Indian Feast Day* (1994; San Jose, Calif., Jan. 6, 1995). **CHAMBER:** Trio for Violin, Viola, and Cello (1959); *Percussion Ego* for 3 Percussion (1963); *Rhapsody* for 4 Bassoons (1963); *Ritmo Indio* for Wind Quintet (Santa Fe, March 8, 1969); *Cacega Ayuwipi* for Chamber Ensemble (Santa Fe, July 28, 1970); *Katcina Dances*, cello-piano suite (Santa Fe, July 28, 1970); *Desert Trilogy* for Octet (Lubbock, Tex., Oct. 28, 1971); *Rio Grande Sonata* for Violin and Piano (Santa Fe, May 15, 1976); *Music for the Earth and the Sky* for Chamber Ensemble (Saarbrücken, May 31, 1986); *Bellum Atramentum*, trio for Oboe, Violin, and Cello (1988; Santa Fe, May 21, 1989); *Capientur a Nullo*, trio for Violin, Cello, and Double Bass (1988); *The Lonely Sentinel* for Wind Sextet (1993). **P i a n o : 4**

American Indian Piano Preludes (1963); *City of Silver: Buenos Aires* (1980); *City of Fire: Los Alamos* (N.Y., Oct. 20, 1984); *City of Light: Paris* (1986; N.Y., Feb. 15, 1987). **VOCAL:** *Espiritu de Santiago* for Chorus, Flute, Piano, and Guitar (1963); *The Gods Will Hear*, cantata for Chorus and Orch. (Liberty, Mo., May 12, 1964); *Mojave Bird Dance Song* for Chorus and Percussion (1970); *Portrait of Will Rogers*, cantata for Narrator, Chorus, and Orch. (Liberty, Mo., April 3, 1972); *Thus Spake Abraham*, cantata for Soloists, Chorus, and Piano (1976; Buenos Aires, Aug. 23, 1980); *Dialogue Differentia* for Mezzo-soprano, Tenor, Baritone, and Orch. (Bonn, June 1, 1989); *Live On, Heart of My Nation*, cantata for Narrator, Soloists, Chorus, and Orch. (McAlester, Okla., April 1, 1990).—**NS/LK/DM**

Ballif, Claude (André François), French composer and pedagogue; b. Paris, May 22, 1924. After training at the Bordeaux Cons. (1942–48), he took courses with Aubin, N. Gallon, and Messiaen at the Paris Cons. (1948–51). He then studied with Blacher and Rufer at the Berlin Hochschule für Musik (1953–55), and also attended Scherchen's classes in Darmstadt. He was associated with the French Radio and Television in Paris (1959–63), and then was a prof. there at the École Normale de Musique (1963–65). After serving as a prof. at the Rheims Cons. (1964–71), he was prof. of analysis (1971–90) and assoc. prof. of composition (1982–90) at the Paris Cons. He subsequently was prof. of composition at the Sevran Cons. from 1990 to 2000. In 1984 he was made a Commandeur des Arts et des Lettres and in 1994 a Commandeur de l'Ordre National du Mérite. As a composer, Bailiff has followed an independent course, developing a system he describes as metatonality, notable for its avoidance of the extremes of diatonicism and chromaticism.

WRITINGS (all publ. in Paris): *Introduction à la métatonalité* (1956); *Berlioz* (1968); *Voyage de mon oreille* (1979); *Économie musicale—Souhaits entre symboles* (1988); *L'Habitant du Labyrinthe* (1992).

WORKS: DRAMATIC: O p e r a : *Dracoula* (1982; rev. 1983; Paris, Sept. 19, 1984); *Il suffit d'un pue d'air* (1990; Montreal, Dec. 11, 1991). **ORCH.:** *Lovecraft* (1955); *Voyage de mon oreille* (1957); *Fantasio* (1957; rev. 1976); *A Cor et à cri* (1962); *Ceci et cela* (1965); *Cinquième Imaginaire* for Chamber Orch. (1968; rev. 1978); *Sixième Imaginaire* for Chamber String Orch. (1974); *Ivre, moi, immobile* for Clarinet and Orch. (1976); *Haut les Rêves* for Violin and Small Orch. (1984); *Le Jouet du jeu* for Oboe and Chamber (1988). **CHAMBER:** 4 quintets (1952, 1954, 1958, 1960); 5 string quartets (1955, 1958, 1959, 1987, 1989); Violin Sonata (1957); Flute Sonata (1958); 19 works entitled *Solfeggietto* for Various Solo Instruments (1961–99); *Le Taille-Lyre* for 7 Instruments (1990); Saxophone Quartet (1995). **KEYBOARD: P i a n o :** 6 sonatas (1957, 1957, 1959, 1960, 1960, 1994). **O r g a n :** 4 sonatas (all 1956). **VOCAL:** *Quatre Antiennes à la Sainte Vierge* for 6 Soloists and Orch. (1952–53); *La Vie du monde qui vient:première symphonie mystique*, requiem for 8 Soloists, 6 Choruses, and Orch. (1953–55; rev. 1972); *Les Battements du coeur de Jésus* for Double Chorus, Trumpet, and Trombone (1971); *Un Coupe de dés* for Chorus, 6 Instruments, and Tape (1980); *Le Livre dur Serviteur* for Baritone, 3 Choruses, and Orch. (1985–88); *La Transfiguration de l'univers* for 3 Choruses and Instruments (1993); *Moments donnés for mandarins* for Mezzo-soprano, Flute, Oboe, and Clarinet (1998).

BIBL.: M. Tosi, *C. B.* (Bezières, 1991).—**NS/LK/DM**

Balling, Michael, German conductor; b. Heidingsfeld am Main, near Würzburg, Aug. 27, 1866; d. Darmstadt, Sept. 1, 1925. He studied viola at the Würzburg Royal Music School. After serving as an orch. and chamber music player, he went to Nelson, New Zealand, in 1892 and organized a music school, an orch., and a choral society. From 1896 he was an asst. conductor at the Bayreuth Festivals, and also appeared as a guest conductor in other German cities, in Spain, and in England. He was conductor of the Hallé Orch. in Manchester from 1912 to 1914. From 1919 he was Generalmusikdirektor in Darmstadt.—**NS/LK/DM**

Ballista, Antonio, Italian pianist and teacher; b. Milan, March 30, 1936. He studied piano and composition at the Milan Cons., graduating in 1955. He subsequently pursued a successful career as a soloist; was particularly noted for his discerning performances of avant-garde music; he also appeared in duo recitals with the pianist Bruno Canino. Ballista was a prof. at the Milan Cons. from 1974.—**NS/LK/DM**

Ballou, Esther (Williamson), American composer, pianist, and teacher; b. Elmira, N.Y., July 17, 1915; d. Chichester, England, March 12, 1973. She studied composition with Luening at Bennington (Vt.) Coll. (graduated, 1937). After further training at Mills Coll. in Oakland, Calif. (1938), she studied composition with Wagenaar at the Juilliard School of Music in N.Y. (graduated, 1943); also received private instruction from Riegger. She made many tours of the U.S. as a pianist with dance companies. She taught at the American Univ. in Washington, D.C. (1959–73). Her *Capriccio* for Violin and Piano was the first score by an American woman composer to be played at the White House in Washington, D.C., in 1963. Her works generally followed along Classical lines.

WORKS: ORCH.: Suite for Chamber Orch. (1939); *Intermezzo* (1943); *Blues* (1944); 2 piano concertos (1945, 1964), *Prelude and Allegro* for Piano and Strings (1951); Concertino for Oboe and Strings (1953); *Adagio* for Bassoon and Strings (1960); *Im memoriam* for Oboe and Strings (1960); Guitar Concerto (1964); *Konzertstück* for Viola and Orch. (1969). **CHAMBER:** *Impertinence* for Clarinet and Piano (1936); *In Blues Tempo* for Clarinet and Piano (1937); *Nocturne* for String Quartet (1937); *War Lyrics* for Piano, Trumpet, and Percussion (1940); *Christmas Variations* for Oboe and Harpsichord (1954); Piano Trio (1955; rev. 1957); *Divertimento* for String Quartet (1958); Violin Sonata (1959); *A Passing Word* for Flute, Cello, Piano, and Oboe (1960); *Capriccio* for Violin and Piano (1963); *Dialogues* for Oboe and Guitar (1966; rev. 1969); *Prism* for String Trio (1969); *Romanzo* for Violin and Piano (1969). **P i a n o :** *Dance Suite* (1937); 2 sonatas for 2 Pianos (1943, 1958); *Bequine* for Piano, 8–Hands (1950; also for 2 Pianos, 1957, and for Orch., 1960); Sonata (1955). **OTHER:** Organ music, choral pieces, and songs.

BIBL.: R. Ringenwald, *The Music of E.W. B.: An Analytical Study* (thesis, American Univ., 1960); J. Heintze, *E.W. B.: A Bio-Bibliography* (Westport, Conn., 1987).—**NS/LK/DM**

Balmer, Luc, Swiss conductor and composer; b. Munich, July 13, 1898. He was the son of the painter Wilhelm Balmer. Following training with Hans Huber,

Ernst Lévy, and Egon Petri at the Basel Cons. (1915–19), he attended Busoni's master class in composition at the Prussian Academy of Arts in Berlin (1921–22). He conducted the Kursaal in Lucerne (1928–32) and at the Zürich Opera (1932–35). Settling in Bern, he conducted at the Opera (1932–35), and then was conductor of the Orch. Assn. (1935–41) and the Music Soc. (1941–64); he also was on the staff of the Bern Radio (1938–68). In 1969 he was awarded the music prize of the City of Bern, and in 1986 the music prize of the Canton of Bern. His compositions, notable for their ludic craftsmanship, were in an accessible style. They include the opera *Die drei gefoppten Ehemänner* (1967–68), Piano Concerto, Violin Concerto, other orch. works, and chamber pieces. —**NS/LK/DM**

Balogh, Ernő, Hungarian-American pianist, teacher, and composer; b. Budapest, April 4, 1897; d. Mitchellville, Md., June 2, 1989. He studied with Bartók (piano) and Kodály (theory) at the Budapest Academy of Music. In 1924 he emigrated to the U.S. and was active as a pianist and teacher. From 1947 to 1960 he was on the faculty of the Peabody Cons. of Music in Baltimore. He wrote some amiable instrumental pieces of brief dimensions, including *Caprice antique* and *Arabesque*, which were performed by Fritz Kreisler. —**NS/LK/DM**

Balokvić, Zlatko, Croatian violinist; b. Zagreb, March 21, 1895; d. Venice, March 29, 1965. He studied at the Zagreb Cons. and with Sevčik in Vienna. He appeared as a soloist with orchs. and as a recitalist in major music centers of the world.—**NS/LK/DM**

Balsam, Artur, Polish-born American pianist and pedagogue; b. Warsaw, Feb. 8, 1906; d. N.Y., Sept. 1, 1994. He studied in Lódź, making his debut there at the age of 12; then enrolled at the Berlin Hochschule für Musik; in 1930 he obtained the prestigious Mendelssohn Prize; in 1932 he made a U.S. tour with Menuhin. With the advent of the anti-Semitic Nazi regime in 1933, he settled in America, where he became a superlative accompanist to celebrated artists; he also played much chamber music and gave occasional solo recitals. He served on the faculties of the Eastman School of Music in Rochester, N.Y., Boston Univ., and the Manhattan School of Music.—**NS/LK/DM**

Balsys, Eduardas, Lithuanian composer and teacher; b. Nikolayev, Dec. 20, 1919; d. Druskininkai, Nov. 3, 1984. He studied composition with Račiunas at the Lithuanian Cons. in Vilnius, graduating in 1950, then took music courses at the Leningrad Cons. (1953). In 1953 he joined the faculty of the Lithuanian Cons., and in 1960 he was appointed chairman of its composition dept. In his music, he adhered to classical forms but made experimental use of certain modern techniques, including dodecaphonic progressions.

WORKS: DRAMATIC: *Eglė žalčių karalienė* (Egle, Queen of Grass Snakes), ballet (Vilnius, 1960; orch. suite, 1961; 4 fragments for Violin and Piano, 1963); *The Journey to Tilže*, opera (1980). **ORCH.:** *Vilnius*, sym. (1950); *Heroic Poem* (1953); 2 violin concertos (1954, 1958); *Folk Dance Suite* (1958); *Dramatic Frescoes* for Violin, Piano, and Orch. (1965); *Symphony-Concerto* for Organ, Percussion, and Orch. (1977); *Sea Reflections* for Strings (1981); *Portraits* (1983). **CHAMBER:** Piano Sonata (1947); *Variations* for Piano (1948); String Quartet (1953); Concerto for Solo Violin (1984). **VOCAL:** 3 cantatas: *Song for My Land* for Chorus and Orch. (1962), *Saulę nešantis* (He Who Carries the Sun) for High Voice, Chorus, Organ, and Percussion (1972), and *Glory to Lenin* for Mixed Chorus, Men's Chorus, and Children's Chorus (1976); *Nelieskite mėlyno gaublio* (Don't Touch the Blue Globe), oratorio for Soloists, Children's Chorus, 2 Pianos, Double Bass, and Percussion (1969).—**NS/LK/DM**

Baltsa, Agnes, prominent Greek mezzo-soprano; b. Lefkas, Nov. 19, 1944. She studied at the Athen Cons. and won the first Callas scholarship, then pursued her training in Munich and Frankfurt am Main. In 1968 she made her operatic debut as Cherubino at the Frankfurt am Main Opera, where she was a member until 1972. In 1970 she sang at the Deutsche Oper in Berlin, appeared as Octavian in Vienna, and made her debut at the Salzburg Festival as Bastien. Her U.S. debut followed in 1971 when she appeared as Carmen in Houston. In 1976 she sang for the first time at Milan's La Scala and London's Covent Garden as Dorabella, returning to Covent Garden in 1984 to portray Romeo in *I Capuleti e i Montecchi*. On Dec. 13, 1979, she made her Metropolitan Opera debut in N.Y. as Octavian, returning to N.Y. in 1987 as Carmen. In 1989 she sang Santuzza in Vienna, and returned there in 1993 as Azucena. Following an engagement as Elisabeth in *Maria Stuarda* in Barcelona in 1993, she sang Dalila in Zürich in 1996. She also pursued a fine concert career. Among her other roles of note were Rosina, Orpheus, Berlioz's Dido, and Strauss's Composer.

BIBL.: C. Baumann, *A. B.: Eine Bildmonographie* (Zürich, 1986).—**NS/LK/DM**

Baltzar, Thomas, German violinist and composer; b. Lübeck, c. 1630; d. London (buried), July 27, 1663. He was a member of a family of German musicians. In 1653 he was made a chamber violinist to Queen Christina of Sweden. About 1655 he went to England, where he established himself as a soloist at private musical gatherings. In 1661 he was named a musician-in-ordinary for the violin in the King's Private Musick. He also composed several works for violin.—**NS/LK/DM**

Bal y Gay, Jesús, Spanish musicologist and composer; b. Lugo, June 23, 1905; d. there, March 3, 1993. He studied in Madrid. He left his homeland in the wake of the Spanish Civil War, and later was on the staff of the Instituto Nacional de Bellas Artes in Mexico City (1949–65). He publ. essays on Spanish music and composed some symphonic and chamber music. —**NS/LK/DM**

Bamberger, Carl, Austrian-born American conductor and pedagogue; b. Vienna, Feb. 21, 1902; d. N.Y., July 18, 1987. He attended the Univ. of Vienna; received training in piano and theory from Schenker and in cello from Buxbaum. He was conductor of the Gdańsk (1924–27) and Darmstadt (1927–31) operas, and then conducted in Russia. In 1937 he settled in N.Y. and became a naturalized American citizen; taught at the Mannes Coll. of Music (1938–75) and was active as a conductor mainly in N.Y. He publ. the manual *The Conductor's Art* (N.Y., 1965).—**NS/LK/DM**

Bamboschek, Giuseppe, Italian-American conductor; b. Trieste, June 12, 1890; d. N.Y., June 24, 1969. He studied at the Trieste Cons., graduating in 1907. In 1913 he went to the U.S. as accompanist for Pasquale Amato; in 1918 he joined the staff at the Metropolitan Opera in N.Y., specializing in the Italian repertoire. After 1929 he was active mainly as a conductor for radio and films.—**NS/LK/DM**

Bamert, Matthias, Swiss conductor and composer; b. Ersigen, July 5, 1942. He studied in Bern, Zürich, Darmstadt, Salzburg, and Paris, his principal composition teachers being Rivier and Boulez. He was first oboist of the Salzburg Mozarteum Orch. (1965–69), and then was asst. conductor to Stokowski with the American Sym. Orch. of N.Y. (1970–71). He received the first George Szell Memorial Award, joining the conducting staff of the Cleveland Orch. in 1971. From 1977 to 1983 he was music director of the Swiss Radio Orch. in Basel, and then was principal guest conductor of the Scottish National Orch. in Glasgow (1985–90). From 1992 to 1998 he was artistic director of the Lucerne Music Festival, and from 1993 to 2000 he was music director of the London Mozart Players.

WORKS: Concertino for English Horn, Piano, and String Orch. (1966); *Septuria Lunaris* for Orch. (1970); *Rheology* for String Orch. (1970); *Mantrajana* for Orch. (1971); *Once Upon an Orch.* for Narrator, 12 Dancers, and Orch. (1975); *Ol-Okun* for String Orch. (1976); *Keepsake* for Orch. (1979); *Circus Parade* for Narrator and Orch. (1979); *Snapshots* for Orch. (1989). —**NS/LK/DM**

Bampton, Rose (Elizabeth), American soprano; b. Cleveland, Nov. 28, 1909. She studied with Queena Mario at the Curtis Inst. of Music in Philadelphia; also took academic courses at Drake Univ. in Des Moines, Iowa, where she obtained a doctorate of fine arts. She sang as a contralto with the Philadelphia Opera (1929–32), then changed to mezzo-soprano and finally to soprano, so that she could sing the roles of both Amneris and Aida. She made her debut at the Metropolitan Opera in N.Y. on Nov. 28, 1932, as Laura in *La Gioconda*, and continued on its staff until 1945 and again from 1947 to 1950. She made annual appearances at the Teatro Colón in Buenos Aires from 1942 to 1948; then returned to N.Y., where she taught voice at the Manhattan School of Music (1962–82) and at the Juilliard School (from 1974). She was married to **Wilfrid Pelletier.** —**NS/LK/DM**

Ban, Joan Albert, Dutch music theorist and composer; b. Haarlem, 1597 or 1598; d. there, July 27, 1644. He was autodidact as a musician. He was active as a priest in Haarlem, where he was made a canon in 1628.

He is historically important for his system of musica flexanima (zielroerende zang or soul-moving singing) in which the text of a score was delineated in musical terms by specific intervals, rhythms, and harmonies; he also worked on the problem of tuning.

WORKS: *Zanh-bloemzel van Ioan Albert Ban...dat is, Staeltjes van den zinroerende zangh* (Amsterdam, 1642).

WRITINGS: *Joannis Alberti Banni dissertatio epistolica de musicae natura, origine, progressu* (Leiden, 1637); *Cort beduydsel vant zingen* (MS, 1642); *Kort sang-bericht van Ioan Albert Ban...op zyne ziel- roerende zangen* (Amsterdam, 1643); *Zangh-bericht* (unfinished; not extant).—**LK/DM**

Banchieri, Adriano (actually, **Tomaso**), important Italian music theorist and composer; b. Bologna, Sept. 3, 1568; d. there, 1634. He entered the Monte Oliveto monastery in 1587. In 1589 he became a novice and received the name Adriano, and in 1590 he completed his vows. He also received instruction in music from Gioseffo Guami. In 1592 he was at the SS. Bartolomeo e Ponziano monastery in Lucca, and in 1593 at S. Benedetto in Siena. He was at S. Michele in Bosco in 1594, where he was made organist in 1596. From 1600 to 1604 he was organist at S. Maria in Regola di Imola. In 1604 he was at the S. Pietro monastery in Gubbia, in 1605 at the church of S. Elena in Venice, and in 1606 at S. Maria in Organo in Venice. He returned to S. Michele in Bosco in 1609. In 1634 he went to the S. Bernardo monastery in Bologna. In 1615 Banchieri helped to organize the Accademia dei Floridi in Bologna, where he was known as "Il Dissonante." He was given the honorary title of Abate Benemerito in 1618. His theoretical writings are of particular significance. He publ. *Cartella, overo Regole utilissime à quelli che desiderano imparare il canto figurato...devise in 2 parti* (Venice, 1601; 2nd ed., rev., 1610; 3rd ed., rev., 1614 as *Cartella musicale*; 4th ed., rev., 1615 as *La cartellina musicale*, op.35; 5th ed., rev., 1623 as *La banchierina, overo Cartella picciola del canto figurato*). In his 1614 edition he was one of the first to advocate the extension of the hexachord by proposing to name the seventh degree of the scale by the syllables *ba* and *bi*, thus corresponding to B-flat and B-sharp, respectively. In his vol. of organ masses, *L'organo suonarino*, op.13 (Venice, 1605; 2nd ed., rev. 1611 as op.25; 3rd ed., rev., 1622 as op.43), he gives instructions for accompaniment and figured bass. His *Terzo libro di nuovi pensieri ecclesiastici* for 1 to 2 Voices and Basso Continuo, op.35 (Bologna, 1613) is one of the earliest examples of the use of the signs *f* and *p* for loudness and softness, respectively. Banchieri also wrote various nonmusical vols. under the pseudonyms Camillo Scaligerri dalla Fratta or Attabalippa dal Peru. He was a distinguished composer of sacred and secular vocal music, as well as of instrumental pieces. His mastery of seconda prattica is manifested in both his sacred and secular output. Among his sacred works were masses, Psalms, and motets. He publ. several vols. of canzonettas and madrigals along the lines of the commedia dell'arte genre, *La pazzia senile: Ragionamenti vaghi, et dilettevoli* for three Voices (Venice, 1598; 2nd ed., rev., 1599) being the best known. G. Vecchi ed. a complete edition of his works in Antiquae musicae italicae, XII (1963 et seq.).

BIBL.: H.-J. Wilbert, *Die Messen des A. B.* (diss., Johannes

Gutenberg Univ., Mainz, 1969); W. May, *A. B.: Late Sacred Motets:The "Seconda Prattica" in Sacred Music* (diss., Tulane Univ., 1975); P. Mecarelli, *"Il zabaione musicale" di A. B.* (Florence, 1987).—**NS/LK/DM**

Band, The, folk-rock revivalists who brought a uniquely American sound to their music. **Membership:** Jaime Robert "Robbie" Robertson, elec./acoustic/bs. gtr., pno., voc. (b. Toronto, July 5, 1944); Richard Manuel, kybd., drm., voc. (b. Stratford, Ontario, April 3, 1944; d. Winter Park, Fla., March 4, 1986); Garth Hudson, kybd., acc., brs., wdwnd. (b. London, Ontario, Aug. 2, 1942); Rick Danko, bs., fid., voc. (b. Simcoe, Ontario, Dec. 9, 1943); Levon Helm, drm., man., voc. (b. Marvell, Ark., May 26, 1943).

The evolution of The Band began when Levon Helm and several other Arkansans moved to Canada in 1958 to back Ronnie Hawkins as The Hawks. Having pursued an unspectacular career as a country musician, Hawkins turned to rock 'n' roll, hitting with "Forty Days" and "Mary Lou" in 1959. One by one, Canadians Rick Danko, Richard Manuel, Garth Hudson and Robbie Robertson joined the group. They recorded a stunning version of "Who Do You Love," featuring Robertson's psychedelic lead guitar work, but the group left Hawkins in early 1964 to tour East Coast clubs as Levon and The Hawks, under Helm's leadership. In 1965, Robertson, Hudson, and Helm assisted white blues artist John Hammond Jr., in recording his *So Many Roads* album.

After the release of his first rock-oriented album, *Bringing It All Back Home*, Bob Dylan recruited the band while in N.J. in the summer of 1965. Helm, Robertson, and Al Kooper backed Dylan at his controversial Forest Hills concert in late August 1965. Without the recalcitrant Helm, the group toured as Dylan's backup band from the fall of 1965 until the spring of 1966. Following Dylan's much-publicized motorcycle accident, Levon Helm was summoned from Ark., and the group and Dylan retired to upstate N.Y. to rehearse and record the so-called *Basement Tapes*. Available for years only on bootleg albums of questionable legality, this material was eventually released officially in 1975.

While in upstate N.Y., the group, known simply as The Band, recorded their first album. Released in mid-1968, *Music from Big Pink* contained one Dylan song, "I Shall Be Released," and two Dylan collaborations, "Tears of Rage" (with Manuel) and "This Wheel's on Fire" (with Danko). It also included several excellent songs by chief songwriter Robertson ("The Weight," "Caledonia Mission," and "Chest Fever") and Manuel ("We Can Talk" and "Lonesome Suzie").

Making their debut in February 1969 at Bill Graham's Winterland in San Francisco, The Band's second album proved their commercial breakthrough and revealed a growing maturation of Robertson's songwriting talents. Generally regarded as the group's masterpiece, The Band included his classic "The Night They Drove Old Dixie Down," as well as "Across the Great Divide," "Up on Cripple Creek" (a major pop hit), and "Rag Mama Rag," a major British hit. Their next album, *Stage Fright*, yielded only one minor hit, "Time to Kill,"

yet contained several memorable cuts, including the title song, "The Shape I'm In," and "Just Another Whistle Stop." In 1970, Robertson began his outside musical activities, producing Jesse Winchester's debut album. The Band's *Cahoots* album contained several intriguing Robertson songs ("Smoke Signal" and "Shootout in Chinatown") as well as the collaborative "Life Is a Carnival." After the live *Rock of Ages* album, the group recorded the amusing *Moondog Matinee*, which consisted primarily of old rock 'n' roll songs. In July 1973, The Band appeared before the largest crowd in rock history with The Grateful Dead and The Allman Brothers at Watkins Glen, N.Y. Recordings from the show were eventually released in 1995.

In 1974, The Band again backed their old mentor and friend Bob Dylan for his *Planet Waves* album and his first tour since 1965. From the tour came *Before the Flood*, an album combining both Dylan and Band favorites. Subsequently, The Band's first album of original material since 1971, *Northern Lights–Southern Cross*, was critically acclaimed as their best since The Band. Consisting entirely of Robertson songs, the album included "Acadian Driftwood," "Ophelia," and "Jupiter Hollow."

Again busy outside the group, Robbie Robertson produced Neil Diamond's *Beautiful Noise* album in 1976. Later that year, The Band announced their retirement after more than 15 years on the road. Only days after recording their final album as a group, *Islands*, they made their final appearance at Bill Graham's Winterland on Thanksgiving night, 1976. Billed as *The Last Waltz*, this final show featured performances by a number of stars and superstars of rock, from Bob Dylan and Eric Clapton to Joni Mitchell, Neil Young, and Van Morrison. Both a film and an album from the show were released the following spring.

Subsequently, both Rick Danko and Levon Helm recorded on their own, Helm initially with The RCO All-Stars (which included Steve Cropper, Paul Butterfield, and Dr. John), and later with his own group. Helm garnered an Academy Award nomination for his supporting role as Loretta Lynn's father in *Coal Miner's Daughter*. Robbie Robertson cowrote, produced, and costarred in the equivocal 1980 film *Carny* with Gary Busey and Jodie Foster. That year, Robertson began working as director Martin Scorsese's musical supervisor, working on *Raging Bull*, 1983's *The King of Comedy*, and 1986's *The Color of Money*. In the meantime, Garth Hudson became Los Angeles' premier sessions accordion player.

The Band reunited, without Robbie Robertson, for touring in 1983, augmented by the Cate Brothers Band. However, while on tour in Fla., Richard Manuel hanged himself in a motel bathroom in Winter Park on the night of March 4, 1986. Levon Helm continued his film work (*Smooth Talk, End of the Line*), whereas Robertson recorded *Robbie Robertson* and *Storyville*. Helm and Rick Danko toured with Ringo Starr during his 1989 American tour. In 1991, Danko, Helm, and Garth Hudson reunited as The Band with three others to tour and later record *Jericho* for Rhino Records. The Band was inducted into the Rock and Roll Hall of Fame in 1994. During the year, a number of Native American musicians billed as The Red Road Ensemble recorded the music, composed by Robertson, for the three-part, six-hour TBS cable network miniseries *The Native Americans*. In 1998, Capitol Records issued Robertson's *Contact from the Underworld of Red Boy*.

One of the most popular bands in the U.S. between the late 1960s and mid-1970s, The Band was ironically manned by four Canadians and only one American. With only an underground reputation despite years of playing together, The Band achieved their first recognition as Bob Dylan's backup band, later breaking through with the landmark *Music from Big Pink* and *The Band* albums. In refreshing contrast to psychedelic music, *The Band* featured a country-gospel sound supplemented by electric instrumentation and loose yet precise musicianship, combined with oblique vocal harmonies and incisive songwriting. Their songs frequently reflected an Americana of yore, as evidenced by the Robbie Robertson classic, "The Night They Drove Old Dixie Down." Following The Band's dissolution with 1976's *The Last Waltz*, the members pursued individual careers, reuniting without Robertson in the early 1980s.

Disc.: *Music from Big Pink* (1968); *The Band* (1969); *Stage Fright* (1970); *Cahoots* (1971); *Rock of Ages* (1972); *Live at Watkins Glen* (1995); *Moondog Matinee* (1973); *Northern Lights–Southern Cross* (1975); *Best* (1976); *Islands* (1977); *Anthology* (1978); *The Last Waltz* (1978); *Jericho* (1993); *High on the Hog* (1996). Bob Dylan: *The Basement Tapes* (rec. 1967; rel. 1975); *Planet Waves* (1974); *Before the Flood* (1974). Rick Danko: *Rick Danko* (1977). **LEVON HELM AND THE RCO ALL-STARS:** *Levon Helm and The RCO All-Stars* (1977). **LEVON HELM:** *Levon Helm* (1978); *American Son* (1980); *Levon Helm* (1982). **ROBBIE ROBERTSON:** *Robbie Robertson* (1987); *Storyville* (1991); *Contact from the Underworld of Red Boy* (1998). **ROBBIE ROBERTSON AND THE RED ROAD ENSEMBLE:** *The Native Americans* (1994).

Bibl.: L. Helm with S. Davis, *This Wheel's on Fire: Levon Helm and the Story of The Band* (N.Y., 1993); B. Hoskyns, *Across the Great Divide: The Band and America* (N.Y., 1993).—**BH**

Bandrowska-Turska, Eva, Polish soprano; b. Kraków, May 20, 1897; d. Warsaw, June 25, 1979. She studied with her uncle, **Alexander Bandrowski-Sas**, then took further instruction with Helena Zboinska-Ruszkowska. She made her debut as a concert singer in 1919, and subsequently appeared in opera; in later years she gained distinction as a solo singer, excelling particularly as a congenial interpreter of the songs of Debussy, Ravel, Roussel, and Szymanowski.

Bibl.: Z. Bieske, *E. B.-T.: Wspomnienia artystki* (Warsaw, 1989).—**NS/LK/DM**

Bandrowski-Sas, Alexander, noted Polish tenor; b. Lubaczów, April 22, 1860; d. Kraków, May 28, 1913. He made his stage debut as a baritone in an operetta production in Lemberg in 1881, using the name Barski. He then studied voice with Sangiovanni in Milan and Salvi in Vienna, and subsequently pursued a successful career as a tenor, using the name Brandt. He sang in Vienna (1890), Berlin (1896, 1898), and Dresden and Munich, and at La Scala in Milan (1896, 1899). From 1889 to 1901 he was a member of the Frankfurt am Main Opera, and also filled engagements in N.Y., Philadelphia, Chicago, and Boston. He retired from the stage in 1904, and then taught voice in Kraków. His niece was **Eva Bandrowska-Turska.—NS/LK/DM**

Banestre, Gilbert, English composer; b. c. 1445; d. London, Aug. 1487. He served as Master of the Children at the Chapel Royal (from 1478). His output includes sacred and secular vocal music.—**LK/DM**

Bangles, The, the "paisley underground" girl group of the 1980s. **Membership:** Susanna Hoffs, gtr., voc. (b. Newport Beach, Calif., Jan.17, 1959); Vicki Peterson, gtr. (b. Los Angeles, Jan. 11, 1958); Michael Steele, bs. (b. June 2, 1954); Debbi Peterson, drm. (b. Los Angeles, Aug. 22, 1961).

Guitarist Susanna Hoffs loved the rock music her parents listened to while she was growing up—The Beatles, The Byrds, and Simon and Garfunkel. She first worked in a band with David Roback (who went on to form Mazzy Star). In 1981, she put an ad in the Orange County weekly, *The Recycler*, and found guitarist Vicki Peterson and her drum playing sister Debbi. Along with bassist Annette Zilinkas, the group, named the Bangs, started playing the Southern Calif. new-wave scene, falling in with the loose affiliation of "paisley underground" bands like Dream Syndicate. They released an independent single, which attracted the attention of both Miles Copeland, who put out an EP on his own Faulty Products label, and the Bangs, a N.Y.–based band who had the name first.

They changed the name of the band to the Bangles. Zelinkas left to join another band and was replaced by former Runaway bassist Michael Steele (b. June 2, 1954). The group signed to Columbia and released their debut, *All over the Place*. While singles like the original "Hero Takes a Fall" and their cover of Katrina and the Waves's "Going Down to Liverpool" failed to chart, the band spent a huge amount of time on the road. The album charted at #80 and the band made a lot of fans.

One of those fans was Prince. Occasionally (and erroneously) linked romantically with Hoffs, Prince brought them the song "Manic Monday," which they recorded for their second album, *Different Light*. The song hit #2 in both the U.S. and England. The follow-up, "If She Knew What She Wants," only broke the top 30, but the next single, "Walk Like an Egyptian" went gold and topped the charts for four weeks, largely due to a very creative video clip. The final single, "Walking Down Your Street," peaked at #11. The album went triple platinum and spent two weeks at #2. The group followed this with a #2 single from the *Less Than Zero* soundtrack, a version of Paul Simon's "Hazy Shade of Winter."

After selling three million albums, most bands would be happy, but there was great dissent in the Bangles after the success of *Different Light*. For one thing, they prided themselves on their songwriting, but their biggest hits were covers. Also, the lead singer on "Manic Monday" and the focus of the "Walk Like an Egyptian" video happened to be Hoffs; this conveyed the message that she was the band's leader. This was only exacerbated when the first two singles from their next album *Everything* featured Hoffs on vocals. "In Your Room" became a #5 hit and "Eternal Flame" topped the charts again, going gold in the process. Despite this, the group was clearly loosing momentum. "Be with You" was a disappointing #30 on the charts, and the last single, "I'll Set You Free," didn't crack the Top 40. By the end of the year, the band had broken up.

Hoffs did some acting (her mother is a film director) and released a solo album, *When You're a Boy*, in 1991, that produced a top 30 single, "My Side of the Bed." She married in 1993, and spent the next few years at home with family before returning to the recording wars with her eponymous second album. Vicky Peterson joined forces with Susan Cowsill and Peter Holsapple in the Continental Drifters, and her sister Debbi recorded with Kindred Spirit.

When they got together, one of their goals was to be the Beatles of the 1980s. In 1999, they sort of got their wish, reforming for a program of Beatles music at the Hollywood Bowl, conducted by Sir George Martin.

DISC.: *All over the Place* (1984); *Different Light* (1985); *Everything* (1988). **SUSANNA HOFFS:** *When You're a Boy* (1991); *Susanna Hoffs* (1996). **KINDRED SPIRIT:** *Kindred Spirit* (1995). **THE CONTINENTAL DRIFTERS:** *The Continental Drifters* (1995).—**HB**

Banister, Henry Charles, English music theorist, teacher, and composer; b. London, June 13, 1831; d. Streatham, near London, Nov. 20, 1897. He studied music with his father, a cellist; then with Cipriani Potter at the Royal Academy of Music, where he twice gained the King's scholarship (1846 and 1848). He was appointed asst. prof. (1853) of harmony and composition at the Royal Academy of Music, and also taught harmony at Guildhall School (from 1880) and at the Royal Normal Coll. for the Blind (from 1881). He publ. *Textbook of Music* (London, 1872), *Some Musical Ethics and Analogies* (1884), *Lectures on Musical Analysis* (1887), *Musical Art and Study* (1888), *George Alexander Macfarren* (1892), *Helpful Papers for Harmony Students* (1895), *The Harmonising of Melodies* (1897), and *The Art of Modulating* (1901). A collection of his lectures, *Interludes*, ed. by Macpherson, appeared in 1898. Banister composed four syms. and five overtures, chamber music, cantatas, piano pieces, and songs.—**NS/LK/DM**

Banister, John, English violinist and composer, father of **John Banister Jr.**; b. London, c. 1625; d. there, Oct. 3, 1679. After he had received some musical instruction from his father, his skill earned him the patronage of King Charles II, who sent him to France for further study. He was later a member of Charles's band, until an outspoken preference for the English over the French musicians playing in it caused his expulsion. Banister was director of a music school, and established the first public concerts not associated with taverns or other gathering places in which music was of only incidental importance, in London (1672–78). He was a prominent figure in the English musical life of his day. He wrote music for Davenant's *Circe* and Shakespeare's *The Tempest* (both 1676) and also contributed to Playford's *Courtly Masquing Ayres* (1662) and to Lock's *Melothesia* (1673); also wrote music for plays by Dryden, Shadwell, and Wycherley.—**NS/LK/DM**

Banister, John Jr., English violinist and composer, son of **John Banister**; b. London, c. 1663; d. there, c. 1725. He studied violin with his father. He served as concertmaster at the Italian Opera in London. He composed mostly for the theater, and contributed to Playford's *Division Violin* (1685), the first violin manual publ. in England.—**NS/LK/DM**

Bank, Jacques, Dutch composer; b. Borne, April 18, 1943. He studied with Jos Kunst and Ton de Leeuw at the Amsterdam Cons., graduating in 1974. In 1989 he received the Matthijs Vermeulen Prize of Amsterdam.

WORKS: *Blind Boy Fuller I* for Recorder, Piano, and Optional Voice, being a recording of *Thousand Women Blues*, sung by Blind Boy Fuller in 1940 in Chicago (1966); *The Memoirs of a Cyclist* for 2 Recorders (1967–70); *Emcée* for Voices (1969); *Put Me on My Bike I* for Baritone, Recorder, and Chorus (1971); *Fan It* for Orch. (1973); *Song of Sitting Bull* for Recorder Player possessing a Baritone Voice and Organ (1974); *Monk's Blues* for Piano, 14 Voices, and 12 Winds (1974); *Die Ouwe* (The Old One) for Bass Recorder, Bass Clarinet, and Piano (1975); *Thomas* for the recorded Voice of poet Dylan Thomas reading his *Lament*, and 19 Instruments (1975); *Pathétique* for Orch. (1976); *Lied* for Countertenor or Mezzo-soprano, Clavichord or Harpsichord, 2 Percussion Players, 2 Violins, Viola, and Cello (1976); *Mezmerized* for Mezzo-soprano or Tenor, 3 Trumpets, 3 Percussion Players, and Piano (1977); *Alexandre's Concerto* for Piano and Orch. (1978); *Muziek voor een slaapstad* for Chorus and Orch. (1979); *Recorders*, concerto for Recorder, Strings, and Percussion (1981); *Coda* for Chorus and Orch. (1983); *Requiem voor een levende* for Narrator, Chorus, and Chamber Ensemble (1985); *Een tanthologie*, opera (1986–87); *Episodes de la vie d'un artiste* for Soloists, Boy's Chorus, Mixed Chorus, and Orch. (1992–93; Rotterdam, June 11, 1994); *Fred Walking Badger and Aaron Rivers are Missing* for Reciter and Ensemble (1995); *Een bevroren trompet in Helsinki* for Chorus and Piccolo Trumpet (1996); *Some Terrible Secret* for Bass Clarinet and Marimba (1997).—**NS/LK/DM**

Banks, Don(ald Oscar), Australian composer; b. Melbourne, Oct. 25, 1923; d. Sydney, Sept. 5, 1980. He took piano lessons as a child and played in dance bands as a youth. He served in the Australian Army (1941–46). After World War II, he studied composition with Nickson and Le Gallienne at the Melbourne Cons. (1947–49). He then went to England, where he studied composition privately in London with Seiber (1950–52), then in Florence with Dallapiccola (1952–53). He remained in England and worked as an arranger and composer of film and television music; was music director of Goldsmiths' Coll. of the Univ. of London (1965–70). In 1971 he returned to Australia and was head of composition and electronic music at the Canberra School of Music (1974–78), and then of composition at the Sydney Conservatorium (1978–80). In 1980 he was made a member of the Order of Australia. In some of his works, he applied serial methods, modified so as not to destroy the sense of tonality; he also made effective use of electronics.

WORKS: ORCH.: *4 Pieces* (1953; London, June 1, 1954); *Episode* for Chamber Orch. (1958); *Elizabethan Miniatures* for Lute, Viola da Gamba, and Strings (1962); *Divisions* (Cheltenham, July 12, 1965); Horn Concerto (1965; London, Feb. 27, 1966); *Assemblies* (Melbourne, Dec. 3, 1966); Violin Concerto (London, Aug. 12, 1966); *Intersections* for Orch. and Tape (1969; London, Jan. 1970); *Meeting Place* for Chamber Orch., Jazz Group, and 2 Synthesizers (London, June 15, 1970); *Nexus* for Jazz Quintet and Orch. (1970; Kassel, April 8, 1971); *Music for Wind Band* (1971); *Prospects* (1974); *Trilogy* (1977). CHAMBER: *Duo* for Violin and Cello (1951–52); *Divertimento* for Flute and String Trio (1951–52); Violin Sonata (1953); *Sonata da Camera*, in memory of Seiber, for 8 Instruments (1961); *Equation I* for 12 Players (1963), *II* for 12 Players (1969), and *III* for Chamber Group, Jazz Quartet, and Synthesizers (1972); Trio for Violin, Horn, and Piano (1962); *Sequence* for Cello (1967); *Prelude, Night Piece and Blues for 2* for Clarinet and Piano (1968); *4 Pieces* for String Quartet (1971); *Take 8* for String Quartet and Jazz Quartet (1973); String Quartet (1976); *4 x 2* for Clarinet(s) and Tape (1977). P i a n o : *Pezzo dramatico* (1956); *Commentary* for Piano and Tape (1971). VOCAL: *5 North Country Folk Songs* for Voice and String Orch. or Piano (1953–54); *Psalm 70* for Voice and Chamber Orch. (1954); *Settings from Roget* for Voice and Jazz Quartet (1966); *Tirade*, triptych for Soprano, Harp, Piano, and 3 Percussionists (1968); *Findings Keepings* for Chorus and Percussion (1969); *Limbo*, cantata for 3 Singers, 8 Instruments, and 2–channel Tape (1971); *Benedictus* for Voices, Jazz Quartet, 5 Synthesizers, Fender Electric Piano, and Tape (1976).
—NS/LK/DM

Bannister, Henry (-Marriott), English music editor and bibliographer; b. Oxford, March 18, 1854; d. there, Feb. 16, 1919. He studied theology, and was ordained priest in 1878. He publ. the valuable editions *Monumenti Vaticani di paleografia musicale latina* (Leipzig, 1913; also in It. tr. by R. Baralli), a catalogue of the music MSS in the Vatican Library, including 141 plates; *Anglo-French Sequelae* (ed. by Dom Anselm Hughes and publ. by The Plainsong and Medieval Music Soc. in 1934); co-ed. Vols. 47, 49, 53, and 54 of *Analecta Hymnica Medii Aevi* (1886–1922); also publ. some MSS of the Abbey of Coupar-Angus in Scotland, with a brief description (Rome, 1910); ed. a Gallican sacramentary, *Missale Gothicum*, with introduction and liturgical notes (London, 1917–19). He was for many years librarian of the Bodleian Library at Oxford.—NS/LK/DM

Banti, Brigida (née **Giorgi**), famous Italian soprano; b. Monticelli d'Ongina, 1759; d. Bologna, Feb. 18, 1806. She sang in Paris cafés, where she attracted the attention of de Vismes, director of the Paris Opéra, who engaged her to sing there. She made her debut on Nov. 1, 1776, singing a song during the intermission. She then studied with Sacchini. In 1779 she went to London for a season, then sang in Vienna (1780), Venice (1782–83), Warsaw (1789), and Madrid (1793–94). Paisiello wrote for her his opera *Giuochi di Agrigento*, and she sang at its premiere (Venice, May 16, 1792). From 1794 to 1802 she sang at King's Theatre in London; then retired. She married the dancer Zaccaria Banti. Her son wrote her biography.

BIBL.: G. Banti, *Vita di B. B.-G.* (Bologna, 1869).
—NS/LK/DM

Bantock, Sir Granville (Ransome), eminent English composer and pedagogue; b. London, Aug. 7, 1868; d. there, Oct. 16, 1946. He was a student of Frederick Corder at the Royal Academy of Music in London (1889–93), where he won the first Macfarren Scholarship. From 1893 to 1896 he was the ed. of the *New Quarterly Musical Review*. In 1894–95 he made a world tour as conductor of the musical comedy *The Gaiety Girl*. From 1897 to 1900 he was director of music of the Tower Orch. in New Brighton, where he won notice as a conductor of contemporary works. From 1900 to 1914 he was principal of the Birmingham and Midland Inst. School of Music. He served as the Peyton Prof. of Music at the Univ. of Birmingham from 1908 to 1934. He subsequently was a teacher and examiner at the Trinity Coll. of Music in London. He was knighted in 1930. Bantock was a prolific composer who often wrote works on a vast scale. Many of his scores were of a programmatic nature, and revealed his fascination for exotic and heroic subjects. An Oriental and Celtic bent was particularly pronounced. His works were brilliantly scored and highly effective in performance, but they are rarely heard today.

WORKS: DRAMATIC: *Aegypt*, ballet (1892); *Eugene Aram*, opera (1892; unfinished); *Caedmar*, opera (London, Oct. 25, 1892); *The Pearl of Iran*, opera (1894); *The ABC, or Flossie the Frivolous*, musical comedy (Wolverhampton, March 21, 1898; in collaboration with others); *Sweet Brier*, musical comedy-drama (1898); *Harlequinade, or Only a Clown*, musical play (1899); *The Great God Pan*, ballet (1915); *The Seal-Woman*, opera (1917–24; Birmingham, Sept. 27, 1924); also incidental music to plays. ORCH.: *The Curse of Kehama* (1894); *Saul*, overture (1897); *Elegiac Poem* for Cello and Orch. (1898); *Helena Variations* (1899; Antwerp, Feb. 21, 1900); *Russian Scenes* (1899); *English Scenes* (1900); 6 tone poems: No. 1, *Thalaba the Destroyer* (1900), No. 2, *Dante* (1901; rev. as *Dante and Beatrice*, 1910; London, May 24, 1911), No. 3, *Fifine at the Fair* (1901; Birmingham, Oct. 2, 1912), No. 4, *Hudibras* (1902), No. 5, *The Witch of Atlas* (Worcester, Sept. 10, 1902), and No. 6, *Lalla Rookh* (1902); *Sapphic Poem* for Cello and Orch. (1906); *The Pierrot of the Minuet*, overture (1908); *3 Dramatic Dances* (1909); *Old English Suite* for Small Orch. (1909); *Oedipus Coloneus*, overture (1911); *From the Far West* for Strings (1912); *From the Scottish Highlands* for Strings (1913); 4 syms.: No. 1, *Hebridean* (1913; Glasgow, Feb. 14, 1916, composer conducting), No. 2, *Pagan* (1923–28; BBC, London, 1936), No. 3, *The Cyprian Goddess: Aphrodite in Cyprus* (1938–39), and No. 4, *Celtic* (1940); *Celtic Poem* for Cello and Orch. (1914); *Dramatic Poem* for Cello and Orch. (1914); *The Land of the Gael* for Strings (1915); *Coronach* for Strings, Harp, and Organ (1918); *Hamabdil* for Cello and Orch. (1919); *Judith* (1919); *Festival Hymn of Judith* (1919); *Wachet auf*, chorale variations (1920); *The Sea Reivers* (London, Feb. 21, 1920); *Caristiona: Hebridean Seascape* (1920); *The Frogs*, overture (1935); *4 Chinese Landscapes* for Small Orch. (1936); *Overture to a Greek Comedy* (1941); *Circus Life*, overture (1941); *2 Heroic Ballads: Cuchullin's Lament and Kishmul's Gallery* (1944); *Hebridean Poem:The Seagull of the Land Under the Waves* (1944); *The Bacchae*, overture (1945); *The Birds*, overture (1946); *The Funeral* (1946). CHAMBER: 2 string quartets (1899, 1933); *Serenade* for Horns (1903); *Pibroch* for Cello and Harp (1917); Viola Sonata (1919); Sonata for Solo Cello (1924); *Salve regina* for String Trio (1924); 3 violin sonatas (1929, 1932, 1940); 2 cello

sonatas (1940, 1945); numerous piano pieces. **VOCAL:** *The Fire Worshippers* for Soloists, Chorus, and Orch. (1892); *Wulstan* for Voice and Orch. (1892); *The Blessed Damozel* for Reciter and Orch. (1892); *Thorvenda's Dream* for Reciter and Orch. (1892); *Christus* for Soloists, Chorus, and Orch. (1901); *The Time Spirit* for Chorus and Orch. (1902); Mass for Men's Chorus (1903); *Ferishtah's Fancies* for Voice and Orch. (1905); *Sappho* for Voice and Orch. (1906); *Sea Wanderers* for Chorus and Orch. (1906); *Omar Khayyam* for Soloists, Chorus, and Orch. (1906); *Atalanta in Calydon*, "sym." for Chorus (1911); *Vanity of Vanities*, "sym." for Chorus (1913); *A Pageant of Human Life*, "sym." for Chorus (1913); *Song of Liberty* for Chorus and Orch. (1914); *Choral Suite from the Chinese* for Men's Chorus (1914); *The Song of Songs* for Soloists, Chorus, and Orch. (1922; radio broadcast, Dec. 11, 1927); *7 Burdens of Isaiah* for Men's Chorus (1927); *The Pilgrim's Progress* for Soloists, Chorus, and Orch. (1928); *Prometheus Unbound* for Chorus and Orch. (1936); *King Solomon* for Narrator, Chorus, and Orch. (1937); *The Sphinx* for Voice and Orch. (1941); *Thomas the Rhymer* for Voice and Orch. (1946); numerous other vocal works, including song cycles and solo songs.
BIBL.: H. Anderton, *G. B.* (London, 1915); M. Bantock, *G. B.: A Personal Portrait* (London, 1972).—**NS/LK/DM**

Banwart, Jakob, German composer; b. Sigmaringen, May 19, 1609; d. Konstanz, c. 1657. He studied with Daniel Bollius, the court organist in Sigmaringen, then continued his education at Dillingen Univ. (1629–31), where he received a master's degree. He was ordained in Konstanz in 1632, and subsequently active as a musician at the court there; in 1641 he became Kapellmeister of the Cathedral. He composed mostly music for the church, but also took time off to write a collection of humorous dialogues, quodlibets, and other pieces which were publ. in his lifetime.—**NS/LK/DM**

Bär, Olaf, prominent German baritone; b. Dresden, Dec 19, 1957. He sang in the Kreuzchor (1966–75) and studied at the Hochschule für Musik in Dresden. In 1982 he won first prize in the Dvořák vocal competition in Karlovy Vary, and, in 1983, first prize in the vocal competition sponsored by the East German opera houses and the Walter Grüner lieder competition in London. In 1981 he made his operatic debut in Dresden, and from 1985 to 1991 he was a principal member of the State Opera there. He made his British debut in a recital at London's Wigmore Hall in 1983, returning to London in 1985 to make his British operatic debut as Strauss's Harlekin at Covent Garden. In 1986 he appeared as Ariadne at the Aix-en-Provence Festival, and as Papageno at the Vienna State Opera and at La Scala in Milan. On March 19, 1987, he made his U.S. debut as Christ in Bach's *St. Matthew Passion* with Solti and the Chicago Sym. Orch., and that same year sang the role of the Count in *Capriccio* at the Glyndebourne Festival. On April 18, 1991, he made his N.Y. recital debut at Alice Tully Hall. He portrayed Mozart's Count at the Netherlands Opera in Amsterdam in 1993. He made his U.S. operatic debut as that composer's Papageno in Chicago in 1996. In addition to his roles in operas by Mozart and Strauss, he has won distinction as a concert and lieder artist.—**NS/LK/DM**

Barab, Seymour, American cellist and composer; b. Chicago, Jan. 9, 1921. He studied with Persichetti,

Volpe, Varese, and Harrison. He played in the Indianapolis Sym. Orch., the Cleveland Orch., the CBS Sym. Orch., the Portland (Ore.) Sym. Orch., the San Francisco Sym., the ABC Sym. Orch., and the Brooklyn Philharmonia; also played in the Galimir String Quartet, the N.Y. Pro Musica, the N.Y. Trio, the New Music Quartet, and the Composers Quartet. He served on the faculties of Black Mountain Coll., Rutgers, the State Univ. of N.J., and the New England Cons. of Music in Boston. As a cellist, Barab commissioned and premiered scores by several American composers. His own large output includes three full-length operas: *Phillips Marshall, Mortals,* and *A Piece of String*; 25 one-act operas; Concerto Grosso for Orch.; *Tales of Rhyme and Reason* for Orch.; Cello Concerto; Concertino for Alto Saxophone and Orch.; Wind Quintet; Quartet for Saxophones; four string quartets; five piano trios; Trio for Flute, Viola, and Harp; choral works; numerous songs.—**NS/LK/DM**

Baranović, Krešimir, Croatian conductor, pedagogue, and composer; b. Šibenik, July 25, 1894; d. Belgrade, Sept. 17, 1975. He studied piano, theory, and composition in Zagreb and in Vienna. He was a theater conductor in Zagreb (1915–27) and toured with Pavlova's ballet group (1927–28). From 1929 to 1940 he was director of the Zagreb Opera. He was a prof. at the Belgrade Academy of Music from 1946 to 1961, and he also was conductor of the Belgrade Phil. from 1952 to 1961.
WORKS: DRAMATIC: Comic Opera: *Striženo-Košeno* (Clipped and Mowed; Zagreb, May 4, 1932); *Nevjesta od Cetingrada* (The Bride from Cetingrad; Belgrade, May 12, 1951). **Ballet:** *Licitarsko srce* (The Gingerbread Heart; 1924); *Kineska priča* (Chinese Tale; Belgrade, April 30, 1955). **ORCH.:** *Pjesma guslara* (Song of the Minstrel; Zagreb, Jan. 25, 1947). **VOCAL:** *Pan* for Narrator, Voices, and Orch. (Belgrade, March 10, 1958); *Oblaci* (The Clouds) for Mezzo-soprano and Orch. (Belgrade, Oct. 31, 1964).—**NS/LK/DM**

Barati, George (real name, **György Baráti**), Hungarian-born American cellist, conductor, and composer; b. Györ, April 3, 1913. After initial training at the Györ Music School (graduated, 1932), he studied at the Franz Liszt Academy of Music in Budapest (graduated, 1935; teacher's diploma, 1937; artist diploma, 1938); he also was a member of the Budapest Concert Orch. (1933–36) and first cellist of the Budapest Sym. Orch. and Municipal Opera orch. (1936–38). In 1939 he emigrated to the U.S., becoming a naturalized citizen in 1944; he studied composition with Georges Couvreur and Henri Switten at Westminster Choir Coll. in Princeton, N.J. (1938–39), and with Sessions at Princeton Univ. (1939–43). He played cello in the Pro Ideale (later Westminster) String Quartet (1936–39), then taught at Princeton Univ. (1939–43). He also conducted the Princeton Ensemble and Choral Union (1941–43) and the Alexandria (La.) Military Sym. Orch. (1944–46). He was a cellist in the San Francisco Sym. Orch. and the Calif. String Quartet (1946–50); he also was music director of the Barati Chamber Orch. of San Francisco (1948–52). From 1950 to 1968 he was music director of the Honolulu Sym. Orch. and Opera, leaving to become executive director of the Montalvo Center for the Arts and conductor of the Montalvo Chamber Orch. in Saratoga, Calif. (1968–78). From 1971 to 1980 he was music director of the Santa Cruz County Sym. Orch. in Aptos, Calif.; he then was music director of the Barati Ensemble (1989–92). In 1991 the George Barati Archive was opened at the Univ. of Calif. at Santa Cruz Library. In 1959 he received the Naumburg Award, in 1962 the Alice M. Ditson Award, and in 1965–66 a Guggenheim fellowship. As a composer, Barati writes fine music in a modern European tradition. During his stay in Hawaii, he studied native melodic and rhythmic patterns of exotic South Sea islands, and these found reflection in some of his works of the period.

WORKS: DRAMATIC: O p e r a : *Noelani* (1968). **B a l - l e t :** *The Love of Don Perlimplin* (1947). **I n c i d e n t a l M u s i c :** *Thirty Pieces of Silver* for Narrator and Chamber Orch. (1951). **F i l m :** *The Ugly Duckling* (1981; arr. as a suite for Narrator and Chamber Orch. or Band, 1982–83); *What Do 2 Rights Make?* (1983). **ORCH.:** *Fever Dreams* (1938); *2 Symphonic Movements* (1941); *Lamentoso* (1943); *Scherzo* (1946); *Configuration* (1947); Chamber Concerto for Flute, Oboe, Clarinet, Bassoon, and Strings (1952); *Tribute* (1952); Cello Concerto (1953; rev. 1957); *The Dragon and the Phoenix* (1960); Sym. (1963); *Polarization* (1965); *Baroque Quartet Concerto* for Flute, Oboe, Harpsichord, Double Bass, and Orch. (1968); *Festival Hula* (1968); *Vaudeville* (1968); Piano Concerto (1973); Guitar Concerto (1976; rev. 1982); *Branches of Time* for 2 Pianos and Orch. (1981); *Confluence* (1982); Violin Concerto (1986); *Serenata Capricciosa* for Chamber Orch. (1990); *Chant of Darkness* (1993); *Seachange* (1993). **CHAMBER:** 3 string quartets (1944, 1961, 1991); Woodwind Quintet (1954); Violin Sonata (1956); Quintet for Oboe and Strings (1961); Harpsichord Quartet for Flute, Oboe, Harpsichord, and Double Bass (1964); Octet for Flute, Oboe, Double Bass, Harpsichord, and String Quartet (1966); *Lumberjack* for Trombone and Piano (1969; rev. 1992); *Hawaiian Forests* for 7 Instruments (1971; rev. 1989); Trio for Flute, Violin, and Guitar (1976; rev. 1979); Triptych for Flute, Oboe, Viola, and Piano (1983); Woodwind Trio (1984); *...And the Shadows Were Filled With Light* for 9 Instruments (1984); *Spring Serenade* for Flute, Viola, and Cello (1987); *Trio Profundo* for Viola, Cello, and Contrabass (1988; rev. 1990); Trio for Clarinet, Violin, and Cello (1988); *Dialogue* for Flute and Piano (1990); *Aquinas Suite* for 3 Unspecified Instruments (1991); *Second Edition*, "encore" for String Quartet (1991); *Spring Rain* for Clarinet and Guitar (1993); piano pieces. **OTHER:** Vocal music.—NS/LK/DM

Barba, Daniel dal
See Dal Barba, Daniel

Barbaia or Barbaja, Domenico,

celebrated Italian impresario; b. Milan, 1778?; d. Posillipo, near Naples, Oct. 19, 1841. He worked as a scullion in local cafes and bars, and is reputed to have been the inventor of barbaiate or granita di caffe, a concoction of coffee or chocolate with whipped cream. In 1808 he obtained the lease of the gambling tables in the foyer of Milan's La Scala, and in 1809 also secured the position of manager of all the royal opera houses in Naples. He became so influential that he was dubbed the "Viceroy of Naples." From 1821 to 1828 he was manager of Vienna's Kärnthnertortheater and Theater an der Wien, and from 1826 to 1832 of Milan's La Scala. In 1811 he engaged Isabella Colbran as a singer in Naples, and she became his mistress only to leave him to marry Rossini in 1822. All the same, he remained a champion of Rossini. Among the other composers he championed were Mercadente, Pacini, Bellini, and Donizetti. Barbaia appears as a character in Auber's opera *La sirène* (1844) and was the inspiration for Emil Lucka's novel *Der Impresario* (Vienna, 1937).—NS/LK/DM

Barbarin, Paul (Adolphe),

drummer, bandleader, composer, uncle of **Danny Barker**; b. New Orleans, May 5, 1901; d. there, Feb. 10, 1969. His father, Isidore, was a local bandleader, playing alto horn with the Onward Brass Band, and three of his brothers were musicians, the most famous being drummer Louis (b. 1902). Paul began on clarinet, then worked as a freight-lift operator at the Hotel St. Charles in New Orleans. With his earnings, he bought his first set of drums. He soon began gigging with local bands. He left New Orleans for Chicago in 1917, working in the stockyards by day and playing club jobs at night. Through 1945, Barbarin spent his professional life alternating between living and working in either Chicago or N.Y. and then returning for a while to his hometown of New Orleans. Some of the highlights of his performing career included a position with King Oliver's band in Chicago from February 1925–summer of 1927; and work with Luis Russell's N.Y.–based band from 1928–January 1932 and again from 1935–late 1938. In between, he gigged with other groups and worked leading various bands in his hometown. He returned to New Orleans in late 1944 pretty much for good, and formed his own band (originally called The Invaders). Besides a brief stint in 1953 with Art Hodes at Jazz Ltd., in Chicago, Barbarin led his own highly successful small band, playing long residencies in New Orleans, but also fulfilling engagements in N.Y., Los Angeles, Toronto, etc. In 1960 he formed the Onward Brass Band, named after the original Onward, which his father had led. In the last decade of his life he was associated with many of the musicians who worked at Preservation Hall, including Sweet Emma Barrett, with whom he recorded. He died while leading the Onward Brass Band in a parade. He was also known for several of his musical compositions, particularly "Bourbon Street Parade" and "The Second Line."

DISC.: *Streets of the City* (1950); *Johnny St. Cyr and His Hot Five* (1950); *Paul Barbarin and Percy Humphrey* (1951); *New Orleans Band* (1951); *New Orleans Jamboree* (1954); *And His Jazz Band* (1954); *And His New Orleans Jazz* (1955); *New Orleans Jazz Band* (1956); *New Orleans Contrasts* (1956); *Bourbon Street* (1962); *And Punch Miller* (1962); *Barbarin's Best at Dixieland Hall* (1964). —JC/LP

Barbarino, Bartolomeo,

Italian organist and composer, known as **Il Pesarino**; b. Fabriano, date unknown; d. probably in Padua, c. 1617. He was an alto at the Santa Casa in Loreto in 1593–94. From 1594 to 1602 he was in the service of Monsignor Giuliano della Rovere in Urbino. He was organist at Pesaro Cathedral from 1602 to 1605, and thereafter was in the service of the Bishop of Padua. Barbarino was one of the earliest composers of monodies. His works, all publ. in Venice, comprise 2 vols. of motets (1610, 1614), 5 vols. of madrigals (1606, 1607, 1610, 1614, 1617), and a vol. of canzonettas (1617).

BIBL.: N. Hockley, *I due primi libri monodici di B. B. (1606 e 1607)* (diss.,Univ. of Parma, 1970).—**LK/DM**

Barbe, Helmut, German organist, choral conductor, pedagogue, and composer; b. Halle an der Saale, Dec. 28, 1927. He was a student at the Berlin Kirchenmusikschule of Herbert Schulze (organ), Gottfried Grote (choral conducting), and Ernst Pepping (counterpoint). In 1952 he became Kantor at St. Nikolai Church in Berlin. From 1955 he was a teacher at the Berlin Kirchenmusikschule. In 1972 he was named Landeskirchenmusikdirektor of West Berlin. From 1975 to 1993 he was a prof. at the Berlin Hochschule der Künste. Barbe incorporated various contemporary techniques into his works, including a modified form of dodecaphony. Among his many choral works are a *Passionsmotette* (1955), a *Magnificat* (1956), *Chinesischen Impressionen* (1964), the *90ᵗʰ Psalm* (1965), the oratorios *Golgotha* (1971), *Tedeum* (1975), and *Potsdamer Tedeum* (1992), and the *Kantate zum Kirchentag 1989: "Der du die Zeit in Handern hast"* (1989). He also wrote the musical *Halleluja Baby* (1956), *Canticum Simeonis*, a concerto for Tenor, Chorus, Celesta, Organ, Percussion, and String Orch. (1958), an Organ Sonata (1964), a Violin Concerto (1966), a Trio for Violin, Cello, and Piano (1969), *Hovs Hallar* for 12 Strings, Percussion, and Organ (1970), and *Herbst* for Chorus and Harp (1988).—**NS/LK/DM**

Barbeau, (Charles) Marius, eminent Canadian anthropologist, ethnologist, and folklorist; b. Ste.-Marie-de-Beauce, Quebec, March 5, 1883; d. Ottawa, Feb. 27, 1969. He studied music with his mother; after taking courses in the humanities at the Collège de Ste.-Anne-de-la-Procatière and in law at Laval Univ., he won a Rhodes scholarship in 1907 and pursued training in anthropology, archeology, and ethnology at Oriel Coll., Oxford (graduated with a B.S. degree and a diploma in anthropology, 1910); also took courses at the Sorbonne and the École d'anthropologie in Paris. In 1911 he became anthropologist and ethnologist at the Museum Branch of the Geological Survey of Canada; after it became the National Museum in 1927, he remained with it until 1948; also taught at the Univ. of Ottawa (1942) and at Laval Univ. (1942–45), where he subsequently served as prof. agrégé. He was founder-director of the Canadian Folk Music Soc. (1956–63). Barbeau collected more than 6,000 melodies and 13,000 texts of French-Canadian folk songs, as well as many thousands of Canadian Indian melodies. He publ. 30 books and 10 song anthologies, some in collaboration with others. Among his most important writings were "Chants populaires du Canada," *Journal of American Folklore* (with E. Massicotte; 1919); *Folksongs of French Canada* (with E. Sapir; New Brunswick, 1925); *Folk- songs of Old Quebec* (Ottawa, 1935); *Where Ancient France Lingers* (Toronto, 1936); *Modalité dans nos mélodies populaire* (Ottawa, 1944); *Jongleur Songs of Old Quebec* (Toronto, 1962). —**NS/LK/DM**

Barbella, Emanuele, Italian violinist, teacher, and composer; b. Naples, April 14, 1718; d. there, Jan. 1, 1777. He spent his entire life in Naples. After training from his father, Francesco Barbella, maestro di violino and composer at the Cons. di S. Maria di Loreto, he studied with Angelo Zaga and Pasqualino Bini before completing his training in theory and composition with Michele Cabbalone and Leonardo Leo. He was first violinist in the orch. of the Teatro Nuovo (1753–56), and then was a member of the royal chapel. From 1761 he played in the orch. of the Teatro San Caro. Barbella wrote the opera *Elmira generosa* (Naples, 1753; in collaboration with N. Logroscino), violin sonatas, duo sonatas, and trio sonatas.—**LK/DM**

Barber, Samuel, outstanding American composer of superlative gifts; b. West Chester, Pa., March 9, 1910; d. N.Y., Jan. 23, 1981. He was the nephew of **Louise Homer** and her husband **Sidney Homer**, who encouraged him in his musical inclination. At the age of six, he began piano lessons, and later had some cello lessons. He was only ten when he tried his hand at composing a short opera, *The Rose Tree*. During his high school years, he gained practical experience as organist at Westminster Presbyterian Church. Even before graduating from high school at age 16, he entered the first class at the newly organized Curtis Inst. of Music in Philadelphia when he was 14, where he was a pupil of Boyle and Vengerova (piano), Scalero (composition), and Reiner (conducting). He also took voice lessons with Emilio de Gogarza and gave recitals as a baritone at the Curtis Inst., where he graduated in 1932. He then went to Vienna to pursue vocal training with John Braun, and also appeared in public as a singer there. In the meantime, his interest in composing grew apace. In 1928 his Violin Sonata won the Bearns Prize of Columbia Univ. It was followed by such enduring scores as his *Dover Beach* for Voice and String Quartet (1931), the *Serenade* for String Quartet (1932), and the Cello Sonata (1932). In 1933 he won the Bearns Prize again for his overture to *The School for Scandal*, which was favorably received at its premiere by the Philadelphia Orch. on Aug. 30 of that year. Then followed the successful premiere of his *Music for a Scene from Shelley* by the N.Y. Phil. on March 24, 1935, under Werner Janssen's direction. Thanks to a Pultizer Traveling Scholarship and a Rome Prize, Barber pursued composition at the American Academy in Rome in 1935 and 1936. During his sojourn there, he wrote his First Sym., which was premiered under Molinari's direction on Dec. 13, 1936. He also wrote his String Quartet in 1936. Rodzinski conducted Barber's First Sym. at the Salzburg Festival on July 25, 1937, the first score by an American composer to be played there. Toscanini conducted the premiere of Barber's (first) *Essay for Orch.* with the NBC Sym. Orch. in N.Y. on Nov. 5, 1938. On the same program, he also conducted the *Adagio* for Strings, a transcription of the second movement of the String Quartet, which was destined to become Barber's most celebrated work, an epitome of his lyrical and Romantic bent. From 1939 to 1942 he taught composition at the Curtis Inst. His most notable work of this period was his Violin Concerto, which was first performed by Albert Spalding with Ormandy and the Philadelphia Orch. on Feb. 7, 1941. With his friend Gian Carlo Menotti, he purchased a house ("Capricorn") in Mount Kisco, N.Y., which was to remain the center of his activities until 1974. In 1943 he was conscripted into the U.S. Army and was assigned to the Army Air Force. During his military service, he composed his Second Sym., which included an electronic instrument producing sound in imitation of radio signals. Koussevitzky conducted its premiere with the Boston Sym. Orch. on March 3, 1944. After his discharge from military service in 1945, Barber revised the score; it was first performed by the Philadelphia Orch. on Jan. 21, 1948. Still dissatisfied with the work, he destroyed the MS except for the second movement, which he revised as *Night Flight*, which was first performed by Szell and the Cleveland Orch. on Oct. 8, 1964. Barber had better luck with his Cello Concerto (1945), which was introduced by Raya Garbousova with Koussevitzy conducting the Boston Sym. Orch. on April 5, 1946. In 1947 it won the N.Y. Music Critics' Circle Award. For Martha Graham, he composed the ballet *Medea* (N.Y., May 10, 1946), which was revised as *The Cave of the Heart* (N.Y., Feb. 27, 1947). He made an orch. suite from the ballet (Philadelphia, Dec. 5, 1947) and the orch. piece, *Medea's Meditation and Dance of Vengeance* (N.Y., Feb. 2, 1956). One of Barber's most distinguished scores, *Knoxville: Summer of 1915* for High Voice and Orch., after James Agee, was first performed by Eleanor Steber with Koussevitzky conducting the Boston Sym. Orch. on April 9, 1948. His remarkable Piano Sonata, premiered by Horowitz in Havana on Dec. 9, 1949, amply utilized contemporary resources, including 12–tone writing. In 1953 he composed the one-act opera *A Hand of Bridge*, scored for four Soloists and Chamber Orch. The work was not performed until June 17, 1959, when it was mounted in Spoleto, Italy, without much impact. In the meantime, Barber composed his finest opera, *Vanessa* (1956–57), to a libretto by Menotti. It was successfuly premiered at the Metropolitan Opera in N.Y. on Jan. 15, 1958, and was awarded the Pulitzer Prize in Music. It was followed by his strikingly brilliant Piano Concerto, which was first performed by John Browning with Leinsdorf conducting the Boston Sym. Orch. at N.Y.'s Lincoln Center for the Performing Arts on Sept. 24, 1962. Barber was awarded his second Pulitzer Prize in Music for this work. A commission from the Metropolitan Opera spurred Barber on to compose his most ambitious work for the stage, the three-act opera *Antony and Cleopatra*. With Zeffirelli as librettist, producer, director, and designer, it was premiered at the opening of the new Metropolitan Opera House in N.Y. on Sept. 16, 1966. Unfortunately, the work found few admirers. Barber revised the score with a revamped libretto by Menotti, and the new version was given a more favorable reception at its first performance by N.Y.'s Opera Theater of the Juilliard School on Feb. 6, 1975.

During the final years of his life, Barber wrote only a handful of works. In 1945, 1947, and 1949 he held Guggenheim fellowships. He was elected to the National Inst. of Arts and·Letters in 1941 and to the American Academy of Arts and Letters in 1958. Barber was one of the most distinguished American composers of the 20th century. He excelled primarily as a melodist, being remarkably sensitive in his handling of vocally shaped patterns. Although the harmonic structures of his music remained fundaméntally tonal, he made free use of chromatic techniques, verging on atonality and polytonality, while his mastery of modern counterpoint enabled him to write canons and fugues in effective neo-Baroque sequences. His orchestration was opulent without being turgid, and his treatment of solo instruments was unfailingly congenial to their nature even though requiring a virtuoso technique.

WORKS: DRAMATIC: O p e r a : *A Hand of Bridge* (1953; Spoleto, June 17, 1959); *Vanessa* (1956–57; N.Y., Jan. 15, 1958, Mitropoulos conducting; rev. 1964); *Antony and Cleopatra* (N.Y., Sept. 16, 1966, Schippers conducting; rev. 1974; N.Y., Feb. 6, 1975, Conlon conducting). **B a l l e t :** *Medea* or *Serpent Heart* (N.Y., May 10, 1946; rev. as *The Cave of the Heart*, N.Y., Feb. 27, 1947; as a ballet suite, Philadelphia, Dec. 5, 1947, Ormandy conducting; as *Medea's Meditation and Dance of Vengeance* for Orch., 1953; N.Y., Feb. 2, 1956, Mitropoulos conducting); *Souvenirs* (1952; N.Y., Nov. 15, 1955; as a ballet suite, 1952; Chicago, Nov. 12, 1953, Reiner conducting; also for Solo Piano or Piano, 4–Hands). **O R C H . :** *Serenade* for Strings (1928; also for String Quartet); *The School for Scandal*, overture (1933; N.Y., March 24, 1935, Janssen conducting); 2 syms.: No. 1 (Rome, Dec. 13, 1936, Molinari conducting; rev. 1942) and No. 2 (Boston, March 3, 1944, Koussevitzky conducting; rev. version, Philadelphia, Jan. 21, 1948, Ormandy conducting; 2nd movement rev. as *Night Flight*, Cleveland, Oct. 8, 1964, Szell conducting); *Adagio* for Strings (arranged from the 2nd movement of the String Quartet, 1936; N.Y., Nov. 5, 1938, Toscanini conducting); (3) *Essay*(s): No. 1 (1937; N.Y., Nov. 5, 1938, Toscanini conducting), No. 2 (N.Y., April 16, 1942, Walter conducting), and No. 3 (N.Y., Sept. 14, 1978, Mehta conducting); Violin Concerto (1939; Philadelphia, Feb. 7, 1941, Spalding soloist, Ormandy conducting); *Funeral March* (1943); *Commando March* for Band (Atlantic City, May 23, 1943, composer conducting; also for Orch., Boston, Oct. 29, 1943, Koussevitzky conducting); *Capricorn Concerto* for Flute, Oboe, Trumpet, and Strings (N.Y., Oct. 8, 1944, Saidenberg conducting); Cello Concerto (1945; Boston, April 5, 1946, Garbousova soloist, Koussevitzky conducting); *Horizon* (c. 1945; Merrick, N.Y., Jan. 19, 1985); *Adventure* for Flute, Clarinet, Horn, Harp, and Exotic Instruments (1954); *Toccata festiva* for Organ and Orch. (Philadelphia, Sept. 30, 1960, Callaway soloist, Ormandy conducting); *Die natalie*, choral preludes for Christmas (Boston, Dec. 22, 1960, Munch conducting); Piano Concerto (N.Y., Sept. 24, 1962, Browning soloist, Leinsdorf conducting); *Fadograph of a Yestern Scene* (Pittsburgh, Sept. 11, 1971, Steinberg conducting); *Canzonetta* for Oboe and Strings (orchestrated by C. Turner, 1977–78; N.Y., Dec. 17, 1981, H. Gomberg soloist, Mehta conducting). **C H A M B E R :** *Serenade* for String Quartet (1928; Philadelphia, May 5, 1930, Swastika Quartet; also for String Orch.); Violin Sonata (Philadelphia, Dec. 10, 1928, Gilbert violinist, composer pianist; not extant); Cello Sonata (1932; N.Y., March 5, 1933, Cole cellist, composer pianist); String Quartet (Rome, Dec. 14, 1936, Pro Art Quartet; 2nd movement arranged as the *Adagio* for Strings, 1936); *Commemorative March* for Violin, Cello, and Piano (n.d.); *Summer Music* for Wind Quintet (1955; Detroit, March 20, 1956); *Canzone (Elegy)* for Flute or Violin and Piano (1962; transcription of the 2nd movement of the Piano Cocnerto): *Mutations from Bach* for 4 Horns, 3 Trumpets, 3 Trombones, and Tuba or Timpani (1967; N.Y., Oct. 7, 1968). **K E Y B O A R D : P i a n o :** *Interlude I (Adagio for Jeanne)* (Philadelphia, May 12, 1932, composer pianist); (4) *Excursions* (1942–44; first complete perf., N.Y., Dec. 22, 1948, Behrend pianist); Sonata (Havana, Dec. 9, 1949, Horowitz pianist); *Souvenirs* (1952; also for Piano, 4–Hands, and as a ballet);

Nocturne: Homage to John Field (San Diego, Oct. 1959, Browning pianist); *Ballade* (Fort Worth, Sept. 11, 1977). **O r g a n :** *Wondrous Love: Variations on a Shape Note Hymn* (Grosse Pointe, Mich., Oct. 19, 1958, Roeckelein organist). **VOCAL:** *10 Early Songs* for Voice and Piano (1925–37; nos. 1–9 first perf., Rome, Jan. 5, 1936, composer singer and pianist); *Dover Beach* for Medium Voice and String Quartet (1931; N.Y., March 5, 1933, Bampton singer, N.Y. Art Quartet); *The Virgin Martyrs* for Women's Voices (1935; CBS, May 1, 1939, composer conducting); *Let Down the Bars, O Death* for Chorus (1936); *I Hear an Army* for Voice and Piano (1936; Philadelphia, March 7, 1937; also for Voice and Orch., CBS, May 5, 1945, Tourel soloist, composer conducting); *God's Grandeur* for Double Chorus (Shippensburg, Pa., Jan. 31, 1938); *Sure on this Shining Night* for Voice and Piano (1938; Philadelphia, April 4, 1941; also for Voice and Orch., CBS, May 5, 1945, Tourel soloist, composer conducting; also for Chorus and Piano); *Nocturne* for Voice and Orch. (1940; CBS, May 5, 1945, Tourel soloist, composer conducting; also for Voice and Piano, Philadelphia, April 4, 1941); *A Stopwatch and an Ordnance Map* for Men's Voices, Brass Ensemble, and Timpani (first perf. without brass, Philadelphia, April 23, 1940, composer conducting; first perf. with brass, N.Y., Dec. 17, 1945, Shaw conducting); *Reincarnations* for Chorus (1940); *Monks and Raisins* for Medium Voice and Piano (1943; also for Medium Voice and Orch., CBS, May 5, 1945, Tourel soloist, composer conducting); *Knoxville: Summer of 1915* for Voice and Orch. (1947; Boston, April 9, 1948, Steber soloist, Koussevitzky conducting; rev. version for Voice and Chamber Orch., Washington, D.C., April 1, 1950); (5) *Mélodies Passagères* for Voice and Piano (1950; first complete perf., Paris, Feb. 1952, Bernac singer, Poulenc pianist); (10) *Hermit Songs* for Voice and Piano (1952–53; Washington, D.C., Oct. 30, 1953, Price singer, composer pianist); *Prayers of Kierkegaard* for Soprano, Chorus, and Orch. (Boston, Dec. 3, 1954, Price soloist, Munch conducting); *Andromache's Farewell* for Soprano and Orch. (1962; N.Y., April 4, 1963, Arroyo soloist, Schippers conducting); *Easter Chorale* for Chorus, Brass Sextet, Timpani, and Organ ad libitum (Washington, D.C., May 7, 1964); *Agnus Dei* for Chorus and Piano or Organ ad libitum (1967; arranged from the 2nd movement of the String Quartet, 1936); *Despite and Still*, song cycle for High or Medium Voice and Piano (N.Y., April 27, 1969, Price singer, Garvey pianist); *The Lovers* for Baritone, Chorus, and Orch. (Philadelpha, Sept. 22, 1971, Krause soloist, Ormandy conducting).

BIBL.: N. Broder, *S. B.* (N.Y., 1954); R. Friedewald, *A Formal and Stylistic Analysis of the Published Music of S. B.* (diss., Univ. of Iowa, 1957); L. Wathen, *Dissonance Treatment in the Instrumental Music of S. B.* (diss., Northwestern Univ., 1960); S. Carter, *The Piano Music of S. B.* (diss., Tex. Tech. Univ., 1980); D. Hennessee, *S. B.: A Bio- Bibliography* (Westport, Conn., 1985); J. Kreiling, *The Songs of S. B.: A Study in Literary Taste and Text-Setting* (Ann Arbor, Mich., 1987); B. Heyman, *S. B.: The Composer and His Music* (Oxford, 1991); P. Wittke, *S. B.: An Improvsatory Portrait* (N.Y., 1994; includes works list by N. Ryan).—**NS/LK/DM**

Barberiis, Melchiore de, Italian lutenist and composer who flourished in Padua in the mid-16th century. He brought out three vols. of pieces for Lute or Guitar (1546, 1549), which contains ricercares, fantasias, canzonas, and dances, as well as arrangements of pieces by Josquin and Févin.—**LK/DM**

Barbetta, Giulio Cesare, Italian lutenist and composer; b. probably in Padua, c. 1540; d. after 1603.

He was one of the leading masters of the lute in his era. Among his works are four books of music in lute tablature (Venice, 1569; 1575, not extant; 1585; 1603).—**LK/DM**

Barbier, René (Auguste-Ernest), Belgian composer and teacher; b. Namur, July 12, 1890; d. Brussels, Dec. 24, 1981. He studied with Gilson at the Brussels Cons. and with Dupuis at the Liège Cons. He taught at the Liège Cons. (1920–49) and at the Brussels Cons. (1949–55); concurrently was director of the Namur Cons. (1923–63). In 1923 he received the Belgian Royal Academy Prize for his symphonic poem *Les Génies du sommeil*, and in 1968 he was elected to membership in the Academy.

WORKS: DRAMATIC: O p e r a : *Yvette* (1910); *La Fête du vieux Tilleul* (1912). **B a l l e t :** *Les Pierres magiques* (1957). **ORCH.:** *Pièce symphonique* for Trumpet and Orch. (1918); 2 piano concertos (1922, 1934); *Les Génies du sommeil*, symphonic poem (1923); *Les Éléments: Suite Platonicienne* (1935); *Poème* for Cello and Orch. (1936); *Fantaisie concertante* for Violin and Orch. (1937); Cello Concerto (1938); *Poco adagio et Allegro brillante* for Clarinet and Orch. (1940); *Diptyque* (1941); *La Musique de perdition*, symphonic poem (1947); *Introduction (Fanfare) et 3 Esquisses symphoniques* (1956); *Pièce concertante* for Violin or Saxophone and Orch. (1958); Guitar Concerto (1960); *3 mouvements symphoniques* for Strings (1962); *Tableau symphonique* (1963); Horn Concerto (1964); *Introduction et Allegro symphonique* (1967); Concerto for Organ, Strings, and Percussion (1967); *Ouverture concertante* (1969); Concertino for 2 Guitars and Strings (1971). **CHAMBER:** Violin Sonata (1914); Piano Quintet (1915); Viola Sonata (1916); Piano Trio (1919); String Quartet (1939); Quartet for 4 Horns (1956); Quartet for 4 Saxophones (1961); Trio for Flute, Cello, and Piano (1971). **VOCAL:** Oratorios and other works.—**NS/LK/DM**

Barbieri, Carlo Emanuele, Italian conductor and composer; b. Genoa, Oct. 22, 1822; d. Pest, Sept. 28, 1867. He was educated at the Naples Cons., where he studied voice with Crescenti and composition with Mercadante. In 1845 he embarked on a career as an opera conductor; eventually settled in Buda, where he conducted at the National Theater from 1862 until his death. He wrote five operas: *Cristoforo Colombo* (Berlin, 1848), *Nisida, la perla di Procida* (1851), *Carlo und Carlin* (1859), *Arabella* (Buda, 1862), and *Perdita, ein Wintermärchen* (Leipzig, 1865).—**NS/LK/DM**

Barbieri, Fedora, Italian mezzo-soprano; b. Trieste, June 4, 1920. She studied in Trieste with Luigi Toffolo and in Milan with Giulia Tess. She made her professional debut as Fidalma in Cimarosa's *Il matrimonio segreto* at Florence's Teatro Comunale in 1940; in 1942 she made her first appearance at Milan's La Scala as Meg Page; in 1950 she first sang at London's Covent Garden as a member of the visiting La Scala company, and returned to Covent Garden as a guest artist in 1957–58 and 1964. From 1947 she sang at the Teatro Colón in Buenos Aires. On Nov. 6, 1950, she made her Metropolitan Opera debut in N.Y. as Eboli, remaining on its roster until 1954, and again for the 1956–57,

1967–68, 1971–72, and 1974–77 seasons. Her large repertory included over 80 roles, both standard and modern, among them Adalgisa, Carmen, Amneris, Santuzza, and Azucena.—NS/LK/DM

Barbieri, Francisco Asenjo, Spanish composer; b. Madrid, Aug. 3, 1823; d. there, Feb. 19, 1894. He studied clarinet, voice, and composition at the Madrid Cons., then engaged in multifarious activities as a café pianist, music copyist, and choral conductor. He found his true vocation in writing zarzuelas, and composed 78 of them. The following, all produced in Madrid, were particularly successful: *Gloria y peluca* (March 9, 1850), *Jugar con fuego* (Oct. 6, 1851), *Los diamantes de la corona* (Sept. 15, 1854), *Pan y Toros* (Dec. 22, 1864), and *El Barberillo de Lavapiés* (Dec. 18, 1874). He also ed. a valuable collection, *Cancionero musical de los siglos XV y XVI*, and publ. a number of essays on Spanish music.

BIBL.: A. Martínez Olmedilla, *El maestro B. y su tiempo* (Madrid, 1941).—NS/LK/DM

Barbieri-Nini, Marianna, Italian soprano; b. Florence, Feb. 18, 1818; d. there, Nov. 27, 1887. She studied with Luigi Barbieri, Pasta, and Vaccai, making her operatic debut in 1840 at La Scala in Milan in Donizetti's *Belisario*. Unfortunately, her peculiarly asymmetrical facial features and an ill-constructed bodily frame produced such a vociferous outburst of revulsion on the part of the notoriously unrestrained Italian opera audiences that she was advised to wear a mask and a bodice to conceal her repellent physique. However, she astutely selected the part of Lucrezia Borgia, a historically celebrated poisoner, in Donizetti's eponymous opera at her next appearance in Florence, and there her ugly countenance fitted the role to a high C. She was also very successful in other bloody roles, among them that of Lady Macbeth in Verdi's opera and of the sympathetic but murderous Gulnara in Verdi's *Il Corsaro*.—NS/LK/DM

Barbirolli, Sir John (actually, **Giovanni Battista**), eminent English conductor of Italian-French descent; b. London, Dec. 2, 1899; d. there, July 29, 1970. He studied cello. He received a scholarship to London's Trinity Coll. of Music in 1910 and another to London's Royal Academy of Music, graduating in 1916. He made his first appearance as a cellist at the age of 12 on Dec. 16, 1911, at the Queen's Hall in London. In 1916 he became a member of the Queen's Hall Orch. In 1923 he joined the International String Quartet and toured with it. In 1924 he organized a chamber orch. in Chelsea, which he conducted for several years. He was a conductor with the British National Opera Co. (1926–29). He gained recognition on Dec. 12, 1927, when he successfully substituted for Beecham at a concert of the London Sym. Orch. In 1928 he was a guest conductor at London's Covent Garden, and a regular conductor there from 1929 to 1933. In 1933 he was named conductor of the Scottish Orch., Glasgow, and the Leeds Sym. Orch. He made his American debut with the N.Y. Phil. on Nov. 5, 1936, and was engaged as its permanent conductor in 1937. However, he failed to impress the N.Y. critics, and

in 1943 he returned to England, where he was named conductor of the Hallé Orch. of Manchester. In 1958 he was appointed its conductor-in-chief. Renewing his American career, he served as conductor of the Houston Sym. Orch. (1961–67), while continuing his tenancy of the Hallé Orch., from which he finally retired in 1968 with the title of Conductor Laureate for Life. He was knighted in 1949 and made a Companion of Honour in 1969. A commemorative postage stamp with his portrait was issued by the Post Office of Great Britain on Sept. 1, 1980. Barbirolli was distinguished primarily in the Romantic repertoire. His interpretations were marked by nobility, expressive power, and brilliance. He had a fine pragmatic sense of shaping the music according to its inward style, without projecting his own personality upon it. However, this very objectivity tempered his success with American audiences, accustomed to charismatic flamboyance. He had a special affinity for English music, and performed many works of Elgar, Delius, and Britten. He conducted the first performances of the 7th and 8th syms. by Vaughan Williams. He also made transcriptions for string orch. and horns of five pieces from the Fitzwilliam Virginal Book (perf. by him under the title *Elizabethan Suite* in Los Angeles, Dec. 4, 1941). For his second wife, Lady Evelyn Barbirolli, he composed an Oboe Concerto on themes by Pergolesi.

BIBL.: C. Rigby, *J. B.* (Altrincham, 1948); M. Kennedy, *Hallé Orch.* (Manchester, 1968; rev. ed., 1976); idem, *B., Conductor Laureate* (London, 1971); C. Reid, *J. B.* (London, 1971); H. Atkins and P. Cotes, *The B.s: A Musical Marriage* (London, 1983). —NS/LK/DM

Barblan, Guglielmo, eminent Italian musicologist; b. Siena, May 27, 1906; d. Milan, March 24, 1978. He first studied jurisprudence, then entered the Rome Cons. as a cello student of Forino and Becker; also took courses in theory at the Bolzano Cons. and attended lectures on musicology by Liuzzi in Rome and Sandberger in Munich. He served as a music critic for *La Provincia di Bolzano* (1932–50), and concurrently lectured on music history at the Bolzano Cons. (1932–49). In 1949 he became head librarian of the Milan Cons.; in 1965 he was appointed prof. of music history there; also taught at the Univ. of Milan from 1961. Barblan's principal contribution as a music scholar was in the field of Italian music history. In addition to his books, he ed. works by Bonporti and Cambini.

WRITINGS: *Un musicista trentino: F.A. Bonporti* (Florence, 1940); *Musiche e strumenti musicali dell'Africa orientale italiana* (Naples, 1941); *L'opera di Donizetti nell'età romantica* (Bergamo, 1948); ed. with A. Della Corte, *Mozart in Italia: I viaggi e le lettere* (Milan, 1956); *Guida al "Clavicembalo ben temperato" di J.S. Bach* (Milan, 1961); with C. Gallico and G. Pannain, *Claudio Monteverdi nel quarto centenario della nascita* (Turin, 1967); ed. *Conservatorio di musica G. Verdi, Milano; Catalogo della biblioteca* (Florence, 1972); with B. Zanolini, *Gaetano Donizetti: Vita e opera di un musicista romantico* (Bergamo, 1983).—NS/LK/DM

Barblan, Otto, Swiss organist, conductor, teacher, and composer; b. Scanfs, March 22, 1860; d. Geneva, Dec. 19, 1943. He studied at the Stuttgart Cons. (1878–84); made his debut as an organist at Augsburg

(1885); taught at Chur (1885–87); then became organist at the Cathedral of Geneva, prof. at the Cons., and conductor of the Société de Chant Sacre (1887). He wrote an *Ode patriotique* (1896); a *Festspiel* (Chur, May 28, 1899) commemorating the 400th anniversary of the battle of Calven, and containing the chorus *Terre des monts*, which attained great popularity, placing it next to the national anthem as a patriotic song; *Post tenebras lux*, cantata for the Calvin jubilee (1909); String Quartet; *Variations and Triple Fugue on B-A-C-H*; *Passion According to St. Luke* (Geneva, April 9, 1919).

BIBL.: E. Perini, *O. B.* (Zürich, 1960).—NS/LK/DM

Barbosa-Lima, Carlos, Brazilian guitarist and teacher; b. São Paulo, Dec. 17, 1944. He began to study the guitar when he was seven and at age 12 he made his debut in São Paulo. His principal teachers were Isaias Savio in Brazil and Andrés Segovia in Spain. In 1967 he made his first tour of the U.S., and subsequently appeared in music centers around the world. From 1982 to 1994 he taught at the Manhattan School of Music in N.Y. He commissioned works from Ginastera, Balada, and Mignone, and made his own effective transcriptions of scores by Bach, Handel, and other masters.—NS/LK/DM

Barbour, J(ames) Murray, American musicologist; b. Chambersburg, Pa., March 31, 1897; d. Homestead, Pa., Jan. 4, 1970. He studied at Dickinson Coll. (M.A., 1920) and Temple Univ. (Mus.B., 1924), then with Kinkeldey at Cornell Univ., where he received the first doctorate in musicology awarded by a U.S. univ. in 1932 with the diss. *Equal Temperament: Its History from Ramis (1482) to Rameau (1737)*; subsequently received a second Ph.D. in music from the Univ. of Toronto in 1936. He taught English at Ithaca Coll. (1932–39); then was a teacher at Mich. State Coll. (later Univ.), where he was a prof. (1954–64). He contributed learned essays to music journals; also publ. *Tuning and Temperament: A Historical Survey* (East Lansing, 1951; 2nd ed., 1953), *The Church Music of William Billings* (East Lansing, 1960), and *Trumpets, Horns and Music* (East Lansing, 1964). Among his compositions are a *Requiem* and some chamber pieces. —NS/LK/DM

Barce, Ramón, Spanish composer and music critic; b. Madrid, March 16, 1928. He studied languages at the Univ. of Madrid but was mainly autodidact in music; then was active with new music groups and as a music critic. He composed theater, orch., chamber, and vocal pieces in a modern idiom.

BIBL.: A. Medina, *R. B. en la vanguardia musical española* (Oviedo, 1983).—NS/LK/DM

Bardi, Giovanni de', Count of Vernio, Italian nobleman, patron of music and art, and composer; b. Florence, Feb. 5, 1534; d. Rome, Sept. 1612. He was the founder of the Florentine Camerata, a group of musicians who met at his home (1576–c. 1582) to discuss the music of Greek antiquity; this led to the beginnings of opera. Count Bardi was descended from an old Guelph banking family; he was a philologist, mathematician, neo-Platonic philosopher, and lover of Dante. He was a member of the Crusca Academy, a literary group founded in 1583 whose ideas had great influence on the Camerata. Bardi is known to have been in Rome in 1567; he lent support to Vincenzo Galilei, a member of the Camerata. In 1580 Bardi married Lucrezia Salvati. The masques of 1589, commemorating the marriage of Grand Duke Ferdinand, were conceived largely by Bardi. In 1592 he left for Rome to become chamberlain at the court of Pope Clement VIII. Caccini was his secretary in 1592. Bardi's writings are: *Discorso sopra il giuoco del calzio fiorentino* (Florence, 1580), *Ristretto delle grandezze di Roma* (Rome, 1600), and *Discorso mandato a Caccini sopra la musica antica* in Doni's *Lyra Barberina* (Florence, 1763). Among his compositions are a madrigal in 4 Voices, *Misere habitator* in Malvezzi's *Intermedi e concerti* (Venice, 1591); the madrigal *Lauro ohime lauro* in *Il lauro secco, lib.* I (Ferrara, 1582). Among contemporary documents that refer to him are Vincenzo Galilei's *Dialogo della musica antica e della moderna* (tr. in part in O. Strunk's Source Readings in Music History, N.Y., 1951; also included is a letter from Bardi's son to G.B. Doni commenting on Bardi's ideas).—NS/LK/DM

Bárdos, Lajos, Hungarian choral conductor, musicologist, and composer; b. Budapest, Oct. 1, 1899; d. there, Nov. 18, 1986. He studied composition with Siklós and Kodály at the Budapest Academy of Music, where he then taught (1928–67). He also conducted Budapest's Cecilia Chorus (1926–41), Palestrina Chorus (1929–33), Chorus (1941–47), and St. Matyas Choir (1942–62). He publ. books on Liszt (1968, 1976), Bartók (1970, 1971), Stravinsky (1971), and Kodály (1972). Among his compositions were choral and chamber pieces.—NS/LK/DM

Barenaked Ladies, clever Canadian band on the razor's edge of pop and novelty. **MEMBERSHIP:** Steven Page, gtr., voc. (b. Scarborough, Ontario, June 22); Ed Robertson, gtr., voc. (b. Ontario, Oct. 25, 1970); Jim Creeggan, acou. bs. (b. Feb. 12, 1970); Andrew Creeggan, kybd. (b. July 4, 1971); Tyler Stewart, drm. (b. Sept. 21, 1967).

Singing guitarists Steven Page and Ed Robertson knew each other from their grade-school days, but only started playing together in their late teens, when they were working at a camp for musically gifted children. They started making demo tapes just for fun in Page's basement. They came up with a name for their act during a Bob Dylan concert. They were so bored that they started making up band names, and came up with Barenaked Ladies. The name reflects their songs, once described as a mixture of intellectual hedonism and vaudeville clowning.

Initially, Page and Robertson played on the street, busking for coins. When they started getting paying gigs, they brought the Creeggan brothers on board—Jim on double bass and Andrew on keyboards. With the addition of drummer Tyler Stewart, they had a road-ready quintet.

Through constant touring, frequently opening for alternative bands Corky and Juice Pigs, they became quite popular. With their concentration on entertaining, they were asked to play at Toronto's annual City Hall New Years Eve Celebration. When the City Council got wind of it, they pulled the plug, saying the band's name objectified women. Suddenly they became a cause cèlébre in the Toronto papers as an illustration of the silliness of political correctness versus common sense. This raised people's curiosity about "the band causing all the furor." Their tape, made as a demo, became the first independent cassette release ever to go platinum in Canada.

Sire Records signed them and released their debut album, *Gordon*. With songs that ranged from the pathos laden "Brian Wilson" to the nutty "Be My Yoko Ono" to the downright strange "Steven Page Is Having a Baby" (Gordon was the baby's name), the album outsold U2 and Michael Jackson in Canada, eventually moving over 800,000 copies (or octuple platinum). They were named group of the year at the Juno Awards (the Canadian Grammys), playing the show dressed as clowns. They took *Gordon* on the road in a show they called "Mr. Rockin's All You Can Eat Salad Bar Tour."

While waiting for a flight back from London's Heathrow Airport after touring Europe, Robertson was notified that his brother had died in a motorcycle accident. They played the next show anyway, rather than canceling a concert for 22,000 people. Adding to their road woes, Page discovered he couldn't write on tour. When the concert jaunt finally ended, he invited his friend Steven Duffy from the English bands Duran Duran, Tin Tin, and Lilac Time to spend a week with him in Toronto. Over the course of the next month and a half, they wrote seven songs together. Four of them made it to the group's next album, *Maybe You Should Drive*. Meanwhile Andrew Creeggin left the group, and was replaced by Kevin Hearn. With all that turmoil, the relatively somber *Maybe You Should Drive* didn't sell well in the U.S. or Canada.

The next two years were tumultuous. When they weren't on the road, they were dealing with a change in management to the company that represented Lillith Fair creator Sarah McLachlan. They finally recorded *Born on a Pirate Ship*. The song "The Old Apartment" charted largely due to a video directed by actor Jason Priestly. It eventually hit the Top 40.

Adding to their popularity in the U.S., the song "Shoebox" was used in an episode of the hit TV series *Friends*. They released a special enhanced EP centered on the song. However, their popularity had ebbed in Canada to the point they couldn't fill Massey Hall in Toronto only two years after selling out two shows. Their next album, the live *Rock Spectacle*, renewed interest in a track from *Gordon*, "Brian Wilson." The song got Adult Album Alternative radio play and the album sold over a million and a half copies.

In 1998, after ten years together, Page and Robertson got something they desperately wanted: a major worldwide hit. "One Week" got frequent MTV play and topped the charts in the U.S. The album that it came from, *Stunt*, went Top Ten. The tune, a rapid-fire patter song, included references to Sting, Yoda, Aquaman, Andrew Lloyd Webber, and Chinese chicken. *Stunt* sold over one and a quarter million records in its first six weeks. By the end of the year it had sold over three million copies in the U.S. However, Hearn came down with leukemia. While his prognosis was good, Chris Brown took over on keyboards as he recovered.

In the wake of the band's new popularity, *Gordon* went gold and *Rock Spectacle* went platinum.

DISC.: *Gordon* (1992); *Maybe You Should Drive* (1994); *Rock Spectacle* (1996); *Shoebox* (1996); *Born on a Pirate Ship* (1996); *Stunt* (1998); *Maroon* (2000).—**HB**

Barenboim, Daniel, greatly talented Israeli pianist and conductor; b. Buenos Aires, Nov. 15, 1942. He began music training with his parents, making his public debut as a pianist in Buenos Aires when he was only seven. During the summers of 1954 and 1955, he studied piano with Edwin Fischer, conducting with Igor Markevitch, and chamber music with Enrico Mainardi at the Salzburg Mozarteum. He also pursued training in theory with Boulanger in Paris (1954–56), was one of the youngest students to receive a diploma from the Accademia di Santa Cecilia in Rome (1956), and took a conducting course with Carlo Zecchi at the Accademia Musicale Chigiana in Siena. In 1955 he made his debut as a soloist with orch. in Paris, and then made his British debut in Bournemouth. In Jan. 1956 he made his first appearance in London as soloist with Krips and the Royal Phil. He made his U.S. debut as soloist in Prokofiev's First Piano Concerto with Stokowski and the Sym. of the Air at N.Y.'s Carnegie Hall on Jan. 20, 1957. Later that year he made his first appearance as a conductor in Haifa. On Jan. 17, 1958, he made his U.S. recital debut in N.Y. In 1960 he played cycles of all the Beethoven piano sonatas in Israel and South America, and later in London (1967, 1970) and N.Y. (1970). From 1965 he was active as a soloist and conductor with the English Chamber Orch. in London. In 1967 he married the renowned English cellist Jacqueline DuPré (b. Oxford, Jan. 26, 1945; d. London, Oct. 19, 1987), with whom he subsequently appeared in numerous concerts until she was tragically stricken with multiple sclerosis in 1973 and was compelled to abandon her career. In 1967 he conducted the Israel Phil. on a tour of the U.S., returning thereafter to appear as a guest conductor with various orchs. He also appeared as a guest conductor throughout Europe. He made his operatic debut in 1973 conducting *Don Giovanni* at the Edinburgh Festival. In 1975 he became music director of the Orchestre de Paris, a position he held until 1989. In 1981 he made his first appearance at the Bayreuth Festival conducting *Tristan und Isolde*. In 1988 he was named artistic director of the new Opéra de la Bastille in Paris by the French minister of culture. However, following the French presidential election, a new minister of culture was appointed and disagreements over artistic policy and remuneration led to Barenboim's abrupt dismissal in Jan. 1989. That same month he was appointed music director of the Chicago Sym. Orch., succeeding Solti. During the 1989–91 seasons, he served as its music director-designate before fully assuming his duties as music director for the orch.'s 100th anniversary season in 1991–92. In 1993 he also became Generalmusikdirektor of the Berlin State Opera. His autobiography appeared as *A Life in Music* (1991). From the earliest years of his professional career as a pianist, Barenboim has been held in the highest esteem. Particularly notable have been his performances of Bach, Mozart, Beethoven, Chopin, and Brahms. In addition to his distinguished appearances as a recitalist and chamber music artist, he has won great admiration as an accompanist. Barenboim's career as a conductor has been less remarkable. While he has maintained an extensive repertoire, he has been most successful with scores from the Romantic and late Romantic eras. He has also championed contemporary works, conducting premieres by such composers as Boulez and Corigliano. —NS/LK/DM

Barere, Simon, virtuoso Russian pianist; b. Odessa, Sept. 1, 1896; d. N.Y., April 2, 1951. He began formal piano study at age 11, and entered the St. Petersburg Cons. as a pupil of Anna Essipova. After her death in 1914, he continued his studies there with Felix Blumenfeld, graduating with the Rubinstein Prize in 1919. Following extensive tours, he went to Berlin in 1929. In 1934 he made his London debut and in 1938 his N.Y. debut. During World War II, he lived in Stockholm; after the War, he resumed touring. On April 2, 1951, he was soloist in Grieg's Piano Concerto with Ormandy and the Philadelphia Orch. at N.Y.'s Carnegie Hall. During the performance, he was fatally stricken with a cerebral hemorrhage. In spite of extensive efforts to save him, he died backstage within minutes. Barere was a master keyboard artist who excelled in the Romantic repertory. —NS/LK/DM

Bargad, Rob, pianist, composer; b. Boston, 1962. He performed in jazz groups while attending New Trier H.S., in suburban Chicago, including a tour of Greece and Romania. He spent a year studying jazz at Ind. Univ., then transferred to Rutgers Univ. (graduating in 1977) to study with Kenny Barron, Paul Jeffrey, John Stubblefield, Ted Dunbar, and Harry Pickens. After moving to N.Y. in 1984, he began freelancing including work in N.J. with Leo Johnson, who introduced him to Jimmy Scott. He worked with Scott for a year and a half, then with Dakota Staton as well as some work with his own Quartet Bargad. In 1987, Paul Jeffrey introduced him to Lionel Hampton, with whom toured extensively throughout the U.S., Europe, and Japan for more than a year, after which he returned to N.Y. In early 1990, Vincent Herring invited him to join the Nat Adderley Quintet, with whom he has toured, recorded nine albums, performed his original compositions, appeared extensively on international radio and TV programs, and participated in numerous clinics for music students. He also toured Europe with the Harper Brothers and Roy Hargrove, and was keyboardist/musical director for Justin Tracy (summer 1997). In the mid-1990s, he worked with Dena DeRose as a composer and lyricist, first for the film *The Four Corners of Nowhere*. His songs and lyrics captured the attention of Shirley Horn, Joyce and Freddy Cole, among others. He has produced albums by Dena DeRose and Justin Tracy, and was musical director and arranger for LaVerne Butler's Day Dreamin.

DISC.: *Better Times* (1994); *The Shadow of Your Smile* (1996). —LP

Bargiel, Woldemar, German composer; b. Berlin, Oct. 3, 1828; d. there, Feb. 23, 1897. He was a half brother of **Clara Schumann.** As a boy he sang at the Berlin Cathedral and studied counterpoint with Dehn, and at the Leipzig Cons. (1846–50) with Hauptmann, Moscheles, Gade, and Rietz. He became prof. at the Cologne Cons. in 1859. He was a teacher and conductor in Rotterdam (1865–75); in 1874 became prof. of composition at the Berlin Hochschule für Musik. He was greatly admired by Schumann and Brahms, and his works, in a Romantic vein, were frequently performed; almost all of his music was publ. during his lifetime. He wrote a Sym., three overtures, String Octet, four string quartets, three piano trios, violin sonatas, numerous piano pieces, and songs.—NS/LK/DM

Bargielski, Zbigniew, Polish composer; b. Lomza, Jan. 21, 1937. He received training in law before studying composition with Szeligowski at the State Higher School of Music in Warsaw (1958–62), musicology with Szabelski at the State Higher School of Music in Katowice (1962–64), and completing his training with Boulanger in Paris (1966–67). In 1977 he settled in Austria. His music makes colorful use of dissonance.

WORKS: DRAMATIC: *Danton, or Some Pictures from the History of the Great French Revolution,* surrealistic historic opera (1968–69); *In a Small Country House,* after Witkiewicz (1979). **ORCH.:** *Sinfonia* (1956); *Parades 1970* (1969–70); *Espace attrapé* (1973); Percussion Concerto (1975); Violin Concerto (1976); *The Valley of Bleaching Bones* for Percussion and Chamber Ensemble (1977); *The Valley of Forgotten Memories* for Improvising Piano and Chamber Ensemble (1981); *Rondo alla Polacca* (1983); *CHAORD* (1990); *Requiem* (1991–92); Trumpet Concerto (1992); *Trigonalis* for Guitar, Accordion, Percussion, and Chamber Orch. (1994); Piano Concertino (1995). **CHAMBER:** *Servet* for Piano, Percussion, and Violin (1966); *Ein Zimmer* for Clarinet, Cello, Trombone, Percussion, and Piano (1972); 4 string quartets (*Alpine,* 1976; *Spring,* 1980; *Still Life with a Shout,* 1985–86; *Le temps ardent,* 1994); 2 wind quintets (*Butterfly Cage,* 1978; *Four Woodwinds with Horn,* 1982); *Dream Bird* for Accordion and Percussion (1980); *Icarus* for Bass Clarinet and Vibraphone (1981); *Epitaphium* for 2 Violins (1981); *Portrait from Memory* for String Sextet (1982); *Submerged Flame* for Violin, Cello, and Accordion (1985); *Labyrinth* for Cello and Accordion (1987); *Birds of Night* for Clarinet Quintet (1987); *Landscape of Remembrance* for Piano Trio (1996); *Tango* for Chamber Ensemble (1997). **Piano:** *7 Studies* (1957); *Vienna Stories* for 2 Pianos (1981); *Panoptikum* for 2 Pianos (1987); *Beethovens Wanderweg zum Fürst Lichnowsky* (1992). **VOCAL:** *Rose Garden* for Baritone and Bass Clarinet, after Eliot (1971); *Another Night, Another Sound* for Mezzo-soprano and Orch. (1981); *Songs of the Sun* for Soloists, Chorus, and Chamber Ensemble (1983); *Nobody's Land,* oratorio (1989); *Orpheus* for Baritone, Crotales, and Violin (1996).—NS/LK/DM

Barié, Augustin, blind French organist and composer; b. Paris, Nov. 15, 1883; d. there, April 22, 1915. He was blind from birth. After studying at the Institution Nationale de Jeunes Aveugles with Adolphe Marty, he was a pupil of Vierne (1904–06). He was organist at St. Germain-des-Prés in Paris at the time of his early demise from a cerebral hemorrhage. His works, which include a Sym. for Organ, an Elegy, and three Pieces, were highly praised.—LK/DM

Barili, Alfredo, Italian-American pianist, composer, and pedagogue; b. Florence, Aug. 2, 1854; d. Atlanta, Ga., Nov. 17, 1935, in an accident when he took a walk and was struck by a bus. He was a scion of an illustrious musical family; his father, Ettore Barili, an excellent musician in his own right, was a half brother of the operatic diva **Adelina Patti.** Alfredo Barili was taken to America in his infancy and was taught piano by his father, making his public debut as a pianist in N.Y. on April 7, 1865. In 1868 the family relocated to Philadelphia, where he studied with Carl Wolfsohn, a German musician who claimed to be the first to perform all 32 piano sonatas of Beethoven in a series of concerts. In 1872 Barili enrolled at the Cologne Cons., studying piano with Friedrich Gernsheim and James Kwast, and composition with Ferdinand Hiller. Returning to the U.S. in 1880, he settled in Atlanta, taught for six years at the Atlanta Female Inst., and in 1886 founded his own "music academy," teaching piano at a fee of $1.50 per lesson. He maintained a cordial relationship with his famous aunt, Adelina Patti, and acted as her piano accompanist at a London concert in 1911. He also composed some perishable salòn music in the approved manner of the time. His piano piece *Cradle Song* went into 26 eds.; also popular among his pupils were his *Danse caprice, Miniature Gavotte,* and *Spanish Serenade.*

BIBL.: N. Orr, *A. B. and the Rise of Classical Music in Atlanta* (Atlanta, 1996).—**NS/LK/DM**

Bar-Illan, David (Jacob), Israeli pianist; b. Haifa, Feb. 7, 1930. He studied at the Haifa Music Inst., and then in N.Y. at the Juilliard School of Music and the Mannes Coll. of Music. In 1946 he made his debut as a soloist with the Palestine Broadcasting Service Orch. After an engagement at London's Wigmore Hall in 1953, he played in the U.S. in 1954. Thereafter he appeared as a soloist with orchs. and as a recitalist in Israel, Europe, and North and South America. From 1980 to 1991 he taught at the Mannes Coll. of Music. During the administration of Israeli Prime Minister Benjamin Netanyahu (1996–99), he served as a spokesman in the prime minister's office. As a pianist, Bar-Illan became particularly well known for his performances of the 19th century repertoire.—**NS/LK/DM**

Barilli, Bruno, Italian writer on music and composer; b. Fano, Dec. 14, 1880; d. Rome, April 15, 1952. He studied in Parma and later in Munich. His collections of essays were publ. under the titles *Il sorcio nel violino* (Milan, 1926) and *Il paese del melodramma* (Lanciano, 1929). He wrote two operas, *Medusa* (1910; Bergamo, Sept. 11, 1938) and *Emiral* (Rome, March 11, 1924).

BIBL.: E. Falqui, ed., *Opere di B. B.* (Florence, 1963). —**NS/LK/DM**

Barjansky, Alexander, Russian cellist; b. Odessa, Dec. 16, 1883; d. Brussels, Jan. 6, 1961. After training in Russia, he pursued his career in Western Europe. He played various new works for cello, among them the premiere of Delius's Cello Concerto (London, Jan. 31, 1921). Barjansky's wife publ. a book about him as *Portraits and Backgrounds* (London, 1940).—**NS/LK/DM**

Bark, Jan (Helge Guttorm), Swedish trombonist and composer; b. Harnosand, April 19, 1934. He was first a jazz trombonist, then studied at the Stockholm Musikhögskolan, taking courses in composition with Larsson and Blomdahl. He was initiated into ultramodern music by Ligeti in Stockholm. In 1962 he made an American trip and worked with avant-garde groups at the Tape Music Center in San Francisco. In 1964 he traveled to the Far East to study oriental music. Returning to Sweden, he joined the radio and television center of the Swedish Broadcasting Service. He was co-founder with Folke Rabe of the Culture Quartet, which explored the potentialities of modern trombone playing. Many of his pieces are of a theatrical, almost exhibitionistic, nature, often with a healthy radical tinge.

WORKS: Piano Sonata (1957); 2 string quartets (1959, 1962); *Metakronismer* for Orch. (1960; Oslo, March 4, 1961); 2 works for the Culture Quartet, in collaboration with Folke Rabe: *Bolos* (1962) and *Polonaise* (1965); *Lamento* for Percussion, Piano, and Double Basses (1962); *Boca Chica* for Chamber Ensemble (1962); *Pyknos* for Orch. (1962); *Eko* for News Broadcaster and 5 Tape Recorders (1962); *Missa Bassa* for Small Orch. with 7 Conductors, 6 of whom also sing (1964; Swedish Radio, April 1, 1967); *Nota* for "choreographic" Chorus (1964); *Ost-Funk* for 8 Jazz Musicians (1964); *Mansbot* for Men's Chorus and 12 Guitars (1964); *Tredjedels Signeri* for 3 Hammond Organs (1967); *Bar,* electronic music (1967); *Light Music* for Chorus (1968); *Lyndon Bunk Johnson,* a "poster" work, composed collectively (1968); *Irk-Ork 1970* for Chamber Ensemble (1970); *Het Jacht von het vliegende Joachim* for Trombone, Cello, and Piano (1971); *Memoria in memoria* for Chamber Group (1974); *Utspel* for Band (1976); *Malumma* for Tuba and Band (1984); *Concerto for Orch.* (1985); various theater pieces and film music. —**NS/LK/DM**

Barkauskas, Vytautas (Pranas Marius), eminent Lithuanian composer and pedagogue; b. Kaunas, March 25, 1931. He settled in Vilnius, where he received training in piano at the J. Tallat-Kelpa Specialized Music H.S. (1949–53), and concurrently took courses in the dept. of physics and mathematics at the State Pedagogical Inst. He then studied composition with Račiunas and orchestration with Balsys at the Lithuanian State Cons. (1953–59), and later attended the orchestration class of J.A. Fortunatov at the Moscow Cons. (1982). In 1961 he became a teacher at the Lithuanian State Cons., where he was made an assoc. prof. in 1974 and a prof. of composition in 1989. In 1972 he was awarded the Lithuanian State Prize and in 1981 he was made a Merited Artist of Lithuania. Barkauskas was an early champion of the avant-garde in Lithuania. His piano cycle *Poetry* (1964) was the first score by a Lithuanian to freely adopt the use of the 12–tone series. In his works, he has expertly balanced serial and tonal techniques.

WORKS: DRAMATIC: *Conflict,* "choreographic scene" for 3 Performers (1965); *Legend about Love,* opera (Vilnius, March 29, 1975). **ORCH.:** *Tone Poem* for Piano and Orch. (1960); 5 syms. (1962, 1971, 1979, 1984, 1986); Concertino for 4 Chamber Groups (1966); *Expressivistic Structures* for Chamber Orch. (1967); *3 Aspects* (1969); *Overture a priori* (1976); *Toccamento* No. 1, concerto for Chamber Orch. (1978); Concerto for Viola and Chamber Orch. (1981); *The Sun,* symphonic picture (1983);

Concerto piccolo for Chamber Orch. (1988); Piano Concerto (1992); *Konzertstück* No. 1 (1992) and No. 2 (1994); *Here and Now* (1998). **CHAMBER:** Piano Trio (1958); *Partita* for Violin (1967); *Intimate Composition* for Oboe and 12 Strings (1968); *Contrast Music* for Flute, Cello, and Percussion (1969); *Pro memoria* for Flute, Bass Clarinet, Piano or Harpsichord, and 5 Percussion (1970); *Monologue* for Oboe (1970); 2 string quartets (1972, 1983); 3 violin sonatas: No. 1, *Sonata Subita* (1976), No. 2, *Dialogue* (1978), and No. 3 (1984); Sextet for 2 Violins, Viola, Cello, Double Bass, and Piano (1985); Doubla Bass Sonata (1987); *Vivo* for 2 Violins, Viola, Cello, Double Bass, and Piano (1990); Trio for Clarinet, Violin, and Piano (1990); *Lare* for Clarinet and Piano (1991); Concert Suite for Cello and Piano (1993); *Intimate Music* for Flute and Percussion (1993); *Modus vivendi* for Violin, Cello, and Piano (1996); Duo for Guitar and Piano (1997); *Toccamento* No. 2 for Viola and Piano Trio (1998). **KEYBOARD: P i a n o :** *Poetry*, cycle (1964); *Variations* for 2 Pianos (1967); *Sonate pathétique* (1969); *5 Pictures of Vytukas* for Piano, 4–Hands (1971); *Legend about Čiurlionis* (1972); *Elegy and Fantastical Toccata* (1972); *Prelude and Fugue* for 2 Pianos (1974); *Polyphonic Suite* (1979); *3 Concert Études* (1981); *Winter 1982* for Piano, 4–Hands (1982); Sonata for 2 Pianos and 3 Performers (1984); *La poème du coeur* (1984); *Sunday Music* for 2 Pianos and 4 Performers (1985); *13 Pieces* (1986); *Vision* (1988); *The Second Legend of Čiurlionis* (1988); *Divertimento* for Piano, 6–Hands (1993); *The Third Legend of Čiurlionis* (1993); *Allegro Brillante* for 2 Pianos (1996). **O r g a n :** *Gloria Urbi* (1972); *Zodiac* (1980); *Credo* (1989); *Inspiration* (1994). **VOCAL:** *Pathetic Thoughts* for Chorus (1962); *Word about Revolution*, cantata-poem for Narrator, Men's Chorus, and Orch. (1967); *La vostra nominanza e color d'erba* for Chamber Chorus and String Quintet (1971); *Prelude and Fugue* for Chorus (1974); *Salute Your Land*, oratorio- mystery for 4 Soloists, Women's Chorus, and Orch. (1976); *Open Window*, 5 sketches for Mezzo-soprano and 5 Instruments (1978); *We Both*, cantata for Soprano, Bass, Chorus, and 5 Instruments (1986); *Hope*, oratorio for 2 Girl's Choruses, Solo Discanto, Men's Vocal Quartet, and Organ (1988).—**NS/LK/DM**

Barkel, Charles, Swedish violinist, conductor, and teacher; b. Stugun, Feb. 6, 1898; d. Stockholm, March 7, 1973. He studied at the Stockholm Cons., the Copenhagen Cons., and with Flesch in Berlin. In 1921 he became a violinist in the Stockholm Concert Soc. Orch. and in 1928 he founded his own string quartet. From 1942 to 1954 he was conductor of the Uppsala Concert Soc. Orch. He also taught violin in Stockholm from 1926 to 1965.—**NS/LK/DM**

Barker, Danny (actually **Daniel Moses**), American guitarist, banjo player, singer, writer; b. New Orleans, Jan. 13, 1909; d. there of cancer, March 14, 1994. In his childhood, Danny Barker learned clarinet, ukulele, and finally banjo from his grandfather, Isadore Barbarin, who played alto horn in the Onward Brass Band. Barker played with the Boozan Kings, and in the early 1920s toured with Little Brother Montgomery and trumpeter Willie Pajeaud. He joined trumpeter Lee Collins and saxophonist David Jones for a 1928 tour of Fla. In 1930 Barker and his wife, singer Louise "Blue Lu" Barker, moved to N.Y. and Danny found work the following year with trumpeter Dave Nelson, trombonist Harry White, and others, including Fats Waller. In the rewarding, personal freedom of N.Y., Barker absorbed everything around him during the Harlem Renaissance, and flourished as a musician. He soon switched from banjo to rhythm guitar, and during the 1930s mainly performed with Sidney Bechet, Fess Williams, Albert Nicholas, and James P. Johnson. In the late 1930s he recorded with his wife and with Henry "Red" Allen, worked in the big bands of Lucky Millinder (1937–38), Benny Carter (1938), and Cab Calloway (1939–46), and began to work with small groups. Barker participated in a Dixieland revival through a series of *This Is Jazz* radio broadcasts and recorded with Mutt Carey and Bunk Johnson. About the same time, he began to play six-string banjo. In 1948 the Barkers spent a long stretch in Calif., where Lu recorded an album for Capitol. Danny recorded various sides in Los Angeles and New Orleans before returning to N.Y. where he performed throughout the 1950s at Ryan's, often with trombonists Conrad Janis and Wilbur DeParis, and with his own band. In 1965 Barker and his wife returned to New Orleans and re-established their careers there. Until 1975 Danny served as assistant curator of the New Orleans Jazz Museum. He continued to work as a bandleader, guitarist, and from 1965 to 1972 led the Onward Brass Band. In later years he also recorded with Wynton Marsalis and the Dirty Dozen Brass Band. His notable compositions are "Don't You Feel My Leg," written for his wife, and "Save the Bones " (for Henry Jones), which was recorded by Nat King Cole. He wrote and lectured about jazz and taught young musicians. When Barker died in 1994 he left a trail of compositions and a discography of considerable range. A distinguished rhythm guitarist, he was also an accomplished six-string guitar player who made over 1,000 recordings as sideman, but only a couple of recordings as leader exist.

DISC.: *Save the Bones* (1991); *Live at the New Orleans Jazz Festival* (1998).

BIBL.: D. Barker, A. Shipton, *A Life in Jazz* (London, 1986); D. Barker, J. Buerkle, *Bourbon Street Black* (N.Y., 1973).—**NAL**

Barkin, Elaine R(adoff), American composer, teacher, and writer on music; b. N.Y., Dec. 15, 1932. She studied with Karol Rathaus at Queens Coll. in N.Y. (B.A., 1954), with Irving Fine at Brandeis Univ. (M.F.A., 1956), Boris Blacher at the Berlin Hochschule für Musik (1957), and Arthur Berger and Harold Shapero at Brandeis Univ. (Ph.D. in composition and theory, 1971). She taught at Queens Coll. (1964–70), Sarah Lawrence Coll. (1969–70), and the Univ. of Mich. (1970–74). In 1974 she joined the faculty of the Univ. of Calif. at Los Angeles, where she taught composition and theory until her retirement as prof. emerita in 1997. From 1963 to 1985 she was an ed. of *Perspectives of New Music*. With Benjamin Boretz and James K. Randall, she became proprietor of the Open Space publication series. With Lydia Hamessley, she ed. the vol. *Audible Traces: Gender, Identity, and Music* (Zürich, 1999). In her early compositions, Barkin utilized serial techniques but later delved into what she describes as "group interactive autonomous alternative music-making culture." She has also pursued an active interest in Indonesian culture and the gamelan.

WORKS: String Quartet (1969); *Plus ça change* for String Orch. and Percussion (1971); *Sound Play* for Violin (1974);

215

Inward and Outward Bound for Chamber Ensemble (1975); *Plein Chant* for Alto Flute (1977); *Ebb Tide* for 2 Vibraphones (1977); *Two Emily Dickinson Choruses* (1977); *"...The Supple Suitor..."*, song cycle for Mezzo-soprano and 5 Players (1978); *De amore*, chamber mini-opera (1980); *Media Speak*, theater piece for 9 Speakers, Saxophone, Tape, and Slides (1981); *At the Piano* for Piano (1982); *"...To Piety More Prone..."*, theater piece for 4 Women Speakers and Tape (1982); *On the Way to Becoming* for Tape (1985); *Rhapsodies* for Flutes and Clarinet (1986); *[Be]coming Together Apart* for Violin and Marimba (1987); *Encore* for Javanese Gamelan (1988); *"Out of the Air..."* for Basset Horn and Tape (1989); *Legong Dreams* for Oboe (1990); *Exploring the Rigors of in Between* for Flute, Horn, Violin, Viola, and Cello (1991); *Gamélange* for Harp and Mixed Gamelan (1993); *"...For My Friends' Pleasure..."* for Harp and Voice (1995); *Touching All Bases/Di Mana-Mana* for Basso Bongo and Gamelan (1996; in collaboration with I Nyoman Wenten); *Poem* for Wind Ensemble (1999).—**NS/LK/DM**

Barlow, Fred, French composer of English and Alsatian descent; b. Mulhouse, Oct. 2, 1881; d. Boulogne, Jan. 3, 1951. He studied in Paris with Jean Huré and his cousin Koechlin.

WORKS: DRAMATIC: Musical Comedy: *Sylvie* (1919–21; Paris, March 2, 1923). **Operetta:** *Mam'zelle Prudhomme* (Monte Carlo, Dec. 22, 1932). **Ballet:** *Gladys, ou La légère incartade* (1915–16; Mulhouse, Jan. 7, 1956); *Polichinelle et Colombine* (1926–27); *La grande Jatte* (1936–38; Paris, July 12, 1950). **CHAMBER:** *Juventa*, violin sonata (1909); *La basilique*, cello sonata (1910–11; rev. 1938–39); *Quatuor des saisons* (1946–47; also for String Orch. and Timpani as *Sinfonietta des saisons*, 1948); also piano music, including a Sonata (1940). **VOCAL:** Songs.—**NS/LK/DM**

Barlow, Harold, American writer on music and composer; b. Boston, May 15, 1915; d. Manhasset, N.Y., Feb. 15, 1993. He studied violin at Boston Univ. (B.M., 1937), and later played in various orchs.; also led a U.S. Army band. He compiled two valuable reference works, for which he designed an original method of indexing melodic themes by letters plus accidentals: *A Dictionary of Musical Themes* (N.Y., 1948) and *A Dictionary of Vocal Themes* (N.Y., 1950), both with S. Morgenstern. He also composed popular songs.—**NS/LK/DM**

Barlow, Howard, American conductor; b. Plain City, Ohio, May 1, 1892; d. Bethel, Conn., Jan. 31, 1972. He received training in law at Columbia Univ. In 1919 he made his debut as a conductor at a MacDowell Colony festival in Peterborough, N.H. He settled in N.Y., where he was founder-conductor of the American National Orch. (1923–25), which was made up entirely of musicians born in the U.S. In 1927 he joined the conducting staff of CBS, where he was general music director from 1932 to 1943. From 1940 to 1943 he also was conductor of the Baltimore Sym. Orch. He was conductor of "The Voice of Firestone" orch. on NBC radio from 1943 to 1961, and also on NBC TV from 1949 to 1961. Barlow commissioned and conducted first performances of many scores by American composers. —**NS/LK/DM**

Barlow, Samuel L(atham) M(itchell), American composer; b. N.Y., June 1, 1892; d. Wyndmoor, Pa.,

Sept. 19, 1982. He studied at Harvard Univ. (B.A., 1914), with Goetschius and Franklin Robinson in N.Y., with Philipp (piano) in Paris, and with Respighi (orchestration) in Rome (1923). He was active in various N.Y. music, civic, and liberal organizations, and also taught. His autobiography appeared as *The Astonished Muse* (N.Y., 1961).

WORKS: DRAMATIC: Opera: *Mon ami Pierrot* (1934; Paris, Jan. 11, 1935); *Amanda* (1936). **Ballet:** *Ballo sardo* (1928). **ORCH.:** *Vocalise* (1926); *Alba*, symphonic poem (1927); Piano Concerto (1930; Rochester, N.Y., Jan. 23, 1931); *Circus Overture* (1930); *Babar*, symphonic concerto with slides (1935); *Biedermeier Waltzes* (1935); *Sousa ad Parnassum* (1939). **CHAMBER:** *Ballad, Scherzo* for String Quartet (1933); *Conversation with Chekov*, piano trio (1940); piano pieces. **VOCAL:** Choruses and songs.—**NS/LK/DM**

Barlow, Stephen, English conductor; b. Seven Kings, Essex, June 30, 1954. He was educated at Trinity Coll., Cambridge, and the Guildhall School of Music and Drama in London. From 1979 to 1985 he was a conductor with the Glyndebourne Festival and the Glyndebourne Touring Opera. He was a conductor with Opera 80 from 1980, and was made its music director in 1987. From 1983 he was also a conductor at the Scottish Opera in Glasgow. In 1989 he made his debut at London's Covent Garden with *Turandot*, and in 1990 made his first appearance at the San Francisco Opera with *Capriccio*. His Australian debut followed in 1991 when he conducted *Die Zauberflöte* in Melbourne. In 1992 he conducted *Faust* at Opera Northern Ireland in Belfast. He conducted *Madama Butterfly* in Auckland in 1994. From 1997 he served as music director of Opera Northern Ireland. He also appeared as a guest conductor with various European and North American orchs. —**NS/LK/DM**

Barlow, Wayne (Brewster), American composer, pedagogue, organist, and choirmaster; b. Elyria, Ohio, Sept. 6, 1912; d. Rochester, N.Y., Dec. 17, 1996. He studied with Rogers and Hanson at the Eastman School of Music in Rochester, N.Y. (B.M., 1934; M.M., 1935; Ph.D., 1937), and also took courses from Schoenberg at the Univ. of Southern Calif. in Los Angeles (1935). He later pursued training in electronic music with Schaeffer at the Univ. of Toronto (1963–64) and postdoctoral research at the univs. of Brussels, Ghent, and Utrecht (1964–65). From 1937 to 1978 he taught at the Eastman School of Music, where he also was director of graduate studies (1955–57; 1973–78) and chairman of its composition dept. and director of the electronic music studio (1968–73). He served as organist and choirmaster at St. Thomas Episcopal Church (1946–76) and at Christ Episcopal Church (1976–78) in Rochester. He was the author of *Foundations of Music* (N.Y., 1953). In his compositions, Barlow follows a varied stylistic path that is basically tonal with free 12–tone development.

WORKS: DRAMATIC: Ballet: *False Faces* (1935); *3 Moods for Dancing* (1940). **ORCH.:** *De Profundis* (1934); 2 sinfoniettas (1936, 1950); *The Winter's Passed* for Oboe and Strings (1938); *Lyrical Pieces* for Clarinet and Strings (1943); *Nocturne* for Chamber Orch. (1946); *Rondo Overture* (1947); *Lento* and *Allegro* (1955); *Night Song* (1958); *Rota* for Chamber Orch. (1959); *Images* for Harp and Orch. (1961); *Sinfonia da camera* for Chamber Orch. (1962); *Vistas* (1963); Concerto for Saxophone and Band (1970); *Hampton Beach,* overture (1971); *Soundscapes* for Tape and Orch. (1972); *Divertissement* for Flute and Chamber Orch. (1980); *Frontiers* for Band (1982). **CHAMBER:** *Prelude, Air, and Variations* for Bassoon, Piano, and String Quartet (1949); Piano Quintet (1951); *Tryptych* for String Quartet (1953); *Intrada, Fugue, and Postlude* for Brass (1959); Trio for Oboe, Viola, and Piano (1964); *Elegy* for Viola and Piano (1967; also for Viola and Orch.); *Duo* for Harp and Tape (1969); *Vocalise and Canon* for Tuba and Piano (1976); *Intermezzo* for Viola and Harp (1980); *Sonatine for 4* for Flute, Clarinet, Cello, and Harp (1984). **KEYBOARD: P i a n o :** Sonata (1948); *Dynamisms* for 2 Pianos (1967). **O r g a n :** *Hymn Voluntaries for the Church Year* (4 vols., 1963–81); *4 Chorale Voluntaries* (1979–80). **VOCAL:** *Zion in Exile,* cantata (1937); *Songs from the Silence of Amor* for Soprano and Orch. (1939); *The 23rd Psalm* for Chorus and Organ or Orch. (1944); *Mass* for Chorus and Orch. (1951); *Poems for Music* for Soprano and Orch. (1958); *Missa Sancti Thomae* for Chorus and Organ (1959); *We All Believe in One True God* for Chorus, Brass Quartet, and Organ (1965); *Wait for the Promise of the Father,* cantata (1968); *Voices of Darkness* for Reader, Piano, Percussion, and Tape (1974); *Voices of Faith* for Reader, Soprano, Chorus, and Orch. (1975); *Out of the Cradle Endlessly Rocking* for Tenor, Chorus, Clarinet, Viola, Piano, and Tape (1978); *The 7 Seals* for Soloists, Chorus, and Orch. (1991). **TAPE:** *Study in Electronic Sound* (1965); *Moonflight* (1970); *Soundprints in Concrete* (1975).—**NS/LK/DM**

Barnes, Milton, Canadian conductor and composer; b. Toronto, Dec. 16, 1931. He studied composition with John Weinzweig and Ernst Krenek, conducting with Victor Feldbrill, Boyd Neel, and Walter Susskind, and piano with Samuel Dolin at the Royal Cons. of Music of Toronto (1952–55). Then he pursued further training in conducting at the Accademia Musicale Chigiana in Siena, at the Berkshire Music Center at Tanglewood, and with Swarowsky at the Vienna Academy of Music (graduated, 1961). He began his career as a jazz drummer and guitarist; during his student days, he composed many dramatic scores for productions at the Univ. of Toronto. He was music director and composer at the Crest Theatre (1961–63), and founder-conductor of the Toronto Repertory Orch. (1964–73). He also was conductor of the St. Catharines (Ontario) Sym. Orch. and Chorus (1964–73) and of the Niagara Falls (N.Y.) Phil. and Chorus (1965–73), and was composer and conductor-in- residence of the Toronto Dance Theatre (1968–73). An eclectic composer, he has utilized classical, jazz, and popular styles.

WORKS: DRAMATIC: *The Spiral Stairs Septet,* ballet suite (1973); *The Dybbuk: A Masque for Dancing* for Tenor and 6 Instruments (1977); music theater pieces; film and television scores. **ORCH.:** 3 syms. (1964, 1973, 1987); *Pinocchio,* symphonic poem (1967); *Shebetim* for Strings (1975); Concerto for Violin and Strings (1975); Viola Concerto (1975); *Maid of the Mist,* symphonic poem (1977); *Channuka Suite* for Orch. or Chamber Orch. (1977); *Divertimento* for Harp and Strings (1978; also for Harp and String Quartet); *Serenade* for String Quartet and String Orch. (1979); Double Concerto for 2 Guitars and Strings (1986); *Three French Canadian Legends* (1986); *Papageno Variations* for String Bass and String Orch. (1988; also for String Bass and Piano); *The Odyssey: A Symphonic Tale* (1990); *Song of*

the Bow, string bass concerto (1991); *Harbord Street* for Flute, Viola, Harp, and Strings (1991; also for Flute, Viola, and Harp); *Variations on a Hebrew Theme* for Strings (1996). **CHAMBER:** *Lamentations of Jeremiah* for Viola or Cello (1959); *Concerto Grosso Sextet* (1973); String Quartet No. 2 (1978); *Anerca I* for Bassoon or String Bass (1979); Octet (1985); *La Rosa Variations* for Cello (1992); *The Classical Cat: Minnie Minou* for Flute, Viola, and Harp (1999). **VOCAL:** *Memorial for Martin Luther King* for Chorus and Piano (1968–98); *Psalms of David* for Soprano, Baritone, Chorus, and Orch. (1973); *Madrigals* for Women's Chorus, 2 Trumpets, and 2 Trombones (1975); *Shir Hashirim* (Song of Songs) for Soprano, Tenor, Women's Chorus, and 7 Instruments (1975); *Rites of Passage,* Requiem for Men's Chorus and Piano (1991); *Fantasy of Jewish Folk Themes* for Tenor, Chorus, and Klezmer Band (1993); *Adioses Cantata* for Mezzo-soprano, Women's Chorus, Flute, Cello, Piano, and Percussion (1994); *Sefarad* for Chorus (1995); *Canciones español* for Soprano, Viola, and Piano (1997).—**NS/LK/DM**

Barnet, Charlie (actually, **Charles Daly**), jazz saxophonist, leader; b. N.Y., Oct. 26, 1913; d. San Diego, Calif., Sept. 4, 1991. He was born into a wealthy family and began playing piano at an early age, picking up the saxophone at 12. He studied at Blair Academy in N.Y., then attended high school in Winnetka, Ill. He went against his family's wishes by refusing to become a lawyer. At 16, he led his own band on the S. S. *Republic* and subsequently led bands on the Cunard, Red Star, and Panama- Pacific liners; he played on many Atlantic crossings (visiting England in the early 1930s), and also performed on Mediterranean and South American cruises. After attending Rumsey Academy and playing in the school band, he left to work for almost a year with Frank Winegar's Pennsylvanians, specializing on tenor sax. He played with Beasley Smith, then gigged his way across the country, performing with Flem Ferguson in Shreveport and Jack Purvis in Kilgore, Tex.

Barnet freelanced on the West Coast, then moved back to N.Y. where he formed his first big band for a three-month residency at Paramount Hotel Grill, N.Y. (spring 1933). During the following year, he led the band at the Park Central Hotel, N.Y., Glen Island Casino, Hotel Roosevelt, and in New Orleans. He formed a new band in spring 1935, disbanded it, then moved to Hollywood for a short- lived acting career, appearing in forgettable flops *Love and Hisses* and *Sally, Irene, and Mary* (both 1936).

Throughout his career, Barnet has done as much as anyone in breaking down racial barriers in music. From the mid-1930s, he employed many African-American musicians including Benny Carter, Garnett Clark, Roy Eldridge, Dizzy Gillespie, Peanuts Holland, Kansas Fields, Al Killian, Frankie Newton, Roger Ramirez, Paul Webster, Trummy Young, Clark Terry, Oscar Pettiford, and Lena Horne. His was also the first white band to play N.Y.'s Apollo Theater. He had nearly 30 big hits between 1936–46, including a version of Ray Noble's "Cherokee," and his own "Skyliner." In fall 1939, Barnet moved to the West Coast; during a residency at the Palomar Ballroom, Los Angeles, the band lost all its instruments and orchestrations in a disastrous fire that October. He continued to lead this unit regularly until 1943, and during the following 10–year period Barnet formed several excellent big bands. In 1949, his group included such modernists as Buddy DeFranco and Dodo Marmarosa. During the 1950s and 1960s, he occasionally organized big bands for specific engagements; the last regular unit played residencies in Las Vegas and N.Y. (late 1966). In his last years, he suffered from Alzheimer's disease, though the immediate cause of death was pneumonia, according to his wife of 33 years, Betty.

Charlie Barnet's film appearances as a musician include *The Fabulous Dorseys* (solo), *Music in Manhattan* (band), *Freddie Steps Out*, and *Juke Box Jenny*. Early in 1967, his specially formed band made a short feature film. A lifelong admirer of Duke Ellington's music, he played chimes on a 1929 Ellington recording of "Ring Dem Bells," and also once subbed on alto for Otto Hardwick with Ellington (March 1943). He also used many Ellington charts in his own groups.

DISC.: "Cherokee" (1939); "Skyliner" (1942); *On the Air!* (1947); *One Night Stand Battle of the Bands* (1949); *Dance with Charlie Barnet* (1952); *Town Hall Jazz Concert* (1955); *Lonely Street* (1956); *More* (1958); *On Stage with Charlie Barnet* (1960); *Jazz Oasis* (1960); *Charlie Barnet* (1963); *Charlie Barnet Big Band: 1967* (1966). D. Ellington: "Ring Dem Bells" (1929).

WRITINGS: With S. Dance, *Those Swinging Years: The Autobiography of Charlie Barnet* (Baton Rouge, 1984).

BIBL.: E. Edwards, *Charlie Barnet and His Orch.* (Whittier, Calif., 1965); C. Garrod, *Charlie Barnet and His Orch.* (Spotswood, N.J., 1973).—JC/LP

Barnett, Bonnie, American singer and composer; b. Chicago, May 2, 1947. She studied at the Univ. of Ill. (B.S., 1968) and with Gaburo, Oliveros, and Erickson at the Univ. of Calif. at San Diego (M.A., 1972). She then moved to San Francisco, where she developed the *TUNNEL HUM Project*, a series of participatory vocal events taking place in acoustically interesting environments. A conducive tonality is established by a group of instrumentalists (E-flat major is used often); the participating hummers then improvise on that tonality, following a written process score. Since 1981 Barnett has produced 29 *Hums* in a variety of contexts, including two satellite-linked live national radio broadcasts (1983, 1984), a Houston subterranean shopping mall (1986), and *Auto Hum*, a live radio broadcast for car-commuter participation throughout Southern Calif. (1985). Her intent is to re-create the participatory pleasures of group vocalizations as a means of "tuning the world"; her *Global Hum*, part of the "Music and Peace" event sponsored by the World Phil. Orch. in Montreal, sent live singers in San Francisco worldwide through satellite broadcast. She was the recipient of a 1983 grant from NPR and a 1984 NEA grant. Since 1986 she has lived in Los Angeles, where she teaches privately and co-hosted the KPFK-radio program "Imaginary Landscape." She also developed a more elaborate *Global Hum* and, eventually, an *Intergalactic Hum*.—NS/LK/DM

Barnett, John (Manley), American conductor; b. N.Y., Sept. 3, 1917. He studied piano, violin, and trumpet. He took courses at Teachers Coll. of Columbia Univ., the Manhattan School of Music, and the Salzburg Mozarteum (1936), and received training in conducting from Walter, Weingartner, Enesco, and Malko. He was asst. conductor of the National Orchestral Assn. in N.Y. (1937–41), and also a conductor with the WPA Federal Music Project there (1939–42), serving concurrently as conductor of the Stamford (Conn.) Sym. Orch. From 1946 to 1956 he was assoc. conductor of the Los Angeles Phil., and from 1956 to 1958 its assoc. music director. In 1947 he organized the Phoenix (Ariz.) Sym. Orch., conducting it until 1949. He later served as music director of the Hollywood Bowl (1953–57) and of the Los Angeles Guild Opera Co. (1954–79). From 1958 to 1972 he was music director of the National Orchestral Assn. in N.Y.; from 1961 to 1971 he held the post of music director of the Phil. Sym. Orch. of Westchester, N.Y. From 1972 to 1978 he served as artistic consultant to the NEA. From 1979 to 1985 he was music director of the Puerto Rico Sym. Orch. in Santurce.—NS/LK/DM

Barolsky, Michael, Lithuanian-born German-Israeli composer; b. Vilnius, July 19, 1947. He studied piano, theory, and ethnology; in 1965 he took lessons in composition with Lutoslawski in Warsaw; in 1968 he went to Moscow and studied privately with Denisov and Schnittke. From 1969 to 1971 he was music adviser at the Lithuanian Radio. In 1971 he emigrated to Germany. In 1972 he attended seminars with Ligeti, Kagel, and Stockhausen in Darmstadt; in 1974 he went to Israel, and taught at the Pedagogic Inst. in Tel Aviv. In 1977 he settled in Cologne on a stipend of the Deutsche Akademie; also worked on electronic music with Humpert. In his compositions, he devotes himself totally to contemporary means of expression, astutely applying the full resources of electronic music.

WORKS: Violin Sonata (1964); String Trio (1964); Woodwind Quartet (1965); *Recitative and Melody* for Flute, Cello, and Piano (1966); Concertino for Violin, Trumpet, Trombone, Piano, and Percussion (1967); *Basso Ostinato* for Cello (1967); *Telefonoballade*, cantata for Baritone, 6 Narrators, and Chamber Ensemble (1969); *Exodus* for Orch. (1970); *Scriptus*, after Kafka's letters, for Baritone, Mime, and Chamber Ensemble (1972); *Dakar* for Percussion, Piano, and Electronics (1972); *Photogenesis I, II, III,* and *IV,* respectively for Harpsichord, Brass Quintet, Bass Flute, and Percussion (1973); *Melos* for Mezzo-soprano, Cello, Piano, Electric Organ, Percussion, and Synthesizer (1975); *Sublimatio* for Flute, Cello, 2 Pianos, Percussion, and Tape (1975); *Cries and Whispers* for Chamber Ensemble and Electronics (1975; Chicago, Jan. 24, 1976); *Blue Eye, Brown Eye*, opera (Tel Aviv, July 29, 1976); *Apocalypse*, song cycle with Electronic Tape (1976); *Iris* for Flute, Oboe, Clarinet, Violin, Cello, and Piano (1976); *Pranah* for Violin and Electronic Tape (1976); *Sternengesang* for Chamber Orch. (1977); *The Book of Emanations* for Orch. (1978); *Ein Stück aus der Nacht* for Actor and Electronics (1978); *Tonus* for Quadraphonic Synthesizer (1979); *Cinderella* for Cello and Piano (1981); *Seelenkalender* for Mezzo-soprano and Piano (1982); *The Book of Changes* for Piano (1983); *Stück-Mund-Stück* for Trombone, Computer Sounds, and Video Tape (1983); *Piccolostück* for Piccolo and Computer Sounds (1983); *Rainbow Music* for 6 Recorders (Bonn, Feb. 12, 1984); *Trioirtrio* for Violin, Cello, and Piano (1984); Cello Concerto (1985); *Computer Time* for Violin, Cello, and Piano (1988); Cello Concerto (1985); *Computer Time* for Violin, Cello, and Piano (1988).—NS/LK/DM

Baron, Samuel, American flutist, conductor, and teacher; b. N.Y., April 27, 1925; d. there, May 16, 1997. He studied at Brooklyn Coll., and was a pupil in flute of Barrère and Lora and in conducting of Schenkman at the Juilliard School of Music in N.Y. (1942–48). He was founder- conductor of the N.Y. Brass Ensemble in 1948, and also played in the N.Y. Woodwind Quintet (1946–49; again from 1980) and other chamber groups. Baron was a member (from 1965) and music director (from 1980) of the Bach Aria Group. He taught at the Yale Univ. School of Music (1965–67), the State Univ. of N.Y. at Stony Brook (from 1966), the Mannes Coll. of Music (1969–72), and the Juilliard School (from 1977). He publ. *Chamber Music for Winds* (N.Y., 1969). —NS/LK/DM

Baroni, Leonora, greatly esteemed Italian singer, lutenist, and viola da gambist, known as **L'Andrianella** and **L'Adrianetta,** daughter of **Andreana Basile;** b. Mantua, Dec. 1611; d. Rome, April 6, 1670. She studied music with her mother at the Gonzaga court in Mantua, where she first attracted attention for her vocal gifts. At age 16, she garnered accolades for her performances in salons throughout Naples. In 1630 she appeared in Genoa, and then in Florence. In 1633 she went to Rome, where she secured her reputation as a brilliant vocal artist in aristocratic circles. Following a sojourn at the French court in Paris (1644–45), she returned to Rome and pursued her career. Her sister, Catarina Baroni (b. Mantua, after 1620; place and date of death unknown), was a singer, harpist, and poet.—NS/LK/DM

Barraqué, Jean, French composer; b. Paris, Jan. 17, 1928; d. there, Aug. 17, 1973. He spent his entire life in Paris, where he received training in counterpoint and harmony from Langlais (1947) and attended Messiaen's classes in analysis at the Cons. (1948–51). After working with Pierre Schaeffer (1951–54), he was a member of the Centre National de la Recherche Scientifique (1961–70). Barraqué was a composer of theosophic aspirations and grandiose musical ideals. He first attracted attention with his expansive Piano Sonata (1950–52). Then followed his *Séquence* for Voice, Percussion, and Several Instruments, after Nietzsche (1950–55). His unfinished magnum opus was inspired by Hermann Broch's philosophical vol. *La Mort de Virgile,* portions of whose text was used in the completed sections *Le Temps Restitué* for Soprano, Chorus, and Orch. (1956–58), *...au delà du hasard* for Four Instrumental Groups, Two Sopranos, and Alto (1959), and *Chant après Chant* for Six Percussion, Voice, and Piano (1965–66). *Discours* for 11 Voices, Piano, and Orch. (begun 1961), *Lysanias* for Soprano, Mezzo-soprano, Baritone, Piano, and Orch. (begun 1966), and *Portiques de Feu* for Chorus and 18 Voices (begun 1968) were never completed. He also wrote a Concerto for Six Instrumental Groups, Vibraphone, and Clarinet (1962–68), and publ. the book *Debussy* (Paris, 1962).—NS/LK/DM

Barraud, Henry, French composer; b. Bordeaux, April 23, 1900; d. Paris, Dec. 28, 1997. He received training in harmony and counterpoint in Bordeaux, and then was a pupil of Dukas (composition), Caussade (fugue), and Aubert (composition and orchestration) at the Paris Cons. (1926–27). In 1937 he was director of music for the Paris International Exposition. He served as head of music (1944–48) and director of the national program (1948–65) of Radiodiffusion Française. He publ. *Berlioz* (Paris, 1955; 3rd ed., 1979), *La France et la musique occidentale* (Paris, 1956), *Pour comprendre les musiques d'aujord'hui* (Paris, 1968), and *Les cinq grands opéras* (Paris, 1972).

WORKS: DRAMATIC: *La Farce du Maître Pathelin,* opéra-comique (1938; Paris, June 24, 1948); *La Kermesse,* ballet (1943–44); *L'Astrologue dans le puits,* ballet (1948); *Numance,* opera (1952; Paris, April 15, 1955); *Lavinia,* opéra-bouffe (1959; Aix-en-Provence, July 20, 1961); *La Fée aux miettes,* radiophonic piece (1968); *Le Roi Gordogane,* chamber opera (1973–74); *Tête d'or,* opera (1980). ORCH.: *Quatre Préludes* for Strings (1928–35); *Poème* (1931); *Concerto da camera* (1934); *Suite pour une comédie de Musset* for Chamber Orch. (1936); *Fantaisie* for Piano and Orch. (1939); *Offrande à une ombre* (1941); *Suite d'orchestre tirée des "Petits métiers"* for Chamber Orch. (1942); 3 syms.: No. 1, *Numance,* after the opera (1952), No. 2 for Strings (1955–56), and No. 3 (1957; Boston, March 7, 1958); *Images pour un poète maudit,* suite for Chamber Orch. (1954); *Rapsodie cartésienne* (1960–61); *Rapsodie dionysienne* (1961); Concerto for Flute and Strings (1962); *Divertimento* (1962); Symphonie concertante for Trumpet and Orch. (1966); *Trois Études* (1966–69); *Une Saison en Enfer* (1968); *Variations à treize* for Chamber Orch. (1969); *Ouverture pour un Opéra interdit* (1971); Concerto for Strings (1972); *Six variations sur l'indicatif "la Trompette de l'aurore"* (1972). CHAMBER: Trio for Oboe, Clarinet, and Bassoon (1935); Trio for Violin, Viola, and Cello (1936); String Quartet (1940); Sonatine for Violin and Piano (1941); Concertino for Piano, Flute, Clarinet, Horn, and Bassoon (1954); *Pièce concertante* for Violin and Piano (1968); Saxophone Quartet (1974); Wind Quintet (1981). P i a n o : *Six Préludes* (1928–35); *Prélude et fugue* for 2 Pianos (1929); *Histoires pour les enfants* (1930); *Premiers pas* (1933); *Six Impromptus* (1941); *Huit Chantefables pour les enfants sages* (1945); *Musique pour petites mains* (1949). VO-CAL: *Chanson villageoise* and *La Ronde des trois filles vaniteuses* for Chorus, Piano, and Orch. (1928–30); *Trois Chansons de Gramadoch* for Voice and Orch. (1935); *Le Feu,* cantata for Chorus and Orch. (1937); *Trois lettres de Mme. de Sévigné* for Soprano or Baritone and Piano (1938; also for Voice and String Orch.); *Noël* for 3 Voices (1945); *Le Testament de François Villon,* chamber cantata for Tenor, Chorus, and Harpsichord (1945); *Le Mystère des Saints Innocents,* oratorio for Baritone, Reciter, Chorus, Children's Chorus, and Orch. (1946–47); *Cantate pour l'Avènement du prince de Monaco* for 4 Voices and Orch. (1950); *Te Deum* for Chorus and Orch. (1955); *Pange lingua (hommage à Rameau),* cantata for Soprano, Baritone, Chorus, and Orch. (1964); *La Divine Comédie,* cantata for 5 Soloists and Orch. (1972–73); *Enfance à Combourg,* choral sym. for Children's Voices, 2 Pianos, and 2 Percussionists, after Chateaubriand (1976).—NS/LK/DM

Barrère, Georges, outstanding French-born American flutist and pedagogue; b. Bordeaux, Oct. 31, 1876; d. Kingston, N.Y., June 14, 1944. He was a student of Joseph-Henri Altès and Paul Taffanel at the Paris Cons. (1889–95), graduating with a premier prix. In 1895 he organized the Société Moderne des Instruments à Vent in Paris, with which he presented more than 80 new compositions; he also was first prize flutist in the

Colonne orch. and the Opéra orch. (1897–1905). He then emigrated to the U.S. in 1905, becoming a naturalized American citizen in 1937. From 1905 to 1928 he was first flutist in the N.Y. Sym. Orch.; he also organized the Barrère Ensemble of Wind Instruments in 1910, which became the Barrère Little Sym. in 1914; also founded the Trio de Lutèce in 1914 and the Barrère-Britt-Salzedo Trio in 1932. He taught at N.Y.'s Inst. of Musical Art (1905–30) and Juilliard School of Music (from 1931). Barrère gave premieres of several scores, including Varèse's *Density 21.5* (N.Y., Feb. 16, 1936). He also composed.

BIBL.: G. Barrère, *G. B.* (N.Y., 1929); *The Platinum Flute and G. B.* (N.Y., 1935).—NS/LK/DM

Barrientos, Maria, celebrated Spanish soprano; b. Barcelona, March 10, 1884; d. Ciboure, France, Aug. 8, 1946. She entered the Barcelona Cons. at age six, where she received training in piano, violin, and composition before graduating at 12; then studied voice with Francesco Bonet. In 1898 she made her operatic debut as Inèz in *L'Africaine*. While still a youth, she appeared in Rome, Berlin, Leipzig, Milan, and other European music centers. On Jan. 31, 1916, she made her Metropolitan Opera debut in N.Y. as Lucia, continuing to sing there until 1920. She then devoted most of her time to concert engagements; she also taught in Buenos Aires (1939–45). In her heyday, Barrientos was acclaimed as one of the finest coloratura sopranos. Among her notable roles were Rosina, Gilda, Amina, Lakmé, Norina, and the Queen of Shemakha.—NS/LK/DM

Barron, Bill (actually, **William Jr.**), tenor and soprano saxophonist, brother of **Kenny Barron;** b. Philadelphia, March 27, 1927; d. Middletown, Conn., Sept. 21, 1989. He took up the saxophone at age 13 and in 1945 was in the concert band alongside Coltrane at the Ornstein School of Music; about 1952, he and Coltrane were taped jamming with Hassaan, but the tape was lost or destroyed. Barron also played with Jimmy Heath, Red Garland, and many others before moving to N.Y. in 1958. He directed the Muse Jazz Workshop at the Children's Museum in Brooklyn and taught at City Coll. in the 1960s and 1970s, then served as chairman of the Wesleyan Univ. Music Department in the mid-1980s. He died after a long illness in 1989. He was a highly original player who never achieved much fame but was well liked and respected by such musician friends as John Coltrane. He was adaptable enough to record in bop and hard bop contexts, yet also work with Cecil Taylor and co-lead a band with Ted Curson.

DISC.: *Tenor Stylings of B.B.* (1961); *Modern Windows* (1961); *Leopard* (1962); *Hot Line* (1962); *West Side Story Bossa Nova* (1963); *Now Hear This* (1964); *Motivation* (1972); *Jazz Caper* (1978); *Variations in Blue* (1984); *Next Plateau* (1987); *Nebulae* (1988).—LP

Barron, Kenny (actually, **Kenneth**), pianist, composer, brother of **Bill Barron;** b. Philadelphia, June 9, 1943. Encouraged by his parents, he began piano studies at the age of 12 with the sister of Ray Bryant. He had his first professional gig two years later with Mel Melvin's Orch. playing alongside his older brother, Bill,

with whom he periodically performed and recorded in later years. Bill also introduced him to Jimmy and Tootie Heath, Coltrane, and Lee Morgan, and he also worked with Philly Joe Jones. In 1961, he moved to N.Y. after high school graduation, worked with Roy Haynes, and at the end of the year joined Gillespie's group, on James Moody's advice, staying until 1966. During this time, he studied recordings of Tommy Flanagan, Hank Jones, and Wynton Kelly. Stints with Freddie Hubbard, Stanley Turrentine, Buddy Rich, Ron Carter, and many others followed.

Barron became one of the most in-demand recording artists in jazz. He made his first album as a leader in 1974, a year after he'd been appointed to the faculty of Rutgers Univ. He became a tenured professor; he retired in June 1999, primarily to keep up with his huge career and long list of gigs. In 1986, he recorded with Stan Getz and toured Europe with him the next year. In 1989, he founded the collective quartet Sphere (dedicated to the music of Thelonious Monk); since then, he often fronts his own trios and quintets. In the early 1990s, Barron hooked up again with Getz, who made his final live recording in a duo with the pianist.

DISC.: *Sunset at Dawn* (1973); *Peruvian Blue* (1974); *Lucifer* (1975); *In Tandem* (1975); *Golden Lotus* (1980); *At the Piano* (1981); *Spiral* (1982); *Green Chimneys* (1983); *Autumn in N.Y.* (1984); *1 + 1 + 1* (1984); *Scratch* (1985); *What If?* (1986); *Two As One* (1986); *Live at Fat Tuesdays* (1988); *Rhythm-A-Ning* (1989); *Only One* (1990); *Live at Maybeck Recital Hall* (1990); *Invitation* (1990); *Quickstep* (1991); *Moment* (1991); *Mitchell's Talking* (1991); *Lemuria- Seascape* (1991); *Sambao* (1993); *Other Places* (1993); *Wanton Spirit* (1994). S. Getz: *Voyage* (1986); *Anniversary* (1987); *Serenity* (1987); *People Time* (1992).—LP

Barroso Neto, Joaquim Antonio, Brazilian teacher and composer; b. Rio de Janeiro, Jan. 30, 1881; d. there, Sept. 1, 1941. He was a pupil of Braga and Nepomuceno, and later acquired a fine reputation as a teacher. He wrote mainly piano pieces in a mildly Romantic manner.

BIBL.: T. Gomes, *B. N.* (Rio de Janeiro, 1939).—NS/LK/DM

Barrueco, Manuel, outstanding Cuban-born American guitarist; b. Santiago de Cuba, Dec. 16, 1952. He began playing the guitar when he was eight and received lessons at the Esteban Salas Cons. in Santiago de Cuba. In 1967 he emigrated with his family to the U.S., and later became a naturalized American citizen. He pursued studies with Aaron Shearer at the Peabody Cons. of Music in Baltimore, where he was awarded his B.M. in 1975. In 1974 he made an auspicious Carnegie Hall recital debut in N.Y., the same year that he became the first guitarist to win the Concert Artist's Guild Award. In addition to recital engagements around the world, he has appeared as a soloist with major orchs. He also teaches at the Peabody Cons. of Music. Barrueco's repertoire includes not only the standard guitar literature but also works by such diverse musicians as Arvo Pärt, Tōru Takemitsu, Roberto Sierra, Steven Stucky, Keith Jarrett, and Chick Corea.—LK/DM

Barry, Gerald (Anthony), Irish composer; b. County Clare, April 28, 1952. He studied at Univ. Coll.,

Dublin (B.Mus., 1973; M.A., 1975), and also studied composition with Peter Schat and organ with Piet Kee in Amsterdam, with Stockhausen and Kagel at the Cologne Hochschule für Musik (1975–80), and received some guidance from Cerha in Vienna (1977). After a brief stint as a lecturer at Univ. Coll., Cork (1982–86), he concentrated on composing. In 1997–98 he was artist-in-residence at the Irish World Music Center at the Univ. of Limerick. He is a member of Aosdána, Ireland's state-sponsored academy of creative artists. Supported by the rudiments of canon technique, Barry's colorfully dissonant music is often aggressive to the point of being visceral.

WORKS: *Things That Gain by Being Painted* for Soprano, Speaker, Cello, and Piano (1977); *Ein Klavier Konzert* for Piano and Orch. (1978); *Décolletage* for Soprano and Actress (1979); _____ for Ensemble (1979; 2nd version, 1987); *Ø* for 2 Pianos (1979); *Sleeping Beauty* for 2 Performers and Bass Drum (1980); *Unkrautgarten*, ballet (1980); *The Intelligence Park*, opera (1981–87); *Sweet Cork* for Soprano, Bass, Recorder, Viol, and Harpsichord (1985); *Of Queens' Gardens* for Chamber Orch. (Dublin, Sept. 29, 1986); *Sweet Punishment* for Brass Quintet (1987); *Chevaux- de-frise* for Orch. (London, Aug. 15, 1988); Oboe Quartet (1988); *Diner* for Orch. (Belfast, Aug. 5, 1988); *Reflections on Guinness* for Orch. (1988); *Children Aged 1–17* for Orch. (1989); *Bob* for 2 Clarinets, Violin, Cello, Piano, and Marimba (1989); *Hard D* for Orch. (1992); Sextet (1992); *The Triumph of Beauty and Deceit*, television opera (1991–92; Channel 4 TV, London, March 6, 1995); 2 pianos quartets (1992, 1996); *The Chair* for Organ (1993); 2 string quartets: No. 1 (1994) and No. 2, *1998* (1999); Octet (1995); Quintet for English Horn, Clarinet/Bass Clarinet, Piano, Cello, and Double Bass (1995); *The Conquest for Ireland* for Bass and Orch. (1995); *The Ring* for Chorus and Brass Band (1996); *La Jalousie Taciturne* for String Orch. (1996); *The Road* for Orch. (1997); *Trumpeter* for Trumpet (1998).—**NS/LK/DM**

Barry, Jeff and **Ellie Greenwich,** songwriting hitmakers of the early 1960s. Jeff Barry (b. N.Y.C., April 3, 1938) and Ellie Greenwich (b. Brooklyn, N.Y., Oct. 23, 1940). While attending Hoftra in the early 1960s, Greenwich became fascinated by rock music. She hung out in record stores, and one of the proprietors introduced her to some record company scouts. They signed her to MCA as Ellie Gaye. While Ellie Gaye's recording career was relatively shortlived, Greenwich started writing songs like Darlene Loves's "Today I Met the Boy I'm Going to Marry." She met another aspiring songwriter, Jeff Barry, at a party not too long after Loves's single came out. Barry had written the tune "Tell Laura I Love Her." The two began writing together. With a handful of songs, they went to the Brill Building, joining such songwriting teams as Leiber and Stoller, Mann and Weill, and King and Goffen.

Barry and Greenwich began writing and producing for wall-of-sound producer Phil Spector's Philles label and working with Leiber and Stoller. In that atmosphere, they wrote songs like "Da Do Ron Ron" and "Be My Baby." They recorded together as The Raindrops, landing a hit with "The Kind of Boy You Won't Forget" (#17, 1963). When Lieber and Stoller formed Red Bird records, Greenwich and Barry wrote and produced there, helping sculpt—along with producer George "Shadow" Morton—the epochal "girl group" sound.

They wrote "Chapel of Love" for the Dixie Cups and "Leader of the Pack" for the Shangri-Las. With such a romantic attitude in their music, it isn't surprising they got married.

As the girl group sound ebbed, Barry and Greenwich created such hits as "Do Wha Diddy," "Hanky Panky," "Then He Kissed Me," "River Deep Mountain High," and the Beach Boys's "I Can Hear Music." However, their marriage fizzled and so did their songwriting partnership and pop success. Greenwich turned her talents to jingles and sang backup for performers ranging from Jim Croce to Blondie. She put together a 1984 musical autobiography called *Leader of the Pack* that ran on Broadway for a while.

Barry wrote a few more hits, including "I Honestly Love You" with Peter Allen and "Sugar Sugar" with Andy Kim. In the early 1990s, he began creating children's records, writing music inspired by children books like the *Clifford the Big Red Dog* and the "Babysitter's Club" series.—**HB**

Barry, Jerome, American baritone; b. Boston, Nov. 16, 1939. He was educated at Northeastern Univ. (B.A. in modern languages, 1961), Tufts Univ. (M.A. in German, 1963), and the Goethe Institut in Germany (certificate, 1962). He pursued vocal training with David Blair McClosky in Boston (1961–64), Romeo Arduini (1966–69), Luigi Ricci (1967–69), and Paolo Silveri (1969–71) in Rome, Jennie Tourel in Jerusalem (1971–74), and Pierre Bernac (1977–79) and Gérard Souzay (1986–97) in Paris. In 1967 he made his operatic debut as Sharpless in Rome, and returned there in 1969 to make his recital debut. In 1972 he made his debut as a soloist with orch. with the Jerusalem Sym. Orch. under Lukas Foss's direction. Thereafter he toured widely as a concert artist. In 1981 he co-founded the Washington (D.C.) Music Ensemble, which he served as director until 1996. He became a senior assoc. in the Voice Treatment Center at the George Washington Univ. Medical Center in 1989. From 1994 he also was director of the Embassy Series of chamber and vocal concerts presented in various embassies in Washington, D.C. Barry's repertoire is particularly notable for its breadth and diversity, enhanced by his command of some 25 languages.—**NS/LK/DM**

Barsanti, Francesco, Italian flutist, oboist, violist, and composer; b. Lucca, c. 1690; d. London, 1772. He was educated at the Univ. of Padua. In 1714 he went to London as an orch. player; after a sojourn in Edinburgh (1735–43), he returned to London. He was an accomplished composer of instrumental music.

WORKS: (6) Sonate for Recorder or Violin and Bass or Basso Continuo, op.1 (London, 1724, 1727); 6 Sonate for Flute and Bass or Basso Continuo, op.2 (London, 1728); (10) Concerti grossi, op.3 (Edinburgh, 1742); 9 overtures, op.4 (Edinburgh, 1743?); 6 Antifone for 5 Voices, op.5 (London, 1750?); 6 Sonatas for 2 Violins, op.6 (London, 1769).—**NS/LK/DM**

Barshai, Rudolf (Borisovich), Russian-born Israeli conductor; b. Labinskaya, Sept. 28, 1924. He

221

studied violin and viola at the Moscow Cons. with Zeitlin (graduated, 1948), and also received training in conducting from Musin in Leningrad. He began his career as a violist and toured throughout Russia. He also was a member of the Borodin and Tchaikovsky string quartets. In 1955 he organized the Moscow Chamber Orch., which became extremely successful. Many Russian composers wrote works for it. In 1976 he emigrated to Israel and led the Israel Chamber Orch. in Tel Aviv until 1981. He also appeared as a guest conductor throughout Europe, North America, and the Far East. From 1982 to 1988 he was principal conductor and artistic advisor of the Bournemouth Sym. Orch. He also was music director of the Vancouver (B.C.) Sym. Orch. (1985–87), president of the Toscanini conducting competition (1986–93), and principal guest conductor of l'Orchestre National de France in Paris (1987–88). —NS/LK/DM

Barsova (real name, **Vladimirova**), **Valeria,** Russian soprano; b. Astrakhan, June 13, 1892; d. Sochi, Dec. 13, 1967. She studied voice with Umberto Mazetti at the Moscow Cons., graduating in 1919; from 1920 to 1948 she was on the staff of the Bolshoi Theater in Moscow. She distinguished herself mainly in the Russian repertoire, but also sang Violetta and Gilda. Her silvery coloratura enabled her to sing such demanding roles as Lakmé. From 1950 to 1953 she taught at the Moscow Cons. She gave solo recitals in Russia and abroad, including England and Germany.

BIBL.: G. Polyanovsky, *V.V. B.* (Moscow and Leningrad, 1941).—NS/LK/DM

Barstow, Dame Josephine (Clare), noted English soprano; b. Sheffield, Sept. 27, 1940. She studied at the Univ. of Birmingham (B.A. in English), the London Opera Centre, and with Eva Turner and Andrew Field. In 1964 she made her operatic debut as Mimi with Opera for All. In 1967 she made her first appearance at the Sadler's Wells Opera in London as Cherubino, and sang with its successor, the English National Opera, from 1974. She also sang with the Welsh National Opera from 1968. In 1969 she joined London's Covent Garden, where she created the roles of Denise in *The Knot Garden* (1970), the Young Woman in *We Come to the River* (1976), and Gayle in *The Ice Break* (1977). On March 28, 1977, she made her Metropolitan Opera debut in N.Y. as Musetta. In 1983 she appeared as Gutrune in the *Ring* cycle at Bayreuth. In 1986 she made her first appearance at the Salzburg Festival creating the role of Benigna in Penderecki's *Die schwarze Maske.* Her appearances in the title role of *Gloriana* with Opera North in Leeds in 1993 and at Covent Garden in 1994 won her critical accolades. She returned to Opera North to reprise her portrayal of Gloriana in 1997. In 1999 she appeared as Poulenc's Mother Marie at the English National Opera. In 1985 she was made a Commander of the Order of the British Empire and in 1995 a Dame Commander of the Order of the British Empire. Barstow is a versatile singer whose repertoire ranges from traditional to contemporary roles.—NS/LK/DM

Bárta, Josef, Bohemian composer; b. Prague, c. 1746; d. Vienna, June 13, 1787. After serving as an organist in Prague, he settled in Vienna. His works include the opera *La Diavolessa* for the Burgtheater (July 18, 1772), several other operas, 13 syms., six string quartets, and six keyboard sonatas.

BIBL.: J. Havlik, *Symfonie Antonina Laubeho a Josefa Bárty* (diss., Univ. of Prague, 1974).—NS/LK/DM

Bárta, Lubor, Czech composer; b. Lubná, Aug. 8, 1928; d. Prague, Nov. 5, 1972. He studied with Řídký at the Prague Academy of Musical Arts (1948–52). His music presented an effective amalgam of modernistic procedures, influenced by Bartók in its rhythms, by Stravinsky in its meters, and by Hindemith in its neo-Classical harmonies.

WORKS: ORCH.: 2 violin concertos (1952, 1970); 3 syms. (1955; *The Bitter Summer,* 1969; 1972); Concerto for Chamber Orch. (1956); Viola Concerto (1957); *Dramatic Suite* (1958); Piano Concerto (1958–59); *From East Bohemia,* symphonic suite (1961); *Concertante Overture* (1964); *Ludi* for 8 Winds and String Orch. (1964); *Musica Romantica* for Strings (1971). **CHAMBER:** 2 violin sonatas (1949, 1959); 2 wind quintets (*Divertimento,* 1949; 1969); 3 string quartets (1950, 1957, 1967); Piano Trio (1955); Trombone Sonatina (1956); Clarinet Sonata (1958); *Ballad and Burlesque* for Cello and Piano (1963); Concertino for Trombone and Piano (1964); Sonata for Solo Guitar (1965); *4 Pieces* for Violin and Guitar (1966); Flute Sonata (1966); *Fragments* for Clarinet and Piano (1967); *Amoroso* for Horn and Piano (1970); Cello Sonata (1971). **KEYBOARD: Piano:** *Variations* (1948); 3 sonatas (1956, 1961, 1971). **Harpsichord:** Sonata (1967). **VOCAL:** 2 cantatas: *Komsomol* (1951) and *Song of the New Age* (1962); songs.—NS/LK/DM

Bartay, Andreas, Hungarian composer, father of **Ede Bartay;** b. Széplak, April 7, 1799; d. Mainz, Oct. 4, 1854. He began his career as a civil servant. At the same time he was engaged in collecting Hungarian folk songs and became interested in music in general. In 1829 he became a director of the first Pest singing academy. In 1834 he publ. one of the earliest collections of Hungarian folk songs and also a Hungarian book on music theory, *Magyar Apollo* (1834). A militant patriot, he participated in the Hungarian struggle for independence of 1848; after its defeat he emigrated to France and eventually to Germany. He wrote three operas: *Aurelia, oder Das Weib am Konradstein* (Pest, Dec. 16, 1837), *Csel* (The Ruse; Pest, April 29, 1839), and *A magyarok Napolyban* (The Hungarians in Naples; unperf.).—NS/LK/DM

Bartay, Ede, Hungarian folk-song collector, son of **Andreas Bartay;** b. Pest, Oct. 6, 1825; d. Budapest, Aug. 31, 1901. He studied law and music and was for many years a practicing piano teacher. In 1876 he was appointed director of the National Cons. in Budapest, a post which he held until his death. In 1863 he founded the Hungarian Pension Fund for Musicians. Like his father, he was a Hungarian patriot. After the defeat of the Hungarian Revolution of 1848 he remained in Budapest, dedicating himself to collecting authentic Hungarian folk songs and dances. He also wrote a Sym., the overture *Pericles,* and many piano pieces. —NS/LK/DM

Bartei, Girolamo, Italian organist and compoer; b. Arezzo, c. 1565; d. c. 1618. He was a member of the Augustinian order. He was maestro di cappella at Arezzo Cathedral (1592–94; 1595–97; 1598) and at Volterra Cathedral (1604–07). In 1608 he went to Rome and served his order as sub-prior at the S. Agostino monastery. Following a stay at the church of S. Agostino, he was sub-prior, organist, and teacher of the professed at the S. Agostino monastery in Orvieto (1616). In 1617–18 he was at the Augustinian monastery of Marino in Rome. He was an accomplished composer of sacred and secular vocal music, and of instrumental music.

BIBL.: F. Coradini, *Il musicista aretino P. B.* (Arezzo, 1923). —LK/DM

Bartha, Dénes, eminent Hungarian musicologist; b. Budapest, Oct. 2, 1908; d. near there, Sept. 7, 1993. He studied at the Univ. of Berlin with Abert, Blume, Hornbostel, Sachs, Schering, and Wolf (Ph.D., 1930, with the diss. *Benedictus Ducis und Appenzeller;* publ. in Wolfenbüttel, 1930). Returning to Budapest, he was a librarian in the music division of the Hungarian National Museum (1930–42), a lecturer (1930–47) and prof. (from 1947) at the Franz Liszt Academy of Music, and a Privatdozent at the Univ. (from 1935). After serving as ed. of *Magyar zénei szemle* (1941–44), he was co-ed. of *Zénei szemle* (1947–49), *Zenetudományi tanulmányok* (1953–61), and *Studia musicologica* (1961–93). He was a visiting prof. at Smith Coll. (1964), Harvard Univ. (summers 1964–65), Cornell Univ. (1965–66), the Univ. of Pittsburgh (1966–67), where he subsequently was the Andrew W. Mellon Prof. (1969–79), and the Univ. of Wash. in Seattle (1980–81). In 1963 he received the Dent Medal of England, and in 1982 the Ehrenkreuz für Kunst und Wissenschaft of Austria. In 1982 he was made a corresponding member of the American Musicological Soc., and in 1990 of the Hungarian Academy of Sciences.

WRITINGS (all published in Budapest unless otherwise given): *Das Musiklehrbuch einer ungarischen Klosterschule aus 1490* (1934); *Lehrbuch der Musikgeschichte* (1935); *Franz Liszt* (Leipzig, 1936); *Beethoven* (1939); with Z. Kodály, *Die ungarische Musik* (1943); *Anthologie der Musikgeschichte* (1948); *J.S. Bach* (1956; 2nd ed., 1960); *Beethoven kilenc szimfóniája* (1956; 5th ed., rev., 1975); with L. Somfai, *Haydn als Opernkapellmeister* (1960); ed. *J. Haydn: Gesammelte Briefe und Aufzeichnungen* (Kassel, 1965); ed. *Zénei Lexikon* (2nd ed., 3 vols., 1965–66).—NS/LK/DM

Barthélémon, François-Hippolyte, French violinist and composer; b. Bordeaux, July 27, 1741; d. London, July 20, 1808. His father was French and his mother Irish. He held posts as violinist in various theater orchs. in London; became acquainted with Haydn during Haydn's London visit in 1792. He was greatly praised as a violinist; Burney speaks of his tone as being "truly vocal." Barthélémon wrote mostly for the stage; among his operas, the most notable are *Pelopida* (London, May 24, 1766); *The Judgement of Paris* (London, Aug. 24, 1768); *Le Fleuve Scamandre* (Paris, Dec. 22, 1768); *The Maid of the Oaks* (The Oaks, near Epsom, June 1774); *Belphegor* (London, March 16, 1778). In addition, he wrote a Violin Concerto, two sets of duos for violins, several string quartets, and catches and glees to English words (many of them publ.). He was married to Mary Young, a noted singer descended from Anthony Young. His daughter contributed a biographical ed. (London, 1827) of selections from Barthélémon's oratorio *Jefte in Masfa.*—NS/LK/DM

Bartholomée, Pierre, Belgian conductor and composer; b. Brussels, Aug. 5, 1937. He studied with Louel, Souffrian, and Stekke at the Royal Cons. in Brussels (1952–57) and privately with Pousseur and Boulez. In 1962 he founded in Brussels an instrumental ensemble, Groupe Musiques Nouvelles, which he conducted until 1977. He also was prof. of analysis at the Royal Cons. in Brussels (from 1972). In 1977 he became music director of the Liège Orch., which post he retained when it became the Orchestre Philharmonique de Liège in 1980, and then the Orchestre Philharmonique de Liège et de la Communaute française de Belgique in 1983.

WORKS: *Chanson* for Cello (1964); *Cantate aux Alentours* for Voices, Instruments, and Live Electronics (1966); *La Ténèbre souveraine* for Soloists, Double Chorus, and Orch. (1967); *Tombeau de Marin* for Violin, 2 Viole da Gamba, and Harpsichord (1967); *Premier alentour* for Flute and 2 Viole da Gamba (1967); *Catalogue* for 4 Harps (1968); *Deuxième alentour: "Cueillir"* for Mezzo-soprano, Piano, and Percussion (1969); *Harmonique* for Orch. (1970); *Fancy I* for Harp and *II* for Instrumental Group (1974–75; can be played together under the title *Sonata quasi una fantasia); Trois pôles entrelacés* for 7 Instruments (1985); *Adieu* for Clarinet and Piano (1987); *Rumeur* for Orch. (1989). —NS/LK/DM

Bartlett, Homer Newton, American organist and composer; b. Olive, N.Y., Dec. 28, 1845; d. Hoboken, N.J., April 3, 1920. He studied piano, organ, and composition in N.Y., where he was organist at the Marble Collegiate Church and the Madison Ave. Baptist Church. Among his works were *La vallière,* opera (1887), *Magic Hours,* operetta (1910), Violin Concerto, Cello Concerto, *Apollo,* symphonic poem (1911), chamber music, piano pieces, organ music, sacred pieces, over 80 songs, and salon pieces, including the once very popular *Grande polka de concert* (1867).—NS/LK/DM

Barto, Tzimon, (real name, **John Barto Smith Jr.**), American pianist, conductor, and composer; b. Eustis, Fla., Jan. 2, 1963. He was five when he began piano studies with his grandmother. After attending the Brevard Music Center (1978–79), he studied at the Tanglewood Inst., where he was named the most outstanding conducting student (1980); then pursued piano training with Adele Marcus at the Juilliard School in N.Y. (1981–84). In 1983 he captured first prize in the Gina Bachauer piano competition in Salt Lake City. In 1985 he made his formal debut as a pianist at the Spoleto Festival of Two Worlds, and subsequently was engaged as a soloist with leading orchs. and as a recitalist in principal music centers; also was active as a guest conductor. While his repertoire ranges from Bach to jazz, he has become particularly known for his performances of the 19th and 20th century piano literature.—NS/LK/DM

Bartók, Béla (Viktor János),

Bartók, Béla (Viktor János), great Hungarian composer; b. Nagyszentmiklós, March 25, 1881; d. N.Y., Sept. 26, 1945. His father was a school headmaster; his mother was a proficient pianist, from whom and he received his first piano lessons. He began playing the piano in public at the age of 11. In 1894 the family moved to Pressburg, where he took piano lessons with László Erkel, son of the famous Hungarian opera composer; he also studied harmony with Anton Hyrtl. In 1899 he enrolled at the Royal Academy of Music in Budapest, where he studied piano with Thomán and composition with Koessler; he graduated in 1903. His earliest compositions reveal the combined influence of Liszt, Brahms, and Richard Strauss; however, he soon became interested in exploring the resources of national folk music, which included not only Hungarian melorhythms but also elements of other ethnic strains in his native Transylvania, including Romanian and Slovak. He formed a cultural friendship with Kodály, and together they traveled through the land collecting folk songs, which they publ. in 1906. In 1907 Bartók succeeded Thomán as prof. of piano at the Royal Academy of Music. His interest in folk-song research led him to tour North Africa in 1913. In 1919 he served as a member of the musical directorate of the short-lived Hungarian Democratic Republic with Dohnányi and Kodály; was also deputy director of the Academy of Music. Bartók was a brilliant pianist whose repertoire extended from Scarlatti to Szymanowski, as well as his own works; he also gave concerts playing works for two pianos with his second wife, **Ditta Pásztory**. In his own compositions, he soon began to feel the fascination of tonal colors and impressionistic harmonies as cultivated by Debussy and other modern French composers. The basic texture of his music remained true to tonality, which he expanded to chromatic polymodal structures and unremittingly dissonant chordal combinations; in his piano works, he exploited the extreme registers of the keyboard, often in the form of tone clusters to simulate pitchless drumbeats. He made use of strong asymmetrical rhythmic figures suggesting the modalities of Slavic folk music, a usage that imparted a somewhat acrid coloring to his music. The melodic line of his works sometimes veered toward atonality in its chromatic involutions; in some instances, he employed melodic figures comprising the 12 different notes of the chromatic scale; however, he never adopted the integral techniques of the 12-tone method.

Bartók toured the U.S. as a pianist from Dec. 1927 to Feb. 1928, and also gave concerts in the Soviet Union in 1929. He resigned his position at the Budapest Academy of Music in 1934, but continued his ethnomusicological research as a member of the Hungarian Academy of Sciences, where he was engaged in the preparation of the monumental Corpus Musicae Popularis Hungaricae. With the outbreak of World War II, Bartók decided to leave Europe; in the fall of 1940 he went to the U.S., where he remained until his death. In 1940 he received an honorary Ph.D. from Columbia Univ.; he also undertook folk-song research there as a visiting assistant in music (1941–42). His last completed score, the *Concerto for Orchestra*, commissioned by Koussevitzky, proved to be his most popular work. His Third Piano Concerto was virtually completed at the time of his death, except for the last 17 bars, which were arranged and orchestrated by his pupil Tibor Serly.

Throughout his life, and particularly during his last years in the U.S., Bartók experienced constant financial difficulties, and complained bitterly of his inability to support himself and his family. Actually, he was apt to exaggerate his pecuniary troubles, which were largely due to his uncompromising character. He arrived in America in favorable circumstances; his traveling expenses were paid by the American patroness Elizabeth Sprague Coolidge, who also engaged him to play at her festival at the Library of Congress in Washington, D.C., for a generous fee. Bartók was offered the opportunity to give a summer course in composition at a midwestern college on advantageous terms, when he was still well enough to undertake such a task, but he proposed to teach piano instead, and the deal collapsed. Ironically, performances and recordings of his music increased enormously after his death, and the value of his estate reached a great sum of money. Posthumous honors were not lacking: Hungary issued a series of stamps with Bartók's image; a street in Budapest was named for him; the centenary of his birth was celebrated throughout the world by concerts and festivals devoted to his works. Forty-three years after his death, his remains were removed from the Ferncliff Cemetery in Hartsdale, N.Y., and taken to Budapest for a state funeral on July 7, 1988.

Far from being a cerebral purveyor of abstract musical designs, Bartók was an ardent student of folkways, seeking the roots of meters, rhythms, and modalities in the spontaneous songs and dances of the people. Indeed, he regarded his analytical studies of popular melodies as his most important contribution. Even during the last years of his life, already weakened by illness, he applied himself assiduously to the arrangement of Serbo-Croatian folk melodies of Yugoslavia from recordings placed in his possession. He was similarly interested in the natural musical expression of children; he firmly believed that children are capable of absorbing modalities and asymmetrical rhythmic structures with greater ease than adults trained in the rigid disciplines of established music schools. His remarkable collection of piano pieces entitled, significantly, *Mikrokosmos*, was intended as a method to initiate beginners into the world of unfamiliar tonal and rhythmic combinations; in this he provided a parallel means of instruction to the Kodály method of schooling.

WORKS: DRAMATIC: *A kékszakállu herceg vará* (Duke Bluebeard's Castle), opera, op.11 (1911; rev. 1912, 1918; Budapest, May 24, 1918, Egisto Tango conducting); *A fából faragott királyfi* (The Wooden Prince), ballet, op.13 (1914–16; Budapest, May 12, 1917, Egisto Tango conducting; orch. suite, 1924; Budapest, Nov. 23, 1931; rev. 1932); *A czodalátos mandarin* (The Miraculous Mandarin), pantomime, op.19 (1918–19; Cologne, Nov. 27, 1926; orch. suite, 1924; rev. 1927; Budapest, Oct. 15, 1928, Ernst von Dohnanyi conducting); *Caprichos*, ballet (N.Y., Jan. 29, 1950; based on *Contrasts* for Violin, Clarinet, and Piano, 1938). **ORCH.:** *Scherzo* (only scored movement of a projected sym. in E-flat major, 1902; Budapest, Feb. 29, 1904); *Kossuth*, symphonic poem (1903; Budapest, Jan. 13, 1904); *Rhapsody* for Piano and Orch., op.1 (1904; Paris, Aug. 1905; composer soloist);

Scherzo for Piano and Orch., op.2 (1904; Budapest, Sept. 28, 1961); 2 suites: No. 1, op.3 (1905; movements 1, 3–5 perf. in Vienna, Nov. 29, 1905; first complete perf., Budapest, March 1, 1909; rev. 1920) and No. 2 for Small Orch., op.4 (1905–07; first perf. of 2nd movement, Scherzo, only; Berlin, Jan. 2, 1909; first complete perf., Budapest, Nov. 22, 1909; rev. 1920, 1943; transcribed for 2 Pianos, 1941); 2 Portraits, op.5 (No. 1, 1907–08; No. 2, 1911; No. 1, Budapest, Feb. 12, 1911; first complete perf., Budapest, April 20, 1916); 2 violin concertos: No. 1 (1907–08; Basel, May 30, 1958, Schneeberger soloist, Paul Sacher conducting) and No. 2 (1937–38; Amsterdam, march 23, 1939, Székely soloist, Mengelberg conducting); 2 Pictures (Deux Images), op.10 (1910; Budapest, Feb. 25, 1913); 4 Pieces, op.12 (1912; orchestrated 1921; Budapest, Jan. 9, 1922); Dance Suite (Budapest, Nov. 19, 1923); 3 piano concertos: No. 1 (1926; Frankfurt am Main, July 1, 1927, composer soloist, Furtwängler conducting), No. 2 (1930–31; Frankfurt am Main, Jan. 23, 1933, composer soloist, Rosbaud conducting), and No. 3 (1945; last 17 measures composed by Tibor Serly; Philadelphia, Feb. 8, 1946, Sándor soloist, Ormandy conducting); Rhapsody No. 1 for Violin and Orch. (1928; also versions for Violin or Cello, and Piano; Königsberg, Nov. 1, 1929, Szigeti soloist, Scherchen conducting) and No. 2 for Violin and Orch. (1928; also for Violin and Piano; Budapest, Nov. 25, 1929, Székely soloist, E. Dohnányi conducting); Music for Strings, Percussion, and Celesta (1936; Basel, Jan. 21, 1937, Paul Sacher conducting); Divertimento for Strings (1939; Basel, June 11, 1940); Concerto for 2 Pianos and Orch. (1940; orchestration of Sonata for 2 Pianos and Percussion; London, Nov. 14, 1942); Concerto for Orchestra (commissioned by Koussevitzky, 1943; perf. under his direction, Boston, Dec. 1, 1944); Viola Concerto (1945; left unfinished in sketches; reconstructed and orchestrated by Tibor Serly, 1947–49; Minneapolis, Dec. 2, 1949, Primrose soloist, Dorati conducting; also arranged by Serly for Cello and Orch.); various orch. transcriptions of Romanian and Hungarian folk and peasant dances, orig. for piano. **CHAMBER:** 3 unnumbered violin sonatas: C minor, op.5 (1895), A major, op.17 (1897), and E minor (1903); Piano Quartet in C minor, op.20 (1898); an unnumbered String Quartet in F major (1898); Duo for 2 Violins (1902); Albumblatt for Violin and Piano (1902); Piano Quintet (Vienna, Nov. 21, 1904); 6 numbered string quartets: No. 1, op.7 (1908; Budapest, March 19, 1910), No. 2, op.17 (1915–17; Budapest, March 3, 1918), No. 3 (1927; London, Feb. 19, 1929), No. 4 (1928; Budapest, March 20, 1929), No. 5 (1934; Washington, D.C., April 8, 1935), and No. 6 (1939; N.Y., Jan. 20, 1941); 2 numbered violin sonatas: No. 1 (1921; Vienna, Feb. 8, 1922) and No. 2 (1922; Berlin, Feb. 7, 1923); Rhapsody No. 1 for Violin and Piano (1928; Budapest, Nov. 22, 1929; Szigeti violinist, composer pianist; also versions for Cello and Piano, and Violin and Orch.) and No. 2 for Violin and Piano (Amsterdam, Nov. 19, 1928; rev. 1944; also a version for Violin and Orch.); 44 Duos for 2 Violins (1931); Sonata for 2 Pianos and Percussion (1937; Basel, Jan. 16, 1938, composer and his wife, Ditta Bartók, soloists; also for Orch. as Concerto for 2 Pianos and Orch.); Contrasts for Violin, Clarinet, and Piano (1938; N.Y., Jan. 9, 1939); Sonata for Solo Violin (1944; N.Y., Nov. 26, 1944, Menuhin soloist). **Piano:** Rhapsody, op.1 (1904; Pressburg, Nov. 4, 1906; composer soloist); 14 Bagatelles, op.6 (Berlin, June 29, 1908); 10 Easy Pieces (1908); 2 Elegies, op.8b (1908–09; Budapest, April 21, 1919; composer soloist); For Children (orig. 85 easy pieces in 4 vols., 1908–09; rev., 1945, reducing the number to 79, divided into 2 vols.); 7 Sketches, op.9 (1908–10; rev. 1945); 3 Burlesques (1908–11); 4 Dirges (1910); Allegro barbaro (1911); 6 Romanian Folk Dances (1909–15); 15 Hungarian Peasant Songs (1914–18); 3 Rondos on Folk Tunes (1916, 1927, 1927);

Romanian Christmas Carols, or Colinde (1915); Sonatina (1915); Suite, op.14 (1916; Budapest, April 21, 1919, composer soloist); 3 Etudes, op.18 (1918); 8 Improvisations on Hungarian Peasant Songs (1920; Budapest, Feb. 27, 1921, composer soloist); Sonata (Budapest, Dec. 8, 1926, composer soloist); Out of Doors (1926); 9 Little Pieces (Budapest, Dec. 8, 1926, composer soloist); Mikrokosmos (153 pieces, 1926–39); Petite Suite (1936); 7 Pieces from Mikrokosmos for 2 Pianos (c. 1939); Suite for 2 Pianos (1941; transcription from Suite No. 2, for Small Orch., op.4). **VOCAL:** 20 Hungarian Folksongs for Voice and Piano (1st 10 by Bartók, 2nd 10 by Kodály; 1906; rev., 1938); 8 Hungarian Folksongs for Voice and Piano (1907–17); 3 Village Scenes for Female Voices and Chamber Orch. (1926; N.Y., Feb. 1, 1927; a transcription of 3 of 5 Village Scenes for Voice and Piano, 1924; Budapest, Dec. 8, 1926); 20 Hungarian Folksongs for Voice and Piano (4 vols., 1929); Cantata Profana for Tenor, Baritone, Chorus, and Orch. (1930; BBC, London, May 25, 1934); 27 Choruses for Women's or Children's Voices (1935); numerous settings of various folk songs.

WRITINGS: Cântece poporale românești din comitatul Bihor (Ungaria)/Chansons populaires roumaines du département Bihar (Hongrie) (Bucharest, 1913; rev. ed. in Eng. as incorporated in B. Suchoff, ed., Rumanian Folk Music, The Hague, vols. I-III, 1967); with Z. Kodály, Erdélyi magyarság népdalok (Transylvanian Folk Songs; Budapest, 1923); "Die Volksmusik der Rumanen von Maramures," Sammelbände für vergleichende Musikwissenschaft, IV (Munich, 1923; in Eng. as incorporated in B. Suchoff, ed., Rumanian Folk Music, The Hague, vol. V, 1975); A magyar népdal (Budapest, 1924; Ger. tr. as Das ungarische Volkslied, Berlin, 1925; Eng. tr. as Hungarian Folk Music, London, 1931; enl. ed., with valuable addenda, as The Hungarian Folk Song, ed. by B. Suchoff, Albany, N.Y., 1981); Népzenenk és a szomszéd népek népzenéje (Our Folk Music and the Folk Music of Neighboring Peoples; Budapest, 1934; Ger. tr. as Die Volksmusik der Magyaren und der benachbarten Völker, Berlin, 1935; French tr. as "La Musique populaire des Hongrois et des peuples voisins," Archivum Europae Centro Orientalis, II; Budapest, 1936); Die Melodien der rumänischen Colinde (Weihnachtslieder) (Vienna, 1935; Eng. tr. in B. Suchoff, ed., Rumanian Folk Music, The Hague, vol. IV, 1975); Miért és hogyan gyűjtsünk népzenét (Why and How Do We Collect Folk Music?, Budapest, 1936; French tr. as Pourquoi et comment recueille-t-on la musique populaire?, Geneva, 1948); with A. Lord, Serbo-Croatian Folk Songs (N.Y., 1951; reprinted in B. Suchoff, ed., Yugoslav Folk Music, vol. I, Albany, N.Y., 1978). The N.Y. Bartók Archive publ. an ed. of Bartók's writings in English trs. in its Studies in Musicology series. The following vols., under the editorship of Benjamin Suchoff, were publ.: Rumanian Folk Music (The Hague, vols. I-III, 1967; vols. IV-V, 1975); Turkish Folk Music from Asia Minor (Princeton, 1976); Béla Bartók's Essays (selected essays; London and N.Y., 1976); Yugoslav Folk Music (4 vols., Albany, N.Y., 1978); The Hungarian Folk Song (Albany, N.Y., 1981).

BIBL.: A. Révész, B. B. utja (Budapest, 1936); D. Dille, B. B. (Antwerp, 1939); M. Seiber, The String Quartets of B. B. (London, 1945); J. Demény, B. (Budapest, 1946); B. Kiss, B. B. müvészete (Cluj, 1946); D. Dille, B. B. (Brussels, 1947); G. Láng, B. élete és müvei (Budapest, 1947); J. Deményi, ed., B. B. levelei (Budapest, 1948–71; 2nd ed., 1976; Eng. tr., 1971); J. Demény, B. élete és müvei (Budapest, 1948); A. Molnár, B. müvészete (Budapest, 1948); S. Moreux, B. B.: Sa vie, ses oeuvres, son langage (Paris, 1949; Eng. tr., London, 1953); B. Rondi, B. (Rome, 1950); H. Stevens, The Life and Music of B. B. (N.Y., 1953; 2nd ed., rev., 1964; 3rd ed., rev. 1993, by M. Gillies); P. Csobádi, B. (Budapest, 1955); E. Lendvai, B. stilusa (Budapest, 1955); F. Bónis, B. élete képekben (Budapest,

1956; 4th ed., 1980; Eng. tr., 1964, as *B. B.: His Life in Pictures*); B. Suchoff, *Guide to B.'s Mikrokosmos* (London, 1957; 3rd ed., N.Y., 1982); B. Szabolcsi, ed., *B.: Sa vie et son oeuvre* (Budapest, 1956; 2nd ed., 1968; Ger. tr., 1957; enl. ed., 1972); J. Szegő, *B. B. a népdalkutató* (Bucharest, 1956); R. Traimer, *B. B.s Kompositionstechnik, dargestellt an seinen sechs Streichquartetten* (Regensburg, 1956); K. Kristóf, *Beszélgetések B. B.* (Budapest, 1957); A. Fassett, *The Naked Face of Genius: B. B.'s American Years* (Boston, 1958; reprint as *B. B.: The American Years*, N.Y., 1970); R. Petzoldt, *B. B., Sein Leben in Bildern* (Leipzig, 1958); W. Reich, *B. B.: Eigene Schriften und Erinnerungen der Freunde* (Basel and Stuttgart, 1958); J. Ujfalussy, ed., *B. breviárium: Levelek, írások, dokumentumok* (Budapest, 1958; 2nd ed., rev., 1974); J. Uhde, *B. B.* (Berlin, 1959); J. Demény, ed., *Ausgewählte Briefe* (Budapest, 1960; Eng. tr., 1971); L. Lesznai, *B. B.: Sein Leben, seine Werke* (Leipzig, 1961; Eng. tr., 1973, as *B.*); B. Szabolcsi, *B. B.: Leben und Werk* (Leipzig, 1961; 2nd ed., 1968); G. Kroó, *B. szinpadi müvei* (Budapest, 1962); V. Bator, *The B. B. Archives: History and Catalogue* (N.Y., 1963); P. Citron, *B.* (Paris, 1963); E. Lendvai, *B. dramaturgiája* (Budapest, 1964); E. Helm, *B. B. in Selbstzeugnissen und Bilddokumenten* (Hamburg, 1965); J. Ujfalussy, *B. B.* (Budapest, 1965; 3rd ed., 1976; Eng. tr., 1972); J. Kárpáti, *B. vonósnégyesei* (Budapest, 1967; rev. ed. as *B. kamarazenéje*, 1976; Eng. tr., 1975; enl. ed. as *B.'s Chamber Music*, 1993); A. Szőllősy, ed., *B. összegyüjtött irásai I* (Budapest, 1967); J. Demény, *B. B. a zongoramüvész* (Budapest, 1968; 2nd ed., 1973); J. Szegő, *B. B. élete* (Budapest, 1969); G. Kroó, *B. kalauz* (Budapest, 1971; Eng. tr., 1974); T. Hundt, *B.'s Satztechnik in den Klavierwerken* (Regensburg, 1971); E. Lendvai, *B. költöi világa* (Budapest, 1971); idem, *B. B.: An Analysis of His Music* (London, 1971); P. Petersen, *Die Tonalität im Instrumentalschaffen von B. B.* (Hamburg, 1971); F. Bónis, *B. B. élete képekben és dokumentumokban* (Budapest, 1972; Eng. tr., 1972, as *B. B.: His Life in Pictures and Documents*); D. Dille, *Thematisches Verzeichnis der Jugendwerke B. B.s 1890–1904* (Budapest, 1974); H. Fladt, *Zur Problematik traditioneller Formtypen dargestellt an Sonatensatzen in den Streichquartetten B. B.s* (Munich, 1974); F. László, ed., *B.-dolgozatok* (Bucharest, 1974); J. McCabe, *B. Orchestral Music* (London, 1974); T. Crow, ed., *B. Studies* (Detroit, 1976); E. Lendvai, *B. and Kodály* (4 vols., Budapest, 1978–80); F. Laszlo, *B. B.: Tanulmányok és tanúságok* (Bucharest, 1980); P. Autexier, ed., *B. B.: Musique de la vie* (Paris, 1981); B. Bartók Jr., *Apám életének krónikája* (Budapest, 1981); idem, *B. B. családi levelei* (Budapest, 1981); T. Tallián, *B. B.* (Budapest, 1981); Y. Queffélec, *B. B.* (Paris, 1981); B. Bartók Jr., *Bartók Béla műhelyében* (Budapest, 1982); H. Milne, *B.: His Life and Times* (Tunbridge Wells, 1982); S. Walsh, *B.'s Chamber Music* (London, 1982); E. Lendvai, *The Workshop of B. and Kodály* (Budapest, 1983); E. Antokoletz, *The Music of B. B.* (Berkeley, Los Angeles, and London, 1984); P. Griffiths, *B.* (London, 1984); G. Ranki, ed., *B. and Kodály Revisited* (Budapest, 1987); E. Antokoletz, *B. B.: A Guide to Research* (N.Y., 1988; 2nd ed., 1997); J. Platthy, *B.: A Critical Biography* (Santa Claus, Ind., 1988); D. Yeomans, *B. for Piano: A Survey of His Solo Literature* (Bloomington, Ind., 1988); M. Gillies, *B. in Britain: A Guided Tour* (Oxford, 1989); D. Dille, *B. B.: Regard sur le passé* (Louvain-la-Neuve, 1990); M. Gillies, *B. Remembered* (London and Boston, 1990); N. John, ed., *The Stage Works of B. B.* (London and Riverrun, N.Y., 1991); P. Wilson, *The Music of B. B.* (New Haven, 1992); J. de Waard, *B.* (Haarlem, 1993); C. Kenneson, *Székely and B.: The Story of a Friendship* (Portland, Ore., 1994); C. Pesavento, *Musik von B. B. als pädagogisches Programm* (Frankfurt am Main, 1994); A. Castronuovo, *B.: Studio biografico e stilistico: Catalogo ragionato delle opere* (Sannicandro Garganico, 1995); P. Ladki, ed., *B. and His World* (Princeton, 1995); B. Suchoff, *B.: The Concerto for Orchestra: Understanding B.'s World* (N.Y., 1995); D. Cooper, *B.:*

Concerto for Orchestra (Cambridge, 1996); L. Somfai, *B. B.: Composition, Concepts, and Autograph Sources* (Berkeley, 1996); F. Hentschel, *Funktion und Beeutung der Symmetrie in den Werken B. B.s* (Lucca, 1997); B. Suchoff, ed., *B. B.: Essays* (Lincoln, Nebr., 1997); J. Frigyesi, *B. B. and Turn-of-the-Century Budapest* (Berkeley, 1998); E. Antokoletz, V. Fischer, and B. Suchoff, eds., *B. Perspectives* (Oxford, 1999).—**NS/LK/DM**

Bartoletti, Bruno, noted Italian conductor; b. Sesto Fiorentino, June 10, 1926. He studied flute at the Florence Cons., and then received training in piano and composition while serving as a flutist in the orch. of the Florence Teatro Comunale. In 1949 he became an asst. conductor there, making his formal debut conducting *Rigoletto* in 1953. In 1954 he made his debut as a sym. conductor at the Maggio Musicale Fiorentino, where he later was director (1957–64). On Oct. 23, 1956, he made his U.S. debut at the Chicago Lyric Opera conducting *Il Trovatore*, and then served as its resident conductor until 1963. With Pino Donati, he was its co-artistic director from 1964 to 1975, and then its sole artistic director from 1975 to 2000 and then served as its music director emeritus. He also was artistic director of the Rome Opera (1965–69), and later artistic advisor (1986–87) and artistic director (1987–92) of the Florence Teatro Comunale. As a guest conductor, he appeared throughout Europe, the U.S., and South America, becoming especially admired for his idiomatic readings of the Italian operatic repertoire; also conducted various French and Russian operas with success.—**NS/LK/DM**

Bartoli, Cecilia, outstanding Italian mezzo-soprano; b. Rome, June 4, 1966. She began vocal training at a very early age with her mother; at the age of nine, sang the off-stage role of the shepherd in *Tosca*. After studying trombone at the Accademia di Santa Cecilia in Rome, she pursued a vocal career, attracting favorable attention when she was 19 on an Italian television special with Ricciarelli and Nucci. Her formal stage debut followed in Verona in 1987. She then received valuable coaching from Karajan and Barenboim. On July 17, 1990, she made her U.S. debut as soloist at the Mostly Mozart Festival in N.Y. During the 1990–91 season, she made successful debuts with the Opéra de la Bastille in Paris as Cherubino, at La Scala in Milan as Isolier in *Le Comte Ory*, at the Maggio Musicale Fiorentino as Dorabella, and at the Teatro Liceo in Barcelona as Rosina. In 1992 she performed admirably as Cherubino and Dorabella in concert performances with Barenboim and the Chicago Sym. Orch., and also appeared as Despina at the Salzburg Festival. On April 23, 1993, she made a sensational U.S. operatic stage debut with the Houston Grand Opera as Rosina. She made her first appearance at the John F. Kennedy Center for the Performing Arts in Washington, D.C., on March 25, 1994. On Sept. 29, 1994, she regaled audiences at the opening of the 1994–95 season of N.Y.'s Carnegie Hall when she appeared as soloist with Marriner and the Academy of St. Martin-in-the-Fields. The event was later telecast to the nation over PBS. She made her debut at the Metropolitan Opera in N.Y. as Despina on Feb. 9, 1996. Her Carnegie Hall recital debut followed on March 28, 1996. In 1998 she appeared as Susanna at the

Metropolitan Opera and as Paisiello's Nina in Zürich. She returned to Zürich in 1999 to portray Donna Elvira. The matchless combination of her vocal perfection and extraordinary dramatic gifts have made Bartoli one of the most heralded singers of her day. Among her other acclaimed operatic roles are Concepción, Bellini's Romeo, Massenet's Charlotte, and Offenbach's Hélène. In addition to opera, she pursues a remarkably successful concert career.

BIBL.: K. Chernin and R. Stendahl, *C. B.: The Passion of Song* (N.Y., 1997); M. Hoelterhoff, *Cinderella & Company: Backstage at the Opera with C. B.* (N.Y., 1999).—NS/LK/DM

Bartolino da Padova (Magister **Frater Bartolinus** de Padua; **Frater carmelitus**), Italian composer who flourished in the second half of the 14th century. He was a member of the Carmelite Order, active in Padua. Some 38 works have been attributed to him, consisting of ballads and madrigals in the style of Jacopo da Bologna. See J. Wolf, ed., *Der Squarcialupi-Codex Pal. 87 der Biblioteca Medicea Laurenziana zu Florenz* (Lippstadt, 1955) and W. Marrocco, ed., *Italian Secular Music*, in Polyphonic Music of the Fourteenth Century, IX (1974).—NS/LK/DM

Bartolomeo degli Organi (Baccio Fiorentino), Italian organist and composer; b. Florence, Dec. 24, 1474; d. there, Dec. 12, 1539. At the age of 13 he became a singer at Ss. Annunziata in Florence. He subsequently served as organist at several Florentine churches, and also was a singer in the service of Lorenzo de' Medici, Duke of Urbino. In 1509 he was appointed principal organist at the Cathedral in Florence. Among his extant compositions are ten Italian secular pieces and several instrumental works. See F. D'Accone, ed., *Music of the Florentine Renaissance*, in Corpus Mensurabilis Musicae, XXXII/2 (1967).—NS/LK/DM

Bartolozzi, Bruno, Italian violinist and composer; b. Florence, June 8, 1911; d. Fiesole, Dec. 12, 1980. After studying violin at the Cherubini Cons. in Florence (1926–30), he was active as a violinist from 1941 to 1965 in the orch. of the Maggio Musicale Fiorentino. He turned to composition quite late in life, and took courses with Fragapane at the Cherubini Cons. (1946–49). In 1964 he was appointed to its faculty. In his music, he followed the modified dodecaphonic techniques as promulgated by Dallapiccola, including triadic constructions. He wrote *New Sounds for Woodwind* (in Eng.; London, 1967; 2nd ed., rev., 1982), demonstrating the possibility of producing simultaneously several pitches on a single woodwind instrument.

WORKS: ORCH.: *Concerto for Orchestra* (1952; Rome, Jan. 18, 1956); *Divertimento* for Chamber Orch. (1953); 2 violin concertos: No. 1 for Violin, Strings, and Harpsichord (San Francisco, Dec. 2, 1957) and No. 2 (1979); *Concertazioni* for Bassoon, Strings, and Percussion (1963; Rome, March 6, 1965); *Memorie* for 3 Guitars and Orch. (1975; Florence, Oct. 7, 1977); *Risonanze* for 18 Instruments and Percussion (1978). **CHAMBER:** *Serenata* for Violin and Guitar (1952); *3 Pieces* for Guitar (1952); *Musica a 5* for Bassoon, Trumpet, Guitar, Violin, and Viola (1953); *Variazioni* for Violin (1957); 2 string quartets (1960,

1979); *Concertazioni* for Oboe, Viola, Guitar, Double Bass, and Percussion (1965); *Andamenti* for Viola (1967); *Collage* for Oboe (1968); *The Hollow Man* for Any Woodwind (1968); *Concertazioni a quattro* for Flute, Oboe, Clarinet, and Bassoon (1969); *Collage* for Bassoon (1969); *Sinaulodia* for 4 Flutes (1969); *Cantilena* for Flute (1970); *Musica per Piero* for 2 Violas (1971); *Auser* for Oboe and Guitar (1973); *Collage* for Clarinet (1973); *Concertazioni* for Clarinet, Horn, Trumpet, Trombone, Guitar, Viola, Cello, Double Bass, and Percussion (1973); *Repitu* for Flute, Viola, Guitar, and Percussion (1975); *Per Olga* for Flute (1976); *The Solitary* for English Horn and Percussion (1976); *Adles* for Guitar (1977); *Atma* for 3 Groups of Solo Instruments (1978). **VOCAL:** *Sentimento del sogno* for Soprano and Orch. (1952); *Immagine* for Soprano and 17 Instruments (1959); *Tres recuerdos del cielo* for Soprano and 10 Instruments (1967; Vienna, Sept. 11, 1968).—NS/LK/DM

Bartoš, Jan Zdeněk, Czech composer; b. Dvůr Králové nad Labem, June 4, 1908; d. Prague, June 1, 1981. He played the violin as a youth, then took composition lessons with Šín and Křička at the Prague Cons., graduating in 1943. He earned his living playing in dance orchs. From 1945 to 1956 he was a member of the Music Section of the Ministry of Education and Culture. In 1958 he was appointed a teacher of composition at the Prague Cons. In his music, he followed the national traditions of the Czech school.

WORKS: DRAMATIC: Opera: *Rýparka* (Ripar's Wife; 1949); *Prokletý zámek* (The Accursed Castle; 1949); *Útok na nebe* (The Attack of Heaven; 1953–54). **Operetta:** *Je libo ananas?* (Do You Like Pineapples?; 1956). **Ballet:** *Hanuman* (1941); *Mirella* (1956); *Král manéžž* (King of the Manege; 1963). **ORCH.:** *Song of St. Matthias*, symphonic poem (1945); 7 syms.: No. 1 (1949–52), No. 2, *da camera* (1956), No. 3, *Giocosa*, for Strings (1964–65), No. 4, *Concertante*, for Oboe d'Amore and Strings (1968), No. 5 for Wind Orch. (1973–74), No. 6 for Wind Quartet and Strings (1977), and No. 7, *Brevis* (1978); *Intermezzo* (1961); *Concerto da camera* for Oboe and Strings (1963); 2 viola concertos (1963, 1970); *Fantasy* for Flute and Orch. (1964); *Inventions* for Bass Clarinet and Strings (1966); Concerto for Accordion and Strings (1966); Horn Concerto (1967); Concerto for Violin and Strings (1970); Concerto-Sym. for Violin and String Orch. (1973); *Fantasy* for Organ and Strings (1975); *Concerto per due Boemi* for Bass Clarinet, Piano, and Strings (1975); Concerto for Violin, Viola, and Strings (1976); *Music* for String Quartet and Orch. (1976); *Rhapsody* for Cello and Strings (1979). **CHAMBER:** Cello Sonata (1938); 2 nonets (1939, 1974); 11 string quartets (1940, 1946, 1948, 1951, 1952, 1956, 1960, 1963, 1970, 1971, 1973); *Partita* for Viola (1944); 3 wind quintets (1946–63); Quintet for Flute, Harp, Viola, Cello, and Guitar (1947); 17 divertimentos for various combinations of instruments (1956–79); Trio for Violin, Viola, and Harp (1961); Double Bass Sonata (1962); *Suite concertante* for Viola, Double Bass, and 9 Wind Instruments (1964); String Trio (1967); 4 piano trios (1968, 1969, 1971, 1979); Sextet for 2 Oboes, English Horn, 2 Bassoons, and Harp (1976); Trombone Sonata (1978); Trio for Viola, Clarinet, and Piano (1980). **Piano:** 2 sonatas (1953, 1959). **VOCAL:** Cantatas; choruses; songs, including *Sonnets of Prague* for Narrator, Tenor, Harp, and String Orch. (1966).—NS/LK/DM

Baryphonus, Henricus (real name, **Heinrich Pipegrop**), German music theorist and composer; b. Wernigerode, Harz, Sept. 17, 1581; d. Quedlinburg, Saxe-Anhalt, Jan. 13, 1655. He studied at the Lateinschule in his native town, and then continued his education at the Univ. of Helmstedt. In 1605 he went to Quedlinburg, where he became cantor at St. Benedicti and a teacher at the Gymnasium; from 1606 was Subkonrector there. He wrote some 17 treatises on music, but only his *Pleiades musicae, quae in certas sectiones distributae praecipuas quaestiones musicas discutiunt* (Halberstadt, 1615) is extant. Only two of his compositions survive.—NS/LK/DM

Barzin, Leon (Eugene), Belgian-born American conductor and teacher; b. Brussels, Nov. 27, 1900; d. Naples, Fla., April 29, 1999. He was taken to the U.S. in 1902 and in 1924 he became a naturalized American citizen. He studied violin with his father and in Belgium with Ysaÿe. In 1919 he became a violist in the N.Y. Phil., where he was principal violist from 1925 to 1929. In 1929 he became asst. conductor of the American Orchestral Soc. in N.Y., which was reorganized as the National Orchestral Assn. in 1930 with Barzin as its music director, a position he held until 1958 and again from 1970 to 1976. Under his leadership, it became an outstanding training ensemble. He also served as music director of the Hartford (Conn.) Sym. Orch. (1938–40), the Ballet Soc. of N.Y. (1947–48), and the N.Y. City Ballet (1948–58). He was a conductor of the Pasdeloup Orch. and a teacher at the Schola Cantorum in Paris (1958–60). In 1960 he was made a member of the Légion d'honneur of France.—NS/LK/DM

Barzun, Jacques (Martin), eminent French-born American historian and educator; b. Créteil, Nov. 30, 1907. He settled in N.Y. and became a naturalized American citizen in 1933. He was educated at Columbia Univ. (A.B., 1927; M.A., 1928; Ph.D., 1932). After serving as a lecturer (1927–29), asst. prof. (1938–42), and assoc. prof. (1942–45) on its faculty, he was a prof. (1945–67), dean of graduate studies (1955–58), and dean of faculties and provost (1958–67) there. In 1967 he was made prof. emeritus. From 1975 to 1993 he also was literary advisor to the publishing firm Charles Scribner's Sons. He was a member of the American Academy and Inst. of Arts and Letters, serving as its president (1972–75; 1977–78). He also was a Chevalier de la Légion d'honneur of France. Among his books dealing with various aspects of music were *Darwin, Marx, Wagner: Critique of a Heritage* (Boston, 1941; rev. ed., 1958), *Berlioz and the Romantic Century* (2 vols., Boston, 1950; 3rd ed., rev., 1969), *Music in American Life* (N.Y., 1956), and *Critical Questions on Music and Letters, Culture and Biography, 1940–1980* (N.Y., 1982).

BIBL.: D. Weiner and W. Keylor, eds., *From Parnassus: Essays in Honor of J. B.* (N.Y., 1976).—NS/LK/DM

Bashkirov, Dmitri (Alexandrovich), Russian pianist and pedagogue; b. Tbilisi, Nov. 1, 1931. He studied in Moscow with Goldenweiser. In 1955 he won second prize in the Long-Thibaud Competition in Paris and in 1970 the Schumann Competition in Zwickau. From 1957 he taught at the Moscow Cons., and also at the Kiev Cons. from 1968. His repertoire ranged from the classics to contemporary scores.—NS/LK/DM

Bashmet, Yuri, outstanding Russian violist; b. Rostov-na-Donu, Jan. 24, 1953. He began his training in Lwów, and then was a student of Borisovski and Druyinine at the Moscow Cons. After winning second prize in the Budapest International Competition in 1975, and first prize in the Munich International Competition in 1976, he pursued a career as a viola virtuoso. In addition to engagements as a soloist with the world's foremost orchs., he also toured widely as a recitalist. In 1984 he founded the Moscow Soloists; also taught at the Moscow Cons. Bashmet's authoritative performances have placed him among the foremost masters of his instrument. He has done much to encourage new works for viola by championing scores by Denisov, Schnittke, and Pettersson.—NS/LK/DM

Basie, Count (real name, **William**), seminal big-band leader, pianist; b. Red Bank, N.J., Aug. 21, 1904; d. Hollywood, Calif., April 26, 1984. His mother was a pianist, but Basie originally played drums in a local kids' band. He later concentrated on piano, taking regular lessons from a local teacher and receiving some instruction from Fats Waller. He worked summers in Asbury Park and played at Leroy's in N.Y. He performed briefly with June Clark's Band and Elmer Snowden, then began a long spell of touring theatres and accompanying variety acts, including Kate Crippen and Her Kids and the Hippity Hop Show. Basie spent two years with the Gonzelle White Show, leaving it in Kansas City in 1927, where he remained; after a serious illness, he began accompanying the Whitman Sisters and working in local theatres. He joined Walter Page's Blue Devils in Dallas in July 1928, remaining with them about a year, and then played briefly with Elmer Payne and his Ten Royal Americans during the summer of 1929. He then joined Bennie Moten's Band; he left Moten early in 1934 to lead own band (under Moten's auspices) in Little Rock, Ark.; he later rejoined Bennie Moten and, after that leader's death in 1935, continued to work for a short time under Buster Moten's leadership. He returned to Kansas City where he worked as a soloist, and then with his own trio, before jointly leading the Barons of Rhythm with altoist Buster Smith. Under Basie's leadership, the band broadcast over Station WSXBY from their residency at the Reno Club, Kansas City; from that time, Bill Basie was dubbed "Count." John Hammond heard the band and initiated their first national tour, which required Basie to expand to a larger group. The band left Kansas City, took up a short residency at the Grand Terrace, Chicago, played at the Vendome Hotel, Buffalo, then into Roseland, N.Y. (December 1936). During the following year, the band was reshuffled and achieved wide success after its residency at Savoy Ballroom, N.Y. in January 1938; this success was consolidated during their stay at The Famous Door from January 1938–January 1939. The band then played in Chicago for six months before returning to N.Y.; afterwards, they left for West Coast engagements in the fall of 1939.

Throughout the 1940s, the Basie Band appeared at most of the major ballrooms and theatres throughout the U.S. Basie also recorded with the Benny Goodman Sextet and made many solo appearances on various radio programs. The Basie Band was featured, along with Mary Lou Williams and Teddy Wilson, at a Fats Waller Memorial concert held at Cafe Society Uptown on Dec. 21, 1943. The band was featured in numerous films during their several Hollywood residencies, among them *Top Man, Choo-Choo Swing, Reveille with Beverly, Stage Door Canteen, Hit Parade of 1943*, and *Made in Paris* (1966). In January 1950, Basie disbanded the big band due to financial problems and began touring with a small band starting in April of that year; they accompanied Billie Holiday at one point. He reformed the big band regularly in 1952, touring Scandinavia (1954) and Europe (1956). Basie did his first tour of Great Britain in April 1957, then returned later that year to play a command performance for the Queen; from then on, he made regular tours of Europe. The "new testament" band (as it was dubbed by Basie biographer Albert Murray) was very successful, notably after vocalist Joe Williams joined; they had hits with "April in Paris" (1956) and with the album *Chairman of the Board* (1960). During 1963, the band toured Japan. From the mid-1960s, the Basie Band frequently toured and recorded with various vocalists, including Frank Sinatra and Tony Bennett. In 1976, Basie suffered a heart attack, but after a period of recuperation, returned to an active career. In 1981, he received the Kennedy Center honors for achievement in the performing arts; at a White House reception that followed, President Ronald Reagan said that Count Basie had revolutionized jazz. In 1985, Reagan awarded him the Medal of Freedom (posth.).

Count Basie's band had a powerful groove that was partly due to his taste as a leader and editor (though not composer) of arrangements. He was a technically accomplished pianist, as he demonstrated on early recordings, but he chose to solo in a sly, concise, and witty style. He was as natural leader, firm but funny and warm, and was one of the most beloved figures in jazz. Billy Mitchell likes to tell about the time that he chided Basie in the middle of a solo for playing a wrong note on the piano. Basie responded "It don't matter none," and kept playing; a half-chorus later, he added, "But if you play one like it, you're fired." After Basie's death, the band continued under various leaders. Thad Jones first took the reins in 1985, but he died soon after in early 1986; he was replaced by Frank Foster, who led the band for nearly a decade until 1995, and then Grover Mitchell took over.

DISC.: *At the Chatterbox* (1937); "One O'Clock Jump" (1937); "Jumpin' at the Woodside," "Good Morning Blues," "Rock-A-Bye Basie," "Jive at Five" (all 1938); *At the Famous Door* (1938); *Lester Leaps In* (1939); *Broadway* (1940); *One Night Stand with Count Basie and His Orch.* (1944); *V Discs, Vol. 1, 2* (1945); *The King, Rambo* (1947); *At Birdland, Vol. 1, 2* (1953); *Swings with Joe Williams* (1955); *April in Paris* (1955); *In London* (1956); *Basie Roars Again!* (1956); *Count Basie at Newport* (1957); *Complete Roulette Studio Count* (1957); *Atomic Mr. Basie* (1957); *Sing Along with Basie* (1958); *Basie Plays Hefti* (1958); *Everyday I Have the Blues* (1959); *Chairman of the Board* (1959); *Basie: Eckstine* (1959); *Basie Swings, Bennett Sings* (1959); *Kansas City Suite: The Music of Benny Carter* (1960); *Chairman of the Board* (1960); *Legend* (1961); *The Count Basie Story* (1961); *First Time! The Count Meets the Duke* (1961); *Basie at Birdland* (1961); *Complete Roulette Live Recordings* (c. 1961); *Sinatra–Basie* (1962); *On My Way and Shoutin' Again* (1962); *Live in Sweden* (1962); *Lil' Ol' Groovemaker* (1962); *Kansas City 7* (1962); *Ella and Basie!* (1963); *Our Shining Hour* (1965); *Basie's Beat* (1965); *Straight Ahead* (1967); *Afrique* (1970); *Bosses* (1973); *Satch and Josh* (1974); *For the First Time* (1974); *Kansas City 3: For the Second Time* (1975); *Fun Time* (1975); *Basie and Zoot* (1975); *Basie Jam at Montreux '75* (1975); *Satch and Josh...Again* (1977); *Prime Time* (1977); *Gifted Ones* (1977); *Basie Jam: Montreux '77* (1977); *Live in Japan* (1978); *Milt Jackson and C. B., Vol. 1* (1978); *C. B. Meets Oscar Peterson* (1978); *On the Road* (1979); *Milt Jackson and C. B., Vol. 2* (1979); *Warm Breeze* (1981); *Kansas City 6* (1981); *Farmers Market Barbecue* (1982); *88 Basie Street* (1983). Moten: "Small Black" (1929); "Moten Swing" (1932).

WRITINGS.: With A. Murray, *Good Morning Blues: The Autobiography of Count Basie* (N.Y., 1985).

BIBL.: A. Morgan, *Count Basie* (Spellmount, N.Y., 1984). —JC/LP

Basile, Andreana, famous Italian contralto and instrumentalist, mother of **Leonora Baroni;** b. Posilipo, c. 1580; d. Rome, c. 1640. She attracted the public by her extraordinary beauty and became known as "la bella Adriana." She often accompanied herself on the harp and guitar. In Naples she married Muzio Baroni, a Calabrian nobleman. In 1610 she was engaged by the court of Vincenzo Gonzaga, the Duke of Mantua, remaining a principal singer at his court until 1624. She was praised by Monteverdi for her musicianship. In 1633 she settled in Rome.—NS/LK/DM

Basili, Francesco, Italian conductor and composer; b. Loreto, Jan. 31, 1767; d. Rome, March 25, 1850. He studied with his father, Andrea Basili, with Giovanni Battista Borghi, and at the Accademia di Santa Cecilia in Rome with Jannaconi. After conducting in Foligno, Macerata, and Loreto, he served as director of the Milan Cons. (1827–37) and maestro di cappella at St. Peter's in Rome (from 1837).

WORKS: DRAMATIC: O p e r a : *La bella incognita* (Rome, Carnival 1788); *La Locandiera* (Rome, Carnival 1789); *Il ritorno di Ulisse* (Florence, Sept. 1, 1798); *Achille all'assedio di Troia* (Florence, Dec. 26, 1798); *Antigona* (Venice, Dec. 5, 1799); *Conviene adattarsi* (Venice, 1801); *L'unione mal pensata* (Venice, Dec. 27, 1801); *Lo stravagante e il dissipatore* (Venice, 1805); *L'ira di Achille* (Venice, Jan. 30, 1817); *L'orfana egiziana* (Venice, Jan. 1818); *Gl'Illinesi* (Milan, Jan. 26, 1819); *Il califfo e la schiava* (Milan, Aug. 21, 1819); *Isaura e Ricciardo* (Rome, Jan. 29, 1820). **OTHER:** Syms.; Piano Concerto; chamber music; numerous sacred works, including oratorios, masses, Magnificats, Psalms, motets, offertories, and cantatas.—NS/LK/DM

Basilides, Mária, Hungarian contralto; b. Jolsva, Nov. 11, 1886; d. Budapest, Sept. 26, 1946. She was a student of József Sík at the Budapest Academy of Music. In 1911 she made her debut in Nougues's *Quo vadis?* at the opening of the Budapest Municipal Theatre, and sang there until 1915. From 1915 until her death she was a member of the Budapest Opera. She also sang in various other European music centers and made frequent appearances as a concert artist, becoming especially known for her idiomatic performances of Bartók and Kodály. Her operatic repertoire was extensive, ranging from Monteverdi to contemporary scores. She was especially admired for her portrayals of roles in operas by Verdi and Wagner.

BIBL.: J. Molnár, *B. M.* (Budapest, 1967).—NS/LK/DM

Basiola, Mario, Italian baritone; b. Annico, July 12, 1892; d. there, Jan. 3, 1965. He was a pupil of Cotogni in Rome. In 1918 he made his operatic debut, and then sang in Barcelona (1920) and Florence (1921) before appearing with the San Carlo Opera Co. in the U.S. (1923–25). On Nov. 11, 1925, he made his Metropolitan Opera debut in N.Y. as Amonasro, remaining on its roster until 1932; he then sang at Milan's La Scala and in Rome (1933–38), and at London's Covent Garden (1939). In 1946 he toured Australia, where he taught until 1951; then settled in Milan as a voice teacher. Among his prominent roles were Rossini's Figaro, Valentin, Iago, Rigoletto, and Scarpia.—NS/LK/DM

Bassani (Bassano, Bassiani), Giovanni Battista, Italian composer, organist, and violinist; b. Padua, c. 1647; d. Bergamo, Oct. 1, 1716. He studied with Legrenzi and Castrovillari in Venice; in 1667 he became a member of the funereally named Accademia della Morte in Ferrara, serving as organist and composer. On July 3, 1677, he became a member of the more cheerful Accademia Filarmonica in Bologna; also served as maestro di cappella and organist of the apocalyptic Confraternita del Finale in Modena (1677–80). In 1680 he became maestro di cappella to the Duke of Mirandola; in 1682 he was appointed principe of the Accademia Filarmonica; in 1683 and 1684 he was maestro di cappella of the Accademia della Morte. In 1687 he was named maestro di cappella of the Ferrara Cathedral, and in 1712 at S. Maria Maggiore in Bergamo; also taught at the music school of the Congregazione di Carita there. He is known to have written at least nine operas, but these are lost; only a few arias from his opera *Gli amori alla moda* (Ferrara, 1688) have survived. Some 15 oratorios have been attributed to him, but these are also lost; however, the texts to three have survived. He also composed masses and other sacred works, secular vocal pieces, and instrumental works, all of which were publ. in his day.—NS/LK/DM

Bassano (also Bassani), Giovanni, Italian violinist, cornet player, singer, and composer; b. 1560 or 1561; d. Venice, Aug. 16, 1617. He learned to play the violin and the cornet. He pursued his career in Venice, where he became a member of the instrumental ensemble at San Marco. He also became a singer (1585) and a teacher (1595) at the seminary there. From 1601 he was in charge of the instrumental ensemble at the Basilica. His writings on ornamentation greatly influenced composers of the Venetian school. As a composer, he excelled in composing motets.

WORKS (all publ. in Venice): **VOCAL: Sacred:** *Motetti per concerti ecclesiastici* for 5 to 8 and 12 Voices (1598); *Concerti ecclesiastici, libro secondo* for 5 to 8 and 12 Voices (1599). **Secular:** *Fantasie per cantar et sonar con ogni sorte d'istrumenti* (1585); *Canzonette* for 4 Voices (1587); *Il fiore dei capricci musicali per sonar ogni sorte di stromenti* for 4 Voices

(1588); *Motetti, madrigali et canzone francese di diversi eccelolenti autori* for 4 to 6 Voices (1591); *Madrigali et canzonette concertate per potersi cantare con il basso & soprno nel liuto & istrumente da pen a con passaggi a ciascuna parte...libro primo* (1602).
—NS/LK/DM

Bassett, Leslie (Raymond), distinguished American composer and teacher; b. Hanford, Calif., Jan. 22, 1923. He received training in piano. He played the trombone in jazz combos, and also was a trombonist during his military service, playing in the 13th Armored Division Band. He then enrolled in Fresno (Calif.) State Coll. (B.A., 1947), and later studied composition with Finney at the Univ. of Mich. (M.M., 1949; D.M., 1956). He also took private lessons with Honegger and Boulanger in Paris in 1950. In 1952 he was appointed to the faculty of the Univ. of Mich., where he was made a prof. in 1965 and was chairman of the composition dept. (1970–85). In 1977 he became the Albert A. Stanley Distinguished Univ. Prof. of Music there, retiring in 1992. He held the American Prix de Rome (1961–63), and received the National Inst. of Arts and Letters Award in 1964. In 1966 he received the Pulitzer Prize in Music for his *Variations* for Orch. He held a Guggenheim fellowship in 1973–74 and again in 1980–81. In 1981 he became a member of the American Academy and Inst. of Arts and Letters. In 1988 he held a Rockefeller Foundation grant for study at its Villa Serbelloni in Bellagio, Italy. In his music, Bassett pursues the ideal of structural logic within the judicial limits of the modern school of composition, with some serial elements discernible in his use of thematic rhythms and motivic periodicity.

WORKS: ORCH.: *5 Movements* (1961; Rome, July 5, 1962); *Variations* (Rome, July 6, 1963); *Colloquy* (1968; Fresno, Calif., May 23, 1969); *Forces* (1972; Des Moines, May 1, 1973); *Echoes from an Invisible World* (1974–75; Philadelphia, Feb. 27, 1976); Concerto for 2 Pianos and Orch. (1976; Midland, Mich., April 30, 1977); *Concerto lirico* for Trombone and Orch. (1983; Toledo, Ohio, April 6, 1984); *From a Source Evolving* (1985; Midland, Mich., Nov. 1, 1986); *Concerto for Orchestra* (1991; Detroit, Feb. 6, 1992); *Thoughts That Sing, Breathe and Burn* (1995; Detroit, Feb. 27, 1997); Alto Saxophone Concerto (1999; Montreal, July 5, 2000). **Band and Wind Ensembles:** *Designs, Images, and Textures* (1964; Ithaca, N.Y., April 28, 1965); *Sounds, Shapes, and Symbols* (1977; Ann Arbor, March 17, 1978); *Concerto grosso* (1982; Ann Arbor, Feb. 4, 1983); *Colors and Contours* (1984; Boulder, Colo., March 1, 1985); *Lullaby for Kirsten* (Ann Arbor, Oct. 4, 1985); *Fantasy* for Clarinet and Wind Ensemble (1986; Ann Arbor, Oct. 2, 1987); *Wood and Reed Transformed* for Bassoon and Wind Ensemble (1998; Ann Arbor, Feb. 12, 1999). **CHAMBER:** 4 string quartets (1951, 1957, 1962, 1978); Horn Sonata (1952); Trio for Viola, Clarinet, and Piano (1953); Quintet for 2 Violins, Viola, Cello, and Double Bass (1954); Viola Sonata (1956); *5 Pieces for String Quartet* (1957); Woodwind Quintet (1958); Violin Sonata (1959); Quintet for 2 Violins, Viola, Cello, and Piano (1962); *Music* for Cello and Piano (1966); Nonet (1967); *Music* for Alto Saxophone and Piano (1968); Sextet for 2 Violins, 2 Violas, Cello, and Piano (1971); *Sounds Remembered* for Violin and Piano (1972); *Wind Music* for Wind Sextet (1975); Sextet for Flutes, Clarinets, and Strings (1979); Trio for Violin, Clarinet, and Piano (1980); *Concerto da camera* for Trumpet and Chamber Ensemble (1981); Duo Concertante for Alto Saxophone and Piano (1984); *Dialogues* for Oboe and Piano (1987);

Brass Quintet (1988); *Duo-Inventions* for 2 Cellos (1988); *Illuminations* for Flute and Piano (1989); *Arias* for Clarinet and Piano (1992); *Narratives* for Guitar Quartet (1993); *Song and Dance* for Tuba and Piano (1993); *Trio-Inventions* for 3 Cellos (1996); *Equale* for 3 Trombones (1996). **KEYBOARD: P i a n o :** *6 Pieces* (1951); *Mobile* (1961); *Elaborations* (1966); (7) *Preludes* (1984); (5) *Configurations* (1987). **O r g a n :** *Voluntaries* (1958); *4 Statements* (1964); *Liturgies* (1980). **VOCAL:** *For City, Nation, World,* cantata for Chorus, Optional Children, Tenor, 4 Trombones, Organ, and Congregation (1959; Buffalo, Feb. 21, 1960); *Moonrise* for Women's Voices and 10 Instruments (1960); *Eclogue, Encomium, and Evocation* for Women's Voices, Piano, Harp, and 2 Percussion (1962); *Prayers for Divine Service* for Men's Voices and Organ (1965); *Notes in the Silence* for Chorus and Piano (1966); *Collect* for Soprano and Tape (1969); *Moon Canticle* for Amplified Speaker, Soprano, Chorus, and Cello (1969); *Celebration in Praise of Earth* for Amplified Speaker, Chorus, and Orch. (1970; Berea, Ohio, Oct. 14, 1971); *Time and Beyond* for Baritone, Clarinet, Cello, and Piano (1973); *A Ring of Emeralds* for Chorus and Piano (1979); *Pierrot Songs* for Soprano, Flute, Clarinet, Violin, Cello, and Piano (1988); *Almighty, Eternal* for Chorus and Organ (1990); *Maker of Our Being* for Chorus and Organ (1993); *2 Stephens Songs* for Baritone and Piano (1996–98). **ELECTRONIC:** *3 Studies in Electronic Sound* (1965); *Triform* (1966). **BIBL.:** E. Johnson, *L. B.: A Bio-Bibliography* (Westport, Conn., 1994).—**NS/LK/DM**

Bassey, Shirley, soulful English diva with a brass band of a voice; b. Tiger Bay, Cardiff, Wales, Jan. 8, 1937. Shirley Bassey was the youngest of seven children in a black family living in a largely white area of Cardiff. Bassey's father left when she was two and she never saw him again, nor did she feel anything in common with her brothers and sisters. Her only solace was her incredibly powerful singing voice that she discovered as a young girl.

By age 14, she was singing at "working men's clubs" on weekends. By 16 she was touring with variety shows throughout the U.K. By 1957, she was in working in the London theater, as part of the revue *Such Is Life*. That year she cut a version of "The Banana Boat Song," already a hit for Harry Belafonte. This started a series of English hits. Her output ranged from theater hits like "As Long As He Needs Me" (from *Oliver*) and "Climb Every Mountain" (from *The Sound of Music*) to the Beatles's "Something." From the early 1960s through the mid-1970s, Bassey was a presence on the English charts.

Bassey's only real hit in America was the theme from the 1965 James Bond film *Goldfinger* (#5), but by then she already had a club following in the U.S. and a huge following nearly everywhere else. She subsequently recorded the themes to two more Bond films, but without enjoying the same chart success.

Bassey has retired nearly as many times as David Bowie, withdrawing to her Swiss retreat; however, she always seems available for the big-ticket concert, TV special, or recording opportunity. These included her 1987 team-up with Yello on "The Rhythm Divine." A decade later, she recorded "History Repeating" with the Propellerheads. The song appeared in the film *Something About Mary* and was also used in an automobile advertisement. Her live shows are lavish affairs, full of extravagant gowns and sets. In a 1998 poll asking "Who is your favorite recording artist?" in the British magazine *MOJO*, she bested the likes of Neil Diamond, Barbra Streisand, Whitney Houston, Bruce Springsteen, Led Zeppelin, Ella Fitzgerald, and Tina Turner.

DISC.: *I'm in the Mood for Love* (1981); *Power of Love* (1992); *Shirley Bassey Sings the Songs of Andrew Lloyd Webber* (1994); *Goldsinger—Best Of* (1995); *Birthday Concert* (1997); *Great Shirley Bassey* (1997); *Original Gold* (1999).—**HB**

Bassi, Amedeo (Vittorio), Italian tenor; b. Montespertoli, near Florence, July 20, 1874; d. Florence, Jan. 14, 1949. He was a pupil of Pavesi in Florence, where he made his operatic debut in 1897 in Marchetti's *Ruy Blas*. He then sang in various Italian opera houses. In 1902 he made his first tour of South America, and in 1908 sang Radamès at the opening of the new Teatro Colón in Buenos Aires. On Dec. 19, 1906, he made his U.S. debut in that same role at N.Y.'s Manhattan Opera House, remaining on its roster until 1908. In 1907 he made his first appearance at London's Covent Garden, and also made appearances with the Chicago Grand Opera Co. (1910–16). He made his Metropolitan Opera debut in N.Y. on March 2, 1911, as Ramerrez in *La Fanciulla del West*. After singing at Milan's La Scala (1921–26), he retired from the operatic stage and sang widely in concerts. He also taught in Florence. His most famous student was Ferruccio Tagliavini. Bassi was particularly known for his roles in Italian operas, but he also sang such Wagnerian roles as Loge, Siegfried, and Parsifal. He created the roles of Lionello in Mascagni's *Amica* (Monte Carlo, March 16, 1905) and Angel Clare in d'Erlanger's *Tess* (Naples, April 10, 1906).—**NS/LK/DM**

Bassi, Carolina Manna, greatly esteemed Italian contralto; b. Naples, Jan. 10, 1781; d. Cremona, Dec. 12, 1862. She was the daughter of the comic bass Giovanni Bassi. With her brother, the comic bass Nicola Bassi (1767–1825), she began her career in her father's company of Raggazi Napoletani at the Teatro San Carlo in Naples in 1789. She subsequently pursued a distinguished career, creating major roles in Meyerbeer's *Semiramide riconosciuta* (Turin, March 1819), *Margherita d'Angiù* (Milan, Nov. 14, 1820), and *L'Esule di Granata* (Milan, March 12, 1821), in Rossini's *Bianca e Falliero, ossia Il consiglio dei tre* (Milan, Dec. 26, 1819), and in operas by Pacini and Mercadante. After retiring from the operatic stage in 1828, she appeared in concerts. —**NS/LK/DM**

Bassi, Luigi, Italian baritone; b. Pesaro, Sept. 4, 1766; d. Dresden, Sept. 13, 1825. He studied with Pietro Morandi in Senigallia, making his debut in Pesaro at the age of 13. He then sang in Florence, and in 1784 went to Prague, where he soon became greatly appreciated. Mozart wrote the part of Don Giovanni for him and heeded his advice in matters of detail. Bassi was in Vienna from 1806 to 1814, then briefly in Prague. In 1815 he joined an Italian opera company in Dresden. —**NS/LK/DM**

Bassini, Achille de
See **De Bassini, Achille**

Bastiaans, Johannes Gijsbertus, Dutch organist and composer; b. Wilp, Oct. 31, 1812; d. Haarlem, Feb. 16, 1875. He studied organ in Deventer and then was a pupil of C.F. Hommert in Rotterdam. He continued his training in Dessau with R. Rümpler (organ) and F. Schneider (organ and theory), and then in Leipzig with C.F. Becker (organ) and Mendelssohn (composition). He served as organist in Deventer (1838–40) and at Amsterdam's Zuiderkerk (1840–58), then was municipal organist in Haarlem (from 1858), where he also was organist at St. Bavo's (from 1868). He championed the music of J.S. Bach. His own works include organ pieces and chorales. He also wrote a treatise on harmony (1867).
BIBL.: J. ten Bokum, *J.G. B. (1812–1875)* (Amsterdam, 1971).—**NS/LK/DM**

Bastianelli, Giannotto, Italian pianist, music critic, and composer; b. San Domenico di Fiesole, June 20, 1883; d. (suicide) Tunis, Sept. 22, 1927. He was mainly autodidact as a musician. After contributing to Florence's *La voce* (1909–15), he was music critic of Florence's *La nazione* (1915–18) and Bologna's *Il resto del Carlino* (1919–23).
WORKS: *La scala*, opera (n.d.; unfinished); *Poema* for String Quartet (c. 1910); Piano Quartet (c. 1910); Violin Sonata (1912); Cello Sonata (1920); 5 piano sonatas (1907–17) and other piano music.
WRITINGS: *Pietro Mascagni* (Naples, 1910); *La crisi musicale europea* (Pistoia, 1912; 2ⁿᵈ ed., rev., 1976); *Musicisti d'oggi e di ieri* (Milan, 1914); *Il Parsifal de Wagner* (Florence, 1914); *L'opera e altri saggi di teoria musicale* (Florence, 1921); M. Donadoni, ed., *La musica pura commentari musicali e altri scritti* (Florence, 1974); M. de Angelis, ed., *Il nouovo dio della musica* (Turin, 1978).—**LK/DM**

Bastianini, Ettore, notable Italian baritone; b. Siena, Sept. 24, 1922; d. Sirmione, Jan. 25, 1967. He studied in Florence with Flaminio Contini. In 1945 he made his operatic debut in the bass role of Colline in Ravenna. He made his first appearance at Milan's La Scala as Tiresias in *Oedipus Rex* in 1948. After additional training from Ricciana Bettarini, he made his debut as a baritone in Bologna in the role of Germont père. He sang Andrei in the rev. version of *War and Peace* in Florence in 1953. On Dec. 5, 1953, he made his Metropolitan Opera debut in N.Y. as Germont père, and was on its roster until 1957 and again in 1959–60 and from 1964 to 1966. In 1954 he sang Posa at his first appearance at the Salzburg Festival. That same year, he made his La Scala debut as a baritone in the role of Onegin, and continued to appear there until 1964. In 1956 he made his debut in Chicago as Riccardo in *I Puritani*. He made his first appearance at London's Covent Garden as Renato in 1962. While he was best known for his Verdi roles, especially Rigoletto and Don Carlo, Bastianini also enjoyed success with his portrayals of Amonasro, Escamillo, and Scarpia.
BIBL.: M. Boagno and G. Starone, *E. B.: Una voce di bronzo e di velluto* (Parma, 1991).—**NS/LK/DM**

Bastin, Jules, Belgian bass; b. Pont, Aug. 18, 1933; d. Brussels, Dec. 2, 1996. He was a student of Frédéric Anspach at the Brussels Cons. In 1960 he made his operatic debut in Brussels as Charon in Monteverdi's *L'Orfeo*, and then sang regularly at the Théâtre de la Monnaie there. In 1972 he first sang with the Covent Garden company in London at a Promenade Concert as Balducci in *Benvenuto Cellini*, and returned to London in 1974 to make his stage debut with the company as Baron Ochs. He appeared as the Monk in *Don Carlo* at his Salzburg Festival debut in 1976. In 1979 he sang the role of the Banker in the Paris premiere of the three-act version of Berg's *Lulu*. He also pursued an active concert career. Among his other roles of note were Osmin, Dr. Bartolo, the Grand Inquisitor, and Varlaam. —**NS/LK/DM**

Baston, Josquin, composer who flourished in the mid- 16ᵗʰ century. He most likely was active in the Netherlands. Among his extant works are 12 Latin motets for four to six Voices, 29 chansons for three to six Voices, and six Dutch songs for four Voices. Some of his works were publ. by Phalèse and Susato.—**NS/LK/DM**

Bate, Jennifer (Lucy), esteemed English organist, teacher, and composer; b. London, Nov. 11, 1944. She received training in piano (1947–60), theory (1959–61), and organ (1960–95), attended the Univ. of Bristol (B.A., Honours, 1966), and worked on early music at the Haslemere Festival with Carl Dolmetsch (1979–93). In 1966 she played at Birmingham Town Hall, and in 1969 made her formal London debut at Westminster Abbey. She made her first appearance in Sweden at Uppsala Cathedral and in France at Notre-Dame Cathedral in Paris in 1970. Following her Italian debut at the Abbey of Vallanbrosa, near Florence, in 1973, she toured widely in Australia and New Zealand in 1974. That year, she also made her first appearance at the London Sir Henry Wood Promenade Concerts at the Royal Albert Hall. She played for the first time in Denmark and Belgium in 1975 as a concert organist, although she had acted as organist in the Church of England in Brussels during the 1960s. In 1976 she made her U.S. debut in Savannah, Ga. After making her German debut at Regensburg Cathedral in 1977, she appeared for the first time in Korea in Seoul in 1978. In 1989 she made her Polish debut in Warsaw at the Autumn Festival. From 1970 she lectured as a guest at colleges and universities worldwide, and from 1977 she gave master classes in organ on a similar basis. She also was a consultant in the restoration and construction of organs from 1975. Bate's repertoire is exhaustive, beginning with early music and extending to contemporary scores. She has played numerous concertos and has surveyed the complete organ works of such diverse masters as Liszt, Franck, and Messiaen, with whom she worked from 1975 until his death in 1992. Among composers who have dedicated works to her are Flor Peeters, William Mathias, and Peter Dickinson. Her own organ works comprise the *Toccata on a Theme of Martin Shaw* (1972), *4 Reflections* (1981–86),

Introduction and Variations on an Old French Carol (1982), *Homage to 1685* (1985), *Il filatoio* (1988), *Canone Inglese* (1996), *Lament* (1997), and *Variations on a Gregorian Theme* (1997).—NS/LK/DM

Bate, Stanley (Richard), English composer and pianist; b. Plymouth, Dec. 12, 1911; d. (suicide) London, Oct. 19, 1959. He studied composition with Vaughan Williams, Morris, and Jacob and piano with Benjamin at the Royal Coll. of Music in London (1932–36), and then pursued composition training with Boulanger in Paris and Hindemith in Berlin. He toured widely as a pianist. In 1938 he married **Peggy Glanville-Hicks;** they divorced in 1948. He wrote music in a finely structured cosmopolitan manner, making use of modern devices but observing the classical forms and shunning doctrinaire systems.

WORKS: DRAMATIC: B a l l e t : *Eros* (1935); *Goyescas* (1937); *Perseus* (1938); *Cap over Mill* (1938); *Highland Fling* (1947); *Troilus and Cressida* (1948); *Dance Variations* (1948). O t h e r : Music for plays and films. ORCH.: 4 syms., including No. 3 (1940; Cheltenham, July 14, 1954) and No. 4 (London, Nov. 20, 1955); 2 sinfoniettas; 3 piano concertos; 3 violin concertos; Viola Concerto (1946); *Concerto grosso* for Piano and Strings (1952); Harpsichord Concerto (1953); Cello Concerto (1953). CHAMBER: Flute Sonata; 2 string quartets; Violin Sonata; Oboe Sonata; 2 piano sonatas and other pieces. VOCAL: Songs. —NS/LK/DM

Bates, Leon, black American pianist; b. Philadelphia, Nov. 3, 1949. He began studying piano and violin when he was 6, and at 7 he gave his first piano recital in Philadelphia. From 1962 to 1967 he was a pupil of Irene Beck at the Philadelphia Settlement Music School; subsequently was a student of Natalie Hinderas at the Esther Boyer Coll. of Music at Temple Univ. in Philadelphia. In 1969 he won the senior student audition of the Philadelphia Orch., and in 1970 he made a highly successful debut with that orch. under Ormandy's direction as soloist in Ravel's G Minor Concerto. In later seasons, he appeared as a soloist with various orchs., as a recitalist, and as a chamber music artist. While blessed with a virtuoso technique, Bates is also capable of the most refined playing. His repertoire is one of great diversity, ranging from the classics to the moderns. He has made a special effort to program works outside the mainstream, including 19th and 20th century American scores, jazz, and works by black and women composers. In 1992 he was soloist in the premiere of Hailstorck's First Piano Concerto.—NS/LK/DM

Bates, William, English composer who flourished in the second half of the 18th century. He wrote popular English operas in the ballad-opera style. His most popular work was *Flora or Hob in the Well*, which he wrote and arranged in 1760 (Covent Garden, April 25, 1770), using seven of John Hippisley's songs from the 1729 *Flora or Hob's Opera*, together with eight new songs of his own and a new overture. Neither of his works is to be confused with Thomas Doggett's 1711 farce with songs, a forerunner of the true ballad opera, variously titled *The Country Wake or Hob* or *The Country Wake*. His

other stage works are *The Jovial Crew* (1760; altered to *The Ladies Frolick* in 1770); *The Theatrical Candidates* (1775); *The Device, or The Marriage Officer* (1777); *Second Thought Is Best* (1778); also a grand opera, *Pharnaces* (London, Feb. 15, 1765).—NS/LK/DM

Bateson, Thomas, English composer; b. Cheshire County; d. probably in Dublin, March 1630. He was organist at Chester Cathedral from 1599 to 1609. In 1609 he became vicar choral and organist of the Cathedral of the Holy Trinity in Dublin. He is said to have been the first music graduate of Trinity Coll., earning his Mus.B. in 1612 and his M.A. in 1622. As a composer, Bateson is especially noted for his madrigals, although they are regarded as inferior to those by Morley or Weelkes. In 1604 he publ. a collection of 29 madrigals for 3 to 6 voices; it included the madrigal *When Oriana walked to take the ayre*, orig. intended for publication in Morley's *Triumphs of Oriana*. A second set of 30 madrigals was publ. in 1618. Both sets are reprinted in *The English Madrigal School* (vols. 21–22), ed. by E.H. Fellowes. —NS/LK/DM

Bath, Hubert, English composer and conductor; b. Barnstaple, Nov. 6, 1883; d. Harefield, Middlesex, April 24, 1945. He was a pupil of Beringer (piano) and Corder (composition) at the Royal Academy of Music in London. He was active as a conductor of popular orch. and choral concerts.

WORKS: DRAMATIC: O p e r a : *Spanish Student* (1904); *Young England*, comic opera (Birmingham, 1915); *Bubbles* (Belfast, Nov. 26, 1923); *The Sire de Maletroit's Door* (n.d.); *The 3 Strangers* (n.d.); *Trilby* (n.d.). ORCH.: *Midshipman Easy*, overture (1911); *The Visions of Hannele*, symphonic poem (1913; rev. 1920); *African Suite* (n.d.); *Pierrette by the Stream*, suite (n.d.); *Woodland Scenes*, suite (n.d.). OTHER: 7 cantatas, chamber music, and songs.—NS/LK/DM

Bathe, William, Irish writer on musical subjects; b. Dublin, April 2, 1564; d. Madrid, June 17, 1614. He studied at Oxford Univ.; instructed Queen Elizabeth in mnemonics and presented her with an Irish harp of his own design. In 1591 he went to Spain; then was in Flanders, where he entered the Jesuit order in 1596; was ordained in Padua in 1599; returned to Spain in 1601; held the post of spiritual director of the Irish Coll. in Lisbon in 1604; eventually went to Madrid, where he remained until his death. His chief merit as a music theorist lay in fixing definite rules for the placing of accidentals and in changing the system of hexachordal modes to scales based on the octave. He was the author of one of the earliest theoretical works on music, *A Brief Introduction to the True Art of Musicke* (London, 1584), as well as *A Brief Introduction to the Skill of Song* (London, c. 1587).—NS/LK/DM

Báthy, Anna, Hungarian soprano; c. Beregszász, June 13, 1901; d. Budapest, May 20, 1962. She went to Budapest, where she studied at the Academy of Music. In 1928 she made her operatic debut as Elisabeth in *Tannhäuser* at the Municipal Theater. In 1929 she joined the Budapest Opera, where she sang mostly Verdi and Wagner roles.

BIBL.: V. Somogyi and I. Molnár, *B. A.* (Budapest, 1969). —NS/LK/DM

Bátiz (Campbell), Enrique, Mexican conductor; b. Mexico City, May 4, 1942. He commenced piano lessons at an early age and made his first public appearance when he was only five; following studies at the Univ. of Mexico (degree, 1959) and Southern Methodist Univ. in Dallas (1960–62), he continued his training at the Juilliard School of Music in N.Y. (1963–65) and undertook postgraduate work at the Warsaw Cons. In 1969 he made his conducting debut in Mexico City, and in 1971 founded the Orquesta Sinfónica del Estado de México, which developed into one of Mexico's leading orchs. From 1983 to 1990 he was artistic director of the Orquesta Filarmónica de la Ciudad de México; he also served (from 1984) as principal guest conductor of the Royal Phil. of London, which he conducted on a major tour of his homeland in 1988. He again served as conductor of the Orquesta Sinfónica del Estado de México from 1990.—NS/LK/DM

Bâton, Charles, le jeune, French vielle (hurdy-gurdy) player and composer; b. Versailles, date unknown; d. Paris, after 1754. He was the son of Henri Bâton, l'aîne (place and date of birth unknown; d. Versailles, c. 1728), the French luthier and musette (bagpipe) and vielle player. Charles continued his father's efforts in making the musette and vielle concert instruments, and wrote a number of works for them, including suites and sonatas.—LK/DM

Bataille, Charles-Amable, French bass and pedagogue; b. Nantes, Sept. 30, 1822; d. Paris, May 2, 1872. He was a pupil of the younger García at the Paris Cons. On June 22, 1848, he made his operatic debut as Sulpice at the Paris Opéra-Comique. He created roles in operas by Thomas, Adam, Halévy, and Meyerbeer. From 1851 he also taught at the Paris Cons. A throat disorder forced him to quit the operatic stage in 1857, but he then sang again from 1860 until retiring permanently in 1863. He publ. a singing method (two vols., 1861, 1863).

BIBL.: J. Joiner, *C.A. B.: Pioneer in Vocal Sciences and the Teaching of Singing* (Lanham, Md., 1998).—NS/LK/DM

Batten, Adrian, English organist and composer; b. Salisbury (baptized), March 1, 1591; d. London, 1637. He studied at Winchester with the Cathedral organist John Holmes, and in 1614 he went to London as vicar choral of Westminster Abbey. In 1626 he became vicar choral and organist at St. Paul's Cathedral. A prolific composer, he left 15 services and 47 anthems in MS. Some of his pieces are included in Boyce's *Cathedral Music.* A modern reprint of one of his services is included in *The Choir;* several anthems have been publ. by Novello. Batten also transcribed into organ score numerous sacred choral works, some of which have come down to us only through his transcriptions. His organ book is described in *Tudor Church Music* (1922, Vol. II).—NS/LK/DM

Battistini, Gaudenzio, Italian composer, grandson of **Giacomo Battistini;** b. Novara, June 30, 1722; d. there, Feb. 25, 1800. He succeeded his father, Giuseppe Battistini, in 1747 as organist of the chapel of S. Gaudenzio in Novara, and served for more than 50 years until his death. He wrote numerous church works in a highly developed polyphonic style. A biographical sketch and examples of his music are found in Vito Fedeli, *Le cappelle musicali di Novara* in Vol. III of *Istituzioni e monumenti dell'arte musicale italiana* (Milan, 1933). —NS/LK/DM

Battistini, Giacomo, Italian organist and composer, grandfather of **Gaudenzio Battistini;** b. 1665; d. Novara, Feb. 5, 1719. He was maestro di cappella at the Novara Cathedral (1694–1706), then at the church of S. Gaudenzio. He is reputed to have been the first to introduce the violoncello into instrumental accompaniment. He composed several masses, motets, and organ works, and also contributed music to the third act of the drama *Antemio in Roma* (1695; with A. Besozzi and D. Erba). See Vito Fedeli, *Le cappelle musicali di Novara* in Vol. III of *Istituzioni e monumenti dell'arte musicale italiana* (Milan, 1933), containing musical illustrations of his Battistini's works.—NS/LK/DM

Battistini, Mattia, celebrated Italian baritone; b. Rome, Feb. 27, 1856; d. Colle Baccaro, near Rieti, Nov. 7, 1928. He studied with V. Persichini and E. Terziani. On Dec. 11, 1878, he made his operatic debut as Alfonso XI in *La Favorite* at the Teatro Argentino in Rome. In 1883 he made his first appearance at London's Covent Garden as Riccardo in *I Puritani,* and he returned to London regularly until 1906. In 1888 he made his debut at Milan's La Scala as Nélusko. He first sang in St. Petersburg in 1893 as Hamlet, and returned there every season until 1914. He also sang in various other European music centers and in South America to great acclaim. Although he never sang in the U.S., he was acknowledged as the foremost Italian baritone of his time. In 1924 he retired from the operatic stage and then appeared in concerts until his farewell in Graz on Oct. 17, 1927. Battistini was a master of bel canto, with a remarkably expressive high register. His operatic repertoire included over 80 roles, among the most celebrated being those in operas by Bellini and Donizetti. He also was renowned for his portrayals of Rossini's Figaro, Rigoletto, Don Giovanni, Amonasro, Ruslan, Iago, Onegin, Rubinstein's Demon, Scarpia, and the tenor role of Werther.

BIBL.: F. Palmegiani, *M. B. (Il re dei baritone)* (Milan, 1948). —NS/LK/DM

Battle, Kathleen (Deanna), outstanding black American soprano; b. Portsmouth, Ohio, Aug. 13, 1948. She studied with Franklin Bens at the Univ. of Cincinnati Coll.-Cons. of Music (B.Mus., 1970; M.Mus., 1971). After making her professional debut as a soloist in the Brahms *Requiem* at the Spoleto Festival in 1972, she pursued further taining with Italo Tajo in Cincinnati. In 1974 she captured first prize in the WGN-Ill. Opera Guild Auditions of the Air and in 1975 first prize in the

Young Artists Awards in Washington, D.C. In 1975 she made her formal operatic debut as Rosina with the Mich. Opera Theatre in Detroit, and later that year her first appearance at the N.Y. City Opera as Mozart's Susanna. On Dec. 22, 1977, she made her Metropolitan Opera debut in N.Y. as the Shepherd in *Tannhäuser*, and quickly established herself as one of its most esteemed artists via such roles as Massenet's and Strauss's Sophie, Despina, Blondchen, Zerlina, and Pamina. She also appeared with other major opera houses in the U.S. and Europe, and toured extensively as a soloist with leading orchs. and as a recitalist. On June 17, 1985, she made her Covent Garden debut in London as Zerbinetta. In 1987 she appeared as soloist at the New Year's Day Concert of the Vienna Phil. conducted by Karajan, which was telecast throughout the world. Although Battle's vocal gifts were undeniable, she acquired a reputation as an extremely temperamental artist. In Jan. 1993 she quit the Metropolitan Opera's production of *Der Rosenkavalier* during rehearsal. During rehearsal for her starring role in its revival of *La Fille du Régiment* on Feb. 7, 1994, general manager Joseph Volpe found her behavior so objectionable that he summarily dismissed her from the Metropolitan Opera roster. She subsequently pursued an active concert career.—NS/LK/DM

Baud-Bovy, Samuel, Swiss music educator; b. Geneva, Nov. 27, 1906; d. there, Nov. 2, 1986. He studied at the Univ. of Geneva; after studying violin with Closset at the Geneva Cons., conducting with Nilius and music history with Adler in Vienna, composition with Dukas and musicology with Pirro in Paris, and conducting with Weingartner in Basel and Scherchen in Geneva, he returned to the Univ. of Geneva to take his doctorat ès lettres in 1936. He was an orch. teacher (1933–73) and a conductor (1942–73) at the Geneva Cons., where he also served as co-principal (1947–57) and principal (1957–70); was also director of studies (from 1931) and an asst. prof. (from 1942) at the Univ. of Geneva. From 1961 to 1963 he was president of the International Soc. for Music Education. He was an authority on Greek folk music, of which he publ. several collections. In addition to many scholarly articles in music journals, he publ. the books *La chanson populaire grecque du Dodécanèse* (Paris, 1936), *Études sur la chanson cleftique* (Athens, 1958), and *Essai sur la chanson populaire grecque* (Athens, 1983).

BIBL.: R. Brandl and E. Konstantinou, eds., *Griechische Musik und Europa: Antike-Byzanz-Volksmusik der Neuzeit: Im Gedenken an S. B.-B.* (Alano, 1988).—NS/LK/DM

Baudo, Serge (Paul), French conductor, nephew of **Paul Tortelier**; b. Marseilles, July 16, 1927. His father was a prof. of oboe at the Paris Cons. He studied conducting with Fourestier and theory with Jean and Noël Gallon at the Paris Cons., winning premiers prix in harmony, percussion, chamber music, and conducting. After serving as conductor of the orch. of Radio Nice (1959–62), he conducted at the Paris Opéra (1962–65). He held the post of first conductor of the Orchestre de Paris from 1967 to 1970. On Sept. 16, 1970, he made his Metropolitan Opera debut in N.Y. conducting *Les Contes*

d'Hoffmann. He was music director of the Lyons Opéra (1969–71), and then of the Orchestre Philharmonique Rhône-Alpes (later known as the Orchestre National de Lyons) from 1971 to 1987. He was also the founder-artistic director of the Berlioz Festival in Lyons (1979–89).—NS/LK/DM

Baudrier, Yves (Marie), French composer; b. Paris, Feb. 11, 1906; d. there, Nov. 9, 1988. He spent his entire life in Paris. While mainly autodidact as a composer, he studied with the organist of Sacre-Coeur, Georges Loth (1929–33), and received advice from Messiaen (1935) before taking lessons in counterpoint with Daniel-Lesur at the Schola Cantorum. With Messiaen, Jolivet, and Daniel-Lesur, he founded the group Le Jeune France in 1936. He also helped to found the IDHEC (Institut des Hautes Études Cinématographiques), with which he was active from 1945 to 1965. He publ. *L'intelligence et la musique* (Paris, 1950).

WORKS: DRAMATIC: *Treize histoires liées par un fil de flûte,* ballet radiophonique (1967); film scores, including *La Bataille du rail* (1945), *Les Maudits* (1947), *Château de verre* (1950), and *Le Monde de silence* (1955); stage and television music. **ORCH.:** *Le Chant de jeunesse* (1935); *Raz de sein,* symphonic poem (1936): *Le musicien dans la cité* (1936–37; rev. 1947 and 1964); *Eleonora* for Ondes Martenot and Chamber Orch. (1938); Suite for Strings (1938); *Le Grand Voilier,* symphonic poem (1939); Sym. (1944); *Prélude à quelque sortilèges* (1953); *Partition trouvée dans une bouteille* (1963). **CHAMBER:** *Deux Images* for Flute and Piano (1938); 2 string quartets (1940; *Autour de Mallarmé,* 1961); Suite for Trumpet (1966); piano music. **VOCAL:** *Agnus Dei* for Chorus and Organ (1938); *Cantate de la Pentecôte* for Women's Chorus and Small Orch. (1952; in collaboration with M. Constant and M. Rosenthal); *Credo adjuva Domine...* for Chorus and Orch. (1960); many songs.

BIBL.: S. Gut, *Le Groupe Jeune France* (Paris, 1977). —NS/LK/DM

Bauer, Billy (actually, William Henry), cool jazz guitarist; b. N.Y., Nov. 14, 1915. He is remembered for a number of innovative sessions with the Tristano school in the late 1940s and early 1950s. He worked with Jerry Wald's Band (1939), then worked with Dick Stabile and Abe Lyman. He played with Woody Herman (1944–46), Benny Goodman (1948), and Chubby Jackson, and also recorded many albums with Lennie Tristano. He did regular TV work in the 1950s, including staff work in Bobby Byme's orch. Bauer played in Europe with Benny Goodman (May 1958); during the late 1950s and early 1960s, he often worked with Lee Konitz, while also leading his own groups, including a long residency at the Sherwood Inn, N.Y. During the 1970s, he maintained a rigorous freelance schedule. He continues to teach at his Long Island home.

DISC.: *Let's Have a Session* (1953); *Plectrist* (1956); *Anthology* (1990).—JC/LP

Bauer, Harold, distinguished English-born American pianist and teacher; b. New Malden, Surrey, April 28, 1873; d. Miami, March 12, 1951. He studied violin with his father and Adolf Politzer; from the age of nine, made appearances as a violinist. When he was 19 he appeared as a pianist in London, and then had lessons from Paderewski in Paris, where he played in 1893. After touring Europe, he made his U.S. debut as soloist with the Boston Sym. Orch. in 1900, and subsequently played in major U.S. cities. In 1912 he was awarded the Gold Medal of the Royal Phil. Soc. of London. During World War I, he settled in the U.S. and became a naturalized American citizen. He was founder-director of the Beethoven Assn. of N.Y. (1918–41), an esteemed chamber music society; he also was active as a teacher. He publ. *Harold Bauer, His Book* (N.Y., 1948). Bauer was particularly known as an interpreter of Beethoven, but he was also admired for his performances of Brahms, Franck, Debussy, and Ravel.—**NS/LK/DM**

Bauer, Marion (Eugenie),

American composer, teacher, and writer on music; b. Walla Walla, Wash., Aug. 15, 1887; d. South Hadley, Mass., Aug. 9, 1955. She began her training with her father, an amateur musician. In 1904 she went to N.Y. to study with Huss; after piano lessons with Pugno in Paris (1905), she returned to N.Y. in 1907 to study theory with Eugene Heffley. In 1910 she went to Germany to pursue composition lessons with Rothwell, and then to Paris in 1923 to complete her training with Gédalge (fugue) and Boulanger (composition). She taught at N.Y. Univ. (1926–51), Chautauqua (from 1928), and the Juilliard School of Music in N.Y. (1940–44). Her music oscillated pleasurably between German Romanticism and Gallic Impressionism.

WRITINGS (all publ. in N.Y.): with E. Peyser, *How Music Grew: From Prehistoric Times to the Present Day* (1925; 2nd ed., rev., 1939); with E. Peyser, *Music through the Ages: A Narrative for Student and Layman* (1932; 2nd ed., rev., 1946; 3rd ed., rev. and enl., 1967 by E. Rogers as *Music Through the Ages: An Introduction to Music History*); *Twentieth Century Music* (1933; 2nd ed., rev., 1947); *Musical Questions and Quizzes: A Digest of Information About Music* (1941); with E. Peyser, *How Opera Grew: From Ancient Greece to the Present Day* (1956).

WORKS: ORCH.: *Indian Pipes* (1927; orch. by M. Bernstein; arr. for Piano, 1928); *Lament on African Themes* for Chamber Orch. (1928); *Symphonic Suite for Strings* (1940); Piano Concerto, *American Youth* (1943); Sym. (1947–50). **CHAMBER:** *Allegro giocoso* for 11 Instruments (1920); Violin Sonata (1922); String Quartet (1928); Sonata for Viola or Clarinet and Piano (1935); Concertino for Oboe, Clarinet, and String Quartet (1939–43); 2 trio sonatas (1944, 1951); *Aquarelle* for Woodwind Ensemble or Chamber Orch. (1948). **Piano:** *In the Country* (1913); *From New Hampshire Woods* (1921); *Sun Splendor* (1926); *Dance Sonata* (1932); 2 *Aquarelles* (1945). **VOCAL:** Many choruses and songs.

BIBL.: N. Stewart, *The Solo Piano Music of M. B.* (diss., Univ. of Cincinnati, 1990).—**NS/LK/DM**

Bauer, Ross,

noteworthy American composer and teacher; b. Ithaca, N.Y., Nov. 19, 1951. He studied at the New England Cons. of Music (B.M., 1976) and with Martin Boykan, Seymour Shifrin, and Arthur Berger at Brandeis Univ. (Ph.D., 1984); also had additional composition training with Berio at the Berkshire Music Center at Tanglewood (summer, 1982). He was a lecturer and leader of the Brandeis Jazz Ensemble at Brandeis Univ. (1985–86), and a founding member of the

Griffin Music Ensemble (1985–94). He was a lecturer at Stanford Univ. (1986–88) and director of its new music ensemble, Alea II. From 1990 to 1994 he was an assoc. prof. at the Univ. of Calif. at Davis, where he became a prof. in 1994; he also founded and directs its Empyrean Ensemble. Among his numerous honors are the Walter Hinrichsen Award from the American Academy and Inst. of Arts and Letters (1984) and a composer's fellowship from the NEA (1986). He also received commissions from the Fromm Music Foundation (1991) and Serge Koussevitzky Foundation (1994), and in 1997 won the Speculum Musicae International Composers' Competition. In 1988 he held a Guggenheim fellowship, and in 1989 he won the League-ISCM National Composer's Competition for his *Chimera* for Nine Players (1987). Bauer describes his music as coming directly out of the tradition as exemplified by the first and second Viennese schools and their descendants in America. His works are freely chromatic, often motoric and sometimes evoke his substantial interest and background in jazz.

WORKS: ORCH.: Concertino for Chamber Orch. (1983); *Sospeso* for Strings (1987); *Neon* (1988); Piano Concerto (1990); *Halcyon Birds* for Chamber Orch. (1993); *Romanza* for Violin and Orch. (1996); *Icons*, bassoon concerto (1997). **CHAMBER:** Trio for Clarinet/Bass Clarinet, Cello and Piano (1980); 3 string quartets (1981, 1987, 2000); *Hang Time* for Clarinet, Violin, and Piano (1984); *Along the Way* for 10 Players (1985); *Deja Vu* for Flute, Clarinet, Violin, Cello, and Piano (1986); *Evanescent Heterophony* for Cello and Piano (1986); *Chimera* for 9 Players (1987); *Fast Gar Nichts...* for String Trio (1988); *Chin Music* for Viola and Piano (1989); *Anaphora* for Flute, Violin, Viola, Cello, and Piano (1991); *Tributaries* for Cello, Percussion, and Piano (1992); *Aplomb* for Violin and Piano (1993); Octet for Clarinet, Bassoon, Horn, String Quartet, and Bass (1994); *Stone Soup* for Flute, Clarinet, Violin, Cello, and Piano (1995); *Motion* for Piano Trio (1998); *Pulse* for Clarinet, Viola, and Piano (1999); *Etudes* for Violin (1999). **Piano:** *Tonarten* (1982); *Birthday Bagatelles* (1993). **VOCAL:** *Four Honig Songs* for Soprano and Piano (1989); *Oda al Olor de la Lena* for Baritone, Alto Flute, Cello, and Percussion, after Neruda (1991); *Ritual Fragments* for Soprano, Flute, Clarinet, Violin, Cello, Percussion, and Piano, after Native American texts (1995); *Eskimo Songs* for Mezzo-soprano, Flute, Cello, and Piano (1996).—**LK/DM**

Bauld, Alison (Margaret),

Australian composer; b. Sydney, May 7, 1944. After training at the National Inst. of Dramatic Art, she studied at the Univ. of Sydney (B.Mus., 1968), and then was a scholarship student of Lutyens and Keller, completing her education at the Univ. of York (Ph.D., 1974). She was music director of the Laban Centre for Dance at the Univ. of London (1975–78) and composer-in-residence at the New South Wales State Conservatorium in Sydney (1978). Later she was a part-time instructor at Hollins Coll. in London. She publ. the piano tutor *Play Your Way* (three vols., 1992).

WORKS: *On the Afternoon of the Pigsty* for Female Speaker, Piano, Alto Melodica, and Percussion (1971); *In a Dead Brown Land* for 2 Mime Actors, 2 Speakers, Soprano, Tenor, Chorus, and 5 Instruments (1971); *Humpty Dumpty* for Tenor, Flute, and Guitar (1972); *Pumpkin 2* for 4 Actors and 5 Instruments (London, June 21, 1973); *Egg* for Tenor, Flute, Cello, and

Percussion (Snape, June 25, 1973); *Mad Moll* for Soprano (1973); *1 Pearl* for Soprano or Countertenor and String Quartet (Southampton, Nov. 11, 1973; also known as *1 Pearl II* for Soprano, Alto Flute, and String Orch., London, April 30, 1976); *Exiles* for 4 Actors, Tenor, Mezzo-soprano, Chorus, Flute, Alto Melodica, Percussion, and String Quartet (1974; Sydney, May 1975); *Concert* for Pianist and Tape (first half for mime only, 2nd half for tape only; Sydney, Dec. 1974); *Van Diemen's Land* for Chorus (London, Nov. 8, 1976); *The Busker's Story* for Alto Saxophone, Bassoon, Trumpet, Violin, and Double Bass (Sydney, Sept. 25, 1978); *Richard III* for Voice and String Quartet (BBC, July 4, 1985); *Monday* for Flute (Sydney, Oct. 1, 1985); *Copy Cats* for Violin, Cello, and Piano (1985; London, Jan. 20, 1988); *Once upon a Time* for 5 Vocal Soloists and Small Chamber Orch. (BBC, Dec. 29, 1986); *Nell*, ballad opera (London, June 1, 1988); *My Own Island* for Clarinet and Piano (1989); *Exult* for Chorus, Organ, and Optional Brass Quintet (1990); *The Witches' Song* for Soprano (Melbourne, May 9, 1990); *Farewell Already* for String Quartet (1993).—NS/LK/DM

Bauldewijn (also Bauldeweyn, Bauldoin, Baudoin, etc.), Noël,

Flemish composer; b. c. 1480; d. Antwerp, 1530. He was magister cantorum at the church of St.-Rombaut in Mechelen (1509–13), then at Notre Dame Cathedral in Antwerp, a post he most likely kept until his death. He wrote masses, motets, and several secular works. For an exposition concerning conflicting attributions of his output, see E. Sparks, *The Music of N. B.* (N.Y., 1972).—NS/LK/DM

Baum, Kurt,

Czech-born American tenor; b. Prague, March 15, 1908; d. N.Y., Dec. 27, 1989. He studied with Garbin in Milan and Scolari in Rome; in 1933, won the Vienna International Competition, then made his operatic debut in the premiere of Zemlinsky's *Der Kreidekreis* in Zürich (Oct. 14, 1933). After singing with the German Theater in Prague (1934–39), he made his U.S. debut as Radames in Chicago in 1939, where he sang until 1941. On Nov. 27, 1941 he made his Metropolitan Opera debut in N.Y. as the Singer in *Der Rosenkavalier*, remaining on its roster until 1962, and again from 1964 to 1966; also made guest appearances at Milan's La Scala (1947–48), the Florence Maggio Musicale (1952), London's Covent Garden (1953), the San Francisco Opera, and in South America.—NS/LK/DM

Baumann, Hermann (Rudolf Konrad),

noted German horn player and pedagogue; b. Hamburg, Aug. 1, 1934. He received training in Hamburg. In 1957 he became first horn in Dortmund, and then held that position with the Stuttgart Radio Sym. Orch. from 1961 to 1967. In 1964 he won the Munich Competition and began to pursue a solo career. In 1969 he became a prof. at the Staatliche Folkwang Hochschule in Essen, and in 1980 at the Stuttgart Hochschule für Musik. In addition to his appearances as a soloist with leading German and European orchs., he also was engaged with minor orchs. in North America. He also appeared in chamber music settings. After an engagement with the Buffalo Phil. on Jan. 12, 1993, he suffered a stroke; however, he was able to resume his career. While his repertoire embraces scores from the Baroque era to the moderns, he has won particular distinction for his performances of Mozart and Richard Strauss.
—NS/LK/DM

Baumann, Max (Georg),

German composer and pedagogue; b. Kronach, Nov. 20, 1917; d. Berlin, July 18, 1999. He was a student of Noetel and Blacher at the Berlin Hochschule für Musik. In 1946 he joined its faculty as a lecturer, and then was a prof. of composition there from 1961 until his retirement in 1979. In 1953 he won the arts prize of the City of Berlin and in 1963 the Prix Italia. He composed much sacred vocal music.

WORKS: DRAMATIC: B a l l e t : *Pelleas und Melisande* (Berlin, Sept. 20, 1954). **ORCH.:** Piano Concerto (1953; Berlin, March 15, 1955); *Petite Suite* for Transverse Flute, Oboe, Bassoon, and Strings (1953); *Perspektiven I* (1957) and *II* (1967); *Orchester-Variationen* (Berlin, Jan. 27, 1959); *Sinfonia piccola* for Strings (1960). **CHAMBER:** Cello Sonata (1947); 3 string quartets (1950, 1951, 1953); Sonata for Solo Violin (Berlin, Dec. 1, 1955); *3 Radierungen* for Violin and Piano (1958); Octet for Strings, Clarinet, Bassoon, and Horn (1964); also organ and piano pieces. **VOCAL:** *Missa 1953* for Chorus (1953); *Schutzengel-Messe* for Chorus and Organ ad libitum (1955); *Kleine Marienmesse* for 2 Soloists and Organ ad libitum (1958); *Passion* for Soprano, Baritone, Speaker, Mixed Chorus, Speaking Chorus, and Orch. (1960); *Libertas cruciata*, cantata for Soloists, Speaker, Chorus, Speaking Chorus, and Orch. (1963); *Deutsche Vesper* for Soprano, Speaker ad libitum, Chorus, and Orch. (1964); *Der Venus süss und herbe Früchte* for Soloists, Speaker, Chorus, and Orch. (1972); *Auferstehung*, oratorio for Soloist, Chorus, Speaking Chorus, and Orch. (1980); *Sonnengesang* for Voice and Piano (1992); other choral works and songs.

BIBL.: A Geck-Böttger and J. Overath, eds., *Te decet hymnus: Festgabe für M. B. zur Vollendung des 75. Lebensjahre* (Sankt Augustin, 1992).—NS/LK/DM

Baumbach, Friedrich August,

German composer and writer on music; b. Gotha (baptized), Sept. 12, 1753; d. Leipzig, Nov. 30, 1813. He was active as a singer, and then as a violinist and music director in Hamburg (1777–89). After serving as music director of the new Riga theater (1782–83), he settled in Leipzig in 1790 and wrote the articles on music for J. Grohmann's *Kurzegefasstes Handwörterbuch über die schönen Künste* (1794). He composed various chamber and vocal works.
—NS/LK/DM

Baumgarten, Karl Friedrich,

German organist, violinist, teacher, and composer; b. Lübeck, c. 1740; d. London, 1824. He studied organ with J.P. Kunzen in Lübeck. About 1758 he settled in London, where he was active as an organist, violinist, and teacher. He served as concertmaster of the Covent Garden orch. (1780–94) and was a violinist in the Duke of Cumberland's band. Among his works were the comic opera *William and Nanny, or The Cottagers* (Covent Garden, 1779), the pantomime *Bluebeard, or The Flight of Harlequin* (Covent Garden, 1791), chamber music, and organ pieces.
—LK/DM

Baumgartner, Rudolf,

Swiss violinist and conductor; b. Zürich, Sept. 14, 1917. He studied at the Univ. of Zürich and pursued training in violin with Stefi Geyer and Paul Müller at the Zürich Cons., with Carl Flesch in Paris, and with Wolfgang Schneiderhan in Vienna. He began his career as a chamber music player,

and also appeared as a soloist. In 1954 he joined the faculty of the Lucerne Cons., where he served as its director from 1960 to 1987. With Schneiderhan, he founded the Lucerne Festival Strings in 1956, and subsequently served as its director. From 1968 to 1980 he was artistic director of the Lucerne Festival.
—NS/LK/DM

Baur, Jürg, German composer and pedagogue; b. Düsseldorf, Nov. 11, 1918. He was a student of Philipp Jarnach (composition) and Mchael Schneider (organ) at the Cologne Cons. (1937–39). During military service in World War II (1939–45), he was taken prisoner-of- war by the Russians. After his release, he returned to Cologne to continue his music training (1946–48), and then studied musicology with Fellerer at the Univ. there (1948–51). He also was a lecturer in theory at the Robert Schumann Cons. in Düsseldorf (1946). From 1952 to 1966 he served as choirmaster at the Pauluskirche in Düsseldorf. In 1965 he became director of the Robert Schumann Cons. there, and in 1969 was made a prof. From 1971 to 1991 he was prof. of composition at the Cologne Hochschule für Musik. In 1957 he received the Robert Schumann Prize of the City of Düsseldorf, in 1980 he was guest of honor of the Villa Massimo in Rome, in 1990 he received the Order of Merit of the State of North-Rhine-Westphalia, in 1994 he received the music award of the City of Duisburg, and in 1997 he received the music award of the Gerhard Maasz Foundation for his life's work and the honorary ring of the German Schubert Soc. In his early works, Baur was much influenced by Bartók and Hindemith. He later pursued a highly personal approach to the utilization of dodecaphony, serialism, and aleatory, which blossomed into an admirably crafted synthesis of styles.

WORKS: ORCH.: Concerto for Strings (1941–48; Bochum, April 11, 1958); Overture (1946–50; Düsseldorf, April 19, 1951); *Partita über "Wie schön leuchtet der Morgenstern"* for Trumpet and Strings (1946–91); *Carmen-Variationen* (1947; Düsseldorf, May 23, 1983); Concerto for Viola and Chamber Orch. (Cologne, April 22, 1951); *Musik* for Strings (1952–53; Duisburg, July 3, 1954); *Sinfonia montana* (1953; Weimar, May 23, 1955)); *Konzert Musik* for Piano and Orch. (1958; Düsseldorf, Jan. 26, 1959); Concertino for Flute, Oboe, Clarinet, Strings, and Timpani (Wuppertal, Aug. 16, 1959); *Concerto romano* for Oboe and Orch. (1960; Münster, Feb. 19, 1961); *Romeo und Julia* (1962–63; Düsseldorf, Sept. 19, 1963); *Piccolo mondo* (1963; first complete perf., Darmstadt, May 21, 1966); *Lo Specchio I* (1965; Düsseldorf, May 5, 1966) and *II* (1966; Munich, July 9, 1967); *Sinfonischer Prolog* (Münster, Nov. 5, 1966); *Pentagram*, concerto for Wind Quintet and Orch. (Essen, Nov. 25, 1966; rev. 1969; Hannover, Feb. 9, 1970); *Abbreviaturen* for 13 Solo Strings (Zagreb, May 7, 1969); *Concerto Ticino* for Clarinet and Orch. (1970; Düsseldorf, Jan. 7, 1971); *Giorno per giorno,* "in memoriam B.A. Zimmermann" (Aachen, June 2, 1971); *Musik mit Robert Schumann* (Hananover, March 13, 1972); *Vier Portraits* for Cello and Orch. (Saarbrücken, Dec. 18, 1972); *Sinfonia breve* (Augsburg, April 8, 1974; rev. 1974; Münster, June 2, 1976); *Triton-Sinfonietta* for Chamber Orch. (1974; Dortmund, Jan. 26, 1975); *Concerto da camera* for Recorder and Chamber Orch. (Essen, May 4, 1975); 2 violin concertos: No. 1, *Ich sag ade* (Bielefeld, June 25, 1976) and No. 2 (Düsseldorf, Nov. 16, 1978); *Sentimento del tempo* for Oboe, Clarinet, Bassoon, and Orch. (Gelsenkirchen, Nov. 24, 1980); *Sinfonische Metamorphosen über Gesualdo* (1981; Bremen, Feb. 1,

1982); 2 syms: No. 1, *Sinfonie einer Stadt (Pathetica)* for the 1,100th anniversary of Duisburg (Duisburg, Sept. 7, 1983) and No. 2, *Aus dem Tagebuch des Alten* (1987; Dortmund, March 14, 1988); *Fresken* for Chamber Orch. (1984; Saarbrücken, Nov. 28, 1985); *Konzertante Fantasie* for Organ and Strings (1984–85; Halle, Jan. 30, 1985); *Sentieri musicale,* sinfonietta (1990; Hannover, April 8, 1991); *Frammenti: Erinnerungen an Schubert* (1995–96; Duisburg, Jan. 15, 1997); *Sinfonia sine nomine* (1997–98; Kiel, June 28, 1999). **CHAMBER:** 2 unnumbered string quartets (1935, 1938); 3 numbered string quartets: No. 1 (1938–46; Düsseldorf, Oct. 19, 1946), No. 2 (1942–46; Düsseldorf, April 30, 1949), and No. 3 (1952; Düsseldorf, April 20, 1954); *Fantasie and Fuge* for String Quartet (1941); Violin Sonata (1943–48; Cologne, May 10, 1950); *Ostinato und Trio* for Flute, Oboe, 2 Clarinets, and 2 Bassoons (1948); *Musik* for Cello and Piano (1950); *Reminiszenzen* for Wind Quintet, "in memoriam Paul Hindemith" (1950–80; Aachen, April 25, 1981); *Fantasie* for Oboe and Piano (1954); *Quintetto sereno* for Flute, Oboe, Clarinet, Horn, and Bassoon (Düsseldorf, May 21, 1958); *Metamorphosen* for Violin, Cello, and Piano (1959–60); *Ballata Romana* for Clarinet and Piano (1960; also for Alto Saxophone and Piano, 1991); *Incontri (Begegnungen),* 3 pieces for Recorder and Piano (1960; also for Flute and Piano); Sonata for Solo Violin (1961–62; Karlsruhe, Nov. 27, 1963); *Divertimento,* 3 fantasies for Harpsichord and Percussion (1961–62; also for Accordion and Percussion, 1990); *Mutazioni* for Recorder (1962) and for Flute (1962); *Dialoge* for Cello and Piano (1962); *Pezzi uccelli* for Recorder (1964); *3 Fantasien* for Guitar (1964); *Kontraste* for Violin, Viola, and Cello (1964); *6 Bagatellen* for Clarinet or Bass Clarinet (1964); Sonata for Solo Viola (1969; Gelsenkirchen, Feb. 14, 1971); *Movimenti* for Violin, Horn, and Piano (1969–70); *Cinque Impressioni* for String Quartet (1970; Munich, Jan. 20, 1971); *Tre studi per quattro* for Recorder Quartet (1972); *Nonett-Skizzen* for Wind Quintet and String Quartet (1973); *Skizzen* for Flute, Oboe, Clarinet, Horn, and Bassoon (Stuttgart, June 17, 1974); *Moments musicaux* for Violin and Piano (1976); *Kontrapunkte 77* for Flute, English Horn, and Bassoon (Düsseldorf, April 1, 1977); *Echoi: Hirtenrufe und Weisen* for 2 Oboes and English Horn (1980); *Pour rien* for 2 Clarinets, 2 Horns, and 2 Bassoon (1980; Krefeld, Sept. 24, 1982); *Ricordi* for 3 Recorders (1983); *Ritratti* for Percussionists, Celesta, and Bass Instrument (Düsseldorf, June 3, 1984); *Cinque foglie* for Saxophone Quartet (1986; Rottenburg, Feb. 1, 1987); *Quintetto pittoresco* for Wind Quintet (1986; Lüdenscheid, Nov. 11, 1987); *Passacaglia* for 4 Trumpets and 4 Trombones (1989; Düsseldorf, May 20, 1990); *Arabesken, Girlanden, Figuren* for Contrabassoon (1990); *Marginalien über Mozart* for Guitar (1991); *Reflexionen* for Guitar and Organ (1991; also for Guitar and Accordion, 1992); *Petite suite* for Flute Quartet (Düsseldorf, Nov. 17, 1992); *Et respice finem* for String Quartet (Saarbrücken, Oct. 27, 1993); *Improvisation und Ostinato* for Bassoon Quartet (Rheinsberg, May 25, 1996); also piano pieces and organ music. **VOCAL:** *Triptychon* for Chorus and Orch. (1948–49); *Im Waldesschatten,* 5 songs for Baritone and Piano (1952; also for Baritone and String Quartet, 1980); *Pfingstmotette: Wer mich liebt* for Baritone and Chorus (1955; Düsseldorf, May 13, 1956); *Vom tiefinnern Sang,* song cycle for Mezzo-soprano and Piano (1957; Düsseldorf, April 25, 1958; also for Mezzo-soprano, Clarinet, and String Quartet, 1989; Bochum, March 12, 1990); *Herb stirb oder singe,* 4 songs for High Voice and Piano (1960; Düsseldorf, June 11, 1961; also for Soprano, Flute, and String Orch., 1964; Baden-Baden, March 29, 1965; also for High Voice, Flute, and String Quartet, Düsseldorf, Sept. 12, 1984); *Mit wechselndem Schlüssel* for Baritone and Piano (1967); *Perché (Warum?)* for Soli, Chorus, and Orch. (1967–68; Düsseldorf, Oct. 24, 1968; also for Soli and

Chorus, 1969; Ludwigsburg, Oct. 24, 1970); *Die Blume des Scharon*, 3 lyric motets for Chorus (1979; Aachen, March 12, 1983); other choral pieces and songs.

BIBL.: J. Scholl, ed., *Der Komponist J. B.: Eine Dokumentation* (Düsseldorf, 1993).—NS/LK/DM

Bausznern, Waldemar von, German composer; b. Berlin, Nov. 29, 1866; d. Potsdam, Aug. 20, 1931. He studied music with Kiel and Bargiel in Berlin. He subsequently was active mainly as a choral conductor. He taught at the Cons. of Cologne (1903–8), at the Hochschule für Musik in Weimar (1908–16), where he also served as director, and at the Hoch Cons. in Frankfurt am Main, where he was a teacher and director (1916–23). He also taught at the Academy of Arts and the Academy for Church and School Music in Berlin. Among his many works were the operas *Dichter und Welt* (Weimar, 1897), *Dürer in Venedig* (Weimar, 1901), *Herbort und Hilde* (Mannheim, 1902), and *Der Bundschuh* (Frankfurt am Main, 1904), as well as eight syms., of which the third and the fifth have choral finales, numerous sacred choral works, four string quartets, two piano quintets, two piano trios, and two violin sonatas. He ed. the score of the opera *Der Barbier von Bagdad* by Peter Cornelius, and completed his unfinished opera *Gunlöd*, which was produced in this version in Cologne in 1906. His syms., academically Romantic in their high-flown idiom, still retain a spark of vitality, to judge by their infrequent performances in Germany.—NS/LK/DM

Bautista, Julián, Spanish composer; b. Madrid, April 21, 1901; d. Buenos Aires, July 8, 1961. He studied violin with Julio Francés, piano with Pilar Fernández de la Mora, and composition with Conrado del Campo at the Madrid Cons., where he taught during the Spanish Civil War. After Madrid fell in 1939, Bautista fled to Argentina, where he was on the faculty of the National Cons. of Buenos Aires. His music, delicately colored and rhythmically robust, invariably reflected Spanish folk melodies.

WORKS: *Juerga*, ballet (1921); *Colores*, 6 piano pieces (1922); Sonatina for String Trio (1924); *Obertura para una ópera grotesca* for Orch. (1932); *Tres ciudades* for Voice and Orch. (1937); *4 poemas gallegos* for Voice, Flute, Oboe, Clarinet, Viola, Cello, and Harp (1946); 2 syms. (*Sinfonia breve*, 1956; 1957); 3 string quartets; songs.—NS/LK/DM

Bauzá, Mario, jazz trumpeter, saxophonist, arranger; b. Havana, Cuba, April 28, 1911; d. N.Y., July 11, 1993. Mario Bauzá was involved in two of the major jazz and Latin trends of the 1930s and 1940s. He was responsible for introducing Dizzy Gillespie to conga legend Chano Pozo and for bringing the standard Cuban rhythm section into line with the big band sound of Cab Calloway and Chick Webb. The meeting of Gillespie and Pozo was influential in the development of a hybrid known as Cubop which included among its proponents Stan Getz and Charlie Parker. The blending of big band arrangements with Cuban rhythms made Bauzá's brother-in-law, Machito (Frank Grillo), the leader of what was arguably the most influential Latin-flavored band in the first half of this century.

Bauzá's first instruments were the clarinet and the bass clarinet, which he played in the Havana Philharmonic. In 1930, shortly after arriving in the United States, Bauzá got a job with Cuarteto Machin playing trumpet, an instrument he learned to play in the two weeks preceding his first job with the band. His first major jazz gig was with Chick Webb in 1933 and from there Bauzá worked briefly with bands led by Don Redman and Fletcher Henderson before joining Cab Calloway's outfit in 1939. In 1940 Bauzá made the move to Machito's newly formed band as the musical director, and there he stayed until 1976. During the late 1970s and early 1980s Bauzá and Graciela (his sister-in-law and former vocalist with Machito) recorded a couple albums for small labels which have since turned into prized collector's items. It was in 1992 that he made a recording featuring Chico O'Farrill's arrangement of "Tanga," a tune originally written by Bauzá back in 1943, and this led to a resurgence in his career.

DISC.: *Tanga* (1992); *My Time Is Now* (1993); *944 Columbus* (1994).—GM

Bavicchi, John (Alexander), American conductor, teacher, and composer; b. Boston, April 25, 1922. He studied at the New England Cons. of Music in Boston with Carl McKinley and Francis Judd Cooke (B.M., 1952), and then attended Harvard Univ. Graduate School, taking courses in theory with Davison, composition with Piston, and musicology with Gombosi (1952–55). He served in the U.S. Navy during World War II, and saw action in Guadalcanal, Okinawa, and Japan (1943–45). Returning to Boston after the War, he devoted himself to teaching, composing, and conducting. Bavicchi lectured on music history at the Cambridge Center for Adult Education (1960–73). He also conducted the Arlington-Belmont Chorale (from 1960), the American Festival Ballet Co. (1962–65), and the Arlington Phil. (1968–82). His music is couched in Classical forms, while presenting a variegated texture of decidedly modernistic invention.

WORKS: ORCH.: Concerto for Clarinet and Strings (1954); Suite No. 1 (1955); *A Concert Overture* (1957); *Fantasy* for Harp and Chamber Orch. (1959); Concertante for Oboe, Bassoon, and Strings (1961); *Caroline's Dance* (1974–75); *Mont Blanc*, overture (1976–77); *Music for Small Orch.* (1981); *Fusions* for Trombone and Orch. (1984–85); *Pyramid* (1986); *Canto I* for String Orch. (1987) and *III* for Concert Band (1991); *Sherbrooke West* (1988) Concerto for Tuba and Concert Band (1988); *Dialogue* for Piano and Orch. (1995); *Icelandic Musings* for Trumpet and Small Orch. (1997); *Tobal II* (1998). **CHAMBER:** 10 trios for a variety of instrumental combinations (1950–83); 2 cello sonatas (1953, 1956); 2 sonatas for Solo Clarinet (1956, 1959); Brass Quartet No. 1 (1956); *A Musical Sketch-book* for Flute, or for Flute, Oboe, Clarinet, Bassoon, and Piano (1960); String Quartet (1960); 2 woodwind quintets (1961, 1973); *Music* for Horn and Piano (1980); Concertino for Tuba and Brass Quartet (1984); Flute Sonata (1986); *Triptych* for Multiple Horns (1987); *Canto II* for Clarinet (1990) and *IV* for Flute, Bassoon, Violin, and Piano (1992); Violin Sonatina (1993); Quintet for Clarinet and Strings (1995); piano pieces. **VOCAL:** *4 Songs* for Contralto and Orch. (1952); *3 Psalms* for Soloists, Chorus, 2 Trumpets, and String Orch. (1963); *There is Sweet Music Here* for Soprano and Orch. (1985); *6 Songs to Poems of William Blake* for Soprano, Violin, and

Piano (1987); *Songs of Remembrance* for Soloists, Chorus, and Orch. (1990); *Talk to Me* for Chorus and Piano (1992); *Infinite Patience* for Mezzo-soprano, Clarinet, and Piano (1992); *Psalm 96* for Chorus and Brass (1996); *The Hallam Songs* for Soprano, Mezzo- soprano, 2 Oboes, and Piano (1999).—NS/LK/DM

Bax, Sir Arnold (Edward Trevor), outstanding English composer; b. London, Nov. 8, 1883; d. Cork, Ireland, Oct. 3, 1953. He entered the Royal Academy of Music in London in 1900 and studied piano with Matthay and composition with Corder there. He won the Academy's Gold Medal as a pianist in 1905, the year in which he completed his studies. After a visit to Dresden in 1905, he went to Ireland. Although not ethnically Irish, he became interested in ancient Irish folklore. He wrote poetry and prose under the name of Dermot O'Byrne, and also found inspiration in Celtic legends for his work as a composer. In 1910 he returned to England. In 1931 he received the Gold Medal of the Royal Phil. Soc. of London. He was awarded honorary degrees from the univs. of Oxford (1934) and Durham (1935). He was knighted at the Coronation of King George VI in 1937, and was made Master of the King's Musick in 1941. Bax was an excellent pianist, but was reluctant to play in public; he also never appeared as a conductor of his own works. His style was rooted in neo- Romanticism, but impressionistic elements are much in evidence in his instrumental compositions. His harmonies are elaborate and rich in chromatic progressions, and his contrapuntal fabric is free and emphasizes complete independence of component melodies. In his many settings of folk songs, he succeeded in adapting simple melodies to effective accompaniments in modern harmonies; in his adaptations of early English songs, he successfully re-created the archaic style of the epoch. He recorded the story of his life and travels in his candid autobiography, *Farewell, My Youth* (London, 1943; ed. by L. Foreman, 1992, as *Farewell, My Youth and Other Writings*).

WORKS: DRAMATIC: B a l l e t : *King Kojata* (1911); *Between Dusk and Dawn* (1917); *The Frog Skin* (1918). I n c i - d e n t a l M u s i c : *The Truth about the Russian Dancers* (1920; rev. 1926); *Golden Eagle* (1945). F i l m : *Malta GC* (1942; orch. suite, 1943); *Oliver Twist* (1948; orch. suite, 1948); *Journey into History* (1952). ORCH.: 12 tone poems: *Cathaleen-ni- Hoolihan* for Small Orch. (1903–05); *A Song of Life and Love* (1905); *A Song of War and Victory* (1905); *Eire: Into the Twilight* (1908), *In the Faery Hills* (1909), and *Rosc-Catha* (1910); *Christmas Eve on the Mountains* (1911; rev. c. 1933); *Nympholept* (1912–15); *The Garden of Fand* (1913–16); *The Happy Forest* (1914–21); *November Woods* (1917); *Tintagel* (1917–19); *The Tale the Pine-trees Knew* (1931); *A Legend* (1944); *Variations: Improvisations* (1904); *A Connemara Revel* (1905); *An Irish Overture* (1906); *Festival Overture* (1911; rev. 1918); *Prelude to Adonais* (1912); *4 Pieces* (also known as *4 Sketches* or *4 Irish Pieces*) (1912–13; rev. 1928); *Spring Fire*, sym. (1913); *Symphonic Scherzo* (arr. from a piano piece; orch. 1917; rev. 1933); *Symphonic Variations* for Piano and Orch. (1918); *Russian Suite* (arr. from piano pieces; 1919); *Summer Music* (1917–20; rev. 1932); *Phantasy*, viola concerto (1920); 7 syms: No. 1 (1921; London, Dec. 4, 1922), No. 2 (1924–25; Boston, Dec. 13, 1929), No. 3 (1929; London, March 14, 1930), No. 4 (1930; San Francisco, March 16, 1932), No. 5 (1931; London, Jan. 15, 1934), No. 6 (1934; London, Nov. 21, 1935), and No. 7 (N.Y., June 9, 1939); *Mediterranean* (arr. from a piano piece; 1922); *Cortège*

(1925); *Romantic Overture* for Chamber Orch. (1926); *Overture, Elegy and Rondo* (1927); *Northern Ballad* Nos. 1 (1927–31) and 2 (1934); *Prelude for a Solemn Occasion* (1927–33); *3 Pieces* (1928); *Overture to a Picaresque Comedy* (1930); *Winter Legends*, sinfonia concertante for Piano and Orch. (1930); Sinfonietta (1932); Cello Concerto (1932); *Rogue's Comedy Overture* (1936); *Overture to Adventure* (1936); *London Pageant* (1937); *Paean* (arr. from a piano piece; 1938); Violin Concerto (1938); *Work in Progress*, overture (1943); *Morning Song: Maytime in Sussex* for Piano and Orch. (c. 1946); Concertante for English Horn, Clarinet, Horn, and Orch. (1948); *Variations on the name Gabriel Fauré* for Harp and Strings (1949; also for Piano); Concertante, concerto for Piano, Left-Hand and Orch. (1949); *Coronation March* (1953). CHAMBER: 2 unnumbered string quartets (1902, 1903); 3 numbered string quartets (1918, 1925, 1936); *Concert Piece* for Violin or Viola and Piano (1903); *Fantasy* for Violin or Viola and Piano (1904); 2 piano trios (1906, 1946); 2 string quintets (1908, 1933); 3 violin sonatas (1910, rev. 1915, 1920, and 1945; 1915, rev. 1920; 1927); *4 Pieces* for Flute and Piano (1912); 2 piano quintets (1915, 1922); *Legend* for Violin and Piano (1915); *4 Pieces* for Violin and Piano (1915); *Ballad* for Violin and Piano (1916); *Elegiac Trio* for Flute, Viola, and Harp (1916); *Im memoriam* for English Horn, Harp, and String Quartet (1917); *Folk Tale* for Cello and Piano (1918); Harp Quintet (1919); Viola Sonata (1922); Oboe Quintet (1922); Cello Sonata (1923); *Fantasy Sonata* for Viola and Harp (1927); Sonatina for Flute and Harp (1928; arr. as the Concerto for Flute, Oboe, Harp, and String Quartet, 1936); *Legend* for Viola and Piano (1929); Nonet for Flute, Oboe, Clarinet, Harp, String Quartet, and Double Bass (1930); Cello Sonatina (1933); Clarinet Sonata (1934); Octet for Horn, Piano, and String Sextet (1934); *Threnody and Scherzo* for Bassoon, Harp, and String Sextet (1936); *Rhapsodic Ballad* for Cello (1939); *Legend-Sonata* for Cello and Piano (1943). P i a n o : *Fantasia* for Piano Duo (1900); 3 unnumbered sonatas; 4 numbered sonatas (1910, rev. 1921; 1919; 1926; 1932); *Concert Valse* (1910); *2 Russian Tone Pictures: May Night in the Ukraine* and *Gopak* (1912); *Toccata* (1913); *The Princess's Rose Garden* (1915); *In a Vodka Shop* (1915); *The Maiden with the Daffodil* (1915); *Apple Blossom Time* (1915); *Sleep Head* (1915); *A Mountain Mood* (1915); *Winter Waters* (1915); *Dream in Exile* (1916); *Nereid* (1916); *Moy Mell (The Pleasant Plain: An Irish Tone Poem)* for Piano Duo (1917); *On a May Evening* (1918); *Whirligig* (1919); *The Slave Girl* (1919); *What the Minstrel Told Us* (1919); *Lullaby* (1920); *Burlesque* (1920); *Ceremonial Dance* (1920); *Country-Tune* (1920); *A Hill Tune* (1920); *Mediterranean* (1920); *Paean* (1920); *Serpent Dance* (1920); *Water Music* (1920); *Hardanger* for Piano Duo (1927); *The Poisoned Fountain* for Piano Duo (1928); *Duo Sonata* (1929); *The Devil that Tempted St Anthony* for Piano Duo (1929); *Red Autumn* for Piano Duo (1931); *O Dame Get Up and Bake Your Pies* (1945). VOCAL: C h o r a l : *Fatherland* for Tenor, Chorus, and Orch. (1907; rev. 1934); *Enchanted Summer* for 2 Sopranos, Chorus, and Orch. (1910); *Of a Rose I Sing a Song* for Chorus, Harp, Cello, and Double Bass (1920); *Now Is the Time of Christymas* for Men's Voices, Flute, and Piano (1921); *Mater ora Filium* for Chorus (1921); *This Worldes Joie* for Chorus (1922); *The Boar's Head* for Men's Voices (1923); *I Sing of a Maiden that is Makeless* for Chorus (1923); *St. Patrick's Breastplate* for Chorus and Orch. (1923); *To the Name above Every Name* for Soprano, Chorus, and Orch. (1923); *Walsinghame* for Tenor, Chorus, and Orch. (1926); *The Morning Watch* for Chorus and Orch. (1935); *5 Fantasies on Polish Christmas Carols* for Unison Treble Voices and Strings (1942); *5 Greek Folksongs* for Chorus (1944); *To Russia* for Baritone, Chorus, and Orch. (1944); *Nunc dimittis* for Chorus and Organ (1944); *Te Deum* for Chorus and Organ (1944); *Gloria* for Chorus and Organ (1945); *Epithalamium* for Chorus and Organ (1947); *Magnificat* for Chorus and Organ (1948); *What is it Like to be Young and Fair* for Chorus (1953); numerous solo songs, some with orch.

BIBL.: R. Hull, *A Handbook on A. B.'s Symphonies* (London, 1932); C. Scott-Sutherland, *A. B.* (London, 1973); L. Foreman, *B.: A Composer and His Times* (London, 1983; 2nd ed., 1988); G. Parlett, *A Catalogue of the Works of Sir A. B.* (Oxford, 1999). —NS/LK/DM

Bay, Emmanuel, Russian pianist; b. Simferopol, Jan. 20, 1891; d. Jerusalem, Dec. 2, 1967. He was a student of Drosdov at the St. Petersburg Cons., graduating with first prize in 1913. After taking a master class with Godowsky in Vienna, he established himself as an excellent accompanist and toured with Zimbalist (1922–29) and Heifetz (1931–51). He also toured with Elman, Milstein, Francescatti, Szigeti, Piatigorsky, Peerce, and Traubel.—NS/LK/DM

Bayle, François, French composer and administrator; b. Tamatave, Madagascar, April 27, 1932. He left Madagascar when he was 14 and settled in Paris, where he taught himself music. From 1958 to 1960 he worked with Pierre Schaeffer at the Groupe de recherches Musicales, and he also worked with Messiaen and Stockhausen. In 1966 he became head of the Groupe de recherches Musicales, where he oversaw its integration with the Institut National de l'Audiovisuel in 1975. He remained its head until 1997 when he founded his own Studio Magison. He won the Grand Prix of the SACEM in 1978, the Grand Prix National du Disque in 1981, the Grand Prix de la Musique de la Ville de Paris in 1996, and the Grand Prix Charles Cros in 1999. Bayle received the Ordre du Mérite in 1976, was made a Commandeur des Arts et Lettres in 1986, and became a member of the Légion d'honneur in 1990. In his compositions, he has explored the use of electronics and other technological modes of expression. His output includes *Trois portraits d'un-Oiseau-Qui-N'existe-Pas* (1963–66), *Espaces in habitables* (1967), *Jeîta* (1970), *L'Expérience Acoustique* (1970–72), *Le Purgatoire, d'après La Divine Comédie de Dante* (1972), *Trois rêves d'oiseau* (1972), *Vibrations composées* (1973), *Grande polyphonie* (1974), *Camera oscura: Sept préludes et labyrinthe* (1976), *Erosphère* (1980), *Son Vitesse-Lumière* (1980–83), *Les couleurs de la nuit* (1982), *Aéroforms* (1983–86), *Motion-Emotion* (1985), *Théâtre d'Ombres* (1988), *Fabulae: Fabula, Onoma, Nola, Sonora* (1990–91), *Le Main Vide: Batoa de pluie, la fleur future, inventions* (1994–95), *Morceaux de ciels* (1997), *Si loin, si proche...* (1998–99), and *La forme du temps est un cercle* (1999–2000).—NS/LK/DM

Bazelaire, Paul, French cellist, pedagogue, and composer; b. Sedan, March 4, 1886; d. Paris, Dec. 11, 1958. He was a student of Delsart and won the premier prix in cello at the Paris Cons. when he was 11, and then took the premier prix in harmony and counterpoint there. He pursued a successful career as a cellist, and also served as a prof. at the Paris Cons. from 1918 to 1957. Among his works were orch. scores, including the *Suite française sur des chants populaires*, the symphonic poem *Cléopâtre* (Paris, Jan. 23, 1908), *Suite grecque* (1910),

and *Rapsodie dans le style russe* for Cello and Orch. (Paris, Feb. 2, 1941), several works for cello and transcriptions for the instrument, and choral pieces. He also publ. the teaching manual *Pédagogie du violoncelle.*—NS/LK/DM

Bazelon, Irwin (Allen), American composer; b. Evanston, Ill., June 4, 1922; d. N.Y., Aug. 2, 1995. He studied piano with Irving Harris and Magdalen Messmann, and composition with Leon Stein. After pursuing his education at De Paul Univ. in Chicago (B.A., 1944; M.A., 1945), he studied composition with Hindemith at Yale Univ., Milhaud at Mills Coll. in Oakland, Calif. (1946–48), and Bloch at the Univ. of Calif. at Berkeley (1947). In 1947 he settled in N.Y. He held fellowships at the MacDowell Colony (1948, 1950, 1951) and at Yaddo (1969). In 1974 he served as composer-in-residence of the Wolf Trap Farm Park in Vienna, Va. He publ. *Knowing the Score: Notes on Film Music* (1975). In his works, Bazelon made use of quaquaversal techniques, ranging from rudimentary triadic progressions to complex dodecaphonic structures infused with syncopated jazz rhythms.

WORKS: ORCH.: *Adagio and Fugue* for Strings (1947); *Concerto Overture* (1951; N.Y., March 21, 1965); *Suite for Small Orch.* (1953); syms.: *Short Symphony: Testament to a Big City* (1961; Washington, D.C., Dec. 4, 1962); No. 1 (1962; Kansas City, Mo., Oct. 26, 1963); No. 3 (1962); No. 4 (1965; 1st movement perf. as *Dramatic Movement for Orchestra*, Seattle, Feb. 21, 1966); No. 5 (1967; Indianapolis, May 8, 1970); No. 6 (1969; Kansas City, Mo., Nov. 17, 1970); No. 7, *Ballet for Orchestra* (1980); No. 8 for Strings (1986); No. 8 1/2 (1988); No. 9, *Sunday Silence* (1992); No. 10 for Narrator, Soprano, Chorus, and Orch. (1995; unfinished); Symphonie concertante for Clarinet, Trumpet, Marimba, and Orch. (1963; Williamston, Mass., April 26, 1985); *Overture to Shakespeare's Taming of the Shrew* (Washington, D.C., May 1964); *Excursion* (1965; Kansas City, Mo., March 5, 1966); *Dramatic Fanfare* (1970); *A Quiet Piece for a Violent Time* (New Orleans, Oct. 28, 1975); *Spirits of the Night* (1976); *De-Tonations* for Brass Quintet and Orch. (1978; N.Y., April 3, 1979); *Memories of a Winter Childhood* (1981; Harrisburg, Pa., Dec. 5, 1989); *Spires* for Trumpet and Small Orch. (1981; Lille, Feb. 6, 1989); *Tides* for Clarinet and Small Orch. (1982); *For Tuba with Strings Attached* for Tuba and Strings (1982; also for Tuba and String Quartet); Piano Concerto, *Trajectories* (1985); *Motivations* for Trombone and Orch. (1986); *Fourscore + 2* for 4 Solo Percussionists and Orch. (1987; Houston, April 26, 1989); *Midnight Music* for Symphonic Wind Band (1990; Machester, England, Oct. 14, 1992); *Prelude to Hart Crane's The Bridge* for Strings (1991); *Entre Nous* for Cello and Orch. (1992; N.Y., Feb. 6, 1994); *Fire and Smoke* for Timpani and Wind Band (1993; Aspen, Colo., July 4, 1994). **CHAMBER:** 3 string quartets (n.d., 1947, 1995); *5 Pieces* for Cello and Piano (1952); Chamber Concerto No. 1 for Flute, Clarinet, Trumpet, Tuba, Violin, Piano, and Percussion (1956; N.Y., Jan. 20, 1957); Brass Quintet (1963; N.Y., March 22, 1964); *Early American Suite* for Flute, Oboe, Clarinet, Bassoon, Horn, and Harpsichord or Piano (1965); Duo for Viola and Piano (1970); *Churchill Downs Chamber Concerto* (N.Y., Oct. 1970); *Propulsions*, percussion concerto for 7 Players (1974; Boston, April 26, 1976); Wind Quintet (N.Y., May 22, 1975); *Concatenations* for Viola and Percussion Quartet (1976; Boston, May 1, 1977); *Double Crossings* for Trumpet and Percussion (1976); *Sound Dreams* for Flute, Clarinet, Viola, Cello, Piano, and Percussion (Boston, Nov. 13, 1977); *Triple Play* for 2 Trombones and Percussion (1977; Sheffield, England, March 11, 1982); *Cross*

Currents for Brass Quintet and Percussion (1978; Cambridge, Mass., Jan. 16, 1981); *3 Men on a Dis-Course* for Clarinet, Cello, and Percussion (1979; N.Y., April 9, 1989); *Partnership* for 5 Timpani and Marimba (N.Y., May 19, 1980); *For Tuba with Strings Attached* for Tuba and String Quartet (1982; N.Y., Jan. 10, 1985; also for Tuba and String Orch.); *Quintessentials* for Flute, Clarinet, Marimba, Percussion, and Brass (Baltimore, Nov. 3, 1983); Suite for Marimba (1983; N.Y., May 21, 1984); *Fusions* for Chamber Group (1983; Pittsburgh, Oct. 22, 1984); *Fairy Tale* for Viola and Chamber Ensemble (N.Y., Oct. 2, 1989); *Alliances* for Cello and Piano (1989); *Bazz Ma Tazz* for 8 Tenor Trombones, 4 Bass Trombones, and 6 Percussion (Boston, April 26, 1993). **P i a n o :** 3 sonatas (1947; 1949–52; 1953); *Piano Suite for Young People* (2 vols., 1951); Sonatina (1952); *5 Pieces* (1952); *Imprints* (1978; N.Y., Feb. 10, 1981); *Re-Percussions* for 2 Pianos (1982; Akron, Ohio, Feb. 9, 1983); *Sunday Silence* (N.Y., Oct. 1, 1990). **VOCAL:** *Phenomena* for Soprano and Chamber Ensemble (1972); *Junctures* for Soprano and Orch. (1979); *Legends and Love Letters* for Soprano and Chamber Ensemble (Washington, D.C., Nov. 5, 1988); *Four...Parts of a World*, song cycle for Soprano and Piano (1991). **OTHER:** Many documentary film scores. **—NS/LK/DM**

Bázlik, Miro, Slovak composer, pianist, and teacher; b. Partizánska L'upča, April 12, 1931. He studied piano with Kafendová at the Bratislava Cons. (1946–51). He then pursued training in mathematical analysis at the Charles Univ. in Prague (1951–56), and concurrently received instruction in composition from Eliáš and in piano from Rauch and Moravec. He completed his study of composition with Cikker at the Bratislava Academy of Music and Drama (1956–61). From 1963 he was active as a composer, pianist, and private teacher of composition. In 1990 he became a lecturer in the mathematics and physics faculty of the Comenius Univ. in Bratislava. In 1974 he won First Prize in the Queen Marie-José Composition Competition in Geneva, and in 1977 the Ján Levoslav Bella Award.

WORKS: DRAMATIC: *Peter and Lucy*, opera (1963–66); *Tempest*, ballet (1977); incidental music; film scores. **ORCH.:** *Baroque Suite* for Small Orch. (1960); *Music for Violin and Orch.* (1961); *Little Concerto Music* for Violin and Strings (1966); *5 Little Elegies* for Strings (1975); *Sonata* for Harpsichord and Strings (1980); *Epoché* for Cello and Orch. (1983; also for Cello, Orch., and Tape); *Ballad*, viola concerto (1984); *Concerto Music* (1985); *Diptych* (1986); *Partita* (1988); *Introid* (1997). **CHAMBER:** 3 *Pieces* for 14 Instruments (1964); 2 string quartets (1965, 1973); *Music to Poetry* for Chamber Ensemble (1966); *Pastorale* for Woodwinds and Harpsichord (1968); 2 wind quintets (1977, 1978); *Quartettino* for String Quartet (1978). **P i a n o :** *Variations and Fugue* (1950); Sonata (1954); *Palette* (1956); *Music to a Poet and a Woman* (1969); *Forget-Me-Nots* (1979); *24 Preludes* (1981–84); *6 Epigrams* (1986). **VOCAL:** *5 Songs on Chinese Poetry* for Alto, Flute, Cello, and Piano (1960); *Twelve*, oratorio for Speaker, Chorus, and Orch., after Blok (1967); Cantata for Chorus and Chamber Orch. (1967); *Canticum 43* for Soprano, Chorus, and Orch. (1968–71); *Suite-Ballad* for Soprano, Nonet, and Percussion (1969); 4 *Folk Songs* for Soprano, Baritone, and Orch. (1986); *Canticum Jeremiae*, chamber oratorio for Soprano, Bass-baritone, Chorus, Violin, and String Orch. (1987); *De Profundis* for Soprano and Orch. (1990); *Apparition d'aprés Stéphane Mallarmé* for Soprano and Chamber Orch. (1995); 3

Songs for Chorus, after Ronsard (1995). **TAPE:** *Spectra* (1970–72); *Triptych* (1971); *Shepherd Ballad* (1977); *Ergodic Composition* (1981); *Shepherd Elegy* (1983); *Ballad about Wood* (1987). **—NS/LK/DM**

Beach, Mrs. H.H.A. (née **Amy Marcy Cheney**), important American composer; b. Henniker, N.H., Sept. 5, 1867; d. N.Y., Dec. 27, 1944. She was descended of early New England colonists, and was a scion of a cultural family. She was educated at a private school in Boston. She studied piano with Ernest Perabo and Carl Baermann, and received instruction in harmony and counterpoint from Junius W. Hill. She made her debut as a pianist in Boston on Oct. 24, 1883, playing Chopin's *Rondo* in E-flat major and Moscheles's G minor concerto under Neuendorff. On March 28, 1885, she made her first appearance with the Boston Sym. Orch. in Chopin's F minor concerto under Gericke. On Dec. 3, 1885, at the age of 18, she married Dr. H.H.A. Beach, a Boston surgeon, a quarter of a century older than she. The marriage was a happy one, and as a token of her loyalty to her husband, she used as her professional name Mrs. H.H.A. Beach. She began to compose modestly, mostly for piano, but soon embarked on an ambitious Mass, which was performed by the Handel and Haydn Soc. in Boston on Feb. 18, 1892, becoming the first woman to have a composition performed by that organization. On Oct. 30, 1896, her *Gaelic Symphony*, based on Irish folk tunes, was performed by the Boston Sym. Orch. with exceptional success. On April 6, 1900, she appeared as soloist with the Boston Sym. Orch. in the first performance of her Piano Concerto. She also wrote a great many songs in an endearing Romantic manner. When her husband died in 1910, she went to Europe. She played her works in Berlin, Leipzig, and Hamburg, attracting considerable attention as the first of her gender and national origin to be able to compose music of a European quality of excellence. She returned to the U.S. in 1914 and lived in N.Y. Her music, unpretentious in its idiom and epigonic in its historical aspect, retained its importance as the work of a pioneer woman composer in America.

WORKS: DRAMATIC: O p e r a : *Cabildo* (1932; Athens, Ga., Feb. 27, 1947). **ORCH.:** *Eilende Wolken, Segler die Lüfte* for Alto and Orch. (N.Y., Dec. 2, 1892); *Bal masque* (N.Y., Dec. 12, 1893); *Gaelic Symphony* (1894; Boston, Oct. 30, 1896); Piano Concerto (1899; Boston, April 6, 1900); *Jephthah's Daughter* for Soprano and Orch. (1903). **CHAMBER:** Violin Sonata (1896; Boston, March 14, 1899); Piano Quintet (1907; Boston, Feb. 27, 1908); *Theme and Variations* for Flute and String Quartet (1916); String Quartet (1929); Piano Trio (1938). **P i a n o :** Many pieces, including the popular *Valse-Caprice* (1889), *Fireflies* (1892), *Ballad* (1894), *The Hermit Thrush at Eve* (1922), and *The Hermit Thrust at Morn* (1922). **VOCAL: CHORAL:** Mass (1890; Boston, Feb. 7, 1892); *Festival Jubilate* for Chorus and Orch. (1891; Chicago, May 1, 1893); *The Chambered Nautilus* (1907); *The Canticle of the Sun* (1928); numerous other choral works, both sacred and secular; many songs, including the favorites *Ecstasy* (1893), *3 Browning Songs* (1900), *June* (1903), and *Shena Van* (1904).

BIBL.: P. Goetschius, *Mrs. H.H.A. B.* (Boston, 1906); E. Merrill, *Mrs. H.H.A. B.: Her Life and Music* (diss., Univ. of Rochester, 1963); M. Eden, *Energy and Individuality in the Art of*

Anna Huntington, Sculptor, and A. B., Composer (Metuchen, N.J., 1987); J. Brown, *A. B. and her Chamber Music: Biography, Documents, Style* (Metuchen, N.J., 1994); W. Jenkins, *The Remarkable Mrs. B., American Composer: A Biographical Account Based on Her Diaries, Letters, Newspaper Clippings, and Personal Reminiscences* (Warren, Mich., 1994); A. Block, *A. B., Passionate Victorian: The Life and Work of an American Composer, 1867–1944* (N.Y., 1998). —NS/LK/DM

Beach Boys, The, pop harmonizers who revolutionized the sound of American rock and roll. **MEMBERSHIP:** Brian Wilson, bs., kybd., voc. (b. Hawthorne, Calif., June 20, 1942); Dennis Wilson, drm., voc. (b. Hawthorne, Dec. 4, 1944; d. Marina del Rey, Calif., Dec. 28, 1983); Carl Wilson, lead gtr., voc. (b. Hawthorne, Dec. 21, 1946; d. Los Angeles, Feb. 6, 1998); Mike Love, lead voc., sax. (b. Los Angeles, March 15, 1941); Al Jardine, rhythm gtr., voc. (b. Lima, Ohio, Sept. 3, 1942). Bruce Johnston (b. Chicago, June 27, 1944) joined in 1965, left in 1972, and returned in 1978.

Formed in 1961 by the Wilson brothers, cousin Mike Love, and friend Al Jardine, as Kenny and The Cadets, and Carl and The Passions, then The Pendletones, The Beach Boys recorded the regional hit "Surfin'" for the small local label X in 1961. They debuted in Long Beach on New Year's Eve 1961, but Jardine soon departed, to be replaced by David Marks for more than a year. Signed to Capitol Records in the summer of 1962, The Beach Boys issued smash hits on the southern Calif. themes of surfing, cars and motorcycles, girls, and high school—virtually all written by Brian Wilson. Early hits included "Surfin' Safari," the remake of Chuck Berry's "Sweet Little Sixteen," and "Surfin' U.S.A.," backed with "Shut Down." Featuring such ballads as the title song (a near-smash hit) and "In My Room" (a major hit) beginning with *Surfer Girl*, the group's first album produced by Brian Wilson, The Beach Boys scored with "Be True to Your School," "Fun, Fun, Fun," and the top hit "I Get Around," backed by the major hit ballad "Don't Worry Baby." "Wendy" proved only a moderate success, but *The Beach Boys Today* contained two near-smash hits, "When I Grow Up (To Be a Man)" and "Dance, Dance, Dance," and the top hit "Help Me, Rhonda."

Conducting their first major U.S. tour in September 1964, *The Beach Boys' Concert* album, recorded in Sacramento, Calif., became the first live album to top the album charts. However, Brian Wilson suffered a nervous breakdown in December and ceased touring with the group. With Carl Wilson becoming the on-stage leader and Al Jardine taking over Brian's falsetto parts, the group was briefly augmented by sessions guitarist Glen Campbell, who was replaced by Bruce Johnston in April 1965. Johnston, an early associate of Sandy Nelson and Phil Spector, had formed a partnership with Terry Melcher in 1963 that yielded hits under the names The Rip Chords ("Hey Little Cobra") and Bruce and Terry ("Summer Means Fun").

Relieved of his arduous touring duties, Brian Wilson concentrated on writing for *The Beach Boys*. With Bruce Johnston's recording debut with the group, the major hit "California Girls," Brian started using elaborate production techniques on the group's recordings. While the rest of The Beach Boys were on tour, Brian began working on his *Pet Sounds* epic, employing scores of studio musicians and utilizing advanced studio techniques. Although perplexed by Brian's work on the album in their absence, the returning group persevered to complete the critically acclaimed masterpiece. However, despite the lush orchestral sound and the inclusion of songs such as "God Only Knows" (with lead vocals by Carl Wilson), "Wouldn't It Be Nice," "I Just Wasn't Made for These Times," "Caroline No," and the folk song "Sloop John B.," *Pet Sounds* sold poorly compared to previous releases.

Severely disappointed, Brian Wilson nonetheless initiated work on the next album, tentatively titled *Smile*, with lyricist Van Dyke Parks. While deeply immersed in the project, Capitol Records issued the monumental single "Good Vibrations." Taking more than six months to complete, using 90 hours of studio time in 17 sessions, "Good Vibrations," with Carl Wilson on lead vocals, became a top hit in the fall of 1966. Meanwhile, the already troubled Brian, working against the perceived competition of Phil Spector and The Beatles, began behaving erratically as rumors of heavy drug use circulated. For whatever reason, *Smile* was not issued. *Smiley Smile* was released in its place on the group's recently formed custom label, Brother Records, distributed by Capitol. The album contained several songs from the abortive Wilson-Parks collaboration, including the major hit "Heroes and Villains."

Pulling out of a scheduled appearance at the Monterey International Pop Festival in June 1967, The Beach Boys met guru Maharishi Mahesh Yogi in December. Their fascination with his transcendental meditation, particularly in the person of Mike Love, culminated in a near-disastrous tour with the Maharishi in the spring of 1968. *Friends* reflected the group's conversion to transcendental meditation, while *20/20*, their final album of new material for Capitol, featured the major hit "Do It Again" and a minor hit remake of the Phil Spector–Jeff Barry–Ellie Greenwich song "I Can Hear Music," with lead vocals by Carl Wilson.

The Beach Boys switched to Warner Brothers/Reprise Records in 1970, reestablishing Brother Records under that company's distributorship. The group appeared to be emerging from their doldrums that year with a successful performance at the Big Sur Folk Festival and the release of the underrated *Sunflower* album, to which Dennis Wilson contributed four songs. However, Brian's withdrawal as songwriter and producer with the *Surf's Up* album and his traumatizing appearance at the Whiskey-A-Go-Go in November 1970 left the rest to their own devices. Two old *Smile* songs, "Surf's Up" and the hastily completed "Sail on Sailor," were later issued as singles. Dennis Wilson appeared with James Taylor in the 1971 film *Two Lane Blacktop* and Johnston left the group in early 1972. By the beginning of 1974, producer James William Guercio (Blood, Sweat and Tears and Chicago) had joined on bass.

The Beach Boys enjoyed a revival with the release of older Capitol material on *Endless Summer* (which remained on the album charts nearly three years) and *Spirit of America*. The Beach Boys toured with Chicago in the spring of 1975, and during 1976, Brian Wilson rejoined the others for an hour-long documentary aired on NBC in August. The album *15 Big Ones*, comprising half new original material and half remade oldies, including a smash hit version of Chuck Berry's "Rock and Roll Music," saw Brian once again producing, though eschewing the production style pioneered with *Pet Sounds*.

Bruce Johnston provided Barry Manilow with the top hit "I Write the Songs" in late 1975 and recorded *Going Public* in 1977. Dennis Wilson recorded *Pacific Ocean Blue*, regarded as a neglected masterpiece, while Mike Love recorded with both Waves and Celebration, who hit with "Almost Summer." For The Beach Boys, neither *M.I.U.* nor *L.A. (Light Album)*, recorded with a returned Bruce Johnston on their new Caribou label, fared particularly well. After Dennis Wilson recorded a second solo album, The Beach Boys issued *Keepin' the Summer Alive*, produced by Johnston. In 1981, Carl Wilson became the first Beach Boy to undertake a solo tour, in support of his Caribou debut.

Mike Love became the front man for The Beach Boys during the 1980s, as Brian Wilson embarked on an unorthodox rehabilitation program under therapist Eugene Landy between 1983 and 1988. Dennis Wilson, the only actual surfer in the group, drowned off Marina del Rey, Calif., on Dec. 28, 1983. The Beach Boys performed at Ronald Reagan's Inaugural Gala in January 1985 and Live Aid the following July. In 1987, they scored a major hit with a remake of the surf classic "Wipeout," recorded with the Fat Boys rap group.

The Beach Boys were inducted into the Rock and Roll Hall of Fame in 1988. During the year, Brian Wilson became the last Wilson brother to release a solo album with the critically acclaimed, but poor-selling, *Brian Wilson* album on Sire Records. However, a second solo album, entitled *Sweet Insanity*, was rejected by Sire. The Beach Boys, without Brian Wilson, scored a top hit with "Kokomo," written by Mike Love, Terry Melcher, John Phillips, and Scott McKenzie, from the soundtrack to the Tom Cruise movie *Cocktail*. Since December 1991, the personal and business affairs of Brian Wilson have been managed by a court-appointed conservator. Producer Don Was directed the film documentary of Brian Wilson's life, *I Just Wasn't Made for These Times*, released in 1995. Wilson also worked with his *Smile* collaborator, songwriter-producer Van Dyke Parks, for *Orange Crate Art* on Warner Brothers Records. In 1999, he released a new solo album, *Imagination*, and embarked on a concert tour of the U.S. Carl Wilson died in Los Angeles on Feb. 6, 1998, from complications of lung cancer at the age of 51.

DISC.: *Surfin' Safari* (1962); *Surfin' U.S.A.* (1963); *Surfer Girl* (1963); *Little Deuce Coupe* (1963); *All Summer Long* (1964); *Christmas Album* (1964); *Concert* (1964); *The Beach Boys Today* (1965); *Summer Days (and Summer Nights)* (1965); *Party!* (1965); *Pet Sounds* (1966); *Smiley Smile* (1967); *Wild Honey* (1967); *Stack-O-Tracks* (1968); *Friends* (1968); *20/20* (1969); *Sunflower* (1970); *Surf's Up* (1971); *In Concert Reprise* (1973); *15 Big Ones* (1976); *The Beach Boys Love You* (1977); *M.I.U.* (1978); *L.A. (Light Album)* (1979); *Keepin' the Summer Alive* (1980); *The Beach Boys* (1985); *Summer in Paradise* (1992); *The Pet Sounds Sessions* (1996). **BRIAN WILSON:** *Brian Wilson* (1988); *I Just Wasn't Made for These Times* (1995); *Imagination* (1999). Van Dyke Parks: *Orange Crate Art* (1995). **CARL AND THE PASSIONS:** *So Tough* (1972). **CARL WILSON:** *Carl Wilson* (1981); *Youngblood* (1983). **DENNIS WILSON:** *Pacific Ocean Blue* (1977); *One of Those People* (1979). **THE VETTES:** *Rev-Up* (1963). **THE DE-FENDERS** : *The Big Ones* (1963); *Drag Beat* (1963). **BRUCE JOHNSTON:** *Surfers Pajama Party* (1963); *Surfin' Round the World* (1963); *Going Public* (1977). **THE RIP CHORDS:** *Hey, Little Cobra (and Other Hot Rod Hits)* (1964); *Three Window Coupe* (1964). **THE CATALINAS:** *Fun, Fun, Fun* (1964).

WRITINGS: B. Wilson with T. Gold, *Wouldn't It Be Nice—My Own Story* (N.Y., 1991).

BIBL.: K. Barnes, *The Beach Boys: A Biography in Words and Pictures* (N.Y., 1976); B. Elliott, *Surf's Up: The Beach Boys on Record, 1961–1981* (Ann Arbor, Mich; 1982); S. Gaines, *Heroes and Villains: The True Story of The Beach Boys* (N.Y; 1986); B. Golden, *The Beach Boys: Southern California Pastoral* (San Bernardino, Calif., 1976); T. White, *The Nearest Faraway Place: Brian Wilson, The Beach Boys, and the Southern California Experience* (N.Y., 1996).—**BH**

Beard, John, renowned English tenor; b. c. 1717; d. Hampton, Feb. 5, 1791. He studied with Bernard Gates at the Chapel Royalm and while still a youth sang in Handel's *Esther* in London (1732). He left the Chapel Royal in 1734, and on Nov. 9 of that year made his debut as Silvio in Handel's *Il Pastor fido* at Covent Garden. He subsequently appeared in about 10 operas, many oratorios, masques, and odes by Handel. In 1761 he became manager of Covent Garden, but continued to make appearances as a singer. He retired in 1767 owing to increasing deafness.—**NS/LK/DM**

Beardslee, Bethany, American soprano; b. Lansing, Mich., Dec. 25, 1927. She studied at Mich. State Univ., then received a scholarship to the Juilliard School of Music in N.Y., making her N.Y. debut in 1949. She soon became known as a specialist in modern music, evolving an extraordinary technique with a flutelike ability to sound impeccably precise intonation. She also mastered the art of *Sprechstimme*, which enabled her to give fine renditions of such works as Schoenberg's *Pierrot Lunaire*, and she also was a brilliant performer of vocal parts in scores by Berg, Webern, and Stravinsky. In 1976 she joined the faculty of Westminster Choir Coll. in Princeton, N.J. In 1981–82 she was a prof. of music at the Univ. of Tex. in Austin. After serving as performer-in-residence at the Univ. of Calif. at Davis (1982–83), she taught at Brooklyn Coll. of the City Univ. of N.Y. (from 1983). She was married to **Jacques-Louis Monod** and, later, to **Godfrey Winham**.—**NS/LK/DM**

Beastie Boys, veteran white rap group who fought for their right to party, but later discovered a social conscience. **MEMBERSHIP:** Michael Diamond, voc., drm. (b. N.Y.C., Nov. 20, 1965); Adam Horovitz, gtr. (b. N.Y.C., Oct. 31, 1966); Adam Yauch, bs. (b. Brooklyn, N.Y., Aug. 5 1964).

BEATLES

Although they were the first rappers to garner a gold and platinum album, the Beastie Boys began life as a four-piece hardcore band with drummer Kate Schellenback and guitarist John Berry. They opened shows at N.Y.'s seminal punk clubs like CBGBs and Max's for the likes of the Bad Brains. The quartet recorded an EP called *Polywog Stew*. They first came to the public fore in 1983, tapping into the burgeoning hip-hop movement with the 12" "Cookie Puss," a crank call set to a reggae-ish hip-hop beat. On the strength of its cheeky humor, it became an underground hit. This brought them to the attention of N.Y.U. student Rick Rubin. They started recording for Def Jam, a label Rubin started out of his dorm room.

Live, they begin to put down their instruments during their sets to MC. Rubin scratched on their next single, the Def Jam release "Rock Hard." By 1985, Columbia Records signed on to distribute Def Jam. The Beasties had a role in the film *Krush Groove* and a slot on the soundtrack. Their tune, "She's on It," merged rap with an AC/DC metal riff and the Beasties's own bad-boy attitude. They took this attitude on the road with Madonna and her "Like a Virgin" tour, followed by a stint on the road with Run DMC. The show featured props like a giant inflatable penis, which garnered them quite a bit of attention in the press.

After all this lead-in, the Beasties's debut album *License to Ill* sold faster than any previous Columbia records debut, shifting a million copies in two months and becoming the first #1 rap album. It eventually sold over eight million copies. They alienated hip-hop purists with the frat-rap "Fight for Your Right (To Party)." They enraged women's groups with tunes like "Girls."

After touring for the album, they parted ways with Def Jam in the wake of royalty feuds and other controversies. They signed with Capital and relocated to Calif., building a studio with a basketball court and skateboard ramp. The first album out of that studio was *Paul's Boutique*, a critically acclaimed album that garnered somewhat disappointing sales initially, but wound up going double platinum.

The group started their own Grand Royal Records, signing Schellenbach's new band Luscious Jackson and Berry's Big Fat Love. After several years of dealing with beats and samples, the trio started honing their chops again. Separately, they also developed other interests. Horovitz acted in several films, including *A Kiss Before Dying* and *Roadside Prophets*. Diamond got involved in X-Large, a b-boy fashion company. Horovitz married actress (Donovan's daughter) Ione Skye; Diamond married filmmaker Tamara Davis, and Yauch was married to Dechen Wangdu. Yauch started exploring Buddhism, and met with the Dalai Lama. So, three years after *Paul's Boutique*, they followed up with *Check Your Head*, a fusion of their punk roots, funk leanings, and hip-hop fortunes. This stance took them out of their old school rap bag and to a place more in line with alternative rock. The album debuted at in the Top Ten. While they had no chart hits, their videos got played heavily on MTV. Eventually the album went triple platinum.

The boys hit the road. They also started a newsletter about Grand Royal Records; it took on a life of its own

and evolved into a magazine. Their growing social consciousness came to the fore with the founding of the Milarepa Foundation, dedicated to promoting universal compassion through music.

Musically, they worked in their studio, first putting together some of their old tracks like "Cookie Puss" and "Polywog Stew" on an album called *Some Old Bullshit*. They then got down to new work, further extending the mix of their own live music with their MC work and samples. The resulting album *Ill Communication* debuted at #1, selling platinum out of the box and rising to triple platinum. It marked a sharp change in attitude. Where at one time (c. *License to Ill*) they rapped, "She'd drop to her knees if we'd only say please," they now maintain "The disrespect of women has got to be through."

The Beastie Boys hit the road, selling out arenas in as few as nine minutes. One dollar from each ticket went to the Milarepa Foundation. The tour took them as far and wide as South America and Southeast Asia.

After the tour, the Beasties took a short trip down memory lane, releasing an eight-track, 11– minute long hardcore EP, *Aglio e Olio*.

In 1996, the Beasties organized the first annual Tibetan Freedom Concert, attracting 100,000 people to San Francisco's Golden Gate Park. They were joined by a diverse line-up of artists ranging from the Skatalites to Yoko Ono, Buddy Guy, The Fugees, and the Red Hot Chili Peppers. The annual event has since played in N.Y. and Washington, D.C. The 1999 show took place simultaneously in Sydney, Amsterdam, Tokyo, and Chicago.

Another EP came out on Grand Royal in 1996. Called *The In Sound from Way Out!*, it consisted of instrumental tracks recorded during the *Check Your Head* and *Ill Communication* sessions. They initially released it to media outlets for use as backdrops for promos and newscasts, but eventually were convinced to put it out.

Late in the 1990s, the Beastie Boys moved back to N.Y., where they recorded *Hello Nasty*. Released in the summer of 1998, this one sold double platinum out of the box, adding another million sales before the year was out. In promoting the album, they made tracks available on their web site for computer download, stirring up considerable consternation at Capitol Records, and proving no matter how much of a social conscience they developed, they were never beyond a little roguish fun.

DISC.: *License to Ill* (1986); *Paul's Boutique* (1989); *Check Your Head* (1992); *Ill Communication* (1994); *Some Old Bullshit* (1994); *Aglio E Olio* (1995); *The In Sound from Way Out!* (1996); *Hello Nasty* (1998).—**HB**

Beatles, The, the most important rock group in history. **MEMBERSHIP:** John Lennon, rhythm gtr., pno., har., voc. (b. Woolton, Liverpool, England, Oct. 9, 1940; d. N.Y.C., Dec. 8, 1980); Paul McCartney, bs., pno., bjo., trpt., voc. (b. Allerton, Liverpool, June 18, 1942); George Harrison, lead gtr., sitar, pno., voc. (b. Wavertree, Liverpool, Feb. 24, 1943); Ringo Starr (b. Richard Starkey), drm., voc. (b. Dingle, Liverpool, July 7, 1940). Early members included Stuart Sutcliffe, bs. (b. Edinburgh, Scotland, June 23, 1940; d. Hamburg, Germany, April 10, 1962); Pete Best, drm. (b. Madras, India, Nov. 24, 1941).

245

The evolution of The Beatles began in 1956 when John Lennon formed a group called The Quarrymen. In July 1957, he met Paul McCartney, who subsequently joined the group. George Harrison joined in August 1958 and, by 1959, they were down to a trio. The group's name changed several times during that year, eventually becoming The Silver Beatles. Bassist Stu Sutcliffe and drummer Pete Best joined the group in January and August 1960, respectively. Subsequently performing in Hamburg, Germany, for three months as The Beatles, the group later backed singer Tony Sheridan in Hamburg in June 1961 and recordings done with Sheridan were later released on albums. In Hamburg, the group completed their musical apprenticeship, playing rigorous night-long shows to unappreciative audiences; live recordings made at the Star Club in 1962 were eventually issued in 1977.

The Beatles returned to England and took up residence at The Cavern, a club in Liverpool, beginning in February 1961. In April, Stu Sutcliffe left the group; he died of a brain hemorrhage in Hamburg on April 10, 1962. In November 1961, record shop owner Brian Epstein discovered the group at The Cavern and attempted to secure them a recording contract. They were initially rejected by Decca and later picked up by the Parlophone subsidiary of EMI (British Capitol) in May 1962. That August, Ringo Starr quit Rory Storm's Hurricanes and replaced Pete Best on drums. Best later recorded an album for Savage Records and served as "technical advisor" for the 1979 Dick Clark production *The Birth of The Beatles*, which aired on ABC-TV. By the late 1990s, Pete Best had formed The Pete Best Combo, recording Best for Music Club Records.

In September, with George Martin producing, The Beatles conducted their first recording session. In October, their first single, "Love Me Do," was issued in Great Britain on Parlophone Records, becoming a modest hit. Their second single, "Please Please Me," quickly proved a smash hit. The Beatles' first British album, *Please Please Me*, issued in March 1963, remained near the top of the charts for six months. Their second album, *With The Beatles*, issued in November, initiated a string of 11 consecutive studio albums of new material to top the British album charts.

In the United States, the next Beatles single, "I Want to Hold Your Hand," backed with "I Saw Her Standing There," was released in January 1964, with heavy promotion by Capitol. The song became a top hit within two weeks and proved to be one of the fastest-selling singles of the 1960s, eventually selling 15 million copies worldwide. In February, The Beatles performed on CBS television's *Ed Sullivan Show* before an estimated audience of 73 million and launched their debut U.S. tour, with massive media coverage.

The dam burst. Nothing could stop The Beatles, and in their wake followed dozens of British groups. Indeed, Lennon and McCartney provided a number of hit songs to up-and-coming British groups, including "Hello Little Girl" for The Fourmost, "Bad to Me" for Billy J. Kramer and The Dakotas, and "It's for You" for Cilla Black. Peter and Gordon scored with their "World without Love" (a top British and American hit) and "I

Don't Want to See You Again," and The Rolling Stones' first major British hit came with Lennon and McCartney's "I Wanna Be Your Man."

For many weeks after the release of "I Want to Hold Your Hand," The Beatles dominated the highest chart positions with the top hits "She Loves You" and "Can't Buy Me Love" (on Capitol), "Please Please Me" and "Do You Want to Know a Secret" (on VeeJay), and "Twist and Shout" and "Love Me Do," backed with "P.S. I Love You" (on Tollie). In March 1964, the group began work on their first film, *A Hard Day's Night*, and John Lennon published his first book, *In His Own Write*. The film premiered in July and the British *A Hard Day's Night* album comprised entirely songs written by Lennon and McCartney. The Beatles' second U.S. tour began in August, and the following February and March they recorded and filmed their second movie, *Help!*, which opened in late July. In June, Lennon published his second book, *A Spaniard in the Works*. Through mid-1965, The Beatles continued their string of hit singles with the top hits "A Hard Day's Night," "I Feel Fine" (backed with "She's a Woman"), "Eight Days a Week," and "Ticket to Ride," and the major hits "And I Love Her," "I'll Cry Instead," and Carl Perkins's "Matchbox" backed with "Slow Down."

Increasing sophistication in the lyrics of Lennon and McCartney became evident after mid-1965. The words to the top hits "Help" and "Yesterday," the smash hit "Nowhere Man" and the major hit "Eleanor Rigby," and songs such as "In My Life" (from *Rubber Soul*) possessed a profound emotional intensity not apparent in earlier work. Completing their third North American tour in August 1965, The Beatles scored a top hit with "We Can Work It Out"/"Day Tripper" at year's end. George Harrison's songwriting ability began to be showcased with *Revolver*, which contained three of his songs: "Taxman," "Love You To," and "I Want to Tell You." The Beatles conducted their final American tour in August 1966 as "Yellow Submarine" (backed with "Eleanor Rigby") was becoming a smash hit.

With the single "Rain" (the flip side of the top hit "Paperback Writer") and songs such as "Tomorrow Never Knows" (from *Revolver*), The Beatles began utilizing involved studio production techniques in their recordings. The contributions of producer-arranger George Martin became particularly strong between 1966 and 1968. Lyrically, the songs of Lennon and McCartney began a tendency toward the bizarre and surreal, often defying logical explanation. This penchant for the surreal, first evident with "Norwegian Wood" (from *Rubber Soul*), continued with "Lucy in the Sky with Diamonds", the quintessential "A Day in the Life" (from *Sgt. Pepper*), and the singles "Strawberry Fields Forever"/"Penny Lane" and "I Am the Walrus."

Focusing their attention on recording, The Beatles' *Sgt. Pepper's Lonely Hearts Club Band* was issued in June 1967, with advance sales of one million plus. It remained on the American album charts for more than three years and eventually sold more then eight million copies in the United States. The first Beatles album to be identical in its British and American versions, *Sgt. Pepper* entailed 700 hours of studio time. As the music industry's first recognized concept album, the record was highly acclaimed by critics and marked perhaps the high point of The Beatles' recording career. The album included "Lucy in the Sky with Diamonds," "With a Little Help from My Friends" (sung by Ringo), Harrison's self-consciously philosophical "Within You, Without You," and the quintessential 1960s production, "A Day in the Life." The singles "All You Need Is Love" and "Hello Goodbye" became top hits before year's end, followed by the smash "Lady Madonna" the next spring.

Individual endeavors by members of The Beatles began in 1967 with the acting debut of John Lennon in the film *How I Won the War* and Paul McCartney's recording of the soundtrack to the film *The Family Way*. During the year, the group scripted, cast, directed, and edited the made-for-television movie *Magical Mystery Tour*, a conspicuous failure in its poor editing and photography. The soundtrack album, released in November in the United States only, included "The Fool on the Hill," "I Am the Walrus," and "All You Need Is Love." In 1968, George Harrison composed, arranged, and recorded his own music for the soundtrack to the film *Wonderwall*. Lennon, now with conceptual artist Yoko Ono, recorded with her the controversial *Two Virgins* album. In July, the animated movie *Yellow Submarine* premiered. It was probably the most artistically successful film with which The Beatles were associated. Furthermore, it was one of the most engaging psychedelic movies of the late 1960s. The soundtrack album included the title song and "All You Need Is Love."

In April 1968, The Beatles had formed their own record company, Apple. The first single for the label, "Hey Jude" (backed with "Revolution"), was released in August and became a top hit. The double-record set entitled *The Beatles* (also known as *The White Album*), issued in November, was the first album on Apple. Disjointed and revealing the tell-tale signs of a Lennon-McCartney rift, the album contained such diverse songs as "Back in the U.S.S.R.," "Blackbird," "Revolution," and Harrison's superlative "While My Guitar Gently Weeps" (recorded, without credit, with Eric Clapton). It remained on the American album charts for nearly three years and sold more than seven million copies in the United States.

During most of 1969, the individual Beatles worked apart. Ringo appeared in the movie *The Magic Christian*. The soundtrack album contained a solo McCartney composition, "Come and Get It," a near-smash hit for Badfinger. In March, John Lennon married Yoko Ono and Paul McCartney married Linda Eastman. The marriages seemed to mark the informal end of The Beatles. During the year, The Beatles scored top hits with "Get Back" and "Come Together" (backed with Harrison's smash hit "Something") and the near-hit "The Ballad of John and Yoko." John Lennon became the first Beatle to perform publicly outside the group in September with The Plastic Ono Band in Toronto.

The only Beatle album release of 1969, *Abbey Road* (named for the studio in which the group had recorded since 1962), was issued in November and became their most popular album, selling more than nine million copies in the United States. It included Lennon's "Come Together," Harrison's "Something" and "Here Comes the Sun," Ringo's "Octopus's Garden," and "She Came in through the Bathroom Window." The *Abbey Road* album was actually the final Beatles recording. *Let It Be*, initially produced by George Martin and later reworked by Phil Spector, was held up by remixing disputes and film editing problems and was eventually issued in May 1970. The album included the top hits "Let It Be," "Get Back," and "The Long and Winding Road," The Beatles' final single release.

On the last day of 1970, Paul McCartney sued for dissolution of The Beatles' partnership, which legally ended on Jan. 9, 1975. Subsequent Beatles album releases were the live sets *Live at Star Club* and *Live at the Hollywood Bowl* (recorded in 1964 and 1965), *Rarities*, and various anthology sets. The individual members of The Beatles recorded a number of albums for Apple in the first half of the 1970s, most notably Paul McCartney's *McCartney* (1970) and *Band on the Run* (with his group, Wings; 1973), George Harrison's *All Things Must Pass* (1970) and *The Concert for Bangladesh* (1972), John Lennon's *Imagine* (1971), and Ringo Starr's *Ringo* (1973).

Throughout the 1970s, rumors persisted that The Beatles would reunite for touring or recordings, but such speculation finally and tragically ended with the murder of John Lennon in N.Y.C. on Dec. 8, 1980. The remaining three, plus Linda McCartney, jointly recorded the 1981 tribute to Lennon, "All Those Years Ago," written by Harrison.

The public's fascination with The Beatles was sustained in the early 1980s through the film documentary *The Compleat Beatles* (1982) and long- time associate Peter Brown's book, *The Love You Make: An Insider's Story of The Beatles* (1983). In August 1985, superstar Michael Jackson purchased the copyrights to 40,000 songs, including over 200 Lennon-McCartney songs. During the 25th anniversary year of The Beatles' first recording, 1987, Capitol Records issued for the first time on CD The Beatles' first seven albums in their British versions (U.S. versions contained one to four fewer songs) and their last five albums (U.S. and British versions were identical). *Sgt. Pepper*, released in June, rapidly became the best-selling CD of all time.

In 1994, the movie *Backbeat* focused on the early days of The Beatles and Stu Sutcliffe in particular. Late in the year, Apple Records issued The Beatles' *Live at the BBC*, 56 songs recorded for broadcast by the radio station between March 1962 and June 1965. Consisting largely of cover songs, the album quickly sold more than five million copies. In November 1995, the three-part special *The Beatles Anthology* aired on ABC television, and the end of the first program featured the debut of "Free As a Bird," a Lennon demonstration record completed by the former Beatles, which became a near-hit. Capitol subsequently issued three double-CD sets of *Anthology* albums that demonstrated the remarkable popularity of a group that had disbanded a quarter of a century ago.

The most important rock group in history, The Beatles' unprecedented commercial success was paralleled by their masterful artistic achievements and widespread cultural impact. Musically, The Beatles were the group that institutionalized many of the advances pioneered in rock music in the late 1950s, from the self-contained music group to the use of sophisticated arrangements and studio production techniques. In encompassing so many diversified forms of music (pop love songs, ballads, novelty songs, folk, country-and-western, rhythm-and-blues) within the basic rock 'n' roll format, The Beatles revitalized rock 'n' roll. Their music exhibited a fresh, clean, exuberant sound that contrasted sharply with the vapid pop ballads and dance songs pervading popular music in the early 1960s. Initiating an eclecticism that was to become one of their trademarks with *Something New*, The Beatles went beyond the standard three-chord progression, often utilizing diminished or augmented seventh and ninth chords while devising intriguing melodies and developing engaging vocal harmonies. Particularly after the *Help!* album, songwriters John Lennon and Paul McCartney brought an unprecedented lyric sophistication to rock music, writing songs of a personal and emotionally evocative nature. Their frequent philosophical concerns in lyrics widened the intellectual boundaries of rock in a manner rivaled only by Bob Dylan. Beginning with the *Revolver* album, perhaps the most innovative rock album ever made, The Beatles introduced novel instrumental combinations into rock, explored elaborate electronic production techniques under George Martin, and sparked the use of the East Indian sitar in rock music. The landmark *Sgt. Pepper* album, regarded by many as the first fully realized concept album and certainly an astounding work, may be the best known rock album of all time; its intricate jacket design also set new standards for the developing field of album artwork.

Within the music industry, The Beatles' enormous success turned the industry away from its preoccupation with individual singers performing songs written by professional songwriters toward music groups performing original material. The consistency of The Beatles' musical performances switched the focus of the consuming public's attention from singles to albums. The Beatles' rise enabled dozens of other British musicians to express themselves musically and achieve popularity, thereby breaking the American stranglehold on British popular music. Perhaps most significantly, the musical and songwriting advances pioneered by The Beatles led critics to view rock music as a valid art form in and of itself, and induced the public to perceive rock music as a total, internally coherent form of conscious experience. In social terms, The Beatles brought public attention to psychedelic drugs, the peace movement, Indian music, and Eastern spiritualism. Moreover, they helped promote a growing youth culture and inspired many young people to begin playing music by and for themselves, making music an essential part of their lifestyle. The Beatles were inducted into the Rock and Roll Hall of Fame in 1988. Producer George Martin was inducted in 1999.

For information on their subsequent careers, see separate entries on John Lennon, Paul McCartney, Ringo Starr, and George Harrison.

DISC.: EARLY BEATLES RECORDINGS: *The Beatles with Tony Sheridan and Their Guests* (1964; reissued as *This Is Where It Started*, 1966); *Live at the Star Club* (1962); *Introducing...The Beatles* (1963); *Jolly What! The Beatles and Frank Ifield* (1964); *Songs, Pictures and Stories of the Fabulous Beatles* (1964); *The Beatles versus The Four Seasons* (1964); *Ain't She Sweet* (1964); *The Early Beatles* (1965); *In the Beginning* (1970). **PETE BEST:** *Best of The Beatles* (1966); *Beyond The Beatles 1964–66* (1996). **PETE BEST COMBO:** *Music Club* (1998). **THE BEATLES:** Note: The album releases for The Beatles through 1966 were significantly different in the U.K. (on Parlophone) and the U.S. (on Capitol). Capitol chose to release the British albums on CD, except in the case of *Meet The Beatles. Please Please Me* (1963); *With The Beatles* (1963); *Meet The Beatles* (1964); *The Beatles' Second Album* (1964); *A Hard Day's Night* (1964); *Something New* (1964); *Beatles for Sale* (1964); *The Beatles' Story* (1964); *Beatles' '65* (1965); *Beatles VI* (1965); *Help!* (1965); *Rubber Soul* (1965); *Yesterday...and Today* (1966); *Revolver* (1966); *Sgt. Pepper's Lonely Hearts Club Band* (1967); *Magical Mystery Tour* (1967); *The Beatles (White Album)* (1968); *Yellow Submarine* (soundtrack; 1969); *Abbey Road* (1969); *Hey Jude* (1970); *Let It Be* (1970); *Live at the BBC* (1994). **BEATLES ANTHOLOGIES:** *1962–1966* (1973); *1967–1970* (1973); *Rock 'n' Roll Music* (1976); *Live at the Hollywood Bowl* (1977); *Love Songs* (1977); *Rarities* (1980); *Reel Music* (1982); *20 Greatest Hits* (1981); *Past Masters–Vol. 1, 2* (1988); *The Ultimate Box Set* (1988); *Anthology 1* (1995); *Anthology 2* (1996); *Anthology 3* (1996); *1* (2000).

WRITINGS: John Lennon, *In His Own Write* (N.Y., 1964); John Lennon, *A Spaniard in the Works* (N.Y., 1965); George Harrison, *I Me Mine* (N.Y., 1980); Pete Best and Patrick Doncaster, *Beatle! The Pete Best Story* (N.Y., 1985); John Lennon, *Skywriting by Word of Mouth, and Other Writings* (N.Y., 1986).

BIBL.: Brian Epstein, *A Cellarful of Noise* (Garden City, N.Y., 1964); Billy Shepherd, *The True Story of The Beatles* (N.Y., 1964); Hunter Davies, *The Beatles: The Authorized Biography* (N.Y., 1968); Edward E. Davis, *The Beatles Book* (N.Y., 1968); Julius Fast, *The Beatles: The Real Story* (N.Y., 1968); Anthony Scaduto, *The Beatles* (N.Y., 1968); Jann Wenner, *Lennon Remembers: The Rolling Stone Interviews* (San Francisco, 1971); Richard Dilello, *The Longest Cocktail Party: A Personal History of Apple* (Chicago, 1972); Peter McCabe and Robert Schonfeld, *Apple to the Core: The Unmaking of The Beatles* (N.Y., 1972); Derek Taylor, *As Time Goes By* (San Francisco, 1973); Wilfrid Mellers, *Twilight of the Gods* (N.Y., 1974); Allan Williams and William Marshall, *The Man Who Gave The Beatles Away* (N.Y., 1975); Harry Castleman and Walter J. Podrazik, *All Together Now: The First Complete Beatles'Discography 1961–1975* (Ann Arbor, Mich., 1976); Harry Castleman and Walter J. Podrazik, *The Beatles Again?* (Ann Arbor, Mich., 1977); Bill Harry, ed., *Mersey Beat: The Beginnings of The Beatles* (London, N.Y., 1977); Nicholas Schaffner, *The Beatles Forever* (N.Y., 1977); Roy Carr and Tony Tyler, *The Beatles: An Illustrated Record* (N.Y., 1975, 1978); J. Philip DiFranco, ed., *The Beatles: A Hard Day's Night* (London, N.Y., 1978); Miles (comp.), *The Beatles in Their Own Words* (N.Y., 1978); George Martin with Jeremy Hornsby, *All You Need Is Ears* (N.Y., 1979); Goldie Friede, Robin Titone, and Sue Weiner, *The Beatles A to Z* (N.Y., 1980); Nicholas Schaffner, *The Boys from Liverpool: John, Paul, George, Ringo* (N.Y., 1980); Tom Schultheiss (compiler), *The Beatles: A Day in the Life: The Beatles Day-by-Day, 1960–1970* (Ann Arbor, Mich., 1980); Geoffry Stokes, *The Beatles* (N.Y., 1980); John Blake, *All You Needed Was Love: The Beatles After The Beatles* (N.Y., 1981); Philip Norman, *Shout! The Beatles in Their Generation* (N.Y., 1981); Charles Reinhart, *You Can't Do That! Beatles Bootlegs and Novelty Records, 1963–80* (Ann Arbor, Mich., 1981);

Bob Woffinden, *The Beatles Apart* (London, N.Y., 1981);Bill Harry, ed., *The Beatles Who's Who* (London, 1982); Jeff Russell, *The Beatles Album File and Complete Discography* (N.Y., 1982); Mark Wallgren, *The Beatles on Record* (N.Y., Schuster, 1982); Peter Brown and Steven Gaines, *The Love You Make: An Insider's Story of The Beatles* (N.Y., 1983); Kevin Howlett, *The Beatles on the Beeb, '62–'65: The Story of Their Radio Career* (Ann Arbor, Mich., 1983); Terence J. O'Grady, *The Beatles, A Musical Evolution* (Boston, 1983); Charles P. Neises, ed., *The Beatles Reader: A Selection of Contemporary Views, News and Reviews of The Beatles in Their Heyday* (Ann Arbor, Mich., 1984); Neville Stannard, *The Long and Winding Road: A History of The Beatles on Record* (N.Y., 1984); John Tobler, *The Beatles* (N.Y., 1984); *Beatlefan: The Authoritative Publication of Record for Fans of The Beatles* (Ann Arbor, Mich., 1985); Carol D. Terry (editor and compiler), *Here, There and Everywhere: The First International Beatles Bibliography, 1962–1982* (Ann Arbor, Mich., 1985); Harry Castleman and Walter J. Podrazik, *The End of The Beatles?* Ann Arbor, Mich., 1985); Robert Cepican, *Yesterday—Came Suddenly: The Definitive History of The Beatles* (N.Y., 1985); Hunter Davies, *The Beatles* (N.Y., 1978, 1985); Geoffrey Guilano, *The Beatles: A Celebration* (N.Y., 1986); Mark Lewisohn, *The Beatles Live!* (N.Y., 1986); Allen J. Wiener, *The Beatles: A Recording History* (Jefferson, N.C., 1986); Derek Taylor, *It Was Twenty Years Ago* (N.Y., 1987); Mark Lewisohn, *Complete Beatles Recording Sessions* (N.Y., 1988); Tim Riley, *Tell Me Why: A Beatles Commentary* (N.Y., 1988); Ray Coleman, *The Man Who Made The Beatles: An Intimate Biography of Brian Epstein* (N.Y., 1989); William J. Dowlding, *Beatlesongs* (N.Y., 1989); William McKeen, *The Beatles: A Bio- Bibliography* (N.Y., 1989); Gareth L. Pawlowski, *How They Became The Beatles: A Definitive History of the Early Years, 1960–1964* (N.Y., 1989); Denny Somach, Kathleen Somach, and Kevin Gunn, *Ticket to Ride* (N.Y., 1989); Edward Gross, *The Fab Films of The Beatles* (Las Vegas, 1990); Mark Lewisohn, *The Beatles: Day by Day, A Chronology 1962–1989* (N.Y., 1990); Mike Clifford, *The Beatles* (N.Y., 1991); Bill Harry, ed., *The Ultimate Beatles Encyclopedia* (N.Y., 1992); Mark Lewisohn, *The Complete Beatles Chronicle* (N.Y., 1992); Allen J. Wiener, *The Beatles: The Ultimate Recording Guide* (N.Y., 1992); Geoffrey Guilano and Brenda Guilano, *The Lost Beatles Interviews* (N.Y., 1994); Ian MacDonald, *Revolution in the Head: The Beatles' Records and the Sixties* (N.Y., 1994); George Martin, *With a Little Help from My Friends: The Making of "Sgt. Pepper"* (Boston, 1994); Steve Turner, *A Hard Day's Write: The Stories Behind Every Beatles Song* (N.Y., 1994); Mark Hertsgaard, *A Day in the Life: The Music and Artistry of The Beatles* (N.Y., 1995); *The Beatles: From Yesterday to Today* (Boston, 1996); Jim O'Donnell, *The Day John Met Paul: A Hour-by-Hour Account of How The Beatles Began* (N.Y., 1996); Brandon Toropov, *Who Was Eleanor Rigby? And 998 More Questions and Answers about The Beatles* (N.Y., 1996); Doug Sulpy and Ray Schweighardt, *Get Back: The Unauthorized Chronicle of The Beatles' Let It Be Disaster* (N.Y., 1997); Richard Buskin, *The Complete Idiot's Guide to The Beatles* (N.Y., 1998).—**BH**

Beattie, Herbert (Wilson), American bass and teacher; b. Chicago, Aug. 23, 1926. He studied voice with John Wilcox at the American Cons. of Music in Chicago and with Dick Marzzolo in N.Y.; he also studied at Colo. Coll. (B.A., 1948), Westminster Choir Coll. (M.M., 1950), and the Salzburg Mozarteum (1955). On Oct. 11, 1957, he made his debut at the N.Y. City Opera as Baron Bouphol in *La Traviata*, where he sang regularly until 1972 and again from 1980 to 1984; he also sang opera in other cities in the U.S. and Europe, and toured as a concert artist. He taught at Syracuse Univ. (1950–52), Pa. State Univ. (1952–53), the Univ. of Buffalo (1953–58), and at Hofstra Univ. (1959–82). Among his best roles were Mozart's Osmin, Sarastro, Leporello, and Don Alfonso, and Rossini's Dr. Bartolo and Mustafà. He also sang in many contemporary operas. —**NS/LK/DM**

Beaulieu (real name, **Martin-Beaulieu**), **Marie-Désiré,** French composer and author; b. Paris, April 11, 1791; d. Niort, Dec. 21, 1863. He studied violin with Kreutzer, composition with Benincori and Abbé Roze; then studied with Mehul at the Paris Cons., winning the Prix de Rome in 1810. He composed the operas *Anacréon* and *Philadelphie*, the oratorios *L'Hymne du matin*, *L'Hymne de la nuit*, etc., and also other sacred music, as well as secular songs. He publ. the essays: *Du rythme, des effets qu'il produit et de leurs causes* (1852), *Mémoire sur ce qui reste de la musique de l'ancienne Grèce dans les premiers chants de l'Église* (1852), *Mémoire sur le caractère que doit avoir la musique de l'Église* (1858), and *Mémoire sur l'origine de la musique* (1859). However, his main contribution to French musical culture was his organizing of annual music festivals in provincial towns. He founded the Association Musicale de l'Ouest in 1835, and in 1860 the Societé des Concerts de Chant Classique, to which he bequeathed 100,000 francs. —**NS/LK/DM**

Beauvarlet-Charpentier, Jean-Jacques, famous French organist; b. Abbeville, June 28, 1734; d. Paris, May 6, 1794. His father was organist of the Hospice de la Charité in Lyons; his mother was the singer Marie Birol, who appeared on the stage under the name Marie Beauvarlet- Charpentier. He succeeded his father as organist in Lyons; from 1763 to 1771 he made appearances there at the Académie des Beaux Arts. He first played in Paris at a Concert Spirituel in 1759; in 1771 he was called to Paris as organist of the Royal Abbey of St. Victor. In 1772 he became organist at St. Paul, and also at St. Eloi des Orfèvres (from 1777) and Notre Dame (from 1783; with three other organists). He was also a composer, but his music attracted little notice. His son, Jacques-Marie Beauvarlet-Charpentier (b. Lyons, July 3, 1766; d. Paris, Sept. 7, 1834), was also an organist and composer.—**NS/LK/DM**

Becerra (-Schmidt), Gustavo, Chilean composer; b. Temuco, Aug. 26, 1925. He studied at the Santiago Cons. with Pedro Allende, and then with Domingo Santa Cruz. In 1949 he graduated from the Univ. of Chile, where he became a prof. in 1952; was its director of the Instituto de Extensión Musical (1959–63) and secretary-general of its music faculty (1969–71). From 1968 to 1970 he served as cultural attaché to the Chilean embassy in Bonn. In 1971 he received the Premio Nacional de Arte in music. His early works are set in the traditional neo-Classical manner, but soon he adopted an extremely radical modern idiom, incorporating dodecaphonic and aleatory procedures and outlining a graphic system of notation, following the pictorial representation of musical sounds of the European avant-garde, but introducing some new elements, such as indication of relative loudness by increasing the size of the notes on a music staff with lines far apart. His works include the opera *La muerte de Don Rodrigo* (1958), three syms. (1955, 1958, 1960), Violin Concerto (1950), Flute Concerto (1957), Piano Concerto (1958), four guitar concertos (1964–70), Concerto for Oboe, Clarinet, and Bassoon, with String Orch. (1970), seven string quartets, Saxophone Quartet, three violin sonatas, Viola Sonata, three cello sonatas, Sonata for Double Bass and Piano, pieces for solo oboe and solo trombone, the oratorios *La Araucana* (1965) and *Lord Cochrane de Chile* (1967), and numerous choral works.—NS/LK/DM

Becher, Alfred Julius, German music critic and composer; b. Manchester, April 27, 1803; d. (executed) Vienna, Nov. 23, 1848. He was the son of a Hanau merchant and was taken to Germany as a child. He studied law in Jena, Berlin, Heidelberg, and Leiden before becoming a confirmed revolutionary. After working as a newspaper ed. and music critic, he taught at the Royal Music School in The Hague (1837–40) and at the Royal Academy of Music in London (1840–41). In 1841 he went to Vienna, where he became a well known music critic. During the Revolution of 1848, he founded the extremist journal *Der Radikale* but was forced into hiding. He was eventually tracked down, court-martialed for treason, and shot. Among his writings was a biography of Jenny Lind (Vienna, 1846; 2nd ed., 1847). He composed a Sym., a *Fantaisie élégiaque* for Violin or Cello and Orch., chamber music, piano pieces, and songs.—NS/LK/DM

Bechet, Sidney (Joseph), masterful and innovative jazz clarinetist, soprano saxophonist; b. New Orleans, May 14, 1897; d. Paris, May 14, 1959. A sensational soloist who had an impact on Ellington and Johnny Hodges, among others, he failed to become as well-established in America as he deserved, primarily because he spent so much of his time in Europe, especially France. And, although he was revered in France as an early jazz master, he was more innovative than he has been given credit for: he recorded the first overdubbed one-man band in 1941, recorded on sarrusophone in 1924, wrote for orchestra, and was, if only on soprano, an influential saxophonist before Coleman Hawkins. He also had a volatile personality and often had difficulty getting along with other musicians.

Bechet was the youngest of seven children; one of his four brothers, Leonard (d. 1952), was once a professional trombonist who left music to become a dentist; another brother, Joseph, played guitar. Bechet took up the clarinet when he was six years old and soon sat in with Freddie Keppard and marched with Manuel Perez. Originally self-taught, he later received instruction from Lorenzo Tio, Big Eye Louis Nelson, and George Baquet, and occasionally subbed for Baquet at the 101 Ranch. He played for a while in the Silver Bells Band led by his brother, Leonard, then had regular engagements with leading New Orleans bands: Buddie Petit's Young Olympians (1909), John Robichaux's Orch., The Olympia (1910), and The Eagle (1911–12). He also doubled at

Fewclothes Cabaret with Bunk Johnson. During these early years Bechet also played cornet regularly for parade work: with Allen's Band c. 1911, also with Jack Carey's Band in 1913.

From 1914 until mid-1917 Bechet spent little time in New Orleans (he once estimated it as four months). He left New Orleans in the spring of 1914 with a travelling show (together with pianist Louis Wade and Clarence Williams); Wade and Bechet cut-out in Galveston, Tex., and joined a touring carnival for two months. During his occasional trips to New Orleans, he played mainly at The Claiborne Street Theatre or at St. Catherine's Hall. During 1916 he also worked with Joe "King" Oliver at Big 25 and at Pete Lala's, and at this time again did parade work on cornet. He left New Orleans permanently in summer of 1917, acting and playing in The Bruce and Bruce Touring Company through Ga., Ala., Ohio, and Ind. He left in the tour in Chicago late in 1917, joined Lawrence Duhe's Band at De Lure Cafe, and later played at Dreamland and at the Monoyram Theatre; he also worked occasionally with King Oliver. He played with Freddie Keppard at The De Luxe, doubling with Tony Jackson at The Pekin Cabaret, At about this time Bechet bought his first soprano saxophone (a curved model), but abandoned his efforts to learn it a few weeks later.

Bechet auditioned for Jim Europe's Band just prior to the leader's death, and subsequently joined Will Marion Cook's Southern Syncopated Orch. in Chicago and journeyed with them to N.Y. He played with Lt. Tim Brymn's orch. in Coney Island, N.Y. and then rejoined Will Marion Cook for a trip to Europe in June 1919. Swiss conductor Ernest Ansermet heard him playing his feature "Characteristic Blues" (which Bechet recorded in 1936) and wrote one of the most famous of all early jazz commentaries, "I wish to set down the name of this artist of genius; as for myself, I shall never forget it." In London, Bechet bought his first straight-model soprano sax, and shortly afterwards he was using it for feature numbers. Bechet remained in London with a breakaway unit from the Southern Syncopated Orch.; this small band, led by drummer Benny Peyton, played at The Embassy Club and Hammersmith Palais. Bechet moved to Paris in spring of 1920 for engagements with the Southern Syncopated Orch., then returned for a residency at the Hammersmith Palais with Benny Peyton's Jazz Kings. However, Bechet had a run-in with the law, and was deported from Great Britain, returning to N.Y. in the fall of 1921. He played with Ford Dabney, then acted and played in Donald Haywood's *How Come?* show.

After touring, Bechet quit the show in N.Y. in the spring of 1923, where he began recording numerous sessions with Clarence Williams, and some with Louis Armstrong as well, often accompanying vaudeville singers. He worked with Mamie Smith and various bands, then toured with Jimmy Cooper's *Black and White Revue*, then with the *Seven Eleven* show (spring 1925). Bechet returned to N.Y., and briefly worked with Duke Ellington (who later wrote "After that we forgot all about the sweet stuff") and with James P. Johnson (temporarily at the Kentucky Club). He led his own

New Orleans Creole Jazz Band at the Rhythm Club, then opened his own Club Basha (pronounced Ba-SHAY, like his name) in N.Y.

In September 1925, Bechet left N.Y. with another touring show, the *Revue Negre*, featuring Josephine Baker (orchestra directed by Claude Hopkins). He left the show in early 1926, and from February until May 1926 toured Russia with a band also featuring Benny Peyton and Frank Withers (trombone). After playing Moscow, the band appeared in Kiev, Kharkov, and Odessa. Bechet returned to Berlin, led his own small band, and then organized a 14–piece orchestra for new edition of *Revue Negre*. After touring Europe during 1927, the orchestra disbanded in Munich. Bechet again led his own small band, this time in Frankfurt-am-Main. In the summer of 1928, he moved to Paris, and joined Noble Sissle at Les Ambassadeurs Club, doubling on E-flat and contra-bass sax. Later that year, Bechet worked at Chez Florence with The International Five (a nine- piece band). He played briefly with Benny Peyton in January 1929, then was jailed in Paris for 11 months after being involved in a shooting incident. Following his inprisonment, Bechet again moved to Berlin, playing residencies at the Wild West Bar and Haus Vaterland. In 1930, he again toured with the *Revue Negre*, but then left the show in Amsterdam, and sailed back to N.Y.

In early 1931, Bechet rejoined Noble Sissle, remaining with him about a year. He traveled with Duke Ellington on a New England tour in May 1932, then organized his own New Orleans Feetwarmers with Tommy Ladnier. They opened at the Savoy, N.Y., in September 1932. The group disbanded early in 1933. After some club work, Bechet left full-time music temporarily, and together with Ladnier opened the Southern Tailor Shop in N.Y. However, he was soon back to music- making; he rejoined Noble Sissle in Chicago in 1934, and except for short periods, remained in the band until October 1938. He then played small jobs in N.Y.–area clubs, leading various pickup bands.

Throughout World War II, Bechet played regularly at Nick's, Ryan's, and various other clubs in N.Y., and also took part in several of Eddie Condon's N.Y. Town Hall concerts. Occasionally, he led own quartet for residencies outside of N.Y. From March 1945, he led a band at the Savoy, Boston, but then returned to N.Y. in January 1946, and began making regular guest star appearances. Bechet made a few trips to Europe in the late 1940s, and then, from the summer of 1951, he made his permanent home in France where he became a celebrity. His most famous compositions are "Petite Fleur" (a worldwide hit by Chris Barber in 1959, with clarinetist Monty Sunshine playing the Bechet part) and "Les Oignons," made in France in 1949 with clarinetist Claude Luter, and said to have sold a million copies by 1955. He returned to the U.S. for various tours and guest-star bookings—late 1951, September 1953 (including first trip to San Francisco)—and toured Britain in September 1956, and Argentina and Chile in spring 1957. Bechet remained musically active until shortly before succumbing to cancer, leading an all-star band at the Brussels International Fair in the summer of 1958. During the last years of his life, his extended works *Nouvelles Orleans*

and the *Night Is a Sorceress* were given public performances. In 1955, he appeared in the French film *Blues*.

DISC.: "Wild Cat Blues" (1923); "Petite Fleur", "Haitian Moods" (both 1923–4); "Jazz from California" (1937); "Summertime" (1939); *Jazz Nocturne, Vol. 1–11* (1945); *Bechet, Bunk and Boston* (1945); *Wingy Manone/Sidney Bechet Together* (1947); *Sidney Bechet's Blue Note Jazzmen* (1950); *Live in N.Y.* (1950); *Bechet in Philadelphia, Vol. 2* (1950); *Days Beyond Recall* (1951); *Wally Bishop's Orch.* (1952); *Jazz Festival Concert Paris* (1952); *In Concert* (1954); *Dixie by the Fabulous Sidney Bechet* (1953); *Sidney Bechet at Storyville* (1955); *Olympia Concert* (1955); *La Nuit Est une Sorciere* (1955); *Jazz a la Creole* (1955); *With Sammy's Price's Blusicians* (1956); *Sidney Bechet Duets* (1956); *Grand Master of the Soprano Sax* (1956); *Young Ideas* (1957); *When a Soprano Meets a Piano* (1957); *Paris Jazz Concert* (1957); *Sidney Bechet in Paris* (1958); *Brussels Fair '58* (1958).

BIBL.: J. Chilton, *Sidney Bechet: The Wizard of Jazz* (Oxford, 1988).—JC/LP

Bechi, Gino, notable Italian baritone; b. Florence, Oct. 16, 1913; d. there, Feb. 2, 1993. He studied in Florence with Frazzi and Di Giorgi and in Alessandria. In 1936 he made his operatic debut as Germont in Empoli, and then sang in Rome (1938–52) and at Milan's La Scala (1939–44; 1946–53), where he acquired an admirable reputation. In 1950 he sang with the La Scala company during its visit to London's Covent Garden, and he returned to London in 1958 to sing at Drury Lane. In 1952 he appeared in Chicago and San Francisco. He also made appearances in musical films. In later years, he was active as a teacher and opera producer. Bechi was best known for his Verdi roles, among them Falstaff, Amonasro, Hamlet, Iago, and Nabucco.—NS/LK/DM

Bechstein, (Friedrich Wilhelm) Carl, German piano manufacturer; b. Gotha, June 1, 1826; d. Berlin, March 6, 1900. He worked in German factories and also in London. In 1853 he set up a modest shop in Berlin, and constructed his first grand piano in 1856; also established branches in France, Russia, and England. After World War I, the London branch continued under the direction of C. Bechstein, grandson of the founder; after his death (1931), it became an independent British firm, Bechstein Piano Co., Ltd. The Bechstein piano possesses a particularly harmonious tone, capable of producing a mellifluous cantilena. For many years it was a favorite instrument of pianists of the Romantic school.

BIBL.: *B.-Chronik* (Berlin, 1926).—NS/LK/DM

Beck, Conrad, distinguished Swiss composer; b. Lohn, June 16, 1901; d. Basel, Oct. 31, 1989. He was a student of Andreae, Laquai, and Baldegger at the Zürich Cons. After further training in Paris and Berlin, he settled in Basel in 1932 and served as director of the music division of the Radio (1939–66). In 1964 he was awarded the arts prize of the city. After composing in a late Romantic style, he developed a highly effective neo-Baroque means of expression.

WORKS: DRAMATIC: *La grande ourse*, ballet (1935–36); *St. Jakob an der Birs*, festival play (1943–44). **ORCH.:** 5 syms.: No. 1 (1925), No. 2, Sinfonietta (1926), No. 3 for Strings (1927),

No. 4, *Concerto for Orch.*, for Strings (1929), and No. 5 (1930); *Aeneas-Silvius-Sinfonie* (1957; Zürich, Feb. 25, 1958); Cello Concerto (1927); Concerto for String Quartet and Orch. (1929); *Innominata* (1931); *Konzertmusik* for Oboe and Strings (1933); Piano Concerto (1933); *Serenade* for Flute, Clarinet, and Strings (1935); *Ostinato* (1935–36); *Rhapsodie* for Piano, 4 Woodwinds, and Strings (1936); Violin Concerto (1940); Flute Concerto (1941); Concerto for Harpsichord and Strings (1942); Viola Concerto (1949); *Mouvement* (1953); *Suite concertante* for Wind, Double Bass, and Percussion (1961); *Concertato* (1964); Clarinet Concerto (1967–68); Chamber Concerto (1971); Concerto for Wind Quintet and Orch. (1976); *Drei Aspekte* for Chamber Orch. (1976); *Cercles* (1978–79); *Nachklänge* (1984). **CHAMBER:** 5 string quartets (1922, 1924, 1926, 1934, 1962); Duo for Violin and Flute (1927); 2 string trios (1928–1946); Duo for Violin and Viola (1934); *3 Bilder aus dem Struwwelpeter* for Flute, Clarinet, Bassoon, and Piano (1934); Violin Sonata (1946); Cello Sonata (1954); Duo for 2 Violins (1960); Sonata for Flute, Oboe, Bassoon, and Violin (1970); piano pieces; organ music. **VOCAL:** *Requiem* (1930); *Oratorium* for Voice, Chorus, and Orch. (1934); *Der Tod zu Basel* for Speaker, Solo Voices, Chorus, and Orch. (1952; Basel, May 22, 1953); *Herbstfeuer* for Alto and Chamber Orch. (1956); *Die Sonnenfinsternis*, cantata for Alto and Chamber Orch. (Lucerne, Aug. 25, 1967); other cantatas, choral pieces, and songs.

BIBL.: W. Schuh and D. Larese, *C. B.: Eine Lebensskizze: Der Komponist und sein Werk* (Amriswil, 1972).—**NS/LK/DM**

Beck (David Campbell),

the artistic nexus of traditional blues and contemporary pop; b. Los Angeles, July 8, 1970 (he took his mother's surname, Hansen, after his parent's divorce). Beck's mother was a Warhol superstar at age 13; her father was one of America's leading FluXus artists, Al Hansen. (FluXus was a Dadaesque art movement of the 1960s that included artists like Yoko Ono among its followers.) Beck's father is an arranger who became an itinerant bluegrass musician during Beck's youth. Beck became as intrigued by the blues of Mississippi John Hurt as he was by the hip-hop and break dancers on the corner, making his music one of the 1990s most satisfying cultural stews.

At age 16, Beck dropped out of school and took his guitar to N.Y.C., where he got involved with the burgeoning "anti-folk" scene. However, Beck did not find an audience for his music like his guitar-strumming comrades Michele Shocked, Roger Manning, Cindy Lee Berryhill, and Ani DeFranco. He returned to Los Angeles where he worked a series of minimum-wage jobs like alphabetizing the pornography section of the local video store. These experiences informed his music, with lyrics that often were improvised.

Beck began playing solo sets at local clubs while bands set up behind him. As his guitar style started to evolve, he recorded a single for Bong Load records called "MTV Makes Me Want to Smoke Crack." His next Bong Load record, 12 inches of alienation called "Loser," caught the ears of radio, with the refrain "I'm a loser baby, why don't you kill me?"

Geffen Record signed Beck after a fierce bidding war. Part of his deal allowed him to record for them and for whomever else he wanted. His first Geffen album, *Mellow Gold* (reputedly made for $300), came out to critical raves, great sales, and ubiquitous play on radio

and MTV for "Loser." The single went gold and reached #10, and the album went platinum and got as high as #13. At the same time, *Stereopathetic Soulmanure* came out on L.A.'s Flipside records and Beck collaborated with K Records's head Calvin Johnson on *One Foot in the Grave*. "Loser" was *Spin's* #1 single of 1994 and was nominated for a Grammy. However, many critics viewed Beck as a one-hit wonder, a slacker novelty act.

The next year, Beck invoked his indie record clause to release two more albums, *Steve Threw Up* and *A Western Field by Moonlight*, which were in the works before he signed with Geffen. As these records hit the stores, Beck was busily at work on his follow-up to *Mellow Gold*. Determined to offer something different, he hooked up with producers The Dust Brothers, who had helped the Beastie Boys realize their artistic watershed, *Paul's Boutique*. The resulting album, *Odelay*, proved an album of unusual artistic and commercial depth, aptly dubbed in *Newsweek* as "American eclectic music." Tunes mixed accordions and turntables, steel guitar, and hardcore funk drums. The album found favor with critics, and music magazines *Spin*, *Rolling Stone*, and *NME* proclaimed Beck "Artist of the Year." *Select* magazine took that a step further, calling him "#1 Most Important Person in the World." The album won Grammy awards for Best Alternative Music Performance and Best Male Rock Vocal Performance. Videos from the album for "Devil's Haircut" and "New Pollution" garnered awards from MTV in several categories. More than that, the album found its audience: *Odelay* sold over two million copies.

Beck went on the road, making a series of successful appearances (he claims not to play live; he just makes random appearances). Meanwhile, artists ranging from Tom Petty and the Heartbreakers to Johnny Cash to the Ska-core Allstars were covering his tunes. Emmylou Harris, Willie Nelson, and Sean "Puff Daddy" Combs sought him out for collaborations. Beck also took time out from music to put together a joint exhibit of his own art along with his grandfather's work.

In 1998, Beck released *Mutations* on Geffen. Produced by Nigel Godrich, who had made Radiohead's *OK Computer*, Beck and the group he appeared with on stage recorded and mixed a track a day for 20 days. While in the studio recording his follow-up to *Mutations*, Beck posted weekly video segments of his work in progress on his official website. Unlike his previous albums, the songs for this one had already been written. Beck worked with strings (arranged by his dad) and even recorded some of the vocals live. The result was more cohesive than any of his previous recordings. The album entered the charts at #13, its peak position. By the middle of 1999, the record had sold over a million copies without any charted singles.

DISC.: *One Foot in the Grave* (1994); *Mellow Gold* (1994); *Stereopathetic Soul Manure* (1994); *Odelay* (1996); *Mutations* (1998).—**HB**

Beck, Franz Ignaz,

German violinist, organist, conductor, teacher, and composer; b. Mannheim, Feb. 20, 1734; d. Bordeaux, Dec. 31, 1809. He studied violin with his father, an oboist and rector of the choir at the court of the Elector Palatine in Mannheim, and later studied there with J. Stamitz. Following service at the court, he went to Venice. About 1760 he went to Marseilles, where he was active in the theater orch. In 1761 he settled in Bordeaux and became a conductor at the Grand Théâtre and organist at the church of St. Seurin. Beck publ. several syms. (1758–66) whose inventive style render them of more than just historical interest in the development of the genre. His other works include the opera *La Belle Jardinière* (Bordeaux, Aug. 24, 1767), the melodrame *Pandore* (Paris, July 2, 1789), a Stabat Mater (1783), violin quartets, and keyboard sonatas.

BIBL.: B. Carrow, *The Relationship Between the Mannheim School and the Music of F. B., Henri Blanchard, and Pierre Gaveaux* (diss., N.Y. Univ., 1956); M. Stahl, *F. B.: Un élève de Stamitz à Bordeaux* (Bordeaux, 1991).—NS/LK/DM

Beck, Jean-Baptiste, Alsatian-American musicologist; b. Gebweiler, Aug. 14, 1881; d. Philadelphia, June 23, 1943. He studied organ before obtaining his Ph.D. at the Univ. of Strasbourg with the diss. *Die Melodien der Troubadours und Trouvères* (1908). He later publ. a somewhat popularized ed. of it in French, *La Musique des troubadours* (Paris, 1910). Beck taught at the Univ. of Ill. from 1911 to 1914; then at Bryn Mawr Coll. from 1914 to 1920. He settled in Philadelphia, where he taught at the Univ. of Pa., and from 1920 at the Curtis Inst. of Music. In 1927 he initiated a project to publ. a Corpus Cantilenarum Medii Aevi, in 52 vols., but was able to bring out only four vols., under the subtitle *Les Chansonniers des troubadours et des trouvères* (all in French), containing phototype reproductions of medieval MSS, transcriptions in modern notation, and commentary: *Le Chansonnier cangé* (2 vols., Philadelphia, 1927) and *Le Manuscrit du roi* (2 vols., Philadelphia, 1938). Beck was an outstanding scholar of medieval vocal music; his application of the modal rhythms of the polyphony of that time to troubadour melodies was an important contribution to the problem of proper transcription into modern notation.—NS/LK/DM

Beck, Jeff, guitar-God with a spotted career; b. Wallington, Surrey, England, June 24, 1944. A competent pianist and guitarist by the age of 11, Jeff Beck performed with early 1960s British bands such as The Nightshifts and The Tridents before replacing Eric Clapton in The Yardbirds in March 1965. Beck played lead guitar with the group through its greatest hit-making period ("Heart Full of Soul," "I'm a Man," "Over Under Sideways Down") and pioneered the use of feedback and effects, particularly with "The Shapes of Things" from 1966. Leaving The Yardbirds that November, he recorded several singles, including the major British hit "Hi Ho Silver Lining," and formed the first of several Jeff Beck Groups with Rod Stewart (vocals), Ron Wood (bass, harmonica), and Mickey Waller (drums). The group proved enormously successful with its blues-oriented material during an American tour in 1968. The tour also introduced American audiences to Rod Stewart, who had been singing almost anonymously with various blues aggregations in Britain for years.

The Jeff Beck Group's debut album, *Truth,* helped pioneer heavy-metal music with songs like "I Ain't Superstitious," "Rock My Plimsoul," and "Beck's Bolero." The group expanded in October 1968 with the addition of sessions keyboardist Nicky Hopkins. After a second album, *Beck-ola,* and the recording of Donovan's major British and moderate American hit "Goo Goo Barabajagal (Love Is Hot)," the group fragmented, with Stewart and Wood joining The Faces, and Hopkins moving to Calif. to join Quicksilver Messenger Service.

An attempt to form a new band with Tim Bogert and Carmine Appice of Vanilla Fudge failed, and a car crash later left Jeff Beck out of commission for 18 months. He reemerged in late 1971 with his second Jeff Beck Group, featuring keyboardist Max Middleton and drummer Cozy Powell. This group recorded two undistinguished albums before disbanding in 1972. With the demise of their second-generation band Cactus, Tim Bogert (bass) and Carmine Appice (drums) joined Beck for the short-lived Beck/Bogert/Appice group, which disbanded in early 1974.

Jeff Beck returned in 1975 with his *Blow by Blow* album, a surprising yet intriguing change of musical direction for Beck. Made with former Beatles producer George Martin, the all-instrumental album had a distinctive jazz (and occasionally disco) flavor and sold remarkably well. *Wired,* recorded with Czech jazz keyboard wizard Jan Hammer, was also well received. Beck subsequently toured with Hammer, releasing a live set from the tour in 1977. After another sabbatical, Beck returned with a new band, the album *There and Back,* and another round of touring as an all-instrumental unit.

In 1983, Jeff Beck joined Eric Clapton, Jimmy Page, and a cast of established British musicians for a brief tour in support of Ronnie Lane's Appeal for Action Research into Multiple Sclerosis. The following year, Beck played on Rod Stewart's *Camouflage* album and its smash hit single "Infatuation," and toured with Stewart before leaving due to "artistic differences." Later he toured and recorded a mini as The Honeydrippers with Robert Plant, Jimmy Page, Brian Setzer, and Cozy Powell. Beck also played on Tina Turner's smash hit "Private Dancer" and Mick Jagger's *She's the Boss* and *Primitive Cool* albums. In 1985, Beck issued his first solo album in five years, *Flash,* which featured Rod Stewart on vocals for "People Get Ready," a minor hit.

Jeff Beck again took several years off, reemerging in 1989 with *Jeff Beck's Guitar Shop,* an all-instrumental album recorded with keyboardist Tony Hymas and drummer Terry Bozzio, and his first major tour in nearly a decade, this time co-headlining with Texas blues guitarist Stevie Ray Vaughan. In 1993, with an ad hoc Big Town Playboys, Beck recorded 15 Gene Vincent songs for *Crazy Legs,* his tribute to the rockabilly star and his guitarist, Cliff Gallup. Jeff Beck toured with Carlos Santana in 1995.

Jeff Beck is one of rock music's most intelligent, innovative, and respected guitarists. One of the first electric guitarists to utilize a fuzztone device and make extensive use of feedback while playing, Beck introduced both modal and East Indian tonalities into rock with The Yardbirds. The debut album by his first Jeff Beck Group introduced American audiences to Rod Stewart, and along with Led Zeppelin's debut album six months later, helped define 1970s heavy-metal music. Moreover, with his *Blow by Blow* album, Beck helped redefine and revitalize the more challenging and ambitious sound of fusion music, a 1970s phenomenon not strictly classifiable as jazz or rock, but containing elements of both. Taking regular extended breaks from recording and touring throughout his career, Jeff Beck is regarded as a musician's musician.

DISC.: THE JEFF BECK GROUP: *Truth* (1968); *Beck-ola* (1969); *Rough and Ready* (1971); *Jeff Beck Group* (1972). BECK, BOGERT AND APPICE: *Beck, Bogert and Appice* (1973). JEFF BECK: *Blow by Blow* (1975); *Wired* (1976); *There and Back* (1980); *Flash* (1985); *Jeff Beck's Guitar Shop* (1989); *Beckology* (1991). Jeff Beck and Jan Hammer: *Live* (1977). The Honeydrippers: *Volume 1* (1984). JEFF BECK AND THE BIG TOWN PLAYBOYS: *Crazy Legs* (1993).—BH

Beck, Johann H(einrich), American violinist, conductor, teacher, and composer; b. Cleveland, Sept. 12, 1865; d. there, May 26, 1924. He studied with Reinecke and Jadassohn at the Leipzig Cons. (1879–82). In 1877 he founded the Schubert String Quartet in Cleveland, and later the Beck String Quartet. He also was conductor of the Detroit Sym. Orch. (1895–96) and orchs. in Cleveland.

WORKS: ORCH.: 4 overtures (1875–85); 2 symphonic poems; 2 scherzos (1885–95; 1889); *Aus meinem Leben*, tone poem (1917). CHAMBER: 4 string quartets (1877–80); String Sextet (1885–86); piano pieces. VOCAL: 4 tone poems for Voice and Orch., including *Elegiac Song* (1877); partsongs; songs. —LK/DM

Beck, Sydney, American music librarian; b. N.Y., Sept. 2, 1906. He studied at the Coll. of the City Univ. of N.Y., at N.Y. Univ., at the Inst. of Musical Art, and at the Mannes Coll. of Music. During this period he took courses in violin and chamber music with Louis Svecenski, in composition with Wagenaar and Weisse, and in musicology with Sachs and Reese. In 1931 he became head of the Rare Book and Manuscript Collections of the N.Y. Public Library, holding this post until 1968. He also taught at the Mannes Coll. of Music (1950–68). In 1968 he was appointed director of libraries at the New England Cons. of Music in Boston, retiring in 1976. He prepared eds. of works by F. Geminiani and J.M. Leclair. —NS/LK/DM

Beck, Thomas Ludvigsen, Norwegian organist, choral conductor, teacher, and composer; b. Horten, Dec. 5, 1899; d. Oslo, Sept. 9, 1963. He studied piano, organ, and composition at the Oslo Cons. and theory in Leipzig. From 1930 he was active as an organist, choral conductor, and teacher in Oslo. He composed several orch. pieces, many cantatas, choruses, songs, and film music.—NS/LK/DM

Becker, Carl Ferdinand, German organist, pedagogue, bibliographer, and composer; b. Leipzig, July 17, 1804; d. there, Oct. 26, 1877. He spent his entire life in Leipzig. After training at the Thomasschule, he was a violinist in the Gewandhaus Orch. (1820–33) and served as organist in various churches. In 1843 he became the first prof. of organ at the Cons. In 1850 he helped to organize the Bach-Gesellschaft. He acquired a valuable collection of early music and musical literature which he gave to the city of Leipzig. Among his writings were *Systematisch-chronologische Darstellung der musikalischen Literatur von der frühesten bis auf die neueste Zeit* (1836; suppl., 1839), *Die Hausmusik in Deutschland im 16., 17., und 18. Jahrhundert* (1840), and *Die Tonwerke des 16. und 17. Jahrhunderts* (1847). He composed piano and organ pieces.—LK/DM

Becker, Constantin Julius, German composer and author; b. Freiberg, Saxony, Feb. 3, 1811; d. Oberlössnitz, Feb. 26, 1859. He studied singing with Anacker and composition with Carl Becker. From 1837 to 1846 he ed. the *Neue Zeitschrift für Musik*, in association with Schumann. In 1843 he settled in Dresden, where he taught singing, composed, and wrote novels on musical subjects. In 1846 he went to Oberlössnitz, where he spent the remainder of his life. He wrote an opera, *Die Erstürmung von Belgrad* (Leipzig, May 21, 1848), a Sym., and various vocal works, but he is best known for his manuals: *Männergesangschule* (1845), *Harmonielehre für Dilettanten* (1842), and *Kleine Harmonielehre* (1844). He also publ. the novel *Die Neuromantiker* (1840) and tr. *Voyage musical* by Berlioz into German (1843). —NS/LK/DM

Becker, Dietrich, German violinist, organist, and composer; b. Hamburg, 1623; d. there, 1679. He began his career as an organist in Ahrensburg, Holstein (1645), and subsequently was active as a violinist in Hamburg. In 1658 he became violinist at the court chapel in Celle. In 1662 he was appointed court violinist in Hamburg. He was named director of the Court Orch. in 1667 and appointed director of music at the Hamburg Cathedral in 1674.

WORKS: *Musicalische Frühlings-Früchte* for 3 to 5 Instruments and Basso Continuo (Hamburg, 1668; 2nd ed., 1673); *Erster Theil...Sonaten und Suiten* for 2 Violins and Basso Continuo (Hamburg, 1674); *Trauer-undBegrabnüss-Musik* for Soprano, Alto, Tenor, Bass, Violin, Bassoon, 3 Viole da Braccio, and Basso Continuo (Glückstadt, 1678); *Ander Theil...Sonaten und Suiten* for 2 Violins and Basso Continuo (Hamburg, 1679); also sacred choral music and songs.—NS/LK/DM

Becker, Frank, American composer; b. Paterson, N.J., March 29, 1944. He studied with Joseph Wood at the Oberlin (Ohio) Coll. Cons. of Music, and composition with Robert Palmer and jazz improvisation with Elston Husk. A Ford Foundation grant took him for two years to Wichita, Kans., where his works were widely performed; he subsequently went to Japan, becoming famous in avant-garde circles as a composer, performer (on synthesizer), and producer. Since his return to the U.S. in 1981, he has written many film and television scores. Among his concert works are *Stonehenge* for Flute and Tape (a mixture of new age, minimalist, and pseudo-Japanese styles) and *Philiapaideia* for Orch. (1973), which won the Prix Francis Salabert in 1975. —NS/LK/DM

Becker, Günther (Hugo), German composer; b. Forbach, Baden, April 1, 1924. He studied conducting with G. Nestler at the Badische Hochschule für Musik in Karlsruhe (1946–49), composition with W. Fortner in Heidelberg, and at the North-West German Academy of Music (1948–56), where he also studied choral conducting with K. Thomas (1953–55). He taught music at the Greek National School Anavryta in Athens (1956–58), and also taught at the Goethe Inst. and the Dorpfeld Gymnasium there (1957–68). He then returned to Germany, where he founded the live electronic group Mega-Hertz (1969), and taught at the summer courses for new music in Darmstadt. He became a lecturer at the Musikhochschule Rheinland of the Robert Schumann Inst. in Düsseldorf (1973) and prof. of composition and live electronics at the Düsseldorf Hochschule für Musik (1974). In 1989 he retired. Becker's works, at first influenced by his sojourn in Greece, eventually gave way to a unique and uncompromising style utilizing all the resources of contemporary compositional processes.

WORKS: ORCH.: *stabil-instabil* (1965; WDR, Cologne, Oct. 28, 1966); *Correspondances I* for Clarinet and Chamber Orch. (Donaueschingen, Oct. 22, 1966); *Griechische Tanzsuite* for Plucked String Orch. (Saarbrücken, Aug. 29, 1967); *Caprices concertants* for Mandolin, Mandola, Guitar, Percussion, and Plucked String Orch. (1968; Hannover, May 18, 1969); *Transformationen* for Orch., Live Electronic Ensemble, and Tape (Warsaw, Sept. 24, 1970); *Attitude* (1972–73; Bonn, June 4, 1973); *Konzert* for Electronic Modulated Oboe and Orch. (1973–74; Munich, April 5, 1974); *In Modo Greco* for Guitar and Plucked String Orch. (1992). **CHAMBER:** 3 string quartets: No. 1 (1963; Darmstadt, July 17, 1964), No. 2 (Darmstadt, Aug. 31, 1967), and No. 3, *Hommage à Joseph Haydn* (Düsseldorf, May 28, 1988); *Correspondances II* for Guitar, Harp, Harpsichord, and String Quartet (1968–69); *Ariosi* for Oboe, English Horn, Clarinet, Bass Clarinet, Vibraphone, and Marimbaphone (1982; Witten, Jan. 26, 1983); *Parenthesen* for String Sextet (1982; Berlin, April 5, 1983); *Un poco giocoso* for Bass Tuba and Chamber Ensemble (1983; Witten, April 27, 1984); *Doppelte Ebenen* for Violin and Viola (1984–85; Düsseldorf, Nov. 9, 1985); *Reverenz 1985* for 4 Players (Düsseldorf, Sept. 8, 1985); *Zeitspuren* for 2 Pianos (1987–88; Düsseldorf, May 21, 1988); *trivalent* for Viola, Cello, and Double Bass (Cincinnati, Nov. 11, 1988); *Hard Times* for Bassoon and Chamber Ensemble (1989–90; Düsseldorf, Jan. 19, 1990); *Oh, Mr. Dolby, What a Terrible Noise* for Bass Clarinet and Tape (1990; Linz, May 27, 1991); *Psychogramme* for Trombone, Accordion, and Percussion (Düsseldorf, Nov. 21, 1992); *Interpolationen* for Organ (Nuremberg, Oct. 1, 1993), *Dumuls...nach dem Grauen* for Speaker and Large Chamber Ensemble (1994–95; Düsseldorf, March 29, 1995); *Dedikation* for Bass Clarinet and Vibraphone (1995; Port Darwin, Australia, July 4, 1997); *Befindlichkeiten* for Alto Saxophone, Cello, and Piano (Wesel, Oct. 12, 1997). **VOCAL:** *Nacht-und Traumgesänge* for Chorus and Orch. (1964; NDR, Hamburg, Feb. 16, 1965); *Ihre Bosheit wird die ganze Erde zu einer Wuste machen,* sacred concerto for Speaker, Alto, Chorus, Organ, Instrumental Ensemble, and Tape (1978; Düsseldorf, Feb. 14, 1979); *Magnum Mysterium— Zeugenaussagen zur Auferstehung,* scenic oratorio (1979–80; Düsseldorf, May 4, 1980).—**NS/LK/DM**

Becker, Gustave Louis, American pianist, teacher, and composer; b. Richmond, Tex., May 22, 1861; d. Epsom, Surrey, England, Feb. 25, 1959. He began piano studies at a youthful age and made his public debut at the age of 11. Following training with C. Sternberg in N.Y. and at the Berlin Hochschule für Musik (1888–91) with Moszkowski and X. Scharwenka, he was active as a pianist and teacher. He composed many vocal and piano pieces, and two suites for String Quartet. He also wrote pedagogical works.—**NS/LK/DM**

Becker, Heinz, German musicologist; b. Berlin, June 26, 1922. He studied clarinet, piano, conducting, and composition at the Berlin Hochschule für Musik, and then pursued musicological studies at the Humboldt Univ. in Berlin (Ph.D., 1951, with the diss. *Zur Problematik und Technik der musikalischen Schlussgestaltung*). In 1956 he joined the musicological inst. of the Univ. of Hamburg as an asst. lecturer, and completed his Habilitation there with his *Studien zur Entwicklungsgeschichte der antiken und mittelalterlichen Rohrblattinstrumente* (1961; publ. in Hamburg, 1966). From 1966 until his retirement in 1987 he was a prof. of musicology at the Ruhr Univ. in Bochum. Becker has distinguished himself particularly as an authority on the life and works of Meyerbeer.

WRITINGS: *Der Fall Heine-Meyerbeer* (Berlin, 1958); ed. *Giacomo Meyerbeer: Briefwechsel und Tagebucher* (4 vols., Berlin, 1960–85); *Geschichte der Instrumentation,* Das Musikwerk series, XXIV (1964); *Beiträge zur Geshichte der Musikkritik* (Regensburg, 1965); *Beiträge zur Geschichte der Oper* (Regensburg, 1969); *Die Couleur Locale in der Oper des 19 Jahrhunderts* (Regensburg, 1976); *Giacomo Meyerbeer in Selbstzeugnissen und Bilddokumenten* (Reinbek, 1980); with G. Becker, *Giacomo Meyerbeer: Ein Leben in Briefen* (Wilhelmshaven, 1983; Eng. tr., 1983, as *Giacomo Meyerbeer: A Life in Letters*); with G. Becker, *Giacomo Meyerbeer-Weltburger der Musik* (Wiesbaden, 1991); *Brahms* (Stuttgart, 1993).

BIBL.: J. Schläder and R. Quandt, eds., *H. B.: Festschrift zum 60. Geburtstag* (Laaber, 1982); S. Döhring and J. Schläder, eds., *H. B. zum 70. Geburtstag: Giacomo Meyerbeer-Musik als Welterfahrung* (Munich, 1995).—**NS/LK/DM**

Becker, Jean, German violinist, father of **(Jean Otto Eric) Hugo Becker;** b. Mannheim, May 11, 1833; d. there, Oct. 10, 1884. He studied with his father, and then with Vincenz Lachner, Hugo Hildebrandt, and Aloys Kettenus. From 1855 to 1865 he was concertmaster of the Mannheim Orch. In 1865 he went to Florence, where he was founder and first violinist in the Florentine String Quartet until 1880. He spent his remaining years touring with his children, Jeanne (b. Mannheim, June 9, 1859; d. there, April 6, 1893), a pianist, Hans (b. Strasbourg, May 12, 1860; d. Leipzig, May 1, 1917), a violist, and Hugo.—**NS/LK/DM**

Becker, (Jean Otto Eric) Hugo, notable German cellist and pedagogue, son of **Jean Becker;** b. Strasbourg, Feb. 13, 1863; d. Geiselgasteig, July 30, 1941. After training from his father, he studied with Kanut Kündinger in Mannheim and Friedrich Grützmacher and Karl Hess in Dresden. He completed his studies with Alfredo Piatti. From 1884 to 1886 he was principal cellist in the orch. of the Frankfurt am Main Opera. He was a member of the Heermann String Quartet from 1890 to 1906, and from 1895 he also served as a prof. at the Frankfurt am Main Hoschule für Musik. Becker played in trios with many artists, including Daniel Quast and Willy Hess, Ernst von Dohnányi and Henri Marteau, Ferruccio Busoni and Eugene Ysaÿe, and Artur Schnabel and Carl Flesch. In 1902 he became a prof. at the Royal Academy of Music in Stockholm. From 1909 to 1929 he was prof. of cello at the Berlin Hochschule für Musik. He composed a Cello Concerto (1898) and variations and études for the cello. He also publ. *Mechanik und Ästhetik des Violoncellspiels* (Vienna, 1929).—NS/LK/DM

Becker, John J(oseph), remarkable American composer; b. Henderson, Ky., Jan. 22, 1886; d. Wilmette, Ill., Jan. 21, 1961. He studied at the Cincinnati Cons. (graduated, 1905), then at the Wisc. Cons. in Milwaukee, where he was a pupil of Alexander von Fielitz, Carl Busch, and Wilhelm Middleschulte (Ph.D., 1923). From 1917 to 1927 he served as director of music at Notre Dame Univ., then was chairman of the fine arts dept. at the Coll. of St. Thomas in St. Paul, Minn. (1929–35). He was subsequently Minn. State Director for the Federal Music Project (1935–41) and prof. of music at Barat Coll. of the Sacred Heart at Lake Forest, Ill. (1943–57). He also taught sporadically at the Chicago Musical Coll. His early works are characterized by romantic moods in a somewhat Germanic manner. About 1930 he was drawn into the circle of modern American music. He was on the editorial board of the *New Music Quarterly*, founded by Cowell, and became associated with Charles Ives. He conducted modern American works with various groups in St. Paul. Striving to form a style that would be both modern and recognizably American, he wrote a number of pieces for various instrumental groups under the title *Soundpiece*. He also developed a type of dramatic work connecting theatrical action with music. Becker's music is marked by sparse sonorities of an incisive rhythmic character contrasted with dissonant conglomerates of massive harmonies.

WORKS: DRAMATIC: *The Season of Pan*, ballet suite for Small Ensemble (c. 1910); *The City of Shagpat*, opera (c. 1926–27; unfinished); *Salome*, film opera (c. 1931; unfinished); *Dance Figure: Stagework No. 1*, ballet for Soprano and Orch. (1932; includes music from *Salome*); *The Life of Man: Stagework No. 4*, ballet for Speaking Chorus and Orch. (1932–43; unfinished); *Abongo, a Primitive Dance: Stagework No. 2*, ballet for Wordless Voices and 29 Percussion Instruments (1933; N.Y., May 16, 1963); *A Marriage with Space: Stagework No. 3*, ballet for Speaking Chorus and Orch. (1935; arr. as Sym. No. 4, *Dramatic Episodes*, 1940); *Nostalgic Songs of Earth*, ballet for Piano (Northfield, Minn., Dec. 12, 1938); *Vigilante 1938*, ballet for Piano and Percussion (Northfield, Minn., Dec. 12, 1938); *Privilege and Privation: Stagework No. 5c*, opera (1939; Amsterdam, June 22, 1982); *Rain Down Death: Stagework No. 5a*, incidental music to the play by A. Kreymborg for Chamber Orch. (1939; also as *A Prelude to Shakespeare* for Orch., 1937, rev. as Suite No. 1 for Orch., 1939); *Dance for Shakespeare's Tempest*, incidental music for Piano and Chamber Orch. (1940; unfinished; arr. by M. Benaroyo as *The Tempest* for 2 Pianos, 1954); *When the Willow Nods: Stagework No. 5b*, incidental music to the play by A. Kreymborg for Speaker and Chamber Orch. (1940; includes music from *4 Dances* for Piano and from *Nostalgic Songs of Earth*; rev. as Suite No. 2 for Orch., 1940); *Antigone*, incidental music to

the play by Sophocles for Orch. (1940–44); *Trap Doors*, incidental music to the play by A. Kreymborg for Speaking Chorus and Piano (n.d.; unfinished); *Deirdre: Stagework No. 6*, opera (1945; unfished); *Julius Caesar*, film score for Brass and Percussion (1949); *Faust: A Television Opera*, monodrama after Goethe for Tenor and Piano (1951; Los Angeles, April 8, 1985); *The Queen of Cornwall*, opera (1956; unfinished); *Madeleine et Judas*, incidental music to the play by R. Bruckberger for Orch. (1958; radio perf., Paris, March 25, 1959); *The Song of the Scaffold*, film score (1959; unfinished). **ORCH.:** Sym. No. 1, *Etude Primitive* (1912; Minneapolis, June 17, 1936); (2) *Cossack Sketches* (1912); *A Tartar Song* (c. 1912); Sym. No. 2, *Fantasia tragica* (1920; not extant; rev. c. 1937); Sym. No. 3, *Symphonia brevis* (1929; first complete perf., Minneapolis, May 20, 1937); *Concerto arabesque* for Piano and 12 Instruments or Small Orch. (1930; St. Paul, Minn., Dec. 7, 1931); Horn Concerto (1933; N.Y., Feb. 8, 1953); *Concertino Pastorale: A Forest Rhapsodie* for 2 Flutes and Orch. (1933; Cincinnati, Jan. 13, 1976); *Mockery: A Scherzo* for Piano and Dance Orch. (1933; first concert perf., N.Y., March 17, 1974); Viola Concerto (1937); Piano Concerto No. 2, *Satirico* (1938; St. Paul, Minn., March 28, 1939); 2 suites: No. 1 (1939; San Francisco, Jan. 15, 1983; from the incidental music to *Rain Down Death*) and No. 2 (1940; from the incidental music to *When the Willow Nods*); Sym. No. 5, *Homage to Mozart* (1942); *Victory March* (1942; from the Sym. No. 6); *The Snow Goose: A Legend of the Second World War* (1944); Violin Concerto (1948; Chattanooga, Jan. 18, 1983). **CHAMBER:** *Sonate American* for Violin and Piano (c. 1925; South Bend, Ind., July 28, 1926); 8 *Soundpieces*: No. 1 for Piano Quartet (1932; N.Y., Nov. 13, 1933; also for Piano and String Quintet, 1933, and for Piano and String Orch., 1935), No. 2a, *Homage to Haydn*: String Quartet No. 1 (1936; also for String Orch., 1936), No. 3: Violin Sonata (1936; St. Paul, Minn., April 1, 1940), No. 4: String Quartet No. 2 (1937; Lake Forest, Ill., Oct. 19, 1947), No. 5: Piano Sonata (1937; St. Paul, Minn., April 13, 1943), No. 6: Sonata for Flute and Clarinet (1942; Chapel Hill, N.C., April 26, 1970), No. 7 for 2 Pianos (1949), and No. 8: String Quartet No. 3 (1959; unfinished). **Piano:** Sonata, *The Modern Man I Sing* (c. 1910); *The Mountains* (c. 1912); *My Little Son, 18 Months Old: Studies in Child Psychology* (1924); *2 Architectural Impressions* (1924); *2 Chinese Miniatures* (1925; arr. for Orch. by R. Kraner, 1928); *4 Dances* (1938). **VOCAL:** *Rouge Bouquet* for Tenor, Men's Voices, Trumpet, and Piano (1917); *Out of the Cradle Endlessly Rocking*, cantata for Speaker, Soprano, Tenor, Chorus, and Orch. (1929; St. Cloud, Minn., July 19, 1931); *Missa symphonica* for Men's Voices (1933); Sym. No. 6, *Out of Bondage*, for Speaker, Chorus, and Orch. (1942); *Mass in Honor of the Sacred Heart* for 3 Equal Voices (1943); *Moments from the Passion* for Solo Voices, Chorus, and Organ (1945); *The 7 Last Words* for Women's or Men's Voices (1947); *Moments from the Liturgical Year* for Speaker, Speaking Chorus, Soloist, and Chorus of 3 Equal Voices (1948); Sym. No. 7 for Speaking Chorus, Women's Voices, and Orch. (1954; unfinished); also many solo songs. **OTHER:** Orchestration of Ives's *General William Booth Enters Into Heaven* for Baritone, Men's Chorus, and Small Orch. (1934–35). —NS/LK/DM

Beckman, Bror, Swedish composer; b. Kristinehamm, Feb. 10, 1866; d. Ljungskile, July 22, 1929. After studying harmony with Julius Bagge and counterpoint with Johan Lindegren (1885–90), he went to Berlin to study orchestration with Franz Mannstädt (1894). In 1910 he became director of the Stockholm Cons., where he also was a prof. from 1911. In 1904 he was made a member of the Royal Swedish Academy of Music. His works include *I sommarnätter* for String Orch. (1890), a Sym. (1895), the symphonic poem *Om lyckan* (1905), pieces for Voice and Orch., a Violin Sonata (1893), piano pieces, and songs.—**LK/DM**

Beckmann, Johann (Friedrich Gottlieb), German organist and composer; b. Celle, Sept. 6, 1737; d. there, April 25, 1792. He pursued his career in Celle, where he was highly esteemed as an organist. He wrote an opera, *Lukas und Hännchen* (Braunschweig, 1768), six harpsichord concertos, 12 keyboard sonatas, and piano pieces.

BIBL.: H. Müller, *J.F.G. B. (1737–1792): Leben und Werk mit thematischen Verzeichnis seiner Werke: Zur Celler Kulturgeschichteim 18. Jahrhundert* (Celle, 1987).—**NS/LK/DM**

Beckwith, John, Canadian composer, teacher, writer on music, and pianist; b. Victoria, British Columbia, March 9, 1927. He studied piano and harmony with Gwendoline Harper. After taking classes at Victoria Coll. (1944–45), he settled in Toronto and studied at the Univ. (M.B., 1947; M.M., 1961). He also pursued piano training with Alberto Guerrero (1945–50). In 1950 he made his debut in a lecture-recital in Toronto. A scholarship award allowed him to study composition with Boulanger in Paris (1950–51). In 1952 he joined the music faculty of the Univ. of Toronto, while also teaching theory at the Royal Cons. of Music of Toronto from 1952 to 1966. He served as dean of the faculty (1970–77), and in 1984 was named the Jean A. Chalmers Prof. of Canadian Music at the Univ. of Toronto, the first position of its kind in a Canadian Univ. In 1990 he retired as prof. emeritus. Active as a reviewer, program annotator, and editor, he made a specialty of the Canadian musical repertoire past and present. He restored Joseph Quesnel's early 19th century musical comedy *Lucas et Cécile* (1992). He ed. Vols 5 and 18 of The Canadian Musical Heritage anthology series (1986, 1995), and publ. *Music Papers: Articles and Talks by a Canadian Composer, 1961–1994* (1997). In 1987 he was made a Member of the Order of Canada. Beckwith's music is marked by pragmatic modernism, in which techniques of serialism, both chromatic and non-chromatic, and structural collage often recur. Many of his works reveal a North American, or specifically Ontarian, origin by their choice of topics, motives, coloration, or sometimes by quotation.

WORKS: DRAMATIC: *Night Blooming Cereus,* chamber opera (1953–58; radio premiere, Toronto, March 4, 1959; stage premiere, Toronto, April 5, 1960); *The Killdeer,* incidental music (1960); *The Shivaree,* opera (1965–66; 1978; Toronto, April 3, 1982); *Crazy to Kill,* opera (1987–88; Guelph, May 11, 1989); *Taptoo!,* opera (1993–95; Montreal, March 17, 1999). **ORCH.:** *Music for Dancing* (1949; rev. 1959); *Montage* (1953); *Fall Scene and Fair Dance* for Violin, Clarinet, and Strings (1956); *Concerto Fantasy* for Piano and Orch. (1958–60); *Flower Variations and Wheels* (1962); *Horn Concertino* (1963); *All the Bees and All the Keys* for Narrator and Orch. (1973); *A Concert of Myths* for Flute and Orch. (1982–83; Calgary, April 15, 1984); *Peregrine* for Solo Viola, Solo Percussion, and Small Orch. (1989; Toronto, March 3, 1990); *Round and Round* (1991–92; Winnipeg, Oct. 9, 1992). **BAND:** *Elastic Band Studies* (1969; rev. 1975); *For Starters* for 11

Brass Instruments (1984). **CHAMBER:** *3 Studies* for String Trio (1955–56); *Circle, with Tangents* for Harpsichord and 12 Solo Strings (Vancouver, July 16, 1967); *Taking a Stand* for 5 Players, 8 Brass Instruments, 14 Music Stands, and 1 Platform (1972); *Musical Chairs* for String Quintet (1973); Quartet for Strings (1977; Montreal, Feb. 10, 1978); *Case Study* for Any 5 Instruments (1980); *Sonatina in 2 Movements* for Trumpet and Piano (1981); *Arctic Dances* for Oboe and Piano (1984); *Coll. Airs* for String Quartet (1990); *Scene* for Clarinet, Trumpet, 2 Percussion, Piano, and Contrabass (1991); *After-images, after Webern* for Guitar and Cello (1994); *Echoes of Thiele* for 8 Instruments (1995; Kitchener, Jan. 17, 1996); *Eureka* for 9 Wind Instruments (Toronto, Oct. 11, 1996); *Lines Overlapping* for Harpsichord and Banjo (1996–97); *Blurred Lines* for Harpsichord and Violin in Quarter Tones (1997); *Ringaround* for Harpsichord and Celtic Harp (1998). **KEYBOARD: Piano:** *Music for Dancing* for Piano, 4–Hands (1948); *Novelette* (1951); *Études* (1983). **Organ:** *Upper Canadian Hymn Preludes* for Organ and Tape (1976–77). **Other Keyboard:** *Keyboard Practice* for 10 Instruments, 4 Players (Toronto, Nov. 24, 1979); *On the Other Hand: 4 Quartertone Studies* for Harpsichord (1997). **VOCAL:** *5 Lyrics of the T'ang Dynasty* for High Voice and Piano (1947); *The Great Lakes Suite* for Soprano, Baritone, Clarinet, Cello, and Piano (1949); *4 Songs to Poems by e.e. cummings* for Soprano and Piano (1950); *Jonah* for 4 Soloists, Chorus, and Small Orch. (1963); *The Trumpets of Summer* for Speaker, 4 Soloists, Chorus, and 6 Instrumentalists (1964); *Sharon Fragments* for Chorus (1966); *Place of Meeting* for 3 Soloists, Chorus, and Orch. (1966–67); *The Sun Dance* for Speaker, 6 Soloists, 2 Choruses, Percussion, and Organ (1968); *Gas!* for 20 Speaking Voices (1969); *3 Motets on Swan's "China"* for Chorus (1980–81); *6 Songs to Poems by e.e. cummings* for Baritone and Piano (1980–82); *Mating* for 20 Solo Voices, Electric Piano, and Percussion (1981–82); *A Little Organ Concert* for Organ, Brass Quintet, and Chorus (1982); *Harp of David* for Chorus (1984–85); *Avowals* for Tenor and Keyboardist (1985); *Les Premiers hivernements* for Soprano, Tenor, and Early Instrumental Ensemble (1986); *Synthetic Trios* for Soprano, Clarinet, and Piano (1987); *beep* for Soprano, Baritone, Chorus, and Percussion (1990); *The Hector* for Soprano/Narrator and Early Instruments (1990); *Stacey* for Soprano and Piano (1997); *Basic Music* for Children's Choir, Youth Choir, and Orch. (Guelph, May 29, 1998). **Collage:** *A Message to Winnipeg* for 4 Narrators, Clarinet, Violin, Piano, and Percussion (1960); *12 Letters to a Small Town* for 4 Narrators, Flute, Oboe, Guitar, and Piano or Harmonium (1961); *Wednesday's Child* for 3 Narrators, Soprano, Tenor, Flute, Viola, Piano, and Percussion (1962); *Canada Dash, Canada Dot* for Folk Singer, 5 Narrators, Soprano, Contralto, Baritone, Bass, and Instruments (1965–67); *The Journals of Susanna Moodie* for 2 Keyboard Players and Percussion (1973); *"In the middle of ordinary noise..."*, auditory masque for Speaker, 2 Singers, 3 Instrumentalists, and Tape (1992).

BIBL.: T. McGee, ed., *Taking a Stand: Essays in Honour of J. B.* (Toronto, 1995).—**NS/LK/DM**

Bečvařovský, Anton Felix (actually, Antonín František), Bohemian organist, teacher, and composer; b. Mladá Boleslav, April 9, 1754; d. Berlin, May 15, 1823. After music studies at the Piarist Coll. of Kosmonosy (1767–74), he completed his training with Kuchař in Prague. He was an organist in Prague before serving as organist at the Hauptkirche and Kapellmeister to the Duke of Braunschweig (1779–96). In 1800 he settled in Berlin as a music teacher. He composed five keyboard concertos (one arranged for two Harpsichords), chamber music, many solo piano pieces, and songs.

BIBL.: O. Kadlec, *A.F. B.:Český hudební emigrant* (diss., Univ. of Prague, 1971).—NS/LK/DM

Beddoe, Dan, Welsh-American tenor; b. Aberaman, March 16, 1863; d. N.Y., Dec. 26, 1937. He won a gold medal and first prize as tenor soloist in the Royal Welsh National Eisteddfod when he was 19, and pursued vocal instruction in Cleveland, Pittsburgh, N.Y., and London. He first attracted notice in the U.S. as a singer with choirs and in oratorio performances. In 1903 he appeared as soloist in the Berlioz Requiem under Damrosch's direction in N.Y., and subsequently toured widely in the U.S. and England. From 1919 to 1935 he also taught at the Cincinnati Cons. of Music.—LK/DM

Bedford, David (Vickerman), English composer, brother of **Steuart (John Rudolf) Bedford;** b. London, Aug. 4, 1937. He was the grandson of **Liza Lehmann.** After training in London at Trinity Coll. of Music and with Berkeley at the Royal Academy of Music (1958–61), he completed his studies with Nono in Venice and worked in the RAI electronic music studio in Milan. Returning to England, he was active as a keyboardist and arranger with Kevin Ayers's rock band The Whole World. He was a teacher (1968–80) and composer-in-residence (1969–81) at Queen's Coll. in London. From 1983 he was assoc. visiting composer at the Gordonstoun School in Scotland. In 1986 he became youth music director of the English Sinfonia in London, serving as its composer-in-assoc. from 1994. Bedford is a remarkably facile composer whose interests range from rock to art music, and from film scores to music for the young.

WORKS: DRAMATIC: Opera: *The Rime of the Ancient Mariner* (1978); *The Death of Baldur* (1979); *Firdiof's Saga* (1980); *The Ragnarok* (1982); *The Camlann Game* (1987); *The Return of Odysseus* (1988); *Anna* (1992–93). **OTHER:** Film scores; television music. **ORCH.:** *This One for You* (1965); *Gastrula* (1968); *Star's End* for Electric Guitar, Electric Bass Guitar, Percussion, and Orch. (1974); *Alleluia Timpanis* (1976); *Prelude for a Maritime Nation* (1981); Sym. for 12 Musicians (1981); *The Valley Sleeper, the Children, the Snakes and the Giant* for Chamber Orch. (1983); 2 syms.: No. 1 (1984) and No. 2 for Wind Band (1987); *Sun Paints Rainbows on the Vast Waves* for Wind Band (1984); *Sea and Sky and Golden Hill* for Wind Band (1985); *Ronde for Isolde* for Orch. or Wind Band (1986); *The Transfiguration* for Chamber Orch., Piano, and Percussion (1988); *Toccata for Tristan* for Brass Band (1989); *In Plymouth Town* for Chamber Orch. (1992); *Allison's Overture* (1992); *Susato Variations* (1992); *Allison's Concerto* for Trumpet and Orch. (1993); *The Goddess of Mahi River* for Sitar, Tabla, Flute, Cello, and Chamber Orch. (1994); Recorder Concerto (1995). **CHAMBER:** *5* for String Quintet (1963); *Trona* for 12 Players (1967); *Pentomino* for Wind Quintet (1968); *Jack of Shadows* for 13 Players (1973); *Pancakes, with Butter, Maple Syrup, and Bacon, and the TV Weatherman* for Brass Quintet (1973); *Circe Variations* for Clarinet, Piano, Violin, and Cello (1976); *Fridiof Kennings* for Saxophone Quartet (1980); String Quartet (1981); Piano Sonata (1981); *Pentaguin* for Flute or Piccolo, Clarinet, Viola, Harp, and Percussion (1985); *For Tess* for Brass Quintet (1985); *Erkenne Mich* for Flute or Alto Flute,

Oboe or English Horn, Bass Clarinet, and Vibraphone (1988); *Backings* for Soprano Saxophone and Tape (1990); *Cadenzas and Interludes* for 2 Clarinets, Viola, Cello, and Double Bass(1992). **OTHER INSTRUMENTAL:** *The Garden of Love* for Flute, Clarinet, Horn, Trumpet, Double Bass, and Rock Band (1969); *The Sword of Orion* for Flute, Clarinet, Violin, Cello, 4 Metronomes, and 32 Percussion Instruments (1970); *With 100 Kazoos* for Flute, Oboe, Clarinet, Bass Clarinet, Horn, Trumpet, Trombone, String Quartet, and 100 Kazoos Played by the Audience (1971); *Nurse's Song with Elephants* for 10 Acoustic Guitars and Singer (1971); *Variations on a Rhythm by Mike Oldfield* for 84 Percussion Instruments and Conductor (1973); *The Ones Who Walk Away From Omelas* for 9 Instruments, Electric Guitar, and Electric Bass Guitar (1976); *Verses and Choruses* for 2 Acoustic Guitars (1986). **VOCAL:** *A Dream of the 7 Lost Stars* for Chorus and Chamber Orch. (1964–65); *Music for Albion Moonlight* for Soprano and 6 Instruments (1965); *That White and Radiant Legend* for Soprano, Speaker, and 7 Instruments (1966); *The Tentacles of the Dark Nebula* for Tenor and 8 Instruments (1969); *Star Clusters, Nebulae, and Places in Devon* for Chorus and Brass or Brass Band (1971); *Holy Thursday with Squeakers* for Soprano, Electric Piano, Viola or Organ, Soprano Saxophone or Bassoon, and Percussion (1972); *When I Heard the Learned Astronomer* for Tenor and 14 Instruments (1972); *12 Hours of Sunset* for Chorus and Orch. (1974); *The Golden Wine is Drunk* for 16 Solo Voices (1974); *The Odyssey* for Chorus and Orch. (1976); *On the Beach at Night* for 2 Tenors, Piano, and Small Organ (1977); *The Way of Truth* for Chorus and Electronics (1977–78); *Of Beares, Foxes, and Many, Many Wonders* for Chorus and Orch. (1978); *The Song of the White Horse* for Chorus and Orch. (1978); *Requiem* for Soprano, Chorus, and Orch. (1980); *Vocoder Sextet* for Vocalist, Vocoder, Flute, Clarinet, Violin, and Viola (1981); *Of Stars, Dreams, and Cymbals* for Chorus (1982); *The Juniper Tree* for Soprano, Recorder, and Harpsichord (1982); *Into Thy Wondrous House* for Soprano, Children's Chorus, Chorus, and Orch. (1987); *The OCD Band and the Minotaur* for Soprano and 6 Instruments (1990); *Touristen Dachau* for Soprano, Men's Voices, and 6 Instruments (1992); *Charm of Grace* for 24 Voices (1994). **Educational:** *Seascapes* for Strings and 4 School Groups (1986); *Frameworks* for 2 Oboes, 2 Horns, Strings, and 4 School Orch. Groups (1989–90).—NS/LK/DM

Bedford, Steuart (John Rudolf), English conductor, brother of **David (Vickerman) Bedford;** b. London, July 31, 1939. He was the grandson of **Liza Lehmann.** He received his training at the Royal Academy of Music in London and at Lancing Coll., Oxford. In 1967 he became conductor of the English Opera Group. After it was renamed the English Music Theatre Co. in 1975, he continued to conduct it until 1980. On June 16, 1973, he conducted the premiere of Britten's *Death in Venice* at the Aldeburgh Festival, where he subsequently conducted regularly. On Oct. 18, 1974, he made his Metropolitan Opera debut in N.Y. conducting the same opera, and remained on its roster until 1977. He was music director of the English Sinfonia from 1981 to 1992. With Oliver Knussen, he served as co-artistic director of the Aldeburgh Festival from 1989. From 1969 to 1980, he was married to **Norma Burrowes.** —NS/LK/DM

Bedos de Celles, Dom François, French organ theorist; b. Caux, near Béziers, Jan. 24, 1709; d. Saint-Denis, Nov. 25, 1779. He became a Benedictine monk at Toulouse in 1726. He wrote an important treatise, *L'Art*

du facteur d'orgues (three vols., Paris, 1766–78); a fourth vol., containing historical notes on the organ, appeared in German (1793); a modern ed. was publ. in Kassel (1934–36; Eng. tr., 1977).—NS/LK/DM

Beecham, Sir Thomas, celebrated English conductor; b. St. Helens, near Liverpool, April 29, 1879; d. London, March 8, 1961. His father, Sir Joseph Beecham, was a man of great wealth, derived from the manufacture of the once-famous Beecham pills; thanks to them, young Beecham could engage in life's pleasures without troublesome regard for economic limitations. He had his first music lessons from a rural organist; from 1892 to 1897 he attended the Rossall School at Lancashire, and later went to Wadham Coll., Oxford. In 1899 he organized, mainly for his own delectation, an amateur ensemble, the St. Helen's Orch.l Soc.; also in 1899 he conducted a performance with the prestigious Halle Orch. in Manchester. In 1902 he became conductor of K. Trueman's traveling opera company, which gave him valuable practical experience with theater music. In 1905 he gave his first professional sym. concert in London, with members of the Queen's Hall Orch.; in 1906 he became conductor of the New Sym. Orch., which he led until 1908; then formed a group in his own name, the Beecham Sym. Orch., which presented its first concert in London on Feb. 22, 1909. In 1910 he presented his first season of opera at London's Covent Garden, and in subsequent seasons conducted there and at other London theaters. In 1915 he organized the Beecham Opera Co., by which time his reputation as a forceful and charismatic conductor was securely established in England. His audiences grew; the critics, impressed by his imperious ways and his unquestioned ability to bring out spectacular operatic productions, sang his praise; however, some commentators found much to criticize in his somewhat cavalier treatment of the classics. In appreciation of his services to British music, Beecham was knighted in 1916; with the death of his father, he succeeded to the title of baronet. But all of his inherited money was not enough to pay for Beecham's exorbitant financial disbursements in his ambitious enterprises, and in 1920 his operatic enterprise went bankrupt. He rebounded a few years later and continued his extraordinary career. On Jan. 12, 1928, he made his U.S. debut as a guest conductor of the N.Y. Phil., at which concert Vladimir Horowitz also made his U.S. debut as soloist. In 1929 he organized and conducted the Delius Festival in London, to which Delius himself, racked by tertiary syphilitic affliction, paralyzed and blind, was brought from his residence in France to attend Beecham's musical homage to him. From 1932 to 1939 he conducted at Covent Garden. In 1932 Beecham organized the London Phil.; contemptuous of general distaste for the Nazi regime in Germany, he took the London Phil. to Berlin in 1936 for a concert which was attended by the Führer in person. As the war situation deteriorated on the Continent, Beecham went to the U.S. in May 1940, and also toured Australia. In 1941 he was engaged as conductor of the Seattle Sym. Orch., retaining this post until 1943; he also filled guest engagements at the Metropolitan Opera in N.Y. from 1942 to 1944. In America he was not exempt from sharp criticism, which he haughtily dismissed as philistine complaints. On his part, he was outspoken in his snobbish disdain for the cultural inferiority of England's wartime allies, often spicing his comments with mild obscenities, usually of a scatological nature. Returning to England, he founded, in 1946, still another orch., the Royal Phil. In 1950 he made an extraordinarily successful North American tour with the Royal Phil. Beecham continued to conduct the orch. until ill health led him to nominate Rudolf Kempe as his successor in 1960. In 1957 Queen Elizabeth II made him a Companion of Honour. Beecham was married three times: to Utica Celestia Wells, in 1903 (divorced in 1942); to Betty Hamby (in 1943), who died in 1957; and to his young secretary, Shirley Hudson, in 1959. He publ. an autobiography, *A Mingled Chime* (London, 1943), and also an extensive biography of Delius (London, 1959; 2nd ed., rev., 1975). To mark his centennial, a commemorative postage stamp with Beecham's portrait was issued by the Post Office of Great Britain on Sept. 1, 1980. In 1964 the Sir Thomas Beecham Soc., dedicated to preserving his memory, was organized, with chapters in America and England. The Soc. publishes an official journal, *Le Grand Baton*, devoted to Beecham and the art of conducting. In spite of the occasional criticism directed at him, Beecham revealed a remarkable genius as an orch. builder. In addition to his outstanding interpretations of Haydn, Mozart, Schubert, Richard Strauss, Delius, and Sibelius, he had a particular affinity for the works of French and Russian composers of the 19th century.

BIBL.: E. Smyth, *B. and Pharaoh* (London, 1935); N. Cardus, *Sir T. B.: A Memoir* (London, 1961); C. Reid, *T. B.: An Independent Biography* (London, 1961); H. Procter-Gregg, ed., *Sir T. B., Conductor and Impresario: As Remembered by His Friends and Colleagues* (Kendal, 1972; 2nd ed., 1976); H. Atkins and A. Newman, *B. Stories* (London, 1978); J. Gilmour, *Sir T. B.: The Seattle Years 1941–1943* (Ocean Shores, Wash., 1978); idem, *Sir T. B.: The North American Tour 1950* (Ocean Shores, Wash., 1979); A. Jefferson, *Sir T. B.: A Centenary Tribute* (London, 1979); special issue of *Le Grand Baton* (March-June 1979); J. Gilmour, *Sir T. B.—50 years in the "New York Times"* (London, 1988).—NS/LK/DM

Beecke, (Notger) Ignaz (Franz) von, German composer and pianist; b. Wimpfen am Neckar, Oct. 28, 1733; d. Wallerstein, Jan. 2, 1803. He was a member of the Zollern Dragoons of the Bavarian Electorate and served in the Seven Years War. During this time, he managed to study with Gluck. While serving as a lieutenant in the Swabian Army, he went to Wallerstein in 1759 and became a courtier in the retinue of Count Philipp Karl of Oettingen-Wallerstein. In 1763 he became a captain and soon was made the count's music director, making the court band an admirable ensemble. He also was the personal adjutant to the young Count Kraft Ernst, who took charge of the government in 1773 and was elevated to the princeship in 1774. Beecke continued to serve the new prince and was made a major in 1792. He also made tours as a pianist, and in 1791 appeared in concert before the King of Prussia in Berlin. Beecke's stage works were influenced by Gluck and his instrumental music by Haydn.

WORKS: DRAMATIC: *Roland*, opera (Paris, after 1770);

Claudine von Villa Bella, Schauspiel mit Gesang (Vienna, June 13, 1780); *Die Jubelhochzeit*, comic opera (Mannheim, June 9, 1782); *Die Weinlese*, Singspiel (Mannheim, Dec. 10, 1782); *Don Quixotte*, Singspiel (1784); *List gegen List* or *Die Glocke*, Singspiel (c. 1785); *Das Herz behält seine Rechte*, Singspiel (Mainz, 1790); *Nina*, Singspiel (Aschaffenburg, 1790); *Die zerstörte Hirtenfeier*, pastorale (Aschaffenburg, 1790). ORCH.: 21 syms.; 3 concertante syms.; 24 keyboard concertos; 2 serenades; 3 wind partitas. CHAMBER: Piano Sextet; Piano Quintet; Quintet for Flute, Oboe, Violin, Viola, and Cello; 15 string quartets; 6 quartets for Flute, Violin, Viola, and Bass; 6 string trios; Piano Trio; 4 duos for Violin and Harpsichord; keyboard pieces, including about 25 piano sonatas and 6 harpsichord sonatas. VOCAL: *Die Auferstehung*, oratorio (Vienna, 1794); Requiem; 2 masses; about 16 cantatas; songs.

BIBL.: F. Munter, *I. v. B. (1733–1803) und seine Instrumentalkompositionen* (diss., Univ. of Munich, 1921); F. Little, *The String Quartet at the Oettingen-Wallerstein Court: I.v. B. and His Contemporaries* (2 vols., N.Y., 1989).—NS/LK/DM

Beecroft, Norma (Marian),

Canadian composer; b. Oshawa, Ontario, April 11, 1934. She studied piano with Gordon Hallett and Weldon Kilburn at the Royal Cons. of Music of Toronto (1952–58), during which period she also studied composition with Weinzweig; following composition training from Copland and Foss at the Berkshire Music Center in Tanglewood (summer 1958), she went to Rome to continue studies with Petrassi at the Accademia di Santa Cecilia (1959–62); she also attended Maderna's classes in Darmstadt (summers 1960–61), and then Schaeffer's electronic music classes at the Univ. of Toronto (1962–63) before working with Davidovsky at the Columbia-Princeton Electronic Music Center (1964). She was active as a producer, host, and commentator for the CBC. With Robert Aitken, she founded the New Music Concerts in Toronto in 1971, which she oversaw until 1989. In her music, Beecroft has followed along modernistic paths. In a number of her works, she has effectively utilized 12–tone techniques and electronics.

WORKS: DRAMATIC: *Undersea Fantasy*, puppet show (1967); *Hedda*, ballet (1982); *The Dissipation of Purely Sound*, radiophonic opera (1988). **ORCH.:** *Fantasy* for Strings (1958); *2 Movements* (1958); *Improvvisazioni Concertanti No. 1* for Flute and Orch. (1961), *No. 2* (1971), and *No. 3* for Flute and Orch. (1973); *Piece Concertante No. 1* (1966); *Jeu de Bach* for Oboe, Piccolo, Trumpet, Strings, and Tape (1985). **CHAMBER:** *Tre Pezzi Brevi* for Flute and Harp, or Guitar, or Piano (1960–61); *Contrasts* for Oboe, Viola, Xylorimba, Vibraphone, Percussion, and Harp (1962); *Rasas I* for Flute, Harp, String Trio, Percussion, and Piano (1968); *II and 7 for 5+* for Brass Quintet and Tape (1975); *Piece for Bob* for Flute and Tape (1975); *Collage '76* for Chamber Ensemble and Tape (1976); *Consequences for 5* for Piano, Synthesizer, and Live Electronics (1977); *Collage '78* for Bassoon, Piano, 2 Percussion, and Tape (1978); *Quaprice* for Horn, Percussion, and Tape (1980); *Cantorum Vitae* for Flute, Cello, 2 Pianos, Percussion, and Tape (1981); *Troissonts* for Viola and 2 Percussion (1981); *Jeu II* for Flute, Viola, and Tape (1985), *III* for Viola and Tape (1987), and *IV (Mozart)* for Fortepiano, Flute, Clarinet, Trumpet, Trombone, Horn, String Quintet, and Tape (1991); *Images* for Wind Quintet (1986); *Accordion Play* for Accordion and 2 Percussion (1989); *Hemispherics* for 9 Instruments (1990). **VOCAL:** *The Hollow Men* for Chorus (1956); *From Dreams of Brass* for Soprano, Narrator, Chorus, Orch., and Tape (1963–64); *Elegy* and *2 Went to Sleep* for Soprano, Percussion or Piano, and Tape (1967); *The Living Flame of Love* for Chorus (1968); *3 Impressions* for Chorus (1973); *Rasas II* (1973; rev. 1975) and *III* (1974) for Voice, Chamber Ensemble, and Tape; *Requiem Mass* for Soloists, Chorus, and Orch. (1989–90). ELECTROACOUSTIC: *Evocations: Images of Canada* (1991).—NS/LK/DM

Beer, Johann,

Austrian-born German music theorist and polemicist; b. St. Georg, Upper Austria, Feb. 28, 1655; d. (accidentally shot while watching a shooting contest) Weissenfels, Aug. 6, 1700. He studied music at the Benedictine monastery in Lambach, then attended classes at Reichersberg, Passau, and the Gymnasium Poeticum in Regensburg. In 1676 he became a student in theology at the Univ. of Leipzig. In 1685 he was appointed Konzertmeister of the court orch. in Weissenfels. His writings are of interest as a curiosity reflecting the musical mores of his time; he publ. polemical pamphlets directed against contemporary writers who deprecated music as dangerous for morals. In such pamphlets he used the pseudonym *Ursus*, Latin for the German *Bär* (which is a homonym of his real name, Beer), i.e., Bear, the ursine animal. One such publication opens with the words "Ursus murmurat" ("The Bear growls"), and another, "Ursus vulpinatur," i.e.,"Bear leads a fox hunt." Both assail a certain Gottfried Vockerodt, who claimed that the depravity of Nero and Caligula was the result of their immoderate love of music. Beer also publ. *Bellum musicum* (Nuremberg, 1719).

BIBL.: R. Alewyn, *J. B.: Studien zum Roman des 17. Jahrhundert* (Leipzig, 1932).—NS/LK/DM

Beer, (Johann) Joseph,

Bohemian clarinetist and composer; b. Grünewald, May 18, 1744; d. Berlin, Oct. 28, 1812. He began his career as a trumpeter. From 1767 to 1777 he was in the service of the Duke of Orléans as a clarinetist. After touring Europe extensively as a virtuoso from 1779, he was active as a chamber musician at the courts in St. Petersburg (1782–92) and Berlin (from 1792). Beer improved the clarinet by adding a fifth key. He also wrote various works for the instrument. —NS/LK/DM

Beer-Walbrunn, Anton,

German composer; b. Kohlberg, Bavaria, June 29, 1864; d. Munich, March 22, 1929. He was a pupil of Rheinberger, Bussmeyer, and Abel at the Akademie der Tonkunst in Munich. From 1901 he was an instructor there, and from 1908 prof. He wrote the operas *Die Sühne* (Lübeck, Feb. 16, 1894), *Don Quijote* (Munich, Jan. 1, 1908), *Das Ungeheuer* (Karlsruhe, April 25, 1914), and *Der Sturm* (1914; after Shakespeare), as well as incidental music to *Hamlet* (1909), two syms., *Mahomet's Gesang* for Chorus and Orch., *Lustspielouvertüre*, Violin Concerto, Piano Quintet, church music, and many compositions for various instruments. He also supervised new eds. of works of Wilhelm Friedemann Bach.—NS/LK/DM

Beethoven, Ludwig van,

great German composer whose unsurpassed genius, expressed with supreme mastery in his syms., chamber music, concertos, and piano sonatas, revealing an extraordinary power of invention, marked a historic turn in the art of composition; b. Bonn, Dec. 15 or 16 (baptized, Dec. 17), 1770; d. Vienna, March 26, 1827. (Beethoven himself maintained, against all evidence, that he was born in 1772, and that the 1770 date referred to his older brother, deceased in infancy, whose forename was also Ludwig.) The family was of Dutch extraction (the surname Beethoven meant "beet garden" in Dutch). Beethoven's grandfather, Ludwig van Beethoven (b. Mechelen, Belgium, Jan. 5, 1712; d. Bonn, Dec. 24, 1773), served as choir director of the church of St. Pierre in Louvain in 1731; in 1732 he went to Liège, where he sang bass in the cathedral choir of St. Lambert; in 1733 he became a member of the choir in Bonn; there he married Maria Poll. Prevalent infant mortality took its statistically predictable tribute; the couple's only surviving child was Johann van Beethoven; he married a young widow, Maria Magdalena Leym (née Keverich), daughter of the chief overseer of the kitchen at the palace in Ehrenbreitstein; they were the composer's parents. Beethoven firmly believed that the nobiliary particle "van" in the family name betokened a nobility; in his demeaning litigation with his brother's widow over the guardianship of Beethoven's nephew Karl, he argued before the Vienna magistrate that as a nobleman he should be given preference over his sister-in-law, a commoner, but the court rejected his contention on the ground that "van" lacked the elevated connotation of its German counterpart, "von." Beethoven could never provide a weightier claim of noble descent. In private, he even tolerated without forceful denial the fantastic rumor that he was a natural son of royalty, a love child of Friedrich Wilhelm II, or even of Frederick the Great.

Beethoven's father gave him rudimentary instruction in music; he learned to play both the violin and the piano; Tobias Friedrich Pfeiffer, a local musician, gave him formal piano lessons; the court organist in Bonn, Gilles van Eeden, instructed him in keyboard playing and in music theory; Franz Rovantini gave him violin lessons; another violinist who taught Beethoven was Franz Ries. Beethoven also learned to play the horn, under the guidance of the professional musician Nikolaus Simrock. Beethoven's academic training was meager; he was, however, briefly enrolled at the Univ. of Bonn in 1789. His first important teacher of composition was Christian Gottlob Neefe, a thorough musician who seemed to understand his pupil's great potential even in his early youth. He guided Beethoven in the study of Bach and encouraged him in keyboard improvisation. At the age of 12, in 1782, Beethoven composed *Nine Variations for Piano on a March of Dressler*, his first work to be publ. In 1783 he played the cembalo in the Court Orch. in Bonn; in 1784 the Elector Maximilian Franz officially appointed him to the post of deputy court organist, a position he retained until 1792; from 1788 to 1792 Beethoven also served as a violist in theater orchs. In 1787 the Elector sent him to Vienna, where he stayed for a short time; the report that he played for Mozart and that Mozart pronounced him a future great composer seems to be a figment of somebody's eager imagination. After a few weeks in Vienna Beethoven went to Bonn when he received news that his mother

was gravely ill; she died on July 17, 1787. He was obliged to provide sustenance for his two younger brothers; his father, who took to drink in excess, could not meet his obligations. Beethoven earned some money by giving piano lessons to the children of Helene von Breuning, the widow of a court councillor. He also met important wealthy admirers, among them Count Ferdinand von Waldstein, who was to be immortalized by Beethoven's dedication to him of a piano sonata bearing his name. Beethoven continued to compose; some of his works of the period were written in homage to royalty, as a cantata on the death of the Emperor Joseph II and another on the accession of Emperor Leopold II; other pieces were designed for performance at aristocratic gatherings.

In 1790 an event of importance took place in Beethoven's life when Haydn was honored in Bonn by the Elector on his way to London; it is likely that Beethoven was introduced to him, and that Haydn encouraged him to come to Vienna to study with him. However that might be, Beethoven went to Vienna in Nov. 1792, and began his studies with Haydn. Not very prudently, Beethoven approached the notable teacher Johann Schenk to help him write the mandatory exercises prior to delivering them to Haydn for final appraisal. In the meantime, Haydn had to go to London again, and Beethoven's lessons with him were discontinued. Instead, Beethoven began a formal study of counterpoint with Johann Georg Albrechtsberger, a learned musician and knowledgeable pedagogue; these studies continued for about a year, until 1795. Furthermore, Beethoven took lessons in vocal composition with the illustrious Italian composer Salieri, who served as Imperial Kapellmeister at the Austrian court. Beethoven was fortunate to find a generous benefactor in Prince Karl Lichnowsky, who awarded him, beginning about 1800, an annual stipend of 600 florins; he was amply repaid for this bounty by entering the pantheon of music history through Beethoven's dedication to him of the *Sonate pathétique* and other works, as well as his first opus number, a set of three piano trios. Among other aristocrats of Vienna who were introduced into the gates of permanence through Beethoven's dedications was Prince Franz Joseph Lobkowitz, whose name adorns the title pages of the six String Quartets, op.18; the *Eroica Symphony* (after Beethoven unsuccessfully tried to dedicate it to Napoleon); the Triple Concerto, op.56; and (in conjunction with Prince Razumovsky) the fifth and sixth syms.—a glorious florilegium of great music. Prince Razumovsky, the Russian ambassador to Vienna, played an important role in Beethoven's life. From 1808 to 1816 he maintained in his residence a string quartet in which he himself played the second violin (the leader was Beethoven's friend Schuppanzigh). It was to Razumovsky that Beethoven dedicated his three string quartets that became known as the Razumovsky quartets, in which Beethoven made use of authentic Russian folk themes. Razumovsky also shared with Lobkowitz the dedications of Beethoven's fifth and sixth syms. Another Russian patron was Prince Golitzyn, for whom Beethoven wrote his great string quartets opps. 127, 130, and 132.

Beethoven made his first public appearance in Vienna on March 29, 1795, as soloist in one of his piano concertos (probably the B-flat major Concerto, op.19). In 1796 he played in Prague, Dresden, Leipzig, and Berlin. He also participated in "competitions," fashionable at the time, with other pianists, which were usually held in aristocratic salons. In 1799 he competed with Joseph Wölffl and in 1800 with Daniel Steibelt. On April 2, 1800, he presented a concert of his works in the Burgtheater in Vienna, at which his First Sym., in C major, and the Septet in E-flat major were performed for the first time. Other compositions at the threshold of the century were the Piano Sonata in C minor, op.13, the *Pathétique*; the C-major Piano Concerto, op.15; "sonata quasi una fantasia" for Piano in C-sharp minor, op.27, celebrated under the nickname *Moonlight Sonata* (so described by a romantically inclined critic but not specifically accepted by Beethoven); the D-major Piano Sonata known as *Pastoral*; eight violin sonatas; three piano trios; five string trios; six string quartets; several sets of variations; and a number of songs.

Fétis was the first to suggest the division of Beethoven's compositions into three stylistic periods. It was left to Wilhelm von Lenz to fully elucidate this view in his *Beethoven et ses trois styles* (two vols., St. Petersburg, 1852). Despite this arbitrary chronological division, the work became firmly established in Beethoven literature. According to Lenz, the first period embraced Beethoven's works from his early years to the end of the 18th century, marked by a style closely related to the formal methods of Haydn. The second period, covering the years 1801–14, was signaled by a more personal, quasi-Romantic mood, beginning with the *Moonlight Sonata*; the last period, extending from 1814 to Beethoven's death in 1827, comprised the most individual, the most unconventional, the most innovative works, such as his last string quartets and the Ninth Sym., with its extraordinary choral finale.

Beethoven's early career in Vienna was marked by fine success; he was popular not only as a virtuoso pianist and a composer, but also as a social figure who was welcome in the aristocratic circles of Vienna; Beethoven's students included society ladies and even royal personages, such as Archduke Rudolf of Austria, to whom Beethoven dedicated the so-called Archduke Trio, op.97. But Beethoven's progress was fatefully affected by a mysteriously growing deafness, which reached a crisis in 1802. On Oct. 8 and 10, 1802, he wrote a poignant document known as the "Heiligenstadt Testament," for it was drawn in the village of Heiligenstadt, where he resided at the time. The document, not discovered until after Beethoven's death, voiced his despair at the realization that the most important sense of his being, the sense of hearing, was inexorably failing. He implored his brothers, in case of his early death, to consult his physician, Dr. Schmidt, who knew the secret of his "lasting malady" contracted six years before he wrote the Testament, i.e., in 1796. The etiology of his illness leaves little doubt that the malady was the dreaded "lues," with symptoms including painful intestinal disturbances, enormous enlargement of the pancreas, cirrhosis of the liver, and, most ominously, the porous degeneration of the roof of the cranium, observ-

able in the life mask of 1812 and clearly shown in the photograph of Beethoven's skull taken when his body was exhumed in 1863. However, the impairment of his hearing may have had an independent cause: an otosclerosis, resulting in the shriveling of the auditory nerves and concomitant dilation of the accompanying arteries. Externally, there were signs of tinnitus, a constant buzzing in the ears, about which Beethoven complained. His reverential biographer A.W. Thayer states plainly in a letter dated Oct. 29, 1880, that it was known to several friends of Beethoven that the cause of his combined ailments was syphilis.

To the end of his life Beethoven hoped to find a remedy for his deafness among the latest "scientific" medications. His Konversationshefte bear a pathetic testimony to these hopes; in one, dated 1819, he notes down the address of a Dr. Mayer, who treated deafness by "sulphur vapor" and a vibration machine. By tragic irony, Beethoven's deafness greatly contributed to the study of his personality, thanks to the existence of the "conversation books" in which his interlocutors wrote down their questions and Beethoven replied, a method of communication which became a rule in his life after 1818. Unfortunately, Beethoven's friend and amanuensis, Anton Schindler, altered or deleted many of these; it seems also likely that he destroyed Beethoven's correspondence with his doctors, as well as the recipes which apparently contained indications of treatment by mercury, the universal medication against venereal and other diseases at the time.

It is remarkable that under these conditions Beethoven was able to continue his creative work with his usual energy; there were few periods of interruption in the chronology of his list of works, and similarly there is no apparent influence of his moods of depression on the content of his music; tragic and joyful musical passages had equal shares in his inexhaustible flow of varied works. On April 5, 1803, Beethoven presented a concert of his compositions in Vienna at which he was soloist in his Third Piano Concerto; the program also contained performances of his Second Sym. and of the oratorio *Christus am Oelberge*. On May 24, 1803, he played in Vienna the piano part of his Violin Sonata, op.47, known as the *Kreutzer Sonata*, although Kreutzer himself did not introduce it; in his place the violin part was taken over by the mulatto artist George Bridgetower. During the years 1803 and 1804 Beethoven composed his great Sym. No. 3, in E-flat major, op.55, the *Eroica*. It has an interesting history. Beethoven's disciple Ferdinand Ries relates that Beethoven tore off the title page of the MS of the score orig. dedicated to Napoleon, after learning of his proclamation as Emperor of France in 1804, and supposedly exclaimed, "So he is a tyrant like all the others after all!" Ries reported this story shortly before his death, some 34 years after the composition of the Eroica, which throws great doubt on its credibility. Indeed, in a letter to the publishing firm of Breitkopf & Härtel, dated Aug. 26, 1804, long after Napoleon'sproclamation of Empire, Beethoven still refers to the title of the work as "really Bonaparte." His own copy of the score shows that he crossed out the designation "Inttitulata Bonaparte," but allowed the words written in pencil, in German, "Geschrieben auf

Bonaparte" to stand. In Oct. 1806, when the first ed. of the orch. parts was publ. in Vienna, the sym. received the title "Sinfonia eroica composta per festeggiare il sovvenire d'un grand' uomo" ("heroic sym., composed to celebrate the memory of a great man"). But who was the great man whose memory was being celebrated in Beethoven's masterpiece? Napoleon was very much alive and was still leading his Grande Armee to new conquests, so the title would not apply. Yet, the famous funeral march in the score expressed a sense of loss and mourning. The mystery remains. There is evidence that Beethoven continued to have admiration for Napoleon. He once remarked that had he been a military man he could have matched Napoleon's greatness on the battlefield. Beethoven and Napoleon were close contemporaries; Napoleon was a little more than a year older than Beethoven.

In 1803 Emanuel Schikaneder, manager of the Theater an der Wien, asked Beethoven to compose an opera to a libretto he had prepared under the title *Vestas Feuer*, but he soon lost interest in the project and instead began work on another opera, based on J.N. Bouilly's *Leonore, ou L'Amour conjugal*. The completed opera was named *Fidelio*, which was the heroine's assumed name in her successful efforts to save her imprisoned husband. The opera was given at the Theater an der Wien on Nov. 20, 1805, under difficult circumstances, a few days after the French army entered Vienna. There were only three performances before the opera was rescheduled for March 29 and April 10, 1806; after another long hiatus a greatly revised version of *Fidelio* was produced on May 23, 1814. Beethoven wrote three versions of the *Overture for Leonore*; for another performance, on May 26, 1814, he revised the Overture once more, and this time it was performed under the title *Fidelio Overture*.

An extraordinary profusion of creative masterpieces marked the years 1802–08 in Beethoven's life. During these years he brought out the three String Quartets, op.59, dedicated to Count Razumovsky; the fourth, fifth, and sixth syms.; the Violin Concerto; theFourth Piano Concerto; the Triple Concerto; the *Coriolan* Overture; and a number of piano sonatas, including the D minor, op.31; No. 2, the *Tempest*; the C major, op.53, the *Waldstein*; and the F minor, op.57, the *Appassionata*. On Dec. 22, 1808, his fifth and sixth syms. were heard for the first time at a concert in Vienna; the concert lasted some four hours. Still, financial difficulties beset Beethoven. The various annuities from patrons were uncertain, and the devaluation of the Austrian currency played havoc with his calculations. In Oct. 1808, King Jerome Bonaparte of Westphalia offered the composer the post of Kapellmeister of Kassel at a substantial salary, but Beethoven decided to remain in Vienna. Between 1809 and 1812, Beethoven wrote his Fifth Piano Concerto; the String Quartet in E-flat major, op.74; the incidental music to Goethe's drama *Egmont*; the seventh and eighth syms.; and his Piano Sonata in E- flat major, op.81a, whimsically subtitled "Das Lebewohl, Abwesenheit und Wiedersehn," also known by its French subtitle, "Les Adieux, l'absence, et le retour." He also added a specific description to the work, "Sonate caractéristique." This explicit characterization was rare with Beethoven; he usually avoided programmatic de-

scriptions, preferring to have his music stand by itself. Even in his Sixth Sym., the *Pastoral*, which bore specific subtitles for each movement and had the famous imitations of birds singing and the realistic portrayal of a storm, Beethoven decided to append a cautionary phrase:"More as an expression of one's feelings than a picture." He specifically denied that the famous introductory call in the Fifth Sym. represented the knock of Fate at his door, but the symbolic association was too powerful to be removed from the legend; yet the characteristic iambic tetrameter was anticipated in several of Beethoven's works, among them the *Appassionata* and the Fourth Piano Concerto. Czerny, who was close to Beethoven in Vienna, claimed that the theme was derived by Beethoven from the cry of the songbird Emberiza, or Emmerling, a species to which the common European goldfinch belongs, which Beethoven may have heard during his walks in the Vienna woods, a cry that is piercing enough to compensate for Beethoven's loss of aural acuity. However that may be, the four-note motif became inexorably connected with the voice of doom for enemies and the exultation of the victor in battle. It was used as a victory call by the Allies in World War II; the circumstance that three short beats followed by one long beat spelled V for Victory in Morse code reinforced its effectiveness. The Germans could not very well jail people for whistling a Beethoven tune, so they took it over themselves as the first letter of the archaic German word "Viktoria," and trumpeted it blithely over their radios. Another famous nicknamed work by Beethoven was the *Emperor Concerto*, a label attached to the Fifth Piano Concerto, op.73. He wrote it in 1809, when Napoleon's star was still high in the European firmament, and some publicist decided that the martial strains of the music, with its sonorous fanfares, must have been a tribute to the Emperor of the French. Patriotic reasons seemed to underlie Beethoven's designation of his Piano Sonata, op.106, as the *Hammerklavier Sonata*, that is, a work written for a hammer keyboard, or fortepiano, as distinct from harpsichord. But all of Beethoven's piano sonatas were for fortepiano; moreover, he assigned the title *Hammerklavier* to each of the 4 sonatas, namely opp. 101, 106, 109, and 110, using the old German word for fortepiano; by so doing, he desired to express his patriotic consciousness of being a German.

Like many professional musicians, Beethoven was occasionally called upon to write a work glorifying an important event or a famous personage. Pieces of this kind seldom achieve validity, and usually produce bombast. Such a work was Beethoven's *Wellingtons Sieg oder Die Schlacht bei Vittoria*, celebrating the British victory over Joseph Bonaparte, Napoleon's brother who temporarily sat on the Spanish throne. In 1814 Beethoven wrote a cantata entitled *Der glorreiche Augenblick*, intended to mark the "glorious moment" of the fall of his erstwhile idol, Napoleon.

Personal misfortunes, chronic ailments, and intermittent quarrels with friends and relatives preoccupied Beethoven's entire life. He ardently called for peace among men, but he never achieved peace with himself. Yet he could afford to disdain the attacks in the press; on the margin of a critical but justified review of his

Wellington's Victory, he wrote, addressing the writer: "You wretched scoundrel! What I excrete [he used the vulgar German word *scheisse*] is better than anything you could ever think up!"

Beethoven was overly suspicious; he even accused the faithful Schindler of dishonestly mishandling the receipts from the sale of tickets at the first performance of the Ninth Sym. He exaggerated his poverty; he possessed some shares and bonds which he kept in a secret drawer. He was untidy in personal habits: he often used preliminary drafts of his compositions to cover the soup and even the chamber pot, leaving telltale circles on the MS. He was strangely naive; he studiously examined the winning numbers of the Austrian government lottery, hoping to find a numerological clue to a fortune for himself. His handwriting was all but indecipherable. An earnest Beethoveniac spent time with a microscope trying to figure out what kind of soap Beethoven wanted his housekeeper to purchase for him; the scholar's efforts were crowned with triumphant success: the indecipherable word was *gelbe*—Beethoven wanted a piece of yellow soap. Q.E.D. The copying of his MSS presented difficulties; not only were the notes smudged, but sometimes Beethoven even failed to mark a crucial accidental. A copyist said that he would rather copy 20 pages of Rossini than a single page of Beethoven. On the other hand, Beethoven's sketchbooks, containing many alternative drafts, are extremely valuable, for they introduce a scholar into the inner sanctum of Beethoven's creative process.

Beethoven had many devoted friends and admirers in Vienna, but he spent most of his life in solitude. Carl Czerny reports in his diary that Beethoven once asked him to let him lodge in his house, but Czerny declined, explaining that his aged parents lived with him and he had no room for Beethoven. Deprived of the pleasures and comforts of family life, Beethoven sought to find a surrogate in his nephew Karl, son of Caspar Carl Beethoven, who died in 1815. Beethoven regarded his sister-in-law as an unfit mother; he went to court to gain sole guardianship over the boy; in his private letters, and even in his legal depositions, he poured torrents of vilification upon the woman, implying even that she was engaged in prostitution. In his letters to Karl he often signed himself as the true father of the boy. In 1826 Karl attempted suicide; it would be unfair to ascribe this act to Beethoven's stifling avuncular affection; Karl later went into the army and enjoyed a normal life.

Gallons of ink have been unnecessarily expended on the crucial question of Beethoven's relationships with women. That Beethoven dreamed of an ideal life companion is clear from his numerous utterances and candid letters to friends, in some of which he asked them to find a suitable bride for him. But there is no inkling that he kept company with any particular woman in Vienna. Beethoven lacked social graces; he could not dance; he was unable to carry on a light conversation about trivia; and behind it all there was the dreadful reality of his deafness. He could speak, but could not always understand when he was spoken to. With close friends he used an unwieldy ear trumpet; but such contrivances were obviously unsuitable in a social

gathering. There were several objects of his secret passions, among his pupils or the society ladies to whom he dedicated his works. But somehow he never actually proposed marriage, and they usually married less hesitant suitors. There remains the famous letter Beethoven addressed to an "unsterbliche Geliebte," the "Immortal Beloved," but her identity remains a matter of much controversy among Beethoven scholars. See G. Altman, *Beethoven: Man of His World: Undisclosed Evidence for His Immortal Beloved* (Tallahassee, 1996).

The so-called third style of Beethoven was assigned by biographers to the last 10 or 15 years of his life. It included the composition of his monumental Ninth Sym., completed in 1824 and first performed in Vienna on May 7, 1824; the program also included excerpts from the *Missa Solemnis* and *Die Weihe des Hauses*. It was reported that Caroline Unger, the contralto soloist in the *Missa Solemnis*, had to pull Beethoven by the sleeve at the end of the performance so that he would acknowledge the applause he could not hear. With the Ninth Sym., Beethoven completed the evolution of the symphonic form as he envisioned it. Its choral finale was his manifesto addressed to the world at large, to the text from Schiller's ode *An die Freude*. In it, Beethoven, through Schiller, appealed to all humanity to unite in universal love. Here a musical work, for the first time, served a political ideal. Beethoven's last string quartets, opp. 127, 130, 131, and 132, served as counterparts of his last sym. in their striking innovations, dramatic pauses, and novel instrumental tone colors.

In Dec. 1826, on his way back to Vienna from a visit in Gneixendorf, Beethoven was stricken with a fever that developed into a mortal pleurisy; dropsy and jaundice supervened to this condition; surgery to relieve the accumulated fluid in his organism was unsuccessful, and he died on the afternoon of March 26, 1827. It was widely reported that an electric storm struck Vienna as Beethoven lay dying; its occurrence was indeed confirmed by the contemporary records in the Vienna weather bureau, but the story that he raised his clenched fist aloft as a gesture of defiance to an overbearing Heaven must be relegated to fantasy; he was far too feeble either to clench his fist or to raise his arm. The funeral of Beethoven was held in all solemnity.

Beethoven was memorialized in festive observations of the centennial and bicentennial of his birth, and of the centennial and sesquicentennial of his death. The house where he was born in Bonn was declared a museum. Monuments were erected to him in many cities. Commemorative postage stamps bearing his image were issued not only in Germany and Austria, but in Russia and other countries. Streets were named after him in many cities of the civilized world, including even Los Angeles.

Beethoven's music marks a division between the Classical period of the 18th century, exemplified by the great names of Mozart and Haydn, and the new spirit of Romantic music that characterized the entire course of the 19th century. There are certain purely external factors that distinguish these two periods of musical evolution; one of them pertains to sartorial matters. Music before Beethoven was *Zopfmusik*, pigtail music. Haydn and

Mozart are familiar to us by portraits in which their heads are crowned by elaborate wigs; Beethoven's hair was by contrast luxuriant in its unkempt splendor. The music of the 18th century possessed the magnitude of mass production. The accepted number of Haydn's syms., according to his own count, is 104, but even in his own catalogue Haydn allowed a duplication of one of his symphonic works. Mozart wrote about 40 syms. during his short lifetime. Haydn's syms. were constructed according to an easily defined formal structure; while Mozart's last syms. show greater depth of penetration, they do not depart from the Classical convention. Besides, both Haydn and Mozart wrote instrumental works variously entitled cassations, serenades, divertimentos, and suites, which were basically synonymous with syms. Beethoven's syms. were few in number and mutually different. The first and second syms. may still be classified as *Zopfmusik*, but with the Third Sym. he entered a new world of music. No sym. written before had contained a clearly defined funeral march. Although the Fifth Sym. had no designated program, it lent itself easily to programmatic interpretation. Wagner attached a bombastic label, "Apotheosis of the Dance," to Beethoven's Seventh Sym. The Eighth Sym. Beethoven called his "little sym.," and the Ninth is usually known as the *Choral* sym. With the advent of Beethoven, the manufacture of syms. en masse had ceased; Schumann, Brahms, Tchaikovsky, and their contemporaries wrote but a few syms. each, and each had a distinctive physiognomy. Beethoven had forever destroyed *Zopfmusik*, and opened the floodgates of the Romantic era. His music was individual; it was emotionally charged; his *Kreutzer Sonata* served as a symbol for Tolstoy's celebrated moralistic tale of that name, in which the last movement of the sonata leads the woman pianist into the receptive arms of the concupiscent violinist. But technically the sonata is very difficult for amateurs to master, and Tolstoy's sinners were an ordinary couple in old Russia.

Similarly novel were Beethoven's string quartets; a musical abyss separated his last string quartets from his early essays in the same form. Trios, violin sonatas, cello sonatas, and the 32 great piano sonatas also represent evolutionary concepts. Yet Beethoven's melody and harmony did not diverge from the sacrosanct laws of euphony and tonality. The famous dissonant chord introducing the last movement of the Ninth Sym. resolves naturally into the tonic, giving only a moment's pause to the ear. Beethoven's favorite device of pairing the melody in the high treble with triadic chords in close harmony in the deep bass was a peculiarity of his style but not necessarily an infringement of the Classical rules. Yet contemporary critics found some of these practices repugnant and described Beethoven as an eccentric bent on creating unconventional sonorities. Equally strange to the untutored ear were pregnant pauses and sudden modulations in his instrumental works. Beethoven was not a contrapuntist by taste or skill. With the exception of his monumental *Grosse Fuge*, composed as the finale of the String Quartet, op.133, his fugal movements were usually free canonic imitations. There is only a single instance in Beethoven's music of the crab movement, a variation achieved by running the

theme in reverse. But he was a master of instrumental variation, deriving extraordinary transformations through melodic and rhythmic alterations of a given theme. His op.120, 33 variations for piano on a waltz theme by the Viennese publisher Diabelli, represents one of the greatest achievements in the art.

When Hans von Bülow was asked which was his favorite key signature, he replied that it was E-flat major, the tonality of the *Eroica*, for it had three flats: one for Bach, one for Beethoven, and one for Brahms. Beethoven became forever the second B in popular music books.

The literature on Beethoven is immense. The basic catalogues are those by G. Kinsky and H. Halm, *Das Werk Beethovens: Thematisch-Bibliographisches Verzeichnis seiner sämtlichen vollendeten Kompositionen*, publ. in Munich and Duisburg in 1955, and by W. Hess, *Verzeichnis der Gesamtausgabe veröffentlichten Werke Ludwig van Beethovens*, publ. in Wiesbaden in 1957. Beethoven attached opus numbers to most of his works, and they are essential in a catalogue of his works.

WORKS: ORCH.: 9 syms.: No. 1, in C major, op.21 (Vienna, April 2, 1800), No. 2, in D major, op.36 (1801–02; Vienna, April 5, 1803), No. 3, in E-flat major, op.55, *Eroica* (1803–04; Vienna, April 7, 1805), No. 4, in B-flat major, op.60 (1806; Vienna, March 5, 1807), No. 5, in C minor, op.67 (sketches from 1803; 1807–08; Vienna, Dec. 22, 1808), No. 6, in F major, op.68, *Pastoral* (sketches from 1803; 1808; Vienna, Dec. 22, 1808), No. 7, in A major, op.92 (1811–12; Vienna, Dec. 8, 1813), No. 8, in F major, op.93 (1812; Vienna, Feb. 27, 1814), and No. 9, in D minor, op.125, *Choral* (sketches from 1815–18; 1822–24; Vienna, May 7, 1824); also a fragment of a Sym. in C minor, Hess 298 from the Bonn period. Sketches for the 1st movement of a projected 10th Sym. were realized by Barry Cooper and performed under the auspices of the Royal Phil. Soc. in London on Oct. 18, 1988. **Incidental Music:** Overture to Collin's *Coriolan*, in C minor, op.62 (1807; Vienna, March 1807); *Egmont*, op.84, to Goethe's drama (with overture; 1809–10; Vienna, June 15, 1810); *Die Ruinen von Athen*, op.113, to Kotzebue's drama (with overture; 1811; Pest, Feb. 10, 1812); *König Stephan*, op.117, to Kotzebue's drama (with overture; 1811; Pest, Feb. 10, 1812); Triumphal March in C major for Kuffner's *Tarpeja* (March 26, 1813); music to Duncker's drama *Leonore Prohaska* (1815); Overture in C major, op.124, to Meisl's drama *Die Weihe des Hauses* (Vienna, Oct. 3, 1822).—Further overtures: 4 overtures written for the opera *Leonore*, later named *Fidelio*: *Leonore* No. 1, in C major, op.138 (1806–07; Feb. 7, 1828), *Leonore* No. 2, op.72a (1804–05; Vienna, Nov. 20, 1805), *Leonore* No. 3, op.72b (1805–06; Vienna, March 29, 1806), and *Fidelio*, op.72c (Vienna, May 26, 1814); *Namensfeier* in C major, op.115 (1814–15; Vienna, Dec. 25, 1815). **Other Works For Orch. or Wind Band:** 12 Minuets, WoO 7 (1795); 12 German Dances (1795); 12 Contredanses (1802?); March "für die böhmische Landwehr' in F major (1809); March in F major (1810); Polonaise in D major, WoO 21 (1810); Écossaise in D major (1810); Écossaise in G major (1810); *Wellingtons Sieg oder Die Schlacht bei Vittoria* (also known as the Battle sym.), op.91 (1813; Vienna, Dec. 8, 1813); March in D major (1816); *Gratulations-Menuet* in E-flat major, WoO 3 (Nov. 3, 1822); March with Trio in C major (1822?). **BALLET:** *Ritterballett* (1790–91; Bonn, March 6, 1791); *Die Geschöpfe des Prometheus*, op.43 (overture, introduction, and 16 numbers; 1800–01; Vienna, March 28, 1801). **W o r k s   F o r   S o l o   I n s t r u m e n t s   a n d   O r c h .:** Piano Concerto in E-flat major (1784); *Romance* in E minor for Piano, Flute, Bassoon, and Orch., Hess 13 (1786; only a fragment extant); Violin Concerto in C major (1790–92; only a portion of the 1st movement extant); Oboe Concerto in F major, Hess 12 (1792?-93?; not extant; only a few sketches survive); Rondo in B-flat major for Piano and Orch. (1793; solo part finished by Czerny); Piano Concerto No. 2, in B-flat major, op.19 (probably begun during the Bonn period, perhaps as early as 1785; rev. 1794–95 and 1798; Vienna, March 29, 1795; when publ. in Leipzig in 1801, it was listed as "No. 2"); Piano Concerto No. 1, in C major, op.15 (1795; rev. 1800; Vienna, Dec. 18, 1795; when publ. in Vienna in 1801, it was listed as "No. 1"); Romance in F major for Violin and Orch., op.50 (1798?; Nov. 1798?); Piano Concerto No. 3, in C minor, op.37 (1800?; Vienna, April 5, 1803); Romance in G major for Violin and Orch., op.40 (1801?- 02); Triple Concerto in C major for Piano, Violin, Cello, and Orch., op.56 (1803–04; Vienna, May 1808); Piano Concerto No. 4, in G major, op.58 (1805–06; Vienna, March 1807); Violin Concerto in D major, op.61 (Vienna, Dec. 23, 1806; cadenza for the 1st movement and 3 cadenzas for the finale; also arranged as a piano concerto in 1807); Fantasia in C minor for Piano, Chorus, and Orch., op.80, Choral Fantasy (Vienna, Dec. 22, 1808); Piano Concerto No. 5, in E-flat major, op.73, "Emperor" (1809; Leipzig, 1810; 1st Viennaperf., Nov. 28, 1811); also 11 cadenzas for piano concertos nos. 1–4, and 2 for Mozart's Piano Concerto No. 20, in D minor, K. 466. **C H A M B E R :** 3 piano quartets: E-flat major, D major, and C major (1785); Trio in G major for Piano, Flute, and Bassoon, WoO 37 (1786); Minuet in A-flat major for String Quartet, Hess 33 (1790); Piano Trio in E-flat major (1791); *Allegretto* in E-flat major for Piano Trio, Hess 48 (1790–92); Violin Sonata in A major, Hess 46 (1790–92; only a fragment is extant); *Allegro and Minuet* in G major for 2 Flutes (1792); Octet in E- flat major for 2 Oboes, 2 Clarinets, 2 Horns, and 2 Bassoons, op.103 (1792–93); Variations in F major on Mozart's "Se vuol ballare" from *Le nozze di Figaro* for Piano and Violin (1792–93); *Rondino* in E-flat major for 2 Oboes, 2 Clarinets, 2 Horns, and 2 Bassoons (1793); Quintet in E-flat major for Oboe, 3 Horns, and Bassoon, Hess 19 (1793); *Rondo* in G major for Piano and Violin (1793–94); String Trio in E-flat major, op.3 (1793; also arranged for Cello and Piano, op.64); 3 piano trios: E- flat major, G major, and C minor, op.1 (1794–95); Trio in C major for 2 Oboes and English Horn, op.87 (1795); String Quintet in E-flat major, op.4 (1795; an arrangement of the Octet, op.103); Variations in C major on Mozart's "La ci darem la mano" from *Don Giovanni* for 2 Oboes and English Horn (1795); Sextet in E-flat major for 2 Horns, 2 Violins, Viola, and Cello, op.81b (1795); Sextet in E-flat major for 2 Clarinets, 2 Horns, and 2 Bassoons, op.71 (1796); Sonatina in C minor for Piano and Mandolin (1796); *Adagio* in E-flat major for Piano and Mandolin (1796); Sonatina in C major for Piano and Mandolin (1796); *Andante and Variations* in D major for Piano and Mandolin (1796); 6 German Dances for Piano and Violin (1796); 2 cello sonatas: F major and G minor, op.5 (1796); Variations in G major on Handel's "See the Conquering Hero Comes" from *Judas Maccabaeus* for Piano and Cello (1796); Variations in F major on Mozart's "Ein Mädchen oder Weibchen" from *Die Zauberflöte* for Piano and Cello, op.66 (1796); Quintet in E-flat major for Piano, Oboe, Clarinet, Horn, and Bassoon, op.16(1796–97; also arranged for Piano and String Trio); Duet in E-flat major for Viola and Cello (1796–97); Serenade in D major for String Trio, op.8 (1796–97); Trio in B- flat major for Piano, Clarinet or Violin, and Cello, op.11 (1797); 3 string trios: G major, D major, and C minor, op.9 (1797–98); 3

violin sonatas: D major, A major, and E-flat major, op.12 (1797–98); March in B-flat major for 2 Clarinets, 2 Horns, and 2 Bassoons (1798); 6 string quartets: F major, G major, D major, C minor, A major, and B-flat major, op.18 (1798–1800); Septet in E-flat major for Clarinet, Horn, Bassoon, Violin, Viola, Cello, and Double Bass, op.20 (1799–1800); Horn (or Cello) Sonata in F major, op.17 (Vienna, April 18, 1800); Violin Sonata in A minor, op.23 (1800–01); Violin Sonata in F major, op.24, Spring (1800–01); Variations in E-flat major on Mozart's "Bei Männern, welche Liebe fühlen" from *Die Zauberflöte* for Piano and Cello (1801); Serenade in D major for Flute, Violin, and Viola, op.25 (1801); String Quintet in C major, op.29 (1801); String Quartet in F major, Hess 34 (an arrangement of the Piano Sonata No. 9, in E major, op.14, No. 1; 1801–02); 3 violin sonatas: A major, C minor, and G major, op.30 (1801–02); 14 Variations in E-flat major for Piano, Violin, and Cello, op.44 (sketches from 1792; 1802?); Violin Sonata in A major, op.47, *Kreutzer* (1802–03; Vienna, May 24, 1803); Trio in E-flat major for Piano, Clarinet or Violin, and Cello, op.38 (an arrangement of the Septet, op.20; 1803); Variations in G major on Müller's "Ich bin der Schneider Kakadu" for Piano, Violin, and Cello, op.121a (1803?; rev. 1816); Serenade in D major for Piano, and Flute or Violin, op.41 (an arrangement of the Serenade in D major, op.25; 1803); *Notturno* in D major for Piano and Viola, op.42 (an arrangement of the Serenade in D major, op.8; 1803); 3 string quartets: F major, E minor, and C major, op.59, *Razumovsky* (1805–06); Cello Sonata in A major, op.69 (1807–08); 2 piano trios: D major and E-flat major, op.70 (1808); String Quartet in E-flat major, op.74, *Harp* (1809); String Quartet in F minor, op.95, *Serioso* (1810); Piano Trio in B-flat major, op.97, *Archduke* (1810–11); Violin Sonata in G major, op.96 (1812); *Allegretto* in B-flat major for Piano Trio (1812); *3 equali* for 4 Trombones: D minor, D major, and B-flat major (1812); 2 cello sonatas: C major and D major, op.102 (1815); String Quintet in C major, op.104 (an arrangement of the Piano Trio, op.1, No. 3; 1817); Prelude in D minor for String Quintet, Hess 40 (1817?); Fugue in D major for String Quintet, op.137 (1817); Movement from an unfinished string quartet (Nov. 28, 1817); 6 National Airs with Variations for Piano, and Flute or Violin, op.105 (1818?); 10 National Airs with Variations for Piano, and Flute or Violin, op.107 (1818); Duet in A major for 2 Violins (1822); String Quartet in E-flat major, op.127 (1824–25); String Quartet in A minor, op.132 (1825); String Quartet in B-flat major, op.130 (with the *Grosse Fuge* as the finale, 1825; *Rondo* finale, 1826); *Grosse Fuge* in B-flat major for String Quartet, op.133 (1825); String Quartet in C-sharp minor, op.131 (1825–26); String Quartet in F major, op.135 (1826); String Quintet in C major, Hess 41 (1826; extant fragment in piano transcription only). **P i a n o   S o n a t a s :** E- flat major, F minor, and D major, *Kurfürstensonaten* (1783); F major (1792); No. 1, in F minor, op.2, No. 1 (1793–95); No. 2, in A major, op.2, No. 2 (1794–95); No. 3, in C major, op.2, No. 3 (1794–95); No. 19, in G minor, op.49, No. 1 (1797); No. 20, in G major, op.49, No. 2 (1795–96); No. 4, in E-flat major, op.7 (1796–97); No. 5, in C minor, op.10, No. 1 (1795–97); No. 6, in F major, op.10, No. 2 (1796–97); No. 7, in D major, op.10, No. 3 (1797–98); C major, WoO 51 (fragment; 1797–98); No. 8, in C minor, op.13, *Pathétique* (1798–99); No. 9, in E major, op.14, No. 1 (1798); No. 10, in G major, op.14, No. 2 (1799); No. 11, in B-flat major, op.22 (1800); No. 12, in A-flat major, op.26, Funeral March (1800–01); No. 13, in E-flat major, op.27, No. 1, "quasi una fantasia" (1800–01); No. 14, in C-sharp minor, op.27, No. 2, "quasi una fantasia," *Moonlight* (1801); No. 15, in D major, op.28, *Pastoral* (1801); No. 16, in G major, op.31, No. 1 (1801–02); No. 17, in D minor, op.31, No. 2, *Tempest* (1801–02); No. 18, in E-flat major, op.31, No. 3

(1801–02); No. 21, in C major, op.53, *Waldstein* (1803–04); No. 22, in F major, op.54 (1803–04); No. 23, in F minor, op.57, *Appassionata* (1804–05); No. 24, in F-sharp minor,op.78 (1809); No. 25, in G major, op.79 (1809); No. 26, in E-flat major, op.81a, "Das Lebewohl, Abwesenheit und Wiedersehn", also known by its French subtitle, "Les Adieux, l'absence, et le retour" (1809); No. 27, in E minor, op.90 (1814); No. 28, in A major, op.101 (1816); No. 29, in B-flat major, op.106, *Hammerklavier* (1817–18); No. 30, in E major, op.109 (1820); No. 31, in A-flat major, op.110 (1821); No. 32, in C minor, op.111 (1821–22). **V a r i a t i o n s F o r P i a n o :** 9 Variations in C minor on a March by Dressler (1782); 24 Variations in D major on Righini's Arietta "Venni amore" (1790–91); 13 Variations in A major on the Arietta "Es war einmal ein alter Mann" from Dittersdorf's *Das rote Käppchen* (1792); 6 Variations in F major on a Swiss Song (1792?; also for Harp); 12 Variations on the "Menuet à la Viganò" from Haibel's *Le nozze disturbate* in C major (1795); 9 Variations in A major on the Aria "Quant' è più bello" from Paisiello's *La molinara* (1795); 6 Variations in G major on the Duet "Nel cor più non mi sento" from Paisiello's *La molinara* (1795); 8 Variations in C major on the Romance "Une Fièvre brûlante" from Grétry's *Richard Coeur de Lion* (1795?); 12 Variations in A major on a Russian Dance from Wranitzky's *Das Waldmädchen* (1796–97); 10 Variations in B-flat major on the Duet "La stessa, la stessissima" from Salieri's *Falstaff* (1799); 7 Variations in F major on the Quartet "Kind, willst du ruhig schlafen" from Winter's *Das unterbrochene Opferfest* (1799); 6 Variations in F major on the Trio "Tandeln und Scherzen" from Süssmayr's *Soliman II* (1799); 6 Variations in G major on an Original Theme (1800); 6 Variations in F major on an Original Theme, op.34 (1802); 15 Variations and a Fugue in E-flat major on an Original Theme, op.35, *Eroica* (1802); 7 Variations in C major on "God Save the King" (1803); 5 Variations in D major on "Rule Britannia" (1803); 32 Variations in C minor on an Original Theme (1806); 6 Variations in D major on an Original Theme, op.76 (1809); 33 Variations in C major on a Waltz by Diabelli, op.120 (1819; 1823). **O t h e r W o r k s F o r P i a n o :** Rondo in C major (1783); Rondo in A major (1783); 2 Preludes through All 12 Major Keys, op.39 (1789; also for Organ); *Allemande* in A major (1793); *Rondo a capriccio* in G major, op.129, "Rage over a Lost Penny" (1795); Fugue in C major, Hess 64 (1795); *Presto* in C minor (1795?); *Allegretto* in C minor (1796–97); *Allegretto* in C minor, Hess 69 (1796–97); Rondo in C major, op.51, No. 1 (1796?–97?); Rondo in G major, op.51, No. 2 (1798?); 7 Bagatelles: E-flat major, C major, F major, A major, C major, D major, and A-flat major, op.33 (1801–02); Bagatelle "Lustig-Traurig" in C major, WoO 54 (1802); *Allegretto* in C major (1803); Andante in F major, "Andante favori" (1803); Prelude in F minor (1804); Minuet in E-flat major (1804); Fantasia in G minor/B-flat major, op.77 (1809); Bagatelle "Für Elise" in A minor (1810); Polonaise in C major, op.89 (1814); Bagatelle in B-flat major (1818); Concert Finale in C major, Hess 65 (1820–21); Allegretto in B minor (1821); 11 Bagatelles: G minor, C major, D major, A major, C minor, G major, C major, A minor, A major, and B-flat major, op.119 (1820–22); 6 Bagatelles: G major, G minor, E-flat major, B minor, G major, and E-flat major, op.126 (1823–24); Waltz in E-flat major (1824); *Allegretto quasi andante* in G minor (1825); Waltz in D major (1825); Écossaise in E-flat major (1825).—For Piano, 4–Hands: 8 Variations in C major on a Theme by Count Waldstein (1792); Sonata in D major, op.6 (1796–97); 6 Variations in D major on "Ich denke dein" (by Beethoven) (1799–1803); 3 Marches: C major, E-flat major, and D major, op.45 (1803?); an arrangement

of the *Grosse Fuge*, op.133, as op.134 (1826). **V O C A L : O p - e r a :** *Fidelio*, op.72 (1st version, 1804–05; Theater an der Wien, Vienna, Nov. 20, 1805; 2nd version, 1805–06; Theater an der Wien, March 29, 1806; final version, Kärnthnertortheater, Vienna, May 23, 1814); also a fragment from the unfinished opera *Vestas Feuer*, Hess 115 (1803). **S i n g s p i e l s :** "Germania," the finale of the pasticcio *Die gute Nachricht* (Kärnthnertortheater, April 11, 1814), and "Es ist vollbracht," the finale of the pasticcio *Die Ehrenpforten* (Kärnthnertortheater, July 15, 1815). **C h o r a l . :** *Cantate auf den Tod Kaiser Joseph des Zweiten* (1790); *Cantate auf die Erhebung Leopold des Zweiten zur Kaiserwurde* (1790); oratorio, *Christus am Oelberge*, op.85 (Vienna, April 5, 1803; rev. 1804 and 1811); Mass in C major, op.86 (Eisenstadt, Sept. 13, 1807); *Chor auf die verbündeten Fürsten "Ihr weisen Gründer"* (1814); cantata, *Der glorreiche Augenblick*, op.136 (Vienna, Nov. 29, 1814); *Meeresstille und glückliche Fahrt*, op.112, after Goethe (1814–15; Vienna, Dec. 25, 1815); Mass in D major, op.123, *Missa Solemnis* (1819–23; St. Petersburg, April 7, 1824); Opferlied, "Die Flamme lodert" (1822; 2nd version, op.121b, 1823–24); Bundeslied, "In allen guten Stunden," op.122, after Goethe (1823–24); Abschiedsgesang, "Die Stunde schlägt" (1814); Cantata campestre, "Un lieto brindisi" (1814); Gesang der Mönche, "Rasch tritt der Tod," from Schiller's *Wilhelm Tell* (1817); Hochzeitslied, "Auf Freunde, singt dem Gott der Ehen" (2 versions; 1819); Birthday Cantata for Prince Lobkowitz, "Es lebe unser theurer Fürst" (1823). **S o l o V o i c e s a n d O r c h . :** Prüfung des Küssens "Meine weise Mutter spricht" for Bass (1790–92); "Mit Mädeln sich vertragen" from Goethe's *Claudine von Villa Bella* for Bass (1790?–92); Primo amore, scena and aria for Soprano (1790–92); 2 arias: "O welch' ein Leben" for Tenor and "Soll ein Schuh nicht drücken" for Soprano, for Umlauf's Singspiel *Die schöne Schusterin* (1795–96); *Ah, perfido!*, scena and aria for Soprano from Metastasio's *Achille in Sciro*, op.65 (1795–96); *No, non turbarti*, scena and aria for Soprano from Metastasio's *La tempesta* (1801–02); "Ne' giorni tuoi felici," duet for Soprano and Tenor from Metastasio's *Olimpiade* (1802–03); *Tremate, empi, tremate* for Soprano, Tenor, and Bass, op.116 (1801–02; 1814); *Elegischer Gesang:*"Sanft wie du lebtest" for Soprano, Alto, Tenor, Bass, and String Quartet or Piano, op.118 (1814). **S o n g s :** More than 80, including the following: *O care selve* (1794); *Opferlied* (1794; rev. 1801–02); *Adelaide*, op.46 (1794–95); 6 Songs, op.48, after Gellert (1802); 8 Songs, op.52 (1790–96); *An die Hoffnung*, op.32 (1805); 6 Songs, op.75 (1809); 4 Ariettas and a Duet for Soprano and Tenor, op.82 (1809); 3 Songs, op.83, after Goethe (1810); *Merkenstein*, op.100 (1814–15); *An die Hoffnung*, op.94 (1815); 6 Songs: *An die ferne Geliebte*, op.98 (1815–16); *Der Mann von Wort*, op.99 (1816); *Der Kuss*, op.128 (1822); arrangements of English, Scottish, Irish, Welsh, Italian, and other folk songs for voice, piano, violin, and cello; numerous canons; etc.

BIBL.: COLLECTED EDITIONS, SOURCE MATE-RIAL: *L. v.B.'s Werke: Vollständige kritisch durchgesehene überall berechtigte Ausgabe*, the first major ed. of his works, was publ. by Breitkopf & Härtel (series 1–24, Leipzig, 1862–65; 25 [suppl.], Leipzig, 1888). An extensive suppl. was ed. by W. Hess, *L. v.B.: Sämtliche Werke: Supplemente zur Gesamtausgabe* (14 vols., Wiesbaden, 1959–71). A new critical ed., *L. v.B.: Werke: Neue Ausgabe sämtlicher Werke* (Munich and Duisburg, 1961 et seq.), is being publ. by the Beethoven- Archiv of Bonn. J. Del Mar has ed. the invaluable New Bärenreiter Urtext Edition of the 9 syms. (9 vols., Kassel, 1996–2000).

The standard thematic and bibliographic index of all of Beethoven's completed publ. works is to be found in G. Kinsky and H. Halm, *Das Werk B.s: Thematisch-*

Bibliographisches Verzeichnis seiner sämtlichen vollendeten Kompositionen (Munich and Duisburg, 1955). An important supplement to this source is K. Dorfmüller, ed., Beiträge zur B.-Bibliographie: Studien und Materialien zum Werkverzeichnis von Kinsky-Halm (Munich, 1978). See also W. Hess, ed., Verzeichnis der nicht in der Gesamtausgabe veröffentlichten Werke L. v.B.s (Wiesbaden, 1957), which lists missing works in the old Leipzig edition. Other sources include the following: The first valuable thematic catalogue, Thematisches Verzeichniss sämmtlicher im Druck erschienen Werke von L. v.B., was publ. by Breitkopf & Härtel (Leipzig, 1851); it was thoroughly rev. and enl. by G. Nottebohm and publ. as Thematisches Verzeichniss der im Druck erschienenen Werke von L. v.B. (Leipzig, 1868; new ed., together with Bibliotheca B.iana, by E. Kastner, Leipzig, 1913; 2nd ed. by T. von Frimmel, Leipzig, 1925); A. Thayer, Chronologisches Verzeichniss der Werke L. v.B.'s (Berlin, 1865); G. Adler, Verzeichniss der musikalischen Autographe von L. v.B....im Besitze von A. Artaria in Wien (Vienna, 1890); A. Artaria, Verzeichnis von musikalischen Autographen...vornehmlich der reichen Bestände aus dem Nachlasse...L. v.B.'s... (Vienna, 1893); W. Haas, Systematische Ordnung B.scher Melodien (Leipzig, 1932); J. Schmidt-Görg, Katalog der Handschriften des B.-Hauses und B.-Archivs Bonn (Bonn, 1935); A. Tyson, The Authentic English Editions of B. (London, 1963); G. Biamonti, Catalogo cronologico e tematico delle opere di B., comprese quelle inedite e gli abbozzi non utilizzati (Turin, 1968); P. Willets, B. and England: An Account of Sources in the British Museum (London, 1970); D. MacArdle, B. Abstracts (Detroit, 1973); H. Goldschmidt, ed., Zu B.: Aufsätze und Dokumente (Berlin, 1984); T. Albrecht, L.v. B.: A Guide to Research (N.Y., 1990); B. Cooper, ed., The B. Compendium: A Guide to B.'s Life and Music (N.Y., 1992); C. Reynolds, L. Lockwood, and J. Webster, eds., B. Forum (7 vols., Lincoln, Nebr., 1992–99). S k e t c h e s a n d A u t o g r a p h s : G. Nottebohm, Ein Skizzenbuch von B. (Leipzig, 1865) and Ein Skizzenbuch von B. aus dem Jahre 1803 (Leipzig, 1880). P. Mies republ. 2 of Nottebohm's eds. as Zwei Skizzenbucher von B. aus den Jahren 1801 bis 1803 (Leipzig, 1924; Eng. tr. as Two B. Sketchbooks, London, 1979). W. Engelmann, ed., B.s eigenhändiges Skizzenbuch zur 9. Symphonie (facsimile; Leipzig, 1913); H. Mersmann, B.s Skizzen (Basel, 1924); P. Mies, Die Bedeutung der Skizzen B.s zur Erkenntnis seines Stiles (Leipzig, 1925; Eng. tr. as B.'s Sketches by D. Mackinnon, London, 1929); K. Mikulicz, Ein Notierungsbuch von B. aus dem Besitze der Preussischen Staatsbibliothek zu Berlin (transcription of the sketchbook of 1800–01; Leipzig, 1927); J. Schmidt-Görg, B.: Drei Skizzenbücher zur Missa Solemnis (facsimile and transcription; Bonn, Vol. I, Ein Skizzenbuch aus den Jahren 1819/20 [1952]; Vol. II, Ein Skizzenbuch zum Credo [1970]; and Vol. III, Ein Skizzenbuch zum Benedictus [1970]); P. Mies, Textkritische Untersuchungen bei B. (Bonn, 1957); D. Weise, B.: Ein Skizzenbuch zur Chorfantasie op.80 und zu anderen Werken (transcription; Bonn, 1957); H. Unverricht, Die Eigenschriften und die Originalausgaben von Werken B.s in ihrer Bedeutung für die moderne Textkritik (Kassel, 1960); D. Weise, B.: Ein Skizzenbuch zur Pastoralsymphonie op.68 und zu den Trios op.70, 1 und 2 (transcription; Bonn, 1961); J. Schmidt-Görg, B.: Ein Skizzenbuch zu den Diabelli-Variationen und zur Missa Solemnis, SV 154 (facsimile and transcription; 2 vols., Bonn, 1968, 1972); D. Johnson, A. Tyson, and R. Winter, eds., The B. Sketchbooks (Berkeley, 1985). C o n v e r s a t i o n B o o k s : D. MacArdle, An Index to B.'s Conversation Books (Detroit, 1962); K.-H. Köhler et al., eds., L. v.B.s Konversation-shefte (10 vols., Leipzig, 1972–93). C o r r e s p o n d e n c e , N o t e b o o k s , a n d O t h e r D o c u m e n t s : L. Nohl, Briefe B.s (Stuttgart, 1865); idem, Neue Briefe B.s (Stuttgart, 1867); idem, B.'s Brevier (Leipzig, 1870; 2nd ed., 1901); idem, Die B.-Feier und die Kunst der Gegenwart (Vienna, 1871); A. Kalischer, ed., B.s sämtliche Briefe (5 vols., Berlin and Leipzig, 1906–08; partial Eng. tr. by J. Shedlock, 2 vols., London and N.Y., 1909; T. von Frimmel edited a 2nd ed. of the German original, Berlin, 1908–11); F. Prelinger, ed., L. v.B.s sämtliche Briefe und Aufzeichnungen (5 vols., Vienna and Leipzig, 1907–11); E. Kastner, ed., L.v.B.s sämtliche Briefe (Leipzig, 1910; 2nd ed. prepared by J. Kapp, Leipzig, 1923); A. Leitzmann, ed., B.s Persönlichkeit (2 vols., Leipzig, 1914; 2nd ed. as L. v.B.: Berichte der Zeitgenossen, 2 vols., Leipzig, 1921); M. Unger, L. v.B. und seine Verleger, S. A. Steiner und Tobias Haslinger in Wien, Ad. Mart. Schlesinger in Berlin, ihr Verkehr und Briefwechsel (Berlin and Vienna, 1921); idem, B.s Handschrift (Bonn, 1926); O. Sonneck, B. Letters in America (N.Y., 1927); G. Kinsky, Die Handschriften zu B.s Egmont-Musik (Vienna, 1933); A. Klarer, ed., Briefe B.s und das Heiligenstädter Testament (Zürich, 1944); H. Freiberger, L. v.B., Ein Bekenntnis, mit Briefen und Zeitdokumenten (Berlin, 1951); H. Müller von Asow, Heiligenstädter Testament (Faksimile) (Hamburg, 1952); D. Weise, ed., B.: Entwurf einer Denkschrift an das Appellationsgericht in Wien vom 18. Februar 1820 (Bonn, 1953); D. MacArdle and L. Misch, eds. and trs., New B. Letters (Norman, Okla., 1957); J. Schmidt-Görg, B. Dreizehn unbekannte Briefe an Josephine Gräfin Deym geb. v. Brunsvik (facsimile; Bonn, 1957); E. Anderson, ed. and tr., The Letters of B. (3 vols., London, 1961); M. Braubach, ed., Die Stammbücher B.s und der Babette Koch. Faksimile (Bonn, 1970); K.-H. Köhler and G. Herre, eds., L. v.B.: Neun ausgewählte Briefe an Anton Schindler (facsimile and transcription; Leipzig, 1971); S. Brandenburg, M. Staehelin et al., eds., L. v.B.: Der Briefwechsel mit dem Verlag Schott (Munich, 1985); S. Brandenburg, ed., B.s Tagebuch (Mainz, 1990); idem, ed., Briefwechsel Gesamtausgabe: L.v. B. im Auftrag des B.-Hauses Bonn (8 vols., Munich, 1996 et seq.). Y e a r b o o k s , H a n d b o o k s , S t u d i e s : G. Nottebohm, B.'s Studien (Leipzig and Winterthur, 1873); T. von Frimmel, Neue B.iana (Vienna, 1888; 2nd ed., 1890); idem, B.-Studien (2 vols., Munich and Leipzig, 1905–06); T. von Frimmel, ed., B.-Jahrbuch (2 vols., Munich and Leipzig, 1908–09); idem, B.-Forschung, Lose Blätter (10 issues, Vienna and Mödling, 1911–25); L. Schiedermair, ed., Veröffentlichungen des B.-Hauses in Bonn (10 vols., Bonn, 1920–34); A. Sandberger, ed., Neues B.-Jahrbuch (10 vols., Augsburg and Braunschweig, 1924–42); T. von Frimmel, B.-Handbuch (2 vols., Leipzig, 1926); P. Mies, J. Schmidt-Görg et al., eds., B.-Jahrbuch (Bonn, 1954 et seq.); P. Nettl, B. Encyclopedia (N.Y., 1956; 2nd ed. as B. Handbook, N.Y., 1967); L. Misch, Neue B.- Studien (Bonn, 1967); E. Schenk, ed., B.-Studien (Vienna, 1970); A. Tyson, ed., B. Studies (N.Y., 1973 et seq.); H. Goldschmidt, ed., Zu B.: Aufsätze und Annotationen (Berlin, 1979); R. Winter and B. Carr, B., Performers, and Critics (Detroit, 1980). B i o g r a p h i c a l : J. Schlosser, L. v.B. (Prague, 1827; Eng. tr. as B.: The First Biography, 1827, 1996); F. Wegeler and F. Ries, Biographische Notizen über L. v.B. (Koblenz, 1838; Nachtrag by Wegeler, Koblenz, 1845; new ed. by A. Kalischer, Berlin and Leipzig, 1906); A. Schindler, Biographie von L. v.B. (Münster, 1840; new ed. by A. Kalischer, Berlin, 1909; Eng. tr. by I. Moscheles as The Life of B., London, 1841, and Boston, n.d. [1841]. The 1860 German ed., publ. in Münster, was tr. and edited by D. MacArdle under the title B. As I Knew Him, London and Chapel Hill, N.C., 1966); W. von Lenz, B.: Eine Kunststudie (2 vols., Kassel, 1855; 2nd ed., Hamburg, 1860; new ed. by A. Kalischer, Berlin and Leipzig, 1908); A. Oulibicheff, B., Ses critiques et ses glossateurs (Leipzig and Paris, 1857); A. Marx, *L. v.B. Leben und Schaffen* (2 vols., Berlin, 1859); A. Thayer, *L. v.B.s Leben* (publ. in a German tr. from the Eng. MS by H. Deiters, 3 vols., Berlin, 1866, 1872, and 1877. After the author's death, Deiters completed vols. IV and V from Thayer's material, but also died before their publication. He had also rev. and enl. Vol. I, Leipzig, 1901. Deiters's MS was rev. and ed. by H. Riemann, Vol. IV, Leipzig, 1907; Vol. V, Leipzig, 1908. Vols. II and III were then rev. and enl. by Riemann and publ. in Leipzig, 1910–11. He completed his task by reediting Vol. I, Leipzig, 1917. Thayer's original Eng. MS was completed by H. Krehbiel and publ. as *The Life of L. v.B.*, 3 vols., N.Y., 1921. It was in turn rev. by E. Forbes and publ. as *Thayer's Life of B.*, 2 vols., Princeton, N.J., 1964; rev. ed., 1967); L. Nohl, *B.s Leben* (publ. in various eds. and formats, Vienna and Leipzig, 1864–77; new ed. by P. Sakolowski,3 vols., Berlin, 1909–13); G. von Breuning, *Aus dem Schwarzspanierhause...* (Vienna, 1874; rev. ed. by A. Kalischer, Berlin and Leipzig, 1907; Eng. tr. as *Memories of B.: From the House of the Blackrobed Spaniards*, 1992); L. Nohl, *Eine stille Liebe zu B.* (Leipzig, 1875; Eng. tr. as *An Unrequited Love*, London, 1876; 2nd Ger. ed., Leipzig, 1902); idem, *B.: Nach den Schilderungen seiner Zeitgenossen* (Stuttgart, 1877; Eng. tr. as *B. as Depicted by His Contemporaries*, London, 1880); W. von Wasielewski, *L. v.B.* (2 vols., Berlin, 1888; 2nd ed., 1895); T. von Frimmel, *B.* (Berlin, 1901; 6th ed., 1922); R. Rolland, *B.* (Paris, 1903); G. Fischer, *B.: A Character Study* (N.Y., 1905); F. Kerst, *B. im eigenen Wort* (Berlin and Leipzig, 1904; Eng. tr. by H. Krehbiel as *B.: The Man and the Artist, as Revealed in His Own Words*, N.Y., 1905); E. Walker, *B.* (London, 1905; 3rd ed., 1920); A. Kalischer, *B. und seine Zeitgenossen* (4 vols., Leipzig, n.d. [1908–10]); P. Bekker, *B.* (Berlin and Leipzig, 1911; Eng. tr. and adaptation by M. Bosman, London, 1925; new Ger. ed., 1927); V. d'Indy, *B.: Biographie critique* (Paris, 1911; Eng. tr. by T. Baker, Boston, 1913; 2nd French ed., 1927); F. Kerst, ed., *Die Erinnerungen an B.* (2 vols., Stuttgart, 1913; 2nd ed., 1925); W. Thomas-San-Galli, *L. v.B.* (Berlin, 1913); A. Hensel, *B. Der Versuch einer musikphilosophischen Darstellung* (Berlin, 1918); La Mara, *B. und die Brunsviks* (Leipzig, 1920); J.-G. Prod'homme, *La Jeunesse de B....* (Paris, 1921; new ed., 1927); W. Schweisheimer, *B.s Leiden: Ihr Einfluss auf sein Leben und Schaffen* (Munich, 1922); T. von Frimmel, *B. im zeitgenössischen Bildnis* (Vienna, 1923); W. Krug, *B.s Vollendung* (Munich, 1924); M. Reinitz, *B. im Kampf mit dem Schicksal* (Vienna, 1924); S. Ley, *B.s Leben in authentischen Bildern und Texten* (Berlin, 1925; 2nd ed., 1970); L. Schiedermair, *Der junge B.* (Leipzig, 1925; 3rd ed., Wilhelmshaven, 1970); G. Adler, *B.s Charakter* (Regensburg, 1927); B. Bartels, *B.* (Hildesheim, 1927); A. de Hevesy, *B.: Vie intime* (Paris, 1926; Eng. tr. as *B. the Man*, London, 1927); S. Ley, *B. als Freund der Familie Wegeler-von Breuning* (Bonn, 1927); E. Newman, *The Unconscious B.: An Essay in Musical Psychology* (N.Y. and London, 1927; 2nd ed., 1969); A. Orel, *B.* (Vienna, 1927); J.-G.Prod'homme, *B. raconte par ceux qui l'ont vu* (Paris, 1927); A. Schmitz, *Das romantische B.bild* (Berlin and Bonn, 1927); W. Turner, *B., The Search for Reality* (London, 1927; 2nd ed., 1933); R. van Aerde, *Les Ancêtres flamands de B.* (Malines, 1927); E. Closson, *L'Élément flamand dans B.* (Brussels, 1928; Eng. tr., London, 1934; 2nd Brussels ed., 1946); R. Rolland, *B.: Les Grandes Époques créatrices* (5 vols. in 7; Paris, 1928–57; in 1 vol. as Edition definitive, Paris, 1966; Eng. tr. of 1st 2 vols. by E. Newman as *B. the Creator*, N.Y., 1929, and *Goethe and B.*, N.Y., 1931); R. Schauffler, *B.: The Man Who Freed Music* (N.Y. and London, 1929); E. Herriot, *La Vie de B.* (Paris, 1929; Eng. tr. as *The Life of B.*, N.Y., 1935); A. Boschot, *B.: La Musique et la vie* (Paris, 1931); R. Specht, *Bildnis B.s* (Hellerau, 1931; Eng. tr., London, 1933); E. Brümmer, *B.: Im Spiegel der zeitgenössischen rheinischen*

Presse (Würzburg, 1932); J. Heer, *Der Graf von Waldstein und sein Verhältnis zu B.* (Leipzig, 1933); E. Bücken, *L. v.B.* (Potsdam, 1934); F. Howes, *B.* (London, 1933); M. Scott, *B.* (London, 1934; rev. ed. by J. Westrup, 1974); C. Carpenter, *French Factors in B.'s Life* (N.Y., 1935); W. Riezler, *B.* (Berlin and Zürich, 1936; 9th ed., 1966; Eng. tr., London, 1938); H. Schultz, *L. v.B., Sein Leben in Bildern* (Leipzig, 1936); H. Kesser, *B. der Europäer* (Zürich, 1937); H. von Hofmannsthal, *B.* (Vienna, 1938); R. Petzoldt, *L. v.B.: Leben und Werk* (Leipzig, 1938); A. Orel, *Grillparzer und B.* (Vienna, 1941); J. Burk, *The Life and Works of B.* (N.Y., 1943); E. Corti, *B.-Anekdoten* (Berlin, 1943); S. Ley, *Aus B.s Erdentagen* (Bonn, 1948); A. Pryce-Jones, *B.* (London, 1948); R. Petzoldt, *L. v.B.: Sein Leben in Bildern* (Leipzig, 1952; 7th ed., 1968); B. Bartels, *B. und Bonn* (Dinkelsbühl, 1954); S. Ley, *B.: Sein Leben in Selbstzeugnissen, Briefen und Berichten* (Vienna, 1954; 2nd ed., 1970); E. and R. Sterba, *B. and His Nephew: A Psychoanalytical Study of Their Relationship* (N.Y., 1954); W. Forster, *B.s Krankheiten und ihre Beurteilung* (Wiesbaden, 1955); S. Ley, *Wahrheit, Zweifel und Irrtum in der Kunde von B.s Leben* (Wiesbaden, 1955); W. Hess, *B.* (Zürich, 1956; 2nd ed., 1976); R. Bory, *La Vie et l'oeuvre de L. v.B.* (Paris, 1960; Eng. tr. as *L. v.B.: His Life and His Work in Pictures*, Zürich and N.Y., 1960); A. Boucourechliev, *B.* (Paris, 1963; 2nd ed., rev., 1976); J. Schmidt-Görg, *B.: Die Geschichte seiner Familie* (Bonn, 1964); J. and B. Massin, *L. v.B.* (Paris, 1967); G. Marek, *B.: Biography of a Genius* (N.Y., 1969); J. Schmidt-Görg and H. Schmidt, eds., *L. v.B.* (Bonn, 1969; Eng. tr., N.Y., 1970); M. Cooper, *B.: The Last Decade, 1817–27* (London, 1970; 2nd ed., rev., 1985); H.C. Robbins Landon, *B.: A Documentary Study* (N.Y. and London, 1970; 2nd ed., rev., 1993 as *B.: His Life, Work, and World*); J. Schmidt-Görg, ed., *Des Bonner Bäckermeisters Gottfried Fischer Aufzeichnung über B.s Jugend* (Bonn and Munich, 1971); F. Knight, *B. and the Age of Revolution* (London, 1973); M. Solomon, *B.* (N.Y., 1977; 2nd ed., rev., 1998); L. Finscher, *L. v.B.* (Darmstadt, 1983); R. James, *B.* (London, 1983); A. Orga, *B.* (Sydney, 1983); D. Matthews, *B.* (London, 1985); C. Dahlhaus, *L. v.B. und seine Zeit* (Laaber, 1987); F. Noli, *B. and the French Revolution* (Tirana, 1991); G. Jeanclaude, *Un amour de B.: Marie Bigot de Morogues, pianiste* (Strasbourg, 1992); K. Küster, *B.* (Stuttgart, 1994); S. Burnham, *B. Hero* (Princeton, 1995); H.-J. Irmen, *B. in seiner Zeit* (Zülpich, 1996); D. Wyn Jones, *The Life of B.* (Cambridge, 1998); A. Werner-Jensen, *L.v. B.* (Stuttgart, 1998). **The Immortal Beloved:** La Mara, *B.s Unsterbliche Geliebte: Das Geheimnis der Gräfin Brunsvik und ihre Memoiren* (Leipzig, 1909); W. Thomas-San-Galli, *Die unsterbliche Geliebte B.s: Lösung eines vielumstrittenen Problems* (Halle, 1909); idem, *B. und die unsterbliche Geliebte: Amalie Sebald/Goethe/Therese Brunsvik und Anderes* (Munich, 1909); M. Unger, *Auf Spuren von B.s "Unsterblicher Geliebten"* (Langensalza, 1911); La Mara, *B. und die Brunsviks* (Leipzig, 1920); O. Sonneck, *The Riddle of the Immortal Beloved* (N.Y., 1927); K. Smolle, *B.s unsterbliche Geliebte* (Vienna, 1947); S. Kaznelson, *B.s ferne und unsterbliche Geliebte* (Zürich, 1954); H. Goldschmidt, *B.-Studien, 2: Um die unsterbliche Geliebte* (Leipzig, 1977); M.-E. Tellenbach, *B. und seine "Unsterbliche Geliebte" Josephine Brunswick* (Zürich, 1983); S. Brandenburg, *B.: Der Brief an die Unsterbliche Geliebte* (Bonn, 1986); G. Altman, *B.: Man of His World: Undisclosed Evidence for His Immortal Beloved* (Tallahassee, 1996). **CRITICAL, ANALYTICAL: General:** I. von Seyfried, ed., *L. v.B.'s Studien im Generalbass, Contrapunct, und in der Compositionslehre* (Vienna, 1832; Eng. tr. by H. Pierson, Leipzig, 1853; new Ger. eds. by G. Nottebohm, Leipzig, 1873, and L. Köhler, Leipzig, 1880); W. von Lenz, *B. et ses trois styles* (2 vols. in 1, St. Petersburg, 1852; new ed. by M.D. Calvocoressi, Paris, 1909); R. Wagner, *B.* (Leipzig, 1870; Eng. tr. by A. Parsons, N.Y., 1872; 3rd ed., 1883); G.

Nottebohm, *B.iana* (Leipzig and Winterthur, 1872; 2nd ed., 1925); L. Nohl, *B., Liszt, Wagner* (Vienna, 1874); E. Mandyczewski, ed., *Zweite B.iana* (Leipzig, 1887; 2nd ed., 1925); D. Mason, *B. and His Forerunners* (N.Y., 1904; 2nd ed., 1930); H. Volkmann, *Neues über B.* (Berlin and Leipzig, 1904); F. Volbach, *B.* (Munich, 1905); R. Rolland, *B.* (N.Y., 1917; 6th ed., 1927); G. Becking, *Studien zu B.s Personalstil: Das Scherzothema* (Leipzig, 1921); H. Mersmann, *B.: Die Synthese der Stile* (Berlin, n.d. [1922]); A. Schmitz, *B.s "zwei Prinzipe"* (Berlin and Bonn, 1923); F. Cassirer, *B. und die Gestalt: Ein Kommentar* (Stuttgart, 1925); A. Halm, *B.* (Berlin, 1926); J.W.N. Sullivan, *B.: His Spiritual Development* (London, 1927; 2nd ed., 1936); T. Veidl, *Der musikalische Humor bei B.* (Leipzig, 1929); A. Schering, *B. in neuer Deutung* (Leipzig, 1934); idem, *B. und die Dichtung* (Berlin, 1936); idem, *Zur Erkenntnis B.s: Neue Beiträge zur Deutung seiner Werke* (Würzburg, 1938); K. Storck and M. Wiemann, *Wege zu B.* (Regensburg, 1938); J. Boyer, *Le "Romantisme" de B.* (Paris, 1939); L. Schrade, *B. in France: The Growth of an Idea* (New Haven, 1942); D. Tovey, *B.* (London, 1944); L. Misch, *B.-Studien* (Berlin, 1950; Eng. tr. as *B. Studies*, Norman, Okla., 1953); K. Schönewolf, *B. in der Zeitenwende* (2 vols., Halle, 1953); L. Ronga, *Bach, Mozart, B.: Tre problemi critici* (Venice, 1956); S. Ley, *Aus B.s Erdentagen* (Siegburg, 1957); L. Misch, *Die Faktoren der Einheit in der Mehrsätzigkeit der Werke B.s* (Munich and Duisburg, 1958); P. Nettl, *B. und seine Zeit* (Hamburg, 1958); D. Arnold and N. Fortune, eds., *The B. Reader* (N.Y., 1971); T. Scherman and L. Biancolli, eds., *The B. Companion* (Garden City, N.Y., 1972); H. Goldschmidt, *Die Erscheinung B.* (Leipzig, 1974); idem, *B.: Werkeinführungen* (Leipzig, 1975); I. Kolodin, *The Interior B.: A Biography of the Music* (N.Y., 1975); J. Crabbe, *B.'s Empire of the Mind* (Newbury, 1982); D. Greene, *Temporal Processes in B.'s Music* (N.Y., 1982); W. Mellers, *B. and the Voice of God* (London, 1983); L. Lockwood and P. Benjamin, eds., *B. Essays: Studies in Honor of Elliot Forbes* (Cambridge, Mass., 1984); G. Pestelli, *The Age of Mozart and B.* (Cambridge, 1984); R. Wallace, *B.'s Critics: Aesthetic Dilemmas and Resolutions During the Composer's Lifetime* (Cambridge, 1986); M. Broyles, *B.: The Emergence and Evolution of B.'s Heroic Style* (N.Y., 1987); A. Comini, *The Changing Image of B.: A Study in Mythmaking* (N.Y., 1987); B. Cooper, *B. and the Creative Process* (Oxford, 1990); A. Boucourechliev, *Essai sur B.* (Arles, 1991); W. Kinderman, ed., *B.'s Compositional Process* (Lincoln, Nebr., 1991); L. Lockwood, *B.: Studies in the Creative Process* (Cambridge, Mass., 1992); R. Hatten, *Musical Meaning in B.: Markedness, Correlation, and Interpretation* (Bloomington, Ind., 1994); E. Rohmer, *De Mozart en B.: Essai sur la notion de profondeur en musique* (Arles, 1996); W. Caplin, *Classical Form: A Theory of Formal Functions for the Instrumental Music of Haydn, Mozart, and B.* (N.Y., 1998). **Orch. Music:** G. Erlanger et al., *B.s Symphonien erläutert* (Frankfurt am Main, 1896); G. Grove, *B.'s Nine Symphonies* (London, 1884; enl. ed. as *B. and His Nine Symphonies*, London, 1896; 3rd ed., 1898); J.-G. Prod'homme, *Les Symphonies de B.* (Paris, 1906; 5th ed., 1949); F. Weingartner, *Ratschläge für Aufführungen der Symphonien B.s* (Leipzig, 1906; 2nd ed., 1916; Eng. tr., N.Y., n.d. [1907]); H. Schenker, *B.s neunte Sinfonie* (Vienna and Leipzig, 1912; 2nd ed., 1969; Eng. tr., 1992); E. Evans Sr., *B.'s Nine Symphonies, fully described and analyzed* (2 vols., London, 1923–24); H. Schenker, *B.s Fünfte Sinfonie* (Vienna, n.d. [1925]; 2nd ed., Vienna, 1970); D. Berg, *B. and the Romantic Symphony* (N.Y., 1927); J. Braunstein, *B.s Leonore-Ouvertüren* (Leipzig, 1927); K. Nef, *Die neun Sinfonien B.s* (Leipzig, 1928); J. Chantavoine, *Les Symphonies de B.* (Paris, 1932); E. Magni Dufflocq, *Le sinfonie di B.* (Milan, 1935); W. Osthoff, *L. v.B.: Klavierkonzert Nr. 3, C-moll op.37* (Munich, 1965); R. Bockholdt, *L. v.B., VI Symphonie F-dur, op.68, Pastorale* (Munich, 1981); A.

Hopkins, *The Nine Symphonies of B.* (London, 1981); L. Della Croce, *L. v.B.: Le nove sinfonie e le altre opere per Orch.* (Pordenone, 1986); M. Geck and P. Schleuning, *Geschrieben auf Bonaparte: B.'s "Eroica"—Revolution, Reaktion, Rezeption* (Reinbek bei Hamburg, 1989); N. Cook, *B.: Symphony No. 9* (Cambridge, 1993); M. Gielen and P. Fiebig, *B. im Gespräch: Die neun Sinfonien* (Stuttgart, 1995); D. Jones, *B.: Pastoral Symphony* (Cambridge, 1995); D. Levy, *B.: The Ninth Symphony* (N.Y., 1995); A. Hopkins, *The Seven Concertos of B.* (Aldershot, 1996); T. Sipe, *B.: Eroica Symphony* (Cambridge, 1998); R. Stowell, *B.: Violin Concerto* (Cambridge, 1998); L. Plantinga, *B.'s Concertos: History, Style, Performance* (N.Y., 1999). **Chamber Music:** T. Helm, *B.s Streichquartette: Versuch einer technischen Analyse im Zusammenhang mit ihrem geistigen Gehalt* (Leipzig, 1885; 3rd ed., 1921); J. Matthews, *The Violin Music of B.* (London, 1902); H. Riemann, *B.s Streichquartette erläutert* (Berlin, 1910); S. Midgley, *Handbook to B.'s Sonatas for Violin and Pianoforte* (London, 1911); O. Rupertus, *Erläuterungen zu B.s Violinsonaten* (Cologne, 1915); H. Wedig, *B.s Streichquartett op.18, 1 und seine erste Fassung* (Bonn, 1922); J. Wetzel, *B.s Violinsonaten, nebst den Romanzen und dem Konzert* (Berlin, 1924); J. de Marliave, *Les Quatuors de B.* (Paris, 1925; Eng. tr. by H. Andrews, London, 1928); M. Herwegh, *Technique d'interprétation sous forme d'essai d'analyse psychologique expérimentale appliqué aux sonates pour piano et violon de B.* (Paris, 1926); W. Hadow, *B.'s Op.18 Quartets* (London, 1926); H. Mersmann, *Die Kammermusik: Vol. II, B.* (Leipzig, 1930); W. Engelsmann, *B.s Kompositionspläne dargestellt in den Sonaten für Klavier und Violine* (Augsburg, 1931); R. Giraldi, *Analisi formale ed estetica dei primi tempi Quartetti Op.18* (Rome, 1933); G. Abraham, *B.'s Second-Period Quartets* (London, 1942); D. Mason, *The Quartets of B.* (N.Y., 1947); I. Mahaim, *B.: Naissance et renaissance des derniers quatuors* (2 vols., Paris, 1964); J. Szigeti, *The Ten B. Sonatas for Piano and Violin* (Urbana, Ill., 1965); P. Radcliffe, *B.'s String Quartets* (London, 1965, and N.Y., 1968); J. Kerman, *The B. Quartets* (N.Y., 1967); H. Truscott, *B.'s Late String Quartets* (London, 1968); C. Wolff, ed., *The String Quartets of Haydn, Mozart, and B.: Studies of the Autograph Manuscripts* (Cambridge, Mass., 1980); M. Rostal, *B.: The Sonatas for Piano and Violin: Some Thoughts on Their Interpretation* (London, 1985); S. Brandenburg and H. Loos, eds., *Beiträge zu B.s Kammermusik: Symposion Bonn 1984* (Munich, 1987); R. Winter and R. Martin, eds., *The B. Quartet Companion* (Berkeley, 1994); L. Ratner, *The B. String Quartets: Compositional Strategies and Rhetoric* (Stanford, 1995); S. Kurth, *B.s Streichquintette* (Munich, 1996); H.-M. Wang, *B.s Violoncell- und Violinsonaten* (Kassel, 1997). **Piano Music:** E. von Elterlein, *B.s Klaviersonaten* (Leipzig, 1856; 5th ed., 1895; Eng. tr., London, 1898); A. Marx, *Anleitung zum Vortrag Beethovenscher Klavierwerke* (Berlin, 1863; 4th ed., 1912); C. Reinecke, *Die Beethovenschen Klaviersonaten* (Leipzig, 1873; Eng. tr., London, 1898); W. Nagel, *B. und seine Klaviersonaten* (2 vols., Langensalza, 1903–05; 2nd ed., 1923–24); H. Schenker, ed., *Die letzten fünf Sonaten von B.: Kritische Ausgabe mit Einführung und Erläuterung* (4 vols., Vienna, 1913–21; new ed., abr., 1971–72); H. Riemann, *L. v.B.s sämtliche Klavier-Solosonaten* (3 vols., Berlin, 1919–20); S. Leoni, *Le sonate per pianoforte di B.* (Turin, 1922); W. Behrend, *L. v.B.s klaversonater...* (Copenhagen, 1923; Eng. tr. as *L. v.B.'s Pianoforte Sonatas*, London, 1927); F. Volbach, *Erläuterungen zu den Klaviersonaten B.s* (3rd ed., Cologne, 1924); A. Milne, *B.: The Pianoforte Sonatas* (London, 1925–28); I. Peters, *B.s Klaviermusik* (Berlin, 1925); J. Johnstone, *Notes on the Interpretation of 24 Famous Pianoforte Sonatas by B.* (London, 1927); D. Tovey, *A Companion to B.'s Pianoforte Sonatas (Bar- to-Bar Analysis)* (London, 1931); H. Westerby, *B. and His Piano Works* (London, 1931); H. Leichtentritt, *The Complete Pianoforte Sonatas* of B. (N.Y., 1936); J.-G. Prod'homme, *Les Sonates pour piano de B. (1782–1823)* (Paris, 1937; 2nd ed., 1950); E. Blom, *B.'s Pianoforte Sonatas Discussed* (London, 1938); E. Fischer, *L. v.B.s Klaviersonaten* (Wiesbaden, 1956; 2nd ed., 1966; Eng. tr., 1959); R. Rosenberg, *Die Klaviersonaten L. v.B.s* (Olten, 1957); J. Cockshoot, *The Fugue in B.'s Piano Music* (London, 1959); R. Reti, *Thematic Patterns in the Sonatas of B.* (London, 1965); W. Newman, *Performance Practices in B.'s Piano Sonatas: An Introduction* (N.Y., 1971); A. Leicher-Olbrich, *Untersuchungen zu Originalausgaben Beethovenscher Klavierwerke* (Wiesbaden, 1976); A. Münster, *Studien zu B.s Diabelli- Variationen* (Munich, 1982); G. Meyer, *Untersuchungen zur Sonatensatzform bei L. v.B.: Die Kopfsätze der Klaviersonaten Op.79 und 110* (Munich, 1985); W. Kinderman, *B.'s Diabelli Variations* (N.Y., 1987); E. McKay, *The Impact of the New Pianofortes on Classical Keyboard Style: Mozart, B. and Schubert* (West Hagley, West Midlands, 1987); J. Goldstein, *A B. Enigma: Performance Practice and the Piano Sonata, Opus 111* (N.Y., 1988); W. Newman, *B. on B.: Playing His Piano Music His Way* (N.Y. and London, 1989); G. Barth, *The Pianist as Orator: B. and the Transformation of Keyboard Style* (Ithaca, N.Y., 1992); M. Frohlich, *B.'s "Appassionata" Sonata* (Oxford, 1992); N. Marston, *B.'s Piano Sonata in E, Op.109* (Oxford, 1995). **V o c a l a n d C h o r a l M u s i c :** M. Bouchor, *La Messe en ré de B.* (Paris, 1886); M. Remy, *Missa solemnis* (Brussels, 1897); R. Sternfeld, *Zur Einführung in L. v.B.s Missa solemnis* (Berlin, 1900); H. de Curzon, *Les Lieder et airs détachés de B.* (Paris, 1905); W. Weber, *B.s Missa solemnis* (Leipzig, 1908); M. Kufferath, *Fidelio de L. v.B.* (Paris, 1913); M. Chop, *L. v.B.: Missa solemnis geschichtlich und musikalisch analysiert* (Leipzig, 1921); H. Böttcher, *B.s Lieder* (Berlin, 1927); idem, *B. als Liederkomponist* (Augsburg, 1928); J. Schmidt, *Unbekannte Manuskripte zu B.s weltlichen und geistlichen Gesangmusik* (Leipzig, 1928); F. Lederer, *B.s Bearbeitungen schottischer und anderer Volkslieder* (Bonn, 1934); A. Schering, *B. und die Dichtung* (Berlin, 1936); W. Hess, *B.s Oper Fidelio und ihre drei Fassungen* (Zürich, 1953); idem, *B.s Bühnenwerke* (Gottingen, 1962); O. Zichenheiner, *Untersuchungen zur Credo-Fuge der Missa Solemnis von L. v.B.* (Munich, 1984); W. Hess, *Das Fidelio-Buch: B.s Oper Fidelio, ihre Geschichte und ihre drei Fassungen* (Winterthur, 1986); W. Drabkin, *B.: Missa Solemnis* (Cambridge, 1991); B. Cooper, *B.'s Folksong Settings: Chronology, Sources, Style* (Oxford, 1994); P. Robinson, ed., *L.v. B.: Fidelio* (Cambridge, 1996). **M i s c e l l a n e o u s :** A. Orel, ed., *Ein Wiener B. Buch* (Vienna, 1921); *B.-Zentenarfeier internationaler musikhistorischer Kongress* (Vienna, 1927); G. Bosse, ed., *B.-Almanach der deutschen Musikbücherei* (Regensburg, 1927); J. Levien, *B. and the Royal Philharmonic Society* (London, 1927); A. Schmitz, ed., *B. und die Gegenwart* (Berlin and Bonn, 1937); L. Bachmann, *B. contra B.: Geschichte eines berühmten Rechtsfalles* (Munich, 1963); S. Kross and H. Schmidt, eds., *Colloquium Amicorum: Joseph Schmidt-Görg zum 70. Geburtstag* (Bonn, 1967); R. Klein, *Beethovenstatten in Österreich* (Vienna, 1970); H. Sittner, ed., *B.-Almanach 1970* (Vienna, 1970); K. Smolle, *Wohnstätten L. v.B.s von 1792 bis zu seinem Tod* (Munich and Duisburg, 1970); P. Lang, ed., *The Creative World of B.* (N.Y., 1971); H. Brockhaus and K. Niemann, eds., *Bericht über den internationalen B.- Kongress 10.-12. Dezember 1970 in Berlin* (Berlin, 1971); C. Dahlhaus et al., eds., *Bericht über den internationalen musikwissenschaftlichen Kongress Bonn 1970* (Kassel, 1971); E. Schenk, ed., *B.-Symposion Wien 1970* (Vienna, 1971); F. Slezak, *B.s Wiener Originalverleger* (Vienna, 1987); B. Bischoff, *Monument für B.: Die Entwicklung der B.-Rezeption Robert Schumanns* (Cologne, 1994).—**NS/LK/DM**

Beffara, Louis-François, French writer on music; b. Nonancourt, Eure, Aug. 23, 1751; d. Paris, Feb. 2, 1838. He was Commissaire de Police in Paris from 1792 to 1816. He left his rare collection of books and MSS to the city of Paris. Practically all of these were burned during the Commune in 1871, but a few are preserved in the Opéra library and at the Bibliothèque Nationale. He wrote a *Dictionnaire de l'Académie royale de Musique* (seven vols.) and seven vols. of rules and regulations of the Académie (Grand Opéra); also a *Dictionnaire alphabétique des acteurs,* etc. (three vols.), *Tableau chronologique des représentations journalières,* etc. (from 1671), *Dictionnaire alphabétique des tragédies lyriques...non représentées à l'Académie,* etc. (five vols.), and *Dramaturgie lyrique étrangère* (17 vols.).—**NS/LK/DM**

Beffroy de Reigny, Louis-Abel, French dramatist and composer who used the pseudonym *Cousin Jacques*; b. Lâon, Nov. 6, 1757; d. Paris, Dec. 17, 1811. He was one of the principal dramatists during the era of the French Revolution. He wrote many popular stage pieces, including the enormously successful *Nicodeme dans la lune* (Paris, 1790).

BIBL.: C. Westercamp, *B. d. R....sa vie et ses oeuvres* (Lâon, 1930).—**LK/DM**

Beglarian, Eve, American composer, performer, and audio producer, daughter of **Grant Beglarian;** b. Ann Arbor, July 22, 1958. She studied music at Princeton Univ. (B.A., 1980) and composition at Columbia Univ. (M.A., 1983), and also had private training in conducting with Jacques Louis Monod in N.Y. (1981–84). She began her career as an "uptown" N.Y. composer, but her shift in the mid-1980s to postminimalist practices and the use of vernacular sources moved her more comfortably "downtown" by the early 1990s. With keyboard player Kathleen Supové she performs in the duo twisted tutu, which blends theater with technology. Among her awards are a Rockefeller Foundation Bellagio Center Residency (1995), the Ford Foundation's Asian-Pacific Performance Exchange APPEX Fellowship (1996–97), and a Rockefeller MAP Grant (1998); from 1985 she has also received annual ASCAP Special Awards. Beglarian currently directs and produces audio books of such authors as Stephen King and Anne Rice for Random House and Simon & Schuster. In 2000 she commenced work on her first opera, *The Man in the Black Suit,* to a libretto by the composer and Grethe Barrett Holby after Stephen King.

WORKS: DRAMATIC: O p e r a : *The Man in the Black Suit,* after Stephen King (2001). **M u s i c T h e a t e r :** *Medea,* 7 odes for Chorus (N.Y., Oct. 17, 1985); *Maiden Songs: Sappho & Alkman* for Voices, Barbitos, and Clarinet (N.Y., May 14, 1987); *Lupie Montana's Shooting Script* (N.Y., Feb. 28, 1993); *typOpera* for Voices and Electronics, after Kurt Schwitters's *Ur Sonata* (Phoenix, April 30, 1994); *No. You Are Not Alone* for Voices, Keyboard, Guitar, Bass, Drums, and Electronics (N.Y., May 23, 1994); Music for *The Bacchae* for Men's Chorus and Chinese Instrumental Ensemble (Beijing, March 14, 1996); *Hildegurls, or The Order of the Virtues* for 4 Singers and Electronics (1996; rev. 1998; N.Y., July 22, 1998); *Open Secrets* for Architectural Space, Homemade Instruments, and Toy Piano (Troy, N.Y., Nov. 18, 1998); *Animal Magnetism* for Voices, Violin, Reeds, and Electronics (1997–2000; Minneapolis, April 7, 2000); *Forgiveness* for Voices, Pipa, Piri, Percussion, and Electronics (1998–2000;

N.Y., March 9, 2000). **D a n c e :** *Your Face Here* for Alto Saxophone, Piano, Voices, and Tape (Durham, N.C., July 14, 1988); *Gizmo* for Sampled Voice and Electronics (N.Y., Dec. 7, 1989); *Overstepping* for Sampled Voices and Electronics (Washington, D.C., May 15, 1991); *Under My Skin* for Percussion and Sampled Sounds (N.Y., March 13, 1992); *Dive Marker* for Sampled Percussion and Electronics (N.Y., Oct. 8, 1992); *Disappearance Act* for Sampled Percussion and Electronics (N.Y., May 6, 1993); *Father/Daughter Dance* for Accordion and Electronics (Washington, D.C., March 20, 1998). **O R C H . :** *Music for Orch.* (1981–82); *FlamingO* for Chamber Orch. (N.Y., Dec. 8, 1995); *The Continuous Life* (2000). **C H A M B E R :** *Uncle Wiggly* for Viola and Tape (1980; Denton, Tex., Nov. 6, 1981); *Quartettsatz* for String Quartet (1981; Trenton, N.J., Jan. 26, 1986); *Five for Clarinet* (1982; N.Y., June 23, 1983); *Clarinet Quartet* for 4 B-flat Clarinets (1983; N.Y., Feb. 4, 1985); *Fresh Air* for Saxophone Quartet and Tape (Yellow Springs, Vt., June 18, 1984); *Michael's Spoon* for 2 Horns and Tape (1984; N.Y., April 7, 1989); *A Big Enough Umbrella* for Viola and Tape (1984; N.Y., Nov. 7, 1985); *Spherical Music* for 12 Marimbas (1985); *Getting to Know the Weather* for Baritone Saxophone (1986); *Machaut in the Machine Age I* for Piano and Percussion (1986; N.Y., May 13, 1987; rev. 1990; Los Angeles, Nov. 6, 1991) and *II* for Bass and MIDI Percussion (Los Angeles, March 22, 1993); *Making Sense of It* for Flute, Clarinet, Violin, Cello, Piano, Percussion, and Tape (1987; N.Y., March 7, 1988); *Born Dancin'* for Electric Cello, Drum Machine, and Actor (Hartford, Ct., Nov. 17, 1989); *Eloise* for Electronic Cello and Sampled Cello Sounds (N.Y., Nov. 17, 1990); *Preciosilla (Margaret's Mix)* for Flute and Tape (N.Y., Feb. 13, 1992); *How I Like That Time* for Violin, 2 Mbiras, and Electronic Tape (N.Y., March 30, 1995); *Wolf Chaser* for Violin, Amplified Bowed Cymbals, and Tape (N.Y., Aug. 10, 1995); *Creating the World* for Violin, Bassoon, Guitar, Electronic Keyboard, Percussion, and Drums (1996); *Play Nice* for Harp and Vibraphone or Toy Piano (N.Y., April 20, 1997); *Elf Again* for Indeterminate Ensemble (N.Y., March 16, 1998). **KEYBOARD: P i a n o :** *Making Hay* for 2 Pianos (Princeton, March 3, 1980); *Miranda's Kiss* (1988; Washington, D.C., May 6, 1990); *Boy Toy/Toy Boy* for 2 Keyboards and Electronics (1997; N.Y., Jan. 22, 1998). **O r g a n :** *Machaut in the Machine Age IV: Ay Mi!* for Processed Electric Chord Organ (N.Y., June 22, 1995); *Wonder Counselor* for Pipe Organ and Electronics (1996). **VOCAL:** *3 Love Songs* for Mezzo- soprano, Clarinet, Viola, and Piano (1981–82; N.Y., Oct. 24, 1982); *Psalm* for Chorus (N.Y., Dec. 17, 1983); *Machaut A Go Go* for Voice, Alto Saxophone, Horn, Trombone, Electric Guitar, Cello, Electric Bass, Harp, and Drums (N.Y., Dec. 8, 1991); *Enough* for Soprano, Piano, and Bass (N.Y., May 25, 1993); *YOursonate* for Voice, Percussion, and Tape (N.Y., Oct. 22, 1993); *The Marriage of Heaven & Hell* for Voice, Flute, Saxophone, Oboe, Bassoon, Viola, Contrabassoon, Piano, and Percussion (Philadelphia, March 25, 1994); *Landscaping for Privacy* for Spoken Voice and Keyboards (N.Y., Oct. 8, 1995); *No Man's Land* for Voice, Amplified Hand Drum, and 2 Electronic Keyboards (N.Y., Jan. 18, 1995); *My Feelings Now* for Voice and Piano (1996); *Non-Jew* for 2 Spoken Voices (N.Y., May 31, 1998); *Written on the Body* for Voice, Keyboards, and Electronics (1999); *Not Worth* for Voice, 2 Bass Clarinets, Viola, Cello, and Bass (1999; N.Y., Feb. 3, 2000); *Just a Little More* for Voice, 2 Keyboards, and Tape (N.Y., March 26, 2000). **ELECTRONIC:** *The Garden of Cyrus* (1984–86; N.Y., March 2, 1987); *Escape to the Stars* (1986); *Eloise Extensions* for Electronic Cello and Sampled Cello Sounds (1991; N.Y., May 27, 1992); *An Elk Revolt* for Electronic Tape (1998).—**LK/DM**

Beglarian, Grant, Georgian-born American arts administrator and composer of Armenian descent, father of **Eve Beglarian;** b. Tiflis, Dec. 1, 1927. He went to Teheran in 1934, and then to the U.S. in 1947, becoming a naturalized American citizen in 1954. After attending Boston Univ. (1947), he studied composition with Finney at the Univ. of Mich. (B.M., 1950; M.M., 1952; D.M.A., 1958) and with Copland at the Berkshire Music Center in Tanglewood (summer 1959). He was president of Music- Book Associates (1954–65) and director of the Contemporary Music Project of the Ford Foundation (1961–69). After serving as dean of the School of Performing Arts at the Univ. of Southern Calif. in Los Angeles (1969–82), he was president of the National Foundation for Advancement in the Arts in Miami (1982–91). Since then, he has served as a consultant to cultural and educational organizations in the U.S. and abroad, most notably the Warsaw Autumn Festival, the Franz Liszt Academy of Music in Budapest, and the American Academy of Art in Giverny, France. He joined the board of the Copland Heritage Assn. in 1996 and chaired its Copland Soc. for the restoration and use of Copland's home for residencies by composers and as a center for promoting the study and performance of works by American composers. In 1958 he won the George Gershwin Award, in 1959 and 1968 he received Ford Foundation Composer awards, and in 1961, 1963, and 1990 he was a resident at the MacDowell Colony.

WORKS: DRAMATIC: *Women of Troy,* incidental music (1949). **ORCH.:** *Symphony in 2 Movements* (1950); *Divertimento* (1957); *Sinfonia* (1961); *A Short Suite* (1968); *Diversions* for Viola, Cello, and Orch. (1972); *Sinfonia* for Strings (1974); *Partita* (1986). **B a n d :** *Prelude and Allegro* (1955); *Overture* (1956); *1st Portrait* (1959); *A Hymn for Our Time* for Multiple Bands (1968). **CHAMBER:** Piano Quintet (1947); String Quartet (1948); Violin Sonata (1949); Cello Sonata (1951); (7) Duos for Flute and Viola (1954); (9) Duets for Violins (1955); *Music* for Bassoon and String Trio (1959); *2 Canzonas* for Trumpets and Trombones (1960); Woodwind Quintet (1966); *Fable, Foibles, and Fancies* for Cello (1971); *Variations on a Paganini Theme* for 3 Cellos (1975); *Ballad* for Cello (1978); *Elegy* for Cello (1979). **O r g a n :** Suite (1956). **VOCAL:** *Tell me Another One* for Baritone and Piano (1949); *12 Hungarian Songs* for Chorus and Orch. (1957); *A Christmas Carol* for Chorus (1959); *Motet* for Chorus (1960); *Nurse's Song* for Chorus and Orch. (1960); *...And All the Hills Echoed* for Bass, Organ, Timpani, and Chorus (1968); *To Manitou* for Soprano and Orch. (1976).—**NS/LK/DM**

Begnis, Giuseppe de, admired Italian bass; b. Lugo, 1793; d. N.Y., Aug. 1849. After serving as a choirboy in Lugo, he made his operatic debut in Modena in 1813 in Pavesi's *Ser Marc'Antonio.* He then sang in various Italian music centers, establishing himself as one of the finest buffo artists of the day. In 1816 he married Giuseppina Ronzi de Begnis, with whom he often appeared in opera. Rossini chose him to create the role of Dandini in *La Cenerentola* (Rome, Jan. 25, 1817), and he subsequently excelled in roles by that composer as well as those by Mayr and Pacini. He and his wife went to Paris in 1819, where he appeared as Don Basilio opposite his wife's Rosina in Rossini's *Il Barbiere di Siviglia* at its first Paris production at the Théâtre-Italien on Oct. 26, 1819. They continued to sing in Paris until 1821, when they went to London. Begnis made his debut there as Don Geronio opposite his wife's Fiorilla in Rossini's *Il Turco in Italia* at the King's Theatre on May 19, 1821. They continued to appear in opera together until their separation in 1825. Begnis remained at the King's Theatre until 1827, but also served as an opera manager in Bath (1823–24) and later in Dublin (1834–37) before settling in N.Y.—**NS/LK/DM**

Béhague, Gerard H(enri), French-born American musicologist; b. Montpellier, Nov. 2, 1937. He studied at the Brazilian Cons. of Music in Rio de Janeiro (diploma, 1958), with Jacques Chailley and Edith Weber at the Univ. of Paris (diploma in musicology, 1963), and with Gilbert Chase, Howard Smither, Peter Hansen, and Norma McLeod at Tulane Univ. (Ph.D., 1966). In 1976 he became a naturalized American citizen. He was an instructor (1966–67), asst. prof. (1967–69), and assoc. prof. (1969–74) at the Univ. of Ill. at Urbana-Champaign. In 1972–73 he held a Guggenheim fellowship. From 1974 he was a prof. at the Univ. of Tex. at Austin, where he was chairman of its music dept. from 1981 to 1989. He served as president of the Soc. for Ethnomusicology from 1979 to 1981. In 1997 the Brazilian government honored him as a Commander of the Order of Rio Branco. He contributed many learned articles to various scholarly books and journals.

WRITINGS: *The Beginnings of Music Nationalism in Brazil* (Detroit, 1971); *Music in Latin America* (Englewood Cliffs, N.H., 1979); ed. *Performance Practice: Ethnomusicological Perspectives* (Westport, Conn., 1984); *Heitor Villa-Lobos: The Search for Brazil's Musical Soul* (Austin, Tex., 1994); ed. *Music and Black Ethnicity: The Caribbean and South America* (Coral Gables, 1994); *Musiques Brésiliennes (De la Cantoria a la Samba-Reggae)* (Paris and Arles, 1999).—**NS/LK/DM**

Beheim, Michel, German minnesinger; b. Sülzbach, near Weinsberg, Sept. 27, 1416; d. there (murdered), 1474. He was active as a soldier and singer in the service of various German, Danish, and Hungarian princes. Beheim was one of the earliest of the Meistersingers who still retained some of the characteristics of the minnesinger. He finally settled in Sülzbach as village major or magistrate. He composed many songs, 11 of which are preserved at Heidelberg and Munich.

BIBL.: A. Kühn, *Rhythmik und Melodik M. B.s* (1907). —**NS/LK/DM**

Behrend, (Gustav) Fritz, German composer and teacher; b. Berlin, March 3, 1889; d. there, Dec. 29, 1972. He studied composition with H. van Eycken, P. Rufer, and Humperdinck, and piano with Breithaupt (1907–11). After serving as a coach at the Braunschweig Hoftheater (1911–12), he taught at the Ochs-Eichelberg Cons. (1918–42) and the Klindworth-Scharwenka Cons. in Berlin (1942–49). His compositions did not meet with favor during the Third Reich, but later they achieved a modicum of recognition.

WORKS: DRAMATIC: *König Renés Tochter* (1919); *Der schwangere Bauer* (1927); *Die lächerlichen Preziösen* (1928; Berlin, May 22, 1949); *Almansor* (1931); *Dornröschen* (1934); *Der Wunderdoktor* (1947); *Der fahrende Schüler im Paradies* (1949); *Der Spiegel* (1950); *Romantische Komödie* (1953). **ORCH.:** 7 syms.; *Rotkäppchensuite* (1912); *Lustspiel Overture* (1913); *Am Rhein*

(1913); *Fantasie* for Piano and Orch. (1919); *Im Hochgebirge* (1920); *Penthesilea* (1926); *Lustspiel Overture* (1937); *Lustige Overture* (1947). **CHAMBER:** 7 string quartets; 2 piano trios (1923, 1929); Violin Sonata (1925); Cello Sonata (1925); Wind Quintet (1951); String Trio; Septet; Octet; piano pieces. **VOCAL:** Over 100 songs.—**NS/LK/DM**

Behrend, Siegfried, German guitarist; b. Berlin, Nov. 19, 1933; d. Hausham, Sept. 20, 1990. His father, a guitar virtuoso, guided his early interest, and at the age of 16 he entered the Klindworth-Scharwenka Cons. in Berlin, where he studied piano, composition, and conducting. He made his debut as a guitarist in Berlin in 1952, then toured Europe. Behrend was particularly known for his performances of contemporary music, and commissioned many works for the guitar. —**NS/LK/DM**

Behrens, Hildegard, noted German soprano; b. Varel, Oldenburg, Feb. 9, 1937. After obtaining a law degree from the Univ. of Freiburg im Breisgau, she studied voice with Ines Leuwen at the Freiburg im Breisgau Staatliche Hochschule für Musik. In 1971 she made her operatic debut as Mozart's Countess at the Freiburg im Breisgau City Theater; that same year she became a member of the opera studio of the Deutsche Oper am Rhein in Düsseldorf, becoming a full-fledged member of the company in 1972; also sang in Frankfurt am Main. In 1976 she made her debut at London's Covent Garden as Giorgetta in *Il Tabarro*. On Oct. 1, 1976, she made her first appearance at the Metropolitan Opera in N.Y. singing *Dich teure Halle* from *Tannhäuser* in a marathon concert, returning to make her formal debut there as Giorgetta on Oct. 15, 1976; in subsequent seasons, she returned to sing such roles as Fidelio, Elettra, Sieglinde, Isolde, Donna Anna, Brünnhilde, Berg's Marie, and Tosca. In 1983 she sang Brünnhilde at the Bayreuth Festival. She made her N.Y. recital debut in 1985. In 1990 she portrayed Salome at Covent Garden. Her characterization of Elektra at the Metropolitan Opera in 1992 was a stunning tour de force. After singing Isolde in Munich in 1996, she appeared as Elektra at Covent Garden in 1997. In 1998 Behrens was bequeathed the Lotte Lehmann Memorial Ring by Leonie Rysanek, and was also awarded the Léonie Sonning Music Prize of Denmark. On July 24, 1999, she created the role of R in Berio's *Cronaca del Lugo* in Salzburg. —**NS/LK/DM**

Behrens, Jack, American composer and teacher; b. Lancaster, Pa., March 25, 1935. He was a student of Bergsma, Persichetti, and Mennin at the Juilliard School of Music in N.Y. (B.S., 1958; M.S., 1959), and then of Kirchner and Sessions at Harvard Univ. (Ph.D., 1973); he also studied with Milhaud at the Aspen (Colo.) Music School (summer 1962) and with Wolpe and Cage in Saskatchewan (summers 1964–65). From 1962 to 1966 he taught at the Univ. of Saskatchewan, where he was head of the theory dept. at its cons. He taught at Simon Fraser Univ. (1966–70) and at Calif. State Coll. in Bakersfield (1970–76). In 1976 he became a member of the faculty of music at the Univ. of Western Ontario, where he was chairman of the theory and composition dept. until 1980; he then served as dean of the faculty (1980–86). Behrens's music is in a sophisticated modern idiom, with judicious use of both serial and aleatoric procedures.

WORKS: DRAMATIC: O p e r a : *The Lay of Thrym* (Regina, Saskatchewan, April 13, 1968). **ORCH.:** Trumpet Concerto (1955); *Introspection* for Strings (1956); *Declaration* (1964); *The Sound of Milo* (1970); Triple Concerto for Clarinet, Violin, Piano, and Orch. (1971); *Fantasy on Francis Hopkinson's My Days Have Been So Wondrous Free* for Small Orch. (1976); *New Beginnings* (1976); *A Greeting* (1977); *Fantasia on a Fragment* for Fortepiano and Chamber Orch. (1984); *Landmarks* (1991). **CHAMBER:** *Quarter-Tone Quartet* for Strings (1960); *Green Centre* for Winds (1964; rev. 1990); *Serenades* for Flute, Clarinet, Piano, Violin, and Cello (1969); *Happy Birthday John Cage I and II* for Solo Instruments (1972); Clarinet Quintet (1974); *Bass Variants* for Double Bass (1977); *Dialogue* for Cello and Piano (1980); String Quartet, *In Nomine* (1980); *Fiona's Flute* for Flute and Piano (1982); *Well-tempered Duo* for Cello and Fortepiano (1984); *Reflections* for Viola and Clarinet (1990); *Reverberations* for Trumpet (1990). **P i a n o :** *Passacaglia* (1964; rev. 1976); *Taos Portraits* (1976); *Music* for 2 Pianos (1979); *Aspects* for 3 Pianos (1983). **VOCAL:** *Early Song* for Tenor or Baritone, Flute, Oboe, Horn, Violin, and Viola (1965); *Looking Back* for Soprano, Flute, and Piano (1979); *A Fable—For the Whaling Fleets* for Narrator, Flute, Clarinet, Violin, Cello, and Piano (1985; rev. 1990); *I Have Mislaid Something* and *The Death of the Loch Ness Monster* for Baritone, Flute, and Piano (1985); many choral pieces.—NS/LK/DM

Beiderbecke, Bix (actually **Leon Bix,** not Bismarck as is sometimes reported), widely admired early jazz cornetist, composer, pianist and a unique stylist; b. Davenport, Iowa, March 10, 1903; d. Queens, N.Y., Aug. 6, 1931. Beiderbecke's parents, German immigrants, were amateur musicians, and he began to play as a small child. His mother was an amateur pianist, and his father had his own merchant's business in Davenport. (He later sent copies of all his records home to his Midwestern German–Protestant family, but they didn't even open the parcels.) His brother brought home records by the Original Dixieland Jazz Band and Bix slowed down the turntable so that he could learn to play the correct solos. He began playing piano at the age of three, and cornet at 14—which, for at least the first eight years, he played left-handed. During his high-school days (1919–21), Beiderbecke began gigging and sitting-in with various bands in the greater Davenport area. In September 1921, he enrolled at Lake Forest Military Academy, near Chicago. While at the Academy, he formed the Cy-Bix Orch. with drummer Walter "Cy" Welge, and also played in the Ten Foot Band in Chicago. Uninterested in his studies, he was expelled from the Academy on May 22, 1922. He briefly returned to Davenport, but then quickly moved back to Chicago to join The Cascades Band. Beiderbecke played on Lake Michigan excursion boats and worked in a quintet at White Lake, Mich., during the summer of 1922. For the next year or so, he worked with various bands in Chicago and, briefly, Syracuse, N.Y., while returning in the summer of 1923 to excursion-boat work in the

Chicago area.

In October 1923, Beiderbecke joined The Wolverines, a semi-pro band popular on college campuses. The band was mostly working in the Ind.–Ohio area, with an occasional date in Chicago. He first recorded with the Wolverines, and soon became friends with songwriter Hoagy Carmichael. During this time, Bix also played briefly with Mezz Mezzrow. The Wolverines came to N.Y. in autumn 1924, to begin a residency at the Cinderella Ballroom on Sept. 12th. However, Bix left The Wolverines in November. He was hired on a try-out basis by bandleader Jean Goldkette, but then returned to Chicago to work for four weeks for Charlie Straight. After being fired by Straight, he gigged in Chicago before spending 18 days as a student at the State Univ. of Iowa from Feb. 2–20, 1925.

In September 1925, Beiderbecke joined Frank Trumbauer in Detroit, who was then leading a band under the auspices of Jean Goldkette. A year later, the pair joined Jean Goldkette's Band until Goldkette temporarily disbanded in September 1927. Through recordings and radio broadcasts with the band, Beiderbecke's initial reputation was made. Beiderbecke also recorded with various accompanists, both under his own name, and with Trumbauer, from summer 1927 on. After a short position in Adrian Rollini Big Band in September 1927, Beiderbecke joined Paul Whiteman's orch. at the Ind. Theatre, Indianapolis on Oct. 31st; he would continue to work with the band on the road and in N.Y. through 1930, except for brief periods of illness. Beiderbecke was a featured soloist in the band, and could be heard on recordings, radio, and in concrts. Beiderbecke also began to make his mark as a composer of advanced music that combined jazz with modern classical influences. Together with Lennie Hayton and Roy Bargy, Beiderbecke played a three-piano version of own composition *In a Mist* at Carnegie Hall on Oct. 7, 1928. The piece showed the influence of European Impressionism.

However, Beiderbecke's health was beginning to fail, and he was absent from Paul Whiteman from November 1928 until March 1929 due to illness. He rejoined the band for a trip to Calif. in May 1929, and then returned to N.Y. Beiderbecke continued to work with Whiteman until suffering another breakdown in health in mid-September. He returned to recuperate in Davenport, and was back to N.Y. in spring of 1930. He did gigs and freelance recordings, including a four- day try-out with the Casa Loma Band in summer of 1930. Except for a brief period from November 1930–January 1931 when he was back in his hometown, Beiderbecke freelanced in N.Y. until his death. He briefly held a regular job on the *Camel Hour* radio show (orch. directed by Charles Previn) that spring, and also played a few university dates. Sometime during the summer of 1931 Bix moved from his 44th Street Hotel apartment to rent the ground-floor apartment of a block in Queens. He had become a serious alcoholic and his death was attributed to that, though the direct cause was pneumonia. He was treated by a doctor during the last few days of his life; he died in the presence of the owner of the apartment, a bass-playing attorney named George Kraslow. Bix was buried at Oakdale Cemetery, Davenport.

Beiderbecke was one of the unique stylists, widely admired by black and white musicians alike for his lyrical reach, unexpected melodic directions, and controlled ("cool," they would later say) and expressive tone. (Armstrong said "He was the only one as serious about his horn as I was." He and Louis admired each other and Louis allegedly once lent him his horn so Bix could sit in.) Not an isolated phenomenon, Beiderbecke was part of a circle of musicians who experimented with wide melodic leaps, a kind of uninflected eighth-note pulse, and compositions using the whole-tone scale. This school, and Beiderbecke himself, had a tremendous impact on musicians growing up in the late 1920s, including Lester Young, Budd Johnson, Eddie Durham, Eddie Barefield, and of course cornetists Jimmy McPartland, Bunny Berigan, Bobby Hackett, and, through Hackett, Miles Davis. Among white musicians he developed a cult following, exemplified to this day in a annual Beiderbecke festival held in Davenport. His early death made him a candidate for legend, exemplified in Dorothy Baker's rather fictional biography, *Young Man with a Horn* (N.Y., 1938), made into a Hollywood film starring Kirk Douglas in 1956.

DISC.: "Singin' the Blues"; "I'm Comin' Virginia"; "Wolverines"; "At the Jazz Band Ball."

BIBL.: R. Berton, *Remembering Bix: A Memoir of the Jazz Age* (1974); R. Sudhalter, P. Evans, *Bix: Man and Legend* (1974); V. Castelli, E. Kaleveld, L. Pusateri, *The Bix Bands: A Bix Beiderbecke Disco-biography* (Milano, 1972); J. P. Perhonis, *The Bix Beiderbecke Story: The Jazz Musician in Legend, Fiction, and Fact* (Univ. of Minn., 1978).—JC/LP

Beinum, Eduard (Alexander) van
See **Van Beinum, Eduard (Alexander)**

Beissel, Johann Conrad,
German-American composer of religious music; founder of the sect of Solitary Brethren of the Community of Sabbatarians; b. Eberbach on the Neckar, Palatinate, March 1, 1690; d. Ephrata, Pa., July 6, 1768. He migrated to America in 1720 for religious reasons. His first attempt to build up a "solitary" residence failed, but in 1732 he started the community at Ephrata, which became a flourishing religious and artistic center. Beissel, who styled himself Bruder Friedsam (Brother Peaceful), was a prolific writer of hymns in fanciful German, publ. in various collections, some printed by Benjamin Franklin, some by the community at Ephrata. He composed tunes for his hymns and harmonized them according to his own rules. His compositions were collected in beautifully illuminated MSS, many of which are preserved at the Library of Congress and the Library of the Historical Soc. of Pa. Beissel was not a trained musician, but had original ideas; his religious fanaticism inspired him to write some startling music; in several of his hymns he made use of an antiphonal type of vocal composition with excellent effect. He left a tract explaining his harmonic theory and his method of singing. Beissel's hymns are collected chiefly in *Zionistischer Weyrauchs Hügel* (1739), *Das Gesang der einsamen und verlassenen Turtel Taube, das ist der christlichen Kirche* (1747), and *Paradisisches Wunder Spiel* (two independent publs., 1754 and 1766). Only texts were printed in these vols., but the 1754 issue was arranged so that the music could be inserted by hand. Beissel's life was first described in the *Chronicon Ephratense*, compiled by the brethren Lamech and Agrippa, publ. at Ephrata in a German ed. in 1786, and in an Eng. tr. by J.M. Hark at Lancaster in 1889.

BIBL.: W.C. Klein, *J.C. B.: Mystic and Martinet* (Philadelphia, 1942).—NS/LK/DM

Bekker, (Max) Paul (Eugen),
eminent German writer on music; b. Berlin, Sept. 11, 1882; d. N.Y., March 7, 1937. He studied violin with Rehfeld, piano with Sormann, and theory with Horwitz. He began his career as a violinist with the Berlin Phil. He was music critic of the *Berliner Neueste Nachrichten* (1906–09) and of the *Berliner Allgemeine Zeitung* (1909–11). In 1911 he became chief music critic of the *Frankfurter Zeitung*. His polemical exchanges with Pfitzner brought him wide recognition. In 1925 he became Intendant of the Kassel City Theater, and in 1927 in Wiesbaden. In 1933 he left Germany, being unable to cope with the inequities of the Nazi regime. He publ. biographies of Oskar Fried (1907) and Jacques Offenbach (1909). His other writings included *Das Musikdrama der Gegenwart* (1909); Beethoven (1911; Eng. tr., 1926); *Das deutsche Musikleben, Versuch einer soziologischen Musikbetrachtung* (1916); *Die Sinfonie von Beethoven bis Mahler* (1918); *Franz Schreker* (1919); *Kunst und Revolution* (1919); *Die Weltgeltung der deutschen Musik* (1920); *Die Sinfonien G. Mahlers* (1921); *Richard Wagner* (1924; Eng. tr., 1931); *Von den Naturreichen des Klanges* (1924); *Musikgeschichte als Geschichte der musikalischen Formwandlungen* (1926); *Das Operntheater* (1930); *Briefe an zeitgenössische Musiker* (1932); *Wandlungen der Oper* (1934; Eng. tr., 1935, as *The Changing Opera*); *The Story of the Orch.* (1936).

BIBL.: B. Cherney, *The B.-Pfitzner Controversy: Its Significance for German Music Criticism During the Weimar Republic* (diss., Univ. of Toronto, 1974); V. Bauer, *P. B.: Eine Untersuchung seiner Schriften zur Musik* (Aachen, 1998).—NS/LK/DM

Bekku, Sadao,
Japanese composer; b. Tokyo, May 24, 1922. He studied theoretical physics at the Univ. of Tokyo (1943–50), and then studied composition with Milhaud, Rivier, and Messiaen at the Paris Cons. (1951–54). Returning to Japan, he became engaged in pedagogy; was also a member of the Japanese section of the ISCM from 1955 (president, 1968–73). His works are set in neo-Classical forms, with occasional use of authentic Japanese modalities. He publ. a book on the occult in music (Tokyo, 1971).

WORKS: O p e r a : *Le Dit les trois femmes*, opera buffa (Rome, 1964); *Prince Arima* (1963–67; Tokyo, March 13, 1967); *Aoi-no-ue* (1979). O R C H .: *Deux prières* (Tokyo, May 10, 1956); *Symphonietta* for Strings (Tokyo, Nov. 27, 1959); 4 syms. (1962, 1977, 1984, 1991); Violin Concerto (Tokyo Radio, Nov. 13, 1969); Viola Concerto (Tokyo, March 3, 1972); Piano Concerto (1981); Cello Concerto (1997). C H A M B E R : Trio for Oboe, Clarinet, and Bassoon (1953); Flute Sonata (1954); 2 *Japanese Suites*: No. 1 for Wind Quintet (1955) and No. 2 for 12 Instruments and Percussion (1958); String Quartet No. 1 (1955); Violin Sonata (1963–67); Viola Sonata (1969; arr. from the Violin Sonata).

Piano : Sonatina (1965); *Kaleidoscope*, suite (1966); *3 Paraphrases* (1968); *Sonatina in Classical Style* (1969). VOCAL: Choruses.—NS/LK/DM

Belafonte, Harry (actually, Harold George Jr.), American singer and actor; b. N.Y., March 1, 1927.

Belafonte was best known for singing such calypso-styled Caribbean folk songs as "Jamaica Farewell, "Mary's Boy Child," and "Banana Boat Song (Day-O)." Albums like *Belafonte, Calypso*, and *Belafonte at Carnegie Hall* made him one of the most successful recording artists of the late 1950s and early 1960s. He expanded from that base to become an internationally popular concert performer as well as a singer, actor, and producer of films; he also became a social activist.

Belafonte's father, Harold George Belafonte, a British subject originally from the island of Martinique, was a cook in the British Royal Navy; his mother, Melvine Love Belafonte, was a Jamaican who worked as a dressmaker and domestic. His parents split up during his childhood, and when he was eight or nine his mother took him and his brother back to Jamaica, where she remarried. The family returned to N.Y. in 1940. He quit high school in 1944 to enlist in the navy and was discharged the following year. In December 1945 he attended a play put on by the American Negro Theatre and eventually joined the troupe. He also attended the dramatic workshop taught by Erwin Piscator at the New School for Social Research on the G.I. Bill. On June 18, 1948, he married Frances Marguerite Byrd, a psychology student at N.Y.U. who later taught there; they had two children and divorced on Feb. 28, 1957.

At the suggestion of his friend Monte Kay, who was involved with the Royal Roost nightclub, Belafonte began singing at the club in January 1949. Kay became his manager, and he recorded his first single, "Lean on Me"/"Recognition" (both music and lyrics by Harry Belafonte), for Jubilee Records. He was then signed by the more prestigious Capitol Records. In the fall of 1949 he was a regular on the variety series *Sugar Hill Times* on network television. But he was uncomfortable singing jazz and pop music, and abandoned his singing career by the end of 1950. He and a couple of friends opened a restaurant, The Sage, in Greenwich Village, which brought him into contact with the emerging folk music scene. He developed an interest in the folk music of the West Indies and put together a club act of such songs that he premiered at the Village Vanguard nightclub in October 1951. After a lengthy engagement there, he moved uptown to the Blue Angel and then to nightclubs around the country.

Belafonte's success as a nightclub performer led to other opportunities. He was signed to a contract by RCA Victor Records and achieved his first chart entry in April 1953 with "Gomen Nasai (Forgive Me)" (music by Raymond Hattori, lyrics by Benedict Myers). That same month, he appeared in his first film, *Bright Road*, in which he sang "Suzanne," a song he wrote with accompanist Millard Thomas. He made his Broadway debut in the revue *John Murray Anderson's Almanac* (N.Y., Dec. 10, 1953), singing the songs "Hold 'em Joe" (music and lyrics by Harry Thomas), "Acorn in the Meadow"

(music and lyrics by Richard Adler and Jerry Ross), and "Mark Twain" (music and lyrics by Harry Belafonte); he won the Tony Award for Outstanding Supporting or Featured Musical Actor.

In October 1954, Belafonte appeared in *Carmen Jones*, the film version of Oscar Hammerstein II's adaptation of Georges Bizet's opera *Carmen* as a contemporary all-black Broadway musical; Belafonte's singing in the demanding role was dubbed. In 1955 he toured the country with dancers Marge and Gower Champion in the revue *3 for Tonight*, which reached Broadway on April 17 for 85 performances and then was broadcast on network television in June, earning him two Emmy nominations: Best Male Singer and Best Specialty Act—Single or Group. In November he returned to television as an actor in an episode of *G.E. Theatre*.

Belafonte's recording career took an upswing with the proliferation of the 12–inch LP in the mid-1950s, and he first reached the album charts in January 1956 with *"Mark Twain" and Other Folk Favorites*, which made the Top Ten. In February 1956, RCA released *Belafonte*, which hit #1 in March and went gold. *Calypso*, released in May, did even better, topping the charts in September, going gold, and becoming the biggest album of the year. With this recording success, Belafonte graduated from clubs to theaters and even larger venues. In June 1956 he sold out Lewisohn Stadium in upper Manhattan, and in July he broke box office records during a two-week engagement at the Greek Theatre in Los Angeles.

For the Christmas season RCA released the Belafonte single "Mary's Boy Child" (music and lyrics by Jester Hairston), which peaked in the Top 40 in December (nearly a year later it hit #1 in the U.K.). The following month, "Jamaica Farewell" (music and lyrics adapted by Lord Burgess from a traditional West Indian folk song), culled from the *Calypso* LP as a single, was just as successful. RCA then released another *Calypso* track, "Banana Boat Song (Day-O)" (music and lyrics by Alan Arkin, Bob Carey, and Erik Darling), giving Belafonte his biggest hit single; it peaked in the Top Ten in February 1957 and sold a million copies.

On March 8, 1957, Belafonte married dancer Julie Robinson; they had two children. He released his third consecutive gold album that month, *An Evening with Harry Belafonte*, and it lodged in the Top Ten. In April he peaked in the Top 40 of the singles charts with "Mama Look at Bubu" (music and lyrics by Lord Melody, a pseudonym for Fitzroy Alexander). He starred in the film *Island in the Sun* in June, and both his recording of the title song and its B-side, "Cocoanut Woman" (both music and lyrics by Harry Belafonte and Lord Burgess), peaked in the Top 40 in July. The songs were featured on his next album, *Belafonte Sings of the Caribbean*, which entered the charts in September and became his fifth consecutive LP to reach the Top Ten.

Belafonte's career was interrupted by a series of eye operations in 1958, though he managed to undertake his first European tour. By the time he returned to record-making with *Belafonte Sings the Blues* in the fall of 1958, his commercial momentum had slowed, and the album missed the Top Ten, as did its follow-ups *Love Is a Gentle Thing* and a duet album with Lena Horne, *Porgy & Bess*, both released in the spring of 1959. Having formed his own film production company, Belafonte was involved in developing both of his next movies, *The World, the Flesh and the Devil*, released in April 1959, and *Odds Against Tomorrow*, released in October. But neither was a success, and he avoided film acting for a decade.

Belafonte's most impressive achievements of 1959 were live performances onstage and on television. His two concerts at Carnegie Hall, April 19–20, were recorded for the double live album *Belafonte at Carnegie Hall*, released in October. The LP reached the Top Ten and went gold, staying in the charts more than three years. On Dec. 10 he starred in a TV special, *Tonight with Belafonte*, which won him an Emmy for Outstanding Performance in a Variety or Musical Program or Series.

Belafonte repeated his successes of 1959 in 1960. On May 2 he again performed at Carnegie Hall, this time with guests Odetta, Miriam Makeba, and the Chad Mitchell Trio; *Belafonte Returns to Carnegie Hall*, another double album, was released in November and became a Top Ten, gold-selling hit, earning Grammy nominations for Album of the Year and Best Vocal Performance, Male. (Belafonte won his first Grammy that year, for Best Folk Performance for the single "Swing Dat Hammer.") His next TV special, *Belafonte*, broadcast on Nov. 20, earned him an Emmy nomination for Outstanding Program Achievement in the Field of Variety.

Belafonte scored his sixth gold album with *Jump Up Calypso*, released in August 1961. *The Midnight Special*, released in April 1962, was his ninth LP to reach the Top Ten; it also earned a Grammy nomination for Best Folk Recording. After that his recordings retreated from the top of the charts, although they continued to sell well. *Belafonte at the Greek Theatre* (1964), which spent more than four months in the charts, was nominated for a Grammy for Best Folk Recording, and the singer won that award the following year for the chart album *An Evening with Belafonte/Makeba*. He also continued to tour regularly and to appear on and produce television shows. But from the mid-1960s on, he devoted much of his attention to social issues, especially civil rights.

After almost three years away from recording records, Belafonte released *Homeward Bound* at the end of 1969; it was his last charting album. He also returned to film for the first time in 11 years, appearing in *The Angel Levine*, released in July 1970. He appeared in the films *Buck and the Preacher* (1972) and *Uptown Saturday Night* (1974), both directed by his friend Sidney Poitier, but did not return to acting full-time.

Belafonte became more active at the end of the 1970s, touring internationally in 1979–83. In August 1981 he released his first U.S. album in many years, *Loving You Is Where I Belong*, and starred in a television movie, *Grambling's White Tiger*, that was broadcast Oct. 4, 1981. He produced the film *Beat Street* in 1984 and was prominently involved in the USA for Africa charity program in 1985, performing on the single "We Are the World" and at the Live Aid concert in Philadelphia on July 13, 1985. He signed to EMI Records and released *Paradise in Gazankulu* (1988) and *Belafonte '89* (1989). In July 1989 he again appeared at the Greek Theatre. In the 1990s he did more film acting, notably in director Robert Altman's *The Player* (1992), *Ready to Wear* (1994), and *Kansas City* (1996), as well as *White Man's Burden* (1995).

DISC.: *"Mark Twain" and Other Folk Favorites* (1956); *Belafonte* (1956); *Calypso* (1956); *An Evening with Harry Belafonte* (1957); *Belafonte Sings of the Caribbean* (1957); *Belafonte Sings the Blues* (1958); *Love Is a Gentle Thing* (1959); *Belafonte at Carnegie Hall* (1959); *Belafonte Returns to Carnegie Hall* (1960); *Jump Up Calypso* (1961); *The Midnight Special* (1962); *Belafonte at the Greek Theatre* (1964); *Homeward Bound* (1969); *Loving You Is Where I Belong* (1981); *Paradise in Gazankulu* (1988). Lena Horne: *Porgy & Bess* (1959).—**WR**

Belaiev (Belaieff), Mitrofan (Petrovich), renowned Russian music publisher; b. St. Petersburg, Feb. 22, 1836; d. there, Jan. 10, 1904. His father, a rich lumber dealer, gave him an excellent education. After his father's death in 1885, Belaiev decided to use part of the income from the business for a music publishing enterprise devoted exclusively to the publication of works by Russian composers (the printing was done in Leipzig); he also established concerts of Russian music in St. Petersburg (ten sym. concerts and four concerts of chamber music each season) and provided funds for prizes awarded for the best compositions. He placed Rimsky-Korsakov, Glazunov, and Liadov on the jury for these multifarious activities. The "Belaiev Editions" became a vital factor in the development of Russian national music. Although a conservative, Belaiev was generous toward representatives of the modern school, such as Scriabin; early in Scriabin's career, Belaiev provided the financial means for him to travel in Europe. The catalogue of Belaiev's publications includes the greatest names in Russian music: Mussorgsky, Rimsky-Korsakov, Borodin, Balakirev, Cui, Scriabin, Glière, Glazunov, Gretchaninov, Liadov, Liapunov, Taneyev, and Nicolas Tcherepnin, as well as many lesser and even obscure composers, such as Akimenko, Alferaky, Amani, Antipov, Artzibushev, Blumenfeld, Kalafati, Kopylov, Sokolov, Steinberg, Wihtol, Zolotarev, and others. The complete list of Belaiev's eds. is available in the *Verzeichnis der in Deutschland seit 1868 erschienenen Werke russischer Komponisten* (Leipzig, 1950). —**NS/LK/DM**

Belcher, Supply, American composer and tunebook compiler; b. Stoughton, Mass., April 9, 1751; d. Farmington, Maine, June 9, 1836. After working as a merchant in Boston, he returned to Stoughton as a farmer and tavern keeper. He also was active as a member of the local musical society. Following a sojourn in Hallowell, Maine (1785–91), he settled in Farmington, where he served as town clerk, magistrate, state representative, selectman, and schoolmaster. Belcher was an accomplished composer and acquired a reputation as the "Handel of Maine." His extant works are found in his tunebook *The Harmony of Maine* (Boston, 1794).

BIBL.: E. Owen, *The Life and Music of S. B.* (diss., Southern Baptist Theological Seminary, 1969).—**NS/LK/DM**

Belcke, Friedrich August, German trombonist; b. Lucka, Altenburg, May 27, 1795; d. there, Dec. 10,

1874. He was a member of the Gewandhaus Orch. in Leipzig (1815) and a chamber musician in Berlin (1816–58). Belcke was the first concert virtuoso on the trombone, for which he wrote concertos and études. **—NS/LK/DM**

Beliczay, Julius (Gyula) von, Hungarian composer; b. Komorn, Aug. 10, 1835; d. Budapest, April 30, 1893. He studied music in Pressburg with Joseph Kumlik, then moved to Vienna, where he had instruction in composition with Franz Krenn and Nottebohm; also took courses in engineering at the Vienna Technische Hochschule (1851–57). He remained in Vienna until 1871, and in 1888 he was appointed prof. of music theory at the National Academy in Budapest. He wrote a Sym., Ave Maria for Soprano, Chorus, and Orch., String Quartet, Serenade for Strings, and a number of piano pieces and songs.

BIBL.: A. Jenetschek, *J. v.B.* (Carlsbad, 1889); I. Sonkoly, *Beliczay Gyula* (Budapest, 1943).**—NS/LK/DM**

Belkin, Boris, Russian-born Israeli, later Belgian violinist; b. Sverdlovsk, Jan. 26, 1948. He began violin lessons at age six and made his debut at seven. After training at Moscow's Central Music School, he completed his studies with Yankelevich and Andrievsky at the Moscow Cons.; he concurrently played throughout the Soviet Union. In 1972 he won first prize in the Soviet National Competition for violinists. In 1974 he emigrated to Israel and became a naturalized citizen. In 1975 he made his North American debut as soloist with the Montreal Sym. Orch. On April 22, 1975, he made his U.S. debut as soloist in the Tchaikovsky Concerto with the N.Y. Phil. He subsequently appeared with principal North American and European orchs. In later years, he made his home in Belgium, becoming a naturalized citizen of that country. He was particularly successful as an interpreter of 19th and 20th century violin masterworks.**—NS/LK/DM**

Bell, Donald (Munro), Canadian bass-baritone; b. South Burnaby, British Columbia, June 19, 1934. He began his studies with Nancy Paisley Benn in Vancouver; after attending the Royal Coll. of Music in London on scholarship (1953–55), he pursued training with Hermann Weissenborn in Berlin (1955–57). He later studied with Judith Boroschek in Düsseldorf (1967–76) and Richard Miller in Oberlin, Ohio (from 1985). He was only 14 when he was engaged to sing with the Vancouver Sym. Orch. In 1955 he appeared at the Glyndebourne Opera and the Berlin State Opera. In 1958 he made his recital debut at London's Wigmore Hall, and then appeared at the Bayreuth Festivals (1958–61). He made his Carnegie Hall debut in N.Y. in 1959. From 1964 to 1967 he was a member of the Deutsche Oper am Rhein in Düsseldorf, where he sang such roles as Don Giovanni, Count Almaviva, Wolfram, Amfortas, Kurwenal, and Gounod's Méphistophélés. He also sang at other European opera houses, but eventually became best known as a concert artist. In addition to the standard repertoire, he devoted much time to furthering the cause of contemporary music. After teaching at Carleton Univ. and the Univ. of Ottawa in 1977, he taught at the Univ. of Calgary from 1982.**—NS/LK/DM**

Bell, Joshua, talented American violinist; b. Bloomington, Ind., Dec. 9, 1967. He first studied violin with Mimi Zweig, making his debut as a soloist with the Bloomington Sym. Orch. in 1975 at the age of seven. He subsequently studied with Gingold at the Ind. Univ. School of Music, and also took summer courses with Galamian and a masterclass with Szeryng. He won the grand prize in the first annual Seventeen Magazine/ General Motors National Concerto Competition in Rochester, N.Y., which led to his appearance as a soloist with the Philadelphia Orch. under Riccardo Muti on Sept. 24, 1982. Bell was the youngest soloist ever to appear with it at a subscription concert. In 1985 he made his Carnegie Hall debut in N.Y. as soloist with the St. Louis Sym. Orch. under Leonard Slatkin, and then toured Europe with them. In 1987 he was awarded the Avery Fisher Career Grant. In subsequent years, Bell appeared as a soloist with principal world orchs., and also gave solo recitals and played in chamber music settings. On Sept. 29, 1993, he was soloist in the premiere of Nicholas Maw's Violin Concerto with Roger Norrington and the Orch. of St. Luke's in N.Y. Bell played the solos in the soundtrack for the film *The Red Violin* (1999), the music by John Corigliano.**—NS/LK/DM**

Bell, W(illiam) H(enry), English composer; b. St. Albans, Aug. 20, 1873; d. Gordon's Bay, Cape Province, South Africa, April 13, 1946. He studied in his hometown. He won the Goss Scholarship for the Royal Coll. of Music in London (1889), where he studied organ with Stegall, violin with Burnett, piano with Izard, and composition with Corder and Stanford. He taught harmony at his alma mater (1903–12). In 1912 he was appointed director of the South African Coll. of Music in Cape Town and then dean of the music faculty at the Univ. of South Africa (1919), retiring in 1936. He was extremely critical of himself as a composer, and destroyed many of his MSS. Among his surviving works are the operas *Hippolytus* (1914) and *Isabeau* (1924). He also composed *Walt Whitman Symphony* (1899), Sym. No. 2 (1917–18), Sym. No. 3 (1918–19), *South African Symphony* (1927), Sym. in F minor (1932), *A Vision of Delight* (1906), *Arcadian Suite* (1908), the symphonic poems *Love among the Ruins* (1908), *The Shepherd* (1908), *La Fée des sources* (1912), and *Veldt Loneliness* (1921), Viola Concerto, and Violin Sonata.

BIBL.: H. du Plessis, ed., *Letters from W.H. B.* (Cape Town and Johannesburg, 1973).**—NS/LK/DM**

Bella, Johann Leopold (Ján Levoslav), Slovak composer; b. Lipto-Szentmiklós, Upper Hungary, Sept. 4, 1843; d. Bratislava, May 25, 1936. He studied theology in Banska Bystrica, then went to Vienna, where he studied composition with Sechter (1863–65). He was ordained a priest in 1866 and served as church music director at Kremnica (1869). In 1873 he received a scholarship to study in Germany and in Prague. In 1881 he relinquished his priesthood, and subsequently was organist at the Protestant church in Hermannstadt, Transylvania, and music director of the municipality there. He went to Vienna in 1921, and in 1928 he returned to Bratislava. He wrote a great quantity of church music in the strict style. He also composed an opera, *Wieland derSchmied* (Bratislava, April 28, 1926), a symphonic poem, *Schicksal und Ideal* (Prague, March 19, 1876), some chamber music, songs, and piano pieces.

BIBL.: D. Orel, *J.L. B.* (Bratislava, 1924); (Prague, 1937); E. Zavárský, *Ján Levoslav B.: Život a dielo* (Bratislava, 1955). —**NS/LK/DM**

Bellaigue, Camille, French music critic; b. Paris, May 24, 1858; d. there, Oct. 4, 1930. Originally a law student, he took music courses at the Paris Cons. with Paḷadilhe and Marmontel. From 1885 was music critic for *La Revue des Deux Mondes*; also wrote for *Le Temps*. He bitterly opposed modern music and was particularly violent in his denunciation of Debussy, his classmate at the Paris Cons. His selected essays are publ. under the following titles: *L'Année musicale* (five vols., 1886–91), *L'Année musicale et dramatique* (1893), *Psychologie musicale* (1894), *Portraits et silhouettes de musiciens* (1896; Eng. tr., 1897; Ger. tr., 1903), *Études musicales et nouvelles silhouettes de musiciens* (1898; Eng. tr., 1899), *Impressions musicales et littéraires* (1900), *Études musicales* (two vols.; 1903, 1907), *Mozart: Biographie critique* (1906), *Mendelssohn* (1907), *Les Époques de la musique* (two vols., 1909), *Gounod* (1910), *Verdi* (1911), *Paroles et musique* (1925), etc.

BIBL.: L. Gillel, *C. B.* (Paris, 1931).—**NS/LK/DM**

Bellasio, Paolo, Italian organist and composer; b. Verona, May 20, 1554; d. Rome, July 10, 1594. He was active as an organist in Rome beginning in 1584. He later traveled to Verona, returning to Rome in 1592. He publ. five books of madrigals (1578) and *Villanelle alla Romana* (1595).—**NS/LK/DM**

Bellère (or **Bellerus,** properly **Beellaerts**), **Jean,** music publisher; b. Liège, 1526; d. Antwerp, Oct. 15, 1595. He was a partner of Pierre Phalèse, *fils*. His son Balthasar Bellère transferred the business to Douai, and printed much music up to 1625. His catalogue of compositions, publ. from 1603 to 1605, was found by Coussemaker in the Douai library.

BIBL.: A. Goovaerts, *De muziekdrukkers Phalesius en Bellerus te Leuven* (Antwerp, 1882).—**NS/LK/DM**

Bellermann, Johann Friedrich, German music scholar, father of **(Johann Gottfried) Heinrich Bellermann;** b. Erfurt, March 8, 1795; d. Berlin, Feb. 5, 1874. He dedicated himself mainly to the study of ancient Greek music, his chief work being *Die Tonleitern und Musiknoten der Griechen,* explanatory of the Greek system of notation (Berlin, 1847). He further wrote *Die alten Liederbücher der Portugiesen* (Berlin, 1840) and *Die Hymnen des Dionysios und Mesomedes* (Berlin, 1840), and ed. essays by authors of classical antiquity: *Anonymi scriptio de musica, Bacchii senioris introductio artis musicae* (Berlin, 1841); also ed. *Fragmentum graecae scriptionis de musica* (Berlin, 1840).—**NS/LK/DM**

Bellermann, (Johann Gottfried) Heinrich, German music teacher and theorist, son of **Johann Friedrich Bellermann;** b. Berlin, March 10, 1832; d.

Potsdam, April 10, 1903. He studied with Eduard Grell. From 1853 he taught singing at Graues Kloster and in 1861 he was appointed Royal Musikdirektor; in 1866 succeeded Marx as prof. of music at Berlin Univ. His book Die Mensuralnoten und Taktzeichen des 15. und 16. Jahrhunderts (Berlin, 1858; 4th enl. ed., Berlin, 1963) gives an excellent exposition of the theory of mensural music; his treatise Der Kontrapunkt (1862; 4th ed., 1901) revives the theories of J.J. Fux's Gradus ad Parnassum. Bellermann attempted to justify his adherence to Fux in a pamphlet, *Die Grösse der musikalischen Intervalle als Grundlage der Harmonie* (Berlin, 1873). He also contributed valuable articles to the *Allgemeine Musikalische Zeitung* (1868–74) and publ. a biography of Eduard Grell (1899).

BIBL.: O. Schneider, *H. B., Gedächtnisrede* (Berlin, 1903). —**NS/LK/DM**

Belletti, Giovanni Battista, famous Italian baritone; b. Sarzana, Feb. 17, 1813; d. there, Dec. 27, 1890. He made his operatic debut in 1837 in Stockholm as Figaro in Rossini's *Il Barbiere di Siviglia*. He made many appearances there with Jenny Lind, and later toured with her in the U.S. He had his greatest successes in dramatic roles in Romantic operas.—**NS/LK/DM**

Bellezza, Vincenzo, Italian conductor; b. Bitonto, Bari, Feb. 17, 1888; d. Rome, Feb. 8, 1964. He studied piano with Alessandro Longo, composition with Nicola d'Arienzo, and conducting with Giuseppe Martucci at the Naples Cons. He made his conducting debut at the Teatro San Carlo in Naples in 1908, then conducted throughout Italy; also had guest engagements at Covent Garden, London (1926–30; 1935–36) and served as guest conductor at the Metropolitan Opera in N.Y. (1926–35). After his return to Italy, he was on the staff of the Rome Opera.—**NS/LK/DM**

Bell'Haver, Vincenzo, Italian organist and composer; b. Venice, c. 1530; d. there, probably in Sept. 1587. He was organist of the church of the Crosieri in Padua by 1567, then organist at the Scuola Grande di S. Rocco in Venice (1568–84), cathedral organist in Padua (1584–85), and first organist at San Marco in Venice (from 1586). He publ. books of madrigals (1567–75), but only book II is extant; single works are also found in contemporary collections.—**NS/LK/DM**

Belli, Domenico, Italian composer; b. c. 1590; d. (buried) May 5, 1627. He lived most of his life in Florence. On Sept. 19, 1619, he and his wife entered the service of the Medici court. As a composer, he was one of the earliest representatives of the new monodic style; Caccini praised his music. However, the claim that his short opera, *Il pianto d'Orfeo,* or *Orfeo Dolente* (Florence, 1616; reprinted Brussels, 1927, in Tirabassi's ed.), was the earliest opera ever written is questionable. Among his instrumental works is *Arie per sonarsi con il chitarrone* (Venice, 1616).—**NS/LK/DM**

Belli, Girolamo, Italian singer and composer; b. Argenta, near Ferrara, 1552; d. probably there, c. 1620.

He was a pupil of Luzzaschi. After serving as a singer at the Gonzaga court in Mantua, he went to Rome. Among his extant works are three books of madrigals for six Voices (1583, 1584, 1590), two books of madrigals for five Voices (1586, 1617), a book of canzonets for four Voices (1596), *Sacrae cantiones* for six Voices (1585), eight Voices (1589), and twn Voices (1594), and two Magnificats for five Voices (1610).—NS/LK/DM

Belli, Giulio, Italian composer; b. Longiano, near Forlì, c. 1560; d. probably in Imola, c. 1621. He was a pupil of Cimello in Naples. In 1579 he entered the Franciscan monastery in Longiano. After serving as maestro di cappella at Imola Cathedral (1582–90) and at S. Maria in Carpi (1590–91), he was named praefectus musices at S. Francesco in Bologna in 1591. About 1594 he went to Venice and became maestro di cappella at the church of the Cà Grande, and then held that post at Montagnana Cathedral in 1596–97, and subsequently at the court of Duke Alfonso II d'Este and at the Accademia della Morte in Ferrara; he also was maestro at Osimo Cathedral in 1599. In 1600 he became maestro di cappella at the cathedral and archiepiscopal seminary in Ravenna, and then at Forlì Cathedral in 1603. In 1606 he resumed his duties at the Cà Grande but then was maestro di cappella at S. Antonio in Padua (1606–08), at S. Francesco in Assisi (1610), again at Imola Cathedral (1611–13), and once more at the Cà Grande (1615). In 1621 he returned to Imola. Among his works, all publ. in Venice, were two books of canzonets for four Voices (1584, 3rd ed., 1595; 1593); books of madrigals for five to six Voices (1589), six Voices (1590), and five to six Voices (1592–93); masses for five Voices (1586), eight Voices (1595; 2nd ed., 1607, with basso continuo), four Voices (1599; 3rd ed., 1615, with basso continuo), and for four to six and eight Voices and Basso Continuo (organ) (1608); Psalms and vespers for five Voices (1592), eight Voices (1596; 3rd ed., 1615, with basso continuo), and for six Voices (1603; 3rd ed., 1607, with basso continuo); *Sacrarum cantionum* for four to six, eight, and 12 Voices (1600); motets and falsi bordoni for eight Voices (1605) and six Voices and Basso Continuo (organ) (1607); falsi bordoni for four Voices and Basso Continuo (organ) (1607); and *Concerti ecclesiastici* for two to three Voices (1613).

BIBL.: A. Brigidi, *Cenni sulla vita e sulle opere di G. B. Longianese* (Modena, 1865).—NS/LK/DM

Bellincioni, Gemma (Cesira Matilda), noted Italian soprano; b. Monza, Aug. 18, 1864; d. Naples, April 23, 1950. She studied with her father, the comic bass Cesare Bellincioni, and her mother, the contralto Carlotta Soroldoni. At age 15, she made her operatic debut in dell'Orefice's *Il segreto della duchessa* at the Teatro della Società Felarmonica in Naples. After further studies with Luigia Ponti and Giovanni Corsi, she sang in Spain and Portugal (1882), and then in Rome (1885). In 1886 she made her first appearance at Milan's La Scala as Violetta, and that same year toured South America, where she became intimate with the tenor Roberto Stagno. In subsequent years, they toured together in opera and concert, although she never appeared in the U.S. On May 17, 1890, she created the role of Santuzza opposite Stagno's Turiddu at the Teatro Costanzi in Rome. On Nov. 17, 1898, she created the role of Fedora at Milan's Teatro Lirico. With Strauss conducting, she was the first to sing Salome in Italy in Turin in 1900, a role she subsequently sang more than 100 times. In 1911 she made her farewell operatic appearance as Salome in Paris, although she came out of retirement to sing opera in the Netherlands in 1924. She taught in Berlin (1911–15), Vienna (1931–32), and at the Naples Cons. (from 1932). Her autobiography was publ. as *Io ed il palcoscenico* (Milan, 1920).

BIBL.: B. Stagno-Bellincioni, *Roberto Stagno e G. B., intimi* (Florence, 1943).—NS/LK/DM

Bellini, Vincenzo, famous Italian composer, a master of bel canto opera; b. Catania, Sicily, Nov. 3, 1801; d. Puteaux, near Paris, Sept. 23, 1835. He was a scion of a musical family; his grandfather was maestro di cappella to the Benedictines in Catania, and organist of the Sacro Collegio di Maria in Misterbianco; his father also served as maestro di cappella. Bellini received his first musical instruction from his father and grandfather, and soon revealed a fine gift of melody. The Duke and Duchess of San Martino e Montalbo took interest in him and in 1819 arranged to have him enter the Real Collegio di Musica di San Sebastiano in Naples, where he studied harmony and accompaniment with Giovanni Furno and counterpoint with Giacomo Tritto; Carlo Conti supervised him as a maestrino and tutor. He further studied the vocal arts with Girolamo Crescentini and composition with Nicola Zingarelli. Under their guidance, he made a detailed study of the works of Pergolesi, Jommelli, Paisiello, and Cimarosa, as well as those of the German classics. While still in school, he wrote several sinfonias, two masses, and the cantata *Ismene* (1824). His first opera, *Adelson e Salvini*, was given at the Collegio in 1825; it was followed by the premiere at the Teatro San Carlo in Naples of his second opera, *Bianca e Gernando* (May 30, 1826), a score later rev. as *Bianca e Fernando* (May 30, 1828). In 1827 Bellini went to Milan, where he was commissioned by the impresario Barbaja to write an opera seria for the famous Teatro alla Scala; it was *Il Pirata*, which obtained fine success at its premiere on Oct. 27, 1827; it was also given in Vienna in 1828. It was followed by another opera, *La Straniera*, which was first given at La Scala on Feb. 14, 1829. It was followed by his *Zaira* (Parma, May 16, 1829). He was then commissioned to write a new opera for the Teatro La Fenice in Venice, on a Shakespearean libretto; it was *I Capuleti ed i Montecchi*; first performed on March 11, 1830, it had a decisive success. Even more successful was his next opera, *La Sonnambula*, which was premiered in Milan on March 6, 1831, with the celebrated prima donna Giuditta Pasta as Amina. Pasta also appeared in the title role of Bellini's most famous opera, *Norma*, first given at La Scala on Dec. 26, 1831, which at its repeated productions established Bellini's reputation as a young master of the Italian operatic bel canto. His following opera, *Beatrice di Tenda* (Venice, March 16, 1833), failed to sustain his series of successes. He then had an opportunity to go to London and Paris, and it was in Paris that he brought out his last opera, *I Puritani* (Jan. 24, 1835), which fully justified the expectations of his admirers. Next to *Norma*, it proved to be one of the greatest masterpieces of Italian operatic art; its Paris production featured a superb cast, which included Grisi, Rubini, Tamburini, and Lablache. Bellini was on his way to fame and universal artistic recognition when he was stricken with a fatal affliction of amebiasis, and died six weeks before his 34th birthday. His remains were reverently removed to his native Catania in 1876.

Bellini's music represents the Italian operatic school at its most glorious melodiousness, truly reflected by the term "bel canto." In his writing, the words, the rhythm, the melody, the harmony, and the instrumental accompaniment unite in mutual perfection. The lyric flow and dramatic expressiveness of his music provide a natural medium for singers in the Italian language, with the result that his greatest masterpieces, *La Sonnambula* and *Norma*, remain in the active repertoire of opera houses of the entire world, repeatedly performed by touring Italian opera companies and by native forces everywhere.

WORKS: DRAMATIC: *Adelson e Salvini*, dramma semiserio (1824–25; Real Collegio di Musica di San Sebastiano, Naples, between Feb. 10 and 15, 1825; 2nd version, 1826; not perf.); *Bianca e Gernando*, melodramma, (1825–26; Teatro San Carlo, Naples, May 30, 1826; rev. version as Bianca e Fernando, Teatro Carlo Felice, Genoa, April 7, 1828); *Il Pirata*, opera seria (Teatro alla Scala, Milan, Oct. 27, 1827); *La Straniera*, opera seria (1828–29; Teatro alla Scala, Milan, Feb. 14, 1829); *Zaira*, opera seria (Teatro Ducale, Parma, May 16, 1829); *I Capuleti ed i Montecchi*, tragedia lirica (Teatro La Fenice, Venice, March 11, 1830); *La Sonnambula*, melodramma (Teatro Carcano, Milan, March 6, 1831); *Norma*, opera seria(Teatro alla Scala, Milan, Dec. 26, 1831); *Beatrice di Tenda*, opera seria (Teatro La Fenice, Venice, March 16, 1833); *I Puritani*, melodramma serio (1834–35; first perf. as I Puritani e i cavalieri at the Théâtre-Italien, Paris, Jan. 24, 1835).

BIBL.: F. Gerardi, *Biografia di V. B.* (Rome, 1835); L. Scuderi, *Biografia di V. B.* (Catania, 1840); F. Cicconetti, *Vita di V. B.* (Prato, 1859); A. Pougin, *B.: Sa vie, ses oeuvres* (Paris, 1868); A. Sciuto, *V. B.: Profilo biografico* (Cantania, 1876); A. Tari, *V. B.: Reminiscenze* (Naples, 1876); F. Florimo, *B.: Memorie e lettere* (Florence, 1882); M. Scherillo, *V. B.: Note aneddotiche e critiche* (Ancona, 1882); G. Salvioli, *Lettere inedite di B.* (Milan, 1884); M. Scherillo, *B.ana: Nuove note* (Milan, 1885); F. Florimo and M. Scherillo, eds., *Album—B.* (Naples, 1886); F. Florimo, ed., *Album B.—Premio B.* (Naples, 1887); A. Amore, *V. B.: Arte—Studi e ricerche* (Catania, 1892); idem, *V. B.: Vita—Studi e ricerche* (Catania, 1894); A. Cametti, *B. a Roma* (Rome, 1900); P. Voss, *V. B.* (Leipzig, 1901); A. Amore, *B.ana (Errori e smentite)* (Catania, 1902); C. Reina, *V. B. (1801–35)* (Catania, 1902; 2nd ed. as *Il cigno catanese: B.—La vita e le opere*, Catania, 1935); W. Lloyd, *V. B.: A Memoir* (London, 1908); I. Pizzetti, *La musica di V. B.* (Milan, 1916); V. Ricci, *V. B.: Impressioni e ricordi, con documenti inediti* (Catania, 1932); L. Cambi, *B.* (Milan, 1934); N. Scaglione, *V. B. a Messina* (Messina, 1934); B. Condorelli, *Il Museo Belliniano: Catalogo storico-iconografico* (Catania, 1935); G. de Angelis, *V. B.: La vita, l'uomo, l'artista* (Brescia, 1935); A. Della Corte and G. Pannain, *V. B.: Il Carattere morale, i caratteri artistici* (Turin, 1935); G. Mezzatesta, *V. B. nella vita e nelle opere* (Palermo, 1935); F. Pastura, ed., *Le lettere di B. (1819–35)* (Catania, 1935); G. Policastro, *V. B. (1801–19)* (Catania, 1935); O. Tiby, *V. B.* (Rome, 1935); I. Pizzetti, ed., *V. B.: L'Uomo, le sue opere, la sua fama* (Milan, 1936); O. Tiby, *V. B.* (Turin, 1938); L. Cambi, ed., *V. B.: Epistolario* (Milan, 1943);

P. Cavazzuti, *B. a Londra* (Florence, 1945); F. Pastura, *B. secondo la storia* (Parma, 1959); idem, *V. B.* (Catania, 1959); L. Orrey, *B.* (London and N.Y., 1969); H. Weinstock, *V. B.: His Life and His Operas* (N.Y.,1971); M. Adamo, *V. B.* (Turin, 1981); G. Tintori, *B.* (Milan, 1983); H.-K. Metzger and R. Riehn, eds., *V. B.* (1985); D. Danzuso, F. Gallo, and R. Monti, *Omaggio a B.* (Milan, 1986); S. Maguire, *V. B. and the Aesthetics of Early Nineteenth-Century Italian Opera* (N.Y. and London, 1989); E. Failla, *V. B.: Critica storia tradizione* (Catania, 1991); C. Osborne, *The Bel Canto Operas of Rossini, Donizetti, and B.* (Portland, Ore., 1994); D. Kimbell, *V. B.: Norma* (Cambridge, 1998).—NS/LK/DM

Bellinzani, Paolo Benedetto, Italian composer; b. probably in Mantua, c. 1690; d. Recanati, Feb. 25, 1757. He became maestro di cappella at the Udine Cathedral in 1715. He received the benefice of S. Ermacora, and subsequently was made a censor in Ferrara. He went to Pergola in 1718. In 1721 he resigned from his position in Udine, and in 1724 became maestro di cappella at the Pesaro Cathedral. He was subsequently maestro di cappella at the Urbino Cathedral (1730–34) and the Ferrara Cathedral (1734–35). From 1737 until his death he was maestro di cappella at the Recanati Cathedral. He composed both sacred and secular vocal works of excellent quality, and also wrote instrumental sonatas.—NS/LK/DM

Belloc-Giorgi, Teresa (née **Maria Teresa Ottavia Faustina Trombetta**), Italian mezzo-soprano of French descent; b. San Benigno Cavanese, near Turin, July 2, 1784; d. San Giorgio Cavanese, May 13, 1855. She made her debut in Turin in 1801, then sang in Paris in 1803, and at La Scala, Milan, from 1804 to 1824. She then toured through Italy, and also appeared in Paris and London. She retired in 1828. Her repertoire comprised roles in 80 operas, Rossini's being her favorites.

BIBL.: C. Boggio, *La cantante T. B.* (Milan, 1895). —NS/LK/DM

Bělohlávek, Jiří, Czech conductor; b. Prague, Feb. 24, 1946. He studied piano with his father, and also took cello lessons at the Prague Cons. and attended Celibidache's master classes in conducting. In 1970 he won first prize in the Czech national competition for young conductors. From 1970 to 1972 he was asst. conductor of the Czech Phil. in Prague. He then was conductor of the Brno State Phil. (1972–77), with which he toured the U.S. In 1977 he was appointed chief conductor of the Prague Sym. Orch., a position he held until 1985. He appeared widely in Europe and abroad as a guest conductor; frequently was conductor with the Czech Phil., serving as its chief conductor from 1990 to 1992. From 1995 he was conductor of the newly founded Prague Chamber Phil.—NS/LK/DM

Bembo, Antonia, Italian-born French composer; b. presumably in Venice, c. 1670; d. place and date unknown. Between 1690 and 1695 she went to Paris. She sang for Louis XIV, and received a pension from him, which enabled her to devote herself to composition. Extant works (in the Paris Bibliothèque Nationale) are

Produzioni armoniche, collection of 40 pieces (motets, duets, soli for soprano, etc., with figured bass or instrumental accompaniment, set to sacred Latin, French, and Italian texts), *Te Deum* for three Voices and String Orch., *Divertimento* for five-voiced Chorus with String Orch., *Te Deum,* with Large Orch., *Exaudiat* for three Voices, two "symphonie" parts, and Basso Continuo, an opera, *L'Ercole Amante* (1707), and *Les Sept Psaumes de David* for various vocal combinations with instrumental accompaniment.—**NS/LK/DM**

Benary, Barbara, American performer, composer, and ethnomusicologist; b. Bay Shore, N.Y., April 4, 1946. She studied music and theater at Sarah Lawrence Coll. (B.A., 1968) and world music at Wesleyan Univ. (M.A., 1971; Ph.D. 1973). She then taught at Rutgers Univ. (1973–80), and in various private and public elementary schools in N.Y. (1984–94). In 1976 she co-founded and served as artistic director of Gamelan Son of Lion, a new music repertory ensemble for which she composed numerous works. Among her awards are grants from Meet the Composer (from 1979), an NEA Consortium Commissioning grant (1981–82), and an NEA Opera-Music Theater grant (1993); in 1997 she received a commission from the Jerome Foundation. Benary has composed works in essentially two genres: ensemble chamber music and theater scores. The styles are various, but have included process and minimalism in her chamber works and the use of ethnic forms and instruments in both her theater and chamber scores. Her stage works have been composed for and performed by such diverse ensembles as the Hudson Vagabond Puppets, Lenox Arts, N.Y. Shakespeare Festival, Odyssey Theatre, Laurel Pawel Dance Co., and Bali-Java Dance Theatre. Currently, Benary manages a N.Y. music booking agency, Lisa Goodman Ensembles.

WORKS: DRAMATIC: O p e r a : *The Only Jealousy of Emer,* after Yeats (1966); *Three Sisters Who Are Not Sisters,* after Gertrude Stein (1970); *Karna: A Shadow Puppet Opera* (1994). **M u s i c   T h e a t e r :** *Javanese Purimspiel* (1997–2001). **T h e a t e r   a n d   D a n c e :** *Interior Castle* (1973); *The Moon's On Fire* (1976); *Sanguine* (1976); *St. George and the Dragon* (1977); *Night Thunks* (1980); *A New Pantheon,* dance drama (1981); *Engineering* (1981); *Mad Damn* (1981); *The Silly Jellyfish* (1981); *The Tempest,* after Shakespeare (1981); *Night Shadow,* dance drama (1982); *Blind,* dance drama (1985); *Children's Ramayana* (1987); *Mythically Speaking,* after Greek Myths (1987); *Hopi Myths* (1989); *Loki and the Hammer: A Norwegian Myth* (1990); *The Picture of Dorian Gray* (1990); *The Island of Dr. Moreau* (1991). **GAMELAN COLLECTION EDS:** *Systems,* a collection of 19 pieces, improvisatory structures for Mixed Ensemble (1973–94) and *Gamelan Works,* a 4–vol. anthology of new work for Javanese Gamelan Percussion Ensemble (1974–94). **O T H E R :** *In Time Enough,* chant (1978); *Solkattu, Singing Braid,* and *Moon Cat Chant* (1980); *Hot-Rolled Steel* (1985); *Slendro Steel* (1992); *Gamelan Round Robin* (1993); *Memorial* (1996); *Angklung Rag (A Rag for Han)* (1996); *Lelambatan Meows* (1997). **W e s t - e r n   I n s t r u m e n t s :** *Barang I, II,* and *IV,* solos and duos for Wind Instruments (1975); *Exlasega* for Concert Band (1980); *Parabola* for Chamber Ensemble (1981); *Four by Four* for Marimba Quartet (1986); *Sun on Snow* for Mixed Ensemble (1985); *Downtown Steel* for Percussion and Winds (1993); *Tintinnalogia,* trio for Violin, Piano, and Percussion (1995); *Aural Shoehorning*

for Woodwind, Percussion, and Gamelan (1997). **VOCAL:** *Dhruva Khanda Alankara* for Chorus (1971–73); *Falling Angels,* vocal sextet (1971–73); *Moot Cat Chant* for Chorus (1971–73); *Srutibox Mass* for Chorus (1974).—**LK/DM**

Benatzky, Ralph (actually, **Rudolf Josef František**), Czech composer; b. Mährisch-Budwitz, June 5, 1884; d. Zürich, Oct. 16, 1957. He studied in Vienna, in Prague with Veit and Klinger, and in Munich with Mottl; he also took a Ph.D. in philology. After conducting at the Kleines Theater in Munich (1910–11), he went to Vienna as music director at the Kabarett Rideamus. He first gained notice as a composer for the theater with his operetta *Der lachende Dreibund* (Berlin, Oct. 31, 1913). His first notable success came with the operetta *Liebe im Schnee* (Vienna, Dec. 2, 1916), which was followed by the successful premieres of *Yuschi tanzt* (Vienna, April 3, 1920), *Apachen* (Vienna, Dec. 20, 1920), *Pipsi* (Vienna, Dec. 30, 1921), *Ein Märchen aus Florenz* (Vienna, Sept. 14, 1923), and *Adieu Mimi* (Vienna, June 9, 1926). From 1924 he also was active at the Grosses Schauspielhaus in Berlin, where he provided music for various productions, including the Johann Strauss pasticcio *Casanova* (Sept. 1, 1928) and *Die drei Musketiere* (Sept. 28, 1929). It was at that theater that he brought out his celebrated operetta *Im weissen Rössl* (Nov. 8, 1930), which was also made into a film in 1935. Among his other theater scores were *Cocktail* (Berlin, Dec. 15, 1930), *Zirkus Aimée* (Basel, March 5, 1932), *Bezauberndes Fräulein* (Vienna, May 24, 1933), *Deux sous de fleurs* (Paris, Oct. 6, 1933), *Das kleine Café* (Vienna, April 20, 1934), *Axel an der Himmelstur* (Vienna, Sept. 1, 1936), *Pairserinnin* (Vienna, May 7, 1937; rev. ver., Lucerne, Dec. 11, 1964), *Majestät-privat* (Vienna, Dec. 18, 1937), and *Der Silberhof* (Mainz, Nov. 4, 1941). During World War II, Benatzky lived in the U.S. After the War, he returned to Europe and finally settled in Switzerland.

BIBL.: F. Hennenberg, *Es muss was Wunderbares sein—: R. B.: Zwischen "Weissem Rössl" und Hollywood* (Vienna, 1996). —**NS/LK/DM**

Benda, Franz (actually, **František**), famous Bohemian violinist and important composer, brother of **Georg Anton (Jíři Antonín)** and father of Friedrich (Wilhelm Heinrich) and Karl Hermann Heinrich Benda; b. Alt-Benatek, Bohemia (baptized), Nov. 22, 1709; d. Neuendorf, near Potsdam, March 7, 1786. In 1718 he became a chorister at the Church of St. Nicolas in Prague. In 1720 he ran away to Dresden, where he sang at the Hofkapelle. In 1723 he returned to Prague. It was not until much later that he began a serious study of music, with Löbel, Koniček, and J.S. Graun at Ruppin. In 1733 he joined the orch. of the Crown Prince (afterward Friedrich II) as first violinist; in 1771 he was named Konzertmeister. During his long years of service for Friedrich II, he accompanied him at his flute concerts. Among his works are 17 violin concertos, 17 syms., numerous solo sonatas, and various pieces of chamber music. His autobiography was publ. in the *Neue Berliner Musikzeitung* in 1856. D. Lee prepared an annotated Eng. tr. as *A Musician at Court: An Autobiography of Franz Benda* (Warren, Mich., 1998).

BIBL.: F. Berten, *F. B.* (Essen, 1928); F. Lorenz, *Die Musiker-familie Benda. Vol. I. F. B. und seine Nachkommen* (Berlin, 1967); D. Lee, *F. B.: A Thematic Catalog of His Works* (N.Y., 1984). —**NS/LK/DM**

Benda, Georg Anton (actually, **Jiří Antonín**), important Bohemian composer, brother of **Franz (František)** and father of Friedrich Ludwig Benda; b. Alt-Benatek (baptized), June 30, 1722; d. Köstritz, Nov. 6, 1795. He studied at the Jesuit college in Jicin (1739–42), and then was a chamber musician in Berlin (1742–49). In 1750 he was appointed Kapellmeister to Duke Friedrich III of Saxe-Gotha. In 1765 he received a ducal stipend to go to Italy for half a year of study; he then resumed his activities at the court of Duke Friedrich III, becoming Kapellmeister again in 1770. He was in hamburg and Vienna (1778–79), and then resigned his post; eventually he went to Köstritz. His works were distinguished for their dramatic use of rapidly alternating moods ("*Affekte*"), which became a characteristic trait of the North German school of composition and exercised considerable influence on the development of opera and ballad forms in Germany; his effective use of melodrama (spoken recitative accompanied by orch.) was an important innovation.

WORKS: DRAMATIC: O p e r a : *Ariadneauf Naxos* (Gotha, Jan. 27, 1775); *Medea* (Leipzig, May 1, 1775); *Philon und Theone*, also known as *Almansor und Nadine* (Gotha, Sept. 20, 1779). **S i n g s p i e l s :** *Der Dorfjahrmarkt* (1775); *Romeo und Julia* (1776); *Der Holzhauer* (1778). **OTHER:** Cantatas; piano concertos; syms.; sonatas; sacred music.

BIBL.: R. Hodermann, *G.A. B.* (Coburg, 1895); F. Brückner, *G.A. B.* (Rostock, 1904); V. Helfert, *G. B. und J.J. Rousseau* (Munich, 1908); Z. Pilková, *Dramaticka tvorba Jiřiho Bendy* (Prague, 1960); F. Lorenz, *Die Musikerfamilie B.* [Vol.] *II. G.A. B.* (Berlin, 1971).—**NS/LK/DM**

Benda, Hans von, German conductor; b. Strasbourg, Nov. 22, 1888; d. Berlin, Aug. 13, 1972. He was a descendant of the Benda family of Bohemia. He studied at the Stern Cons. in Berlin; also at the Univs. of Berlin and Munich. He was director of music of the Berlin Radio (1926–33); then Intendant of the Berlin Phil. (1934–39); in 1939 he organized the Berlin Chamber Orch., with which he toured throughout Europe, South America, and the Far East. From 1954 to 1958 he served as director of music of Radio Free Berlin.—**NS/LK/DM**

Bendel, Franz, German pianist, teacher, and composer; b. Schönlinde, Bohemia, March 23, 1833; d. Berlin, July 3, 1874. He studied with Proksch in Prague and Liszt in Weimar. From 1862 he taught at Kullak's Academy in Berlin. He wrote syms., a Piano Concerto, masses, chamber music, piano pieces, and songs. —**NS/LK/DM**

Bendeler, Johann Philipp, German organ theorist; b. Riethnordhausen, near Erfurt (baptized), Nov. 20, 1654; d. Quedlinburg, Dec. 26, 1709. He went to Quedlinburg in 1681 as an instructor at the Gymnasium there, and in 1687 added the duties of cantor, which post he held for the rest of his life. As an organ theorist he belongs, with Werckmeister, to the middle German group whose ideas were realized in the organs of Arp Schnitger. His most important work is *Organopoeia* (c. 1690; reprinted in 1739 as *Orgelbaukunst*; facsimile ed., Amsterdam, 1972), a treatise on organ building. Other works are *Collegium Musicum de Compositione* (mentioned in Mattheson's *Ehrenpforte*), *Melopeia practica* (1686), and *Aerarium melopoeticum* (1688). In addition, he wrote two books on mathematics.

BIBL.: C. Mahrenholz, *Die Berechnung der Orgelpfeifenmensuren* (Kassel, 1938).—**NS/LK/DM**

Bendinelli, Agostino, Italian composer and teacher; b. Lucca, April 26, 1635; d. there, c. 1703. He was active as canon of St. John Lateran in Rome, and also served as superintendent of the monastery of S. Frediano in Lucca and as prior of S. Agostino in Piacenza and S. Leonardo in Lucca. His most famous pupil was G.M. Bononcini. His only extant publication is his *Psalmi vespertini ternis, quaternis, quinisque vocibus ad organum concinendi una cum litanis BVM, op. 1* (Bologna, 1671).—**NS/LK/DM**

Bendinelli, Cesare, Italian trumpeter; d. probably in Munich, 1617. He became a trumpeter in Vienna in 1567. He was called to Munich in 1580 as chief trumpeter at the court, a post he held until his death. He prepared the earliest known trumpet method, *Tutta l'arte della trombetta* (publ. in Documenta Musicologica, second series, V, 1975; Eng. tr., 1976).—**NS/LK/DM**

Bendix, Otto, Danish pianist, teacher, and composer, brother of **Victor Emanuel Bendix;** b. Copenhagen, July 26, 1845; d. San Francisco, March 1, 1904. He was a pupil of Niels Gade, then studied with Kullak in Berlin and Liszt at Weimar. He taught piano at the Copenhagen Cons., and was oboist in a theater orch. He went to the U.S. in 1880, settling in Boston as a piano teacher at the New England Cons. In 1895 moved to San Francisco, where he established his own music school; gave successful concerts in Europe and America. Bendix publ. some piano pieces.—**NS/LK/DM**

Bendix, Victor Emanuel, Danish pianist and conductor, brother of **Otto Bendix;** b. Copenhagen, May 17, 1851; d. there, Jan. 5, 1926. He studied at the Copenhagen Cons. with Gade and J.P.E. Hartmann, and also took piano lessons with Liszt in Weimar. Returning to Copenhagen, he was appointed to the piano faculty of the Royal Academy of Music. In 1897 he organized the Copenhagen Phil. Concerts and conducted them for many years. He wrote four syms. in a Romantic vein, a Piano Concerto, and much choral music.—**NS/LK/DM**

Bendl, Karl (Karel), Czech composer and conductor; b. Prague, April 16, 1838; d. there, Sept. 20, 1897. He studied at the Prague Organ School withBlažek, Pietsch, and Zvonar. In 1864–65 he was active as a conductor in Brussels, Amsterdam, and Paris. Returning to Prague in 1865, he conducted the male choral society Hlahol for 12 years; also was briefly deputy conductor at the Provisional Theater in Prague. He subsequently served as an organist at the church of St. Nicholas in Prague. He was an ardent supporter of Dvořák and Smetana in the cause of creating a national school of Czech music.

WORKS: DRAMATIC: Opera: *Lejla* (1867; Prague, Jan. 4, 1868); *Břetislav* (1869; Prague, Sept. 18, 1870); *Starý ženich* (1871–74); *Die Wunderblume* (1876; Czech Radio, Prague, Aug. 30, 1940, in Czech); *Indická princezna*, operetta (1876–77; Prague, Aug. 26, 1877); *Černohorci* (1881; Prague, Oct. 11, 1881); *Karel Škréta* (1883; Prague, Dec. 11, 1883); *Gina* (1884; not perf.); *Dítě Tabora* (1886–88; Prague, March 13, 1892); *Máti Míla* (1893–95; Prague, June 25, 1895); *Švanda dudák* (1895–96; Prague, April 29, 1907). **Ballet:** *Česká svatba* (1894; Prague, Feb. 13, 1895). **OTHER:** 2 masses; 2 cantatas; about 450 songs and choruses.

BIBL.: E. Krasnohorska, *Z mládí Karla Bendla* (Prague, 1897; 2nd ed. as *Z mého mládí*, 1920); J. Polák, *Karel B.* (Prague, 1938). —NS/LK/DM

Bendler, Salomon,

famous German bass, son of **Johann Philipp Bendeler;** b. Quedlinburg, 1683; d. Braunschweig, 1724. He studied with his father, then sang throughout Germany and Italy, and later made appearances in London (1712–17). Upon his return to Germany, he became a chamber singer at the court in Braunschweig, where he remained until his death. —NS/LK/DM

Ben-Dor, Gisèle (née Buka),

Uruguayan conductor of Polish descent; b. Montevideo, April 26, 1955. Her parents emigrated to Uruguay after World War II. She commenced piano lessons at age 4 with Gloria Rodriguez and Santiago Baranda Reyes at the J.S. Bach Cons. She later received instruction in harmony and counterpoint from Yolanda Rizzardini. She was only 12 when she began conducting, and at 14 she was made music director of her school's choral and instrumental ensembles. In 1973 she accompanied her family to Israel, where she studied piano with Enrique Barenboim and composition with Arthur Gelbrun. She then studied orchestral conducting with S. Ronley Riklis and choral conducting with Avner Itai. She also trained with Mendi Rodan in Jerusalem. Following further studies with Franco Ferrara at the Accademia Musicale Chigiana in Siena (1980), she completed her education at the Yale School of Music (M.A., 1982). In 1982 she made a notably successful debut with the Israel Phil. She subsequently appeared with other Israeli orchs. She was a Fellow Conductor of the Los Angeles Phil. Inst. and at the Berkshire Music Center in Tanglewood in 1985, and was awarded the Leonard Bernstein fellowship. In 1986 she won the Bartók Prize of the Hungarian TV conductor's competition. In 1987–88 she was asst. conductor of the Louisville Orch. From 1988 to 1991 she was resident conductor of the Houston Sym. Orch., where, during her tenure, she also served as music director of the Houston Youth Sym. and as acting music director of the Orch. at the Shepherd School of Music at Rice Univ. In 1991 she became music director of the Boston ProArte Chamber Orch. and of the Annapolis Sym. Orch. In Dec. 1993 she made an auspicious debut with the N.Y. Phil. when she was called in at the last minute to substitute for an ailing Kurt Masur. She conducted the concert without benefit of rehearsals and without scores, winning audience acclaim. In 1994 she became music director of the Santa Barbara Sym. Orch. while retaining her posts in Annapolis until 1997 and in Boston until 2000. As a guest conductor, she appeared widely in North America, Europe, and Israel.—NS/LK/DM

Benedetti, Michele,

Italian bass; b. Loreto, Oct. 17, 1778; place and date of death unknown. He settled in Naples, where he appeared in the first Italian mounting of *La vestale* in 1811. He won the esteem of Rossini, who chose him to create there the roles of Elmiro Barberigo in *Otello, ossia Il Moro di Venezia* (1816), Idraste in *Armida* (1817), Mosè in *Mosè in Egitto* (1818), Ircano in *Ricciardo eZoraide* (1818), Douglas d'Angus in *La donna del lago* (1819), and Leucippo in *Zelmira* (1822). He also created roles in operas by Pacini, Mayr, Mercadante, and Bellini. —NS/LK/DM

Benedict, Sir Julius,

German-English conductor and composer; b. Stuttgart, Nov. 27, 1804; d. London, June 5, 1885. He was the son of a Jewish banker, and from his earliest childhood he showed a decisive musical talent. He took lessons with J.C.L. Abeille in Stuttgart, then had further instruction with Hummel at Weimar. Hummel introduced him to Weber, and he became Weber's private pupil. In 1823, Benedict was appointed conductor of the Kärnthnertortheater in Vienna, and in 1825 he obtained a similar post at the Teatro San Carlo in Naples and also at the Fondo Theater there. He produced his first opera, *Giacinta ed Ernesto*, in Naples in 1827. His second opera was *I Portoghesi in Goa*, produced in Naples on June 28, 1830. In 1834 Benedict went to Paris, and in 1835 he proceeded to London, where he remained for the rest of his life. In 1836 he became music director at the Opera Buffa at the Lyceum Theatre. He conducted opera at the Drury Lane Theatre from 1838 to 1848. His first opera in English, *The Gypsy's Warning*, was produced at Drury Lane under his direction on April 19, 1838. He also conducted at Covent Garden, led the Monday Popular Concerts, served as music director of the Norwich Festivals (1845–78), and conducted the Liverpool Phil. Soc. (1876–80). In recognition of his services, he was knighted in 1871. From 1850 to 1852 he accompanied Jenny Lind on her American tours. His reputation as a conductor and composer was considerable, in both Europe and America. Among his operas the most successful was *The Lily of Killarney*, which was produced at Covent Garden on Feb. 8, 1862; it was also staged in America and Australia. His other operas were *The Brides of Venice* (Drury Lane, April 22, 1844), *The Crusaders* (Drury Lane, Feb. 26, 1846), *The Lake ofGlenaston* (1862), and *The Bride of Song* (Covent Garden, Dec. 3, 1864). He also wrote the cantatas *Undine* (1860), *Richard Coeur-de-Lion* (1863), *The Legend of St. Cecilia* (1866), and *Graziella* (1882), an oratorio, *St. Peter* (1870), a Sym., two piano concertos, and other instrumental works. He publ. biographies of Mendelssohn (London, 1850) and Weber (London, 1881; 2nd ed., 1913), both comprised of information from his personal acquaintances.—NS/LK/DM

Benelli, Antonio Peregrino (Pellegrino), Italian tenor and composer; b. Forli, Romagna, Sept. 5, 1771; d. Börnichau, Saxony, Aug. 16, 1830. In 1790 he was first tenor at the Teatro San Carlo in Naples. He held the same position in London in 1798, and in Dresden from 1801 to 1822, when his voice failed. He then taught singing at the Royal Theater School in Berlin until 1829. His most valuable work is a vocal method, *Gesangslehre* (Dresden, 1819; orig. publ. in Italian as *Regole per il canto figurato*, 1814); he also wrote *Bemerkungen über die Stimme in the Allgemeine Musikalische Zeitung* (Leipzig, 1824). He composed many vocal pieces and some piano works.—NS/LK/DM

Benestad, Finn, important Norwegian musicologist; b. Kristiansand, Oct. 30, 1929. He was educated at the Univ. of Oslo (M.A., 1953; Ph.D., 1961, with the diss. *Johannes Haarklou: Mannen og verket*; publ. in Oslo, 1961). After working as a teacher (1950–59) and a music critic (1953–61) in Oslo, he served as prof. of musicology at the Univ. of Trondheim (1961–64) and at the Univ. of Oslo (1965–98). He also was a Fulbright scholar at the Univ. of Calif. at Los Angeles (1968–69). He was chairman of the Edvard Grieg Committee in Oslo from 1980, where he oversaw the completion of Grieg's complete works in 20 vols. in 1995. In 1979 he was made a member of the Norwegian Academy of Science and Letters.

WRITINGS (all publ. in Oslo unless otherwise given): *Waldemar Thrane: an pionér i norsk musikkliv* (1961); *Musikklaere* (1963; 5th ed., 1977); *Musikkhistorisk oversikt* (1965; 3rd ed., 1976); ed. with P. Krømer, *Festschrift til Olav Gurvin* (Oslo and Drammen, 1968); ed. *Norsk musikk: Studier i Norge*, vol. VI (1968); ed. *Skolens visebok* (1972); with others, *Aschehougs musikkverk* (1973–77); *Musikk og tanke: Hovedretninger i musikkestetikkens historie fra antikken til vår egen tid* (1976; 2nd ed., 1977); with D. Schjeldrup-Ebbe, *Edvard Grieg: Mennesket og kunstneren* (1980; Eng. tr., 1987, as *Edvard Grieg: The Man and the Artist*); with D. Schjeldrup-Ebbe, *Johan Svendsen: Mennesket og kunstneren* (1990; Eng. tr., 1995, as *Johan Svendsen: The Man, the Maestro, the Music*);with D. Schjelderup-Ebbe, *Edvard Grieg Chamber Music: Nationalism, Universality, Individuality* (Oxford, 1993).—NS/LK/DM

Benet, John, English composer who flourished in the 15th century. His extant works (masses, mass movements, and motets) number 21 pieces. His motets *Lux fulget ex Anglia* and *Tellus purpurium* are in B. Trowell, *Music Under the Plantagenets* (diss., Univ. of Cambridge, 1960), and his isorythmic motet *Gaude pia Magdalena* is in Early English Church Music, VIII (1968); other works have also been publ. in modern eds.—NS/LK/DM

Benevoli, Orazio, Italian composer; b. Rome, April 19, 1605; d. there, June 17, 1672. He was the son of a French baker who Italianized his name when he settled in Rome. He studied with Vincenzo Ugolini and sang in the boy's choir in the school "dei francesi" in Rome (1617–23); also had some instruction from Lorenzo Ratti. After completion of his studies he had successive posts as maestro di cappella, serving at S. Maria in Trastevere (1624–30), S. Spirito, Sassia

(1630–38), and S. Luigi dei Francesi (1638–44). In 1644 he went to Vienna, where he served at the Court until 1646. He then returned to Rome as maestro di cappella at S. Maria Maggiore, and was also attached to the Vatican. His music shows influences of the Palestrina style, combined with polychoral techniques of the Venetians; some of his sacred works call for 12 separate choirs. A considerable controversy arose when some music historians attributed to Benevoli the composition of the *Missa salisburgensis*, containing 53 separate parts, which was cited as an example of Benevoli's extraordinary contrapuntal skill. Such a Mass was indeed commissioned by Salzburg in 1628, but it was not composed by Benevoli; whoever wrote it, its performance did not take place until about 1682. This Mass and a hymn in 56 voices were reprinted in Denkmäler der Tonkunst in Österreich; another Mass, which really was composed by Benevoli and was performed at the S. Maria sopra Minerva Church in Rome in 1650, is set for 12 choirs of four voices each.

BIBL.: L. Feininger, ed., *O. B.: Opera omnia* (Rome, 1966 et seq.).—NS/LK/DM

Bengtsson, Gustaf Adolf Tiburt(ius), Swedish conductor and composer; b. Vadstena, March 29, 1886; d. there, Oct. 5, 1965. He studied at the Stockholm Cons., then in Berlin with Juon and in Leipzig with Riemann. Subsequently he was active in Karlstad as a composer and teacher, and later as a conductor in Linköping (1943–49).

WORKS: 3 syms. (1908, 1910, 1921); Violin Concerto; Cello Concerto; *Sinfonia concertante* for Violin, Viola, and Orch.; *Canone concertante* for Violin, Viola, and Chamber Orch. (1950); *Vettern*, symphonic poem (1950); String Quartet (1907); Piano Trio (1916); Violin Sonata; songs.—NS/LK/DM

Bengtsson, (Lars) Ingmar (Olof), eminent Swedish musicologist; b. Stockholm, March 2, 1920; d. there, Dec. 3, 1989. He studied piano at the Stockholm Musikhögskolan and musicology at the univs. of Stockholm, Uppsala (Ph.D., 1955, with diss. *J.H. Roman och hans instrumentalmusik: Käll och stilkritiska studier*; publ. in Uppsala, 1955), and Basel. He appeared as a pianist and harpsichordist (1942–55); wrote music criticism for Stockholm's *Svenska Dagbladet* (1943–59); was a lecturer (1947–61) and a prof. (1961–85) at the Univ. of Uppsala. He served as president of the Swedish Soc. of Musicology (1961–85) and as ed.-in-chief of its journal, *Svensk tidskrift för musikforskning* (1962–71). In 1963 he became chairman of the complete ed. of Berwald's works. In 1965 he founded the Swedish Archives of the History of Music. He was honored with a Festschrift on his 50th (1970) and 65th (1985) birthdays.

WRITINGS: *Bach och hans tid* (Stockholm, 1946); *Från visa till symfoni* (Stockholm, 1947; 5th ed., 1973); with R. Danielson, *Handstilar och notpikturer i Kungl.: Musikaliska akademiens Romansamling* (Uppsala, 1955); *Modern nordisk musik: Fjorton tonsättare om egna verk* (Stockholm, 1957); *Musikvetenskap: En oversikt* (Stockholm, 1973; 2nd ed., 1977); *Mr. Roman's Spuriosity Shop: A Thematic Catalogue of 503 Works (1213 Incipits and Other Excerpts) from ca. 1680–1750 by More Than Sixty Composers* (Stockholm, 1976); *Beräkning av intervall, stämningar, tempereringar m. m. med hjälp av räknedosa: Ett kompendium* (Uppsala, 1978); *Musik-videnskab—nu og i fremtiden* (Copenhagen, 1978); with E. Lomnäs and N. Castegren, *Franz Berwald: Die Dokumente seines Lebens* (Kassel, 1979); *Något om det heroiska i 1800–taets dikt och ton* (Lund, 1984).—NS/LK/DM

Ben-Haim (real name, **Frankenburger**), **Paul,** eminent German-born Israeli composer and teacher; b. Munich, July 5, 1897; d. Tel Aviv, Jan. 14, 1984. He studied piano, composition (with Klose), and conducting at the Munich Academy of Arts (1915–20). He was asst. conductor to Walter and Knappertsbursch (1920–24) before serving as conductor n Augsburg (1924–31). With the advent of the Nazi regime in 1933, he emigrated to Tel Aviv and changed his surname to the Hebrew Ben-Haim. He was director of the Jerusalem Academy of Music (1949–54). In 1957 he was awarded the Israel State Prize. An automobile accident in 1972 brought a premature end to his creative work. Although his output followed generally along late Romantic lines, he also was influenced by the indigenous music of the Middle East, particularly of his adopted homeland. He was especially successful as a composer of vocal works.

WORKS: ORCH.: *Concerto Grosso* (1931); *Pan,* symphonic poem (1931); 2 syms.: No. 1 (1940; Tel Aviv, June 5, 1941) and No. 2 (1945; Tel Aviv, Feb. 2, 1948); *Evocation* for Violin and Orch. (1942); Concerto for Strings (1947); Piano Concerto (1949; Tel Aviv, Feb. 1, 1950); *Fanfare to Israel* (1950; also for Band); *From Israel* (1951); *The Sweet Psalmist of Israel* (1953; Tel Aviv, Oct. 18, 1956); *To the Chief Musician* (1958); Violin Concerto (1960; Tel Aviv, March 20, 1962); *Dance and Invocation* (1960; Tel Aviv, Feb. 2, 1961); *Capriccio* for Piano and Orch. (Tel Aviv., Sept. 25, 1960); Cello Concerto (1962; Limburg, Dec. 14, 1967); *The Eternal Theme* (1965; Tel Aviv, Feb. 12, 1966); *Divertimento* for Flute and Chamber Orch. (1971–72). **CHAMBER:** String Trio (1927); String Quartet (1937); Clarinet Quintet (1941); *Serenade* for Flute and String Trio (1952); Sonata for Solo Violin (1953); *3 Pieces* for Cello (1973); piano pieces, including a Sonata (1953). **VOCAL:** *Yoram,* oratorio (1931); Liturgical Cantata for Baritone, Chorus, and Orch. or Organ (1950); *A Book of Verses* for Chorus (1958); *Vision of a Prophet,* cantata for Tenor, Chorus, and Orch. (1959); *Lift up Your Heads,* motet for Soprano and 8 Instruments (1961); *3 Psalms* for Solo Voices, Chorus, and Orch. (1962); *A Hymn to the Desert* for Soprano, Baritone, Chorus, and Orch. (1963); *Myrtle Blossoms from Eden* for Soprano or Tenor, Alto or Baritone, and Piano or Chamber Orch. (1966); *Kabbalai Shabbat* (Friday Evening Service) for Soprano, Tenor, Chorus, and Organ or 9 Instruments (1967); *6 Sephardic Songs* for Chorus (1971).

BIBL.: J. Hirschberg, *P. B.-H.* (Tel Aviv, 1983; Eng. tr., 1990); H. Guttmann, *The Music of B.-H.: A Performance Guide* (Metuchen, N.J., 1992).—NS/LK/DM

Benincori, Angelo Maria, Italian violinist, teacher, and composer; b. Brescia, March 28, 1779; d. Belleville, near Paris, Dec. 30, 1821. He studied violin with Rolla and counterpoint with Ghiretti in Parma, playing at the court when he was eight; then completed his training with Cimarosa in Italy. After a sojourn in Spain, and then in Vienna (1800–03), he settled in Paris. Although Benincori attempted to establish himself as a dramatic composer, he was unsuccessful and was compelled to teach violin. Upon the death of Isouard in

1818, he was given the task of completing that composer's opera *Aladin, ou La lampe merveilleuse,* but Benincori died before finishing the score. Habeneck then finished the opera, which was successfully premiered in Paris on Feb. 6, 1822. Benincori wrote six operas and various chamber pieces, including nine string quartets (three not extant) and three piano trios.—NS/LK/DM

Benjamin, Arthur, admired Australian pianist, teacher, and composer; b. Sydney, Sept. 18, 1893; d. London, April 9, 1960. After studies in Brisbane, he completed his training at the Royal Coll. of Music in London with Frederick Cliffe (piano) and Stanford (composition). He taught at the Sydney Cons. (1919–21) and the Royal Coll. of Music(from 1926). After pursuing his career in Vancouver, British Columbia (1939–46), he returned to England. Benjamin was an adept composer who produced works in a readily accessible style.

WORKS: DRAMATIC: Opera: *The Devil Take Her* (London, Dec. 1, 1931); *Prima Donna* (1933; London, Feb. 23, 1949); *A Tale of 2 Cities* (1949–50; BBC, London, April 17, 1953); *Mañana,* television opera (1956); *Tartuffe* (1960; completed by A. Boustead; London, Nov. 30, 1964). **Ballet:** *Orlando's Silver Wedding* (London, May 1951). **ORCH.:** Piano Concertino (1927); *Light Music,* suite (1928–33); Violin Concerto (1932); *Heritage,* ceremonial march (1935); *Romantic Fantasy* for Violin, Viola, and Orch. (1937; London, March 24, 1938); *Overture to an Italian Comedy* (London, March 2, 1937); *Cotillon,* suite (1938); *2 Jamaican Pieces* (1938; includes the highly popular *Jamaican Rumba;* also for 1 or 2 Pianos); *Prelude to Holiday* (1940; Indianapolis, Jan. 17, 1941); Sonatina for Chamber Orch. (1940); Concerto for Oboe and Strings (transcribed from Cimarosa, 1942); Sym. No. 1 (1944–45; Cheltenham, June 30, 1948); Suite for Flute and Strings (transcribed from Scarlatti, 1945); *Elegy, Waltz and Toccata,* viola concerto (1945; also for Viola and Piano); *From San Domingo* (1945); *Caribbean Dance* (1946); *Ballade* for Strings (1947); *Concerto quasi una fantasia* for Piano and Orch. (Sydney, Sept. 5, 1950); Harmonica Concerto (London, Aug. 15, 1953); *North American Square Dances* for 2 Pianos and Orch. (Pittsburgh, April 1, 1955). **CHAMBER:** *3 Pieces* for Violin and Piano (1919); 2 string quartets (*Pastorale Fantasia,* 1924; 1959); Violin Sonatina (1924); Cello Sonatina (1938); *Le Tombeau de Ravel: Valse Caprice* for Clarinet or Viola and Piano (1949); *Divertimento* for Wind Quintet (1960). **Piano:** Suite (1927); *2 Jamaican Songs* for 2 Pianos (1949). **VOCAL:** *3 Impressions* for Voice and String Quartet (1920); choral music; songs. —NS/LK/DM

Benjamin, George (William John), English composer, teacher, conductor, and pianist; b. London, Jan. 31, 1960. He began piano studies at age seven and composition lessons at age nine. After training with Gellhorn in London (1974–76), he studied with Messiaen (composition) and Loriod (piano) at the Paris Cons. (1976–78), and then with A. Goehr at King's Coll., Cambridge (1978–82). He also had lessons with Robin Holloway. In 1979 he made his debut in London as a pianist. From 1984 to 1987 he pursued research in electronic music at IRCAM in Paris. In 1986 he became a prof. of composition at the Royal Coll. of Music in London, where from 1994 he was the Royal Consort Prof. of Composition. He also was active as a performer and lecturer in Great Britain, Europe, the U.S., and the

Far East. From 1993 to 1996 he was principal guest artist at the Hallé Orch. in Manchester. He was the featured composer at the Salzburg Festival in 1995 and at the Tanglewood Festival in 1999. In 2000 he became composer-in-residence of the Berlin Phil. In 1996 he was named a Chevalier de l'Ordre des Arts et des Lettres of France. Benjamin has exploited the full range of compositional expression, from the traditional to a sophisticated use of electronics.

WORKS: ORCH.: *Altitude* for Brass Band (1977; York, May 12, 1979); *Ringed by the Flat Horizon* (1979–80; Cambridge, March 5, 1980); *At First Light* for Chamber Orch. (London, Nov. 23, 1982); *Fanfare for Aquarius* (London, Oct. 18, 1983); *Jubilation* (London, Sept. 16, 1985, composer conducting); *Antara* for Instrumental Ensemble and Electronics (1985–87; Paris, April 25, 1987, composer conducting); *Sudden Time* (1989–93; London, July 21, 1993, composer conducting); *3 Inventions* for Chamber Orch. (1993–95; first complete perf., Salzburg, July 27, 1995, composer conducting); *Palimpsest* (1998–99; London, Feb. 2, 2000). **CHAMBER:** Violin Sonata (1976–77; London, May 27, 1977, composer pianist); Octet for Flute, Clarinet, Celesta, Percussion, Violin, Viola, Cello, and Double Bass (1978; London, Feb. 24, 1979); *Flight* for Flute (1978–79; Paris, March 21, 1980); Duo for Cello and Piano (N.Y., Nov. 5, 1980, composer pianist); *Viola, Viola* for 2 Violas (Tokyo, Sept. 16, 1997). **P i a n o :** Sonata (1977–78; Paris, May 18, 1978, composer pianist); *Sortilèges* (1981; Cheltenham, July 15, 1982); *3 Studies* (1982–84; first complete perf., London, Feb. 4, 1986, composer pianist). **VOCAL:** *A Mind of Winter* for Soprano and Orch., after Wallace Stevens (1980–81; Snape Maltings, June 26, 1981); *Upon Silence* for Mezzo-soprano and 5 Viols, after Yeats (London, Oct. 30, 1990; rev. for Mezzo-soprano and 7 Strings, 1991; Paris, March 21, 1992); *Sometime Voices* for Baritone, Chorus, and Orch. (Manchester, Sept. 11, 1996). **T a p e :** *Panorama* (1985). **OTHER:** Transcription of Purcell's *Fantasia VII* for Clarinet, Violin, Cello, and Celesta (Aldeburgh Festival, June 16, 1995). **—NS/LK/DM**

Benjamin, William E(mmanuel), Canadian music theorist, musicologist, and composer; b. Montreal, Dec. 7, 1944. He studied composition with Anhalt at McGill Univ. in Montreal (Mus.B., 1965) and with Babbitt, Cone, Westergaard, and Randall at Princeton Univ. (M.F.A., 1968; Ph.D., 1976, with the diss. *On Modular Equivalence as a Musical Concept*). After teaching at Wellesley Coll. (1970–72) and the Univ. of Mich. (1972–78), he was assoc. (1978–83) and then full (from 1983) prof. at the Univ. of British Columbia, where he was head of the music school (1984–91). His writings on theory and analysis have been publ. in various journals. In his music, he strives to fashion a rational multidimensional musical space, in which dynamics, rhythm, and tonality are functional components in free serial arrangements.

WORKS: *A Midsummer Night's Dream*, incidental music to Shakespeare's play (1964); *The King of Siam*, incidental music to L. Angel's play (1965); *Mah Tovu*, hymn for Chorus (1965); *Variations* for 4 Players (1967); *At Sixes and Sevens*, sextet for Strings and Clarinets (1968); *2 Movements* for String Trio (1972); Piano Concerto (1970–75); *Square Waves* for Concert Band (1976–77); *2 Poems* for Contralto and Chamber Ensemble (1981); *The Unveiling*, incidental music to L. Angel's play (1982); *Sequences* for Guitar (1982).**—NS/LK/DM**

Bennard, George, American hymn composer; b. Youngstown, Ohio, Feb. 4, 1873; d. Reed City, Mich., Oct. 10, 1958. He served as a Salvation Army officer from 1892 to 1907; subsequently traveled as an evangelist in the U.S. and Canada. He wrote a number of sacred songs, among them *God Bless Our Boys, The Old Rugged Cross*, and *Sweet Songs of Salvation*.**—NS/LK/DM**

Bennet, John, English composer; b. probably in Lacashire, c. 1577; d. place and date unknown. He publ. a fine vol. of *Madrigalls to Foure Voyces* (1599) and also contributed the madrigal *All creatures now are merry minded* to *The Triumphs of Oriana* (1601) and six songs to Ravenscroft's *A Briefe Discourse* (1614). His works were ed. by E. Fellowes in The English Madrigal School (1913–24; 2nd ed., rev., 1956 by T. Dart as The English Madrigalists).**—NS/LK/DM**

Bennet, Sir Richard Rodney, eminent English composer; b. Broadstairs, March 29, 1936. He began composing in his youth, and then studied with Howard Ferguson and Lennox Berkeley at the Royal Academy of Music in London (1953–56). After further training in Paris with Boulez on a French government scholarship (1957–59), he returned to London. From 1963 to 1965 he was prof. of composition at the Royal Academy of Music. In 1983 he became vice president of the Royal Coll. of Music. He held the International Chair of Composition at the Royal Academy of Music in 1995. In 1977 he was made a Commander of the Order of the British Empire and in 1998 he was knighted. Bennett is a remarkable composer whose prolific output reveals a facile and inventive mind. He has written scores in all of the principal genres in a style that has incorporated traditional, atonal, and jazz elements.

WORKS: DRAMATIC: O p e r a : *The Ledge* (London, Sept. 11, 1961); *The Midnight Thief*, children's opera (1963); *The Mines of Sulphur* (1963–65; London, Feb. 24, 1965); *A Penny for a Song* (London, Oct. 31, 1967); *All the King's Men*, children's opera (1968; Coventry, March 28, 1969); *Victory* (1969–70; London, April 13, 1970). **B a l l e t :** *Jazz Calendar* (1963–64); *Isadora* (1980; London, April 30, 1981); *Noctuary* (1981; Armidale, Australia, June 3, 1985). **F i l m :** Many, including *Far From the Madding Crowd* (1967); *Nicholas and Alexandra* (1971); *Murder on the Orient Express* (1973); *Enchanted April* (1992); *Four Weddings and a Funeral* (1994); *Swann* (1996). **O t h e r :** Radio and television scores. **ORCH.:** Horn Concerto (1956); *Journal* (1960); *Calendar* for Chamber Ensemble (London, Nov. 24, 1960); *Suite française* for Chamber Orch. (1961); *Nocturnes* for Chamber Orch. (1962); *Aubade* (London, Sept. 1, 1964); 3 syms.: No. 1 (1965; London, Feb. 10, 1966), No. 2 (1967; N.Y., Jan. 18, 1968), and No. 3 (Worcester, Aug. 24, 1987); Piano Concerto (Birmingham, Sept. 19, 1968); Concerto for Guitar and Chamber Ensemble (London, Nov. 18, 1970); Concerto for Viola and Chamber Orch. (York, July 3, 1973); *Concerto for Orch.* (1973; Denver, Feb. 25, 1974); Violin Concerto (1975; Birmingham, March 25, 1976); *Zodiac* (Washington, D.C., March 30, 1976); *Serenade* (1976; London, April 24, 1977); *Acteon* for Horn and Orch. (London, Aug. 12, 1977); *Music for Strings* (1977; Cheltenham, July 7, 1978); Concerto for Double Bass and Chamber Orch. (Isle of Man, Aug. 1978); *Sonnets to Orpheus* for Cello and Orch. (Edinburgh, Sept. 3, 1979); Harpsichord Concerto (St. Louis, Dec. 4, 1980); *Anniversaries* (London, Sept. 9, 1982); *Freda's*

Fandango (1982; Cheltenham, July 2,1983); *Memento* for Flute and Strings (Windsor, Nov. 10, 1983); *Sinfonietta* (1984; St. Ives, Huntingdon, Feb. 16, 1985); *Moving into Aquarius* (1984; London, Jan. 23, 1985; in collaboration with Thea Musgrave); *Reflections on a Theme of William Walton* for 11 Solo Strings (London, May 20, 1985); *Dream Dancing* for 13 Players (London, May 28, 1986); Concerto for Clarinet and Strings (1987; Keele, Feb. 15, 1988); Concerto for Saxophone and Strings (London, Oct. 14, 1988); *Diversions* (1989; London, March 17, 1990); Concerto for Percussion and Chamber Orch. (Kirkwall, Orkney Islands, June 27, 1990); *Concerto for Stan Getz* for Tenor Saxophone, Timpani, and Strings (1990; London, Aug. 1, 1992); *Celebration* (1991; Hagerstown, Md., March 14, 1992); *Variations on a Nursery Tune* (London, Aug. 1, 1992); Concerto for Bassoon and Strings (1994; London, April 4, 1995); *Partita* (London, Oct. 19, 1995); *Reflections on a 16th Century Tune* for Strings (Portsmouth, April 10, 1999); *Rondel* for Large Jazz Ensemble (London, May 1, 1999); Flute Concerto (London, Aug. 12, 1999). **Wind and Brass Ensembles:** *Morning Music* for Symphonic Wind Ensemble (1986; Boston, July 25, 1987); Concerto for 10 Brass Players (1988; London, June 27, 1989); *Flowers of the Forest* for Brass Band (London, Aug. 6, 1989); *The Four Seasons* (Cheltenham, July 16, 1991); Concerto for Trumpet and Wind Orch. (Manchester, Sept. 17, 1993). **CHAMBER:** 4 string quartets (1952, 1953, 1960, 1964); Sonatina for Solo Flute (1954); *4 Improvisations* for Violin (1955); *Winter Music* for Flute and Piano (1960); Oboe Sonata (1961); Sonata for Solo Violin (1964); *Conversations* for 2 Flutes (1964); Trio for Flute, Oboe, and Clarinet (1965); Wind Quintet (1967–68); *5 Impromptus* for Guitar (1968); *Commedia I* for 6 Players (1972), *II* for Flute, Cello, and Piano (1972; N.Y., April 5, 1973), *III* for 10 Players (London, Feb. 25, 1973), and *IV* for Brass Quintet (1973; London, April 27, 1974); *Scena II* for Cello (1973; Bangor, Wales, April 25, 1974) and *III* for Clarinet (1977; London, Jan. 13, 1978); Oboe Quartet (Kings Lynn, July 28, 1975); *Travel Notes 1* for String Quartet (1975) and *2* for Flute, Oboe, Clarinet, and Bassoon (1976); Horn Sonata (1978; Edinburgh, Sept. 6, 1979); Violin Sonata (1978; London, Jan. 17, 1979); *Metamorphoses* for String Octet (Fishguard Festival, Wales, July 21, 1980); *Six Tunes for the Instruction of Singing Birds* for Flute (Norfolk, Aug. 15, 1981); *Music for String Quartet* (1981; Portsmouth, April 1, 1982); Sonatina for Solo Clarinet (1981; Northumberland, March 1983); *After Syrinx I* for Oboe and Piano (1982; Seaton, Devon, Oct. 13, 1983) and *II* for Marimba (N.Y., May 21, 1984); *Summer Music* for Flute and Piano (London, Nov. 23, 1982); Concerto for Wind Quintet (1983; Roehampton, Aug. 15, 1984); Sonata for Solo Guitar (1983; Cheltenham, July 17, 1985); *Serenade* for Ondes Martenot and Piano (1984); *Romances* for Horn and Piano (1985; N.Y., Feb. 25, 1986); Duo Concertante for Clarinet and Piano (1985; Cheltenham, July 17, 1986); *Sonata After Syrinx* for Flute, Viola, and Harp (1985; London, May 20, 1986); *Sounds and Sweet Aires* for Flute, Oboe, and Piano (1985; WUNC Radio, Chapel Hill, N.C., April 26, 1986); *Tender is the Night* for Ondes Martenot and String Quartet (1985); *Lamento d'Arianna* for String Quartet (Bromsgrove Festival, May 7, 1986); Sonata for Wind Quintet and Piano (1986; N.Y., April 21, 1987); Soprano Saxophone Sonata (1986; London, Nov. 23, 1988); *After Ariadne* for Viola and Piano (1986; Cheltenham, July 7, 1987); *Arethusa* for Oboe, Violin, Viola, and Cello (Manchester, Aug. 16, 1989); *A Book of Hours* for Chamber Group (London, Sept. 16, 1991); Cello Sonata (1991; Harrogate, Aug. 11, 1992); *Capriccio* for Cello and Piano (Ryedale Festival, Aug. 7, 1991); Bassoon Sonata (1991; Seaton, Feb. 11, 1993); *Arabesque* for Oboe (1992; Birmingham, Feb. 2, 1993); Clarinet Quintet (Warwick, July 3, 1992); Saxo-

phone Quartet (Cheltenham, July 12, 1994); *Three Piece Suite* for Alto Saxophone and Piano (Loughborough, March 21, 1996; transcription of 3 movements from the *Four Piece Suite* for 2 Pianos, 1974); *Rondel* for Viola (1997). **KEYBOARD: Piano:** Sonata (1954); *5 Studies* (1962–64); *Capriccio* for Piano, 4–Hands (1968); *Scena I* (1974); *Four Piece Suite* for 2 Pianos (1974); *Kandinsky Variations* for 2 Pianos (London, Dec. 1, 1977); *Impromptu on the Name of Haydn* (1981; BBC, March 31, 1982); *Noctuary* (1981; Armidale, Australia, June 3, 1985); *Tango After Syrinx* (1985); *Tender is the Night* (BBC Radio 2, June 30, 1985); *Suite for Skip and Sadie* for Piano Duet (1986); *Three Romantic Pieces* (BBC, Birmingham, Oct. 28, 1988); *Excursions* (1993; Surrey, Feb. 6, 1994); *Impromptu on a Theme of Henri Dutilleux* (1994). **Organ:** *Alba* (Bradford, Nov. 3, 1973). **VOCAL:** *The Approaches of Sleep* for Soprano, Alto, Tenor, Bass, and Chamber Ensemble (1959–60); *London Pastoral* for Tenor and Chamber Orch. (1962); *Crazy Jane* for Soprano, Clarinet, Cello, and Piano, after Yeats (1968; BBC TV, May 26, 1970); *A Garland for Marjory Fleming* for Soprano and Piano, after Marjory Fleming (1969; BBC, Edinburgh, Dec. 2, 1970); *Sonnet Sequence* for Tenor and String Orch. (Milton Keynes, Dec. 20, 1974); *Spells* for Soprano, Chorus, and Orch. (1974; Worcester, Aug. 28, 1975); *Time's Whiter Series* for Countertenor and Lute (1974; Aldeburgh, June 6, 1975); *The Little Ghost Who Died for Love* for Soprano and Piano (1976; London, Jan. 31, 1977); *Just Friends in Print* for Voice and Piano (1979); *Nonsense* for Chorus and Piano Duet (1979; rev. version, Chester, July 18, 1984); *Puer Nobis* for Chorus (Aberdeen, Dec. 21, 1980); *Vocalese* for Soprano and Piano (1981; London, March 1, 1983); *Letters to Lindbergh* for Women's Voices and Piano Duet (Sevenoaks, May 16, 1982); *Sea-Change* for Chorus and Tubular Bells ad libitum (1983; Worcester, Aug. 23, 1984); *Lullay Mine Liking* for Chorus (Broadstairs, Dec. 23, 1984); *this is the garden* for High Voice and Piano (1984; Brighton, May 13, 1985); *And Death Shall Have No Dominion* for Men's Chorus and Horn (1986; London, July 7, 1988); *Dream-Songs* for Soprano or Unison High Voices and Piano (1986; Mont Albert, Australia, March 24, 1990); *Nowel* for Chorus (Cambridge, Dec. 24, 1986); *Missa Brevis* for Chorus (1990; Canterbury, Feb. 10, 1991); *Sermons and Devotions* for 6 Men's Voices, after Donne (1992; Berlin, March 18, 1993); *A History of Thé Dansant* for Mezzo-soprano and Piano (Norfolk, Aug. 13, 1994); *Calico Pie* for Chorus, after Edward Lear (1994; Manchester, May 14, 1995); *A Contemplation Upon Flowers* for Chorus (1999); *A Good Night* for Chorus (Godalming, July 18, 1999).

BIBL.: S. Craggs, *R.R. B.: A Bio-Bibliography* (Westport, Conn., 1990).—**NS/LK/DM**

Bennett, Joseph, English critic and writer on music; b. Berkeley, Gloucestershire, Nov. 29, 1831; d. Purton, June 12, 1911. After serving in various musical positions in London, he wrote music criticism for the *Sunday Times, Pall Mall Gazette,* and the *Graphic.* He was annotator of the programs of the Phil. Soc. (1885–1903) and of the Saturday Popular Concerts, and also wrote libretti for several English composers.

WRITINGS: *Letters from Bayreuth* (1877); *The Musical Year* (1883); with F.R. Spark, *History of the Leeds Musical Festivals, 1858–1889* (1892); *Story of Ten Hundred Concerts* (1887; an account of the origin and rise of the Saturday Popular Concerts, 1857–87); *Forty Years of Music* (1908).—**NS/LK/DM**

Bennett, Robert Russell, American orchestrator, arranger, and composer; b. Kansas City, Mo., June

15, 1894; d. N.Y., Aug. 18, 1981. He was a member of a musical family: his father played in the Kansas City Phil. and his mother was a piano teacher. He studied in Kansas City with Carl Busch (1912–15), in Paris with Boulanger (1926–31), and in Berlin and London. In 1919 he orchestrated his first theatrical songs, and during the next 40 years reigned as the leading orchestrator of Broadway musicals. In all, he orchestrated about 300 such works, including ones by Kern, Gershwin, Porter, Rodgers, Berlin, and Loewe. His own music reveals not only a mastery of orchestration but a facile flow of melodies and rhythms in luscious harmonies. He publ. a book on orchestration, *Instrumentally Speaking* (N.Y., 1975).

WORKS: DRAMATIC: *Columbine,* pantomime ballet (1916); *Endimion,* operetta-ballet (1926; Rochester, N.Y., April 5, 1935); *An Hour of Delusion,* opera (1928); *Hold Your Horses,* musical play (N.Y., Sept. 25, 1933); *Maria Malibran,* opera (1934; N.Y., April 8, 1935); *The Enchanted Kiss,* opera (1944; WOR Radio, N.Y., Dec. 30, 1945); *Crystal,* opera (1972); incidental music and radio scores. **ORCH.:** Sym. No. 1 (1926); *Charleston Rhapsody* for Small Orch. (1926; N.Y., Feb. 18, 1931; rev. 1933); *Paysage* (1927; Rochester, N.Y., Dec. 15, 1933); *Abraham Lincoln Symphony: A Likeness in Symphony Form* (1929; Philadelphia, Oct. 24, 1931); *Sights and Sounds* (1929; Chicago, Dec. 13, 1938); March for 2 Pianos and Orch. (Los Angeles, July 18, 1930; rev. 1950); *An Early American Ballade on Melodies of Stephen Foster* for Small Orch. (CBS, N.Y., April 15, 1932); Concerto Grosso for Dance Band and Orch. (Rochester, N.Y., Dec. 9, 1932); *6 Variations in Fox-trot Time on a Theme by Jerome Kern* for Chamber Orch. (N.Y., Dec. 3, 1933); *Adagio Eroico: To the Memory of a Soldier* (1932; Philadelphia, April 25, 1935); *Hollywood: Introduction and Scherzo* (NBC, Nov. 15, 1936); *8 études* (CBS, July 17, 1938); Concerto for Viola, Harp, and Orch. (1940; WOR Radio, N.Y., Feb. 27, 1941; rev. as Concerto for Harp, Cello, and Orch., 1959; N.Y., July 31, 1960); *Classic Serenade* for Strings (WOR Radio, N.Y., March 30, 1941); *Antique Suite* for Clarinet and Orch. (WOR Radio, N.Y., April 6, 1941); *Noctune and Appassionata* for Piano and Orch. (WOR Radio, N.Y., Aug. 18, 1941); *Symphony in D for the Dodgers:* Sym. No. 3 (WOR Radio, N.Y., May 16, 1941); Violin Concerto (WOR Radio, N.Y., Dec. 26, 1941); *The 4 Freedoms: A Symphony After 4 Paintings by Norman Rockwell* (NBC, N.Y., Sept. 26, 1943); Sym. No. 6 (1946); *A Dry Weather Legend* for Flute and Orch. (1946; Knoxville, Tenn., Feb. 19, 1947); *Overture to an Imaginary Drama* (Toronto, May 14, 1946); Piano Concerto (1947); *Concert Variations on a Crooner's Theme* for Violin and Orch. (Louisville, Nov. 30, 1949); *Overture to the Mississippi* (Boston, Jan. 14, 1950); *Kansas City Album: 7 Songs for Orch.* (1949; Kansas City, Mo., Feb. 6, 1950); Concerto for Violin, Piano, and Orch. (1958; Portland, Ore., March 18, 1963); *A Commemoration Symphony: Stephen Collins Foster* for Soprano, Tenor, Chorus, and Orch. (Pittsburgh, Dec. 30, 1959); *Armed Forces Suite* (1959); Sym. No. 7 (1962; Chicago, April 11, 1963); *Harmonica Concerto* (1971). **WIND BAND OR ORCH.:** *Tone Poems* (1939); *Suite of Old American Dances* (1949); *Rose Variations* (1955); *Concerto grosso* (1957); *Symphonic Songs* (1957); *Ohio River Suite* (1959); *West Virginia Epic* (1960); *Kentucky* (1961); *Overture to Ty, Tris and Willie* (1961); *3 Humoresques* (c. 1961); *Twain and the River* (1968); *Zimmer's American Greeting* (1974); *Autobiography* (1976). **CHAMBER:** Violin Sonata (1927); *Water Music* for String Quartet (1937); *Dance Scherzo* for Flute, Oboe, Clarinet, Horn, and Bassoon (1937); *Hexapoda* for Violin and Piano (1940); Clarinet Quartet (1941); *A Song Sonata* for Violin and Piano (1947); Trio for Flute, Cello, and

Piano (1950); String Quartet (1956); Trio for Harp, Cello, and Flute (c. 1960); Quintette for Accordion and String Quartet (1962); *Arabesque* for 2 Trumpets, Horn, Trombone, and Bass Trombone (1978); piano pieces; organ music. **VOCAL:** Choral works; songs.

BIBL.: G. Ferencz, *R.R. B.: A Bio-Bibliography* (Westport, Conn., 1990).—**NS/LK/DM**

Bennett, Sir William Sterndale, distinguished English pianist, conductor, and composer; b. Sheffield, April 13, 1816; d. London, Feb. 1, 1875. His father, Robert Bennett, an organist, died when he was a child, and he was then placed in the care of his grandfather, John Bennett, who was also a musician. At the age of eight he was admitted to the choir of King's Coll. Chapel, Cambridge, and at ten he became a pupil at the Royal Academy of Music in London, where he studied theory with Charles Lucas and piano with William Henry Holmes, and played violin in the academy orch. under Cipriani Potter; he later studied music theory there with William Crotch. Soon he began to compose; he was 16 years old when he was the soloist in the first performance of his Piano Concerto No. 1 in Cambridge on Nov. 28, 1832. In 1836 he made an extensive visit to Leipzig, where he became a close friend of Mendelssohn and Schumann; also appeared as a pianist and conductor of his own works with the Gewandhaus Orch. there. He continued to compose industriously, and played his Piano Concerto No. 4 with the Gewandhaus Orch. in Leipzig on Jan. 17, 1839. He visited Germany again in 1841–42. From 1843 to 1856 he gave a series of chamber music concerts in London; in 1849 he founded the Bach Soc. From 1856 to 1866 he conducted the Phil. Soc. of London; concurrently he held the post of prof. of music at the Univ. of Cambridge; in 1866 he assumed the position of principal of the Royal Academy of Music. His reputation as a composer grew; Mendelssohn and Schumann were eloquent in praising his works. He amassed honors: in 1856 he received the honorary degree of D.Mus. from the Univ. of Cambridge, which also conferred on him the degree of M.A. in 1867; he received the degree of D.C.L. from the Univ. of Oxford in 1870; in a culmination of these honors, he was knighted by Queen Victoria in 1871. The final honor was his burial in Westminster Abbey.

WORKS: ORCH.: Sym. No. 1, in E-flat major (London, June 16, 1832); Piano Concerto No. 1, in D minor, op.1 (Cambridge, Nov. 28, 1832); Sym. No. 2, in D minor (1832–33); *The Tempest,* overture (1832); *Parisina,* overture, op.3 (London, March 1835); Piano Concerto No. 2, in E-flat major, op.4 (1833; London, May 24, 1834); Overture in D minor (1833); Sym. No. 4, in A major (1833–34; London, Jan. 5, 1835); *The Merry Wives of Windsor,* overture (1834); Piano Concerto No. 3, in C minor, op.9 (1834; London, May 16, 1835; the original slow movement was rejected by the composer and replaced by a *Romanza;* the *Adagio* in G minor for Piano and Orch. was first perf. in Manchester on June 18, 1981; Sym. No. 5, in G minor (1835; London, Feb. 8, 1836); Piano Concerto No. 4, in F minor (London, July 1, 1836; rev. 1838; Leipzig, Jan. 17, 1839); *The Naiads,* overture, op.15 (1836; London, Jan. 25, 1837); *The Wood Nymphs,* overture, op.20 (1838; Leipzig, Jan. 24, 1839); *Caprice* in E major for Piano and Orch., op.22 (London, May 25, 1838); *Concert-Stück* in A major for Piano and Orch. (1841–43; London, June 5, 1843); *Marie du Bois*, overture (1843; rev. 1844; London, June 25, 1845); *Paradise and the Peri*, fantasia-overture, op.42 (London, July 14, 1862); Sym. No. 6, in G minor, op.43 (London, June 27, 1864). **CHAMBER:** String Quartet; Piano Sonata in A-flat major, op.46, known as *The Maid of Orleans* (1873); numerous piano pieces; pedagogical works for piano. **VOCAL:** *Zion*, oratorio (1839); *The May Queen*, op.39, pastoral for Soprano, Alto, Tenor, Bass, Chorus, and Orch. (Leeds Festival, Sept. 8, 1858); *Ode for the Opening of the International Exhibition*, op.40 (London, May 1, 1862); *Ode on the Installation of the Duke of Devonshire* (Cambridge, May 10, 1862); *The Woman of Samaria*, cantata, op.44 (Birmingham Festival, Aug. 28, 1867); also music to Sophocles' *Ajax* (1872?); anthems; songs.

BIBL.: J.R. Sterndale Bennett, *The Life of W. S. B.* (Cambridge, 1907); R. Williamson, *W. S. B.: A Descriptive Thematic Catalog* (Oxford, 1996).—NS/LK/DM

Bennett, Tony (originally, **Anthony Dominick Benedetto**), celebratory American singer; b. Queens, N.Y., Aug. 3, 1926. Bennett, a husky-voiced tenor shading to baritone in later life, continued to extol the virtues of the classic pop songwriters far into the rock era, eventually developing a new audience not yet born when he scored his initial flurry of pop hits. Those recordings, such as "Because of You," "Cold, Cold Heart," and "Rags to Riches," established him as a major pop singer of the early 1950s. A decade later, with his signature song, "I Left My Heart in San Francisco," and other recordings, he became a leading classic pop interpreter just before the second wave of rock 'n' roll arrived with The Beatles. Like many of his contemporaries and predecessors, he moved more toward jazz in the 1970s, but in the 1980s he mounted a stunning commercial comeback culminating in a performance on MTV that led to a gold record and Album of the Year Grammy in 1994.

Bennett's father, John Benedetto, was an Italian immigrant who ran a grocery in Manhattan on the eventual site of the building housing Columbia Records. He died when Bennett was nine, and Bennett's mother, Anna Suraci Benedetto, went to work in the garment industry to support the family. He attended the H.S. of Industrial Arts in Manhattan, studying music and painting, and later remembered the influence of a music teacher named Mr. Sondberg. By his teens he was singing in clubs in Queens. Drafted into the army in 1944, he served in Europe in the last days of World War II and was discharged in 1946. Using the G.I. Bill, he studied voice at the American Theater Wing with Peter D'Andrea and Miriam Spier.

In 1949, after years of struggling for a foothold in the entertainment business, Bennett was hired to perform in a revue at the Greenwich Village Inn, where he was seen by Bob Hope. Hope put him onstage at the Paramount Theater in Times Square and gave him his stage name. He was signed to Columbia Records by Mitch Miller in 1950 and released his first single, "The Boulevard of Broken Dreams" (music by Harry Warren, lyrics by Al Dubin). That summer he appeared on the television series *Songs for Sale*.

Bennett made his commercial breakthrough with "Because of You" (music by Dudley Wilkinson, lyrics by

Arthur Hammerstein), which topped the charts in September 1951 and sold a million copies. He followed it with "Cold, Cold Heart" (music and lyrics by Hank Williams), another gold record that hit #1 in November. On Feb. 12, 1952, he married Patricia Ann Beech; they had two sons, D'Andrea (Danny) and Daegal, and divorced in 1971. He continued to reach the charts over the next two years but didn't score another big hit until "Rags to Riches" (music and lyrics by Richard Adler and Jerry Ross) went to #1 in 1953 and was a million-seller; it was immediately followed by another gold single, "Stranger in Paradise" (music and lyrics by Robert Wright and George Forrest, music based on the first theme from the Polovetsian Dances from Alexander Borodin's opera *Prince Igor*).

Bennett scored three more Top Ten hits through the end of the decade, but the rise of rock 'n' roll after 1955 limited his commercial success. Meanwhile, he toured clubs nationally. He hosted the summer replacement series for Perry Como in 1956 (*The Tony Bennett Show*) and (*Perry Presents*) in 1959. He also performed with jazz musicians, notably on two albums backed by Count Basie's orchestra.

Bennett released the album *I Left My Heart in San Francisco* in June 1962 (title song music by George Cory, lyrics by Douglass Cross). The album hit the Top Ten and went gold, and the single hit the Top 40 and won him Grammys for Record of the Year and Best Solo Vocal Performance, Male. From then on the song was identified with him. The result was a considerable career resurgence. His next single, "I Wanna Be Around" (music and lyrics by Johnny Mercer and Sadie Vimmerstedt), was another Top 40 hit that brought a Record of the Year Grammy nomination, and the *I Wanna Be Around* album reached the Top Ten.

Bennett's albums of the mid-1960s regularly placed among the 50 best-sellers. He earned Grammy nominations for Best Vocal Performance, Male, in 1964 for "Who Can I Turn To (When Nobody Needs Me)" (music and lyrics by Leslie Bricusse and Anthony Newley) and in 1965 for "The Shadow of Your Smile (theme from *The Sandpipers*)" (music by Johnny Mandel, lyrics by Paul Francis Webster). His 1965 compilation album *Tony's Greatest Hits, Volume III* went gold. Bennett began living with Sandra Grant in the late 1960s, and she bore him a daughter, Joanna, in 1970. Following his divorce from his first wife, they were married on Dec. 29, 1971. They had a second daughter, Antonia, and later divorced.

Bennett's record sales began to fall off in 1967, and by the end of the decade Columbia was pressuring him to record the songs of contemporary rock performers. He acceded on such albums as *Tony Bennett Sings the Great Hits of Today!*, but he was unhappy with the approach, and it did not restore his commercial fortunes. In 1972 he left Columbia for MGM/Verve, and made one album, *The Good Things in Life*. In 1975 he recorded an album with jazz pianist Bill Evans for Fantasy Records and formed his own label, Improv Records, for which he recorded several albums. When the label foundered in the late 1970s, he was without a record contract. But he continued to tour regularly, playing concert halls and hotel/casinos around the world.

With the upsurge of interest in classic pop in the 1980s, Bennett, by now being managed by his son Danny, re-signed to Columbia in 1986 and released *The Art of Excellence*, his first chart album in more than 13 years. He followed it with a series of carefully considered collections largely devoted to pop standards. *Perfectly Frank* (1992), an album of songs associated with Frank Sinatra, went gold and won a Grammy for Best Traditional Pop Vocal Performance. *Steppin' Out* (1993), an album of songs associated with Fred Astaire, won the same award the following year.

Bennett appeared on the *Unplugged* series on the cable music network MTV in 1994. The resulting *MTV Unplugged* album went gold and won Grammys for Album of the Year and, for the third year in a row, Best Traditional Pop Vocal Performance. Bennett won the same vocal performance Grammy in 1996 for *Here's to the Ladies* and in 1997 for *Tony Bennett on Holiday*, an album of songs associated with Billie Holiday. In 1998 he released *The Playground*, which earned a Grammy nomination for Best Musical Album for Children.

WRITINGS: With W. Friedwald, *The Good Life.* (N.Y., 1998).

DISC.: *I Left My Heart in San Francisco* (1962); *Tony's Greatest Hits, Volume III* (1965); *The Art of Excellence* (1986); *Perfectly Frank* (1992); *Steppin' Out* (1993); *MTV Unplugged* (1994); *Here's to the Ladies* (1996); *Tony Bennett on Holiday* (1997); *The Playground* (1998).

BIBL.: T. Jasper, *T. B.: A Biography* (London, 1984).—**WR**

Bennewitz (real name, **Benevic**), **Anton(ín),** Czech violinist and pedagogue; b. Přívaty, near Litomysl, March 26, 1833; d. Dosky, near Litoměřice, May 29, 1926. He was a pupil of M. Mildner at the Prague Cons. (1846–52), where he served as prof. of violin (from 1865) and as director (1882–1901). His students included Ševčík, Suk, Karel Hoffmann, Haliř, F. Ondříček, and Nedbal.—**NS/LK/DM**

Benoît, Camille, French writer on music and compoer; b. Roanne, Loire, Dec. 7, 1851; d. Paris, July 1, 1923. He studied with Franck (1872). From 1883 he wrote articles on music, and in 1888 he joined the staff of the Louvre in Paris, becoming keeper of antiquities in 1895. Collections of his articles on music appeared in *Souvenirs* (1884) and *Musiciens, poètes et philosophes* (1887). Among his compositions were an unfinished opera, *Cléopâtre* (1889), two symphonic poems, *Merlin l'enchanteur* and *La nuit* (unfinished), and *Eleison* for Solo Voices, Chorus, and Orch. (1890).—**LK/DM**

Benoit, Peter (Léopold Léonard), eminent Flemish composer; b. Harlebeke, Belgium, Aug. 17, 1834; d. Antwerp, March 8, 1901. He studied at the Brussels Cons. with Fétis (1851–55); while there he earned his living by conducting theater orchs. and wrote music for Flemish plays. At the age of 22 he produced his first opera in Flemish, *Het dorp in't gebergte* (A Mountain Village), staged in Brussels on Dec. 14, 1856. With his cantata *Le Meurtre d'Abel* Benoit obtained the Belgian Prix de Rome (1857); however, he did not go to Italy, but traveled instead in Germany. As part of his duties he submitted a short *Cantate de Noël* to Fétis, who praised Benoit's music; he also wrote the essay *L'École de musique flamande et son avenir*, proclaiming his fervent faith in the future of a national Flemish school of composition, of which he was the most ardent supporter. His one-act opera *Roi des Aulnes* was presented in Brussels (Dec. 2, 1859). The Théâtre-Lyrique of Paris tentatively accepted it, and Benoit spent many months in Paris awaiting its production, which never took place; in the meantime he acted as second conductor at the Bouffes-Parisiens. In 1863 he returned to Belgium, where he produced his second Flemish opera, *Isa* (Brussels, Feb. 24, 1867). In 1867 he founded the Flemish Music School in Antwerp; he militated for many years to obtain official status for it. In 1898 it was finally granted, and the school became the Royal Flemish Cons. Benoit remained its director to the end of his life. In Belgium Benoit is regarded as the originator of the Flemish musical tradition in both composition and education; but although he cultivated the Flemish idiom in most of his works, his musical style owes much to French and German influences. Apart from his successful early operas, he wrote the opera *Pompeja* (1895), which was not produced. He also composed the Flemish oratorios *Lucifer* (Brussels, Sept. 30, 1866; highly successful; considered his masterpiece), *De Schelde* (1868), and *De Oorlog* (War; 1873), a dramatic musical score, *Charlotte Corday* (1876), an historical music drama, *De Pacificatie van Ghent* (1876), a children's oratorio, *De Waereld in* (In the World; 1878), the oratorio, *De Rhijn* (1889), and the cantatas *Hucbald* (1880) and *De Genius des Vaderlands* (1880). Of his church music, the most important is his *Quadrilogie religieuse* (Antwerp, April 24, 1864), of which the component parts had been separately performed in 1860, 1962, and 1863; also *Drama Christi* (1871). Benoit wrote relatively little instrumental music; his symphonic poems for piano with orch. and for flute with orch. have been performed. He also composed many songs in French and in Flemish. In his propaganda for national Flemish music, Benoit contributed numerous papers and articles, among them *Considérations à propos d'un projet pour l'institution de festivals en Belgique* (1874), *Verhandeling over de nationale Toonkunde* (two vols., Antwerp, 1877–79), *De Vlaamsche Muziekschool van Antwerpen* (1889; a history of the Flemish Music School), and *De Oorsprong van het Cosmopolitisme in de Muziek* (1876). In 1880 he was elected a corresponding member of the Belgian Royal Academy, and in 1882, a full member.

BIBL.: L. Mortelmans, *P. B.* (Antwerp, 1911); H. Baggaert, *P. B.: Een kampion der nationale gedachte* (Antwerp, 1919); J. Horemans, *P. B.* (Antwerp, 1934); A. Pols, *Het leven van P. B.* (Antwerp, 1934); C. van den Borren, *P. B.* (Brussels, 1942); R. Boschvogel, *P. B.* (Tiel, 1944); A. Corbet, *P. B.: Leven, werk en beteekenis* (Antwerp, 1944); G.-M. Matthijs, *P. B.* (Brussels, 1944); F. van der Mueren, *P. B. in het huidig perspectief* (Antwerp, 1968); H. Willaert, *P. B., de levenswekker* (Brussels, 1984).—**NS/LK/DM**

Benson, George, pop-jazz guitarist; b. Pittsburgh, March 22, 1943. He began learning the guitar at age eight. Having moved to N.Y., he first recorded as sideperson to Jack McDuff; he then recorded under his own name for Columbia, where he introduced his singing on "Willow Weep for Me." He began to make his mark during the 1960s and early 1970s with his jazz-flavored guitar work. Under the name George "Bad" Benson, he scored his first British hit single with "Supership" (1975). His breakthrough came with the jazz-funk LP *Breezin'* (1976), when it became apparent that this skillful guitarist was a strong singer too. "This Masquerade," a remake of the Leon Russell song, became the first U.S. Top Ten hit for Benson. The Stevie Wonder-ish vocals of Benson were pushed to the forefront on the next hit "The Greatest Love of All," the theme from the Mohammed Ali movie *The Greatest*. In 1980, Benson teamed up with the Quincy Jones, whose jazz-tinged, soul-inflected sound made *Give Me the Night* a major commercial triumph; the album's title track was Benson's first Top Ten single in the U.K. and reached #4 in the U.S. This success with its financial rewards gave Benson the kind of security needed to tempt him back to jazz with Tenderly and Big Boss Band with the Count Basie Orch. One of the most popular jazz guitarists of all time, he has had such success as a commercial singer that few people remember his spectacular drive and fluency as a jazz instrumentalist. Nevertheless, his singing is gorgeous and heartfelt.

DISC.: *Beyond the Blue Horizon* (1971); *White Rabbit* (1973); *Breezin'* (1976); *In Flight* (1977); *Weekend in L.A.* (1977); *Give Me the Night* (1980); *Tenderly* (1989); *Big Boss Band* (1990); *Love Remembers* (1993); *That's Right* (1996); *Essentials: The Very Best of George Benson* (1998); *The George Benson Anthology* (2000). —MM/LP

Benson, Joan, American keyboard player and teacher; b. St. Paul, Minn., Oct. 9, 1929. She studied at the Univ. of Ill. (B.Mus., M.Mus., 1951) and at Ind. Univ. (1953), then went to Europe, where she received additional instruction from Edwin Fischer, Guido Agosti et al., returning to the U.S. in 1960. She pursued a successful career as a versatile keyboard artist, becoming especially well known as a clavichordist and fortepianist through numerous tours of the U.S., Europe, and the Far East. Her repertoire extends from Renaissance pieces to modern music. As a teacher, she served on the faculties of Stanford Univ. (1970–76) and the Univ. of Ore. (1976–87).—NS/LK/DM

Benson, Warren (Frank), American composer and teacher; b. Detroit, Jan. 26, 1924. He studied percussion and horn at Detroit's Cass Technical H.S. before pursuing training in theory at the Univ. of Mich. (B.M., 1949; M.M., 1951).After teaching percussion at the Univ. of Mich. (1943) and playing timpani in the Detroit Sym. Orch. (1946), he was a Fulbright music teacher at Anatolia Coll. in Salonica, Greece (1950–52). Returning to the U.S., he was director of the band and orch. at Mars Hill (N.C.) Coll. (1952–53). He served as prof. of music and composer-in-residence at Ithaca (N.Y.) Coll. (1953–67), where he was founder-director of its percussion ensemble. From 1967 until his retirement in 1993 he was prof. of composition at the Eastman School of Music in Rochester, N.Y. From 1986 to 1988 he was also the Algur H. Meadows Distinguished Visiting Prof. of Composition at Southern Methodist Univ. in Dallas. In 1981–82 he held a Guggenheim fellowship. Benson has

described his output as inclusive in nature, ranging from the tonal to the atonal in a style that remains uniquely his own. In addition to his idiomatic scores for percussion and wind ensemble, he has composed song cycles of high quality. He also publ. a vol. of verse entitled "...And My Daddy Will Play the Drums" (1999).

WORKS: DRAMATIC: *Odysseus*, dance-drama (Salonica, Greece, May 1951); *Bailando*, ballet (1965). **ORCH.:** *A Delphic Serenade* (1953); *5 Brief Encounters* for Strings (1961); Sym. for Drums and Wind Orch. (1962); *Theme and Excursions* for Strings (1963); *Chants and Graces* for Strings, Piccolo, Harp, and Percussion (1964); Horn Concerto (1971); *The Man With the Blue Guitar* (1980); *Beyond Winter: Sweet Aftershowers* for Strings (1981); Concertino for Flute, Strings, and Percussion (1983). **Band:** *Transylvania Fanfare*, concert march (1953); *Night Song* (1958); *Juniperus* (1959); *Polyphonies* for Percussion (1960); *Remembrance* (1963); *The Leaves Are Falling* (1964); *Ginger Marmalade* (1978); Sym. No. 2, *Lost Songs* (1983); *Dawn's Early Light* (1987); *Meditation on I am for Peace* (1990). **WIND ENSEMBLE:** *Star-Edge* for Alto Saxophone and Wind Ensemble (1965); *Recuerdo* for Oboe, English Horn, and Wind Ensemble (1965); *Helix* for Tuba and Wind Ensemble (1966); *The Solitary Dancer* (1966); *The Mask of Night* (1968); *The Passing Bell* (1974); *Wings* (1984); *Other Rivers* (1984); *Danzón- memory* (1991); *Adagietto* (1991); *Dux Variations* (1992); *Divertissement* (1993); *The Drums of Summer* (1997); *Daughter of the Stars (A Reminiscence on Shenandoah)* (1998). **CHAMBER:** *Marche* for Woodwind Quintet (1955); Quintet for Oboe or Soprano Saxophone and Strings (1957); Percussion Trio (1957); Trio for Clarinet, Cello, and Piano (1959); *3 Pieces* for Percussion Quartet (1960); *Streams* for 7 Percussion (1961); *Wind Rose* for Saxophone Quartet (1967); 2 string quartets (1969, 1985); *Capriccio* for Piano Quartet (1972); *The Dream Net* for Alto Saxophone and String Quartet (1976); *Largo Tah* for Bass Trombone and Marimba (1977); *Winter Bittersweet* for 6 Percussion (1981); *Elegy* for Horn and Organ (1982); *Thorgard's Song* for Horn, Crotales, Chimes, Glockenspiel, and Vibraphone (1982); *Fair Game* for Clarinet, Trumpet, Violin, Cello, Piano, and Percussion (1986); *The Red Lion* for Vibraphone and Piano (1988); *Steps* for Brass Quintet (1988); many pieces for Solo Instrument. **VOCAL:** *Psalm XXIV* for Women's Voices and String Orch. (1957); *Love Is* for Antiphonal Choruses (1966); *Shadow Wood* for Soprano and Wind Ensemble or Chamber Orch. (1969; rev. 1992); *Nara* for Soprano, Flute, Piano and 2 Percussion (1970); *Songs of O* for Chorus, Brass Quintet, and Marimba (1974); *The Beaded Leaf* for Bass and Wind Orch. (1974); *Of Rounds* for Antiphonal Choruses and Chamber Ensemble (1975); *Earth, Sky, Sea* for Chorus, Flute, Bass Trombone, and Marimba (1975); *5 Lyrics of Louise Bogan* for Mezzo-soprano and Flute (1978); *Meditation, Prayer, and Sweet Hallelujah* for Antiphonal Choruses and Piano (1979); *Songs for the End of the World* for Mezzo-soprano, English Horn, Horn, Cello, and Marimba (1980); *Moon, Rain, and Memory Jane* for Soprano and 2 Cellos (1984); *Dos Antifonas Lindas* for Soprano, Mezzo-soprano, and Viola (1985); *Songs and Asides About Love* for Baritone, Viola, and Guitar (1999); *Love and the Lady* for Mezzo-soprano and Cello (1999); many other vocal works.

Bent, Ian (David), esteemed English musicologist; b. Birmingham, Jan. 1, 1938. He was educated at the Univ. of Cambridge (B.A., 1961; B.M., 1962; M.A., 1965; Ph.D., 1969, with the diss. The Early History of the English Chapel Royal, c. 1066–1327). From 1965 to 1975 he was a lecturer at King's Coll., Univ. of London, and then a prof. of music and head of the music dept. at the

Univ. of Nottingham from 1975 to 1987. In 1982–83 he was a visiting prof. at Harvard Univ. In 1986 he became a prof. at Columbia Univ., where he was made the Anne Parsons Bender Prof. of Music in 1990. With his first wife, Margaret Bent, and B. Trowell, he edited the rev. ed. of Dunstable's works in the Musica Britannica series, VIII (1970). In 1986 he became general ed. of the series Cambridge Studies in Music Theory and Analysis. From 1990 he was active in the collaborative Eng. translations of Schenker's *The Masterworks in Music* (1994–97) and *Der Tonwille* (2001 et seq.). Bent has devoted much of his research to the history of music theory in the 18th, 19th, and 20th centuries. He has contributed articles to many scholarly books and journals. He also served as a senior consulting ed. (1971–80) and area ed. (1994–2000) of *The New Grove Dictionary of Music and Musicians*, to which he contributed.

WRITINGS: Ed. *Source Materials and the Interpretation of Music: A Memorial Volume to Thurston Dart* (London, 1981); *Analysis* (London and N.Y., 1987); *Music Analysis in the Nineteenth Century* (2 vols., Cambridge, 1994); ed. *Music Theory in the Age of Romanticism* (Cambridge, 1996).—**NS/LK/DM**

Bent, Margaret (Hilda), English musicologist; b. St. Albans, Dec. 23, 1940. She was an organ scholar at Girton Coll., Cambridge (B.A., 1962; B.Mus., 1963), and also studied with Dart, receiving her Ph.D. in 1969 from the Univ. of Cambridge with the diss. *The Old Hall Manuscript: A Palaeographical Study*. She taught at King's Coll. (1965–75); also, concurrently, at Goldsmiths' Coll. from 1972. In 1975 she joined the faculty of Brandeis Univ. at Waltham, Mass. She joined the faculty of Princeton Univ. in 1981; she also served as president of the American Musicological Soc. (1985–86). In 1992 she became senior research fellow of All Souls Coll., Oxford. With A. Hughes, she ed. *The Old Hall Manuscript* in the Corpus Mensurabilis Musicae series, XLVI (1969–73); with her former husband, **Ian Bent**, and B. Trowell, she ed. the revised edition of Dunstable's works in the Musica Britannica series; also publ. a valuable study, *Dunstaple* (London, 1981).—**NS/LK/DM**

Bentoiu, Pascal, Romanian composer and writer on music; b. Bucharest, April 22, 1927. He was a pupil of M. Jora in Bucharest (1943–48). After working at the Inst. for Folklore there (1953–56), he pursued research in ethnomusicology and aesthetics. He publ. three books on aesthetics: *Imagine şi sens* (Bucharest, 1971), *Deschideri spre lumea muzicii* (Bucharest, 1973), and *Gîndirea muzicală* (Bucharest, 1975), and a study of Enesco's works, *Capodopere enesciene* (Bucharest, 1984). As a composer, he won the State Prize in 1964, the Prix Italia of the RAI in 1968, and the Enesco Prize of the Romanian Academy in 1974. He was president of the Romanian Composers Union from 1990.

WORKS: DRAMATIC: O p e r a : *Amorul doctor* (The Love Doctor; 1964; Bucharest, Dec. 23, 1966); *Jertfirea Iphigeniei* (The Immolation of Iphigenia; Bucharest, Sept. 1968); *Hamlet* (1969; Bucharest, Nov. 19, 1971). **ORCH.:** Concert Overture (1948; rev. 1961); 2 piano concertos (1954, 1960); *Suite Transylvania* (1955); *Luceafarul* (The Morning Star), symphonic poem (1957); Violin Concerto (1958); *Bucharest Images* (1959); 8 syms.

(1965, 1974, 1976, 1978, 1979, 1985, 1986, 1987); *Eminesciana III* (1976); Cello Concerto (1989). **CHAMBER:** Piano Sonata (1947; rev. 1957); 6 string quartets (1953–82); Violin Sonata (1962). **VOCAL:** Various works.—**NS/LK/DM**

Benton, Brook (Benjamin Peay), one of the pioneer soul singers of the 1950s; b. Camden, S.C., Sept. 9 (or 19), 1931; d. N.Y.C., April 9, 1988. In the late 1940s and early 1950s, Brook Benton toured the gospel circuit with the Camden Jubilee Singers, the Bill Landford Spiritual Singers and the Golden Gate Quartet. Signed as solo artist to Epic Records in 1953, Benton also recorded for the RCA subsidiary Vik before meeting songwriter Clyde Otis around 1957. Benton, Otis and arranger Belford Hendricks subsequently formed a songwriting partnership. Recording hundreds of demonstration records with Otis, the pair co-wrote Nat "King" Cole's "Looking Back," and Benton co-wrote Clyde McPhatter's "A Lover's Question" and The Diamonds' "The Stroll," all smash hits from 1958. In 1959 Otis persuaded Mercury Records to sign Benton. Over the next four years the team provided Benton with a number of hit recordings on Mercury, including the top R&B and smash pop hit "It's Just a Matter of Time," "Endlessly," "Thank You Pretty Baby," "Kiddio" and "The Boll Weevil Song." Other hits recorded by Benton included "So Many Ways" (a top R&B and smash pop hit) and the pop and R&B smash "Hotel Happiness." "So Close," "Think Twice" and "Lie to Me" became R&B smashes.

In late 1959 Brook Benton recorded *The Two of Us* with Dinah Washington, and the album yielded two huge hits with "Baby (You've Got What It Takes)" and "A Rockin' Good Way." He continued to record for Mercury with modest commercial success, switching to RCA in 1965 and Reprise in 1967. He eventually scored his final smash hit on Cotillion with Tony Joe White's "Rainy Night in Georgia" in 1970. He later recorded for MGM and All Platinum and maintained his career on the club circuit. On April 9, 1988, Brook Benton died in N.Y. at the age of 56 of complications from spinal meningitis.

DISC.: *At His Best* (1959); *It's Just a Matter of Time* (1959); *Endlessly* (1959); *So Many Ways I Love You* (1960); *Songs I Love to Sing* (1960); *If You Believe* (1961); *The Boll Weevil Song* (1961); *There Goes That Song Again* (1962); *Lie to Me* (1962); *Best Ballads of Broadway* (1963); *Born to Sing The Blues* (1964); *On The Country Side* (1964); *This Bitter Earth* (1964); *Mother Earth* (1966); *Mother Nature, Father Time* (1965); *That Old Feeling* (1966); *My Country* (1966); *Laura, What's He Got That I Ain't Got* (1967); *Do Your Thing* (1969); *Today* (1970); *Home Style* (1970); *Gospel Truth* (1971); *Story Teller* (1972); *Something for Everyone* (1973); *This Is Brook Benton* (1976).—**BH**

Benton, Rita, American musicologist and music librarian; b. N.Y., June 28, 1918; d. Paris, March 23, 1980. She studied with Friskin (piano diploma, 1938) and Wagenaar (theory) at the Juilliard School of Music in N.Y., at Hunter Coll. in N.Y. (B.A., 1939), and musicology at the Univ. of Iowa (M.A., 1951; Ph.D., 1961), where she was a music librarian (from 1953) and a member of the music dept. faculty (from 1967). In 1962–63 she was president of the Music Library Assn. She ed. *Fontes artis musicae* (from 1976), publ. a catalogue of Pleyel's works (N.Y., 1977), and was general ed. of the *Director of Music Research Libraries*. J. Halley collaborated with her on the study *Pleyel as Music Publisher: A Documentary Sourcebook of Early 19th-century Music* (Stuyvesant, N.Y., 1990). **—NS/LK/DM**

Bentonelli (real name, **Benton**), **Joseph (Horace),** American tenor; b. Sayre, Okla., Sept. 10, 1898; d. Oklahoma City, April 4, 1975. Following the frequent practice among American singers, he adopted an Italian-sounding name when he embarked on a singing career. He was a student of Jean de Reszke in Paris. In 1925 he made his public debut with the de Reszke Ensemble in Nice. In 1934 he appeared at the Chicago Opera. On Jan. 10, 1936, he made his Metropolitan Opera debut in N.Y. as Massenet's Des Grieux, singing there until 1937. His repertoire included many leading Italian roles.**—NS/LK/DM**

Bentzon, Jørgen, Danish composer, cousin of **Niels Viggo Bentzon;** b. Copenhagen, Feb. 14, 1897; d. Horsholm, July 9, 1951. He studied composition with Carl Nielsen (1915–18). At the same time, he took courses in jurisprudence; subsequently he was attached to the Ministry of Justice in Denmark, and served as clerk of records of the Danish Supreme Court. He also taught piano and theory at a People's School of Music in Copenhagen. As a composer, he followed the Romantic trends current in Scandinavia; an influence of Nielsen pervades his music.

WORKS: O p e r a : *Saturnalia* (Copenhagen, Dec. 15, 1944). **ORCH.:** *Dramatic Overture* (1923); *Variations on a Danish Folktune* for Piano, Strings, and Percussion (1928); 3 chamber concertos: No. 1, *Symphonic Trio,* for 3 instrumental groups of Violins, Horns, and Cellos (1928–29), No. 2, *Intermezzo Espressivo,* for Oboe, Clarinet, Horn, Bassoon, Strings, and Percussion (1935), and No. 3, for Clarinet and Chamber Orch. (1941); *Fotomontage,* overture (1934); *Variations* for Chamber Orch. (1935); *Cyklevise-Rhapsody* (1936); *Sinfonia seria* for School Orch. (1937); *Sinfonia buffa* for School Orch. (1939); 2 syms.: No. 1, *Dickens-Symphonie* (1939–40) and No. 2 (1946–47); Sinfonietta for Strings (1943). **CHAMBER:** 5 string quartets (1921–28); String Trio (1921); Sonatina for Flute, Clarinet, and Bassoon (1924); *Variazioni interrotti* for Clarinet, Bassoon, and String Trio (1925); Duo for Violin and Cello (1927); *Racconti 1–6* for 3 to 5 Instruments (1935–50). **P i a n o :** *Variations* (1921); Sonata (1946). **VOCAL:** *En romersk Fortaelling* (A Roman Tale), cantata for Soloists, Chorus, and Piano (1937); *Mikrofoni No. 1* for Baritone, Flute, and Piano Trio (1937–39); songs; choruses. **—NS/LK/DM**

Bentzon, Niels Viggo, prominent Danish pianist, pedagogue, and composer, cousin of **Jørgen Bentzon;** b. Copenhagen, Aug. 24, 1919; d. there, April 25, 2000. He began his piano training with his mother, and then took lessons with the jazz pianist Leo Mathisen; he subsequently studied piano with Christiansen, organ with Bangert, and theory with Jeppesen at the Copenhagen Cons. (1938–42). In 1943 he made his debut as a pianist, and later toured Europe and the U.S. He taught

at the Århus Cons. (1945–49) and the Royal Danish Cons. of Music in Copenhagen (from 1949). Although a prolific composer, Bentzon also found time to write music criticism, publ. poetry, and paint. He publ. *Tolvtoneteknik* (Copenhagen, 1953) and *Beethoven: en skitse af et geni* (Copenhagen, 1970). His compositions followed along avant-garde lines for the most part, encompassing happenings, audio-visual scores, and graphic notation.

WORKS: DRAMATIC: O p e r a : *Faust III* (1961–62; Kiel, June 21, 1964); *Automaten* (1973; Kiel, May 3, 1974). **B a l l e t :** *Metafor* (Copenhagen, March 31, 1950); *Kurtisanen* (The Courtesan; Copenhagen, Dec. 19, 1953); *Døren* (The Door; Copenhagen, Nov. 14, 1962); *Jenny von Westphalen* (Århus, Sept. 9, 1965); *Jubilacumsballet 800* (1968); *Duell* (Stockholm, Nov. 12, 1977). **ORCH.:** 22 numbered syms. (1942–91); 8 piano concertos (1947–82); 4 violin concertos (1951–76); 3 cello concertos (1956–82); 2 flute concertos (1963, 1976); concertos for Oboe (1952), Accordion (1962), Clarinet (1970–71), Viola (1973), Tuba (1975), etc. **CHAMBER:** 11 string quartets (1940–76); 7 violin sonatas (1940–73); 5 wind quintets (1941–57); 4 cello sonatas (1946–72); 8 sonatas for different solo wind instruments (1947–73); 4 quartets for 4 Flutes (1974–77); Harp Sonata (1986); *Trio Quartetto* for Violin, Cello, and Piano (1991); Quartet for Clarinet, Violin, Viola, and Cello (1993). **KEYBOARD:** 15 numbered piano sonatas (1940–81) and numerous other piano pieces; organ music. **OTHER:** Various vocal works and occasional pieces.**—NS/LK/DM**

Benucci, Francesco, famous Italian bass; b. c. 1745; d. Florence, April 5, 1824. He began his career in 1769. In 1783 he went to Vienna, where he created the roles of Figaro in *Le nozze di Figaro* (Vienna, May 1, 1786) and Guglielmo in *Così fan tutte* (Vienna, Jan. 26, 1790). He visited London in 1788–89, then lived again in Vienna. In 1795 he returned to Italy.**—NS/LK/DM**

Benvenuti, Tommaso, Italian opera composer; b. Cavarzere (Venice), Feb. 4, 1838; d. Rome, Feb. 26, 1906. When he was 18 years old, his opera *Valenzia Candiano* was announced for performance in Mantua, but was taken off after a rehearsal. The following year, he succeeded in having his second opera, *Adriana Lecouvreur,* produced in Milan (Nov. 26, 1857). Other productions followed: *Guglielmo Shakespeare* (Parma, Feb. 14, 1861), *La Stella di Toledo* (Milan, April 23, 1864), *Il Falconiere* (Venice, Feb. 16, 1878), *Beatrice di Suevia* (Venice, Feb. 20, 1890), and *Le baruffe Chiozzotte,* opera buffa (Florence, Jan. 30, 1895). Although Benvenuti's operas are workmanlike and effective, they failed to hold the stage after initial successes.**—NS/LK/DM**

Ben-Yohanan, Asher, Israeli composer and pedagogue; b. Kávala, Greece, May 22, 1929. He settled in Palestine in 1935 and studied composition with Ben-Haim in Tel Aviv. After training from Copland at the Berkshire Music Center in Tanglewood (summer, 1958), he studied with Reese and La Rue at N.Y. Univ. (1958–61). He continued his training with Nono in Venice, and in Darmstadt (1966), and then studied at the Univ. of Mich. (M.M., 1970). In 1970–71 he was the Morse fellow in composition and a teacher at the Univ. of Cincinnati Coll.-Cons. of Music. He taught theory and literature at the Israel Cons. of Music (1962–69) and at the Telma Yellin Music and Arts School (1964–87), where he also was head of the music dept. (until 1975). In 1973 he became prof. of theory and composition at Bar-Ilan Univ. From 1989 to 1992 he was chairman of the Israel Composers' League. Ben-Yohanan's works have been widely performed in Israel and in many other countries throughout the world.

WORKS: ORCH.: *Independence Day Parade* for Wind Band (1956); *Festive Overture* (1957); *2 Movements* (1959); *Music* (1967); Concertino for Strings (1973); *Variations* (1980; rev. 1989); *Meditations* for Chamber Orch. (1992). **CHAMBER:** String Quartet (1962–64); *Chamber Music for 6* (1968); *Quartetto Concertato* for Piano, Clarinet, Trombone, and Cello (1969–70); *Meditations on a Folk Song* for Piano, Flute, and Clarinet (1972); *3 Pieces for 3 Woodwinds* for Oboe, Clarinet, and Bassoon (1978); Woodwind Quintet (1985); *Divertimento* for Brass Trio (1988–89); *Hidden Feelings* for Harp (1990). **VOCAL:** *Ode to Jerusalem* for Chorus (1954); *Mosaic* for Soprano and 10 Players (1970–71); *Four Summer Songs* for Baritone and Piano (1974); *Three Songs Without Titles* for Soprano and Piano (1983); *Yefeh Nof* (O Fair Sight) for Chorus (1984).—**NS/LK/DM**

Benzell, Mimi, American soprano; b. Bridgeport, Conn., April 6, 1922; d. Manhasset, Long Island, N.Y., Dec. 23, 1970. Her grandfather was a singer of Jewish folk songs in Russia before his emigration to America. She studied at Hunter Coll. of the City Univ. of N.Y. and with Olga Eisner at the Mannes Coll. of Music in N.Y. In 1944 she made her operatic debut in Mexico City. On Dec. 3, 1944, she made her first appearance at the Metropolitan Opera in N.Y. in a concert, and then returned there to make her formal operatic debut as the Queen of the Night on Jan. 5, 1945; she remained on its roster until 1949. In subsequent years she pursued a career as a singer of popular music, winning her greatest success in the Broadway musical *Milk and Honey* (1961–63).—**NS/LK/DM**

Benzi, Roberto, French conductor; b. Marseilles, Dec. 12, 1937. He began music training as a small child and in 1948 appeared as a youthful conductor in Bayonne and of the Colonne Orch. in Paris. He pursued academic studies at the Sorbonne in Paris and was a conducting pupil of Cluytens (1947–50). In 1954 he made his debut as an opera conductor, and in 1959 he made his first appearance at the Paris Opéra conducting *Carmen.* He subsequently made guest appearances in Europe, Japan, and North and South America. On Dec. 11, 1972, he made his Metropolitan Opera debut in N.Y. conducting *Faust.* From 1973 to 1987 he was music director in Bordeaux, and then was principal conductor and artistic advisor of Arnhem's Het Gelders Orch. from 1989. In 1966 he married **Jane Rhodes.**—**NS/LK/DM**

Berardi, Angelo, Italian organist, theorist, and composer; b. S. Agata, Feltria, c. 1630; d. Rome, April 9, 1694. He was a student of Mario Scacchi. He served as maestro di cappella and organist at Tivoli (1673–79), and then was at the Spoleto Cathedral (1681) and at the college of S. Angelo in Viterbo (1687). In 1693 he was a canon and maestro di cappella at S. Maria in Trastevere, Rome.

WRITINGS (all publ. in Bologna): *Ragionamenti musicali* (1681); *Documenti armonici* (1687); *Arcani musicale* (1690); *Il Perché musicale ovvero Staffetta armonica* (1693).

WORKS: *Missa pro defunctis* (1663); *Salmi concertati* (Bologna, 1668); *Concentus cum Missa* (Bologna, 1669); *Musiche diverse variamente concertate per camera* (Bologna, 1689); many canons.—**NS/LK/DM**

Berardi, Sangeeta Michael, avant-garde guitarist; b. Waterbury, Conn., Sept. 2, 1939. He began playing guitar at age 10, and started gigging at about 14, but his musical progress was delayed when he was arrested for armed robbery at 18. While in prison, he resumed the guitar and on his release in 1960 began gigging at Providence Coll. and elsewhere while attending the Univ. of Conn. (B.A., English). In 1963, he moved to Chicago where he worked with Baby Face Willette and Joe Diorio, with whom he studied informally. In 1964, he was back in Conn., where he studied with Bertram Turetzky. He led bands in N.Y. with Perry Robinson, Dewey Johnson, and others (1965–8), while studying with Ronnie Ball. He led groups in Woodstock, New Paltz and N.Y., and co-led bands with Sonny Simmons and with Sunny Murray (1968–9). In the spring to fall of 1968, he was the music director at Group 212, a multimedia arts cooperative near Woodstock, bringing Archie Shepp, Murray, and many others and paving the way for the Creative Music Studio. He appeared at N.Y. loft festivals (1970–2) with his own groups and co-led one with Marzette Watts at the East Village Inn, and played in the groups of David Izenson, Roswell Rudd, and Alice Coltrane. In 1972, he began a weekly concert and workshop series on the SUNY New Paltz campus; he later moved to San Francisco where he led bands and performed with Shepp and Pharoah Sanders. From 1975, he became heavily involved with yoga and the music of India. In 1980, he moved back to N.Y. and opened up his 7th Avenue loft as a workshop/performance space featuring Rashied Ali, Sanders, Dave Schnitter, Joe Lovano, and many others until the building closed in 1984. In 1985, he appeared in San Francisco with Shepp. From 1985–8, he concentrated on writing prose and poems and drawing. From 1988–93, Berardi was in El Cerrito, Calif., making occasional appearances. Back on the East Coast, a severe back injury curtailed his playing during 1994–5, but in 1996 he began performing again.

DISC.: R. Ali: *The Godz* (1966); *Rock and Other Four Letter Words* (1968); *Soundtrack for "Brand X"* (1968); *Sangeeta: Divine Song* (1979).—**LP**

Berberian, Cathy (actually, **Catherine**), versatile American mezzo-soprano; b. Attleboro, Mass., July 4, 1925; d. Rome, March 6, 1983. She studied singing, dancing, and the art of pantomime; took courses at Columbia Univ. and N.Y. Univ.; then studied voice in Milan with Giorgina del Vigo. In 1957 she made her debut in a concert in Naples; attracted wide attention in 1958, when she performed John Cage's *Fontana Mix*, which demanded a fantastic variety of sound effects. Her vocal range extended to three octaves, causing one bewildered music critic to remark that she could sing both *Tristan* and *Isolde*. Thanks to her uncanny ability to produce ultrahuman (and subhuman) tones, and her willingness to incorporate into her professional vocalization a variety of animal noises, guttural sounds, grunts and growls, squeals, squeaks and squawks, clicks and clucks, shrieks and screeches, hisses, hoots, and hollers, she instantly became the darling of inventive composers of the avant-garde, who eagerly dedicated to her their otherwise unperformable works. She married one of them, **Luciano Berio**, in 1950, but their marriage was dissolved in 1964. She could also intone classical music. Shortly before her death, she sang her own version of the *Internationale* for an Italian television program commemorating the centennial of the death of Karl Marx (1983). She was an avant-garde composer in her own right; she wrote multimedia works, such as *Stripsody*, an arresting soliloquy of labial and laryngeal sounds, and an eponymously titled piano piece, *Morsicat(h)y*. Her integrity as a performer is reflected in her life-long insistance that her objective was always to meet the challenge of the new art of her time.—**NS/LK/DM**

Berbiguier, Antoine (Benoît-) Tranquille,

French flutist and composer; b. Calderousse, Vaucluse, Dec. 21, 1782; d. Pont-Levoy, near Blois, Jan. 28, 1833. He studied with Wunderlich at the Paris Cons. He composed numerous works for flute, including ten concertos and many chamber pieces.—**NS/LK/DM**

Berchem, Jacquet or Jachet de,

Flemish composer; b. Berchem-lez-Anvers, c. 1505; d. c. 1565. He was active in Venice until serving as maestro di cappella in Verona from 1546 until about 1550. He may have subsequently been in the service of Alfonso II d'Este in Florence. Berchem was a significant composer of madrigals, of which he publ. three vols. (Venice, 1546, 1555, 1561). The latter vol. includes his *Capriccio*, after Ariosto's *Orlando furioso*, which constitutes one of the earliest madrigal cycles. Among his other works were two masses, nine motets, and several chansons.

BIBL.: D. Hall, *The Italian Secular Vocal Works of J. B.* (diss., Ohio State Univ., 1973); G. Nugent, *The J. Motets and their Authors* (diss., Princeton Univ., 1973).—**NS/LK/DM**

Berens, (Johann) Hermann,

German pianist and pedagogue; b. Hamburg, April 7, 1826; d. Stockholm, May 9, 1880. He studied with his father, Karl Berens of Hamburg, then had instruction with Reissiger in Dresden, and later with Czerny in Vienna. In 1847 he emigrated to Sweden. After serving as music director to the Hussar regiment in Orebro (1849–60), he was music director at Mindre Teatern in Stockholm (from 1860). In 1861 he was appointed to the staff of the Stockholm Cons.; in 1868 was named prof. there. He wrote an operetta, *En sommarnattsdröm* (1856), and the operas *Violetta* (1855), *Lully och Quinault* (1859), *En utflykt i det gröne* (1862), and *Riccardo* (1869), which sank without a trace. But his collection of piano studies, *Neueste Schule der Geläufigkeit*, modeled after Czerny's studies, remained popular with piano students and teachers for many years.—**NS/LK/DM**

Berenstadt, Gaetano,

German castrato alto who flourished in the first half of the 18th century. In 1711 he sang in Novara and Bologna, and then entered the service of the Grand Duchess of Tuscany. After appearances in Düsseldorf (1712–14), he made his London debut in Handel's *Rinaldo* on Jan. 5, 1716. He also gave concerts there. In 1717 he sang in Dresden and served as virtuoso to the King of Poland and Elector of Saxony. After singing in Rome (1719–20) and Venice (1721), he returned to London and appeared with the Royal Academy of Music (1722–24), creating roles in Handel's *Ottone* (Jan. 23, 1723), *Flavio* (May 25, 1723), and *Giulio Cesare* (Feb. 20, 1724). In 1726 he sang in Rome and in 1726–27 in Naples. He then served as a member of the royal chapel in the latter city from 1727 to 1734. He also sang in Florence (1727–28; 1729–30; 1733–34) and Rome (1728–29; 1732).—**NS/LK/DM**

Berezovsky, Maximus (Sozontovich),

Russian tenor and composer; b. Glukhov, Oct. 27, 1740; d. (suicide?) St. Petersburg, April 2, 1777. He studied at the Kiev Ecclesiastic Academy, then was chorister at the Court Chapel in St. Petersburg. He attracted attention by his lyric voice, and in 1765 was sent by the Russian government to Bologna for further study. He became a pupil of Padre Martini, and wrote an opera, *Demofoonte* (1773), which was produced in Bologna. Upon his return to Russia, he was unable to compete with Italian musicians who had acquired all the lucrative positions in the field of vocal teaching and opera. He became despondent and apparently cut his own throat. —**NS/LK/DM**

Berezowsky, Nicolai,

talented Russian-born American composer; b. St. Petersburg, May 17, 1900; d. (suicide?) N.Y., Aug. 27, 1953. He studied piano, violin, and voice at the Imperial Chapel in St. Petersburg. After graduating in 1916, he obtained work as a violinist in the orch. of the provincial opera theater in Saratov, on the Volga River, where he played until 1919. The then joined the orch. of the Bolshoi Theater in Moscow. He crossed the border to Poland in 1920, managed to obtain an American visa, and arrived in N.Y. in 1922. He was engaged as a violinist in the orch. of the Capital Theater; in 1923 he joined the N.Y. Phil., remaining there until 1929. At the same time he took violin lessons with Paul Kochanski and studied composition with Rubin Goldmark. In 1928 he became an American citizen. He began to compose in larger forms; his Clarinet Sextet was performed at a chamber music festival in Washington, D.C., on Oct. 7, 1926. In 1929 his *Hebrew Suite* was conducted by Mengelberg with the N.Y. Phil. Soon Berezowsky obtained other opportunities; Koussevitzky let him conduct the Boston Sym. in performances of his First Sym. in 1931 and his Fourth Sym. in 1943; Koussevitzky himself conducted Berezowsky's second and third Syms. The famous German violinist Carl Flesch played the solo part of Berezowsky's Violin Concerto with the Dresden Phil. in 1930; Primrose played his Viola Concerto in 1942; and Piatigorsky performed his *Concerto lirico* with Koussevitzky and the Boston Sym. Berezowsky continued to play violin and conduct. From 1932 to 1936 and from 1941 to 1946 he was violinist and asst. conductor with CBS, and from 1935 to 1940 was a member of the Coolidge String Quartet. He held a Guggenheim fellowship in 1948. His cantata *Gilgamesh* (1947) was favorably received, and his children's opera *Babar the Elephant* (1953) had numerous performances. His music possesses a Romantic quality, ingratiatingly Russian in color, and in his later works he introduced fine impressionistic harmonies.˙ He died of intestinal congestion apparently caused by a suicidal dose of powerful sedative drugs. His first wife (he was married twice) wrote a sweet little memoir, *Duet with Nicky*, describing his happier days.

WORKS: DRAMATIC: Children's Opera: *Babar the Elephant* (N.Y., Feb. 21, 1953). **ORCH.:** Sinfonietta (NBC, N.Y., May 8, 1932; won a prize); 4 syms.: No. 1 (Boston Sym., March 16, 1931, composer conducting), No. 2 (Boston Sym., Feb. 16, 1934), No. 3 (Rochester, N.Y., Jan. 21, 1937), and No. 4 (Boston Sym. Orch., Oct. 22, 1943, composer conducting); *Hebrew Suite* (1929); *Christmas Festival Overture* (N.Y., Dec. 23, 1943); *Soldiers on the Town* (N.Y., Nov. 25, 1943); Violin Concerto (Dresden, April 29, 1930; Carl Flesch, soloist, composer conducting); *Concerto lirico* for Cello and Orch. (Boston, Feb. 22, 1935; Piatigorsky, soloist, Koussevitzky conducting); Viola Concerto (CBS Orch., N.Y., Oct. 11, 1941); Harp Concerto (Philadelphia, Jan. 26, 1945); *Passacaglia* for Theremin and Orch. (N.Y., Feb. 29, 1948); *Fantaisie* for 2 Pianos and Orch. (N.Y., Feb. 12, 1932); *Introduction and Waltz* for Orch. (N.Y., Oct. 15, 1939); *Theme and Variations*, sextet for Strings, Clarinet, and Piano (Washington, D.C., Oct. 7, 1926); *Sextet Concerto* for Strings (1953). **CHAMBER:** Duo for Clarinet and Viola (1931); Woodwind Quintet (1941). **VOCAL:** *Gilgamesh*, cantata (N.Y., May 16, 1947).

BIBL.: A. Berezowsky, *Duet with Nicky* (N.Y., 1943). —NS/LK/DM

Berg, Alban (Maria Johannes),

greatly significant Austrian composer whose music combined classical clarity of design and highly original melodic and harmonic techniques that became historically associated with the Second Viennese School; b. Vienna, Feb. 9, 1885; d. there, Dec. 24, 1935. He played piano as a boy and composed songs without formal training. He worked as a clerk in a government office in Lower Austria; in 1904 he met Schoenberg, who became his teacher, mentor, and close friend; he remained Schoenberg's pupil for six years. A fellow classmate was Webern; together they initiated the radical movement known to history as the New or Second Viennese School of composition. In Nov. 1918 Schoenberg organized in Vienna the Soc. for Private Musical Performances (Verein für Musikalische Privataufführungen) with the purpose of performing works unacceptable to established musical society. So as to emphasize the independence of the new organization, music critics were excluded from attendance. The society was disbanded in 1922, having accomplished its purpose. In 1925 Berg joined the membership of the newly created ISCM, which continued in an open arena the promotion of fresh musical ideas.

Berg's early works reflected the Romantic style of Wagner, Wolf, and Mahler; typical of this period were his *Three Pieces for Orch.* (1913–15). As early as 1917 Berg began work on his opera *Wozzeck* (after the romantic play by Büchner), which was to become his masterpiece. The score represents an ingenious synthesis of Classical forms and modern techniques; it is organized as a series of purely symphonic sections in traditional Baroque forms, among them a passacaglia with 21 variations, a dance suite, and a rhapsody, all cast in a setting marked by dissonant counterpoint. Its first production at the Berlin State Opera on Dec. 14, 1925, precipitated a storm of protests and press reviews of extreme violence; a similarly critical reception was accorded to *Wozzeck* in Prague on Nov. 11, 1926. Undismayed, Berg and his friends responded by publishing a brochure incorporating the most vehement of these reviews so as to shame and denounce the critics. Stokowski, ever eager to defy convention, gave the first U.S. performance of *Wozzeck* in Philadelphia on March 19, 1931; it aroused a great deal of interest and was received with cultured equanimity. Thereafter, performances of *Wozzeck* multiplied in Europe, and in due time the opera became recognized as a modern masterpiece. Shortly after the completion of *Wozzeck*, Berg wrote a *Lyric Suite* for String Quartet in six movements; it was first played in Vienna by the Kolisch Quartet on Jan. 8, 1927; in 1928 Berg arranged the second, third, and fourth movements for String Orch., which were performed in Berlin on Jan. 31, 1929. Rumors of a suppressed vocal part for the sixth movement of the suite, bespeaking Berg's secret affection for a married woman, Hanna Fuchs-Robettin, impelled Douglas M. Greene to institute a search for the original score; he discovered it in 1976 and, with the help of George Perle, decoded the vocal line in an annotated copy of the score that Berg's widow, understandably reluctant to perpetuate her husband's emotional aberrations, turned over to a Vienna library. The text proved to be Stefan Georg's rendition of Baudelaire's *De Profundis clamavi* from *Les Fleurs du mal*. Indeed, Berg inserted in the score all kinds of semiotical and numerological clues to his affection in a sort of symbolical synthesis. The *Lyric Suite* with its vocal finale was performed for the first time at Abraham Goodman House, N.Y., by the Columbia String Quartet and Katherine Ciesinski, mezzo-soprano, on Nov. 1, 1979.

Berg's second opera, *Lulu* (1928–35), to a libretto derived from two plays by Wedekind, was left unfinished at the time of his death; two acts and music from the *Symphonische Stücke aus der Oper Lulu* of 1934 were performed posthumously in Zürich on June 2, 1937. Again, Berg's widow intervened to forestall any attempt to have the work reconstituted by another musician. However, Berg's publishers, asserting their legal rights, commissioned Friedrich Cerha to re-create the third act from materials available in other authentic sources, or used by Berg elsewhere; the task required 12 years (1962–74) for its completion. After Berg's widow died in 1976, several opera houses openly competed for the Cerha version of the work; the premiere of the complete opera, incorporating this version, was first presented at the Paris Opéra on Feb. 24, 1979; the first U.S. performance followed in Santa Fe, N.Mex., on July 28, 1979. As in *Wozzeck*, so in *Lulu*, Berg organized the score in a series of classical forms; but while *Wozzeck* was written ˙before Schoenberg's formulation of the method of composition in 12 tones related solely to one another, *Lulu* was set in full-fledged dodecaphonic techniques; even so, Berg allowed himself frequent divagations, contrary to the dodecaphonic code, into triadic tonal harmonies.

Berg's last completed work was a Violin Concerto commissioned by Louis Krasner, who gave its first performance at the Festival of the ISCM in Barcelona on April 19, 1936. The score bears the inscription "Dem Andenken eines Engels," the angel being the daughter of Alma Mahler and Walter Gropius who died at an early age. The work is couched in the 12–tone technique, with free and frequent interludes of passing tonality.

WORKS: O p e r a : *Wozzeck*, after Büchner, op.7 (1917–22; Berlin, Dec. 14, 1925, E. Kleiber conducting); *Lulu*, after Wedekind (1928–35; Acts 1and 2 complete, with Act 3 in short score; Acts 1 and 2, with music from the *Symphonische Stücke aus der Oper Lulu* [1934] to accompany the Act 3 death of Lulu, Zürich, June 2, 1937; 2nd version, with Act 3 realized by Friedrich Cerha, Paris, Feb. 24, 1979, Boulez conducting). **OTHER WORKS:** 70 lieder, including settings of Ibsen, Goethe, Rückert, Heine, Burns, and Rilke (1900–05); *7 frühe Lieder* for Voice and Piano (1905–08; rev. and orchestrated 1928; Vienna, Nov. 6, 1928); *Variations on an Original Theme* for Piano (Vienna, Nov. 6, 1928); Piano Sonata, op.1 (1907–08; Vienna, April 24, 1911; rev. 1920); *4 Lieder* for Medium Voice and Piano, op.2 (1908–09; rev. 1920); String Quartet, op.3 (1910; Vienna, April 24, 1911; rev. 1924); *5 Orchesterlieder nach Ansichtskartentexten von Peter Altenberg*, op.4 (1912; 2 numbers perf. in Vienna, March 31, 1913, Schoenberg conducting; first complete perf., Rome, Jan. 24, 1953, Horenstein conducting); *4 Stücke* for Clarinet and Piano, op.5 (1913; Vienna, Oct. 17, 1919); *3 Stücke* for Orch., op.6. (1913–15; rev. 1929; first complete perf., Oldenburg, April 14, 1930); *3 Bruchstücke from Wozzeck* for Soprano and Orch., op.7 (1923; Frankfurt am Main, June 11, 1924, Scherchen conducting); *Kammerkonzert* for Piano, Violin, and 13 Wind Instruments (the thematic material based on letter-notes in the names of Schoenberg, Webern, and Berg; 1923–25; Berlin, March 27, 1927, Scherchen conducting; its *Adagio*, scored for Violin, Clarinet, and Piano, was arranged in 1934); *Lyrische Suite* for String Quartet (1925–26; Vienna, Jan. 8, 1927, Kolisch Quartet; movements 2–4 arranged for String Orch., 1928; Berlin, Jan. 31, 1929, Horenstein conducting; with newly discovered vocal finale, N.Y., Nov. 1, 1979, Columbia String Quartet, K. Ciesinski mezzo-soprano); *Der Wein*, concert aria for Soprano and Orch., after Baudelaire (1929; Königsberg, June 4, 1930); *Symphonische Stücke aus der Oper Lulu* or *Lulu-Symphonie (Suite)*, in 5 movements, with soprano soloist in no. 3, *Lied der Lulu* (Berlin, Nov. 30, 1934, Kleiber conducting); Violin Concerto, *Dem Andenken eines Engels* (1935; Barcelona, April 19, 1936; L. Krasner soloist, Scherchen conducting); also piano arrangements of Schreker's *Der ferne Klang* (1911) andSchoenberg's *Gurrelieder* (1912), and the last 2 movements of the String Quartet, op.10, for Voice and Piano. He also made an arrangement for chamber ensemble of J. Strauss's waltz *Wine, Women, and Song*. A historical-critical complete edition of his works began publication in Vienna in 1995.

WRITINGS: Berg contributed articles to many contemporary music journals; also wrote analyses for Schoenberg's *Gurrelieder, Kammersymphonie,* and *Pelleas und Melisande.*

BIBL.: W. Reich, *A. B.: Mit B.s eigenen Schriftem und Beiträgen von Theodor Wiesengrund-Adorno und Ernst Křenek* (Vienna, 1937); R. Leibowitz, *Schoenberg et son école* (Paris, 1947; Eng. tr., 1949, as *Schoenberg and His School*); H. Redlich, *A. B.: Versuch einer Würdigung* (Vienna, 1957; abr. Eng. tr., 1957, as *A. B.: The Man and His Music*); W. Reich, ed., *A. B.: Bildnis im Wort: Selbstzeugnisse und Aussagen der Freunde* (Zürich, 1959); K. Vogelsang, *A. B.: Leben und Werk* (Berlin, 1959); W. Reich, *A. B.: Leben und Werk* (Zürich, 1963; Eng. tr., 1965, as *The Life and Work of A. B.*); H. Berg, ed., *A. B.: Briefe an seine Frau* (Vienna, 1965; Eng. tr., 1971, as *A. B.: Letters to His Wife*); T. Adorno, *A. B., der Meister des Kleinsten Übergangs* (Vienna, 1968; rev. ed., 1978); G. Ploebsch, *A. B.s "Wozzeck": Dramaturgie und Musikalischer Aufbau* (Strasbourg, 1968); K. Schweizer, *Die Sonatensatzform im Schaffen A. B.s* (Stuttgart, 1970); M. Carner, *A. B.: The Man and the Work* (London, 1975; 2nd ed., rev., 1983); E. Hilmar, *Wozzeck von A. B.* (Vienna, 1975); V. Scherleiss, *A. B.* (Hamburg, 1975); D. Jarman, *The Music of A. B.* (Berkeley, 1979); K. Monson, *A. B.* (Boston, 1979); F. Grasberger and R. Stephan, eds., *Die Werke von A. B.: Handschriftenkatalog* (Vienna, 1981); R. Klein, ed., *A. B. Symposion, Wien 1980: Tagungsbericht* (Vienna, 1981); G. Perle, *The Operas of A. B.* (2 vols., Berkeley, 1981, 1985); J. Schmalfeldt, *B.'s Wozzeck: Harmonic Language and Dramatic Design* (London, 1983); E. Berg, *Der unverbesserliche Romantiker: A. B., 1885–1935* (Vienna, 1985); R. Hilmar, ed., *Katalog der Schriftstücke von der Hand A. B.s, derfremdschriftlichen und gedruckten Dokumente zur Lebensgeschichte und zu seinem Werk* (Vienna, 1985); P. Petersen, *A. B., Wozzeck: Eine semantische Analyse unter Einbeziehung der Skizzen und Dokumente aus dem Nachlass B.s* (Munich, 1985); J. Brand, C. Hailey, and D. Harris, eds., *The B.- Schönberg Correspondence* (N.Y., 1986); S. Rode, *A. B. und Karl Kraus: Zur geistigen Biographie des Komponisten der "Lulu"* (Frankfurt am Main, 1988); P. Hall, *A View of B.'s Lulu Through the Autograph Sources* (diss., Yale Univ., 1989); D. Jarman, *A. B.: "Wozzeck"* (Cambridge, 1989); idem ed., *The B. Companion* (Boston, 1990); H.-U. Fuss, *Musikalisch-dramatische Prozesse in den Opern A. B.s* (Hamburg, 1991); D. Gable and R. Morgan, eds., *A. B.: Historical and Analytical Perspectives* (Oxford, 1991); D. Jarman, *A. B.: Lulu* (Cambridge, 1991); R. Lorkovi, *Das Violinkonzert von A. B.: Analysen, Textkorrekturen, Interpretationen* (Winterthur, 1991); A. Pople, *B.: Violin Concerto* (Cambridge, 1991); C. Flores, *A B.: Musik als Autobiographie* (Wiesbaden, 1992); A. von Massow, *Halbwelt, Kultur und Natur in A. B.s "Lulu"* (Stuttgart, 1992); W. Gratzer, *Zur "wunderlichen Mystik" A. B.s: Eine studie* (Vienna, 1993); E. Buch, *Histoire d'un secret: À propos de la Suite lyrique d'A. B.* (Arles, 1995); S. Morgenstern, *A.B. und seine Idole: Erinnerungen und Briefe* (Luneburg, 1995); G. Perle, *"Style and Idea" in the Lyric Suite of A. B.* (Stuyvesant, N.Y., 1995); M. von Borries, *A. B.'s "Drei Orchesterstücke, op.6" als ein Meisterwerk atonaler Symphonik* (Weimar, 1996); P. Hall, *A View of B.'s Lulu Through the Autograph Sources* (Berkeley, 1996); D. Headlam, *The Music of A. B.* (New Haven, 1996); U. Krämer, *A. B. als Schüler Arnold Schönbergs: Quellenstudien und Analysen zum Frühwerk* (Vienna, 1996); J.-P. Olive, *A. B., le tissage et le sens* (Paris, 1997); A. Pople, ed., *The Cambridge Companion to B.* (Cambridge, 1997); S. Bruhn, ed., *Encrypted Messages in A. B.'s Music* (N.Y., 1998); B. Simms, ed., *Schoenberg, B., and Webern: A Companion to the Second Viennese School* (Westport, Conn.,1999).—NS/LK/DM

Berg, Bob (actually, **Robert**), American jazz tenor saxophonist; b. N.Y., April 7, 1951. Berg's reputation as a world class tenor player has been carefully constructed through stints with Miles Davis and Chick Corea, as well as his own groups, including a fusion band he co- leads with long time collaborator, guitarist Mike Stern. While at Juilliard, Berg was offered a tour with organist Jack McDuff, which launched his career as a jazz musician. In 1973 he joined Horace Silver's band and remained there for three years. Pianist Cedar Walton's quartet, Eastern Rebellion was Berg's next stop, where he replaced George Coleman for nearly five years. In 1984 Berg joined Miles Davis for three years, touring the world with the Davis group. After leaving Davis, he embarked on a solo recording career, as well as an ongoing collaboration with guitarist Mike Stern. Concurrently, from 1992–96, Berg was part of Chick Corea's Acoustic Quartet, also recording for Corea's Stretch Records. A free-jazz player with energy and style in the 1960s, Berg assimilated the Coltrane influence and became a respected orthodox hard-bop soloist in the 1970s. When he joined Davis in the mid-1980s, he began playing fusion music as well. His later releases successfully balance traditional and contemporary elements.

DISC.: *Short Stories* (1988); *Cycles* (1989); *In the Shadows* (1990); *Backroads* (1991); *Games* (1992); *Virtual Reality* (1993); *Riddles* (1994); *Steppin'—Live in Europe* (1994); *Another Standard* (1997); *Enter the Spirit* (1997).—**BP**

Berg, (Carl) Natanael, Swedish composer; b. Stockholm, Feb. 9, 1879; d. there, Oct. 14, 1957. He was a pupil of Julius Günther (voice) and J.Lindegren (counterpoint) at the Stockholm Cons. (1897–1900), but was essentially autodidact in composition; held state composer's fellowships for further studies in Berlin and Paris (1908–09), and in Vienna (1911–12); also took a degree in veterinary medicine (1902) and served as a veterinary surgeon in the Swedish Army until 1939. In 1918 he helped to found the Soc. of Swedish Composers, serving as its chairman until 1924. In 1932 he was elected a member of the Royal Swedish Academy of Music in Stockholm. His music is indulgent, reminiscent in its tumescent harmonies of Richard Strauss.

WORKS: DRAMATIC: O p e r a (all first perf. in Stockholm): *Leila* (1910; Feb. 29, 1912); *Engelbrekt* (1928; Sept. 21, 1929); *Judith* (1935; Feb. 22, 1936); *Brigitta* (1941; Jan. 10, 1942); *Genoveva* (1944–46; Oct. 25, 1947). **P a n t o m i m e B a l l e t :** *Alvorna* (1914); *Sensitiva* (1919); *Hertiginnans friare* (The Duchesse's Suitors; 1920). **ORCH.:** symphonic poems: *Traumgewalten* (1910); *Varde ljus!* (1914); *Reverenza* (1949); 5 syms.: No. 1, *Alles endet was entstehet* (1913), No. 2, *Arstiderna* (The Tides; 1916), No. 3, *Makter* (Power; 1917), No. 4, *Pezzo sinfonico* (1918; rev. 1939), and No. 5, *Trilogia delle passioni* (1922); Violin Concerto (1918); *Serenade* for Violin and Orch. (1923); Suite (1930); Piano Concerto (1931). **CHAMBER:** Piano Quintet (1917); 2 string quartets (1917, 1919). **VOCAL:** *Saul och David* for Baritone and Orch. (1907); *Eros' vrede* (Love's Wrath) for Baritone and Orch. (1911); *Mannen och kvinnan* (Man and Woman) for Soloists, Chorus, and Orch. (1911); *Predikaren* (The Preacher) for Baritone and Orch. (1911); *Israels lovsång* (Israel's Hymns), for Soloists, Chorus, and Orch. (1915); *Höga Visan* (The Song of Solomon) for Soloists, Chorus, and Orch. (1925); songs. —**NS/LK/DM**

Berg, Gunnar (Johnsen), Danish composer; b. St. Gallen (of Danish parents), Jan. 11, 1909; d. Bern, Aug. 25, 1989. He was taken to Denmark when he was 12 and began piano lessons. In 1936 he became a student in counterpoint of Jeppesen at the Copenhagen Cons. He later received training in piano from Koppel and Elisabeth Jürgens, and in theory from Herbert Rosenberg. In 1948 he went to Paris to study composition with Honegger at the École Normale de Musique, and he also

received training in analysis from Messiaen. Upon his return to Denmark in 1958, he became active in avant-garde circles. Although he was awarded an annual grant by the Danish government in 1965 to pursue creative work, he became frustrated by the lack of acceptance of his music in Denmark and in 1980 he returned to Switzerland. Berg was the first Danish composer to write a serial composition in 1950 with his Suite for Cello. After 1958, he employed a *sui generis* serial technique in which each theme was a "cell" consisting of five to ten notes, a model suggested by the experiments in cellular biology of the German bacteriologist Georg Gaffky (1850–1918).

WORKS: DRAMATIC: B a l l e t : *Mouture* (1953; rev. 1987). **ORCH.:** *Hymnos* for Strings (1946); *Passacaille* (1948; Århus, Sept. 7, 1980); *Essai acoustique III* for Piano and Orch. (1954); *5 études* for Double String Orch. (1955–56; Stockholm, Sept. 26, 1960); *El triptico gallego* (1957; first complete perf., Copenhagen, May 31, 1960); *Mutationen* (1958; Danish Radio, Nov. 1, 1978); *37 Aspects* for Chamber Orch. (1959); *Pour piano et orchestre* (1959; Danish Radio, Sept. 29, 1966); *Frise* for Piano and Chamber Orch. (Copenhagen, May 17, 1961); *Uculang* for Piano and Orch. (1967; Danish Radio, April 15, 1969); *Aria* for Flute and Orch. (1980–81; Danish Radio, Feb. 2, 1984); *Etincelles* for Harpsichord andBrass Ensemble (1984–85). **CHAMBER:** *Duetto* for Flute and Oboe (1937); *Caprice* for Violin and Piano (1941; rev. 1951); Sonata for Flute and Clarinet (1942; rev. 1951); Sonata for Solo Violin (1945; rev. 1982); *Pièce* for Trumpet, Violin, and Piano (1949); Suite for Cello (1950); *Filandre* for Flute, Clarinet, and Violin (1953); *Prosthesis* for Saxophone and Piano (1954); *Trio d'Anches* for Oboe, Clarinet, and Bassoon (1955); *Belem* for Percussion and Piano, 4–Hands (1956); *9 Duos* for Recorder and Cello (1957; rev. for Recorder and Guitar, 1984); *Petite Musique* for Flute, String Quartet, and Piano (1958; rev. 1960); *Pour 2 violoncelles et piano* (1958; rev. 1987); *Pour clarinette et violon* (1959); *Pour violon et piano* (1960); *Pour quintette à vent* (1962); *Pour quatuor à cordes* (1964–66); *Random* for Cello and Percussion (1968); *Tronqué* for Xylophone, Cello, and Piano (1969); *Agregats I* for Ondes Martenot (1970); *Monologue* for Trumpet (1975); *Fresques I- IV* for Guitar (1976–78); *Mouvements* for String Quartet (1979); *Melos I* for Guitar (1979); *Aerophones I-II* for Winds (1982–83); *Ar-Goat* for 2 Guitars (1984). **KEYBOARD: P i a n o :** *Fantaisie* (1936; rev. 1968); *La Boite à musique* (1938); *Toccata-Interludium-Fuga* (1938); *Feldspath* (1942–44); *Variations sur une daina lithuanienne* (1946); Sonata (1945–47); *Cahier pour Léonie* (1951); *Cosmogonie* for 2 Pianos (1952); *Eclatements I-XV* (1954–61; 1987–88); *Gaffky's I-X* (1958–59). **O r g a n :** *Pour orgue* (1960); *Tantum ergo* (1978); *Melos II* (1979). **VOCAL:** *Le chemin de fer* for Voice, Flute, Clarinet, Violin, and Piano, 4–Hands (1945; rev. 1950); *Tøbrud* for Voice, Violin, Clarinet, and Piano (1961); *Hyperion* for Voice and 10 Instruments (1977); *Graphos* for Voice, 2 Cellos, Percussion, and Piano (1987); solo songs.—**NS/LK/DM**

Berg, Josef, Czech composer; b. Brno, March 8, 1927; d. there, Feb. 26, 1971. He studied with Petrželka at the Brno Cons. (1946–50). He was music ed. of Brno Radio (1950–53), and also wrote simple music for the Folk Art ensemble. Later he began using 12–tone techniques. His most original works are the operas *Odysseů návrat* (Odysseus's Return; 1962), *Evropská turistika* (European Tourism; 1963–64), *Eufrides před branami Thymen* (Euphrides in Front of the Gates of Tymenas; 1964), and *Johannes Doktor Faust* (1966). He also wrote three syms.

(1950, 1952, 1955), Viola Sonata (1958), *Fantasia* for two Pianos (1958), Sextet for Piano, Harp, and String Quartet (1959), *Songs of the New Werther* for Bass-baritone and Piano (1962), Nonet for two Harps, Piano, Harpsichord, and Percussion (1962), *Sonata in Modo Classico* for Harpsichord and Piano (1963), *Organ Music on a Theme of Gilles Binchois* (1964), String Quartet (1966), *2 Canti* for Baritone, Instrumental Ensemble, Organ, and Metronome (1966), *Ó Corino* for four Solo Voices and Classical Orch. (1967), and *Oresteia* for Vocal Quartet, Narrator, and Instrumental Ensemble (1967).

BIBL.: M. Štědroň, *J. B.* (Brno, 1992).—NS/LK/DM

Berganza (Vargas), Teresa, admired Spanish mezzo- soprano; b. Madrid, March 16, 1935. She was a pupil of Lola Rodriguez Aragón in Madrid. After winning the singing prize at the Madrid Cons. in 1954, she made her debut in a Madrid concert in 1955; in 1957 she made her operatic debut as Dorabella at the Aix-en-Provence Festival. In 1958 she made her British debut as Cherubino at the Glyndebourne Festival, and that same year she sang at the Dallas Civic Opera. In 1960 she made her first appearance at London's Covent Garden as Rosina, and in 1962 her debut at the Chicago Lyric Opera as Cherubino, a role she repeated for her Metropolitan Opera debut in N.Y. on Oct. 11, 1967; she remained on its roster until 1969. She toured widely as a concert artist, winning particular distinction for her Spanish song recitals. In 1992 she participated in the gala ceremonies at the Olympic Games in Barcelona. She appeared in recital at London's Wigmore Hall in 1997 and at N.Y.'s Alice Tully Hall in 1999. In addition to her roles in operas by Mozart and Rossini, she was esteemed for her portrayals of Monteverdi's Octavia, Purcell's Dido, and Bizet's Carmen. Her career is the subject of her book *Meditaciones de na Cantante* (Madrid, 1985).—NS/LK/DM

Berge, Sigurd, Norwegian composer; b. Vinstra, July 1, 1929. He studied composition with Thorleif Eken at the Oslo Cons. and with Finn Mortensen (1956–59), and later took courses in electronic music in Stockholm, Copenhagen, and Utrecht. From 1959 he taught at the Sagene Coll. of Education. He served as chairman of the Norwegian Composers Union (1985–88). His output ranges from traditional works to electronic pieces.

WORKS: *Dances from Gudbrandsdal* for Orch. (1955–56); *Divertimento* for Violin, Viola, and Cello (1956); *Episode for* Violin and Piano (1958); *Pezzo orchestrale* (1958); *Rāga*, concerto-study in Indian music, for Oboe and Orch. (1959); *Sinus* for Strings and Percussion (1961); *Tamburo piccolo* for Strings and Percussion (1961); *Chroma* for Orch. (1963); *A* for Orch. (1964–65); *B* for Orch. (1965–66); Flute Solo (1966); Oboe Solo (1966); *Yang Guan* for Wind Quintet (1967); *Ballet* for 2 Dancers and Percussion (1967–68); *Gamma* for 7 Instruments (1970); *Epsilon* for Chamber Orch. (1970); *Delta* for Jazz Trio and Tape (1970); *Horn Call* for Horn (1972); *Between Mirrors* for Violin and Chamber Orch. (1977); *Music for* Orch. (1978); *Gudbrandskalsspelet*, music drama (1980); *Wind*, ballet (1981); *Music* for 4 Horns (1984); numerous electronic pieces.—NS/LK/DM

Bergel, Erich, Romanian-born German conductor; b. Rosenau, June 1, 1930; d. Ruhpolding, May 3, 1998.

He studied in Bucharest. In 1959 he was appointed conductor of the Cluj Phil., but was shortly afterward (May 9, 1959) arrested and incarcerated on charges of subversive activities. After his release from prison on Oct. 4, 1962, he was engaged as a trumpet player by the Cluj Phil. In 1966 he became its conductor. In 1971 he left Romania and settled in West Germany. In 1975 he made his U.S. debut as guest conductor with the Houston Sym. Orch., serving as its principal guest conductor from 1979 to 1981. He publ. a disquisition on Bach's *Art of the Fugue* (Bonn, 1979; 1st vol.only).—NS/LK/DM

Berger, Andreas, German composer; b. Dolsenhaim, near Altenburg, Saxony, 1584; d. Ulm, Jan. 10, 1656. In 1606 he became a tenor at the court chapel in Stuttgart, where from 1608 to 1612 he was court composer. From 1624 to 1634 he served as Kapellmeister to Count Ludwig Eberhard of Öttingen. He subsequently held posts as a public official in Augsburg, Leutkirch, and Ulm. He composed both sacred and secular vocal music.—NS/LK/DM

Berger, Arthur (Victor), respected American composer and writer on music; b. N.Y., May 15, 1912. He studied piano (1923–28) and began composing while still in high school. After attending the City Coll. of N.Y. (1928–30), he studied composition with Vincent Jones at N.Y. Univ. (B.S., 1934). He then continued his training at the Longy School of Music in Cambridge, Mass. (1935–37), and concurrently was a pupil of Piston, Davison, and Leichtentritt at Harvard Univ. (M.A., 1937). After further studies with Boulanger at the École Normale de Musique in Paris (1937–39), he taught at Mills Coll. in Oakland, Calif. (1939–42), where he also had composition lessons with Milhaud; then taught at Brooklyn Coll. (1942–43), the Juilliard School of Music in N.Y., Brandeis Univ. (1953–80), and at the New England Cons. of Music in Boston (from 1979). He served as ed. of the *Musical Mercury* (1934–37) and as co-founder and ed. of *Perspectives of New Music* (1962–63); also was a music critic for the *Boston Transcript* (1943–47), *N.Y. Sun* (1943–46), and *N.Y. Herald Tribune* (1946–53). In addition to many articles in journals, he publ. a monograph on Copland (N.Y., 1953). In 1960 he held a Fulbright fellowship and in 1975–76 a Guggenheim fellowship. His musical idiom reveals the influence of divergent schools, including a *sui generis* serialism and the neo-Classical pragmatism of Stravinsky. His works, in whatever idiom, are characterized by strong formal structures; the title of one of his most cogent scores, *Ideas of Order* (1952), is a declaration of principles.

WORKS: ORCH.: *Serenade Concertante* for Violin and Chamber Orch. (1944; Rochester, N.Y., Oct. 24, 1945); *3 Pieces* for Strings (1945; N.Y., Jan. 26, 1946); *Ideas of Order* (1952; N.Y., April 11, 1953); *Polyphony* (Louisville, Nov. 17, 1956); Chamber Concerto (1960; N.Y., May 13, 1962; 3rd movement rev. as *Movement* for Orch., 1964; 1st, 2nd, and 3rd movements rev. as *Perspectives I, II,* and *III*, 1978). **CHAMBER:** Woodwind Quartet (1941); *3 Pieces* for String Quartet (1945); Duo No. 1 for Violin and Piano (1948), No. 2 for Violin and Piano (1950), No. 3 for Cello and Piano (1951), and No. 4 for Oboe and Clarinet (1952; arr. for Clarinet and Piano, 1957); *Chamber Music* for 12 Instruments (1956); String Quartet (1958); Septet for Flute, Clarinet, Bassoon,

Violin, Viola, Cello, and Piano (1965–66; Washington, D.C., Nov. 25, 1966); Trio for Guitar, Violin, and Piano (1972); Piano Trio (1980); Woodwind Quintet (1984); *Diptych* for Flute, Clarinet, Violin, Cello, and Piano (1990); *Collage III* for Flute, Clarinet, Violin, Cello, Percussion, and Piano (1992). **P i a n o :** 2 Episodes (1933); *Entertainment Pieces*, ballet music (1940); *Fantasy* (1942); *Rondo* (1945); *Capriccio* (1945); *3 Bagatelles* (1946); *Partita* (1947); *Intermezzo* (1948); 4 2-part inventions (1948–49); 1-part invention (1954); *3 Pieces* for 2 Prepared Pianos (1961); *5 Pieces* (1969); *Composition* for Piano, 4–Hands (1976); *An Improvisation for A*[aron] *C*[opland] (1981). **VOCAL:** *Words for Music, Perhaps* for Soprano or Mezzo-soprano, Flute, Clarinet, and Cello (1939–40); *Garlands* for Mezzo-soprano and Piano (1945); *Psalm XCII* for 4 Voices (1946); *Boo Hoo at the Zoo: Tails of Woe* for 2 Voices (1978); *5 Songs* for Tenor and Piano (1978–79); *Love, Sweet Animal* for 4 Voices and Piano, 4–Hands (1982); *Ode of Ronsard* for Soprano and Piano (1987).—**NS/LK/DM**

Berger, Dave, jazz composer, trumpeter, educator; b. N.Y., March 30, 1949. He studied at Berklee Coll. of Music until 1966, earned a B.M. at Ithaca Coll. (1967–71), studied at the Eastman School of Music (on and off, 1967–81), including work with Rayburn Wright (1970–1) and Jimmy Maxwell (1972–80), and earned an M.M. in Jazz Composition at the Manhattan School of Music (1985–6). He first played trumpet with big bands, but has worked most often as a composer and orchestrator, collaborating on albums and with the bands of Gerry Mulligan, Clark Terry, Buddy Rich, Chuck Israels, Quincy Jones, Lee Konitz, Mercer Ellington, Thad Jones and Mel Lewis, and singers Carol Channing and Leslie Uggams. He served as conductor, transcriber and arranger for the Lincoln Center Jazz Orch. (1988–94). He has scored such films as *Brighton Beach Memoirs* and *The Cotton Club* and Broadway shows including *Sophisticated Ladies, Best Little Whorehouse in Texas,* and *Jerry's Girls;* he has written music for TV's *Tonight Show* and PBS specials. He worked with Wynton Marsalis on the *Marsalis on Music* series for PBS-TV, *Blood on the Fields* for Columbia Records and NPR, and the *Making the Music* series for NPR. For choreographer Donald Byrd, Berger created "The Harlem Nutcracker," which includes 28 minutes of Ellington and Strayhorn's "Nutcracker" and an additional 90 minutes of his own interpretations of the unused Tchaikovsky themes in the Ellington style; this was performed in N.Y. and on tour (1996–8). Since 1985, he has taught at the Manhattan School of Music, where he conducted two concerts of Duke Ellington's sacred music (December 1993) with Marsalis, Jon Hendricks, William Warfield, and choreographer Mercedes Ellington. He has also taught at William Paterson Coll. (1986–93), New School for Social Research (1987–9), Long Island Univ. (1985–8), Montclair State Coll. (1985–7), Jersey City State Coll. (1979–82), and at numerous clinics and workshops. His second jazz symphony, "Self Portraits in Blue," was completed with the help of an NEA award around 1997. He conducted *Live from Lincoln Center: A Classical Jazz Christmas* (PBS-TV, 1989). He is a noted Ellington specialist who has transcribed over 300 of his works (and about 200 other big band classics). Berger was perhaps the first to publish scores and accurate parts of Ellington's recordings for public performance.—**LP**

Berger, Erna, distinguished German soprano; b. Cossebaude, near Dresden, Oct. 19, 1900; d. Essen, June 14, 1990. She was a student of Böckel and Melita Hirzel in Dresden. In 1925 she made her operatic debut as the first boy in *Die Zauberflöte* at the Dresden State Opera, where she sang until 1930. In Berlin she sang at the City Opera (1929) and the State Opera (from 1934); also appeared at the Bayreuth (1930–33) and Salzburg (1932–54) festivals. In 1934 she made her debut at London's Covent Garden as Marzelline, and sang there until 1938 and again in 1947. On Nov. 21, 1949, she made her Metropolitan Opera debut in N.Y. as Sophie, remaining on its roster until 1951. In 1955 she retired from the operatic stage but pursued a career as a lieder artist until 1968. From 1959 she was a prof. of voice at the Hamburg Hochschule für Musik. In 1985 the Berlin State Opera made her an honorary member. Her autobiography was publ. as *Auf Flügeln des Gesanges* (Zürich, 1988). Berger was an outstanding coloratura soprano. Among her other roles were the Queen of the Night, Rosina, Martha, Gilda, and Zerbinetta.

BIBL.: K. Höcker, *E. B.: Die singende Botschafterin* (Berlin, 1961).—**NS/LK/DM**

Berger, Francesco, English pianist and composer; b. London, June 10, 1834; d. there, April 25, 1933. He studied harmony with Luigi Ricci in Trieste, piano with Karl Lickl in Vienna; later studied with Hauptmann and Plaidy at Leipzig. Returning to London, he was a prof. of piano at the Royal Academy of Music and at the Guildhall School of Music. He made frequent concert tours through Great Britain and Ireland, and was for some years director and, from 1884 to 1911, honorary secretary of the Phil. Soc. He composed an opera, *Il Lazzarone,* a Mass, overtures and incidental music to Wilkie Collins's *The Frozen Deep* and *The Lighthouse,* many songs, and piano pieces. He publ. *First Steps at the Pianoforte, Reminiscences, Impressions and Anecdotes, Musical Expressions, Phrases and Sentences,* and a *Musical Vocabulary in 4 Languages* (1922). In 1931 he publ. his memoirs, entitled (with reference to his age) *97.* —**NS/LK/DM**

Berger, Jean, German-born French, later American conductor, teacher, and composer; b. Hamm, Sept. 27, 1909. He studied musicicology with Wellesz at the Univ. of Vienna and with Besseler at the Univ. of Heidelberg (Ph.D., 1931), and then composition with Aubert and Capdevielle in Paris, where he conducted the choir Les Compagnons de la Marjolaine and in 1935 became a naturalized citizen. After teaching at the Conservatorio Brasileiro de Música in Rio de Janeiro (1939–41), he settled in the U.S., becoming a naturalized citizen in 1943. He taught at Middlebury (Vt.) Coll. (1948–59), the Univ. of Ill. in Urbana (1959–61), and the Univ. of Colo. (1961–68). In 1964 he founded the John Sheppard Music Bress in Boulder. He wrote mainly choral music in an accessible style. His best known work is the *Brazilian Psalm* for Chorus (1941).

WORKS: DRAMATIC: *Pied Piper,* musical play for Dancers, Solo Voices, Choruses, and Small Orch. (1968); *Birds of a Feather: An Entertainment* (1971); *Yiphth and his Daughter,* opera

(1972); *The Cherry Tree Carol*, liturgical drama (1975). **ORCH.:** *Caribbean Concerto* for Harmonica and Orch. (St. Louis, March 10, 1942, Larry Adler soloist); *Creole Overture* (1949); *Petit Suite for Strings* (1952); *Short Overture* for Strings (1958); *Divertissement for Strings* (1970); *Short Symphony* (1974); *Diversion for Strings* (1977). **CHAMBER:** Suite for Flute and Piano (1955); Divertimento for 3 Treble Instruments (1957); *6 Short Pieces* for Woodwind Quintet (1962); *Partita* for Woodwind Quintet (1970); piano pieces. **VOCAL:** *Le Sang des autres* (1937); *Brazilian Psalm* (1941); *Vision of Peace* (1949); *Magnificat* for Soprano, Chorus, Flute, and Percussion (1960); *Fiery Furnace*, dramatic cantata (1962); *Song of Seasons* for Soloists, Choruses, and Orch. (1967); *The Exiles* for 2 Voices, 2 Pianos, and Percussion (1976); also songs.—**NS/LK/DM**

Berger, Kenny, jazz baritone saxophonist, clarinetist, flutist, bass clarinetist, bassoonist, composer; b. N.Y., Dec. 19, 1947. He grew up in Brooklyn, attended Mannes Coll. of Music as bassoon major (1965–8), Univ. of Ill. as a composition major (1986), and earned his B.A. at S.U.N.Y. Empire State Coll. He has been an active freelancer around N.Y. for many years, appearing with the Thad Jones–Mel Lewis Jazz Orch., Lee Konitz Nonet, Julius Hemphill Sextet, National Jazz Ensemble, Bobby Previte Septet, Duke Ellington Orch., Toshiko Akiyoshi Jazz Orch., Duke Pearson Big Band, Gil Goldstein Zebra Coast Orch., Ned Rothenberg's Powerlines Ensemble, Phil Woods, Dizzy Gillespie, Gerry Mulligan, Roy Eldridge, Dr. John, Alvin Ailey Dance Theater, Orch. of St. Luke's, Liza Minelli, James Taylor, Paul Simon, Frank Sinatra, Mel Torme, Bill Cosby, Sarah Vaughan, Ray Charles, Tony Bennett, the Saturday Night Live Band, and others. He has written and arranged for some of those groups as well. Berger teaches at Jersey City State Coll. and has taught at William Paterson Coll. (1993–5), at Western Wash. Univ. (1991), and Long Island Univ. (1991).

DISC.: J. McNeil–K. Berger: *Hip Deep* (1996); *Brooklyn Ritual* (1997).—**LP**

Berger, Ludwig, German composer, pianist, and teacher; b. Berlin, April 18, 1777; d. there, Feb. 16, 1839. He studied flute and piano. He went to Berlin in 1799, where he received instruction in harmony and counterpoint with Gürrlich. In 1804 he went to Russia, but fled in the face of Napoleon's invasion in 1812. In 1815 he returned to Berlin and was active mainly as a teacher, numbering among his students Mendelssohn, Henselt, and Taubert. He wrote a Piano Concerto, seven piano sonatas, songs, and numerous piano works.

BIBL.: L. Rellstab, *L. B.* (Berlin, 1846); D. Siebenkäs, *L. B.: Sein Leben und seine Werke unter besonderer Berücksichtigung seines Liedschaffens* (Berlin, 1963).—**NS/LK/DM**

Berger, Roman, Slovak composer and writer on music; b. Cieszyn, Poland, Aug. 9, 1930. He was the son of an evangelical pastor. His youth was disrupted by the Nazi attack on Poland in 1939, and he later was sent to the Auschwitz and Dachau concentration camps. Following his liberation at the end of World War II, he entered the State Higher School of Music in Katowice in 1945. In 1952 he and his family were forced to leave Poland, and they settled in Bratislava, where he studied piano (graduated, 1956) and composition (graduated, 1965) at the Academy of Music and Drama. He also worked at the Cons. there until 1966. In 1967–68 he was secretary of the composers' section of the Union of Slovak Composers. From 1969 to 1971 he worked in the dept. of theory at the Academy of Music and Drama, but then was expelled from the Union of Slovak Composers and was left unemployed. In 1980 he was able to find employment in the Art History Inst. of the Slovak Academy of Sciences. However, his theoretical writings led him to be classified as a dissident and subjected to harassment by the Communist authorities. With the collapse of the Communist regime in the wake of the "Velvet Revolution" in 1989, he served as a member of the advisory board of the Ministry of Culture until 1991, the year he left his position at the Slovak Academy of Sciences. In 1967 he received the Ján Levoslav Bella Prize for composition, in 1967 the prize and in 1990 the diploma of the Czechoslovak Music Critics for composition, and in 1988 the Herder Prize of the Univ. of Vienna for his compositions and writings on theory. His works are formally well disciplined, melodically atonal, and harmonically complex.

WORKS: DRAMATIC: Stage music and film scores. **ORCH.:** *Suite in the Old Style* (1963–78); *Transformation* (1965); *Memento* (1973). **CHAMBER:** *Romance* for Violin and Piano (1960); Trio for Flute, Clarinet, and Bassoon (1962); *Convergencies I* for Violin (1969), *II* for Viola (1970), and *III* for Cello (1975); Violin Sonata (1983); *Adagio* (No. 1) *for Jan Branny* (1987), No. 2, *Repentance* (1988–89), and No. 3 (1988, 1994) for Violin and Piano. **KEYBOARD: Piano:** *Fantasia quasi una sonata* (1955); *3 Inventions* (1959–61); *Sonata 1960* (1960); *Suite* (1961); *Sonata da camera* (1971); *Inventions II*, 10 studies (1987–90); *November-Music I* (1989). **Organ:** *Exodus II* (1981) and *IV-Finale* (1982). **VOCAL:** *Lullaby* for Mezzo-soprano and Chamber Orch. (1962); *In the Silence so Dearly Redeemed* for Chorus (1962); *Black and Red* for Chorus and Percussion (1967); *Litany to Trees* for Men's Chorus (1975); *De profundis* for Bass, Piano, Cello, and Live Electronics (1980); *Wiegenlied* for Alto and Piano (1992). **Electroacoustic:** *Elegy in memoriam Ján Rúčka* (1969); *En passant* (1970); *Epitaph for Mikuláš Kopernik* (1972); *Transgressus I* (1993).—**NS/LK/DM**

Berger, Rudolf, Czech baritone and tenor; b. Brünn, April 17, 1874; d. N.Y., Feb. 27, 1915. He was a pupil of Adolf Robinson in Brünn. In 1896 he made his debut as a baritone in Brünn, and then sang at the Berlin Royal Opera (from 1898) and at the Bayreuth Festivals (1901–08). He also made guest appearances in Vienna, London (Covent Garden), Paris, and Prague. After further studies with Oscar Saenger in N.Y., he concentrated on Heldentenor roles from 1909. On Feb. 5, 1914, he made his Metropolitan Opera debut in N.Y. as Siegmund, and remained on its roster until his death. In 1913 he married **Marie Rappold**.—**NS/LK/DM**

Berger, Theodor, Austrian composer; b. Traismauer an der Donau, May 18, 1905; d. Vienna, Aug. 21, 1992. He was a pupil of Korngold and Schmidt at the Vienna Academy of Music (1926–32). Under the influence of his teachers, he evolved a new Romantic style of composition.

WORKS: DRAMATIC: Ballet: *Homerische Sinfonie* (1948); *Heiratsannoncen* (1958). **ORCH.:** *Malinconia* for Strings (1938); *Ballade* (1941); *Legende vom Prinzen Eugen* (1942); *Rondino giocoso* for Strings (1947); *Concerto manuale* for 2 Pianos, Marimbaphone, Metallophone, Strings, and Percussion (1951); *La parola* (1954); Violin Concerto (1954); *Sinfonia Parabolica* (1956); *Sinfonia Macchinale* (1956); *Symphonischer Triglyph* (1957); *Jahreszeiten*, sym. (1958). **CHAMBER:** 2 string quartets (1930, 1931). **VOCAL:** *Frauenstimmen im Orchester* for Women's Chorus, Harps, and Strings (1959); *Divertimento* for Men's Chorus, 7 Wind Instruments, and Percussion (1968).—**NS/LK/DM**

Berger, Wilhelm Georg, Romanian composer; b. Rupea, Dec. 4, 1929; d. Bucharest, March 8, 1993. He studied at the Bucharest Cons. (1948–52). From 1948 to 1957 he was a violist in the Bucharest Phil.

WORKS: ORCH.: *Symphonic Variations* (1958); Concerto for Strings (1958); 17 syms.: No. 1, *Lyric* (1960), No. 2, *Epic* (1963), No. 3, *Dramatic* (1964), No. 4, *Tragic* (1965), No. 5, *Solemn Music* (1968), No. 6, *Harmony* (1969), No. 7, *Energetic* (1970), No. 8, *The Morning Star*, with Chorus (1971), No. 9, *Melodie* (1973–74), No. 10, with Solo Organ (1975–76), No. 11, *Sarmizegetusa* (1976), No. 12, *To the Star*, for Strings (1978), No. 13, *Sinfonia solemnis* (1980), No. 14 (1980–84), No. 15 (1984–86), No. 16 (1986), and No. 17 (1986); 2 viola concertos (1960, 1962); *Rhapsodic Images* (1964); Violin Concerto (1965; Brussels, Jan. 11, 1966); Cello Concerto (1967); *Meditations*, cycle of variations for Chamber Orch. (1968); *Variations* for Wind Orch. (1968); Concerto for 2 Violas and Orch. (1968); *Concert Music* for Flute, Strings, and Percussion (1972); Concerto for Violin, Viola, and Orch. (1977); *Faust*, dramatic sym. (1981); *Horia*, symphonic poem (1985). **CHAMBER:** Viola Sonata (1953); 15 string quartets (1954, 1955, 1957, 1959, 1961, 1965, 1966, 1966, 1967, 1967, 1967, 1967, 1979, 1980, 1983); Nonet (1957); 2 violin sonatas (1959, 1977); Quintet for 2 Violins, Viola, Cello, and Piano (1968); Trio for Piano, Violin, and Cello (1977); Concerto for Solo Organ (1981); *7 Serious Pieces* for String Quartet (1986); *7 Dramatic Pieces* for String Quartet (1986). **VOCAL:** *Stefan Furtună*, oratorio (1958); songs.—**NS/LK/DM**

Berggreen, Andreas Peter, Danish composer; b. Copenhagen, March 2, 1801; d. there, Nov. 8, 1880. He studied law and turned to music late in life; occupied various teaching posts in Copenhagen. His opera *Billedet og Busten* (The Portrait and the Bust) was produced in Copenhagen on April 9, 1832; he also wrote incidental music to plays. His most important contribution to music literature is the compilation of 11 vols. of folk songs, *Folke-sang og melodier, faedre landske og fremmede* (Copenhagen, 1842–55; 2nd ed., enl., 1861–71). He further publ. 14 vols. of songs for use in schools (1834–76) and ed. church anthems. Among his students was Niels Gade.

BIBL.: C. Skou, *A.P. B.* (Copenhagen, 1895).—**NS/LK/DM**

Berghaus, Ruth, German opera director; b. Dresden, July 2, 1927; d. Zeuthen, Jan. 25, 1996. She received training in dance at the Palucca School in Dresden (1947–50). In 1964 she became a choreographer with the Berliner Ensemble, serving as its Intendant (1971–77). She garnered notoriety as an opera director at the Berlin State Opera with her staging of *Il barbiere di Siviglia*.

From 1980 to 1987 she was an opera director at the Frankfurt am Main Opera, where she oversaw outstanding productions of *Parsifal* (1982) and the *Ring* cycle (1985–87); also was active as a guest director in other European opera centers, including Brussels, Hamburg, Munich, and Vienna. In her productions, Berghaus has pursued a radical course laden with symbolism and satire. She was married to **Paul Dessau**.

BIBL.: S. Neef, *Das Theater der R. B.* (Berlin, 1989); K. Bertisch, *R. B.* (Frankfurt am Main, 1990).—**NS/LK/DM**

Berghem, Jachet (de)
See **Berchem, Jachet (de)**

Bergiron de Briou, Nicolas-Antoine, Seigneur du Fort Michon, French composer; b. Lyons, Dec. 12, 1690; d. there, before April 27, 1768. He studied classical literature and law at the Univ. of Paris. With J.P. Christin, he established in 1713 the Académie des Beaux-Arts in Lyons, with which he remained associated in various capacities until 1764. He composed a number of cantatas and motets, divertissements, and several operas.—**NS/LK/DM**

Berglund, Joel (Ingemar), Swedish bass-baritone; b. Torsåker, June 4, 1903; d. Stockholm, Jan. 21, 1985. He was a pupil of John Forsell at the Stockholm Cons. (1922–28). In 1928 he made his operatic debut as Lothario in *Mignon* at the Royal Opera in Stockholm, where he was a member until 1949; he then made guest appearances there until 1964. He also sang in Venice, Chicago, Bayreuth (as the Dutchman, 1949), and other operatic centers. On Jan. 9, 1946, he made his Metropolitan Opera debut in N.Y. as Hans Sachs, remaining on its roster until 1949. He served as director of the Royal Opera in Stockholm (1949–52), and continued to make appearances in opera until his retirement in 1970. —**NS/LK/DM**

Berglund, Paavo (Allan Engelbert), prominent Finnish conductor; b. Helsinki, April 14, 1929. After violin lessons from his grandfather, he pursued training at the Sibelius Academy in Helsinki, Vienna, and Salzburg. In 1949 he began his career as a violinist in the Finnish Radio Sym. Orch. in Helsinki. In 1952 he became conductor of the Helsinki Chamber Orch. In 1956 he was made assoc. conductor and in 1962 principal conductor of the Finnish Radio Sym. Orch. He was principal conductor of the Bournemouth Sym. Orch. (1972–79) and music director of the Helsinki Phil. (1975–79); then was principal guest conductor of the Scottish National Orch. in Glasgow (1981–85). He served as the conductor of the Stockholm Phil. from 1987 to 1991. Berglund has won distinction for his interpretations of the 20th-century masters of the sym., ranging from Sibelius to Shostakovich. He conducts left-handed.—**NS/LK/DM**

Bergman, Alan and **Marilyn (Keith),** American lyricists. Husband-and-wife lyric-writing team. Alan Bergman (b. Brooklyn, Sept. 11, 1925) and Marilyn

Bergman (b. Brooklyn, Nov. 10, 1929) wrote lyrics for songs used in at least 50 feature films released between 1960 and 1996. Usually known for wistful romantic ballads, they were particularly associated with Barbra Streisand, and their work with her on the films *The Way We Were* and *Yentl* brought them both of their Grammys and two of their three Academy Awards; their first Oscar came for the standard "The Windmills of Your Mind." They worked with many different composers, finding greatest success with Michel Legrand and Marvin Hamlisch.

Alan Bergman was the son of Samuel Bergman, a clothing salesman, and Ruth Margulies Bergman. In 1942 he enrolled at the Univ. of N.C. at Chapel Hill, majoring in music and theater arts. In 1943 he joined the army, where he wrote and directed shows in the Special Services division during World War II. Discharged in 1945, he returned to college; he graduated with a B.A. degree in 1948 and earned a master's degree from U.C.L.A. in 1949. That year he moved to Philadelphia, where he became a television director. He began writing songs, and after receiving encouragement from Johnny Mercer, he moved to Los Angeles in 1953, later becoming a writer of special material on the variety series *Shower of Stars* and other programs. He met Marilyn Keith through composer Lew Spence, with whom both had collaborated.

Bergman and Keith had similar backgrounds: both were born and raised in Brooklyn, and Keith's father, Albert A. Katz, also worked in the clothing business. Keith had private study in the piano as a child, intending to become a concert pianist. By the time she enrolled at N.Y.U. in 1945 she was a premedical student, but later concentrated on English and psychology. She left without a degree after being injured in a fall and joined her family, which had moved to Los Angeles. Encouraged by lyricist Bob Russell, she began to write lyrics and had amassed enough credits to join ASCAP by 1953.

Bergman and Keith teamed up, initially finding work writing television theme songs for such series as *Oh! Susanna* (1956) and *The Nat King Cole Show* (1956). Their first song success came with "Yellow Bird," a song adapted by Norman Luboff from a West Indian folk tune, for which they provided lyrics. The Norman Luboff Choir recorded it for their 1957 chart album *Calypso Holiday*. The Mills Brothers' single entered the charts in January 1959, but the song became best known for an instrumental version by the Arthur Lyman Group that reached the Top Ten in July 1961. Meanwhile, the lyricists married on Feb. 9, 1958, and had a daughter in 1960.

Frank Sinatra recorded the Bergmans' "Nice 'n' Easy" (music by Lew Spence) and used it as the title track for a chart-topping, gold-selling album in 1960. It was also released as a single that made the charts, and it earned the songwriters their first Grammy nomination for Song of the Year. That December, along with Spence, they had the title song in the film *The Marriage-Go-Round*, sung on the soundtrack by Tony Bennett.

Although they continued to place songs with middle-of-the-road performers, the Bergmans had trouble scoring hits during the 1960s, when the charts were dominated by rock acts who generated their own material. Collaborating with composer Sammy Fain, they wrote the songs for a Broadway musical, *Something More*, in 1964, but it closed after 15 performances. They began to focus more on Hollywood, and from 1966 to 1996 they averaged between one and two films per year. In an era when film musicals were becoming rare, this usually meant writing a title or theme song heard under the credits or in a key sequence in a nonmusical film. Teaming up with Quincy Jones, they wrote a title song for the drama *In the Heat of the Night* (1967), performed on the soundtrack by Ray Charles, whose recording peaked in the Top 40 in September 1967.

The Bergmans diverged from their usually romantic lyrics with "The Windmills of Your Mind," written for the 1968 film *The Thomas Crown Affair*, which marked the beginning of a long-term collaboration with Michel Legrand. The abstract lyric's extended series of similes for round objects suggested the influence of rock writers such as Bob Dylan and Paul Simon. On April 14, 1969, it won them their first Academy Award, for Best Song. Two months later, Dusty Springfield's recording peaked in the Top 40.

The Bergmans earned Oscar nominations for Best Song for the next four years in a row. In 1969 they were nominated for "What Are You Doing the Rest of Your Life?" (music by Michel Legrand) from *The Happy Ending*; in 1970 for "Pieces of Dreams" (music by Michel Legrand) from *Pieces of Dreams*; in 1971 for "All His Children" (music by Henry Mancini) from *Sometimes a Great Notion*, sung on the soundtrack and recorded for a Top Ten country hit by Charley Pride; and in 1972 for "Marmalade, Molasses and Honey" (music by Maurice Jarre) from *The Life and Times of Judge Roy Bean*. They earned a second Grammy nomination in 1972 for Song of the Year for "The Summer Knows" (music by Michel Legrand) from *Summer of '42* (1971).

The Way We Were, starring Barbra Streisand and Robert Redford, was released in September 1973 with a title song written by the Bergmans with Marvin Hamlisch. Streisand's recording of the song hit #1 in February 1974, selling two million copies. It went on to win the Academy Award for Best Song and the Grammy for Song of the Year, and the Bergmans also shared with Hamlisch the Grammy for Best Album of Original Score Written for a Motion Picture or TV Special.

Turning to television, the Bergmans wrote songs with Billy Goldenberg for the highly rated and critically acclaimed television musical *Queen of the Stardust Ballroom*, broadcast in February 1975. It was adapted for the stage, opened on Broadway in December 1978 under the title *Ballroom*, and ran 116 performances.

While continuing to write for various films in the 1970s, the Bergmans enjoyed a special relationship with Barbra Streisand after "The Way We Were." Their song "I Believe in Love" (music by Kenny Loggins) was featured in the Streisand-starring remake of *A Star Is Born* in 1976 and became a chart single for Kenny Loggins in 1977. Also in 1977, they collaborated with Neil Diamond on "You Don't Bring Me Flowers," a heart-breaking ballad featured on his album *I'm Glad You're Here with Me Tonight*. Streisand covered the song on her 1978 *Songbird* album, and after an enterprising disc jockey edited the two recordings together, the singers recorded a duet version that hit #1 in December 1978 and sold two million copies.

Meanwhile, after being shut out of Oscar nominations for five years, the Bergmans earned a 1978 nod for "The Last Time I Felt Like This" (music by Marvin Hamlisch) from *Same Time, Next Year*. They were nominated again the following year for "I'll Never Say Goodbye" (music by David Shire) from *The Promise*. In 1982 they occupied a remarkable three out of the five Best Song nominations—"It Might Be You" (music by Dave Grusin) from *Tootsie*, a Top 40 hit for Stephen Bishop; "If I Were in Love" (music by John Williams) from *Yes, Giorgio*; and "How Do You Keep the Music Playing?" (music by Michel Legrand) from *Best Friends*, a chart single for James Ingram and Patti Austin—without winning the Oscar.

In 1983 the Bergmans collaborated with Michel Legrand on a full-scale film musical, Barbra Streisand's *Yentl*. Released in the fall, it spawned a million-selling soundtrack album. "The Way He Makes Me Feel" reached the Top 40 and topped the adult contemporary charts, and "Papa, Can You Hear Me?" was also an adult contemporary hit. Both songs earned Academy Award nominations, but the Bergmans instead won their third Oscar for the song score as a whole.

The Bergmans' work was heard less often in films after the mid-1980s. They continued to work with Barbra Streisand, writing "Two People" (music by Barbra Streisand) for her 1987 film *Nuts* and "Places That Belong to You" (music by James Newton Howard) for 1991's *The Prince of Tides*. In 1989 they earned another Academy Award nomination for Best Song for "The Girl Who Used to Be Me" (music by Marvin Hamlisch) from *Shirley Valentine*. Marilyn Bergman was elected president of ASCAP in March 1994, a position she still held five years later.

WORKS (only works for which Alan and Marilyn Bergman were the primary, credited lyricists are listed): **STAGE** (dates refer to N.Y. openings): *Something More* (Nov. 19, 1964); *Ballroom* (Dec. 14, 1978). **FILM**: *Yentl* (1983). **TELEVISION**: *Queen of the Stardust Ballroom* (Feb. 13, 1975); *Sybil* (Nov. 14–15, 1976). —WR

Bergman, Erik (Valdemar), eminent Finnish composer, conductor, music critic, and pedagogue; b. Nykarleby, Nov. 24, 1911. He received training in musicology at the Univ. of Helsinki (1931–33) and in composition from Furuhjelm at the Helsinki Cons. (diploma, 1938). Following further studies with Tiessen at the Berlin Hochschule für Musik (1937–39), he studied with Vogel in Switzerland. Returning to Helsinki, he was conductor of the Catholic Church Choir (1943–50), the Akademiska Sangföreningen at the Univ. (1950–69), and the Sällskapet Muntra Musikanter (1951–78). As a music critic, he wrote for the *Nya Pressen* (1945–47) and *Hufvudstadsbladet* (1947–76). From 1963 to 1976 he was prof. of composition at the Sibelius Academy. In 1961 he received the International Sibelius Prize of the Wihuri Foundation. In 1982 he was made a Finnish Academician. In 1994 he was awarded the Nordic Council Music

Prize for his opera *Det sjungande trädet* (The Singing Tree), which received its premiere in Helsinki on Sept. 3, 1995. Bergman ranks among the foremost Finnish composers of his era. He cultivates varied techniques, ranging from medieval modality to serialism. His major works have evolved along expressionistic lines.

WORKS: DRAMATIC: Opera: *Det sjungande tradet* (The Singing Tree; 1986–88; Helsinki, Sept. 3, 1995). **ORCH.**: Suite for Strings (1938); *Burla* (1948); *Tre aspetti d'una serie dodecafonica* (Helsinki, Nov. 8, 1957); *Aubade* (1958; Helsinki, Nov. 20, 1959); *Simbolo* (1960; Helsinki, March 14, 1961); *Circulus* (Helsinki, May 21, 1965); *Colori ed improvvisazioni* (1973; Zeeland, Jan. 23, 1974); *Dualis* for Cello and Orch. (Helsinki, Sept. 19, 1978); *Birds in the Morning* for Flute and Orch. (Warsaw, Sept. 18, 1979); *Arctica* (Utrecht, Nov. 2, 1979; based on *Lapponia* for Mezzo-soprano, Baritone, and Chorus, 1975); Piano Concerto (1980–81; Helsinki, Sept. 16, 1981); *Ananke* (1981–82; Helsinki, Oct. 6, 1982); Violin Concerto (1982; Mainz, May 11, 1984); *Tutti e soli* for Chamber Orch. (Helsinki, April 3, 1990); *Sub Luna*, 4 noctures (Helsinki, Aug. 21, 1991); *Poseidon* (1992; Washington, D.C., March 3, 1994); *Fanfare* for Chamber Orch. (Porvoo, June 18, 1993); *Musica Marina* for Strings (Jakobstad, May 20, 1994). **CHAMBER**: Piano Trio (1937); Violin Sonata (1943); Suite for Guitar (1949); *3 Fantasies* for Clarinet and Piano (Helsinki, May 14, 1954); *Concertino da camera* for 8 Instruments (Helsinki, Nov. 24, 1961); *Soltafara* for Alto Saxophone and Percussion (1977; Helsinki, Jan. 16, 1978); *Dialogue* for Flute and Guitar (Savonlinna, July 22, 1977); *Midnight* for Guitar (London, Dec. 9, 1977); *Silence and Eruptions* for 10 Instruments (1979; Stockholm, May 16, 1980); *Janus* for Violin and Guitar (Jyväskylä, July 2, 1980); *Mipejupa* for Flute, Alto Saxophone, Guitar, and Percussion (Helsinki, June 20, 1981); String Quartet (Kuhmo, July 27, 1982); *Borealis* for 2 Pianos and Percussion (Washington, D.C., Nov. 19, 1983); *Quo Vadis* for Cello and Piano (1983; Helsinki, Aug. 31, 1984); *etwas rascher* for Saxophone Quartet (1985; Savonlinna, Aug. 10, 1986); *Karanssi* for Clarinet and Cello (Warsaw, Sept. 15, 1990); *Mana* for Violin, Cello, Clarinet, and Piano (Washington, D.C., Sept. 27, 1991); *Quint-essence* for Saxophone Quartet and Percussion (1993); *Attention!* for 5 Percussion (1993; Helsinki, Aug. 22, 1995); *Now* for Viola and Piano (1994; Lapland Festival, July 6, 1995); *Una Fantasia* for String Quartet and Piano (1994; Kuhmo, July 21, 1995). **KEYBOARD: Piano**: *Intervalles* (1949; Zürich, Oct. 19, 1951); Sonatina (1950); *Espressivo* (Helsinki, Dec. 5, 1952); *Aspekter* (1963); *A propos de B-A-C-H* (Helsinki, March 21, 1977); *Omaggio a Christoforo Colombo* (Helsinki, Nov. 29, 1991). **Organ**: *Exsultate* (1954). **Harpsichord**: *Energien* (1970; Helsinki, Nov. 26, 1971). **VOCAL**: *Majnätter* (May Nights) for Soprano and Orch. (Stockholm, May 20, 1946); *Ensamhetens sånger* (Songs of Solitude) for Mezzo-soprano, Baritone, and Orch. (1947); *Rubaiyat* for Baritone, Men's Chorus, and Orch. (1953); *Adagio* for Baritone, Men's Chorus, Flute, and Vibraphone (1957; Helsinki, May 10, 1958); *Svanbild* (Swan Picture) for Baritone, Vocal Quartet, and Men's Chorus (1958; Helsinki, April 15, 1959); *Aton* for Baritone, Reciter, Chorus, and Orch. (1959; Helsinki, April 29, 1960); *3 Galgenlieder* for Baritone, 2 Reciters, and Men's Choruses (1959); *4 Galgenlieder* for 3 Reciters and Speaking Chorus (1960; Zürich, Dec. 3, 1961); *Bauta* for Men's Chorus, Baritone, and Percussion (Helsinki, Nov. 25, 1961); *Sela* for Baritone, Chorus, and Chamber Orch. (Helsinki, Nov. 18, 1962); *Fåglarna* (Birds) for Baritone, Men's Chorus, Percussion, and Celesta (1962; Helsinki, April 6, 1963); *Barnets drom* (Child's Dream) for Child Reciter, 2 Men Speakers, Men's Chorus, and Recorder (Helsinki, Nov. 30, 1963); *Ha Li Bomp* for

Reciter, Tenor, and Men's Chorus (1964; Helsinki, April 10, 1965); *En sådan Kväll* (Such an Evening) for Soprano and Chorus (1965; Turku, June 11, 1966); *Snö* (Snow) for Tenor, Men's Chorus, and Flute (1966); *Springtime* for Baritone and Chorus (1966; London, Feb. 22, 1967); *Jesurun* for Baritone, Men's Chorus, 2 Trumpets, 2 Trombones, and 3 Percussion (1967; Helsinki, May 10, 1968); *Annonssidan* (Small Ads) for Baritone, 3 Tenors, 25 Reciters, and Men's Chorus (1969); *Nox* for Baritone, Chorus, Flute, English Horn, and Percussion (Goteborg, April 20, 1970); *Requiem över en död diktare* (Requiem for a Dead Poet) for Baritone, Chorus, 2 Trumpets, 2 Trombones, 2 Percussion, and Organ (1970; Stockholm, May 19, 1975); *Missa in honorem Sancti Henrici* for Soloists, Chorus, and Organ (Helsinki, Sept. 5, 1971); *Hathor Suite* for Soprano, Baritone, Chorus, Flute, English Horn, Harp, and 2 Percussion (Helsinki, Nov. 27, 1971); *Bardo Thödol* for Reciter, Mezzo-soprano, Baritone, Chorus, and Orch. (1974; Helsinki, May 19, 1975); *Lapponia* for Mezzo-soprano, Baritone, and Chorus (Cambridge, Nov. 30, 1975; reworked as *Arctica* for Orch., 1979); *Bon Appetit!* for Reciter, Baritone, and Men's Chorus (1975); *Noa* for Baritone, Chorus, and Orch. (1976; Helsinki, Oct. 25, 1977); *Bim Bam Bum* for Reciter, Tenor, Men's Chorus, Flute, and Percussion (1976; Uppsala, April 23, 1977); *Voices in the Night* for Baritone and Men's Chorus (1977; Reykjavík, May 9, 1979); *Triumf att finnas till* (Triumph of Being Here) for Soprano, Flute, and Percussion (1978; Cologne, Jan. 25, 1979); *Gudarnas spar* (Tracks of the Gods) for Alto, Baritone, and Chorus (1978; Helsinki, March 2, 1980); *Tipitaka Suite* for Baritone and Men's Chorus (1980; Turku, April 3, 1982); *4 Vocalises* for Mezzo-soprano and Men's Chorus (1983; Helsinki, Nov. 24, 1986); *Lemminkainen* for Reciter, Mezzo-soprano, Baritone, and Chorus (1984; Helsinki, May 8, 1985); *Svep* (Sweep) for Reciter, Mezzo-soprano, Baritone, Chorus, and Instrumental Ensemble (1984; Helsinki, Feb. 5, 1985); *Bygden* (The Village) for Reciter, Soprano, Baritone, Chorus, Child Soprano, Children's Chorus, Instruments, Cowbells, Bottles, Gongs, etc. (1985); *Forsta maj* (May Day) for Tenor and Men's Chorus (1985; Helsinki, March 7, 1988); *Tule armaani* (Come, My Love) for Baritone and Men's Chorus (1988; Helsinki, Nov. 23, 1989); *Careliana* for 6 Men's Voices (1988; Joensuu, June 11, 1989); *Petrarca Suite* for Baritone and Chorus (Helsinki, Dec. 12, 1991); *Nein zur Lebensangst* for Reciter and Chamber Chorus (1991); *Tapiolassa* for Alto and Children's Chorus (1991; Helsinki, Nov. 23, 1993); *Den heliga oron* for Mezzo-soprano and String Qurtet (1994; Korsholm, June 19, 1995); *Aggadot* for Vocal Quartet and Instrumental Ensemble (1994; Joensuu, June 21, 1995); various other mixed and men's choruses; solo songs.

BIBL.: J. Parsons, *E. B.: A Seventieth Birthday Tribute* (London, 1981).—**NS/LK/DM**

Bergmann, Carl, German cellist and conductor; b. Ebersbach, Saxony, April 12, 1821; d. N.Y., Aug. 10, 1876. He was a pupil of Zimmerman in Zittau and of Hesse in Breslau; in consequence of his involvement in the revolutionary events of 1848–49, he went to America. In 1850 he joined the traveling Germania Orch. as a cellist; later became its conductor; also led the Handel and Haydn Soc. of Boston (1852–54). In 1854 he went to N.Y. and became conductor of the German men's chorus Arion. On April 21, 1855, he made an impressive debut as a guest conductor of the N.Y. Phil., and was named its sole conductor for the 1855–56 and 1858–59 seasons; then shared the conductorship with Theodore Eisfeld. In 1865 he became permanent conductor of the N.Y. Phil., a position he held until he retired in March 1876.

He continued to perform as a cellist, taking part in the Mason-Thomas chamber music concerts; furthermore, he led a series of Sacred Concerts, in programs of both choral and orch. music. He was a progressive musician, and presented works of Berlioz, Liszt, and Wagner at the time when their music did not suit the tastes of the American public.—**NS/LK/DM**

Bergmans, Paul (Jean Étienne Charles Marie), Belgian librarian and musicologist; b. Ghent, Jan. 23, 1868; d. there, Nov. 14, 1935. He was educated at the Univ. of Ghent; also took courses in piano and violin at the Ghent Cons., and received private instruction in theory from Waelput. From 1885 until his death he wrote music criticism for *Flandre Ibérale*; in 1892 he became assistant librarian and in 1919 chief librarian at the Univ. of Ghent; in 1919 he also became the first holder of its chair in musicology, the first in a Belgian univ. In 1920 he was elected a member of the Académie Royale de Belgique.

WRITINGS: *Pierre Josephe Le Blau: Carillonneur de la ville de Gand au XVIIIᵉsiècle* (Ghent, 1884); *Hendrick Waelput* (Ghent, 1886); *Variétés musicologiques* (Ghent, 1891–1901; Antwerp, 1920); *Analecte belgiques* (Ghent, 1896); *Les imprimeurs belges à l'étranger* (Ghent, 1897; 2ⁿᵈ ed., 1922); *La vie musicale gantoise au XVIIIᵉ siècle* (Ghent, 1897); *L'organiste des archiducs Albert et Isabelle: Peter Philips* (Ghent, 1903); *Nicolas Maiscocque: Musicien montois due XVIIᵉ siècle* (Ghent, 1909); *Mélanges iconographiques, bibliographiques et historiques* (Ghent, 1912); *Les musiciens de Courtrai et du Courtraisis* (Ghent, 1912); *La biographie du compositeur Corneille Verdonck* (Brussels, 1919); *Henri Vieuxtemps* (Turnhout, 1920); *Le baron Limnander de Nieuwenhove* (Brussels, 1920); *Quatorze lettres inédites du compositeur Philippe de Monte* (Brussels, 1921); *Tielman Susato* (Antwerp, 1923); *Les origines belges de Beethoven* (Brussels, 1927); *Une famille de musiciens belges du XVIIIᵉ siècle: Les Loeillet* (Brussels, 1928); *La typographie musicale en Belgique au XVIᵉ siècle* (Brussels, 1930).—**NS/LK/DM**

Bergonzi, Carlo, Italian violin maker; b. Cremona, c. 1683; d. there, 1747. He began manufacturing violins about 1720, working independently of Stradivarius and other violin makers of his time. His son, Michael Angelo Bergonzi, continued the trade, as did his grandsons, Carlo, Nicola, and Zosimo Bergonzi.—**NS/LK/DM**

Bergonzi, Carlo, eminent Italian tenor; b. Polisene, near Parma, July 13, 1924. He studied with Grandini in Parma, where he also took courses at the Boito Cons. During World War II, he was imprisoned for his fervent anti-Fascist stance. After his liberation, he made his operatic debut in the baritone role of Rossini's Figaro in Lecce in 1948. In 1951 he made his debut as a tenor singing Andrea Chénier in Bari. He made his first appearance at Milan's La Scala in 1953 creating the title role in Napoli's *Masaniello*, and that same year he made his London debut as Alvaro at the Stoll Theatre. In 1962 he returned to London to make his Covent Garden debut in the same role. In 1955 he made his U.S. debut as Luigi in *Il Tabarro* at the Chicago Lyric Opera. On Nov. 13, 1956, he made his Metropolitan Opera debut in N.Y. as Radames, remaining on its roster until 1972, and again for the 1974–75, 1976–77, and 1978–83 seasons. He

gave his farewell N.Y. concert at Carnegie Hall on April 17, 1994; he then bade farewell to Europe that same year in a series of concerts. He was blessed with a voice of remarkable beauty and expressivity. Among his many outstanding roles were Pollione, Rodolfo, Alfredo, Canio, Manrico, Nemorino, and Cavaradossi.
—NS/LK/DM

Bergsma, William (Laurence), notable American composer and pedagogue; b. Oakland, Calif., April 1, 1921; d. Seattle, March 18, 1994. His mother, a former opera singer, gave him piano lessons; he also practiced the violin. After the family moved to Redwood City, Bergsma entered Burlingame H.S., where he had theory lessons. In 1937 he began to take lessons in composition with Hanson at the Univ. of Southern Calif. in Los Angeles. He composed a ballet, *Paul Bunyan*, and Hanson conducted a suite from it with the Rochester Civic Orch. in Rochester, N.Y., on April 29, 1939. Bergsma also took courses at Stanford Univ. (1938–40); from 1940 to 1944 he attended the Eastman School of Music in Rochester, studying general composition with Hanson and orchestration with Bernard Rogers. He graduated in 1942, receiving his M.M. degree in 1943. In 1944 Bergsma became an instructor in music at Drake Univ. in Des Moines. In 1946 and in 1951 he held Guggenheim fellowships. In 1946 he was appointed to the faculty of the Juilliard School of Music in N.Y., where he taught until 1963. From 1963 to 1971 Bergsma served as director of the School of Music of the Univ. of Wash. in Seattle, remaining as a prof. there until 1986. In 1967 he was elected to membership in the National Inst. of Arts and Letters. During his teaching activities he continued to compose, receiving constant encouragement from an increasing number of performances. His style of composition is that of classical Romanticism, having a strong formal structure without lapsing into modernistic formalism. The Romantic side of his music is reflected in his melodious lyricism. He never subscribed to fashionable theories of doctrinaire modernity.

WORKS: DRAMATIC: O p e r a : *The Wife of Martin Guerre* (N.Y., Feb. 15, 1956); *The Murder of Comrade Sharik* (1973; rev. 1978). B a l l e t : *Paul Bunyan* (San Francisco, June 22, 1939); *Gold and the Senor Commandante* (Rochester, N.Y., May 1, 1942). ORCH.: Sym. for Chamber Orch. (Rochester, N.Y., April 14, 1943); 2 numbered syms.: No. 1 (1946–49; Radio Hilversum, April 18, 1950) and No. 2, *Voyages* (Great Falls, Mont., May 11, 1976); *Music on a Quiet Theme* (Rochester, N.Y., April 22, 1943); *A Carol on Twelfth Night*, symphonic poem (1953); *Chameleon Variations* (1960); *In Celebration: Toccata for the 6th Day*, commissioned for the inaugural-week concert of the Juilliard Orch. during the week of dedication of Phil. Hall at Lincoln Center for the Performing Arts (N.Y., Sept. 28, 1962); *Documentary 1* (1963; suite from a film score) and *2* (1967); *Serenade, To Await the Moon* for Chamber Orch. (La Jolla, Calif., Aug. 22, 1965); Violin Concerto (Tacoma, Wash., May 18, 1966); *Dances from a New England Album, 1852* for Small Orch. (1969); *Sweet Was the Song the Virgin Sung: Tristan Revisited*, variations and fantasy for Viola and Orch. (1977); *In Campo Aperto* for Oboe Concertante, 2 Bassoon, and Strings (1981). CHAMBER: *Showpiece* for Violin and Piano (1934); Suite for Brass Quartet (1940); 6 string quartets (1942, 1944, 1953, 1970, 1982, 1991); *Pieces for Renard* for Recorder and 2 Violas (1943); Concerto for

Wind Quintet (1958); *Fantastic Variations on a Theme from Tristan und Isolde* for Viola and Piano (Boston, March 2, 1961); *Illegible Canons* for Clarinet and Piano (1969); *Changes for 7* for Wind Quintet, Percussion, and Piano (1971); *Clandestine Dialogues* for Cello and Percussion (1972); *Blatant Hypotheses* for Trombone and Piano (1977); Quintet for Flute and Strings (1979); *The Voice of the Coelacanth* for Horn, Violin, and Piano (1980); *Masquerade* for Wind Quintet (1986); *A Lick and a Promise* for Saxophone and Chimes (1988). P i a n o : *3 Fantasies* (1943; rev. 1983); *Tangents* (1951); *Variations* (1984). VOCAL: *In a Glass of Water* (1945); *On the Beach at Night* (1946); *Confrontation*, from the Book of Job, for Chorus and 22 Instruments (Des Moines, Iowa, Nov. 29, 1963); *Wishes, Wonders, Portents, Charms* for Chorus and Instruments (N.Y., Feb. 12, 1975); *In Space* for Soprano and Instruments (Seattle, May 21, 1975); *I Told You So*, 4 songs for Voice and Percussion (1986).—NS/LK/DM

Berigan, Bunny (Rowland Bernard), well-known jazz trumpeter, singer, leader; b. Hilbert, Wisc., Nov. 2, 1908; d. N.Y., June 2, 1942. His powerful, clearly conceived solos made him a favorite of musicians as well as the public, winning a jazz poll in 1939 with five times as many votes as his nearest competitor. His brother Don was a drummer, their mother played piano. Bunny began on violin, then switched to trumpet (continuing to double until 1927). At 13 played locally with Merrill Gwen and his Pennsy Jazz Band; during the early 1920s sat in with the New Orleans Rhythm Kings in Wisc. Though not a student at the Univ. of Wisc., he played regularly in the college dance bands throughout his teens. He played in local bands including those led by Jesse Cohen and Cy Mahlberg (1926). Resident at The Chanticleer Ballroom in Madison with local leaders, then played in N.Y. and Philadelphia (1928). He returned to Wisc. before making another trip to N.Y. to play with violinist Frank Cornwell's Band at The Hofbrau (early 1929), then returned home again before journeying once more to N.Y. to join Hal Kemp at the Hotel Taft in the spring of 1930. He was with Hal Kemp in Europe from May until September 1930. He then returned to the U.S. and began freelancing in N.Y. prior to joining Fred Rich Orch.; during the early 1930s, he did extensive studio work, including radio and recording sessions with Benny Krueger, Ben Selvin, etc. He worked in Dorsey Brothers' Band for the Broadway show *Everybody Welcome* (1931), doubled studio work and freelance work until spending summer season with Smith Ballew. He joined Paul Whiteman from late 1932 until late 1933, a month with Abe Lyman, then CBS studio work and occasional gigs with the Dorseys, Benny Goodman, etc. He played regularly with Benny Goodman from June until September 1935, left Goodman in Calif., home to Wisc., then back to N.Y. to resume at CBS studios. Active as A.R.C. staff man during 1936, combining this with short spells with Red McKenzie, Red Norvo, Ray Noble, and leading his own pick-up bands. CBS work in early 1937, recording work with Tommy Dorsey, then from spring 1937 leading own big band, which bankruptcy eventually caused him to disband in spring of 1940. He was with Tommy Dorsey from March until August 1940, then formed own small band for residency at 47 Club, N.Y. Soon reverted to leading a big band, extensive touring and summer

1941 residency in Columbus, Ohio. He went to Hollywood in late 1941 to record part of soundtrack for the film *Syncopation* (sharing trumpet work with George Thow), then returned to big band until contracting pneumonia in April 1942. He left the hospital on May 8, 1942, and continued one-nighters until May 30th. He was a serious alcoholic, which exacerbated his condition, and he suffered a severe hemorrhage and was admitted to the N.Y. Polyclinic Hospital, where he died three days later.

DISC.: B. Goodman: "King Porter Stomp" (1935). T. Dorsey: "Marie " (1937); "Song of India" (1937); "I Can't Get Started" (1937).—JC/LP

Beringer, Oscar, German-born English pianist and pedagogue; b. Furtwangen, Baden, July 14, 1844; d. London, Feb. 21, 1922. His father, a political refugee, settled in London in 1849. Oscar Beringer received his rudimentary education at home, then enrolled in the Leipzig Cons., where he studied with Plaidy, Moscheles, and Reinecke (1864–66); he further studied in Berlin with Tausig. In 1869 became a prof. at Tausig's Schule des Hoheren Klavierspiels. He returned to London in 1871, and in 1873 established there an Academy for the Higher Development of Pianoforte Playing, organized on the model of Tausig's Berlin school. From 1885 he was also a prof. at the Royal Academy of Music. He was a pianist of great perfection of method; his book of technical exercises is valuable for students. Among his publ. compositions are a Piano Concerto, 2 piano sonatinas, various minor piano pieces, and songs. He also publ. *Fifty Years' Experience of Pianoforte Teaching and Playing* (1907).—NS/LK/DM

Berio, Luciano, eminent Italian composer, conductor, and pedagogue; b. Oneglia, Oct. 24, 1925. Following initial training from his father, Ernesto Berio, he entered the Milan Cons. in 1945 to study composition with Paribeni and Ghedini, obtaining his diploma in 1950. He married **Cathy Berberian** in 1950 (marriage dissolved in 1964), who became a champion of his most daunting vocal works. In 1952 he attended Dallapiccola's course at the Berkshire Music Center in Tanglewood. After attending the summer course in new music in Darmstadt in 1954, he returned to Milan and helped to organize the Studio di Fonologia Musicale of the RAI with Maderna, remaining active with it until 1961. In 1956 he founded the journal *Incontri Musicali*, and also served as director of the concerts it sponsored until 1960. He taught composition at the Berkshire Music Center (1960, 1982), the Dartington Summer School (1961–62), Mills Coll. in Oakland, Calif. (1962–64), and Harvard Univ. (1966–67). From 1965 to 1972 he taught composition at the Juilliard School of Music in N.Y., where he also conducted the Juilliard Ensemble. From 1974 to 1979 he worked at IRCAM in Paris. He also gave increasing attention to conducting, eventually appearing as a guest conductor with leading European and North American orchs. In 1987 he became founder-director of Tempo Reale in Florence, a research, educational, and composition center. During the 1993–94 academic year, he was the Charles Eliot Norton Prof. of

Poetry at Harvard Univ., and then served as its Distinguished Composer-in-Residence from 1994. In 1980 he was awarded an honorary doctorate from the City Univ. of London. He received the Premio Italia in 1982 for his *Duo*. In 1989 he was awarded the Ernst von Siemens-Musikpreis of Munich. He won the Premium Imperiale of Japan in 1996.

From the very beginning of his career as a composer, Berio embraced the ideals of the avant-garde. His early use of 12–tone writing was followed by imaginative explorations of aleatory, electronics, objets trouvés, and other contemporary means of expression. As one of the principal composers of his era, Berio has demonstrated a remarkable capacity for infusing new life into established forms. The theatrical nature of much of his music has rendered his vocal scores among the most challenging and significant works of their time. These works, like most of his output, have set daunting hurdles of virtuosity for the performer while demanding a level of tolerance from both critics and audiences alike.

WORKS: DRAMATIC: *Allez Hop,* racconto mimico for Mezzo-soprano, 8 Mimes, Ballet, and Orch. (1952–59; Venice, Sept. 23, 1959; rev. 1968); *Passaggio,* messa in scena for Soprano, 2 Choruses, and Orch. (1961–62; Milan, May 6, 1963); *Laborintus II* for Voices, Instruments, and Tape (1965); *Il combattimento di Tancredi e Clordina,* after Monteverdi (1966); *Opera* for 10 Actors, 2 Sopranos, Tenor, Baritone, Vocal Ensemble, Orch., and Tape (1969–70; Santa Fe, N.Mex., Aug. 12, 1970; rev. version, Florence, May 28, 1977); *Per la dolce memoria de quel giorno,* ballet (1974); *La vera storia,* opera (1977–78; Milan, March 9, 1982); *Un re in ascolto,* azione musicale (1979–83; Salzburg, Aug. 7, 1984); *Duo,* imaginary theater for radio for Baritone, 2 Violins, Chorus, and Orch. (1982); *Naturale,* theater piece (1985–86; *Wir Bauen eine Stadt,* children's opera, after Hindemith (1987); *Outis,* opera (Milan, Oct. 2, 1996); *Cronaca del Lugo,* music theater piece (Salzburg, July 24,1999). **ORCH.:** *Preludio a una festa marina* for Strings (1944); Concertino for Clarinet, Violin, Harp, Celesta, and Strings (1951; rev. 1970); *Variazioni* for Chamber Orch. (1953–54; Hamburg, Feb. 23, 1955); *Nones* (1954; Rome, Oct. 15, 1955); *Mimusique No. 2* (1955); *Allelujah I* (1955–56) and *II* (1957–58; Rome, May 17, 1958); *Variazoni* for 2 Basset Horns and Strings, after Mozart (1956); *Divertimento* (Rome, Dec. 2, 1957; in collaboration with B. Maderna); *Tempi concertati* for Flute, Violin, 2 Pianos, and Other Instruments (1958–59); *Quaderni I* (1959), *II* (1961), and *III* (1962); *Chemins I* for Harp and Orch. (1965; based on *Sequenza II*), *III* for Viola and Orch. (1968; rev. 1973; based on *Chemins II*), *IIB* (1970), *IIC* for Bass Clarinet and Orch. (1972), *IV* for Oboe and Strings (1975; based on *Sequenza VII*), and *V* for Guitar and Chamber Orch. (1992); *Bewegung* (1971); *Still* (1971–73); Concerto for 2 Pianos and Orch. (1972–73; *Points on the Curve to Find...* for Piano and 23 Instruments (1974); *Eindrücke* (1973–74); *Il ritorno degli snovidenia* for Cello and 30 Instruments (1976–77); *Encore* (1978); 2 piano concertos: No. 1 (1979) and No. 2, *Echoing Curves* (1988); *Entrata* (San Francisco, Oct. 1, 1980); *Accordo* for 4 Wind Bands (1981); *Corale* for Violin, 2 Horns, and Strings (1981; based on *Sequenza VIII*); *Fanfara* (1982); *Requies* (1983–84; Lausanne, March 26, 1984; rev. 1985); *Voci* for Viola and 2 Instrumental Groups (1984); *Formazioni* (1986; Amsterdam, Jan. 15, 1987; rev. 1988); *Continuo* (1989); *Festum* (Dallas, Sept. 14, 1989); *Récit (Chemins VII)* for Alto Saxophone and Orch. (Milan, Oct. 12, 1996); *ekphrasis (continuo II)* (1996; Gran Canaria Festival, Jan. 24, 1997); *Alternatim,* double concerto for Clarinet, Viola, and

Orch. (1996–97; Amsterdam, May 16, 1997); *Solo* for Trombone and Orch. (Zürich, Dec. 7, 1999). **CHAMBER**: *Divertimento* for Violin, Viola, and Cello (1947; rev. 1985); *Tre pezzi* for 3 Clarinets (1947); Wind Quintet (1948); Wind Quartet (1950–51; rev. 1951 as *Opus Number Zoo* for Wind Quintet); Sonatina for Flute, 2 Clarinets, and Bassoon (1951); *Due Pezzi* for Violin and Piano (1951; rev. 1966); *Study* for String Quartet (1952; rev. 1985); 2 string quartets (1956; 1986–93); *Serenata* for Chamber Ensemble (1957); *Sequenza I* for Flute (1958), *II* for Harp (1963), *V* for Trombone (1966), *VI* for Viola (1967), *VII* for Oboe (1969), *VIII* for Violin (1976), *IXa* for Clarinet (1980), *IXb* for Alto Saxophone (1981), *X* for Trumpet and Piano Resonance (1985), *XI* for Guitar (1987–88), and *XII* for Accordion (1995); *Differences* for Flute, Clarinet, Harp, Viola, Cello, and Tape (1958); *Sincronie* for String Quartet (1963–64); *Gesti* for Recorder (1966); *Chemins II* for Viola and 9 Instruments (1967; based on *Sequenza VI*); *Memory* for Electric Piano and Electric Harpsichord (1970); *Autre Fois* for Flute, Clarinet, and Harp (1971); *Musica leggera* for Flute, Viola, and Cello (1974); *Les Mots sont allés* for Cello (1978); *Duetti* for 2 Violins (1979–82); *Lied* for Clarinet (1983); *Call-St. Louis Fanfare* for 5 Winds (1985; rev. 1987); *Ricorrenze* for Wind Quintet (1985–87); *Comma* for Clarinet (1987); *Psy* for Double Bass (1989); *Brin* for Guitar (1994; also for Piano, 1990); *Glosse* for String Quartet (Regio Emilia, June 22, 1997). **KEYBOARD: P i a n o :** *Pastorale* (1937); *Toccata* for Piano Duet (1939); *Petite Suite* (1947); *Cinque variazioni* (1952–53; rev. 1966); *Wasserklavier* (1965); *Sequenza IV* (1965–66); *Erdenklavier* (1969); *Luftklavier* (1985); *Feuerklavier* (1989); *Leaf* (1990); *Brin* (1990; also for Guitar, 1994). **O r g a n :** *Fa-Si* for Organ and Registration Assistants (1975). **H a r p s i c h o r d :** *Rounds* (1966). **VOCAL:** *O bone Jesu* for Chorus (1946); *4 canzoni popolari* for Woman's Voice and Piano (1946–47); *Trio liriche greche* for Voice and Piano (1946–48); *Due canti siciliani* for Tenor and Men's Chorus (1948); *Ad Hermes* for Voice and Piano (1948); *Due pezzi sacri* for 2 Sopranos, Piano, 2 Harps, Timpani, and 12 Bells (1949); *Magnificat* for 2 Sopranos, Chorus, and Orch. (1949); *Opus Number Zoo* for Reciters and Wind Quintet (1951; rev. 1970; based on the Wind Quintet); *Deus meus* for Voice and 3 Instruments (1951); *El Mar la Mar* for Soprano, Mezzo-soprano, and 7 Instruments (1952); *Chamber Music* for Woman's Voice, Clarinet, Cello, and Harp (1953); *Epifanie* for Soprano or Mezzo-soprano and Orch. (1959–61; rev. 1965); *Circles* for Woman's Voice, Harp, and 2 Percussionists (1960); *Folk Songs* for Mezzo-soprano and 7 Instruments (1964; also for Mezzo-soprano and Orch., 1973); *Sequenza III* for Voice (1965); *O King* for Voice and 5 Instruments (1968); *Questo vuol dire che* for 3 Women's Voices, Small Chorus, and Tape(1968); *Sinfonia* for 8 Voices and Orch. (1968–69); *Air* for Soprano and Orch. (1969); *Melodrama* for Tenor and Instrumental Ensemble, after *Opera* (1970); *Agnus* for 2 Sopranos and 3 Clarinets (1971); *Bewegung II* for Baritone and Orch. (1971); *Recital for Cathy* for Mezzo-soprano and 17 Instruments (1971); *E Vó* for Soprano and Instrumental Ensemble (1972); *Cries of London* for 6 Voices (1973–74; also for 8 Voices, 1974–76); *Calmo (in memoriam Bruno Maderna)* for Mezzo-soprano and Chamber Orch. (1974; rev. 1988–89); *Coro* for 40 Voices and Instrumental Ensemble (1974–77); *Scena de La vera storia* for Mezzo-soprano, Bass, Chorus, and Orch. (1981); *Ecce: musica per musicologi* for Women's Voices, Men's Voices, and Bells (1987); *Ofanim* for Woman's Voice, 2 Children's Choruses, 2 Instrumental Groups, and Computer (1988–97); *Canticum novissimi testamenti II* for Soprano, Alto, Tenor, Bass, 4 Clarinets, and Saxophone Quartet (1989); *Epiphanies* for Soprano or Mezzo-soprano and Orch. (1991–92); *Echo* for Soprano and Flute (Salzburg, Aug. 17, 1999).

ELECTRONIC: *Mutazioni* (1954); *Perspectives* (1957); *Momenti* (1957); *Thema (Omaggio a Joyce)* (1958); *Visage* (1961); *Chants parallèles* (1975); *Diario imaginario* (1975). **OTHER:** *Brahms-Berio, Op.120, No. 1* for Clarinet or Viola and Orch. (1984–85); *Schubert-Berio: Rendering* for Orch. (1989; a restoration of fragments from a Schubert sym.); arrangements of various other works, including those by Verdi, Mahler, Weill, and Falla.

BIBL.: R. Dalmonte and B. Varga, *L. B.: Two Interviews* (London, 1985); D. Osmond-Smith, *B.* (Oxford, 1991); F. Menezes Filho, *L. B. et la phonologie: Une approche jakobsonienne de son oeuvre* (Frankfurt am Main, 1993).—**NS/LK/DM**

Bériot, Charles (-Auguste) de, celebrated Belgian violinist, pedagogue, and composer, b. Louvain, Feb. 20, 1802; d. Brussels, April 8, 1870. After initial instruction from a provincial teacher, he was left to perfect his technique on his own. In 1821 he went to Paris, where he briefly attended Baillot's class as the Cons.; that same year, he made a successful debut in Paris. In 1826 he made his first appearance in London, where he garnered great praise. He then served as solo violinist to the King of the Netherlands until 1830. In 1826 he met **María Malibran**, with whom he lived until her marriage to her first husband was annulled in 1836 and at which time the two were married. From 1829 to 1836 he toured widely, and gave joint concerts with Malibran in France, England, Italy, and Belgium. After her death in 1836, he withdrew from public appearances until 1838. He then gave joint concerts in Austria and Italy with Pauline García, his late wife's sister. In 1840 he played in Russia. In 1843 he became a prof. of violin at the Brussels Cons., a post he retained until failing eyesight and paralysis of the left arm compelled him to retire in 1852. His most renowned pupil was Henri Vieuxtemps. Bériot's playing was greatly admired for its combination of technical brilliance and warmth of tone. He publ. 10 violin concertos (Nos. 1, 7, and 9 are still used in violin courses), *12 Airs variés*, duos brillants for Violin and Piano, 11 sets of variations for Violin, etc. His pedagogical works are still useful, the most notable being his *Méthode de Violon* (Paris, 1858).—**NS/LK/DM**

Berkeley, Michael (Fitzhardinge), English composer, son of **Sir Lennox (Randall Francis) Berkeley;** b. London, May 29, 1948. He was a chorister at Westminster Cathedral under the tutelage of George Malcolm. He also studied with his father at the Royal Academy of Music and then privately with Richard Rodney Bennett. He received the Guinness Prize for his *Meditations* for Chamber Orch. (1977). Berkeley was assoc. composer to the Scottish Chamber Orch. (1979) and composer-in-residence at the London Coll. of Music (1987–88). From 1994 to 1997 he was co-artistic director of the Spitalfields Festival. In 1995 he became artistic director of the Cheltenham Festival. His anti-nuclear oratorio *Or Shall We Die?* (1982) brought him to international attention. His music is austere while still projecting a firm relationship to the English New Romantic movement.

WORKS: DRAMATIC: *The Mayfly*, children's ballet (London, Sept. 30, 1984); *Baa-Baa Black Sheep*, opera (Cheltenham, July 7, 1993). **ORCH.:** *Meditations* for Chamber Orch.

(1977); *Fantasia Concertante* for Chamber Orch. (1977); Concerto for Oboe and Chamber Orch. (Burnham Market, Aug. 20, 1977); *Primavera* (London, May 18, 1979); *Uprising,* sym. for Chamber Orch. (Edinburgh, Dec. 18, 1980); *Flames* (1980; Liverpool, Jan. 10, 1981); *The Vision of Piers the Ploughman* for Chamber Orch. (1981); *Gregorian Variations* (London, April 22, 1982); *The Romance of the Rose* for Chamber Orch. (1982); Concerto for Cello and Chamber Orch. (London, Feb. 20, 1983); Concerto for Horn and Chamber Orch. (Cheltenham, July 17, 1984); Organ Concerto (Cambridge, July 23, 1987); *Coronach* for Strings (1988); *Entertaining Master Punch* for Chamber Orch. (1991); Clarinet Concerto (1991); *Elegy* for Flute and Strings (1993); Viola Concerto (1994); *Secret Garden* (1997); *Garden of Earthly Delights* (1998). **CHAMBER:** String Trio (1978); Violin Sonata (1979); *American Suite* for Flute or Recorder and Cello or Bassoon (1980); Chamber Sym. (London, Aug. 1, 1980); 5 string quartets (1981, 1984, 1987, 1995, 1997); Piano Trio (1982); *Music from Chaucer* for Brass Quintet (1983); Clarinet Quintet (1983); *Fierce Tears* for Oboe and Piano (1984); *A Mosaic for Father Popieluszko* for Violin and Guitar (1985); *For the Savage Messiah* for Piano Quartet and Bass (1985). **S o l o I n s t r u m e n t s :** *Strange Meeting* for Piano (1978); Organ Sonata (1979); *Iberian Notebook* for Cello (1980); *Worry Beads* for Guitar (1981); Guitar Sonata (1982); *The Snake* for English Horn (1990). **VOCAL:** *The Wild Winds* for Soprano and Small Orch. (London, Dec. 19, 1978); *Rain* for Tenor, Violin, and Cello (1979); *At the Round Earth's Imagin'd Corners* for Chorus (1980); *The Crocodile and Father William* for Chorus (1982); *Or Shall We Die?,* oratorio for Soprano, Baritone, Chorus, and Orch. (London, Feb. 6, 1983); *Songs of Awakening Love* for Soprano and Small Orch. (Cheltenham, July 15, 1986); *Verbum caro factum est* for Baritone, Chorus, and Organ (1987; Birmingham, Jan. 7, 1988); *The Red Macula* for Chorus and Orch. (Leeds, May 5, 1989); *Stupendous Stranger* for Chorus and Brass (1990).—**NS/LK/DM**

Berkeley, Sir Lennox (Randall Francis), eminent English composer and teacher, father of **Michael (Fitzhardinge) Berkeley;** b. Boars Hill, May 12, 1903; d. London, Dec. 26, 1989. He was educated at Merton Coll., Oxford (1922–26), and then studied composition with Boulanger in Paris (1927–32). Returning to London, he worked for the BBC (1942–45) before serving as a prof. of composition at the Royal Academy of Music (1946–68). In 1957 he was made a Commander of the Order of the British Empire, in 1970 he received an honorary D. Mus. from the Univ. of Oxford, and in 1974 he was knighted. In his early works, Berkeley was influenced by the Parisian neo-Classicists and the music of Britten. He later developed a complex individual style that was broadly melodious, richly harmonious, and translucidly polyphonic.

WORKS: DRAMATIC: O p e r a : *Nelson* (1949–54; London, Sept. 22, 1954; orch. suite, 1955); *A Dinner Engagement* (Aldeburgh Festival, June 17, 1954); *Ruth* (London, Oct. 2, 1956); *Castaway* (Aldeburgh Festival, June 3, 1967). **B a l l e t :** *The Judgement of Paris* (1938). Also incidental music for plays and film scores. **ORCH.:** *Introduction and Dance* for Small Orch. (1926); 2 suites (1927, 1953); Concertino for Chamber Orch. (London, April 6, 1927); 2 sinfoniettas (1929, 1950); Sym. for Strings (1930–31; London, Dec. 14, 1931); 2 overtures (1934, Barcelona, April 23, 1936; 1947); *Mont Juic,* suite (1937; in collaboration with Britten); *Introduction and Allegro* for 2 Pianos and Orch. (1938); *Serenade* for Strings (1939); 4 syms.: No. 1 (1940; London, July 8, 1943), No. 2 (1956–58; Birmingham, Feb.

24, 1959), No. 3 (Cheltenham, July 9, 1969), and No. 4 (1976–78; London, May 30, 1978); Cello Concerto (1939; Cheltenham, July 17, 1983); *Divertimento* (1943); *Nocturne* (1946); Piano Concerto (1947); Concerto for 2 Pianos and Orch. (1948); Flute Concerto (1952; London, July 29, 1953); Concerto for Piano and Double String Orch. (1958; London, Feb. 11, 1959); *Overture for Light Orch.* (1959); *Suite: A Winter's Tale* (1960); *5 Pieces* for Violin and Orch. (1961; London, July 3, 1962); Concerto for Violin and Chamber Orch. (1961); *Partita* for Chamber Orch. (1964–65); *Windsor Variations* for Chamber Orch. (1969); *Dialogue* for Cello and Chamber Orch. (1970); *Palm Court Waltz* (1971); Sinfonia concertante for Oboe and Chamber Orch. (1973); *Antiphon* for Strings (1973); *Voices of the Night* (Birmingham, Aug. 22, 1973); Suite for Strings (1973–74); Guitar Concerto (London, July 4, 1974). **CHAMBER:** *Serenade* for Flute, Oboe, Violin, Viola, and Cello (1929); Suite for Flute, Oboe, Violin, Viola, and Cello (c. 1930); 2 violin sonatas (1931, c. 1933); 3 string quartets (1935, 1942, 1970); Trio for Flute, Oboe, and Piano (1935); Sonatina for Recorder or Flute and Piano (1939); String Trio (1943); Viola Sonata (1945); *Elegy* for Violin and Piano (1950); Trio for Violin, Horn, and Piano (1954); Sextet for Clarinet, Horn, and String Quartet (1955); Concertino for Recorder or Flute, Violin, Cello, and Harpsichord or Piano (1955); *Allegro* for 2 Treble Recorders (c. 1955); *Diversions* for 8 Instruments (1964); Quartet for Oboe and String Trio (1967); *Introduction and Allegro* for Double Bass and Piano (1971); Duo for Cello and Piano (1971); Quintet for Winds and Piano (1974–75); Flute Sonata (1978); also many piano pieces, including a Sonata (1941–45); harpsichord music; organ pieces. **VOCAL:** *Jonah,* oratorio (1933–35); *Domini est Terra* for Chorus and Orch. (London, June 17, 1938); *4 Poems of St. Teresa of Avila* for Contralto and Strings (1947); *Stabat Mater* for 6 Solo Voices and 12 Instruments (1947; arranged for Voices and Small Orch. by M. Berkeley, 1978); *Colonus' Praise* for Chorus and Orch. (1948); *Variations on a Theme by Orlando Gibbons* for Tenor, Chorus, Strings, and Organ (1951); *4 Ronsard Sonnets:* Set 1 for 2 Tenors and Piano (1952) and Set 2 for Tenor and Orch. (London, Aug. 9, 1963); *Batter My Heart* for Soprano, Chorus, Organ, and Chamber Orch. (1962); *Signs in the Dark* for Chorus and Strings (1967); *Magnificat* for Chorus and Orch. (London, July 8, 1968); *Una and the Lion* for Soprano, Recorder, Viola da Gamba, and Harpsichord (1978–79); many other choral works and songs.

BIBL.: P. Dickinson, *The Music of L. B.* (London, 1988). —**NS/LK/DM**

Berlijn, Anton (real name, **Aron Wolf**), Dutch composer and conductor; b. Amsterdam, May 2, 1817; d. there, Jan. 18, 1870. He was a pupil of his father, in Berlin of L.C. Erk and F. Schneider, in Kassel of Spohr, and in Leipzig of G.W. Finck. After serving as director of the Amsterdam theater, he conducted singing societies and was director of music at the synagogue. He composed over 500 works, including 6 operas, among them *Die Bergknappen* (1841) and *Proserpina, Le lutin de Culloden* (1842), a melodrama, *Ben-Leil,* 7 ballets, 2 syms., a *Grande ouverture triomphale* (1842), an oratorio, *Moses auf nebo* (1843), partsongs for Men's Voices, solo songs, and a String Quartet.

BIBL.: P. Böhm, *Nachruf an den verstorbenden Komponist A.W. B.* (Amsterdam, n.d.).—**NS/LK/DM**

Berlin, Irving (originally, **Baline, Israel**), adaptable Russian-born American songwriter; b. Mohilev, May 11, 1888; d. N.Y., Sept. 22, 1989. The most sucessful songwriter of the first half of the 20th century, Berlin counted among his 1,500 published songs such standards as "Alexander's Ragtime Band," "Oh, How I Hate to Get Up in the Morning," "A Pretty Girl Is Like a Melody," "Always," "Blue Skies," "Russian Lullaby," "Puttin' on the Ritz," "Cheek to Cheek," and "Change Partners." Writing for Tin Pan Alley, Broadway, and Hollywood, he developed his style from the ethnic novelty lyrics and ragtime music popular in the early part of the century to the more sophisticated compositions expected of songwriters of the 1920s and 1930s. Several of his songs transcended even the status of standards to become definitive expressions of popular culture: "God Bless America" is universally accepted as a second U.S. national anthem; "There's No Business Like Show Business" became the theme song for the field of popular entertainment; and "White Christmas," the best-selling record of all time, spoke for millions during World War II, becoming as much a part of the holiday season as Santa Claus. Writing any one of those songs would have marked Berlin as a major figure; writing all of them made him the most pervasive figure in popular music.

Berlin and his five older siblings were brought to the U.S. in September 1893 by his parents, Moses (b. January 1846; d. July 19, 1901) and Lena Lipkin Baline (b. August 1849; d. July 21, 1922), settling in N.Y. His father had been a cantor in Russia; in the U.S. he found only part-time work as a kosher-poultry inspector. Berlin, who had no formal musical training, left school and home at 13. He became a street entertainer, a song plugger, and finally a singing waiter at the Pelham Café in Chinatown. After gaining attention for the often risqué parodies of popular songs he sang, he was asked to collaborate with the café's pianist, Nick Michaelson, on a song. The result was his first published effort, "Marie from Sunny Italy" (1907), for which he changed his name to Irving Berlin.

Berlin began his long relationship with publisher/composer Ted Snyder with his second publication, "Dorando" (1908), the first song for which he wrote both words and music. It was published by Ted Snyder's Seminary Music Company (later, [Henry] Waterson and Snyder)—a company in which Berlin would become a partner three years later—and before long Berlin was working for and collaborating with Snyder. (Unable to read or write music, Berlin composed by playing the black keys on the piano, using a special lever to transpose from one musical key to another; his compositions were transcribed by an assistant.)

"She Was a Dear Little Girl" (1909; music by Snyder) was Berlin's first song to be interpolated into a Broadway musical. Berlin's first major record hit came that October with "My Wife's Gone to the Country, Hurrah! Hurrah!" (music by Snyder, lyrics by Berlin and George Whiting). A string of Berlin hits in 1910 included most notably "That Mesmerizing Mendelssohn Tune" (the tune in question was "Spring Song"). Meanwhile, Berlin and Snyder appeared together in the revue Up and Down Broadway (N.Y., July 18, 1910), performing their songs "That Beautiful Rag" and "Sweet Italian Love."

Beginning a relationship with the noted Broadway impressario Florenz Ziegfeld, Berlin contributed several songs to the Ziegfeld Follies of 1911 (N.Y., June 26, 1911), the most successful of which was "Woodman, Woodman, Spare That Tree" (lyrics by Vincent Bryan), written for blackface performer Bert Williams and generating a hit recording for him two years later.

"Alexander's Ragtime Band" (1911), the most successful song of Berlin's early career, was popularized by vaudeville star Emma Carus, leading to a series of popular recordings. The song's stirring music and mild syncopation made it more of a march than a ragtime tune, strictly speaking, but it ushered in a fashion for ragtime and crowned its songwriter as king of the genre; he quickly took advantage of the situation by churning out more ragtime-styled songs. A sheet-music million-seller, "Alexander's Ragtime Band" was successfully revived on record by Bessie Smith in 1927, the Boswell Sisters in 1935, and Louis Armstrong in 1937. Thanks to its success, in December 1911, Berlin was made a partner in his publishing firm, which was renamed Waterson, Berlin and Snyder. (In June 1919 he formed his own publishing company, Irving Berlin Inc., and in 1944 the Irving Berlin Music Corporation.)

In February 1912, Berlin married Dorothy Goetz, the sister of one of his collaborators. The couple honeymooned in Cuba, where Mrs. Berlin was taken ill with typhoid fever; she died at the age of 20 on July 17. Henry Burr scored a massive hit in April 1913 with "When I Lost You," unmistakably a musical comment on Berlin's bereavement and his first important ballad; the song also sold over two million copies of sheet music.

Berlin's major effort for 1914 was his first full score for a Broadway revue, Watch Your Step, which starred the popular dance team Vernon and Irene Castle. Running for 175 performances, the show produced three hits. Also in 1914, composer Victor Herbert encouraged Berlin to join the newly formed American Society of Composers, Authors, and Publishers (ASCAP) as a charter member; Berlin remained active in ASCAP for decades to come. He had great success in 1915 with songs from the revue Stop! Look! Listen!, including "I Love a Piano" and "The Girl on the Magazine Cover."

Berlin joined the Army in 1917 as the U.S. entered World War I. Stationed at Camp Upton on Long Island, he maintained his ties to Tin Pan Alley and Broadway but devoted most of his time to writing an army show, Yip! Yip! Yaphank. He appeared in the show, singing "Oh, How I Hate to Get Up in the Morning," which was second only to George M. Cohan's "Over There" as the most memorable song of World War I. The show's other major hit was "Mandy," though it did not take off until after it was included in Berlin's score for the Ziegfeld Follies of 1919, subsequently selling a million copies of sheet music. "God Bless America," written for the show, mysteriously was dropped by Berlin; it was put "in the trunk" for later use.

Ben Selvin's recording of "Mandy" began with an excerpt from the major song Berlin wrote for the 1919 Follies, "A Pretty Girl Is Like a Melody," which became a best-selling record on its own and the theme song for all future *Follies.* "You'd Be Surprised," a comic song added after the show's opening and also interpolated into other shows, was a third hit from the 1919 *Follies*, a sheet-music million-seller and a popular record for Eddie Cantor, who sang it in the show. The success of Berlin's songs in the 1919 Follies led Ziegfeld to commision him to again write the bulk of the score for the next year's edition, whose best-remembered hit is "The Girl of My Dreams."

The year 1921 brought "All by Myself," one of Berlin's all-time biggest hits, which enjoyed enough record covers to sell a million records as well as a million copies of sheet music. But Berlin was spending most of his time preparing for the opening of the Music Box Theatre, which he and producer Sam H. Harris had built in N.Y. The first edition of the *Music Box Revue* ran 440 performances and generated three hits, most notably "Say It with Music." Three more *Revue*s would run through 1925, but none was as successful as the first one. During this period, Berlin had hits with "What'll I Do?," a wistful ballad interpolated into the third *Revue* that sold over a million copies on disc and in sheet music, and "All Alone," the biggest record hit of 1925. Meanwhile, Berlin's score for the musical comedy *The Cocoanuts* was overshadowed by the antics of the Marx Brothers, who helped carry the show to a run of 377 performances.

It has been suggested that the romantic mood of songs like "All by Myself," "What'll I Do?," "All Alone," and "Remember" were influenced by the ups and downs of Berlin's romance with Ellin Mackay, the daughter of millionaire Clarence Mackay, who opposed the match. For months their courtship and marriage were fodder for the tabloids, who milked the Jewish immigrant-weds-millionaire-heiress angle. There can be no doubt that "Always," his next ballad hit, was written for her: he assigned rights for the song to her as a wedding present. They were married Jan. 4, 1926, and had three daughters as well as a son who died in infancy. "Always" went some way toward recompensing Mrs. Berlin for the loss of her inheritance. (She and Berlin were later reconciled with Mackay, who was ruined in the 1929 stock market crash.) Its theme of romantic contentment was continued in Berlin's other hits of 1926, notably the standard "Blue Skies," written for Belle Baker to sing in the musical *Betsy* (N.Y., Dec. 28, 1926) and subsequently a best-selling record for many artists.

In 1927, Berlin became the first songwriter to compose all the songs in an edition of the *Follies*. The revue, which ran a disappointing 167 performances, brought two record hits to its star, Ruth Etting, particularly "Shaking the Blues Away," also an instrumental hit for Paul Whiteman. Jolson sang "Blue Skies" in October in *The Jazz Singer*, the first motion picture with synchronized sound, which opened the door to film music for many songwriters. Berlin was quick to jump on the movie bandwagon, abandoning Broadway for more than four years. However, Berlin eventually was frustrated by his treatment in Hollywood, where songs were used rather indiscriminately in films good, bad, and indifferent, and many songs written were dropped from the finished product. In the face of such cavalier treatment, Berlin left Hollywood in 1931, not writing for another movie for four years.

Berlin returned to Broadway in 1931 with *Face the Music*, a modestly successful musical satire that ran for 165 performances. He had greater success with 1933's *As Thousands Cheer*, a revue mounted at the Music Box, which, at 400 performances, was Berlin's longest-running show yet. Its hits were "Easter Parade" (which reused the music of "Smile and Show Your Dimple"), recorded by Clifton Webb, from the show, on vocals, and "Heat Wave," recorded by Ethel Waters, also featured in the show, among others.

Berlin returned to Hollywood in 1935 for the Astaire–Ginger Rogers film musical *Top Hat*. All five of the songs he wrote for the film became record hits for Astaire. "Cheek to Cheek" topped the hit parade for weeks and was also recorded by Phil Ohman and His Orch., Duchin, Lombardo, and the Boswell Sisters, on its way to becoming one of the biggest hits of the year. It was Berlin's first song to be nominated for an Academy Award. He wrote seven more songs the next year for the Astaire-Rogers film *Follow the Fleet*, and Astaire had five more hits, including the film's most popular song, "I'm Putting All My Eggs in One Basket."

Like other Broadway songwriters, Berlin had expressed reservations about the Swing-band arrangements employed on some of the covers of his songs. The most radical of these had to be Tommy Dorsey and His Orch.'s uptempo revival of "Marie" in March 1937, complete with slang interjections shouted by the band. But the record became a massive hit, selling a million copies. Many more Berlin songs entered the jazz repertoire, either as instrumental or vocal hits.

Berlin wrote the original story on which the 1938 film *Alexander's Ragtime Band* was based, earning himself an Oscar nomination in the process. He was also nominated again in the best song category for "Now It Can Be Told," but most of the songs used were vintage Berlin compositions like the title song, which became a best-seller all over again in a recording by Crosby and Connee Boswell.

Carefree reunited Berlin with Astaire and Rogers with the usual felicitous results: Four of the five songs Berlin wrote became hits (even though only three of them were actually sung in the film). Astaire topped the hit parade with "Change Partners," even though a version by Jimmy Dorsey and His Orch. with Bob Eberly on vocals was equally popular.

In November 1938, Berlin responded to a request to write a patriotic song for the 20th anniversary observance of Armistice Day by giving "God Bless America," a song written for but not used in *Yip! Yip! Yaphank*, to Kate Smith to sing on her radio show. Smith's recording of the song became a hit in April 1939 and enjoyed revivals in 1940 and 1942, but it was less important as a record hit than as an acknowledged national treasure. Berlin assigned his publishing royalties to the Boy Scouts, the Girl Scouts, and the Campfire Girls. He was awarded a medal of honor by Congress for writing the song.

Berlin returned to Broadway for the first time in six-and-a-half years with *Louisiana Purchase*, a politically tinged satirical musical that ran 444 performances (the longest run of the 1939–40 season). Berlin's activities slowed in the war years; he had a new film and a new show to work on in 1941, though neither were ready until mid-1942. In the meantime, "Easter Parade" enjoyed another revival and earned a gold record in an instrumental performance by Harry James and His Orch. at Eastertime in 1942.

The 1942 service show *This Is the Army*, which again featured Berlin singing "Oh, How I Hate to Get Up in the Morning," ran for 113 performances on Broadway before taking off for a tour of the war zones over the next few years. The month after *This Is the Army* opened on Broadway, *Holiday Inn* opened in movie theaters. Given the summer season, the first hit from the film was not "White Christmas" but "Be Careful, It's My Heart," recorded both by Crosby, who starred in the picture, and by Tommy Dorsey, with vocals by his departing boy singer, Frank Sinatra. But at the start of the fall, Crosby's recording of "White Christmas" began to assert its seasonal dominance for the first time, becoming a chart-topping gold record and the biggest hit of 1942. That, of course, was only the beginning. Sinatra had a gold-selling chart record with it in 1944, and Jo Stafford's 1946 cover reached the Top Ten. But it was the Crosby recording, reissued year after year, that was the most successful, topping the charts again in 1945 and 1946 (with a new version cut in 1947), earning another gold record during the 1955 Christmas season and continuing to chart nearly every year for more than 40 years.

On his fifth try, Berlin won the Academy Award for Best Song of 1942 for "White Christmas." In 1974, Crosby's recording was among the first entered in the NARAS Hall of Fame. The release of the film *Christmas Holiday* in December 1944 revived interest in "Always," which was featured in the film, leading to four hit recordings.

The death of Jerome Kern, who had been scheduled to write the songs for a musical based on the life of Wild West sharpshooter Annie Oakley, left the assignment to Berlin. *Annie Get Your Gun* ran for 1,147 performances on Broadway, making it the biggest hit of the 1945–46 season and the biggest show hit of Berlin's career. It generated five chart hits; the show's cast album, prominently featuring Ethel Merman, also charted. Oddly, "There's No Business Like Show Business" did not become a record hit but has become one of Berlin's best-known compositions. The film version of *Annie Get Your Gun* was one of the biggest box office hits of 1950, and its soundtrack album also became a chart hit, as did the soundtrack of a 1957 TV version starring Mary Martin. The show became a long-running success on tour, returning to Broadway for revivals in February 1952 and May 1966, the latter again starring Merman.

Like *Alexander's Ragtime Band*, *Blue Skies* (1946), starring Crosby and Astaire, and *Easter Parade* (1947), starring Astaire and Judy Garland, contained a combination of Berlin evergreens and a handful of newly written songs. Berlin's catalog continued to bring cur-

rent success, as indicated by the surprising revival of "I've Got My Love to Keep Me Warm" in the winter of 1948–49. Les Brown recorded an instrumental version in 1946, and when it was reissued in late 1948 it topped the charts, attracting successful cover records by the Mills Brothers among others.

At 308 performances, the 1949 Broadway show *Miss Liberty* was a relative disappointment for Berlin, although the musical spawned three moderate hits and the original cast album sold well. Berlin returned to Broadway a year later with unusual speed, reteaming with Merman for another political satire, *Call Me Madam*, which ran a more satisfying 644 performances and launched the hit "You're Just in Love."

Berlin was less active in the 1950s, but he had two films in release in the last quarter of 1954, both combining new songs with past favorites. Paramount's *White Christmas* became the highest-grossing motion picture of the year and brought a Top Ten hit to Eddie Fisher and a seventh Best Song Oscar nomination to Berlin for "Count Your Blessings (Instead of Sheep)." 20th Century-Fox's *There's No Business Like Show Business* produced a Top Ten soundtrack album. From this point on, Berlin was more or less in retirement.

In 1962, at age 74, Berlin returned to work for a final Broadway show, *Mr. President*, considered a disappointment, though it ran for 265 performances and had a cast album that stayed in the charts nearly six months. Berlin spent the remainder of his life in growing seclusion. Unable to adapt to popular trends, he guarded his own works carefully. Although a 100th birthday gala was held for him in N.Y., he declined to attend. He died of natural causes at the age of 101.

WORKS: MUSICALS (dates refer to N.Y. openings): *Watch Your Step* (Dec. 8, 1914); *Stop! Look! Listen!* (Dec. 25, 1915). Victor Herbert: *The Century Girl* (Nov. 6, 1916). George M. Cohan: *The Cohan Revue of 1918* (Dec. 31, 1917); *Yip! Yip! Yaphank* (Aug. 19, 1918); *Ziegfeld Follies of 1919* (June 23, 1919); *Ziegfeld Follies of 1920* (June 22, 1920); *Music Box Revue* (first edition) (Sept. 22, 1921); *Music Box Revue* (second edition) (Oct. 23, 1922); *Music Box Revue* (third edition) (Sept. 22, 1923); *Music Box Revue* (fourth edition) (Dec. 1, 1924); *The Cocoanuts* (Dec. 8, 1925); *Ziegfeld Follies of 1927* (Aug. 16, 1927); *Face the Music* (Feb. 17, 1932); *As Thousands Cheer* (Sept. 30, 1933); *Louisiana Purchase* (May 28, 1940); *This Is the Army* (July 4, 1942); *Annie Get Your Gun* (May 16, 1946); *Miss Liberty* (July 15, 1949); *Call Me Madam* (Oct. 12, 1950); *Mr. President* (Oct. 20, 1962). **FILMS:** *The Cocoanuts* (1929); *Hallelujah!* (1929); *Puttin' on the Ritz* (1930); *Mammy* (1930); *Reaching for the Moon* (1930); *Top Hat* (1935); *Follow the Fleet* (1936); *On the Avenue* (1937); *Alexander's Ragtime Band* (1938); *Carefree* (1938); *Second Fiddle* (1939); *Louisiana Purchase* (1941); *Holiday Inn* (1942); *This Is the Army* (1943); *Blue Skies* (1946); *Easter Parade* (1948); *Annie Get Your Gun* (1950); *Call Me Madam* (1953); *White Christmas* (1954); *There's No Business Like Show Business* (1954). **NOTABLE SONGS:** "Marie from Sunny Italy" (1907); "Dorando" (1908); "Oh, How That German Could Love" (1909); "My Wife's Gone to the Country, Hurrah! Hurrah!" (1909); "Sadie Salome, Go Home" (1909); "That Mesmerizing Mendelssohn Tune" (1910); "The Grizzly Bear" (1910); "Call Me Up Some Rainy Afternoon" (1910); "Alexander's Ragtime Band" (1911); "The Ragtime Mocking Bird" (1912); "That Mysterious Rag" (1912); "Everybody's Doin' It Now" (1912); "The Ragtime Violin" (1912); "I'm Afraid, Pretty

Maid, I'm Afraid" (1912); "The Ragtime Jockey Man" (1912); "Ragtime Soldier Man" (1912); "When the Midnight Choo Choo Leaves for Alabam'" (1913); "When I Lost You" (1913); "At the Devil's Ball" (1913); "Snookey Ookums" (1913); "The Pullman Porters on Parade" (1913); "That International Rag" (1913); "The Syncopated Walk" (1914); "Play a Simple Melody" (1914); "The Minstrel Parade" (1914); "When I Leave the World Behind" (1915); "When I Get Back to the U.S.A." (1915); "I Love a Piano" (1915); "The Girl on the Magazine Cover" (1915); "Let's All Be Americans Now" (1917); "Smile and Show Your Dimple" (1918); "I'm Gonna Pin a Medal on the Girl I Left Behind" (1918); "They Were All Out of Step but Jim" (1918); "Oh, How I Hate to Get Up in the Morning" (1918); "Mandy" (1918); "A Pretty Girl Is Like a Melody" (1919); "You'd Be Surprised" (1919); "I'll See You in C-U-B-A" (1919); "I've Got My Captain Working for Me Now" (1920); "Nobody Knows (And Nobody Seems to Care)" (1920); "Tell Me, Little Gypsy" (1920); "The Girl of My Dreams" (1920); "After You Get What You Want, You Don't Want It" (1920); "Home Again Blues" (1921); "Say It with Music" (1920); "Everybody Step" (1920); "They Call It Dancing" (1920); "All by Myself" (1921); "Say It with Music" (1921); "Everybody Step" (1921); "They Call It Dancing" (1921); "Some Sunny Day" (1922); "School House Blues" (1922); "Pack Up Your Sins (And Go to the Devil)" (1922); "Crinoline Days" (1922); "Lady of the Evening" (1922); "Porcelain Maid" (1922); "An Orange Grove in California" (1923); "Learn to Do the Strut" (1923); "What'll I Do?" (1923); "Lazy" (1923); "All Alone" (1925); "Remember" (1925); "Always" (1926); "At Peace with the World" (1926); "How Many Times (Have I Said I Love You)?" (1926); "Blue Skies" (1926); "Because I Love You" (1927); "Russian Lullaby" (1927); "Shaking the Blues Away" (1927); "It All Belongs to Me" (1927); "The Song Is Ended (But the Melody Lingers On)" (1928); "Marie" (1928); "How About Me?" (1929); "Where Is the Song of Songs for Me?" (1929); "When My Dreams Come True" (1929); "Puttin' on the Ritz" (1930); "With You" (1930); "Let Me Sing and I'm Happy" (1930); "When the Folks High Up Do the Mean Low Down" (1930); "Reaching for the Moon" (1931); "Let's Have Another Cup o' Coffee" (1932); "Soft Lights and Sweet Music" (1932); "Say It Isn't So" (1932); "How Deep Is the Ocean? (How High Is the Sky?)" (1932); "Maybe It's Because I Love You Too Much" (1933); "Easter Parade" (1933); "Heat Wave" (1933); "I Never Had a Chance" (1934); "No Strings" (1934); "The Piccolino" (1935); "Top Hat, White Tie and Tails" (1935); "Cheek to Cheek" (1935); "Isn't This a Lovely Day to Be Caught in the Rain?" (1935); "I'm Putting All My Eggs in One Basket" (1935); "This Year's Kisses" (1936); "You're Laughing at Me" (1937); "I've Got My Love to Keep Me Warm" (1937); "Slummin' on Park Avenue" (1937); "Now It Can Be Told" (1938); "My Walking Stick" (1938); "The Yam" (1938); "I Used to Be Color-Blind" (1938); "Change Partners" (1938); "The Night Is Filled with Music" (1938); "Back to Back" (1939); "I'm Sorry for Myself" (1939); "Winter Comes" (1939); "I Poured My Heart into a Song" (1940); "You're Lonely and I'm Lonely" (1940); "I Left My Heart at the Stage Door Canteen" (1942); "Be Careful, It's My Heart" (1942); "White Christmas" (1942); "Abraham" (1942); "They Say It's Wonderful" (1945); "The Girl That I Marry" (1945); "Doin' What Comes Natur'lly" (1945); "I Got the Sun in the Morning" (1945); "Who Do You Love, I Hope" (1945); "There's No Business Like Show Business" (1945); "You Keep Coming Back Like a Song" (1946); "Let's Take an Old-Fashioned Walk" (1949); "Homework" (1949); "Just One Way to Say I Love You" (1949); "You're Just in Love" (1950); "Count Your Blessings (Instead of Sheep)" (1954).

BIBL.: A. Woollcott, *The Story of I. B.* (N.Y., 1925); D. Jay, *The I. B. Sonography* (New Rochelle, N.Y., 1969); M. Freedland, *I. B.* (N.Y., 1974); I. Whitcomb, *I. B. & Ragtime America* (London, 1987); V. Motto, *The I. B. Catalogue* (Quicksburg, Va., 1988); L. Bergreen, *As Thousands Cheer: The Life of I. B.* (N.Y., 1990); M. Barrett (his daughter), *I. B.: A Daughter's Memoir* (N.Y., 1994); C. Hamm, *I. B.: Songs from the Melting Pot: The Formative Years, 1907–1914* (N.Y., 1997); P. Furia, *I. B.: A Life in Song* (N.Y., 1998). —WR

Berlin, Johan Daniel, German-born Norwegian organist and composer; b. Memel, May 12, 1714; d. Trondheim, Nov. 4, 1787. He studied organ with his father. In 1730 he proceeded to Copenhagen, where he continued his studies with Andreas Berg. In 1737 he became a city musician in Trondheim, a position he held until 1767; he was also organist at the city Cathedral from 1740 until his death. In addition to his various musical duties for the city, he collected musical instruments and wrote several treatises on music. He was a founding member of the Royal Norwegian Scientific Assoc. (1760). He composed some organ music, but few of his works are extant.

BIBL.: K. Michelesen, *J.D. B.* (diss., Univ. of Trondheim, 1971).—NS/LK/DM

Berlinski, Herman, German-born American organist and composer; b. Leipzig, Aug. 18, 1910. He studied piano, theory, and conducting at the Leipzig Cons. (1927–32) and composition with Boulanger and piano with Cortot at the Paris École Normale de Musique (1934–38). In 1941 he settled in the U.S., and in 1947 became a naturalized American citizen. He pursued training in organ with Joseph Yasser at the Jewish Theological Seminary of America in N.Y. (Doctor of Sacred Music degree, 1960). From 1954 to 1960 he was asst. organist, and from 1960 to 1963 organist at N.Y.'s Temple Emanu-El; subsequently served as minister of music of the Washington, D.C., Hebrew Congregation (1963–77). On Nov. 14, 1981, he appeared in his native city of Leipzig for the first time in 48 years as a recitalist at the new Gewandhaus. His extensive output reflects dedication to liturgical musical expression.

WORKS: ORCH.: *Symphonic Visions* (1949); *Concerto da camera* (1952); Organ Concerto (1965); *Prayers for the Night* (1968). **CHAMBER:** *Chazoth*, suite for String Quartet and Ondes Martenot (1938); Flute Sonata (1941; rev. 1984); *Hassidic Suite* for Cello and Piano (1948); *Quadrille*, woodwind quartet (1952); String Quartet (1953); *Le Violon de Chagall*, violin sonata (1985); many organ pieces, including *The Burning Bush* (1956) and 11 sinfonias (1956–78). **VOCAL: Oratorios:** *Kiddush Ha-Shem* (1954–60); *Job* (1968–72; rev. 1984); *The Trumpets of Freedom* (Washington, D.C., Dec. 5, 1988). **Cantatas:** *The Earth Is the Lord's* (1966); *Sing to the Lord a New Song* (1978); *The Beadle of Prague* (1983); *The Days of Awe* (1965–85; Washington, D.C., Sept. 22, 1985). **Other Vocal:** Songs. —NS/LK/DM

Berlioz, (Louis-) Hector, great French composer who exercised profound influence on the course of modern music in the direction of sonorous grandiosity, and propagated the Romantic ideal of program music, unifying it with literature; b. La Côte-Saint-André, Isère, Dec. 11, 1803; d.Paris, March 8, 1869. His father was a medical doctor who possessed musical inclinations. Under his guidance, Berlioz learned to play the flute, and later took up the guitar; however, he never became an experienced performer on any instrument. Following his father's desire that he study medicine, he went to Paris, where he entered the École de Médecine; at the same time, he began taking private lessons in composition from Jean François Le Sueur. In 1824 he abandoned his medical studies to dedicate himself entirely to composition; his first important work was a *Messe solennelle*, which was performed at a Paris church on July 10, 1825; he then wrote an instrumental work entitled *La Révolution grecque*, inspired by the revolutionary uprising in Greece against the Ottoman domination. He was 22 years old when he entered the Paris Cons. as a pupil of his first music teacher, Le Sueur, in composition, and of Anton Reicha in counterpoint and fugue. In 1826 Berlioz wrote an opera, *Les Francs- juges*, which never came to a complete performance. In 1827 he submitted his cantata *La Mort d'Orphée* for the Prix de Rome, but it was rejected. On May 26, 1828, he presented a concert of his works at the Paris Cons., including the *Resurrexit* from the *Messe solennelle*, *La Révolution grecque*, and the overtures *Les Francs-juges* and *Waverley*. Also in 1828 he won the second prize of the Prix de Rome with his cantata *Herminie*. In 1828–29 he wrote *Huit scenes de Faust*, after Goethe; this was the score that was eventually revised and produced as *La Damnation de Faust*. In 1829 he applied for the Prix de Rome once more with the score of *La Mort de Cléopâtre*, but no awards were given that year. He finally succeeded in winning the 1st Prix de Rome with *La Mort de Sardanapale*; it was performed in Paris on Oct. 30, 1830. In the meantime, Berlioz allowed himself to be passionately infatuated with the Irish actress Harriet Smithson after he attended her performance as Ophelia in Shakespeare's *Hamlet*, given by a British drama troupe in Paris on Sept. 11, 1827. He knew no English and Miss Smithson spoke no French; he made no effort to engage her attention personally; conveniently, he found a surrogate for his passion in the person of Camille Moke, a young pianist. Romantically absorbed in the ideal of love through music, Berlioz began to write his most ambitious and, as time and history proved, his most enduring work, which he titled *Symphonie fantastique*; it was to be an offering of adoration and devotion to Miss Smithson. Rather than follow the formal subdivisions of a sym., Berlioz decided to integrate the music through a recurring unifying theme, which he called an *idée fixe*, appearing in various guises through the movements of the *Symphonie fantastique*. To point out the personal nature of the work he subtitled it "Épisode de la vie d'un artiste." The artist of the title was Berlioz himself, so that in a way the sym. became a musical autobiography. The 5 divisions of the score are: I. *Reveries, Passions*; II. *A Ball*; III. *Scene in the Fields*; IV. *March to the Scaffold*; V. *Dream of a Witches' Sabbath*. Berlioz supplied a literary program to the music: a "young musician of morbid sensibilities" takes opium to find surcease from amorous madness. Berlioz himself, be it noted, never smoked opium, but this hallucinogenic substance was in vogue at the time, and was the subject of several mystic novels and pseudo-scientific essays. In the *Symphonie fantastique* the object of the hero's passion haunts him through the device of the *idée fixe*; she appears first as an entrancing, but unattainable, vision; as an enticing dancer at a ball; then as a deceptive pastoral image. He penetrates her disguise and kills her, a crime for which he is led to the gallows. At the end she reveals herself as a wicked witch at a Sabbath orgy. The fantastic program design does not interfere, however, with an orderly organization of the score, and the wild fervor of the music is astutely subordinated to the symphonic form. The *idée fixe* itself serves merely as a recurring motif, not unlike similar musical reminiscences in Classical syms. Interestingly enough, in the *March to the Scaffold* Berlioz makes use of a section from his earlier score *Les Francs-juges*, and merely inserts into it a few bars of the *idée fixe* to justify the incorporation of unrelated musical material. No matter; *Symphonie fantastique* with or without Miss Smithson, with or without the idee fixe, emerges as a magnificent tapestry of sound; its unflagging popularity for a century and a half since its composition testifies to its evocative power. The work was first performed at the Paris Cons. on Dec. 5, 1830, with considerable success, although the Cons.'s director, the strict perfectionist Cherubini, who failed to attend the performance, spoke disdainfully of it from a cursory examination of the score. Nor did Miss Smithson herself grace the occasion by her physical presence. Incongruously, the publ. score of the *Symphonie fantastique* is dedicated to the stern Russian czar Nicholas I. That this apotheosis of passionate love should have been inscribed to one of Russia's most unpleasant czars is explained by the fact that Berlioz had been well received in Russia in 1847. Berlioz followed the *Symphonie fantastique* with a sequel entitled *Lélio, ou Le Retour à la vie*, purported to signalize the hero's renunciation of his morbid obsessions. Both works were performed at a single concert in Paris on Dec. 9, 1832, and this time La Smithson made her appearance. A most remarkable encounter followed between them; as if to prove the romantic notion of the potency of music as an aid to courtship, Berlioz and Smithson soon became emotionally involved, and they were married on Oct. 3, 1833. Alas, their marriage proved less enduring than the music that fostered their romance. Smithson broke a leg (on March 16, 1833) even before the marriage ceremony; and throughout their life together she was beset by debilitating illnesses. They had a son, who died young. Berlioz found for himself a more convenient woman companion, one Maria Recio, whom he married shortly after Smithson's death in 1854. Berlioz survived his second wife, too; she died in 1862.

Whatever the peripeteias of his personal life, Berlioz never lost the lust for music. During his stay in Italy, following his reception of the Prix de Rome, he produced the overtures *Le Roi Lear* (1831) and *Rob Roy* (1831). His next important work was *Harold en Italie*, for the very unusual setting of a solo viola with orch.; it was commissioned by Paganini (although never performed by him), and was inspired by Lord Byron's poem *Childe Harold*. It was first performed in Paris on Nov. 23, 1834. Berlioz followed it with an opera, *Benvenuto Cellini*

(1834–37), which had its first performance at the Paris Opéra on Sept. 10, 1838. It was not successful, and Berlioz revised the score; the new version had its first performance in Weimar in 1852, conducted by Liszt. About the same time, Berlioz became engaged in writing musical essays; from 1833 to 1863 he served as music critic for the *Journal des Débats*; in 1834 he began to write for the *Gazette Musicale*. In 1835 he entered a career as conductor. In 1837 he received a government commission to compose the *Grande messe des morts (Requiem)*, for which he demanded a huge chorus. The work was first performed at a dress rehearsal in Paris on Dec. 4, 1837, with the public performance following the next day. On Dec. 16, 1838, Berlioz conducted a successful concert of his works in Paris; the legend has it that Paganini came forth after the concert and knelt in homage to Berlioz; if sources (including Berlioz himself) are to be trusted, Paganini subsequently gave Berlioz the sum of 20,000 francs. In 1839 Berlioz was named asst. librarian of the Paris Cons. and was awarded the Order of the Légion d'Honneur. On Nov. 24, 1839, Berlioz conducted, in Paris, the first performance of his dramatic sym. *Roméo et Juliette*, after Shakespeare; the work is regarded as one of the most moving lyrical invocations of Shakespeare's tragedy, rich in melodic invention and instrumental interplay. In 1840 Berlioz received another government commission to write a *Grande symphonie funèbre et triomphale*. This work gave Berlioz a clear imperative to build a sonorous edifice of what he imagined to be an architecture of sounds. The work was to commemorate the soldiers fallen in the fight for Algeria, and if contemporary reports can be taken literally, he conducted it with a drawn sword through the streets of Paris, accompanying the ashes of the military heroes to their interment in the Bastille column. The spirit of grandiosity took possession of Berlioz. At a concert after the Exhibition of Industrial Products in 1844 in Paris he conducted Beethoven's Fifth Sym. with 36 double basses, Weber's *Freischütz Overture* with 24 French horns, and the *Prayer of Moses* from Rossini's opera with 25 harps. He boasted that his 1,022 performers achieved an ensemble worthy of the finest string quartet. For his grandiose *L'Impériale*, written to celebrate the distribution of prizes by Napoleon III at the Paris Exhibition of Industrial Products in 1855, Berlioz had 1,200 performers, augmented by huge choruses and a military band. As if anticipating the modus operandi of a century thence, Berlioz installed 5 subconductors and, to keep them in line, activated an "electric metronome" with his left hand while holding the conducting baton in his right. And it was probably at Berlioz's suggestion that Vuillaume constructed a monstrous Octo-bass, a double bass 10 feet high, for use in a huge orch.; it was, however, never actually employed. Such indulgences generated a chorus of derision on the part of classical musicians and skeptical music critics; caricatures represented Berlioz as a madman commanding a heterogeneous mass of instrumentalists and singers driven to distraction by the music. Berlioz deeply resented these attacks and bitterly complained to friends about the lack of a congenial artistic environment in Paris.

But whatever obloquy he suffered, he also found satisfaction in the pervading influence he had on his contemporaries, among them Wagner, Liszt, and the Russian school of composers. Indeed, his grandiosity had gradually attained true grandeur; he no longer needed huge ensembles to exercise the magic of his music. In 1844 he wrote the overture *Le Carnaval romain*, partially based on music from his unsuccessful opera *Benvenuto Cellini*. There followed the overture *La Tour de Nice* (later rev. under the title *Le Corsaire*). In 1845 he undertook the revision of his early score after Goethe, which now assumed the form of a dramatic legend entitled *La Damnation de Faust*. The score included the *Marche hongroise*, in which Berlioz took the liberty of conveying Goethe's Faust to Hungary. The march became extremely popular as a separate concert number. In 1847 Berlioz undertook a highly successful tour to Russia, and in the following year he traveled to England. In 1849 he composed his grand *Te Deum*; he conducted its first performance in Paris on April 28, 1855, at a dress rehearsal; it was given a public performance two days later, with excellent success. In 1852 he traveled to Weimar at the invitation of Liszt, who organized a festival of Berlioz's music. Between 1850 and 1854 he wrote the oratorio *L'Enfance du Christ*; he conducted it in Paris on Dec. 10, 1854. Although Berlioz was never able to achieve popular success with his operatic productions, he turned to composing stage music once more between 1856 and 1860. For the subject he selected the great epic of Virgil relating to the Trojan War; the title was to be *Les Troyens*. He encountered difficulties in producing this opera in its entirety, and in 1863 divided the score into two sections: *La Prise de Troie* and *Les Troyens à Carthage*. Only the second part was produced in his lifetime; it received its premiere at the Théâtre-Lyrique in Paris on Nov. 4, 1863; the opera had 22 performances, and the financial returns made it possible for Berlioz to abandon his occupation as a newspaper music critic. His next operatic project was *Béatrice et Bénédict*, after Shakespeare's play *Much Ado about Nothing*. He conducted its first performance in Baden-Baden on Aug. 9, 1862. Despite frail health and a state of depression generated by his imaginary failure as composer and conductor in France, he achieved a series of successes abroad. He conducted *La Damnation de Faust* in Vienna in 1866, and he went to Russia during the 1867–68 season. There he had a most enthusiastic reception among Russian musicians, who welcomed him as a true prophet of the new era in music.

Posthumous recognition came slowly to Berlioz; long after his death some conservative critics still referred to his music as bizarre and willfully dissonant. No cult comparable to the ones around the names of Wagner and Liszt was formed to glorify Berlioz's legacy. Of his works only the overtures and the *Symphonie fantastique* are accorded frequent hearings. His *Requiem* stands as one of the greatest scores of its kind, but its demands on performers renders it a work generally reserved for special occasions. Performances of his operas are infrequent.

WRITINGS: *Grand traité d'instrumentation et d'orchestration modernes* (Paris, 1843; numerous subsequent eds.; Eng. tr., 1948; eds. covering modern usages were publ. in German by F.

Weingartner, Leipzig, 1904, and R. Strauss, Leipzig, 1905); *Le Chef d'orchestre, Théorie de son art* (Paris, 1855; Eng. tr. as *The Orchestral Conductor, Theory of His Art*, N.Y., 1902); *Voyage musical en Allemagne et en Italie, Études sur Beethoven, Gluck, et Weber. Mélanges et nouvelles* (2 vols., Paris, 1844); *Les Soirées de l'orchestre* (Paris, 1852; Eng. tr. as *Evenings in the Orch.*, tr. by C. Roche, with introduction by Ernest Newman, N.Y., 1929; new Eng. tr. as *Evenings with the Orch.* by J. Barzun, N.Y., 1956; 2nd ed., 1973); *Les Grotesques de la musique* (Paris, 1859); *À travers chants:Études musicales, adorations, boutades, et critiques* (Paris, 1862); *Les Musiciens et la musique* (a series of articles collected from the *Journal des Débats*; with introduction by A. Hallays, Paris, 1903); *Mémoires de Hector Berlioz* (Paris, 1870; 2nd ed. in 2 vols., Paris, 1878; new annotated ed. by P. Citron, Paris, 1991; Eng. tr., London, 1884; new tr. by R. and E. Holmes, with annotation by Ernest Newman, N.Y., 1932; another Eng. tr. by D. Cairns, N.Y., 1969; corrected ed., 1975). An incomplete ed. of literary works of Berlioz was publ. in German by Breitkopf & Härtel: *Literarische Werke* (10 vols. in 5, Leipzig, 1903–04) and *Gesammelte Schriften* (4 vols., Leipzig, 1864). For his music criticism, see H. Cohen and Y. Gérard, eds., *H. B.: La critique musicale, 1823–1863* (Paris, 1996 et seq.).

WORKS: DRAMATIC: O p e r a : *Estelle et Némorin* (1823; not perf.; score destroyed); *Les Francs-juges* (1826; not perf.; rev. 1829 and 1833; overture and 5 movements extant); *Benvenuto Cellini* (1834–37; Opéra, Paris, Sept. 10, 1838; rev. 1852; Weimar, Nov. 17, 1852); *La Nonne sanglante* (1841–47; score unfinished); *Les Troyens* (1856–58; rev. 1859–60; divided into 2 parts, 1863: I, *La Prise de Troie* [first perf. in German, Karlsruhe, Dec. 6, 1890]; II, *Les Troyens à Carthage* [first perf., Théâtre-Lyrique, Paris, Nov. 4, 1863]; first perf. of both parts in French, with major cuts, Brussels, Dec. 26–27, 1906; first complete perf., sans cuts, alterations, etc., in Eng., Glasgow, May 3, 1969; in French, Royal Opera House, Covent Garden, London, Sept. 17, 1969); *Béatrice et Bénédict* (1860–62; Baden-Baden, Aug. 9, 1862). **ORCH.: S y m s . :** *Symphonie fantastique: Épisode de la vie d'un artiste*, op.14a (Paris, Dec. 5, 1830; rev. 1831); *Harold en Italie* for Solo Viola and Orch., op.16 (Paris, Nov. 23, 1834); *Roméo et Juliette* for Solo Voices, Chorus, and Orch., op.17 (Paris, Nov. 24, 1839); *Grande symphonie funèbre et triomphale*, op.15 (Paris, July 28, 1840). **OTHER:** *Waverley*, overture, op.1 (1827–28; Paris, May 26, 1828); *Rob Roy*, full title *Intrata di Rob Roy Macgregor*, overture (1831; Paris, April 14, 1833); *Le Roi Lear*, overture, op.4 (1831; Paris, Dec. 22, 1833); *Rêverie et caprice*, romance for Violin and Orch., op.8 (1841); *Le Carnaval romain*, overture, op.9 (Paris, Feb. 3, 1844); *La Tour de Nice*, overture (1844; Paris, Jan. 19, 1845; rev. 1851–52 as *Le Corsaire*, op.21; Braunschweig, April 8, 1854); *Marche troyenne* (arranged from Act I of *Les Troyens*; 1864). **VOCAL: M a j o r C h o r a l W o r k s :** *Mass* (1824; Saint-Roch, July 10, 1825); *La Révolution grecque*, scène héroïque (1825–26; Paris, May 26, 1828); *La Mort d'Orphée*, monologue et bacchanale (1827; Paris, Oct. 16, 1932); *Huit scènes de Faust* (1828–29; 1 movement only perf., Paris, Nov. 29, 1829); *La Mort de Sardanapale* (Paris, Oct. 30, 1830); *Fantaisie sur la Tempête de Shakespeare* (1830; perf. as *Ouverture pour la Tempête de Shakes-peare*, Paris, Nov. 7, 1830); *Le Retour à la vie*, op.14b, monodrame lyrique (1831–32; Paris, Dec. 9, 1832; rev. 1854 as *Lélio, ou Le Retour à la vie*); *Grande messe des morts (Requiem)*, op.5 (1837; Paris, Dec. 4 [dress rehearsal], Dec. 5 [public perf.], 1837; rev. 1852 and 1867); *La Damnation de Faust*, légende dramatique, op.24 (1845–46; Paris, Dec. 6, 1846); *Te Deum*, op.22 (1849; Paris, April 28 [dress rehearsal], April 30 [public perf.], 1855); *L'Enfance du Christ*, trilogie sacrée, op.25 (1850–54; Paris, Dec.

10, 1854). **SOLO VOICE AND ORCH.:** *Herminie*, scène lyrique (1828); *La Mort de Cléopâtre*, scène lyrique (1829). **S o n g s :** More than 40, including 9 songs after Thomas Moore (1829; 3 orchestrated); *La Captive*, op.12 (1832; orchestrated 1834 and 1848); *Les Nuits d'été*, 6 songs, op.7 (1840–41; orchestrated 1843–56); *La Mort d'Ophélie* (1842; orchestrated 1848; publ. as *Tristia*, no. 2, 1849).

BIBL.: COLLECTED EDITIONS, SOURCE MATE-RIAL: The first major ed. of Berlioz's works (*Benvenuto Cellini, Les Troyens*, and several other scores excepted) was edited by C. Malherbe and F. Weingartner (20 vols., Leipzig, 1900–07); see Supplement 5 in J. Barzun's *B. and the Romantic Century* (2 vols., Boston, 1950; 3rd ed., rev., 1969) for an extensive enumeration of its musical and other errors. A new critical ed. of all of the extant works, the *New B. Edition*, under the general editorship of H. Macdonald, began publication in Kassel in 1967. The definitive catalog is D. Holoman, *Catalogue of the Works of H. B.* (Kassel, 1987). The standard bibliography is C. Hopkinson, *A Bibliography of the Musical and Literary Works of H. B. 1803–1869...* (Edinburgh, 1951; 2nd ed. with additions and corrections by R. Macnutt, Tunbridge Wells, 1980). Another valuable source is M. Wright, *A Bibliography of Critical Writings on H. B.* (1967). **CORRESPONDENCE:** D. Bernard, ed., *Correspondance in-édite de B.* (Paris, 1879; Eng. tr. as *Life and Letters of B.*, I, 1882); *Lettres intimes* (Paris, 1882; Eng. tr. as *Life and Letters of B.*, II, 1882); La Mara, ed., *Briefe von H. B. an die Fürstin Carolyne Sayn-Wittgenstein* (Leipzig, 1903); J. Tiersot, ed., *H. B.: Les Années romantiques (1819–1842)* (Paris, 1904), *H. B.: Le Musicien Errant (1842–1852)* (Paris, 1919), and *H. B.: Au Milieu du Chemin (1852–1855)* (Paris, 1930); J. Barzun, ed. and tr., *Nouvelles lettres de B., 1830–1868; New Letters of B., 1830–1868* (N. Y., 1954); P.Citron, H. Macdonald et al., eds., *Correspondance générale de H. B.* (6 vols., Paris, 1972–95). **BIOGRAPHICAL:** W. Neumann, *B.: Eine Biographie* (Kassel, 1855); E. de Mirecourt, *B.* (Paris, 1856); A. Jullien, *H. B.: La Vie et le combat; Les OEuvres* (Paris, 1882); J. Bennett, *B.* (London, 1883); E. Hippeau, *B. intime, d'après des documents nouveaux* (Paris, 1883; 2nd ed., 1889); A. Jullien, *H. B.: Sa vie et ses oeuvres* (Paris, 1888); M. Brenet, *Deux pages de la vie de B.* (Paris, 1889); E. Hippeau, *B. et son temps* (Paris, 1890); L. Pohl, *H. B.: Leben und Werke* (Leipzig, 1900); A. Hahn et al., *H. B.: Sein Leben und seine Werke* (Leipzig, 1901); G. Allix, *Sur les éléments dont s'est formée la personnalité artistique de B.* (Grenoble, 1903); R. Louis, *H. B.* (Leipzig, 1904); J.-G. Prod'homme, *H. B. (1803–1869): Sa vie et ses oeuvres* (Paris, 1904; 3rd ed., 1927); A. Boschot, *La Jeunesse d'un romantique: H. B., 1803–31* (Paris, 1906; rev. ed., 1946), *Un Romantique sous Louis-Philippe: H. B., 1831–42* (Paris, 1908; rev. ed., 1948), and *Le Crépuscule d'un romantique: H. B., 1842–69* (Paris, 1913; rev. ed., 1950); B. Schrader, *B.* (Leipzig, 1907); A. Coquard, *B.* (Paris, n.d.); P.-L. Robert, *Étude sur H. B.* (Rouen, 1914); J. Kapp, *B.: Eine Biographie* (Berlin and Leipzig, 1917; 7th ed., 1922); A. Boschot, *Une Vie romantique: H. B.* (Paris, 1919); P.-M. Masson, *B.* (Paris, 1923); E. Rey, *La Vie amoureuse de B.* (Paris, 1929); L. Constantin, *B.* (Paris, 1934); W. Turner, *B.: The Man and His Work* (London, 1934); T. Wotton, *H. B.* (London, 1935); J. Elliot, *B.* (London, 1938; 4th ed., rev., 1967); E. Lockspeiser, *B.* (London, 1939); G. de Pourtalès, *B. et l'Europe romantique* (Paris, 1939; rev. ed., 1949); P. Mouthier, *H. B.* (Dilbeck, 1944); J. Daniskas, *H. B.* (Stockholm, 1947; Eng. tr., 1949); F. Knuttel, *H. B.* (The Hague, 1948); J. Barzun, *B. and the Romantic Century* (2 vols., Boston, 1950; 3rd ed., rev., 1969); A. Ganz, *B. in London* (London, 1950); T. Tienot, *H. B.: Esquisse biographique* (Paris, 1951); H. Kühner, *H. B.: Charakter und Schöpfertum* (Olten, 1952); H. Barraud, *H. B.* (Paris, 1955; 2nd ed., 1966); C. Ballif, *B.* (Paris, 1968); S. Demarquez, *H.*

B.: L'Homme et son oeuvre (Paris, 1969); J. Crabbe, H. B.: Rational Romantic (London, 1980); H. Macdonald, B. (London, 1982); R. Clarson-Leach, B.: His Life and Times (Tunbridge Wells, 1983); W. Dömling, H. B. und seine Zeit (Laaber, 1986); D. Cairns, B. (2 vols., London, 1989, 2000); D. Holoman, B. (Cambridge, Mass., 1989); J.-P. Maassakker, B. à Paris (Paris, 1993); A. Ramaut, H. B., compositeur romantique français (Arles, 1993); P. Bloom, The Life of B. (Cambridge, 1998). CRITICAL, ANALYTICAL: A. Ernst, L'OEuvre dramatique de H. B. (Paris, 1884); R. Pohl, H. B.: Studien und Erinnerungen (Leipzig, 1884); J.-G. Prod'homme, La Damnation de Faust (Paris, 1896); E. Destranges, Les Troyens de B.:Étude analytique (Paris, 1897); J.-G. Prod'homme, L'Enfance du Christ (Paris, 1898); J. Tiersot, B. et la société de son temps (Paris, 1904); P. Magnette, Les Grandes Étapes dans l'oeuvre de B., I: Symphonie fantastique (1829–32) (Liège, 1908); E. Bernoulli, H. B. als Ästhetiker der Klangfarben (Zürich, 1909); A. Boschot, Le Faust de B. (Paris, 1910; rev. ed., 1946); P.-L. Robert, H. B.: Les Troyens (Rouen, 1920); T. Mantovani, La dannazione di Faust di Ettore B. (Milan, 1923); J. Tiersot, La Damnation de Faust de B. (Paris, 1924); A. Boschot, H. B.: Critique musical (Brussels, 1938); H. Bartenstein, H. B.' Instrumentationskunst und ihre geschichtlichen Grundlagen (Leipzig, 1939; rev. ed., 1974); F. Schlitzer, Il Grande Requiem di Ettore B. (Naples, 1939); H. Macdonald, B. Orchestral Music (London, 1969); E. Cone, B.: Fantastic Symphony (N.Y., 1971); A. Dickinson, The Music of B. (London, 1972); B. Primmer, The B. Style (London, 1973); W. Dömling, H. B.: Die symphonisch-dramatischen Werke (Stuttgart, 1979); F. Piatier, Benvenuto Cellini de B. ou Le Mythe de l'artiste (Paris, 1979); M. Clavaud, H. B.: Visages d'un masque (Lyons, 1980); D. Holoman, The Creative Process in the Autograph Musical Documents of H. B., ca. 1818–1845 (Ann Arbor, 1980); C. Berger, Phantastik als Konstruktion: H. B.'s "Symphonie fantastique" (Kassel, 1983); J. Rushton, The Musical Language of B. (Cambridge, 1983); K. Murphy, H. B. and the Development of French Music Criticism (Ann Arbor, 1988); P. Bloom, ed., B. Studies (Cambridge, 1992); J. Rushton, B.: Roméo et Juliette (Cambridge, 1994).—NS/LK/DM

Berman, Lazar (Naumovich), brilliant Russian pianist; b. Leningrad, Feb. 26, 1930. He began music training in infancy with his mother, and at the age of 3 began piano lessons with Savshinsky. At age 7, he made his debut at the All-Union Festival for young performers in Moscow, where, at age 9, he became a pupil of Alexander Goldenweiser at the Central Music School, and later at the Cons. (graduated, 1953; master classes, 1953–57); he also studied at the Cons. with Theodore Gutmann. In 1951 he won the World Youth and Student Festival prize in East Berlin, and in 1956 took fifth prize at the Queen Elisabeth of Belgium competition in Brussels and third prize at the Liszt competition in Budapest. From 1957 he pursued his career in earnest. In 1958 he made his London debut, but it was not until a highly successful tour of Italy in 1970 that he made his mark in the West. In 1971 he made his U.S. debut as soloist with the N.J. Sym. Orch., and returned in 1976 to tour the U.S. to great critical acclaim. In subsequent years, he toured throughout the world. His titanic technique, astounding in bravura passages, does not preclude the beauty of his poetic evocation of lyric moods. His performances of Schumann, Liszt, Tchaikovsky, Scriabin, and Prokofiev are particularly compelling. —NS/LK/DM

Bermudo, Juan, Spanish music theorist; b. Ecija, Seville, c. 1510; d. Andalusia, after 1555. He first studied theology and devoted himself to preaching. He later turned to music and studied at the Univ. of Alcalá de Henares. He spent 15 years as a Franciscan monk in Andalusia. In 1550 he entered the service of the Archbishop of Andalusia, where Cristóbal de Morales was choir director. The writings of Bermudo constitute an important source of information on Spanish instrumental music of the 16th century. His most comprehensive work is the Declaración de instrumentos musicales (Osuna, 1549 and 1555). It deals with theory, in which his authorities were Gaffurius, Glareanus, and Ornithoparchus; instruments, including problems of tuning, technique of performance, and repertoire; and critical evaluation of contemporary composers, showing familiarity with the works of Josquin Des Prez, Willaert, and Gombert. Bermudo also wrote El Arte tripharia (Osuna, 1550). Thirteen organ pieces by him are included in F. Pedrell, Salterio Sacro-Hispano.

BIBL.: R. Stevenson, J. B. (The Hague, 1960).—NS/LK/DM

Bernabei, Ercole, Italian composer, father of **Giuseppe Antonio Bernabei;** b. Caprarola, Papal States, 1622; d. Munich (buried), Dec. 6, 1687. He was a pupil of Orazio Benevoli, whom he succeeded in 1672 as chapel master at the Vatican; in 1674 he became court conductor in Munich. He wrote 5 operas, which were produced in Munich, and publ. a book of madrigals, Concerto madrigalesco (1669). Other works include masses, offertories, Psalms, and other sacred music.

BIBL.: R. Casimiri, E. B., Maestro di cappella musicale lateranse (Rome, 1920); R. de Rensis, E. B. (Rome, 1920). —NS/LK/DM

Bernabei, Giuseppe Antonio, Italian composer, son of **Ercole Bernabei;** b. Rome, 1649; d. Munich, March 9, 1732. He studied with his father, and served with him as a vice-Kapellmeister in Munich beginning in 1677. After his father's death in 1687, he assumed his post as principal Kapellmeister. He wrote 15 operas and much sacred music.

BIBL.: K. Forster, G.A. B. als Kirchenkomponist (Munich, 1933).—NS/LK/DM

Bernac (real name, Bertin), Pierre, eminent French baritone and teacher; b. Paris, Jan. 12, 1899; d. Villeneuve-les-Avignon, Oct. 17, 1979. He received private voice lessons in Paris. He began his career as a singer rather late in life, being first engaged in finance as a member of his father's brokerage house in Paris. His musical tastes were decidedly in the domain of modern French songs; on May 2, 1926, he made his debut recital in Paris with a program of songs by Francis Poulenc and Georges Auric; at other concerts he sang works by Debussy, Ravel, Honegger, and Milhaud. Eager to learn the art of German lieder, he went to Salzburg to study with Reinhold von Warlich. Returning to Paris, he devoted himself to concerts and to teaching. He became a lifelong friend to Poulenc, who wrote many songs for him and acted as his piano accompanist in many tours through Europe and America. He also conducted master classes in the U.S. and was on the faculty of the American Cons. at Fontainebleau. He publ. a valuable manual, *The Interpretation of French Song* (N.Y., 1970; 2nd ed., 1976), and a monograph, *Francis Poulenc: The Man and His Songs* (N.Y., 1977).—NS/LK/DM

Bernacchi, Antonio Maria, celebrated Italian castrato alto; b. Bologna (baptized), June 23, 1685; d. there, March 13, 1756. He studied voice with Pistocchi and G.A. Ricieri. In 1700 he was sopranist at the church of S. Petronio in Bologna. He made his operatic debut in Genoa in 1703, and between 1709 and 1735 had a number of engagements in Venice. Between 1712 and 1731 he made several appearances in Bologna. He also sang in Munich (1720–27). In 1716–17 he sang in London, and in 1729 he was engaged by Handel as a substitute for Senesino for the London seasons of the Italian Opera; however, he failed to please British opera-goers and returned to his native town of Bologna, where he opened a singing school. In his singing he cultivated the style of vocal embellishments in the manner of the French roulades.—NS/LK/DM

Bernal Jiménez, Miguel, Mexican composer; b. Morelia, Michoacán, Feb. 16, 1910; d. León, Guanajuato, July 12, 1956. He received training in music in Morelia, and later studied composition, organ, and Gregorian chant at the Pontifical Inst. of the Sacred Heart in Rome (1928–33). After returning to Morelia, he became director of the Escuela Nacional in 1936 and of the Las Rosas Cons. in 1945. From 1952 until his death he was head of the music faculty of Loyola Univ. in New Orleans. His Organ Concertino is a nearly exclusive Mexican example of the genre.

WORKS: DRAMATIC: *Tata Vasco*, opera-symphonic drama (1940–41); *Tingambato*, ballet (1943); *El Chueco*, ballet (1950–51); *Los tres galanes de Juan*, ballet (1952). ORCH.: *Noche en Morelia*, symphonic poem (1941); *Michoacán*, suite (1942); *Tres cartas de México* (1944); *Sinfonía México*, symphonic poem (1946); Organ Concertino (1949); *Angelus* (1950); *Navidad en Pátzcuaro* (1953). CHAMBER: *Cuarteto virreinal* for String Quartet (1939). Organ: 2 sonatas (1942). VOCAL: *Sinfonía Hidalgo* for Chorus and Orch. (1953); *El himno de los bosques* for Narrator, Chorus, and Orch. (orchestrated by Manuel Enríquez, 1991). —LK/DM

Bernard der Deutsche, important German organist who was known as **Bernardo di Steffanino Murer**; b. place and date unknown; d. 1459. He served as an organist at San Marco. He was the reputed inventor of organ pedals.—NS/LK/DM

Bernardi, Bartolomeo, Italian violinist and composer; b. Bologna, c. 1660; d. Copenhagen, May 23, 1732. He received an invitation from the Danish Court to serve as a violinist and composer, and began his work there on Jan. 1, 1703; after an absence of several years (1705–10), he returned to Copenhagen and was appointed director of court music. In Copenhagen he produced 2 operas, *Il Gige fortunato* (Aug. 26, 1703) and *Diana e la Fortuna* (Oct. 10, 1703); he also wrote an opera, *La Libussa*, for a production in Prague in 1703; the music of these operas is lost. His trio sonatas were publ. in Bologna (1692, 1696).—NS/LK/DM

Bernardi, Francesco
See **Senesino**

Bernardi, Mario (Egidio), Canadian conductor of Italian descent; b. Kirkland Lake, Ontario, Aug. 20, 1930. He studied piano, organ, and composition with Bruno Pasut at the Manzato Cons. in Treviso (1938–45), and took his examination at the Venice Cons. (1945). He was a student of Lubka Kolessa (piano) and Ettore Mazzoleni (conducting) at the Royal Cons. of Music of Toronto (1948–51) before completing his conducting studies with Leinsdorf at the Salzburg Mozarteum (1959). He began his career as a church organist and concert pianist, and also was a coach and conductor with the Royal Cons. Opera School in Toronto (from 1953). In 1957 he made his debut as an opera conductor with *Hänsel und Gretel* with the Canadian Opera Co. in Toronto. In 1963 he made his first appearance at Sadler's Wells Opera in London, where he became its music director in 1966. In 1967 he made his U.S. debut conducting *La Bohème* at the San Francisco Opera. In 1969 he became the founding music director of the National Arts Centre Orch. in Ottawa, a position he held until 1982. He led it on various tours of Canada, the U.S., Mexico, and Europe. From 1971 to 1982 he also was artistic director of its notable successful opera festival. In 1983 he became principal conductor of the CBC Vancouver Orch. He also was music director of the Calgary Phil. from 1984 to 1993. On Jan. 19, 1984, he made his Metropolitan Opera debut in N.Y. conducting *Rinaldo*. He also appeared as a guest conductor of the Vancouver Opera, Calgary Opera, Montreal Opera, Houston Grand Opera, Lyric Opera of Chicago, St. Louis Opera, Santa Fe Opera, and at London's Covent Garden, as well as with various North American and European orchs. During the 1997–98 season, he conducted Canada's National Youth Orch. on a coast-to-coast tour. In 1972 he was made a Companion of the Order of Canada and in 1998 he received the Jean E. Chalmers National Music Award.—NS/LK/DM

Bernardi, Stefano, Italian composer and music theorist; b. Verona, c. 1585; d. probably in Salzburg, 1636. He sang at Verona Cathedral in his youth, and then served as chaplain there in 1603. In 1610 he was maestro di cappella at the church of the Madonna dei Monti in Rome, and then held that position at Verona Cathedral from 1611 to 1622. After serving the Archduke Carl Joseph, Bishop of Breslau and Bressanone (1622–24), he went to Salzburg. In 1627 he was awarded a Doctor of Law degree. His Te Deum for 12 Choirs was composed for the consecration of Salzburg Cathedral in 1628. He publ. the treatise *Porta musicale per la quale li principiante con facile brevita all'acquisto delle perfette regole del contrapunto vien inrodotto*, op.2 (Verona, 1615). His 3 vols. of madrigals for 5 Voices (Venice, 1611, 1616, 1619) demonstrate his transition from the prima to seconda prattica styles. In his *Salmi concertati* for 5 Voices and Basso Continue (Venice, 1627), he anticipated the solo concerto by utilizing a soprano voice opposite a four-part ripieno. Among his other works were masses, Psalms, and motets.

BIBL.: F. Posch, *S. B.s weltliche Vokal- und Instrumental-Werke* (Salzburg, 1935).—**NS/LK/DM**

Bernart de Ventadorn, troubadour poet and composer who flourished in the second half of the 12th century. His vita states that he was born in the castle of Ventadorn in the province of Limousin, and later was in the service of the Duchess of Normandy, Eleanor of Aquitaine, and of Raimon V, Count of Toulouse. He is believed to have entered a monastery in Dordogne, where he lived until his death. Some 45 poems are attributed to him, and 18 survive with complete melodies.

BIBL.: S. Nichols and J. Galm, eds., *The Songs of B. d.V.* (Chapel Hill, N.C., 1962); M. Lazar, *B. d.V.—Chansons d'amour* (Paris, 1966).—**NS/LK/DM**

Bernasconi, Andrea, Italian composer; b. probably in Marseilles, c. 1706; d. Munich, Jan. 27?, 1784. It is known that he was maestro di cappella at the Ospedale della Rieta in Venice during the season 1746–47. In 1753 he was in Munich, where he taught music to Princess Maria Anna Josepha (1754–55) and Princess Josepha Maria (1754–65); he also gave musical instruction to the Elector, Maximilian III Joseph. He was appointed Kapellmeister at the Munich court in 1755. He wrote a number of operas and pasticcios, some of which were produced in Munich. He also composed sacred music.

BIBL.: E.J. Weiss, *A. B. als Opernkomponist* (diss., Univ. of Munich, 1923).—**NS/LK/DM**

Bernasconi, Antonia, German soprano, stepdaughter of Andrea Bernasconi; b. Stuttgart, c. 1741; d. probably in Vienna, c. 1803. She was the daughter of a valet in the service of the Duke of Württemberg. After her father's death, her mother married Andrea Bernasconi. Antonia received her vocal training from him and made her debut as Aspasia in his *Temistocle* in Munich on Jan. 21, 1762. About 1765 she went to Vienna, where she won accolades at the first performance of Gluck's *Alcestis* (Dec. 16, 1767). Mozart wrote the role of Aspasia for her in his *Mitridate* (Dec. 1770). After appearances in Venice (1771–72), Naples (1772–73; 1774–75), and at the King's Theatre in London (1778–80), she returned to Vienna to sing in 1781. —**NS/LK/DM**

Berne, Tim, eclectic jazz alto saxophonist; b. Syracuse, N.Y., Jan. 16, 1954. He didn't begin playing alto until 19, when he was attending Lewis and Clark Coll. in Ore. He was deeply affected by Julius Hemphill's album *Dogon A.D.*, which established his direction. He moved to N.Y. (1974), sought Hemphill out, and entered into an apprenticeship with the elder musician. The "lessons" they had together lasted for hours and covered everything from composition to record promotion to recording to pasting up handbills to aspects of magic and spirituality and, sometimes, even playing the saxophone; Berne was also greatly helped by studies with Anthony Braxton. He established his own label and made his first two recordings on the West Coast before moving back to N.Y. He has worked with Vinny Golia, Alex Cline, Roberto Miranda, Olu Dara, Ed Schuller, John Zorn, Marilyn Crispell, and Paul Motian, among others; Berne also headed the group Miniature with Hank Roberts and Joey Baron. From 1994–7, his group Bloodcount performed over 250 concerts worldwide. Many of his recordings were released on his own labels, Empire and Screwgun. In 1996, his string quartet piece, "dry ink, silence," was premiered by the Kronos Quartet at the Brooklyn Academy of Music. This and the *Visible Man* (1992) were supported by Readers Digest/Meet the Composer grants; he has also received awards from the N.Y. State Council on the Arts, N.Y. State Foundation for the Arts, and been in residence at the MacDowell Colony. Berne is a hard driving eclectic whose albums have included strains of free jazz, hard bop, rock, pop, fusion, various international, even contemporary classical elements.

DISC.: *Five Year Plan* (1979); *7x* (1980); *Songs and Rituals in Real Time* (1981); *Theoretically* (1983); *Mutant Variations* (1983); *Ancestors* (1983); *Fulton Street Maul* (1986); *Sanctified Dreams* (1988); *Fractured Fairy Tales* (1989); *Pace Yourself: Tim Berne's Caos* (1990); *Diminutive Mysteries* (1992); *Nice View* (1993); *Poisoned Minds* (1994); *Lowlife* (1994); *Unwound* (1996); *Memory Select* (1994).—**LP**

Berners, Lord (Sir Gerald Hugh Tyrwhitt-Wilson, Baronet), eccentric English composer, writer, and painter; b. Arley Park, Bridgnorth, Sept. 18, 1883; d. Farringdon House, Berkshire, April 19, 1950. He was mainly self-taught, although he received some music training in Dresden and England, and advice and encouragement from Stravinsky. He served as honorary attaché to the British diplomatic service in Constantinople (1909–11) and Rome (1911–19). Returning to England, he joined the literary smart set; he was on close terms with George Bernard Shaw, H.G. Wells, and Osbert Sitwell. He publ. half a dozen novels, including *The Girls of Radcliff Hall* (1937), *The Romance of a Nose* (1942), and *Far from the Madding War*, in which he portrays himself as Lord Fitzcricket. Berners affected bizarre social behavior; his humor and originality are reflected in his compositions, many of which reveal a subtle gift for parody. He wrote 2 autobiographical vols., *First Childhood* (London, 1934) and *A Distant Prospect* (London, 1945); he also had successful exhibitions of his oil paintings in London (1931, 1936).

WORKS: DRAMATIC: O p e r a : *Le Carrosse du Saint-Sacrement* (Paris, April 24, 1924). **B a l l e t :** *The Triumph of Neptune* (London, Dec. 3, 1926); *Luna Park* (London, March 1930); *A Wedding Bouquet* (London, April 27, 1937); *Cupid and Psyche* (London, April 27, 1939); *Les Sirènes* (London, Nov. 12, 1946). **ORCH.:** 3 pieces: *Chinoiserie, Valse sentimentale,* and *Kasatchok* (1919); *Fantaisie espagnole* (1920); *Fugue* (1928). **P i a n o :** *3 Little Funeral Marches* (1914); *Le Poisson d'or* (1914); *Fragments psychologiques* (1915); *Valses bourgeoises* for Piano Duet (1915). **OTHER:** Film scores, including *Nicholas Nickleby* (1947); songs, including *Lieder Album,* to texts by Heine (1913; *Du bist wie eine Blume* is set in accordance with the suggestion that the poem was not addressed to a lady but to a small white pig).

BIBL.: J. Holbrooke, *B.* (London, 1925); H. Bridgeman and E. Drury, *The British Eccentric* (N.Y., 1975).—**NS/LK/DM**

Bernet, Dietfried, Austrian conductor; b. Vienna, May 14, 1940. He studied at the Vienna Academy of Music and received training in conducting from Swarowsky and Mitropoulos. In 1962 he won first prize in the Liverpool conducting competition, and then was a conductor in Vienna at the State Opera and at the Volksoper from 1964. In 1973 he made his U.S. debut as a guest conductor with the Chicago Sym. Orch. He also was a guest conductor with various other orchs. on both sides of the Atlantic, and appeared with opera companies in Munich, Hamburg, Cologne, Stuttgart, London, Barcelona, Venice, Glyndebourne, and Geneva. In 1995 he was made chief guest conductor of the Royal Opera in Copenhagen.—NS/LK/DM

Bernet Kempers, Karel Philippus, Dutch musicologist; b. Nijkerk, Sept. 20, 1897; d. Amsterdam, Sept. 30, 1974. He studied with Sandberger at the Univ. of Munich (Ph.D., 1926, with the diss. *Jacobus Clemens non Papa und seine Motetten*; publ. in Augsburg, 1928) and completed his Habilitation at the Univ. of Amsterdam in 1929 with his *Herinnerignsmotieven, leidmotieven, grondthema's*. He taught music history at the Royal Cons. in The Hague (1929–49) and at the Amsterdam Cons. (1934–53); was also privatdozent (1929–38), lecturer (1938–46), reader (1946–53), and prof. (1953–63) in musicology at the Univ. of Amsterdam. He was the ed. of the complete works of Clemens non Papa.

WRITINGS: *De italiaanse opera van Peri tot Puccini* (Amsterdam, 1929; Eng. tr., 1947); *Muziekgeschiedenis* (Rotterdam, 1932; 6th ed., 1965); *Meesters der Muziek* (Rotterdam, 1939; 6th ed., 1958); *Panorama der Muziek* (Rotterdam, 1948).—NS/LK/DM

Bernhard, Christoph, German music theorist, singer, and composer; b. Kolberg, Jan. 1, 1628; d. Dresden, Nov. 14, 1692. He was a student of Siefert in Danzig and of Schütz in Dresden, where he then was a singer and teacher of singing to the choirboys (1649–55) and Second Kapellmeister (1655–63) at the electoral court. From 1664 to 1674 he was Kantor at the Johannisschule and municipal director of church music in Hamburg. He also was associated with Weckmann and his collegium musican concerts there. In 1674 he was recalled to Dresden as tutor to the Elector's grandsons. He also acted as Second Kapellmeister at the electoral court under Schütz. Upon the latter's death in 1674, he continued in that capacity until finally being made First Kapellmeister in 1681. He retired in 1688. Bernhard was a significant music theorist. In his *Tractatus compositionis augmentatus* he delineated three compositional styles according to the relationship of words and music, place of performance, and types of dissonance employed. His other treatises included *Ausführlicher Bericht vom Gebrauche der Con- und Dissonantien* and *Von der Singe-Kunst oder Manier*. His compositions included various sacred works, including a vol. of 20 concertos for 1 to 4 Voices as *Geistliche Harmonien* (Dresden, 1665) and *Prudentia prudentiana* (Hamburg, 1669). Bernhard was also commissioned by Schütz in 1672 to compose a funeral motet for 5 Voices to be performed at Schütz's funeral.

BIBL.: R. Streetman, *C. B.* (diss., North Tex. State Univ. 1967).—NS/LK/DM

Bernheimer, Martin, German-born American music critic; b. Munich, Sept. 28, 1936. He was taken to the U.S. as a child in 1940 and became a naturalized citizen in 1946. He studied at Brown Univ. (Mus.B., 1958); after attending the Munich Hochschule für Musik (1958–59), he studied musicology with Reese at N.Y. Univ. (M.A., 1961), where he also taught (1959–62). He was contributing critic of the *N.Y. Herald-Tribune* (1959–62), contributing ed. of the *Musical Courier* (1961–64), temporary music critic of the *N.Y. Post* (1961–65), Kolodin's assistant at the *Saturday Review* (1962–65), and music ed. and chief music critic of the *Los Angeles Times* (from 1965). As a critic, Bernheimer possesses a natural facility and not infrequently a beguiling felicity of literary style; he espouses noble musical causes with crusading fervor, but he can also be aggressively opinionated and ruthlessly devastating to composers, performers, or administrators whom he dislikes; as a polemicist, he is a rara avis among contemporary critics, who seldom rise to the pitch of moral or musical indignation; he also possesses a surprising knowledge of music in all its ramifications, which usually protects him from perilous pratfalls. In 1974 and 1978 he won the ASCAP-Deems Taylor Award, and in 1982 the Pulitzer Prize for distinguished criticism.—NS/LK/DM

Bernier, Nicolas, French organist, teacher, music theorist, and composer; b. Mantes-la-Jolie, June 5 or 6, 1665; d. Paris, July 6, 1734. He was a student of Caldara in Rome. From 1694 to 1698 he was maître at Chartes Cathedral before being called to Paris in 1698 as maître de musique at St. Germain l'Auxérrois. He subsequently held that position at Sainte-Chapelle from 1704 to 1726, and from 1723 he was one of the 3 sous-maîtres at the Chapelle Royale. Bernier was the son-in-law of Marin Marais. He was one of the first French composers to cultivate the secular cantata. He publ. 8 vols. of Cantates françoises, the most notable being *Les nuits de Sceaux* (Paris, 1715). Among his sacred vocal output were many motets. He also wrote a treatise on counterpoint as *Principes de composition* (Eng. tr., 1964, by P. Nelson).

BIBL.: P. Nelson, *N. B. (1665–1734): A Study of the Composer and his Sacred Works* (diss., Univ. of N.C., 1958).—NS/LK/DM

Bernier, René, Belgian composer; b. Saint Gilles, March 10, 1905; d. Brussels, Sept. 8, 1984. He studied at the Brussels Cons. and with Gilson. With 7 other pupils of Gilson, he formed the Groupe des Synthetistes in 1925 with the aim of combining Classical forms with modern techniques. He was prof. of music history at the Mons Cons. (1945–70). In 1963 he was made a member of the Belgian Royal Academy.

WORKS: DRAMATIC: Ballet: *Le Bal des ombres* (1954); *Symphonie en blanc* (1961; based on the *Sinfonietta* for String Orch., 1957); *Tanagras* (1969). ORCH.: *Mélopées et Rythmes* (1932); *Ode à une Madone* (1938; rev. 1955); *Le Tombeau devant l'Escaut*, symphonic poem (1952); *Notturno* (1955); *Bassonniere* for Bassoon and Orch. (1956); *Sinfonietta* for Strings (1957); *Homage à sax* for Saxophone and Orch. (1958); *Reverdies* for Clarinet and Orch. (1960); *Interludes* (1966); *Ménestraudie* for Violin and Orch. (1970). CHAMBER: *Sonata à deux* for Flute and Harp (1939); Trio for Flute, Cello, and Harp (1942); piano pieces. **VOCAL:** *Présages* for Voice and Orch. (1942–46); *Liturgies* for Chorus (1968); *Agnus Dei* for Voice and Keyboard Instrument (1983; also for Chorus and String Orch.); solo songs. **—NS/LK/DM**

Berno von Reichenau, writer on music; b. c.970; d. Reichenau, June 7, 1048. He may have been of German birth. After serving at the Prüm monastery, Emperor Henry II made him abbot of Reichenau in 1008, a position he held until his death. He traveled to Rome in 1014 for the coronation of Emperor Henry II, was again in Italy with the emperor in 1023, and returned to Rome in 1027 for the coronation of Emperor Conrad II. Berno's most distinguished student was Hermannus Contractus. His major work is a tonary in which he treats the subjects of transposition and the so-called middle modes. An early MS source also attributes several compositions to him.

BIBL.: H. Oesch, *B. und Hermann von Reichenau als Musiktheoretiker*, Publikationen der schweizerischen musikforschenden Gesellschaft, 2nd series, IX (Bern, 1961).**—NS/LK/DM**

Bernstein, Lawrence F., American musicologist; b. N.Y., March 25, 1939. He studied at Hofstra Univ. (B.S., 1960) and with LaRue and Reese at N.Y. Univ. (Ph.D., 1969, with the diss. *Cantus Firmus in the French Chanson for Two and Three Voices, 1500–1550*). He taught at the Univ. of Chicago (1965–70). Bernstein was assoc. prof. (1970–81) and prof. (from 1981) of music at the Univ. of Pa., where he also was chairman of the music dept. (1972–73; 1974–77) and later was the Karen and Gary Rose Term Prof. of Music. He also served as a visiting prof. at Columbia Univ. (1979), Princeton Univ. (1980), Rutgers Univ. (1982–83), and N.Y. Univ. (1982–83). He served as supervising ed. of the Masters and Monuments of the Renaissance series (from 1970), to which he contributed, as ed.-in-chief of the *Journal of the American Musicological Society* (1975–77), as a member of the editorial board of the New Josquin Edition (1982–92), and as general ed. of the American Musicological Soc. Monuments series (from 1990). In 1987–88 he held a Guggenheim fellowship. In addition to contributions to journals and other publications, he wrote articles for *The New Grove Dictionary of Music and Musicians* (1980).**—NS/LK/DM**

Bernstein, Leonard (actually, **Louis**), prodigiously gifted American conductor, composer, pianist, and teacher; b. Lawrence, Mass., Aug. 25, 1918; d. N.Y., Oct. 14, 1990. He was born into a family of Russian-Jewish immigrants. When he was 16, he legally changed his given name to Leonard to avoid confusion with another Louis in the family. He was 10 when he began piano lessons with Frieda Karp. At age 13, he began piano training with Susan Williams at the New England Cons. of Music in Boston. When he was 14, he commenced piano studies with Heinrich Gebhard and his assistant, Helen Coates. In 1935 he entered Harvard Univ., where he took courses with Edward Burlingame Hill (orchestration), A. Tillman Merritt (harmony and counterpoint), and Piston (counterpoint and fugue). He graduated cum laude in 1939. On April 21, 1939, he

made his first appearance as a conductor when he led the premiere of his incidental music to Aristophanes' *The Birds* at Harvard Univ. He then enrolled at the Curtis Inst. of Music in Philadelphia, where he studied with Reiner (conducting), Vengerova (piano), Thompson (orchestration), and Renée Longy (score reading), receiving his diploma in 1941. During the summers of 1940 and 1941, he was a pupil in conducting of Koussevitzky at the Berkshire Music Center at Tanglewood, returning in the summer of 1942 as Koussevitzky's assistant. In 1942–43 he worked for the N.Y. publishing firm of Harms, Inc., using the pseudonym Lenny Amber (Amber being the Eng. tr. of the German Bernstein).

In Aug. 1943 Artur Rodzinski, then music director of the N.Y. Phil., appointed Bernstein as his asst. conductor. On Nov. 14, 1943, Bernstein substituted at short notice for ailing guest conductor Bruno Walter in a N.Y. Phil. concert which was broadcast to the nation by radio. He acquitted himself magnificently and was duly hailed by the press as a musician of enormous potential. Thus the most brilliant conducting career in the history of American music was launched, and Bernstein was engaged to appear as a guest conductor with several major U.S. orchs. On Jan. 28, 1944, he conducted the premiere of his First Sym., *Jeremiah*, with the Pittsburgh Sym. Orch. The score was well received and won the N.Y. Music Critics' Circle Award for 1944. That same year he brought out his ballet *Fancy Free*, followed by the musical *On the Town*, which scored popular and critical accolades. In 1945 he became music director of the N.Y. City Sym. Orch., a post he held until 1948. On May 15, 1946, he made his European debut as a guest conductor of the Czech Phil. in Prague. In 1947 he appeared as a guest conductor of the Palestine Sym. Orch. in Tel Aviv. During Israel's War of Independence in 1948, he conducted a series of concerts with it as the renamed Israel Phil. He then completed his Second Sym. for Piano and Orch., *The Age of Anxiety*, a score which reflected the troubled times. It was given its first performance by Koussevitzky and the Boston Sym. Orch. on April 8, 1949, with the composer at the piano. In 1951 Bernstein composed his first opera, *Trouble in Tahiti*. During the Israel Phil.'s first tour of the U.S. in 1951, he shared the conducting duties with Koussevitzky. Upon the latter's death that year, he was named his mentor's successor as head of the orch. and conducting depts. at the Berkshire Music Center, where he was active until 1953 and again in 1955. He also taught intermittently at Brandeis Univ. from 1951 to 1954. In 1953 he produced his successful Broadway musical *Wonderful Town*.

Bernstein was the first American conductor ever to appear as a guest conductor at Milan's La Scala when he led Cherubini's *Medea* in Dec. 1953. In 1954 he wrote the score for the Academy Award winning film *On the Waterfront*. That same year he made an indelible impact as an expositor/performer on the *Omnibus* television program. Returning to the theater, he composed his comic operetta *Candide*, after Voltaire, in 1956. Bernstein was appointed co-conductor (with Mitropoulos) of the N.Y. Phil. in 1956, and in 1958 he became its music director, the first American-born and trained conductor to attain that prestigious position. In 1957 he brought out his musical *West Side Story*, a significant social drama abounding in memorable tunes, which proved enduringly popular; in its film incarnation (1961), it won no less than 11 Academy Awards, including best film of the year. In the meantime, Bernstein consolidated his protean activities as music director of the N.Y. Phil. through his concerts at home and abroad, as well as his numerous recordings, radio broadcasts, and television programs. Indeed, he acquired a celebrity status rarely achieved by a classical musician. His televised N.Y. Phil. Young People's Concerts (1958–72) were extremely successful with viewers of all ages. In 1959 he took the N.Y. Phil. on a triumphant tour of 17 European and Near East nations, including the Soviet Union. On Jan. 19, 1961, he conducted the premiere of his *Fanfare* at the Inaugural Gala for President John F. Kennedy in Washington, D.C. Bernstein led the gala opening concert of the N.Y. Phil. in its new home at Phil. Hall at N.Y.'s Lincoln Center for the Performing Arts on Sept. 23, 1962. He then took the orch. on a transcontinental tour of the U.S. in 1963. On Dec. 10, 1963, he conducted the first performance of his Third Sym., *Kaddish*, with the Israel Phil. in Tel Aviv. The score reflects Bernstein's Jewish heritage, but is also noteworthy for its admixture of both 12–tone and tonal writing. On March 6, 1964, he made his Metropolitan Opera debut in N.Y. conducting *Falstaff*, which work he also chose for his Vienna State Opera debut on March 14, 1966. In 1967 he appeared for the first time as a guest conductor of the Vienna Phil. In subsequent years he became closely associated with it, appearing not only in Vienna but also on extensive tours, recordings, and films.

In 1969 Bernstein retired as music director of the N.Y. Phil. and was accorded the title of laureate conductor. Thereafter he made regular appearances with it in this honored capacity. From 1970 to 1974 he served as advisor at Tanglewood. For the opening of the John F. Kennedy Center for the Performing Arts in Washington, D.C., he composed his theater piece, *Mass* (Sept. 8, 1971), a challenging and controversial liturgical score. During the 1973–74 academic year, he was the Charles Eliot Norton Prof. of Poetry at Harvard Univ., where he gave a series of lectures later publ. as *The Unanswered Question* (1976). He returned to the genre of the musical in 1976 with his *1600 Pennsylvania Avenue*, but the work was notsuccessful. On Jan. 19, 1977, he conducted at the Inaugural Concert for President Jimmy Carter in Washington, D.C. In 1983 Bernstein completed work on his opera *A Quiet Place*, which he considered his most important creative achievement. However, its premiere in Houston on June 17, 1983, was not a success. He then revised the work and incorporated it into his earlier opera *Trouble in Tahiti*. The revised version was premiered at Milan's La Scala on June 19, 1984, the first opera by an American composer ever accorded such a distinction. All the same, the opera remained problematic. In July–August 1985 he toured as conductor with the European Community Youth Orch. in a "Journey for Peace" program to Athens, Hiroshima, Budapest, and Vienna. Bernstein also conducted celebratory performances of Beethoven's Ninth Sym. to mark the opening of the Berlin Wall, first at the Kaiser Wilhelm Memorial Church in West Berlin (Dec. 23, 1989), and then at the Schauspielhaus Theater in East Berlin (telecast to the world, Dec. 25, 1989).

Increasingly plagued by ill health, Bernstein was compelled to announce his retirement from the podium on Oct. 9, 1990. His death just 5 days later (of progressive emphysema, complicated by a chronic pleurisy, eventuating in a fatal heart attack) shocked the music world and effectively brought to a close a unique era in the history of American music. Bernstein was afforded innumerable honors at home and abroad. Among his foreign decorations were the Order of the Lion, Commander, of Finland (1965); Chevalier (1968), Officier (1978), and Commandeur (1985), of the Légion d'honneur, of France; Cavaliere, Order of Merit, of Italy (1969); Grand Honor Cross for Science and Art of Austria (1976); and the Grand Order of Merit of the Italian Republic (1988). In 1977 he was made a member of the Swedish Royal Academy of Music in Stockholm, in 1981 of the American Academy and Inst. of Arts and Letters in N.Y., in 1983 of the Vienna Phil., and in 1984 of the N.Y. Phil. In 1987 he was awarded the Gold Medal of the Royal Phil. Soc. of London. He was made president of the London Sym. Orch. in 1987 and laureate conductor of the Israel Phil. in 1988. His 70th birthday was the occasion for an outpouting of tributes from around the world, highlighted by a major celebration at Tanglewood from Aug. 25 to 28, 1988. Bernstein's extraordinary musical gifts were ably matched by an abundance of spiritual and sheer animal energy, a remarkable intellect, and an unswerving commitment to liberal, and even radical, political and humanitarian ideals. As a composer, he revealed a protean capacity in producing complex serious scores on the one hand, and strikingly original and effective works for the Broadway musical theater on the other. All the same, it was as a nonpareil conductor and musical expositor that Bernstein so profoundly enlightened more than one generation of auditors. Ebullient and prone to podium histrionics of a choreographic expressivity, he was a compelling interpreter of the Romantic repertory. Bernstein had a special affinity for the music of Mahler, whose works drew from him unsurpassed readings of great beauty and searing intensity. He was also a convincing exponent of Haydn, Mozart, and Beethoven. Fortunately, many of Bernstein's greatest performances have been captured on recordings and video discs as a testament to the life and work of one of the foremost musicians of the 20th century.

WORKS: DRAMATIC: *The Birds*, incidental music to Aristophanes' play (1938; Cambridge, Mass., April 21, 1939, composer conducting); *The Peace*, incidental music to Aristophanes' play (1940; Cambridge, Mass., May 23, 1941); *Fancy Free*, ballet (N.Y., April 18, 1944, composer conducting); *On the Town*, musical comedy (Boston, Dec. 13, 1944, Goberman conducting); *Facsimile*, ballet (N.Y., Oct. 24, 1946, composer conducting; 2nd version as *Parallel Lives*, Milwaukee, Oct. 19, 1986; 3rd version as *Dancing On*, Zagreb, March 31, 1988); *Peter Pan*, incidental music to Barrie's play (N.Y., April 24, 1950); *Trouble in Tahiti*, opera (1951; Waltham, Mass., June 12, 1952, composer conducting); *Wonderful Town*, musical comedy (New Haven, Conn., Jan. 19, 1953); *The Lark*, incidental music to Anouilh's play, adapted by Lillian Hellman (Boston, Oct. 28, 1955); *Salomé*, incidental music to Wilde's play (CBS-TV, N.Y., Dec. 11, 1955;

withdrawn); *Candide*, comic operetta (Boston, Oct. 29, 1956; rev. version, N.Y., Dec. 20, 1973, Mauceri conducting; operatic version, N.Y., Oct. 13, 1982, Mauceri conducting; rev., Glasgow, May 17, 1988, Mauceri conducting); *West Side Story*, musical (Washington, D.C., Aug. 19, 1957); *The Firstborn*, incidental music to Christopher Fry's play (N.Y., April 29, 1958; withdrawn); *Mass*, theater piece for Singers, Players, and Dancers (Washington, D.C., Sept. 8, 1971, Peress conducting; chamber version, Los Angeles, Dec. 26, 1972); *Dybbuk*, ballet (N.Y., May 16, 1974, composer conducting; retitled *Dybbuk Variations for Orch.*); *By Bernstein*, musical cabaret (N.Y., Nov. 23, 1975; withdrawn); *1600 Pennsylvania Avenue*, musical (Philadelphia, Feb. 24, 1976; concert version as *The White House Cantata*, London, July 1997); *A Quiet Place*, opera (Houston, June 17, 1983, DeMain conducting; withdrawn; rev. version, incorporating *Trouble in Tahiti*, Milan, June 19, 1984, Mauceri conducting). **F i l m :** *On the Waterfront* (1954). **ORCH.:** 3 syms.: No. 1, *Jeremiah*, for Mezzo-soprano and Orch. (1942; Pittsburgh, Jan. 28, 1944, Tourel soloist, composer conducting), No. 2, *The Age of Anxiety*, for Piano and Orch. (Boston, April 8, 1949, composer soloist, Koussevitzky conducting; rev. version, N.Y., July 15, 1965, Entremont soloist, composer conducting), and No. 3, *Kaddish*, for Speaker, Soprano, Chorus, Boys' Choir, and Orch. (Tel Aviv, Dec. 12, 1963, Tourel soloist, composer conducting; rev. version, Mainz, Aug. 25, 1977, Caballé soloist, composer conducting); *Suite from Fancy Free* (1944; Pittsburgh, Jan. 14, 1945, composer conducting; withdrawn); *3 Dance Variations from Fancy Free* (N.Y., Jan. 21, 1946, composer conducting); *3 Dance Episodes from On the Town* (1945; San Francisco, Feb. 13, 1946, composer conducting); *Facsimile*, choreographic essay (1946; Poughkeepsie, N.Y., March 5, 1947, composer conducting); *Prelude, Fugue, and Riffs* for Clarinet and Jazz Ensemble (1949; CBS-TV, N.Y., Oct. 16, 1955, Benny Goodman soloist, composer conducting); *Serenade* for Violin, Harp, Percussion, and Strings (Venice, Sept. 12, 1954, Isaac Stern soloist, composer conducting); *Symphonic Suite from On the Waterfront* (Tanglewood, Aug. 11, 1955, composer conducting); *Overture to Candide* (1956; N.Y., Jan. 26, 1957, composer conducting); *Symphonic Dances from West Side Story* (1960; N.Y., Feb. 13, 1961, Foss conducting); *Fanfare* for the inauguration of President John F. Kennedy (Washington, D.C., Jan. 19, 1961, composer conducting); *Fanfare* for the 25th anniversary of N.Y.'s H.S. of Music and Art (N.Y., March 24, 1961); *2 Meditations from Mass* (Austin, Tex., Oct. 31, 1971, Peress conducting; *Meditation III from Mass* (Jerusalem, May 21, 1972, composer conducting; withdrawn); *Dybbuk Variations* (Auckland, New Zealand, Aug. 16, 1974, composer conducting); *3 Meditations from Mass* for Cello and Orch. (Washington, D.C., Oct. 11, 1977, Rostropovich soloist, composer conducting); *Slava!*, "a political overture" for Rostropovich (Washington, D.C., Oct. 11, 1977, Rostropovich conducting); *CBS Music* for the 50th anniversary of CBS (1977; CBS-TV, N.Y., April 1, 1978; withdrawn); *Divertimento* (Boston, Sept. 25, 1980, Ozawa conducting); *A Musical Toast*, in memory of Kostelanetz (N.Y., Oct. 11, 1980, Mehta conducting); *Halil*, nocturne for Flute and Orch. (Jerusalem, May 27, 1981, Rampal soloist, composer conducting). **C H A M B E R :** Trio for Violin, Cello, and Piano (1937); Violin Sonata (1940); *4 Studies* for 2 Clarinets, 2 Bassoons, and Piano (c. 1940); Clarinet Sonata (1941–42; Boston, April 21, 1942, David Glazer clarinetist, composer pianist); *Brass Music* (1948); *Shivaree* for Double Brass Ensemble and Percussion (1969); *Red, White, and Blues* for Trumpet and Piano (1984; transcribed by P. Wastall from the song in *1600 Pennsylvania Avenue*). **P i a n o :** Sonata (1938); *Scenes from the City of Sin* for Piano, 4–Hands (1939); *7 Anniver-*

saries (1943; Boston, May 14, 1944, composer pianist); *4 Anniversaries* (Cleveland, Oct. 1, 1948, Educie Podis pianist); *5 Anniversaries* (1949–51); *Touches* (1981); *Moby Diptych* (1981); *13 Anniversaries* (1988); *For Nicky, in Ancient Friendship* for Nicolas Slonimsky's 95th birthday (Los Angeles, April 27, 1989). **V O C A L :** *Hashkiveinu* for Cantorial Solo (Tenor), Chorus, and Organ (N.Y., May 11, 1945); *Yigdal* for Chorus and Piano (1950); *Harvard Choruses* for Men's Voices and Band (N.Y., March 7, 1957, Woodworth conducting; withdrawn); *Chichester Psalms* for Boy Soloist, Chorus, and Orch. (N.Y., July 15, 1965, composer conducting); *Suite from Candide* for Soloists, Chorus, and Orch. (Bloomington, Ind., April 9, 1977, Mauceri conducting); *Songfest* for 6 Singers and Orch. (first complete perf., Washington, D.C., Oct. 11, 1977, composer conducting); *Olympic Hymn* for Chorus and Orch. (Baden-Baden, Sept. 23, 1981, Shallon conducting; withdrawn); *Jubilee Games* for Baritone and Orch. (N.Y., Sept. 13, 1986, composer conducting; rev. version, incorporating *Opening Prayer*, retitled as *Benediction*, Tel Aviv, May 31, 1988, composer conducting); *Opening Prayer* for Baritone and Orch. (N.Y., Dec. 15, 1986, composer conducting; retitled as *Benediction* and incorporated in the rev. version of *Jubilee Games*, Tel Aviv, May 31, 1988, composer conducting; in spite of this revision, *Opening Prayer* remains an independent work as well); *Missa brevis* for Countertenor or Septet of Solo Voices, Chorus, and Percussion (Atlanta, April 21, 1988, Shaw conducting). **S o n g s** (all for Voice and Piano unless otherwise given): *I Hate Music*, cycle of 5 children's songs (Lenox, Mass., Aug. 24, 1943, Tourel soloist, composer pianist); *Afterthought* (1945; N.Y., Oct. 24, 1948; withdrawn); *La Bonne Cuisine*, "4 recipes" (1947; N.Y., Oct. 10, 1948); *2 Love Songs*, after Rilke (1949; No. 1, N.Y., March 13, 1949; No. 2, N.Y., March 13, 1963); *Silhouette* (1951; Washington, D.C., Feb. 13, 1955); *On the Waterfront* (1954; withdrawn); *Get Hep!* (1955; withdrawn); *So Pretty* (N.Y., Jan. 21, 1968, Streisand soloist, composer pianist); *An Album of Songs* (1974; withdrawn); *My New Friends* (1979); *Piccola Serenata*, vocalise for Karl Böhm's 85th birthday (Salzburg, Aug. 27, 1979, Ludwig soloist, composer pianist); *Sean Song* for Voice and Violin, Viola, Cello, Harp, or Piano (1986); *My 12–tone Melody* for Irving Berlin's 100th birthday (N.Y., May 11, 1988, composer singer and pianist); *Arias and Barcarolles* for 4 Soloists and Piano, 4–Hands (N.Y., May 9, 1988, Tilson Thomas and composer pianists).

WRITINGS: *The Joy of Music* (N.Y., 1959); *Leonard Bernstein's Young People's Concerts for Reading and Listening* (N.Y., 1961; rev. ed., 1970, as *Leonard Bernstein's Young People's Concerts*); *The Infinite Variety of Music* (N.Y., 1966); *The Unanswered Question: Six Talks at Harvard* (Cambridge, Mass., and London, 1976); *Findings* (N.Y., 1982).

BIBL.: J. Briggs, *L. B., The Man, His Work and His World* (Cleveland and N.Y., 1961); A. Holde, *L. B.* (Berlin, 1961); J. Gruen and K. Hyman, *The Private World of L. B.* (N.Y., 1968); P. Robinson, *B.* (N.Y., 1982); P. Gradenwitz, *L. B.: Eine Biographie* (Zürich, 1984; 2nd ed., 1990; Eng. tr., 1986); M. Freedland, *L. B.* (London, 1987); J. Peyser, *L. B.: A Biography* (N.Y., 1987; rev. ed., 1998); J. Gottlieb, ed., *L. B.: A Complete Catalog of His Works: Celebrating His 70th Birthday, August 25, 1988* (N.Y., 1988); J. Flugel, ed., *B. Remembered: A Life in Pictures* (N.Y., 1991); S. Chapin, *L. B.: Notes From a Friend* (N.Y., 1992); M. Secrest, *L. B.: A Life* (N.Y., 1994); W. Burton, ed., *Conversations About B.* (Oxford, 1995); P. Myers, *L. B.* (London, 1998).—**NS/LK/DM**

Bernstein, Martin, American musicologist; b. N.Y., Dec. 14, 1904; d. there, Dec. 19, 1999. He was educated at N.Y. Univ. (B.S., 1925; B.Mus., 1927), and played the double bass in the N.Y. Sym. Orch. (1925–26), the N.Y. Phil. (1926–28), and the Chautauqua Sym. Orch. (1929–36). He was a member of the faculty of N.Y. Univ. (1926–72); then a prof. of music at Lehman Coll., City Univ. of N.Y. (1972–73). He publ. *Score Reading* (1932; 2nd ed., rev., 1947) and the successful textbook *An Introduction to Music* (N.Y., 1937; 3rd ed., rev., 1966, and 4th ed., rev., 1972 with M. Picker). A brother, Artie (actually, Arthur) Bernstein (b. N.Y., Feb. 3, 1909; d. Los Angeles, Jan. 4, 1964), a classically trained cellist, became a leading jazz bassist in the 1930s and '40s, playing with many big bands, including Jimmy Dorsey's; from 1939 to 1941 he was part of the Benny Goodman Sextet; after World War II, he became a studio musician.

BIBL.: E. Clinkscale and C. Brook, eds., *A Musical Offering: Essays in Honor of M. B.* (N.Y., 1977).—**NS/LK/DM**

Bernuth, Julius von, German conductor; b. Rees, Aug. 8, 1830; d. Hamburg, Dec. 24, 1902. He was a practicing lawyer. He studied music with Taubert and Dehn in Berlin, and at the Leipzig Cons., where he founded a chamber music society, Aufschwung (1857), and the Dilettanten-Orchester-Verein (1859). From 1867 to 1894 he was conductor of the Hamburg Phil. Orch. In 1873 he founded a cons. in Hamburg.—**NS/LK/DM**

Béroff, Michel, French pianist; b.Épinal, May 9, 1950. After training at the Nancy Cons. (premier prix, 1962; prix d'excellence, 1963), he completed his studies with Loriod at the Paris Cons. (premier prix, 1966). In 1967 he made his Paris debut and won first prize in the Messiaen competition in Rouen; thereafter he toured internationally, appearing as a soloist with major orchs. and as a recitalist. While his large repertory embraces works from Mozart to the contemporary period, he has won particular notice for his performances of scores by Debussy, Stravinsky, Prokofiev, Bartók, and Messiaen. —**NS/LK/DM**

Berr (original name, Beer), Friedrich, German clarinetist and bassoonist; b. Mannheim, April 17, 1794; d. Paris, Sept. 24, 1838. He studied with Fétis and Reicha in Paris, and settled there in 1823. He served as the second clarinetist at the Théâtre-Italien, becoming first clarinetist in 1828. In 1831 he was appointed to the faculty of the Paris Cons., and in 1836 he became director of the new School of Military Music. He was the author of a *Traité complet de la clarinette à 14 clefs* (1836), and the composer of many works for clarinet and bassoon and some 500 pieces of military music. —**NS/LK/DM**

Berry, Chu (actually, Leon Brown), jazz tenor saxophonist; b. Wheeling, W.Va., Sept. 13, 1908; d. Conneaut, Ohio, Oct. 30, 1941. He came from a musical family; his brother, Nelson, was a tenor sax player. He took up sax after hearing Coleman Hawkins playing on a Fletcher Henderson summer tour. He played alto sax at high school, and later, during his three years at W.Va. State Coll., played alto and tenor with Edwards' Collegians, also worked with Perry Smith and with Fleming Huff in Ohio; he was offered a career as a professional football player, but decided on music. While with Edwards' Collegians in Bluefield, W.Va., was sent for by Sammy Stewart. Traveled to join the band in Columbus, Ohio (1929). At the time of his joining he sported a goatee beard and moustache; lead alto Billy Stewart began calling him "Chu-Chin-Chow"; this was later shortened to "Chu." (In the late 1930s a photograph was published showing "Chu" wearing a sweater clearly marked "Chew"—it is impossible to ascertain whether Leon or the knitter decided on this spelling.) "Chu" traveled to N.Y. with the Sammy Stewart Band for their Savoy Ballroom residency (February–April 1930), he left the band later that year at the Arcadia Ballroom. During the early 1930s worked short spells with several bandleaders including: Cecil Scott, Otto Hardwick at the Hot Feet Club), Kaiser Marshall, Walter Pichon, and Earl Jackson's Band at the Lennox Club, with Benny Carter in summer of 1932, and again in 1933, also with Charlie Johnson late 1932 to early 1933. He joined Teddy Hill's Band and remained until late 1935. Became a regular member of Fletcher Henderson's Band in late 1935, after having previously worked for Henderson on broadcasts and other dates from the spring of 1934. He left Fletcher Henderson to join Cab Calloway in July 1937. He remained with Calloway until the time of his death (other than absence for a tonsillectomy in June 1939). After playing a one-nighter with Calloway in Brookfield, Ohio, "Chu," Andy Brown, and Lammar Wright set out by car for the next night's venue in Toronto, Ontario. Near Conneaut, Ohio, the car skidded on the road and hit a concrete bridge. Brown and Wright were only slightly hurt, but "Chu" received severe head injuries. He died four days later without regaining consciousness.

DISC.: *Sittin' In* (1938). The Chocolate Dandies: "Krazy Kapers" (1933). Teddy Wilson: "Blues in C# Minor" (1935–36). L. Hampton: "Hot Mallets" (1939). Wingy Manone: "Limehouse Blues" (1941).—**JC/LP**

Berry, Chuck (actually, Charles Edward Anderson), American rock 'n' roll songwriter, singer, and guitarist; b. St. Louis, Mo., Oct. 18, 1926. Berry's songs, such as "Roll over Beethoven," "Rock & Roll Music," "Sweet Little Sixteen," "Johnny B. Goode," and "Memphis, Tennessee," with their articulate, teen-oriented lyrics and distinctive guitar chords, created a basic repertoire for rock 'n' roll. He was an immediate influence on the Beach Boys, The Beatles, and the Rolling Stones, all of whom recorded his songs, and through them and others on all subsequent rock music. As a performer and recording artist himself, despite a career bedeviled by legal problems, he was an international concert attraction for more than 40 years, able to use pickup groups wherever he went because all rock musicians knew his material. He placed numerous recordings of his own compositions in the charts from the 1950s to the 1970s.

Berry was the son of Henry and Martha Berry; his father was a carpenter. He sang in a church choir as a child, began studying the piano at eight, and took up the guitar at the start of his teens, studying with Ira Harris. He attended Sumner H.S. in St. Louis, receiving instruction from the music teacher, Julia Davis. He was playing in local groups, notably one led by Ray Bands, by 1942. In 1944 he was convicted of armed robbery, and he spent three years in a reformatory. Upon his release in 1947, he went to work in an automobile manufacturing plant while studying cosmetology at the Poro School of Beauty Culture at night; upon graduation, he became a hairdresser. On Oct. 28, 1948, he married Themetta Suggs Toddy, with whom he had four children, among them a daughter named Ingrid who later sang with him.

In 1952, Berry began playing local clubs with a trio including pianist Johnnie Johnson and drummer Ebby Hardy. In 1955 he went to Chicago and auditioned for Chess Records, which released his debut single, "Maybellene" (music and lyrics credited to Chuck Berry, Russ Frato, and Alan Freed, though Berry was the sole author); it topped the R&B charts in August and peaked in the pop Top Ten in September, launching Berry's career. ("Maybellene" was inducted into the Grammy Hall of Fame in 1988.) Before the end of the year, he was back in the R&B Top Ten with "Thirty Days (To Come Back Home)," and "No Money Down" reached the R&B Top Ten early in 1956, but he didn't score another pop hit until his fourth single, "Roll over Beethoven," which was in the pop Top 40 in June 1956. ("Roll over Beethoven" was inducted into the Grammy Hall of Fame in 1990.) Both sides of his next single, "Too Much Monkey Business"/"Brown Eyed Handsome Man," reached the R&B Top Ten without crossing over to the pop charts. In December 1956 he appeared in the film Rock, Rock, Rock!, singing his next, noncharting single, "You Can't Catch Me."

Zeroing in on teen concerns, Berry's seventh single, "School Day," hit #1 on the R&B charts in April 1957 and peaked in the pop Top Ten in May. His less successful eighth single, "Oh Baby Doll," was featured along with its B-side, "La Jaunda," in his next film appearance, Mr. Rock and Roll in October. "Rock & Roll Music" was a return to form, peaking in the pop Top Ten in December. "Sweet Little Sixteen" did even better, topping the R&B charts and peaking in the pop Top Ten in March 1958. (His performance of it at the 1958 Newport Jazz Festival that July turned up in the September 1959 concert film Jazz on a Summer's Day.) "Johnny B. Goode" was his third consecutive pop Top Ten in June.

Berry's record sales cooled in the second half of 1958, but he reached the R&B Top Ten and the pop Top 40 with "Carol" later in the year and achieved similar success with "Almost Grown" in the spring of 1959. He sang both the B-side of the latter single, "Little Queenie," and "Memphis, Tennessee," the B-side of his next single, the Top 40 hit "Back in the U.S.A.," in the film Go, Johnny, Go!

Berry was arrested and indicted in December 1959 for transporting a minor across state lines for immoral purposes, a charge originating with a girl he had brought from Tex. to work in his St. Louis nightclub who had been arrested for prostitution. After two trials he was convicted in October 1961, given a two-year sentence, and sent to prison in February 1962. Mean-

while, his songs were taken up by various performers. The Velaires reached the charts with "Roll over Beethoven" in August 1961; Jerry Lee Lewis revived "Sweet Little Sixteen" for a chart entry in September 1962; and in May 1963 the Beach Boys hit the Top Ten by borrowing the music from "Sweet Little Sixteen" for "Surfin' U.S.A." (lyrics by Brian Wilson). Two months later, Lonnie Mack's instrumental treatment of "Memphis, Tennessee" was in the Top Ten. Chess Records capitalized on Berry's growing popularity with the album Chuck Berry on Stage, actually consisting of studio recordings with audience sounds overdubbed, which became his first chart LP in August.

British performers also recorded Berry songs, notably the Rolling Stones, whose first single, "Come On," which entered the U.K. charts in July 1963 and made the Top 40, was a cover of a noncharting 1961 Berry single. Dave Berry, who borrowed his stage name from his idol, made the British charts in September with "Memphis, Tennessee," which also got into the Top 40. In October a Chuck Berry single containing the 1960 B-side "Let It Rock" and "Memphis, Tennessee" entered the U.K. charts on its way to the Top Ten. In November The Beatles' cover of "Roll over Beethoven" appeared on their second British album, With the Beatles; released as a single in North America in December, it made the U.S. charts in March 1964.

Berry was released from prison in October 1963 and began to take advantage of the rise in his fortunes brought about by the many covers of his work. His first newly recorded single, "Nadine (Is It You?)," peaked in the Top 40 in May 1964; "No Particular Place to Go" hit the Top Ten in July; and "You Never Can Tell" was a Top 40 hit in September, with "Little Marie" and "Promised Land" both reaching the charts before the end of the year. The LPs Chuck Berry's Greatest Hits and St. Louis to Liverpool also reached the charts. Meanwhile, Berry revivals continued apace: Tommy Roe reached the charts in April 1964 with "Carol"; Johnny Rivers had a Top-Ten hit with "Memphis, Tennessee" in July and a Top 40 hit with "Maybellene" in September; Dion took "Johnny B. Goode" back into the charts in August; and Bill Black's Combo had an instrumental chart entry with "Little Queenie" in October. Berry performed that same month at the all-star T.A.M.I. Show, released as a film in November.

Both Berry's own recording career and the spate of revivals fell off after 1964, as contemporary performers, influenced by The Beatles, began to focus on performing their own compositions, although the Dave Clark Five's revival of his 1958 B-side, "Reelin' and Rockin'," peaked in the Top 40 in May 1965. In 1966, Berry switched from Chess to Mercury Records, for which he recorded several commercially unsuccessful albums. He spent much of his money building Berry Park, an amusement park in Wentzville, Mo., near St. Louis. In July 1969, Buck Owens topped the country charts with a revival of "Johnny B. Goode." Berry appeared at the Toronto Peace Festival that September, his performance filmed for the 1970 movie Sweet Toronto. Having re-signed to Chess Records, he recorded the album Back Home in December, which featured the single "Tulane." Johnny

Winter revived "Johnny B. Goode" for a chart entry in January 1970.

Berry's next Chess album, *San Francisco Dues*, released in September 1971, did not chart, but in February 1972 he traveled to England where his performance at the Lancaster Arts Festival was taped along with some studio recordings for *The London Chuck Berry Sessions*, released in May. Included on the album was a live take of "My Ding-A-Ling," a comically smutty sing-along; released as a single in June, it hit #1 in October and sold a million copies, while the LP hit the Top Ten and went gold. His greatest commercial success, this brought several albums of his older recordings into the charts; a live version of "Reelin' and Rockin'" with new, suggestive lyrics peaked in the Top 40 in February 1973; and Berry's next album, *Chuck Berry/Bio*, reached the charts in September 1973.

The resurgence in Berry's popularity, part of an overall nostalgia for 1950s rock 'n' roll in the early 1970s, led to another wave of successful revivals of his songs that lasted through the 1970s. The Electric Light Orch. reached the charts in April 1973 with "Roll over Beethoven"; the Beach Boys enjoyed a Top 40 reissue of "Surfin' U.S.A. in August 1974 and revived "Rock & Roll Music" for a Top Ten hit in August 1976; Elvis Presley took "Promised Land" into the Top 40 in December 1974; Leif Garrett had a Top 40 hit with "Surfin' U.S.A." in October 1977; and Linda Ronstadt had a Top 40 hit with "Back in the U.S.A." in October 1978. In the U.K., a Berry compilation album, *Motorvatin'*, reached the charts in February 1977 and hit the Top Ten, and the Steve Gibbons Band charted in August 1977 with a cover of "Tulane" that became a Top 40 hit. Berry, meanwhile, was seen performing in the films *Let the Good Times Roll* (1973), *Alice in the Cities* (1974), and *American Hot Wax* (1978).

Berry was convicted of tax evasion in 1979, and he served a 100–day prison sentence that ended in November. While he was incarcerated, his last album of newly recorded material, *Rockit*, was released by Atco Records. He continued to tour in the 1980s, and in 1986 his 60th birthday was marked by an all-star concert in St. Louis filmed for the movie biography *Chuck Berry: Hail! Hail! Rock 'n' Roll*, released the following year along with his autobiography. Meanwhile, his work continued to draw attention: Peter Tosh had yet another chart version of "Johnny B. Goode" in 1983; and the three-CD box set reissue *Chuck Berry—The Chess Box* won the 1989 Grammy for Best Historical Album. Berry continued to perform during the 1990s.

WRITINGS: *C. B.: The Autobiography* (N.Y., 1987).

DISC.: *Rock and Roll Music* (1957); *Sweet Little Sixteen* (1957); *One Dozen Berrys* (1958); *After School Session* (1958); *Pickin' Berries* (1959); *Chuck Berry Is on Top* (1959); *Rockin' at the Hops* (1960); *New Juke Box Hits* (1961); *Chuck Berry Twist* (1962); *Check Berry on Stage* (live; 1963); *Chuck & Bo, Vols. 1, 2* (1963); *This Is Chuck Berry* (1963); *Latest and Greatest* (1963); *St. Louis to Liverpool* (1964); *Promised Land* (1964); *Chuck & Bo, Vol 3* (1964); *You Never Can Tell* (1964); *Chuck Berry in London* (1965); *In Memphis* (live; 1967); *Live at the Fillmore Auditorium* (1967); *Back Home* (1970); *San Francisco Dues* (1971); *The London Chuck Berry Sessions* (1972); *Chuck Berry/Bio* (1973).

BIBL.: H. De Witt, *C. B.: Rock 'n' Roll Music* (Fremont, Calif., 1981; 2nd ed., rev., 1985); K. Reese, *C. B.: Mr. Rock n' Roll* (London and N.Y., 1982); D. Cohen and J. Green, *Send More C. B.* (South Bend, Ind., 1990).—**WR**

Berry, Wallace (Taft), American composer and music theorist; b. La Crosse, Wisc., Jan. 10, 1928; d. Vancouver, British Columbia, Nov. 16, 1991. He studied with Stevens at the Univ. of Southern Calif. in Los Angeles (B.Mus., 1949; Ph.D., 1956) and with Boulanger at the Paris Cons. (1953–54); then taught at the Univ. of Southern Calif. (1956–57), the Univ. of Mich. (1957–77), and (from 1978) the Univ. of British Columbia, where he was also head of the music dept. (1978–84). He served as president of the Soc. for Music Theory (1982–85). He publ. *Form in Music* (Englewood Cliffs, N.J., 1966; 2nd ed., rev., 1985), *Eighteenth-Century Imitative Counterpoint: Music for Analysis* (with E. Chudacoff; N.Y., 1969), *Structural Functions in Music* (Englewood Cliffs, N.J., 1975; 2nd ed., 1987), and *Musical Structure and Performance* (New Haven, Conn., 1989).

WORKS: DRAMATIC: *The Admirable Bashville*, chamber opera (1954). **ORCH.:** *4 Movements* for Chamber Orch. (1954); *Fantasy* (1958); *5 Pieces* for Small Orch. (1961); Piano Concerto (1964); *Canto Elegiaco* (1968); *Intonation: Victimis hominum inhumanitatis, in memoriam* (1972); *Acadian Images: 2 Movements* (1977–78). **CHAMBER:** Clarinet Sonata (1950); Suite for String Trio (1950); *3 Pieces on Arabic Songs* for Flute, Oboe, and Tom-tom (1950); Piano Quintet (1951); *Divertimento* for Harpsichord, Oboe, English Horn, and Cello (1952); 4 string quartets (1960, 1964, 1966, 1984); *Threnody* for Violin (1963–64); *Divertimento* for Wind Quintet, Piano, and Percussion (1964); Composition for Piano and Electronic Sounds (1967); Trio for Piano, Violin, and Cello (1970); *3 Essays in parody* for Treble Instrument and Piano (1973); *Anachronisms* for Violin and Piano (1973); Piano Sonata (1975). **VOCAL:** *Spoon River*, 6 songs for Soprano, Bass-baritone, and Orch. (1952); *Canticle on a Judaic Text* for Soprano or Tenor and Orch. (1953); *No Man is an Island* for Chorus (1959); *3 Songs of April* for Soprano or Tenor and String Quartet (1959); *Heaven-haven* for Chorus (1960); *Spring Pastoral* for Chorus (1960); *Des visages de France* for Soprano, Mezzo-soprano, and Ensemble (1967); *Credo in unam vitam* for Tenor, Horn, Cello, and Chamber Ensemble (1969); *Lover of the Moon Trembling Now at Twilight* for Soprano or Tenor and Ensemble (1971); *Of the Changeless Night and the Stark Ranges of Nothing* for Mezzo-soprano, Cello, and Piano (1978–79); *The Moment: Summer's Night* for Mezzo-soprano and Piano (1985). —**NS/LK/DM**

Berry, Walter, admired Austrian bass-baritone; b. Vienna, April 8, 1929; d. Oct. 27, 2000. He studied engineering at the Vienna School of Engineering before pursuing vocal training with Hermann Gallos at the Vienna Academy of Music. In 1950 he made his debut at the Vienna State Opera in Honegger's *Jeanne d'Arc*, and subsequently sang there regularly; he also appeared at the Salzburg Festivals (from 1952). In 1957 he made his U.S. debut as Mozart's Figaro in Chicago. He made his Metropolitan Opera debut in N.Y. as Barak on Oct. 2, 1966, remaining on its roster until 1974 and returning for its 1975–76 and 1977–78 seasons. In 1976 he made his first appearance at London's Covent Garden as Barak. He also sang in Berlin, Munich, Paris, Tokyo, Buenos

Aires, and elsewhere. In 1957 he married **Christa Ludwig**, with whom he appeared in opera and concert; they were divorced in 1970. In 1963 he was made an Austrian Kammersänger. Among his other roles were Leporello, Papageno, Telramund, Wotan, Escamillo, Baron Ochs, Wozzeck, and Dr. Schön.

BIBL.: P. Lorenz, *Christa Ludwig-W. B.: Eine Künstler Biographie* (Vienna, 1968).—NS/LK/DM

Bertali, Antonio, influential Italian composer; b. Verona, March 1605; d. Vienna, April 17, 1669. He was a student of Stefano Bernardi in Verona (1611–22). In 1622 he entered the service of Archduke Carl Joseph, Bishop of Breslau and Bressanone, the brother of Emperor Ferdinand II of Austria. In 1624 he went to Vienna, where he became a composer and violinist in the service of the imperial court. He composed much sacred and secular music, and was called upon to write works for various important official functions. Among the latter were the cantata *Donna real* for the marriage festivities of the future Emperor Ferdinand III and the Spanish Infanta Maria in 1631, the *Missa Ratisbonensis* for the imperial diet in Regensburg in 1636, and the *Requiem pro Ferdinando III* in 1637. In 1649 he was appointed imperial court Kapellmeister by Emperor Ferdinand III, and thereafter did much to establish the Italian style of opera in Vienna. He composed at least 10 operas, but only three complete scores are extant. Bertali's extant instrumental sonatas are notable, particularly his writing for large ensembles in which he deftly combined Venetian polychoral writing with the sonata concertata. Among his sacred works were many oratorios, masses, Magnificats, Te Deums, Psalms, and motets.

BIBL.: C. LaRoche, *A. B. als Opern- und Oratorienkomponist* (diss., Univ. of Vienna, 1919).—NS/LK/DM

Bertalotti, Angelo Michele, Italian composer and teacher; b. Bologna, April 8, 1666; d. there, March 30, 1747. He studied in Bologna, then sang in the choirs of S. Luigi dei Francesi and S. Agostino in Rome (1687–90). In 1693 he became singing master at the Scuole Pie in Bologna, where he was a member of the choir of S. Petronio from 1705. He publ. *Regole facilissime* (1706 and subsequent eds.). His *Solfeggi a canto e alto dati alle stampe per comodo delli putti delle Scuole pie* (1744; rev. ed., 1764) retains its value as a choral method.
—NS/LK/DM

Bertani, Lelio, Italian composer; b. Brescia, c. 1550; d. there, c. 1620. He was appointed maestro di cappella at the Brescia Cathedral in 1584 and remained there until c. 1590; from 1598 to 1604 he held a similar post at the Padua Cathedral. His madrigals were greatly appreciated.

WORKS: *Il primo libro de madrigali* for 5 Voices (Brescia, 1584); *Il primo libro de madrigali* for 6 Voices (Venice, 1585); *Madrigali spirituali* for 3 Voices (Brescia, 1585).—NS/LK/DM

Berté, Heinrich, Hungarian composer; b. Galgócz, May 8, 1857; d. Perchtoldsdorf, near Vienna, Aug. 23, 1924. He was a student in Vienna of Hellmesberger,

Fuchs, and Bruckner, and in Paris of Delibes. He began his career composing mainly ballets, but from 1904 he devoted much time to operettas. While success eluded him as a composer of original scores, he achieved phenomenal success with the Schubert pasticcio *Das Dreimäderlhaus* (Vienna, Jan. 15, 1916). It subsequently was heard all over the world in tr. as *Lilac Time, Blossom Time, Chanson d'amour,* etc. His nephew, Emil Berté (b. Vienna, Dec. 6, 1898; d. there, Jan. 17, 1968), was also a composer. He prepared the Schubert pasticcio *Der Musikus von Lichtenthal* (Vienna, March 30, 1928). His original scores for the theater included *Musik in Mai* (Vienna, May 13, 1927), *Steppenkinder* (Augsburg, Dec. 15, 1929), *Das Kaiserliebchen* (Vienna, Jan. 4, 1930), and *Melodie aus Wien* (Linz, Oct. 22, 1955).

WORKS: DRAMATIC: Musical Theater: *Bureau Malicorne* (Baden bei Wien, Feb. 22, 1887); *Die Schneeflocke* (Prague, Oct. 4, 1896); *Der neue Burgermeister* (Vienna, Jan. 8, 1904); *Die Millionenbraut* (Munich, April 3, 1904); *Der Stadtregent* (Munich, April 1, 1905); *Der schöne Gardist* (Breslau, Oct. 12, 1907); *Der kleine Chevalier* (Dresden, Nov. 30, 1907); *Die Wunderquelle* (Holle, Nov. 1, 1908); *Der Glücksnarr* (Vienna, Nov. 7, 1908); *Der erste Kuss* (Hamburg, Nov. 14, 1909); *Kreolenblut* (Hamburg, Dec. 25, 1910); *Der Märchenprinz* (Hannover, Feb. 28, 1914); *Das Dreimäderlhaus* (Vienna, Jan. 15, 1916); *Tavasz es szerelem* or *Lenz und Liebe* (Budapest, Sept. 15, 1917); *Die drei Kavaliere* (Hamburg, Nov. 5, 1919); *Kulissengeheimnisse* (Hamburg, Jan. 28, 1920).—NS/LK/DM

Berteau, Martin, famous French cellist; b. c. 1700; d. Angers, Jan. 23, 1771. He studied the bass viol with Kozecz in Germany, then took up the cello, achieving mastery of its technique. He is regarded as the protagonist of the French school of cello playing. He also composed a number of effective pieces for cello.
—NS/LK/DM

Bertheaume, Isidore, French violinist; b. Paris, c. 1752; d. St. Petersburg, March 20, 1802. A precocious musician, he joined the orch. of the Paris Opéra in 1767 and served there until 1769 and again from 1775 to 1781. He conducted the Concert Spirituel during the Revolution (1789–91), then left France and went to Germany. In 1801 he emigrated to Russia, where he served as first violinist in the Imperial Orch. in St. Petersburg. He composed 2 syms. concertantes for 2 Violins, 6 sonatas for Clavecin, with Violin, violin concertos, and other works for violin.—NS/LK/DM

Berti, Carlo, Italian composer and organist; b. probably in Florence, c. 1555; d. Mantua, before Sept. 2, 1602. He became a novice in the Servite order at Ss. Annunziata in Florence (1577), and was ordained at the convent of the order in 1580. In 1592 he became maestro di cappella at Ss. Annunziata, remaining there until 1598. He went to Mantua in 1601. Only 3 books of his sacred music are extant, all publ. in Venice (1592, 1593, 1596).

BIBL.: D. Nutter, *The Life and Works of C. B.* (diss., Rosary Coll., 1970).—NS/LK/DM

Berti, Giovanni Pietro, Italian singer, organist, and composer; d. Venice, 1638. He was a tenor in the choir of S. Marco in Venice. He was named second organist there in 1624, and remained at that post until his death. His songs, particularly his strophic arias, are of considerable historical importance; 56 songs for solo voice and continuo are extant.

BIBL.: D. Nutter, *The Life and Works of C. B.* (diss., Rosary Coll., 1970).—**NS/LK/DM**

Bertin, Louise (-Angélique), French composer; b. Les Roches, near Paris, Feb. 15, 1805; d. Paris, April 26, 1877. She was a pupil of Fétis. She composed the operas *Guy Mannering* (Les Roches, Aug. 25, 1825), *Le Loup-garou* (Paris, March 10, 1827), *Fausto* (Paris, March 7, 1831), and *La Esmeralda* (to a libretto adapted by Victor Hugo from his novel *Notre-Dame de Paris*; Paris, Nov. 14, 1836). She also wrote a number of instrumental works, of which *6 Ballades* for Piano was publ. —**NS/LK/DM**

Bertin de la Doué, Thomas, French composer; b. Paris, c. 1680; d. there, 1745. He was maître de musique to the Princess of Orléans, then held the post of organist at the Théatins church in Paris. He also served as violinist and keyboard musician with the Paris Opéra orch. (1714–34). As a composer, he was best known for his opera- ballet *Ajax* (Paris, April 30, 1716).—**NS/LK/DM**

Bertini, (Benoît-) Auguste, French pianist, brother of **Henri (-Jérôme) Bertini;** b. Lyons, June 5, 1780; d. London, 1830. He took lessons with Clementi in London from 1793 to 1799. In 1806 he returned to Paris, where he publ. a didactic tract, *Stigmatographie, ou L'Art d'écrire avec des points, suivie de la mélographie, nouvel art de noter la musique* (Paris, 1812), in which he claimed to simplify musical notation. In London he publ., in 1830, another didactic pamphlet, extravagantly titled *New System for Learning and acquiring extraordinary facility on all musical instruments* (3rd ed., 1849).—**NS/LK/DM**

Bertini, Domenico, Italian composer and pedagogue; b. Lucca, June 26, 1829; d. Florence, Sept. 7, 1890. He studied at the Lucca Music School, and later with Michele Puccini. In 1857 he was director of the music inst. and maestro di cappella at Massa Carrara. He settled in Florence (1862) as a singing teacher and music critic; became director of the Cherubini Soc. He contributed to musical periodicals, including *Boccherini* of Florence and *La Scena* of Venice; also wrote a *Compendio de' principi di musica, secondo un nuovo sistema* (1866). He composed 2 operas, masses and other sacred pieces, and chamber music.—**NS/LK/DM**

Bertini, Gary, Russian-born Israeli conductor and composer; b. Brichevo, May 1, 1927. He was taken to Palestine as a child and began violin lessons at age 16. After studies at the Milan Cons. (diploma, 1948), he continued his training with Seter and Singer at the Tel Aviv Coll. of Music (diploma, 1951). He then went to Paris, where he studied at the Cons. and the École Normale de Musique, his principal mentors in composition being Honegger, Messiaen, and Boulanger. He

also studied musicology at the Sorbonne with Chailley. Returning to Israel in 1954, he was music director of the Rinat (later Israel Chamber) Choir (1955–72), the Israel Chamber Ensemble Orch. (1965–75), and the Jerusalem Sym. Orch. (1977–86). He also served as principal guest conductor of the Scottish National Orch. in Glasgow (1971–81) and as artistic advisor of the Israel Festival (1976–83) and of the Detroit Sym. Orch. (1981–83). From 1983 to 1991 he was chief conductor of the Cologne Radio Sym. Orch. He also was Intendant and Generalmusikdirektor of the Frankfurt am Main Opera from 1987 to 1991, concurrently serving as chief conductor of its Museumgesellschaft concerts. In 1994 he became artistic director of the New Israeli Opera in Tel Aviv. In 1997 he became music director of the Rome Opera. He also was music director of the Tokyo Metropolitan Sym. Orch. from 1998. Bertini has become well known for conducting 20th-century scores, including many first performances. As a composer, he has written stage music, incidental scores, orch. works, chamber music, and songs. In 1978 he was awarded the Israel State Prize for composition.—**NS/LK/DM**

Bertini, Giuseppe, Italian musicographer, son of **Salvatore Bertini;** b. Palermo, Jan. 20, 1759; d. there, March 15, 1852. He studied at the Scuole Pie degli Scolopi, and later entered the priesthood without abandoning his work in musical lexicography. He compiled the *Dizionario storico-critico degli scrittori di musica* (Palermo, 1814–15), which is still of some value for its entries on obscure Italian musicians.—**NS/LK/DM**

Bertini, Henri (-Jérôme), known as "Bertini le jeune," pianist and composer, brother of **August (Benoît) Bertini;** b. London, Oct. 28, 1798; d. Meylau, near Grenoble, Oct. 1, 1876. When 6 months old, he was taken to Paris, where he was taught music by his father and his elder brother. At age 12 he made a concert tour through the Netherlands and Germany; then studied in Paris and Great Britain. He lived in Paris as a concert pianist from 1821 to 1859, when he retired to his estate at Meylau. He wrote valuable technical studies, some of which have been publ. in eds. by G. Buonamici and by Riemann; also arranged Bach's *48 Preludes and Fugues* for Piano, Four-Hands. He composed much chamber music and many piano pieces.—**NS/LK/DM**

Bertini, Salvatore, Italian composer, father of **Giuseppe Bertini;** b. Palermo, 1721; d. there, Dec. 16, 1794. He studied in Palermo before entering the Jesuit Coll. in Naples; subsequently took music courses with Fago and Leo at the Turchini Cons. In 1748 he was appointed substitute maestro di cappella at the Cappella Palatina in Palermo; was named maestro there in 1778. He composed mostly for the church.—**NS/LK/DM**

Bertinotti (-Radicati), Teresa, Italian soprano; b. Savigliano, 1776; d. Bologna, Feb. 12, 1854. She studied with La Barbiera in Naples. She married the singer Felice Radicati in 1801, and toured with him in a vocal duo, visiting Austria and Germany. She sang at the King's Theatre in London from 1810 to 1812, then was in Lisbon from 1812 to 1814. Upon her husband's death in 1820, she retired from the stage and devoted herself to teaching voice.—NS/LK/DM

Bertoldo, Sperindio (Sper'in Dio), Italian organist and composer; b. Modena, c. 1530; d. Padua, Aug. 13, 1570. He served as chief organist at the Cathedral of Padua. His surviving compositions include 2 books of madrigals in 5 Voices, publ. in Venice (book 1, 1561; book 2, 1562); the first book includes an *Echo a 6 voci* and a *Dialogo a 8 voci*. Several other madrigals are included in a collection by Cipriano and Annibale (Venice, 1561). Bertoldo's *Toccate, ricercari e canzoni francese...per sonar d'organo* (Venice, 1591) was publ. posth. Two ricercari for Organ are included in L. Torchi, *L'Arte musicale in Italia* (vol. III).—NS/LK/DM

Bertolli, Francesca, Italian contralto; d. Bologna, Jan. 9, 1767. She sang in Bologna in 1728, then was engaged by Handel in 1729 for his Royal Academy of Music operatic performances in London at the King's Theatre. In 1733 she left Handel's company to join his rival's establishment, the Opera of the Nobility. In 1736–37 she was again a member of Handel's company, after which she returned to Italy and soon retired. She was noted for her performances of male roles in lieu of castrati.—NS/LK/DM

Berton, Henri-Montan, French conductor and composer, son of **Pierre-Montan Berton;** b. Paris, Sept. 17, 1767; d. there, April 22, 1844. He was a pupil of Rey and Sacchini. In 1782 he joined the orch. of the Paris Opéra as a violinist, and in 1795 he was appointed to the staff of the Paris Cons., where, in 1818, he succeeded Méhul as prof. of composition. From 1807 to 1809 he conducted at the Opéra-Bouffe, and in 1809 became chorus master at the Paris Opéra. In 1815 he was elected a member of the French Academy. He wrote 47 operas, of which the most successful were *Montano et Stéphanie* (1799), *Le Délire* (1799), and *Aline, reine de Colconde* (1803); also several oratorios, 8 cantatas, and 4 ballets.

BIBL.: D. Raoul-Rochette, *Notice historique sur la vie et les ouvrages de M. B.* (Paris, 1846); H. Blanchard, *H.-M. B.* (Paris, 1839).—NS/LK/DM

Berton, Pierre-Montan, French tenor, conductor, and composer, father of **Henri-Montan Berton;** b. Maubert-Fontaines, Ardennes, Jan. 7, 1727; d. Paris, May 14, 1780. He studied organ, harpsichord, and composition at the Senlis Cathedral choir school, and then completed his training in Paris. After singing at the Paris Opéra and in Marseilles, he became director of the Bordeaux Grand Théâtre. In 1755 he returned to Paris as conductor of the Opéra, serving as its general director (1775–78). Under his leadership, the Paris Opéra orch. attained notable distinction. Berton was an adept arranger of the operas of Lully, Rameau, and Gluck, in which he interpolated his own music.

WORKS: DRAMATIC: Opera-ballet: *Deucalion et Pyrrha* (Paris, Sept. 30, 1755). **Opera:** *Silvie* (Fontainebleau, Oct. 17, 1765); *Érosine* (Paris, Aug. 29, 1766); *Théonis,*

ou Le toucher (Paris, Oct. 11, 1767; in collaboration with Trial); *Adèle de Ponthieu* (Paris, Dec. 1, 1772; in collaboration with Laborde); *Linus* (unfinished). **VOCAL:** A cantata, a motet, and songs.—NS/LK/DM

Bertoni, Ferdinando (Gioseffo), esteemed Italian composer, organist, and pedagogue; b. Salò, near Venice, Aug. 15, 1725; d. Desenzano, Dec. 1, 1813. He was a student of Padre Martini in Bologna. He settled in Venice, where he successfully brought out his first opera in 1745, and soon established an enviable reputation as a composer for the theater. In 1752 he was appointed to the post of first organist at San Marco, where he succeeded Galuppi as maestro di cappella in 1785. He also was maestro di cappella at the Mendicanti (1757–97). As a teacher, he numbered among his pupils Calegari, Mayr, and Pacchierotti. In 1773 he was elected a member of the Accademia Filarmonica in Bologna, and in 1804 of the Accademia degli Unanimi in Salò. Bertoni was one of the leading Venetian opera composers of his day. Many of his operas were performed abroad, including several during his two visits to London (1778–81; 1781–83). He also was admired for his sacred music.

WORKS: DRAMATIC (all first perf. in Venice unless otherwise given): **Comic Opera:** *La vedova accorta* (Carnival 1745); *La pescatrici* (Dec. 26, 1751); *I bagni d'Abano* (Feb. 1753; in collaboration with Galuppi); *La moda* (Carnival 1754); *La vicende amorose* (1760); *La bella Girometta* (1761); *L'ingannatore ingannato* (Carnival 1764); *L'anello incantato* (1771); *L'orfane svizzere* (Livorno, Carnival 1774); *La governante* (London, May 15, 1779); *Il duca di Atene* (London, May 9, 1780); *Il convito, or The Banquet* (London, Nov. 2, 1782). **Opere Serie:** *Il Cajetto* (Carnival 1746); *Orazio e Curiazio* (1746); *Armida* (Dec. 26, 1746); *Ipermestra* (Genoa, Carnival 1748); *Antigono* (1752); *Ginevra* (1753); *Sesostri* (Turin, Dec. 26, 1754); *Antigona* (Genoa, Carnival 1756); *Lucio Vero* (Turin, Carnival 1757); *Il Vologeso* (Padua, 1759); *Ifigenia in Aulide* (Turin, 1762); *Achille in Sciro* (Carnival 1764); *Il Bajazetto* (Parma, May 3, 1765); *Olimpiade* (Carnival 1765); *Tancredi* (Turin, Dec. 26, 1766); *Ezio* (Carnival 1767); *Semiramide riconosciuta* (Naples, May 30, 1767); *Scipione nelle Spagne* (Milan, Jan. 30, 1768); *Alessandro nell'Indie* (Genoa, 1769); *Il trionfo di Clelia* (Padua, June 10, 1769); *Eurione* (Udine, Aug. 1770); *Decebalo* (Treviso, Oct. 1770); *Andromaca* (Dec. 26, 1771); *Narale* (May 25, 1774); *Aristo e Temira* (Jan. 3, 1776); *Orfeo ed Euridice* (Jan. 3, 1776); *Creonte* (Modena, Jan. 27, 1776); *Artaserse* (Forlì, 1776); *Telemaco ed Eurice nell'isola di Calipso* (Dec. 26, 1776); *Medonte* (Turin, Dec. 26, 1777); *Quinto Fabio* (Milan, Jan. 31, 1778); *Demofoonte* (London, Nov. 28, 1778); *Armida abbandonata* (Dec. 26, 1780); *Cago Mario* (1781); *Cimene* (London, Jan. 7, 1783); *Eumene* (Dec. 26, 1783); *Nitteti* (Feb. 6, 1789); *Angelica e Medoro* (Carnival 1791). **Other:** 18 occasional dramatic pieces and some 50 oratorios. **INSTRUMENTAL:** Sinfonias; string quartets; trio sonatas; harpsichord sonatas. **SACRED VOCAL:** Some 50 oratorios; several masses and mass movements; Requiem; 87 motets; more than 40 Psalms and Psalm verses; 17 hymns and canticles; 9 marian antiphons.

BIBL.: G. Bustico, *Per la storia del melodramma: F. B. e Rubinelli* (Salò, 1913); I. Haas, *F. B.: Leben und Instrumentalwerk* (Vienna, 1958).—NS/LK/DM

Bertouch, Georg von, German-born Norwegian composer and soldier; b. Helmershausen, June 19, 1668;

d. Christiania, Sept. 14, 1743. After a sojourn in Italy, he joined the Danish army and spent his last years as commander of Akershus Castle in Christiania. Among his works are sacred cantatas and 24 sonatas, the latter greatly influenced by Bach's 48 Preludes and Fugues. —LK/DM

Bertouille, Gérard, Belgian composer; b. Tournai, May 26, 1898; d. Brussels, Dec. 12, 1981. He studied with Absil, Bourguignon, Marsick, and Souris. His music followed a median path in a restrained modern idiom.

WORKS: ORCH.: *Ouverture* (1937); *Prélude et Fugue* (1939); Sinfonietta (1942); 2 violin concertos (1942, 1970); 2 piano concertos (1946, 1953); 2 trumpet concertos (1946, 1973); 3 syms. (1947, 1955, 1977); *Sinfonia da Requiem* (1957); *Fantaisie-Passacaille* (1963); *Fantaisie Lyrique* (1969); Concerto for Strings (1974); Concerto for Flute, Oboe, and Strings (1977); *Ouverture romantique* for Band (1978). CHAMBER: 5 violin sonatas (1936, 1942, 1946, 1953, 1971); 6 string quartets (1939, 1941, 1942, 1953, 1953, 1957); 2 string trios (1943, 1945); Quartet for Flute and String Trio (1948); Trio for 2 Violins and Piano (1955); Wind Quintet (1969); *Fantaisie* for Piano Quartet (1978); piano music, including 2 sonatas (1945, 1978). VOCAL: *Requiem des hommes d'aujourd'hui* (1950); *Les Tentations de St. Antoine,* choreographic poem for Mezzo-soprano, Baritone, and Orch. (1958–59); songs. —NS/LK/DM

Bertram, Theodor, German baritone; b. Stuttgart, Feb. 12, 1869; d. (suicide) Bayreuth, Nov. 24, 1907. He studied with his father, the baritone Heinrich Bertram, and made his debut as the Hermit in *Der Freischütz* in Ulm in 1889. He then sang at the Hamburg Opera (1891) and the Berlin Kroll Opera (1892), and was a member of the Munich Court Opera (1893–99). He made his Metropolitan Opera debut in N.Y. on Jan. 6, 1900, as the Flying Dutchman, remaining on the roster for a year. He also sang at Covent Garden, London (1900, 1903, 1907), and at Bayreuth (1901–06). He was married to the soprano **Fanny Moran-Olden;** following her death, he became despondent and hanged himself.—NS/LK/DM

Bertrand, Aline, notable French harpist; b. Paris, 1798; d. there, March 13, 1835. She studied at the Paris Cons. with Nadermann, then with Bochsa (1815), making her debut in 1820. She then toured Europe, winning special acclaim upon her appearance in Vienna (1828). She publ. *Fantaisie sur la Romance de Joseph* (on themes of Méhul's opera) for Harp, and various other arrangements.—NS/LK/DM

Bertrand, Antoine de, French composer; b. Fontanges, between 1530 and 1540; d. Toulouse, between 1580 and 1582. He settled in Toulouse about 1560, where he became associated with the Ronsardist poets. He later was influenced by the Jesuits.

WORKS: VOCAL: S e c u l a r : *Les amours de P. Ronsard* for 4 Voices (35 chansons; Paris, 1576; ed. in Monuments de la musique française au temps de la renaissance, IV-V, 1926); *Second livre des amours de P. de Ronsard* for 4 Voices (25 chansons; Paris, 1578; ed. in ibid., VI, 1927); *Tiers livre de chansons* for 4 Voices (24 chansons and 1 Italian madrigal; Paris, 1578; ed. in ibid., VII, 1927). S a c r e d : *Premier livre de sonets chrestiens mis en musique* for 4 Voices (Lyons, 1580); *Second livre de sonets*

chrestiens mis en musique for 4 Voices (Lyons, 1580); (27) *Airs spirituels contenant plusieurs hymnes et cantiques* for 4 to 5 Voices (Paris, 1582).

BIBL.: J. Vaccaro, *A. d. B.* (diss., Univ. of Tours, 1965). —NS/LK/DM

Berutti (originally, **Beruti**), **Arturo,** Argentine composer of Italian descent; b. San Juan, March 27, 1862; d. Buenos Aires, Jan. 3, 1938. He received his early training in music with his father; then went to Leipzig, where he became a student of Jadassohn. He subsequently lived in Italy, where he composed 3 operas: *La Vendetta* (Vercelli, May 21, 1892), *Evangelina* (Milan, Sept. 19, 1893), and *Taras Bulba* (Turin, March 9, 1895). Returning to Argentina in 1896, he premiered the following operas in Buenos Aires: *Pampa* (July 27, 1897), *Yupanki* (July 25, 1899), *Khrise* (June 21, 1902), *Horrida Nox* (the opera by a native Argentine composer, written to a Spanish libretto, to be produced in Argentina; July 7, 1908), and *Los Heroes* (Aug. 23, 1919).—NS/LK/DM

Berwald, Franz (Adolf), outstanding Swedish composer, cousin of **Johan Fredrik Berwald;** b. Stockholm, July 23, 1796; d. there, April 3, 1868. His father, Christian Friedrich Berwald (1740–1825), was a German musician who studied with Franz Benda and settled in Stockholm in the 1770s as a member of the orch. of the Royal Chapel. Franz received training in violin from his father and cousin, and in composition from J.B.E. du Puy. He was a violinist and violist in the orch. of the Royal Chapel in Stockholm (1812–28). In 1819 he toured Finland with his brother, Christian August Berwald, and Russia. In 1829 he went to Berlin and in 1835 opened an orthopedic establishment, which soon flourished. In 1841 he went to Vienna, where he obtained short-lived success as a composer with his symphonic poems. He then returned to Stockholm and secured a foothold as a composer with his operettas and cantatas. On Dec. 2, 1843, his cousin conducted the premiere of his *Sinfonie sérieuse* (his only acknowledged sym. performed in his lifetime), but poor execution of the score did little to further his cause. In 1846 he returned to Vienna, where Jenny Lind sang in his stage cantata *Ein ländliches Verlobungfest in Schweden* at the Theater an der Wien. In 1847 he was elected an honorary member of the Salzburg Mozarteum. In 1849 he returned to his homeland in hopes of securing the position of either conductor of the Royal Opera in Stockholm or director of music in Uppsala. Hopes dashed, he became manager of a glassworks in Sandö, Ångermanland (1850–58) and part owner of a sawmill (1853), and briefly operated a brick factory. Berwald was shunned by the Swedish musical establishment (which he disdained), and his extraordinary gifts as a composer went almost totally unrecognized in his lifetime. Finally, in 1864, he was made a member of the Swedish Royal Academy of Music in Stockholm. In the last year of his life he was named to its composition chair, only to be unseated, however briefly, on a second vote demanded by his enemies. Berwald's masterpiece is his *Sinfonie singulière* (1845), a singular work of notable distinction, which was not performed until 70 years after its composition. He also wrote 3 other fine syms. and a number of worthy chamber music pieces. His output reveals the influence of the German Romantic school in general, but with an unmistakably individual voice.

WORKS: DRAMATIC (all are operas unless otherwise given): *Gustaf Wasa* (unfinished; concert perf. of Act 1, Stockholm, Feb. 12, 1828; scene and aria from Act 2, Stockholm, Nov. 18, 1828); *Cecilia* (1829; not extant); *Leonida* (1829; only fragments extant); *Der Verräter* (1830; not extant); *Donna Isabella* (1830; not extant); *Trubaduren* (1830; not extant); *Estrella da Soria* (1841, 1848; rev. version, Stockholm, April 9, 1862); *Jag går i kloster*, operetta (excerpts, Stockholm, Dec. 2, 1843); *Modehandlerskan*, operetta (excerpts, Stockholm, March 26, 1845; in collaboration with others); *Slottet Lochleven* (1863; not extant); *Drottningen av Golconda* (1864–65; Stockholm, April 3, 1968). **ORCH.:** Sym. in A major (1820; Stockholm, March 3, 1821; discarded by Berwald; only fragments extant); *Sinfonie sérieuse* (No. 1) in G minor (1842; Stockholm, Dec. 2, 1843); *Sinfonie capricieuse* (No. 2) in D major (1842; perf. ed. by Ernst Ellberg, Stockholm, Jan. 9, 1914; critical ed. by Nils Castegren, 1968); *Sinfonie singulière* (No. 3) in C major (1845; Stockholm, Jan. 10, 1905); *Sinfonie* in E-flat major ("No. 4," or *Sinfonie naïve*, the latter title unauthorized; 1845; Stockholm, April 9, 1878); Violin Concerto (Stockholm, March 3, 1821); *Concertstück* for Bassoon and Orch. (1827); Piano Concerto (transcription for 2 pianos by Gustaf Heintze, Stockholm, Dec. 14, 1904; with orch., Stockholm, April 27, 1908). **Symphonic Poems:** *Elfenspiel and Erinnerung an die norwegischen Alpen* (Vienna, March 6, 1842); *Ernste und heitere Grillen* (Stockholm, May 19, 1842); *Bayaderen-Fest* (Stockholm, Dec. 6, 1842); *Wettlauf* (1842). **CHAMBER:** 2 piano quintets; 3 string quartets; 5 piano trios; Septet. **OTHER:** Vocal music.

BIBL.: A. Hillman, *F. B.* (Stockholm, 1920); R. Layton, *B.* (Stockholm, 1956; Eng. tr., London, 1959); I. Bengtsson, N. Castegren, and E. Lömans, eds., *F. B.: Die Dokumente seines Lebens* (Kassel, 1979); I. Andersson, *F. B.* (Stockholm, 1996). **—NS/LK/DM**

Berwald, Johan Fredrik (Johann Friedrich), Swedish violinist and composer, cousin of **Franz (Adolf) Berwald;** b. Stockholm, Dec. 4, 1787; d. there, Aug. 26, 1861. He was a member of a musical family of German nationality that settled in Sweden. A precocious musician, he played the violin in public at the age of 5; took lessons in composition with Abbé Vogler during the latter's stay in Sweden. At 16 he went to St. Petersburg and served as concertmaster in the Russian Imperial Court Orch. (1803–12). Returning to Sweden, he was appointed chamber musician to the King of Sweden, a post he held from 1815 until 1849; also conducted (from 1819) the Royal Orch. in Stockholm. He wrote his first sym. when he was 9 years old, but in his mature years he devoted himself mainly to theatrical productions. One of his light operas, *L'Héroïne de l'amour*, to a French libretto, was produced in St. Petersburg in 1811. In Stockholm he was also active as a teacher; among his pupils was his cousin Franz Berwald.**—NS/LK/DM**

Besanzoni, Gabriella, Italian mezzo-soprano; b. Rome, Sept. 20, 1888; d. there, June 6, 1962. She studied with Hilde Brizzi and Alessandro Maggi. In 1911 she made her operatic debut as a soprano in the role of Adalgisa in Viterbo; in 1913 she sang in Rome as Ulrica; appeared at the Teatro Colón in Buenos Aires from 1918. On Nov. 19, 1919, she made her Metropolitan Opera debut in N.Y. as Amneris, singing there for only one season. From 1923 to 1932 she appeared at Milan's La Scala, making her farewell appearance in Rome in 1939 in her finest role, Carmen. Among her other roles were Isabella, Cenerentola, Dalila, and Mignon.**—NS/LK/DM**

Besard, Jean-Baptiste, French lutenist, anthologist, music theorist, and composer; b. Besançon, c. 1567; d. after 1617. He was educated at the Univ. of Dôle (Licentiate and Doctor of Laws, 1587), and then pursued the study of medicine in Rome, where he also claimed to have studied with Lorenzini. In 1613 he inherited letters of nobility from his father. He was mainly active in the fields of law and medicine, but he also taught lute and composed. He publ. an exhaustive anthology, *Thesaurus harmonicus* (10 vols., Cologne, 1603), which includes works by some 21 composers, including some of his own. It also includes his valuable treatise on lute playing, *De modo in testudine libellus*, which was tr. into Eng. in R. Dowland's *Varietie of Lute Lessons* (London, 1610). He also brought out a second anthology, *Novus partus, sive Concertationes musicae* (Augsburg, 1617), which includes works by some 12 composers, including several of his own. It also includes a rev. ed. of his treatise on lute playing as *Ad artem testudinis*, which appeared in a Ger. tr. as *Isagoge in artem testudinariam* (Augsburg, 1617).

BIBL.: J. Garton, *J.-B. B.'s Thesaurus harmonicus* (diss., Ind. Univ., 1952); J. Sutton, *J.-B.˙B.'s Novus partus of 1617* (diss., Univ. of Rochester, 1962).**—NS/LK/DM**

Besler, Samuel, German composer; b. Brieg, Silesia, Dec. 15, 1574; d. Breslau, July 19, 1625. He settled in Breslau, where he was Kantor of St. Bernhard by 1602 and rector of its school by 1609. He was held in high esteem in Breslau, where he composed much sacred music. Among his works were the St. Mark and St. Luke Passions (1612) and large works for double choir, which were composed for state occasions. He also wrote collections of carols and graces (1602–15).**—NS/LK/DM**

Besozzi, Alessandro, celebrated Italian oboist; b. Parma, July 22, 1702; d. Turin, July 26, 1793. He was a musician at the ducal chapel in Parma (1728–31). He made concert tours with his brother, Girolamo (see 3 below), appearing with him in Paris in 1735; he then lived in Turin. He publ. numerous trio sonatas for Flute, Violin, and Cello, 6 violin sonatas (with Basso Continuo), etc. Other members of the family who specialized in wind instruments were: **(1) Antonio Besozzi,** oboist, nephew of Alessandro (b. Parma, 1714; d. Turin, 1781); **(2) Carlo Besozzi,** oboist, son of Antonio (b. Naples, c. 1738; d. Dresden, March 22, 1791); played in the Dresden orch. (1754); wrote several oboe concertos; **(3) Girolamo Besozzi,** bassoonist, brother of Alessandro (b. Parma, April 17, 1704; d. Turin, 1778); **(4) Gaetano Besozzi,** oboist, nephew of Alessandro (b. Parma, 1727; d. London, 1794); **(5) Girolamo Besozzi,** oboist, son of Gaetano (b. Naples, c. 1750; d. Paris, 1785); **(6) Henri Besozzi,** flutist, son of Girolamo; played at the Opéra-

Comique; **(7) Louis-Désiré,** son of Henri (b. Versailles, April 3, 1814; d. Paris, Nov. 11, 1879), a student of Le Sueur and Barbereau; he won the Prix de Rome in 1837, defeating Gounod.—**NS/LK/DM**

Bessaraboff, Nicholas (actually, **Nikolai**), Russian-born American writer on music; b. Voronezh, Feb. 12, 1894; d. N.Y., Nov. 10, 1973. He was trained as a mechanical engineer and a draftsman, but he also played the horn and became interested in the mechanics and acoustics of musical instruments. After the completion of his studies at the polytechnical inst. in St. Petersburg, he was sent in 1915 with a group of other Russian engineers to the U.S. in order to expedite the shipping of American military equipment for the Russian armed forces during World War I. He remained in the U.S. after the Russian Revolution of 1917, becoming a naturalized American citizen in 1927. He worked as a draftsman in Rochester, N.Y., at the same time doing extensive reading on the subject of musical instruments. In 1931 he moved to Boston, where he began cataloguing the collection of instruments in the Boston Museum of Fine Arts. In 1941 he publ. his magnum opus, *Ancient European Musical Instruments, An Organological Study of the Musical Instruments in the Leslie Lindsey Mason Collection at the Museum of Fine Arts, Boston.* In 1945 he officially changed his name to Nicholas Bessaraboff Bodley, adopting the maiden name of his American wife, Virginia Bodley.—**NS/LK/DM**

Besseler, Heinrich, eminent German musicologist; b. Dortmund-Hörde, April 2, 1900; d. Leipzig, July 25, 1969. He was a pupil of Gurlitt at the Univ. of Freiburg im Breisgau (Ph.D., 1923, with the diss. *Beiträge zur Stilgeschichte der deutschen Suite im 17. Jahrhundert;* Habilitationsschrift, 1925, *Die Motettenkomposition von Petrus de Cruce bis Philipp von Vitry (ca. 1250–1350),* Adler at the Univ. of Vienna, and Ludwig at the Univ. of Göttingen. He was a reader at the Univ. of Heidelberg (1928–48) and then prof. of musicology at the univs. of Jena (1948–56) and Leipzig (1956–65). Besseler was a distinguished authority on the music of the Middle Ages and the Renaissance. He wrote the important and influential study *Die Musik des Mittelalters und der Renaissance* (Potsdam, 1931), contributed valuable articles to various music journals and to *Die Musik in Geschichte und Gegenwart,* and ed. the collected works of Dufay, Ockeghem, and others of their era. His other writings include *Johann Sebastian Bach* (Stuttgart, 1935; 2nd ed., 1955); *Zum Problem der Tenorgeige* (Heidelberg, 1949); *Bourdon und Fauxbourdon: Studien zum Ursprung der niederländischen Musik* (Leipzig, 1950); *Fünf echte Bildnisse Johann Sebastian Bachs* (Kassel, 1956); with M. Schneider, *Musikgeschichte in Bildern* (Leipzig, 1961–68; W. Bachmann, co.-ed., 1968–69).

BIBL.: *Festschrift H. B. zum 60. geburtstag* (Leipzig, 1961). —**NS/LK/DM**

Best, Matthew, English conductor and bass; b. Farnborough, Feb. 6, 1957. He was a choral scholar at King's Coll., Cambridge (M.A.), and studied with Otakar Kraus, at the National Opera Studio (1978–80), and with Robert Lloyd and Patrick Maguigan. In 1973 he founded the Corydon Singers, which he subsequently conducted in an expansive repertoire. In 1978 he made his operatic debut as Seneca in Monteverdi's *L'incoronazione di Poppea* with the Cambridge Univ. Opera Soc. From 1980 to 1986 he was a member of the Royal Opera at London's Covent Garden. In 1982 he won the Kathleen Ferrier Prize. From 1998 he served as principal conductor of the Hanover Band in Hove, Sussex. His appearances as a bass took him to London, Glyndebourne, Leeds, Cardiff, Frankfurt am Main, Salzburg, and other music centers. As a conductor, he led various choral performances and appeared as a guest conductor with many orchs.—**NS/LK/DM**

Best, W(illiam) T(homas), eminent English organist; b. Carlisle, Aug. 13, 1826; d. Liverpool, May 10, 1897. He studied organ in Liverpool, and held various posts as a church organist in Liverpool and London. At his numerous concerts he introduced arrangements of symphonic works, thus enabling his audiences to hear classical works in a musicianly manner at a time when orch. concerts were scarce. His own works, popular in type, though classical in form, included sonatas, preludes, fugues, concert studies, etc. for organ. He publ. *Handel Album* (20 vols.), *Arrangements from the Scores of the Great Masters* (5 vols.), *Modern School for the Organ* (1853), *The Art of Organ Playing* (1870), etc.

BIBL.: J. Mewburn Levien, *Impressions of W.T. B.* (London, 1942).—**NS/LK/DM**

Bethune (Green), Thomas, blind black American pianist and composer, known as **Blind Tom**; b. Columbus, Ga., May 25, 1849; d. Hoboken, N.J., June 13, 1908. He was born blind in slavery and was purchased with his parents in 1850 by the Columbus journalist, lawyer, and politician James N. Bethune. At the age of 4, he began studying music with his master's daughter. In 1857 he was taken on his first tour of Ga. by his master. At 9, he was "leased" to the Savannah planter Perry Oliver, who took him on a major tour of the slave states highlighted by a command performance at Willard Hall in Washington, D.C. In 1861 Blind Tom was returned to Bethune, who took him on tours of the South to raise funds for the Confederate cause. After the close of the Civil War in 1865, Bethune won a guardianship trial over Blind Tom. Bethune then took him to Europe with W.P. Howard serving as his music tutor. During his European sojourn, Blind Tom won testimonials from Charles Hallé, Ignaz Moscheles et al. Bethune then took him on various tours of the U.S. and Canada. He also received additional music training from Joseph Poznanski in N.Y. Bethune's son's widow won legal custody of Blind Tom in 1887, and subsequently oversaw his tours. He made his last appearance on the vaudeville circuit in 1905. In his heyday, a typical Blind Tom appearance consisted of performances of works by Bach, Beethoven, Chopin, Liszt, and other masters, improvisational feats, and some of his own works. His output included over 100 piano pieces in a salon manner, among them *The Rainstorm* (1865), *The Battle of Manassas* (1866), *March Timpani* (1880), *Blind Tom's Mazurka* (1888), and *Grand March Resurrection* (1901). He also wrote vocal pieces.

BIBL.: G. Southall, *B. T.: The Post-Civil War Enslavement of a Black Musical Genius* (Minneapolis, 1979); idem, *The Continuing "Enslavement" of B. T., 1865–1887* (Minneapolis, 1982). —**NS/LK/DM**

Bettinelli, Bruno, respected Italian composer and teacher; b. Milan, June 4, 1913. He studied harmony and counterpoint with Paribeni and orchestration with Bossi at the Milan Cons., taking diplomas in piano in 1931 and in composition and conducting in 1937; then pursued advanced training in composition with Frazzi at the Accademia Musicale Chigiana in Siena (1940). In 1941 he joined the faculty of the Milan Cons., where he was a prof. of composition from 1957 until his retirement in 1979. In 1961 he was made a member of the Accademia di Santa Cecilia in Rome and of the Accademia di Luigi Cherubini in Florence. In his extensive output, he reveals particular skill in instrumental writing which reflects the best in the central European tradition with infusions of contemporary techniques, including the 12–tone method.

WORKS: O p e r a : *Il pozzo e il pendolo* (1957; Bergamo, Oct. 24, 1967); *La Smorfia* (Como, Sept. 30, 1959); *Count Down* (1969; Milan, March 26, 1970). **ORCH.:** *Movimento sinfonico* Nos. 1 (1938) and 2 (1945); *Sinfonia da camera* (1938); *Corale ostinato* (1938); *Due invenzioni* for Strings (1939); 7 syms. (1939; 1943; 1946; *Sinfonia breve*, 1954; 1975; 1976; 1978); 4 concertos (1940, 1951, 1964, 1988); *Fantasia concertante* for String Quartet and Orch. (1949); 2 piano concertos (1953, 1968); *Musica* for Strings (1958); *Preludio elegiaco* (1959); *Episodi* (1961); Concerto for 2 Pianos and Orch. (1962); *Varianti* (1970); *Musica per 12* (1973); *Studio* (1974); *Contrasti* (1979); *Divertimento* for Harpsichord and Orch. (1979); Concerto for Guitar, Strings, and Vibraphone (1981); Violin Concerto (1982–83); *Alternanze* (1983); *Omaggio a Stravinskij* for Chamber Orch. (1984); *Strutture* for Strings (1985); *Tre studi d'interpretazione* for Strings (1986). **CHAMBER:** 2 string quartets (1935, 1960); Cello Sonata (1951); *Improvvisazione* for Violin and Piano (1968); *Studio da concerto* for Clarinet (1971); Octet for 2 Flutes, Oboe, 2 Clarinets, 2 Bassoon, and Horn (1975); Violin Sonata (1980); Quintet for Flute, Oboe, Clarinet, Bassoon, and Horn (1984); *Ricercare a tre* for Piano, Clarinet, and Cello (1988); Trio for Violin, Cello, and Piano (1991); piano pieces; organ music; guitar pieces. **VOCAL:** *Messa di Requiem* (1942–43); *Cinque liriche di Montale* for Soprano and Chamber Ensemble (1948); *Sono una creatura*, cantata for Chorus and Orch. (1971); *In Nativitate Domini*, cantata for Soprano and Orch. (1982); *Terza Cantata* for Chorus and Orch. (1982–83); *Salmo IV*, cantata for Chorus and Orch. (1992); many other choral pieces and songs.

BIBL.: N. Castiglioni, *B. B.* (Milan, 1955); E. Gabellich, *Linguaggio Musicale di B. B.* (Milan, 1989).—**NS/LK/DM**

Bettoni, Vincenzo, Italian bass; b. Melegnano, July 1, 1881; d. there, Nov. 4, 1954. He made his operatic debut as Silva in 1902 in Pinerolo. In 1905 he made his first appearance at Milan's La Scala, where he was regularly engaged from 1926 to 1940. He also sang at the Teatro Colón in Buenos Aires from 1910. In 1923 he appeared as Gurnemanz in the first Spanish mounting of *Parsifal* in Barcelona. In 1934 he sang Don Alfonso in

the first season of the Glyndebourne Festival. He first appeared at London's Covent Garden in 1935. Bettoni was especially admired for his portrayals of roles in Rossini's operas.—**NS/LK/DM**

Betts, Lorne, Canadian composer, music critic, and teacher; b. Winnipeg, Aug. 2, 1918; d. Hamilton, Ontario, Aug. 5, 1985. He studied piano, organ, and theory in Winnipeg, and was a pupil of Weinzweig in Toronto (1947–53) before settling in Hamilton, Ontario.

WORKS: DRAMATIC: O p e r a : *Riders to the Sea* (1955); *The Woodcarver's Wife* (1960). **ORCH.:** *Sinfonietta* (1952); 2 syms. (1954, 1961); 2 piano concertos (1955, 1957); *2 Abstracts* (1961); *Kanadario: Music for a Festival Occasion* (1966); *Variants* (1969); Suite (1975); Concerto for Cello, Piano, and Orch. (1976). **CHAMBER:** Violin Sonata (1948); Clarinet Sonata (1949); 3 string quartets (1950, 1951, 1970); String Trio (1959); Quartet for Flute, Clarinet, Bass Clarinet, and Celesta (1960); piano pieces, including a Sonata (1950). **VOCAL:** Choral works and songs. —**NS/LK/DM**

Betz, Franz, noted German baritone; b. Mainz, March 19, 1835; d. Berlin, Aug. 11, 1900. He studied in Karlsruhe. In 1856 he made his operatic debut as the Herald in *Lohengrin* in Hannover, and then sang in Altenburg, Gera, Cöthen, and Rostock. On May 16, 1859, he made his first appearance at the Berlin Royal Opera as Don Carlos in *Ernani*, and remained one of its principal members until 1897. He was particularly esteemed for his Wagnerian roles, and was chosen to create the roles of Hans Sachs in Munich (1868) and the Wanderer in *Siegfried* at Bayreuth (1876). Among his other prominent roles were Don Giovanni, Pizzaro, Amonasro, and Falstaff. His wife was the soprano Johanne Betz (1837–1906).—**NS/LK/DM**

Beurhaus, Friedrich, German music theorist; b. Immecke, near Meinerzhagen, 1536; d. Dortmund, Aug. 6, 1609. He was educated in Münster and Dortmund, and then received his M.A. in 1560 from the Univ. of Cologne. Subsequently he was cantor in several towns before taking up the post of cantor of the Reinoldi school in Dortmund in 1567; was named its rector in 1582. He publ. the important treatise *Musicae erotematum libri duo, ex optimis huius artis scriptoribus vera perspicuaque methodo descripto* (Dortmund, 1573; 2nd ed. as *Erotematum musicae libri duo*, 1580; 4th ed., 1591; facsimile ed., prepared by W. Thoene, in *Beiträge zur rheinischen Musikgeschichte*, Cologne, 1959).—**NS/LK/DM**

Beversdorf, (Samuel) Thomas, American composer and teacher; b. Yoakum, Tex., Aug. 8, 1924; d. Bloomington, Ind., Feb. 15, 1981. He studied trombone and baritone horn with his father, a band director; later studied composition with Kennan, DeLamarter, and Donato at the Univ. of Tex. (B.M., 1945), Rogers and Hanson at the Eastman School of Music in Rochester, N.Y. (M.M., 1946; D.M.A., 1957), Honegger and Copland at the Berkshire Music Center in Tanglewood (summer, 1947), and privately with Fuleihan. He was a trombonist in the Rochester (N.Y.) Phil. (1945–46), the Houston Sym. Orch. (1946–48), and the Pittsburgh Sym. Orch.

(1948–49). After teaching at the Univ. of Houston (1946–48), he was a prof. of music at the Ind. Univ. School of Music in Bloomington (1951–77).

WORKS: DRAMATIC: *Threnody: The Funeral of Youth,* ballet (Bloomington, Ind., March 6, 1963; also as *Variations for Orch.*); *The Hooligan,* opera (1964–69); *Metamorphosis,* opera (1968); *Vision of Christ,* mystery play (Lewisburg, Pa., May 1, 1971). **ORCH.:** 4 syms.: No. 1 (1946), No. 2 (1950), No. 3 for Winds and Percussion (Bloomington, Ind., May 9, 1954; also for Full Orch., Bloomington, Ind., Oct. 10, 1958), and No. 4 (1958); *Essay on Mass Production* (1946); *Mexican Portrait* (1948; rev. 1952); Concerto Grosso for Oboe and Chamber Orch. (1948; Pittsburgh, April 28, 1950); Concerto for 2 Pianos and Orch. (1951; Bloomington, Ind., March 17, 1967); *New Frontiers* (Houston, March 31, 1953); Violin Concerto, *Danforth* (1959); *Murals, Tapestries, and Icons* for Symphonic Band, Electric Bass, and Electric Piano (1975); Concerto for Tuba and Wind Orch. (Bloomington, Ind., Feb. 11, 1976). **CHAMBER:** Horn Sonata, *Christmas* (1945); 2 string quartets (1951, 1955); Tuba Sonata (1956); Trumpet Sonata (1962); Violin Sonata (1964–65); Flute Sonata (1965–66); Cello Sonata (1967–69); *La Petite Exposition* for Violin or Clarinet and 11 Strings (Dallas, Feb. 28, 1976); Sonata for Violin and Harp (1976–77); *Corelliana Variations* for 2 Flutes and Cello (1980).—**NS/LK/DM**

Bevin, Elway, Welsh organist and composer; b. c. 1554; d. (buried) Bristol, Oct. 19, 1638. He may have been a pupil of Tallis. After serving as vicar-choral at Wells Cathedral (1579–80), he was master of the choristers (1585–89) and then organist at Bristol Cathedral. In 1605 he was made a Gentleman Extraordinary of the Chapel Royal. He publ. the valuable tract *A Briefe and Short Instruction in the Art of Musicke* (London, 1631). His extant works include a Dorian or Short Service, 2 incomplete evening services, 5 anthems, and 2 secular songs.

BIBL.: G. Hooper, *E. B.* (Bristol, 1971).—**NS/LK/DM**

Beyer, Frank Michael, German composer and pedagogue; b. Berlin, March 8, 1928. He received early music training from his father, a writer and amateur pianist; following studies in sacred music, he was a pupil of Pepping at the Berlin Staatliche Hochschule für Musik (1952–55). He was an asst. prof. (1960–68) and prof. (from 1968) at the Berlin Hochschule der Künste, and founder of the "musica nova sacra" concert series. He was a member of the Berlin Akademie der Künste, serving as director of its contemporary music section.

WORKS: DRAMATIC: Ballet: *Geburt des Tanzes* (1987; Berlin, March 27, 1988); *Das Fenster* (1991). **ORCH.:** *Concerto for Orch.* (1957); *Ode* (1963); Flute Concerto (1964); Organ Concerto (1967); *Versi* for Strings (Berlin, Oct. 7, 1968); *Rondeau imaginaire* (1972; Berlin, Sept. 20, 1973); *Concertino a tre* for Chamber Orch. (Schwetzingen, May 22, 1974); *Diaphonie* (1975; Nuremberg, Feb. 26, 1976); *Streicherfantasien* (1977; Berlin, March 12, 1980; also for String Quintet, Berlin, Sept. 18, 1978); *Griechenland* for 3 String Groups (1981; Berlin, June 22, 1982); *Deutsche-Tänze* for Cello, Double Bass, and Chamber Orch. (1982; Berlin, June 14, 1984; arranged from *Deutsche Tänze* for Cello and Double Bass, Vienna, Nov. 10, 1980); *Notre-Dame-Musik* (1983–84; Saarbrücken, Nov. 2, 1984); *Mysteriensonate* for Viola and Orch. (1986; Berlin, May 16, 1987); Concerto for Oboe and Strings (1986; Berlin, Oct. 7, 1987); *Musik der Frühe,* violin

concerto (1993); *Canto di giorno* for Cello and Orch. (Berlin, April 16, 1999). **CHAMBER:** 3 string quartets (1957, 1969, 1985); Concerto for Organ and 7 Instruments (1966–69; arranged as Concerto for 5 Instruments, 1968); Wind Quintet (1972); Violin Sonata (1977); *De lumine* for 7 Players (1978); Trio for Oboe, Viola, and Harp (1980); *Passacaglia fantastica* for Violin, Cello, and Piano (1984); Sym. for 8 Players (Berlin, Feb. 6, 1989); *Sanctus* for Saxophone Quartet (1989); *Canciones* for Clarinet and Ensemble (1991); Clarinet Quintet (1992); *Nachstück* for Oboe and Piano (1993); *Nänie* for 2 Guitars (1994); piano pieces; organ works. **VOCAL:** Choral music, including *Maior Angelis,* cantata (1970).—**NS/LK/DM**

Beyer, Johanna Magdalena, German-American composer and musicologist; b. Leipzig, July 11, 1888; d. N.Y., Jan. 9, 1944. She studied piano and theory in Germany. In 1924 she went to America and studied at the David Mannes School in N.Y. receiving a teacher's certificate in 1928. She also took private lessons with Rudhyar, Crawford, Seeger, and Cowell. She wrote music and several plays for various projects in N.Y. During Cowell's term in San Quentin prison (1937–41), Beyer acted as his secretary and cared for his scores. Her compositional style was dissonant counterpoint.

WORKS: ORCH.: *March* for 14 Instruments (1935); *Cyrnab* for Chamber Orch. (1937); *Fragment* for Chamber Orch. (1937); *Symphonic Suite* (1937); *Dance for Full Orchestra (Status Quo)* (1938); *Elation* for Concert Band (1938); *Reverence* for Winds (1938); *Symphonic Movement I* (1939) and *II* (1941); *Symphonic Opus 3* (1939) and *5* (1940). **CHAMBER:** *Suite* for Clarinet *I* (1932) and *Ib* (1933); *Percussion Suite* (1933); Quintet for Woodwinds (1933); *Suite* for Clarinet and Bassoon (1933); *IV* for Percussion Ensemble (1935); Clarinet Sonata (1936); *Suite* for Bass Clarinet and Piano (1936?); *Movement* for Double Bass and Piano (1936); *Suite* for Violin and Piano (1937); *Suite* for Oboe and Bassoon (1937); *Movement* for Woodwinds (1938); *March* for 30 Percussion Instruments (1939); *Percussion,* op. 14 (1939); *Six Pieces* for Oboe and Piano (1939); *Three Movements* for Percussion Ensemble (1939); *Waltz* for Percussion Ensemble (1939); Trio for Woodwinds (1940?); 4 string quartets (1933–34; 1936; *Dance,* 1938; 1943?); *Music of the Spheres (Status Quo)* (1938). **Piano:** *Gebrauschs-Musik* (1934); *Clusters* or *New York Waltzes* (1931, 1936); *Winter Ade and five other folk song settings* (1936); *Movement* for 2 Pianos (1936); *Dissonant Counterpoint* (1936?); *Suite for Piano* (1939); Sonatina (1943); *Prelude and Fugue* (n.d.); *Piano-Book, Classic-Romantic-Modern* (n.d.). **VOCAL: Choral:** *The Robin in the Rain* (1935); *The Federal Music Project* (1936); *The Main-Deep* (1937); *The People, Yes* (1937); *The Composers' Forum Laboratory* (1937). **Songs:** *Sky-Pieces* (1933); 3 Songs (*Timber Moon; Stars, Songs, Faces; Summer Grass*) for Soprano, Piano, and Percussion (1933); *Ballad of the Star-Eater* for Soprano and Clarinet (1934); 3 Songs (*Total Eclipse; Universal-Local; To Be*) for Soprano and Clarinet (1934); *Have Faith!* for Soprano and Flute (3 versions; 1936–37). —**NS/LK/DM**

Bezekirsky, Vasili, Russian violinist; b. Moscow, Jan. 26, 1835; d. there, Nov. 8, 1919. He studied violin in Moscow, and in 1858 went to Brussels, where he took violin lessons with Leonard and lessons in composition with Damcke. Returning to Moscow in 1860, he was concertmaster at the Bolshoi Theater (1861–91); from

1882 to 1902 he was prof. at the Moscow Phil. Inst. As a violin virtuoso, he was greatly regarded in Russia. Tchaikovsky wrote about him: "Although not a Czar of the first magnitude, Bezekirsky is brilliant enough on the dim horizon of present violin playing." Bezekirsky was also a composer; he wrote a Violin Concerto (Moscow, Feb. 26, 1873) and contributed cadenzas to the violin concertos of Beethoven and Brahms. He publ. a vol. of reminiscences, *From the Notebook of an Artist* (St. Petersburg, 1910).—NS/LK/DM

Bhatkhande, Vishnu Narayan, eminent Indian musicologist; b. Bombay, Aug. 10, 1860; d. there, Sept. 19, 1936. He studied jurisprudence, and concurrently investigated the systems of Indian ragas. While earning a living as a lawyer, he traveled throughout India to collect authentic ragas. In 1910 he abandoned his legal practice and dedicated himself exclusively to Indian folk music. His compilations of ragas are invaluable resources. He publ. *Hindusthāni sangit paddhati* (4 vols., Marathi, 1910–32), *Śrimal-laksya saṅgitam* (Bombay, 1910), and *Kramik pustak mālikā* (6 vols., Marathi, 1919–37).—NS/LK/DM

Bialas, Günter, German composer and pedagogue; b. Bielschowitz, Silesia, July 19, 1907; d. Glonn, July 8, 1995. His father was the business manager of a local theater, and Bialas absorbed much music through personal connections with professional organizations. He studied in Breslau (1925–27) and with Trapp in Berlin (1927–33). After teaching composition at the Weimar Hochschule für Musik (1947), he was a teacher (1947–50) and a prof. (1950–59) of composition at the North-West German Academy of Music in Detmold; then was prof. of composition at the Munich Hochschule für Musik (1959–72). In 1967 he received the music prize of the Bavarian Academy of Fine Arts, and in 1971 the Culture Prize of Upper Silesia. He developed a style using serial procedures, with diversions into medieval and African modes.

WORKS: DRAMATIC: Opera: *Hero und Leander* (Mannheim, Sept. 8, 1966); *Die Geschichte von Aucassin und Nicolette* (1967–69; Munich, Dec. 12, 1969); *Der gestiefelte Kater* (1973–74; Schwetzingen, May 15, 1975; rev. version, Munich, July 18, 1987). **Ballet:** *Meyerbeer-Paraphrasen* (1971; Hamburg, May 12, 1974). **ORCH.:** *Kleine Konzertmusik* (1935); Viola Concerto (1940); Violin Concerto (1949); *Sinfonia piccola* (1960); Clarinet Concerto (1961); 2 cello concertos (1962, 1993); *Music in 2 Movements* for Harp and Strings (1966); *Concerto Lirico* for Piano and Orch. (1967); *Musik* for 11 Strings (1969); Chamber Concerto for Harpsichord or Piano and 13 Strings (1973); *Introitus—Exodus* for Organ and Orch. (1976); *Der Weg nach Eisenstadt*, "Haydn-Fantasy" for Small Orch. (1980); *Marschfantasie* (1988). **CHAMBER:** 3 string quartets (1936, 1949, 1969); Viola Sonata (1946); Violin Sonata (1946); Flute Sonata (1946); *Partita* for 9 Winds (1963); *Pastorale and Rondo*, nonet (1969); *Romanza e Danza*, octet (1971); *Assonanzen* for 12 Cellos (1978); Quintet for Harp and String Quartet (1983); *Andante (Herbstzeit)*, piano quartet (1984); 9 Bagatelles for Wind Trio, String Trio, and Piano (1984); 6 Bagatelles for Saxophone Quartet (1985–86); *Kunst des Kanons*, 10 pieces for 2 to 4 Saxophones (1992). **VOCAL:** *Indianische Kantate* for Baritone, Chamber Choir, and 8 Instruments (1951); *Oraculum*, cantata for Soprano,

Tenor, Chorus, and Orch. (1953); *Symbolum* for Men's Chorus and Wind Quintet (1967); *Lamento di Orlando* for Baritone, Chorus, and Orch. (1986); *Matratzengruft*, Liedenspiel (1992).

BIBL.: G. Speer and H.-J. Winterhoff, *G. B. Meilensteine eines Komponistenlebens: Festschrift zum 70. Geburtstag* (Kassel, 1977); *G. B. zum 80. Geburtstag* (Dülmen, 1987); M. Holl and H. Schafer, *Wort und Musik: Ausstellung zum 85. Geburtstag von G. B.: Bayerische Staatsbibliothek München, Musikabteilung, 15. July bis 4. September 1992* (Munich, 1992).—NS/LK/DM

Bianchi, Antonio, Italian baritone and composer; b. Milan, 1758; d. after 1817. He sang in Milan and Genoa, and then was a court singer to the Prince of Nassau Weilburg. From 1792 to 1797 he was a member of the Königlisches National theater in Berlin, where his opera *Die Insel der Alcina* was premiered on Feb. 16, 1794. He subsequently sang in other German cities and was co-director of a touring opera troupe. His best known roles were in comic operas by Cimarosa, Sarti, and Paisiello.—LK/DM

Bianchi, Francesco, Italian composer; b. Cremona, c. 1752; d. (suicide) London, Nov. 27, 1810. He studied in Naples with Jommelli and Cafaro. He wrote nearly 80 operas, some quite pleasing, but ephemeral. His first was *Giulio Sabino* (Cremona, 1772); it was followed by *Il Grand Cidde* (Florence, 1773). From 1775 to 1778 he was in Paris serving as maestro al cembalo at the Comédie-Italienne, where he produced his opera *La Réduction de Paris* (Sept. 30, 1775). In 1778 he went to Florence, and in 1783 he became 2nd maestro at the Cathedral of Milan, a post he held until 1793, He concurrently worked in Venice from 1785 to 1791, and again from 1793 to 1797, when he served as second organist at S. Marco. He subsequently was in Naples, where he produced his most significant opera, *La Vendetta de Nino* (Nov. 12, 1790). In 1794 he went to London, where he officiated as conductor at the King's Theatre (1795–1801); several of his operas were produced there under his supervision. Apart from his operas, he wrote instrumental music, and publ. a theoretical treatise, *Dell'attrazione armonica*, which was publ. in excerpts, in Eng., in the *Quarterly Musical Magazine and Review* (1820–21). Bianchi was also a successful teacher, numbering among his English pupils Henry Bishop. —NS/LK/DM

Bianchi, Valentina, Russian soprano; b. Vilnius, 1839; d. Kurland, March 11, 1884. She studied at the Paris Cons., and made her debut as a soprano in Frankfurt am Main (1855). She sang at Schwerin (1855–61), St. Petersburg (1862–65), and Moscow (until 1867), and retired in 1870. She married chief forester von Fabian in 1865. Her range was extraordinary, extending from low alto through high soprano notes.—NS/LK/DM

Bianchini, Domenico, Italian lutenist and composer; b. c. 1510; d. Venice, c. 1576. He worked as a mosaicist at S. Marco in Venice (1540–76). As a composer, he publ. *Intabolatura de lauto...di recercari, motetti, madrigali, napolitane et balli, libro primo* (Venice, 1546). —NS/LK/DM

Bianco, Pietro Antonio, Italian singer and composer; b. Venice, c. 1540; d. Graz (buried), Feb. 2, 1611. He was a canon at S. Salvatore in Venice. He became a tenor at the Hofkapelle in Graz in 1578, being named Hofkapellmeister there in 1595. He composed both secular and religious vocal music.—NS/LK/DM

Bibalo, Antonio (Gino), Italian-born Norwegian composer of Slovak descent; b. Trieste, Jan. 18, 1922. After training with Luciano Gante (piano) and Giulio Viozzi (composition) at the Trieste Cons. (graduated, 1946), he went to London in 1953 to complete his composition studies with Elisabeth Luytens. In 1956 he settled in Norway and in 1967 became a naturalized Norwegian citizen. In 1991 he was awarded Norway's Prize for Culture for his opera *Macbeth* and was decorated with the St. Olaf Knight Cross of the King of Norway. In his music, Bibalo demonstrates a capacity for inventive tonal, melodic, and rhythmic writing with occasional excursions into serialism.

WORKS: DRAMATIC: O p e r a : *The Smile at the Foot of the Ladder,* after Henry Miller (1958–62; first complete perf. as *Das Lächeln am Fusse der Leiter,* Hamburg, April 6, 1965); *Frøken Julie* (Miss Julie), after Strindberg (Århus, Sept. 8, 1975); *Askeladden* (Numskull Jack; 1976; Norwegian Radio, Dec. 26, 1977); *Gespenster* (Ghosts), after Ibsen (Kiel, June 21, 1981); *Macbeth,* after Shakespeare (1989; Oslo, Sept. 29, 1990); *Die Glasmanenagerie,* after Tennessee Williams (Trier, Nov. 3, 1996; in Eng. as *The Glass Menagerie,* Oslo, Oct. 9, 1998). **B a l l e t :** *Pinocchio* (1967; Hamburg, Jan. 17, 1969); *Nocturne for Apollo* (1969); *Flammen* (1974). **ORCH.:** *Pitture Astratte* (1950–58); 2 piano concertos: No. 1 (1955; Oslo, Aug. 1, 1972) and No. 2 (1971; Bergen, April 27, 1972); 2 concerti da camera: No. 1 for Piano, Timpani, and Strings (1954) and No. 2 for Violin, Harpsichord, and Strings (1974); *Fantasia* for Violin and Orch. (1954); *Pour "Marguerite Infante"* (1955–70); *Concerto Allegorico* for Violin and Orch. (1957); *Serenata* for Chamber Orch. (1966); *Ouverture pour "Le Serviteure de deux maîtres"* (1968); 2 syms.: No. 1, *Sinfonia Notturna* (1968) and No. 2 (1978–79); *Per Clavicembalo, violino concertante e orchestra d'archi* (1974); *Freithoff Suite* (1974); *Musica* for Oboe, Strings, Percussion, and Harp (1986); Concertante for Wind Quintet and Orch. (1990); *5 Frammenti sinfonici* (1997). **CHAMBER:** *Autunnale* for Flute, Vibraphone, Double Bass, and Piano (1968); *Sonatina 1 A: Semplie* (1971) and *2 A: Astrale* (1972) for Flute, Oboe, Clarinet, Horn, and Bassoon; String Quartet (1972); *Sonata: Quasi una fantasia* for Accordion (1977); Sonata for Solo Violin (1978); *Study in Blue* for Guitar (1983); *The Savage,* "4 impressions" for 6 Players (1982–83); *Hvitt Landskap* for Violin, Cello, Flute, Clarinet, Piano, and Tape (1984); *Racconto d'una Stagione Alta* for Cello and Piano (1986); *4 Morceau* for 7 Players (1990); *Invenzione Evolutiva* for Double Bass (1990). **KEYBOARD: P i a n o :** *3 Hommages* (1953); *4 Balkan Dances* (1956; also for Orch.); *Toccata* (1957); 2 sonatas (1974; *La Notte,* 1975); *Piano "Solo" in the Evening* (1977). **O r g a n :** *Prelude ed Elegia* (1989). **VOCAL:** *Elegie einer Raum-Zeit* for Soprano, Baritone, Chorus, and Orch. (1963); *Nocturne for Apollo: A Ballet of Requiem* for Chorus, Tape, and Orch. (1969); *Serenata* for Baritone and Men's Chorus (1971); *Cantico* for Mezzo-soprano and Tape (1983); *2 Intermezzi* for Baritone and Flute (1984–85); *Nocturne* for Voice and Piano (1988).—NS/LK/DM

Biber, Heinrich Ignaz Franz von, outstanding Bohemian composer and violinist; b. Wartenberg, Aug. 12, 1644; d. Salzburg, May 3, 1704. He was in the service of Prince Bishop Karl, Count Liechtenstein-Kastelkorn of Olmütz, by about 1665. In 1670 he settled in Salzburg as a member of the archbishop's Kapelle, where he was made Vice-Kapellmeister in 1679 and Kapellmeister in 1684. In 1690 he was ennobled by Emperor Leopold I. Biber was a remarkable composer of both secular and sacred music, and was a virtuoso violinist who excelled in scordatura. His *Mystery* and *Rosary Sonatas* for Violin and Continuo (c. 1676), composed as postludes for the services of the Rosary Mysteries at Salzburg Cathedral, are notable examples of scordatura. His 8 sonatas for Solo Violin and Continuo (1681) are also fine scores. Among his other chamber works are 2 collections of music for 1 or 2 Violins, 2 Violas, and Bass (1680, 1683). He also publ. a collection of music for Trumpets and Strings (1676). Among his finest sacred works are the 32-part *Vesperae* (1693), the *Missa Sancti Henrici* (1701), the 36-part *Missa Alleluja,* and the Requiems in A major and F minor. An anonymous 53-part *Missa salisburgensis* (1682) may be his as well. He also wrote the operas *Chi la dura la vince* (1687), *Alessandro in Pietra* (1689; not extant), and *L'ossequio di Salisburgo* (1699; not extant), as well as several school dramas.

BIBL.: E. Luntz, *H.I.F. B.* (Vienna and Leipzig, 1906); E. Dann, *H. B. and the Seventeenth-century Violin* (diss., Columbia Univ., 1968); P. Eder et al., eds., *H.F. B., 1644–1704: Musik u. Kultur im hochbarocken Salzburg: Studien und Quellen* (Salzburg, 1994).—NS/LK/DM

Bible, Frances, American mezzo-soprano; b. Sackets Harbor, N.Y., Jan. 26, 1927. She studied with Belle Julie Soudant and Queena Mario at the Juilliard School of Music in N.Y. (1939–47). She made her operatic debut as the Shepherd in *Tosca* at the N.Y. City Opera on Oct. 7, 1948, subsequently attaining a prominent place on its roster, singing principal roles there regularly until 1977. She was later a teacher (1979–82) and artist-in-residence (1982–83) at Rice Univ. in Houston. She was best known for her trouser and contemporary roles.—NS/LK/DM

Bielawa, Herbert, American composer, pianist, and teacher; b. Chicago, Feb. 3, 1930. He studied music at home; from 1954 to 1956 he served in the U.S. Army in Germany, stationed in Frankfurt am Main, where he also studied conducting with Bruno Vondenhoff. He took courses in piano with Soulima Stravinsky at the Univ. of Ill. (B.M., 1954); then enrolled at the Univ. of Southern Calif. in Los Angeles, and took courses in composition with Dahl (1960–61), Stevens (1961–64), and Kohs (1961–63); also studied music for cinema with Rosza and Raksin. In 1966 he was appointed to the faculty of San Francisco State Univ., where, in 1967, he established the Electronic Music Studio; he retired in 1991. In his music, he makes unprejudiced use of the entire field of practical resources.

WORKS: *Concert Piece* for Orch. (1953); *Essay* for String Orch. (1958); *A Bird in the Bush,* chamber opera (1962); *Abstractions* for String Orch. (1965); *4 Legends* for Violins and Cellos (1967); *Divergents* for Orch. (1969); *Fluxbands* for 10 Instruments

(1981); Duo for Violin and Harpsichord (1984); String Quartet (1989); *50/50* for Flute, Oboe, Clarinet, Bassoon, and Piano (1991); keyboard pieces; choral works; songs; electronic music. —NS/LK/DM

Bierdiajew, Walerian, Polish conductor; b. Grodno, March 7, 1885; d. Warsaw, Nov. 28, 1956. He studied composition with Reger and conducting with Nikisch at the Leipzig Cons. He began his conducting career in Dresden in 1906; in 1908 he became regular conductor at the Maryinsky Opera Theater in St. Petersburg; then conducted in various Russian opera houses; from 1921 to 1925 he lived in Poland; from 1925 to 1930 he was again engaged as a conductor in Russia. In 1930 he was appointed prof. of conducting at the Warsaw Cons., and from 1947 to 1949 he was conductor of the Kraków Phil. He then taught at the Poznán Cons. (1949–54) and at the Warsaw Cons. (1954–56); also was director of the Warsaw Opera (1954–56).—NS/LK/DM

Bierey, Gottlob Benedikt, German conductor and composer; b. Dresden, July 25, 1772; d. Breslau, May 5, 1840. He was a pupil of Christian E. Weinlig at Dresden, then director of a traveling opera troupe. He was appointed Kapellmeister at Breslau in 1808, succeeding Weber; retired in 1828. He composed 26 operas and operettas, 10 cantatas, masses, orch. and chamber music, etc.—NS/LK/DM

Bigard, Barney (Albany Leon), noted New Orleans–style clarinetist, b. New Orleans, March 3, 1906; d. Culver City, Calif., June 27, 1980. His uncle, Emile Bigard was a violinist; his brother, Alex, a drummer. Barney was one of the most highly regarded jazz clarinetists, whose unique "woodsy" sound was featured with Ellington for about 12 years and Armstrong for about nine. The Bigard brothers are cousins of Natty Dominique. He started on E-flat clarinet at the age of seven, lessons from Lorenzo Tio Jr. He first worked as a photo-engraver, did some parade work on clarinet, but began specializing on tenor sax. In late 1922 he joined Albert Nichoias Band at Tom Anderson's Cabaret, in the following year worked with Oke Gaspard's Band at the Moulin Rouge. He left in the summer of 1923, played briefly with Amos White at the Spanish Fort, before returning to work for Albert Nicholas and Luis Russell at Tom Anderson's Cabaret. He went to Chicago in late 1924 to join King Oliver after two months with Dave Peyton joined Oliver for residency at The Plantation, playing tenor until Darnell Howard left the band, from then on specialized on clarinet. He left Chicago with Oliver in April 1927, played in St. Louis and N.Y., then after a brief tour left Oliver to join Charlie Elgar at the Eagle Ballroom in Milwaukee (summer 1927). He returned to N.Y. to join Luis Russell for two months, then joined Duke Ellington in December 1927. Bigard remained with Duke until June 1942 (except for brief absence in summer of 1935). He left in Calif., formed his own small band in August 1942, disbanded to join Freddie Slack in November 1942, left in summer of 1943, did some studio work including a soundtrack for the film *I Dood It*, then formed his own small band for Los Angeles residencies. He led a small band at Onyx in N.Y., from autumn 1944 until early 1945. He returned to Los Angeles, did film–studio work and led a small band in L.A. He played regularly with Kid Ory during 1946, and also took part in filming of *New Orleans*. He joined Louis Armstrong for debut of the All Stars in August 1947, remaining with him until the summer of 1952. Returning to the West Coast, some free–lancing and led a small band, then rejoined Armstrong in spring 1953 until August 1955; led a small band, then played with Ben Pollack's Band (late 1956), also did studio work including an appearance in the film *St. Louis Blues*. He was on tour with Cozy Cole's Band from November 1958 until March 1959. Following a spell in New Orleans Creole Jazz Band, he led his own band at Ben Pollack's Club before playing again with Louis Armstrong's All Stars from April 1960 until September 1961. He joined Johnny St. Cyr's Young Men of New Orleans" playing at Disneyland; worked briefly with Muggsy Spanier in San Francisco during the autumn of 1962. Since then he has left full-time music, playing mainly in and around Los Angeles, including some gigs with Rex Stewart in 1966 and 1967 and appearancesd with Art Hodes on Chicago TV (February 1968). He recovered from cataract operation (1971) and toured with Hodes, Eddie Condon, Wild Bill Davison (October 1971). He toured Europe with the Pelican Trio in summer of 1978.

DISC.: Ellington: "Mood Indigo" (1959).

BIBL.: B. Bigard, *With Louis and the Duke: The Autobiography of a Jazz Clarinetist* (N.Y., 1985).—JC/LP

Biggs, E(dward George) Power, eminent English-born American organist; b. Westcliff on Sea, Essex, March 29, 1906; d. Boston, March 10, 1977. He studied at the Royal Academy of Music in London, graduating in 1929. In 1930 he emigrated to the U.S. and became a naturalized citizen in 1937. After making his N.Y. recital debut in 1932, he launched a career as one of the most distinguished concert organists of his time. He became particularly popular via his weekly CBS radio broadcasts (1942–58), his extensive recital tours, and his numerous recordings. His repertoire was vast, ranging from the great masters of the past to scores commissioned from contemporary composers, among them Piston, Harris, Hanson, and Quincy Porter; Britten also wrote a work for him. Biggs refused to perform on electronic organs, which in his opinion vulgarized and distorted the classical organ sound. His own style of performance had an unmistakable austerity, inspired by the Baroque school.

BIBL.: B. Owen, *E. P. B.: Concert Organist* (Bloomington, Ind., 1987).—NS/LK/DM

Bignami, Carlo, Italian violinist and composer; b. Cremona, Dec. 6, 1808; d. Voghera, Oct. 2, 1848. He studied violin with his father and elder brother. He played in theater orchs. in Cremona and Milan, and in 1829 was appointed director of the Teatro Sociale in Mantua; then was in Milan and Verona. Returning to Cremona in 1837 as director and first violinist of the orch., he made it one of the best in Lombardy. Paganini called him "*il primo violinista d'Italia,*" but he may have meant this phrase to express his low opinion of other Italian violinists in comparison. Bignami wrote a number of violin pieces, including a Concerto, a *Capriccio*, *Studi per violino*, *Grande Adagio*, *Polacca*, fantasias, variations, etc.—**NS/LK/DM**

Bigot, Eugène, French conductor; b. Rennes, Feb. 28, 1888; d. Paris, July 17, 1965. He studied violin and piano at the Rennes Cons. and later at the Paris Cons. In 1913 he was named chorus master at the Théâtre des Champs Élysées in Paris; subsequently toured Europe with the Ballets Suédois; also conducted the Paris Cons. Orch. (1923–25); then served as music director at the Théâtres des Champs-Élysées (1925–27). In 1935 he became president and director of the Concerts Lamoureux in Paris, a post he held until 1950; he also was principal conductor of the Paris Opéra-Comique (1936–47). From 1947 until his death he was chief conductor of the Paris Radio Orch.—**NS/LK/DM**

Bigot (de Morogues), Marie (née **Kiene**), pianist; b. Colmar, Alsace, March 3, 1786; d. Paris, Sept. 16, 1820. After her marriage in 1804, she lived in Vienna, where she was known and esteemed by Haydn and Beethoven. In 1808 she went to Paris, where she gave piano lessons from 1812. Mendelssohn was briefly her pupil in Paris at the age of 7.

BIBL.: G. Jeanclaude, *Un amour de Beethoven: M. B. de Morogues, pianiste* (Strasbourg, 1992).—**NS/LK/DM**

Bijvanck, Henk, Dutch composer; b. Kudus, Java, Nov. 6, 1909; d. Heemstede, near Haarlem, Sept. 5, 1969. He studied composition with Franz Schmidt and piano with Andrassy in Vienna, where he was active as a pianist. He then taught piano at the Amsterdam Music Lyceum (1945–47). His works include a Piano Concerto (1943), *Liberation Symphony* (1944), *Lourdes Symphony* (1952), Sym. No. 2 (1965), chamber music, and vocal works.—**NS/LK/DM**

Bildstein, Hieronymus, important Austrian organist and composer; b. Bregenz, c. 1580; d. c. 1626. After studying music in Bregenz, he went to Konstanz, where he was active as court organist. He wrote 25 motets publ. as *Orpheus christianus seu Symphoniarum sacrarum prodromus, 5–8 vocum cum basso generali* (Regensburg, 1624), publ. in a modern ed. in Denkmäler der Tonkunst in Österreich, CXXII (1971) and CXXVI (1976).—**NS/LK/DM**

Bilhon (Billhon, Billon), Jhan (Jean, Jan, Jehan, Joannes) de (du), French or Flemish composer who flourished from 1534 to 1556. His extant works include a Mass, a Magnificat, and other sacred works (publ. 1534–56).—**NS/LK/DM**

Bilk, (Mr.) Acker (Bernard Stanley), jazz clarinetist; b. Pensford, Somerset, England, Jan. 29, 1929. He played piano as a child but took up clarinet while serving in Egypt with the Royal Engineers (1948). He soon formed his own band in Bristol. In 1954, he played with Ken Colyer in London, then continued to lead his Paramount Jazz Band in Bristol area; the band also toured Poland (summer 1956). The band, with personnel changes, played a residency in London (summer 1957) and became fully professional in October 1957; soon afterwards, they played dates in Düsseldorf, Germany. Having debuted in early 1960 with the bluesy album *Summer Set,* he became one of the most successful artists of the traditional jazz boom. The album *Stranger on the Shore* spent 55 weeks in the U.K. chart and topped the U.S. listing. He was thrilled when Duke Ellington recorded "Stranger on the Shore" (1964). Album success followed in the company of Chris Barber and Kenny Ball. His band toured internationally, including Germany, Australia, Kuala Lumpur, and France. He maintained his reputation with cabaret and TV appearances, and returned to the charts with mid-1970s albums *Aria* and *Sheer Magic*. The band's wide-ranging schedule continued through the 1990s. Bilk also played a series of duo dates with Humphrey Lyttelton (1993–94).

DISC.: *Summer Set* (1960); *Stranger on the Shore* (1961); *Expo 70* (1970); *Regal Starline* (1970); *Pye* (1972). S. Tracey: *We Love You Madly* (1968).

BIBL.: L., Peter, P. Gwynn-Jones, *The Book of Bilk, Or 41 Characters in Search of an Acker* (London, 1963); G. Williams, *Acker Bilk* (London, 1962).—**MM/JC-B**

Billings, William, pioneer American composer of hymns and anthems and popularizer of "fuging tunes" b. Boston, Oct. 7, 1746; d. there, Sept. 26, 1800. A tanner's apprentice, he acquired the rudiments of music from treatises by Tans'ur. He compensated for his lack of education by a wealth of original ideas and a determination to put them into practice. His first musical collection, *The New England Psalm Singer* (Boston, 1770), contained what he described at a later date as "fuging pieces...more than twenty times as powerful as the old slow tunes." The technique of these pieces was canonic, with "each part striving for mastery and victory." His other publ. books were *The Singing Master's Assistant* (1778), *Music in Miniature* (1779), *The Psalm Singer's Amusement* (1781), *The Suffolk Harmony* (1786), and *The Continental Harmony* (1794). In one instance, he harmonized a tune, Jargon, entirely in dissonances; this was prefaced by a "Manifesto" to the Goddess of Discord. There was further a choral work, *Modern Music,* in which the proclaimed aim was expressed in the opening lines: "We are met for a concert of modern invention—To tickle the ear is our present intention." Several of his hymns became popular, particularly *Chester* and *The Rose of Sharon*; an interesting historical work was his *Lamentation over Boston,* written in Watertown while Boston was occupied by the British. However, he could not earn a living by his music. Appeals made to provide him and his large family with funds bore little fruit, and Billings died in abject poverty. The combination of reverence and solemnity with humor makes the songs of Billings unique in the annals of American music, and aroused the curiosity of many modern American musicians. Henry Cowell wrote a series of "fuging tunes" and William Schuman's *New England Triptych* is based on 3 Billings tunes. John Cage's *Apartment House 1776,* written to commemorate the bicentennial of the American Revolution, is comprised of 44 "rewritten" four-part choral works by Billings and other American composers. K. Kroeger and H. Nathan ed. *The Complete Works of William Billings* (4 vols., Charlottesville, Va., 1977–90).

BIBL.: J. Barbour, *The Church Music of W. B.* (East Lansing, 1960); D. McKay and R. Crawford, *W. B. of Boston* (Princeton, 1975); H. Nathan, *W. B., Data and Documents* (Detroit, 1976). —**NS/LK/DM**

Billington, Elizabeth (née **Weichsel**), famous English soprano; b. London, Dec. 27, 1765; d. near Venice, Aug. 25, 1818. Her mother, a singer, was a pupil of Johann Christian Bach, and Elizabeth, too, had some lessons with him. She received her early musical training from her father, a German oboist. She also studied with James Billington, a double-bass player by profession, whom she married on Oct. 13, 1783. Her operatic debut took place in Dublin (1784), as Eurydice in Gluck's opera. She went to London, where she appeared as Rosetta in *Love in a Village* at Covent Garden on Feb. 13, 1786. Her success was immediate: she was reengaged at Covent Garden and also sang at the Concerts of Antient Music in London. Her career was briefly disrupted by the publication, in 1792, of anonymous Memoirs attacking her private life. This was immediately followed by an equally anonymous rebuttal, "written by a gentleman," defending her reputation. In 1794 she went to Italy, where she sang for the King of Naples. He made arrangements for her appearances at the San Carlo, where she performed in operas by Bianchi, Paisiello, Paer, and Himmel, all written specially for her. After her husband died in 1794, she remained in Italy for 2 more years, then lived in France, where she married M. Felissent. Returning to London in 1801, she sang alternately at Drury Lane and Covent Garden, with great acclaim, at 4,000 guineas a season. This period was the peak of her success. She retired in 1809, except for occasional performances. After a temporary separation from Felissent, she returned to him in 1817. They settled at their estate at St. Artien, near Venice. —**NS/LK/DM**

Billroth, Theodor, eminent German surgeon and amateur musician; b. Bergen, on the island of Rugen, April 26, 1829; d. Abazzia, Feb. 6, 1894. He received a thorough musical education, and was an intimate friend of Hanslick and Brahms. The musical soirees at his home in Vienna were famous. Almost all the chamber music of Brahms was played there (with Billroth as violist) before a public performance. He wrote the treatise *Wer ist musikalisch?* (1896, ed. by Hanslick). Billroth originated two crucial intestinal surgical operations, known in medical literature as Billroth I and Billroth II.

BIBL.: I. Fischer, *T. B. und seine Zeitgenossen* (1929); A. Frankel, *T. B.* (1931); O-G. Gottlieb, *B. und Brahms im Briefwechsel* (1935).—**NS/LK/DM**

Bilse, Benjamin, German conductor; b. Liegnitz, Aug. 17, 1816; d. there, July 13, 1902. He was "Stadtmusikus" at Liegnitz (1843), and brought his orch. to a

remarkable degree of perfection. He then lived in Berlin (1868–84) and conducted at the Concerthaus, retiring in 1894 with the title "Hofmusikus." He composed salon music.—**NS/LK/DM**

Bilson, Malcolm, distinguished American pianist, fortepianist, and pedagogue; b. Los Angeles, Oct. 24, 1935. He studied at Bard Coll. (B.A., 1957), the Vienna Academy of Music (1959), the Paris École Normale de Musique (1960), and the Univ. of Ill. (M.M., 1962; D.M.A., 1968). In 1968 he joined the faculty of Cornell Univ. as an asst. prof., and subsequently served there as an assoc. prof. (1970–75), prof. (from 1975), and as the Frederick J. Whiton Prof. of Music (from 1990). As a performing artist, Bilson has championed the cause of playing works of the Classical and Romantic eras on original instruments or modern replicas. In addition to many recital and chamber music performances, he has appeared as a soloist with both period and modern instrument orchs. on both sides of the Atlantic. He is particularly esteemed for his insightful interpretations of works by Haydn, Mozart, Beethoven, Schubert, Mendelssohn, and Schumann.—**NS/LK/DM**

Bilt, Peter van der, Dutch bass-baritone; b. Jakarta, Dutch East Indies, Aug. 30, 1936; d. Amsterdam, Sept. 25, 1983. He studied in Amsterdam, where he made his operatic debut as Dulcamara in 1960. After appearing as Rossini's Don Basilio at the San Francisco Opera in 1963, he joined the Deutsche Oper am Rhein in Düsseldorf in 1964; made guest appearances in Vienna, Munich, Edinburgh, Los Angeles, and other music centers. Among his prominent roles were Don Giovanni, Figaro, Don Pasquale, Beckmesser, and Gianni Schicchi. He also sang widely in concerts.—**NS/LK/DM**

Bimstein, Phillip (Kent), noteworthy American composer and politician, b. Chicago, Nov. 20, 1947. He studied theory and composition at the Chicago Cons. of Music (B.M., 1972). In the 1980s he led the new wave band Phil 'n' the Blanks, whose 3 albums and 6 videos were college radio and MTV hits. After further studies at the Univ. of Calif. at Los Angeles in composition, orchestration, and conducting, Bimstein took a hiking trip to southern Utah, where he remained, becoming a two-term mayor (1993–2001) of the town of Springdale, and an outspoken advocate of Utah's wilderness. His *Dark Winds Rising* for String Quartet and Tape (1992) is based on the controversy regarding a proposed toxic waste incinerator on the Kaibab Paiute Reservation. He received grants from the NEA (1991, 1993, 1995) and a Meet the Composer "New Residency Award" (1997–99). In 1992 he won the Prix Ars Electronica for his *Garland Hirschi's Cows*. In 2000 he was elected to the board of the American Music Center. Bimstein classifies his work as "alternative classical," his compositions often mixing traditional orchestral instruments with digitally sampled natural sounds or voices.

WORKS: *The Louie Louie Variations* for Clarinet, Cello, Piano, and Marimba (1989; also for String Quartet, and for Mandolin Quartet); *Garland Hirschi's Cows* for Digital Sampler (1990); *Koulangatta* for String Quartet and Harmonica (1990; in collaboration with C. Siegel); *Dark Winds Rising* for String Quartet and Tape (1992; also for Wind Quintet and Tape); *Bim* for Saxophone, Violin, Cello, Piano, and Percussion (1993); *Vox Dominum* for Digital Sampler (1994); *Liquid Interior* for Digital Sampler (1994); *The Door* for Digital Sampler (1994); *5.7 Wild!* for Violin, Alto Saxophone, and Bass (1996); *Casino* for Wind Quintet and Tape (1996); *Rockville Utah 1926* for String Quartet (1997); *Variations on "Come Come Y Saints"* for Brass Quintet (1997); *Half Moon at Checkerboard Mesa* for Oboe and Frogs, Crickets, and Coyotes on Tape (1997; also for Flute, Clarinet, Bassoon, Horn, Trombone, Violin, and Tape); *Grand Staircase* for Wind Quintet (1998); *Refuge* for String Quartet and Tape (1999); *Busy Wushy Rag* for Wind Quintet and Tape (2000).—**LK/DM**

Binchois (Binch, Binche), Gilles (de), important Franco-Flemish composer; b. probably in Mons, Hainaut, c. 1400; d. Soignies, near Mons, Sept. 20, 1460. His father was most likely Jean de Binch, counselor to 2 rulers of Hainaut. Binchois may have been in the service of William de la Pole, the Earl of Suffolk, in Paris in 1424; by the close of that decade he was in the service of the Burgundian court, where he advanced from fifth to second chaplain, retaining the latter position until his death. He greatly distinguished himself as a composer of both sacred and secular works, many of which have been publ. since the 19th century; the most important modern eds. are those by W. Rehm in *Die Chansons von G. B. (1400–1460)* (Mainz, 1957) and P. Kaye in *The Sacred Music of G. B.* (Oxford, 1992).

BIBL.: W. Rehm, *Das Chansonwerk von G. B.* (diss., Univ. of Freiburg, 1952); J. Kreps, *G. d. B., 1460–1960* (Louvain, 1960); J. Boucher, *The Religious Music of G. B.* (diss., Boston Univ., 1963). —**NS/LK/DM**

Binder, Christlieb Siegmund, German organist and composer; b. Dresden (baptized), July 29, 1723; d. there, Jan. 1, 1789. He became a court musician in Dresden in 1751, where he played the pantoleon. In 1764 he was made second organist and in 1787 first organist at the Catholic court chapel. He wrote prolifically, in an "elegant style" akin to that of C.P.E. Bach. Some of his compositions have been reprinted by O. Schmid in *Musik am sächsischen Hofe*, IV and VI (Leipzig, 1903–4).

WORKS: Sonatas for harpsichord solo, and for harpsichord in various combinations with violin and cello; 76 organ preludes; harpsichord concertos; quartets with harpsichord; and trio sonatas for 2 Violins with basso continuo.

BIBL.: H. Fleischer, *C.S. B. (1723–1789)* (Regensburg, 1941). —**NS/LK/DM**

Binenbaum, Janco, Bulgarian-French composer; b. Adrianopol, Dec. 28, 1880; d. Chevreuse, Seine-et-Oise, Feb. 4, 1956. He studied in Munich with Rheinberger and others; was active as a piano teacher in Germany and France, eventually settling in Chevreuse. He wrote a considerable amount of symphonic and chamber music in an impressionistic vein, colored with Balkan rhythms, none of which was publ., and little ever performed. Nonetheless, Binenbaum found sincere admirers of his works, among whom M.D. Calvocoressi was the most vocal.—**NS/LK/DM**

Binet, Jean, Swiss composer; b. Geneva, Oct. 17, 1893; d. Trélex, Feb. 24, 1960. He studied in Geneva at the Univ. and at the Institut Jaques-Dalcroze; after training with Otto Barban, William Montillet, and George Templeton Strong, he completed his studies with Bloch in N.Y., whom he helped to found the Dalcroze Rhythmic School and then the Cleveland Cons. He taught the Dalcroze method in Brussels (1923–29) before settling in Trélex; later was president of the Société Suisse des Auteurs et Editeurs (1951–60). His output was marked by a refined Gallic quality.

WORKS: DRAMATIC: Ballet: *L'Ile enchantée* (1947); *Le printemps* (1950). **Other:** Incidental music. **ORCH.:** Concertino for Small Orch. (1927); *Suite d'airs et danses populaires suisses* for Small Orch. (1931); *Divertissement* for Violin and Small Orch. (1934; also for Violin and Piano); *4 danses* (1936); *3 pièces* for Strings (1939); *Cartes postales* for Small Orch. (1940); *Musique de mai* (1943); *6 pièces enfantines* for Small Orch. (1947); *Prélude symphonique* (1949); *Petit concert* for Clarinet and Strings (1950; also for Clarinet and Piano); *Suite grisonne* for Small Orch. (1951). **CHAMBER:** String Quartet (1927); Flute Sonatine (1942); *Kaval* for Flute and Piano (1945); *Sonate brève* for Violin and Piano (1946); *3 dialogues* for 2 Flutes (1957); *Variations sur un chant de Noël* for Bassoon and Piano (1957). **VOCAL:** Choral music and songs.

BIBL.: *Hommage à J. B.* (Nyon, 1961).—**NS/LK/DM**

Bing, Sir Rudolf (Franz Joseph), prominent Austrian-born English opera manager; b. Vienna, Jan. 9, 1902; d. N.Y., Sept. 2, 1997. He studied at the Univ. of Vienna and took singing lessons. After working at the Darmstadt Landestheater (1928–30) and the Berlin Städtische Oper (1930–33), he went to England and joined the Glyndebourne Festival in 1934, where he then was its general manager (1936–49). In 1947 he also helped to found the Edinburgh Festival, which he led as artistic director until 1949. In 1946 he became a naturalized British subject. From 1950 to 1972 he was general manager of the Metropolitan Opera in N.Y. His tenure there was a distinguished, if at times controversial, one. His self assurance and acerbic wit added color to his clashes with the board of directors, celebrated artists, and the press. In 1971 he was knighted. He publ. the books *5,000 Nights at the Opera* (N.Y., 1972) and *A Knight at the Opera* (N.Y., 1981). His last years were blighted by Alzheimer's disease.—**NS/LK/DM**

Bingham, Seth (Daniels), American organist and composer; b. Bloomfield, N.J., April 16, 1882; d. N.Y., June 21, 1972. He studied with Horatio Parker, and later in Paris with d'Indy, Widor (composition), and Guilmant (organ). Returning to America, he graduated from Yale Univ. (B.A., 1904; M.B., 1908), where he then taught until 1919. He was an instructor and associate prof. at Columbia Univ. until 1954. His music is contrapuntal, occasionally chromatic, and, in later works, highly modal.

WORKS: DRAMATIC: Opera: *La Charelzenn* (1917). **ORCH.:** *Wall Street Fantasy* (1912; perf. as *Symphonic Fantasy* by the N.Y. Phil., Feb. 6, 1916); *Memories of France*, orch. suite (1920); *Wilderness Stone* for Narrator, Soli, Chorus, and Orch. (1933); Concerto for Organ and Orch. (Rochester, Oct. 24, 1946); *Connecticut Suite* for Organ and Strings (Hartford, March 26, 1954). **CHAMBER:** *Tame Animal Tunes* for 18 Instruments (1918); Concerto for Brass, Snare Drum, and Organ (Minneapolis, July 12, 1954). O r g a n : *Suite* (1926); *Pioneer America* (1928); *Harmonies of Florence* (1929); *Carillon de Château-Thierry* (1936); *Pastoral Psalms* (1938); *12 Hymn-Preludes* (1942); *Variation Studies* (1950); *36 Hymn and Carol Canons* (1952).—**NS/LK/DM**

Bini, Pasquale, Italian violinist, teacher, and composer; b. Pesaro, June 21, 1716; d. there, April 1770. At 15, he became a pupil of Tartini in Padua. After winning success as a violinist in Rome (c. 1734), he returned to Padua to complete his training with Tartini. He then was again in Rome until returning to Pesaro in 1747. In 1754 he became director of concerts and chamber music to the Duke of Württemberg. About 1759 he returned to Pesaro. He wrote concertos and sonatas for violin. —**LK/DM**

Binički, Stanislav, Serbian composer and conductor; b. Jasika, near Kruševca, July 27, 1872; d. Belgrade, Feb. 15, 1942. He studied at the Univ. of Belgrade, and later took courses in composition with Rheinberger in Munich. Returning to Belgrade, he helped organize the Serbian School of Music; was also active as an opera conductor. He composed a number of incidental pieces for the theater, the opera *Na uranku* (Dawn; Belgrade, Jan. 2, 1904), and choruses and songs.—**NS/LK/DM**

Binkerd, Gordon (Ware), American composer and teacher; b. Lynch, Nebr., May 22, 1916. He studied piano in S.Dak., and composition with Rogers at the Eastman School of Music in Rochester, N.Y., and with Piston at Harvard Univ. From 1949 to 1971 he was a member of the faculty of the Univ. of Ill. He received a Guggenheim fellowship in 1959.

WORKS: ORCH.: 4 syms.: No. 1 (Urbana, March 20, 1955), No. 2 (Urbana, April 13, 1957), No. 3 (N.Y., Jan. 6, 1961), and No. 4 (St. Louis, Oct. 12, 1963; dismembered and reduced to a *Movement for Orch.*); *A Part of Heaven*, 2 romances for Violin and Orch. (1972). CHAMBER: Cello Sonata (1952); Trio for Clarinet, Viola, and Cello (1955); 2 string quartets (1956, 1961); Violin Sonata (1977); String Trio (1979). P i a n o : 4 sonatas (1955, 1981, 1982, 1983). VOCAL: Choral works; songs. —**NS/LK/DM**

Binkley, Thomas (Eden), American lutenist, wind player, and music scholar; b. Cleveland, Dec. 26, 1931; d. Bloomington, Ind., April 28, 1995. He studied at the Univ. of Ill. (B.M., 1956), then pursued postgraduate studies at the Univ. of Munich (1957–58) and the Univ. of Ill. (1958–59). His principal mentors were Dragan Plamenac, Claude Palisca, John Ward, Thrasybulos Georgiades, and George Hunter. From 1960 to 1980 he was director of the Studio der fruhen Musik in Munich; also taught and performed in the medieval program at the Schola Cantorum Basiliensis in Basel (1973–77). In 1979 he became prof. of music and director of the Early Music Inst. at the Ind. Univ. School of Music in Bloomington. He served as general ed. of its book series Music: Scholarship and Performance, and of its monograph series Early Music Inst. Publications. He ed. the vol. *Willi Apel, Medieval Music: Collected Articles and Reviews* (Wiesbaden, 1986), and contributed articles to other publications. As a performing musician, he made appearances in major music centers in America and Europe.—**NS/LK/DM**

Binns, Malcolm, English pianist and fortepianist; b. Gedling, Nottingham, Jan. 29, 1936. He studied at the Royal Coll. of Music in London. He made his debut in London in 1957; subsequently appeared with the leading English orchs. and gave recitals. His vast repertory ranges from early music on the fortepiano to contemporary scores on the concert grand.—**NS/LK/DM**

Bioni, Antonio, Italian composer; b. Venice, 1698; d. after 1739. He was a pupil of Giovanni Porta. Among his works are 33 stage pieces, most of which were first performed at the Ballhaus Theater in Breslau, where he was impresario, composer, and arranger (1730–34); three of these scores were written for Prague. In 1731 he became composer to the Mainz electoral court. Among his other works are a serenata for the Archduchess Maria Theresia, *La pace fra la virtù e la bellezza* (Vienna, 1739), and a Mass.—**LK/DM**

Biordi, Giovanni, Italian composer; b. Rome, 1691; d. there, March 11, 1748. He was maestro di cappella at Tivoli Cathedral (1714–16), and in 1717 became a chapel singer to the Pope. He was named maestro di cappella at the church of S. Giacomo degli Spagnuoli in Rome in 1722, and remained in this post until his death. He also was a voice teacher at the Papal Coll. from 1724; was named secretary (1730) and then chamberlain (1737) of the Sistine Chapel. He composed many sacred works.—**NS/LK/DM**

Bird, Arthur, American pianist, organist, music critic, and composer; b. Belmont, Mass., July 23, 1856; d. Berlin, Dec. 22, 1923. He began his training with his father and uncle, both composers and compilers of hymn tunes. By age 15 he was an organist in Brookline and Cambridge, Mass. After studies with Haupt, Löschhorn, and Rohde at the Berlin Hochschule für Musik (1875–77), he was a church organist in Halifax, Nova Scotia (1877–81). From 1881 to 1886 he was again in Berlin for composition studies with H. Urban, and also spent several months with Liszt. After serving as director of the Milwaukee Music Festival in 1886, he settled in Berlin and wrote for such American journals as the *Etude* and Chicago's *Musical Leader*. In his articles, he violently attacked Richard Strauss and other composers of the day. In 1898 he was elected a member of the National Inst. of Arts and Letters. His works were written in a conservative, late Romantic style. Much of his music was publ. abroad, which accounted in large measure for his relative obscurity in America. He was a major composer of pieces for the American reed organ (harmonium) in the 1890s, but composed little after 1900.

WORKS: DRAMATIC: C o m i c O p e r a : *Daphne, or The Pipes of Arcadia* (1893–94; Waldorf-Astoria Hotel, N.Y., Dec. 13, 1897). B a l l e t : *Volksfest* (1886); *Rübezahl* (1887–88; rev. 1891). ORCH.: 2 serenades (1882, 1882); Concert Overture (1884); *Eine Carneval Szene* (1884; Sonderhausen, June 3, 1886); 3 *Little Suites* (1884; 1884–85; 1890); Sym. (1885; Berlin, Feb. 4, 1886); *Melody and Spanish Dance* for Violin and Chamber Orch. (1885); *Introduction and Fugue* (1886; rev. for Organ and Orch., 1888); 2 *Episodes* (1887–88); 2 *Poems* (1888); 2 *Pieces* for Strings

(1888); *Romance* for Violin and Chamber Orch. (1890); *Variations on an American Folk Song* for Flute and Chamber Orch. (1891); Symphonic Suite (c. 1910; rev. 1918). **CHAMBER:** *Andante and Allegro* for Violin and Piano (1878); *Adagio* for Flute, Violin, Cello, and Piano (1879); *Nonet (Marche miniature)* for Woodwinds (1887); Suite for 10 Instruments (1889); Serenade for 10 Wind Instruments (1889). **KEYBOARD: P i a n o :** Sonata (1883); *American Melodies* for Piano, 4–Hands (1887); *Theme and Variations* (1889); several sets of pieces. **O r g a n :** 4 sonatas (1882); *3 Oriental Sketches* (1898); *Concert Fantasia* (1904); 30 pieces of manual music for Harmonium. **VOCAL:** Various works.

BIBL.: W. Loring Jr., *The Music of A. B.* (Atlanta, 1974). —**NS/LK/DM**

Biret, Idil, remarkable Turkish pianist; b. Ankara, Nov. 21, 1941. She began her music studies when she was only 3. Her talent prompted the Turkish government to send her to Paris to study at the Cons., where she was a student of Jean Doyen (piano), Nadia Boulanger (accompaniment), and Jacques Février (chamber music), and where she took premiers prix in all three at age 15. When she was 11, Kempff invited her to perform Mozart's E-flat major Concerto for 2 Pianos and Orch., K.365/316a, with him in Paris. She continued her training with Kempff, and also received advice from Cortot. In 1954 and again in 1964 she won the Lily Boulanger Memorial Fund Award. From the time she was 15 she began to tour widely as a soloist with orchs., as a recitalist, and as a chamber music player. In 1959 she was awarded the Harriet Cohen/Dinu Lipatti Gold Medal. In 1973 she performed all of the Beethoven violin sonatas with Menuhin at the Istanbul Festival. She was named a Chevaliere de l'Ordre du Merité in 1976 by the French government. In 1986 she played Liszt's formidable transcriptions of all of the Beethoven syms. at the Montepellier Festival, which she also recorded. She has won notable distinction for her performances of the standard repertoire, but she has also played much contemporary music. Her recordings of the complete piano works of Chopin (1992) and the complete solo piano music of Brahms (1995) have secured her reputation as a pianist of the first rank. —**LK/DM**

Biriukov, Yuri, Russian composer; b. Moscow, April 1, 1908; d. there, Nov. 1, 1976. He studied piano with Feinberg and composition with Miaskovsky at the Moscow Cons., graduating in 1936. Among his works are 2 operas, *Peasant Gentlewoman* (1947) and *Knight of the Golden Star* (1956), a ballet, *The Cosmonauts* (1962), a musical, *The Blue Express* (1971), a Sym. on Ingush themes (1968), 3 piano concertos (1941, 1945, 1970), 24 preludes and 4 toccatas for Piano, and much music for the theater and films.—**NS/LK/DM**

Birkenstock, Johann Adam, German violinist and composer; b. Alsfeld, Feb. 19, 1687; d. Eisenach, Feb. 26, 1733. He studied in Kassel with Ruggiero Fedeli, then in Berlin with Volumier and in Bayreuth with Fiorelli. After being employed in the Kassel Court Orch.

(1709–30), in 1730 went to Eisenach, where he served as Kapellmeister. His sonatas for violin with basso continuo (Amsterdam, 1722) are included in several anthologies.—**NS/LK/DM**

Birnbach, Heinrich, German pianist, music pedagogue, and composer, son of **Karl Joseph Birnbach;** b. Breslau, Jan. 8, 1793; d. Berlin, Aug. 24, 1879. He studied piano with his father. He taught in Breslau from 1814 to 1821, then settled in Berlin as a music teacher and founded a music inst. Among his pupils were Nicolai, Kücken, and Dehn. He composed 2 syms., 2 overtures, concertos for oboe, clarinet, and guitar, piano concertos, a Piano Quintet, piano sonatas, piano duos, etc. He also publ. a treatise, *Der vollkommene Kapellmeister* (1845).—**NS/LK/DM**

Birnbach, Karl Joseph, German composer, father of **Heinrich Birnbach;** b. Köpernick, Silesia, 1751; d. Warsaw, May 29, 1805. During the last years of his life he was conductor at the German Theater in Warsaw. A prolific composer, he wrote 2 operas, 10 syms., 16 piano concertos, 10 violin concertos, cantatas, masses, chamber music, piano pieces.—**NS/LK/DM**

Birnie, Tessa (Daphne), New Zealand pianist and conductor; b. Ashburton, July 19, 1934. She studied piano with Paul Schramm in Wellington, then took lessons with Lefébure in Paris and K.U. Schnabel in Como. She subsequently toured as a pianist in Australia and Asia, and also played in the U.S. She organized the Sydney Camerata Orch. in 1963, appearing with it as both pianist and conductor. She was founder-president of the Australian Soc. of Keyboard Music and founder of the journal Key Vive Music. In 1985 she was awarded the Medal of the Order of Australia.—**NS/LK/DM**

Birtner, Herbert, German musicologist; b. Hamburg, June 16, 1900; d. in battle at Voronezh, Russia, Sept. 27, 1942. He first studied medicine, then took courses in musicology with Gurlitt and Kroyer. He was an asst. lecturer at the Univ. of Leipzig (1924–28), and then a prof. at the Univ. of Marburg (1938–40). In 1940 he was drafted into the German army. He contributed important studies on the music of the Reformation. His publ. works include *Joachim à Burck als Motettenkomponist* (Leipzig, 1924) and *Studien zur niederlandisch-humanistischen Musikanschauung* (Marburg, 1929). —**NS/LK/DM**

Birtwistle, Sir Harrison (Paul), eminent English composer; b. Accrington, Lancashire, July 15, 1934. He was a student of Frederick Thurston (clarinet) and Richard Hall (composition) at the Royal Manchester Coll. of Music (1952–60), and then of Reginald Kell (clarinet) at the Royal Academy of Music in London (1960–61). After serving as director of music at the Cranbourne Chase School in Dorset (1962–65), he was a visiting prof. at Princeton Univ. (1966). Returning to England, he co-founded with Peter Maxwell Davies the Pierrot Players in 1967, a contemporary music ensemble, with which he remained active until 1970. He was a visiting prof. of music at Swarthmore Coll. (1973–74) and the State Univ. of N.Y. at Buffalo (1975). Returning once more to England, he was active as music director at the National Theater in London from 1975. In 1987 he received the Grawemeyer Award of the Univ. of Louisville for his opera *The Mask of Orpheus*. He was knighted in 1988. In 1995 he was awarded the Siemens Prize. In his compositions, Birtwistle departed completely from the folkloric trends popular in modern English music and adopted an abstract idiom, one marked by an expert handling of various elements in a thoroughly contemporary idiom. His operas constitute a significant contribution to the British stage.

WORKS: DRAMATIC: *Punch and Judy*, tragical comedy or comical tragedy (1966–67; Aldeburgh, June 8, 1968; rev. version, London, March 3, 1970); *Down by the Greenwood Side*, dramatic pastorale (1968–69; Brighton, May 8, 1969); *The Mask of Orpheus*, opera (1973–75; 1981–84; London, May 21, 1986); *Pulse Field: Frames, Pulses, and Interruptions*, ballet (Snape, June 25, 1977); *Bow Down*, music theater (London, July 4, 1977); *Yan, Tan, Tethera*, opera (1983–84; London, Aug. 7, 1986); *Gawain*, opera (1990–91; London, May 30, 1991); *The Second Mrs. Kong*, opera (1993–94; Glyndebourne, Oct. 21, 1994); *The Last Supper*, opera (1999; Berlin, April 18, 2000); incidental music. **ORCH.:** *Chorales* (1960–63; London, Feb. 14, 1967); *3 Movements with Fanfares* (London, July 8, 1964); *Nomos* for Amplified Flute, Amplified Clarinet, Amplified Horn, Amplified Bassoon, and Orch. (1967–68; London, Aug. 23, 1968); *An Imaginary Landscape* (London, June 2, 1971); *The Triumph of Time* (1971–72; London, June 1, 1972); *Grimethorpe Aria* for Brass Band (Harrogate, Aug. 15, 1973); *Melencolia I* for Clarinet, Harp, and 2 String Orchs. (Glasgow, Sept. 18, 1976); *Earth Dances* (1985–86; London, March 14, 1986); *Endless Parade* for Trumpet, Vibraphone, and Strings (1986–87; Zürich, May 1, 1987); *Machaut à ma Manière* (1988); *Salford Toccata* for Brass Band (Salford, April 12, 1989); *Gawain's Journey* (Vienna, Oct. 21, 1991); *Antiphonies* for Piano and Orch. (1992; Paris, May 5, 1993); *The Cry of Anubis* for Tuba and Orch. (1994; London, Jan. 16, 1995); *Panic* for Alto Saxophone, Drummer, and Wind, Brass, and Percussion Orch. (London, Sept. 16, 1995). **CHAMBER:** *Refrains and Choruses* for Wind Quintet (1957; Cheltenham, June 11, 1959); *3 Sonatas for 9 Instruments* (Aldeburgh, June 17, 1960); *The World Is Discovered* for 12 Instruments (London, March 5, 1961); *Entr'actes* for Flute, Viola, and Harp (1962; used in *Entr'actes and Sappho Fragments*, 1964); *Tragoedia* for 10 Instruments (Devon, Aug. 20, 1965); *Verses* for Clarinet and Piano (London, Oct. 1965); *Chorale from a Toy Shop* for Flute, Oboe or Clarinet, Clarinet or English Horn, Horn or Trombone, and Bassoon or Tuba (1967; Lewes, March 28, 1979; also for 2 Trumpets, Horn, Trombone, and Tuba, London, May 19, 1978); *3 Lessons in a Frame* for Piano, Flute, Clarinet, Violin, Cello, and Percussion (Cheltenham, July 17, 1967); *Linoi* for Clarinet and Piano (London, Oct. 11, 1968; 2nd version for Clarinet, Piano, Dancer, and Tape, London, April 22, 1969; 3rd version for Clarinet, Piano, and Cello, Sheffield, Nov. 12, 1973); *4 Interludes for a Tragedy* for Clarinet and Tape (without tape, London, Oct. 18, 1968; with tape, London, Feb. 10, 1969); *Verses* for Ensembles (1968–69; London, Feb. 12, 1969); *Some Petals from my Twickenham Herbarium* for Piccolo, Clarinet, Viola, Cello, Piano, and Bells (London, April 22, 1969); *Medusa* for Chamber Ensemble and Tape (Sheffield, Oct. 22, 1969; rev. version, London, March 3, 1970); *8 Lessons* for Keyboards (London, Jan. 13, 1970); *Signals* for Clarinet and Electronics (Edinburgh, Aug. 25, 1970); *Dinah*

and Nick's Love Song for 3 Melody Instruments and Harp (1970; Sheffield, Oct. 26, 1972); *Tombeau in memoriam Igor Stravinsky* for Flute, Clarinet, Harp, and String Quartet (1971; London, June 17, 1972); *Chanson de Geste* for Amplified Sustaining Instrument and Tape (Perugia, July 1973); *For O, for O the Hobby Horse Is Forgot* for 6 Percussionists (1976; Tokyo, Feb. 10, 1978); *Silbury Air* for 15 Instruments (London, March 9, 1977); *Carmen Arcadiae Mechanicae Perpetuum* for 14 Instruments (1977; London, Jan. 24, 1978); Clarinet Quintet (1980; Huddersfield, Nov. 21, 1981); *Pulse Sampler* for Oboe and Claves (Huddersfield, Nov. 20, 1981); *Duets for Storab* for 2 Flutes (1983; London, March 25, 1984); *Secret Theatre* for 14 Instruments (London, Oct. 18, 1984); *Fanfare for Will* for 3 Trumpets, 4 Horns, 3 Trombones, and Tuba (London, July 10, 1987); *Ritual Fragment* for 14 Instruments (London, May 6, 1990); *An Interrupted Endless Melody* for Oboe and Piano (1991); *9 Movements* for String Quartet (1991–96; first complete perf., London, April 29, 1996); *5 Distances* for Flute, Oboe, Clarinet, Bassoon, and Horn (1992; London, May 7, 1993); *Hoquetus Petrus* for 2 Flutes and Piccolo Trumpet (Chicago, March 30, 1995); Piece for Piano and 12 Winds (London, April 26, 1996). **VOCAL:** *Monody for Corpus Christi* for Soprano, Flute, Horn, and Violin (1959; London, April 5, 1960); *Narration: A Description of the Passing of a Year* for Chorus (1963; London, Feb. 14, 1964); *Entr'actes and Sappho Fragments* for Soprano and 6 Instruments (Cheltenham, July 11, 1964); *Ring a Dumb Carillon* for Soprano Playing Suspended Cymbals, Clarinet, and Percussion (1964–65; London, March 19, 1965); *Carmen Paschale*, motet for Chorus and Organ ad libitum (Aldeburgh, June 17, 1965); *The Visions of Francesco Petrarca* for Baritone, Mime Ensemble, Chamber Ensemble, and School Orch. (1965–66; York, June 15, 1966); *Monodrama* for Soprano, Speaker, and Chamber Ensemble (London, May 30, 1967); *Cantata* for Soprano and Chamber Ensemble (London, June 12, 1969); *Nenia: The Death of Orpheus* for Soprano, 3 Bass Clarinets, Piano, and Crotales (London, Nov. 20, 1970); *Meridian* for Mezzo-soprano, 2 3-part Soprano Choruses, and Instruments (1970–71; London, Feb. 26, 1971); *Prologue* for Tenor and 7 Instruments (London, April 18, 1971); *The Fields of Sorrow* for 2 Sopranos, Chorus, and 16 Instruments (Dartington, Aug. 7, 1971; rev. 1972); *Epilogue* for Baritone, Horn, 4 Trombones, and 6 Tam-tams (London, April 23, 1972); *La Plage: 8 Arias of Remembrance* for Soprano, 3 Clarinets, Piano, and Marimba (Sheffield, Oct. 26, 1972); *...agm...* for 16 Voices and 3 Instrumental Groups (1978–79; Paris, April 9, 1979); *Chorale Fragments from...agm...* for 16 Voices (London, April 5, 1979); *On the Sheer Threshold of the Night*, madrigal for 4 Solo Voices and Chorus (Hessian Radio, Frankfurt am Main, May 10, 1980); *Songs by Myself* for Soprano and 7 Instruments (London, Oct. 18, 1984); *Words Overheard* for Soprano and Chamber Orch. (Glasgow, Nov. 17, 1985); *4 Songs of Autumn* for Soprano and String Quartet (1987; London, Jan. 24, 1988); *An die Musik* for Soprano and 10 Instruments (London, May 4, 1988); *White and Light* for Soprano and 5 Instruments (Brighton, May 13, 1989); *9 Settings of Celan* for Soprano, 2 Clarinets, Viola, Cello, and Double Bass (1989–96; first complete perf., Witten, April 28, 1996); *4 Poems by Jaan Kaplinski* for Soprano and 13 Instruments (Aldeburgh, June 19, 1991); *Tenebrae* for Soprano and 5 Instruments (London, Sept. 18, 1992); *Night* for Soprano, 2 Choruses, Cello, and Double Bass (London, Sept. 18, 1992). **Tape:** *Chronometer* (1971–72; London, April 24, 1972). **OTHER:** Pieces for young people; electronic music; arrangements.

BIBL.: M. Hall, *H. B.* (London, 1984).—NS/LK/DM

Bischof, Rainer, Austrian composer; b. Vienna, June 20, 1947. He studied law, philosophy, art history, and pedagogy at the Univ. of Vienna (Ph.D., 1973), composition at the Vienna Academy of Music (1965), and privately with Apostel (1967–72). After serving as president of the Austrian Composers Union (1984–86), he was a lecturer on aesthetics at the Vienna Hochschule für Musik (from 1987) and general secretary of the Vienna Sym. Orch. (from 1988). His music follows the tenets of the Second Viennese School.

WORKS: CHAMBER Opera: *Das Donauergeschenk* (1990; Vienna, June 22, 1991). ORCH.: *Deduktion* for String Orch. (1973–74); *Orchesterstücke* (1976–82); Concerto for Flute and Strings (1978–79; Innsbruck, Jan. 22, 1981); Double Concerto for Violin, Cello, and Orch. (1979–80; Zürich, June 9, 1983); Organ Concerto (1983–86; Vienna, March 5, 1987); *Largo Desolato* for Strings (1985); *Come uno sviluppo...stracci*, chamber sym. (1988–89); *Studie in PP* (1991). CHAMBER: Duo for Flute and Clarinet (1970); *Thema und 7 Variationen* for Oboe and Cello (1970); Wind Quartet for Flute, Clarinet, Horn, and Bassoon (1971); *Charakteristische Differenzen* for Violin and Piano (1974); *Studien zum Flöten- Konzert* for Flute (1978); *Musik* for 6 Recorders (1982–83); *Viola Tricolor*, 32 variations for Viola (1982); String Quartet (1983–86); *Trio Fragile 1985* for Violin, Cello, and Piano (1985); *Mallet Ricarcare* for Xylophone, Vibraphone, and Marimbaphone (1988); *Nightwoods* for Saxophone Quartet (1988); *Trio 89* for Violin, Cello, and Piano (1989); String Trio (1989–90); String Sextet (1989–90); *Hawa Naschira* for Violin (1990–91). VOCAL: Various works, including song cycles.—NS/LK/DM

Bischoff, John, innovative American composer, live- electronic music performer, and programmer; b. San Francisco, Dec. 7, 1949. He studied composition at the San Francisco Cons. of Music (1968–70), Calif. Inst. of the Arts (B.F.A., 1971), and Mills Coll. (M.F.A., 1973), where he received the Elizabeth Mills Crothers Prize in Composition (1973). His teachers in composition and electronic music have included Robert Moran, James Tenney, and Robert Ashley. From 1975 to 1992 he served as head technician and a faculty member at the City Coll. of San Francisco, and in 1992 he joined the faculty at Mills Coll. as an instructor and studios coordinator for its Center for Contemporary Music. He also serves as treasurer of Ubu Inc./Artifact Recordings in Berkeley (from 1989). Beginning in 1973, Bischoff created electronic music for both himself as solo performer and for computer network bands, and from 1976 toured widely, appearing throughout the U.S. and Europe; in 1998 he performed at the seventh International Festival of Electroacoustic Music in Havana, Cuba. He was a founding member of The League of Automatic Music Composers, the first computer network band, and in 1985 became a founding member of The Hub, a computer music band whose members design and build their own hardware and software instruments. He has also contributed several seminal articles on digital music, artistic software design, and computer applications to several respected journals. In 1989 he began creating software tools using the HMSL language which enable him to execute random searches for sonic textures on a MIDI synthesizer, and to recall and transform those textures in a strikingly idiomatic fashion. A sampling of such works comprise his noteworthy CD recording *The Glass Hand* (1996), lauded by critics as "transcending the mechanical and suffused with an organic quality." —LK/DM

Bishop, Anna (née **Ann Riviere**), famous English soprano; b. London, Jan. 9, 1810; d. N.Y., March 18, 1884. She studied piano with Moscheles and voice with **Henry Bishop** in London, marrying the latter in 1831. On April 20, 1831, she made her debut in a London concert. In 1839 she toured with the harpist Bochsa, and then returned to London to appear at Her Majesty's Theatre. After she and Bochsa became intimate, they headed for the Continent and toured widely in concerts. In 1843 she was made prima donna assoluta at the Teatro San Carlo and the Teatro Fondo in Naples. In 1846 she returned to London to sing at the Drury Lane Theatre. In 1847 she made her U.S. debut in N.Y. as Linda di Chamounix. She created the title role of *Martha* in the first U.S. performance of that opera in N.Y. in 1850. After Bochsa's death in 1856, she married the N.Y. diamond merchant Martin Schulz. In subsequent years she toured as a concert artist all over the world, making her farewell appearance in N.Y. in 1883. She was greatly praised for her superb vocal technique.—NS/LK/DM

Bishop, Sir Henry (Rowley), English conductor and composer; b. London, Nov. 18, 1786; d. there, April 30, 1855. He studied harmony with Francesco Bianchi. From 1810 to 1824 he was music director at London's Covent Garden. In 1813 he also helped to organize the Phil. Soc. of London, with which he appeared as a conductor. In 1824 he became music director at London's Drury Lane Theatre, where he brought out his most ambitious operatic effort, *Aladdin* (April 29, 1826), which proved a failure. From 1830 to 1840 he was music director at London's Vauxhall Gardens, and then again at Covent Garden in 1840–41; also conducted London's Concerts of Antient Music (1840–48). He was prof. of music at the univs. of Edinburgh (1841–43) and Oxford (from 1848), where he was made B.Mus. (1839) and D.Mus. (1853). In 1842 he was knighted. He was married to the singers Sarah Lyon (1809) and **Anna Bishop** (1831), but the latter left him to become intimate with the harpist Bochsa. Bishop's various stage pieces, most of which were merely incidental settings or adaptations to spoken plays, were undistinguished. He remains best known for his famous song "Home, Sweet Home" from his stage piece *Clari, or The Maid of Milan* (London, May 3, 1823), and for several glees.

BIBL.: R. Northcott, *The Life of Sir H.R. B.* (London, 1920). —NS/LK/DM

Bishop, Stephen
See **Kovacevich, Stephen**

Bishop-Kovacevich, Stephen
See **Kovacevich, Stephen**

Bispham, David (Scull), American baritone; b. Philadelphia, Jan. 5, 1857; d. N.Y., Oct. 2, 1921. He first sang as an amateur in church choruses in Philadelphia. In 1886 he went to Italy, where he studied with Vannuccini in Florence and Francesco Lamperti in Milan; later studied in London with Shakespeare and Randegger. He made his operatic debut as Longueville in Messager's *La Basoche* (English Opera House, London, Nov. 3, 1891), in which his comic acting ability, as well as his singing, won praise. He made his first appearance in serious opera as Kurwenal in *Tristan und Isolde* (Drury Lane, June 25, 1892). He was particularly effective in the Wagnerian baritone roles; made his American debut with the Metropolitan Opera in N.Y. as Beckmesser (Nov. 18, 1896), and was on the Metropolitan roster 1896–97, 1898–99, and 1900–03. He was a strong advocate of opera in English. A Soc. of American Singers was organized under his guidance, presenting light operas in the English language. He publ. an autobiography, *A Quaker Singer's Recollections* (N.Y., 1920). A Bispham Memorial Medal Award was established by the Opera Soc. of America in 1921 for an opera in English by an American composer.—NS/LK/DM

Bissell, Keith (Warren), Canadian composer, music educator, and conductor; b. Meaford, near Owen Sound, Ontario, Feb. 12, 1912; d. Newmarket, near Toronto, May 9, 1992. He was a composition student of Leo Smith at the Univ. of Toronto (B.Mus., 1942), and later studied with Gunild Keetman and Orff in Munich (1960). After teaching in Toronto schools (1934–48), he was asst. supervisor (1948) and then supervisor (1949–55) of school music in Edmonton. From 1955 to 1976 he served as supervisor of school music in Scarborough (part of Metropolitan Toronto), where he introduced the Orff Schulwerk method. He also was conductor of the Scarborough Orff Ensemble (1960–73). In addition to his works for professional performance, he wrote much music for the young.

WORKS: DRAMATIC: *His Majesty's Pie,* operetta (1964); *The Centennial Play,* incidental music (1967); *A Musical Play,* operetta (1977); *The Miraculous Turnip,* children's opera (1980). ORCH.: *3 Pieces* for Strings (1960); *Under the Apple Boughs* for Horn and Strings (1962); Concertino for Piano and Strings (1962); *Adagio* for Small Orch. (1963); *Little Suite* for Trumpet and Strings (1963); *Divertimento* for Strings (1964); *Canada 1967* (1967); *Andante e Scherzo* for Chamber Orch. (1971); *Variations on a Canadian Folk Song* for Strings (1972); *3 Commentaries on Canadian Folk Songs* for Strings (1973); *Andante and Allegro* for Oboe and Strings (1976). CHAMBER: *Ballad* for Violin and Piano (1947); Violin Sonata (1948); *A Folk Song Suite* for Winds (1960); *Little Suite* for Trumpet and Piano (1962); *Serenade* for Wind Quintet (1972); Trio Suite for Trumpet, Horn, and Trombone (1973); Suite for Bassoon, String Quartet, and Percussion (1977); Suite for Brass Quintet (1977); Suite for Winds (1978); Horn Sonata (1978); *In the Modes* for Recorder and Percussion (1982); *3 Pieces* for 4 Recorders (1986). VOCAL: *People Look East,* cantata for Soloists, Chorus, and 4 Instruments (1965); *Let There Be Joy,* cantata for Soloists, Chorus, and 5 Instruments (1965); *Canada, Dear Home/Canada douce patrie* for Chorus and Orch. (1966); *A Bluebird in March* for Chorus and Orch. (1967); *The Passion According to St. Luke* for Soloists, Chorus, and Orch. (1970); *How the Loon Gots Its Necklace* for Narrator, String Quintet, and Percussion (1971); *Cantate Domino* for Women's Chorus and Chamber Orch. (1977); *Anniversary Cantata* for Chorus and Orch. (1978); *A Celebration of the Nativity* for

Soloists, Chorus, and Chamber Orch. (1978); *Great Little One: Music for the Nativity* for Chorus and Orch. (1983); choruses; arrangements.

BIBL.: M. Irving, *K. B.: His Life, Career and Contribution to Music Education from 1912–76* (thesis, Univ. of Western Ontario, 1982).—NS/LK/DM

Bitetti (Ravina), Ernesto (Guillermo), Argentine guitarist and teacher; b. Rosario, July 20, 1943. He studied guitar in Santa Fe; completed his education at the Univ. Nacional del Litoral (M. Mus., 1964). He made his debut in Rosario in 1958; then toured in the U.S., Europe, the Middle East, and the Orient. He taught at the Ind. Univ. School of Music in Bloomington from 1989. Several composers wrote guitar pieces especially for him.—NS/LK/DM

Bitter, Carl Hermann, German writer on music; b. Schwedt-an-der-Oder, Feb. 27, 1813; d. Berlin, Sept. 12, 1885. He studied at the Univ. of Berlin and at Bonn Univ. He pursued a career in government, serving in the finance dept.; in 1879 he was appointed Prussian Minister of Finance by Bismarck. He retired in 1882. He publ. a book on Bach in 2 vols. (Berlin, 1865; 2nd ed., 1880; abr. Eng. ed., 1873). Other books were *Mozarts Don Juan und Glucks Iphigenia in Taurus* (Berlin, 1866), *C.Ph.E. Bach und W.Fr. Bach und deren Brüder* (2 vols., Berlin, 1868), *Beiträge zur Geschichte des Oratoriums* (Berlin, 1872), and *Die Reform der Oper durch Gluck und R. Wagner's Kunstwerke der Zukunft* (Braunschweig, 1884). —NS/LK/DM

Bittner, Julius, Austrian composer; b. Vienna, April 9, 1874; d. there, Jan. 9, 1939. He first studied law; then music with Bruno Walter and Josef Labor. He was a magistrate in Vienna until 1920 while at the same time composing industriously. He devoted most of his energy to opera and also wrote his own librettos. He also composed 2 syms., sacred choruses, and numerous songs for his wife, Emilie Bittner, a contralto. During his last years, he suffered from a crippling illness, necessitating the amputation of both legs.

WORKS: DRAMATIC: O p e r a : *Die rote Gret* (Frankfurt am Main, Oct. 26, 1907); *Der Musikant* (Vienna, April 12, 1910); *Der Bergsee* (Vienna, Nov. 9, 1911; rev. 1938); *Der Abenteurer* (Cologne, Oct. 30, 1913); *Das höllisch Gold* (Darmstadt, Oct. 15, 1916); *Das Rosengärtlein* (Mannheim, March 18, 1923); *Mondnacht* (Berlin, Nov. 13, 1928); *Das Veilchen* (Vienna, Dec. 8, 1934). OTHER: Operettas, ballets, and mimodramas.

BIBL.: R. Specht, *J. B.* (Munich, 1921); U. Bittner, *J. B.* (Vienna, 1969).—NS/LK/DM

Bizet, Georges (baptismal names, **Alexandre-César-Léopold**), great French opera composer; b. Paris, Oct. 25, 1838; d. Bougival, June 3, 1875. His parents were both professional musicians: his father, a singing teacher and composer; his mother, an excellent pianist. Bizet's talent developed early in childhood. At the age of 9, he entered the Paris Cons., his teachers being Marmontel (piano), Benoist (organ), Zimmerman (harmony), and Halévy (composition), whose daughter, Geneviève, married Bizet in 1869. In 1852 he won a first prize for piano, in 1855 for organ and for fugue, and in 1857 the Grand Prix de Rome. Also in 1857 he shared (with Lecocq) a prize offered by Offenbach for a setting of a one-act opera, *Le Docteur Miracle*; Bizet's setting was produced at the Bouffes-Parisiens on April 9, 1857. Instead of the prescribed Mass, he sent from Rome during his first year a two-act Italian opera buffa, *Don Procopio* (not produced until March 10, 1906, when it was given in Monte Carlo in an incongruously ed. version); later he sent 2 movements of a sym., an overture (*La Chasse d'Ossian*), and a 1–act opera (*La Guzla de l'Émir*; accepted by the Paris Opéra-Comique, but withdrawn by Bizet prior to production). Returning to Paris, he produced a grand opera, *Les Pêcheurs de perles* (Théâtre-Lyrique, Sept. 30, 1863); but this work, like *La Jolie Fille de Perth* (Dec. 26, 1867), failed to win popular approval. A one-act opera, *Djamileh* (Opéra-Comique, May 22, 1872), fared no better. Bizet's incidental music for Daudet's play *L'Arlésienne* (Oct. 1, 1872) was ignored by the audiences and literary critics; it was not fully appreciated until its revival in 1885. But an orch. suite from *L'Arlésienne* brought out by Pasdeloup (Nov. 10, 1872) was acclaimed; a second suite was made by Guiraud after Bizet's death. Bizet's next major work was his masterpiece, *Carmen* (based on a tale by Mérimée, text by Halévy and Meilhac), produced, after many difficulties with the management and the cast, at the Opéra-Comique (March 3, 1875). The reception of the public was not enthusiastic; several critics attacked the opera for its lurid subject, and the music for its supposed adoption of Wagner's methods. Bizet received a generous sum (25,000 francs) for the score from the publisher Choudens and won other honors (he was named a Chevalier of the Légion d'Honneur on the eve of the premiere of *Carmen*); although the attendance was not high, the opera was maintained in the repertoire. There were 37 performances before the end of the season; the original cast included Galli-Marie as Carmen, Lhérie as Don José, and Bouhy as Escamillo. Bizet was chagrined by the controversial reception of the opera, but it is a melodramatic invention to state (as some biographers have done) that the alleged failure of Carmen precipitated the composer's death (he died on the night of the 31st perf. of the opera). Soon *Carmen* became a triumphant success all over the world; it was staged in London (in Italian at Her Majesty's Theatre, June 22, 1878), St. Petersburg, Vienna, Brussels, Naples, Florence, Mainz, N.Y. (Academy of Music, Oct. 23, 1878), etc. The Metropolitan Opera produced *Carmen* first in Italian (Jan. 9, 1884), then in French, with Calvé as Carmen (Dec. 20, 1893). It should be pointed out that the famous *Habanera* is not Bizet's own, but a melody by the Spanish composer Yradier; Bizet inserted it in *Carmen* (with slight alterations), mistaking it for a folk song. Bizet also wrote an operetta, *La Prêtresse* (1854); the operas *Numa* (1871) and *Ivan le Terrible*, in 4 acts (Bordeaux, Oct. 12, 1951; the score was believed to have been destroyed by Bizet, but was discovered among the MSS bequeathed to the Paris Cons. by the second husband of Bizet's widow); the cantatas *David* (1856) and *Clovis et Clothilde* (1857); *Vasco da Gama*, symphonic ode, with Chorus (1859); *Souvenirs de Rome*, symphonic suite in 3 movements (Paris, Feb. 28, 1869; publ. in 1880

as a four-movement suite, *Roma*); orch. overture, *Patrie* (Paris, Feb. 15, 1874); *Jeux d'enfants*, suite for Piano, Four-Hands; about 150 piano pieces of all kinds (Bizet was a brilliant pianist); etc. Bizet's First Sym., written at the age of 17, was discovered in the Bizet collection at the Paris Cons. in 1933, and was given its first performance by Felix Weingartner in Basel on Feb. 26, 1935; it rapidly became popular in the concert repertoire. Bizet also completed Halévy's biblical opera, *Noë* (1869).

BIBL.: E. Galabert, *G. B.* (Paris, 1877); C. Pigot, *B. et son oeuvre* (1886; new ed., 1911); C. Bellaigue, *B.* (1891); P. Voss, *B.* (Leipzig, 1899); A. Weissmann, *B.* (Berlin, 1907); H. Gauthier-Villars, *B.: Biographie critique* (Paris, 1911); R. Brancour, *La Vie et l'oeuvre de B.* (Paris, 1913); J. Rabe, *B.* (Stockholm, 1925); D.C. Parker, *B., His Life and Works* (London, 1926); E. Istel, *B. und Carmen* (Stuttgart, 1927); R. Laparra, *B. et l'Espagne* (Paris, 1934); M. Cooper, *B.* (London, 1938); W. Dean, *G. B.: His Life and Work* (London, 1948; 3rd ed., 1975); M. Curtiss, *B. and His World* (N.Y., 1958); J. Roy, *B.* (Paris, 1983); G. Corapi, *Invito all'ascolto di G. B.* (Milan, 1992); R. Stricker, *G. B.: 1838–1875* (Paris, 1999). —NS/LK/DM

Bjerre, Jens, Danish organist and composer; b. Århus, Oct. 13, 1903; d. Copenhagen, Jan. 3, 1986. He studied piano, organ, and theory at the Copenhagen Cons. (1919–23), and piano with Lévy in Paris. He was organist at Copenhagen's St. Stefanskirke (1933–55) and Garnisonskirke (1955–72).

WORKS: DRAMATIC: Ballet: *Kameliadamen* (1958; Copenhagen, March 27, 1960); *Den hvide souper* (The White Supper; Danish Radio and TV, Dec. 27, 1964). **Other:** Incidental music. **ORCH.:** *Madrigal con Variazioni* (1948; Danish Radio, June 10, 1958); *Ouverture Parisienne* (1949). **CHAMBER:** *Mosaique musicale I* for Flute, Violin, and Cello (1936), *II* for English Horn, Violin, and Cello, (1955), and *III* for Flute, Violin, and Cello (1974); 2 violin sonatinas (1941, 1945); *Duo Concertante* for Cello and Piano (1942); *Serenade* for Flute, Oboe, and Viola (1943); Piano Trio (1946); Sonata for Solo Cello (1947); *Diapsalmata* for Cello and Piano (1953); *Dionysian Suite* for Oboe (1962); Trio for Flute, Cello, and Piano (1969); *Interludium* for Flute and Organ (1980). **Organ:** *Toccata con fughetta e ciacone* (1956). **VOCAL:** Choruses and songs.—NS/LK/DM

Bjoner, Ingrid, Norwegian soprano; b. Kraakstad, Nov. 8, 1927. She studied pharmacy at the Univ. of Oslo (graduated, 1951) and pursued vocal training at the Oslo Cons. with Gudrun Boellemose, at the Frankfurt am Main Hochschule für Musik with Paul Lohmann, and in N.Y. with Ellen Repp. After making her operaric debut as the 3rd Norn and Gutrune with the Norwegian Radio in Oslo in 1956, she made her stage debut as Mozart's Donna Anna with the Norwegian National Opera in Oslo in 1957. She sang at the Stockholm Drottningholm Court Theater (1957), the Wuppertal Theater (1957–59), the Deutsche Oper am Rhein in Düsseldorf (1959–61), the Bayreuth Festival (1960), and the Bavarian State Opera in Munich (from 1961). On Oct. 28, 1961, she made her Metropolitan Opera debut in N.Y. as Elsa in *Lohengrin*, remaining on its roster until 1968 and returning again in 1971–72 and 1974–75. In 1967 she sang at London's Covent Garden and in 1974 she returned to N.Y. to sing the Duchess of Parma in the U.S. premiere of Busoni's *Doktor Faust* at Carnegie Hall.

In subsequent years, she concentrated her career on European engagements. She also toured throughout the world as a concert singer. Later she served as a prof. at the Royal Danish Cons. of Music in Copenhagen (from 1991) and at the Norwegian Academy of Music in Oslo (from 1992). Bjoner was especially admired for her roles in operas by Wagner, Verdi, and Richard Strauss. She also won praise as Beethoven's Leonore, Iphigenia, and Turandot.—NS/LK/DM

Björkander, Nils (Frank Frederik), Swedish pianist, teacher, and composer; b. Stockholm, June 28, 1893; d. Södertalje, March 5, 1972. He studied piano and counterpoint at the Stockholm Cons. (1910–16). In 1917 he founded his own music school. In 1920 he made his debut as soloist in Beethoven's Third Piano Concerto in Stockholm. He wrote mainly for piano, his best known score being *Fyra Skärgärdsskisser* (4 Sketches from the Skerries; 1923; also arranged for orch. by others). His other piano pieces include an *Impromptu* and a Sonatina. He also wrote a Duo for Flute and Piano, a Duo for Violin and Piano, and songs.—LK/DM

Björling, Jussi (actually, **Johan Jonatan**), eminent Swedish tenor; b. Stora Tuna, Feb. 5, 1911; d. Siarö, near Stockholm, Sept. 9, 1960. He studied voice with his father, a professional singer, making his first public appearance in 1916 as a member of the Björling Male Quartet, which included his father, David Björling (1873–1926), and 2 other brothers, Johan Olof "Olle" (1909–65) and Karl Gustaf "Gösta" (1912–57), both of whom pursued careers as singers; another brother, Karl David "Kalle" (1917–75), was also a singer. The Björling Male Quartet gave concerts throughout Sweden (1916–19); made an extensive tour of the U.S. (1919–21); then continued to sing in Sweden until 1926. Jussi Björling had an excellent professional training with John Forsell at the Royal Academy of Music in Stockholm. He made his operatic debut as the Lamplighter in *Manon Lescaut* at the Royal Theater in Stockholm on July 21, 1930, and remained there until 1939; also sang as a guest artist with the Vienna State Opera and the Dresden State Opera, and at the Salzburg Festival. He made his professional U.S. debut in a concert broadcast from Carnegie Hall in N.Y. on Nov. 28, 1937, and his first appearance with the Metropolitan Opera as Rodolfo in *La Bohème* on Nov. 24, 1938; he continued to sing there until 1941, when his career was interrupted by World War II. He resumed his appearances at the Metropolitan Opera in 1945 and sang there until 1954, and then again in 1956–57 and 1959. On March 15, 1960, he suffered a heart attack as he was preparing to sing the role of Rodolfo at the Royal Opera House, Covent Garden, London, but in spite of his great discomfort, went through with the performance. He appeared for the last time at a concert in Stockholm on Aug. 20, 1960. Björling was highly regarded for his fine vocal technique and his sense of style. He excelled in Italian and French roles, and also essayed some Russian operas. He wrote an autobiography, *Med bagaget i strupen* (Stockholm, 1945). The Jussi Björling Memorial Archive was founded in 1968.

BIBL.: J. Porter and H. Henrysson, *A J. B. Discography* (comprehensive, with biographical profile; Indianapolis, 1982; 2nd ed., rev., 1993); A.-L. Björling and A. Farkas, *J.* (Portland, Ore., 1996).—NS/LK/DM

Björling, Sigurd, Swedish baritone; b. Stockholm, Nov. 2, 1907; d. Helsingborg, April 8, 1983. He was a student of Louis Condé (1928–30), then of Torsten Lennartson at the Cons. (1933–34) and the Royal Opera School (1934–36) in Stockholm. In 1934 he made his operatic debut as Billy Jackrabbit in *La Fanciulla del West* in Stockholm, where he continued to sing regularly until 1973. He also made guest appearances in various European opera centers. In 1950 he made his U.S. debut as Kurwenal with the San Francisco Opera. In 1951 he appeared at London's Covent Garden as Amfortas. On Nov. 15, 1952, he made his Metropolitan Opera debut in N.Y. as Telramund, singing there until 1953.—NS/LK/DM

Björnsson, Árni, Icelandic composer; b. Loni i Kelduhverfi, Dec. 23, 1905; d. Reykjavík, July 3, 1995. He studied theory, composition, piano, and organ at the Reykjavík Coll. of Music, and later went to England, where he enrolled at the Royal Manchester Coll. of Music. Subsequently he returned to Reykjavík, where he joined the faculty of the Coll. of Music. He composed orch. pieces and much choral music in a general Romantic vein.—NS/LK/DM

Blacher, Boris, remarkable German composer; b. Newchwang, China (of half-German, quarter-Russian, and quarter-Jewish ancestry), Jan. 19, 1903; d. Berlin, Jan. 30, 1975. His family moved to Irkutsk, Siberia, in 1914, remaining there until 1920. In 1922 Blacher went to Berlin, where he studied architecture and then took a course in composition with F.E. Koch. From 1948 until 1970 he was prof. at the Hochschule für Musik in West Berlin, and from 1953 to 1970 served as its director. A prolific composer, Blacher was equally adept in classical and experimental forms and procedures. He initiated a system of "variable meters," with time signatures following the arithmetical progression, alternatively increasing and decreasing, with permutations contributing to metrical variety. For the theater he developed a sui generis "abstract opera," incorporating an element of organized improvisation. In 1960 he was appointed director of the Seminar of Electronic Composition at the Technological Univ. in Berlin, and subsequently made ample use of electronic resources in his own compositions.

WORKS: DRAMATIC: O p e r a : *Habemeajaja* (1929; not extant); *Fürstin Tarakanowa* (1940; Wuppertal, Feb. 5, 1941); *Romeo und Julia* (1943; Berlin Radio, 1947); *Die Flut* (1946; Berlin Radio, Dec. 20, 1946; stage premiere, Dresden, March 4, 1947); *Die Nachtschwalbe*, "dramatic nocturne" (Leipzig, Feb. 22, 1948; aroused considerable commotion because of its subject, dealing with prostitutes and pimps); *Preussisches Märchen*, ballet-opera (1949; Berlin, Sept. 23, 1952); *Abstrakte Oper No. 1* (Frankfurt Radio, June 28, 1953; stage premiere, Mannheim, Oct. 17, 1953; rev. version, Berlin, Sept. 30, 1957); *Rosamunde Floris* (Berlin, Sept. 21, 1960); *Zwischenfälle bei einer Notlandung*, "reportage in 2 phases and 14 situations" for Singers, Instruments, and

Electronic Devices (1965; Hamburg, Feb. 4, 1966); *200,000 Taler* (Berlin, Sept. 25, 1969); *Yvonne, Prinzessin von Burgund* (1972; Wuppertal, Sept. 15, 1973); *Das Geheimnis des entwendeten Briefes* (1974; Berlin, Feb. 14, 1975). **B a l l e t :** *Fest im Süden* (Kassel, Feb. 4, 1935); *Harlekinade* (1939; Krefeld, Feb. 14, 1940); *Das Zauberbuch von Erzerum* (1941; Stuttgart, Oct. 17, 1942; rev. version as *Der erste Ball*, Berlin, June 11, 1950); *Chiarina* (1946; Berlin, Jan. 22, 1950); *Hamlet* (1949; Munich, Nov. 19, 1950); *Lysistrata* (1950; Berlin, Sept. 30, 1951); *Der Mohr von Venedig* (Vienna, Nov. 29, 1955); *Demeter* (1963; Schwetzingen, June 4, 1964); *Tristan* (Berlin, Oct. 10, 1965). **I n c i d e n t a l M u - s i c :** *Romeo and Juliet* (1951); *Lulu* (1952); *Georges Dandin* (1955); *War and Peace* (1955); *Robespierre* (1963); *Henry IV* (1970). **ORCH.:** Concerto for 2 Trumpets and 2 String Orchs. (1931); *Kleine Marchmusik* (Berlin, Nov. 22, 1932); *Capriccio* (1933; Hamburg, May 14, 1935); Piano Concerto (Stuttgart, Nov. 13, 1935); *Divertimento* for Wind Instruments (1936; Berlin, Feb. 24, 1937); *Geigenmusik* for Violin and Orch. (1936); *Concertante Musik* (Berlin, Dec. 6, 1937); Sym. (1938; Berlin, Feb. 5, 1939); *Concerto da camera* for 2 Violins, Cello, and Strings (1939); *Hamlet*, symphonic poem (Berlin, Oct. 28, 1940); Concerto for Strings (1940; Hamburg, Oct. 18, 1942); *Partita* for Strings and Percussion (1945); *16 Variations on a Theme of Paganini* (Leipzig, Nov. 27, 1947); Concerto for Jazz Orch. (1947); 2 piano concertos: No. 1 (1947; Göttingen, March 20, 1948) and No. 2 (Berlin, Sept. 15, 1952); Violin Concerto (1948; Munich, Nov. 17, 1950); Concerto for Clarinet, Bassoon, Horn, Trumpet, Harp, and Strings (Berlin, June 14, 1950); *Dialog* for Flute, Violin, Piano, and Strings (1950); *Orchester-Ornament*, based on "variable meters" (Venice Festival, Sept. 15, 1953); *Studie im Pianissimo* (1953; Louisville, Sept. 4, 1954); *Zwei Inventionen* (Edinburgh Festival, Aug. 28, 1954); Viola Concerto (1954; Cologne, March 14, 1955); *Orchester-Fantasie* (1955; London, Oct. 12, 1956); *Hommage à Mozart* (Berlin, Dec. 10, 1956); *Music for Cleveland* (Cleveland, Nov. 21, 1957); *Musica giocosa* (Saarbrücken, April 30, 1959); *Variations on a Theme of Muzio Clementi* for Piano and Orch. (Berlin, Oct. 4, 1961); *Konzertstück* for Wind Quintet and Strings (Donaueschingen, Oct. 19, 1963); Cello Concerto (1964; Cologne, March 19, 1965); *Virtuose Musik* for Violin, 10 Wind Instruments, Percussion, and Harp (1966; Hanover, N.H., Aug. 19, 1967); arrangement of Bach's *Das musikalische Opfer* (1966); *Collage* (1968; Vienna, Oct. 5, 1969); Concerto for Trumpet and Strings (1970; Nuremberg, Feb. 11, 1971); Concerto for Clarinet and Chamber Orch. (1971; Schwetzingen, May 12, 1972); *Stars and Strings* for Jazz Ensemble and Strings (1972; Nuremberg, Jan. 12, 1973); *Poème* (1974; Vienna, Jan. 31, 1976); *Pentagram* for Strings (1974; Berlin, April 4, 1975). **CHAMBER:** 5 string quartets: No. 1 (1930; Frankfurt am Main, Dec. 6, 1939), No. 2 (1940; Venice, 1941), No. 3 (1944), No. 4 (1951; Berlin, Jan. 25, 1953), and No. 5, *Variationen über einen divergierenden c-moll-Dreiklang* (1967; Berlin, March 8, 1968); Cello Sonata (1940); *Divertimento* for Trumpet, Trombone, and Piano (Berlin, Jan. 23, 1948); *Divertimento* for 4 Woodwinds (Munich, Sept. 28, 1951); Violin Sonata (1951; Berlin, Jan. 27, 1952); *2 Poems* for Vibraphone, Double Bass, Percussion, and Piano (1957; N.Y., Nov. 14, 1958); *Perpetuum mobile* for Violin (1963); Octet for Clarinet, Bassoon, Horn, and String Quintet (1965; Saarbrücken, Oct. 19, 1966); *4 Ornamente* for Violin and Piano (N.Y., Nov. 5, 1969); Piano Trio (1970); Sonata for 2 Cellos and 11 Instruments (Berlin, Dec. 26, 1972); *Blues espagnola and Rumba philharmonica* for 12 Cellos (1972; Tokyo, Oct. 28, 1973); Duo for Flute and Piano (1972); Quintet for Flute, Oboe, and String Trio (1973); *Tchaikovsky Variations* for Cello and Piano (1974). **P i a n o :** 2 sonatinas (1940, 1941); *3 pièces* (1943); *Ornamente, 7 Studies* (1950); Sonata

(1951); 24 preludes (1974). **VOCAL:** *Jazz-Koloraturen* for Soprano, Saxophone, and Bassoon (1929); *5 Sinnsprüche Omars des Zeltmachers* for Voice and Piano (1931); *Der Grossinquisitor*, oratorio (1942; Berlin, Oct. 14, 1947); 4 choruses to texts by Villon (1944); *Es taget vor dem Walde*, cantata (Berlin, June 29, 1946); *Francesca da Rimini* for Soprano and Violin (1954); *Traume vom Tod und vom Leben*, cantata (Wuppertal, June 5, 1955); *13 Ways of Looking at a Blackbird* for Voice and Strings (1957; Vienna, Jan. 11, 1959); *Après-lude*, 4 lieder for Voice and Piano (1958); *Die Gesänge des Seeraubers O'Rourke und seiner Geliebten Sally Brown* for Soprano, Cabaret Singer, Baritone, Speaker, Chorus, and Orch. (1958; Vienna, Oct. 5, 1959); *Requiem* for Soprano, Baritone, Chorus, and Orch. (1958; Vienna, June 11, 1959); *Jüdische Chronik* for Soloists, Chorus, and Orch. (1961; Cologne, Jan. 14, 1966; in collaboration with Dessau, K.A. Hartmann, Henze, and Wagner-Regeny); 5 Negro spirituals for Voice and Instruments (1962; Vienna, March 9, 1963); *Parergon to Eugene Onegin* for Mezzo-soprano and Chamber Ensemble (1966); *Nursery Rhymes* (1967); *For 7* for Soprano, Percussion, and Double Bass (1973). **ELECTRONIC:** *Multiple Raumperspektiven* (1962); *Elektronische Studie über ein Posaunenglissando* (1962); *Persische elektronische Impulse* (1965); *Elektronisches Scherzo* (1965); *Musik für Osaka* (1969); *Ariadne*, duodrama for 2 Speakers and Electronics (1971).

BIBL.: H. Stuckenschmidt, *B. B.* (Berlin, 1973); H. Henrich, *B. B., 1903–1975: Dokumente zu Leben und Werk* (Berlin, 1993); J. Hunkemöller, *B. B., der Jazz-Komponist* (Frankfurt am Main, 1994); C. Grafschmidt, *B. B.s variable Metrik und ihre Ableitungen: Voraussetzungen, Ausprägungen, Folgen* (Frankfurt am Main, 1996).—NS/LK/DM

Blachly, Alexander, distinguished American choral conductor and musicologist; b. Washington, D.C., Nov. 13, 1944. He was educated at Haverford Coll. (B.A. in music composition, 1967) and at Columbia Univ. (M.A., 1971, with the thesis *The Motets of Philippe de Vitry*; Ph.D., 1995, with the diss. *Mensuration and Tempo in 15ᵗʰ-Century Music: Cut Signatures in Theory and Practice*). In 1971–72 he was director of the Columbia Univ. Collegium Musicum, where he was an assoc. prof. in music from 1972 to 1974. He was director of the Diller-Quaille Renaissance Choir (1972–75) and of the Josquin Choir (1975–78) in N.Y. In 1972 Blachly founded and subsequently served as the consummate director of Pomerium, a professional a cappella vocal ensemble devoted to the masters of the Renaissance, among them Du Fay, Ockeghem, Josquin, and Lassus. He conducted his ensemble on both sides of the Atlantic at various festivals and concerts, including appearances in N.Y., Philadelphia, Boston, Cleveland, Utrecht, Antwerp, and Regensburg. From 1976 to 1988 he was an instructor in musicology and performance at Sarah Lawrence Coll., and from 1982 to 1985 he was director of the N.Y. Univ. Collegium Musicum. He was director of Ancient Voices and the Penn Madrigal Singes at the Univ. of Pa. from 1985 to 1993. Blachly became director of choral music and assoc. prof. of music at the Univ. of Notre Dame in 1993. Throughout the years, he continued to tour and record with Pomerium in performances marked by historically informed and beautifully rendered interpretations. Blachly has contributed valuable articles to various books and journals, and has also ed. *Orlande de Lassus: Motets for the Christmas Season* (Vol. I, N.Y., 1999).

In 1992 he was honored with the Noah Greenberg Award of the American Musicological Soc. and in 1999 his Pomerium was nominated for a Grammy Award. —**LK/DM**

Blachut, Beno, Czech tenor; b. Wittkowitz, June 14, 1913; d. Prague, Jan. 10, 1985. He was a pupil of Luis Kadeřábek at the Prague Cons. (1935–39). In 1938 he made his operatic debut as Jeník in *The Bartered Bride* in Olomouc, where he sang until 1941; then was a leading member of the Prague National Theater; also sang in concerts. He was particularly esteemed for his portrayals of roles in operas by Smetana, Dvořák, and Janáček. —**NS/LK/DM**

Black, Andrew, British baritone; b. Glasgow, Jan. 15, 1859; d. Sydney, Australia, Sept. 15, 1920. He studied singing in London with Randegger and Welch, then in Milan with Scafati. He made his London debut at the Crystal Palace on July 30, 1887. In 1893 he was appointed prof. of singing at the Royal Manchester Coll. of Music. In 1913 he settled in Australia.—**NS/LK/DM**

Black, Frank, American conductor; b. Philadelphia, Nov. 28, 1894; d. Atlanta, Jan. 29, 1968. He studied piano with Raphael Joseffy in N.Y., then devoted himself chiefly to conducting radio orchs. In 1928 he organized the music dept. of NBC, a post he held until 1948. —**NS/LK/DM**

Black, Stanley, English pianist and conductor; b. London, June 14, 1913. He studied at the Matthay School of Music in London, and began his career as a jazz pianist and arranger. He then was a conductor of the BBC Dance Orch. (1944–52), and subsequently worked as a music director for films. In 1968–69 he was principal conductor of the BBC Northern Ireland Orch.; also appeared as a guest conductor with various orchs. in England. In 1971 he served as assoc. conductor of the Osaka Phil. In 1986 he was made an Officer of the Order of the British Empire.—**NS/LK/DM**

Blackburn, Bonnie J., American musicologist; b. Albany, N.Y., July 15, 1939. She was educated at Wellesley Coll. (B.A., 1961) and the Univ. of Chicago (M.A., 1963; Ph.D., 1970, with the diss. *The Lupus Problem*). After serving as a research asst. at the Univ. of Chicago (1963–76), she returned there as a visiting assoc. prof. in 1986. In 1987 she was a lecturer at Northwestern Univ., and in 1989–90 she was a visiting assoc. prof. at the State Univ. of N.Y. at Buffalo. From 1964 to 1976 she was asst. ed. of the Monuments of Renaissance Music series, and in 1993 she became its general ed. In 1988–89 she held a Guggenheim fellowship. In 1971 she married **Edward Lowinsky**. After his death, she married the classicist Leofranc Holford-Strevens. In addition to her books and editions, she contributed articles to various learned books and journals.

WRITINGS: Ed. with E. Lowinsky, *Josquin des Prez: Proceedings of the International Josquin Festival-Conference* (London,

1976); ed. *Johannis Lupi Opera omnia* (3 vols., Stuttgart, 1980–89); *Music for Treviso Cathedral in the Late Sixteenth Century: A Reconstruction of the Lost Manuscripts 29 and 30* (London, 1987); ed. *Music in the Culture of the Renaissance and Other Essays by Edward E. Lowinsky* (2 vols., Chicago, 1989); ed. with E. Lowinsky and C. Miller, *A Correspondence of Renaissance Musicians* (Oxford, 1991); with L. Holford-Strevens, *The Oxford Companion to the Year* (Oxford, 1999).—**NS/LK/DM**

Blackhall, Andrew, Scottish composer; b. 1535 or 1536; d. Jan. 31, 1609. He was canon at the Abbey of Holyroodhouse in Edinburgh, and then was made minister in Liberton (1564), Ormiston (1567), and at the Inveresk parish Church in Musselburgh (1574). In 1582 he was granted a pension by King James VI. His extant works comprise 2 anthems, Psalms, a canticle, and a part song.—**LK/DM**

Blackman, Cindy, American jazz drummer; b. Yellow Springs, Ohio, Nov. 18, 1959. Cindy Blackman can be a flashy drummer at times but her basic training and technique is solid, befitting an artist who learned her skills at the Univ. of Hartford (classical percussion) and the Berklee Coll. of Music (with Alan Dawson and Lennie Nelson). After moving to N.Y.C. in 1982, Blackman achieved the respect of her jazz compatriots through work with Jackie McLean, Sam Rivers, Ted Curson, and Joe Henderson. She has also garnered some notoriety through her recording and touring with rock musician Lenny Kravitz. As a leader Blackman has recorded four albums for Muse, featuring a variety of new and established talent including Kenny Barron, Ron Carter, Jacky Terrasson, and the Roney brothers, Wallace and Antoine.

DISC.: *Arcane* (1988); *Trio + Two* (1990); *Code Red* (1990); *Telepathy* (1992); *Sax Storm* (1993); *The Oracle* (1995); *In the Now* (1998); *Works on Canvas* (1999).—**GM**

Blackwood, Easley, American pianist, teacher, and composer; b. Indianapolis, April 21, 1933. He studied piano in his hometown and appeared as a soloist with the Indianapolis Sym. Orch. at age 14. He studied composition during summers at the Berkshire Music Center (1948–50), notably with Messiaen in 1949, and also with Bernhard Heiden at Ind. Univ. and Hindemith at Yale Univ. (1949–51; M.A., 1954). He then went to Paris to study with Boulanger (1954–56). In 1958 he was appointed to the faculty of the Univ. of Chicago, from which he retired in 1997. Blackwood's music is marked by impassioned Romantic eclat and is set in a highly evolved chromatic idiom. He is also an accomplished pianist, particularly notable for his performances of modern works of transcendental difficulty. He publ. *The Structure of Recognizable Diatonic Tunings* (Princeton, N.J., 1986).

WORKS: ORCH.: 5 syms.: No. 1 (1954–55; Boston, April 18, 1958), No. 2 (1960; Cleveland, Jan. 5, 1961), No. 3 for Small Orch. (1964; Chicago, March 7, 1965), No. 4 (1973), and No. 5 (1978); Chamber Sym. for 14 Wind Instruments (1955); Clarinet Concerto (Cincinnati, Nov. 20, 1964); *Symphonic Fantasy* (Louisville, Sept. 4, 1965); Concerto for Oboe and Strings (1966); Violin Concerto (Bath, England, June 18, 1967); Concerto for Flute and

Strings (Hanover, N.H., July 28, 1968); Piano Concerto (1969–70; Highland Park, Ill., July 26, 1970). **CHAMBER:** Viola Sonata (1953); 2 string quartets (1957, 1959); Concertino for 5 Instruments (1959); 2 violin sonatas (1960, 1973); *Fantasy* for Cello and Piano (1960); *Pastorale and Variations* for Wind Quintet (1961); Sonata for Flute and Harpsichord (1962); *Fantasy* for Flute, Clarinet, and Piano (1965); Piano Trio (1968); Cello Sonata (1985); Clarinet Sonata (1994); Piccolo Clarinet Sonatina (1994). **KEYBOARD: P i a n o :** 3 *Short Fantasies* (1965); Sonata (1996). **O r g a n :** *Symphonic Episode* (1966). **VOCAL:** *Un Voyage à Cythère* for Soprano and 10 Players (1966); 4 *Letter Scenes from Gulliver's Last Voyage* for Mezzo-soprano, Baritone, and Tape (1972). **OTHER:** 12 *Microtonal Études* for Synthesizer (1982).—**NS/LK/DM**

Blaes, Arnold Joseph, noted Belgian clarinetist; b. Brussels, Dec. 1, 1814; d. there, Jan. 11, 1892. He studied with Bachmann at the Brussels Cons., winning first prize there in 1834. He traveled on concert tour in Europe, and, while in Russia, married **Elisa Blaes** (née Meerti) in 1843. He taught at the Brussels Cons. from 1844 to 1871. His autobiography appeared as *Souvenirs de ma vie artistique* (Brussels, 1888). —**NS/LK/DM**

Blagrove, Henry Gamble, English violinist; b. Nottingham, Oct. 20, 1811; d. London, Dec. 15, 1872. He was extremely precocious in his development, and at the age of 12 was admitted to the Royal Academy of Music in London at its opening in 1823. From 1832 to 1834 he was in Germany and took lessons with Spohr in Kassel. He is credited with having established the first regular series of chamber music concerts in London in 1835.—**NS/LK/DM**

Bláha, Ivo, Czech composer and teacher; b. Litomyšl, March 14, 1936. He was a student of Řídký and Sommer at the Prague Academy of Musical and Dramatic Arts (M.A., 1958), where he pursued postgraduate studies with Hlobil (1965–70); he also worked under Herzog and Kabeláč at the experimental studio of the Czech Radio in Plzeň (1969–70). He taught composition (1964–72) and was a reader on the film and television faculty (from 1967) of the Prague Academy of Musical and Dramatic Arts. In 1988 he completed his Habilitation there as a Dozent, and later was head of its dept. of sound creation of its film and television faculty (from 1993).

WORKS: DRAMATIC: Film and television scores. **ORCH.:** *Concerto for Orchestra* (1957); Percussion Concerto (1964); Violin Concerto (1968); *Per archi,* sinfonia (1977). **CHAMBER:** Wind Quintet (1956); 3 string quartets (1957, 1966, 1983); 3 *Pieces* for Violin and Piano (1961); *Spring Plays,* suite for Wind Quintet (1962); *Sonatina semplice* for Trombone and Piano (1963); *Solitude,* sonata for Solo Violin (1965); *Music for 5 Wind Instruments* (1965); *Music to Pictures of a Friend* for Flute, Oboe, and Clarinet (1971); Cello Sonata (1972); 2 *Inventions* for Flute (1974); *Variations on a Czech Folk Song* for 3 Flutes (1975); Duo for Bass Clarinet and Piano (1975); *With Respect for Old Maestros* for Violin and Piano (1978); *Violin* for Violin (1979); *Sonnets* for Brass Ensemble (1980); *Sonata transparenta* for Flute and Piano (1982); 2 sets of *Zoolessons* for Guitar (1984, 1987); *Imagination* for Violin and Piano (1988); *Sonata introspettiva* for

Solo Viola (1989). **KEYBOARD: P i a n o :** 3 *Toccata Studies* (1967); *Rays* (1976); *Prelude for Cat* (1979). **O r g a n :** *Hymnus* (1980); *Vaults* (1986). **VOCAL:** *What's Beauty in the World,* cantata cycle for Children's Chorus and Chamber Orch. or Wind Quintet or Piano (1958); *Sentences About Life, Death, and Eternal Time* for Men's Chorus (1968); *Cet amour* for Speaker, Flute, Oboe, Clarinet, and Tape (1973–75); *Moravian Lullabies* for Soprano, Flute, and Piano (1982); various children's choral pieces.—**NS/LK/DM**

Blahetka, Marie Léopoldine, Austrian pianist and composer; b. Guntramsdorf, near Vienna, Nov. 15, 1811; d. Boulogne, France, Jan. 12, 1887. She was a piano pupil of Kalkbrenner and Moscheles, and also studied composition with Sechter. In 1840 she settled in Boulogne. She wrote a romantic opera, *Die Räuber und die Sänger,* which was produced in Vienna in 1830, and a considerable number of salon pieces for piano. —**NS/LK/DM**

Blainville, Charles-Henri de, French cellist and music theorist; b. probably in or near Rouen, 1710; d. Paris, c. 1770. His claim to musicological attention resides in his "discovery" of a third "mode hellénique" (actually the Phrygian mode), which he put to use in a sym. in 1751. Rousseau, always eager to welcome a "historical" discovery, expressed his admiration for Blainville. Among Blainville's theoretical writings are *L'Harmonie théorico-pratique* (1746), *Essai sur un troisième mode,* expounding the supposed "mode hellenique" (1751), *L'Esprit de l'art musical* (1754), and *Histoire générale, critique et philologique de la musique* (1767). He composed 5 syms., publ. a book of sonatas "pour le dessus de viole avec la basse continue," and arranged Tartini's sonatas in the form of concerti grossi. —**NS/LK/DM**

Blake, David (Leonard), English composer and teacher; b. London, Sept. 2, 1936. He studied at Gonville and Caius Coll., Cambridge (1957–60). After receiving a Mendelssohn scholarship, he studied with Eisler in East Berlin at the Deutsche Akademie der Künste (1960–61). He was a Granada Arts Fellow (1963–64), lecturer (1964–71), senior lecturer (1971–76), prof. (from 1976), and head of the music dept. (1980–83) at the Univ. of York. He edited the vol. *Hanns Eisler: A Miscellany* (1995). After working with tonal and 12–tone systems, his works since the late 1970s have been written in a chromatically tonal idiom.

WORKS: DRAMATIC: **O p e r a :** *Toussaint* (1976; London, Sept. 28, 1977; rev. 1982; London, Sept. 6, 1983); *The Plumber's Gift* (1985–88; London, May 25, 1989); *The Fabulous Adventures of Alexander the Great* (1996; Mitilene, July 11, 1998); *Scoring a Century* (1999). **ORCH.:** Chamber Sym. (York Minster, June 1966); *Metamorphoses* (York Minster, March 1971); Violin Concerto (London, Aug. 19, 1976); *Sonata alla Marcia* (London, May 17, 1978); *Scherzi ed Intermezzi* (Bedford, Nov. 17, 1984); *Pastoral Paraphrase* for Bassoon and Orch. (York, Feb. 22, 1989); *Mill Music* for Brass Band (Norwich, Oct. 13, 1990); Cello Concerto (1992; Cheltenham, July 4, 1993); *Nocturne* for Strings (1994; Swaledale Festival, June 9, 1996; also as *A Little More Night Music* for Saxophone Quartet 1990). **CHAMBER:** 3 string quartets: No. 1 (1962), No. 2 (York, July 5, 1973), and No. 3

(1982; Cambridge, April 18, 1983); *Sequence* for 2 Flutes (1967); Nonet (London, June 21, 1971; rev. 1978); *Scenes* for Cello (London, Oct. 13, 1972); *Arias* for Clarinet (1978; Newcastle, Jan. 23, 1979); *Cassation* for Winds (Sheffield, May 19, 1979; 3 movements arranged as *Scherzo and Two Dances* for Chamber Ensemble, 1981; York, Jan. 16, 1982); Clarinet Quintet (1980; Bradford, Jan. 29, 1981); *Capriccio* for Chamber Ensemble (1980; York, Jan. 14, 1981); *Fantasia* for Violin (York, Nov. 21, 1984); *Seasonal Variants* for Chamber Ensemble (Norwich, Oct. 18, 1985); *A Little More Night Music* for Saxophone Quartet (1990; Bielefeld, Feb. 3, 1991; also as *Nocturne* for String Orch., 1994). **VOCAL:** *Three Choruses to Poems by Robert Frost* (1964; London, May 1966); *Beata L'Alma* for Soprano and Piano (1966; Harrogate Festival, Aug. 1967); *What is the Cause?* for Chorus (Harrogate Festival, Aug. 1967); *The Almanack* for Chorus (1968); *Lumina* for Soprano, Baritone, and Orch., after Pound (1969); *The Bones of Chuang Tzu* for Baritone and Piano (Aldeburgh Festival, June 17, 1972; also for Baritone and Chamber Orch., 1973; Glasgow, March 25, 1975); *In Praise of Krishna* for Soprano and Orch. (Leeds, March 7, 1973); *Toussaint Suite* for Mezzo-soprano, Baritone, and Orch. (1977; London, Nov. 17, 1983); *Song of the Common Wind* for Mezzo-soprano and Orch., from *Toussaint* (1977; York, Dec. 4, 1991); *From the Mattress Grave* for High Voice and Orch., after Heine (1978; Durham, Feb. 3, 1979); *Change is going to come* for Mezzo-soprano, Baritone, Chorus, Clarinet, Trumpet, Piano, and Viola (London, Nov. 14, 1982); *Rise, Dove* for Baritone and Orch., after Aimé Césaire (Manchester, Dec. 21, 1983); *Three Ritsos Choruses* for Men's Voices and Guitars (1992; also for Chorus and Guitars or Orch., 1993).—NS/LK/DM

Blake, Eubie (actually, **James Hubert**), noteworthy ragtime pianist, composer; b. Baltimore, Md., Feb. 7, 1883; d. N.Y., Feb. 12, 1983. Both his parents were former slaves. Relatives and friends called him Hubie (from Hubert), which was abbreviated to Eubie. He grew up in an atmosphere of syncopated music and sentimental ballads played on music boxes, and had some lessons from a friendly church organist in Baltimore. At the age of 15, he got a regular job as a pianist in a "hookshop" (a sporting house) run by Aggie Sheldon, a successful madam, which provided him with tips from both the inmates and their customers. Blake improvised rag music (his long fingers could stretch to 12 white keys on the keyboard) and soon began to compose in earnest. In 1899, he wrote his "Charleston Rag," which became a hit. In 1901, he toured for a while with a medicine show, then worked as accompanist for Madison Reed. He worked mainly at the Goldfield Hotel, Baltimore (1907–15), then while playing at River View Park, began a long association with Noble Sissle. They moved together to N.Y. and worked as partners for many years: composing, performing as The Dixie Duo, and as joint orchestra leaders. They wrote and produced an all-black musical, *Shuffle Along*, which opened in N.Y. on May 23, 1921, billed as "a musical melange." The score included the song "I'm Just Wild about Harry," which became a hit and was later used as a campaign song for Harry Truman in 1948. They appeared in Europe and were successful in the U.K.; "You Were Meant for Me" was introduced by Noel Coward and Gertrude Lawrence in a 1923 London revue. Blake teamed with Spencer Williams on *Chocolate Dandies* in 1924, then returned to N.Y. (1926); he re-

mained in the U.S. when Sissle returned to Europe. During the late 1920s and early 1930s, Blake wrote for many shows and revues, ranging from the *Blackbirds* (teamed with Andy Razaf) to Olsen and Johnson's *Atrocities of 1932*. Another hit song was "Memories of You," which he wrote for *Blackbirds of 1930*. Blake resumed his partnership with Noble Sissle; in World War II they toured with their own show for the U.S.O. Though professionally inactive from 1946, he appeared occasionally on TV shows with Sissle and made several concert appearances. In 1949, he took courses in the Schillinger System of Composition at N.Y.U. In 1969, he recorded the album *The 86 Years of Eubie Blake*, and in 1972 he formed his own record company. He was a great success at the New Orleans Jazz Fest (1969), and at festivals in Southern Calif. (1971) and Newport (1971). He was featured at many jazz festivals during the 1970s, both in the U.S. and Europe. Blake played at President Jimmy Carter's White House Jazz Party (1978). In old age, he had a whole new career, playing piano and reminiscing; he said that if he'd known he was going to live that long he'd have taken better care of himself. As his centennial approached, there was a growing appreciation of his natural talent, and a Broadway musical billed simply *Eubie!* was produced with resounding success. In 1981, he received the Medal of Freedom from President Reagan. He made his last public appearance at the age of 99, at Lincoln Center on June 19, 1982. His compositions include: "Memories of You," "I'm Just Wild about Harry," "You're Lucky to Me," and "Love Will Find a Way."

DISC.: "Charleston Rag" (1921); *The 86 Years of Eubie Blake* (1969).

BIBL.: A. Rose, *E. B.* (N.Y., 1979).—JC/MM/NS

Blake, Ran, jazz pianist, composer; b. Springfield, Mass., April 20, 1935. He studied at Bard Coll. (B.A., 1960) and at Columbia Univ. (1960–2), where he attended classes in improvisation with William Russo; he also studied at the School of Jazz, Lenox, Mass., and with Oscar Peterson, Mal Waldron, and Mary Lou Williams. His most influential mentor was Gunther Schuller, who inculcated him in "third stream" music (1960–67); he also took straight jazz instruction at the Lenox School of Jazz. Blake teamed with singer Jeanne Lee at Bard in 1957, experimenting with duo improvisations. The 1961 duo album was the recording debut for each of them and won the 1963 RCA Album First Prize in Germany and the 1980 Prix Billie Holiday and is included in the Académie du Jazz. He is well known as an educator, having started out as a protégé of Gunther Schuller at New England Cons. and working his way up to director since 1973 of the Third Stream Department, a category which involves incorporation of world music into free improvisations and an emphasis on ear training and transcribing solos by ear. He primarily records and performs solo, with occasional guests. He was voted #2 in the 1985 *Down Beat* International Critics Poll, and has performed at festivals throughout the U.S., Canada, Europe, South America, and Mexico. He received fellowships from the Guggenheim Foundation, and the NEA. He won a MacArthur "genius" grant in 1988. He is a unique solo pianist who does not work with standard jazz rhythm sections but prefers to explore striking harmonies and sonorities alone or in duets.

DISC.: *Newest Sound Around* (1961); *R.B. Plays Solo Piano* (1965); *Blue Potato* (1969); *Breakthru* (1975); *Third Stream Today* (1977); *Third Stream Recompositions* (1977); *Take Two* (1977); *Take One* (1977); *Portfolio of Doktor Mabuse* (1977); *Rapport* (1978); *Film Noir* (1980); *Improvisations* (1981); *Duke Dreams* (1982); *Suffield Gothic* (1983); *Painted Rhythms: The Complete R.B., Vols. 1 and 2* (1985); *Short Life of Barbara Monk* (1986); *You Stepped out of a Cloud* (1989); *Masters from Different Worlds* (1989); *That Certain Feeling* (1990); *Epistrophy* (1991); *Round About* (1992).—**LP/NS**

Blake, Rockwell (Robert), gifted American tenor; b. Plattsburgh, N.Y., Jan. 10, 1951. He studied voice with Renata Booth as part of his high school education. Following attendance at the State Univ. of N.Y. at Fredonia, he receivd a scholarship to pursue vocal training at the Catholic Univ. of America in Washington, D.C.; completed his vocal studies in N.Y. He began his career singing with various small opera companies, first attracting notice when he appeared as Lindoro with the Washington, D.C., Opera in 1976; then sang with the Hamburg State Opera (1977–79) and the Vienna State Opera (1978). In 1978 he became the first recipient of the Richard Tucker Award. On Sept. 23, 1979, he made his N.Y. City Opera debut as Count Ory, and on Feb. 2, 1981, his Metropolitan Opera debut in N.Y. as Lindoro. He sang at the Chicago Lyric Opera and at the Rossini Opera Festival in Pesaro in 1983, at the San Francisco Opera in 1984, at the Paris Opéra in 1985, at the Paris Opéra-Comique and the Bavarian State Opera in Munich in 1987, and in Montreal and at the Salzburg Festival in 1989. In 1990 he appeared in the leading tenor role in Pergolesi's *Annibal* in Turin. In 1992 he sang James V in *La Donna del Lago* at Milan's La Scala. He sang in *Semiramide* at the Rossini Festival in Pesaro in 1994. In 1996 he was engaged as Jupiter in the French premiere of Handel's *Semele* in Aix-en-Provence. He also sang widely in concerts. Blessed with a remarkable coloratura, Blake won notable distinction as a true tenore di grazia, excelling in Mozart and Rossini.—**NS/LK/DM**

Blakey, Art (Buhaina, Abdullah ibn), famed bebop drummer, leader; b. Pittsburgh, Oct. 11, 1919; d. of lung cancer in N.Y., Oct. 16, 1990. He worked in steel mills as a youth, taught himself to play piano, and performed at night in local clubs. He claimed that he switched to drums after hearing his local competition, Errol Garner, on piano; it is also said that when the regular drummer was too sick to play for a ruthless gangster, Blakey had to step in to prevent disaster. He worked with several bands in and around Pittsburgh before moving to N.Y. and working with Mary Lou Williams (1942). He joined Fletcher Henderson (1943) for a year, then led his own band in Boston before joining Billy Eckstine's Big Band in 1944. After leaving Eckstine (1947), Blakey led his own group, The Seventeen Messengers, and played on many freelance recording dates, including important early work with Monk, and longer stints with Lucky Millinder and Buddy De

Franco (1952–53). A man of great warmth and also volatile temper, it is said that he punched Charlie Parker in March 1955 and that this helped precipitate the latter's death. On occasion, he would lead a group of his own out of N.Y.; when Horace Silver asked him to put a group together for some recordings, the Jazz Messengers were formed. Initially they were a co-operative consisting of Blakey, Silver, Hank Mobley, Doug Watkins and Kenny Dorham (later replaced by Donald Byrd), but when the other four left in 1956, it was Blakey who inherited the Jazz Messenger's name, and he continued to lead that group, with many international tours. In 1971–72, he temporarily disbanded the group for The Giants of Jazz tour with Gillespie and Monk. Blakey was an amazing talent scout and the Jazz Messengers was the first gig of note for a remarkable number of famous jazz players, including Wayne Shorter, Freddie Hubbard, Woody Shaw, Terence Blanchard, Keith Jarrett, Joanne Brackeen, Jackie McLean, Lee Morgan, Curtis Fuller, Bobby Timmons, Cedar Walton, Branford and Wynton Marsalis, Mulgrew Miller, James Williams, Donald Brown, and Johnny Griffin. A daughter, Evelyn, appears occasionally as a vocalist around N.Y. Blakey won a Grammy in 1984 for the album *N.Y. Scene.*

DISC.: *New Sounds* (c. 1947); *Africaine* (c. 1950); *A.B./Sabu* (1953); *A Night at Birdland, Vols. 1–3* (1954); *Jazz Messengers at the Cafe Bohemia, Vols. 1, 2, 3* (1955); *Jazz Messengers* (1956); *Hard Bop* (1956); *Drum Suite* (1956); *Theory of Art* (1957); *Ritual: The Modern Jazz Messengers* (1957); *Reflections on Buhaina* (1957); *Orgy in Rhythm, Vol. 1, 2* (1957); *Mirage* (1957); *Midnight Session with the Jazz* (1957); *Jazz Messengers Play Lerner and Loewe* (1957); *Hard Drive* (1957); *Hard Bop Academy* (1957); *Dawn on the Desert* (1957); *Cu-Bop* (1957); *A.B.'s Jazz Messengers with T. Monk* (1957); *A.B. and His Rhythm* (1957); *A.B. Big Band* (1957); *Paris 1958* (1958); *Moanin'* (1958); *Live in Holland* (1958); *Holiday for Skins, Vol. 1, 2* (1958); *Des Femmes Disparaissent* (1958); *Au Club Saint-Germain, Vol. 1* (1958); *Paris Olympia* (1958); *Les Liaisons Dangereuses* (soundtrack; 1959); *Paris Jam Session* (1959); *Paris Concert* (1959); *Live in Stockholm* (1959); *Live in Copenhagen* (1959); *Live in Lausanne: 1960, Pt. 1* (1960); *Night in Tunisia* (1960); *Meet You at the Jazz Corner of the World* (1960); *Live in Stockholm* (1960); *Like Someone in Love* (1960); *Big Beat* (1960); *Witch Doctor* (1961); *Roots and Herbs* (1961); *Pisces* (1961); *Paris Jazz Concert* (1961); *Freedom Rider* (1961); *Day with A.B. and the Jazz Messengers* (1961); *Buhaina's Delight* (1961); *A.B.!!!!!* (1961); *Three Blind Mice, Vols. 1 and 2* (1962); *Thermo* (1962); *Caravan* (1962); *African Beat* (1962); *Ugetsu* (1963); *Selections from the film "Golden Boy"* (1963); *Jazz Message* (1963); *Kyoto* (1964); *Indestructible* (1964); *Free for All* (1964); *Blues Bag* (1964); *A.B. and the Jazz Messengers* (1964); *Soul Finger* (1965); *Let's Make It* (1965); *Tough!* (1966); *Hold On, I'm Coming* (1966); *Buttercorn Lady* (1966); *A. B. Live!* (1968); *Mellow Blues* (1969); *Art Blakey and the Jazz Messengers* (1970); *For Minors Only* (1971); *Child's Dance* (1972); *Art's Break* (1972); *Buhaina* (1973); *Anthenagin* (1973); *Percussion Discussion* (1976); *Backgammon* (1976); *In My Prime, Vol. 1* (1977); *Gypsy Folk Tales* (1977); *Reflections in Blue* (1978); *In This Korner* (1978); *In My Prime, Vol. 2* (1978); *One by One* (1979); *Live at Montreux and Northsea* (1980); *Live at Bubba's* (1980); *Jazzbuhne Berlin '80* (1980); *And the Jazz Messengers Big Band* (1980); *Straight Ahead* (1981); *Killer Joe: Art Blakey and George Kawaguchi* (1981); *In Sweden* (1981); *Album of the Year* (1981); *Oh, by the Way* (1982); *Keystone 3* (1982); *Art Blakey and the All Star Messengers* (1982); *Aurex Jazz Festival '83*

(1983); *Super Live* (1984); *N.Y. Scene* (1984); *New Year's Eve at Sweet Basil* (1985); *Live at Ronnie Scott's* (1985); *Live at Kimball's* (1985); *Farewell* (1985); *Dr. Jeckyl* (1985); *Buhaina: The Continuing Message* (1985); *Blue Night* (1985); *Standards* (1988); *Not Yet* (1988); *Magical Trio* (1988); *I Get a Kick out of Bu* (1988); *Feel the Wind* (1989); *Three Blind Mice, Vol. 2* (1990); *Chippin' In* (1990). Bluesiana Triangle: *Bluesiana Triangle* (1990); *Bluesiana 2* (1991). Dr. John: *Dr. John and Friends* (1992).

BIBL.: J. Ramsay, *Art Blakey's Jazz Messages* (Warner Bros., 1994).—LP

Blamont, François Colin de, French composer; b. Versailles, Nov. 22, 1690; d. there, Feb. 14, 1760. He was a pupil of Délalande. He became superintendent of the King's music. Among his works were many court ballets, cantatas, and motets. He also publ. *Essai sur les goûts anciens et modernes de la musique française* (1754). —NS/LK/DM

Blanchard, Esprit Joseph Antoine, French composer; b. Pernes, Comtat-Venaissin, Feb. 29, 1696; d. Versailles, April 19, 1770. He studied with Poitevin at the choir school of the St. Sauveur Cathedral in Aix-en-Provence. In 1717 he became maître de musique to the chapter of St. Victor in Marseilles; was then maître de chapelle at the Toulon, Besançon, and Amiens cathedrals. He succeeded Bernier as sous-maître at the Chapelle du Roi in Versailles in 1738, where he was maître de chapelle from 1761 to 1765. He wrote mainly sacred choral music for performance at the churches where he was employed.—NS/LK/DM

Bland, Bobby "Blue" (originally Robert Calvin), American blues singer; b. Rosemark, Tenn., Jan. 27, 1930. Bland, a soulful baritone, was a reliable presence on the R&B charts for almost 30 years, making him one of the most successful blues singers of the second half of the 20th century. Among his biggest hits were "Farther Up the Road," "I Pity the Fool," and "That's the Way Love Is."

After spending his childhood in the rural town of Rosemark near Memphis, Bland moved with his mother to the city in the mid-1940s. While working at a garage, he began singing, first with a gospel group and then with the Beale Streeters, a loose affiliation of blues performers including B. B. King and Roscoe Gordon, each of whom also employed him as a valet and chauffeur. His recording of "I Love You Till the Day I Die" appeared on the B-side of Gordon's single "Booted," which was released on both Chess Records and the RPM subsidiary of Modern Records and hit #1 on the R&B charts in March 1952. He made further recordings for Modern, then signed to Duke Records, but he was drafted and spent the next two and a half years in the army, during which time Duke was acquired by Houston-based record executive Don Robey.

Bland was discharged in 1955 and went back to recording for Duke. He also began to tour in a revue headlined by Junior Parker and featuring a band led by trumpeter Joe Scott who helped organize his recording sessions. In 1957 he had his first R&B hit with "Farther Up the Road" (music and lyrics by Don Robey and J.

Veasey), which hit #1 in September 1957. From then on he reached the R&B charts every year through 1982, scoring 24 Top Ten hits and topping the charts with "I Pity the Fool" (March 1961) and "That's the Way Love Is" (March 1963). Both songs were credited to "Deadric Malone," a pseudonym for Robey, who reportedly bought the songs—and many others that Bland recorded—from their original writers, who included members of his band.

Bland's recordings also crossed over to the pop charts, where he peaked in the Top 40 with "Turn On Your Love Light" (music and lyrics by Deadric Malone and Joe Scott; January 1962), "Call on Me" (music and lyrics by Deadric Malone; February 1963), "That's the Way Love Is" (March 1963), and "Ain't Nothing You Can Do" (music and lyrics by Deadric Malone and Joe Scott; April 1964). He also placed several albums in the pop charts, notably *Call on Me/That's the Way Love Is* (1963), which charted for six months.

Bland continued to tour with Junior Parker until the early 1960s, when he went out on his own with a band led by Joe Scott, performing hundreds of shows each year. In 1968 the band broke up and Bland fell out with Robey, ceasing to record, though Duke continued to issue previously recorded tracks and score hits. After marrying a college student named Marty who bore him a daughter, and giving up drinking, Bland returned to recording for Duke in the early 1970s. The label was sold to ABC/Dunhill Records, which attempted to update his sound for the soul era, resulting in his first pop chart albums in a decade, *His California Album* (1973) and *Dreamer* (1974). The label also teamed him up with B. B. King for two live albums, the first of which, *Together for the First Time... Live* (1974), went gold.

Bland's record sales gradually diminished after the mid-1970s, though he continued to record regularly on MCA Records after the label absorbed ABC in 1979. In 1985 he switched to the independent Malaco label, which recorded him in a more traditional blues vein. He remained with the label, and on the road, in the 1990s.

DISC.: "Little" Junior Parker: *Blues Consolidated* (1958), *Barefoot Rock and You Got Me* (1960). B.B. King: *Together for the First Time...Live* (1974); *Together Again—Live* (1976). *Two Steps from the Blues* (1961); *Here's the Man!!!* (1962); *Call on Me* (1963); *Ain't Nothin' You Can Do* (1964); *The Soul of the Man* (1966); *Touch of the Blues* (1967); *Spotlighting the Man* (1968); *His California Album* (1973); *Dreamer* (1974); *Get on Down with B.B.* (1975); *Reflections in Blue* (1977); *Come Fly with Me* (1978); *I Feel Good I Feel Fine* (1979); *Sweet Vibrations* (1980); *You Got Me Loving You* (1981); *Try Me, I'm Real* (1981); *Here We Go Again* (1982); *Tell Mr. Bland* (1983); *Members Only* (1985); *After All* (1986); *Blues You Can Use* (1987); *Midnight Run* (1989); *Portrait of the Blues* (1991); *Sad Street* (1995); *Live on Beale Street* (1998); *Memphis on Monday Morning* (1998).—WR

Blangini, (Giuseppe Marco Maria) Felice, Italian composer; b. Turin, Nov. 18, 1781; d. Paris, Dec. 18, 1841. He was a choirboy at Turin Cathedral. In 1799 his family moved to Paris, where he gave concerts. He wrote fashionable *romances*, and came into vogue as an opera composer when he completed Della-Maria's opera *La Fausse Duègne* (1802); he was also popular as a singing teacher. After producing an opera in Munich, he was appointed court Kapellmeister (1805). He later was Generalmusikdirektor at Kassel (1809), and upon his return to Paris in 1814, he was made superintendent of the King's music, court composer, and prof. of singing at the Cons., positions which he held until 1830. His works include 30 operas, 4 masses with Orch., 170 nocturnes for 2 Voices, 174 romances for 1 Voice, etc. See his autobiography, *Souvenirs de F. B.*, ed. by M. de Villemarest (Paris, 1834).—NS/LK/DM

Blank, Allan, American composer and teacher; b. N.Y., Dec. 27, 1925. He studied at the H.S. of Music and Art in N.Y.; subsequently at the Juilliard School of Music (1945–47), Washington Square Coll. (B.A., 1948), the Univ. of Minn. (M.A., 1950), and the Univ. of Iowa. He was a violinist in the Pittsburgh Sym. Orch. (1950–52). After teaching instrumental music in N.Y. high schools (1956–65), he taught at Western Ill. Univ. in Macomb (1966–68), Paterson (N.J.) State Coll. (1968–70), Lehman Coll. of the City Univ. of N.Y. (1970–77), and Va. Commonwealth Univ. in Richmond (1978–96). He was also conductor (1984) and music director (1986–89) of the Richmond Community Orch. In his works, Blank strives for lyrical and dramatic expressivity complemented by clarity of line and richness of content.

WORKS: DRAMATIC: *Aria da capo*, chamber opera (1958–60); *The Magic Bonbons*, opera (1980–83); *The Noise*, opera (1985–86); incidental music to *Othello* (1983) and *Measure for Measure* (1984). ORCH.: *Concert Piece* for Band (1960–63); *Music for Orch.* (1964–67); *Some Thank-You Notes* for Jazz Band (1970); *6 Miniatures and a Fantasia* (1972); *6 Significant Landscapes* for Chamber Orch. (1972–74); *Divertimento* for Tuba and Band (1979); *Kreutzer March* for Band (1981); Concertino for Bassoon and Strings (1984); Concertino for Strings (1987); *Overture for a Happy Occasion* (1987); Concerto for Clarinet and Strings (1990); Concerto for Contrabass and Strings (1995); Violin Concerto (1995); *Statements and Interactions* for Horn and Strings (1995); *Music for Small Orch.* (1995); Saxophone Concerto (1999). CHAMBER: 5 string quartets (1958, 1981, 1989, 1998, 1998); Wind Quintet (1968–70); *Bicinium I to VII* for Various Instruments (1974–93); Trio for Trumpet, Horn, and Trombone (1975); *An American Medley* for Brass Quintet, Flute, and Percussion (1976); *Paganini Caprices* for 4 Horns, 3 Trumpets, 3 Trombones, and Tuba (1976); *Music for Tubas* (1977); *4 Inventions* for Bassoon and Piano (1979); *Fantasy on Cantillation Motives* for Violin, Viola, and Cello (1983); Trio for Flute, Cello, and Piano (1983), 2 Studies for Brass Quintet (1984); Concertino for 5 Players (1984–86); *Polymorphics* for Double Wind Quintet (1988); *Nocturne* for Bassoon and Harp (1988); Sonata for Solo Violin (1990); *Divertimento* for Woodwind Quintet (1991); *3 Windgrams* for Flute, Clarinet, and Bassoon (1991); *Introduction and 3 Episodes* for Flute, Clarinet, and Bassoon (1991); *Around the Turkish Lady* for Alto Saxophone (1991); *4 Studies* for Contrabass (1992); *3 Bouquets* for Bassoon and Contrabass (1992); *The 3 Graces* for 3 Flutes (1992); *A Twosome Frolic* for Violin and Cello (1993); *Elegy* for Violin and Organ (1993); 5 Pieces for Clarinet (1993); *Dualisms* for Violin and Organ (1994); 2 Pieces for Alto Saxophone and Piano (1996); Trio for Flute, Bassoon, and Piano (1997); Trio for Flute, Violin, and Harpsichord (1997); 3 Duos for 2 Flutes (1998); Duos for 2 Bassoons (1999). PIANO: *Rotation* (1959–60); *Restatement of Romance* (1973); Sonata (1992). VOCAL: *Esther's Monologue*, cantata for Soprano, Oboe, Viola, and Cello (1970); *Lines from Proverbs* for Chorus (1973); *Coali-*

tions for Soprano and 6 Instrumentalists (1975); *2 Holy Sonnets by John Donne* for Alto, Oboe, English Horn, Viola, and Harp (1977); *American Folio* for Chorus, Piano, and/or Optional Instruments (1979); *Some Funnies and Poems* for Narrator and Piano (1982); *Lines by Horace* for Chorus (1989); *Peace Cantata* for Chorus and Orch. or Piano (1989); *Friday Evening Service* for Soloist, Chorus, Organ, Flute, and Cello (1990); *A Shout of Praise* for Chorus (1993); *The Tide Rises, the Tide Falls* for Chorus and Piano (1994); *Poems from the Holocaust* for Soprano, Contrabass, and Piano (1996); *A Noiseless Patient Spider* for Bass-baritone and Piano (1999).—NS/LK/DM

Blankenburg, Quirin van (full name, **Quirinus Gerbrandszoon van Blankenburg**), Dutch organist; b. Gouda, 1654; d. The Hague, May 12, 1739. He studied organ with his father and served as a church organist in Rotterdam (1671–76) and in Gorinchem (1676–81). Later on he went to Leiden for further study at the univ. there; his next engagement was as organist at the Hoofkerk in The Hague (1687–1702); he was then employed at the Nieuwe Kerk. He publ. *Elementa musica* (The Hague, 1729), and also compiled *Clavicembel en Orgelboek der gereformeerde Psalmen en Kerkgezangen* (The Hague, 1732; 3rd ed., 1772) and a method for flute.—NS/LK/DM

Blankenburg, Walter, German theologian and musicologist; b. Emleben, near Gotha, July 31, 1903; d. Schlüchtern, March 10, 1986. He was born into a family of Lutheran ministers. He received a classical education in Gotha and Altenburg (1914–22), and then pursued training in theology (1922–29) with Büchsel and Althaus in Rostock, Heim in Tübingen, and Barth and Hirsch in Göttingen. He also studied musicology and history with Ludwig and Brandl in Göttingen, with Gurlitt, Besseler, and Ritter in Freiburg im Breisgau, and with Schering and Blume in Berlin before completing his education with Zenck at the Univ. of Göttingen (Ph.D., 1940, with the diss. *Die innere Einheit Bachs Werke*). From 1930 to 1933 he was a music teacher in Rotenburg am Fulda and Kassel, and then was a pastor in Vaake from 1930 to 1937. He also was director of the Kasseler Singgemeinde Music in Schlüchtern, and then was music director of the Evangelische Landeskirche of Kurhessen-Waldeck. He was ed. of the *Zeitschrift für Hausmusik* (1933–41), co-ed. of *Kirchenchordienst* (1935–42), and an ed. (1941–52) and ed.-in-chief (from 1952) of *Musik und Kirche*. In 1962 he was awarded an honorary doctorate in theology by the Univ. of Marburg. He was the author of the study *Einführung in Bachs h-moll Messe* (Kassel, 1950; 3rd ed., rev., 1974). With A. Dürr, he ed. Bach's *Weihnachtsoratorium* for the Neue Bach-Ausgabe (2nd series, VI, Kassel, 1960). He contributed many articles to journals and other publications, including the vols. *Geschichte der evangelischen Kirchenmusik* (Kassel, 2nd ed., rev., 1965; Eng. tr., 1974, as *Protestant Church Music: A History*) and *Kirchenmusik im Spannungsfeld der Gegenwart* (Kassel, 1968). Blankenburg's study *Johann Walter: Lebun und Werk* was ed. by F. Brusniak and publ. posthumously (Tutzing, 1991).—NS/LK/DM

Blanter, Matvei (Isaakovich), Russian composer; b. Pochep, Feb. 10, 1903; d. Moscow, Sept. 24,

1990. He was a student of G. Conus in Moscow. Among his works were an operetta, *On the Banks of the Amur* (1939), incidental music, and songs.

BIBL.: V. Zak, *M. B.* (Moscow, 1971).—**NS/LK/DM**

Blanton, Jimmy (actually, James), innovative

jazz bassist, famous for his work with Duke Ellington; b. Chattanooga, Tenn., Oct. 5, 1918; d. Monrovia, Calif., July 30, 1942. His hard-swinging lines introduced a chromaticism not typical of jazz bass before him, and through exposure with Ellington, who always appreciated bassists, he became the role model for the entire next generation. His mother was a pianist, who led her own band in Tenn. for many years. Jimmy started on violin during early childhood, did first gig at a local store, at the age of eight. He studied theory with an uncle, who specialized in teaching the mathematical aspects of music. Blanton switched to string bass while studying at Tenn. State Coll.; played in the State Collegians and gigged with local bands led by "Bugs" Roberts and drummer Joe Smith. During college summer vacations he played with Fate Marable on the riverboats; left college during his third year and moved to St. Louis. He joined Jeter-Pillars Orch. in late 1937 (playing a three-string bass), and continued to work in Fate Marable's Cotton Pickers during summer months. In autumn 1939, while playing at the Coronado Hotel Ballroom, St. Louis, he was signed by Duke Ellington, bought a four-string bass on hire-purchase (guarantor Gene Porter), and began working with Duke (sharing bass duties with Billy Taylor until Taylor left in January 1940). While working with Ellington in L.A., Blanton was taken seriously ill (entered L.A. Hospital in late 1941, where tuberculosis was diagnosed). In the spring of 1942 he was moved from the hospital to the Duarte Sanitarium, near L.A., where he spent the last few months of his life.

DISC.: Duke Ellington: "Plucked Again/Blues" (1930); "Pitter Panther Patter/Sophisticated Lady" (1940); "Body and Soul/Mr. J. B. Blues" (1940); "Jack the Bear" (1940); "Conga Brava/Ko-Ko" (1940); "Concerto for Cootie" (1940); "Sepia Panorama/Harlem Air Shaft" (1940); "In a Mellotone" (1940). B. Bigard: "Lost in Two Flats" (1939). Cootie Williams: "Black Butterfly" (1940). J. Hodges: "Squatty Roo" (1941).

BIBL.: I. Kanth, *A Discography of Jimmy Blanton* (Stockholm, 1970).—**JC/LP**

Blaramberg, Pavel (Ivanovich), Russian com-

poser; b. Orenburg, Sept. 26, 1841; d. Nice, March 28, 1907. His father was a geographer of French origin and his mother was Greek. At the age of 14 he went to St. Petersburg, where he later became a functionary of the Central Statistical Committee. He was largely self-taught in music, apart from occasional advice from Balakirev and Rimsky-Korsakov. In 1878 he settled in Moscow as an instructor at the newly founded Phil. Inst. In 1898 he went to the Crimea, then to France.

WORKS: DRAMATIC: O p e r a : *The Mummers* (1881); *Russalka* (Moscow, April 15, 1888); *Maria Tudor,* after Hugo (produced as *Mary of Burgundy* on account of the censor's objection to the original libretto; Moscow, Oct. 29, 1888); *Tushintsy* (Moscow, Feb. 5, 1895); *The Waves* (1902). **OTHER:**

The Dying Gladiator, symphonic poem (1882); Sym. (1886); songs.—**NS/LK/DM**

Blass, Robert, American bass of German parents; b.

N.Y., Oct. 7, 1867; d. Berlin, Dec. 3, 1930. He went to Leipzig in 1887 to study violin, but then pursued vocal instruction from Stockhausen in Frankfurt am Main. In 1892 he made his operatic debut as King Heinrich in Weimar, and then sang in various German opera centers. In 1899 he appeared at London's Covent Garden. On Nov. 13, 1900, he made his Metropolitan Opera debut as Hermann in *Tannhäuser* during the company's visit to San Francisco. He first sang on the stage of the Metropolitan Opera in N.Y. as Rocco on Dec. 28, 1900, and remained on its roster until 1910 and again from 1920 to 1922. In 1901 he appeared as Gurnemanz and Hagen at Bayreuth and sang at the Berlin Deutsches Opernhaus from 1913 to 1919.—**NS/LK/DM**

Blasters, The, first recognized for their authentic,

original re-creations of the sound and spirit of vintage rockabilly and rhythm and blues; formed in 1979 in Downey, Calif. **MEMBERSHIP:** Phil Alvin, lead voc., rhythm gtr. (b. Los Angeles, March 6, 1953); Dave Alvin, rhythm gtr. (b. Los Angeles, Nov. 11, 1955); John Bazz, bs. (b. July 6, 1952); Bill Bateman, drms. (b. Orange, Calif., Dec. 16, 1951). Later members include Gene Taylor, pno. (b. Tyler, Tex., July 2, 1952); Lee Allen, tenor sax.; Steve Berlin, bar. sax. (b. Philadelphia, Pa., Sept. 14, 1955).

The Blasters soon expanded their repertoire into the realm of socially conscious songs concerned with the plight of common people, leading to comparisons with Bruce Springsteen and John Mellencamp. Centered around lead vocalist Phil Alvin and songwriter Dave Alvin, one of the most talented brother duos of the 1980s, the group were a fixture in the Los Angeles alternative-rock scene. The group endured after Dave Alvin departed in 1985 to join X and that band's folk- and country-style spinoff the Knitters before launching his own career as one of America's most compelling songwriters.

The Blasters were initially comprised of brothers Phil and Dave Alvin, bassist John Bazz, and drummer Bill Bateman. Developing a local reputation during the waning days of punk music, the Blasters toured the United States as opening act for Queen in 1980. Rockabilly singer Shakin' Stevens scored a major British hit with Dave Alvin's "Marie Marie." The group recorded their debut album, *American Music,* for the small independent label Rollin' Rock. They added pianist Gene Taylor to rerecord the album for another Los Angeles independent label, Slash. Released as simply *The Blasters,* the album sold remarkably well after Warner Bros. picked up distribution of the label. The album featured the celebratory classic "American Music," the nostalgic but rocking "Border Radio," and "Marie Marie," all written by Dave Alvin and performed in an exciting, bare-bones style. The Blasters toured tirelessly to establish themselves as one of this country's most engaging live bands, and next recorded the EP *Over There* live in London.

The Blasters won their greatest critical acclaim with 1983's *Non Fiction*, recorded with short-time members Lee Allen (tenor saxophone) and Steve Berlin (baritone saxophone). Songs such as "Boomtown," "Fool's Paradise," and "Jubilee Train" revealed a concern for the plight of the common man; the album also included "Long White Cadillac" (later covered by Dwight Yoakam) and the ballad "Leaving." Returning to the basic quintet of the Alvins, Taylor, Bazz, and Bateman, the Blasters recorded *Hard Line*, which included the rocking "Trouble Bound," the ominous "Dark Night," the blatantly political "Common Man," John Mellencamp's "Colored Lights," and "Just Another Saturday Night," cowritten by Dave Alvin and John Doe of X.

During his free time Dave Alvin had been playing with John Doe, Exene Cervenka, and D. J. Bonebrake of X in an acoustic folk and country group called the Knitters. The group toured and then recorded *Poor Little Critter on the Road* for Slash. Alvin quit the Blasters in 1985, and the remaining quartet added guitarist Michael "Hollywood Fats" Mann, but he died of a heart attack soon after at age 32. Dave rejoined the group for their 1987 European tour, after which the group added guitarist Greg Hormel. In 1986 Phil Alvin recorded the eclectic *Un' Sung Stories* for Slash.

Dave Alvin joined X in 1985, staying on through the recording of *See How We Are*, which included his "Fourth of July." He left X in 1987 to pursue a solo career, recording *Every Night about This Time* in England. The album was picked up by Epic in the United States and released as *Romeo's Escape*. In the 1990s Alvin recorded for the Oakland-based independent label Hightone, but his albums were sorely neglected despite his excellent songwriting. In 1994, with singer-songwriter Tom Russell, Alvin coproduced the Merle Haggard tribute album *Tulare Dust*, featuring artists such as Dwight Yoakam, Robert Earl Keen, Joe Ely, Marshall Crenshaw, Iris DeMent, and Katy Moffatt. Touring with Russell and Peter Case under the Tulare Dust banner, Alvin concluded the tour in April 1995 with a live version of the album performed by many of the artists at San Francisco's Fillmore Auditorium; Haggard himself closed the show.

DISC.: THE BLASTERS: *American Music* (1980); *The B.* (1981); *Over There* (1982); *Non Fiction* (1983); *Hard Line* (1985); *Collection* (1991). **PHIL ALVIN:** *Un' Sung Stories* (1986). **THE KNITTERS:** *Poor Little Critter on the Road* (1985). **X (WITH DAVE ALVIN):** *See How We Are* (1987). **DAVE ALVIN:** *Romeo's Escape* (1987); *Blue Blvd* (1991); *Museum of the Heart* (1993); *King of California* (1994). **VARIOUS ARTISTS:** *Tulare Dust: A Song-Writer's Tribute to Merle Haggard* (1994).—**BH**

Blatný, Josef, Czech organist, pedagogue, and composer, father of **Pavel Blatný**; b. Brünn, March 19, 1891; d. there (Brno), July 18, 1980. He studied composition with Janáček at the Brünn Organ School (1909–12), and then was his assistant; subsequently was prof. of organ at the Brno Cons. (1928–56) and teacher of organ improvisation at the Janáček Academy of Music and Dramatic Arts in Brno (1947–55).

WORKS: *Sinfonia brevis* for String Orch. (1957); *2 Symphonic Dances* (1959); Chamber Sym. (1961); 3 violin sonatas (1925,

1957, 1968); 3 string quartets (1928, 1954, 1962); Suite for 2 Flutes, Clarinet, and Bassoon (1947); Piano Trio (1950); Piano Quartet (1968); Piano Sonata (1960); organ pieces; vocal music. —**NS/LK/DM**

Blatný, Pavel, Czech pianist, conductor, teacher, and composer, b. Brno, Sept. 14, 1931. He began music studies with his father, and then had instruction in piano and theory at the Brno Cons. (1950–55) and in musicology at the Univ. of Brno (1954–58). He also took composition lessons with Bořkovec at the Prague Academy of Music (1955–59) and attended summer courses of new music at Darmstadt (1965–69). In 1968 he traveled to the U.S. and took lessons in jazz piano and composition at the Berklee Coll. of Music in Boston. He wrote a vast number of works, some of them paralleling the development of "third-stream music" initiated in the U.S. by Schuller. He also gave countless piano recitals in programs of modern music, conducted a great many concerts, and participated in programs of the Czech Radio. In 1971 he was appointed chief of the music division of the television station in Brno. He also taught at the Janáček Academy of Music and Dramatic Arts in Brno (from 1979). He retired from these posts in 1991. In his later compositions, he turned to "serious" music, albeit with tonal manifestations.

WORKS: DRAMATIC: *Prohádky lesa (Studánka a Domeček)* (Forest Tales [The Well and Little House]), 2 television operas for children (1975); 3 musicals. 3rd-stream Music: *Per orchestra sintetica* for Jazz and Classic Wind Orch. (1960); Concerto for Jazz Orch. (1962–64); *Étude* for Quarter Tone Trumpet (1964); *Tre per S+H* for Jazz Septet (1964); *Dialogue* for Soprano Saxophone and Jazz Orch. (1959–64); *10'30"* for Sym. Orch. (1965); *D-E-F-G-A-H- C* for Jazz Orch. (1968); *Quattro per Amsterdam* for Soprano, Chamber Orch., and Jazz Orch. (1969); *3 Pieces for E. Verschuaeren* for Big Band (1971); *Suite for Gustav Brom* (1972); *3 Sketches* for Chorus and Jazz Orch. (1973); *4 Movements* for Big Band (1973); *In Modo Classico* for String Quartet and Jazz Orch. (1973); *In Modo Archaico* for Piano and Jazz Orch. (1974); Concertino for Clarinet and Jazz Orch. (1974); *Picture* for Jazz Orch. (1976); *Trumpeters* for Jazz Orch. (1977); *Chime* for Jazz Orch. (1978); *Intermezzo* for Vocalist and Jazz Trio (1978); *Uno pezzo per due Boemi* for Bass Clarinet and Piano (1981); *Collage* for Jazz Orch. (1981); *Signals* for Big Band (1983); *Nenia* for Jazz Orch. (1985); *Jazz Roll Call* for Jazz Orch. (1986); *Dialogue* for Cello and Jazz Trio (1987); *Litany* for Jazz Orch. (1990). **ORCH.:** *Music* for Piano and Orch. (1955); *Concerto for Orch.* (1956); Concerto for Chamber Orch. (1958); *Movement* for Strings (1976); *Circle* for Strings (1977); *2 Movements* for Brass Ensemble (1979); *Zvony* (The Bells), symphonic movement (1981); *Hommage à Gustav Mahler* (1982); Sym. (1984); *Collage—hommage à J.S. Bach* (1984); *Nenia for my Mother* (1985); *Jubilee Collage* (1986); *Anti-Variations on a Theme of Antonín Dvořák* (1990); *Věta* (1995); *Ein Lied* (1995). **CHAMBER:** Suite for Winds and Piano (1958); *Suite 12* for Bass Clarinet and Piano (1961); *Debate* for Violin, Accordion, and Guitar (1971); *Scene for Brasses* for Brass Quintet (1972); *2: 3* for Wind Quintet (1975); *Due pezzi per quintetto d'ottoni* (1978); *Musica cameralis per Ars cameralis* for Clarinet, Viola, and Piano (1981); *Groping* for Flute and Guitar (1982); *Circle* for Saxophone Quartet (1983); *...And a Little Song...* for Bass Clarinet and Piano (1986); *Dialogue* for Flute and Piano (1990); *Measures* for 4 Bassoons (1997); *Prologue* and *Epilogue* for Wind Ensemble (1997). **VOCAL**: Cantatas: *The Willow Tree* (1980); *Christmas Eve* (1982); *The Noonday Witch* (1982); *The Water Sprite* (1988); *The Peculiar Loves* (1989); Mass (1993); songs.—**NS/LK/DM**

Blatt, František Tadeáš, Bohemian clarinetist and composer; b. Prague, 1793; d. there, March 9, 1856. He studied clarinet with Václav Farník and composition with Dionys Weber at the Prague Cons. He was a member of the orch. at the Prague Opera, and also taught at the Prague Cons. He publ. a method for clarinet (1828) and also composed a number of works for the clarinet; other works include duets, trios, and piano music.—**NS/LK/DM**

Blaukopf, Kurt, Austrian musicologist; b. Czernowitz, Feb. 15, 1914; d. Vienna, June 14, 1999. He studied with Bricht (theory) and Scherchen (conducting) in Vienna (1932–37), and with Gerson-Kiwi (music history) in Jerusalem (1940–42). He was ed. of the periodicals *Phono* (1954–65) and *HiFi Stereophonie* (from 1965) in Vienna. In 1962 he became a lecturer in music sociology and in 1968 a prof. at the Vienna Academy of Music. In 1974 he was made an honorary prof. of the Univ. of Vienna, where he was awarded an honorary doctorate in 1994.

WRITINGS: *Grosse Dirigenten* (Teufen, 1952; 2nd ed., 1957; Eng. tr., 1955); *Musiksoziologie* (Cologne, 1952; 2nd ed., 1972); *Grosse Virtuosen* (Teufen, 1954; Fr. tr., 1955); *Werktreue und Bearbeitung* (Karlsruhe, 1968); *Gustav Mahler, oder Zeitgenosse dur Zukunft* (Vienna, 1969; Eng. tr., 1973); *Gustav Mahler: Sein Leben, sein Werk und seine Welt in zeitgenossischen Bildern und Texten* (Vienna, 1976; 2nd ed., 1994; Eng. tr., 1976, as *Gustav Mahler: A Documentary Study*; rev. and enl. ed., 1991, as *Mahler: His Life, Work and World*); *Massenmedium Schallplatte* (Wiesbaden, 1977); *Musik im Wandel der Gesellschaft: Grundzüge der Musiksoziologie* (Munich, 1982; Eng. tr., 1992, as *Musical Life in a Changing Society: Aspects of Music Sociology*); with H. Blaukopf, *Die Wiener Philharmoniker: Wesen, Werden, Wirken eines Grossen Orchesters* (Vienna, 1986; 2nd ed., 1992, as *Die Wiener Philharmoniker: Welt des Orchesters, Orchester der Welt*); *Pioniere empiristischer Musikforschung* (Vienna, 1995); *Die Aesthetik Bernard Bolzanos* (Sankt Augustin, 1996); *Unterwegs zur Musiksoziologie: Auf der Suche nach Heimat und Standort* (Graz, 1998).

BIBL.: I. Bontinck and O. Brusatti, eds., *Festschrift K. B.* (Vienna, 1975).—**NS/LK/DM**

Blauvelt, Lillian Evans, American soprano; b. Brooklyn, March 16, 1874; d. Chicago, Aug. 29, 1947. She received violin lessons and made her debut at a recital in N.Y.'s Steinway Hall when she was 8; then entered the National Cons. of Music of America there at age 15 to pursue vocal training with Bouhy and Fürsch-Madi; continue studies in Paris with Bouhy before making her operatic debut in Gounod's *Mireille* in Brussels on Sept. 6, 1891. In 1899 she sang before Queen Victoria and in 1902 sang the coronation ode for Edward VII, who presented her with the Coronation Medal. In 1903 she made her first appearance at London's Covent Garden as Gounod's Marguerite. In later years, she appeared mainly in concerts. Following further training with

Alexander Savine, whom she married in 1914, she created the title role in his opera *Xenia* (Zürich, May 29, 1919). She spent her last years as a voice teacher in N.Y. and Chicago.—**NS/LK/DM**

Blavet, Michel, renowned French flutist and composer; b. Besançon (baptized), March 13, 1700; d. Paris, Oct. 28, 1768. He was self-taught as a musician, mastering both bassoon and flute. He went to Paris in 1723 with Duke Charles-Eugène Lévis, and made his debut at the Concert Spirituel in 1726, remaining as its most celebrated artist for some 25 years. He was acknowledged as the foremost flute virtuoso of his time.

WORKS: **DRAMATIC**: *Floriane, ou La Grotte des spectacles*, comédie-ballet (Château de Berny, Aug. 25, 1752); *Les Jeux olympiques*, ballet héroïque (Château de Berny, Aug. 25, 1753); *La Fête de Cythère*, opera (Château de Berny, Nov. 19, 1753). **CHAMBER**: 6 Sonates for 2 Flutes, op.1 (Paris, 1728; ed. by H. Ruf, Mainz, 1967); [6] *Sonates melées de pièces* for Flute and Basso Continuo, op.2 (Paris, 1732; ed. by W. Kolneder, Heidelberg, 1969); [6] Sonates for Flute and Basso Continuo, op.3 (Paris, 1740). **OTHER**: Flute Concerto (ed. in Florilegium Musicum, XI, Lorrach and Baden, 1956); instrumental and vocal music in anthologies of his day.—**NS/LK/DM**

Blaze (called **Castil-Blaze**), **François-Henri-Joseph,** French writer on music, father of **Henri Blaze, Baron de Bury;** b. Cavaillon, Vaucluse, Dec. 1, 1784; d. Paris, Dec. 11, 1857. He studied with his father, a lawyer and amateur musician, then went to Paris in 1799 as a law student; held various administrative posts in provincial towns in France. At the same time he studied music and compiled information on the opera in France. The fruit of this work was the publication in 2 vols. of his book *De l'opéra en France* (Paris, 1820, 1826). He became music critic of the influential Paris *Journal des Débats* in 1822, signing his articles "XXX." He resigned from this post in 1832 but continued to publish books on music, including valuable compilations of musical lexicography: *Dictionnaire de musique moderne* (2 vols., 1821; 2nd ed., 1825; 3rd ed., edited by J.H. Mees, 1828); *Chapelle-musique des Rois de France* (1832); *La Danse et les ballets depuis Bacchus jusqu'à Mlle. Taglioni* (1832); *Mémorial du Grand Opéra* (1847); *Molière musicien* (1852); *Théâtres lyriques de Paris* (2 vols., 1855–56); *Sur l'opéra français: Vérités dures mais utiles* (1856); *L'Art des jeux lyriques* (1858); tr. into French many librettos of German and Italian operas. He himself wrote 3 operas and also compiled a collection *Chants de Provence*. Some of his popular ballads attained considerable popularity. —**NS/LK/DM**

Blaze, Henri, Baron de Bury, French music critic, son of **François-Henri-Joseph Blaze;** b. Avignon, May 17, 1813; d. Paris, March 15, 1888. He wrote many essays for the *Revue des Deux Mondes* and other periodicals, which were subsequently collected as *Musiciens contemporains* (1856), *Meyerbeer et son temps* (1865), *Musiciens du passé, du présent, etc.* (1880), and *Goethe et Beethoven* (1882). His most valuable book is *La Vie de Rossini* (1854).—**NS/LK/DM**

Blažek, Zdeněk, Czech composer and teacher; b. Žarošice, May 24, 1905; d. Prague, June 19, 1988. He was a pupil of Petrželka at the Brno Cons. (1924–29) and of Suk at the Prague Cons. (1933–35). Returning to Brno, he was a teacher (1941–61) and director (1947–57) at the Cons., and then a teacher at the Purkyně Univ. (1961–70). His music evolved from Moravian folksongs.

WORKS: DRAMATIC: Opera: *Verchovina* (The Highlands; 1950–51; Brno, 1956); *R.U.R.* (1975). **ORCH.:** Suite for Strings (1934); *Funereal Music* for Strings, 2 Harps, Gong, and Timpani (1968); *Divertimento* for Strings (1971); *Lyric Suite* (1980); Horn Concerto (1981); *Malá*, suite for Chamber Orch. (1983); Bassoon Concerto (1985); Chamber Sym. with Solo Baritone (1986). **CHAMBER:** 8 string quartets (1943, 1947, 1956, 1967, 1969, 1977, 1981, 1986); String Quintet (1949); *4 Romantic Compositions* for Horn and Piano (1952); *4 Compositions* for Violin and Piano (1954); Horn Sonata (1964); Wind Quintet (1971); Violin Sonata (1982). **VOCAL:** 3 cantatas: *Song of My Native Land* (1938), *Ode to Poverty* (1958), and *Home* (1962); Requiem (1978); *Czech Christmas Mass* for Soloists, Chorus, and Orch. (1984); choruses; songs.—**NS/LK/DM**

Blech, Harry, English violinist and conductor; b. London, March 2, 1910; d. there, May 9, 1999. He studied at Trinity Coll. of Music in London and at the Royal Manchester Coll. of Music. In 1929–30 he was a violinist in the Hallé Orch. in Manchester, and then in the BBC Sym. Orch. in London from 1930 to 1936. In 1933 he founded the Blech String Quartet, serving as its first violinist until it disbanded in 1950. In 1942 he founded the London Wind Players and in 1946 the London Symphonic Players. He founded the London Mozart Players in 1949, serving as its conductor until 1984 when he was made its conductor laureate. In 1952 he founded the London Mozart Choir and from 1961 to 1965 he was director of the Royal Academy of Music Chamber Orch. in London. He was made an Officer in 1962 and a Commander in 1984 of the Order of the British Empire. As a conductor, Blech became well known for his performances of composers of the Classical era, particularly Haydn and Mozart.—**NS/LK/DM**

Blech, Leo, eminent German conductor and composer; b. Aachen, April 21, 1871; d. Berlin, Aug. 25, 1958. As a young man he was engaged in a mercantile career. He then studied briefly at the Hochschule für Musik in Berlin, and returned to Aachen to conduct at the Municipal Theater (1893–99); also took summer courses in composition with Humperdinck (1893–96). He was subsequently engaged as opera conductor in Prague (1899–1906), and then became conductor at the Berlin Royal Opera in 1906; was named Generalmusikdirektor in 1913. In 1923 he became conductor of the Deutsches Opernhaus in Berlin; in 1924 was with the Berlin Volksoper, and in 1925 with the Vienna Volksoper. In 1926 he returned to Berlin as a conductor with the Staatsoper, remaining there until 1937; then went to Riga as a conductor of the Riga Opera (1937–41). From 1941 to 1949 he conducted in Stockholm. In 1949 he returned to Berlin and served as Generalmusikdirektor of the Stadtische Oper there, remaining at that post until 1953. He was considered a fine interpreter of the standard German and Italian repertoire, particularly in the works of Wagner and Verdi. His own music is in the Wagnerian tradition. His knowledge and understanding of instrumental and vocal resources enabled him to produce competent operas; however, after initial successes, they suffered total oblivion.

WORKS: DRAMATIC: Opera: *Aglaja* (1893); *Cherubina* (1894); *Das war ich*, "opera-idyl" (Dresden, Oct. 6, 1902); *Alpenkönig und Menschenfeind* (Dresden, Oct. 1, 1903; rewritten and produced as *Rappelkopf*, Berlin Opera, 1917); *Aschenbrodel* (Prague, 1905); *Versiegelt* (Hamburg, 1908; N.Y., 1912); *Die Strohwitwe*, operetta (Hamburg, 1920). **OTHER:** 3 symphonic poems: *Die Nonne, Waldwanderung*, and *Trost in der Natur*; *10 Kleinigkeiten* for Piano, 4-Hands; music for children; choruses; songs; piano pieces.

BIBL.: E. Rychnowsky, *L. B.* (Prague, 1905); W. Jacob, *L. B.* (Hamburg, 1931).—**NS/LK/DM**

Bledsoe, Jules, black American baritone and composer; b. Waco, Tex., Dec. 29, 1898; d. Los Angeles, July 14, 1943. He studied at the Chicago Musical Coll. (B.A., 1919), then in Paris and Rome. Returning to America, he distinguished himself as a fine performer in musical comedies and opera. He sang the central role in the premiere of Jerome Kern's *Show Boat* (1927), appeared in grand opera as Rigoletto and Boris Godunov, and sang the title role in Gruenberg's *Emperor Jones*. As a composer, he wrote an *African Suite* for Orch. and several songs in the manner of Negro spirituals.—**NS/LK/DM**

Blegen, Judith, American soprano; b. Lexington, Ky., April 27, 1940. She studied violin and voice at the Curtis Inst. of Music in Philadelphia (1959–64). In 1963 she went to Italy, where she studied with Luigi Ricci; then sang at the Nuremberg Opera (1963–66). She made a successful appearance at the Santa Fe Opera on Aug. 1, 1969, in the role of Emily in Menotti's satirical opera *Help! Help! the Globolinks!*, which was written especially for her. She made her Metropolitan Opera debut on Jan. 19, 1970, in N.Y. as Papagena, returning there regularly in subsequent seasons to sing such roles as Zerlina, Marzelline, Gilda, Sophie, Blondchen, Adele, Oscar, and Juliette. In 1975 she made her first appearance at London's Covent Garden, and in 1977 at the Paris Opéra.—**NS/LK/DM**

Blewitt, Jonathan, English composer; b. London, July 19, 1782; d. there, Sept. 4, 1853. He studied with his father, and with Battishill, and was an organist at several churches; served as conductor at the Theatre Royal in Dublin. Returning to London (1825), he was appointed music director at Sadler's Wells Theatre. He composed many popular ballads, and also authored a treatise on singing, *The Vocal Assistant*.—**NS/LK/DM**

Bley, Paul, jazz pianist; b. Montreal, Canada, Nov. 10, 1932. He led his own quartet in a hotel in 1945, playing Montreal nightclubs in the wake of Oscar Peterson; he was soon accompanying visiting artists such as Ben Webster, Charlie Parker (1953), Lester Young, and Roy Eldridge. Bley's debut album (1953) was a trio album produced by and featuring Charles Mingus and Art Blakey. He left Montreal for N.Y. (1954), where he studied at the Juilliard School and formed a band with Donald Byrd, Doug Watkins, Art Taylor, and

Jackie McLean. He then moved to Calif., playing with Chet Baker, and then forming a trio with Charlie Haden and Billy Higgins. They were joined by Don Cherry and Ornette Coleman for an engagement at the Hillcrest, Los Angeles; he later issued two LPs from these gigs. Apparently Bley returned to Canada for a while, because he got a visa to go to N.Y. at the end of 1959, and played there with Rene Thomas; he then joined Mingus around May 1960. Bley worked with George Russell, and recorded with D. Ellis (1961–62). In 1961, he formed a trio with Steve Swallow and Pete La Roca and then toured Europe with Swallow in the Jimmy Giuffre trio, which reunited for a tour and recordings in the mid-1990s. While married to Carla Bley, he was a founding member of the Jazz Composers Guild, along with Bill Dixon, Archie Shepp, and Sun Ra; it failed but led to the more successful Jazz Composers Association formed by Carla and Mike Mantler. He has had a particular empathy with great bassists, recording with Mingus, Charlie Haden, Scott La Faro, Gary Peacock, and Dave Holland. He teamed with singer Annette Peacock in the 1970s and they experimented with synthesizers; he was the first jazz artist to perform publicly on the synthesizer. In 1974, he established the Improvising Artists record label with video artist Carol Goss. His recording *Fragments* emphasized his connection to Bill Evans. The low-key beauty of this kind of music has influenced New Age music. In 1996, he toured with Evan Parker and Barre Phillips. An intense, controlled, lyrical perfectionist, Bley has influenced and been admired by Keith Jarrett, Chick Corea, and others, just as they shared his colleagues Charlie Haden, Barry Altschul, and others. His concept of the interactive trio developed just after that of Bill Evans, and the two shared Gary Peacock and Paul Motian. His importance has been little acknowledged, partly because of the subtlety of his music and perhaps partly because he has not successfully promoted himself.

Disc.: *Introducing Paul Bley* (1953); *Paul Bley* (1954); *Solemn Meditation* (1958); *Live at the Hillcrest Club* (1958); *Footloose* (1962); *Floater Syndrome* (1962); *Syndrome* (1963); *Paul Bley with Gary Peacock* (1963); *Turning Point* (1964); *Paul Bley Quartet* (1964); *Barrage* (1964); *Copenhagen and Haarlem* (1965); *Closer* (1965); *Ramblin'* (1966); *Ballads* (1967); *Mr. Joy* (1968); *Synthesizer Show* (1970); *Solo Piano* (1972); *Paul Bley and Scorpio* (1972); *Open for Love* (1972); *I'm the One* (1972); *Alone Again* (1974); *Japan Suite* (1975); *Axis* (1977); *Virtuosi* (1978); *Quiet Song* (1978); *Ramblings* (1980); *Tango Palace* (1983); *Sonor* (1983); *My Standard* (1985); *Hot* (1985); *Solo* (1987); *Live at Sweet Basil* (1988); *Life of a Trio: Saturday and Sunday* (1989); *Blues for Red* (1989); *Paul Bley/NHØP* (1990); *Fragments* (1986); *Changing Hands* (1991); *Synth Thesis* (1993); *Outside In* (1994). C. Parker: *In Montreal* (1953).—**LP**

Bleyer, Georg, German composer, poet, and court functionary; b. Tiefurt, near Weimar (baptized), Oct. 28, 1647; d. c. 1694. He studied law and music in Jena (1664–66). He was named chamber secretary at the court in Rudolstadt, and was awarded the garland of poet laureate in 1672. He then was active as a musician in Darmstadt at the court (1677–78). He composed sacred vocal music, and also publ. a collection of dances for 4 and 5 instruments as *Lust-Music* (2 vols., Leipzig, 1670).

Bibl.: C. Höfer, *G. B.: Ein thüringischer Tonsetzer und Dichter der Barockzeit* (Zeitschrift des Vereins für thüringische Geschichte, suppl. XXIV, Jena, 1941).—**NS/LK/DM**

Bleyer, Nicolaus, German violinist and composer; b. Stolzenau, Feb. 2, 1591; d. Lübeck, May 3, 1658. He studied with Brade (1614–17), and then joined the orch. of Count Ernst in Bückeburg. He settled in Lübeck as town musician in 1621, remaining there until his death. About 1628 he publ. *Erster Theil neuer Paduanen, Galliarden, Balletten, Mascarden und Couranten.*—**NS/LK/DM**

Blind Tom
See **Bethune, Thomas Greene**

Bliss, Philip P(aul), prominent American gospel hymn composer and hymnbook compiler; b. Clearfield County, Pa., July 9, 1838; d. in a train accident near Ashtabula, Ohio, Dec. 29, 1876. After pursuing a career as a singing-school teacher, director of musical conventions, and concert singer, he was active in the evangelistic field from 1874. Although he wrote almost 100 secular songs, it was as the author and/or composer of over 300 sacred works that established his reputation. The designations "gospel song" and "gospel hymn" were first used in his compilations *Gospel Songs* (Cincinnati, 1874) and *Gospel Hymns and Sacred Songs* (Cincinnati, 1875). His memoirs were ed. by D. Whittle (N.Y., 1877).

Bibl.: B. Neil, *P.P. B. (1838–1876): Gospel Hymn Composer and Compiler* (diss., New Orleans Baptist Theological Seminary, 1977); D. Smucker, *P.P. B. and the Musical, Cultural and Religious Sources of the Gospel Music Tradition in the United States, 1850–1876* (diss., Boston Univ., 1981).—**NS/LK/DM**

Bliss, Sir Arthur (Drummond), eminent English composer; b. London, Aug. 2, 1891; d. there, March 27, 1975. He studied counterpoint with Charles Wood at the Univ. of Cambridge (Mus.B., 1913), and then pursued training with Stanford, Vaughan Williams, and Holst at the Royal Coll. of Music in London (1913–14). While serving in the British Army during World War I, he was wounded in 1916 and gassed in 1918. After the Armistice, he gained recognition as something of an *enfant terrible* with his *Madame Noy* for Soprano and 7 Instruments (1918) and *Rout* for Soprano and 10 Instruments (1920). With such fine scores as *A Colour Symphony* (1921–22), the *Introduction and Allegro* for Orch. (1926), the Oboe Quintet (1927), and the Clarinet Quintet (1932), he rose to prominence as a composer of great distinction. His music for H.G. Well's film *Things to Come* (1934–35) and the *Music* for Strings (1935) added luster to his reputation, which was further enhanced by his outstanding ballets *Checkmate* (1937), *Miracle in the Gorbals* (1944), and *Adam Zero* (1946). After a sojourn as a teacher in Berkeley, Calif. (1939–41), Bliss served as director of music for the BBC in London (1942–44). In 1950 he was knighted and in 1953 he was made the Master of the Queen's Music. In 1969 he was made a Knight Commander of the Royal Victorian Order and in 1971 a Companion of Honour. G. Roscow ed. *Bliss on*

Music: Selected Writings of Arthur Bliss (1920–1975) (Oxford, 1991).

WORKS: DRAMATIC: O p e r a : *The Olympians* (1944–49; London, Sept. 29, 1949); *Tobias and the Angel* (1958–59; BBC-TV, London, May 19, 1960). **B a l l e t :** *Checkmate* (Paris, June 15, 1937); *Miracle in the Gorbals* (London, Oct. 26, 1944); *Adam Zero* (London, April 10, 1946); *The Lady of Shalott* (1957–58; Berkeley, Calif., May 2, 1958). **I n c i d e n t a l M u s i c :** *As You Like It* (1919); *The Tempest* (1921); *King Solomon* (1924). **F i l m :** *Things to Come* (1934–35); *Conquest of the Air* (1936–37); *Caesar and Cleopatra* (1944); *Men of Two World* (1945); *Presence au combat* (1945); *Christopher Columbus* (1949); *The Beggar's Opera* (1952–53); *Seven Waves Away* (1956). **ORCH.:** *2 Studies* (1920; London, Feb. 17, 1921); *Mêlée fantasque* (London, Oct. 13, 1921); *A Colour Symphony* (1921–22; Gloucester, Sept. 7, 1922; rev. version, London, April 27, 1932); *Twone, the House of Felicity* (London, March 15, 1923); *Elizabethan Suite* for Strings (1923); *Introduction and Allegro* (London, Sept. 8, 1926); *Hymn to Apollo* (Amsterdam, Nov. 28, 1926); *Music for Strings* (Salzburg, Aug. 11, 1935); Piano Concerto (1938–39; N.Y., June 10, 1939); *The Phoenix March: Homage to France, Aug. 1944* (Paris, March 11, 1945); Processional for the coronation of Queen Elisabeth II (London, June 2, 1953); Violin Concerto (1953–54; London, May 11, 1955); *Meditations on a Theme by John Blow* (Birmingham, Dec. 13, 1955); *Edinburgh*, overture (Edinburgh, Aug. 20, 1956); *Discourse* (Louisville, Oct. 23, 1957; rev. version, London, Sept. 28, 1965); *March of Homage in Honour of a Great Man* for Sir Winston Churchill (1961–62; BBC, London, March 30, 1962); Cello Concerto (1969–70; Aldeburgh, June 24, 1970); *Metamorphic Variations* (1972; London, April 21, 1973). **B r a s s a n d M i l i t a r y B a n d :** *Kenilworth Suite* (1936); *The First Guards*, march (1956); *The Belmont Variations* (1962); *The Linburn Air*, march (1964); various fanfares for royal and other occasions. **CHAMBER:** Violin Sonata (c. 1914); 4 string quartets: No. 1 (Cambridge, May 30, 1914), No. 2 (1923–24), No. 3 (1940–41; N.Y., Jan. 13, 1944), and No. 4 (Edinburgh, Sept. 1, 1950); Piano Quartet (London, April 22, 1915); Piano Quintet (Paris, Nov. 26, 1919); *Conversations* for Flute, Oboe, Violin, Viola, and Cello (1920; London, April 20, 1921); *Allegro* for 2 Violins, Viola, and Piano (1923–24); *Andante tranquillo e legato* for Clarinet (1926–27); Oboe Quintet (Venice, Sept. 11, 1927); Clarinet Quintet (London, Dec. 19, 1932); Viola Sonata (London, May 9, 1933). **P i a n o :** *Bliss* (1923); *Masks* (1924); *Toccata* (c. 1925); *2 Interludes* (1925); Suite (1925); *The Rout Trot* (1927); *Study* (1927); Sonata (1952; London, April 24, 1953); *Miniature Scherzo* (1969); *Triptych* (1970); *A Wedding Suite* (1973). **VOCAL:** *Madame Noy* for Soprano and 7 Instruments (1918; London, June 23, 1920); *Rhapsody* for Mezzo-soprano, Tenor, and 7 Instruments (1919; London, Oct. 6, 1920); *Rout* for Soprano and 10 Instruments (London, Dec. 15, 1920); *2 Nursery Rhymes* for Soprano, Clarinet, and Piano (1920); Concerto for Piano, Tenor, Strings, and Percussion (London, June 11, 1921); *The Women of Yueh*, song cycle for Voice and Ensemble (N.Y., Nov. 11, 1923); *Pastoral: Lie Strewn the White Flocks* for Mezzo-soprano, Chorus, Flute, Timpani, and String Orch. (1928–29; London, May 8, 1929); *Serenade* for Baritone and Orch. (1929; London, March 18, 1930); *Morning Heroes*, sym. for Orator, Chorus, and Orch., dedicated to the composer's brother and all others who perished in battle (1929–30; Norwich, Oct. 22, 1930); *The Enchantress*, scene for Contralto and Orch. (Manchester, Oct. 2, 1951); *A Song of Welcome* for Soprano, Baritone, Chorus, and Orch. (London, May 15, 1954); *The Beatitudes*, cantata for Soprano, Tenor, Chorus, Organ, and Orch. (1960–61; Coventry, May 25, 1962); *Mary of Magdala*, cantata for Contralto, Bass, Chorus, and Orch. (1962; Worcester, Sept. 2, 1963); *The Golden Cantata* for Tenor, Chorus, and Orch. (1963; Cambridge, Feb. 18, 1964); *A Knot of Riddles*, song cycle for Baritone and 11 Instruments (Cheltenham, July 11, 1963); *The World Is Charged with the Grandeur of God*, cantata for Chorus, 2 Flutes, 3 Trumpets, and 4 Trombones (Blythburgh, June 27, 1969); *2 Ballads* for Children's or Women's Chorus and Piano or Small Orch. (1970); *Shield of Faith*, cantata for Soprano, Baritone, Chorus, and Organ (1974; Windsor, April 26, 1975); also unaccompanied vocal pieces.

BIBL.: S. Craggs, *A. B.: A Bio-Bibliography* (N.Y., 1988); idem, *A. B.: A Source Book* (Aldershot, 1996); J. Sugden, *Sir A. B.* (London, 1997).—NS/LK/DM

Blitheman, John, English organist and composer; b. c. 1525; d. London, May 23, 1591. He was from 1558 a Gentleman of the Chapel Royal, and also held an annuity from Christ Church, Oxford. John Bull is said to have been one of his pupils. He composed liturgical organ music and several vocal pieces. See D. Stevens, ed., *The Mulliner Book*, in the Musica Britannica series, 1 (1951; 2nd ed., rev., 1962).—NS/LK/DM

Blitzstein, Marc, significant American composer; b. Philadelphia, March 2, 1905; d. Fort de France, Martinique, Jan. 22, 1964. He studied piano and organ with Sternberg in Philadelphia. In 1921 he entered the Univ. of Pa. on a scholarship, but left the following year when he failed to meet the physical education requirements. He then studied piano with Siloti in N.Y. From 1924 1926 he was a composition student of Scalero at the Curtis Inst. of Music in Philadelphia. After further training with Boulanger in Paris and Schoenberg in Berlin (1926–28), he returned to the U.S. and wrote a few generic instrumental works in either a late Romantic or a more modern, Copland- influenced jazz style. However, he soon turned to creating works for the theater à la Brecht and Weill, in which "art for society's sake" and "social consciousness" of a fervent left-wing persuasion became the norm. Particularly notable was his play in music, *The Cradle Will Rock* (N.Y., June 16, 1937). In 1940–41 and 1941–42 he held Guggenheim fellowships. From 1942 to 1945 he served in the U.S. Army Air Force in England, where he was music director of the American Broadcasting Station for Europe. Upon his return to the U.S., he resumed composing for the theater. However, in the 1950s he was unable to sustain his musical standing as his unique blending of musical theater and opera went out of fashion, as did his penchant for social protest. During the last decade of his life, his works became more conventional. In 1959 he was elected to membership in the National Inst. of Arts and Letters. In 1960 he received a Ford Foundation grant to compose an opera on the subject of Sacco and Vanzetti for the Metropolitan Opera in N.Y., but the work was never finished. Two other operas were also left incomplete. Blitzstein died from injuries sustained after a savage beating by 3 sailors in an alley. Three arias, 1 each from his 3 unfinished operas, were premiered at a memorial concert conducted by Bernstein in N.Y., April 19, 1964. Blitzstein remains best known for his adaptation of Weill's *Die Dreigroschenoper* as *The Threepenny Opera* (Waltham, Mass., June 14, 1952). It opened off Broadway on March 10, 1954, and had a remarkable 6–year N.Y. run, becoming a classic of the American theater.

WORKS: DRAMATIC: R a d i o : *Svarga*, ballet (1924–25); *Jig-Saw*, ballet (1927–28); *Triple Sec*, opera- farce (1928; Philadelphia, May 6, 1929); *Parabola and Circula*, opera- ballet (1929); *Cain*, ballet (1930); *The Harpies*, satirical chamber opera (1931; N.Y., May 25, 1953); *The Condemned*, choral opera (1932); *The Cradle Will Rock*, "play in music" in 10 scenes with "social significance" (1936–37; N.Y., June 16, 1937, composer at the piano); *I've Got the Tune*, "radio song-play" (CBS, N.Y., Oct. 24, 1937); *No for an Answer*, short opera (1938–40; N.Y., Jan. 5, 1941); *The Guests*, ballet (1946–48; N.Y., Jan. 20, 1949; incorporates the unperformed ballet *Show*, 1946); *Regina*, musical theater to Hellman's play *The Little Foxes* (1946–49; tryout, New Haven, Oct. 6, 1949; N.Y. premiere, Oct. 31, 1949; rev. 1953 and 1958 for N.Y. opera house perfs.); *Reuben Reuben*, musical play (1949–55; Boston, Oct. 10, 1955); *Juno*, musical play (1957–59; N.Y., March 9, 1959); *Sacco and Vanzetti*, opera (1959–64; unfinished); *The Magic Barrel*, opera (1962–64; unfinished); *Idiots First*, opera (1962–64; unfinished but completed by L. Lehrman, 1973; piano score, Ithaca, N.Y., Aug. 1974). **I n c i d e n t a l   M u s i c   T o :** Shakespeare's *Julius Caesar* (1937), Büchner's *Danton's Death* (1938), Shaw's *Androcles and the Lion* (1946), Hellman's *Another Part of the Forest* (1946), Shakespeare's *King Lear* (2 versions, 1950, 1955), Jonson's *Volpone* (1956), Shakespeare's *A Midsummer Night's Dream* (1958) and *A Winter's Tale* (1958), and Hellman's *Toys in the Attic* (1960). **F i l m :** *Hände* (1927); *Surf and Seaweed* (1931); *The Spanish Earth* (1936–37; in collaboration with V. Thomson); *Valley Town* (1940); *Native Land* (1940–41); *Night Shift* (1942); *The True Glory* (1944–45; not used). **OTHER:** Tr. and adaptation of Weill's *Dreigroschenoper* as *The Threepenny Opera* (1950–52; Waltham, Mass., June 14, 1952). **ORCH.:** *Sarabande* (1926); *Romantic Piece* (1930); Piano Concerto (1931; first perf. with orch., Brooklyn, Jan. 24, 1986); *Surf and Seaweed*, suite from the film (1931); *Orch. Variations* (1934; N.Y., Oct. 9, 1988); *Freedom Morning* (London, Sept. 28, 1943); *Native Land*, suite from the film (1946; rev. 1958); *Lear: A Study* (1957–58; N.Y., Feb. 27, 1958; includes music from the 2 incidental scores to *King Lear*). **CHAMBER:** String Quartet, *The Italian* (1930); *Serenade* for String Quartet (1932; in 3 uncontrasted movements all marked Largo); *Discourse* for Clarinet, Cello, and Piano (1933; unfinished). **P i a n o :** Sonata (1927); *Percussion Music for the Piano* (1928–29); *Scherzo* (1930); *Piano Solo* (1933); *Le monde libre* (1944); *The Guests*, suite from the ballet (1946–48). **V O - CAL:** *Gods* for Mezzo-soprano and Strings, after Whitman (originally for Voice and Piano, 1926; rescored 1927; Philadelphia, Feb. 15, 1928); *A Word Out of the Sea*, cantata for Women's Chorus and Instrumental Ensemble, after Whitman (1928; 3 extant movements); *Is Five*, 5 songs for Soprano and Piano, after e.e. cummings (1929); *Invitation to Bitterness* for Men's Chorus and Supplementary Altos (1939); *The Airborne Symphony*, cantata for Tenor, Bass, Narrator, Men's Chorus, and Orch. (1943–46; N.Y., April 1, 1946, Orson Welles narrator, Bernstein conducting); *This is the Garden*, cantata (1956–57; N.Y., May 5, 1957); *Six Elizabethan Songs* for Voice and Piano (1958); *From Marion's Book*, 7 songs for Voice and Piano, after e.e. cummings (1960).

BIBL.: R. Dietz, *The Operatic M. B.* (diss., Univ. of Iowa, 1970); E. Gordon, *Mark the Music: The Life and Work of M. B.* (N.Y., 1989).—NS/LK/DM

Blitzstein, Marc(us Samuel),

astringent American composer, lyricist, and librettist; b. Philadelphia, March 2, 1905; d. Fort-de-France, Martinique, Jan. 22, 1964. Blitzstein was a notable composer of contemporary classical music and wrote the music, lyrics, and books of several operalike Broadway musicals. But he is best known for his libretto and English lyrics for the Off-Broadway production of Kurt Weill and Bertolt Brecht's *The Threepenny Opera*, including "Mack the Knife," which became a standard.

Blitzstein was the son of Russian immigrants Samuel Marcus and Anna Lewytski (later Levitt) Blitzstein; his father worked in the family's bank. A musical prodigy, Blitzstein began picking out tunes on the piano at age three, gave his first public performance at seven, and appeared as a soloist with the Philadelphia Orch. at 16. He attended the Univ. of Pa. (1921–23) while studying piano with Alexander Siloti, then enrolled at the Curtis Inst. of Music (1924–26), where he studied composition with Rosario Scalero. In 1926 he went to Paris and studied with Nadia Boulanger, and in 1927 he enrolled at the Akademie der Künste in Berlin and studied with Arnold Schoenberg.

After completing his studies, Blitzstein returned to the U.S., where he composed classical works, lectured, and wrote music criticism. His satiric one-act opera *Triple-Sec* (libretto by Ronald Jeans) was premiered in Philadelphia on May 6, 1929, then interpolated into the Broadway revue *The Garrick Gaieties* (N.Y., June 4, 1930), marking his musical theater debut. Although homosexual, he married writer (Maria Luisa) Eva Goldbeck on March 2, 1933; they remained married until her death on May 26, 1936.

By the mid-1930s, Blitzstein had begun writing works reflective of his left- wing political views; by 1938 he had joined the Communist party. His first major foray into musical theater was the pro-union *The Cradle Will Rock*. The show was initially sponsored by Federal Theatre Project of the U.S. government's Works Progress Administration, but when budget cuts forced its cancellation, producer John Houseman and director Orson Welles put it on anyway in a celebrated performance with the composer at the piano and the actors in the audience. After brief runs in June and December 1937, it reopened on Broadway Jan. 3, 1938, for a profitable run of 108 performances; Musicraft Records' release of a seven-disc 78–rpm album of the show in April 1938 marked the first full-length cast recording of a Broadway musical. In the meantime, Blitzstein had written and performed in a musical for radio, *I've Got the Tune*; composed incidental music for a production of *Julius Caesar* (N.Y., Nov. 11, 1937) by Orson Welles's Mercury Theatre. He contributed a sketch to Harold Rome's revue *Pins and Needles* (N.Y., Nov. 27, 1937). He also composed incidental music for the Mercury Theatre production of *Danton's Death* (N.Y., Nov. 2, 1938).

Blitzstein's follow-up to *The Cradle Will Rock* was 1941's *No for an Answer*, which was mounted for three minimally staged performances but, despite critical acclaim, never had a full-scale production due to its political content. The composer served in the army air force during World War II; he spent his time in England, writing his *Airborne* symphony (premiered by the N.Y. City Symphony, conducted by Leonard Bernstein, at the City Center in N.Y. on April 1, 1946). His next musical, *Regina*, based on Lillian Hellman's play *The Little Foxes*, ran for 56 performances in late 1949. The following year, Blitzstein directed Benjamin Britten's children's show, *Let's Make an Opera* (N.Y., Dec. 13, 1950), and he provided incidental music for a Broadway production of *King Lear* (N.Y., Dec. 25, 1950).

The first performance of Blitzstein's adaptation of *The Threepenny Opera* was a concert version conducted by Bernstein at Brandeis Coll. on June 14, 1952. The show was then produced Off-Broadway in 1954 for 96 performances, returning in 1955 for a record-breaking run of 2,611 performances. "Mack the Knife" was recorded by Louis Armstrong for a Top 40 hit in March 1956; Bobby Darin's recording sold a million copies and was the biggest hit of 1959; and Ella Fitzgerald revived it again for a Top 40 hit in July 1960.

Blitzstein's next musical, *Reuben Reuben*, opened in Boston on Oct. 10, 1955, but closed without going to Broadway. *Juno*, based on Sean O'Casey's play *Juno and the Paycock*, for which Blitzstein wrote music and lyrics, got to Broadway in 1959, but only for 16 performances. Blitzstein worked for several years on a musical about the executed anarchists Sacco and Vanzetti, but it was left unfinished when he was robbed and beaten to death at the age of 58.

WORKS (only works for which Blitzstein was a primary composer or lyricist are listed): **MUSICALS/REVUES:** *The Cradle Will Rock* (N.Y., June 16, 1937); *No for an Answer* (N.Y., Jan. 5, 1941); *Regina* (N.Y., Oct. 31, 1949); *The Threepenny Opera* (N.Y., March 10, 1954); *Juno* (N.Y., March 9, 1959). **RADIO:** *I've Got the Tune* (CBS, Oct. 24, 1937).

BIBL.: E. Gordon, *Mark the Music: The Life and Work of M. B.* (N.Y., 1989).—**WR**

Bloch, Augustyn (Hipolit), Polish composer and organist; b. Grudziądz, Aug. 13, 1929. He was a student of Feliks Rączkowski (organ, 1950–55) and Tadeusz Szeligowski (composition, 1952–59) at the State Higher School of Music in Warsaw. From 1954 to 1977 he composed music for various plays and radio dramas for the Theatre of the Polish Radio in Warsaw. He was vice president of the Polish Composers' Union from 1977 to 1979, and again from 1983 to 1987. From 1979 to 1987 he was chairman of the repertoire committee of the Warsaw Autumn International Festival of Contemporary Music. In 1971 and 1985 he received the Minister of Culture and Art Award, in 1975 the Prime Minster's Award, in 1981 the Polish Composers' Union Award, and in 1989 the Brighton Festival Award. He also was decorated with the Cavalier's (1969) and Officer's (1979) Cross of the Polonia Restituta Order.

WORKS: DRAMATIC: *Voci*, ballet (1962; Warsaw, Sept. 20, 1967); *Oczekiwanie* (Awaiting), ballet (1963; Warsaw, Sept. 19, 1964); *Byk* (The Bull), ballet (Amsterdam, June 24, 1965); *Ajelet, córka Jeftego* (Ayelet, Jephthah's Daughter), mystery-opera (1967; Warsaw, Sept. 22, 1968); *Gilgamesz* (Gilgamesh), ballet-pantomime (1968; concert version, Warsaw, Sept. 28, 1969); *Pan Zagłoba* (Sir Zagłoba), musical (1971); *Bardzo śpiąca królewna* (Very Sleeping Beauty), opera-ballet-pantomime (1973; Warsaw, Sept. 29, 1974); *Zwierciadło* (Looking Glass), ballet-pantomime (1975); *Głos milczenia* (The Voice of Silence), ballet-pantomime (1977); *Bajka o skrzypcowej duszy* (Tale of a Violin's Soul), children's musical (1978). **ORCH.:** Concertino for Violin, Strings, Piano, and Percussion (1958); *Dialoghi* for Violin and Orch.

(1964; Warsaw, Sept. 22, 1966); *Enfiando* (Bonn, Oct. 12, 1970); *Oratorium* for Organ, Strings, and Percussion (1982; Warsaw, Sept. 24, 1983); *Zostań Panie z nami (Bleibe bei uns, Herr)* (Abide With Us, Lord; 1986); *Wzwyż* (Upwards; 1993); *Hac festa die* for Organ, Chorus, and Orch. (1996); *Drei Stücke Saxophon-Kammer-Orchester* (1998). **CHAMBER:** *Elegia* for Violin and Piano (1954); *Clarinetto divertente* for Clarinet (1976; Leningrad, Feb. 13, 1978); *Warstwy czasu* (The Layers of Time) for 15 Strings (Warsaw, Sept. 20, 1978); *Chodzenie po klawiszach na cztery małe ręce i perkusję też niedużą* (Walking on the Keys for Four Small Hands and Percussion, Also of Small Proportions) for Piano and Percussion (Łódź, Nov. 1981); *Notes* for Alto Saxophone (1981); *Jazda na gapę przez Europę na cztery małe ręce i perkusję też niedużą* (A Free Trip Around Europe for Four Small Hands and Percussion, Also of Small Proportions) for Piano and Percussion (1981); *Supplicazioni* for Cello and Piano (1983); *A Due* for Saxophone, Bass Clarinet, Vibraphone, and Marimbaphone (1984); *Musica* for Clarinet and 4 Stringed Instruments (1984–85); *Duetto* for Violin and Cello (1986; Hitzacker, July 26, 1987); *Skrzypce i organy (Geige und Orgel)* (Violin and Organ; 1988); *Musica* for 13 Brass Instruments (1988); Trio for Violin, Cello, and Piano (1992); *Infiltrazione: Béla Bartók in memoriam* for 2 Violins (1995). **KEYBOARD: Piano:** *Wariacje fortepianowe "Karol Szymanowski in memoriam"* (Pianos Variations "Karol Szymanowski in memoriam;" 1953); *Filigranki* (Filigrees; 1978). **Organ:** *Fantasia* (1953); Sonata (1954); *Jubilate* (Warsaw, Sept. 24, 1975); *Forte, piano e forte* (1985). **VOCAL:** *Espressioni* for Soprano and Orch. (1959; Lódź, Jan. 1960); *Impressioni poetiche* for Men's Chorus and Orch. (1959); *Medytacje* (Meditations) for Soprano, Organ, and Percussion (Warsaw, Nov. 20, 1961); *Depesza* (A Cable) for Children's Chorus, 2 Pianos, and Percussion (1963); *Salmo gioioso* for Soprano and 5 Winds (1970); *Poemat o Warszawie* (A Poem of Warsaw) for Narrator, Chorus, and Orch. (1974; Warsaw, Jan. 17, 1975); *Wordsworth Songs* for Baritone and Chamber Orch. (Warsaw, Sept. 23, 1976); *Taka sobie muzyka* (Just So Music), song cycle for Soprano and Orch. (1976–77; Poznań, April 24, 1977); *Anenaiki* for Chorus (Warsaw, May 12, 1979); *Carmen biblicum* for Soprano and 9 Instruments (Witten, April 19, 1980); *Albowiem nadejdzie światłość Twoja (Denn Dein Licht kommt)* (For Thy Light is Come) for Reciter, Organ, Chorus, and Orch. (1987; Hamburg, June 29, 1988); *Exaltabo Te, Domino* for Chorus (Warsaw, June 1, 1988); *Lauda* for Soprano, Alto, Percussion, and 4 Stringed Instruments (1988); *Litania Ostrobramska* (Litany of Ostra Brama) for Chorus and Orch. (1989; Bydgoszcz, Sept. 9, 1990); *Nie zabijaj! (Du sollst nicht töten!)* (Thou Shalt Not Kill!) for Baritone, Cello, Chorus, and Orch. (1989–90); *Wypłoszona* (Scared Out) for Baritone, Viola, Cello, and Piano (1994); *Oratorium Gedanense 1997* for Organ, Chorus, and Orch. (1996–97).

BIBL.: D. Gojowy, ed., *A. B.: Ein Komponistenleben in Polen* (Cologne, 1999).—**NS/LK/DM**

Bloch, Ernest, remarkable Swiss-born American composer of Jewish descent, father of **Suzanne Bloch;** b. Geneva, July 24, 1880; d. Portland, Ore., July 15, 1959. He studied solfeggio with Jaques-Dalcroze and violin with Louis Rey in Geneva (1894–97); then went to Brussels, where he took violin lessons with Ysaÿe and studied composition with Rasse (1897–99); while a student, he wrote a string quartet and a "symphonie orientale," indicative of his natural attraction to non-European cultures and coloristic melos. In 1900 he went to Germany, where he studied theory with Knorr at the

Hoch Cons. in Frankfurt am Main and took private lessons with Thuille in Munich; there he began the composition of his first full-fledged sym., in C-sharp minor, with its 4 movements orig. bearing titles expressive of changing moods. He then spent a year in Paris, where he met Debussy; Bloch's first publ. work, *Historiettes au crépuscule* (1903), shows Debussy's influence. In 1904 he returned to Geneva, where he began the composition of his only opera, *Macbeth*, after Shakespeare; another opera, *Jézabel*, on a biblical subject, never materialized beyond a few initial sketches. As a tribute to his homeland, he outlined the orch. work *Helvetia*, based on Swiss motifs, as early as 1900, but the full score was not completed until 1928. During the season 1909–10, Bloch conducted symphonic concerts in Lausanne and Neuchâtel. In 1916 he was offered an engagement as conductor on an American tour accompanying the dancer Maud Allan; he gladly accepted the opportunity to leave war-torn Europe, and expressed an almost childlike delight upon docking in the port of N.Y. at the sight of the Statue of Liberty. Allan's tour was not successful, however, and Bloch returned to Geneva; in 1917 he received an offer to teach at the David Mannes School of Music in N.Y., and once more he went to America; he became a naturalized American citizen in 1924. This was also the period when Bloch began to express himself in music as an inheritor of Jewish culture, explicitly articulating his racial consciousness in several verbal statements. His *Israel Symphony*, *Trois poèmes juifs*, and *Schelomo*, a "Hebrew rhapsody" for Cello and Orch., mark the height of Bloch's greatness as a Jewish composer. In America, he found sincere admirers and formed a group of greatly talented students, among them Sessions, Bacon, Antheil, Moore, Rogers, Thompson, Porter, Stevens, Herbert Elwell, Isadore Freed, Jacobi, and Kirchner. From 1920 to 1925 he was director of the Inst. of Music in Cleveland, and from 1925 to 1930, director of the San Francisco Cons. When the magazine *Musical America* announced in 1927 a contest for a symphonic work, Bloch won first prize for his "epic rhapsody" entitled simply *America*; Bloch fondly hoped that the choral ending extolling America as the ideal of humanity would become a national hymn; the work was performed with a great outpouring of publicity in 5 cities, but as happens often with prizewinning works, it failed to strike the critics and the audiences as truly great, and in the end remained a mere by-product of Bloch's genius. From 1930 to 1939 Bloch lived mostly in Switzerland; he then returned to the U.S. and taught classes at the Univ. of Calif. at Berkeley (1940–52); finally retired and lived at his newly purchased house at Agate Beach, Ore. In 1937 he was elected a member of the National Inst. of Arts and Letters, and in 1943 of the American Academy of Arts and Letters. In 1947 he was awarded the first Gold Medal of the American Academy of Arts and Sciences. In 1952 he received 2 N.Y. Music Critic's Circle awards for his String Quartet No. 3 and Concerto Grosso No. 2.

In his harmonic idiom, Bloch favored sonorities formed by the bitonal relationship of 2 major triads with the tonics standing at the distance of a tritone, but even the dissonances he employed were euphonious. In his last works of chamber music, he experimented for the first time with thematic statements of 12 different notes, but he never adopted the strict Schoenbergian technique of deriving the entire contents of a composition from the basic tone row. In his early Piano Quintet, Bloch made expressive use of quarter tones in the string parts. In his Jewish works, he emphasized the interval of the augmented second, without a literal imitation of Hebrew chants. Bloch contributed a number of informative annotations for the program books of the Boston Sym., N.Y. Phil., and other orchs.; he also contributed articles to music journals, among them "Man and Music" in *Musical Quarterly* (Oct. 1933). An Ernest Bloch Soc. was formed in London in 1937 to promote performances of his music, with Albert Einstein as honorary president and with vice-presidents including Sir Thomas Beecham, Havelock Ellis, and Romain Rolland.

WORKS: DRAMATIC: Opera: *Macbeth* (1904–09; Paris, Nov. 30, 1910). **ORCH.:** *Vivre-Aimer*, symphonic poem (1900; Geneva, June 23, 1901); Sym. in C-sharp minor (1901–02; first complete perf., Geneva, 1910); *Hiver-printemps*, symphonic poems (1904–05; Geneva, Jan. 27, 1906); *Trois Poèmes juifs* (1913; Boston, March 23, 1917); *Schelomo*, Hebrew rhapsody for Cello and Orch. (1915–16; N.Y., May 3, 1917); Suite for Viola and Orch. (1919); *In the Night* (1922; orchestration of piano piece); *Poems of the Sea* (1922; orchestration of piano piece); *Concerto Grosso* No. 1 for Strings and Piano Obbligato (1924–25; Cleveland, June 1, 1925) and No. 2 for String Quartet and String Orch. (1952; BBC, London, April 11, 1953); *4 Episodes* for Chamber Orch. (1926); *Helvetia, the Land of Mountains and its People*, symphonic fresco (1900–1929; Chicago, Feb. 18, 1932); *Voice in the Wilderness*, symphonic poem with Cello Obbligato (1936; Los Angeles, Jan. 21, 1937); *Evocations*, suite (1937; San Francisco, Feb. 11, 1938); Violin Concerto (1937–38; Cleveland, Dec. 15, 1938); *Bal Shem Suite* for Violin and Orch. (1939; N.Y., Oct. 19, 1941; orchestration of 1923 chamber piece); *Suite symphonique* (1944; Philadelphia, Oct. 26, 1945); *Concerto symphonique* for Piano and Orch. (1947–48; Edinburgh, Sept. 3, 1949); Concertino for Flute, Viola, and Strings (1948); *Scherzo fantasque* for Piano and Orch. (1948; Chicago, Dec. 2, 1950); *Suite hébraique* for Viola or Violin and Orch. (1951; Chicago, Jan. 1, 1953); *In Memoriam* (1952); *Sinfonia breve* (1952; BBC, London, April 11, 1953); Sym. for Trombone and Orch. (1953–54; Houston, April 4, 1956); Sym. in E-flat major (1954–55; London, Feb. 15, 1956); *Proclamation* for Trumpet and Orch. (1955); *Suite Modale* for Flute and Strings (1956; Kentfield, Calif., April 11, 1965); *2 Last Poems* ("Maybe") for Flute and Chamber Orch.: *Funeral Music* and *Life Again?* (1958; anticipatory of death from terminal cancer). **CHAMBER:** 5 string quartets (1916, 1945, 1952, 1953, 1956); Suite for Viola and Piano (1919; also orchestrated); 2 violin sonatas (1920; *Poème mystique*, 1924); 2 piano quintets: No. 1 with the use of quarter tones (N.Y., Nov. 11, 1923) and No. 2 (N.Y., Dec. 6, 1957); *Baal Shem*, "3 Pictures of Chassidic Life" for Violin and Piano (1923; orchestrated 1939); *From Jewish Life* for Cello and Piano (1924); *Méditation hébraïque* for Cello and Piano (1924); *3 Nocturnes* for Piano Trio (1924); *Nuit exotique* for Violin and Piano (1924); *In the Mountains* for String Quartet (1925); *Night* for String Quartet (1925); *Paysages* for String Quartet (1925); *Prelude* for String Quartet (1925); *Abodah* for Violin and Piano (1929); *Melody* for Violin and Piano (1929); *2 Pieces* for String Quartet (1938, 1950); *Meditation and Processional* for Viola and Piano (1951); 3 suites for Cello (1956, 1956, 1957); 2 suites for Violin (1958); Suite for Viola (1958; last movement incomplete). **KEYBOARD: Piano:** *Ex-Voto* (1914); *4 Circus Pieces* (1922); *In the Night* (1922; orchestrated); *Poems of the Sea* (1922; orchestrated); *Danse sacrée* (1923); *Enfantines* (1923); *Nirvana* (1923); *5 Sketches in Sepia* (1923); Sonata (1935); *Visions et Prophéties* (1936; piano reduction to parts of *Voice in the Wilderness*). **O r g a n :** *6 Preludes* (1949); *4 Wedding Marches* (1950). **VOCAL:** *Historiettes au crépuscule*, 4 songs for Mezzo-soprano and Piano (1903); *Poèmes d'automne*, songs for Mezzo-soprano and Orch. (1906); *Prelude and 2 Psalms* (Nos. 114 and 137) for Soprano and Orch. (1912–14); *Psalm 22* for Alto or Baritone and Orch. (1914); *Israel*, sym. for 5 Soloists and Orch. (1912–16; N.Y., May 3, 1917, composer conducting); *America: An Epic Rhapsody* for Chorus and Orch. (1926; N.Y., Dec. 20, 1928); *Avodath Hakodesh* for Baritone, Chorus, and Orch. (1930–33; Turin, Jan. 12, 1934).

BIBL.: M. Chiesa, *Bibliografia delle opere musicali di E. B.* (Turin, 1931); idem, *E. B.* (Turin, 1933); D. Kushner, *E. B. and His Music* (Glasgow, 1973); S. Bloch and I. Heskes, *E. B., Creative Spirit: A Program Source Book* (N.Y., 1976); R. Strassburg, *E. B., Voice in the Wilderness: A Biographical Study* (Los Angeles, 1977); D. Kushner, *E. B.: A Guide to Research* (N.Y., 1988); W. Matz, *Musica humana: Versuch über E. B.s Philosophie der Musik* (Frankfurt am Main and N.Y., 1988).—**NS/LK/DM**

Bloch, Suzanne, Swiss-American lutenist and harpsichordist, daughter of **Ernest Bloch;** b. Geneva, Aug. 7, 1907. She went to the U.S. with her father; studied there with him and with Sessions; then in Paris with Boulanger. She became interested in early music, which she championed on original instruments. With I. Heskes, she publ. *Ernest Bloch, Creative Spirit: A Program Source Book* (N.Y., 1976).—**NS/LK/DM**

Blochwitz, Hans Peter, German tenor; b. Garmisch-Partenkirchen, Sept. 28, 1949. He received an engineering degree in computer science; after singing in amateur choruses and occasional concerts, he pursued a vocal career. In 1984 he made his operatic debut as Lensky at the Frankfurt am Main Opera; then sang in Brussels, Geneva, Hamburg, Milan, and Vienna. In 1987 he made his U.S. debut as the Evangelist in Bach's *St. Matthew Passion* with Solti and the Chicago Sym. Orch. In 1989 he made his first appearance at London's Covent Garden as Mozart's Ferrando, and that same year made his U.S. operatic debut in San Francisco as Mozart's Idamanto. On Sept. 27, 1990, he appeared as Don Ottavio at his debut at the Metropolitan Opera in N.Y., and the following month made his U.S. recital debut in La Jolla, Calif.; subsequently sang in opera and concert on both sides of the Atlantic. In 1993 he was a soloist in Beethoven's Ninth Sym. at the London Promenade Concerts. He was engaged to sing the title role in Henze's *Der Junge Lord* in Munich in 1995. His impressive oratorio and concert repertoire ranges from Bach and Handel to Zemlinsky and Britten, with a noteworthy regard for the lieder of Schubert and Schumann. Among his operatic roles are Mozart's Tito, Tamino, and Belmonte, as well as Rossini's Count Almaviva and Donizetti's Nemorino.—**NS/LK/DM**

Block, Michel, Belgian-born American pianist and teacher; b. Antwerp, June 12, 1937. He grew up in Mexico, making his debut as a soloist with the National Orch. in Mexico when he was 16. He then went to N.Y., where he studied at the Juilliard School of Music. He made his N.Y. debut in 1959, then made a successful career as soloist with orchs. in the U.S. and Europe. In 1978 he became a teacher at the Ind. School of Music in Bloomington. In 1987 he became a naturalized American citizen.—**NS/LK/DM**

Blockx, Jan, significant Flemish composer; b. Antwerp, Jan. 25, 1851; d. Kapellenbos, near Antwerp, May 26, 1912. He studied organ with Callaerts and composition with Benoit. In 1885 he became a lecturer at the Flemish Music School; also was music director of the Cercle Artistique and other societies in Belgium. With Benoit, he is regarded as the strongest representative of the national Flemish school of composition. While the melodic and rhythmic materials in his music strongly reflect Flemish folk elements, the treatment, contrapuntal and harmonic, is opulent, approaching Wagnerian sonorities.

WORKS: DRAMATIC: O p e r a : *Jets vergeten* (Antwerp, Feb. 19, 1877); *Maître Martin* (Brussels, Nov. 30, 1892); *Herbergprinses* (Antwerp, Oct. 10, 1896; produced in French as *Princesse d'auberge*, N.Y., March 10, 1909); *Thyl Uylenspiegel* (Brussels, Jan. 12, 1900); *De bruid der zee* (Antwerp, Nov. 30, 1901); *De kapel* (Antwerp, Nov. 7, 1903); *Baldie* (Antwerp, Jan. 25, 1908; rev. and perf. under the title *Liefdelied*; Antwerp, Jan. 6, 1912). **B a l l e t :** *Milenka* (1887). **OTHER:** *Rubens*, overture for Orch.; *Romance* for Violin and Orch.; several choral works with Orch., among them *Vredezang, Het droom vant paradies, De klokke Roelandt, Op den stroom*, and *Scheldezang*.

BIBL.: L. Solvay, *Notice sur J. B.* (Brussels, 1920); F. Blockx, *J. B.* (Brussels, 1943).—**NS/LK/DM**

Blodek, Wilhelm (actually, **Vilém**), Czech composer; b. Prague, Oct. 3, 1834; d. there, May 1, 1874. He studied with J.F. Kittl and A. Dreyschock. He taught for 3 years in Poland, then returned to Prague, and became a prof. of flute at the Prague Cons. (1860–70). In 1870 he became insane and spent the rest of his life in an asylum. His opera in the Czech language, *V studni* (In the Well), was produced with excellent success in Prague (Nov. 17, 1867); it was also given in German under the title *Im Brunnen* (Leipzig, 1893). His second opera, *Zitek*, remained unfinished at his death; it was completed by F.X. Vana, and produced in Prague at the centennial of Blodek's birth (Oct. 3, 1934). Blodek also wrote a Sym. in D minor (1859) and a Flute Concerto (1862).

BIBL.: R. Budiš, *V. B.* (Prague, 1964).—**NS/LK/DM**

Blom, Eric (Walter), eminent English writer on music; b. Bern, Switzerland, Aug. 20, 1888; d. London, April 11, 1959. He was of Danish and British descent on his father's side; his mother was Swiss. He was educated in England. He was the London music correspondent for the *Manchester Guardian* (1923–31); then was the music critic of the *Birmingham Post* (1931–46) and of *The Observer* in 1949; ed. *Music & Letters* from 1937 to 1950 and from 1954 to the time of his death; he was also ed. of the Master Musicians series. In 1955 he was made a Commander of the Order of the British Empire in recognition of his services to music and received the honorary degree of D.Litt. from Univ. of Birmingham. In his writings, Blom combined an enlightened penetration of musical aesthetics with a literary capacity for presenting his subjects and stating his point of view in a brilliant journalistic manner. In his critical opinions, he never concealed his disdain for some composers of great fame and renown, such as Rachmaninoff. In 1946 he was entrusted with the preparation of a newly organized and greatly expanded ed. of *Grove's Dictionary of Music and Musicians*, which was brought out under his editorship in 1954, in 9 vols., and for which Blom himself wrote hundreds of articles and tr. entries by foreign contributors. In 1946 Blom publ. his first lexicographical work, *Everyman's Dictionary of Music*, which went through several eds. before being thoroughly rev. by D. Cummings in 1988 as *The New Everyman Dictionary of Music*. His other books include *Stepchildren of Music* (1923); *The Romance of the Piano* (1927); *A General Index to Modern Musical Literature in the English Language* (1927; indexes periodicals for the years 1915–26); *The Limitations of Music* (1928); *Mozart* (1935; 6th ed., rev., 1974 by J. Westrup); *Beethoven's Pianoforte Sonatas Discussed* (1938); *A Musical Postbag* (1941; collected essays); *Music in England* (1942; rev. 1947); *Some Great Composers* (1944); *Classics, Major and Minor, with Some Other Musical Ruminations* (London, 1958).—NS/LK/DM

Blomberg, Erik,

Swedish composer and teacher; b. Järnskog, May 6, 1922. He was a student of Erland von Koch and Gunnar Bucht at the Stockholm Musikhögskolan (graduated, 1954), and then devoted himself to composing and teaching. His compositions are in a progressive, post-Webern style.

WORKS: ORCH.: 11 syms.: No. 1, *4 dramatiska skisser* (1966), No. 2, *3 studier i melodik* (1968), No. 3, *Associationskedjor* (1971), No. 4 (1973), No. 5 (1974), No. 6 (1982), No. 7 (1984), No. 8, *Liten* (1992), No. 9 (1995), No. 10 (1998), and No. 11 (1999); *Dialog* for Piano and Orch. (1969); *Uppsaliensisk festmusik 1977* for Strings (1976); *Flykt* (1979); *Intoning* (1981); *Uttoning* (1981); *Sjuttonårsmelodik* (1992); *Artonårsmelodik* for Violin and Orch. (1992); *Chaconne* (1993); *Dansscen* (1993); *Lek* (1993); *Kväde 3* (1993); *Polonäs* (1994); *Studie* for Viola and Strings (1996); *Omvandlingar* (1997); *Defilering* (1997). **OTHER:** *Kompriment 1–20* for Various Instrumental Formations, ranging from small groups to orch. (1971–78); chamber music; piano pieces; much vocal music, including choral works and songs.—NS/LK/DM

Blomdahl, Karl-Birger,

significant Swedish composer; b. Växjö, Oct. 19, 1916; d. Kungsängen, near Stockholm, June 14, 1968. He studied composition with Hilding Rosenberg and conducting with Tor Mann in Stockholm; in 1946 he traveled in France and Italy on a state stipend; in 1954–55 he attended a seminar at Tanglewood on a grant of the American-Scandinavian Foundation. Returning to Sweden, he taught composition at the Stockholm Musikhögskolan (1960–64); in 1964 he was appointed music director at the Swedish Radio. He was an organizer (with Bäck, Carlid, Johanson, and Lidholm) of a "Monday Group" in Stockholm, dedicated to the propagation of an objective and abstract idiom as distinct from the prevalent type of Scandinavian romanticism. Blomdahl's early works are cast in a neo-Classical idiom, but he then turned to more advanced techniques, including the application of elec-

tronic resources. His Third Sym., *Facetter* (Facets), utilizes dodecaphonic techniques. In 1959 he brought out his opera *Aniara*, which made him internationally famous; it pictures a pessimistic future when the remnants of the inhabitants of the planet Earth, devastated by atomic wars and polluted by radiation, are forced to emigrate to saner worlds in the galaxy; the score employs electronic sounds, and its thematic foundation is derived from a series of 12 different notes and 11 different intervals. At the time of his death, Blomdahl was working on an opera entitled *The Saga of the Great Computer*, incorporating electronic and concrete sounds, and synthetic speech.

WORKS: DRAMATIC: *Vaknatten* (The Wakeful Night), theater music (1945); *Aniara*, opera (1957–59; Stockholm, May 31, 1959); *Minotaurus*, ballet (Stockholm, April 5, 1958); *Spel för åtta* (Game for 8), ballet (Stockholm, June 8, 1962; also as a choreographic suite for Orch., 1964); *Herr von Hancken*, comic opera (Stockholm, Sept. 2, 1965). **ORCH.:** *Symphonic Dances* (Göteborg, Feb. 29, 1940); Concert Overture (Stockholm, Feb. 14, 1942); Viola Concerto (Stockholm, Sept. 7, 1944); 3 syms.: No. 1 (1944; Stockholm, Jan. 26, 1945), No. 2 (1947; Stockholm, Dec. 12, 1952), and No. 3, *Facetter* (Facets; 1950; Frankfurt am Main, June 24, 1951); Concerto Grosso (Stockholm, Oct. 2, 1945); Concerto for Violin and Strings (Stockholm, Oct. 1, 1947); *Pastoral Suite* for Strings (1948); *Prelude and Allegro* for Strings (1949); Chamber Concerto for Piano, Winds, and Percussion (Stockholm, Oct. 30, 1953); *Sisyfos*, choreographic suite (Stockholm, Oct. 20, 1954; also as a ballet, Stockholm, April 18, 1957); *Fioriture* (Cologne, June 17, 1960); *Forma ferritonans* (Oxelösund, June 17, 1961). **CHAMBER:** Trio for Oboe, Clarinet, and Bassoon (1938); 2 string quartets (1939, 1948); 2 suites for Cello and Piano (1944, 1945); String Trio (1945); *Little Suite* for Bassoon and Piano (1945); *Dance Suite No. 1* for Flute, Violin, Viola, Cello, and Percussion (1948) and *No. 2* for Clarinet, Cello, and Percussion (1951); Trio for Clarinet, Cello, and Piano (1955). **Piano:** *3 Polyphonic Pieces* (1945). **VOCAL:** *I speglarnas sal* (In the Hall of Mirrors), oratorio for Soloists, Chorus, and Orch. (1951–52; Stockholm, May 29, 1953); *Anabase* for Baritone, Narrator, Chorus, and Orch. (Stockholm, Dec. 14, 1956); *...resan i denna natt* (...the voyage in this night), cantata for Soprano and Orch. (Stockholm, Oct. 19, 1966). **ELECTRONIC:** *Altisonans* (1966).

BIBL.: G. Bucht, ed., *"Facetter" av och om K.-B. B.* (Stockholm, 1970; contains a complete catalogue of works with dates of first perfs.).—NS/LK/DM

Blomstedt, Herbert (Thorson),

prominent American-born Swedish conductor; b. Springfield, Mass. (of Swedish parents), July 11, 1927. He took courses at the Stockholm Musikhögskolan and at the Univ. of Uppsala; after conducting lessons with Markevitch in Paris, he continued his training with Morel at the Juilliard School of Music in N.Y. and with Bernstein at the Berkshire Music Center in Tanglewood, where he won the Koussevitzky Prize in 1953. In 1954 he made his professional conducting debut with the Stockholm Phil., then was music director of the Norrkoping Sym. Orch. (1954–61); he subsequently held the post of first conductor of the Oslo Phil. (1962–68) while being concurrently active as a conductor with the Danish Radio Sym. Orch. in Copenhagen, where he served as chief conductor from 1967 to 1977. From 1975 to 1985 he was chief conductor of the Dresden Staatskapelle, with which he toured Europe and the U.S. (1979, 1983). From 1977 to 1983 he was chief conductor of the Swedish Radio Sym. Orch. in Stockholm. From 1985 to 1995 he was music director of the San Francisco Sym., leading it at its 75th-anniversary gala concert in 1986 and on a tour of Europe in 1987. In 1996 he became chief conductor of the North German Radio Sym. Orch. in Hamburg. He has also appeared as a guest conductor with many of the principal orchs. of the world. —NS/LK/DM

Blondeau, Pierre-Auguste-Louis, French violist and composer; b. Paris, Aug. 15, 1784; d. there, 1865. He studied at the Paris Cons. with Baillot, Gossec, and Méhul, winning the Prix de Rome in 1808 with his cantata, *Maria Stuart.* He was violist in the Grand Opera Orch. until 1842. He wrote an opera, *Alla fontana*, a ballet, 3 overtures, church music, chamber music, piano pieces, and songs. He also a number of theoretical works.—NS/LK/DM

Blondie, the most commercially successful group to emerge from the late-1970s N.Y. punk scene. **MEMBERSHIP:** Deborah Harry, voc. (b. Miami, Fla., July 1, 1945); Chris Stein, gtr. (b. Brooklyn, N.Y., Jan. 5, 1950); Jimmy Destri, kybd. (b. Brooklyn, N.Y., April 13, 1954); Gary Valentine, bs.; Clem Burke, drms. (b. N.Y., Nov. 24, 1955). Later members include Frank Infante, bs., gtr.; Nigel Harrison, bs. (b. Stockport, England, April 24, 1951).

Blondie crafted a series of excellent pop singles between 1979 and 1982 under producer Mike Chapman. Remarkably eclectic musically, Blondie scored the first crossover hit between New Wave and disco with "Heart of Glass," promoted reggae with "The Tide Is High," and helped introduce rap with "Rapture." The group's success opened the door for tough, aggressive female vocalists such as Pat Benatar, Joan Jett, and Chrissie Hynde, and the up-front sexuality of lead vocalist Deborah Harry set the stage for the rise of Madonna.

Deborah Harry was adopted by the Harry family of Hawthorne, N.J., at age three months. She grew up in Hawthorne and attended Centenary Coll. for two years before moving to Manhattan. In 1968 she recorded an album with the folk-rock group Wind in the Willows. Later Harry worked as a Playboy "bunny" and waited tables at Max's Kansas City, one of the N.Y. clubs that served as the base for the emerging punk movement. In the early 1970s she helped form the glitter-rock group the Stilettos, recruiting guitarist Chris Stein in late 1973. Harry and Stein subsequently formed Angel and the Snakes, then changed the group's name to Blondie.

Adding Farfisa organist Jimmy Destri, Blondie won a local cult following through appearances at CBGB's, another important punk club on N.Y.'s Lower East Side, and Max's Kansas City. Debuting on the West Coast as the opening act for the Ramones at Los Angeles's Whisky a-Go-Go in early 1977, Blondie recorded their first album for the small Private Stock label. Achieving hits in Great Britain, Europe, and Australia with "In the Flesh" and "Rip Her to Shreds," Blondie was picked up by Chrysalis Records, for whom they recorded *Plastic Letters* with producer Richard Gottehrer.

Original bassist Gary Valentine was replaced first by Frank Infante, and then by Englishman Nigel Harrison; Infante switched to guitar after Harrison joined the band. Under producer Mike Chapman they cut their next album, *Parallel Lines*, which established Blondie in the United States. The album included "Hanging on the Telephone" and yielded the major hits "One Way or Another" and the disco-style "Heart of Glass." Established as headliners, Blondie toured America in 1979, and next recorded the hard-rocking *Eat to the Beat*, which produced the three hits "Dreaming," "The Hardest Part," and "Atomic." In early 1980 the group scored big with "Call Me," the theme to the film *American Gigolo*, recorded under disco producer Giorgio Moroder. That year Harry demonstrated her acting ability in two movies, *Union City* with Pat Benatar and *Roadie* with Meat Loaf and others. The diverse album *Autoamerican* produced two top hits for Blondie: a remake of the Paragons' reggae song "The Tide Is High," and the early rap song "Rapture." Following Debbie Harry's debut solo album *KooKoo* and the group effort *The Hunter*, Blondie disbanded in 1983.

Debbie Harry was largely out of the public view between 1983 and 1985, save for her costarring role in the disturbing David Cronenberg film *Videodrome*, while she cared for Chris Stein, who was afflicted with a debilitating illness. Harry reemerged in 1986 with the album *Rockbird*, recorded with Stein, guitarist Nile Rodgers (Chic), and producer-keyboardist Seth Justman (J. Geils Band). The album produced minor hits with "French Kissing" and the Harry-Stein composition "In Love with Love." Debbie Harry subsequently appeared in the films *Hairspray* and *Tales from the Darkside*, and in the Showtime cable-TV thriller *Intimate Stranger*; she recorded *Def, Dumb and Blonde* for Sire under producer Mike Chapman, and *Once More into the Bleach* for Chrysalis. In 1994 Harry contributed one song to the Jazz Passengers' *In Love* album and toured as the group's lead vocalist.

DISC.: WIND IN THE WILLOWS: *Wind in the Willows* (1968). **BLONDIE:** *B.* (1977); *Parallel Lines* (1978); *Plastic Letters* (1978); *Eat to the Beat* (1979); *Autoamerican* (1980); *Best* (1981); *The Hunter* (1982); *B. and Beyond: Rarities and Oddities* (1993); *The Platinum Collection* (1994). **DEBBIE HARRY:** *KooKoo* (1981); *Rockbird* (1986); *Def, Dumb and Blonde* (1989).

BIBL.: L. Bangs, *B.* (N.Y., 1980).—BH

Blood, Sweat and Tears, influential late 1960s–early 1970s group bringing big-band instrumentation into a rock context. **MEMBERSHIP:** Al Kooper, kybd., voc. (b. Brooklyn, N.Y., Feb. 5, 1944); Steve Katz, gtr. voc. (b. Brooklyn, May 9, 1945); Jerry Weiss, trpt., flugelhorn (b. N.Y.C., May 1, 1946); Randy Brecker, trpt., flugelhorn (b. Philadelphia, Nov. 27, 1945); Fred Lipsius, alto sax., pno. (b. N.Y.C., Nov. 19, 1944); Dick Halligan, trpt., flt., kybd. (b. Troy, N.Y., Aug. 29, 1943); Jim Fielder, bs. (b. Denton, Tex., Oct. 4, 1947); Bobby Colomby, drm., voc. (b. N.Y.C., Dec. 20, 1944); Al Kooper, Jerry Weiss, and Randy Brecker left after the first album, to be replaced by David Clayton-Thomas, voc. (née David Tomsett; b.

Surrey, England, Sept. 13, 1941); Lew Soloff, trpt., flugel-horn (b. Brooklyn, Feb. 20, 1944); Chuck Winfield, trpt., flugelhorn (b. Monessen, Pa., Feb. 5, 1943); Jerry Hyman, trmb., rec. (b. Brooklyn, May 19, 1947).

Blood, Sweat and Tears was formed in 1968 by Al Kooper, Steve Katz, and Bobby Colomby following Katz and Kooper's departure from The Blues Project. These founders recruited additional musicians Jim Fielder, Jerry Weiss, Randy Brecker, Fred Lipsius, and Dick Halligan. Although their debut album on Columbia, *Child Is Father to the Man,* failed to generate any hit singles, it contained a number of excellent Al Kooper compositions ("I Love You More Than You'll Ever Know," "My Days Are Numbered," and "I Can't Quit Her"), as well as early versions of Harry Nilsson's "Without Her" and Randy Newman's "Just One Smile."

In mid-1968, Kooper left Blood, Sweat and Tears to accept a lucrative offer from Columbia Records to become a producer. Weiss and Brecker also left, to be replaced by Lew Soloff, Chuck Winfield, and Jerry Hyman. The lead vocalist role was taken over by David Clayton-Thomas. Clayton-Thomas had worked around Toronto for ten years, recording five Canadian gold-award records with The Bossmen. The new lineup's first album exploded onto the music scene in early 1969. In addition to including Steve Katz' beautiful "Sometimes in Winter" and a remake of Billie Holiday's "God Bless the Child," the album yielded three smash hit singles with Laura Nyro's "And When I Die," Brenda Hollway's "You've Made Me So Very Happy" and Clayton-Thomas' "Spinning Wheel." Blood, Sweat and Tears' next album contained two hit singles, "Hi-De-Ho" and "Lucretia MacEvil," plus the elaborately arranged "Symphony/Sympathy for the Devil" and "40,000 Headmen." Their next album included only one moderate hit, "Go Down Gamblin.'"

A series of defections soon struck Blood, Sweat and Tears, effectively crippling the group. Clayton-Thomas and Lipsius departed at the end of 1971, with Clayton Thomas pursuing an undistinguished solo career. Halligan also left, followed by Katz and Winfield in 1973. The group persevered with new personnel and a succession of lead vocalists—Bobby Doyle, Jerry Fisher, and Jerry La Croix.

Clayton-Thomas subsequently rejoined Blood, Sweat and Tears in July 1974. By then, only Bobby Colomby remained from the original group. Personnel shifts continued to plague Blood, Sweat and Tears, and, in 1976, Colomby left. On Jan. 31, 1978, one-year member Gregory Herbert was found dead in an Amsterdam hotel room during the group's European tour. By 1980, David Clayton-Thomas was the only "original" member left in Blood, Sweat and Tears, although another edition of the group toured the United States in 1988. Blood, Sweat and Tears also appeared at Woodstock '94.

The first major rock group to successfully augment its sound with horns, Blood, Sweat and Tears displayed an early amalgamation of jazz, rock, and, later, classical music. Following the departure of keyboardist-vocalist Al Kooper after their first album, Blood, Sweat and Tears evolved into an enormously popular, highly arranged pop band fronted by vocalist David Clayton-

Thomas that set the standard for the blending together of rock, pop, and jazz music.

DISC.: BLOOD, SWEAT AND TEARS *Child Is Father to the Man* (1968); *Blood, Sweat and Tears* (1969); *3* (1970); *4* (1971); *Greatest Hits* (1972); *New Blood* (1972); *No Sweat* (1973); *Mirror Image* (1974); *New City* (1975); *More Than Ever* (1976); *Brand New Day* (1978); *Blood, Sweat and Tears* (1980); *Nuclear Blues* (rec. 1980; rel. 1995); *Live* (rec. 1982; rel. 1994). DAVID CLAYTON-THOMAS: *I Got a Woman* (1969); *Magnificent Sanctuary Band* (1972); *Tequila Sunrise* (1972); *Harmony Junction* (1973); *Clayton* (1978).—BH

Bloom, Jane Ira, innovative jazz soprano saxophonist, composer; b. Boston, Jan. 12, 1955. From 1968, she studied with Herb Pomeroy and Joseph Viola at Berklee, Donald Sinta at the Hartt Coll. of Music, and George Coleman in N.Y. From 1973–77, she studied at Yale (B.A., M.M.). Moving to N.Y., Bloom steadily built up a reputation and has worked primarily as a leader. Among her honors have been grants from the Ford and Rockefeller Foundations and three fellowships from the N.E.A. She has composed and performed scores for the Pilobolus Dance Company and for the NBC movie *Shadow of a Doubt.* She has been profiled on CBS's *Sunday Morning,* appeared on CNBC's *America After Hours* (1996), NPR's "Women in Jazz" film series, and the PBS series *Behind the Scenes.* Winner of the Downbeat International Critics Poll for soprano saxophone (1983–94), Bloom was cited for her work by *Time* magazine in its 1990 "Women: The Road Ahead" issue and included in *Life* magazine's 1996 Second Great Day group photo of jazz musicians. In 1989, she was the first musician ever commissioned by the NASA Art Program and in 1998 the International Astronomical Union named an asteroid in her honor. She is currently on the faculty of the jazz education program at the N.J. Performing Arts Center. Bloom plays major venues and festivals in the U.S. and Europe and toured Australia and Brazil in 1998. A highly original composer, she is one of the few to exclusively play soprano saxophone and uses electronics live.

DISC.: *We Are* (1978); *Second Wind* (1980); *Mighty Lights* (1982); *As One* (1984); *Modern Drama* (1987); *Slalom* (1988); *Art and Aviation* (1992); *The Nearness* (1996). C. Laine: *Jazz.* J. Clayton: *All Out.*—LP

Bloomfield, Theodore (Robert), American conductor; b. Cleveland, June 14, 1923; d. 1998. He studied conducting with Maurice Kessler and piano at the Oberlin (Ohio) Coll.-Cons. of Music (Mus.B., 1944), then took courses in conducting at the Juilliard Graduate School in N.Y. with Edgar Schenkman; also studied piano with Arrau and conducting with Monteux. In 1946–47 he was apprentice conductor to Szell at the Cleveland Orch., then conducted the Cleveland Little Sym. and the Civic Opera Workshop (1947–52). He was subsequently music director of the Portland (Ore.) Sym. (1955–59) and of the Rochester (N.Y.) Phil. (1959–63). He then was first conductor of the Hamburg State Opera (1964–66) and Generalmusikdirektor of Frankfurt am Main (1966–68). From 1975 to 1982 he was chief conductor of the (West) Berlin Sym. Orch.—NS/LK/DM

Blow, John, great English composer and organist; b. Newark-on-Trent, Nottinghamshire (baptized), Feb. 23, 1649 (1648, Julian calendar); d. Westminster (London), Oct. 1, 1708. In 1660–61 he was a chorister at the Chapel Royal, under Henry Cooke; he later studied organ with Christopher Gibbons. His progress was rapid, and on Dec. 3, 1668, he was appointed organist of Westminster Abbey. In 1679 he left this post and Purcell, who had been Blow's student, succeeded him. After Purcell's untimely death in 1695, Blow was reappointed, and remained at Westminster Abbey until his death; he was buried there, in the north aisle. He married Elizabeth Braddock in 1674; she died in 1683 in childbirth, leaving 5 children. Blow held the rank of Gentleman of the Chapel Royal from March 16, 1674; on July 23, 1674, he succeeded Humfrey as Master of the Children of the Chapel Royal; was Master of the Choristers at St. Paul's (1687–1703); in 1699 he was appointed Composer of the Chapel Royal. He held the honorary Lambeth degree of D.Mus., conferred on him in 1677 by the Dean of Canterbury. While still a young chorister of the Chapel Royal, Blow began to compose church music; in collaboration with Humfrey and William Turner, he wrote the *Club Anthem* ("I will always give thanks"); at the behest of Charles II, he made a two-part setting of Herrick's poem "Goe, perjur'd man." He wrote many secular part-songs, among them an ode for New Year's Day 1681/82, "Great sir, the joy of all our hearts," an ode for St. Cecilia; 2 anthems for the coronation of James II; *Epicedium for Queen Mary* (1695); *Ode on the Death of Purcell* (1696). Blow's collection of 50 songs, *Amphion Anglicus*, was publ. in 1700. His best- known work is *Masque for the Entertainment of the King: Venus and Adonis*, written c. 1685; this is his only complete score for the stage, but he contributed separate songs for numerous dramatic plays. Purcell regarded Blow as "one of the greatest masters in the world." Fourteen large works by Blow, anthems and harpsichord pieces, have been preserved; 11 anthems are printed in Boyce's *Cathedral Musick* (1760–78). Selected anthems are publ. in Musica Britannica, 7. The vocal score of his masque *Venus and Adonis* was publ. by G.E.P. Arkwright in the Old English Edition (No. 25; 1902); the complete score was publ. by the Editions de l'Oiseau Lyre, as ed. by Anthony Lewis (Paris, 1939).

BIBL.: B. Wood, *J. B.'s Anthems with Orch.* (diss., Cambridge Univ., 1977).—**NS/LK/DM**

Blue Öyster Cult, mainstays of heavy-metal music during the 1970s, the group formed as Soft White Underbelly on Long Island in 1968. **MEMBERSHIP:** Donald "Buck Dharma" Roeser, lead gtr., voc., kybd., bs.; Allen Lanier, kybd., gtr., voc.; Eric Bloom, gtr., synthesizer., voc.; Joe Bouchard, bs., voc. (b. Watertown, N.Y., Nov. 9, 1948); and Albert Bouchard, drms., voc. (b. Watertown, N.Y., May 24, 1947).

Blue Öyster Cult featured a deafening yet frequently melodic triple- guitar attack on songs often concerned with death and destruction. The group took the name Stalk Forest before becoming Blue Öyster Cult in 1971. A variety of band members passed through these early incarnations, including the rock critic R. Meltzer, who has since gone on to be one of the group's strongest

champions. The final lineup included frontmen guitarist-songwriter Donald "Buck Dharma" Roeser, guitarist-keyboardist Allen Lanier, and guitarist-vocalist Eric Bloom. The band spent the early 1970s touring as a support act to Alice Cooper, finally breaking through in 1976 with the album *Agents of Fortune*, which featured their only major hit, "(Don't Fear) The Reaper." A special guest on the album was Lanier's then-girlfriend, Patti Smith, the N.Y. punk diva who contributed some vocals and songs to the effort. Blue Öyster Cult established themselves as exciting live performers, as evidenced by their best-selling live set, *On Your Feet or On Your Knees*, as well as two other live discs. The group pursued a more pop sound with the 1981 departure of drummer-songwriter Albert Bouchard. He eventually returned to the otherwise intact group in 1988 for the album *Imaginos*. The band soldiered on into the early 1990s, although the Bouchard brothers Joe and Albert had jumped ship by 1994.

DISC.: BLUE ÖYSTER CULT: *B. Ö. C.* (1972); *Tyranny and Mutation* (1973); *Secret Treaties* (1974); *On Your Feet or On Your Knees* (1975); *Agents of Fortune* (1976); *Spectres* (1977); *Some Enchanted Evening* (1978); *Mirrors* (1979); *Cultosaurus Erectus* (1980); *Fire of Unknown Origin* (1981); *Extraterrestrial Live* (1982); *The Revolution by Night* (1983); *Club Ninja* (1986); *Imaginos* (1988); *Career of Evil: The Metal Years (1974–1986)* (1990); *Cult Classic* (1994); *Workshop of the Telescopes* (1995). **BUCK DHARMA:** *Flat Out* (1982).—**BH**

Blues Traveler, the archetypal rock band in atypical times (formed Princeton, N.J., c. 1983). **MEMBERSHIP:** John Popper, voc., har. (b. Cleveland, Ohio,1967); Chan Kinchla, gtr; Bobby Sheehan, bs; Brendan Hill, drms.

In many ways, Blues Traveler led the "movement" of "jam bands" like Phish and the Spin Doctors that flew in the face of the prevailing alternative sounds of the late 1980s and early 1990s. Fronted by harmonica virtuoso and vocalist John Popper, the band plays a loose-limbed rock that owes as much to the Grateful Dead as it does to Bruce Springsteen. Like both of the latter, they often play sets that run to three or more hours. Popper also peppers his lyrics with references to Cyrano de Bergerac and Rudyard Kipling. The band came together when Popper, who had moved from Cleveland to Conn., finally landed in Princeton, N.J. He met drummer Brendan Hill in high school, and they started playing as the Blues Band. They added the "Traveler" part after seeing the film *Ghostbusters*—the villain who takes the form of the marshmallow man is Gozer The Traveler. Six foot, five inch Chan Kinchla joined the band when a knee injury curtailed his participation in football and his disaffection with the limited vocabulary of punk led him to explore other avenues for his guitar playing.

The trio moved to Brooklyn, N.Y., attending classes at Manhattan's New School for Social Research. Adding bassist Bobby Sheehan in 1987, they started playing clubs in the East Village and cutting demo tapes, which they sold from the stage. One person who became aware of the group and befriended them was *Late Night with David Letterman* band leader Paul Shaffer. Another was impresario Bill Graham. He booked them with bands like the Allman Brothers and Santana, getting them a far higher profile. This eventually landed them at A&M Records, who put out their eponymous debut in 1990. Shaffer helped get them booked on the Letterman Show, where they became regulars.

In addition to appearing on Letterman over a dozen times, the band played over 800 concerts in three years. In answer to Jane's Addictions successful alternative music festival Lollapalooza, Blues Traveler created the HORDE (Horizons of Rock Developing Everywhere) tour in 1992, headlining Spin Doctors, Phish, and Widespread Panic, among others. Over the intervening years, artists ranging from the Allman Brothers to Bruce Hornsby to Smashing Pumpkins to Neil Young have joined the HORDE.

Blues Traveler's first three albums sold modestly with *Save His Soul* actually charting at #73. Immediately before the album came out, Popper was in a serious motorcycle accident. After six months of recovery, the band hit the road again, with Popper taking the stage in a wheelchair for the second annual HORDE.

Their fourth album—aptly titled *Four*—sold over six million copies when the band's song "Run-Around" became ubiquitous on pop and rock radio (it peaked at #8, #27 sales and #3 airplay) and won a Best Rock Performance, Duo or Group, with Vocal Grammy. The follow-up single, "Hook" topped out at #23 and the album peaked at #9.

The band appeared over the closing credits of the movie *Kingpin*. They played "But Anyway" dressed in Amish garb. Popper also had a cameo in the Howard Stern movie *Private Parts*.

Blues Traveler put out the double-live album *Live from the Fall*, which captured the spirit of their set but failed to chart. They followed this a year later with *Straight on Till Morning*. In addition to the radio track single "Carolina Blues," the album featured strings and other production touches the band had previously avoided. The songwriting was more structured and the playing reflected the band's maturing status.

DISC.: *Blues Traveler* (1990); *Travelers and Thieves* (1991); *Save His Soul* (1993); *Four* (1994); *Live from the Fall* (1996); *Straight on Till Morning* (1997).—**HB**

Blum, Robert (Karl Moritz),

Swiss composer and teacher; b. Zürich, Nov. 27, 1900; d. there, Dec. 10, 1994. He was a student of Andreae, Baldegger, Jarnach, Laquai, and Vogler at the Zürich Cons. (1912–22). After attending Busoni's master class in composition at the Prussian Academy of Arts in Berlin (1923), he returned to Switzerland and conducted various amateur orchs. and choirs. From 1943 to 1976 he taught counterpoint and composition at the Zürich Cons. In his extensive output, Blum utilized various contemporary means of expression, from polytonal to 12–tone writing.

WORKS: DRAMATIC: *Amarapura*, opera (1924); film music. **ORCH.:** 10 syms. (1924–80); *4 Partite* (1929, 1935, 1953, 1967); *Passionskonzert* for Organ and Strings (1943); *Lamentatio angelorum* for Chamber Orch. (1943); *Overture on Swiss Folk Songs* (1944); Viola Concerto (1951); *Concerto for Orch.* (1955); Oboe Concerto (1960); *Christ ist erstanden* (1962); Triple Concerto for Violin, Oboe, Trumpet, and Chamber Orch. (1963);

Concertante Symphonie for Wind Quintet and Chamber Orch. (1964). **CHAMBER:** 3 string quartets; Flute Quartet (1963); Sonata for Flute and Violin (1963); *Divertimento* for 10 Instruments (1966); *Le Tombe di Ravenna* for 11 Winds (1968); Quartet for Clarinet and String Trio (1970); piano pieces; organ music. **VOCAL:** Oratorios; cantatas; Psalms; hymns; songs.

BIBL.: G. Fierz, *R. B.: Leben und Werk* (Zürich, 1967); G. Lehmann, *Zur Musik von R. B.* (Baden, 1973).—**NS/LK/DM**

Blume, (Ferdinand Anton) Clemens,

German music scholar; b. Billerbeck, Jan. 31, 1862; d. Königstein, April 8, 1932. He studied theology, and then taught it at the Catholic Univ. in Frankfurt am Main. He was regarded as an authority on texts of medieval Latin hymns. His books include *Cursus Sanctus Benedicti* (liturgical hymns of the sixth to ninth centuries; 1908), *Guide to Chevalier's "Repertorium Hymnologicum"* (1911), and, his standard work, *Analecta hymnica medii aevi* (1896–1922; Vols. 1–48 co-ed. with C.M. Dreves; some vols. with H.M. Bannister). A selection from this valuable sourcebook of hymnological research was extracted as *Ein Jahrtausend lateinischer Hymnendichtung* (2 vols., 1909). Blume also publ. *Unsere liturgischen Lieder* (Pustet, 1932).—**NS/LK/DM**

Blume, Friedrich,

eminent German musicologist and editor; b. Schluchtern, Jan. 5, 1893; d. there, Nov. 22, 1975. He was the son of a Prussian government functionary. He first studied medicine in Eisenach; in 1911 he went to the Univ. of Munich, where he began musicological studies; then went to the univs. of Leipzig and Berlin. During World War I, he served in the German army; he was taken prisoner by the British and spent 3 years in a prison camp in England. In 1919 he resumed his studies at the Univ. of Leipzig, where he took his Ph.D. in 1921 with the diss. *Studien zur Vorgeschichte der Orchestersuite im 15. und 16. Jahrhundert* (publ. in Leipzig, 1925); in 1923 he became a lecturer in music at the Univ. of Berlin; in 1925 he completed his Habilitation there with *Das monodische Prinzip in der protestantischen Kirchenmusik* (publ. in Leipzig, 1925); was made Privatdozent there that same year; also lectured in music history at the Berlin-Spandau School of Church Music from 1928 to 1934. In 1934 he joined the faculty of the Univ. of Kiel, where he was prof. from 1938 until his retirement in 1958; was then made prof. emeritus. In 1952 he was made a corresponding member of the American Musicological Soc. Blume was an authority on Lutheran church music; his *Die evangelische Kirchenmusik* was publ. in Bucken's *Handbuch der Musikwissenschaft*, X (1931; 2nd ed., rev., as *Geschichte der evangelischen Kirchenmusik*, 1965; Eng. tr., 1974, as *Protestant Church Music: A History*). He prepared a collected edition of the works of M. Praetorius (21 vols., Berlin, 1928–41); was general ed. of Das Chorwerk, a valuable collection of early polyphonic music (1929–38); also ed. of Das Erbe deutscher Musik (1935–43). In 1943 he was entrusted with the preparation of the monumental encyclopedia *Die Musik in Geschichte und Gegenwart* (14 vols., Kassel, 1949–68); following its publication, he undertook the further task of preparing an extensive supplement, which contained numerous additional articles and corrections; its publication was continued after his death by his daughter, Ruth Blume. He also wrote *Wesen und Werden deutscher Musik* (Kassel, 1944); *Johann Sebastian Bach im Wandel der Geschichte* (Kassel, 1947; Eng. tr., 1950, as *Two Centuries of Bach*); *Goethe und die Musik* (Kassel, 1948); *Was ist Musik?* (Kassel, 1959); *Umrisse eines neuen Bach-Bildes* (Kassel, 1962). His life's work was a study in the practical application of his vast erudition and catholic interests in musicological scholarship.

BIBL.: A. Abert and W. Pfannkuch, eds., *Festschrift F. B. zum 70. Geburtstag* (Kassel, 1963).—NS/LK/DM

Blumenfeld, Felix (Mikhailovich), Russian composer and conductor; b. Kovalevka, near Kherson, April 19, 1863; d. Moscow, Jan. 21, 1931. He studied piano in Elizavetgrad, then went to St. Petersburg, where he studied composition with Rimsky-Korsakov. Upon graduation in 1885, he joined the staff of the Cons. and taught there until 1905, and again from 1911 to 1918. From 1895 to 1911 he was the conductor at the Imperial Opera in St. Petersburg; he was also a guest conductor in the Russian repertoire in Paris during the "Russian seasons" in 1908. He was a pianist of virtuoso caliber, and also active as an accompanist for Chaliapin and other famous singers. From 1918 to 1922 he was a prof. of piano at the Cons. of Kiev, and from 1922 to his death he taught at the Moscow Cons. Among his piano students was Vladimir Horowitz. As a composer, Blumenfeld excelled mainly in his piano pieces and songs, many publ. by Belaiev. He also wrote a sym., entitled *To the Beloved Dead*, a String Quartet, and other pieces. —NS/LK/DM

Blumenfeld, Harold, American composer; b. Seattle, Oct. 15, 1923. He studied composition with Hindemith at Yale Univ. (M.B., 1949; M.M., 1950), took courses in conducting with Bernstein and operatic stage direction with Goldovsky at the Berkshire Music Center at Tanglewood, and in 1948–49 attended the Univ. and Cons. in Zürich. In 1951 he joined the faculty of Washington Univ. in St. Louis, where he founded the Opera Theatre of St. Louis, directing it through 1971. In 1971–72 he was a visiting prof. at Queens Coll. of the City Univ. of N.Y., and then was again on the faculty of Washington Univ. until 1989. He received an award from the American Academy and Inst. of Arts and Letters in 1977 and an opera fellowship from the NEA in 1979. Blumenfeld has concentrated his compositional efforts on vocal and dramatic music for various media.

WORKS: DRAMATIC: Opera: *Amphitryon Five* (1962; rev. 2001); *Fourscore: An Opera of Opposites*, after Nestroy (1980–86); *Breakfast Waltzes*, after Molnar (1991; Des Moines, July 12, 1997); *Seasons in Hell: A Life of Rimbaud* (1992–94; Cincinnati, Feb. 8, 1996); *Borgia Infami*, after Klabund and Hugo (1998–99). **ORCH.:** *Miniature Overture* (1958); *Illuminations: Symphonic Fragments after Rimbaud* (1992; Cincinnati, April 15, 1993); *Voci Luminose* for 2 Violins and Orch. (Umeå, Sweden, Nov. 8, 1996). **VOCAL:** *3 Scottish Poems* for Chorus (n.d.); *4 Tranquil Poems* for Men's Chorus, after D.H. Lawrence (n.d.); *War Lament* for Chorus and Guitar, after Sassoon (1970); *Eroscapes* for Medium Voice and 9 Instruments (1971); *Song of Innocence* for Mixed Chorus, Chamber Chorus, Soloists, and Orch., after Blake (1973); *Starfires* for Soprano, Tenor, and Orch.

(1975); *Rilke* for Voice and Guitar (1975); *Voyages* for Baritone, Viola, Guitar, and 2 Percussion, after Hart Crane (1977); *Silentium: 9 Songs* for Medium Voice and Piano, after Osip Mandelstam (1979); *Circle of the Eye*, 11 songs for Medium Voice and Piano, after Tom McKeown (1979); *La Voix reconnue* for Soprano, Tenor, and Chamber Ensemble, after Verlaine (1980); *La Face cendrée* for Mezzo-soprano, Cello, and Piano, after Rimbaud (1981); *Charioteer of Delphi* for Baritone, Viola, and Guitar, after Merrill (1985); *Carnet de damné* for Mezzo-soprano and 8 Players, after Rimbaud (1987); *Ange de flamme et de glace* for Medium Voice, 7 Players, and Tape, after Rimbaud (1990); *Mythologies* for Baritone, Woman Speaker, Flute, Clarinet, 3 Cellos, and 2 Percussion, after Derek Walcott (1990); *Songs of Cassis* for Baritone and Piano (1995); *A l'Ouest de la lune* for Soprano, Tenor, Flute, Clarinet, Viola, and Cello, after Verlaine (1995); *Vers Sataniques* for Baritone, Soprano, and Orch., after Baudelaire (1997).—NS/LK/DM

Blumental, Felicja, Polish-born Brazilian pianist; b. Warsaw, Dec. 28, 1908; d. Tel Aviv, Dec. 31, 1991. She studied composition with Szymanowski and piano with Drzewiecki and Joseph Goldberg at the Warsaw Cons. In 1942 she emigrated to Brazil and became a naturalized Brazilian citizen; in 1962 she returned to Europe. She became particularly known for her performances of works by rarely heard composers of the past, especially Clementi, Czerny, and Hummel. She also commissioned scores from Villa-Lobos, Lutosławski, and Penderecki. —NS/LK/DM

Blüthner, Julius (Ferdinand), celebrated German piano maker; b. Falkenhain, near Merseburg, March 11, 1824; d. Leipzig, April 13, 1910. In 1853 he founded his establishment at Leipzig with 3 workmen, and by 1897 it had grown to a sizable company, producing some 3,000 pianos yearly. Blüthner's specialty was the "Aliquotflügel," a grand piano with a sympathetic octave-string stretched over and parallel with each unison struck by the hammers. He was awarded many medals for his contributions to the advancement of piano construction. He was co-author, with H. Gretschel, of *Lehrbuch des Pianofortebaus in seiner Geschichte, Theorie und Technik* (Weimar, 1872; 4th ed., 1921). —NS/LK/DM

Boatwright, Helen (née **Strassburger**), American soprano and teacher; b. Sheboygan, Wisc., Nov. 17, 1916. She began her training with Anna Shram Irving, and later studied with Marion Sims at Oberlin (Ohio) Coll. After making her operatic debut as Anna in an English language production of Nicolai's *Die lustigen Weiber von Windsor* at the Berkshire Music Center in 1942, she appeared in opera in Austin and San Antonio (1943–45). In 1943 she married **Howard Boatwright**, with whom she often appeared in concert. She taught in New Haven (1945–64), and in 1965 became adjunct prof. of voice at Syracuse Univ. In 1967 she made her N.Y. recital debut at Town Hall. She was prof. of voice at the Eastman School of Music in Rochester, N.Y. (1972–79) and at the Peabody Cons. of Music in Baltimore (1987–89); also gave master classes.—NS/LK/DM

Boatwright, Howard (Leake Jr.), American violinist, conductor, music educator, and composer; b.

Newport News, Va., March 16, 1918; d. Syracuse, N.Y., Feb. 20, 1999. He studied violin with Israel Feldman in Norfolk. At age 17, he made his debut as soloist with the Richmond (Va.) Sym. Orch. From 1943 to 1945 he taught violin at the Univ. of Tex. in Austin, and then studied composition with Hindemith at Yale Univ. (1945–48), where he subsequently taught (1948–64). He concurrently served as music director at St. Thomas' Church in New Haven, Conn. (1949–64). From 1964 to 1972 he was dean of the music school at Syracuse Univ., and then taught theory there. He continued to give violin recitals, usually with his wife, **Helen Boatwright**, whom he married in 1943. From 1950 to 1962 he was concertmaster of the New Haven Orch., and from 1957 to 1960 conducted the Yale Univ. Sym. He became greatly interested in the musical folklore of Eastern nations. In 1959 he went to India on grants from the Fulbright and Rockefeller foundations, and wrote 2 valuable monographs, *A Handbook of Staff Notation for Indian Music* and *Indian Classical Music and the Western Listener*, both publ. in Bombay in 1960. In his compositions, he revived the modalities of early church music, using modern harmonies and linear counterpoint. His best works were of this type, mostly written for chorus.

WORKS: ORCH.: *Variations* for Chamber Orch. (1949); Sym. (1976). **CHAMBER:** 2 string quartets (1947, 1975); *Serenade* for 2 String Instruments and 2 Wind Instruments (1952); Clarinet Quartet (1958); 12 pieces for Violin (1977); Clarinet Sonata (1980). **VOCAL:** Mass in C (1958); *The Passion According to St. Matthew* for Chorus (1962); *Canticle of the Sun* for Chorus (1963); *6 Prayers of Kierkegaard* for Soprano and Piano (1978); other choral works and songs.—**NS/LK/DM**

Boatwright, McHenry, black American bass-baritone; b. Tennile, Ga., Feb. 29, 1928; d. N.Y., Nov. 5, 1994. He studied piano (B.Mus., 1950) and voice (B.Mus., 1954) at the New England Cons. of Music in Boston. In 1953 and 1954 he received Marian Anderson awards. In 1956 he made his formal concert debut in Boston, and in 1958 his first N.Y. concert appearance. After making his operatic debut as Arkel in *Pelléas et Mélisande* at the New England Opera Theater in 1958, he appeared with various opera companies and as a soloist with orchs. He created the central role in Schuller's opera *The Visitation* (Hamburg, Oct. 12, 1966). —**NS/LK/DM**

Boccherini, (Ridolfo) Luigi, famous Italian cellist and composer; b. Lucca, Feb. 19, 1743; d. Madrid, May 28, 1805. He was the son of Leopoldo Boccherini, a double bass player in the Cappella Palatina in Lucca, from whom he may have received his initial instruction in cello before studying the instrument with Domenico Francesco Vannucci at the seminary school of Lucca Cathedral. In 1753–54 he completed his training as a cellist under Giovanni Battista Costanzi in Rome. On Aug. 4, 1756, Boccherini made his debut at the age of 13 playing a cello concerto at the church of San Romano in Lucca. In 1758 he and his father were engaged as members of the orch. of the Théâtre Allemande in Vienna, where they were engaged again in 1760–61 and 1763–64. Boccherini also made highly successful concert appearances during these years in both Vienna and Italy. In 1764 he became a cellist in the Cappella Palatina, where he remained until his father's death in 1766. He and the orch.'s concertmaster, Filippo Manfredi, decided to seek their fortune abroad and eventually made their way to Paris, where Boccherini was already esteemed via the publication of his first trios and quartets in 1767. On March 20, 1768, Boccherini played a cello sonata at the Concerts spirituels. Later that year he and Manfredi were called to Madrid as members of the orch. of the Compagnia dell'Opera Italiana dei Sitios Reales. In 1770 Boccherini was appointed Compositore e virtuoso di camera to the Infante Don Luis Antonio Jaime de Borbon, brother of King Carlos III, in Aranjuez. In 1776 Boccherini's patron chose to marry beneath his social class, and the court degraded him to the status of a count and compelled him to move to Arenas de San Pedro. Boccherini remained in his patron's service there until the count's death in 1785. He then returned to Madrid. On Jan. 21, 1786, he was named court composer to Crown Prince Friedrich Wilhelm of Prussia, who became King Friedrich Wilhelm II in Aug. of that year. There is no evidence, however, that Boccherini ever visited Prussia during his service to the Prussian monarch. Indeed, that same year, he accepted the position of Direttore di concerto of the orch. of the Countess Maria Josefa of Benavente, Duchess of Osuna. Boccherini's service to the Prussian court ended with the death of King Friedrich Wilhelm III in 1797. After the Countess left Madrid in 1798, Boccherini apparently lost her financial support as well. However, in 1800–01 he was employed by Lucien Bonaparte, the French ambassador to Madrid. His last years were plagued by poor health.

Boccherini was a prolific composer whose varied output reflected his assured handling of the classical style. He was especially known for his instrumental music, including some 30 syms., 11 cello concertos, 125 string quintets, 91 string quartets, 48 string trios, 24 quintets for Strings and Flute or Oboe, 21 violin sonatas, 16 sextets, 6 cello sonatas, 2 octets, and much guitar music. He also wrote a zarzuela, *La Clementina* (1786), and a Stabat mater for Soprano and Strings, a Christmas cantata, and other sacred works.

BIBL.: D. Cerù, *Cenni intorno alla vita e le opere di L. B.* (Lucca, 1864); H. Schletterer, *B.* (Leipzig, 1882); G. Malfatti, *L. B. nell'arte, nella vita e nelle opere* (Lucca, 1905); L. Parodi, *L. B.* (Genoa, 1913); A. Bonaventura, *B.* (Milan and Rome, 1931); G. de Rothschild, *L. B.* (Paris, 1962; Eng. tr., 1965); Y. Gérard, *Thematic, Bibliographical and Critical Catalogue of the Works of L. B.* (London, 1969); P. Carmirelli, ed., *Le opere complete di L. B.* (Rome, 1970); M. Ophee, *L. B.'s Guitar Quintets: New Evidence* (Boston, 1981); L. della Croce, *Il divino B.: Vita, opere, epistolario* (Padua, 1988); L. Olschki, ed., *Atti del convegno internazionale di studi: L. B. e la musica strumentale* (Florence, 1994).—**NS/LK/DM**

Bochsa, (Robert-) Nicolas-Charles, celebrated French harpist; b. Montmédy, Meuse, Aug. 9, 1789; d. Sydney, Australia, Jan. 6, 1856. He first studied music with his father, and played in public at the age of 7. He wrote a sym. when he was 9, and an opera, *Trajan*, at 15. He then studied with Franz Beck in Bordeaux, and later at the Paris Cons. with Méhul and Catel (1806). His harp teachers were Nadermann and Marin. Of an

inventive nature, Bochsa developed novel technical devices for harp playing, transforming the harp into a virtuoso instrument. He was the court harpist to Napoleon, and to Louis XVIII. He wrote 7 operas for the Opéra-Comique (1813–16), several ballets, an oratorio, and a great number of works for the harp; also a method for harp. In 1817 he became involved in some forgeries, and fled to London to escape prison. He became very popular as a harp teacher in London society; organized a series of oratorio productions with Sir George Smart (1822). He was also the first prof. of harp at the Academy of Music in London, but in 1827 he lost his position when he committed bigamy. However, he obtained a position as conductor of the Italian Opera at the King's Theatre (1826–30). Another scandal marked Bochsa's crooked road to success and notoriety when he eloped with the soprano Anna Bishop, the wife of Henry Bishop, in Aug. 1839. He gave concerts with her in Europe, America, and Australia, where he died.
—NS/LK/DM

Bock, Jerry (actually, Jerrold Lewis), and Sheldon (Mayer) Harnick,

American songwriting team. Composer Bock (b. New Haven, Conn., Nov. 23, 1928) and lyricist Harnick (b. Chicago, April 30, 1924) wrote the songs for seven musicals that opened on Broadway between 1958 and 1970. Their greatest success was *Fiddler on the Roof*, a warmhearted examination of the breakdown of tradition set in a turn-of-the-century Russian Jewish village that became the longest-running Broadway production up to its time; they also scored a hit with the award-winning *Fiorello!*, a musical biography of N.Y. mayor Fiorello La Guardia.

Both men worked extensively before launching their partnership. Harnick studied violin in high school, where he also began to write sketches and songs. He attended Northwestern Univ., but his education was interrupted by World War II; he was drafted into the army in 1943, serving in the Signal Corps in Ga., where he wrote for USO shows. In 1946 he was discharged, and he returned to Northwestern, where he met his first wife and graduated with a bachelor of music degree.

Harnick first worked as a violinist in bands in Chicago, then in 1950 moved to N.Y. to try to become a songwriter. He placed satirical songs and sketches in the Broadway revue *New Faces of 1952* (N.Y., May 16, 1952); his song "Boston Beguine" was featured in the film version of the show, *New Faces*, released in 1954. Meanwhile, he contributed songs to the revues *Two's Company* (N.Y., Dec. 15, 1952) and *John Murray Anderson's Almanac* (N.Y., Dec. 10, 1953). Up to this point he had been writing his own music, but he collaborated with composer David Baker on the songs for his first full-length book musical, a show based on the Horatio Alger stories, initially called *Horatio* (Dallas, March 8, 1954). After mounting a tryout in Tex., the songwriters began holding backers auditions for it in N.Y. (Seven years later the show finally ran Off-Broadway for a few weeks under the title *Smiling, the Boy Fell Dead* [N.Y., April 19, 1961].)

Harnick continued to write for revues, contributing songs and sketches to the *Shoestring Revue* (N.Y., Feb. 28, 1955), which ran Off-Broadway, and songs to the Off-Broadway shows *The Littlest Revue* (N.Y., May 22, 1956) and *Shoestring '57* (N.Y., Nov. 5, 1956). He met Jerry Bock on the opening night of the Harry Warren musical *Shangri-La* (N.Y., June 13, 1956), to which he had contributed uncredited additional lyrics.

Bock was the son of George Joseph Bock, an automotive parts salesman, and Rebecca Alpert Bock. His family moved to N.Y. when he was two. He began taking piano lessons at nine and wrote the music and lyrics for his first musical, *My Dream*, in 1945 during his senior year at Flushing H.S.; it was performed as a benefit to raise money for recreational equipment for a Navy hospital ship. He began attending the Univ. of Wisc. in the fall of 1945, starting as a journalism major but quickly transferring to the School of Music. In his third year he wrote another musical, *Big as Life*, with lyrics by Jack Royce, which was staged on campus in May 1948 and performed around Wisc. and in Chicago. Bock and Royce's score won a competition sponsored by BMI, and several of the songs were published. Bock was sufficiently encouraged that he and fellow student Larry Holofcener, who had become his lyricist, moved to N.Y. in 1949 to try to become songwriters.

Bock and Holofcener were hired to write songs for the network television variety series *The Admiral Broadway Revue*, starring Sid Caesar and Imogene Coca, which ran from January to June 1949, broadcasting live for an hour on Friday nights. In February 1950 the series returned to the air under the title *Your Show of Shows*, and it ran for 90 minutes on Saturday nights until June 1954. Bock and Holofcener wrote one song, and Bock wrote music for two others, for the Broadway revue *Talent 50* (N.Y., April 28, 1950). On May 28, 1950, Bock married Patti Faggen; they had two children.

Bock and Holofcener contributed three songs to the revue *Catch a Star!* (N.Y., Sept. 6, 1955), which led to their first assignment to write a book musical. They were joined by George David Weiss, and all three were credited with writing music and lyrics for the songs for *Mr. Wonderful* (N.Y., March 22, 1956), a star vehicle for Sammy Davis Jr., based roughly on his life. The show ran 383 performances, and the score was recorded for a cast album that spent a month in the charts, while two of its songs became Top 40 hits: Sarah Vaughan, Peggy Lee, and Teddi King each had popular singles with the title song, and Eydie Gorme scored with a version of "Too Close for Comfort." Notwithstanding this achievement, Bock and Holofcener split up, so that Bock was looking for a new lyric collaborator when he met Harnick.

Bock and Harnick's first Broadway musical, *The Body Beautiful* in January 1958, was a failure, running only 60 performances, but their second, *Fiorello!* (November 1959), was a hit. It ran 795 performances, winning the Pulitzer Prize for drama and the Tony Award for Best Musical. The cast album hit the Top Ten and earned a Grammy nomination in its category.

Harnick and Ogden Nash wrote lyrics to the Serge Prokofiev music for a television version of *Peter and the Wolf* (May 3, 1959) starring Art Carney and the Baird Marionettes. The next Bock-Harnick musical was *Ten-*

derloin (October 1960), another period story set in N.Y. By opening night Bobby Darin had made a Top 40 hit out of "Artificial Flowers" from the score, and the cast album spent eight months in the charts, but the show ran only 216 performances, closing at a loss. In April 1962, Harnick, having been divorced from his first wife since the late 1950s, married comedienne Elaine May (real name Berlin); they divorced after a year, and Harnick later married actress Margery Gray.

Bock and Harnick's fourth Broadway musical, She Loves Me (April 1963), based on the 1937 play Parfumerie by Miklos Nikolaus Lazlo, ran 302 performances, which was not enough to turn a profit. But the much-admired score was recorded for a two-LP cast album that spent five months in the charts and won the Grammy for Best Score from an Original Cast Show Album. The songwriters next wrote a revue, To Broadway with Love (N.Y., April 21, 1964), that was performed at the N.Y. World's Fair and recorded as an album.

Then came Fiddler on the Roof (September 1964), based on the stories of Sholom Aleichem. It ran for 3,242 performances, until July 1972, and won the Tony Award for Best Musical. The title song was recorded for a chart single by the Village Stompers, and Roger Williams reached the charts with "Sunrise, Sunset" from the score, which also featured "If I Were a Rich Man" and "Tradition," songs fashioned for star Zero Mostel. The Broadway cast album reached the Top Ten and sold two million copies, earning a Grammy nomination in its category. The show was produced successfully all over the world, notably in the U.K., where the West End version starring Israeli actor Chaim Topol opened Feb. 16, 1967, and ran 2,030 performances.

The Apple Tree (October 1966), Bock and Harnick's sixth Broadway show, was an experimental effort presenting three separate short musicals with the same cast. It ran 463 performances, and its cast album, a Grammy nominee, spent two months in the charts. The songwriters next turned to television, penning songs for a musical version of the film The Canterville Ghost that was broadcast in November 1966. Their final musical together, The Rothschilds (October 1970) traced the history of the wealthy European banking family; it ran 505 performances, its cast album earning a Grammy nomination in its category. In November 1971, United Artists released a three-hour movie version of Fiddler on the Roof starring Topol that became the top grossing film of the year. The two-LP soundtrack album went gold.

Bock and Harnick were unable to find a project they both wanted to work on in the early 1970s, though they combined a final time for Regards to the Lindsay Years (Dec. 14, 1973)—a theatrical salute to N.Y. mayor John Lindsay that was recorded for an album. Prior to that, Bock wrote the music and lyrics for an autobiographical concept album, Album Leaves, released in 1972, and a second LP, Trading Dreams, in 1974. During this period he worked on a murder-mystery musical called Caper that was never produced. He also worked with the Musical Theatre Lab, a workshop for aspiring composers and lyricists. In 1992 he scored the film A Stranger Among Us.

Harnick's initial efforts after his partnership with Bock were both children's shows done by the Baird Marionettes. His version of Pinocchio (N.Y., Dec. 15, 1973), with music by Mary Rodgers, ran for 134 performances Off-Broadway, while Alice in Wonderland (N.Y., Feb. 19, 1975), with music by Joe Raposo, for which Harnick provided the voice of the White Rabbit, ran Off-Broadway for 51 performances. He wrote the lyrics and libretto for the opera Captain Jinks of the Horse Marines (Kansas City, Sept. 20, 1975), with music by Jack Beeson, then returned to Broadway, collaborating with Richard Rodgers on the musical Rex (N.Y., April 25, 1976). It ran only 49 performances but the cast album earned a Grammy nomination in its category.

Harnick wrote a well-received new English version of Franz Lehár's Die lüstige Witwe (The Merry Widow) for the N.Y. City Opera in 1978. His translations of Jacques Demy's lyrics for the songs of Michel Legrand were heard in a theatrical production of the film The Umbrellas of Cherbourg (N.Y., Jan. 2, 1979) for 36 performances Off-Broadway. He and Legrand then collaborated on a musical version of Charles Dickens's novella A Christmas Carol that had regional tryouts in 1981 and 1982 without coming to Broadway. He did an English translation of Georges Bizet's Carmen produced by Peter Brook in Paris in 1983. Dragons (N.Y., May 12, 1984), a musical for which he wrote the music, lyrics, and libretto, was given a workshop production of six performances Off-Broadway. He wrote the lyrics to Joe Raposo's music for a stage version of A Wonderful Life (Washington, D.C., Nov. 15, 1991), and his work finally was heard again on Broadway when he contributed additional lyrics to Cyrano, The Musical (N.Y., Nov. 21, 1993), a show imported from the Netherlands, which ran 137 performances. He collaborated with Michel Legrand on the score of the animated children's film Aaron's Magic Village, which opened in September 1997.

WORKS (only works for which Bock and Harnick, working together, were primary, credited songwriters are listed): MUSICALS/REVUES (dates refer to N.Y. openings): The Body Beautiful (Jan. 23, 1958); Fiorello! (Nov. 23, 1959); Tenderloin (Oct. 17, 1960); She Loves Me (April 23, 1963); Fiddler on the Roof (Sept. 22, 1964); The Apple Tree (Oct. 18, 1966); The Rothschilds (Oct. 19, 1970). TELEVISION: The Canterville Ghost (Nov. 2, 1966). FILM: Fiddler on the Roof (1971).—WR

Bockelmann, Rudolf (August Louis Wilhelm),

German bass-baritone; b. Bodenteich, April 2, 1892; d. Dresden, Oct. 9, 1958. He studied in Celle and with Lassner, Soomer, and Scheidemantel in Leipzig. In 1920 he made his operatic debut in Celle. In 1921 he sang the Herald in Lohengrin at the Leipzig Opera, where he appeared until 1926. From 1926 to 1932 he sang at the Hamburg City Theater. He also appeared at the Bayreuth Festivals (1928–42), London's Covent Garden (1929–30; 1934–38), and the Chicago Opera (1930–32). From 1932 to 1945 he was a member of the Berlin State Opera. Guest engagements also took him to Milan, Paris, Rome, Vienna, and Munich. His Nazi inclinations precluded engagements outside Germany after World War II. After teaching voice in Hamburg, he went to Dresden in 1955 as a prof. at the Hochschule für Musik. He was particularly esteemed as a Wagnerian, winning praise for his portrayals of Hans Sachs, Wotan, Kurwenal, Gunther, and the Dutchman.—NS/LK/DM

Bodanzky, Artur, famous Austrian conductor; b. Vienna, Dec. 16, 1877; d. N.Y., Nov. 23, 1939. He studied at the Vienna Cons., and later with Zemlinsky. He began his career as a violinist in the Vienna Court Opera Orch. In 1900 he received his first appointment as a conductor, leading an operetta season in Budweis; in 1902 he became assistant to Mahler at the Vienna Court Opera; conducted in Berlin (1905) and in Prague (1906–9). In 1909 he was engaged as music director at Mannheim. In 1912 he arranged a memorial Mahler Festival, conducting a huge ensemble of 1,500 vocalists and instrumentalists. He conducted *Parsifal* at Covent Garden in London in 1914. His success there led to an invitation to conduct the German repertoire at the Metropolitan Opera in N.Y.; he opened his series with *Götterdämmerung* (Nov. 18, 1915). From 1916 to 1931 he was director of the Soc. of Friends of Music in N.Y.; from 1919 to 1922 he also conducted the New Sym. Orch. He made several practical arrangements of celebrated operas (*Oberon, Don Giovanni, Fidelio,* etc.), which he used for his productions with the Metropolitan Opera. His style of conducting was in the Mahler tradition, with emphasis on climactic effects and contrasts of light and shade.—NS/LK/DM

Böddecker, Philipp Friedrich, German organist, bassoonist, and composer; b. Hagenau, Alsace (baptized), Aug. 5, 1607; d. Stuttgart, Oct. 8, 1683. He first studied in Stuttgart with J.U. Steigleder. From 1626 to 1629 he served as organist and singing master in Buchsweiler, Alsace, and then was organist and bassoonist at the courts in Darmstadt and Durlach. In 1638 he became organist at Frankfurt am Main's Barfüsserkirche, in 1642 he was appointed organist at the Strasbourg Cathedral, and in 1648 received the post of organist and director of music at the Univ. of Strasbourg. In 1652 he settled in Stuttgart as organist at the collegiate church there. He publ. the treatise *Manuductio nova methodica-practica bassum generalem* (Stuttgart, 1701). He composed *Melos irenicum* for 6 Soloists, Chorus, and Instruments (Strasbourg, 1650) and 8 sacred concertos. His son, Philipp Jakob Böddecker (b. Frankfurt am Main, 1642; d. Stuttgart, Feb. 1, 1707), was also an organist and composer; he succeeded his father as organist at the collegiate church in Stuttgart (from 1686). —NS/LK/DM

Bode, Johann Joachim Christoph, German instrumentalist and composer; b. Barum, Jan. 12, 1730; d. Weimar, Dec. 13, 1793. He began his career as a bassoon player, and also played cello in the Collegium Musicum in Helmstedt and oboe in Celle. In 1757 he went to Hamburg, where he was active as a teacher, writer, publisher, and translator; in 1778 he settled in Weimar as a diplomat. As a composer, he wrote several syms., a Cello Concerto, a Violin Concerto, a Bassoon Concerto, and songs.

BIBL.: E. Greeven, *J.J.C. B., Ein Hamburger Uebersetzer, Verleger und Drucker* (Weimar, 1938).—NS/LK/DM

Bodenschatz, Erhard, German theologian and music editor; b. Lichtenberg, 1576; d. Gross-Osterhausen, near Querfurt, 1636. He was a pupil of Calvisius in Pforta, then studied theology in Leipzig. In 1600 he became cantor in Schulpforta, in 1603 he was pastor in Rehausen, and in 1608, in Gross-Osterhausen, where he remained until his death. He publ. several valuable collections of motets and hymns. Particularly important is *Florilegium portense* in 2 parts: the first part orig. contained 89 motets (Leipzig, 1603; 2nd ed., with 120 motets, 1618) and the 2nd part (Leipzig, 1621) contained 150 motets, all by contemporary composers. There have been several reprints. He also publ. *Florilegium selectissimorum hymnorum* in 4 vols. (Leipzig, 1606). Bodenschatz's own compositions are not distinctive.

BIBL.: O. Riemer, *E. B. und sein Florilegium portense* (Leipzig, 1928).—NS/LK/DM

Bodin, Lars-Gunnar, Swedish composer; b. Stockholm, July 15, 1935. He studied composition with Lennart Wenström (1956–60), and attended the Darmstadt summer courses (1961). In 1972 he was composer-in-residence at Mills Coll. in Oakland, Calif. In 1978 he became director of the Stockholm Electronic Music Studio. In collaboration with the Swedish concrete poet and composer Bengt Emil Johnson, he produced a series of "text-sound compositions."

WORKS: DANCE: *Place of Plays* (1967); *...from one point to any other point* (1968); *Händelser och handlingar* (1971). **CHAMBER:** *Music for 4 Brass Instruments* (1960); *Arioso* for Clarinet, Trombone, Cello, Piano, and Percussion (1962); *Semikolon: Dag Knutson in memoriam* for Horn, Trombone, Electric Guitar, Piano, and Organ (1963); *Calendar Music* for Piano (1964). **LIVE AND ELECTRONIC:** *My World—Is Your World* for Organ and Tape (1966); *Primary Structures* for Bassoon and Tape (1976); *Enbart för Kerstin* for Mezzo-soprano and Tape (1979); *Anima* for Soprano, Flute, and Tape (1984); *On Speaking Terms* for Trombone and Tape (1984); *Diskus* for Wind Quintet and Tape (1987). **ELECTRONIC:** *Place of Plays* (1967); *Winter Events* (1967); *Toccata* (1969); *Traces I* (1970) and *II* (1971); *Från borjan till slut* (1973); *Syner (Jorden, himlen, vindaran)* (1973); *Epilogue: Rapsodie de la seconde récolte* (1979); *Mémoires d'un temps avant la destruction* (1982); *For Jon II: Retrospective Episodes* (1986); *Wonder-Void* (1990); *Divertimento för Dalle* (1991); *Pour traverser la membrane de l'espace-temps* (1992); *Best Wishes from the Lilac Grove* (1994). **INTERMEDIA:** *Clouds* (1973–76). **TEXT-SOUND:** *Semikolon* (1965); *Fikonsnackarna* (1966); *En aptitretar—inga hundar i Kina* (1966); *Cybo I* and *II* (both 1967); *Dedicated to You I* (1970), *II* (1972), and *III* (1973); *For Jon (Fragments of a Time to Come)* (1977); *Nästan* (1977); *Plus* (1977); *For Jon III (They Extracted Their Extremities Plus for John)* (1982).—NS/LK/DM

Bodinus, Sebastian, German violinist and composer; b. c. 1700; d. c. 1760. He was in the service of the Margrave Carl Wilhelm of Baden-Durlach before serving as first violinist at the Württemberg court (1723–28). He then served intermittently as Konzertmeister in

Karlsruhe (1728–33; 1736–38; 1747–52). Among his output were syms., concertos, and much chamber music of high quality, including quartets, trios, sonatas, and solo sonatas.—LK/DM

Bodky, Erwin, German-American music scholar; b. Ragnit, March 7, 1896; d. Lucerne, Dec. 6, 1958. He studied piano and theory in Berlin with Dohnányi and Juon, and later attended classes of Richard Strauss and Busoni at the Meisterschule für Komposition (1920–22). He subsequently taught at the Scharwenka Cons. in Berlin. With the advent of the Nazi regime in 1933, Bodky went to Amsterdam, where he remained until 1938. He then emigrated to the U.S., and taught at the Longy School of Music in Cambridge, Mass. (1938–48). In 1949 he was appointed a prof. at Brandeis Univ.

WRITINGS: *Der Vortag alter Klaviermusik* (Berlin, 1932); *Das Charakterstück* (Berlin, 1933); *The Interpretation of J.S. Bach's Keyboard Works* (Cambridge, Mass., 1960; Ger. tr., Tutzing, 1970).

BIBL.: H. Slosbert et al., eds., *E. B.: A Memorial Tribute* (Waltham, Mass., 1965).—NS/LK/DM

Bodley, Nicholas Bessaraboff
See **Bessaraboff, Nicholas**

Bodley, Seóirse, Irish composer, teacher, conductor, and pianist; b. Dublin, April 4, 1933. He studied in Dublin at the Royal Irish Academy of Music and at Univ. Coll. (B.M., 1955). Following training in Stuttgart (1957–59) with J.N. David (composition), Alfred Kreutz (piano), and Hans Müller-Kray (conducting), he returned to Dublin and took his D.Mus. at Univ. Coll. (1960). In 1959 he joined its faculty, where he also conducted its chorus and orch., and founded its electroacoustic studio. He appeared as a conductor with other Dublin ensembles, introducing many works to the city. His 2nd Sym., *Ceol,* inaugurated the National Concert Hall in Dublin on Sept. 9, 1981. Bodley was founding chairman of the Folk Music Soc. of Ireland and of the Assn. of Irish Composers. In 1982 he was made a member of Aosdána, Ireland's official body of distinguished artists. While Bodley has composed a number of works in which traditional Irish music is discernable, he has also written scores in an avant-garde mode, including serial techniques and novel instrumental combinations.

WORKS: ORCH.: *Music for Strings* (Dublin, Dec. 10, 1952); 5 syms.: No. 1 (1958–59; Dublin, Oct. 23, 1960), No. 2, *I Have Loved the Lands of Ireland* (1980; Dublin, Jan. 9, 1981), No. 3, *Ceol,* for Soprano, Mezzo-soprano, Tenor, Baritone, Semichorus, Children's Chorus, Orch., Speaker, and Audience (1980; Dublin, Sept. 9, 1981), No. 4 (1990–91; Parma, June 21, 1991), and No. 5, *The Limerick* (Limerick, Oct. 4, 1991); *Divertimento* for Strings (1961; Dublin, June 15, 1992); 2 chamber syms.: No. 1 (Paris, 1964, composer conducting) and No. 2 (Dublin, June 17, 1982, composer conducting); *Configurations* (1967; Dublin, Jan. 29, 1969); *A Small White Cloud Drifts Over Ireland* (1975; Dublin, Jan. 5, 1976); *Sinfonietta* (1999). CHAMBER: 2 string quartets: No. 1 (1968; Dublin, Jan. 6, 1969) and No. 2 (1992; Dublin, May 21, 1993); *September Preludes* for Flute and Piano (1973; Dublin, Jan. 7, 1974); *Celebration Music* for 3 Trumpets and String Quartet (Dublin, Nov. 11, 1983; also for 3 Trumpets and String

Orch.); *Trio* for Flute, Violin, and Piano (Dublin, July 6, 1986); *Phantasms* for Flute, Clarinet, Harp, and Cello (Dublin, Oct. 27, 1989); *Brass Quintet* (1995). PIANO: *The Narrow Road to the Deep North* for 2 Pianos (Belfast, Feb. 17, 1972); *Aislingi* (Kilkenny, Aug. 29, 1977); *News from Donabate* (1999). VOCAL: *An Bás is an Bheatha* (Life and Death), song cycle for Chorus (1960; Dublin, Jan. 21, 1961); *Never to have lived is best,* song cycle for Soprano and Orch. (Dublin, June 11, 1965); *Ariel's Songs* for Soprano and Piano (1969; Dublin, Jan. 7, 1970); *Meditations on Lines from Patrick Kavanagh* for Alto and Orch. (1971; Dublin, June 30, 1972); *A Chill Wind* for Chorus (1977; Dublin, Jan. 12, 1978); *A Girl,* song cycle for Mezzo-soprano and Piano (Dublin, Oct. 17, 1978); *The Radiant Moment* for Chorus (Cork, April 26, 1979); *A Concert Mass* for Soprano, Mezzo-soprano, Tenor, Bass, Chorus, and String Orch. (1984; Dublin, May 4, 1990, composer conducting); *The Naked Flame* for Mezzo-soprano or Baritone and Piano (1987; Dublin, April 7, 1988); *Carta Irlandesa* (New from Ireland) for Mezzo-soprano or Baritone and Piano (Sligo, Sept. 4, 1988, composer pianist); *Fraw Musica* for Mezzo-soprano, Chorus, Flute, Bassoon, Organ, and Orch. (Torgau, Germany, Oct. 5, 1996); *Pax Bellumque* for Soprano, Flute, Clarinet, Violin, and Piano (1997). ELECTROACOUSTIC: *The Banshee* for Soprano, Mezzo-soprano, Tenor, Bass, and Electronics (Belfast, April 25, 1983).—NS/LK/DM

Body, Jack (actually, **John Stanley**), New Zealand composer, ethnomusicologist, teacher, and experimental photographer; b. Te Aroha, Oct. 7, 1944. He studied with Ronald Tremain and Robin Maconie at the Univ. of Auckland (B.M., 1966; M.M., 1967), at Lilburn's electronic music studio in Wellington, in Cologne (1968), and with Koenig at the Inst. of Sonology in Utrecht (1969). After serving as a guest lecturer at the Akademie Musik Indonesia in Yogyakarta (1976–77), he became a lecturer at the Victoria Univ. of Wellington School of Music in 1980. Body is an active champion of New Zealand musical life through his editorship of the Waiteata Music Press, which publishes scores by New Zealand composers, and as a producer of CDs of New Zealand music. As a composer, he has ranged widely over genres, from the use of traditional instruments to electroacoustic means. He has been notably influenced by the music of Southeast Asia and East Asia, most especially of Indonesia, and has demonstrated a remarkable capacity for synthesizing non-Western musical materials with contemporary compositional techniques. In his experimental photography, he has explored relationships between sound and image.

WORKS: DRAMATIC: Opera: *Alley* for Baritone, Actor, Beijing Opera Singer, 2 Folk Singers, Chorus, and 16 Instrumentalists (1997). ORCH.: *Hello François* (1976); *Melodies* (1983); *Little Elegies* (1985); *Poems of Solitary Delights* for Orch. and Voice (1985); *Pulse* (1995); *Fours on My Teaching* for Orch. and Speaker (1997). CHAMBER: *Turtle Time* for Harp, Piano, Harpsichord, Organ, and Speaker (1968); *The Caves of Ellora* for Piano and Brass Ensemble (1979); *3 Transcriptions* for String Quartet (1987); *Interior* for Chamber Ensemble and Tape (1987); *Epicycle* for String Quartet (1989); *African Strings,* transcriptions for 2 Guitars (1990); *Arum Manis* for String Quartet and Tape (1991); *The Garden* for Chamber Ensemble (1996); *Campur Sari* for String Quartet and Javanese Musician (1996). PIANO: *4 Stabiles* (1968); *5 Melodies* (1982); *3 Rhythmics* for Piano Duet (1986); *Sarajevo* (1996). VOCAL: *Carol to St. Stephen* for 3 Soloists and Chorus (1975); *Marvel not Joseph* for 2 Soloists and

Chorus (1976); *Vox Populi* for Chorus and Tape (1981); *Love Sonnets of Michelangelo* for Soprano and Mezzo-soprano (1982); *5 Lullabies* for Chorus (1988); *Wedding Song for St. Cecilia* for Chorus (1993). **ELECTROACOUSTIC:** *Krytophones* (1973); *Musik dari Jalan* (Music from the Street; 1975); *Duets and Choruses* (1978); *Musik Anak- anak* (Children's Music; 1978); *Fanfares* (1981); *Jangkrik Genggong* (1985); *Musik mulut* (Mouth music; 1989); *Vox Humana* (1991). **SOUND IMAGE INSTALLATIONS:** *Runes* (1984–85); *Citywalk* (1989); *Bloodlines* (1990); *Sun and Steel: Homage to Mishima* (1995). **OTHER:** *Encounters* for 4 Track Tape and Actors/Participants (1980). —NS/LK/DM

Boeck, August de, Belgian composer; b. Merchtem, May 9, 1865; d. there, Oct. 9, 1937. He studied organ at the Brussels Cons., and subsequently was church organist in Brussels; later taught harmony at the Royal Flemish Cons. at Antwerp and at the Brussels Cons. In 1930 he returned to his native town. He wrote operas and incidental music for stage plays, *Rapsodie Dahomeenne* for Orch., on exotic African themes (1893), an orch. fantasy on Flemish folk songs (1923), and many songs to French and Flemish texts. Much of his orch. music is infused with impressionistic colors.

BIBL.: F. Rasse, *A. D.B.* (Brussels, 1943).—NS/LK/DM

Boehe, Ernst, German composer and conductor; b. Munich, Dec. 27, 1880; d. Ludwigshafen, Nov. 16, 1938. He studied with Rudolf Louis and Thuille in Munich. In 1907 he was assoc. conductor, with Courvoisier, of the Munich Volkssymphoniekonzerte; from 1913 to 1920 was court conductor at Oldenburg; then conducted concerts in Ludwigshafen. His works are of a programmatic type, the orchestration emphasizing special sonorities of divided strings, massive wind instruments, and various percussive effects; his tone poems show a decisive Wagnerian influence, having a system of identification motifs. His most ambitious work was an orch. tetralogy on Homer's Odyssey, under the general title *Odysseus' Fahrten*, comprising *Odysseus' Ausfahrt und Schiffbruch* (Munich, Feb. 20, 1903; Philadelphia, Dec. 3, 1904), *Die Insel der Kirke, Die Klage der Nausikaa,* and *Odysseus' Heimkehr.* He also composed the symphonic poem *Taormina* (Essen, 1906; Boston Sym., Nov. 29, 1907).—NS/LK/DM

Boehm, Karl
See **Böhm, Karl**

Boehm, Theobald, famous German flutist and flute manufacturer; b. Munich, April 9, 1794; d. there, Nov. 25, 1881. He was the son of a goldsmith and learned mechanics in his father's workshop. He also studied flute, and eventually established himself as one of the greatest flute virtuoso of his era. In 1818 he became a court musician in Munich. He opened a factory in Munich in 1828 and introduced his first flute in 1832. His system of construction marked a new departure in the making of woodwind instruments. To render the flute acoustically perfect, he fixed the position and size of the holes so as to obtain, not convenience in fingering, but purity and fullness of tone; all holes are covered by keys, whereby prompt and accurate "speaking" is assured; and the bore is modified, rendering the tone much fuller and mellower. He publ. *Über den Flötenbau und die neuesten Verbesserungen desselben* (Mainz, 1847; ed. by K. Ventzke as *On the Construction of Flutes/Über den Flötenbau,* Baren, the Netherlands, 1982) and *Die Flöte und das Flötenspiel* (Munich, 1871).

BIBL.: C. Welch, *History of the B. Flute* (London, 1883). —NS/LK/DM

Boëllmann, Léon, French composer; b. Ensisheim, Alsace, Sept. 25, 1862; d. Paris, Oct. 11, 1897. He studied organ with Gigout, and later was an organ teacher in Paris. He left 68 publ. works, his *Variations symphoniques* for Cello and Orch. becoming part of the repertoire of cello players. He wrote a sym., *Fantaisie dialoguee,* for Organ and Orch., *Suite gothique* for Organ, Piano Quartet, Piano Trio, Cello Sonata, and *Rapsodie carnavalesque* for Piano, Four-Hands. He also publ. a collection of 100 pieces for organ under the title *Heures mystiques.*

BIBL.: P. Locard, *L. B.* (Strasbourg, 1901).—NS/LK/DM

Boëly, Alexandre Pierre François, French organist and composer; b. Versailles, April 19, 1785; d. Paris, Dec. 27, 1858. His father, a court musician, gave him his first instruction in music. Boëly studied piano and organ, and then occupied various positions as a church organist in Paris. As a teacher, he exercised a profound influence; Franck and Saint-Saëns owed much to him in the development of their style of composition for organ.—NS/LK/DM

Boesch, Christian, Austrian baritone; b. Vienna, July 27, 1941. He pursued his training at the Vienna Hochschule für Musik, and in 1966 made his operatic debut at the Bern Stadttheater. He became a member of the Vienna Volksoper in 1975, later scoring notable success at the Salzburg Festival in 1978 for his portrayal of Papageno, a role he also chose for his Metropolitan Opera debut in N.Y. on Feb. 17, 1979. He later sang Wozzeck and Masetto at the Metropolitan.—NS/LK/DM

Boesch, Rainer, Swiss composer, pianist, and teacher; b. Männedorf, Aug. 11, 1938. He received training in piano at the Geneva Cons. (diploma, 1960) and the Neuchâtel Cons. (diploma, 1965), and then in composition with Messiaen at the Paris Cons. (1966–68), where he received the premier prix in 1968 with the first electro-acoustic piece ever presented there. After serving as director of the Lausanne Cons. (1968–72), he headed the new music dept. of the Institut de Hautes Études Musicales (1973–75). He settled in Geneva, where he founded the Studio ESPACES in 1976, a teaching and research organization. He also taught at the Institut Jaques-Dalcroze from 1976, overseeing its research center from 1989. In 1985 he co-founded the Swiss Centre for Computer Music, which he subsequently served as co-director. Boesch's large output embraces avant-garde usages, with a special regard for multimedia and electronic works.

WORKS: Cello Sonata (1955); Piano Pieces (1955–92); String Quartet (1960–61); *Désagrégation* for 12 Clarinets, 2 Tubas, Percussion, and Tape (1968); *Florès* for Instrumental Ensemble (1968); *Cendres*, piano concerto (1968–69); *Fêtes* for Chorus, Mimes, and Tape (1972); *Mécaniques* for Tape (1973); *Espaces*, opera (1975); *Transparences* for Orch. (1977); *Schriftzeichen für Kathrin* for Women's Voices, Piano, Orch., and Tape (1977); *Tissages* for Orch. (1978); *"***" (Suite II)*, multimedia piece (1978–89); Wind Quintet (1980); *Kreise* for Wind Orch. (1986); *Clavirissima* for Piano and Computer (1987); *Solisti* for Flute, Bassoon, 2 Saxophones, Double Bass, and Piano (1991).
—NS/LK/DM

Boesmans, Philippe, Belgian composer; b. Tongeren, May 17, 1936. He studied composition with Froidebise and Pousseur, and piano at the Liège Cons. (1954–62). His music adheres to the abstract trends of cosmopolitan modernism, with structural formulas determining the contents.

WORKS: *Étude I* for Piano (1963); *Sonance I* for 2 Pianos (1964) and *II* for 3 Pianos (1967); *Impromptu* for 23 Instruments (1965); *Correlations* for Clarinet and 2 Instrumental Ensembles (Brussels, Sept. 16, 1967); *Explosives* for Harp and 10 Instrumentalists (1968); *Verticles* for Orch. (1969); *Blocage* for Voice, Chorus, and Chamber Ensemble (1970); *Upon La, Mi* for Voice, Amplified Horn, and Instrumental Ensemble (1970); *Fanfare* for 2 Pianos (1971); *Intervalles I* for Orch. (1972), *II* for Orch. (1973), and *III* for Voice and Orch. (1974); *Sur Mi* for 2 Pianos, Electric Organ, Crotale, and Tam-Tam (1974); *Multiples* for 2 Pianos and Orch. (1974); *Element—Extensions* for Piano and Chamber Orch. (1976); *Doublures* for Harp, Piano, Percussion, and 4 Instrumental Groups (1977); *Attitudes*, musical spectacle for Voice, 2 Pianos, Synthesizer, and Percussion (1977); Piano Concerto (1978); Violin Concerto (1979; Liège, Feb. 22, 1980); *Conversions* for Orch. (1980); *La Passion de Gilles*, opera (Brussels, Oct. 18, 1983); *Ricercar sconvolto* for Organ (1983); *Extase* for Orch. (1985); String Quartet (1989); *Reigen*, opera (1992).—NS/LK/DM

Boësset, Antoine, Sieur de Villedieu, French composer; b. Blois, 1586; d. Paris, Dec. 8, 1643. He was active in various positions at the French court from 1613, where he won distinction as a composer of airs de cour (publ. in 9 vols., 1617–42). Among his other works were vocal pieces for ballets de cour and sacred music. His son, Jean-Baptiste (de) Boësset, Sieur de Dehault (b. Paris, 1614; d. there, 1685), was also a composer who was in the service of the French court for about 50 years. He wrote airs de cour and ballets.

BIBL.: N. Dufourcq, *J.-B. d. B.* (Paris, 1962).—NS/LK/DM

Boethius, Anicius Manlius Severinus, Roman philosopher, theologian, man of letters, and statesman; b. Rome, c.480; d. (executed) c. 524. He was of a distinguished Roman family and received a thorough academic education. In 510 he became consul, and about 520 was made magister officium to King Theodoric. When the senator Albinus was charged with treason, Boethius defended him and was himself charged with treason, imprisoned with Albinus in Pavia, and executed. It was during his imprisonment that Boethius wrote his most celebrated work, *De consolatione philosophiae*. However, his importance to music history rests upon his treatise *De institutione musica* (first publ. in his collected works, Venice, 1491–92; 2nd ed., 1498–99; edited by Glarean, Basel, 1546; 2nd ed., 1570; Eng. tr., with notes, by C. Bower and C. Palisca, as *Fundamentals of Music*, New Haven and London, 1989). This treatise is noteworthy for its view that music is all-pervasive in the universe (musica mundana), that it is one of the major vivifying links between man's soul and his physical being (musica humana), and that it can be divined in some instruments (musica instrumentalis). By delineating what he called a Perfect System of Greek theory, Boethius produced one of the most influential works of its kind, one that had a profound impact on the late Middle Ages and the early Renaissance.

BIBL.: G. Pietzsch, *Studien zur Geschichte der Musiktheorie im Mittelalter: Die Klassifikation der Musik von B. bis Ugolino von Orvieto* (Halle, 1929); H. Potiron, *La notation grecque et B.* (Rome, 1951); idem, *B.: Theoretician de la musique grecque* (Paris, 1954).
—NS/LK/DM

Boettcher, Wilfried, German cellist and conductor; b. Bremen, Aug. 11, 1929; d. Uzes-Saint Siffret, France, Aug. 22, 1994. He studied cello with Arthur Troester at the Hamburg Hochschule für Musik (diploma, 1955) and with Fournier in Paris (1955–56). He was first cellist in the Bremen Radio Orch. (1948–50) and in the Hannover Opera orch. (1956–58). From 1958 to 1965 he was a prof. of cello at the Vienna Academy of Music. In 1959 he founded Die Wiener Solisten, which he conducted until 1966. From 1965 to 1974 he was a prof. at the Hamburg Hochschule für Musik. He also was chief conductor of the Hamburg Sym. Orch. (1967–71), and a conductor at the Hamburg State Opera (1970–73). From 1974 to 1978 he was principal guest conductor of the RAI Orch. in Turin. He also was a conductor at the Berlin Deutsche Oper (1975–82) and the Vienna State Opera (1977–82). In later years, he became closely associated as a conductor with several British orchs.—NS/LK/DM

Boetticher, Wolfgang, German musicologist; b. Bad Ems, Aug. 19, 1914. He studied with Schering, Schünemann, and Blume at the Univ. of Berlin (Ph.D., 1939, with the diss. *Robert Schumann: Einführung in Persönlichkeit und Werk*; publ. in Berlin, 1941; Habilitation, 1943, with *Studien zur solistischen Lautenpraxis des 16. und 17. Jahrhunderts*; publ. in Berlin, 1943). In 1948 he joined the faculty of the Univ. of Göttingen, where he was prof. of musicology from 1956 to 1959. From 1958 he also taught at the Technical Univ. in Clausthal. Boetticher is an authority on the music of both the Renaissance and the 19th century. His writings on lute music, Orlando di Lasso, and Robert Schumann are particularly valuable. He ed. compositions of Lasso in the new critical edition of that composer's works (Vols. I, XIX, Munich, 1959–90) and the Urtext edition of Schumann's complete piano works (24 vols., Munich, 1972–96).

WRITINGS: *Robert Schumann in seinen Schriften und Briefen* (Berlin, 1942); *Orlando di Lasso und seine Zeit* (2 vols., Kassel and Basel, 1958; new ed. with suppl., 1998; Vol. III, index of works, 1999); *Von Palestrina zu Bach* (Stuttgart, 1959; 2nd ed., enl., 1981);

Dokumente und Briefe um Orlando di Lasso (Kassel, 1960); *Aus Orlando di Lassos Wirkungskreis, Neue archivalische Studien zur Münchener Musikgeschichte* (Kassel and Basel, 1963); *Neue Forschungsergebnisse im Gebiet der musikalischen Renaissance* (Göttingen, 1964); *Robert Schumanns Klavierwerke: Entstehung, Urtext, Gestalt: Untersuchungen anhand unveröffentlicher Skizzen und biographischer Dokumente* (Wilhelmshaven, 1976 et seq.); *Die Familienkassette Schumanns in Dresden: Unbekannte Briefe an Robert und Clara Schumann* (Leipzig, 1979; 2nd ed., 1982); *Einführung in die musikalische Romantik* (Wilhelmshaven, 1983); *Geschichte der Motette* (Darmstadt, 1989; new ed., Wilhelmshaven, 2000).

BIBL.: H. Hüschen and D.-R. Moser, eds., *Covivium musicorum: Festschrift W. B. zum sechzigsten Geburtstag* (Berlin, 1974). —NS/LK/DM

Bofill, Angela, jazz singer; b.N.Y.,1954. Migrating between contemporary jazz and slick pop, Bofill's biggest successes came within the realm of the latter, though at both the beginning of her professional career (with Dizzy Gillespie, Cannonball Adderley, and others) and then after its commercial success waned, she performed in genuine jazz contexts. The Hispanic multi-instrumental prodigy grew up in the Bronx and performed on the Latin music scene, most notably with the salsa band led by Ricardo Morrero known simply as The Group. Flutist Dave Valentin of that band introduced her to the owners of GRP, who launched her career with an album that made the jazz charts. After her second album for GRP, she disputed her royalties and subsequently her contract was moved to Arista, which promoted her solely as an R&B artist and similarly focused the production on her albums. Though she never broke through to the mainstream, she had a number of R&B hits and her mid-1980s albums charted consistently. She had the greatest success with Narada Michael Walden, who like Bofill directed jazz chops in a commercial direction. By the latter part of the decade, however, her sound was no longer current, and later efforts to update it came off awkwardly. Finally on her Shanachie album she returned to her old style, at least sounding comfortable again.

DISC.: *Angie* (1978); *Angel of the Night* (1979); *Something About You* (1981); *Too Tough* (1983); *Teaser* (1983); *Let Me Be the One* (1984); *Tell Me Tomorrow* (1985); *Intuition* (1988); *Love Is in Your Eyes* (1991); *I Wanna Love Somebody* (1993); *Love in Slow Motion* (1996).—SH

Bogusławski, Edward, Polish composer and pedagogue; b. Chorzów, Silesia, Sept. 22, 1940. He received training in theory (1959–64; degree, 1964) and composition (with Bolesław Szabelski, 1961–66; graduated, 1966) at the State Higher School of Music in Katowice, and then completed his studies with Haubenstock-Ramati in Vienna (1967). In 1963 he joined the faculty of the State Higher School of Music in Katowice, where he was dean of the faculty of music education (1971–72), dean of the faculty of composition, conducting, and theory (1971–75; 1990–96), and a prof. (from 1983). From 1984 he also was head of the faculty of theory and music teaching at the Higher School of Pedagogy in Częstochowa. In 1966 he won first prize in the Malawski Composers' Competition in Kraków, and in 1975 first prize in the National Composers' Compe-

tition. He also received the Minister of Culture and Arts Award twice.

WORKS: DRAMATIC: *Sonata Belzebuba* (Beelzebub's Sonata), chamber opera (1976–77; Wrocław, Nov. 19, 1977); *Gra snów* (The Game of Dreams), musical drama (1985). **ORCH.:** *Sygnały* (Signals; 1965–66; Warsaw, June 3, 1966); *Intonazioni II* (1966; Paris, Nov. 15, 1967); Concerto for Oboe, Oboe d'amore, English Horn, Musette, and Orch. (1967–68; Warsaw, Sept. 24, 1970); *Sinfonia* for Chorus and Orch. (1968–69; Katowice, May 28, 1969); *Capriccioso notturno* (1972; Warsaw, Jan. 12, 1973); *Pro Varsovia* (1973–74; Warsaw, Jan. 17, 1975); Concerto for Instrumentalists, Soprano, and Orch. (1975–76); *Musica concertante* for Alto Saxophone and Orch. (1980; Warsaw, Sept. 20, 1983); Piano Concerto (1981; Katowice, Dec. 3, 1982); *Symphonie concertante* for Violin and Chamber Orch. (1982); *Polonia*, symphonic poem for Violin and Orch. (Katowice, Oct. 5, 1984); *Les Extrêmes se touchent* (1986); *Play* for Flute and Chamber Orch. (1988–89; Poznań, April 7, 1991); Guitar Concerto (Katowice, Oct. 2, 1992); *Concerto classico* for Strings (1995); Organ Concerto (Kraków, Oct. 25, 1996); *Musica* for Strings (1997). **CHAMBER:** *Intonazioni I* for 9 Instruments (1963); 2 string quartets (1964–75; 1995); *Szkice* (Essays) for Oboe and Piano (1965); *Metamorfozy* (Metamorphoses) for Oboe, Clarinet, Violin, Viola, and Cello (1967; Bayreuth, Aug. 18, 1969); *Wersje* (Versions) for 6 Instruments (1968); *Musica per Ensemble MW-2* for Flute, Cello, and 2 Pianos (Kraków, Sept. 17, 1970); Trio for Flute, Oboe, and Guitar (1971; Nice, June 1, 1973); *Impromptu I* for Flute, Viola, and Harp (1972; Lisbon, April 12, 1974) and *II* for Oboe, Clarinet, Bassoon, and Piano (1999); *Musica notturna* for Oboe and Piano (1974; Siena, July 2, 1976); *Divertimento I* for Chamber Ensemble (1975), *II* for Accordion Quintet (1982), and *III* for Violin, Cello, and Accordion (1986); *Preludi e cadenza* for Violin (Warsaw, April 23, 1979); *Kwartet dziecięcy* (Children's Quartet) for 4 Violins (1979; Łódź, Sept. 20, 1981); *Preludi e cadenza* for Violin and Piano (1983; Katowice, March 20, 1985); *Capriccioso* for Accordion (1985; Białystok, Aug. 25, 1986); *Nokturny* (Nocturnes) for Harp (1986; Vienna, July 22, 1987); *Dialogues* for Saxophone and Vibraphone (1987); *Continuo I* for Accordion Quintet (1987; Rotterdam, Feb. 13, 1989) and *II* for Accordion (1988; Białystok, April 10, 1989); *Musica* for Guitar (1993); Piano Trio (1993); *Elegia* for Cello and Piano (1994). **KEYBOARD: P i a n o :** *Per pianoforte* (1968; Warsaw, Oct. 27, 1969); *Solo per pianoforte* (Cieszyn, Dec. 6, 1995). **O r g a n :** *Prelude* (Katowice, Oct. 19, 1994); *Inwokacja* (Invocation; 1996). **VOCAL:** *Apokalypsis* (Apocalypse) for Reciter, Chorus, and Instrumental Ensemble (1965; Warsaw, Dec. 17, 1966); *Canti* for Soprano and Orch. (1967; Warsaw, Sept. 29, 1968); *Kontemplacje* (Contemplations) for Soprano and Piano (1969); *L'Être* for Soprano, Flute, Cello, and 2 Pianos (1973); *Ewokacja* (Evocation) for Baritone and Orch. (1974); *Sonet* (Sonnet) for Soprano, Flute, Cello, and 2 Pianos (1980); *Gaude Mater Polonia* for Soprano, Chorus, and Orch. (1990; Częstochowa, May 1, 1991); *Lacrimosa* for Soprano and Piano (1991); *Dies irae* for Chorus, Percussion, and Piano (1992; Wrocław, Feb. 25, 1994); *Oda* (Ode) for Reciter, Chorus, Piano, and Orch. (1994); *Agnus Dei* for Soprano and Piano (1995; Chorzów, Oct. 9, 1997); *Et in terra pax* for Chorus (1995; Gliwice, Nov. 11, 1999); *Requiem* for Soprano, Chorus, Percussion, and Organ (1995–96); *Pater noster* for Chorus (1996); *Pieśni Safony* (Sappho's Songs) for Woman Reciter, Flute, Percussion, and 2 Accordions (1998); *Strofy* (Strophes) for 2 Choruses and Organ (1999). —NS/LK/DM

Boháč, Josef, Czech composer; b. Vienna, March 25, 1929. After training in Vienna, he was a student of

Petrželka at the Janáček Academy of Music and Dramatic Art in Brno (1955–59). He later was active with Czech TV and the music publishing concern Panton. As a composer, he followed the median line of Central European modernism, with occasional resort to serial methods.

WORKS: DRAMATIC: *Námluvy* (The Courtship), comic opera (1967; Prague, March 18, 1971); *Goya*, opera (1972–77; Ostrava, Sept. 30, 1978); *Oči* (Eyes), television opera (1973; Czech TV, Prague, Oct. 5, 1974); *Zvířatka a Petrovští* (The Little Animals and Petrovští), opera (1980); *Zlatá svatba* (The Golden Wedding), comic opera (1981); *Rumcajs*, opera (1985). **ORCH.:** *Rhapsody* (1955); *Symphonic Overture* (1964); *Sinfonietta concertante* (1964–65); *Fragment* (1969); *Elegy* for Cello and Chamber Orch. (1969); *Suita drammatica* for Strings and Timpani (1969–70); *Southern Rainbow*, suite (1971); *February Overture* (1973); Piano Concerto (1974); Concerto for Violin and Chamber Orch. (1978); *Concertino Pastorale* for 2 Horns and Orch. (1978); *Concerto for Orch.* (1983); *Dramatic Variants* for Viola and Orch. (1983). **CHAMBER:** Suite for String Quartet (1953); Cello Sonata (1954); String Trio (1965); *Sonetti per Sonatori* for Flute, Bass Clarinet, Percussion, and Piano (1974); *Sonata Giovane* for Piano (1983). **VOCAL:** *My Lute Sounds*, monodrama for Tenor, Soprano, and Nonet or Piano (1971); *Sonata Lirica* for Soprano, Strings, and Vibraphone (1982).—NS/LK/DM

Böhm, Georg, German organist; b. Hohenkirchen, Thuringia, Sept. 2, 1661; d. Lüneburg, May 18, 1733. He studied at the Univ. of Jena. He was in Hamburg in 1693, and in 1698 he became organist at the Johanneskirche in Lüneburg. His organ preludes and harpsichord pieces are exemplars of keyboard works of his time; Bach himself was influenced by Böhm's style of writing. A complete ed. of Böhm's work was begun by Johannes Wolgast in 1927 in 2 vols.; a rev. ed. of both vols. was publ. in Wiesbaden in 1952 and 1963, respectively.

BIBL.: J. Wolgast, *G. B.* (Berlin, 1924).—NS/LK/DM

Böhm, Joseph, violinist; b. Budapest, March 4, 1795; d. Vienna, March 28, 1876. He was a pupil of his father, and at 8 years of age he made a concert tour to Poland and St. Petersburg, where he studied for some years under Pierre Rode. His first concert at Vienna (1815) was very successful; after a trip to Italy, he was appointed (1819) violin prof. at the Vienna Cons.; retired in 1848. He taught many distinguished pupils, including Joachim, Ernst, Auer, Rappoldi, and Hellmesberger (Sr.).—NS/LK/DM

Böhm, Karl, renowned Austrian conductor; b. Graz, Aug. 28, 1894; d. Salzburg, Aug. 14, 1981. He studied law before enrolling at the Graz Cons., where he took lessons in piano and theory; subsequently he studied musicology with Mandyczewski at the the Univ. of Vienna. After service in the Austrian Army during World War I, he made his debut as a conductor at the Graz Opera in 1917. He then completed his training in law at the Univ. of Graz (Dr.Jur., 1919). In 1920 he was appointed first conductor at the Graz Opera. Although he never took formal lessons in conducting, he soon acquired sufficient technique to be engaged at the

Bavarian State Opera in Munich (1921). In 1927 he was appointed Generalmusikdirektor in Darmstadt; having already mastered a number of works by Mozart, Wagner, and Richard Strauss, he included in his repertoire modern operas by Krenek and Hindemith. In 1931 he conducted *Wozzeck* by Berg, a performance which Berg himself warmly praised. From 1931 to 1933 Böhm held the post of Generalmusikdirektor of the Hamburg Opera; from 1934 to 1943 he was music director of the Dresden State Opera, where he gave the first performances of *Die Schweigsame Frau* (June 24, 1935) and *Daphne* (Oct. 15, 1938), which Strauss dedicated to him. In 1943 he became director of the Vienna State Opera, but his tenure was a brief one due to its closure by the Nazis in 1944 and by its destruction by Allied bombing during the closing weeks of World War II in 1945. The rumors were rife of his at least passive adherence to the Nazis, although he categorically denied that he was ever a member of the party. After the War, he was not allowed by the Allied authorities to give performances pending an investigation of his political past; he was cleared and resumed his career in 1947. From 1950 to 1953 he conducted the German repertoire at the Teatro Colón in Buenos Aires. He then served again as director of the Vienna State Opera from 1954 to 1956. On Nov. 5, 1955, he conducted Beethoven's *Fidelio* at the opening of the reconstructed Vienna State Opera House. He made his first appearance in the U.S. with the Chicago Sym. Orch. on Feb. 9, 1956; on Oct. 31, 1957, he made his first appearance at the Metropolitan Opera in N.Y. with Mozart's *Don Giovanni*. He continued to conduct occasional performances at the Metropolitan until 1978. In 1961 he took the Berlin Phil. to the U.S., and in 1963–64 he made a tour in Japan with it. In 1975 he conducted an American tour with the Deutsche Oper of Berlin. In 1979 he took the Vienna State Opera on its first U.S. tour. He also conducted radio and television performances. Böhm received numerous honors and tokens of distinction, among them the Golden Mozart Memorial Medal from the International Mozarteum Foundation in Salzburg, the Brahms Medal from Hamburg, and the Brückner Ring from the Vienna Sym. Orch. On his 70th birthday, a Böhm Day was celebrated in Vienna, and he was granted the rare honorary title of Generalmusikdirektor of Austria; both his 80th and 85th birthdays were observed in Salzburg and Vienna. In 1977 he was elected president of the London Sym. Orch. Böhm was admired for his impeccable rendition of classical opera scores, particularly those of Mozart, in which he scrupulously avoided any suggestion of improper romanticization; he was equally extolled for his productions of the operas of Wagner and Richard Strauss, and he earned additional respect for his authoritative performances of the Austro-German orch. repertoire. He publ. *Begegnung mit Richard Strauss* (Munich, 1964) and a personal memoir, *Ich erinnere mich ganz genau* (Zürich, 1968; Eng. tr., 1992, as *A Life Remembered: Memoirs*).

BIBL.: F. Endler, *K. B.: Ein Dirigentenleben* (Hamburg, 1981); H. Hoyer, *K. B. an der Wiener Staatsoper: Eine Dokumentation* (Vienna, 1981).—NS/LK/DM

Böhme, Kurt (Gerhard), distinguished German bass; b. Dresden, May 5, 1908; d. Munich, Dec. 20, 1989.

He was a student of Adolf Kluge at the Dresden Cons. In 1930 he made his operatic debut as Caspar in *Der Freischütz* at the Dresden State Opera, where he remained as one of its principal artists until 1950; then was a member of the Bavarian State Opera in Munich. In 1936 he made his first appearance at London's Covent Garden with the visiting Dresden State Opera; later made regular appearances there from 1956 to 1970; he also was a guest artist in Vienna, Bayreuth, and Milan. On Nov. 11, 1954, he made his Metropolitan Opera debut in N.Y. as Pogner, and was again on its roster in 1956–57. Böhme was especially admired for his Wagnerian roles, but he also won great acclaim as Baron Ochs.—NS/LK/DM

Bohnen, (Franz) Michael, noted German bass-baritone; b. Cologne, May 2, 1887; d. Berlin, April 26, 1965. He received training from Fritz Steinbach and Schulz-Dornburg at the Cologne Cons. In 1910 he made his operatic debut as Caspar in *Der Freischütz* in Düsseldorf. After singing in Wiesbaden (1912–13), he was a highly respected member of the Berlin Royal (later State) Opera from 1913 to 1921. He also made debuts in 1914 at London's Covent Garden and the Bayreuth Festival. On March 1, 1923, he made his Metropolitan Opera debut in N.Y. as the Tourist/Francesco in Schillings' *Mona Lisa*, remaining on its roster until 1932. On Jan. 19, 1929, he sang the leading role there in the U.S. premiere of Krenek's *Jonny spielt auf.* From 1933 to 1945 he sang at the Berlin Deutsches Opernhaus, and subsequently served as Intendant at the renamed Städtische Oper from 1945 to 1947. He was equally well versed in baritone and bass roles, numbering among his finest Sarastro, Wotan, King Marke, Hagen, Gurnemanz, Méphistophélès, Baron Ochs, and Scarpia.—NS/LK/DM

Böhner, (Johann) Ludwig, German pianist and composer; b. Töttelstädt, Jan. 7, 1787; d. Gotha, March 28, 1860. Following his musical training, he attained the position of music director in Nuremberg. As a pianist, he scored his first major success at the Gewandhaus in Leipzig on May 16, 1814. Concert tours then followed in Germany, and he also played in Austria, Denmark, and Switzerland. Böhner's early success as a pianist and his genuine talent as a composer were compromised in later years by his growing eccentricity and ill health. He led a wandering life in his native Thuringia, being compelled to sell himself and his scores virtually for alms. His final appearance as a pianist took place in Arnstadt in Aug. 1859. Böhner wrote a romantic opera, *Die Mädchen in einsamen Mühlenthale* (1810–13), which he later reworked as the comic opera *Der Dreiherrenstein* (Meiningen, April 7, 1848). Its overture reveals a command of orchestral writing, as does his Grosse Ouvertüre for the concert hall (1812). He also wrote a well-crafted Sym. (1844), several piano concertos, and a number of variations for different solo instruments and orch.

BIBL.: K. Bolt, *J.L. B.: Leben und Werk* (Hildburghausen, 1940).—NS/LK/DM

Boieldieu, François-Adrien, celebrated French opera composer; b. Rouen, Dec. 16, 1775; d. Jarcy, near Grosbois, Oct. 8, 1834. His father was a clerical functionary who at one time served as secretary to Archbishop Larochefoucauld; his mother owned a millinery shop; the parents were divorced in 1794. Boieldieu received his musical instruction from Charles Broche, then was apprenticed to Broche as an asst. organist at the church of St. André in Rouen. When he was 17 his first opera, *La Fille coupable* (to his father's libretto), achieved a production in Rouen (Nov. 2, 1793). He composed patriotic pieces which were in demand during the revolutionary period. His *Chant populaire pour la Fête de la Raison* for Chorus and Orch. was presented at the Temple of Reason (former cathedral) in Rouen on Nov. 30, 1793. His second opera, *Rosalie et Myrza*, was also staged in Rouen (Oct. 28, 1795). He was befriended by the composer Louis Jadin and the piano manufacturer Erard; he met Cherubini and Méhul, and made a tour in Normandy with the tenor Garat. A facile composer, Boieldieu produced one opera after another and had no difficulties in having them staged in Paris. Particularly successful was *Le Calife de Bagdad* (Paris, Sept. 16, 1800), which appealed to the public because of its exotic subject and pseudo-oriental arias. On March 19, 1802, Boieldieu married the dancer Clotilde Mafleurai, but separated from her the following year. Opportunely, he received an invitation to go to Russia. His contract called for an attractive salary of 4,000 rubles annually, in return for writing operas for the Imperial theaters in St. Petersburg. He attended to his duties conscientiously, and produced operas every year. His salary was raised, but Boieldieu decided to leave Russia in 1811 and return to Paris. His estranged wife died in 1826, and Boieldieu married the singer Jenny Phillis. True to his custom, he resumed composing operas for the Paris theaters. In 1817 he was appointed prof. of composition at the Paris Cons.; he resigned in 1826. In 1821 he was named a Chevalier of the Légion d'honneur. After a number of insignificant productions, he achieved his greatest success with his Romantic opera *La Dame blanche*, fashioned after Walter Scott's novels *The Monastery* and *Guy Mannering*; the dramatic subject and the effective musical setting corresponded precisely to the tastes of the public of the time. It was produced at the Opéra-Comique in Paris on Dec. 10, 1825, and became a perennial success in Paris and elsewhere; it was produced in London on Oct. 9, 1826, and in N.Y. on Aug. 24, 1827. In 1833 he received a grant of 6,000 francs from the French government and retired to his country house at Jarcy, where he died. During the last years of his life he became interested in painting; his pictures show a modest talent in landscape. He was also successful as a teacher, numbering among his pupils Fétis, Adam, and P.J.G. Zimmerman. Boieldieu composed about 40 operas, of which several were written in collaboration with Méhul, Berton, Hérold, Cherubini, Catel, Isouard, Kreutzer, and Auber; 9 of these operas are lost. Boieldieu's significance in the history of French opera is great, even though the nationalistic hopes of the French music critics and others that he would rival Rossini did not materialize; Boieldieu simply lacked the tremendous power of invention, both in dramatic and comic aspects, that made Rossini a magician of 19th-century opera. Boieldieu's natural son, Adrien-Louis-

Victor Boieldieu (b. Paris, Nov. 3, 1815; d. Quincy, July 9, 1883), was also a composer; his mother was Thérèse Regnault, a singer. He wrote 10 operas, including *Marguerite*, which was sketched by his father but left incomplete, and *L'Aïeule*.

WORKS: DRAMATIC: Opera: *La Fille coupable* (Rouen, Nov. 2, 1793); *Rosalie et Myrza* (Rouen, Oct. 28, 1795); *La Famille suisse* (Paris, Feb. 11, 1797); *Zoraine et Zulnare* (Paris, May 10, 1798); *La Dôt de Suzette* (Paris, Sept. 5, 1798); *Beniowski* (Paris, June 8, 1800); *Le Calife de Bagdad* (Paris, Sept. 16, 1800); *Ma tante Aurore* (Paris, Jan. 13, 1803); *Aline, reine de Golconda* (St. Petersburg, March 17, 1804); *Abderkhan* (St. Petersburg, Aug. 7, 1804); *La Jeune Femme colère* (St. Petersburg, April 30, 1805); *Un Tour de soubrette* (St. Petersburg, April 28, 1806); *Télémaque dans l'isle de Calypso* (St. Petersburg, Dec. 28, 1806); *Les Voitures versées* (St. Petersburg, April 16, 1808); *Rien de trop ou Les Deux Paravents* (St. Petersburg, Jan. 6, 1811); *Jean de Paris* (Paris, April 4, 1812); *Le Nouveau Seigneur de village* (Paris, June 29, 1813); *La Fête du village voisin* (Paris, March 5, 1816); *Le Petit Chaperon rouge* (Paris, June 30, 1818); *La Dame blanche* (Paris, Dec. 10, 1825). The following operas were products of collaboration: *La Prisonnière*, with Cherubini (1799); *Le Baiser et la quittance*, with Méhul, Kreutzer, and others (1803); *Bayard à Mézières*, with Cherubini, Catel, and Isouard (1803); *Les Béarnais, ou Henry IV en voyage*, with Kreutzer (1814); *Angéla, ou L'Atelier de Jean Cousin*, with Mme. Gail, a pupil of Fétis (1814); *Charles de France, ou Amour et gloire*, with Hérold (1816); *Blanche de Provence, ou La Cour des fées*, with Cherubini, Berton, and others (1821); *Les Trois Genres*, with Auber (1824); *La Marquise de Brinvilliers*, with Berton and others (1831). **INSTRUMENTAL:** Piano Concerto (1797); Harp Concerto (1800); Duo for Violin and Piano; 4 duos for Harp and Piano; 4 piano sonatas; numerous songs.

BIBL.: G. Favre, *B.: Sa vie, son oeuvre* (2 parts, 1944–45). —NS/LK/DM

Bois, Rob du,

Dutch composer; b. Amsterdam, May 28, 1934. He had piano lessons as a child, and then studied law. Bois was mainly audodidact as a composer.

WORKS: ORCH.: Piano Concerto (1960; rev. 1968); *Cercle* for Piano, 9 Winds, and Percussion (1963); *Simultaneous* (1965); *Breuker Concerto* for 2 Clarinets, 4 Saxophones, and 21 String Players (1968); *A Flower Given to My Daughter* (1970); *Le Concerto pour Hrisanide* for Piano and Orch. (1971); *Allegro* for Strings (1973); *3 pezzi* (1973); Suite No. 1 (1973); Violin Concerto (1975); *Skarabee* (1977); *Zodiak* for Various Instruments (1977); Concerto for 2 Violins and Orch. (1979); *Sinfonia da camera* for Wind Orch. (1980); *My Daughter's Flower* for Brass Band (1982); *Luna* for Alto Flute and Orch. (1987–88); *Elegia* for Oboe d'Amore and Strings (1995; also for Oboe d'Amore, Violin, Viola, and Cello, 1980). **CHAMBER:** 4 string quartets (1960–90); 7 pastorales: No. 1 for Oboe, Clarinet, and Harp (1960; rev. 1969), No. 2 for Recorder, Flute, and Guitar (1963; rev. 1969), No. 3 for Clarinet, Bongos, and Double Bass (1963; rev. 1969), No. 4 for Guitar (1963), No. 5 for String Quartet (1964; rev. 1966), No. 6 for Piano (1964), and No. 7 for Recorder (1964); Trio for Flute, Oboe, and Clarinet (1961); *Rondeaux per deux* for Piano and Percussion (1962; 2nd series for Piano, 4–Hands, and Percussion, 1964); *3 Pieces* for Flute, Oboe, and Cello (1962); *Chants et contrepoints* for Wind Quintet (1962); *Espaces à remplir* for 11 Musicians (1963); Oboe Quartet (1964); 7 Bagatelles for Flute and Piano (1964); String Trio (1967); *Musica per quattro* for Horn, 2 Trumpets, and Trombone (1967); *Rounds* for Clarinet and Piano (1967); *Ranta Music* for Percussionist (1968); *Musique d'atelier* for Clarinet, Trombone, Cello, and Piano (1968); *Enigma* for Flute, Bass

Clarinet, Piano, and Percussion (1969); *Trio agitato* for Horn, Trombone, and Tuba (1969); *Reflexions sur le jour ou Pérotin le Grand ressuscitera* for Wind Quintet (1969); *Polonaise* for a Pianist and a Percussionist (1971); *Fusion pour deux* for Bass Clarinet and Piano (1971); *The Dog Named Boo Has a Master Called Lobo* for Clarinet, Violin, and Piano (1972); *Because It Is* for 4 Clarinets (1973); *The 18th of June, Springtime, and Yet Already Summer* for 4 Saxophones (1974); *Melody* for Bass Clarinet and String Quartet (1974); *Springtime* for Piano and Wind Instruments (1978); *His Flow of Spirits is Something Wonderful* for Piano and Wind Instruments (1978); *Elegia* for Oboe d'Amore, Violin, Viola, and Cello (1980; also for Oboe d'Amore and String Orch., 1995); 2 violin sonatas (1980, 1992); *Hyperion* for Clarinet, Horn, Viola, and Piano (1984); *Das Liebesverbot* for 4 Wagner Tubas (1986); *Symphorine* for Flute (1987); *Thalatta, thalatta* for 4 Bass Flutes (1987); *Vertiges* for Double Bass and Wind Ensemble (1987); *Fünf* for Oboe, Clarinet, and Bassoon (1996); *Fleeting* for Clarinet Ensemble (1997).—NS/LK/DM

Boise, Otis Bardwell,

American organist, teacher, and composer; b. Oberlin, Ohio, Aug. 13, 1844; d. Baltimore, Dec. 2, 1912. He was a pupil of Moscheles and Richter in Leipzig (1861–64), and of Kullak in Berlin (1864). He was an organist in Cleveland (1865–70) and N.Y. (1870–80). After teaching in Berlin (1888–1901), he taught at the Peabody Cons. of Music in Baltimore. His works include syms., overtures, and piano concertos. He publ. *Harmony Made Practical* (N.Y., 1900) and *Music and Its Masters* (N.Y., 1902).—NS/LK/DM

Boismortier, Joseph Bodin de,

French composer; b. Thionville, Moselle, Dec. 23, 1689; d. Roissy-en-Brie, Oct. 28, 1755. He lived in Metz and Perpignan before settling in Paris in 1724. A prolific composer of instrumental music, he wrote more than 100 opus numbers; of these there are several for block flutes (i.e., recorders) and transverse flutes; 2 suites for clavecin; trio sonatas, among them one with the viola da gamba (1732; modern ed., Mainz, 1967); collections of pieces designed for amateurs, scored with a drone instrument, either the musette or the vielle, and publ. under such coaxing titles as "Gentillesses," or "Divertissements de campagne." He also wrote 3 ballet-operas: *Les Voyages de l'Amour* (1736), *Don Quichotte* (1743), and *Daphnis et Chloé* (1747), and a number of cantatas.—NS/LK/DM

Boito, Arrigo (baptismal name, Enrico),

important Italian poet and opera composer; b. Padua, Feb. 24, 1842; d. Milan, June 10, 1918. He studied at the Milan Cons. with Alberto Mazzucato and Ronchetti-Monteviti. His 2 cantatas, *Il 4 Giugno* (1860) and *Le Sorelle d'Italia* (1861), written in collaboration with Faccio, were performed at the Cons., and attracted a great deal of favorable attention; as a result, the Italian government granted the composers a gold medal and a stipend for foreign travel for 2 years. Boito spent most of his time in Paris, and also went to Poland to meet the family of his mother (who was Polish); he also visited Germany, Belgium, and England. He was strongly influenced by new French and German music. Upon his return to Milan, he undertook the composition of his first and most significant large opera, *Mefistofele*, which contains elements of conventional Italian opera but also dramatic ideas stemming from Beethoven and Wagner. It was performed for the first time at La Scala (March 5, 1868). A controversy followed when a part of the audience objected to the unusual treatment of the subject and the music, and there were actual disorders at the conclusion of the performance. After the 2nd production, the opera was taken off the boards, and Boito undertook a revision to effect a compromise. In this new version, the opera had a successful run in Italian cities; it was also produced in Hamburg (1880), in London (in Italian, July 6, 1880), and in Boston (in Eng., Nov. 16, 1880). It was retained in the repertoire of the leading opera houses, but its success never matched that of Gounod's *Faust*. Boito never completed his 2nd opera, *Nerone*, on which he worked for more than half a century (from 1862 to 1916). The orch. score was revised by Toscanini and performed by him at La Scala on May 1, 1924. There are sketches for an earlier opera, *Ero e Leandro*, but not enough material to attempt a completion. Boito's gift as a poet is fully equal to that as a composer. He publ. a book of verses (Turin, 1877) under the anagrammatic pen name of Tobia Gorrio; he wrote his own librettos for his operas and made admirable trs. of Wagner's operas (*Tristan und Isolde; Rienzi*). He wrote the librettos of *Otello* and *Falstaff* for Verdi, which are regarded as his masterpieces; also for *Gioconda* by Ponchielli, *Amleto* by Faccio, etc. Boito also publ. novels. He held various honorary titles from the King of Italy; in 1892 he was appointed inspector-general of Italian conservatories; was made honorary D.Mus. by the Univ. of Cambridge and the Univ. of Oxford; in 1912 he was made a senator by the King of Italy. Boito's letters were ed. by R. de Rensis (Rome, 1932), who also ed. Boito's articles on music (Milan, 1931).

BIBL.: A. Boccardi, *A. B.* (Trieste, 1877); R. Giani, *Il Nerone di A. B.* (Turin, 1901); M. Risolo, *Il primo Mefistofele di A. B.* (Naples, 1916); A. Pompeati, *A. B.* (Florence, 1919); C. Ricci, *A. B.* (Milan, 1919); V. Gui, *Il Nerone di A. B.* (Milan, 1924); A. Bonaventura, *A. B.; Mefistofele* (Milan, 1924); F. Ballo, *A. B.* (Turin, 1938); R. de Rensis, *A. B.; Aneddoti e bizzarrie poetiche e musicali* (Rome, 1942); P. Nardi, *Vita di A. B.* (Verona, 1942; 2nd ed., Milan, 1944); M. Vajro, *A. B.* (Brescia, 1955); G. Mariani, *A. B.* (Parma, 1973); G. Scarsi, *Rapporto poesia-musica in A. B.* (Rome, 1973); G. Morelli, ed., *A. B.* (Florence, 1994); D. Del Nero, *A. B.: Un artista europeo* (Florence, 1995); H. Helbling, *A. B.: Ein Musikdichter der italienischen Romantik* (Munich, 1995).—NS/LK/DM

Bok, Mary Louise Curtis, munificent American music patroness; b. Boston, Aug. 6, 1876; d. Philadelphia, Jan. 4, 1970. She inherited her fortune from Cyrus H.K. Curtis, founder of the Curtis Publishing Co. In 1917 she founded the Settlement School of Music in Philadelphia. In 1924 she established in Philadelphia the Curtis Inst. of Music and endowed it initially with a gift of $12.5 million in memory of her mother. The school had a faculty of the most distinguished American and European musicians, and it provided tuition exclusively on a scholarship basis; many talented composers and performers were among its students, including Bernstein, Barber, and Foss. She was first married to Edward W. Bok, in 1896, who died in 1930; in 1943 she married the eminent Russian-born American violinist and pedagogue Efrem Zimbalist (b. Rostov-na-Donu, April 21, 1889; d. Reno, Nev., Feb. 22, 1985), who was director of the Curtis Inst. from 1941 until 1968. In 1932 she received an honorary doctorate from the Univ. of Pa., and, in 1934, an honorary doctorate from Williams Coll.

BIBL.: E. Viles, *M. L. C. B. Zimbalist: Founder of the Curtist Institute of Music and Patron of American Arts* (diss., Bryn Mawr Coll., 1983).—NS/LK/DM

Bokemeyer, Heinrich, German music theorist and composer; b. Immensen, near Lehrte, Lower Saxony, March 1679; d. Wolfenbüttel, Dec. 7, 1751. He attended the St. Martin's and St. Catherine's Church School in Braunschweig, and in 1702 went to the Univ. of Helmstedt. Returning to Braunschweig in 1704, he served as cantor at St. Martin's; concurrently studied composition with Georg Oesterreich. In 1712 he became cantor in Husum, and in 1717 he repaired to Wolfenbüttel, where in 1720 he became cantor at the ducal palace. He was a founding member of Mizler's Societät der Musikalischen Wissenschaften of Leipzig. Few of his compositions are extant, but several of his theoretical treatises survive. He collected a large music library. See H. Kummerling, *Katalog der Sammlung Bokemeyer* (Kassel, 1970).—NS/LK/DM

Bokor, Margit, Hungarian soprano; b. Losoncz, near Budapest, 1905; d. N.Y., Nov. 9, 1949. She received her training in Budapest and Vienna. After making her operatic debut in Budapest (1928), she sang in Berlin (1930) and then with the Dresden State Opera (1931–35), where she created the role of Zdenka in Strauss's *Arabella* in 1933. Following appearances at the Salzburg Festival (from 1934) and the Vienna State Opera (1935–38), she settled in the U.S. After appearances in Chicago and Philadelphia, on April 6, 1947, she made her N.Y. City Opera debut as the Composer in *Ariadne*. —NS/LK/DM

Bolcom, William (Elden), prominent American composer, pianist, and teacher; b. Seattle, May 26, 1938. He studied at the Univ. of Washington in Seattle with George Frederick McKay and John Verrall (B.A., 1958), took a course in composition with Darius Milhaud at Mills Coll. in Oakland, Calif. (M.A., 1961), and attended classes in advanced composition with Leland Smith at Stanford Univ. (D.M.A., 1964). He also studied at the Paris Cons. with Milhaud and Jean Rivier (1959–61; 1965–66; 2nd prix in composition, 1965). In 1964–65 and 1968–69 he held Guggenheim fellowships. He taught at the Univ. of Washington in Seattle (1965–66) and at Queens Coll. of the City Univ. of N.Y. (1966–68). In 1969–70 he served as composer-in-residence at the N.Y. Univ. School of the Arts. In 1973 he joined the faculty of the Univ. of Mich. as an asst. prof., subsequently serving there as an assoc. prof. (1977–83), prof. (1983–94), the Ross Lee Finney Distinguished Univ. Prof. of Music in Composition (from 1994), and as chairman of the composition dept. (from 1998). He was composer-in-residence of the Detroit Sym. Orch. (1987–88), Ithaca Coll. (1990–91), and the N.Y. Phil. (1995). In 1988 he won the Pulitzer Prize in Music for his *12 New Etudes* for Piano, and in 1993 he was elected a member of the American Academy and Inst. of Arts and Letters. He is also active as a pianist, recording and giving recitals of ragtime works. In 1975 he married **Joan Morris**, with whom he appears in concerts and with whom he has recorded some 20 albums. He publ., with Robert Kimball, a book on the black American songwriting and musical comedy team of Noble Sissle and Eubie Blake, *Reminiscing with Sissle and Blake* (N.Y., 1973; reissued, 1999). He also ed. the collected essays of George Rochberg under the title *The Aesthetics of Survival: A Composer's View of Twentieth-Century Music* (Ann Arbor, 1984). Bolcom's thorough knowledge and appreciation of the music of America, both past and present, has been an important factor in his own development as a composer. His diverse output utilizes styles ranging from romantic to modern, including elements of such popular genres as country and rock.

WORKS: DRAMATIC: *Dynamite Tonite*, actors' opera (N.Y. Dec. 21, 1963); *Greatshot*, actors' opera (1969); *Theatre of the Absurd* for Actor and Chamber Group (1970; San Francisco, March 2, 1979); *The Beggar's Opera*, adaptation of John Gay's work, adding to already-arranged work by Milhaud, for Actors and Chamber Orch. (1978; Minneapolis, Jan. 27, 1979); *Casino Paradise*, musical theater opera (1986–90; Philadelphia, April 4, 1990); *McTeague*, opera (1991–92; Chicago, Oct. 31, 1992); *A View from the Bridge*, opera after Arthur Miller (Chicago, Oct. 9, 1999). **ORCH.:** 7 syms.: No. 1 (Aspen, July 1957), No. 2, *Oracles* (1964; Seattle, May 2, 1965), No. 3 for Chamber Orch. (St. Paul, Sept. 15, 1979), No. 4 for Medium Voice and Orch., after Roethke (1986; St. Louis, March 13, 1987), No. 5 (1989; Philadelphia, Jan. 11, 1990), No. 6 (1996–97; Washington, D.C., Feb. 26, 1998), and No. 7 (2002); *Concertante* for Violin, Flute, Oboe, and Orch. (1961); *Concerto-Serenade* for Violin and Strings (1964); *Fives* for Violin, Piano, and 3 String Orchs. (1966); *Humoresk* for Organ and Orch. (1969; N.Y., Dec. 3, 1979); *Commedia for "Almost" 18th Century Orch.* (1971; St. Paul, March 1972); *Summer Divertimento* for Chamber Orch. (Portland, Ore., Aug. 9, 1973); Piano Concerto (Seattle, March 8, 1976); *Ragomania* (Boston, May 4, 1982); Violin Concerto (Stuttgart, June 3, 1984); *Fantasia concertante* for Viola, Cello, and Orch. (1985; Salzburg, Jan. 26, 1986); *Seattle Slew*, dance suite (1985–86; Seattle, March 5, 1986); *Spring Concertino* for Oboe and Chamber Orch. (1986–87; Midland, Mich., Nov. 7, 1987); *Fanfare: Converging on the Mountain* (1989; Aspen, July 16, 1991); *MC-MXC Tanglewood* (Tanglewood, Aug. 4, 1990); Clarinet Concerto (1990; N.Y., Jan. 3, 1992); *Lyric Concerto* for Flute and Orch. (St. Louis, Oct. 27, 1993); *GAEA*, concerto for 2 Left-Handed Pianists and Orch. (1995; Baltimore, April 11, 1996); *Gala Variation* (St. Louis, May 19, 1996); *Classical Action Samba* (N.Y., May 12, 1997). **Concert Band:** *Broadside* (1981); *Liberty Enlightening the World* (1985); Concert Suite for Saxophone and Band (1999). **CHAMBER:** 10 string quartets (1950–88); 4 violin sonatas: No. 1 (1956; rev. 1984), No. 2 (1978; Washington, D.C., Jan. 12, 1979), No. 3, *Sonata Stromba* (1992; Aspen, July 12, 1993), and No. 4 (1995; Ann Arbor, Jan. 26, 1997); Concert Piece for Clarinet and Piano (1958; Oakland, Calif., April 30, 1959); *Décalge* for Cello and Piano (1961; Stanford, Jan. 1962); *Pastorale* for Violin and Piano (1961); *Session I* for Chamber Group (Berlin, May 12, 1965), *II* for Violin and Viola (1966), *III* for Chamber Group (1967), and *IV* for Chamber Group (1967); *Dream Music No. 2* for Harpsichord and Percussion (1966); *Dark Music* for Timpani and Cello (1969; Washington, D.C., May 31,

1970); *Duets for Quintet* for Flute, Clarinet, Violin, Cello, and Piano (1970); *Whisper Moon* for Alto Flute, Clarinet, Violin, Cello, and Piano (N.Y., April 1971); *Fancy Tales* for Violin and Piano (1971); *Duo Fantasy* for Violin and Piano (Portland, Ore., Aug. 6, 1973); *Seasons* for Guitar (1974; Ann Arbor, Nov. 15, 1975); 2 piano quartets: No. 1 (1976; N.Y., Oct. 23, 1977) and No. 2 (Washington, D.C., Dec. 10, 1996); *Afternoon Cakewalk*, rag suite of Joplin, Lamb, Scott, and Bolcom for Clarinet, Violin, and Piano (N.Y., Nov. 1, 1979); Brass Quintet (Aspen, July 7, 1980); *Aubade* for Oboe and Piano (Helsinki, Sept. 1982); *Orphee-Serenade* for Chamber Ensemble (1984; N.Y., April 13, 1985); *Lilith* for Alto Saxophone and Piano (1984); *Five Fold Five* for Woodwind Quintet and Piano (Saratoga Springs, N.Y., Aug. 14, 1987); *3 Rags* for String Quartet (1989); Cello Sonata (1989; Boston, May 3, 1990); Trio for Clarinet, Violin, and Piano (London, March 25, 1994); Suite No. 1 for Cello (1994–95; Tanglewood, July 12, 1996); *Tres piezas lindas* for Flute and Guitar (St. Paul, March 11, 1995); *Spring Trio* for Violin, Cello, and Piano (Charlottesville, Va., Sept. 15, 1996); *Celestial Dinner Music* for Flute and Harp (1996). **KEYBOARD: Piano:** *Romantic Pieces* (1959); *12 Etudes* (1959–60); Fantasy-Sonata No. 1 (1961); *Interlude* for 2 Pianos (1963); *Dream Music No. 1* (Berlin, Sept. 21, 1965); *Brass Knuckles* (1968); *Garden of Eden*, suite (1968); *Dream Shadows*, rag (1970); *The Poltergeist*, rag (1970); *Seabiscuits Rag* (1970); *Graceful Ghost*, rag (1970); *Raggin' Rudi*, rag (1972); *12 New Etudes* (1977–86; first complete perf., N.Y., Oct. 12, 1987); *Fields of Flowers* (1978); *Monsterpieces (and Others)* for Children (1980); *3 Dance Portraits* (1986; Charlemont, Mass., July 1987); *Rag Tango (Homage to Ernesto Nazareth)* (1988); *Recuerdos* for 2 Pianos (Miami, Dec. 17, 1991); Sonata for 2 Pianos (1993; Lafayette, Ind., April 6, 1994); *Haunted Labyrinth* (1994); *9 Bagatelles* (1996; Fort Worth, May 1997). **Organ:** *Chorale Prelude on Abide With Me* (Everett, Wash., Oct. 19, 1970); *Hydraulis* (1971); *Mysteries* (1976); *Gospel Preludes* (4 vols., 1979–84). **OTHER:** *Black Host* for Organ, Chimes, Cymbals, Bass Drum, and Tape (1967); *Praeludium* for Organ and Vibraphone (1969); *Revelation Studies* for 2 Carillon Players (1976). **VOCAL:** *Songs of Innocence and of Experience* for Soloists, Chorus, and Orch., after Blake (1956–81; Stuttgart, Jan. 8, 1984); *Cabaret Songs* for Medium Voice and Piano (4 vols., 1963–96); *Satires* for Madrigal Group (1970); *Open House* for Tenor and Chamber Orch. (St. Paul, Oct. 8, 1975); *I Will Breathe a Mountain* for Medium Voice and Piano (1990; N.Y., March 26, 1991); *The Mask* for Chorus and Piano (Philadelphia, Oct. 12, 1990); *Let Evening Come* for Soprano, Viola, and Piano (N.Y., April 19, 1994); *A Whitman Triptych* for Mezzo-soprano and Orch., after Whitman (San Francisco, June 24, 1995); *Turbulence: A Romance* for Soprano, Baritone, and Piano (1996; Minneapolis, April 27, 1997); *Briefly it Enters* for Soprano and Piano (Ann Arbor, Sept. 29, 1996).—**NS/LK/DM**

Boldemann, Laci, Finnish-born Swedish composer; b. Helsinki, April 24, 1921; d. Munich, Aug. 18, 1969. He studied piano and conducting at the Royal Academy of Music in London. At the outbreak of World War II in 1939, he went to Sweden and pursued piano training with Gunnar de Frumerie. After being compelled to return to Germany for army service, he saw action in the campaigns in the Soviet Union, Poland, and Italy before being captured by the Allies. He was a prisoner-of-war in the U.S. for 2 years; upon his release at the end of the War, he returned to Sweden to pursue his career as a composer. He was also active as a teacher and from 1963 to 1969 was secretary and treasurer of the

Swedish Composers' Soc. Boldemann's output was the work of a solid craftsman who placed great store in lyrical invention.

WORKS: DRAMATIC: *Svart är vitt, sa kejsaren* (Black Is White, Said the Emperor), fairy tale opera (1964; Stockholm, Jan. 1, 1965); *Dårskapens timme* (Hour of Madness), opera-musical (Malmö, March 22, 1968); *Och så drommer han om Per Jonathan* (And He Dreams of Per Jonathan), operatic scene (Stockholm, Nov. 29, 1969). **ORCH.:** *La Danza*, overture (1949–50); Sinfonietta for Strings (1954); *Fantasia Concertante* for Cello and Orch. (1954); Piano Concerto (1956); Violin Concerto (1959); Sym. (1963; Munich, Jan. 13, 1964); Trumpet Concerto (1968; Malmö, Feb. 11, 1969); *Med bleck och med trä*, little wind overture (1969). **CHAMBER:** Violin Sonata (1950); *6 Small Pieces without Pedal* for Piano (1950); String Quartet (1950–57); *Canto elegiaco* for Cello and Piano (1962). **VOCAL:** *Lieder der Vergänglichkeit*, cantata for Baritone and Strings (1951); *4 Epitaphs* for Soprano and Strings (1952); *Notturno* for Soprano and Orch. (1958); *John Bauer*, oratorio (1967); songs.—**NS/LK/DM**

Bolden, Buddy (Charles Joseph),

New Orleans cornetist, leader, and perhaps the most legendary figure in all jazz; b. New Orleans, Sept. 6, 1877; d. Jackson, La., Nov. 4. 1931. His legendary status is due partly because he preceded the known jazz artists and by some accounts, was a powerful player, but he never recorded (despite rumors) and did not perform publicly after 1907. Because he was in fact a generation older than all other jazz artists it is certain that he did not begin by playing the same music as they (this is simple logic), so it is likely that he should be considered an inspiration to some early jazz players rather than a founder or inventor of the medium. Despite intensive research by Danny Barker and others, few hard facts emerge that detail his career. Guitarist Louis Keppard remembered playing with Bolden's Band at the Globe Hall in New Orleans in 1895. Bunk Johnson said that he played second with Bolden at about that time, but Big Eye Louis Deslisle said that Bolden was "just beginning on cornet" in 1900. George Baquet said that he first sat in with Bolden at the Oddfellows Hall in 1905. Every scrap of information that comes to light seems, in some small way, to contradict the previous story. Chilton says confusion arises from the fact that informants are not all talking about the same man, and their appraisals of Bolden's musical skills range from the ecstatic to the unprintable. Certainly there was more than one cornetist called Bolden from the Crescent City; in 1908 a New Orleans cornetist, Charles Bolden, visited N.Y. with a travelling minstrel show. The "real" Bolden did at one time run his own barber-shop in New Orleans, also led his own band, and they were regularly featured with Buddy Bottley. During his heyday Bolden is alleged to have simultaneously put out six bands bearing his name, making brief appearances with each of them. Later, he was deposed, and his musicians worked under Frankie Dusen's leadership. Bolden's last known job was with Allen's Brass Band in 1907. He is said to have been permanently committed to the East La. State Hospital on June 5, 1907, however, bassist Bob Lyons remembered seeing Bolden in New Orleans at the celebrations marking the end of World War I. It seems possible that Bolden was released from the mental home for brief periods, but spent his last years there. Henry "Red" Allen went to see Bolden (who was a friend of his father) in the home, c. 1928. Red said that he failed to gain any comprehension from Bolden who just shuffled about without saying a word. Bolden is also the subject of the novel *Coming Through Slaughter* by Michael Ondaatje, author of *The English Patient*.

DISC.: *Instrumental History of Jazz* (1997). Planet Gong: *Floating Arnachy Live '77* (1978).

BIBL.: D. Barker, A. Shipton, *Buddy Bolden and the Last Days of Storyville* (London, N.Y., 1998); D. M. Marquis, *In Search of Buddy Bolden, First Man of Jazz* (Baton Rouge, La. State Univ., 1978); D.M. Marquis, *Finding Buddy Bolden, First Man of Jazz: The Journal of a Search* (Goshen, Ind., 1978).—**JC/LP**

Bolet, Jorge, brilliant Cuban-born American pianist; b. Havana, Nov. 15, 1914; d. Mountain View, Calif., Oct. 16, 1990. After training in Havana, he enrolled at the age of 12 as a scholarship student at the Curtis Inst. of Music in Philadelphia, where he studied with Saperton (piano) and Reiner (conducting); he also studied piano with Godowsky (1932–33) and Rosenthal (1935). In 1935 he made his European debut in Amsterdam, and in 1937 his U.S. debut in Philadelphia. He then continued his training with Serkin. In 1937 he received the Naumburg Prize, which led to his successful N.Y. debut that same year. In 1938 he won the Josef Hofmann Award. After serving as Serkin's assistant at the Curtis Inst. (1939–42), he served in the military during World War II. Following the War, he pursued additional training with Chasins and then began to tour. However, it was not until the early 1960s that he gained wide recognition as a virtuoso in the grand Romantic manner. In subsequent years he toured all over the globe. He also served as prof. of music at the Ind. Univ. School of Music in Bloomington (1968–77), and then as head of the piano dept. at the Curtis Inst. (from 1977).—**NS/LK/DM**

Bolling, Claude, pop-jazz pianist, composer, leader; b. Cannes, France, April 10, 1930. He began formal piano training at age 12, receiving thorough grounding in the classical repertoire while mastering the jazz idiom; later he studied harmony and composition with Maurice Durufle in Paris, where he immersed himself in the jazz scene. Bolling became a prominent figure in the crossover movement when he composed his "Sonata for Two Pianists" (1970) for Jean-Bernard Pommier. His "Suite for Flute and Jazz Piano Trio," written in 1975 for Jean-Pierre Rampal, became an internationally successful recording, attaining gold-record status in 1981. He also wrote "California Suite" (1976), "Suite for Violin and Jazz Piano Trio" (1978), "Suite for Chamber Orch. and Jazz Piano Trio" (1983), and "Suite for Cello and Jazz Piano Trio" (1984). A light classical player and swing-oriented jazz musician, he has had great success with a pieces that blend jazz and classical material and helped to spur a trend for classical artist to get more involved with jazz.

DISC.: *Claude Bolling Plays Duke Ellington* (1956); *Bolling's Band's Blowing* (1963); *Original Ragtime* (1966); *Suite for Flute and*

Jazz Piano (1975); *Concerto for Classical Guitar and Jazz Piano* (1978); *Toot Suite* (1980); *Live at the Meridien* (1984); *Bolling Plays Ellington, Vol. 1 and 2* (1991); *Black, Brown and Beige* (1993). —NS/LP

Bollius, Daniel, German organist and composer; b. Hechingen, c. 1590; d. Mainz, c. 1642. He studied at the Univ. of Dillingen. He was court organist in Sigmaringen from 1613 to 1619, and in 1626 he was appointed organist to the elector of Mainz. His oratorio, *Representatio harmonica conceptionis et nativitatis S. Joannis Baptistae,* is historically significant as an early example of the Italian oratorio form in Germany.—NS/LK/DM

Bologna, Jacopo da
See **Jacopo da Bologna**

Bolshakov, Nikolai, Russian tenor; b. Kharkov, Nov. 23, 1874; d. Leningrad, Jan. 20, 1958. He studied in St. Petersburg, making his debut there with the Kharkov Opera Co. in 1899. In 1902 he went to Milan, where he studied voice with A. Brogi. He then sang with the Maryinsky Theater in St. Petersburg (1906–29), participated in the spectacles of Diaghilev's "Russian Seasons" in Paris and London (1911–13), and also gave recitals. From 1923 to 1953 he taught voice at the Leningrad Cons. He was noted for his interpretations of Faust and Don José.—NS/LK/DM

Bolton, Ivor, English conductor; b. Lancashire, May 17, 1958. He was educated at Clare Coll., Cambridge (Mus.B.; M.A.), at the Royal Coll. of Music in London, and at the National Opera Studio. In 1981–82 he was conductor of the Schola Cantorum at Oxford. From 1982 to 1990 he was music director at St. James's, Piccadilly. He was founder-director of the St. James's Baroque Players in London from 1984, and also founder-music director of the Lufthansa Festival of Baroque Music from 1985. After serving as chorus master at the Glyndebourne Festival (1985–88), he returned there to conduct Gluck's *Orfeo* in 1989. From 1990 to 1993 he was music director of the English Touring Opera. He made his first appearance at the English National Opera in London conducting *Xerxes* in 1992, the same year he became music director of the Glyndebourne Touring Opera. From 1993 to 1996 he also was chief conductor of the Scottish Chamber Orch. in Glasgow. In 1995 he made his debut at London's Covent Garden conducting the premiere of Goehr's *Arianna.* He was a conductor at the Munich Festival in 1997. In addition to various guest conducting engagements with opera companies, he also appeared as a guest conductor with many British orchs. —NS/LK/DM

Bolzoni, Giovanni, Italian composer and conductor; b. Parma, May 14, 1841; d. Turin, Feb. 21, 1919. He studied at the Parma Cons. He was active as a conductor in Perugia, served as director and prof. of composition at the Liceo Musicale in Turin (1887–1916), and also conducted at the Teatro Regio there (1884–89). His most successful operas were *Il matrimonio civile* (Parma, 1870),

La stella delle Alpi (Savona, 1876), and *Jella* (Piacenza, 1881). A melodious minuet from one of his string quartets became a perennial favorite in numerous arrangements.—NS/LK/DM

Bomtempo, João Domingos, Portuguese pianist; b. Lisbon, Dec. 28, 1775; d. there, Aug. 18, 1842. He studied in Paris, then went to London, where he stayed until 1811. Returning to Lisbon, he was active on the concert stage. In 1816 he went to London again, and finally went back to Portugal in 1820. In 1822 he founded a phil. society in Lisbon, and in 1833 became director of the Lisbon Cons. He wrote 6 syms., 4 piano concertos, 14 piano sextets, a Piano Quintet, and several piano sonatas; also an opera, *Alessandro in Efesso.* He publ. a piano method (London, 1816).

BIBL.: M.A. de Lima Cruz, *D. B.* (Lisbon, 1937). —NS/LK/DM

Bon, Maarten, Dutch pianist and composer; b. Amsterdam, Aug. 20, 1933. He graduated from the Muzieklyceum in Amsterdam in 1954. He studied piano with T. Bruins and Spaanderman, and composition with Baaren, and then gave recitals with his wife, the violinist Jeannelotte Hertzberger. His compositions, often whimsical, include *Caprichoso y Obstinato* for Flute (1965); *Disturbing the Peace,* improvisation for 9 Players, more or less (1968–69); *Let's Go Out for a Drive (and Pollute the Air),* improvisation for Trombone, 3 Pianists, and Conductor (1970–74); *Free or Not* for 21 Wind Players (1972); *Sieben, jedenfalls sieben* for Chamber Ensemble (1976); *Display IV* for 6 Pianos and Piano Tuner (1980; rev. 1982) and *V* for 12 Cellos (1983); *Boréal* for Violin and Percussion Ensemble (1981); Solo for Clarinet (1983–86); *Canon a tre voci* for 3 Cellos (1988–93); *Song (without words) Nos. 1–5* for Various Instruments (1991–93); *5 Easy Pieces* for String Quartet (1996); *About Synchronicity* for 4 Pianos (1996).—NS/LK/DM

Bon, Willem Frederik, Dutch composer and conductor; b. Amersfoort, June 15, 1940; d. Nijeholtpade, April 14, 1983. He studied clarinet, conducting, and composition at the Amsterdam Cons. and the Royal Cons. of Music at The Hague, receiving a conducting diploma in 1971. In 1972 he became conductor of the Eindhoven Baroque Ensemble, and in 1973 was named an asst. conductor of the Concertgebouw Orch. in Amsterdam. At the time of his death, he taught composition at the Groningen Cons.

WORKS: DRAMATIC: *Erik's wonderbaarlijke reis* (Erik's Miraculous Journey), instrumental opera for Children, Narrator, and Orch. (1979). ORCH.: *Dialogues and Monologues* for Piano and Orch. (1968); *Nocturnes* for Strings (1968); *Variations on a Theme of Sweelinck* for Chamber Orch. (1969); 2 syms.: No. 1, *Usher Symphony,* after Poe (1968–70; originally intended as an opera) and No. 2, *Les Predictions* (1970); Concerto for Strings (1970); *Games* for 6 Wind Instruments, Piano, and Strings (1970); *To Catch a Heffalump* for Orch. and Tape (1971); *Circe,* prelude (1972); *Passacaglia in Blue* for 12 Wind Instruments and Double Bass (1972); *Aforismen* for 15 Strings (1972); Concerto for Oboes (Oboe, Oboe d'Amore, and Heckelphone) and Strings (1974); Sym. for Strings (1982). CHAMBER: 2 wind quintets (1963–66; 1969); Cello Sonata (1966); *Sunphoneion I* for Flute,

Vibraphone, and Piano (1968); *Sans paroles* for Clarinet, Bass Clarinet, and String Trio (1970); *Petite trilogie* for Trumpet (1970); Sonata for Solo Bassoon (1970); *Riflessioni* for Flute and Harp (1971); *5 tours de passe- passe* for Flute and Piano (1971); *Allegorie* for Harp (1972); *3 Saturnien* for Piano Trio (1981). **P i a n o :** *Miniatures* (1966). **V O C A L :** *3 poèmes de Verlaine* for Mezzo-soprano, Flute, Cello, and Piano (1967); *Missa brevis* for Chorus and 9 Wind Instruments (1969); *Jadis et naguere* for Mezzo-soprano, Clarinet, Violin, and Piano (1970); *1999, 4 Prophesies of Nostradamus* for Soprano and Orch. (1973); *Le Grand Age Millième*, 4 quatrains after Nostradamus, for Men's Chorus (1974); *Les Quatre Saisons de Verlaine*, each for a different Vocal Soloist and Orch.: *Le Printemps* for Soprano, *L'Été* for Alto, *L'Automne* for Baritone, and *L'Hiver* for Tenor (1976–79); *Silence*, after Poe, for Mezzo-soprano, Wind Quintet, and Piano (1978); *Dag* (Hello), 4 songs for Mezzo-soprano and Percussion (1979). **—NS/LK/DM**

Bona (or **Buona**), **Valerio,** Italian composer; b. Brescia, c. 1560; date of death unknown, but he was still living in 1619. He was a Franciscan monk, serving as maestro di cappella at the cathedrals of Vercelli (1591) and Mondovi, and at the Church of S. Francesco in Milan (1596), musician at S. Francesco in Brescia (1611), and prefect at S. Fermo Maggiore in Verona (1614). He was a prolific composer, in polyphonic style, of sacred and secular vocal music (masses, litanies, Lamentations, motets, madrigals, etc.), many of which he wrote for 2 choirs. Also a theorist, he publ. *Regole del contrapunto, et compositione brevemente raccolte da diuersi auttori* (Casale, 1595), *Esempii delli passagi delle consonanze, et dissonanze* (Milan, 1596), etc.**—NS/LK/DM**

Bona, Giovanni, Italian cardinal; b. Mondovi, Oct. 12, 1609; d. Rome, Oct. 28, 1674. His tract *De divina psalmodia...tractatus historicus, symbolicus, asceticus* (Rome, 1653) contains valuable information on church music. A complete ed. of his works was publ. in Rome in 1747.**—NS/LK/DM**

Bonaventura, Anthony di, American pianist and teacher, brother of **Mario di Bonaventura;** b. Follansbee, W.Va., Nov. 12, 1930. A precocious talent, he made his debut at age 13 as soloist in the Beethoven Third Piano Concerto with the N.Y. Phil. At age 18, he became a pupil of Vengerova at the Curtis Inst. of Music in Philadelphia, graduating at 24. He then launched an ambitious career as a soloist with American and European orchs.; also played numerous recitals. He commissioned several composers of the avant-garde to write special works for him, among them Berio, Kelemen, and Ligeti. In 1973 he was appointed to the piano faculty of Boston Univ.**—NS/LK/DM**

Bonaventura, Arnaldo, Italian musicologist; b. Livorno, July 28, 1862; d. Florence, Oct. 7, 1952. He studied law, violin, and theory, but made musicology his career. He was a prof. of music history and librarian at the Florence Istituto Musicale until 1932, and then became director and prof. of music history and aesthetics at the Florence Cons.

WRITINGS: *Manuale di storia della musica* (Livorno, 1898; 10th ed., 1920); *Elementi di estetica musicale* (Livorno, 1905; 3rd ed., 1926, as *Manuale di estetica musicale*); *Dante e la musica* (Livorno, 1904); *Storia degli stromenti musicali* (Livorno, 1908; many other eds.); *Niccolo Paganini* (Modena, 1911; 3rd ed., 1925); *Saggio storico sul teatro musicale italiano* (Livorno, 1913); *Storia e letteratura del pianoforte* (Livorno, 1918); *Verdi* (Paris, 1923); *Bernardo Pasquini* (Ascoli Piceno, 1923); *Manuale di cultura musicale* (Livorno, 1924); *"Mefistofele" di Boito* (Milan, 1924); *Giacomo Puccini: L'uomo-l'artista* (Livorno, 1925); *Storia del violino, dei violinisti e della musica per violino* (Milan, 1925); *L'opera italiana* (Florence, 1928); *Domenico del Mela* (Burgo San Lorenzo, 1928); *Musicisti livornesi* (Livorno, 1930); *Boccherini* (Milan and Rome, 1931); *Rossini* (Florence, 1934).**—NS/LK/DM**

Bonaventura, Mario di, American conductor, music educator, and music publisher, brother of **Anthony di Bonaventura;** b. Follansbee, W.Va., Feb. 20, 1924. He studied violin, was a pupil in composition in Paris of Boulanger (1947–53), and in conducting at the Salzburg Mozarteum and in Paris of Markevitch; received instruction in piano accompaniment at the Paris Cons., and won the Lili Boulanger Memorial Prize in composition (1953). He was music director of the Ft. Lauderdale Sym. Orch. (1959–62); then taught at Dartmouth Coll. (1962–74), where he served as director of its Congregation of the Arts, a summer contemporary music festival (1963–70). After serving as vice-president and director of publications at G. Schirmer/Associated Music Publishers, N.Y. (1974–79), he was director of the Boston Univ. School of Music (1980–82).**—NS/LK/DM**

Bonavia, Ferruccio, Italian-English writer on music and composer; b. Trieste, Feb. 20, 1877; d. London, Feb. 5, 1950. He studied violin in Trieste and Milan, and in 1898 he went to England, where he earned his living as a violinist. He mastered the English language and became music critic of the *Manchester Guardian* and of the *London Daily Telegraph*. He publ. a monograph on Verdi (London, 1930; 2nd ed., 1947), miniature biographies of Mozart (1938) and Rossini (1941), and a fanciful book of imaginary conversations, *Musicians in Elysium* (1949). He composed a Violin Concerto, a String Octet, a String Quartet, and some songs.**—NS/LK/DM**

Bonci, Alessandro, Italian tenor; b. Cesena, Feb. 10, 1870; d. Viserba, Aug. 8, 1940. He studied with Pedrotti and Coen in Pesaro, and with Delle Sedie in Paris. On Jan. 20, 1896, he made his operatic debut as Fenton in Parma; after appearances at Milan's La Scala (1897) and London's Covent Garden (debut as Rodolfo, 1900), he toured throughout Europe. On Dec. 3, 1906, he sang Lord Arthur Talbot in *I Puritani* at the opening of the new Manhattan Opera House in N.Y. On Nov. 22, 1907, he made his Metropolitan Opera debut in N.Y. as the Duke of Mantua, and remained on its roster until 1910. He later sang in Chicago (1919–21) and at the Teatro Costanzi in Rome (1922–23) before settling in Milan as a voice teacher. Among his best roles were Count Almaviva, Ottavio, Wilhelm Meister, and Rodolfo. He also appeared in German lieder recitals.
—NS/LK/DM

Bond, Chapel, English organist and composer; b. Gloucester (baptized), Dec. 14, 1730; d. Coventry, Feb.

14, 1790. He studied with Martin Smith, the Cathedral organist, and when he was 19 he became organist at St. Michael and All Angels in Coventry; from 1752 he also served as organist at Holy Trinity, retaining both posts until his death. He composed a number of effectively written instrumental pieces, including concerti grossi and concertos for trumpet and bassoon.—NS/LK/DM

Bond, Victoria, American conductor and composer; b. Los Angeles, May 6, 1945. Her father was a physician and an opera singer and her mother was a pianist. Following initial music instruction from her mother, she attended the Mannes School of Music in N.Y. and pursued piano training with Nadia Reisenberg. Returning to Los Angeles, she studied composition with Dahl at the Univ. of Southern Calif. (B.M.A., 1968), and also worked with Paul Glass. Upon returning to N.Y., she pursued studies in composition with Sessions and in conducting with Morel, Ehrling, Karajan, Slatkin, and Blomstedt at the Juilliard School (M.M.A., 1975; D.M.A., 1977), where she also was an assistant to Boulez and the first woman to take a doctorate in orchestral conducting. She was an Exxon-Arts Endowment conductor with the Pittsburgh Sym. Orch. (1978–80), and concurrently was music director of the Pittsburgh Youth Orch. She was music director (1982–85) and artistic director (1986–88) of the Bel Canto Opera Co. in N.Y., and also was music director of the Empire State Youth Orch. in Albany (1984–86). In 1985–86 she was an asst. conductor at the N.Y. City Opera. From 1986 to 1995 she was artistic director of Opera Roanoke, and from 1989 to 1995 she was music director of the Roanoke Sym. Orch. In 1997 she became artistic advisor of the Wuhan Sym. Orch. in China and in 1998 artistic director of the Harrisburg (Pa.) Opera. As a guest conductor, she appeared widely in the U.S., Europe, and Asia, making special effort to champion out-of-the-ordinary repertoire, including scores by women composers.

WORKS: DRAMATIC: O p e r a : *Gulliver,* after Swift (1987; Louisville, March 17, 1988); *Travels* (1994; Roanoke, May 18, 1995, composer conducting); *Mrs. Satan* (1999–2000; N.Y., April 27, 2000). M u s i c a l : *Everyone is Good for Something* (1986). B a l l e t : *Equinox* (Philadelphia, Oct. 13, 1977); *Other Selves* (Lenox, Mass., Aug. 21, 1979); *Sandburg Suite* (1980); *Great Galloping Gottschalk* (1981; Miami, Jan. 12, 1982); *Rage* (1993). ORCH.: *C-A-G-E-D* for Strings (Cabrillo, Calif., Aug. 17, 1974); *Equinox,* suite from the ballet (1977; Dublin, July 7, 1982, composer conducting); Concertino (1980); *The Frog Prince* (Albany, N.Y., April 28, 1984, composer conducting); *What's the Point of Counterpoint?* for Narrator and Orch. (1985); *Ringing* (Houston, July 4, 1986, composer conducting); Piano Concerto, *Black Light* (1988; rev. 1997); *Urban Bird* (San Francisco, April 3, 1993); *Thinking Like a Mountain* (Shanghai, Dec. 4, 1994, composer conducting); *Variations on a Theme of Brahms* (N.Y., Feb. 6, 1998). B a n d : *White on Black* (1983). CHAMBER: Duet for Flute and Viola (1969; Los Angeles, Oct. 25, 1970); *Can(n)ons* for Clarinet and Violin (Los Angeles, Oct. 25, 1970); Cello Sonata (Los Angeles, June 20, 1971); *Conversation Piece* for Viola and Vibraphone (N.Y., Aug. 15, 1975); *Notes From Underground* for Alto Saxophone and Piano (Kingsport, Tenn., Oct. 9, 1985); *Hot Air* for Woodwind Quintet (1991; Pittsburgh, March 6, 1992); *Dreams of Flying* for String Quartet (1994; Sofia, Sept. 3, 1995);

Chi for Bamboo Flute and Zheng (N.Y., April 16, 1997); *Moli Hua* for Viola (1999). KEYBOARD: P i a n o : *Potirion Sotiriu* (1999). O r g a n : *D-Day* (Roanoke, June 6, 1994). VOCAL: *Suite aux Troubadours* for Soprano and Instruments (Los Angeles, Oct. 25, 1970); *From an Antique Land,* song cycle for Soprano and Piano, after Millay, Shelley, and Hopkins (1972; N.Y., Nov. 10, 1976); *Peter Quince at the Clavier* for Soprano and Piano, after Wallace Stevens (N.Y., April 16, 1978); *Tarot* for Soprano, Chorus, and Percussion Ensemble (Fairmont, W.Va., April 17, 1978); *Molly Manybloom* for Soprano and String Quartet, after James Joyce (1990; Albany, N.Y., March 10, 1991); *A Modest Proposal* for Tenor and Orch. (1999; Cleveland, Feb. 7, 2000, composer conducting).—NS/LK/DM

Bondeville, Emmanuel (Pierre Georges) de, French composer; b. Rouen, Oct. 29, 1898; d. Paris, Nov. 26, 1987. He studied organ in Rouen and composition at the Paris Cons. He served as music director of the Eiffel Tower radio station (1935–49), artistic director of the Monte Carlo Opera (1945–49), and director of the Paris Opéra (1952–70). In 1959 he was elected a member of the Académie des Beaux-Arts of the Institut de France.

WORKS: DRAMATIC: O p e r a : *L'École des maris* (Paris, June 19, 1935); *Madame Bovary* (Paris, June 1, 1951); *Antoine et Cléopâtre* (Rouen, March 10, 1974). ORCH.: Symphonic triptych after Rimbaud's *Illuminations*: *Le Bal des pendus* (Paris, Dec. 6, 1930), *Ophélie* (Paris, March, 29, 1933) and *Marine* (Paris, March 11, 1934); *Symphonie lyrique* (1957); *Symphonie choréogaphie* (1965). OTHER: Choral pieces; songs; Piano Sonata.—NS/LK/DM

Bondon, Jacques (Lauret Jules Désiré), French composer; b. Boulbon, Bouches-du-Rhône, Dec. 6, 1927. He studied violin and painting. In 1945 he settled in Paris, where he was a student of Dandelot, Koechlin, Milhaud, and Rivier. In 1963 he became a member of the music committee of the ORTF. In 1981 he became director of the Georges Bizet Cons. In 1979 he won the Henri Dauberville prize of the Institut de France.

WORKS: DRAMATIC: O p e r a : *La nuit foudroyée* (1964); *Mélusine au rocher* (1964; Luxembourg, Oct. 30, 1969); *Les arbres* (1969); *Ana et l'albatros* (Metz, Nov. 21, 1970); *I-330* (1974; Nantes, May 20, 1975). ORCH.: *La coupole* (1953); *Le taillis ensorcelé* (1954); Ondes Martenot Concerto (1955); *Concert de printemps* (1957); *Suite indienne* (1958); *Giocoso* for Violin and Strings (1960); *Fleurs de feu* (1964); *Concerto de Mars* for Guitar and Orch. (1965); *Ivanhoë* (1966); *Concerto de Molines* for Violin and Orch. (1967); *Symphonie latine* (1973); *Chant et danse* for Trombone and Small Orch. (1974); *Concerto solaire* for 7 Brass Instruments and Orch. (1974); *Lumières et formes animées* for Strings (1974); *Concerto d'octobre* for Clarinet and Strings (1976); *Concerto con fuoco* for Guitar and Strings (1980); *Concerto pour un ballet* for Flute and Orch. (1982). *Trois images concertantes* for Bassoon and Orch. (1982); *Concerto cantabile* for Cello and Orch. (1995); *Concerto vivo* for Harp and Orch. (1997); *Concerto deciso* for Trombone and Orch. (1997); *Concerto des offrandes* for Clarinet and Orch. (1998); Piano Concerto (1999). CHAMBER: *Sonatine d'ete* for Violin and Piano (1953); *Kaléidoscope* for Chamber Ensemble (1957); String Quartet (1959); *Le Maya* for 10 Percussion, Ondes Martenot, and Harp (1965); *Le soleil multicolore* for Flute, Viola, and Harp (1970); *Swing No. 1* for Flute and

Harp (1972) and *No. 2* for Guitar (1972); *Musique pour un jazz différent* for Percussion Quartet (1973); Symphonie concertante for 11 Instruments (1978); *Le tombeau de Schubert* for String Quartet and Piano (1979); *Movimenti* for Clarinet or Saxophone Quartet (1980); *Lever du jour* for Trumpet and Organ (1982); *Les folklores imaginaires No. 1* for Wind Quintet (1985), *No. 2* for Guitar, Flute, and Violin (1986; also for Piano, Flute, and Violin), and *No. 3* for 2 Guitars (1989); *Musiques pour un regard* for String Sextet (1988); *Sonate à cinq* for Flute, Harp, Violin, Viola, and Cello (1992); *Sinfonia* for 16 Instruments (1993); *Danses fantastiques* for Violins and Piano (1996). **VOCAL:** *Le pain de serpent* for Soprano and Chamber Ensemble (1957); *Le résurrection*, oratorio for 4 Soloists, Chorus, and Orch. (1975); *Les monts de l'étoile* for Soprano and String Quartet (1977; also for Soprano and Orch., 1978); *Le chemin de croix*, oratorio for 3 Soloists, Chorus, and Orch. (1989).—**NS/LK/DM**

Bonds, Margaret (Allison), black American pianist, teacher, and composer; b. Chicago, March 3, 1913; d. Los Angeles, April 26, 1972. She first studied with her mother, then had training in piano and composition from Florence Price; also studied with William Dawson. Following studies at Northwestern Univ. (B.M., 1933; M.M., 1934), she went to N.Y. and pursued training with Djane Herz (piano) and Starer (composition) at the Juilliard Graduate School. She also had some training from Roy Harris. In 1933 she became the first black soloist to appear with the Chicago Sym. Orch. when she played Florence Price's Piano Concerto at the World's Fair. She subsequently made tours of North America. In Chicago she founded the Allied Arts Academy. After working in N.Y. as a theater music director and as a teacher, she settled in Los Angeles. As a composer, Bonds became best known for her spirituals for Solo Voice and/or Chorus, and also for her popular songs. Among her other works were the theater scores *Shakespeare in Harlem, Romey and Julie*, and *U.S.A.*, ballets, *Montgomery Variations* for Orch. (1965; dedicated to Martin Luther King Jr.), *Credo* for Baritone, Chorus, and Orch. (1972), choruses, song cycles, and piano pieces.—**LK/DM**

Bonelli (Bunn), Richard, American baritone; b. Port Byron, N.Y., Feb. 6, 1887; d. Los Angeles, June 7, 1980. He studied at Syracuse Univ. and with Arthur Alexander and Jean de Reszke in Paris. On April 21, 1915, he made his operatic debut as Valentine at the Brooklyn Academy of Music. After appearances at the Monte Carlo Opera, Milan's La Scala, and in Paris, he sang with the Chicago Opera (1925–31). On Dec. 1, 1932, he made his Metropolitan Opera debut in N.Y. as Germont, remaining on its roster until 1945. Thereafter he taught at the Curtis Inst. of Music in Philadelphia and in N.Y. He was best known for his Verdi roles, but also was praised for his portrayals of Wolfram, Tonio, and Sharpless.—**NS/LK/DM**

Bonfichi, Paolo, Italian organist and composer; b. Livraga, near Lodi, Oct. 6, 1769; d. Lodi, Dec. 29, 1840. He was self-taught as a keyboard performer; attended the Univ. of Parma, where he studied figured bass. He entered the order of Servi di Maria in 1787, but returned

to music while in Rome as a student of counterpoint with Guglielmo. He then lived in a monastery in Poïna (1796–1805); subsequently was in Milan; in 1829 became maestro di cappella at the Santa Casa of Loreto, where he remained until 1839. He composed mainly music for the church, including oratorios and cantatas.
—**NS/LK/DM**

Bonhomme, Pierre, South Netherlands composer; b. c. 1555; d. Liège, June 12, 1617. He was educated in Liège, receiving the tonsure in 1579. In 1594 was awarded a canonry at the collegiate church of Sainte-Croix in Liège, where he spent the rest of his life. He publ. *Melodiae sacrae* for 5 to 9 Voices (Frankfurt, 1603) and *Missae* for 6, 8, 10, and 12 Voices (Antwerp, 1616).—**NS/LK/DM**

Boni, Guillaume, French composer who flourished in the second half of the 16th century. He was maître de chapelle at the Cathedral in Toulouse. His sacred vocal works include motets and Psalms; he also composed secular sonnets after Ronsard.—**NS/LK/DM**

Bonini, Severo, Italian composer, organist, and writer on music; b. Florence, Dec. 23, 1582; d. there, Dec. 5, 1663. He received the habit of the Vallombrosan Benedictines in 1595 and professed in 1598. He then studied theology and other subjects at the Univ. at Passignano; subsequently resided in an abbey in Florence. In 1611 he became organist at the abbey of S. Trinita, and in 1613 he assumed a similar position at S. Mercuriale in Forlì. In 1615 he was made camarlingo at the abbey of S. Michele in Forcole, Pistoia, and in 1619 at S. Mercuriale in Forlì. In 1623 he became curate at S. Martino in Strada, where he remained until 1637. In 1640 he was named organist and maestro di cappella at S. Trinita, posts he retained until his death. He wrote a valuable treatise on the beginnings of monody and opera, *Discorsi e regole sovra la musica et il contrappunto* (modern ed. and tr. by M. Bonino, Provo, Utah, 1978).

WORKS: *Madrigali e canzonette spirituali* for Voice and Instruments (Florence, 1607); *Il primo libro delle canzonette affettuose in stile moderno* for 4 Voices (Florence, 1608; not extant); *Il primo libro de' motetti* for 3 Voices, Organ, and Instruments (Venice, 1609); *Il secondo libro de' madrigali e motetti* for 1 and 2 Voices and Instruments (Florence, 1609); *Lamento d'Arianna in stile recitativo* for 1 and 2 Voices (Venice, 1613); *Affetti spirituali* for 2 Voices (Venice, 1615); *Serena aleste*, Motetti for 1 to 3 Voices (Venice, 1615).

BIBL.: M. Bonino, *Don S. B. (1582–1663): His "Discorsi e regole"* (diss., Univ. of Southern Calif., 1971).—**NS/LK/DM**

Boninsegna, Celestina, Italian soprano; b. Reggio Emilia, Feb. 26, 1877; d. Milan, Feb. 14, 1947. Without the benefit of vocal training, she made her debut at the age of 15 at Reggio Emilia as Norina; then enrolled at the Pesaro Cons.; her official debut took place in Fano in 1896, when she appeared as Gilda; then sang in Milan, Rome, Genoa, and South America; also at London's Covent Garden (1904, 1905). On Dec. 21, 1906, she made her Metropolitan Opera debut in N.Y. as Aida, but remained on the roster for only that 1 season. In 1909–10 she sang with the Boston Opera. Following her retirement, she taught voice; spent her last years in the Casa di Riposo in Milan.—NS/LK/DM

Bónis, Ferenc, Hungarian musicologist; b. Miskolc, May 17,1932. He studied composition with Szervánszky and musicology with Bartha, Kodály, and Szabolcsi at the Budapest Academy of Music (Ph.D., 1958, with the diss. *Mosonyi Mihály*). He was an ed. (1950–52; 1957–70) and director of programs in music for young audiences (1970–96) with the Hungarian Radio. From 1961 to 1973 he pursued musicological research at the Hungarian Academy of Sciences. He was made a lecturer at the Budapest Academy of Music in 1972 and the Univ. of Cologne in 1996. He became ed. of *Magyar Zenetudomány* in 1959, and also of *Magyar Zenetörteneti Tanulmányok* in 1968. In 1989 he became president of the Ferenc Erkel Soc., and also of the Hungarian Kodály Soc. in 1992.

WRITINGS: *Erkel Ferenc* (1953); *Bartók élete képekben* (1956; Ger. tr., 1964; Fr. tr., 1964; Eng. tr., 1964, as *Béla Bartók: His Life in Pictures*); *Kadosa Pál* (1965); ed. *Tóth Aladár válogatott zenekritikai* (1968); *Bartók Bélá élete képekben és dokumentumokban* (1972; Ger. tr., 1972; Eng. tr., 1972, as *Béla Bartók: His Life in Pictures and Documents*; Russ. tr., 1981; Japanese tr., 1981); *Tizenhárom találkozás Ferencsik Jánossal* (1984); *Kodály Zoltán Psalmus Hungaricusa* (1987); *Hódolat Bartóknak és Kodálynak* (1991); *Bartók-Lengyel, A csodálatos mandarin* (1992); *The Dance Suite of Béla Bartók* (1998; also in Hungarian and Ger.); *Mozarttól- Bartókig* (2000).—NS/LK/DM

Bon Jovi, the band that defined mid-1980s pop-metal. **MEMBERSHIP:** Jon Bon Jovi (real name, John Francis Bongiovi), gtr., voc. (b. Pert Amboy, N.J., March 2, 1962); Richie Sambora, gtr. (b. Woodbridge, N.J., July 11, 1959); David Bryan, kybd. (b. Feb. 7, 1962); Alec John Such, bs. (b. Yonkers, N.Y., Nov. 14, 1956); Tico Torres (real name, Hector Torres), drm. (b. N.Y.C., Oct. 7, 1953). The son of a hairdresser and former Playboy Bunny–turned-florist, John Bongiovi slept through his SATs, having played a gig the night before. He decided he didn't need to take the test to become a rock star. In his case, he was right.

Bongiovi started playing the guitar in grade school, but got serious about it early in high school. He had trouble making small talk and used his guitar- playing skills as a means to pick up girls. He started playing in clubs and dances with various bands, several including keyboard player David Bryan Rashbaum. By age 16, he was hanging out with Southside Johnny and jamming with Bruce Springsteen and the E Street Band.

John's uncle, Tony Bongiovi, owned and operated the Power Station, one of the top studios of the 1970s and 1980s, and hired John to sweep floors in the studio and let him sleep in the top floor apartment. Tony had young John sing a tune on the Star Wars Christmas Album, "Christmas with the Stars" in 1978. During downtime, John recorded demos. One tune, "Runaway," recorded with members of the E Street Band, started getting radio play in the N.Y. area. He was signed to PolyGram worldwide and put together a band

of friends from the Jersey shore. These including drummer Tico Torres, bassist Alec John Such, Rashbaum, and guitaist Dave Sabo, who was replaced by Richie Sambora and later joined Skid Row. Rashbaum lost his last name, becoming David Bryan and Bongiovi changed his name to the less ethnic Jon Bon Jovi.

The group recorded their eponymous debut, released in 1984. The first single, a cover of "She Don't Know Me" recorded at the insistence of the album's producer, hit #48. The follow-up, "Runaway" actually cracked the Top 40, spending a week at #39. The album sold respectably, hitting #43. The band toured relentlessly behind the album, a habit they maintained through the mid-1990s.

The next album, 1985's *7800 Fahrenheit*, succumbed to the sophomore jinx, peaking at #37 as a result of the band's constant touring, but producing no chart singles. For their third album, the band took several steps. They brought in professional songwriter Desmond Child to help polish their songs, then tested them for teen audiences, basing what they used on the reaction. They recorded in Vancouver, spending much of their down time in strip clubs. From a shower act at one of these clubs came the title *Slippery When Wet*. The lead single from the album, "You Give Love a Bad Name" topped the U.S. charts, as did the follow-up, "Livin' on a Prayer." "Wanted Dead or Alive" came in at #7. The album topped the charts, sold 11 million copies, and suddenly Bon Jovi was the biggest name in pop music, and pop metal became the sound of young America circa 1986.

The band took to the road for nearly two years. They went into the studio and followed up with the world-wide chart topper N.J. This one sold six million copies on the strength of singles like the #1 hits "I'll Be There for You" and "Bad Medicine," the #3 "Born to Be My Baby," and the Top Ten hits "Lay Your Hands on Me" and "Living in Sin."

After another grueling world tour, the band announced that they were taking a break. Bon Jovi recorded music for the soundtrack of the movie *Young Guns*, including the chart topping single "Blaze of Glory," which became the title track of the album. The album charted at #3, and the follow-up single "Miracle" topped out at #12. He made a cameo appearance in the film, and was so intrigued by acting, he started taking lessons with renowned teacher Harold Guskin.

Sambora also recorded a solo album, the hard rocking *Stranger in Town*, which charted at #36. Bryan did an album of more textural music during the hiatus, as well. The band also received an MTV Lifetime Achievement Award, an odd thing considering how they usually made very simple performance style clips.

After four years away from each other, they came back together re-energized. Leaning more on the power ballads than the rockers, the single "Keep The Faith" and album of the same name both did better overseas than in the U.S., though the album did sell two million copies and reach #5. "Bed of Roses" hit #10 on the charts and "In These Arms" #27. "I'll Sleep When I'm Dead," however, barely cracked the Hot 100, and "I

Believe" and "Dry County" didn't.

After another exhausting world tour, the band took another break. During this hiatus, Bon Jovi tested his acting skills in a few independent films, in addition to modeling for Versace.

The #4 single "Always" heralded the greatest hits-plus package *Cross Road*. The other single "Someday I'll Be Saturday Night" didn't chart in the U.S., but went to ten in England. The band's next album, *These Days*, had a similar fate. While it clocked in at a respectable #9 in the U.S., it topped the English charts. "This Ain't a Love Song" hit #14, but the other two singles, which went Top Ten over there didn't even chart in the U.S.

The band went on two more grueling world tours. In 1984, they played to audiences in 37 countries—45 the next year. Bon Jovi made three more films and then returned to music with *Destination Anywhere*. Produced by Eurythmic Dave Stewart and Steve Lironi, the album featured hard rock licks and computer loops. Sambora released his *Undiscovered Soul* a year later. The band expected to regroup for an album due just at the turn of the millenium.

DISC.: BON JOVI: *Bon Jovi* (1984); *Slippery When Wet* (1986); *Bon Jovi Live* (1987); *New Jersey* (1988); *Keep The Faith* (1993); *These Days* (1995). **JON BON JOVI:** *Young Guns II: "Blaze of Glory" (Music from...)* (1990); *Destination Anywhere* (1997). **RICHIE SAMBORA:** *Stranger in Town* (1991); *Undiscovered Soul* (1998). **DAVID BRYAN:** *Netherworld* (1992). —HB

Bonner, Eugene (MacDonald), American composer and music critic; b. Jacksonville, N.C., 1889; d. Taormina, Sicily, Dec. 8, 1983. He studied at the Peabody Cons. of Music in Baltimore and received training in piano with Bachner and Hutcheson, in organ with Philips, and in composition with Bois and Brockway; during a European sojourn (1911–17), pursued studies in composition and instrumentation with Scott, Lehmann, and Bedford; during a second European sojourn, took courses in instrumentation and conducting with Wolff in Paris (1921–27). Returning to the U.S., he became music ed. of *Outlook Magazine* (1927–29); subsequently was a music critic for the *Brooklyn Eagle*, the *Daily Mirror*, *Cue Magazine*, and the *N.Y. Herald Tribune*, and managing ed. of the *Musical Record*. In 1955 he settled in Taormina.

WORKS: DRAMATIC: O p e r a : *Barbara Frietchie* (1921); *Celui qui Épousa une Femme Muette* (1923); *The Venetian Glass Nephew* (1927); *The Gods of the Mountain* (1936); *Frankie and Johnnie* (1945). **I n c i d e n t a l M u s i c T o :** *The Young Alexander* (1929). **ORCH.:** *White Nights* (1925); *Taormina*, little suite (1939); Concertino for Piano and String Orch. (1945). **CHAMBER:** Piano Quintet (1925); *Suite Sicilienne* for Violin and Piano (1926). **VOCAL:** *Whispers of Heavenly Death*, 3 songs for Voice and Orch. (1922); *Flutes* for Voice and 4 Instruments (1923).—NS/LK/DM

Bonnet, Joseph (Élie Georges Marie), eminent French organist, pedagogue, and composer; b. Bordeaux, March 17, 1884; d. Ste. Luce-sur-Mer, Quebec, Aug. 2, 1944. He studied with his father, organist at Ste. Eulalie; at the age of 14, he was appointed regular organist at St. Nicholas, and soon after at St. Michel; entered the class of Guilmant at the Paris Cons. and graduated with first prize. In 1906 he won the post of organist at St. Eustache over many competitors. After extensive tours on the Continent and in England, he became organist of the Concerts du Conservatoire as successor to Guilmant in 1911, which position he retained until 1939. He made his American debut in N.Y. (Jan. 30, 1917), followed by successful tours of the U.S. In 1940 he fled France and went to the U.S., finally settling in Quebec as a teacher at the Cons. He wrote many pieces for his instrument, and ed. for publication all the works played in his series of N.Y. concerts as *Historical Organ Recitals* (6 vols.); also publ. an anthology of early French organ music (N.Y., 1942). —NS/LK/DM

Bonney, Barbara, admired American soprano; b. Montclair, N.J., April 14, 1956. She received training in Canada and with Walter Raninger at the Salzburg Mozarteum. In 1979 she became a member of the Darmstadt Opera, where she made her first appearance as Anna in *Die lustigen Weiber von Windsor*; among her subsequent roles were Blondchen, Adina, Cherubino, Gilda, Massenet's Manon, and Natalie in Henze's *Der Prinz von Homburg*. In 1983–84 she appeared with the Frankfurt am Main Opera, the Hamburg State Opera, and the Bavarian State Opera in Munich. In 1984 she made her first appearance at London's Covent Garden as Sophie. In 1985 she made her debut at Milan's La Scala as Pamina. She made her Metropolitan Opera debut in N.Y. on March 3, 1988, as Najade in *Ariadne auf Naxos*, where she returned to sing Adele and Sophie. In 1989 she made her first appearance at the Chicago Lyric Opera as Adele. In 1991 she sang in the Mozart Bicentenary Gala at Covent Garden. After singing Sophie at the Metropolitan Opera that year, she returned there as Adina in 1996 and as Susanna in 1997. She was engaged in 1997 as a soloist in the centenary performance of the Brahms *Requiem* in Vienna. On Aug. 7, 1997 she made her N.Y. recital debut at Alice Tully Hall, followed by her Carnegie Hall recital debut on Jan. 31, 1998. In addition to her distinguished operatic career, Bonney has won acclaim for her appearances as a soloist with the world's leading orchs. and as a recitalist. She has made frequent appearances with her husband **Håkan Hagegård.**—NS/LK/DM

Bonno, Giuseppe, noted Austrian composer of Italian descent; b. Vienna, Jan. 29, 1711; d. there, April 15, 1788. His father, Lucrezio Bonno, was the imperial footman. Giuseppe Bonno began his musical studies with Johann Georg Reinhardt, the court organist. Charles VI sent Bonno to Naples in 1726 for further musical education; there he studied composition with Durante and Leo. His first opera, *Nigella e Nise*, was performed in Naples in 1732. In 1736 he returned to Vienna, where he brought out his second opera, *L'amore insuperabile*. In 1737 he was made a court scholar in composition, and in 1739 was named court composer. In 1739 he brought out his oratorio *Eleazaro*, which proved highly successful. He subsequently joined Gluck and Dittersdorf as a Kapellmeister to Field Marshall Joseph

Friedrich, Prince of Sachsen-Hildburghausen, in Schlosshof and Mannersdorf. In 1774 he succeeded Gassmann as Imperial Court Kapellmeister. Bonno was greatly esteemed as a teacher; Dittersdorf and Marianne di Martinez were among his pupils. He was a friend of the Mozart family, and recognized the budding genius of Mozart at an early date.

WORKS: DRAMATIC (all first perf. at the Burgtheater in Vienna unless otherwise given): *Nigella e Nise*, pastorale (Naples, 1732); *L'amore insuperabile*, festa di camera (July 26, 1736); *Trajano*, festa di camera (Oct. 1, 1736); *La gara del genio con Giunone*, serenata (Laxenburg, May 13, 1737); *Alessandro Severo*, festa di camera (Oct. 1, 1737); *La generosità di Artaserse*, serenata (Nov. 4, 1737); a pastorale (Nov. 19, 1737); *La pace richiamata*, festa di camera (July 26, 1738); *La pietà di Numa*, festa di camera (Oct. 1, 1738); *La vera nobiltà*, festa di camera (July 26, 1739); *Il natale di Numa Pompilio*, festa di camera (Oct. 1, 1739); *Il nume d'Atene*, festa di camera (Nov. 19, 1739); *La generosa Spartana*, serenata (Laxenburg, May 13, 1740); *Il natale di Giove*, azione teatrale (Favorita, Vienna, Oct. 1, 1740); *Il vero omaggio*, componimento drammatico (Schloss Schönbrunn, Vienna, March 13, 1743); *La danza*, cantata (April 1744); *Danae*, opera (1744; not extant); *Ezio*, opera (1749; not extant); *Il Re pastore*, dramma per musica (Schloss Schönbrunn, Vienna, Oct. 27, 1751); *L'Ero cinese*, opera (Schloss Schönbrunn, Vienna, May 13, 1752); *L'isola disabitata*, azione teatrale (Sept. 23, 1754); *Didone abbandonata*, opera (1752; not extant); *Colloquio amoroso fra Piramo e Tisbe* (1757); *Complimento*, for the Prince of Sachsen-Hildburghausen (1761; not extant); *L'Atenaide ovvero Gli affetti più generosi*, azione teatrale (1762); *Il sogno di Scipione* (1763); also, in collaboration with others, *Catone in Utica* (1742) and *L'Armida placata* (Oct. 8, 1750). **ORATORIOS** (all perf. in Vienna): *Eleazaro* (1739); *San Paolo in Athene* (March 31, 1740); *Isacco figura del redentore* (March 18, 1759); *Il Giuseppe riconosciuto* (March 20, 1774). **OTHER:** Masses and instrumental works.

BIBL.: A. Schienerl, *Die kirchlichen Kompositionen des G. B.* (diss., Univ. of Vienna, 1925); K. Breitner, *G. B. und sein Oratorienwerk* (diss., Univ. of Vienna, 1961).—NS/LK/DM

Bononcini, Antonio Maria,

Italian opera composer, son of **Giovannia Maria** and brother of **Giovanni Bononcini;** b. Modena, June 18, 1677; d. there, July 8, 1726. He studied with his father. His first success came with the production of his opera *Il trionfo di Camilla, regina dei Volsci* (Naples, Dec. 26, 1696). This opera was produced in many other theaters in Italy, sometimes under different titles, as *Amore per amore, La fede in cimento*, etc. It was presented in London (March 31, 1706) with great acclaim. In 1702 Bononcini was in Berlin; from 1704 to 1711 he was in Vienna, where he produced the operas *Teraspo* (Nov. 15, 1704), *Arminio* (July 26, 1706), *La conquista delle Spagne di Scipione Africano* (Oct. 1, 1707), *La presa di Tebe* (Oct. 1, 1708), and *Tigrane, re d'Armenia* (July 26, 1710). Returning to Italy, he produced the following operas in Milan: *Il Tiranno eroe* (Dec. 26, 1715), *Sesostri, re di Egitto* (Feb. 2, 1716), and *Griselda* (Dec. 26, 1718). In his native town of Modena, he directed his operas *L'enigma disciolto* (Oct. 15, 1716) and *Lucio Vero* (Nov. 5, 1716). His last opera, *Rosiclea in Dania*, was staged in Naples (Oct. 1, 1721). He wrote 19 operas in all, and 3 oratorios. His most famous opera, *Il trionfo di Camilla*, has often been erroneously attributed to his brother; several songs from it were publ. in London by Walsh.

BIBL.: L.F. Valdrighi, *I B. da Modena* (Modena, 1882). —NS/LK/DM

Bononcini, Giovanni,

Italian composer, son of **Giovanni Maria** and brother of **Antonio Maria Bononcini;** b. Modena, July 18, 1670; d. Vienna, July 9, 1747 (buried July 11). His first teacher was his father, and he also studied with G.P. Colonna in Bologna and took cello lessons from Giorgio. In 1687 he was a cellist in the chapel of S. Petronio in Bologna; in the same year he became maestro di cappella at S. Giovanni in Monte. He publ. his first work, *Trattenimenti da camera* for String Trio, in Bologna at the age of 15. This was followed in quick succession by a set of chamber concertos, "sinfonie" for small ensembles, masses, and instrumental duos (1685–91). In 1691 he went to Rome, where he produced his first opera, *Serse* (Jan. 25, 1694), and shortly afterward, another opera, *Tullo Ostilio* (Feb. 1694). In 1698 he went to Vienna as court composer, where he brought out his operas *La fede pubblica* (Jan. 6, 1699) and *Gli affetti piu grandi vinti dal piu giusto* (July 26, 1701). He spent 2 years (1702–04) at the court of Queen Sophie Charlotte in Berlin. At her palace in Charlottenburg he produced, in the summer of 1702, the opera *Polifemo*, as well as a new opera, *Gli amori di Cefalo e Procri* (Oct. 16, 1704). After the Queen's death (Feb. 1, 1705) the opera company was disbanded. Bononcini returned to Vienna and staged the following operas: *Endimione* (July 10, 1706), *Turno Aricino* (July 26, 1707), *Mario fuggitivo* (1708), *Abdolonimo* (Feb. 3, 1709), and *Muzio Scevola* (July 10, 1710). In 1711 Bononcini returned to Italy with his brother (who had also been in Vienna). In 1719 he was in Rome, where he produced the opera *Erminia*. In 1720 he received an invitation to join the Royal Academy of Music in London, of which Handel was director, and the Italian Opera Co. connected with it. A famous rivalry developed between the supporters of Handel, which included the King, and the group of noblemen (Marlborough, Queensberry, Rutland, and Sunderland) who favored Bononcini and other Italian composers. Indicative of the spirit of the time was the production at the King's Theatre of the opera *Muzio Scevola*, with the first act written by Amadei, the second by Bononcini (he may have used material from his earlier setting of the same subject), and the third by Handel (April 15, 1721). By general agreement Handel won the verdict of popular approval; this episode may have inspired the well-known poem publ. at the time ("Some say, compar'd to Bononcini, That Mynheer Handel's but a ninny," etc.). Other operas brought out by Bononcini in London were *Astarto* (Nov. 19, 1720), *Crispo* (Jan. 10, 1722), *Farnace* (Nov. 27, 1723), *Calpurnia* (April 18, 1724), and *Astianatte* (May 6, 1727). He then suffered a series of setbacks: first the death of his chief supporter, Marlborough (1722), and then the revelation that a madrigal he had submitted to the Academy of Music was an arrangement of a work by Lotti, which put Bononcini's professional integrity in doubt. To this was added his strange association with one Count Ughi, a self-styled alchemist who claimed the invention of a philosopher's stone, and who induced Bononcini to invest his earnings in his scheme for making gold. After his London debacle, Bononcini went (in 1732) to Paris, where he was engaged as a cellist at the court of Louis XV. He was referred to in *Le Mercure de France* (Feb. 7, 1735) as the composer of 78 operas. In 1735 he was in Lisbon; in 1737, in Vienna, where he produced the oratorio *Ezechia* (April 4, 1737) and a *Te Deum* (1740). Reduced to poverty, he petitioned the young Empress Maria Theresa for a pension, which was granted in Oct. 1742, giving him a monthly stipend of 50 florins, received regularly until his death on July 9, 1747, at the age of 77. This date and the circumstances of his last years in Vienna were first made known in the valuable paper by Kurt Hueber, *Gli ultimi anni di Giovanni Bononcini, Notizie e documenti inediti*, publ. by the Academy of Sciences, Letters and Arts of Modena (Dec. 1954). Among Bononcini's works, other than operas, are 7 oratorios (including *Ezechia*; all on various biblical subjects), and instrumental works publ. in London by Walsh: several suites for Harpsichord; *Cantate e Duetti*, dedicated to George I (1721); Divertimenti for Harpsichord (1722); *Funeral Anthem for John, Duke of Marlborough* (1722); 12 Sonatas or Chamber Airs for 2 Violins and a Bass (1732); etc.

BIBL.: K. Hueber, *Die Wiener Opern G. B.s von 1697 bis 1710* (diss., Univ. of Vienna, 1955); L. Lindgren, *A Bibliographic Scrutiny of Dramatic Works Set by G. and His Brother Antonio Maria Bononcini* (diss., Harvard Univ., 1972).—**NS/LK/DM**

Bononcini, Giovanni Maria, Italian composer, father of **Giovanni** and **Antonio Maria Bononcini;** b. Montecorone, Sept. 23, 1642; d. Modena, Nov. 18, 1678. In 1671 he was awarded a ducal appointment as violinist at the Cathedral of Modena. He also served as chamber musician to the Dowager Duchess Laura d'Este. He had 8 children, of whom the only 2 who survived infancy were Giovanni and Antonio Maria Bononcini. He publ. 11 sets of instrumental works: *I primi frutti del giardino musicale* (Venice, 1666); *Varii fiori* (Bologna, 1669); *Arie, correnti, sarabande, gighe e allemande* (Bologna, 1671); *Sonate* (Venice, 1672); *Ariette, correnti, gighe, allemande e sarabande* (Bologna, 1673); *Trattenimenti musicali* (Bologna, 1675); *Arie e correnti* (Bologna, 1678); also the vocal works *Cantate da camara* for Solo Voice and 2 Violins (Bologna, 1677) and *Madrigali* for 5 Voices (Bologna, 1678). He further publ. a didactic manual, *Musico prattico* (Bologna, 1673; Ger. tr., Stuttgart, 1701).

BIBL.: W. Klenz, *G.M. B. of Modena: A Chapter in Baroque Instrumental Music* (Durham, N.C., 1962).—**NS/LK/DM**

Bonporti, Francesco Antonio, Italian composer; b. Trento (baptized), June 11, 1672; d. Padua, Dec. 19, 1748. He studied theology in Innsbruck and Rome. In 1695 he returned to Trento, where he was ordained a priest and served as a cleric at the Cathedral. He publ. 3 sets of 10 trio sonatas each (Venice, 1696, 1698, and 1703); 10 sonatas for Violin and Bass (Venice, 1707); 10 "concerti a 4" and 5 "concertini" for Violin and Bass; 6 motets for Soprano, Violin, and Bass. He also wrote 2 sets of minuets (50 in each set), which are lost. Four of his "invenzioni" were mistaken for Bach's works and were included in the Bachgesellschaft ed. (XLV, part 1, p. 172). Henry Eccles publ. the fourth of these pieces as his

own, incorporating it in his Violin Sonata No. 11.

BIBL.: G. Barblan, *Un Musicista trentino, F.A. B.* (Florence, 1940); G. Barblan, ed., *F.A. B. nel 3 centenario della nascita* (Trent, 1972); L. Feininger, *F.A. B.: Catalogus thematicus operum omnium* (Trent, 1975).—**NS/LK/DM**

Bonsel, Adriaan, Dutch flutist and composer; b. Hilversum, Aug. 4, 1918. He studied at the Amsterdam Cons., and appeared as a flute soloist in recitals and with various orchs.

WORKS: ORCH.: Suite for Flute and Strings (1946); *Folkloristic Suite* (1948); Clarinet Concerto (1950); 2 syms. (1956, 1957); *Divertimento* for Small Orch. (1957); *S.O.S.*, overture (1962); *Vrede-Oorlog-Vrede? (Peace-War-Peace?) Moto-perpetuo?* (1975); *Suite voor bamboe* (1988); Sinfonietta for Amateu Orch. (1990). **CHAMBER:** 2 wind quintets (1949, 1953); *Elegy* for Viola (1961); *Concert Études* for Flute (1963); *Musica* for Flute, Cello, and Piano (1971); *Anthriscus Sylvestris*, divertimento for 12 Flutes (1974); Octet for Winds (1975); *Intrada* for Horn, 2 Trumpets, 2 Trombones, and Tuba (1982); 3 pieces for Flute (1984).—**NS/LK/DM**

Bontempi (real name, Angelini), Giovanni Andrea, Italian singer and composer; b. Perugia, c. 1624; d. Torgiano, July 1, 1705. He was a castrato, and sang in the choir of S. Marco in Venice (1643–50). After studies with Mazzocchi, he was appointed joint Kapellmeister in Dresden, with Schütz and Vincenzo Albrici, in 1656. He assumed the name Bontempi after his patron, Cesare Bontempi. In 1680 he returned to Italy; sang at the Collegiata di S. Maria at Sapello, near Foligno, in 1682; was maestro di cappella there during the first half of 1686. He was one of the earliest composers of Italian operas and oratorios. His first opera, *Il Paride in musica*, to his own libretto, was produced in Dresden, on Nov. 3, 1662; it was the first Italian opera ever produced there. Two later operas, both produced in Dresden, were *Apollo e Dafne*, written in collaboration with Peranda and produced in Dresden on Sept. 3, 1671, and *Giove e Io* (also with Peranda), produced in Dresden on Jan. 16, 1673. He also composed an oratorio, *Martirio di San Emiliano*. Bontempi publ. the treatises *Nova quatuor vocibus componendi methodus* (Dresden, 1660), *Tractus in quo demonstrantur occultae convenientiae sonorum systematis participati* (Bologna, 1690), and *Historia musica, nella quale si ha piena cognitione della teorica e della pratica antica della musica harmonica secondo la dottrina de' Greci* (Perugia, 1695).

BIBL.: G.B. Rossi Scotti, *Di G.A. B. di Perugia* (1878); F. Briganti, *G.A. Angelini-B. (1624–1705), Musicista, letterato, architto: Perugia-Dresda* (Florence, 1956).—**NS/LK/DM**

Bonvin, Ludwig, Swiss-American organist, conductor, music scholar, and composer; b. Sierre, Feb. 17, 1850; d. Buffalo, Feb. 18, 1939. He was mainly autodidact as a musician. He studied medicine in Vienna and law in Switzerland before entering his noviate in a German Jesuit order in Exaeten, the Netherlands, in 1874, where he was active as organist and choirmaster. After his ordination in England in 1885, he settled in Buffalo in 1887, where he was active with various academic institutions until 1929. He championed the cause of applying mensural rhythm to Gregorian chant and publ. the study *Musical Accents in Gregorian Chant* (1932). In his own works, he pursued a late Romantic style. Several of his works were publ. under the pseudynyms J.B. Rainer, B. von Siders, and Georges De'Sierre. Among his extensive output were a Sym., 6 tone poems, 17 pieces for chamber ensembles, 10 masses and other choral works with orch., numerous sacred and secular choruses, 11 song cycles, piano pieces, and organ works.—LK/DM

Bonynge, Richard (Alan), noted Australian conductor; b. Sydney, Sept. 29, 1930. He studied piano at the New South Wales Conservatorium of Music in Sydney and at the Royal Coll. of Music in London, beginning his career as a pianist. After marrying **Joan Sutherland** in 1954, he devoted himself to helping her master the bel canto operatic repertoire. In 1962 he made his conducting debut in a concert with his wife in Rome; he then made his debut as an opera conductor with a performance of *Faust* in Vancouver (1963). He made his first appearance at London's Covent Garden in 1964, leading a performance of *I Puritani*. On Dec. 12, 1966, he made his Metropolitan Opera debut in N.Y., conducting *Lucia di Lammermoor*, with his wife in the title role. In subsequent years he conducted concerts and operas throughout the world. He was music director of the Australian Opera in Sydney from 1976 to 1986. In 1977 he was made a Commander of the Order of the British Empire.

BIBL.: Q. Eaton, *Sutherland & B.: An Intimate Biography* (N.Y., 1987).—NS/LK/DM

Booker, James, American jazz pianist; b. New Orleans, La., Dec. 17, 1939; d. there, Nov. 8, 1983. The troubled, flamboyant master of New Orleans piano, James Carroll Booker had so much technique and energy that other keyboard players were in awe. On a good night Booker could take those 88s and drive tunes into an ever-widening spiral of improvisation that left performers such as Mac Rebennack (a.k.a. Dr. John) and Allen Toussaint with their jaws hanging to the floor. Trained in the classics and picking up R&B licks on the side, Booker had the kind of technical grounding which let him segue from Chopin to bop-influenced riffs and traditional New Orleans habanera-tinged barrelhouse with ease. Rebennack has called Booker a genius, and few who have heard him on a good night would deny the possibility.

In 1960 Booker had a Top 40 hit with "Gonzo," a raucous organ instrumental released on Don Robey's Peacock label. He also did a lot of session work for Imperial, King, and Reprise in addition to working with Fats Domino, Sam Cooke, Aretha Franklin, B.B. King, Little Richard, Wilson Pickett, Joe Tex, and Lloyd Price, among others. Still, idiosyncrasies and drug dependency had derailed other major talents, keeping them from a life their abilities deserved, and Booker was no exception to the rule. A convicted felon and drug addict, having spent time at L.A.'s Angola State Prison and the Anchora Mental Institution, Booker's offstage behavior often interfered with his onstage responsibilities. The

last year of his life found him working a day job in the New Orleans city hall.

DISC.: *Junco Partner* (1976); *King of the New Orleans Keyboard* (1976); *New Orleans Piano Wizard: Live!* (1977); *Resurrection of the Bayou Maharajah* (1977); *Classified* (1982); *Spiders on the Keys* (1993); *The Lost Paramount Tapes* (1995); *Gonzo: More Than All the 45's* (1996).—GM

Booker T. and the MGs, best remembered historically as the studio band for Stax/Volt Records during the 1960s, the band created the so-called Memphis Sound, illustrated in the hit recordings of Carla and Rufus Thomas, Otis Redding, and Sam and Dave, among others. **MEMBERSHIP:** Booker T. Jones, kybd., gtr., bs. (b. Memphis, Tenn., Nov. 12, 1944); Steve Cropper, lead and rhythm gtr. (b. Willow Springs, Mo., Oct. 21, 1941); Donald "Duck" Dunn, bs. (b. Memphis, Tenn., Nov. 24, 1941); Al Jackson Jr., drms. (b. Memphis, Tenn., Nov. 27, 1935; d. there, Oct. 1, 1975).

Perhaps the last rock band to issue albums comprised entirely of instrumentals, Booker T. and the MGs featured cohesive yet spare sound on hits of their own, such as "Green Onions," "Hang 'Em High," and "Time Is Tight." They were also one of the few multiracial bands, with two black men (Jones and Jackson) and two white.

In 1962 Booker T. and the MGs (for *Memphis* Group) formed as the house band for Memphis's Stax Records. Steve Cropper and Donald "Duck" Dunn had been members of the Mar-Keys since the late 1950s, and both played on the group's 1961 instrumental hit "Last Night." Dunn remained with the Mar-Keys until 1964 while also playing as part of the MGs. In the early 1960s Booker T. and the MGs provided the instrumental backing for hits by Carla Thomas ("Gee Whiz") and her father Rufus Thomas ("Walking the Dog"). Their reputation as a band in their own right was established in 1962 with the smash instrumental hit "Green Onions."

Over the next seven years Booker T. and the MGs recorded independently and backed various Stax/Volt artists while individual members pursued solo projects. Booker T. Jones cowrote with artist-producer William Bell the oft-recorded blues classic "Born under a Bad Sign." In 1966 Jones received a degree in music from Ind. Univ. In the meantime, Steve Cropper supervised the recordings of Otis Redding and cowrote hits by Wilson Pickett ("In the Midnight Hour"), Eddie Floyd ("Knock on Wood"), and Redding ("[Sittin' on the] Dock of the Bay"). Al Jackson produced recordings by blues guitarist Albert King. Booker T. and the MGs also served as the backing band for Sam and Dave's two biggest hits, "Hold On! I'm Coming" and "Soul Man." On their own, Booker T. and the MGs scored major hits with "Groovin'" and "Soul Limbo" and near-smashes with "Hang 'Em High" and "Time Is Tight," the latter from the soundtrack to *Uptight*, scored by Booker T. In 1969 Steve Cropper recorded the album *With a Little Help from My Friends*, as well as *Jammed Together* with Albert King and gospel patriarch "Pop" Staples.

By 1970 Booker T. and the MGs had abandoned their role as Stax house band, officially disbanding in 1972. Booker Jones moved to Calif. and joined A&M Records as a staff producer. There he supervised recording sessions for Rita Coolidge, his wife Priscilla (Rita's sister), and Bill Withers. In the early 1970s Jones recorded three albums with his wife, plus the solo album *Evergreen.* Cropper continued with session and production chores at Stax/Volt Records until 1975, when Stax/Volt folded. He then moved to Los Angeles.

The original members of Booker T. and the MGs were planning a reunion when Al Jackson was shot to death in Memphis. The band reunited, with Willie Hall (formerly of the Bar-Kays) succeeding Jackson on drums, for the album *Universal Language.* In 1977 Jones, Cropper, and Dunn recorded and toured with Levon Helm's RCO All-Stars. Also in 1977–1978, Cropper and Dunn re-created their distinctive 1960s sound behind the Blues Brothers (John Belushi and Dan Aykroyd) on tours and albums, as well as in the popular 1980 movie *The Blues Brothers.* In 1988 Booker T., Steve Cropper, and Duck Dunn reunited and joined drummer Anton Fig to perform at Atlantic Records' 40th anniversary show at Madison Square Garden; that lineup subsequently stayed together for several years to perform as Booker T. and the MGs. In October 1992 Jones, Cropper, and Dunn, with session drummer Jim Keltner, served as the house band for the four-hour Bob Dylan tribute staged at Madison Square Garden. In 1994 Booker T., Cropper, and Dunn recorded their first album in 17 years, *That's the Way It Should Be,* with session drummers.

DISC.: THE MAR-KEYS: *Last Night* (1961); *Do the Pop-Eye* (1962); *The Great Memphis Sound* (1966); *Damifiknew* (1969); *The Memphis Experience* (1971); *Damnifiknew/The Memphis Experience* (1994). **BOOKER T. AND THE MGS/THE MAR-KEYS:** *Back to Back* (1967). **VARIOUS ARTISTS:** *The Complete Stax-Volt Singles, 1959–1968* (1991). **BOOKER T. AND THE MGS:** *Green Onions* (1962); *Soul Dressing* (1965); *And Now!* (1966); *In the Christmas Spirit* (1966); *Hip Hug-Her* (1967); *Best* (1968); *Doin' Our Thing* (1968); *Soul Limbo* (1968); *The Booker T. Set* (1969); *Uptight* (soundtrack; 1969); *Greatest Hits* (1970); *McLemore Avenue* (1970); *Melting Pot* (1971); *Universal Language* (1977); *Free Ride* (1978); *Groovin'* (1993); *That's the Way It Should Be* (1994); *Very Best* (1994). **STEVE CROPPER:** *With a Little Help from My Friends* (1969); *Playin' My Thang* (1981); *Night After Night* (1982). **STEVE CROPPER/ALBERT KING/"POP" STAPLES:** *Jammed Together* (1969). **PRISCILLA JONES:** *Gypsy Queen* (1971). **BOOKER T. AND PRISCILLA JONES:** *Booker T. and Priscilla* (1971); *Home Grown* (1972); *Chronicles* (1973). **THE MGS:** *The MGs* (1973). **BOOKER T. JONES:** *Evergreen* (1974); *Try and Love Again* (1978); *The Best of You* (1980); *Booker T. Jones* (1981); *The Runaway* (1989). **LEVON HELM AND THE RCO ALL-STARS:** *Levon Helm and the RCO All-Stars* (1977). **THE BLUE BROTHERS:** *Briefcase Full of Blues* (1978); *The Blues Brothers* (soundtrack; 1980); *Made in America* (1980); *Best* (1981); *The Definitive Collection* (1992); *Red, White and Blues* (1992).—**BH**

Bookspan, Martin, American music critic, administrator, and broadcaster; b. Boston, July 30, 1926. He was educated at the Boston Music School (violin and theory) and Harvard Coll. (B.S. in German literature, 1947). He was executive director of the New England Opera Theater (1952–54); from 1956 to 1968, held various administrative positions with WQXR Radio in N.Y.

In 1968 he was named coordinator for the sym. and concert activities of ASCAP. He was host and commentator for the Boston Sym. and Pops radio broadcasts (1957–68); from 1975 to 1988 he was host, commentator, and executive producer for the N.Y. Phil. radio broadcasts; from 1976 also commentator for the "Live from Lincoln Center" PBS telecasts. He was a permanent member of the panel of critics for the "First Hearing" radio program; was a contributing ed. to *Stereo Review Magazine* (1958–76); also wrote for the *N.Y. Times* (1963–65). He publ. *101 Masterpieces of Music and Their Composers* (N.Y., 1968), *Zubin: The Zubin Mehta Story* (N.Y., 1978), and *André Previn: A Biography* (Garden City, N.Y., 1981).—**NS/LK/DM**

Boone, Charles, American composer and writer on music; b. Cleveland, June 21, 1939. He studied with Schiske at the Vienna Academy of Music (1960–61), took private lessons with Krenek and Weiss in Los Angeles (1961–62), and attended the Univ. of Southern Calif. in Los Angeles (B.M., 1963) and San Francisco State Coll. (M.A., 1968). He served as chairman of the San Francisco Composers' Forum and coordinator of the Mills Coll. Performing Group and Tape Music Center. From 1975 to 1977 he was composer-in-residence in Berlin under the sponsorship of the Deutscher Akademischer Austauschdienst. In addition to composing, Boone has been active as a writer on contemporary music. His music creates a sonic environment on purely structural principles, employing serial matrices, coloristic contrasts, and spatial parameters of performing instruments, with resulting styles ranging from lyrical pointillism to static sonorism. Electronic resources make up part of his musical equipment.

WORKS: *3 Motets* for Chorus (1962–65); *Oblique Formation* for Flute and Piano (1965); *Starfish* for Flute, Clarinet, 2 Percussion, 2 Violins, and Piano (1966); *A Cool Glow of Radiation* for Flute and Tape (1966); *The Edge of the Land* for Orch. (1968); *Not Now* for Clarinet (1969); *Zephyrus* for Oboe and Piano (1970); *Vermilion* for Oboe (1970); *Quartet* for Clarinet, Violin, Cello, and Piano (1970); *Chinese Texts* for Soprano and Orch. (1971); *First Landscape* for Orch. (1971); *Vocalise* for Soprano (1972); *Second Landscape* for Chamber Orch. (1973; also for Orch., 1979); *Raspberries* for 3 Percussion (1974); *Linea Meridiana* for 10 Instruments (1975); *San Zeno/Verona* for Chamber Ensemble (1976); *Fields/Singing* for Soprano and Chamber Ensemble (1976); *Shunt* for 3 Percussion (1978); *String Piece* for String Orch. (1978); *Streaming* for Flute (1979); *Little Flute Pieces* (1979); *Springtime* for Oboe (1980); *Winter's End* for Soprano, Countertenor, Viola da Gamba, and Harpsichord (1980); *Slant* for Percussion (1980); *The Watts Tower* for Percussion (1981); *Trace* for Flute and 10 Instruments (1981–83); *Weft* for 6 Percussion (1982); *Drum Bug* for Mechanical Woodblocks (1983); *The Khaju Bridge* for Soprano, Trumpet, Double Bass, Electric Organ, Percussion, and Tape (1984); *Drift* for Flute, Oboe, Clarinet, Piano, Violin, Viola, Cello, and Double Bass (1984); *Solar One* for Flute and Trumpet (1985); *The Timberline, and Other Pieces* for Carillon (1987–89); *Silence and Light* for String Quartet (1989–90); *Morphosis* for Percussion Quartet (1989–90).—**NS/LK/DM**

Boone, Pat (Charles Eugene), American singer and actor; b. Jacksonville, Fla., June 1, 1934. Boone was one of the most successful recording artists of the second half of the 1950s and the only one who effectively straddled the conflicting styles of traditional pop and emerging rock 'n' roll. Though his well-articulated tenor and relaxed singing style marked him as a successor to Bing Crosby and Perry Como, his initial success came with his covers of recordings by such artists as Fats Domino and Little Richard. Among the 60 recordings he placed in the singles charts between 1955 and 1969, there were ten gold records and six #1 hits, the most popular being "I Almost Lost My Mind," "Love Letters in the Sand," and "April Love."

Boone was the son of Archie and Margaret Prichard Boone; his father was a building contractor and his mother a registered nurse. The family moved to Nashville, Tenn., in 1936, where he grew up, first performing publicly at age ten. In high school he had his own local radio show, *Youth on Parade*. He enrolled at David Lipscomb Coll. in Nashville and married Shirley Foley, the daughter of Red Foley, on Nov. 7, 1953. They had four daughters, among them the singer Debby Boone. Finding a job at a television station in Fort Worth, Tex., he moved to Denton, Tex., and transferred to North Tex. State Coll. His singing brought him to the attention of the network television talent show *The Original Amateur Hour*, and he appeared on the show and won three times. He was signed to Republic Records and made a few singles for the label.

In 1954, Boone appeared on *Arthur Godfrey's Talent Scouts*, a rival show to *The Original Amateur Hour*, and was equally successful. He signed to Dot Records, whose president, Randy Wood, was finding success having Caucasian pop singers cover songs previously done by African Americans for the R&B market. Recording cover versions of hits was a common practice in the record business, but at a time when R&B music was starting to cross over to the pop charts, whites sometimes denied blacks the opportunity to score hits themselves. At the same time, whites popularized the material, and given that many of the songs were written by black artists, also brought them publishing income.

For Boone's first Dot single, Wood chose "Two Hearts" (music and lyrics by Otis Williams and Henry Stone), a Top Ten R&B hit for the Charms. Boone's cover peaked in the Top 40 in April 1955. His next single, a cover of Fats Domino's #1 R&B hit "Ain't That a Shame" (music and lyrics by Dave Bartholomew and Fats Domino), topped the charts in September and sold a million copies. Arthur Godfrey invited him to become a regular on his series *Arthur Godfrey and His Friends*, and Boone moved to the N.Y. area, transferring to Columbia Coll. (Though his career forced him to take occasional leaves of absence, he graduated magna cum laude with a B.S. degree in 1958.)

Boone had three more songs in the charts before the end of 1955. He had ten in 1956, including the million-selling #1 hits "I Almost Lost My Mind" (music and lyrics by Ivory Joe Hunter, whose original version had been a #1 R&B hit in 1950), "Don't Forbid Me" (music and lyrics by Charles Singleton), and the million-sellers "I'll Be Home" (music and lyrics by Stan Lewis and Ferdinand Washington; a Top Ten R&B hit for the

Flamingos) and "Friendly Persuasion (Thee I Love)" (music by Dmitri Tiomkin, lyrics by Paul Francis Webster). He ranked second only to Elvis Presley as the most successful singles artist of that year.

Success brought further opportunities. Boone was signed to a seven-year contract with 20th Century-Fox Pictures and began shooting his first film, *Bernardine*, which opened in July 1957. His second, *April Love*, appeared in November. In October he began hosting his own television series, the half-hour musical variety program *The Pat Boone–Chevy Showroom*; it ran for three seasons, through 1960. Meanwhile, his recording career continued apace: He placed eight songs in the charts in 1957, among them the #1 million- sellers "Love Letters in the Sand" (music by J. Fred Coots, lyrics by Nick Kenny and Charles Kenny) and "April Love" (music by Sammy Fain, lyrics by Paul Francis Webster), as well as two other million-sellers, "Why Baby Why" (music and lyrics by Luther Dixon and Larry Harrison) and "Remember You're Mine" (music and lyrics by Kal Mann and Bernie Lowe). He also released his only gold album, *Pat's Great Hits*. Again, he ranked second only to Elvis Presley as the year's top recording artist.

Focusing primarily on his television show and his recordings in 1958, Boone had only one film role, *Mardi Gras*, released in November. He had nine songs in the charts, four of them in the Top Ten, and one, "A Wonderful Time Up There" (music and lyrics by Lee Roy Abernathy), a million-seller. He also published his first book, *'Twixt Twelve and Twenty*, which offered advice to teenagers.

Boone's career began to decline in 1959. Though he continued with his television series and appeared in another film, the science fiction story *Journey to the Center of the Earth*, among his seven chart songs there were no Top Ten hits. By 1960 he was having trouble getting into the Top 40. He scored a surprise #1 hit in June 1961 with "Moody River" (music and lyrics by Gary D. Bruce) and a final Top Ten with 1962's novelty "Speedy Gonzales" (music and lyrics by Buddy Kaye, David Hess, and Ethel Lee), but he was only in the charts rarely after the early 1960s. Similarly, his film career largely subsided after his appearances in *All Hands on Deck* (1961) and a remake of Richard Rodgers and Oscar Hammerstein II's *State Fair* (1962).

After his commercial peak, Boone spent much of his time on entertainment activities related to religion, writing books, and touring and recording with his family. In 1982 he and his wife hosted the television series *Together with Pat and Shirley Boone* on the Christian Broadcasting Network, and starting in 1983 he began broadcasting a Christian radio show on stations across the country. He also made occasional recordings, placing a few singles in the country charts in the 1970s, and some personal appearances, notably a run in the title role of *The Will Rogers Follies* in a production in Branson, Mo., in 1994. In 1997, Hip-O Records released his tongue-in-cheek album *Pat Boone in a Metal Mood: No More Mr. Nice Guy*, on which he covered heavy-metal songs. But heavy-metal fans were not intrigued, and some of his Christian fans were offended.

WRITINGS: *The P. B. Book* (London, 1958); *'Twixt Twelve and*

Twenty (Englewood Cliffs, N.J., 1958); *Between You, Me and the Gatepost* (Englewood Cliffs, N.J., 1960); *The Real Christmas* (Westwood, N.J., 1961); *The Care and Feeding of Parents* (Englewood Cliffs, N.J., 1967); *A New Song* (Carol Stream, Ill., 1970; rev. ed., 1988); *Dr. Balaam's Talking Mule* (Van Nuys, Calif., 1974); *A Miracle a Day Keeps the Devil Away* (Old Tappan, N.J., 1974); *My Faith* (1976); with D. O'Neill, *P. B. Devotional Book* (Van Nuys, Calif., 1977); *My Brother's Keeper; Get Your Life Together* (1978); *Together: 25 Years with the B. Family* (Nashville, 1979); *Pray to Win: God Wants You to Succeed* (N.Y., 1980); with S. Boone, *The Honeymoon Is Over* (Nashville, 1977); *The Marriage Game* (1984); *P. B.'s Favorite Bible Stories for the Very Young* (N.Y., 1984); *P. B.'s Favorite Bible Stories* (Altamonte Springs, Fla., 1989); *Let Me Live: The Anthem of the Unborn Child*.

DISC.: *Pat Boone* (1956); *Howdy!* (1956); *Pat* (1957); *Pat's Great Hits* (1957); *A Closer Walk with Thee* (1957); *Four by Pat* (1957); *Hymns We Love* (1957); *Pat Boone Sings Irving Berlin* (1957); *Star Dust* (1958); *Yes Indeed!* (1958); *Tenderly* (1959); *Side by Side* (1959); *He Leadeth Me* (1959); *Pat Boone Sings* (1959); *White Christmas* (1959); *Moonglow* (1960); *Hymns We Have Loved* (1960); *This and That* (1960); *Great! Great! Great!* (1960); *Moody River* (1961); *My God and I* (1961); *I'll See You in My Dreams* (1962); *State Fair* (1962); *I Love You Truly* (1963); *Days of Wine and Roses* (1963); *The Star Spangled Banner* (1963); *Pat Boone Sings Guess Who?* (1963); *Tie Me Kangaroo Down, Sport* (1963); *Sing Along without Pat Boone* (1963); *The Touch of Your Lips* (1964); *Pat Boone* (1964); *Ain't That a Shame* (1964); *The Lord's Prayer* (1964); *Boss Beat!* (1964); *Near You* (1965); *Blest Be Thy Name* (1965); *Memories* (1966); *Wish You Were Here, Buddy* (1966); *Christmas Is a Comin'* (1966); *I Was Kaiser Bill's Batman* (1967); *Look Ahead* (1968); *In the Holy Land* (1972); *I Love You More and More Each Day* (1973); *Born Again* (1973); *All in the Boone Family* (1973); *Something Supernatural* (1975); *Texas Woman* (1976); *The Country Side of Pat Boone* (1977); *Pat Boone Sings Golden Hymns* (1984); *Family Christmas* (1995); *Pat Boone in a Metal Mood: No More Mr. Nice Guy* (1997).

BIBL.: J. Bales, *P. B. and the Gift of Tongues* (Searcy, Ark., 1970); B. Evans, *Joy!: Correspondence with P. B.* (Carol Stream, Ill., 1973).—**WR**

Booren, Jo van den, Dutch composer; b. Maastricht, March 14, 1935. He studied trumpet with Marinus Komst and composition with Kees van Baaren and Klaus Huber.

WORKS: ORCH.: *Suite dionysienne* for English Horn and String Orch. (1963–64); *Capriccio* for Brass Orch. (1968); 3 syms.: No. 1, *Sinfonia jubilata* (1975), No. 2 (1983), and No. 3, *Short Symphony* (1987); *Display* for Saxophone Quartet and Symphonic Band (1986); *Passage* (1987); Concerto for Saxophone Quartet and Orch. (1989); *Rofena* for Wind Orch. (1990); Flute Concerto (1991); Organ Concerto (1991); 2 violin concertos: No. 1 for Violin and Brass Band (1992) and No. 2 for Violin and String Orch. (1993); *Cirkels I* for Accordion Orch. (1993) and *II* for Wind Band and String Orch. (1993); Double Concerto for Violin, Cello, and Orch. (1998); *La soledad sonara* (1999; also for Organ, 1996). **CHAMBER:** Trio for Oboe, Clarinet, and Bassoon (1960); Sonata for 3 Clarinets (1962); *Estremi* for Oboe, Violin, Viola, and Cello (1967); *Spectra* for Wind Quintet (1967); *Spiel I* for Oboe and Electronic Sound (1969); *Strofa I* for Cello (1969), *II* for Trumpet (1970), and *III* for Horn (1972); *Equilibrio* for Flute (1970); *Ballade* for Oboe (1971); *Intrada Festiva* for 4 Horns, 4 Trumpets, and 4 Trombones (1971); *Akirob* for Flute, Violin, and Viola (1972); *Potpourri 1973* for Brass Quintet (1973); 3 flute quartets (1978, 1980, 1980); Sextet for 2 Clarinets, 2

Bassoon, and 2 Horns (1987); Sonata for Solo Violin (1988); *Meditazione I* (1990; rev. 1994), *II* (1994), and *III* (1996) for Ensemble; *Discourse and Reflection* for 4 Trombones (1993); *Primavera* for Oboe, Violin, and Piano (1994); *Askesis* for Piano (1995); *Cyberphony No. 1* for Loudspeakers (1996); *La soledad sonara* for Organ (1996; also for String Orch., 1999).
—**NS/LK/DM**

Boosey & Hawkes, English music publishers. Thomas Boosey was a London bookseller and a continental traveler from 1792. He was often asked to handle music, and in 1816 founded a music publishing house on Holles Street. On the Continent he met eminent musicians of the time; he visited Vienna and negotiated about publication with Beethoven (who mentions Boosey's name in one of his letters to the Phil. Soc. in London). Boosey's main stock consisted of Italian and French operas. He owned copyrights of Bellini, Donizetti, and Verdi (until 1854), and publ. inexpensive English eds. of standard European works. In the 1820s he put his son, Thomas, in charge of musical publications. In 1846 the firm of Boosey & Sons began publishing band music; in 1855 (in conjunction with the flutist R.S. Pratten) the manufacture of improved flutes was begun; in 1868 the firm acquired Henry Distin's factory for musical instruments, and supplied band instruments for the British and Colonial armies. It was this development that eventually brought about the merger of Boosey and Hawkes. William Henry Hawkes was a trumpeter-in- ordinary to Queen Victoria. He established in 1865 a workshop of band instruments and an ed. of concert music for orch. and became a strong competitor of Boosey & Sons from 1885 on. Economic pressure forced the amalgamation of the 2 firms in 1930, combining valuable eds. covering a whole century of music. A branch of Boosey & Sons had been established in N.Y. (1892), discontinued in 1900, and reestablished in 1906; after the merger, Boosey & Hawkes opened offices in N.Y., Chicago, and Los Angeles. In Canada, the business was inaugurated in 1913; a Paris branch, the Editions Hawkes, was started in 1922; further affiliates were established in Australia (1933), India (1937), Argentina (1945), South Africa (1946), and Germany (1950). After World War II, the factories for the manufacture of band instruments in London were greatly expanded; quantity production of wind instruments, harmonicas, and drums enabled the firm to extend the market to all parts of the world. In 1927 the firm acquired the American rights of Enoch & Sons; in 1943 the catalogue of Adolph Fürstner, containing all the operas of Richard Strauss, was bought for certain territories; in 1947 the Koussevitzky catalogue (Édition Russe de Musique and Édition Gutheil) was purchased, including the major output of Stravinsky, Prokofiev, and Rachmaninoff. It also publ. works by Mahler, Bartók, Britten, Maxwell Davies et al. Carl Fischer obtained a controlling interest in the firm in 1986. Boosey & Hawkes merged with **Bote & Bock** in 1996.—**NS/LK/DM**

Borca, Karen, jazz bassoonist; b. Green Bay, Wisc., Sept. 5, 1948. She studied music with her mother, a schoolteacher who played and taught classical and stride piano. She played alto saxophone for 10 years and began bassoon in high school, continuing at the Univ. of Wisc. (B.M., 1971); there Alec Wilder and members of the N.Y. Woodwind Quintet encouraged her to go to N.Y. to study before returning to Wisc. In the 1970–71 school year, Cecil Taylor taught there and she played in and assisted with his big band. In 1971–73, she was a teaching assistant to Taylor at Antioch Coll., rehearsing student groups, and has since performed with him in various contexts. She taught music in public schools in 1972 in Antioch, and in N.Y. on a part time basis since 1974. Through Taylor, she met Jimmy Lyons and in the fall of 1974 became his assistant at Bennington Coll., notating and rehearsing his works, followed by their marriage and over 12 years of touring with Lyons. She has also led her own groups since 1972.

DISC.: Linny Lyons: *Wee Sneezawee* (1983); *Give It Up* (1985). Cecil Taylor Segments II: *Winged Serpent (Sliding Quadrants)* (1984). *Critics Picks, Vol. 3* (1998). Joe Morris: *Many Rings* (1999).—**LP**

Borck, Edmund von, talented German composer; b. Breslau, Feb. 22, 1906; d. in battle near Nettuno, Italy, Feb. 16, 1944. He studied composition in Breslau (1920–26), and music history at the Univ. of Berlin. He held several positions as opera conductor in Berlin and Frankfurt am Main, then taught theory and composition in Berlin until drafted into the army in 1940. His progress as a composer was rapid; his early works indicated an innate and original creative ability, and his death in combat was a great loss to German music. His style of composition is neo-Classical, with strong contrapuntal structure; the rather austere and reticent mode of expression assumes in Borck's music a colorful aspect through a variety of melodic and rhythmic devices, often in a rhapsodically romantic vein.

WORKS: Alto Saxophone Concerto (1932); Violin Sonata (1932); *Orchesterstücke* (1933); *Ländliche Kantate* (1934); *Concerto for Orch.* (1936); Sextet for Flute and Strings (1936); *Kleine Suite* for Flute (1938); *2 Fantasiestücke* for Orch. (1940); Piano Concerto (1941); *Orphika*, "an Apollonian transformation" for Orch. (1941); *Napoleon*, opera (1942).—**NS/LK/DM**

Borde, Jean Benjamin de la
See **La Borde, Jean Benjamin de**

Borden, David, American composer, pianist, and teacher; b. Boston, Dec. 25, 1938. After studies at Boston Univ. (1956–58), he took degrees at the Eastman School of Music (B.M., 1961; M.M., 1963) and Harvard Univ. (M.A., 1965). He also studied on a Fulbright scholarship at the Hochschule für Musik in Berlin (1965–66). Upon his return to the U.S., he was composer-in-residence for the Ithaca City School District in N.Y. (1966–68), and in 1968 joined the faculty at Cornell Univ., first as a composer-pianist for dance in its dept. of physical education (1968–88), and later as a senior lecturer in its music dept. (from 1988), where he also served as director of its Digital Music Program. Among his specialty courses are MIDI techniques, counterpoint combined with electronic sequencing, and collaborative music composition using digital instruments. Borden worked closely with electronic music pioneer Robert

Moog, through which he discovered new ways of using Moog's huge modular synthesizer and four-track Scully tape recorder in performance as well as in his own compositions. Through contact with Gordon Mumma and David Tudor, a sustained interest in live electronic music emerged as well. In 1968 Borden founded Mother Mallard (initially Mother Mallard's Portable Masterpiece Co.), the first all-synthesizer performance group whose personnel initially included Borden, Steve Drews, and Bard Prentiss (a sculptor), and was later joined by Linda Fisher; Fisher was still later replaced by Judy Borsher. The group performed extensively in the succeeding decades, giving lively performances of works by such senior contemporaries as Robert Ashley, Allen Bryant, Daniel Lentz, Steve Reich, Philip Glass, Terry Riley, Jon Hassel, Morton Feldman, and John Cage. In 1974 Mother Mallard started its own recording label, Earthquack Records.

WORKS: *The Continuing Story of Counterpoint, Parts 1–12* for Synthesizers, Soprano, Woodwinds, and Electric Guitar (1976–87; Bowling Green, Ind., Oct. 9, 1995); *Anagram Portraits* for Various Ensembles (1984 et seq.); *The Vermeer Variations* for Flute, Oboe, Cello, and Harpsichord (1985); *Trains* for Synthesizers, Soprano, Clarinet, and Electric Guitar (1987); *The Boston Elegies* for Synthesizers, Woodwinds, and Electric Guitar (1988); *Cayuga Night Music* for Synthesizers, Sampler, Soprano Voice, and Soprano Saxophone (1988–93); *Angels* for Mixed Amplified Vocal Ensemble, Soprano, Tenor, and Baritone Soloists, Synthesizers, Woodwinds, and Electric Guitar (1989–90); *Birthday Variations* for Various Ensembles (1990 et seq.); *Variations on a Theme of Philip Glass* for Synthesizers, 2 Sopranos, Woodwinds, and Electric Guitar (1991); *Infinity Variations 1* for Chamber Orch. (1992) and *2, Silent Stars,* for 2 Fortepianos and Chamber Orch. (1994–95; Houghton, Mich., Oct. 22, 1995); *Notes From Vienna* for Electric Guitar and Wind Ensemble (1993–94; Ithaca, N.Y., March 12, 1994); *The Perilous Night Companion* for Electroacoustic Ensemble (1999).—**LK/DM**

Bordes, Charles (Marie Anne), French choral conductor; b. Roche-Corbon, near Vouvray-sur-Loire, May 12, 1863; d. Toulon, Nov. 8, 1909. He studied piano with Marmontel and composition with César Franck. In 1894, in association with Guilmant and Vincent d'Indy, he organized the Schola Cantorum in Paris, and in subsequent years organized chapters of it in Avignon and Montpellier. He made numerous tours with his choral group. In 1889 he was commissioned by the French government to make a study of Basque folk songs; he publ. 100 of these in *Archives de la tradition basque.* He also wrote several pieces based on Basque motifs, among them *Suite basque* for Flute and String Quartet (1888) and *Rapsodie basque* for Piano and Orch. (1890). He also ed. several anthologies of early French music, publ. by the Schola Cantorum.

BIBL.: C. B., *In memoriam* (Paris, Schola Cantorum, 1909); P. Alibert, *C. B. à Maguelonne* (Paris, 1926); P. Dowd, *C. B. and the Schola Cantorum of Paris* (diss., Catholic Univ. of America, Washington, D.C., 1969).—**NS/LK/DM**

Bordogni, Giulio Marco, Italian tenor and singing teacher; b. Gazzaniga, near Bergamo, Jan. 23, 1789; d. Paris, July 31, 1856. He was a pupil of Simon Mayr. He made his operatic debut in 1808 at La Scala, Milan.

From 1819 to 1833 he was engaged at the Théâtre-Italien in Paris. He later devoted himself primarily to teaching, joining the staff of the Paris Cons. in 1820. He publ. a collection of 36 vocalises, in 2 vols., which became a standard book of vocal exercises throughout Europe. —NS/LK/DM

Bordoni, Faustina

See **Hasse, Faustina** (née **Bordoni**)

Boretz, Benjamin (Aaron), American composer, writer on music, and teacher; b. N.Y., Oct. 3, 1934. He studied piano and cello, and received lessons in conducting from Julius Rudel and in harpsichord from Erwin Bodky. He was educated at Brooklyn Coll. (B.A., 1954), Brandeis Univ. (M.F.A., 1957), and Princeton Univ. (M.A., 1960; Ph.D., 1970). Among his composition mentors were Arthur Berger, Irving Fine, Lukas Foss, Darius Milhaud, and Roger Sessions. He taught at N.Y. Univ. (1964–69) and Columbia Univ. (1969–72). In 1973 he joined the faculty of Bard Coll., where he taught until becoming prof. emeritus in 1997. He also was founder-director of its Music Program Zero (1989–97). From 1962 to 1969 he was music critic of *The Nation*. With Berger, he founded *Perspectives of New Music* in 1961, and served as its co-ed. until 1964, and then as its ed. until 1983, and again in 1994–95. He was a visiting prof. at the Univ. of Calif. at Los Angeles and at Santa Barbara in 1991–92. In 1998 he became co-ed. of *Open Space Magazine*. In addition to his writings in various books and journals, he publ. the vols. *Language, as a Music* (1980), *Talk: If I Am a musical thinker* (1985), *Music Columns from The Nation, 1962–68* (1980), and *Meta-Variations: Studies in the Foundations of Musical Thought* (1994).

WORKS: Concerto Grosso for String Orch. (1954); *Nocturne* for Strings (1955); *Partita* for Piano (1955); *Divertimento* for Chamber Ensemble (1956); Violin Concerto (1956–57); *2 Movements* for String Quartet (1958–59); *3 Poems of John Donne* for Voice and Piano (1960); *Group Variations I* for Chamber Orch. (1964–67) and *II* for Computer (1970–72); *Liebeslied* for Piano (1974); *...my chart shines high where the blue milk's upset...* for Piano (1976); *Language, as a Music* for Speaker, Piano, and Tape (1978); *Passage, for Roger Sessions* for Piano (1979); *Soliloquy* for Keyboard (1980); *Converge* for Orch. (1981); *forM(a music)* for Voice and Keyboard (1982); *Two (Seattle)* for Improvising Keyboards (1983; in collaboration with J.K. Randall); *ONE: An Exercise* for 8 Piano Solo Sound Sessions (1985); *To Open* for Improvising Ensemble (1987); *Please Think: Here are Five Texts Conjoined for Your Reflection* for Speaker, Piano, Improvising Ensemble, and Audience (1988); *ForM(a Music)* for Tape (1989); *Frontier Music* for Orch. (1990); *Lament for Sarah* for Piano (1990); *WAIT (Four Speculative Pieces)* for Ensemble (1991); *INHABIT (Three Speculative Pieces)* for Ensemble (1992); *The Purposes and Politics of Engaging Strangers* for 2 or More Speaking and Playing Performers and Audience and Video Tape (*Phase I*, 1991, *II*, 1992, and *III*, 1993); *music/consciousness/gender* for Live Speaker, Recorded Speakers, and Audio and Video Tape (1994–95); *echoic/anechoic* for Piano (1997); *Black/Noise I* for Computer-processed Piano (1998) and *II* and *III* for Computer-processed Speaker and Video Images (1998); *UN(-): 1* for Chamber Orch. (1999; also for Ensemble, 2000).—NS/LK/DM

Borg, Kim, Finnish bass, teacher, and composer; b. Helsinki, Aug. 7, 1919; d. April 28, 2000. He studied voice with Heikki Teittinen in Helsinki (1936–41; 1945–47), where he also received training in theory and composition with Leo Funtek and Aarre Merikanto, and then pursued vocal studies with Andrejewa de Skilondz in Stockholm (1950–59). He also studied biochemistry at the Helsinki Inst. of Technology (diploma, 1946). In 1947 he made his formal concert debut in Helsinki, and in 1951 his formal operatic debut in Århus as Colline in *La Bohème*. In addition to his concert appearances, he sang regularly in opera in Helsinki and Copenhagen (1952–70), Stockholm (1963–75), and Hamburg (1964–70). On Oct. 30, 1959, he made his Metropolitan Opera debut in N.Y. as Count Almaviva, remaining on its roster until 1962. In 1961 he appeared as Boris Godunov in Moscow. He retired from the stage in 1980. From 1972 to 1989 he was a prof. at the Royal Danish Cons. of Music in Copenhagen. He publ. the books *Suomalainen laulajanaapinen* (ABC for a Finnish Singer; Helsinki, 1972) and *Muistelmia* (Memoirs; Helsinki, 1992). Among his compositions were 2 syms., Sinfonietta for Strings, a Trombone Concerto, a Concerto for Double Bass and Strings, chamber music, a *Stabat Mater*, and songs. He also prepared orchestrations of Mussorgsky's *Songs and Dances of Death* and *Without Sun*, and of Wolf's *Michelangelo Lieder*. In addition to Boris Godnunov, he also had success in such roles as Osmin, Don Giovanni, King Marke, Hans Sachs, Don Carlos, Pimen, Gremin, Rossini's Don Basilio, and Debussy's Arkel.—NS/LK/DM

Borgatti, Giuseppe, Italian tenor, father of **Renata Borgatti;** b. Cento, March 17, 1871; d. Reno, Lago Maggiore, Oct. 18, 1950. He studied with Alessandro Busi in Bologna, making his operatic debut as Faust in Castelfranco Veneto in 1892; in 1896 he sang the title role in *Andrea Chenier* at Milan's La Scala; also sang in Wagner's operas. He retired from the stage in 1914 owing to glaucoma, becoming totally blind in 1923. He publ. an autobiography, *La mia vita d'artista* (Bologna, 1927).—NS/LK/DM

Borgatti, Renata, Italian pianist, daughter of **Giuseppe Borgatti;** b. Bologna, March 2, 1894; d. Rome, March 10, 1964. She pursued a fairly successful career mainly in recital, presenting programs of the complete works of Debussy. After the end of World War II, she lived in Rome.—NS/LK/DM

Borghi, Adelaide, Italian mezzo-soprano; b. Bologna, Aug. 9, 1829; d. there, Sept. 28, 1901. Acting on the advice of Pasta, she trained herself for the stage, making her debut at Urbino (1846) in Mercadante's *Il Giuramento*. She toured through Italy and in Vienna and Paris (1854–56), sang with the Grand Opéra in Paris (1856–59), and appeared in London with great success (1860) before returning to Italy.—NS/LK/DM

Borghi, Giovanni Battista, Italian composer; b. Camerino, Macerata, Aug. 25, 1738; d. Loreto, Feb. 25, 1796. He studied at the Cons. della Pietà dei Turchini in Naples (1757–59). From 1759 to 1778 he was maestro di cappella at the Macerata Cathedral; from 1778, at S.

Casa of Loreto. He composed some 25 operas, including *La morte di Semiramide* (Milan, Feb. 9, 1791), which was moderately successful. He also wrote a number of oratorios and other sacred works.—NS/LK/DM

Borgioli, Armando, Italian baritone; b. Florence, March 19, 1898; d. in an air raid on the Milan-Modena train near Codogno, Jan. 20, 1945. He made his debut as Amonasro at the Teatro Carcano in Milan in 1925, and then sang at Milan's La Scala and London's Covent Garden. On Jan. 22, 1932, he made his Metropolitan Opera debut in N.Y., as Carlo in *La forza del destino*, remaining on the company's roster until 1935. He was best known for his dramatic roles in Verdi's operas. —NS/LK/DM

Borgioli, Dino, Italian tenor; b. Florence, Feb. 15, 1891; d. there, Sept. 12, 1960. He studied in Florence with Eugenio Giachetti. In 1914 he made his operatic debut as Arturo in *I Puritani* at Milan's Teatro Corso; appeared in various Italian opera houses, including Milan's La Scala (debut as Ernesto in *Don Pasquale*, 1918). After singing with Melba on her farewell tour of Australia (1924), he made his first appearance at London's Covent Garden as Edgardo in 1925, continuing to sing there until 1939. In 1932 he sang Cavaradossi in San Francisco, a role he again sang in Chicago in 1933. On Dec. 31, 1934, he made his Metropolitan Opera debut in N.Y. as Rodolfo, but sang with the company for only that 1 season. In 1937 he sang Ottavio at the Glyndebourne Festival. From 1939 he taught voice in London, eventually retiring to Florence. His roles in operas by Mozart and Rossini were particularly esteemed. —NS/LK/DM

Bori, Lucrezia (real name, **Lucrecia Borja y Gonzalez de Riancho**), distinguished Spanish soprano; b. Valencia, Dec. 24, 1887; d. N.Y., May 14, 1960. She studied at the Valencia Cons. and with Melchior Vidal in Milan. She made her operatic debut in Rome at the Teatro Adriano on Oct. 31, 1908, as Micaëla; then sang in Milan, in Naples, and, in 1910, in Paris as Manon Lescaut with the Metropolitan Opera Co.; then made a European tour. In 1911 she sang at La Scala in Milan; made her debut at the Metropolitan Opera in N.Y. as Manon Lescaut on Nov. 11, 1912, and sang there until the end of the 1914–15 season. After a period of retirement occasioned by a vocal affliction, she reappeared in 1919 at Monte Carlo as Mimi, returning to the Metropolitan in 1921 in the same role. Thereafter she appeared in N.Y. with increasing success and popularity until the end of the 1935–36 season, when she retired from opera. Among her finest roles were Juliette, Despina, Massenet's Manon, Mélisande, Violetta, Norina, and Mimi.—NS/LK/DM

Borkh, Inge (real name, **Ingeborg Simon**), famous German soprano; b. Mannheim, May 26, 1917. She first appeared as a stage actress, then decided upon a singing career. She studied at the Milan Cons. and at the Mozarteum in Salzburg. She made her debut as Czipra in Johann Strauss's *Zigeunerbaron* at the Lucerne

Opera in 1940, remaining a member there until 1944; then sang at the Bern Opera until 1951. She made her American debut at the San Francisco Opera in 1953; on Jan. 24, 1958, she appeared at the Metropolitan Opera in N.Y. as Salome, returning to its roster for the 1960–61 and 1970–71 seasons. In 1959 she made her first appearance at London's Covent Garden, also as Salome. She made her farewell operatic appearance at the Munich Festival in 1988. Her other notable roles included Leonore, Eglantine, Lady Macbeth, and Elektra. She wrote *Ich komm' vom Theater nicht los: Erinnerungen und Einsichten* (Berlin, 1996).—NS/LK/DM

Bořkovec, Pavel, Czech composer; b. Prague, June 10, 1894; d. there, July 22, 1972. He originally studied philosophy, and turned to composition rather late in life; took lessons with Křička and Foerster in 1919. From 1925 to 1927 he attended master classes of Suk at the Prague Cons. From 1946 to 1964 he was on the faculty of the Academy of Musical Arts in Prague. His early works were in the manner of Dvořák and Suk; later he experienced the influence of neo-Classicism and adopted dissonant counterpoint.

WORKS: DRAMATIC: O p e r a : *The Satyr* (1937–38; Prague, Oct. 8, 1942); *Paleček* (Tom Thumb; 1945–47; Prague, Dec. 17, 1958). B a l l e t : *Krysař* (The Pied Piper; 1939; concert perf., Prague, Jan. 15, 1941; first stage perf., Oct. 8, 1942). ORCH.: *Stmívaní* (Twilight), symphonic poem (1920); 3 syms. (1926–27; 1955; 1959); *The Start*, symphonic allegro (1929; Prague, March 26, 1930); 2 piano concertos (1931; 1949–50); Violin Concerto (1933); *Partita* (1936); Concerto Grosso for 2 Violins, Cello, Orch., and Piano (1941–42); *2 Symphoniettas* for Chamber Orch. (1944; 1963–68); Cello Concerto (1950–51). CHAMBER: Piano Quartet (1922); 5 string quartets (1924; 1928; 1940; 1947; 1961–62); Sonata for Solo Viola (1931); Wind Quintet (1932); 2 violin sonatas (1934, 1956); Nonet (1941–42); Violin Sonatina (1942); *Intermezzo* for Horn and Piano (1965). P i a n o : Suite (1930); *Partita* (1935); 2 Pieces (1941–42). VOCAL: *Jen jedenkrat* (Only Once), melodrama (1921); *Stadion* (The Stadium) for Voice, Wind Quintet, and Piano (1929); *Love Songs* for Voice and Piano or Small Orch., after Goethe and Villon (1932); 5 *Songs*, after Pasternak (1935); 6 *Madrigals about Time* for Chorus (1957); *Silentium Turbatum*, symphonic movement for Alto, Orch., and Electric Guitar (Prague, Feb. 28, 1965); *Te Deum* for Soli, Chorus, and Orch. (1968).—NS/LK/DM

Bornefeld, Helmut, German organist and composer; b. Stuttgart-Untertürkheim, Dec. 14, 1906; d. Heidenheim, Feb. 11, 1990. He studied organ, piano, and composition at the Hochschule für Musik in Stuttgart, and then was organist and choirmaster in Heidenheim. With Siegfried Reda, he organized the Heidenheim Arbeitstage für Neue Kirchenmusik in 1946, and remained actively engaged in its activities until 1960. His compositions include numerous sacred and secular choral pieces, chamber music, and organ pieces.

WRITINGS: *Das Positiv* (Kassel, 1941); *Orgelbau und neue Orgelmusik* (Kassel, 1952); *Orgelspiegel* (Kassel, 1966). —NS/LK/DM

Borodin, Alexander (Porfirievich), celebrated Russian composer; b. St. Petersburg, Nov. 12,

1833; d. there, Feb. 27, 1887. He was the illegitimate son of a Georgian prince, Gedianov; his mother was the wife of an army doctor. In accordance with customary procedure in such cases, the child was registered as the lawful son of one of Gedianov's serfs, Porfiry Borodin; hence, the patronymic, Alexander Porfirievich. He was given an excellent education; learned several foreign languages, and was taught to play the flute. He played four-hand arrangements of Haydn's and Beethoven's syms. with his musical friend M. Shchiglev. At the age of 14, he tried his hand at composition; wrote a piece for flute and piano and a String Trio on themes from *Robert le Diable*. In 1850 he became a student of the Academy of Medicine in St. Petersburg, and developed a great interest in chemistry; he graduated in 1856 with honors, and joined the staff as asst. prof.; in 1858 he received his doctorate in chemistry; contributed several important scientific papers to the bulletin of the Russian Academy of Sciences; traveled in Europe on a scientific mission (1859–62). Although mainly preoccupied with his scientific pursuits, Borodin continued to compose. In 1863 he married Catherine Protopopova, who was an accomplished pianist; she remained his faithful companion and musical partner; together they attended concerts and operas in Russia and abroad; his letters to her from Germany (1877), describing his visit to Liszt in Weimar, are of great interest. Of a decisive influence on Borodin's progress as a composer was his meeting with Balakirev in 1862; later he formed friendships with the critic Stasov, who named Borodin as one of the "mighty 5" (actually, Stasov used the expression "mighty group" or "handful"), with Mussorgsky and other musicians of the Russian national school. He adopted a style of composition in conformity with their new ideas; he particularly excelled in a type of Russian orientalism which had a great attraction for Russian musicians at the time. He never became a consummate craftsman, like Rimsky-Korsakov; although quite proficient in counterpoint, he avoided purely contrapuntal writing; his feeling for rhythm and orch. color was extraordinary, and his evocation of exotic scenes in his orch. works and in his opera *Knyaz' Igor'* (Prince Igor) is superb. Composition was a very slow process for Borodin; several of his works remained incomplete, and were ed. after his death by Rimsky-Korsakov and Glazunov.

WORKS: DRAMATIC: *Bogatïri* (The Bogatirs), opera-farce (Moscow, Nov. 18, 1867); *Mlada*, opera-ballet (1872; Act 4 only; other 3 three acts by Rimsky-Korsakov, Cui, and Mussorgsky); *Knyaz' Igor'* (Prince Igor), opera (1869–70; unfinished; completed and partially orchestrated by Rimsky-Korsakov and Glazunov; St. Petersburg, Nov. 16, 1890). **ORCH.:** 3 syms.: No. 1 in E-flat major (1862–67; St. Petersburg, Jan. 16, 1869), No. 2 in B minor (1869–76; St. Petersburg, March 10, 1877), and No. 3 in A minor (1882; 1886–87; 1st and 2nd movements only finished; ed. and orchestrated by Glazunov; St. Petersburg, Nov. 5, 1887); *V sredney Azii* (In Central Asia), musical picture (St. Petersburg, April 20, 1880). **CHAMBER:** Concerto for Flute and Piano (1847; not extant); Trio for 2 Violins and Cello (1847; not extant); Trio for 2 Violins and Cello (c. 1850–60; fragment extant); Quartet for Flute, Oboe, Viola, and Cello (1852–56); String Quintet (1853–54); Grand Trio for 2 Violins and Cello (1859–62; 3rd movement unfinished); Trio for 2 Violins and Cello (c. 1860);

Cello Sonata (c. 1860); String Sextet (1860–61; 3rd and 4th movements not extant); Piano Trio (1860–61); Piano Quintet (1862); 2 string quartets (1874–79; 1881); Scherzo for String Quartet (1882; No. 3 in the 2nd set of *Les vendredis*, in collaboration with Glazunov, Rimsky-Korsakov et al.); *Serenata alla spagnola* for String Quartet (1886; 3rd movement for the String Quartet on the name B-la-f [Belaiev]; in collaboration with Liadov, Glazunov, and Rimsky-Korsakov). **Piano:** *Polka Hélène* for Piano, 4–Hands (1843); *Fantasia on a Theme of Hummel* (1849); *Le courant* (1849); *Adagio poetico* (1849); Scherzo (1852; not extant); Allegreto for Piano, 4–Hands (1861; arranged from the 3rd movement of the String Quintet); Scherzo for Piano, 4–Hands (1861); Tarantella for Piano, 4–Hands (1862); *Polka, Marche funèbre, Requiem,* and *Mazurka* for Piano, 3–Hands (1874–78; for the collection *Paraphrases*; in collaboration with Liadov et al.); *Petite Suite* (1885; orchestrated by Glazunov); Scherzo (1885; orchestrated by Glazunov for inclusion in the *Petite Suite*). **VOCAL:** Choruses and songs.

BIBL.: V. Stasov, *A.P. B.: Evo zhizn', perepiska i muzïkal'nïye stat'i* (A.P. B.: Life, Correspondence and Articles on Music; St. Petersburg, 1880); A. Habets, *A. B. d'après la biographie et la correspondance publiées par M. Wladimir Stassoff* (Paris, 1893; Eng. tr., 1895); E. Braudo, *A.P. B.: Evo zhizn' i tvorchestvo* (A.P. B.: Life and Works; Petrograd, 1922); S. Dianin, ed., *Pis'ma A.P. B.* (A.P. B.'s Letters; Moscow and Leningrad, 1928–50); L. Solovtsova, *Kamerno-instrumental'naya muzïka A.P. B.* (A.P. B.'s Instrumental Chamber Music; Moscow, 1952); S. Dianin, *B.: Zhizneopisaniye, materialï i dokumentï* (B.: Biography, Materials and Documents; Moscow, 1955; partial Eng. tr., 1963); A. Sokhor, *A.P. B.: Zhizn', deyatel'nost', muzïkal'noye tvorchestvo* (A.P. B.: Life, Works, Musical Compositions; Moscow, 1965); L. Velluz, *Du laboratoire au Prince Igor, Pages sur B.* (Paris, 1971); G. Golovinsky, *Kamernïye ansambli B.* (B.'s Chamber Music; Moscow, 1972); M. Bobéth, *B. und seine Oper Fürst Igor: Geschichte-Analyse-Konsequenzen* (Munich and Salzburg, 1982); M. Ilin and E. Segal, eds., *A.P. B., 1833–1887: Pis'ma* (A.P. B., 1833–1887: Letters; Moscow, 1989); S. Neef, *Die Russischen Fünf: Balakirew, B., Cui, Mussorgski, Rimski-Korsakow: Monographien, Dokumente, Briefe, Programme, Werke* (Berlin, 1992); A. Gaub and M. Unseld, *Ein Fürst, zwei Prinzessinnen und vier Spieler: Anmerkungen zum Werk A. B.s* (Berlin, 1994).—**NS/LK/DM**

Borodina, Olga (Vladimirovna), notable Russian mezzo-soprano; b. Minsk, July 29, 1963. She studied at the Leningrad Cons. and in San Francisco. In 1987 she won the All-Union Glinka Competition in her homeland and the Rosa Ponselle Competition in the U.S., and in 1989 the Francisco Vignas Competition in Barcelona. In 1987 she joined the Kirov Opera, where she made her formal operatic debut as Siebel in *Faust*. Her appearances with the company on tour were warmly received, including visits to Hamburg in 1990, Edinburgh in 1991, and N.Y., Paris, and Palermo in 1992. In 1992 she made her debut at London's Covent Garden as Dalila, and in 1993 she appeared as Marina in Berlin. In 1995 she sang for the first time at the San Francisco Opera as Cenerentola, and returned there as Carmen in 1996. In 1997 she sang Marina in Salzburg, which role she chose for her Metropolitan Opera debut in N.Y. on Dec. 19 of that year. Her subsequent engagements took her to most of the principal operatic centers of the world. In addition to her admired Russian roles, particularly Marina, Olga, and Marfa, she has won acclaim for her characterizations of Rosina, Marguerite in *La Damnation de Faust*, and Angelina.—NS/LK/DM

Boronat, Olimpia, highly esteemed Italian soprano; b. Genoa, 1867; d. Warsaw, 1934. She was a pupil of Leoni at the Milan Cons. After appearing throughout Italy (from 1885), she toured in Spain, Portugal, and South America. In 1890 she became a member of the St. Petersburg Imperial Opera, where she was notably successful. In 1893 she married the Polish nobleman Rzewuski and retired from the stage. In 1901 she resumed her career and sang with renewed success in Russia. She also sang in Poland and then in Italy (from 1909). In 1922 she retired for good and settled in Warsaw as a voice teacher. Among her outstanding roles were Rosina, Elvira in *I Puritani*, Ophélie in *Hamlet*, and Violetta.—NS/LK/DM

Boroni, Antonio, Italian composer; b. Rome, 1738; d. there, Dec. 21, 1792. He studied with Martini in Bologna and with Abos and Lorenzo Fago at the Conservatorio Pieta dei Turchini in Naples (1757–58). He then devoted himself to writing operas. After composing works for Turin, Treviso, and Venice, he accompanied the Bustelli opera troupe to Prague (1767–68) and Dresden (1768–70). He served as Kapellmeister in Stuttgart (1770–77), then returned to Rome as maestro di cappella at St. Peter's (from 1778). He also held similar posts at S. Luigi de' Francesi and at S. Apollinare, the church of the Collegio Germanica (from c. 1790).

WORKS: DRAMATIC: *La Moda*, dramma giocoso (Turin, 1761; rev. Venice, 1769); *Demofoonte*, opera seria (Treviso, Carnival 1762); *L'amore in musica*, dramma giocoso (Venice, Oct. 15, 1763); *La Pupilla rapita*, dramma giocoso (Venice, 1763; in collaboration with S. Laurenti); *Sofonisba*, dramma per musica (Venice, Ascension 1764); *Siroe*, dramma per musica (Venice, 1764); *Le Villeggiatrici ridicole*, dramma comico (Venice, 1765); *La notte critica*, dramma giocoso (Venice, Carnival 1766); *Artaserse*, dramma per musica (Prague, Jan. 1767); *Didone*, dramma per musica (Prague, Carnival 1768); *Il carnevale*, dramma giocoso (Dresden, 1769); *Le Orfane svizzere*, dramma giocoso (Venice, 1770); *Le Contadine furlane*, dramma giocoso (Venice, Carnival 1771); *Le Déserteur*, opéra-comique (Stuttgart, 1774–75); *L'Amour fraternel*, opéra-comique (Stuttgart, 1774–75); *Zémire et Azor*, opéra-comique (Stuttgart, 1774–75); *L'isola disabitata*, intermezzo (Stuttgart, Dec. 31, 1775); *Enea nel Lazio*, dramma per musica (Rome, Carnival 1778). **OTHER:** Sym. (1772) and other orch. works; much sacred music.—NS/LK/DM

Borosini, Francesco, Italian tenor; b. Modena, c. 1690; d. c. 1750. From 1712 to 1731 he sang at the imperial court in Vienna. He also made appearances in Italy and in 1724–25 in London, where he appeared in operas by Handel and Ariosti. In 1725 he created the role of Grimoaldo in Handel's *Rodelinda*. He was married to the Italian soprano Rosa (née d'Ambreville) Borosini (b. Modena, June 27, 1698; d. after 1740). She launched her career in 1713, and later sang in Vienna (1721–40).—NS/LK/DM

Borowski, Felix, English-American composer, music critic, and teacher; b. Burton, March 10, 1872; d.

Chicago, Sept. 6, 1956. He studied violin with his father, a Polish émigré; took lessons with various teachers in London, and at the Cologne Cons.; then taught in Aberdeen, Scotland. His early *Russian Sonata* was praised by Grieg, which provided impetus to his progress as a composer. In 1897 he accepted a teaching engagement at the Chicago Musical Coll.; was its president from 1916 to 1925. Subsequently he became active in musical journalism; in 1942 he was appointed music ed. of the *Chicago Sun*; also served as program annotator for the Chicago Sym. Orch. (from 1908). He also taught musicology at Northwestern Univ. (1937–42). Among his many musical works, the violin piece *Adoration* became widely popular. Borowski revised G.P. Upton's *The Standard Operas* in 1928, and *The Standard Concert Guide* in 1930.

WORKS: DRAMATIC: *Boudour*, ballet-pantomime (Chicago, Nov. 25, 1919); *Fernando del Nonsensico*, satiric opera (1935). **ORCH.:** Piano Concerto (Chicago, 1914); *Allegro de concert* for Organ and Orch. (Chicago, 1915); *Peintures* (Chicago, Jan. 25, 1918); *Le Printemps passionne*, symphonic poem (Evanston, Ill., 1920); *Youth*, fantasy-overture (Evanston, Ill., May 30, 1923); *Ecce Homo*, symphonic poem (N.Y., Jan. 2, 1924); *Semiramis*, symphonic poem (Chicago, Nov. 13, 1925); 3 syms.: No. 1 (Chicago, March 16, 1933), No. 2 (Los Angeles, July 22, 1936), and No. 3 (Chicago, March 29, 1939); *The Little Match Girl* for Narrator and Orch., after Andersen (1943); *Requiem for a Child* (1944); *The Mirror*, symphonic poem (Louisville, Nov. 27, 1954). **CHAMBER:** 3 string quartets; many pieces for violin, organ, and piano. **VOCAL:** Songs.—NS/LK/DM

Borris, Siegfried, respected German music scholar, pedagogue, and composer; b. Berlin, Nov. 4, 1906; d. there, Aug. 23, 1987. He studied economics at the Univ. of Berlin (1925–27), where he then pursued training in musicology with Schering (Ph.D., 1933, with the diss. *Kirnbergers Leben und Werk*); he also studied composition with Hindemith at the Berlin Hochschule für Musik (1927–29), where he subsequently taught (1929–33). After teaching privately, he rejoined its faculty as a lecturer in music history in 1945; he also was director of Berlin's Julius Stern Inst. from 1967. He composed in an accessible style, highlighted by an effective use of folk music.

WORKS: DRAMATIC: 2 radio operas: *Hans im Glück* (1947) and *Hirotas und Gerline* (1948); *Die Rübe*, Märchenoper (1953); *Frühlingsgesellen*, Liederspiel (1951); *Ruf des Lebens*, scenic cantata (1954); *Das letzte Spiel*, ballet (1955). **ORCH.:** Suite (1938); 5 syms. (1940, 1940, 1942, 1943, 1943); *Aeolische Suite* for Strings (1943); Concertino for English Horn and Strings (1949); *Divertimento* for 5 Winds and Strings (1951); Concerto for Harpsichord, Flute, Bassoon, and Strings (1952); Concertino for Flute and Strings (1953); Concertino for Accordion and Orch. (1955); Concerto for Violas da Gamba, 3 Woodwind Instruments, and Strings (1957); Piano Concerto (1962); *Hymnus* for Oboe and Orch. (1964); *Concerto for Orch.* (1964); Organ Concerto (1965); Saxophone Concerto (1966); Horn Concerto (1967); Concerto for Strings (1968); *Evolution* for 19 Winds, 3 Double Basses, Harp, and Percussion (1972). **CHAMBER:** Oboe Quartet (1938); Wind Quintet (1938); 3 string quartets (1938, 1941, 1953); Wind Octet (1941); Octet for Clarinet, Bassoon, Horn, and Strings (1960); Piano Quintet (1960); Wind Sextet (1966); also 15 sonatas, 16 duos, 16 trios, and many keyboard pieces. **VOCAL:** Sacred works, including *Missa "Dona nobis pacem"* (1953), *Weihnachtsmotette* (1955), and *Psalm CXXXV* for Solo Voices, Chorus, and Orch. (1963); secular works, including 14 sets of lieder.

WRITINGS: *Praktische Harmonielehre* (Berlin, 1938; 2ⁿᵈ ed., rev., 1972); *Der grosse Acker* (Berlin, 1946); *Beiträge zu einer neuen Musikkunde* (Berlin, 1947–48); *Einführung in die moderne Musik* (Halle, 1951); *Klingende Elementarlehre* (Berlin, 1951; 2ⁿᵈ ed., 1973); *Modern Jazz* (Berlin, 1962); *Die Oper im 20. Jahrhundert* (Wolfenbüttel, 1962–73); *Der Schlüssel zur Musik von heute* (Düsseldorf, 1967); *Musikleben in Japan* (Kassel, 1967); *Die grossen Orchester* (Düsseldorf, 1969).—NS/LK/DM

Borroff, Edith, American musicologist, composer, and writer; b. N.Y., Aug. 2, 1925. She was educated at the Oberlin (Ohio) Cons., the American Cons. of Music in Chicago (B.Mus., 1946; M.M., 1948), and the Univ. of Mich. (Ph.D., 1958, with the diss. *The Instrumental Music of Jean-Joseph Cassanea de Mondonville*). She taught at Milwaukee-Downer Coll. (1950–54), Hillsdale (Mich.) Coll. (1958–62), the Univ. of Wisc. (1962–66), Eastern Mich. Univ. (1966–72), and the State Univ. of N.Y. at Binghamton (1973–92). In addition to her books and articles on various aspects of music, she also wrote poetry and fiction.

WRITINGS: *Elisabeth Jacquet de La Guerre* (1966); *The Music of the Baroque* (1970); *Music in Europe and the United States: A History* (1971; 2ⁿᵈ ed., 1990); *Notations and Editions (A Book in Honor of Louise Cuyler)* (1974); with M. Irvin, *Music in Perspective* (1976); *Three American Composers* (1986); *American Opera: A Checklist* (1992); *Music Melting Round: A History of Music in the United States* (1995); *Keep Trying!: My Life* (1999).

WORKS: DRAMATIC: *Spring Over Brooklyn*, musical (1954); *Pygmalion*, incidental music to Shaw's play (1955); *La Folle de Chaillot*, incidental music to Giraudou's play (1962); *The Sun and the Wind*, musical fable (1974–76). **ORCH.:** Concerto for Marimba and Small Orch. (1981). **B a n d :** *Variations* (1968). **C H A M B E R :** 4 string quartets (n.d., 1943, 1943, 1974); Trio for Violin, Viola, and Cello (1943); Variations for Cello and Piano (1944); Clarinet Quintet (1948); 2 cello sonatas (1949, 1993); *Vorspiel über das Thema "In dulci jubilo"* for 2 Flutes, 2 Horns, and Piano (1951); *Sonatina Giocosa* for Viola and Piano (1953; also for Violin and Piano, 1980); Horn Sonata (1955); *Variations and Theme* for Oboe and Piano (1956); *Voices in Exile*, 3 canons for Flute and Viola (1962); *IONS: 14 Pieces in the Form of a Sonnet* for Flute and Piano (1968); *Game Pieces*, suite for Woodwind Quintet (1980); *Divertimento* for Flute (1980); Trio for Tenor Saxophone, Piano, and Percussion (1982); Trio for Violin, Cello, and Piano (1983); Suite for Percussion, 8 canons for 6 Players (1984); *The Elements*, sonata for Violin and Cello (1987); *Comic Miniatures*, suite for Violin and Piano (1988); *Mottoes*, suite for 8 Saxophones (1989); *5 Pieces* for Viola and Piano (1989); *2 Pieces from the Old Rag Bag: Sad Sack and Ragamuffin* for 4 Saxophones (1989); *An Historical Anagram*, 11 pieces for 2 Recorder Players (1991); *32 Variations in the Form of a Sonata* for Clarinet and Piano (1991); *Rondelay* for 2 Violins (1992); Sonata for Violin, Cello, and Piano (1995); *Interactions*, suite for 2 Oboes (1996); *Theme, Variations, and Coda*, quintet for Clarinet, Violin, Viola, Cello, and Piano (1997); Suite for Recorder and Piano (1998); Trio for Viola, Horn, and Piano (1999). **KEYBOARD: P i a n o :** Suite (1949); *2 Rags* (1952, 1972); *Sonata on English Folk Tunes* for Piano, 4–Hands (1978); *Fantasy* for 2 Pianos (1985); *Variations on a Trill* (1985); *International Suite* (1994). **H a r p s i c h o r d :** (2) *Figures of Speech* (1987, 1990). **O r g a n :** *Passacaglia* (1946); 3 Chorale Preludes (1948, 1949, 1982); *Organ Prelude in Dorian* (1950); *Variations on Two American Tunes* (1982); *An American Olio, or, General Ruckus* for 2 Players at 1 Console (1983); *DIPTYCH* (1985); *Honors for His Name: A Celebration of Praises* (1985); *Wings of Love*, sonata (1989); *Meditation and Toccata* (1989); *Aria* (1993). **VOCAL: C h o r a l :** 3 *Madrigals* for Women's Voices (1951); *Missa Patrinae Rerum Domini* for Chorus (1961; also for Soprano and Organ); *Psalm of Praise* (1972); *The Poet* for Women's Voices and Piano (1973); *Choral Trilogy* (1986); *Light in Dark Places: Slavery and Freedom in Nineteenth-Century America* (1988); *A Joyful Noise for Chorus*, Soloists, Piano, and 3 Trumpets (1992). **S o n g s :** Many, including: *7 Early Songs* (1947–50); *Modern Love*, 7 songs after Keats and Shelley (1979); *Food and Gladness*, 7 songs (1986); *A House of Love*, 5 songs (1986); *Changeling* for Soprano, Oboe, Bassoon, and Piano (1990); *5 Whitman Songs* for Tenor and Piano (1990); *Trilogy*, 3 songs for Baritone, Horn, and Piano (1998).

BIBL.: J. Regier, *The Organ Compositions of E. B.: An Introduction* (diss., Univ. of Okla., 1993).—NS/LK/DM

Bortkiewicz, Sergei (Eduardovich), Russian pianist and composer; b. Kharkov, Feb. 28, 1877; d. Vienna, Oct. 25, 1952. He was a pupil of Liadov at the St. Petersburg Cons. (1896–99), and later studied with Jadassohn in Leipzig (1900–02). He made his debut as a pianist in Munich in 1902, and subsequently made concert tours of Germany, Australia, Hungary, France, and Russia. From 1904 to 1914 he lived in Berlin, and taught at the Klindworth-Scharwenka Cons.; then returned to Russia; was in Vienna from 1920 to 1929, in Berlin from 1929 to 1934, and again in Vienna from 1934. His compositions include an opera, *Acrobats*, 2 syms., *Austrian Suite* and *Yugoslav Suite* for Orch., 4 piano concertos, Violin Concerto, Cello Concerto, piano pieces, and songs. He was the author of the book *Die seltsame Liebe Peter Tschaikowskys und der Nadezhda von Meck* (1938).—NS/LK/DM

Bortniansky, Dimitri (Stepanovich), Russian composer; b. Glukhov, Ukraine, 1751; d. St. Petersburg, Oct. 10, 1825. He was a choirboy in the court chapel, where he attracted the attention of Galuppi, who was at the time conductor there; was sent to Italy, where he studied with Galuppi and with other Italian masters in Venice, Bologna, Rome, and Naples (1769–79). In Italy he produced his operas *Creonte* (Venice, Nov. 26, 1776; lost) and *Quinto Fabio* (Modena, Dec. 26, 1778). In 1779 he returned to St. Petersburg and became director of vocal music at the court chapel (1796); as a conductor of the chapel choir he introduced radical reforms for improvement of singing standards; composed for his choir a number of sacred works of high quality, among them a Mass according to the Greek Orthodox ritual; 35 sacred concerti in 4 parts; 10 Psalms in 8 parts; 10 concerti for Double Choir; etc. He also continued to compose for the stage; produced the comic operas, in French, *Le Faucon* (Gatchina, Oct. 22, 1786) and *Le Fils rival* (Pavlovsk, Oct. 22, 1787). His sacred choral works are publ. in 10 vols., ed. by Tchaikovsky.

BIBL.: B. Dobrohotov, *D. B.* (Moscow, 1950).—NS/LK/DM

Börtz, Daniel, Swedish composer; b. Osby, Hässleholm, Aug. 8, 1943. He studied composition privately with Fernström and Rosenberg, and then at the Stockholm Musikhögskolan with Blomdahl (1962–65) and Lidholm (1965–68); he also received training in violin from Barkel and Grünfarb, and later in electronic music from Koenig at the Univ. of Utrecht. From 1972 to 1979 he was secretary of the Swedish Composer's Soc. He taught at the Stockholm Musikhögskolan from 1987. Börtz's works, which reflect the state of contemporary usages, nevertheless display an individualistic approach to melodic and harmonic writing.

WORKS: DRAMATIC: *Muren—Vägen—Ordet*, liturgical opera (1971–72); *Landskab med flod*, chamber opera (1972); *Den heliga Birgittas död och Mottagande i himmelen*, liturgical opera (Lund, Oct. 7, 1973); *Bacchanterna*, opera (1988–90; Stockholm, Nov. 2, 1991). ORCH.: *Intrada* (1964); *In memoriam di* (1969); 11 syms. (1973; 1974–75; 1975–76; 1976–77; 1980–81; 1981–83; 1984–86; 1987–88; 1990–91; 1992; 1993–94); Concerto for Violin, Bassoon, and Chamber Orch. (1974); *Concerto grosso* No. 1 (1977–78) and No. 2 for Wind Orch. (1981); *October Music* for Strings (1978); Concerto for Bassoon, Winds, and Percussion (1978–79); Concerto for Cello and Chamber Orch. (1980); Concerto for Piano, Percussion, and Chamber Orch. (1981–82); Violin Concerto (1985); Oboe Concerto (1986); *Parodos* (1987). CHAMBER: *5 Preludes* for Flute (1964); *Monologhi I* for Cello (1965–66), *II* for Bassoon (1966), *III* for Violin (1967), and *IV* for Piano and Tape (1970); 3 string quartets (1966; 1971; 1985–87). VOCAL: *Il canto dei canti di Salomone* for Soprano and Instruments (1965); *Voces* for 3 Voices, Orch., and Tape (1968); *Josef K* for Narrator, 8 Soli, Chorus, and Orch., after Kafka (1969); *Night Winds* for Vocal Quartet (1972); *Nightflies* for Mezzo-soprano and Chamber Ensemble (1973); *Fläcker av liv* for 2 Narrators, Soli, Chorus, and Orch. (1979–80).—NS/LK/DM

Borup-Jørgensen, (Jens) Axel, Danish composer; b. Hjørring, Nov. 22, 1924. He studied with Rachlew (piano), and with Schierbeck and Jersild (orchestration) at the Royal Danish Cons. of Music in Copenhagen (1946–51); later attended the summer sessions in new music at Darmstadt (1959, 1962). His works came to reflect the ideals of Fortner, Ligeti, and Stockhausen.

WORKS: ORCH.: Concertino for Piano, Flute, Bassoon, and Strings (1948–49); *Fantasy* for Flute and Strings (1949); Clarinet Concerto (1949–50); *Chamber Concerto* for Violin and Small Orch. (1951); *Sommasvit* for Strings (1957); *Cretaufoni* (1960–61); *Insulae* for Strings (1961–62); *Stykker* (1963–65); *Marin* (1963–70); *Nordic Summer Pastorale* for Small Orch. (1964); *Déjà vu* for Guitar and Strings (1983). CHAMBER: 5 string quartets (1950; 1951; 1954–55; 1960; 1965); Viola Sonata (1952–53); *Partita* for Viola (1953–54); *Improvisations* for String Quartet (1955); *Music* for Percussion and Viola (1955–56); *Microorganisms* for String Quartet (1956); Sonatina for 2 Violins (1958); *Sonata breve* for Viola and Piano (1959–60); *Mobile* for Viola, Marimba, and Piano (1961); *Vinterstykke* for String Quartet (1967); *Tagebuch im Winter* for Flute, String Quartet, and Piano (1970–72); *Distichon* for Violin and Piano (1972–73); *Malinconia* for String Quartet (1972–74); *Recostruzioni* for Wind Quintet (1973–74); *Carambolage* for Piano, Electric Guitar, and Percussion (1976–77); *Musica Autumnalis* for Winds, Percussion, and Electric Organ (1977); Piano Quintet (1978); *Periphrasis* for Flute and Percussion (1979); *Favola* for Flute and Harp (1980); *La Primavera* for 2 Percussionists (1982); *Coast of Sirens* for 7 Instruments and Tape (1985). PIANO: *7 Preludes* (1958–59); *Winter Pieces* (1959); *Vinter-epigrammer* (1975); *Epigrammer*

(1976); *Thalatta, Thalatta* (1988); Trio for Clarinet, Cello, and Piano (1988–90); 2 *Movements* for Harp (1993). VOCAL: *Pocket Oratorium* for 16 Voices and Instruments (1963–64); *Marin* for 24 Men's Voices (1969); songs.—NS/LK/DM

Borwick, Leonard, English pianist; b. Walthamstow, Feb. 26, 1868; d. Le Mans, France, Sept. 15, 1925. He studied with Clara Schumann in Frankfurt am Main, making his debut there (1889). He then performed in London (May 8, 1889), and made a concert tour in America and Australia (1911); also played in Europe. His programs included classics and moderns; in the last years of his career he played much music of Debussy and Ravel. He made a transcription for piano of Debussy's *L'Après-midi d'un faune.*—NS/LK/DM

Bos, Coenraad Valentyn, Dutch pianist and pedagogue; b. Leiden, Dec. 7, 1875; d. Chappaqua, N.Y., Aug. 5, 1955. He was a pupil of Julius Rontgen at the Amsterdam Cons. (1892–95), and later studied in Berlin. With Jan van Veen (violin) and Jan van Lier (cello), he formed a trio in Berlin that enjoyed an enviable reputation during its active period (1896–1910). His masterly accompaniments on a tour with Ludwig Wüllner attracted more than ordinary attention, and made him one of the most celebrated accompanists both in Europe and in the U.S., where he eventually settled. He was the accompanist of Culp, Hempel, Traubel, Kreisler, Schumann-Heink, Casals, Gerhard, Thibaud, Farrar, and many others. He taught at the Juilliard School of Music in N.Y. from 1934 to 1952. In collaboration with Ashley Pettis, he publ. *The Well-Tempered Accompanist* (1949).—NS/LK/DM

Bosch, Pieter Joseph van den, Netherlands organist; b. Hoboken, c. 1736; d. Antwerp, Feb. 19, 1803. He became organist at the Antwerp Cathedral in 1765, remaining at this post until 1797. He composed a number of keyboard works.—NS/LK/DM

Boschi, Giuseppe Maria, Italian bass who flourished in the late 17th century and the first half of the 18th century. He married the contralto Francesca Vanini in 1698. After singing in Venice (1707; 1708–09), he went to London with his wife and made his first appearance there in Mancini's *Idaspe fedele* on Nov. 19, 1710. On Feb. 24, 1711, he created the role of Argante in Handel's *Rinaldo*. After singing again in Venice (1713–14), he appeared in Dresden (1717–20), after which he was called to London by Handel to serve as one of the principal members of his Royal Academy of Music opera productions (1720–28). He subsequently returned once more to Venice, where he sang in opera (1728–29) and later in the choir at San Marco.—NS/LK/DM

Boschot, Adolphe, French music critic; b. Fontenay-sous-Bois, near Paris, May 4, 1871; d. Paris, June 1, 1955. He was music critic of *Echo de Paris* from 1910, and of *Revue Bleue* from 1919; founded, with Théodore de Wyzewa, the Paris Mozart Soc.; was elected to the Institut de France in 1926, succeeding Widor as permanent secretary of the Académie des Beaux-Arts. His greatest work is an exhaustive biography of Berlioz in three vols.: *La Jeunesse d'un romantique, Hector Berlioz, 1803–31* (Paris, 1906; rev. ed., 1946), *Un Romantique sous Louis- Philippe, Hector Berlioz, 1831–42* (Paris, 1908; rev. ed., 1948), and *Le Crépuscule d'un romantique, Hector Berlioz, 1842–69* (Paris, 1913; rev. ed., 1950). Other books are *Le Faust de Berlioz* (1910; new ed., 1945); *Carnet d'art* (1911); *Une Vie romantique, Hector Berlioz* (an abridgement of his three-vol. work, 1919; 27th ed., 1951; also in Eng.; definitive ed., 1965); *Chez les musiciens* (3 vols., 1922–26); *Entretiens sur la beauté* (1927); *La Lumière de Mozart* (1928); *Le Mystère musical* (1929); *La Musique et la vie* (2 vols., 1931–33); *Théophile Gautier* (1933); *Mozart* (1935); *La Vie et les oeuvres d'Alfred Bruneau* (1937); *Musiciens-Poètes* (1937); *Maîtres d'hier et de jadis* (1944); *Portraits de musiciens* (3 vols., 1946–50); *Souvenirs d'un autre siècle* (1947). Boschot tr. into French the librettos of several of Mozart's operas. He was also prominent as a poet; publ. the collections *Poèmes dialogués* (1901) and *Chez nos poètes* (1925).—NS/LK/DM

Boscovich, Alexander Uriah, significant Israeli composer; b. Klausenburg, Transylvania, Aug. 16, 1907; d. Tel Aviv, Nov. 13, 1964. He studied in Budapest; later enrolled at the Vienna Academy of Music, where he studied piano with Victor Ebenstein and composition with Richard Stöhr; then went to Paris, where he took courses with Dukas and Boulanger; also had a few lessons in piano with Cortot. From 1930 to 1938 he was engaged as conductor at the State Opera in Cluj; in 1938 he emigrated to Palestine; taught at the Tel Aviv Cons. (1945–64); wrote music criticism for the Israeli newspaper *Haaretz*. In his music, Boscovich incorporated quasi-oriental motifs in the framework of Western music; in several works, he made use of authentic Jewish folk songs, adorning them with modernistic harmonies. In this manner he wrote his most popular piece, *Chansons populaires juives* for Orch. (Haifa, March 15, 1938; orig. entitled *The Golden Chain*). Other works: Violin Concerto (1942); Oboe Concerto (1943); *Adonai Ro'i* (The Lord Is My Shepherd) for Alto Voice and Orch. (1946); *Semitic Suite* for Piano (1947; also for 2 Pianos, and for Orch.); *Piccola suite* for Flute, Snare Drum, and String Orch. (1956–57); *Psalm* for Violin and Piano (1957; contains thematic material from the Violin Concerto); *Cantico di ma'alot* (Song of Ascent) for Orch. (1960); *Bal Yisrael* (Daughter of Israel), cantata for Tenor, Chorus, and Orch. (1960–61); *With Joy and Gladness* for 2 Violins, with optional Drum and Triangle (1961); *Piece* for Oboe and Harpsichord (1961–62); *Lament* for Violin or Cello, and Piano (1962); *Concerto da camera* for Violin and Chamber Ensemble (1962); *Ornaments* for Flute and 4 Orch. Groups (1964).—NS/LK/DM

Bose, Fritz, German musicologist; b. Messenthin, July 26, 1906; d. Berlin, Aug. 16, 1975. He studied at the Humboldt Univ. in Berlin, where his teachers included Abert and Schering (musicology), Hornbostel (ethnomusicology), and Sachs (organology); received his Ph.D. there in 1934 with the diss. *Die Musik der Uitoto* (publ. in Berlin, 1934). He was a lecturer of the Univ. of Berlin from 1934 to 1945; in 1953 he was named director of the

history dept. of the Institut für Musikforschung in Berlin, retiring in 1971; he also taught at the Technical Univ. of Berlin (1963–67). In 1966 he founded the Deutsche Gesellschaft für Musik des Orients, which he headed until 1972. He also served as ed. of the *Jahrbuch für musikalische Volks- und Völkerkunde* from 1963 until his death. He wrote the study *Musikalische Völkerkunde* (Freiburg im Briesgau and Zürich, 1953).—NS/LK/DM

Bose, Hans-Jürgen von, German composer and teacher; b. Munich, Dec. 24, 1953. He went to Frankfurt am Main and studied at the Hoch Cons. (1969–72) and with Hans Engelmann (composition) and Klaus Billing (piano) at the Hochschule für Musik (1972–75). In 1980 and 1985 he held scholarships at the Villa Massimo in Rome. In 1986 he was elected a member of the Akademie der Künste in Berlin. In 1992 he became a teacher of composition at the Munich Hochschule für Musik.

WORKS: DRAMATIC: *Blütbund*, chamber opera (1974; Hamburg, June 8, 1977); *Das Diplom*, chamber opera (1975; Ulm, Nov. 26, 1976); *Die Nacht aus Blei*, ballet (1980–81; Berlin, Nov. 1, 1981); *Die Leiden des jungen Werthers*, lyrical scenes (1983–84; Schwetzingen, April 30, 1986); *Chimäre*, opera (Aachen, June 11, 1986); *Werther- Szenen*, ballet (1988; Schweinfurt, April 26, 1989); *63: Dream Palace*, opera (1989; Munich, May 6, 1990); *Medea*, ballet (Zürich, Feb. 20, 1994); *Schlachthof 5*, opera after Vonnegut's *Slaughterhouse 5* (1994–95; Munich, July 1, 1996). **ORCH.:** *Morphogenesis* (1975; Baden-Baden, Sept. 12, 1976); Sym. No. 1 (1976; Munich, March 10, 1978); *Musik für ein Haus voll Zeit* for Large Chamber Orch. (1978; Kiel, April 9, 1979); *Travesties in a Sad Landscape* for Chamber Orch. (London, Nov. 19, 1978); *Symphonic Fragment* for Tenor, Baritone, Bass, Chorus, and Orch. (Darmstadt, June 1, 1980); *Variationen* for 15 Strings (1980; Frankfurt am Main, March 29, 1981; rev. 1990; Berlin, Jan. 25, 1991); *Idyllen* (1982–83; Berlin, April 23, 1983); *Symbolum* for Organ and Orch. (1985; Munich, May 27, 1988); *Labyrinth I* (1987; Stuttgart, March 4, 1991); *...Other Echoes Inhabit the Garden* for Oboe and Orch. (Donaueschingen, Oct. 16, 1987); *Prozess* for Chamber Orch. (1987–88; Radio France, Paris, March 5, 1988); *Zwei Studien* (Saarlandischer Rundfunk, Saarbrucken, May 28, 1989); *Scene* for Chamber Orch. (1991); *Concertino per il H.W.H.* for Chamber Orch. (Munich, Sept. 29, 1991); *Scene* for Chamber Orch. (London, Oct. 8, 1991); *Salut für Billy Pilgrim*, piano concerto (1995). **CHAMBER:** 4 string quartets: No. 1 (1973), No. 2 (1976–77), No. 3 (1986–89; Saarbrücken, May 25, 1989), and No. 4, with Sampler (1996); *Threnos—Hommage à Bernd Alois Zimmermann* for Viola and Cello (1975); Sonata for Solo Violin (1975); String Trio (1978); *Solo* for Cello (1978–79); *...vom Wege abkommen* for Cello (1981–82); *Drei Studien* for Violin and Piano (1986; Paris, April 24, 1988); *Drei Epitaphe* for Wind Sextet (Berlin, Sept. 12, 1987); Nonett (Salzburg, Aug. 21, 1988); *Befragung* for Clarinet, 2 Violins, Viola, Cello, and Double Bass (1988; Mönchengladbach, June 5, 1989); *Edge* for Violin (Berlin, Nov. 17, 1989). **Piano:** *Labyrinth II* (1987; Frankfurt am Main, Jan. 8, 1988); *Origami*, 2 episodes for Piano, 4–Hands (1991; Deutschlandsberg, Oct. 18, 1992). **VOCAL:** *Todesfuge* for Baritone, Chorus, and Organ (1972; Frankfurt am Main, Nov. 10, 1991); 3 Songs for Tenor and Chamber Orch. (1977); *Guarda el canto* for Soprano and String Quartet (1981–82); *Sappho-Gesänge* for Mezzo-soprano and Piano or Chamber Orch. (1982); *...im Wind gesprochen* for Soprano, 2 Narrators, Chorus, Organ, and Chamber Orch. (1984–85; Stuttgart, Sept. 20, 1985); *Sonnet XLII* for Baritone and String Quartet, after Shakespeare (1985; Hamburg, Feb. 7, 1986); *5 Gesänge* for Baritone and 10 Instruments, after Garcia Lorca (1986; Cologne, Feb. 6, 1987); *Karfreitags-Sonett* for Chorus (1986); *Sechs deutsche Volkslieder* for Baritone and 8 Instruments (Berlin, Oct. 18, 1988); *Vier Lieder* for Soprano and 10 Instruments (Berlin, Oct. 18, 1988); *Achalm* for Soprano and 7 Instruments (Frankfurt am Main, Sept. 8, 1989); *Love after Love* for Soprano and Orch. (1990–91; Hamburg, Oct. 13, 1991); *Ein Brudermord* for Baritone, Accordion, Cello, and Tape (Stuttgart, Nov. 8, 1991); *In hora mortis* for Speaker and String Orch. (1991; Cologne, March 10, 1992); *Siete Textos de Miguel Angel Bustos* for Soprano, Accordion, and Cello (Digne-les-Bains, Oct. 11, 1991).—**NS/LK/DM**

Bose, Sterling (Belmont) (Boze, Bozo), early jazz trumpeter, cornetist (singer); b. Florence, Ala., Feb. 23, 1906; d. St. Petersburg, Fla., June 1958. He sat in with various New Orleans bands in early 1920s (including Tom Brown's). Late in 1923 he moved to St. Louis; gigged with various bands, then with Crescent City Jazzers and Arcadia Serenaders until 1927. He joined Jean Goldkette in Detroit and during winter 1927–28 played a season for Goldkette at Pla-Mor Ballroom, Kansas City. Then he worked for Radio WGN house band in Chicago until autumn 1930. He joined Ben Pollack in November 1930; played there on and off until May 1933. He was with Eddie Sheasby in Chicago. Then in N.Y., he did extensive studio work with Victor Young. He joined Joe Haymes' Band in spring of 1934; remained when Tommy Dorsey assumed leadership in 1935. He was with Ray Noble in early 1936, occasionally did vocals with the Noble Band (i.e. "Big Chief de Sota" recording). He was with Benny Goodman in August and September 1936; left through illness. Early in 1937 he was a member of Lana Webster Band in N.Y., then joined the Glenn Miller Orch. until October 1937, then was with the Bob Crosby Band until early in 1939. He played regularly at Nick's in N.Y.; had a short spell with Bobby Hackett Big Band in spring of 1939. He was a member of short lived Bob Zurke Big Band until April 1940, then he spent six months with Jack Teagarden until taking his own trio into Muggsy McGraw's Club in Chicago (December 1940). He played with Bud Freeman's Big Band in Chicago (February 1942). He moved back to N.Y. during early 1943, and worked with Geory Brunis at Famous Door, then with Bobby Sherwood's Band from July until November 1943. He performed regularly with the Miff Mole Band at Nick's: also with Art Hodes at same venue in June 1944, and briefly with Horace Heidt in August 1944, then freelanced in N.Y. before moving back to Chicago in 1945. Freelanced in Chicago, N.Y., and Mobile before moving to Fla.; had occasional work with the Tiny Hill Band. From March 1948, he led his own band at the Municipal Ballroom, St. Petersburg, Fla., then various club residencies before playing at Soreno Lounge, St. Petersburg, from 1950–57. Bose suffered a long illness before dying of self-inflicted gun-shot wounds.

DISC.: Arcadian Serenaders: "You Gotta Know How/Angry" (1925). J. Goldkette: "Just Imagine", "My Blackbirds Are Bluebirds Now/Don't Be Like That" (1928). J. Teagarden: "Rockin' Chair/Loveless Love", "You Rascal, You" (1931). B. Pollack: "Two Tickets to Georgia" (1933). Dorsey Brothers Orch.: *Harlem Lullaby* (1933). J. Mercer: "Lord, I Give You My Children/The Bathtub Ran Over Again" (1934). Tommy

Dorsey: *Having a Wonderful Time* (1935). R. Noble: "Big Chief De Sota" (1936). Bob Crosby and His Orch.: *South Rampart Street Parade* (1936). Bing Crosby: "I'm Prayin' Humble" (1938). B. Zurke: "Between the Devil and the Deep Blue Sea/I've Found a New Baby" (1939).—**JC/LP**

Bösendorfer, firm of piano makers at Vienna, specializing in concert grands. It was established by Ignaz Bösendorfer (b. Vienna, July 27, 1794; d. there, April 14, 1859) in 1828, and later managed by his son Ludwig (b. Vienna, April 10, 1835; d. there, May 9, 1919). The firm, retaining its original name, was taken over by Carl Hutterstrasser (1863–1942). The Bösendorfer Saal (opened by Hans von Bülow in 1872, and used until 1913) was one of the finest chamber music concert halls in Europe.—**NS/LK/DM**

Boskovsky, Willi, noted Austrian violinist and conductor; b. Vienna, June 16, 1909; d. Visp, Switzerland, April 21, 1991. He entered the Vienna Academy of Music at age 9 to study violin with Mayrecker and Moravec, graduating at 17 with the Fritz Kreisler Prize. He made appearances as a soloist until 1939, although he joined the Vienna Phil. in 1933; from 1939 to 1971 he was one of its concertmasters. In 1937 he founded the Boskovsky Quartet, and in 1948 the Vienna Octet, with which he remained active until 1958. From 1954 to 1979 he served as conductor of the New Year's Day Concerts of the Vienna Phil., which brought him international recognition through its radio and television broadcasts. From 1969 he also was chief conductor of the Vienna Strauss Orch., and likewise conducted the Vienna Mozart Ensemble.—**NS/LK/DM**

Bosmans, Henriëtte (Hilda), Dutch pianist and composer; b. Amsterdam, Dec. 5, 1895; d. there, July 2, 1952. She studied piano with her mother at the Amsterdam Cons., and embarked on a career as a pianist. In 1927 she took lessons in composition with Pijper. In her music, she cultivated an agreeable neo-Classical idiom, with coloristic éclat, suggesting the techniques and devices of French Impressionism. She wrote many songs to texts by French poets.

WORKS: Violin Sonata (1918); Cello Sonata (1919); Piano Trio (1921); 2 cello concertos (1922, 1924); *Poem* for Cello and Orch. (1926); String Quartet (1928); Concertino for Piano and Orch. (1928; Geneva, April 6, 1929); *Konzertstück* for Flute and Orch. (1929); *Konzertstück* for Violin and Orch. (1934); *Doodenmarsch* (March of the Dead) for Narrator and Chamber Orch. (1946); piano pieces.—**NS/LK/DM**

Bosseur, Jean-Yves, French composer and musicologist; b. Paris, Feb. 5, 1947. He received training in composition from Stockhausen and Pousseur in Cologne before taking his Ph.D. at the Univ. of Paris I. After working as a producer for Radio France, he was prof. of musicology at the Univ. of Paris IV. He also was co-founder of the Groupe Intervalles. In addition to many articles, he publ. a number of books, among them *Musique, passion d'artistes* (1988; Eng. tr., 1991), *Le sonore et le visuel* (1992; Eng. tr., 1993), *John Cage* (1995), *Le temps de la prendre: Journal musical (1967/...)* (1997), and *Musique et arts plastiques: Interactions au Xe siècle* (1998).

WORKS: ORCH.: *In extremis* (1975; rev. 1989); *Traverses* for Flute Quartet and String Orch. (1982; Dôle, March 1984); *Eisleriana* for Harmony Orch. (1995; Thouars, Feb. 1996). CHAMBER: *Un arraché de partout* for 4 Trumpets, 4 Trombones, Hammond Organ, 2 Electric Guitars, Xylophone, Marimbaphone, Vibraphone, and 2 Percussion (1967); *Alto molto* for Viola (1975; rev. 1992); *Alliages de cuivre* for Trumpet, Horn, Trombone, and Tuba (1981); *Byrdy* for Instrument(s) (1986–87); *Stream* for Accordion (1988); *Quinaire* for Flute, Clarinet, Violin, Cello, and Piano (Paris, Dec. 1989); *Hong-Kong Variations* for 7 Instruments (1990); *Portrait de Geneviève Asse* for Harpsichord, Flute, and Cello (1991); *En quête de tango* for 7 Instruments (Brussels, April 1994); *Morty's* for Violin, Cello, Flute, Clarinet(s), and Piano (1996; Paris, Jan. 1997); *Liptov* for 7 Instruments (1997); *Patchwork* for 11 Instruments (1998); *O.D. (Portrait d'Olivier Debré)* for Instrumental Ensemble (Paris, June 1999). Piano: *Portrait de Jiri Kolar* (1978–83; Paris, Sept. 1985); *Seul* (Brussels, Sept. 1981); *Empreintes nocturnes* (1981; Paris, Sept. 1982). VOCAL: *Quelques pages du Livre des Questions* for Soprano and 9 Instruments, after Edmond Jabès (1979–80; Paris, Jan. 1980); *Satie's Dream* for Soprano and 5 Instruments, after Kenneth White (1980–81; Brussels, Oct. 1981); *Portrait d'Albert Ayme* for Soprano and 5 Instruments, after Michel Butor (1980–81; Paris, Nov. 1981); *The Sun-Moon Sequence* for Soprano and 4 Instruments, after Kenneth White (Châtenay-Malabry, Dec. 1982); *Les Tarots-musiciens* for Soprano and 5 Players, after Michel Butor (Nice, June 1983); *Allégories* for Soprano and 5 Instruments, after Claude Melin (Metz, Nov. 1983); *Faïences* for Soprano, Mezzo-soprano, and 3 Clarinets, after Paul Louis Rossi (1990–91; Périgueux, May 1993); *Aubade* for Mezzo-soprano, Flute(s), Clarinet(s), and Piano (1993–94; Quimper, March 1994); *Teneur* for Soprano, 2 Pianos, Clarinet, and Cello, after Ludovic Janvier (1994; Radio France, Feb. 1995); Mass for 5 Soloists, Chorus, and 6 Instruments (1994–95; Valence, June 1995); *Memorandum I* for Vocal Soloist(s) (1996; Paris, April 1999) and *II* for Mezzo-soprano, Bass Clarinet or Cello, and Piano (1998).—NS/LK/DM

Bossi, (Marco) Enrico,

Italian composer, father of **(Rinaldo) Renzo Bossi**; b. Salo, Brescia, April 25, 1861; d. at sea (en route from America to Europe), Feb. 20, 1925. Son and pupil of the organist Pietro Bossi of Morbegno (1834–96), he studied at the Liceo Rossini in Bologna (1871–73), and at Milan (1873–81) under Sangali (piano), Fumagalli (organ), Campanari (violin), Boniforti (counterpoint), and Ponchielli (composition). He subsequently was maestro di cappella and organist at Como Cathedral (1881–89). He then was prof. of organ and harmony in the Royal Cons. San Pietro at Naples (until 1896), prof. of advanced composition and organ at the Liceo Benedetto Marcello in Venice (1896–1902), and director of the Liceo Musicale at Bologna (1902–12). After a brief period of retirement from teaching, he was director of the Music School of the Accademia di Santa Cecilia in Rome (1916–23). He toured Europe, England, and the U.S. as a pianist and organist. He also wrote *Metodo di studio per l'organo moderno* (in collaboration with G. Tebaldini; Milan, 1893).

WORKS: DRAMATIC: Opera: *Paquita* (Milan, 1881); *Il Veggente* (Milan, 1890; rewritten and produced as *Il Viandante*, Mannheim, 1896); *L'Angelo della notte*. OTHER: *Intermezzi Goldoniani* for String Orch.; *Concertstück* for Organ and Orch.; *Inno di Gloria* for Chorus and Organ; *Tota pulchra* for Chorus and Organ; *Missa pro Sponso et Sponsa* (Rome, 1896); *Il Cieco* for Solo, Chorus, and Orch. (1897); *Canticum Canticorum*, biblical cantata; *Il Paradiso Perduto* for Chorus and Orch. (Augsburg, 1903); *Surrexit pastor*, motet; *Giovanna d'Arco*, mystery play (Cologne, 1913); *Primavera classica* for Chorus; String Trio; Piano Trio; etc.

BIBL.: E. Dagnino, *M.E. B., Cenni biografici* (Rome, 1925); G.C. Paribeni, L. Orsini, and E. Bontempelli, *M.E. B.: Il Compositore, l'organista, l'uomo* (Milan, 1934); F. Mompellio, *M.E. B.* (Milan, 1952; contains list of works).—NS/LK/DM

Bossi, (Rinaldo) Renzo,

Italian conductor and composer, son of **(Marco) Enrico Bossi**; b. Como, April 9, 1883; d. Milan, April 2, 1965. He studied in Venice and in Leipzig, and took a course in conducting with Nikisch. He conducted at various cities in Italy. In 1916 he was appointed instructor at the Verdi Cons. in Milan. His biographical data and a complete list of works are appended to F. Mompellio's monograph on Enrico Bossi (Milan, 1952). See also S. Pintacuda, *R. B.* (Milan, 1955).

WORKS: DRAMATIC: Opera: *Passa la ronda* (Milan, March 3, 1919); *Volpino il calderaio* (Milan, Nov. 13, 1925); *La rosa rossa* (Parma, Jan. 9, 1940). Ballet: *Il trillo del diavolo* (1948). OTHER: Sym.; Violin Concerto; many minor pieces for various instruments.—NS/LK/DM

Bostic, Earl,

jazz/R&B alto saxophonist, arranger, leader; b. Tulsa, Okla., April 25, 1913; d. Rochester, N.Y., Oct. 28, 1965. He started on alto and clarinet while at local Booker T. Washington School. He worked with Terrence Holder's Band (1931–2), briefly with Bernie Moten early in 1933, then enrolled at Xavier Univ. in New Orleans; while there became proficient on several instruments; worked with Joe Robichaux (c. 1934). He left La., and worked with Ernie Fields' Band before joining Clarence Olden's Band in Columbus, Ohio. He played and arranged for a band jointly led by Charlie Creath and Fate Marable 1935–36, then joined Marion Sears' Band in Cleveland, subsequently was with Clyde Turpin in Buffalo. He relocated to N.Y. in January 1938, then joined Don Redman in April. He briefly played with Edgar Hayes, then led his own band at Small's (occasionally playing trumpet, guitar, and baritone sax); he also worked with Lips Page Band at Mime's Club, N.Y., during 1941, and later led his own band at that same venue. He was briefly with Lips Page, then joined Lionel Hampton in June 1943; he left the next year and formed his own band, residing at Small's from August 1944. He occasionally worked out-of-town gigs, including residency at Club Bengasi, Wash., during 1947. From the early 1950s, he enjoyed tremendous international success as a popular recording artist. "Flamingo" was a #1 R&B hit in 1951 and there were many others. He toured coast-to-coast extensively. An automobile accident rendered him inactive from December 1951 until April 1, 1952, when he resumed touring with a new band including John Coltrane on tenor and backup group vocals. A new group in December 1952 included Blue Mitchell, and Stanley Turrentine later played with the band. After moving to Los Angeles, Bostic suffered a serious heart attack in 1956, and was inactive for three years. He resumed touring in 1959, but work was again curtailed by illness. After a period of semi-retirement, he began a residency at the Midtown Tower Hotel in Rochester; after playing the opening night, he suffered another heart attack and died two days later. Earl Bostic was a prolific arranger during the early 1940s, scoring for Artie Shaw, Hot Lips Page, Paul Whiteman, Louis Prima, and others.

Disc.: *Alto-Tude* (1957); *Ain't Misbehavin'* (1959); *Jazz As I Feel It* (1963); *E.B. Plays Bossa Nova* (1963); *New Sound* (1964). **—JC/LP**

Boston, an MIT grad's high-tech idea of a rock band. **Membership:** Tom Scholz, voc., various inst. (b. Toledo, Ohio, March 10, 1947); Barry Goudreau, gtr. (b. Boston, Nov. 29, 1951); Brad Delp, voc. (b. Boston, June 12, 1951); Fran Sheehan, bs. (b. Boston, March 26, 1949); Sib Hashian, drm. (b. Boston, Aug. 17, 1949).

Boston started in the Tom Scholz's basement. Scholz had moved to Boston after earning a full scholarship to MIT, graduating with a 4.8 GPA. Polaroid signed him up to work on their ill-fated instant sound movies (obviated by the rise of videotape). During his off-hours, he recorded his songs, paying meticulous attention to the sound. By the time the Boston demos reached Epic Records, they had been in the works for six years. Epic signed the "band," which forced Scholz to put a band together! He brought in some local scene bar band cronies—Brad Delp, voc. (b. Boston, June 12, 1951); Fran Sheehan, bs. (b. Boston, March 26, 1949); Barry Goudreau, gtr. (b. Boston, Nov. 29, 1951); Sib Hashian, drm. (b. Boston, Aug. 17, 1949)—to work as the actual band, but in the studio, nearly everything is played by Scholz. He took a leave of absence from Polaroid to promote Boston's debut—and never returned.

Capitalizing on this element of Scholz's past, Epic's marketing department began selling Boston's debut with the slogan "better music through science," in an ad featuring the 6' 5" Scholz in a space suit. One critic called the band's sound "non-violent hard rock." On the strength of the singles "More Than a Feeling" (#5), "Long Time," and "Peace of Mind," along with album rock staples like "Rock and Roll Band," Boston's debut sold over 16 million records, holding the record for sales by a debut album for nearly a quarter of a century. The album got as high as #3 on the LP charts. The band went on tour, opening for the likes of Sammy Hagar, even though their album sold much faster than his. Scholz brought some of his technical inventions on tour to help them approximate the band's studio sheen.

Epic released the follow-up *Don't Look Back* in 1978. The title track went to #4, and the album topped the charts for two weeks. A second single, "A Man I'll Never Be," went top 30. However, "Feeling Satisfied" didn't fare that well. The band toured through 1979 and then disappeared for eight years.

In part, the layoff was due to a wave of legal problems. A management deal went sour. Then Scholz started having problems with his record company. First, they refused to let him produce a record for Hagar, ordering him into the studio to complete an album for Boston. Goudreau, growing impatient for a new Boston project, recorded his own solo album with the help of

Delp and Hashian. The album bombed, but Scholz took exception to his record company marketing it as "Almost Boston."

Scholz's work on the third Boston album did not proceed quickly enough for Epic Records, who needed their million-selling acts to record with somewhat more regularity. By 1982, the company started to withhold royalties in hopes that might motivate Scholz to finish the third Boston album. When Scholz complained, they laid a $20 million breach of contract suit on him. Scholz countersued, and the artist and his label spent the next five years in various legal wrangling. The record company got an injunction preventing the release of any Boston album, which didn't get lifted until 1985.

In the meantime, Scholz formed Scholz Research and Development and started to work on technological solutions to problems he had as a musician. He came out with the Rockman line of amplifiers, effects, and personal practice units. They had 3,000 orders before the first unit left the factory and did millions of dollars worth of business a year, helping to finance the third Boston album. In the mean time, Godreau left the band to form Orion The Hunter, a band featuring vocalist-guitarist Fran Cosmo.

By 1986, Boston's *Third Stage* came out, zooming to the top of the charts and staying there for four weeks. The single "Amanda" topped the charts, and the followup, "We're Ready," reached #9. The album became the first compact disc to go gold, and sold four million copies in four weeks. The band toured off and on through 1989.

In 1990, Scholz started working on a fourth recording. None of the original members of the band remained. Hashian, Sheehan, and percussionist Jim Masdea sued Scholz for royalties (he settled out of court). He finally won his suits against the record company, but lost against his old manager. Meanwhile, Delp and Goudreau, along with several others, formed a band called RTZ. Their first album *Return to Zero*, spent the years 1991–92 on the verge of breaking through, but never quite made it.

Four years in the making, Boston next released *Walk On*. Fran Cosmo replaced Brad Delp. The record debuted at #7, got as high as #5, then plummeted off the charts. Still the band did a spectacular tour, featuring a massive pipe organ that Scholz would swing to on a rope during the show. Another tour in 1996 got cancelled when Scholz hurt his hand playing basketball.

The band hit the road in 1997, supporting a Greatest Hits package. Delp returned to the fold and shared vocal and guitar chores with Cosmo. Boston went into the studio sometime in 1998, but as of yet, nothing has been released.

Disc.: *Boston* (1976); *Don't Look Back* (1978); *Third Stage* (1986); *Walk On* (1994); *Greatest Hits: Rock & Roll Band* (1997). **—HB**

Bostridge, Ian (Charles), English tenor; b. London, Dec. 25, 1964. He was educated at St. John's Coll., Oxford (M.A., Ph.D. in history, 1990), St. John's Coll., Cambridge (M.Phil. in history and the philosophy of science), and Corpus Christi Coll., Oxford (postdoctoral fellow in history). In 1993 he made his professional debut in opera in a minor role in a concert performance of *Tristan und Isolde* at London's Royal Festival Hall. His stage debut followed in 1994 as Britten's Lysander with the Australian Opera during its visit to the Edinburgh Festival. He made his first appearance at London's Covent Garden in *Salome* in 1995, and also sang in recital at London's Wigmore Hall. In 1996 he portrayed Tamino at his debut with the English National Opera in London. For the bicentenary Schubert concerts at Wigmore Hall, he was engaged to sing *Die schöne Müllerin* in 1997. He also returned to Covent Garden that year as Britten's Quint. He made his first recital tour of the U.S. in 1998, and also sang Monteverdi's Nerone at the Munich Festival. In 1999 he made his Carnegie Hall debut in N.Y. as soloist with the Academy of St. Martin-in-the- Fields under Marriner's direction. Among his other roles are Orfeo, Belmonte, Vasek, and Tom Rakewell. His concert and lieder repertoire ranges from Bach to Henze. He has contributed reviews and articles to various periodicals, and has also publ. books on witchcraft (1997) and on the vocal art (1999).—LK/DM

Boswell, Connee (actually, Constance Foore), American singer and actress; b. Kansas City, Dec. 2, 1907; d. N.Y., Oct. 11, 1976.

With her siblings as the Boswell Sisters in the early 1930s and as a solo performer thereafter, Boswell was a popular jazz-oriented vocalist on records, radio, film, and television. Her biggest solo hits included "On the Beach at Bali-Bali," "On the Isle of May," and "Let It Snow! Let It Snow! Let It Snow!," as well as several duets with Bing Crosby.

Boswell grew up in New Orleans. She was struck by polio as a child, the illness complicated by a fall that kept her in a wheelchair for life. Nevertheless, she studied music and cello with Otto Finck and, like her sisters, performed with the New Orleans Philharmonic Orch. She turned to popular music and learned to play saxophone, trombone, and guitar. When she and her sisters formed a singing trio, it was she who wrote the group's arrangements. On their first recording, for Victor in 1925, she was allowed a solo side, "Cryin' Blues," and while the group experimented with different vocal blends, she usually sang lead.

When the sisters moved to N.Y. and signed to Brunswick Records, Boswell also recorded solo, scoring her first hit with "Say It Isn't So" (music and lyrics by Irving Berlin) in October 1932. In 1935 she married Harold Leedy, the group's manager; they remained married until his death in the early 1970s. Both of her sisters also married in 1935, and they retired in 1936, leaving her to turn to solo work full-time.

Having followed record executive Jack Kapp from Brunswick to Decca, Boswell continued to record, placing "On the Beach at Bali-Bali" (music and lyrics by Al Sherman, Jack Meskill, and Abner Silver) in the hit parade for 11 weeks during the summer of 1936. She became a regular guest on the *Kraft Music Hall* radio series hosted by Bing Crosby and recorded a series of popular duets with him, notably "Bob White (Whatcha Gonna Swing Tonight?)" (music by Bernard Hanighen, lyrics by Johnny Mercer; 1937) and "Alexander's Ragtime Band" (music and lyrics by Irving Berlin; 1938). She also made her first solo appearance in a film, *Artists and Models* (August 1937), in which she sang the Academy Award–nominated "Whispers in the Dark" (music by Frederick Hollander, lyrics by Leo Robin).

Boswell spent nine weeks in the hit parade in the spring of 1940 with "On the Isle of May" (music by André Kostelanetz, adapted from the Andante Cantabile movement in Tchaikovsky's String Quartet in D Major, lyrics by Mack David). She appeared in the films *Kiss the Boys Goodbye* (August 1941) and *Syncopation* (May 1942) and had a Top Ten hit with "Let It Snow! Let It Snow! Let It Snow!" (music by Jule Styne, lyrics by Sammy Cahn) in February 1946, backed by Russ Morgan and His Orch. (By this time she had changed the spelling of her first name from Connie to Connee.) She also appeared in the film *Swing Parade of 1946*.

Boswell was less active from the 1950s on, though she scored a final Top Ten hit with "If I Give My Heart to You" (music and lyrics by Jimmie Crane, Al Jacobs, and Jimmy Brewster) in October 1954. She concluded her recording career with a look back to her jazz roots, the LP *Connee Boswell and the Original Memphis Five in Hi-Fi*, released by RCA Victor in 1956. She made her last film appearance in *Senior Prom* in December 1958, then costarred in the dramatic TV series *Pete Kelly's Blues* from April to September 1959. She continued to appear as a guest star on television into the 1960s. She died of cancer at the age of 68 in 1976.

DISC.: "On the Beach at Bali-Bali" (1936); "On the Isle of May" (1940); "Let It Snow! Let It Snow! Let It Snow!" (1946); "If I Give My Heart to You" (1954); *Connee Boswell and the Original Memphis Five in Hi-Fi* (1956).—WR

Boswell Sisters, The, American vocal group.

The Boswell Sisters were the most successful singing group of the first half of the 1930s, injecting a distinctly jazz flavor into their intricate arrangements and improvised harmonies. They scored a series of record hits between 1931 and 1936, the most popular of which was "The Object of My Affection." They also made personal appearances and performed on radio and in films.

MEMBERSHIP: Martha (b. Kansas City, 1905; d. July 2, 1958); Constance, known as Connie, then Connee (b. Kansas City, Dec. 2, 1907; d. N.Y., Oct. 11, 1976); and Helvetia, known as Vet (b. Birmingham, Ala., 1909; d. Nov. 12, 1988). Their parents and their aunt and uncle—two brothers who had married two sisters—were a singing quartet. Raised in New Orleans, the sisters learned to play musical instruments (Martha, pno.; Connie, cello; Vet, vln.) and played in the New Orleans Philharmonic Orch. They turned to singing and playing popular music, as Connie learned to play saxophone and guitar, Vet banjo and guitar. But soon Martha's piano was their only onstage instrument. They first appeared at the Orpheum Theatre in New Orleans in 1925, then on local radio. They made their first recordings the same year for a field representative from Victor Records. Both original compositions, the issued songs were "Nights When I'm Lonely," credited to the trio, and "Cryin' Blues," credited to Connie alone.

The Boswell Sisters had their first out-of-town booking in Chicago in 1928, and this led to radio appearances in L.A. in 1930; they recorded again for Victor and for OKeh during the year. But they first gained national attention in early 1931, when they moved to N.Y., began appearing on Rudy Vallée's network radio show, and signed to Brunswick Records. They scored their first hit in April 1931 with "When I Take My Sugar to Tea" (music and lyrics by Sammy Fain, Irving Kahal, and Pierre Norman Connor), on which they were accompanied by the studio band led by Tommy and Jimmy Dorsey. They appeared regularly on Bing Crosby's radio show and were featured with him on records, notably a 12–inch disc containing "Gems from *George White's Scandals*" in the fall of 1931, and in the October 1932 film *The Big Broadcast*. They toured Europe in 1933 and appeared in two more films in 1934, *Moulin Rouge* in February and *Transatlantic Merry-Go-Round* in October. They scored their biggest hit with "The Object of My Affection" (music and lyrics by Pinky Tomlin, Coy Poe, and Jimmie Grier) in January 1935.

All three sisters married during 1935: Vet to John Paul Jones; Martha to record executive George Lloyd; and Connie to Harold Leedy, the group's manager. The breakup of the group was precipitated by Vet's pregnancy. They made their final recordings in early 1936, and "I'm Gonna Sit Right Down and Write Myself a Letter" (music by Fred E. Ahlert, lyrics by Joe Young) spent six weeks in the hit parade starting in February. Martha and Vet retired, while Connie, the group's lead singer, who had made solo records throughout the group's tenure, launched a solo career. Martha lived in Peekskill, N.Y., until her death in 1958 at 53. Connie (who had changed the spelling of her name to "Connee" in the 1940s) died of cancer in 1976 at 68. Vet, who had moved to Peekskill after the death of her husband in the early 1970s, died in 1988.—**WR**

Bote & Bock, German music publishers. The firm was established in Berlin in 1838 by Eduard Bote (retired 1847) and Gustav Bock (b. April 1, 1813; d. April 27, 1863). The directorship was assumed after Bock's death by his brother Eduard Bock (d. March 31, 1871), followed by his son Hugo Bock (b. Berlin, July 25, 1848; d. there, March 12, 1932), who handled the affairs of the firm for over 60 years. He acquired for the firm a great number of operas and operettas, and also a number of instrumental works by celebrated 19th century composers. In 1904 Bock purchased the catalogue of Lauterbach & Kuhn of Leipzig, including the works of Max Reger (from op.66 on). His successor was his son Gustav Bock (b. Berlin, July 17, 1882; d. July 6, 1953), who headed the firm until 1938, and again from 1947. The headquarters of the firm remained in Berlin. In 1996 the firm merged with **Boosey & Hawkes**.

BIBL.: *B. & B., Musikverlag, Berlin, 1838–1938* (Berlin, 1938); H. Kunz, ed., *125 Jahre B. & B., 1838–1963* (Berlin, 1963); idem, ed., *Festschrift zum 150 jährigen Firmenjubiläum* (Berlin, 1988). —**NS/LK/DM**

Botstein, Leon, Swiss-born American educator, historian, and conductor; b. Zürich, Dec. 14, 1946. After graduating from the H.S. of Music and Art in N.Y. (1963), he studied history at the Univ. of Chicago (B.A., 1967) and Harvard Univ. (M.A., 1968; Ph.D., 1985). In 1969 he was a lecturer in history at Boston Univ. From 1970 to 1975 he was president of Franconia (N.H.) Coll., and also founder-principal conductor of the White Mountain Festival of the Arts (1973–75). In 1975 he became president of Bard Coll. in Annandale-on-Hudson, N.Y., and also of Simon's Rock Coll. of Bard in Great Barrington, Mass., in 1979. He was co-conductor (1982–89) and conductor (1989–92) of the Hudson Valley Phil. Chamber Orch. in Poughkeepsie, N.Y., and principal guest conductor of the Hudson Valley Phil. there (1991–92). In 1990 he became artistic director of the Bard Music Festival. He became music director of the American Sym. Orch. in 1992 and artistic director of the American Russian Young Artists Orch. in 1995, both based in N.Y. He also became the revitalizing ed. of the *Musical Quarterly* in 1992. In 1993 he was made a Fellow of the American Academy of Arts and Sciences. Botstein's provocative articles, essays, and reviews, ranging from the current state of education in America to music history, have appeared in various newspapers, magazines, and professional journals.

WRITINGS: *Judentum und Modernität: Essays zur Rolle der Juden in der deutschen und österreichischen Kultur 1848–1938* (Vienna, 1991); *Jefferson's Children: Education and the Promise of American Culture* (N.Y., 1997); *The Compleat Brahms* (N.Y., 1999). —**NS/LK/DM**

Botstiber, Hugo, Austrian music scholar; b. Vienna, April 21, 1875; d. Shrewsbury, England, Jan. 15, 1941. He was a pupil of R. Fuchs, Zemlinsky, H. Rietsch, and G. Adler in Vienna, where he subsequently held administrtive posts until emigrating to England in 1939. He ed. the *Musikbuch aus Österreich* (1904–11); publ. *Joseph Haydn und das Verlagshaus Artaria* (with Franz Artaria; Vienna, 1911); *Geschichte der Ouvertüre* (Leipzig, 1913); and *Beethoven im Alltag* (Vienna, 1927); completed C. Pohl's biography of J. Haydn (Vol. III, Leipzig, 1927). Of particular interest to American musicians is his article "Musicalia in der New York Public Library" in the bulletin of the Société Internationale de Musique (Oct. 1903), calling international attention for the first time to the important music collection of the N.Y. Public Library.—**NS/LK/DM**

Bottenberg, Wolfgang (Heinz Otto), German-born Canadian composer and teacher; b. Frankfurt am Main, May 9, 1930. He studied theology and philosophy at the Vallender Theologische Hochschule (1952–57), during which time he taught himself music theory and organ performance. In 1958 he emigrated to Canada and in 1964 he became a naturalized Canadian citizen. He studied theory and piano with Robert Stangeland at the Univ. of Alberta (B.Mus., 1961) before completing his training with Huston, Takács, and Cooper at the Univ. of Cincinnati (M.Mus., 1962; D.M.A., 1970). From 1965 to 1973 he taught at the Acadia Univ. in Wolfville, Nova Scotia. In 1973 he joined the faculty of Concordia Univ. in Montreal, where he served as a prof. from 1993 until his retirement in 1997. As a researcher,

Bottenberg has worked on a project to evaluate the implications of reading early music from its original mensural notation. In 1993 he issued the first scholarly and complete CD recordings of the compositions of Friedrich Nietzsche. Bottenberg's music has been significantly influenced by Gregorian chant, Renaissance and Baroque polyphony, and by neo-tonal composers such as Hindemith, but he also makes use of serial, aleatoric, and minimalistic techniques.

WORKS: DRAMATIC: Opera: *Inook* (1986). **ORCH.:** *Passacaglia* for Chamber Orch. (1961; rev. 1971); *Fantasia* for Trumpet and Small Orch. (1966); *A Suite of Carols* (1967; orchestration of 3 *English Carols* for Piano Duet, 1963); *Sinfonietta* (1970; orchestration of Sonata for Piano Duet, 1961); *Fantasia Serena* (1973; Halifax, Dec. 1, 1980); Concerto for Organ and Small Orch. (1975; Guelph, July 18, 1979); Concertino for Tenor Saxophone and Strings (1989); *Festival Overture* (1990); *Prelude, Aria, and Fugue* for Strings (1992; Montreal, April 22, 1993). **CHAMBER:** *Sonata with Variations on a South German Folk Song* for 2 Alto Recorders and Piano (1959; rev. 1972); Quartet for Flute, 2 Clarinets, and Bassoon (1960); Trio for Flute, Clarinet, and Piano (1960–63); Trio for Flute, Clarinet, and Bassoon (1963); *Variables* for Recorder Player, Woodwind Quartet, and String Quintet (1964); Trio for 3 Recorders (1964); *Ciacona* for Alto Recorder and Harpsichord or Piano (1964; rev. 1977); String Quartet (1968); *Divertimento* for Flute Quartet (1968); *Dialogue* for Alto Recorder and Harpsichord or Piano (1971; rev. 1972); Octet (1972; Montreal, Feb. 21, 1985); *Fa So La Ti Do Re* for Soprano Saxophone or Clarinet and String Quartet (1972; Radio Hilversum, Jan. 17, 1984); Sonata for Flute and Clarinet (1972); *Partita* for Guitar, Recorder Quartet, and Viola da Gamba (1978); *Sonata Modalis* for Clarinet or Viola and Piano (Montreal, Nov. 22, 1979); *Overture for Broken Consort* for Flute, Clarinet, Violin, Cello, and Guitar (1981; San Francisco, March 29, 1982); *Fanfare* for Brass Quintet (1982); *5 for 5* for Woodwind Quintet (1983; Montreal, Feb. 21, 1985); *Reflections of Summer* for Flute, Viola, and Guitar (1983); *Canzona Festiva "O Canada"* for 16 Horns (Montreal, Dec. 15, 1989); Suite for Recorder Quartet and Optional Percussion (Montreal, May 17, 1989); Trio for Viola, Cello, and Piano (1991); *Toccata* for Clarinet and 4 Sound Tracks (1991; also for 5 Clarinets); *Partita* for 4 Guitars (1993); *2 Preludes and Fugues* for String Quartet (1995); *Variations* for Guitar and Piano (1995); Sonatina for Flute and Piano (1996); *Variations* for Cello and Piano (1996); *Illuminations* for Cello and Piano (1996); *Canzona* for Flute and Piano (1996); Suite for Piano Trio (1998). **KEYBOARD: Piano:** Sonata for Piano Duet (1961; orchestrated as Sinfonietta, 1970); *3 English Carols* for Piano Duet (1963; orchestrated as *A Suite of Carols*, 1967); *Moods of the Modes* (1973); *3 Sketches* (1981); Pieces for Piano Duet (1988); *Elements of Nature* for 2 Pianos (1990); *Drawings of Paul Klee* (1998). **Organ:** *Triptych* (1967); Sonata *"Ave Maris Stella"* (1990); *Partita "Es ist ein Ros entsprungen"* (1999). **VOCAL:** *Duineser Kantate/Duino Cantata* for Baritone, Chorus, and Small Orch. (1962); *The World is a Rainbow*, secular cantata for Soprano or Tenor or Boy Soprano, Chorus, and Woodwind Quintet (1966); *Those Passions...Which Yet Survive*, cantata for Bass and 7 Instruments (1968); *Ritual* for Chorus and Orch. (1970); *Eine Weihnachtliche Hausmusik* for Medium Voice, 2 Alto Recorders, and Piano or Piano Duet (1973); *Canadian Madrigals* for Chorus (1983); *Cunctipotens Genitor Deus* for Chorus and Orch. (1990); songs.

WRITINGS: *Building a Treble Viola da Gamba* (Montreal, 1980); ed. *Florilegium Cantionum Mensuralium* (2 vols., Montreal, 1982); *Reading Early Music from Original Notation* (Montreal, 1983).—NS/LK/DM

Bottesini, Giovanni, Italian double-bass virtuoso, conductor, and composer; b. Crema, Dec. 22, 1821; d. Parma, July 7, 1889. He took lessons in double-bass playing with Rossi at the Milan Cons. (1835–39). He played in various orchs. In 1847 he visited the U.S., and in 1848 he went to England, where he appeared as a cello soloist, making his independent concert debut in London on June 26, 1849. In 1853 he was once more in America; also was active as a conductor in Paris, in Russia, and in Scandinavian countries. In 1871 he was invited by Verdi to conduct the world premiere of *Aida* in Cairo. He eventually retired to Parma as director of the cons. there. Bottesini was the first great virtuoso on the double bass, regarded as an unwieldy instrument, and thus became a legendary paragon for the few artists who essayed that instrument after him; thus Koussevitzky was often described as the Russian Bottesini during his early career as a double-bass player. Bottesini was the composer of a number of passable operas which had several performances in his lifetime. He also wrote a valuable *Metodo complete per contrabasso*, in 2 parts, treating the double bass as an orch. and as a solo instrument (in Eng., adapted by F. Clayton, London, 1870).

WORKS: DRAMATIC: Opera: *Cristoforo Colombo* (Havana, 1847); *L'Assedio di Firenze* (Paris, Feb. 21, 1856); *Il Diavolo della notte* (Milan, Dec. 18, 1858); *Marion Delorme* (Palermo, Jan. 10, 1862); *Vinciguerra il bandito* (Monte Carlo, Feb. 22, 1870); *Ali Baba* (London, Jan. 18, 1871); *Ero e Leandro* (Turin, Jan. 11, 1879); *La Regina di Nepal* (Turin, Dec. 26, 1880). **OTHER:** Oratorio, *The Garden of Olivet* (Norwich Festival, Oct. 12, 1887); overtures; string quartets; effective pieces for double bass, such as *Carnevale di Venezia* and *Tarantella*.

BIBL.: C. Lesei, *G. B.* (Milan, 1886); A. Carniti, *In memoria di G. B.* (Crema, 1922).—NS/LK/DM

Bottje, Will Gay, American flutist, teacher, and composer; b. Grand Rapids, June 30, 1925. He studied flute (B.S., 1947) and received instruction in composition (M.S., 1948) from Giannini at the Juilliard School of Music in N.Y. He then pursued training with Badings in Holland and Boulanger in Paris (1952–53), and subsequently was a pupil of Rogers and Hanson (composition), Joseph Mariano (flute), and Paul White (conducting) at the Eastman School of Music in Rochester, N.Y. (D.M.A., 1955); later worked at the Univ. of Utrecht electronic music studios (1962–63) and at the Stockholm Stiftlesen (1973). He taught at the Univ. of Miss. (1955–57) before serving as prof. of theory and composition at Southern Ill. Univ. in Carbondale (1957–81), where he founded an electronic music studio (1965). His music is of a highly experimental nature, awash with corrosive dissonances in a manner influenced primarily by developments cultivated in the Northern avant-garde music laboratories.

WORKS: DRAMATIC: Opera: *Altgeld* (Carbondale, Ill., March 6, 1968); *Root!* (1971). **ORCH.:** 7 syms. (1946–70); *The Ballad Singer* (1951); Concerto for Flute, Trumpet, Harp,

Strings, and Percussion (1955); Piccolo Concertino (1956); *Theme and Variations* (1958); Concerto for Trumpet, Trombone, and Winds (1959); Piano Concerto (1960); Sinfonietta (1960); Sinfonia Concertante for Brass Quintet and Winds (1961); *Rhapsodic Variations* for Viola, Piano, and Strings (1962); *Chiaroscuros* (1975); *Mutations* for Small Orch. (1977); Tuba Concerto (1977); *Songs From the Land Between the Rivers* (1980); Concerto for Oboe, Bassoon, and Orch. (1981); *Scenes From the West Shore* (1983); *Commentaries* for Guitar and Orch. (1983); Concerto for 2 Flutes and Orch. (1984); Concerto for Oboe, Violin, and Orch. (1984). **CHAMBER:** 4 string quartets (1950, 1959, 1962, 1982); Quintet for Flute and Strings (1954); 2 wind quintets (1957, 1984); Trumpet Sonata (1959); Cello Sonata (1959); Saxophone Quartet (1963); *Modalities I* for Saxophone Quartet and Tape (1970) and *II* for Clarinet and Tape (1971); *Modules I* for Clarinet and Piano (1973) and *II* for Double Bass and Piano (1976); Sym. for Cello and Piano, 4–Hands (1978–79); Guitar Sonata (1980); Oboe Sonata (1981); Harpsichord Sonata (1981). **VOCAL:** Song cycles.—NS/LK/DM

Bottrigari, Ercole, Italian music theorist; b. Bologna (baptized), Aug. 24, 1531; d. San Alberto, near Bologna, Sept. 30, 1612. He was an illegitimate son of the nobleman Giovanni Battista Bottrigari. He studied mathematics and music in the house of his father, and learned to sing and play several instruments; his house teacher was Bartolomeo Spontone. In 1551 he married a rich lady. In his residence he met many celebrated poets of the day, including Tasso. Having acquired profound learning in several scientific and artistic disciplines, he devoted much of his energies to theoretical musical subjects. He publ. numerous papers, many of a polemical nature.

WRITINGS: *Il Patricio ovvero De' tetracordi armonici di Aristosseno* (Bologna, 1593); *Il Desiderio ovvero De' concerti di vari stromenti musicali* (Venice, 1594, without Bottrigari's name, but under the pseudonym Alemanno Benelli, anagram of the name of his friend Annibale Melone; 2nd ed. with Bottrigari's name, Bologna, 1599; modern reprint, with introduction and annotations by Kathi Meyer, 1924; 3rd ed., Milan, 1601, under the name of Melone); *Il Melone, Discorso armonico* (Ferrara, 1602). He left trs. of Boetius and other writers in MS, preserved in the library of the Liceo Musicale in Bolonga.

BIBL.: *Notizie biografiche intorno agli studi ed alla vita del Cavaliere B.* (Bologna, 1842).—NS/LK/DM

Boucher, Alexandre-Jean, famous French violinist; b. Paris, April 11, 1778; d. there, Dec. 29, 1861. A brilliant violin virtuoso, he styled himself "l'Alexandre des violons." Boucher began his career at the age of 6, playing with the Concert Spirituel in Paris. He was soloist in the court of Charles IV of Spain (1787–1805); also traveled extensively on the Continent and in England. He wrote 2 violin concertos.—NS/LK/DM

Boucourechliev, André, Bulgarian-born French composer and writer on music; b. Sofia, July 28, 1925; d. Boulogne-Billancourt, Nov. 13, 1997. He enrolled at the Sofia Cons. in 1946 and studied piano with Pelischek. After winning first prize in the National Competition for Musical Interpretation in 1948, he was awarded a French government grant to pursue training at the École

Normale de Musique in Paris with Gronoli (piano; licence de concert diploma, 1951) and with Dandelot (harmony). He also received private instruction in counterpoint from Vaurabourg-Honegger. In 1954 he attended the summer courses in new music in Darmstadt, and in 1955–56 he was a student in Gieseking's master classes in piano in Saarbrücken. After teaching piano at the École Normale de Musique from 1952 to 1960, he devoted himself mainly to composing and writing. In 1956 he became a naturalized French citizen. In 1976 he won the Grand Prix musical of Paris and in 1984 the Grand Prix national de musique. Among his compositions, the series entitled *Archipel* is particularly noteworthy.

WORKS: *Étude I* for Tape (1956); *Musique à trois* for Flute, Clarinet, and Harpsichord (1957); *Texte I* (1958) and *II* (1960) for Tape; Piano Sonata (1959); *Tic-tac* for Tape (1959); *Signes* for Flute, Piano, and 2 Percussion (1961); *Grodek* for Soprano, Flute, and 3 Percussion, after Georg Trakl (1963); *Musique nocturnes* for Clarinet, Harp, and Piano (1966); *Archipel I* for 2 Pianos and 2 Percussion ad libitum (1967), *II* for String Quartet (1968), *III* for Piano and 6 Percussion (1969), *IV* for Piano (1970), and *V* for 6 Instruments (1970–71); *Ombres: Hommage à Beethoven* for 11 Strings (Toulouse, June 8, 1970); *Tombeau "à la memoire de Jean-Pierre Guézec"* for Clarinet and Percussion or Piano (1971); *Anarchipel* for Harp, Harpsichord, Organ, Piano, and 2 Percussion (1972); *Faces* for Orch. (1972); *Amers* for Orch. (1973); *Thrène* for Reciter, Chorus, and Tape, after Mallarmé (1973–74); Piano Concerto (1974–75); *Orion I* for Organ (1979), *II* for Piano, Brass, and Percussion (1982), and *III* for Piano (1982); *Ulysse* for Flute and Percussion (1981); *Nocturnes* for Clarinet and Piano (1984); *Lit de neige* for Soprano and 19 Instruments (1984); *Le Miroir* for Mezzo-soprano and Orch. (1987); *Chevelure de Bérénice* for Instrumental Ensemble (1987); String Quartet No. 2 (1991).

WRITINGS: *Schumann* (Paris, 1956; new ed., 1995; Eng. tr., 1959); *Chopin: Eine Bildbiographie* (Munich, 1962); *Beethoven* (Paris, 1963; 2nd ed., rev., 1976); *Stravinski* (Paris, 1982; Eng. tr., 1987); *Essai sur Beethoven* (Arles, 1991); *Dire la musique* (Paris, 1995); *Debussy: La révolution subtile* (Paris, 1998).

BIBL.: A. Girardot, *Esthétique de B. à travers ses "Archipels"* (diss., Univ. of Paris, 1974).—NS/LK/DM

Boudreau, Robert (Austin), American trumpeter and conductor; b. Bellingham, Mass., April 25, 1927. He studied trumpet with Georges Mager of the Boston Sym. Orch. and with William Vacchiano at the Juilliard School of Music in N.Y. He then taught music at Ithaca Coll. (1951–52), Lehigh Univ. (1952–53), and Duquesne Univ. (1955–57). In 1957 he founded in Pittsburgh the American Wind Sym. Orch., specializing in contemporary music; it commissioned works from numerous composers with its performances taking place aboard the *Point Counterpoint II*, a floating arts center. —NS/LK/DM

Boughton, Rutland, English composer; b. Aylesbury, Jan. 23, 1878; d. London, Jan. 24, 1960. He studied at the Royal Coll. of Music in London with Stanford and Davies; without obtaining his diploma, he engaged in professional activity; was for a time a member of the orch. at the Haymarket Theatre in London; taught at the Midland Inst. in Birmingham (1905–11); also conducted a choral society there. He became a firm believer in the universality of arts along Wagnerian lines; formed a partnership with the poet Reginald Buckley; their book of essays, *The Music Drama of the Future*, expounding the neo-Wagnerian idea, was publ. in 1911. To carry out these plans, Boughton organized stage festivals at Glastonbury, helped by his common-law wife, Christina Walshe. Boughton's opera, *The Immortal Hour*, was performed there on Aug. 26, 1914; his choral music drama, *The Birth of Arthur*, had a performance there in 1920; these productions were staged with piano instead of an orch. After an interruption during World War I, Boughton continued the Glastonbury festivals until 1926. In 1927 he settled in the country, in Gloucestershire. He continued to compose, however, and produced a number of stage works, as well as instrumental pieces. His ideas of universal art had in the meantime been transformed into concepts of socialist realism, with an emphasis on the paramount importance of folk music as against formal constructions. He publ. *The Death and Resurrection of the Music Festival* (1913); *The Glastonbury Festival Movement* (1922); *Bach, the Master* (1930); *Parsifal: A Study* (1920); *The Nature of Music* (1930); *The Reality of Music* (1934).

WORKS: DRAMATIC: *The Birth of Arthur* (1909; Glastonbury, Aug. 16, 1920); *The Immortal Hour* (1913; Glastonbury, Aug. 26, 1914); *The Round Table* (Glastonbury, Aug. 14, 1916); *The Moon Maiden*, choral ballet for girls (Glastonbury, April 23, 1919); *Alkestis*, music drama (Glastonbury, Aug. 26, 1922); *The Queen of Cornwall*, music drama (Glastonbury, Aug. 21, 1924); *May Day*, ballet (1926); *The Ever Young*, music drama (1928; Bath, Sept. 9, 1935); *The Lily Maid*, opera (Gloucester, Sept. 10, 1934); *Galahad*, music drama (1944); *Avalon*, music drama (1946). **ORCH.:** *The Skeleton in Armour*, symphonic poem with Chorus (1898); *The Invincible Armada*, symphonic poem (1901); *A Summer Night* (1902); 3 syms. (*Oliver Cromwell*, 1904; *Deirdre*, 1927; 1937); *Love and Spring* (1906); *Midnight* (1907); Trumpet Concerto (1943). **CHAMBER:** Violin Sonata (1921); Quartet for Oboe and Strings (1930); String Trio (1944); Piano Trio (1948); Cello Sonata (1948). **VOCAL:** *Song of Liberty* for Chorus and Orch. (1911); *Bethlehem*, choral drama (1915); *Pioneers* for Tenor, Chorus, and Orch. (1925); many choral pieces.

BIBL.: *The Self-Advertisement of R. B.* (c. 1909); M. Hurd, *Immortal Hour: The Life and Period of R. B.* (London, 1962; 2nd ed., rev. and enl., 1993, as *R. B. and the Glastonbury Festivals*). **—NS/LK/DM**

Boughton, William (Paul), English conductor; b. Birmingham, Dec. 18, 1948. He studied cello at the Guildhall School of Music in London, with Maurice Eisenberg in the U.S., and with Milos Sadlo at the Prague Academy of Music; after a brief career as a cellist with the Royal Phil., the London Sinfonietta, and several BBC orchs., he turned to conducting. In 1980 he founded the English String Orch. in Worcester, which made a major tour of Europe in 1986; he also was artistic director of the Malvern Festival (1983–88) and principal conductor of the Jyväskylä Sym. Orch. in Finland (1986–93). He appeared as guest conductor with many British orchs. His repertoire ranges from Haydn to Tippett.**—NS/LK/DM**

Bouhy, Jacques (-Joseph André), Belgianborn French baritone; b. Pepinster, June 18, 1848; d.

Paris, Jan. 29, 1929. He studied at the Liège Cons., then entered the Paris Cons., where he studied piano, organ, and theory of composition, as well as singing. He made his debut as Méphistophélès in Gounod's *Faust* at the Paris Opéra on Aug. 2, 1871, and on March 3, 1875, he sang Escamillo in the first performance of *Carmen* at the Opéra-Comique in Paris. He appeared at Covent Garden, London, on April 22, 1882, then sang at various opera houses in Europe, including that in St. Petersburg. In 1885 he went to N.Y. and served as director of the N.Y. Cons. (until 1889); was again in N.Y. from 1904 to 1907; then returned to Paris and settled there as a singing teacher.**—NS/LK/DM**

Boulanger, Lili (Juliette Marie Olga), talented French composer, sister of **Nadia (Juliette) Boulanger;** b. Paris, Aug. 21, 1893; d. Mézy, Seine-et-Oise, March 15, 1918. She studied composition with Vidal at the Paris Cons. (1909–13), attracting considerable attention when she won the Grand Prix de Rome at graduation with her cantata *Faust et Hélène*, becoming the first woman to receive this distinction. Her early death at the age of 24 was lamented by French musicians. Her talent, delicate and poetic, continued the tradition of French Romanticism on the borderline of Impressionism. Besides her prize-winning cantata, she wrote 2 symphonic poems, *D'un soir triste* and *D'un matin de printemps*; her opera to Maeterlinck's play *La Princesse Maleine* remained incomplete. She also wrote several choral works with orch.: *Soir sur la plaine*; *Hymne au soleil*; *La Tempête*; *Les Sirenes*; *Sous bois*; *La Source*; *Pour les funérailles d'un soldat*; *3 psaumes*; *Vieille prière bouddhique*; *Pie Jesu*, sacred chorus for Voice, Strings, Harp, and Organ; cycle of 13 songs to texts of Francis Jammes, *Clairieres dans le ciel*; some flute pieces.

BIBL.: E. Lebeau, *L. B.* (Paris, 1968); L. Rosenstiel, *The Life and Works of L. B.* (Rutherford, 1978); P. Gallo, *L. B.: L'innocenza del sogno simbolista* (Treviso, 1996).**—NS/LK/DM**

Boulanger, Nadia (Juliette), illustrious French teacher, sister of **Lili (Juliette Marie Olga) Boulanger;** b. Paris, Sept. 16, 1887; d. there, Oct. 22, 1979. Both her father and grandfather were teachers at the Paris Cons.; her mother, the Russian Countess Myshetskaya, was a professional singer, and it was from her that Boulanger received her first music lessons. She entered the Paris Cons., where she studied organ with Guilmant and Vierne, and composition with Fauré; she graduated with prizes in organ and theory; in 1908 she received the 2nd Prix de Rome for her cantata *La Sirène*; she completed the composition of the opera by Raoul Pugno, *La Ville Morte*, left unfinished at his death; also composed cello music, piano pieces, and songs. Realizing that she could not compare with her sister Lili in talent as a composer, she devoted herself to teaching, and it was in that capacity that she found her vocation. She was assistant in a harmony class at the Paris Cons. (1909–24); was engaged as a teacher at the École Normale de Musique in Paris (1920–39); when the American Cons. was founded in 1921 at Fontainebleau, she joined its faculty as a teacher of composition and orchestration, becoming its director in 1950. She also had a large class of private pupils from all parts of the world, many of whom achieved fame; among Americans who went to Paris to study with her were Copland, Harris, Piston, Thomson, Carter, Diamond, Siegmeister, Irving Fine, Easley Blackwood, Berger, Vincent, and Shapero; others were Markevitch, Françaix, Lennox Berkeley, and Dinu Lipatti. Not all of her students were enthusiastic about her methods; some of them complained about the strict, and even restrictive, discipline she imposed on them; but all admired her insistence on perfection of form and accuracy of technique. Her tastes were far from the catholicity expected of teachers; she was a great admirer of Stravinsky, Debussy, and Ravel, but had little appreciation of Schoenberg and the modern Vienna School. She visited the U.S. several times; played the organ part in Copland's Organ Sym. (which she advised him to compose) with the N.Y. Sym. Orch., under the direction of Walter Damrosch (Jan. 11, 1925), and was the first woman to conduct regular subscription concerts of the Boston Sym. Orch. (1938) and of the N.Y. Phil. (Feb. 11, 1939). During World War II, she stayed in America and taught classes at Radcliffe Coll., Wellesley Coll., and the Juilliard School of Music in N.Y. Returning to Paris in 1946, she took over a class in piano accompaniment at the Cons., and also continued her private teaching as long as her frail health permitted. Her 90th birthday was celebrated in Sept. 1977, with sincere tributes from her many students in Europe and America.

BIBL.: A. Kendall, *The Tender Tyrant. N. B.: A Life Devoted to Music* (London, 1977); B. Mosaingeon, *Mademoiselle: Entretiens avec N. B.* (Luynes, 1980; Eng. tr., 1985); L. Rosenstiel, *N. B.: A Life in Music* (N.Y., 1982); J. Spycket, *N. B.* (Lausanne, 1987; Eng. tr., 1992).—NS/LK/DM

Boulez, Pierre, greatly significant French composer and conductor; b. Montbrison, March 26, 1925. He received training in piano, and pursued his secondary studies in Montbrison and St.-Etienne. After studying advanced mathematics in Lyons (1941), he went to Paris in 1942. In 1944 he entered the harmony class of Messiaen at the Cons. In 1946 he became music director of the Renaud-Barrault theater company. Boulez conducted concerts at the Petit-Marigny, which became the "Domaine Musical" concerts in 1955. He led these influential concerts of contemporary music until 1967. From 1955 to 1960 he gave summer courses in musical analysis in Darmstadt. In 1959 he began a close association with the Südwestfunk in Baden-Baden, where he programmed much contemporary music. From 1960 to 1962 he gave courses in musical analysis and composition in Basel, and then was a visiting prof. at Harvard Univ. in 1962–63. In 1965 he appeared as a guest conductor at the Monday Evening Concerts in Los Angeles. That same year, he gave a conducting course in Basel. In 1966 Boulez made his debut at the Bayreuth Festival conducting *Parsifal*, and then took the company to Japan for performances of *Tristan und Isolde*. From 1967 he appeared as a guest conductor with the Cleveland Orch., serving as its principal guest conductor from 1969 to 1971. He conducted *Pelléas et Mélisande* at London's Covent Garden in 1969. From 1971 to 1975 Boulez served as chief conductor of the BBC Sym. Orch. in London, and from 1971 to 1977 as music director of

the N.Y. Phil. His tenure in N.Y. proved controversial in some quarters for his uncompromising advocacy of 20th century music. He led the orch. on tours of Japan in 1974 and of Europe in 1975. In 1971 Boulez was asked by the French President Pompidou to organize the Institut de Recherche et Coordination Acoustique/Musique (IRCAM) in Paris, which under his guidance became one of the world's leading centers for experimental music. In 1976 he founded and became president of the Ensemble Inter/Contemporain (EIC) in Paris, with which he subsequently conducted numerous performances of contemporary music. That same year, he conducted the centenary *Ring* cycle at the Bayreuth Festival, which he conducted again each summer from 1977 to 1980. Boulez was named a prof. at the Collège de France by decree of the French President in 1976. On Feb. 24, 1979, he conducted the first performance of the complete version of Berg's *Lulu* at the Paris Opéra. He made a major tour of the U.S. with the Ensemble Inter-Contemporain in 1986, which he subsequently took to Australia and New Zealand in 1988, Russia in 1990, and Canada in 1991. In 1992 he appeared as both a conductor and composer at the Salzburg Festival. On Dec. 7, 1992, he conducted Debussy's *La Mer* as part of the 150th anniversary concert of the N.Y. Phil., which was televised live to the nation by PBS. He conducted the Ensemble Inter/Contemporain on another tour of the U.S. in 1993, at the Salzburg Festival and in Berlin in 1994, and in South America in 1996. Boulez was appointed principal guest conductor of the Chicago Sym. Orch. in 1995. He also held the Carnegie Hall Composer's Chair from 1999 to 2003.

As a composer, Boulez's influence on the course of art music in the second half of the 20th century has been especially significant via his espousal of avant-garde techniques. His works, challenging to his auditors as well as his performers, are often difficult to describe, even in the familiar terms of dissonant counterpoint, free serialism, or indeterminism. As a conductor, he has demonstrated an acute analytical approach to not only contemporary scores but also to standard works of the past. His undemonstrative podium manner lends itself well to the clarity and lucidity he brings to his interpretations.

Among Boulez's many honors are the Praemium Imperiale Prize of Japan (1989), Grammy Awards (3 in 1994, 2 in 1995, and 2 in 1996), the Edison and *Gramophone* awards (1995), and the Berlin Kunstpreis and Polar Prize of Sweden (1996).

WRITINGS: *Penser la musique aujourd'hui* (1963); *Relevés d'apprenti* (1966; Eng. tr., 1991, *Stocktakings from an Apprenticeship*).

WORKS: DRAMATIC: *Le Soleil des Eaux,* music for a radio play for Voice and Orch. (1948; rev. as a cantata for Soprano, Tenor, Bass, and Chamber Orch., 1948; withdrawn; rev. for Soprano, Tenor, Bass, Chorus, and Orch., 1958; rev. for Soprano, Chorus, and Orch., 1965); *L'Orestie,* incidental music (1948); *Symphonie Mécanique,* film music for Tape (1955); *Le Crépuscule de Yang Kouï-Fe,* incidental music for radio (1967); *Ainsi parla Zarathoustra,* incidental music (1974). **ORCH.:** *Polyphonie X* for 18 Solo Instruments (Donaueschingen, Oct. 6, 1951); *Doubles* (1957–58; Paris, March 16, 1958; expanded as

Figures-Doubles-Prismes, 1963 and 1968); *Poésie pour pouvoir* for 2 Orchs. and Tape (Donaueschingen, Oct. 19, 1958, composer and H. Rosbaud conducting); *Tombeau* (1959–62); *Domaines* for Clarinet and 21 Instruments (1961–68; Brussels, Dec. 20, 1968, composer conducting; also for Solo Clarinet, 1961); *Éclat* for 15 Instruments (Los Angeles, March 26, 1965; expanded as *Éclats/Multiples* for 27 Instruments, 1966–in progress); *Livre pour Cordes* (1968; based on *Livre pour quatuor* for String Quartet, 1948–49); *...explosante-fixe...* (1971; also for 2 Instruments and Electronics, 1972, and for Flute and Electronics, 1989); *Mémoriales* (1973–75); *Rituel in memoriam Bruno Maderna* (1974–75; London, April 2, 1975, composer conducting); *Notations* (Paris, June 18, 1980; based on *12 Notations* for Piano, 1945); *Répons* for 24 Players, 6 Instrumental Soloists, Chamber Ensemble, Computers, and Live Electronics (Donaueschingen, Oct. 18, 1981); *Initiale,* fanfare for 7 Brass Instruments (1987); *Dérive II* for 11 Instruments (1988) and *III,* fanfare for Brass Instruments, for Solti's 80th birthday (Chicago, Nov. 21, 1992, composer conducting); *Notations VII* (1997–98; Chicago, Jan. 14, 1999). **CHAMBER:** Flute Sonatine (1946); *Livre pour quatuor* for String Quartet (1948–49; rev. 1989; also as *Livre pour Cordes* for Orch., 1968); *Strophes* for Flute (1957); *Domaines* for Clarinet (1961; also for Clarinet and 21 Instruments, 1961–68); *Messagesquisse* for Solo Cello and 6 Cellos (1976); *Pour le docteur Kalmus* for Clarinet, Flute, Violin, Cello, and Piano (1977); *Dérive I* for Flute, Clarinet, Violin, Cello, Vibraphone, and Piano (1984); *Dialogue de l'ombre double* for Clarinet and Electronics (1984); *Mémoriale ("...explosante fixe..." originel)* for Flute and 8 Instruments (1985); *Anthèmes* for Violin and Electronics (1991); *Sur Incises* for 3 Pianos, 3 Percussionists, and 3 Harps (1994–98). **Piano:** *12 Notations* (1945; utilized in *Notations* for Orch., 1980); 3 sonatas: No. 1 (1946), No. 2 (1946–48; Paris, April 29, 1950), and No. 3 (1955–57); Sonata for 2 Pianos (Paris, April 29, 1950); *Structures I* (1951–53) and *II* for 2 Pianos (1956–61). **VOCAL:** *Le Visage nuptial* for Soprano, Alto, 2 Ondes Martenot, Piano, and Percussion (1946–47; rev. for Soprano, Alto, Women's Chorus, and Orch., 1951–52, and for Soprano, Mezzosoprano, Chorus, and Orch. 1985–89); *Le Soleil des Eaux,* cantata for Soprano, Tenor, Bass, and Chamber Orch. (1948; withdrawn; based on music for a radio play for Voice and Orch., 1948; rev. for Soprano, Tenor, Bass, Chorus, and Orch., 1958; rev. for Soprano, Chorus, and Orch., 1965); *Le Marteau sans Maître* for Alto, Alto Flute, Guitar, Vibraphone, Xylorimba, Percussion, and Viola (1953–55; rev. 1957); *Improvisation sur Mallarmé* for Soprano, Harp, Bells, Vibraphone, and Percussion (1957; also for Soprano and Orch., 1962), *II* for Soprano, Celesta, Harp, Piano, Bells, Vibraphone, and Percussion (1957), and *III* for Soprano and Orch. (1959; rev. 1983–84); *Pli selon pli (Don, Improvisation sur Mallarmé I-III, Tombeau)* for Soprano and Orch. (1957–90); *Don* for Soprano and Piano (1960; also for Soprano and Orch., 1962, rev. 1989–90); *Tombeau* for Soprano and Orch. (1959–60); *cummings ist der dichter* for 16 Solo Voices and 24 Instruments (1970; rev. 1986). **Tape:** *Études I, sur un son, II, sur sept songs* (1951–52).

BIBL.: A. Goléa, *Rencontres avec P. B.* (Paris, 1958); J. Peyser, *B., Composer, Conductor, Enigma* (N.Y., 1976); R. Miller, *Pli selon pli: P. B. and the "New Lyricism"* (diss., Case Western Reserve Univ., 1978); P. Griffiths, *B.* (N.Y., 1979); D. Jameux, *P. B.* (Paris, 1984; Eng. tr., 1990); J. Hausler, ed., *Festschrift P. B.* (Vienna, 1985); T. Hirsbrunner, *P. B. und sein Werk* (Laaber, 1985); W. Glock, ed., *P. B.: A Symposium* (London, 1986); P. Stacey, *B. and the Modern Concept* (Lincoln, Nebr., 1987); L. Koblyakov, *P. B.: A World of Harmony* (Chur and N.Y., 1990); J.-J. Nattiez and F. Davoine, eds., *P. B./John Cage: Correspondance et documents* (Winterthur, 1990; Eng. tr., 1993); G. Born, *Rational Music: IRCAM, B., and the Institutionalisation of the Avant-Garde* (Berkeley, 1995); M. Breatnach, *B. and Mallarmé: A Study in Poetic Influence* (Aldershot, 1996).—**NS/LK/DM**

Boulnois, Joseph, French composer; b. Paris, Jan. 28, 1884; killed in battle at Chalaines, Oct. 20, 1918. He studied piano and composition at the Paris Cons. He later became a church organist, and from 1909 he was choir leader at the Opéra-Comique. He wrote an opera, *L'Anneau d'Isis,* a *Symphonie funèbre,* a Cello Sonata, and various pieces for organ, piano, and voice. His works remain mostly in MS. There has been a revival of interest in his music, which has resulted in some performances of his songs and choruses.—**NS/LK/DM**

Boult, Sir Adrian (Cedric), eminent English conductor; b. Chester, April 8, 1889; d. London, Feb. 22, 1983. His mother, a professional writer on music, gave him piano lessons; at age 12 he received some instruction in music from a science teacher, H.E. Piggott, at the Westminster School in London. At 19 he entered Christ Church, Oxford, and sang in the Oxford Bach Choir; then he studied with Hans Sitt at the Leipzig Cons. (1912–13), and also attended rehearsals and concerts of that city's Gewandhaus Orch. under Nikisch and sang in the Gewandhaus Choir. Upon his return to England, he took his D.Mus. at Oxford and joined the staff of London's Covent Garden in 1914. In 1916 he appeared as guest conductor with the Liverpool Phil. and in 1918 with the London Sym. Orch. During the autumn season of 1919, he was principal conductor of Diaghilev's Ballets Russes in London, and from 1919 to 1924 he was conductor of the British Sym. Orch., an ensemble made up of former soldiers in the British army. In 1919 he also became a teacher of conducting at the Royal Coll. of Music in London, a post he retained until 1930. From 1924 to 1930 he was music director of the City of Birmingham Orch.; he also was music director of the Bach Choir from 1928 to 1931.

In 1930 he was appointed director of music for the BBC in London, and retained that important position until 1942. He was also charged with organizing the BBC Sym. Orch., which he conducted in its first concert on Oct. 22, 1930. He subsequently served as its chief conductor until 1950. Under his discerning guidance, it became one of the principal radio orchs. in the world. He led it on several tours abroad, including a notably successful one to Paris, Vienna, Zürich, and Budapest in 1936. During these years, he also appeared as guest conductor with the Vienna Phil. (1933), the Boston Sym. Orch. (1935), the NBC Sym. Orch. in N.Y. (1938), the N.Y. Phil. (leading it in the premieres of Bax's Seventh Sym. and Bliss's Piano Concerto at the 1939 World's Fair, June 9 and 10, respectively), the Chicago Sym. Orch. (1939), and the Concertgebouw Orch. of Amsterdam (1945). From 1942 to 1950 he was assoc. conductor of the Henry Wood Promenade Concerts in London. He was music director of the London Phil. from 1950 to 1957 and led it on a major tour of the Soviet Union in 1956. In 1959–60 he was again music director of the City of Birmingham Sym. Orch., and from 1962 to 1966 he once more taught conducting at the Royal Coll. of Music. In 1937 he was knighted, and in 1969 was made a Companion of Honour. In 1944 he was awarded the Gold Medal of the Royal Phil. Soc. He was conductor at the coronations of King George VI in 1937 and Queen Elizabeth II in 1953.

Boult's style of conducting was devoid of glamorous self-assertion; his ideal was, rather, to serve music with a minimum of display, and for this he was greatly respected by the musicians he led. Throughout his long and distinguished career he championed the cause of British music. He was particularly esteemed for his performances of the works of Vaughan Williams, whose *Pastoral Symphony* (Jan. 26, 1922), Fourth Sym. (April 10, 1935), and Sixth Sym. (April 21, 1948) received their premiere performances under his direction in London.

WRITINGS: *The Point of the Stick: A Handbook on the Technique of Conducting* (Oxford, 1920); *Thoughts on Conducting* (London, 1963); *My Own Trumpet*, an autobiography (London, 1973).

BIBL.: J. Moore, ed., *Music and Friends: Letters to A. B.* (London, 1979); H. Simeone and S. Mundy, eds., *Sir A. B., Companion of Honour: A Tribute* (Tunbridge Wells, 1980); M. Kennedy, *A. B.* (London, 1987).—**NS/LK/DM**

Bour, Ernest, French conductor; b. Thionville, April 20, 1913. He attended the Univ. and took courses in piano, organ, and theory at the Cons. in Strasbourg. His mentors were Fritz Münch and Hermann Scherchen. He was chief conductor of the Strasbourg Radio from 1935 to 1939. From 1941 to 1947 he was music director of the Mulhouse Orch. He served as chief conductor of the Strasbourg Municipal Orch. from 1950 to 1954, of the Südwestfunk Sym. Orch. in Baden-Baden from 1964 to 1979, and of the Netherlands Radio Chamber Orch. in Hilversum from 1976 to 1987. He also appeared as a guest conductor throughout Europe, where he became known as a champion of contemporary music. —**NS/LK/DM**

Bourdin, Roger, French baritone; b. Lavallois, June 14, 1900; d. Paris, Sept. 14, 1973. He studied at the Paris Cons. He made his operatic debut as Lescaut in *Manon* in 1922 at the Paris Opéra-Comique; also sang at the Paris Opéra. He made his Covent Garden debut in London in 1930 as Debussy's Pélleas. He was married to Geori Boué.—**NS/LK/DM**

Bourgault-Ducoudray, Louis-Albert, French composer; b. Nantes, Feb. 2, 1840; d. Paris, July 4, 1910. At the age of 18 he composed his first opera, *L'Atelier de Prague* (Nantes, 1858). He was a pupil of Ambroise Thomas at the Paris Cons., taking the Grand Prix de Rome in 1862 with a cantata, *Louise de Mézières*. He founded an amateur choral society in Paris (1868). He spent some time in research in Greece, after which he publ. *Souvenirs d'une mission musicale en Grèce, 30 mélodies populaires de Grèce et de l'Orient*, and *Études sur la musique ecclésiastique grecque* (1877). He was appointed prof. of music history at the Paris Cons. in 1878.

WORKS: DRAMATIC: O p e r a : *Thamara* (Paris Opéra, Dec. 28, 1891); *Michel Colomb* (Brussels, May 7, 1887); *Anne de*

Bretagne (Nantes, Dec. 1892); *Myrdhin* (Nantes, March 28, 1912); *L'Atelier de Prague* (Nantes, 1858). **ORCH.:** *Le Carnaval d'Athènes* (from his *Danses grecques*, orig. for Piano, 4–Hands); *Rapsodie cambodgienne.* **P i a n o :** Various pieces. **VOCAL:** *François d'Amboise*, cantata (1866); *Stabat Mater* (1868); *La Conjuration des fleurs; Symphonie religieuse;* etc.; numerous songs, including *30 mélodies populaires de la Basse-Bretagne*, with French trs. (1885).

BIBL.: M. Emmanuel, *Éloge funèbre de L.-A. B.- D.* (Paris, 1911; with complete catalogue of works).—**NS/LK/DM**

Bourgeois, Loys, French composer and music theorist; b. Paris, c. 1512; d. there, c. 1560. By 1545 he was in Geneva as maître des enfants at St. Pierre and at St. Gervais. In 1547 he was made a citizen of Geneva. Following his request for payment for "improving" the Calvinist Psalter, most likely in the Psalms tr. by Marot and de Béze (publ. in Geneva, 1551; reprint 1554), he was arrested on Dec. 3, 1551, for having failed to obtain authorization from the Genevan council. The next day Calvin secured his release. In 1552 he obtained a leave of absence from his duties and returned to France, and later that year the Genevan council dismissed him from his duties. After living in Lyons, he went to Paris in 1560. In addition to his work on the Calvinist Psalter, he wrote *Le droict chemin* (Geneva and Lyons, 1550; Eng. tr. by B. Rainbow as *The Direct Road to Music*, Kilkenny, 1982), the earliest treatise in French devoted to singing and sight-reading.

WORKS: (50) *Pseaulmes de David...à voix de contrepoinct égal consonante au verbe* for 4 Voices (Lyons, 1547; rev. as *Pseaulmes LXXXIII de David* for 4 Voices, Lyons, 1554; 37 Psalms ed. by K. Bernet Kempers as *37 Psalmen...van Loys Bourgeois*, Delft, 1937); *Le premier livre des [24] pseaulmes...en diversité de musique* for 4 Voices (Lyons, 1547; ed. in Monuments de la musique suisse, III, Basel, 1960); *Quatre-vingt-trois psalmes de David...dont la basse contre tient le sujet* for 4 to 6, and 8 Voices (Paris, 1561; not extant).

BIBL.: P.-A. Gaillard, *L. B.: Sa vie, son oeuvre comme pédagogue et compositeur* (Lausanne, 1948).—**NS/LK/DM**

Bourgeois, Thomas-Louis (-Joseph), French singer and composer; b. Fontaine-L'Eveque, Oct. 24, 1676; d. Paris, 1750. He was maître de musique at the Strasbourg Cathedral (1703–06), and then sang with the Paris Opéra (1708–11). From 1715 to 1721 he was in the service of the Duke of Bourbon. As a composer, he produced a number of fine cantatas, of which 19 are extant; he also wrote divertissements and ballets. —**NS/LK/DM**

Bourguignon, Francis de, Belgian composer; b. Brussels, May 29, 1890; d. there, April 11, 1961. He was a student of Dubois and Tinel (composition) and de Greef (piano) at the Brussels Cons. After touring extensively as a pianist, he pursued composition studies with Gilson in Brussels (1925). With 7 other students of Gilson, he formed the Groupe des Synthétistes to promote contemporary music. From 1939 to 1955 he taught at the Brussels Cons.

WORKS: DRAMATIC: *La Mort d'Orphé*, ballet (1928); *Congo*, radio play (1936); *Le Mauvais Pari*, chamber opera (1937). **ORCH.:** Piano Concertino (1927); *2 esquisses sud-américaines* (1928); *Fête populaire* (1929); *Le Jazz vainqueur*, symphonic poem

(1929); *Prélude and Dance* (1929); *Éloge de la folie* (1934); Sym. (1934); *Oiseaux de nuit* (1937); *Puzzle*, suite (1938); *Fantasy on 2 Themes of Eugène Ysaÿe* for Piano and Orch. (1938); Sinfonietta (1939); *Berceuse* (1940); Suite for Viola and Orch. (1940); *Juventus*, suite (1941); *Recuerdos: 2 impressions sud-américaines* (1943); *Concerto Grosso* (1944); Violin Concerto (1947); Piano Concerto (1949); *Récitatif et Ronde* for Trumpet and Orch. (1951); Concertino for Piano and Chamber Orch. (1952); Concerto for 2 Pianos and Orch. (1953); *Ouverture martiale* (1960). **CHAMBER:** String Trio; Piano Trio; 2 string quartets; Oboe Quintet; piano suites. **VOCAL:** *La Nuit*, oratorio (1945); choral pieces; songs.

BIBL.: A. Vandernoot, *F. d.B.* (Brussels, 1949).—**NS/LK/DM**

Bournonville, Jacques de, French harpsichordist and composer; b. probably in Amiens, c. 1675; d. Paris, c. 1754. He was either the grandson or the great-grandson of **Jean de Bournonville**. He studied with Bernier, and subsequently established himself as a harpsichord player. His motets for 1 and 2 voices with continuo were publ. in 1711.—**NS/LK/DM**

Bournonville, Jean de, French composer, father of **Valentin de Bournonville;** b. Noyon, c. 1585; d. Paris, May 27, 1632. In 1612 he was appointed director of music at the choir school of the collegiate church of St. Quentin, and then was active in Amiens (1618–31). In 1631 he was named director of the choir school of the Sainte-Chapelle. He composed masses, Psalms, motets, and other church music.—**NS/LK/DM**

Bournonville, Valentin de, French composer, son of **Jean de Bournonville;** b. probably in St. Quentin, c. 1610; d. probably in Chartres, Dec. 1663. He studied with his father, and became active as a musician in Amiens. In 1646 he became maître de musique at Notre Dame in Paris. In 1653 he was appointed choir director of the school in Chartres. In 1662 he returned to his former post at Notre Dame in Paris.—**NS/LK/DM**

Bousset, Jean-Baptiste, French composer and singer; b. Dijon, 1662; d. Paris, Oct. 3, 1725. He was active as maître de musique at the chapel of the Louvre, the Académie Française, and the Académies des Sciences et des Inscriptions. He publ. 40 books of airs sérieux et à boire (Paris, 1690–1709), 2 books, both titled *Eglogue bachique* (Paris, 1693, 1695), and a book of cantatas (Paris, before 1710); his motets and an opera are lost. His son, René Drouard de Bousset (b. Paris, Dec. 11, 1703; d. there, May 19, 1760), was also a musician who was active in Paris as an organist and composer. —**NS/LK/DM**

Boutmy, family of South Netherlands musicians:

(1) Jacques-Adrien Boutmy, organist; b. Ghent, Jan. 16, 1683; d. Brussels, Sept. 6, 1719. He was organist at St. Nicholas in Ghent, and then at the collegiate church of SS. Michel et Gudule in Brussels from 1711.

(2) Josse (actually, **Charles Joseph) Boutmy,** organist, harpsichordist, and composer, brother of the preceding; b. Ghent, Feb. 1, 1697; d. Brussels, Nov. 27, 1779. He was active in Brussels, where he became a citizen in 1729. In 1736 he entered the service of the Prince of Thurn and Taxis. From 1744 to 1777 he was organist at the court chapel, where he also taught. He was married twice and had 16 children, 3 of whom are listed below. Boutmy became best known as a composer of harpsichord music and publ. the vols. *Première livre de pièces* (Paris, 1738), *Second livre de pièces* (Paris, c. 1742), and *Troisième livre de pièces* (Brussels, c. 1750). Portions of the first and third vols. were ed. in Monumenta Musicae Belgicae, V (1943).

(3) Guillaume Boutmy, organist, harpsichordist, organ builder, and composer; b. Brussels, June 15, 1723; d. there, Jan. 22, 1791. He pursued his career in Brussels, where he was in the service of the Prince of Thurn and Taxis. In 1752 he became a postal official. From 1760 to 1776 he taught organ and harpsichord at the court, and also was active as an organ builder. He publ. 6 harpsichord sonatas.

(4) Jean-Joseph Boutmy, organist, harpsichordist, and composer; b. Brussels, April 29, 1725; d. Kleve, 1782. He went to Ghent as a harpsichord teacher, and then was organist at St. Baaf Cathedral there (1757–59). He later was organist to the Portuguese ambassador in The Hague. Among his works are 6 harpsichord concertos and 6 divertissements for Harpsichord and Violin Accompaniment ad libitum. He also publ. *Traité abrégé de la basse continue* (The Hague, c. 1760).

(5) Laurent-François Boutmy, organist, harpsichordist, pianist, and composer; b. Brussels, June 19, 1756; d. there, Nov. 3, 1838. He studied with his father. After a sojourn in Rotterdam (1779–83), he was again in Brussels. In 1789 he went to Ermonenville, France, but Revolution forced him to go to London in 1793, where he was active as a harpsichord and piano teacher. He later was piano teacher to Princess Marianne in the Netherlands. He wrote the opera *Armide, ou Les statues* and various keyboard pieces.—**NS/LK/DM**

Bouvet, Charles (René Clement), French musicologist; b. Paris, Jan. 3, 1858; d. there, May 24, 1935. He studied at the Paris Cons. He organized the Fondation J.S. Bach (1903–11), and in 1924 was appointed archivist of the Paris Opéra. He ed. works of Bonporti and Couperin, and also publ. *Une Dynastie de musiciens français: Les Couperin...* (1919), *L'Opéra* (1924), and *Massenet* (1929).—**NS/LK/DM**

Bouzignac, Guillaume, French composer; b. c. 1587; d. c. 1643. He was a choirboy at Narbonne. In 1609 he was the "maître des enfants' at the Grenoble Cathedral. His creative period comprises the years 1610–40; he wrote a number of effective motets in the popular French style, distinguished by dramatic expression, as well as religious works. H. Quittard publ. several of these pieces in his "Un Musicien oublié du XVIIᵉ siècle," *Bulletin de la Société Internationale de Musique* (Paris, 1905).

BIBL.: M. Leroux, *G. B. (ca. 1587–ca. 1643):Étude musicologique* (Béziers, 1993).—**NS/LK/DM**

Bovet, Joseph, Swiss priest, teacher, conductor, and composer; b. Sales, Gruyère, Oct. 7, 1879; d. Clarens,

Feb. 10, 1951. He studied in Romont, Fribourg, and Einsiedeln, and at the Seckau Benedictine monastery, then became a priest and taught music at the Fribourg diocesan seminary. He was made conductor at the Fribourg Cathedral and conducted various choral groups; from 1909 to 1923 he was also conductor of the Fribourg sym. concerts. He wrote much church music for choral forces, music for plays, and part songs.

BIBL.: *Hommage à l'abbe B.* (Fribourg, 1947); R. Loup, *L'abbe B.: Barde du pays* (Lausanne, 1952).—NS/LK/DM

Bovicelli, Giovanni Battista, Italian singer, music theorist, and composer who flourished in the late 16th century. He wrote the important treatise *Regole, passaggi di musica, madrigali et motetti passeggiati* (Venice, 1594; ed. by N. Bridgman, Kassel, 1957), notable for its treatment of singing and improvised vocal ornamentation.—NS/LK/DM

Bovy, Vina (real name, **Malvina Johanna Pauline Félicité Bovi van Overberghe**), Belgian soprano; b. Ghent, May 22, 1900; d. there, May 16, 1983. She studied piano and voice at the Ghent Cons. (1915–17). In 1917 she made her debut in *Hänsel und Gretel* in Ghent; sang at the Théâtre Royal de la Monnaie in Brussels (1920–23) and at the Teatro Colón in Buenos Aires (1927); had guest engagements in Barcelona, Madrid, Monte Carlo, Venice, Milan, Rome, and Paris. On Dec. 24, 1936, she made her Metropolitan Opera debut in N.Y. as Violetta, remaining on its roster until 1938. From 1947 to 1955 she was director of the Ghent Opera. Among her best roles were Gilda, Manon, Lakmé, Juliette, Pamina, Desdemona, and Elsa.

BIBL.: J. Deleersnyder, *V. B.* (Ghent, 1965).—NS/LK/DM

Bovy-Lysberg, Charles-Samuel, Swiss pianist and composer; b. Lysberg, near Geneva, Feb. 1, 1821; d. Geneva, Feb. 15, 1873. He went to Paris and was one of the few young pianists to study with Chopin (1835). Returning to Switzerland, he settled at Dardagny, near Geneva, in 1848; taught piano at the Geneva Cons., and gave recitals in the French cantons. His opera, *La Fille du carillonneur*, was produced in Geneva in 1854. He also wrote a romantically inspired piano sonata, *L'Absence*, but he became known chiefly by his effective salon pieces for piano (numbering about 130), among them *La Napolitaine, Le Réveil des oiseaux, Le Chant du rouet, Idylle, Les Ondines, Sur l'onde*, etc. His real name was Bovy, but he hyphenated it with Lysberg, the name of his birthplace.—NS/LK/DM

Bowen, (Edwin) York, English composer and teacher; b. London, Feb. 22, 1884; d. Hampstead, Nov. 23, 1961. He studied at the Royal Academy of Music in London, where he won the Erard and Sterndale Bennett scholarships; his teachers were T. Matthay (piano) and F. Corder (composition). Upon graduation, he was appointed instructor in piano there. A prolific composer, Bowen wrote 3 syms.; 3 piano concertos; Violin Concerto; Viola Concerto; Rhapsody for Cello and Orch.; symphonic poems (*The Lament of Tasso, Eventide*, etc.); orch. suites; many practical piano pieces in miniature

forms. Bowen was the author of a manual, *Pedalling the Modern Pianoforte* (London, 1936).

BIBL.: M. Watson, *Y. B.: A Centenary Tribute* (London, 1984).—NS/LK/DM

Bowen, Ralph (Michael), jazz educator, b. Guelph, Ontario, Canada, Dec. 23, 1961. His grandfather led a dance band in Canada; his brother plays saxophone and his wife is a professional violinist. He started on clarinet as a young teen, and then studied sax with Pat LaBarbera from 1978–83. He played around Toronto from 1979–84 with various groups, and also led his own ensembles. He continued his studies in the early 1980s at the Univ. of Ind. and Rutgers Univ. (B.Music, 1989), and was part of the group Out of the Blue with fellow students Mike Mossman and others from 1985–90. Bowen and Mossman played as a team with Michel Camilo (from 1986) and Horace Silver (from 1988). Bowen has since played with pianist Renee Rosnes' band and several other groups. He began teaching at his alma mater part time in the late 1980s, became head ("convenor") of the jazz program there in the mid-1990s, and in 1997 became a full-time professor.

DISC.: *Movin' On* (1992).—LP

Bowers, Thomas J., esteemed black American tenor; b. Philadelphia, c. 1823; d. there, Oct. 3, 1885. He studied organ with his brother, John C. Bowers, succeeding him as organist of Philadelphia's St. Thomas's African Episcopal Church (c. 1838). After vocal training with Elizabeth Taylor Greenfield, he began a North American duo-recital tour with her with a performance at Philadephia's Sansom St. Hall (1854). Critics hailed him as the "American Mario" and the "colored Mario."—NS/LK/DM

Bowie, David (originally, **Jones, David**), rock's English master of image and sound manipulation; b. Brixton, London, England, Jan. 8, 1947. David Bowie has pursued an erratic career based very much on image, as opposed to musical substance. His successes have totally transformed the way in which musical heroes are regarded by the consuming public, in terms of shock value, cleverness, and timeliness rather than substance or talent. Tapping musical wellsprings as diverse as folk, pop, disco, and punk, Bowie has demonstrated the uncanny ability to exploit virtually every musical trend without mastering any. Nonetheless, Bowie can be seen as a genius of performance art and astute for his choices of musical collaborators, be it Mick Ronson, Brian Eno, or Nile Rodgers.

David Bowie achieved his earliest major success at the hands of producer-guitarist Mick Ronson, with the classic *Hunky Dory, Ziggy Stardust*, and *Aladdin Sane* albums and tours. Bowie was thereby established as the first star of glitter rock, with its ambivalent sexuality, bizarre costuming and cosmetics, contrived theatricality, and elaborate stage lighting and presentation. This achievement helped open rock and pop to artists unafraid to display their flamboyance (Kiss, The New York Dolls), androgyny (Boy George, Michael Jackson), and openly gay sexuality (Queen). During the 1970s Bowie established a vital link between music, dance, acting, mime, and street theater that presaged the development of performance art in the 1980s. His electronic and synthesizer experiments of the late 1970s opened the door for the synthesizer-dominated pop sound of the 1980s and the ambient sound of the 1990s. His 1980 album *Scary Monsters* inspired a new generation of performers such as Ultravox and Duran Duran, yet he garnered his most widespread popularity with 1983's *Let's Dance* album and Serious Moonlight tour, both in a more pop vein, thanks to the influence of producer Nile Rodgers. Abandoning more than 20 years of hits following 1990's Sound + Vision tour, David Bowie explored heavy metal with Tin Machine before reemerging in 1993 with the jazz-soul-hip-hop sound of *Black Tie White Noise*.

David Jones took up saxophone at age 12, later forming a number of groups, including David Jones and the Lower Third. Scoring several minor British hits in 1967, he changed his name to David Bowie to avoid confusion with Davy Jones of the Monkees. After a first album heavily influenced by the British music hall tradition, Bowie shifted to a hippie image for his first episode in science fiction, *Space Oddity*, an album not released in the United States until 1972. The title song became a smash hit in Great Britain and eventually became his first major American hit in 1973. Nonetheless, he "retired" for 18 months to run an Arts Lab in Beckenham, South London, before reemerging with *The Man Who Sold the World*, recorded with guitarist Mick Ronson and drummer Woody Woodmansey. With the British cover (banned in the United States) depicting Bowie as a drag queen with a striking resemblance to Lauren Bacall, the album earned him the beginnings of an English following and introduced the concept of glitter rock. Switching to RCA Records, Bowie managed a moderate hit with "Changes" from *Hunky Dory*.

Arranged by Mick Ronson, *The Rise and Fall of Ziggy Stardust and the Spiders from Mars* was the first of four concept albums that brought Bowie widespread publicity and acclaim and his first recognition in the United States. With Bowie becoming rock star Ziggy Stardust, and Mick Ronson, Woody Woodmansey, and bassist Trevor Bolder becoming the Spiders from Mars, the album featured the minor hit "Starman" and Bowie classics such as "Star," "Suffragette City," and "Rock 'n' Roll Suicide." The 1972 Ziggy Stardust tour of the United States introduced American audiences to Bowie's peculiar, camp mixture of makeup, costume and set changes, and elaborate lighting and staging. The follow-up album, *Aladdin Sane*, generated a minor hit with "Jean Genie."

At this same time David Bowie composed and produced Mott the Hoople's first hit, "All the Young Dudes," and produced Lou Reed's *Transformer* and Iggy Pop's *Raw Power*. Following his final album with the Spiders from Mars and the conclusion of his British tour of 1973, Bowie announced his retirement. However, he was soon back with *Diamond Dogs*, his first album without the services of Mick Ronson, and its minor hit "Rebel Rebel."

Young Americans revealed another image shift, with Bowie embracing the sound of Philadelphia soul. With a new, sophisticated playboy look, he hit with "Young Americans" and "Fame," coauthored by John Lennon. Bowie continued his soul persona with *Station to Station* and the smash "Golden Years." Later in 1976 he revealed a talent for acting, in the title role of Nicolas Roeg's *The Man Who Fell to Earth*, portraying a space voyager stranded on Earth.

Bowie's next three studio albums featured a spare, minimalist sound created by avant-garde keyboardist Brian Eno. Although the albums failed to sell spectacularly, they influenced an entire generation of European rock bands who used electronic synthesizers and sparse arrangements in their playing. In 1980 Bowie received rave reviews for his performance on tour and on Broadway as the grossly deformed John Merrick in Bernard Pomerance's *The Elephant Man*. He recorded *Scary Monsters* without Brian Eno, but with former King Crimson guitarist Robert Fripp. The album included "Ashes to Ashes," promoted with one of the most expensive videos to date, and the minor hit "Fashion." Bowie's next major hit, "Under Pressure," was recorded with Queen.

Bowie switched to EMI America Records and enlisted Nile Rodgers and Tony Thompson of Chic for his 1983 album *Let's Dance*. The title song and hits "China Girl" and "Modern Love" featured Stevie Ray Vaughan on guitar. Playing stadiums rather than arenas, the subsequent Serious Moonlight tour established Bowie as a performing act, without the theatrical effects of earlier tours. In 1984 "Blue Jean" became a near-smash hit from *Tonight*, and the following year Bowie and Mick Jagger hit with a remake of "Dancing in the Street," with all proceeds donated to Live Aid. Bowie later acted in the 1986 film *Labyrinth* and recorded its soundtrack.

David Bowie returned to his theatrics for the 1987 Glass Spider tour, supported by guitarist Peter Frampton, who played on *Never Let Me Down* and its two major hits "Day-In Day-Out" and the title cut. In late 1988 Bowie formed Tin Machine as an integrated band under the influence of punk and heavy-metal music. However, their albums generated little interest, and in 1990 Bowie conducted his Sound + Vision tour with guitarist Adrian Belew as a recapitulation of his career to date. He eventually reemerged with his first solo album in six years, *Black Tie White Noise*, but within months his new label, Savage Records, had ceased operations. Bowie attempted to woo a younger crowd by touring in 1995 with Nine Inch Nails; the audience seemed more interested in the young rockers, though, and Bowie's new material was mostly ignored.

DISC.: EARLY DAVID BOWIE: *The World of D. B.* (1967); *Images, 1966–1967* (1973); *Starting Point* (1977); *Love You Till Tuesday* (1984); *Early On (1964–1966)* (1991). **DAVID BOWIE:** *Space Oddity* (1969); *The Man Who Sold the World* (1970); *Hunky Dory* (1971). **DAVID BOWIE AND THE SPIDERS FROM MARS:** *The Rise and Fall of Ziggy Stardust and the Spiders from Mars* (1972); *Aladdin Sane* (1973); *Pin Ups* (1973). **THE SPIDERS FROM MARS:** *The Spiders from Mars* (1976). **DAVID BOWIE:** *Diamond Dogs* (1974); *David Live* (1974); *Young Americans* (1975); *Changesonebowie* (1976);

Station to Station (1976); *Heroes* (1977); *Low* (1977); *Stage* (1978); *Lodger* (1979); *Scary Monsters* (1980); *Changestwobowie* (1981); *Christiane F.* (sountrack; 1982); *In Bertolt Brecht's "Baal"* (1982); *Golden Years* (1983); *Let's Dance* (1983); *Ziggy Stardust: The Motion Picture* (1983); *Fame and Fashion (All-Time Greatest Hits)* (1984); *Tonight* (1984); *Labyrinth* (sountrack; 1986); *Never Let Me Down* (1987); *Sound + Vision* (1989); *Changesbowie* (1990); *Bowie: The Singles* (1993); *Black Tie White Noise* (1993); *Jump* (1994); *Outside* (1995). **DAVID BOWIE/EUGENE ORMANDY AND THE PHILADELPHIA ORCH.:** *D. B. Narrates Prokofiev's "Peter and the Wolf"* (1978). **TIN MACHINE:** *Tin Machine* (1989); *Tin Machine II* (1991); *Oy Vey, Baby* (1992).

BIBL.: G. Tremlett, *The D. B. Story* (London, 1974); V. Clair, *D. B.! The King of Glitter Rock* (N.Y., 1977); D. Fletcher, *David Robert Jones Bowie: The Discography of a Generalist, 1962–1979* (Chicago, 1979); Miles and C. Charlesworth, *D. B. Black Book: The Illustrated Biography* (London, 1980); Carr et al., *B.: An Illustrated Record* (N.Y., 1981); C. Charlesworth, *D. B.: Profile* (N.Y., 1981); K. Cann, *D. B.: A Chronology* (London, 1983); K. Lynch, *D. B.: A Rock 'n' Roll Odyssey* (London, 1984); J. Hopkins, *B.* (N.Y., 1985); P. Gillman and L. Gillman, *Alias D. B.* (N.Y., 1990); A. Bowie, with P. Carr, *Backstage Passes: Life on the Wild Side with D. B.* (N.Y., 1993).—BH

Bowie, Joseph, jazz/funk trombonist, percussionist, brother of **Lester Bowie;** b. St. Louis, Mo., 1953. He studied piano and worked with Paramounts, Lamontes, and Oliver Sain. He was Music Director for Fontella Bass. A member of BAG, he also formed Defunkt, which managed to successfully merge funk beats, rock energy, jazz techniques and soloing, with an unpredictable, free-wheeling avant-garde aesthetic. They were popular during the early and mid-1980s, disbanded, then reunited in early 1990s.

DISC.: *Defunkt: Defunkt* (1980); *A Defunkt Anthology* (1981); *Thermonuclear Sweat* (1982); *In America* (1988); *Avoid the Funk* (1988); *Heroes* (1990); *Crisis* (1992); *Live at the Knitting Factory* (1991).—LP

Bowles, Paul (Frederic), American man of letters and composer; b. N.Y., Dec. 30, 1910; d. Tangier, Nov. 18, 1999. He became fascinated with pictorial arts, belles lettres, and the vocal projection of poetry as a child, and when he was 8 he also began to study music. At 17, he had his first poem publ. in the literary review *transition*. In 1929 he made his way to Paris, where he was dazzled by its intellectual resplendence and the insouciant millieu of the Left Bank. Returning to N.Y., his hypnopomping musical talent manifested itself and in 1930 he became a student of Copland. In 1931 he returned to Paris, where he continued his studies with Copland and had a few lessons with Boulanger. He became a habitué of the circle surrounding Gertrude Stein and Alice B. Toklas, but his wanderlust led him to visit Berlin and North Africa. The latter sojourn proved the turning point in his artistic career, both as a composer and as a man of letters. After composing several orch., chamber, and vocal scores, Bowles attracted attention with his ballet *Yankee Clipper* (1936). During the following 2 decades, he proved adept at composing film scores and incidental music for plays. In 1941 he received a Guggenheim fellowship, which resulted in his opera *The Wind Remains* (1941–43), after García Lorca.

His psychological attraction to exotic lands prompted him to return to North Africa in 1947, which remained the center of his activities for the rest of his life with occasional sojourns to various lands abroad. Among his later compositions was the opera *Yerma* (1948–55), also after García Lorca. As a composer, he found his métier in works reflecting American, Mexican, and North African elements. Bowles soon became best known, however, as a writer, when in 1949 he publ. the first of his many bone-chilling novels, *The Sheltering Sky*. He also wrote short stories and made trs. of native works about North Africa. His autobiography was publ. as *Without Stopping* (1972). The vol. *Paul Bowles: Music* (1995) is a collection of essays, interviews, and reviews. Bowles was married to the novelist and playwright Jane Auer, who died in 1973.

WORKS: DRAMATIC: O p e r a : *Denmark Vesey* (1938); *The Wind Remains* (1941–43); *Yerma* (1948–55). B a l - l e t : *Yankee Clipper* (1936); *The Ballroom Guide* (1937); *Pastorela* (1941); *Colloque sentimental* (1944). Also incidental music to plays and various film scores. ORCH.: *Iquitos* (1933); *Pastorale, Havanaise et Divertissement* (1933); *Suite* (1933); *Romantic Suite* (1939); *Concerto for 2 Pianos, Winds, and Percussion* (1947); *Danza mexicana* (1947). CHAMBER: *Sonata for Oboe and Clarinet* (1930); *Flute Sonata* (1932); *Violin Sonata* (1934); *Piano Trio* (1936); *Melodia* for 11 Instruments (1937); *Music for a Farce* for Clarinet, Trumpet, Percussion, and Piano (1938); *Prelude and Dance* for Wind, Brass, Percussion, and Piano (1947); many piano pieces, including *Sonata for 2 Pianos* (1949). VOCAL: *Scènes d'Anabase* for Tenor, Oboe, and Piano (1932); *Par le détroit*, cantata for Soprano, 4 Men's Voices, and Harmonium (1933); *3 Pastoral Songs* for Tenor, Piano, and Strings (1944); *A Picnic Cantata* for 4 Soloists, 2 Pianos, and Percussion (1952); many songs for Voice and Piano; see P. Garland, ed., *Paul Bowles: Selected Songs* (Santa Fe, N.Mex., 1984).

BIBL.: C. Sawyer-Lauçanno, *An Invisible Spectator: A Biography of P. B.* (N.Y., 1989).—NS/LK/DM

Bowlly, Al, one of the all-time most popular British pop vocalists, guitarist, banjo player, pianist; b. Maputo, Mozambique, Jan. 7, 1898; d. London, April 17, 1941. Born to a Greek father and a Lebanese mother, he grew up in Johannesburg and learned to play the ukelele. Bowlly toured Africa and India as a banjo/guitarist and was a resident at Raffles in Singapore. He made his first records in Berlin (1927), then freelanced in London, making 678 sides (1930–4), mainly with the Roy Fox and Ray Noble bands. His best-known records are Noble compositions; "The Very Thought of You" and others also did well in the U.S. Noble took Bowlly with him to N.Y. (1934), where Glenn Miller was Noble's arranger. Bowlly sang an early lyric to a Miller tune that later became "Moonlight Serenade." He was successful in the U.S. but returned to London (1937) to tour with his own Radio City Rhythm Makers and team up with Maltese singer Jimmy Messini in Radio Stars With Two Guitars. Bowlly worked with West Indian bandleader Ken "Snakehips" Johnson (1940–41). A bomb hit the Cafe de Paris, killing Johnson and many others in March 1941; Bowlly was killed by another in April. He made the U.K. Top Ten album chart in 1978 as the featured singer in the *Pennies from Heaven* soundtrack.

DISC.: *Al Bowlly with Ray Noble* (1931); *On the Sentimental*

Side (1978); *One & Only* (1980); *Goodnight Sweetheart–1931 Sessions* (1982); *The Golden Age of Al Bowlly* (1983); *A Million Dreams–Solos 1932–33* (1984); *The Dance Band Days* (1984); *The Al Bowlly Circle* (1984); *Sweet As a Song* (1895); *Sentimentally Yours* (1986); *20 Golden Pieces of Al Bowlly* (1986); *My Song Goes Round the World* (1986); *The London Sessions 1928–30* (1986); *Al Bowlly in New York* (1987); *Something to Sing About* (1987); *Flowers for Madame 1935–37* (1988); *The Very Thought of You* (1988); *Proud of You* (1989); *Proud of You* (1992); *Just a Bowl of Cherries* (1993); *Love Is the Sweetest Thing* (1995); *The Dance Band Years* (1997); *Goodnight Sweetheart* (1997); *HMV Sessions, Vol. 1: 1930–1934* (1998); *HMV Sessions, Vol. 2: 1930–1934* (1999); *Marvelous Melodies of Peter Mendoza* (1999); *Right from the Heart* (1999); *Sweet Someone* (2000); *Dance Band Years* (2000); *Al Bowlly* (2000); *1931–1934* (2000); *Love Is the Sweetest Thing [Past Perfect]* (2000); *Al Bowlly & the Great British Bands* (2000).

BIBL.: S. Colin, T. Staveacre, *Al Bowlly* (1979).—**MM/JC-B/LP**

Bowman, James (Thomas),

notable English countertenor; b. Oxford, Nov. 6, 1941. He was educated at New Coll., Oxford (Dip.Ed., 1964; M.A. in history, 1967) and received vocal instruction in London from De Rentz and Manen. In 1967 he made his operatic debut as Britten's Oberon at Aldeburgh with the English Opera Group. From 1967 he sang with the group regularly in London, and also was a member of the Early Music Consort (1967–76). In 1970 he appeared in *Semele* at the Sadler's Wells Opera there, and continued to sing there after it became the English National Opera in 1974. He sang Endymion in *La Calisto* at the Glyndebourne Festival in 1970, and sang there regularly until 1974. On July 12, 1972, he created the role of the Priest in Maxwell Davies's *Taverner* at London's Covent Garden. Britten then wrote the role of Apollo for him in *Death in Venice* (Aldeburgh, June 16, 1973). On July 7, 1977, he created the role of Astron in Tippett's *The Ice Break* at Covent Garden. In 1979 he appeared at the Opéra-Comique in Paris and in 1983 he sang in Geneva. He was engaged as Jommelli's Fetonte at Milan's La Scala in 1988. In 1992 he portrayed Britten's Oberon at the Aix-en-Provence Festival. In 1996 he sang Daniel in Handel's *Belshazzar* at the Göttingen Festival. He was made a Commander of the Order of the British Empire in 1997.—**NS/LK/DM**

Boxberg, Christian Ludwig,

German composer; b. Sondershausen, April 24, 1670; d. Görlitz, Dec. 1, 1729. He studied at the Thomasschule in Leipzig, and from 1692 to 1702 was organist in Grossenhain; also was active as a librettist, composer, and singer at the Leipzig Opera. In 1702 he became organist at Ss. Peter and Paul in Görlitz. He wrote librettos for the operas of N.A. Strungk. His own operas include *Orion* (Ansbach, 1697), *Die verschwiegene Treue* (Ansbach, 1698), *Sardanapolus* (Ansbach, 1698), and *Amyntas und Phyllis* (Leipzig, 1700). He also composed numerous cantatas.

BIBL.: H. Mersmann, *C.L. B. und seine Oper "Sardanapolus," Ansbach, 1698* (diss., Univ. of Berlin, 1916).—**NS/LK/DM**

Box Tops, The,

hit-making Memphis group that issued one of the shortest hits of all time and started the career of power-pop legend Alex Chilton (b. Memphis,

Tenn., Dec. 28, 1950), formed 1965, Memphis, Tenn.

Alex Chilton is one of rock's great underground legends, certainly revered among his peers. So much so, The Replacements once recorded a song called "Alex Chilton." Not bad for someone who hadn't had a chart hit for 15 years before the song (and hasn't had one since).

Chilton, son of a Memphis jazz musician, was 16 when a local Memphis band called the Devilles— guitarists Gary Talley (b. Aug. 17, 1950) and Billy Cunningham (b. Jan. 23, 1950), bassist John Evans (b. 1949), and drummer Danny Smyth (b. 1949)—took him on as lead singer. The band's management hooked them up with legendary producer Chips Moman, who had just left Muscle Shoals studios to establish his own American Sound studios. Moman's partner, songwriter Dan Penn, produced the group's first recording. They cut a song that ran a minute and 52 seconds, including a sound-effects recording of a jet engine grafted onto the beginning. That song, "The Letter," topped the charts for a solid month during the summer of 1967. Over the next three years, the Box Tops recorded half a dozen more Top 40 hits: "Neon Rainbow" (#24), "Cry Like a Baby" (two weeks at #2), "Choo Choo Train" (#26), "I Met Her in Church" (#36), "Sweet Cream Ladies, Forward March" (#28) and "Soul Deep" (#18). However, after "The Letter," the studio Box Tops were only Chilton and the American Sound house band. Live, when the original band played, they couldn't live up to these standards. Several members opted for college and Chilton moved on.

Ironically, Chilton is less legendary for his work with the hit-making Box Tops than he is for Big Star, the band that he formed afterwards with guitarist Chris Bell (b. Memphis, Tenn., Jan. 12, 1951, d. there, Dec. 27, 1978), Jody Stephens (b. Memphis, Tenn., Oct. 4, 1952), and Andy Hummel (b. Memphis, Tenn., Jan. 26, 1951). Heavily influenced by "British revolution" bands like The Beatles, The Kinks, and The Who, their three records became word-of-mouth legends over the course of years, influencing artists ranging from Paul Westerberg to The Bangles. On release, however, they sold very poorly, largely due to erratic distribution. In fact, the group broke up after the pristine pop of *#1 Record*, when Bell became disillusioned with the poor sales. He died in a car accident in 1978. A gig at a rock writer's convention lured the remaining band members back together, which resulted in the rawer, Bell-less record, *Radio City*. They went into the studio again with session players like Steve Cropper, but the record, *3rd/Sister Lover*, didn't come out until years later.

Chilton hit lean times after Big Star, turning to drink and working odd jobs like cab driver and yard man in N.Y. During that period, young musicians were discovering his music, but he wasn't getting any offers to record, and his sporadic live shows varied with his level of sobriety. He recorded a couple of spotty albums, including *Like Flies on Sherbert*, played guitar in Tav Falco's Panther Burns, and produced the Cramps' *Songs the Lord Taught Us*.

Early in the 1980s, Chilton got clean and sober and started performing in his new home of New Orleans, working with a soul band playing four nights a week for tourists. A booking agent heard that he had become active again and offered him some shows in N.Y. This resulted in a new recording contract and the album *Feudalist Tarts,* which once again provided fodder for the critics and cultists, but earned no real sales. Still, it marked a comeback for Chilton, who went on to record *High Priest* in Memphis using mostly local musicians. It included a motley mix of material, such as "Come by Here," a gospel take on the campfire staple "Cumbaya," and a cover of that hoary chestnut "Volare." Similarly, *Cliches* found him recording solo acoustic guitar versions of songs by Ray Charles and Cole Porter, and *1970* covering songs from the era of his greatest stardom. 1995's *A Man Called Destruction,* named for the pianist in Howlin' Wolf's band, demonstrated that Chilton could still write biting, bracing music of his own.

Chilton and Stephens revived Big Star, fleshing the band out with John Auer and Ken Stringfellow of The Posies, initially to play one show at the Univ. of Mo. that was recorded for release. This led to a continuing on and off relationship. The Original Box Tops have also gotten back together, playing about 20 gigs a year on the oldies circuit. Chilton also continues to tour, playing his own music, and the legend continues to grow.

DISC.: *Best of The Box Tops* (1996). BIG STAR: *Third* (1978); *Live* (1992); *Columbia–Live at Missouri University* (1993); *Nobody Can Dance* (1999). ALEX CHILTON: *Live in London* (1982); *Bach's Bottom* (1975); *Live in London* (1980); *Like Flies on Sherbert* (1980); *Feudalist Tarts/No Sex* (1985); *High Priest/Black List* (1987); *19 Years—A Collection* (1991); *Cliches* (1994); *Man Called Destruction* (1995); *1970* (1996).—HB

Boyce, William, significant English organist and composer; b. London (baptized), Sept. 11, 1711; d. Kensington, Feb. 7, 1779. As a youth he was a chorister in St. Paul's Cathedral under Charles King. He then studied organ with Maurice Greene, the cathedral organist. From 1734 to 1736 he was organist at the Earl of Oxford's Chapel, then at St. Michael's, Cornhill, from 1736 to 1768. Concurrently he was named in 1736 composer to the Chapel Royal. In 1759 he was Master of the King's Musick. An increasing deafness forced him to abandon active musical duties after 1769. His main task consisted in providing sacred works for performance; he also contributed incidental music to theatrical productions. He conducted the Festivals of the Three Choirs (Gloucester, Worcester, Hereford) in 1737, and served as Master of the Royal Band in 1755. His magnum opus was the compilation of the collection *Cathedral Music,* in 3 vols. (1760, 1768, and 1773; 2nd ed., 1788; later eds., 1844 and 1849). This collection comprises morning and evening services, anthems, and other church music by a number of British composers, namely Aldrich, Batten, Bevin, Blow, Bull, Byrd, Child, Clarke, Creyghton, Croft, Farrant, Gibbons, Goldwin, Henry VIII, Humfrey, Lawes, Locke, Morley, Mundy, Purcell, Rogers, Tallis, Turner, Tye, Weldon, and Wise. Of his own music, there are remarkable instrumental works: 12 overtures (London, 1770; reprinted in Musica Britannica, vol. XIII); 12 sonatas for 2 Violins and Bass (London, 1747); 8 syms. (London, 1760; modern ed. by M. Goberman, Vienna, 1964); 10 voluntaries for Organ or Harpsichord (London, 1779). Two overtures erroneously attributed to Boyce, and publ. in Lambert's ed. under the titles *The Power of Music* and *Pan and Syrinx,* were works by John Stanley, not by Boyce. His stage works include the following, all produced in London: *The Chaplet* (Dec. 2, 1749), *The Roman Father* (Feb. 24, 1750; not extant), *The Shepherd's Lottery* (Nov. 19, 1751), and *Harlequin's Invasion* (with M. Arne and T. Aylward, Dec. 31, 1759). Several of his vocal works were publ. in *Lyra Britannica* (1745–55); there were also 15 anthems (1780) and a collection of anthems (1750), which were republ. in Novello's ed. in 4 vols.; also, various songs were orig. publ. in the anthologies *The British Orpheus, The Vocal Musical Mask,* and others.—NS/LK/DM

Boyd, Anne (Elizabeth), Australian composer; b. Sydney, April 10, 1946. She studied flute at the New South Wales Cons. (1960–63) and composition at the Univ. of Sydney (1963–66); concluded her studies at York Univ. in England (Ph.D., 1972). She was a lecturer at the Univ. of Sussex (1975–77); served as head of the music dept. at the Univ. of Hong Kong (1980–88). She composed two children's operas, *The Little Mermaid* (1978) and *The Beginning of the Day* (1980), and *The Rose Garden,* theater piece (1972).—NS/LK/DM

Boydell, Brian (Patrick), Irish composer and teacher; b. Dublin, March 17, 1917. He studied at the Evangelical Church Music Inst. of the Univ. of Heidelberg, with Hadley and Howells at the Royal Coll. of Music in London (1938–39), at the Royal Irish Academy of Music in Dublin, and at the Univ. of Dublin (Mus.D., 1959). From 1962 to 1982 he was prof. of music at the Univ. of Dublin. He was made a Commendatore della Repubblica Italiana for his services to Italian Renaissance music (1983), was awarded an honorary D.Mus. of the National Univ. of Ireland, and was made a member of Aosdána for general contributions to the creative arts in Ireland. He publ. *A Dublin Musical Calendar 1700–1760* (1988) and *Rotunda Music in Eighteenth-Century Dublin* (1992). His music reveals an assured command of traditional compositional techniques.

WORKS: ORCH.: Sym. for Strings (1945); *5 Joyce Songs* (1946); *In Memoriam Mahatma Gandhi* (1948); Violin Concerto (1953); *The Wooing of Etain,* 2 suites (1954); *Elegy and Capriccio* for Clarinet and Strings (1955); *Megalithic Ritual Dances* (1956); *Meditation and Fugue* (1956); *Ceól Cas Corach* (1958); *Shielmartin Suite* (1958); *Richard's Riot* (1961); *Symphonic Inscapes* (1968); *Jubilee Music* (1976); *Partita Concertante* for Violin, Harp, and Orch. (1978); *A Wild Dance for Ceól Chumann na nóg* (1982); *Masai Mara* (1988). CHAMBER: Oboe Quintet (1940); String Trio (1944); Cello Sonata (1945); 3 string quartets (1950, 1957, 1969); Quintet for Flute, Harp, and String Trio (1960); *4 Sketches* for 2 Irish Harps (1962); *A Pack of Fancies for a Travelling Harper* (1970); *5 Mosaics* for Violin and Piano or Harp (1972); *5 Blows* for Brass Quintet (1984); *An Album of Pieces for the Irish Harp* (1989); *Adagio and Scherzo* for String Quartet (1991); *Viking-Lip-Music* for 11 Brasses and 2 Percussionists (1996). KEYBOARD: Many piano pieces. VOCAL: *An Easter Carol* for Chorus (1940); *Shatter Me, Music* for Chorus (1952); *The Deer's Cry* for Baritone and Orch. (1957); *Noël* for Chorus and Orch. (1960); *Mors et vita* for Soloists, Chorus, and Orch. (1960–61); *A Terrible*

Beauty is Born for Narrator, Soloists, Chorus, and Orch. (1965); *4 Yeats Poems* for Soprano and Orch. (1965); *Mouth Music* for Chorus (1974); *The Small Bell*, cantata (1980); *The Carlow Cantata or The Female Friend* (1985); *Under No Circumstances: An Historical Entertainment* for 2 Soloists, Narrator, Chorus, and Orch. (1987; Dublin, March 10, 1988); songs.—NS/LK/DM

Boyden, David D(odge), American musicologist; b. Westport, Conn., Dec. 10, 1910; d. Berkeley, Sept. 18, 1986. He studied at Harvard Univ. (A.B., 1932; M.A., 1938), then joined the faculty of the Univ. of Calif. at Berkeley, remaining there until 1975. He publ. *A Manual of Counterpoint Based on Sixteenth-century Practice* (N.Y., 1944; 2nd ed., 1953), *The History and Literature of Music, 1750 to the Present* (N.Y., 1948), *An Introduction to Music* (N.Y., 1956; 2nd ed., 1970), and *The History of Violin Playing from Its Origins to 1761* (London, 1965). —NS/LK/DM

Boykan, Martin, American composer, teacher, and pianist; b. N.Y., April 12, 1931. He studied composition with Piston at Harvard Univ. (B.A., 1951), Copland at the Berkshire Music Center at Tanglewood (summers, 1949–50), and Hindemith at the Univ. of Zürich (1951–52) and Yale Univ. (M.M., 1953). He also had lessons in piano from Steuermann. From 1957 to 1970 he was active as a pianist. In 1957 he joined the faculty of Brandeis Univ., where he later was a prof. of composition. He also was a visiting prof. of composition at Columbia Univ. (1988–89) and N.Y. Univ. (1993). In 1994 he was a senior Fulbright lecturer at Bar-Ilan Univ. in Israel. He held Fulbright (1953–55) and Guggenheim (1984) fellowships. In 1986 and 1988 he received awards from the American Academy of Arts and Letters. His music is marked by a predominate lyrical line and emotional breadth.

WORKS: ORCH.: Concerto for 13 Players (1971); Sym. for Baritone and Orch. (1989; Salt Lake City, April 9, 1993). **CHAMBER:** Trio for Violin, Viola, and Cello (1948); String Quartet (1949); 4 numbered string quartets (1967, 1974, 1984, 1995–96); Flute Sonata (1950); Duo for Violin and Piano (1951); Flute Quintet (1953); 2 trios for Violin, Cello, and Piano (1975, 1997); *Nocturne* for Cello, Piano, and Percussion (1991); *Eclogue* for Flute, Horn, Viola, Cello, and Piano (1991); *Echoes of Petrarch* for Flute, Clarinet, and Piano (1992); Cello Sonata (1992); *Impromptu* for Violin (1993); Violin Sonata (1994); Sonata for Solo Cello (1998); *Flume* for Clarinet and Piano (1998); *Romanza* for Flute and Piano (1999). **KEYBOARD: P i a n o :** 2 sonatas (1986, 1990); *Pastorale* (1993); *Usurpations*, 5 bagatelles (1997). **O r g a n :** *Prelude* (1964). **VOCAL:** *Psalm 128* for Chorus (1965); *Elegy* for Soprano and 6 Instruments (1982); *Shalom Rav* for Baritone, Chorus, and Organ (1985); *Epithalamion* for Baritone, Violin, and Harp (1987); *Voyages* for Soprano and Piano (1992); *Sea Gardens*, 4 songs for Soprano and Piano (1993); *3 Psalms* for Soprano and Piano (1993); *Ma'ariv* Settings for Chorus and Organ (1995); *3 Shakespeare Songs* for Chorus (1996); *Psalm 121* for Soprano and String Quartet (1997).—NS/LK/DM

Boyle, George Frederick, American pianist, teacher, and composer; b. Sydney, Australia, June 29, 1886; d. Philadelphia, June 20, 1948. He received his early musical training from his parents, and in 1905

went to Berlin, where he took piano lessons with Busoni. He began his career as an accompanist. In 1910 he settled in the U.S., where he taught piano at the Peabody Cons. of Music in Baltimore (1910–22), the Curtis Inst. of Music in Philadelphia (1924–26), and the Inst. of Musical Art in N.Y. (1927–39). He wrote *Aubade* for Orch. (St. Louis, March 5, 1916), Piano Concerto (Worcester Festival, Sept. 28, 1911), Cello Concerto (Washington, D.C., Feb. 7, 1918), 3 piano trios, Violin Sonata, Viola Sonata, Cello Sonata, about 100 piano pieces, and 50 songs.

BIBL.: I. Peery, *G.F. B.: Pianist, Teacher, Composer* (diss., Peabody Cons. of Music, 1987).—NS/LK/DM

Boyvin, Jacques, French organist and composer; b. Paris, c. 1649; d. Rouen, June 30, 1706. He studied in Paris, then was organist at the Hopital des Quinze-Vingts (1663–74). From 1674 until his death he was organist at Notre Dame Cathedral in Rouen; also served at St. Herbland (1697–1702). He composed mainly for organ; his organ works were publ. in Paris in 2 books (1689–90; 1700). See A. Guilmant and A. Pirro, eds., *J. B.: OEuvres complètes d'orgue* (Paris, 1905).—NS/LK/DM

Bozay, Attila, Hungarian composer and teacher; b. Balatonfűzfő, Aug. 11, 1939; d. Gönc, Sept. 14, 1999. He studied in Budapest at the Bartók Cons. (1954–57) and then with Farkas at the Academy of Music, graduating in 1962. After serving as a music producer for the Hungarian Radio (1963–66), he went to Paris on a UNESCO scholarship in 1967. Returning to Budapest, he devoted himself fully to composition and later taught at the Academy of Music. In 1968 and 1979 he received the Erkel Prize. In 1984 he was made a Merited Artist by the Hungarian government. In 1988 he received the Bartók-Pásztory Award.

WORKS: O p e r a : *Küngisz királynö* (Queen Kungisz; 1968–69); *Csongor és Tünde* (1979–84; Budapest, Jan. 20, 1985). **ORCH.:** *Pezzo concertato No. 1* for Viola and Orch. (1965) and *No. 2* for Zither and Orch. (1974–75); *Pezzo sinfonico No. 1* (1967) and *No. 2* (1975–76); *Pezzo d'archi* (1968; rev. 1974); *Gyermekdalok* (Children's Songs) for 18 Strings (1976); *Variazioni* (1977); *Improvisations No. 3* for Prepared Piano and Strings (1987). **CHAMBER ENSEMBLE:** *Sorozat* (Series; 1970); *A malom* (The Mill; 1972–73). **CHAMBER:** Duo for 2 Violins (1958); *Episodi* for Bassoon and Piano (1959); Trio for Violin, Viola, and Cello (1960; rev. 1966); Wind Quintet (1962); 2 string quartets (1964, 1971); *Két tétel* (2 Movements) for Oboe and Piano (1970); *Improvisations No. 2* for Recorders and String Trio (1976); *Tükor* (Mirror) for Zither and Cimbalom (1977); Violin Sonata (1987–88); various pieces for Solo Instrument, including many for Piano. **VOCAL:** *Papírszeletek* (Paper Slips) for Soprano, Clarinet, and Cello (1962); *Kiáltások* (Outcries) for Tenor, Violin, Cello, Clarinet, Horn, and Piano (1963); *Trapéz és korlát* (Trapeze and Parallel Bars), cantata for Tenor, Chorus, and Orch. (1966); *Lux perpetua*, motet for Chorus (1969); *Két tájkép* (2 Landscapes) for Baritone, Flute, and Zither (1970–71); 24 Children's or Women's Choruses (1985).—NS/LK/DM

Božič, Darijan, Slovenian composer; b. Slavonski Brod, April 29, 1933. He studied composition with Škerjanc and conducting with Švara at the Ljubljana

Academy of Music (1958–61). Upon graduation, he served as an opera conductor and artistic director of the Slovenian Phil. (1970–74); later was a prof. at the Univ. of Maribor (from 1988). His music was at first influenced by jazz; subsequently he adopted radical serial techniques.

WORKS: DRAMATIC: *Baletska jednočinka*, ballet (1957); *Humoreske*, opera (1958); *Spoštovanja vredna vlačuga*, opera (1960); *Polineikes*, collage (1966); *Gluha okna*, ballet (1967); *Ares Eros*, opera (1970); *Lizistrata*, opera (1975); *King Lear*, opera (1985). **ORCH.:** Piano Concerto (1956); Saxophone Concerto (1958); Trombone Concerto (1960); Trumpet Concerto (1961); Sym. (1964–65); *Audiostructures* for Piano and Orch.; *Audiospectrum* (1972). **CHAMBER:** *Sonata in Cool I* for Flute and Piano (1961), *II* for Clarinet and Piano (1961), and *III* for Flute, Bass Clarinet, and Harp (1965); *Pop-art-music* for String Quartet, Piccolo, and 2 Metronomes (1969); *Audiogemi I-IV* for String Quartet (1974). **VOCAL:** *Trije dnevni Ane Frank* (3 Days of Anne Frank) for 2 Narrators and Synthetic Sound (1963); *Gregora strniše* for Narrator and 7 Instruments (1965); *Kriki* (Cries) for Narrator, Brass Quintet, and Tape (1966); *Requiem (to the Memory of a Murdered Soldier—My Father)*, sound collage for Narrator, Chorus, Instruments, and Concrete Sounds (1969). —NS/LK/DM

Bozza, Eugène, French composer and conductor; b. Nice, April 4, 1905; d. Valenciennes, Sept. 28, 1991. He studied at the Paris Cons., and received the Grand Prix de Rome in 1934. From 1939 to 1948 he was conductor of the Opéra-Comique in Paris. He then moved to Valenciennes, where he was appointed director of the local cons.

WORKS: DRAMATIC: *Fête romaine*, ballet (1942); *Jeux de plage*, ballet (1946) *Léonidas*, opera (1947); *Beppo ou le Mort dont personne ne voulait*, comic opera (1963); *La Duchesse de Langeais*, lyric drama (Lille, 1967). **ORCH.:** Violin Concerto (1938); Saxophone Concerto (1939); *Rhapsodie niçoise* for Violin and Orch. (1942); Concertino for Bassoon and Chamber Orch. (1944); *Ballade* for Trombone and Orch. (1944); Cello Concerto (1947); Sym. (1948); *5 Mouvements* for Strings (1970). **CHAMBER:** *Luciolles* for 6 Clarinets; *Suite française* for 5 Woodwind Instruments; *3 Pieces* for 5 Trombones; other compositions for unusual instrumental combinations.—NS/LK/DM

Brackeen, Charles, American tenor saxophonist and jazz reed player; b. Eufala, Okla., March 13, 1940. Charles Brackeen lived on a cattle and hog farm in Eufaula until he was 11, then moved to Paris, Tex., internalizing the capacious Southwest tenor sound and incantational Amerindian rhythms in his mind's ear. He played piano and violin from a young age, on which he'd accompany his aunt at church services, and began playing saxophone at age 10. At 14 he moved to N.Y., where various "hip" relatives gradually introduced him to the music of Charlie Parker, Stan Getz, Sonny Rollins, and John Coltrane. During a late-teens sojourn to Los Angeles he met Ornette Coleman, Don Cherry, Billy Higgins, Paul Bley, and other pioneers of New Jazz. During the 1960s and early 1970s in N.Y., tenor/soprano saxophonist Brackeen established himself as a thoroughly individual and personal voice in the avant-garde realm. During the 1980s, he was sought out by the manager of the Silkheart label and invited to record

three dates between 1986–87. Although Brackeen has had long hiatuses from recording, his documented work is highly energetic and invigorating.

DISC.: *Rhythm X* (1968); *Bannar* (1987); *Attainment* (1987); *Worshippers Come Nigh* (1987).—**TP**

Brackeen, JoAnne (nee **Grogan**), jazz pianist, composer; b. Ventura, Calif., July 26, 1938. She is mostly self-taught as a jazz musician. While a student at the Los Angeles Cons., she listened to her parents' records of pianist Frankie Carle, then directly imitated his solos, and later solos of Charlie Parker, Bud Powell, and John Coltrane. Brackeen played with Teddy Edwards, Harold Land, Dexter Gordon, and Charles Lloyd in Los Angeles during the late 1950s. She moved to N.Y. with then husband Charles Brackeen in the 1960s. She played with Art Blakey (1970–72) and toured with Stan Getz in the late 1970s; she also worked with Joe Henderson and Pharoah Sanders. Since then, Brackeen has led several trios, and done solo and combo dates. She usually plays her own compositions. Terence Blanchard, Branford Marsalis, Jack DeJohnette, Eddie Gomez, Cecil McBee, and Al Foster are among the musicians who have worked with her. She is an Associate Professor (part time) of piano at Berklee. In 1996, she gave 20 international concerts including the Smithsonian, the Kennedy Center, Avery Fisher Hall, and others. She has numerous commissions for compositions. She is also a member of the advisory board for *Keyboard* magazine.

DISC.: *Snooze* (1975); *Tring-A-Ling* (1977); *Mythical Magic* (1978); *Aft* (1979); *Ancient Dynasty* (1980); *Special Identity* (1981); *Havin' Fun* (1985); *Fi-Fi Goes to Heaven* (1986); *Live at Maybeck Recital Hall* (1989); *Wish List* (1991); *Where Legends Dwell* (1991); *Breath of Brazil* (1991); *Take a Chance* (1993); *After Dark* (1993); *Turnaround* (1995).—**LP/MM**

Bradbury, William Batchelder, American composer, teacher, piano manufacturer, and music publisher; b. York County, Maine, Oct. 6, 1815; d. Montclair, N.J., Jan. 7, 1868. He studied in Boston with Sumner Hill and at Lowell Mason's Academy of Music. After teaching music in Machias, Maine (1836–38) and at St. John's, New Brunswick (1838–40), he went to Brooklyn as choirmaster of the first Baptist Church. In 1841 he became organist at N.Y.'s Baptist Tabernacle. He also was instrumental in organizing music instruction in the N.Y. public schools. He then pursued training in piano with E. Wenzel, harmony with Hauptmann, and composition with Moscheles in Leipzig (1847–49). He subsequently was active as a teacher, choirmaster, music ed., and composer in N.J. and N.Y. With his brother, Edward Bradbury, and F.C. Lighte, he founded a piano manufacturing business in N.Y. in 1854. In 1861 he also founded his own music publishing concern in N.Y., where he brought out various sacred and secular collections which sold into the millions. He composed 2 cantatas, 30 anthems, 79 other sacred choral pieces, and 921 hymn tunes. Among his most successful hymns were *He Leadeth Me, Jesus Loves Me, Just as I Am without One Plea, Saviour, Like a Shepherd Lead Us*, and *Sweet Hour of Prayer*.

BIBL.: A. Wingard, *The Life and Works of W.B. B. (1816–1868)* (diss., Southern Baptist Theological Seminary, 1973).
—NS/LK/DM

Brade, William, English-born German violinist and composer; b. 1560; d. Hamburg, Feb. 26, 1630. He settled in Germany about 1590, and thereafter was a court musician in various localities, including Brandenburg, Copenhagen, Bückeburg, Hamburg, Güstrow, and Berlin. He composed a number of popular collections of dances.

WORKS: *Newe ausserlesene Paduanen, Galliarden, Canzonen, Allmand und Coranten...auff allen musicalischen Instrumenten lieblich zu gebrauchen* (Hamburg, 1609); *Newe ausserlesene Paduanen und Galliarden...auff allen musicalischen Instrumenten und insonderheit auff Fiolen lieblich zu gebrauchen* (Hamburg, 1614); *Newe ausserlesene liebliche Branden, Intraden, Mascharaden, Balletten, All'manden, Couranten, Volten, Aufzüge und frembde Tänze...insonderheit auff Fiolen zu gebrauchen* (Hamburg and Lubeck, 1617); *Melodieuses paduanes, chansons, galliardes* (Antwerp, 1619); *Newe lustige Volten, Couranten, Balletten, Paduanen, Galliarden, Masqueraden, auch allerley arth newer frantzösischer Täntze* (Berlin, 1621).

BIBL.: C. Huber, *The Life and Music of W. B.* (diss., Univ. of N.C., 1965).**—NS/LK/DM**

Braden, Don, contemporary American jazz saxophonist; b. Cincinnati, Ohio, Nov. 20, 1963. Don Braden started playing contemporary jazz professionally at age 15 after two years of learning to play tenor sax in Louisville, Ky. After time at Harvard (during which he studied with Jerry Bergonzi and Bill Pierce), he moved to N.Y. in 1984 and began gigging with a variety of mainstream artists, starting with the Harper Brothers Quintet and Lonnie Smith. After one album for a Sony subsidiary, Braden was dropped, but caught a break when he was picked to provide the music for jazz-lover Bill Cosby's TV show *Cosby*. In 1998, Braden began teaching at William Paterson Univ.

DISC.: *Time Is Now* (1991); *Wish List* (1991); *Landing Zone* (1994); *Organic* (1995); *The Voice of the Saxophone* (1997).**—SH**

Bradford, Perry (John Henry) (Mule), pioneering jazz leader, composer, pianist; b. Montgomery, Ala., Feb. 14, 1893; d. Queens, N.Y., April 20, 1970. Family moved to Atlanta, Ga., when Perry was six. By 1906 he was working with minstrel shows; he joined Allen's New Orleans Minstrels in 1907. He left to work as a solo pianist, and played in Chicago (1909). In 1910, he visited N.Y., and toured theatre circuits for several years, as a soloist and in double acts; he also began prolific composing. He settled in N.Y., and became musical director for Mamie Smith; Bradford was responsible for Mamie's recording debut—generally accepted as the first recording featuring an African-American blues singer. Mamie's 1921 recording of Bradford's composition "Crazy Blues" sold over a million copies. He toured with Mamie Smith during the early 1920s, and also led own recording bands featuring Louis Armstrong, Buster Bailey, Johnny Dunn, James P. Johnson, and others. He ran his own publishing company in N.Y., and also pioneered the use of African-

American performers on commercial radio. Bradford composed many big-selling numbers, including "You Can't Keep a Good Man Down," "Evil Blues," and "That Thing Called Love."

DISC.: "Stomp Off," "Static Strut" (both 1926); *P.B. Story* (1957).

BIBL.: P. Bradford, *Born with the Blues* (1965).**—JC/LP**

Bradley, Gwendolyn, black American soprano; b. N.Y., Dec. 12, 1952. She received training at the N.C. School of the Arts in Winston-Salem, N.C., the Curtis Inst. of Music in Philadelphia, and the Philadelphia Academy of Vocal Arts. In 1976 she made her operatic debut as Verdi's Nannetta at the Lake George (N.Y.) Opera, and on Feb. 20, 1981, she made her first appearance at the Metropolitan Opera in N.Y. as the Nightingale in *L'Enfant et les sortilèges*, returning there to sing such roles as Blondchen, Gilda, and Offenbach's Olympia in subsequent years. She made her European debut at the Corfu (Greece) Festival in 1981, and later was guest artist with opera companies in Cleveland, Philadelphia, Amsterdam, Glyndebourne, Hamburg, Berlin, Monte Carlo, and Nice. She also appeared as a soloist with many distinguished orchs. and as a recitalist.
—NS/LK/DM

Bradley, Will (originally, **Schwichtenberg, Wilbur**), jazz trombonist, leader; b. Newton, N.J., July 12, 1912; d. Flemington, N.J., July 15, 1989. Raised in Washington, N.J., he played in the local high school band. He moved to N.Y. in 1928 and did local gigs before joining Milt Shaw's Detroiters; he then worked with Red Nichols and later joined the CBS studio staff (1931–34). He was with Ray Noble (1935–36), then returned to studio work, until forming his own band (July 1939); he changed his name because Wilbur Schwichtenberg wouldn't fit on a marquee. This band, which was co-led with Ray McKinley, remained together until June 1942. It was a white jazz-orientated dance band whose big hit "Beat Me Daddy, Eight to the Bar" fueled the boogie-woogie fad. (Nicolas Slonimsky used the name of this piece to illustrate the American meaning of the word "bar" to a sceptical British musicologist.) "Celery Stalks at Midnight" was one of the 78s smashed by juvenile delinquents in the 1955 movie *Blackboard Jungle*. Through the 1950s, Bradley worked regularly in N.Y. studios, occasionally organizing his own bands for specific engagements. He did a brief spell of touring with the Sauter-Finegan Band (1953). In later years, he composed several extended classical works. His son, Will Bradley Jr. (b. N.Y., Feb. 15, 1938), was a jazz drummer who played from about 1954 on with Woody Herman (recording in 1956), Tony Scott, J. R. Monterose, George Wallington, and Tony Fruscella.

DISC.: *Beat Me Daddy, Eight to the Bar* (1940); *Dixieland Jazz All-Time Greats* (1953); *Boogie Woogie* (1955); *Big Band Boogie* (1959); *Celery Stalks at Midnight* (1985).**—JC/MM**

Bradshaw, Merrill (Kay), American composer and pedagogue; b. Lyman, Wyo., June 18, 1929. He was educated at Brigham Young Univ. (A.B., 1954; M.A., 1955) and the Univ. of Ill. (M.M., 1956; D.M.A., 1962).

From 1957 he taught at Brigham Young Univ. As a member of the Mormon Church, he contributed a great deal to the formulation of classical Mormon music.

WORKS: DRAMATIC: Musical: *The Title of Liberty* (1975). **ORCH.:** Piano Concerto (1955); 5 syms.: No. 1 (1957), No. 2 (1962), No. 3 (1967), No. 4 (1968), and No. 5 (1978; Auckland, New Zealand, July 4, 1979); *Facets* (1965); *Feathers* (1968); *4 Mountain Sketches* (1974); *Nocturnes and Revels* (1974); *Lovers and Liars* (1976); *Homages*, viola concerto (Provo, July 14, 1979); Violin Concerto (Provo, March 5, 1981). **CHAMBER:** *Dialogue* for Flute and Horn (1956); 2 string quartets (1957, 1969); Violin Sonata (1957); Suite for Viola (1967); Suite for Oboe and Piano (1966); Brass Quintet (1969); Nocturne for 2 Horns and Strings (1977). **Piano:** *6 Bagatelles* (1958); *Moments* (1968); *20 Mosaics* (1972); *6 plus 4* for 10 Pianos (1976). **VOCAL:** *The Restoration*, oratorio (Provo, March 23, 1974); *Love and Death, 4 Elizabethan Lyrics* for Soprano, Viola, and Strings (Provo, Sept. 10, 1982); choruses; hymns; Psalms; ballads. —NS/LK/DM

Bradshaw, Tiny (Myron), jazz/R&B singer, drummer, pianist, bandleader; b. Youngstown, Ohio, Sept. 23, 1905; d. Cincinnati, Ohio, Nov. 26, 1958. He majored in psychology at Wilberforce Univ., Ohio. He began his singing career with Horace Henderson's Collegians and subsequently worked in N.Y. with Marion Hardy's Alabamians, The Savoy Bearcats, The Mills Blue Rhythm Band (1932). He sang with Luis Russell, then left to form his own band, which made its debut at the Renaissance Ballroom, N.Y., in 1934; later that year, they recorded for Decca. After residencies in Philadelphia, Chicago, and the Savoy, N.Y., the band achieved national fame with several big-selling records. He switched from big band in the mid-1940s, leading groups of essentially jazz-trained musicians into the developing field that came to be known as R&B. His small combo was said to be Buddy Holly's favorite; its R&B hits in the late 1940s and early 1950s usually featured raunchy sax solos by Sil Austin or Red Prysock, both of whom went off and started similar successful combos of their own. Bradshaw continued to lead throughout the 1940s and early 1950s, including a U.S.O. tour of Japan in late 1945. His band had five Billboard hits (and also recorded the original "Train Kept A-Rollin'") with King Records. Bradshaw's band produced such saxophone stars as Sonny Stitt, Prysock, and Austin; among the vocalists to record with the group were Roy Brown, Arthur Prysock, Lonnie Johnson, and Tiny Kennedy. He worked regularly in Chicago, until suffering two strokes that forced his retirement.

DISC.: *Breakin' up the House* (1985).—JC/MM

Brady, Tim, jazz guitarist, composer; b. Toronto, July 11, 1956. He studied at Concordia Univ. and the New England Cons. (M.M. in jazz guitar and composition). He led jazz groups in Toronto (1980–6), including a 10 piece, 7 piece, trio and quartet, all at various times; he also worked for the Canadian Broadcasting Corporation, and played jazz festivals (Ottawa, Edmonton, Vancouver, Montreal) and club dates. Brady did special projects in Toronto with Gil Evans (1983) and Kenny Wheeler (1984). Since the 1980s, he has worked mainly in composed new music and electroacoustics; very occasionally, he uses improvisation in composed works. Brady still plays jazz at home, and his composed music betrays a strong jazz influence in the harmonic and melodic constructions, but he does not use the blues or 32-bar forms. He is an innovative composer admired by fellow guitarists but not yet known much outside that circle.

DISC.: *Chalk Paper* (1983); *Vision* (1984); *Inventions* (1991); *Imaginary Guitars* (1995).—LP

Braein, Edvard Fliflet, Norwegian composer and conductor; b. Kristiansund, Aug. 23, 1924; d. Oslo, April 30, 1976. He was of a musical family; his grandfather was an organist and choirmaster, and his father, Edvard Braein (1887–1957), was a composer, organist, and conductor. He studied at the Oslo Cons., graduating in 1943; then studied conducting with Grüner-Hegge and composition with Brustad; later took private lessons with Rivier in Paris (1950–51). Upon returning to Oslo, he was active mainly as a choral conductor.

WORKS: DRAMATIC: *Anne Pedersdotter*, opera (Oslo, 1971); *Den stundeslose* (The Wastrel), opera buffa (Oslo, 1975); *The Little Matchstick Girl*, ballet (1976; unfinished). **ORCH.:** *Towards the Sea* for Chamber Orch. (1947); Concert Overture (1948); 3 syms. (1949–50; 1951–54; 1967); *Serenade* (1951–52); *Adagio* for Strings (1953); *Capriccio* for Piano and Orch. (1956–57); *Divertimento* for Flute and Orch. (1958); *Symphonic Prelude* (1959); *Largo* for Strings (1960–61); *Intrata* (1961); *Overture in Miniature* (1962); *Little Serenade* (1963); *Ritmico e melodico* (1971); *Til Arendal*, festival overture (1972); *Havljom* (Echo from the Sea; 1973). **CHAMBER:** Violin Sonata (1940); *The Merry Musicians* for Clarinet, Violin, Viola, and Cello (1947); Divertimento for Clarinet, Violin, Viola, and Cello (1962); String Trio (1964); *Humoresque* for Chamber Ensemble (1966).—NS/LK/DM

Braga, Gaetano, Italian cellist and composer; b. Giulianova, Abruzzi, June 9, 1829; d. Milan, Nov. 21, 1907. He studied at the Naples Cons. with C. Gaetano (1841–52). He made tours as a cellist in Europe and America, and lived mostly in Paris and London. His *Leggenda valacca*, known in English as *Angel's Serenade*, orig. written for voice with cello (or violin) obbligato, attained tremendous popularity and was arranged for various instrumental combinations. Braga wrote several operas: *Alina, or La spregiata* (1853), *Estella di San Germano* (Vienna, 1857), *Il ritratto* (Naples, 1858), *Margherita la mendicante* (Paris, 1859), *Mormile* (La Scala, Milan, 1862), *Ruy Blas* (1865), *Reginella* (Lecco, 1871), and *Caligola* (Lisbon, 1873).

BIBL.: V. Bindi, *G. B.: Da ricordi della sua vita* (Naples, 1927). —NS/LK/DM

Braga Santos, (José Manuel) Joly
See **Santos, (José Manuel) Joly Braga**

Bragard, Roger, Belgian musicologist; b. Huy, Nov. 21, 1903; d. Brussels, Dec. 15, 1985. He studied philology at the Univ. of Liège, then went to Paris, where he studied musicology with Pirro and composition with d'Indy. Returning to Belgium, he taught music history at the Brussels Cons. He publ. the valuable *Histoire de la musique belge* (3 vols., 1946, 1949, 1956).—NS/LK/DM

Braham (real name, **Abraham**), **John,** renowned English tenor; b. London, March 20, 1774; d. there, Feb. 17, 1856. He studied with Leoni in London, with Rauzzini in Bath, and with Isola in Genoa. He made his debut at Covent Garden (April 21, 1787); then appeared at Drury Lane in 1796, in the opera *Mahmoud* by Storace. He was subsequently engaged to sing at the Italian Opera House in London. In 1798 he undertook an extensive tour in Italy, and also appeared in Hamburg. Returning to England in 1801, he was increasingly successful. Endowed with a powerful voice of 3 octaves in compass, he knew no difficulties in operatic roles. He was the original Huon in Weber's *Oberon* (1826). As a ballad writer, he was very popular; he wrote much of the music for the operatic roles which he sang; often he added portions to operas by other composers, as in *The Americans* (1811), with its famous song *The Death of Nelson*; contributed incidental music to 12 productions. In 1831 he entered upon a theatrical business venture; he acquired the Colosseum in Regent's Park; in 1836 he had the St. James's Theatre built, but failed to recoup his investment and lost much of his considerable fortune. He made an American tour from 1840 to 1842 despite the weakening of his voice with age; however, his dramatic appeal remained undiminished and he was able to impress the American public in concert appearances. He then returned to London, making made his final appearance in 1852.

BIBL.: J. Mewburn Levien, *The Singing of J. B.* (London, 1945).—NS/LK/DM

Braham, David, English composer and conductor; b. near London, 1834; d. N.Y., April 11, 1905. He learned to play the violin in his youth and began his career playing in London music halls. In 1856 he settled in N.Y., where he played in orchs. and began to compose songs and theater pieces. He worked as musical director for several theaters, including the Theatre Comique from 1865, where he had his first success as a composer with the burlesque *Pluto* (Feb. 1, 1868). In 1872 he began composing scores to lyrics by Edward Harrigan, who was to become his son-in-law. He served as musical director of the Harrigan and Hart team until the duo broke up in 1885, and he continued to work with Harrigan for some more years until devoting his remaining years to the Grand Opera House and Wallack's Theater. Among his most famous songs for the Harrigan and Hart team were "The Mulligan Guards" (1874), "The Regular Army O! (1874), "Slavery Days" (1876), "The Babies on Our Block" (1879), "Hang the Mulligan Banner Up" (1880), "The Mulligan Braves" (1880), "Paddy Duffy's Cart" (1881), "Just Across from Jersey" (1883), and "Poverty's Tears Ebb and Flow" (1885). In all, he had some 200 songs publ.—LK/DM

Brahms, Johannes, great German composer, the preeminent guardian of the classical tradition in the late Romantic era; b. Hamburg, May 7, 1833; d. Vienna, April 3, 1897. His father, who played the double bass in the orch. of the Phil. Soc. in Hamburg, taught Brahms the rudiments of music. In 1840 he began to study piano with Otto F.W. Cossel, and made his first public appear-ance as a pianist with a chamber music group at the age of 10. Impressed with his progress, Cossel sent Brahms to his own former teacher, the noted pedagogue Eduard Marxsen, who accepted him as a scholarship student, without charging a fee. Marxsen not only oversaw Brahms's training in piano but encouraged him to pursue intensive studies in the music of Bach and Beethoven. Brahms later remembered his mentor with the dedication of his Second Piano Concerto. At the age of 13, Brahms was on his own, and had to eke out his meager subsistence by playing piano in taverns, restaurants, and other establishments, some of ill repute. On Sept. 21, 1848, at the age of 15, Brahms played a solo concert in Hamburg under an assumed name. On April 14, 1849, he gave his first concert under his own name. In 1853 he met the Hungarian violinist Eduard Reményi, with whom he embarked on a successful concert tour. While in Hannover, Brahms formed a friendship with the famous violin virtuoso Joseph Joachim, who gave him an introduction to Liszt in Weimar. Of great significance was his meeting with Schumann in Düsseldorf. In his diary of the time, Schumann noted: "Johannes Brahms, a genius." He reiterated his appraisal of Brahms in his famous article "Neue Bahnen," which appeared in the *Neue Zeitschrift für Musik* on Oct. 28, 1853; in a characteristic display of metaphor, he described young Brahms as having come into life as Minerva sprang in full armor from the brow of Jupiter. Late in 1853, Breitkopf & Härtel publ. his 2 piano sonatas and a set of 6 songs. Brahms also publ., under the pseudonym of G.W. Marks, a collection of 6 pieces for piano, Four-Hands, under the title *Souvenir de la Russie* (Brahms never visited Russia). Schumann's death in 1856, after years of agonizing mental illness, deeply affected Brahms. He remained a devoted friend of Schumann's family; his correspondence with Schumann's widow Clara reveals a deep affection and spiritual intimacy, but the speculation about their friendship growing into a romance exists only in the fevered imaginations of psychologizing biographers. Objectively judged, the private life of Brahms was that of a middle-class bourgeois who worked systematically and diligently on his current tasks while maintaining a fairly active social life. He was always ready and willing to help young composers (his earnest efforts on behalf of Dvořák were notable). Brahms was entirely free of professional jealousy; his differences with Wagner were those of style. Wagner was an opera composer, whereas Brahms never wrote for the stage. True, some ardent admirers of Wagner (such as Hugo Wolf) found little of value in the music of Brahms, while admirers of Brahms (such as Hanslick) were sharp critics of Wagner, but Brahms held aloof from such partisan wranglings with the exception of a publ. letter in 1880.

From 1857 to 1859 Brahms was employed in Detmold as court pianist, chamber musician, and choir director. In the meantime he began work on his first Piano Concerto. He played it on Jan. 22, 1859, in Hannover, with Joachim as conductor. Other important works of the period were the 2 serenades for orch. and the first String Sextet. He expected to be named conductor of the Hamburg Phil. Soc., but the directoriat preferred to engage, in 1863, Julius Stockhausen in that capacity. Instead, Brahms accepted the post of conductor of the Singakademie in Vienna, which he led from 1863 to 1864. In 1869 he decided to make Vienna his permanent home. As early as 1857 he began work on his choral masterpiece, *Ein deutsches Requiem*; he completed the score in 1868, and conducted its first performance in the Bremen Cathedral on April 10, 1868, although the first 3 movements had been given by Herbeck and the Vienna Phil. on Dec. 1, 1867. In May 1868 he added another movement to the work (the fifth, "Ihr habt nun Traurigkeit") in memory of his mother, who died in 1865; the first performance of the final version was given in Leipzig on Feb. 18, 1869. The title of the German Requiem had no nationalistic connotations; it simply stated that the text was in German rather than Latin. His other important vocal scores include *Rinaldo*, a cantata; the *Liebeslieder* waltzes for Vocal Quartet and Piano, Four-Hands; the *Alto Rhapsody*; the *Schicksalslied*; and many songs. In 1869 he publ. 2 vols. of *Hungarian Dances* for Piano Duet; these were extremely successful. Among his chamber music works, the Piano Quintet in F minor; the String Sextet No. 2, in G major; the Trio for Horn, Violin, and Piano; the 2 String Quartets, op.51; and the String Quartet op.67 are exemplary works of their kind. In 1872 Brahms was named artistic director of the concerts of Vienna's famed Gesellschaft der Musikfreunde; he held this post until 1875. During this time, he composed the *Variations on a Theme by Joseph Haydn*, op.56a. The title was a misnomer; the theme occurs in a Feld-partita for Military Band by Haydn, but it was not Haydn's own; it was orig. known as the St. Anthony Chorale, and in pedantic scholarly eds. of Brahms it is called St. Anthony Variations. Otto Dessoff conducted the first performance of the work with the Vienna Phil. on Nov. 2, 1873.

For many years friends and admirers of Brahms urged him to write a sym. He clearly had a symphonic mind; his piano concertos were symphonic in outline and thematic development. As early as 1855 he began work on a full-fledged sym.; in 1862 he nearly completed the first movement of what was to be his First Sym. The famous horn solo in the finale of the First Sym. was jotted down by Brahms on a picture postcard to Clara Schumann dated Sept. 12, 1868, from his summer place in the Tirol; in it Brahms said that he heard the tune played by a shepherd on an Alpine horn; and he set it to a rhymed quatrain of salutation. Yet Brahms was still unsure about his symphonic capacity. The great C-minor Sym., his First, was completed in 1876 and first performed at Karlsruhe on Nov. 4, 1876, conducted by Dessoff. Hans von Bülow, the German master of the telling phrase, called it "The 10th," thus placing Brahms on a direct line from Beethoven. It was also Bülow who cracked a bon mot that became a part of music history, in referring to the 3 B's of music, Bach, Beethoven, and Brahms. The original saying was not merely a vacuous alphabetical generalization; Bülow's phrase was deeper; in answering a question as to what was his favorite key, he said it was E-flat major, the key of Beethoven's *Eroica*, because it had 3 B's in its key signature (in German, B is specifically B-flat, but by extension may signify any flat)—1 for Bach, 1 for Beethoven, and 1 for Brahms. The

witty phrase took wing, but its sophisticated connotation was lost at the hands of professional popularizers.

Brahms composed his Second Sym. in 1877; it was performed for the first time by the Vienna Phil. on Dec. 30, 1877, under the direction of Hans Richter, receiving a fine acclaim. Brahms led a second performance of the work with the Gewandhaus Orch. in Leipzig on Jan. 10, 1878. Also in 1878 Brahms wrote his Violin Concerto; the score was dedicated to Joachim, who gave its premiere with the Gewandhaus Orch. on Jan. 1, 1879. Brahms then composed his Second Piano Concerto, in B-flat major, and was soloist in its first performance in Budapest, on Nov. 9, 1881. There followed the Third Sym., in F major, first performed by the Vienna Phil., under the direction of Richter, on Dec. 2, 1883. The Fourth Sym., in E minor, followed in quick succession; it had its first performance in Meiningen on Oct. 25, 1885. The symphonic cycle was completed in less than a decade; it has been conjectured, without foundation, that the tonalities of the 4 syms. of Brahms—C, D, F, and E—correspond to the fugal subject of Mozart's Jupiter Sym., and that some symbolic meaning was attached to it. All speculations aside, there is an inner symmetry uniting these works. The 4 syms. contain 4 movements each, with a slow movement and a scherzo-like Allegretto in the middle of the corpus. There are fewer departures from the formal scheme than in Beethoven, and there are no extraneous episodes interfering with the grand general line. Brahms wrote music pure in design and eloquent in sonorous projection; he was a true classicist, a quality that endeared him to the critics who were repelled by Wagnerian streams of sound, and by the same token alienated those who sought something more than mere geometry of thematic configurations from a musical composition.

The chamber music of Brahms possesses similar symphonic qualities; when Schoenberg undertook to make an orch. arrangement of the Piano Quartet of Brahms, all he had to do was to expand the sonorities and enhance instrumental tone colors already present in the original. The string quartets of Brahms are edifices of Gothic perfection; his 3 violin sonatas, his Second Piano Trio (the first was a student work and yet it had a fine quality of harmonious construction), all contribute to a permanent treasure of musical classicism. The piano writing of Brahms is severe in its contrapuntal texture, but pianists have continued to include his rhapsodies and intermezzos in their repertoire; and Brahms was able to impart sheer delight in his Hungarian rhapsodies and waltzes; they represented the Viennese side of his character, as contrasted with the profound Germanic quality of his syms. The song cycles of Brahms continued the evolution of the art of the lieder, a natural continuation of the song cycles of Schubert and Schumann.

Brahms was sociable and made friends easily; he traveled to Italy, and liked to spend his summers in the solitude of the Austrian Alps. But he was reluctant to appear as a center of attention; he declined to receive the honorary degree of Mus.D. from the Univ. of Cambridge in 1876, giving as a reason his fear of seasickness in crossing the English Channel. He was pleased to receive the Gold Medal of the Phil. Soc. of London in 1877. In 1879 the Univ. of Breslau proffered him an honorary degree of Doctor of Philosophy, citing him as "Artis musicae severioris in Germania nunc princeps." As a gesture of appreciation and gratitude he wrote an *Akademische Festouvertüre* for Breslau, and accepted the invitation to conduct its premiere in Breslau on Jan. 4, 1881. In 1887 he was presented with the Prussian Order "Pour le Mérite." In 1889 he received the freedom of his native city of Hamburg; also in 1889, Franz Joseph, the Emperor of Austria, made him a Commander of the Order of Leopold. With success and fame came a sense of self- sufficiency, which found its external expression in the corpulence of his appearance, familiar to all from photographs and drawings of Brahms conducting or playing the piano. Even during his Viennese period, Brahms remained a sturdy Prussian; his ideal was to see Germany a dominant force in Europe philosophically and militarily. In his workroom he kept a bronze relief of Bismarck, the "Iron Chancellor," crowned with laurel. He was extremely meticulous in his working habits (his MSS were clean and legible), but he avoided wearing formal dress, preferring a loosely fitting flannel shirt and a detachable white collar, but no cravat. He liked to dine in simple restaurants, and he drank a great deal of beer. He was indifferent to hostile criticism; still, it is amazing to read the outpouring of invective against Brahms by George Bernard Shaw and by American critics; the usual accusations were of dullness and turgidity. When Sym. Hall was opened in Boston in 1900 with the lighted signs "Exit in Case of Fire," someone cracked that they should more appropriately announce "Exit in Case of Brahms." Yet, at the hands of various German conductors, Brahms became a standard symphonist in the U.S. as well as in Europe. From the perspective of a century, Brahms appears as the greatest master of counterpoint after Bach; one can learn polyphony from a studious analysis of the chamber music and piano works of Brahms; he excelled in variation forms; his piano variations on a theme of Paganini are exemplars of contrapuntal learning, and they are also among the most difficult piano works of the 19th century. Posterity gave him a full measure of recognition; Hamburg celebrated his sesquicentennial in 1983 with great pomp. The 100th anniversary of his death was widely commemorated in 1997. Brahms had lived a good life, but died a bad death, stricken with cancer of the liver.

Works: ORCH.: 2 piano concertos: No. 1, in D minor, op.15 (1854–58; Hannover, Jan. 22, 1859, Brahms, soloist, Joachim conducting) and No. 2, in B-flat major, op.83 (1878–81; Budapest, Nov. 9, 1881, Brahms soloist, Erkel conducting); 4 syms.: No. 1, in C minor, op.68 (1855–76; Karlsruhe, Nov. 4, 1876, Dessoff conducting), No. 2, in D major, op.73 (Vienna, Dec. 30, 1877, Richter conducting), No. 3, in F major, op.90 (Vienna, Dec. 2, 1883, Richter conducting), and No. 4, in E minor, op.98 (1884–85; Meiningen, Oct. 17, 1885, Brahms conducting [private perf.]; public perf., Oct. 25, 1885, Bülow conducting); 2 serenades: No. 1, in D major, op.11 (first version, for small orch., 1857–58; Hamburg, March 28, 1859, Joachim conducting; 2nd version, for larger orch., 1859; Hannover, March 3, 1860, Joachim conducting) and No. 2, in A major, op.16 (1858–59; Hamburg, Feb. 10, 1860, composer conducting; rev.

1875); *Variations on a Theme by Joseph Haydn*, op.56a (the theme, from the St. Anthony Chorale, is not by Haydn; Vienna, Nov. 2, 1873, Dessoff conducting); Violin Concerto in D major, op.77 (1878; Leipzig, Jan. 1, 1879, Joachim, soloist, composer conducting); *Akademische Festouvertüre*, op.80 (1880; Breslau, Jan. 4, 1881, composer conducting); *Tragische Ouvertüre*, op.81 (Vienna, Dec. 26, 1880, Richter conducting; rev. 1881); Concerto in A minor for Violin, Cello, and Orch., op.102, the *Double Concerto* (Cologne, Oct. 18, 1887, Joachim, violinist, Hausmann, cellist, Wüllner conducting); also 3 Hungarian Dances arranged for Orch. (1873): No. 1, in G minor; No. 3, in F major; No. 10, in F major. **CHAMBER:** Piano Trio No. 1, in B major, op.8 (1853–54; N.Y., Nov. 27, 1855; rev. 1889); Sextet No. 1, in B-flat major, for 2 Violins, 2 Violas, and 2 Cellos, op.18 (1858–60; Hannover, Oct. 20, 1860); Piano Quartet No. 1, in G minor, op.25 (Hamburg, Nov. 16, 1861); Piano Quartet No. 2, in A major, op.26 (1861–62; Vienna, Nov. 29, 1862); Piano Quintet in F minor, op.34 (1861–64; Paris, March 24, 1868); Sextet No. 2, in G major, for 2 Violins, 2 Violas, and 2 Cellos, op.36 (1864–65; Vienna, Feb. 3, 1867); Cello Sonata No. 1, in E minor, op.38 (1862–65); Trio in E-flat major for Violin, Horn or Viola, and Piano, op.40 (Karlsruhe, Dec. 7, 1865); String Quartet No. 1, in C minor, op.51 (1865?-73?; Vienna, Dec. 1, 1873); String Quartet No. 2, in A minor, op.51 (1865?-73?; Vienna, Oct. 18, 1873); Piano Quartet No. 3, in C minor, op.60 (1855–75; Ziegelhausen, Nov. 18, 1875); String Quartet No. 3, in B-flat major, op.67 (Berlin, Oct. 1876); Violin Sonata No. 1, in G major, op.78 (1878–79; Vienna, Nov. 29, 1879; also arranged for cello and publ. in 1897); Piano Trio No. 2, in C major, op.87 (1880–82; Frankfurt am Main, Dec. 28, 1882); Quintet No. 1, in F major, for 2 Violins, 2 Violas, and Cello, op.88 (Frankfurt am Main, Dec. 28, 1882); Cello Sonata No. 2, in F major, op.99 (Vienna, Nov. 24, 1886); Violin Sonata No. 2, in A major, op.100 (Vienna, Dec. 2, 1886); Piano Trio No. 3, in C minor, op.101 (Budapest, Dec. 20, 1886); Violin Sonata No. 3, in D minor, op.108 (1886–88; Budapest, Dec. 22, 1888); Quintet No. 2, in G major, for 2 Violins, 2 Violas, and Cello, op.111 (Vienna, Nov. 11, 1890); Trio in A minor for Clarinet or Viola, Cello, and Piano, op.114 (Berlin, Dec. 1, 1891); Quintet in B minor for Clarinet and String Quartet, op.115 (Berlin, Dec. 1, 1891); 2 sonatas: No. 1, in F minor, and No. 2, in E-flat major, for Clarinet or Viola, and Piano, op.120 (1894; Vienna, Jan. 7, 1895); also a Scherzo in C minor for Violin and Piano, a movement from the Sonata in A minor by Brahms, Schumann, and A. Dietrich. In 1924 a copy from the original score of a Trio in A major, presumably composed by Brahms when he was about 20 years old (see letter to R. Schumann, 1853), was discovered in Bonn; it was publ. in 1938. **KEY-BOARD: Piano Solo:** Scherzo in E-flat minor, op.4 (1851; Vienna, March 17, 1867); Sonata No. 1, in C major, op.1 (1852–53; Leipzig, Dec. 17, 1853); Sonata No. 2, in F-sharp minor, op.2 (1852; Vienna, Feb. 2, 1882); Sonata No. 3, in F minor, op.5 (1853; Vienna, Jan. 6, 1863); *Variations on a Theme by Schumann* in F-sharp minor, op.9 (1854; Berlin, Dec. 1879); 4 Ballades, op.10: D minor, D major, B minor, and B major (1854); Gavotte in A minor (1854); Gavotte in A major (1855); 2 Gigues: A minor and B minor (1855); 2 Sarabandes: A minor and B minor (1855; Vienna, Jan. 20, 1856); *Variations [13] on a Hungarian Song* in D major, op.21 (1853; London, March 25, 1874); *Variations [11] on an Original Theme* in D major, op.21 (1857; Copenhagen, March 1868); *Variations [25] and Fugue on a Theme by Handel* in B-flat major, op.24 (Hamburg, Dec. 7, 1861); *Variations [28] on a Theme by Paganini* in A minor, op.35 (1862–63; Zürich, Nov. 25, 1865); 16 Waltzes, op.39 (1865); 8 Piano Pieces, op.76 (1871–78; Leipzig, Jan. 4, 1880); 2 Rhapsodies: B minor and G minor, op.79 (1879; Krefeld, Jan. 20, 1880); *Fantasien* [7], op.116 (1892); 3 Intermezzos: E-flat major, B-flat minor, and C-sharp minor, op.117 (1892); Piano Pieces [6], op.118 (1892; London, Jan. 1894); Piano Pieces [4], op.119 (1892; London, Jan. 1894); also 5 *Studien* for Piano (I, Study after Frédéric Chopin, in F minor, an arrangement of Chopin's Étude No. 2, op.25; II, Rondo after Carl Maria von Weber, in C major, an arrangement of the finale of Weber's *Moto perpetuo*, op.24; III and IV, Presto after J.S. Bach, in G minor, 2 arrangements of the finale of BWV 1001; V, *Chaconne* by J.S. Bach, in D minor, an arrangement of the finale of BWV 1016); Theme and Variations in D minor (an arrangement of the slow movement of the Sextet No. 1; 1860; Frankfurt am Main, Oct. 31, 1865); Gavotte in A major (an arrangement from Gluck's *Paris ed Elena*; Vienna, Jan. 20, 1856; publ. 1871); 10 Hungarian Dances (an arrangement of nos. 1–10 from the original version for Piano, 4–Hands; publ. 1872); 51 Exercises (publ. 1893); cadenzas to concertos by Bach (Harpsichord Concerto No. 1, in D minor, BWV 1052), Mozart (Piano Concertos Nos. 17, in G major, K. 453; 20, in D minor, K. 466; and 24, in C minor, K. 491), and Beethoven (Piano Concerto No. 4, in G major, op.58). **4 – h a n d s :** *Variations on a Theme by Schumann* in E-flat major, op.23 (1861; Vienna, Jan. 12, 1864); 16 Waltzes, op.39 (1865; Vienna, March 17, 1867); *Liebeslieder*, 18 waltzes, op.52a (1874; an arrangement from the original version for 4 Voices and Piano, 4–Hands); *Neue Liebeslieder*, 15 waltzes, op.65a (1877; an arrangement from the original version for 4 Voices and Piano, 4–Hands); Hungarian Dances (21 dances in 4 books; 1852–69). **2 P i a n o s :** Sonata in F minor, op.34b (1864; Vienna, April 17, 1874); Variations on a Theme by Haydn, op.56b (1873; Vienna, March 17, 1882); also arrangements of Joachim's *Demetrius* Overture and Overture to *Henry IV.* **O r - g a n :** Fugue in A-flat minor (1856); *O Traurigkeit, O Herzeleid*, chorale prelude and fugue in A minor (1856; Vienna, Dec. 2, 1882); 2 preludes and fugues: A minor and G minor (1856–57); 11 *Choralvorspiele*, op.122 (1896). **VOCAL: C h o r a l :** *Mass: Kyrie* for Chorus and Keyboard, and *Sanctus, Benedictus*, and *Agnus Dei* for Chorus a cappella or with accompaniment (1856); *Geistliches Lied* for Chorus and Organ or Piano, op.30 (1856); *Ein deutsches Requiem* for Soprano, Baritone, Chorus, and Orch., op.45 (1857–68; 1st 3 movements, under Herbeck, Vienna, Dec. 1, 1867; movements 1–4 and 6, under Brahms, Bremen, April 10, 1868; first complete perf., under Reinecke, Leipzig, Feb. 18, 1869); *Ave Maria* for Women's Voices, and Orch. or Organ, op.12 (1858); *Begräbnisgesang* for Choir and Wind Instruments, op.13 (1858; Hamburg, Dec. 2, 1859); *Marienlieder* for Chorus, op.22 (Hamburg, Sept. 19, 1859); 4 Songs for Women's Voices, 2 Horns, and Harp, op.17 (1859–60); *Der 13. Psalm* for Women's Voices and Organ or Piano, with Strings ad libitum, op.27 (1859; Hamburg, Sept. 19, 1864); 2 Motets for Chorus, op.29 (1860; Vienna, April 17, 1864); 3 Sacred Choruses for Women's Voices, op.37 (1859–63); 5 *Soldatenlieder* for Men's Chorus, op.41 (1861–62); 3 Songs for Chorus with Piano ad libitum, op.42 (1859–61); 12 Songs and Romances for Women's Voices, with Piano ad libitum, op.44 (1859–63); *Rinaldo*, cantata for Tenor, Men's Chorus, and Orch., op.50, after Goethe (1863–68; Vienna, Feb. 28, 1869); *Rhapsodie* for Contralto, Men's Chorus, and Orch., op.53, after Goethe's *Harzreise im Winter* (1869; Jena, March 3, 1870); *Schicksalslied* for Chorus and Orch., op.54 (1868–71; Karlsruhe, Oct. 18, 1871); *Triumphlied* for Chorus, Baritone, and Orch., op.55 (1870–71; Karlsruhe, June 5, 1872); 7 Songs for Chorus, op.62 (1874); *Nänie* for Chorus and Orch., op.82, after Schiller (1880–81; Zürich, Dec. 6, 1881); 2 Motets for Chorus, op.74 (1877; Vienna, Dec. 8, 1878); *Gesang der Parzen* for Chorus and Orch., op.89, after Goethe's *Iphigenie auf Tauris*

(Basel, Dec. 10, 1882); 6 Songs and Romances for Chorus, op.93a (1883–84; Krefeld, Jan. 27, 1885); *Tafellied* for Chorus and Piano, op.93b (1884; Krefeld, Jan. 28, 1885); 5 Songs for Chorus, op.104 (1888; Vienna, April 3, 1889); *Fest- und Gedenksprüche* for a Double Chorus, op.109 (1886–88; Hamburg, Sept. 14, 1889); 3 Motets for Chorus, op.110 (1889; Cologne, March 13, 1890); also 13 Canons for Women's Voices, op.113 (1860–67); *Deutsche Volkslieder* (26 songs arranged for 4-part Chorus; 1854–73; publ. in 2 books, 1864 and 1926–27). **Q u a r t e t s :** For Soprano, Alto, Tenor, Bass, and Piano: 3 Quartets, op.31 (1859–63); *Liebeslieder*, 18 waltzes, with Piano, 4–Hands, op.52 (1868–69; Vienna, Jan. 5, 1870); 3 Quartets, op.64 (1862–74); *Neue Liebeslieder*, 15 waltzes, with Piano, 4–Hands, op.65 (1874; Mannheim, May 8, 1875); 4 Quartets, op.92 (1877–84); *Zigeunerlieder*, op.103 (1887); 6 Quartets, op.112 (1888–91); also *Liebeslieder*, Nos. 1, 2, 4–6, 8, 9, and 11 from op.52 and No. 5 from op.65, with Orch. (1870); *Kleine Hochzeitskantate* (1874). **D u e t s :** With Piano Accompaniment: 3 Duets for Soprano and Alto, op.20 (1858–60; Vienna, Jan. 29, 1878); 4 Duets for Alto and Baritone, op.28 (1860–62; Vienna, Dec. 18, 1862); 4 Duets for Soprano and Alto, op.61 (1874); 5 Duets for Soprano and Alto, op.66 (1875; Vienna, Jan. 29, 1878); 4 Ballads and Romances, op.75 (1877–78). **S o n g s :** With Piano Accompaniment: 6 Songs, op.7 (1851–52); 6 Songs, op.3, for Tenor or Soprano (1852–53); 6 Songs, op.6, for Soprano or Tenor (1852–53); 8 Songs and Romances, op.14 (1858); 5 Poems, op.19 (1858); Romances [15] from L. Tieck's "Magelone" (1861–68); Songs [9], op.32 (1864); 7 Songs, op.48 (1855–68); 4 Songs, op.43 (1857–64); 5 Songs, op.47 (1860–68); 4 Songs, op.46 (1864–68); 5 Songs, op.49 (1868); Songs [8], op.57 (1871); Songs [8], op.58 (1871); Songs [8], op.59 (1871–73); Songs [9], op.63 (1874); 4 Songs, op.70 (1875–77); 9 Songs, op.69 (1877); 5 Songs, op.72 (1876–77); 5 Songs, op.71 (1877); 6 Songs, op.86 (1877–79); 6 Songs, op.85 (1877–82); Romances and Songs [15] for 1 or 2 Female Voices, op.84 (1881); 2 Songs for Alto, Viola, and Piano, op.91 (publ. 1884); 5 Songs, op.94 (1884); 7 Songs, op.95 (1884); 4 Songs, op.96 (1884); 6 Songs, op.97 (1884–85); 5 Songs, op.105 (1886); 5 Songs, op.106 (1886); 5 Songs, op.107 (1886); *Vier ernste Gesänge* for Baritone, op.121 (1896); also *Mondnacht* (1854); *Regenlied* (1872); 5 *Songs of Ophelia* for Soprano, with Piano ad libitum (1873); 14 *Volkskinderlieder*, arrangements for Voice and Piano (1858); 28 *Deutsche Volkslieder*, arrangements for Voice and Piano (1858; publ. 1926); arrangement of Schubert's *Memnon* for Voice and Orch. (1862); arrangement of Schubert's *An Schwager Kronos* for Voice and Orch. (1862); arrangement of Schubert's *Geheimes* for Voice, Horn, and Strings; 8 *Gypsy Songs*, an arrangement of op.103, nos. 1–7 and 11, for Voice and Piano (1887); 49 *Deutsche Volkslieder*, arrangements for Voice and Piano (1894).

BIBL.: COLLECTED WORKS, SOURCE MATE- RIAL: H. Gál and E. Mandyczewski prepared the Gesellschaft der Musikfreunde of Vienna edition; it was publ. as *J. B.: Sämtliche Werke* (26 vols., Leipzig, 1926–28). A new historical-critical edition of the complete works, the *J. B. Gesamtausgabe*, with editorial coordination by the Research Center in Kiel in conjunction with the Gesellschaft der Musikfreunde, began publication in Munich in 1997. When completed, this monumental edition will consist of approximately 65 vols. A thematic catalogue was prepared by N. Simrock, *Thematisches Verzeichniss sämmtlicher im Druck erschienenen Werke von J. B.* (Berlin, 1897; 3rd ed., 1909; Eng. tr. and aug. ed. by J. Braunstein as *Thematic Catalogue of the Collected Works of B.*, N.Y., 1956; rev. by M. McCorkle, N.Y., 1973). The standard thematic and bibliographic catalogue is found in M. McCorkle, *J. B. Thematisch-Bibliographisches Werkverzeichnis* (Munich, 1983). Other sources include A. von Ehrmann, *J. B.: Thematisches Verzeichnis* (Leipzig, 1933); L. Koch, *B.- Bibliografia* (Budapest, 1943); G. Bozarth, E. Auman, and W. Parsons, *The Musical Manuscripts and Letters of J. B. in the Collections of the Music Division, Library of Congress* (Washington, D.C., 1983); R. Pascall, ed., *B.: Biographical, Documentary and Analytical Studies* (Cambridge, 1983); M. Musgrave, ed., *B. 2.: Biographical, Documentary and Analytical Studies* (Cambridge, 1987); S. Antonicek and O. Biba, eds., *B.-Kongress, Wien 1983: Kongressbericht* (Tutzing, 1988); T. Quigley, *J. B.: An Annotated Bibliography of the Literature Through 1982* (Metuchen, N.J., 1991); T. Quigley and M. Ingraham, *J. B.: An Annotated Bibliography of the Literature From 1982 to 1996 With an Appendix on B. and the Internet* (Lanham, Md., 1998); L. Botstein, *The Compleat B.* (N.Y., 1999). **C o r r e s p o n d e n c e :** A major ed. of his correspondence was publ. by the Deutsche Brahmsgesellschaft as *J. B.: Briefwechsel* (16 vols., Berlin, 1906–22). See also B. Litzmann, ed., *Clara Schumann-J. B.: Briefe aus den Jahren 1853–1896* (2 vols., Leipzig, 1927; Eng. tr., n.d.); K. Stephenson, ed., *J. B.: Heimatbekenntnisse in Briefen an seine Hamburger Verwandten* (Hamburg, 1933); O.-G. Billroth, *Billroth und B. im Briefwechsel* (Vienna, 1935); R. Litterscheid, ed., *J. B. in seinen Schriften und Briefen* (Berlin, 1943); E. Müller von Asow, ed., *J. B. und Mathilde Wesendonck: Ein Briefwechsel* (Vienna, 1943); H. Barkan, ed., *J. B. and Theodore Billroth: Letters from a Musical Friendship* (Norman, Okla., 1957); K. Stephenson, *J. B. und Fritz Simrock, Weg einer Freundschaft: Briefe des Verlegers an den Komponisten* (Hamburg, 1961); K. Stephenson, *J. B. in seiner Familie: Der Briefwechsel* (Hamburg, 1973). **BIOGRAPHICAL:** H. Reimann, *J. B.* (Berlin, 1897; 6th ed., 1922); A. Dietrich, *Erinnerungen an J. B. in Briefen, besonders aus seiner Jugendzeit* (Leipzig, 1898; Eng. tr. by D. Hecht in *Recollections of J. B.*, London, 1899); J. Widmann, *J. B. in Erinnerungen* (Berlin 1898; 5th ed., 1947; Eng. tr. by D. Hecht in *Recollections of J. B.*, London, 1899); J. Widmann, *Sizilien und andere Gegenden Italiens: Reisen mit J. B.* (Frauenfeld, 1898; 3rd ed., 1912); W. Hübbe, *B. in Hamburg* (Hamburg, 1902); M. Kalbeck, *J. B.* (8 vols., Berlin, 1904–14); H. Antcliffe, *B.* (London, 1905); J. Erb, *B.* (London, 1905); R. von der Leyen, *J. B. als Mensch und Freund* (Düsseldorf and Leipzig, 1905); F. May, *The Life of J. B.* (2 vols., London, 1905; 2nd ed., 1948; 3rd ed., rev., 1977); G. Henschel, *Personal Recollections of J. B.* (Boston, 1907); W. Pauli, *Moderne Geister: B.* (Berlin, 1907); H. Colles, *J. B.* (London, 1908; 2nd ed., 1920); R. von Perger, *B.* (Leipzig, 1908); J. Fuller Maitland, *B.* (London, 1911); W. Thomas-San-Galli, *J. B.* (Munich, 1912; 5th ed., 1922); L. Misch, *J. B.* (Bielefeld, 1913; 2nd ed., 1922); E. Lee, *B.: The Man and His Music* (London, 1915); W. Niemann, *J. B.* (Berlin, 1920; Eng. tr., N.Y., 1929); P. Landormy, *B.* (Paris, 1921; rev. ed., 1948); G. Ophüls, *Erinnerungen an J. B.* (Berlin, 1921); W. Nagel, *J. B.* (Stuttgart, 1923); J. Pulver, *J. B.* (London, 1926; new ed., 1933); J. Cooke, *J. B.* (Philadelphia, 1928); M. Komorn, *J. B. als Chordirigent in Wien und seine Nachfolger* (Vienna, 1928); R. Specht, *J. B.: Leben und Werk eines deutschen Meisters* (Hellerau, 1928; Eng. tr., 1930); G. Ernest, *J. B.* (Berlin, 1930); P. Mies, *J. B.* (Leipzig, 1930); A. von Ehrmann, *J. B.: Weg, Werk und Welt* (Leipzig, 1933); R. Fellinger, *Klänge um B.* (Berlin, 1933); R. Hill, *B.* (London, 1933; 2nd ed., 1941); E. Hirschmann, *J. B. und die Frauen* (Vienna, 1933); L. Koch, *B. in Ungarn* (Budapest, 1933); J. Müller-Blattau, *J. B.* (Potsdam, 1933); W. Murdoch, *B.: With an Analytical Study of the Complete Pianoforte Works* (London, 1933); R. Schauffler, *The Unknown B.: His Life, Character and Works, Based on New Material* (N.Y., 1933); W. Schramm, *J. B. in Detmold* (Leipzig, 1933); K. Stephenson, *J. B.' Heimatbekenntnis* (Hamburg, 1933); E. Blom, *J. B.* (N.Y., 1934); R. Hernried, *J. B.* (Leipzig, 1934); K. Geiringer, *J. B.: Leben und Schaffen eines deutschen Meisters* (Vienna, 1935; Eng.

tr., London and N.Y., 1936; 3rd ed., rev. and enl., N.Y., 1981); K. Huschke, *J. B. als Pianist, Dirigent und Lehrer* (Karlsruhe, 1935); R. Lienau, *Erinnerungen an J. B.* (Berlin, 1935); K. Huschke, *Frauen um B.* (Karlsruhe, 1937); A. Orel, *J. B.s Leben in Bildern* (Leipzig, 1937); R. Gerber, *J. B.* (Potsdam, 1938); M. Goss and R. Schauffler, *B., the Master* (N.Y., 1943); K. Laux, *Der Einsame: J. B., Leben und Werk* (Graz, 1944); W. and P. Rehberg, *J. B.: Sein Leben und Werk* (Zürich, 1947; 2nd ed., 1963); J. Culshaw, *B.: An Outline of His Life and Music* (London, 1948); P. Latham, *B.* (London, 1948; rev. ed. by J. Westrup, London, 1975); A. Orel, *J. B.: Ein Meister und sein Weg* (Vienna, 1950); F. Grasberger, *J. B.: Variationen um sein Wesen* (Vienna, 1952); L. Henning, *Die Freundschaft Clara Schumanns mit J. B.* (Zürich, 1952); C. Rostand, *B.* (2 vols., Paris, 1954–55); L. Berger, *Vom Menschen J. B.* (Tübingen, 1959); F. Müller-Blattau, *J. B.* (Königstein, 1960); H. Gál, *J. B.: Werk und Persönlichkeit* (Frankfurt am Main, 1961; Eng. tr. as *J. B.: His Work and Personality*, N.Y., 1963); J. Laufer, *B.* (Paris, 1963); J. Bruyr, *B.* (Paris, 1965); W. Siegmund- Schultze, *J. B.* (Leipzig, 1966); Y. Tiénot, *B.: Son vrai visage* (Paris, 1968); K. Dale, *B.: A Biography with a Survey of Books, Editions & Recordings* (Hamden, Conn., and London, 1970); R. Heuberger, *Erinnerungen an J. B.: Tagebuchnotizen aus den Jahren 1875–97* (Tutzing, 1971; 2nd ed., 1976); J. Burnett, *B.: A Critical Study* (London, 1972); J. Chissell, *B.* (London, 1977); K. Hocker, *J. B.: Begegnung mit dem Menschen* (Berlin, 1983); R. and K. Hofmann, *J. B.: Zeittafel zu Leben und Werk* (Tutzing, 1983); C. Schmidt, *J. B. und seine Zeit* (Laaber, 1983); P. Holmes, *B.: His Life and Times* (Southborough, 1984); J. Forner, *J. B. in Leipzig: Geschichte einer Beziehung* (Leipzig, 1987); I Keys, *J. B.* (London, 1989); W. Frisch, ed., *B. and His World* (Princeton, 1990); M. MacDonald, *B.* (London, 1990); M. Audiberti, *B., un génie ordinaire* (Paris, 1991); H. Becker, *B.* (Stuttgart, 1993); C. Schmidt, *J. B.* (Stuttgart, 1994); W. Gürtelschmied, *J. B.: Sein Werk, sein Leben* (Vienna, 1997); S. Kross, *J. B.: Versuch einer kritischen Dokumentar-Biographie* (Bonn, 1997 et seq.); H. Schaefer, *J. B.: Ein Führer durch Leben und Werk* (Berlin, 1997); J. Swafford, *J. B.: A Biography* (N.Y., 1997). **CRITICAL, ANALYTICAL:** L. Köhler, *J. B. und seine Stellung in der Musikgeschichte* (Hannover, 1880); E. Krause, *J. B. in seinem Werken* (Hamburg, 1892); W. Nagel, *B. als Nachfolger Beethovens* (Leipzig, 1892); G. Ophuls, *B.-Texte* (Berlin, 1898; 3rd ed., 1923); R. Barth, *J. B. und seine Musik* (Hamburg, 1904); G. Jenner, *J. B. als Mensch, Lehrer und Kunstler: Studien und Erlebnisse* (Marburg, 1905; 2nd ed., 1930); W. Thomas-San-Galli, *J. B. Eine musikpsychologische Studie* (Strasbourg, 1905); J. Knorr and H. Riemann, *J. B. Symphonien und andere Orchesterwerke erläutert* (Berlin, 1908); M. Burkhardt, *J. B.: Ein Führer durch seine Werke* (Berlin, 1912); E. Evans, *Historical, Descriptive and Analytical Account of the Entire Works of J. B.* (London; Vol. I, vocal works, 1912; Vols. II and III, chamber and orch. works, 1933 and 1935; vol. IV, piano works, 1936); W. Nagel, *Die Klaviersonaten von J. B.: Technisch-ästhetische Analysen* (Stuttgart, 1915); M. Kalbeck, *B. als Lyriker* (Vienna, 1921); M. Friedlander, *B.' Lieder* (Berlin and Leipzig, 1922; Eng. tr., London, 1928); P. Mies, *Stilmomente und Ausdrucksstilformen im B.schen Lied* (Leipzig, 1923); H. Meyer, *Linie und Form: Bach, Beethoven, B.* (Berlin, 1930); E. Markham Lee, *B.'s Orchestral Works* (London, 1931); H. Drinker, *The Chamber Music of B.* (Philadelphia, 1932); W. Blume, *B. in der Meininger Tradition* (Stuttgart, 1933); P. Browne, *B.: The Symphonies* (London, 1933); H. Colles, *The Chamber Music of B.* (London, 1933); D. Mason, *The Chamber Music of B.* (N.Y. and London, 1933; 2nd ed., 1950); F. J. Harrison, *B. and His Four Symphonies* (London, 1939); S. Drinker, *B. and His Women's Choruses* (Merion, Pa., 1952); I. Fellinger, *Über die Dynamik in der Musik von J. B.* (Berlin, 1961); A. Mitschka, *Der Sonatensatz in den Werken von*

J. B. (Gütersloh, 1963); C. Dahlhaus, *B., Klavierkonzert Nr. 1 d-moll op.15, Meisterwerke der Musik* (III, Munich, 1965); W. Moritz, *J. B. und sein Verhältnis zum deutschen Volkslied* (Tutzing, 1965); J. Wetschky, *Die Kanontechnik in der Instrumentalmusik von J. B.* (Regensburg, 1967); S. Helms, *Die Melodienbildung in den Liedern von J. B. und ihr Verhältnis zu den Volksliedern und volkstümlichen Weisen* (Bamberg, 1968); J. Horton, *B. Orchestral Music* (London, 1968); K. Blum, *Hundert Jahre "Ein deutsches Requiem" von J. B.* (Tutzing, 1971); M. Harrison, *The Lieder of B.* (N.Y., 1972); E. Sams, *B. Songs* (London, 1972); R. Jacobson, *The Music of J. B.* (London, 1977); A. Craig Bell, *The Lieder of B.* (Darley, Harrogate, 1979); C. Floros, *B. und Bruckner: Studien zur musikalische Exegetik* (Wiesbaden, 1980); J. Dunsby, *Structural Ambiguity in B.* (Ann Arbor, 1981); V. Hancock, *B.'s Choral Compositions and His Library of Early Music* (Ann Arbor, 1983); H. Mayer, *Ein Denkmal für J. B.: Versuche über Musik und Literatur* (Frankfurt am Main, 1983); W. Frisch, *B. and the Principle of Developing Variation* (Berkeley, 1984); M. Musgrave, *The Music of B.* (London, 1985); J. Kraus, *J. B. als Klavierkomponist: Wege und Hinweise zu seiner Klaviermusik* (Wilhelmshaven, 1986; Eng. tr., 1988); M. Rohn, *Die Coda bei J. B.* (Hamburg, 1986); P. Gülke, *B., Bruckner: Zwei Studien* (Kassel, 1989); G. Bozarth, ed., *International B. Conference (1983: Washington, D.C.): B. Studies: Analytical and Historical Perspectives: Papers Delivered at the International B. Conference, Washington, DC, 5–8 May 1983* (Oxford, 1990); J. Jost, ed., *B. als Liedkomponist: Studien zum Verhältnis von Text und Vertonung* (Stuttgart, 1992); U. Mahlert, *J. B.: Klavierkonzert B-Dur, op.83* (Munich, 1994); M. Musgrave, *The Music of B.* (Oxford, 1994); L. Stark, *A Guide to the Solo Songs of J. B.* (Bloomington, Ind., 1995); A. Craig Bell, *B.: The Vocal Music* (Madison, N.J., 1996); W. Frisch, *B.: The Four Symphonie* (N.Y., 1996); M. Musgrave, *B.: A German Requiem* (Cambridge, 1996); R. Ulm, ed., *J. B.: Das symphonische Werk: Entstehung, Deutung, Wirkung* (Kassel, 1996); D. Brodbeck, *B.: Symphony No. 1* (Cambridge, 1997); G.-H. Falke, *J. B.: Wiegenlieder meiner Schmerzen: Philosophie des musikalischen Realismus* (Berlin, 1997); C. Floros, *J. B., "frei aber einsam:" Eine Leben für eine poetische Musik* (Zürich, 1997); J. Frorner, *B.: Eine Sommerkomponist* (Frankfurt am Main, 1997); W. Gieseler, *Die Harmonik bei J. B.* (Essen, 1997); H.-W. Heister, ed., *J. B., oder, die Relativierung der "absoluten" Musik* (Hamburg, 1997); R. Knapp, *B. and the Challenge of the Symphony* (Stuyvesant, N.Y., 1997); K. Körner, *Die Violinsonaten von J. B.: Studien* (Augsburg, 1997); H. Stekel, *Sehnsucht und Distanz: Theologische Aspekte in den wortgebundenen religiösen Komposition von J. B.* (Frankfurt am Main, 1997); C. Lawson, *B.: Clarinet Quintet* (Cambridge, 1998); L. Stark, *B.'s Vocal Duets and Quartets With Piano: A Guide With Full Texts and Translations* (Bloomington, Ind., 1998).—**NS/LK/DM**

Brăiloiu, Constantin, distinguished Romanian-born French ethnomusicologist; b. Bucharest, Aug. 25, 1893; d. Geneva, Dec. 20, 1958. He studied music in Lausanne, with Gédalge at the Paris Cons. (1912–14), and in Romania. After a period as a composer and music critic, he turned to ethnomusicological research. In 1921 he became a prof. of music history and aesthetics at the Académie Royale de Musique in Bucharest, and later taught at the Académie de Musique Religieuse de la Sainte Patriarchie (1929–35). In 1926 he became secretary-general of the Soc. of Romanian Composers, where he founded its folklore archives in 1928; it later became the Institutul de Folclor şi Etnografie. From 1943 to 1946 he served as attaché at the Romanian Embassy in Bern. With Eugène Pittard, he founded the

international folk music archives in Geneva in 1944. In 1948 he went to Paris and in 1956 he became a naturalized French citizen. He was a member of the Centre National de la Recherche Scientifique, and pursued research at the Musée de l'Homme and at the Sorbonne's Inst. of Musicology. His article "Esquisse d'une méthode de folklore musical (organisation d'archives)," *Revue de Musicologie*, XI (1931; Eng. tr. in *Ethnomusicology*, XIV, 1970) is a valuable guide to his approach to the synoptic transcription of music. Among his other important articles were "Le rythme aksak," *Revue de Musicologie*, XXX (1951), "Sur une mélodie russe," *Musique russe* (vol. II, Paris, 1953), and "Le rythme enfantin: Notions liminaires," *Cercle international d'études ethnomusicologiques: Wegimont 1954*. He also engaged in valuable fieldwork, which he preserved on recordings.

BIBL.: E. Comişel, *C. B., 1893–1958* (Bucharest, 1996). —**NS/LK/DM**

Brailowsky, Alexander, noted Russian-born French pianist; b. Kiev, Feb. 16, 1896; d. N.Y., April 25, 1976. After study with his father, a professional pianist, he continued his training at the Kiev Cons., graduating with a gold medal in 1911. Following advanced studies with Leschetizky in Vienna (1911–14) and Busoni in Zürich, he completed his training with Plante in Paris, where he made his debut in 1919. In 1926 he became a naturalized French citizen. He presented a complete cycle of Chopin's works in Paris (1924), which he repeated several times. He made a highly successful world tour; made his American debut at Aeolian Hall in N.Y. on Nov. 19, 1924; made a coast-to-coast tour of the U.S. in 1936; first gave the Chopin cycle in America during the 1937–38 season, in 6 recitals in N.Y. In 1960 he played the Chopin cycle again in N.Y. and Brussels in honor of the 150th anniversary of Chopin's birth. —**NS/LK/DM**

Brain, Alfred (Edwin), English-born American horn player and teacher, brother of **Aubrey (Harold)** and uncle of **Dennis Brain;** b. London, Oct. 24, 1885; d. Los Angeles, March 29, 1966. After studying horn with his father, he pursued training with Borsdorf at the Royal Academy of Music in London (1901–04). He played in the Scottish Orch. in Glasgow (1904–08); then was principal horn in the Queen's Hall Orch. (1908–16; from 1919) and also was a member of the London Sym. Orch. (from 1919). After serving as co-principal horn in the N.Y. Sym. Orch. (1922–23), he was first horn in the Los Angeles Phil. (1923–34; 1936–37) and the Cleveland Orch. (1934–36); was again a member of the Los Angeles Phil. (1943–44); also played in Hollywood film studios. In 1930 he became a naturalized American citizen. —**NS/LK/DM**

Brain, Aubrey (Harold), English horn player and teacher, brother of **Alfred (Edwin)** and father of **Dennis Brain;** b. London, July 12, 1893; d. there, Sept. 20, 1955. He studied horn with his father, and then at the Royal Coll. of Music in London with Borsdorf (1911–13). In 1911 he was made principal horn in the New Sym. Orch. in London; in 1913 he played in the orch. of the

Beecham Opera Co. From 1922 to 1930 he was a member of the orch. of the Royal Phil. Soc. and the Queen's Hall Orch. in London; also pursued a solo career from 1923, and held the posts of co-principal (1923–24), principal (1924–28), and again co-principal (1928–29) horn in the London Sym. Orch. From 1930 to 1945 he was principal horn in the BBC Sym. Orch. in London. He later played in the Philharmonia Orch. in London (1948–50). From 1923 to 1955 he was prof. of horn at the Royal Academy of Music in London.—NS/LK/DM

Brain, Dennis, phenomenal English horn player, son of **Aubrey (Harold)** and nephew of **Alfred (Edwin) Brain**; b. London, May 17, 1921; d. in an automobile accident in Hatfield, Sept. 1, 1957. He received piano lessons as a child and took up the bugle in his school cadet band. In 1936 he began studying the horn at home with his father, who continued as his teacher when he entered the Royal Academy of Music in London that same year; he also had instruction there in piano, organ, and conducting. While still a student, he launched his professional career in 1938 playing second horn to his father in a concert under Adolf Busch in London. With the outbreak of World War II in 1939, he enlisted in the Royal Air Force and played principal horn in its sym. orch. for the duration of the conflict. In the meantime, he completed his training at the Royal Academy of Music in 1940. From 1942 to 1947 he was principal horn in the National Sym. Orch. in London; he also was a valuable member of the New London Orch., the London Wind Players, and the London Baroque Ensemble. In 1945 he became principal horn of the Philharmonia Orch. in London, a post he held with great distinction for the rest of his life. He also served as principal horn of the Royal Phil. in London from 1946 to 1948, and again from 1950 to 1954. From 1949 he was principal horn of the London Mozart Players. In addition to his various orch. duties, he toured as a virtuoso soloist and was active with his own wind quintet and trio. Brain was duly recognized as the foremost horn player of his time, and following his tragic death he became a legend. His lips were insured for £10,000. Among his legendary performances captured on recordings are the 4 Mozart and the 2 Strauss horn concertos, all of which were classical best-sellers in his lifetime and remain unsurpassed for their perfection of execution. From 1942 several noted composers wrote works especially for him, among them Britten (*Serenade* for Tenor, Horn, and Strings), Seiber (*Notturno* for Horn and Strings), Hindemith (Horn Concerto), Jacob (Horn Concerto), Arnold (2nd Horn Concerto), and Searle (*Aubade* for Horn and Orch.). It can only be imagined how profoundly the modern horn repertoire would have been enhanced in succeeding decades had Brain lived an average lifetime.

BIBL.: S. Pettitt, *D. B.: A Biography* (London, 1976). —NS/LK/DM

Braithwaite, (Henry) Warwick, New Zealand conductor, father of **Nicholas (Paul Dallon) Braithwaite**; b. Dunedin, Jan. 9, 1896; d. London, Jan. 18, 1971. He studied at the Royal Academy of Music in London; won the Challen Gold Medal and the Battison Hayes Prize. He began his career as a conductor with the O'Mara Opera Co.; then conducted with the British National Opera Co. He was asst. music director of the BBC; then went to its Cardiff studio in Wales as music director; also conducted the Cardiff Musical Soc. (1924–31). He was a founder of the Welsh National Orch. From 1932 to 1940 he was a conductor at the Sadler's Wells Opera in London; then he led the Scottish Orch. in Glasgow (1940–46). Later he was a ballet conductor at the Royal Opera, Covent Garden, in London (1950–53); then conducted the National Orch. of New Zealand and served as artistic director of the National Opera of Australia (1954–55). From 1956 to 1960 he was music director of the Welsh National Opera; then was again a conductor at Sadler's Wells until 1968. He publ. *The Conductor's Art* (London, 1952). —NS/LK/DM

Braithwaite, Nicholas (Paul Dallon), English conductor, son of **(Henry) Warwick Braithwaite**; b. London, Aug. 26, 1939. He studied at the Royal Academy of Music in London, at the Bayreuth Festival master classes, and with Swarowsky in Vienna. He was assoc. conductor of the Bournemouth Sym. Orch. (1967–70), assoc. principal conductor of the Sadler's Wells Opera in London (1970–74), and music director of the Glyndebourne Touring Opera (1976–80). After serving as principal guest conductor of the Manchester Camerata (1977–84), he was its principal conductor (1984–91). He also was music director of the Stora Theater Opera and Ballet in Göteborg (1981–84), chief conductor of the Adelaide Sym. Orch. (1987–91), and dean of the Victorian Coll. of the Arts in Melbourne (1988–91). He then was chief conductor of the Tasmanian Sym. orch. (from 1991).—NS/LK/DM

Brambilla, Marietta, Italian contralto, sister of **Teresa Brambilla**; b. Cassano d'Adda, June 6, 1807; d. Milan, Nov. 6, 1875. She was a member of a musical family; her 4 sisters were singers. She studied at the Milan Cons., making her debut in London in 1827; then sang in Italy, Vienna, and Paris. She eventually settled in Milan as a teacher. She publ. collections of vocalises. —NS/LK/DM

Brambilla, Teresa, Italian soprano, sister of **Marietta Brambilla**; b. Cassano d'Adda, Oct. 23, 1813; d. Milan, July 15, 1895. She studied singing at the Milan Cons., making her debut in 1831 in Milan and traveling through Europe, including Russia. Her appearances at La Scala were highly successful. After several seasons in Paris, she was engaged at the Teatro La Fenice in Venice, where she created the role of Gilda in *Rigoletto* (March 11, 1851).—NS/LK/DM

Branchu, Alexandrine Caroline (née **Chevalier de Lavit**), famous French soprano; b. Cap Français, Santo Domingo, Nov. 2, 1780; d. Passy, Oct. 14, 1850. She was a pupil of Garat at the Paris Cons. In 1799 she married the ballet dancer Branchu, and that same year made her debut at the Théâtre Feydeau in Paris. From 1801 to 1826 she was one of the leading

members of the Paris Opéra. She sang principal roles in the premieres of Cherubini's *Anacréon* (1803) and *Les Abencérages* (1813), winning the composer's approbation. She was also highly regarded for her portrayals of Gluck's Alcestis, Iphigenia, and Armida, and of Piccinni's Dido.—**NS/LK/DM**

Branco, Luis de Freitas
See **Freitas Branco, Luis de**

Brancour, René, French music critic; b. Paris, May 17, 1862; d. there, Nov. 16, 1948. Educated at the Paris Cons., he became curator of its collection of musical instruments. In 1906, he began a course of lectures on aesthetics at the Sorbonne; also wrote newspaper criticism. A brilliant writer, he poured invective on the works of composers of the advanced school; his tastes were conservative, but he accepted French music of the Impressionist period. He wrote biographies of Felicien David (1911) and Méhul (1912) in the series Musiciens Célèbres; of Massenet (1923) and Offenbach (1929) in Les Maîtres de la Musique. Other books were *La Vie et l'oeuvre de Georges Bizet* (1913), *Histoire des instruments de musique* (1921), and *La Marseillaise et le chant du départ.* —**NS/LK/DM**

Brand, Max(imilian), Austrian-born American composer; b. Lemberg, April 26, 1896; d. Langenzersdorf, near Vienna, April 5, 1980. He became a student of Schreker in Vienna in 1919, and continued as his student in Berlin in 1920. He also received instruction from Alois Hàba and Erwin Stein. Brand's early use of 12-tone methods is revealed in his *Fünf Balladen nach Gedichten von Else Lasker-Schüler* (1927). He scored a sensation when he brought out his first opera, *Maschinist Hopkins* (Duisburg, April 13, 1929), which subsequently was performed throughout Europe. This expressionistic score of the "machine era" served as a remarkable precursor to Berg's *Lulu*. Brand pursued his interest in avant-garde expression by founding Vienna's Mimoplastisches Theater für Ballett and by serving as co-director of the Raimund Theater, where he oversaw the Wiener Opernproduktion company. He also was associated with Eisler in producing experimental films. As a Jew, Brand's works were banned by the Nazis in Germany in 1933. After the Anschluss in Austria in 1938, he was compelled to flee to Brazil. In 1940 he went to the U.S. and in 1944 became a naturalized American citizen. He was active in N.Y. as director of the Music and Theatre Wing, Caravan of East and West. Around 1958 he began to experiment with electronics. In 1975 he returned to Austria and was active in his own electronic music studio.

WORKS: DRAMATIC: *Maschinist Hopkins*, opera (1928; Duisburg, April 13, 1929); *Kleopatra*, opera (1932–38); *Requiem*, opera (1933); *Die Chronik*, scenic cantata (1938); *The Gate*, scenic oratorio (N.Y., May 23, 1944); *Stormy Interlude*, opera (1955); ballets; incidental music. **ORCH.:** *Eine Nachtmusik* for Chamber Orch. (1923); *The Wonderful 1–Hoss Shay*, symphonic poem (Philadelphia, Jan. 20, 1950); *Night on the Bayous of Louisiana*, tone poem (1953). **CHAMBER:** String Trio (1923); *Piece* for Flute and Piano (1940). **VOCAL:** *Nachtlied* for Soprano and

Orch. (1922); *Kyrie Eleison* for Chorus (1940); songs. **ELECTRONIC:** *The Astronauts, An Epic in Electronics* (1962); *Ilian 1 & 2* (1966).

BIBL.: T. Brezinka, *M. B., 1896–1980: Leben und Werk* (Munich, 1995).—**NS/LK/DM**

Brandl, Johann Evangelist, German composer; b. Kloster Rohr, near Regensburg, Nov. 14, 1760; d. Karlsruhe, May 25, 1837. He studied in various religious schools and monasteries as a youth, then decided to devote himself to music, becoming proficient as an organist and violinist. He was attached to the court of the Archduke of Baden as music director.

WORKS: DRAMATIC: Opera: *Germania* (1800); *Triumph des Vaterherzens* (Karlsruhe, Jan. 15, 1811); *Omar der Gute* (Karlsruhe, Aug. 24, 1811); *Nanthild, das Mädchen von Valbella* (Karlsruhe, May 19, 1813). **ORCH.:** "Grande Symphonie;" Bassoon Concerto. **CHAMBER:** String quartets and quintets. **VOCAL:** Oratorios; masses; songs.

BIBL.: O. Danzer, *J.E. B.s Leben und Werke* (Leipzig, 1936). —**NS/LK/DM**

Brandt, Jobst vom (or **Jodocus de Brant**), German musician; b. Waldershof, near Marktredwitz, Oct. 28, 1517; d. Brand, near Marktredwitz, Jan. 22, 1570. In 1530 he enrolled at Heidelberg Univ. In 1548 he had become Captain of Waldsassen and Administrator of Liebenstein. Brandt was one of the most important composers of the Senfl school. His music is distinguished by deep feeling and a skillful use of counterpoint.

WORKS: *45 Psalmen und Kirchengesänge* (Eger, 1572–73); 55 vocal pieces in G. Forster's collection *Ein Auszug guter alter und neuer teutscher Liedlein* (III, Wittenberg, 1549; IV-V, 1556). —**NS/LK/DM**

Brandt, Marianne (real name, **Marie Bischoff**), Austrian contralto; b. Vienna, Sept. 12, 1842; d. there, July 9, 1921. She studied voice in Vienna, and later with Pauline Viardot-García in Baden-Baden (1869–70). She made her debut as Rachel in *La Juive* in Olmütz on Jan. 4, 1867, then sang in Hamburg and at the Berlin Royal Opera (1868–82). In 1872 she appeared in London. She made her American debut as Leonore at the Metropolitan Opera in N.Y. on Nov. 19, 1884, and remained on its staff until 1888; also sang Italian roles in operas by Verdi and Meyerbeer. In 1890 she settled in Vienna as a singing teacher.—**NS/LK/DM**

Brandts-Buys, Jan (Willem Frans), Dutch composer; b. Zutphen, Sept. 12, 1868; d. Salzburg, Dec. 7, 1933. He was a pupil of M. Schwarz and A. Urspruch at the Raff Cons. in Frankfurt am Main. He lived for a time in Vienna, and later settled in Salzburg. His first opera, *Das Veilchenfest* (Berlin, Dec. 3, 1909), met with opposition; a second opera, *Das Glockenspiel* (Dresden, Dec. 4, 1913), was received more kindly; while a third, *Die drei Schneider von Schönau* (Dresden, April 1, 1916), was quite successful. Subsequent operas were *Der Eroberer* (Dresden, Jan. 14, 1918), *Micarême* (Vienna, Nov. 14, 1919), *Der Mann im Mond* (Dresden, June 18, 1922), *Traumland* (Dresden, Nov. 24, 1927), and *Ulysses* (German radio, March 12, 1937). He also wrote a ballet, *Machinalität* (Amsterdam, 1928); 2 piano concertos; a *Konzertstück* for Cello and Orch.; chamber music; piano pieces; songs.—**NS/LK/DM**

Brandukov, Anatol (Andreievich), eminent Russian cellist; b. Moscow, Dec. 22, 1856; d. there, Feb. 16, 1930. He studied cello at the Moscow Cons. with Fitzenhagen (1868–77), and also attended Tchaikovsky's classes in harmony. In 1878 he undertook a concert tour of Europe; lived mostly in Paris until 1906. His artistry was appreciated by Tchaikovsky, who dedicated his *Pezzo capriccioso* for Cello and Orch. to him; he also enjoyed the friendship of Saint-Saëns and Liszt. In 1906 he returned to Moscow, where he was prof. at the Phil. Inst.; from 1921 to 1930 he taught cello at the Moscow Cons. He composed a number of cello pieces and made transcriptions of works by Tchaikovsky, Rachmaninoff, and others.

BIBL.: L. Ginsburg, *A.A. B.* (Moscow, 1951).—**NS/LK/DM**

Brandy, (actually, Norwood, Brandy) soulful, intelligent teen hitmaker and actress; b. McComb, Miss., Feb. 11, 1979. Brandy's father was the church music director, so it's not surprising that Brandy Norwood and her brother, Willie Ray Jr., had musical talent and performed in the church choir. Recognizing the depth of their children's talent, the Norwood family relocated to L.A. by the time Brandy started school. As a member of a youth choir, she performed on several award shows. By the time she was 11, she had done several commercials, soloed for Arsenio Hall, and did backing vocals for the teen soul group Immature.

Although she started off as a singer—and was signed to Atlantic Records—Brandy made her first real professional mark as an actress, playing Danesha on the 1993 ABC TV series *Thea*. The show was shortlived, but Brandy would maintain a strong presence in both music and television from that point forward.

During the show's hiatus, Brandy recorded her eponymous debut for Atlantic. Her first single, "I Wanna Be Down" topped the R&B charts for four weeks, rising to #6 on the pop charts and going gold. The album earned two Grammy nominations and four Soul Train Awards, among others. It also turned out three more pop hits: the platinum "Baby," which hit #4 pop and spent four weeks at #1 R&B; "Best Friend," which peaked at #34; and "Brokenhearted," which went gold and hit #9 pop. In 1994, she was named Best New R&B Artist at the American Music Awards, *Billboard* Music Awards, and the NAACP Image Awards. The album stayed on the charts for 84 weeks.

As she received all these awards for her music, Brandy once again was acting. She got her own series, *Moesha*. Initially ordered by CBS, it was picked up by the fledgling UPN network and quickly became one of their biggest series. Along with her platinum-selling single, "Sitting in My Room," from the *Waiting to Exhale* soundtrack, it also kept Brandy in the public eye, despite a four-year gap between her first and second album.

That sophomore effort, 1998's *Never Say Never*, featured "The Boy Is Mine," a duet with fellow teen sensation Monica. They debuted at #1, and won a Grammy for R&B Performance by a Duo or Group with Vocal. Brandy also found time to star in a television revival of Rodgers and Hammerstein's *Cinderella* with Whitney Houston that gave ABC its highest ratings in 10 years and sold a million copies on home video. Her next appearance was in the high grossing, gross-out teen slasher film *I Still Know What You Did Last Summer*. She also co-starred with Diana Ross in the TV movie *Double Platinum*, and was named a spokes-model for Candie's shoes and Cover Girl Cosmetics.

DISC.: *Brandy* (1994), *Never Say Never* (1998).—**HB**

Brannigan, Owen, English bass; b. Annitsford, March 10, 1908; d. Newcastle upon Tyne, May 9, 1973. He studied at the Guildhall School of Music in London (1934–42), where he won its gold medal in 1942. In 1943 he made his operatic debut as Sarastro with the Sadler's Wells Opera in London, where he sang until 1948 and again from 1952 to 1958; also appeared at the Glyndebourne Festivals (1947–49), at London's Covent Garden, and with the English Opera Group. He became closely associated with the music of Britten, in whose operas he created Swallow in *Peter Grimes* (1945), Collatinus in *The Rape of Lucretia* (1946), Superintendent Budd in *Billy Budd* (1947), Noye in *Noye's Fludde* (1958), and Bottom in *A Midsummer Night's Dream* (1960). He also sang in oratorio, concerts, and lighter fare. In 1964 he was made a member of the Order of the British Empire. —**NS/LK/DM**

Brant, Henry, remarkable and innovative American composer; b. Montreal (of American parents), Sept. 15, 1913. He received rudimentary instruction in music from his father, Saul Brant (1882–1934), a concert violinist, and began to compose when he was only 8. After studies at the McGill Conservatorium in Montreal (1926–29), he went to N.Y. and continued his training with Leopold Mannes at the Inst. of Musical Art (1929–34). He also received private instruction from Riegger and Antheil. He likewise studied conducting with Fritz Mahler. During the 1930s and 1940s, Brant was active as a composer and conductor for radio, films, ballet, and jazz groups in N.Y. while pursuing experimental composition for the concert hall. He taught orchestration and conducted ensembles at Columbia Univ. from 1945 to 1952 and at the Juilliard School of Music from 1947 to 1955. From 1957 to 1980 he taught composition at Bennington (Vt.) Coll., and then settled in Santa Barbara in 1981. In 1947 and 1956 he held Guggenheim fellowships. He was the first American composer to win the Prix Italia in 1955. In 1979 he was elected to membership in the American Academy and Inst. of Arts and Letters. He received grants from the Fromm (1989) and Koussevitzky (1995) foundations. In 1998 he was awarded an honorary Doctor of Fine Arts degree from Wesleyan Univ. His MSS were deposited at the Paul Sacher Foundation in Basel in 1998.

Brant is a pioneer of spatial music, in which performing forces are placed at specified widely separated points in space on the stage, in the balconies, and in the aisles, with the object of making contrasted, high-impact textures clear and intelligible for the listener. An audacious explorer of sonic potentialities, he has introduced unusual acoustic timbres into large and small ensembles, and complete orchestral ensembles, each comprising only a single tone quality. His vocal writing frequently involves a notated form of scat singing, much expanded in its range of expression, and often deployed in complex polyphony. He also employs jazz and other popular genres simultaneously with classical materials, and utilizes intact original idioms from other cultures—African, Indian, and Indonesian—as well. In conducting his spatial music, he uses an appropriate body language, turning at 90, 135, and 180 angles to address his performers. He also gives cues by actually imitating the appearance of the entering instruments, miming the violin bow, a trombone slide, a piccolo, a drum, etc. by the movement of his body or by facial movements. Brant has expounded the rationale of spatial music in his article "Space as an Essential Aspect of Musical Composition" in B. Childs and E. Schwartz, eds., *Contemporary Composers on Contemporary Music* (N.Y., 1967; 2nd ed., rev., 1998). His experiments have convinced him that space exerts specific influences on harmony and polyphony and has come to view space as music's inescapable fourth dimension, the other three being the familiar pitch, time-measurement, and tone-quality. His works exclude electronic materials and do not permit amplification. He finds that recordings do not adequately suggest the spatial resonances, definitions, and contrasts in his music, and thus are only fully intelligible when heard live.

WORKS: SPATIAL: *Antiphony I* for 5 Orch. Groups or Chamber Ensemble (1953); *December* for Soprano, Tenor, Man and Woman Speakers, Choruses, Woodwinds, Brass, Percussion, and Organ (1954); *Grand Universal Circus* for 8 Solo Voices, Chorus, and Orch. (1956); *On the Nature of Things* for String Orch., Solo Winds, and Glockenspiel (1956); *In Praise of Learning* for 16 Sopranos and 16 Percussionists (1958); *Mythical Beasts* for Soprano or Mezzo-soprano and 16 Instruments (1958); *The Children's Hour* for 6 Voices, Chorus, 2 Trumpets, 2 Trombones, Organ, and Percussion (1958); *Atlantis* for Mezzo-soprano, Speaker, Chorus, Orch., Band, and Percussion Group (1960); *Headhunt* for Trombone, Bass Clarinet, Bassoon, Cello, and Percussion (1962); *The Fourth Millennium* for 2 Trumpets, Horn, Euphonium, and Tuba (1963); *Voyage Four* for Orch., Organ, and Soprano (1963); *Odyssey—Why Not?* for Solo Flute, Flute Obbligato, and 4 Orch. Groups (1965); *Windjammer* for Horn, Piccolo, Oboe, Bass Clarinet, and Bassoon (1969); *Kingdom Come* for Orch., Circus Band, and Organ (1970); *Immortal Combat* for 2 Bands (1972); *An American Requiem* for 16 Woodwinds, 14 Brass, Percussion, Organ, Church Bells, and Optional Soprano (1973); *Sixty* for 3 Wind Ensembles (1973); *Prevailing Winds* for Wind Quintet (1974); *Solomon's Gardens* for 7 Solo Voices, Chorus, 24 Hand-bells, and 3 Instruments (1974); *A Plan of the Air* for Soprano, Alto, Tenor, Bass, Organ, Orch. Wind Groups, and Percussion (1975); *Curriculum I* for Baritone and 8 Instruments (1975) and *II* for Small Orch. Groups (1978); *Homage to Ives* for Baritone, Piano, and 3 Orch. Groups (1975); *Spatial Concerto—Questions from Genesis* for Piano, 8 Sopranos, 8 Altos, and Orch. (1976); *Antiphonal Responses* for 3 Solo Bassoons, Piano, Orch., and 8 Instruments Obbligati (1978); *Trinity of*

Spheres for 3 Orch. Groups (1978); *Orbits* for 80 Trombones, Organ, and Soprano (1979); *The Glass Pyramid* for Unison Strings, Horn, E-flat Clarinet, Chimes, 2 Pianos, English Horn, Bassoon, and Contra-bassoon (1980); *Inside Track* for Solo Piano, Sopranino Obbligato, 3 Small Ensembles, and Projected Images (1982); *Meteor Farm* for Orch., 2 Choruses, 2 Percussion Groups, Jazz Orch., Javanese Gamelan Orch., West African Drumming Ensemble, South Indian Soloists, and 2 Western Solo Sopranos (1982); *Desert Forests* for Large and Small Orch. Groups and Improvising Pianist (1983); *Litany of Tides* for Solo Violin, 4 Soprano Voices, and 2 Orchs. (1983); *Bran(d)t aan de Amstel* for 100 Flutes, 4 Jazz Drummers, 3 Choruses, 4 Street Organs, 4 Church Carillons, and 4 Concerto Bands (1984); *Mass in Gregorian Chant* for Multiple Flutes (1984); *Western Springs* for 2 Orchs., 2 Choruses, and 2 Jazz Combos (1984); *Northern Lights over the Twin Cities* for Large Chorus, Small Chorus, 5 Solo Singers, Concert Band, Jazz Ensemble, Bagpipe Group, Chamber Orch., 5 Pianos, and Large Percussion Ensemble (1985); *Autumn Hurricanes* for Men's and Women's Choruses, 3 Solo Singers, Woodwind Ensemble, Jazz Ensemble, Brass Ensemble, Percussion Ensemble, String Orch., and 4 Pianos (1986); *Ghost Nets* for Double Bass and 2 Chamber Orchs. (1988); *Flight Over a Global Map* for 50 Trumpets (1989); *Rainforest* for 4 Solo Singers, String Ensemble, Piano, Harp, Percussion, Woodwind Quartet, and Brass Trio (1989); *Rosewood* for Guitar Orch. (1989); *Prisons of the Mind* for 2 Orchs., 2 Concert Bands, 2 Brass Sextets, and 2 Steel-drum Ensembles (1990); *Skull & Bones* for Chorus, Orch., Large Jazz Band, Large Flute Ensemble, and 5 Solo Voices (1991); *The Old Italians Dying* for Narrator and 2 Orchs. (1991); *500: Hidden Hemisphere* for 3 Concert Bands and Caribbean Steel-drum Ensemble (1992); *Fourscore* for 4 Quartets of Violin, Viola, Tenor Cello, and Cello (1993); *Homeless People* for Piano, String Quartet, and Accordion (1993); *Seventy* for 3 Concert Bands (1994); *Dormant Craters* for 16 Percussion (1995); *Plowshares and Swords*, total orch. environment (1995); *Festive 80* for 26 Brass, 18 Woodwinds, and 4 Percussionists (1997); *Mergers* for Orch., Organ, Mezzo-soprano, and Baritone (1998). **NON-SPATIAL:** *Angels and Devils* for Flute Solo and Flute Orch. (1932); *Partita* for Flute and Piano (1932); *Requiem in Summer* for Woodwind Quintet (1934); Duo for Cello and Piano (1937); *Hommage aux Frères Marx* for Tin Whistle and Chamber Ensemble (1938; publ. as *The Marx Brothers*, 1996); *Two Lyric Interludes* for String Orch. (1938); *Whoopee in D* for 10 Instruments or Orch. (1938); Clarinet Concerto (1939); Concerto for Saxophone or Trumpet and 9 Instruments (1941); *Fantasy & Caprice*, violin concerto (1941); 2 syms.: No. 1 (1945) and No. 2, *Promised Land* (1947); Jazz Clarinet Concerto (1946); *All Souls' Carnival* for Flute, Violin, Cello, Piano, and Accordion (1949); *Street Music* for Winds and Percussion (1949); *Millennium I* for 8 Trumpets, Chimes, and Glockenspiel (1950); *Origins* for Percussion Orch. and Optional Organ (1952); *Signs and Alarms* for 3 Woodwinds, 5 Brass, and 2 Percussion (1954); *Ice Age* for Ondes Martenot or Clarinet, Piano, and Percussion (1953); *Conversations in an Unknown Tongue* for Violin, Viola, Tenor Cello, and Cello (1958); *Sky Forest* for Accordion Quartet (1960); *Concerto with Lights* for Violin Solo, 10 Instruments, and 5 Musicians (1961); *Feuerwerk—Words Over Fireworks* for Solo Woman Speaker and 9 Instruments (1961); *From Bach's Menagerie* for 4 Saxophones (1963); *Consort for True Violins* (1965); *The Big Haul* for Cello (1973); *The Thunderbolt* for Men's Chorus and Percussion (1980). **OTHER:** Orchestration of Ives's *Concord Sonata* as *A Concord Symphony* (Ottawa, June 16, 1995); Completion of Schubert's B minor Sym. (Vienna, Oct. 14, 1997).—**NS/LK/DM**

Brant, Jan, Polish composer and theologian; b. probably in Poznan, 1554; d. Lwów, May 27, 1602. He entered the Jesuit order in 1571, and was ordained in 1578; he then studied theology in Rome. He returned to Poland in 1584, and subsequently held positions in a number of Polish convents. Some of his MSS were discovered in 1972 in the archives of the Univ. of Uppsala.—NS/LK/DM

Brant, Per, Swedish violinist, composer, and poet; b. Uppland, Dec. 1714; d. Stockholm, Aug. 9, 1767. He settled in Stockholm in 1727. In 1735 he joined the royal chapel, where he was made Konzertmeister in 1738 and Kapellmeister in 1745. From 1758 until at least 1765 he served as principal court Kapellmeister. Various works attributed to him have also been claimed for Johan Helmich Roman.—LK/DM

Branzell, Karin Maria, noted Swedish contralto; b. Stockholm, Sept. 24, 1891; d. Altadena, Calif., Dec. 14, 1974. She was a pupil of Thekla Hofer in Stockholm, Louis Bachner in Berlin, and Enrico Rosati in N.Y. In 1912 she made her operatic debut as Prince Sarvilaka in d'Albert's *Izeÿl* in Stockholm, where she sang at the Royal Opera until 1918; then was a member of the Berlin State Opera until 1923. On Feb. 6, 1924, she made her Metropolitan Opera debut in N.Y. as Fricka in *Die Walküre*, and remained on the roster until 1944; sang there again in 1951. She also appeared at the Bayreuth Festivals (1930–31), London's Covent Garden (1935; 1937–38), and the San Francisco Opera (1941). In later years she taught at the Juilliard School of Music in N.Y. The exceptional range of her voice allowed her to sing both contralto and soprano roles. Although especially known for such Wagnerian roles as Ortrud, Venus, Erda, Brangäne, and the *Walküre* Brünnhilde, she also was admired as Amneris, Dalila, Herodias, and Clytemnestra.—NS/LK/DM

Braslau, Sophie, American contralto; b. N.Y., Aug. 16, 1892; d. there, Dec. 22, 1935. She studied with Arturo Buzzi-Peccia. On Nov. 27, 1913, she made her Metropolitan Opera debut in N.Y. as the voice in *Parsifal*, followed by her formal debut there the next day as Fyodor in *Boris Godunov*; remained on its roster until 1920, creating Cadman's Shanewis on March 23, 1918. She gave concerts throughout the U.S., and in 1931 made a tour of Europe. In 1934 she sang for the last time in N.Y.—NS/LK/DM

Brassart, Johannes or **Jean,** composer who flourished in the first half of the 15th century. He was active in Liège at the collegiate church of St. Jean l'Evangeliste (1422–31) and at St. Lambert Cathedral (1428–31). In 1431 he was in Rome as a member of the papal choir. After serving at the chapel of the Council of Basel (1433–34), he was rector capelle to the emperors Sigismund, Albert II, and Friedrich III (1434–43?). He also was a canon in the church of Our Lady in Tongres. Among his extant works are 10 mass movements, 8 Introit settings, 4 motets, and 10 other sacred pieces. See K. Mixter, ed., *J. B.: Opera omnia,* Corpus Mensurabilis Musicae, XXXV/1–2 (1965–71).—LK/DM

Brassin, Louis, French pianist; b. Aix-la-Chapelle, June 24, 1840; d. St. Petersburg, May 17, 1884. He was a pupil of Moscheles at the Leipzig Cons., and made concert tours with his brothers Leopold and Gerhard. He then taught at the Stern Cons. in Berlin (1866), the Brussels Cons. (1869–79), and the St. Petersburg Cons. He publ. the valuable *École moderne du piano,* and also composed 2 piano concertos, salon pieces for piano, and songs. His effective piano transcription of the Magic Fire music from *Die Walküre* is well known.—NS/LK/DM

Brätel, Ulrich, German composer; b. c. 1495; d. Stuttgart, 1544 or 1545. After working at the Vienna, Hungarian, Polish, and Heidelberg courts, he was in the service of Duke Ulrich of Württemberg in Stuttgart (from 1534). He composed many works for the Reformed church liturgy, secular vocal pieces, and instrumental music.—LK/DM

Braud (Breaux), Wellman, jazz bassist; b. St. James Parish, La., Jan. 25, 1891; d. La., Oct. 27, 1966. A major force in the early Ellington band, he was one of those who brought, at Ellington's instigation, a New Orleans influence into the music. He began playing violin at the age of seven, later played violin and bass in string trios in New Orleans, including residency at Tom Anderson's Cabaret; he also learned to play the trombone. He moved to Chicago in 1917, toured with John H. Wickliffe's Band, then joined the Original Creole Orch. at the Pekin Cafe, Chicago; played with this band at Dreamland and De Lure Cafe, then joined Charlie Elgar's Orch. c. 1922. He traveled to London with the Plantation Orch. in March–May 1923, doubling string bass and trombone. He returned to N.Y., worked a spell with Wilbur Sweatman, then played for various revues, including *7–11 Burlesque Company* (1926), and Vaughn's *Lucky Sambo* (1926–27). He joined Duke Ellington in mid-1927 and remained until May 1935 (sharing bass duties with Billy Taylor for last few months). He left to organize a band with Jimmy Noone for residency at their own short-lived Vodvil Club on 132nd Street, N.Y., with Kaiser Marshall Band, then late in 1935 became player-manager of The Spirits of Rhythm. He formed his own trio in 1937, which he led for several years, combining this work with many other bands including: Hot Lips Page (1938), Edgar Hayes (1939), Sidney Bechet (1940–41), Al Sears (1943), Garvin Bushell (1944), etc. He subbed in Duke Ellington's Orch. (summer 1944), then worked regularly in N.Y. with Garvin Bushell's Band (1944). He left full-time music to manage a pool hall and meat-marketing business, but continued to do regular gigs, including week-end work with Bunk Johnson in N.Y. (November 1947). In early 1956 he returned to full-time music and joined Kid Ory (touring Europe with Ory later that year). During the 1960s he lived in Calif.; worked with Joe Darensbourg (1960). He suffered a mild heart attack in the summer of 1961, and celebrated his return to good health by sitting in with Duke Ellington in autumn 1961. He worked regularly accompanying folksinger Barbara Dane in San Francisco, with brief spells of semi-retirement. In the early autumn of 1966 he toured Ore. with pianist Kenny Woodson. Shortly afterward he suffered a fatal heart attack at his home in Los Angeles.

Disc.: Duke Ellington: *Saturday Night Function* (1929); "Misty Mornin'/Saratoga Swing" (1929); *Double Check Stomp* (1930). S. Greer: *Saturday Night Function* (1929). J.R. Morton: "Sweet Substitute/Panama" (1940). Bechet-Spanier Big Four: "Sweet Lorraine/Lazy River" (1940). B. Johnson: *Last Testament of a Great Jazzman* (1947). K. Ory: *The Legendary Kid.*—JC/LP

Braun, family of German musicians:

(1) Anton Braun, instrumentalist and composer; b. Ober-Beisheim, near Bad Hersfeld, Jan. 20, 1729; d. Kassel, April 26, 1798. He settled in Kassel about 1743 and became an oboist in the military band. In 1760 he was made first violinist and copyist of the court orch. Five of his children became musicians:

(2) Johann Braun, violinist and composer; b. Kassel, Aug. 29, 1753; d. Berlin, Jan. 1, 1811. He studied with his father, and then with C.A. Pesch (violin) and J.G. Schwanenberg (theory and composition) in Braunschweig. Returning to Kassel, he was first violinist in the court orch. from about 1780 until it was disbanded in 1785. After serving as a music teacher at the court, he was called to Berlin in 1788 as Konzertmeister to Queen Friederike of Prussia. Among his extant works are Simphonie concertante for 2 Horns and Orch., 2 cello concertos, a Concerto for Clarinet, 2 Horns, and Orch., and 12 string trios.

(3) Johann Friedrich Braun, oboist and composer; b. Kassel, Sept. 15, 1758; d. Ludwigslust, Sept. 15, 1824. He studied with his father and with C.S. Barth in Kassel before completing his training with the oboist Carlo Besozzi in Dresden. From 1777 he was oboist in the Ludwigslust court orch. He also made tours as a virtuoso in Germany and Denmark. In 1786 he married the court singer Friederice Louise Ulrica Kunzen, the daughter of C.A. Kunzen. He wrote a Sinfonia at 8, at least 6 oboe concertos, and various chamber pieces featuring the oboe and other instruments. He had two sons who became musicians: **(a) Carl Anton Philipp Braun** (b. Ludwigslust, Dec. 26, 1798; d. Rommehed, Sweden, June 11, 1835), an oboist and composer. He studied oboe with his father. In 1807 he was called to Copenhagen by his uncle, F.L.A. Kunzen, the court conductor, to serve as a chamber musician at the royal court. After giving concerts in Germany (1811–13), he settled in Stockholm as a member of the court orch. (1815). Later he was conductor of the military band. He composed 6 syms., other orch. works, much chamber music, and some vocal pieces. **(b) Wilhelm Theodor Johannes Braun** (b. Ludwigslust, Sept. 20, 1796; d. Schwerin, May 12, 1867), an oboist and composer. He studied with his father. In 1824 he married his cousin, the singer Kathinka Braun. In 1825 he was named his father's successor in Ludwigslust, where his wife became court singer. After the court was removed to Schwerin in 1837, he remained in its service there until 1856. He wrote an Oboe Concerto, a Clarinet Concerto, 6 overtures, and other orch. works, much chamber music, and various keyboard pieces.

(4) Maria Louise Braun, singer, mandolinist, and pianist; b. Kassel, Oct. 22, 1762; d. Munich, April 7, 1834. She pursued her career in Kassel until her marriage in 1797.

(5) Moriz Braun, violinist and bassoonist; b. Kassel, May 7, 1765; d. Würzburg, Nov. 16, 1828. He joined the Kassel court orch. as a violinist when he was twelve. After suffering a finger injury, he took up the bassoon, and from 1787 played in the Würzburg archiepiscopal court orch. He also made successful tours in Germany. He had two children who became musicians: Katharina Maria Louise Braun (b. Würzburg, March 24, 1799; d. Ludwigslust, June 8, 1832), a singer, who in 1824 married her cousin, the oboist and composer Wilhelm Theodor Johannes Braun. In 1825 she went with him to Ludwigslust, where she became a court singer. Joseph Braun (b. Würzburg, 1804; d. there, April 4, 1861), a bassoonist and composer. He served as a musician at the Fürstenberg court in Donaueschingen.—LK/DM

Braun, Carl, German bass; b. Meisenheim, Prussia, June 2, 1885; d. Hamburg, April 19, 1960. He studied with Hermann Gausche in Kreuznach and later with Eugen Robert Weiss. He sang at the Wiesbaden Opera (1906–11) and at the Vienna Court Opera (1911–12); then was engaged at the Berlin City Opera (1912–14). He also appeared at the Bayreuth Festivals (1906–31). On Feb. 8, 1913, he made his American debut at the Metropolitan Opera in N.Y. as King Marke, but was dismissed as an enemy alien in the spring of 1917 when the U.S. entered the war against Germany. In 1922–23 he made a South American tour; also sang in the U.S. in 1928 and 1931. In 1933 he was engaged as a stage director at the German Opera in Berlin, and in 1935–36 held similar posts at the Berlin Volksoper and at the Danzig Municipal Theater. In 1937 he retired from the stage and was thereafter active mainly as a concert agent in Hamburg. He was particularly esteemed for his Wagnerian roles. —NS/LK/DM

Braun, Peter Michael, German composer, teacher, pianist, and conductor; b. Wuppertal, Dec. 2, 1936. He was a pupil of Martin, Bernd Alois Zimmermann, and Eimert at the Cologne Hochschule für Musik and of Giselher Klebe at the Detmold Hochschule für Musik. In 1978 he became a prof. of composition and theory at the Heidelberg-Mannheim Hochschule für Musik. He publ. a book on harmony and music theory (Cologne, 2000). His style is governed by structural and spectral considerations.

Works: DRAMATIC: Opera: *Eichendorff* (1974–92); *Die Schöne lau* (1984–86); *Die Juden* (1994–95). **ORCH.:** *Seliger Kontrapunkt* for Strings (1952; 1988–91); *Scherzo* (1956–91); *Exkursion* (1958–71); *Interstellar* for 4 Orch. Groups (1959); *Transfer* (1965–68); *Variété* (1965–69); *Landschaft* (1966–71); *Problems and Solutions* for Strings (1973–74); *Junctim* (1974–75; rev. 1988); *Ambiente* (1974–76); *Serenata Palatina* (1975–82); *Ballett* for Orch. and Speaker ad libitum (1980–87); *Recherche* (1983–85). **CHAMBER:** *Zwei Fantasien* for 4 Recorders (1952–83); *Fantasie-Quartett* for Horns (1952–84); String Quartet (1957); Piano Trio (1958); *Terms* for Chamber Ensemble (1962–71); *Miró* for Flute and Piano, after 3 paintings of Joan Miró (1976; rev. 1989); *Drei Choräle* for 4 Trombones or 3 Cellos and Double Bass or 4 Bassoons and Contrabassoon (1979); *Man liebt Brahms*, 2 retrospectives for Violin and Cello (1986; also for Violin and

Harp, 1987); Duo for Violin and Piano (1988; also for Flute and Piano, 1989); *Kontemplation "on minimal art"* for Flute or Violin and Piano (1988); *Arc-en-ciel* for Bass or Alto Flute (1992); piano pieces; organ music. **VOCAL:** *Entelechie* for 6 Solo Voices or Chorus and Orch. (1972); *Kashima Kiko* for Alto or Baritone and Small Orch. (1977); *Arie* for Soprano and Orch. (1977–80); *Alborada* for Soprano and Orch. (1987); choral pieces; songs. **ELECTRONIC:** *Ereignisse: Hommage à Edgard Varèse* (1966–68); *Essay*, 3 pieces (1971); *Klangsonden* (1976). —NS/LK/DM

Braun, Wilhelm
See **Brown, William**

Braunfels, Walter, German composer and pedagogue; b. Frankfurt am Main, Dec. 19, 1882; d. Cologne, March 19, 1954. He studied piano in Vienna with Leschetizky and composition in Munich with Thuille. In 1925 he became a co-director of the Hochschule für Musik in Cologne. With the advent of the Nazi regime in 1933, he was compelled to abandon teaching; after the collapse of the Third Reich in 1945, he reorganized the Hochschule für Musik in Cologne and served as its director until 1950. He excelled mainly as an opera composer; the following operas are notable: *Falada* (Essen, May 24, 1906); *Prinzessin Brambilla* (Stuttgart, March 25, 1909; rev. 1931); *Ulenspiegel* (Stuttgart, Nov. 9, 1913); *Die Vögel*, after Aristophanes (Munich, Dec. 4, 1920; his most successful opera); *Don Gil von den grünen Hosen* (Munich, Nov. 15, 1924); *Der glaserne Berg* (Krefeld, Dec. 4, 1928); *Galatea* (Cologne, Jan. 26, 1930); *Der Traum, Ein Leben* (1937); *Die heilige Johanna* (1942); also a mystery play, *Verkündigung*, after Paul Claudel (1936). He further wrote 2 piano concertos; Organ Concerto; *Revelation of St. John* for Tenor, Double Chorus, and Orch.; piano music and songs. He believed in the artistic and practical value of Wagnerian leading motifs; in his harmonies he was close to Richard Strauss, but he also applied impressionistic devices related to Debussy.—NS/LK/DM

Bravničar, Matija, Slovenian composer and teacher; b. Tolmin, Feb. 24, 1897; d. Ljubljana, Nov. 25, 1977. After service in the Austrian army (1915–18) he was a violinist at the opera theater in Ljubljana; meanwhile he studied composition at the Cons. there, graduating in 1932. He was director of the Ljubljana Academy of Music (1945–49) where he later taught composition (1952–68); was president of the Soc. of Slovenian Composers (1949–52) and of the Union of Yugoslavian Composers (1953–57). In his works, he cultivated a neo-Classical style, with thematic material strongly influenced by the melorhythmic inflections of Slovenian folk music.

WORKS: DRAMATIC: *Pohujšanje v dolini Sentflorijanski* (Scandal in St. Florian's Valley), opera buffa (Ljubljana, May 11, 1930); *Stoji, stoji Ljubljanca*, satirical revue (Ljubljana, Dec. 2, 1933); *Hlapec Jernij in njegova pravica* (Knight Jernej and His Justice), opera (Ljubljana, Jan. 25, 1941). **ORCH.:** *Hymnus Slavicus* (1931; Ljubljana, May 14, 1932); *Kralj Matjaž* (King Mattias), overture (Ljubljana, Nov. 14, 1932); *Slavik Dance Burlesques* (1932); *Divertissements* for Piano and Strings (1933);

Belokranjska rapsodija (1938); *Simfonična antiteza* (Symphonic Antithesis; 1940; Ljubljana, Feb. 9, 1948); 3 syms.: No. 1 (1947; Ljubljana, Feb. 20, 1951), No. 2 (1951; Ljubljana, Oct. 27, 1952), and No. 3 (1956); *Kurent*, symphonic poem (1950); *Plesne metamorfoze* (1955); *Marcia-Rondo* (1960); Violin Concerto (1961); Horn Concerto (1963); *Fantasia rapsodica* for Violin and Orch. (1967); *Simfonični plesi* (Symphonic Dances; 1969). **CHAMBER:** *Elegie* for Horn and Piano (1929); 2 wind quintets (1930, 1968); Trio for Flute, Clarinet, and Bassoon (1930); *Dialog* for Cello and Piano (1965); Sonata for Solo Violin (1966); piano pieces.—NS/LK/DM

Braxton, Anthony, avant-garde jazz alto saxophonist, contrabass clarinetist, composer, pianist; b. Chicago, June 4, 1945. He studied at Chicago School of Music (1959–63), and began playing alto saxophone at age 17, influenced by Roscoe Mitchell. His other early influences included Paul Desmond, Warne Marsh, Charlie Parker, John Coltrane, Ornette Coleman, Eric Dolphy, and composer-theorists such as John Cage and Karlheinz Stockhausen. Braxton studied harmony, composition, and philosophy. In 1966, he joined AACM and taught harmony. His album *For Alto* was the first complete LP for unaccompanied saxophone. In 1967, he formed Creative Construction Company with Leroy Jenkins and Leo Smith; they joined Steve McCall in Paris (1969) for concerts and recordings. Braxton moved to N.Y. where he played in the improvisation ensemble Musica Elettronica Viva (1970). In 1970–71, he toured in Circle with Chick Corea, Dave Holland, and Barry Altschul. His output in the 1970s included compositions for his various groups as well as for large band and piano, for 100 tubas, and for four amplified shovels and a coal pile. *For Four Orchestras*, a two-hour piece that was recorded by four conductors and 160 musicians in 1978, is a prime example of Braxton's more complex works, which revolve around theater, dance, opera, and multiple orchestras. Unfortunately, Braxton had to finance the *Four Orchestras* recording himself, and by the early 1980s the Braxton family was living in poverty in upstate N.Y., in a telephoneless house heated by burning logs in a fireplace. However in 1990, he was hired as a full-time professor at Wesleyan Univ., and in 1994 he received a five-year MacArthur Foundation fellowship. The prize came shortly after the second book about him was published. Braxton is one of the most discussed figures in the avant-garde. He is often lampooned for his cerebral way of discussing music and his drawings and diagrams that serve as titles for many of his pieces, and for his rather heavy tonguing, but in performance, he is thoroughly intense and emotionally committed.

DISC.: *Three Compositions of New Jazz* (1968); *For Alto Saxophone* (1968); *Together Alone* (1971); *Complete Braxton* (1971); *Saxophone Improvisations* (1972); *Quartet Live at Moers New Jazz* (1974); *N.Y.* (1974); *In the Tradition, Vols. 1–2* (1974); *Montreux / Berlin Concerts* (1975); *Dortmund* (1976); *Creative Orchestra Music* (1976); *For Four Orchestras* (1978); *Birth and Rebirth* (1978); *Alto Saxophone Improvisations* (1978); *With Robert Schumann String Quartet* (1979); *For Two Pianos* (1980); *Open Aspects* (1982); *Seven Standards* (1985); *Six Monk's Compositions* (1987); *Voigt Kol Nidre* (1988); *London Solo* (1988); *Ensemble* (1988); *19 (Solo) Compositions* (1988); *Vancouver Duets* (1989); *Tristano Compositions* (1989);

Eugene (1989); *Willisau* (1991); *Wesleyan* (1992); *Twelve Compositions* (1993); *Charlie Parker Project* (1993); *Composition 174 for 10 percussionists and tape* (1995); *Composition 175* (1995); *Trilium M* (1995); *Two Lines* (1995); *Knitting Factory* (1995).—**LP/NS**

Bread, one of the defining bands in 1970s soft, middle-of-the-road rock, formed 1969, L.A. **MEMBERSHIP:** David Gates, voc., gtr., kybd. (b. Tulsa, Okla., Dec. 11, 1940); James Griffin, voc., gtr; (b. Nashville, Tenn.); Rob Royer, kybd.; Mike Botts, drm. (b. Sacramento, Calif.).

David Gates' father, who directed the band and orchestra for the local high school, warned his son against playing music for a living, but Gates went after it anyway. He hooked up with his girlfriend's brother, Leon Russell. Their band backed the likes of Chuck Berry and Carl Perkins when they came to town. They also made money by booking halls and playing dances.

Russell moved to Calif., and Gates followed. He started picking up session work, and even some production, including the first single for Captain Beefheart. One of those jobs for a duo called Pleasure Faire intrigued him. They decided to join forces. Pleasure Faire's members were fairly well known in the L.A. music community. James Griffin (b. Nashville, Tenn.) and Rob Royer had cowritten "For All We Know" for the film *Lover's and Other Strangers*, which would win an Oscar later that year. Royer had also recorded an album for Reprise. They changed the name of the band to Bread.

Their first record didn't even break the Top 100. Deciding to give it one more shot before calling it a day, they added drummer Mike Botts (b. Sacramento, Calif.) and recorded *On the Water*. The album generated the #1 hit "Make It with You." It became the first of a dozen hit singles and seven gold albums for the band. While they recorded some more up-tempo pop like "Let Your Love Go" (later used to advertise furniture) and "Mother Freedom," they only managed to hit #28 and #37 respectively. It was the band's soft hits that made their name. "If" (#4, 1971), one of the biggest wedding songs of the 1970s, would be covered by some 200 artists ranging from Frank Sinatra and Johnny Mathis to the Baja Marimba Band and Telly Savalas. Other hits included "It Don't Matter to Me" (#10, 1970) and "Baby I'm-a Want You" (#3 and gold, 1971).

Royer left the band in 1971 to write screenplays. Replacing him with Larry Knechtel, Bread continued their hit streak: "Everything I Own" (#5, 1972), "Diary" (#15, 1972), "The Guitar Man" (#11, 1972), "Sweet Surrender" (#15, 1972), and "Aubrey" (#15, 1973). However, Griffin and Gates ceased to get along and the group broke up.

Gates had a minor solo hit, "Never Let Her Go" (#29, 1975), but the band reformed in 1976, recording the #9 hit "Lost without Your Love." The reunion didn't last. Botts joined Linda Ronstadt's band. Gates had a couple of more hits, the theme song from the Neil Simon film *The Goodbye Girl* (#15, 1978) and "Took the Last Train" (#30, 1978). He continued to record and produce, recording *Love Is Always 17* in 1994 and working on country artist Billy Dean's 1998 LP. In 1997, Bread went out on a year-long 25th anniversary tour.

DISC.: *Bread* (1969); *On the Waters* (1970); *Manna* (1971); *Baby I'm-a Want You* (1972); *Best of Bread* (1972); *Guitar Man* (1972); *Best of Volume 2* (1974); *Anthology* (1985).—**HB**

Bream, Julian (Alexander), noted English guitarist and lutenist; b. London, July 15, 1933. He was educated at the Royal Coll. of Music in London. He made his debut at the age of 17. In 1960 he founded the Julian Bream Consort; also directed the Semley Festival of Music and Poetry from 1971. Through his numerous concerts and recordings, he has helped to revive interest in Elizabethan lute music. He was named an Officer of the Order of the British Empire in 1964, and a Commander of the Order of the British Empire in 1985.

BIBL.: T. Palmer, *J. B.: A Life on the Road* (London, 1982); S. Button, *J. B.: The Foundations of a Musical Career* (Aldershot, 1997).—**NS/LK/DM**

Brecker, Michael, pop-jazz tenor saxophonist, brother of **Randy Brecker;** b. Philadelphia, March 29, 1949. He grew up in a musical family and his father is a jazz pianist. As a child, he shared his brother's love of R&B; he began playing the clarinet at seven, switched to alto sax, and then tenor. He studied under Vince Trombetta and Joe Allard and Charles Banacos in the mid 1960s, and cut his teeth in local bands before being turned onto jazz through the recordings of Miles Davis, Cannonball Adderley, and John Coltrane while studying at the Univ. of Ind. Michael originally intended to become a doctor, but one of his teachers convinced him that he should be in music. In 1970, after about one semester, he left college and joined Randy in N.Y.; his first professional work was with Edwin Birdsong in another R&B outfit which also featured Billy Cobham, who soon became a close friend and accomplice of both brothers. They also both made the first of a number of hard-driving recordings with Hal Galper, first as part of his Guerrilla Band and later as part of an acoustic jazz group. Later that year, the Breckers formed the fusion group Dreams, which recorded two albums for Columbia Records before disbanding in 1971. Michael and Randy would continue to work in tandem, teamed together in 1973 as the front line for Horace Silver's quintet, and again in 1974 recording and touring with Cobham. In 1975, they formed a funk-based band and released their debut album as The Brecker Brothers. Over the next six years, The Brecker Brothers would release six widely acclaimed albums, earning seven Grammy nominations along the way. Described by the *New York Times* as having "the most valid blend of jazz and rock than any group has yet achieved," the two brothers created, according to *Down Beat*, "the most widely recognized and most influential horn sound of the 1970s." That sound appeared to be a development of wind parts to be found in early Kool and the Gang and instrumental JB's albums c. 1969–74. During the late 1970s, Michael became one of the most sought after session musicians and played on a freelance basis with everyone from Charles Mingus, James Taylor, Horace Silver, Eric Clapton, John Lennon, Yoko Ono's touring group, and a series of Average White Band albums. In

1977, Michael and Randy opened up a jazz club in lower Manhattan called Seventh Avenue South, a place where all the great names on the scene would stop by and play. Around 1979–80, he was recruited by Joni Mitchell to join with an all-star band including Pat Metheny and Jaco Pastorius to tour and record Joni's acclaimed album *Shadows and Light* and a concert video. At Seventh Avenue South, the band Steps evolved through some informal late-night jams between Michael, Mike Mainieri, Steve Gadd, Don Grolnick, and Eddie Gomez. Conceived in 1979 as an acoustic ensemble, the quintet grew into a high-powered fusion band with the advent of MIDI technology and later changed their name to Steps Ahead. Brecker consulted with Nyle Steiner, inventor of the EWI (electronic wind instrument), a wind-driven synth controller that put MIDI at his fingertips and used his own custom built model until Akai released the EWI commercially. He recorded six albums with the band, three under the name Steps, and three under the name Steps Ahead. Michael also continued touring and recording as a soloist and sideman on various projects, working with Pat Metheny, Chick Corea, Jaco Pastorius and arranger Claus Ogerman. During the period 1980–81, he overcame a longstanding problem with heroin addiction by going through a rehab program. His busy studio schedule has included work with Frank Sinatra, Billy Joel, Steely Dan, and Bruce Springsteen. He took up the role of bandleader on *Michael Brecker*, an album released in 1987 that was named "Jazz Album of the Year" by both *Downbeat* and *Jazziz* magazines, and nominated for two grammys; it was the No. 1 album on *Billboard*'s Jazz Chart for 21 weeks. In 1988, Brecker's second solo album, *Don't Try This at Home*, won the Grammy for "Best Jazz Instrumental Performance." In addition to headlining around the world with his own band, Brecker took time out that year for a stint as featured soloist with Herbie Hancock's Headhunters II band. He toured with Paul Simon as featured soloist to support the *Rhythm of the Saints* album. Once back home in 1992, Michael reunited with his brother Randy for a much anticipated world tour and GRP recording, *Return of the Brecker Brothers*. Three Grammy nominations and a year of touring later, the brothers returned to the studio in the fall of 1994 to record *Out of the Loop*. This time not only did they win the Grammy for Best Contemporary Jazz Performance, Michael won a Grammy for Best Instrumental Composition for "African Skies." In addition to touring throughout the U.S. and Europe in 1995, the Brecker Brothers were the first international contemporary jazz group to perform in the People's Republic of China, playing before sell-out crowds in Beijing and Shanghai. In 1995, he toured with McCoy Tyner. In the summer of 1997, he played with Pat Metheny at the Montreal Jazz Festival and in Japan in August 1997. As of June 1998, he has appeared on over 450 albums. A true virtuoso, Brecker has gone from early work in fusion and jazz-rock to one of the most in-demand studio musicians, accompanying all kinds of artists, to one of the most influential saxophonists today in all idioms including acoustic jazz. Heavily influenced by Coltrane, he uniquely adapted many of Coltrane's methods for use in fusion and funk contexts.

DISC.: *Michael Brecker* (1987); *Don't Try This at Home* (1988); *Now You See It ... Now You Don't* (1990); *The Michael Brecker Band Live* (1993); *The Cost of Living* (1994); *Two Block from the Edge* (1998). R. Brecker: *Score* (1968); *Dreams: Dreams* (1970); *Imagine My Suprise* (1972). H. Silver: *In Pursuit of the 27th Man* (1972). H. Galper: *The Guerilla Band* (1973); *Reach Out* (1976); *Speak with a Single Voice* (1978); *Brecker Brothers: Back to Back* (1975); *Brecker Brothers* (1975); *Heavy Metal Be–Bop* (1978); *Détente* (1980); *Don't Stop the Music* (1980); *Straphanging* (1980); *Return of the Brecker Brothers* (1992); *Out of the Loop* (1994); *Live* (1994). B. Springsteen: *Born to Run* (1975). B. Cobham: *Crosswind* (1974); *Funky Thide of Sings* (1975). C. Ogerman: *Gate of Dreams* (1976); *Cityscape* (1982); *Featuring Michael Brecker* (1991). J. Brackeem: *Tring-A-Ling* (1977). C. Mingus: *Me, Myself and Eye* (1978); M. Nock: *In Out and Around* (1978). P. Metheny: *1980–81* (1980); J. Mitchell: *Shadows and Light* (1980). H. Hancock: *Magic Windows* (1981); *Steps: Smokin' in the Pit* (1981); *Step By Step* (1981); *Paradox* (1982); *Steps Ahead* (1983). C. Corea: *Three Quartets* (1981). F. Sinatra: *L.A. Is My Lady* (1984); *Steps Ahead: Smokin' in the Pit: Live!* (1982); *Modern Times* (1984); *Live in Tokyo* (1986); *N.Y.C.* (1989); *Vibe* (1994); *Magnetic* (1986); *Yin-Yang* (1992). D. Grolnick: *Hearts and Numbers* (1985); *Weaver of Dreams* (1990). P. Simon: *Rhythm of the Saints* (1990). H. Hancock: *The Herbie Hancock Quartet Live* (1998).

BIBL.: C. Coan, *Michael Brecker Solos* (Hal Leonard, 1995). —LP/DD

Brecker, Randy, pop-jazz trumpeter, flugelhornist, brother of **Michael Brecker;** b. Philadelphia, Nov. 27, 1945. His first instrument was the piano, which his father played professionally; his love of R&B led him to take up the trumpet while in high school. While studying classical trumpet at school, Randy would play with local R&B bands at night. He attended the Univ. of Ind. but quit early to pursue a career as a professional musician; in 1966, he moved to N.Y. and a year later joined Blood, Sweat and Tears, before playing with Horace Silver, Art Blakey, and Duke Pearson. He was first spotted around N.Y. in a prize-winning youth quintet along with David Liebman and Cameron Brown, then featured with Duke Pearson's big band and other groups. At he same time, he was playing with rock and pop luminaries such as Janis Joplin and Stevie Wonder and this diversity informed his next move. In 1970, his brother Michael had joined him in N.Y. and together they formed the jazz-rock group Dreams; although they had very little success at this time, they found universal critical acclaim and commercial success in their subsequent fusion band, The Brecker Brothers. (See entry for Michael Brecker.) He then worked with Billy Cobham, Larry Coryell, and Lew Tabackin, before forming a band which he led with his wife, Eliane Elias. In 1998, he earned a Grammy nomination for Best Contemporary Jazz Performance. His record release party for *Into the Sun* at SOB's was aired on NHK television in Japan; he co-headlined a tour of the U.K. with Billy Cobham in 1998.

DISC.: *Score* (1969); *Imagine My Surprise* (1971); *Detente* (1979); *Amanda* (1985); *In the Idiom* (1986); *Toe to Toe* (1990); *Live at Sweet Basil* (1992); *Into the Sun* (1998).

BIBL.: M. A. Davison, *A Motivic Study of Twenty Improvised Solos of Randy Brecker Between the Years 1970–1980* (Univ. of Wisc., 1987).—LP

Brecknock, John, English tenor; b. Long Eaton, Nov. 29, 1937. He studied with Frederic Sharp and Dennis Dowling at the Birmingham School of Music. In 1967 he made his debut as Alfred in *Die Fledermaus* at the Sadler's Wells Opera in London, and continued to sing with fine success; also appeared at the Glyndebourne Festival (1971) and at London's Covent Garden (debut as Fenton, 1974). On March 23, 1977, he made his Metropolitan Opera debut in N.Y. as Tamino. He also appeared in various European operatic centers. Although best known for such roles as Mozart's Belmonte and Ottavio, Rossini's Count Almaviva and Comte Ory, and Verdi's Duke of Mantua, he also sang in contemporary roles.—NS/LK/DM

Bredemeyer, Reiner, German composer; b. Velez, Colombia, Feb. 2, 1929. He studied composition with Karl Höller at the Akademie der Tonkunst in Munich (1949–53); then took courses with Wagner-Regény at the Akademie der Künste in East Berlin (1955–57). In 1961 he was appointed conductor of the German Theater in East Berlin; in 1978 he joined the faculty of the Akademie der Künste there. In his music he is an astute experimenter, but he adheres to the tenets of classical forms and avoids the extremes of modernism.

WORKS: DRAMATIC: *Leben der Andrea,* opera after Brecht's *Galileo* (1971); *Die Galoschenoper,* after *The Beggar's Opera* (1978); *Candide,* after Voltaire (1981–82; Halle, Jan. 12, 1986). **ORCH.:** *Integration* (1961); *Variante* (1962); Violin Concerto (1963); *Komposition* for 56 Strings (1964); *Spiel* (1964); *Schlagstück* 3 for Orch. and 3 Percussion Groups (1966); *Bagatellen für B.* for Piano and Orch. (1970); *Spiel zu 45* (1970); *Piano und...,* piano concerto (1972); *Oktoberstück* (1973); Sym. (1974); *Anfangen—aufhören* (1974); Double Concerto for Harpsichord, Oboe, and Orch. (1974); *2 tempi* for Flute, Recorder, and Strings (1976); *Auftakte* for 3 Orch. Groups (1976); Concerto for Oboe and Strings (1977); *4 Pieces* (1979); *9 Bagatelles* for Strings (1984); *3 Pieces* for 2 Orch. Groups (1986); Horn Concerto (1986); *Sonatas I-III* (1988); *Vermasseltes Doppel, NOK,* oboe concerto (1994). **CHAMBER:** Quintet for Flute, Clarinet, Violin, Cello, and Double Bass (1956); Concertino for 12 (1957); Octet (1959); 2 woodwind quintets (1959, 1969); *Schlagstück 1* for Percussionist (1960), 2 for Piano and Percussion (1965), and 5 for Piano and Percussion (1970); 3 string quartets (1961, 1968, 1983); String Quintet (1962); *5 Pieces* for Oboe and 3 Bassoons (1964); *6 Serenades* for various instrumental combinations (1966–80); *Pointing* for 18 String Instruments (1966); Sonata for Violin, Viola, and Piano (1967); *Schlagquartett* for Piano, Double Bass, and 2 Percussionists (1967); *Ab 14* for Piano and 13 String Instruments (1971); *(Cello)²*for Cello and Tape (1971); *8 Pieces* for String Trio (1971); *6 Solos* for Various Instruments (1973–80); *(Oboe)²*for Oboe and Tape (1975); *Grosses Duet* for 2 Instrumental Groups (1975); *Piano und...⁵*for Piano, Flute, Horn, Trombone, Cello, and Double Bass (1976); *Interludium* for Soprano Saxophone, Flute, Cello, Double Bass, and Percussion (1977); *Piano und...⁶*for Piano, 2 Cellos, Wind Instrument, and 3 Percussionists (1977); *Still Leben? mit Gitarre* for Guitar and 4 Trombones (1978); *5 Blechstücke* for 2 Trumpets and 2 Trombones (1979); *D für Paul Dessau* for 15 String Instruments (1980); *Septet 80* for 2 Oboes, Cello, Double Bass, Percussion, Trombone, and Harpsichord (1980); *Septet 87* for 2 Guitars, Percussion, and String Quartet (1987); *Vorwahl 522 (Kein Anschluss unter dieser Nummer?)* for Chamber Ensemble (1989). **VOCAL:** *Cantata* for Alto and Women's Chorus (1961); *Wostock* for Chorus and Orch.

(1961); *Karthago* for Chorus and Chamber Ensemble (1961); *Sätze und Sentenzen* for Chorus and Orch. (1963); *Canto* for Alto, Men's Chorus, and 10 Instruments (1965); *Synchronisiert-Asynchron* for Soprano, Oboe, Bassoon, Cello, Piano, Percussion, and Tape (1975); *Zum 13. 7. (Für Schönberg)* for Woman's Voice, Clarinet, Saxophone, and Percussion (1976); *Cantata 2* for 16 Voices and 16 Instruments (1977); *Madrigal, Rezitativ und Arie* for Tenor and 8 Instruments (1979); *Das Alltägliche* for Soprano, Tenor, and Orch. (1980); *Musica Vivarese* for Soprano, Bass Chorus, and Instruments (1982); *Die Winterreise* for Baritone, Horn, and Piano, after Wilhelm Müller (1984); *Lieder auf der Flucht* for Mezzo-soprano and Piano (1986); *Die schöne Müllerin* for Baritone, String Quartet, and Horn Quartet, after Müller (1986; Berlin, Feb. 21, 1987); *Post-modern* for Chorus and 4 Horns (1988).—NS/LK/DM

Brediceanu, Tiberiu, Romanian composer, administrator, and music editor; b. Lugoj, Transylvania, April 2, 1877; d. Bucharest, Dec. 19, 1968. He studied music mainly in Romania. He was director of the Astra Cons. in Brasov (1934–40) and director-general of the Romanian Opera in Bucharest (1941–44). He publ. valuable collections of Romanian songs and dances, including 170 Romanian folk melodies, 810 tunes of the Banat regions, and 1,000 songs of Transylvania.

WORKS: DRAMATIC: Opera: *Poemul muzical etnografic* (1905; rev. and retitled *Romania in port, joc si cintec,* 1929); *La şezătoare* (1908). **Other Dramatic:** *Seara mare,* lyric scene (1924); *Învierea,* pantomime (1932). **ORCH.:** *La seceriş* (1936); *4 Symphonic Dances* (1951). **CHAMBER:** 2 suites for Violin and Piano; piano pieces. **VOCAL:** Songs.—NS/LK/DM

Bree, Jean Bernard van (Johannes Bernardus van), Dutch violinist and composer; b. Amsterdam, Jan. 29, 1801; d. there, Feb. 14, 1857. He was a pupil of Bertelman. In 1820–21 he played in the orch. of the Théâtre Français in Amsterdam, and in 1830 he became conductor of the Felix Meritis Soc. In 1841 he founded the Cecilia Soc. in Amsterdam, and later he became director of the Music School of the Soc. for the Promotion of Music.

WORKS: DRAMATIC: Opera: *Sappho* (in Dutch; Amsterdam, March 22, 1834); *Le Bandit* (in French; Amsterdam, Dec. 22, 1835); *Nimm dich in Acht* (in German; 1845). **Other Dramatic:** 2 melodramas. **OTHER:** Several masses; cantatas; overtures; chamber music.

BIBL.: H. Beijermann, *J.B. v.B.* (1857).—NS/LK/DM

Bregman, Buddy, jazz/pop composer, arranger, conductor, TV and film producer, director, author; b. Chicago, July 9, c. 1937. He was from a well-to-do family. His mother's brother is songwriter Jule Styne; another uncle was saxophone player Maurie Stein. Bregman studied piano and clarinet with Mossaiye Bogaslowski and Buck Wells at age 5 and 11 respectively. He wrote arrangements from age 11, inspired by listening to Herman, Kenton, and others. He went to college at UCLA at 15. While there, at age 17, a classmate's father paid for a session and he had a hit with the Lieber & Stoller song, "I Need Your Lovin'" (1954). Norman Granz heard the flip side "Bernie's

Tune," and in 1956 asked Bregman to work for a new label he was starting, which would end up being Verve. Among Bregman's first projects were two of the tracks from the album *The Greatest with Count Basie and Joe Williams*—"Come Rain or Come Shine" and "I Can't Believe That You're in Love with Me." Among his best known albums are *The Cole Porter Songbook* and *Rodgers and Hart Songbook*—both double albums with Ella Fitzgerald—and Bing Crosby's *Bing Sings Whilst Bregman Swings*; all of these eventually went platinum. At Verve, Bregman also worked with Fred Astaire, Oscar Peterson, and Anita O'Day. He arranged albums for Decca with Jerry Lewis, Sammy Davis Jr., and arranged for Bobby Darin at Atlantic. He also scored/orchestrated many major studio films, including *Pajama Game, Crime in the Streets,* and *Secret of the Purple Reef.* After his tenure at Verve, he concentrated on producing and directing in TV and films. He directed music for TV shows of Frank Sinatra, Ethel Merman, Victor Borge, and for Judy Garland's U.S. tour. He produced and directed a series of TV specials in England, France, and Germany and worked for the BBC, directing series and major specials. He then wrote the Royal Shakespeare Company's first stage musical, *Jump Jim Crow.* Upon his return to the U.S. in the 1980s, he continued to produce and direct for TV.

Disc.: *Swingin' Kicks* (1956); *Dig Buddy Bregman in Hi Fi* (1956); *Swingin' Standards* (1959). A. O'Day: *Rules of the Road* (1993).—**LP**

Brehm, Alvin, American double bass player, conductor, and composer; b. N.Y., Feb. 8, 1925. He studied with Fred Zimmerman (double bass) and Giannini (orchestration) at the Juilliard School of Music in N.Y. (1942–43), and then with Riegger (composition) at Columbia Univ. (M.A., 1951). After making his debut as a double-bass player (1942), he performed with the Pittsburgh Sym. Orch. (1950–51), the Contemporary Chamber Ensemble (1969–73), the Group for Contemporary Music (1971–73), the Philomusica Chamber Music Soc. (1973–83), and the Chamber Music Soc. of Lincoln Center (1984–89). After making his debut as a conductor (1947), he was active in promoting contemporary music. He was founder-conductor of the Composer's Theatre Orch. (1967), and also taught at the State Univ. of N.Y. at Stony Brook (1968–75), the Manhattan School of Music (1969–75), and the State Univ. of N.Y. at Purchase (from 1981), where he also was head of its music division (1981–90).

Works: Dramatic: *The Final Theory,* chamber opera (1994). **Orch.:** *Hephaestus Overture* (1966); Concertino for Violin and Strings (N.Y., April 22, 1975); Piano Concerto (N.Y., Nov. 1979); Double Bass Concerto (N.Y., Nov. 1982); Tuba Concerto (1982). **Chamber:** *Divertimento* for Trumpet, Horn, and Trombone (1962); *Dialogues* for Bassoon and Percussion (1964); *Divertimento* for Woodwind Quintet (1965); Brass Quintet (N.Y., Feb. 1967); *Colloquy and Chorale* for Bassoon Quartet (1974); Cello Sonata (1974); *Quarks* for Flute, Bassoon, String Quartet, and Piano (N.Y., Feb. 1976); Sextet for Piano and Strings (N.Y., April 1976); *A Pointe at His Pleasure* for Renaissance Instruments (1979); *AYU Variations* for Flute and Guitar (1980); *Tre canzone* for Viola and Piano (N.Y, Nov. 1980); *La bocca della verità* for Flute, Clarinet, Violin, Cello, and Piano (N.Y., Oct.

1983); Sextet for Woodwind Quintet and Piano (1984); *Children's Games* for Flute, Clarinet, Violin, Viola, Cello, and Piano (1984–85); *Circles* for Piano (1991); *Lion's Den* for Violin and Percussion (1992); *By the Numbers* for Piano (1995). **Vocal:** Song Cycle for Soprano and 10 Instruments, after García Lorca (N.Y., Nov. 1973).—**NS/LK/DM**

Brehme, Hans (Ludwig Wilhelm), German composer; b. Potsdam, March 10, 1904; d. Stuttgart, Nov. 10, 1957. He studied piano in Berlin with Wilhelm Kempff, taught at Stuttgart and elsewhere. A highly diligent composer, he wrote music in many genres; the idiom of his compositions is fundamentally Classical, with a generous admixture of moderately modern harmonies. He wrote an opera, *Der Uhrmacher von Strassburg* (1941), an operetta, *Versiegelten Bürgermeister* (1944), 2 syms., 2 piano concertos, Flute Concerto, *Triptycon* for Orch., on a theme by Handel (highly successful), Sextet for Flute, Clarinet, Horn, Violin, Viola, and Cello, Clarinet Quintet, Saxophone Sonata, and several works for Accordion.—**NS/LK/DM**

Bréhy, Hercule, Belgian organist and composer; b. Brussels (baptized), Sept. 13, 1673; d. there (buried), Feb. 28, 1737. He was active as an organist in Brussels, and from 1705 until his death singing master at Ste. Gudule. His works include masses, motets, and Lamentations.—**NS/LK/DM**

Breil, Joseph Carl, American composer; b. Pittsburgh, June 29, 1870; d. Los Angeles, Jan. 23, 1926. He studied voice in Milan and Leipzig, and for a time sang in various opera companies. He was the composer of one of the earliest motion picture scores, *Queen Elizabeth* (Chicago, 1912); he also wrote the music for D.W. Griffith's film *The Birth of a Nation* (1915), as well as the words and music for the comic operas *Love Laughs at Locksmiths* (Portland, Maine, Oct. 27, 1910), *Prof. Tattle* (1913), and *The Seventh Chord* (1913). His serious opera, *The Legend,* was produced by the Metropolitan Opera in N.Y. on March 12, 1919. His opera *Asra* (after Heine) had a single performance, in Los Angeles (Nov. 24, 1925).—**NS/LK/DM**

Breitengraser, Wilhelm, German composer; b. Nuremberg, c. 1495; d. there (buried), Dec. 23, 1542. He studied at the Univ. of Leipzig, and then was active as a teacher and musician in Nuremberg. His works include masses, Psalms, and hymns.—**NS/LK/DM**

Breitkopf & Härtel, important German firm of book and music publishers. As an established printing firm in Leipzig, it was bought in 1745 by Bernhard Christoph Breitkopf (b. Klausthal Harz, March 2, 1695; d. Leipzig, March 23, 1777). His son, Johann Gottlob Immanuel (b. Nov. 23, 1719; d. Jan. 28, 1794), entered the business in 1745; it was his invention which made the basis for the firm's position in the publication of music. In 1756 he devised a font with much smaller division of the musical elements, and this greatly reduced the cost of printing chords (and hence piano music). The firm soon began to issue numerous piano reductions of popular operas for amateur consumption. The earliest music publications, such as the *Berlinische Oden und Lieder* (3 vols., 1756, 1759, 1763), were made by Johann Gottlob Immanuel Breitkopf himself, and bore the imprint "Leipzig, Druckts und Verlegts Johann Gottlob Immanuel Breitkopf"; from 1765 to 1777 the firm name appears as "Bernhard Christoph Breitkopf und Sohn"; from 1777 to 1787 (after Christoph's death) Johann's name again appears alone; his second son, Christoph Gottlob (b. Leipzig, Sept. 22, 1750; d. there, April 4, 1800), joined the firm in 1787; from 1787 to 1795 publications were issued as "im Breitkopfischen Verlage" (or Buchhandlung, or Musikhandlung); in 1795 (the year after Immanuel's death) Christoph Gottlob Breitkopf took as his partner his close friend Gottfried Christoph Härtel (b. Schneeberg, Jan. 27, 1763; d. Cotta, near Leipzig, July 25, 1827); since 1795 the firm has been known as Breitkopf & Härtel, although no Breitkopf has been actively associated with the firm since Christoph Gottlob's death in 1800. Härtel's tremendous energy revitalized the firm. He added a piano factory; founded the important periodical *Allgemeine musikalische Zeitung* (1798; ed., J.F. Rochlitz); introduced pewter in place of the harder copper for engraving music; used Senefelder's new lithographic process for either title pages or music where suitable; issued so-called "complete" eds. of the works of Mozart, Haydn, Clementi, and Dussek. The firm also began the practice of issuing catalogues with thematic indexes and keeping stocks of scores. From 1827 to 1835 Florenz Härtel was head of the firm; Hermann Härtel (b. Leipzig, April 27, 1803; d. there, Aug. 4, 1875) and his brother, Raimund Härtel (b. Leipzig, June 9, 1810; d. there, Nov. 9, 1888), together dominated the book business of Leipzig (and thus all Germany) for many years; the sons of 2 sisters of Raimund and Hermann, Wilhelm Volkmann (b. Halle, June 12, 1837; d. Leipzig, Dec. 24, 1896) and Dr. Oskar von Hase (b. Jena, Sept. 15, 1846; d. Leipzig, Jan. 26, 1921), succeeded them. After Wilhelm Volkmann's death, his son, Dr. Ludwig Volkmann (1870–1947), headed the firm jointly with von Hase; von Hase's son Hermann (1880–1945) entered the firm in 1904 and was a co-partner from 1910 to 1914. Hermann von Hase publ. essays tracing the relation of J. Haydn, C.P.E. Bach, and J.A. Hiller to the firm; in 1915 he became a partner in the book business of K.F. Koehler. His brother Dr. Hellmuth von Hase (b. Jan. 30, 1891; d. Wiesbaden, Oct. 18, 1979) became director of the firm in 1919. The old house was destroyed during the air bombardment of Dec. 4, 1943; it was rebuilt after the war. In 1950 Dr. von Hase moved to Wiesbaden, where he established an independent business, reclaiming the rights for the firm in West Germany. Important enterprises of the firm throughout its existence are eds. of Bach, Beethoven, Berlioz, Brahms, Chopin, Gluck, Grétry, Handel, Haydn, Lassus, Liszt, Mendelssohn, Mozart, Palestrina, Schein, Schubert, Schumann, Schütz, Victoria, and Wagner. The German government supported the publication by Breitkopf & Härtel of the 2 series of Denkmäler Deutscher Tonkunst (1892–1931 and 1900–1931). Other publications of the firm are *Der Bär*, yearbook (since 1924); *Katalog des Archivs von Breitkopf und Härtel*, ed. by Dr. F.W. Hitzig (2 vols., 1925–26); *Allgemeine musikalische Zeitung* (weekly; 1798–1848 and 1863–65); *Monatshefte für Musikgeschichte* (1869–1905); *Mitteilungen des Hauses Breitkopf und Härtel* (1876–1940; resumed in 1950); *Vierteljahrsschrift für Musikwissenschaft* (1869–1906); *Zeitschrift der Internationalen Musikgesellschaft* (monthly; Oct. 1899–Sept. 1914); *Sammelbände der Internationalen Musikgesellschaft* (quarterly; 1899–1914); *Korrespondenzblatt des Evangelischen Kirchengesangvereins für Deutschland* (monthly; 1886–1922); *Zeitschrift für Musikwissenschaft* (monthly; 1919–35); *Archiv für Musikforschung* (1936–43).

BIBL.: B. Brook, ed., *The B. Thematic Catalogue...1762–1787* (N.Y., 1966); R. Elvers, ed., *B. & H. 1719–1969. Ein historischer Überblick zum Jubiläum* (Wiesbaden, 1968); I. Hempel, ed., *Pasticcio auf das 250 jahrige Bestehen des Verlages B. & H.* (Leipzig, 1968); O. von Hase, *B. & H. Gedenkschrift und Arbeitsbericht* (3 vols.: I, 1542–1827; II, 1828–1918; III, 1918–68; Wiesbaden, 1968).
—NS/LK/DM

Brelet, Gisèle (Jeanne Marie Noémie), French musicologist and pianist; b. Fontenay-le-Comte, Vendée, March 6, 1915; d. Sèvres, June 21, 1973. She studied piano at the Nantes Cons. and at the Paris Cons., and also took courses in biology and philosophy at the Sorbonne in Paris (Ph.D., 1949). In 1950 she became director of the Bibliothèque Internationale de Musicologie. She wrote the studies *Esthétique et création musicale* (Paris, 1947), *Le Temps musical* (Paris, 1949), and *L'Interprétation créatrice* (Paris, 1951).—NS/LK/DM

Brema, Marie (real name, Minny Fehrmann), English mezzo-soprano; b. Liverpool (of a German father and an American mother), Feb. 28, 1856; d. Manchester, March 22, 1925. She was a pupil of Henschel (1890). Under the name Bremer (in honor of her father's native city of Bremen), she made her concert debut in London singing Schubert's *Ganymed* on Feb. 21, 1891. Her operatic debut followed on Oct. 19, 1891, when she sang Lola in the first English performance of *Cavalleria rusticana* at London's Shaftesbury Theatre. She was the first English-born singer to appear at the Bayreuth Festival when she sang Ortrud in 1894, and returned there to sing Fricka in the *Ring* cycle in 1896 and Kundry in 1897. During the 1894–95 season, she toured in the U.S. with the Damrosch Opera Co. On Nov. 27, 1895, she made her Metropolitan Opera debut in N.Y. as Brangäne, remaining on its roster until 1896 and appearing there again from 1898 to 1900. In 1900 she was soloist in the premiere of Elgar's *The Dream of Gerontius*. She created the role of Beatrice in Stanford's *Much Ado About Nothing* at London's Covent Garden in 1901, and in 1902 she sang Brünnhilde in the first French mounting of *Götterdämmerung* in Paris. She oversaw opera productions in English at London's Savoy Theatre in 1910, where she also sang Orfeo. From 1913 until her death she was prof. of voice and director of the opera class at the Royal Manchester Coll. of Music.
—NS/LK/DM

Brémond, François, French horn player and pedagogue; b. Nimes, Nov. 1, 1844; d. Houilles, near

Paris, July 15, 1925. He studied at the Paris Cons. with J.-B. Mohr, winning a premier prix in 1869. From 1878 to 1888 he was principal horn of the Société des Concerts du Conservatoire in Paris; was also principal horn of the orch. at the Opéra-Comique. In 1891 he joined the faculty of the Paris Cons. He preferred to play the natural horn, and in later years took up the valve horn as well.—NS/LK/DM

Brendel, (Karl) Franz, German writer on music; b. Stolberg, Nov. 26, 1811; d. Leipzig, Nov. 25, 1868. He was educated at the univs. of Leipzig and Berlin. He studied piano with Wieck and through him entered the Schumann circle; ed. Schumann's periodical *Neue Zeitschrift für Musik* from 1845 until his death in 1868, and also was co-editor, with R. Pohl, of the monthly *Anregungen für Kunst*. In 1846 he joined the faculty of the Leipzig Cons.; was also one of the founders, in 1861, of the Allgemeiner Deutscher Musikverein. In his articles he boldly championed the cause of the new German music, as symbolized by the works of Wagner and Liszt. He publ. a successful general music history, *Geschichte der Musik in Italien, Deutschland und Frankreich von den ersten christlichen Zeiten bis auf die Gegenwart* (1852; 7th ed., edited by Kienzl, 1888; new aug. ed., edited by R. Hovker, 1902, and reissued in 1906). He also publ. a treatise commenting on "the music of the future," *Die Musik der Gegenwart und die Gesamtkunst der Zukunft* (1854), and other similar publications dealing with new developments in German music.—NS/LK/DM

Brendel, Alfred, great Austrian pianist; b. Wiesenberg, Jan. 5, 1931. He studied in Zagreb with S. Deželić (piano, 1937–43) and F. Dugan (harmony), and in Graz with L Kaan (piano, 1943–47) and A. Michl (composition). He pursued his training in piano with P. Baumgartner in Basel, and also attended the master classes of E. Fischer in Lucerne and E. Seuermann in Salzburg. In 1947 he was awarded his state diploma in Vienna, and in 1948 he made his formal debut in Graz. He captured 4th prize in the Busoni competition in Bolzano in 1949. His appearances at the Vienna and Salzburg Festivals in 1960 were noteworthy and led to frequent engagements there and at other major festivals. In 1962 he garnered critical acclaim when he gave a complete cycle of the Beethoven piano sonatas in London, a cycle he repeated there (1977; 1982–83; 1992–95). He also gave the cycle in Vienna (1965; 1982–83), Rome (1970), Amsterdam, Paris, and Berlin (1982–83), N.Y. (1983), and in 14 European and 4 North American cities (1992–96). Brendel settled in London in 1974. As a soloist, he was engaged by many of the foremost conductors and orchs. of his time, and he also was active as a chamber music artist. In 1983 his series of master classes appeared on BBC TV in London. He gave a series of Schubert recitals throughout Europe and North America in 1987–88. In 1991 he was soloist in Beethoven's *Choral Fantasy* at the gala concert celebrating the centenary of N.Y.'s Carnegie Hall. Brendel was the first to record all of Beethoven's piano music, for which he was awarded the Grand Prix du Disque of France in 1965. He also won numerous other recording prizes. Among his many other honors were membership in the American Academy of Arts

and Sciences (1984), Commandeur des Arts et des Lettres of France (1985), honorary knighthood from Queen Elizabeth II of England (1989), Orden pour le Mérite für Wissenschaften und Künste of Germany (1991), and the Gold Medal of the Royal Phil. Soc. of London (1993). In his interpretations, Brendel has combined intellectual discernment and refined expression in his mastery of the Viennese classical tradition. In addition to his remarkable performances of Beethoven and Schubert, he has also demonstrated penetrating insights into the works of Bach, Mozart, and Liszt. His interests also include Stravinsky, Bartók, and Schoenberg. Brendel is also an engaging and often witty writer. In addition to his contributions to various periodicals, he has publ. the books *Musical Thoughts and Afterthoughts* (1976; 2nd ed., 1982), *Music Sounded Out: Essays, Lectures, Interviews, Afterthoughts* (1990), *Fingerzeig* (1996), and *Störendes Lachen während des Jaworts* (1997).—NS/LK/DM

Brendel, Wolfgang, German baritone; b. Munich, Oct. 20, 1947. After vocal studies, he began his career in Kaiserslautern. He joined the Bavarian State Opera in Munich in 1971, and became Kammersänger there in 1977. On Nov. 20, 1975, he made his Metropolitan Opera debut in N.Y. as Count Almaviva in *Le nozze di Figaro*; then appeared at the San Francisco Opera as Rodrigo in *Don Carlo* (1979), at Milan's La Scala as Count Almaviva (1981), at the Chicago Lyric Opera as Miller in *Luisa Miller* (1982), and at the Bayreuth Festival as Wolfram in *Tannhäuser* (1985). He made his debut at London's Covent Garden as Conte Di Luna in *Il Trovatore* on Oct. 12, 1985. In 1990 he sang Eugene Onegin in Chicago. He portrayed Amfortas at La Scala in 1992. In 1997 he appeared as the Dutchman at the Deutsche Oper in Berlin. He appeared in opera centers throughout Europe and the U.S.; his most noted roles include Rossini's Figaro, Papageno, Eugene Onegin, Amfortas, Silvio, and Pelléas.—NS/LK/DM

Brendler, (Frans Fredric) Eduard, German-born Swedish flutist and composer; b. Dresden, Nov. 4, 1800; d. Stockholm, Aug. 16, 1831. He made his debut as a flutist in Stockholm when he was 10, and later pursued a commercial career while continuing his interest in music. In 1823 he became a flutist in the Harmonisk Sallskap orch. His works include instrumental and choral pieces. His opera, *Ryno*, was completed by Prince Oscar in 1832 and was first performed at the Royal Opera in 1834. His early death was regretted by his admirers in Sweden.—NS/LK/DM

Brennan, John Wolf, Irish-Swiss composer and pianist; b. Dublin, Feb. 13, 1954. He moved to Switzerland as a youth, and began playing bass and guitar as a teenager in Lucerne. He studied musicology, film, and literature at the Univ. of Fribourg and attended the Swiss Jazz school in Berne (1975–79), continuing his studies in piano, composition, and theory in Lucerne, Dublin, and N.Y. (1979–84). From 1984 Brennan formed various duets, quartets, and quintets with a number of European jazz virtuosos. In 1993 he formed the "Groupe Lacroix," a cooperative of six Swiss and Austrian com-

445

posers who perform their own works. From the mid-1980s, Brennan worked internationally as a jazz musician, conductor, music director for radio and television, piano teacher, and leader of improvisation workshops. In 1999 he performed in a festival of his works held in Chicago to celebrate Swiss Days. Brennan is a unique musician, equally comfortable in the worlds of jazz and concert music. From an early influence as diverse as Miles Davis and the Beatles, Brennan's music evolved into a high-art synthesis of John Cage, Henry Cowell, Pierre Henri, and free-jazz, which at times involves theatrical techniques such as musique concrète, bowing of piano strings, and multiphonics. His titles reflect his proclivity for word play.

WORKS: DRAMATIC: Theater Music: *Swiss-Timing* (1981); *Romeo and Julia in Willisau* (1982); *Festspiel Sempach* (1986); *De Zeigerdieb* (1987); *Sri Salami* (1989); *Adrift* (1990); *K's Kilimandjaro* (1992); *Totentanz* (1993); *Moskau-Petuschki* (1994). **Radio:** *Wort Zeichen Klang* for Voice, Flute, Double Bass, Piano, Sound Objects, and Sound Installation (1995–96; Lucerne, June 13, 1997). **CHAMBER:** *Ex Aequo* for Viola and Percussion (1986); Brass Variations for Brass Quintet (1988); *Twelfth Night*, 6 songs for Saxophone Quartet (1990); *Dance, You Monster, to My Soft Song*, after the Klee painting, for Jazz Orch. (1990); Sonatina for Viola, Trumpet, Piano, and Contrabass (1991); *Tango neon* for Ensemble (1991); *Atanos* for Alto Saxophone, Piano, and Contrabass (1993); *Frictions* for Flute, Bass Clarinet, Vibraphone, and String Trio (1993); *Diálogos* for 2 Cellos (1994); *Epithalamium* for Nonet (1994); *A Golly Gal's Way to Galway Bay* for Flute Ensemble (1995); *Leave it in Limbo* for Horn (1996); *Olos* for Clarinet (1996); *Alef Bet* for Oboe, Bassoon, and Piano, or for Piano Trio (1996); *Rhap.s.odie* for Violin and Piano (1996); *Nearly Charming* for Octet (1997); *Tango* for Cello (1998); *Monumentum* for Bass Clarinet, Piano, and Percussion (1998); *N-gl*, after an angel painting by Klee, for Oboe, Bassoon, and Viola (1999). **KEYBOARD: Piano:** *Treiblinge*, 13 pieces (1982); *Capriccio* (1990); *Sonata Pentatonica* (1993); 4 solo-piano "programs" of pieces: *The Beauty of Fractals* (1988), *Iritations* (1991; with sound objects), *Text, Context, Co-Text & Co-Co Text* (1993), and *The Well-Prepared Clavier* for Piano, Partially Prepared (1997–98; includes his cycle *Seven Studies* for Prepared Piano); *Kyoto* (1997); *Kla4* for 2 Pianos (1999); *Silly Blooze* (1999–2000). **Organ:** *Pandämonium* (1994); *5 Interludien* (1997); *4 Solo Pieces* (1999). **VOCAL:** *Bestiarium*, 13 songs for Soprano and Piano (1983; rev. 1990); *OrganIC VoICes*, cycle for Voice and Organ (1990–91; with trumpet and percussion); *SprüchGägeSprüch*, "dialectic cantata" for 2 Choruses, String Quartet, and Percussion (1991); *Euratorium* for Chorus, Orch., and Alpine Horn (1993); *Fraeschber's Traum* for Soprano, String Trio, and Bass Clarinet (1997); *Through the Ear of a Raindrop* for Voice and 5 Instruments (1997); *Abel, steh auf!*, cantata for Women's Chorus and Brass Quartet (1999–2000).—**LK/DM**

Brent, Charlotte, English soprano; b. c. 1735; d. London, April 10, 1802. She studied with Arne, making her operatic debut in his Eliza at the Smock Alley Theatre in Dublin on Nov. 29, 1755; then sang at London's Drury Lane Theatre and at Covent Garden. She was noted for her performances of Polly in *The Beggar's Opera* and for corresponding roles in Handel's operas.—**NS/LK/DM**

Brenta, Gaston, Belgian composer; b. Brussels, June 10, 1902; d. there, May 30, 1969. He studied theory with Gilson; in 1925 he and 7 other pupils of Gilson formed the Belgian Groupe des Synthétistes, advocating a more modern approach to composition. From 1931 he was associated with the Belgian Radio; from 1953 to 1967 he was music director of the French Services there. His music follows the traditions of cosmopolitan Romanticism, with exotic undertones.

WORKS: DRAMATIC: *Le Khâdi dupé*, opera (Brussels, Dec. 16, 1929); 2 radio dramas: *Aucassin et Nicolette* (1934) and *Heracles* (1955); 3 ballets: *Zo'har* (1928); *Florilège de Valses* (1940); *Candide* (1955); *Le Bal chez la Lorette* (1954), which forms a part of *Les Bals de Paris*, a large ballet consisting of passages contributed by several Belgian composers. **ORCH.:** *Variations sur un thème congolais* (1926); *Nocturne* (1934); *Arioso et Moto Perpetuo* (1940); *War Music* (1946); Sym. (1946); *In Memoriam Paul Gilson* (1950); *Farandole burlesque* (1951); 2 piano concertos (1952, 1968); Concertino for Trumpet, Strings, and Timpani (1958); *Saxiana*, concertino for Saxophone, Strings, Timpani, and Piano (1962); *Airs variés pour de belles écouteuses* for Bassoon and Strings (1963); *Pointes sèches de la Belle Époque* for Piano and Strings (1964); *Matinee d'été* (1967). **CHAMBER:** String Quartet (1939); *Melopée* for Violin and Piano (1945); *Le Soldat fanfaron*, suite for Quintet (1952); Concertino for 5 Winds, Double Bass, Piano, and Percussion (1963); piano pieces.—**NS/LK/DM**

Bresgen, Cesar, Austrian composer and teacher of German descent; b. Florence, Oct. 16, 1913; d. Salzburg, April 7, 1988. He studied organ, piano, conducting, and composition at the Munich Academy of Music (1930–36), his mentors being Emmanuel Gatscher, Gottfried Rüdinger, and Joseph Haas. In 1936 he won the Felix Mottl Prize for composition. After working in the music division of the Bavarian Eadio in Munich, he settled in Salzburg in 1939 and organized his own music school; he also taught composition at the Mozarteum. He served in the army during World War II, and then was a church organist and choir director in Mittersill. In 1947 he returned to the Salzburg Mozarteum as prof. of composition. In 1974 he was awarded the Austrian State Prize for music. He publ. the books *Musikalische Dokumentation* (Vienna, 1982) and *Die Improvisation in der Musik* (Wilhelmshaven, 1983), as well as folk song collections. As a composer, Bresgen acquired a notable facility for writing effective *Gebrauchsmusik*.

WORKS: DRAMATIC: *Der Goggolore*, Singspiel (1937–39; unfinished); *Dornröschenm*, Singspiel (Strasbourg, April 15, 1942); *Paracelsus*, opera (1942–43); *Das Urteil des Paris*, komisches Singspiel (Göttingen, Jan. 31, 1943); *Der Igel als Brautigam*, children's opera (Esslingen, Nov. 3, 1948; rev. version, Nuremburg, Nov. 13, 1951); *Visiones amantis* or *Der Wolkensteiner*, Ludus tragicus (1951; Bremen Radio, Feb. 17, 1964; first stage perf., Innsbruck, Dec. 20, 1971); *Niño fliegt mit Niña*, "insect comedy" for Children (Munich, May 14, 1953); *Brüderlein Hund*, children's opera (Nuremberg, Nov. 12, 1953); *Der ewige Arzt*, Mystereinspiel (Schwyz, Feb. 10, 1956); *Ercole*, opera (Hamburg Radio, 1956); *Der Mann im Mond*, musical fairy tale (Nuremberg, May 22, 1960); *Die alte Lokomotive*, scenic cantata (Munich, Oct. 7, 1960); *Die Schattendiebe* or *Ali und der Bilderdiebel*, children's Singspiel (Vienna, April 13, 1962); *Bastian der Faulpelz*, musical pantomime (Hamburg, 1966); *Trubloff*, Singspiel (1970); *Der Engel von Pra*, opera (Salzburg, Dec. 25, 1978; rev. 1985); *Pilatus*, opera (Villach, Aug. 2, 1980); *Krabat*, Singspiel

(1982); *Albolina, oder der Kampf der Geister um die Morgenrote,* musical fairy tale (Villach, July 12, 1987). **ORCH.:** Chamber Concerto for Guitar and Small Orch. (1962); *Elegie* for 12 Cellos (1979); *Ballade* for Violin, Harpsichord, and 13 Strings (1983); *Impressioni nella notte* for Small Orch. (1984); Clarinet Concerto (1986); *Magnalia Dei,* symphonic metamorphosis for Orch. and Speaker (1987). **OTHER:** Chamber music and choral pieces.

BIBL.: D. Larese, *C. B.* (Amriswil, 1968); R. Lück, *C. B.* (Vienna, 1974).—**NS/LK/DM**

Bresnick, Martin, American composer and teacher; b. N.Y., Nov. 13, 1946. He studied at the H.S. of Music and Art in N.Y., and then with Arnold Franchetti at the Hartt School of Music in Hartford, Conn. (B.A., 1967), Leland Smith and John Chowning at Stanford Univ. (M.A., 1968; D.M.A., 1972), Einem and Cerha at the Vienna Academy of Music on a Fulbright fellowship (1969–70), and with Ligeti. After teaching at the San Francisco Cons. of Music (1971–72) and Stanford Univ. (1972–75), he became a prof. of composition at the Yale Univ. School of Music in 1975. In 1993 he was the Valentine Prof. of Music at Amherst Coll. and in 1998 the Mary Duke Biddle Prof. of Music at Duke Univ. He received grants from the NEA (1974, 1979, 1990), held the Rome Prize (1975–76) and MacDowell Colony (1977) fellowships, took first prize in the Premio Ancona (1980) and the International Sinfonia Musicale Competition (1982), and won the Elise L. Stoeger Prize for Chamber Music of the Chamber Music Soc. of Lincoln Center (1996) and the Charles Ives Living Award of the American Academy of Arts and Letters (1998). Bresnick's music is marked by a fine command of structure and carefully wrought expressivity.

WORKS: ORCH.: *Ocean of Storms* (1970); *Wir Weben, Wir Weben* for Strings (1978; also for Chamber Ensemble or String Sextet); *One* (1986); *Little Suite* for Amateur String Orch. (1987); *Pontoosuc* (1989); *Angelus Novus* (1991); *Sinfonia* (1992); *On an Overgrown Path* for Chamber Orch. (1996). **CHAMBER:** 3 string quartets (1968, 1984, 1992); *Musica* for 9 Instruments (1972); *B.'s Garlands* for 8 Cellos (1973); *Conspiracies* for Flute and Tape (1979); *Bread & Salt* for 14 Instruments (1984); *Just Time* for Woodwind Quintet (1985); Trio for Violin, Cello, and Piano (1988); *The Bucket Rider* for 6 Players (1995); Trio for Clarinet, Viola, and Piano (1997); *Pine Eyes* for Bass Clarinet, Piano, 2 Percussion, and Narrator (1998); *Bird as Prophet* for Violin and Piano (1999). **VOCAL:** *Where is the Way* for Chorus (1970); *Ants* for Soprano, Mezzo- soprano, Tenor, Baritone, 5 Actor- Mimes, Woodwind Quintet, String Quartet, Double Bass, Percussion, and Harp (1976); *Der Signál* for Soprano, Alto, Mezzo- soprano, Narrator or Tape, and 8 Instruments (1982); *3 Choral Songs* (1986); *New Haven, Woodstock* for Chorus (1993); *Falling* for Mezzo-soprano and Piano or Orch. (1994). **OTHER:** Film scores, including *Arthur & Lillie* (1975) and *The Day After Trinity* (1981).—**NS/LK/DM**

Bressler, Charles, American tenor; b. Kingston, Pa., April 1, 1926; d. N.Y., Nov. 28, 1996. After studies with Lucia Dunham, Sergius Kagen, and Marjorie Schloss at the Juilliard School of Music in N.Y. (graduated, 1950; postgraduate diploma, 1951), he became a founding member of the N.Y. Pro Musica, with which he toured widely (1953–63). He also was a founding member of the N.Y. Chamber Soloists (from 1957);

likewise appeared with the Santa Fe Opera and the Washington (D.C.) Opera Soc., and toured Europe as a concert artist. He taught at various schools, including N.Y.'s Mannes Coll. of Music (from 1966) and Manhattan School of Music (from 1978). He was best known for his performances of early music, but also had success in contemporary roles.—**NS/LK/DM**

Bressler-Gianoli, Clotilde, Italian contralto; b. Geneva (of Italian parents), June 3, 1875; d. there, May 12, 1912. She received her primary training at the Geneva Cons., then enrolled at the Milan Cons., where she studied singing with Sangiovanni, Giocosa, and Ronconi. She made her operatic debut at the age of 19 in Geneva in *Samson et Dalila;* later sang at La Scala in Milan, at the Opéra-Comique in Paris, and with the San Carlo Co. at New Orleans. Her best roles were Carmen and Mignon.—**NS/LK/DM**

Bretan, Nicolae, remarkable Romanian composer; b. Năsăud, April 6, 1887; d. Cluj, Dec. 1, 1968. He studied at the Klausenburg Cons., composition and voice with Farkas, and violin with Gyémánt (1906–08); then at the Vienna Academy of Music (1908–09) and at the Magyar Királyi Zeneakademia in Budapest (1909–12) with Siklos (theory) and Szerémi (violin). His primary career was that of an opera singer, performing baritone parts at the opera houses in Bratislava, Oradea, and Cluj between 1913 and 1944, also acting as a stage director. At the same time, he surprisingly asserted himself as a composer of operas and lieder in an effective veristic manner, marked by a high degree of professional expertise and considerable originality.

WORKS: DRAMATIC: Opera: *Luceafărul* (The Evening Star; in Romanian; tr. by the composer into Hungarian and German; Cluj, Feb. 2, 1921); *Golem* (in Hungarian; tr. by the composer into Romanian and German; Cluj, Dec. 23, 1924); *Eroii de la Rovine* (in Romanian; Cluj, Jan. 24, 1935); *Horia* (in Romanian; also tr. into German by the composer; Cluj, Jan. 24, 1937); *Arald* (in Romanian; 1939). **OTHER:** *Requiem;* mystery play, *An Extraordinary Seder Evening* (in Hungarian; also tr. into Eng.); *Mein Liederland,* about 230 songs to Romanian, Hungarian, and German texts.—**NS/LK/DM**

Bretón y Hernández, Tomás, Spanish composer; b. Salamanca, Dec. 29, 1850; d. Madrid, Dec. 2, 1923. As a youth he played in restaurants and theaters. He graduated from the Madrid Cons. (1872), then conducted at the Madrid Opera. In 1901 he joined the faculty of the Madrid Cons. A fertile composer, he contributed greatly to the revival of the zarzuela. He was at his best in the one-act comic type (*género chico*). Among his operas and zarzuelas (all produced in Madrid) are *Los amantes de Teruel* (1889), *Juan Garín* (1892), *La Dolores* (1895), *El Domingo de Ramos* (1896), *La Verbena de la Paloma* (1894), *Raquel* (to his own libretto; Jan. 20, 1900), *El caballo del señorito* (1901); *Farinelli* (1903); and *Tabaré* (1913). He also wrote an oratorio, *Apocalipsia* (Madrid, 1882), and works for Orch., including *Ecenas Andaluzas, Funeral March for Alfonso XII,* and a Violin Concerto.

BIBL.: A. Salcedo, *T. B.: Su vida y sus obras* (Madrid, 1924).—**NS/LK/DM**

Brett, Charles (Michael), English countertenor; b. Maidenhead, Oct. 27, 1941. He studied with Julian Smith (1957–60) and John Whitworth (1958–60), and at King's Coll., Cambridge (B.A., 1963; M.A., 1967), where his mentors were Willcocks, Dart, and Leppard. In 1964 he made his debut as a soloist with the Monteverdi Choir and Orch. under Gardiner's direction in Cambridge, and subsequently was engaged to sing around the globe with many of the leading conductors and orchs. He made his recital debut in 1968 at the Winter Gardens in Malvern. Following his operatic debut as Angelica in Fux's *Vinitrice di Alcina* at the Graz Opera in 1984, he sang in Handel's *Semele* in Ludwigsburg (1985), Gluck's *La clemenza di Tito* in Tourcoing and on tour in France (1986), and Britten's *A Midsummer Night's Dream* in Aachen (1987–88). In 1995 he directed a production of *Dido and Aeneas* at the Cervantino Festival in Mexico. —NS/LK/DM

Brett, Philip, English-born American musicologist; b. Edwinstowe, Oct. 17, 1937. He studied at King's Coll., Cambridge (B.A., 1958; Mus.B., 1961), and after a brief period at the Univ. of Calif. at Berkeley, completed his training at Cambridge (Ph.D., 1965). He joined the faculty at the Univ. of Calif. at Berkeley in 1966, where he was a prof. (1978–90) and chairman of the music dept. (1988–90). In 1979 he became a naturalized American citizen. He was prof. of music at the Univ. of Calif. at Riverside from 1991. With Thurston Dart, he prepared The English Madrigalists (1956; a rev. ed. of Fellowes's The English Madrigal School); he also was general ed. of the new critical edition of the works of Byrd. He publ. the useful study *Peter Grimes* (Cambridge, 1983).—NS/LK/DM

Breuer, Hans (real name, **Johann Peter Joseph**), German tenor; b. Cologne, April 27, 1868; d. Vienna, Oct. 11, 1929. He studied voice at the Cologne Cons. (1890–92), making his operatic debut in 1896 as Mime at Bayreuth, and appearing there regularly until 1914. He also sang at the Vienna Court Opera from 1900 until his death. He made his Metropolitan Opera debut in N.Y. in *Die fliegender Holländer* on Jan. 6, 1900. —NS/LK/DM

Breval, Jean-Baptiste Sebastien, outstanding French cellist and composer; b. Paris, Nov. 6, 1753; d. Colligis, Aisne, March 18, 1823. He studied cello with Jean-Baptiste Cupis, making his debut in 1778 at a Concert Spirituel performing one of his own sonatas. He subsequently was a member of its orch. (1781–91), and then played in the orch. of the Théâtre Feydeau (1791–1800). He composed a great quantity of instrumental music, including syms., cello concertos, string quartets, trios, duos, and sonatas. He also wrote an opéra-comique, *Ines et Leonore, ou La Soeur jalouse,* performed in Versailles on Nov. 14, 1788.—NS/LK/DM

Bréval, Lucienne (real name, **Berthe Agnes Lisette Schilling**), Swiss-born French soprano; b. Männedorf, Nov. 4, 1869; d. Paris, Aug. 15, 1935. She studied piano at the Lausanne Cons. and the Geneva Cons. and voice with Wartot at the Paris Cons., making her operatic debut at the Paris Opéra as Selika in *L'Africaine* on Jan. 20, 1892; subsequently was a principal singer there for 25 years. In 1899 she sang at London's Covent Garden, and on Jan. 16, 1901, made her Metropolitan Opera debut in N.Y. as Chimène in *Le Cid*, remaining on the company's roster until 1902. She excelled in the French repertoire.—NS/LK/DM

Brevik, Tor, Norwegian composer, conductor, and music critic; b. Oslo, Jan. 22, 1932. He studied violin, viola, and theory at the Oslo Cons. before completing his training in Sweden. In 1958 he founded the Oslo Youth Chamber Orch. He was also active as a music critic.

WORKS: DRAMATIC: *Contrasts*, ballet (1964); *Da kongen kom til Spilliputt*, opera (1973). **ORCH.:** *Adagio and Fugue* for Strings (1958); *Overture* (1958); *Serenade* for Strings (1959); *Chaconne* (1960); Concertino for Clarinets and Strings (1961); *Canto elegiaco* (1964); Chamber Concerto for Strings (1967); *Intrada* (1969); *Romance* for Violin and Orch. (1972; also for Violin and Piano); *Andante cantabile* for Violin and Strings (1975); Viola Concerto (1982); Sinfonietta (1989); *Sinfonia Brevik* (1991); *Music* (1993). **CHAMBER:** *Music* for Violin (1963); *Divertimento* for Wind Quintet (1964); *Adagio religioso* for Horn (1967); String Quartet (1967); *Music* for 4 Strings (1968); Septet (1977); *Fantasy* for Flute (1979); *Serenade* for 10 Winds (1994). **VOCAL:** *Elegy* for Soprano, Viola, Double Bass, and Percussion (1964); *Light of Peace* for Soloists, Chorus, and String Quartet or Orch. (1980); choruses; songs.—NS/LK/DM

Bréville, Pierre (-Onfroy de), French composer, teacher, and music critic; b. Bar-le-Duc, Feb. 21, 1861; d. Paris, Sept. 24, 1949. He studied at the Paris Cons. with Dubois (1880–82) and later with Franck. He was a prof. of counterpoint at the Paris Schola Cantorum from 1898 to 1902; was active also as a music critic. He completed (with d'Indy and others) Franck's unfinished opera *Ghiselle*; in his own music, he followed the traditions of French Romanticism. His opera, *Eros Vainqueur*, was premiered in Brussels on March 7, 1910; he also wrote an overture to Maeterlinck's play *La Princesse Maleine*, and to his *Les Sept Princesses*; also composed the orch. suites *Nuit de decèmbre* and *Stamboul*, as well as numerous choral pieces.—NS/LK/DM

Brewer, Sir (Alfred) Herbert, English organist, choirmaster, and composer; b. Gloucester, June 21, 1865; d. there, March 1, 1928. After serving as a chorister at Gloucester Cathedral (1877–80), he was an organ scholar at Exeter Coll., Oxford (1883). He then was a student at the Royal Coll. of Music in London (1883–85). He was organist at Bristol Cathedral (1885) and St. Michael's, Coventry (1886–92), after which he served as organist and choirmaster at Gloucester Cathedral from 1896 until his death. In 1926 he was knighted. Among his works were the cantatas *Emmaus* (1901; partly scored by Elgar) and *The Holy Innocents* (1904), patriotic odes, such as *England, My England*, songs, and organ pieces.

BIBL.: A. Brewer, *Memories of Choirs and Cloisters: Fifty Years of Music* (London, 1931).—NS/LK/DM

Brewer, Teresa (originally Theresa Breuer), vocalist who spanned jazz, country, and MOR pop in a 60-year career; b. Toledo, Ohio, May 7, 1931. Breuer's father worked as a glass inspector for the Libby-Owens Co., and no one else in her family was particularly musical. However, Theresa was a precocious performer. Her mother got her onto the radio by the time she was two years old, singing "Take Me Out to the Ballgame" on WSPD's *Uncle August's Kiddie Show*. Before she was 10, she became a regular on "Major Bowes Amateur Hour," earning about $100 a week, the most of anyone in her touring unit. When she turned 12, however, her parents decided she should stay closer to home and concentrate on her school work. She continued performing on local radio, eventually getting her own show billing her as "Toledo's Miss Talent."

In 1948, Breuer and three other local entertainers won a local competition and were flown out to N.Y. to compete in a national contest. Winning that event earned Breuer an acetate recorder and a week's engagement at the Latin Quarter. She changed her name to Brewer thinking it would appear more theatrical on the Latin Quarter Marquee. In the wake of many more talent competition wins, she earned a regular role at the Latin Quarter and appearances at other local clubs, including the Sawdust Trail. At that club she was signed by an agent, who introduced Brewer to the record companies.

One of the early American signings on London records, Brewer put out three singles that went nowhere. Next, she returned to the studio with The Dixieland All Stars to record "Copenhagen," with a throwaway B-side. Disc jockeys picked up on the infectious B-side, a tune called "Music, Music, Music." It spent four weeks on the top of the charts, selling over a million copies in 1950.

This started a period Brewer refers to as her "Ootsy-poo period." Her next hit, also with the Dixieland All Stars, was the #17 "Choo'n Gum." London also saddled her with tunes like "Molasses, Molasses" and other music she felt should have been children's records. Her final hit for London, however, was "Longing for You." A variation on Oskar Strauss's "Dream Waltz," she brought it to #23 on the charts. She also married and had a daughter.

At the ripe old age of 20, Brewer moved on to Coral records. Here she worked with producer Bob Theile. Her first hit introduced in 1952 was "Gonna Get Along without You Now," a tune she took to #25 but that would chart higher for later singers. Her duet with Don Cornell, "You'll Never Get Away Again," went to #17. Her third hit of 1952, "Till I Waltz Again with You," became one of the biggest hits of the year, topping the charts for seven weeks and going gold. She was named the country's most popular female singer in a poll taken by Paramount pictures, who cast her in *Those Redheads from Seattle*.

Brewer received good reviews for her acting debut, and Paramount offered her a seven-year contract. However, she turned it down, not wanting to uproot her family (now three children) from their home in suburban New Rochelle. Instead, she worked on television,

still based largely in N.Y during the 1950s. She co-starred with Mel Torme on the network series "Summertime USA," and continued to record. 1953's "Dancin' with Someone (Longin' for You)" hit #17 and "Into Each Life Some Rain Must Fall" went to #23. She recorded her next tune, "Richochet," while suffering from a cold, but it didn't stop it from spending two weeks at #2 and going gold. This was followed by a song from the film *Those Redheads from Seattle*, "Baby, Baby, Baby," which rose to #12.

Brewer's next single, 1954's "Bell Bottom Blues" backed with "Our Heart Breaking Waltz," became one of those rare double A-sided singles, with the former rising to #17 and the latter hitting #23. For her next record she started dabbling in country. The tune "Jilted" hit #6. She followed this with 1955's "Let Me Go Lover," the theme to a popular TV show, which also hit #6. She headlined supper clubs around the country, rising to the ranks of headliner at her old haunt, the Latin Quarter, where she broke house records.

As the 1950s progressed and rock and roll took over, Brewer started doing MOR covers of hits by rock and R&B artists. In 1955, she had a hit with "Pledging My Love" (#17, equal to Johnny Aces's original). In 1956 she took Ivory Joe Hunter's "A Tear Fell" to #5 (Hunter got to #15 R&B) and Fats Domino's "Bo Weevil" to #17 (Domino only got to #35). In 1957 she took Hunter's "Empty Arms" to #13 (Hunter's version didn't chart pop) and Sam Cooke's "You Send Me" to #8 (Cooke had topped the charts with it). She also recorded tunes that were in the style of her older hits, like "A Sweet Old Fashioned Girl," which she took to #7 in 1956. While Brewer last hit the Top 40 in 1960, with "Anymore" (#31), she continued to record and appear, usually on television so she could be at home. Through the 1960s, she recorded occasionally, played live occasionally and spent most of her time with her family.

In the 1970s, she was reunited with Thiele. He convinced her to perform for his new Flying Dutchman label and got her excited about recording—and other things. She wound up divorcing her husband of over 20 years to marry Thiele. While she didn't have any hits, her albums for Flying Dutchman included sessions with the Count Basie Orch., Stephane Grappelli, and the final recording Duke Ellington ever did. She cut a rock record that had an electric version of "Music, Music, Music." As her family grew older, she started performing live more frequently, interrupted only by Thiele's passing in 1996. She continues to headline casinos and clubs into her 60s, not having lost a note since she was two.

DISC.: *Midnight Cafe* (1982); *Good Ship Lollipop* (1983); *Best of Teresa Brewer* (1989); *16 Most Requested Songs* (1991); *Music! Music! Music! The Best* (1995); *Good News* (1996).—**HB**

Brewster, William Herbert Sr., black American gospel singer and songwriter; b. Somerville, Tenn., July 2, 1897; d. Memphis, Oct. 14, 1987. He was educated at Roger Williams Coll. in Nashville, Tenn. (B.A., 1922). In 1928 he became pastor of the East Trigg Baptist Church in Memphis. He was founder-director of the Brewster Theological Clinic there, which maintained branches in many other U.S. cities. He possessed a fine baritone voice and toured with his own group, the Brewster Ensemble. He composed over 200 gospel songs, the most popular being "Move on Up a Little Higher" (1946) and "Surely, God is Able" (1949). He also wrote over 15 biblical music dramas.

BIBL.: *A Retrospective of Gospel Music Composer Reverend W.H. B.* (Washington, D.C., 1982).—**NS/LK/DM**

Brey, Carter, American cellist; b. Glen Ridge, N.J., Sept. 19, 1954. He was a student of Laurence Lesser (1972–74) and Stephen Kates (1974–76) at the Peabody Inst. in Baltimore, and of Aldo Parisot (1977–78) at Yale Univ. After winning first prize in the duo category with pianist Barbara Weintraub at the Munich International Competition in 1978, he took third prize in the first Rostropovich International Cello Competition in Paris in 1981. In 1982 he won the Young Concert Artists Auditions and made his formal debut at the Kennedy Center in Washington, D.C. In 1984 he received an Avery Fisher Career Grant. From 1983 he pursued a career as a soloist with the major orchs., as a recitalist, and as a chamber music player. He became principal cellist of the N.Y. Phil. in 1996.—**NS/LK/DM**

Brian, (William) Havergal, English composer of extreme fecundity and longevity; b. Dresden, Staffordshire, Jan. 29, 1876; d. Shoreham-by-the-Sea, Sussex, Nov. 28, 1972. He studied violin, cello, and organ with local teachers; left school at age 12 to earn his living and help his father, who was a potter's turner. At the same time he taught himself elementary theory and also learned French and German without an instructor. From 1904 to 1949 he engaged in musical journalism. He attained a reputation in England as a harmless eccentric possessed by inordinate ambitions to become a composer; he attracted supporters among English musicians, who in turn were derided as gullible admirers of a patent amateur. But Brian continued to write music in large symphonic forms; some of his works were performed, mostly by non- professional organizations; amazingly enough, he increased his productivity with age; he wrote 22 syms. after reaching the age of 80, and 7 more after the age of 90. The total number of syms. at the time of his death was 32. Finally, English musicians, critics, conductors, and concert organizations became aware of the Brian phenomenon, and performances, mostly posthumous, followed. A Havergal Brian Soc. was formed in London, and there were a few timorous attempts to further the Brian cause outside of England. The slow acceptance of Brian's music was not due to his overindulgence in dissonance. Quite the contrary is true; Brian was not an innovator; he followed the Germanic traditions of Richard Strauss and Mahler in the spirit of unbridled grandiosity, architectural formidability, and rhapsodically quaquaversal thematicism. Brian's modernism tended to be programmatic, as in the ominous whole-tone progressions in his opera *The Tigers,* illustrating the aerial attacks on London by zeppelins during World War I. Brian's readiness to lend his MSS to anyone showing interest in his music resulted in the loss of several of his works; a few of them were retrieved after years of search.

WORKS: O p e r a : *The Tigers,* to his own libretto (1916–19; lost until 1977; BBC, May 3, 1983); *Turandot,* to a German libretto after Schiller (1950–51); *The Cenci,* after Shelley (1952); *Faust,* after Goethe (1955–56); *Agamemnon,* to an English libretto after Aeschylus (1957; London, Jan. 28, 1972). **ORCH.:** *Tragic Prelude* (1899–1900; not extant); *Burlesque Variations on an Original Theme* (1903; lost until 1974; Hull, March 13, 1980); *For Valour,* concert overture (1904; rev. 1906; London, Oct. 8, 1907); *Hero and Leander,* symphonic poem (1904–05; Hanley, Dec. 3, 1908; not extant); 5 English Suites: No. 1 (1904–06; Leeds, Jan. 12, 1907), No. 2, *Night Portraits* (1915; not extant), No. 3 (1919–21; Bournemouth, March 16, 1922), No. 4, *Kindergarten* (1924; London, July 5, 1977), and No. 5, *Rustic Scenes* (1953); *Fantastic Variations on an Old Rhyme* (1907; 1st movement of *A Fantastic Symphony;* rev. 1912; Brighton, April 28, 1921); *Festal Dance* (1908; 3rd movement of *A Fantastic Symphony;* Birmingham, Dec. 14, 1914)); *In Memoriam* (1910; Edinburgh, Dec. 26, 1921); *Comedy Overture* No. 1: *Doctor Merryheart* (1911–12; Birmingham, Jan. 3, 1913), No. 2: *The Tinker's Wedding* (1948; BBC, Glasgow, June 25, 1950, and No. 3: *The Jolly Miller* (1962; Philadelphia, Nov. 15, 1974); 32 syms.: No. 1, *The Gothic,* in 2 parts of 3 movements each (Part II is a setting of the *Te Deum)* for 4 Vocal Soloists, 4 Mixed Choruses, Children's Chorus, 4 Brass Bands, and Very Large Orch. (1919–27; amateur perf., London, June 24, 1961; professional perf., London, Oct. 30, 1966), No. 2 (1930–31; Brighton, May 19, 1973), No. 3 (1931–32; BBC, Oct. 18, 1974), No. 4, *Das Siegeslied,* a German setting of *Psalm 68* in the Lutheran version, for Soprano, Double Mixed Chorus, and Orch. (1932–33; BBC, July 3, 1967), No. 5, *Wine of Summer,* for Baritone and Orch. (1937; London, Dec. 11, 1969), No. 6, *Tragica* (1948; BBC, Sept. 21, 1966), No. 7 (1948; BBC, March 13, 1968), No. 8 (1949; BBC, Feb. 1, 1954), No. 9 (1951; BBC, March 22, 1958), No. 10 (1953–54; BBC, Nov. 3, 1958), No. 11 (1954; BBC, Nov. 5, 1959), No. 12 (1957; BBC, Nov. 5, 1959), No. 13 (1959; BBC, May 14, 1978), No. 14 (1959–60; BBC, May 10, 1970), No. 15 (1960; BBC, May 14, 1978), No. 16 (1960; BBC, June 18, 1975), No. 17 (1960–61; BBC, May 14, 1978), No. 18 (1961; London, Feb. 26, 1962), No. 19 (1961; BBC, Dec. 31, 1976), No. 20 (1962; London, Oct. 5, 1976), No. 21 (1963; BBC, May 10, 1970), No. 22, *Brevis* (1964–65; BBC, Aug. 15, 1971), No. 23 (1965; Galesburg, Ill., Oct. 4, 1973), No. 24 (1965; BBC, June 18, 1975), No. 25 (1965–66; BBC, Dec. 31, 1976), No. 26 (1966; Stoke on Trent, May 13, 1976), No. 27 (1966; BBC, March 18, 1979), No. 28 (1967; BBC, Oct. 5, 1973), No. 29 (1967; Stoke on Trent, Nov. 17, 1976), No. 30 (1967; London, Sept. 24, 1976), No. 31 (1968; London, March 18, 1979), and No. 32 (1968; London, Jan. 28, 1971); 2 violin concertos: No. 1 (1934; stolen and presumed destroyed) and No. 2 (1934–35; London, June 20, 1969); *Elegy* (1954; London, Feb. 17, 1977); Cello Concerto (1964; London, Feb. 5, 1971); *Concerto for Orch.* (1964; Leeds, April 12, 1975); *Ave Atque Vale,* legend (1968). **CHAMBER:** *Legend* for Violin and Piano (1919); *Festival Fanfare* for Brass (1967; originally *Fanfare for the Brass;* Urbana, Ill., May 7, 1972). **P i a n o :** *3 Illuminations* (1916); *Double Fugue* in E major (1924); *Prelude and Fugue* in C minor (1924); *Prelude and Fugue* in D major and D minor (1924); *John Dowland's Fancy,* prelude (1934). **VOCAL:** *Requiem* for Baritone, Chorus, and Orch. (1897; not extant); *Psalm 23* for Tenor, Chorus, and Orch. (1904; full score not extant; reconstructed 1945; Hove, March 10, 1973); *By the Waters of Babylon* for Baritone, Chorus, and Orch. (1905; rev. 1909; Hanley, April 18, 1907; full score not extant); *Carmilhan,* dramatic ballad for Soloists, Chorus, and Orch. (1906; not extant); *The Vision of Cleopatra,* cantata for Soloists, Chorus, and Orch. (1907; Southport, Oct. 14, 1909; full score destroyed by fire); *Pilgrimage to*

Kevlaar, ballad for Chorus and Orch. (1913–14; not extant); *Prometheus Unbound*, lyric drama for Soloists, Double Chorus, and Orch., after Shelley (1937–44; full score not extant); choruses; over 100 songs.

BIBL.: R. Nettel, *Ordeal by Music: The Strange Experience of H. B.* (London, 1945); L. Foreman, ed., *H. B.: A Collection of Essays* (London, 1969); M. MacDonald, *H. B.: Perspective on the Music* (London, 1972); idem, *The Symphonies of H. B.* (3 vols., London, 1974–83); K. Eastaugh, *H. B.: The Making of a Composer* (London, 1976); L. Foreman, *H. B. and the Performance of His Orchestral Music: A History and a Sourcebook* (London, 1976); R. Nettel, *H. B. and His Music* (London, 1976); P. Rapoport, *Opus Est* (London, 1979); J. Schaarwächter, ed., *HB: Aspects of H. B.* (Aldershot, 1997).—**NS/LK/DM**

Briccetti, Thomas (Bernard), American conductor and composer; b. Mt. Kisco, N.Y., Jan, 14, 1936; d. Perugia, May 27, 1999. He studied piano with Jean Dansereau and composition with Barber, Mennin, and Hovhaness, and attended the Eastman School of Music in Rochester, N.Y. (1955). In 1959–60 he held the Prix de Rome, and then Ford Foundation Composer's fellowships (1961–63). He was music director of the St. Petersburg (Fla.) Sym. Orch. (1963–68) and the Florida Sun Coast Opera (1964–68). He was assoc. conductor of the Indianapolis Sym. Orch. (1968–72). From 1971 to 1978 he was music director of the Ft. Wayne (Ind.) Phil., and also of the Cleveland Inst. of Music Univ. Circle Orch. (1972–75). He was music director of the Omaha Sym. Orch. and Nebr. Sinfonia (1975–83). After serving as principal guest conductor of the Stavanger Sym. Orch. and Radio Ensemble (1986–87), he was artistic director of the Orch. Stabile in Bergamo (from 1988) and principal conductor of the Orch. Sinfonica in Umbria (from 1988). His compositions included *Eurydice*, opera; Sym.; Violin Concerto; *The Fountain of Youth*, overture; *Illusions*, symphonic poem; String Quartet; Flute Sonata; Piano Sonata; choral music; songs.—**NS/LK/DM**

Brice, Carol (Lovette Hawkins), black American contralto; b. Sedalia, N.C., April 16, 1918; d. Norman, Okla., Feb. 15, 1985. She received training at Palmer Memorial Inst. in Sedalia, at Talladega (Ala.) Coll. (B.Mus., 1939), and from Francis Rogers at the Juilliard School of Music in N.Y. (1939–43). She first attracted attention when she sang in *The Hot Mikado* at the N.Y. World's Fair (1939); she was also chosen to sing at a concert for President Roosevelt's third inauguration in 1941 and was the first black American to win the Naumburg Award (1943). Among her many stage roles were Addie in *Regina*, Maude in *Finian's Rainbow*, Maria in *Porgy and Bess*, Queenie in *Showboat*, and Harriet Tubman in *Gentlemen, Be Seated*. She was a member of the Vienna Volksoper (1967–71), then taught at the Univ. of Okla. (from 1974). With her husband, the baritone Thomas Carey, she founded the Cimarron Circuit Opera Co.—**NS/LK/DM**

Bricken, Carl Ernest, American composer, conductor, and pianist; b. Shelbyville, Ky., Dec. 28, 1898; d. Sweet Briar, Va., Jan. 25, 1971. He studied with Scalero at the Mannes School of Music in N.Y., and also pursued

training at Yale Univ., in Vienna, and with Cortot at the École Normale de Musique in Paris. He taught at the Mannes School of Music (1925–28) and at the Inst. of Musical Art in N.Y.; in 1931 he organized the music dept. at the Univ. of Chicago, and was its chairman until becoming prof. of music at the Univ. of Wisc. in 1938. After serving as conductor of the Seattle Sym. Orch. (1944–48), he taught at Sweet Briar Coll. (1954–63) before devoting himself to painting. He wrote 3 syms., and other orch. works, chamber music, and piano pieces.—**NS/LK/DM**

Bricktop
See **Smith, Ada (Beatrice Queen Victoria Louise Virginia)**

Brico, Antonia, Dutch-American pianist, conductor, and teacher; b. Rotterdam, June 26, 1902; d. Denver, Aug. 3, 1989. She studied at the Univ. of Calif. at Berkeley (graduated, 1923); after piano studies with Stojowski in N.Y., she studied conducting at the Berlin Hochschule für Musik and privately with Muck. Overcoming general skepticism concerning women conductors, she raised funds to conduct a special concert of the Berlin Phil. on Jan. 10, 1930, which aroused some curiosity. On Aug. 1, 1930, she conducted the Los Angeles Phil. at the Hollywood Bowl. She then pursued her career in N.Y., where she was founder-conductor of the Women's Sym. Orch. (1934–38). In 1938 she became the first woman to conduct the N.Y. Phil. In 1941 she settled in Denver, where she founded and conducted her own semiprofessional Antonia Brico Sym. Orch., making her last appearance on the podium in 1985. In the film documentary *Antonia* (1974), she eloquently pleaded for the feminist cause in music and especially in conducting.—**NS/LK/DM**

Bridge, Frank, distinguished English composer; b. Brighton, Feb. 26, 1879; d. Eastbourne, Jan. 10, 1941. He studied composition with Stanford at the Royal Coll. of Music in London (1899–1903). He was active as a violinist and violist in several string quartets, among them the Joachim, Grimson, and English string quartets. In 1910–11 he was conductor of the New Sym. Orch. in London, and in 1913 he conducted at Covent Garden there. In 1923 he toured the U.S. conducting his own works. As a composer, Bridge received recognition only in the last years of his life. After his death, greater appreciation arose, particularly in his homeland. In his early works, he followed the paths of Delius, Ireland, and Bax. After World War I, he pursued a more adventuresome route, influenced by the Second Viennese School, although never embracing serialism. Among his most remarkable advanced works are the third and fourth string quartets. Britten, his ardent student and admirer, composed his *Variations on a Theme of Frank Bridge* after the latter's *Idyll* No. 2 for String Quartet.

WORKS: DRAMATIC: *The 2 Hunchbacks*, incidental music (London, Nov. 15, 1910, composer conducting); *The Pageant of London* (1911); *Threads*, incidental music (London, Aug. 23, 1921); *In the Shop*, children's ballet (1921); *The Christmas Rose*, opera (1919–29; London, Dec. 8, 1931, composer conducting).

ORCH.: *Berceuse* for Violin and Strings (1901; London, June 20, 1902); *Coronation March* (1901); *Valse intermezzo à cordes* for Strings (1902); *Trois Morceau d'orchestre* (1902); *Serenade* (1903); *Symphonic Poem* (1903; London, May 20, 1904, composer conducting); *Norse Legend* (1905); *Rosemary* (1906); *Dramatic Overture* (c. 1906); *Isabella* (London, Oct. 3, 1907); *Dance Rhapsody* (London, July 21, 1908, composer conducting); *An Irish Melody* for Strings (1908; also for String Quartet); Suite for Strings (1909–10); *The Sea* (1911; London, Sept. 24, 1912); *Dance Poem* (1913; London, March 16, 1914, composer conducting); *Lament* for Strings (London, Sept. 15, 1915); *Summer* (1914–15; London, March 13, 1916, composer conducting); *2 Poems* (1915; London, Jan. 1, 1917, composer conducting); *2 Old English Songs* for Strings (London, Sept. 26, 1916, composer conducting); *Sir Roger de Coverley* (London, Oct. 21, 1922, composer conducting; also for String Orch., 1938); *Vignettes de danse* for Small Orch. (1925; BBC, Glasgow, May 12, 1941); *Canzonetta* for Small Orch. (1926); *There is a willow grows aslant a brook* for Small Orch. (London, Aug. 20, 1927, composer conducting); *Enter Spring* (Norwich, Oct. 27, 1927, composer conducting); *Oration, concerto elegiaco* for Cello and Orch. (1930; BBC, Jan. 16, 1936, Florence Hooten soloist, composer conducting); *Phantasm* for Piano and Orch. (1931; London, Jan. 10, 1934, Kathleen Long soloist, composer conducting); *Todessehnsucht (Come Sweet Death)* for Strings (1936); *Rebus* (1940; London, Feb. 23, 1941); Sym. for Strings (1940; unfinished; 1st movement, Aldeburgh Festival, June 20, 1979). **CHAMBER:** 2 piano trios: No. 1 (London, Nov. 14, 1900) and No. 2 (1928–29; London, Nov. 4, 1929); String Quintet (London, Dec. 4, 1901); *Scherzo phantastick* for 2 Violins, Viola, and Cello (1901; London, June 27, 1907); 1 unnumbered string quartet (1900; London, March 14, 1901); 4 numbered string quartets: No. 1 (1906; London, June 16, 1909), No. 2 (1914–15; London, Nov. 4, 1915), No. 3 (1925–27; Vienna, Sept. 17, 1927), and No. 4 (1937; Pittsfield, Mass., Sept. 23, 1938); Piano Quartet (1902; London, Feb. 23, 1903); 2 violin sonatas: No. 1 (1904) and No. 2 (1932; London, Jan. 18, 1934); *Elégie* for Cello and Piano (1904; Kensington, March 6, 1908); 2 piano quintets: No. 1 (1905; London, May 28, 1907) and No. 2 (London, May 29, 1992); *Phantasie* for String Quartet (1905; London, June 22, 1906); String Sextet (1906–12; London, June 18, 1913); *3 Idylls* for String Quartet (1906; London, March 8, 1907); *Phantasy* for Piano Trio (1907; London, April 27, 1909); *Allegro appassionato* for Viola and Piano (c. 1907; London, Nov. 24, 1909); 3 sets of *Miniatures* for Violin, Cello, and Piano (c. 1908; Exeter, Nov. 7, 1913); *Phantasy* for Piano Quartet (1910; London, Jan. 21, 1911); *2 Pieces* for 2 Violas (1911–12; London, March 18, 1912); Cello Sonata (1913–17; London, July 13, 1917); *Rhapsody* for 2 Violins and Viola (1928; Aldeburgh Festival, June 24, 1965); *Divertimenti* for Flute, Oboe, Clarinet, and Bassoon (1934; rev. 1937–38; Washington, D.C., April 14, 1940); Viola Sonata (c. 1935; unfinished). **KEYBOARD: Piano:** *2 capriccios* (1905); *Dramatic fantasia* (1906); *3 sketches* (1906); *3 Poems* (1913–14); *4 Characteristic Pieces* (1917); *A Fairy Tale* (1917); 3 sets of *Miniature pastorals* (1917, 1921, 1921); *3 Improvisations* for Piano, left-hand (1918); *The Hour Glass* (1919–20); Sonata (1924; London, Oct. 15, 1925, Myra Hess pianist); *In Autumn* (1924); *Winter pastoral* (1925). **Organ:** *3 Pieces* (c. 1905); 2 books of *Organ Pieces* (1905, 1912); *Lento: Im memoriam C(harles) H(ubert) H(astings) P(arry)* (1918); *3 Pieces* (1939). **VOCAL:** *Music when soft voices die* for Chorus (1904); *A Prayer* for Chorus and Orch. (1916; London, Jan. 1919, composer conducting; also for Chorus and Organ); *A Litany* for Women's Chorus (1918); *Evening Primrose* for Women's Chorus and Piano (1923); *Golden Slumbers* for Women's Voices (1923); solo songs.

BIBL.: P. Pirie, *F. B.* (London, 1971); A. Payne and L. Foreman, *F. B.* (London, 1976); P. Hindmarsh, *F. B.: A Thematic Catalogue* (London, 1983); A. Payne, *F. B.: Radical and Conservative* (London, 1984); K. Little, *F. B.: A Bio-Bibliography* (N.Y., 1991).—NS/LK/DM

Bridge, Joseph (Cox), English organist and composer, brother of **Sir (John) Frederick Bridge;** b. Rochester, Aug. 16, 1853; d. St. Albans, March 29, 1929. He studied with his brother and with John Hopkins. From 1877 to 1925 was organist of Chester Cathedral; in 1879 he revived the Chester Triennial Music Festival and became its conductor until 1900. He also founded (1883) and conducted for 20 years the Chester Musical Soc., and from 1908 was a prof. of music at Durham Univ.

WORKS: Oratorio, *Daniel* (1885); 2 cantatas: *Rudel* (1891) and *Resurgam* (1897); *Evening Service*, with Orch. (1879); Requiem Mass (1900); operetta, *The Belle of the Area*; Sym. (1894); String Quartet; Cello Sonata; anthems, organ music, piano pieces, songs.—NS/LK/DM

Bridge, Sir (John) Frederick, English organist, conductor, and composer, brother of **Joseph (Cox) Bridge;** b. Oldbury, near Birmingham, Dec. 5, 1844; d. London, March 18, 1924. At the age of 14 he was apprenticed to John Hopkins, organist of Rochester Cathedral, and later studied under John Goss. He was principal organist at Westminster Abbey (1882–1918), and took the degree of D.Mus. at Oxford in 1874 with his oratorio Mount Moriah. He then taught harmony and organ at various music schools, including the Royal Coll. of Music (from 1883). He was conductor of the Highbury Phil. Soc. (1878–86), the Madrigal Soc., and the Royal Choral Soc. (1896–1922); also served as chairman of Trinity Coll. of Music. He was knighted in 1897. He publ. primers on counterpoint, canon, organ accompaniment, and other subjects; also *A Course of Harmony* (with Sawyer; 1899), *Samuel Pepys, Lover of Music* (1903), an autobiography, *A Westminster Pilgrim* (1918), *12 Good Musicians from John Bull to Henry Purcell* (1920), *The Old Cryes of London* (1921), and *Shakespearean Music in the Plays and Early Operas* (1923); also ed. selected motets of Orlando Gibbons (1907).

WORKS: 4 cantatas: *Boadicea* (1880), *Rock of Ages* (1885), *Callirrhoe* (1888), and *The Lobster's Garden Party, or The Selfish Shellfish* (1904); dramatic oratorio, *The Repentance of Nineveh* (Worcester, 1890); concert overture, *Morte d'Arthur* (1896); choral ballades.—NS/LK/DM

Bridgetower, George (Auguste Polgreen), violinist; b. Biala, Poland, Oct. 11, 1778; d. Peckham, Surrey, Feb. 28, 1860. His father was an Abyssinian; his mother, of Polish extraction. He studied with Giornovichi. As a youth he went to England and entered the service of the Prince of Wales. In 1791, at the age of 13, he played in the violin section of the Haydn-Salomon Concerts in London. On Oct. 4, 1807, he was elected to the membership of the Royal Soc. of Musicians in London. In 1811 he received his Bachelor of Music degree from Cambridge Univ. From about 1829 to 1843 he resided mostly in Paris and Rome, eventually returning to England, where he married and settled in

Surrey. His name is historically important because of his association with Beethoven; it was Bridgetower who gave the first performance, from MS, of the *Kreutzer Sonata*, with Beethoven himself at the piano, in Vienna on May 24, 1803. Beethoven spelled his name in a German orthography as Brischdower.—**NS/LK/DM**

Briegel, Wolfgang Carl, German organist and composer; b. Königsberg, May 1626; d. Darmstadt, Nov. 19, 1712. He received his musical training in Nuremberg; from 1645 to 1650 he was active in Schweinfurt. In 1650 he was appointed cantor at the court of Gotha, and in 1671 he went to Darmstadt, where he served as court Kapellmeister until his death. He dedicated himself primarily to sacred choral composition, and publ. a number of collections for the Lutheran church service, among them *Evangelische Gespräch*, in 3 parts (1660, 1662, 1681), *Geistliche Arien*, in 2 parts (1660–61), *Evangelischer Blumengarten*, in 4 parts (1666–69), *Evangelischer Palmen-Zweig* (1685), *Evangelische Harpfen* (1685), *Apostolische Chormusik* (1697), and *Letzter Schwanengesang* (1709). He also wrote instrumental works in dance forms, for instruments and voices, under such inviting Baroque titles as *Musicalisches Tafelkonfekt* (1672); a Singspiel, *Das triumphierende Siegespiel der wahren Liebe*; and other theatrical music.

BIBL.: K.F. Hirschmann, *W.C. B.* (Giessen, 1936); E. Noack, *W.C. B.: Ein Barock-Komponist in seiner Zeit* (Berlin, 1963).
—**NS/LK/DM**

Briggs, Pete, jazz tuba player, bassist; b. Charleston, S.C., c. 1904. He was a distant relative of Arthur Briggs. He toured with the Jim Jam Jazzers in the early 1920s, then worked with the Lucky Boy Minstrels (late 1923). He worked in Chicago with Carroll Dickerson (c. 1926), with Louis Armstrong's Stompers at the Sunset Cafe (1927), also doubled with Jimmie Noone at the Apex Club (1927). Briggs took part in Louis Armstrong's Hot Seven recordings (1927). He was with Carroll Dickerson (1928), to N.Y. with Dickerson and Louis Armstrong (1929). He soon joined Edgar Hayes' Orch. at the Alhambra, N.Y. (1929–30). During the 1930s worked for several years in N.Y. in Vernon Andrade's Orch. He was with Herman Autrey's Band in Philadelphia (1943–44). He left music to run his own farm.—**JC/LP**

Brilioth, Helge, Swedish tenor; b. Vaxjo, May 7, 1931. He studied at the Stockholm Musikhögskolan, the Accademia di Santa Cecilia in Rome, and the Salzburg Mozarteum. In 1958 he made his operatic debut in the baritone role of Bartolo in Paisiello's *Il Barbiere di Siviglia* in Stockholm; then sang in Bielefeld (1962–64). After further training in Stockholm, he made his debut as a tenor there in 1965 in the role of Don José. In 1969 he made his first appearance at the Bayreuth Festival as Siegmund. He sang Siegfried in *Götterdämmerung* at the Salzburg Easter Festival in 1970. On Nov. 14, 1970, he made his Metropolitan Opera debut in N.Y. as Parsifal, where he remained on the roster until 1974. He subsequently concentrated his career in Europe.—**NS/LK/DM**

Brimfield, William, jazz trumpeter; b. Chicago, Ill., April 8, 1938. He began studying piano and violin.

In 1957, he studied with Fred Anderson. In 1961, on discharge from the army, he met Richard Muhal Abrams. Along with Anderson, Brimfield joined the Joseph Jarman Sextet. He has played with George Hunter, Red Saunders, Lionel Hampton, Abrams big band, Edwin Daugherty's Third World. He is a member of AACM.—**LP**

Brindle, Reginald Smith
See **Smith Brindle, Reginald**

Brînduş, Nicolae, Romanian composer, pianist, writer on music, and teacher; b. Bucharest, April 16, 1935. He studied piano (1952–57) and composition (1960–64) at the Bucharest Univ. of Music, and then attended intermittent summer courses in new music in Darmstadt (1969–80). Later he worked at IRCAM in Paris (1985). After serving as pianist of the Ploieşti Phil. (1960–69), he taught chamber music at the Bucharest Univ. of Music (1969–81). In 1981 he became an ed. of the journal *Musica*. He also was a prof. of chamber music at the Bucharest Cons. from 1992. From 1993 he lectured on contemporary music in N.Y., Washington, D.C., Los Angeles, Northampton, Reno, Hong Kong, Israel, China et al. After serving on the executive committee of the ISCM (1991–93), he was president of its Romanian section (from 1994). He publ. the theoretical vol. *Interferenţe* (Interrelations; Bucharest, 1984). Among his honors are the prizes of the Romanian Composers and Musicologists Union (1974), the Romanian Radio and TV (1975, 1977), and the Romanian Academy (1977). In his compositions, Brînduş has explored the utilization of modal and serial elements, improvisation, and electronics. He is also a leading advocate of the syncretic form known as instrumental theater.

WORKS: DRAMATIC: *Logodna* (The Betrothal), opera-pantomime (1964–66; Bucharest, Feb. 9, 1975); *La Tigănci* (With the Gypsy Girls), opera (1978–85; Bucharest, June 19, 1987). **Instrumental Theater:** *Kitsch-N* for Clarinet and Tape (1974; Warsaw, Sept. 1979); *Infrarealism* for Voice, Clarinet, and Piano (1975; Warsaw, Sept. 1981); *Languir me fais* for Percussionist (1979); *Prolegomene I* (1981) and *II* (1988) for Tenor and Piano or Bass and Double Bass; *Ouvédennerode* for Saxophone, Bass, and Tape (1993). **ORCH.:** *6 Miniatures* (1962–70; Braşov, June 4, 1970); *3 Pieces* (1964; Cluj-Napoca, May 14, 1966); *Music* for Chamber Orch. (1964; Tîrgu Mureş, May 5, 1966); *Phtora I-Durations* (1968; Bucharest, May 10, 1973); *Inscription* (1969; Arad, June 4, 1971); *Antiphonia* for String Chamber Orch. (Zagreb, May 4, 1971); *Match II- Monody I and Polyphony IV* for Chamber Orch. and Tape (Warsaw, Sept. 1973); 2 piano concertos: No. 1, *Dialogos* (1978; Iaşi, May 1979) and No. 2 (1993; Chişinău, April 1995); *Sineuphonia I* for 2 Organs, Orch., and Tape (1986–87; Chişinău, April 1994). **CHAMBER:** *Cantus Firmus-Phtora III* for Keyboard Instrument(s) and Other Instruments or Voices (1970); *Waves* for Piano, Violin, Viola, Cello, Clarinet, and Percussion (Darmstadt, July 1972); *Melopedia and Fugue* for Bassoon (1981); *Rhythmòdia*, concerto for Solo Percussion (1982); *K-N Comment 1988* for Flute and Tape (1988); *K-N Comment 1999* for Instrumental Ensemble (1999). **Piano:** *Pieces* (1962); *Ostinato* (1962); Sonata for 2 Pianos (1963). **VOCAL:** *The Ballad Symphony* (1964–78); *7 Psalms* for Baritone, Piano, and Percussion (1965); *Mărturie*, cantata for Chorus and

Orch. (1967; Bucharest, Feb. 16, 1971); *Domnişoara Huş*, cantata for Voices and Orch. (1968; Bucharest, Feb. 12, 1970); *Oratorio*, after the Thomas Evangile (1995–98). ELECTRONIC: *Ekstasis 256/n* (1997); *Apocalypse* (1999).—**NS/LK/DM**

Brioschi, Antonio, Italian composer who flourished in the first half of the 18ᵗʰ century. He was one of the earliest composers of Classical syms., some of which date from the early 1730s. A number of his syms. were publ. in his lifetime in Paris and London. He also wrote trio sonatas, some of which were publ. with G.B. Sammartini's in the 1740s.—**LK/DM**

Bristow, George Frederick, American violinist, organist, conductor, teacher, and composer; b. Brooklyn, Dec. 19, 1825; d. N.Y., Dec. 13, 1898. His father was the clarinetist, conductor, and composer William Richard Bristow (1803–67). He studied piano and violin with his father and W. Musgriff. It is believed that he later received lessons in violin from Ole Bull and in harmony, counterpoint, and orchestration from Henry Charles Timm. At age 13, he became a violinist in the Olympic Theatre Orch. in N.Y. In 1843 he joined the N.Y. Phil., playing in the first violin section until 1879. He also played in the orchs. that accompanied Jenny Lind (1850–51) and Marietta Alboni (1852), and in Jullien's orch. (1853–54). He was conductor of the N.Y. Harmonic Soc. (1851–63) and the Mendelssohn Soc. (1867–71), and also was active as a church organist and choirmaster. From 1854 he taught in the N.Y. public schools, and also privately. Bristow was notably active in N.Y. in promoting the cause of American music. All the same, his extensive output reflects European models, being well-crafted although lacking in originality. As a pedagogue, he publ. *Cantara, or Teacher of Singing* (with F. Nash; 1866; 2ⁿᵈ ed., enl., 1868), *George F. Bristow's New and Improved Method for the Reed or Cabinet Organ* (1887), and *Bristow's Two-part Vocal Exercises* (1890–95).

WORKS: Opera: *Rip Van Winkle* (1852–55; N.Y., Sept. 27, 1855; rev. 1878–82); *King of the Mountains* (1894; unfinished). ORCH.: 5 syms.: No. 1 in E-flat major (1848), No. 2 in D minor, *Jullien* (c. 1853; N.Y., March 1, 1856), No. 3 in F-sharp minor (1858; N.Y., March 26, 1859), No. 4, *Arcadian* (Brooklyn, Feb. 8, 1872), and No. 5, *Niagara*, for Soloists, Chorus, and Orch. (1893; N.Y., April 11, 1898); 4 overtures: E-flat major (1845; N.Y., Nov. 14, 1847), *Winter's Tale* (1856), *Columbus* (1861; N.Y., Nov. 17, 1866), and *Jibbenainosay* (N.Y., March 6, 1889). CHAMBER: *Duetto concertante* for Violin and Piano (1844; rev. as *La cracovian* for Violin and Orch., 1850); 2 string quartets (c. 1849, 1849); 3 duos for Violin and Viola; piano pieces; organ music. VOCAL: Sacred: *Gloria Patri, Praise to God* for Soloists, Chorus, and Orch. (1860; N.Y., March 2, 1861); *Daniel*, oratorio for Soloists, Chorus, and Orch. (1866; N.Y., Dec. 30, 1867); Mass for Soloists, Chorus, and Orch. (1885); various anthems, services, hymns, and chants. Secular: *The Pioneer*, cantata for Soloists, Chorus, and Orch. (c. 1872); *The Great Republic, Ode to the American Union* for Soloists, Chorus, and Orch. (Brooklyn, May 10, 1879).

BIBL.: D. Rogers, *Nineteenth-century Music in New York City as Reflected in the Career of G.F. B.* (diss., Univ. of Mich., 1967); B. Kauffman, *The Choral Works of G.F. B. (1825–1898) and William H.*

Fry (1815–1864) (diss., Univ. of Ill., 1975); K. Gombert, *"Leonora" by William Henry Fry and "Řip Van Winkle" by G.F. B.: Examples of Mid-nineteenth-century American Opera* (diss., Ball State Univ., 1977).—**NS/LK/DM**

Britain, Radie, American composer and teacher; b. Silverton, Tex., March 17, 1899; d. Palm Springs, Calif., May 23, 1994. After studying piano at the American Cons. in Chicago (B.M., 1924), she studied theory and composition with Noelte in Munich and organ with Dupré in Paris (1924–26); then continued her studies with Noelte in Chicago, and also had instruction in piano from Godowsky and organ from Yon. She taught harmony and composition at Chicago's Girvin Inst. of Music (1930–34); after teaching at the Chicago Cons. (1934–39), she taught piano and composition in Hollywood (1940–60). She publ. the book *Composer's Corner* (1978). Her autobiography appeared posthumously as *Ridin' Herd to Writing Symphonies* (Lanham, Md., 1996). Most of her compositions followed along traditional lines, inspired by various American subjects.

WORKS: DRAMATIC: *Ubiquity*, musical drama (1937); *Happyland*, children's operetta (1946); *Carillon*, opera (1952); *The Spider and the Butterfly*, children's operetta (1953); *Kuthara*, chamber opera (1960; Santa Barbara, June 24, 1961); *The Dark Lady Within*, drama with music (1962); *Western Temperament*, drama with music (telecast, Omaha, June 2, 1963); 4 ballets. ORCH.: *Prelude to a Drama* (1928; Chicago, Jan. 31, 1937); *Symphonic Intermezzo* (Chicago, Jan. 8, 1928); *Heroic Poem* (1929; Rochester, N.Y., March 3, 1932); *Rhapsodic Phantasie* for Piano and Orch. (1933; Chicago, April 24, 1938); *Nocturn* for Small Orch. (1934; Chicago, Nov. 10, 1940); *Light* (1935; Chicago, Nov. 29, 1938); *Southern Symphony* (1935; Chicago, March 4, 1940); *Ontonangon Sketches* (1939); *Saturnale* (1939); Suite for Strings (1940; Rochester, N.Y., Oct. 23, 1945); *Phantasy* for Oboe and Orch. (1942; Amarillo, Tex., April 22, 1958); *We Believe* (1942; Madrid, March 19, 1961); *Serenata Sorrentina* for Small Orch. (1946; Amarillo, Tex., April 8, 1947); *Cactus Rhapsody* (1953; Washington, D.C., April 4, 1960); *Cowboy Rhapsody* (Amarillo, Tex., April 11, 1956); *Cosmic Mist Symphony* (1962; Houston, April 18, 1967); *Pyramids of Giza* (1973; N.Y., Feb. 20, 1976); *Anwar Sadat (In Memory)* (1982); *Earth of God* for Strings (1984); *Sam Houston* (1987); *Texas* (1987). CHAMBER: Epic Poem for String Quartet (1927); String Quartet (1934; Chicago, Nov. 3, 1940); *Chipmunks* for Woodwind, Harp, and Percussion (1940); *Phantasy* for Oboe and Piano (1942; also for Oboe, Harp, and Piano); Serenade for Violin and Piano (1944); *Barcarola* for Violin and Piano (1948; also for Voice and 8 Cellos, 1958); *In the Beginning* for 4 Horns (1962); *Hebraic Poem* for String Quartet (1976); *Ode to NASA* for Brass Quintet (1981); *Soul of the Sea* for Cello and Piano (1984); many piano pieces, including a Sonata (1958). VOCAL: Choral works, songs cycles, and solo songs.

BIBL.: W. and N. Bailey, *R. B.: A Bio-Bibliography* (N.Y., 1990).—**NS/LK/DM**

Britten, (Edward) Benjamin, Lord Britten of Aldeburgh, outstanding English composer; b. Lowestoft, Suffolk, Nov. 22, 1913; d. Aldeburgh, Dec. 4, 1976. He grew up in moderately prosperous circumstances; his father was an orthodontist, his mother an amateur singer. He played the piano and improvised facile tunes; many years later he used these youthful inspirations in a symphonic work which he named

Simple Symphony. In addition to piano, he began taking viola lessons with Audrey Alston. At the age of 13, he was accepted as a pupil in composition by Frank Bridge, whose influence was decisive on Britten's development as a composer. In 1930 he entered the Royal Coll. of Music in London, where he studied piano with Arthur Benjamin and Harold Samuel, and composition with John Ireland until 1933. He progressed rapidly; even his earliest works showed a mature mastery of technique and a fine talent for lyrical expression. His *Fantasy Quartet* for Oboe and Strings was performed at the Festival of the ISCM in Florence on April 5, 1934. He became associated with the theater and the cinema and began composing background music for films. In 1936 he met Peter Pears. From 1937 they appeared in joint recitals, remaining intimate as well as professional companions until Britten's death. With the outbreak of World War II in 1939, Britten went to the U.S.; he returned to England in the spring of 1942; was exempted from military service as a conscientious objector. After the War, he organized the English Opera Group (1947), and in 1948 the Aldeburgh Festival, in collaboration with Eric Crozier and Pears; this Festival became an important cultural institution in England, serving as the venue for the first performances of many of Britten's own works, often under his direction; he also had productions at the Glyndebourne Festival. In his operas, he observed the economic necessity of reducing the orch. contingent to 12 performers, with the piano part serving as a modern version of the Baroque ripieno. This economy of means made it possible for small opera groups and univ. workshops to perform Britten's works; yet he succeeded in creating a rich spectrum of instrumental colors, in an idiom ranging from simple triadic progressions, often in parallel motion, to ultrachromatic dissonant harmonies; on occasion he applied dodecaphonic procedures, with thematic materials based on 12 different notes; however, he never employed the formal design of the 12–tone method of composition. A sui generis dodecaphonic device is illustrated by the modulatory scheme in Britten's opera *The Turn of the Screw*, in which each successive scene begins in a different key, with the totality of tonics aggregating to a series of 12 different notes. A characteristic feature in his operas is the inclusion of orch. interludes, which become independent symphonic poems in an impressionistic vein related to the dramatic action of the work. The cries of seagulls in Britten's most popular and musically most striking opera, *Peter Grimes*, create a fantastic quasi-surrealistic imagery. Britten was equally successful in treating tragic subjects, as in *Peter Grimes* and *Billy Budd*, comic subjects, exemplified by his *Albert Herring*, and mystical evocation, as in his *The Turn of the Screw*. He was also successful in depicting patriotic subjects, as in *Gloriana*, composed for the coronation of Queen Elizabeth II. He possessed a flair for writing music for children, in which he managed to present a degree of sophistication and artistic simplicity without condescension. In short, Britten was an adaptable composer who could perform a given task according to the specific requirements of the occasion. He composed a "realization" of Gay's *Beggar's Opera*. He also wrote modern "parables" for church perfor-

mance, and produced a contemporary counterpart of the medieval English miracle play *Noye's Fludde*. Among his other works is the remarkable *War Requiem*, a profound tribute to the dead of many wars. In 1952 Britten was made a Companion of Honour, in 1965 he received the Order of Merit, and in 1976 he became the first English composer to be created a life peer, becoming Lord Britten of Aldeburgh. In collaboration with Imogen Holst, Britten wrote *The Story of Music* (London, 1958) and *The Wonderful World of Music* (Garden City, N.Y., 1968; rev. ed., 1970).

WORKS: O p e r a : *Paul Bunyan* (N.Y., May 5, 1941; rev. 1974; BBC, Feb. 1, 1976; Aldeburgh, June 14, 1976); *Peter Grimes* (London, June 7, 1945); *The Rape of Lucretia* (Glyndebourne, July 12, 1946); *Albert Herring* (Glyndebourne, June 20, 1947, composer conducting); *The Beggar's Opera*, a realization of the ballad opera by John Gay (Cambridge, May 24, 1948, composer conducting); *The Little Sweep*, or *Let's Make an Opera*, "an entertainment for young people" with optional audience participation (Aldeburgh, June 14, 1949); *Billy Budd* (1st version in 4 acts; London, Dec. 1, 1951, composer conducting; rev. version in 2 acts, 1960; BBC, Nov. 13, 1960); *Gloriana* (London, June 8, 1953); *The Turn of the Screw*, chamber opera (Venice, Sept. 14, 1954, composer conducting); *Noye's Fludde*, children's opera (Aldeburgh, June 18, 1958); *A Midsummer Night's Dream* (Aldeburgh, June 11, 1960, composer conducting); *Curlew River*, church parable (Aldeburgh, June 12, 1964, composer conducting); *The Burning Fiery Furnace*, church parable (Aldeburgh, June 9, 1966, composer conducting); *The Prodigal Son*, church parable (Aldeburgh, June 10, 1968, composer conducting); *Owen Wingrave* (BBC-TV, May 16, 1971, composer conducting; stage premiere, London, May 10, 1973); *Death in Venice* (Aldeburgh, June 16, 1973); 2 realizations of operas by Purcell: *Dido and Aeneas* (London, May 1, 1951, composer conducting) and *The Fairy Queen*, a shortened version for concert perf. (Aldeburgh, June 25, 1967); a ballet, *The Prince of the Pagodas* (London, Jan. 1, 1957, composer conducting). **ORCH.:** *Sinfonietta* (1932; London, Jan. 31, 1933); Double Concerto for Violin, Viola, and Chamber Orch. (1932); *Simple Symphony* (Norwich, March 6, 1934, composer conducting); *Soirées musicales*, suite from Rossini (1936); *Variations on a Theme of Frank Bridge* for Strings (Salzburg, Aug. 27, 1937); *Mont Juic*, suite of Catalan dances (1937; BBC, Jan. 8, 1938; in collaboration with L. Berkeley); Piano Concerto (London, Aug. 18, 1938; rev. 1945; with an added 3rd movement, Cheltenham, July 2, 1946); Violin Concerto (1939; N.Y., March 28, 1940); *Young Apollo* for Piano, String Quartet, and Strings (Toronto, Aug. 27, 1939); *Canadian Carnival* (1939; BBC, June 6, 1940); *Sinfonia da Requiem* (1940; N.Y., March 29, 1941); *An American Overture* (1942); *Diversions* for Piano, Left-Hand, and Orch. (1940; Philadelphia, Jan. 16, 1942; rev. 1954); *Matinées musicales*, suite from Rossini (1941); *Scottish Ballad* for 2 Pianos and Orch. (Cincinnati, Nov. 28, 1941); *Prelude and Fugue* for 18 Strings (London, June 23, 1943); *4 Sea Interludes*, from *Peter Grimes* (Cheltenham, June 13, 1945); *The Young Person's Guide to the Orch.*, variations and fugue on a theme of Purcell (Liverpool, Oct. 15, 1946); Symphonic Suite from *Gloriana* (Birmingham, Sept. 23, 1954); *Pas de six* from *The Prince of the Pagodas* (Birmingham, Sept. 26, 1957); *Cello Symphony* (1963; Moscow, March 12, 1964, Rostropovich soloist, composer conducting); *The Building of the House*, overture for the opening of the Maltings concert hall (Aldeburgh, June 2, 1967, composer conducting); *Suite on English Folk Tunes* (1974; Aldeburgh, June 13, 1975); *Lachrymae, Reflections on a Song of John Dowland* for Viola and Strings (1976; Recklinghausen, May 3, 1977).

CHAMBER: *Quartettino* for String Quartet (1930; London, May 23, 1983); 1 unnumbered string quartet (1931; rev. 1974; Aldeburgh, June 7, 1975); 3 numbered string quartets: No. 1 (Los Angeles, Sept. 21, 1941), No. 2 (London, Nov. 21, 1945), and No. 3 (1975; Aldeburgh, Dec. 19, 1975); *Phantasy* in F minor for String Quintet (July 22, 1932); *Phantasy* for Oboe and String Trio (1932; Florence, April 5, 1934); Suite for Violin and Piano (1935; London, Jan. 27, 1936); *2 Insect Pieces* for Oboe and Piano (1935; Manchester, March 7, 1979); *3 Divertimenti* for String Quartet (London, Feb. 25, 1936); *Temporal Variations* for Oboe and Piano (London, Dec. 15, 1936); *Lachrymae, Reflections on a Song of John Dowland* for Viola and Piano (Aldeburgh, June 20, 1950); *6 Metamorphoses* for Oboe (Thorpress, June 14, 1951); *Alpine Suite* for 3 Recorders (1955); Cello Sonata (Aldeburgh, July 7, 1961); *Nocturnal* for Guitar (1963; Aldeburgh, June 12, 1964); *3 Suites* for Cello: No. 1 (1964; Aldeburgh, June 27, 1965), No. 2 (1967; Aldeburgh, June 17, 1968), and No. 3 (1971; Aldeburgh, Dec. 21, 1974); *Gemini Variations* for Flute, Violin, and Piano, 4–Hands (Aldeburgh, June 19, 1965); Suite for Harp (Aldeburgh, June 24, 1969). **P i a n o :** 5 waltzes (1923–25; rev. 1969); *Holiday Diary*, suite (1934); *Sonatina romantica* (1940; Aldeburgh, June 16, 1983). **VOCAL:** *A Hymn to the Virgin*, anthem for Mixed Voices (1930; Lowestoft, Jan. 5, 1931); *A Boy Was Born*, choral variations (1933; BBC, Feb. 23, 1934; rev. 1955); *Friday Afternoons* for Children's Voices (1935); *Te Deum in C* (1935; London, Jan. 27, 1936); *Our Hunting Fathers*, symphonic cycle for High Voice and Orch. (Norwich, Sept. 25, 1936, composer conducting); *On This Island*, 5 songs, after Auden (BBC, London, Nov. 19, 1937); *4 Cabaret Songs*, after Auden (1937–39); *Ballad of Heroes* for High Voice, Chorus, and Orch. (London, April 5, 1939); *Les Illuminations* for High Voice and Strings, after Rimbaud (1939; London, Jan. 30, 1940); *7 Sonnets of Michelangelo* for Tenor and Piano (1940; London, Sept. 23, 1942); *Hymn to St. Cecilia* for Chorus (London, Nov. 22, 1942); *A Ceremony of Carols* for Treble Voices and Harp (Norwich, Dec. 5, 1942); *Rejoice in the Lamb* for Chorus, Soloists, and Organ (Northampton, Sept. 21, 1943); *Serenade* for Tenor, Horn, and Strings (London, Oct. 15, 1943); *Festival Te Deum* (1944; Swindon, April 24, 1945); *The Holy Sonnets of John Donne* for High Voice and Piano (London, Nov. 22, 1945); *Canticle I, "My Beloved Is Mine"* for High Voice and Piano (Aldeburgh, Nov. 1, 1947); *A Charm of Lullabies* for Mezzo-soprano and Piano (1947; The Hague, Jan. 3, 1948; orchestrated by Colin Matthews; Indianapolis, Jan. 17, 1991, Forrester soloist, Leppard conducting); *Saint Nicolas*, cantata (Aldeburgh, June 5, 1948); *Spring Symphony* for Soloists, Chorus, and Orch. (Amsterdam, July 9, 1949); *5 Flower Songs* for Chorus (Dartington, South Devon, April 3, 1950); *Canticle II, Abraham and Isaac* (Nottingham, Jan. 21, 1952); *Choral Dances* from *Gloriana* (1953); *Winter Words* for High Voice and Piano, after Thomas Hardy (Harewood House, Leeds, Oct. 8, 1953); *Canticle III, Still Falls the Rain*, for Tenor, Horn, and Piano, after Edith Sitwell (London, Jan. 28, 1955); *Songs from the Chinese* for High Voice and Guitar (1957; Aldeburgh, June 17, 1958); *Nocturne* for Tenor, Obbligato Instruments, and Strings, after English poems (Leeds, Oct. 16, 1958); *6 Hölderlin Fragments* for Voice and Piano (Schloss Wolfsgarten, Nov. 20, 1958); *Cantata accademica* for Soloists, Chorus, and Orch. (1959; Basel, July 1, 1960); *Missa Brevis in D* for Boy's Voices and Organ (London, July 22, 1959); *War Requiem* for Soloists, Chorus, and Orch., after the Latin Requiem Mass and Wilfred Owen (Coventry, May 30, 1962, composer conducting); *Cantata Misericordium* for Soloists, Small Chorus, and Orch. (Geneva, Sept. 1, 1963); *Songs and Proverbs of William Blake* for Baritone and Piano (Aldeburgh, June 24, 1965); *Voices for Today*,

anthem for Chorus (triple premiere, N.Y., Paris, and London, Oct. 24, 1965); *The Poet's Echo* for High Voice and Piano, after Pushkin (Moscow, Dec. 2, 1965); *The Golden Vanity*, vaudeville for Boy's Voices and Piano (1966; Aldeburgh, June 3, 1967); *Children's Crusade*, ballad for Children's Voices and Orch., after Brecht (1968; London, May 19, 1969); *Who Are These Children?*, song cycle for Tenor and Piano (1969; Edinburgh, May 4, 1971); *Canticle IV, Journey of the Magi* for Tenor, Countertenor, Baritone, and Piano, after T.S. Eliot (Aldeburgh, June 26, 1971); *Canticle V, The Death of St. Narcissus* for Tenor and Harp, after T.S. Eliot (1974; Schloss Elmau, Bavaria, Jan. 15, 1975); *Sacred and Profane*, 8 medieval lyrics for Chorus (Aldeburgh, Sept. 14, 1975); *A Birthday Hansel* for Voice and Harp, after Robert Burns (1975; Cardiff, March 19, 1976); *Phaedra*, cantata for Mezzo-soprano and Chamber Orch. (1975; Aldeburgh, June 16, 1976); *Welcome Ode* for Children's Chorus and Orch. (1976; Ipswich, July 11, 1977); *8 British Folksongs* arranged for Voice and Orch.; *6 French Folksongs* arranged for Voice and Orch.; 6 vols. of British folk-song arrangements, with Piano Accompaniment (1943–61); realizations of Purcell's *Orpheus Brittanicus*, with Peter Pears; *4 chansons françaises* for High Voice and Orch. (1928; first perf. in concert form at Aldeburgh, June 10, 1980).

BIBL.: E. White, *B. B.* (London, 1948; 3rd ed., rev., 1983); D. Mitchell and H. Keller, eds., *B. B.: A Commentary of His Works from a Group of Specialists* (London, 1952); *Tribute to B. B. on His 50th Birthday* (London, 1963); I. Holst, *B.* (London, 1966; rev. ed., 1970); M. Hurd, *B. B.* (London, 1966); P. Young, *B.* (London, 1966); P. Howard, *The Operas of B. B.* (N.Y., 1969); A. Kendall, *B. B.* (London, 1973); D. Mitchell, *B. B., 1913–1976; A Pictorial Biography* (N.Y., 1978); P. Evans, *The Music of B. B.* (London, 1979); D. Herbert, ed., *The Operas of B. B.* (London, 1979); A. Blyth, *Remembering B.* (London, 1981); R. Duncan, *Working with B.: A Personal Memoir* (Welcombe, Devon, 1981); C. Headington, *B.* (London, 1981); M. Kennedy, *B.* (London, 1981; rev. ed., 1993); A. Whittall, *The Music of B. and Tippett: Studies in Themes and Techniques* (Cambridge, 1982; 2nd ed., 1990); P. Brett, *Peter Grimes* (Cambridge, 1983); C. Palmer, ed., *The B. Companion* (London, 1984); B. Britten, *My Brother B.* (Bourne End, 1987); S. Corse, *Opera and the Uses of Language: Mozart, Verdi, and B.* (London and Toronto, 1987); J. Evans, P. Reed, and P. Wilson, eds., *A B. Source Book* (Aldeburgh, 1987); D. Mitchell, *B. B.: Death in Venice* (Cambridge, 1987); P. Reed, *The Incidental Music of B. B.: A Study and Catalogue of His Music for Film, Theatre and Radio* (diss., Univ. of East Anglia, 1988); D. Mitchell and P. Reed, eds., *Letters from a Life: Selected Letters and Diaries of B. B.* (2 vols., Berkeley, 1991); H. Carpenter, *B. B.: A Biography* (London, 1992); P. Banks, ed., *B.'s 'Gloriana': Essays and Sources* (Woodbridge, Suffolk, 1993); M. Cook and P. Reed, eds., *B. B.: Billy Budd* (Cambridge, 1993); M. Saremba, *Elgar, B. & Co.: Eine Geschichte der britischen Musik in zwölf Portraits* (Zürich, 1994); P. Banks, ed., *The Making of Peter Grimes: The Facsimile of B.'s Composition Draft: Studies* (2 vols., Woodbridge, Suffolk, 1995); W. Godsalve, *B.'s A Midsummer Night's Dream: Making an Opera from Shakespeare's Comedy* (Madison, N.J., 1995); C. Mark, *Early B. B.: A Study of Stylistic and Technical Evolution* (Hamden, Conn., 1995); P. Reed, ed., *On Mahler and B.: Essays in Honour of Donald Mitchell on his Seventieth Birthday* (Woodbridge, Suffolk, 1995); M. Cooke, *B.: War Requiem* (Cambridge, 1996); X. de Gaulle, *B. B., ou, L'impossible quiétude* (Arles, 1996); P. Hodgson, *B. B.: A Guide to Research* (N.Y., 1996); M. Wilcox, *B. B.'s Operas* (Bath, 1997); M. Cooke, *B. and the Far East: Asian Influences in the Music of B. B.* (Woodbridge, 1998).—NS/LK/DM

Brixi, Franz (actually, **František**) **Xaver,** Bohemian organist and composer, son of **Šimon Brixi;** b. Prague, Jan. 2, 1732; d. there, Oct. 14, 1771. He spent his entire life in Prague, where he studied with Segert. After serving as a church organist, he became Kapellmeister at St. Vitus's Cathedral in 1759. He composed numerous sacred works, including masses, offertories, and anthems, as well as orch. music and keyboard pieces.

BIBL.: O. Kamper, *F.X. B.* (Prague, 1926).—**NS/LK/DM**

Brixi, Šimon, Czech organist and composer, father of **Franz (František) Xaver Brixi;** b. Vikava, Oct. 28, 1693; d. Prague, Nov. 2, 1735. He settled in Prague, where he studied law at the Charles Univ. After completing his musical training, he became organist at the Týn Church. In 1725 he was made a music teacher at St. Martin's school and organist at the church, serving as its choirmaster from 1727. He was an accomplished composer of sacred music.—**LK/DM**

Brixi, Viktorin (Ignác), Czech organist and composer; b. Plzeň, June 26, 1716; d. Poděbrady, March 30, 1803. He began his musical training with his uncle, Viktorin Zádolský, the Skalsko parish priest. After further studies with Josef Hojer, the Čelákovice organist, he completed his education at the Piarist Gymnasium in Kosmonosy. He settled in Poděbrady as a schoolmaster, where he later was organist and choirmaster at the church. Brixi composed mainly sacred music.—**LK/DM**

Brkanović, Ivan, Croatian composer; b. Skaljari, Dec. 27, 1906; d. Zagreb, Feb. 20, 1987. He studied with Bersa at the Zagreb Academy of Music (graduated, 1935) and Léfebre at the Paris Schola Cantorum. He then taught in Zagreb secondary schools (1935–51) and was a visiting prof. at the Sarajevo Academy of Music (1957–62). His works utilized thematic materials derived from national folk music, but his harmonic idiom followed along modern lines.

WORKS: DRAMATIC: O p e r a : *Ekvinocij* (Equinox; 1945; Zagreb, Oct. 4, 1950); *Zlato Zadra* (The Gold of Zadar; Zagreb, April 15, 1954). **B a l l e t :** *Heloti* (1959; Zagreb, March 17, 1963). **ORCH.:** 5 syms. (1935, 1946, 1947, 1948, 1949); Concertino for Strings (1955); *Sarajevska svita* (1957; Zagreb, Jan. 20, 1958). **CHAMBER:** 2 string quartets (1933, 1938); piano pieces. **VOCAL:** *Triptych* for Soloists, Chorus, and Orch. (1936); *Dalmatinski diptihon* for Soloists, Chorus, and Orch. (1953); 3 cantatas: *Bosnanska sjeÃ©anja* (1961), *Zelena zmija lujbavi* (1964), and *Snatrenje* (1967); *Ho po mukah Ambroza Matije Gupca zvanog Beg* (The Torturous Journey of Ambrose Matija Gubec, Named Beg), scenic oratorio (Zagreb, Dec. 13, 1974). —**NS/LK/DM**

Broadfoot, Eleanora
See **Cisneros, Eleanora de** (née **Broadfoot)**

Broadstock, Brenton, (Thomas), Australian composer and teacher; b. Melbourne, Dec. 12, 1952. He studied at Monash Univ. (B.A., 1976), Memphis (Tenn.) State Univ. (M.M., 1980), the Univ. of Sydney (with Sculthorpe; postgraduate composition diploma, 1981), Trinity Coll. in London (A.Mus., 1981), and the Univ. of Melbourne (D.Mus., 1989). In 1988 he served as the first composer-in-residence of the Melbourne Sym. Orch. and in 1989 joined the faculty of the Univ. of Melbourne. He publ. the vol. *Sound Ideas: Australian Composers born since 1950* (Sydney, 1995). In 1994 he received the Paul Lowin Song Cycle Prize and in 1999 the Don Banks Award. In his music, Broadstock follows a stylistically diverse course frequently marked by adventuresome harmonies, dense and complex textures, and aleatoric structures. In his opera *Fahrenheit 451* (1992), he explores the potentials of electronic sound. He also reveals a deep social consciousness in such scores as his first 3 syms.: No 1, *Toward the Shining Light* (1988), was prompted by the severe mental and physical handicaps of his first-born son; No. 2, *Stars in a Dark Night* (1989), was inspired by the letters of Ivor Gurney; and No. 3, *Voices from the Fire* (1991), was his coming to terms with genocide.

WORKS: DRAMATIC: *Fahrenheit 451*, opera (1992); *That Eye the Sky*, film score (1993). **ORCH.:** *Festive Overture* (1981); *The Mountain* (1984); *Expedition* for Strings (1985); *Aurora Australis* (1985); Tuba Concerto (1985); *Battlements* (1986); Piano Concerto (1987); 5 syms.: No. 1, *Toward the Shining Light* (Melbourne, May 21, 1988), No. 2, *Stars in a Dark Night* (Melbourne, Nov. 11, 1989), No. 3, *Voices from the Fire* (1991; Melbourne, July 2, 1992), No. 4 (Melbourne, July 1995), and No. 5 (Krasnoyarsk, May 1999); *Nearer and Farther* for Horn and Strings (1991); *In a Brilliant Blaze* for Chamber Orch. (1993). **B r a s s B a n d :** *St. Aelred*, rhapsody (1981); *Click*, festival march (1982); *Rutherford Variations* (1990). **CHAMBER:** 4 string quartets (n.d., 1981, n.d., 1990); *Aureole 1* for Flute and Piano (1982), *2* for Bass Clarinet (1983), *3* for Oboe and Piano (1984), and *4* for Piano (1984); *Beast from Air* for Trombone and Percussion (1985); Wind Quartet, *Down the Emperor's Road* (1986); *And No Birds Sing* for Flute, Clarinet, Violin, Piano, and Percussion (1987); *In Chains* for Alto Flute and Guitar (1990); *Deserts Bloom...Lakes Die* for Wind Octet and Double Bass (1990); *Pennscapes* for Clarinet, Viola, Cello, and Piano (1994); *Celebration* for Flute, Clarinet, Piano, 2 Violins, Viola, and Cello (1994–95). **P i a n o :** *In the Silence of Night* (1989); *Giants in the Land* (1991; also for Organ). **VOCAL:** *Eheu Fugaces* for Soprano, Flute, Clarinet, Violin, Cello, Piano, and Percussion (1981); *Bright Tracks* for Soprano and String Trio (1994). —**NS/LK/DM**

Broadwood & Sons, family of English piano manufacturers. The firm was founded in London in 1728 by Burkhard Tschudi or Shudi (b. Schwanden, Switzerland, March 13, 1702; d. London, Aug. 19, 1773). John Broadwood (b. Cockburnspath, Scotland, 1732; d. London, 1812), a Scottish cabinetmaker, was Shudi's son-in-law and successor; in 1773 he began to build square pianos modeled after Zumpe's instruments; in 1780 he marketed his own square pianos, which he patented in 1783; in these, he dispensed with the old clavichord arrangement of the wrest-plank and tuning-pins and transformed the harpsichord pedals into damper and piano pedals; another important invention came in 1788, when he divided the long bridge, which until then had been continuous. Broadwood's improvements were soon adopted by other manufacturers. In 1794 the range of the keyboard was extended to 6 octaves. John Broadwood's sons, James Shudi Broadwood (b. London, Dec. 20, 1772; d. there, Aug. 8, 1851) and Thomas Broadwood, were admitted to the firm in 1795 and 1807, respectively, and the business was then carried on under the name of John Broadwood & Sons. Beethoven received a Broadwood piano in 1817. Henry John Tschudi Broadwood (d. Feb. 8, 1911), great-grandson of the founder, patented the so-called "barless" grand piano; he became a director of John Broadwood & Sons, Ltd., established in 1901.

BIBL.: W. Dale, *Tschudi, the Harpsichord Maker* (London, 1913); D. Wainwright, *B., by Appointment: A History* (London, 1982).—NS/LK/DM

Broche, Charles, French organist and composer; b. Rouen, Feb. 20, 1752; d. there, Sept. 30, 1803. He studied with Desmazures at the Rouen Cathedral, then served as church organist in Lyons (1771–72); later went to Bologna, where he studied with Padre Martini. He returned to Rouen in 1777 and succeeded Desmazures as cathedral organist there. Among his pupils was Boieldieu. He publ. 3 piano sonatas (1782) and wrote some organ pieces.—NS/LK/DM

Brockway, Howard A., American pianist, teacher, and composer; b. Brooklyn, Nov. 22, 1870; d. N.Y., Feb. 20, 1951. He studied with K. Barth (piano) and O. Boise (composition) in Berlin (1890–95). He taught privately in N.Y. (1895–1903; 1910–25), and at the Peabody Cons. in Baltimore (1903–10) and the David Mannes School of Music in N.Y. (from 1925). With L. Wyman, he ed. 2 vols. of Appalachian folk songs: *Lonesome Tunes* (N.Y., 1916) and *20 Kentucky Mountain Songs* (Boston, 1920).

WORKS: Sym. (Berlin, Feb. 23, 1895); *Sylvan Suite* for Orch. (Boston, April 6, 1901); *Cavatina* and *Romanza* for Violin and Orch.; Suite for Cello and Orch.; Violin Sonata; *Moment musical* for Violin and Piano; many piano pieces.—NS/LK/DM

Brod, Max, significant Czech-born writer and composer; b. Prague, May 27, 1884; d. Tel Aviv, Dec. 20, 1968. In Prague he associated himself with Kafka and other writers of the New School, and himself publ. several psychological novels. He studied music at the German Univ. in Prague and became a music critic for various Czech and German publs. In 1939 he emigrated to Tel Aviv, where he continued his literary and musical activities. Among his compositions are *Requiem Hebraicum* (1943), *2 Israeli Peasant Dances* for Piano and Small Orch. (Tel Aviv, April 24, 1947), several piano suites, and 14 song cycles. He wrote an autobiography, *Streitbares Leben* (Munich, 1960), a biography of Janáček (Prague, 1924), and a book on music in Israel (Tel Aviv, 1951). —NS/LK/DM

Brodie, Paul (Zion), noted Canadian saxophonist and teacher; b. Montreal, April 10, 1934. He studied saxophone with Larry Teal at the Univ. of Mich. in Ann Arbor (M.Mus., 1958) and with Marcel Mule in Paris (1959), making his N.Y. recital debut in 1960 at Town Hall. He taught briefly at the Royal Cons. of Music of Toronto (1959–60), then became founder-director of the Brodie School of Music and Modern Dance in Toronto (1961–79); he was also on the faculty of the Univ. of Toronto (1968–73). In 1969 he helped to found the World Saxophone Congress. From 1972 to 1979 he toured with his own Paul Brodie Saxophone Quartet, and then devoted himself to touring as a soloist around the globe. From 1982 he taught at York Univ.—NS/LK/DM

Brodsky, Adolf, famous Russian violinist; b. Taganrog, April 2, 1851; d. Manchester, England, Jan. 22, 1929. A precocious violinist, he made his public debut at the age of 9 in Odessa. He was then sent to Vienna, where he studied with Joseph Hellmesberger Sr., and played the second violin in his string quartet. From 1866 to 1868 he was a violinist in the Vienna Court Orch. In 1873 he returned to Moscow, where he studied with Ferdinand Laub, whom he succeeded in 1875 as prof. at the Moscow Cons. In 1881 he made a European tour, and on Dec. 4, 1881, in Vienna, he gave the world premiere of Tchaikovsky's Violin Concerto, which Tchaikovsky in gratitude dedicated to him, after it had been rejected by Leopold Auer as unplayable. He was praised for his virtuosity, but Tchaikovsky's Violin Concerto was damned as badly written for the violin; the review by Eduard Hanslick, which described the music as emitting a stench, became notorious for its grossness, and caused Tchaikovsky great pain. From 1883 to 1891 Brodsky taught violin at the Leipzig Cons., and also organized a string quartet there (with Hugo Becker, Hans Sitt, and Julius Klengel), which enjoyed an international reputation. In 1891 he went to America and served as concertmaster of the N.Y. Sym. Orch. until 1894. In 1895 he went to England, where he became concertmaster of the Halle Orch. in Manchester (1895–96). He also taught violin at the Royal Manchester Coll. of Music, becoming principal in 1896. In England he changed the spelling of his first name to *Adolph*. His wife publ. *Recollections of a Russian Home* (London, 1904).—NS/LK/DM

Brodsky, Vera
See **Lawrence, Vera Brodsky**

Brogi, Renato, Italian composer; b. Sesto Fiorentino, Feb. 25, 1873; d. San Domenico di Fiesole, Florence, Aug. 25, 1924. He studied music in Florence, then at the Milan Cons., winning the Steiner Prize in Vienna with his opera *La prima notte* (Florence, Nov. 25, 1898). He also composed the operas *L'Oblio* (Florence, Feb. 4, 1890) and *Isabella Orsini* (Florence, April 24, 1920) and the operettas *Bacco in Toscana* and *Follie Veneziane* (both produced in Florence, 1923). Other works included a Violin Concerto, String Quartet, Piano Trio, and songs. —NS/LK/DM

Brogue, Roslyn, American composer; b. Chicago, Feb. 16, 1919; d. Beverly, Mass., Aug. 1, 1981. She studied languages at the Univ. of Chicago and music at Radcliffe Coll. (Ph.D., 1947). In 1944 she married her private student **Ervin Henning.** Her music followed dodecaphonic precepts.

WORKS: Trio for Oboe, Clarinet, and Bassoon (1946); *Suite for Small Orch.* (1947); *Suite* for Recorders (1949); Piano Quartet (1949); String Quartet (1951); Trio for Violin, Clarinet, and Piano (1953); many songs with varied instrumental accompaniments. **—NS/LK/DM**

Broman, Natanael, Swedish pianist and composer; b. Kolsva, Dec. 11, 1887; d. Stockholm, Aug. 27, 1966. He studied at the Stockholm Cons. (1902–11) and later in Berlin. From 1925 to 1951 he was in charge of the music division of Stockholm Radio. He was highly regarded as a pianist. In his compositions, he followed the neo-Romantic trend with a strong undertow of Scandinavian melos. He composed a symphonic poem, *Fritiof och Ingeborg* (1912); some violin pieces; and a number of songs.**—NS/LK/DM**

Broman, Sten, eminent Swedish violinist, conductor, music critic, and composer; b. Uppsala, March 25, 1902; d. Lund, Oct. 29, 1983. He studied violin with Marteau, conducting with Zemlinsky, and composition with Finke at the German Academy of Music in Prague; pursued training in musicology with Wagner at the Univ. of Fribourgh and with Sachs at the Univ. of Berlin; in 1926 he received his licentiate degree from the Univ. of Lund. He was the influential music critic of *Sydsvenksa Dagbladet* (1930–67); in 1937 he founded the Skåne Quartet, and later was a member of the Piano Quartet (1948–51); also conducted the Malmö Phil. Soc. (1946–66). From 1930 to 1962 he was president of the Swedish section of the ISCM. As a composer, he followed a median line of Scandinavian Romanticism; beginning around 1960 he adopted serial techniques and later experimented with electronic sound.

WORKS: DRAMATIC: *Malmö Dances,* ballet (1952); film music. **ORCH.:** *Choral Fantasia* (1931); *Gothic Suite* for Strings (1932); 9 syms.: No. 1, *Sinfonia ritmica* (Malmo, March 20, 1962), No. 2 (Stockholm, Nov. 16, 1963), No. 3 (Malmö, April 27, 1965), No. 4 (1965; Detroit, Nov. 17, 1966), No. 5 for Soprano and Orch. (Stockholm, April 19, 1968), No. 6, with Taped Organ Sounds (Lund, Sweden, Oct. 13, 1970), No. 7, with Electronic Sound (Stockholm, May 5, 1972), No. 8 (Stockholm, April 5, 1975), and No. 9 (Swedish Radio, June 15, 1977); *Sententia crevit* for Orch. and Concrete Sound Tape (Lund, June 13, 1968); Overture (1979). **CHAMBER:** *Canon* for Piano (1929); 4 string quartets (1929, 1933, 1970, 1973); Duo for Violin and Viola (1932); 3 suites for Viola and Piano (1935, 1937, 1942); Sextet for Strings, Percussion, and Piano (1963); Septet for Percussion, Celesta, and Piano (1968); Brass Concerto (Malmö, Nov. 11, 1971). **VOCAL:** *Musica Cathedralis* for Soprano, Bass, 3 Choruses, Orch., 2 Organs, and Tape (Lund, April 4, 1973).**—NS/LK/DM**

Bronarski, Ludwik (Ryszard Marian), Polish-Swiss musicologist; b. Lemberg, April 13, 1890; d. Fribourg, Nov. 9, 1975. He traveled to Vienna, where he studied musicology with Adler and Dietz at the Univ. (1909–13), later completing his training with Peter Wagner at the Univ. of Fribourg (Ph.D., 1919, with the diss. *Die Lieder der heiligen Hildegard;* publ. in Zürich, 1922); he subsequently received a law diploma (1926). He taught at the Fribourg Cons. (1946–67). With J. Turcyń-

ski, he ed. the Paderewski edition of Chopin's works (21 vols., Warsaw, 1949–63).

WRITINGS: *Harmonika Chopina* (Warsaw, 1935); *Études sur Chopin* (2 vols., Lausanne, 1944–46; 2nd ed., 1947–48); *Chopin et l'Italie* (Lausanne, 1946); *Szkice Chopinowskie* (Chopin Sketches; Kraków, 1961).**—NS/LK/DM**

Bronfman, Yefim, admired Russian-born Israeli, later American pianist; b. Tashkent, April 10, 1958. He began his training with his mother, a piano teacher; after the family emigrated to Israel in 1973, he took up formal study at the Rubin Academy of Music in Tel Aviv. In 1976 he appeared at the Marlboro (Vt.) Music Festival; then pursued additional training with Serkin at the Curtis Inst. of Music in Philadelphia and at the Juilliard School in N.Y. As a soloist with the Israel Phil., he toured the U.S. (1976), Australia (1978), and South America (1979); also appeared as a soloist with major U.S. and European orchs. In 1982 he made his N.Y. recital debut. He became a naturalized American citizen in 1989. In 1991 he was awarded the Avery Fisher Prize, giving his first recital at N.Y.'s Avery Fisher Hall in 1993. His expansive repertoire extends from Scarlatti to works from the contemporary era.**—NS/LK/DM**

Bronner, Georg, German organist and composer; b. Hamburg (baptized), Feb. 17, 1667; d. there (buried), March 8, 1720. In 1688 he became sacristan at the Heilig Geist hospital in Hamburg. In 1689 he also assumed the post of organist there, remaining in both positions until 1719. A number of his sacred works are extant. **—NS/LK/DM**

Brons, Carel, Dutch composer; b. Groningen, Jan. 1, 1931; d. Hilversum, May 16, 1983. He studied piano with Luctor Ponse, organ with Cor Batenburg, and theory with Johan Vetter (1949–55). He worked for Radio Holland (1954–72), and from 1958 also was music director of the Hilversum Radio. He adopted versatile idioms in his compositions, making occasional use of serial methods.

WORKS: ORCH.: *Varianten* (1966; orchestration of organ work); *Epitaphium* (1967); *Music for Strings* (1969); *They Are Telling Us* for 2 Harps and Chamber Orch. (1976–78); *Symphonic Fantasy* for Organ and Orch. (1980). **CHAMBER:** *Balletto* for Wind Quintet (1961); *Dialogs I* for Oboe and Piano (1962) and *II* for Flute and Harp (1967); 3 string quartets (1962, 1969, 1977); *Serenata I* for Flute (1963), *II* for Oboe, Clarinet, and Bassoon (1964), and *III* for 4 Clarinets (1974); *Mutazione* for Wind Quintet (1964); *Monologue I* for Oboe (1967), *II* for Flute (1967), *III* for Clarinet (1968), *IV* for Bassoon (1968; rev. 1974), and *V* for Trumpet (1970); Concertino for Clarinet, Violin, and Piano (1977); *Gentle Vision* for Flute and Piano (1978); *Threnody* for Flute (1978); *Ballade '81* for Saxophone Quartet (1981); *Springtime Music* for 11 Instruments (1982–83). **KEYBOARD: Piano:** *Imaginations I-III* (1966, 1966, 1974); *Telling a Story I* (1970) and *2* for Young Pianists (1978). **Organ:** *Invenzione* (1963); *Reflecties* (1965); *Varianten* (1965; orchestrated 1966); *Prismen* (1967); *Astrabikon* (1968); *Cyclus* (1969); *Litany* (1971); *Reflections* for 2 Organs (1975); Suite (1979); *Structures in Music* (1980). **VOCAL:** *Vox mea,* cantata for Soprano, Chorus, Instrumental Soloists, and Orch. (1974–76).**—NS/LK/DM**

Bronsart (von Schellendorf), Hans, German pianist and composer; b. Berlin, Feb. 11, 1830; d. Munich, Nov. 3, 1913. He studied piano with Kullak in Berlin and took lessons with Liszt in Weimar. In 1857 he undertook a concert tour through Germany, France, and Russia; from 1860 to 1867 he was active as a conductor in Leipzig, Dresden, and Berlin. He was the dedicatee and first performer of Liszt's Second Piano Concerto. In his compositions he followed the Romantic trend in Schumann's tradition. His most successful was his youthful Piano Trio, his first opus number (1856); some of his piano pieces retained their popularity for a brief while. He also wrote a dramatic tone poem, *Manfred*, for Chorus and Orch., to his own text (Weimar, Dec. 1, 1901); 2 programmatic syms.; and choruses. In 1861 he married **Ingeborg Bronsart (von Schellendorf)** (née Starck).—NS/LK/DM

Bronsart (von Schellendorf), Ingeborg (née **Starck**), German pianist and composer; b. St. Petersburg (of Swedish parents), Aug. 24, 1840; d. Munich, June 17, 1913. She studied piano with Liszt at Weimar. In 1861 she married **Hans Bronsart (von Schellendorf)**. She composed 4 operas: *König Hjarne* (Berlin, Feb. 14, 1891), *Jery und Bätely* (Weimar, April 26, 1873), *Die Sühne* (Dessau, April 11, 1909), and *Die Göttin zu Sais*; also piano concertos, piano sonatas, salon pieces, violin pieces, cello pieces, and songs.—NS/LK/DM

Bronskaya, Evgenya (Adolfovna), outstanding Russian soprano; b. St. Petersburg, Feb. 1, 1882; d. there (Leningrad), Oct. 12, 1953. She first studied with her mother, E. de Hacke; then in Milan with Teresa Arkel; made her operatic debut in Tiflis in 1901; subsequently sang in Kiev (1902–03) and in Moscow (1904–05). From 1907 to 1910 she sang with a traveling Italian opera troupe, performing in Italy, France, and the U.S. (Boston, Chicago, and Philadelphia). Returning to Russia, she was a member of the Maryinsky Theater in St. Petersburg (1910–23); from 1923 to 1950 she taught voice at the Leningrad Cons. She was a brilliant coloratura soprano, particularly impressive in the roles of Lucia, Gilda, and Violetta.—NS/LK/DM

Brook, Barry S(helley), eminent American musicologist; b. N.Y., Nov. 1, 1918; d. there, Dec. 7, 1997. He studied piano privately with Mabel Asnis, then entered the Manhattan School of Music, where he was a student of Louise Culver Strunsky in piano, of Hugh Ross in conducting, and of Sessions in composition. He subsequently studied at the City Coll. of the City Univ. of N.Y. (B.S., social sciences, 1939), then took courses in musicology with Lang at Columbia Univ. (M.A., 1942, with the diss. *Clément Janequin*). From 1942 to 1945 he was a member of the U.S. Air Corps. Selecting as his major subject French music history, he went to Paris, where he studied at the Sorbonne (Ph.D., 1959, with the diss. *La Symphonie française dans la seconde moitié du XVIIIᵉsiècle*). In 1945 he became a prof. at Queens Coll. of the City Univ. of N.Y. He also was a lecturer at Brooklyn Coll. (1945–46) and a prof. at Hunter Coll. (1954) of the City Univ. of N.Y. In 1967 he became a prof. of music and executive officer of the Ph.D. program at the Graduate School and Univ. Center of the City Univ. of N.Y., leaving these posts in 1989 to become director of the Univ.'s Center for Music Research and Documentation. He also taught at the Institut de Musicologie at the Univ. of Paris (1967–68), the Eastman School of Music in Rochester, N.Y. (1973), the Univ. of Adelaide (1974), the Juilliard School in N.Y. (from 1977), the Centre National de la Recherche Scientifique in Paris (1983), and the Univ. of Ala. (1987). He served as ed. in chief of *RILM* [Répertoire International de Littérature Musicale] *Abstracts of Music Literature* (from 1966), *The Symphony 1720–1840* (61 vols., N.Y., 1979–86), and *French Opera in the 17ᵗʰ and 18ᵗʰ Centuries* (75 vols., N.Y., 1984 et seq.); with F. Degrada and H. Hucke, he was general ed. of *Giovanni Battista Pergolesi Complete Works/Opere Complete* (18 vols., N.Y., 1986 et seq.). In 1954–55 he held a Ford Foundation fellowship, in 1958–59 a Fulbright Research scholarship, and in 1961–62 and 1966–67 Guggenheim fellowships. In 1965 he became the first American to receive the Dent Medal of the Royal Musical Assn. of England, in 1972 he was made a Chevalier de l'Ordre des Arts et des Lettres of France, in 1978 he was awarded the Smetana Medal of Czechoslovakia, and in 1989 he became the first non-Scandinavian musicologist to be elected to membership in the Royal Swedish Academy of Music. In 1997 he was made an honorary memory of the American Musicological Soc. Brooks especially distinguished himself as an authority on 17ᵗʰ and 18ᵗʰ century music and on musical bibliography.

WRITINGS: *La Symphonie française dans la seconde moitié du XVIIIᵉ siècle* (3 vols., Paris, 1962); *The Breitkopf Thematic Catalogue, 1762–1787* (N.Y., 1966); ed. *Musicology and the Computer; Musicology 1960–2000: A Practical Program* (N.Y., 1970); ed. with E. Downes and S. Van Solkema, *Perspectives in Musicology: The Inaugural Lectures of the Ph.D. Program in Music at the City University of New York* (N.Y., 1972; 2ⁿᵈ ed., rev., 1975); *Thematic Catalogues in Music: An Annotated Bibliography* (N.Y., 1972; 2ⁿᵈ ed., 1997, with R. Viano).—NS/LK/DM

Brook, Peter (Stephen Paul), noted English theater and opera producer; b. London, March 21, 1925. He was educated at Magdalen Coll., Oxford. His career in the theater commenced at the age of 17 when he staged a performance of Marlowe's *The Tragedie of Dr. Faustus*. After producing plays in Birmingham, Stratford, and London, he served as director of productions at the Royal Opera in London from 1947 to 1950. His productions there included *Boris Godunov* and *La Bohème* in 1948, and *Le nozze di Figaro* and *Salome* in 1949. In 1953 he staged *Faust* at the Metropolitan Opera in N.Y., returning there in 1957 to produce *Eugene Onegin*. In 1962 he became co-director of the Royal Shakespeare Theatre. From 1971 he was also active in Paris with his Centre International de Créations Théâtrales, with which he attempted to synthesize theatrical elements in a total media art. His compressed version of *Carmen* as *La tragédie de Carmen* was produced in Paris in 1981 and in N.Y. in 1983, and won him an Emmy Award and the Prix Italia in 1984. His similar treatment of *Pelléas et Mélisande* as *Impressions de Pelléas* was first mounted in Paris in 1992. Brook's autobiography, *The Shifting Point*, appeared in 1988. Among his other writings are *The*

Empty Space (N.Y., 1978), *The Open Door: Thoughts on Acting and Theater* (N.Y., 1993), and *Threads of Time* (Washington, D.C., 1998). In 1965 he was made a Commander of the Order of the British Empire. He was made an Officier of the Légion d'honneur of France in 1995, and in 1998 Queen Elizabeth II made him a Companion of Honour.

BIBL.: A. Hunt and G. Reeves, *P. B.* (Cambridge, 1995). —NS/LK/DM

Brooks, Garth, 1990s country sensation who broke through big time on the pop charts; b. Luba, Okla., Feb. 7, 1962. Brooks's mother, Coleen, was a small-time country singer who worked sporadically in their native Okla. on recordings and radio. Brooks himself grew up interested in sports, playing football, basketball, and track in high school, and entering Okla. State on a track-and-field scholarship, with a specialty in javelin throwing. His guitar playing career began in high school and continued in college, where he worked college-area clubs performing a mix of James Taylor folk-pop and country. He made his first trip to Nashville in 1985, without success, returning home with his college-sweetheart wife, Sandy Mahl. Returning to Nashville in 1987, Brooks attracted the attention of Capitol Records and producer Allen Reynolds.

His first album was successful, but the followup, *No Fences*, really began Garthmania. It sold 700,000 copies in its first ten days of release, and stayed on the pop charts for over a year. His third album, *Ropin' the Wind*, entered the pop charts in the #1 position, the first country album ever to do so. Brooks's hit singles from these albums combined country bathos ("If Tomorrow Never Comes," a ten-hanky weeper about a husband's realization of the value of his marriage), with neo-honky tonk ("Friends in Low Places," a cleverly humorous song with its tip-of- the-hat bass vocals recalling George Jones), and even the feminist "The Thunder Rolls," a story of a cheating husband (whose message is made graphic in a video that ruffled quite a few conservative Nashville feathers with its depiction of a physically abusive husband).

Brooks's performing style captured the attention of the major media. Learning a lesson from the arena rock stars of his youth, Brooks built a special set featuring large ramps enclosing the band (enabling him to dramatically charge up and down around his backup musicians), and even installed a rope so he could swing out over the audience, in shades of Ozzy Osbourne–like theatrics! With his portable mike neatly hooked to his ten-gallon hat, Brooks is one of the most mobile and energetic of all country performers, although recently he has descended into such schmaltzy tactics as waving and winking at the audience, and blowing air kisses at his fans.

Brooks 1992 album, *The Chase*, reflects a further nudging towards mainstream pop, particularly in the anthemic single "We Shall Be Free," whose vaguely liberal politics also sent shivers of despair through the conservative Nashville musical community. Less successful than his previous releases (although still selling several million copies), Brooks followed it with 1993's *In Pieces*, featuring a safer selection of high-energy honky-tonk numbers and even the odd "American Honky-Tonk Bar Association," in which Brooks beats up on welfare recipients, a shameless attempt to cater to Country's traditionally conservative audience.

During the mid-1990s, Brooks seemed obsessed with topping The Beatles's record of selling over 100 million albums; by this time, he had already passed 60 million, and set himself the goal of beating The Beatles by the year 2000. To meet this goal, Garth began a series of clever, if stunt-like promotions with his 1994 *The Hits* collection, originally issued for a "limited time only." Blue-light shoppers were thrilled, and the CD sold like crazy. That same year, Brooks teamed with the burghers of burgerland, McDonalds, to release *The Garth Brook's Collection*, only available to buyers of the Big Mac (and only for a "limited time"). And, if that was enough reworking of his back catalogue, he also originally packaged his *Hits* collection with a second CD entitled *CD Zooming*, which featured snippets from *all* of his work to date.

Garth's mid-1990s work has been less-inspired than his earlier work. When he tried to break out of the box with 1995's *New Horses*, his fans didn't tolerate the dreamy folk-flavored material ("Ireland") or country-styled reworkings of rock songs (Aerosmith's "The Fever"). In 1996, Garth claimed his label was not adequately promoting his records, withholding his next record, and even lobbying successfully for new management. 1997's *Sevens* returned Brooks to more comfortable country ground, but by now the formulas were beginning to wear thin. Nonetheless, record sales were up.

In 1998, in another unusual marketing gambit aimed at getting Garth over the 100–million album mark, he issued *The Limited Series*, a boxed set "limited" to two million copies, featuring all of his previous albums, each with one additional cut.

Garth Brook's career took a surreal turn in 1999 when he issued the album *Garth Brooks in ... the Life of Chris Gaines*. Supposedly a "greatest hits" album by an 1980s-era pop rocker, the album was a "pre-soundtrack" to a film Brooks says he will make about the fictional rocker. Not surprisingly, given Brooks's love of mainstream pop-rock of the 1970s and 1980s, Gaines's "hits" are very much in a mainstream mold, given a competent if not inspired production by pop producer Don Was. Brooks's vocals lose their country warble, and he even attempts some R&B-flavored falsetto.

The album was greeted by mixed reaction. Some critics lambasted the singer for not having enough courage to "go pop" under his own name. Few thought the music was inspired, and the hubris of labeling new material "greatest hits" which have never been actually on the charts undoubtedly annoyed many rock and country writers. The record's sales were pitiful by Brooksian standards, a clear sign that his fans were not yet ready for Garth-without-a-hat. He followed up with a hastily assembled album of Christmas standards, which also failed to make much of an impact among the record-buying public.

Nonetheless, Brooks's phenomenal success in the 1990s is a combination of genuine talent, shrewd marketing, and being "in the right place at the right time (with the right act)." His neo-country act draws so much on mid-1970s folk-rock and even arena rock (in its staging) that it's hard to think of him as a pure country artist. The fact that several of his albums have shot to the top of the pop charts, outgunning Michael Jackson, Guns 'n' Roses, and Bruce Springsteen, underscores the fact that Brooks is a pop artist dressed in a cowboy hat. Still, Brooks draws on genuine country traditions, particularly the honky tonk sound of George Jones, and he's managed to popularize country music without diluting the sound.

DISC.: *Garth Brooks* (1989); *No Fences* (1990); *Ropin' the Wind* (1991); *Beyond the Season* (1992); *The Chase* (1992); *In Pieces* (1993); *The Hits* (1994); *Fresh Horses* (1995); *Sevens* (1997); *In the Life of Chris Gaines* (1999).—RC

Brooks, Patricia, American soprano; b. N.Y., Nov. 7, 1937; d. Mount Kisco, N.Y., Jan. 22, 1992. She studied at the Manhattan School of Music in N.Y.; also took dance lessons with Martha Graham. She made her operatic debut as Marianne in *Der Rosenkavalier* at the N.Y. City Opera on Oct. 12, 1960; also sang with opera companies in San Francisco, Chicago, New Orleans, Philadelphia, Houston, and Santa Fe. She made her Covent Garden debut in London in 1969 as Shemakha in *The Golden Cockerel*. In 1978 she retired from the operatic stage and taught at the State Univ. of N.Y. in Purchase until 1981. Among her best roles were Gilda, Lucia, Violetta, Massenet's Manon, Sophie, and Mélisande. —NS/LK/DM

Broome, (William) Edward, English-born Canadian choral conductor, organist, teacher, and composer; b. Manchester, Jan. 3, 1868; d. Toronto, April 28, 1932. He studied in Wales with Roland Rogers (organ and piano, 1876–90) and Jules Riviere (conducting); was awarded a piano diploma from the Royal Academy of Music in London (1884) and was made a Fellow of the Guild of Organists (1889). After settling in Canada, he was awarded the B.Mus. from Trinity Coll., Toronto (1901) and the D.Mus. from the Univ. of Toronto (1908). He served as organist-choirmaster at churches in Brockville, Ontario (1893–95), Montreal (1895–1906), Toronto (1906–25), and Calgary (1926–27). From 1907 he taught at the Toronto Cons. of Music. In 1910 he founded the Toronto Oratorio Soc., which he conducted until 1925. He won 8 first prizes in composition in the Welsh Eisteddfods, including one for his dramatic cantata *The Siege of Cardiff Castle* (1908). Among his other works were the cantata *The Hymn of Trust* (1910), various other sacred pieces, and songs.—NS/LK/DM

Broqua, Alfonso, Uruguayan composer; b. Montevideo, Sept. 11, 1876; d. Paris, Nov. 24, 1946. He studied with d'Indy at the Schola Cantorum in Paris, where he settled. His works are characterized by a fine feeling for exotic material, which he presented in the brilliant manner of French modern music.

WORKS: DRAMATIC: *Cruz del Sur*, opera (1918); *Thelen at Nagouëy*, Inca ballet (1934); *Isabelle*, romantic ballet (1936).

OTHER: *Tabaré*, poetic cycle for Soloists, Women's Chorus, and Piano or Orch. (1908); *Poema de las Lomas*, triptych for Piano (1912); Piano Quintet; *3 cantos del Uruguay* for Voice, Flute, and 2 Guitars (1925); *Cantos de Parana* for Voice and Guitar (1929); *Evocaciones Criollas*, 7 pieces for Guitar (1929); *3 préludes Pampéens* for Piano (1938; also for orch.).—NS/LK/DM

Brosa, Antonio, Spanish violinist; b. Canonja, Tarragona, June 27, 1894; d. Barcelona, March 26, 1979. He studied in Barcelona and Brussels, and then went to London, where he founded the Brosa String Quartet in 1925. After making tours of Europe and the U.S. with it until 1938, he concentrated on a career as a soloist. He lived in the U.S. during World War II, returning to Europe in 1946. He was the soloist in the premiere of Britten's Violin Concerto in N.Y. on March 28, 1940. —NS/LK/DM

Broschi, Carlo
See **Farinelli**

Broschi, Riccardo, Italian composer, brother of **Carlo Broschi;** b. Naples, c. 1698; d. Madrid, 1756. He studied at the Cons. di Santa Maria di Loreto in Naples, where he brought out several operas in which his brother sang. He later settled in Spain with his brother. —NS/LK/DM

Brosmann (a Sancto Hieronymo), Damasus, Moravian composer; b. Fulnek, Sept. 7, 1731; d. Pribor, Sept. 16, 1798. He studied violin and cello with Weissgraber in Fulnek, then devoted himself to the Piarist calling, serving in various capacities in Moravian towns. He wrote mostly sacred music.

BIBL.: C. Gardavsky, *D. B. a S.H.* (diss., Univ. of Brno, 1937).—NS/LK/DM

Brossard, Sébastien de, French composer; b. Dompierre, Orne (baptized), Sept. 12, 1655; d. Meaux, Aug. 10, 1730. He studied theology at Caen (1670–76); was then in Paris (1678–87); in 1687 he went to Strasbourg; in 1689 became maître de chapelle at the Strasbourg Cathedral; in 1698 received a similar post at the Cathedral of Meaux; in 1709 he became canon there. His fame rests upon the authorship of what was erroneously regarded as the earliest dictionary of musical terms; it was in fact preceded by many publications: by the medieval compilation *De musica antica et moderna* (c. 1100), the last section of which is a vocabulary of musical terms (to be found in Lafage's *Essais de dipthérographie musicale*, vol. I, pp. 404–7); by Joannes Tinctoris's *Terminorum musicae diffinitorium* (c. 1475); and by Janowka's *Clavis ad thesaurum magnae artis musicae* (1701); Brossard had access to none of these, however. The title of Brossard's own vol. is *Dictionnaire de musique, contenant une explication des termes grecs, latins, italiens et français les plus usités dans la musique*, etc. (Paris, 1703; 2nd ed., 1705; there is an Amsterdam reprint, marked 6th ed., but this designation is erroneous; Eng. tr. by Grassineau, 1740). Brossard also wrote *Lettre à M. Demotz sur sa nouvelle méthode d'écrire le* *plain-chant et la musique* (1729); a considerable variety of church music, including *Canticum Eucharisticum* on the Peace of Ryswick (1697; new ed. by F.X. Mathias); motets; etc. He brought out several vols. of *Airs sérieux et à boire*. His library of MSS was acquired by Louis XV in 1724, and formed the nucleus of the music collection of the Bibliothèque Nationale.

BIBL.: M. Brenet, *S. d.B.* (Paris, 1896).—**NS/LK/DM**

Bros y Bertomeu, Juan (Joaquin Pedro Domingo), Spanish composer; b. Tortosa (baptized), May 12, 1776; d. Oviedo, March 12, 1852. He studied with Queralt in Barcelona, and served as asst. maestro de capilla there at the church of S. Maria del Mar and as organist of the chapel of S. Severo. From 1806 to 1823 he was maestro de capilla at the Cathedral of Leon; in 1824 was named maestro de capilla at the Cathedral of Oviedo. He wrote mostly church music.—**NS/LK/DM**

Brott, Alexander, prominent Canadian conductor, violinist, teacher, and composer, father of **Boris** and **Denis Brott;** b. Montreal, March 14, 1915. Following violin lessons with Alfred De Seve, he studied with Maurice Onderet (violin) and Douglas Clarke (composition) at the McGill Cons. (Licentiate in Music, 1932) in Montreal; subsequently pursued training with Jacobsen (violin), Willeke (chamber music), Wagenaar (composition), and Stoessel (conducting) at the Juilliard School of Music in N.Y. (1934–39). He was a violinist in the Montreal Orch. (1930–34; 1939–41); then was concertmaster (1945–48) and asst. conductor (intermittently 1948–61) of the Montreal Sym. Orch. From 1939 to 1985 he was on the faculty of McGill Univ. In 1939 he founded the McGill String Quartet and in 1945 the McGill Chamber Orch. He appeared as a guest conductor throughout North America and Europe. From 1965 to 1981 he was artistic director of the Kingston (Ontario) Sym. In 1985 he founded the Montreal Young Virtuosi. In 1979 he was made a member of the Order of Canada, and in 1987 Chevalier de l'Ordre national du Québec. In his music he follows the Romantic tradition, with impressionistic harmonies imparting an aura of modernity.

WORKS: DRAMATIC: B a l l e t : *Le Corriveau* (1966). **ORCH.:** *Oracle* (1938); *War and Peace* (1944); *Concordia* (1946); *From Sea to Sea*, suite (1947); Concerto for Violin and Chamber Orch. (Montreal, March 7, 1950); *Delightful Delusions* (1950); *Prelude to Oblivion* for Chamber Orch. (1951); *Fancy and Folly* (1953); *Scherzo* (1954); *Analogy in Anagram* (1955); *Arabesque* for Cello and Chamber Orch. (1957); *3 Astral Visions* for Strings (1959); *Spheres in Orbit* (1960); *Martlet's Muse* (1962); *Circle, Triangle, 4 Squares* for Strings (1963); *Profundium Praedictum* for Double Bass or Viola or Cello, and String Orch. (1964); *Paraphrase in Polyphony*, variants based on a recently unearthed 10–bar canon written by Beethoven in 1825 (Montreal, Nov. 3, 1967); *The Young Prometheus*, 12 preludes and fugues based on Beethoven sketches (1969); *The Emperor's New Clothes* for Narrator and Orch. (Kingston, Ontario, Feb. 21, 1971); *Cupid's Quandary*, violin concerto (1975); *Evocative Provocations*, cello concerto (1975); *Hymn II Her* for Flute, Bassoon, and Strings (1977); *My Mother—My Memorial* (1978); *Curioso Furioso* for Strings (1982); *Trivial Trifles* for Strings (1984). **CHAMBER:** Quintet for Recorder and String Quartet (1940); String Quartet (1941); *Critic's Corner* for String Quartet and Percussion (1950);

5 Miniatures for 8 Players (1950); *Vignettes en caricature* for Piano (1952); *Sept for 7* for Narrator, String Trio, Clarinet, Saxophone, and Piano (1955); *3 Acts for 4 Sinners* for Saxophone Quartet (1961); *Mutual Salvation Orgy* for Brass Quintet (1962); *Berceuse* for Saxophone Quartet (1962); *3 on a Spree* for Flute, Oboe, and Harp (1963); *Mini-Minus* for Clarinet, Bassoon, Trumpet, Trombone, Violin, Double Bass, and Percussion (1968); *Spasms for 6* for 6 Percussionists (1971); *Saties-Faction* for String Quartet (1972); *Shofar* for Cello (1976); *Double Entente* for String Quartet (1976); *Prisms* for Flute and Guitar (1984). **V O C A L:** *Israel* for Chorus and Orch. (1956); *The Vision of Dry Bones* for Baritone, Piano, and Strings (1958); *World Sophisticate* for Soprano, Brass Quintet, and Percussion (1962); *Centennial Celebration* for Narrator, Women's Chorus, and Strings (1967).—**NS/LK/DM**

Brott, Boris, Canadian conductor, son of **Alexander** and brother of **Denis Brott;** b. Montreal, March 14, 1944. He received training in violin from his father, and took courses at the Montreal Cons. (1957–61). After conducting studies with Monteux in Hancock, Maine (summer 1956), he pursued training with Markevitch at the Instituto Nacional de Bellas Artes in Mexico City, where he took first prize in the Pan-American conducting competition in 1958. He was founder-conductor of the Phil. Youth Orch. in Montreal (1959–61). After winning third prize in the Liverpool conducting competition in 1962, he was asst. conductor of the Toronto Sym. Orch. (1963–65). From 1964 to 1969 he was music director of the Northern Sinfonia Orch. in Newcastle upon Tyne, and also was a conductor of the Royal Ballet at London's Covent Garden (1966–68). From 1967 to 1972 he was music director of Lakehead Univ. in Thunder Bay, Ontario. In 1968 he was one of the four first prize winners in the Mitropoulos conducting competition in N.Y., and in 1968–69 he was an asst. conductor of the N.Y. Phil., where he profited from the tutelage of Bernstein. In 1969 he became music director of the Hamilton (Ontario) Phil., a post he retained until 1990. In 1970–71 he was interim music director of the Kitchener Waterloo Sym. Orch. in Ontario. From 1970 to 1973 he was music director of the Regina (Saskatchewan) Sym. Orch. He served as chief conductor of the BBC Welsh Sym. Orch. in Cardiff from 1972 to 1977, and also was principal conductor of the CBC Winnipeg Orch. from 1976 to 1983. He was founder-conductor and music advisor of Symphony Nova Scotia in Halifax from 1983 to 1986. In 1988 he founded the Boris Brott Summer Music Festival in Hamilton, subsequently serving as its artistic director. With his father, he served as co- conductor of the McGill Chamber Orch. in Montreal from 1989. He likewise was music director of the Ventura County (Calif.) Sym. Orch. from 1992. As a guest conductor, he appeared with leading orchs. around the world. In 1987 he received the Order of Canada and in 1990 he was made a Knight of Malta. —**NS/LK/DM**

Brott, Denis, Canadian cellist and teacher, son of **Alexander** and brother of **Boris Brott;** b. Montreal, Dec. 9, 1950. He studied with Walter Joachim at the Montreal Cons. (1959–67), Nelsova in Aspen (1963–68), Starker at Ind. Univ. (1968–71), and Piatigorsky at the Univ. of Southern Calif. in Los Angeles (1971–75); he then completed his training with Rose in N.Y., Gendron in Paris, and Navarra in Siena. In 1967 he won first prize at the Merriweather Post Competition in Washington, D.C.; then placed first in the Montreal Sym. Orch. Concours that same year, which led to his debut with that orch. in the Dvořák Concerto (1967). During his seasons at the Marlboro (Vt.) Festival (1972–75), he attended Casal's master classes. He toured widely as a soloist in North America and Europe; from 1980 to 1989 he was a member of the Orford String Quartet. He taught at the Univ. of N.C. (1975–77), the Royal Cons. of Music of Toronto (from 1978), the Univ. of Toronto (1980–89), and the Montreal Cons. (from 1989).—NS/LK/DM

Brouwenstijn, Gré (actually, **Gerarda Demphina Van Swol**), Dutch soprano; b. Den Helder, Aug. 26, 1915; d. Amsterdam, Dec. 14, 1999. She studied at the Amsterdam Music Lyceum. In 1940 she made her operatic debut as one of the three ladies in *Die Zauberflöte* in Amsterdam. In 1946 she became a member of the Netherlands Opera in Amsterdam. In 1951 she made her debut at London's Covent Garden as Aida, and continued to make regular appearances there until 1964. She also sang at the Bayreuth Festivals (1954–56), at the Teatro Colón in Buenos Aires (1958), and at the Lyric Opera in Chicago (1959). In 1971 she gave her farewell performance in *Fidelio* in Amsterdam. Brouwenstijn was particularly esteemed for her Verdi and Wagner roles.—NS/LK/DM

Brouwer, Leo, noted Cuban guitarist, conductor, and composer; b. Havana, March 1, 1939. He began music training in Havana, where he made his debut as a guitarist in 1955. In 1959 he went to the U.S. to study composition at the Juilliard School of Music in N.Y. and guitar at the Hartt School of Music in Hartford, Conn. Returning to Havana, he became a leading figure in avant-garde music circles. He also pursued a distinguished career as a guitar virtuoso, traveling all over the world. He likewise appeared as a conductor in his homeland and abroad. In 1972 he was in Berlin under the auspices of the Deutscher Akademischer Austauschdienst. In 1984 a guitar competition was founded in his honor in Japan. He served as music director of the Orquesta de Córdoba in Spain from 1992. In 1998 he received the Manuel de Falla Prize. He was awarded the National Music Prize of Cuba in 1999. Brouwer started composing in 1955 in a style that adapted sounds of popular Cuban culture. A second compositional period evolved around 1962. He became the first Cuban composer to embrace aleatory and open forms, and his *Sonograma I* was the first example of indeterminate music by a Cuban composer. Then, after 1973, he entered his third period, a self-described "New Simplicity" that fused his avant-garde techniques with previous styles of popular and classical music. Unique in his output are his 8 guitar concertos, which fall mostly in his third period: No. 1 (1972), No. 2, *Concierto de Liège* (1980–81), No. 3, *Concierto Elegiaco* (1985), No. 4, *Concierto de Toronto* (1987), No. 5, *Concierto de Helsinki* (1992), No. 6, *Concierto de Bolos* (1996), No. 7, *La Habana* (1997–98), and No. 9, *Cantata de Perugia* (1999). Among

his other works are: *3 danzas concertants* for Guitar and String Orch. (1958); Sonata for Solo cello (1960); *Variantes* for Percussionist (1962); *Sonograma I* for Prepared Piano (1963), *II* for Orch. (1964), and *III* for 2 Pianos (1968) *Homage to Mingus* for Jazz Band and Orch. (1965); *Dos conceptos del tiempo* for 10 Players (1965); *Conmutaciones* for Prepared Piano and Percussion (1966); *La tradicíon se rompe...pero cuesta trabajo* for Orch. (1967–69); *El reino de esto mondo* for Wind Quintet (1968); *Cantigas del tiemp nuevo*, cantata for Narrator, Children's Chorus, and Small Ensemble or Orch. (1969); *Exaedros I* for Ensemble or Orch. (1969) and *II* for Percussionist and 2 Orch. Groups (1970); *Sonata "pian e forte"* for Piano (1970); *Per sonore a tres* for Guitar, Flute, and Viola (1970); *Per sonore a due* for Guitar and Tape (1971); Concerto for Flute and String Orch. (1972); Violin Concerto (1975–76); *Canción de gesta* for Chamber Orch. (1979); *Baladas del Decamerón Negro* for Guitar (1981); *Manuscrito antiguo encontrado en una botella* for Piano Trio (1982); *Cuban Landscape with Rumba* for Guitar Quartet (1985); Guitar Sonata (1990); Double Concerto for Guitar, Violin, and Orch. (1995); *Hika: In Memoriam Takemitsu* for Guitar (1996); Triple Concerto for Violin, Cello, and Orch. (1997).—NS/LK/DM

Brouwer, Margaret, American composer and teacher; b. Ann Arbor, Feb. 8, 1940. She was educated at the Oberlin (Ohio) Cons. of Music (B.M., 1962), Mich. State Univ. (M.M., 1963), and Ind. Univ. (D.M., 1988). She taught at Ind. Univ. (1985–88) and Washington and Lee Univ. (1988–96). From 1993 to 1997 she was composer-in-residence of the Roanoke Sym. Orch. In 1996 she was appointed to the Vincent K. and Edith H. Smith Chair in Composition and was made head of the composition dept. at the Cleveland Inst. of Music. She held residencies at the Va. Center for the Arts (1990), the Rockefeller Foundation Bellagio Center in Italy (1994), and at the MacDowell Colony (1999). In 1999 she was awarded the Cleveland Arts Prize.

WORKS: ORCH.: *Currents and Cross Currents* (1988); *Third from the Sun* (1988; rev. 1991; N.Y., Jan. 31, 1992); *Fractal Images* (1990; Lexington, Va., March 1, 1991); *Then the Bells...* for Chamber Orch. (1991); *Shifting Circles* (Roanoke, May 3, 1993); *Silence Beyond...* for Wind Ensemble or Concert Band (1993); Chamber Concerto (1993; Baltimore, Feb. 6, 1994); Clarinet Concerto (1994; Roanoke, Jan. 27, 1997); *Prelude and Vivace* for Clarinet and Chamber Ensemble (Pittsburgh, April 11, 1996); *Remembrances* (Roanoke, March 18, 1996); *Pluto: A Sequel* (Roanoke, March 17, 1997); Sym. No. 1, *Lake Voices* (Akron, Oct. 25, 1997). **CHAMBER:** *Dream Drifts* for Viola, Piano, and Tape Delay (Dallas, April 2, 1983); *Ilumyst* for 7 Instruments (Bloomington, Ind., Nov. 6, 1984); *Mountains of the Moon* for String Quartet (New Milford, Conn., Aug. 14, 1985); *Aurolucent Echoes* for 7 Players (1985; Bloomington, Ind., Feb. 25, 1986); *Timespan* for Brass Quintet (1986; San Francisco, Oct. 6, 1987); Violin Sonata (Interlochen, Mich., Aug. 6, 1987); *SCHerZOID* for Horn (Moscow, Idaho, April 18, 1989); *2 Pieces* for Viola (1989; Dallas, May 7, 1990); *Skyriding* for Flute, Violin, Cello, and Piano (Lexington, Va., May 3, 1992); *Diary of an Alien* for Flute (Lexington, Va., Jan. 28, 1994); *Tolling the Spirits* for Brass Quintet (Philadelphia, Oct. 29, 1994); *Crosswinds* for String Quartet (N.Y., April 11, 1995); *A Little Renaissance Music* for Violin, Oboe, Clarinet, Cello, and Double Bass (Bennington, Vt.,

Aug. 17, 1996); Horn Sonata (Iowa City, Oct. 18, 1996); *Demeter Prelude* for String Quartet (Reston, Va., June 20, 1997); *Celebration* for Brass Quintet (Lexington, Va., Sept. 9, 1998); Piano Sonata (Cleveland, Feb. 2, 1999). **VOCAL:** *Rapunzel* for Soprano and 5 Players (Evansville, Ind., Sept. 10, 1988); 2 Songs for Soprano and 6 Instruments (Richmond, Va., Nov. 11, 1990); *Washington and Lee Hymn* for Chorus (1990; Lexington, Va., March 19, 1991); *Missa Brevis* for Men's Chorus (1991; Lexington, Va., March 20, 1992).—**LK/DM**

Brown, A(lfred) Peter, learned American musicologist; b. Chicago, April 30, 1943. He was educated at Northwestern Univ. (B.M.E., 1965; M.M., 1966; Ph.D., 1970, with the diss. *The Solo and Ensemble Keyboard Sonatas of Joseph Haydn: A Study in Structure and Style*). He also attended the Domaine School of Conductors in Hancock, Maine (1965) and pursued postdoctoral studies at N.Y. Univ. (1970). He was a lecturer at Ind. Univ. Northwest (1967–69) and was asst. prof. at the Univ. of Hawaii (1969–74). In 1972–73 he was an American Council of Learned Societies fellow, and in 1978–79 he held a Guggenheim fellowship. He was asst. prof. (1974–77), assoc. prof. (1977–81), and prof. of music (from 1981) at Ind. Univ., where he also was chairman of the musicology dept. (from 1997). In 1981 he was a visiting scholar at the Univ. of Mo. in Columbia, in 1984 he directed an NEH Summer Seminar for Coll. Teachers on Haydn, in 1989 he was a member of the faculty of the Aston Magna Academy, in 1991 he was the Ida Beam Distinguished Visiting Prof. at the Univ. of Iowa, and in 1993 he was the Distinguished Alumane Lecturer at the Northwestern Univ. School of Music. Brown has devoted much of his research to the elucidation of 18th century music, on which he has written authoritative books and articles in scholarly journals. His edition of Haydn's *The Creation* has been recorded by Hogwood, Solti, Weil, and Gardiner.

WRITINGS: With J. Berkenstock and C. Brown, *Joseph Haydn in Literature: A Bibliography* (Munich, 1974); *Carlo d'Ordonez (1734–1786): A Thematic Catalog* (Detroit, 1978); with P. Alexander, *Seven Symphonies of Carlo d'Ordonez: An Edition*, in B. Brook, ed., *The Symphony* (N.Y., 1979); *The String Quartets Opus 1 of Carlo d'Ordonez: A Critical Edition* (Madison, Wisc., 1980); *Performing Haydn's The Creation: Reconstructing the Earliest Renditions* (Bloomington, Ind., 1985); *Haydn's Keyboard Music: Sources and Style* (Bloomington, Ind., 1986); with R. Griscom, *The French Music Publisher Guera of Lyon: A Dated List* (Detroit, 1987); *Haydn's The Creation: A New Performing Edition* (Oxford, 1995); *The Symphony from Sammartini to Lutosławski* (5 vols., Bloomington, Ind., 1999 et seq.).—**NS/LK/DM**

Brown, Bobby, the singer who went from teen sensation to controversial R&B star, inventing New Jack Swing in the process; b. Boston, Mass., Feb. 5, 1969. Bobby Brown grew up in the projects in the Roxbury section of Boston. His father was a construction worker and his mother taught grade school. They sang in church, and listened to blues and R&B at home. Brown saw music as his way out of the projects. He formed the vocal group New Edition with four of his Roxbury friends, sharing lead vocal duty with Ralph Tresvant for five years before going solo in 1986 at age 17. Despite the group's success, his solo debut, *King of Stage*, sold

disappointingly, with the single "Girlfriend" a comparatively middling R&B hit.

In 1988, he hooked up with producers Teddy Riley and L.A. Reid and Babyface. The album they produced, the chart-topping, sextuple platinum *Don't Be Cruel*, helped change the face of popular music, fusing melodic, soulful songs with hip-hop rhythms, bringing the hybrid style new jack swing to a pop audience. The title track went gold, topped the R&B charts, and hit #8 on the pop charts. The gold follow-up single, "My Prerogative," topped both the pop and R&B charts. "Roni" went to #3; "Every Little Step" went gold, topped the R&B chart, and hit #3 pop; "Rock Witcha" went gold and hit #7 pop. Brown also had a platinum single with the #2 pop tune "On Our Own," featured in the film *Ghostbusters II*. He topped the pop charts again on a gold duet with Glen Medeiros, "She Ain't Worth It."

A remix album followed, went to #9, and sold platinum. However, Brown's rise to super pop stardom wasn't without controversy. His hip-shaking live show proved too much for the authorities in Columbus, Ga., who cited him in violation of the city's lewd behavior act and fined him $600. This was not the last of his legal difficulties (though it was the least). Brown fathered several children with various girlfriends, and did some time in drug rehab. Then he married Whitney Houston in a lavish wedding at Houston's N.J. estate in 1992.

After the wedding, Brown finally released a new album, *Bobby*. The album debuted at #2 and eventually sold two million copies. The singles "Humping Around" (#3 pop/#1R&B) and "Good Enough" (#7 pop) both went gold. "Get Away" hit #14. The album also included a duet with Houston, "Something in Common."

Brown joined the chart-topping New Edition reunion in 1996 before returning to his solo career with *Forever* in 1997, but the album didn't even go gold. Earlier that year, his recording studio in Atlanta went bankrupt. Beset by rumors of marital difficulty, Brown and Houston remain wed, although Brown's career seems now to have stalled, while Houston continues to top the charts while also developing a successful acting career.

DISC.: *King of Stage* (1986); *Don't Be Cruel* (1988); *Dance!...Ya Know It* (1989); *Bobby* (1992); *Remixes in the Key of B* (1993); *Forever* (1997).—**HB**

Brown, Chris, innovative American composer, performer, and teacher; b. Mendota, Ill., Sept. 9, 1953. After studies in composition and electronic music with Williams Brooks and Gordon Mumma at the Univ. of Calif. at Santa Cruz (B.A., 1974), he studied computer music with David Rosenboom at Mills Colege in Oakland, Calif. (M.F.A. in electronic music and recording media, 1985), where, from 1987, he served on its faculty. Brown is noted for his invention of unusual electroacoustic instruments, which are put to use in his *Alternating Currents* (1983), and for his use of live, interactive electronics to extend the sonorities of traditional acoustic instruments, as in his *Iceberg* (1985), *Hall of Mirrors* (1987), and *Lava* (1992). His *Snakecharmer* (1986) contrasts the mechanical qualities of automated electronic sound environments and the spontaneity of free improvisation, while his *Chain Reaction* (1990), *Wheelies* (1992), *Talking Drum* (1995), and *Role'm* (1998) explore applications of new technology in performance in such a way as to change the role of musicians one to another as well as to audiences. Brown is also an avid performer, and many of his works with interactive electronics were composed for the ensemble Room, with which he performed, along with William Winant, Larry Ochs, and Scot Gresham-Lancaster. Brown is also a founding member of The Hub, a computer music band whose members designed and built their own hardware and software instruments. Their sharing of musical information and ensuing interaction in live performance created a new genre known as "Computer Network Music." —LK/DM

Brown, Cleo(patra), jazz pianist, singer; b. Meridian, Miss., Dec. 8, 1909; d. Denver, Colo., April 15, 1995. She was a creative two-handed pianist who was admired by Dave Brubeck, but whose singing overshadowed her instrumental ability. Her brother, Everett, was a pianist; their father was the pastor of the Pilgrim Baptist Church in Meridan. In 1919 when the family moved to Chicago, Cleo studied music and began playing piano for a touring show. During the late 1920s she played several residencies in and around Chicago, and also gigged with various bands. In 1932, while playing and singing in a local rumba band, she was signed by Texas Guinan and began appearing regularly on Chicago radio programs. She then had her own series on WABC, led her own group at Three Deuces, Chicago, made extensive recordings, and appeared regularly in N.Y. and Hollywood during the late 1930s. After working as a piano teacher, she was taken seriously ill and was in a Calif. sanatorium from late 1940 until 1942. In the late 1940s, she moved to Los Angeles, making her last jazz recording in 1949. In 1973, she settled in Denver, where she found religion and focussed on writing and performing hymns and gospel material under the name of C. Patra Brown. She made a late-life appearance on Marian McPartland's Piano Jazz series in 1987.

Disc.: *The Feminine Touch* (1953); *Living in the Afterglow* (1987); *Boogie Woogie* (1988); *The Legendary Cleo Brown* (1996). —JC/LP

Brown, Clifford (Brownie), important and widely influential 1950s-era jazz trumpeter; b. Wilmington, Del., Oct. 30, 1930; d. in an automobile accident on the Pennsylvania Tpke. near Bedford, Pa., June 26, 1956. He studied at Del. State Coll. and Md. State Coll. and gained experience playing in college jazz bands. He worked and recorded with Chris Powell. Later, Brown joined Tadd Dameron and toured Europe with Lionel Hampton's orch. (1953). Upon returning to the U.S., he worked with Art Blakey. Brown joined the Max Roach Quintet (1954), with Richie Powell on piano, and Harold Land, who was replaced by Sonny Rollins in late 1955. The group was sometimes billed as the Brown–Roach Quintet and sometimes as Roach–Brown, presumably so they could share equal billing. Brown was a capable

pianist who recorded himself in rehearsal and several hours of these rehearsals exist on tape. His solo trumpet practicing on "Cherokee" has been issued. Through such documents we can study the development of his style which took off from Fats Navarro and Miles Davis and certainly, but less explicitly, from Dizzy Gillespie. "Cherokee" was almost his theme song and he recorded it many times between 1953–55 in different versions. The group and Brown were becoming the hottest attractions in jazz when he and Powell were killed. Their car, driven by Powell's wife who also died, went off the road in the middle of the night on the way from Philadelphia to their next gig. This was front page news in the black press and jazz press and a tragedy whose impact is still felt. According to recent research, the session issued as "the end" was not his last date, but made on June 27, 1955. Brown is still studied and emulated by young trumpeters and by any musicians interested in perfectly phrased melodic lines that swing delicately and yet scream with intensity and blues when called for.

Disc.: *Swedish All-Stars* (1953); *Stockholm Sweetnin'* (1953); *Quartet in Paris, Vols. 1 and 2* (1953); *New Star on the Horizon* (1953); *"Joy Spring"* (1953); *The Complete Blue Note/Pacific Jazz Clifford Brown* (1953); *Clifford Brown / Gigi Gryce Sextet* (1953); *Clifford Brown and His Ensemble* (1954); *Clifford Brown Ensemble* (1954); *Clifford Brown All Stars* (1954); *Clifford Brown and Max Roach* (1954); *Brown and Roach, Inc.* (1954); *Best Coast Jazz with All-Stars* (1954); *All Stars* (1954); *Study in Brown* (1955); *Live at the Bee Hive* (1955); *Clifford Brown with Strings* (1955); *Beginning and the End* (1955); *Pure Genius* (1956); *At Basin Street* (1956).

Bibl.: B. Weir, D. N. Baker, *Jazz Style of Clifford Brown* (Hialeah, Fla.); D. Baker, *The Jazz Style of Clifford Brown: A Musical and Historical Perspective* (Warner Bros., 1982).—LP

Brown, David (Clifford), English musicologist; b. Gravesend, July 8, 1929. He studied at the Univ. of Sheffield (B.A., 1951; B.Mus., 1952); then was music librarian at the Univ. of London Library, Senate House (1959–62). In 1962 he was appointed a lecturer at the Univ. of Southampton; was prof. of musicology there from 1983 to 1989. He was awarded a Ph.D. in 1971 by the Univ. of Southampton for his book *Thomas Weelkes: A Biographical and Critical Study* (London, 1969). He also wrote *John Wilbye* (London, 1974) and then specialized in Russian music; publ. *Mikhail Glinka* (London, 1974) and an extended four-vol. biography of Tchaikovsky (1978–91), the merits of which are marred by an easy acceptance of the questionable theory that Tchaikovsky committed suicide. Later he publ. *Tchaikovsky Remembered* (London and Boston, 1993). He contributed articles on Russian music to *The New Grove Dictionary of Music and Musicians* (1980).—NS/LK/DM

Brown, Earle (Appleton Jr.), significant American composer; b. Lunenburg, Mass., Dec. 26, 1926. He took courses in engineering and mathematics at Northeastern Univ. in Boston, and then studied theory with Kenneth McKillop (from 1946) and composition with Roslyn Brogue (from 1947), graduating from the Schillinger School in 1950. From 1952 to 1955 he was associated with the Project for Music for Magnetic Tape in N.Y. He soon adopted the most advanced compositional techniques, experimenting with serial methods as well as aleatory forms. He was fascinated by the parallelism in abstract expressionism in painting, mobile sculptures, and flexible musical forms, which prompted him to develop the idea of graphic notation in 1952 and of open from in 1953. Brown professes no *parti pris* in his approach to techniques and idioms of composition, whether dissonantly contrapuntal or serenly triadic. Rather, his music represents a mobile assemble of plastic elements, in open-ended or closed forms. As a result, his usages range from astute asceticism and constrained constructivism to soaring sonorism and lush lyricism, *sine ira et studio*. Brown has had many lectureships and received many honors. He served as composer-in-residence at the Peabody Cons. in Baltimore (1968–73), the Aspen (Colo.) Music Festival (1971, 1975, 1981), the Rotterdam Phil. and Cons. (1974), the Calif. Inst. of the Arts (1974–83), the American Academy in Rome (1987) et al. He also was a visiting prof. at the Basel Academy of Music (1975), the State Univ. of N.Y. at Buffalo (1975), the Univ. of Calif. at Berkeley (1976), the Univ. of Southern Calif. in Los Angeles (1978), Yale Univ. (1980–81; 1986–87) et al. In 1965–66 he held a Guggenheim fellowship. He was given an honorary doctorate in music by the Peabody Cons. in 1970. From 1986 to 1989 Brown was president of the American Music Center in N.Y.

Works: *Fugue* for Piano (1949); *Home Burial* for Piano (1949); Trio for Clarinet, Bassoon, and Piano (1949; unfinished); *Passacaglia* for Piano (1950); *Strata* for 2 Pianos (1950); String Quartet (1950); *3 Pieces* for Piano (1951); *Perspectives* for Piano (1952); *Music* for Violin, Cello, and Piano (1952); *Folio* for Unspecified Instruments (1952–53: *October 1952, November 1952 [Synergy], December 1952, MM 87 and MM 135,* and *Music for Trio for 5 Dancers;* arranged for Chamber Ensemble, 1981); *Music for "Tender Buttons"* for Speaker, Flute, Horn, and Harp (1953); Octet I (1952–53) and II (1957) for 8 Tapes; *25 Pages* for 1 to 25 Pianos (1953; N.Y., April 14, 1954); *4 Systems* for Unspecified Instruments (1954; arranged for Chamber Ensemble, 1981); *Indices* for Chamber Orch. (1954); *Music* for Cello and Piano (1954–55); *4 More* for Piano (1956); *Pentathis* for Flute, Bass Clarinet, Trumpet, Trombone, Harp, and Piano Quartet (1957–58); *Holograph I* for Flute, Piano, and Percussion (1959); *Available Forms I* for 18 Musicians (1961) and II for Large Orch. and 2 Conductors (1962); *Light Music* for Large Orch., Lights, and Electronics (1961); *Novara* for Flute, Bass Clarinet, Trumpet, Trombone, Harp, and Piano Quartet (1962); *From Here* for 4 Sopranos, 4 Altos, 4 Tenors, 4 Basses, and 20 Instruments (1963); *Times 5* for Flute, Trombone, Harp, Violin, Cello, and 4–track Tape (1963); *Corroboree* for 3 or 2 Pianos (1964); *9 Rarebits* for 1 or 2 Harpsichords (1965); *String Quartet 1965* (1965); *Calder Piece* for 4 Percussion and Mobile (1963–66); *Modules I-II* (1966) and III (1969) for Orch.; *Event: Synergy II* for 11 Woodwind and 8 Strings (1967–68); *Small Piece for Large Chorus* (1969–70); *Syntagm III* for Flute, Bass Clarinet, Vibraphone, Marimba, Harp, Piano, Violin, and Cello (1970); *New Piece Loops* for 17 Instruments (1971–72); *Time Spans* for Large Orch. (1972); *Centering* for Violin and Chamber Orch. (1973); *Sign Sounds* for 18 Instruments (1972); *Cross Sections and Color Fields* for Orch. (1975); *Windsor Jambs (Transients)* for Mezzo-soprano, Flute, Clarinet, Piano, Percussion, Violin, Viola, and Cello (1980); *Folio II* for Unspecified Instruments (1981); *Sounder Rounds* for Orch. (1982; Saarbrücken, May 12, 1983, composer conducting); *Tracer* for Flute, Oboe, Bassoon, Violin, Cello, Double Bass, and 4–Track Tape (1984; Berlin, Feb. 8, 1985).

Bibl.: P. Quist, *Indeterminate Form in the Works of E. B.* (diss., Peabody Cons. of Music, 1984).—NS/LK/DM

Brown, Eddy, American violinist; b. Chicago, July 15, 1895; d. Abano Terme, Italy, June 14, 1974. He was given his first violin lessons by his father; then was taken to Europe, and studied in Budapest with Hubay. He won a violin competition at the age of 11 playing the Mendelssohn Concerto in Budapest. He then proceeded to London, and eventually to Russia, where he became a pupil of Auer. Returning to the U.S. in 1915, he made several transcontinental tours; was a soloist with the N.Y. Phil., the Chicago Sym. Orch., the Philadelphia Orch., and the Boston Sym. Orch. In 1922 he founded the Eddy Brown String Quartet; in 1932 he became president of the Chamber Music Soc. of America, which he organized. He became active in educational programs over the radio; was music director of the Mutual Broadcasting System (1930–37) and of station WQXR in N.Y. (1936–55). From 1956 to 1971 he was artistic coordinator of the Univ. of Cincinnati Coll.-Cons. of Music. —NS/LK/DM

Brown, Howard Mayer, American musicologist; b. Los Angeles, April 13, 1930; d. Venice, Feb. 21, 1993. He studied composition with Piston and musicology with Gombosi at Harvard Univ. (B.A., 1951; M.A., 1954; Ph.D., 1959, with the diss. *Music in the French Secular Theater, 1400–1550;* publ. in Cambridge, Mass., 1963); also studied in Vienna (1951–53) and later held a Guggenheim fellowship in Florence (1963–64). He was a member of the faculty at Wellesley Coll. (1958–60). In 1960 he was appointed to the staff of the Univ. of Chicago, where he subsequently was made a prof. (1967) and chairman of the music dept. (1970). From 1972 to 1974 he taught at King's Coll., Univ. of London, and then returned to the Univ. of Chicago. In 1989 he was made an honorary member of the American Musicological Soc. He publ. *Instrumental Music Printed before 1600: A Bibliography* (Cambridge, Mass., 1965), *Embellishing Sixteenth-Century Music* (London, 1976), and *Music in the Renaissance* (Englewood Cliffs, N.J., 1976; 2nd ed., 1999, with L. Stein). In 1970 he was named ed. of the compendium *Italian Opera, 1640–1770: Major Unpublished Works in a Central Baroque and Early Classical Tradition* (N.Y., 1977 et seq.). With S. Sadie, he ed. *Music Before 1600* (Basingstoke, 1989) and *Music After 1600* (Basingstoke, 1989).—NS/LK/DM

Brown, Iona, esteemed English violinist and conductor; b. Salisbury, Wiltshire, Jan. 7, 1941. She studied violin as a child. In 1955 she joined the National Youth Orch. of Great Britain, remaining its member for 5 years. She also studied with Hugh Maguire in London, Remy Principe in Rome, and Henryk Szeryng in Paris and Nice. From 1963 to 1966 she played in the Philharmonia Orch. of London. In 1964 she joined the Academy of St. Martin-in- the-Fields, and served as its director from 1974. In 1980 she was named music director of the Norwegian Chamber Orch. in Oslo. She also was music advisor (1986–87) and music director (1987–92) of the

Los Angeles Chamber Orch., and music director of the Sonderjyllands Sym. Orch. in Sønderborg (from 1997). She was made an Officer of the Order of the British Empire in 1986.—NS/LK/DM

Brown, James, "The Godfather of Soul"; b. Macon, Ga., May 3, 1928 (although some sources claim May 3, 1933, in Barnwell, S.C.). Raised in Augusta, James Brown took up keyboards, then drums and bass, at an early age. Dropping out of school in the seventh grade, Brown spent a delinquent youth, serving four years in reform school for petty theft beginning in 1949. Upon release, he joined pianist Bobby Byrd's Gospel Starlighters. Evolving into The Famous Flames and concentrating on rhythm-and-blues music, the group played around Ga. and came to the attention of Ralph Bass of Cincinnati's King Records. He signed them to a recording contract in January 1956 after hearing their first demonstration record. Rerecorded with Byrd and former Gospel Starlighters Sylvester Keels and Nafloyd Scott, the song, "Please, Please, Please," became a smash rhythm-and-blues hit in April.

James Brown quickly became the undisputed leader of The Famous Flames. Their next hit, 1958's "Try Me," topped the R&B charts and filtered into the pop charts. A series of smash rhythm-and-blues hits began in 1960 with "Think," followed by "I Don't Mind," "Baby, You're Right," "Lost Someone," and "Night Train." Brown organized the James Brown Revue with dozens of singers, musicians, and dancers, and, with a tightly rehearsed and choreographed stage act polished to near perfection, they played to sellout, box-office record audiences in ghetto areas across the country in the early 1960s. The live recording of their show at Harlem's Apollo Theatre on Oct. 24, 1962, reflected Brown's mastery of showmanship and effectively established him as an important artist, and the resulting album is regarded as a classic.

During 1962, James Brown reluctantly recorded several songs with vocal chorus and strings at the insistence of King Records. One of the songs, "Prisoner of Love," became a major pop hit. By 1964, however, Brown had deemphasized vocals in favor of strong hard polyrhythms. He brought a set of recently recorded songs to the Smash subsidiary of Mercury Records in Chicago. One of them, "Out of Sight," became a major pop hit and Brown's first record to sell in large quantities to whites. Brown eventually returned to King with complete control over all aspects of his recording career, with releases on Smash restricted to instrumentals and recordings by members of the Revue.

With The Famous Flames, James Brown became perhaps the earliest purveyor of bottom-heavy funk music. Over the years, his groups included saxophonists Maceo Parker (1964–70, 1973–76, and 1984–88, the last as band director) and Alfred "Pee Wee" Ellis (1965–70), guitarist Jimmy Nolen (1965–70, 1972–83), trombonist Fred Wesley (1968–76), and bassist William "Bootsy" Collins (1969–71). All except Nolen recorded albums on their own after leaving Brown.

Eschewing club engagements in favor of concert auditoriums, Brown scored a top rhythm-and-blues and near-smash pop hit in 1965 with the seminal "Papa's Got a Brand New Bag," recorded with Nolen, Parker, and new band leader Nat Jones. Adding Ellis, Brown followed up with the top R&B and smash pop hits "I Got You (I Feel Good)" and "It's a Man's Man's World," and the rhythm-and-blues smashes "Ain't That a Groove (Part 1)," "Don't Be a Drop- Out," "Bring It Up," and "Let Yourself Go." Ellis took over as musical director and chief musical collaborator in 1967. Buying three Southern radio stations, Brown subsequently achieved top R&B and near- smash pop hits with the funk masterpiece "Cold Sweat" and "I Got the Feelin,'" and rhythm-and-blues smashes with "I Can't Stand Myself," "There Was a Time," "Licking Stick (Part1)," and "Licking Stick (Part 2)."

By the late 1960s, James Brown was producing the entire show for the Revue—songs, costumes, routines, choreography, and lighting. Credited with helping quell riots after the assassination of Dr. Martin Luther King Jr., Brown issued one of the first anthems of black pride in 1968, "Say It Loud, I'm Black and I'm Proud," a top R&B and major pop hit. Performing at President Richard Nixon's inaugural celebration in January 1969, Brown scored the top R&B and major pop hit "Give It Up or Turnit a Loose" and the smash R&B and major pop hit "I Don't Want Nobody to Give Me Nothing." He next returned to more conventional hits based on the dance style called the Popcorn, beginning with the top R&B and major pop hit "Mother Popcorn," followed by the smash R&B and major pop hit "Ain't It Funky Now (Part 1)" and the seminal "Funky Drummer."

In mid-1970, The Famous Flames broke up, to be replaced by The JBs, centered around pianist Bobby Byrd, guitarist Jimmy Nolen, saxophonist "Pee Wee" Ellis, trombonist Fred Wesley, and new bassist William "Bootsy" Collins. Scoring his final smash R&B hits on King with "Get Up I Feel Like Being a Sex Machine," "Super Bad," "Get Up, Get Into It, Get Involved," and "Soul Power," Brown switched to Polydor Records in 1971, bringing with him his entire back catalog and forming his own label, People, for the classic "Hot Pants" and recording by the JBs. However, Ellis and Collins soon left the JBs, with Fred Wesley replacing Ellis as band leader. Nonetheless, top rhythm- and-blues hits continued through 1974 with "Make It Funky (Part 1)," "Talking Loud and Say Nothing (Part 1)," "Get on the Good Foot (Part 1)," "The Payback (Part 1)," "My Thang," and "Papa Don't Take No Mess (Part 1)." Smash R&B hits of the era included ""King Heroin," "There It Is (Part 1)," "I Got a Bag of My Own," ""I Got Ants in My Pants," and "Funky President (People It's Bad)." In 1973, Brown and Wesley scored the music to the movies *Black Caesar* and *Slaughter's Big Rip-Off.*

In the early 1970s, Maceo Parker, Pee Wee Ellis, and Fred Wesley recorded as Maceo and The King's Men and Maceo and The Macks. The JBs recorded a number of albums for People Records in the first half of the 1970s. Parker, Wesley and Bootsy Collins all joined George Clinton's Parliament–Funkadelic aggregation in the 1970s, with Wesley recording one spin-off album as The Horny Horns. Collins later went on to his own successful funk career, and Parker, Wesley, and Ellis recorded successful jazz albums in the 1990s.

James Brown began having tax disputes with the Treasury Department in 1975 and scored his last smash rhythm-and-blues hit for 12 years with "Get Up Offa That Thing" in 1976. Enduring diminished popularity, particularly with the rise of disco music, Brown even utilized the services of an outside producer for the first time for *The Original Disco Man* in 1979. Touring the rock club circuit for the first time in 1980, he was introduced to a new generation of fans with his appearance in *The Blues Brothers* movie. He began playing the supper club circuit in 1983, but long-time guitarist Jimmy Nolen died in Atlanta on Dec. 18, 1983. Brown scored a minor R&B hit with hip-hop pioneer Afrika Bambaataa on "Unity" in 1984 and experienced a revival of interest in his music with the 1986 smash pop and near-smash R&B hit "Living in America" from the movie *Rocky IV*.

In 1986, James Brown was inducted into the Rock and Roll Hall of Fame and switched to Scotti Brothers Records. He soon became beset by personal, health, and financial troubles, yet scored a smash rhythm-and-blues hit with "I'm Real" in 1988. However, his September 1988 arrest in S.C. following a two-state car chase by police resulted in a prison term of more than two years beginning in December. Paroled in February 1991, James Brown quickly resumed touring and recording. Brown was the opening act for Woodstock '99.

Probably the single most popular black artist among blacks until the mid-1970s, James Brown may very well be the last vaudeville performer, with his high-powered, histrionic, and intensely dramatic stage show. In fact, his performance style influenced generations of performers, from Mick Jagger and Sly Stone to Michael Jackson and Prince. His classic 1962 album, *Live at the Apollo*, is regarded by some as the greatest in-concert album ever recorded and was likely the first album bought in mass quantities by blacks. With his unique mixture of gospel, blues, and even jazz, and the powerful choreographed playing of The Fabulous Flames, Brown reinvigorated soul music in the 1960s and opened the door for soul shouters such as Wilson Pickett and Otis Redding. One of the first rock entertainers to gain complete control over his career, James Brown was certainly the first black artist to achieve independence from his record company in matters of arrangements, production, and packaging. In emphasizing polyrhythms from the late 1960s to early 1970s with instrumentalists Maceo Parker, Fred Wesley, and William "Bootsy" Collins, Brown Africanized American rhythm-and-blues and originated funk music later pursued by Sly Stone and George Clinton. That influence extended into the 1980s and 1990s with the development of hip-hop and rap music, which regularly mimicked his style and sampled his early recordings. Moreover, Brown was one of the first blacks to champion black self-pride and political consciousness in the 1960s, while at the same time establishing himself as one of the nation's first black entrepreneurs. Inducted into the Rock and Roll Hall of Fame in its inaugural year, 1986, James Brown endured a rocky period of health, financial, and legal problems in the late 1980s.

Disc.: *Please, Please, Please* (1959); *Try Me* (1960); *Think!* (1960); *The Always Amazing* (1961); *Jump Around/Night Train* (1962); *Shout and Shimmy/Good Good Twistin'* (1962); *Tour the U.S.A.* (1962); *"Live" at the Apollo* (1963); *Prisoner of Love* (1963); *Pure Dynamite!* (1964); *Showtime* (1964); *Papa's Got a Brand New Bag* (1965); *Grits and Soul* (1965); *Today and Yesterday* (1965); *I Got You (I Feel Good)* (1966); *Mighty Instrumental* (1966); *It's a Man's World* (1966); *Christmas Songs* (1966); *Plays New Breed* (1966); *Handful of Soul* (1966); *Presenting ... The James Brown Show* (1966); *Raw Soul* (1967); *Live at the Garden* (1967); *Cold Sweat* (1967); *Plays the Real Thing* (1967); *Sings Out of Sight* (1968); *Live at the Apollo, Volume 2* (1968); *I Can't Stand Myself When You Touch Me* (1968); *I Got the Feelin'* (1968); *Nothing but Soul* (1968); *Thinking about Little Willie John and a Whole New Thing* (1968); *A Soulful Christmas* (1968); *Say It Loud, I'm Black and I'm Proud* (1969); *Gettin' Down to It* (1969); *Popcorn* (1969); *It's a Mother* (1969); *Ain't It Funky* (1970); *It's a New Day* (1970); *Soul on Top* (1970); *Sex Machine* (1970); *Sho Is Funky Down Here* (1971); *Hey America!* (1971); *Super Bad* (1971); *Hot Pants* (1971); *Revolution of the Mind (Live at the Apollo, Vol. III)* (1971); *Love Power Peace: Live at the Olympia, Paris, 1971* (1992); *There It Is* (1972); *Get on the Good Foot* (1972); *Black Caesar* (music from the soundtrack; 1973); *Slaughter's Big Rip-Off* (music from the soundtrack; 1973); *The Payback* (1974); *It's Hell* (1974); *Reality* (1975); *Sex Machine Today* (1975); *Everybody's Doin' the Hustle* (1975); *Hot* (1976); *Get Up Offa That Thing* (1976); *Body Heat* (1977); *Mutha's Nature* (1977); *Sex Machine Recorded Live at Home* (1977); *Jam 1980s* (1978); *Take a Look at Those Cakes* (1979); *The Original Disco Man* (1979); *People* (1980); *Live ... Hot on the One* (1980); *Soul Jubilee* (recorded 1984; 1996); *Living in America* (1985); *Gravity* (1986); *I'm Real* (1988).
JAMES BROWN AND FRIENDS: *Soul Session Live* (1989); *Love Overdue* (1991); *Universal James* (1992); *Live at the Apollo 1995* (1995); *Hooked on Brown* (1996); *Soul Classic, Volume 1* (1972); *Soul Classic, Volume 2* (1973); *Solid Gold: 30 Golden Hits* (1977); *Best (1956–1971)* (1981); *Roots of a Revolution (1956–1964)* (1984); *Ain't That a Groove (1966–1969)* (1984); *Doin' It to Death (1969–1973)* (ND); *Dead on the Heavy Funk (1974–1976)* (1985); *James Brown's Funky People* (recorded 1971–1975; 1986); *In the Jungle Groove* (1986); *The of JB II (Cold Sweat and Other Soul Classics)* (1988); *James Brown's Funky People, Part II* (1988): *Motherlode* (1988); *Messing with the Blues (1957–1975)* (1990); *Star Time* (1991); *20 All-Time Greatest Hits* (1991); *Soul Pride: The Instrumentals (1960–1969)* (1993); *James Brown's Funky Christmas* (1995); *Foundations of Funk: A Brand New Bag, 1964–1969* (1996); *Funk Power 1970: A Brand New Thang* (1996); *Make It Funky/The Big Payback: 1971–1975* (1996); *JB40: 40th Anniversary Collection* (1996); *1975–1983: Dead on the Heavy Funk* (1998); *Say It Live and Loud* (1998); *Spank* (ND); *Federal Years, Volume 1* (1984); *Federal Years, Volume 2* (1984); *Greatest Hits (1964–1968)* (1986); *Santa's Got a Brand New Bag* (1988); *Soul Syndrome* (1991); *James Brown Is Back* (1991); *Greatest Hits of the Fourth Decade* (1992); *Sex Machine* (1998).
Writings: With Bruce Tucker, *J. B.: The Godfather of Soul* (N.Y., 1986, 1990, 1997).
Bibl.: Cynthia Rose, *Living in America: The Soul Saga of J. B.* (1990).—**BH**

Brown, John, English writer; b. Rothbury, Northumberland, Nov. 5, 1715; d. (suicide) Newcastle upon Tyne, Sept. 23, 1766. He became vicar of Great Horkesley, Essex, in 1754, and of St. Nicholas's, Newcastle, in 1758. He is the author of *Dissertation on the Rise, Union, and Power, the Progressions, Separations and Corruptions of Poetry and Music, to which is prefixed The Cure* *of Saul, A Sacred Ode* (London, 1763). A revised ed. was publ. in 1764 as *The History of the Rise and Progress of Poetry, through Its Several Species* (Fr. tr., Paris, 1768; Ger. tr., Leipzig, 1769; It. tr., 1772).—**NS/LK/DM**

Brown, Lawrence, jazz trombonist; b. Lawrence, Kans., Aug. 3, 1907; d. Los Angeles, Sept. 5, 1988. His brother, Harold, is a professional pianist; their father was a minister. Lawrence started on piano, violin, and tuba, then specialized on trombone. While studying medicine at Pasadena Junior Coll., he played in school orchestra. Professional at 19 with Charlie Echols' Band, left after six months to join Paul Howard, with whom he recorded in 1929. He worked with Leon Herriford and Curtis Mosby's Blue Blowers before rejoining Paul Howard. He worked as a "house-man" at Sebastian's Cotton Club in Culver City, playing with various leaders including Les Hite, with whom he accompanied Louis Armstrong (on records). In the spring of 1932, he was signed by impresario Irving Mills and joined Duke Ellington. He remained with Duke until March 1951 (except for a brief absence in the summer of 1943). He was with Johnny Hodges' Small Band until spring of 1955, did studio work in N.Y. (including a spell at CBS), then rejoined Ellington in May 1960. Other than brief absences, he worked regularly with Duke throughout the 1960s, and also led his own recording bands. He left Duke early in 1970, and worked for the U.S. government (1971), retiring in 1974 He moved to Calif., were he worked as a part-time business consultant.

DISC.: *Slide Trombone Featuring Lawrence* (1955); *Inspired Abandon* (1965). Ellington: "Rose of the Rio Grande" (1938). —**JC/LP**

Brown, Les(ter Raymond), pop-jazz bandleader of the "Band of Renown," arranger, composer; b. Reinerton, Pa., March 14, 1912. He formed a band at Duke Univ. in the early 1930s. In 1938, he led Les Brown and his Band of Renown, which became the most popular white dance band in the U.S. in the 1940s and early 1950s. Doris Day was his vocalist; their biggest hits together included "My Dreams Are Getting Better All the Time" and "Sentimental Journey" (both #1 in 1945), plus instrumentals "I've Got My Love to Keep Me Warm" (#1 in 1948; the last big instrumental hit of the Swing era), "Bizet Has His Day," and "Leap Frog." He had quit in 1946, but a March 1947 ballroom gig forced him to form a new band. He eventually worked in radio and TV, playing with Bob Hope, Steve Allen, and Dean Martin. He remained one of the most popular leaders on the West Coast. His albums during the 1980s included long-time vocalist Jo Ann Greer, and Butch Stone on baritone sax and vocals. His orch. was strictly a dance group, with lightweight arrangements and novelty tunes.

DISC.: *Over the Rainbow* (1951); *Lullaby in Rhythm* (1954); *Cool Classics* (1955); *Composer's Holiday* (1957); *Les Brown Goes Direct to Disc* (1977); *Twilight Time; Sentimental Journey* (1977). —**MM/LP**

Brown, Marion (Jr.), jazz alto saxophonist; b. Atlanta, Ga., Sept. 8, 1935. He studied music and history and economics at Clark Coll. and Howard Univ. He reportedly played with Johnny Hodges in the 1950s before moving to N.Y. His first job was with Archie Shepp. He led his own groups on and off from 1965. He recorded with B. Dixon and John Coltrane, played with Sun Ra, then toured Europe, where he played and recorded with Gunter Hampel and Jeanne Lee. On his return, he became involved in education and formed a duo with trumpeter L. Smith in the 1970s; he also performed solo. His recordings reflect his interest in and absorption with African and African-American folk music and traditional rhythms and songs. In the 1990s, he occasionally performed and read his poetry at Studio 5C in N.Y. He was reported ill in 1999 and living at the Bethany Methodist Home, Brooklyn.

DISC.: Coltrane: *Ascension* (1965); *Why Not?* (1966); *Three for Shepp* (1966); *Marion Brown Quartet* (1966); *Juba-Lee* (1966); *Porto Nova* (1967); *Afternoon of a Georgia Faun* (1970); *Geechee Recollections* (1973); *Duets* (1973); *Sweet Earth Flying* (1974); *Vista* (1975); *La Placita / Live in Willisau* (1977); *Reed 'n Vibes* (1978); *Back to Paris* (1980); *Gemini* (1983); *Recollections: Ballads and Blue* (1985); *Native Land* (1990).

WRITINGS: *Recollections: Essays, Drawings, Miscellanea* (Frankfurt, Schmitt, 1984).—**LP**

Brown, Maurice J(ohn) E(dwin), English writer on music; b. London, Aug. 3, 1906; d. Marlborough, Sept. 27, 1975. He was educated at the Univ. of London (B.Sc., 1929; B.Mus., 1939); then pursued a career as a high- school and grammar-school teacher; concurrently devoted himself to research, studying various aspects of the life and works of Schubert; his *Schubert: A Critical Biography* (London, 1958; Ger. tr., 1969) is a standard source; he was also an authority on Chopin. In addition to many articles for music periodicals, he wrote *Schubert's Variations* (London, 1954); *Chopin: An Index of His Work in Chronological Order* (London, 1960); *Essays on Schubert* (London, 1966); with O.E. Deutsch, *Schubert: Die Erinnerungen seiner Freunde* (Leipzig, 1966); *Schubert Songs* (London, 1967); *Schubert Symphonies* (London, 1970).—**NS/LK/DM**

Brown, Merton (Luther), American composer; b. Berlin, Vt., May 5, 1913. He studied both piano and violin; moved to N.Y. in 1935 and took piano lessons with Anne Hull, and studied composition privately with Riegger (1939–42) and Ruggles (1943–45). From 1949 to 1967 he lived in Rome; then settled in Boston. His music is set in dense, dissonant counterpoint without negating the lyrical flow of melody.

WORKS: *Consort for 4 Voices*, scored for 2 Pianos (N.Y., April 21, 1947); *Piano Sonata* (1948); *Chorale* for Strings (1948); *Duo in 3 Movements* for Violin and Piano (1956); *Concerto breve per archi* (Naples, Jan. 23, 1960); *Metamorfosi per piano* (1965); *Dialogo* for Cello and Piano (1970); *Concertino* for String Orch. (1974); *Divertimento* for Piano, 4–Hands (1975); *5 Pieces* for Clarinet and Piano (1976); *Psalm 13* (1976).—**NS/LK/DM**

Brown, Newel Kay, American composer and pedagogue; b. Salt Lake City, Feb. 29, 1932. He studied composition with Robertson at the Univ. of Utah (B.F.A., 1953; M.F.A., 1954) and with Hanson, Barlow, and

Rogers at the Eastman School of Music in Rochester, N.Y. (Ph.D., 1967). From 1961 to 1967 he taught at Centenary Coll. for Women at Hackettstown, N.J.; from 1967 to 1970 he was on the faculty of Henderson State Coll., Arkadelphia, Ark.; in 1970 he became prof. of composition at North Tex. State Univ. in Denton. As a member of the Mormon Church, he wrote a number of choral works which entered the permanent repertoire; his Mormon children's choral work *I Hope They Call Me on a Mission* (1968) was tr. into 17 languages.

WORKS: Saxophone Sonata (1968); *4 Pieces* for Flute and Clarinet (1968); Suite for 2 Trumpets (1968); Trombone Sonata (1969); Woodwind Quintet (1969); *Hopkins Set* for Baritone and Trombone (1971); *Postures* for Bass Trombone and Piano (1972); *Glaser Set* for Mezzo-soprano, Trumpet, Clarinet, and Piano (1974); *Anagrams* for Trumpet, Marimba, and Percussion (1977); *Windart I* for Tuba, Soprano, and Piano (1978) and *II* for Euphonium, 6 Clarinets, Vibraphone, and Percussion (1980); *4 Meditations* for Bass Voice, Alto Saxophone, and Percussion (1981); numerous sacred songs and choruses.—**NS/LK/DM**

Brown, Pete (James Ostend), jazz alto saxophonist; b. Baltimore, Md., Nov. 9, 1906; d. N.Y., Sept. 20, 1963. His father was originally from Barbados and played trombone; his mother was a pianist. Pete's cousin Estelle Carroll was a singer. He played piano from the age of eight, took up the ukelele soon after, and then specialized on violin. He played in local a moviehouse band from the age of 12, and was a featured soloist at high school concerts. He began working in a Baltimore theatre orchestra, switching to alto and tenor saxophone in 1924. He played with a number of local bands through early 1927, when he joined Banjo Bernie Robinson in Atlantic City; that June, he moved to N.Y. with the band (where Pete began doubling on trumpet in 1928). From c. 1930–35, he worked on and off with Charlie Skeets. From c. 1933–May 1937, he worked in Fred Moore's Trio (with Don Frye) at various N.Y. clubs, and then became an original member of the John Kirby Band. He left Kirby in May 1938, and formed his own band that played many residencies in N.Y. During this period, he played on several recordings organized by Leonard Feather, and also recorded with Willie "The Lion" Smith (1937), and Frankie Newton. He co-led a band with Newton in early 1940, then led his own band at various clubs from 1941–43. During 1943, he was with Frankie Newton in Boston and then briefly fronted Louis Jordan's group while the leader did a solo tour. From 1944 through the 1950s, he continued to lead his own small groups, but persistent ill health curtailed regular playing in the later years of his life. He was featured at the Newport Jazz Festival in 1957, and continued playing until his death, with regular stints at the Village Vanguard and other N.Y. clubs. From the late 1950s, he doubled on tenor sax. He regularly gave sax instruction from the 1930s; his pupils include Cecil Payne and Flip Phillips.

DISC.: *Peter the Great* (1954); *From the Heart* (1959).—**JC/LP**

Brown, Pud (Albert), early jazz reeds player; b. Wilmington, Del., Jan. 22, 1917; d. May 27, 1996. Both parents (and brothers and sisters) were musical. First toured in Brown Family Band in 1927, billed as "World's Youngest Saxophone Player." He worked in theatre orchestras during the early 1930s, then did spells with Count Balooki, Marshall Van Poole, Lou Clanc, and Phil Levant. Brown moved to Chicago and worked with Bud Freeman, Jimmy Dorsey, Bud Jacobson, and Pete Daily. He gigged in Shreveport, La., from 1945–49, then moved to Los Angeles. In Calif. from 1949–73, he worked with Nappy Lamare, Jack Teagarden, Teddy Buckner, and Kid Ory, also led his own band. He began doubling Shreveport in 1973; worked a on cornet and trumpet in the early 1960s. Brown recorded with his own all-star band in 1977. During his career, he occasionally played string-bass.—**JC/LP**

Brown, Ray(mond Matthews), renowed jazz bassist; b. Pittsburgh, Oct. 13, 1926. He is one of the most recorded bassists in jazz. He moved to N.Y. around 1945 and performed and recorded with Dizzy Gillespie, Charlie Parker, and Bud Powell in the late 1940s. Brown played in Gillespie's big band (1946–47) and is seen onscreen with the band in the film *Jivin' in Bebop*. He was married to Ella Fitzgerald and accompanied her (1948–52). In 1951, he performed and recorded with the Milt Jackson Quartet, forerunner of the Modern Jazz Quartet. He was a member of the Oscar Peterson trio (1951–66), which brought him international recognition and a popular following; for more than a decade, he dominated jazz popularity polls for the double bass. He played on numerous albums on Norman Granz's Verve label. Following the example of Oscar Pettiford, he took up the cello. In 1960, he had a hybrid instrument combining features of the cello and double bass made for him, which was a forerunner of the piccolo bass. After leaving Peterson, Brown settled on the West Coast and became active as a freelance and studio musician, recording frequently for the Concord label; he co-led a group with Milt Jackson, recorded two albums with Jimmie Rowles and at least nine albums with the L.A. Four. Brown also managed other artists, including Quincy Jones, and produced concerts at the Hollywood Bowl. He did hundreds of recording sessions as a sideman, many for Granz's Pablo Records. He recorded as a leader for the Verve (1956–65) and Concord (1975–present) labels. In 1972, he recorded an album with Duke Ellington, in which the two men recreated the latter's well-known performances with Jimmy Blanton. During the late 1980s, he toured in a trio with Gene Harris and Mickey Roker; in the 1990s, the trio's personnel was often Benny Green and Geoff Keezer.

DISC.: *Bass Hit!* (1956); *This Is Ray Brown* (1958); *Ray Brown with the All Star Big Band* (1962); *Featuring Cannonball Adderley* (1962); *Much in Common* (1964); *Ray Brown with Milt Jackson* (1965); *As Good As It Gets* (1977); *Live at the Concord Jazz Festival* (1979); *Ray Brown Three* (1982); *Milt Jackson–Ray Brown Jam* (1982); *Red Hot Ray Brown Trio* (1985); *Two Bass Hits* (1991). D. Gillespie: "One Bass Hit" (1946); "Two Bass Hit" (1947). O. Peterson: *The Oscar Peterson Trio at the Stratford Shakespearean Festival* (1956); *Porgy and Bess* (1959); *Some of My Best Friends Are* (1994). J. Rowles: *Jazz Cello* (1960); *Brown's Bag* (c. 1976); *As Good as It Gets* (c. 1978); *Tasty!* (1979). D. Ellington: *This One's for Blanton* (1972). L. A. Four: *Montage* (1981); *Soular Energy* (1984); *Don't Forget the Blues* (1985).—**LP/MM**

Brown, Rayner, American organist, teacher, and composer; b. Des Moines, Iowa, Feb. 23, 1912; d. Los Angeles, June 16, 1999. He studied at the Univ. of Southern Calif. in Los Angeles (B.Mus., 1938; M.Mus., 1947); his mentors included Dahl, Eisler, and Cailliet. He was organist at Wilshire Presbyterian Church (1941–77) and a prof. of music at Biola Univ. in La Mirada, Calif. (1950–77).

WORKS: ORCH.: 6 syms. (1952, 1957, 1958, 1980, 1982, 1982); 7 organ concertos (1959, 1966, 1980, 1980, 1982, 1983, 1986); Concerto for Clarinet and Wind Orch. (1979); Concerto for Bass Trombone and Wind Orch. (1981); Clarinet Concerto (1984); Concerto for Violin, Harp, and Orch. (1987); Concert for Organ Duet and Orch. (1989); also various pieces for Wind Orch. and band music. **CHAMBER:** 3 sonatas for Flute and Piano (1944, 1959, 1985); Quartet for Violin, Viola, Cello, and Piano (1947); String Quartet (1953); 4 brass quintets (1957, 1960, 1981, 1985); Violin Sonata (1977); Sonata for 6 Trombones (1980); Tuba Quartet (1980); Trio for Cello, Trumpet, and Piano (1982); Sonata for Violin and Harp (1986); Sonata for English Horn and Organ (1989); Sonata for Harp and Organ (1990); various piano pieces; numerous organ works, including 35 sonatinas (1945–80) and 20 sonatas (1958–87). **VOCAL:** Cantatas and other pieces.—NS/LK/DM

Brown, Ruth (nee Alston Weston), American R&B singer and actress; b. Portsmouth, Va., Jan. 12, 1928. Brown was the daughter of Leonard Weston, a dock worker, and Martha Jane Alston Weston. Her father served as a church choir director, and she received her first musical instruction singing spirituals in church. She began singing secular music while working at a USO club during World War II and around 1945 joined the Raleigh Randolph band, where she met and teamed up with trumpeter/vocalist Jimmy Earle Brown as Brown and Brown. She married Brown, but the marriage was annulled when she found out he was already married; nevertheless, they stayed together and went out on their own, with Jimmy Brown forming his own group in 1947. The following year they separated and she began to perform alone. While appearing at the Frolic Show Bar in Detroit she was hired by bandleader Lucky Millinder, who fired her a month later, on July 4, 1948, stranding her in Washington, D.C. She found work singing in the Crystal Caverns, a club run by Cab Calloway's sister, Blanche Calloway, who became her manager. This led to an engagement at the Apollo Theatre in N.Y. and a contract offer from recently formed Atlantic Records.

On Oct. 28, 1948, Brown traveled north for the Apollo performance but was involved in an automobile accident in which both of her legs were broken, and she was hospitalized for months. But she signed to Atlantic on Jan. 12, 1949, and on May 25, 1949, did her first recording session, from which came "So Long" (music and lyrics by Russ Morgan, Remus Harris, and Irving Melsher), which entered the R&B charts in September and peaked in the Top Ten. Her next few singles were not successful, but Atlantic released "Teardrops from My Eyes" (music and lyrics by Rudolph Toombs) in the fall of 1950 and it hit #1 in December. That year she became involved with Willis Jackson, who became her common-law husband until 1955.

Brown scored two R&B Top Ten hits in 1951 and another two in 1952, the most successful of them being the million-seller "5–10–15 Hours" (music and lyrics by Rudolph Toombs), which hit #1 in May 1952. "(Mama) He Treats Your Daughter Mean" (music and lyrics by Herb Lance and Johnny Wallace) topped the R&B charts in March 1953, the first of her three Top Ten hits that year. She had only two Top Ten hits in 1954, but both of them hit #1, "Oh What a Dream" (music and lyrics by Chuck Willis) in September and "Mambo Baby" (music and lyrics by Charlie Singleton and Rosemarie McCoy) in November.

In January 1955, Brown gave birth to a son, Ronald David Jackson, actually the issue of a brief liaison with boxing trainer Drew "Bundini" Brown. That year she married saxophone player Earl Swanson, with whom she had a second son, Earl Swanson Jr., in 1957, after which they separated and divorced. From 1958 to 1962 she lived with trumpeter Danny Moore. She placed six recordings in the R&B charts in 1955, five of which reached the Top Ten, but she began to perform less frequently. She had four more R&B Top Tens through the end of the decade, two of which, "Lucky Lips" (music and lyrics by Jerry Leiber and Mike Stoller; 1957) and "This Little Girl's Gone Rockin'" (music and lyrics by Bobby Darin; 1958) also made the pop Top 40.

Brown scored a final R&B Top Ten hit, "Don't Deceive Me" (music and lyrics by Chuck Willis), in 1960, then switched from Atlantic to Philips Records, but she stopped reaching the charts. In 1963 she married Bill Blunt, a police officer, moved to Long Island, and semi-retired from music, though she continued to perform and make recordings occasionally. In 1966 she and Blunt separated, later divorcing, and she began to work outside music to support her family. Her performance of "Yesterday" (music and lyrics by John Lennon and Paul McCartney) on the Skye Records album *Black Is Brown and Brown Is Beautiful* brought her a 1969 Grammy nomination for Best Rhythm & Blues Vocal Performance, Female.

Brown resumed her career in 1975 as her sons began attending college. She moved to L.A., where she appeared in the play *Selma* portraying Mahalia Jackson. She began performing in Las Vegas and appeared there in a touring production of the Frank Loesser musical *Guys and Dolls* (Feb. 14, 1977). She was cast in the television series *Hello, Larry,* a situation comedy that ran from January 1979 to April 1980, and in April 1981 was part of the one-month tryout of the TV series *Checking In.* She also appeared in the 1981 film *Under the Rainbow.* She made her Broadway debut in the musical *Amen Corner* (N.Y., Nov. 10, 1983), which ran 28 performances. In 1984 she appeared in the musical revue *Black and Blue* in Paris. She was in the Off-Broadway musical *Staggerlee* (N.Y., March 18, 1987), which ran 118 performances. In 1988 she had a small part in the film *Hairspray.*

Brown repeated her role in the Broadway version of *Black and Blue* (N.Y., Jan. 26, 1989), which ran 824 performances, winning a Tony as Best Actress in a Musical. She won a 1989 Grammy for Best Jazz Vocal Performance, Female, for her album *Blues on Broadway,* released by Fantasy Records, and with costar Linda

Hopkins was nominated for the 1990 Grammy for Best Traditional Blues Recording for "'Tain't Nobody's Business if I Do" from the cast album for *Black and Blue*.

DISC.: *Ruth Brown Sings Favorites* (1956); *Ruth Brown* (1957); *Late Date with Ruth Brown* (1959); *Along Comes Ruth* (1962); *Gospel Time* (1962); *Ruth Brown '65* (1964); *Fine Brown Frame* (1968); *The Big Band Sound of Thad Jones and Mel Lewis featuring Miss Ruth* (1968); *Black Is Brown and Brown Is Beautiful* (1969); *Takin' Care of Business* (1980); *Have a Good Time* (live; 1988); *Blues on Broadway* (1989); *Brown, Black & Beautiful* (1990); *Fine and Mellow* (1991); *Songs of My Life* (1993); *Live in London* (1996); *R+B = Ruth Brown* (1997); *Good Day for the Blues* (1999).

WRITINGS: With Andrew Yule, *Miss Rhythm: The Autobiography of Ruth Brown, Rhythm & Blues Legend* (N.Y., 1996).—**WR**

Brown, Steve (Theodore),

early jazz bassist, brother of **Tom Brown;** b. New Orleans, Jan. 13, 1890; d. Detroit, Sept. 15, 1965. Steve originally played tuba in his brother's band, then string bass. In May 1915, the band went to Chicago. He continued to work with his brother while playing with other local bands over the next decade. In 1923, Brown joined the New Orleans Rhythm Kings replacing Arnold Loyacano. He was with Jean Goldkette from 1924–28, with a brief respite to play with Paul Whiteman (October 1927–February 1928). In 1929, he settled in Detroit, freelancing with many local bands, also occasionally leading his own band in the 1930s and 1940s. In the 1950s, he played with several Dixieland revival bands. His popping sound and tricky rhythms enlivened recordings of the Wolverines and Whiteman.

DISC.: Wolverines: *Tiger Rag*. Whiteman: *From Monday On*.
—**JC/LP**

Brown, Tom (Red),

early jazz trombonist; brother of **Steve Brown;** b. New Orleans, June 3, 1888; d. March 25, 1958. His early nickname was "Red." He began on violin at nine, later played trombone in Papa Jack Laine's Reliance Bands, and led his own band from c. 1910. He took his own Brown's Ragtime Band to open at Lamb's Cafe, Chicago, on May 15, 1915. A newspaper ad for the band is the first known printed use of the word jazz in connection with music, but it was spelled "Jad"! During the following year, he led novelty band The Five Rubes, and played dates at N.Y.'s Century Theatre early in 1916. He returned to Chicago, and led his own band at Camel Gardens and on variety tours. During this period, he made many freelance recordings in Chicago and N.Y. He worked in Chicago for Ray Miller c. 1922–3, then returned to New Orleans and played for various local bandleaders. He worked regularly on string bass during the 1930s including a long spell in Val Barbara's Orch. He also worked as a radio repair person and owned his own radio and music shop. Through the 1940s and 1950s, he continued to gig on trombone and string bass in New Orleans and Eunice, La., in a Dixieland-revival style.

DISC.: *Tom Brown's Band from Dixie Land* (1954); *Tom Brown and His New Orleans Jazz* (1958).—**JC/LP**

Brown, William,

flute player and composer who settled in America in the middle of the 18th century. He gave a concert on the flute in Baltimore on Jan. 30, 1784, and then went to Philadelphia, where he participated in numerous benefit concerts. In 1785 he established a series of Subscription Concerts in N.Y. and Philadelphia (with Alexander Reinagle and Henri Capron). He composed 3 Rondos for the Pianoforte or Harpsichord (dedicated to Francis Hopkinson). He was probably a German; may be identical with Wilhelm Braun of Kassel.—**NS/LK/DM**

Browne, Jackson,

perhaps the most stimulating and profound male song-poet of the 1970s, established the singer-songwriter genre with subtle, honest songs with romantic, spiritual, or apocalyptic themes; b. Heidelberg, Germany, Oct. 9, 1948.

Exhibiting a feel for both folk and rock music, his compelling sound featured multi-instrumentalist David Lindley, who introduced unusual stringed instruments, including the lap steel guitar, into rock music. A political activist since the late 1970s, Browne possesses a social awareness that came to the forefront in his music with 1986's *Lives in the Balance*, addressing the then-current crisis in Nicaragua.

Born in Germany but raised in Los Angeles, Jackson Browne first sang at "hoots" in Orange County in 1966. He wrote his first song in high school and was signed to a songwriting contract by Elektra Records in September 1966, then released. Browne played folk clubs around N.Y. during winter 1967, often accompanying Nico (of Velvet Underground fame) and Tim Buckley. Returning to Los Angeles, he served a brief tenure with the Nitty Gritty Dirt Band. Folk singer Tom Rush became the first major artist to showcase Browne's songs, recording "Shadow Dream Song" in 1967 and "These Days" in 1968. Browne's first performing success came in the fall of 1969, when he opened for Linda Ronstadt at the Troubadour Club in Los Angeles. He completed his first concert tour in 1970, opening for Laura Nyro.

By 1971 Jackson Browne had initiated his own recording career with the invaluable assistance of multi-instrumentalist David Lindley (formerly with Kaleidoscope). "Doctor My Eyes" became a smash hit from his debut album, which also contained "Jamaica Say You Will" and "Rock Me on the Water." During spring 1972 Browne toured with songstress Joni Mitchell, and later that year his song "Take It Easy" (cowritten with Glenn Frey) launched the Eagles on their spectacularly successful career. Coming nearly two years later, his second album included the minor hit "Redneck Friend" as well as his own versions of "Take It Easy" and "These Days." By 1974 Browne was touring as a headline act with a band formed around David Lindley. Browne's *Late for the Sky* album, though yielding no hit single, was his most poignant and penetrating work to date, featuring visions of death, apocalypse, and resigned hope; it contained most notably "Fountain of Sorrow," "The Late Show," "For a Dancer," and "Before the Deluge."

Another two years elapsed before the release of *The Pretender*. Although displaying a degree of melodic and rhythmic repetition, the album again included a number of honest and moving songs, from the hit "Here Comes Those Tears Again" to "The Fuse" to the title song.

Browne's next, the live *Running on Empty*, displayed a wide range of moods and material. This album yielded a near-smash hit with the anthemic title song and a major hit with a remake of Maurice Williams's 1960 "Stay."

A leader of the antinuclear movement, Jackson Browne helped found MUSE (Musicians United for Safe Energy) in 1979 and was one of the major backers of the *No Nukes* concert, movie, and album. His 1980 album *Hold Out* included the major hits "Boulevard" and "That Girl Could Sing" and introduced Browne to the arena-rock crowd. Browne was involved in the production of Warren Zevon's first two albums and coproduced David Lindley's album *El Rayo X* from 1981, the year they parted company. In September 1981 Browne was one of the demonstrators arrested at California's Diablo Canyon nuclear-power plant.

In 1982 Browne scored a major hit with "Somebody's Baby" from the Sean Penn film *Fast Times at Ridgemont High*, and the following year he hit with "Tender Is the Night" and the satirical "Lawyers in Love" from his next album of the same title. In 1984 and 1985 he visited Central America to learn more about the turmoil engulfing the region. Browne subsequently became involved with Little Steven (Van Zandt of Bruce Springsteen's E Street Band) in Artists United Against Apartheid, while managing a pop hit with "You're a Friend of Mine," recorded with Clarence Clemons. The politically charged *Lives in the Balance* focused largely on his social concerns, whether foreign or domestic, and yielded two hits, "For America" and "In the Shape of a Heart."

Browne toured in 1986 and 1988, releasing another collection of socially conscious songs in 1989 on the album *World in Motion*, including "The Word Justice," "Anything Can Happen," and Little Steven's "I Am a Patriot." Following his breakup with actress Darryl Hannah in 1992, Browne recorded *I'm Alive*, an album pervaded with songs of lost love. By this time he was unable to equal his earlier chart success, although his core audience continued to buy his albums and attend his concerts.

DISC.: *J. B.* (1972); *For Everyman* (1973); *Late for the Sky* (1974); *The Pretender* (1976); *Running on Empty* (1977); *Hold Out* (1980); *Lawyers in Love* (1983); *Lives in the Balance* (1986); *World in Motion* (1989); *I'm Alive* (1993).

BIBL.: Crowe, Cameron. "A Child's Garden of J. B." *Rolling Stone*, no. 161 (May 23, 1974), pp 38–40.—**BH**

Browning, John, brilliant American pianist; b. Denver, May 22, 1933. His father was a professional violinist, his mother an accomplished pianist. Browning studied with her from childhood; played a Mozart piano concerto at the age of 10, and was accepted as a student by Rosina Lhévinne, who was giving a master course in Denver at the time. The family later moved to Los Angeles, where Browning became a private student of Lee Pattison. He soon moved to N.Y., where he entered the class of Lhévinne at the Juilliard School of Music; in 1954 he received the $2,000 Steinway Centennial Award. In 1955 he won the Leventritt Award. He made his N.Y. Phil. debut in 1956; then went to Brussels to compete for the International Piano Competition

sponsored by Queen Elisabeth; he won second prize, after Vladimir Ashkenazy, who received first prize. Returning to the U.S., he developed a nonstop career of uninterrupted successes. On Sept. 24, 1962, he gave the premiere of Samuel Barber's Piano Concerto with the Boston Sym. Orch., conducted by Erich Leinsdorf at Lincoln Center for the Performing Arts in N.Y. The work became his honorific cachet; it was modern, it was difficult to play, but he performed it hundreds of times in subsequent years. He also performed virtually the entire standard repertoire of piano concertos from Beethoven to Prokofiev. His engagements as a recitalist took him all over the globe, and he frequently appeared with the foremost orchs. as a soloist.—**NS/LK/DM**

Brownlee, John (Donald Mackensie), Australian baritone; b. Geelong, Jan. 7, 1900; d. N.Y., Jan. 10, 1969. He was a pupil of Gilly in Paris, where he made his operatic debut as Nilakantha in *Lakmé* at the Théâtre-Lyrique in 1926. On June 8, 1926, he first appeared at London's Covent Garden as Marcello during Melba's farewell concert. From 1927 to 1936 he was a member of the Paris Opéra; also sang at the Teatro Colón in Buenos Aires (1931) and the Glyndebourne Festivals (1935–39). On Feb. 17, 1937, he made his Metropolitan Opera debut in N.Y. as Rigoletto, and continued to sing there until 1957. He also sang in Chicago (1937–38; 1945), San Francisco (1940–50), and again at Covent Garden (1949–50). From 1953 to 1967 he was president of the American Guild of Musical Artists. He founded the Empire State Music Festival near Ellenville, N.Y., in 1955. In 1956 he became president of the Manhattan School of Music, and then was its president from 1966 until his death. Among his most prominent roles were Don Giovanni, Count Almaviva, Papageno, Alfonso, Iago, and Scarpia.—**NS/LK/DM**

Brubeck, Dave (originally David Warren), American jazz pianist, bandleader, and composer; b. Concord, Calif., Dec. 6, 1920. Brubeck's father, Howard Peter Brubeck, was a cattle rancher; his mother, Elizabeth Ivey Brubeck, was a piano teacher. Though he began taking piano lessons from his mother at the age of four and played in bands as a teenager, he entered the Coll. of the Pacific as a veterinary major, intending to follow his father into the cattle business. Nevertheless, he had become a music major by the time he graduated in 1942. After graduation he went into the army, where he led a service band. He married Iola Marie Whitlock on Sept. 21, 1942. They had six children, of whom four (David Darius, Christopher, Daniel, and Matthew) became professional musicians and played with their father.

Upon his discharge from the service in 1946, Brubeck studied composition with Darius Milhaud at Mills Coll. for three years; he also studied piano with Fred Saatman in 1949. During this period he formed an octet that performed occasionally, though he more frequently appeared with the rhythm section of the group as the Dave Brubeck Trio. He made his first recordings in 1949 for the Coronet label, and in 1950 helped found Fantasy Records, for which he recorded exclusively until 1954 and occasionally thereafter.

The Dave Brubeck Trio broke up after Brubeck was injured in a swimming accident in 1950. When he recovered in 1951 he organized a quartet featuring Paul Desmond, alto sax. (real name Paul Emil Breitenfeld, b. 1924; d. 1977), Bob Bates. bs., and Joe Dodge, drm. The personnel of the rhythm section varied over the next several years; the definitive version of the group featured drummer Joe Morello, who joined in 1956, and bass player Eugene Wright, who joined in 1958. The quartet rose in prominence through its appearances, notably at colleges, to the point that it was signed by Columbia Records and released its first major-label album, the live recording *Jazz Goes to College*, in June 1954. On Oct. 8, 1954, Brubeck was featured on the cover of *Time* magazine, and by the end of that month the album was in the charts, where it reached the Top Ten. Follow-up albums *Dave Brubeck at Storyville, Brubeck Time*, and *Jazz: Red, Hot and Cool* all made the Top Ten in 1955.

The Dave Brubeck Quartet continued to release charting albums in the late 1950s while touring extensively in the U.S. and around the world. In October 1960 the group released *Time Out*, an album on which each song was performed in a different time signature, among them "Take Five" (music by Paul Desmond), which was in 5/4, and "Blue Rondo à la Turk" (music by Dave Brubeck), which was in 9/8. "Blue Rondo à la Turk" earned Brubeck a Grammy nomination for Best Jazz Composition, More Than 5 Minutes. In July 1961, Columbia released "Take Five" as a single; it reached the Top 40 by October, earning a Grammy nomination for Record of the Year, and *Time Out* vaulted into the Top Ten, going gold and remaining in the charts for more than three years. In November, Columbia released *Time Further Out*, which hit the Top Ten in February 1962. The chart single "Unsquare Dance" (music by Dave Brubeck) drawn from the album, earned Brubeck a Grammy nomination for Best Original Jazz Composition.

Brubeck made his sole screen appearance in the film *All Night Long*, released in the U.S. in February 1962. For the next several years he toured extensively while releasing two or three albums a year, several of which made the charts. *Dave Brubeck at Carnegie Hall*, a double live album recorded Feb. 21, 1963, earned a Grammy nomination for Best Instrumental Jazz Performance, Soloist or Small Group. Brubeck wrote music for the network television series *Mr. Broadway*, which ran from September to December 1964. "Theme from *Mr. Broadway*," included on the album *Jazz Impressions of New York*, was nominated for a Grammy for Best Original Jazz Composition.

Brubeck's record sales fell off after the mid-1960s. The quartet disbanded in December 1967, ostensibly so that Brubeck could devote himself more to the kind of jazz-based classical compositions he had been writing since the early 1960s. But by May 1968 he was back on the road with a new group featuring baritone saxophonist Gerry Mulligan, bass player Jack Six, and drummer Alan Dawson. Their album *Compadres* earned a 1968 Grammy nomination for Best Instrumental Jazz Performance, Small Group or Soloist with Small Group. They also performed and recorded backed by the Cincinnati Symphony Orch.

Brubeck parted ways with Columbia Records in 1971 and signed to Atlantic Records. For his fall 1972 tour of Europe, his group was joined by Paul Desmond, resulting in the 1973 album *We're All Together Again (For the First Time)*. Brubeck launched a new group in 1973, Two Generations of Brubeck, featuring his sons David Darius (electric kybd.), Christopher (bs. gtr.), and Daniel (drm.), along with such other performers as alto saxophonist Jerry Bergonzi.

Brubeck continued to tour and to release at least an album a year in the mid-1970s. *1975: The Duets*, released on Horizon Records, paired him once again with Paul Desmond and reached the pop charts. In March 1976 he reassembled the Dave Brubeck Quartet of 1958–67 for a concert tour to mark the 25th anniversary of the founding of the group. This resulted in the 1977 album *25th Anniversary Reunion*; but Desmond's death on May 30, 1977, put an end to the group.

Brubeck organized a new Dave Brubeck Quartet, initially featuring Jerry Bergonzi, Christopher Brubeck, and drummer Butch Miles, and began recording for the Concord Jazz label, switching to MusicMasters in 1987 and to Telarc in 1993. He wrote the score for the 1984 film *Ordeal by Innocence*. Health problems forced him to cut back on his performing schedule somewhat in the 1990s, but he continued to work regularly. In September 1997 his quartet, featuring alto saxophonist and flautist Bobby Militello, bass player Jack Six, and drummer Randy Jones, recorded *So What's New?*, an album of new compositions released by Telarc in April 1998.

Following the demise of the Swing Era and the limited appeal of bebop, the Dave Brubeck Quartet achieved widespread popular success with its small-group "cool" jazz in the second half of the 1950s and the first half of the 1960s. Brubeck's classically informed musical experimentation, notably performing pieces in unusual time signatures, was offset by the lyricism of the quartet's alto saxophonist, Paul Desmond, resulting in a remarkable 21 pop-chart albums between 1954 and 1976, among them the gold-selling *Time Out*, which featured the Top 40 hit "Take Five."

DISC: *Jazz at Oberlin* (1953); *Jazz Goes to College* (1954); *Jazz at the College of the Pacific* (1954); *D. B./Paul Desmond* (with Paul Desmond; 1954); *Brubeck Time* (1955); *Brubeck Plays Brubeck* (1956); *Dave Digs Disney* (1957); *In Europe* (1958); *Newport 1958* (1959); *Time Out* (1960); *Time Further Out* (1961); *Countdown Time in Outer Space* (1962); *D. B.'s Greatest Hits* (1966); *Adventures in Time* (1972); *Two Generations of Brubeck—Brother the Great Spirit Made Us All* (1973); *1975: The Duets* (with Paul Desmond; 1975); *Time Signatures: A Career Retrospective* (1992); *A D. B. Christmas* (1996); *Love Songs* (2000); *One Alone* (2000).

BIBL.: H. Brubeck, *D. B.* (1961); *Biography of D. B.* (1972); Ilse Storb and Klaus Fischer, *D. B.: Improvisations and Compositions: The Idea of Cultural Exchange* (N.Y.; 1994); Fred M. Hall, *It's about Time: The D. B. Story* (Fayetteville, Ark., 1996).—**WR**

Bruce, (Frank) Neely, American pianist, conductor, music scholar, and composer; b. Memphis, Tenn., Jan. 21, 1944. He studied piano with Roy McAllister at the Univ. of Ala. (B.M., 1965); then was a pupil in piano (M.M., 1966) of Soulima Stravinsky and in composition (D.M.A., 1971) of Ben Johnston at the Univ. of Ill., where he also taught (1968–74). In 1974 he joined the faculty at Wesleyan Univ., where he also conducted the Wesleyan Singers. In 1977 he founded the American Music/ Theatre Group, an ensemble devoted to the performance of American music from all eras.

WORKS: DRAMATIC: *Pyramus and Thisbe*, chamber opera (1964–65); *The Trials of Psyche*, opera (1970–71); *Americana, or, A New Tale of the Genii*, opera (1978–83); incidental music to plays and films; dance scores. ORCH.: *Quodlibet on Christmas Tunes* for Chamber Orch. (1963); Percussion Concerto (1967); Concerto for Violin and Chamber Orch. (1974); *Atmo-Rag* for Chamber Orch. (1987); *Santa Ynez Waltz* for Chamber Orch. (1989); *Trio for 3 Rock Bands* (1988–94); *Orion Rising* (1988–97); *1, 2, Ready, Go!* for Chamber Orch. (1991); *Barnum's Band* for Large Wind Ensemble (1991–92); *Songs of Zion Recycled* for Tuba and Orch. (1992–93; Hartford, Ct., June 5, 1993). CHAMBER: Trio for Violin, Viola, and Cello (1963); Quintet for Flute, Clarinet, English Horn, Bass Clarinet, and Bassoon (1967); *Rondo* for Flute, Tuba, and Piano (1976); *Jesus Christ is Risen Today*, Easter partita for 2 Horns, 2 Trumpets, 2 Trombones or Baritone Horns, and Organ (1980); *The Hartford and Middletown Waltzes* for Violin and Piano (1986); *Music for Emeline* for 8 Instruments (1989); *Narrative Objects* for Oboe, Clarinet, Bassoon, and 2 Alto Saxophones (1991); *Brass Bouquet* for Brass Instruments (1992); *Analogues* for Violin and Alto Saxophone (1993); *Wild Oysters II* for Electric Cello (1993); *4 + 1* for String Quartet and Piano (1994). KEYBOARD: P i a n o : *Variations on a Polonaise* (1969); 6 sonatas; *Introduction and Variations* (1978); *Furniture Music in the Form of 50 Rag Licks* (1980); 9 nocturnes; *Siagi Tamu Tango, or, Tango Rue Jardin* (1984); *Homage to Charlie* (1985); *Piano Rock Album* (1989–91); *2 Moods* (1990). O r g a n : *Variations and Interludes* (1968); *Homage to Maurice* (1986); *Pink Music* (1989–92). H a r p s i c h o r d : *A Book of Pieces for the Harpsichord* (1968–85). VOCAL: *Psalms of the Nativity*, oratorio for Mezzo-soprano, Tenor, Baritone, Chorus, and Chamber Orch. (1972–89); *There was a child went forth...* for Men's Chorus, Piano, Percussion, and Flute (1972); *A Feast of Fat Things*, cantata for Soprano and 7 Instruments (1977); *Perfumes and Meanings* for 16 Solo Voices (1980); *The Plague: A Commentary on the Work of the Fourth Horseman* for 4 Solo Voices and Tape (1983–84); *6 Whitman Settings* for 12 Solo Singers and 12 Instruments (1986–87); *The Dream of the Other Dreamers* for 4 Singers and 2 SPX 90s (1987); *Hamm Harmony*, 38 Psalm and fuguing tunes (1988–92); *8 Ghosts* for 4 Singers and 4 SPX 90s (1989); *2+2+2* for 6 Singers (1989); *Hugomotion*, oratorio for Soloists, Chorus, and Orch. (1989–95); *Emily's Flowers*, 24 vocal pieces (1991–92); *Tanglewood*, oratorio for Soloists, 2 Choruses, and Orch. (1993); also various solo songs in sets or cycles.—NS/LK/DM

Bruch, Max (Christian Friedrich),

distinguished German composer, conductor, and pedagogue; b. Cologne, Jan. 6, 1838; d. Friedenau, near Berlin, Oct. 2, 1920. His mother was a soprano and singing teacher, and it was from her that he first studied piano. He was only 9 when he wrote his first composition. He soon began taking theory lessons with Heinrich Breidenstein in Bonn. After winning the Mozart Foundation prize of Frankfurt am Main in 1852, he went there to study composition with Hiller and piano with Reinecke and Ferdinand Breunung (1853–57). He then composed his first opera, *Scherz, List und Rache*, after Goethe, which

was premiered in Colgne on Jan. 14, 1858. After studying philosophy, art, and architecture at the Univ. of Bonn (1859), he devoted himself fully to a musical career. He then composed the opera *Die Loreley* (Mannheim, June 14, 1863). While staying in Mannheim, he received instruction in conducting and orchestration from Franz Lachner. With his choral work *Frithjof*, which he conducted at its premiere in Aachen on Nov. 20, 1864, Bruch established himself as a composer of effective choral works. *Frithjof* was subsequently given in other German cities, as well as in Vienna with much success. From 1865 to 1867 Bruch was director of the Royal Inst. for Music and of the subscription concerts in Koblenz. While in Koblenz, Bruch wrote his most celebrated score, his First Violin Concerto (Koblenz, April 24, 1866). It subsequently was played by all the leading violin virtuosos of the day and became a standard repertory piece. From 1867 to 1870 he served as first court conductor in Sondershausen. He then went to Berlin, where his opera *Hermione* was premiered on March 21, 1872. While it proved a failure, Bruch found success with his secular oratorio *Odysseus* (Barmen, Feb. 8, 1873). In 1878 he became conductor of the Stern'schen Gesangverein in Berlin. In 1880 he was named musical director of the Liverpool Phil. Soc., which position he held until 1883. During this period, Bruch brought out 2 of his finest works, the so-called *Scottish Fantasy* for Violin and Orch. and *Kol Nidrei* for Cello and Orch. The latter, based on a traditional Jewish melody, led to the erroneous assumption that Bruch was Jewish. In fact, he was descended from a long-standing Protestant family.

In 1883 Bruch toured the U.S. as a conductor of various choral organizations. From 1883 to 1890 he was conductor of the Breslau Concert Soc. He then completed work on his Third Violin Concerto, which was a great success at its premiere in Düsseldorf on May 31, 1891. In 1892 Bruch became a prof. and director of the master class in composition at the Berlin Royal Academy of Arts, remaining there until his retirement in 1911. In 1893 he received an honorary D.Mus. degree from the Univ. of Cambridge and in 1918 honorary doctorates in philosophy and theology from the Univ. of Berlin. In 1881 he married the young contralto Clara Tuczek (b. Berlin, Feb. 15, 1864; d. there, Aug. 27, 1919), who occasionally sang at his concerts. Bruch's music, although imitative in its essence, retains a great eclectic charm. He was a thorough master of harmony, counterpoint, and instrumentation. His choral output was highly regarded in his homeland, particularly his secular works. While most of his music is now forgotten, his violin concertos, the *Scottish Fantasy*, and *Kol Nidrei* remain as notable examples of his gifts and continue to find their way occasionally into the concert hall.

WORKS: DRAMATIC: O p e r a : *Scherz, List und Rache* (Cologne, Jan. 14, 1858); *Die Loreley* (Mannheim, June 14, 1863); *Hermione* (Berlin, March 21, 1872). ORCH.: 3 syms.: No. 1, in E-flat major (Sondershausen, July 26, 1868, composer conducting), No. 2, in F minor (Sondershausen, Sept. 4, 1870, composer conducting), and No. 3, in E major (N.Y., Dec. 17, 1882, Damrosch conducting); 3 violin concertos: No. 1, in G minor (1864–66; Koblenz, April 24, 1866, Königslöw soloist, composer conducting; definitive version, Bremen, Jan. 7, 1868, Joachim soloist, Reinthaler conducting), No. 2, in D minor (London,

Nov. 4, 1877, Sarasate soloist, composer conducting), and No. 3, in D minor (1890–91; Düsseldorf, May 31, 1891, Joachim soloist, composer conducting); *Romanze* for Violin and Orch. (1874); *Fantasia for the Violin and Orch. with Harp, freely using Scottish Folk Melodies* (1879–80; Liverpool, Feb. 22, 1881, Joachim soloist, composer conducting); *Kol Nidrei* for Cello and Orch. (Liverpool, Nov. 2, 1880); *Adagio appassionata* for Violin and Orch. (1891); *Canzone* for Cello and Orch. (1891); *Adagio on Celtic Themes* for Cello and Orch. (1891); *Ave Maria* for Cello and Orch. (1892); *In Memoriam* for Violin and Orch. (1893); *Serenade* for Violin and Orch. (1899; Paris, May 15, 1901, Débroux soloist, Chevillard conducting); *Suite [No. 1] für grosses Orchester nach russischen Volksmelodien* (1903), No. 2 (1906; rewritten as Serenade for String Orch., on Swedish melodies, 1916), and No. 3 for Organ and Orch. (1904–15; rewritten as Concerto for 2 Pianos and Orch.; unauthorized version, drastically altered by the performers, Philadelphia, Dec. 29, 1916, O. and R. Sutro soloists, Stokowski conducting; authorized version, Berlin, May 6, 1974, Nathan Twining and Martin Berkofsky soloists, Doráti conducting); *Konzertstück* for Violin and Orch. (Norfolk, Conn., June 8, 1911, Maud Powell soloist); *Romanze* for Viola and Orch. (1911); Double Concerto for Clarinet, Viola, and Orch. (1911; Wilhelshaven, March 5, 1912). **CHAMBER:** Septet for Clarinet, Horn, Bassoon, 2 Violins, Cello, and Double Bass (1849); Piano Trio (1858); 2 string quartets (1859, 1860); Piano Quintet (1886); *Swedish Dances* for Violin and Piano (1892); *4 Pieces* for Cello and Piano (1896); *8 Trio Pieces* for Clarinet, Viola, and Piano (1910); String Quintet (1919); String Octet (1920); piano pieces. **VOCAL: A c c o m p a n i e d   S a c r e d   C h o - r a l :** *Jubilate* (1858); *Die Flucht der heiligen Familie* (1863); *Gesang der heiligen drei Könige* (1863); *Rorate coeli* (Krefeld, Feb. 22, 1869); *Die Flucht nach Aegypten* (1869); *Morgenstunde* (1869); *Messensätze: Kyrie, Sanctus, und Agnus Dei* (1870); *Gruss an die heilige Nacht* (1892); *Hymne* (1893); *Moses: Ein biblisches Oratorium* (1894; Barmen, Jan. 19, 1895); *Sei getreu bis an den Tod* (1896); *Osterkantate* (Cologne, Nov. 17, 1908); *Das Wessobrunner Gebet* (1909). **U n a c c o m p a n i e d   S a c r e d   C h o - r a l :** *Christkindlieder* (1918). **A c c o m p a n i e d   S e c u - l a r   C h o r a l :** *Die Birken und die erlen* (1857); *Frithjof* (Aachen, Nov. 20, 1864); *Schön Ellen* (Koblenz, Feb. 22, 1867); *Salamis* (1868); *Normannenzug* (1869); *Römische Leichenfeier* (1869); *Das Lied vom deutschen Kaiser* (1871); *Dithyrambe* (1871); *Odysseus* (1871–72; Barmen, Feb. 8, 1873); *Arminius* (Zürich, Jan. 21, 1877); *Das Lied von der Glocke* (Cologne, May 12, 1878); *Achilleus* (Bonn, June 28, 1885); *Drei Hebraische Gesange* (1888); *Das Feuerkreuz* (1888); *Leonidas* (Vienna, Oct. 8, 1893); (3) *Neue Männerchöre* (1896); *Gustav Adolf* (1897–98; Barmen, May 22, 1898); *Der letzte Abschied des Volkes* (1900); *Damajanti* (1902; Cologne, Oct. 20, 1903); *Die Macht des Gesanges* (1911); *Heldenfeier* (1914–15); *Der Stimme der Mutter Erde* (1916); *Trauerfeier für Mignon* (Berlin, April 5, 1919). **O t h e r   V o c a l :** *Die Priesterin der Isis in Rom* for Solo Voice and Orch. (1870); *Szene der Marfa* for Mezzo-soprano and Orch. (1906); various lieder.

BIBL.: F. Gysi, *M. B.: 110 Neuhjahrsblatt der allgemeinen Musikgesellschaft in Zürich* (Zürich, 1922); H. Pfitzner, *Meine Beziehungen zu M. B.: Persönliche Erinnerungen* (Munich, 1938); W. Lauth, *M. B.s Instrumentalmusik* (diss., Univ. of Cologne, 1967); D. Kämper, ed., *M. B. Studien, zum 50 Todestag des Komponisten* (Cologne, 1970); K. Fellerer, *M. B.* (Cologne, 1974); S. Luyken, *M. B.* (Cologne, 1984); C. Fifield, *M. B.: His Life and Works* (London, 1988); M. Schwarzer, *Die Oratorien von M. B.: Eine Quellenstudie* (Kassel, 1988); U. Baur, *M. B. und Koblenz (1865–1867): Eine Dokumentation* (Mainz, 1996).—**NS/LK/DM**

Bruck (or Brouck), Arnold von (known also as **Arnold de Bruges** and **Arnoldo Flamengo**), Flemish composer; b. Bruges, c. 1500; d. Linz, Feb. 6, 1554. He served as a choirboy in the chapel of Charles V. In 1527 he was named court Kapellmeister to Ferdinand I. He retired on Dec. 31, 1545. Many of his motets, hymns, and German part-songs are preserved in MS collections of the 16th century. See also O. Wessely, ed., *A. v. B.: Sämtliche lateinschule Motetten*, Denkmäler der Tonkunst in Österreich, XCIX (1961).

BIBL.: O. Wessely, *A. v.B.: Leben und Umwelt* (Habilitationsschrift, Univ. of Vienna, 1958).—**NS/LK/DM**

Bruck, Charles, Romanian-born French conductor and pedagogue; b. Timişoara, May 2, 1911; d. Hancock, Maine, July 16, 1995. He studied at the Vienna Cons., then took courses with Perlemuter (piano) and Boulanger (composition) at the Paris École Normale de Musique; he also received instruction in conducting from Monteux (1934). In 1939 he became a naturalized French citizen. After winning the conducting competition of the Orch. Symphonique de Paris (1936), he served as its asst. conductor; he later conducted at the Cannes and Deauville Casinos (1949–50), the Netherlands Opera in Amsterdam (1950–54), the Strasbourg Radio Sym. Orch. (1955–65), and the Orch. Philharmonique de l'ORTF in Paris (1965–70). Subsequently he was director of Monteux's conducting school in Hancock, Maine until his death.—**NS/LK/DM**

Bruckner, (Josef) Anton, great Austrian composer; b. Ansfelden, Sept. 4, 1824; d. Vienna, Oct. 11, 1896. He studied music with his father, a village schoolmaster and church organist; also took music lessons at Hörsching with his cousin Johann Baptist Weiss. After his father's death in 1837, Bruckner enrolled as a chorister at St. Florian, where he attended classes in organ, piano, violin, and theory. In 1840–41 he attended the special school for educational training in Linz, where he received instruction from J.N.A. Dürrnberger; he also studied music theory with Leopold Edler von Zenetti in Enns. While in his early youth, Bruckner held teaching positions in elementary public schools in Windhaag (1841–43) and Kronstorf (1843–45); later he occupied a responsible position as a schoolteacher at St. Florian (1845–55); also served as provisional organist there (1848–51). Despite his professional advance, he felt a lack of basic techniques in musical composition, and at the age of 31 went to Vienna to study harmony and counterpoint with Simon Sechter. He continued his studies with him off and on until 1861. In 1856 he became cathedral organist in Linz, having successfully competed for this position against several applicants. Determined to acquire still more technical knowledge, he sought further instruction and began taking lessons in orchestration with Otto Kitzler, first cellist of the Linz municipal theater (1861–63). In the meantime, he undertook an assiduous study of the Italian polyphonic school, and of masters of German polyphony, especially Bach. These tasks preoccupied him so completely that he did not engage in free composition until he was nearly 40 years old. Then he fell under the powerful influence of Wagner's music, an infatuation that diverted him from his study of classical polyphony. In 1865 he attended the premiere of *Tristan und Isolde* in Munich, and met Wagner. He also made the acquaintance of Liszt in Pest, and of Berlioz during his visit in Vienna. His adulation of Wagner was extreme; the dedication of his Third Sym. to Wagner reads:"To the eminent Excellency Richard Wagner the Unattainable, World- Famous, and Exalted Master of Poetry and Music, in Deepest Reverence Dedicated by Anton Bruckner." Strangely enough, in his own music Bruckner never embraced the tenets and practices of Wagner, but followed the sanctified tradition of German polyphony. Whereas Wagner strove toward the ideal union of drama, text, and music in a new type of operatic production, Bruckner kept away from the musical theater, confining himself to symphonic and choral music. Even in his harmonic techniques, Bruckner seldom followed Wagner's chromatic style of writing, and he never tried to emulate the passionate rise and fall of Wagnerian "endless" melodies depicting the characters of his operatic creations. To Bruckner, music was an apotheosis of symmetry; his syms. were cathedrals of Gothic grandeur; he never hesitated to repeat a musical phrase several times in succession so as to establish the thematic foundation of a work. The personal differences between Wagner and Bruckner could not be more striking: Wagner was a man of the world who devoted his whole life to the promotion of his artistic and human affairs, while Bruckner was unsure of his abilities and desperately sought recognition. Devoid of social graces, being a person of humble peasant origin, Bruckner was unable to secure the position of respect and honor that he craved. A signal testimony to this lack of self-confidence was Bruckner's willingness to revise his works repeatedly, not always to their betterment, taking advice from conductors and ostensible well- wishers. He suffered from periodic attacks of depression; his entire life seems to have been a study of unhappiness, most particularly in his numerous attempts to find a woman who would become his life companion.

A commanding trait of Bruckner's personality was his devout religiosity. To him the faith and the sacraments of the Roman Catholic Church were not mere rituals but profound psychological experiences. Following the practice of Haydn, he signed most of his works with the words *Omnia ad majorem Dei gloriam*; indeed, he must have felt that every piece of music he composed redounded to the greater glory of God. His original dedication of his Te Deum was actually inscribed "an dem lieben Gott." From reports of his friends and contemporaries, it appears that he regarded each happy event of his life as a gift of God, and each disaster as an act of divine wrath. His yearning for secular honors was none the less acute for that. He was tremendously gratified upon receiving an honorary doctorate from the Univ. of Vienna in 1891; he was the first musician to be so honored there. He unsuccessfully solicited similar degrees from the univs. of Cambridge, Philadelphia, and even Cincinnati. He eagerly sought approval in the public press. When Emperor Franz Josef presented him with a snuffbox as a sign of Imperial favor, it is said that Bruckner pathetically begged the Emperor to order

Hanslick to stop attacking him. Indeed, Hanslick was the nemesis of the so-called New German School of composition exemplified by Wagner and Liszt, and to a lesser extent, also by Bruckner. Wagner could respond to Hanslick's hostility by caricaturing him in the role of Beckmesser (whom he had originally intended to name Hanslich), and Liszt, immensely successful as a virtuoso pianist, was largely immune to critical attacks. But Bruckner was highly vulnerable. It was not until the end of his unhappy life that, thanks to a group of devoted friends among conductors, Bruckner finally achieved a full recognition of his greatness.

Bruckner himself was an inadequate conductor, but he was a master organist. In 1869 he appeared in organ recitals in France, and in 1871 he visited England, giving performances in the Royal Albert Hall and the Crystal Palace in London. He was also esteemed as a pedagogue. In 1868 he succeeded Sechter as prof. of harmony, counterpoint, and organ at the Vienna Cons.; also in 1868 he was named provisional court organist, an appointment formally confirmed in 1878. Concurrently he taught piano, organ, and theory at St. Anna Coll. in Vienna (1870–74). In 1875 he was appointed lecturer in harmony and counterpoint at the Univ. of Vienna. In failing health, Bruckner retired from the Vienna Cons. in 1891 and a year later relinquished his post as court organist; in 1894 he resigned his lecturer's position at the Univ. of Vienna. The remaining years of his life he devoted to the composition of his Ninth Sym., which, however, remained unfinished at his death.

Bruckner's syms. constitute a monumental achievement; they are characterized by a striking display of originality and a profound spiritual quality. His sacred works are similarly expressive of his latent genius. Bruckner is usually paired with Mahler, who was a generation younger, but whose music embodied qualities of grandeur akin to those that permeated the symphonic and choral works of Bruckner. Accordingly, Bruckner and Mahler societies sprouted in several countries, with the express purpose of elucidating, analyzing, and promoting their music.

The textual problems concerning Bruckner's works are numerous and complex. He made many revisions of his scores, and dejectedly acquiesced in alterations suggested by conductors who expressed interest in his music. As a result, conflicting versions of his syms. appeared in circulation. With the founding of the International Bruckner Soc., a movement was begun to publ. the original versions of his MSS, the majority of which he bequeathed to the Hofbibliothek in Vienna. A complete ed. of Bruckner's works, under the supervision of Robert Haas and Alfred Orel, began to appear in 1930; in 1945 Leopold Nowak was named its editor in chief. For a complete catalogue of his works, see R. Grasberger, ed., *Werkverzeichnis A. B.* (Tutzing, 1977).

WORKS: Bruckner rejected his first sym. as a student work; it is in F minor and is known as his *Schul-Symphonie* or *Studien-Symphonie* (Study Sym.; 1863; movements 1, 2, and 4 first perf. under Moissl, Klosterneuburg, March 18, 1924; movement 3 first perf. under Moissl, Klosterneuburg, Oct. 12, 1924). Another sym. in D minor apparently held some interest for him, as he marked it No. 0, "Die Nullte" (1869; movements 3 and 4 first perf. under Moissl, Klosterneuburg, May 17, 1924; first complete perf. under Moissl, Klosterneuburg, Oct. 12, 1924). The following list of his 9 syms. is the standard canon: No. 1, in C minor (Version I, "Linz," 1865–66; first perf., with minor additions and alterations, under Bruckner, Linz, May 9, 1868; Version II, "Vienna," 1890–91, a thorough revision; first perf. under Richter, Vienna, Dec. 13, 1891); No. 2, in C minor (Version I, 1871–72; first perf., with minor revisions, under Bruckner, Vienna, Oct. 26, 1873; Version II, 1876–77, with cuts and alterations); No. 3, in D minor, the "Wagner" Sym. (Version I, 1873; first perf. in the Nowak ed. under Schonzeler, Adelaide, March 19, 1978; Version II, 1876–77, a thorough revision; first perf. under Bruckner, Vienna, Dec. 16, 1877; Version III, 1888–89, a thorough revision; first perf. under Richter, Vienna, Dec. 21, 1890; a 2nd Adagio [1876] was first perf. under C. Abbado, Vienna, May 24, 1980); No. 4, in E-flat major, the "Romantic" Sym. (Version I, 1874; first perf. in the Nowak ed. under K. Woss, Linz, Sept. 20, 1975; Version II, 1877–78, with Finale of 1880, a thorough revision with a new Scherzo; first perf. under Richter, Vienna, Feb. 20, 1881; Version III, 1887–88, a major revision by Löwe, including a new Finale; first perf. under Richter, Vienna, Jan. 22, 1888); No. 5, in B-flat major (1875–76; minor revisions, 1876–78; first perf. in a recomposed version by F. Schalk, under his direction, Graz, April 8, 1894; first perf. in the Haas ed. under Hausegger, Munich, Oct. 20, 1935); No. 6, in A major (1879–81; Adagio and Scherzo under Jahn, Vienna, Feb. 11, 1883; with major cuts, under Mahler, Vienna, Feb. 26, 1899; first complete perf. under Pohlig, Stuttgart, March 14, 1901); No. 7, in E major (1881–83; first perf. under Nikisch, Leipzig, Dec. 30, 1884); No. 8, in C minor (Version I, 1884–87; first perf. in the Nowak ed. under Schönzeler, BBC, London, Sept. 2, 1973; Version II, 1889–90, a thorough revision; first perf. under Richter, Vienna, Dec. 18, 1892; first perf. in the Haas ed. [a composite version of I and II] under Furtwängler, Hamburg, July 5, 1939); No. 9, in D minor (movements 1–3, 1887–94; Finale [unfinished], 1894–96; first perf. in a recomposed version by Löwe, under his direction, Vienna, Feb. 11, 1903, with Bruckner's *Te Deum* substituted for the Finale; first perf. in the Haas ed. under Hausegger, Munich, April 2, 1932). Other major works are 3 masses: D minor (1864; Linz, Nov. 20, 1864; rev. 1876 and 1881); E minor (1866; Linz, Sept. 29, 1869; rev. 1869, 1876, and 1882); F minor (1867–68; Vienna, June 16, 1872; many revisions); String Quintet in F major (1878–79); *Te Deum* (1881; rev. 1883–84; first perf. with orch. under Richter, Vienna, Jan. 10, 1886); Psalm 150 (1892; Vienna, Nov. 13, 1892). Selected minor works are a Mass in C major (1842?); *Requiem* in D minor (1848–49; St. Florian, March 13, 1849); *Missa Solemnis* in B-flat minor (1854; St. Florian, Sept. 14, 1854); *Apollomarsch* for Military Band (1862; authenticity not established); March in D minor for Orch. (1862); 3 orch. pieces in E-flat major, E minor, and F major (1862); String Quartet in C minor (1862); Overture in G minor (1862–63; Klosterneuburg, Sept. 8, 1921); *Germanenzug* for Men's Chorus and Brass Instruments (1863); March in E-flat major for Military Band (1865); *Abendzauber* for Men's Chorus and 4 Horns (1878); *Intermezzo* for String Quintet (1879); *Helgoland* for Men's Chorus and Orch. (1893); other choral settings; motets; etc.

BIBL.: BIOGRAPHICAL: F. Brunner, *Dr. A. B.* (Linz, 1895); R. Louis, *A. B.* (Munich, 1905; 3rd ed., 1921); F. Gräflinger, *A. B.: Bausteine zu seiner Lebensgeschichte* (Munich, 1911; rev. ed., 1927); M. Morold, *A. B.* (Leipzig, 1912; 2nd ed., 1920); E. Decsey, *A. B.: Versuch eines Lebens* (Berlin, 1920; 3rd ed., 1930); F. Gräflinger, *A. B.: Sein Leben und seine Werke* (Regensburg, 1921); A. Göllerich and M. Auer, *A. B.: Ein Lebens- und Schaffensbild* (4

vols., Regensburg, 1922–37; 2nd ed., 1938); K. Grunsky, *A. B.* (Stuttgart, 1922); H. Tessmer, *A. B.* (Regensburg, 1922); R. Wetz, *A. B.: Sein Leben und Schaffen* (Leipzig, 1923); J. Daninger, *A. B.* (Vienna, 1924); G. Gräner, *A. B.* (Leipzig, 1924); E. Kurth, *A. B.* (2 vols., Berlin, 1925); A. Orel, *A. B.: Ein Österreichischer Meister der Tonkunst* (Altötting, 1926); F. Gräflinger, *A. B.: Leben und Schaffen* (Berlin, 1927); M. Auer, *A. B.: Sein Leben und Werk* (Vienna, 1931; 6th ed., 1966); G. Engel, *The Life of A. B.* (N.Y., 1931); R. Haas, *A. B.* (Potsdam, 1934); A. Orel, *A. B., 1824–1896: Sein Leben in Bildern* (Leipzig, 1936); W. Wiora, *A. B.* (Berlin, 1936; rev. ed., 1959); E. Schwanzara, *B.s Stamm- und Urheimat* (Berlin, 1937); K. Laux, *A. B.: Leben und Werk* (Leipzig, 1940; 2nd ed., 1947); W. Wolff, *A. B.: Rustic Genius* (N.Y., 1942); A. Machabey, *La Vie et l'oeuvre d'A. B.* (Paris, 1945); W. Reich, ed., *A. B.: Ein Bild seiner Persönlichkeit* (Basel, 1953); H. Redlich, *B. and Mahler* (London, 1955; rev. ed., 1963); P. Benary, *A. B.* (Leipzig, 1956); W. Abendroth, *B.: Eine Bildbiographie* (Munich, 1958); E. Doernberg, *The Life and Symphonies of A. B.* (London, 1960); L. Nowak, *A. B.: Musik und Leben* (Vienna, 1964); G. Wehle, *A. B. im Spiegel seiner Zeitgenossen* (Garmisch- Partenkirchen, 1964); J. Lassl, *Das kleine Brucknerbuch* (Salzburg, 1965; 2nd ed., 1972); H.-H. Schönzeler, *B.* (N.Y., 1970; rev. ed., 1978); J. Gallios, *B.* (Paris, 1971); L. Nowak, *A. B.: Musik und Leben* (Linz, 1973); H. Fischer, *A. B.: Sein Leben* (Salzburg, 1974); D. Watson, *B.* (London, 1975); P. Langevin, *A. B., Apogée de la symphonie* (Lausanne, 1977); M. Wagner, *B.: Monographie* (Mainz, 1983); M. Hansen, *A. B.* (Leipzig, 1987); S. Martinotti, *A. B.* (Pordenone, 1990); U. Harten, ed., *B.-Ikonographie* (Graz, 1990); E. Maier, *A. B.: Stationen eines Lebens* (Linz and Munich, 1996); H. Schaefer, *A. B.: Ein Führer durch Leben und Werk* (Berlin, 1996); F. Scheder, *A. B. Chronologie* (Tutzing, 1996); C. Howie, P. Hawkshaw, and T. Jackson, eds., *Perspectives on B.* (Brookfield, Vt., 2000). **CRITICAL, ANALYTICAL:** A. Halm, *Die Symphonie A. B.s* (Munich, 1914; 2nd ed., 1923); A. Knapp, *A. B.: Zum Verständnis seiner Persönlichkeit und seiner Werke* (Düsseldorf, 1921); A. Orel, *Unbekannte Frühwerke A. B.s* (Vienna, 1921); E. Schwebsch, *A. B.: Ein Beitrag zur Erkenntnis von Entwicklungen in der Musik* (Stuttgart, 1921; 2nd ed., 1923); K. Kobald, ed., *In memoriam A. B.* (Vienna, 1924); O. Lang, *A. B.: Wesen und Bedeutung* (Munich, 1924; 3rd ed., 1947); K. Singer, *B.s Chormusik* (Stuttgart, 1924); A. Orel, *A. B.: Das Werk, der Kunstler, die Zeit* (Vienna, 1925); R. Wickenhausen, *A. B.s Symphonien: Ihr Werden und Wesen* (Leipzig, 1926–27); M. Auer, *A. B. als Kirchenmusiker* (Regensburg, 1927); H. Grunsky, *Das Formproblem in A. B.s Symphonien* (Augsburg, 1929); F. Grüninger, *A. B.: Der metaphysische Kern seiner Persönlichkeit und Werke* (Augsburg, 1930); H. Grunsky, *Formenwelt und Sinngefüge in den B.-Symphonien* (2 vols., Augsburg, 1931); K. Grunsky, *Fragen der B.-Auffassung* (Stuttgart, 1936); A. Köberle, *Bach, Beethoven, B. als Symbolgestalten des Glaubens* (Berlin, 1936; 4th ed., 1941); F. Grüninger, *Der Ehrfürchtige: A. B.s Leben dem Volke erzählt* (Freiburg im Breisgau, 1937); O. Loerke, *A. B.: Ein Charakterbild* (Berlin, 1938; 3rd ed., 1943); W. Abendroth, *Die Symphonien A. B.s: Einführungen* (Berlin, 1940; 2nd ed., 1942); F. Wohlfahrt, *A. B.s symphonisches Werk* (Leipzig, 1943); P. Raabe, *Wege zu B.* (Regensburg, 1944); D. Newlin, *B., Mahler, Schoenberg* (N.Y., 1947; rev. ed., 1978); L. Nowak, *Te Deum laudamus: Gedanken zur Musik A. B.s* (Vienna, 1947); E. Refardt, *Brahms, B., Wolf: Drei Wiener Meister des 19. Jahrhunderts* (Basel, 1949); F. Grüninger, *Der Meister von Sankt Florian—Wege zu A. B.* (Augsburg, 1950); E. Schenk, *Um B.s Persönlichkeit* (Vienna, 1951); G. Engel, *The Symphonies of A. B.* (N.Y., 1955); I. Krohn, *A. B.s Symphonien: Eine Untersuchung über Formenbau und Stimmungsgehalt* (3 vols., Helsinki, 1955–57); N. Tschulik, ed., *A. B. im Spiegel seiner Zeit* (Vienna, 1955); M.

Dehnert, *A. B.: Versuch einer Deutung* (Leipzig, 1958); R. Simpson, *B. and the Symphony* (London, 1963); F. Grasberger, ed., *B.-Studien: Leopold Nowak zum 60. Geburtstag* (Vienna, 1964); H. Winterberger, *A. B. in seiner Zeit* (Linz, 1964); R. Simpson, *The Essence of B.: An Essay towards the Understanding of His Music* (London, 1967; rev. ed., 1992); O. Wessely, ed., *B.-Studien* (Vienna, 1975); P. Barford, *B. Symphonies* (London, 1978); C. Röthig, *Studien zur Systematik des Schaffens von A. B. auf der Grundlage zeitgenössischer Berichte und autographer Entwürfe* (Kassel, 1978); C. Floros, *Brahms und B.: Studien zur musikalische Exegetik* (Wiesbaden, 1980); W. Notter, *Schematismus und Evolution in der Sinfonik A. B.s* (Munich, 1983); T. Röder, *Auf dem Weg zur B.- Symphonie: Untersuchungen zu den ersten beiden Fassungen von A. B.s dritter Symphonie* (Wiesbaden, 1987); H.-H. Schönzeler, *Zu B.s IX Symphonie: Die Krakauer Skizzen/B.s 9th Symphony: The Crakow Sketches* (Vienna, 1987); C.-H. Mahling, ed., *A. B. Studien zu Werk und Wirkung. Walter Wiora zum 30. Dezember 1986* (Tutzing, 1988); P. Gülke, *Brahms, B.: Zwei Studien* (Kassel, 1989); S. Lieberwirth, *B. und Leipzig: Vom Werden und Wachsen einer Tradition* (Leipzig, 1990); W. Steinbeck, *A. B.: Neunte Symphonie D-Moll* (Munich, 1993); E. Herhaus, *Phänomen B.: Hörfragmente* (Wetzlar, 1995); R. Boss, *Gestalt und Funktion von Fuge und Fugato A. B.* (Tutzing, 1997); T. Jackson and P. Hawkshaw, eds., *B. Studies* (N.Y., 1997); C. Brüstle, *A. B. und die Nachwelt: Zur Rezeptionsgeschichte des Komponisten in der ersten Hälfte des 20. Jahrhunderts* (Stuttgart, 1998). **CORRESPONDENCE:** F. Gräflinger, ed., *A. B.: Gesammelte Briefe* (Regensburg, 1924); M. Auer, ed., *A. B.: Gesammelte Briefe*, new series (Regensburg, 1924); A. Orel, *B.-Brevier: Briefe, Dokumente, Berichte* (Vienna, 1953). **PERIODICALS:** *B. Blätter: Mitteilungen der Internationalen B.-Gesellschaft* (1929–37; renamed *Mitteilungen der Deutschen B.-Gesellschaft*, 1939–40); *Chord and Discord* (1931–41; 1947 et seq.); *Mitteilungsblatt der Internationalen B.-Gesellschaft* (1971 et seq.); *B.-Jahrbuch* (1980 et seq.). —NS/LK/DM

Brückner-Rüggeberg, Wilhelm, German conductor and pedagogue; b. Stuttgart, April 15, 1906; d. Hamburg, April 1, 1985. He studied with August Schmid-Lindner and Siegmund von Hausegger in Munich, where he began his career as chorus master at the Bavarian State Opera in 1928. After conducting in various German music centers, he was a guest conductor with the Hamburg State Opera in 1936–37; subsequently was on its roster from 1938 to 1971. He taught at the Hamburg Hochschule für Musik, becoming a prof. in 1955. —NS/LK/DM

Brudieu, Joan, French-Catalonian composer; b. in the diocese of Limoges, c. 1520; d. Urgel, between April 22 and May 10, 1591. In 1539 he became choirmaster at the Urgel Cathedral, a post he held until 1577. He then served as maestro de capilla and organist at Santa Maria del Mar in Barcelona (1578–79), and subsequently resumed his Urgel post. His extant works include a four-part Requiem Mass and Spanish madrigals. —NS/LK/DM

Bruggen, Frans, distinguished Dutch recorder player, flutist, and conductor; b. Amsterdam, Oct. 30, 1934. He studied the recorder with Kees Otten and flute at the Amsterdam Muzieklyceum; in addition, took courses in musicology at the Univ. of Amsterdam. He then launched a major career as a virtuoso performer of music for the recorder; as a flute soloist, he was equally at home in performances of the Baroque masters and contemporary avant-garde composers; also gave informative lectures and illustrative performances of recorder music in Europe, and taught at the Royal Cons. in The Hague. In 1981 he founded the Orch. of the 18th Century, which he conducted with fine success on both sides of the Atlantic. He also was artistic director of the Netherlands Radio Chamber Orch. in Hilversum (1991–94) and joint principal guest conductor of the Orch. of the Age of Enlightenment in London (from 1992).—NS/LK/DM

Bruhns, Nicolaus, German violinist, organist, and composer; b. Schwabstedt, 1665; d. Husum, March 29, 1697. He studied organ and composition with Buxtehude in Lübeck, and then traveled to Copenhagen, where he served as a church organist. In 1689 he moved to Husum and was appointed organist at the Cathedral there. He was reputed to be an inventive virtuoso who could play the violin while providing the basso continuo on organ pedals. He was a reputable composer, his 12 church cantatas being particularly notable; he also wrote fugues and chorales for organ.
    BIBL.: H. Kolsch, *N. B.* (Kassel, 1958); M. Geck, *N. B.: Leben und Werk* (Cologne, 1968).—NS/LK/DM

Brüll, Ignaz, Austrian pianist and composer; b. Prossnitz, Moravia, Nov. 7, 1846; d. Vienna, Sept. 17, 1907. He studied in Vienna with Epstein (piano) and Dessoff (composition). He subsequently made extended recital tours, settling eventually in Vienna, where he was a prof. of piano at the Horak Inst. (1872–78). He was an intimate friend of Brahms, who greatly valued his advice.
    WORKS: DRAMATIC: O p e r a : *Die Bettler von Samarkand* (1864); *Das goldene Kreuz* (Berlin, Dec. 22, 1875); *Der Landfriede* (Vienna, Oct. 4, 1877); *Bianca* (Dresden, Nov. 25, 1879); *Königin Marietta* (Munich, 1883); *Gloria* (Hamburg, 1886); *Das steinerne Herz* (Vienna, 1888); *Gringoire* (Munich, March 19, 1892); *Schach dem Könige* (Munich, 1893); *Der Husar* (Vienna, 1898); *Rübezahl* (unfinished). **B a l l e t :** *Ein Märchen aus der Champagne* (1896). **OTHER:** *Im Walde*, overture; 3 serenades and a Dance Suite for Orch.; 2 piano concertos; Violin Concerto; piano pieces; songs.
    BIBL.: H. Schwarz, *I. B. und sein Freundeskreis* (1922). —NS/LK/DM

Brumby, Colin (James), Australian composer, conductor, and teacher; b. Melbourne, June 18, 1933. He was educated at the Univ. of Melbourne Conservatorium of Music (B.Mus., 1957; D.Mus., 1971). He also received training in composition in Santiago de Compostela (1962), London (1962–64), and Rome (1972–73), and studied computer music at Stanford Univ. (1974). He was music director of the Victorian Chamber Players (1956), the South Melbourne Sym. Orch. (1957), and the Queensland Opera (1969–71). In 1964 he joined the faculty of the Univ. of Queensland, where he was an assoc. prof. from 1977 as well as music director of its Musical Soc. (1966–68; 1977–86). After composing in an approved atonal style, Brumby forsook that path in 1974 to embrace an adventuresome tonal style. In both atonal and tonal scores, melodic writing is a salient feature.

WORKS: DRAMATIC: O p e r a : *The 7 Deadly Sins* (Brisbane, Sept. 12, 1970); *The Marriage Machine* (1971; Sydney, Jan. 28, 1972); *La Donna* (1986); *Lorenzaccio* (1986–87); *Fire on the Wind* (1990); *Summer Carol* (1990); *The Heretic* (1998–99). **B a l - l e t :** *Bunyip*, television ballet (1966); *Cinderella*, after Rossini (Brisbane, Dec. 10, 1975); *Masques* (Brisbane, Aug. 18, 1980); *Alice, Memories of Childhood* (1987). Also operettas for children, incidental music, and film scores. **ORCH.:** Concerto for Viola and Strings (1960); *Antipodea* (1962); *Partite* for Clarinet and Strings (Brisbane, June 20, 1962); *Fibonacci Variations* (1964); *Mediterranean Suite* (1964); 2 violin concertos: No. 1 (1969; Brisbane, Feb. 28, 1970) and No. 2 (Brisbane, Aug. 1983); *Litanies of the Sun* (1970; Brisbane, May 28, 1971); *The Phoenix and the Turtle* (Canberra, Oct. 6, 1974); Horn Concerto (1974; Brisbane, April 2, 1975); Flute Concerto (1976; Brisbane, Feb. 23, 1977); *Entradas* (1978); *Musagettes* (Brisbane, Oct. 2, 1978); *Festival Overture on Australian Themes* (1981; Adelaide, Feb. 17, 1982); 2 syms.: No. 1 (Brisbane, April 7, 1982) and No. 2, *Mosaics of Ravenna* (1993); *Paean* (Sydney, July 3, 1982); Bassoon Concerto (Adelaide, Nov. 16, 1983); *South Bank Overture* (1984; Brisbane, April 23, 1985); Guitar Concerto (Brisbane, May 22, 1985); Piano Concerto (Perth, Sept. 17, 1985); Oboe Concertino (Brisbane, June 29, 1987); Clarinet Concerto (1988; Brisbane, July 21, 1989); *Scena* for English Horn and Strings (1988); Viola Concerto, *Tre aspetti di Roma* (1990); Trumpet Concerto (1991); *West End Overture* (1993); Concerto for Organ and Strings (1994). **CHAMBER:** *4 Exotic Pieces* for Flute and Harp (1961); Wind Quintet (1964); String Quartet (1969); *Player Chooses* for 3 Instruments and Keyboard (1973); *Chiaroscuro* for Clarinet, Cello, and Piano (1977); Suite for Double Basses (1978); *Haydn Down Under* for Bassoon and String Quartet (1980); *The 7 Ages of Man* for Wind Quintet and Optional Narrator (1981); Slarinet Sonatina (1982); Bassoon Sonata (1984); Piano Quartet (1985); Flute Sonatina (1985); *4 Aphorisms* for Clarinet and Piano (1986); *Mundoolun* for English Horn and Piano (1988); *Borromeo Suite* for Flute and Guitar (1990); *Gardens of the Villa Taranto* for Flute and Guitar (1991); *Aubade* for Violin and Piano (1991); *Capriccio* for Bassoon (1995); *Aria* for Violin and Piano (1996); *Little Waltz* for Violin and Piano (1996); *Menteith* for Flute and Piano (1997). **VOCAL:** *3 Italian Songs* for High Voice and String Quartet (1968); *Gilgamesh* for Narrator, Chorus, Brass, and Percussion (1968); *Charlie Bubble's Book of Hours* for Soloists, Chorus, and Orch. (1969); *Bring Out Your Christmas Masks* for Soloists, Chorus, Dancers, Actors, Orch., and Organ (Brisbane, Dec. 10, 1969); *Ballade for St. Cecilia* for Soloists, Chorus, and Orch. (1970); *Celebrations and Lamentations* for 4 Choruses, Wind, Brass, and Percussion (Brisbane, May 25, 1972); *This Is the Vine* for Soloists, Chorus, and Orch. (1972; Melbourne, Feb. 24, 1973); *Orpheus Beach* for Soprano, Baritone, and Orch. (Brisbane, Oct. 10, 1978); *3 Baroque Angels* for Chorus and Orch. (1979); *Festival Mass* for Chorus, Wind, Brass, and Percussion (Brisbane, Aug. 11, 1984); *Psalm 148* for Chorus and Band (Brisbane, Aug. 11, 1984); *Great Is Truth and Mighty Above All Things* for Baritone, Chorus, and Orch. (Brisbane, May 10, 1985); *Stabat mater dolorosa* for Soprano, Baritone, and String Trio (1986); *The Ballad of Sydney Hospital*, cantata for Mezzo-soprano, Baritone, Chorus, and Orch. (Sydney, Nov. 15, 1988); *The Ballad of Charlie Blow*, cantata for Women's Chorus, Mixed Chorus, and Orch. (1988); *Canti Pisani* for Medium Voice and Orch. (1989); *A Special*

Inheritance, cantata for Women's Voices and Orch. (1990); *The Trenchant Troubadour*, song cycle for Medium Voice and Piano (1991); *Song of Mary* for Women's Voices and String Orch. (1995); *Justorum animae* for Chorus (1996).—**NS/LK/DM**

Brumel, Antoine, celebrated French composer; b. 1460; d. after 1520. He served as a chorister at the Cathedral of Notre Dame in Chartres in 1483, and in 1486 he became a Master of the Innocents at St. Peter's in Geneva, where he remained until 1492. In 1497 he was Canon at Laon Cathedral. He was a singer at the ducal court in Chambery in 1501, then took up his duties at the court of Alfonso I, Duke of Ferrara, in Aug. 1506, remaining in his service there until the chapel was disbanded in 1510. A number of his sacred works were publ. during his lifetime; other pieces are scattered in various anthologies. A complete ed. of his works was begun by A. Carapetyan in 1951 in Rome under the aegis of the American Inst. of Musicology. He composed masses, motets, Magnificats, and other sacred works. B. Hudson ed. the collection *A. Brumel: Opera omnia*, Corpus Mensurabilis Musicae, V/1–6 (1969–72).
—**NS/LK/DM**

Brun, Fritz, Swiss conductor, teacher, and composer; b. Lucerne, Aug. 18, 1878; d. Grosshochstetten, Nov. 29, 1959. He studied in Lucerne (1892–95) and at Cologne (1896–1901), then settled in Bern (1909), where he taught at the Cons. and conducted the Bern Sym. Orch. until 1943.

WORKS: ORCH.: 10 syms. (1908–53); *Variations* for Piano and String Orch. (1944); Piano Concerto (1944); Cello Concerto; *Rhapsodie* for Orch. (1958). **CHAMBER:** 4 string quartets (1898, 1921, 1943, 1949); Violin Sonata (1906); Cello Sonata (1953).

BIBL.: *Kleine Festgabe für F. B.* (Bern, 1941).—**NS/LK/DM**

Brün, Herbert, German composer and teacher; b. Berlin, July 9, 1918. In 1936 he went to Jerusalem, where he studied with Wolpe and Pelleg at the Cons. until 1938; after attending Columbia Univ. in N.Y. (1948–49), he pursued research on the applications of electroacoustic and electronic methods of sound production in Paris, Cologne, and Munich (1955–62). He taught at the Univ. of Ill. (1963–88). Among his writings are *Über Musik und Zum Computer* (1971) and *My Words and Where I Want Them* (1986). In his music, he explores the potentialities of computers as a catalytic factor for advanced techniques; the titles of his works often suggest paradoxical logic.

WORKS: Concertino for Orch. (1947); 3 string quartets (1952, 1957, 1961); *Mobile* for Orch. (1958); *Gestures for 11* for 11 Instruments (1964); *Soniferous Loops* for Instruments and Tape (1964); *Non sequitur*, group of works for Varying Ensembles (1966); Trio for Trumpet, Trombone, and Percussion (1968); Nonet (1969); *6 for 5 by 3 in Pieces* for Oboe, English Horn, Clarinet, and Bass Clarinet (1971); *Twice Upon 3 Times* for Bass Clarinet and Tuba (1980). **ELECTRONIC:** *Anepigraphe* (1958); *Klänge unterwegs* (1962); *Futility 1964* (1964); *Infraudibles* (1968); *Piece of Prose* (1972); *Dust* (1976); *More Dust* (1977); *Dustiny* (1978); *A Mere Ripple*˙ (1979); *U-turn-to* (1980); *I Told You So* (1981). **C o m p u t e r :** *Mutatis mutandis* (1968); *Polyplots* (1971); *Links* (1973).—**NS/LK/DM**

Bruneau, (Louis-Charles-Bonaventure-) Alfred, French opera composer; b. Paris, March 3, 1857; d. there, June 15, 1934. In 1873 he entered the Paris Cons., where he was a pupil of Franchomme. He won the first cello prize in 1876, and later studied harmony with Savard and composition with Massenet; in 1881 he won the Prix de Rome with his cantata *Sainte-Geneviève*. He was a music critic for *Gil Blas* (1892–95), then for *Le Figaro* and *Le Matin*. In 1903–04 he was first conductor at the Opéra-Comique. In 1900 he was made a member of the "Conseil Superieur" at the Paris Cons., and in 1909 succeeded Reyer as inspector of music instruction. He made extensive tours of Russia, England, Spain, and the Netherlands, conducting his own works. He was made a Knight of the Légion d'honneur in 1895, received the title "Commandeur de St.-Charles" in 1907, and became a member of the Académie des Beaux Arts in 1925. His role in the evolution of French opera is of great importance; he introduced realistic drama on the French musical stage, working along lines parallel with Zola in literature. He used Zola's subjects for his most spectacular opera, *L'Ouragan*, and also for the operas *Messidor* and *L'Enfant-Roi*. In accordance with this naturalistic trend, Bruneau made free use of harsh dissonance when it was justified by the dramatic action of the plot. He publ. *Musiques d'hier et de demain* (1900), *La Musique française* (1901), *Musiques de Russie et musiciens de France* (1903; German tr. by M. Graf in *Die Musik*, Berlin, 1904), *La Vie et les oeuvres de Gabriel Fauré* (1925), and *Massenet* (1934).

WORKS: DRAMATIC: O p e r a (all first perf. in Paris unless otherwise given): *Kérim* (June 9, 1887); *Le Rêve* (June 18, 1891); *L'Attaque du Moulin* (Nov. 23, 1893); *Messidor* (Feb. 19, 1897); *L'Ouragan* (April 29, 1901); *Lazare* (1902); *L'Enfant-Roi* (March 3, 1905); *Naïs Micoulin* (Monte Carlo, Feb. 2, 1907); *La Faute de l'Abbé Mouret* (March 1, 1907); *Les Quatre Journees* (Dec. 25, 1916); *Le Roi Candaule* (Dec. 1, 1920); *Angelo, tyran de Padoue* (Jan. 16, 1928); *Virginie* (Jan. 7, 1931). **B a l l e t :** *L'Amoureuse Leçon* (Feb. 6, 1913); *Les Bacchantes* (after Euripides; Oct. 30, 1912). **OTHER:** 2 overtures: *Ode héroïque* and *Léda*; 2 symphonic poems: *La Belle au Bois dormant* and *Penthésilée*, with Chorus; a Requiem; *Lieds de France* and *Chansons à danser* (both to poems by C. Mendès); *Les Chants de la vie* (to poems by H. Bataille, F. Gregh, etc.); *Le Navire* for Voice and Orch.; pieces for various combinations of string and wind Instruments.

BIBL.: A. Boschot, *La Vie et les oeuvres d'A. B.* (Paris, 1937). —NS/LK/DM

Brunelle, Philip, American conductor, organist, and choral scholar; b. Faribault, Minn., July 1, 1934. He was educated at the Univ. of Minn. From 1968 to 1985 he was music director of the Minn. Opera, where he conducted operas by various American composers. In 1969 he was named organist and choirmaster at the Plymouth Congregational Church in Minneapolis, where he quickly organized and became artistic director of the Plymouth Music Series of Minn., a distinguished and innovative series widely known for its diversified programming. As a guest conductor, Brunelle appeared with various American orchs. and opera companies. After making his European conducting debut at the Aldeburgh Festival in 1983, he made guest conducting appearances in several European music centers. In 1991 he founded and served as artistic director of the Ensemble Singers, which also made occasional appearances with his Plymouth Music Series. In 1994 he conducted the Ensemble Singers in successful engagements in Nuremburg, Leipzig, and Prague. In addition to his performing career, Brunelle served as a visiting prof. at the Univ. of Minn. School of Music and contributed a regular column to *The American Organist*. He has prepared eds. of several major choral works. In 1982 he was awarded the Kodály Medal by the Hungarian government. In 1988 he received Sweden's Stig Anderson Award and in 1989 the King of Sweden presented him with the Royal Order of the Polar Star. He was awarded honorary doctorates from St. Olaf Coll. in Northfield, Minn. (1988), Gustavus Adolphus Coll. in St. Peter, Minn. (1993), and St. John's Univ. and United Theological Seminary (1999). Brunelle's repertoire is expansive, ranging from early music to contemporary scores. Among modern composers he champions are Copland, Argento, Hemberg, Shchedrin, Susa, and Larsen.—NS/LK/DM

Brunelli, Antonio, Italian music theorist and composer; b. Pisa, c. 1575; d. there, c. 1630. He was a pupil of G.M. Nanini. He served as an organist at S. Miniato in Tuscany from 1604 to 1607, then went to Prato, where he served as maestro di cappella at the Cathedral. On April 12, 1612, he was appointed maestro di cappella of the Grand Duke of Tuscany. Between 1605 and 1621 he publ. motets, canzonette, Psalms, madrigals, Requiems, and others sacred works, some of which were included in Donfried's *Promptuarium musicum* (1623). He publ. the theoretical treatises *Regole utilissime per li scolari che desiderano imparare a cantare* (Florence, 1606; one of the first publ. methods for voice), *Esercizi ad 1 e 2 voci* (Florence, 1607), and *Regole et dichiarazioni de alcuni contrappunti doppii* (Florence, 1610).—NS/LK/DM

Brunetti, family of Italian musicians:

(1) Giovan Gualberto Brunetti, composer; b. Pistoia, April 24, 1706; d. Pisa, May 20, 1787. He studied with Atto Gherardeschi, in Pisa with Clari (1723–28), and in Naples at the Turchini Cons. (1728–33). After serving as maestro di cappella to the Duke of Monte Nero, he was secondo maestro at the Turchini Cons. (1745–54). He then was maestro di cappella in Pisa (from 1754). In 1756 he was made a member of Bologna's Accademia Filarmonica. He was ordained a priest in 1764.

WORKS: DRAMATIC: O p e r a : *Amore imbratta il senno* (Naples, 1733); *Don Pasquino* (Naples, 1735); *Il corrivo* (Naples, 1736); *Ortensio* (Naples, Carnival 1739); *Alessandro nell'Indie* (Pisa, Carnival 1763); *Arminio* (Luca, 1763); *Temistocle* (Lucca, 1776). Also *Ester*, oratorio (Florence, 1758).

(2) Antonio Brunetti, violinist, son of the preceding; b. Naples, c. 1740; d. Salzburg, Dec. 25, 1786. He was Hofmusikdirektor and Hofkonzertmeister in Salzburg from 1776, succeeding Mozart as Konzertmeister in 1777. His intimacy with Maria Judith Lipps, the sister-in-law of Michael Haydn, resulted in the illegitimate birth of a child in 1778. Later that year they were finally married. Mozart wrote his works K.261, 269, 373, and 379 for Brunetti but personally loathed him.

(3) Giuseppe Brunetti, composer, brother of the preceding; b. Naples, c. 1741; d. after 1780. He was active mainly in Pisa (1754–75), Siena (1779), and Florence (1780). He wrote the operas *Didone* (Siena, 1759) and *Galatea* (Braunschweig, 1762).

(4) Antonio Brunetti, composer, probably son of the preceding; b. c. 1767; d. after 1845. He was maestro di cappella at Chieti Cathedral (1790–1800), at Urbino Cathedral (1810–16), and in Macerata (1816–26). In 1826 he was recalled to his former position at Urbino Cathedral, but in 1827 he resigned without having assumed his duties.

WORKS: DRAMATIC: O p e r a : *Lo sposo di tre e marito di nessuno* (Bologna, 1786); *La stravaganza in campagna* (Venice, 1787); *Il Bertoldo* (Florence, Carnival 1788); *Vologeso re de' Parti* (Florence, 1789); *Le nozze per invito, ossia Gli amanti capricciosi* (Rome, 1791); *Fatima* (Brescia, 1791); *Li contrasti per amore* (Rome, 1792); *Il pazzo glorioso* (Rome, Carnival 1797); *Il libretto alla moda* (Naples, Carnival 1808); *La colomba contrastata, ossia La bella carbonara* (Rimini, Carnival 1813); *Amore e fedeltà alla prova* (Bologna, May 1814); *La fedeltà coniugale* (Parma, Jan. 30, 1815). —NS/LK/DM

Brunetti, Domenico, Italian composer; b. Bologna, c. 1580; d. there, April or May 1646. He was organist at the Church of S. Domenico (c. 1609), then maestro di cappella at the Bologna Cathedral (1618). With F. Bertacchi he founded the Accademia dei Filaschici (1633), which later was absorbed into the Accademia Filarmonica. His publications include *Euterpe* (Venice, 1606), *Varii Concentus unica, voce, duabus, tribus, quatuor vel pluribus cum gravi et acuto ad Organum* (Venice, 1609), and *Canticum Deiparae Virginis Octies iuxta singulos Rhytmorum Sacrorum* (Venice, 1621). Several of his compositions (motets, madrigals, etc.) were publ. in contemporary collections (1611–26) of A. Schadeo, G. Donfried, A.N. di Treviso, F. Sammaruco, Z. Zanetti, and G.P. Biandra.—NS/LK/DM

Brunetti, Gaetano, Italian violinist and composer; b. probably in Fano, 1744; d. Colmenar de Orejo, near Madrid, Dec. 16, 1798. He most likely was a student of Nardini in Livorno. About 1762 he went to Madrid, where he became a violinist in the Royal Chapel in 1767. From 1788 he was director of the Royal Chamber Orch. Brunetti was held in high esteem at the court, for which he composed some 450 works.

WORKS: DRAMATIC: O p e r a : *El Faetón* (not extant); *El Jason* (Madrid, Oct. 4, 1768; not extant). **ORCH.:** 28 syms.; 4 sinfonie concertante; 6 overtures; 18 minuets; 12 contradanses; 7 marches; variations. **CHAMBER:** 12 sextets; 66 quintets; 44 string quartets; 70 minuets for String Quartet; 30 string trios; 64 sonatas for Violin and Bass; 23 divertimenti for Violin, Viola, and Cello; 6 divertimenti for Violin and Viola; 6 duos for 2 Violins; 4 duets for 2 Violins. **VOCAL:** Mass for 8 Voices and Orch.; Miserere for 4 Voices and Instruments; 3 Lamentations; 6 concert arias.

BIBL.: A. Belgray, *G. B.: An Exploratory Bio-bibliographical Study* (diss., Univ. of Mich., 1970).—NS/LK/DM

Bruni, Antonio Bartolomeo, Italian violinist and composer; b. Cuneo, Jan. 28, 1757; d. there, Aug. 5, 1821. He studied with Pugnani in Turin. In 1780 he went to Paris, and on May 15, 1780, appeared as a violinist at the Concert Spirituel; then served as a member of the orch. of the Comédie-Italienne (1781–89). He was subsequently director of the orch. of the Opéra-Comique (1799–1801); then at the Opéra-Italienne (1801–6). He wrote 22 operas, of which the most successful were *Célestine* (Paris, Oct. 15, 1787), *Claudine* (Paris, March 6, 1794), and *La Rencontre en voyage* (Paris, April 28, 1798). He also wrote music for the violin, and publ. methods for both violin and viola (the latter reprinted in 1928).

BIBL.: G. Cesari, H. Closson, L. de La Laurencie, A. Della Corte, and C. Zino, *A.B. B., musicista cuneese* (Turin, 1931). —NS/LK/DM

Brunis (originally **Brunies**), **Georg(e Clarence),** pioneering New Orleans trombonist; b. New Orleans, Feb. 6, 1902; d. Chicago, Nov. 19, 1974. Henry Brunies Sr., a baker who played violin, and his wife, Elizabeth, a pianist, had six sons and a daughter, all of whom were musical. The daughter, Ada, played guitar, and the oldest son, Rudy (1884–1955), played double bass, although he earned his living as a brewer. The second son, Richie (Richard) Brunies (b. New Orleans, Nov. 29, 1889; d. New Orleans, March 28, 1961), played cornet in Fischer's Brass Band (1907–8) and also in Papa Jack Laine's Reliance Brass Band. Trombonist Henny Brunies (b. New Orleans, 1891. d. there, 1932) played in brass bands in New Orleans but also toured Calif. and performed and recorded in Chicago (1923–26) with a group led by his brother Merritt. Abbie (Albert) Brunies (b. New Orleans, Jan. 19, 1900; d. Oct. 2, 1978) was yet another cornet player. Georg shortened the spelling of his name on the advice of a numerologist to make it 11 rather than 13 letters.

At the age of eight, Georg was playing alto horn in Papa Jack Laine's Reliance Brass Band, and also worked with the family band. He first played trombone around age ten in a band led by Laine's son, Alfred "Pantsy" Laine and his Wampas Cats. During his teens, he played at Brunnin's Hall and at Martin's, near Lake Pontchartrain, with Leon Roppolo. He moved to Chicago c. 1919 to work in a band led by New Orleans drummer Joe "Ragababy" Stevens. After playing on the S.S. *Capitol*, Brunis returned to Chicago c. 1921, and joined Paul Mares's Friar's Society Orch. and thus became a founder-member of the New Orleans Rhythm Kings. He left the N.O.R.K. in 1924, briefly worked with Eddie Tancil's Band in Chicago, and then joined Ted Lewis (1924–34), including a trip to Europe. From 1936, Brunis was virtually a "house-musician" at Nick's, in N.Y., playing with many New Orleans revivalists through the late 1940s. In June 1949, he moved back to Chicago and was in residence at the Club IIII from 1951 to 1959. During the late 1950s and early 1960s, he also led in Madison, Wisc., and in Cincinnati. He continued to work through the mid-1960s, briefly living in Biloxi, Miss., where his family had a band in 1965, and then returned to Chicago. He played at the 1968 New Orleans Jazz Festival with Art Hodes. He became seriously ill in the late 1960s but resumed blowing and began working with Smokey Stover's Band in September 1969.

He continued to play with Stover and other Dixieland-revival bands until his death.

DISC.: *King of the Tailgate Trombone* (1950); *Georg Brunis & The Original New Orleans Rhythm Kings* (1954); *Georg Brunis and His Rhythm Kings* (1964); *Georg Brunis and His New Rhythm* (1965).—**JC/LP**

Brunner, Adolf, Swiss composer; b. Zürich, June 25, 1901; d. Thalwil, Feb. 15, 1992. He studied with his uncle, the composer Hans Lavater, and then in Berlin with Jarnach and at the Hochschule für Musik with Schreker and Gmeindl (1921–25), where he received training in composition and conducting. He completed his studies in Paris and Italy. From 1949 to 1960 he was director of the dept. of politics and current affairs of Radio Zürich. In 1955 he founded the Swiss Soc. for Protestant Church Music. He publ. *Wesen, Funktion und Ort der Musik im Gottesdienst* (Zürich, 1956; 2nd ed., rev. and enl., 1968). Brunner was especially known for his attempts to renew Protestant church music via his many sacred works.

WORKS: ORCH.: Sym. Orch. Piece and Suite (1924–25); *Concertante Music* (1928–59); *Partita* for Piano and Orch. (1938–39); Concerto grosso for Strings and Timpani (1943–44); Concerto for Large Orch. (1955–56). **CHAMBER:** String Trio (1928); Flute Sonata (1933–34); Violin Sonata (1948); String Quartet (1961–62). **KEYBOARD:** Piano Pieces, including a Sonata (1933); organ music. **VOCAL:** Mass for 4 Voices (1933); *Das Gleichnis von den 10 Jungfrauen* for Chorus and Orch. (1938–39); *Jesus und die Ehebrecherin* for Chorus and Orch. (1939); *Jesus und die Samariterin am Brunnen* for 3 Voices, Flute, 5 Strings, and Orch. (1939); *Das Gespräch Jesu mit Nikodemus* for 2 Voices, Oboe, Strings, and Organ (1947); *Das Weihnachtsevangelium* for Chorus and Strings (1963); *St. Mark Passion* for 4 Solo Voices, Chorus, Organ, and Orch. (1970–71).

BIBL.: B. Billeter, *A. B.* (Zürich, 1972).—**LK/DM**

Brunold, Paul, French pianist, organist, and writer on music; b. Paris, Oct. 14, 1875; d. there, Sept. 14, 1948. He was a pupil of Marmontel (piano) and Lavignac (theory) at the Paris Cons., and later studied with Paderewski. In 1915 he became organist at St. Gervais, in Paris. With H. Expert, he ed. the *Anthologie des maîtres français du clavecin des XVIIe et XVIIIe siècles*; with A. Tessier, he brought out a complete edition of Chambonnières's works; he also ed. 2 vols. of works by Dieupart (*6 Suites pour clavecin* and *Airs et Chansons*). He publ. the book *Histoire du grand orgue de l'Église St. Gervais à Paris* (1934).—**NS/LK/DM**

Brunswick, Mark, American composer and teacher; b. N.Y., Jan. 6, 1902; d. London, May 25, 1971. He studied with Goldmark and Bloch; then lived in Europe (1925–38), during which time he studied with Boulanger in Paris and was active in Vienna. Returning to the U.S., he served as chairman of the National Committee for Refugee Musicians (1938–43); was president of the American section of the ISCM (1941–50) and of the Coll. Music Assn. (1953). After teaching at Black Mountain Coll. (1944) and Kenyon Coll. (1945), he was chairman of the music dept. at the City Coll. of N.Y. (1946–67).

WORKS: DRAMATIC: Opera: *The Master Builder*, after Ibsen. (1959–67; unfinished). **ORCH.:** Sym. (1945; Minneapolis, March 7, 1947); *Air with Toccata* for Strings (1967). **CHAMBER:** *2 Movements* for String Quartet (1926); *Fantasia* for Viola (1932); *7 Trios* for String Quartet (1956); Septet for Wind Quintet, Viola, and Cello (1957); Quartet for Violin, Viola, Cello, and Double Bass (1958). **VOCAL:** *Lysistrata* for Soprano, Women's Voices, and Orch. (1930); *Eros and Death*, choral sym. for Mezzo-soprano, Chorus, and Orch. (1932–54); *4 Madrigals and a Motet* (1960); *5 Madrigals* for Chorus (1965); songs.
—**NS/LK/DM**

Bruscantini, Sesto, Italian baritone; b. Porto Civitanova, Dec. 10, 1919. He studied law, then went to Rome to study music with Luigi Ricci. He made his debut at La Scala in Milan in 1949, singing the bass role of Don Geronimo in Cimarosa's *Il matrimonio segreto*. He then sang at several festivals in Glyndebourne (1951–54). In 1952 he appeared at the Salzburg Festival. In 1961 he made his U.S. debut with the Chicago Lyric Opera. On Feb. 2, 1981, he made his Metropolitan Opera debut in N.Y. as Taddeo in *L'Italiana in Algeri*, and sang there until 1983. He was particularly renowned for his buffo roles. In 1953 he married **Sena Jurinac**.

BIBL.: A. Foresi, ed., *Una Vita per l'opera: Conversazioni con S. B.* (Lucca, 1997).—**NS/LK/DM**

Brusilovsky, Evgeni (Grigorievich), Russian composer and pedagogue; b. Rostov-na-Donu, Nov. 12, 1905; d. Moscow, May 9, 1981. He studied composition with Maximilian Steinberg at the Leningrad Cons., graduating in 1931. In 1933 he was commissioned by the Leningrad Union of Composers to go to Kazakhstan to promote music education there and to help native composers write music based on their own ethnic sources. Brusilovsky taught at the Alma-Ata Cons. of Music. He wrote a number of works making use of native motifs; particularly notable are his operas on folk subjects.

WORKS: DRAMATIC: Opera (all first perf. in Alma-Ata): *Kyz-Zhybek* (1934); *Zhalbyr* (1935; 2nd version, 1938; 3rd version, 1946); *Er-Targyn* (1937; 2nd version, 1954); *Ayman-Sholpan* (1938); *Altyn Styk* (1940); *Guard, Alga!* (1942); *Amangeldy* (1945); *Dudaray* (1953); *The Inheritors* (1963). **Ballet:** *Bayan-Slu* (1971). **ORCH.:** 8 syms. (1931, 1932, 1944, 1957, 1961, 1965, 1969, 1972); Piano Concerto (1948); Trumpet Concerto (1967); Viola Concerto (1969). **CHAMBER:** 2 string quartets (1944, 1952); piano pieces; educational studies for various instruments. **VOCAL:** Numerous choruses and songs.
—**NS/LK/DM**

Brusilow, Anshel, American violinist, conductor, and teacher; b. Philadelphia, Aug. 14, 1928. He studied violin with Zimbalist at the Curtis Inst. of Music in Philadelphia (1943) and with Jani Szanto at the Philadelphia Musical Academy (diploma, 1947), and conducting with Monteux (1944–54). In 1944 he made his debut as a violinist with Ormandy and the Philadelphia Orch. He served as concertmaster of the New Orleans Sym. Orch. (1954–55), assoc. concertmaster of the Cleveland Orch. (1955–59), and concertmaster of the Philadelphia Orch. (1959–66). Brusilow also was founder- conductor of the Philadelphia Chamber Orch. (1961–65) and the Chamber Sym. of Philadelphia (1966–68). After serving as resident conductor (1970–71) and executive director and conductor (1971–73) of the Dallas Sym. Orch., he taught at North Tex. State Univ. in Denton (1973–82), Southern Methodist Univ. in Dallas (1982–89), and the Univ. of North Tex. at Denton (from 1989). From 1992 he also was music director of the Richardson (Tex.) Sym. Orch.—NS/LK/DM

Bruson, Renato, distinguished Italian baritone; b. Este, near Padua, Jan. 13, 1936. He received training at the Padua Cons. In 1961 he made his operatic debut as Count Di Luna in Spoleto, and then sang in various Italian music centers. On Feb. 1, 1969, he made his Metropolitan Opera debut in N.Y. as Enrico in *Lucia di Lammermoor*. In 1972 he made his first appearance at Milan's La Scala as Antonio in *Linda di Chamounix*. He made his debut at London's Covent Garden as Renato in *Un ballo in maschera* in 1976. In 1982 he sang Falstaff in Los Angeles. He appeared as Don Giovanni at the Berlin Deutsche Oper in 1988. In 1990 he sang Montfort in *Les Vêpres siciliennes* at N.Y.'s Carnegie Hall. He appeared as Germont at Covent Garden in 1995. In 1997 he was engaged as Macbeth in Monte Carlo. His guest engagements also took him to Vienna, Munich, Chicago, Hamburg, Paris, San Francisco, and other cities.

BIBL.: T. Tegano, *R. B.: L'interprete e i personaggi* (It. and Eng., Parma, 1998).—NS/LK/DM

Brusselmans, Michel, Belgian composer; b. Paris (of Belgian parents), Feb. 12, 1886; d. Brussels, Sept. 20, 1960. He studied with Huberti, Tinel, and Gilson at the Brussels Cons.; won the Agniez Prix in 1914 for his symphonic poem *Helène de Sparte*. In 1922 he became ed. for the Paris music publisher Jamin, and spent most of his life in France. His music is Romantic in inspiration and programmatic in content.

WORKS: DRAMATIC: Ballet: *Les Néréides* (1911); *Kermesse flamande* (1912); *Les Sylphides* (on themes of Chopin). **ORCH.:** *Ouverture fériale* (1908); *Scènes Breugheliennes* (1911); *Hélène de Sparte*, symphonic poem (1914); *Télémaque a Gaulus* for Chamber Orch. (1923); 3 syms. (1924; 1934; *Levantine*, 1956–57); *Esquisses flamandes* (1927); *Légende du gapeau* for Horn and Orch. or Piano (1930); *Rhapsodie flamande* (1931); *Scènes provençales* (1931); *Suite phrygienne* (1932); *Suite d'après les Caprices de Paganini* (1936); *Suite divertissement* (1937); *Rhapsodie* for Horn and Orch. (1938); Organ Concerto (1938); *Ouverture héroïque* (1942); Sinfonietta (1954). **CHAMBER:** Violin Sonata (1915); Cello Sonata (1916); *Prelude and Fugue* for 8 Winds (1923); *Visages de Paris* for Piano (1946). **VOCAL:** *Jésus*, oratorio (1936); *Psaume LVI* for Soprano, Chorus, and Orch. (1954); songs.—NS/LK/DM

Brustad, Bjarne, Norwegian violinist, violist, conductor, and composer; b. Christiania, March 4, 1895; d. there (Oslo), May 22, 1978. He studied at the Christiania Cons., then took violin lessons with Flesch in Berlin (1915–16). From 1919 to 1922 he was a violinist in the Oslo Phil., and from 1929 to 1943 he played first viola there. He also conducted orchs. in Oslo; in 1951 he

received a government life pension. His music is Romantic in its essence, and traditional in form.

WORKS: DRAMATIC: Opera: *Atlantis* (1945). **ORCH.:** 4 violin concertos (1922–61); Concertino for Viola and Chamber Orch. (1932); 9 syms. (1948, 1951, 1953, 1957, 1967, 1970, 1971, 1972, 1973); Clarinet Concerto (1970). **CHAMBER:** 3 string quartets (1919, 1929, 1959); 3 sonatas for Solo Violin (1935, 1956, 1957); Trio for Clarinet, Violin, and Viola (1938); Trio for Clarinet, Violin, and Bassoon (1947); Violin Sonata (1950); *Divertimento* for Flute (1958).—NS/LK/DM

Bruynèl, Ton, Dutch composer; b. Utrecht, Jan. 26, 1934. He studied piano at the Utrecht Cons., and then worked in the studio for electronic music at the Univ. of Utrecht. In 1957 he organized a private electronic music studio. Most of his compositions involve instruments in combination with electronics, and some require theatrical visualizations.

WORKS: *Resonance I* (1960–62) and *II* (1963), theater pieces; *Reflexes* for Birma Drum (1961); *Relief* for Organ and 4 Sound Tracks (1964); *Mobile* for 2 Sound Tracks (1965); *Milieu* for 2 Sound Tracks and Organ (1965–66); *Arc* for Organ and 4 Sound Tracks (1966–67); *Mekaniek* for Wind Quintet and 2 Sound Tracks (1967); *Decor*, ballet score (1967); *Signs* for Wind Quintet, 2 Sound Tracks, and Video Projection (1969); *Ingredients* for Piano and Sound Tracks (1970); *Intra I* for Bass Clarinet and Sound Track (1971); *Elegy* for Woman's Voice and 2 Sound Tracks (1972); *Looking Ears* for Bass Clarinet, Grand Piano, and Sound Tracks (1972); *Phases* for 4 Sound Tracks and Orch. (Utrecht, Jan. 10, 1975); *Soft Song* for Oboe and 2 Sound Tracks (1975); *Dialogue* for Bass Clarinet and Sound Tracks (1976); *Translucent I* for String Quartet and Sound Tracks (1977) and *II* for String Orch. and Sound Tracks (1978); *Toccare* for Piano and Sound Tracks (1979); *From the Tripod* for Loudspeakers, Women, and Listeners (1981); *John's Lullaby* for Chorus, Tape, and Orch. (1985); *Continuation* for Chorus and Tape (1985); *Nocturno en Pedraza* for Flute and Sound Tracks (1988); *Ascolta* for Soloist and Chorus (1989); *Tarde* for Cello (1992); *Le Jardin* for Alto Flute, Harpsichord, and Woman's Voice (1992).—NS/LK/DM

Bruzdowicz, Joanna, Polish-born French composer; b. Warsaw, May 17, 1943. She studied piano with Irena Protasewicz and Wanda Losakiewicz, and composition with Sikorski at the Warsaw Cons. (M.A., 1966). She then pursued training in composition in Paris with Boulanger, Messiaen, and Schaeffer (1968–70), where she was active with the Groupe de Recherches Musicales of the ORTF. In 1975 she became a naturalized French citizen but also retained her Polish citizenship. She was active as a composer, music critic, and teacher. Her output ranges the spectrum from traditional scores to electronic pieces.

WORKS: DRAMATIC: Opera: *In der Strafkolonie* or *La Colonie Pénitentiaire* (Tours, 1972; rev. version, Liège, Oct. 9, 1986); *Les Troyennes* (Paris, 1973; Polish version, Warsaw, July 20, 1979); *Bramy Raju* (The Gates of Paradise; Warsaw, Nov. 1987); *Tides and Waves* (1991–92; Gdańsk, June 1, 1997). **Ballet:** *Le Petit Prince* (Brussels, Dec. 10, 1976). **Children's Musical:** *En attendant Anaïs* (Brussels, Dec. 6, 1987). Many film and theater scores. **ORCH.:** *Impressions* (1966); *Suite in memoriam Sergei Prokofiev* (1966–67); *Eclairs* (1969); Piano Concerto (1974; Paris, Feb. 23, 1975); Sym. (Paris, April 30, 1975); Violin Concerto (1975; Radio France, Feb. 11, 1978); *Aquae sextiae*, suite for Winds (Aix-en-Provence, July 12, 1978); Double

Bass Concerto (1982; Lódź, March 1984); *4 Season's Greetings* for Soloists and String Chamber Orch. (1988–89; Poznań, April 2, 1989); *The Cry of the Phoenix*, cello concerto (Lublin, Sept. 16, 1994); Sym. for 2 Guitars, Percussion, and String Quintet or Chamber Orch. (1999). **CHAMBER:** Wind Quintet (1966); *Per Due* for Violin and Piano (1966); *Epigrams* for Violin (1966); *Esquisses* for Flute, Viola, Cello, and Piano (1969); *Stigma* for Cello (1969; Paris, Dec. 1970); *Episode* for Piano and 13 Strings (1973); *Ette* for Clarinet (1974); *Einklang* for Harpsichord and Organ (1975); Trio for Variable Instrumentation (1975); *Fantasia Hermantica on the Theme S'A'B'B'E* for Viola and Piano (1979); *Tre contre tre* for Flute, Oboe, Viola, and 3 Percussion (1979); *Marlos Grosso Brasileiras* for Flute, Violin, Harpsichord, and Tape (1980); *Trio dei Due Mondi* for Violin, Cello, and Piano (1980; Radio Fance, Jan. 1981); *Dum Spiro Spero* for Flute and Tape (Brussels, May 1981); *Para y contra* for Double Bass and Tape (Brussels, Sept. 1981); *Trio per Trio* for Flute, Violin, and Harpsichord (Brussels, Sept. 15, 1981); *Dreams and Drums* for Percussionist (Santa Barbara, Calif., March 1982); 2 string quartets: No. 1, *La Vita* (Brussels, April 1983) and No. 2, *Cantus Aeternus* (Warsaw, May 10, 1988); *Oracle* for Bassoon and Tape (1982; Paris, March 1983); *Aurora Borealis* for Harp and Organ (Bergen, May 22, 1988); Sonata for Solo Violin, *Il Ritorno* (Zagreb, April 25, 1990); *Je me souviens* for Marimba (Montreal, Dec. 17, 1990); Violin Sonata, *Spring in America* (N.Y., April 20, 1994); *Song of Hope and Love* for Cello and Piano (Washington, D.C., June 22, 1997). **PIANO:** *Erotiques* (1966); *Esitanza* for 2 Pianos or Piano 4–Hands (1973); *An der Schönen Blauen Donau* for 2 Pianos and Tape (1973–74); *October Sonata* (1978). **VOCAL:** *Niobe* for Speaker, Soprano, and 5 Instruments (1966); *Sketches from the Harbor* for Mezzo-soprano, Flute, Piano, and 3 Percussion (1967); *Jour d'ici et d'ailleurs* for Vocal Quartet, Chorus, Speaker, and Chamber Ensemble (1971); *A Claire Voix* for Chorus, 4 Instruments, and Tape (1973); *Urbi et Orbi*, cantata for Tenor, Children's Chorus, 2 Trumpets, 2 Trombones, and Organ (Stuttgart, June 23, 1985); *La Espero*, cantata for Soprano, Baritone, and 7 Instruments (Kraków, March 25, 1990); *On Prayer* for Soprano and Piano (WFMT, Chicago, Nov. 21, 1990); *Stabat Mater* for Chorus (Los Angeles, April 3, 1993); *World*, 5 songs for Soprano and Piano, after Czesław Miłosz (1995–96; Chicago, May 18, 1996). **OTHER:** *Ek- Stasis*, electroacoustic piece with mimes (1969); *Phobos*, electronic piece (1969); *Homo Faber*, electronic trilogy (1971–75); *Inner Space-Outer Space*, electronic piece (1978); *Bartókalia*, electronic piece (1979); *Neue Kinderszenen*, electronic suite for children (1980).—**NS/LK/DM**

Bryant, Boudleaux (Diadorius) and Felice (Matilda Genevieve Scaduto),

American songwriters. Together and separately, the husband-and-wife team of Boudleaux (b. Shellman, Ga., Feb. 13, 1920; d. Gatlinburg, Tenn., June 30, 1987) and Felice Bryant (b. Milwaukee, Aug. 7, 1925) wrote music and lyrics for numerous pop and country hits of the 1950s and 1960s. They were most closely associated with the Everly Brothers and wrote such hits as "Bye Bye Love," "Wake Up Little Susie," and "All I Have to Do Is Dream" for the duo. They also wrote hits for a variety of country artists, including "Hey, Joe!" for Carl Smith, "Midnight" for Red Foley, and "Come Live with Me" for Roy Clark.

Boudleaux's father, Daniel Green Bryant, was a lawyer; his mother, Louise Farham Bryant, played guitar and mandolin. He studied the violin from the ages of 5 to 18 with the intention of becoming a concert artist. In 1938 he played with the Atlanta Philharmonic Symphony and other orchestras. From 1939 he also played with country and jazz bands. He began to write during this period, composing the instrumental "Mississippi Muddle" while working with Hank Penny and His Radio Cowboys. In 1945, while playing in a jazz band at the Schroeder Hotel in Milwaukee, he met Matilda Scaduto, an elevator operator.

Matilda was the daughter of Salvatore and Katherine Loverdi Scaduto. An aspiring singer, she had sung on local radio when she was six, and she received voice training as a child. She had worked in musicals at a local theater and performed with the USO. She also wrote poetry and lyrics. She and Bryant married on Sept. 5, 1945, and eventually had two sons. They began writing songs together, but did not achieve significant success until they submitted "Country Boy" to publisher Wesley Rose, who arranged to have it recorded by "Little" Jimmy Dickens. Dickens's recording reached the country charts in June 1949 and hit the Top Ten. He returned to the country Top Ten with the Bryants' "A-Sleeping at the Foot of the Bed," which reached the charts in January 1950.

The Bryants moved to Nashville in 1950 and took up songwriting full-time. In 1952 they scored three Top Ten country hits: "Somebody's Stolen My Honey," recorded by Ernest Tubb, "It's a Lovely, Lovely World," recorded by Carl Smith (both of which were written by Boudleaux alone), and "Our Honeymoon," also recorded by Carl Smith. Tony Bennett recorded their "Have a Good Time" for a pop hit in August 1952. Boudleaux cowrote "Midnight" with Chet Atkins, and Red Foley recorded it for a #1 country hit in January 1953. Boudleaux and Atkins also wrote "How's the World Treating You?"; Eddy Arnold recorded it for a Top Ten country hit in 1953. The Bryants wrote "Just Wait 'Til I Get You Alone," and Boudleaux collaborated with Carl Smith on "Orchids Mean Goodbye"; these songs were released on either side of a single in the spring of 1953, and both made the country Top Ten. But the most successful Bryant composition of 1953 was Boudleaux's "Hey, Joe!," which hit #1 for Carl Smith in August and was covered by Frankie Laine for a Top Ten pop hit.

Boudleaux's "Back Up, Buddy" was recorded by Carl Smith for a country Top Ten hit in 1954, and the Bryants' "Out behind the Barn" also hit the country Top Ten for Jimmy Dickens that year. Boudleaux wrote two Top Ten country hits in 1955 for Eddy Arnold—"I've Been Thinking" and "The Richest Man (in the World)"—as well as a pop- chart entry for Frankie Laine, "Hawk-Eye." The Bryants had a British success in March 1956, when Alma Cogan reached the U.K. charts with "Willie Can."

The Bryants were signed to a ten-year songwriting contract at Acuff-Rose by Wesley Rose, the son of Fred Rose, who had died in 1954. The Bryants were assigned to write for the Everly Brothers. "Bye Bye Love," their first song to be recorded by the brothers, hit #1 on the pop and country charts in July 1957, also reaching the Top Ten of the R&B charts and selling a million copies. Even more successful was the follow-up, "Wake Up Little Susie," another million-seller that topped the pop, country, and R&B charts in October 1957. The Everlys' third single, a revival of the 1955 R&B hit "This Little Girl of Mine" (music and lyrics by Ray Charles), was less successful, but their fourth, Boudleaux's ballad "All I Have to Do Is Dream," topped the pop, country, and R&B charts in the spring of 1958 and sold a million copies.

Their fifth single combined two Boudleaux songs, the uptempo "Bird Dog" and the ballad "Devoted to You." The former hit #1 on the pop and country charts and the Top Ten of the R&B charts in the summer of 1958; the latter reached the Top Ten of all three charts; and the single was a million-seller. The Everlys' sixth single featured the Bryants' "Problems," which reached the Top Ten of the pop charts in December 1958 and also made the country charts, and "Love of My Life," a Top 40 pop hit. In addition to their Everly Brothers successes, the Bryants were represented in the country Top Ten in 1958 by Jim Reeves's recording of their "Blue Boy." The Everlys' seventh single again consisted of two Bryant songs, "Take a Message to Mary" and "Poor Jenny," both of which reached the pop Top 40 in April 1959. At the same time Buddy Holly reached the charts for the last time with the Bryants' "Raining in My Heart," one of the last songs he recorded before his death.

The Everly Brothers emphasized their own songwriting after 1959, though they scored two more pop hits with Bryant compositions: "Always It's You," a chart entry in May 1960, and "Like Strangers," which reached the Top 40 in November, and their 1958 recording of "All I Have to Do Is Dream" briefly returned to the pop charts in July 1961. Without the Everlys, the Bryants continued to score crossover hits in the early 1960s, reaching the pop and country Top Ten with Boudleaux's "Let's Think about Living," recorded by Bob Luman, in the fall of 1960; the pop Top 40 and the country Top Ten with "My Last Date (With You)" (music by Floyd Cramer, lyrics by Boudleaux Bryant and Skeeter Davis), recorded by Skeeter Davis, in January 1961; and the pop Top Ten and the top of the easy-listening charts with Boudleaux's instrumental "Mexico," recorded by Bob Moore and His Orch., in October 1961. They also enjoyed several revivals of their work: the Louvin Brothers reached the country charts with "How's the World Treating You?" in September 1961; Sue Thompson reached the pop Top 40 in July 1962 with "Have a Good Time" and had a pop-chart entry with "Willie Can" in January 1963; and Richard Chamberlain hit the pop Top 40 with "All I Have to Do Is Dream" in March 1963.

While the Bryants never again scored hits with the frequency they had from the early 1950s to the early 1960s, for the next 20 years they continued to reach the pop and country charts with a combination of newly written songs and newly covered old songs that had not been hits the first time around. The new songs included: "Baltimore," a Top Ten country hit for Sonny James in 1964; "I Love to Dance," a Top Ten country hit for Ernest Ashworth in 1964; "Break Away (From That Boy)," a Top 40 pop hit for the Newbeats in 1965; Boudleaux's "Take Me As I Am (Or Let Me Go)," a Top Ten country hit for Ray Price in 1968; "Rocky Top," a Top 40 country

hit for the Osborne Brothers in 1968; "Come Live with Me," a #1 country hit for Roy Clark that also made the pop charts for him and for Ray Charles in 1973; "Sweet Deceiver" and Boudleaux's "Tryin' to Forget about You," both country chart entries for Cristy Lane in 1977; "(I Need You) All the Time," a Top 40 country hit for Eddy Arnold in 1977; and "I Can Hear Kentucky Calling Me," a country chart entry for the Osborne Brothers and for Chet Atkins in 1980.

Songs enjoying a delayed success were Felice's 1955 composition "We Could," a pop-chart entry in 1964; the 1960 song "She Wears My Ring," a Top Ten country hit for Ray Price in 1968; Boudleaux's 1960 composition "Love Hurts," which reached the U.S. pop charts and the Top Ten of the U.K. charts for Jim Capaldi in 1975; and the 1969 song "Penny Arcade," a Top Ten country hit for Cristy Lane in 1978.

The Bryants were also represented in the charts in the late 1960s, 1970s, and early 1980s by numerous revivals of their previous hits. These included "Raining in My Heart," a Top 40 country hit for Ray Price in 1969 and a country- and pop-chart entry for Leo Sayer in 1978; "All I Have to Do Is Dream," a Top Ten country and Top 40 pop hit for Glen Campbell and Bobbie Gentry in 1970, a pop- and country-chart entry for the Nitty Gritty Dirt Band in 1975, and a country-chart entry for Nancy Montgomery and pop-chart entry for Andy Gibb and Victoria Principal, both in 1981; "Rocky Top," a Top 40 country hit for Lynn Anderson in 1970; "We Could," a Top Ten country hit for Charley Pride in 1974; "Love Hurts," a million-selling Top Ten pop hit for Nazareth in 1976; "Take Me as I Am (Or Let Me Go)," a Top 40 country hit for Mack White in 1976 and for Bobby Bare in 1981; "Devoted to You," a Top 40 pop and country hit for Carly Simon and James Taylor in 1978; "Bye Bye Love," a country-chart entry for Billy Walker and Barbara Fairchild in 1980; "Hey, Joe!" (as "Hey Joe [Hey Moe]"), a Top Ten country hit for Joe Stampley and Moe Bandy in 1981; and "Wake Up Little Susie," a Top 40 pop hit for Simon and Garfunkel in 1982.

The Bryants, who had moved from Nashville to Gatlinburg in 1978, opened a motel there called the Rocky Top Village Inn in 1982; that same year "Rocky Top" was named the official state song of Tenn. Boudleaux Bryant died of cancer at age 67 in 1987.

Disc.: *Boudleaux Bryant's Best Sellers* (1963); *All I Have to Do Is Dream* (1979); *Surfin' on a New Wave* (1979).—**WR**

Bryant, Clora, jazz trumpeter, singer; b. Denison, Tex., May 30, 1929. Her mother died when she was about three years old, and her father raised her and her siblings. The entire family was musical: her father whistled and performed birdcalls; her mother was a singer; and her brother Fred played trumpet and brother Mel was a singer/dancer. She began playing trumpet, studying on her own and in school; by her last year of high school, she was in a school dance band. In September 1943, she attended Prairie View State Coll. because of their all-black female band, the Prairie View Coll. Co-eds. She joined the band, and in the summer of 1944 toured the U.S., including an appearance as the headline group at the Apollo in Harlem. In January 1945, she moved to Los Angeles, where she worked with a black swing combo that played at a white club in Norwalk. Soon, she was playing trumpet in an all-black woman quintet called the Queens of Swing, which included saxophonist Minnie Hightower. They toured throughout the west and northwest. By early 1946, she had returned to Los Angeles to join the Darlings of Rhythm, an all-woman big band that had been founded by Clarence Love in 1944. She married in 1948; her husband, bassist Joe Stone, was often on the road with T-Bone Walker and Jimmy Witherspoon, while she jammed and gigged around Los Angeles. During the late 1950s and 1960s, she toured major U.S. cities, often performing her tribute to Louis Armstrong. In Las Vegas, she worked behind Damita Jo, Harry James, and Sammy Davis Jr., accompanying Davis in the film *Pepe* (1960). In the early 1960s, she also played a stint in New Orleans with Horace Henderson's band. She toured with Billy Williams (c. 1962–64) and with her brother, actor and singer Mel Bryant (c. 1964–66). When her fourth child was born in 1969, she began attending UCLA to study music especially black music history, working on and off toward a B.A. She composed the suite "To Dizzy with Love" (1975) and has won two NEA awards for composition and performance. Around 1980, she had taken over the late Blue Mitchell's chair in Bill Berry's big band. She toured Europe with Johnny Otis and Jeannie and Jimmy Cheatham, and toured Russia in 1989. In 1993 she directed and performed in memory of Gillespie at a Trumpet Summit along with Clark Terry, Jon Faddis, Freddie Hubbard, and others.

DISC.: *Gal with a Horn* (1957).—**LP**

Bryant, Dave, avant-garde jazz keyboardist; b. Petersburg, Va., May 27, 1958. He attended Shenandoah Coll. and Cons. of Music in Winchester, Va. (1976–78). He moved to Boston to attend Berklee (1978–82; B.M., Jazz Piano Performance). He then began studies with Ornette Coleman in 1983. Bryant released a self-titled debut album with his trio Shock Exchange (1986), featuring John Turner and Chris Bowman. In 1990 Bryant joined on as an official member of Prime Time, marking Ornette Coleman's first extended work with a keyboard instrument in decades. In June 1995 he recorded a project at Harmolodic Studios with long-time associates Turner, Bowman, George Garzone, Bob Gullotti, and recording engineer Roger Nichols. He is a faculty member at the Longy School of Music.

DISC.: *Shock Exchange* (1986).—**LP**

Bryant, Ray (Raphael), jazz pianist, composer; b. Philadelphia, Dec. 24, 1931. Bryant hails from a musical family; his older brother was jazz bassist Tommy (Thomas) Bryant (b. Philadelphia, May 21, 1930; d. there Jan. 1, 1982), and he is the uncle of Kevin and Robin Eubanks. He first worked with Tiny Grimes in the late 1940s, but made his first major impression on the jazz scene in 1953 when working as house bass player at Philadelphia's Blue Note club, accompanying Miles Davis, Lester Young, and Charlie Parker on their performances. From 1956 to 1957, he accompanied Carmen

McRae, while also freelancing with others. In 1959 he moved to N.Y., where he became house bassist for several small jazz labels, and began leading his own trio. He enjoyed some early 1960s hits with the jazz-funk numbers "Madison Time" and "Little Susie." He has continued to work primarily in a trio setting, while also doing sessions accompanying various other jazz musicians.

DISC.: *Meet Betty Carter and Ray Bryant Trio* (1955); *Ray Bryant Trio* (1956); *Alone with the Blues* (1958); *Little Susie* (1959); *Con Alma* (1960); *Madison Time* (1960); *Slow Freight* (1966); *Solo Flight* (1976); *Montreux '77* (1977); *Plays Basie and Ellington* (1987); *Ray Bryant Trio Today* (1987); *Ray Bryant Trio* (1993).—**LP**

Bryant, Willie (actually, **William Steven**), jazz band leader, singer; b. New Orleans, Aug. 30, 1908; d. Los Angeles, Feb. 9, 1964. His family moved to Chicago in 1912. He made a short-lived attempt to play trumpet, then worked as a candy-seller at the Grand Theatre, Chicago. In 1926 he began working as a soft-shoe dancer in the Whitman Sisters' Show, did extensive touring throughout the 1920s and into the early 1930s, and also partnered with Leonard Reed in a vaudeville dance act. He had a solo spot in "Chocolate Revue" (1934), and also partnered with Bessie Smith in "Big Fat Ma and Skinny Pa" stage feature. Following a brief spell as vocalist with Buck and Bubbles' Band, Bryant formed his own big band (late 1934–38). From January 1939 Bryant worked as an actor, master of ceremonies, and disc jockey. He did U.S.O. tours during World War II, re-formed his band 1946–48, then resumed compere work. He moved to Calif. in the 1950s, and dee-jayed programs in San Francisco and Los Angeles. He died of a heart attack in 1964.

DISC.: *All of Me* (1934); *Blues Around the Clock* (1945); *1935–1935, Vol. 4* (1995); *Willis Bryant & His Orchestra* (1996); *Keep a Song in Your Soul* (1998).—**JC/LP**

Bryars, (Richard) Gavin, significant English composer and teacher; b. Goole, Yorkshire, Jan. 16, 1943. He studied composition privately with Cyril Ramsey (1959–61) and George Linstead (1963–65) in England, and with Ben Johnston (1968) in the U.S.; also at the Univ. of Sheffield (B.A. in philosophy, 1964) and at the Northern School of Music (1964–66). After teaching at the Northampton Coll. of Technology (1966–67), the Portsmouth Coll. of Art (1969–70), and the Leicester Polytechnic (1970–85), he was prof. of music at De Montford Univ. (1985–96). In 1981 he founded his own Gavin Bryars Ensemble, with which he toured widely. Bryar's output is generally experimental in nature. His works are indeterminate, replete with repetition, and often utilize electronics. His warmth and humor is evidenced in his *The Sinking of the Titanic* (1969), a multimedia, meditative collage work composed of excerpts from pieces the drowning orch. might have been playing. His poignant *Jesus' Blood Never Failed Me Yet*, originally composed for Ensemble and Tape (1971), became an international success in its later version for Orch. and Tape (1994), incorporating the raspy voice of Tom Waits. Bryars has also collaborated with a number of well-known musicians, including Eno, Reich, and

Cardew, as well as with the preeminent American theater director, Robert Wilson.

WORKS: DRAMATIC: O p e r a : *Irma* (1977; realization of a work by Tom Phillips); *Medea* (1982; rev. version, Lyons, Oct. 23, 1984; rev. 1995); *Doctor Ox's Experiment* (1994–96; London, June 15, 1998). **O t h e r :** Theater music, dance scores, and incidental music. **ORCH.:** *2nd Suite from Irma* for Piano and Strings (1978); *3 Studies on Medea* (1983); *Eglisak* for Chamber Orch. (1984–85; Strasbourg, Oct. 10, 1985); *By the Vaar* for Double Bass, Bass Clarinet, Percussion, and Strings (London, April 6, 1987); *The Green Ray* for Soprano Saxophone and Chamber Orch. (Swanage, July 6, 1991); *The North Shore* for Viola, Strings, Harp or Piano, and Percussion (London, July 30, 1994; also for Viola and Piano, 1993); *Jesus' Blood Never Failed Me Yet* for Orch. and Tape (Winnipeg, Feb. 5, 1994; also for Ensemble and Tape, 1971); *The East Coast* for Bass Oboe and Chamber Orch. (1994; Winnipeg, Jan. 24, 1995); Cello Concerto, *Farewell to Philosophy* (London, Nov. 24, 1995); *Epilogue from Wonderlawn* for Viola, Cello, Electric Guitar or Piano or Harp, and Strings (1995; also for Viola, Cello, Double Bass, and Electric Guitar, 1994); *The Sinking of the Titanic* for Orch. and Tapes (1995; Glasgow, March 14, 1997; also for Ensemble, 1969); *Allegrasco* for Soprano Saxophone or Clarinet and Strings (Riga, Feb. 1998; also for Soprano Saxophone or Clarinet and Piano or Ensemble, 1983). **INSTRUMENTAL:** *The Sinking of the Titantic* for Ensemble (1969; London, Dec. 11, 1972); *The Squirrel and the Ricketty-Racketty Bridge* for 2 Guitars (1 Player) or Multiples of Same (1971; London, Dec. 11, 1972); *Jesus' Blood Never Failed Me Yet* for Ensemble and Tape (1971; London, Dec. 11, 1972; also for Orch. and Tape, 1994); *The Cross-Channel Ferry* for Up to 12 Players (Paris, Nov. 16, 1979); *Les Fiançailles* for Piano, String Quintet, and 2 Percussionists (Vienna, May 22, 1983); *Allegrasco* for Soprano Saxophone or Clarinet and Piano (Leicester, Dec. 7, 1983; also for Clarinet or Soprano Saxophone and Ensemble, Ghent, Nov. 10, 1986); 3 string quartets: No. 1, *Between the National and the Bristol* (Vienna, Oct. 8, 1985), No. 2 (Huddersfield, Dec. 1, 1990), and No. 3 (Cheltenham, July 15, 1998); *Viennese Dance No. 1* for Horn, Percussion, and Optional String Trio (1985; Paris, Nov. 20, 1986), and No. 4, *A Man in a Room, Gambling* for Pre-recorded Voice and String Quartet (London, April 17, 1992); *Sub Rosa* for Clarinet, Recorder, Vibraphone, Piano, Violin, and Double Bass (Ghent, Nov. 10, 1986); *The Old Tower of Löbenicht* for Violin or Viola, Bass Clarinet, Tenor Horn, Cello, Double Bass, 2 Percussionists, Piano, and Electric Guitar (London, June 13, 1987); *Alaric I or II* for Saxophone Quartet (Leicester, Oct. 3, 1989); *After the Requiem* for Electric Guitar, 2 Violas, and Cello (1990); *4 Elements* for Ensemble (1990; Oxford, Nov. 16, 1994); *A Man in a Room Gambling* for String Quartet and Prerecorded Voice (London, April 17, 1992); *Die Letzten Tage* for 2 Violins (Seville, April 19, 1992); *Aus den Letzten Tagen* for 2 Violins, Cello, Clarinet, 2 Percussionists, and Electric Keyboard (1992); *The Archangel Trip* for Ensemble (Bristol, April 18, 1993); *The North Shore* for Viola and Piano (Edinburgh, Oct. 19,1993; also for Viola, String Orch., Harp or Piano, and Percussion, 1994); *3 Elegies* for 9 Clarinets (1993); *Epilogue from Wonderlawn* for Viola, Cello, Double Bass, and Electric Guitar (Amsterdam, May 21, 1994; also for Viola, Cello, Electric Guitar or Piano or Harp, and Strings, 1995); *One last bar then Joe can sing* for Percussion Ensemble (London, Nov. 10, 1994); *The South Downs* for Cello and Piano (Bath, March 22, 1995); *In Nomine* for Viol Consort, after Purcell (London, May 2, 1995). **P i a n o :** *Out of Zaleski's Gazebo* for 2 Pianos, 6– or 8–Hands (Louvain, Dec. 12, 1977); *My First Homage* for 2 Pianos (N.Y., Nov. 11, 1978).

VOCAL: *On Photography* for Chorus, Harmonium, and Piano (1983); *Effarene* for Soprano, Mezzo-soprano, 2 Pianos, and 2 Percussionists (London, March 23, 1984); *Pico's Flight* for Soprano and Orch. (Egham, Feb. 25, 1986; also for Soprano and Chamber Orch., Leicester, Feb. 11, 1990); *Glorious Hill* for Male Alto, 2 Tenors, and Baritone (Lewes, Aug. 10, 1988); *Incipit Vita Nova* for Male Alto, Violin, Viola, and Cello (Leicester, April 1, 1989); *Cadman Requiem* for Alto, 2 Tenors, Baritone, 2 Violas, Cello, and Optional Double Bass (Lyons, May 17, 1989; also for Alto, 2 Tenors, Baritone, and Viol Consort, Nov. 17, 1997); *The Black River* for Soprano and Organ, after Jules Verne (Leicester, Jan. 22, 1991); *The White Lodge* for Low Mezzo-soprano, Electronics, and Tape (London, Sept. 21, 1991; also for Low Contralto, 2 Violins, Viola, Cello, 2 Double Basses, 2 Percussionists, and Electric Keyboard, Paris, Dec. 9, 1992); *The War in Heaven* for Soprano, Male Alto, Semi Chorus, Chorus, and Orch. (London, April 29, 1993); *The Adnan Songbook* for Soprano and Ensemble (1995–96; first complete perf., London, July 20, 1996); *The Island Chapel* for Mezzo-soprano, Electric Keyboard, and Cello (St. Ives, April 26, 1997; also for Mezzo-soprano and Chamber Orch., Turin, April 18, 1998); *Expressa Solis* for Men's Voices (Cambridge, July 29, 1997); *3 Poems of Cecco Angiolieri* for Soli and Chorus (Cambridge, Aug. 2, 1997); *And so ended Kant's travelling in this world* for Chorus (Cambridge, Aug. 2, 1997).—NS/LK/DM

Brymer, Jack, English clarinetist and teacher; b. South Shields, Jan. 27, 1915. He was educated at Goldsmiths' Coll., Univ. of London. Following service in the Royal Air Force in World War II (1940–45), he was principal clarinet in the Royal Phil. in London (1946–63), the BBC Sym. Orch. in London (1963–72), and the London Sym. Orch. (1972–87). He also was a member of the Wigmore, Prometheus, and London Baroque ensembles. Brymer was director of the London Wind Soloists, with which he championed the complete chamber music for winds of J.C. Bach, Haydn, Mozart, and Beethoven. He also was active as a mainstream jazz artist. He was a prof. at the Royal Academy of Music in London (1950–58), the Royal Military School of Music in Kneller Hall (1969–73), and at the Guildhall School of Music and Drama in London (from 1981). In 1960 he was made an Officer of the Order of the British Empire. He publ. the books *The Clarinet* (1976), an autobiography, *From Where I Sit* (1979), and *In the Orch.* (1987).—NS/LK/DM

Bryne, Albert or **Albertus,** English organist and composer; b. probably in London, c. 1621; d. Westminster, 1671. He was a pupil of John Tomkins, whom he succeeded as organist at St. Paul's Cathedral in 1638. In 1649 he lost his position with the coming of the Commonwealth, but regained it at the Restoration in 1660. From 1666 to 1668 he was organist at Westminster Abbey. He was a distinguished composer of harpsichord suites; he also wrote anthems and services.—LK/DM

Bryn-Julson, Phyllis (Mae), esteemed American soprano; b. Bowdon, N.Dak., Feb. 5, 1945. She studied piano, organ, violin, and voice at Concordia Coll., Moorehead, Minn.; then spent several summers at the Berkshire Music Center at Tanglewood and completed her studies at Syracuse Univ. On Oct. 28, 1966, she made her formal debut as soloist in Berg's *Lulu Suite* with the Boston Sym. Orch., and in 1976 made her operatic debut as Malinche in the U.S. premiere of Sessions's *Montezuma* in Boston. She often appears in recital with her husband, the organist Donald Sutherland. In addition to teaching at Kirkland-Hamilton Coll. in Clinton, N.Y., and at the Univ. of Md., she conducted master classes on both sides of the Atlantic. She is particularly renowned as a concert singer, at ease with all periods and styles of music.—NS/LK/DM

Bryson, Jeanie, jazz singer, daughter of **Dizzy Gillespie;** b. N.Y., March 10, 1958. Her mother was Connie Bryson, a songwriter and pianist; her father was the famous jazz trumpeter Dizzy Gillespie (her parents were never married). She was raised in East Brunswick, N.J., and began playing piano while in the first grade. She attended Livingston Coll. (Rutgers Univ.), where she studied harmony with Kenny Barron but focused primarily on ethnomusicology. From 1981 to 1987 she was a postal worker by day and singer by night. She went full-time as a vocalist in the late 1980s, and toured Europe in 1992–93. She made her solo recording debut in 1993, and continues to record and perform.

DISC.: *I Love Being Here with You* (1993); *Tonight I Need You So* (1994); *Some Cats Know* (1996).—LP

Bryson, Peabo (Pepo Bryson), one of the great singers of romantic soul, known for a smooth baritone and good looks; b. Greenville, S.C., April 13, 1951. Bryson was born into a musical family, and decided he wanted to sing by the age of four. His father left home when Bryson was five, and he lived with his mother and grandfather on the grandfather's farm, where he worked hard, claiming to have slaughtered his share of pigs and removed the chitterlings.

By the age of 14, Bryson was on the road as a backup singer for Al Freeman and the Upsetters. Three years later he worked as a backup singer for Mose Dillard and Textile Display. Dillard continuously introduced him from the stage as "Peabo," and Bryson decided to go with this new name. He was "discovered" singing with Dillard in an Atlanta club by Bang Records, and he worked there as a writer, producer, and arranger from 1970–76. In 1976, he finally released his own record, *Peabo*. The R&B chart success of the singles "I Can Make It Better" and "Underground Music" impressed Capitol records. They signed him that year.

Bryson's first two records with Capitol, *Reaching for the Sky* and *Crosswinds*, went gold. The title track "Reaching for the Sky," the classic "Feel the Fire," and his single from *Crosswinds*, "So into You," hit the R&B Top Ten. Bryson began recording a series of duets on Capitol, starting with "Gimme Some Time" with Natalie Cole. The album *Born to Love* went gold on the strength of his #16 duet with Roberta Flack, "Tonight I Celebrate My Love."

Bryson moved on to Elektra, taking his music in a more pop direction. "If Ever You're in My Arms Again" went #10 on the pop charts, topping the adult-

contemporary (AC) charts for a month, but Bryson was uncomfortable with the style. He also had a substantial R&B hit in "Without You," a duet with Regina Belle. However, the album *Take No Prisoners* tried to capitalize on prevailing musical trends, pairing Bryson with guitarist Eddie Van Halen. The album lost sight of Bryson's musical strengths, and he went to Columbia for one album. *Can You Stop the Rain* went gold and topped the R&B charts on the strength of the #1 title track and the Grammy nominated "Lost in the Night."

Yet it was his duets with women that brought Bryson to the pinnacle of his career, in the unlikely venue of Disney Films. He earned a best Pop Performance Grammy for his duet with Celine Dion on the 1993 #9 single "Beauty and the Beast" from the Disney film of the same name. The following year, he topped the charts with his duet with Regina Belle on "A Whole New World," which they performed over the end credits of the movie *Aladdin*; the song also won a Grammy award. The movie themes and other tunes comprised the album *Through the Fire*. Without question, 1994 was a banner year for the singer; he became the first artist in *Billboard* history to top four charts simultaneously: Contemporary Jazz for his recording with sax player Kenny G on the tune "By the time the Night Is Over"; Pop and Adult Contemporary charts with "A Whole New World"; and Classical Crossover for his recording of music from *The King and I*.

Following these successes, Bryson took a break from recording, thought that break marked one of the busiest periods of his career. He cowrote the theme to the soap opera *All My Children* as well as two songs from the *Barney* movie. He expanded his reach from the concert stage to the dramatic stage, first touring with the musical *Raisin*, then playing the Wizard in a touring company of *The Wiz*. In 1998, he appeared in the Mich. Opera Theater's 100th anniversary production of *Porgy and Bess*. In 1999, Bryson returned to the pop world, signing with Adult Contemporary label Private Music and releasing the album *Unconditional Love*.

DISC.: *Peabo* (1976); *Reaching for the Sky* (1977); *Crosswinds* (1978); *Paradise* (1980); *I Am Love* (1981); *Turn Back the Hands of Time* (1981); *Don't Play with Fire* (1982); *Straight from the Heart* (1984); *Peabo Bryson Collection* (1984); *Take No Prisoners* (1985); *Positive* (1988); *All My Love* (1989); *Can You Stop the Rain* (1993); *Through the Fire* (1994); *Unconditional Love* (1999). Natalie Cole: *We're the Best of Friends* (1979). Roberta Flack: *Live and More* (1980); *Born to Love* (1983).—HB

Bubalo, Rudolph, American composer and teacher; b. Duluth, Oct. 21, 1927. He studied at the Univ. of Minn. (1945–48), the Chicago Musical Coll. (B.M. in composition, 1954), the Univ. of Ill. (1952–53), Roosevelt Univ. (M.M. in composition, 1956), Case Western Reserve Univ. (1957–59), and Kent State Univ. (1965). His principal mentors were Becker, Jirak, Krenek, and Rieti. He was asst. director of the electronic music studio (1967–68) and a teacher (1968–69) at the Cleveland Inst. of Music, and also taught at Case Western Reserve Univ. (1968–69). From 1965 to 1967 he was a lecturer at Cleveland State Univ., where he was a prof. from 1969 until his retirement as a prof. emeritus in 1997. In 1970 he was awarded the Cleveland Arts Prize, and in 1978, 1984, and 1993–94 he held NEA grants.

WORKS: ORCH.: *Spacescape* for Orch. and Tape (1974); *Modules* for Large Jazz Orch. and Tape (1975); *Trajectories* for Orch. and Tape (1978); Clarinet Concerto (1982); *Symmetricality* for Piano and Orch. (1982); *Strata* for Chamber Orch. (1983); Concertino for Chamber Orch. (1984); *Offset I*, 3 pieces for Orch. and Synthesizers (1988); Cello Concerto (1991–92); Violin Concerto (1994–95). **CHAMBER:** *Theme and Variations* for Clarinet and String Quartet (1953); 2 string quartets (1954, 1956); *Divertimento* for Brass and Timpani (1955); 3 Pieces for Brass Quintet (1959); *Improvisations* for Piano (1961); 5 Pieces for Brass Quintet and Percussion (1964); *Valence II* for Clarinet, Bassoon, and Tape (1966); *Soundposts* for Violin, Clarinet, and Piano (1968); *Conicality* for Saxophone Quartet (1977); *Organic Concretion* for Alto Saxophone, Percussion, Organ, and Tape (1979).—**LK/DM**

Bucchi, Valentino, Italian composer and pedagogue; b. Florence, Nov. 29, 1916; d. Rome, May 9, 1976. He studied composition with Frazzi and Dallapiccola, and music history with Torrefranca at the Univ. of Florence, graduating in 1944; subsequently held teaching posts at the Florence Cons. (1945–52; 1954–57), the Venice Cons. (1952–54), and the Perugia Cons. (1957–58); was music director of the Accademia Filarmonica Romana (1958–60) and artistic director of the Teatro Comunale in Bologna (1963–65); was director of the Florence Cons. (1974–76). In his works, he continued the national Italian tradition of the musical theater, while attempting to modernize the polyphony of the Renaissance along the lines established by Malipiero.

WORKS: DRAMATIC: Opera: *Il giuoco del barone* (Florence, Dec. 20, 1944); *Il Contrabasso*; (Florence, May 20, 1954); *Una notte in Paradiso* (Florence, May 11, 1960); *Il coccodrillo* (Florence, May 9, 1970). **Ballet:** *Racconto siciliano* (Rome, Jan. 17, 1956); *Mirandolina* (Rome, March 12, 1957). **ORCH.:** *Ballata del silenzio* (1951); *Concerto lirico* for Violin and Strings (1958); *Concerto grottesco* for Double Bass and Strings (1967). **CHAMBER:** String Quartet (1956); Solo Clarinet Concerto (1969); *Ison* for Cello (1971). **VOCAL:** *Colloquio corale* for Narrator, Soloist, Chorus, and Orch. (1971).—**NS/LK/DM**

Bucci, Mark, American composer; b. N.Y., Feb. 26, 1924. He attended St. John's Univ. in N.Y. (1941–42); after private training in composition from Serly (1942–45), he continued his studies with Jacobi and Giannini at the Juilliard School of Music in N.Y. (B.S., 1951) and with Copland at the Berkshire Music Center in Tanglewood. In 1953–54 and 1957–58 he held Guggenheim fellowships. His modern, lyrical style is particularly effective in his stage works.

WORKS: DRAMATIC: Opera: *The Boor* (N.Y., Dec. 29, 1949); *The Dress* (N.Y., Dec. 8, 1953); *Sweet Betsy from Pike* (N.Y., Dec. 8, 1953); *Tale for a Deaf Ear* (Tanglewood, Aug. 5, 1957); *The Hero* (N.Y., Sept. 24, 1965); Midas (1981). **Musicals:** *Caucasian Chalk Circle* (1948); *The Thirteen Clocks* (1953); *The Adamses* (1956); *Time and Again* (1958); *The Girl from Outside* (1959); *Chain of Jade* (1960); *Pink Party Dress* (1960); *The Old Lady Shows Her Medals* (1960); *Cheaper by the Dozen* (1961); *Johnny Mishuga* (1961); *Our Miss Brooks* (1961); *The Best of Broadway* (1961); *Ask Any Girl* (1967); *Second Coming* (1976). **Incidental Music To:** *Cadenza* (1947); *Elmer and Lily* (1952); *Summer Afternoon* (1952); *The Western* (1954); *The Sorcerer's*

Apprentice (1969). **OTHER:** Film scores; Concerto for Kazoo and Orch. (1959; N.Y., March 26, 1960; renamed *Concerto for a Singing Instrument*); Flute Concerto; choral music; songs. —**NS/LK/DM**

Bucenus, Paulus, esteemed German composer who flourished in the second half of the 16th century. He matriculated at the Univ. of Greifswald in 1567. About 1570 he became Kantor at the Thorn Gymnasium; by 1576 he was Kantor at the Riga Cathedral. He was a notable composer of sacred music. His works include the *St. Matthew Passion* for 6 Voices (1578) and the 2 extensive collections *Tomi musici operis ecclesiae rigensis* (1583–84), which includes 24 masses, 100 motets, and various other liturgical pieces.

BIBL.: G. von Keussler, *P. Bucaenus* (Riga, 1931).—**LK/DM**

Buchanan, Isobel, Scottish soprano; b. Glasgow, March 15, 1954. She studied at the Royal Scottish Academy of Music and Drama in Glasgow, graduating in 1974. In 1976 she made her operatic debut as Pamina with the Australian Opera in Sydney, where she sang until 1978 when she made her Glyndebourne Festival debut in the same role and as Micaëla at the Vienna State Opera. In 1979 she appeared at London's Covent Garden and at the Santa Fe (N.Mex.) Opera. In 1981 she sang at the Aix-en-Provence Festival. In subsequent years, she appeared with various opera companies and toured widely as a concert artist. Among her most admired roles are Adina, Zerlina, Donna Elvira, Susanna, and Fiordiligi.—**NS/LK/DM**

Buchbinder, Rudolf, Austrian pianist; b. Leitmeritz, Dec. 1, 1946. He studied with Bruno Seidlhofer at the Vienna Academy of Music; in 1965 he made a tour of North and South America; in 1966 he won a special prize awarded at the Van Cliburn Competition; then made a tour with the Vienna Phil., and also appeared as a soloist in Paris, Milan, Madrid, and London. In 1975 he made a tour of Japan and the U.S. with the Vienna Sym. Orch.; in addition, he taught piano at the Basel Academy of Music. He subsequently toured extensively, appearing as a soloist with leading orchs and as a recitalist.—**NS/LK/DM**

Buchla, Donald (Frederick), American electronic-instrument designer and builder, composer, and performer; b. Southgate, Calif., April 17, 1937. After studying physics at the Univ. of Calif. at Berkeley (B.A., 1961), he became active with the San Francisco Tape Music Center, where in 1966 he installed the first Buchla synthesizer. That same year he founded Buchla Associates in Berkeley for the manufacture of synthesizers. In addition to designing and manufacturing electronic instruments, he also installed electronic-music studios at the Musikhögskolan in Stockholm and at IRCAM in Paris, among other institutions. In 1975 he became co-founder of the Electric Weasel Ensemble, a live electronic-music group, and in 1978 he became co-director of the Artists' Research Collective in Berkeley. He held a Guggenheim fellowship in 1978.

WORKS: With electronic instruments: *Cicada Music* for some 2,500 Cicadas (1963); *5 Video Mirrors* for Audience of 1 or More (1966); *Anagnorisis* for 1 Performer and Voice (1970); *Harmonic Pendulum* for Buchla Series 200 Synthesizer (1972); *Garden* for 3 Performers and Dancer (1975); *Keyboard Encounter* for 2 Pianos (1976); *Q* for 14 Instruments (1979); *Silicon Cello* for Amplified Cello (1979); *Consensus Conduction* for Buchla Series 300 Synthesizer and Audience (1981); also an orchestration of D. Rosenboom's *How Much Better If Plymouth Rock Had Landed on the Pilgrims* for 2 Buchla Series 300 Synthesizers (1969). **—NS/LK/DM**

Buchner, Hans, German organist; b. Ravensburg, Württemberg, Oct. 26, 1483; d. probably in Constance, mid-Feb. 1538. His father, an organist, gave Buchner his first instruction. He became organist at the Cathedral of Constance on June 19, 1506, and was given permanent employment in 1512. His magnum opus was a *Fundamentum*, a manual for composition and improvisation on the organ (1551).**—NS/LK/DM**

Buchner, Philipp Friedrich, German organist; b. Wertheim, Sept. 11, 1614; d. Würzburg, March 23, 1669. He was a chorister in Frankfurt am Main, where he then served as organist in the Barfüsserkirche (1634–36). Subsequently he was engaged as Kapellmeister in Kraków (c. 1637–47). In 1648 he was in Mainz. His *Concerti ecclesiastici* was publ. in 2 books (Venice, 1642, 1644); he also wrote instrumental music for violins, violas, and cembalo.**—NS/LK/DM**

Bucht, Gunnar, Swedish composer, musicologist, and pedagogue; b. Stocksund, Aug. 5, 1927. He studied composition with Blomdahl (1947–51) and also took courses in musicology at the Univ. of Uppsala (Ph.D., 1953). He later pursued training in composition with Orff in Germany (1954), Petrassi in Italy (1954–55), and Deutsch in Paris (1961–62). He taught at the Univ. of Stockholm (1965–69), and then was in the diplomatic service as cultural attaché at the Swedish Embassy in Bonn (1970–73). From 1975 to 1985 he was a prof. of composition at the Stockholm Musikhögskolan, serving as its director from 1987 to 1993. From 1963 to 1969 he was chairman of the Soc. of Swedish Composers. In 1964 he was elected to membership in the Royal Swedish Academy of Music in Stockholm. His music retains traditional forms while adopting diverse modern techniques.

WORKS: D R A M A T I C: *Tronkrävarna* (The Pretenders), opera (1961–64; Stockholm, Sept. 10, 1966); *Jerikos murar* (The Walls of Jericho), opera-oratorio (1966–67; reworked as an electronic piece). **ORCH.:** *Introduction and Allegro* for Strings (1950); *Meditation* for Piano and Orch. (1950); 12 syms.: No. 1 (1952; Swedish Radio, Dec. 6, 1953), No. 2 (1953), No. 3 (1954; Swedish Radio, April 17, 1955), No. 4 (1957–58; Stockholm, April 3, 1959), No. 5 (1960; Stockholm, Jan. 14, 1962), No. 6 (1961–62; Stockholm, Nov. 20, 1963), No. 7 (1970–71; Norrköping, March 26, 1972), No. 8 (1982–83; Stockholm, Sept. 13, 1984), No. 9 (1988–90; Stockholm, Oct. 31, 1990), No. 10, *Sinfonie gracieuse ou l'Apothéose de Berwald* (1993), No. 11 (1993–94), and No. 12, *Mouvements sonores et accentués* (1997); 2 cello concertos (1954; 1989–90); *Symphonic Fantasy* (1955); *Divertimento*

(1955–56); *Couplets et Refrains* (1960); *Strangaspel* for Strings (1965); *Winter Organ* (1974); *Journées Oubliées* (1975; Stockholm, April 25, 1976); *Au delà* (1977; Stockholm, March 14, 1979); Violin Concerto (1978; Stockholm, Nov. 5, 1980); *The Big Band—and After* (1979; Swedish Radio, April 3, 1981); *Georgica* (1980; Swedish Radio, Feb. 11, 1983); *Ein Clairobscur* for Chamber Orch. (1980–81); Sinfonia Concertante for Flute, Viola, Harp, and Orch. (1981–82; Norrköping, Jan. 13, 1983); *Fresques mobiles* (1985–86; Swedish Radio, Jan. 28, 1989); *Tonend bewegte Formen* (1987); *Konsert för Arholma* for Strings (1989); Piano Concerto (1994); *Rörelser i rummet* (1996); *Concerto de Marle* for Viola and Orch. (1998). **CHAMBER:** String Quintet (1949–50); 3 string quartets (1951, 1959, 1997); *5 Bagatelles* for String Quartet (1953); Sonata for Piano and Percussion (1955); *Quintetto amichevole* for Winds (1976); *A huit mains* for Flute, Violin, Cello, and Harpsichord (1976); *Bald från mitt gulsippeänge* for Clarinet and Piano (1985; also for Harpsichord, 1988); *Unter vollem Einsatz* for Organ and 5 Percussion (1986–87); *Coup sur coup* for 6 Percussionists (1995). **P i a n o :** *Theme and Variations* (1949); 2 sonatas (1951, 1959). **VOCAL:** *La fine della diaspora* for Chorus and Orch. (1958; Stockholm, Oct. 4, 1963); *Eine lutherische Messe* for Soloists, Mixed and Children's Choruses, and Orch. (1972–73); *Music for Lau* for Children's Chorus, Winds, Percussion, Double Basses, and Tape (1974–75); *Panta rei* for Soloists, Chorus, and Orch. (1998–99); cantatas; choruses; songs.**—NS/LK/DM**

Büchtger, Fritz, German composer; b. Munich, Feb. 14, 1903; d. in an automobile accident in Starnberg, Dec. 26, 1978. He was a student of Beer-Walbrunn and Waltershausen at the Munich Akadamie der Tonkunst (1923–26). He was active as a choral conductor and teacher, and also in the promotion of contemporary music until the advent of the Nazi regime, when he was compelled to change course. After the collapse of the Third Reich, he again embraced the cause of contemporary music, helping to found the Studio for New Music in Munich in 1948. In 1953 he became president of the Musikalischen Jugend Deutschlands, and was a prominent figure in music education. In 1953 he received the music prize of the City of Munich and in 1977 the Schwabinger Kunstpreis. In his music, Büchtger developed a dodecaphonic technique which he adroitly utilized even in his sacred music.

WORKS: D R A M A T I C: *O Mensch, gib acht!*, Kalenderspiel (1939); *Der Spielhansl*, musical play (1946). **ORCH.:** *Muzik zu einer Feier* for Strings (1932); *Musik* for Little Orch. (1935); *Kleines festliches Vorspiel* (1939); Concerto for Strings (1952); *Studien* (1956); Concerto for Orchestra (1957); Concertino I for Oboe, Violin, Cello, and Strings (1960) and II for Piano, Winds, Strings, Vibraphone, and Percussion (1962); Concerto for Violin and Strings (1963); *Stufen* (1966); *Musik* for Strings (1967); *Schichten-Bögen* (1969); *Ascensio* (1973). **CHAMBER:** 6 string quartets (1948, 1958, 1967, 1969, 1972, 1973); *Strukturen* for Nonet (1968); *Stück* for Oboe and String Quartet (1971); Quartet for Violin, Viola, Cello, and Piano (1972); *Nyktodia* for Wind Octet (1972); Piano Trio (1974); piano pieces; organ music. **VOCAL: C a n t a t a s :** *Der Name des Menschen* for Chorus and Orch. (1931); *Flamme* for Baritone, Chorus, and Orch. (1932); *Bergfahrt* for Baritone, Men's Chorus, Piano, and Small Orch. (1939); *Es werden Zeichen geschehen* for Chorus and Small Orch. (1969). **O r a t o r i o s :** *Der weisse Reiter* for Baritone, Chorus, and Orch. (1948); *Das gläserne Meer* for Baritone, Chorus, and Orch. (1953); *Die Auferstehung* for Chorus and Orch. or Strings and Organ (1954); *Die Verklärung* for Baritone,

Women's Voices, and Strings (1956); *Die Himmelfahrt Christi* for Baritone, Chorus, and Orch. or Strings and Organ (1957); *Pfingsten* for Baritone, Chorus, and Orch. (1957); *Das Weihnachtsoratorium* for Voices, Flute, Oboe, and Strings (1959); *Johannes der Taufer* for Baritone, Chorus, and Orch. (1961). O t h e r : *Serenata im Walde* for Men's Chorus and Orch. (1935); *Hymnen an das Licht* for Baritone or Medium Woman's Voice and Orch. (1938); *Drusus* for Soloists, Chorus, and Orch. (1943); *Das Gesicht des Hesekiel* for Baritone, Women's Voices, and 15 Instruments (1972); numerous choruses and solo songs.

BIBL.: L. Wismeyer, *F. B.* (Regensburg, 1963); A. Ott, ed., *F. B. 1973* (Munich, 1974; new ed., 1988, as *F. B. 1903–1978*); K. Hübler, *F. B. und die neue Musik in München* (Munich, 1983); K.-R. Danler et al., *F. B.* (Tutzing, 1989).—**NS/LK/DM**

Buck, Dudley, American organist, pedagogue, and composer; b. Hartford, Conn., March 10, 1839; d. West Orange, N.J., Oct. 6, 1909. He began piano lessons at age 16. After attending Trinity Coll. in Hartford (1855–57), he pursued studies at the Leipzig Cons. with Plaidy and Moscheles (piano), Schneider (organ), Hauptmann (composition), and Rietz (instrumentation). Returning to Hartford in 1862, he was active as a church organist and music teacher. After a Chicago sojourn (1869–71), he went to Boston as organist of the Music Hall and as a teacher at the New England Cons. of Music. In 1875 he became asst. conductor of the Theodore Thomas Orch. in N.Y. He subsequently served as organist and choirmaster at the Holy Trinity Church, and as music director of Brooklyn's Apollo Club until 1903. In 1898 he was elected to membership in the National Inst. of Arts and Letters. He publ. *Illustrations in Choir Accompaniment with Hints in Registration* (N.Y., 1877) and *The Influence of the Organ in History* (London, 1882). In his day, he was particularly successful as a composer of sacred music, organ pieces, and secular cantatas.

WORKS: D R A M A T I C : *Deseret, or A Saint's Affliction,* comic opera (N.Y., Oct. 11, 1880); *Serapis,* opera (1889). **ORCH.:** *In Springtime,* sym. (not extant); *Romanza* for 4 Horns and Orch. (c. 1875); *Marmion,* overture (1878); *Festival Overture on...The Star-Spangled Banner* (c. 1879); *Canzonetta et bolera* for Violin and Orch. (1887; also for Violin and Piano). **CHAMBER:** *Concert Variations on The Last Rose of Summer* for String Quintet (1875); *Romanza and Scherzo* for 6 Instruments (1883); *3 Fantasias for Clarinet and Piano.* O r g a n : *Grand Sonata* (1866); *Concert Variations on The Star-Spangled Banner* (1868); *Impromptu-pastorale* (1868); *At Evening* (1871); *Variations on a Scotch Air* (1871); *Sonata No. 2* (1877); *Variations on The Last Rose of Summer* (1877); *Variations on Old Folks at Home* (1888). **VOCAL: S a c r e d :** *The 46th Psalm* for Solo Voices, Chorus, and Orch. (1872); 4 cantatas: *The Story of the Cross* (1892), *The Triumph of David* (1892), *The Coming of the King* (1895), and *Christ, the Victor* (1896); 55 anthems; choruses; etc. S e c u l a r : Numerous cantatas, including *The Legend of Don Munio* (1874), *The Centennial Meditation of Columbia* (1876), *Scenes from The Golden Legend* (1879), *The Voyage of Columbus* (1885), and *The Light of Asia* (1886); various choruses; songs.

BIBL.: *D. B.: A Complete Bibliography* (N.Y., 1910); W. Gallo, *The Life and Church Music of D. B.* (diss., Catholic Univ. of America, 1968).—**NS/LK/DM**

Buck, Sir Percy Carter, English organist and teacher; b. London, March 25, 1871; d. there, Oct. 3, 1947.

He studied at the Guildhall School of Music and the Royal Coll. of Music in London; subsequently served as a church organist. From 1901 to 1927 he was music director at the Harrow School; was prof. of music at Trinity Coll. in Dublin (1910–20) and at the Univ. of London (1925–37); also taught at the Royal Coll. of Music in London. He was knighted in 1937. His works include an overture for Orch., *Coeur de Lion*; String Quartet; Piano Quintet; sonatas; piano pieces; etc. He was the author of *Ten Years of University Music in Oxford* (1894; with Mee and Woods); *Unfigured Harmony* (1911); *Organ Playing* (1912); *First Year at the Organ* (1912); *The Organ: A Complete Method for the Study of Technique and Style; Acoustics for Musicians* (1918); *The Scope of Music* (1924); *Psychology for Musicians* (1944); also was ed. of the introductory vol. and vols. I and II of the second edition of the *Oxford History of Music.*—**NS/LK/DM**

Bücken, Ernst, eminent German musicologist; b. Aachen, May 2, 1884; d. Overath, near Cologne, July 28, 1949. He studied musicology at the Univ. of Munich with Sandberger and Kroyer; also took courses in composition with Courvoisier; received his Ph.D. there in 1912 with the diss. *Anton Reicha; Sein Leben und seine Kompositionen* (publ. in Munich, 1912); completed his Habilitation at the Univ. of Cologne in 1920 with his *Der heroische Stil in der Oper* (publ. in Leipzig, 1924); was a prof. there from 1925 to 1945; then retired to Overath. His elucidation of musical styles remains an important achievement in his work as a musicologist; as such, he ed. the monumental Handbuch der Musikwissenschaft in 10 vols., which began publication in 1927; for this series he contributed *Musik des Rokokos und der Klassik* (1927), *Die Musik des 19. Jahrhunderts bis zur Moderne* (1929–31), and *Geist und Form im musikalischen Kunstwerk* (1929–32); he was also editor of the series Die Grossen Meister der Musik from 1932. His further writings include *Tagebuch der Gattin Mozarts* (Munich, 1915); *München als Musikstadt* (Leipzig, 1923); *Führer und Probleme der neuen Musik* (Cologne, 1924); *Musikalische Charakterköpfe* (Leipzig, 1924); ed. *Handbuch der Musikerziehung* (Potsdam, 1931); *Ludwig van Beethoven* (Potsdam, 1934); *Richard Wagner* (Potsdam, 1934; 2nd ed., 1943); *Deutsche Musikkunde* (Potsdam, 1935); *Musik aus deutscher Art* (Cologne, 1936); *Musik der Nationen* (Leipzig, 1937; 2nd ed., rev. as *Geschichte der Musik,* ed. by J. Volckers, 1951); ed. *Richard Wagner: Die Hauptschriften* (Leipzig, 1937); *Das deutsche Lied: Probleme und Gestalten* (Hamburg, 1939); *Robert Schumann* (Cologne, 1940); *Wörterbuch der Musik* (Leipzig, 1940); *Musik der Deutschen: Eine Kulturgeschichte der deutschen Musik* (Cologne, 1941); *Wolfgang Amadeus Mozart: Schöpferische Wandlungen* (Hamburg, 1942); *Richard Strauss* (Kevelaar, 1949).—**NS/LK/DM**

Buckley, Emerson, American conductor; b. N.Y., April 14, 1916; d. Miami, Nov. 17, 1989. He studied at Columbia Univ. (B.A., 1936), where he began his career as conductor of its Grand Opera (1936–38). He subsequently was conductor of the Palm Beach (Fla.) Sym. Orch. (1938–41), the N.Y. City Sym. Orch. (1941–42), the San Carlo Opera in N.Y. (1943–45), and WOR Radio in N.Y. (1945–54). In 1950 he became music director of the

Miami Opera, and from 1973 to 1985 he was its artistic director and resident conductor; also served as music director of the Fort Lauderdale Sym. Orch. (later the Phil. Orch. of Florida) from 1963 to 1986. In 1963 he received the Alice M. Ditson Award for conducting. He was principally known as a favorite conductor on tour with Pavarotti. With his silver hair and goatee he cut a striking figure when he appeared in Pavarotti's film *Yes, Giorgio!* (1982); the film was unsuccessful, but Buckley's appearance produced an impression. He was also the conductor in a film documentary about Pavarotti, entitled *A Distant Harmony.*—NS/LK/DM

Buckley, John, Irish composer; b. Templeglantine, County Limerick, Dec. 19, 1951. He studied flute with Doris Keogh (1969–71) and composition with James Wilson (1971–75) at the Royal Irish Academy of Music in Dublin, and subsequently studied composition with Alun Hoddinott in Cardiff (1978–79). Buckley taught briefly in Ireland before becoming a full-time composer in 1982. In 1984 he was elected a member of Ireland's state-sponsored academy of creative artists, Aosdána. His works were performed at ISCM festivals in 1985, 1994, and 1999. Buckley's music explores timbral and dynamic properties of chromatically tonal music.

WORKS (all first perf. in Dublin): OPERA: *The Words upon the Window-Pane,* chamber opera (Oct. 17, 1991). ORCH.: *Taller than Roman Spears* (1977; rev. 1986); *Fornocht do chonac thú,* ballet music (1980); Concerto for Chamber Orch. (1981); Sym. No. 1 (1983–88; June 3, 1988); Organ Concerto (June 26, 1992); Concerto for Alto Saxophone and Strings (1997); *A Mirror into the Light* (1999). CHAMBER: Sonata for English Horn and Piano (1973; also for Saxophone and Piano, 1990); *Sequence* for Clarinet, Bassoon, and Piano (1974); 2 brass quintets (1974, 1986); Wind Quintet (1976; rev. 1985); *"Why Not?" Mr. Berio* for Trombone and Piano (1977); Sonata for Solo Violin (1983); *Boireann* for Flute and Piano (1983); *A Summer Ghost* for Flute, Cello, and Piano (1986); 2 guitar sonatas (1989, 1998); Sonata for Solo Horn (1993); *In Lines of Dazzling Light* for Clarinet, Bassoon, Horn, Violin, and Piano (1995); Saxophone Quartet (1996). KEYBOARD: P i a n o : *Islands* (1979); *Winter Music* (1988). O r g a n : *At the Round Earths Imagin'd Corners* (1985). VO-CAL: *Auburn Elegy* for Chorus, 2 Flutes, and Clarinet (1973); *A Thin Halo of Blue* for Chorus, Narrator, Tape, and Orch. (1990–91); *De Profundis* for Soloists, Chorus, and Small Orch. (1993; March 25, 1994); *Rivers of Paradise* for 2 Speakers and Orch. (1993); *Maynooth Te Deum* for Soloists, Mixed Chorus, Chamber and Men's Choruses, and Orch. (Nov. 16, 1995). —LK/DM

Buckner, Milt(on Brent), jazz pianist, organist, vibraphonist, arranger; b. St. Louis, July 10, 1915; d. Chicago, July 27, 1977. He was orphaned at the age of nine and raised in Detroit. He received musical education from his uncle, trombonist John Tobias. In 1930 he did first arrangements for Earl Walton's Band. He studied at the Detroit Inst. of Arts for two years, and during this time gigged with the Harlem Aristocrats, Mose Burke, and the Dixie Whangdoodles; he later played and arranged for McKinney's Cotton Pickers. He worked mainly in Detroit throughout the 1930s with various local bands. He is said to have pioneered the "locked hands" piano style, both hands playing parallel

chords, as early as 1934. He joined Lionel Hampton in November 1941 as assistant director and staff arranger (he wrote "Hamp's Boogie Woogie" and many more), and remained with Hampton until September 1948. He left to form his own sextet, and later led his own big band, before rejoining Lionel Hampton from July 1950 until August 1952. He then switched primarily to playing Hammond organ, often performing in a trio setting, from the early 1950s through the end of his career. During the late 1960s and 1970s, he made several tours of Europe. Besides working on his own, he also partnered during this period with Illinois Jacquet, Jo Jones, and Buddy Tate.

His brother, Ted (Theodore Guy) Buckner (b. St. Louis, Dec. 14, 1913; d. April 12, 1976), was an alto and soprano saxophonist best remembered for his long stint with the Jimmie Lunceford band from 1937 to 1943.

DISC.: "Hamp's Boogie Woogie" (1941); *Milt Buckner Piano* (1946); *Rockin' Hammond* (1956); *Milt Buckner* (1967); *Play Chords* (1973).—JC/LP

Buckner, Thomas, leading American baritone, composer, and producer; b. N.Y., Aug. 13, 1941. After brief studies at Yale Univ., he took both B.A. (1964) and M.A. (1965) degrees in English literature at the Univ. of Santa Clara in Calif.; also took courses in linguistics at Stanford Univ. He then devoted himself to vocal training, numbering among his mentors W.A. Mathieu, Martial Singher, Alden Gilchrist, Marion Cooper, and Raymond Beegle; also studied Indian music with Ali Akbar Kahn at the American Soc. for Eastern Arts in Berkeley, Calif. (1967–67). Buckner was active in Berkeley from 1967 to 1983, where he founded and directed the 1750 Arch Concerts (1972–80) and 1750 Arch Records (1973–83); he also was co-founder/director (with Robert Hughes) of the 23–piece Arch Ensemble, which specialized in 20th-century music. From 1989 he curated the World Music Institute's "Interpretations" series in N.Y. While Buckner's repertoire spans the ages, he has become a stalwart proponent of the avant-garde, appearing in first performances of works by Annea Lockwood, Henry Threadgill, Somei Satoh, Jin Hi Kim, and David Behrman, among many others; he is known particularly for his lengthy association with Robert Ashley, in whose *Perfect Lives* trilogy (*Atalanta [Acts of God]* [1982], and *eL/Aficionado* [1987] and *Improvement [Don Leaves Linda]* [1984–85] from *Now Eleanor's Idea*) he created critically acclaimed leading roles. In 1995 he performed the leading role in David First's opera *Manhattan Book of the Dead.* Through these and other performances, including a number of noteworthy recitals in N.Y. and frequent appearances with the improvisational group "Act of Finding," the experimental group "Roscoe Mitchell New Chamber Ensemble," and the pianist Joseph Kubera, Buckner has earned the critical sobriquet "*the* voice of the Downtown (N.Y.) new music scene." Among his many recordings are 2 solo compilations, *Full Voice Spectrum* (1992) and *Sign of Our Times* (1995), both featuring works written especially for him, as well as *Pilgrimage* (1995; with the Roscoe Mitchell New Chamber Ensemble") and *Act of Finding* (1995; with Ratzo B. Harris, Bruce Arnold, and Tom Hamilton). As a composer, Buckner creates primarily structured improvisations, in both solo (*Resonances*, 1995) and ensemble (*In Moments of Great Passion* for Improvising Baritone and String Orch., after John Ralston Saul's *Voltaire's Bastards*; N.Y., Dec. 19, 1995) settings. —**NS/LK/DM**

Buczek, Barbara, Polish composer; b. Kraków, Jan. 9, 1940; d. there, Jan. 21, 1993. She spent her entire career in Kraków, where she studied piano with Kazimierz Mirski and was a student of Maria Bilińska-Riegerowa at the music school. She then pursued training with Ludwik Stefanski (piano diploma, 1965) and Boguslaw Schaeffer (composition diploma, 1974) at the Academy of Music, where she later served on the faculty.

WORKS: ORCH.: *3 Pieces* for Chamber Orch. (1968); *Metaphonie* (1970); *2 Impressions* (1970); *Anekumena*, concerto for 89 Instruments (1974; Warsaw, Sept. 25, 1975); *Labirynt* (1974); *Assemblage* for Alto Flute and Strings (1975); *Simplex* (1976); Violin Concerto (1979; Turin, June 13, 1986); *Dikolon* (Salzburg, May 11, 1985); Concerto for Cello, Chorus, and Orch. (1985); *Les sons esoteriques* for Flute, Orch., and Tape (1985; Salzburg, Aug. 5, 1989); *Fantasmagorie* for Chamber Orch. (1992). **CHAMBER:** 2 string quartets (1968; *Transgressio*, 1985); Wind Quintet (1969; Kraków, April 3, 1980); Quintet for Saxophone, Flute, Horn, Cello, and Vibraphone (1971); Sextet for Violin, Flute, Soprano, Cello, and 2 Pianos (1974); Duodecet for Strings (1976; Gdańsk, Jan. 20, 1984); *Eidos I* for Violin (1977), *II* for Tuba (1977; also for Tuba and Piano, 1984), *III* for Bassoon (1979), and *IV* for Piano (1992); *Hypostase I*, quintet for Soprano, Flute, Vibraphone, Cello, and Saxophone (1978; Kraków, Feb. 4, 1980), *II* for Violin Sextet (1985; Salzburg, June 27, 1990), and *III* for Mezzo-soprano and Chamber Group (1985); *Primus inter pares* for Flute, Saxophone, Clarinet, Trombone, Violin, and Double Bass (1985). **VOCAL:** Vocal Concerto for 12 Voices (1969); *Desunion* for Soprano and Double Bass (1982); *Motet* for Reciters, Baritone, Instruments, and Tape (1984).—**NS/LK/DM**

Buczynski, Walter (Joseph), Canadian composer, pianist, and teacher; b. Toronto, Dec. 17, 1933. After studies with Earle Moss (piano) and Ridout (theory) at the Royal Cons. of Music of Toronto, he had lessons in composition with Milhaud and Charles Jones at the Aspen (Colo.) Music School (summer 1956); he then studied piano with Lhévinne in N.Y. (1958–59) and Drzewiecki in Warsaw (1959, 1961), and composition with Boulanger in Paris (1960, 1962). He taught piano and theory at the Royal Cons. of Music of Toronto (from 1962), and piano, theory, and composition at the Univ. of Toronto (from 1969); until 1977 he also pursued an active career as a pianist. His early penchant for satirical and humorous expression eventually mellowed as he pursued a more lyrical but still adventuresome path.

WORKS: DRAMATIC: *Mr. Rhinoceros and His Musicians*, children's opera (1965); *Do Re Mi*, children's opera (1967); *From the Buczynski Book of the Living*, chamber opera (1972); *Naked at the Opera*, chamber opera (1978). **ORCH.:** *Beztitula* for Piano and Orch. (1964); *4 Arabesques and Dance* for Flute and Strings (1964); *3 Thoughts* (1964); *Triptych* (1964); *4 Movements* for Piano and Strings (1969); *7 Miniatures* (1970); *A Work for Dance* (1970); *Zeroing In No. 2 (Distractions and Then)* (1971), *No. 4 (Innards and Outards)* for Soprano, Piano, and Orch. (1972), and *No. 3* for String Quartet and Orch. (1973); *3 against Many* for Flute, Clarinet, Bassoon, and Orch. (1973); *Ars Romantica* for Chamber

Orch. (1976); *Lyric I* for Piano and Orch. (1976), *II* for Piano and Orch. (1983), *III* for Cello and Orch. (1984), *V* for Oboe and Strings (1988), and *VII* for Viola and Orch. (1991); *Rhapsody* for 2 Horns and Strings (1976); *3 Serenades* (1976); *Legends* for Strings (1976); Piano Concerto (1979); Violin Concerto (1980); *Rhapsody* for 2 Horns and Strings (1976); *3 Serenades* (1976); *Legends* for Strings (1976); Piano Concerto (1979); Violin Concerto (1980); *Fantasy on Themes from the Past* for Accordion and Strings (1980; rev. 1984); *Prayer and Dance* for Clarinet, String Quartet, and String Orch. (1982); Sym. (1986). **CHAMBER:** Trio for Violin, Cello, and Piano (1954); *Divertimento* for Violin, Cello, Clarinet, and Bassoon (1957); *Elegy: In Memoriam Kathleen Parlow* for Violin and Piano (1963); *Trio/67* for Mandolin, Clarinet, and Cello (1967); Duo for Double Bass and Piano (1974); *Quartet/74* for Flute, Clarinet, Cello, and Harpsichord (1974); Sextet for Flute, Clarinet, Violin, Cello, and 2 Percussion (1974); *Trio/74* for Harp, Bass Clarinet, and Double Bass (1974); *Olympics '76* for Brass Quintet (1976); *Sonata Belsize* for Accordion (1977); Violin Sonata (1979); *...Winds...* for Flute, Cello, Celesta, Harpsichord, and Percussion (1982); Cello Sonata (1982); Sonata for Violin and Cello (1983); Piano Quintet (1984); *Gemini Quartet* for Oboe, Violin, Viola, and Cello (1986); *Divertissement No. 2* for Harp, Accordion, and Vibraphone (1987) and *No. 3: Impressions and Memories* for Percussion Quintet (1988); String Quartet No. 3 with Soprano (1987). **P i a n o :** *Aria and Toccata* (1963); *Amorphus* (1964); Suite (1964); 3 sonatas (1967, 1972, 1991); *Zeroing In* for Pianist-Speaker and Tape (1971) and *No. 5 (Dictionary of Mannerisms)* (1972); *27 Pieces for a 27 Minute Show* (1973); *Zeroing In—Zeroing Out* for Piano and Tape (1977); *Monogram* (1978); *Lyric Ii* (1984); *August Collection*, 24 preludes (1987); *Mosaics* (1988). **VOCAL:** *Mass with Outside Prayers* for Chorus and Wind Quintet (1976); *The Tales of Nanabozho* for Speaker and Wind Quintet (1976); *Psalm 51* for Soloists, Chorus, and Orch. (1977); *Missa brevis* for Chorus, String Quartet, and Brass Quartet (1977); *Resurrection II* for Baritone, Clarinet, Violin, Viola, Cello, Accordion, and Percussion (1980); *Songs of War* for Tenor, Baritone, and Piano (1983); *Remembrances of Latin Texts* for Chorus (1988).—**NS/LK/DM**

Budd, Harold (Montgomery), highly original American composer, pianist, and poet; b. Los Angeles, May 24, 1936. He grew up in Los Angeles and the Mojave desert town of Victorville. He studied composition and acoustics with Gerald Strang and Aurelio de la Vega at San Fernando Valley State Coll. (later Calif. State Univ. at Northridge; B.A., 1963) and with Dahl at the Univ. of Southern Calif. in Los Angeles (M.Mus., 1966). From 1970 to 1976 he taught at the Calif. Inst. of the Arts. He received NEA grants in 1974 and 1979. In 1992 he made a tour of Europe with Bill Nelson; another followed, in 1994, with Hector Zazou. Budd's compositions from the early 1970s, including his *Madrigals of the Rose Angel* (1972) for Topless Female Chorus, Harp, Percussion, Celesta, and Lights, challenged the avant-garde with their prettiness and surface decoration. By the early 1980s, he began to use the recording studio as an instrument, producing 7 albums in rapid succession, including two on his own Cantil label, *The Serpent (In Quicksilver)* (1981), and *Abandoned Cities* (1984), as well as collaborations with Brian Eno, *The Plateaux of Mirror* (1980) and *The Pearl* (1984), and The Cocteau Twins, *The Moon And The Melodies* (1986). His later *Lovely Thunder* (1986), co-produced with Michael Hoenig, was his last album before departing for London, where he resided from 1987 to 1990; *The White Arcades* (1988) is his sole recorded work as an expatriate. He also created two gallery installations, including "Blue Room with Flowers and Gong" for Los Angeles's Inst. of Contemporary Art, for which his *Gypsy Violin* (1985) was composed. Upon his return to the U.S., Budd composed the pieces comprising his *By the Dawn's Early Light* (1991), a recording which signals both his departure from studio-produced albums and a return to more formal modes of composition: through-composed text settings and predetermined structures. The genesis of this work, scored for Guitar, Pedal Steel Guitar, Viola, Harp, and Voice, is a journal of poems Budd had written which were sparked to life by his discovery in Japan of a book of pastels and "poems" by the Italian artist Sandro Chia, which had a profound effect. Other recordings of the period include *The Pavilion of Dreams* (1978), *Lovely Thunder* (1986), *Music For 3 Pianos* (1992; with Ruben Garcia and Daniel Lentz), *She Is A Phantom* (1994), *Through The Hill* (1994; with Andy Partridge), *Glyph* (1995; with Hector Zazou), *Walk Into My Voice: American Beat Poetry* (1995; with Lentz), and the critically acclaimed *Luxa* (1996).

Although Budd is best known for his recordings, his career as a composer predates his recorded works by nearly two decades. To this earlier period belong such minimalist scores as *Analogies from Rothko* for Orch. (1964); *September Music* (1967); *November* (1967); *Black Flowers*, "quiet chamber ritual for 4 performers," to be staged in semidarkness on the threshold of visibility and audibility (1968); *Intermission Piece* (1968); *One Sound* for String Quartet glissando (1968); *Mangus Colorado* for Amplified Gongs (1969; Buffalo, Feb. 4, 1970); *Lovely Thing* for Piano, with instructions to the player:"Select a chord—if in doubt call me (in lieu of performance) at 213–662–7819 for spiritual advice" (Memphis, Tenn., Oct. 23, 1969); *Lovely Thing* for Strings (1969); *California 99* (1969); *The Candy-Apple Revision* (1970; an unspecified D-flat major chord); and *Lirio*, a 24–hour marathon for Solo Gong (1971).—**NS/LK/DM**

Budden, Julian (Midforth), English musicologist; b. Holylake, Cheshire, April 9, 1924. He was educated at Queen's Coll., Oxford (B.A., 1948; M.A., 1951) and the Royal Coll. of Music, London (B.Mus., 1955); from 1951 he worked for the BBC, serving as a producer for music programs (1955–70), chief producer for opera (1970–76), and music organizer for external services (1976–83). His studies of 19th-century Italian opera are important; especially valuable is *The Operas of Verdi* (3 vols., London, 1973–81; rev. ed., 1992). He also publ. the biography *Verdi* (London, 1985; rev. ed., 1993). In 1991 he received the Order of the British Empire. —**NS/LK/DM**

Buelow, George J(ohn), American musicologist; b. Chicago, March 31, 1929. He studied piano with Ganz at the Chicago Musical Coll., where he received M.B. (1950) and M.M. (1951) degrees; then studied musicology with Martin Bernstein, Sachs, and Reese at N.Y. Univ. (Ph.D., 1961, with the diss. *Johann David Heinichen, "Der General-bass in der Composition": A Critical Study*

with Annotated Translation of Selected Chapters). In 1961 he joined the faculty of the Univ. of Calif. at Riverside; then was prof. of music at the Univ. of Ky. in Louisville (1968–69) and Rutgers Univ. (1969–77). In 1977 he became prof. of musicology at Ind. Univ. in Bloomington. He is particularly noted for his studies of 17th- and 18th-century German music. He publ. *Thorough-bass Accompaniment according to Johann David Heinichen* (Berkeley, 1966; 3rd ed., rev., 1992), *New Mattheson Studies* (with H. Marx; Cambridge, 1984), and *The Late Baroque Era: From the 1680s to 1740* (Basingstoke, 1993).

BIBL.: T. Mathiesen and B. Rivera, eds., *Festa Musicologica: Essays in Honor of G.J. B.* (Stuyvesant, N.Y., 1995).—**NS/LK/DM**

Buffalo Springfield, distinctive folk-rock pioneers. **MEMBERSHIP:** Neil Young, first lead gtr., voc.(b. Toronto, Ontario, Can., Nov. 12, 1945); Stephen Stills, second lead gtr., kybd., voc. (b. Dallas, Jan. 3, 1945); Richie Furay, rhythm gtr., voc. (b. Yellow Springs, Ohio, May 9, 1944); Bruce Palmer, bs. (b. Liverpool, Nova Scotia, Can., Sept. 1946); Dewey Martin, drm. (b. Chesterville, Ontario, Can., Sept. 30, 1942). Jim Messina (b. Maywood, Calif., Dec. 5, 1947) sang and played bass with the group during its last months of existence.

Also known as The Herd in their early days, Buffalo Springfield formed in Los Angeles in the spring of 1966. Neil Young had played in several Canadian groups, including The Squires, and manned The Mynah Birds with Bruce Palmer and future funk star Rick James in the Detroit area before moving to Los Angeles in 1965. Stephen Stills and Richie Furay had been members of the N.Y.–based Au Go-Go Singers. Canadian Dewey Martin had played with the bluegrass group The Dillards and toured with Roy Orbison.

Performing an extended engagement as the house band at Los Angeles' Whiskey A-Go-Go, Buffalo Springfield were featured at a July 1966 Hollywood Bowl concert and later toured with The Byrds and The Beach Boys. Signed to the Atco subsidiary of Atlantic Records, their third single, Stills's "For What It's Worth," became the group's best-selling single and launched their popular recording career. Their debut album contained seven Stills songs, including the country-flavored "Go and Say Goodbye" and "Hot Dusty Roads," and five Neil Young songs, including the beautiful love song "Do I Have to Come Right Out and Say It" and "Flying on the Ground Is Wrong," both sung by Richie Furay. Relations between Stills and Young grew increasingly tense and Young left the group in the spring of 1967 for several months. Thus, Buffalo Springfield performed at the June 1967 Monterey International Pop Festival without Young.

Neil Young returned for the gutsier *Buffalo Springfield Again*, which contained a wider range of material, from the rock-and-roll of Young's psychedelic "Mr. Soul" and Stills's "Bluebird" and "Rock and Roll Woman" to the major production efforts of Young's "Expecting to Fly" and "Broken Arrow." Jim Messina handled part of the engineering duties along with playing some bass. Palmer departed in early 1968, and, amidst reports of dissension and group infighting, *Last Time Around* was produced by Jim Messina, who also played bass, sang, and contributed "Carefree Country Day." Other outstanding songs on the album included "On the Way Home" and "I Am a Child" by Young, "Pretty Girl Why" and "Four Days Gone" by Stills, and Furay's "Kind Woman." Buffalo Springfield performed their last concert at Long Beach, Calif., in May 1968.

Subsequently, Jim Messina and Richie Furay formed Poco, whereas Neil Young recorded solo before joining Steve Stills in Crosby, Stills, Nash and Young. Stills later recorded solo and Messina dueted with Kenny Loggins. In the mid 1970s Furay helped form the Souther-Hillman-Furay Band. Young has enjoyed an incredibly diverse solo career.

One of the first American groups to combine electric instrumentation and drums with distinctive, incisive songwriting and intricate vocal harmonies, Buffalo Springfield (along with The Byrds) pioneered both folk-rock and country-rock. Although the group featured three excellent singer-songwriter-guitarists, they failed to garner major commercial success during their existence, perhaps due to their inability to transfer the tension and excitement of their live shows onto recordings. Buffalo Springfield nonetheless produced the masterful *Buffalo Springfield Again* and became a rock legend, and the influence of their key members is still felt today through various aggregations and solo endeavors. Buffalo Springfield were inducted into the Rock and Roll Hall of Fame in 1997.

DISC.: *Buffalo Springfield* (1967); *Buffalo Springfield Again* (1967); *Last Time Around* (1968); *Retrospective* (1969); *Expecting to Fly* (1970); *Buffalo Springfield* (1973). **THE AU GO-GO SINGERS (WITH STEVE STILLS AND RICHIE FURAY):** *They Call Us the Au Go-Go Singers* (1964). **DEWEY MARTIN:** *Medicine Ball* (1970). **BRUCE PALMER:** *The Cycle Is Complete* (1971).—**BH**

Buffardin, Pierre-Gabriel, French flutist; b. Provence, c. 1690; d. Paris, Jan. 13, 1768. He joined the Dresden Court Orch. in 1715, returning to France in 1750. He was highly regarded as a teacher, numbering among his pupils Johann Jacob Bach (brother of J.S. Bach) and J.J. Quantz.—**NS/LK/DM**

Buffett, Jimmy, one of the most amusing singer-songwriters to emerge in the 1970s, appealed to country and rock audiences with an intriguing variety of songs, alternately silly and sentimental, about sailing, partying, and womanizing, all portraying his unique, laid-back lifestyle; b. Mobile, Ala., Dec. 25, 1946.

Achieving only one major hit in 25 years of recording (1977's "Margaritaville"), Buffett nonetheless established himself as one of the most popular touring acts of the 1980s and 1990s.

Jimmy Buffett began sidelining as a folk singer while attending the Univ. of Southern Miss., from which he was graduated with a degree in history and journalism. After working in New Orleans he moved to Nashville in 1969, ultimately settling in Key West, Fla., in 1971. Recording two obscure albums for the Barnaby label, Buffett assembled the Coral Reefers as his backup band and switched to Dunhill Records (absorbed by MCA, as

was his later label, ABC). He gained his first recognition with songs such as "Railroad Lady," cowritten with Jerry JeffWalker, and "Why Don't We Get Drunk and Screw" from his debut album. His first moderate hit, the ballad "Come Monday," came in 1974.

Throughout the 1970s Buffett recorded best-selling albums that featured fun ditties such as Lord Buckley's "God's Own Drunk," "My Head Hurts, My Feet Stink and I Don't Love Jesus," "Margaritaville" (his only major hit), "Livingston Saturday Night," "Cheeseburger in Paradise," "Fins," and "Volcano," and moving ballads such as "A Pirate Looks at Forty," "Havana Daydreamin'," and "Treat Her Like a Lady." He also recorded songs by excellent contemporary songwriters such as Jesse Winchester ("Defying Gravity") and Steve Goodman ("Door Number Three" and "Banana Republics"). Buffett appeared in and performed the music for the 1975 film *Rancho Deluxe*. He toured tirelessly and established himself with legions of fans who made him one of the best-drawing pop acts of the 1980s and 1990s.

During the 1980s Buffett continued to record his own compositions, including fan favorites such as "Coconut Telegraph," "It's My Job," "Growing Older but Not Up," "Where's the Party," and "Gypsies in the Palace," as well as Rodney Crowell's "Stars on the Water" and Van Morrison's "Brown Eyed Girl." In 1989 he published a collection of short stories, *Tales from Margaritaville*, followed by the novel *Where Is Joe Merchant?* in 1992, the year he founded Margaritaville Records, distributed by MCA, for subsequent recordings.

DISC.: *Down to Earth* (1970); *High Cumberland Jubilee* (1977); *Before the Salt: Early J. B.* (1979); *A White Sports Coat and a Pink Crustacean* (1973); *Living and Dying in 3/4 Time* (1974); *A-1–A* (1974); *Rancho Deluxe* (sountrack; 1975); *Havana Daydreamin'* (1976); *Changes in Latitudes, Changes in Attitudes* (1977); *Son of a Son of a Sailor* (1978); *You Had to Be There* (1978); *Volcano* (1979); *Coconut Telegraph* (1981); *Somewhere Over China* (1982); *One Particular Harbor* (1983); *Riddles in the Sand* (1984); *Last Mango in Paris* (1985); *Songs You Know by Heart (Greatest Hits)* (1985); *Floridays* (1986); *Hot Water* (1988); *Off to See the Lizard* (1989); *Feeding Frenzy* (1990); *Boats Beaches Bars and Ballads* (1992); *Before the Beach* (1993); *Fruitcakes* (1994).—**BH**

Bughici, Dumitru, Romanian composer; b. Iași, Nov. 14, 1921. He received initial training at the Iași Cons. (1935–38), and later studied at the Leningrad Cons. (1950–55), where his teachers included Schnittke and Arapov. In 1955 he joined the faculty of the Bucharest Cons. In 1988 he went to Jerusalem, where he was active as a teacher and composer.

WORKS: DRAMATIC: Ballet: *The Fight of Light Against Darkness* (1965); *Energy* (1965); *The Liberation of the Village* (1980). **ORCH.:** *The Poem of New Life* (1953); 2 violin concertos (1955, 1977); *Evocation*, symphonic poem (1956); 4 sinfoniettas (1958, 1962, 1969, 1979); *The Heroic Poem* (1959); 11 syms. (1961; 1964, rev. 1967; 1966; 1972; 1977; 1978–79; 1983; 1984; 1985; 1985; 1987–90); *Bolero* (1963); *The Monument*, symphonic poem (1964); *Partita* (1965); *Dramatic Dialogues* for Flute and Strings (1967); *Sonata* for Strings (1970); *Melody, Rhythm, Color*, jazz concerto (1970); *A Poem to Love* (1971); *Symphonic Fantasia in Jazz Rhythm* (1974); Cello Concerto (1974); Trumpet Concerto (1975); Piano Concertino (1975); *5 Musical Images* (1977); *Choreographic Tableaux*, symphonic suite (1978); *Simfonie*

497

Concertante No. 1 for String Quartet and Orch. (1979–80) and No. 2 for Flute, Oboe, Clarinet, Bassoon, Strings, and Percussion (1980–81); Flute Concerto (1985). **CHAMBER:** Suite for Violin and Piano (1953); Scherzo for Cello and Piano (1953); 5 string quartets (1954; 1968; 1971; 1976–77; 1978); 3 trios for Violin, Cello, and Piano (1961 1976, 1983); 2 violin sonatas (1963, 1981); Sonata for Solo Violin (1968); *Quartet-Fantasia* (1968–69); *Triptych* for Violin and Piano (1970); 2 brass quintets (1975, 1981); *Fantasia* for Xylophone and Double Bass (1980); Septet (1980–81); piano pieces.—NS/LK/DM

Buhlig, Richard, American pianist and teacher; b. Chicago, Dec. 21, 1880; d. Los Angeles, Jan. 30, 1952. He studied in Chicago, and in Vienna with Leschetizky (1897–1900); made his recital debut in Berlin (1901); then toured Europe and the U.S. (American debut with the Philadelphia Orch. in N.Y., Nov. 5, 1907). In 1918 he was appointed teacher of piano at the Inst. of Musical Arts in N.Y. He eventually settled in Los Angeles as a performer and teacher.—NS/LK/DM

Bujarski, Zbigniew, Polish composer and pedagogue; b. Muszyna, Aug. 21, 1933. He received training in conducting (1955–58) and in composition (with Stanisław Wiechowicz, 1956–50) at the State Higher School of Music in Kraków. In 1972 he joined its faculty, where he served as dean of the dept. of composition, conducting, and theory (1978–86) and as a prof. of composition (from 1992). In 1979 and 1987 he received the Minister of Culture and Arts Award, Second Class, in 1984 he was honored with the Award of the Polish Composers' Union and the City of Kraków Award, and in 1991 he received the Alfred Jurzykowski Foundation Award of the U.S.

WORKS: ORCH.: *Tryptyk* for Strings and Percussion (1958); *Strefy* (Zones; 1961; Kraków, June 15, 1962); *Kinoth* for Chamber Orch. (1963); *Contraria* (1965; Warsaw, Sept. 22, 1966); *Musica domestica* for 18 Strings (Warsaw, Sept. 22, 1977); *Concerto per archi I* for Violin and Strings (1979; Warsaw, Sept. 10, 1980) and *II* for Cello and Strings (1992; Kraków, Nov. 27, 1993); *Similis Greco I* (Warsaw, Sept. 23, 1979), *II, Lumen* (1997; Kraków, May 31, 1998), and *III, Narodzenie* (The Birth) for Chorus and Orch. (1981; Warsaw, Sept. 21, 1986); *Veni Creator Spiritus* (1988; Kraków, Nov. 17, 1989); *Scolaresca* for Strings (1993; Kraków, June 4, 1995); *Pawana dla "oddalonej"* (Pavane for a Remote One) for Strings (1994; Kraków, June 4, 1995). **CHAMBER:** 3 string quartets: No. 1, *Kwartet na otwarcie domu* (Quartet for a Housewarming; Lusławice- Dwór, Aug. 29, 1980), No. 2, *Kwartet na Adwent* (Quartet for Advent; 1984; Warsaw, Feb. 25, 1985), and No. 3, *Kwartet na Wielkanoc* (Quartet for Easter; 1989; Kraków, Feb. 27, 1994); *Lęk ptaków I* (The Fear of Birds) for Violin, Viola, and Percussionist (1993; Kraków, Jan. 17, 1994), *II* for 2 Clarinets and Percussion (1994; Kraków, June 9, 1995), and *III* for Clarinet, Bass Clarinet, Violin, Viola, and Percussion (Kraków, Dec. 7, 1995); *Cassazione per Natale* for Winds and Percussion (1996). **Organ:** *Veni Creator Spiritus* (Gdańsk, Aug. 9, 1983). **VOCAL:** *Krzewy płonące* (Burning Bushes) for Voice and Piano or Chamber Ensemble (1958); *Synchrony I* for Soprano and Chamber Ensemble (1959; also for Soprano, Chorus, and Orch., 1960); Chamber Piece for Voice, Flute, Harp, Piano, and Percussion (1963); *El Hombre*, oratorio for Soprano, Mezzo- soprano, Baritone, Chorus, and Orch. (1969–73; Warsaw, Sept. 21, 1974); *Da Bóg nam kiedyś...* (One Day God Will Give Us...) for Baritone and Piano (1983); *Ogrody* (The Gardens) for Soprano and Orch. (1987; Kraków, May 5, 1989); 5 Songs for Soprano, String Orch., and Vibraphone (1994–96; Kraków, May 20, 1997).—NS/LK/DM

Buketoff, Igor, American conductor; b. Hartford, Conn., May 29, 1915. He studied at the Univ. of Kans. (1931–32), the Juilliard School of Music in N.Y. (B.S., 1935; M.S., 1941), and the Los Angeles Cons. In 1942 he won the first Alice M. Ditson Award for Young Conductors. He was music director of the Chautauqua Opera (1941–47), the N.Y. Phil. Young People's Concerts (1948–53), the Fort Wayne (Ind.) Phil. (1948–66), the Iceland Sym. Orch. in Reykjavík (1964–65), the St. Paul (Minn.) Opera (1968–74), and the Tex. Chamber Orch. (1980–81). He also taught at the Juilliard School of Music (1935–45), the Chautauqua School of Music (1941–47), Columbia Univ. (1943–47), Butler Univ. (1953–63), and the Univ. of Houston (1977–79). Buketoff was notably active in the promotion of contemporary music.—NS/LK/DM

Bukofzer, Manfred F(ritz), eminent German-born American musicologist; b. Oldenburg, March 27, 1910; d. Oakland, Calif., Dec. 7, 1955. He studied at the Hoch Cons. in Frankfurt am Main, and at the univs. of Heidelberg, Berlin, and Basel (Ph.D., 1936, with the diss. *Geschichte des englischen Diskants und des Fauxbourdons nach den theoretischen Quellen*; publ. in Strasbourgh, 1936); also took courses with Hindemith in Berlin. He lectured in Basel (1933–39); also at Oxford and Cambridge Univs. In 1939 he settled in the U.S., becoming a naturalized American citizen in 1945. He taught at Case Western Reserve Univ. in Cleveland (1940–41). In 1941 he became a member of the faculty of the Univ. of Calif. at Berkeley where, a year before his untimely death, he was appointed chairman of its music dept. His numerous publications are distinguished by originality of historical and musical ideas coupled with precision of factual exposition; having mastered the English language, he was able to write brilliantly in British and American publications; he was also greatly esteemed as a teacher. Bukofzer ed. the works of Dunstable (Vol. VIII of Musica Britannica, 1953; 2nd ed., rev., 1970 by M. Bent, I. Bent, and B. Trowell).

WRITINGS: *Sumer Is Icumen In: A Revision* (Berkeley, 1944); *Music in the Baroque Era* (N.Y., 1947); *Studies in Medieval and Renaissance Music* (N.Y., 1950); *The Place of Musicology in American Institutions of Higher Learning* (N.Y., 1957); *Music of the Classic Period, 1750–1827)* (Berkeley, 1958).—NS/LK/DM

Bull, Edvard Hagerup
See **Hagerup Bull, Edvard**

Bull, John, famous English organist and composer; b. probably in Old Radnor, Radnorshire, c. 1562; d. Antwerp, March 12, 1628. He became a chorister at Hereford Cathedral in 1573. In 1574 he joined the Children of the Chapel Royal and studied music with William Blitheman and Willian Hunnis. In 1582 he became organist at Hereford Cathedral, and in 1583 he also became its master of the choristers. In 1586 he received his B.Mus. and in 1592 his D.Mus. from the Univ. of Oxford. He was sworn in as a Gentleman of the Chapel Royal in Jan. 1586, becoming its organist in 1591. In 1596, on Queen Elizabeth's recommendation, he was appointed prof. of music at Gresham Coll., and on March 6, 1597, was elected first public lecturer there. He got into difficulties with Gresham Coll. when he impregnated premaritally a maiden named Elizabeth Walter, and was forced to resign on Dec. 20, 1607; he hastened to take a marriage license 2 days later. In 1610 he entered the service of Prince Henry, but in 1613 was charged with adultery and had to flee England. In Sept. 1615 he became asst. organist at the Antwerp Cathedral in Belgium, and was named its principal organist on Dec. 29, 1617. In the Netherlands he became acquainted with the great Dutch organist and composer Sweelinck; both he and Bull exerted considerable influence on the development of contrapuntal keyboard music of the time. Bull also composed many canons and anthems. Various works previously attributed to him are now considered doubtful. For a modern edition of his keyboard works, see *J. B.: Keyboard Music* in Musica Britannica, XIV (ed. by T. Dart, F. Cameron, and J. Steele, 1960; 2nd edition, rev., 1967) and XIX (ed. by T. Dart, 1963; 2nd edition, rev., 1970).

BIBL.: W. Cunningham, *The Keyboard Music of J. B.* (Ann Arbor, 1984).—NS/LK/DM

Bull, Ole (Bornemann), eccentric Norwegian violinist and composer; b. Bergen, Feb. 5, 1810; d. Lyso, near Bergen, Aug. 17, 1880. He was extremely precocious, and played the violin experimentally even before acquiring the rudiments of music. At the age of 9, he played solos with the Bergen Harmonic Soc. His teachers were then Niels Eriksen and J.H. Poulsen; later he had regular instruction with M. Ludholm. Ignoring academic rules, he whittled the bridge almost to the level of the fingerboard, so as to be able to play full chords on all 4 strings. He was sent by his father to Christiania to study theology, but failed the entrance examinations; instead, he organized a theater orch., which he led with his violin. In 1829 he played in Copenhagen; that same year, he was sent to Kassel to seek advice from Spohr. In 1831 he went to Paris, where he heard Paganini and became obsessed with the idea of imitating his mannerisms and equaling his success, a fantasy devoid of all imagined reality because of Bull's amateurish technique. In 1833 he gave his first Paris concert but it was not until an appearance at the Paris Opéra in 1835 that he won a following. By then he had developed a personal type of playing that pleased the public, particularly in localities rarely visited by real artists. On May 21, 1836, he made his London debut. During the 1836–37 season, he played 274 concerts in England and Ireland. In 1840 he played Beethoven's *Kreutzer Sonata* in London, with Liszt at the piano. On July 23, 1849, he announced the formation of a Norwegian Theater in Bergen, which was opened on Jan. 2, 1850. While he failed to impress most of the serious musicians and critics in Europe, he achieved his dream of artistic success in America; he made 5 concert tours across the U.S. from 1843, playing popular selections

and his own compositions on American themes with such fetching titles as *Niagara, Solitude of the Prairies,* and *To the Memory of Washington,* interspersing them with his arrangements of Norwegian folk songs. He entertained a strong conviction that Norway should generate its own national art, but the practical applications of his musical patriotism were failures because of his lack of formal study and a concentration on tawdry effects; still, it may be argued that he at least prepared the ground for the emergence of true Norwegian music; indeed, it is on his recommendation that Grieg was sent to study at the Leipzig Cons. Characteristically, Bull became attracted by the ideas of communal socialism. In 1852 he purchased 11,144 acres in Pa. for a Norwegian settlement, but his lack of business sense led his undertaking to disaster. The settlement, planned on strict socialist lines, was given the name Oleana, thus establishing a personal connection with the name of its unlucky founder. Oleana soon collapsed, but Bull earned admiration in Norway as a great national figure. Many of his violin pieces, mostly sentimental or strident in nature, with such titles as *La preghiera d'una madre, Variazioni di bravura, Polacca guerriera,* etc., were publ., but they sank into predictable desuetude.

BIBL.: J. Lie, *O. B.s breve i utdreg* (Copenhagen, 1881); S. Bull (his 2nd wife), *O. B.: A Memoir* (Boston, 1883; Ger. ed., Stuttgart, 1886); O. Vik, *O. B.* (Bergen, 1890); C. Aarvig, *Den unge O. B.* (Copenhagen, 1935); A. Björndal, *O. B. og Norsk folkemusik* (Bergen, 1940); M. Smith, *The Life of O. B.* (Princeton, 1943); Z. Hopp, *Eventyret om O. B.* (Bergen, 1945); Ola Linge, *O. B.* (Oslo, 1953); I. Bull, *O. B. Returns to Pennsylvania* (N.Y., 1961); E. Haugen and C. Cai, *O. B.: Romantisk musiker og kosmopolitisk nordmann* (Oslo, 1992; Eng. tr., 1992, as *O. B.: Norway's Romantic Musician and Cosmopolitan Patriot*).—NS/LK/DM

Bullant, Antoine, French bassoonist and composer; b. c. 1750; d. St. Petersburg, June 1821. He went to Paris about 1771, where he was active as a bassoonist and composer. In 1780 he settled in St. Petersburg. In 1783–84 he was court bassoonist, and then joined the imperial theater orch. in 1787. He composed the popular comic opera *Sbitenshchik* (The Hot-Mead Vendor; St. Petersburg, 1784). He also wrote the comic opera *Vinetta, ili Taras v ulye* (Vinetta, or Taras in the Beehive; 1799), 5 syms., chamber music, and vocal works. —LK/DM

Buller, John, English composer; b. London, Feb. 7, 1927. He studied music as a child, beginning formal composition lessons in 1959 with Anthony Milner in London. He served as composer-in-residence at the Univ. of Edinburgh (1975–76) and at Queens Univ. in Belfast (1985–86).

WORKS: *The Cave* for Flute, Clarinet, Trombone, Cello, and Tape (1970); *2 Night Pieces from Finnegans Wake* for Soprano, Flute, Clarinet, Piano, and Cello (1971); *Finnegans Floras* for 14 Voices, Hand Percussion, and Piano (1972); *Poor Jenny* for Flutes and Percussion (1973); *Le terrazze* for 14 Instruments and Tape (1974); *The Mime of Mick, Nick, and the Maggies* for Soprano, Tenor, Baritone, Chorus, Orch., and Speaker or Tape (1976; London, Feb. 6, 1978); *Proença* for Mezzo-soprano, Electric Guitar, and Orch. (London, Aug. 6, 1977); *Sette spazi* for 2 Clarinets, Violin, Cello, and Piano (1978); *The Theatre of Memory*

for Orch. (London, Sept. 7, 1981); *Kommos* for Voices and Electronics (St. Bartholomew's Festival, June 21, 1982); *Towards Aquarius* for 15 Players and Tape (London, Nov. 1, 1983); *A la fontana del vergier* for Countertenor, 2 Tenors, and Baritone (1984); *Of 3 Shakespeare Sonnets* for Mezzo-soprano, Flute, Clarinet, Harp, 2 Violins, Viola, and Cello (London, June 12, 1985); *Bakxai*, opera (1991–92); *Bacchae Metrics* for Orch. (1993).
—NS/LK/DM

Bullis, Thomas, English organist and composer; b. Ely (baptized), Nov. 8, 1657; d. there (buried), Aug. 24, 1712. He was the son of the English composer Thomas Bullis (b. Ely [baptized], Aug. 26, 1627; d. there (buried), Jan. 23, 1708). He was a chorister and lay clerk under John Ferrabosco at Ely Cathedral, where he also acted occasionally as organist. He was also active at Holy Trinity in Ely. Bullis composed a number of fine services and anthems.—LK/DM

Bullock, Chick (Charles), jazz-pop singer; b. Butte, Mont., Sept. 16, 1908; d. Calif., Sept. 15, 1981. He was one of the most recorded singers of all time. He began singing in a vaudeville theater to accompany the projection of series of photographs and also took small acting roles in silent films. Success with his first recording coupled with a disfiguring eye ailment caused him to concentrate on radio and recording work. Between 1930 and 1941, he made hundreds of recordings, many as leader of his studio band, the Levee Loungers. Among the sidemen in this group at various times were several major jazz musicians, including Bunny Berigan, Bill Coleman, Jack Teagarden, the Dorsey brothers, Joe Venuti, and Eddie Lang. "Back Home Again in Indiana" (1940) is a particularly good example of a fine ensemble. Bullock also recorded as a sideman with others, notably Duke Ellington (1931) and Adrian Rollini. He seemingly shunned all personal publicity. He moved to the West Coast c. 1945 and was engaged primarily in real estate; he appeared on a "Tribute to Bunny Berigan" radio program in the mid-1950s. By the 1970s, he was retired.

DISC.: "Back Home Indiana" (1940).

BIBL.: P. Murphy, *Chick Bullock: A Discography of His Recordings* (Melbourne, Australia, 1983).—JC/LP

Bullock, Sir Ernest, English organist and educator; b. Wigan, Sept. 15, 1890; d. Aylesbury, May 24, 1979. He studied organ with Bairstow in Leeds; also took courses at the Univ. of Durham (B.Mus., 1908; D.Mus., 1914). After serving as suborganist at Manchester Cathedral (1912–15), he was organist and choirmaster at Exeter Cathedral (1919–27). In 1928 he was named organist and Master of the Choristers at Westminster Abbey, and as such participated in several coronations. He became Gardiner Prof. of Music at the Univ. of Glasgow in 1941. He was then director of the Royal Coll. of Music in London from 1952 until his retirement in 1960. He was knighted by King George VI in 1951.
—NS/LK/DM

Bülow, Hans (Guido) von, celebrated German pianist and conductor of high attainment; b. Dresden, Jan. 8, 1830; d. Cairo, Feb. 12, 1894. At the age of 9 he began to study piano with Friedrich Wieck and theory with Max Eberwein; then went to Leipzig, where he studied law at the univ. and took a music course with Moritz Hauptmann; he also studied piano with Plaidy. From 1846 to 1848 he lived in Stuttgart, where he made his debut as a pianist. In 1849 he attended the Univ. of Berlin; there he joined radical social groups; shortly afterward he went to Zürich and met Wagner, who was there in exile. After a year in Switzerland, where he conducted theater music, Bülow proceeded to Weimar, where he began to study with Liszt. In 1853 he made a tour through Germany and Austria as a pianist. In 1855 he was appointed head of the piano dept. at the Stern Cons. in Berlin, retaining this post until 1864. He married Liszt's natural daughter, Cosima, in 1857. In 1864 he was called by Ludwig II to Munich as court pianist and conductor; the King, who was a great admirer of Wagner, summoned Wagner to Munich from exile. Bülow himself became Wagner's ardent champion; on June 10, 1865, he conducted at the Court Opera in Munich the first performance of *Tristan und Isolde*, and on June 21, 1868, he led the premiere of *Die Meistersinger von Nürnberg*. It was about this time that Wagner became intimate with Cosima; after her divorce she married Wagner, in 1870. Despite this betrayal, Bülow continued to conduct Wagner's music; his growing admiration for Brahms cannot be construed as his pique against Wagner. It was Bülow who dubbed Brahms "the third B of music," the first being Bach, and the second Beethoven. In fact, the context of this nomination was more complex than a mere alphabetical adumbration; according to reports, Bülow was asked to name his favorite key; he replied that it was E-flat major, the key signature of the *Eroica*, with the 3 B's (German colloquialism for flats) signifying Bach, Beethoven, and Brahms. Then he was asked why he did not instead nominate Bruckner for the third B, and he is supposed to have replied that Bruckner was too much of a Wagnerian for him. Bülow was indeed renowned for his wit and his aptitude for alliterative punning; his writings are of elevated literary quality. In 1872 Bülow lived in Florence; then resumed his career as a pianist, winning triumphant successes in England and Russia; during his American tour in 1875–76 he gave 139 concerts; he revisited America in 1889 and 1890. An important chapter in his career was his conductorship in Meiningen (1880–85). In 1882 he married a Meiningen actress, Marie Schanzer. He was conductor of the Berlin Phil. from 1887 to 1893, when a lung ailment forced him to seek a cure in Egypt. He died shortly after his arrival in Cairo.

As a conductor, Bülow was an uncompromising disciplinarian; he insisted on perfection of detail, and he was also able to project considerable emotional power on the music. He was one of the first conductors to dispense with the use of the score. His memory was fabulous; it was said that he could memorize a piano concerto by just reading the score, sometimes while riding in a train. The mainstay of his repertoire was Classical and Romantic music, but he was also receptive toward composers of the new school. When Tchaikovsky, unable to secure a performance of his First Piano Concerto in Russia, offered the score to Bülow, he accepted it, and gave its world premiere as soloist with a pickup orch. in Boston, on Oct. 25, 1875; however, the music was too new and too strange to American ears of the time, and the critical reactions were ambiguous. Bülow encouraged the young Richard Strauss, and gave him his first position as conductor. Bülow was a composer himself, but his works belong to the category of "Kapellmeister Musik," competent, well structured, but devoid of originality. Among his compositions was incidental music to Shakespeare's *Julius Caesar*. He made masterly transcriptions of the prelude to Wagner's *Meistersinger* and the entire opera *Tristan und Isolde*; also arranged for piano the overtures to *Le Corsaire* and *Benvenuto Cellini* by Berlioz. He annotated and edited Beethoven's piano sonatas; these eds. were widely used by piano teachers, even though criticism was voiced against his cavalier treatment of some passages and his occasional alterations of Beethoven's original to enhance the resonance. His writings were publ. by his widow, Marie von Bülow, under the title *Briefe und Schriften H. v.B.s* (8 vols., Leipzig, 1895–1908; vol. III, republ. separately in 1936, contains selected essays, while the other vols. contain letters); selected letters in Eng. tr. were publ. by C. Bache, *The Early Correspondence of H. v.B.* (London, 1896).

BIBL.: E. Zabel, *H. v.B.* (Hamburg, 1894); R. Sternfeld, *H. v.B.* (Leipzig, 1894); T. Pfeiffer, *Studien bei H. v.B.* (Berlin, 1894; 6th ed., 1909); H. Heimann, *H. v.B.: Sein Leben und sein Wirken* (Berlin, 1909); R. Du Moulin-Eckart, *H. v.B.* (1921); M. von Bülow, *H. v.B. in Leben und Wort* (1925); L. Schemann, *H. v.B. im Lichte der Wahrheit* (Regensburg, 1935); W. Stresemann, *The Berlin Philharmonic from B. to Karajan* (in Ger. and Eng.; Berlin, 1979); H. Müller and V. Gerasch, eds., *Beiträge zum Kolloquium, H.v. B., Leben, Wirken und Vermächtnis* (Meiningen, 1994). —NS/LK/DM

Bumbry, Grace (Melzia Ann), greatly talented black American mezzo-soprano and soprano; b. St. Louis, Jan. 4, 1937. She attended Boston Univ. and Northwestern Univ., and pursued vocal training with Lehmann at the Music Academy of the West in Santa Barbara (1955–58) and with Bernac in Paris. With Martina Arroyo, she was co-winner of the Metropolitan Opera auditions in 1958. In 1960 she made a notably successful operatic debut as Amneris at the Paris Opéra. In 1961 she became the first black American singer to appear at the Bayreuth Festival when she sang Venus in *Tannhäuser*. In 1963 she made her Covent Garden debut in London as Eboli, and her Chicago Lyric Opera debut as Ulrica. In 1964 she sang Lady Macbeth at her first appearance at the Salzburg Festival. She made her Metropolitan Opera debut in N.Y. as Eboli on Oct. 7, 1965, and subsequently sang there regularly. From 1970 she concentrated on the soprano repertoire. Among her distinguished roles at the Metropolitan were Carmen (1967), Santuzza (1970), Tosca (1971), Salome (1973), Venus (1977), Leonora in *Il Trovatore* (1982), and Gershwin's Bess (1985). In 1990 she sang Berlioz's Cassandre at the opening of the new Opéra de la Bastille in Paris. She also appeared as a soloist with major orchs. and as a recitalist.—NS/LK/DM

Bunch, John, talented American piano player and musical director; b. Tipton, Ind., Dec. 1, 1921. Bunch began playing piano in a small Ind. town in the early 1930s and, by age 12, was appearing in clubs all over the state that officially honored him at the 1996 Elkhart Jazz Festival. An Army Air Force enlistee in 1942, Bunch was shot down and captured during his 17th mission over Germany. He passed time as a prisoner playing with the camp band and wrote his first arrangement there. Upon his return to the U.S., Bunch entered Ind. Univ., graduating in 1950. He mostly put music aside until age 34, when he headed for Calif. and a spot in Woody Herman's band, followed by band work with Benny Goodman and Maynard Ferguson, and subsequent dates around N.Y.C. with Urbie Green. In December 1966, Bunch joined Tony Bennett as accompanist and musical director for six years, and was appropriately referred to by the singer as "Gentleman John Bunch." In 1972, Bunch returned to jazz full-time. As well as working solo over the years, he worked with the Scott Hamilton Quintet, frequently returned to the Benny Goodman fold, and played mostly in small groups. He currently works with guitarist Bucky Pizzarelli and bassist Jay Leonhart in a powerhouse combine dubbed New York Swing. Bunch has been around long enough to come under the spell of Fats Waller and Teddy Wilson, but was young enough to adopt some Bud Powell mannerisms and sophisticated harmonies. Bunch remains very much a melody player with a delicate keyboard touch and yet can swing with the best.

DISC.: *John Bunch Play Kurt Weil* (1975); *John's Bunch* (1975); *Jubilee* (1977); *John's Other Bunch* (1977); *Slick Funk* (1977); *The Best Thing for You* (1987); *NY Swing* (1992); *Plays Rodgers and Hart* (1993); *Plays Cole Porter* (1994); *Plays Jerome Kern* (1994); *Struttin'* (1995); *Solo* (1996); *New York Swing: Live at the Norway* (1997); *World War II Love Songs* (1999).—JTB

Bunger, Richard Joseph
See **Evans, Richard (Joseph) Bunger**

Bungert, (Friedrich) August, German composer; b. Mülheim an der Ruhr, March 14, 1845; d. Leutesdorf am Rhein, Oct. 26, 1915. He studied at the Cologne Cons. (1860–62), in Paris, and with Kiel in Berlin. His most ambitious project was the operatic tetralogy after Homer, *Die Odyssee* (4 parts first perf. in Dresden: *Kirke*, Jan. 24, 1898; *Nausikaa*, March 20, 1901; *Odysseus' Heimkehr*, Dec. 12, 1896; *Odysses' Tod*, Oct. 30, 1903). The companion to this Wagnerian-inspired effort, *Die Ilias*, never appeared. He also wrote a comic opera, *Die Studenten von Salamanka* (Leipzig, 1884), a mystery play, *Warum? woher? wohin?* (1908), incidental music to Goethe's *Faust*, orch. works, including *Zeppelins erste grosse Fahrt* (Koblenz, Dec. 1, 1909), *Symphonia Victrix*, *Tasso, Hohes Lied der Liebe*, and *Auf der Wartburg*, choral pieces, songs, a Piano Quartet, and piano pieces.

BIBL.: M. Chop, *A. B.: Ein deutscher Dichterkomponist* (Berlin, 1916).—NS/LK/DM

Bunin, Revol, Russian composer; b. Moscow, April 6, 1924; d. there, July 4, 1976. He was a pupil of Litinsky, Shebalin, and Shotakovich at the Moscow Cons. (graduated, 1945).

WORKS: DRAMATIC: *Masquerade*, opera (1944); film scores. **ORCH.**: 8 syms. (1943, 1945, 1957, 1959, 1961, 1966, 1968, 1970); Viola Concerto (1953); Concerto for Piano and Chamber Orch. (1963); Concertante Sym. (1972). **CHAMBER**: 2 string quartets (1943, 1956); Piano Quintet (1946). **VOCAL**: Songs.—NS/LK/DM

Bunn, Teddy (actually, **Theodore Leroy**), jazz guitarist, singer; b. Long Island, N.Y., c. 1909; d. Lancaster, Calif., July 20, 1978. His brother, Kenneth, was a violinist; their mother played the organ, their father was an accordionist. He played without a pick, using his thumb and forefinger to solo in a heavily melodic, rather than chordal fashion. Bunn taught himself the guitar. Although Teddy specialized on guitar, he did work briefly on banjo with Cecil Scott in N.Y. (January 1929). He recorded with Duke Ellington in 1929, and later deputized for Fred Guy on a tour of New England with Duke Ellington; he worked in the Washboard Serenaders during the early 1930s, then c. 1932 joined the group known as Ben Bernie's Nephews; this unit moved to N.Y. to play a long residency at Chick Groman's Stables and changed their name to the Spirits of Rhythm. They also worked in Philadelphia and Chicago as well as touring. Bunn left in 1937, worked briefly in the original John Kirby Band (May 1937), then led his own trio and duo at various N.Y. clubs before rejoining the Spirits of Rhythm in April 1939. He made prolific freelance recordings in the 1930s with Jimmie Noone, Johnny Dodds, Trixie Smith, Mezz Mezzrow and Tommy Ladnier, and J. C. Higginbothan and Sidney Bechet. After residency at N.Y.'s World Fair, the group moved to Calif. in 1940, and for a period of ten years disbanded and re-formed with great regularity. Bunn also recorded in 1940 with Lionel Hampton, where he began using electric rather than acoustic guitar. Bunn was briefly absent from the music scene in 1942, then led his own Waves of Rhythm (1944). During the 1940s and 1950s, he primarily worked on the West Coast, sometimes on his own, and on various occasions with Edgar Hayes. In the late 1950s toured with a "rock 'n' roll" show. During the 1960s, he played less regularly through recurring illness, and finally retired from music in the 1970s.

DISC.: SIDNEY BECHET: *1924–1938* (1924). *Complete, Vols. 1–2* (1932); *Masterpieces, Vol. 7* (1932); *In New York (1937–1940* (1937); *Teddy Bunn 1930–1939* (1989); *The Spirit of Rhythm 1932–1934* (1989).—**JC/LP**

Bunnett, Jane, Canadian jazz soprano saxophonist and flutist; b. Toronto, Ontario, Canada, Oct. 22, 1956. Bunnett was originally trained as a classical pianist but had to give up that career option when tendinitis made it too difficult for her to play. Traveling to San Francisco to recoup her energies, Bunnett heard a series of concerts by Charles Mingus at Keystone Corners which inspired her to change her instrumental focus to the flute. She is also a gifted soprano saxophone player, having studied with Steve Lacy and won a couple of *Down Beat* polls for the instrument. Another crucial element in her musical history revolves around her discovery of Cuban rhythms and musicians. Before this time, she was a fairly straight-ahead post-bop player with interesting, if conventional, ideas. Bunnett's exposure to Cuban music has opened up new vistas in her playing and widened her compositional palette. Her album *Spirits of Havana* featured a large group, including several Cuban percussionists. She also appeared with a Cuban group at the 1998 Caramoor festival in N.Y. and elsewhere. Bunnett and her trumpet-playing husband Larry Cramer are raising money to send technicians to Cuba to repair Cuban musicians' antiquated Soviet-era instruments.

DISC.: *In Dew Time* (1988); *New York Duets* (1989); *Spirits of Havana* (1991); *Live at Sweet Basil* (1991); *The Water Is Wide* (1994); *Rendez-Vous Brazil/Cuba* (1995); *Jane Bunnett & the Cuban Piano Masters* (1996); *Chamalongo* (1998).—**GM**

Buonamente, Giovanni Battista, Italian composer; b. c. 1600; d. Assisi, Aug. 29, 1642. He was musicista da camera at the Austrian court in Vienna from 1626 to 1631; then served in a similar position at the Basilica of S. Francesco in Assisi, beginning in 1633. His importance rests on his sonatas for violin, some of which are the earliest examples of this form; he publ. 7 books of such works in Venice (1626–37); also wrote trio sonatas for 2 violins and bass.—**NS/LK/DM**

Buonamici, Giuseppe, Italian pianist; b. Florence, Feb. 12, 1846; d. there, March 17, 1914. He first studied with his uncle, Giuseppe Ceccherini, then at the Munich Cons. with Hans von Bülow and Rheinberger (1868–70). In 1873 returned to Florence, where he was active as a teacher and choral conductor. He publ. a compilation of the technical figures found in Beethoven's piano music, in the form of daily studies; ed. the *Biblioteca del Pianista* and the complete Beethoven sonatas. He also publ. piano pieces of his own.—**NS/LK/DM**

Burbure de Wesembeek, Léon-Philippe-Marie, Belgian music scholar; b. Dendermonde, Aug. 16, 1812; d. Antwerp, Dec. 8, 1889. A scion of an aristocratic family, he studied law at the Univ. of Ghent; he also received an excellent musical education at home with private teachers. In 1846 he settled at Antwerp, and became the keeper of Archives at the Cathedral. He made a profound study of materials on early music accessible to him, and publ. a number of valuable monographs dealing with the Renaissance music guilds of Antwerp, on lute makers, etc. He also composed some 200 works, including an opera, 25 orch. pieces, numerous choral works, etc.

WRITINGS: *Aperçu sur l'ancienne corporation des musiciens instrumentistes d'Anvers, dite de St. Job et de Ste. Marie-Madeleine* (Brussels, 1862); *Recherches sur les facteurs de clavecins et luthiers d'Anvers, depuis le XVIe jusqu'au XIXᵉ siècle* (Brussels, 1869); *Notice sur Charles-Louis Hanssens* (Brussels, 1872); *Charles Luython (1550–1620), compositeur de musique de la Cour impériale* (Brussels, 1880); *Les OEuvres des anciens musiciens belges* (Brussels, 1882).

BIBL.: F.A. Gevaert, *Notice sur le Chevalier Léon de Burbure* (Brussels, 1893).—**NS/LK/DM**

Burch(ell), John (Alexander), jazz pianist, composer; b. London, Jan. 6, 1932. He studied piano from age 12, performed in Army bands, then gigged around London. In the late 1950s, he worked with own trio on U.S. bases in Europe. He played with the Jazzmakers in summer 1960, then joined the Don Rendell Quartet (early 1961–late 1962); afterwards, he led his own octet, which continued to flourish intermittently through the 1970s and 1980s and included, at various times, Ray Warleigh, Peter King, Dick Morrissey, and Hank Shaw. He also freelanced with Tommy Whittle and others; played at Ronnie Scott's with Roland Kirk (1966) and Freddie Hubbard (1967); and toured with Hubbard. As a composer, Burch's most famous piece was "Preach and Teach," which was a hit for R&B singer Georgie Fame in 1966, and was later recorded by Buddy Rich for his album *Mercy, Mercy* (1968). He taught regularly at jazz summer schools including the Barry Summer School (1975) and the NYJO Easter Jazz Course (1974). In the mid-1970s, he was occasionally leading a trio, octet, or quintet. He often worked with Ray Warleigh, Kathy Stobart (from around 1978), and Georgie Fame. In 1980–81, he toured and recorded with Eddie "Cleanhead" Vinson. He worked regularly in Dick Morrissey's Quartet from the mid-1980s through to the 1990s, and remains active freelancing.

DISC.: D. RENDELL: *Roarin'* (1961); "Preach and Teach" (1966).—**LP**

Burchuladze, Paata, Russian bass; b. Tbilisi, Feb. 12, 1951. He studied at the Tbilisi Cons. In 1975 he made his operatic debut as Gounod's Méphistophélès in Tbilisi, and then sang throughout Russia and in Italy, where he pursued further training. In 1983 he made his British debut as a soloist in Elgar's *The Dream of Gerontius* at the Lichfield Festival, and in 1984 he made his first appearance at London's Covent Garden as Verdi's Ramfis. In 1987 he sang Mozart's Commendatore at the Salzburg Festival. He made his Metropolitan Opera debut in N.Y. as Rossini's Don Basilio on Oct. 21, 1989. In 1994 he appeared as Boris Godunov at the New Israeli Opera in Tel Aviv. He sang Verdi's Zaccaria at the Verona Arena in 1996. In 1997 he appeared as Banquo in Hamburg.—**NS/LK/DM**

Burck (real name, **Moller**), **Joachim à,** German organist and composer; b. Burg, near Magdeburg, 1546; d. Mühlhausen, Thuringia, May 24, 1610. In 1563 he settled in Mühlhausen. He became organist at the Protestant Church of St. Blasius in 1566.

WORKS: *Harmoniae sacrae* (5 books of motets; Nuremberg, 1566); *Die deutsche Passion* (Wittenberg, 1568); *Crepundia sacra* (4 books; Mühlhausen, 1578); several books of motets, odes, and German songs, reprinted in various collections.—**NS/LK/DM**

Burganger, Judith, American pianist and teacher; b. Buffalo, March 17, 1939. She was educated at the Stuttgart Staatliche Hochschule für Musik (diploma, 1961; M.M., 1965). After winning first prize in the Munich Competition, she appeared as a soloist with several major U.S. orchs., gave recitals, and played in chamber music concerts. She also was active as a teacher.—**NS/LK/DM**

Burge, David (Russell), American pianist, teacher, writer, and composer; b. Evanston, Ill., March 25, 1930. He was educated at Northwestern Univ. (B.M., 1951; M.M., 1952), the Eastman School of Music in Rochester, N.Y. (D.M.A. and Artist's Diploma, 1956), and the Cherubini Cons. in Florence on a Fulbright scholarship (1956–57). Thereafter he pursued a highly active career as a pianist, giving numerous concerts in the U.S. as well as in Europe, the Near East, the Far East, and Australia. After serving as an assoc. prof. at Whitman Coll. (1957–62), he was a prof. at the Univ. of Colo. (1962–75) and music director of the Boulder Phil. (1965–72). In 1975 he was artist-in-residence at the Univ. of Calif. at Davis. From 1975 to 1993 he was a prof. at the Eastman School of Music, where he was also chairman of the piano dept. from 1975 to 1987. He was prof. of composition at the Univ. of Pa. in 1977, and served on the faculties of the Banff Centre in Canada (1983–84; 1986) and at the Chautauqua Institution in N.Y. (1986–90). From 1989 to 1994 he was music chair of the National Assn. for Advancement in the Arts in Miami. He wrote music criticism for the San Diego *Union-Tribune* from 1994 to 1996. In 1995 he became composer-in-residence of the San Diego Ballet. In 1978 and 1979 he won the Deems Taylor Award for music journalism. In addition to his many articles and reviews in various publications, Burge also wrote the study *Twentieth-Century Piano Music* (1990) and the novel *Vanishing Spring* (1999). As a pianist, he has won particular distinction as an indefatigable and persuasive exponent of contemporary music. He has given the premieres of many new works, including scores by Krenek, Persichetti, Berio, Crumb, William Albright, and Ward-Steinman.

WORKS: DRAMATIC: *Blood Wedding*, songs and incidental music after García Lorca (1951); *Infernal Machine*, songs and incidental music after Cocteau (1952); *Popoff*, music comedy after Chekhov (1961); *Intervals*, chamber opera (1961); *Twone in Sunshine*, "entertainment for theater" (1969); *Liana's Song*, ballet for Piano, 4–Hands (1995); *Luna Lunera*, ballet (1996); *Loteria*, ballet (1998). **ORCH.:** Piano Concerto (1956); Concerto for Viola and Small Orch. (1959); *Serenade No. 1* for Violin and Orch. (1960); *"...that no one knew"* for Violin and Orch. (1969); *Dances of Love and Laughter* for Piano and Orch. (1998). **CHAMBER:** 2 string quartets (1950, 1969); Woodwind Quintet (1955); Piano Quintet (1958); *Sources I* for Flute and Piano (1964), *II* for Violin, Celesta, and Piano (1965), and *III* for Clarinet and Percussion (1967); *2 Pieces* for Cello and Piano (1982); Violin Sonata (1994; rev. 1999); *Moku* (Island) for 3 Percussionists (1998). **Piano:** 4 sonatas (1948, 1958, 1959, 1962); *Go-hyang* (Ancestral Home; 1994); *24 Preludes* (1996). **VOCAL:** *Pie Jesu* for Soprano and Piano (1952); *Vanishing Spring* for Soprano and Piano (1953); *Portami il Girasole* for Soprano and Piano (1957); *Gloria del distesso mezzogiorno* for Soprano, Violin, and Cello (1985); *Songs of Love and Sorrow* for Soprano and Piano (1989); *Candytata* for Soprano and Piano (1993); *Life Begins at 40* for Mezzo-soprano and Piano (1998).—**NS/LK/DM**

Burgess, Anthony (real name, **John Anthony Burgess Wilson**), celebrated English novelist, critic, and composer; b. Manchester, Feb. 25, 1917; d. London, Nov. 22, 1993. He studied language and literature at the Univ. of Manchester (B.A., 1940); he also played piano in jazz combos and taught himself to compose by a close study of the Classical masters. He was active as a teacher in England and the Far East; later was writer-in- residence at the Univ. of N.C. at Chapel Hill (1969–70), visiting prof. at Princeton Univ. and Columbia Univ. (1970), and distinguished prof. at City Coll. of the City Univ. of N.Y. (1972–73). As a novelist, Burgess made a notable impression with his disturbing *A Clockwork Orange* (1962), which was followed by such novels as the *Napoleon Symphony* (1974) and his major literary achievement, *Earthly Powers* (1980). Among his other writings were *This Man and Music* (1982) and the autobiography, *Little Wilson and Big God* (1987). As a composer, he produced a respectable body of works notable for being refreshingly rhythmical and tonal, but not without quirky quartal harmonies and atonal diversions.

WORKS: DRAMATIC: O p e r a : *Blooms of Dublin* (1981). ORCH.: Sym. (1937); Sinfonietta for Jazz Combo (1941); *Gibraltar*, symphonic poem (1944); Cello Concerto (1944); *Song of a Northern City* for Piano and Orch. (1947); *Ascent of F6* for Dance Band (1947); *The Adding Machine* for Dance Band (1949); *Partita* for Strings (1951); *Ludus Multitonalis* for Recorder Consort (1951); Concertino for Piano and Percussion (1951); *Sinfoni Melayu* (1956); Concerto for Flute and Strings (1960); *Passacaglia* (1961); Sym. in C (1975); Piano Concerto (1976); *A Glasgow Overture* (1985); *Mr. Burgess's Almanac* (1988); *Petite Symphonie pour Strasbourg* (1988); *Concerto Grosso* for 4 Guitars and Orch. (1988); *Marche pour une Révolution* (1989). CHAMBER: Cello Sonata (1944); *Cyrano de Bergerac* for Flute, Trumpet, Cello, Percussion, and Keyboard (1970); 2 guitar quartets (1984, 1987). P i a n o : 2 sonatas (1946, 1951). VOCAL: *The Brides of Enderby* for Voice, Flute, Oboe, Cello, and Piano (1976); *Man Who Has Come Through* for Voice, Flute, Oboe, Cello, and Piano (1984); *La Piaggia del Pineto* for Voice and Piano (1988). —NS/LK/DM

Burgess, Sally, South African-born English mezzo-soprano; b. Durban, Oct. 9, 1953. She was a student of Alan at the Royal Coll. of Music in London, and later pursued private training with Studholme, Salaman, and Veasey. In 1976 she began her career as a soprano with her formal debut as a soloist in the Brahms *Requiem* in London. In 1977 she made her first appearance at the English National Opera there as Bertha in *Euryanthe*, returning there in subsequent years to sing such roles as Zerlina, Cherubino, Micaëla, Massenet's Charlotte, Mimi, and Strauss's Composer. In 1978 she made her Wigmore Hall Recital debut in London, and thereafter became well known via her many concert engagements. In 1983 she made her debut as a mezzo-soprano at London's Covent Garden as Siebel. She also appeared that year at Glyndebourne as Smeraldina in Prokofiev's *The Love for 3 Oranges*. In 1986 she sang Carmen at the English National Opera, and also appeared with Opera North. She sang Fricka in *Die Walküre* at Glasgow's Scottish Opera in 1991, returning there in 1992 as Annius in *La Clemenza di Tito*. In 1991 she also sang in the premiere of Paul McCartney's *Liverpool Oratorio*. She portrayed Dalila in Nantes in 1994. In 1996 she sang

Strauss's Herodias at the English National Opera and Isabella in *The Voyage* at the Metropolitan Opera. In 1997 she appeared in the premiere of *Twice Through the Heart* at the Aldeburgh Festival.—NS/LK/DM

Burghauser, Jarmil, distinguished Czech composer, conductor, and musicologist; b. Písek, Oct. 21, 1921. After training in composition with Křička (1933–37) and Jeremiáš (1937–40), he pursued studies in conducting at the Prague Cons. with Doležil and Dědeček (graduated, 1944), and then at its master school with Talich (graduated, 1946); subsequently he took courses in musicology and psychology at the Charles Univ. in Prague, but quit his studies in protest against the Communist coup in 1948; it was not until 1991 that he presented his diss. and was awarded his Ph.D. He served as chorus master and conductor at the National Theater in Prague from 1946 to 1950, and thereafter devoted himself principally to composition and scholarship. Following the Soviet-bloc invasion of his homeland in 1968 and the restoration of hard-line Communist rule, he became suspect. Although he had done valuable work on the critical edition of Dvořák's works, his name was not acknowledged in the new vols. In order to get his music before the public, he took the pseudonym Michal Hájků. From 1978 to 1989 to was choirmaster at St. Margaret's church in Prague. Following the overthrow of the Communist regime by the "Velvet Revolution" in 1989, Burghauser became a leading figure in the restoration of the musical life of his country by serving as chairman of the Guild of Composers and as a member of the rehabilitation committee of the Ministry of Culture. In addition to his valuable work on the critical edition of Dvořák's compositions, he also ed. works for the critical editions of the music of Janáček, Smetana, and Fibich. In his own compositions, he developed a style which he described as harmonic serialism. Under his pseudonym, he composed an interesting series of works in the style of earlier periods which he called "Storica apocrifa della musica Boema."

WORKS: DRAMATIC: *Lakomec* (The Miser), opera (1949; Liberec, May 20, 1950); *Karolinka a lhář* (Caroline and the Liar), opera (1950–53; Olomouc, March 13, 1955); *Honza a čert* (Honza and the Devil), ballet (Ostrava, Nov. 23, 1954; rev. 1960); *Sluha dvou pánů* (Servant of 2 Masters), ballet (1957; Prague, May 9, 1958); *Most* (The Bridge), anti-opera (1963–64; Prague, March 31, 1967); *Tristam a Izalda*, ballet (1969). ORCH.: Syms.: No. 1 (1933; rev. 1974); No. 2 (1935; rev. 1979); No. 3 (1936; rev. 1959); *Indiánská symfonie* (1974); Sinfonia in F (1980); *Jarní rondo* (Spring rondo) for Small Orch. (1937; rev. 1970); Suite for Chamber Orch. (1939; rev. 1977); Concerto for Wind Quintet and Strings (1942; Prague, Feb. 12, 1948); Toccata for Small Orch. (1947); *Symphonic Variations on We Greet the Spring* (1952); Symphonic Suite (1955); *Sedem reliefu* (7 Reliefs; 1962; Prague, Feb. 19, 1963); *Cesty* (Ways) for Strings, Percussion, and Bowed Instruments (1964; Prague, Feb. 21, 1965); *Barvy v čase* (Colors in Time) for Small Orch. (Wexford, Ireland, Oct. 25, 1967); *Strom života* (The Tree of Life; 1968; Graz, Oct. 22, 1969); *Rožmberská suita* (Rožmberk Suite) for Small Orch. (1972); Concerto for Guitar and Strings (1978); *Ciaconna per il fine d'un tempo* for Piano and Orch. (1982). CHAMBER: *Romance* for Violin and Piano (1933; rev. 1984); 5 trios for 2 Oboes and Bassoon (1933–83); 5 string quartets (1934, rev. 1953; 1937, rev. 1953; 1941;

1944; 1944–51); 2 suites for 6 Clarinets (1938, 1970); 2 trios for Flute, Viola, and Guitar (1938, rev. 1967; 1962); 2 piano trios (1938, rev. 1982; 1940); Nonet (1942); *Možnosti* (Possibilities) for Clarinet, Cimbalom, and Percussion (1965); *10 Sketches* for Flute (1965); *Patero zamyšlení* (5 Reflections) for Violin and Guitar (1966); *Pět barevných střepin* (5 Colored Splinters) for Harp (1966); Violin Sonata, *Neveselé vyprávění* (Cheerless Tale; 1970); *Stanze dell'ansietà e speranza* for Flute, Oboe, Violin, Viola, Cello, and Harpsichord (1971); *Soumraky a svítání* (Dusks and Dawns) for Bass Clarinet and Piano (1971); *Plochy a čáry* (Areas and Lines) for Violin, Guitar, and Cello (1972); *Jitřní hudba* (Morning Music) for Flute and Guitar (1974); *Partita* for 2 Flutes, Guitar, and Cello (1976); *Lobkovitz Trio* for Flute, Guitar, and Cello (1977); *Vchynice Trio* for Flute, Violin, and Cello (1978); *Parthia czeská* for Recorder, Lute, and Viola da Gamba (1978); *Coree regales* for Early Instruments (1978); *Sonata da chiesa* for Flute, Oboe, Violin, Viola, Cello, and Harpsichord (1979); String Trio (1982); *Alejí času* (By the Alley of Time) for Trumpet, Horn, and Trombone (1982); *Pianot, rabbia e conforto* for Cello and Piano (1982); *Tre ricercari* for 9 Instruments (1983); Viola Sonata (1985); *Recitativo e terzetto* for Flute, Violin, and Cello (1989); *Tesknice* (Nostalgia) *II* for Violin and Cimbalom (1989); numerous works for 1 or 2 Guitars. **VOCAL:** *Utrpení a vzkříšení* (Suffering and Resurrection), vocal sym. (1937–46; Prague, May 26, 1946); *Věčná oblaka* (Eternal Clouds), cantata (1942); *Tajemný trubač* (The Mystic Trumpeter), cantata after Walt Whitman (1944); *Česká* (Czech), cantata (1952); *Země zamyšlená* (Thoughtful Earth), cantata (1966; Prague, March 24, 1968); *Pašije podle Lukáše* (St. Luke Passion) for Soloists and Chorus (1977); *Proprium de Nativiatate* for Soloists, Chorus, and Orch. (1978); *Missa brevis pastoralis* for Soloists, Chorus, and Orch. (1980); *V zemi české* (In the Czech Country) for Reciters, Chorus, and Orch. (1982); choruses; song cycles.

WRITINGS (all publ. in Prague): *Orchestrace Dvořákových Slovanských tanců* (Orchestration of Dvořák's Slavonic Dances; 1959); *Antonín Dvořák: Tematický katalog, bibliografie, přehled života a díla* (Antonín Dvořák: Thematic Catalog, Bibliography, Survey of Life and Work; 1960); *Nejen pomníky* (Not Monuments Only; 1966); *Antonín Dvořák* (1966); with A. Špelda, *Akustické základy orchestrace* (Acoustic Basis of Orchestration; 1967; Ger. tr., 1971); completion of J. Rychlík's *Moderní instrumentace* (Modern Instrumentation; 1968); *Česká interpretační tradice* (Czech Tradition of Interpretation; 1982).—NS/LK/DM

Burghersh, Lord John Fane, 11th Earl of Westmorland, English politician, general, diplomat, and amateur musician; b. London, Feb. 3, 1784; d. Wansford, Northamptonshire, Oct. 16, 1859. He was educated at Harrow and at Trinity Coll., Cambridge (M.A., 1808), where he received training in music from Hague. He was active in several military campaigns during the Napoleonic wars, and served as aide-de-camp to the Duke of Wellington, his wife's uncle; he also was a member of Parliament for Lyme Regis (1806–16). In 1822 he was made privy councillor, in 1825 a major general, in 1838 a lieutenant general, and in 1854 a general; he was also the British envoy in Florence (1814–30), resident minister in Berlin (1841–51), and ambassador in Vienna (1851–55). Through his persistent efforts, the Royal Academy of Music was organized in

London in 1822, and he ruled the institution with an iron hand for the rest of his life. His compositions were disdained in his day and are now mercifully forgotten. —NS/LK/DM

Burgmüller, family of German musicians:

(1) Johann August Franz Burgmüller, organist and conductor; b. Magdeburg, April 28, 1766; d. Düsseldorf, Aug. 21, 1824. After touring as a theater conductor, he settled in Düsseldorf. In 1818 he founded the Lower Rhine Music Festival, which he served as director. He also was the first music director of Düsseldorf. He had two sons:

(2) (Johann) Friedrich (Franz) Burgmüller, composer; b. Regensburg, Dec. 4, 1806; d. Beaulieu, near Paris, Feb. 13, 1874. He studied with Spohr in Kassel, and then settled in Paris and adopted a light style of composition. His ballet *La Peri* (Paris, Feb. 22, 1843) won great popularity. With Flotow and Delvedez, he wrote the ballet *Lady Henriette* (Paris, Feb. 21, 1844). Among his other works were many salon pieces and didactic studies.

(3) (August Joseph) Norbert Burgmüller, composer; b. Düsseldorf, Feb. 8, 1810; d. Aachen, May 7, 1836. He was a child prodigy who began composing at an early age. He received training from his father, and in Kassel with Spohr and Hauptmann. Burgmüller composed a Sym., a Piano Concerto, chamber music, piano pieces, and songs. A second Sym., in B minor, the same key as Schubert's Eighth Sym., was left unfinished. Schumann thought highly of Burgmüller's talent and completed the third movement, a scherzo, of the score, which received many performances in this form.

BIBL.: H. Eckert, *N. B.* (Augsburg, 1932).—NS/LK/DM

Burgon, Geoffrey (Alan), English composer; b. Hambledon, July 15, 1941. He was a student of Peter Wishart (composition) and Bernard Brown (trumpet) at the Guildhall School of Music and Drama in London. After playing trumpet in various orchs., jazz ensembles, and theater orchs. (1964–71), he devoted himself to composing and to conducting for films and television. His scores for the television series *Tinker, Tailor, Soldier, Spy* (1979) and *Brideshead Revisited* (1981) established his reputation. He has demonstrated special talent in composing works for vocal forces.

WORKS: DRAMATIC: O p e r a : *Hard Times* (1991). M u s i c T h e a t e r : *Epitaph to Sir Walter Raleigh* (1968; London, Feb. 8, 1969); *Joan of Arc* (1970); *The Fall of Lucifer* (1977); *Mirandola* (1980–81); *Orpheus* (Wells, July 17, 1982). B a l l e t : *The Golden Fish* (1964); *Ophelia* (1964); *The Calm* (1974); *Running Figures/Goldberg's Dream* (Leeds, March 25, 1975); *Step at a Time* (London, Nov. 4, 1976); *Persephone* (1979); *Lamentations and Praises* (Jerusalem, Aug. 7, 1979); *Mass* (1984; London, Sept. 16, 1985); *The Trial of Prometheus* (1988); film and television scores. ORCH.: Concerto for Strings (1963; Bath, June 6, 1977); *5 Pieces* for Strings (1967); *Gendling* (London, July 11, 1968); *Alleluia Nativitas* (London, Feb. 17, 1970); *Cantus Alleluia* (1973; London, April 10, 1974); *May Day Prelude* (London, May 1, 1977); *Brideshead Variations* (London, March 21, 1982; also for Brass or Concert Band); Trumpet Concerto, *The Turning World* (London, July 15, 1993); *Suite from Martin Chuzzlewit* (Birmingham, Nov. 20, 1994); *Paradise Dances* for Brass Band (London, Nov. 24, 1994); *City Adventures* for Percussion and Orch. (London, Aug. 26, 1996); Piano Concerto (Singapore, Oct. 24, 1997). **CHAMBER**: *Fanfares and Variants* for 2 Trumpets and 2 Trombones (1969); *Gloria* for 6 Instruments (1973); *3 Nocturnes* for Harp (1974); *4 Guitars* (1977); *4 Horns* (1977); Oboe Quartet (1980); *Sanctus Variations* for 2 Trumpets and Organ (1980); *Chamber Dances* (1981–82); *Little Missenden Variations* for Clarinet, English Horn, Horn, and Bassoon (1984); *Fanfare* for Horns, Trumpets, Trombones, and Tuba (1985); *The Wanderer* for Clarinet and String Quartet (1997–98; London, March 18, 1998). **VOCAL**: *Cantata on Medieval Latin Texts* for Countertenor, Flute, Oboe, and Bassoon (1964); *Acquainted with Night* for Countertenor, Strings, Harp, and Percussion (1965); *The Think on Dredful Domeday* for Voices and Orch. (1969); *Magnificat* for Voices and Orch. (1970); *The Golden Eternity* for Voices and Orch. (1970); *This Endris Night* for Tenor, Women's Voices, and Brass (1972); *Canciones del Alma* for 2 Countertenors and 13 Solo Strings (1975); *Requiem* for Soprano, Countertenor, Tenor, Chorus, and Orch. (Hereford, Aug. 26, 1976); *Veni Spiritus* for Soprano, Baritone, Chorus, and Orch. (1978–79); *Magnificat and Nunc Dimittis* for 2 Sopranos, Trumpet, Organ, and Strings (1979); *Hymn to St. Thomas of Hereford* for Chorus and Orch. (1981; Hereford, Aug. 22, 1982); *The World Again* for Soprano and Orch. (1982–83; London, Oct. 9, 1984); *Revelations* for Soprano, Tenor, Baritone, Chorus, and Orch. (1984; London, April 13, 1985); *Title Divine* for Soprano and Orch. (1986; London, April 22, 1987); *A Vision* for Tenor and String Orch. (1991); *First Was the World* for Countertenor or Mezzo-soprano, Chorus, and Orch. (London, June 8, 1994); *Almost Peace*, 3 songs for Soprano and Instrumental Ensemble (BBC Radio 3, Oct. 1, 1995); *Merciless Beauty* for Countertenor and Orch. (1996; Woodburn Festival, Oct. 18, 1997).—NS/LK/DM

Burgstaller, Alois, German tenor; b. Holzkirchen, Sept. 21, 1871; d. Gmund, April 19, 1945. He was trained as a watchmaker, and also sang; encouraged by Cosima Wagner, he made a serious study of singing, and performed the roles of Siegfried, Siegmund, Erik, and Parsifal at the Bayreuth Festivals (1896–1902). He made his American debut at the Metropolitan Opera in N.Y. as Siegmund in *Die Walküre* on Feb. 12, 1903; remained on its roster until his final appearance, again as Siegmund, on Jan. 14, 1909. He also sang the title role in the first staged American performance of *Parsifal*, in N.Y., on Dec. 24, 1903, in violation of the German copyright; as a result, he was permanently banned from Bayreuth. In 1910 he returned to Germany.—NS/LK/DM

Burian, Emil František, Czech composer and stage director; b. Pilsen, June 11, 1904; d. Prague, Aug. 9, 1959. His father was a baritone and his mother a singing teacher. He received his training at the Prague Cons. where he attended Foerster's masterclass in composition (graduated, 1927). Even before graduating, he was active in avant-garde quarters in Prague as a stage director, dramatist, actor, and musician. With his mother, he presented concerts of new music from 1920. In 1924 he organized Přítomnost, a soc. for contemporary music. In 1927 he organized the Voice Band, which sang according to prescribed rhythm but without definite pitch. It attracted considerable attention at the Sienna ISCM Festival on Sept. 12, 1928. Between 1929

and 1932 he was active in Brno and Oloumoc. In 1933 he founded his own D 34 theater in Prague. During the Nazi occupation, Burian's theater was shut down and he was placed in a concentration camp. After his liberation, he was a director in Brno (1945–46). In 1946 he returned to Prague and served that year as director of the Karlín musical theater. His long-standing commitment to the political Left led to his being made a deputy in the post-World War II National Assembly. As a composer, he followed an eclectic path, finding inspiration in Czech folk art, jazz, the music of Les Six, and Dada. Between the 2 World Wars, he was one of the leading figures in the Czech avant-garde. After World War II and the installation of the Communist regime, he embraced the tenets of socialist realism. His writings, all publ. in Prague, include *O moderní ruské hudbě* (1926); *Polydynamika* (1926); *Jazz* (1928); *Památník bratří Burianů* (Almanac of the Burian Brothers; 1929); *Pražská dramaturgie* (1938); *Emil Burian* (1947); *Karel Burian* (1948); *Divadlo za našich dnů* (The Theater of Our Days; 1962).

WORKS: DRAMATIC: O p e r a : *Alladine a Palomid* (1923; rev. version, Prague, Oct. 14, 1959); *Před slunce východem* (Before Sunrise; Prague, Nov. 24, 1925); *Bubu z Montparnassu* (Bubu from Montparnasse (1927; Prague, March 20, 1999); *Mastičkář* (The Quack; Prague, May 23, 1928; rev. by R. Krátký, 1955); *Milenci z kiosku* (The Lovers from the Market Stall; Prague, Nov. 13, 1935); *Maryša* (Brno, April 16, 1940); *Opera z pouti* (Country Fair Scenes; Prague, Jan. 28, 1956); *Račte odpusdit* (Please Forgive Me; Prague, Oct. 13, 1956). **OTHER:** Ballets and film scores. **ORCH.:** *Suita poetica* (5 separate movements: 1925, 1947, 1950, 1951, 1953); Suite for Oboe and Strings (1928); *Reminiscence*, symphonic suite (1929–36); 2 syms. (*Sirène*, 1947; 1948); Accordion Concerto (1949); *Overture to Socialism* (1950). **CHAMBER:** Trio for Flute, Viola, and Cello (1924); *From Youth*, string sextet (1924); Duo for Violin and Cello (1925); 8 string quartets (1927, 1929, 1940, 1947, 1947, 1948, 1949, 1951); *Variations* for Wind Quintet (1928); *Of Warm Nights*, suite for Violin and Piano (1928); *Passacaglia* for Violin and Viola (1929); *4 Pieces* for Wind Quintet (1929); Wind Quintet (1930); Suite for Cello and Piano (1935); *Sonata romantica* for Violin and Piano (1938); *Lost Serenade* for Flute and Piano (1940); Duo for Violin and Piano (1946); *Fantasie* for Violin and Piano (1954). **P i a n o :** *American Suite* for 2 Pianos (1926); Sonata (1927); *Echoes of Czech Dances* (1953); Sonatina (1954). **VOCAL:** *Cocktails*, song cycle for Voice and Jazz Band (1926); *Requiem* for Voice Band and Jazz Band (1927); *May*, cantata for Voice Band, Harp, 2 Pianos, and Timpani (1936); *Children's Songs*, song cycle for Voice and Chamber Orch. (1937).

BIBL.: B. Srba, *Poetické divadlo E.F. B.a* (The Poetic Theater of E.F. B.; Prague, 1971); I. Kladiva, *E.F. B.* (Prague, 1982). —NS/LK/DM

Burke, Johnny (John), light-hearted American lyricist; b. Antioch, Calif., Oct. 3, 1908; d. N.Y., Feb. 25, 1964. Burke wrote songs for at least 43 motion pictures between 1930 and 1956. Most of the films were released by Paramount, starred Bing Crosby, and had music by James Van Heusen. Burke's other most frequent collaborators included Arthur Johnston and James V. Monaco. He sometimes composed his own music, but with Van Heusen he wrote such songs as the Academy Award-winning "Swinging on a Star," "Moonlight Becomes You," and "Sunday, Monday or Always," all of which were million-sellers. With others he wrote such hits as "Pennies from Heaven," "I've Got a Pocketful of Dreams," "Scatterbrain," and "Only Forever." His whimsical, optimistic words helped set the tone for the popular music of the late 1930s and 1940s.

The son of William Burke, Johnny Burke grew up in Chicago and attended Crane Coll. in the city as well as the Univ. of Wisc. at Madison, studying piano and drama. He became a pianist in dance bands and in 1926 took a job as a piano salesman with the music-publishing company Irving Berlin Inc. in Chicago, later moving to the N.Y. office. In N.Y. he also worked as an entertainer in vaudeville, film, and the legitimate theater, and he turned to songwriting, initially as a composer. He was hired by the Fox movie studio and went to Hollywood where he wrote "Boop-Boop-a-Doopa-Doo Fox Trot" (lyrics by George A. Little), which was sung in the February 1930 release *Let's Go Places* by actress Dixie Lee, who seven months later married Bing Crosby.

Burke earned his first screen credit as a primary songwriter for the June 1930 release *Rough Romance*, but with the decline in interest in musicals in Hollywood in the early 1930s, he returned to N.Y. to write for Tin Pan Alley; he also switched to lyric writing. More than three years passed before he scored his first hit, "Shadows on the Swanee" (music by Harold Spina, lyrics also by Joe Young), recorded by Isham Jones and His Orch., in September 1933. The same trio of writers was also responsible for "Annie Doesn't Live Here Anymore," which became a hit for Guy Lombardo and His Royal Canadians in November.

Burke formed his first songwriting partnership with Harold Spina, and the two wrote a spate of hits over the next two years: "The Beat o' My Heart," recorded by Ben Pollack and His Orch. (March 1934); "I've Got a Warm Spot in My Heart for You," by Pollack (July 1934); "Irresistible," by Hal Kemp and His Orch. (October 1934); "It's Dark on Observatory Hill," by the Dorsey Brothers Orch. (January 1935); and "You're So Darn Charming," by Kemp (August 1935).

In 1936, Burke signed to Paramount Pictures, where he would work for the next 20 years, and moved to Hollywood. He was teamed with composer Arthur Johnston, and their first project was a Mae West vehicle, *Go West, Young Man*, which was released in November. No hits emerged from that film, but Burke and Johnston's next assignment was more successful. They were lent, along with Bing Crosby, to Columbia Pictures and had five songs in *Pennies from Heaven*, including the title song, which topped the hit parade for Crosby and earned an Academy Award nomination. Burke and Johnston were among the several songwriters who contributed to the August 1937 Crosby picture *Double or Nothing*. One of their songs was "The Moon Got in My Eyes," which Crosby took into the hit parade in September.

By the end of 1937, Burke had acquired a new collaborator, James V. Monaco. Burke became, and would remain for the next 16 years, Crosby's primary lyricist. The first project for the new team was the May 1938 release *Doctor Rhythm*; among Burke and Monaco's

four songs was "On the Sentimental Side," which Crosby took into the hit parade even before the film opened. *Sing, You Sinners*, which followed only three months later, featured "I've Got a Pocketful of Dreams," with which Crosby topped the hit parade in October, in close competition with a version by Russ Morgan and His Orch.

East Side of Heaven, the next Crosby film with songs by Burke and Monaco, opened in April 1939; none of its songs became hits. On June 10, 1939, Burke married Bessie Patterson, who had come to Hollywood as the winner of a beauty contest that entitled her to a bit part in the 1936 Crosby film *Rhythm on the Range* and then attended the Univ. of Southern Calif. The couple later divorced. In total, Burke married four times, divorced three times, and had four children.

Burke had began to collaborate with other writers by the summer of 1939. He worked with James Van Heusen for the first time, writing "Oh, You Crazy Moon," which Tommy Dorsey and His Orch. took into the hit parade in September. Burke returned to Monaco for the next Crosby film, *The Star Maker*, which opened in August and gave Crosby three hit parade entries, "Go Fly a Kite," "A Man and His Dream," and "An Apple for the Teacher" (the last in a duet with Connee Boswell), all in September. Crosby was back in the hit parade in October with "What's New?" The song had begun life as an instrumental that Robert Haggart, of Bob Crosby's orchestra, had developed from a solo by the band's trumpeter, Billy Butterfield, in 1938 and was initially titled "I'm Free." Burke then added lyrics to create a song that went on to become a standard. Burke had yet another hit parade entry and one of the biggest hits of the year in November 1939 with "Scatterbrain" (music and lyrics by Burke, Carl Bean, Kahn Keene, and Frankie Masters). It was recorded by Frankie Masters and His Orch. and was at the top of the charts in December–January 1940.

Burke returned to working with Monaco at Paramount for *Road to Singapore*, the first of the Bing Crosby–Bob Hope "road" pictures, released in March. Crosby had an entry in the hit parade from that film in April with "Too Romantic." That same month Crosby's next film, *If I Had My Way*, opened, but no hits emerged from the Burke-Monaco score. Burke returned to moonlighting with Van Heusen and scored a #1 hit in June with "Imagination," recorded by Glenn Miller and His Orch. Miller also made the hit parade in June with "Devil May Care," which Burke wrote with Harry Warren.

Monaco had already completed his contract with Paramount and left the studio by the time his final film with Burke and Crosby, *Rhythm on the River*, was released in August. It was one of their more successful scores, providing Crosby with his biggest hit of the year, the chart-topping, Oscar-nominated "Only Forever," as well as the chart entry "That's for Me."

With the departure of Monaco, Burke arranged for Van Heusen to be signed to Paramount as his new full-time partner. Their first effort, *Love Thy Neighbor*, a vehicle for radio comedians Jack Benny and Fred Allen released in December 1940, did not produce any hits, perhaps because of the dispute between ASCAP and the radio networks that caused ASCAP songs to be banned from airplay in early 1941. The ban was still on in April, when Burke and Van Heusen's score to the second Crosby-Hope road picture *Road to Zanzibar* went unnoticed; but in July 1943, during the musicians' union recording ban, Tommy Dorsey's 1941 recording of one of its songs, "It's Always You," with a vocal by Frank Sinatra, belatedly reached the Top Ten.

Crosby next made two pictures for which he did not need his contract writers, *Birth of the Blues*, which featured a score full of old jazz songs, and *Holiday Inn*, which featured songs by Irving Berlin. Burke and Van Heusen were lent out to RKO for two Kay Kyser vehicles, *Playmates*, released in December 1941, and *My Favorite Spy*, released in May 1942. Back at Paramount they drew the third Crosby-Hope road picture, *Road to Morocco*, released in November 1942. Crosby scored the highest charting recording of "Moonlight Becomes You" from the score; Glenn Miller's recording also made the Top Ten; and the version by Harry James and His Orch. sold a million copies. Crosby also had a chart entry with "Constantly" from the film.

The combination of the U.S. entry into World War II in December 1941 and the beginning of the recording ban in August 1942 slowed work for the songwriters, who had only one film, the Crosby vehicle *Dixie*, in 1943. Released in June, it contained "Sunday, Monday or Always," which Crosby recorded a cappella backed by a vocal group; the disc topped the charts and sold a million copies. "If You Please" from the film also made the charts for Crosby.

Burke and Van Heusen's first assignment for 1944 was to add music to the movie version of the Kurt Weill–Ira Gershwin musical *Lady in the Dark*. Released in February, it contained "Suddenly It's Spring," which Glen Gray and the Casa Loma Orch. recorded for a hit. The team's next Crosby film was *Going My Way*, released in May; it became the top box office hit of the year and featured "Swinging on a Star," which became the biggest hit of the year in Crosby's recording, selling a million copies, and won the Academy Award. Crosby also scored minor hits with the title song and "The Day after Forever." Burke and Van Heusen wrote songs for two more films during the year: *And the Angels Sing*, featuring Betty Hutton, contained "His Rocking Horse Ran Away," which Hutton recorded for a Top Ten hit, and "It Could Happen to You," a Top Ten hit for Jo Stafford; and *Bell of the Yukon*, featuring Dinah Shore, contained "Sleigh Ride in July," which Shore recorded for a Top Ten hit and which earned an Academy Award nomination, and "Like Someone in Love," a chart entry for Crosby.

Burke and Van Heusen's movie schedule was light in 1945 as they concentrated on writing their first Broadway musical, *Nellie Bly*. But they did score a few hits: "Yah-Ta-Ta Yah-Ta-Ta (Talk, Talk, Talk)," a novelty song crafted for Crosby and Judy Garland, reached the Top Ten in June; "A Friend of Yours," from the Crosby-produced film *The Great John L.*, was a Top Ten hit for Tommy Dorsey in July; and "Aren't You Glad You're You?" their sole contribution to *The Bells of St. Mary's*

(the December sequel to *Going My Way*), was a Top Ten hit for Crosby and an Academy Award nominee. (Van Heusen also wrote the music to lyrics by actor Phil Silvers, reportedly assisted by Burke and Sammy Cahn, for "Nancy [With the Laughing Face]," a tribute to Frank Sinatra's four-year-old daughter, which Sinatra recorded for a Top Ten hit in December.)

Nellie Bly opened on Broadway in January 1946; it was a flop, running only 16 performances, and none of its songs became hits at the time, although "Harmony" was interpolated into the October 1947 film *Variety Girl*, where it was sung by Bing Crosby and Bob Hope; it was then recorded for a minor hit by Johnny Mercer and the King Cole Trio.

Road to Utopia, the fourth Crosby-Hope road picture, opened in February 1946, as usual with a Burke–Van Heusen score. The risqué "Personality" emerged as a major hit, with three Top Ten renditions, the most successful being the #1 version by Johnny Mercer. *Welcome Stranger*, released in August 1947, was not exactly another sequel to *Going My Way*, but it reteamed Crosby with Barry Fitzgerald in a similar scenario. It was similarly successful, too, becoming the top-grossing film of the year, though none of its Burke–Van Heusen songs became hits. *Road to Rio*, the fifth Crosby-Hope road picture, released in February 1948, also became the top grossing film of its year, and its Burke–Van Heusen score included "But Beautiful," which became a minor hit for Frank Sinatra. For *The Emperor Waltz*, the Crosby film released in June 1948 that was one of the ten most successful films of the year, Burke wrote lyrics for song adaptations of music by Richard Heuberger and Johann Strauss. Also successful was Crosby's filming of *A Connecticut Yankee in King Arthur's Court*, released in April 1949, with a Burke–Van Heusen score that included two chart entries, "Once and for Always" (for Jo Stafford) and "If You Stub Your Toe on the Moon" (for Tony Martin).

Burke and Van Heusen continued to write songs for Crosby films into the early 1950s. Burke scored hits in 1953 with two adaptations of classical music: "Wild Horses," a Top Ten hit for Perry Como in March, was based on Robert Schumann's "Wilder Reiter," while "Now That I'm in Love," a chart single for Patti Page in May, was adapted from Gioachino Rossini's "The William Tell Overture." Burke and Van Heusen wrote the songs for and coproduced their second Broadway musical, *Carnival in Flanders*, in September 1953, but it was a failure. After providing lyrics to Van Heusen's music for his 24th Bing Crosby film, *Little Boy Lost*, released later that month, Burke became inactive, reportedly due to illness; Van Heusen formed a partnership with Sammy Cahn.

Burke returned to work with the film *The Vagabond King*, released in September 1956, writing lyrics to music by Rudolf Friml. In 1959 he wrote lyrics for the Erroll Garner instrumental "Misty," resulting in a Top 40 hit for Johnny Mathis; the song enjoyed Top 40 revivals in 1963, for Lloyd Price, in 1966, for Richard "Groove" Holmes, and in 1975, for Ray Stevens. In 1961, Burke wrote music as well as lyrics for his third Broadway musical, *Donnybrook!*, based on the 1952 film *The Quiet*

Man; it ran 68 performances and the cast album spent two months on the charts. Big Dee Irwin with Little Eva revived "Swinging on a Star" for a Top 40 hit in 1963.

Burke died in 1964 at age 55. In 1983, Linda Ronstadt, accompanied by the Nelson Riddle Orch., revived "What's New?" as a Top 40 single and as the title track of an album that sold three million copies. *Swinging on a Star*, subtitled "The Johnny Burke Musical," which was conceived, written, and directed by Michael Leeds, opened on Broadway in 1995 and played for 97 performances, earning a Tony Award nomination for Best Musical.

WORKS (only works for which Burke was a primary, credited songwriter are listed): **MUSICALS/REVUES:** *Nellie Bly* (N.Y., Jan. 21, 1946); *Carnival in Flanders* (N.Y., Sept. 8, 1953); *Donnybrook!* (N.Y., May 18, 1961); *Swinging on a Star* (N.Y., Oct. 22, 1995). **FILMS:** *Rough Romance* (1930); *Go West, Young Man* (1936); *Pennies from Heaven* (1936); *Doctor Rhythm* (1938); *Sing, You Sinners* (1938); *East Side of Heaven* (1939); *The Star Maker* (1939); *Road to Singapore* (1940); *If I Had My Way* (1940); *Rhythm on the River* (1940); *Love Thy Neighbor* (1940); *Road to Zanzibar* (1941); *Playmates* (1941); *My Favorite Spy* (1942); *Road to Morocco* (1942); *Dixie* (1943); *Going My Way* (1944); *And the Angels Sing* (1944); *Belle of the Yukon* (1945); *Road to Utopia* (1946); *London Town* (aka *My Heart Goes Crazy*; 1946); *Cross My Heart* (1946); *Welcome Stranger* (1947); *Road to Rio* (1948); *A Connecticut Yankee in King Arthur's Court* (1949); *Top o' the Morning* (1949); *Riding High* (1950); *Mr. Music* (1950); *Road to Bali* (1953); *Little Boy Lost* (1953).—**WR**

Burke, Solomon, the original soul singer (b. Philadelphia, Pa., 1936). By the age of 12, Solomon Burke was a bishop in the church where both his grandmother and mother were ministers. Called "The Wonder Boy Preacher," Burke's ministry took him all over the northeast and earned him a regular spot on the radio by the late 1940s. He also performed with a group called the Gospel Cavaliers. In his late teen years, he signed on with Apollo Records, singing gospel, R&B, and various other styles. He had some minor successes like "You Can Run (But You Can't Hide)," and even made occasional national TV appearances. After leaving the label in a money dispute, he moved back to Philadelphia, eventually reduced to begging on street corners. His grandmother took him back in and helped him learn a trade; Burke is a licensed mortician.

One of Burke's Apollo recordings, "Be Bop Grandma," brought him to the attention of Atlantic Records. Unable to call himself—as the bishop of a church—an R&B singer (the elders forbade it), he coined the term "soul singer." His first Atlantic record was the country tune "Just Out of Reach (Of My Two Open Arms)." When radio programmers ignored the record, a chance meeting with the song's publisher, Gene Autry, got it on some of the stations Autry owned. This started the ball rolling. The tune eventually wound up on the R&B, country, and pop charts (#24). Burke recorded four more top-40 pop hits for Atlantic: "If You Need Me" (#37, 1963), "Goodbye Baby (Baby Goodbye)" (#33, 1964), "Got to Get You Off My Mind" (#22 pop, #1 R&B, 1965), and "Tonight's the Night" (#28, 1965). He also had 15 R&B hits, including the seminal "Everybody Needs Somebody to Love," later covered note for

note by the Blues Brothers, right down to the "I'm so happy to be here tonight" introduction. Moving on to Bell records in the late 1960s, Burke cut the Memphis soul classic *Proud Mary*, making the title track a minor hit. He took to performing on stage wearing a purple, fur-fringed robe and a crown: he was the king of soul music.

Burke's pop and soul recordings became somewhat spotty after that, though some high points include a record with the group Swamp Dogg, *From the Heart*. He made several strong gospel records for Savoy into the 1980s. He also explored acting, taking a role in *The Big Easy* and several Italian films. In the late 1980s, Burke signed with Bullseye Records, who recognized his real milieu: live performance. The 1988 album *Soul Alive* reintroduced the energized singer to contemporary audiences. The band featured several of his 21 children. He followed this up with a stunning studio album, *Change Is Gonna Come*. His most recent album, 1997's *Definition of Soul*, featuring four of his offspring, lives up to the name.

Burke claimed that as of Jan. 1, 2000, he would give up the music business to concentrate on his ministry. His Solomon's Temple: The House of God for All People has over 300 ordained ministers whose job is to "feed the hungry, educate the uneducated and be God's workers in the vineyard." The church has 40,000 parishioners in close to 200 churches across North America and Jamaica. He also owns funeral parlors in Calif., Pa., and N.C.; two of his children have turned the mortuary business into a franchise.

DISC.: *Solomon Burke* (1962); *If You Need Me* (1963); *Rock 'n'Soul* (1964); *The Rest of Solomon Burke* (1965); *I Wish I Knew* (1968); *King Solomon* (1968); *Proud Mary* (1969); *King Heavy* (1972); *Electronic Magnetism* (1972); *I Have a Dream* (1974); *Back to My Roots* (1975); *Music to Make Love To* (1975); *Sidewalks, Fences & Walls* (1979); *Lord We Need a Miracle* (1979); *King of Rock 'n'Soul* (1981); *Soul Alive* (1988); *Best of Solomon Burke* (1991); *Home in Your Heart—Best Of* (1992); *Live at House of Blues* (1994); *Definition of Soul* (1997); *Very Best of Solomon Burke* (1998); *King of Rock 'N' Soul* (1998); *Not by Water But Fire This Time* (1999). —**HB**

Burkhard, Paul, Swiss conductor and composer; b. Zürich, Dec. 21, 1911; d. Zell, Sept. 6, 1977. He was trained at the Zürich Cons. After working at the Bern City Theater (1932–34), he was resident composer at the Zürich Theater (1939–44). From 1944 to 1957 he conducted the Zürich Radio Orch. As a composer, he was successful mainly with light theater pieces. His *Der schwarze Hecht* (Zürich, April 1, 1939) was partially reworked by Erik Charell as *Feuerwerk* (Munich, May 16, 1950), and became internationally known via its song, *O, mein Papa*. Among his other theater pieces were *Hopsa* (Zürich, Nov. 30, 1935; rev. version, Wiesbaden, Oct. 12, 1957), *Dreimal Georges* (Zürich, Oct. 3, 1936), *Die Frauen von Coraya* or *Der Paradies der Frauen* (Stettin, Feb. 19, 1938), *Casanova in der Schweiz* (Zürich, 1942), *Tic-Tac* (1942), *Die Pariserin* (1946; Zürich, Dec. 31, 1957), *Die kleine Niederdorfoper* (Zürich, Dec. 31, 1951), *Bunbury* (1963; Basel, Oct. 7, 1965), *Die Schneekönigin* (Zürich, 1964) and *Regenbogen* (Basel, Nov. 30, 1977). He also wrote various works for young people, including the

Christmas opera *Ein Stern geht auf aus Jakob* (Hamburg, Dec. 6, 1970) and religious plays.

BIBL.: P. Flury and P. Kaufmann, *O mein Papa...P. B.: Leben und Werk* (Zürich, 1979).—NS/LK/DM

Burkhard, Willy, significant Swiss composer and pedagogue; b. Leubringen bei Biel, April 17, 1900; d. Zürich, June 18, 1955. After graduating from the Muristalden teachers's training college, he took up music studies with E. Graf in Bern; he then pursued training with Karg- Elert and Teichmüller in Leipzig (1921), Courvoisier in Munich (1922–23), and d'Ollone in Paris (1923–24). He taught theory at the Bern Cons. (1928–33), and later theory and composition at the Zürich Cons. (1942–55). His music was neo-Classical in form and strongly polyphonic; his astringent linear idiom was tempered by a strong sense of modal counterpoint. He made an especially important contribution to church music.

WORKS: DRAMATIC: O p e r a : *Die Schwarze Spinne* (1947–48; Zürich, May 28, 1949; rev. 1954). **ORCH.:** 2 violin concertos: No. 1 (1925) and No. 2 (1943; Zürich, Jan. 26, 1946); 2 syms. (1926–28; Sym. in 1 Movement, 1944); *Ulenspiegel Variations* (1932); *Fantasy* for Strings (1934); *Small Serenade* for Strings (1935); Concerto for Strings (1937); *Toccata* for Strings (1939); *Laupen-Suite* (1940); Concertino for Cello and Strings (1940); Organ Concerto (1945); *Hymne* for Organ and Orch. (1945); *Concertante Suite* (1946); *Piccola sinfonia giocosa* for Small Orch. (1949); *Fantasia mattutina* (1949); *Toccata* for 4 Winds, Percussion, and Strings (Zürich, Dec. 7, 1951); *Sonata da camera* for Strings and Percussion (1952); Viola Concerto (1953); Concertino for 2 Flutes, Harpsichord, and Strings (1954). **CHAMBER:** String Trio (1926); Piano Trio (1936); Violin Sonatina (1936); Suite for 2 Violins (1937); Sonata for Solo Viola (1939); String Quartet in 1 Movement (1943); *Serenade* for 8 Instruments (1945); *Romance* for Horn and Piano (1945); Violin Sonata (1946); Cello Sonata (1952); *Serenade* for Flute and Clarinet (1953); Suite for Flute (1954–55). **KEYBOARD: P i a n o :** Sonata (1942); *6 Preludes* (1954–55). **O r g a n :** *Fantasie* (1931); *Choral- Triptychon* (1953). **VOCAL: O r a t o r i o s :** *Das Gesicht Jesajas* (1933–35; Basel, Feb. 18, 1936); *Das Jahr* (1940–41; Basel, Feb. 19, 1942). **C a n t a t a s :** *Biblische Kantate* (1923); *Till Ulenspiegel* (1929); *Vorfrühling* (1930); *Spruchkantate* (1933); *Genug ist nicht genug* (1938–39; Basel, June 11, 1940); *Lob der Musik* (1939); *Cantate Domino* (1940); *Heimatliche Kantate* (1940); *Psalmen-Kantate* (1952); various other cantatas. **OTHER:** *Te Deum* for Chorus, Trumpet, Trombone, Kettledrum, and Organ (1931); *Das ewige Brausen* for Bass and Chamber Orch. (1936); *Psalm 93* for Chorus and Organ (1937); *Kreuzvolk der Schweiz* for Chorus and Organ (1941); *Magnificat* for Soprano and Strings (1942); *Cantique de notre terre* for Soloists, Chorus, and Orch. (1943); *Mass* for Soprano, Bass, Chorus, and Orch. (Zürich, June 28, 1951); *Psalm 148* for Chorus and Instruments (1954).

BIBL.: H. Zurlinden, *W. B.* (Erlenbach, 1956); E. Mohr, *W. B.: Leben und Werk* (Zürich, 1957); S. Burkhard and F. Indermühle, *W. B. (17. April 1900–18. Juni 1955) Werkverzeichnis* (Liebefeld, 1968).—NS/LK/DM

Burlas, Ladislav, Slovak composer and musicologist; b. Trnava, April 3, 1927. He first studied music with Mikuláš Schneider-Trnavský, and then went to Bratislava to pursue training in philosophy, history, and musicology at the Comenius Univ. (1946–51). He con-

currently studied composition with Alexander Moyzes at the Cons., and subsequently at the Academy of Music and Drama (1951–55). He later was awarded his C.Sc. degree (1960) and his Dr.Sc. degree (1985). From 1951 he taught in Bratislava at the Teachers' Training Coll., the Comenius Univ., and the Academy of Music and Drama. From 1960 to 1988 he also was active with the Slovak Academy of Sciences, and from 1966 he served as senior lecturer in music theory at the Prague Academy of Music. In 1990 he became a lecturer in the faculty of philosophy in Bratislava, and was named a prof. in 1993. Among his writings are books on J.L. Bella (1953), Alexander Moyzes (1956), contemporary music theory (1978), and the theory of music education (1997). In 1968 and 1980 he won prizes of the Union of Slovak Composers, in 1985 he won the prize of the Ministry of Culture, and in 1988 he won the National Prize of the Slovak Republic.

WORKS: ORCH.: Symphonic Triptych (1957); *Epitaph* (1958); *Bagatelles* for Strings (1959); *Planctus* for Strings (1968); Concertino for Winds and Percussion (1971); *Music* for Violin and Orch. (1977); Organ Concerto (1983). **CHAMBER:** *A Singing Heart* for String Sextet (1960); Sonatina for Solo Violin (1968); 3 string quartets (1969, 1972, 1977); *Sonata Concertante* for Violin (1974); *Cadence* for Violin (1974); Sonata for Solo Violin (1975); *Poetical Music* for Wind Quintet (1983). **P i a n o :** Sonatina (1978); *Lyrical Music* (1979); *To Matica slovenská*, sonata (1988). **VOCAL:** *Miners' Cantata* for Soloists, Chorus, and Orch. (1955); *Wedding Songs from Horehronie* for Chorus and Orch. (1955); *Metamorphoses of Beauties* for Chorus and Violin (1964); *The Bells* for Chorus (1969); *6 Love Poems* for Chorus (1975); *To Meet a Human Being* for Mezzo- soprano, Baritone, Chorus, and Orch. (1984).—NS/LK/DM

Burleigh, Cecil, American composer, violinist, and teacher; b. Wyo., N.Y., April 17, 1885; d. Madison, Wisc., July 28, 1980. He studied violin and theory as a child; after training with Anton Witek (violin) and Leichtentritt (composition) at the Klindworth-Scharwenka Cons. in Berlin (1903–05), he studied with Émile Sauret (violin) and Borowski (composition) at the Chicago Musical Coll. (1905–07). From 1907 to 1909 he toured as a soloist with orchs. and as a recitalist in North America. He taught violin at the Western Inst. of Music and Drama in Denver (1909–11), violin and theory at Morningside Coll. in Sioux City, Iowa (1911–14), and at Mont. State Univ. in Missoula. In 1919 he went to N.Y. to study violin with Auer, composition with Bloch, and orchestrtion with Rothwell, concurrently pursuing his career as a violinist. He taught violin, theory, and composition at the Univ. of Wisc. in Madison from 1921 to 1955.

WORKS: ORCH.: 3 violin concertos: No. 1 (1912), No. 2, *Indian* (1918; Cleveland, March 13, 1921), and No. 3 (1927); *Mountain Pictures* (1917–19); *Evangeline* (1918); *The Village Dance* (1921; based on a piano piece); 2 *Sketches from the Orient* for Band (1927; based on a piano piece); *Leaders of Men* (1943); 3 syms.: *Creation*, *Prophecy*, and *Revelation* (c. 1944; Madison, Wisc., May 1, 1955); *From the Muses* for Small Orch. (1945). **CHAMBER:** 4 *Rocky Mountain Sketches* for Violin and Piano (1914); *Scherzando fantastique* for Violin and Piano (1921); 2 violin sonatas (*The Ascension*, 1914; *From the Life of St. Paul*, 1926); 6 *Nature Studies* for Violin and Piano (1915); 4 *Prairie Sketches* for Violin and Piano (1916); *Hymn to the Ancients* for

Piano Quintet (1940); 2 *Essays* for String Quartet, *Illusion* and *Transition* (1945); piano pieces. **VOCAL:** About 65 songs.

BIBL.: J. Howard, *C. B.* (N.Y., 1929).—**NS/LK/DM**

Burleigh, Henry Thacker,

black American baritone and songwriter; b. Erie, Pa., Dec. 2, 1866; d. Stamford, Conn., Sept. 12, 1949. He studied at the National Cons. in N.Y. In 1894 he became baritone soloist at St. George's Church in N.Y., retiring in 1946 after 52 years of service. He gained wide popularity for his arrangements of *Heav'n, Heav'n, Deep River,* and *Go Down Moses.* On May 16, 1917, the National Assn. for the Advancement of Colored People awarded him the Spingarn Medal for highest achievement by an American citizen of African descent during the year 1916. His works also included 6 *Plantation Melodies* for Violin and Piano (1901), *Southland Sketches* for Violin and Piano, *From the Southland* for Piano, *Jubilee Songs of the United States of America* (1916), and *Old Songs Hymnal* (1929).
—**NS/LK/DM**

Burmeister, Joachim,

German music theorist and composer; b. Luneburg, March 5, 1564; d. Rostock, May 5, 1629. He received a master's degree from the Univ. of Rostock, where he publ. the treatises *Hypomnematum Musicae Poeticae* (1599; Eng. tr., New Haven, 1993) and *Musicae Practicae sive artis canendi ratio* (1601). He composed several sacred songs, which were publ. in 1601.

BIBL.: M. Ruhnke, *J. B.* (Kassel, 1955).—**NS/LK/DM**

Burnette, Johnny, and Dorsey Burnette.

MEMBERSHIP: Johnny Burnette, gtr., voc. (b. Memphis, Tenn., March 25, 1934; d. Clear Lake, Calif., Aug. 1, 1964); Dorsey Burnette, bs., voc. (b. Memphis, Dec. 28, 1932; d. Canoga Park, Calif., Aug. 19, 1979). With electric lead guitarist Paul Burlison (b. Brownsville, Tenn., Feb. 4, 1929) and brother Dorsey, Johnny Burnette founded the pioneering but largely overlooked rockabilly group The Johnny Burnette Rock 'n Roll Trio in the early 1950s. Although they never enjoyed national acclaim, the group provided some of the wildest rockabilly of the era. Disbanding the group in 1957, the brothers moved to Calif., where they wrote hits for Ricky Nelson and launched their own solo careers.

Johnny and Dorsey Burnette began playing in bands with electric lead guitarist Paul Burlison while still in high school. In 1952 all three worked as electricians for Crown Electric Company, which later employed a truck driver named Elvis Presley. Officially formed in 1953, The Johnny Burnette Rock 'n Roll Trio auditioned for Sam Phillips's Sun Records following the local success of Presley's "That's Alright Mama." Although they were not signed, they persevered, traveling to N.Y. in late 1955, where they won *The Ted Mack Amateur Hour* television competition three times in a row. Soon signed to Coral Records, the group recorded their first single in N.Y.C. in May 1956. The wild rockabilly classic "Tear It Up" became a regional hit in Boston and Baltimore, but failed to make the national charts.

The group toured nationally and finished their first album in Nashville at The Barn under producer Owen Bradley. They returned to the Nashville studio in July, recording "The Train Kept A-Rollin'." Years later The Yardbirds would re-record the song, recreating it virtually note-for-note. The group toured with Carl Perkins and Gene Vincent and appeared in the 1957 film *Rock, Rock, Rock.* The group went into the studio for the third and final time in March 1957, but Dorsey Burnette soon departed, to be replaced by Bill Black's brother Johnny. The Johnny Burnette Rock 'n Roll Trio officially disbanded in the fall of 1957.

Dorsey and Johnny Burnette moved to Calif. in 1958, where they concentrated on songwriting and recording demonstration records. They provided Ricky Nelson with two of his most boisterous hits, "Waitin' in School" and "Believe What You Say." Dorsey supplied Nelson with "It's Late" while Johnny furnished him with "Just a Little Too Much." Johnny Burnette recorded for Freedom and Liberty, while Dorsey recorded for Era and later Dot. The most interesting of these recordings were "Way in the Middle of the Night," "Sweet Baby Doll," and "Cincinnati Fireball."

In 1960 Dorsey scored hits with "Tall Oak Tree" and "Hey Little One" on Era, while Johnny hit with "Dreamin'" and the classic "You're Sixteen" on Liberty. The following year Johnny had success with "Little Boy Sad," the forlorn "Big Big World," and "God, Country and My Baby," but on Aug. 1, 1964, he died in a boating accident on Clear Lake in Calif. Dorsey switched to country music in the 1960s and achieved a number of moderate country-and-western hits between 1972 and his Aug. 19, 1979 death from a heart attack in Canoga Park, Calif.

Dorsey Burnette's son Billy (b. Memphis, May 8, 1953) played in his father's band in the 1970s and had modest recording success in the country field in the early 1980s. He was a member of Fleetwood Mac from 1987 to 1993, returning for their 1994 tour. Johnny Burnette's son Rocky (Jonathan Burnette, b. Memphis, June 12, 1953) had a smash pop hit in 1980 with "Tired of Toein' the Line." Each recorded an album in the 1990s.

DISC.: JOHNNY BURNETTE AND THE ROCK AND ROLL TRIO: *Johnny Burnette and The Rock and Roll Trio* (1956); *Vol. 2* (1957). **JOHNNY BURNETTE:** *Dreamin'* (1960); *Johnny Burnette* (1961); *Johnny Burnette Sings* (1961); *Roses Are Red* (1962); *Hits and Other Favorites* (1963); *The Johnny Burnette Story* (1966); *Dreamin'* (1967). **DORSEY BURNETTE:** *Tall Oak Tree* (1960); *Dorsey Burnette Sings* (1963); *Here and Now* (1972); *Dorsey Burnette* (1973). **BILLY BURNETTE:** *Billy Burnette* (1972); *Billy Burnette* (1979); *Between Friends* (1979); *Billy Burnette* (1980); *Gimme You* (1981); *Coming Home* (1993). **ROCKY BURNETTE:** *The Son of Rock and Roll* (1980); *Tear It Up* (1996).—**BH**

Burney, Charles,

celebrated English music historian; b. Shrewsbury, April 7, 1726; d. Chelsea, April 12, 1814. He was a pupil of Edmund Baker (organist of Chester Cathedral), of his eldest half brother, James Burney, and, from 1744 to 1747, of Arne in London. In 1749 he became organist of St. Dionis-Backchurch, and harpsichord player at the subscription concerts in the King's Arms, Cornhill. He resigned these posts in 1751, and until 1760 was organist at King's Lynn, Norfolk, where he planned and began work on his *General History of Music*. He returned to London in 1760; received the degrees of B.Mus. and D.Mus. from Oxford Univ. in 1769. Having exhausted such material as was available in London for his *History of Music*, he visited France, Switzerland, and Italy in 1770 and Germany, the Netherlands, and Austria in 1772, consulting the libraries, attending the best concerts of sacred and secular music, and forming contacts with the leading musicians and scholars of the period (Gluck, Hasse, Metastasio, Voltaire et al.). The immediate result of these journeys was the publication of *The Present State of Music in France and Italy*, etc. (1771, in diary form) and *The Present State of Music in Germany, the Netherlands*, etc. (1773). His *General History of Music* appeared in 4 vols. (1776–89; new ed. by Frank Mercer in 2 vols. with "Critical and Historical Notes," London and N.Y., 1935), the first vol. concurrently with the complete work of his rival, Sir John Hawkins. From 1806 he received a government pension. Other publications: *La musica che si canta annualmente nelle funzioni della settimana santa nella Cappella Pontificia, composta de Palestrina, Allegri e Bai* (1771; a book of sacred works with Burney's preface); *An Account of the Musical Performances in Westminster Abbey...in Commemoration of Handel* (1785); *Memoirs of the Life and Writings of the Abate Metastasio* (3 vols., 1796); the articles on music for Rees's *Cyclopedia*; etc. He composed, for Drury Lane, music to the dramas *Alfred* (1745), *Robin Hood* and *Queen Mab* (1750), and *The Cunning Man* (1765; text and music adapted from *Le Devin du village* by Rousseau); also sonatas for piano and for violin; violin and harpsichord concertos; cantatas; flute duets; etc. Burney's daughter, Frances Burney (b. King's Lynn, Norfolk, June 13, 1752; d. London, Jan. 6, 1840), wrote the novel *Evelina* and *Memoirs of Dr. Burney* (3 vols., 1832), the latter a highly bowdlerized version; she destroyed much of the original MS, but fragments were discovered 120 years later; S. Klima, G. Bowers, and K. Grant ed. and annotated a new edition as *Memoirs of Dr. C. B., 1726–1769* (1988).

BIBL.: C. Ricci, *B., Casanova e Farinelli in Bologna* (Milan, 1920); C.H. Glover, *Dr. C. B.'s Continental Travels, 1770–72* (compiled from Burney's journals and other sources; London, 1927); P.A. Scholes, *The Great Dr. B.* (Oxford, 1948); R. Lonsdale, *Dr. C. B.: A Literary Biography* (London, 1965).—**NS/LK/DM**

Burno, Dwayne, fusion-jazz bassist; b. Philadelphia, June 10, 1970. He began playing the bass, self taught, at the age of 16. His first major gig was with Donald Harrison in 1989. In 1990 he played with Jesse Davis and moved to N.Y. later that year to work with Betty Carter. After leaving Carter in late 1991, he played with Roy Haynes, Joe Henderson, Joe Chambers, Herbie Hancock, Barry Harris, Arthur Taylor, and Wynton Marsalis. He has shared the stage with Mulgrew Miller, Abbey Lincoln, Steve Turre, Benny Green, Cyrus Chestnut, Eric Reed, Steve Wilson, Jacky Terrason, Roy Hargrove, Joshua Redman, Jon Faddis, Ralph Moore, Stephen Scott, and a host of others. He also leads a group featuring Kevin Hays, Steve Nelson, Dion Parson, and Myron Walden.—**LP**

Burr, Henry (Harry H. McClaskey), popular Canadian ballad singer; b. St. Stephen, New Brunswick, Can., Jan. 15, 1882; d. Chicago, April 6, 1941. Burr is said to have appeared on upwards of 12,000 recordings, making his tenor voice the most-recorded in history. He was second only to Billy Murray as the most successful recording artist of the first two decades of the 20th century in the U.S., reportedly selling ten million records.

Burr made his debut in 1898 and moved to N.Y. to study voice after being discovered by Giuseppe Companari, formerly of the Metropolitan Opera. He turned to popular music when he began recording in 1903, assuming his stage name to do so. (In later years he sometimes recorded under his real name as well.) His solo hits included "Come Down, Ma Ev'ning Star" (1903), "In the Shade of the Old Apple Tree" (recorded under the pseudonym "Irving Gillette") (1905), "Love Me and the World Is Mine" (1906), "To the End of the World with You" (1909), "I Wonder Who's Kissing Her Now" (1909), "Meet Me To-Night in Dreamland" (1910), "When I Lost You" (1913), "Last Night Was the End of the World" (1913), "The Song That Stole My Heart Away" (1914), "M-O-T-H-E-R (A Word That Means the World to Me)" (1916), "Good-Bye, Good Luck, God Bless You (Is All That I Can Say)" (1916), "I'm Sorry I Made You Cry" (1918), "Beautiful Ohio" (1919), "Oh! What a Pal Was Mary" (1919), and "My Buddy" (1922). "Just a Baby's Prayer at Twilight (For Her Daddy over There)" (1918) was his biggest solo hit, reportedly selling over a million copies.

In 1904, Burr formed the Columbia Male Quartet, subsequently called the Peerless Quartet, with Albert Campbell, Steve Porter, and Tom Daniels. The group's major hits included "You're the Flower of My Heart, Sweet Adeline" (1904), "Let Me Call You Sweetheart" (1911), "I Didn't Raise My Boy to Be a Soldier" (1915), "My Bird of Paradise" (1915), "The Lights of My Home Town" (1916), George M. Cohan's "Over There" (1917), and "I Don't Know Where I'm Going but I'm on My Way" (1918). After Frank Stanley replaced Daniels in 1906, he and Burr made a series of duet records together until Stanley's death in 1910. Burr then assumed leadership of the Peerless Quartet and sang lead on nearly all its records. He assembled a new edition of the group in 1925 and maintained it until 1928.

Burr and Campbell launched a series of successful duet recordings in 1911. Their major hits include "When I Was Twenty-One and You Were Sweet Sixteen" (1912), "The Trail of the Lonesome Pine" (1913), "I'm on My Way to Mandalay" (with Will Oakland; 1914), "Close to My Heart" (1915), "There's a Quaker Down in Quaker Town" (1916), "Lookout Mountain" (1917), "Till We Meet Again" (1919), and "I'm Forever Blowing Bubbles" (1919). They also recorded with the Columbia Orch. Burr, Campbell, and John Meyer (who had replaced Stanley in the Peerless Quartet) recorded as the Sterling Trio starting in 1916. Burr also made successful records with Helen Clark, Frank Croxton (a replacement member of the Peerless Quartet), Marcia Freer (on Irving Berlin's "What'll I Do?" [1924]), Ada Jones, Roger Wolfe Kahn and His Orch., Art Landry and His Orch., Murray (their sole duet being "I Wonder Where My Baby Is To-Night?" [1926]), Lieutenant Gitz Rice of the First Canadians (on the World War I song "Life in a Trench in Belgium" [1918]), Andrea Sarto, Elizabeth Spencer, Elise Stevenson, and Caroline Vaughan.

From 1921 to 1925, Burr managed the Eight Popular (or Famous) Victor Artists, a touring package that included the Peerless Quartet and Murray and that played around the U.S. for 15 years. Though his recording career declined after the mid-1920s, Burr became a popular radio entertainer, appearing on NBC's *National Barn Dance* for seven years, among other programs.—WR

Burrell, Dave (Herman Davis, II), jazz pianist, composer; b. Middletown, Ohio, Sept. 10, 1940. He studied at Berklee School of Music, then Univ. of Hawaii. He moved to N.Y. where he worked with G. Logan, Marion Brown, Pharoah Sanders, Sonny Murray, Archie Shepp, and Sonny Sharrock. He performed at the Pan-African Festival in Algiers (1969). He has been active in musical, educational, and cultural circles, particularly in the 1970s. He taught for two years at Queens Coll. He has recorded albums with Shepp, Sanders, and Brown. In the mid-1990s, he became the head of UCLA's jazz program.

DISC.: *High* (1965); *La Vie de Boheme* (1969); *In: Sanity* (1976); *High One High Two* (1977); *Lush Life* (1978); *In Concert* (1991); *Jelly Roll Joys* (1991); *Brother to Brother* (1993).—LP

Burrell, Kenny (actually, **Kenneth Earl**), jazz guitarist; b. Detroit, July 31, 1931. Encouraged and coached by his older brother, Billy, Kenny began playing guitar at 12; he played both bass and guitar in the high school band. Soon he was freelancing with Tommy Flanagan, Yusef Lateef, Pepper Adams, Elvin Jones, and others. He made his recording debut with Dizzy Gillespie's sextet (1951). Burrell completed his formal training at Wayne State Univ. (B.A., Music Composition and Theory). Upon his graduation in 1955, he toured with Oscar Peterson, then moved to N.Y. where he played with Benny Goodman; he also has led his own combos since 1951. In 1960, he was in a play in N.Y. called *The Long Dream* with Golson, Roach, Hank Jones, Dizzy Reece, and Joya Sherill. He soon became internationally in demand for club, concert, and studio work, as well as college seminars and festivals. Burrell recorded on Verve with Astrud Gilberto, Gil Evans, Stan Getz, and others; one of his most popular albums was *Guitar Forms* (1964), arranged by Evans. He has made over 70 albums as a leader and played on more than 200 as a sideman, with both jazz artists and popular singers such as Tony Bennett, James Brown, and Sammy Davis Jr. He played banjo with Mercer Ellington. Burrell began leading seminars at colleges in the early 1970s, and has taught courses on Duke Ellington's music at various campuses in Los Angeles. He was in residence at William Paterson Coll. in 1995–96. He divides his time between playing and recording as director of USC's Jazz Studies Department.

DISC.: *For Charlie Christian and Benny Goodman* (1956); *Introducing Kenny Burrell* (1956); *Monday Stroll* (1956); *All Day Long* (1957); *Blue Moods* (1957); *Cats* (1957); *Kenny Burrell, Vol. 2* (1957); *Blue Lights, Vols. 1, 2* (1958); *Kenny Burrell and John Coltrane* (1958); *Night at the Vanguard* (1959); *Bluesy Burrell* (1962); *Guitar Forms* (1964); *Man at Work* (1966); *Blues: the Common Ground* (1967); *Ode to 52nd Street* (1967); *Ellington Is Forever, Vols. 1, 2* (1975); *Live at the Village Vanguard* (1978); *For Duke* (1981); *Generation* (1986); *Midnight at the Village Vanguard* (1995). JAZZ HERITAGE ALL-STARS LIVE AT THE BLUE NOTE: *Jazzmen: Detroit* (1956).—LP

Burrian, Carl
See **Burian, Karl**

Burritt, Lloyd (Edmund), Canadian composer; b. Vancouver, June 7, 1940. He was a student of Coulthard (composition) and Hultberg (electronic music) at the Univ. of British Columbia (B.M., 1963; M.M., 1968); he also took courses in composition with Jacob and Howells at the Royal Coll. of Music in London (1963–65) and in conducting with Schuller, Leinsdorf, Bernstein, and Dee Hiatt at the Berkshire Music Center in Tanglewood (summers, 1965–66). His works follow an expressionist path.

WORKS: DRAMATIC: Music Theater and Multimedia: *Acid Mass* for Film, Tape, and Dancers (1969); *Electric Soul*, tape piece for Dancers (1970); *Electric Chair* for Actress, Alto Saxophone, and Tape (1971); *Altar of the Sun* for Actors, Singers, Dancers, Chorus, Flute, Horn, Percussion, and Piano (North Vancouver, April 3, 1983; concert version as *Francis of Assisi Suite*); *The Hobbit* for Actors, Singers, Dancers, Chorus, Flute, Horn, Percussion, and Piano (North Vancouver, Dec. 19, 1984; concert version as *The Hobbit Suite*). ORCH.: Sym. (1964); *Assassinations* for Orch. and Tape (Vancouver, Dec. 1, 1968); *Electric Tongue* for Orch. and Tape (Vancouver, May 30, 1969); *Cicada* for Orch. and Tape (Calgary, April 5, 1970; also for Concert Band); *New York* for Orch. and Tape (1970); *Overdose* for Orch. and Tape (Ottawa, Feb. 15, 1971); *Spectrum* for Strings, Piano, and Tape (Vancouver, Aug. 13, 1972); *Symphonic Overture* (1980). CHAMBER: Piano Sonatina (1961); Violin Sonata (1963); *Icon* for Organ and Tape (1970); *Memo to RCCO* [Royal Coll. of Canadian Organists] for Organ and Tape (1972); *Memo to NFBC* [National Film Board of Canada] for Keyboard and Tape (1972). VOCAL: *3 Autumn Songs* for Mezzo-soprano and Orch. (1965; Vancouver, Feb. 27, 1968; also for Mezzo-soprano and Piano); *Landscapes* for Soprano, Alto, and Tape (1967; also as *Landscapes 3* for Soprano, Violin, and Tape); *The Hollow Men* for Girl and Boy Speakers, Soprano, Alto, Tenor, Bass, Semi-Chorus, Chorus, 13 Instrumentalists, and Tape (Vancouver, April 5, 1968); *Once Again...Pop!* for Non-singing Chorus and Tape (1969); *4 Winter Haiku* for Baritone and Tape (1969); *Rocky Mountain Grasshopper* for Chorus, Concert Band, and Tape (North Vancouver, May 27, 1971); *David* for Boy Soprano, Tenor, Baritone, Children's Voices, Chorus, Orch., and Tape (Vancouver, Nov. 5, 1977); *Rise of the Phoenix* for Voice or Voices and Instruments (1979); *Song for Marshall McLuhan* for Bass-baritone, Chorus, and Orch. (Vancouver, April 30, 1986); *Crystal Earth* for Soprano, Chorus, and Concert Band (1987; North Vancouver, Oct. 24, 1988).—NS/LK/DM

Burroughs, Alvin ("Mouse"), jazz drummer; b. Mobile, Ala., Nov. 21, 1911; d. Chicago, Aug. 1, 1950. He is best known for his work with the Earl Hines big band. He was raised in Pittsburgh and at age 16 made his debut (with Roy Eldridge) in a kids' band at Sharon, Pa. He worked with Walter Page's Blue Devils in 1928–29, with Alphonse Trent (1930). Burroughs settled in Chicago, played with various leaders including pianist Hal Draper's Arcadians in 1935; he was with Horace Henderson from July 1937 until 1938; he was with Earl Hines from September 1938 until late 1940; and he was with Milton Larkin's Band at Rhumboogie, Chicago (1941), with Benny Carter in late 1942. Burroughs his led own band, then worked with Henry "Red" Allen from 1945 until April 1946. He played with Bill Harris and Gene Ammons. Jo Jones credits him with using a coin in his hand to produce the first sizzle cymbal effect; this technique is heard on his 1947 work with Gene Ammons. Burroughs soon joined George Dixon's Quartet and was a member of this group until he suffered a fatal heart attack.

DISC.: B. HARRIS: *Small Herd on Keynote* (1945). G. AMMONS: *Jug Sessions* (1947).—JC/LP

Burrowes, Norma (Elizabeth),

Welsh soprano; b. Bangor, April 24, 1944. She studied at the Queen's Univ. in Belfast and with Flora Nielsen and Rupert Bruce-Lockhart at the Royal Academy of Music in London. In 1970 she made her professional operatic debut as Zerlina with the Glyndebourne Touring Opera Co., and that same year she made her first appearance at London's Covent Garden as Fiakermilli in *Arabella*. From 1971 she sang at the Sadler's Wells (later the English National) Opera in London, and also appeared at the Salzburg, Glyndebourne, Aix-en-Provence, and other festivals. On Oct. 12, 1979, she made her Metropolitan Opera debut in N.Y. as Blondchen. She also toured widely as a concert singer. In 1982 she retired from the operatic stage. From 1969 to 1980 she was married to Steuart Bedford.—NS/LK/DM

Burrows, (James) Stuart,

Welsh tenor; b. Pontypridd, Feb. 7, 1933. He was educated at Trinity Coll., Carmarthen. After winning a prize at the National Eisteddfod of Wales in 1959, he appeared as a concert singer. In 1963 he made his operatic debut as Ismaele in *Nabucco* at the Welsh National Opera in Cardiff. In 1967 he made his first appearance at London's Covent Garden as Beppe, and subsequently sang there regularly. He made his U.S. debut as Tamino at the San Francisco Opera that same year. In 1970 he sang for the first time at the Vienna State Opera and the Salzburg Festival. On April 13, 1971, he made his Metropolitan Opera debut in N.Y. as Ottavio, and continued to make occasional appearances there until 1982. He also toured extensively as a concert artist. Among his other esteemed roles were Faust, Alfredo, Belmonte, Lensky, Ernesto, and Rodolfo.
—NS/LK/DM

Burt, Francis,

English composer and teacher; b. London, April 28, 1926. He studied with Ferguson and Berkeley at the Royal Academy of Music in London (1948–51), and then with Blacher in Berlin (1951–54). After winning the Mendelssohn Scholarship in 1954, he completed his studies in Rome (1954–55). In 1956 he settled in Vienna, where he was a prof. of composition at the Hochschule für Musik and Darstellende Kunst from 1973 to 1993. In 1973 he received the Körner Prize. He was awarded the Würdigungspreis for music in 1978 and in 1981 he received the music prize of the City of Vienna. He was awarded the Great Silver Medal of Honor in 1992 for services to the Republic of Austria.

WORKS: DRAMATIC: O p e r a : *Volpone or The Fox*, after Ben Jonson (1952–58; Stuttgart, June 2, 1960; rev. 1960–61; Oldenburg, Feb. 8, 1963); *Barnstable oder Jemand auf dem Dachboden* (1967–69; Kassel, Nov. 30, 1969). **B a l l e t :** *Der Golem* (1959–63; Hannover, Jan. 31, 1965). **ORCH.:** *Jamben* (1953; Baden-Baden, Aug. 24, 1955); *Espressione orchestrale* (1958–59; Vienna, Dec. 18, 1959); *Fantasmagoria* (London, Aug. 23, 1963); *Morgana* (1983–86; Vienna, May 16, 1986); *Blind Visions* for Oboe and Small Orch. (1994–95; Vienna, Nov. 3, 1995). **CHAMBER:** 2 string quartets: No. 1 (1951–52; Berlin, Jan. 7, 1953) and No. 2 (1992–93; London, June 16, 1995); *Serenata Notturna* for Oboe, Clarinet, and Bassoon (1952); Duo for Clarinet and Piano (1954); *For William* for 9 Players (BBC, London, April 10, 1988); *Echoes* for 9 Players (1988–89; Vienna, March 1, 1989); *Für AlFrED SCHLEE* for String Quartet (Vienna, Nov. 18, 1991); *Hommage à Jean-Henri Fabre* for 5 Players (1993–94; ORF, Vienna, Oct. 24, 1994). **P i a n o :** *Three Little Piano Pieces for J. J.* (1949); *Musik* for 2 Pianos (1952; Berlin, Feb. 27, 1953). **VOCAL:** *Two Songs of David* for Chorus (1951); *Hüte* in the collection *Sieben Lieder nach Gedichten von Carl Sandburg* for Medium Voice and Piano (1952; with 6 other composers); *The Skull*, cantata for Tenor and Piano, afer Cyril Tourneur (1953–54; also for Tenor and Orch., 1955; WDR, Cologne, Dec. 10, 1956); *Bavarian Gentians* for Vocal Quartet and Piano, after D. H. Lawrence (Dartington, Aug. 1956); *Unter der blanken Hacke des Monds* for Baritone and Orch., after Peter Huchel (1974–76; Munich, Nov. 18, 1976); *Und GOtt der HErr sprach* for Mezzo-soprano, Baritone, Bass, 2 Choruses, and Orch. (1976–83; Vienna, Jan. 25, 1984).

BIBL.: H. Krones, *Musikalisches Dokumentation F. B.* (Vienna, 1980).—NS/LK/DM

Burtius (also known as Burci or Burzio), Nicolaus,

Italian theorist; b. Parma, c. 1445; d. there, after 1518. He studied with J. Gallicus. He received first clerical Orders in Parma in 1472, then studied ecclesiastical law in Bologna. In 1487 he publ. *Musices Opusculum*, which was one of the earliest printed books on music, containing mensural notes printed from woodblocks. In this work Burtius supported the Guidonian system, opposing the innovations introduced by Ramos de Pareja.—NS/LK/DM

Burton, Gary,

world-class jazz vibraphone player; b. Anderson, Ind., Jan. 23, 1943. His parents wanted him to study an instrument other than piano, which his older sister played, and he became interested in marimba after attending a concert when he was six. After two years, he added vibraphone; on both, he played popular sheet music. Burton had some training on piano, but is self-taught on vibes with his four-mallet approach. In high school, he became excited about jazz after hearing a Benny Goodman record. He attended Berklee Coll. from 1960–61; in 1961 he released his first album as a bandleader. He joined George Shearing (1963) and the group recorded an album of Burton's tunes. Leading his own small groups, Burton made 12 albums on RCA in the 1960s, including *Duster*, which many consider to be one of the first jazz-rock albums; he recorded seven albums on Atlantic (1967–71), and 12 on ECM (1972–82). Carla Bley wrote "A Genuine Tong Funeral" for him. He has helped foster the careers of many other artists, from Larry Coryell to Tommy Smith. He returned to Berklee Coll. as a faculty member in 1971, and was appointed dean of curriculum there in 1985; in the late 1990s, he was named executive vice president of the school. He discovered Pat Metheny, invited him to Berklee Coll., and featured him on a recording in 1975. He has had a long- term association with Chick Corea, including duet tours and recordings in the 1970s and 1980s. In 1995 Burton announced that he was gay and addressed the issue with admirable candor and openness in interviews.

DISC.: *New Vibe Man in Town* (1961); *Who Is Gary Burton?* (1962); *Something's Coming* (1963); *3 in Jazz* (1963); *Groovy Sound of Music* (1964); *Tennessee Firebird* (1966); *Time Machine* (1966); *Duster* (1967); *Lofty Fake Anagram* (1967); *Country Roads and Other Places* (1968); *Gary Burton in Concert* (1968); *Good Vibes* (1969); *Paris Encounter* (1969); *Throb* (1969); *Alone at Last* (1971); *Gary Burton and Keith Jarrett* (1971); *Turn of the Century* (1971); *Crystal Silence* (1972); *New Quartet* (1973); *Seven Songs for Quartet and Chamber Orchestra* (1973); *Hotel Hello* (1974); *Matchbook* (1974); *Ring* (1974); *Dreams So Real* (1975); *Passengers* (1976); *Chick Corea and Gary Burton* (1978); *Duet* (1979); *In Concert* (1979); *Real Life Hits* (1984); *Gary Burton and the Berklee All Stars* (1985); *Whiz Kids* (1986); *New Tango* (1988); *Reunion* (1989); *Alive* (1991); *Live in Tokyo* (1992); *Six Pack* (1992); *It's Another Day* (1993); *Face to Face* (1994). **G. SHEARING:** *Out of the Woods* (1963).

BIBL.: S. Balcomb, *The Music of Gary Burton* (Hal-Leonard, 1989).—**LP/MM**

Burton, John, English organist, harpsichordist, and composer; b. Yorkshire, 1730; d. probably in Portici, near Naples, Sept. 3, 1782. He was a pupil of Keeble. In 1754 he toured Germany with notable success, and later was active mainly in London. Among his works are a keyboard concerto, 10 sonatas for Harpsichord, or Organ, or Piano (1766), 6 sonatas for Piano, or Harpsichord, or Organ and Violin (c. 1770), and 12 *Italian Canzonetts* for Voice and Harpsichord (c. 1770).—**LK/DM**

Burton, Stephen Douglas, American composer and teacher; b. Whittier, Calif., Feb. 24, 1943. He studied at the Oberlin (Ohio) Coll. Cons. of Music (1960–62), with Henze at the Salzburg Mozarteum, and at the Peabody Cons. of Music in Baltimore (M.M., 1974). In 1969 he was awarded a Guggenheim fellowship. After teaching at the Catholic Univ. of America in Washington, D.C. (1970–74), he joined the faculty of George Mason Univ. in Fairfax, Va., in 1974, serving as a prof. there from 1983. In 1996 he was selected as its Heritage Chair in Music, a lifetime appointment. He publ. the widely used book *Orchestrtion* (1982). With Gillian Anderson, during the years 1997–99, he restored the original film scores for *Ben Hur* (1926), *The Passion of Joan of Arc* (1928), Cecil B. deMille's *The Ten Commandments* (1923), which reopened the restored Grauman's Egyptian Theater in Hollywood in 1998, and Douglas Fairbanks Sr.'s, *Robin Hood* (1923?). While Burton's music draws upon the totality of modern resources, it remains faithful to the directness, energy, and spirit of the American experience.

WORKS: DRAMATIC: *The Nightingale and the Rose,* chamber ballet (1968; also as *Eurydice* for Violin, Clarinet, Trombone, Piano or Celesta, and Percussion, 1977); *No Trifling with Love*, opera (1970); *An American Triptych*, 3 1-act operas: *Maggie*, after Crane, *Dr. Heidegger's Experiment*, after Hawthorne, and *Benito Cereno*, after Melville (1974–75; Alexandria, Va., July 29, 1988); *The Starchild*, children's opera (1975); *The Duchess of Malfi*, opera (1975–78; Vienna, Va., Aug. 18, 1978); *Finisterre*, dance piece (Newport, R.I., Aug. 21, 1977); *The Merchant of Venice*, incidental music to Shakespeare's play (1988); *Brotherhood*, music theater (1991–92). **ORCH.:** *Sinfonia per Roma* (1963); Concerto for Violin and Chamber Orch. (1965; also as Concerto for Violin and Piano); 7 syms.: No. 1 (1967; Berlin, Jan. 31, 1968), No. 2, *Ariel*, for Baritone or Mezzo-soprano and Baritone and Orch., to poems by Sylvia Plath (Washington, D.C., Oct. 19, 1976), No. 3, *Songs of the Tulpehocken*, for Tenor and Orch. (Reading, Pa., Feb. 22, 1976), No. 4, *Homage to Bach*, for Organ and Orch. (1980), No. 5, *Prelude* (1981), No. 6, *I Have a Dream*, for Soprano, Narrator, Chorus, and Orch. (Washington, D.C., May 17, 1987), and No. 7, *The Tempest: Homage to Shakespeare* (Long Island, N.Y., March 1988); *Dithyramb* (Washington, D.C., Oct. 10, 1972); *Stravinskyiana*, flute concerto (Chicago, Feb. 14, 1972; also for Flute and Piano); *Variations on a Theme by Mahler* for Chamber Orch. (Washington, D.C., Oct. 10, 1982); *Fanfare for Peace* (Washington, D.C., Sept. 1983); *Pied Piper Overture* (Washington, D.C., Feb. 1, 1983); *Ode* (1986). **CHAMBER:** *Notturno/Elegy* for Cello (1972); *Partita* for Violin (1972); *Burlesque* for Clarinet, Piano, and String Quartet (1972); String Quartet, *Quartet Fantasy* (Washington, D.C., Feb. 9, 1974); Trio for Violin, Cello, and Piano (1975); *Rhapsody* for Alto Saxophone and Piano (London, July 28, 1975); *3 Poems* for Flute (1976); *Fantocciata*, trio sonata/collage for Flute, Oboe, and Harpsichord or Piano (1976); *Divertimento* for Wind Quintet (1976); *Dances* for Flute and Guitar (1984). **VOCAL:** *Ode to a Nightingale* for Soprano and Orch. (1962; Berlin, Oct. 9, 1963); *Requiem Mass* for 6 Soloists, Chorus, and Orch., in memory of President John F. Kennedy (1963); *6 Hebrew Melodies after George, Lord Byron* for Medium Voice and String Quintet (1967; also for Medium Voice and Piano, 1973); *Sérénade* for Soprano, Flute, Harp, and String Quartet (1967); *Los Desastres de la Guerra* for Men's Chorus, Organ, Piano, and Percussion (1971); *Sechs Lieder nach Gedichten von Hermann Hesse* for High Voice and Piano (Washington, D.C., May 26, 1974; also for High Voice and 13 Instruments, 1977); *Requiescat* for Chorus (1975); *From Noon to Starry Night* for Chorus and Chamber Orch. (1989); *The Burning Babe*, cantata for Vocal Quartet or Chamber Chorus, Recorder, Oboe d'amore, Renaissance Harpsichord, and Renaissance String Quintet (1998; N.Y., Jan. 1999).—**NS/LK/DM**

Bury, Bernard de, French composer; b. Versailles, Aug. 20, 1720; d. there, Nov. 19, 1785. He was a student of his father, Jean-Louis Bury, who served as ordinaire de la musique du roi, and of Collin de Blamont. In 1741 he purchased the reversion of Marguérite-Antoinette Couperin's post of keyboard player to the chambre du roi. In 1751 he became surintendant de la musique du roi, and in 1779 he was granted a royal pension. In 1785 he was ennobled by King Louis XVI. Bury was held in high favor by the French court.

WORKS: DRAMATIC: *Les caractères de la folie*, opéra-ballet (Paris, Aug. 20, 1743); *Jupiter vainqueur des Titans*, tragédie lyrique (Versailles, Dec. 11, 1745); *La nymphe de Versailles*, divertissement (Versailles, March 19, 1746); *Titon et l'Aurore*, pastorale héroïque (Versailles, Jan. 14, 1750); *La parque vaincue*, divertissement (Versailles, 1751); *Palmyre*, ballet héroïque (Fontainebleau, Oct. 24, 1765); *Zénis et Almesie*, ballet héroïque (Fontainebleau, Nov. 2, 1765; in collaboration with J. de La Borde). **OTHER:** A cantata, motet, and harpsichord pieces.—**LK/DM**

Bury, Edward, Polish composer and teacher; b. Gniezno, Sept. 18, 1919; d. Kraków, Feb. 13, 1995. He studied composition with Sikorski and conducting at the Warsaw Cons. (1937–44). From 1945 to 1954 he taught at the Kraków State Higher School of Music. He publ. books on conducting (1961) and score reading (1971).

WORKS: ORCH.: *Czech Fantasy* for Piano and Orch. (1948); *Little Suite* (1950); *Triptych* (1952); Violin Concerto (1954); *Concert Overture* (1954); *Suita giocosa* (1956); *Maski* (Masks), fantastic suite (1957); 8 syms.: No. 1, *Symfonia wolności* (Freedom Sym.; 1960), No. 2 for 6 Concertante Instruments and Orch. (1962), No. 3, *Mówi Prezydent John F. Kennedy* (President John F. Kennedy Speaks) for Male Speaker, Women's Speaking Chorus, Mixed Chorus, and Orch. (1964), No. 4, *De timpani a tutti*, for Bass, Chorus, Tape, and Orch. (1966–67), No. 5, *Bohaterska* (Heroic; 1969), No. 6, *Pacem in terris*, to a text from the encyclical of Pope John XXIII, for Narrator, Church Bells, and Orch. (1972), No. 7 (1977), and No. 8 (1980). **OTHER:** Chamber music; piano pieces; *The Millennium Hymn* for Chorus and Orch. (1965); choruses.—**NS/LK/DM**

Burzio, Eugenia, Italian soprano; b. Milan, June 20, 1872; d. there, May 18, 1922. She studied in Milan with Aversa and Benvenuti. In 1903 she made her operatic debut in Turin, and then sang in Parma and Palermo (from 1904). In 1906 she made her first appearance at Milan's La Scala as Katusha in Alfano's *Risurrezione*, and in 1907 scored a fine success there as Catalani's Loreley. She also sang at the Teatro Colón in Buenos Aires (from 1909). In 1919 she made her final stage appearance as Ponchielli's Marion Delorme at Milan's Teatro Lirico. Although most successful in verismo roles, Burzio was also praised for her portrayals of Gluck's Armide, Pacini's Saffo, and Bellini's Norma.—**NS/LK/DM**

Busby, Thomas, English writer on music; b. Westminster, Dec. 1755; d. London, May 28, 1838. He was a chorister in London, then studied with Battishill (1769–74). He served as church organist at St. Mary's, Newington, Surrey, and St. Mary Woolnoth, Lombard Street. He obtained the degree of B.Mus. from Cambridge Univ. in 1801. In collaboration with Arnold, he publ. *A Complete Dictionary of Music* (1801); he then publ. *A Grammar of Music* (1818) and *A General History of Music* (2 vols., compiled from Burney and Hawkins; London, 1819; reprinted 1968). In 1825 he brought out a set of 3 little vols. entitled *Concert Room and Orchestra Anecdotes of Music and Musicians, Ancient and Modern*, a compilation of some topical value, even though many of the stories are apocryphal. He also publ. *A Musical Manual, or Technical Directory* (1828). His anthology of

sacred music, *The Divine Harmonist* (1788), is valuable. His own compositions (oratorios and odes) are imitative of Handel. A melodrama, *Tale of Mystery*, with Busby's music, was produced at Covent Garden (Nov. 13, 1807).—**NS/LK/DM**

Busch, Adolf (Georg Wilhelm), noted German violinist, brother of **Hermann** and **Fritz Busch;** b. Siegen, Westphalia, Aug. 8, 1891; d. Guilford, Vt., June 9, 1952. He studied in Cologne and Bonn; then served as concertmaster of the Vienna Konzertverein (1912–18); subsequently taught at the Hochschule für Musik in Berlin. In 1919 he organized the Busch Quartet and the Busch Trio (with his younger brother, Hermann, and his son-in-law, Rudolf Serkin). The Busch Quartet gained renown with the appointment of Gosta Andreasson and Karl Doktor as members; Busch's brother Hermann became cellist in the Busch Trio in 1926 and in the Busch Quartet in 1930. Adolf Busch went to Basel in 1927; in 1939 he emigrated to America. In 1950 he organized the Marlboro School of Music in Vt. His *Adolf Busch: Briefe, Bilder, Erinnerungen* (Walpole, N.H., 1991) was publ. posthumously in German and in English.—**NS/LK/DM**

Busch, Carl (Reinholdt), Danish-American conductor and composer; b. Bjerre, March 29, 1862; d. Kansas City, Mo., Dec. 19, 1943. He studied at the Royal Cons. in Copenhagen with Hartmann and Gade (1882–85), at the Brussels Cons. (1885), and with Godard in Paris (1886). In 1887 he went to Kansas City, where he was active as founder-conductor of the Sym. Orch. (1911–18); he also appeared as a guest conductor throughout the U.S. and Europe and was active as a teacher in Chicago, Salt Lake City, and South Bend, Ind. He received knighthoods from the kings of Denmark and Norway. A number of his compositions dealt with American subjects, most notably the American Indian.

WORKS: ORCH.: Sym. (1898); 6 suites (1890–1928); 2 rhapsodies (1897); 14 pieces for Strings (1897–1918); 4 symphonic poems (1898–1924); Cello Concerto (1919). **CHAMBER:** 4 string trios (1893–1926); String Quartet (1897); Violin Sonata (1897); 44 string solos (1893–1926); 8 woodwind solos (1893–1940); 24 string etudes (1909); 26 pieces for Woodwind Ensemble (1930–43). **VOCAL:** 22 cantatas (1894–1929); numerous choral works; many songs. **OTHER:** Band music.

BIBL.: M. Barney, *Sir C. B.* (Kansas City, Mo., 1942); D. Lowe, *Sir C. B.: His Life and Work as a Teacher, Conductor, and Composer* (diss., Univ. of Mo., 1972).—**NS/LK/DM**

Busch, Fritz, eminent German conductor, brother of **Adolf (Georg Wilhelm)** and **Hermann Busch;** b. Siegen, Westphalia, March 13, 1890; d. London, Sept. 14, 1951. He studied at the Cologne Cons. with Steinbach, Boettcher, Uzielli, and Klauwell; was then conductor of the Deutsches Theater in Riga (1909–10); in 1912 he became music director of the city of Aachen, and then of the Stuttgart Opera in 1918. In 1922 he was named Generalmusikdirektor of the Dresden State Opera; during his tenure, he conducted many notable productions, including the premieres of Strauss's *Intermezzo* and *Die Aegyptische Helena*. On Nov. 27, 1927, he made his U.S. debut as a guest conductor with the N.Y. Sym. Orch. In 1933 he was dismissed from his Dresden post by the Nazi government; leaving Germany, he made many appearances as a conductor with the Danish Radio Sym. Orch. and the Stockholm Phil.; from 1934 to 1939 he served as music director of the Glyndebourne Festivals; from 1940 to 1945 he was active mainly in South America. On Nov. 26, 1945, he made his first appearance with the Metropolitan Opera in N.Y., conducting *Lohengrin*; he continued on its roster until 1949. He was equally distinguished as an operatic and symphonic conductor, becoming particularly renowned for his performances of Mozart. He wrote an autobiography, *Aus dem Leben eines Musikers* (Zürich, 1949; Eng. tr., 1953, as *Pages from a Musician's Life*).

BIBL.: G. Busch, *F. B., Dirigent* (Frankfurt am Main, 1970); B. Dopheide, *F. B.* (Tutzing, 1970).—**NS/LK/DM**

Busch, Hermann, noted German cellist, brother of **Adolf (Georg Wilhelm)** and **Fritz Busch;** b. Siegen, Westphalia, June 24, 1897; d. Bryn Mawr, Pa., June 3, 1975. He studied at the Cologne Cons. and the Vienna Academy of Music; played cello in the Vienna Sym. Orch. (1923–27); in 1926 he became a member of the Busch Trio; was also a member of the renowned Busch Quartet from 1930 until the death of his brother Adolf in 1952. During his last years of life, he taught at the Marlboro School of Music in Vt.—**NS/LK/DM**

Bush, Alan (Dudley), English composer and teacher; b. London, Dec. 22, 1900; d. Watford, Oct. 31, 1995. He was a student of Corder (composition) and Matthay (piano) at the Royal Academy of Music in London (1918–22); also received private training in piano from Moiseiwitsch (1924–29) and Schnabel (1928), and in composition from Ireland (1927–32); also studied musicology with Wolf and Blume at the Univ. of Berlin (1929–31). From 1925 to 1978 he was prof. of composition at the Royal Academy of Music. He also was active as a pianist and conductor. In 1935 he joined the Communist Party, to which he remained deeply committed. In 1936 he founded the Workers' Music Assn., which he served as president from 1941 to 1976. In 1947–48 he was chairman of the Composers Guild of Great Britain. He publ. *Strict Counterpoint in the Palestrina Style* (London, 1948), *In My Seventh Decade* (London, 1970), and *In My Eighth Decade* (London, 1980). His early works were highly modern, utilizing a thematic style in which every note retains thematic importance. After World War II, tonal elements were added.

WORKS: DRAMATIC: O p e r a: *Wat Tyler* (1948–51; [East] Berlin Radio, April 3, 1952); *Men of Blackmoor* (1954–55; Weimar, Nov. 18, 1956); *The Sugar Reapers* (1961–63; Leipzig, Dec. 11, 1966); *Joe Hill: The Man Who Never Died* (1966–68; East Berlin, Sept. 29, 1970); also operas for young people. **B a l l e t:** *His Wars or Yours* (1935); *Mining* (1935). **ORCH.:** *Symphonic Impressions* (1927; London, Nov. 11, 1930); *Dance Overture* for Military Band (1930; orchestrated 1935); Piano Concerto, with Baritone Solo and Men's Chorus in the finale (1937); 4 syms.: No. 1 (1941; London, July 24, 1942), No. 2, *Nottingham* (Nottingham, June 27, 1949), No. 3, *Byron Symphony*, for Baritone, Chorus, and Orch. (1959–60), and No. 4, *Lescaux Symphony* (1983); *Meditation on a German Song of 1848* for Violin and Strings (1941; also for Violin and Piano); *Overture: Festal Day*

(1942); *Fantasia on Soviet Themes* (1942; London, July 27, 1945); *English Suite* for Strings (1945–46); *Overture "Resolution"* (1946); *Homage to William Sterndale Bennett* for String Orch. (1946); *Piers Plowman's Day* (1946–47; Prague Radio, Oct. 16, 1947); Violin Concerto (London, July 16, 1948); Concert Suite for Cello and Orch. (1952); *Defender of Peace* (Vienna Radio, May 24, 1952); *Dorian Passacaglia and Fugue* (1959); *Variations, Nocturne and Finale on an English Sea-Song* for Piano and Orch. (1962); *Partita Concertante* (1965); *Time Remembered* for Chamber Orch. (1969); *Africa* for Piano and Orch. (1972); *Concert Overture for an Occasion* (1972); *Liverpool Overture* (1973); *Festival March for British Youth* (1973); *Song Poem and Dance Poem* for Strings (1986). **CHAMBER:** String Quartet (1923; London, Dec. 4, 1924); Piano Quartet (1924); *Dialectic* for String Quartet (1929; London, March 22, 1935); *3 Concert Studies* for Piano, Violin, and Cello (1947); *Autumn Poem* for Horn and Piano (1954); *3 African Sketches* for Flute and Piano (1960); *Prelude, Air, and Dance* for Violin, String Quartet, and Percussion (1963–64); *Serenade* for String Quartet (1969); *Suite of 6* for String Quartet (1975); Concertino for 2 Violins and Piano (1981); Piano Quintet (1984); Octet (1985); many piano pieces, including 3 sonatas (1921, 1970, 1986). **VOCAL:** *The Winter Journey* for Soprano, Baritone, Chorus, String Quintet, and Harp (1946); *Lidice* for Chorus (1947); *Voices of the Prophets* for Tenor and Piano (1953); *The Ballad of Freedom's Soldier* for Tenor, Bass-Baritone, Chorus, and Orch. (1953); *The Alps and Andes of the Living World* for Speaker, Tenor, Chorus, and Orch. (1968); *Africa Is My Name* for Mezzo-soprano, Chorus, and Piano and Orch. (1976); *The Earth in Shadow* for Chorus and Orch. (1982); *Mandela Speaking* for Chorus and Orch. (1985); many other choral works and songs.

BIBL.: R. Stevenson, ed., *Time Remembered—A. B.: An 80th Birthday Symposium* (Kidderminster, 1981).—**NS/LK/DM**

Bush, Geoffrey, English composer and teacher; b. London, March 23, 1920; d. there, Feb. 24, 1998. He received training in composition from Ireland and then pursued his education at Balliol Coll., Oxford (B.Mus., 1940; D.Mus., 1946). After lecturing in the extra-mural dept. at the Univ. of Oxford (1947–52), he tutored in the extra-mural dept. at the Univ. of London (1952–80), where he subsequently served as music consultant (1984–87). He also was a visiting prof. at King's Coll., Univ. of London (1969–89). In 1957 he was chairman of the Composers Guild of Great Britain. He ed. works for Musica Britannica and for the collected edition of Elgar's works. He publ. *Musical Creation and the Listener* (London, 1954; rev. 1967), *Left, Right and Centre: Reflections on Composers and Composing* (London, 1983), and *An Unsentimental Education and Other Musical Recollections* (London, 1990). His works were written in an engaging neo- Classical style.

WORKS: DRAMATIC: *The Blind Beggar's Daughter*, opera (1952; rev. 1964); *If the Cap Fits*, opera (Cheltenham, July 12, 1956); *The Equation*, opera (1967; BBC Radio, Feb. 7, 1976); *Lord Arthur Savile's Crime*, theater piece (1972; BBC Radio, July 27, 1986); *The Cat who went to Heaven*, music theater (1974); *Love's Labours Lost*, opera (1988). **ORCH.:** *Natus est Immanuel* for Strings (1939); *Rhapsody* for Clarinet and Strings (1940; also for Clarinet and String Quartet or Piano); *The Spanish Rivals*, overture (1941); *Divertimento* for Strings (1943); Sinfonietta Concertante for Cello and Small Orch. (1943; BBC, Sept. 28, 1945); *In Praise of Salisbury* (1944); *The Rehearsal*, overture (1945); Concerto for Oboe and Strings (1948); *2 Miniatures* for Strings (1948); *Yorick*, overture (1949); Concertino No. 1 for Piano and

Orch. (1953; London, Feb. 11, 1961); 2 syms.: No. 1 (Cheltenham, July 8, 1954) and No. 2, *The Guilford* (1957); Concerto for Light Orch. (1958); *Hornpipe for St. Cecilia's Day* (Birmingham, Nov. 22, 1960); *Old London*, suite for Concert Band (1961); Concerto for Trumpet, Piano, and Strings (1962; London, Dec. 16, 1963); *Finale for a Concert* (1964); *Music* (1967); *Consort Music: 6 Victorian Sketches* for Strings (1987). **CHAMBER:** Violin Sonata (1945; BBC, Oct. 31, 1949); Trio for Oboe, Bassoon, and Piano (Canterbury, Nov. 18, 1952); *Dialogue* for Oboe and Piano (London, March 25, 1960); *Homage to Matthew Locke* for 3 Trumpets and 3 Trombones (1962); Wind Quintet (1963); Concertino No. 2 for Piano and 12 Players (1976); *Tributes: 5 Respectful Pieces* for Clarinet and Piano (1986); *Pavans and Galliards* for Wind Quintet (1992); piano pieces; organ music. **VOCAL:** *A Christmas Cantata* for Soprano, Chorus, Oboe, and Strings (1947); *A Summer Serenade* for Tenor, Chorus, Piano, Timpani, and Strings (1948); *Twelfth Night, an Entertainment* for Tenor, Chorus, and Chamber Orch. (1950); *Farewell, Earth's Bliss* for Baritone and String Quartet or String Orch. (1950); *In Praise of Mary* for Soprano, Chorus, and Orch. (Hereford, Sept. 7, 1955); *Songs of Wonder* for High Voice and Piano or String Orch. (1959); *A Lover's Progress* for Tenor, Oboe, Clarinet, and Bassoon (London, April 26, 1961); *Cantata Piccola* for Baritone, Chorus, Strings, and Harpsichord or Piano (1965); *Daffydd in Love* for Baritone, Chorus, and Piano (1974); *Phantoms* for Soprano, Girl's or Boy's Chorus, and Instrumental Ensemble or Brass Band (1978); *Love's Labours Lost* for Soprano, Baritone, and Orch. (1986); *4 Chaucer Settings* for Baritone, Oboe, and Piano (1987); many other choral pieces; various other songs, including *Archy at the Zoo* for High Voice and Piano (1994).—**NS/LK/DM**

Bush, Kate (Catherine),

reclusive English thrush who gave art rock a good name; b. Bexleyheath, Kent, England, July 30, 1958. Kate Bush's physician father allowed her the liberty to study music and dance. She and her brother had bands through most of their teens. One of them came to the attention of Pink Floyd's David Gilmore, who served as a mentor and put her in the studio. By the time she turned 19, her single "Wuthering Heights" had already reached #1 in England, where it caused a major increase in sales of the Emily Brontë book of the same name.

Most Americans first became aware of Kate Bush when she appeared on *Saturday Night Live* at the behest of Eric Idle. She offered a combination of modern dance and classical/romantic pop that flew in the face of new wave in 1978. Her voice, clearly as much a product of careful classical training as her body, soared and dipped like a kite in a windstorm, exhibiting nearly all of her four-octave range. It was one of the most atypical musical moments in the show's history. It was also the last time Kate Bush performed live in the U.S.

Her appearance coincided with the release of her debut album, *The Kick Inside*. In addition to "Wuthering Heights," "The Man with the Child in His Eyes" (#6 U.K., #85 U.S.) solidified her status as a bona fide star in Europe, while she established a core cult following in America. Both songs showed off Bush's startling voice but only hinted at a rock aesthetic. The album went to #3 in England, but didn't chart in America.

Lionheart, released a scant 11 months later, was a continuation of *The Kick*, concentrating on the quasi-arias befitting an art-rock diva. However, there was little on this record that really cut loose. Even the (U.K. #14) hit, "Wow," still relied on heavy orchestrations. The album went to #6 in the U.K. and again did not chart in America.

The irony of "Wow" is that the song deals with performing, something Bush had minimal experience with. She had played some 30 dates in Europe before deciding that touring was too exhausting. Fortunately, before reaching this conclusion, a video was made of her show. In performance, Bush wore a headset mike, allowing her freedom of movement. Wearing a body stocking and brief shorts, her live music was even more rococo than her recordings. However, as the live EP *Kate Bush on Stage* illustrates, it freed her band up, and every now and again they really stretch out and rock. The reggae beat of "Those Heavy People" became more pronounced, the chords in "James and the Cold Gun" crunchier (with an extended guitar solo tossed in at the end), and the break in "Don't Put Your Foot on the Heartbreak" damn near boogies. The album reached #10 in the U.K.

The powerful chords and a blaring guitar solo carry over to "Violin" on her next studio album, 1980's U.K. chart-topping release, *Never for Ever*. Max Middleton's keyboards added the same jazzy inflections to Bush's music that he had brought to Jeff Beck a decade earlier, albeit in a much lower-key setting. Also low key but evident is the presence of what was then the latest in musical technology, a Fairlight musical computer, able to emulate any sound in a single bound. Again, the record sold to a cult following in America (which included a young Tori Amos). Two U.K. hits, "Army Dreamers" and "Breathing," hit #16. The other single from the album, the #5 U.K. hit "Babooshka," illuminated Bush's future direction. It rocks on the chorus, with the keys and bass giving the song a jazzy air. Like Peter Gabriel—Bush was a featured artist on his third eponymous solo album that same year—she was learning/creating a new contemporary vocabulary for progressive rock.

This vocabulary became manifest on her next album, *The Dreaming*. Given Bush's previous work, *The Dreaming* might have been made by a different artist. The album kicked off with the rip-snorting, soulful rocker, "Sat in Your Lap" (#11 U.K.), a song that interestingly dealt with peaking too soon, having success too young. Synthetics and samples replaced the strings, but the most notable change is in Bush's voice and attitude. The high end of her range is reserved for backing vocals more often than not, and her middle range, while less exotic, serves the material better. At age 24, Kate Bush, artist, was introduced to the world.

Bush took three years to make her next album, *Hounds of Love*, with most of that time spent putting together her own studio, where she could experiment at her leisure. Not as consistently satisfying as *The Dreaming*, the high points offer some of her best material ever. The album did produce the one thing that had eluded her during her entire career: an American hit. "Running up That Hill" made the top 30, as did the album. They fared better in England, where the single rose to #3 and the album topped the charts.

Five years later, after a chart-topping greatest hits album, a video, and a new record deal, Bush made one of the most stunningly voluptuous records ever, *The Sensual World*, which she called, "my most personal and female album." James Joyce's *Ulysses* is the inspiration for the title track, with Kate as everyone's favorite "yes" girl, Molly Bloom. "Deeper Understanding" offers a love song to her computer. The album explored the emerging influence "indigenous" music had on pop, using Uilleann pipes and the unearthly harmonies of The Trio Bulgarka. *The Sensual World* rocked more consistently and more convincingly than any of Bush's previous albums. It hit #3 in the U.K. and rose to #43 in the U.S. as well.

The Red Shoes (1993) featured heavy stars including Prince, Eric Clapton, and Jeff Beck. Ironically, none of them performed on the hits "Rubberband Girl" (#12 U.K., #88 U.S.), "Moments of Pleasure," or "The Red Shoes" (#26 U.K.). Intensely visual, as her initial performance demonstrated, Bush traded in dancing for film, directing most of her videos. She actually brought the two back together in 1995, directing a 50–minute film, *The Line, the Cross & the Curve*, based on the album and starring Bush and Miranda Richardson.

Bush takes a good deal of time between projects because she can: *Cosmopolitan* proclaimed her one of England's richest female pop singers. She can also do what interests her. On the 1994 tribute *The Glory of Gershwin*, she sang "The Man I Love," and more recently she performed "Brazil" on Michael Kamen's *Opus*. She took up painting, and a pair of her canvases painted black with a small, red, battery-operated flashing light went for 1,150 pounds at a charity auction.

London Times critic David Sinclair thought he was making a joke when he observed upon the release of *The Red Shoes*, "If her work rate gets any slower, we'll be lucky to see another Kate Bush album this side of the millennium." Actually, he was correct.

DISC.: *The Kick Inside* (1978); *Lionheart* (1978); *Never for Ever* (1980); *The Dreaming* (1982); *Hounds of Love* (1985); *Whole Story* (1986); *The Sensual World* (1989); *Red Shoes* (1993).—**HB**

Bushell, Garvin (Payne),

early jazz clarinetist, saxophonist, flutist, oboist, bassonist; b. Springfield, Ohio, Sept. 25, 1902; d. Las Vegas, Nev., Oct. 31, 1991. Bushell's astounding career took him from Fats Waller recordings in 1926 to John Coltrane in 1961. Both parents taught singing; his uncle was a clarinetist. He started on piano at six and clarinet at 13. He studied at Wilberforce Univ., and during summer vacations played for traveling tent shows. In 1919 he moved to N.Y. Through the 1920s he worked with various artists, including tours with Mamie Smith and Ethel Waters (1921–22), a long stint with Sam Wooding (1925–28, including a trip to Europe in spring 1925), and freelance recording work. In the 1930s he worked with a number of big bands, including Fletcher Henderson (summer 1935–early 1936), Cab Calloway (Feb. 1936–Nov. 1937), and then Chick Webb (Dec. 1937–1939). During the 1940s, Bushell led his own bands in Philadelphia (late 1941), N.Y. (1943–44), and Calif. (Oct. 1944), and also gigged and recorded with Bunk Johnson in Nov. and Dec. 1947. In the 1950s, he was based in N. J., where he continued to lead his own band. He worked with Wilbur de Paris Band from September 1959 until summer of 1964 (including overseas tours); toured Africa with Paul Taubman's Concert Orch. in September 1964. On Nov. 3, 1961, he played English horn and contrabassoon with John Coltrane for a live recording at the Village Vanguard. He was with Cab Calloway in 1966. Bushell moved to Puerto Rico in spring of 1967, where he was mainly active as a music teacher; in the early 1980s, he settled in Las Vegas.

DISC.: "Royal Garden Blues" (1921); "Shim-me-King's Blues" (1921); "By the Waters of the Minnetonka" (1926); "Dreaming of a Castle in the Air" (1926); "Sergeant Dunn's Bugles Call Blues" (1928); "Buffalo Blues" (1928); "Louisiana Sugar Babes" (1928); "Sippi" (1928); "Keep It to Yourself" (1930); "New Orleans Hop Scop Blues" (1930); "Baby, What Else Can I Do?" (1939); "I Just Got a Letter" (1939). **WILBUR DEPARIS:** *The Wild Jazz* (1960). *Wilbur DePairs on the Riviera* (1960). **JOHN COLTRANE:** *The Other Village Vanguard Tapes* (1961).—**JC/LP**

Bushkin, Joe (Joseph),

jazz pianist, trumpeter; b. N.Y., Nov. 7, 1916. His father, who ran a barbershop in N.Y., arrived from Kiev, Russia, in 1909. Bushkin's first gigs were college dates on Long Island with a band led by Benny Goodman's brother, Irving. In 1932 he began working at the Roseland Ballroom, N.Y., with Frank LaMarr's Band. He became intermission pianist at the Famous Door in 1935; that same year, he accompanied Billie Holiday on a recording session. The late 1930s were occupied with band work, including on and off work with Eddie Condon (1936–37), Joe Marsala (doubling on trumpet; 1937–early 1938), Bunny Berigan (April 1938–Aug. 1939), and Muggsy Spanier's Ragtimers (through Dec. 1939). He joined Tommy Dorsey on Jan. 20, 1940, where he recorded what became his signature song, "Oh! Look at Me Now" in 1941. During the war years, he was in the Air Force, working with the Winged Victory Show as its musical director, and also playing with the show's band, the Winged Pigeons. After being released from duty in February 1946, Bushkin did studio work, then worked with Benny Goodman from spring until November 1946. After a brief stint in Rio de Janeiro in Bud Freeman's Trio in winter/spring 1947, he returned to N.Y. A dislocated shoulder interrupted his career for a while, and then he resumed studio work. He acted and played in the Broadway play *The Rat Race* (October 1949 until May 1950); a decade later, he appeared in the film version. During the early 1950s, he played long residencies at various N.Y. clubs. He visited Europe early in 1953, then returned to the U.S. to tour with Louis Armstrong's All Stars (April–June 1953). Bushkin continued to lead his own small groups throughout the 1950s and 1960s, and was also regularly featured on TV shows. In the 1960s he relocated to Marin County, Calif., and then, in the summer of 1965, he moved to Hawaii for two and a half years, playing a residency at the Gauguin Club, and also touring the Hawaiian Islands for U.S. State Department. During the late 1960s through the mid-1970s, he lived in Santa Barbara, Calif., working occasionally. He was Bing Crosby's accompanist on tour in 1976 and in

London 1977, and resumed working in N.Y. clubs during the 1980s and 1990s.

DISC.: "Oh! Look at Me Now" (1941); *I Love a Piano* (1950); *Piano Moods* (1950); *After Hours* (1951); *Bushkin-Safranski-Wilson Groups* (1955); *Bushkin Spotlights Berlin* (1956); *Night Sounds of San Francisco* (1965); *Road to Oslo and Play It Again Joe* (1977). —JC/LP

Busnois, Antoine,

greatly significant composer; b. probably in Busnes, France, c. 1430; d. probably in Bruges, before Nov. 6, 1492. By 1460 he was active at the church of St. Martin in Tours, where he was a chori clerk and "heuriers" (clericos de choro et pannis); he received minor orders and was elevated to sub-deacon at the church of St. Venant there in 1465. He most likely was a priest by 1470, and subsequently held several minor benefices. He formally entered the service of Charles the Bold of Burgundy in 1467. After Charles's death in 1477, he entered the service of his daughter, Marie of Burgundy; following her marriage to Maximilian I of Austria that same year, he was active mainly in his household chapel until 1483. He spent his last years as rector cantoriae at the church of St. Sauveur in Bruges. Busnois was a master of imitative polyphony and varied contrapuntal techniques. Among his extant works are 7 chansons in early publications of Petrucci (1501–3), the masses *L'Homme armé, O crux lignum,* and *Regina coeli,* and some Magnificats, motets, and other chansons.

BIBL.: C. Brooks, *A. B. as a Composer of Chansons* (diss., N.Y. Univ., 1951); P. Higgins, *A. B. and Musical Culture in Late Fifteenth- Century France and Burgundy* (diss., Princeton Univ., 1986); C. Goldberg, *Die Chansons von A. B.: Die Ästhetik der höfischen Chansons* (Frankfurt am Main, 1994).—**NS/LK/DM**

Busoni, Ferruccio (Dante Michelangiolo Benvenuto),

greatly admired Italian-German pianist, pedagogue, and composer; b. Empoli, near Florence, April 1, 1866; d. Berlin, July 27, 1924. Busoni grew up in an artistic atmosphere: his father played the clarinet and his mother, Anna Weiss, was an amateur pianist. He learned to play the piano as a child; at the age of 8, he played in public in Trieste. He gave a piano recital in Vienna when he was 10, and included in his program some of his own compositions. In 1877 the family moved to Graz, where Busoni took piano lessons with W. Mayer. He conducted his *Stabat Mater* in Graz at the age of 12. At 15 he was accepted as a member of the Accademia Filarmonica in Bologna; he performed there his oratorio *Il sabato del villaggio* in 1883. In 1886 he went to Leipzig and undertook a profound study of Bach's music. In 1889 he was appointed a prof. of piano at the Helsinki Cons., where among his students was Sibelius (who was a few months older than his teacher). At that time, Busoni married Gerda Sjostrand, whose father was a celebrated Swedish sculptor; their 2 sons became well-known artists. In 1890 Busoni participated in the Rubinstein Competition in St. Petersburg, winning first prize with his *Konzertstück* for Piano and Orch. On the strength of this achievement, he was engaged to teach piano at the Moscow Cons. (1890–91). He then accepted the post of prof. at the New England Cons. of Music in

Boston (1891–94); however, he had enough leisure to make several tours, maintaining his principal residence in Berlin. During the season of 1912–13, he made a triumphant tour of Russia. In 1913 he was appointed director of the Liceo Musicale in Bologna. The outbreak of the World War I in 1914 forced him to flee to the U.S.; after a tour of the country, he moved to neutral Switzerland. In 1923 he went to Paris, and then returned to Berlin, remaining there until his death. In various cities, at various times, he taught piano in music schools; among his students were Brailowsky, Ganz, Petri, Mitropoulos, and Grainger. Busoni also taught composition, numbering Weill, Jarnach, and Vogel among his pupils. He exercised great influence on Varèse, who was living in Berlin when Busoni was there; Varèse greatly prized Busoni's advanced theories of composition.

Busoni was a philosopher of music who tried to formulate a universe of related arts; he issued grandiloquent manifestos urging a return to classical ideals in modern forms; he sought to establish a unifying link between architecture and composition; in his eds. of Bach's works, he included drawings illustrating the architectonic plan of Bach's fugues. He incorporated his innovations in his grandiose piano work *Fantasia contrappuntistica,* which opens with a prelude based on a Bach chorale and closes with a set of variations on Bach's acronym, B-A-C-H (i.e., B-flat, A, C, B-natural). In his theoretical writings, he proposed a system of 113 different heptatonic modes, and also suggested the possibility of writing music in exotic scales and subchromatic intervals; he expounded those ideas in his influential essay *Entwurf einer neuen Aesthetik der Tonkunst* (Trieste, 1907; Eng. tr. by T. Baker, N.Y., 1911). Busoni's other publications of significance were *Von der Einheit der Musik* (1923; in Italian, Florence, 1941; in Eng., London, 1957) and *Über die Möglichkeiten der Oper* (Leipzig, 1926). Despite Busoni's great innovations in his own compositions and his theoretical writing, however, the Busoni legend is kept alive not through his music but mainly through his sovereign virtuosity as a pianist. In his performances, he introduced a concept of piano sonority as an orch. medium; indeed, some listeners reported having heard simulations of trumpets and French horns sounded at Busoni's hands. The few extant recordings of his playing transmit a measure of the grandeur of his style, but they also betray a tendency, common to Busoni's era, toward a free treatment of the musical text, surprisingly so, since Busoni preached an absolute fidelity to the written notes. On concert programs Busoni's name appears most often as the author of magisterial and eloquent transcriptions of Bach's works. His gothic transfiguration for piano of Bach's *Chaconne* for Unaccompanied Violin became a perennial favorite of pianists all over the world.

Busoni was honored by many nations. In 1913 he received the order of Chevalier de la Légion d'honneur from the French government, a title bestowed on only 2 Italians before him: Rossini and Verdi. In 1949 a Concorso Busoni was established. Another international award honoring the name of Busoni was announced by the Accademia di Santa Cecilia of Rome, with prizes given for the best contemporary compositions; at its opening session in 1950, the recipient was Stravinsky.

WORKS: O p e r a : *Sigune* (1885–88); *Die Brautwahl* (1906–11; Hamburg, April 12, 1912); *Arlecchino* (1914–16; Zürich, May 11, 1917, composer conducting); *Turandot* (1916–17; Zürich, May 11, 1917, composer conducting); *Doktor Faust* (1916–23; unfinished; completed by Jarnach, 1924–25; Dresden, May 21, 1925). **O R C H .:** *Symphonic Suite* (Trieste, June 9, 1883; *Introduction and Scherzo* for Piano and Orch. (1882–84); *Concert Fantasy* for Piano and Orch. (1888–89; Leipzig, June 10, 1890, composer soloist, Reinecke conducting; rev. as *Symphonic Tone Poem*, Boston, April 14, 1893; *Konzertstück* for Piano and Orch. (1889–90; St. Petersburg, Aug. 27, 1890, coposer soloist, Moritz Köhler conducting); Suite No. 2, *Geharnischte* (1894–95; Berlin, Oct. 8, 1897, composer conducting; rev. 1903; Berlin, Dec. 1, 1904, composer conducting); Violin Concerto (1896–97; Berlin, Oct. 8, 1897, Henri Petri soloist, composer conducting); *Lustspielouvertüre* (Berlin, Oct. 8, 1897, composer conducting; rev. 1904; Berlin, Jan. 11, 1907, composer conducting; Concerto for Piano, Men's Chorus, and Orch. (1901–04; Berlin, Nov. 10, 1904, composer soloist, Muck conducting); *Turandot*, incidental music (1905; Berlin, Oct. 26, 1911; not extant); *Turandot*, suite from the opera (Berlin, Oct. 21, 1905, composer conducting); *Berceuse élégiaque: Des Mannes Wiegenlied am Sarge seiner Mutter* (1909; N.Y., Feb. 21, 1911, Mahler conducting); *Die Brautwahl*, suite from the opera (1912; Berlin, Jan. 3, 1913, Fried conducting); *Nocturne symphonique* (1912–13; Berlin, March 12, 1914, composer conducting); *Indianische Fantasie* for Piano and Orch. (1913–14; Berlin, March 12, 1914, composer soloist, Alexis Birnbaum conducting); *Rondò arlecchinesco* (1915; Rome, March 5, 1916, composer conducting); *Gesang vom Reigen der Geister*, study for Small Orch. from the *Indianisches Tagebuch* No. 2 (1915); Concertino for Clarinet and Small Orch. (Zürich, Dec. 9, 1918); *Sarabande und Cortège*, 2 studies for *Doktor Faust* (1918–19; Zürich, March 31, 1919); *Divertimento* for Flute and Orch. (1920; Berlin, Jan. 13, 1921, Henrik de Vries soloist, composer conducting); *Tanzwalzer* (1920; Berlin, Jan. 13, 1921, composer conducting); *Romanza e scherzoso* for Piano and Orch. (Basel, Dec. 10, 1921). **C H A M B E R :** 1 unnumbered Violin Sonata (1876); 2 numbered violin sonatas: No. 1 (c. 1889) and No. 2 (Helsinki, Sept. 30, 1898); 4 string quartets (1876; 1881; c. 1884; Leipzig, Jan. 28, 1888); Concerto for Piano and String Quartet (1878); Suite for Clarinet and Piano (1878); Suite for Clarinet and String Quartet (1878–81); *Solo dramatique* for Clarinet and Piano (1879); Serenade for Cello and Piano (1883); Short Suite for Cello and Piano (1885); 4 *Bagatelles* for Violin and Piano (1888); *Kultaselle*, 10 short variations on a Finnish folk song for Cello and Piano (1889); *Albumleaf* for Flute or Muted Violin and Piano (1916); *Elegy* for Clarinet and Piano (1919–20). **P i a n o :** 8 sonatas (1875, 1877, 1877, 1877, 1880, 1880 [not extant], 1883, n.d.); 5 *Pieces* (1877); *Suite campestre* (1878); (4) *Danze antiche* (1878–79); *3 Pieces in the Old Style* (1880); 24 *Préludes* (1881); *Una festa di villaggio*, 6 pieces (1881); *Danza notturna* (1882); *Macchiette medioevali* (1882–83); 5 *Études* (c. 1882–88); 6 *Elegies* (1907); *Fantasia nach Johann Sebastian Bach* (London, Oct. 16, 1909, composer pianist); *An die Jugend*, 4 pieces (1909); *Fantasia contrappuntistica*, after J.S. Bach (Basel, Sept. 30, 1910, composer pianist); 6 sonatinas (1910, 1912, 1915, 1917, 1918, 1920); *Indianisches Tagebuch*, book I (1915); *Improvisation* on the Bach chorale *Wie wohl ist mir, o Freund der Seele* for 2 Pianos (1916); 3 *Albumleaves* (1917, 1921, 1921); *Klavierübung in fünf Teilen* (1, 1917; 2, 1917–18; 3, 1919–21; 4, 1897; 5, 1922); *Nocturne* (1918); *Toccata* (1920); *Perpetuum mobile* (1922); 5 *kurze Stücke zur Pflege des polyphonischen Spiels* (1923); *Prélude et étude en arpèges* (1923); *Klavierübung in zehn Büchern* (1923–24). **V O C A L :** Mass for 4 Voices (1879); *Requiem* for Soloists, Chorus, and Orch. (1881); 4 *Pieces* for Soloists, Men's Chorus, and Orch. (1882); *Il sabato del villaggio*, cantata for Soloists, Chorus, and Orch. (1882; Bologna, March 22, 1883); 2 *Songs* for Voice and Piano, after Byron (1883); *So lang man jung* for Tenor, Men's Chorus, and Orch. (1884); *Unter den Linden* for Voice and Small Orch. (1893); *Altoums Gebet* for Baritone and Small Orch. (1917); *Lied des Méphistophélès* for Baritone and Small Orch., after Goethe (1918); *Lied des Unmuts* for Baritone and Piano or Orch. (1918); *Zigeunerlied* for Baritone and Orch. (1923); *Schlecter Trost* for Baritone and Orch. (1924). **OTHER :** Cadenzas to concertos by Mozart, Beethoven, Weber, and Brahms; transcriptions of numerous works by J.S. Bach, Mozart, Liszt et al.

BIBL.: H. Leichtentritt, *F. B.* (Leipzig, 1916); H. Pfitzner, *Futuristengefahr* (Munich, 1917); G. Selden-Goth, *F. B.* (Vienna, 1922); S. Nadel, *F. B.* (Leipzig, 1931); E. Dent, *F. B., A Biography* (London, 1933); A. Santelli, *B.* (Rome, 1939); G. Guerrini, *F. B., La vita, la figura, l'opera* (Florence, 1944); H. Stuckenschmidt, *F. B., Zeittafel eines Europaers* (Zürich, 1967; Eng. tr., *F. B.: Chronicle of a European*, London, 1970); H. Meyer, *Die Klaviermusik F. B.s* (Zürich, 1969); H. Kosnick, *B., Gestaltung durch Gestalt* (Regensburg, 1971); J. Kindermann, *Thematisch-chronologisches Verzeichnis der musikalischen Werke von F. B.* (Regensburg, 1980); S. Sablich, *B.* (Turin, 1982); A. Beaumont, *B. the Composer* (London, 1985); L. Sitsky, *B. and the Piano: The Works, the Writings, and the Recordings* (N.Y., 1986); A. Beaumont, ed. and tr., *F. B.: Selected Letters* (London, 1987); A. Riethmüller, *F. B.s Poetik* (Mainz and London, 1988); M.-A. Roberge, *F. B.: A Bio-Bibliography* (N.Y., 1991).—NS/LK/DM

Bussani, Dorothea, Austrian soprano; b. Vienna, 1763; d. after 1810. In 1786 she married the Italian bass **Francesco Bussani.** She created the roles of Cherubino in Mozart's *Le nozze di Figaro* (Vienna, May 1, 1786) and Despina in his *Così fan tutte* (Vienna, Jan. 26, 1790), opposite her husband's roles as Bartolo and Antonio. She made appearances in Italy with her husband between 1795 and 1805; subsequently appeared in Lisbon and London until she disappeared from the scene in 1810.—NS/LK/DM

Bussani, Francesco, Italian bass; b. Rome, 1743; d. after 1807. He sang tenor roles, then turned to bass. He was active from 1783 to 1794 in Vienna, where he married **Dorothea Bussani** in 1786. He created the roles of Bartolo and Antonio in Mozart's *Le nozze di Figaro* (Vienna, May 1, 1786) and Don Alfonso in *Così fan tutte* (Vienna, Jan. 26, 1790), opposite his wife as Cherubino and Despina. He returned to Italy with her in 1795 and continued to make appearances there until they went to Lisbon in 1807.—NS/LK/DM

Busse, Henry, early jazz trumpeter; b. Magdeburg, Germany, May 19, 1894; d. Memphis, April 23, 1955. He came to the U.S. in 1916, played with Paul Whiteman (1918–28), then formed his own dance band with a characteristic shuffle beat and his muted "sweet jazz" horn. He co-wrote "Wang Wang Blues" and "Hot Lips" (1920), which were big hits for Whiteman; he later recorded both tunes himself (1935). He led Busse's Buzzards, who actively recorded and performed in the 1920s, 1930s, and 1940s; violinist Joe Venuiti recorded with them in mid-1920s. Busse made the switch to swing and big band as well as traditional jazz in the 1940s.

DISC.: "Wang Wang Blues" (1935); "Hot Lips" (1935). —**MM/LP**

Büsser, (Paul-) Henri, esteemed French conductor, pedagogue, and composer; b. Toulouse, Jan. 16, 1872; d. Paris, Dec. 30, 1973. He received initial music instruction as a choirboy at the Toulouse Cathedral under Aloys Kunc; at age 13, he was taken to Paris, where he studied with A. Georges at the School of Religious Music; he then pursued training at the Cons. (1889–92) as a pupil of Franck and Widor (organ) and Guiraud (composition); he also received advice from Gounod. In 1892 he became organist at St. Cloud, near Paris. In 1893 he won the Prix de Rome with his cantata *Antigone.* Returning to Paris, he became conductor at the Théâtre du Chateau d'Eau in 1900, and at the Opéra-Comique in 1902; he was conductor at the Opéra (1905–39; 1946–51). In 1904 he became head of the vocal ensemble class at the Cons., and subsequently was prof. of composition there from 1931 to 1948. In 1938 he was elected to membership in the Académie. He married **Yvonne Gall** in 1958. Büsser was an accomplished composer for the theater. He also orchestrated Debussy's *Petite Suite* (1907), *Printemps* (1912), *La cathédrale engloutie* (1917), and other pieces. His writings comprise *Traité d'instrumentation* (with Guiraud; Paris, 1933), *De "Pelléas" aux "Indes galantes"* (Paris, 1955), and *Gounod* (Lyons, 1961).

WORKS: DRAMATIC: *Les accordailles,* opéra comique (1890); *Les Marivaudages,* pantomime (1891); *Daphnis et Chloé,* scenic pastorale (c. 1896; Paris, Dec. 14, 1897); *Le miracle des perles,* drame lyrique (1898); *Blanc et noir,* pantomime (Paris, 1900); *Colomba,* drame lyrique (c. 1910; Nice, Feb. 4, 1921); *Les noces corinthiennes,* tragédie lyrique (1916–18; Paris, May 10, 1922); *La pie borgne,* comédie lyrique (Aix-les-Bains, Aug. 5, 1927); *La carosse du Saint-Sacrement,* comédie lyrique (Paris, June 2, 1948); *Roxelane,* comédie lyrique (Mulhouse, Jan. 31, 1948); *Diafoirus 60,* farce musicale (Lille, April 4, 1963); *La Vénus d'Ille,* drame lyrique (Lille, April 15, 1964). **ORCH.:** *A la villa Médicis* (c. 1895); *Suite funambulesque* (1900); *Hercule au jardin des Hespérides* (1900). **OTHER:** Magnificat; masses; motets; choruses; songs; piano pieces; organ music.—**NS/LK/DM**

Bussotti, Sylvano, important Italian composer, opera director, and stage designer; b. Florence, Oct. 1, 1931. He began violin lessons at a very early age and also took up painting while still a youth. At the age of 9, he entered the Florence Cons., where he was a student in harmony and counterpoint of Roberto Lupi and in piano of Dallapiccola. His training there was soon interrupted by World War II. After the War, he pursued composition study on his own (1949–56) before continuing his training in Paris with Max Deutsch (1956–58). He also attended courses in new music at Darmstadt (summers, 1958–61). In 1964–65 he was active in the U.S. on a Rockefeller Foundation grant. In 1972 he studied in Berlin under the auspices of the Deutscher Akademischer Austauschdienst. He taught at the Academy of Fine Arts in L'Aquila (1971–74), and then served as artistic director of the Teatro La Fenice in Venice (1975). He was artistic consultant to the Puccini Festival in Torre del Lago (1979–81), and later its artistic director. From 1980 he taught at the Fiesole School of Music. He publ. *I miei teatri: Diario segreto, diario pubblico, alcuni saggi* (Palermo, 1981). Bussotti's early interest in painting continued later in life; his visual works have been exhibited around the globe. As a composer, he found his exploration of serialism, indeterminacy, and other modern means of expression too restrictive. He thus charted a revolutionary course which led him to embrace an anarchistic aestheticism. In 1976 he established his own production company, "Bussottioperaballet," which, from 1984 to 1992, operated asa festival in Genazzano. From his *Lorenzaccio* (1972), much of Bussotti's energies have gone into operas, both his own (which often draw heavily upon earlier compositions) and the standard repertory, which he has explored as a director and stage designer in most luxurious terms. He has also continued to create films and to write poetry, and has elevated himself to Italian celebrity status through his flamboyant direction of the musical section of the Venice Biennale, of which his last, highly controversial term was 1991.

WORKS: DRAMATIC: *Juvenilia,* ballet (1951–53; Segromigno, Aug. 5, 1983); *La Passion selon Sade,* chamber mystery (Palermo, Sept. 5, 1965); *Lorenzaccio,* romantic melodrama (1968–72; Venice, Sept. 7, 1972); *Raramente,* choreographic mystery (Florence, Feb. 4, 1971); *Bergkristall,* ballet (1972–74; concert premiere, North German Radio, Hamburg, May 15, 1973; stage premiere, Rome, June 8, 1974); *Syro-Sadun-Settimino,* monodance (Royan, March 1974); *Oggetto amato,* dance piece (1975; Milan, April 7, 1976); *Phaidra/Heliogabalus,* ballet (1975–80; Turin, Feb. 15, 1981); *Nottetempo,* lyric drama (Milan, April 7, 1976); *Le rarita', potente,* lyric representation (1976–78; Treviso, Oct. 12, 1979); *Autotono,* divertimento (1977; Treviso, Oct. 12, 1979); *Le Racine,* theater piece (Milan, Dec. 9, 1980); *Miró, L'uccello luce,* ballet-pantomime (Venice, Sept. 25, 1981); *Cristallo di Rocca,* ballet (Milan, June 10, 1983); *Phèdre,* lyric tragedy (Rome, April 19, 1988); *L'Ispirazione,* melodrama (Florence, May 25, 1988). **ORCH.:** *...et due voci* (1958–85); *I semi di Gramsci,* symphonic poem for String Quartet and Orch. (1962–71; Rome, April 22, 1972); *Lorenzaccio Symphony I* for Soprano and Orch. (Royan, March 28, 1974) and *II* (Rome, Dec. 17, 1978); *Il catalogo è questo I-IV* (1976–88); *Le bal Miró* (1981; Rome, Dec. 20, 1986); *Timpani* (1985; Rome, Jan. 12, 1986); *Nuit du faune, Concerti con figuro* (1991). **CHAMBER:** *Breve* for Ondes Martenot (1958–72); *Phrase à trois* for String Trio (1960); *mit einem gewissen sprechenden Ausdruck* for Chamber Orch. (1961–63); *Fragmentations* for Harp (1962); *Rara (eco sierologico)* for Violin, Viola, Cello, Double Bass, and Guitar (1964–67); *Rara (dolce)* for Flute and Mime (1966); *Solo* for Various Instrumental Combinations (1967; Danish Radio, Feb. 3, 1968); *Marbre pour cordes* for 11 Strings (London, Nov. 10, 1967); *Ultima rara (pop song)* for Solo Guitar or Guitar and 3 Speakers (1969); *Quartetto Gramsci* for String Quartet (1971; Siena, Aug. 26, 1974); *Rondò di scena* for 4 Flutes (1975); *Ripetente* for 8 Instrumentalists (Milan, Feb. 12, 1976); *Gran Duo* for Cello and Piano (1977–78); *Passo d'uomo* for Piccolo, Timpani, and Percussion (Rome, Dec. 17, 1978); *Tramonto* for Flute, Horn, and Clarinet (1978; L'Aquila, March 5, 1979); *"Dai, dimmi, su!"* for 11 Instruments (1978); *3 Lovers' Ballet* for Violin, Cello, and Piano (1978); *Brutto, ignudo* for Bass Clarinet (1979); *Accademia* for Flute and Piano (1980; Fiesole, June 22, 1981); *Nudo disteso* for Viola (1980); *Naked Angel Face* for Double Bass (Pisa, Nov. 13, 1982); *La vergine ispirata* for Harpsichord and Another Harmony Instrument (1982; Paris, March 21, 1983); *Due concertanti I* for Piccolo and Double Bass (1983); *Qu'un corps défiguré* for Viola, Oboe, Bassoon, Trombone, and Percussion (Rome, June 14, 1986); *Concerto a L'Aquila* for Piano and 9 Instruments (London, July 5, 1986); *Andante favorito* for String Quartet (1988). **P i a n o :** *La Recherche de bal perdu* (1953–57); *Musica per amici* (1957; rev. 1971); *Piano Pieces for David Tudor* (1959); *Pour clavier* (1961); *Tableaux vivants* for 2 Pianos (1964); *Foglio d'album* (1970); *Novelletta* (1972–73); *Brillante* (1975); *Olof Palme* (1987). **VOCAL:** *Nympheo* for Voices and Instruments (1937–84); *Autunno* for 4 Voices (1950–53); *Poesia di depisis* for Soprano and 15 Instruments (1954; Siena, Aug 27, 1975); *Nottetempo con lo scherzo e una rosa* for Voice and Chamber Orch. (1954–57); *El carbonero* for 5 Voices (1957); *Due voci* for Soprano, Ondes Martenot, and Orch. (1958); *Pièces de chair II* for Baritone, Woman's Voice, Piano, and Instruments (1958–60; Paris, Oct. 22, 1970); *Torso (Letture di Braibanti)* for Voice and Orch. (1960–63); *Memoria* for Voices and Orch. (1962); *Siciliano* for 12 Men's Voices (1962); *Il nudo* for Voice and 5 Instruments (1963); *"Extraits de concert"* for Voice and Ensemble (1965; Milan, Feb. 28, 1966); *Cinque frammenti all'Italia* for Mixed Voices and Chorus (1967–68; Venice, Sept. 14, 1968); *Julio Organum Julii* for Reciter and Organ (1968); *The Rara Requiem* for Vocal Group, Chorus, Guitar, Cello, Wind Orch., Piano, Harp, and Percussion (Venice, Sept. 13, 1969; rev. 1970); *Aria di Mara* for Soprano and Orch. (Milan, July 9, 1973); *Lachrimae* for Voices (1978); *Citazione con quartina per Maurice* for Baritone and Piano (1981); *In memoriam (Cathy Berberian)* for Voice, Flute, Viola, and Piano (Genazzano, Sept. 8, 1984); *Pianino* for Boy's Voice and Piano (1987); *Lingue ignote* for Bass and 7 Instruments (1993–94); *Furioso* for Mezzo-soprano and Orch. (Vienna, May 28, 1994); *Unerbittliches Denkgesetz* for Bass, Flute, Trumpet, and Piano (Rome, Jan. 20, 1994). **BIBL.:** F. Degrada, *S. B. e il suo teatrale* (Milan, 1976); M. Bucci, *L'opera di S. B.* (Florence, 1988).—NS/LK/DM

Bustini, Alessandro, Italian composer and teacher; b. Rome, Dec. 24, 1876; d. there, June 23, 1970. He studied at the Accademia di Santa Cecilia in Rome with Sgambati (piano), Renzi (organ), and Falchi (composition), graduating in 1897. He was subsequently appointed to its faculty, and was its president from 1952 to 1964. His works, all written in the traditional Italian manner, include the opera *Maria Dulcis* (Rome, April 15, 1902), 2 syms. (1899, 1909), *Le Tentazioni*, symphonic poem (1914), *Le Stagioni* for Violin and Chamber Orch. (1934), 2 string quartets, songs, and piano works. —NS/LK/DM

Buswell, James Oliver (IV), American violinist, conductor, and teacher; b. Fort Wayne, Ind., Dec. 4, 1946. He studied violin with Galamian at the Juilliard School of Music in N.Y., then pursued academic training at Harvard Univ. (B.A., 1970). In 1963 he made his debut as a violinist in St. Louis, and in 1967 made his N.Y. recital debut; subsequently toured as a soloist, recitalist, and chamber music player; later was a member of the Buswell-Parnas-Luvisi Trio, and also made appearances as a conductor. He taught at the Univ. of Ariz. in Tucson (1972–73), the Ind. Univ. School of Music in Bloomington (1974–86), and the New England Cons. of Music in Boston (from 1986).—NS/LK/DM

Buths, Julius (Emil Martin), German conductor, pianist, music educator, and composer; b. Wiesbaden, May 7, 1851; d. Düsseldorf, March 12, 1920. He was a pupil of Hiller in Cologne and Kiel in Berlin. He conducted in Wiesbaden (1871–72), Breslau (1875–79), and Elberfeld (1879–90), then settled in Düsseldorf, where he was music director (1890–1908). He also conducted the Lower Rhine Music Festivals and was music director of the Düsseldorf Cons. (from 1902). He wrote a Piano Concerto and chamber pieces. —NS/LK/DM

Butler, Jerry, one of the most engaging soul music singer-songwriters to emerge in the late 1950s; b. Sunflower, Miss., Dec. 8, 1939. After moving to Chicago with his family at the age of three, Jerry Butler began singing in gospel groups as a child. He sang with Curtis Mayfield in the Northern Jubilee Gospel Singers, and during 1957, he and Mayfield joined The Roosters. By 1958, they had changed their name to The Impressions and signed with VeeJay Records. Featuring Butler's soothing baritone, The Impressions' first single, "For Your Precious Love" (coauthored by Butler) became a smash R&B and pop hit.

Leaving The Impressions after the solitary hit, Jerry Butler scored a top R&B and pop hit in late 1960 with "He Will Break Your Heart," cowritten by Butler and Mayfield. Butler and Mayfield also cowrote the near-smash R&B and major pop hits "Find Another Girl" and "I'm-a Telling You." With the success of Butler's vocals on Henry Mancini's "Moon River" and Burt Bacharach's "Make It Easy on Yourself" (both major crossover hits), he was established as a purveyor of smooth soul ballads on the American supper club circuit. Subsequent hits included "Need to Belong" and "Let It Be Me," recorded with Betty Everett. Butler's moderate hit, "I Don't Want to Hear It Anymore," was one of the first Randy Newman songs to make the charts and Butler later wrote "I've Been Loving You Too Long (To Stop Now)" for and with Otis Redding.

With the demise of VeeJay Records in 1966, Jerry Butler moved to Mercury Records, where he worked with songwriter-producers Kenny Gamble and Leon Huff. The collaboration resulted in a number of hits for Butler through 1969. These included the top R&B hits "Hey Western Union Man" and "Only the Strong Survive" (also a smash pop hit), as well as the hits "Never Give You Up," "Moody Woman," and "What's the Use of Breaking Up." His 1969 album *The Iceman Cometh*, the most successful of his career, contained three of the hits and provided Butler with the "Iceman" nickname, denoting his cool sophisticated style.

Jerry Butler stayed with Mercury Records when Kenny Gamble and Leon Huff moved to Columbia Records in 1970. He established the Songwriters' Workshop in Chicago and recorded an album with Gene Chandler. With Brenda Lee Eager, Butler scored a major R&B hit with "Power of Love" and his last major pop/R&B hit with "Ain't Understanding Mellow." "If It's Real What I Feel" and "One Night Affair" also became R&B hits on Mercury in the early 1970s. Butler subsequently switched to Motown Records, where he achieved a R&B hit with "I Wanna Do It to You" and recorded two albums with Thelma Houston. In 1978, he reunited with Kenny Gamble and Leon Huff at Philadelphia International Records for two albums and the major rhythm-and-blues hit "(I'm Just Thinking About) Cooling Out." Elected as a Cook County (Chicago) commissioner in 1986, Jerry Butler returned to recording in the 1990s with *Time and Faith* and *Simply Beautiful.*

DISC.: THE IMPRESSIONS WITH JERRY BUTLER: *The Impressions* (1963); *For Your Precious Love* (1963). **JERRY BUTLER:** *Jerry Butler Esquire* (1959); *He Will Break Your Heart* (1961); *Love Me* (1961); *Aware of Love* (1962); *Moon River* (1963); *Folk Songs* (1963); *Giving Up on Love/Need to Belong* (1963); *Soul Artistry* (1967); *Mr. Dream Merchant* (1968); *Golden Hits* (live; 1968); *The Soul Goes On* (1968); *Gift of Love* (1968); *Starring Jerry Butler* (1969); *Very Best* (1969); *The Iceman Cometh* (1969); *Ice on Ice* (1969); *You and Me* (1970); *Sings Assorted Sounds* (1970); *Sagittarius Movement* (1971); *Spice of Life* (1972); *Power of Love* (1974); *Sweet Sixteen* (1974); *Love's on the Menu* (1976); *Suite for the Single Girl* (1977); *It All Comes Out in My Song* (1977); *Nothing Says I Love You Like I Love You* (1978); *The Best Love I Ever Had* (1980); *Only the Strong Survive—The Great Philadelphia Hits* (1984); *Best, 1958–1969* (1985); *Gold* (1987); *Time and Faith* (1992); *The Iceman* (1992); *Iceman: The Mercury Years Anthology* (1992); *Simply Beautiful* (1995). **JERRY BUTLER AND BETTY EVERETT:** *Delicious Together* (1964); *Starring Jerry Butler and Betty Everett* (1968); *Together* (1970). **JERRY BUTLER AND GENE CHANDLER:** *One and One* (1971). **JERRY BUTLER AND BRENDA LEE EAGER:** *The Love We Have* (1973). **JERRY BUTLER AND THELMA HOUSTON:** *Thelma and Jerry* (1977); *Two to One* (1978).—**BH**

Butt, Dame Clara (Ellen), notable English contralto; b. Southwick, Sussex, Feb. 1, 1872; d. North Stoke, Oxfordshire, July 13, 1936. She studied with J.H. Blower at the Royal Coll. of Music in London; later took lessons with Bouhy in Paris and Gerster in Berlin. She made her operatic debut as Ursula in Sullivan's *Golden Legend* (London, Dec. 7, 1892); then sang at the music festivals at Hanley and Bristol. She visited the U.S. in 1899 and 1913; in 1913–14 she made a world tour with her husband, R. Kennerley Rumford, a baritone. Several composers wrote works for her, among them Elgar (*Sea-Pictures* and H. Bedford (*Romeo and Juliet*). In 1920 she was made a Dame Commander of the Order of the British Empire.

BIBL.: W. Ponder, *C. B.* (London, 1928).—**NS/LK/DM**

Butt, John, English organist, harpsichordist, clavichordist, conductor, and musicologist; b. Solihull, Nov. 11, 1960. He learned to play the organ in his youth and began giving recitals when he was 13. He was educated at the Univ. of Cambridge (B.A. in music, 1982; M.Phil. in musicology, 1984; M.A., 1986; Ph.D. in musicology, 1987, with the diss. *The Significance and Incidence of Articulation Marks in the Primary Sources of J.S. Bach;* basically rewritten and publ. as *Bach Interpretation,* Cambridge, 1990). In 1986–87 he lectured at the Univ. of Aberdeen, and then was a research fellow at Magdalene Coll., Cambridge (1987–89). In 1989 he made his first appearances as an organ recitalist in the U.S. in Berkeley and San Francisco. He was an asst. prof. (1989–92) and assoc. prof. (1992–97) at the Univ. of Calif. at Berkeley,

where he also served as univ. organist (1989–97) and director of its chamber chorus (1991–97). In 1995 he made his N.Y. recital debut as an organist. From 1995 to 1997 he was director of the Philharmonia Baroque Chorale. In 1997 he became a lecturer at the Univ. of Cambridge, and founder-director of its mixed choir, the King's Voices. As a performing musician, his repertoire includes works by Bach, Telemann, Purcell, Frescobaldi, Pachelbel, Kuhnau et al. He has contributed articles and reviews to scholarly journals, and also served as consultant ed. and contributor to the *Oxford Companion to Bach* (Oxford, 1999). He publ. *Bach: Mass in B Minor* (Cambridge, 1991), *Music Education and the Art of Performance in the German Baroque* (Cambridge, 1994), and the *Cambridge Companion to Bach* (Cambridge, 1997). —**LK/DM**

Butterfield, Billy (actually, Charles William), jazz trumpeter, flugelhornist; b. Middletown, Ohio, Jan. 14, 1917; d. North Palm Beach, Fla., March 18, 1988. Husband of vocalist Dotty Dare Smith. He started on violin, then bass and trombone before specializing on trumpet. He attended high school in Wyo., then studied medicine at Transylvania Coll.; he also played in college dance bands. His first break came when he was hired by Bob Crosby (Sept. 1937–June 1940); he then joined Artie Shaw (Sept. 1940–Feb. 1941), soloing on Shaw's recording of "Star Dust." He also played with Shaw's Gramercy Five. He was with Benny Goodman from March 1941 until early 1942, then joined Les Brown's Band before becoming a studio musician at CBS and NBC until he joined the Army. After being demobilized in late 1945, he formed his own band. Throughout the late 1940s and 1950s, he played club work in the N.Y. area and also did occasional tours, particularly for college audiences. He recorded with many leaders, along with several brief stints with Benny Goodman (including Newport Jazz Festival in 1958). Early in 1959, he moved to Smithfield, Va., where he began teaching music, as well as leading his own band. In the mid-1960s, he moved to Fla. From 1968 to early 1973, he worked regularly in the World's Greatest Jazzband. In the later 1970s through most of the 1980s, he continued performing and doing studio sessions.

DISC.: *Stardusting* (1950); *Billy Butterfield* (1954); *Billy Butterfield at Amherst* (1955); *Billy Butterfield at Princeton* (1955); *Billy Butterfield at Rutgers* (1955); *Billy Butterfield Goes to NYU* (1955); *N.Y. Land Dixie* (1955); *They're Playing Our Song* (1956); *Session at Riverside* (1957); *Songs Bix Beiderbecke Played* (1969).—**JC/LP**

Butterfield, Erskine, blues-jazz pianist, organist, singer, composer; b. Syracuse, N.Y., Feb. 9, 1913; d. N.Y., July 1961. Butterfield began playing piano at the age of nine, attended school in Newark, N.J., then became a full-time music student. He worked with Noble Sissle, briefly with The Savoy Sultans, then led his own band before joining the NBC studio staff in 1938. After service in the army during WWII, Butterfield led his own trio in Minneapolis, then resumed studio work in N.Y. He led different editions of his Blue Boys band.

DISC.: *Piano Cocktail.*—**JC/LP**

Butterfield, Paul, pioneering white blues revivalist and harmonica player; b. Chicago, Dec. 1942; d.

North Hollywood, Calif., May 4, 1987. Paul Butterfield grew up in Chicago and studied classical flute as a child. He later took up guitar and harmonica, mastering blues harmonica by his late teens. Meeting vocalist Nick Gravenites, the two began playing on college campuses. Butterfield subsequently met guitarist Elvin Bishop, who was attending the Univ. of Ill. on a scholarship, and the two began frequenting Chicago-area black blues clubs, where they were befriended by Muddy Waters. In 1963, Butterfield, Bishop, bassist Jerome Arnold, and drummer Sam Lay began playing at Big John's on Chicago's North Side. Mike Bloomfield, a respected blues guitarist, joined the group in late 1964. Signed to Elektra Records in 1964, The Paul Butterfield Blues Band's initial recordings were not issued until 1995.

The Paul Butterfield Blues Band brought electric instrumentation to the Newport Folk Festival in June 1965, both on their own and backing Bob Dylan. Augmented by keyboardist Mark Naftalin (who subsequently became a permanent member), the group's self-titled debut album featured Chicago blues fare played with rock instruments, a pioneer of the blues-rock genre. Replacing Sam Lay with jazz drummer Billy Davenport, their second album, *East–West*, included more blues standards and Gravenite's "Born in Chicago" plus Mike Bloomfield's exotic 13–minute title cut, which explored both Eastern and Western music and popularized extended guitar improvisation. In early 1967, Bloomfield departed to form The Electric Flag with Nick Gravenites and Buddy Miles. The Paul Butterfield Blues Band performed at the Monterey International Pop Festival in June 1967 and the remaining original members (Butterfield, Bishop, and Naftalin) regrouped, adding a three-piece horn section for *The Resurrection of Pigboy Crabshaw* in one of the first instances of horns augmenting a rock band.

Mark Naftalin left The Paul Butterfield Blues Band after *Pigboy Crabshaw* and Elvin Bishop left after *In My Own Dream*. In 1969, Butterfield, Mike Bloomfield, and Sam Lay helped record Muddy Waters's *Fathers and Sons*. That August, The Paul Butterfield Blues Band performed at the Woodstock Music and Art Fair. As the only original member left, Butterfield persevered with a series of guitarists, bassists, and drummers, eventually disbanding the group in the fall of 1972. He then moved to Woodstock, N.Y., and formed Paul Butterfield's Better Days with vocalist-guitarist Geoff Muldaur and guitarist Amos Garrett, recording two albums for Bearsville Records. Better Days broke up in 1974. Butterfield appeared on The Band's *Last Waltz* in 1976 and later toured with Levon Helm and The RCO All-Stars and the Danko-Butterfield Band, with The Band's Rick Danko. Paul Butterfield died of drug-related heart failure in his apartment in North Hollywood, Calif.

Elvin Bishop and Mark Naftalin had moved to the San Francisco Bay area by 1968. Elvin Bishop recorded two albums for Bill Graham's short-lived Fillmore label before switching to Epic in 1972 and Capricorn in 1974. His Capricorn debut, *Let It Flow*, featured favorites like "Stealin' Watermelons" and the minor hit "Travelin' Shoes." His biggest success came in 1976 with the smash hit "Fooled Around and Fell in Love," sung by Mickey

Thomas, who later joined The Jefferson Starship. Playing West Coast engagements during the 1980s, Bishop ultimately returned to recording in 1988 with the Chicago- based blues label Alligator Records.

Mark Naftalin pursued sessions work, recording over 100 albums with others, including John Lee Hooker, Percy Mayfield, James Cotton, and Big Joe Turner. He also put together his own Rhythm & Blues Revue and produced concerts, festivals, and radio shows. His *Blues Power Hour* radio show (on San Francisco's KALW-FM since 1984) has run almost continuously since 1979. Naftalin served as associate producer of the Monterey Jazz Festival's Blues Afternoon from 1982 to 1991 and produced the Marin County Blues Festival beginning in 1981. In the 1990s, Naftalin's Winner Records issued archival recordings of The Paul Butterfield Blues Band.

With The Paul Butterfield Blues Band, Paul Butterfield legitimized white blues starting with their debut album, and he laid the foundation for the blues revival of the late 1960s. One of the first white bands to play the blues with rock instrumentation, The Paul Butterfield Blues Band brought much-deserved recognition to black blues performers and paved the way for blues-rock bands such as Cream and The Electric Flag. The Paul Butterfield Blues Band was the first band to bring electric instrumentation to the Newport Folk Festival in 1965 and Butterfield became known as one of America's leading white blues harmonica players. The band's *East–West* album was one of the first recordings to explore the fusion of Western and Eastern musical styles and to feature extended guitar improvisation. The Paul Butterfield Blues Band's *Pigboy Crabshaw* album was one of the first to augment electric instrumentation with horns, several months before Blood, Sweat and Tears. Furthermore, members Mike Bloomfield, Elvin Bishop, and Mark Naftalin later moved to the San Francisco Bay Area, where they helped establish a regional blues scene second only to that of Chicago.

DISC.: THE PAUL BUTTERFIELD BLUES BAND: *The Paul Butterfield Blues Band* (1965); *East–West* (1966); *The Resurrection of Pigboy Crabshaw* (1967); *In My Own Dream* (1968); *Keep on Moving* (1969); *Live* (1970); *Sometimes I Feel Like Smiling* (1971); *Golden Butter* (1972); *Better Days* (1973); *It All Comes Back* (1973); *The Original Lost Elektra Sessions* (recorded 1964; 1995); *Strawberry Jam* (recorded 1966–68; 1995); *East–West Live* (recorded 1966–67; 1996); *Born in Chicago—The Best of the Butterfield Blues Band: The Elektra Years* (1998). **PAUL BUTTERFIELD:** *Put It in Your Ear* (1976); *North South* (1981); *The Legendary Paul Butterfield Rides Again* (1986). **SAM LAY:** *In Bluesland* (1970); *Stone Blues* (1996). **SAM LAY BLUES BAND:** *Shuffle Master* (1993). **ELVIN BISHOP:** *The Elvin Bishop Group* (1969); *Feel It!* (1970); *Rock My Soul* (1972); *The Best of Elvin Bishop: Crabshaw Rising* (1972); *Let It Flow* (1974); *Juke Joint Jump* (1975); *Struttin' My Stuff* (1975); *Hometown Boy Makes Good!* (1976); *Raisin' Hell* (live; 1977); *Big Fun* (1988); *Don't Let the Bossman Get You Down!* (1991); *Sure Feels Good: The Best of Elvin Bishop* (1992); *The Best of Elvin Bishop: Tulsa Shuffle* (1994); *Ace in the Hole* (1995); *The Skin I'm In* (1998).—**BH**

Butterley, Nigel (Henry), Australian composer, pianist, and teacher; b. Sydney, May 13, 1935. He attended the New South Wales State Conservatorium of

Music in Sydney (1952–55), his principal mentors being Frank Warbick (piano) and Raymond Hanson (composition), and later pursued training in composition with Priaulx Rainier in London (1962). In 1966 he won the Prix Italia for his choral work *In the Head the Fire*. He was active as a pianist, especially as a proponent of contemporary music. He also was on the music staff of the Australian Broadcasting Commission. From 1973 to 1991 he was a lecturer at the Newcastle Conservatorium. In 1991 he received an Australian Creative Artists' Fellowship and was made a Member of the Order of Australia. In 1996 he was awarded an honorary D.M. degree by the Univ. of Newcastle. As a composer, Butterley pursues a thoroughly individualistic style, notable for its assured technical command and penchant for lyricism.

WORKS: DRAMATIC: *In the Head the Fire*, radio piece (1966); *Watershore*, radio piece (1978); *Lawrence Hargrave Flying Alone*, opera (Sydney, Sept. 24, 1988). **ORCH.**: *Meditations of Thomas Traherne* (1968); *Pentad* (1968); *Refractions* (1969); *Explorations* for Piano and Orch. (1970); Violin Concerto (1970; rev. 1975); *Fire in the Heavens* (1973); Sym. (1980); *Goldengrove* for Strings (1982; rev. 1993); *In Passing* (1982); *From Sorrowing Earth* (Sydney, Aug. 21, 1991); *Poverty* (1992). **CHAMBER**: *Laudes* for 8 Instruments (1963); 4 string quartets (1965, 1974, 1980, 1995); *The White-Throated Warbler* for Sopranino Recorder or Flute or Piccolo and Harpsichord or Piano (1965); *Variations* for Wind Quintet and Piano (1967); *Voices* for Wind Quintet (1971); *Fanfare and Processional* for 4 Trumpets, 2 Trombones, and 2 Timpani (1977); *Evanston Song* for Flute and Piano (1978); Trio for Clarinet, Cello, and Piano (1979); *Forest I* for Viola and Piano (1990) and *II* for Trumpet and Piano (1993); *The Wind Stirs Gently* for Flute and Cello (1992); *Of Wood* for Cello (1995). **KEYBOARD: Piano**: *Arioso, Toccata, Comment on a Popular Song* (1960); *Grevillea* (1962; rev. 1985); *Letter From Hardy's Bay* (1971); *Uttering Joyous Leaves* (1981); *Lawrence Hargrave Flying Alone* (1981); *Il Gubbo* (1987). **Organ**: *3 Pieces* (1961, 1979, 1989). **VOCAL**: *The True Samaritan* for Chorus (1958; rev. 1976); *Carmina: 4 Latin Poems of Spring* for Medium Voice and Wind Quintet (1968; rev. 1990); *Sometimes with One I Love* for Soprano, Baritone, Male Speaker, Flute, Clarinet, Horn, 2 Cellos, and Piano (1976); *The Owl* for Soprano, Flute, Clarinet, Violin or Viola, Cello, Piano, and Percussion (1983); *There Came a Wind like a Bugle* for Chorus (1987); *The Woven Light* for Soprano and Orch. (1994); *Spring's Ending* for Chorus (1997); *Towards Autumn* for Women's Voices, Flute, Clarinet, and Chinese Gong (1998); various other choral pieces and songs. —NS/LK/DM

Butterworth, George (Sainton Kaye),

talented English composer; b. London, July 12, 1885; d. in the battle of the Somme, near Pozières, Aug. 5, 1916. He learned to play the organ at school in Yorkshire, then studied with Dunhill at Eton (1899–1904) and at Trinity Coll., Oxford (1904–08). He then taught at Radley and wrote music criticism for *The Times* of London; with C. Sharpe and Vaughan Williams, he became an ardent collector of folk songs, which were incorporated into several of his compositions; also helped to prepare Vaughan Williams's *London Symphony*, which was dedicated to his memory. To strengthen his technique, he studied with Parratt (organ), Sharpe (piano), and Wood (harmony) at the Royal Coll. of Music in London (1910–11). At the outbreak of World War I, he enlisted in the British army and was posthumously awarded the Military Cross for bravery. His death was greatly lamented. Before he left for France, he destroyed many of his MSS, including those of a Violin Sonata and a *Barcarolle* for Orch. that had been much praised.

WORKS: ORCH.: *2 English Idylls* (Oxford, Feb. 8, 1912); *A Shropshire Lad*, rhapsody (originally titled *The Cherry Tree*, prelude; Leeds, Oct. 2, 1913); *The Banks of Green Willow*, idyll (West Kirby, Feb. 27, 1914). **CHAMBER**: Suite for String Quartet (n.d.). **VOCAL**: *I fear thy kisses*, after Shelley (1909); 6 songs from *A Shropshire Lad*, after Housman (London, June 20, 1911); *Requiescat*, after Wilde (1911); *Bredon Hill*, after Housman (1912); *I will make you brooches*, after Stevenson (n.d.); *Love blows as the wind blows*, after Henley, for Baritone and String Quartet or Piano or Orch. (1914). **Choral**: *On Christmas Night* (1902); *We et up in the morn* (1912); *In the highlands*, after Stevenson (1912); *11 Folk Songs from Sussex* (1912); *Morris Dances* (with Sharpe; 1913).

BIBL.: *G. B. 1885–1916* (1916); I. Copley, *G. B. and His Music: A Centennial Tribute* (London, 1985); M. Barlow, *Whom the Gods Love: The Life and Music of G. B.* (London, 1997). —NS/LK/DM

Butting, Max,

German composer; b. Berlin, Oct. 6, 1888; d. there, July 13, 1976. He studied organ in Berlin and composition in Munich. Returning to Berlin, he was a successful teacher, but in 1933 was deprived of his various positions for political reasons, being the former ed. of a socialist publication. He was able to return to his professional activities after the end of World War II. In 1948 he was appointed a lecturer in the music division of the East Berlin Radio; in 1968 he received an honorary doctor's degree from Humboldt Univ. in East Berlin. His music is animated by polyphonic purposefulness and is marked by rhythmic vitality and lyric meditation. Since many of his works were destined for amateur performances, Butting shunned modernistic involvements; however, in his ninth and tenth syms. he applied dodecaphonic structures.

WORKS: Opera: *Plautus im Nonnenkloster* (Leipzig, Oct. 3, 1959). **ORCH.**: 10 syms. (1922–63); *Sinfonietta, with Banjo* (1929); Flute Concerto (1950); *Symphonic Variations* (1953); Sinfonietta (1960); Piano Concerto (1965); *Legende* (1966); *Triptychon* (1967); *Concert Overture* (1973). **CHAMBER**: 10 string quartets (1914–71); String Quintet (1916); Quintet for Violin, Viola, Cello, Oboe, and Clarinet (1921); Wind Quintet (1925); Piano Trio (1947); String Trio (1952); many piano pieces. **VOCAL**: Choruses; songs.

BIBL.: D. Brennecke, *Das Lebenswerk M. B.s* (Leipzig, 1973). —NS/LK/DM

Buttstett, Johann Heinrich,

German organist and composer; b. Bindersleben, near Erfurt, April 25, 1666; d. Erfurt, Dec. 1, 1727. He studied with Johann Pachelbel, and was appointed organist at the Reglerkirche in Erfurt in 1684. In 1691 became organist at the Predigerkirche there, a post he held for 36 years, until his death. He publ. *Musicalische Clavier-Kunst und Vorraths-Kammer* for Harpsichord (Leipzig, 1713), and also composed several masses and many chorale preludes for organ. His *Ut, mi, sol, re, fa, la, tota musica et harmonia aeterna* (Erfurt, 1716) is a polemical pamphlet directed against Mattheson.

BIBL.: E. Ziller, *J.H. B.* (diss., Univ. of Halle, 1934).
—NS/LK/DM

Buttykay (real name, **Gálszécsy és Buty-kai**), **Ákos,** Hungarian pianist, teacher, and composer; b. Halmi, July 22, 1871; d. Debrecen, Oct. 26, 1935. He studied in Budapest, where he took courses in law and also attended the Academy of Music; he pursued training in piano and composition in Weimar. After touring as a pianist, he taught piano at the Budapest Academy of Music (1907–22). He won success as a theater composer with his operetta *A bolygó görög* (The Wandering Greek; Budapest, Oct. 19, 1905). After composing the theater scores *A harang* (Budapest, Feb. 1, 1907), *Csibészkirály* (Budapest, Feb. 21, 1907), and *Hamupipőke* (Budapest, Oct. 26, 1912), he composed his most successful operetta, *Az ezüst sirály* (The Silver Seagull; Budapest, Feb. 6, 1920). His *Olivia hercegnő* was chosen to open the new Fővariosi Operettszinház in Budapest on Dec. 23, 1922. Among his other works were 2 syms. (1900, 1902); *Magyar Suite* for Orch. (1900); *Magyar Rhapsody* for Orch. (1931); chamber music; piano pieces; songs.—NS/LK/DM

Buus, Jacques (Jachet de or **van Paus; Jacobus Bohusius; Jacob Buus),** Flemish organist and composer; b. c. 1500; d. Vienna, late Aug. 1565. His first publications were 2 French songs, printed in Lyons in 1538. In 1541 he went to Italy and was engaged as asst. organist at S. Marco in Venice. In 1550 he settled in Vienna. He publ., in Venice, 2 books of instrumental *Canzoni francese* (1543, 1550), 2 books of *Ricercari* (1547, 1549), and 1 book of *Motetti* (1549). Several of his madrigals were publ. in various collections of the period, and also reprinted in a number of anthologies.

BIBL.: W. Breitner, *Jacob Buus als Motettenkomponist* (Tutzing, 1977).—NS/LK/DM

Buxtehude, Dietrich, significant Danish-born German organist and composer; b. probably in Helsingborg, c. 1637; d. Lübeck, May 9, 1707. His father, Johannes Buxtehude (1601–74), an organist of German extraction, was active in Holstein, which was under Danish rule. After receiving a thorough education, in all probability from his father, Dietrich became organist at St. Mary's in Helsingborg (1657 or 1658), and then at St. Mary's in Helsingør (1660). On April 11, 1668, he was appointed organist and Werkmeister in succession to the recently deceased Franz Tunder at St. Mary's in Lübeck, subject to the condition that he would abide by the custom of marrying the predecessor's unmarried daughter; he did so, marrying Anna Margaretha on Aug. 3, 1668. He continued the Abendmusiken, concerts consisting of organ music and concerted pieces for chorus and orch., held annually in Lübeck in late afternoon on 5 of the 6 Sundays immediately preceding Christmas. Mattheson and Handel visited Buxtehude on Aug. 17, 1703, with the ostensible purpose of being considered as his successor; but it is a valid surmise that the notorious marriage clause, which would have com-

pelled the chosen one to marry Buxtehude's daughter, allegedly lacking in feminine charm, deterred them from further negotiations. In 1705 J.S. Bach made a pilgrimage allegedly to hear the Abendmusik, to study with Buxtehude, and possibly to investigate the impending opening; though details of Bach's trip are subject to speculation, there can be no doubt that Buxtehude exercised a profound influence on Bach, as both organist and composer. Buxtehude's daughter, 1 of 7, eventually married her father's successor, Johann Christian Schieferdecker, on Aug. 29, 1707. Buxtehude exerted a major influence on the organists who followed him by virtue of the significant role he played in the transitional period of music history from Froberger to the contrapuntal mastery of Bach. Though little of his music exists in MS, many composers were known to have made copies of his works for their own study. His major student was Nicolaus Bruhns. Buxtehude appears prominently in the painting *Domestic Music Scene* (1674) by Johannes Voorhout. For a detailed compilation of Buxtehude's works, see G. Karstädt, ed., *Thematisch-systematisches verzeichnis der musikalische Werke von D. B.: B.-Werke-Verzeichnis* (Wiesbaden, 1974). Editions of his works include: P. Spitta, ed., *D. B.: Werke für Orgel* (1875–76; rev. and aug., 1903–04, by M. Seiffert; suppl., 1939, by M. Seiffert); M. Seiffert, ed., *D. B.: Abendmusiken und Kirchenkantate,* in Denkmäler Deutscher Tonkunst, XIV (1903; 2nd ed., rev., 1957, by H.J. Moser); W. Gurlitt, ed., *D. B.: Werke* (Klecken and Hamburg, 1925–28); E. Bandert, ed., *D. B.: Klavervaerker* (Copenhagen, 1942); J. Hedar, ed., *D. B.: Orgelwerke* (Copenhagen, 1952); K. Beckmann, ed., *D. B.: Sämtliche Orgelwerke* (Wiesbaden, 1972); K. Snyder, general ed., *D. B.: The Collected Works* (18 vols., N.Y., 1987 et seq.; includes rev. ed. of Gurlitt's vols.).

WORKS (the Buxtehude-Werke-Verzeichnis [BuxWV] number follows the work): **VOCAL: 4 1 A r i a s :** *An filius non est Dei,* 6; *Att du, Jesu, will mig hora,* 8; *Bedenke, Mensch, das Ende,* 9; *Das neugeborne Kindelein,* 13; *Dein edles Herz,* 14; *Du Lebensfürst, Herr Jesu Christ,* 22; *Entreisst euch, meine Sinnen,* 25; *Fallax mundus, ornat vultus,* 28; *Jesu, dulcis memoria,* 56; *Jesu, Komm, mein Trost und Lachen,* 58; *Jesu, meine Freud und Lust,* 59; *Jesulein, du Tausendschon,* 63; *Kommst du, Licht der Heiden,* 66; *Lauda Sion Salvatorem,* 68; *Mein Gemüt erfreuet sich,* 72; *Meine Seele, willtu ruhn,* 74; *Fried- und Freudenreiche Hinfahrt,* 76; *Nun freut euch, ihr Frommen, mit mir,* 80; *O fröhliche Stunden, o fröhliche Zeit,* 84; *O fröhliche Stunden, o herrlich Zeit,* 85; *O Gottes Stadt,* 87; *O Jesu mi dulcissime,* 88; *O lux beata Trinitas,* 89; *O wie selig sind,* 90; *Pange lingua,* 91; *Salve, desiderium,* 93; *Schwinget euch himmelan,* 96; *Surrexit Christus hodie,* 99; *Was frag' ich nach der Welt,* 104; *Was mich auf dieser Welt betrübt,* 105; *Welt, packe dich,* 106; *Wenn ich, Herr Jesu, habe dich,* 107; *Wie schmeckt es so lieblich und wohl,* 108; *Wie soll ich dich empfangen,* 109; *Wie wird erneuet, wie wird erfreuet,* 110; *Auf, Saiten, auf!,* 115; *Auf! stimmet die Saiten,* 116; *Deh credete il vostro vanto,* 117; *Gestreuet mit Blumen,* 118; *Klinget für Freuden,* 119; *O fröhliche Stunden, o herrlicher Tag,* 120. **3 C a n o n s :** *Canon duplex per Augmentationem,* 123; *Divertisons nous aujourd'hui,* 124; *Canon quadruplex,* 124a. **2 0 C a n - t a t a s :** *Alles, was ihr tut,* 4; *Drei schöne Dinge sind,* 19; *Eins bitte ich vom Herrn,* 24; *Frohlocket mit Händen,* 29; *Fürchtet euch nicht,* 30; *Gott fähret auf mit Jauchzen,* 33; *Gott hilf mir,* 34; *Herr, auf dich traue ich,* 35; *Herr, wenn ich nur dich habe,* 39; *Ich habe Lust abzuscheiden,* 46; *Ich habe Lust abzuschieden,* 47; *Ich halte es dafür,*

48; *Ich suchte des Nachts*, 50; *Ihr lieben Christen, freut euch nun*, 51; *Ist es recht*, 54; *Je höher du bist*, 55; *Membra Jesu nostri*, 75 (cycle of 7 cantatas); *Nichts soll uns scheiden*, 77; *O Gott, wir danken deiner Güt'*, 86; *Schlagt, Künstler, die Pauken*, 122. **16 Chorale Settings**: *All solch dein Güt' wir preisen*, 3; *Befiehl dem Engel, dass er komm*, 10; *Du Friedefürst, Herr Jesu Christ*, 20; *Du Friedefürst, Herr Jesu Christ*, 21; *Erhalt uns, Herr, bei deinem Wort*, 27; *Gen Himmel zu dem Vater mein*, 32; *Herren vår Gud*, 40; *Herzlich lieb' hab ich dich, o Herr*, 41; *Herzlich tut mich verlangen*, 42; *In dulci jubilo*, 52; *Jesu, meine Freude*, 60; *Nimm von uns, Herr, du treuer Gott*, 78; *Nun lasst uns Gott dem Herren*, 81; *Wachet auf, ruft uns die Stimme*, 100; *Wär Gott nicht mit uns diese Zeit*, 102; *Walts Gott, mein Werk ich lasse*, 103. **6 Ciacconas**: *Herr, wenn ich nur dich hab'*, 38; *Jesu dulcis memoria*, 57; *Jesu, meines Lebens Leben*, 62; *Laudate pueri Dominum*, 69; *Liebster, meine Seele saget*, 70; *Quemadmodum desiderat cervus*, 92. **27 Concertos**: *Afferte Domino gloriam honorem*, 2; *Also hat Gott die Welt geliebet*, 5; *Aperite mihi portas justitiae*, 7; *Canite Jesu nostro*, 11; *Cantate Domino*, 12; *Der Herr ist mit mir*, 15; *Dixit Dominus, Domino meo*, 17; *Domine, salvum fac regem*, 18; *Ecce nunc benedicite Domino*, 23; *Fürwahr, er trug unsere Krankheit*, 31; *Herr, nun lässt du deinen Diener*, 37; *Ich bin die Auferstehung*, 44; *Ich bin eine Blume zu Saron*, 45; *Ich sprach in meinem Herzen*, 49; *In te, Domine, speravi*, 53; *Jubilate Domino*, 64; *Lauda anima mea Dominum*, 67; *Lobe den Herren, meine Seele*, 71; *Mein Herz ist bereit*, 73; *Nun danket alle Gott*, 79; *O clemens, o mitis*, 82; *O dulcis Jesu*, 83; *Salve Jesu*, 94; *Schaffe in mir, Gott*, 95; *Sicut Moses exaltavit serpentem*, 97; *Singet dem Herrn*, 98; *Benedicam Dominum*, 113. **4 Dialogues**: *Herr, ich lasse dich nicht*, 36; *Jesu, meiner Freuden Meister*, 61; *Wo ist doch mein Freund gelieben?*, 111; *Wo soll ich fliehen hin?*, 112. **Liturgical**: *Missa alla brevis*, 114. **2 Parodies**: *Erfreue dich, Erde!*, 26 (of 122); *Klinget mit Freuden*, 65 (of 119). **KEYBOARD**: 12 canzoni, 166–176, 225; 9 chorale fantasias, 188, 194–196, 203–204, 210, 218, 223; 32 chorale preludes, 178, 180, 182–187, 189–193, 197–202, 206, 208–209, 211–212, 214–215, 217, 219–222, 224; 6 chorale variations, 177, 179, 181, 205, 207, 213; 2 ciacconas, 159–160; Passacaglia, 161; Praeambulum, 158; 20 praeludia, 136–153, 162–163; 19 suites, 226–244; 5 toccatas, 155–157, 164–165; 6 variation sets, 145–150. **CHAMBER**: 16 sonatas for Violin, Viola da Gamba, and Continuo, 252–265, 272–273 (252–258 publ. as op.1, c. 1694; 259–265 publ. as op.2, 1696); 3 sonatas for 2 Violins, Viola da Gamba, and Continuo, 266, 269, 271; Sonata for Viola da Gamba, Violone, and Continuo, 267. **Doubtful and Lost Works: VOCAL**: *Accedite gentes, accurite populi*, 1 (doubtful); *Die ist der Tag*, 16 (not extant); *Heut triumphieret Gottes Sohn*, 43 (doubtful); *Wachet auf, ruft uns die Stimme*, 101 (doubtful). **KEYBOARD**: 7 suites, "Die Natur oder Eigenschafft der Planeten," 251 (not extant); Sonata for Viola da Gamba and Continuo, 268 (doubtful).

BIBL.: H. Jimmerthal, *B.* (Lübeck, 1877); C. Steihl, *Die Organisten an der Marienkirche und die Abendmusiken in Lübeck* (Leipzig, 1886); A. Pirro, *B.* (Paris, 1913); S. Hagen, *D. B.* (Copenhagen, 1920); W. Stahl, *Franz Tunder und D. B.* (Leipzig, 1926); idem, *B.* (Kassel, 1937); C.-A. Moberg, *D. B.* (Helsingborg, 1946); J. Hedar, *D. B.s Orgelwerke* (Stockholm, 1951); F. Hutchins, *D. B.: The Man, His Music, His Era* (Paterson, N.J., 1955); H.J. Moser, *D. B.: Der Mann und sein Werk* (Berlin, 1957); S. Sørensen, *D. B.s vokale kirkenmusik* (Copenhagen, 1958); N. Friis, *D. B.* (Helsingør, 1960); M. Geck, *Die Vokalmusik D. B. und der frühe Pietismus* (Kassel, 1965); G. Karstadt, *Der Lübecker Kantatenband D. B.* (Lübeck, 1971); S. Sørenson, *Das B. bild im Wandel der Zeit* (Lübeck, 1972); H. Wettstein, *D. B. (1637–1707): Eine Bibliographie: Mit einem Anhang über Nicolaus Bruhns* (Freiburg im Breisgau, 1979; 2nd ed., rev., 1989 as *D. B. [1637–1707]: Bibliographie zu seinem Leben und Werk*); L. Archbold, *Style and Structure in the Praeludia of D. B.* (Ann Arbor, 1985); C. Defant, *Kammermusik und Stylus phantasticus: Studien zu D. B.s Triosonaten* (Frankfurt am Main, 1985); K. Snyder, *D. B.: Organist in Lübeck* (N.Y., 1987); A. Edler and F. Krummach, eds., *D. B. und die europäische Musik siner Zeit* (Kassel, 1990); G. Webber, *North German Church Music in the Age of B.* (Oxford, 1996); M. Belotti, *Die freien Orgelwerke D. B.s:Überlieferungsgeschischtliche und stilkritische Studien* (Frankfurt am Main, 1997); M. Schneider, *B.s Choralfantasien: Textdeutung oder "phantastischer Stil"?* (Kassel, 1997).—NS/LK/DM

Buzzcocks, The, the English band that captured punk lightning in a pop bottle, formed 1975, in Manchester, England. **MEMBERSHIP:** Pete Shelly (real name, Peter McNeish), voc., gtr. (b. April 17, 1955); Howard Devoto (real name, Howard Trotter), voc. gtr. (b. Manchester, England, 1955); Steve Diggle, bs.; John Maher, drm.

Peter McNeish had played heavy metal in bands through high school. Howard Traford was fascinated by the music of the Stooges and the MC5. They met at the Bolton Inst. of Technology's electronic music society in 1975 and formed a band with a drummer, covering Brian Eno, the Stooges, and others, but never performed live and eventually broke up. McNeish and Traford remained friends, however, and when the Sex Pistols first hit in 1975, the pair went down to London to see the first flowerings of punk. The show convinced them they could start a similar scene in Manchester. They changed their names to Pete Shelly and Howard Devoto, and so the Buzzcocks were formed.

They set up their initial gig by booking the Sex Pistols in Manchester, with the intention of sharing the bill, but their bass player and drummer left just before the show. There they met Steve Diggle, who joined the band on bass. They recruited drummer John Maher through an ad in *Melody Maker*, and were ready to actually open for the Pistols the next time they came through Manchester. The Pistols asked them along on their Anarchy tour.

Shortly thereafter, with funding from Shelly's father, they cut *Spiral Scratch*, the first so-called do-it-yourself (D.I.Y.) record of the punk era. After its release, Devoto left the band to go back to school, forming Magazine later in the year. Shelly took over lead vocals, Diggle took over on guitar, and the bassist who punked out on them before the Pistols' show rejoined the band. *Spiral Scratch* sold out its initial pressing, and record companies started taking interest in the Buzzcocks' apolitical songs of romantic frustration. They signed with United Artists, who guaranteed them creative control. They took advantage of that with their first single, "Orgasm Addict." The government-owned BBC radio found it too explicit and wouldn't play it. Their next single, "What Do I Get," hit #37 despite the raunchily titled B-side, "Oh Shit." Neither saw American releases.

This set the stage for their debut album, 1978's *Another Music in a Different Kitchen*. The album hit #15 on the U.K. charts, despite the lack of a hit single ("I Don't Mind" topped out at #55). They released the single "Love You More"/"Noise Annoys" four months later, and it hit #34. Just half a year after their debut, they pumped out another album, *Love Bites*. Concurrently, they released the single "Have You Ever Fallen in Love with Someone You Shouldn't've." The single rose to #12, while the album peaked at #13. The band toured relentlessly and partied with nearly the same passion.

By the time they released *A Different Kind of Tension* in 1979, the cracks were beginning to show. They showed even further on their first American tour. The last straw came when EMI bought United Artists and refused to fund the band's next studio project. In revenge, the group released a compilation of singles, most of which had not been on previous albums.

Shelly went solo, recording the critically acclaimed but small-selling album, *Homosapien*. Diggle and Maher formed Flag of Convenience. By 1986, Shelly had released two more albums. One of them, *XL1* actually charted. Flag of Convenience became known as FOC.

Although they might have lacked chart success, the enormous influence the band had on both sides of the Atlantic began to show. The grunge movement paid homage to them as influences while bands from Heaven 17 and Fine Young Cannibals to Naked Raygun started covering their songs.

In 1992, the Buzzcocks were the subject of a boxed set, *Progress* and a tribute album. By 1993, Maher was back in the fold, and the band released the album *Trade Test Transmission* and toured with Nirvana.

By 1995, Garvey had left the band to be with his family, and Maher to devote his time to car racing. They were replaced by bassist Tony Arber and drummer Phil Barker. For their next album, the Buzzcocks sought out Neill King to produce *All Set*. Ironically, he had been a gofer at the studio when they recorded *A Different Kind of Tension*. Although none of their records have sold especially well, their impact continues to be substantial.

DISC.: *Another Music in a Different Kitchen* (1978); *Love Bites* (1978); *A Different Kind of Tension* (1979); *The Peel Sessions* (1979); *Singles Going Steady* (1979); *Lest We Forget* (1980); *Buzzcocks Pts. 1–3* (1980); *Operators Manual (Buzzcocks Best)* (1991); *Product* (box set; 1989); *Entertaining Friends: Live at the Hammersmith* (1992); *Trade Test Transmissions* (1993); *French* (1996); *All Set* (1996); *Modern* (1999).—HB

Buzzolla, Antonio, Italian composer and conductor; b. Adria, March 2, 1815; d. Venice, March 20, 1871. He received his early education from his father, a theater conductor, and then was a student at the Naples Cons. as a student of Donizetti and Mercadante (1837–39). He was then active as a theater conductor in Italy, Germany, and France, returning to Venice in 1847. He wrote the operas *Ferramondo* (Venice, Dec. 3, 1836), *Mastino I della Scala* (Venice, May 31, 1841), *Gli Avventurieri* (Venice, May 14, 1842), *Amleto* (Venice, Feb. 24, 1848), and *Elisabetta di Valois* (Venice, Feb. 16, 1850). He also wrote an opera in Venetian dialect, *La Puta onorata*, which remained incomplete. In 1855 he was appointed maestro di cappella at S. Marco, for which he wrote much sacred music.

BIBL.: F. Passadore and L. Sirch, *A. B.: Una vita musicale nella Venezia romantica* (Rovigo, 1994).—NS/LK/DM

Byard, Jaki (John A. Jr.), jazz pianist, tenor saxophonist, composer; b. Worcester, Mass., June 15, 1922; found dead in Queens, N.Y., Feb. 11, 1999. After playing trumpet and piano as a child, Byard learned trombone while in the Army. After touring and recording stints with Earl Bostic during the 1940s and 1950s, Byard moved to Boston, where he was a mainstay of the jazz scene. He had stints as a saxophonist and composer in Herb Pomeroy's big band, worked with Maynard Ferguson (1959–62), then Charles Mingus (on and off from 1963 to 1970). He said that Mingus hired him for Town Hall Concert because he needed somebody who could play "old-fashioned." He also led his own groups, including one in 1965 with Joe Farrell at the Hartford Jazz Society. When Duke Ellington became sick just before he died, Byard played piano in the Ellington Orch. He also headed the Apollo Stompers, a sorely underrated aggregation, in Boston and N.Y. Byard was also prominently involved in jazz education, teaching at Berklee and the New England Cons. of Music, among other institutions. He was found dead from a gunshot wound to the head at his Queens home. There was no weapon found at the scene, which eliminated the suspicion of suicide. Police investigated the shooting, but the mystery remains unsolved.

DISC.: *Blues for Smoke* (1960); *Here's Jaki* (1961); *Out Front!* (1961); *Live! at Lennie's, Vols. 1, 2* (1965); *Freedom Together* (1966); *On the Spot* (1967); *Sunshine of My Soul* (1967); *J. B. Experience* (1968); *With Strings* (1968); *Solo Piano* (1969); *There'll Be Some Changes Made* (1972); *Family Man* (1978); *Live at the Royal Festival Hall* (1983); *Phantasies, Vol. 1* (1984); *Phantasies, Vol. 2* (1988); *Live at Maybeck Recital Hall, V* (1991). **R. BLAKE:** *Improvisations* (1994).—LP

Byas, Don (Carlos Wesley), talented jazz tenor saxophonist; b. Muskogee, Okla., Oct. 21, 1912; d. Amsterdam, Aug. 24, 1972. Byas was quite an astonishing player who surely would have been even better known and more influential in the U.S. had he not spent most of his career in Europe. He began on violin, then switched to alto sax. As a teenager, Byas worked with Benny Moten and Terrence Holder, also played in Oklahoma City with Walter Page's Blue Devils (c. 1929). In 1931–32 he led his own band, Don Carlos and his Collegiate Ramblers (based at Langston Coll., Okla.). In 1933 he left Okla. for Calif. with Bert Johnson and his Sharps and Flats; Byas changed to tenor sax with this band. From mid-1935 through winter 1937, Byas was based in Los Angeles, playing with various bands, and then moved to N.Y. with Eddie Mallory's Band (March 1937), accompanying Ethel Waters; he remained with this band for about 18 months. He held chairs with various bands between 1939 and early 1941, when he joined Count Basie, with whom he worked from January 1941 until November 1943, and then worked briefly with Dizzy Gillespie. During 1944–fall 1946, he gigged around N.Y., briefly leading his own band. In September 1946 Byas went to Europe as a member of Don Redman's Band and lived in Europe until his death. He was regularly featured at jazz festivals throughout Europe and continued his prolific recording career. In 1970 he returned to the U.S. to play the Newport Jazz Festival and several club dates. He made a tour of Japan in 1971 with Art Blakely, and then returned to his home in the Netherlands, where he died of lung cancer.

DISC.: "Midnight at Minton's" (1941); "Candy" (1945); "I Got Rhythm" (1945); "Living My Life" (1946); *On Blue Star* (1950); *Tenderly* (1951); *Tenor Saxophone Concerto* (1951); *Don Byas with Beryl Booker* (1954); *Jazz from Saint-Germain Des Pre* (1955); *Tribute to Cannonball* (1961); *Night in Tunisia* (1963); *Anthropology* (1963); *Don Byas Meets Ben Webster* (1968).

BIBL.: W. Van Eyle, *Don Byas Discography* (Netherlands, 1967).—JC/LP

Bychkov, Semyon, Russian-born American conductor; b. Leningrad, Nov. 30, 1952. He was the brother of **Yakov Kreizberg**. He attended the Glinka Choir School in Leningrad as a youth; subsequently studied with Ilya Musin at the Leningrad Cons., graduating in 1974. In 1975 he emigrated to the U.S., where he received an Artist Diploma from the Mannes Coll. of Music in N.Y. in 1976. From 1980 to 1985 he was music director of the Grand Rapids Sym. Orch. In 1983 he became a naturalized American citizen. After serving as assoc. conductor (1980–81) and principal guest conductor (1981–85) of the Buffalo Phil., he was its music director (1985–89). He subsequently was music director of the Orchestre de Paris (from 1989), and also was principal guest conductor of the orch. of the Maggio Musicale Fiorentino (from 1992) and of the St. Petersburg Phil. (from 1992).—NS/LK/DM

Bylsma, Anner, Dutch cellist; b. The Hague, Feb. 17, 1934. He studied cello with Carel Boomkamp at the Royal Cons. of Music in The Hague, receiving the Prix d'excellence in 1957; subsequently won the Pablo Casals Competition in Mexico City (1959). After serving as principal cellist of Amsterdam's Concertgebouw Orch. (1962–68), he devoted himself to an international career as a soloist and recitalist. He taught at his alma mater and at Amsterdam's Sweelinck Cons., and was the Erasmus Scholar at Harvard Univ. in 1982. His repertoire is comprehensive, ranging from the Baroque and early Classical periods (utilizing original instruments) to contemporary scores.—NS/LK/DM

Byrd, Charlie (actually, **Charles L.**), pop-jazz guitarist; b. Chuckatuck, Va., Sept. 16, 1925; d. Annapolis, Md., Dec. 1, 1999 (some sources say Nov. 30, 1999, or Dec. 2, 1999). Taught by his father, Byrd learned how to play the guitar at age nine and eventually played in various school, college, and U.S. Army bands. While stationed in France, he met the famed jazz guitarist Django Reinhardt, influencing him to pursue his interest in the music. After World War II, Byrd settled in N.Y., where he spent the 1950s building a strong reputation in both the jazz and classical fields; he also studied with André Segovia in 1954. Byrd played with Woody Herman in 1959, then embarked upon a U.S. government–sponsored tour of South America (1961), during which he discovered and adopted the bossa nova sound. This style and its accompanying dance became a fashionable

new craze in both the U.S. and the U.K. in the early 1960s, largely due to the exposure Byrd gave the style on his return to the U.S. In 1962 he teamed with Stan Getz and released an album of bossa nova with an instrumental single called "Desafinado." It reached the top 20 on both sides of the Atlantic, as did the duo's album *Jazz Samba*. Charlie Byrd was never a chart star again, but he continued to be active in the music business. He ran his own club, the Byrd Cage, in Washington, D.C., which saw him remaining loyal to both wings of his musical self. In 1973 he formed the Great Guitars trio with Barney Kessel and Herb Ellis; they made five albums together and also toured extensively through the next decade. Byrd died of cancer in 1999. His brother, Joe, is a professional bassist who worked in Byrd's group for many years, and his other brother, Jack, is an amateur guitarist.

DISC.: *Blues for Night People* (1957); *Jazz Recital* (1957); *Midnight Guitar* (1957); *Byrd's Word* (1958); *Jazz at the Show Boat, Vols. 1, 2, 3* (1959); *Mr. Guitar* (1959); *Charlie's Choice* (1960); *Guitar Artistry of Charlie Byrd* (1960); *Blues Sonata* (1961); *Charlie Byrd at the Village Vanguard* (1961); *In Greenwich Village* (1961); *Bossa Nova Pelos Passaros* (1962); *Jazz Samba* (1962); *Latin Impressions* (1962); *Byrd at the Gate* (1963); *Once More! Bossa Nova* (1963); *Brazilian Byrd* (1964); *Solo Flight* (1965); *Music for "Villa Lobos"* (1967); *Great Guitars* (1974); *Great Guitars at the Winery* (1980); *Great Guitars at Charlie's* (1982); *Washington Guitar Quartet* (1992); *Great Guitars II* (1995).—MM/LP

Byrd, Donald(son Toussaint L'ouverture, II), jazz-funk trumpeter, flugelhornist, educator; b. Detroit, Dec. 9, 1932. He studied at Wayne State Univ. in Detroit (B.M., 1954) and at the Manhattan School of Music (M.A., Music Education); he then studied composition with Boulanger in Paris (1962–63). Byrd came to fame with Art Blakey and Horace Silver's hard bop bands during the 1950s, and recorded extensively for the Blue Note, Savoy, and Prestige labels. He also worked with Red Garland, Jackie McLean, Max Roach, and Sonny Rollins. He teamed up with Pepper Adams to co-lead a group (1958–61), which Herbie Hancock joined in 1961. In 1962 Byrd began experiencing problems with his teeth and at the same time, began work on streamlining and simplifying his style. He also concentrated on beauty of tone and on writing challenging harmonic studies such as "Fly Little Bird Fly." He served on the faculties of Rutgers Univ., the Hampton Inst., Howard Univ., and N.C. Central Univ. Byrd moved toward a more funk-based sound and launched the Blackbyrds in 1973, a band that consisted of students at Howard Univ. Their aim was to experiment with Byrd's musical ideas, as a way of complementing and enhancing their studies. In 1973 Byrd recorded the *Black Byrd* album, a huge seller whose single "Walking in Rhythm" was among the first jazz-funk hits; it set the trend for their other such releases. Success continued with the release of *Street Lady*, which further helped lay the foundation of contemporary dance. Consequently, Byrd's work has experienced a great resurgence in popularity during the 1990s; his work is the most sampled of all the Blue Note artists. Byrd also guested on Guru's *Jazzmatazz* album and tour (1993). He has performed exclusively with a mute since the 1980s. He currently teaches at Del. State Univ.

DISC.: *Byrd Jazz* (1955); *Byrd's Eye View* (1955); *Byrd's Word* (1955); *First Flight* (1955); *Long Green* (1955); *Jazz Message Of ...* (1956); *Two Trumpets* (1956); *Byrd Blows on Beacon Hill* (1957); *Gigi Gryce-Donald Byrd Jazz Lab* (1957); *Jazz Eyes* (1957); *Jazz Lab* (1957); *Byrd in Paris, Vols. 1 and 2* (1958); *Off to the Races* (1958); *Fuego* (1959); *Byrd in Flight* (1960); *Donald Byrd at the Half Note Café* (1960); *Cat Walk* (1961); *Chant* (1961); *Free Form* (1961); *Royal Flush* (1961); *Jazz Message* (1962); *New Perspective* (1963); *I'm Tryin' to Get Home* (1964); *Up with Donald Byrd* (1964); *Mustang!* (1966); *Fancy Free* (1969); *Black Byrd* (1972); *Street Lady* (1973); *Harlem Blues* (1987); *Getting Down to Business* (1989); *City Called Heaven* (1991). **D. PEARSON:** *Wahoo* (1964).—**MM/LP**

Byrd, William, great English composer; b. probably in Lincoln, c. 1540; d. Stondon Massey, Essex, July 4, 1623. There are indications that Byrd studied music with Tallis. On March 25, 1563, Byrd was appointed organist of Lincoln Cathedral. In 1570 he was sworn in as a Gentleman of the Chapel Royal, while retaining his post at Lincoln Cathedral until 1572. He then assumed his duties, together with Tallis, as organist of the Chapel Royal. In 1575 Byrd and Tallis were granted a patent by Queen Elizabeth I for the exclusive privilege of printing music and selling music paper for a term of 21 years. However, the license proved unprofitable and they successfully petitioned the Queen in 1577 to give them an annuity in the form of a lease. In 1585, after the death of Tallis, the license passed wholly into Byrd's hands. The earliest publication of the printing press of Byrd and Tallis was the first set of *Cantiones sacrae* for 5 to 8 Voices (1575), printed for them by Vautrollier and dedicated to the Queen. Works issued by Byrd alone under his exclusive license were *Psalmes, Sonets and Songs* (1588), *Songs of Sundrie Natures* (1589), and 2 further vols. of *Cantiones sacrae* (1589, 1591). Many of his keyboard pieces appeared in the MS collection *My Ladye Nevells Booke* (1591) and in Francis Tregian's *Fitzwilliam Virginal Book* (c. 1612–19), among others. During the winter of 1592–93, he moved to Stondon Massey, Essex. He subsequently was involved in various litigations and disputes concerning the ownership of the property. Between 1592 and 1595 he publ. 3 masses, and between 1605 and 1607 he brought out 2 vols. of Gradualia. His last collection, *Psalmes, Songs and Sonnets*, was publ. in 1611. Byrd was unsurpassed in his time in compositional versatility. His masterly technique is revealed in his ecclesiastical works, instrumental music, madrigals, and solo songs.

WORKS (all publ. in London): *Cantiones, quae ab argumento sacrae vocantur* for 5 to 8 Voices (with Tallis, 1575); *Psalmes, Sonets and Songs* for 5 Voices (1588); *Liber primus sacrarum cantionum* (*Cantiones sacrae*) for 5 Voices (1589); *Songs of Sundrie Natures* for 3 to 6 Voices (1589); *Liber secundus sacrarum cantionum* (*Cantiones sacrae*) for 5 to 6 Voices (1591); *Mass for 4 Voices* (publ. without title page; c. 1592); *Mass for 3 Voices* (publ. without title page; c. 1593); *Mass for 5 Voices* (publ. without title page; c. 1595); *Gradualia ac cantiones sacrae* for 3 to 5 Voices (1605); *Gradualia seu cantionum sacrarum, liber secundus* for 4 to 6 Voices (1607); *Psalmes, Songs and Sonnets...* for 3 to 6 Voices (1611). He also wrote a *Short Service* for 4 to 6 Voices; a *2nd Service* for 1 to 5 Voices and Organ; a *3rd Service* for 5 Voices; a *Great Service* for 5 to 10 Voices; *1st Preces and Psalms 47, 54, and*

100; and *2nd Preces and Psalms 114, 55, 119, and 24*; several other works are incomplete. His keyboard music appeared in *My Ladye Nevells Booke* (1591), *The Fitzwilliam Virginal Book* (c. 1612–19), *Parthenia* (c. 1612–13), *Will Forster's Book* (1624), and other contemporary collections. Modern eds. of Byrd's works have been publ. in several series, including the Tudor Church Music and Musica Britannica series. E. Fellowes was a pioneer in the field; he brought out many of the works in his series on the English madrigalists, and also planned a complete ed. of the music, which was continued by T. Dart and others. Their efforts culminated in The Byrd Edition, ed. by P. Brett, which commenced appearing in 1971.

BIBL.: E. Fellowes, *The English Madrigal Composers* (Oxford, 1921; 2nd ed., 1948); idem, *W. B.: A Short Account of His Life and Work* (Oxford, 1923; 2nd ed., 1928); F. Howes, *W. B.* (London, 1928); E. Fellowes, *W. B.* (Oxford, 1936; 2nd ed., 1948); H. Andrews, *The Technique of B.'s Vocal Polyphony* (London, 1966); I. Holst, *B.* (London, 1972); O. Neighbour, *The Consort and Keyboard Music of W. B.* (Berkeley, 1978); J. Kerman, *The Music of W. B.: Vol. I, The Masses and Motets of W. B.* (London, 1981); R. Turbet, *W. B.: A Guide to Research* (N.Y., 1987); A. Brown and R. Turbet, eds., *B. Studies* (Cambridge, 1991); R. Turbet, *W. B. (1543–1623): Lincoln's Greatest Musician* (Lincoln, 1993); J. Harley, *W. B.: Gentleman of the Chapel Royal* (Aldershot, 1997). —**NS/LK/DM**

Byrds, The, the most important group in the creation of both folk-rock and country-rock. **MEMBERSHIP:** Roger McGuinn (real name, James Joseph McGuinn III), lead electric 12–string gtr., voc. (b. Chicago, July 13, 1942); Gene Clark (real name, Harold Eugene Clark), rhythm gtr., har., voc. (b. Tipton, Mo., Nov. 17, 1941; d. Sherman Oaks, Calif., May 24, 1991); David Crosby (real name, Van Cortland), rhythm gtr., voc. (b. Los Angeles, Aug.14, 1941); Chris Hillman, bs., mdln., voc. (b. Los Angeles, Dec. 4, 1942); Mike Clarke (b. N.Y., June 3, 1944; d. Treasure Island, Fla., Dec. 19, 1993). Gene Clark left in March 1966. David Crosby left in October 1967. Gram Parsons (real name, Cecil Connor III), gtr., voc. (b. Winter Haven, Fla., Nov. 5, 1946; d. Joshua Tree, Calif., Sept. 19, 1973), was a member in 1968. Other later members included Clarence White, gtr., voc., (b. Lewiston, Maine, June 7, 1944; d. Palmdale, Calif., July 14, 1973); John York, bs. (b. White Plains, N.Y., Aug. 3, 1946); Skip Battin, bs. (b. Gallipolis, Ohio, Feb. 2, 1934); Kevin Kelly, drm. (b. Calif., 1945); Gene Parsons, drm. (b. April 9, 1944).

The Byrds formed in L.A. in the summer of 1964. Jim McGuinn had made his debut at the Gate of Horn in Chicago in the late 1950s, later backing the Limeliters and Judy Collins. He performed as a solo folk artist in Greenwich Village and played as accompanist to the Chad Mitchell Trio beginning in 1960, helping record their *Mighty Day on Campus* and *At the Bitter End* albums. After working with Bobby Darin in N.Y. in 1962, he returned to solo work at the Troubadour in L.A., where he met Gene Clark in 1964. Clark had played in bands since the age of 13 and was a member of the New Christy Minstrels in the early 1960s. McGuinn and Clark began working as a duo and were later joined by David Crosby. Crosby had sung in coffeehouses in N.Y. and Calif. in the early 1960s and served a short-lived stint in Les Baxter's Balladeers.

Crosby introduced them to producer Jim Dickson and the trio recorded "The Only Girl I Adore."

McGuinn, Clark, and Crosby subsequently formed the Jet Set, recording "You Movin'" and "The Only Girl" with sessions musicians. They subsequently recruited drummer Michael Clarke and bluegrass prodigy Chris Hillman. Hillman had formed the Scottsville Squirrel Barkers in 1961, and, later, the Hillmen with Gosdin brothers Vern and Rex. Recordings made by the Hillmen between 1963 and 1964 were later issued on Together Records after the success of the Byrds.

In 1964, with the assistance of Dickson, the group recorded a demonstration tape at World Pacific Studios (later issued as *Preflyte*). Initially signed to Elektra Records as the Beefeaters, the group's first single, "Please Let Me Love You," flopped and they subsequently signed with Columbia Records in November 1964, thus becoming the first rock act signed by the mainstream label. Soon changing their name to the Byrds, the group recorded Bob Dylan's "Mr. Tambourine Man" at the urging of Dickson. Ironically, only McGuinn actually played an instrument on the recording, his electric 12–string guitar. With McGuinn singing lead and Crosby and Clark providing harmonies, the instrumentation was done by L.A. studio stalwarts Leon Russell, Larry Knechtel, and Hal Blaine. The single, issued in March 1965, became a top British and American hit and launched the Byrds into international prominence. Debuting that month at Ciro's in L.A., the original group remained far more effective as a recording group than a performing one.

All of the Byrds actually played on their debut album, save the songs "Mr. Tambourine Man" and "I Knew I'd Want You." The album contained four Dylan songs, including the moderate American and near-smash British hit "All I Really Want to Do," plus Gene Clark's classic "I'll Feel a Whole Lot Better," and Jackie DeShannon's "Don't Doubt Yourself, Babe." Their second album yielded a top American hit with the title song, "Turn! Turn! Turn!" (adapted by Pete Seeger from the Biblical Book of Ecclesiastes), and contained two more Dylan songs, McGuinn's "It Won't Be Wrong," and Clark's "Set You Free This Time," a minor hit.

Conflicts in the group soon became apparent as Crosby and McGuinn frequently disagreed on the Byrds' direction, sometimes coming to actual blows. However, the first defection was Gene Clark in March 1966. He soon recorded his debut album with Gosdin brothers Vern and Rex, augmented by Hillman, Clarke, Clarence White, and Doug Dillard. It included "Echoes," "Tried So Hard," and "So You Say You Lost Your Baby." With Dillard, Clark subsequently formed Dillard and Clark, recording two neglected albums for A&M Records that are regarded as the earliest example of newgrass, a progressive variation of traditional bluegrass. Their debut, recorded with future Flying Burrito Brother and Eagle Bernie Leadon, featured the Clark-Leadon composition, "Train Leaves Here This Mornin'." Fiddler Byron Berline joined for the second album. Never afforded the attention of other former Byrds, Clark recorded the solo albums *White Light*, *No Other*, and *Two Sides to Every Story* during the 1970s.

Having lost one of their singers and their principal songwriter, the Byrds realigned, with Hillman taking up vocals and McGuinn and Crosby writing more songs. At the same time, the group started experimenting with a more sophisticated sound, as McGuinn immersed himself in the music of jazz saxophonist John Coltrane. The result was the major hit single "Eight Miles High," written by McGuinn, Crosby, and Gene Clark and recorded shortly before Clark's departure. With three-part harmony and an almost imperceptible melody, the song featured McGuinn playing his electric 12–string modally (rather than in a major or minor scale). The first psychedelic hit song, with its apparent reference to the LSD experience, "Eight Miles High" had the dubious distinction of being one of the first singles of the 1960s to be banned from airplay. The eclectic *Fifth Dimension* album also included McGuinn and Crosby's psychedelic "I See You," the moderate hit "Mr. Spaceman," and the bluesy "Hey Joe."

The Byrds' increasing musical sophistication was evident with the release of *Younger Than Yesterday*. Although marred by two overdone production numbers, the album yielded a pair of hits with Dylan's "My Back Pages" and McGuinn and Hillman's bitterly satiric "So You Want to Be a Rock 'n' Roll Star." It contained Crosby's beautiful "Everybody's Been Burned," two McGuinn-Crosby collaborations, "Why" and "Renaissance Faire," and four Hillman songs, including the country-flavored "Time Between." The Byrds performed at the Monterey International Pop Festival in June 1967, but by then the rift between McGuinn and Crosby had become irreparable. When Crosby refused to sing two Gerry Goffin-Carole King compositions, he was summarily paid off and fired in October. Crosby later produced Joni Mitchell's debut album and helped form the quintessential 1960s acoustic guitar-vocal harmony group, Crosby, Stills and Nash. Crosby's subsequent career is chronicled under Crosby, Stills and Nash.

Recorded with the assistance of outside musicians, *The Notorious Byrd Brothers* was critically hailed and marked the beginning of a trend toward simplicity rather than sophistication in the music of the Byrds. The album contained the two disputed Goffin-King songs, "Wasn't Born to Follow" and "Goin' Back," a minor hit, and McGuinn and Hillman's "Change Is Now." Mike Clarke departed in late 1967, to be replaced by Hillman's cousin Kevin Kelly.

McGuinn, now using the first name Roger, recruited singer-songwriter- guitarist Gram Parsons in February 1968, lending the Byrds a country music orientation. They soon appeared at the Grand Ole Opry in Nashville and their next album, *Sweetheart of the Rodeo*, openly embraced country-western music. Hailed as the first country-rock album, *Sweetheart* was years ahead of its time and proved a commercial flop. It contained Dylan's "Nothing Was Delivered" and "You Ain't Going Nowhere," a minor hit, and two excellent Parsons songs, "Hickory Wind" and "One Hundred Years from Now." The Byrds subsequently began to deteriorate. Gram Parsons quit in July 1968, followed in October by Chris Hillman. The two soon formed the Flying Burrito Brothers with Chris Ethridge. Hillman's career with and after the Flying Burrito Brothers is chronicled under the Flying Burrito Brothers.

McGuinn, the only original member left, put together a new group with another bluegrass prodigy, Clarence White. White had been playing bluegrass music with his brothers Roland and Eric since the mid-1950s, initially as the Three Little Country Boys, later as the Country Boys. By the early 1960s, the Country Boys had evolved into the Kentucky Colonels, one of the most popular West Coast bluegrass bands, rivaled only by Hillman's groups. After the Kentucky Colonels disbanded around 1967, Clarence White had pursued session work before joining Gene Parsons, Gib Guilbeau, Sneaky Pete Kleinow, and others in the group Nashville West. For McGuinn's newest Byrds, White recommended John York and Gene Parsons. Parsons (no relation to Gram) had played with Guilbeau in the duo Cajun Gib and Gene before joining Nashville West.

The new lineup of the Byrds recorded *Dr. Byrds and Mr. Hyde*, which included McGuinn's "Bad Night at the Whiskey," McGuinn and Gram Parsons' "Drug Store Truck Driving Man," and the instrumental "Nashville West." The Byrds' nosedive into obscurity was arrested briefly by the surprise popularity of the Peter Fonda-Dennis Hopper film *Easy Rider*. The best-selling soundtrack album contained three songs sung by McGuinn, including the minor hit "The Ballad of Easy Rider." The obvious follow-up album *The Ballad of Easy Rider* yielded the Byrds' final (minor) hit, "Jesus Is Just All Right."

John York left in September 1968, and was replaced by Skip Battin. Years earlier, Battin had been half of the duo Skip and Flip, who hit with a remake of Marvin and Johnny's "Cherry Pie" in 1960. The Byrds' (*Untitled*), half live and half studio material, included "Truck Stop Girl" (written by Lowell George and Bill Payne of Little Feat) and several McGuinn-Jaques Levy collaborations, most notably "Lover of the Bayou" and "Chestnut Mare." Defections continued and, finally, in February 1973, McGuinn disbanded the Byrds. The original group did reassemble briefly for 1973's rather crassly commercial reunion album, which featured McGuinn's "Born to Rock 'n' Roll." The Byrds were inducted into the Rock and Roll Hall of Fame in 1991.

Clarence White quickly joined David Grisman, Peter Rowan, Richard Greene, and others in Muleskinner, recording one album on Warner Brothers. He formed the New Kentucky Colonels with brother Roland, touring Sweden, and started work on a solo album. However, on July 14, 1973, he was killed when struck by a drunk driver while loading equipment in Palmdale, Calif.

Gene Parsons recorded the impressive *Kindling* album before joining the later-day edition of the Flying Burrito Brothers for *Flying Again* and *Airborne*. He joined Sierra Records in 1980 and later recorded with Meridian Green, whom he married in 1986.

Roger McGuinn recorded a number of albums for Columbia in the 1970s, most notably the overlooked *Cardiff Rose*. Produced by Mick Ronson, the album contained two previously unrecorded songs, Joni Mitch-

ell's "Dreamland" and Bob Dylan's "Up to Me." McGuinn toured with Dylan's Rolling Thunder Revue in late 1975, forming a new band, Thunderbyrd, in 1977. That spring Chris Hillman's band toured Europe with Gene Clark's band and McGuinn's Thunderbyrd, leading to a jam session among the three at London's Hammersmith Odeon. Later, Clark joined McGuinn onstage at the Troubadour in L.A. They subsequently toured as a duo, becoming a trio when Hillman joined. The three, playing acoustic guitars, opened the Canadian leg of Eric Clapton's Slowhand tour. In late 1978, the three recorded the highly polished *McGuinn, Clark and Hillman* album for Capitol Records, and managed a moderate hit with McGuinn's "Don't Write Her Off."

Gene Clark toured with John York and others as the Byrds from 1985–87. In 1987, he recorded the solo album *Firebyrd* for Takoma Records and *So Rebellious a Lover* with Carla Olson of the Textones. In January 1989, David Crosby, Roger McGuinn, and Chris Hillman played three Calif. club dates to establish their right to the Byrds' name and prevent Gene Clark and Mike Clarke from touring under the name. On May 24, 1991, Clark was found dead in his home in Sherman Oaks. Roger McGuinn, who did not record during the 1980s, finally reemerged in 1991 with *Back from Rio*, recorded with the assistance of Elvis Costello and Tom Petty. Michael Clarke died of liver failure on Dec. 19, 1993, in Treasure Island, Fla.

The Byrds are often considered as influential as the Beatles and the Rolling Stones. Producing a remarkable body of work from 1965–68, the Byrds were noteworthy for their spirit of adventure and innovation, and were one of the first rock groups to experiment with studio technology. Presenting the first substantial challenge to the popularity of the Beatles and the Rolling Stones in the mid-1960s, the Byrds' recording of Bob Dylan's "Mr. Tambourine Man" marked the first time his still-acoustic music had been adapted to rock and launched folk-rock. Ostensibly, their recording inspired Dylan to take up electric guitar. The Byrds' 1966 hit "Eight Miles High" was the first hit psychedelic song and showcased Roger McGuinn's chiming 12–string electric guitar playing (a sound later emulated by Tom Petty and R.E.M.). The song was also one of the first to be banned for radio airplay due to its supposed reference to drugs. Anchored by the excellent songwriting of Roger McGuinn, David Crosby, Gene Clark, and Chris Hillman, the Byrds were an inspiration to the singer-songwriter movement that proved so popular in the 1970s. Moreover, their attention to melody and harmony opened rock to the gentle sophistication later explored by groups such as Crosby, Stills and Nash. The Byrds' 1968 *Sweetheart of the Rodeo* album, one of the first albums recorded in Nashville by an established rock group, introduced Gram Parsons to rock audiences and pioneered country-rock. The Byrds were inducted into the Rock and Roll Hall of Fame in 1991.

Although talented songwriter Gene Clark languished in obscurity after leaving the group, others, particularly Gram Parsons, Chris Hillman, and David Crosby went on to spectacularly influential and successful careers. Parsons and Hillman formed the Flying

Burrito Brothers, the group that laid the foundation for dozens of bands that explored country and rock during the 1970s. David Crosby helped found Crosby, Stills and Nash, who blended acoustic instrumentation with electric backing on engaging melodies and impeccable harmonies and helped define the singer-songwriter movement of the 1970s.

DISC.: THE CHAD MITCHELL TRIO (WITH JIM MCGUINN): *A Mighty Day on Campus* (1962); *Live at the Bitter End* (1962). **THE SCOTTSVILLE SQUIRREL BARKERS (WITH CHRIS HILLMAN):** *Blue-Grass Favorites* (1963). **THE HILLMEN:** *The Hillmen* (recorded 1963–1964; 1969). **THE BYRDS:** *Mr. Tambourine Man* (1965); *Turn! Turn! Turn!* (1965); *Fifth Dimension* (1966); *Younger Than Yesterday* (1967); *Greatest Hits* (1967); *Sweetheart of the Rodeo* (1968); *Preflyte* (1968); *Notorious Byrd Brothers* (1968); *Dr. Byrds and Mr. Hyde* (1969); *Ballad of Easy Rider* (1969); *(Untitled)* (1970); *Byrdmaniax* (1971); *Farther Along* (1971); *Best (Greatest Hits, Volume 2)* (1971); *Clark, Hillman, Crosby, McGuinn, Clarke* (1973); *The Byrds Play Dylan* (1979); *The Original Singles (1965–1967)* (1981); *Very Best* (1986); *In the Beginning* (1988); *The Byrds: Box Set* (1990); *20 Essential Tracks from the Boxed Set: 1965–1990* (1991). **GENE CLARK:** *Early L.A. Sessions* (1972); *Gene Clark with the Gosdin Brothers* (1967); *White Light* (1971); *No Other* (1974); *Two Sides to Every Story* (1977); *Firebyrd* (1987). **DILLARD AND CLARK:** *The Fantastic Expedition of Dillard and Clark* (1968); *Through the Morning, Through the Night* (1970). **GENE CLARK AND CARLA OLSON:** *So Rebellious a Lover* (1987). **THE KENTUCKY COLONELS (WITH CLARENCE WHITE):** *New Sound of Bluegrass* (1963); *Livin' in the Past* (1975); *Scotty Stoneman with the Kentucky Colonels—Live in L.A.* (1975); *Long Journey Home* (live; 1964); *Appalachian Swing!* (1964); *The Kentucky Colonels* (1974); *The White Brothers (The New Kentucky Colonels) Live in Sweden* (1977); *The Kentucky Colonels Featuring Clarence White* (1980); *On Stage* (1984). **NASHVILLE WEST (WITH CLARENCE WHITE AND GENE PARSONS):** *Nashville West* (1978); *Nashville West Featuring Clarence White* (1997). **MULESKINNER (WITH CLARENCE WHITE):** *Muleskinner* (1973); *Muleskinner Live: Original Television Soundtrack* (1992). **MCGUINN, CLARK AND HILLMAN:** *McGuinn, Clark and Hillman* (1979); *City* (1980). **MCGUINN AND HILLMAN:** *McGuinn and Hillman* (1980). **SKIP BATTIN:** *Skip Battin* (1973). **GENE PARSONS:** *Kindling* (1973); *Melodies* (1980); *The Kindling Collection* (1995). **GENE PARSONS AND MERIDIAN GREEN:** *Birds of a Feather* (1987). **ROGER MCGUINN:** *Roger McGuinn* (1973); *Peace on You* (1974); *Roger McGuinn and Band* (1975); *Cardiff Rose* (1976); *Thunderbyrd* (1977); *Born to Rock & Roll* (1991); *Back from Rio* (1990); *Live from Mars* (1996).

BIBL.: John Rogan, *Timeless Flight: The Definitive Biography of The Byrds* (London, 1981).—**BH**

Byrne, David, Scottish-born American musician; b. Dumbarton, May 14, 1952. He was taken to the U.S. when he was 6. In 1970–71 he attended the R.I. School of Design, where he developed his dominant conviction that dance, song, instrumental music, drama, and cinema were parts of a total art. As his own medium he selected modern dance music and vocal works, stretching in style from folk music to rock. He frequented the popular cabarets and dance halls of N.Y., where he absorbed the essence of urban folklore and the rhythmic ways of natural musicians. He joined the group Talking

Heads in 1975 as lead singer, guitarist, and composer, which made a specialty of exotic rhythms, especially Caribbean dance tunes, merengue, salsa, bomba, and cha-cha; from Colombia they took cambia; from Brazil, the classical samba. Much of the music that Byrne concocts of these elements is multilingual; one of his albums is titled *Speaking in Tongues* (1983). Byrne also favors African sounds, such as that of the Nigerian juju. The titles of his own songs are fashionably nonsensical, e.g., "Stop Making Sense," which seems to make plenty of sense to his public. He is an accomplished guitarist, and as a performer displays unbounded physical energy, allowing himself a free voice that ranges from a hiccup to a cry, while urging the accompanying chorus to intone such anarchistic declarations as "Don't Want to Be Part of Your World." The devotion that Byrne has for modern dance is exemplified by the remarkable score he wrote for *The Catherine Wheel*, choreographed by Twyla Tharp; it possesses the widely differing ingredients of new-wave rock and spiritual soul music, masculine and rough on the one hand and elegiac and devotional on the other. The resulting complex has also the additional element of African percussion. Taken as a whole, it represents a synthesis of urban beat and a largely unrelated Eastern rhythms. Talking Heads disbanded in 1989. His 1989 album, *Rei Momo* (promoted in concert at the Brooklyn Academy of Music as part of the New Music America Festival), consists of songs that, backed by a 16–piece band, combine Latin and pop styles. In 1992 he brought out the succesful album *Uh-Oh*. It was followed by his *David Byrne* album in 1994. There is a hypnopompic quality in his inspiration as a composer, asymptotically lying in both reality and irreality, like a half-waking state.

DISC.: *My Life in the Bush of Ghosts* (1981); *The Catherine Wheel* (Broadway score; 1981); *The Last Emperor* (soundtrack, with Ryuichi Sakamoto; 1987); *Rei Momo* (1989); *The Forest* (1991); *Uh-Oh* (1992); *David Byrne* (1994); *Feelings* (1997); *In Spite of Wishing and Wanting* (1999). **TALKING HEADS:** See separate entry.—**NS/LK/DM**

Byron, Don, innovative jazz clarinetist, bass clarinetist; b. Bronx, N.Y., Nov. 8, 1958. His father was from the Caribbean and played bass in calypso bands. Don started playing clarinet at age seven, attending Music and Arts H.S.; he concentrated on classical music while also getting involved in local Latin bands and arranging for them. He attended the Manhattan School of Music for a year before transferring to the New England Cons. (c. 1977–78), where he studied alto saxophone (and classical clarinet, with Joe Allard). While in Boston, Byron pursued his steadily broadening interests, including the conservatory's Klezmer band and Latin bands, in some of which he played piano; he also worked in Gunther Schuller's New England Ragtime Ensemble. Back in N.Y. after graduating, he was recruited for Hamiet Bluiett's group Clarinet Family, comprised of eight clarinets and a rhythm section. Other engagements followed with Geri Allen, the Ellington Band under Mercer Ellington, Mario Bauza, Bobby Previte, the David Murray Big Band, Reggie Workman, Craig Russell, Uri Caine, Ralph Peterson's Fo'tet, and Bill

Frisell. Byron has also pursued his Klezmer activities, even forming his own group that pays tribute to Mickey Katz. He has attracted much attention as perhaps the only African American in that field on a regular basis (as opposed to the many blacks, even Charlie Parker, who have played at an occasional bar mitzvah.) He pursues his classical side by leading Semaphore, a new chamber music ensemble, and plays Latin music with Music for Six Musicians. He has remained an independent thinker and an outspoken eclectic, moving into the music of Raymond Scott and composing his own unique pieces. In 1999 he was composing music to accompany the silent Ernie Kovacs "Eugene" comedy shows, to be performed live in 2000.

Disc.: *Tuskegee Experiments* (1990); *Plays the Music of Mickey Katz* (1993); *Music for Six Musicians* (1995); *Bug Music* (1996); *No Vibe Zone* (1996).—**LP**

Byström, Oscar (Fredrik Bernadotte), Swedish pianist, organist, conductor, teacher, and composer; b. Stockholm, Oct. 13, 1821; d. there, July 22, 1909. He studied piano with his father, Thomas Byström (1772–1839), a piano pedagogue at the Stockholm Cons. He pursued training with Erik Drake at the cons. and with Arrhén von Kapfelman at the military cadet college in Stockholm. He then entered the military and served in the Svea Artillery Regiment, attaining the rank of captain by the time of his retirement in 1871. Byström also pursued an active career as a musician, becoming well known as a pianist and teacher. He also ran a lime works on the island of Gotland and invented the hydropyrometer, an instrument designed to measure pressure in blast furnaces. In 1862 it won a medal at the World Exhibition in London. In 1864 Byström was elected to membership in the Royal Academy of Music in Stockholm, where he became inspector of the Cons. in 1867. From 1872 to 1876 he also was director of the Turku Musical Soc. in Finland. Thereafter he became active in the movement to reform chorale singing, and gave numerous motet concerts of historical programs throughout Sweden. He publ. several collections of early Gregorian melodies of medieval Sweden and early chorale melodies. In 1871 he publ. a vol. on theory. Byström's output reveals the influence of Berwald, and is marked by a sure hand for form, melody, and harmony.

Works: DRAMATIC: *Herman Vimpel*, operetta (1873; Helsinki, May 28, 1875); *Cervantes*, opera (unfinished). **ORCH.:** 3 waltzes (1851; also for Piano); Overture (c. 1855); Sym. (1870–72; first complete perf., Stockholm, Oct. 19, 1874; rev. 1895); *Andantino* (Turku, May 31, 1876). **CHAMBER:** Piano Trio (1850); Duo for Cello and Piano (1851); 2 string quartets (1856, rev. 1895; c. 1865). **VOCAL:** Choral works.
—**NS/LK/DM**

Caamaño, Roberto, Argentine composer, pedagogue, and pianist; b. Buenos Aires, July 7, 1923. He studied piano and composition at the Conservatorio Nacional de Música in Buenos Aires. He toured as a pianist in Latin America, North America, and Europe (1944–61). He concentrated his activities in Buenos Aires, where he was on the faculties of the Universidad del Litoral (1949–52), the Conservatorio Nacional de Música (1956–74), and the Universidad Católica Argentina (from 1964); he also was artistic director of the Teatro Colón (1961–64). In 1969 he became a member of the Accademia Nacional de Bellas Artes. In 1971 he received the Gran Premio of the Argentine Sociedad de Autores y Compositores. He publ. the valuable compendium *Historia del Teatro Colón* (three vols., Buenos Aires, 1969) and *Apuntes para la formación del pianista profesional* (Buenos Aires, 1979).

WORKS: ORCH.: *Variaciones americanas* (1953–54; Buenos Aires, July 10, 1955); Bandoneón Concerto (Buenos Aires, Aug. 2, 1954); 2 piano concertos: No. 1 (1957; Washington, D.C., April 18, 1958) and No. 2 (Buenos Aires, Aug. 9, 1971); *Tripartita* for Wind Orch. (1966); Harp Concerto (1973–74; Washington, D.C., May 1, 1974); Guitar Concerto (Buenos Aires, Nov. 30, 1974). CHAMBER: 2 string quartets (1945, 1947); Piano Quintet (1962); various piano pieces. VOCAL: *Magnificat* for Chorus and Orch. (1954; Louisville, Ky., March 25, 1955); *Cantata de la paz* for Chorus and Orch. (Buenos Aires, July 3, 1966); *Canto a San Martin* for Reciter, Chorus, and Orch. (1979; Buenos Aires, June 13, 1980); *Te Deum* for Chorus and Orch. (1980; Buenos Aires, Nov. 28, 1981); songs.—NS/LK/DM

Caballé, Montserrat, celebrated Spanish soprano; b. Barcelona, April 12, 1933. She was a pupil of Eugenia Kemeny, Conchita Badia, and Napoleone Annovazzi at the Barcelona Conservatorio del Liceo; after her graduation in 1953, she made her operatic debut in Reus, near Barcelona, in *La Serva padrona*. She then sang in Basel (1956–59) and Bremen (1959–62), and also made guest appearances in Vienna as Salome and Donna Elvira (1958), Milan's La Scala as a Flowermaiden in *Parsifal* (1960), where she sang major roles from 1969,

and Mexico City as Massenet's Manon (1962). She made a brilliant U.S. debut on April 20, 1965, when she substituted for Marilyn Horne in a concert performance of *Lucrezia Borgia* at N.Y.'s Carnegie Hall. After appearing as the Marschallin and the Countess at the Glyndebourne Festival (summer 1965), she made her Metropolitan Opera debut in N.Y. on Dec. 22, 1965, as Gounod's Marguerite. In subsequent years, she returned to the Metropolitan Opera regularly, eliciting extraordinary praise for such roles as Desdemona, Norma, Violetta, Liù, Mimi, Aida, Adriana Lecouvreur, and Tosca, among others. She also sang with various other opera companies, including debut appearances as Violetta at the Chicago Lyric Opera (1970) and London's Covent Garden (1972). In addition, she toured extensively as a concert artist. Her performances of operas in concert allowed her to survey not only Wagner but roles seldom heard. On Sept. 24, 1989, she created the role of Queen Isabella in Balada's *Cristóbal Colón* in Barcelona, where, in 1992, she also appeared at the opening gala ceremonies at the Olympic Games. The great beauty of Caballé's voice was ably complemented by an extraordinary vocal technique, one equally suited for the opera house and concert hall. Few singers of her day could match her command of such a large repertory, which ranged from standard to contemporary opera, and from art songs to zarzuela. In 1964 she married the Spanish tenor Bernabé Martí (b. 1934).

BIBL.: R. Pullen and S. Taylor, *M.C.: Casta diva* (London, 1994).—NS/LK/DM

Caballero, M(anuel) F(ernández), Spanish conductor and composer; b. Murcia, March 14, 1835; d. Madrid, Feb. 26, 1906. He had lessons in piano, violin, and flute, received instruction in composition from José Calvo, and studied harmony and composition with Indalecio Soriano Fuertes. In 1850 he enrolled at the Madrid Cons., where he studied with José Vega, Pedro Albéniz (piano), and Eslava (counterpoint and fugue), taking first prize for composition in 1856. He began his career playing violin in the orch. of the Teatro Real in Madrid, and then was active as a conductor in various theaters there. After conducting in Cuba (1864–71), he settled in Madrid and devoted himself to conducting and composing zarzuelas. In 1891 he was elected to membership in the Academy of Fine Arts. He wrote almost 200 zarzuelas, the most memorable being *La viejecita* (Madrid, April 29, 1897) and *Gigantes y cabezudos* (Madrid, Nov. 29, 1898). He also wrote masses and other sacred works, dances, and songs.—NS/LK/DM

Cabanilles, Juan Bautista José, Spanish organist and composer; b. Algemesí, province of Valencia, Sept. 4, 1644; d. Valencia, April 29, 1712. He studied for the priesthood at Valencia and probably received his musical training at the Cathedral there. He was appointed organist of the Valencia Cathedral May 15, 1665 (succeeding J. de la Torre), and retained that post until his death. He was ordained a priest on Sept. 22, 1668. He was the greatest of the early Spanish composers for organ, and the most prolific. He composed chiefly "tientos," remarkable for the ingenious use of the variation form (on liturgical or popular themes). A complete ed. of his works, in four vols., has been edited by H. Anglès (Barcelona, 1927–52). The *Obras vocales* are edited by J. Climent (Valencia, 1971).

BIBL.: A. Garcia Ferreras, *J.B. C.: Sein Leben und sein Werk* (Regensburg, 1973).—NS/LK/DM

Cabel, Marie (-Josèphe), Belgian soprano; b. Liège, Jan. 31, 1827; d. Maisons-Laffitte, May 23, 1885. She was a pupil of Bouillon in Liège, then studied with F. Cabel and L.J. Cabel, becoming the latter's wife in 1847. She subsequently completed her training at the Paris Cons. In 1849 she made her operatic debut at the Paris Opéra- Comique in Halévy's *Val d'Andorre*. After appearances in Brussels, Lyons, Strasbourg, and London, she returned to Paris as a member of the Opéra-Comique in 1856, where she created Meyerbeer's Dinorah (April 4, 1859). She retired in 1877. Cabel's roles in French opera were particularly admired.—NS/LK/DM

Cabezón (Cabeçon), Antonio de, great Spanish organist and composer; b. Castrillo de Matajudios, near Burgos, 1510; d. Madrid, March 26, 1566. He became blind in infancy; went to Palencia about 1521 to study with the Cathedral organist Garcia de Baeza and with Tomás Gómez. He was appointed organist to the court of the Emperor Charles V and Empress Isabella (1526); after her death, Cabezón entered the service of Prince Philip and accompanied him to Italy, Germany, the Netherlands (1548–51), and England (1554); he returned to Spain (1556) and remained court organist until his death. His keyboard style greatly influenced the development of organ composition on the Continent and the composers for the virginal in England; Pedrell called him "the Spanish Bach." The series Libro de Cifra Nueva (1557), which contains the earliest eds. of Cabezón's works, was reprinted by H. Anglès in *La música en la corte de Carlos V* (1944). His son and successor at the court of Philip II, Hernando (b. Madrid; baptized, Sept. 7, 1541; d. Valladolid, Oct. 1, 1602), publ. his instrumental works as *Obras de música para tecla, arpa y vihuela* (Madrid, 1578). This vol. contains exercises in two and three parts, arrangements of hymn tunes, four-part "tientos," arrangements of motets in up to six parts by Josquin and other Franco-Flemish composers, and variations on tunes of the day (*El caballero*, etc.). See Cabezón's *Collected Works* (C. Jacobs, ed.; N.Y., 1967–76).

BIBL.: S. Kastner, *A. d.C.* (Barcelona, 1952); M. Kastner, *A. und Hernando d.C.: Ein Chronik* (Tutzing, 1977).—NS/LK/DM

Caccini, Francesca (nicknamed "La Cecchina"), Italian composer, daughter of **Giulio Caccini**; b. Florence, Sept. 18, 1587; d. c. 1640. She was probably the first woman composer of operas. Her opera-ballet *La liberazione di Ruggiero dall'isola d'Alcina* was produced at a palace near Florence on Feb. 2, 1625, and a book of songs from it was publ. in the same year. A modern reprint, ed. by D. Silbert, was publ. in Northampton, Mass. (1945). Caccini wrote further a *Ballo delle zingare* (Florence, Feb. 24, 1615) in which she acted as one of the gypsies. Her sacred opera *Il martirio di Sant'Agata* was produced in Florence, Feb. 10, 1622. —NS/LK/DM

Caccini, Giulio, Italian composer (called **Romano**, because he lived mostly in Rome), father of **Francesca Caccini**; b. probably in Tivoli, Oct. 8, 1551; d. Florence (buried), Dec. 10, 1618. He was a pupil of Scipione delle Palla in singing and lute playing. His first compositions were madrigals in the traditional polyphonic style, but the new ideas generated in the discussions of the artists and literati of the "Camerata," in the houses of Bardi and Corsi at Florence, inspired him to write vocal soli in recitative form (then termed "musica in stile rappresentativo"), which he sang with consummate skill to his own accompaniment on the theorbo. These first compositions in a dramatic idiom were followed by his settings of separate scenes written by Bardi, and finally by the opera *Il combattimento d'Apolline col serpente* (poem by Bardi). Next was *Euridice* (1600; poem by Rinuccini) and *Il rapimento di Cefalo* (in collaboration with others; first perf., Oct. 9, 1600, at the Palazzo Vecchio in Florence). Then followed *Le nuove musiche*, a series of madrigals for Solo Voice, with Bass (Florence, 1602; new eds., Venice, 1607 and 1615; a modern ed. of the 1602 publ., prepared by H. Wiley Hitchcock [Madison, Wisc., 1970], includes an annotated Eng. tr. of Caccini's preface, realizations of the solo madrigals, airs, and the final section of *Il rapimento di Cefalo*, an introductory essay on Caccini, the music, the poetry, MSS, other eds., and a bibliography. A tr. of the preface is also available in O. Strunk, *Source Readings in Music History* [N.Y., 1950]). The song *Amarilli mia bella* from the first series became very popular. Caccini also publ. *Fuggilotio musicale* (Venice, 2nd ed., 1613; including madrigals, sonnets, arias, etc.). From 1565 Caccini lived in Florence as a singer at the Tuscan court. He was called, by abbate Angelo Grillo, "the father of a new style of music" Bardi said of him that he had "attained the goal of perfect music." But his claim to priority in writing vocal music in the "stile rappresentativo" is not supported by known chronology. Caccini's opera *Il rapimento di Cefalo* was performed three days after Peri's path-breaking *Euridice*; the closeness in time of operatic productions by both Caccini and Peri is further emphasized by the fact that when Peri produced *Euridice* in Florence (1600), he used some of Caccini's songs in the score. Caccini later made his own setting of *Euridice* (1600), but it was not produced until Dec. 5, 1602. On the other hand, Caccini was undoubtedly the first to publish an operatic work, for his score of *Euridice* was printed early in 1601, before the publication of Peri's work of the same title.

BIBL.: A. Ehrichs, *G. C.* (Leipzig, 1908); F. Schmitz, *G. C., Nuove musiche (1602/1614): Texte und Musik* (Pfaffenwiler, 1995).
—**NS/LK/DM**

Caceres, Ernie (actually, **Ernesto**), jazz clarinetist, saxophonist; b. Rockport, Tex., Nov. 22, 1911; d. San Antonio, Tex., Jan. 10, 1971. He was the brother of Emilio (violin) and Pinero (trumpet and piano), who died in 1960. He played clarinet from an early age; also studied guitar and saxophone. He worked with local bands from 1928, then worked with family trio. After a long spell with brother Emilio's small band including residencies in Detroit and N.Y., he joined Bobby Hackett in summer 1938 and played tenor sax in Jack Teagarden's Band from February 1939. In the early 1940s, he played with various bands, including Glenn Miller (Feb. 1940–summer 1942), Benny Goodman (Oct.–mid-1944; except for Dec. 1943, when he was with Tommy Dorsey), and Woody Herman (mid-1944–45). From mid-1945–46, he played in a U.S. Army service band. After the war, he worked in the N.Y. area, taking part in many recordings with Eddie Condon alumni during the 1940s and 1950s. He had regular TV work with Garry Moore Orch. from 1950 until 1956. He also led his own small groups, did freelance session work, recordings, etc., during this period. During the early 1960s worked regularly with Billy Butterfield (with whom he had worked previously in 1947). Around 1963, he settled in San Antonio, Tex., where he continued to work with local bands. Caceres died of throat cancer.

DISC.: Emilio Caceres: *No More Blues* (1937); *Ernie and Emilio Caceres* (1969). Bobby Hackett, Eddie Condon: *Jam Session* (1948). Metronome All Stars: *Victory Ball* (1949).—**JC/LP**

Cacioppo, George (**Emanuel**), innovative American composer; b. Monroe, Mich., Sept. 24, 1927; d. Ann Arbor, Mich., April 4, 1984. He studied with Ross Lee Finney at the Univ. of Mich. in Ann Arbor (M.A., 1952) and later with Roberto Gerhard there (1960); also with Leon Kirchner at the Berkshire Music Center in Tanglewood. In 1960 he helped to organize the ONCE Festival in Ann Arbor, with which he was active until 1968; was an announcer and engineer at the Univ. of Mich. radio station (1960–84), and also taught periodically at the Univ. (1970–80). His interests in astronomy, mathematics, and poetry consumed him after 1970. His compositions written between 1960 and 1970 concern themselves with pitch relationships and with total-sound spectrums.

WORKS: *Fantasy* for Violin and Piano (1950); *Music for 2 Trumpets and Strings* (1951); Piano Sonata: *In Memoriam Béla Bartók* (1951); *Overture and Elegy* for Orch. (1952–53); String Trio (1960); *Bestiary I: Eingang* for Soprano, Piano, and 4 Percussionists (1961); 11 piano pieces for any number of pianos, with their realizations on tape sounding synchronously, or non-synchronously, and lasting any practical, or impractical, length of time, 2 of which are subtitled: No. 3, *Cassiopeia* (1962) and No. 11, *Informed Sources* (1970); *2 Worlds* for Soprano and 7 Instruments (1962); *Mod 3* for Flute, Double Bass, and Percussion (1963); *Moved Upon Silence* for 6 Percussionists (1963); *The Advance of the Fungi* for Textless Men's Chorus, 3 Clarinets, 3 Trombones, 2 Horns, and Percussion (1964); *Time on Time in Miracles* for Soprano, 2 Horns, 2 Trombones, Cello, Piano, and Percussion (1964); *Holy Ghost Vacuum, or America Faints* for Electric Organ (Ann Arbor, March 29, 1966, composer organist); *K* for Live Electric Organs, Pianos, and Sound Modifiers (1967; rev. as *K–2*, 1968); *Dream Concert* for Organ, Voice, and Percussionist (1976).—**NS/LK/DM**

Cadman, Charles Wakefield, important American composer; b. Johnstown, Pa., Dec. 24, 1881; d. Los Angeles, Dec. 30, 1946. His great-grandfather was the hymn composer Samuel Wakefield (1799–1895). After studies with William Steiner (organ), Edwin L. Walker (piano), and Leo Oehmler (theory), he received training in theory and conducting from Luigi von Kunits and Emil Paur. From 1908 to 1910 he was music ed. and critic of the *Pittsburgh Dispatch*. His interest in American Indian music resulted in various lecture-performance tours in the U.S. and Europe with the Cherokee-Creek Indian Princess Tsianina Redfeather. In 1916 he settled in Los Angeles as a composer and teacher. Cadman wrote an opera based on the life of Redfeather, *Shanewis or The Robin Woman*, which was premiered at the Metropolitan Opera in N.Y. on March 23, 1918.

WORKS: DRAMATIC: *The Land of the Misty Water*, opera (1909–12; rev. as *Ramala*); *Shanewis or The Robin Woman*, opera (N.Y., March 23, 1918); *The Sunset Trail*, operatic cantata (Denver, Dec. 5, 1922); *The Garden of Mystery*, opera (N.Y., March 20, 1925); *The Ghost of Lollypop Bay*, operetta (1926); *Lelawala*, operetta (1926); *A Witch of Salem*, opera (Chicago, Dec. 8, 1926); *The Belle of Havana*, operetta (1928); *South in Sonora*, operetta (1932); *The Willow Tree*, radio score (NBC, Oct. 3, 1932); film scores. **ORCH.:** *Thunderbird Suite* (1914); *Oriental Rhapsody* (1917); *Prairie Sketches* (1923; arranged from a piano piece, 1906); *To a Vanishing Race* for Strings (1925); *Hollywood Suite* (1932); *Dark Dancers of the Mardi Gras* for Piano and Orch. (1933); *Trail Pictures* (1934); *American Suite* for Strings (1936); *Suite on American Folktunes* (1937); Sym., *Pennsylvania* (1939–40; Los Angeles, March 7, 1940); *Aurora Borealis* for Piano and Orch. (1944); *A Mad Empress Remembers* for Violin and Orch. (1944); *Huckleberry Finn Goes Fishing*, overture (1945). **CHAMBER:** Piano Trio (1914); Violin Sonata (1932); Piano Quintet (1937). **KEYBOARD: P i a n o :** *Melody* (1905); *Prairie Sketches* (1906; also for Orch., 1923); *Idealized Indian Themes* (1912); Sonata (1915); *Oriental Suite* (1921). **VOCAL:** *The Vision of Sir Launfal* for Men's Chorus (1909); *The Father of Waters* for Chorus (1928); *The Far Horizon* for Chorus (1934); sacred anthems; song cycles; numerous solo songs.

BIBL.: N. Fielder, *Complete Musical Works of C.W. C.* (Los Angeles, 1951; catalog); H. Perison, *C.W. C.: His Life and Works* (diss., Eastman School of Music, 1978).—**NS/LK/DM**

Caduff, Sylvia, Swiss conductor; b. Chur, Jan. 7, 1937. She studied at the Lucerne Cons., receiving a

piano diploma in 1961. She then attended Karajan's conducting classes at the Berlin Cons., and continued conducting studies with Kubelik, Matačić, and Otterloo in Lucerne, Salzburg, and Hilversum. She made her debut with the Tonhalle Orch. of Zürich. After winning first prize in the 1966 Mitropoulos conducting competition in N.Y., she was an asst. conductor under Bernstein with the N.Y. Phil. (1966–67). She then taught conducting at the Bern Cons. (1972–77). In 1977 she became the first woman in Europe to be appointed a Generalmusikdirektor, when she took that position with the orch. of the city of Solingen. She left that position in 1985.
—NS/LK/DM

Caesar, Johann Melchior, German composer; b. Saverne, Alsace, c. 1648; d. Augsburg, Oct. 18, 1692. He received training in Saverne and at the Univ. of Würzburg. He served as cathedral Kapellmeister in Breslau (1667–79), Würzburg (1679–83), and Augsburg (from 1683). Among his works were masses, Psalms, and other sacred pieces, secular vocal music, and various dance suites.—NS/LK/DM

Cafaro, Pasquale, Italian composer; b. San Pietro in Galatina, Lecce, Feb. 8, 1716; d. Naples, Oct. 23, 1787. He studied at the Naples Cons., where he was made secondo maestro in 1759; he also was maestro di cappella soprannumeriario (1768–71) and then primo maestro (from 1771) of the Royal Chapel.

WORKS: DRAMATIC: Opera: *Ipermestra* (Naples, Dec. 18, 1751); *La disfatta di Dario* (Naples, Jan. 20, 1756); *L'incendio di Troia* (Naples, Jan. 20, 1757); *Arianna e Teseo* (Naples, Jan. 20, 1766); *Creso, ultimo rè della Lidia* (Turin, 1768); *L'Olimpiade* (Naples, Jan. 12, 1769); *Antigono* (Naples, Aug. 13, 1770). OTHER: 5 oratorios; cantatas; a *Stabat Mater*.
—NS/LK/DM

Caffarelli (real name, **Gaetano Majorano**), Italian castrato soprano; b. Bitonto, April 12, 1710; d. Naples, Jan. 31, 1783. A poor peasant boy endowed with a beautiful voice, he was discovered by a musician, Domenico Caffarelli, who taught him, and later sent him to Porpora at Naples. In gratitude to his patron, he assumed the name of Caffarelli. He studied for five years with Porpora, who predicted a brilliant career for him. Caffarelli became a master of pathetic song, and excelled in coloratura as well; read the most difficult music at sight, and was an accomplished harpsichord player. His debut at the Teatro Valle (Rome, 1724) in a female role was a triumph. From 1737 to 1745 he sang in London, then in Paris and Vienna. His last public appearance took place on May 30, 1754, in Naples. He was in Lisbon during the earthquake of 1755; he retired from the opera in 1756. Upon his return to Naples, he bought the dukedom of Santo-Durato with the fortune he had amassed during his career, and assumed the title of duke.—NS/LK/DM

Caffi, Francesco, Italian judge, writer on music, and composer; b. Venice, June 14, 1778; d. Padua, Jan. 24, 1874. He studied counterpoint with Matteo Rauzzini, Simone Mayr, and Giuseppe Scatena, and singing and harpsichord with Francesco Gardi. He was a judge of the Milan court of appeals from 1827 to 1840, and then was presiding judge of the Rovigo court from 1840 to 1850. Among his works were stage pieces, an Oboe Concerto, an oratorio, and cantatas.

WRITINGS (all publ. in Venice unless otherwise given): *Della vita e del comporre di Bonaventura Furlanetto detto Musin* (1820); *Della vita e del comporre di Benedetto Marcello* (1830); *Lettera di Francesco Caffi ad Emmanuele Cicogna intorno alla vita ed al comporre di Antonio Lotti* (1835); *Della vita e delle opere del prete Gioseffo Zarlino* (1836); *Biografia di Domenico Dragonetti* (1846); *Lo Stabat di Rossini* (1847); *Storia della musica sacra nella già cappella ducale di San Marco in Venezia dal 1318 al 1797* (2 vols., 1854–55); *Della vita e delle opere di Giammatteo Asola* (Padua, 1862).
—NS/LK/DM

Cage, John (Milton Jr.), singularly inventive and much beloved American composer, writer, philosopher, and visual artist of ultramodern tendencies; b. Los Angeles, Sept. 5, 1912; d. N.Y., Aug. 12, 1992. His father, John Milton Cage Sr., was an inventor, and his mother, Lucretia Harvey, was active as a clubwoman and columnist in Southern Calif. He studied piano with his Aunt Phoebe and Fannie Charles Dillon in Los Angeles, showing particular interest in the music of Edvard Grieg. He had early aspirations to be either a minister or a writer, and, representing Los Angeles H.S. in 1927, won the Southern Calif. Oratorical Contest at the Hollywood Bowl with his essay "Other People Think," a plea for Pan-American conscience by the (North) American people. After brief studies at Pomona Coll. in Claremont, Calif. (1928–30), he traveled to Europe, where he studied architecture with Ernö Goldfinger and piano with Lazare Lévy in Paris; also traveled throughout Biskra, Majorca, Madrid, and Berlin (1930–31), painting, writing poetry, and producing his first musical compositions, which he abandoned prior to his return to Calif. He continued writing, painting, and composing on his own, supporting himself as a gardener in an auto court in Santa Monica and also lecturing on modern art and music to housewives. He then studied composition with Richard Buhlig, developing a method of composition employing two twenty-five tone ranges, which appear in his early *Solo with Obbligato Accompaniment of Two Voices in Canon, and Six Short Inventions on the Subjects of the Solo* (1933–44; rev. 1963). At the suggestion of Henry Cowell, he pursued studies in harmony with Adolph Weiss; he also studied modern harmony, contemporary music, and Oriental and folk music with Cowell at the New School for Social Research in N.Y. Cage's studies culminated with counterpoint lessons from Schoenberg (1934), both privately and at the Univ. of Southern Calif.; he also attended Schoenberg's classes in counterpoint and analysis at the Univ. of Calif., Los Angeles. On June 7, 1935, Cage married Xenia Andreyevna Kashevaroff. Through his brief association with the filmmaker Oskar Fischinger, Cage became interested in noise, subsequently developing methods of writing complex rhythmic structures for percussion music; he then joined a modern dance group at the Univ. of Calif., Los Angeles, as an accompanist and percussion composer. He and Xenia also studied bookbinding with Hazel Dreis, and formed a quartet of bookbinders for playing percussion music.

During the summer of 1937, Cage was on the faculty of Mills Coll. in Oakland, Calif., where he worked as a composer for Marian Van Tuyl. He then moved to Seattle as composer-accompanist for Bonnie Bird's modern dance classes at the Cornish School, where he met Merce Cunningham, who was a dance student there. He organized a percussion orchestra, collected musical instruments, and made tours throughout the Northwest; it was in Seattle that Cage also met Morris Graves, and arranged for an exhibition of his work; he also arranged exhibitions of the work of Alexej Jawlensky, Kandinsky, Klee, and Mark Tobey. In 1939 he gave concerts of percussion music with Lou Harrison in San Francisco; he also worked as a recreational leader for the Works Progress Administration there, and composed his *First Construction (in Metal)* for six Percussionists (Seattle, Dec. 9, 1939). He began developing Cowell's piano technique of making use of tone clusters and playing directly on the body of the instrument or on the strings, which culminated in his invention of the "prepared piano;" by placing objects (screws, copper coins, rubber erasers, etc.) on and between the piano strings, he was able to significantly alter the tone color of individual keys and thus transform the piano into a percussion orchestra. His first prepared piano piece was music to accompany a dance by Syvilla Fort, *Bacchanale* (1938; rev. version, Seattle, April 28, 1940). The instrument rapidly gained acceptance among avant-garde composers, and in 1949, after the N.Y. premiere by Maro Ajemian of his *Sonatas and Interludes* for Prepared Piano (1946–48), he received a grant from the Guggenheim Foundation and a $1,000 award from the National Academy of Arts and Letters for having "extended the boundaries of music."

In 1941 Cage went to Chicago, where, at the invitation of László Moholy-Nagy, he taught a class in experimental music at the School of Design. He also accompanied dance classes of Katherine Manning there, and gave a concert of percussion music at the Arts Club. Commissioned by CBS ("Columbia Workshop") to create a radio program, he composed *The City Wears a Slouch Hat* for four Percussion and Sound Effects, to a text by Kenneth Patchen (Chicago, May 31, 1942). He then moved to N.Y. (1942), where he began a lengthy association with Cunningham, who had since relocated to N.Y. to perform with Martha Graham; Cage and Cunningham would collaborate for nearly 50 years on works that introduced radical innovations in musical and choreographic composition. When the Merce Cunningham Dance Co. was formed in 1953, Cage served as its first music director, a position he maintained for more than 30 years. It was also during this period that Cage met Marcel Duchamp through Max Ernst and Peggy Guggenheim. He became interested in chess, and later played demonstration games with Duchamp on a chessboard designed by Lowell Cross to operate on aleatory principles with the aid of a computer (*Reunion*; Toronto, March 5, 1968). During this period Cage also gave a concert at the Museum of Modern Art, the first in a series of N.Y. recitals that established his reputation. After his divorce from Xenia in 1945, he moved to N.Y.'s Lower East Side; having a "crisis of faith" about com-

position, he began what became a life-long study of Eastern philosophies, first (Indian philosophy and music) with the visiting Indian musician and teacher Gira Sarabhai, and then (Zen Buddhism) with Daisetz Teitaro Suzuki, whose classes he attended at Columbia Univ. He also made numerous tours with Cunningham, and received an important commission from Lincoln Kirstein and the Ballet Soc., resulting in *The Seasons* (N.Y., May 18, 1947). In 1948 Cage taught at Black Mountain Coll. in N.C., where he met R. Buckminster Fuller, Richard and Louise Lippold, Elaine and Willem de Kooning, and Joseph Albers, among others. In 1949 he spent three months in Europe, where he appeared in concerts and dance recitals with Cunningham; he also met Pierre Boulez; their subsequent correspondence was publ. as *Pierre Boulez/John Cage: Correspondance et documents* (J.-J. Nattiez and F. Davoine, eds., Winterthur, 1990). Returning to N.Y., Cage participated in the formation, with Robert Motherwell and others, of the Artists Club. Dating from this period are also his "Lecture on Nothing" and "Lecture on Something," and his *String Quartet in Four Parts* (1949–50).

In 1950 Cage began developing means for composition with chance operations. He came under the influence of the *I Ching*, or "Book of Changes," one of the most influential books in the Chinese canon, which became his sole director as a composer, poet, and visual artist for the remainder of his life. An extremely significant collaboration stemming from this period, and extending throughout the decade in the realization of the first of his *I Ching* chance-determined compositions, was with the pianist David Tudor, who was able to reify Cage's exotic inspirations, works in which the performer shares the composer's creative role. Tudor also became closely associated with the Merce Cunningham Dance Co., and thus he and Cage had a close working relationship of some forty years' duration. In 1950 Cage completed a score for Herbert Matter's film, *Works of Calder* for Prepared Piano and Tape (1949–50), which received first prize from the Woodstock Art Film Festival. He also composed his *Concerto for Prepared Piano and Chamber Orchestra* (1950–51; N.Y., Jan. 1952) as well as his *Imaginary Landscape No. 4* for 24 Performers on 12 Radios, commissioned by the New Music Soc. and presented at Columbia Univ.'s McMillin Theater on May 10, 1951. It was during this period as well that he began a life-long friendship with Robert Rauschenberg. In 1952, at Black Mountain Coll., Cage presented a theatrical event historically marked as the earliest Happening; participants in this prototypical adventure included Cunningham, Charles Olson, Rauschenberg, M.C. Richards, and Tudor. Cage's seminal *Music of Changes* was given its premiere performance by Tudor at the Cherry Lane Theater on Jan. 1, 1952. In this year, he also composed his first piece for tape as a score for a dance by Jean Erdman, *Imaginary Landscape No. 5* (N.Y., Jan. 18, 1952). Influenced at the Black Mountain Happening by Rauschenberg's all-black and all-white paintings, Cage composed his notoriously tacet *4'33"* (1952); the ultimate freedom in musical expression, Cage's work is heard in three movements (indicated by the pianist's closing and reopening of the piano key cover), during which no sounds are intentionally produced. It was first performed by Tudor in Woodstock, N.Y., on Aug. 29, 1952. A decade later Cage created a second "silent" piece, 0'00", "to be played in any way by anyone," presented for the first time in Tokyo on Oct. 24, 1962. Any sounds produced by the listeners are automatically regarded as integral to the piece, so that the wisecrack about the impossibility of arriving at a fair judgment of such a silent piece, since one cannot tell what music is not being played, is invalidated by the uniqueness of Cage's art.

In 1954 Cage moved with Tudor, Richards, and Karen Weinrib to a cooperative community established by Paul and Vera Williams in Rockland County, N.Y. He also made a concert tour of Europe (Donaueschingen, Cologne, Paris, Brussels, Stockholm, Zürich, Milan, and London) with Tudor, and, upon his return, met Jasper Johns, who would remain a life-long friend and associate. He also began work on his *Music for Piano* series (ranging from *Music for Piano 1*, 1952, to *Music for Piano 85* for Piano and Electronics, 1962), using the imperfections in manuscript paper to guide his composition. From 1956 to 1960 he taught occasional classes at the New School for Social Research, where his students included George Brecht, Al Hansen, Dick Higgins, Toshi Ichiyanagi, Allan Kaprow, and Jackson Mac Low. In 1958 an historically significant 25-year retrospective concert of his music was given at N.Y.'s Town Hall. He then spent a summer in Europe teaching a class in experimental music at Darmstadt and giving concerts and lectures elsewhere, including "Indeterminacy, New Aspects of Form in Instrumental and Electronic Music" at the Brussels World Fair. In Italy he composed *Fontana Mix* for any Sound Sources or Actions (1958; Rome, Jan. 5, 1959); he also appeared on an Italian quiz show, "Lascia o Raddoppia," as a mushroom expert, winning $6,000; in his five performances he presented his *Amores* for Prepared Piano and three Percussionists (1936; rev. version, N.Y., Feb. 7, 1943), *Sounds of Venice* for Various Stage Properties and Tape (Milan, Jan. 1959), and *Water Walk* for Piano and Various Stage Properties (Milan, Jan. 1959).

Returning to N.Y. in 1959, Cage again taught at the New School for Social Research, this time three specific courses: (1) mushroom identification, (2) the music of Virgil Thomson, and (3) experimental composition. In 1960–61 he was a fellow at the Center for Advanced Studies at Wesleyan Univ. in Middletown, Conn., where he completed his first book, *Silence* (1961), which has since become a classic study in 20th-century musical aesthetics. He also met Norman O. Brown. In 1961 he was commissioned by the Montreal Festivals Soc. to write the orch. piece *Atlas Eclipticalis* for One to 86 Specified Instruments (1961–62; Montreal, Aug. 3, 1961). In 1962 he founded, with Esther Dam, Ralph Ferrara, Lois Long, and Guy G. Nearing, the N.Y. Mycological Soc. He also made an extensive concert tour of Japan with Tudor. In 1963 he directed the first N.Y. performance of *Vexations* by Erik Satie, a composer to whom he expressed almost life-long devotion. He also made a world tour with the Merce Cunningham Dance Co. Other activities in the late 1960s included the formation, with Johns, of the philanthropic Foundation for Contemporary Performance Arts in N.Y.; he also was

composer-in-residence at the Univ. of Cincinnati. In 1967 he publ. *A Year From Monday*. It was during this period also that he met the controversial Canadian media philosopher Marshall McLuhan, whose ideas resonated strongly in Cage, as well as Wendell Berry, who introduced him to the *Journals* of Henry David Thoreau, which subsequently appeared, in various guises, in many of Cage's works. He also was an assoc. at the Center for Advanced Study at the Univ. of Ill., where he created *HPSCHD* for One to Seven Amplified Harpsichords and One to 51 Tapes (1967–69; Champaign-Urbana, Ill., May 16, 1969; in collaboration with L. Hiller). In 1969 he was an artist-in-residence at the Univ. of Calif., Davis; he also publ. *Notations* (with A. Knowles), and executed his first visual work (with Calvin Sumsion), *Not Wanting to Say Anything About Marcel*, at Hollander's Workshop in N.Y. In 1970 he again, this time as an advanced fellow, at the Center for Advanced Studies at Wesleyan Univ.

Throughout the 1970s Cage traveled extensively and produced works in a variety of media. With Lois Long he publ. *Mushroom Book*, and also made a European tour with Tudor. In 1973 he publ. *M: Writings '67- '72*. In 1974–75 he composed his *Etudes Australes* (Witten, April 23 and 25, 1982), using star charts as his guide; in 1978 he created color etchings entitled *Score without Parts (40 Drawings by Thoreau): Twelve Haiku*, incorporating drawings by Thoreau. Also from the 1970s were his *Child of Tree* (Detroit, Mich., March 8, 1975) and *Branches* (1976), both scored for Percussion and Amplified Plant Materials, as well as his *Lecture on the Weather* for 12 Amplified Voices, optionally with Instruments, Tape, and Film (1975; Toronto, Feb. 26, 1976), a lavish audio-visual work commissioned by the Canadian Broadcasting Corp. on the occasion of American's Bicentennial, combining collages of spoken texts by Thoreau, a film by Luis Frangella, and weather recordings by Marianne Amacher. He also composed *Renga* for 78 Instruments or Voices or combinations thereof (1975–76; Boston, Sept. 29, 1976) and *Apartment House 1776* for four Voices, optionally on Tape, and any number of Instruments (Boston, Sept. 29, 1976). He then began reading the works of James Joyce, being particularly influenced by *Finnegans Wake*. On the advice of Yoko Ono, he also began following the macrobiotic diet, which significantly improved his health. In 1977 he began work on his mammoth *Freeman Etudes* for Violin, composed for Paul Zukofsky and dedicated to Betty Freeman and completed with the assistance of James Pritchett only shortly before their premiere in Zürich on June 29, 1991; also from this period was his *Inlets* for three Performers using Water-filled Conch Shells, Blown Conch Shell, and the sound of fire (Seattle, Sept. 10, 1977). At the encouragement of Kathan Brown in 1978, Cage began making prints at Crown Point Press in Oakland (later San Francisco), Calif.; Cage returned there annually until his death in 1992, producing such works as *Seven Day Diary* (1978), *Dereau* (1982), *Where There Is Where There—Urban Landscape* (1987), *Dramatic Fire* (1989), and *Smoke Weather Stone Weather* (1991); Cage also produced a series of unique pencil rock tracings on handmade Indian paper, entitled *Where R = Ryoanji* (1983–92). Also in 1978 was the publication of his *Writing Through*

Finnegans Wake (with A. Knowles) and the composition of his lively *Alla Ricerca del Silenzio Perduto* (a.k.a. *Il Treno*) for Prepared Train (1977; Bologna and vicinity, June 26–28, 1978).

In 1979 Cage worked at Paris's IRCAM (with David Fullemann) to complete his *Roaratorio, an Irish Circus on Finnegans Wake*, a quintessential realization of his __, __ *Circus on* __ for Voice, Tape, and any number of Musicians, optionally on tape, a means of translating any book into music; the work was commissioned by Klaus Schöning at the WDR, Cologne, and premiered in Donaueschingen on Oct. 20 of that same year. In 1980 his *Third* and *Fourth Writings Through Finnegans Wake* appeared; in 1981–82 he composed his fanciful hörspiel, *James Joyce, Marcel Duchamp, Erik Satie: Ein Alphabet* (WDR, Cologne, July 6, 1982). In 1981 he wrote *Composition in Retrospect* (Cambridge, Mass., 1993), and also composed *Thirty Pieces for Five Orchestras* (Pont-à-Mousson, Nov. 22, 1981) and *Dance/4 Orchestras* (Mission San Juan Bautista, Calif., Aug. 22, 1982). He also gave a night-long reading of his *Empty Words: Writings '73-'78* (Middletown, Conn., 1979) over National Public Radio. In 1982 his scores and prints were exhibited for the first time at the Whitney Museum of American Art in N.Y. and at the Philadelphia Museum of Art. In 1984 he began extensive work with the computer, employing programs made for him by Andrew Culver and Jim Rosenberg, producing his first computer-assisted mesostic poem, after Allen Ginsburg's *Howl*.

In 1987 several large-scale works were completed and premiered, including Cage's only installation, *Voiceless Essay*, based on texts from Thoreau's *Essay on Civil Disobedience* and ambient sounds. He also completed *Europeras 1 & 2* for any number of Voices, Chamber Orch., Tape, and Organ ad libitum (1984–87; Frankfurt am Main, Dec. 12, 1987), a chance-determined, musicodramatic staged collage self-referentially comprised of excerpts from extant operas across historical time. The scheduled opening of *Europeras 1 & 2* on Nov. 15, 1987 was delayed and its location changed due to a fire, reportedly set by a vagrant in search of food, which devastated the Frankfurt am Main Opera House. He also produced works for and attended numerous 75th birthday celebrations worldwide, including a week-long event at the Los Angeles Festival. Also from this year was his *Two* for Flute and Piano, the first in a series of "number pieces," each utilizing a flexible notation system of his devising called "time-bracket notation;" "time-bracket notation" would be his method of choice for virtually all compositions henceforth. In 1988 he extended his activities as a visual artist further with a series of watercolors with Ray Kass at the Mountain Lake Workship in Roanoke, Va. In 1988–89 he held the prestigious Charles Eliot Norton Chair at Harvard Univ., for which he wrote and delivered six large-scale, quasi-autobiographical mesostic poems incorporating the writings of Fuller, Thoreau, McLuhan et al.; these poems (or lectures), with texts from interspersed seminars with students, were later publ. as *I-VI* (Boston, 1990). In 1989 a joint exhibition, "Dancers on a Plane: John Cage, Merce Cunningham, Jasper Johns," was presented in London and Liverpool. In 1990 Cage's watercolors were exhibited as "New River Watercolors"

at the Phillips Collection in Washington, D.C. Cage also saw the premiere of his *Fourteen* for Piano and Small Orch. (Zürich, May 12, 1990) and his *Europeras 3 & 4* for at least six Voices, two Pianos, at least six Performers with 12 Gramophones and one Phonograph, and Tape and Light Operators at London's Almeida Music Festival (June 17, 1990). His *Europera 5* followed in 1991, a somewhat diminutive version in the *Europeras* series for two Voices, Piano, Phonograph, and Sound and Light Operators (Buffalo, N.Y., April 18, 1991). The Scottish National Orch. produced a week of Cage music. Cage also began designing, in collaboration with curator Julie Lazar, his continually changing work for museum, *Rolywholyover A Circus*, which was seen successively, after his death, in Los Angeles, Houston, N.Y., Mito (Japan), and Philadelphia. In 1991 Cage attended the John Cage-James Joyce Zürich June Festival, where his *Europeras 1 & 2* was performed at the Zürich Opera; also premiered there was *Beach Birds*, his final collaboration with Cunningham. During this period, Cage also made suites of handmade paper and edible drawings with Bernie Toale at Rugg Toad Papers in Boston, Mass.

In 1992, the last year of his life, Cage attended innumerable 80th birthday celebrations around the world. He also composed a remarkable number of scores, including orch. works for the Hessischer Rundfunk (Frankfurt am Main), the Westdeutscher Rundfunk (Cologne), and the American Composers Orch. (N.Y.)., as well as some 20 compositions, most of them "number pieces," for various smaller ensembles. He also completed his first and only film, the strikingly minimalist *One11*, with Henning Lohner. Shortly before his 80th birthday and his scheduled departure for Frankfurt am Main to attend the extensive birthday celebrations planned in both Frankfurt and Cologne, on Aug. 11, 1992, Cage collapsed in the N.Y. loft he shared with Cunningham; he died peacefully the following afternoon, on Aug. 12, 1992, without gaining consciousness, of a massive stroke.

Cage's influence, while unquestionably profound, has likely yet to be fully felt. With the passing years, he departed from the pragmatism of precise musical notation and circumscribed ways of performance, electing instead to mark his creative intentions in graphic symbols, pictorial representations, generalized and often poetic instructions, and flexible time relationships. His principal contribution to the history of music was his establishment of the principle of indeterminacy in composition; by adapting Zen Buddhist meditative practices to composition, Cage succeeded in bringing both authentic spiritual ideas and a liberating attitude of play to the enterprise of Western art. His aesthetic of chance also, uniquely, produced a body of what might be called "once-only" works, any two performances of which can never be the same. In an effort to reduce the subjective element in composition, Cage developed methods of selecting the components of his pieces by chance, early on through the throwing of coins or dice and later through the use of various random number generators on the computer, and especially the program known as *IC*, designed by Cage's assistant, Andrew Culver, to simulate the coin oracle of the *I Ching*; the result is a system of total serialism, in which all elements pertaining to acoustical pulses, pitch, noise, duration, relative loudness, tempi, combinatory superpositions, etc., are determined by referring to previously drawn correlating charts. Thus, Cage's works did not originate in psychology, motive, drama, or literary purpose, but, rather, were just sounds, free of judgments about whether they are musical or not, free of fixed relations, and free of memory and taste.

Cage was also a brilliant writer, much influenced by the manner, grammar, syntax, and glorious illogic of Gertrude Stein. While his books did not appear until the early 1960s (with the exception of the co-authored *Virgil Thomson: His Life in Music*; with K. Hoover, N.Y., 1959), he was early on a frequent reviewer and contributor on music and dance to such periodicals as *Perspectives of New Music* and *Modern Music*, the latter under the guiding editorship of his close friend, Minna Daniel (née Lederman); he also was an assoc. ed. of the short-lived magazine *Possibilities*. Of singular importance to the field, however, was his development of a style of poetry he called "mesostic" (the name suggested by Norman O. Brown, to differentiate from the clearly related "acrostic"), which uses an anchoring, generating string of letters down the center of the page that spell a name, a word, or line of text relating (or not) to the subject matter of the poem. Cage's mesostic poems, analogously indeterminate with respect to their composition to his musical works of the period, were eventually also composed via computer, the "source material" pulverized and later enhanced by Cage into semi-coherent, highly evocative poetic texts; the most extensive example is found in the six lectures comprising the aforementioned *I-VI*, composed for Harvard Univ. He also collaborated on a number of other projects, including *The First Meeting of the Satie Society*, with illustrations by Johns, Cy Twombly, Rauschenberg, Sol LeWitt, Mell Daniel, Thoreau, and Cage himself, coordinated by Benjamin Schiff and publ. in 1993 by the Limited Editions Club.

Cage was elected to the American Academy and Inst. of Arts and Letters in 1968 and to the American Academy of Arts and Sciences in 1978; he was inducted into the more exclusive branch of the Academy, the American Academy of Arts and Letters, in 1989. In 1981 he received the Mayor's Award of Honor in N.Y.C. He was named Commander of the Order of Arts and Letters by the French Minister of Culture in 1982, and received an Honorary Doctorate of Performing Arts from the Calif. Inst. of the Arts in 1986. In the summer of 1989 he was guest artist at International Festivals in Leningrad and Moscow, at which he presented works entitled *Music for ____* (1984; rev. 1987), incorporating flexible time-bracket notation, which he conducted chironomically. In late 1989 he traveled to Japan to receive, in traditional and quite formal Japanese dress, the highly prestigious and lucrative Kyoto Prize.

WORKS: DRAMATIC: *Music for Marriage at the Eiffel Tower* for Piano and Toy Instruments (Seattle, March 24, 1939; in collaboration with H. Cowell and G. McKay); *The City Wears a Slouch Hat*, music for a radio play for 4 Percussion and Sound Effects, to a text by K. Patchen (Chicago, May 31, 1942); *Works of Calder*, music for a film for Prepared Piano and Tape (1949–50); *Black Mountain Piece* for 3 Voices, Piano, Dancer,

Gramophone, Radios, Films, Slides, and Painter (Black Mountain, N.C., Summer, 1952); *Water Music* for Piano and Various Stage Properties (N.Y., May 2, 1952); *Sounds of Venice* for Various Stage Properties and Tape (Milan, Jan. 1959); *Water Walk* for Piano and Various Stage Properties (Milan, Jan. 1959); *Theatre Piece* for 1 to 8 Performers (N.Y., March 7, 1960); *Mewanemoose-icday*, musical exhibition around the music of Erik Satie (Davis, Calif., Nov. 21, 1969); *Dialogue* for 2 Performers (c. 1970); *Song Books* for Any Number of Performers (Paris, Oct. 26, 1970); *Demonstration of the Sounds of the Environment* for 300 people silently following a chance-determined path (Milwaukee, Fall 1971); *Alla Ricerca del Silenzio Perduto* for Prepared Train (1977; Bologna and vicinity, June 26–28, 1978); *Silent Environment* for an indeterminate closed space (1979; Berlin, Jan. 20, 1980); *Evéne/EnvironneMetzment* for an audience possibly producing sounds (Metz, Nov. 21, 1981); *Europeras 1 & 2* for any number of Voices, Chamber Orch., Tape, and Organ ad libitum (1985–87; Frankfurt am Main, Dec. 12, 1987); *Europeras 3 & 4* for at least 6 Voices, 2 Pianos, at least 6 Performers with 12 Gramophones and 1 Phonograph, and Tape and Light Operators (London, June 17, 1990); *Europera 5* for 2 Voices, Piano, Phonograph, and Sound and Light Operators (Buffalo, N.Y., April 18, 1991). **Radio Plays:** *James Joyce, Marcel Duchamp, Erik Satie: Ein Alphabet* (1981–82; WDR, Cologne, July 6, 1982); *Klassik nach Wunsch* (WDR, Cologne, April 23, 1982); *Fifteen Domestic Minutes* (National Public Radio, Nov. 5, 1982); *HMCIEX* (1983–84; WDR, Cologne, July 10, 1984); *Empty Mind* (WDR, Cologne, Feb. 15, 1987). **Film:** *One[11]* (1992; may be performed with *103* for Orch.). **ORCH.:** *The Seasons* (N.Y., May 18, 1947); *Concerto for Prepared Piano and Chamber Orchestra* (1950–51; N.Y., Jan. 1952); *Etcetera* for Chamber Orch. (Paris, Nov. 6, 1973); *Exercise* (Rome, 1973; rev. 1984); *Quartets I-VIII* for Small Orch. (1976; Aptos, Calif., Aug. 20, 1977); *Quartets I-VIII* for Chamber Orch. (1976; St. Paul, Minn., May 31, 1978); *Quartets I-VIII* for Full Orch. (1976; Bonn, Dec. 9, 1977); *Quartets I, V and VI* for Concert Band and 12 Amplified Voices (1976); *Thirty Pieces for Five Orchestras* (Pont-à-Mousson, Nov. 22, 1981); *Dance/4 Orchestras* (Mission San Juan Bautista, Calif., Aug. 22, 1982); *A Collection of Rocks* for Chorus and Orch. (1984; Zagreb, April 19, 1985); *Etcetera 2/4 Orchestras* (1985; Tokyo, Dec. 8, 1986); *Twenty-Three* for Strings (Putney, Vt., July 1988); *1O1* (1988; Boston, April 6, 1989); *108* (Stuttgart, Nov. 30, 1991); *103* (1991; Cologne, Sept. 19, 1992; may be performed with the film *One[11]*); *Twenty-Eight* for 28 Woodwind and Brass Instruments, *Twenty-Six* for 26 Violins, and *Twenty-Nine* for 2 Timpani, 2 Percussion, Piano, 10 Violas, 8 Cellos, and 6 Double Basses (1991; Frankfurt am Main, Sept. 5, 1992); *Eighty* (1992); *Sixty-Eight* (Frankfurt am Main, Nov. 6, 1992); *Fifty-Eight* for Concert Band (Graz, Oct. 11, 1992); *Seventy-Four* (N.Y., Nov. 8, 1992). **CHAMBER:** *Sonata for Clarinet* (1933); *Allemande* for Clarinet (1934); *Duet for Flutes* (1934); *Six Short Inventions* for Alto Flute, Clarinet, Trumpet, Violin, 2 Violas, and Cello (1934–58; N.Y., May 15, 1958); *Quest* for Various Amplified Objects and Piano (Los Angeles, April 28, 1935); *Three Pieces for Flute Duet* (1935); *String Quartet* (1936); *Amores* for Prepared Piano and 3 Percussionists (1936; rev. version, N.Y., Feb. 7, 1943); *Music for Wind Instruments* for Flute, Oboe, Clarinet, Horn, and Bassoon (1938); *Fads and Fancies in the Academy* for Piano and 4 Percussionists (Oakland, Calif., July 27, 1940); *Four Dances* for Voice, Prepared Piano, and Percussion (1942–43; N.Y., Jan. 16, 1943); *She Is Asleep* for 4 Percussionists, Voice, and Prepared Piano (1943; N.Y., May 15, 1958); *Four Walls* for Piano and Voice (Steamboat Springs, Colo., Aug. 22, 1944); *Prelude for Six Instruments in A minor* for Flute, Bassoon, Trumpet, Piano, Violin, and Cello (1946); *Nocturne for Violin and*

Piano (N.Y., Oct. 23, 1947); *String Quartet in Four Parts* (1949–50; Black Mountain, N.C., Aug. 12, 1950); *Six Melodies for Violin and Keyboard* for Violin and Piano (1950; Cambridge, Mass., Nov. 1959); *Sixteen Dances* for Flute, Trumpet, 4 Percussion, Piano, Violin, and Cello (1950–51; N.Y., Jan. 21, 1951); *Inlets* for 3 Performers using Water-filled Conch Shells, Blown Conch Shell, and the sound of fire (Seattle, Sept. 10, 1977); *Cheap Imitation* for Violin (Nov. 5, 1977); *Chorals for Violin Solo* (1978); *Pools* for Performer using Water-filled Conch Shells and Tape (1977–78; Amsterdam, June 15, 1978); *Sounday* for Violin, Piano, Voice, 9 Performers with Amplified Plant Materials and Water-filled Conch Shells, Blown Conch Shell, and Tape (1977–78; Amsterdam, June 15, 1978); *Freeman Etudes* for Violin (1977–90; Zürich, June 29, 1991); *Thirty Pieces for String Quartet* (1983; Darmstadt, July 27, 1984); *Haikai* for Flute and Zoomoozophone (1984; N.Y., March 9, 1985); *Eight Whiskus* for Violin (1985; N.Y., April 23, 1986); *Improvisation A + B* for Voice, Clarinet, Trombone, Percussion, and Cello (1986); *Haikai* for Gamelan (1986); *Two* for Flute and Piano (1987); *Seven* for Flute, Clarinet, Percussion, Piano, Violin, Viola, and Cello (Boston, Nov. 18, 1988); *Four* for String Quartet (1989); *Three* for 3 Recorder Players (1989; Speyer, July 27, 1990); *Fourteen* for Piano, Flute, Bass Flute, Clarinet, Bass Clarinet, Horn, Trumpet, 2 Percussionists, 2 Violins, Viola, Cello, and Double Bass (Zürich, May 12, 1990); *One⁶* for Violin (1990); *Seven²* for Bass Flute, Bass Clarinet, Bass Trombone, 2 Percussionists, Cello, and Double Bass (Erlangen, Sept. 25, 1990); *One⁸* for Cello (Stuttgart, Nov. 30, 1991); *Eight* for Flute, Oboe, Clarinet, Bassoon, Horn, Trumpet, Trombone, and Tuba (Washington, D.C., May 14, 1991); *Five²* for English Horn, 2 Clarinets, Bass Clarinet, and Timpani (1991; Cologne, Jan. 19, 1992); *Four³* for 1 or 2 Pianos, 12 Rainsticks, and Violin or Oscillator (Zürich, June 20, 1991); *One⁹* for Shō (1991; Japan, Jan. 18, 1992); *Two³* for Shō and Water-filled Conch Shells (1991); *Two⁴* for Violin and Piano or Shō (Washington, D.C., Nov. 15, 1991); *Five³* for Trombone and String Quartet (1991; Middelburg, The Netherlands, June 28, 1992); *Five⁴* for 2 Saxophones and 3 Percussionists (1991; Witten, April 25, 1992); *Five⁵* for Flute, 2 Clarinets, Bass Clarinet, and Percussion (1991); *Four⁵* for Saxophone Quartet or multiples thereof (1991); *Ten* for Flute, Oboe, Clarinet, Trombone, Percussion, Piano, and String Quartet (1991; Amsterdam, Feb. 24, 1992); *Two⁵* for Trombone and Piano (1991; Frankfurt am Main, Jan. 30, 1992); *One¹⁰* for Violin (1992; Baltimore, Md., April 4, 1993); *Two⁶* for Violin and Piano (Orléans, Dec. 5, 1992); *Thirteen* for Flute, Oboe, Clarinet, Bassoon, Trumpet, Trombone, Tuba, 2 Xylophones, and String Quartet (1992; Gütersloh, Feb. 17, 1993). **PERCUSSION:** *Quartet* (1935; Seattle, 1938); *Trio* (1936); *Imaginary Landscape No. 1* for 4 Percussionists (Seattle, Spring 1939); *First Construction (in Metal)* for 6 Percussionists (Seattle, Dec. 9, 1939); *Second Construction* for 4 Percussionists (Portland, Ore., Feb. 14, 1940); *Imaginary Landscape No. 2* for 4 Percussionists (Seattle, May 7, 1940; withdrawn); *Living Room Music* for 4 Percussionists (1940); *Third Construction* for 4 Percussionists (San Francisco, May 14, 1941); *Double Music* for 4 Percussionists (San Francisco, May 14, 1941; in collaboration with L. Harrison); *Imaginary Landscape No. 3* for 6 Percussionists (Chicago, March 1, 1942); *Imaginary Landscape No. 2* for 5 Percussionists (San Francisco, May 7, 1942); *Credo in Us* for 4 Percussionists (Bennington, Vt., Aug. 1, 1942); *27'10.554" for a Percussionist* (1956; Munich, Feb. 2, 1962); *Child of Tree* for Percussionist using Amplified Plant Materials (Detroit, Mich., March 8, 1975); *Branches* for any number of Percussionists using Amplified Plant Materials (1976); *R/13 (Where R = Ryoanji)* for Percussionist using found objects (Viitasaari, July 1983); *But what about the noise of crum-*

pling paper which he used to do in order to paint the series of "Papiers froissés" or tearing up paper to make "Papiers déchirés?" Arp was stimulated by water (sea, lake, and flowing waters like rivers), forests. for 3 to 10 Percussionists (1985); *One⁴* for Percussionist (1990); *Three²* for 3 Percussionists (1991); *Six* for 6 Percussionists (1991; The Hague, June 19, 1992); *Four⁴* for 4 Percussionists (1991; N.Y., Summer 1992). **KEYBOARD: Piano and Prepared Piano:** *Etudes* (c. 1931); *Three Easy Pieces* (1933); *Music for Xenia* (1934); *Two Pieces for Piano* (c. 1935; rev. 1974); *Metamorphosis* (Seattle, Oct. 10, 1938); *Bacchanale* (1938; rev. version, Seattle, April 28, 1940); *Four Songs of the Moment* (Seattle, May 7, 1940); *Spiritual* (Seattle, May 7, 1940); *Jazz Study* (c. 1942); *Dance* (1942); *Opening Dance* (Minneapolis, Minn., Feb. 20, 1942); *Totem Ancestor* (N.Y., Oct. 20, 1942); *And the Earth Shall Bear Again* (N.Y., Dec. 6, 1942); *Primitive* (1942); *In the Name of the Holocaust* (1942; Chicago, Feb. 14, 1943); *Shimmera* (1942; Chicago, Feb. 14, 1943); *Lidice* (N.Y., Jan. 20, 1943); *Ad Lib* (Chicago, Feb. 14, 1943); *Our Spring Will Come* (1943); *A Room* (1943); *Chess Pieces* (1943); *Meditation* (1943); *Tossed As It Is Untroubled* (1943; N.Y., April 5, 1944); *Triple-Placed No. 1* (1943; N.Y., April 5, 1944); *The Perilous Night* (1943–44; N.Y., April 5, 1944); *Prelude for Meditation* (1944); *Root of an Unfocus* (N.Y., April 5, 1944); *Spontaneous Earth* (N.Y., April 5, 1944); *Tripled-Paced No. 2* (1944); *The Unavailable Memory of* (N.Y., April 5, 1944); *A Valentine Out of Season* (1944); *A Book of Music* for 2 Prepared Pianos (1944; N.Y., Jan. 21, 1945); *Crete* (c. 1945); *Dad* (c. 1945); *Thin Cry* (c. 1945); *Soliloquy* (N.Y., Jan. 9, 1945); *Experiences No. 1* for 2 Pianos (N.Y., Jan. 9, 1945); *Mysterious Adventure* (N.Y., Jan. 9, 1945); *Three Dances* for 2 Prepared Pianos (1944; rev. version, N.Y., Jan. 21, 1945); *Daughters of the Lonesome Isle* (1945; Bronxville, N.Y., Feb. 27, 1946); *The Feast* (1946); *Foreboding* (1946); *Ophelia* (Bronxville, N.Y., Feb. 27, 1946); *Encounter* (N.Y., May 12, 1946); *Two Pieces for Piano* (1946); *Sonatas and Interludes* (1946–48; Black Mountain, N.C., April 6, 1948); *Music for Marcel Duchamp* (1947); *Dream* (Black Mountain, N.C., Aug. 20, 1948); *Orestes* (Black Mountain, N.C., Aug. 20, 1948); *Suite for Toy Piano* (Black Mountain, N.C., Aug. 20, 1948); *Haikus* (1950–51); *Music of Changes* (1951; N.Y., Jan. 1, 1952); *Waiting* (N.Y., Feb. 4, 1952); *Seven Haiku* (1951–52); *Two Pastorales* (1951–52; N.Y., Feb. 10, 1952); *For M.C. and D.T.* (Norwalk, Conn., Aug. 1952); *Music for Piano 1* (N.Y., Dec. 16, 1952); *Music for Piano 2* (1953; N.Y., Jan. 10, 1954); *Music for Piano 4–19* for any number of Pianos (Baton Rouge, La., June 23, 1953); *Music for Piano 3* (1953); *Music for Piano 20* (1953); *34'46.776" for a Pianist* and *31'57.9864" for a Pianist* (Donaueschingen, Oct. 17, 1954); *Music for Piano 21–36/37–52* for any number of Pianos (New City, N.Y., Oct. 15, 1955); *Music for Piano 53–68* for any number of Pianos (Notre Dame, Ind., May 18, 1956); *Music for Piano 69–84* for any number of Pianos (1956); *Winter Music* for 1 to 20 Pianos (1956–57; N.Y., Jan. 12, 1957); *For Paul Taylor and Anita Dencks* (N.Y., Oct. 20, 1957); *TV Köln* (Cologne, Oct. 6 or 7, 1958); *Music for Amplified Toy Pianos* (Middletown, Conn., Feb. 25, 1960); *Music for Piano 85* for Piano with Electronics (1962); *Electronic Music for Piano* for any number of Pianos with Electroncis (Stockholm, Sept. 1964); *Cheap Imitation* (1969; N.Y., Jan. 8, 1970); *Etudes Australes* (1974–75; Witten, April 23 and 25, 1982); *Furniture Music Etcetera* for 2 Pianos (1980); *Perpetual Tango* (1984); *One* (1987; Essen, Feb. 27, 1988); *Swinging* (1989); *Two²* for 2 Pianos (1989; N.Y., May 4, 1990); *One²* for Pianist using 1 to 4 Pianos (Huddersfield, Nov. 21, 1989); *The Beatles 1962–1970* for Piano and Tapes (1990); *One⁵* (1990). **O r g a n :** *Some of The Harmony of Maine* (1978; Essen, Nov. 8, 1980); *Souvenir* (1983; San Francisco, June 29, 1984); *Organ²/ASLSP* (Metz, Nov. 21,

1987). **CARILLON:** *Music for Carillon No. 1* (1952; N.Y., May 15, 1958), *No. 2* (1954), *No. 3* (1954), *No. 4* (1961), and *No. 5* (1967). **VOCAL:** *Greek Ode* for Voice and Piano (Santa Monica, Calif., Nov. 1932); *The Preacher* for Voice and Piano (Santa Monica, Calif., Nov. 1932); *Three Songs* for Voice and Piano (1932–33); *Five Songs for Contralto* for Voice and Piano (1938); *Ho to AA* for Voice and Piano (1939); *A Chant with Claps* for Voice with Handclaps (c. 1940); *America Was Promises* for Voice and Piano, 4-Hands (Seattle, May 7, 1940); *The Wonderful Widow of Eighteen Springs* for Voice and Piano (N.Y., May 5, 1942); *Forever and Sunsmell* for Voice and 2 Percussionists (N.Y., Oct. 20, 1942); *Experiences No. 2* for Voice (1948); *A Flower* for Voice and Piano (1950); *Solo for Voice 1* (N.Y., May 25, 1958); *Aria* for Voice (1958; Rome, Jan. 5, 1959); *Solo for Voice 2* (Lenox, Mass., Aug. 12, 1960); *Sixty-Two Mesostics re Merce Cunningham* for Voice (1971); *Les Chants de Maldoror Pulvérisés par l'Assistance Même* for a Francophone Audience of no more than 200 persons (1971); *Lecture on the Weather* for 12 Amplified Voices, with optional Instruments, Tape, and Film (1975; Toronto, Feb. 26, 1976); *Hymns and Variations* for 12 Amplified Voices (Bonn, June 10, 1979); *Litany for the Whale* for 2 Voices (1980); *Ear for Ear* for 2 or More Voices (N.Y., April 8, 1983); *Nowth upon Nacht* for Voice and Piano (1984); *Eight Whiskus* for Voice (1984; N.Y., May 14, 1985); *Selkus²* for Voice (1984); *Mirakus²* for Voice (1984); *Sonnekus²* for Voice (Bonn, March 31, 1985); *Wishing Well* for 4 Voices (1986); *Four Solos for Voice* for any solo from or combination of Soprano, Mezzo-soprano, Tenor, and Bass (N.Y., June 29, 1988); *Four²* for Chorus (1990); *One¹²* for Voice (Perugia, June 22, 1992). **TAPE:** *Imaginary Landscape No. 5* (N.Y., Jan. 18, 1952); *Williams Mix* (1952; Urbana, Ill., March 22, 1953); *Music for The Marrying Maiden* (N.Y., June 15, 1960); *Rozart Mix* (Waltham, Mass., May 1965); *Bird Cage* (1972); *Newport Mix* (Cincinnati, Spring 1967); *Cassette* (N.Y., Dec. 7, 1977); *Improvisation III* (N.Y., Feb. 26, 1980); *Improvisation IV* (London, June 30, 1980; rev. 1982); *Instances of Silence* (March 16, 1982); *Stratified Essay* (1987); *Voiceless Essay* (1987); *Mozart Mix* (1991). **ELECTRONIC MEDIA:** *Imaginary Landscape No. 4* for 24 Performers on 12 Radios (N.Y., May 10, 1951); *Speech 1955* for 5 Radios and Newsreader (1955); *WBAI* for Tapes and Phonodiscs or Amplifiers (N.Y., Feb. 1960); *Cartridge Music* for 1 to 40 Players using Amplified Small Sounds and Piano or Cymbal (Bremen, Sept. 15, 1960); *Variations V* for any number of Performers using Photo-electric Cells and Electronic Sound Sources (N.Y., July 23, 1965); *Variations VI* for any number of Performers using Photo-electric Cells and Electronic Sound Sources (Washington, D.C., April 27, 1966); *Reunion* for Electronic Chessboard and Electronic·Equipment activited by a game of chess (Toronto, March 5, 1968); *0'00" No. 2* for Amplified Playing Area activated by a game involving 2 or more persons (1968); *Program (KNOBS) for the Listener* for Phonodisc and Amplifier (1969; in collaboration with L. Hiller); *33 1/3* a large number of Phonodiscs and at least 12 Turntables to be operated by the audience (Davis, Calif., Nov. 21, 1969); *Variations VII* for any number of Musicians using Photo-electric Cells and Electronic Equipment (N.Y., Oct. 15, 1966; rev. 1972); *Telephones and Birds* for 3 Performers using Telephones and Tapes (N.Y., Jan. 18, 1977); *Address* for Phonodiscs and 12 Turntables to be operated by the audience, 5 Performers using Cassette Machines, and Electric Bell (N.Y., Dec. 7, 1977); *Paragraphs of Fresh Air* for Voice and 4 Instrumentalists also operating Tapes, Cassettes, Phonodiscs or Microphones, and Telephone (1979); *Concerto Grosso* for 4 Television Sets and 12 Radios (1979; Berlin, Jan. 20, 1980); *Rocks* for any combination of at least 6 Radios, Television Sets, Phonodiscs, and Cassettes ad libitum with machines emitting relatively

fixed sounds (1986); *Sculptures Musicales* for any number of groups of indeterminate Sound Sources, each group consisting of at least 3 different sounds (Berkeley, Sept. 23, 1989); *One³* for Performer amplifying the sound of an auditorium to feedback level (Kyoto, Nov. 1989). **VARIABLE INSTRUMENTATION:** *In a Landscape* for Piano or Harp (Black Mountain, N.C., Aug. 20, 1948); *59 1/2" for a String Player* for Violin, Viola, and Cello or Double Bass (1953; San Antonio, May 7, 1962); *26'1.1499" for a String Player* for Violin, Viola, and Cello or Double Bass (1953–55; New City, N.Y., Oct. 15, 1955); *Radio Music* for 1 to 8 Radios (N.Y., May 30, 1956); *Concert for Piano and Orchestra* for any solo from or combination of Piano, Flute, Clarinet, Bassoon, Trumpet, Trombone, Tuba, 3 Violins, 2 Violas, Cello, and Double Bass, with optional Conductor (1957–58; N.Y., May 15, 1958); *Atlas Eclipticalis* for 1 to 86 Specified Instruments (Montreal, Aug. 3, 1961); *HPSCHD* for 1 to 7 Amplified Harpsichords and 1 to 51 Tapes (1967–69; Champaign-Urbana, Ill., May 16, 1969; in collaboration with L. Hiller); *Cheap Imitation* for 24 to 95 Specified Instruments (1970–72; The Hague, May 13, 1972 [declared public rehearsal by the composer]); *Etudes Boreales* for Cello and/or Piano (1978); *A House Full of Music* for Music School Students performing their repertoire simultaneously (1981–82; Bremen, May 10, 1982); *Postcard from Heaven* for 1 to 20 Harps (Minneapolis, Sept. 1982); *Musicircus for Children* for Children performing their repertoire simultaneously (Turin, May 19, 1984); *Aslsp* for Piano or Organ (Coll. Park, Md., July 14, 1985); *Ryoanji* for any solo from or combination of Voice, Flute, Oboe, Trombone, Double Bass ad libitum with Tape, and Obbligato Percussionist or any 20 Instruments (1983–85); *Hymnkus* for any solo from or combination of Voice, Alto Flute, Clarinet, 2 Saxophones, Bassoon, Trombone, 2 Percussionists, Accordion, 2 Pianos, Violin, and Double Bass (1986); *Music for ____* for any solo from or combination of Voice, Flute, Oboe, Clarinet, Horn, Trumpet, Trombone, 4 Percussionists, 2 Pianos, 2 Violins, Viola, and Cello (New Milford, Conn., Aug. 15, 1984; rev. 1987); *composed Improvisation* for any solo from or combination of Snare Drum, Steinberger Bass Guitar, and One-sided Drums, with or without Jangles (1987–90); *Scottish Circus* for any Scottish or Irish Folk Instruments (Glasgow, Sept. 20, 1990). **INDETERMINATE SOUND SOURCES:** Music-based mathematical formulae (1930–31); *Sonata for Two Voices* (1933); *Solo with Obbligato Accompaniment of Two Voices in Canon, and Six Short Inventions on the Subjects of the Solo* (1933–44; rev. 1963); *Composition for Three Voices* (1934); *Party Pieces* for any Instruments encompassing specified ranges (c. 1945; in collaboration with H. Cowell, L. Harrison, and V. Thomson); *4'33"* (Woodstock, N.Y., Aug. 29, 1952); *Haiku* (1958); *Variations I* (Greensboro, N.C., March 15, 1958); *Music Walk* for 1 or More Performers at a single Piano using Radios and other Auxiliary Sound Sources (Düsseldorf, Oct. 14, 1958); *Fontana Mix* for any Sound Sources or Actions (1958; Rome, Jan. 5, 1959); *Variations II* (N.Y., March 24, 1961); *0'00"* for 1 Performer (Tokyo, Oct. 24, 1962); *Variations III* (1962–63; Berlin, Jan. 1963); *Variations IV* (Los Angeles, July 17, 1963); *Musicircus* for any number of Performers willing to perform in the same place and time (Champaign-Urbana, Ill., Nov. 17, 1967); *Variations VIII* for any number of Performers possibly producing sounds with machines (1968; rev. 1976 and 1978); *Sound Anonymously Received* for Unsolicited Instrument (Davis, Calif., Nov. 21, 1969; rev. 1978); *Score (40 Drawings by Thoreau) and 23 Parts* for any Instruments or Voices or combinations thereof and Tape (Saint Paul, Minn., Sept. 28, 1974); *Renga* for 78 Instruments or Voices or combinations thereof (1975–76; Boston, Sept. 29, 1976); *Apartment House 1776* for 4

Voices, optionally on Tape, and any number of Instruments (Boston, Sept. 29, 1976); *49 Waltzes for the Five Boroughs* (1977); *A Dip in the Lake* (1978); ___, ___ *Circus on* __ for Voice, Tape, and any number of Musicians, optionally on tape (Donaueschingen, Oct. 20, 1979); *Vis-à-Vis* for 2 Musicians (1986; in collaboration with T. Takemitsu); *Five* for 5 Voices or Instruments or combination thereof encompassing specified ranges (Middelburg, The Netherlands, June 27, 1988); *Five Stone Wind* for 3 Performers (Avignon, July 30, 1988); *One⁷* (1990); *Five Hanau Silence* for environmental sounds of Hanau (1991); *Four⁶* (1990–92; N.Y., July 23, 1992).

WRITINGS: With K. Hoover, *Virgil Thomson: His Life and Music* (N.Y., 1959); *Silence: Lectures and Writings* (Middletown, Conn., 1961); *A Year from Monday: New Lectures and Writings* (Middletown, Conn., 1967); *To Describe the Process of Composition Used in Not Wanting to Say Anything about Marcel* (Cincinnati, 1969); with A. Knowles, *Notations* (N.Y., 1969); *M: Writings '67-'72* (Middletown, Conn., 1973); *Writings through Finnegans Wake* (N.Y., 1978; includes *Writing for the Second Time through Finnegans Wake*); *Empty Words: Writings '73-'78* (Middletown, Conn. 1979); with D. Charles, *For the Birds* (Boston, 1981); with S. Barron, *Another Song* (N.Y., 1981); W. Diamond and C. Hicks, eds., *John Cage: Etchings 1978–1982* (Oakland, Calif., 1982); with L. Long, *Mud Book* (N.Y., 1982; 2nd ed., 1988); *Themes and Variations* (N.Y., 1982); *X: Writings '79-'82* (Middletown, Conn., 1983); *I-VI* (Cambridge, Mass., 1990); *Composition in Retrospect* (Cambridge, Mass., 1993); R. Kostelanetz, ed., *John Cage, Writer: Previously Uncollected Pieces* (N.Y., 1993).

BIBL.: S. Kubota, *Marcel Duchamp and J. C.* (N.Y., 1968); R. Kostelanetz, ed., *J. C.* (N.Y., 1970; new ed., 1991); E. Snyder, *J. C. and Music since World War II: A Study in Applied Aesthetics* (diss., Univ. of Wisc., 1970); W. Duckworth, *Expanding Notational Parameters in the Music of J. C.* (diss., Univ. of Ill., 1972); R. Bunger, *The Well-Prepared Piano* (Colorado Springs, Colo., 1973; 2nd ed., San Pedro, Calif., 1981); J. Davies, *Two aspects of the American avant-garde: Charles Ives and J. C.* (diss., Univ. of Wales, Cardiff, 1973); L. Ferrero, *Le Idée di J. C.* (diss., Univ. of Turin, 1974); M. Nyman, *Experimental Music: C. and Beyond* (N.Y., 1974); J. Francis, *Structure in the Solo Piano Music of J. C.* (diss., Fla. State Univ., 1976); D. Charles, *Gloses sur J. C.* (Paris, 1978); H.-K. Metzger and R. Riehn, *J. C.* (Munich, 1978); M. Fürst-Heidtmann, *Das präparierte Klavier des J. C.* (Regensburg, 1979); M. Perloff, *The Poetics of Indeterminacy: Rimbaud to Cage* (Princeton, N.J., 1980); F. Bayer, *De Schönberg à Cage: Essai sur la notion d'espace sonore dans la musique contemporaine* (Paris, 1981); P. Griffiths, *C.* (N.Y., 1981); W. Diamond and C. Hicks, eds., *John Cage: Etchings 1978–1982* (Oakland, Calif., 1982); M. Froment-Meurice, *Les intermittences de la raison: Penser C., entendre Heidegger* (Paris, 1982); P. Gena and J. Brent, eds., *A J. C. Reader: In Celebration of His 70th Birthday* (N.Y., 1982); H. Kepler, *J. C. und der Zen- Buddhismus* (diss., Univ. of Marburg, 1982); K. Schöning, *Roaratorio: Eine irischer Circus über Finnegans Wake* (Königstein, 1982); T. DeLio, *Circumscribing the Open Universe: Essays on C., Feldman, Wolff, Ashley and Lucier* (Washington, D.C., 1984); D. Campana, *Form and Structure in the Music of J. C.* (diss., Northwestern Univ., 1985); T. Holmes, *Annotated Discography of the Music of J. C.* (Cherry Hill, N.J., 1986); J. Petkus, *The Songs of J. C. (1932–1970)* (diss., Univ. of Conn., 1986); S. Hilger, *C. and Cunningham: Eine Entwicklungsgeschichte von Musik und Tanz auf dem Weg einer beziehungsreichen Beziehungslosigkeit* (diss., Univ. of Bonn, 1987); R. Kostelanetz, ed., *Conversing with C.* (N.Y., 1987); E. Pedrini, *J. C. Happening and Fluxus* (Florence, 1988); J. Pritchett, *The Development of Chance Techniques in the Music of J. C., 1950–1956* (diss., N.Y.U., 1988); R. Fleming and W. Duck-

worth, eds., *J. C. at Seventy- Five* (London and Toronto, 1989); H.-K. Metzger and R. Riehn, eds., special issue of *Musik-Konzept* (2 vols.; Frankfurt am Main, 1990; includes list of works, discography, and extensive bibliography); J.-J. Nattiez and F. Davoine, eds., *Pierre Boulez/J. C.: Correspondance et documents* (Winterthur, 1990; Eng. tr., 1993; Ger. tr., 1995; Japanese tr., 1996); W. Fetterman, *J. C.'s Theatre Pieces: Notations and Performances* (diss., N.Y.U., 1992); L. Kuhn, *J. C.'s "Europeras 1 & 2": The Musical Means of Revolution* (diss., Univ. of Calif., Los Angeles, 1992); D. Revill, *The Roaring Silence: J. C.: A Life* (N.Y., 1992); *Rolywholyover A Circus*, "box" accompanying the Los Angeles Museum of Contemporary Art exhibition of the same name (N.Y., 1992; contains new and reprinted essays by C., A. d'Harnoncourt, J. Lazar, L. Kuhn, J. Retallack, M. Swed, M. McLuhan, A. Weil, E. Snyder, and D.T. Suzuki); J.-Y. Bosseur, *J. C.* (Paris, 1993); R. Kostelanetz, ed., *Writings About J. C.* (Ann Arbor, 1993); J. Pritchett, *The Music of J. C.* (Cambridge, 1993); J. Corbett, *Extended Play: Sounding Off from John Cage to Dr. Funkenstein* (Durham, N.C., 1994); G. Leonard, *Into the Light of Things: The Art of the Commonplace from Wordsworth to J. C.* (Chicago, 1994); M. Perloff and C. Junkerman, *J. C: Composed in America* (Chicago, 1994); W. Duckworth, *Talking Music: Conversations with J. C., Philip Glass, Laurie Anderson, and Five Generations of American Experimental Composers* (N.Y., 1995); R. Kostelanetz, *C. Ex(Plain)ed* (N.Y., 1995); J. Retallack, *MUSICAGE: C. Muses on Art, Music, Poetry* (Middletown, Conn., 1995); P. van Emmerik, *Thema's en Variaties: Systematische Tendensen in de Compositietechnieken van J. C.* (diss., Univ. of Amsterdam, 1996); D. Patterson, *J. C., 1942–1954: A Language of Changes* (diss., Columbia Univ., 1996); R. Kostelantz, *Writings About J. C.* (Ann Arbor, Mich., 1996); A. Rich, *American Pioneers: Ives to C. and Beyond* (N.Y., 1996); J. Rivest, *Le Concert for Piano and Orchestra de John Cage ou les limites de l'indétermination* (diss., Univ. of Montreal, 1996); Y. Suenobu, *J. C. Remembered* (Tokyo, 1996); H. Lindenberger, *Opera in History: From Monteverdi to C.* (Stanford, Calif., 1998); C. Shultis, *Silencing the Sounded Self: J. C. and the American Experimental Tradition* (Boston, 1998).—**NS/LK/DM**

Cahill, Teresa (Mary), English soprano; b. Maidenhead, July 30, 1944. She trained at the Guildhall School of Music and the Royal Academy of Music in London. In 1967 she made her operatic debut as Rosina with the Phoenix Opera Co. in London; from 1970 she appeared at the Glyndebourne Festivals and at Covent Garden in London; also sang with the Welsh National Opera in Cardiff and Scottish National Opera in Glasgow. In 1972 she appeared for the first time at the Santa Fe Opera, in 1976 at Milan's La Scala, and in 1981 with the Philadelphia Opera. She also pursued an active career as a concert singer. Her operatic repertoire includes roles in operas by Mozart, Verdi, and R. Strauss. —**NS/LK/DM**

Cahn, Sammy (Samuel Cohen), romantic American lyricist; b. N.Y., June 18, 1913; d. Los Angeles, Jan. 15, 1993. Remarkably prolific, in a career lasting more than 50 years—from the 1930s to the 1980s—Cahn wrote lyrics for songs used in at least 137 motion pictures. He maintained long-running collaborations with composers Saul Chaplin, Jule Styne, and James Van Heusen, but also worked with many others. He earned 26 Academy Award nominations for Best Song, far more than any other songwriter, and he won four Oscars, for

"Three Coins in the Fountain," "All the Way," "High Hopes," and "Call Me Irresponsible." Among his other major hits were "I've Heard That Song Before," "It's Been a Long, Long Time," and "Let It Snow! Let It Snow! Let It Snow!" He enjoyed a special relationship with Frank Sinatra, who recorded many more of his songs than those of any other lyricist. Though Cahn prided himself on being a professional able to turn out lyrics on demand, he was also a craftsman noted for intricate internal rhymes, and an unabashed romantic whose songs were mostly devoted to hopeful declarations of love.

Cahn was the son of Polish immigrants Abraham and Elka Riss Cohen; his father ran a restaurant. Cahn took violin lessons as a child, and as a teenager he joined the group Frankie Miggs and His Pals of Harmony. He wrote both music and lyrics to his first published song, "Shake Your Head from Side to Side," but soon entered into a songwriting partnership with the group's pianist, Saul Kaplan, whom he persuaded to change his name to Chaplin. (Cahn changed his own name from Cohen to Kahn to avoid confusion with a comedian named Sammy Cohen, then altered the spelling to Cahn to avoid confusion with lyricist Gus Kahn.)

Cahn and Chaplin began writing special material—comic dialogue, song parodies, etc.—for vaudeville performers. (Cahn continued to write special material for performers throughout his career, usually without credit or payment.) Their first song success came with "Rhythm Is Our Business," written for and recorded by Jimmie Lunceford and His Orch., which became a best-seller in August 1935. (In return for his sponsorship, Lunceford was "cut in" on the writing of the song, which was credited as music by Lunceford, lyrics by Cahn and Chaplin.) The two wrote a follow-up, "(If I Had) Rhythm in My Nursery Rhymes" (music credited to Lunceford and Chaplin, lyrics to Cahn and Don Raye), which was recorded by Tommy Dorsey's Clambake Seven and spent five weeks in the hit parade starting in January 1936. They returned to the hit parade in August with their revision of the 1931 song "Till the Real Thing Comes Along" (music and lyrics by L. E. Freeman and Mann Holiner); as "Until the Real Thing Comes Along" it was recorded by Andy Kirk and His Twelve Clouds of Joy and spent 11 weeks in the chart. "If It's the Last Thing I Do" (music and lyrics by Cahn and Chaplin) was recorded by Tommy Dorsey and His Orch. and spent seven weeks in the hit parade starting in November.

Cahn and Chaplin first topped the hit parade in January 1938 with "Bei Mir Bist Du Schön," recorded by the Andrews Sisters with a competing version by Guy Lombardo and His Royal Canadians. The songwriters were credited with writing the English lyrics for the song, which had music by Sholom Secunda and had been featured in the 1933 Yiddish musical *I Would If I Could*, with Yiddish lyrics by Jacob Jacobs. Meanwhile, Cahn and Chaplin were working for the Vitagraph studios in Brooklyn, writing songs for film shorts. One of these, "Please Be Kind," was recorded by Red Norvo and His Orch. with Mildred Bailey on vocals and topped the hit parade in May. The following April,

Larry Clinton and His Orch. spent a week in the chart with Cahn and Chaplin's "I Want My Share of Love."

Warner Bros., Vitagraph's parent company, closed the studio, and Cahn and Chaplin were sent to Hollywood. There they made their first notable contributions to feature films with two songs in the September 1940 release *Ladies Must Live,* one of which was "I Could Make You Care," recorded for a minor hit by Tommy Dorsey with Sinatra on vocals. But the songwriters stayed at Warner Bros. only briefly before moving to the low-budget Republic studios and then the slightly more prestigious Columbia Pictures. They wrote songs for half a dozen films released during 1941 and another couple released in the first several months of 1942 without scoring any hits. This led them to decide to split up.

In 1942, Cahn accepted an offer to collaborate with Jule Styne on songs for the film *Youth on Parade* at Republic. Released at the end of the year, the film featured "I've Heard That Song Before," which was recorded by Harry James and His Orch., resulting in a chart-topping million-seller that was the biggest hit of 1943. The song was Cahn's first to be nominated for an Academy Award. He and Styne formed a songwriting partnership. Their next hit was the war-themed song "Vict'ry Polka," recorded by Crosby and the Andrews Sisters; it made the Top Ten in January 1944. Also reflecting on the war was "I'll Walk Alone," sung by Dinah Shore in the all-star April 1944 film *Follow the Boys* and recorded by her for a #1 hit, which brought the team its second Academy Award nomination. Signing to Columbia Pictures, they wrote the songs for the Kay Kyser vehicle *Carolina Blues* which was released in Dec. and featured "There Goes That Song Again," taken into the Top Ten by Russ Morgan and His Orch. Also included in the score, though not written for the film, was "Poor Little Rhode Island," which became a hit for Guy Lombardo and was adopted as R.I.'s state song.

Cahn and Chaplin attempted to mount a Broadway musical, *Glad to See You,* in the fall of 1944. It closed out of town on New Year's Eve after tryouts in Philadelphia and Boston, but Jimmy Dorsey and His Orch. recorded "Can't You Read Between the Lines?" for a Top Ten hit, and the score also featured "Guess I'll Hang My Tears Out to Dry," which went on to become a standard.

Sinatra took Cahn and Styne's "Saturday Night (Is the Loneliest Night of the Week)" into the Top Ten in March 1945. The same month saw the release of the film *Tonight and Every Night,* which featured "Anywhere," their third Academy Award nominee. May saw the release of *Thrill of a Romance,* for which Cahn, Axel Stordahl, and Paul Weston wrote "I Should Care"; Sinatra recorded it for a Top Ten hit. In July, Sinatra starred in the movie musical *Anchors Aweigh* one of the most successful films of the year, with a Cahn-Styne score that included "What Makes the Sunset?" which he recorded for a minor hit, and "I Fall in Love Too Easily," another Academy Award nominee. On Sept. 5, Cahn married actress Gloria Delson, with whom he had two children. They divorced on April 13, 1964. He and Styne ended 1945 with a song for the G.I.s returning after the war, "It's Been a Long, Long Time." Recordings by

Crosby with Les Paul and His Trio and by Harry James each topped the charts in November and Dec.

Cahn wrote the lyrics for songs used in four movie musicals released during 1946, but all his hits for the year came from independent songs. The seasonal "Let It Snow! Let It Snow! Let It Snow!" (music by Styne), recorded by Vaughn Monroe and released in Dec. 1945, went to #1 in January, and Sinatra took "Day by Day" (music and lyrics by Cahn, Stordahl, and Weston) into the Top Ten in March, "Five Minutes More" (music by Styne) to #1 in September, and "The Things We Did Last Summer" (music by Styne) into the Top Ten in Dec. Sinatra starred in *It Happened in Brooklyn*, released in March 1947, and recorded two of the songs from the Cahn-Styne score on a single: "I Believe" hit the Top Ten, and "Time after Time," also a chart entry, went on to become a much-revived standard. Cahn and Styne were successful in their second attempt at a Broadway show in the fall, as *High Button Shoes* ran 727 performances, making it the biggest musical hit of the 1947–48 season.

Cahn and Styne returned to Hollywood and signed to Warner Bros., where they wrote the songs for *Romance on the High Seas*, released in June 1948. The film featured "It's Magic," sung by Doris Day, who became a movie star as a result of her performance. Her recording reached the Top Ten, and the song was Cahn's fifth to be nominated for an Academy Award. "Put 'Em in a Box, Tie 'Em with a Ribbon (And Throw 'Em in the Deep Blue Sea)," also heard in the film, was recorded for a chart entry by Eddy Howard. Cahn and Styne's score for *Two Guys from Texas*, released in August, included "Ev'ryday I Love You (Just a Little Bit More)," which provided a chart entry for Vaughn Monroe. *It's a Great Feeling*, released in August 1949, marked the formal end of Cahn and Styne's partnership, as Styne moved to N.Y. and worked in the theater, while Cahn remained in Hollywood. But the break was amicable, and the two worked together occasionally thereafter. The title song from *It's a Great Feeling* brought them another Academy Award nomination.

Always Leave Them Laughing, a vehicle for comedian Milton Berle released in November 1949, featured songs with lyrics by Cahn and music by Cahn, Berle, or Heindorf; it marked the beginning of a six-year period during which Cahn had no permanent writing partner. His next hit was the novelty song "Go to Sleep, Go to Sleep, Go to Sleep" (music by Fred Spielman), which peaked in the Top Ten for Mary Martin and Arthur Godfrey in April 1950. The nearest Cahn had to a regular collaborator during the early 1950s was composer Nicholas Brodszky, with whom he teamed up to write the songs for the September 1950 release *The Toast of New Orleans*, a vehicle for opera singer Mario Lanza. Lanza's recording of "Be My Love" from the score became a chart-topping million-seller, and the song brought Cahn his seventh Oscar nomination. He earned his eighth, again with Brodszky, for "Wonder Why," featured in the July 1951 release *Rich, Young and Pretty*. Vic Damone, who appeared in the film, recorded the song for a chart entry, and the soundtrack album was a Top Ten hit.

Cahn enjoyed two song revivals in 1952. Jane Froman sang "I'll Walk Alone" on the soundtrack of her film biography, *With a Song in My Heart*, a box office hit released in April. Her recording of the song made the charts, but it was outdistanced by a Top Ten rendition by Don Cornell. And in October, Ralph Flanagan and His Orch. peaked in the Top Ten with their recording of "I Should Care." Cahn's most successful new song for the year was the title tune of the Lanza vehicle *Because You're Mine*, written with Brodszky and released in September. Lanza's recording of the song reached the Top Ten, and his *Because You're Mine* album went to #1; the song also earned an Oscar nomination.

Hollywood grew less interested in original movie musicals in the early 1950s and more interested in title songs for nonmusical movies. Cahn, with his ability to write quickly and to order, responded well to this trend. He again teamed up with Styne to write "Three Coins in the Fountain," the title song for a film romance. Released in May 1954 with Sinatra singing the song during the credits, the picture became a box office hit; the song was taken into the Top Ten by Sinatra, but to #1 and to million-seller status by the Four Aces; with it, Cahn finally won the Academy Award for Best Song on his tenth nomination. He also enjoyed more hits during the year: Nat "King" Cole recorded "Make Her Mine" (music by Chester Conn) for a chart entry in July; the Four Aces made the charts with "It's a Woman's World" (music by Cyril J. Mockridge), the theme from the September film release *Woman's World* and the DeCastro Sisters peaked in the Top Ten with "Teach Me Tonight" (music by Gene de Paul) in December.

In 1955, the year he finally found a new regular writing partner, Cahn collaborated with six different composers on songs for six films and a television musical, as well as a seventh composer for an independent hit. With Brodszky he wrote "I'll Never Stop Loving You" for the Ruth Etting film biography *Love Me or Leave Me*, starring Day and released in May. Day's recording of the song made the charts, and the songwriters earned another Academy Award nomination. In July, Cahn had songs in *Ain't Misbehavin'*, written with Johnnie Scott, and *How to Be Very, Very Popular* with Styne. In August came the box office hit *Pete Kelly's Blues*, starring Jack Webb, Peggy Lee, and Ella Fitzgerald. Cahn collaborated with Heindorf on the title song, which became an instrumental chart record for Ray Anthony, and the film generated three Top Ten albums: one on Columbia Records featuring Heindorf's score, one on Decca sung by Lee and Fitzgerald, and one on RCA with Webb's narration. Also in August, the Dean Martin–Jerry Lewis comedy *You're Never Too Young* was released with songs by Cahn and Arthur Schwartz.

But it was Cahn's sixth songwriting partner of 1955 who would prove the most significant. At the behest of Frank Sinatra, he began working with James Van Heusen, who had been freelancing with different lyricists since the demise of his partnership with Johnny Burke. Cahn and Van Heusen wrote songs for a musical version of Thornton Wilder's play *Our Town*, broadcast on television in September and featuring Sinatra. From their score, "Love and Marriage" became a Top Ten hit for Sinatra, and the song won an Emmy Award for Best Musical Contribution. Also in September, Sinatra charted with "Same Old Saturday Night," which Cahn wrote with Frank Reardon. In November came the Sinatra film *The Tender Trap*, for which Cahn and Van Heusen wrote "(Love Is) The Tender Trap." Sinatra took the song into the Top Ten, and it earned Cahn his second Oscar nomination of the year.

The success of "Love and Marriage" and "(Love Is) The Tender Trap" led Cahn and Van Heusen to form a permanent partnership, but unlike Cahn's previous teamings with Chaplin and Styne, this one was not exclusive, at least for Cahn. Throughout the 14 years he wrote with Van Heusen, Cahn continued to work with other composers as well. He contributed songs to nine films released in 1956, working with five different composers, and wrote an independent song with two other songwriters that was a hit during the year. Among the highlights: his title song for the February release *Forever Darling* (music by Bronislau Kaper) became a Top 40 hit for the Ames Brothers; from his score for the March release *Meet Me in Las Vegas,* on which he collaborated with Brodszky, the Four Aces scored chart entries with "If You Can Dream" and "The Gal with the Yaller Shoes"; the Lanza vehicle *Serenade,* released in March, with songs by Cahn and Brodszky, resulted in a Top Ten Lanza LP of the songs; the title song to *The Man with the Golden Arm* (music by Van Heusen), not actually heard in the motion picture itself, was recorded as an instrumental theme by several artists, including Richard Maltby, while Dick Jacobs and His Orch. had the most successful vocal version, a Top 40 single in April; Perry Como scored a Top 40 hit with the title song of the July release *Somebody Up There Likes Me* (music by Kaper); Tony Martin reached the charts with "It's Better in the Dark" (music by Van Heusen) in September; Frank Sinatra hit the Top Ten in December with "Hey! Jealous Lover" (music and lyrics by Cahn, Kay Twomey, and Bee Walker); and *Written on the Wind,* which opened at the end of the year, featured a title song (music by Victor Young) that was nominated for an Academy Award and became a Top 40 hit for the Four Aces.

Cahn was equally busy in 1957, working with eight collaborators on seven motion pictures as well as writing an original children's musical for records, *Ali Baba and the Forty Thieves* (music by Mary Rodgers), recorded by Crosby and released on Golden Masterpiece Records in October. His greatest success for the year came with Van Heusen on "All the Way," a song written for the Sinatra film *The Joker Is Wild,* which opened in September. Sinatra recorded the song for a Top Ten hit, and it won Cahn his second Academy Award.

Cahn contributed music to eight films in 1958 and wrote songs for records, nightclub acts, and television. He used Van Heusen more frequently, notably on the title songs for two Sinatra albums, "Come Fly with Me" and "Only the Lonely" (both albums topped the charts, and the latter went gold), and on "To Love and Be Loved," the Oscar-nominated theme from the Sinatra film *Some Came Running.* But he also worked with five other composers, most successfully with Alex North on the title song from the film *The Long Hot Summer,* which

was recorded for a chart entry by Jimmie Rodgers. In 1959, Cahn collaborated with Van Heusen on seven of the nine films he worked on, and his only notable song during the year not by Van Heusen was the title song from *The Best of Everything* (music by Alfred Newman), which was recorded for a chart entry by Johnny Mathis and nominated for an Academy Award. With Van Heusen, Cahn won the 1959 Academy Award for Best Song for "High Hopes" from the Sinatra film *A Hole in the Head,* a box office success. Sinatra enjoyed a Top 40 hit with the song, which also was nominated for a Grammy Award for Song of the Year. Cahn and Van Heusen again wrote title songs for two Sinatra albums during the year, *Come Dance with Me* and *No One Cares;* both hit the Top Ten, and the former went gold. Meanwhile, Louis Prima and Keely Smith revived "Bei Mir Bist Du Schön" and the McGuire Sisters rerecorded "Teach Me Tonight" in a cha-cha treatment for chart entries.

Cahn collaborated with Van Heusen on all seven of the 1960 films to which he contributed. Their major success of the year was "The Second Time Around," from the Crosby vehicle *High Time,* which earned Academy and Grammy Award nominations for Best Song and became a chart record for Sinatra. They also enjoyed chart entries with Andy Williams's recording of the title song from *Wake Me When It's Over,* and with revivals of "The Last Dance" by the McGuire Sisters (earlier recorded by Sinatra) and "Time after Time," by Frankie Ford.

Cahn's songwriting opportunities for the movies began to diminish after 1960, though he worked regularly in Hollywood for the next four years. He contributed only title songs to three motion pictures released during 1961, among them "Pocketful of Miracles" (music by Van Heusen), which was nominated for an Academy Award and which Sinatra recorded for a Top 40 hit. Cahn and Van Heusen also wrote the title song for Sinatra's Top Ten 1961 album *Ring-a-Ding Ding!* In 1962, Patti Page charted with the title song from the film *Boys' Night Out* (music by Van Heusen); on the charts again were "Teach Me Tonight" (a Top 40 hit by George Maharis) and "It's Magic" (by the Platters). Cahn and Van Heusen had songs in four films released in 1963, their greatest success for the year coming with "Call Me Irresponsible" from the Jackie Gleason–starring *Papa's Delicate Condition,* which the two had actually written in the 1950s when Fred Astaire was attached to the project. The song won the Academy Award and was nominated for a Grammy Award for Song of the Year. Jack Jones recorded it for a chart entry.

In 1964, Cahn and Van Heusen scored the Sinatra movie musical *Robin and the 7 Hoods,* which brought them an Oscar nomination for the song "My Kind of Town" and a charting soundtrack album that earned a Grammy nomination. They were also nominated for the Academy Award for their title song for the film *Where Love Has Gone,* which was recorded for a chart entry by Jones. And Gloria Lynne had a chart revival of "I Should Care."

Cahn and Van Heusen wrote the title song for Frank Sinatra's August 1965 album *September of My Years.* The

LP reached the Top Ten and went gold, and the song was nominated for a Grammy Award for Song of the Year. With less work forthcoming from Hollywood, the songwriters accepted an offer to write a Broadway musical, resulting in *Skyscraper,* which ran 248 performances and produced a cast album that charted for two months. They followed it in November 1966 with another show, *Walking Happy,* which ran 161 performances. In Dec., Chris Montez reached the Top 40 with another revival of "Time after Time."

Returning to Hollywood, Cahn found occasional work in the movies. His and Van Heusen's title song for the box office hit *Thoroughly Modern Millie,* which starred Julie Andrews, earned an Academy Award nomination in 1967, and the soundtrack album spent more than six months in the charts. *Star!,* which opened in October 1968, also starring Andrews, was an expensive flop, but the Cahn-Van Heusen title song earned another Oscar nomination. Cahn teamed up again with Styne for the Broadway musical *Look to the Lilies* in 1970, but it was unsuccessful. On Aug. 2, 1970, he married fashion consultant Virginia "Tita" Basile Curtis.

Cahn earned his 25th Academy Award nomination for "All That Love Went to Waste" (music by George Barrie), used in the 1973 film *A Touch of Class.* In November 1973, Sinatra reached the charts with "Let Me Try Again (Laisse Moi le Temps)," a French song composed by Michel Jourdan for which Cahn and Paul Anka had fashioned an English lyric about Sinatra's return to performing after a brief retirement. In 1974, Cahn starred in an autobiographical revue, *Words and Music,* singing many of his best-known songs and telling stories about his career. The show ran on Broadway for 127 performances, after which he toured with it throughout the U.S. and in England. He earned his final Oscar nomination for "Now That We're in Love" (music by George Barrie) from the 1975 film *Whiffs.* He continued to write songs during the 1980s, placing his last in a motion picture with "How Much I Care" (music by Clint Eastwood) in *Heartbreak Ridge* in 1987. He died in 1993 of congestive heart failure at 79.

WORKS (only works for which Cahn was a primary, credited lyricist are listed): **FILMS:** *Ladies Must Live* (1940); *Rookies on Parade* (1941); *Time Out for Rhythm* (1941); *Two Latins from Manhattan* (1941); *Go West, Young Lady* (1941); *Honolulu Lu* (1941); *Blondie Goes to College* (1942); *Youth on Parade* (1942); *Johnny Doughboy* (1943); *Lady of Burlesque* (1943); *Thumbs Up* (1943); *Pistol Packin' Mama* (1943); *Step Lively* (1944); *Carolina Blues* (1944); *Tonight and Every Night* (1945); *Anchors Aweigh* (1945); *Tars and Spars* (1946); *Cinderella Jones* (1946); *The Kid from Brooklyn* (1946); *Earl Carroll Sketch Book* (1946); *Ladies' Man* (1947); *It Happened in Brooklyn* (1947); *Romance on the High Seas* (1948); *Two Guys from Texas* (1948); *It's a Great Feeling* (1949); *Always Leave Them Laughing* (1949); *The Toast of New Orleans* (1950); *West Point Story* (1950); *Rich, Young and Pretty* (1951); *Double Dynamite* (1951); *She's Working Her Way Through College* (1952); *Because You're Mine* (1952); *April in Paris* (1952); *Peter Pan* (1953); *Small Town Girl* (1953); *Three Sailors and a Girl* (1953); *You're Never Too Young* (1955); *The Court Jester* (1956); *Meet Me in Las Vegas* (1956); *Serenade* (1956); *Pardners* (1956); *The Opposite Sex* (1956); *Ten Thousand Bedrooms* (1957); *This Could Be the Night* (1957); *The Joker Is Wild* (1957); *Paris Holiday* (1958); *Rock-a-Bye Baby* (1958); *Say One for Me* (1959); *A Hole in the Head* (1959);

Journey to the Center of the Earth (1959); *Ocean's Eleven* (1960); *Let's Make Love* (1960); *High Time* (1960); *Boys' Night Out* (1962); *The Road to Hong Kong* (1962); *Papa's Delicate Condition* (1963); *Come Blow Your Horn* (1963); *Honeymoon Hotel* (1964); *Robin and the 7 Hoods* (1964); *The Pleasure Seekers* (1964); *Thoroughly Modern Millie* (1967); *The Bobo* (1967); *The Great Bank Robbery* (1969); *Journey Back to Oz* (1974); *Whiffs* (1975); *The Duchess and the Dirtwater Fox* (1976); *The Stud* (U.K., 1978; U.S., 1980); *Heidi's Song* (1982). **MUSICALS/REVUES** (dates refer to N.Y. openings): *High Button Shoes* (Oct. 9, 1947); *Skyscraper* (Nov. 13, 1965); *Walking Happy* (Nov. 26, 1966); *Look to the Lilies* (March 29, 1970); *Words and Music* (April 16, 1974). **TELEVISION:** *Our Town* (Sept. 9, 1955); *Jack and the Beanstalk* (Feb. 26, 1967); *The Night the Animals Talked* (1971); *Saturday Night* (1977).

WRITINGS: *I Should Care: The S. C. Story* (N.Y., 1974); *The Songwriter's Rhyming Dictionary* (N.Y., 1983); *S. C. Songbook* (1986); *The New S. C. Songbook* (1989); *S. C.'s Rhyming Dictionary* (1995).—**WR**

Caiazza, Nick (actually, **Nicholas**), tenor saxophonist, clarinetist; b. New Castle, Pa., March 20, 1914; d. Melrose, Mass., Dec. 1981. He received his first musical instruction from Ralph Gaspare. He left home in 1932, toured the Middle West with the Keystone Serenaders. He toured with Joe Haymes in 1936–37; worked with Muggsy Spanier Ragtimers (Nov.–Dec. 1939), then with Woody Herman (early 1940), before joining Will Bradley-Ray McKinley Band. He worked at Nick's with Bobby Hackett (late 1940), then stinted with Dick Roger's Band before joining the Muggsy Spanier Big Band from April 1941. He left during spring 1942; was briefly with Teddy Powell, then with Alvino Rey until touring with the Chico Marx Band in summer 1943. During 1944 and 1945 he made many 'V' Disc recordings with Louis Armstrong, Jack Teagarden, Hot Lips Page, and others. He worked as radio staff musician from the mid-1940s. From 1950 until 1959 he was on Paul Whiteman's ABC studio staff; during this period he also worked with Tommy Dorsey, Ray McKinley, Benny Goodman, and Billy Butterfield; recorded with the N.Y. Philharmonic Orch. He studied composition with Paul Creston in N.Y.; in 1960 moved to Boston. Several of his extended compositions have been publicly performed. During the late 1960s he taught at the Berklee School of Music.—**JC/LP**

Cailliet, Lucien, exceptional French-born American composer, arranger, and conductor; b. Châlons-sur-Marne, May 22, 1891; d. Woodland Hills, Calif., Jan. 3, 1985. He gained experience as an instrumentalist and bandmaster in the French Army, and received training at the Dijon Cons. and from Fauchet, Caussade, and Pares at the Paris Cons. (graduated, 1913). In 1915 he emigrated to the U.S. and in 1923 became a naturalized citizen. In 1919 he joined the Philadelphia Orch. as a clarinetist, and also was active with it as an arranger (several of his arrangements appeared under Stokowski's cognomen, with the approval of Cailliet). He also taught at the Curtis Inst. of Music in Philadelphia. In 1937 he was awarded a doctorate in music by the Philadelphia Musical Academy. From 1938 to 1945 he taught orchestration, counterpoint, and conducting at the Univ. of Southern Calif. in Los Angeles. Between

1945 and 1957 he wrote some 25 film scores for Hollywood. He also made appearances as a guest conductor. From 1957 to 1976 he was educational and musical director of the G. Leblanc Corp. He prepared an orchestration of Mussorgsky's *Pictures at an Exhibition* (1937). Among his original works were *Memories of Stephen Foster* for Orch. (1935), *Variations on "Pop Goes the Weasel"* for Orch. (1938), band music, and clarinet pieces. For a complete list of his works, see L. Fisher, "L. C.: His Contribution to the Symphonic Band, Orchestra, and Ensemble Literature," *Journal of Band Research*, XVIII/2 (1983).—NS/LK/DM

Cain, Jackie (actually, **Jacqueline Ruth**), jazz singer; b. Milwaukee, Wisc., May 22, 1928. Her family moved to Chicago when she was a youngster; she began performing while still in high school, studying voice with Don Maya in 1947–48. Since 1947 she has worked in duet with pianist/vocalist Roy Kral (b. Chicago, Ill., Oct. 10, 1921), as Jackie and Roy. They first met while both were performing in George Davis's group, and then worked with Charlie Ventura (1948–49). She married Kral in 1949; they then led their own small groups. Together, they have co-authored a number of popular songs, with Cain writing lyrics to Kral's melodies.—LP

Cairns, David (Adam), distinguished English music critic and writer on music; b. Loughton, Essex, June 8, 1926. He was educated at Trinity Coll., Oxford, and was the Jane Eliza Procter Fellow at Princeton Univ. in 1950–51. From 1958 to 1962 he was music critic of the *Evening Standard* and of the *Spectator*. After serving as arts ed. of the latter (1961–62), he was asst. music critic of the *Financial Times* (1962–67) and music critic of the *New Statesman* (1967–70). From 1968 to 1973 he was classical music program coordinator for Philips Records. He was a freelance music critic from 1973 to 1985. In 1985 he was Distinguished Visiting Prof. at the Univ. of Calif. at Davis. In 1985 he became music critic of the *Sunday Times*. In 1992 he was a visiting scholar at the Getty Center for the History of Art and Humanities, and in 1993 a visiting resident fellow at Merton Coll., Oxford. He was made a Chevalier (1975) and an Officier (1991) of l'Ordre des Arts et des Lettres of France, and in 1997 he was made a Commander of the Order of the British Empire. Cairns is an authority on Berlioz. He tr. Berlioz's *Les Soirées de l'orchestre* (1963), ed. and tr. Berlioz's memoirs (1969; 4th ed., 1990), and publ. a valuable biography of Berlioz (two vols., 1989, 2000). He also publ. *Responses: Musical Essays and Reviews* (1973).—NS/LK/DM

Calabro, Louis, American composer, conductor, and teacher; b. N.Y., Nov. 1, 1926; d. Bennington, Vt., Oct. 21, 1991. He studied with Persichetti at the Juilliard School of Music in N.Y. (graduated, 1952; postgraduate diploma, 1953). From 1955 he taught at Bennington (Vt.) Coll. He also was founder-conductor of the Sage City Sym. in North Bennington from 1971. He received Guggenheim fellowships in 1954 and 1959, NEA fellowships in 1973 and 1976, and the Vt. Governor's Award

for the Arts in 1991. His autobiography, *Cosmos: A Life* (1986), remains unpublished.

WORKS: ORCH.: Concerto Grosso (1950); *Statement* (1951); Piano Concerto (1953); 3 syms. (1956–62); Triple Concerto for 3 Cellos and Orch. (1971); *Young Pianist's Concertino* (1972); *Threnody* for Strings (1973); *Invention* for Band (1975); *Eos* for English Horn and Strings (1977); *The Paradisa Bird* for Orch. and Narrator (1983); Double Concerto for Viola, Cello, and Orch. (1986); Fugue for Strings (1991). **CHAMBER:** Trio for Clarinet, Cello, and Piano (1949); Trio for Violin, Cello, and Piano (1952); Violin Sonata (1953); 2 string quartets (1954, 1968); *Bodas de Sangre* for Chamber Group (1955); Sonata for Solo Cello (1956); *Dynamogeny* for Viola and Piano (1958); *Co- Instances: Music without Order* for Chamber Group (1958; rev. 1978); *Environments* for Brass Choir (1969); *Memoirs—Part 1* for Bassoon and Percussion (1973); *Music for Folks* for 4 Cellos (1975); *Rare Birds* for Flute and Narrator (1976); *Kusehani* for Chamber Group (1976); *10 Lyric Duets* for Flute (1977); *Epiphany* for 12 Cellos (1978); *13 Ways of Looking at a Tone Row*, trio for Flute, Clarinet, and Viola (1985); Double Bass Duo (1985); *Isoquinto*, woodwind quintet (1986); *Sonata Fantasia* for Tuba and Piano (1987); *Antiphon Ritmico* for 8 Cellos (1988); *More Music for Folks* for 4 Cellos (1988); *Sonata India* for Cello and Percussion (1990); *Variations* for Viola (1990). **KEYBOARD: Piano:** Sonata (1954); *Diversities* (1966); *Variations* (1968); *Finneganations* (1981); *3 Dances* for 2 Pianos (1986); *Hanon Sampler* (1991). **VOCAL:** *Dada Cantatadada*, oratorio for Blues Singer and Orch. (1964); *Epitaphs* for Chorus and Orch. (1967); *Latitude 15.09 N* for Chorus and Orch. (1970); *The Floods Are Risen* for Chorus and Small Orch. (1973); *Voyage* for Chorus and Orch. (1975); *Lunarlied* for Chorus and Orch. (1976); *Missa Brevis* for Chorus and String Orch. (1983); *Primavera* for Chorus, Children's Chorus, and Piano (1987); *7 Deadly Modes* for Chorus and Piano (1991); songs.—NS/LK/DM

Caldara, Antonio, important Italian composer; b. Venice, c. 1670; d. Vienna, Dec. 28, 1736. He was a choirboy under Giovanni Legrenzi at San Marco in Venice, where he received training in composition, viola da gamba, cello, and keyboard playing. In 1699 he became maestro di cappella da chiesa a dal teatro to the Duke of Mantua, where he had the opportunity to hone his skills as a dramatic composer. In 1708 he went to Rome, where his Lenten oratorio *Il martirio di S. Caterina* was given at the palace of Cardinal Ottoboni. Following a sojourn in Spain, where his *Il più bel nome* (Barcelona, Aug. 2, 1708) was the first Italian opera to be performed in that country, he returned to Rome as maestro di cappella to prince Rusopoli. During this time, Caldara's Venetian style was refined to embrace galant modes of expression. In 1716 he was called to Vienna to serve as vice-Kapellmeister under Fux at the court, where he concentrated much of his compositional energies on the creation of operas. His style was further refined to a greater use of contrapuntal writing. Caldara was a prolific composer of vocal music, producing some 3,400 works, with his historical significance resting mainly upon his contributions to the development of opera and oratorio.

WORKS: DRAMATIC (all are drammi per musica and were 1st perf. in Vienna unless otherwise given): *L'Argene*, trattenimento per musica (Venice, 1689); *Il Tirsi*, drama pastorale (Venice, 1696; in collaboration with others); *La promessa serbata al primo* (Venice, 1697); *L'ingratitudine gastigata* (Venice,

1698?); *L'oracolo in sogno* (Mantua, June 6, 1699; Act 2 by A. Quintavalle and Act 3 by C.F. Pollarolo); *La Partenope* (Mantua, May 1701; rev. Ferrara, May 1709); Opera pastorale (Manuta, 1701; rev. as the drama pastorale *La costanza in amor vince l'inganno*, Rome, Feb. 9, 1711); *Farnace* (Venice, 1703); *Gli equivoci del sembiante* (Casale, 1703); *Paride sull'Ida, overo Gl'amori di Paride con Enone*, favola pastorale (Mantua, 1704); *L'Arminio* (Genoa, Carnival 1705); *Il selvaggio eroe*, tragicomedia eroico-pastorale (Venice, Nov. 20, 1707); *Il più bel nome*, componimento da camera (Barcelona, Aug. 2, 1708); *Sofonisba* (Venice, 1708); *L'inimico generoso* (Bologna, May 11, 1709); *Il nome più glorioso*, componimento da camera (Barcelona, Nov. 4, 1709); *L'Atenaide* (1709; Act 1 by A.S. Fiorè and Act 3 by Gasparini; rev. as *Teodosio ed Eudossa*, Braunschweig, Sept. 12, 1716; in collaboration with Fux and Gasparini); *L'Anagilda, o vero La fede ne' tradimenti* (Rome, Jan. 4, 1711); *Giunio Bruto, overo La caduta de' Tarquinii* (1711; not perf.; Act 1 by C.F. Cesarini and Act 3 by A. Scarlatti); *Tito e Berenice* (Rome, Carnival 1714); *L'Atenaide* (Nov. 19, 1714; Act 1 by M.A. Ziani and Act 2 by A. Negri); *Il giubilo della salza*, festa (Salzburg, 1716); *Il maggior grande*, componimento per musica da camera (Oct. 1, 1716); *Pipa e Barlafuso*, intermezzo (Nov. 19, 1716); *Caio Marzio Coriolano* (Aug. 28, 1717); *Il Tiridate, overo La verità nell'inganno* (Nov. 11, 1717); *Ifigenia in Aulide* (Nov. 5, 1718); *Sirita* (Aug. 21, 1719); *Dafne*, dramma pastorale (Salzburg, Oct. 4?, 1719); *Lucio Papirio dittatore* (Nov. 4, 1719); *Apollo in cielo*, componimento da camera (Nov. 4, 1720); *Psiche*, componimento da camera (Nov. 19, 1720; in collaboration with Fux); *Gli eccessi dell'infedeltà* (Salzburg, 1720); *L'inganno tradito dall'amore* (Salzburg, 1720); *Il germanico Marte* (Salzburg, Oct. 4, 1721); *Ormisda, re di Persia* (Nov. 4, 1721); *Nitocri* (Aug. 30, 1722); *Camaide, imperatore della China, overo Li figliuoli rivali del padre* (Salzburg, Oct. 4?, 1722); *Scipione nelle Spagne* (Nov. 4, 1722); *La contesa de' numi*, servigio di camera (Prague, Oct. 1, 1723); *La concordia de' pianetti*, componimento teatrale (Nov. 19, 1723); *Euristeo* (May 16, 1724); *Andromaca* (Aug. 28, 1724); *Giangiur, imperatore del Mogol* (Nov. 4, 1724); *Il finto Policare*, tragicommedia per musica (Salzburg, 1724); *Semiramide in Ascalone* (Aug. 28, 1725); *Astarto* (Salzburg, Oct. 4, 1725); *Il Venceslao* (Nov. 4, 1725); *Amalasunta* (Jaroměřice?, 1726); *I due dittatori* (Nov. 4, 1726); *L'Etearco* (Slzburg, 1726); *Don Chisciotte in corte della duchessa*, opera serioridicola (Feb. 6, 1727); *Imeneo*, pastorale (Aug. 28, 1727); *Ornospade* (Nov. 4, 1727); *La verità nell'inganno, ossia Arsinoe* (Salzburg, Nov. 15, 1727); *La forza dell'amicizia, ovvero Pilade ed Oreste* (Graz, Aug. 17, 1728; Act 1 by G. Reutter); *Amor non ha legge*, favola pastorale (Jaroměřice, 1728); *Mitridate* (Nov. 4, 1728); *I disingannati*, commedia per musica (Feb. 8, 1729); *Enone*, pastorale (Aug. 28, 1734); *Caio Fabbrizio* (Nov. 13, 1729); *Sancio Pansa, governatore dell'isola Barattaria*, commedia per musica (1730; rev. Jan. 27, 1733); *La pazienza di Socrate con due mogli*, scherzo drammatico (Jan. 17, 1731; in collaboration with G. Reutter); *Il Demetrio* (Nov. 4, 1731); *Livia*, festa teatrale (Nov. 19, 1731); *L'asilo d'amore*, festa teatrale (Linz, Aug. 28, 1732); *Adriano in Siria* (Nov. 9, 1732); *L'olimpiade* (Aug. 30, 1733); *Demofoonte* (Nov. 4, 1733); *La clemenza di Tito* (Nov. 4, 1734); *Le cinesi*, componimento drammatico (Carnival 1735); *Il natale di Minerva Tritonia*, festa per musica (Aug. 28, 1735); *Scipione Africano il maggiore*, festa di camera (Nov. 4, 1735); *Achille in Sciro* (Feb. 13, 1736); *Ciro riconosciuto* (Aug. 28, 1736); *Il Temistocle* (Nov. 4, 1736). **OTHER:** Over 40 oratorios (1697–1735); masses; mass sections; cantatas; motets; Psalms; vespers; hymns; antiphons; canons; madrigals; (12) *Suonata a 3* for 2 Violins, Cello, and Organ (Venice, 1693); (12) *Suonate da camera* for 2 Violins and Basso Continuo (Venice, 1699).

BIBL.: L. Posthorn, *A. C.s Instrumental-Musik* (diss., Univ. of Vienna, 1920); M. Barnes, *The Trio Sonatas of A. C.* (diss., Fla. State Univ., 1960); E. Fissinger, *Selected Sacred Works of A. C.* (diss., Univ. of Ill., 1965); U. Kirkendale, *A. C.: Sein Leben und seine venezianische- römischen Oratorien* (Graz, 1966); J. Wagner, *The Keyboard Works of A. C.* (diss., Washington Univ., St. Lous, 1966); U. Kirkendale, *A. C.: La vita* (Florence, 1971); B. Pritchard, ed., *A. C.: Essays on His Life and Times* (London, 1987). —NS/LK/DM

Caldwell, Happy (actually, **Albert W.**), jazz tenor saxophonist, clarinetist; b. Chicago, Ill., July 25, 1903; d. N.Y., Dec. 29, 1978. He attended Wendell Phillips H.S. in Chicago and studied pharmacy. He took up clarinet in 1919. He played clarinet in Eighth Ill. Regimental Band; after Army service he took lessons from his cousin, Buster Bailey. He returned to studies until 1922, then joined Bernie Young's Band in Chicago; made his first records with Young in 1923 ("Dearborn Street Blues"), and began doubling tenor c. 1923. He toured in Mamie Smith's Jazz Hounds, then remained in N.Y. (1924). After a summer season at Asbury Park, he joined Bobby Brown's Syncopators (1924). In April 1925 he worked with Elmer Snowden and other leaders. He was with Willie Gant's Ramblers (summer 1926); worked with Cliff Jackson, and toured with Keep Shufflin' revue (early 1927). He was with Arthur Gibbs' Orch. (summer 1927–summer 1928), recorded with Louis Armstrong (1929); also worked with Elmer Snowden again, Charlie Johnson, Fletcher Henderson, and others through the early 1930s. He played regularly with Vernon Andrade's Orch. (1929–33). He was with Tiny Bradshaw (1934) and Louis Metcalfe (1935), then led his own band, mainly in N.Y. He recorded with Jelly Roll Morton (1939), and with Willie Gant (1940). After leading his Happy Pals at Minton's in early 1941, he moved to Philadelphia for three years; occasionally led his own band, but also worked with Eugene "Lonnie" Slappy and his Swingsters and Charlie Gaines. He returned to N.Y. in January 1945. He was active with own band throughout the 1950s and 1960s; also gigged with Louis Metcalf and Jimmy Rushing. He took a day job as custodian at N.Y.'s City Coll. in the early 1970s, but continued to gig locally. He toured Scandinavia in 1975. His name was sometimes misspelled as "Cauldwell."—JC/LP

Caldwell, Sarah, remarkable American conductor and operatic impresario; b. Maryville, Mo., March 6, 1924. She studied at the Univ. of Ark. and at Hendrix Coll., and then was a violin pupil of Richard Burgin at the New England Cons. of Music in Boston. She also studied viola with Georges Fourel at the Berkshire Music Center in Tanglewood (summer, 1946), where she returned in 1947 to stage Vaughan Williams's *Riders to the Sea*. After studying with and serving as assistant to Boris Goldovsky, she was head of the Boston Univ. opera workshop (1952–60). In 1958 she founded the Boston Opera Group, which became the Opera Co. of Boston in 1965, which played a prominent role in the musical life of the city for some 25 years, disbanding in 1991. In addition to standard operatic fare, Caldwell conducted the U.S. stage premieres of such modern operas as Schoenberg's *Moses und Aron* (Nov. 30, 1966), Prokofiev's *War and Peace* (May 8, 1974), Sessions's *Montezuma* (March 31, 1976), and Tippett's *The Ice Break* (May 18, 1979). She also was the first woman to conduct at the Metropolitan Opera in N.Y. (*La Traviata*, Jan. 13, 1976). She returned to the Metropolitan Opera in 1978 to conduct *L'Elisir d'Amore*. She also appeared as a guest conductor with various U.S. orchs. In 1999 she became a prof. at the Univ. of Ark. at Fayetteville.—NS/LK/DM

Calegari, Antonio, Italian organist, conductor, music theorist, and composer; b. Padua, Feb. 17, 1757; d. there, July 22, 1828. He studied with Scalabrin and Betoni in Venice; was active as a composer there and in Padua. He was a conductor at the Teatro Nuovo in Padua (c. 1790–96), then was made organist (1801) and maestro di cappella (1814) at the church of S. Antonio there. He brought out three operas in Venice: *Le Sorelle rivali* (1784), *L'amor soldato* (1786), and *Il matrimonio scoperto* (1789); the authorship of all three is dubious, the last perhaps attributable to Luigi Caligari. Antonio Calegari publ. a curious treatise on composition, *Gioco pittagorico musicale* (Venice, 1801), which was republ. in Paris, during his residence there, as *L'Art de composer la musique sans en connaître les éléments* (1802). A harmonic system, *Sistema armonico* (1829), and a vocal method, *Modi generali del canto* (1836), were publ. posth. —NS/LK/DM

Calegari, Francesco Antonio, Italian composer, music theorist, and teacher; b. Venice, 1656; d. there, Nov. 12, 1742. After taking his vows as a Franciscan at the Palma del Friuli convent in Venice, he obtained his bachelor's degree at the Franciscan seminary in Assisi and then studied counterpoint with Lotti. He was maestro di cappella at S. Francesco in Bologna (1700–01), S. maria Gloriosa dei Frari in Venice (1701–03; 1727–42), and the basilica of S. Antonio in Padua (1703–27). Calegari wrote much sacred music and several treatises, the most important being *Ampla dimonstrazione degli armoniali musicali tuoni* (1732), which concerns dissonance in figured basses.

BIBL.: W. Schutt, *F.A. C. (d. 1742): Music Theorist and Composer* (diss., Catholic Univ. of America, 1969).—LK/DM

Callas, Maria (real name, **Maria Anna Sofia Cecilia Kalogeropoulos**), celebrated American soprano; b. N.Y., Dec. 3, 1923; d. Paris, Sept. 16, 1977. Her father was a Greek immigrant. The family returned to Greece when she was 13. She studied voice at the Royal Academy of Music in Athens with Elvira de Hidalgo, and made her debut as Santuzza in the school production of *Cavalleria rusticana* in Nov. 1938. Her first professional appearance was in a minor role in Suppe's *Boccaccio* at the Royal Opera in Athens when she was 16; her first major role, as Tosca, was there in July 1942. She returned to N.Y. in 1945. Callas auditioned for the Metropolitan Opera and was offered a contract, but decided instead to go to Italy, where she made her operatic debut in the title role of *La Gioconda* (Verona, Aug. 3, 1947). She was encouraged in her career by Tullio Serafin, who engaged her to sing Isolde and Aida

in various Italian productions. In 1951 she became a member of La Scala in Milan. She was greatly handicapped by her absurdly excessive weight (210 lbs.); by a supreme effort of will, she slimmed down to 135 pounds; with her classical Greek profile and penetrating eyes, she made a striking impression on the stage; in the tragic role of Medea in Cherubini's opera she mesmerized the audience by her dramatic representation of pity and terror. Some critics opined that she lacked a true bel canto quality in her voice and that her technique was defective in coloratura, but her power of interpretation was such that she was soon acknowledged to be one of the greatest dramatic singers of the century. Her personal life was as tempestuous as that of any prima donna of the bygone era. In 1949 she married the Italian industrialist Giovanni Battista Meneghini, who became her manager, but they separated ten years later. Her romance with the Greek shipping magnate Aristotle Onassis was a recurrent topic of sensational gossip. Given to outbursts of temper, she made newspaper headlines when she walked off the stage following some altercation, or failed to appear altogether at scheduled performances, but her eventual return to the stage was all the more eagerly welcomed by her legion of admirers. After leaving La Scala in 1958, she returned there from 1960 to 1962. She also sang at London's Covent Garden (1952–53; 1957–59; 1964), in Chicago (1954–56), and Dallas (1958–59). Perhaps the peak of her success was her brilliant debut at the Metropolitan Opera in N.Y. as Norma on Oct. 29, 1956. Following a well-publicized disagreement with its management, she quit the company only to reach an uneasy accommodation with it to return as Violetta on Feb. 6, 1958; that same year she left the company again, returning in 1965 to sing Tosca before abandoning the operatic stage altogether. In 1971–72 she gave a seminar on opera at the Juilliard School in N.Y., which was enthusiastically received. In 1974 she gave her last public performances in a series of concerts with Giuseppe di Stefano. She died of a heart attack in her Paris apartment. Her body was cremated and her ashes scattered on the Aegean Sea. Callas was nothing short of a phenomenon, one whose popularity has only increased with time. One radio commentator's characterization of Callas was that "If an orgasm could sing, it would sound like Maria Callas." She excelled particularly in roles by Rossini, Bellini, Donizetti, and Verdi.

BIBL.: E. Gara and R. Hauert, *M. C.* (Geneva, 1957; Eng. tr., 1958); E. Callas, *My Daughter M. C.* (N.Y., 1960); G. Jellinek, *C.: Portrait of a Prima Donna* (N.Y., 1960; 2nd ed., 1986); S. Galatopoulos, *C.—La Divina: Art That Conceals Art* (London, 1963; 3rd ed., rev. and aug., 1976, as *C.: Prima donna assoluta*); J. Ardoin and G. Fitzgerald, *C* (N.Y., 1974); H. Wisneski, *M. C.: The Art Behind the Music* (N.Y., 1975); J. Ardoin, *The C. Legacy: The Complete Guide to Her Recordings* (N.Y., 1977; 2nd ed., rev., 1982; new ed., 1991); P.-J. Rémy, *M. C.: A Tribute* (N.Y., 1978); S. Linakis, *Diva: The Life and Death of M. C.* (Englewood Cliffs, N.J., 1980); C. Verga, *M. C.: Mito e malinconia* (Rome, 1980); C. Chiarelli, *M. C.: Vita, immagini, parole, musica* (Venice, 1981); G. Menghini, *M. C. mia moglie* (Milan, 1981; Eng. tr., 1982); A. Stassinopoulos, *M. C.: The Woman Behind the Legend* (N.Y., 1981); D. Lowe, ed., *C., as They Saw Her* (N.Y., 1986); R. La Rochelle, *C.: La diva et le vinyle* (Montreal, 1987); N. Stancioff, *M. C. Remem-*

bered (N.Y., 1987); J. Callas, *Sisters: A Revealing Portrait of the World's Most Famous Diva* (London and N.Y., 1989); J. Kesting, *M. D.* (Düsseldorf, 1990; Eng. tr., 1993); R. Allegri, *La vera storia di M. C.: Con documenti inediti* (Milan, 1991); A. Petrolli, *La divina C.: Vita ed arte* (Trento, 1991); M. Di Stefano, *C. nemica mia* (Milan, 1992); M. Scott, *M.M. C.* (Boston, 1992); E. Kanthou, *M. C.* (Wilhelmshaven, 1993); F. Rohmer, *C.: Gesichter eines Mediums* (Munich, 1993); B. Tosi, *Casta diva: L'incomparable C.* (Parma, 1993); D. Lelait, *M. C.: J'ai vécu d'art, j'ai vécu d'amour* (Paris, 1997); D. Bret, *M. C.: The Tigress and the Lamb* (N.Y., 1998); S. Galatopoulos, *M. C.: Sacred Monster* (N.Y., 1999).—**NS/LK/DM**

Callaway, Paul (Smith), American organist and conductor; b. Atlanta, Ill., Aug. 16, 1909; d. March 21, 1995. After attending Westminster Coll. in Fulton, Mo. (1927–29), he studied organ with Noble in N.Y. (1930–35), with Sowerby in Chicago (1936), and with Dupré in Paris. He was organist and choirmaster at St. Thomas's Chapel in N.Y. (1930–35) and at St. Mark's Chapel in Grand Rapids (1935–39); then was organist and music director of the Cathedral Church of St. Peter and St. Paul in Washington, D.C. (1939–42; 1946–77). He also was music director of the Opera Soc. of Washington, D.C. (1956–57) and of the Lake George Opera Festival in Glens Falls, N.Y. (1967–77).—**NS/LK/DM**

Callcott, John Wall, English organist and composer; b. London, Nov. 20, 1766; d. Bristol, May 15, 1821. Early in life he developed a particular talent for composing glees and catches. He won three prize medals at a contest of the Catch Club of London (1785) for his catch *O Beauteous Fair*, a canon, *Blessed Is He*, and a glee, *Dull Repining Sons of Care*. He received his Mus.Bac. and Mus.Doc. from the Univ. Oxford (1785, 1800). He was a co-founder of the Glee Club (1787). During Haydn's visit to London in 1791, Callcott took a few lessons with him and wrote a sym. in imitation of his style. His mind gave way from overwork on a projected biographical dictionary of musicians, and he was institutionalized just before he reached the quirky letter Q. He recovered, but not sufficiently to continue his work, and was released in 1812. In addition to numerous glees, catches, and canons, he wrote *A Musical Grammar* (London, 1806), a standard elementary textbook that went through numerous eds. in England and America. A three-vol. collection of glees, catches, and canons, with a biographical memoir, was publ. posthumously by his son-in-law, William Horsley (London, 1824). —**NS/LK/DM**

Callender, Red (actually, **George Sylvester**), famed jazz bassist, tuba player; b. Haynesville, Va., March 6, 1916; d. Los Angeles, Calif., March 8, 1992. He learned to play several instruments while a student. At 15 he worked with Banjo Bernie's Band; he moved to Calif. in the mid-1930s. He was with Louis Armstrong in Los Angeles (November 1937), subsequently with Nat "King" Cole and various bands in Calif. During this time he had long spells of studio work, and led his own trio at Suzi-Q Club in Hollywood. He worked in Lee and Lester Young's band in 1941–42 in Los Angeles. He was with Errol Garner's Trio (late 1946), Johnny Otis

(1947), then led his own band in Hawaii until 1950. He returned to Hollywood, spent two years with Jerry Fielding, then had extensive freelance work in film, TV, and recording studios, occasionally leading small groups through the 1950s and 1960s. His 1954 album, *Red Callender Speaks Low,* was a landmark in jazz recording in its emphasis on the bass as a solo instrument. During the 1970s, he toured Europe with the Legends of Jazz tour in 1978 and 1979. He founded the group Wind Coll. in Los Angeles in the 1980s. He remained active composing, teaching, and performing until a year before his death.

DISC.: *Red Callender Speaks Low* (1954); *Swingin' Suite* (1956); *Lowest* (1958); *Night Mist Blues* (1984).

WRITINGS: R. Callender and E. Cohen, *Unfinished Dream* (London, 1985).—**JC/LP**

Calligaris, Sergio, Argentine-born Italian pianist, teacher, and composer; b. Rosario, Jan. 22, 1941. He commenced piano lessons with Domingo Scarafia and began touring when he was 13. In 1964 he became a student of Arthur Loesser at the Cleveland Inst. of Music (artist's diploma, 1966), where he also taught, and then completed his training with Guido Agosti at the Accademia di Santa Cecilia in Rome. In 1969 he became a teacher of piano at Calif. State Univ. in Los Angeles. In 1973 he founded the American Academy of the Arts in Verona, serving as its first artistic director. In 1974 he became a naturalized Italian citizen and began teaching at the Cons. of San Pietro a Majello in Naples. From 1977 he taught at the Alfredo Casella Cons. in L'Aquila. His playing is distinguished by a Romantic elan and virtuoso technique. As a composer, he blends Romantic and post-Romantic styles into a thoroughly contemporary idiom.

WORKS: ORCH.: Concerto for Strings (1989); *Danze Sinfoniche: Omaggio a Bellini* (Catania, Oct. 4, 1990); Piano Concerto (1992); *Toccata, Adagio, and Fugue* for Strings (L'Aquila, Oct. 8, 1997); Double Concerto for Violin, Piano, and Strings (1997). **CHAMBER:** *Tema e Sete Variazioni,* trio for Oboe or Violin, Bassoon or Cello, and Harpsichord or Piano (1958; rev. 1976); Cello Sonata (1978); Suite for Cello and Harpsichord or Piano (1981); *Suite Classica* for Flute or Violin and Piano (1983); *Suite da Requiem No. 1* for Violin, Horn, and Piano (1984) and *No. 2* for 2 Pianos, 4 Timpani ad libitum, and Chorus ad libitum (1985); Suite for Cello (1991); Clarinet Sonata (1997). **KEYBOARD: Piano:** *Scherzo* (1957); *Siciliana* (1977); *Il quaderno pianistico di Renzo* (1978); *24 studi* (1978–80); *Scene coreografiche* for Piano Duet or 2 Pianos (1979); *Preludio, Sarabanda, and Finale* (1980); *Passacaglia* for 3 Pianos, after Bach (1983); *BHS,* divertimento on music by Bach, Handel, and Scarlatti for 2 Pianos and Women's Voices ad libitum (1984–85); *Vivaldiana,* divertimento on themes by Vivaldi for 2 Pianos (1986); *Due danze concertanti* for 2 Pianos (1986). **OTHER:** Various vocal pieces.—**NS/LK/DM**

Calloway, Blanche, jazz singer, leader, sister of **Cab Calloway;** b. Baltimore, Md., 1902; d. there, Dec. 16, 1978. She was featured at N.Y.'s Ciro Club during the mid-1920s, then did extensive touring with traveling revues and played residencies in Chicago. She fronted Andy Kirk's Band for residency at Pearl Theatre, Philadelphia (1931); from then on led her own touring band until September 1938, when bankruptcy (filed under married name of Blanche Calloway Pinder) forced her to disband. She worked as a solo artist for several years. During the early 1960s, she was the director of a Fla. radio station.—**JC/LP**

Calloway, Cab(ell III), flamboyant American singer, bandleader, and songwriter; b. Rochester, N.Y., Dec. 25, 1907; d. Greenburgh, N.Y., Nov. 18, 1994. Calloway was an exuberant entertainer whose dancing and mugging tended to overshadow his abilities as a singer and bandleader, though he scored a series of hits, especially in the 1930s, and fronted a worthy jazz ensemble, especially in the 1940s. Primarily a live performer, he also had a successful career in films and on the legitimate stage. Among his biggest hits were "Minnie the Moocher" and "(Hep-Hep!) The Jumpin' Jive."

Calloway was the son of Cabell Calloway II, a lawyer, and Eulalia Reed Calloway, a teacher. In his youth, the family moved to Baltimore, and he was a boy soprano in the church choir, later singing in the Baltimore Melody Boys, a quartet. The family moved to Chicago, and he had a band while attending Douglass H.S., from which he graduated in 1927. He enrolled as a pre-law student at Crane Coll. in Chicago but began to appear in the all-black revue *Plantation Days* at the Loop Theatre with his older sister Blanche, herself a singer and bandleader. He also worked as a relief drummer and master of ceremonies at the Sunset Café. In 1928 he began singing with and fronting the band the Alabamians.

Also in 1928, Calloway entered into a common-law marriage with Wenonah Conacher; they had a daughter. He later married a second woman, with whom he adopted a second daughter. In 1942 he met a woman named Nuffie, with whom he fathered two more daughters, Chris and Lael, before arranging a divorce from his wife and marrying Nuffie in 1949. They had a third daughter, Cabella. Both Chris and Lael Calloway became performers and appeared with their father.

In the fall of 1928, Calloway went to N.Y. and worked with the band the Missourians. Back in Chicago in April 1929, he and the Alabamians appear at the Merry Gardens. But he returned to N.Y. and appeared in the all-black Broadway revue *Hot Chocolates*, which opened June 20 and ran 228 performances. In October he and the Alabamians appeared in N.Y. at the Savoy Ballroom, but the group broke up after the unsuccessful engagement. Acquiring Irving Mills of the Mills Music publishing company as his manager, Calloway returned to the Missourians and reorganized them. Recording for Brunswick as the Jungle Band, they scored their first hit in December 1930 with "St. Louis Blues" (music and lyrics by W. C. Handy).

In February 1931, as Cab Calloway and His Orch., the group headlined at the Cotton Club, replacing Duke Ellington. On March 9 they recorded "Minnie the Moocher" (music and lyrics by Calloway, Mills, and Clarence Gaskill, based on the traditional song "Willy the Weeper"); it became a best-seller in April and was Calloway's signature song from then on. Calloway continued to appear at the Cotton Club regularly

throughout the 1930s, and his major hits of the period, many of them featured in the club's revues, included "St. James Infirmary" (music and lyrics by Joe Primrose; 1931), "Kickin' the Gong Around" (music by Harold Arlen, lyrics by Ted Koehler; 1931), "Trickeration" (music by Arlen, lyrics by Koehler; 1931), "Minnie the Moocher's Wedding Day" (music by Arlen, lyrics by Koehler; 1932), "Moon Glow" (music and lyrics by Will Hudson, Eddie DeLange, and Irving Mills; 1934), and "Chinese Rhythm" (1934). In 1939 he scored a million-seller with "(Hep-Hep!) The Jumpin' Jive" (music and lyrics by Calloway, Jack Palmer, and Frank Froeba). He also appeared in the films *The Big Broadcast* (1932), *International House* (1933), *The Singing Kid* (1936), and *Manhattan Merry-Go-Round* (1937).

In the 1940s, Calloway led a celebrated band anchored by such notable instrumentalists as Dizzy Gillespie, Chu Berry, and Milt Hinton. He reached the Top Ten of the pop charts in March 1942 with "Blues in the Night" (music by Arlen, lyrics by Johnny Mercer) and the Top Ten of the R&B charts in February 1946 with "The Honeydripper" (music and lyrics by Joe Liggins), and he appeared in the films *Stormy Weather* (1943) and *Sensations of 1945* (1944).

The decline of the Swing Era forced Calloway to break up his big band in April 1948, though he reformed it on a temporary basis for specific engagements. For the most part he led bands ranging in size from four to seven pieces for the next several years. In June 1952 he was cast in a touring production of *Porgy and Bess* that played in the U.S. and Europe for more than two years, finishing in August 1954. He appeared in the W. C. Handy film biography *St. Louis Blues* in 1958, in the film *The Cincinnati Kid* in 1965, in an all-black replacement cast in the Broadway musical *Hello, Dolly!* in 1967, and in the Broadway revue *Bubbling Brown Sugar* in the late 1970s. He continued to record occasionally, and last reached the R&B charts with a rerecording of "Minnie the Moocher" in 1978.

Calloway made his final film appearance in *The Blues Brothers* in 1980 but remained active until shortly before his death following a stroke at age 86 in 1994.

DISC.: *Hi De Ho Man: Classics* (1974); *Cab Calloway and Co.* (1985); *Best of the Big Bands: Cab Calloway* (1990); *Best of the Big Bands: Cab Calloway Featuring Chu Berry* (1993); *Are You Hep to the Jive?: 22 Sensational Tracks* (1994); *Cocktail Hour: Cab Calloway and His Orchestra* (2000).

WRITINGS: *The New Cab Calloway's Hepsters Dictionary* (N.Y., 1944); with B. Rollins, *Of Minnie the Moocher and Me* (N.Y., 1976).—**WR**

Calvé (real name, **Calvet de Roquer**), **(Rosa-Noémie) Emma,** famous French soprano; b. Décazeville, Aveyron, Aug. 15, 1858; d. Millau, Jan. 6, 1942. She studied voice with Puget in Paris and with Marchesi and Laborde. She made her operatic debut as Marguerite in Gounod's *Faust* at the Théâtre Royal de la Monnaie in Brussels on Sept. 23, 1881; then sang at the Opéra-Comique in Paris 3 years later. She sang at La Scala in Milan and at other Italian opera houses from 1886; appeared at Covent Garden in London from 1892 to 1904. She made her American debut at the Metropolitan Opera in N.Y. as Santuzza on Nov. 29, 1893, and remained on its staff until 1904; her greatest role was that of Carmen. Subsequently she sang at the Manhattan Opera (1907–09), in Boston (1912), and in Nice (1914) before retiring from the operatic stage; she continued to give concerts until 1927. Her life was made the subject of a novel by Gustav Kobbé, *Signora, A Child of the Opera House* (N.Y., 1903). She publ. an autobiography, in Eng., *My Life* (N.Y., 1922); she later publ. an additional vol. of memoirs, *Sous tous les ciels j'ai chanté* (Paris, 1940).

BIBL.: A. Gallus, *E. C., Her Artistic Life* (N.Y., 1902). —NS/LK/DM

Calvisius, Sethus (real name, **Seth Kallwitz**), German music theorist; b. Feb. 21, 1556; d. Leipzig, Nov. 24, 1615. He supported himself while studying in the Gymnasia of Frankenhausen and Magdeburg, and the Univs. at Helmstadt and Leipzig. In Leipzig he became music director at the Paulinerkirche (1581). From 1582 to 1592 he was cantor at Schulpforta, then cantor of the Thomasschule at Leipzig, and in 1594 became music director at the Thomaskirche and Nicolaikirche there. Calvisius was not only a musician, but a scholar of high attainments. His writings are valuable sources: *Melopoeia seu melodiae condendae ratio* (1582; 2nd ed., 1592); *Compendium musicae practicae pro incipientibus* (1594; 3rd ed. as *Musicae artis praecepta nova et facillima*, 1612); *Harmoniae cantionum eccle siasticarum a M. Luthero et aliis viris piis Germaniae composi tarum 4 voc.* (1596); *Exercitationes musicae duae* (1600); *Auserlesene teutsche Lieder* (1603); *Exercitatio musicae tertia* (1611); *Biciniorum libri duo* (1612).—NS/LK/DM

Calvocoressi, Michel Dimitri, eminent Greek writer on music; b. Marseilles, Oct. 2, 1877; d. London, Feb. 1, 1944. He studied music in Paris, but was mostly autodidact; also pursued study in the social sciences. In 1914 he settled in London. He wrote music criticism and correspondences for French and other journals. He mastered the Russian language and became an ardent propagandist of Russian music; made excellent trs. into English and French of Russian and German songs. Among his books are *La Musique russe* (Paris, 1907); *The Principles and Methods of Musical Criticism* (London, 1923; rev. 1933); *Musical Taste and How to Form It* (London, 1925); *Musicians' Gallery: Music and Ballet in Paris and London* (London, 1933); also monographs on Liszt (Paris, 1906), Mussorgsky (Paris, 1908), Glinka (Paris, 1911), Schumann (Paris, 1912), and Debussy (London, 1941); a new extensive biography of Mussorgsky was posth. publ. (London, 1946). With G. Abraham, he publ. the valuable *Masters of Russian Music* (London, 1936).—NS/LK/DM

Calzabigi, Ranieri (Simone Francesco Maria) di, Italian poet and music theorist; b. Livorno, Dec. 23, 1714; d. Naples, July 1795. In 1750 he went to Paris, then proceeded to Brussels in 1760. From 1761 until 1772 he remained in Vienna, and was in Pisa by 1775. He engaged in polemics regarding the relative merits of French and Italian operas, lending energetic support to Gluck in his ideas of operatic reform. He

wrote for Gluck the libretti of *Orfeo, Alceste,* and *Paride ed Elena*. He publ. *Dissertazione su le poesie drammatiche del Sig. Abate Pietro Metastasio* (1755), a controversial work concerning Metastasio and Hasse. A. Bellina ed. his *Scritti teatrali e letterari* (two vols., Rome, 1994).

BIBL.: G. Lazzeri, *La vita e l'opera letteraria di R. C.* (Città di Castello, 1907).—LK/DM

Cambefort, Jean de, French singer and composer; b. c. 1605; d. Paris, May 4, 1661. He was a singer in Richelieu's private chapel. After Richelieu's death in 1642, Cambefort entered the service of Cardinal Mazarin. In 1644 he was named maître des enfants de la chambre du roi. In 1650 he become compositeur de la musique de la chambre to Louis XIV, and later served as surintendant de la musique de roi. He was highly regarded at the court as both a singer and as a composer of ballets de cour, airs de cour, and sacred works. —NS/LK/DM

Cambert, Robert, French composer; b. Paris, c. 1628; d. London, c.Feb. 1677. He was a pupil of Chambonnières. In 1652 he became organist at St. Honore in Paris. He then was made composer to the queen mother, Anne of Austria, in 1662. His first venture on the lyric stage was *La Pastorale,* written with the librettist Perrin and successfully produced at the Château d'Issy in 1659; it was followed by *Ariane, ou Le Mariage de Bacchus* (rehearsed in 1661) and *Adonis* (1662; not perf.; MS lost). In 1669 Perrin received letters patent for establishing the Académie Royale de Musique (the national operatic theater, now the Grand Opéra); he brought out, in collaboration with Cambert, the opera *Pomone* (1671); another opera, *Les Peines et les plaisirs de l'amour,* was written, and produced in Paris in March 1671, before Lully secured the patent. In 1673, after Lully secured the patent in violation of the agreement with Molière, Cambert went to London. With his former pupil Louis Grabu, he founded a Royal Academy of Musick in 1674 for the production of stage works.

BIBL.: A. Pougin, *Les Vrais Créateurs de l'opéra français, Perrin et C.* (Paris, 1881).—NS/LK/DM

Cambini, Giuseppe Maria (Gioacchino), Italian composer; b. Livorno, Feb. 13?, 1746; d. probably in Paris, 1825. Nothing is known about his early years with any certainty. By 1767 he was a violist in a quartet with Boccherini, Manfredi, and Nardini. He settled in Paris about 1770. On May 20, 1773, he appeared as a violinist at the Concert Spirituel, his only known public appearance there. He subsequently devoted himself to composition. About 1787 he became director of the Théâtre des Beaujolais, where seven of his opéras-comiques were premiered. In 1791 he became conductor of the Théâtre Louvois, where he was active until 1794. Cambini was a prolific composer. Hundreds of his works were publ. in Paris between 1773 and 1789. Of his 14 stage works, only *La statue* (Paris, Aug. 2[?], 1784) and *Le tuteur avare* (Paris, March 1, 1788) are extant in full. Although he had some success as a composer for the stage, he won great popularity with his instrumental music. He wrote over 80 symphonies concertantes, which secured his reputation. He also composed several syms. and concertos, and numerous quintets, quartets, trios, duos, and solo pieces, as well as sacred and secular vocal works. He likewise publ. methods for the violin (Paris, c. 1795) and the flute (Paris, 1799). —NS/LK/DM

Cambreling, Sylvain, French conductor; b. Amiens, July 2, 1948. He received training in music at the Paris Cons. In 1975 he became asst. conductor of the Orchestre de Lyon, and also conducted opera in Lyon. Beginning with the 1979–80 season, he appeared regularly as a conductor at the Paris Opéra. In 1981 he became joint music director (with John Pritchard) of the Théâtre Royal de la Monnaie in Brussels. He also conducted at the Glyndebourne Festival, the Frankfurt am Main Opera, La Scala in Milan, in the U.S., and in Canada. On Jan. 9, 1986, he made his Metropolitan Opera debut in N.Y. conducting *Roméo et Juliette*. From 1993 to 1997 he was chief conductor of the Frankfurt am Main Opera. He became chief conductor of the SWR (South West Radio) Sym. Orch. of Baden-Baden and Freiburg im Breisgau in 1998.—NS/LK/DM

Camden, Archie (actually, **Archibald Leslie**), virtuoso English bassoonist; b. Newark-upon-Trent, March 9, 1888; d. Wheathampstead, Feb. 16, 1979. He studied at the Royal Manchester Coll. of Music. In 1906 he joined the Hallé Orch. of Manchester, where he played first bassoon from 1914 to 1933. During the same period, he taught bassoon at the Royal Manchester Coll. of Music. In 1933 he joined the BBC Sym. Orch. in London, then played with the Royal Phil. (1946–47). He finally was a member of the London Mozart Players (1954–71). Camden did much to establish the bassoon as a solo instrument. His performances of works by Vivaldi, Mozart, and Weber were outstanding. His autobiography was publ. as *Blow by Blow* (London, 1982).—NS/LK/DM

Cameo, one of the most adventurous funk bands of the 1980s, formed in 1974, in N.Y. **MEMBERSHIP:** Larry Blackmon, drm. (b. N.Y.C., May 24, 1956); Greg Johnson, kybd.; Nathan Leftenant, horns, voc.; Tomi Jenkins, voc.

Taking a cue from the Ohio Players, Larry Blackmon originally called his band the New York City Players. While maintaining his day job as a tailor, he attended classes at the Juilliard School of Music. The group's membership ranged from six to twelve players, earning a good reputation that eventually got them signed to Casablanca Records' Chocolate City subsidiary (home of Parliament). They changed their name to the less-derivative Cameo after the African silhouette jewelry popular at the time. Their debut, *Cardiac Arrest*, produced the modest R&B hit "Rigor Mortis." The day Blackmon heard it on the radio while waiting on a customer at work, he put down his chalk, walked out, and never came back.

Between 1979–82, the band had a series of Top Ten R&B singles, and the albums *Secret Omen, Cameosis,* (#25 pop), *Feel Me, Knights of the Sound Table,* and *Alligator Woman* (#23 pop) all went gold, despite a lack

of crossover success. Dissatisfied with this situation, as well as with conditions in the North—and recognizing Atlanta as a major hub for their touring schedule—Blackmon stripped the band down to himself, Leftenant, and Jenkins and moved there in 1980. There, he started his own Atlanta Artists label.

With the retooled business and band came a retooled sound. No longer horn-oriented, the band instead played a slinky synthesizer funk that Blackmon presciently referred to as black rock. The title track to the gold *Single Life* was a #1 hit in England. The title track to the gold follow-up, *She's Strange,* topped the R&B charts and hit #47 pop.

The next album, 1986's *Word Up,* finally crossed the band over to the pop charts. The title track topped the R&B charts and was a #6 pop hit. "Candy" also topped the R&B charts, hitting #21 pop. "Back and Forth" got as high as #50 pop, #3 R&B. The album peaked at #8. Suddenly, Blackmon was doing Coke commercials. He also became an in-demand producer, working on Bobby Brown's debut and even working with Miles Davis.

Yet the band's popularity was short-lived. Cameo's 1988 release *Machismo* was the band's last gold record. In the early 1990s, Blackmon spent several years working in the Warner Bros. A&R department. The 1996 album *Nasty* was released without major label distribution. By 1998, Blackmon was hosting a radio show on Saturday nights out of Miami.

DISC.: *Cardiac Arrest* (1977); *We All Know Who We Are* (1977); *Secret Omen* (1979); *Cameosis* (1980); *Knights of the Sound Table* (1981); *Feel Me* (1981); *Alligator Woman* (1982); *She's Strange* (1984); *Word Up* (1986); *Machismo* (1988); *Real Men...Wear Black* (1990); *Emotional Violence* (1992); *The Best of Cameo* (1993); *In the Face of Funk* (1994); *The Best of Cameo: Vol. 2* (1996); *Nasty* (1996); *The Ballads Collection* (1998); *Greatest Hits* (1998); *The 12" Collection and More* (1999).—HB

Camerloher, Placidus Cajetan von, German composer; b. Murnau, Aug. 9, 1718; d. Freising, July 21, 1782. He studied at the Ettal Ritterakademie and in Munich. In 1744 he took holy orders and became Kapellmeister to the Freising court. He also was made prebendary at the monastery of St. Veit in 1748 and at St. Andreas in 1752, and likewise served as director of chamber music in Liège. His output included Singspiels, many syms., chamber music, and sacred pieces.

BIBL.: B. Ziegler, *P.v. C. (1718–82)* (Freising, 1919). —LK/DM

Cameron, (George) Basil, English conductor; b. Reading, Aug. 18, 1884; d. Leominster, June 26, 1975. He studied with Noble in York (1900–1902) and with Joachim (violin) and Bruch (composition) at the Berlin Hochschule für Musik (1902–06). After playing violin in the Queen's Hall Orch. in London, he Germanized his name as Basil Hindenberg and was conductor of the Torquay orch. (1912–16). With the outbreak of World War I in 1914, he deemed it prudent to revert to his real name. After conducting the Hastings orch. (1923–30), he served as co-conductor (with Dobrowen) of the San Francisco Sym. Orch. (1931–34). From 1932 to 1938 he was conductor of the Seattle Sym. Orch. He then returned to England and conducted at the London Promenade Concerts. After World War II, he appeared as a guest conductor in England and on the Continent. In 1957 he was made a Commander of the Order of the British Empire.—**NS/LK/DM**

Campagnoli, Bartolommeo, renowned Italian violinist; b. Cento di Ferrara, Sept. 10, 1751; d. Neustrelitz, Germany, Nov. 6, 1827. He studied in Bologna with Dall'Ocha and in Florence with Nardinim, and for several years gave concerts in Italy. He became music director to the Duke of Kurland in Dresden (1779–97), and then was concertmaster at the Gewandhaus in Leipzig (1797–1818). He made several successful concert tours while in his service. From 1797 to 1818 he was active as a violinist in Leipzig. He composed 41 *Capricci per l'alto viola* (rev. by E. Kreuz and A. Consolini as *Caprices pour le viola*, 1922), a Violin Concerto, études for violin, and chamber music. He was the author of several pedagogic manuals for the violin, including *Nouvelle méthode de la mécanique progressive du jeu de violon* (1791; Eng. tr., 1856), and *Metodo per violino* (1797).

BIBL.: G. Atti, *Biografia di B. C.* (Bologna, 1892). —**NS/LK/DM**

Campanari, Giuseppe, Italian baritone, brother of **Leandro Campanari;** b. Venice, Nov. 17, 1855; d. Milan, May 31, 1927. He was a cellist in the orch. of Milan's La Scala, but also studied voice. After playing cello in the Boston Sym. Orch. (1884–93), he made his operatic debut as Tonio with Hinrich's Opera Co. in N.Y. on June 15, 1893. On Nov. 30, 1894, he made his Metropolitan Opera debut in N.Y. as Di Luna, and continued on its roster until 1912. In addition to Italian roles, he also appeared there as Papageno, Valentin, Nélusko, Escamillo, Kothner, and Nevers.—**NS/LK/DM**

Campanari, Leandro, Italian violinist and conductor, brother of **Giuseppe Campanari;** b. Rovigo, Oct. 20, 1857; d. San Francisco, April 22, 1939. He studied in Padua, and also attended the Milan Cons., graduating in 1877. After a tour of Europe, he went to the U.S. in 1881 and settled in Boston, where he organized the Campanari String Quartet. He became a proficient conductor and was in charge of the Grand Orch. Concerts at La Scala in Milan from 1897 till 1905. In Feb. 1907 he was engaged to complete the season of the Philadelphia Orch. after the sudden illness of the regular conductor, Fritz Scheel. However, Campanari failed to impress the orch. or the audience, and was not reengaged. —**NS/LK/DM**

Campanella, Michele, Italian pianist; b. Naples, June 5, 1947. He was educated at the Naples Cons., winning the Casella Competition while a student there in 1966. He then taught at the Milan Cons. (1969–73), and subsequently made tours as soloist with leading orchs. of Europe and the U.S. From 1987 he taught master classes at the Accademia Musicale Chigiana in Siena. His performances of the Romantic and modern repertoire have won critical praise.—**NS/LK/DM**

Campanini, Cleofonte, eminent Italian-American conductor, brother of **Italo Campanini;** b. Parma, Sept. 1, 1860; d. Chicago, Dec. 19, 1919. He studied violin at the Parma Cons. and later at the Milan Cons., making his conducting debut with *Carmen* at Parma (1882). He conducted the first American performance of *Otello* at the N.Y. Academy of Music (April 16, 1888) while his brother, Italo, was impresario. Between 1888 and 1906, he conducted in Italy, in England, and in South America. A larger field opened to him in 1906, when Hammerstein engaged him for the new Manhattan Opera House in N.Y. Differences with Hammerstein led him to resign in 1909. In the following year he was engaged as principal conductor of the newly formed Chicago Opera Co.; in 1913 he was appointed general director, which post he held until his death. Among opera conductors he occupied a place in the first rank; he seemed to be equally at home in all styles of music. He introduced many new operas in the U.S., among them Massenet's *Hérodiade*, Debussy's *Pelléas et Mélisande*, Charpentier's *Louise*, Wolf-Ferrari's *Il segreto di Susanna*, et al. On May 15, 1887, he married, in Florence, **Eva Tetrazzini** (sister of **Luisa Tetrazzini**). —**NS/LK/DM**

Campanini, Italo, famous Italian tenor, brother of **Cleofonte Campanini;** b. Parma, June 30, 1845; d. Corcagno, near Parma, Nov. 22, 1896. In his early years he was an apprentice in his father's blacksmith shop. He joined Garibaldi's army and was wounded in the Italian struggle for unification. Subsequently, he studied with Griffini and Lamperti, then appeared at Bologna in *Lohengrin* (Nov. 1, 1871), which started him on the road to fame. He made his London debut as Gennaro in *Lucrezia Borgia* (May 4, 1872), and his American debut, also as Gennaro, at the N.Y. Academy of Music (Oct. 1, 1873). He appeared in *Faust* at the opening of the Metropolitan Opera (Oct. 22, 1883); was on its roster until 1894. He was briefly active as an impresario; brought over his brother Cleofonte Campanini to conduct the American premiere of Verdi's *Otello* at the N.Y. Academy of Music (April 16, 1888).—**NS/LK/DM**

Campbell, Glen (G. Travis C.), country-pop vocalist and guitarist; b. Delight, Ark., April 22, 1936. Best-known for a string of mid-1960s crossover hits, Campbell has soldiered on in the country market, although with diminishing success.

Campbell was encouraged by other musicians in his family to take up the guitar at age four. By his teens, he was touring with his own country band, the Western Wranglers. At age 24, Campbell relocated to L.A., where he quickly found employment as a session guitarist, and scored a minor solo hit in 1961 with "Turn Around Look at Me." Campbell worked comfortably in pop, country, and rock, and briefly toured as bassist for the Beach Boys after founder Brian Wilson suffered a nervous breakdown.

In the mid-1960s, Campbell signed to Capitol Records as a solo artist. The company first tried to promote him as an instrumentalist, releasing an LP of 12-string guitar instrumentals aimed at a general pop market. However, it was Campbell's clear tenor, with only a hint of a country twang, which would gain him his hits as a pop crooner. His first hit, a cover of John Hartford's "Gentle on My Mind," came in 1967, and was followed by a string of Jimmy Webb-penned soft-country hits ("By the Time I Get to Phoenix," "Wichita Lineman," "Galveston"). These songs all had pop arrangements, replete with string sections and vocal choruses, giving them an appeal for both pop and country audiences. Campbell's career was furthered by his exposure as the host for a summer replacement program for the popular Smothers Brothers TV show, followed by his own variety show in 1969, plus film roles, most notably with John Wayne in *True Grit*.

Soon after, the hits stopped. Campbell returned to the charts in the mid- 1970s as a more country-oriented performer with "Rhinestone Cowboy" and "Southern Nights," but then lapsed again into obscurity. Although he continues to perform both as a vocalist and instrumentalist, Campbell has failed to capitalize on his earlier success.

DISC.: *Big Bluegrass Special* (1962); *Gentle on My Mind* (1967); *By the Time I Get to Pheonix* (1967); *Wichita Lineman* (1968); *Galveston* (1969); *The Glen Campbell Goodtime Album* (1970); *Glen Campbell's Greatest Hits* (1971); *Best of Glen Campbell* (1976); *The Very Best of Glen Campbell* (1987); *Greatest Country Hits* (1990); *Classics Collection* (1990); *Gentle on My Mind: The Collection* (1997).—RC

Campbell, John (Elwood II),

jazz pianist, vibraphonist, bassist, drummer; b. Bloomington, Ill., July 7, 1955. Campbell's grandfather played piano and organ semi-professionally, an uncle was a school band director, and his younger brother is an amateur drummer. He started piano at seven and as a teenager he taught himself drums, bass, and vibraphone. He performed at school dances and had a gig at a pizza parlor. He attended Ill. State Coll. (1973–75), and gigged locally. In 1976 he moved to Chicago, where he led a quartet (1978–c. 1982). His trio worked at the Jazz Showcase backing up Eddie Jefferson, Eddie Harris, James Moody, Red Rodney, and Bunky Green. He played with Stan Getz (1984), worked and recorded on occasion with Clark Terry (from 1984), and toured with Mel Tormé (1986–90). He then worked with Milt Jackson, Moody, Cleo Laine and Johnny Dankworth, Greg Gisbert, and Jerry Dodgion (1993–97); he also played solo at the Four Seasons. He moved back to Chicago in 1997, where he continues to freelance.

DISC.: *After Hours* (1988); *Turning Point* (1990); *Live at Maybeck Recital Hall* (1993).—LP

Campbell, Roy,

performer, composer, arranger, music director, and teacher; b. Los Angeles, Calif., Sept. 29, 1952. He has been a fixture on the underground music scene for over two decades. Playing trumpet, flugelhorn, and flute, he has accrued credits in the David Murray Octet and Billy Bang's group, as well as recording albums as leader for the Delmark label and for the Swedish label, Silkheart. His family moved to N.Y. when he was a child and he began playing piano at age six and switched to trumpet in high school. As a

member of the Jazzmobile Workshop from 1971 to 1973, he pursued advanced trumpet studies with Lee Morgan and Kenny Dorham. An eclectic musician, he has dabbled in an array of musical genres, including R&B, funk, bebop, standards, and has found his home in the avant garde, to which he brings all of these influences in collaborations with Cecil Taylor, Sunny Murray, Henry Threadgill, Jemeel Moondoc, Craig Harris, Woody Shaw, and others. His expertise in orchestration (he's written for 15- to 20-piece orchestras), past collaborations with leading jazz innovators, and ability to draw inspiration from a variety of sources, set him apart from the trumpet herd. In the late 1980s and early 1990s he split his time between N.Y. and Rotterdam, where he toured with bass saxophonist Klaas Hekman and took over the helm of the Thelonious New World Orch. there. He now leads a N.Y.–based trio with fluctuating personnel, plays in William Parker's Little Huey Creative Music Orch., and co-leads the group Other Dimensions in Music with Daniel Carter (alto/tenor saxophones, flute, trumpet), William Parker (bass), and Rashid Bakr.

He has forged a solid second outing as leader with *La Tierra del Fuego (The Land of Fire)* (1994), composing all but one of the seven tunes. Campbell composes on Spanish motifs, at times inflecting haunting or fiery rhythms laden with percussion. The centerpiece of the album is the 17-minute title tune, a three-movement suite that builds on Spanish folk melodies and third world sounds. The leader creates festive colors and pleasing textures that make this session eminently more interesting than those of most young trumpet players recording today. It's a tough choice between his two Delmark albums and *New Kingdom* (1992): his debut album for the label could just as easily be a first pick since it was so highly praised by fans and critics when it came out. Delmark is a fitting choice for his innovative music that seems to draw, in part, from AACM (Association for the Advancement of Creative Musicians) influences as well as from the N.Y.C. avant-garde scene. He mostly adheres to melody frameworks as he generates open and muted trumpet/flugelhorn smears, sputters, splashes, splats, and straight-up renderings, leading innovative trio settings with William Parker (bass) and Zen Matsuura (drums). The group expands to a quintet featuring Ricardo Strobert (alto sax, flute) and Bryan Carrott (vibes), and a sextet with guesting tenor saxophonist Zane Massey (on two tracks). In addition to his accomplished trumpet skills, his talents as composer are impressive; he wrote five of the album's eight tunes. (Parker contributes two originals, Massey one.)

DISC.: *Communion* (1995).—NAL

Campbell-Tipton, Louis,

American composer; b. Chicago, Nov. 21, 1877; d. Paris, May 1, 1921. After studies in Chicago and Boston, he pursued training with Gustav Schreck and Carl Reinecke at the Leipzig Cons. (1896–99). From 1901 to 1904 he taught theory and composition at the Chicago Musical Coll., and then settled in Paris and devoted himself to composing and teaching. The early German influence on his works eventually gave way to French Impressionism. He composed effective piano pieces (*Sonata Heroic*, 1904; *2 Legends*, 1908; *Etude en octaves*, 1912), and songs (*4 Sea*

Lyrics; The Opium Smoker; A Memory; all 1907). Among his other works were pieces for violin and piano, mostly notably *Suite pastorale, Romanza appassionata,* and *Lament.*—**NS/LK/DM**

Campion, François, French instrumentalist, theorbist, and composer of English descent; b. Rouen, c. 1686; d. Paris, Jan. or Feb. 1748. He was a theorbist and guitarist at the Académie Royale de Musique in Paris (1703–19), and also active as a lutenist. Among his works, all publ. in Paris, were *Nouvelles découvertes...contenant plusieurs suites de pièces sur 8 manières d'accorder* for Guitar, op.1 (1705), *Avantures pastorales meslées de vers,* op.3 (1719; 54 airs), and *Second recueil d'airs,* op.5 (1734).

WRITINGS (all publ. in Paris): *Traité d'accompagnement et de composition selon la règle des octaves de musique,* op.2 (1716); *Lettres du Sieur Campion à un philosophe disciple de la règle de l'octave* (1729); *Addition au traité de l'accompagnement et de composition par la règle de l'octave,* op.4 (1730); *Lettre de Monsieur l'abbé Carbasus à Monsieur D+++, auteur du Temple du Goust, sur la mode des instruments de musique* (1739).—**NS/LK/DM**

Campion (Campian), Thomas, English physician, poet, composer, and dramatist; b. London, Feb. 12, 1567; d. there, March 1, 1620. He studied at Cambridge from 1581 to 1584, residing at Peterhouse; entered Gray's Inn on April 27, 1586. He received his M.D. degree from the Univ. of Caen in France on Feb. 10, 1605. He was first called a "Doctor of Physick" in an English publication in Barnabe Barnes's *Four Books of Offices* in 1606. Earlier evidence of his having studied medical science is an oblique reference of Philip Rosseter in 1601, speaking of Campion's poetry and music as "the superfluous blossoms of his deeper studies." Campion was primarily a lyric poet, and his music was to enhance the beauty of the poetry by supplying unobtrusive and simple harmonies. In this he differed from such contemporaries as John Dowland, who contrived elaborate lute accompaniments.

WORKS: 3 songs (1596); *A Booke of Ayres, Set Foorth to Be Sung to the Lute Orpherian, and Base Violl* (1601; consists of 2 separate books, one by Campion and one by Rosseter; Campion wrote both the words and the music for his half of the work); *First and Second Books of Airs* (1613?); *Third and Fourth Books of Airs* (1617?); songs for masques at the marriages of Sir James Hay (1607), Princess Elizabeth (1613), and Robert, Earl of Somerset (1613); songs for a masque at Caversham House (1613); *Songs of Mourning* (for Prince Henry; 1613; words by Campion, music by John Coperario); *A New Way for Making Foure Parts in Counterpoint* (1618; also in Playford's *Introduction to the Skill of Musick,* with additions by Christopher Simpson, 1655 and following years). Campion also publ. *Poemata,* a vol. of Latin epigrams and elegiacs (1595; reprinted 1619), *Observations on the Art of English Poesie* (1602; condemns "the vulgar and unartificial custom of riming"), etc. The 4 books of airs and the songs from Rosseter's *Booke of Ayres* are reprinted in E.H. Fellowes, *English School of Lutenist Song-Writers.*

BIBL.: M. Kastendieck, *England's Musical Poet, T. C.* (Oxford, 1938); W.R. Davis, ed., *The Works of T. C.; Complete Songs, Masques, and Treatises* (Garden City, N.Y., 1967); E. Lowbury, T. Salter, and A. Young, *T. C.: Poet, Composer, Physician* (N.Y.,1970); W. Davis, *T. C.* (Boston, 1987); M. Pilkington, *C., Dowland and the Lutenist Songwriters* (London, 1989).—**NS/LK/DM**

Campoli, Alfredo, Italian-born English violinist; b. Rome, Oct. 20, 1906; d. London, March 27, 1991. He was a pupil of his father, a prof. at the Accademia di Santa Cecilia in Rome, and then settled in England while still a child. After making his London debut at the age of ten, he toured throughout England, receiving the gold medal at the London Music Festival in 1919. In 1938 he made his first appearance at the London Promenade Concerts. He also was active with his own orch., which featured lighter works. From 1945 he pursued a career as a violin virtuoso, making his U.S. debut in N.Y. in 1953. In subsequent years, he toured the globe. He was admired for his finely wrought interpretations of the standard repertory, but he also promoted 20th century English works, including those by Elgar and Bliss.

BIBL.: D. Tunley, *The Bel Canto Violin: The Life and Times of A. C. 1906–1991* (London, 1999).—**NS/LK/DM**

Campora, Giuseppe, Italian tenor; b. Tortona, Sept. 30, 1923. He studied voice in Genoa and Milan. In 1949 he made his operatic debut in Bari as Rodolfo; in 1951 he joined Milan's La Scala and also sang with other Italian opera houses. He made his Metropolitan Opera debut in N.Y. as Rodolfo on Jan. 20, 1955, and remained on the roster until 1959; was again on its roster from 1963 to 1965. Among his best known roles were Enzo, Massenet's Des Grieux, Gounod's Faust, Cavaradossi, Edgardo, and Alfredo.—**NS/LK/DM**

Camporese, Violante, Italian soprano; b. Rome, 1785; d. there, 1839. She studied in Paris with Crescentini, and sang before Napoleon. On Jan. 11, 1817, she made her London debut at the King's Theatre as Cimarosa's Penelope, and continued to sing there until 1823 in such roles as Donna Anna, Dorabella, and Susanna. From 1817 to 1829 she appeared at Milan's La Scala, where she created the role of Bianca in Rossini's *Bianca e Faliero* (Dec. 26, 1819). She was held in high esteem as a Mozartian.—**NS/LK/DM**

Campos-Parsi, Héctor, Puerto Rican composer; b. Ponce, Oct. 1, 1922. He studied in Ponce, then at the Univ. of Puerto Rico in Río Piedras (1938–44). After taking courses at the New England Cons. of Music in Boston (1947–50) and with Copland and Messiaen at the Berkshire Music Center in Tanglewood (summers 1949–50), he studied with Boulanger in Fontainebleau (1951–53). Returning to Puerto Rico in 1955, he was active as a composer, poet, journalist, music critic, television commentator, and concert manager. In some of his works, he utilized Puerto Rican folk music. In other pieces, he embraced aleatory procedures and electronics.

WORKS: DRAMATIC: B a l l e t : *Incidente* (1949); *Melos* (1951); *Juan Bobo y las fiestas* (1957); *Urayoán* (1958); *Areyto boriken* (1974); *De Diego* (1974). ORCH.: *Divertimento de Sur* for Flute, Clarinet, and Strings (1953); *Oda a Cabo Rojo* (1959); *Rapsodia elegíaca* for Strings (1960); *Kollagia* for Orch., Percussion, and Tape (1963); *Dúo trágico* for Piano and Orch. (1964); *Tiempo sereno* for Strings (1983); *Trés Madrigales* for Soprano and Strings (1983); *Tissú* for Accordion and Small Orch. (1984); *Tureyareito* (1984); *Eglogas* for Baritone and Strings (1988).

CHAMBER: *Serenata* for String Trio (1949); Violin Sonata (1949); *Música* for 3 Violins (1949); String Quartet (1950); *Dialogantes* for Violin and Piano (1952); Violin Sonatina (1953); *Música per la stagione estiva* for 2 Flutes and Piano (1956); *El secreto* for Flute, Oboe, 2 Clarinets, Cello, and Piano (1957); *Petroglifos* for Piano Trio (1966); *Arawak* for Cello and Tape (1970); *Sleeping Beauty* for Flute, Harp, and 2 Pianos (1978); *Fanfare for an American Festival* for 3 Trumpets, 2 Trombones, and Percussion (1982); *Sonetos Sagrados* for Soprano, Flute, Oboe, Clarinet, Bassoon, and Horn (1986); piano pieces.

BIBL.: F. Caso, *H. C.-P. in the History of Twentieth-Century Music in Puerto Rico* (diss., Ind. Univ., 1972).—**NS/LK/DM**

Campra, André, important French composer; b. Aix-en-Provence (baptized), Dec. 4, 1660; d. Versailles, June 29, 1744. He stududied with Guillaume Poitevin; then embraced an ecclesiastical vocation; was made chaplain at Aix on May 27, 1681; served as maître de musique at St. Étienne in Toulouse from 1683 to 1694, and at Notre Dame from 1694 to 1700; then was active at the Paris Opéra. In 1722 he was made maître de musique to the Prince of Conti. In 1723 he received a court appointment as sous-maître with Bernier and Gervais. In 1730 he was appointed inspecteur général of the Académie Royale de Musique in Paris. Campra was esteemed as a composer of both stage works and sacred music.

WORKS (all 1st perf. in Paris unless otherwise given): **DRAMATIC:** *L'Europe galante,* opéra-ballet (Oct. 24, 1697); *Le Carnaval de Venise,* ballet (Jan. 20, 1699; Act 3 includes the Italian opera *Orfeo nell'inferni*); *Hésione,* tragédie lyrique (Dec. 20, 1700); *Aréthuse, ou La Vengeance de l'Amour,* tragédie lyrique (July 14, 1701); *Tancrède,* tragédie lyrique (Nov. 7, 1702); *Les Muses,* opéra-ballet (Oct. 28, 1703); *Iphigénie en Tauride,* tragédie lyrique based on the unfinished work of Desmarets (May 6, 1704); *Télémaque,* extracts from operas by Campra et al. (Nov. 11, 1704); *Alcine,* tragédie lyrique (Jan 15, 1705); *Hippodamie,* tragédie lyrique (March 6, 1708); *Les Fêtes vénitiennes,* opéra-ballet (June 17, 1710); *Idomenée,* tragédie lyrique (Jan. 12, 1712); *Les Amours de Vénus et de Mars,* ballet (Sept. 6, 1712); *Téléphe,* tragédie lyrique (Nov. 28, 1713); *Camille, reine des volsques,* tragédie lyrique (Nov. 9, 1717); *Ballet représenté à Lion devant M. le marquis d'Harlincourt,* ballet (Lyons, May 17, 1718; not extant); *Les Âges,* opéra-ballet (Oct. 9, 1718); *Achille et Deidamie,* tragédie lyrique (Feb. 24, 1735). **OTHER:** Several divertissements (most of them not extant); 3 books of *Cantates françoises* (1708, 1714, 1728); 5 books of motets (1695–1720); Mass (1700); 2 books of Psalms (1737–38).

BIBL.: A. Pougin, *A. C.* (Paris, 1861); M. Barthélemy, *A. C.* (Paris, 1957); C. Castle, *The Grand Motets of A. C.* (diss., Univ. of Mich., 1962); J. Anthony, *The Opera-Ballet of A. C.: A Study of the First Period French Opera-Ballet* (diss., Univ. of Southern Calif., 1964); A. Baker, *The Church Music of A. C.* (diss., Univ. of Toronto, 1978).—**NS/LK/DM**

Camps, Pompeyo, Argentine composer; b. Paraná, Oct. 27, 1924; d. Buenos Aires, Nov. 3, 1997. After playing piano in bands in his native town, he settled in Buenos Aires in 1947, where he studied with Jaime Pahissa and adopted his "intertonal system" of convertible counterpoint. In 1964 Camps modified this technique by incorporating serial procedures. He was also active as a music critic.

WORKS: Piano Sonata (1954); 2 string quartets (1957, 1974); *La pendiente,* opera (1959); *Fantasia* for Strings (1961); *The Ballad of Reading Gaol* for Men's Chorus, Narrator, and Orch. (1964); *Sinfónia para un poeta* for Baritone and Orch. (1967); *Tríptico arcáico* for Flute, Viola, Cello, and Guitar (1961); *Danzas* for Percussion (1966); *Reflejos* for 13 Brasses and Percussion (1968); *Ciudad sin tregua* for String Quartet (1974); songs; piano pieces.—**NS/LK/DM**

Candeille, (Amélie) Julie, French pianist, harpist, singer, actress, composer, and writer, daughter of **Pierre Joseph Candeille;** b. Paris, July 31, 1767; d. there, Feb. 4, 1834. She received most of her musical training from her father, but also studied piano with Holaind and singing with Legros. At age 14 she joined the Paris Opéra, and at 15 appeared as Gluck's Iphigénie there. In 1783 she appeared as an instrumentalist at the Concert Spirituel. By 1785 she was a member of the Comédie Française, where she was active as both a performer and a composer. In 1816 she was granted a pension by Louis XVIII. Her most successful work was the comédie *Catherine, ou La belle fermière* (Paris, Nov. 27, 1792). In addition to other stage pieces, she also composed orch. works, chamber music, piano pieces, and songs. Among her writings were novels, dramas, and her memoirs, the last included in L. Aillaud, "J. C.," *Chronique mondaine, littéraire et artistique* (Nîmes, Oct. 27, 1923-Jan. 12, 1924). —**NS/LK/DM**

Candeille, Pierre Joseph, French singer and composer, father of **(Amélie) Julie Candeille;** b. Estaires, Dec. 8, 1744; d. Chantilly, April 24, 1827. He received his training at the song school of the collegiate church of St. Pierre in Lille. After settling in Paris, he was a basse taille in the chorus of the Opéra (1767–71; 1773–81) and of the Concert Spirituel (1769–71; 1773–81), and later wawas chorus master of the Opéra (1800–02; 1804–05). He wrote about 20 stage works, of which the most successful was the opera *Castor et Pollux* (Paris, June 14, 1791). He also wrote four syms. and sacred vocal pieces.—**NS/LK/DM**

Caniglia, Maria, Italian soprano; b. Naples, May 5, 1905; d. Rome, April 16, 1979. She was a pupil of Roche at the Naples Cons. In 1930 she made her operatic debut in Turin as Chrysothemis, and later that year made her first appearance at Milan's La Scala as Maria in Pizzetti's *Lo Straniero.* She continued to sing at La Scala until 1943, and again from 1948 to 1951; also appeared with the company on its visits to London's Covent Garden (1937, 1939, 1950). On Nov. 21, 1938, she made her Metropolitan Opera debut in N.Y. as Desdemona, but returned to Europe in 1939. In 1939 she married **Pino Donati.** Among her best known roles were Tosca, Aida, Alice Ford, the 3 Leonoras, Maria Boccanegra, and Adriana Lecouvreur. She also created the title role in Respighi's *Lucrezia* (Milan, Feb. 24, 1937).—**NS/LK/DM**

Canis, Cornelius or **Corneille,** Flemish composer; b. Flanders, c. 1515; d. Prague, Feb. 15, 1561. He was in the service of the imperial court by 1542. In 1547 he was made maistre des enfans, and later was maître de chapelle and the retainer of several royal prebends. In 1557 he became chaplain of St. Martin and canon of Notre Dame in Courtrai. His extant works comprise 2 masses, 32 motets, and 29 chansons.

BIBL.: W. Wells, *The Sacred Music of C. C., Flemish Composer, 1510/1520–1561* (diss., Stanford Univ., 1968).—**LK/DM**

Cannabich, prominent family of German musicians:

(1) Martin Friedrich Cannabich, flutist and composer; b. c. 1675; d. after 1759. He was a member of the Mannheim Court Orch., and also flute teacher to the Elector Carl Theodor. He was one of the earliest composers of the Mannheim school. Among his publ. works were *Six Solos for a German Flute, Violin or Harpsichord* (London, c. 1740) and a vol. of six flute sonatas (Paris, 1751).

(2) (Johann) Christian (Innocenz Bonaventura) Cannabich, distinguished violinist, conductor, teacher, and composer, son of the preceding; b. Mannheim (baptized), Dec. 28, 1731; d. Frankfurt am Main, Jan. 20, 1798. He studied with Johann Stamitz and was admitted to the Mannheim Court Orch. as a "scholar" when he was only 12; by the time he was 16 he was a full-fledged member of the orch. In 1750 he was sent by the Elector to study with Jommelli in Rome. After a sojourn in Stuttgart with his teacher (1753–54), he went to Milan. Returning to Mannheim, he was court ballet composer and maestro de' concerti by 1758. He made visits to Paris in 1764, 1766, and 1772, appearing in the latter year at the Concert Spirituel. In 1774 he was appointed court director of instrumental music and was given complete charge of the Mannheim Court Orch. Under his discerning guidance, it reached unprecedented renown. In 1778 he moved with the court to Munich, where he added most of the Mannheim players to the Munich Court Orch. During the last years of his life, the court musical establishment was cut back and Cannabich found it necessary to tour as a concert violinist in order to supplement his income. Mozart was befriended by Cannabich, and was the piano teach of Cannabich's daughter, for whom he composed his sonata, K.284b/309. Cannabich was highly influential as a violin teacher, and is generally regarded as the father of the Mannheim violin style. As a conductor, he developed the method of even bowing. His extensive output as a composer reveals him to have been a skillful craftsman in the galant style of the era. Among his works were the operas *Azakia* (Mannheim, 1778) and *Le croisée* (Paris, 1778), the melodrama *Elektra* (Mannheim, Sept. 4, 1781), about 40 ballets, some 100 syms., two flute concertos, a Keyboard Concerto, and much chamber music.

BIBL.: H. Hofer, *C. C.: Biographie und vergleichende Analyse seiner Sinfonien* (diss., Univ. of Munich, 1921); R. Kloiber, *Die dramatischen Ballette von C. C.* (diss., Univ. of Munich, 1928).

(3) Carl (Konrad) Cannabich, violinist and composer, son of the preceding; b. Mannheim (baptized), Oct. 11, 1771; d. Munich, May 1, 1806. After studies with his father, he was a pupil in Munich of Friedrich Eck (violin) and Joseph Grätz (composition). In 1778 he became a violinist in the Munich Court Orch. under his father. After serving as conductor in Frankfurt am Main in 1796, he became Konzertmeister of the Munich Court Orch. in 1798. In 1800 he was made court music director in Munich. His works reveal the influence of Mozart.

WORKS: DRAMATIC: O p e r a : *Orfeo* (Munich, 1802); *Palmer und Amalie* (Munich, Aug. 1803). **ORCH.:** Sym.; 3 violin concertos; 2 concertos for 2 Violins and Orch.; *Rondeau varie* for Violin and Orch. **KEYBOARD: P i a n o :** Several pieces, including a Sonata. **VOCAL:** *Mozarts Gedaechtnis Feyer seinen Manen gewidmet* for Solo Voices, Chorus, and Orch. (1797); choruses; songs.—**NS/LK/DM**

Canned Heat, a legendary blues-rock group, formed in L.A. in 1965. **MEMBERSHIP:** Bob "The Bear" Hite, voc., har., gtr. (b. Torrance, Calif., Feb. 26, 1945; d. North Hollywood, Calif., April 5, 1981); Alan "Blind Owl" Wilson, gtr., har., voc. (b. Boston, Mass., July 4, 1943; d. Topanga, Calif., Sept. 3, 1970); Henry Vestine, gtr. (b. Washington D.C., Dec. 25, 1944; d. Paris, Oct. 20, 1997); Larry Taylor, bs. (b. Brooklyn, June 26, 1942); Frank Cook, drm. Cook was replaced by Adolpho "Fito" de la Parra (b. Mexico City, Feb. 8, 1946) in 1968 and Vestine was replaced by Harvey Mandel (b. Detroit, March 11, 1945) in 1969. In 1970, Mandel departed and Vestine returned.

Originally formed as a jug band, Canned Heat became a popular white blues- and-boogie band as they played local L.A. clubs. Members Bob "The Bear" Hite and Alan "Blind Owl" Wilson were blues scholars and record collectors, and the group's recordings reflected their enthusiasm for the music. Debuting at the Monterey International Pop Festival in June 1967, Canned Heat signed with Liberty Records. Their debut album featured "Rollin' and Tumblin,'" while their second and most successful disc, with new drummer Fito de la Parra, included "Amphetamine Annie" and yielded a major hit with "On the Road Again." The album remained on the album charts for an entire year. Touring Europe in the fall of 1968, the band scored a near-smash hit with "Going up the Country." However, Henry Vestine departed in July 1969, to be replaced by Harvey Mandel.

Canned Heat appeared at the Woodstock Music and Art Fair in August 1969, and the following spring Taylor left and Vestine returned. The group appeared at the Isle of Wight Festival in August 1970, but, on Sept. 3, founding member Alan Wilson was found dead of a drug overdose in the garden of Hite's Topanga Canyon home. Their version of Wilbert Harrrison's "Let's Work Together" soon became a major hit, but the group was subsequently plagued by personnel changes. In 1971, they backed blues great John Lee Hooker for *Hooker 'N' Heat*. Nonetheless, the band's popularity faded and they were without a major record label following 1974's *One More River to Cross* for Atlantic. Since Hite's death of a drug-related heart attack on April 5, 1981, Canned Heat has been led by Fito de la Parra for engagements on the Calif. bar circuit. The group released several albums on small labels in the 1990s. While touring with the group, Vestine died of apparent respiratory failure in a hotel near Paris, France, on Oct. 20, 1997, at the age of 52.

DISC.: *Canned Heat* (1967); *Boogie with Canned Heat* (1968); *Living the Blues* (1968); *Hallelujah* (1969); *Vintage Heat* (1970); *The*

Canned Heat Cookbook/Best Of (1970); *Hooker 'n' Heat* (with John Lee Hooker; 1970); *Live in Europe* (1970); *Future Blues* (1970); *Live at the Topanga Corral* (1971); *Historical Figures and Ancient Heads* (1972); *New Age* (1973); *One More River to Cross* (1974); *The Very Best of Canned Heat* (1975); *Human Condition* (1978); *Hooker 'n' Heat Live* (1981); *The Best of Canned Heat* (1987); *Reheated* (1990); *Burnin' Live* (1992); *Uncanned: The Best of Canned Heat* (1994); *Internal Combustion* (1994).—**BH**

Cannon, Freddie "Boom Boom," (Freddy Picariello), the first "everyman" rock star; b. Lynn, Mass., Dec. 4, 1940.

A fixture on the oldies circuit as long as such a thing existed, during the late 1950s and early 1960s, Freddy Cannon had eight Top 40 singles. The son of a dance-band leader, Cannon worked with the Boston-area vocal group the G-Clefs and recorded with the Spindrifts. Boston DJ Jack McDermott took a song Freddy and his mother wrote to producers Bob Crewe and Frank Slay. Titled "Rock 'n' Roll Baby," Crewe and Slay added their own touches to the tune and retitled it "Tallahassee Lassie"; they also dubbed the songwriter Freddy Cannon. The record came out on Swan, a label partly owned by "American Bandstand" host Dick Clark, and (not surprisingly) Cannon became a fixture on the program. The tune hit #6 on the charts. They followed that up with a reworking of the hoary Crescent City chestnut "Way Down Yonder in New Orleans." It became Cannon's biggest hit, reaching #3 towards the end of 1959 and going gold.

Between 1960 and 1965, Cannon had six more Top 40 hits. They ranged from a rock remake of Red Foley's "Chattanooga Shoeshine Boy" to the #3 hit by Chuck Barris, "Palisades Park." One of the few rock singers to survive the British revolution, Cannon hit #16 in 1964 with his Warner Bros. debut, "Abigail Beecher." Dick Clark once again helped him to his final Top 40 single in 1965, "Action," the theme to Clark's television show *Where the Action Is.*

Cannon continued to record through the 1980s and 1990s, including a 1981 record with the Belmonts (Dion's old backing group), "Let's Put the Fun Back in Rock and Roll" and a charity Christmas trio with Johnny Tillotson and Brian Hyland on the *Christmas Album, A Gift of Hope* that also featured Frank Sinatra, Hank Williams Jr., Dionne Warwick, Willie Nelson and other notables. Not bad company for someone who hadn't had a hit in nearly a quarter century.

DISC.: *Happy Shades of Blue* (1960); *The Explosive Freddy Cannon* (1960); *Freddy Cannon Favourites* (1961); *Twistin' All Night Long* (1961); *Freddie Cannon at Palisades Park* (1962); *Freddie Cannon Steps Out* (1963); *Bang On* (1963); *Freddie Cannon* (1964); *Steps Out* (1964); *Sings Abigall Beecher* (1964); *Action!* (1965); *Palisades Park* (1985); *Big Blast From Boston: Best Of* (1995).—**HB**

Cannon, (Jack) Philip, English composer and teacher; b. Paris (of English-French parents), Dec. 21, 1929. He was educated in England; studied composition with Imogen Holst; then at the Royal Coll. of Music in London with Gordon Jacob and Vaughan Williams. He subsequently took lessons with Hindemith. From 1957 to 1959 he lectured at the Univ. of Sydney; in 1960 he joined the staff of the Royal Coll. of Music in London.

WORKS: 2 Rhapsodies for Piano (1943); 2 string quartets (1944, 1964); String Trio (1945); *In the Time of the Breaking of Nations* for Voice and Piano Quintet (1945); *Fantasia* for String Quartet (1946); Sextet for Flute, Oboe, and String Quartet (1946); Sinfonietta for Chamber Orch. (1947); *Symphonic Study: Spring* for Orch. (1949); *Songs to Delight* for Women's Chorus and Strings (1950); Sinfonietta for Strings (1952); *5 Chansons de Femme* for Soprano and Harp (1952); *L'Enfant s'amuse*, suite for Piano (1954); *Sonatine champêtre* for Piano (1959); Sonata for 2 Pianos (1960); *Son of Science*, cantata for Boy's Voices, Chorus, Tenor, Piano, Percussion, and Strings (Aylesbury, Dec. 2, 1961); *Fanfare to Youth* for 8 Trumpets (1963); *Morvoren*, opera (London, July 15, 1964); *Kai-kaus (A Persian Suite)* for Chamber Group (1965); *Lacrimae mundi* for Piano Trio (1974); *Son of Man* for Chorus and Orch. (Liverpool, June 26, 1975); *Lord of Light*, oratorio (1980).—**NS/LK/DM**

Cantelli, Guido, brilliant Italian conductor; b. Novara, April 27, 1920; d. in an airplane crash in Orly, near Paris, Nov. 24, 1956. A gifted child, he was given a place in his father's military band when he was a small boy; appeared as organist at the local church from age 10, and made his debut as a pianist at age 14. He pursued formal studies with Pedrollo and Ghedini at the Milan Cons. He then was conductor of Novara's Teatro Coccia in 1941, but was compelled to give up his post and join the Italian army in 1943. When he refused to support the Fascist cause, he was sent to the Nazi-run Stettin labor camp (1943–44); after being transferred to Bolzano, he escaped to Milan, but was captured and sentenced to death. He was saved by the liberation of his homeland in 1944. After World War II, he conducted at Milan's La Scala; Toscanini heard his performances and was sufficiently impressed to invite him as guest conductor with the NBC Sym. Orch. in N.Y. He made his American debut on Jan. 15, 1949, and subsequently conducted there regularly. From 1951 he also made appearances as a conductor with the Philharmonia Orch. in London. Cantelli was one of the most gifted conductors of his generation. A perfectionist, he conducted both rehearsals and concert and operatic performances from memory. He was able to draw the most virtuosic playing from his musicians. A few days before his death, he was appointed artistic director of La Scala.

BIBL.: L. Lewis, *G. C.: Portrait of a Maestro* (London, 1981). —**NS/LK/DM**

Cantelo, April (Rosemary), English soprano; b. Purbrook, April 2, 1928. She studied piano and voice at the Royal Coll. of Music in London; was subsequently a member of the New English Singers and the Deller Consort; also appeared in opera with the Glyndebourne Opera and the English Opera Group; she also gave solo recitals. From 1949 to 1964 she was married to **Sir Colin Davis.**—**NS/LK/DM**

Canteloube (de Malaret), (Marie-) Joseph, French pianist, composer, and writer on music; b. Annonay, near Tournon, Oct. 21, 1879; d. Grigny, Seine-et-Oise, Nov. 4, 1957. His name was simply Canteloube, but he added "de Malaret" after the name of his

ancestral estate. He studied piano in Paris with Amélie Doetzer and composition with d'Indy at the Schola Cantorum. He became an ardent collector of French folk songs and arranged and publ. many of them for voice with instrumental accompaniment. His *Chants d'Auvergne* (four sets for Voice, with Piano or Orch., 1923–30) are frequently performed. Among his other albums, *Anthologie des chants populaires français* (four sets, 1939–44) is a comprehensive collection of regional folk songs. He also publ. a biography of d'Indy (Paris, 1949).

WORKS: DRAMATIC: Opera: *Le Mas* (1910–13; Paris, April 3, 1929); *Vercingetorix* (1930–32; Paris, June 26, 1933). **ORCH.:** *Vers la princesse lointaine*, symphonic poem (1910–11); 3 symphonic sketches: *Lauriers* (Paris, Feb. 22, 1931), *Pièces françaises* for Piano and Orch. (1935), and *Poème* for Violin and Orch. (1937). **CHAMBER:** *Rustiques* for Oboe, Clarinet, and Bassoon (1946).

BIBL.: L. Boursiac, *C.* (Toulouse, 1941); F. Gougniaud-Taginel, *J. C.: Chantre dela terre* (Béziers, 1988).—**NS/LK/DM**

Cantor, Eddie (Isidore Itzkowitz),

energetic American comedian, singer, and actor; b. N.Y., Jan. 31, 1892; d. Beverly Hills, Oct. 10, 1964. Cantor's brash comic style enabled him to conquer the fields of musical theater, records, film, radio, and television in a career that spanned more than 50 years. He was one of the stars of the *Ziegfeld Follies of 1918* (N.Y., June 16, 1918) and the *Ziegfeld Follies of 1919* (N.Y., June 16, 1919), the latter of which found him singing Irving Berlin's "You'd Be Surprised," which became a popular record for him. He had a hit with "Makin' Whoopee," but his biggest record came in August 1925 with "If You Knew Susie."

His parents, Russian immigrants, died by the time he was three, and he was raised by his grandmother, Esther Kantrowitz, a peddler, later deriving his stage name from hers. He began working in vaudeville in 1907; in 1912 he joined Gus Edwards's *Kid Kabaret*, staying for two years. Part of his performance was an impression of blackface entertainer Eddie Leonard, singing Leonard's signature song "Ida, Sweet As Apple Cider." The song became a Cantor favorite when he married Ida Tobias on June 9, 1914. (They had five daughters and remained married until her death in 1962.) While on his honeymoon in London, he appeared in the revue *Not Likely*.

Cantor was in the musical *Canary Cottage* in L.A. in 1916 when he was tapped by impresario Florenz Ziegfeld to appear in the *Ziegfeld Midnight Frolic*. He attracted attention with his presentation of "Oh, How She Could Yacki, Hacki, Wicki, Wacki, Woo," which led Ziegfeld to put him in the *Ziegfeld Follies of 1917* (N.Y., June 12, 1917), where he sang "That's the Kind of a Baby for Me," which became his first recording for Victor. He appeared in the revue *Broadway Brevities of 1920* (N.Y., Sept. 29, 1920), followed by *The Midnight Rounders of 1921* (N.Y., Feb. 7, 1921) and *Make It Snappy* (N.Y., April 13, 1922), meanwhile continuing to record and scoring a best-seller with "Margie" in March 1921. Returning to Ziegfeld, he appeared in the *Ziegfeld Follies of 1923* (N.Y., Oct. 20, 1923) and in the Ziegfeld-produced book musical *Kid Boots* (N.Y., Dec. 13, 1923), which ran 479 performances. The month it opened he had the double-

sided record hit "No, No, Nora"/"I've Got the Yes! We Have No Bananas Blues."

Cantor made his feature-film debut in a silent version of *Kid Boots* in 1926, followed by *Special Delivery* (for which he also wrote the story) in 1927, the year he made his final Follies appearance, the *Ziegfeld Follies of 1927* (N.Y., Aug. 16, 1927). *Whoopee* (N.Y., Dec. 4, 1928) was nearly as successful onstage as *Kid Boots* and gave him one of his biggest record hits in "Makin' Whoopee." He co-wrote the libretto for *Earl Carroll's Sketch Book* (N.Y., July 1, 1929), though he did not appear in the revue; it ran 392 performances. After losing a fortune in the 1929 stock market crash, Cantor made at least some of the money back by writing a book, *Caught Short*, about the experience. (A movie based on the book came out in 1930.) He then went to Hollywood and made a series of musical comedy films: *Glorifying the American Girl* (1929); *Whoopee!* (1930); *Palmy Days* (1931); *The Kid from Spain* (1932) (featuring the record hit "What a Perfect Combination"); *Roman Scandals* (1933); *Kid Millions* (1934) (featuring the record hit "Okay, Toots"); *Strike Me Pink* (1936); and *Ali Baba Goes to Town* (1937).

Cantor had a popular radio show starting in 1931, but he was blacklisted by radio in 1939 after giving a speech at the N.Y. World's Fair in which he denounced fascism. When world events vindicated his position, he returned to the air. After another film, *Forty Little Mothers*, in 1940, he made his last appearance in a Broadway musical with *Banjo Eyes* (N.Y., Dec. 21, 1941). His other films of the 1940s were *Thank Your Lucky Stars* (1943), *Show Business* (1944, which he produced), *Hollywood Canteen* (1944), and *If You Knew Susie* (1948, which he produced).

In September 1952, Cantor began hosting *The Colgate Comedy Hour* on television. The show lasted until 1954, when he hosted the *Eddie Cantor Comedy Theatre* for an additional year. He played himself in the film *The Story of Will Rogers* (1952). He dubbed the voice of Keefe Braselle in the film *The Eddie Cantor Story* (1953). The last decade of his life he was largely inactive due to a heart condition.

WRITINGS: With D. Freedman, *My Life Is in Your Hands* (N.Y., 1928); *Caught Short: A Saga of Wailing Wall Street* (N.Y., 1929); *Between the Acts* (N.Y., 1930); *Yoo Hoo, Prosperity! The Eddie Cantor Five-Year Plan* (N.Y., 1931); *Your Next President* (N.Y., 1932); *Ziegfeld, The Great Glorifier* (N.Y., 1934), ed., *World's Book of Best Jokes* (Cleveland, 1943); with J. Ardmore, *Take My Life* (N.Y., 1957); P. Rosenteur, ed., *The Way I See It* (Englewood Cliffs, N.J., 1959); *As I Remember Them* (N.Y., 1963).

BIBL.: G. Koseluk, *E. C.: A Life in Show Business* (Jefferson, N.C., 1995); H. Goldman, *Banjo Eyes: E. C. and the Birth of Modern Stardom* (N.Y., 1997).—**WR**

Capecchi, Renato,

Italian baritone; b. Cairo (of Italian parents), Nov. 6, 1923; d. Milan, June 30, 1998. He was a student in Milan of Ubaldo Carrozzi. After making his debut on the Italian Radio (1948), he made his stage debut as Amonasro in 1949 in Reggio Emilia. From 1950 he sang at Milan's La Scala. On Nov. 24, 1951, he made his Metropolitan Opera debut in N.Y. as Germont père, remaining on its roster until 1954. In 1975 he returned there, and then made occasional visits until

1994. Between 1953 and 1983 he was a regular guest at the Verona Arena. In 1962 he made his debut at London's Covent Garden as Melitone, and sang there again in 1973. In 1977 and 1980 he appeared as Falstaff at Glyndebourne. His guest appearances took him not only all over Italy but to Berlin, Paris, Munich, Moscow, Stuttgart, Stockholm, and other European music centers. His vast repertoire included hundreds of roles, ranging from the traditional to the contemporary. He was particularly successful as a buffo artist, winning special praise for his portrayals of Rossini's Figaro, Dr. Bartolo, Dulcamara, Don Pasquale, and Gianni Schicchi. —NS/LK/DM

Capers, Valerie, pianist and vocalist; b. N.Y., May 24, 1935. While she has not recorded much, she has certainly made her mark on the scene. And when she does record, it is with a sturdy two-handed, dramatic approach and the ultimate sensitivity to her material. Before losing her sight at the age of six, she was playing piano and picking up songs by ear. Encouraged by a supportive family, she graduated from the N.Y. Inst. for the Education of the Blind where she began classical piano studies. She received her B.S. and M.S. degrees, in 1959 and 1960, respectively, from Juilliard School of Music, the first blind graduate. Although she was playing classical repertoire, she ventured into jazz with encouragement from her brother, Bobby Capers, then a saxophonist/flutist with Mongo Santamaria. She began her career in jazz as composer-arranger for Mongo Santamaria's Afro-Cuban-jazz band, contributing his hits, *El Toro* (recorded on his *Live at the Village Gate* album), *Uh-Huh*, and the bossa nova, *Sarai*. She formed her own trio and made her 1967 recording debut on Atlantic with *Portrait in Soul*, and recorded a 1982 album, *Affirmation*. In between, she worked with Ray Brown, Slide Hampton, James Moody, Max Roach, Dizzy Gillespie, and others. She has appeared at Newport, Kool, JVC, North Sea, and other festivals, and performs regularly in N.Y. clubs. She has conducted various performances, including the 1978 Christmas jazz cantata *Sing About Love* at Carnegie Hall and her own "opertorio" *Sojourner* which premiered at N.Y.'s St. Peter's Church (1981). Her teaching credentials include stints at the Manhattan School of Music and her current position as Professor Emeritus and Artist-in-Residence at Bronx Community Coll. of the C.U.N.Y., where she was Chairman of the Department of Music and Art (1987–95). She has received numerous awards, honors, and music grants and, in 1996, was awarded an honorary Doctor of Fine Arts degree from Susquehanna Univ. for her achievements as a scholar, educator, and musician. Fifteen years after her 1982 recording, she made her only album currently in print.

DISC.: *Come on Home* (1995).—NAL

Capet, Lucien, distinguished French violinist and teacher; b. Paris, Jan. 8, 1873; d. there, Dec. 18, 1928. He studied at the Paris Cons. From 1896 to 1899 he was concertmaster of the Lamoureux Orch. From 1899 to 1903 he taught violin at the Cons. of Ste. Cécile in Bordeaux. In 1904 he founded the celebrated Capet Quartet, and played first violin in it until 1921, specializing particularly in the later Beethoven quartets. In 1924 he was appointed director of the Inst. de Violon in Paris. He composed *Le Rouet*, symphonic poem, *Prélude religieux* for Orch., *Devant la mer* for Voice and Orch., *Poème* for Violin and Orch., five string quartets, two violin sonatas, and six violin études. He publ. *La Technique supérieure de l'archet* (Paris, 1916) and *Les 17 Quatuors de Beethoven*, as well as a philosophical work, *Espérances.*—NS/LK/DM

Caplet, André, French composer and conductor; b. Le Havre, Nov. 23, 1878; d. Paris, April 22, 1925. He studied violin in Le Havre, and played in theater orchs. there and in Paris. He entered the Paris Cons. (1896), where he studied with Leroux and Lenepveu. In 1901 he received the Grand Prix de Rome for his cantata *Myrrha*. His *Marche solennelle* for the centennial of the Villa Medicis was performed in Rome (April 18, 1903). He was active in France as a choral and operatic conductor; conducted the first performance of Debussy's *Le Martyre de St. Sébastien* (Paris, May 22, 1911); also conducted the Boston Opera Co. (1910–14) and in London at Covent Garden (1912). Caplet was wounded in action while serving in the French Army during World War I, which seriously impaired his life and greatly curtailed his subsequent musical activities. His music is unequivocally impressionistic, with a lavish use of whole-tone scales and parallel chord formations; he combined this impressionism with neo-archaic usages and mystic programmatic ideas. He was a close friend of Debussy, with whom he collaborated on several of his orch. works and even completed sections left unfinished by Debussy. Their correspondence was publ. in Monaco in 1957.

WORKS: *Rêverie* for Flute and Piano (1897); *Myrrha*, cantata (1901); Double Wind Quintet (Paris, March 9, 1901); *Marche solennelle* (Rome, April 18, 1903); *Elégie* for Cello and Piano (1903); *The Masque of the Red Death* for Harp and Orch. (Paris, March 7, 1909; arranged as *Conte fantastique* for Harp and String Quartet, 1919; Paris, Dec. 29, 1923); Septet for 3 Women's Voices and String Quartet (1909); *Inscriptions champêtres* for Chorus (1914); *Douaumont* for Military Band (1917); Mass for 3 Voices (1920); *Hymne à la naissance du matin* for Chorus and Orch. (1920); *Epiphanie* for Cello and Orch. (Paris, Dec. 29, 1923); *Le miroir de Jésus* for Mezzo-soprano, Women's Chorus, Harp, and Strings (1923; Paris, May 1, 1924); *A la française* and *A l'espagnole*, divertissements for Harp (1924); various choral works, songs, and piano pieces.

BIBL.: *A. C.* (Paris, 1976).—NS/LK/DM

Capobianco, Tito, Argentine-born American opera director and administrator; b. La Plata, Aug. 28, 1931. He received training in law and philosophy in La Plata and in music at the Univ. of Buenos Aires. In 1953 he launched his career as an opera director with a production of *Pagliacci* in La Plata. Moving to Buenos Aires, he was technical director at the Teatro Colón (1958–62) and general director of the Teatro Argentino (1959–61); subsequently was artistic director of the Cincinnati Opera Festival (1961–65) and the Cincinnati Opera (1962–65). In 1966 he began staging operas at the N.Y.C. Opera, where he was resident stage director from 1967. In 1975 he organized the Las Palmas Festival in the

Canary Islands. He also became artistic director of the San Diego Opera in 1975, serving as its general director from 1977. In 1983 he became general director of the Pittsburgh Opera, and in 1997 he was made its artistic director. He was prof. of acting and interpretation at the Academy of Vocal Arts in Philadelphia (1962–68); in 1967 he founded the American Opera Center at the Juilliard School of Music in N.Y., serving as its director until 1969. He was director of opera studies and festival stage director at the Music Academy of the West in Santa Barbara (from 1983), and prof. of acting, staging, and interpretation at the Graduate School of Music at Yale Univ. (from 1983). In many of his operatic stagings, he collaborated with his wife, the choreographer Elena Denda.—NS/LK/DM

Capocci, Filippo, Italian organist, teacher, and composer, son of **Gaetano Capocci;** b. Rome, May 11, 1840; d. there, July 25, 1911. He studied organ and harmony with his father, and then piano at the Accademia di Santa Cecilia in Rome (diploma, 1861). In 1873 he was made organist at St. John Lateran in Rome, succeeding his father as maestro direttore de cappella there in 1898. He also taught organ at the Accademia di Santa Cecilia. He wrote the oratorio *S. Atanasio* (1863) and various organ pieces.

BIBL.: A. De Santi, *Il maestro F. C.* (Rome, 1888).—LK/DM

Capocci, Gaetano, Italian organist, composer, and teacher, father of **Filippo Capocci;** b. Rome, Oct. 16, 1811; d. there, Jan. 11, 1898. He studied music with Valentino Fioravanti and organ with Sante Pascoli; at the same time he took courses in theology. In 1830 he was appointed organist and music director at the Church of S. Maria in Rome. He then was organist at S. Maria Maggiore (from 1839) and at S. Giovanni in Laterano (from 1855). He had numerous students, among them Margherita of Savoy, the future Queen of Italy. His chief merit as a composer was a successful revival of the Classical oratorio. He wrote the oratorios *Il Battista* (Rome, March 31, 1833) and *Assalonne* (Rome, Dec. 8, 1842), as well as numerous sacred choruses and organ pieces.—NS/LK/DM

Capoianu, Dumitru, Romanian composer; b. Bucharest, Oct. 19, 1929. He studied at the Bucharest Cons. (1941–53) with Jora, Mendelsohn, Vancea, Andricu, and Rogalski. From 1969 to 1973 he was manager of the Georges Enesco Phil.

WORKS: DRAMATIC: Musicals, ballets, and film scores. **ORCH.:** 2 suites (1953, 1954); *Divertissement* for 2 Clarinets and Strings (1956); Violin Concerto (1957); *Cinematographic Variations* (1965); *Moto perpetuo* for Solo Violin or Group of Violins and Orch. (1972); *Chemari '77* (1977); *Muzica de ambianta* (1980); *Faţete*, symphonic jazz suite (1986). **CHAMBER:** Wind Quintet (1950); Viola Sonata (1952); 2 string quartets (1954, 1959); Trio for Violin, Viola, and Cello (1968); Sonata for Solo Harp (1978); *Arcuri*, trio for Viola, Cello, and Piano (1982); Sonata for Solo Cello (1982). **VOCAL:** *Valses ignobles et sentimentales du tout...* for Mezzo- soprano and String Orch. (1986); choral pieces; solo songs.—NS/LK/DM

Capoul, (Joseph-Amédée-) Victor, French tenor; b. Toulouse, Feb. 27, 1839; d. Pujaudran-du-Gers,

Feb. 18, 1924. He was a student of Revial and Mocker at the Paris Cons. On Aug. 26, 1861, he made his operatic debut as Daniel in Adam's *Le Châlet* at the Paris Opéra-Comique. After a decade there, he sang at the Academy of Music in N.Y. (1871–74) and at London's Drury Lane (1871–75). On April 5, 1877, he made his first appearance at London's Covent Garden as Fra Diavolo, where he sang until 1879. He made his Metropolitan Opera debut in N.Y. as Faust on Oct. 27, 1883, remaining on its roster until 1884 and again in 1891–92 and 1895–96. From 1897 to 1905 he was stage manager at the Paris Opéra. His other prominent roles included Count Almaviva, Wilhelm Meister, Edgardo, and Roméo. —NS/LK/DM

Capp, Frank, big band and small ensemble drummer; b. Worcester, Mass., Aug. 20, 1931. He was 19 when he replaced Shelly Manne in the Stan Kenton band in 1951. He then joined the bands of Neal Hefti, Billy May, Benny Goodman, and Bob Florence. He also worked and/or recorded with major jazz stars, including Ella Fitzgerald, Benny Goodman, Andre Previn, Art Pepper, and Turk Murphy, and played in bands of the *Merv Griffin*, *Red Skelton*, and *Steve Allen* TV shows.

Always in demand as a studio musician, he is known for laying down a solid beat while accenting the melody of each song. He worked for Warner Bros. Studio and fueled combos for vocalists Peggy Lee and Shirley Horn, pianist Roger Kellaway, trumpeter Ruby Braff, and trombonists Al Grey and Rob McConnell. He performs in small combos at jazz parties and festivals around the nation, as well as leading the Frank Capp Juggernaut big band. Juggernaut effectively emulates the tight section work and exciting solos of the Basie bands, and has earned fans and record-chart recognition via tours to England and Japan. Juggernaut originated as a one-nighter in 1975 when he was contracting for the Neal Hefti band and the leader decided to break up the orchestra. He has continued to lead Juggernaut after Pierce's death in 1992, with Gerald Wiggins at the piano. Vocalists Joe Williams, Ernie Andrews, and Ernestine Anderson have performed with Juggernaut, but the main focus is on instrumental power and polish. The band's changing cast of musicians has included trumpeters Blue Mitchell, Snooky Young, Conte Candoli, Bobby Shew, Bill Berry, Carl Saunders and Frank Szabo; saxophonists Marshal Royal, Red Holloway, Bob Cooper, Lanny Morgan, Plas Johnson, Richie Kamuca, Pete Christlieb, Jack Nimitz, Jackie Kelso and Rickey Woodard; trombonists Buster Cooper, Thurman Green and George Bohanon; and bassists Chuck Berghofer and Bob Maize.

DISC.: *Juggernaut* (1977); *Live at the Alley Cat* (1987); *The Capp-Pierce Juggernaut: Live at the Century Plaza* (1987); *Juggernaut Strikes Again!* (1990); *Frank Capp Trio Presents Rickey Woodard* (1991); *The Frank Capp Juggernaut: In a Hefti Bag* (1995); *Frank Capp Quartet Featuring Rickey Woodard: Quality Time* (1995); *Frank Capp Juggernaut: Play It Again, Sam* (1997).—PM

Cappuccilli, Piero, admired Italian baritone; b. Trieste, Nov. 9, 1929. He studied with Luciano Doaggio in Trieste. In 1957 he made his operatic debut at Milan's

Teatro Nuovo as Tonio. On March 26, 1960, he made his Metropolitan Opera debut in N.Y. as Germont père, but then pursued his career in Europe. In 1964 he made his first appearance at Milan's La Scala as Donizetti's Ashton, and subsequently sang there regularly with notable success. He made his debut at London's Covent Garden as Germont père in 1967, and returned there in 1976 as a member of the La Scala company. In 1969 he made his first appearance at the Chicago Lyric Opera as Francesco in *I Due Foscari*. He made his debut at the Salzburg Festival as Posa in 1975. In 1978 he sang Simon Boccanegra in Paris. While continuing to sing in various Italian operatic centers, he also appeared as a guest artist throughout Europe. Among his other fine roles were Iago, Renato, Rigoletto, Nabucco, Escamillo, and Macbeth.—**NS/LK/DM**

Capricornus, Samuel Friedrich, Bohemian-born German composer; b. Schertitz, Dec. 21, 1628; d. Stuttgart, Nov. 10, 1665. He received training in music, theology, languages, and philosophy. In 1651 he became director of music of the churches and at the gymnasium in Pressburg. From 1657 he served as Kapellmeister at the Württemberg court in Stuttgart. He composed operas, ballets, instrumental pieces, and sacred vocal works.

> **BIBL.:** H. Buchner, *S.F. C.* (diss., Univ. of Munich, 1922). —**LK/DM**

Caprioli, Alberto, Italian composer, conductor, teacher, and writer on music; b. Bologna, Nov. 16, 1956. He studied composition with Margola (1973–79) and Togni (diploma, 1983) and conducting with Guarino (1977–78) at the Padua Cons. He also studied conducting with Tito Gotti at the Bologna Cons. (diploma, 1979), with Kondrashin in Hilversum (1978), and with Suitner (1979–83) and Cerha (diploma, 1983) at the Vienna Academy of Music. His training in composition was completed with Schaeffer at the Salzburg Mozarteum (1986–88). He also pursued studies in the humanities at the Univ. of Bologna (Ph.D.). In 1980 he became a teacher of conducting at the Bologna Cons., where he held that chair from 1989. From 1990 he was one of the collaborators on the critical edition of Maderna's works. In 1992 he founded the Progetto Esperia in Bologna, a new music laboratory. His writings have appeared in various publications, and range from studies on Schumann and Hölderlin to Nono and Boulez. In his music, Caprioli has followed a contemporary path which includes the use of tape and live electronics.

> **WORKS: CHAMBER:** Trio for Piano, Violin, and Cello (Austrian Radio, Salzburg, Sept. 28, 1984); *del celeste confine* for String Quartet (1985; Kraków, April 7, 1987); *Serenata per Francesca* for 6 Players (Austrian Radio, Salzburg, Sept. 27, 1985); *A la dolce ombra* for Violin, Cello, and Piano (1985; Perugia, Jan. 28, 1987); *Dialogue* for Double Bass and 2 String Quartets (Undine, Oct. 2, 1986); *Symphoniae I/II* (Salzburg, May 5, 1988) and *III* (Salzburg, Aug. 4, 1989) for Violin; *Due Notturni d'obliò* for Chamber Ensemble (Stuttgart, Sept. 10, 1988); *...il vostro pianto aurora o luna* for Flute, Clarinet, Horn, Guitar, and Vibraphone (Paris, Dec. 11, 1988); *Intermedio I* for Amplified Flute and Live Electronics (Klagenfurt, March 9, 1989); *Vor dem singenden Odem (alla memoria di Luigi Nono)* for Flute, Clarinet,

Violin, Cello, and Piano (Perugia, May 31, 1990; rev. version, Bologna, April 8, 1992); *"John-Cage"-Variations* for Bass Flute, Bass Clarinet, Violin, Cello, and Piano (Trieste, Sept. 25, 1991); *À quinze ans* for Cello (Bratislava, Oct. 22, 1991); *Anges*, paraphrase after Schumann, for Alto Flute, Viola, and Harp (Siena, Aug. 26, 1993); *Folâtre (Notturno di rosa)* for 2 Guitars (1993); *Evaernesto*, duo concertante for Flute, Clarinet, and Chamber Ensemble (Vienna, Oct. 28, 1995); *Elegia per Carlo Michelstaedter* for Oboe and Instruments (Bologna, Feb. 25, 1998); *Era* for Alto Saxophone and Brass Quintet (Berlare, March 6, 1999). **KEYBOARD: Piano:** *Elegia* (1974; Ravenna, Feb. 22, 1987); *Sette Frammenti dal diario* (1974; South German Radio, Stuttgart, June 24, 1987); *Les Adieux de vent* (1974; Bologna, Sept. 6, 1988); *Per lo dolce silentio de la notte* for Piano and Tape (Salzburg, May 25, 1987). **VOCAL:** *Abendlied (omaggio a Gustav Mahler)* for Soprano and Orch. (1977; Parma, May 5, 1978); *Sonetti di Shakespeare* for Voice and Chamber Ensemble (Austrian Radio, Salzburg, Oct. 4, 1983); *Sette frammenti dal Kyrie per Dino Campana* for Soli, Chorus, and Orch. (Stuttgart, Aug. 25, 1991); *L'ascesa degli angeli ribelli* for Voice and Instruments (Bologna, Feb. 8, 1994); *Dittico baciato* for Chorus and Orch. (Bologna, Nov. 15, 1994); *Canto* for Reciter and Orch. (Bologna, May 18, 1998). —**NS/LK/DM**

Caproli or **Caprioli, Carlo,** Italian organist, violinist, and composer, known as **Carlo Del Violino**; b. Rome, c. 1617; d. probably there, c. 1693. After serving as second organist at the Collegio Germanico in Rome (1643–45), he was second violinist (1649–61) and then first violinist (1661–70) at S. Luigi dei Francesi. In 1653–54 he also was in the service of Prince Ludovisio Pamphili. Following a sojourn at the French court, where he brought out the successful opera *Le nozze di Peleo e di Theti* (Paris, April 14, 1654; music not extant) and was honored with the title of maître de la musique du cabinet du Roy, he returned to Rome and was in the service of Cardinal Antonio Barberini from 1654 until about 1664. He gained distinction as a composer of cantatas, and he also wrote several oratorios.—**LK/DM**

Capron, Henri, French-born American cellist, singer, impresario, and composer who flourished in the late 18th century. After training in Paris, he settled in America and became manager of subscription concerts in Philadelphia in 1785. With Reinagle, he was co-manager of subscription concerts in N.Y. (1788–89), and then sole manager (1791–92; 1793–94), at which he appeared as both a cellist and a singer. He also was a cellist in the Old American Co. orch. He returned to Philadelphia in 1793 and became co-manager with John Christopher Moller of a music store, which publ. a periodical collection of music in the *Moller and Capron's Monthly Numbers*. In 1794 he became principal of a French boarding school. His extant works comprise *A New Contredance* and some songs.—**NS/LK/DM**

Captain Beefheart (Don Van Vliet), protopunk, gravel-voiced singer of enigmatic lyrics; b. Glendale, Calif., Jan. 15, 1941. Captain Beefheart moved with his family to the desert town of Lancaster, Calif., at age 13 and became friends with Frank Zappa in high school. Teaching himself harmonica and saxophone, Beefheart performed with several R&B bands before forming the first edition of His Magic Band in 1964. Gaining a reputation in area desert towns, the group recorded Bo Diddley's "Diddy Wah Diddy" for A&M Records, and the single became a regional hit. However, material for a first album was rejected by A&M as "too negative," and Van Vliet retreated to Lancaster. By 1965, he had assembled a new Magic Band with lead guitarist Ry Cooder and drummer John French to rerecord the material for Buddah Records, which released it as *Safe As Milk*. Winning considerable critical acclaim in the United States and Europe, the album spurred a successful tour of Europe in early 1966.

With the departure of Cooder, Beefheart's band was crippled, since the lead guitar parts, complex and erratic, were personally taught by Van Vliet over long periods of time. Nonetheless, with new guitarist Jeff Cotton, sessions for the next album began in April 1968. The album was ultimately released in altered form as *Strictly Personal*. Most of the album's contents were later reissued in unaltered form as *I May Be Hungry but I Sure Ain't Weird* in 1992. *Mirror Man*, also recorded in 1968, was not issued until 1970.

A disappointed Van Vliet subsequently accepted Zappa's offer to make a new album, free of all artistic restrictions, for Zappa's Straight Records. Following Van Vliet's lead, the members of the reorganized Magic Band took on bizarre names: guitarist-flutist Bill Harkleroad became Zoot Horn Rollo; guitarist Jeff Cotton became Antennae Jimmy Semens; and bassist Mark Boston became Rockette Morton. Joining them was an unidentified drummer (John French, known as Drumbo) and the Mascara Snake on vocals and clarinet. *Trout Mask Replica*, produced by Zappa, was hailed as one of the most advanced concepts in rock music but proved a commercial failure.

Beefheart subsequently performed the vocals on "Willie the Pimp" for Zappa's album *Hot Rats*, and switched his own group to Reprise for *Lick My Decals Off, Baby*. In 1971, they made one of their infrequent tours of the U.S. to befuddled fans. Art Tripp (also known as Ed Marimba) was added on drums and marimba for *The Spotlight Kid* and *Clear Spot*. Moving to Mercury Records, the band recorded the softer and more accessible *Unconditionally Guaranteed*. Thereafter, the band quit and Beefheart recorded *Bluejeans and Moonbeams* with session musicians.

On May 20 and 21, 1975, Beefheart recorded *Bongo Fury* with Zappa and the Mothers at the Armadillo World Headquarters in Austin, Tex. By 1976, Beefheart had assembled a new Magic Band for occasional club appearances. During 1977 and 1978, the group successfully toured Europe and played sold-out engagements at N.Y.'s Bottom Line and Hollywood's Roxy. Subsequent album releases were *Shiny Beast (Bat Chain Puller)*, *Doc at the Radar Station* (hailed as perhaps the best of Beefheart's later career), and *Ice Cream for Crow*. The group successfully toured Europe and the U.S. in 1980, but disbanded in 1982. Van Vliet, an accomplished artist for many years, retired from music in 1985 to pursue painting as a full-time profession. He has since exhibited his works at galleries in the U.S. and Europe, including the San Francisco Museum of Modern Art in 1989.

An early associate of both Zappa and Cooder, Captain Beefheart and His Magic Band played a curious mix of delta blues, rock 'n' roll and avant-garde jazz that explored the farthest reaches of rock music in the 1960s and 1970s. The band's unique sound, passed over by all but the most progressive of fans, was characterized by Beefheart's incredible voice (growling and gravelly, yet with a range of more than four octaves), intricate arrangements, enigmatic lyrics (generally written by Beefheart), and early use of the theremin, an electronic instrument. Perhaps best known for 1969's *Trout Mask Replica*, Beefheart and His Magic Band are an acknowledged influence on punk and new wave music.

DISC.: *Safe As Milk* (1965); *Strictly Personal* (1968); *Trout Mask Replica* (1969); *Mirror Man* (1970); *Lick My Decals Off, Baby* (1970); *The Spotlight Kid* (1972); *Clear Spot* (1972); *Unconditionally Guaranteed* (1974); *Bluejeans and Moonbeams* (1974); *Bongo Fury* (with Frank Zappa and the Mothers; 1975); *Shiny Beast (Bat Chain Puller)* (1978); *Doc at the Radar Station* (1980); *Ice Cream for Crow* (1982); *The Dust Blows Forward* (box set; 1999); *Grow Fins: Rarities 1965–1982* (box set; 1999).—**BH**

Cara, Marchetto, Italian singer, lutenist, and composer; b. probably in Verona, c. 1470; d. Mantua, c. 1525. By 1494 he was in the service of the court in Manta, where he was made maestro di cappella in 1511; he also was active in other Italian cities. He was a leading composer of frottolas, of which 85 such works are extant. Among his other works are a *Salve regina* for three Voices, seven *laudi*, and various madrigals.

BIBL.: W. Prizer, *M. C. and the North Italian Frottola* (diss., Univ. of N.C., 1974).—**LK/DM**

Caracciolo, Franco, Italian conductor; b. Bari, March 29, 1920. He studied composition and piano at the Cons. in San Pietro a Majella in Naples and conducting with Molinari at the Accademia di Santa Cecilia in Rome. In 1949 he went to Naples as conductor of the Alessandro Scarlatti Orch. In 1964 he settled in Milan as principal conductor of RAI, retiring in 1987. In his programs, Caracciolo revived many of the forgotten orch. works of Italian composers; he also conducted contemporary works.—**NS/LK/DM**

Caradori-Allan, Maria (Caterina Rosalbina née de Munck), Alsatian soprano; b. Milan (of Alsatian parents), 1800; d. Surbiton, Surrey, Oct. 15, 1865. She received her musical training from her mother, whose name she chose as her own for professional purposes. After appearances in France and Germany, she made her London debut as Cherubino at the King's Theatre on Jan. 12, 1822. She continued to sing in London until 1827, and then again from 1834, becoming particularly known as a concert and oratorio artist. She created the role of Giulietta in Bellini's *I Capuleti e i Montecchi* (Venice, March 11, 1830) and sang in the premiere of Mendelssohn's *Elijah* (Birmingham Festival, Aug. 26, 1846). Among her finest operatic roles were Zerlina, Amina, and Rosina.—**NS/LK/DM**

Carafa (de Colobrano), Michele (Enrico-Francesco-Vincenzo-Aloisio- Paolo), Italian composer; b. Naples, Nov. 17, 1787; d. Paris, July 26,

1872. He was a son of Prince Colobrano, Duke of Alvito, and began to study music at an early age. Though he became an officer in the army of Naples, and fought in Napoleon's Russian campaign, he devoted his leisure time to music, and after Waterloo adopted it as a profession. In 1827 he settled in Paris, succeeding Le Sueur as a member of the Academy (1837). In 1840 was appointed a prof. of composition at the Paris Cons.

WORKS: DRAMATIC: O p e r a : *Gabriella di Vergy* (Naples, July 3, 1816); *Ifigenia in Tauride* (Naples, June 19, 1817); *Berenice in Siria* (Naples, July 29, 1818); *Elisabetta in Derbyshire* (Venice, Dec. 26, 1818); the following operas were produced at the Opéra-Comique in Paris: *Jeanne d'Arc* (March 10, 1821); *Le Solitaire* (Aug. 17, 1822); *Le Valet de chambre* (Sept. 16, 1823); *L'Auberge supposée* (April 26, 1824); *Sangarido* (May 19, 1827); *Masaniello* (Dec. 27, 1827; on the same subject as Auber's *La Muette de Portici*, staged at the Paris Opéra 2 months later; yet Carafa's *Masaniello* held the stage in competition with Auber's famous opera for 136 nights); *La Violette* (Oct. 7, 1828); *Jenny* (Sept. 26, 1829); *Le Livre de l'ermite* (Aug. 11, 1831); *La Prison d'Edimbourg* (July 20, 1833); *Une Journée de la Fronde* (Nov. 7, 1833); *La Grande Duchesse* (Nov. 16, 1835); *Thérèse* (Sept. 26, 1838). Also ballets, cantatas, and much church music. **—NS/LK/DM**

Carapetyan, Armen, eminent Persian-born American musicologist of Armenian descent; b. Isfahan, Oct. 11, 1908; d. Francestown, N.H., Sept. 5, 1992. He studied at the American Coll. in Tehran (diploma, 1927); after receiving training in violin and composition in Paris and N.Y., he continued composition studies with Malipiero; then took courses in musicology at Harvard Univ. (M.A., 1940; Ph.D., 1945, with the diss. *The "Musica nova" of Adriano Willaert, with Reference to the Humanistic Society of Sixteenth- Century Venice*). In 1945 he became founder-director of the American Inst. of Musicology with headquarters in Rome and Cambridge, Mass., where he diligently pursued his labors until 1980; he served as general ed. of Corpus Mensurabilis Musicae, Corpus Scriptorum de Musica, and Musicological Studies and Documents, and was ed. of the journal *Musica Disciplina* (from 1946). He contributed numerous important articles on the music of the Middle Ages and the Renaissance to U.S. and European journals. In 1979 he was made an honorary member of the American Musicological Soc.**—NS/LK/DM**

Cardan, Jerome, Italian physician and music theorist; b. Pavia, Sept. 24, 1501; d. Rome, Sept. 20, 1576. He studied music in Milan and medicine at the Univ. of Padua (M.D., 1526). From 1562 to 1571 he was prof. of medicine at the Univ. of Bologna. He wrote two valuable treatises on music, both entitled *De musica* (1546, 1574); see C. Miller, *The Writings of J. C. on Music*, Musicological Studies and Documents, XXXII (1973).

BIBL.: J. Eckman, *J. C.* (Baltimore, 1946).**—LK/DM**

Cardew, Cornelius, English composer of extreme avant-garde tendencies; b. Winchcombe, Gloucester, May 7, 1936; d. in a road accident in London, Dec. 13, 1981. He studied composition with Ferguson at the Royal Academy of Music in London (1953–57); in 1957

he went to Cologne and worked at the electronic studio there as an assistant to Stockhausen (1958–60). Returning to England, he organized concerts of experimental music. From 1963 to 1965 he had private lessons with Petrassi in Rome. In 1967 he was appointed to the faculty of the Royal Academy of Music in London. In 1969, together with Michael Parsons and Howard Skempton, he organized the Scratch Orch., a heterogeneous group for performances of new music, militantly latitudinarian and disestablishmentarian. Under the influence of the teachings of Mao Zedong, Cardew renounced his modernistic past as a bourgeois deviation detrimental to pure Marxism, and subsequently attacked his former associate, Stockhausen, in a book ominously entitled *Stockhausen Serves Imperialism* (London, 1974). He also repudiated his own magnum opus, *The Great Learning*, which was orig. performed at the 1968 Cheltenham Festival, scored for a non-singing chorus to the words of Ezra Pound's tr. of Confucius, a chorus which was admonished to bang on tapped stones, to whistle and shriek, but never to stoop to vocalizing. In the revised version of the work, he appended to the title the slogan "Apply Marxism-Leninism-Mao Zedong Thought in a living way to the problems of the present." This version was first performed by the Scratch Orch. at a Promenade Concert in London on Aug. 24, 1972. His other works include *Volo Solo* for Any Handy Musical Instrument (1965); *Three Winter Potatoes* for Piano and various assorted Concrete Sounds, as well as for Newspapers, Balloons, Noise, and People Working (London, March 11, 1968); *The East is Red* for Violin and Piano (1972); and *The Old and the New* for Soprano, Chorus, and Orch. (1973). He also publ. several pamphlets containing some confusing confutations of Confucius. In addition, he compiled a seminal manual, *Scratch Music* (London, 1970).**—NS/LK/DM**

Cardon, Jean-Baptiste, French harpist, teacher, and composer; b. Mons, South Netherlands, 1760; d. St. Petersburg, March 11, 1803. He was the son of the violinist and composer Jean-Baptiste (actually, Jean-Guillain) Cardon (b. Mons, Jan. 18, 1732; d. Versailles, Oct. 18, 1788). He was taken by his family to Paris when he was about a year old. While still a young man, he acquired a notable reputation as a harp teacher. In the wake of the French Revolution, he went to Russia and served as harpist to the royal family and as a theater musician (1790–93). Among his works were symphonies concertantes, a Harp Concerto, chamber music, and solo harp pieces. His works for the harp proved influential. **—LK/DM**

Cardoso, Manuel, distinguished Portuguese composer; b. Fronteira, near Portalegre (baptized), Dec. 11, 1566; d. Lisbon, Nov. 24, 1650. After studies with Manuel Mendes and Cosme Delgado at the Évora Cathedral choir school, he was made a member of the Carmelite order (1588) and took his vows (1589) at Lisbon's Convento do Carmo, where he was active as an organist and choirmaster. He wrote much sacred music, most of which perished in the devastating Lisbon earthquake and fire of 1755. His extant works, all publ. in Lisbon, include *Cantica BVM* for four to five Voices

(1613), *Missae* for four to six Voices, lib. 1 (1625), *Missae* for four to six Voices, lib. 2 (1636), *Missae de BVM* for four to six Voices, lib. 3 (1636), and *Livro de varios motetes officio da semana santa e outras cousas* for four Voices (1648), all of which have been ed. in Portugaliae Musica, series A, V-VI, XIII, XX, XXII, XXVI (1962–74).

BIBL.: M. de Sampayo Ribeiro, *Frei M. C.: Contribuição para o estudo da sua vida e da sua obra*, Achegas para a História da Música em Portugal, VI (Lisbon, 1961).—**NS/LK/DM**

Cardus, Sir (John Frederick) Neville, English writer on music and cricket; b. Manchester, April 3, 1888; d. London, Feb. 28, 1975. He studied singing, then turned to journalism; wrote essays on numerous subjects, but primarily on cricket and music. In 1917 he joined the staff of the *Manchester Guardian*; then was its chief music critic (1927–39); from 1939 to 1947 he was in Australia, writing on cricket and music for the *Sydney Morning Herald*. Returning to London, he became music critic for the *Manchester Guardian* in 1951. He received the Wagner Medal of the City of Bayreuth in 1963, and in 1967 he was knighted. His literary style is quasi-Shavian in its colloquial manner and stubborn persuasion.

WRITINGS: *Music for Pleasure* (1942); *Ten Composers* (1945; 2nd ed., Aug., 1958 as *A Composers' Eleven*); *Autobiography* (1947); *Second Innings: More Autobiography* (1950); *Talking of Music* (1957); *Sir Thomas Beecham: A Memoir* (1961); *Gustav Mahler: His Mind and His Music* (1965); *The Delights of Music: A Critic's Choice* (1966); *Full Score* (1970).

BIBL.: R. Daniels, ed., *Conversations with C.* (London, 1976); C. Brookes, *His Own Man: The Life of N. C.* (London, 1985). —**NS/LK/DM**

Carelli, Emma, esteemed Italian soprano; b. Naples, May 12, 1877; d. in an automobile accident in Montefiascone, near Rome, Aug. 17, 1928. She was a pupil of her father, the composer B. Carelli, at the Cons. San Pietro a Majella in Naples. In 1895 she made her operatic debut in Altamura in Mercadante's *La Vestale*. After singing in various Italian opera houses, she made her debut at Milan's La Scala in 1899 as Desdemona; in 1901 she was the first to sing the role of Tatiana in Italy. She then sang throughout Europe, and also appeared at the Teatro Colón in Buenos Aires and in Rio de Janeiro. In 1910 she married Walter Mocchi, the director of Rome's Teatro Costanzi, where she was the first to sing Elektra in Italy in 1912. She succeeded her husband as its director (1912–26). Among her most acclaimed roles were Iris and Zazá.—**NS/LK/DM**

Carena, Maria, Italian soprano; b. Turin, 1891; d. there, Oct. 9, 1966. She studied in Turin with Virginia Ferni-Germano, and made her operatic debut there in 1917 as Leonora in *Il Trovatore*. Following appearances in Rome, Naples, and Milan, she sang in Buenos Aires (1919), Lisbon (1920), and Madrid (1920–21). In 1922 she made her first appearance at Milan's La Scala as Suor Angelica, and continued to sing there until 1932. In 1924 she sang in the premiere of Boito's *Nerone* at La Scala. In 1932 she scored a fine success as Giulia in *La Vestale* in Rome.—**NS/LK/DM**

Carestini, Giovanni, greatly renowned Italian castrato alto; b. Filottrano, near Ancona, c. 1705; d. probably there, c. 1760. He studied in Milan, then made his operatic debut in a female role in A. Scarlatti's *Griselda* in Rome (1721), where he continued to sing until 1723. He sang in Venice (1723–26), Parma and Genoa (1726), Rome (1727–30), Milan (1727–32), Naples (1728–29), where he found a rival in Bernacchi, and again in Venice (1729, 1731); he also served as chamber virtuoso to the Duke of Parma. From 1731 to 1741 he was in the service of the Elector of Bavaria in Munich, but he remained active in other music centers. He made his London debut in the pasticcio *Semiramide riconosciuta* (Oct. 30, 1733); there Handel chose him to create the leading male roles in his *Arianna in Creta* (Jan. 26, 1734), *Il Parnasso in festa* (March 13, 1734), *Ariodante* (Jan. 8, 1735), and *Alcina* (April 16, 1735), as well as the completely revised role of Mirtillo in *Il Pastor fido* (May 18, 1734). After appearances in Venice (1735) and Naples and Bologna (1736), he sang once again in London (1739–40). On Dec. 26, 1740, he sang in the inaugural performance at Turin's Teatro Regio of Feo's *Arsace*; he also sang in Reggio (1741), Milan (1742–44), where he created the principal roles in Gluck's *Demofoonte* (Jan. 6, 1743) and *Sofonisba* (Jan. 13, 1744), Padua (1743), and Venice (1743–45). He entered the service of the Elector of Saxony in Dresden in 1747. After serving Frederick the Great in Berlin (1750–54), he went to St. Petersburg, where he won the approbation of the Empresess Elizabeth.—**NS/LK/DM**

Carewe, John (Maurice Foxall), English conductor; b. Derby, Jan. 24, 1933. After studies with W. Goehr, Deutsch, and Boulez at the Guildhall School of Music in London, and with Messiaen at the Paris Cons., he organized the New Music Ensemble (1958). He was also on the staff of Morley Coll. (1958–66) and was principal conductor of the BBC Welsh Sym. Orch. in Cardiff (1966–71); he subsequently was music director of the Brighton Phil. Soc. (1974–87) and principal conductor of the Fires of London (1980–84). In 1993 he became music director of the City Theater and Robert Schumann Phil. in Chemnitz.—**NS/LK/DM**

Carey, Henry, English composer; b. probably in Yorkshire, c. 1687; d. (suicide) London, Oct. 5, 1743. He was a natural son of Henry Savile, Lord Eland. He studied music with Linnert, Roseingrave, and Geminiani. He settled around 1710 in London, where he was active as a poet, librettist, playwright, and composer. He wrote six ballad-operas, of which *The Contrivances* (Drury Lane, London, June 20, 1729) achieved the greatest success. He wrote the words of the popular song *Sally in Our Alley* and composed a musical setting for it, but his setting was replaced in 1790 by the tune *What Though I Am a Country Lass*, which has since been traditionally sung to Carey's original poem; also popular was his intermezzo with singing, *Nancy, or The Parting Lovers* (1739). He publ. a collection of 100 ballads, *The Musical Century* (two vols., 1737 and 1740); also six Cantatas (1732) and three Burlesque Cantatas (1741). Carey's claim to the authorship of *God Save the King* was put forth by his son, George Savile Carey

(1743–1807), more than 50 years after his father's death, without any supporting evidence; many anthologies still list Carey's name as the author of the British national anthem. For a complete account of this misattribution, see P.A. Scholes, *God Save the Queen!* (London, 1954). See also W. Cummings, "God Save the King," *The Origin and History of the Music and Words* (London, 1902), O.G. Sonneck, *Report on the Star- Spangled Banner* (1909), F.S. Boas and J.E. Borland, *The National Anthem* (London, 1916), J.A. Fuller Maitland, "Facts and Fictions about God Save the King," *Musical Quarterly* (Oct. 1916), and E.A. Maginty, "America: The Origin of Its Melody," ibid. (July 1934).—**NS/LK/DM**

Carey, Mariah, the most successful female artist of the 1990s, her six-octave voice selling over 80 million albums worldwide; b. N.Y.C., March 22, 1970. Mariah Carey's mother, Patricia Carey, was a solist with the N.Y.C. Opera in the late 1960s and early 1970s, and continued to work as a vocal coach. Her father, a black Venezuelan aeronautical engineer, divorced her mom when she was just three years old. From a very young age, Mariah was convinced she would be a star. She left her home in Long Island the day after graduating high school to prove it.

While waiting tables, Mariah hooked up with Ben Margulies, a friend of her older brother's. They started writing songs together and cut a demo tape. Through another friend, she found out that dance artist Brenda K. Starr was looking for a background vocalist. Carey sought and got the job. Starr became her mentor, taking her to music business parties and events. At one such soiree, Starr gave Carey's demo to Columbia records president Tommy Mattola. Legend has it that Mattola popped the tape into his limo's cassette player and liked what he heard so much he had his driver go back to the party so he could start the signing process.

Carey's eponymous 1990 debut generated four chart-topping singles in a row, "Vision of Love" (also #1 R&B), "Love Takes Time" (also #1 R&B), "Someday," and "I Don't Wanna Cry" (also #1 AC). All but the last went gold. The album went octuple platinum and stayed on the top of the album charts for 11 weeks. At the Grammy's that year, Mariah took home the Best New Artist and Best Pop Vocal Performance Female statuettes.

Carey managed to avoid the Best New Artist curse, however, following that success up with *Emotions* a little over a year later. The gold title track topped both the pop and R&B charts, "Can't Let Go" hit #2 pop and topped the AC charts, and "Make It Happen" got as high as #5. The album sold four million copies and rose as high as #4.

Despite her enormous success, Carey had yet to appear widely in concert, creating rumors that her phenomenal vocal range was somehow manufactured in the studio. Admittedly not fond of performing live, Carey had only done so in limited settings—for video cameras in upstate N.Y., at trade events promoting her records, and small "boutique" concerts. Her next recording, however, was a live performance for MTV's *Unplugged* series. The triple platinum EP featured her

version of the Jackson 5's "I'll Be There" that topped the pop and AC charts. It also helped launch the career of her background singer, Trey Lorenz.

In 1993 Carey became Mrs. Tommy Mattola. She also released her third studio album, *Music Box*. The first single from the album, "Dreamlover" spent eight weeks at the top of the pop charts and sold platinum. "Hero" also went platinum and spent four weeks atop the charts. The gold "Without You" only got as high as #3 and "Anytime You Need a Friend" rose to #12. The album sold 10 million copies and spent eight weeks at #1.

The next year, Carey duetted with Luther Vandross on "Endless Love," taking the tune to a gold #2. After releasing a triple platinum Christmas record in 1994, she followed with *Daydream*. The album featured a series of duets, pairing Carey with rapper ODB from the Wu Tang Clan, on the double platinum single "Fantasy." The single became only the second in chart history to enter at #1. Her next single, another double platinum duet from the album, "One Sweet Day" found Carey accompanied by the vocal group Boyz II Men. It also entered the charts at #1 and stayed there for a record-breaking 16 weeks. The album sold over 10 million copies and topped the charts.

Having sold 80 million records worldwide, Carey next tried her hand at a custom label. She started Crave records through Sony Music. However, she was unable to translate her hit-making talents to other artists. Within two years, the operation had shuttered. Shortly after, Carey and Mattola separated and divorced.

Back to her forte of recording, Carey's next album, *Butterfly*, entered the charts at #1, as did the debut single from the record, "Honey." "My All" also topped the charts and sold platinum. The album featured a who's who of the hip-hop scene, including Missy "Misdemeanor" Elliott, members of Bone Thugs-N-Harmony, and Sean "Puffy" Combs.

Carey next released a collection of her chart-topping singles, simply called *Ones*. The album went triple platinum and topped off at #4 on the charts. It featured the #1 platinum single "I Still Believe."

Carey and Whitney Houston performed a duet on "When You Believe" for the *Prince of Egypt* soundtrack. The record, pairing the two most successful female artists in pop music history, reached #1 and went gold. In fall 1999 Carey returned once again to the top of the charts with "Heartbreaker," featuring the rapper Jay-Z. This was her fourteenth #1 single, giving her a total of over 60 weeks at the #1 position, a new record for a pop act. Her record label bragged that Carey was the only artist to have a #1 pop song in every year of the decade of the 1990s, a feat matched only once before: by Paul Whiteman's jazz orchestra in the 1920s!

One of the most ambitious singers working in pop music, Carey's technique and talent often get lost in the gloss of her popularity. Unlike many of her contemporaries, Carey writes or co-writes the bulk of her material. She has also directed many of her videos, all of which tend to focus on her considerable physical charms. She has a reputation for being in the studio and in control from the beginning of a project until the end. Her success only *looks* easy.

DISC.: *Mariah Carey* (1990); *Emotions* (1991); *Mariah Carey MTV Unplugged* (1992); *Music Box* (1993); *Merry Christmas* (1994); *Daydream* (1995); *Butterfly* (1997); *No. 1's* (1998).—**HB**

Carey, Mutt (actually, **Thomas;** aka **Papa**), early jazz trumpeter; b. Hahnville, La., 1891; d. Elsinore, Calif., Sept. 3, 1948. Brother of Jack (trombonist, leader) and Peter (alto horn); several other brothers were also musicians. He started on drums and guitar, then played alto horn before changing to cornet c. 1912. He played cornet in the Crescent Orch. (led by his brother Jack) from 1913; also did regular parade work with other bands before joining Kid Ory in 1914 (replacing Lewis Matthews). In 1917 he toured with the "Mack and Mack" show (along with Johnny Dodds and Steve Lewis), played briefly in Chicago with Lawrence Duhe's Band, then returned to New Orleans (1918). He worked with Chris Kelly (on second trumpet) at the Bulls' Club, then joined Wade Whaley's Band in Bucktown. Went to Calif. in November 1919 to join Kid Ory. In 1925, when Ory left for Chicago, he handed the leadership of his band to Carey, who subsequently led his own big band, the Jeffersonians, during the late 1920s and 1930s. The band did regular work at Hollywood film studios, including providing atmosphere music on silent- film sets. During the early 1940s Carey worked as a Pullman-porter but continued gigging. He rejoined Kid Ory in 1944, continued day work for a while, then resumed full-time music and played regularly for Kid Ory until summer 1947. He led his own recording band in N.Y. in late 1947, then returned to Calif. and gigged with his own band. Carey played with Louis Armstrong's group in the mid-1940s. He was organizing a new band at the time of his death. He appears briefly in the film *New Orleans.*

DISC.: *Mutt Carey Plays the Blues* (1954).—**JC/LP**

Carhart, George, jazz guitarist, banjoist, band leader; b. July 21, 1905; d. N.Y., Sept. 1984. Taught by Elmer Snowden, Carhart played in the school band at George Washington High in N.Y. He played various summer seasons, then organized his own all-star band that played regularly in Europe during the late 1920s (some of the musicians employed were Bud Freeman, Danny Polo, Jack Purvis, and Dave Tough). He continued to lead bands during the 1930s and played on several liner cruises. He retired in the 1940s.—**JC/LP**

Caridis, Miltiades, Greek conductor; b. Gdańsk (of Greek parents), May 9, 1923; d. Athens, March 1, 1998. He studied at the Athens Cons. and with Swarowsky at the Vienna Academy of Music, where he received his conducting diploma in 1947. He also studied conducting with Karajan and Scherchen. He conducted opera in Graz (1945–59), Bregenz (1947–48), and Cologne (1959–62). Caridis was chief conductor of the Philharmonia Hungarica in Marl kreis Recklinghausen (1960–67), with which he toured the U.S. in 1964 and 1967. After serving as chief conductor of the Oslo Phil.

(1969–75), he was Generalmusikdirektor of the Duisburg Sym. Orch. (1975–81). He then was chief conductor of the Niederösterreichisches Tonkünstler Orch. in Vienna (1981–85).—**NS/LK/DM**

Carissimi, Giacomo, important Italian composer and teacher; b. Marino, near Rome (baptized), April 18, 1605; d. Rome, Jan. 12, 1674. He was a singer and organist at Tivoli Cathedral (1623–27). Following a sojourn in Assisi (1628–29), he settled in Rome and became maestro di cappella at the Jesuit Collegio Germanico in 1629. He also was active at the collegiate church of S. Apollinare. In 1637 he became a priest. He was made maestro di cappella del concerto di camera to the exiled Queen Christina of Sweden in 1656. Carissimi was a distinguished composer of oratorios, motets, and cantatas, and his works reveal his mastery of concertato writing. His MSS were lost after the Jesuit order was dissolved in 1773 but his output is known to have included 14 oratorios, among them *Baltazar, Jephte, Jonas,* and *Judicium.* His motets were publ. in three vols. (Cologne, 1665–66). L. Bianchi et al. ed. his complete works (1951–73). Carissini was the author of the treatise *Ars cantandi* (Italian original not extant; German tr., Augsburg, 1692).

BIBL.: G. Rose, *The Cantatas of C.* (diss., Yale Univ., 1960); L. Bianchi, *C., Stradella, Scarlatti e l'oratorio musicale* (Rome, 1969); I. Buff, *The Chamber Duets and Trios of C.* (diss., Univ. of Rochester, 1973); C. Sartori, *C.: Catalogo delle opere attribuite* (Milan, 1975); A. Jones, *The Motets of C.* (diss., Univ. of Oxford, 1979); G. Dixon, *C.* (Oxford, 1986).—**NS/LK/DM**

Carl, William Crane, influential American organist and pedagogue; b. Bloomfield, N.J., March 2, 1865; d. N.Y., Dec. 8, 1936. He studied with Samuel P. Warren. In 1882 he became organist of the First Presbyterian Church in Newark. After further training with Guilmant in Paris (c. 1890), he went to N.Y. as organist of the Old First Presbyterian Church in 1892. He also organized the Guilmant Organ School in 1899. Carl toured throughout the U.S. and overseas as a distinguished recitalist in an expansive repertoire. He ed. various vols. of organ music, several of which include his own transcriptions. He also publ. the organ method *Master-Studies for the Organ* (1907).—**NS/LK/DM**

Carlid, Göte, Swedish composer; b. Högbo, Dec. 26, 1920; d. Stockholm, June 30, 1953. He was a philosophy student at the Univ. of Uppsala; then served as a municipal librarian in Enköping (1946–48) and Sollentuna (1948–50). As a composer, he was largely autodidact, but from the outset he adopted a modern idiom, making use of impressionistic and expressionistic techniques. His last works before his early death show a learned approach to many of the problems of new music.

WORKS: *Monologues* for Piano (1944–50); *Notturno* for String Orch. (1945); *3 Songs* for Woman's Voice, Flute, Clarinet, and Cello (1946–49); *Small Pieces* for Piano (1947); Piano Sonata (1948); *Quartetto elegiaco* for String Quartet (1948); *A Little Tea Music* for Flute, 2 Clarinets, and Cello (1949); *Mass* for Strings (1949); *Triad* for Saxophone and Piano (1950); *Hymnes à la beauté* for Chorus and Orch. (1952); *The Music Bus* for Soli, Children's Chorus, and Instruments (1952).—**NS/LK/DM**

Carlisle, Una Mae, jazz pianist, singer, composer; b. Xenia, Ohio, Dec. 26, 1915; d. N.Y., Nov. 7, 1956. Carlisle was of American Indian and Afro-American ancestry. She was discovered by Fats Waller while he was working in Cincinnati in late 1932; she worked with him for a while, then was featured as a solo act. She worked and recorded in Europe (1937–39), appearing in England, France, and Germany; she returned to the U.S. on the eve of the Second World War. With Waller, she recorded "I Can't Give You Anything but Love" (1939), singing straight to his wisecracks. She recorded solo on Bluebird, backed by Lester Young, Benny Carter, and Slam Stewart; her own "Walking by the River" was a hit (1941), as was "I See a Million People." She had her own radio and TV series in the late 1940s. She suffered for many years with mastoid trouble, which forced her to retire in 1954.

DISC.: *The Complete Una Mae Carlisle* (1994).—JC/LP

Carlos, Wendy (née **Walter**), American organist, composer, and electronics virtuoso; b. Pawtucket, R.I., Nov. 14, 1939. He played piano as a child, and later studied with Ron Nelson at Brown Univ. (A.B., 1962) and with Luening, Ussachevsky, and Beeson at Columbia Univ. (M.A., 1965). In 1964 he began working with Robert Moog in perfecting the Moog Synthesizer. The result of their experiments with versified tone-colors was a record album under the title *Switched-On Bach* (1968), which became unexpectedly successful, selling some million copies and garnering three Grammy Awards. This was followed in 1969 by the *Well-Tempered Synthesizer*, engineered entirely by Carlos. Then, at the age of 32, he suddenly became aware of his unique sexual duality, and underwent a transsexual operation. On St. Valentine's Day, Feb. 14, 1979, he officially changed his first name from Walter to Wendy. She/he described his sexual tergiversation in a candid interview in *Playboy* (May 1979), illustrated with "before and after" photographs. In 1979 the two-LP set appeared, *Switched-On Brandenburgs*. In the 1980s Carlos explored alternate scales and tunings, combining music from old world cultures in her *Beauty in the Beast* (1987). In 1992 she brought out the album *Switched-On Bach 2000,* a surround sound reworking of the earlier *Switched-on Bach* utilizing the unequal temperaments of Bach's time. From 1992 to 1995 she collaborated with Larry Fast in developing a state-of-the-art digital process of sound-track restoration and surround stereo conversion called Digi-Surround Stereo Sound.

WORKS: *Noah,* opera (1964–65); *Timesteps* for Synthesizer (1970); *Sonic Seasonings* for Synthesizer and Tape (1971); *Pompous Circumstances* for Synthesizer or Orch. (1974–75); *Variations on Dies irae* for Orch. (1980); *Digital Moonscapes,* introducing the "LSI Phil. Orch.," which digitally replicates orchestral timbres (1983); *Land of the Midnight Sun* (1986); *Tales of Heaven and Hell* (1998); film scores, including *A Clockwork Orange* (1971), *The Shining* (1978–80), *TRON* (1981–82), and *Woundings* (1998); also some chamber music and other pieces.—NS/LK/DM

Carlson, Claudine, French-American mezzo-soprano; b. Mulhouse, Feb. 26, 1937. She studied in Calif. and at the Manhattan School of Music in N.Y. with Jennie Tourel and Esther Andreas; then embarked on a successful career as a concert singer. On April 18, 1968, she made her first appearance at the N.Y.C. Opera as Cornelia in *Giulio Cesare.* She made her Metropolitan Opera debut in N.Y. as Geneviève in *Pelléas et Mélisande* on Oct. 11, 1977, and sang there again in 1981. Gifted with a voice of fine quality, she gained particular renown in the French repertoire.—NS/LK/DM

Carlstedt, Jan, Swedish composer; b. Orsa, June 15, 1926. He studied composition with Lars-Erik Larsson at the Stockholm Musikhogskolan (1948–52), then pursued studies at the Royal Coll. of Music in London (1952–53) and in Rome (1953–54). Returning to Stockholm, he became active in furthering the cause of modern music; was founder-chairman of the Contemporary Music Assn. in Stockholm (1960) and secretary of the Soc. of Swedish Composers (1961–63). In 1964 he was elected a member of the Royal Swedish Academy of Music in Stockholm.

WORKS: ORCH.: 2 syms.: No. 1 (1952–54; rev. 1960; Stockholm, Oct. 4, 1961) and No. 2, in memory of Martin Luther King Jr. (1968; N.Y., Dec. 20, 1970); Sonata for String Orch. (1956); *Trittico* for Oboe and String Orch. (1980); *Intrada* (1985); *Metamorphosi* for Strings (1986). **CHAMBER:** 6 string quartets (1951–52; 1966; 1967; 1972; 1977; 1998); String Trio (1955–56); Sonata for 2 Violins (1956); *12 Miniatures* for Violin, Clarinet, and Cello (1958); 8 Duets for 2 Violins (1958); Sinfonietta for Wind Quintet (1959); Sonata for Solo Violin (1959); *Ballata* for Cello (1960); *Divertimento* for Oboe and String Trio (1962); Wind Quintet (1962); *Pentastomos* for Wind Quintet (1972–73); *Metamorfoser* for Flute, Oboe, Violin, and Cello (1974); *Nocturne* for 4 Cellos (1983). **VOCAL: Chorus:** *Missa pro defunctis: Lacrimosa* (1989); *Ballad to Stephen Foster* (1990); *Angelus* (1997). —NS/LK/DM

Carmichael, Hoagy (actually, **Hoagland Howard**), rustic American composer, singer, and actor; b. Bloomington, Ind., Nov. 22, 1899; d. Rancho Mirage, Calif., Dec. 27, 1981. Carmichael differed from many of his songwriting contemporaries in that his work was imbued with jazz and blues; he rarely wrote for the theater or composed whole film scores, preferring to compose mostly individual songs for Tin Pan Alley and the movies; he never formed a permanent partnership with a lyricist, although he worked frequently with Johnny Mercer and Frank Loesser and sometimes wrote his own lyrics; and he pursued a parallel career as a performer that included work as a singer, pianist, bandleader, character actor, and radio and TV host. Thus in several ways he was a prototype for later generations of singer-songwriters, although he was atypical of his own time. His songs, with their long melodic lines containing few repeated notes, were equally at home on Hollywood sound stages, on the hit parade, and in jazz clubs. Among his many hits were "Star Dust," "Georgia on My Mind," and "Heart and Soul."

Carmichael was the son of Howard Clyde and Lida Robison Carmichael; his mother was the pianist at a silent-movie theater, and he learned the piano at her side. When he was 16, the family moved to Indianapolis, where he studied with ragtime and jazz pianist Reginald DuValle. He began playing professionally in dance bands while still in high school, but he entered Ind. Univ. to become a lawyer. Nevertheless, he financed his education by working as a musician, becoming pianist and director of Carmichael's Collegians in 1923. He also booked bands, including the Wolverine Orch., which featured his friend, cornetist Bix Beiderbecke. Encouraged by Beiderbecke, he wrote his first composition, "Riverboat Shuffle," and the Wolverines recorded it for Gennett Records on May 6, 1924. That brought the tune to the attention of N.Y. publisher Mills Music, which published it in 1925 with Irving Mills and Wolverines pianist Dick Voynow cut in as co-composers. The song was then recorded by Isham Jones and His Orch., who scored a hit with it in July 1925. Meanwhile, Carmichael had launched his own recording career with his "Washboard Blues," which he cut for Gennett as the pianist with Curtis Hitch's Happy Harmonists on May 19, 1925.

Despite these efforts, Carmichael maintained his ambition to become a lawyer, and when he earned his LL.B. degree in 1926, he moved to Fla. to practice law. The same year, however, Mills Music published "Washboard Blues" (again appending Irving Mills's name), and it was recorded by Red Nichols and His Five Pennies for a hit in April 1927. This second recording success convinced Carmichael to become a professional composer and musician. He moved back to Bloomington in the summer of 1927, where he wrote "Star Dust," which he recorded at dance tempo with a five-piece band on Oct. 31. Meanwhile, "Riverboat Shuffle" had been given a new recording by Frankie Trumbauer and His Orch., including Beiderbecke, on May 9, and it became a hit again in September, with yet another successful recording by Nichols in January 1928. There was also a hit revival of "Washboard Blues," recorded Nov. 18, 1927, by Paul Whiteman and His Concert Orch., with Carmichael sitting in on piano and vocals (a lyric had been added by Fred B. Callahan), that became popular in March 1928.

"Star Dust" was published by Mills as an instrumental in January 1929, when it was spelled "Stardust"; the two spellings have been used interchangeably ever since. As "Star Dust," it was republished with a lyric added by Mitchell Parish in May. Carmichael moved to N.Y. and played piano on the first successful recording of the song—an instrumental credited to Irving Mills and His Hotsy Totsy Band that became popular in January 1930. This version was again up-tempo, but Isham Jones next recorded the tune at what is now its familiar slow ballad pace, and his version established "Star Dust" as a major hit, becoming a best-seller in April 1931 and inspiring many cover records. Bing Crosby had the most successful vocal recording.

Carmichael's next hit was "Georgia on My Mind" (lyrics by Stuart Gorrell). He had recorded the song himself in September 1930, but it was made into a popular recording for the first time by Frankie Trumbauer in August 1931. The second time came soon after: Mildred Bailey scored her first hit recording with the song in January 1932. Another Carmichael song with

which Bailey became associated was "Rockin' Chair" (lyrics by Carmichael), but it was the Mills Brothers' recording that made it a hit in May 1932, leading to the successful reissue of an earlier recording by Louis Armstrong and His Orch. from December 1929 on which Armstrong and Carmichael duetted. This was followed by the belated issue of Carmichael's November 1930 recording of "Lazy River" (music and lyrics by Carmichael and Sidney Arodin), which became a hit in June 1932. "Lazybones," Carmichael's next hit, was his first with lyricist Johnny Mercer; it became a best-seller for Ted Lewis and His Band in July 1933. In September the Dorsey Brothers Orch. had an instrumental hit with "Old Man Harlem" (music and lyrics by Carmichael and Rudy Vallée).

Through the intercession of Bing Crosby, Carmichael was invited to make his first contribution to a motion picture in 1935, interpolating "Moonburn" (lyrics by Edward Heyman) into Paramount's film version of Cole Porter's musical *Anything Goes*, which starred Crosby and was released in February 1936. On March 14, 1936, Carmichael married Ruth Mary Meinardi, a model. They had two sons and divorced in 1955.

Carmichael next wrote several songs for the Broadway revue *The Show Is On*, including the title song and "Little Old Lady" (lyrics by Stanley Adams), which reached the hit parade for the Abe Lyman Orch. in March 1937. Paramount offered Carmichael a contract, and he moved to Hollywood. He made his first film appearance in *Topper*, which opened in July 1937, and had a song in that production as well as in *Every Day's a Holiday*, released at the end of the year. For the unproduced *Romance in the Rough*, he wrote "The Nearness of You" (lyrics by Ned Washington), which would become a hit later.

Carmichael contributed music to five Paramount features released in 1938, and two of the songs from those films made the hit parade in the fall: "Small Fry" (lyrics by Frank Loesser), from the Bing Crosby film *Sing, You Sinners*, as recorded by Crosby and Johnny Mercer; and "Two Sleepy People" (lyrics by Mercer) from the Bob Hope film *Thanks for the Memory*, recorded by Fats Waller's Orch. But Carmichael's most successful composition of the period was the independently published "Heart and Soul" (lyrics by Loesser), recorded by the Larry Clinton Orch., which also played it in a Paramount short, *A Song Is Born*; it went on to become a favorite of piano students everywhere.

Although Carmichael contributed to such Paramount features as *St. Louis Blues* and *Some Like It Hot* in 1939 and even appeared in a short, *Paramount Presents Hoagy Carmichael*, his major song successes of the year were independent efforts. "I Get Along without You Very Well" (lyrics by Carmichael, based on a poem by Jane Brown Thompson), recorded by the Red Norvo Orch., was in the hit parade in March and April 1939, and "Blue Orchids" (lyrics by Carmichael) topped the hit parade for the Glenn Miller Orch. in November. The year 1939 was also when Carmichael published the novelty song "Hong Kong Blues" (lyrics by Carmichael), although it did not become a hit for him until later.

Carmichael and Mercer wrote the songs for the Broadway musical *Walk with Music* in 1940, but it flopped, running only 55 performances. Nevertheless, Carmichael continued to score hits with his back catalog. In August, Glenn Miller finally made a Top Ten hit of "The Nearness of You," and on Oct. 7, Artie Shaw and His Orch. recorded an instrumental version of "Star Dust" that turned it into one of the century's most popular songs. The Shaw recording made the Top Ten in January 1941 and sold over a million copies; thereafter, "Star Dust" was recorded well over a thousand times, making it one of the most successful songs of the century.

Carmichael earned his first credits for scoring complete motion pictures in 1941, placing five songs in United Artists' *Road Show* in February and three in Paramount's animated feature *Mr. Bug Goes to Town* in December. Among Carmichael's notable songs of 1942 were the wistful "Baltimore Oriole" and "The Lamplighter's Serenade," both with lyrics by Paul Francis Webster, but his major hit of the year was "Skylark" (lyrics by Mercer), which had four chart recordings, the most successful of which was Glenn Miller's, a Top Ten hit in May.

Carmichael scored Paramount's *True to Life*, released in August 1943, contributing four songs with lyrics by Johnny Mercer. But he gained much more recognition for his next film assignment, *To Have and Have Not* (1944), starring Humphrey Bogart and Lauren Bacall. In his second acting role, Carmichael performed "Hong Kong Blues" and his subsequent recording became a Top Ten hit in October 1945. The same month, his song "Doctor, Lawyer, Indian Chief" (lyrics by Paul Francis Webster) was sung by Betty Hutton in the film *The Stork Club*. Hutton's recording topped the charts in February 1946 in competition with other renditions, including Carmichael's, which was popular too.

Carmichael continued to appear in films. In 1945 he had been in *Johnny Angel*; in 1946 he was in *The Best Years of Our Lives* and *Canyon Passage*, for which he also wrote the songs, among them "Ole Buttermilk Sky" (music and lyrics by Carmichael and Jack Brooks), which attracted six chart recordings (one, of course, by Carmichael), the most popular of which was by Kay Kyser, who topped the charts with it in December. The song earned Carmichael his first Academy Award nomination.

Carmichael marked other milestones in 1946. He published the first of his two books of memoirs, *The Stardust Road*, and he scored his first hit with a song he had not written himself. Released in November, his version of the novelty song "Huggin' and Chalkin'" (music and lyrics by Clancy Hayes and Kermit Goell) outdistanced three others to reach the top of the charts in February 1947.

Jo Stafford had a minor hit with "Ivy" (lyrics by Carmichael), written as a promotional song for the Universal film of the same name, in May 1947, and Carmichael appeared and placed a song in RKO's *Night Song* in November. "Bubble-Loo Bubble-Loo" (lyrics by Webster) was a minor hit for Peggy Lee in August 1948. For the most part, however, Carmichael turned his attention to orchestral works in the late 1940s, and the Indianapolis Symphony Orch. performed his "tone picture" *Brown County Autumn* in 1949. His other notable work of the period was the *Johnny Appleseed Suite*. He returned to film work with *Johnny Holiday*, appearing in the Christmas 1949 release and contributing a song. He also appeared, without singing, in *Young Man with a Horn* (1950), a film loosely based on the life of Bix Beiderbecke.

Carmichael spent part of 1950 writing a score for *The Keystone Girl*, a proposed film biography of silent-film director Mack Sennett, and although it was never produced, he was able to salvage several of the songs for later use, including "In the Cool, Cool, Cool of the Evening" (lyrics by Mercer), which was featured in the Bing Crosby film *Here Comes the Groom* in September 1951 after it had already become a hit for Crosby and co-star Jane Wyman; it won the 1951 Academy Award for Best Song.

Meanwhile, Carmichael himself had returned to the charts in May 1950 with "The Old Piano Roll Blues" (music and lyrics by Cy Coben) in a duet with Cass Daley. Carmichael and Daley had a second hit in April 1951 with a revival of the 1914 song "The Aba Daba Honeymoon" (music and lyrics by Arthur Fields and Walter Donovan), inspired by its use in the Debbie Reynolds film *Two Weeks with Love*.

Carmichael provided the songs and appeared in RKO's *The Las Vegas Story* in early 1952. He also appeared in *Belles on Our Toes* in April. The duo of Perry Como and Eddie Fisher had the most popular version of his "Watermelon Weather" (lyrics by Paul Francis Webster) in June, and in October the Four Aces scored a hit revival of "Heart and Soul." Bob Manning brought "The Nearness of You" back into the charts in April 1953.

Carmichael and lyricist Harold Adamson wrote nine songs for *Gentlemen Prefer Blondes*, but only two remained when the film was released in July 1953. In September one of Carmichael's discarded songs from *The Keystone Girl* turned up in *Those Redheads from Seattle*. Meanwhile, Carmichael had launched a career as a TV host with *Saturday Night Revue*, a 90-minute variety show on NBC that ran during the summer of 1953 and was supposedly broadcast from Carmichael's penthouse apartment.

Carmichael was less active, especially as a songwriter, after the mid-1950s. He placed a song in *Three for the Show* (1954) and scored *Timberjack* (1955), in which he also appeared. Billy Ward and His Dominoes had a gold-selling revival of "Star Dust" in 1957. Carmichael was a regular on the Western TV series *Laramie* during the 1959–60 season.

The songwriter's most popular songs enjoyed further revivals in the early 1960s. Ray Charles topped the charts in 1960 with a definitive version of "Georgia on My Mind." (Michael Bolton confirmed the power of Charles's interpretation by taking a virtual carbon-copy performance into the Top 40 in 1990.) In 1961 the Cleftones and Jan and Dean each had Top 40 records with "Heart and Soul," and Bobby Darin and Si Zentner and His Orch. each scored with "Lazy River." Nino Tempo and April Stevens reached the Top 40 in 1964 with "Star Dust." Carmichael himself took on one last film assignment, writing a couple of songs for the 1962 film *Hatari!*, the soundtrack for which reached the Top Ten. Willie Nelson, a singer whose delivery was similar to Carmichael's self-described "flatsy through the nose" approach, scored his biggest success with his 1978 album of standards, *Star Dust*, which sold four million copies and contained his country-chart-topping rendition of "Georgia on My Mind."

Carmichael died of a heart attack at the age of 82, survived by his sons and his second wife, Dorothy Wanda McKay, whom he had married in 1977.

WORKS (only those works for which Carmichael was the primary, credited composer are listed): **MUSICALS/ REVUES**: *Walk with Music* (N.Y., June 4, 1940). **FILMS**: *Road Show* (1941); *Mr. Bug Goes to Town* (a.k.a. *Hoppity Goes to Town*; 1941); *True to Life* (1943); *To Have and Have Not* (1944); *Canyon Passage* (1946); *The Las Vegas Story* (1952); *Timberjack* (1955).

WRITINGS: *The Stardust Road* (N.Y., 1946); with Stephen Longstreet, *Sometimes I Wonder: The Story of H. C.* (N.Y., 1965).

DISC.: *Old Rockin' Chair* (1955); *Hoagy Sings Carmichael* (1956); *Stardust Road* (1958); *Legend of Hoagy Carmichael* (1961); *I Can Dream, Can't I?* (1963); *Stardust* (1929).

BIBL.: J. Hasse, *The Works of H. C.* (Cincinnati, 1983); R. Schiff, ed., *H. C.: The Star Dust Melodies of...* (Melville, N.Y., 1983).—**WR**

Carmichael, Judy, American pianist; b. Pico Rivera, Calif., Nov. 27, 1952. Born into a musical family, she began to study piano at an early age. When her grandfather offered $50 to the first grandchild who could play "Maple Leaf Rag," she taught herself the piece and collected the reward. While attending college at Cal State Fullerton, she took a part-time job playing ragtime piano on the Balboa Pavilion Queen Riverboat. Since she drew larger crowds than the regular pianist, she soon took over on a full-time basis. Because she was so consistently booked as a pianist, after two years of college, she dropped out, and at the age of 21, first heard Fats Waller's recordings, and began to move from the ragtime style into stride. In 1977 she was hired to play stride piano at Disneyland. She made her first recording for the Progressive label in 1980 and moved on to N.Y. the following year. Bringing the freshness to the stride music that is so deeply ingrained in her soul, Carmichael plays beyond interpretation, with both authority and authenticity, almost as if she invented the musical style herself. She plays clubs, concert halls and festivals around the world. In addition to recording for Progressive/Statiras and other labels, she has recorded for her own label, C&D Productions.

DISC.: *Judy Carmichael...and Basie Called Her Stride* (1983); *Pearls* (1993); *Chops* (1996).—**SKB**

Carmirelli, Pina (actually, **Giuseppina**), Italian violinist; b. Varzi, Jan. 23, 1914; d. Carpena, Feb. 27, 1993. She studied at the Milan Cons., graduating in 1930, and at the Accademia di Santa Cecilia in Rome. She began her concert career in 1937; in 1949 she founded the Boccherini Quintet, and in 1954 the Car-

mirelli Quartet, with which she toured throughout Europe. From 1975 to 1986 she was concertmaster of I Musici. She was also active as a teacher in Italy and the U.S.—**NS/LK/DM**

Carner, Mosco, Austrian-born English writer on music and conductor; b. Vienna, Nov. 15, 1904; d. Cornwall, Aug. 3, 1985. He studied at the New Vienna Cons., and then musicology with Adler at the Univ. of Vienna (Ph.D., 1928, with the diss. *Studien zur Sonatenform bei Robert Schumann*). After conducting opera in Opava (1929–30) and Gdańsk (1930–33), he emigrated to England and became a naturalized British subject. He devoted himself mainly to writing music criticism in London, and later was music critic of *Time and Tide* (1949–62) and the *Evening News* (1957–61).

WRITINGS (all publ. in London unless otherwise given): *Dvořák* (1941); Vol. 2 of *A Study of 20th- Century Harmony* (1942); *Of Men and Music* (1944); *The Waltz* (1948); *Puccini: A Critical Biography* (1958; 3rd ed., rev., 1992); *Alban Berg: The Man and the Work* (1975; 2nd ed., rev., 1983); *Madam Butterfly* (1979); *Major and Minor* (1980); *Hugo Wolf Songs* (1982); *Tosca* (Cambridge, 1985).—**NS/LK/DM**

Carnes, Kim, raspy voiced singer and hit songwriter best-remembered for the hit "Bette Davis Eyes"; b. Los Angeles, July 20, 1945. By her 20s, Kim Carnes was playing the night clubs of Los Angeles, singing backup on record dates, acting in films, and writing songs. Eventually her tunes were performed by artists ranging from Frank Sinatra to Kenny Rogers. She met Rogers when both were members of the folk group The New Christy Minstrels during the mid-1960s. After a stab at acting in the forgettable *C'mon, Let's Live a Little* (co-starring fellow pop chanteuse Jackie DeShannon), she married frequent collaborator Dave Ellingson. Together, they wrote "Nobody Knows" for the 1971 film *Vanishing Point*. Her debut solo album, *Rest on Me*, appeared shortly after, producing the minor AC hit "You're a Part of Me." She recut the song with Gene Cotton for her eponymous sophomore album, and that version broke the Top 40, spending three weeks and peaking at #36. Her next album, *Sailin'*, featured her composition "Love Comes from Unexpected Places," which won best song at the 1977 American Song Festival and was covered by Barbra Streisand.

Carnes's big break came when Rogers asked Carnes and Ellingson to write the bulk of his *Gideon* album. He also asked Kim to sing with him on "Don't Fall in Love with a Dreamer." The tune peaked at #4 in the spring of 1980, setting up Carnes's own cover of the Miracles "More Love" (from *Romance Dance*) two months later. That single got as high as #10. This all built up to the release the following year of *Mistaken Identity*. The album featured her biggest hit, "Bette Davis Eyes," which she co-wrote with (oddly enough) Jackie DeShannon. It became one of the longest running #1 singles in *Billboard* chart history. At the 1982 Grammies, it won Song of the Year and Record of the Year.

However, Carnes was unable to produce a followup to this smash. Her next two singles from *Mistaken Identity* were disappointing. Similarly, the title track from her next album, 1982's *Voyeur*, only hit #28 and the follow-up to that, "Does It Make You Remember" only scraped the Top 40, hitting #36. Her 1983 effort, *Café Racers*, proved even more discouraging, with "Invisible Hands" spending a couple of weeks at #40 and nothing else getting any higher. Carnes's last pop hurrah was the minor hit, "Crazy in the Night (Barking at Airplanes)" from the 1985 *Barking at Airplanes* album.

Carnes continued recording into the 1990s, although with diminishing returns. Her country-ish 1988 effort, *View from the House*, spawned "Speed of the Sound of Loneliness," a country hit featuring Lyle Lovett on backing vocals. In the mid-1990s, Carnes and Ellingson moved to Nashville to pursue a career as songwriters. They started writing for artists such as Vince Gill and Reba McEntire, who both took her "The Heart Won't Lie" to the high reaches of the Country charts in 1994.

DISC.: *Rest on Me* (1972); *Kim Carnes* (1975); *Sailin'* (1976); *St. Vincent's Court* (1979); *Romance Dance* (1980); *Kim Carnes & the Hate Boys* (1981); *Mistaken Identity* (1981); *Voyeur* (1982); *Cafe Racers* (1983); *Barking at Airplanes* (1985); *Light House* (1986); *View from the House* (1988); *Best of You* (1988); *Crazy in the Night* (1990); *Gypsy Honeymoon: Best of Kim Carnes* (1993); *Bette Davis Eyes* (1998); *King Biscuit Flower Hour* (live; 1998); *Mistaken Identity Collection* (1999).—**HB**

Carney, Harry (Howell), jazz baritone saxophonist, clarinetist; b. Boston, Mass., April 1, 1910; d. N.Y., Oct. 8, 1974. His brother, Ray, was a pianist. Harry began on piano, then specialized on clarinet before taking up alto saxophone. He joined the Knights of Pythias student band at 13. He worked in Boston with Bobby Sawyer and pianist Walter Johnson, journeyed to N.Y. (with boyhood friend Charlie Holmes) early in 1927, gigged with Fess Williams at the Savoy Ballroom, and worked at the Bamboo Inn with banjo-guitarist Henri Saparo, briefly with pianist Joe Steele. He joined Duke Ellington during the last week of June 1927, playing first date at a one-nighter at Nuttings-on-the-Charles, near Boston. Except for a brief absence, he worked regularly with Duke Ellington. He originally played alto with the band, but soon began specializing on baritone sax. In 1944 he began doubling on bass clarinet. He was a pioneer in using circular breathing, a technique allowing the soloist to hold notes for inordinate periods. He was also Ellington's driver and confidant. He continued to play with the Ellington Orch until his death, and was given co-composer credit for Ellington's "Rockin' in Rhythm."

DISC.: *Harry Carney with Strings* (1954); *Moods for Girl and Boy* (1954).—**JC/LP**

Caro, Paul, German composer; b. Breslau, Oct. 25, 1859; d. there, June 23, 1914. He was a student of Bruckner at the Vienna Cons. (1880–85). Among his works were two operas, *Hero und Leander* (Breslau, May 31, 1912) and *Die Hochzeit von Ulfosti*, five syms., two serenades for Strings, 34 string quartets, piano pieces, a Requiem, cantatas, and songs.—**LK/DM**

Caron, Philippe, composer who flourished in the second half of the 15th century. He may have studied in Cambrai and possibly was in the service of Charles the Bold. His extant works, five masses and several chansons, have been publ. by the Inst. of Mediaeval Music (Brooklyn, 1971–76).—**NS/LK/DM**

Caron, Rose (Lucille) (née **Meuniez**), French soprano; b. Monerville, Nov. 17, 1857; d. Paris, April 9, 1930. She entered the Paris Cons. in 1880, leaving in 1882 to study with Marie Sasse in Brussels, where her debut was made as Alice in *Robert le Diable* (1883). She sang for two years at the Paris Opéra, and again in Brussels, creating Lorance (in *Jocelyn*), Richilde, and Salammbô (1890); in 1890 she returned to the Paris Opéra, where she sang Sieglinde (1893) and Desdemona (1894) in the first performances of *Die Walküre* and *Otello* in France; in 1898 she sang Fidelio at the Opéra-Comique. From 1900 she appeared almost exclusively on the concert stage. In 1902 she was appointed a prof. of singing at the Paris Cons.—**NS/LK/DM**

Carpenter, John Alden, important American composer; b. Park Ridge, Ill., Feb. 28, 1876; d. Chicago, April 26, 1951. He studied in Chicago with Amy Fay and W.C.E. Seeboeck, and then with J.K. Paine at Harvard Univ. (B.A., 1897). During a trip to Rome (1906), he had some lessons with Elgar, and then completed his training in Chicago with B. Ziehn (1908–12). He was employed in his father's shipping supply business, later serving as its vice-president (1909–36). In subsequent years, he devoted himself entirely to composition. In 1918 he was elected a member of the National Inst. of Arts and Letters, and received its Gold Medal in 1947. In 1942 he was elected a member of the American Academy of Arts and Leters. Carpenter gained success as a composer with his first orch. score, the humorous suite *Adventures in a Perambulator* (1914). Adopting mildly modernistic technques, he was notably successful in his works on American subjects with a tinge of ragtime and jazz elements. His "jazz pantomime" *Krazy Kat* (1921), after the well-known comic strip by George Herriman, proved an immediate success. It was followed by his *Skyscrapers* (1923–24), "a ballet of American life," which retains its historial interest as a period piece. Among his orch. works, the most notable is his symphonic poem *Sea Drift* (1933), after Whitman. Carpenter also distinguished himself as a composer of songs.

WORKS: DRAMATIC: *The Birthday of the Infanta,* ballet (1917; rev. version, Chicago, Dec. 23, 1919; suite, 1930, rev. 1940; concert suite, 1949); *Krazy Kat,* "jazz pantomime" (Chicago, Dec. 23, 1921; rev. 1940); *Skyscrapers,* ballet (1923–24; N.Y., Feb. 19, 1926); incidental music. **ORCH.:** Suite (c. 1906–09); *Berceuse* for Small Orch. (1908); *Adventures in a Perambulator,* suite (1914; Chicago, March 19, 1915); Piano Concertino (1915; Chicago, March 10, 1916; rev. 1948); 2 syms.: No. 1, *Sermons in Stones* (Norfolk, Conn., June 5, 1917; rev. version, Chicago, Oct. 24, 1940) and No. 2 (N.Y., Oct. 22, 1942); *A Pilgrim Vision,* symphonic poem (Philadelphia, Nov. 23, 1920); *Jazz Orchestra Pieces: Oil and Vinegar* (1925–26); *Patterns* for Piano and Orch. (Boston, Oct. 21, 1932); *Sea Drift,* symphonic poem after Whitman (Chicago, Nov. 30, 1933; rev. 1944); Violin Concerto (1936; Chicago, Nov. 18, 1937); *Danza* (1937; also for Piano, 1947); *The*

Anxious Bugler, symphonic poem (N.Y., Nov. 17, 1943); *Blue Gal* for Cello and Orch. (1943); *The 7 Ages*, suite after Shakespeare (N.Y., Nov. 29, 1945); *Carmel Concerto* for Piano and Orch. (1948). **C H A M B E R :** Violin Sonata (1911; N.Y., Dec. 11, 1912); String Quartet (1927); Piano Quintet (1934). **KEYBOARD: P i - a n o :** Sonata (1897); *Polonaise américaine* (1912); *Little Indian* (1916); *Little Dancer* (1917); *Tango américaine* (1920); *Diversions* (1922). **V O C A L :** *Songs of Faith* for Chorus and Orch. (1931; rev. 1936); *Song of Freedom* for Chorus and Orch. (1941); *Song of David* for Women's Voices, Cello, and Orch. (1951; unfinished); song cycles, including *Gitanjali* (1913) and *Water Colors* (1918); many solo songs.

BIBL.: O T. Pierson, *The Life and Music of J.A. C.* (diss., Univ. of Rochester, 1952); J. O'Connor, *J.A. C.: Bio-Bibliography* (Westport, Conn., 1994).—**NS/LK/DM**

Carpenter, Wingie (actually, **Theodore**), jazz trumpeter, singer; b. St. Louis, Mo., April 15, 1898; d. summer 1975. He had his left arm amputated after being involved in an accident during his early teens; the operation was performed by Doc Cheatham's uncle, a noted surgeon. He took up trumpet some time later; by 1920 he was working in traveling carnival shows, touring with Herbert's Minstrel Band in 1921. He settled in Cincinnati for a while, worked with Wes Helvey, Clarence Paige, and Zack Whyte, and worked with Speed Webb (1926), later playing residency in Buffalo with Eugene Primus (1927). From late 1926 until 1928 he worked on and off with the Whitman Sisters' Show (usually with pianist Troy Snapp's Band). During the early 1930s he was featured with Smiling Billy Steward's Celery City Serenaders. He also worked with another Fla. band, led by Bill Lacey. In the mid-1930s he did regular touring with various bandleaders, including Jack Ellis, Dick Bunch, and Jesse Stone. He settled in N.Y. and worked with Campbell "Skeets" Albert and Fitz Weston. He was mainly active as leader of his own small band from 1939 through the 1960s.—**JC/LP**

Carpenters, The, one of the most popular easy-listening acts of the 1970s. **MEMBERSHIP:** Karen Carpenter, voc., drm. (b. New Haven, Conn., March 2, 1950; d. Downey, Calif., Feb. 4, 1983); Richard Carpenter, kybd., voc. (b. New Haven, Conn., Oct. 15, 1946).

The Carpenters scored an impressive string of hits with the compositions of songwriters such as Burt Bacharach, Paul Williams, Leon Russell, Carole King, and Neil Sedaka. Featuring the full, resonant, yet spiritless alto voice of Karen Carpenter and the delicate harmony of brother Richard, the duo ultimately had more Top 20 singles than even the Everly Brothers and sold more than 80 million records. A longtime sufferer of anorexia nervosa, Karen died in 1983 at age 32 of heart failure due to the condition.

Karen and Richard Carpenter moved with their family to Downey, Calif., in 1963. Richard began playing piano at age nine and completed his musical education at Calif. State Univ., Long Beach, whereas Karen took up drums while in high school. They formed the Carpenter Trio with bassist Wes Jacobs in 1965, winning a Battle of the Bands contest at the Hollywood Bowl in 1966. Although signed to RCA Records, no recordings were

ever released, and the trio disbanded.

By the late 1960s Karen and Richard had formed a duo to pursue their interest in vocal harmonies and were signed to A&M Records by Herb Alpert on the strength of a demonstration tape. Their first hit came in 1970, with Burt Bacharach's "Close to You." Subsequent early–1970s hits included "For All We Know" two Paul Williams-Roger Nichols compositions, "We've Only Just Begun" and "Rainy Days and Mondays," and Leon Russell and Bonnie Bramlett's "Superstar." *A Song for You* provided six hits: "Bless the Beasts and the Children," "Hurting Each Other," Carole King's "It's Going to Take Some Time," "Goodbye to Love," "Top of the World," and the Williams-Nichols composition "I Won't Last a Day without You." Other major hits through 1976 were "Sing," "Yesterday Once More," "Only Yesterday," Neil Sedaka's "Solitaire," and "I Need to Be in Love." Although the Carpenters' popularity waned in the late 1970s, they managed a major hit in 1981 with "Touch Me When We're Dancing."

While working on *Voice of the Heart*, Karen Carpenter died at her parents' Downey home of heart failure due to anorexia nervosa on Feb. 4, 1983, at age 32. The Karen Carpenter Memorial Foundation was formed to aid in the research of anorexia, and a music scholarship fund in her name was established at Calif. State Univ., Long Beach. Richard worked as a staff producer at A&M. The 1988 made-for-TV movie *The Karen Carpenter Story* portrayed her life and death. The posthumusly released album *Lovelines* contained 10 previously unreleased songs, including four by Karen from a never-completed solo album. In 1994 A&M issued a Carpenters tribute album, with their songs being covered by contemporary acts such as Sonic Youth, the Cranberries, Sheryl Crow, Matthew Sweet, and Babes in Toyland.

DISC.: THE CARPENTERS: *Ticket to Ride* (1969); *Close to You* (1970); *The C.* (1971); *A Song for You* (1972); *Now and Then* (1973); *The Singles: 1969–1973* (1973); *Horizon* (1975); *A Kind of Hush* (1976); *Passage* (1977); *A Christmas Portrait* (1978); *Made in America* (1981); *Voice of the Heart* (1983); *An Old-Fashioned Christmas* (1985); *Yesterday Once More* (1985); *Lovelines* (1989); *From the Top: The Ultimate Retrospective* (1991). **TRIBUTE ALBUM:** *If I Were a Carpenter* (1994).

BIBL.: Ray Coleman, *The C.: The Untold Story* (N.Y., 1994). —**BH**

Carpentras (real name, **Elzéar Genet**), French composer; b. Carpentras, c. 1470; d. Avignon, June 14, 1548. In 1505 he became a chaplain in Avignon. In 1508 he was the leading singer in, and from 1513 to 1521 maestro di cappella of, the Pontifical Chapel in Rome; in 1521 he was sent to Avignon on negotiations connected with the Holy See; in 1524 he made his last visit to Rome; in 1526 he returned to Avignon. Four vols. of his works (masses, 1532; Lamentations, 1532; hymns, 1533; Magnificats, 1537) were publ. in Avignon. His works, severe and dignified in style, were highly esteemed by his contemporaries. They have been ed. by A. Seay in Corpus Mensurabilis Musicae, LVIII (1972–73). —**NS/LK/DM**

Carr, prominent family of English-American music publishers and musicians:

(1) Joseph Carr, music publisher; b. England, 1739; d. Baltimore, Oct. 27, 1819. He was active as a music publisher in London before settling in Baltimore in 1794, where he continued his music publishing business. In addition to bringing out European and American works, including the first edition of *The Star-Spangled Banner* (1814), he publ. the *Musical Journal for the Piano Forte* (1800–04) and *Carr's Musical Miscellany* (from 1812). He had two sons:

(2) Benjamin Carr, organist, music publisher, and composer; b. London, Sept. 12, 1786; d. Philadelphia, May 24, 1831. After working with his father in London and studying music with Samuel Arnold and Charles and Samuel Wesley, he went to Philadelphia in 1793, where he founded a flourishing music publishing concern. In 1794–95 he was active as an actor and singer with the Old American Co. in N.Y., and also pursued his music business there until 1797. However, he made Philadelphia the center of his activities. In addition to his business affairs, he also was organist at St. Augustine's Catholic Church (from 1801) and at St. Peter's Episcopal Church, appeared as a singer and conductor, taught, and was a promoter of music in general, being the founder of the Musical Fund Soc. of Philadelphia in 1820. So pervasive was Carr's influence on the city that he became known as the "Father of Philadelphia Music." As a music publisher, he was most influential through the vast amount of American and European music he brought out. He ed. his father's *Musical Journal for the Piano Forte* (1800–04) and *Carr's Musical Miscellany* (1812–25). As a composer, he wrote one of the earliest American operas, *The Archers, or Mountaineers of Switzerland* (N.Y., April 18, 1796). He also composed the pastoral opera *Philander and Silvia, or Love Crown'd at Last* (London, Oct. 16, 1792); incidental music to *Macbeth* (N.Y., Jan. 14, 1795); various instrumental pieces, mostly for piano, including *Federal Overture* (1794); 6 sonatas (1796); *Dead March and Monody for General Washington*, with voices (1800); *The Siege of Tripoli: Historical Naval Sonata* (1804); sonatinas; waltzes; marches; variations; sacred vocal works, including masses, Psalms, anthems, hymns, and chants; secular vocal works, including ballads; several pedagogical works.

BIBL.: R. Smith, *The Church Music of B. C.* (diss., Southwestern Baptist Theological Seminary 1969); C. Sprenkle, *The Life and Works of B. C.* (diss., Peabody Cons. of Music, 1970).

(3) Thomas Carr, organist, music publisher, and composer; b. England, 1780; d. Philadelphia, April 15, 1849. He went with his father to Baltimore in 1794, where he was active in the family music publishing concern and served as organist at Christ Church (1798–1811). Upon his father's death, he took charge of the music publishing concern. After selling out in 1822, he settled in Philadelphia and was active as a publisher and teacher. Francis Scott Key asked him to prepare the music for *The Star-Spangled Banner* (1814), for which he adapted the English drinking song *To Anacreon in Heaven.*—**NS/LK/DM**

Carr, Mancy (Peck), early jazz banjo player, guitarist; b. Charleston, W. Va., c. 1900; d. unknown. He is chiefly remembered for his recorded work with Louis

Armstrong in 1928 and 1929. He worked with Carroll Dickerson in 1924, then played in Lottie Hightower's Night Hawks (1925) before rejoining Carroll Dickerson; worked with that leader for several years and went with him (and Louis Armstrong) to N.Y. in 1929. He returned to Chicago, then moved back to W.Va. and worked there with his brother. He is thought to have died many years ago. He has mistakenly been referred to as a white musician. In some jazz histories, his name was misspelled as "Cara."—**JC/LP**

Carreño, (Maria) Teresa, famous Venezuelan pianist; b. Caracas, Dec. 22, 1853; d. N.Y., June 12, 1917. As a child, she studied with her father, an excellent pianist. Driven from home by a revolution, the family settled in N.Y. in 1862, where she studied with Gottschalk. At the age of eight, she gave a public recital in N.Y. (Nov. 25, 1862). She began her career in 1866, after studying with G. Mathias in Paris and A. Rubinstein. She lived mainly in Paris from 1866 to 1870; then in England. She developed a singing voice and made an unexpected appearance in opera in Edinburgh as the Queen in *Les Huguenots* (May 24, 1872) in a cast that included Tietjens, Brignoli, and Mario; was again in the U.S. in 1876, when she studied voice in Boston. For the Bolivar centenary celebration in Caracas (Oct. 29, 1885), she appeared as singer, pianist, and composer of the festival hymn, written at the request of the Venezuelan government; hence the frequent but erroneous attribution to Carreño of the national hymn of Venezuela, *Gloria al bravo pueblo* (the music of which was actually composed in 1811 by J. Landaeta, and officially adopted as the Venezuelan national anthem on May 25, 1881). In Caracas she once again demonstrated her versatility, when for the last three weeks of the season she conducted the opera company managed by her husband, **Giovanni Tagliapietra**. After these musical experiments, she resumed her career as a pianist; made her German debut in Berlin, Nov. 18, 1889; in 1907 toured Australia. Her last appearance with an orch. was with the N.Y. Phil. (Dec. 8, 1916); her last recital appearance was in Havana (March 21, 1917). She was married four times: to **Émile Sauret** (June 1873), Tagliapietra (1876), **Eugène D'Albert** (1892–95), and Arturo Tagliapietra, a younger brother of Giovanni (June 30, 1902). She was greatly venerated in Venezuela; her mortal remains were solemnly transferred from N.Y., where she died, and reburied in Caracas, on Feb. 15, 1938.

BIBL.: M. Milinowski, *T. C.* (New Haven, 1940); A. Marquez Rodriguez, *Esbozo biográfico de T. C.* (Caracas, 1953); R. Marciano, *T. C.* (Kassel, 1990).—**NS/LK/DM**

Carreras, José (Maria), celebrated Spanish tenor; b. Barcelona, Dec. 5, 1946. He studied with Jaime Puig at the Barcelona Cons. before completing his training with Juan Ruax. In 1970 he made his operatic debut as Flavio in *Norma* in Barcelona, and later that year appeared as Gennaro opposite Caballé's Lucrezia Borgia. In 1971 he won the Verdi Competition in Parma, where he made his Italian debut as Rodolfo. He also made his first appearance in London that year singing Leicester in a concert performance of *Maria Stuarda*. On March 15,

1972, he made his U.S. debut as Pinkerton at the N.Y.C. Opera, where he remained on the roster until 1975. In 1973 he sang for the first time at the San Francisco Opera as Rodolfo. He made his Metropolitan Opera debut in N.Y. on Nov. 18, 1974, as Cavaradossi, and subsequently returned there regularly. In 1975 he sang for the first time at Milan's La Scala as Riccardo. In 1976 he made his first appearances at the Salzburg Festival (as Don Carlos) and at the Chicago Lyric Opera (as Riccardo). In addition to his engagements with principal opera houses of the world, Carreras pursued a notably successful career as a concert artist. However, in 1987 he was stricken with acute lymphocytic leukemia. Following exhaustive medical treatment, he was able to resume his career in 1988 when he appeared at a special Barcelona outdoor concert before an audience of 150,000 admirers. That same year he founded the José Carreras Leukemia Foundation in Barcelona. In 1989 he appeared in recitals in Seattle and N.Y., and also returned to the operatic stage as Jason in Cherubini's *Medea* in Mérida, Spain. On Sept. 24, 1989, he created the title role in Balada's *Cristóbal Colón* in Barcelona. On July 7, 1990, he appeared in a spectacular concert with fellow tenors Plácido Domingo and Luciano Pavarotti in Rome, with Zubin Mehta conducting. The event was telecast live to the world and subsequently became a best-selling video and compact disc. The "three tenors" subsequently staged such extravaganzas throughout the world. In 1998 he sang Wolf-Ferrari's Sly in Zürich, a role he reprised at the Washington (D.C.) Opera in 1999 in his first U.S. stage appearance in 12 years. His autobiography was publ. as *Singen mit der Seele* (Munich, 1989; Eng. tr., 1991, as *Singing from the Soul*). The title aptly describes his approach not only to singing but to living the life of one of the world's favorite tenors.

BIBL.: J. Pérez Senz, *J. C. El placer de cantar: Un retrato autobiográfico* (Barcelona, 1988); M. Lewis, *The Private Lives of the Three Tenors: Behind the Scenes with Plácido Domingo, Luciano Pavarotti, and J. C.* (N.Y., 1996).—NS/LK/DM

Carrillo (-Trujillo), Julián (Antonio), innovative Mexican composer; b. Ahualulco, San Luis Potosí, Jan. 28, 1875; d. Mexico City, Sept. 9, 1965. He was of Indian extraction, and lived mostly in Mexico City, where he studied violin with Pedro Manzano and composition with Melesio Morales. He graduated from the National Cons. in 1899 and received a government stipend for study abroad as a winner of the President Diaz Prize. He took courses at the Leipzig Cons. with Hans Becker (violin), Jadassohn (theory), and Hans Sitt (orchestration). He also played violin in the Gewandhaus Orch. under Nikisch. From 1902 to 1904 he studied at the Ghent Cons., winning 1st prize as violinist. He returned to Mexico in 1905 and made numerous appearances as a violinist. He also conducted concerts. Carrillo served as general inspector of music and director of the National Cons. (1913–14; 1920–24). He visited the U.S. many times, and conducted his works in N.Y. and elsewhere. During his years in Leipzig, he wrote a Sym., which he conducted there in 1902; at the same time, he began experimenting with fractional tones and developed a theory which he named *Sonido 13*, symbolically indicating divisions beyond the 12 notes of the chromatic scale. He further devised a special number notation for quarter tones, eighth tones, and sixteenth tones, and constructed special instruments for their realization, such as a harpzither with 97 strings to the octave. He also publ. several books dealing with music of fractional tones, and ed. a monthly magazine, *El Sonido 13*, in 1924–25. His music was championed by Stokowski, who often premiered his works; the two toured Mexico in 1930–31 with the Thirteenth Sound Orch., which Carrillo had founded. In the 1940s he patented plans for 15 microtonal pianos, known as metamorphosing pianos. They were finally exhibited and won a Gold Medal at the World's Fair in Brussels in 1958, where one of them was used in the premiere of his piano concerto *Metamorfoseador Carillo*.

WORKS: DRAMATIC: OPERA: *Oina a Príncipe Ossian* (1902); *Matilda o México en 1810* (1909); *Xúlitil* (1921; rev. 1947). **ORCH.:** 4 suites for Chamber Orch. (*Bagatelas*, 1896; rev. 1932; *Los naranjos*, c. 1903; *Impresiones de la Habana*, 1929; arrangement of *6 Preludes* for Piano, 1944); 3 numbered syms. (1901; 1905; *Atonal*, 1945); 2 *marchas nupciales* for Chamber Orch. (1909); *8 de septiembre*, fantasy for Piano and Orch. (1930); *Xochimilco*, symphonic poem (1935); Triple Concerto for Flute, Violin, Cello, and Orch. (1942); *Trozo sinfónico atonal* (1961). 3 *Columbia* syms., in quarter, eighth, and sixteenth tones (1926, 1926, 1931); Concertino for 6 Instruments (Piccolo, Horn, Harp, Violin, Cello, and Guitar) in quarter, eighth, and sixteenth tones, with Orch. in normal tuning (1926; Philadelphia, March 4, 1927); *Serenata* for quarter-tone Cello with Orch. in normal tuning (1926); *Nocturno al Río Hudson* for Orch. in quarter, eighth, and sixteenth tones (1927); *Capricho* for Horn in sixteenth tones and Orch. in normal tuning (1929); Concerto for Cello in quarter and eighth tones and Orch. in normal tuning (1945); *Horizontes*, symphonic poem for Violin, Cello, and Harp in quarter and sixteenth tones and Orch. in normal tuning (1947; Pittsburgh, Nov. 30, 1951); Concerto, *Metamorfoseador Carrillo*, for Metamorphosing Piano in third tones and Orch. in normal tuning (1948; Brussels, Nov. 9, 1958); 2 concertos for Violin in quarter tones and Orch. in normal tuning (1949, 1964); *Balbuceos* for Metamorphosing Piano in sixteenth tones and Chamber Orch. in normal tuning (1958; Houston, March 18, 1960). **CHAMBER:** *Stella (Berceuse)* for Flute, Horn, English Horn, Harp, and Cello (1897); String Sextet (1900); unnumbered String Quartet in E-flat (1903); 6 sonatas for Solo Violin (*Paganini*, 1903; 1909; n.d.; 1963; n.d.; n.d.); *Tema con variaciones* for Violin and Piano (1910); Piano Quintet (1913); 4 numbered string quartets, subtitled *Atonal* (a *Debussy*, c. 1927; c. 1930; 1932; a *Beethoven*, 1955); unnumbered String Quartet, on a 6-tone scale (1937); unnumbered String Quartet, on a 7-tone scale (c. 1940). 2 of 5 separate pieces under the collective title *5 primeras composiciones*, all in quarter, eighth, and sixteenth tones: *Preludio* for Cello and Small Ensemble and *Hoja de album* for 6 Instruments (1922–58); 8 unnumbered string quartets in quarter tones (c. 1924; c. 1925; c. 1925; *Meditación*, 1926; *En secreto*, 1926; 1962; 1964; 1964); *Sonata casi-fantasia* for 7 Instruments in quarter, eighth, and sixteenth tones (1925); *Serenata* for Cello in quarter tones, with English Horn, Harp, and String Quarter in normal tuning (1926); 3 *Estudios en forma de sonatina* for Solo Violin in quarter tones (1927); Sonata for Solo Cello in quarter tones (1927); *Fantasia Sonido 13* for String Quartets, Wind Quintet, Trumpet, Trombone, and Harps in quarter, eighth, and sixteenth tones (1930); *Amanecer en Berlin 13*, sonata for Solo Zither-Harp in quarter tones (1931; rev. 1957); 4 *Casi-sonatas* for Solo Cello in quarter tones (1959); Sonata for Guitar in quarter tones (1960); 3

Casi-sonatas for Solo Violin in quarter tones (1960); 4 *Casi-sonatas* for Solo Viola in quarter tones (1961). **KEYBOARD: PIANO:** *En el bosque,* waltz (1896); *6 Preludes* (1920). **VOCAL:** *Misa* for Chorus and Orch. (1896); *Requiem* for Chorus and Orch. (1900); *Misa al Sagrado Corazón de Jesús* for Men's Chorus and Orch. (1918); *Pequeño requiem atonal* for 24 Solo Voices, 4 Mixed Choruses, and Orch. (1956); choruses and songs. *Preludio a Colón* for Soprano and 5 Instruments, *Ave Maria* for Chorus and 6 Instruments, and *Tepepán* for Soprano with Chorus and Harp (3 pieces from the cycle *5 Primera composiciones,* all in quarter, eighth, and sixteenth tones, 1922–25); *"I Think of You"* for Soprano Singing in English and in quarter tones with Trumpet and Zither-Harp in sixteenth tones (1929); *Misa a S. S. Juan XXIII* for Chorus singing in quarter tones (1962); *Misa No. 2* for Men's Chorus singing in quarter tones (1965).

WRITINGS: *Julián Carrillo, Su vida y su obra* (Mexico City, 1945); *Leyes de metamorfósis musicales* (Mexico City, 1949). **—NS/LK/DM**

Carrington, Terri Lyne,

jazz drummer, composer, vocalist; b. Medford, Mass., Aug. 4, 1965. Her father worked part-time as a tenor saxophonist in the Boston area and helped to promote her when she was young. A one-time protegé of Alan Dawson at Berklee, Carrington played at Boston clubs and jazz functions as a child and later as a teen. At 17, she won a young talent award from the NAJE (1983). In late 1986 or early 1987, she moved to N.Y.; she has since played with Herbie Hancock, Al Jarreau, Stan Getz, Wayne Shorter, David Sanborn, Dianne Reeves, and Joe Sample. Her album *Real Life Story* was nominated for a Grammy Award. She had a four-month gig as drummer on the Arsenio Hall Show and currently is concentrating on producing.

DISC.: *Real Life Story* (1989).—**LP**

Carroli, Silvano,

Italian baritone; b. Venice, Feb. 22, 1939. He trained at the opera school of the Teatro La Fenice in Venice and with Marcello and Mario del Monaco. After making his operatic debut as Schanuard in Venice in 1963, he sang in various Italian music centers. In 1972 he made his U.S. debut as Tonio in Dallas. As a member of Milan's La Scala company, he toured the U.S. in 1976 and Japan in 1981. In 1977 he made his debut at London's Covent Garden as Jack Rance, and returned there in later seasons. In 1978 he made his first appearance at the Chicago Lyric Opera. On Oct. 28, 1983, he made his Metropolitan Opera debut in N.Y. as Don Carlo in *La forza del destino.* In 1984 he sang at the Paris Opéra. His guest engagements also took him to Vienna, Barcelona, Brussels, Munich, and Berlin. Carroli is especially associated with roles in Italian opera, but he also sings roles to fine effect in operas by Mozart and Wagner.—**NS/LK/DM**

Carroll, Barbara (actually, Coppersmith, Barbara Carole),

jazz pianist; b. Worcester, Mass., Jan. 25, 1925. Carroll began playing piano at age 5; after spending a year at the New England Cons., she toured with a trio with the U.S.O. during World War II. After the war, she settled in N.Y., where she began leading her own trio and made her recording debut in 1949. She married trio member bassist Joe Shulman in 1954, and they worked together until his death three years later. During the 1960s, she remarried and retired from music making; returned to performing in 1976. She has played regularly at N.Y.'s Carlyle Hotel since 1978. Carroll has spent so much time in hotel lounges that few people remember that she is a fine jazz improviser.

DISC.: *Barbara Carroll Trio* (1951); *Piano Panorama* (1951); *Just Plain Blue* (1954); *We Just Couldn't Say Goodbye* (1956); *Barbara Carroll* (1976); *Live at the Carlyle* (1991).—**LP**

Carron (real name, Cox), Arthur,

English tenor; b. Swindon, Dec. 12, 1900; d. there, May 10, 1967. He joined London's Old Vic Theatre in 1929; also sang in London at the Sadler's Wells Opera until 1935 and at Covent Garden (1931, 1939). In 1936 he went to the U.S., where he won the Metropolitan Opera Auditions of the Air, and made his debut with the Metropolitan on May 29, 1936, as Canio in *Pagliacci;* he was chosen to sing the role of Nolan in the world premiere of Walter Damrosch's *The Man without a Country* on May 12, 1937; remained on the roster of the Metropolitan until 1946; then returned to England, where he sang at Covent Garden until 1951. Among his other roles were Tristan, Tannhäuser, Siegmund, Otello, and Manrico. **—NS/LK/DM**

Cars, The,

edgy band that helped bring new-wave music to pop radio (formed Boston, Mass., 1975). **MEMBERSHIP:** Ric Ocasek (real name, Richard Otcasek), gtr., voc. (b. Baltimore, Md., March 23, 1949); Benjamin Orr (real name, Orzechowski), bs., voc. (b. Cleveland, Ohio, Aug. 9, 1955; d. Atlanta, Ga., Oct. 10, 2000); Elliot Easton (real name, Shapiro), gtr. (b. Brooklyn, Dec. 18, 1953); Greg Hawkes, kybd. (b. Baltimore, Md.); David Robinson, drm.

Ric Ocasek and session musician Ben Orr started playing together in the early 1970s as Milkwood. They recorded two LPs for Paramount with Greg Hawkes on keyboards. They added guitarist Elliot Easton to the band and changed the group's name to Cap'n Swing. With the addition of former Modern Lovers' drummer David Robinson, they changed their name one final time to the Cars, and started playing regularly at Boston clubs like the Rat. They opened a concert for Bob Seger, and got their demo version of "Just What I Needed" added to the playlist at Boston radio station WCOZ. It became the station's #1 request.

With all this buzz, the Cars were signed to Elektra records who put them in the studio with producer Roy Thomas Baker. Two weeks later, they delivered their eponymous debut album. The sound had the aural austerity of the growing new-wave, with the clean, arch elements of Roxy Music. The album became a staple on Album Rock radio, with such synth-heavy tunes as "Moving in Stereo" and the singles "Just What I Needed" and "My Best Friend's Girl" reached #27 and #35, respectively, on the pop charts. The album eventually sold six million copies and hit #18 on the charts.

Capitalizing on this sound and success, the group quickly released their next album, *Candy-O.* The single "Let's Go" climbed up to #14, and the album went to

#3, ultimately selling over three million copies. The group played for half a million fans in N.Y.'s Central Park. They were asked to host the late night weekend TV show *The Midnight Special*, which they accepted provided they could have control over the selection of the other performers. It was probably the only time the band Suicide ever appeared on commercial TV!

The Cars's next release, 1980's *Panorama*, went to #5 on the strength of the single "Touch and Go" which hit #37. The band had started to sound a little tired and formulaic, so the group took a year off. They bought Intermedia Studio's in Boston, refitted it to their desires, and opened it as Synchro Sound. Ocasek produced albums by model Bebe Buell and the avant rock duo Suicide there.

The Cars got back together with producer Baker at Synchro and recorded the upbeat *Shake It Up* in 1981. The album rose to #9, on the strength of the #4 title track and considerable album rock play for "Since You're Gone," and sold platinum. After spending close to a year on the road, the group took another hiatus. Ocasek recorded his solo debut, *Beatitude*, which climbed to #28. Hawkes also put out a solo record, *Niagra Falls*.

The band went to England to record with producer Robert John "Mutt" Lange. The result, 1984's *Hearbeat City*, earned the band as many hits as their previous three records combined. With a video that made use of state-of-the-art special effects, "You Might Think" became a high rotation clip on MTV and went to #7. "Magic" followed at #12. Ben Orr's vocals took the ballad "Drive" to #3. The album hit #5 and sold five million copies. In 1985, the band cut two additional tracks for a *Greatest Hits* collection: "Tonight She Comes" went to #7, and "I'm Not the One" topped out at #32.

Another hiatus followed, during which Easton released *Change, No Change*, which hit a lackluster #99 on the album charts. Orr released *The Lace*, which got as high as #92, but the single "Stay the Night" rose to #24. Hawkes recorded a couple of film scores. Ocasek released his second solo album, *This Side of Paradise*, which rose to #32 on the strength of the #15 single "Emotion in Motion."

After three years away from each other, the Cars made 1987's *Door to Door*. A much more live sounding album, it reprised a couple of the songs they used to play as Cap'n Swing. However, the album was not very successful, topping out at #26, while the single "You are the Girl" topped out at #17. By this time life within the band became "redundant, envious and business-oriented" according to Ocasek, and the band broke up.

Ocasek released three more solo albums, but mostly became a successful producer, working with acts ranging from nerd rockers Weezer to pop sensations Hanson. Orr played with a series of bands and continued to try and get a solo deal, performing live throughout New England. Hawkes created several CDs of synth and sound effects for sampling. Easton worked with his own band, the Tiki Love Gods, and became the lead guitarist for Creedence Clearwater Revisited. Frequent overtures to reunite the Cars generally fall apart, allegedly owing to bad blood between Orr and Ocasek.

DISC.: *Cars* (1978); *Candy-O* (1979); *Panorama* (1980); *Shake It Up* (1981); *Heartbeat City* (1984); *Greatest Hits* (1985); *Door to Door* (1987); *Just What I Needed: Cars Anthology* (1995). Ric Ocasek: *Beatitude* (1983); *This Side of Paradise* (1986); *Troublizing* (1997). Ben Orr: *The Lace* (1986). Greg Hawkes: *Niagra Falls* (1983). Elliot Easton: *Change, No Change* (1985).—**HB**

Carse, Adam (von Ahn), English composer and writer on music; b. Newcastle upon Tyne, May 19, 1878; d. Great Missenden, Buckinghamshire, Nov. 2, 1958. He studied with F. Corder and Burnett at the Royal Academy of Music in London. From 1909 to 1922 he taught music at Winchester Coll., then taught harmony and composition at the Royal Academy of Music (1923–40). He assembled a collection of about 350 wind instruments, which he presented to the Horniman Museum in London in 1947. A catalog of this collection was publ. in 1951.

WORKS: 2 symphonic poems: *The Death of Tintagiles* (London, 1902) and *In a Balcony* (London, Aug. 26, 1905); 2 syms. (London, July 3, 1906; London, Nov. 19, 1908, rev. 1909); 2 orch. suites: *The Merry Milkmaids* (1922) and *The Nursery* (1928); *Judas Iscariot's Paradise*, ballade for Baritone, Chorus, and Orch. (1922); 2 sketches for Strings (1923); *Barbara Allen* for Strings; *Norwegian Fantasia* for Violin and Orch.; *The Lay of the Brown Rosary*, dramatic cantata; numerous choruses; chamber music; piano pieces; songs.

WRITINGS: *The History of Orchestration* (London, 1925); *Orchestral Conducting* (London, 1929); *Musical Wind Instruments* (London, 1939); *The Orchestra in the 18th Century* (Cambridge, 1940; 2nd ed., 1950); *The Orchestra from Beethoven to Berlioz* (Cambridge, 1948); *The Orchestra* (London, 1948); *18th Century Symphonies* (London, 1951); *The Life of Jullien* (Cambridge, 1951). —**NS/LK/DM**

Cartan, Jean, talented French composer; b. Nancy, Dec. 1, 1906; d. Bligny, March 26, 1932. His father was the famous mathematician Elie Cartan. He studied with Marcel Rousseau; then with Dukas at the Paris Cons. His works, composed within the brief period of six years, showed extraordinary promise, and his death at the age of 25 was mourned as a great loss to French music. He left a cantata, *Pater Noster*, two string quartets, a Sonatina for Flute and Clarinet (Oxford, July 25, 1931), piano pieces, and several cycles of songs. —**NS/LK/DM**

Carte, Richard D'Oyly, English impresario; b. London, May 3, 1844; d. there, April 3, 1901. He studied at Univ. Coll. in London. He wrote an opera, *Dr. Ambrosias*, and later turned to music management, representing, among others, Gounod, Adelina Patti, and the tenor Mario. He then became interested in light opera and introduced in England Lecocq's *Giroflé-Girofla*, Offenbach's *La Périchole*, and other popular French operettas. His greatest achievement was the launching of comic operas by Gilbert and Sullivan; he commissioned and produced at the Royalty Theatre their *Trial by Jury* (1875) and then formed a syndicate to stage other productions of their works at the London Opéra Comique Theatre. Dissension within the syndicate induced him to build the Savoy Theatre (1881), which subsequently became celebrated as the home of Gilbert and Sullivan productions, with Carte himself as the leading "Savoyard." He successfully operated the Savoy Theatre until his death; the enterprise was continued by his wife (Helen Lenoir) until her death in 1913; thereafter by his sons, and finally by his granddaughter; it was disbanded in 1982, but was revived in 1998. In 1887 Carte attempted to establish serious English opera through the building of a special theater (now known as the Palace Theatre), and the production in 1891 of Sullivan's grand opera *Ivanhoe*, followed by commissions to other English composers to write operas. D'Oyly Carte introduced many improvements in theatrical management, including the replacement of gaslight by electric illumination.

BIBL.: F. Cellier and C. Bridgeman, *Gilbert, Sullivan and d'O. C.*(London, 1914).—NS/LK/DM

Carter, Benny (actually, Bennett Lester; aka "The King"),

legendary, long-careered jazz alto and tenor saxophonist, trumpeter, clarinetist, bandleader, arranger, composer, trombonist, pianist, clarinetist; b. N.Y., Aug. 8, 1907. His father, Norell Carter (b. in or near Clarksburg, W. Va., c. 1877), a janitor and later a postal clerk, was a self-taught guitarist, his mother Sadie Bennett (b. Richmond, Va., c. 1877; d. N.Y. 1926) played piano and organ. He had two older sisters, Edna (b. c. 1900) and Alice (b. c. 1904). When he was perhaps one year old, the family moved to the San Juan Hill area of Manhattan. He sang in the choir at an Episcopal church. On July 4, 1917 or 1918, he accidentally shot a girl in the back with a BB gun and was sent to a reformatory for a few weeks, after which his mother sent him to live for a year or two with her relatives near Pittsburgh. He then returned to school in N.Y.; he was later expelled for punching a teacher who called him a "nigger." Carter studied piano with his mother from age ten, then with a neighborhood teacher. Inspired by his cousin, Theodore "Cuban" Bennett, an accomplished trumpet player, he saved up for eight months and at age 13 paid $33 for a second-hand trumpet; after one weekend of abortive blowing, he returned to the shop and after some difficulty got the owner to exchange it for a saxophone on the advice of local musician Harold Proctor. He took lessons from Arthur Reeves (a particular inspiration), and also taught himself from books.

By age 15, Carter was sitting in at Harlem night spots, despite parental objections. When his family moved to Harlem in 1923, he became even more involved in the jazz scene. Probably his first regular paying job was in 1923 when Miley invited him to sub for Ben Whittet at John O'Connors' Club in Harlem. He joined June Clark's Band (August 1924) and switched to alto sax. Soon afterwards, he worked with Billy Paige's Broadway Syncopators at the Capitol, N.Y.; they quickly disbanded and Benny played with Lois Deppe's Serenaders, then on baritone with Earl Hines at the Grape Arbor in Pittsburgh (late 1924). He also worked with Willie "the Lion" Smith in a trio and sat in with William (later Count) Basie. Carter began to teach himself composition and arranging by taking published stock arrangements and studying the parts spread out on the floor without a score. Initially, he wrote without a score as well. In summer 1925 he met Rosa Lee Jackson and they were married a few weeks later; she died of pneumonia in 1928. In 1925 he went to Wilberforce Coll., Ohio, to join Horace Henderson's (Wilberforce) Collegians (he never enrolled there despite what has often been stated). He left Henderson in 1926 and during that summer worked with Billy Fowler's Band in Baltimore and N.Y. After a brief stint with James P. Johnson, he worked two weeks in Duke Ellington's Band, then spent a short spell with Fletcher Henderson, producing his first recorded arrangement, "P.D.Q. Blues," written in 1927, the same year he published his first composition, "Nobody Knows," co-written with Fats Waller. Carter then spent over a year with Charlie Johnson, with whom he made his first surviving recordings (1928), including two of his arrangements ("Charleston is the Best Dance After All"). He rejoined Horace Henderson in Detroit, then toured briefly with Fletcher Henderson (autumn 1928) before forming his own band (late 1928) in N.Y. and on tour. He worked again with Fletcher Henderson (from January 1930), writing many arrangements. Carter joined Chick Webb (c. March 1931) and left during summer 1931 to spend a year as the musical director of McKinney's Cotton Pickers. From this period onward, he regularly doubled on trumpet. While working with McKinney, he also played dates with Don Redman and Fletcher Henderson.

Carter began rehearsing his own band in the summer of 1932, with Dicky Wells, Chu Berry, and Sid Catlett (Teddy Wilson joined in 1933); he led this band in N.Y. (from c. September 1932), including benefits for the Scottsboro Nine defense fund on Oct. 7, 1932 and March 8, 1933, touring, and local residencies at Lafayette Theatre and Savoy Ballroom. In January 1934, his band opened the Apollo Theater in Harlem. He recorded with Fletcher Henderson (September 1934), and arranged for Duke Ellington and Benny Goodman. Carter disbanded his group and worked on trumpet with Willie Bryant (spring 1935), and then with Charlie Barnet, before receiving an invitation to Europe. After emigration delays, Carter joined Willie Lewis's Band in Paris (summer 1935). At Leonard Feather's suggestion, he took an appointment as staff arranger for the radio BBC Dance Orch. (1936) in London. He frequently toured Europe, playing Scandinavia (autumn 1936), Amsterdam (March 1937), France, and led the first International (and interracial) Band at Scheveningen, Holland (summer 1937); he led a band at Boeuf sur le Toit in Paris before returning to the U.S. in May 1938. He organized his own big band (November 1938), which was frequently resident at the Savoy Ballroom, N.Y. (March 1939–January 1941). In the fall of 1941, he led a sextet that included Dizzy Gillespie and Kenny Clarke and performed at clubs on 52nd Street. During this period, his arrangements were featured on recordings by Goodman, Glenn Miller, Gene Krupa, and Tommy Dorsey; his well known "When Lights Are Low" was first recorded in London with singer Elizabeth Welch (1936), then done as an instrumental by Lionel Hampton (1939).

In February 1942 Carter re-formed a big band; on tour in Hollywood, he decided to settle in the L.A. area, where he has lived ever since. He played on and helped to orchestrate the soundtrack of *Stormy Weather* (1943), leading to other soundtrack work; he was one of the first African-Americans to work in this area. Carter led his own band at Billy Berg's Club, Los Angeles, followed by residencies at the Hollywood and Casa Manana. He started a residency at the Apollo, N.Y. (1944); he was billed as "The Amazing Man of Music." In 1945 he had residencies at the Trocadero, Hollywood, Plantation Club. During this period, his band included (at times) Miles Davis, J. J. Johnson, Art Pepper, and Max Roach; the band broke up in 1946. He reorganized a new seven-piece band (1947) and continued to do occasional tours, but from the late 1940s through the early 1970s he worked mainly as a composer-arranger for the film and later TV industry.

In 1950, he chaired the committee that negotiated the successful effort to combine the black musicians local 767 of Los Angeles with the white local 47. He led his own bands in and around Hollywood during the 1950s. In the 1950s and 1960s, he also did brief overseas tours with Norman Grant's Jazz at the Philharmonic. In the late 1950s and 1960s, he did arrangements for various singers, including Billie Holiday, Ella Fitzgerald, Sarah Vaughan, Lou Rawls, Ray Charles, Peggy Lee, Louis Armstrong, Pearl Bailey, Billy Eckstine, and Mel Tormé; he also played trombone on Capitol records by Julia Lee. Carter restricted his playing to the alto sax during the 1960s. He subbed with Duke Ellington as a favor for a few nights early in 1968, and later that year played solo dates in the U.K. During the past 25 years, Carter has arranged and composed music for dozens of important films, among them *The Snows of Kilimanjaro, The View from Pompey's Head, As Thousands Cheer,* and *Clash by Night.* He also wrote music for more than two dozen theatrical films, including *An American in Paris, The Sun Also Rises,* and *The Guns of Navarone.* In 1975 he traveled throughout the Middle East on a tour sponsored by the U.S. State Department, and around 1976 he resumed an extremely busy full-time jazz career including frequent visits to Europe and Japan. He played at President Jimmy Carter's White House Jazz Party (June 1978). In the 1970s, he became involved in education, conducting seminars and workshops at many universities. He has received honorary doctorates from Harvard, Princeton, New England Cons., and Rutgers Univ. Other honors include induction into the Black Film Makers Hall of Fame (1978), the coveted Golden Score award of the American Society of Music Arrangers (1980), and appointment to the music advisory panel of the NEA. He also led an orch. for the 1984 inaugural of President Reagan and played at the White House in 1989 as a guest of President Bush. In 1987 Carter received a Grammy Lifetime Achievement Award from the National Academy of Recording Arts and Sciences. That year he recorded *Central City Sketches* with the American Jazz Orch., nominated for a Grammy in 1988. Carter placed first in the 1989 Down Beat International Critics Poll in the arranger's category. Carter celebrated his 82nd birthday with a concert in Lincoln Center's Alice Tully Hall. Summer 1991 saw the premiere of a suite

called "Good Vibes," which Lincoln Center had commissioned from Carter for this occasion. He wrote the "Peaceful Warrior Suite" for Martin Luther King, commissioned by the Library of Congress for a big band, strings, and Joe Williams and Marlena Shaw. In 1990 Carter was named Jazz Artist of the Year in both the Down Beat and Jazz Times International Critics' polls. He received a Kennedy Center honor on Dec. 8, 1996.

DISC.: *Symphony in Riffs* (1930); *Chocolate Dandies* (1933); *When Lights are Low* (1936); *Crazy Rhythm* (1937); *All of Me* (1940); *New Jazz Sounds* (1954); *Urbane Mr. Carter* (1954); *Jazz Giant* (1957); *Aspects* (1958); *Swingin' the Twenties* (1958); *Further Definitions* (1961); *B.B.B. & Co.* (1962); *Additions to Further Definition* (1966); *Live and Well in Japan* (1977); *Montreux* (1977); *Gentleman and His Music* (1985); *Central City Sketches* (1987); *Cookin' at Carlos 1* (1988); *Over the Rainbow* (1988); *My Man Benny, My Man Phil* (1989); *Devil's Holiday* (1991); *Harlem Renaissance* (1992); *B.C. Songbook Vols. 1, 2* (1995); *Another Time, Another Place* (1996); *Journey to Next* (1996).

BIBL.: J. Evensmo, *The Alto Saxophone, Trumpet, and Clarinet of B. C., 1927–1946* (Hosle, Norway, 1982); M. Berger, *B. C.: A Life in American Music* (Metuchen, N.J., 1982); *Benny Carter Plays Standards* (Milwaukee, WI, 1996).—JC/LP

Carter, Betty (originally, Jones, Lillie Mae; aka Lorene Carter and "Bette Bebop"), jazz

singer; b. Flint, Mich., May 16, 1929; d. Brooklyn, N.Y., Sept. 26, 1998. Carter turned professional in 1946 after studying piano at the Detroit Cons. She began singing in local jazz clubs, sharing bills with Charlie Parker, Miles Davis, and Dizzy Gillespie. Using the name Lorene Carter, she toured with Lionel Hampton (1948–51, first appearing on surviving Armed Forces Jubilee broadcasts with the Hamptones, a vocal trio, from October 1948 onward); Hampton dubbed her "Betty Bebop," a name she was not happy with. Thereafter, she was known as Betty Carter. She also worked with Miles Davis, Sonny Rollins, and others. Her 1960 recorded duet with Ray Charles, "Baby It's Cold Outside" and tour with Charles helped to build her name, but the 1960s were mainly tough times for her. She lived in Newark from the late 1960s and formed a trio that became increasingly successful on college campuses in the 1970s. She had a great ear for talent and her trios over the years featured pianists John Hicks, Mulgrew Miller, Cyrus Chestnut, bassists Buster Williams, Dave Holland, drummers Jack DeJohnette, Lewis Nash, Eric Harland and many others. The distinctiveness and individuality of her albums and her refusal to compromise led to the inability to secure recording dates on major labels, and she issued and distributed her recordings from 1969 through the 1980s on her own Bet-Car label, including the Grammy-nominated *The Audience with Betty Carter.* Carter gained widespread acclaim at the Newport Jazz Festivals at Carnegie Hall (1977, 1978). A contract with Verve in the late 1980s gave her widespread exposure, as did an appearance on the Cosby Show and Saturday Night Live. Her first album on Verve, *Look What I Got,* was on Billboard's Top Ten jazz albums in early 1989 and won a Grammy for Best Female Jazz Vocalist. In 1993 Carter founded Jazz Ahead, a music program that brings about 20 young musicians from across the country to N.Y. every year during spring break; it is capped by a weekend of concerts at the Brooklyn Academy of Music. In 1996 Carter was invited by President Clinton to perform for him at a private party at the White House; that August she participated in the President's satellite-linked birthday party, beamed into Radio City Music Hall from a stage in Washington, D.C. Carter also appeared in Verve's 50th Anniversary celebration at Carnegie Hall. She holds an honorary doctorate from Williams Coll. and won the National Medal of Arts (1997). She succumbed to pancreatic cancer in 1998.

DISC.: *Meet Betty Carter* (1955); *Social Call* (1955); *I Can't Help It* (1958); *Out There* (1958); *Modern Sound of Betty Carter* (1960); *Ray Charles and Betty Carter* (1961); *Round Midnight* (1962); *Inside Betty Carter* (1965); *Finally, Betty Carter* (1969); *At the Village Vanguard* (1970); *Betty Carter, Vols. 1, 2* (1971); *Betty Carter Album* (1972); *Now It's My Turn* (1976); *What a Little Moonlight Can Do* (1976); *Audience with Betty Carter* (1979); *Whatever Happened to Love* (1982); *Jazzbuhne Berlin '85* (1985); *In the Mood for Swing* (1987); *Look What I Got* (1988); *Droppin' Things* (1990); *It's Not About the Melody* (1992); *Feed the Fire* (1993); *I'm Yours, You're Mine* (1996).

BIBL.: William R. Bauer, *Betty Carter: A Bibliography and Style Analysis* (CUNY, 1996).—**LP**

Carter, Elliott (Cook Jr.),

outstanding American composer and teacher; b. N.Y., Dec. 11, 1908. After graduating from the Horace Mann H.S. in N.Y. in 1926, Carter entered Harvard Univ., majoring in literature and languages; at the same time, he studied piano at the Longy School of Music in Cambridge, Mass. In 1930 he devoted himself exclusively to music at Harvard, taking up harmony and counterpoint with Piston, and orchestration with Hill, and also attended in 1932 a course given there by Holst. He obtained his M.A. in 1932, and then went to Paris, where he studied with Boulanger and at the École Normale de Musique, receiving a *licence de contrepoint*; in the interim, he learned mathematics, Latin, and Greek. In 1935 he returned to the U.S. He was music director of the Ballet Caravan (1937–39) and gave courses in music and also in mathematics, physics, and classical Greek at St. John's Coll. in Annapolis, Md. (1940–44). He then taught at the Peabody Cons. of Music in Baltimore (1946–48). He was on the faculty of Columbia Univ. (1948–50), Queens Coll. of the City Univ. of N.Y. (1955–56), and Yale Univ. (1960–62). In 1963 he was composer-in-residence at the American Academy in Rome, and in 1964 held a similar post in West Berlin. In 1967–68 he was a prof.-at-large at Cornell Univ. He held Guggenheim fellowships in 1945–46 and 1950–51, and the American Prix de Rome in 1953. In 1965 he received the Creative Arts Award from Brandeis Univ. In 1953 he received first prize in the Concours International de Composition pour Quatuor a Cordes in Liège for first String Quartet; in 1960 he received the Pulitzer Prize in Music for his second String Quartet, which also received the N.Y. Music Critics Circle Award and was further elected as the most important work of the year by the International Rostrum of Composers. He again won the Pulitzer Prize in Music, for his third String Quartet, in 1973. In 1985 he was awarded the National Medal of Arts by President Ronald Reagan. In 1987 he was made a Dommandeur dans l'Ordre des Arts des Lettres of France. In 1991 he was named a Commendatore of the Order of Merit in Italy. Carter's reputation as one of the most important American composers grew with each new work he produced; Stravinsky was quoted as saying that Carter's Double Concerto was the first true American masterpiece. The evolution of Carter's compositional style is marked by his constant preoccupation with taxonomic considerations. His early works are set in a neo-Classical style. He later absorbed the Schoenbergian method of composition with 12 equal tones. Finally he developed a system of serial organization in which all parameters, including intervals, metric divisions, rhythm, counterpoint, harmony, and instrumental timbres, become parts of the total conception of each individual work. In this connection, he introduced the term "metric modulation," in which secondary rhythms in a polyrhythmic section assume dominance expressed in constantly changing meters, often in such unusual time signatures as 10/16, 21/8, etc. Furthermore, he assigns to each participating instrument in a polyphonic work a special interval, a distinctive rhythmic figure, and a selective register, so that the individuality of each part is clearly outlined, a distribution which is often reinforced by placing the players at a specified distance from one another. E. and K. Stone ed. *The Writings of E. C.: An American Composer Looks at Modern Music* (N.Y., 1977). J. Bernard ed. *E. C.: Collected Essays and Lectures, 1937–1995* (Rochester, N.Y., 1997).

WORKS: DRAMATIC: O p e r a : *Tom and Lily* (1934; withdrawn); *What Next?* (Berlin, Sept. 16, 1999). **B a l l e t :** *Pocahontas* (Keene, N.H., Aug. 17, 1936; withdrawn; orch. version, 1938–39; N.Y., May 24, 1939); *The Minotaur* (N.Y., March 26, 1947). **INCIDENTAL MUSIC TO:** Sophocles's *Philoctetes* (1931; Cambridge, Mass., March 15, 1933); Plautus's *Mostellaria* (Cambridge, Mass., April 15, 1936); Shakespeare's *Much Ado About Nothing* (1937; withdrawn). **ORCH.:** Sym. (1937; withdrawn); *Prelude, Fanfare, and Polka* for Small Orch. (1938); Sym. No. 1 (1942; Rochester, N.Y., April 27, 1944; rev. 1954); *Holiday Overture* (1944; rev. 1961); *Elegy* for Strings (1952; N.Y., March 1, 1953; arranged from the *Elegy* for Cello and Piano, 1943); *Variations for Orchestra* (1954–55; Louisville, April 21, 1956); Double Concerto for Harpsichord, Piano, and 2 Chamber Orchs. (N.Y., Sept. 6, 1961); Piano Concerto (1964–65; Boston, Jan. 6, 1967); *Concerto for Orchestra* (1968–69; N.Y., Feb. 5, 1970); *A Symphony of 3 Orchestras* (1976; N.Y., Feb. 17, 1977); *Penthode* for 5 Instrumental Quartets (1984–85; London, July 26, 1985); *3 Occasions* (1986–89; 1, *A Celebration of Some 100 x 150 Notes*, 1986; Houston, April 10, 1987; 2, *Remembrance*, Tanglewood, Aug. 10, 1988; 3, *Anniversary*, London Oct. 5, 1989); Oboe Concerto (1986–87; Zürich, June 17, 1988); Violin Concerto (San Francisco, May 2, 1990); *Partita* (1993; Chicago, Feb. 17, 1994); *Adagio Tenebroso* (1994; London, Sept. 13, 1995). **CHAMBER:** *Canonic Suite* for 4 Alto Saxophones (1939; rev. for 4 Clarinets, 1955–56; rev. for 4 Saxophones, 1981); *Pastoral* for English Horn or Viola or Clarinet and Piano (1940); *Elegy* for Cello and Piano (1943; arranged for String Quartet, 1946, for String Orch., 1952, and for Viola and Piano, 1961); Piano Sonata (1945–46; N.Y. radio broadcast, Feb. 16, 1947); Woodwind Quintet (1948; N.Y., Feb. 21, 1949); Cello Sonata (1948; N.Y., Feb. 27, 1950); *8 Etudes and a Fantasy* for Flute, Oboe, Clarinet, and Bassoon (1949–50; N.Y., Oct. 28, 1952); *8 Pieces for 4 Timpani* for 1 Performer (1950–66); 4 string quartets: No. 1 (1950–51; N.Y., Feb. 26, 1953), No. 2 (1959;

N.Y., March 25, 1960), No. 3 (1971; N.Y., Jan. 23, 1973), and No. 4 (Miami, Sept. 17, 1986); Sonata for Flute, Oboe, Cello, and Harpsichord (1952; N.Y., Nov. 19, 1953); *Canon for 3: In memoriam Igor Stravinsky* for 3 Equal Instruments (1971; N.Y., Jan. 23, 1972); Duo for Violin and Piano (1973–74; N.Y., March 21, 1975); Brass Quintet for 2 Trumpets, Horn, and 2 Trombones (BBC, London, Oct. 20, 1974); *A Fantasy About Purcell's "Fantasia Upon One Note"* for 2 Trumpets, Horn, and 2 Trombones (1974; N.Y., Jan. 13, 1975); *Birthday Fanfare for Sir William Glock's 70th* for 3 Trumpets, Vibraphone, and Glockenspiel (London, May 3, 1978); *Night Fantasies* for Piano (Bath, June 2, 1980); Triple Duo for Violin, Cello, Flute, Clarinet, Piano, and Percussion (1982–83; N.Y., April 23, 1983); *Changes* for Guitar (N.Y., Dec. 11, 1983); *Canon for 4: Homage to William* [Glock] for Flute, Bass Clarinet, Violin, and Cello (Bath, June 8, 1984); *Esprit rude/esprit doux* for Flute and Clarinet (1984; Baden-Baden, March 31, 1985); *Riconoscenza per Goffredo Petrassi* for Violin (Pontino, June 15, 1984); *Birthday Flourish* for 5 Trumpets or Brass Quintet (San Francisco, Sept. 14, 1988); *Enchanted Preludes* for Flute and Cello (N.Y., May 16, 1988); *Con leggerezza pensosa* for Clarinet, Violin, and Cello (Latina, Italy, Sept. 29, 1990); Quintet for Piano and Winds (1991; Cologne, Sept. 13, 1992); *Scrivo in Vento* for Flute (Avignon, July 20, 1991); *Bariolage* for Harp (Geneva, March 23, 1992); *Immer Neu* for Oboe and Harp (Sermoneta, Italy, June 30, 1992); *Immer Song* for Oboe (Witten, April 25, 1992); 3 preceding works constitute *Trilogy* for Oboe and Harp (Sermoneta, June 30, 1992); *Gra* for Clarinet (Sermoneta, June 4, 1993); *Figment* for Cello (1994; N.Y., May 8, 1995). **VOCAL:** 11 madrigals for 3 to 8 Voices (1937); *Heart Not So Heavy as Mine* for Chorus (1938; N.Y., March 31, 1939); *The Defense of Corinth* for Speaker, Men's Voices, and Piano, 4-Hands (1941; Cambridge, Mass., March 12, 1942); 3 poems of Robert Frost for Mezzo-soprano or Baritone and Piano (1943; also for Soprano or Tenor and Chamber Orch., 1975); *Warble for Lilac Time* for Soprano or Tenor and Piano or Small Orch. (1943; Saratoga Springs, N.Y., Sept. 14, 1946; rev. 1954); *Voyage* for Mezzo-soprano or Baritone and Piano (1943; N.Y., March 16, 1947; also for Small Orch., 1975; rev. 1979); *The Harmony of Morning* for Women's Voices and Small Orch. (1944; N.Y., Feb. 25, 1945); *Musicians Wrestle Everywhere* for Mixed Voices and Strings ad libitum (1945; N.Y., Feb. 12, 1946); *A Mirror on Which to Dwell* for Soprano and 9 Players (1975; N.Y., Feb. 24, 1976); *Syringa* for Mezzo-soprano, Bass, and 11 Players (N.Y., Dec. 10, 1978); *In Sleep, in Thunder* for Tenor and 14 Players (1981; London, Oct. 27, 1982); *Of Challenge and of Love* for Soprano and Piano (1995).

BIBL.: A. Edwards, *Flawed Words and Stubborn Sounds: A Conversation with E. C.* (N.Y., 1971); *E. C.: A 70th Birthday Tribute* (London, 1978); D. Schiff, *The Music of E. C.* (N.Y., 1983; 2nd ed., 1998); C. Rosen, *The Musical Languages of E. C.* (Washington, D.C., 1984); D. Harvey, *The Later Music of E. C.: A Study in Music Theory and Analysis* (N.Y., 1989); E. Restagno, *E. C.: In Conversation with Enzo Restagno for Settemre Musica 1989* (N.Y., 1991); A. Edwards, C. Rosen, and H. Holliger, *Entretiens avec E. C.* (Geneva, 1992); J. Link, *E. C.: A Guide to Research* (N.Y., 2000).—**NS/LK/DM**

Carter, James, jazz saxophonist; b. Detroit, Mich., Jan. 3, 1969. Carter's musical education consisted of private studies with local bop-scene veteran Donald Washington as well as tenures at the prestigious Blue Lake Fine Arts Camp. Carter first came to national attention touring with Wynton Marsalis while only 17. Since then, he has worked with Lester Bowie, Julius Hemphill, the Charles Mingus Big Band, the Lincoln Center Jazz Orch., and Kathleen Battle, among many others. He appeared in *Jazz at Lincoln Center: The City of Jazz* (PBS, 1994), in the film *Kansas City* (1995), and in *Live at Newport 1996* (PBS). He is one of a few of the younger players to embrace the avant-garde jazz stylings of the 1960s and 1970s. Although he is a favorite of critics and audiences, many musicians find his style bizarre and grand-standing.

DISC.: *JC on the Set* (1993); *Jurassic Classics* (1994); *The Real Quietstorm* (1994); *Conversin' with the Elders* (1996). L. Bowie: *Lester Bowie's New York Organ Ensemble—The Organizer* (1991). F. Lowe: *Inappropriate Choices* (1991). J. Hemphill: *The Fat Man and the Hard Blues* (1991); *Five Chord Stud* (1993). Various artists: *Kansas City Soundtrack* (1995).—**LP**

Carter, John (Wallace), jazz clarinetist, alto saxophonist, composer; b. Fort Worth, Tex., Sept. 24, 1929; d. Los Angeles, Calif., March 31, 1991. He grew up in Fort Worth with Ornette Coleman, Charles Moffett, and Dewey Redman; he started playing clarinet as a child, gigging from the age of 14 around Fort Worth and Dallas. He was a prodigy, graduating from high school at 15 and college at 19; B.A. in Music at Lincoln Univ. After college Carter took a teaching job in the Fort Worth school systems, which he kept through the 1950s while earning his M.A. at Univ. of Colo. (1956); during that time, he also played in jazz and blues groups throughout the Southwest. In 1961 he moved to Los Angeles and again took a job as a public school teacher. He started working with Bobby Bradford; they founded an avant-garde jazz group in 1965, which they co-led, called the New Arts Jazz Ensemble (1965–73). Carter and Bradford also worked and recorded with Horace Tapscott in the early 1970s. Carter led his own groups from 1973 until he joined James Newton's woodwind quintet (1980) and recorded with British drummer John Stevens. In 1974 he dropped playing saxophone to focus on the clarinet. He gave many educational lectures and performed in concerts. Although he and Bradford recorded albums and toured Europe in the early 1970s, Carter continued to teach most of the time in Los Angeles. In the early 1980s, with his four children grown, he finally quit teaching to devote all his energies to being a full-time musician. He formed his own record label and recorded with James Newton, Bradford, and a group he founded called Clarinet Summit (1984–87), for which he recruited Alvin Batiste, Jimmy Hamilton, and David Murray. He was also commissioned by N.Y.'s Public Theater to compose a five-part suite, *Roots and Folklore: Episodes in the Development of American Folk Music*, which he began in 1982 and completed in 1989. Tracing the history of slavery from Africa to the migrations of the African-American populations from the rural South to urban centers after World War II, this monumental work combined traditional themes with brilliant orchestration for a bebop-flavored octet.

DISC.: *Flight for Four* (1969); *Seeking* (1969); *Self-Determination Music* (1969); *West Coast Hot* (1969); *Secrets* (1972); *Suite of Early American Folk Pieces for Solo Clarinet* (1979); *Dauwhe* (1982); *Clarinet Summit* (1984); *Castles of Ghana* (1985); *Dance of the Love Ghosts* (1985); *Fields* (1988); *Shadows on a Wall* (1989).—**LP/MS**

Carterette, Edward C(alvin), learned American experimental psychologist, ethnomusicologist, and musicologist; b. Mount Tabor, N.C., July 10, 1921; d. Los Angeles, July 7, 1999. He studied mathematics at the Univ. of Chicago, psychology at Harvard Univ., and experimental and mathematical psychology at Ind. Univ. (Ph.D., 1957). He concurrently worked in the Brain Wave Laboratory of Mass. General Hospital in Boston, in the Acoustics Laboratory of the Mass. Inst. of Technology, and in the Hearing and Communication Laboratory of Ind. Univ. In 1956 he joined the faculty of the dept. of psychology at the Univ. of Calif. at Los Angeles, where he was made a prof. in 1968 and an adjunct prof. of ethnomusicology and systematic musicology in 1988. He retired as prof. emeritus in 1991. He served as co-ed. of the Handbook of Perception series (nine vols., 1973–78) and as ed. of the Handbook of Perception and Cognition series (2nd ed., 17 vols., 1994–99), and also was assoc. ed. of the journals *Perception and Psychophysics* (1972–93) and of *Music Perception* (1982–99). Carterette's publications numbered around 200 and were notable for their catholicity. In music he wrote on such diverse subjects as acoustics, musical expression, and hearing in orchestral players. —NS/LK/DM

Carter Family, The seminal American country-music group. **MEMBERSHIP:** A(lvin) P(leasant) (Delaney) Carter, voc., fdl. (b. near Maces Springs, Va., Dec. 15, 1891; d. Kingsport, Tenn., Nov. 7, 1960); his wife, Sara Elizabeth (Dougherty) Carter, voc., autoharp, gtr. (b. Flat Woods, Va., July 21, 1898; d. Lodi, Calif., Jan. 8, 1979); and his sister-in-law (and Sara's cousin) songwriter ("Mother") Maybelle (Addington) Carter, voc., gtr. (b. Nickelsville, Va., May 10, 1909; d. Nashville, Oct. 23, 1978).

A. P., the son of Robert and Molly Bayes Carter, was selling fruit trees when he met Sara, who had been raised by her aunt and uncle, Milburn and Melinda Nickels, after her mother died when she was an infant. They married on June 18, 1915, and eventually had three children: Gladys, Janette, and Joe. Maybelle, the daughter of Hugh Jack and Margaret Addington, who owned a general store and a mill, married A. P.'s brother Ezra, a railroad mail clerk, on March 23, 1926, and they had three daughters: Helen, June, and Anita.

The Carter Family first auditioned for Brunswick Records; then, on July 31, 1927, for Victor Records in Bristol, Tenn., for A&R executive Ralph Peer. They recorded six songs for Victor on Aug. 1–2. Among them was "Bury Me under the Weeping Willow," which became a hit. They went to Camden, N.J., for a second Victor session in May 1928 that produced the million-seller "Wildwood Flower" and the hits "Keep on the Sunny Side" and "Little Darling Pal of Mine." Their February 1929 recording session in Camden resulted in the hit "I'm Thinking Tonight of My Blue Eyes." "Worried Man Blues" was a hit in September 1930, and "Lonesome Valley" in April 1931.

The Carters' repertoire consisted of songs they had collected, adapted, and written, although they were credited to A. P. as original compositions on the Victor discs. Nevertheless, the Carters' arrangements and performances were highly original, especially Maybelle's guitar playing, featuring what came to be called the Carter Lick, used in country music ever after.

In the early 1930s A. P. and Sara separated, and they eventually divorced, although they continued to perform together. After a final RCA Victor recording session in December 1934, they contracted to the American Record Corporation (ARC) (later Columbia Records) and recorded 40 sides in May 1935, many of them repeats of songs done for Victor, although "Can Will the Circle Be Unbroken (Bye and Bye)," released on Banner Records, became a hit in August. From June 1936 to June 1938 they were contracted to Decca Records, recording 60 songs. Between 1938 and 1941 they spent their winters in Tex., broadcasting over the Mexican radio stations XERA, XEG, and XENT, sponsored by the Consolidated Royal Chemical Corporation of Chicago. (These powerful stations, located just south of the U.S. border, could be picked up in much of the country.) On the broadcasts (some of which were transcribed on disc and later released commercially), they frequently included their children.

Sara married A. P.'s cousin, Coy Bayes, on Feb. 20, 1939, and the couple moved to Calif., although she continued to perform with the family. The Carters recorded 20 sides for Columbia's OKeh label on Oct. 3, 1940, and another 13 for RCA Victor's Bluebird label on Oct. 14, 1941. These were the last of their 273 commercial recordings. Starting in late 1942 and running until March 1943, they appeared on WBT, Charlotte, N.C. At this point the group broke up; A. P. went back to Maces Springs and opened a store, Sara retired to Calif.

Maybelle carried on: On June 1, 1943, "the Carter Sisters and Mother Maybelle" began broadcasting on WRNL, Richmond, Va. They moved to WRVA's *Old Dominion Barn Dance* in 1946, to WNOX's *Tennessee Barn Dance* in 1948, and to KWTO Springfield's *Ozark Jubilee* in 1949. In 1950 they reached the pinnacle of country radio programs, WSM Nashville's *Grand Ole Opry*. A. P. and Sara, with their children Janette and Joe, formed the A. P. Carter Family in 1952 for recordings on the local Acme Records label; A. P. also opened the Summer Park arena in the Clinch Mountains, in which the group performed. They stayed active until 1956.

After A. P.'s death, Maybelle and her daughters began billing themselves as the Carter Family, and the earlier trio began to be referred to as the Original Carter Family. In the mid-1960s, Sara and Maybelle appeared together at the Newport Folk Festival and recorded the Columbia album *An Historic Reunion*. The Original Carter Family became the first group inducted into the Country Music Hall of Fame in November 1970.

The Carter Family had a tremendous influence on country, folk, and pop music. Their repertoire provided hits for many artists: Roy Acuff (who had earlier adapted the tune of "I'm Thinking Tonight of My Blue Eyes" for his "Great Speckle Bird") had a million-seller with "Wabash Cannonball" in 1938; "I'm Thinking Tonight of My Blue Eyes" was a Top Ten Country hit for Gene Autry in 1944; "Wildwood Flower" hit the Country Top Ten in an instrumental version by Hank Thompson and His Brazos Valley Boys with Merle Travis in 1955; Mac Wiseman had a Top Ten Country hit with "Jimmy Brown the Newsboy" and the Kingston Trio had a Top 40 pop hit with their version of "Worried Man Blues," "A Worried Man," in 1959; and Lester Flatt, Earl Scruggs, and the Foggy Mountain Boys had a Top 40 Country hit with "You are My Flower" in 1964. In addition to these specific hits, the Carters' songs were endlessly performed, recorded, and adapted by other artists. Woody Guthrie employed many of their melodies for his songs, notably borrowing the tune of "When the World's on Fire" for his "This Land is Your Land."

The Carters' rural background and rudimentary musical style formed the basis for traditional country music and bluegrass and remain the defining elements of those genres. The Nitty Gritty Dirt Band's gold-selling 1972 triple-LP (now a double CD) album *Will the Circle Be Unbroken*, featuring a guest appearance by Mother Maybelle Carter and including such Carter songs as the title track, "Keep on the Sunny Side," "You are My Flower," "Wabash Cannonball," "I'm Thinking Tonight of My Blue Eyes," and "Wildwood Flower," underscored the Carter Family's ongoing influence on country and pop music.

BIBL.: J. Atkins, *The Carter Family* (London, 1973); M. Orgill, *Anchored in Love: The Carter Family Story* (1975); R. Krishef, *The Carter Family: Country Music's First Family* (Minneapolis, 1978); Janette Carter (A. P. and Sara's daughter), *Living with Memories* (N.Y., 1983); June Carter Cash (Maybelle's daughter), *From the Heart* (N.Y., 1987).—**WR**

Carulli, Ferdinando, Italian guitar player and composer; b. Naples, Feb. 20, 1770; d. Paris, Feb. 17, 1841. He went to Paris in 1808 and prospered there as a guitar teacher. He is generally regarded as the first guitarist to use his instrument for artistic performances. He publ. a method, *L'Harmonie appliquée à la guitarre* (Paris, 1825). His works number nearly 400 items, including concertos, quartets, trios, duos, fantasias, variations, and solos of all descriptions. In 1830 he composed a piece of program music for guitar entitled *Les Trois Jours*, descriptive of the days of the July 1830 revolution.—**NS/LK/DM**

Caruso, Enrico (actually, **Errico**), great Italian tenor; b. Naples, Feb. 25, 1873; d. there, Aug. 2, 1921. While attending the Scuola sociale e serale in Naples, he received some training in oratorio and choral singing. By the age of 11, he was serving as principal soloist in its choir. He also received lessons from Amelia Tibaldi Nicola. In 1891 he began vocal training with Guglielmo Vergine, who remained a mentor until 1895. In 1894 he was engaged to sing in *Mignon* at the Teatro Mercadante in Naples, but at the piano rehearsal he proved a dismal failure at sight-reading and was dismissed. Caruso finally made his operatic debut at the Teatro Nuovo in Naples in Mario Morelli's *L'Amico Francesco* on March 15, 1895. He then sang Turiddu and Faust in Caserta, and subsequently Faust, the Duke of Mantua, and Alfredo at the Teatro Bellini in Naples. After successful appearances in Cairo as Edgardo, Enzo Grimaldo, and Puccini's Des Grieux, he returned to Naples to sing

Bellini's Tebaldo at the Teatro Mercadente. While engaged in Salerno (1896–97), he received vocal coaching from the conductor Vincenzo Lombardi. On May 29, 1897, he scored a fine success as Enzo Grimaldo at the opening of the Teatro Massimo in Palermo. He then won accolades as Rodolfo at the Teatro Goldoni in Livorno on Aug. 14, 1897. During the 1897–98 season, he sang at the Teatro Lirico in Naples with increasing success. The decisive turning point in his career came at that theater on Nov. 17, 1898, when he created the role of Loris in Giordano's *Fedora*. On Jan. 27, 1899, he made his first appearance in St. Petersburg as Alfredo, where he sang until 1900. He sang Loris at his debut in Buenos Aires on May 14, 1899, and continued to appear there until 1901, returning again in 1915 and 1917. On March 6, 1900, he made his first appearance in Moscow at a concert at the Bolshoi Theater, and then made his stage debut there as Radames on March 11. Caruso first sang at La Scala in Milan on Dec. 26, 1900, as Rodolfo. After appearing in the premiere of Mascagni's *Le Maschere* there on Jan. 17, 1901, he scored an enormous success there as Nemorino on Feb. 17. On March 11, 1902, he sang in the premiere of Franchetti's *Germania* there. His La Scala success prompted the Gramophone & Typewriter Co. of England to make a series of recordings of him in Milan in 1902–03. Caruso's fame was greatly enhanced through these and other recordings, especially those made with the Victor Talking Machine Co. of the U.S. between 1904 and 1920. On May 14, 1902, he made a notable British debut as the Duke of Mantua at Covent Garden in London. He appeared there again from 1904 to 1907, and in 1913–14. On Nov. 6, 1902, he sang in the premiere of Cilea's *Adriana Lecouvreur* at the Teatro Lirico in Milan. Caruso made an auspicious U.S. debut as the Duke of Mantua at the Metropolitan Opera in N.Y. on Nov. 23, 1903. For the rest of his career, he remained a stellar artist on its roster, appearing not only with the company in N.Y. but widely on tour. In his 18 seasons with the company, he sang 39 roles in 862 performances.

In addition to the Italian repertoire, Caruso won great success in such French roles as Massenet's Des Grieux, Saint-Saëns's Samson, Bizet's Don José, and Meyerbeer's Raoul. He also created the role of Ramerrez in Puccini's *La Fanciulla del West* on Dec. 10, 1910. Caruso chose his famous portrayal of the Duke of Mantua for his debut appearances at the Dresden Court Opera (May 8, 1904), the Vienna Court Opera (Oct. 6, 1906), and the Berlin Royal Opera (Oct. 23, 1907). His success in Vienna led Emperor Franz Joseph I to make him an Austrian Kammersänger in 1906, and he returned there to sing in 1907 and again from 1911 to 1913. He also continued to appear at the Berlin Royal Opera until 1909. In 1910 Kaiser Wilhelm II made him a German Kammersänger. From 1911 to 1913 he again sang at the Berlin Royal Opera. With the outbreak of World War I in 1914, Caruso concentrated his career mainly on the Metropolitan Opera, where he had become an idolized figure. He also made various appearances as a concert artist. On Dec. 11, 1920, while singing Nemorino at the Brooklyn Academy of Music, he was stricken with a throat hemorrhage. He managed to sing through the first act, but the remainder of the performance had to be cancelled. Although in great physical distress, he insisted on meeting his contractual obligation to sing Eléazar at the Metropolitan on Christmas Eve, 1920. This was his last public appearance. A severe pleurisy necessitated several debilitating surgeries. On May 28, 1921, he set sail to his beloved Italy, where he died eight weeks later.

Caruso was richly blessed with a voice of extraordinary beauty and refinement, with unsurpassed breath control and impeccable intonation. Following surgery to remove a node from his vocal cords in 1909, his voice took on the darker characteristics of the baritone range. Caruso's earnings were astounding in his day. During his highest paid season at the Metropolitan (1907–08), he received $140,000. His concert fees were most lucrative, and eventually reached $15,000 per appearance. His recordings likewise became a gold mine. For his last contract with the Victor Talking Machine Co. in 1919, he was guaranteed an annual payment of $100,000 per year, in addition to royalties. In spite of his great wealth, however, he never lost his common touch and gave generously to various causes. And as much as he loved to sing, he loved life even more. Unfortunately, his private life was wracked by numerous ill-fated love affairs, several of which led to unsavory court proceedings and widespread press coverage and gossip. In 1897 he became intimate with the soprano (Vittoria Matilde) Ada Giachetti (b. Florence, Dec. 1, 1874; d. Rio de Janeiro, Oct. 16, 1946), the wife of the wealthy manufacturer Gino Botti. Their liaison produced two sons, the younger of whom, Enrico (Roberto Giovanni) Caruso Jr. (b. Castello, near Florence, Sept. 7, 1904; d. Jacksonville, Fla., April 9, 1987), had a brief career as a tenor and actor. Caruso was also attracted to Ada's younger sister, the soprano Rina Giachetti, with whom he became intimate in 1906. It was also in 1906 that he was accused of making improper advances to a woman at N.Y.'s Central Park Zoo, which became known as the "monkey-house incident." Although Caruso pleaded not guilty and had a corroborating eye-witness, he was found guilty as charged and fined $10. He lost on appeal and paid the fine in 1907. In 1908 Ada deserted him for the family chauffeur. The bitter conflict which ensued between them culminated in a rancorous court battle in Milan in 1912. Caruso found solace in Rina, then in Dorothy Park Benjamin, whom he married in N.Y. on Aug. 20, 1918. Caruso's colorful life was the subject of the fictionalized film biography, *The Great Caruso* (1951), starring Mario Lanza. On Feb. 27, 1987, the U.S. Postal Service issued a commemorative stamp in his honor, with appropriate ceremonies at the Metropolitan Opera in N.Y., attended by his son, Enrico Caruso Jr.

BIBL.: S. Fucito and B. Beyer, *C. and the Art of Singing* (N.Y., 1922); P. Key, *E. C.: A Biography* (Boston, 1922); D. Caruso and T. Goddard, *Wings of Song: The Story of C.* (N.Y., 1928; British ed., 1928, as *Wings of Song: An Authentic Life Story of E. C.*); N. Daspuro, *E. C.* (Milan, 1938); P. Suardon, *E. C.* (Milan, 1938); D. Caruso, *E. C.: His Life and Death* (N.Y., 1945); H. Steen, *C.: Eine Stimme erobert die Welt* (Essen-Steele, 1946); E. Gara, *C.: Storia di un emigrante* (Milan, 1947); T. Ybarra, *C.: The Man of Naples and the Voice of Gold* (N.Y., 1953); J.-P. Mouchon, *E. C., 1873–1921, sa vie et sa voix:Étude psycho-physiologique, physique, phonétique et esthétique* (Langres, 1966; Eng. tr., 1974); S. Jackson, *C.* (N.Y., 1972); H. Greenfield, *C.* (N.Y., 1983); M. Scott, *The Great C.* (N.Y., 1988); E. Caruso Jr. and A. Farkas, *E. C.: My Father and My Family* (Portland, Ore., 1990); S. Fucito, *C. and the Art of Singing* (Mineola, N.Y., 1995); P. Gargano, *Una vita, una leggenda: E. C., il pió grande tenore del mondo* (Milan, 1997); J. Laurens, *C.: Son àme, ses techniques, sa voix* (Paris, 1997).—NS/LK/DM

Caruso, Luigi, Italian composer; b. Naples, Sept. 25, 1754; d. Perugia, 1822. He was a student of his father, a church musician, and of Sala. He was maestro di cappella in Cingoli (1790–96?), Fabriano (1796?–98), Perugia (1798–1808), Urbino (1808–10), and again in Perugia (from 1810), where he also was director of the music school. His large output included over 60 operas, as well as oratorios.—NS/LK/DM

Carvalho (real name, **Carvaille**), **Léon,** distinguished French baritone and opera manager; b. Port-Louis, near Paris, Jan. 18, 1825; d. Paris, Dec. 29, 1897. He studied at the Paris Cons. He began his career as a singer; in 1853 he married the French soprano **Caroline Carvalho**. From 1856 to 1868 he was director of the Théâtre-Lyrique, and from 1869 to 1875 chief producer at the Paris Opéra; concurrently was manager of the Théâtre du Vaudeville (1872–74). He then acted as stage manager at the Opéra, and from 1876 to 1887 was director of the Opéra-Comique, succeeding du Locle. After the fire at the Opéra-Comique in 1887, in which 131 persons perished, he was arrested and sentenced to six months' imprisonment, but was acquitted on appeal, and reinstated in 1891. He had the reputation of an enlightened administrator, encouraging young artists and young composers.—NS/LK/DM

Carvalho, Caroline (née **Caroline-Marie Félix-Miolan**), French soprano; b. Puys, Seine-Inférieure, Dec. 31, 1827; d. near Dieppe, July 10, 1895. She entered the Paris Cons. at 12; studied under Duprez. She made her operatic debut on Dec. 14, 1849, in *Lucia di Lammermoor* at the Opéra-Comique, where she was engaged from 1849 to 1855; from 1856 to 1867 she sang at the Théâtre-Lyrique, where she created the soprano parts in Gounod's *Faust*, *Roméo et Juliette*, and *Mireille*, and in Clapisson's *La Fanchonette*. From 1868 to 1885 she sang at the Paris Opéra and at the Opéra-Comique; also appeared in London, Berlin, Brussels, St. Petersburg, etc. She retired in 1885. In 1853 she married **Léon Carvalho**.

BIBL.: E. Accoyer-Spoll, *Mme. C.* (Paris, 1885). —NS/LK/DM

Carvalho, Eleazar de, Brazilian conductor and composer; b. Iguatú, July 28, 1912; d. São Paulo, Sept. 15, 1996. His father was of Dutch extraction and his mother was part Indian. He studied in Fortaleza at the Apprentice Seaman's School; later joined the National Naval Corps in Rio de Janeiro and played tuba in the band. In 1941 he became asst. conductor of the Brazilian Sym. Orch. in Rio de Janeiro. In 1946 he went to the U.S. to study conducting with Koussevitzky at the Berkshire Music Center in Tanglewood, and Koussevitzky invited him to conduct a pair of concerts with the Boston Sym. Orch. Carvalho demonstrated extraordinary ability and musicianship by leading all rehearsals and the concerts without score in a difficult program; his sense of perfect pitch was exceptional. He subsequently conducted a number of guest engagements with orchs. in America and in Europe. From 1963 to 1968 he was music director of the St. Louis Sym. Orch.; during his tenure, he introduced many modern works into his programs, much to the discomfiture of the financial backers of the orch. From 1969 to 1973 he was conductor of the Hofstra Univ. Orch. in Hempstead, N.Y., which offered him a more liberal aesthetic climate; then returned to Brazil, where he became artistic director of the São Paulo State Sym. Orch. He married the Brazilian composer and pianist of French and Portuguese descent **Jocy de Oliveira**.

WORKS: DRAMATIC: O p e r a : *Descuberta do Brasil* (Rio de Janeiro, June 19, 1939); *Tiradentes* (Rio de Janeiro, Sept. 7, 1941). ORCH.: *Sinfonia branca* (1943); 3 symphonic poems: *A Traicao* (1941), *Batalha Naval de Riachuelo* (1943), and *Guararapes* (1945); 3 overtures. CHAMBER: 2 trios; 2 string quartets; Violin Sonata. VOCAL: Songs.—NS/LK/DM

Carvalho, João de Sousa, eminent Portuguese pedagogue and composer; b. Estremoz, Feb. 22, 1745; d. Alentejo, 1798. He studied at the Colégio dos Santos Reis in Vila Viçosa and with Cotumacci at the Cons. di S. Onofrio in Naples, then settled in Lisbon, where he became a member of the Brotherhood of St. Cecilia and prof. of counterpoint (1767), mestre (1769–73), and mestre de capela (1773–98) at the Seminario Patriarcal. He was the most gifted Portuguese composer of his day, excelling in both sacred and secular vocal music. In 1778 he became music teacher to the royal family.

WORKS: DRAMATIC: O p e r a (all 1st perf. in Lisbon unless otherwise given): *La Nitteti* (Rome, Carnival 1766; not extant); *L'amore industrioso* (1769); *L'Eumene* (June 6, 1773); *L'Angelica* (July 25, 1778); *Perseo* (July 5, 1779); *Testoride argonauta* (July 5, 1780); *Seleuco rè di Siria* (July 5, 1781); *Everardo II rè di Lituania* (July 5, 1782); *Penelope nella partenza da Sparta* (Dec. 17, 1782); *Tomiri amazzone guerriéra* (Dec. 17, 1783); *L'Endimione* (July 25, 1783); *Adrasto rè degli Argivi* (July 5, 1784); *Nettuno ed Eglé* (April 25?, 1785); *Alcione* (July 25, 1787); *Numa Pompilio II rè dei romani* (June 24, 1789).—NS/LK/DM

Carver, Robert, Scottish composer; b. 1487; d. after 1546. He was a Monk of Scone Abbey. He developed a melismatic style of composition, and wrote masses on the medieval song "L'Homme arme" and many motets, one of them in 19 independent parts. He is regarded as an equal of Dunstable in melodic and rhythmic excellence. Vol. 1 of his collected works was publ. by the American Inst. of Musicology, ed. by Denis Stevens, in 1959.

BIBL.: D. Ross, *Musick Fyne: R. C. and the Art of Music in Sixteenth Century Scotland* (Edinburgh, 1993).—NS/LK/DM

Carver, Wayman (Alexander), early jazz flutist, saxophonist, clarinetist; b. Portsmouth, Va., Dec. 25, 1905; d. Atlanta, Ga., May 6, 1967. Carver was one of the first flutists in jazz, as featured on Chick Webb recordings and in a film with Cab Calloway. His father was a clarinetist; his Uncle D. D. Copeland, a flutist, led a municipal band. Wayman played flute from an early age. He toured for several years with J. Neal Montgomery's Collegiate Ramblers, then formed his own band. Carver moved to N.Y., played with Elmer Snowden in 1931–32, and then led own band before joining Benny Carter in 1933. He was with Chick Webb from 1934 and remained when Ella Fitzgerald became leader. He left in February 1940, then returned to Ella in 1941. He left full-time music, became active as a teacher and arranger, and was later appointed Associate Professor of Music at Clark Coll., Atlanta, a post he held until his death.—JC/LP

Carvin, Michael (Wayne), jazz drummer; b. Houston, Tex., Dec. 12, 1944. His father was a drummer who taught him the basics prior to Carvin joining Earl Grant's big band in the mid-1960s. After a tour of duty in Vietnam, Carvin played with B. B. King. During the 1970s, he worked with Freddie Hubbard (1973–74), Hampton Hawes (1971–72), Dexter Gordon (1971), Pharoah Sanders (1974–76), McCoy Tyner (1974), Jackie McLean (1973–80), and Alice Coltrane (1976–77), as well as leading his own quintet from 1976 to 1979. In the 1980s he spent time with the Bridgewater Bros. (1980–85), Cecil Taylor (1981), Slide Hampton (1981–83), James Moody (1981–84), Illinois Jacquet (1985–86), and Dakota Staton (1986–88). The early 1990s found him working with Abbey Lincoln and Claudio Roditi. At the same time, he has been active as a freelance musician in the studio. Besides his performing work, Carvin has been active as a jazz educator, founding the Michael Carvin School of Drumming in 1985 and authoring a jazz drum instruction book.

DISC.: *Antiquity* (1974); *Camel* (1975); *First Time* (1986); *Between Me and You* (1988); *Revelation* (1989); *Each One Teach One* (1992). H. Hawes: *Live at Montmartre* (1971). D. Gordon: *A Little Night Music* (1971). J. McLean: *New York Calling* (1974).—LP

Cary, Annie Louise, notable American contralto; b. Wayne, Maine, Oct. 22, 1841; d. Norwalk, Conn., April 3, 1921. She was a pupil of J.Q. Wetherbee and Lyman Wheeler in Boston, and of Giovanni Corsi in Milan. In 1867 she made her operatic debut as Azucena in Copenhagen. After additional training from Viardot-García in Baden-Baden, she sang in Hamburg, Stockholm, Brussels, and London. On Sept. 19, 1870, she made her U.S. debut in a N.Y. recital. She sang Amneris in the U.S. premiere of *Aida* at the N.Y. Academy of Music on Nov. 28, 1873. Following a tour of Europe (1875–77), she returned to the U.S. and became the first American woman to sing a Wagnerian role when she appeared as Ortrud in 1877. After singing with Clara Louise Kellog's opera company, she was a member of J.H. Mapleson's company (1880–82). She also made various appearances as a concert and oratorio singer in the U.S.—NS/LK/DM

Cary, Dick (actually **Richard Durant**), jazz pianist, alto horn player, trumpeter, arranger; b. Hartford, Conn., July 10, 1916; d. Glendale, Calif., April 6, 1994. He played violin from early childhood, appearing with the Hartford Symphony Orch. while in high school. Later he specialized on piano, worked with Joe Marsala (1942), and played solo residency at Nick's in N.Y. in 1942–43. He arranged for Benny Goodman in 1943, played for a month in the Casa Loma Band (August 1943), then worked with Brad Gowans before serving in the U.S. Army (1944–46), during which time he recorded V-discs with Muggsy Spanier and Wild Bill Davison in 1944 and 1945. After the war, he played in Billy Butterfield's Band in 1946 and recorded with him playing alto horn, then led his own band in Meridan, Conn. (late 1946). He was the original pianist in Louis Armstrong's All Stars (Aug. 1947–Jan. 1948). He also worked with Jimmy Dorsey (1949 and spring 1950) and Tony Parenti (late 1949). He did studio work during the early 1950s (including a stint in Jerry Jerome's TV Band), while also working with Muggsy Spanier (late 1952) and with Eddie Condon at his N.Y. club and on Condon's TV show, playing alto horn as well as piano. He was with Bobby Hackett Band (alto horn and arranger) from November 1956. He worked with Max Kaminsky during 1958, and was also active as arranger and composer. He moved to Los Angeles in 1959, did prolific composing and freelance arranging, and worked with Bob Crosby, Red Nichols, and Ben Pollack. He toured Far East with Eddie Condon in spring 1964, then worked for a while in Los Angeles with Matty Matlock. He temporarily ceased doubling on brass in the early 1960s, but continued to work regularly on piano; was featured at several U.S. jazz festivals in the late 1960s. Occasionally, he led his own band (1970–71), playing trumpet, alto horn, and piano. He toured Europe (1977) and America in the 1970s and 1980s, working with the Barrelhouse Jazzband in 1975 and heading his own groups. For over 20 years, he sponsored an informal Tuesday night get-together for L.A.-based jazz players at his home; the group played out at the L.A. Classic Jazz Festival in 1992. He also did some arrangements for the Rochester Symphony Orch.

DISC.: *Dixieland Goes Progressive* (1957); *Hot and Cool* (1958); *Dick Cary and His Dixieland Doo* (1959); *Amazing Dick Cary* (1975); *California Doings* (1981).—JC/LP

Caryll, Ivan (real name, **Felix Tilkin**), Belgian-born American conductor and composer; b. Liège, May 12, 1861; d. N.Y., Nov. 29, 1921. He studied at the Liège Cons. and the Paris Cons. In 1882 he went to London, where he established himself as a theater conductor. In 1887 he became music director of the Prince of Wales Theatre. In 1889 he was named music director of the Lyric Theatre, where he scored his first major success as a composer of light theater music with his burlesque *Little Christopher Columbus* (Oct. 10, 1893; known in the U.S. as *Little Christopher*). In 1894 he became composer-in-residence and music director of the Gaiety Theatre. He brought out several successful stage works, often with contributions with Lionel Monckton, including *The Shop Girl* (Nov. 24, 1894), *The Circus Girl* (Dec. 5, 1896), *A Runaway Girl* (May 21, 1898), *The Messenger Boy* (Feb. 3, 1900), *The Toreador* (June 17, 1901), and *The Orchid* (Oct. 28, 1903). Among Caryll's other successful scores were *The Gay Parisienne* (April 4, 1896; known in the U.S. as *The Girl from Paris*), *The Ladies' Paradise* (March 11, 1901), *The Girl from Kays* (Nov. 15,

1902; in collaboration with Cecil Cook), *The Duchess of Dantzic* (Oct. 17, 1903), *The Earl and the Girl* (Dec. 10, 1903), *The Cherry Girl* (Dec. 21, 1903), *The New Aladdin* (Sept. 29, 1906), *The Girls of Gottenberg* (May 15, 1907), and *Our Miss Gibbs* (Jan. 23, 1909). From 1899 Caryll likewise was conductor of his own light orch. In 1910 he went to the U.S., eventually becoming a naturalized American citizen. Settling in N.Y., his success continued in his adopted homeland with such scores as *The Pink Lade* (March 13, 1911), *Oh! Oh! Delphine* (Sept. 30, 1912), *The Little Café* (Nov. 10, 1913), *Chin-Chin* (Oct. 20, 1914), *Jack o'Lantern* (Oct. 16, 1917), *The Girl Behind the Gun* (Sept. 16, 1918), *Tip-Top* (Oct. 5, 1920), *Kissing Time* (Oct. 11, 1920), and *The Hotel Mouse* (March 13, 1922; rev. version of *Little Miss Raffles*, Stamford, Conn., Dec. 1, 1921). Caryll also wrote numerous songs, dances, and salon pieces.—LK/DM

Casadesus, François Louis, French conductor and composer, brother of **Henri Casadesus** and **Marius Casadesus;** b. Paris, Dec. 2, 1870; d. there, June 27, 1954. He studied at the Paris Cons. He conducted the Opéra and the Opéra-Comique of Paris on tour in France (1890–92); in 1895 he conducted the Opéra on a European tour; he was the founder and director (1918–22) of the American Cons. at Fontainebleau; later was active as a radio conductor and wrote music criticism. A collection of valedictory articles was publ. in honor of his 80th birthday (Paris, 1950).

WORKS: DRAMATIC: O p e r a : *Cachaprès* (Brussels, 1914); *La Chanson de Paris* (1924); *Bertran de Born* (Monte Carlo, 1925); *Messie d'Amour* (Monte Carlo, 1928). ORCH.: *Symphonie scandinave*; *Au beau jardin de France* for Orch.; Sym.; smaller compositions for orch. VOCAL: Numerous songs. —NS/LK/DM

Casadesus, Gaby (née **Gabrielle L'Hôte**), French pianist and teacher; b. Marseilles, Aug. 9, 1901; d. Paris, Nov. 12, 1999. She studied with Louis Diémer and Marguerite Long at the Paris Cons., where she won the premier prix in 1917. She then toured widely as a soloist, and later in duo concerts with her husband, **Robert Casadesus.** She served on the faculties of the Salzburg Mozarteum, the Paris Schola Cantorum, and the American Cons. in Fontainebleau. In 1975 she helped organize the Robert Casadesus International Piano Competition in Cleveland, which became the Cleveland International Piano Competition in 1994. Her career is the subject of the vol. *Mes noces musicales: Conversation avec Jacqueline Muller* (Paris, 1989). —NS/LK/DM

Casadesus, Henri, French violinist, brother of **François Casadesus** and **Marius Casadesus;** b. Paris, Sept. 30, 1879; d. there, May 31, 1947. He studied with Lavignac and Laforge in Paris; from 1910 to 1917 he was a member of the Capet Quartet; he was a founder and director of the Société Nouvelle des Instruments Anciens, in which he played the viola d'amore; subsequently toured in the U.S. His collection of rare and ancient instruments were housed in the museum of the Boston Sym. Orch.—NS/LK/DM

Casadesus, Jean-Claude, French conductor, nephew of **Robert (Marcel) Casadesus** and **Gaby Casadesus;** b. Paris, Dec. 7, 1935. He studied at the Paris Cons.; in 1959 he received the premier prix as a percussion player there; he was then engaged as timpanist of the Concerts Colonne (until 1968) and of the Domaine Musical in Paris; also studied conducting with Dervaux at the École Normale de Musique in Paris (premier prix, 1965) and with Boulez in Basel. In 1969 he became resident conductor of the Opéra and of the Opéra-Comique in Paris. In 1971 he became asst. conductor to Dervaux with the Orchestre Philharmonique des Pays de la Loire in Angers. In 1976 he founded the Lille Phil.; also appeared as a guest conductor with various orchs. and opera houses in Europe. He was made an officer of the National Order of Merit for his services to French culture.—NS/LK/DM

Casadesus, Jean (Claude Michel), French pianist, son of **Robert (Marcel) Casadesus** and **Gaby Casadesus;** b. Paris, July 7, 1927; d. in an automobile accident near Renfrew, Ontario, Canada, Jan. 20, 1972. He studied piano with his parents; at the outbreak of World War II, he went to the U.S. and studied at Princeton Univ. He won the contest for young soloists held by the Philadelphia Orch. in 1946; then appeared as soloist with the N.Y. Phil. and with major European orchs.—NS/LK/DM

Casadesus, Marius, French violinist and composer, brother of **François Casadesus** and **Henri Casadesus;** b. Paris, Oct. 24, 1892; d. there, Oct. 13, 1981. He studied at the Paris Cons., graduating in 1914 with the premier prix in violin; subsequently toured in Europe and America; gave numerous sonata recitals with his nephew, **Robert Casadesus.** He was a founding member of the Société Nouvelle des Instruments Anciens (1920–40), organized with the purpose of reviving early string instruments, such as the Quinton and Diskantgambe. He wrote a number of pieces for the violin, some choral music, and songs, but his most notorious contribution to violin literature was the so-called *Adelaide Concerto,* supposedly composed by Mozart when he was 10 years old and dedicated to the oldest daughter of Louis XV, Adelaide (hence the nickname). It was performed in Paris on Dec. 24, 1931, with considerable publicity, but skepticism arose when Casadesus failed to produce either the MS or a contemporary copy of it. In 1977, in the course of a litigation for his copyright as the arranger of the "Adelaide Concerto," Casadesus admitted that the piece was entirely of his own hand. —NS/LK/DM

Casadesus, Robert (Marcel), eminent French pianist and composer; b. Paris, April 7, 1899; d. there, Sept. 19, 1972. A scion of a remarkable musical family, he absorbed music at home from his earliest childhood. His uncles were **Henri Casadesus, Marius Casadesus,** and **François Casadesus;** another uncle, Marcel Louis Lucien (1882–1917), was a cellist, and his aunt Rose was a pianist. He received his formal musical education studying piano with Diemer and composition with

Leroux at the Paris Cons. From 1922 he toured extensively; after the outbreak of World War II in 1939, he went to the U.S.; taught classes at various schools. After the war, he taught at the American Cons. at Fontainebleau. He was a prolific composer; wrote seven syms., of which the last was performed posth. in N.Y. on Nov. 8, 1972. He appeared with his wife, **Gaby Casadesus,** in his Concerto for two Pianos and Orch. with the N.Y. Phil. on Nov. 25, 1950. He also wrote a Concerto for 3 Pianos and String Orch., which he performed for the first time with his wife and his son Jean in N.Y., July 24, 1965. As a pianist, Casadesus was distinguished for his Gallic sense of balance and fine gradation of tonal dynamics. In 1975 the first Robert Casadesus International Piano Competition was held in Cleveland to honor his memory. In 1994 it was reorganized as the Cleveland International Piano Competition.

BIBL.: S. Stookes, *The Art of R. C.* (London, 1960). —NS/LK/DM

Casals, Pablo (actually, **Pau Carlos Salvador Defilló**), great Spanish cellist; b. Vendrell, Catalonia, Dec. 29, 1876; d. San Juan, Puerto Rico, Oct. 22, 1973. Legend has it, supported by Casals himself, that he was conceived when Brahms began his B-flat Major Quartet, of which Casals owned the original MS, and that he was born when Brahms completed its composition. This legend is rendered moot by the fact that the quartet in question was completed and performed before Casals was even born. But even the ascertainable facts of the life of Casals make it a glorious tale. His father, the parish organist and choirmaster in Vendrell, gave Casals instruction in piano, violin, and organ. When Casals was 11, he first heard the cello performed by a group of traveling musicians, and decided to study the instrument. In 1888 his mother took him to Barcelona, where he enrolled in the Escuela Municipal de Música. There he studied cello with José García, theory with José Rodoreda, and piano with Joaquín Malats and Francisco Costa Llobera. His progress as a cellist was nothing short of prodigious, and he was able to give a solo recital in Barcelona at the age of 14, on Feb. 23, 1891; he graduated with honors in 1893. Albéniz, who heard him play in a café trio, gave him a letter of introduction to Count Morphy, the private secretary to María Cristina, the Queen Regent, in Madrid. Casals was asked to play at informal concerts in the palace, and was granted a royal stipend for composition study with Tomás Bretón. In 1893 he entered the Cons. de Música y Declamación in Madrid, where he attended chamber music classes of Jésus de Monasterio. He also played in the newly organized Quartet Soc. there (1894–95). In 1895 he went to Paris and, deprived of his stipend from Spain, earned a living by playing second cello in the theater orch. of the Folies Marigny. He decided to return to Spain, where he received, in 1896, an appointment to the faculty of the Escuela Municipal de Música in Barcelona; he was also principal cellist in the orch. of the Gran Teatro del Liceo. In 1897 he appeared as soloist with the Madrid Sym. Orch., and was awarded the Order of Carlos III from the Queen. His career as a cello virtuoso was then assured. In 1899 he played at the Crystal Palace in London, and later for Queen Victoria at her summer residence at Cowes, Isle of Wight. On Nov. 12, 1899, he appeared as a soloist at a prestigious Lamoureux Concert in Paris, and played with Lamoureux again on Dec. 17, 1899, obtaining exceptional success with both the public and the press. He toured Spain and the Netherlands with the pianist Harold Bauer (1900–1901); then made his first tour of the U.S. (1901–2). In 1903 he made a grand tour of South America. On Jan. 15, 1904, he was invited to play at the White House for President Theodore Roosevelt. In 1906 he became associated with the talented young Portuguese cellist Guilhermina Suggia, who studied with him and began to appear in concerts as Mme. P. Casals-Suggia, although they were not legally married. Their liaison was dissolved in 1912; in 1914 Casals married the American socialite and singer Susan Metcalfe; they were separated in 1928, but did not divorce until 1957. Continuing his brilliant career, Casals organized, in Paris, a concert trio with the pianist Cortot and the violinist Thibaud; they played concerts together until 1937. Casals also became interested in conducting, and in 1919 he organized, in Barcelona, the Orquesta Pau Casals and led its first concert on Oct. 13, 1920. With the outbreak of the Spanish Civil War in 1936, the Orquesta Pau Casals ceased its activities. Casals was an ardent supporter of the Spanish Republican government, and after its defeat vowed never to return to Spain until democracy was restored. He settled in the French village of Prades, on the Spanish frontier; between 1939 and 1942 he made sporadic appearances as a cellist in the unoccupied zone of southern France and in Switzerland. So fierce was his opposition to the Franco regime in Spain that he declined to appear in countries that recognized the totalitarian Spanish government, making an exception when he took part in a concert of chamber music in the White House on Nov. 13, 1961, at the invitation of President John F. Kennedy, whom he admired. In 1950 he resumed his career as conductor and cellist at the Prades Festival, organized in commemoration of the bicentennial of the death of Bach; he continued leading the Prades Festivals until 1966. He made his permanent residence in 1956, when he settled in San Juan, Puerto Rico (his mother was born there when the island was still under Spanish rule). In 1957 an annual Festival Casals was inaugurated there. During all these years, he developed energetic activities as a pedagogue, leading master classes in Switzerland, Italy, Berkeley, Calif., and Marlboro, Vt., some of which were televised. Casals was also a composer; perhaps his most effective work is *La sardana*, for an ensemble of cellos, which he composed in 1926. His oratorio *El pessebre* (The Manger) was performed for the first time in Acapulco, Mexico, on Dec. 17, 1960. One of his last compositions was the *Himno a las Naciones Unidas* (Hymn of the United Nations); he conducted its first performance in a special concert at the United Nations on Oct. 24, 1971, two months before his 95th birthday. On Aug. 3, 1957, at the age of 80, Casals married his young pupil Marta Montañez; following his death, she married the pianist Eugene Istomin, on Feb. 15, 1975. Casals did not live to see the liberation of Spain from the Franco dictatorship, but he was posthumously honored by the Spanish government of King Juan Carlos I, which issued in 1976 a commemorative postage stamp in honor of his 100th birthday.

BIBL.: L. Littlehales, *P. C.* (N.Y., 1929; rev. ed., 1948); A. Conte, *La Légende de P. C.* (Perpignan, 1950); J. Corredor, *Conversations with C.* (London, 1956); A. Seiler, *C.* (Olten, 1956); P. and A. Kahn, *Joys and Sorrows: Reflections by P. C. as Told to Albert E. Kahn* (N.Y., 1970); H. Kirk, *P. C. A Biography* (N.Y., 1974); D. Blum, *C. and the Art of Interpretation* (London, 1977); J. Lloyd Webber, ed., *Song of the Birds: Sayings, Stories, and Impressions of P. C.* (London, 1985); J. Corredor, *P. C.* (Barcelona, 1991); J. Hargrove, *P. C.: Cellist of Conscience* (Chicago, 1991); R. Baldock, *P. C.* (London, 1992); H. Garza, *P. C.* (N.Y., 1993); D. Goodnough, *P. C.: Cellist for the World* (Springfield, N.J., 1997). —NS/LK/DM

Casanova, André, French composer; b. Paris, Oct. 12, 1919. He studied at the École Normale de Musique in Paris, and also with René Leibowitz. In 1966 he won the Queen Marie-José composition competition and in 1979 the Prix de la Fondation Durand of the French Institut.

WORKS: DRAMATIC: O p e r a : *La Clé d'Argent* (1965); *Le Bonheur est dans le Crime* (1969); *La Coupe d'Or* (1970); *Dumala* (1994–95); *La Murmure de la Mer* (1997–98). **ORCH.:** 4 numbered syms.: No. 1 (1949), No. 2 for Chamber Orch. (1952; Nice, Feb. 20, 1971), No. 3, *Dithyrambe*, for Tenor and Orch. (1964; Paris, Feb. 13, 1973), and No. 4 for Soprano and Orch. (1992); *Ballade* for Clarinet and Chamber Orch. (1954–55); Piano Concertino (1958); *Notturno* (1959); *Capriccio* for Oboe and Chamber Orch. (1960); *Anamorphoses* (1961); Violin Concerto (1963); Concerto for Trumpet and Strings (1966); *Strophes* (1968); Organ Concerto (1972); *Épisodes* for Violins and Strings (1972); Guitar Concerto (1973); *Récitatifs* (1973); *Idylles* (1976); *Partita* (1979); *Sinfonia* for Chamber Orch. (1981); Cello Concerto (1982–83); *Ein musikalisches Opfer* (1984); *Rhapsodie concertante* for Viola and Chamber Orch. (1987); Piano Concerto (1988–89); *Ephemeris* (1989); *Petite Symphonie* for Chamber Orch. (1993); *Duo concertant* for Oboe, Clarinet, and Chamber Orch. (1993); *Stances* (1996); *Impromptu* (1996); *Elementa* (1997–98); *An easy game* for Bassoon and Strings (1998); *Abrériation* for Strings (1998); *Instants* (1999). **CHAMBER:** 6 string quartets (1967, 1985, 1986, 1990, 1991, 1992); Quintet for Piano and Strings (1970); Sextet for Clarinet, Bassoon, Horn, Violin, Viola, Cello, and Double Bass (1985); Violin Sonata (1987–88); Quintet for 2 Violins, Viola, and 2 Cellos (1988); *4 Pieces* for Oboe, Clarinet, and Bassoon (1993); Quintet for 2 Violins, 2 Violas, and Cello (1996); Quartet for Violin, Viola, Cello, and Piano (1999); piano pieces. **VOCAL:** *Cavalier seul* for Baritone and Strings (1964); *Rituels* for Voice and Instrumental Ensemble (1972–82); *Esquisses pour une tragédie* for Soprano, Baritone, and Instrumental Ensemble (1979); *Deutsche Gesänge* for Baritone and Orch. (1980); *Liederkreis* for Alto and Piano (1993).—NS/LK/DM

Casella, Alfredo, outstanding Italian composer and teacher; b. Turin, July 25, 1883; d. Rome, March 5, 1947. He began to play the piano at the age of four and received his early instruction from his mother. In 1896 he went to Paris, and studied with Diémer and Fauré at the Cons. He won the premier prix in piano in 1899. He made concert tours as a pianist in Europe, and appeared as a guest conductor with European orchs. He taught piano classes at the Paris Cons. from 1912 to 1915. Returning to Rome, he was appointed a prof. of piano at the Accademia di Santa Cecilia. In 1917 he founded the Società Nazionale di Musica (later the Società Italiana di Musica Moderna; from 1923 the Corporazione delle Musiche Nuove, Italian section of the ISCM). On Oct. 28, 1921, Casella made his American debut with the Philadelphia Orch. in the triple capacity of composer, conductor, and piano soloist; he also appeared as a guest conductor in Chicago, Detroit, Cincinnati, Cleveland, and Los Angeles; was conductor of the Boston Pops from 1927 to 1929, introducing a number of modern works, but failing to please the public. In 1928 he was awarded the first prize of $3,000 from the Musical Fund Soc. in Philadelphia; in 1934 he won the Coolidge Prize. In 1938 he returned to Italy. Apart from his activities as pianist, conductor, teacher, and composer, Casella was a prolific writer on music, and contributed numerous articles to various publications in Italy, France, Russia, Germany, and America; he possessed an enlightened cosmopolitan mind, which enabled him to penetrate the musical cultures of various nations; at the same time, he steadfastly proclaimed his adherence to the ideals of Italian art. In his music, he applied modernistic techniques to earlier forms; his style may be termed neo-Classical, but in his early years he cultivated extreme modernism.

WORKS: DRAMATIC: O p e r a : *La donna serpente* (Rome, March 17, 1932); *La favola d'Orfeo* (Venice, Sept. 6, 1932); *Il deserto tentato* (Florence, May 6, 1937). **B a l l e t :** *Il convento veneziano* (1912; Milan, Feb. 7, 1925); *La Giara,* "choreographic comedy" (Paris, Nov. 19, 1924); *La camera dei disegni,* for children (Rome, 1940); La rosa del sogno (Rome, 1943). **ORCH.:** 3 syms. (1905; 1908–09; Chicago, March 27, 1941); Suite in C (1909); *Italia,* rhapsody (Paris, April 23, 1910); *Le Couvent sur l'eau,* symphonic suite based on the ballet *Il convento veneziano* (Paris, April 23, 1914); *Elegia eroica* (Rome, Jan. 21, 1917); *Pagine di guerra* (1916); *Pupazzetti,* 5 pieces for Puppets (1918); *A notte alta* for Piano and Orch. (1921; also for Piano, 1917); *Partita* for Piano and Orch. (N.Y., Oct. 29, 1925); *Scarlattiana,* on themes by Scarlatti, for Piano and Orch. (N.Y., Jan. 22, 1927); *Concerto romano* for Organ and Orch. (N.Y., March 11, 1927); Violin Concerto (Moscow, Oct. 8, 1928); *Introduzione, Aria e Toccata* (Rome, April 5, 1933); Concerto for Trio and Orch. (Berlin, Nov. 17, 1933); Concerto (Amsterdam, 1937); *Paganiniana,* on themes by Paganini (Vienna, 1942). **CHAMBER:** *Barcarola e scherzo* for Flute and Piano (1904); 2 cello sonatas (1907, 1927); *Siciliana e burlesca* for Flute and Piano (1914; also for Piano Trio, 1917); *5 pezzi* for String Quartet (1920); Concerto for String Quartet (1923–24; also for String Orch.); *Serenata* for Clarinet, Bassoon, Trumpet, Violin, and Cello (1927); *Sinfonia* for Clarinet, Trumpet, Cello, and Piano (1932); Piano Trio (1933). **KEYBOARD: P i a n o :** Many pieces, including 2 series of stylistic imitations, *À la manière de...:* Wagner, Fauré, Brahms, Debussy, Strauss, and Franck (1911), and (in collaboration with Ravel) Borodin, d'Indy, Chabrier, and Ravel (1913); Sonatina (1916); *A notte alta* (1917; also for Piano and Orch., 1921); *11 pezzi infantili* (1920); *2 ricercari sul nome Bach* (1932); 3 pieces for Pianola (1918). **VOCAL:** *Notte di Maggio* for Voice and Orch. (Paris, March 29, 1914); *L'Adieu à la vie,* cycle of 4 Hindu lyrics after Tagore's *Gitanjali* (1915; also for Voice and Orch., 1926); *4 favole romanesche* (1923); *Ninna nanna popolare genovese* (1934); *3 canti sacri* for Baritone and Orch. (1943); *Missa solemnis pro pace* (1944).

WRITINGS: *L'evoluzione della musica* (publ. in Italian, French, and Eng. in parallel columns; 1919); *Igor Stravinsky* (1926; new ed., 1951); *"21 & 26"* (1931); *Il pianoforte* (1938); *I segreti della Giara* (1941; Eng. tr., 1955, as *Music in My Time: The Memoirs of Alfredo Casella*); *La tecnica dell'orchestra contemporanea* (completed by V. Mortari; 1950).

BIBL.: L. Cortese, *A. C.* (Genoa, 1935); F. d'Amico & G. Gatti, eds., *A. C.* (Milan, 1958); R. Calabretto ed., *A. C.: Gli anni di Parigi: Dai Documenti* (Florence, 1997).—**NS/LK/DM**

Casey, Al(bert Aloysius),

famed jazz guitarist; b. Louisville, Ky., Sept. 15, 1915. Casey is best known for his fine and swinging acoustic work with Fats Waller, and he later turned to the electric guitar. His father was a drummer. He started on violin at the age of 8, then played ukulele. He moved to N.Y. in 1930, studied guitar while at the DeWitt Clinton H.S., and received some tuition from James Smith. His first professional work with Fats Waller was in 1934; he worked regularly with Fats throughout the 1930s and recorded over 230 songs with him. He was with Teddy Wilson Big Band in 1939–40, then with Buster Harding's Quartet at Nick's, N.Y., in May 1940. He worked with Fats Waller again from October 1940 until 1942. During these years he also recorded with Billie Holiday, Teddy Wilson, Earl Hines, Sid Catlett, and Chu Berry. He led his own trio from 1943, playing at clubs in L.A., N.Y., Chicago, and elsewhere. He was featured at Metropolitan Opera House concert in January 1944, played briefly in Clarence Profit's Trio (early 1944), with Billy Kyle Trio (1949), and others. He did extensive freelance work in the 1950s, then worked regularly in King Curtis All Stars until 1961, then played long residency with Curley Hammer's Sextet in N.Y. Resident at Baby Grand, Harlem (1971). He returned to basic blues and jazz in the 1970s and 1980s, playing with Helen Humes and the Harlem Blues and Jazz Band.

DISC.: *Al Casey Quartet* (1960); *Buck Jumpin'* (1960); *Al Casey* (1961); *Surfin' Hootenanny* (1963); *Jumpin' with Al* (1973); *Guitar Odyssey* (1976); *Best of Friends* (1981); *Genius of Jazz Guitar* (1981); *Al Casey Remembers King Curtis* (1985); *Jivin' Around* (1995).—**JC/LP**

Casey, Bob (actually, Robert Hanley),

jazz bassist, guitarist; b. Johnson County, Ill., Feb. 11, 1909; d. March 9, 1986. He began on tenor-banjo at 14, self-taught. He played weekend dances in southern Ill.; with The Egyptian Transportation System Orch. (1926–27), then moved to St. Louis in December 1927, playing with Joe Gill (1929–31), and Joe Reichman (1932). He began playing bass in 1929, and doubled guitar for several years. He moved to Chicago, with Wingy Manone (1933), Russ Kettler, and the King's Jesters, was also staff musician at NBC Chicago. He was with Muggsy Spanier from July 1939. After Muggsy disbanded, he returned to Chicago, performed briefly with Pete Daily, then with Gus Arnheim and Charlie Spivak. He joined Brad Gowans at Nick's, N.Y., in October 1943, spending several years at Nick's and at Condon's Club; also worked with Art Hodes and Bobby Hackett. He moved to Fla. in 1957 and played with Dukes of Dixieland (1962). He emerged from semi-retirement to play dates in N.Y. (1971).—**JC/LP**

Casey, Floyd, early jazz drummer, washboard player; b. Poplar Bluffs, Mo., 1900; d. N.Y., Sept. 7, 1967. He worked regularly on the riverboats during the early 1920s; was with Ed Allen's Whispering Gold Band in 1922. He played in St. Louis with Dewey Jackson (c. 1921), and with saxist Jimmy Powell's Jazz Monarchs (c. 1925–26); moved to N.Y. and from 1927 was featured on many recordings with Clarence Williams. He worked with trombonist George Wilson at Capitol Palace, N.Y., in 1927. During the 1930s he played many "taxi-dance" jobs in N.Y. He was with Jimmy Reynold's Band in 1941, worked in Ed Allen's Band, then (with Ed Allen) played in a band led by pianist Benton Heath at the New Gardens, N.Y., for many years. He recorded with Allen and Elmer Snowden in 1961.—JC/LP

Cash, Johnny, deep-voiced country singer; b. Kingsland, Ark., Feb. 26, 1932. Johnny Cash grew up in Dyess, Ark., where he had moved at the age of three. Following his discharge from the Air Force in July 1954, he traveled to Memphis and eventually auditioned for Sam Phillips of Sun Records in March 1955. Signed to Sun, Cash managed pop hits with his own "I Walk the Line," "Ballad of a Teenage Queen," "Guess Things Happen That Way," and "The Ways of a Woman in Love." In 1957 W. S. Holland joined his backup band, becoming one of the first drummers in country music. In August 1958 Johnny Cash switched to Columbia Records and soon hit with "Don't Take Your Guns to Town." Moving to Calif., Cash started working with June Carter, of the legendary Carter Family, in 1961. He began feeling the strain of constant touring and the collapse of his first marriage and grieved the death of friend Johnny Horton. As a consequence, Cash started taking amphetamines and tranquilizers to cope with his hectic life.

In 1963 Johnny Cash scored his first major pop hit on Columbia with "Ring of Fire." He soon began hanging out on the periphery of the Greenwich Village folk music scene, and his next hit, "Understand Your Man," had a distinctive folk feel to it. In 1964 he appeared with Bob Dylan at the Newport Folk Festival. During this time, Cash recorded a number of folk songs, including Peter LaFarge's "Ballad of Ira Hayes" and Dylan's "Don't Think Twice, It's Alright," and, with June Carter, "It Ain't Me, Babe," another country and pop hit.

Despite increasing popular success, Johnny Cash's life seemed to deteriorate. In October 1965 he was arrested at El Paso International Airport in possession of hundreds of stimulants and tranquilizers. After being found near death in a small Ga. town in 1967, Cash decided to reform. With June Carter providing moral support, he cleaned up his act. The couple scored a smash country hit with "Jackson" in 1968, the year they married. In 1970, they hit the pop charts with Tim Hardin's "If I Were a Carpenter."

Johnny Cash began a series of successful TV appearances in 1967, and his 1968 *Johnny Cash at Folsom Prison* remained on the album charts for more than two years and revitalized his career. The album yielded a top country hit and moderate pop hit with "Folsom Prison Blues." In early 1969 Cash scored another top country and moderate pop hit with Carl Perkins's "Daddy Sang Bass." Cash's penchant for novelty songs culminated in his biggest pop hit, "A Boy Named Sue," from *Johnny Cash at San Quentin,* another best-seller. The 1969 debut show for his ABC network TV series featured a film of Cash and Bob Dylan recording "Girl from the North Country." The song later appeared on Dylan's first country album, *Nashville Skyline.* Later shows featured artists such as Gordon Lightfoot, Kris Kristofferson, Waylon Jennings, and Joni Mitchell. During the 1969 Newport Folk Festival, Johnny Cash introduced Kris Kristofferson, later recording his "Sunday Morning Coming Down" and bolstering his early career.

Johnny Cash again demonstrated his social consciousness in the early 1970s with the hits "What is Truth" and "Man in Black." He also narrated and co-produced the soundtrack to the Christian epic *Gospel Road* and assisted in the production of *The Trail of Tears,* a dramatization of the tragedy of the Cherokee Indians, broadcast on public television (PBS). Cash scored another pop novelty hit with "One Piece at a Time" in 1976 and hit the country charts in 1978 with "There Ain't No Good Chain Gangs," recorded with Waylon Jennings. His last major country hit came in 1981 with "The Baron." Future country star Marty Stuart was a member of Cash's band from 1979 to 1985.

In 1985 Johnny Cash joined Waylon Jennings, Willie Nelson, and Kris Kristofferson to tour and record as the Highwaymen. They hit the top of the country charts with Jimmy Webb's "The Highwayman." The following year, Cash reunited with old Sun Records alumni Carl Perkins, Jerry Lee Lewis, and Roy Orbison for *Class of '55,* contributing "I Will Rock & Roll with You." Cash was dropped from the Columbia Records roster in 1986 and he subsequently signed with Mercury Records, switching to American Records in 1993. In 1990 he joined Jennings, Nelson, and Kristofferson as the Highwaymen for another album and round of touring. Cash sang "The Wanderer" with U2, included on their *Zooropa* album. In 1994 he recorded the moody, acoustic *American Recordings* album for American Records under producer Rick Rubin, best known for his work with Run-D.M.C., Public Enemy, and the Red Hot Chili Peppers. The following year, Cash once again joined the Highwaymen, to tour and record for Liberty Records *The Road Goes on Forever.* However, he retired from active performing in 1997, after announcing he was suffering from a degenerative nerve disease. Helping to broaden the scope of country-and-western music and popularize country music with rock and pop fans, Johnny Cash became the first international country star and may have done more to popularize country music than anyone since Hank Williams. Indeed, his TV series (1969–71) was instrumental in widening the audience for country music. Additionally, he was instrumental in introducing Bob Dylan and Kris Kristofferson to broader public acceptance. Johnny Cash was inducted into the Rock and Roll Hall of Fame in 1992.

WRITINGS.: *Man in Black* (Grand Rapids, Mich., 1975); *Man in White: A Novel* (San Francisco, 1986); with Patrick Carr, *Cash: The Autobiography* (San Francisco, 1997).

DISC.: *The Fabulous Johnny Cash* (1958); *Hymns by Johnny Cash* (1959); *Songs of Our Soil* (1959); *Now, There Was a Song!* (1960); *Ride This Train* (1960); *Hymns from the Heart* (1962); *The Sound of Johnny Cash* (1962); *Blood, Sweat and Tears* (1963); *Christmas Spirit* (1963); *Ring of Fire* (1963); *Bitter Tears—Ballads of the American Indian* (1964); *I Walk the Line* (1964); *Ballads of the True West* (1965); *Orange Blossom Special* (1965); *Everybody Loves a Nut* (1966); *Mean as Hell* (1966); *That's What You Get for Lovin' Me* (1966); *From Sea to Shining Sea* (1967); *Greatest Hits* (1967); *At Folsom Prison* (1968); *At San Quentin* (1969); *The Holy Land* (1969); *Johnny Cash* (1969); *Hello, I'm Johnny Cash* (1970); *I Walk the Line* (soundtrack, 1970); *The Johnny Cash Show* (1970); *Walls of a Prison* (1970); *The World of Johnny Cash* (1970); *Greatest Hits, Vol. 2* (1971); *Man in Black* (1971); *America: A 200-Year Salute in Story and Song* (1972); *Folsom Prison Blues* (1972); *Johnny Cash Songbook* (1972); *A Thing Called Love* (1972); *Any Old Wind That Blows* (1973); *Ballad of the American Indians* (1973); *Gospel Road* (soundtrack, 1973); *Five Feet High and Rising* (1974); *The Junkie and the Juicehead Minus Me* (1974); *That Ragged Old Flag* (1974); *John R. Cash* (1975); *Look at Them Beans* (1975); *Sings Precious Memories* (1975); *One Piece at a Time* (1976); *Strawberry Cake* (1976); *Last Gunfighter Ballad* (1977); *The Rambler* (1977); *Gone Girl* (1978); *Greatest Hits, Vol. 3* (1978); *I Would Like to See You Again* (1978); *A Believer Sings the Truth* (1979); *Silver* (1979); *Classic Christmas* (1980); *Rockabilly Blues* (1980); *The Baron* (1981); *Encore* (1981); *This Is Johnny Cash* (1981); *The Adventures of Johnny Cash* (1982); *Biggest Hits* (1982); *Johnny 99* (1983); *Believe in Him* (1986); *Classic Cash* (1988); *Columbia Records 1958–1986* (1987); *Johnny Cash Is Coming to Town* (1987); *Water from the Wells of Home* (1988); *Boom Chick a Boom* (1990); *Patriot* (rec. 1964–76, rel. 1990); *Best* (1991); *Greatest Hits* (1991); *The Mystery of Life* (1991); *The Essential Johnny Cash (1955–83)* (1992); *The Gospel Collection* (1992); *American Recordings* (1994); *Personal Christmas Collection* (1994); *Wanted Man* (1994); *Live Recording* (1996); *The Man in Black* (1996); *Golden Hits* (1998); *Unchained* (1998). June Carter: *Carryin' On* (1967); *Give My Love to Rose* (1972); *The Johnny Cash Family* (1972); *Johnny Cash and His Woman* (1973); *Super Hits* (1994). Jerry Lee Lewis and Carl Perkins: *The Survivors* (1982). Waylon Jennings: *Heroes* (1986). Jerry Lee Lewis, Roy Orbison, and Carl Perkins: *Class of '55* (1986). Willie Nelson, Waylon Jennings, and Kris Kristofferson: *The Highwaymen* (1985); *Highwayman II* (1990); *The Road Goes on Forever* (1995).

BIBL.: Albert Govoni, *A Boy Named Cash* (N.Y., 1970); Christopher Wren, *Winners Got Scars, Too: The Life and Legends of Johnny Cash* (N.Y., 1971); Charles P. Conn, *The New Johnny Cash* (N.Y., 1973; Old Tappan, N.J., 1978).—**BH**

Cash, Rosanne, married to singer-songwriter Rodney Crowell from 1979 to 1992, began achieving success in the early 1980s as a purveyor of highly personal, country-style material played in a rock, almost New Wave style; b. Memphis, Tenn., May 24, 1955.

Garnering the most public attention for a female country singer since Emmylou Harris, Cash pioneered this "new country" woman's sound and style, and opened the door for other intelligent songwriters such as Mary-Chapin Carpenter and Shawn Colvin.

Rosanne Cash, **Johnny Cash**'s daughter by Vivian Liberto, moved to Ventura, Calif., with her mother in 1966, when her parents divorced. After high school she toured with her father's road show for three years with stepsisters Rosey Nix and Carlene Carter. She attended Vanderbilt Univ. and studied for six months in Lee Strasberg's noted drama school in Hollywood. She met Rodney Crowell in 1977, married him in 1979, and made her first recordings (with Crowell producing) in Germany that year. Signed to Columbia Records, her first album, *Right or Wrong*, launched her recording career, producing three major country hits with "No Memories Hangin' Around" (in duet with Bobby Bare), "Couldn't Do Nothin' Right," and "Take Me, Take Me." With Crowell as her producer, Cash became fully established as a country artist with *Seven Year Ache*. The album yielded three top country hits with her title song (also a major pop hit), Leroy Preston's "My Baby Thinks He's a Train," and her "Blue Moon with Heartache."

After 1982's *Somewhere in the Stars*, which featured the country hits "Ain't No Money," "I Wonder," and "It Hasn't Happened Yet." Rosanne Cash underwent treatment for cocaine addiction, and her marriage nearly ended. This led to an almost three-year exile from recording. She rebounded with 1985's *Rhythm and Romance*, largely produced by David Malloy. The album contained four country hits: "I Don't Know Why You Don't Want Me" (cowritten by Cash and Crowell), "Never Be You" (written by Tom Petty and Benmont Tench), "Hold On," and "Second to No One." *King's Record Shop*, again produced by Crowell, was more issue oriented and yielded four more top country hits: "The Way We Make a Broken Heart" (by John Hiatt), "Tennessee Flat Top Box" (a major hit for her father in 1962), "If You Change Your Mind" (by Cash and Hank DeVito), and "Runaway Train" (by John Stewart). She also had a top country hit in 1988 with "It's Such a Small World," a duet with Crowell.

Rosanne Cash transcended the country field with 1990's introspective *Interiors*, which she wrote and produced. Hailed by some as the album of her career, it did not produce any pop hits, yet it did establish her in the front ranks of intelligent female singer-songwriters. Following her divorce from Rodney Crowell in spring 1992, Cash recorded *The Wheel*, a semiconfessional album that featured "Seventh Avenue," "Roses in the Fire," and "The Truth About You."

DISC.: *Right or Wrong* (1980); *Seven Year Ache* (1981); *Somewhere in the Stars* (1982); *Rhythm and Romance* (1985); *King's Record Shop* (1987); *Hits, 1979–1989* (1989) *Interiors* (1990); *The Wheel* (1993); *Retrospective* (1995); *10-Song Demo* (1995).—**BH**

Casini, Giovanni Maria, Italian organist and composer; b. Florence, Dec. 16, 1652; d. there, Feb. 25, 1719. He studied composition in Florence, and later in Rome with Matteo Simonelli and Bernardo Pasquini (organ). He became a priest and served as organist and maestro di cappella at Florence Cathedral from 1703; retired in 1711 owing to ill health. As a keyboard composer, Casini represents the late Baroque style.

WORKS: *Canzonette spirituali* (Florence, 1703); a collection of motets for 4 Voices, op.1 (Rome, 1706); *Responsori per la Settimana Santa*, op.2 (Florence, 1706); *Pensieri per l'organo*, op.3 (Florence, 1714); several oratorios.—**NS/LK/DM**

Casken, John (Arthur), English composer and teacher; b. Barnsley, Yorkshire, July 15, 1949. He was a student of Joubert and Dickinson at the Univ. of Birmingham (1967–71), and of Dobrowolski in Warsaw (1971–73), where he also profited from consultations with Lutosławski. In 1973 he became a lecturer at the Univ. of Birmingham. He held a research fellowship at the Huddersfield Polytechnic in 1980. In 1981 he became a lecturer at the Univ. of Durham. he was made a prof. of music at the Univ. of Manchester in 1992. His first opera, *Golem* (London, June 28, 1989), received the first Britten Award for Composition. Casken's early works were influenced by Lutosławski but he has since tended toward eclecticism with inspiration derived from landscape, poetry, and painting.

WORKS: DRAMATIC: *Golem*, opera (1986–88; London, June 28, 1989); *Soul Catcher*, ballet music (1988); *God's Liar*, opera (2000). ORCH.: *Tableaux des Trois Ages* (1976–77; Birmingham, Sept. 27, 1977); *Masque* for Oboe and Small Orch. (Eton, Oct. 9, 1982); *Erin* for Double Bass and Small Orch. (1982–83; York, Jan. 22, 1988); *Orion Over Farne* (Glasgow, Sept. 17, 1984; rev. 1986); *Maharal Dreaming* (Darlington, May 12, 1989); Concerto for Cello and Chamber Orch. (1990–91; Wotersen, Germany, July 7, 1991); *Darting the Skiff* for Strings (1992–93; Cheltenham, July 13, 1993, composer conducting); *Bougie-wougie*, overture (1994); Violin Concerto (1994–95; London, July 26, 1995); *Sortilège* (1995–96; London, April 9, 1996); *Distant Variations* for Saxophone Quartet and Wind Orch. (1996; London, March 10, 1997); *Après un silence* for Violin and Chamber Orch. (1998; Newcastle, March 24, 1999; also for Violin and Chamber Ensemble or Piano). CHAMBER: *Jadu* for 2 Cellos (1973); *Kagura* for 13 Wind Instruments (1972–73; Birmingham, May 1973); *Music for the Crabbing Sun* for Flute, Oboe, Cello, and Harpsichord (1974–75; London, Oct. 30, 1976); *Music for a Tawny-Gold Day* for Viola, Alto Saxophone, Bass Clarinet, and Piano (1975–76; Amsterdam, Sept. 1976); *Thymehaze* for Treble Recorder and Piano (Birmingham, Oct. 29, 1976); *Amarantos* for 9 Players (1977–78; London, Dec. 12, 1978); *A Belle Pavine* for Violin and Tape (York, June 14, 1980; rev. 1992); 2 string quartets: No. 1 (1981–82; London, Feb. 2, 1982) and No. 2 (1993; Manchester, Feb. 5, 1994; rev. 1996); *Piper's Linn* for Northumbrian Small Pipes and Tape (1983–84); *Clarion Sea* for Brass Ensemble (1984–85; Birmingham, May 5, 191985); *Vaganza* for Large Ensemble (St. Albans Festival, July 12, 1985); *Salamandra*, fire-haunt for 2 Pianos (Huddersfield, Nov. 20, 1986); Piano Quartet (1989–90; Birmingham, Nov. 24, 1990; rev. 1997); *Cor d'oeuvre* for Horn and Ensemble (Manchester, Nov. 4, 1993); *Infanta Marina* for Small Ensemble (1993–94; London, March 1, 1994; rev. 1997); *A Spring Cadenza* for Cello (1994; Sydney, July 31, 1995); *Fanfare* for 11 Brass Players (1995); *Après un silence* for Violin and Piano (1998; Dublin, Feb. 21, 1999; also for Violin and Chamber Orch. or Ensemble). VOCAL: *Ia Orana, Gaugin* for Soprano and Piano (1978; Leicester, Jan. 18, 1979); *Firewhirl* for Soprano and 7 Players (1979–80; Bath Festival, May 25, 1980); *To Fields We Do Not Know* for Chorus (1983–84; BBC Radio 3, Oct. 24, 1985); *The Land of Spices* for Chorus (1990); *A Gathering* for Chorus (Cambridge, Dec. 24, 1991); *Sharp Thorne* for 4 Solo Voices (1991–92; Durham, March 3, 1992); *Still Mine* for Baritone and Orch. (1991–92; London, July 31, 1992); *Sunrising* for Chorus (Durham, May 15, 1993); *A Song of Chimes* for Chorus and Organ (London, Oct. 27, 1996).—NS/LK/DM

Cassado (Moreau), Gaspar, distinguished Spanish cellist; b. Barcelona, Sept. 30, 1897; d. Madrid, Dec. 24, 1966. He was the son of Joaquin Cassadó (Valls) (b. Mataró, near Barcelona, Sept. 30, 1867; d. Barcelona,

March 25, 1926), a well-known organist and composer. Gaspar Cassado studied cello with Casals. He toured Europe, and made his U.S. debut in N.Y. on Dec. 10, 1936; made a U.S. tour in 1949. He composed a Cello Sonata, a Cello Concerto, and other pieces for his instrument. His *Catalonian Rhapsody* for Orch. was performed by the N.Y. Phil. on Nov. 8, 1928. He also made arrangements for cello and orch. of a Mozart horn concerto and Weber's Clarinet Concerto.—NS/LK/DM

Cassel, (John) Walter, American baritone and teacher; b. Council Bluffs, Iowa, May 15, 1910; d. Bloomington, Ind., July 2, 2000. He studied voice with Harry Cooper in Council Bluffs, where he also received training in trumpet and piano; after attending Creighton Univ. in Omaha, he pursued vocal studies with Frank La Forge in N.Y. In 1938 he began singing on radio shows, and on Dec. 12, 1942, made his Metropolitan Opera debut in N.Y. as Brétigny in *Manon*, remaining on its roster until 1945, and then again from 1954 to 1970 and in 1973–74. On March 21, 1948, he made his first appearance at the N.Y.C. Opera as Escamillo, singing there regularly until 1954, and then intermittently until 1969. He taught at Ind. Univ. in Bloomington (from 1974). While he proved equally at home in both serious and light roles, he was best known for his roles in operas by Wagner and R. Strauss. He sang the role of Horace Tabor in the first performance of Douglas Moore's *The Ballad of Baby Doe* (1956).—NS/LK/DM

Cassilly, Richard, American tenor; b. Washington, D.C., Dec. 14, 1927; d. Boston, Jan. 30, 1998. He studied at the Peabody Cons. of Music in Baltimore. After singing Michele in Menotti's *The Saint of Bleecker Street* in N.Y. (1955), he made his N.Y.C. Opera debut as Vakula in Tchaikovsky's *The Golden Slippers* (Oct. 13, 1955); was on its roster until 1959, and again from 1960 to 1963 and from 1964 to 1966. He made his European debut in Sutermeister's *Raskolnikoff* in Geneva (1965) and that same year sang at the Hamburg State Opera, where he appeared regularly (1966–77). He was concurrently a member of London's Covent Garden (1968–78) and also sang in major European opera centers. He made his Metropolitan Opera debut in N.Y. as Radames on Jan. 20, 1973. He resumed his association with the Metropolitan Opera in 1978, and subsequently appeared there in such roles as Tannhäuser, Don José, Tristan, Samson, Otello, Jimmy Mahoney in *Mahagonny*, and Captain Vere in *Billy Budd*. From 1986 he was prof. of voice at Boston Univ.—NS/LK/DM

Cassiodorus, Flavius Magnus Aurelius, Roman historian, statesman, and monk; b. Scyllacium (Squillace), Bruttii, c.485; d. Vivarese, Calabria, c.580. He held various civil offices under Theodoric and Athalaric until c.540. He founded the monasteries of Castellum and Vivarium; at the latter, he wrote his *De artibus ac disciplinis liberalium litterarum*; the section treating of music, *Institutiones musicae*, a valuable source, is printed in Gerbert's *Scriptores ecclesiastici de musica sacra potissimum* (vol. I, 1784); a partial reproduction is to be found in Strunk's *Source Readings in Music History* (N.Y., 1950).
—NS/LK/DM

Cassuto, Álvaro (Leon), Portuguese conductor and composer; b. Oporto, Nov. 17, 1938. He studied violin and piano as a small child, then took courses in composition with Artur Santos and Lopes Graça. In the summers of 1960 and 1961 he attended classes in new music in Darmstadt with Ligeti, Messiaen, and Stockhausen, and at the same time had instruction in conducting with Karajan. He further studied conducting with Pedro de Freitas Branco in Lisbon and Franco Ferrara in Hilversum. In 1964 he took his Ph.D. in law at the Univ. of Lisbon and in 1965 his M.A. in conducting at the Vienna Academy of Music. In 1969 he received the Koussevitzky Prize at Tanglewood. He served as an asst. conductor of the Gulbenkian Orch. in Lisbon (1965–68) and with the Little Orch. in N.Y. (1968–70). In 1970 he was appointed permanent conductor of the National Radio Orch. of Lisbon, and in 1975 was elected its music director. In 1974 he was appointed a lecturer in music and conductor of the Sym. Orch. of the Univ. of Calif. at Irvine, remaining there until 1979. From 1979 to 1985 he was music director of the R.I. Phil. in Providence, and from 1981 to 1987 the music director of the National Orchestral Assn. in N.Y. In 1987 he founded the Nova Filarmonia Portuguesa in Lisbon, which he conducted until 1993. In 1993 he founded the Portuguese Sym. Orch. in Lisbon at the behest of the Portuguese government, serving as its artistic director and principal conductor. He also was guest conductor of numerous orchs. in Europe, South America, and the U.S. A progressive-minded and scholarly musician, Cassuto amassed a large repertoire of both classical and modern works, displaying a confident expertise. He is also a composer of several orch. works in a modern idiom, as well as of chamber pieces.

WORKS: *Sinfonia breve No. 1* (Lisbon, Aug. 29, 1959) and *No. 2* (1960); *Variations* for Orch. (1961); *Permutations* for 2 Orchs. (1962); String Sextet (1962); Concertino for Piano and Orch. (1965); *Cro (mo-no)fonia* for 20 String Instruments (1967); *Canticum in Tenebris* for Soloists, Chorus, and Orch. (1968); *Evocations* for Orch. (1969); *Circle* for Orch. (1971); *In the Name of Peace,* opera (1971); *Song of Loneliness* for 12 Players (1972); *To Love and Peace,* symphonic poem (1973); *Homage to My People,* suite for Band, on Portuguese folk songs (1977); *Return to the Future* for Orch. (1985); *4 Seasons or Movements* for Piano and Orch. (1987).—**NS/LK/DM**

Castagna, Bruna, Italian mezzo-soprano; b. Bari, Oct. 15, 1905; d. Pinamar, Argentina, July 10, 1983. She was a student of Scognamiglio in Milan. In 1925 she made her operatic debut as the Nurse in *Boris Godunov* in Mantua; that same year she made her first appearance at Milan's La Scala as Suzuki, and then sang there until 1928 and again from 1932 to 1934; also appeared at the Teatro Colón in Buenos Aires (1927–30). On March 2, 1936, she made her Metropolitan Opera debut in N.Y. as Amneris, remaining there until 1940, and then returning in 1943 and 1945. She eventually settled in Argentina. In addition to her roles in Verdi's operas, she became well known for her portrayals of Carmen, Adalgisa, Santuzza, and Dalila.—**NS/LK/DM**

Castello, Dario, significant Italian composer who flourished in the early 17th century. He was active in Venice, where he led his own ensemble of wind players. He also was a musician in the chapel of the Doge and at San Marco. Castello publ. two vols. of instrumental sonatas (Venice, 1621, 1629). They constitute an important contribution to the development of a true instrumental style, and are marked by virtuoso writing in which the traditional canzona style serves as the foundation of an exploration of the stil moderno. —**NS/LK/DM**

Castelmary, Armand (real name, **Comte Armand de Castan**), French bass; b. Toulouse, Aug. 16, 1834; d. on the stage of the Metropolitan Opera just after Act 1 of *Martha* in N.Y., Feb. 10, 1897. He was a member of the Paris Opéra (1863–70), where he created the roles of Don Diego in *L'Africaine* (April 28, 1865), the Grand Inquisitor in *Don Carlos* (March 11, 1867), and Hamlet in Thomas's opera (March 9, 1868). In 1870 he made his U.S. debut in New Orleans. From 1889 to 1896 he sang at London's Covent Garden. On Nov. 29, 1893, he made his Metropolitan Opera debut in N.Y. as Vulcan in *Philémon et Baucis,* remaining on its roster until his death. He was particularly esteemed for his portrayal of Méphistophélès in the operas by Gounod and Boito. From 1864 to 1867 he was married to **Marie Sass.**—**NS/LK/DM**

Castelnuovo-Tedesco, Mario, greatly significant Italian-born American composer; b. Florence, April 3, 1895; d. Los Angeles, March h 16, 1968. He studied piano with Edoardo del Valle, and then continued his training at the Florence Cons., where he took diplomas in piano (1910) and in composition in Pizzetti's class (1913). He attained considerable eminence in Italy between the two world wars, and his music was often heard at European festivals. Political events forced him to leave Italy; in 1939 he settled in the U.S. and in 1946 became a naturalized American citizen. He became active as a composer for films in Hollywood, but continued to write large amounts of orch. and chamber music. His style is remarkably fluent and adaptable, often reaching rhapsodic eloquence.

WORKS: DRAMATIC: *La mandragola,* opera (Venice, May 4, 1926); *The Princess and the Pea,* overture with Narrator (1943); *Bacco in Toscana,* dithyramb for Voices and Orch. (Milan, May 8, 1931); *Aucassin et Nicolette,* puppet show with Voices and Instruments (1938; Florence, June 2, 1952); *All's Well That Ends Well,* opera (1959); *Saul,* biblical opera (1960); *Il Mercante di Venezia,* opera (Florence, May 25, 1961); *The Importance of Being Earnest,* chamber opera (1962); *The Song of Songs,* scenic oratorio (Hollywood, Aug. 7, 1963); *Tobias and the Angel,* scenic oratorio (1965). **Biblical Oratorios:** *Ruth* (1949); *Jonah* (1951). **ORCH.:** 3 violin concertos: No. 1, *Concerto italiano* (1925; Rome, Jan. 31, 1926), No. 2, *The Prophets* (N.Y., April 12, 1933), and No. 3 (1939); 2 piano concertos: No. 1 (Rome, Dec. 9, 1928) and No. 2 (N.Y., Nov. 2, 1939); *Variazioni sinfoniche* for Violin and Orch. (1930); Cello Concerto (1934; N.Y., Jan. 31, 1935); 2 guitar concertos (1939, 1953); *Cipressi* (Boston, Oct. 25, 1940; arranged from the piece piece, 1920); *Poem* for Violin and Orch. (1942); *The Birthday of the Infanta* (1942; New Orleans, Jan. 28, 1947); *Indian Songs and Dances,* suite (Los Angeles, Jan. 7, 1943); *An American Rhapsody* (1943); *Serenade* for Guitar and Orch. (1943); *Octoroon Ball,* ballet suite (1947); *Noah's Ark,* movement for Narrator and Orch., from *Genesis*, a suite, with other movements by Schoenberg, Stravinsky, Toch, Milhaud, Tansman, and N. Shilkret, who commissioned the work (Portland, Ore., Dec. 15, 1947); Concerto for 2 Guitars and Orch. (1962); overtures. **CHAMBER:** *Signorine: 2 profili* for Violin and Piano (1918); *Ritmi* for Violin and Piano (1920); *Capitan Fracassa* for Violin and Piano (1920); *Notturno adriatico* for Violin and Piano (1922); *I nottambuli* for Cello and Piano (1927); Cello Sonata (1928); 2 piano trios (1928, 1932); 3 string quartets (1929, 1948, 1964); *Sonata quasi una fantasia* for Violin and Piano (1929); *The Lark* for Violin and Piano (1930); 2 piano quintets (1932, 1951); *Toccata* for Cello and Piano (1935); *Capriccio diabolico* for Guitar (1935; later arranged as a guitar concerto); Concertino for Harp and 7 Instruments (1937); *Ballade* for Violin and Piano (1940); *Divertimento* for 2 Flutes (1943); Sonata for Violin and Viola (1945); Clarinet Sonata (1945); Sonatina for Bassoon and Piano (1946); Quintet for Guitar and Strings (1950); Sonata for Viola and Cello (1950); *Fantasia* for Guitar and Piano (1950); *Concerto da camera* for Oboe and Strings (1950); Sonata for Violin and Cello (1950); Sonata for Cello and Harp (1966); numerous guitar pieces. **KEYBOARD: P i a n o :** *English Suite* (1909); *Questo fu il carro della morte* (1913); *Il raggio verde* (1916); *Alghe* (1919); *I naviganti* (1919); *La sirenetta e il pesce turchino* (1920); *Cantico* (1920); *Vitalba e Biancospino* (1921); *Epigrafe* (1922); *Alt-Wien* (1923); *Piedigrotta* (1924); *Le stagioni* (1924); *Le danze del Re David* (1925); *3 poemi campestri* (1926); *3 corali su melodie ebraiche* (1926); Sonata (1928); *Crinoline* (1929); *Candide*, 6 pieces (1944); *6 canoni* (1950). **VOCAL: S o n g s :** *Le Roy Loys* (1914); *Ninna-Nanna* (1914); *Fuori i barbari* (1915); *Stelle cadenti* (1915); *Coplas* (1915); *Briciole* (1916); *3 fioretti di Santo Francesco* (1919; also with Orch.); *Girotondo de golosi* (1920); *Etoile filante* (1920); *L'infinito* (1921); *Sera* (1921); 33 Shakespearean songs (1921–25); *2 preghiere per i bimbi d'Italia* (1923); *1830* (1924); *Scherzi*, 2 series (1924–25); *Indian Serenade* (1925); *Cadix* (1926); *3 Sonnets from the Portuguese* (1926); *Laura di Nostra Donna* (1935); *Un sonetto di Dante* (1939); *Recuerdo* (1940); *Le Rossignol* (1942); *The Daffodils* (1944). **C h o r a l :** 2 madrigals (1915); *Lecho dodi*, synagogue chant for Tenor, Men's Voices, and Organ (1936); *Sacred Synagogue Service* (1943); *Liberty, Mother of Exiles* (1944).

BIBL.: N. Rossi, *Complete Catalogue of Works by M. C.-T.* (N.Y., 1977); B. Scalin, *Operas by M. C.-T.* (diss., Northwestern Univ., 1980).—NS/LK/DM

Castil-Blaze
See **Blaze, François-Henri-Joseph**

Castle, Lee (originally, Castaldo, Aniello),
jazz trumpeter, leader; b. N.Y., Feb. 28, 1915; d. Hollywood, Fla., Nov. 16, 1990. His brother Charles is a trombonist. He played in junior bands on drums, began on trumpet at 15, and became professional at 18. He worked in the mid-1930s with Joe Haymes, Dick Stabile, and Artie Shaw, before joining Red Norvo in July 1937. He joined Tommy Dorsey in September 1937, leaving the band when Tommy sent him to study with the Dorseys' father in Lansford, Pa., and returned in late 1938. He played briefly with Glenn Miller, then with Jack Teagarden from April–December 1939. He led his own band in 1940, was briefly with Will Bradley, then joined Artie Shaw in early 1941. H led his own band from March 1942—adopting the name Castle at this point—signed the band over to Richard Himber in late

1942, then joined Benny Goodman until late 1943 (appearing in the films *Stage Door Canteen* and *The Girls They Left Behind*). He again led big bands in the 1940s, forming the Dixieland outfit in 1949. He was with Artie Shaw (1950), then the Dorsey Brothers (from 1953); fronted Jimmy Dorsey's Band during that leader's last illness. Shortly after Jimmy Dorsey's death in 1957, the band was divided into two memorial orchestras, one under each brother's name. Castle assumed leadership of the Jimmy Dorsey Orch., which he continued to lead into the 1980s.

DISC.: *The Lee Castle Jazztette* (1952); *Dixieland Heaven* (1957). A. Shaw: *Sugar Foot Stomp* (1936). T. Dorsey: *I Never Knew* (1938); *Sentimental and Swinging* (1955). W. Bradley: *Basin Street Bougie* (1941). J. Dorsey: *So Rare*; *Sophisticated Swing* (both 1956).—JC/LP

Castleman, Charles (Martin),
American violinist and teacher; b. Quincy, Mass., May 22, 1941. He began violin lessons at the age of four with Ondříček. When he was only six he appeared as a soloist with Fiedler and the Boston Pops Orch. At nine, he made his solo recital in Boston. He was a student of Galamian at the Curtis Inst. of Music in Philadelphia (1957–63), and also received coaching from Gingold, Szeryng, and Oistrakh. He likewise pursued his education at Harvard Univ. and the Univ. of Pa. In 1964 he made his formal debut at N.Y.'s Town Hall. In 1970 he organized the Quartet Program, an innovative workshop in solo and chamber music performances. It celebrated its 30th anniversary under his direction in 1999. From 1972 to 1975 he was a member of the New String Trio of N.Y. In 1975 he became prof. of violin at the Eastman School of Music in Rochester, N.Y. He also played in the Raphael Trio from 1975, which made tours of the U.S. in a series of Haydn, Beethoven, and Dvořák cycles. The trio also played much contemporary music, including Bischof's *Trio 89* at the Vienna Festival in 1989. On May 2, 1981, Castleman was soloist in the premiere of Amram's Violin Concerto with the St. Louis Sym. Orch. under Slatkin's direction. That same year, he performed all of Ysaÿe's 6 Sonatas for Solo Violin at N.Y.'s Alice Tully Hall. His engagements as a soloist have led to appearances with orchs. in Boston, Chicago, N.Y., Philadelphia, Mexico City, Moscow, and elsewhere. He has also appeared at many festivals in the U.S. and abroad. As a teacher, he has presided over numerous master classes around the globe.—NS/LK/DM

Castro, Jean de,
South Netherlands composer; b. Liège, c. 1540; d. c. 1600. He was active in Antwerp. After sojourns in Germany and France, he was again in Antwerp by 1586. He later was in the service of the courts in Düsseldorf and Cologne. He publ. 29 vols. of music (1571–1600), among which were various sacred works, madrigals, chansons, and odes.

BIBL.: M. Oebel, *Beiträge zu einer Monographie über J.d. C. (ca.1540–1610)* (Regensburg, 1928).—NS/LK/DM

Castro, José María,
Argentine cellist, conductor, and composer, brother of **Juan José Castro** and **Washington Castro;** b. Avellaneda, near Buenos Aires, Dec.

15, 1892; d. Buenos Aires, Aug. 2, 1964. He studied cello and composition in Buenos Aires. From 1913 he played in orchs. and chamber music ensembles, and later was solo cellist in the Orquesta Filharmónica of the Asociación del Profesorado Orquestal (1922–27). He was titular conductor of the Orquesta Filarmónica in Buenos Aires (1930–42), and also conducted the municipal band there (1933–53).

WORKS: DRAMATIC: B a l l e t : *Georgia* (1937; Buenos Aires, June 2, 1939); *El sueño de la botella* (1948); *Falarka* (La Plata, Oct. 27, 1951). M o n o d r a m a : *La otra voz* (1953; Buenos Aires, Sept. 24, 1954). ORCH.: *Concerto grosso* (1932; Buenos Aires, June 11, 1933); *Obertura para una ópera cómica* (1934; Buenos Aires, Nov. 9, 1936); Piano Concerto (Buenos Aires, Nov. 17, 1941; rev. 1955); *Concerto for Orchestra* (1944); Concerto for Cello and 17 Instruments (1945; Buenos Aires, April 8, 1949); *Tres pastorales* (Buenos Aires, Sept. 30, 1945); *El libro de los sonetos* (1947); *Suite de cinco piezas* (1948); *Arietta con variazioni* (1948); *Preludio y Toccata* (1949); *Tema coral con variaciones* (1952; Buenos Aires, June 27, 1954); Concerto for Violin and 18 Instruments (1953; Buenos Aires, July 6, 1954); Piano Concerto (1955); *Diez improvisaciones breves* (1957; Buenos Aires, May 9, 1959); *Preludio, Tema con variaciones y Final* (1959; Buenos Aires, Aug. 18, 1960); *Sinfonía de Buenos Aires* (1963; Buenos Aires, June 26, 1966). CHAMBER: Concerto for Violin and Piano (1917); Violin Sonata (1918); Sonata Cello and Violin (1933); Sonata for 2 Cellos (1938); 3 string quartets (1943, 1947, 1956); *Tres estudios* for Cello and Piano (1946); *Tres piezas* for Cello and Piano (1947); *Sonata poética* for Violin and Piano (1957); many solo piano pieces, including 6 sonatas (1919; 1924; 1927; 1931; *Sonata de Primavera*, 1939; *Sonata dramática*, 1944). VOCAL: *Cinco liricas* for Voice and Orch. (1958); *Con la patria adentro* for Tenor and Orch. (1964; Buenos Aires, Aug. 26, 1965); many songs with piano.—NS/LK/DM

Castro, Juan José,

eminent Argentine composer and conductor, brother of **José Maria Castro** and **Washington Castro;** b. Avellaneda, near Buenos Aires, March 7, 1895; d. Buenos Aires, Sept. 3, 1968. After study in Buenos Aires, he went to Paris, where he took a course in composition with d'Indy. Returning to Argentina in 1929, he organized in Buenos Aires the Orquesta de Nacimiento, which he conducted; in 1930 he conducted the ballet season at the Teatro Colón; conducted opera there from 1933; also became music director of the Asociación del Profesorado Orquestal and Asociación Sinfónica, with which he gave first local performances of a number of modern works. In 1934 he received a Guggenheim Foundation grant. From 1947 to 1951 he conducted in Cuba and Uruguay; from 1952 to 1953 he was principal conductor of the Victorian Sym. Orch. in Melbourne, Australia; from 1956 to 1960 he was conductor of the Orquesta Sinfónica Nacional in Buenos Aires; from 1959 to 1964 he was director of the Puerto Rico Cons. in San Juan. Castro was proficient in all genres of composition, but his works were rarely performed outside South America, and he himself conducted most of his symphonic compositions. His most notable success outside his homeland came when he won the prize for the best opera in a La Scala competition in Milan with his *Prosperpino e lo straniero* (in Spanish as *Prosperpina y el extranjero*) in 1952.

WORKS: DRAMATIC: O p e r a : *La Zapatera prodigiosa*

(Montevideo, Dec. 23, 1949); *Prosperpina e lo straniero* (Milan, March 17, 1952); *Bodas de sangre* (Buenos Aires, Aug. 9, 1956); *Cosecha negra* (1961). B a l l e t : *Mekhano* (Buenos Aires, July 17, 1937); *Offenbachiana* (Buenos Aires, May 25, 1940). ORCH.: *Dans le jardin des morts* (Buenos Aires, Oct. 5, 1924); *A una madre* (Buenos Aires, Oct. 27, 1925); *La Chellah*, symphonic poem (Buenos Aires, Sept. 10, 1927); 5 syms.: No. 1 (1931), No. 2, *Sinfonía biblica*, for Chorus and Orch. (1932), No. 3, *Sinfonía Argentina* (Buenos Aires, Nov. 29, 1936), No. 4, *Sinfonía de los campos* (Buenos Aires, Oct. 29, 1939), and No. 5 (1956); *Allegro, Lento y Vivace* (1931); *Anunciación, Entrada a Jerusalem, Golgotha* (Buenos Aires, Nov. 15, 1932); Piano Concerto (1941); *Corales criollos No. 3*, symphonic poem (1953); *Suite introspectiva* (1961; Los Angeles, June 8, 1962); Violin Concerto (1962). CHAMBER: Violin Sonata (1914); Cello Sonata (1916); String Quartet (1942). KEYBOARD: P i a n o : 2 sonatas (1917, 1939); *Corales criollos Nos. 1 and 2* (1947). VOCAL: *Epitafio en ritmos y sonidos* for Chorus and Orch. (1961); *Negro* for Soprano and Orch. (1961); songs.

BIBL.: R. Arizaga, *J.J. C.* (Buenos Aires, 1963).
—NS/LK/DM

Castro, Washington,

Argentine conductor, teacher, and composer, brother of **José Maria Castro** and **Juan José Castro;** b. Buenos Aires, July 13, 1909. He studied cello; from 1947 he devoted himself mainly to conducting and teaching.

WORKS: ORCH.: *Sinfonía primaveral* (1956); Piano Concerto (1960); *Sinfonía breve* for Strings (1960); *Concerto for Orchestra* (1963); *Rhapsody* for Cello and Orch. (1963); *3 Pieces* (1970). CHAMBER: 3 string quartets (1945, 1950, 1965); piano pieces. VOCAL: Songs.—NS/LK/DM

Castrucci, Pietro,

Italian violinist and composer; b. Rome, 1679; d. Dublin, Feb. 29, 1752. He most likely was a student of Corelli. In 1715 he went to London, where he was concertmaster of Handel's opera orch. until 1737. His brother, Prospero, also was active as a violinist in London. Pietro acquired a notable reputation as a violinist, and also attracted attention as the inventor of the violetta marina, a stringed instrument resembling the viola d'amore. Handel wrote two obbligato parts for "violette marine per gli Signori Castrucci" in the hero's sleep aria in *Orlando*, and also a part for the instrument in *Sosarme*. In his last years, Castrucci's fortunes declined and he settled in Dublin in 1750, where he died in poverty. He publ. two vols. of 12 sonatas each for Violin and Basso Continuo (London, 1718, 1734), two vols. of Solos (sonatas) for Flute and Basso Continuo (London, 1723, 1725), and 12 Concerti grossi (London, 1736). He also contributed six sonatas or solos for Flute and Basso Continuo to the collection by Geminiani (London, c. 1720).—NS/LK/DM

Catalani, Alfredo,

greatly talented Italian composer; b. Lucca, June 19, 1854; d. Milan, Aug. 7, 1893. He studied music with his father, a church organist; in 1872 studied with Fortunato Magi and Bazzini at the Istituto Musicale Pacini in Lucca. He then went to Paris, where he attended classes of Bazin (composition) and Marmontel (piano). He returned to Italy in 1873, and in 1886 he became the successor of Ponchielli as prof. of composition at the Milan Cons. It was in Milan that he became acquainted with Boito, who encouraged him in his composition. He also met young Toscanini, who became a champion of his music. Catalani was determined to create a Wagnerian counterpart in the field of Italian opera, and he selected for his libretti fantastic subjects suitable for dramatic action. After several unsuccessful productions he finally achieved his ideal in his last opera, *La Wally*; he died of tuberculosis the year after its production.

WORKS: DRAMATIC: Opera: *La Falce* (Milan, July 19, 1875); *Elda* (Turin, Jan. 31, 1880; rev. as *Loreley*, Turin, Feb. 16, 1890); *Dejanice* (Milan, March 17, 1883); *Edmea* (Milan, Feb. 27, 1886); *La Wally* (Milan, Jan. 20, 1892). **ORCH.:** *Sinfonia a piena orchestra* (1872); *Il Mattino*, romantic sym. (1874); *Ero e Leandro*, symphonic poem (Milan, May 9, 1885). **OTHER:** Piano pieces and songs.

BIBL.: D. Pardini, *A. C.* (Lucca, 1935); A. Bonaccorsi, *A. C.* (Turin, 1942); C. Gatti, *A. C.* (Milan, 1953).—**NS/LK/DM**

Catalani, Angelica,

famous Italian soprano; b. Sinigaglia, May 10, 1780; d. Paris, June 12, 1849. She was educated in the convent of S. Lucia di Gubbio in Rome, and received vocal training from her father and from Morandi. After making her operatic debut as Mayr's Lodoïska at the Teatro La Fenice in Venice in 1795, she sang at La Pergola in Florence (1799), La Scala in Milan (1801), and in Lisbon (from 1801). In 1806 she made her London debut at the King's Theatre in Portugal's *Semiramide*, and soon became one of the most highly acclaimed and paid prima donnas of the era. She became well known for her roles in operas by Paër, Paisiello, and Piccinni. In 1812 she sang Susanna in the first London staging of *Le nozze di Figaro*. After serving as manager of the Théâtre-Italien in Paris (1814–17), she toured extensively in Europe. In 1821 she retired from the operatic stage but continued to appear in concerts until 1828. Catalani captivated her audiences by the sheer beauty and range of her coloratura.

BIBL.: H. Satter, *A. C.* (Frankfurt am Main, 1958); M. Zurletti, *C.* (Turin, 1982).—**NS/LK/DM**

Catán, Daniel,

Mexican composer; b. Mexico City, April 3, 1949. He studied philosophy in England (1967–70) before turning to music. After attending the Univ. of Southampton (1970–73), he studied composition with Boretz and Babbitt at Princeton Univ. (1973–77), where he received his Ph.D. Catán taught composition at the Cons. Nacional in Mexico City. In 1987–88 he was resident composer of the Welsh National Opera in Cardiff. In 1994 his opera *La hija de Rappaccini* was the first opera by a Mexican composer to be staged in the U.S.

WORKS: DRAMATIC: Opera: *Encuentro en al ocaso*, chamber opera (1978–79; Mexico City, Aug. 2, 1980); *La hija de Rappaccini*, after Hawthorne by way of O. Paz (1983–89; Mexico City, April 25, 1991); *Florencia en al Amazones* (1994–96; Houston, Oct. 25, 1996). **Musical Play:** *El medallón de Mantelillos* (Mexico City, Dec. 9, 1982). **Ballet:** *Ausencia de flores* (1982–83; Guadalajara, Nov. 23, 1983). **ORCH.:** *Hetaera Esmeralda* (1975); *El árbol de la vida* (1980); *En un doblez del tiempo* (1982); *Tu So, To Rise, Tu Sonrise* (1991). **CHAMBER:** Quintet for Oboe, Clarinet, Violin, Cello, and Piano (1972); Piano Trio (1982). **KEYBOARD: Piano:** *Variaciones* (1971). **VOCAL:** *Ocaso de medianoche* for Mezzo-soprano and Orch. (1977); *Mariposa de obsidiana* for Soprano, Chorus, and Orch. (1984).—**LK/DM**

Catel, Charles-Simon,

French composer and pedagogue; b. l'Aigle, Orne, June 10, 1773; d. Paris, Nov. 29, 1830. He studied in Paris with Gossec and Gobert at the École Royale de Chant. He served as accompanist and teacher there (1787), and also was accompanist at the Opéra and asst. conductor (to Gossec) of the band of the Garde Nationale (1790). In 1795, on the establishment of the Cons., he was appointed prof. of harmony, and was commissioned to write a *Traité d'harmonie* (publ. 1802), a standard work at the Cons. for 20 years thereafter. In 1810, with Gossec, Méhul, and Cherubini, he was made an inspector of the Cons., resigning in 1816. He was named a member of the Académie des Beaux-Arts in 1817. As a composer, Catel was at his best in his operas, written in a conventional but attractive style of French stage music of the time.

WORKS: DRAMATIC: Opera (all 1st perf. at the Paris Opéra and the Opéra-Comique): *Sémiramis* (May 4, 1802); *L'Auberge de Bagnères* (April 23, 1807); *Les Artistes par occasion* (Jan. 22, 1807); *Les Bayadères* (Aug. 8, 1810); *Les Aubergistes de qualité* (June 11, 1812); *Bayard a Mézières* (Feb. 12, 1814); *Le Premier en date* (Nov. 3, 1814); *Wallace, ou Le Ménestrel écossais* (March 24, 1817); *Zirphile et Fleur de Myrte, ou Cent ans en jour* (June 29, 1818); *L'Officier enlevé* (May 4, 1819). **OTHER:** Several syms. and chamber works.

BIBL.: J. Carlez, *C.:Étude biographique et critique* (Caen, 1895); F. Hellouin and J. Picard, *Un Musicien oublié: C.* (Paris, 1910); S. Suskin, *The Music of C.-S. C. for the Paris Opéra* (diss., Yale Univ., 1972).—**NS/LK/DM**

Catlett, Sid(ney) (aka "Big Sid"),

early jazz drummer, composer; b. Evansville, Ind., b. Jan. 17, 1910; d. Chicago, Ill., March 25, 1951. After a brief spell on piano, he played drums in school band. His family moved to Chicago, where he attended the Tilden H.S., receiving drum tuition from Joe Russek. He played with local musicians, then came to N.Y. in 1931 to join Elmer Snowden. He worked with Snowden until 1932, when he joined Benny Carter (through 1933) and Rex Stewart (1933–34). He moved back to Chicago in summer 1934, worked with various leaders and briefly led his own band. He played with Fletcher Henderson out of St. Louis from February–September 1936, then joined Don Redman, staying with him through 1938. He was with Louis Armstrong from late 1938 until early 1941, briefly with Roy Eldridge, then worked on and off with Benny Goodman from June until October 1941. He rejoined Louis Armstrong from late 1941 until summer 1942, then was with Teddy Wilson from c.August 1942 until early 1944. Led own quartet from spring 1944 until 1947 for residencies in N.Y., Chicago, San Francisco, and L.A.; he also toured with "Concert Varieties" and subbed for Sonny Greer with Duke Ellington (1945). He briefly led own big band in late 1946. He was with Louis Armstrong All Stars from August 1947; was forced to quit touring through illness (spring 1949). He became resident drummer at Jazz Ltd., Chicago, from spring 1949; worked with Muggsy Spanier, Sidney Bechet, and others there. He also worked in N.Y. with Eddie Condon in 1949 and took part in Carnegie Hall concert with John Kirby (December 1950). He was ill with pneumonia early in 1951, returning to play at Jazz Ltd. He attended an Easter weekend jazz concert at the Chicago Opera House, and while talking to Slam Stewart in the wings, he suffered a fatal heart attack. He appeared on screen in the short film *Jammin' the Blues* (1944), but as was the practice then, no sound was recorded during filming. His drum work was dubbed in at a post-synchronization session by Jo Jones; where Catlett appears on screen, Jones's playing is heard!

With C. Parker: *Salt Peanuts* (1945). L. Young: *Complete Lester Young* (1943). D. Gillespie: *Shaw' Nuff* (1945); *Groovin' High* (1945). H. Jones: *Carnegie Hall Concert* (1947). L. Armstrong: *Satchmo at Symphony Hall* (1947).—JC/LP

Caturla, Alejandro Garcia, Cuban composer; b. Remedios, March 7, 1906; d. there (assassinated), Nov. 12, 1940. He studied with Pedro Sanjuán in Havana, then with Nadia Boulanger in Paris (1928). He was founder (1932) and conductor of the Orquesta de Conciertos de Caibarién (chamber orch.) in Cuba. He served as district judge in Remedios. In Caturla's music, primitive Afro-Cuban rhythms and themes are treated with modern techniques and a free utilization of dissonance.

WORKS: Suite of 3 Cuban dances: *Danza del tambor, Motivos de danzas,* and *Danza Lucumi* (Havana, 1928); *Bembe* for 14 Instruments (Paris, 1929); *Dos poemas Afro-Cubanos* for Voice and Piano (Paris, 1929; also arranged for Voice and Orch.); *Yambo-O,* Afro- Cuban oratorio (Havana, Oct. 25, 1931); *Rumba* for Orch. (1931); *Primera suite cubana* for Piano and 8 Wind Instruments (1930); *Manita en el Suelo,* "mitologia bufa Afro-Cubana" for Narrator, Marionettes, and Chamber Orch. (1934). —NS/LK/DM

Caurroy, François-Eustache du
See **Du Caurroy, François-Eustache, Sieur de St.-Frémin**

Caustun, Thomas, English composer; b. c. 1523; d. London, Oct. 28, 1569. About 1550 he was made a Gentleman of the Chapel Royal. His fine anthems and services for men's voices were publ. in Day's *Certaine Notes* (London, 1565). He also contributed to Day's *The Whole Psalmes in Foure Partes* (London, 1563).—LK/DM

Cavaillé-Coll, Aristide, celebrated French organ builder; b. Montpellier, Feb. 4, 1811; d. Paris, Oct. 13, 1899. His father, Dominique Hyacinthe (1771–1862), was also an organ builder. Aristide went to Paris in 1833. He built the organ at St.-Denis, and thereafter many famous organs in Paris (St.-Sulpice, Madeleine, etc.), the French provinces, Belgium, the Netherlands, and elsewhere. He invented the system of separate wind chests with different pressures for the low, medium, and high tones; also the "flûtes octaviantes." He publ. *Études expérimentales sur les tuyaux d'orgues* (report for the Académie des Sciences, 1849) and *Projet d'orgue monumental pour la Basilique de Saint-Pierre de Rome* (1875).

BIBL.: A. Peschard, *Notice biographique sur A. C.-C. et les orgues électriques* (Paris, 1899); C. and E. Cavaille-Coll, *A. C.- C.: Ses origines, sa vie, ses oeuvres* (Paris, 1928).—NS/LK/DM

Cavalieri, Catarina (real name, **Franziska Cavalier**), Austrian soprano of Italian descent; b. Wahring, near Vienna, Feb. 19, 1760; d. Vienna, June 30, 1801. She studied with Salieri, making her operatic debut as Sandrina in Anfossi's *La finta giardiniera* at the Italian Opera in Vienna on April 29, 1775; subsequently sang with notable success at the German Opera there. Salieri, with whom she maintained a liaison, composed several operas for her. Mozart, too, composed the roles of Constanze in *Die Entführung aus dem Serail* (July 16, 1782) and Mme. Silberklang in *Der Schauspieldirektor* (Feb. 7, 1786) for her, as well as the extra aria "Mi tradi" (K. 540c) in *Don Giovanni,* for the first Vienna performance in 1788. In a letter of May 21, 1785, Mozart described her as "a singer of whom Germany might well be proud." She retired from the stage in 1793. —NS/LK/DM

Cavalieri, Emilio de', Italian composer; b. Rome, c. 1550; d. there, March 11, 1602. He was born into a noble family. After serving as organist and supervisor of the Lenten music at the Oratorio del Crocifisso in S. Marcello in Rome (1578–84), he went to Florence in 1588 as a court overseer and diplomat to Ferdinando de' Medici. In 1589 he composed music for and supervised the celebrated intermedi presented at his patron's wedding. He subsequently composed sets of Lamentations and responses for Holy Week (c. 1599). Upon his return to Rome, he composed his most significant work, *Rappresentatione di Anima, et di Corpo...per recitar cantando* (Collegio Sacro, Feb. 1600). This score is historically significant as the earliest dramatic piece set entirely to music, and its printed score (Rome, 1600) was the earliest to use a figured bass. See T. Read, *A Critical Study and Performance Edition of Emilio de' Cavalieri's Rappresentazione di anima e di corpo* (diss., Univ. of Southern Calif., 1969).—NS/LK/DM

Cavalieri, Lina (actually, **Natalina**), famous Italian soprano; b. Viterbo, Dec. 25, 1874; d. in an air raid on Florence, Feb. 8, 1944. As a young woman of striking beauty, she became the cynosure of the Paris boulevardiers via her appearances in cafés (1893) and at the Folies-Bergère (1894). During a trip to Russia in 1900, she married Prince Alexander Bariatinsky, who persuaded her to take up an operatic career. After studying in Paris, she made a premature debut as Nedda at the Teatro São Carlo in Lisbon (1900); at her second appearance, the audience's disapproval brought the performance to a halt. She and the Prince then parted company, but she continued vocal studies with Maddalena Mariani-Masi in Milan, returning successfully to the stage as Mimi at the Teatro San Carlo in Naples (1900); she then sang in St. Petersburg and Warsaw (1901). In 1905 she was chosen to create the role of L'Ensoleillad in Massenet's *Chérubin* in Monte Carlo, and on Dec. 5, 1906, she made her Metropolitan Opera debut in N.Y. as Fedora, winning subsequent praise for her dramatic portrayals there of Tosca and Mimi. In 1907, after divorcing her husband, she contracted a lucrative marriage with the American millionaire Winthrop Chandler, but left him in a week, precipitating a sensational scandal that caused the Metropolitan to break her contract; she made her farewell appearance there in a concert on March 8, 1908. She sang at London's Covent Garden (1908), N.Y.'s Manhattan Opera House (1908), the London Opera House (1911), and the Chicago Grand Opera (1913–14; 1921–22). She married **Lucien Muratore** in 1913, but abandoned him in 1919; she then married Paolo D'Arvanni, making her home at her Villa Cappucina near Florence. Among her other fine roles were Adriana Lecouvreur, Manon Lescaut, and Salomé in *Hérodiade*. She publ. an autobiography, *La mie veritá* (1936). She was the subject of an Italian film under the telling title *La Donna più bella dello mondo* (1957), starring Gina Lollobrigida.—**NS/LK/DM**

Cavalli (real name, Caletti), Pier Francesco,

historically significant Italian opera composer; b. Crema, Feb. 14, 1602; d. Venice, Jan. 14, 1676. His father, Giovanni Battista Caletti (known also as Bruni), was maestro di cappella at the Cathedral in Crema; he gave him his first instruction in music; as a youth he sang under his father's direction in the choir of the Cathedral. The Venetian nobleman Federico Cavalli, who was also mayor of Crema, took him to Venice for further musical training; and as it was a custom, he adopted his sponsor's surname. In December 1616 he entered the choir of S. Marco in Venice, beginning an association there which continued for the rest of his life; he sang there under Monteverdi; also served as an organist at Ss. Giovanni e Paolo (1620–30). In 1638, he turned his attention to the new art form of opera, and helped to organize an opera company at the Teatro San Cassiano. His first opera, *Le nozze di Teti e di Peleo*, was performed there on Jan. 24, 1639; nine more were to follow within the next decade. In 1639 he successfully competed against three others for the post of second organist at S. Marco. In 1660 Cardinal Mazarin invited him to Paris, where he presented a restructured version of his opera *Serse* for the marriage festivities of Louis XIV and Maria Theresa. He also composed the opera *Ercole amante* while there, which was given at the Tuileries on Feb. 7, 1662. He returned to Venice in 1662; on Jan. 11, 1665, he was officially appointed first organist at S. Marco; on Nov. 20, 1668, he became maestro di cappella there. After Monteverdi, Cavalli stands as one of the most important Venetian composers of opera in the mid-17th century. In recent years several of his operas have been revived; Raymond Leppard ed. *L'Ormindo* (London, 1969) and *Calisto* (London, 1975); Jane Glover ed. *L'Eritrea* (London, 1977).

WORKS: DRAMATIC: O p e r a : *Le nozze di Teti e di Peleo* (Venice, Jan. 24, 1639); *Gli amori d'Apollo e di Dafne* (Venice, 1640); *Didone* (Venice, 1641); *Amore innamorato* (Venice, Jan. 1, 1642; music not extant); *La virtù de' strali d'Amore* (Venice, 1642); *Egisto* (Venice, 1643); *L'Ormindo* (Venice, 1644); *Doriclea* (Venice, 1645); *Titone* (Venice, 1645; music not extant); *Giasone* (Venice, Jan. 5, 1649); *Euripo* (Venice, 1649; music not extant); *Orimonte* (Venice, Feb. 20, 1650); *Oristeo* (Venice, 1651); *Rosinda* (Venice, 1651); *Calisto* (Venice, 1652); *L'Eritrea* (Venice, 1652); *Veremonda l'amazzone di Aragona* (Naples, Dec. 21, 1652); *L'Orione* (Milan, June 1653); *Ciro* (composed by Francesco Provenzale; prologue and arias added by Cavalli for Venice, Jan. 30, 1654); *Serse* (Venice, Jan. 12, 1655); *Statira principessa di Persia* (Venice, Jan.

18, 1656); *Erismena* (Venice, 1656); *Artemisia* (Venice, Jan. 10, 1657); *Hipermestra* (Florence, June 12, 1658); *Antioco* (Venice, Jan. 21, 1659; music not extant); *Elena* (Venice, Dec. 26, 1659); *Ercole amante* (Paris, Feb. 7, 1662); *Scipione Affricano* (Venice, Feb. 9, 1664); *Mutio Scevola* (Venice, Jan. 26, 1665); *Pompeo Magno* (Venice, Feb. 20, 1666); *Eliogabalo* (composed in 1668; not perf.); *Coriolano* (Piacenza, May 27, 1669; music not extant); *Massenzio* (composed in 1673; not perf.; music not extant). The following operas have been ascribed to Cavalli but are now considered doubtful: *Narciso et Ecco immortalati*; *Deidamia*; *Il Romolo e 'l Remo*; *La prosperita infelice di Giulio Cesare dittatore*; *Torilda*; *Bradamante*; *Armidoro*; *Helena rapita da Theseo*; also *La pazzia in trono, overo Caligola delirante*, which is a spoken drama with some music. None of the music is extant for any of these works.

BIBL.: H. Prunières, *C. et l'opéra venetien au dix-septième siècle* (Paris, 1931); E. Rosand, *Aria in the Early Operas of F. C.* (diss., N.Y.U., 1971); L. Bianconi, *F. C. und die Verbreitung der venezianischen Oper in Italien* (diss., Univ. of Heidelberg, 1974); J. Glover, *C.* (N.Y., 1978).—**NS/LK/DM**

Cavallini, Ernesto,

outstanding Italian clarinetist; b. Milan, Aug. 30, 1807; d. there, Jan. 7, 1874. At the age of 10, he entered the Milan Cons. as a pupil of Benedetto Carulli. Following concert tours of Italy, he played in the La Scala orch. and taught in Milan. He gave concerts in Paris (1842) and London (1842, 1845), and then was solo clarinetist at the St. Petersburg court (1852–70) before returning to Milan. A masterful performer, he was acclaimed as the Paganini of the clarinet. He composed a number of works for his instrument.—**LK/DM**

Cavallo, Enrica,

Italian pianist and teacher; b. Milan, May 19, 1921. She studied at the Milan Cons. After her marriage to **Franco Gulli**, they formed the noted Gulli-Cavallo Duo in 1947 and subsequently toured all over the world. From 1973 to 1991 she also taught at the Ind. Univ. School of Music in Bloomington.—**NS/LK/DM**

Cavazzoni (also called da Bologna and d'Urbino), Marco Antonio,

Italian composer and singer, father of **Girolamo Cavazzoni;** b. Bologna, c. 1490; d. c. 1570 (the date appearing on his will is April 3, 1569). He went to Urbino about 1510 and became acquainted with Cardinal Pietro Bembo. He then became a musician in the private chapel of Pope Leo X (1515). In Venice (1517) he was employed by Francesco Cornaro, nephew of the Queen of Cyprus. Returning to Rome (1520), he was again in the employ of Pope Leo X. From 1522 to 1524. From 1528 to 1531 he was in Venice, and in 1536–37 was organist at Chioggia. From 1545 to 1559 he was a singer at S. Marco (Venice), where Adriaen Willaert was maestro di cappella. As a youth wrote a Mass, *Domini Marci Antonii*, so named because he derived its theme from the solmization syllables of his Christian names. His most important work is a collection of keyboard pieces, *Recerchari, motetti, canzoni, Libro I* (Venice, 1523). The ricercari are toccata-like rather than contrapuntal, and the motets and canzonas are instrumental transcriptions of vocal pieces. Modern reprints (with biographical notes) are found in Benvenuti's *I classici musicali italiani* (Milan, 1941) and in K. Jeppesen, *Die italienische Orgelmusik am Anfang des Cinquecento* (Copenhagen, 1943).—**NS/LK/DM**

Cavazzoni, Girolamo, Italian organist and composer, son of **Marco Antonio Cavazzoni;** b. Urbino, c. 1520; d. Venice, c. 1577. He was a godson of Cardinal Pietro Bembo. He was organist at S. Barbara in Mantua until 1577, where he supervised the building of the organ in 1565–66. His *Intavolatura cioe Ricercari, Canzoni, Hinni, Magnificati* (Venice, 1542) contains the first examples of the polyphonic ricercare of the 16th century. His organ ricercari, though related to the motet, differ from it in their extension of the individual sections by means of more numerous entries of the subject and more definite cadences between sections. The two canzonas from the same work mark the beginnings of an independent canzona literature for the keyboard. Reprints of Cavazzoni's works are found in L. Torchi, *L'arte musicale in Italia* (vol. III), Tagliapietra, *Antologia di musica* (vol. I), Davison and Apel, *Historical Anthology of Music,* and Schering, *Geschichte der Musik in Beispielen.* O. Mischiati ed. his organ works (two vols., Mainz, 1959 and 1961).—NS/LK/DM

Cavendish, Michael, English composer; b. c. 1565; d. London, July 5?, 1628. He was a member of the nobility. He publ. a vol. of 20 ayres for the lute or with three other voices, and eight madrigals (1598; ed. by E. Fellowes in The English School of Lutenist-songwriters, second series, VII, 1926, and in The English Madrigalists, rev. by T. Dart, XXXVI, 1961).—LK/DM

Cavos, Catterino, Italian-Russian composer; b. Venice, Oct. 30, 1775; d. St. Petersburg, May 10, 1840. He studied with Francesco Bianchi. His first work was a patriotic hymn for the Republican Guard, performed at the Teatro La Fenice (Sept. 13, 1797); he then produced a cantata, *L'Eroe* (1798). That same year he received an invitation to go to Russia as conductor at the Imperial Opera in St. Petersburg. He was already on his way to Russia when his ballet *Il sotterraneo* was presented in Venice (Nov. 16, 1799). He remained in St. Petersburg for the rest of his life. His Russian debut as a composer was in a collaborative opera, *Rusalka* (adapted from Das Donauweibchen by F. Kauer; Nov. 7, 1803). This was followed by the operas *The Invisible Prince* (May 17, 1805), *The Post of Love* (1806), *Ilya the Bogatyr* (Jan. 12, 1807), *3 Hunchback Brothers* (1808), *The Cossack Poet* (May 27, 1812), and several ballets. His most significant work was *Ivan Susanin,* which he conducted at the Imperial Theater on Oct. 30, 1815. The subject of this opera was used 20 years later by Glinka in his opera *A Life for the Czar;* the boldness of Cavos in selecting a libretto from Russian history provided the necessary stimulus for Glinka and other Russian composers. (Cavos conducted the premiere of Glinka's opera.) His subsequent operas were also based on Russian themes: *Dobrynia Nikitich* (1818) and *The Firebird* (1822). Cavos was a notable voice teacher, numbering among his pupils several Russian singers who later became famous.—NS/LK/DM

Cazden, Norman, American pianist, musicologist, and composer; b. N.Y., Sept. 23, 1914; d. Bangor, Maine, Aug. 18, 1980. He studied piano with Ernest Hutcheson and composition with Bernard Wagenaar at the Juilliard

Graduate School (teacher's diploma, 1932); then attended City Coll. in N.Y. (B.S., 1943); he later studied composition with Piston and Copland and took courses in musicology at Harvard Univ. (Ph.D., 1948, with the diss. *Musical Consonance and Dissonance*). From 1926 he was active as a pianist. He taught at the Univ. of Maine in Orono (1969–80). He wrote *A Book of Nonsense Songs* (N.Y., 1961), and, with H. Haufrecht and N. Studer, *Folk Songs of the Catskills* (Albany, 1982). His compositions reflect some interesting technical ideas in a general format of acceptable modernity.

WORKS: DRAMATIC: *The Lonely Ones,* ballet (1944); *Dingle Hill,* dramatic cantata (1958); incidental music to *The Merry Wives of Windsor* (1962) and *The Tempest* (1963). **ORCH.:** *6 Definitions* (1930–39); *Preamble* (1938); *On the Death of a Spanish Child* (1939); *3 Dances* (1940); *Stony Hollow* (1944); Sym. (1948); *3 Ballads* (1949); *Songs from the Catskills* for Band (1950); *Woodland Valley Sketches* (1960); *Adventure* (1963); Chamber Concerto for Clarinet and Strings (1965); Viola Concerto (1972). **CHAMBER:** String Quartet (1936); Concerto for 10 Instruments (1937); 3 chamber sonatas for Clarinet and Viola (1938); Quartet for Clarinet and String Trio (1939); String Quintet (1941); Horn Sonata (1941); Flute Sonata (1941); Suite for Violin and Piano (1943); Suite for 2 Trumpets, Horn, Baritone Horn, Trombone, and Tuba (1954); Quintet for Oboe and String Quartet (1960); *2 Elizabethan Suites* for 2 Trumpets, Horn, Trombone, and Tuba (1964) and for String Quartet (1965); Wind Quintet (1966); Piano Trio (1969); Bassoon Sonata (1971); English Horn Sonata (1974); Tuba Sonata (1974). **OTHER:** Choral works and folk-music arrangements.—NS/LK/DM

Cazzati, Maurizio, Italian organist and composer; b. Lucera, near Reggio Emilia, c. 1620; d. Mantua, 1677. He entered the priesthood and in 1641 served as organist and maestro di cappella at the church of S. Andrea in Mantua. After working at the court of the Duke of Sabioneta in Bozzolo (1647–48), he was maestro di cappella of the Accademia della Morte in Ferrara until 1653, and then at S. Maria Maggiore in Bergamo. By 1657 he was in Bologna, where he became maestro di cappella at S. Petronio. He instituted many reforms during his tenure and did much to advance the cause of instrumental liturgical music. He engaged in disputes with various musicians, most bitterly with Arresti. After being dismissed from his post in 1671, he returned to Mantua as maestro di cappella to the Duchess Anna Isabella Gonzaga. He wrote five operas and 11 oratorios. He publ. 66 vols. of music, including ten instrumental, 43 sacred vocal, and nine secular vocal collections.

BIBL.: U. Brett, *Music and Ideas in Seventeenth-Century Italy: The C.-Arresti Polemic* (N.Y. and London, 1989).—LK/DM

Cebotari (real name, **Cebutaru**), **Maria,** outstanding Moldavian soprano; b. Kishinev, Bessarabia, Feb. 23, 1910; d. Vienna, June 9, 1949. She sang in a church choir; from 1924 to 1929 she studied at the Kishinev Cons.; then went to Berlin, where she took voice lessons with Oskar Daniel at the Hochschule für Musik. In 1929 she sang with a Russian émigré opera troupe in Bucharest and in Paris. In 1931 she made an auspicious debut as Mimi at the Dresden State Opera, where she was a principal member until 1943; also appeared at the Salzburg Festival. In 1936 she joined the Berlin State Opera, singing with it until 1944; from 1946 she was a member of the Vienna State Opera. She also filled guest engagements in other European opera houses. She had a large repertoire which included the standard soprano roles, among them Violetta, Madama Butterfly, Pamina, and Manon; she also gave brilliant performances in modern operas; Richard Strauss greatly prized her abilities, entrusting to her the role of Aminta in the premiere of his *Die schweigsame Frau* (Dresden, June 24, 1935). Thanks to her cosmopolitan background, she sang the part of Tatiana in Russian in Tchaikovsky's opera *Eugene Onegin* and the part of Antonida in Glinka's *A Life for the Czar*. She also appeared in films. She was married to the Russian nobleman Count Alexander Virubov; after their divorce in 1938, she married the film actor Gustav Diessl.

BIBL.: A. Mingotti, *M. C., Das Leben einer Sängerin* (Salzburg, 1950).—NS/LK/DM

Ceccato, Aldo,
Italian conductor; b. Milan, Feb. 18, 1934. He studied at the Verdi Cons. in Milan (1948–55), with Albert Wolff and Willem van Otterloo in the Netherlands (1958), and at the Berlin Hochschule für Musik (1959–62). In 1960 he served as assistant to Celibidache at the Accademia Musicale Chigiana in Siena. In 1964 he won first prize in the RAI conducting competition. In 1969 he made his U.S. debut at the Chicago Lyric Opera and his first appearance at London's Covent Garden. He was music director of the Detroit Sym. Orch. (1973–77) and Generalmusikdirektor of the Hamburg State Phil. (1975–83), and then was music director of the Bergen Sym. Orch. (1985–89) and chief conductor of the Hannover Radio Orch. (1985–89). He subsequently was chief conductor of the Slovak Phil. in Bratislava (1990–91), the RAI Orch. in Turin (from 1990), and the Orquesta Nacional de España in Madrid (1991). From 1997 to 2000 he was chief conductor of the Brno Phil. His father-in-law was **Victor de Sabata**. —NS/LK/DM

Cecchino, Tomaso,
Italian composer; b. Verona, c. 1580; d. Hvar, Aug. 31, 1644. After serving as temporary maestro di cappella at Split Cathedral (1603–07; 1613–14), he was maestro di cappella at Hvar Cathedral from 1614 until his death. Many of his sacred and secular vocal pieces were esteemed and were widely disseminated during his lifetime.—LK/DM

Ceely, Robert (Paige),
American composer and teacher; b. Torrington, Conn., Jan. 17, 1930. He studied at the New England Cons. of Music (B.Mus., 1954), with Milhaud and Kirchner at Mills Coll. (M.A., 1955), with Sessions at the Berkshire Music Center at Tanglewood (1955), and with Sessions, Babbitt, and Cone (analysis) and Strunk (musicology) at Princeton Univ. (1957–59). He also attended the summer courses in new music in Darmstadt (1962, 1964), and seminars in electronic music and digital sound synthesis in the U.S. He taught at the U.S. Naval School of Music (1955–57), Robert Coll. in Istanbul (1961–63), the New England Cons. of Music (1967–97), where he also was founder-director of its

electronic music studio (1995–97), Emmanuel Coll. (1969–73), and Northeastern Univ. (1984–85). He publ. *Electronic Music Resource Book* (1983).

WORKS: DRAMATIC: *Kyros,* theatrical documentary for Viola, Optics, and Tape (1969); *Beyond the Ghost Spectrum,* ballet (1969); *Automobile Graveyard,* opera after Fernando Arrabal (Boston, Feb. 21, 1995). **CHAMBER:** String Trio (1953); Wind Quintet (1954); *Composition for 10 Instruments* (1963); *Logs* for 2 Double Basses (1968); *Slide Music* for Trombone Quartet (1974); *Rituals* for 40 Flutes (1978); *Bottom Dogs* for 4 Double Basses (1981); *Roundels* for Wind Ensemble and Tape (1981); *Totems* for Oboe and Tape (1982); *Dialogues* for Flute (1983); *Pitch Dark* for Jazz Ensemble (1985); *Synoecy* for Clarinet and Tape (1986); *Timeshares* for Percussion Ensemble (1989); *Post hoc, ergo propter hoc* for Bass Clarinet (1989); *Harlequin* for Double Bass and Tape (1990); *Hypallage* for Trumpet and Tape (1990); *Roundels, Book 4, La Valse Twist* for Wind Ensemble (1993); *Group Sax* for 5 Saxophonists (Boston, Feb. 6, 1996); *Music for Ten* for 10 Instruments (Cambridge, Mass., Feb. 10, 1996); *Auros* for Oboe, Clarinet, Piano, Violin, and Cello (Cambridge, Mass., March 29, 1997); *Wieman's treibt, so geht's* for Bass Clarinet and Tape (Boston, April 3, 1997); *Gymel* for 2 Oboes (Cambridge, Mass., May 16, 1998); *Triple Double* for Oboe, English Horn, Bassoon, and Tape (Brookline, Mass., May 10, 1999). **KEYBOARD: Piano:** *Piano Piece* (1980); *Minute Rag* (in honor of Gunther Schuller's 60th birthday; 1985); *Special K,* variations (1989); *Asyndeton* for Piano and Tape (1993). **TAPE:** *Stratti* (1963); *Elegia* (1964); *Vonce* (1967); *Mitsyn 1971* (1971); *La Fleur, les fleurs* (1975); *Infractions* for Tape (1985); *Enchanted Cycles* for Computer-generated Tape (Boston, May 2, 1996). **VOCAL:** *Flee, Floret, Florens* for 15 Solo Voices (1979).—NS/LK/DM

Celestin, Papa (actually, Oscar Phillip),
early jazz trumpeter, leader, singer; b. La Fourche Parish, Napoleonville, La., Jan. 1, 1884; d. New Orleans, La., Dec. 15, 1954. As a youth, he was nicknamed "Sonny"; as the years went by, his nickname matured to "Papa." Following early efforts on the guitar and mandolin, he worked for a few years as a cook on the Texas and Pacific Railroad. He settled in St. Charles, La., and began playing trombone and trumpet in the local brass band. He moved to New Orleans in 1906 and joined the Ind. Brass Band on cornet. Later he worked in Ailen's Brass Band and with Jack Carey, the Olympia Band, and other local bands, before leading his own band at Tuxedo Hall, New Orleans, from 1910 until the hall closed in 1913. He led his own band at Villa Cafe, then co-led a band with trumpeter and bassist Ricard Alexis, later billed as the Original Tuxedo Brass Band. In about 1917 he helped trombonist William Ridgely organize the Original Tuxedo Orch.; the two men co-led on and off until splitting up in 1925, then Celestin led his own Tuxedo Jazz Orch., which did several recording sessions in the late 1920s, played regularly in New Orleans, and also toured throughout the Gulf Coast states until the early 1930s. Celestin then left full- time music but continued to lead his own band in New Orleans, including a residency at the Pelican Roof in 1939. He worked in the local shipyards during World War II, until being seriously injured by a hit-and-run motorist in 1944. He began playing more regularly from 1946, recommenced recording in 1947. During the late 1940s he led at the Paddock, New Orleans, and also made

regular radio and TV appearances and occasional tours. In May 1953 he went to Washington to play for President Eisenhower; later that year the band appeared in the film *Cinerama Holiday*.

DISC.: *1950's Radio Broadcasts* (1950); *The Battle of the Bands* (1950); *Marie Laveau* (1950); *Papa's Golden Wedding* (1954). —JC/LP

Celibidache, Sergiu, transcendently endowed Romanian conductor; b. Roman, June 28, 1912. He studied at the Berlin Hochschule für Musik, where his teachers included Kurt Thomas, Heinz Thiessen, Fritz Stein, and Heinz Gmeindl; he also took courses in musicology with Schering and Schünemann at the Univ. of Berlin. In 1945 he was appointed conductor of the Berlin Phil. as successor to Furtwängler; he continued in that capacity until Furtwängler formally resumed his position in 1952. After engagements as a guest conductor throughout Europe, he was chief conductor of the Swedish Radio Sym. Orch. in Stockholm (1964–71), the Stuttgart Radio Sym. Orch. (1971–77), and the Orch. National de France in Paris (1973–75). In 1979 he became Generalmusikdirektor of the Munich Phil. He also went to the U.S., where he was engaged as conductor of the student orch. at the Curtis Inst. of Music in Philadelphia (1983–84). So remarkable was his progress with this student group that he was engaged to make a formal U.S. debut as a conductor with it at Carnegie Hall in N.Y. on Feb. 27, 1984, at which he astonished the audience and the critics with his mastery of a diversified program of works by Rossini, Wagner, Debussy, and Prokofiev. In 1989 he took the Munich Phil. on an 11-city tour of the U.S., winning extraordinary acclaim. A cosmopolitan existentialist, Celibidache lectured on musical phenomenology at the Univ. of Mainz; he also composed in his leisure time, producing four syms., a Piano Concerto, and a variety of minor pieces. In spite of his cult-like following, however, Celibidache's career remained a singular one. After leaving his Berlin post, his appointments and guest engagements were confined to orchs. of the second rank due to his exorbitant demand for unlimited rehearsal time. He also disdained commercial recordings so that his performances were preserved only with thanks to the radio stations which taped his concerts throughout his career. In 1988 he relented and allowed video discs to be made of several of his performances.

BIBL.: K. Weiler, *C.: Musiker und Philosoph* (Munich, 1993); K. Umbach, *C., der andere Maestro: Biogjraphische Reportagen* (Munich, 1995); V. Cosma, *S. C.: Concertul de adio: Schiţă biografică, repertoriu şi antologie de texte* (Bucharest, 1998). —NS/LK/DM

Celis, Frits, Belgian conductor and composer; b. Antwerp, April 11, 1929. He studied composition at the Royal Flemish Cons. in Antwerp and harp at the Brussels Cons.; also attended the summer conducting course at the Mozarteum in Salzburg (1949–51) and similar courses at the Hochschule für Musik in Cologne (1953–54). He then conducted at the Théâtre Royal de la Monnaie in Brussels (1954–59). In 1960 he was appointed to the faculty of the Royal Flemish Cons. of Antwerp.

WORKS: *Music* for Strings (1951); Violin Sonata (1951); String Trio (1958); *De Geestelijke bruiloft* for Voice, and Piano or Chamber Orch. (1958); Cello Sonata (1963); *Élégie* for Orch. (Antwerp, Dec. 8, 1967); *3 Symphonic Movements* (1969); *Toccata* for Oboe and Piano (1972); *Episodes* for Viola and Harpsichord (1973); *Variazioni* for Chamber Orch. (1974); Trio for Flute, Viola, and Harp (1977); 3 syms.: No. 1 (1979), No. 2 (1986), and No. 3, *Incanti* (1987); *Cantilena* for Orch. (1980); *Preludio e Narrazione* for Soprano and Orch. (1983); *Musica per Undici* for 10 Percussionists and Synthesizer (1984); Sonatina for Oboe, Clarinet, and Bassoon (1986); *Incantations* for Clarinet Choir (1987); *A Hypocritical Funeral March* for Brass Quartet (1987); Quartet for Flute, Violin, Viola, and Cello (1987); choruses; songs. —NS/LK/DM

Cellarius, Simon, German composer and clergyman; b. probably in Saxony, date unknown; d. Kohren, 1544. He was Kantor at St. Mary's in Zwickau in 1521–22, and then active as a Protestant clergyman. Cellarius was one of the finest early composers of Protestant church music. Among his extant works are motets, Psalms, and hymns.—LK/DM

Cellier, Alexandre (-Eugène), French organist, writer on music, and composer; b. Molières-sur-Cèse, Gard, June 17, 1883; d. Courbevoie, March 4, 1968. He was a pupil of Diemer (piano), Guilmant (organ), Leroux (harmony), and Widor (composition) in Paris. At 18, he was made organist at the Chapelle Milton. After serving as organist at the Temple de la Rédemption, he became organist at the Étoile in 1910. He publ. in Paris *L'orgue moderne* (1913), *Les Passions et l'Oratorio de noël de J.S. Bach* (1929), *L'orgue: Ses éléments, son histoire et son esthétique* (1933), and *Traité de la registration d'orgue* (1957). In addition to various organ pieces, he composed orch. works, chamber music, and piano pieces.—LK/DM

Cellier, Alfred, English conductor and composer; b. London, Dec. 1, 1844; d. there, Dec. 28, 1891. He was a chorister at London's Chapel Royal and a student of Thomas Helmore. After working as a church and concert organist, he went to Belfast in 1866 as conductor of the Phil. He had his first success as a composer with his operetta *Charity Begins at Home* (London, Feb. 7, 1872). Following a period as music director at London's Court Theatre, he held that position at Manchester's Prince's Theatre (1871–75), where he brought out his successful comic opera *The Sultan of Mocha* (Nov. 16, 1874). Returning to London, he composed for various theaters and in 1877 he became a conductor at the Opéra Comique. From 1878 he conducted Richard D'Oyley Carte's company in performances throughout England, the U.S., and Australia. His own success as a composer culminated in his comic opera *Dorothy* (London, Sept. 25, 1886), which scored the longest run on the 19th century British musical stage. Its song *Queen of My Heart* was the popular favorite for years.

WORKS: DRAMATIC (all 1st perf. in London unless otherwise given): *Charity Begins at Home*, operetta (Feb. 7, 1872); *Dora's Dream*, operetta (July 3, 1873); *Topsyturveydom* (March 21, 1874); *The Sultan of Mocha*, comic opera (Manchester, Nov. 16,

607

1874; rev. version, London, Sept. 21, 1887); *Tower of London*, comic opera (Manchester, Oct. 4, 1875; rev. as *Doris*, London, April 20, 1889); *Nell Gwynne*, opera (Manchester, Oct. 17, 1876; rev. as *Dorothy*, London, Sept. 25, 1886); *2 Foster Brothers*, operetta (March 12, 1877); *The Spectre Knight*, operetta (Feb. 9, 1878); *Belladonna, or The Little Beauty and the Great Beast*, opera (Manchester, April 27, 1878); *After All*, vaudeville (Dec. 23, 1878); *In the Sulks*, vaudeville (Feb. 21, 1880); *The Masque of Pandora* (Boston, Jan. 10, 1881); *Too Soon* (N.Y., Feb. 18, 1883); *The Carp* (Feb. 13, 1886); *Mrs. Jarramie's Genie*, operetta (Feb. 14, 1888; in collaboration with F. Cellier); *The Mountebanks*, comic opera (Jan. 4, 1892; completed by I. Caryll); incidental music. —NS/LK/DM

Cerha, Friedrich, notable Austrian composer, conductor, and pedagogue; b. Vienna, Feb. 17, 1926. He began violin lessons at the age of six and began to compose when he was nine. He studied composition with Uhl and violin with Prihoda at the Vienna Academy of Music (1946–51), and also pursued training in musicology and philosophy at the Univ. of Vienna (Ph.D., 1950). In 1956 he attended the summer courses in new music in Darmstadt, and in 1957 he held a Rome fellowship. With Kurt Schwertsik, he founded the new music ensemble "die reihe" in Vienna in 1958, and remained associated with it for over 40 years. In 1959 he became a lecturer at the Vienna Academy of Music, where he served as a prof. from 1976 to 1988. From 1960 he was active as a conductor, becoming particularly known for his programming of contemporary works. In 1970–71 he was in Berlin on a Deutscher Akademischer Austauschdienst fellowship. Cerha received the Prize of the City of Vienna in 1974 and was awarded the Great Austrian State Prize in 1986 for his contributions to music. In his large output, he has created scores notable for their innovative blending of traditional idioms and contemporary techniques. He also completed the third act of Berg's unfinished opera *Lulu* (1962–78), which was first given in its finished version in Paris on Feb. 24, 1979.

WORKS: DRAMATIC: *Spiegel*, theater piece (1960–61); *Netzwerk*, theater piece (1962–67, 1980; Vienna, May 31, 1981); *Baal*, opera after Brecht (1974–80; Salzburg, Aug. 7, 1981); *Der Rattenfänger*, theater piece after Zuckmayer (1984–86; Graz, Sept. 26, 1987). **ORCH.:** *Sinfonia in un Movimento* (1947–49; Innsbruck, June 3, 1959); Concerto for Strings (1947–50; Vienna, Dec. 5, 1993, composer conducting); *Triptychon* for Flute, Oboe, Clarinet, Horn, and Strings (1948–51; Vienna, Dec. 5, 1993); Piano Concerto (1951–54; Vienna, Oct. 16, 1998); *Relazioni fragili* for Harpsichord and Chamber Ensemble (1956–57; Vienna, May 16, 1960, composer conducting); *Espressioni fondamentali* (1957; Berlin, Nov. 17, 1960); *Mouvements I-III* for Chamber Orch. (1959; Berlin, Oct. 4, 1962, composer conducting); *Intersecazioni* for Violin and Orch. (1959–73; Graz, Oct. 16, 1973); *Fasce* (1959–74; Graz, Oct. 8, 1975); *Spiegel I-VII* for Orch. and Tape (1960–61; 1st complete perf., Graz, Oct. 9, 1972, composer conducting); *Phantasma 63* (Vienna, May 25, 1963, composer conducting); *Symphonien* for Winds and Timpani (1964; Baden-Baden, Nov. 27, 1970); *Catalogue des objets trouvés* for Chamber Orch. (1969; Vienna, March 16, 1970, composer conducting); *Langegger Nachtmusik I* (1969; Berlin, Oct. 1, 1970, composer conducting), *II* (Hamburg, April 20, 1970, composer conducting), and *III* (1990; Berlin, April 27, 1991, composer conducting); Sym. (1975; Royan, March 25, 1976, composer conducting);

Concerto for Violin, Cello, and Orch. (1975; Vienna, April 26, 1976, composer conducting); Double Concerto for Flute, Bassoon, and Orch. (1982; Graz, Oct. 7, 1983); *Monumentum für Karl Prantl* (1988; Salzburg, Aug. 12, 1989); *Phantasiestück in C.'s Manier* for Cello and Orch. (Vienna, Nov. 24, 1989, composer conducting; expanded as a Cello Concerto, 1996; Berlin, Sept. 11, 1998); *Impulse* (1992–93; Vienna, April 13, 1996); Viola Concerto (1993; Vienna, April 2, 1995, composer conducting); Concerto for Violin, Accordion, and Chamber Orch. (1994; Vienna, March 11, 1996, composer conducting); *Jahr lang ins Ugewisse hinab* (1995–96; Vienna, May 14, 1997, composer conducting). **CHAMBER:** *Arie und Fuge* for 8 Winds (1946–47; Vienna, Feb. 21, 1991); 3 violin sonatas: No. 1 (1947; Vienna, Feb. 24, 1951), No. 2 (1953; Innsbruck, May 30, 1956), and No. 3 (1954; Vienna, April 22, 1959); *Konzertante Tafelmusik* for Oboe, Clarinet, Bassoon, and Trumpet (1947–48; Vienna, April 26, 1957; rev. version as *Divertimento* for 8 Winds and Percussion, 1954; Vienna, April 30, 1955); Sonata for Violin and Guitar (1951; Vienna, Jan. 28, 1953); Viola Sonata (1951; Vienna, May 25, 1952); *Ricercar, Toccata und Passacaglia* for Flute, Viola d'Amore, and Lute (1951; Vienna, Feb. 2, 1956; also for Flute, Viola d'Amore, and Harpsichord, 1952); *Deux éclats en reflexion* for Violin and Piano (1956; Vienna, March 25, 1957); *Formation et solution* for Violin and Piano (1956–57; Darmstadt, Sept. 12, 1958); *Enjambements* for Chamber Ensemble (1959); *Curriculum* for 13 Winds (1971–72; N.Y., Feb. 18, 1973); 3 string quartets: No. 1 (1989; Salzburg, Feb. 1, 1991), No. 2 (1989–90; Evian, May 12, 1991), and No. 3 (1991–92; Vienna, May 3, 1992); *Quellen* for Chamber Ensemble (Klosterneuburg, Nov. 22, 1992); *Für K* for Chamber Ensemble (St. Pölten, Sept. 25, 1993); Saxophone Quartet (1995; Vienna, March 16, 1996); *Acht Sätze nach Hölderlin- Fragmenten* for String Sextet (1995; Cologne, Oct. 3, 1996); *Sechs Stücke* for Violin (1997; 1st complete perf., Vienna, March 24, 1998). **KEYBOARD: P i a n o :** *Klavierübung in barocken Formen für R. C.* (1954); *Slowakische Erinnerungen aus der Kindheit* (1956–89; Vienna, April 20, 1994); *Klavierstücke 58* (1958); *Elegie* (1963); *Adaxl-Suite* (1970, 1987); *Netzwerk- Fantasie* (1988; Vienna, Nov. 26, 1989). **VOCAL:** *Sechs Lieder* for Voice and Piano (1945–47; Vienna, May 1, 1949); *Ein Buch von der Minne* for Voice and Piano (1946–64); *Sonnengesang des heiligen Franz von Assisi* for Soloists, Chorus, and String Orch. (1948–52; Vienna, May 25, 1954); *Zehn Rubaijat des Omar Chajjam* for Chorus (1949–55; Vienna, Dec. 7, 1956); *An die Herrscher der Welt*, cantata for 3 Soloists and Chorus (1951; Vienna, Jan. 24, 1988); *Exercises* for Baritone, Speaker, and Instrumental Ensemble (1962–67; Vienna, March 26, 1968; rev. 1987); *Verzeichnis* for 16 Voices or Chorus (1969; Bremen, June 30, 1970); *Keintate I* (1980–81; Vienna, June 19,1983) and *II* (1983–85; Vienna, June 10, 1991) for Medium Voice and Instruments; *Baal- Gesänge* for Baritone and Orch. (1981; Hamburg, Jan. 22, 1982, composer conducting); *Nachtgesang* for Tenor and Orch. (1984; Stuttgart, April 18, 1986, composer conducting); *In memoriam Ernst Kein* for Medium Voice and Instruments (1985; Krems, June 18, 1996, composer conducting); *Eine Art Chansons* for Chansonnier, Percussion, Piano, and Double Bass (1985–87; St. Pölten, June 28, 1988); *"bevor es zu spät ist"* for Tenor and Orch. (1988–97); *Requiem für Rilke* for Tenor and Orch., after *Der Rattenfänger* (1989; Vienna, May 15, 1991; composer conducting); Requiem for Chorus and Orch. (1994; Stuttgart, Aug. 16, 1995); *Lichtenberg-Splitter* for Baritone and Instrumental Ensemble (1997; Vienna, Jan. 16, 1998, composer conducting); Song Cycle for Baritone and Orch. (1999; Las Palmas, Jan. 15, 2001). **OTHER:** Completion of Act III of Berg's opera *Lulu* (1962–78; Paris, Feb. 24, 1979).—NS/LK/DM

Cerone, Domenico Pietro, Italian tenor and music theorist; b. Bergamo, 1566; d. Naples, 1625. In 1592 he went to Spain and became a singer in the court choir. He later was appointed teacher of plainsong to the clergy of the church of the Annunciation at Naples. From 1610 until his death, he sang in the Royal Chapel Choir there. He publ. the manual *Regole per il canto fermo* (Naples, 1609) and *El Melopeo y Maestro, tractado de musica teorica y practica* (Naples, 1613). This treatise, written in Spanish and numbering 1,160 pages, contains a compendium of early music theory. Its pedantic exposition and inordinate length were the main target of Eximeno's satirical novel *Don Lazarillo Vizcardi*; Book XII is publ. in Eng. in O. Strunk's *Source Readings in Music History* (N.Y., 1950).

BIBL.: F. Pedrell, *P. Antonio Eximeno* (1920); G. Pannain, *L'oratorio dei Filippini* (1934).—NS/LK/DM

Cerquetti, Anita, Italian soprano; b. Montecosaro, near Macerata, April 13, 1931. After training in Perugia, she made her operatic debut in 1951 as Aida in Spoleto. She then sang in various Italian opera houses. In 1955 she made her U.S. debut at the Chicago Lyric Theatre. In 1958 she scored a major success when she substituted for Callas in the role of Norma at the Rome Opera, and that same year she made her first appearance at Milan's La Scala as Abigaille. Her promising career was cut short by a debilitating illness which compelled her to retire in 1961.

BIBL.: E. Trovato, *A. C.: Umiltà e fierezza* (Parma, 1996). —NS/LK/DM

Certon, Pierre, significant French composer; b. c. 1510; d. Paris, Feb. 22, 1572. He was made matins clerk at Notre Dame in Paris (1529), then clerk (1532) and master of the choristers (1536) at the Sainte-Chapelle. He was "compositeur de musique de la chapelle du Roy" from c. 1570 and also held a canonry at Notre Dame in Melun. For modern editions of his works, see F. Lesure and R. de Morcourt, eds., *Psaumes de P. C. réduits pour chant et luth par G. Morley* (Paris, 1957), A. Seay, ed., *P. C.: Zehn Chansons zu 4 Stimmen*, Das Chorwerk, LXXXII (1961), A. Agnel, ed., *Chansons de P. C., Cahiers de polyphonie* (Paris, 1965), H. Expert and A. Agnel, eds., *P. C.: Chansons polyphoniques publiées par P. Attaingnant*, Maîtres Anciens de la Musique Française, I-III (Paris, 1967–68).

WORKS: MASSES: *Missae tres...* for 4 Voices (Paris, 1558); others in contemporary collections. **MOTETS:** *Recens modulorum editio...24 motettorum, liber secundus* (Paris, 1542); others in contemporary collections. **PSALMS, CHANSONS, AND SPIRITUELLES** *Trente et un pseaumes* for 4 Voices (Paris, 1546); *Premiere livre de* [13] *psalmes...reduitz en tabulature de leut par Maistre G. Morlaye* (Paris, 1554); *Cinquante pseaulmes de David* for 4 Voices (Paris, 1555); *Les Meslanges: 15 chansons spirituelles* for 4, 5, and 6 Voices (Paris, 1570). **CHANSONS** *Premier livre de* [16] *chansons* for 4 Voices (Paris, 1552); *Les Meslanges: 84 chansons* (Paris, 1570); others in contemporary collections.

BIBL.: S. Van Solkema, *The Liturgical Music of P. C.* (diss., Univ. of Mich., 1962).—NS/LK/DM

Červený, Wenzel Franz (Václav František), Bohemian inventor of brass instruments; b. Dubeč, Sept. 27, 1819; d. Königgrätz, Jan. 19, 1896. He was a good performer on most brass instruments when he was only 12 years old. He learned his trade with Bauer, a musical instrument maker in Prague, and worked at various times in Brünn, Bratislava, Vienna, and Budapest. In 1842 he established his own shop at Königgrätz. He invented the following instruments: Cornon (1844), Contrabass (1845), Phonikon (1848), Baroxiton (1853), Contrafagotto in metal (1856), Althorn obbligato (1859), Turnerhorn, Jägerhorn, army trombones (1867), and Primhorn (1873). After the success of the Primhorn, he created the complete Waldhorn quartet, which he considered his greatest achievement. Then followed the Subcontrabass and the Subcontrafagotto, and finally an entire family of improved cornets ("Kaiserkornette") and the "Triumph" cornet. His "roller" cylinder- mechanism is an invention of the greatest importance. He also improved the Euphonion, the Russian Signal-horns, the Screw-drum, and the church kettledrum. His instruments took 1st prizes at exhibitions in Europe and America.—NS/LK/DM

Cervetti, Sergio, Uruguayan-born American composer and teacher; b. Dolores, Nov. 9, 1940. He received training in piano from José Maria Martino Rodas in Mercedes and from Hugo Balzo in Montevideo, and in composition from Carlos Estrada at the National Cons. in Montevideo and from Guido Santórsola. From 1962 to 1967 he pursued studies at the Peabody Cons. of Music in Baltimore, where he had further training in composition from Stefans Grové and Ernst Krenek. In 1969–70 he was composer-in-residence at the Deutscher Akademischer Austauschdienst in West Berlin. With the dancer Kenneth Rinker, he co-founded the Berlin Dance Ensemble, with whom he collaborated in various dance scores in subsequent years. In 1970 he went to N.Y. and worked in electronic music with Davidovsky and Ussachevsky at Columbia Univ., and also taught at Brooklyn Coll. From 1972 to 1997 he was a prof. at the Tisch School of the Arts at N.Y.U., where he taught advanced courses in electronic and 20th century music. In 1979 he became a naturalized American citizen. In his early works, Cervetti employed serial and expressionist styles. Around 1970 he became more adventuresome and turned to aleatory and electronics with minimalist and nationalistic excursions. His *Inez de Castro*, which was premiered by Ballet Hispanico in N.Y. in Oct. 1988, was chosen to open the U.S. Pavilion at the Seville World's Fair in 1992. This remarkable score has subsequently been performed all over the globe.

WORKS: ORCH.: *Orbitas* (1967); *Plexus* for Small Orch. (1971); *Trumpet Concerto* (1977); *Las Indias Olvidadas*, concerto for Harpsichord and 11 Instruments (1990; Alicante, Sept. 27, 1992); *Piano Concerto* (1994). **CHAMBER:** *String Trio* (1963); *Cinco Episodios*, piano trio (1966); *Zinctum* for String Quartet (1968); *...de la tierra...* for Ensemble (1972); *El Rio de los Pajaros Pintados* for Bandoneon and Tape (1978); *Music for Rachel* for Ensemble (1979); *3rd String Quartet* (1990). **KEYBOARD: Piano:** 2 sonatas (1964, 1989); *Estudios Australes* (1989). **Harpsichord:** *Candombe* (1984); *Llanto y Muerte* (1988); *Alberada y Hard Rock* (1993). **VOCAL:** *El Carro de Heno* for

Chorus and Orch. (1967); *Cantata Duraciones* (1967); *Lux Lucet in Tenebris* for Chorus (1970); *4 Fragments of Pablo Neruda* for Soprano, Oboe, Guitar, Cello, and Percussion (1970); *Madrigal III* (1975) and *IV* (1985); *4 Fragments of Isadora*, song cycle for Soprano and Piano (1979); *7 Songs of Orfila Bardesio* for Voice and Piano (1989); *Leyenda* for Soprano and Orch. (1991); *El Triunfo de la Muerte*, song cycle for Voice and Piano (1993); *No Longer Very Clear*, aria for Soprano, String Quartet, and Harpsichord (WNYC-FM, N.Y., June 13, 1994). ELECTROACOUSTIC: *Wind Devil* (1983); *Manhattan* (1984); *Enclosed Time* (1985); *Night Trippers* (1986); *Transatlantic Light* (1987); *The Hay Wain* (1987); *Inez de Castro* (N.Y., Oct. 1988). OTHER: *Cocktail Party* for Amplified Instruments, Piano obbligato, and a "variable number of guests" (1970).—NS/LK/DM

Cesti, Antonio (baptismal name, **Pietro**), renowned Italian composer, uncle of **Remigo Cesti;** b. Arezzo (baptized), Aug. 5, 1623; d. Florence, Oct. 14, 1669. Although earlier reference works give his name as Marc' Antonio Cesti, this rendering is incorrect; he adopted the name Antonio when he joined the Franciscan order. He was a choirboy in Arezzo before joining the Franciscan order in Volterra in 1637; he served his novitiate at S. Croce in Florence and then was assigned to the Arezzo monastery. He is reported to have received his musical training from Abbatini in Rome and Città di Castello (1637–40) and from Carissimi in Rome (1640–45). While in Volterra, he was accorded the patronage of the Medici family. His first opera, *Orontea* (Venice, Jan. 20, 1649), was highly successful. He was active at the court of Archduke Ferdinand Karl in Innsbruck from 1652 to 1657, then was a tenor in the Papal Choir in Rome (1659–60). After being released from his vows, he quit the Papal Choir with the intention of returning to his court duties in Innsbruck. In spite of a threat of excommunication, he went to Innsbruck in 1661. Thanks to the intervention of the court, he was eventually released from his post in the Papal Choir and remained in Innsbruck until the death of the Archduke in 1665 led to the removal of its musical entourage to Vienna in 1666. He was made "Capelan d'honore und intendenta delle musiche theatrali" at the Vienna court in 1666, and in 1668 returned to Italy and served as maestro di cappella at the Tuscan court in Florence during the last year of his life. Cesti was one of the most important composers of secular vocal music of his time. See D. Burrows, ed., *A. C.: The Italian Cantata,* I, Wellesley Edition, V (1963).

WORKS: DRAMATIC: Opera: *Orontea* (Venice, Jan. 20, 1649); *Alessandro vincitor di se stesso* (Venice, 1651); *Il Cesare amante* (Venice, 1651); *La Cleopatra* (Innsbruck, 1654); *L'Argia* (Innsbruck, 1655); *La Dori* (Innsbruck, 1657); *La magnanimità d'Alessandro* (Innsbruck, 1662); *Il Tito* (Venice, Feb. 13, 1666); *Nettunno e Flora festeggianti* (Vienna, July 12, 1666); *Le disgrazie d'Amore* (Vienna, Feb. 19, 1667); *La Semirami* (Vienna, July 9, 1667); *Il pomo d'oro* (Vienna, July 13–14, 1668); also several doubtful works. OTHER: Over 60 secular cantatas; some sacred vocal music.

BIBL.: C. Schmidt, *The Operas of A. C.* (diss., Harvard Univ., 1973).—LK/DM

Cesti, Remigio, Italian composer, nephew of **Antonio Cesti;** b. Arezzo, c. 1635; d. Florence, c. 1713. He

became a member of the Dominican order in 1649. After serving as organist to the Knights of St. Stephen in Pisa (1663), he was maestro di cappella in Pisa, Volterra, Arezzo, and Faenza. From 1671 he held ecclesiastical posts in Arezzo and Siena. Among his extant works are the opera *Il principe generoso* (Vienna, 1665) and sacred pieces.—NS/LK/DM

Chabrier, (Alexis-) Emmanuel, famous French composer; b. Ambert, Puy de Dôme, Jan. 18, 1841; d. Paris, Sept. 13, 1894. He studied law in Paris (1858–61), and also studied composition with Semet and Hignard, piano with Edouard Wolff, and violin with Hammer. He served in the government from 1861, at the same time cultivating his musical tastes; with Duparc, d'Indy, and others he formed a private group of music lovers, and was an enthusiastic admirer of Wagner. He began to compose in earnest, and produced two light operas: *L'Étoile* (Paris, Nov. 28, 1877) and *Une Éducation manquée* (Paris, May 1, 1879). In 1879 he went to Germany with Duparc to hear Wagner's operas. Returning to Paris, he publ. some piano pieces; then traveled to Spain; the fruit of this journey was his most famous work, the rhapsody *España* (Paris, Nov. 4, 1883), which produced a sensation when performed by Lamoureux in 1884. Another work of Spanish inspiration was the *Habanera* for Piano (1885). In the meantime he served as chorus master for Lamoureux; this experience developed his knowledge of vocal writing; he wrote a brief cantata for mezzo-soprano and women's chorus, *La Sulamite* (March 15, 1885), and his operas *Gwendoline* (Brussels, April 10, 1886), *Le Roi malgré lui* (Opéra-Comique, Paris, May 18, 1887), and *Briseis* (concert perf., Paris, Jan. 31, 1897; stage perf., Royal Opera, Berlin, Jan. 14, 1899). In his operas Chabrier attempted a grand style; his idiom oscillated between passionate Wagnerianism and a more conventional type of French stage music; although these operas enjoyed a succès d'estime, they never became popular, and Chabrier's place in music history is secured exclusively by his *España*, and other piano pieces such as *Bourrée fantasque* (1891; orchestrated by Felix Mottl). His *Joyeuse Marche* for Orch. (orig. entitled *Marche française*, 1888) is also popular. Other works are *Ode à la musique* for Voices and Orch. (1890), *10 pièces pittoresques* for Piano (1880; four of them orchestrated and perf. as *Suite pastorale*), *3 valses romantiques* for two Pianos (1883), and songs.

BIBL.: R. Martineau, *E. C.* (Paris, 1911); G. Servières, *E. C.* (Paris, 1912); J. Desaymard, *C. d'après ses lettres* (Paris, 1934); F. Poulenc, *E. C.* (Paris, 1961); R. Myers, *E. C. and His Circle* (London, 1969); F. Robert, *E. C.: L'Homme et son oeuvre* (Paris, 1970); R. Delage, *C.* (Geneva, 1982).—NS/LK/DM

Chadabe, Joel, American composer; b. N.Y., Dec. 12, 1938. He studied with Will Mason at the Univ. of N.C. at Chapel Hill (B.A., 1959) and Carter at Yale Univ. (M.M., 1962), then taught at the State Univ. of N.Y. at Albany (from 1965), served as consultant to Bennington (Vt.) Coll. (from 1971), and was president of Intelligent Computer Music Systems, Inc. (from 1986). In 1964 he held a Ford Foundation fellowship, later receiving grants, commissions, or awards from the NEA (1976, 1985, 1988), Rockefeller Foundation (1977), N.Y. Foundation for the Arts (1985), and the Fulbright Commission (travel grant, 1988). From 1978 to 1987 he was president of Composer's Forum, Inc. In 1994, with Paul Lansky and Neil Rolnick, he founded the Electronic Music Foundation in Albany, N.Y. His articles on electronic music have appeared in various journals, including *Computer Music Journal* and *Contemporary Music Review*. He publ. the book *Electric Sound: The Past and Promise of Electronic Music* (Upper Saddle River, N.J., 1997). His compositions make use of a variety of electronic and computer technologies.

WORKS: *Prelude to Naples* for 4 Instruments (1965); *Street Scene* for English Horn, Tape, and Projections (1967); *Ideas of Movement at Bolton Landing* for Electronic Sounds on Tape (1971); *Shadows and Lines* for Electronic Sounds on Tape (1972); *Flowers* for Stringed Instrument and Electronic Sounds on Tape (1975); *Settings for Spirituals* for Singer and Computer-generated Accompaniment (1977); *Solo for Computer/Synthesizer* (1978; rev. 1981); *Scenes from Stevens* for Computer/Synthesizer System (1979); *Rhythms* for Computer/Synthesizer System and Percussion (1980); *Variation* for Piano (1983); *Follow Me Softly* for Computer/Synthesizer System and Percussion (1984); *The Long Ago and Far Away Tango* for Piano (1984); *Bar Music* for Computer/Synthesizer (1985); *Several Views of an Elusive Lady* for Soprano and Electronic Sounds on Tape (1985); *Many Mornings Many Moods* for Percussion, Electronics, and Orch. (1988); *After Some Songs* for Computer/Synthesizer and Solo Instruments (1994).—NS/LK/DM

Chad and Jeremy,

folky English duo that rode the British invasion to hitsville. **MEMBERSHIP:** Chad Stuart, voc., gtr. (b. Durham, England, Dec. 10, 1943); Jeremy Clyde, voc., gtr. (b. Buckinghamshire, England, March 22, 1944). Chad Stuart and Jeremy Clyde met while studying at London's Central School of Speech and Drama. They had a mutual interest in folk music and started playing together just as the Beatles were scoring their first hits. Never a huge act, Chad and Jeremy had only one hit in England. However, they managed to ride the coattails of Beatlemania to score seven Top 40 American singles, making the Mersey sound even safer for mainstream pop ears. Following on the heels of the Nov. 21, 1964 debut "Yesterday's Gone," their career peaked later that year with the #7 "Summer Song," still a fixture on oldies radio, especially during the hot months. With its acoustic guitars and subdued two-part harmony, it appealed strongly to middle-of-the-road pop fans.

During 1964–66, Chad and Jeremy appeared on American TV regularly, guesting on shows ranging from the music show *Hullabaloo* to the campy 1960s TV series *Batman*. As they recorded more, their music became more ambitious, like the concept albums *Of Cabbages and Kings* and *The Ark*. These albums sold poorly, however, and failed to produce hits, so they broke up to pursue other interests in 1967.

Clyde became an actor noted for his appearances on the British stage and the 1960s TV show *Rowan and Martin's Laugh-In*. Stuart started writing musicals, worked as a producer for A&M Records, was the musical director for the *Smothers Brothers* TV show, and did some acting as well. During the mid-1980s, they were reunited when they happened to star together in a

London run of the play *Pump Boys and Dinettes*. They recorded a comeback album and hit the oldies circuit, where they still pop up from time to time.

DISC.: *British Folk Artist Concert* (live; 1964); *Yesterday's Gone* (1964); *Before & After* (1965); *Chad & Jeremy Sing for You* (1965); *I Don't Want to Lose You Baby* (1965); *Distant Shores* (1966); *More* (1966); *Of Cabbages & Kings* (1967); *The Ark* (1968); *Three in the Attic* (1969); *Chad Stuart & Jeremy Clyde* (1983).—HB

Chadwick, George Whitefield,

eminent American composer and teacher; b. Lowell, Mass. Nov. 13, 1854; d. Boston, April 4, 1931. He began musical training with his brother. From the time he was 15, he was active as an organist, and in 1872 he became a Congregational church organist. He also pursued organ training with Dudley Buck and Eugene Thayer at the New England Cons. of Music in Boston. After serving as a prof. of music at Olivet Coll. in Mich. (1876–77), he went to Leipzig to study privately with Jadassohn, and then entered the Cons. there in 1878. His *Rip Van Winkle* overture and his Second String Quartet were selected as the finest works at the annual Cons. concerts in 1879. He then pursued training with Rheinberger at the Munich Hochschule für Musik (1879–80). Upon his return to Boston in 1880, he devoted himself mainly to composing and teaching. He also was active as an organist, as a pianist (prinicipally in programs of his own works), and as a symphonic and choral conductor. He served as director and conductor of the Springfield (1890–99) and Worcester (1897–1901) festivals. In 1882 he became a teacher at the New England Cons. of Music. In 1897 he became its director, and proceeded to make it one of the most distinguished conservatories in the U.S. Many noted American composers were Chadwick's pupils. In 1898 he was elected a member of the National Inst. of Arts and Letters, and in 1909 of the American Academy of Arts and Letters, which awarded him its gold medal in 1928. Chadwick was one of the leading American composers of his day. While he is usually regarded as a pillar of the "Boston Classicists," his most important works actually reveal attempts to find a new American style, albeit one reflecting the tenets of late Romanticism. Among his most important works were the verismo opera *The Padrone* (1912–13), the Second Sym. (1883–85), the *Symphonic Sketches* (1895–1904), the symphonic ballad *Tom O'Shanter* (1914–15), the Fourth String Quartet (1896), and various songs.

WORKS: DRAMATIC: *The Peer and the Pauper*, comic operetta (1884); *A Quiet Lodging*, operetta (Boston, April 1, 1892); *Tabasco*, burlesque opera (1893–94; Boston, Jan. 29, 1894); *Judith*, lyric drama (1899–1900; Worcester Festival, Sept. 23, 1901); *Everywoman: Her Pilgrimage in Quest of Love*, incidental music (1910; Hartford, Conn., Feb. 9, 1911); *The Padrone*, opera (1912–13; concert perf., Thomaston, Conn., Sept. 29, 1995); *Love's Sacrifice*, pastoral opera (1916–17; Chicago, Feb. 1, 1923). **ORCH.:** *Rip Van Winkle*, overture (Leipzig, March 18, 1879; rev. 1920s); *Schön München*, waltz (1880; Boston, Jan. 7, 1881); 3 syms.: No. 1 (1881; Boston, Feb. 23, 1882). No. 2 (1883–85; 1st complete perf., Boston, Dec. 10, 1886), and No. 3 (1893–94; Boston, Oct. 19, 1894); *Andante* for Strings (Boston, April 13, 1892); *Thalia: Overture to an Imaginary Comedy* (1882; Boston, Jan. 12, 1883); *Melpomene: Overture to an Imaginary Tragedy* (Boston, Dec. 23, 1887); *A Pastoral Prelude* (1890; Boston, Jan. 30, 1892);

Serenade (1890); *Tabasco March* for Band or Orch. (Boston, Jan. 29, 1894); *Symphonic Sketches* (1895–1904; Boston, Feb. 7, 1908); *Adonais*, overture (1899; Boston, Feb. 2, 1900); *Euterpe*, overture (1903; Boston, April 22, 1904); *Cleopatra*, symphonic poem (1904; Worcester Festival, Sept. 29, 1905); Sinfonietta (Boston, Nov. 21, 1904); *Suite symphonique* (1905–09; Philadelphia, March 29, 1911); *Theme, Variations, and Fugue* for Organ and Orch. (Boston, Nov. 13, 1908); *Everywoman Waltz* (1909); *Aphrodite*, symphonic fantasy (1910–11; Norfolk Festival, June 4, 1912); *Tam O'Shanter*, symphonic ballad (1914–15; Norfolk Festival, June 3, 1915); *Angel of Death*, symphonic poem (1917–18; N.Y., Feb. 9, 1919); *Jericho March* (c. 1919); *Elegy: In Memoriam Horatio Parker* (1920); *Anniversary Overture* (Norfolk Festival, June 7, 1922); *Tre pezzi* (1923). **CHAMBER:** 5 string quartets: No. 1 (Leipzig, May 29, 1878), No. 2 (1878; Leipzig, May 30, 1879), No. 3 (c. 1885; Boston, March 9, 1887), No. 4 (Boston, Dec. 21, 1896), and No. 5 (1898; Boston, Feb. 12, 1901); Piano Quintet (1887; Boston, Jan. 23, 1888); *Romanze* for Cello and Piano (1911); *Easter Morn* for Violin or Cello and Piano (c. 1914); *Fanfare* for 3 Trumpets, 3 Trombones, and Timpani (Boston, Nov. 3, 1925); piano pieces; organ music. **VOCAL: C h o r u s a n d O r c h.:** *The Viking's Last Voyage* (Boston, April 22, 1881); *Dedication Ode* (1883); *Lovely Rosabelle*, ballad (Boston, Dec. 10, 1899); *The Pilgrims* (1890; Boston, April 2, 1891); *Phoenix expirans*, cantata (1891; Springfield Festival, May 5, 1892); *Ode* for the Opening of the World's Columbian Exposition (Chicago, Oct. 21, 1892); *The Lily Nymph*, dramatic cantata (1894–95; N.Y., Dec. 7, 1895); *Ecce jam noctis* (New Haven, Conn., June 30, 1897); *Noel* (1907–08; Norfolk Festival, June 2, 1909); *Land of Our Hearts* (1917; Norfolk Festival, June 4, 1918); *Fathers of the Free* (c. 1927); *Commemoration Ode* (c. 1928); many other accompanied and unaccompanied choral works, both sacred and secular. **S o l o V o i c e a n d O r c h.:** *The Miller's Daughter* for Baritone and Orch. (1886; San Francisco, May 18, 1887); *Lochinar* for Baritone and Orch. (Springfield Festival, May 7, 1896); *Aghadoe* for Alto and Orch. (1910). Also many solo songs with piano or organ accompaniment. **WRITINGS:** *Harmony: A Course of Study* (Boston, 1897; many subsequent eds.); *Key to the Textbook on Harmony* (Boston, 1902). **BIBL.:** V. Yellin, *The Life and Operatic Works of G.W. C.* (diss., Harvard Univ., 1957); idem, *C.: Yankee Composer* (Washington, D.C., and London, 1990); B. Faucett, *G.W. C: His Symphonic Works* (Lanham, Md., 1996); idem, *G.W. C.: A Bio-Bibliography* (Westport, Conn., 1998).—**NS/LK/DM**

Chailley, Jacques, eminent French musicologist and composer; b. Paris, March 24, 1910; d. Montpellier, Jan. 21, 1999. He studied composition with Boulanger, Delvincourt, and Busser, musicology with Pirro, Rokseth, and Smijers, and conducting with Mengelberg and Monteux; he also took courses in medieval French literature at the Sorbonne in Paris (1932–36; Ph.D., 1952, with two dissertations: *L'École musicale de Saint-Martial de Limoges jusqu'à la fin du XIᵉsiècle* [publ. in Paris, 1960] and *Chansons de Gautier du Coinci* [publ. as *Les Chansons à la Vierge de Gautier de Coinci* in *Monuments de la musique ancienne*, XV, 1959]). He was general secretary (1937–47), vice-principal (1947–51), and prof. of the choral class (1951–53) at the Paris Cons.; from 1952 to 1979 he was director of the Inst. of Musicology at the Univ. of Paris; also taught at the Paris Lycée La Fontaine (1951–69); from 1962 to 1981 he was director of the Schola Cantorum. He wrote authoritatively on many subjects,

including medieval music, the music of ancient Greece, music history, and the music of Bach, Mozart, Wagner, and others.

WORKS: DRAMATIC: *Les perses*, incidental music for Ondes Martenot and Percussion, after Aeschylus (1936); *Pan et la Syrinx*, opera (1946); *Thyl de Flandre*, opera (1949–53; Brussels, Oct. 1, 1957); *La Dame à la licorne*, ballet (1953). **ORCH.:** 2 syms.: No. 1 (1942–45; 1ˢᵗ complete perf., Toulouse, March 4, 1948) and No. 2 (1980–84). **CHAMBER:** String Quartet (1936); Viola Sonata (1939–41); *Chant funèbre* for Cello and Piano (1945); *Suite sans prétention pour Monsieur de Molière* for 3 Ondes Martenot and Wind Quintet (1955); *Prélude et allegro* for Viola and Cello (1976). **KEYBOARD: P i a n o :** *Sonata breve* (1960). **VOCAL:** *Cantique de soleil* for Contralto, Ondes Martenot, and Orch. (1934); *Symphonies mariales*, oratorio (1965); *Messe française* for 2 Soloists and Congregational Men's Chorus (1976); *Casa Dei*, oratorio (1991).

WRITINGS (all publ. in Paris unless otherwise given): *Petite Histoire de la chanson populaire française* (1942); with H. Challan, *Théorie complète de la musique* (1949); *Histoire musicale du Moyen Âge* (1950; 3ʳᵈ ed., 1984); *Les Notations musicales nouvelles* (1950); *La Musique médiévale* (1951); *Traité historique d'analyse musicale* (1951; 2ⁿᵈ ed., 1977, as *Traité historique harmonique*); *Formation et transformations du langage musical* (1954); *Chronologie musicale: I, années 300 à 1599* (1955); ed. *Précis de musicologie* (1958; 2ⁿᵈ ed., rev., 1984); *L'Imbroglio des modes* (1960); *40,000 ans de musique: L'Homme à la découverte de sa musique* (1961; Eng. tr., 1964, as *40,000 Years of Music: Man in Search of Music*); *Les Passions de J.S. Bach* (1963; 2ⁿᵈ ed., rev., 1984); *Tristan et Isolde de Wagner* (1963; 2ⁿᵈ ed., 1972); *Alia musica* (1965); *Expliquer l'harmonie?* (Lausanne, 1967); *La Musique et le signe* (Lausanne, 1967); "*La Flûte enchantée,*" *opéra maçonnique: Essai d'explication du livret et de la musique* (1968; 2ⁿᵈ ed., aug., 1983; Eng. tr., 1971, as *The Magic Flute, Masonic Opera*); "*L'Art de la fugue*" *de J.S. Bach. Étude critique des sources* (I, 1971, II, 1972); *Le "Carnaval" de Schumann* (1971); *Cours d'histoire de la musique* (4 vols., 1972–90); *Les Chorals d'orgue de Bach* (1974); *La Musique* (Tours, 1975); *Le Voyage d'hiver de Schubert* (1975); *Solfège-déchiffrage pour les jeunes pianistes* (1975); *Traité d'harmonie au clavier* (1977); *Parsifal de R. Wagner, opéra initiatique* (1979); *La Musique grecque antique* (1979); *De la musique à la musicologie...a l'occasion de son 70ᵉ anniversaire* (1980); *Eléments de philologie musicale* (2 vols., 1985); with J. Viret, *Le Symbolisme de la gamme* (1988); *Propos sans orthodoxie* (1989); *La musique et son langage* (1996).—**NS/LK/DM**

Chailly, Luciano, prominent Italian music administrator, teacher, and composer, father of **Riccardo Chailly;** b. Ferrara, Jan. 19, 1920. He studied violin in Ferrara (diploma, 1941) and pursued academic training at the Univ. of Bologna (B.A., 1943). After composition studies with R. Bossi at the Milan Cons. (diploma, 1945), he studied with Hindemith in Salzburg (1948). He was director of music programming for the RAI (1950–67), and artistic director of Milan's La Scala (1968–71), Turin's Teatro Regio (1972), Milan's Angelicum (1973–75), and Verona's Arena (1975–76). He was again associated with La Scala (from 1977) and was artistic director of the Genoa Opera (1983–85); he also taught at the Milan Cons. (1968–83). In 1989–90 he was artistic director of the RAI orch. and choir in Turin. His music is composed in a communicative neo-Classical idiom, with some dodecaphonic incrustations and electronic effects.

WORKS: DRAMATIC: O p e r a : *Ferrovia soprelevata* (Bergamo, Oct. 1, 1955); *Una domanda di matrimonio* (Milan, May 22, 1957); *Il canto del cigno* (Bologna, Nov. 16, 1957); *La riva delle Sirti* (Monte Carlo, March 1, 1959); *Procedura penale* (Como, Sept. 30, 1959); *Il mantello* (Florence, May 11, 1960); *Era proibito* (Milan, March 5, 1963); *L'Idiota* (1966–67; Rome, Feb. 14, 1970); *Vassiliev* (Genoa, March 16, 1967); *Markheim* (Spoleto, July 14, 1967); *Sogno (ma forse no)* (Trieste, Jan. 28, 1975); *Il libro dei reclami* (Vienna, May 29, 1975); *La Cantatrice calva* (Vienna, Nov. 5, 1985). **B a l l e t :** *Fantasmi al Grand-Hotel* (Milan, 1960); *Il cappio* (Naples, 1962); *L'urlo* (Palermo, 1967); *Shee* (Melbourne, 1967); *Anna Frank* (Verona, 1981); *Es-Ballet* (1983). **INSTRU-MENTAL:** *Toccata* for Orch. (1948); *12 Sonate tritematiche* (for various instrumentations; 1951–61); *Sequenze dell'artide* for Orch. (1961); *Piccole serenate* for Strings (1967); *Contrappunti a quattro dimensioni* for Orch. (1973); *Newton- Variazioni* for Chamber Orch. (1979); *Es-Konzert* for Orch. (1980); *Psicosi* for Instruments and Percussion (1980); *Es-Kammerkonzert* for Small Instrumental Group (1983); chamber works; piano pieces. **OTHER:** Choral works; songs; music for television.

BIBL.: R. Cresti, *Linguaggio musicale di L. C.* (Milan, 1993). **—NS/LK/DM**

Chailly, Riccardo,

noted Italian conductor, son of **Luciano Chailly;** b. Milan, Feb. 20, 1953. He studied composition with his father, and then with Bruno Bettinelli at the Milan Cons.; he also studied conducting with Piero Guarino in Perugia, Franco Caracciolo in Milan, and Franco Ferrara in Siena. He was asst. conductor of the sym. concerts at Milan's La Scala (1972–74); his international career began with his U.S. debut at the Chicago Lyric Opera conducting *Madama Butterfly* (1974); he subsequently was a guest conductor at the San Francisco Opera, Milan's La Scala, London's Covent Garden, and the Vienna State Opera. He made his Metropolitan Opera debut in N.Y. with *Les Contes d'Hoffmann* on March 8, 1982. From 1982 to 1989 he was chief conductor of the (West) Berlin Radio Sym. Orch., which he led on its first tour of North America in 1985; he also was principal guest conductor of the London Phil. (1982–85) and artistic director of the Teatro Comunale in Bologna (1986–89). In 1988 he became chief conductor of the Concertgebouw Orch. of Amsterdam, which was renamed the Royal Concertgebouw Orch. that same year by Queen Beatrix in honor of its 100th anniversary. Chailly is one of the leading conductors of his generation, and has won praise for his performances in both the opera pit and the concert hall.**—NS/LK/DM**

Chalabala, Zdeněk,

noted Czech conductor; b. Uherské Hradiště, April 18, 1899; d. Prague, March 4, 1962. He studied composition with Novák in Prague, then took courses in violin, conducting, and composition at the Brno Cons., where his principal teachers were Janáček and Neumann. He was conductor of the Slovak Phil. in Brno (1924–25), the National Theater in Brno (1925–29), where he served as music director (1929–36), and the Prague National l Theater (1936–45), and chief conductor of the Ostrava Opera (1945–49), the Brno National Theater (1949–52), and the Slovak National Theater in Bratislava (1952–53). In 1953 he returned to the Prague National Theater as chief conductor, a post he held with distinction until his death.**—NS/LK/DM**

Chaliapin, Feodor (Ivanovich),

celebrated Russian bass; b. near Kazan, Feb. 13, 1873; d. Paris, April 12, 1938. He was born into a poverty- ridden peasant family, and thus was compelled to work in menial jobs from an early age and had little opportunity for formal schooling. While still a youth, he began to travel with various opera and operetta companies as a chorister and eventually appeared in stage roles. In 1890 he made his formal operatic debut as the Stolnik in *Halka* with the Semyonov-Smarsky company in Ufa. During his travels, he was accompanied by the writer Maxim Gorky, who also sang in a chorus; together they made their way through the Russian provinces, often walking the railroad tracks when they could not afford the fare. Chaliapin's wanderings took him to Tiflis, where his extraordinary vocal gifts deeply impressed the tenor and vocal pedagogue Dimitri Usatov (1847–1913), who taught him free of charge in 1892–93. After appearances in Tiflis in 1893–94, Chaliapin went to St. Petersburg and sang with Panayev's company in 1894. He then was a member of the St. Petersburg Imperial Opera from 1894 to 1896. He subsequently went to Moscow, where he sang with Mamontov's company (1896–99), producing a great impression with his portrayals of Boris Godunov, Ivan Susanin, Varlaam, Dosifey, Ivan the Terrible, Holofernes in Serov's *Judith*, the Viking Guest in *Sadko*, and the Miller in Dargomyzhsky's *Rusalka*. On Dec. 7, 1898, he created the role of Salieri in Rimsky-Korsakov's *Mozart and Salieri* with Mamontov's company. During this time, Chaliapin also acquired fame as a concert singer. In 1899 he joined Moscow's Bolshoi Theater, where he served as its principal bass until 1914. His first appearance outside his homeland was at Milan's La Scala in 1901 when he sang Boito's Mefistofele. He returned to La Scala in 1904, 1908, 1912, 1929–30, and 1933. From 1905 to 1937 he made frequent appearances in Monte Carlo, where he created the title role in Massenet's *Don Quichotte* on Feb. 19, 1910. On July 25, 1905, he made his London debut at a private concert, and returned there to sing in the Russian seasons at Drury Lane in 1913 and 1914. He made his Metropolitan Opera debut in N.Y. as Mefistofele on Nov. 20, 1907. However, his dramatic characterizations failed to evoke sympathetic response from N.Y. audiences and critics, so he went to Paris to sing in Diaghilev's Russian seasons in 1908, 1910, and 1913. After the Russian Revolution, he became soloist and artistic director of the Petrograd Opera in 1918. He also was made a People's Artist by the Soviet government, but he soon became estranged by the course of events in his homeland and in 1921 settled in Paris. On Dec. 9, 1921, he made a triumphant return to the Metropolitan Opera with his compelling portrayal of Boris Godunov, and thereafter sang there with notable acclaim until 1929. From 1922 to 1924 he also sang with the Chicago Opera. In 1926 and in 1928–29 he appeared at London's Covent Garden, and in 1931 he returned to London to sing at the Lyceum Theatre. On March 3, 1935, he gave his farewell concert performance in N.Y.; his operatic farewell followed in Monte Carlo in 1937 when he once again sang Boris Godunov. Chaliapin made many recordings and appeared in film versions of *Tsar Ivan the Terrible* (1915) and *Don Quixote* (1933). He wrote *Stranitsiiz moyey zhizni:*

Avtobiografiya (Leningrad, 1926; Eng. tr., 1927, as *Pages from My Life*) and *Maska i dusha: Moi sorok let na teatrakh* (Paris, 1932; Eng. tr., 1932, as *Man and Mask*). Chaliapin was one of the foremost singing actors ever to grace the operatic stage. He dominated every scene in which he appeared as much by his remarkable dramatic gifts as by his superlative vocal prowess. Even in his last years, when this prowess declined, he never failed to move audiences by the sheer intensity of his performances.

BIBL.: M. Yankovsky, C. (Leningrad, 1972); V. Borovsky, C.: *A Critical Biography* (N.Y., 1988).—**NS/LK/DM**

Challis, Bill (actually, William H.),

jazz arranger; b. Wilkes-Barre, Pa., July 8, 1904; d. there, Oct. 4, 1994. Originally a saxophonist and clarinetist, he was a self-taught pianist. He played "C" melody sax at high school (1921); later studied economics and philosophy at Bucknell Univ. and led his own student band. He graduated in June 1925 and joined Dave Harmon's Band as saxist/arranger. He submitted arrangements to Jean Goldkette and was asked to join Goldkette's organization as staff arranger (autumn 1926). A recorded chart on "Blue Room" caught the ear of young Benny Carter. Challis worked for a year with Goldkette, then joined Paul Whiteman until the spring of 1930. Occasionally he led a radio orchestra in the 1930s, but was mainly active as a freelance arranger for Fletcher Henderson, Frank Trumbauer, the Dorsey brothers, Lennie Hayton, the Casa Loma Band, Nat Shilkret, and others. He continued to work through the 1960s, 1970s, and 1980s, including arrangements for Bobby Hackett, Bucky Pizzarelli (arranging Bix Beiderbecke's piano compositions for guitar quintet), and Manhattan Transfer. Among his last projects was recreating the original Goldkette charts for Vince Giordano's Nighthawks in 1986; they were subsequently recorded and issued two years later.

DISC.: *Goldkette Project* (1988); *Bill Challis and His Orchestra 1936* (1988); *More 1936* (1988).—**JC/LP**

Chaloff, Serge,

bebop baritone saxophonist; b. Boston, Mass., Nov. 24, 1923; d. there, July 16, 1957. His mother, Madame Margaret Chaloff, was a highly respected music teacher, and his father, Julius, was a concert pianist who recorded piano rolls, taught at New England Cons., and played piano in the Boston Symphony Orch. His brother Richard is an audio expert who recorded Serge at home on piano and tenor saxophone in the early 1940s. Serge studied piano and clarinet but was self-taught on baritone saxophone. He played with Boyd Raeburn, Georgie Auld, and Jimmy Dorsey; after joining Woody Herman's Second Herd (1947), he became a star. He was the anchor in the famous "Four Brothers" reed section and featured on the up-tempo "Man, Don't Be Ridiculous." Chaloff spent two years with Herman and another with Basie before returning to Boston. He did some teaching and made a few releases as a leader before his death. He was a heroin addict and later cleaned up; he died due to complications from spinal paralysis. He was the first major bop player on the baritone saxophone and displaced Harry Carney in Down Beat polls three years in a row. One of the most admired players on his instrument, he had a light sound and great fluency.

DISC.: *Boston* (1950); *Boston Blow-Up* (1955); *Blue Serge* (1956); *Serge Chaloff and Boots Mussull: New Stars—New Sounds, Vol. 2* (1949); *Fable of Mable* (1954).—**LP**

Chambers, Henderson (Charles),

jazz trombonist; b. Alexandria, La., May 1, 1908; d. N.Y., Oct. 19, 1967. He attended local school, then studied at Leland Coll., in Baker, La. He began playing trombone with the student band at Morehouse Coll., Atlanta. His first professional work was with Neil Montgomery in 1931. He was with Doc Banks in Nashville (1932), then worked in saxist Jack Jackson's Pullman Porters; later fronted by Speed Webb (1933). He was with Zack Whyte (1934), then played in Ky. with Al Sears' Band (1935–36) and Tiny Bradshaw (1937–38). He moved to N.Y. in 1939, worked with Chris Columbus Band at Savoy Ballroom until late 1940, then with Louis Armstrong from January 1941 until 1943. He was with Don Redman in 1943, joined Ed Hall Sextet in summer of 1944, worked on and off with Ed Hall for four years, and also played with Don Redman, Sy Oljver, and other leaders. He was with Lucky Millinder (1950–53), Count Basie, Jerry Relding (1954), did occasional tours with Cab Calloway; also worked with Doc Cheatham in Boston (late 1955). Occasionally with Duke Ellington in 1957, he also did regular freelance studio work, and played with a band led by Mercer Ellington (1959). He toured with Ray Charles (1961–late 1963), then with Count Basie from January 1964 until 1966. During the last years of his life, he assisted Edgar Battle in running a big rehearsal band. He died of a heart attack.—**JC/LP**

Chambers, Joe (actually, Joseph Arthur),

jazz drummer, composer; b. Stoneacre, Va., June 25, 1942. He started playing in 1951, and turned professional three years later; he played frequently in Philadelphia with his family. He worked in the JFK Quintet in the D.C. area (1960–63), then moved to N.Y. (1963), studied composition and played with Jimmy Giuffre, James Brown, the Shirelles, Eric Dolphy (1963), Donald Byrd, Freddie Hubbard (1964–66), Wayne Shorter (1965–67), Herbie Hancock, Charles Lloyd, Archie Shepp, and Joe Henderson, among many others He worked with Bobby Hutcherson (1965–70), writing some much admired compositions for him. He was a founding member of Max Roach's M'Boom in 1970. From 1971 to 1973, he worked with Charles Mingus, and then in 1974 began leading his own groups. Also in 1974, he performed his classical-jazz suite, *The Almoravid*, at Carnegie Hall. In 1975 he received a composition grant from the NEA. In the early 1980s, he worked with Chet Baker and Ray Mantilla's Space Station. He has taught at the New School for Social Research since 1986 and has not performed or recorded very often since.

DISC.: *Almoravid* (1973); *New World* (1976); *Double Exposure* (1977); *N.Y. Concerto* (1981); *Phantom of the City* (1991). JFK Quintet: *New Jazz Frontiers from Washington* (1961); *Young Ideas* (1962). B. Hutcherson: *Dialogue* (1965). J. Henderson: *Mode for Joe* (1966). McCoy Tyner: *Tender Moments* (1967). L. Konitz: *Figure and Spirit* (1976).—**LP**

Chambers, Paul (Laurence Dunbar Jr.),

noted jazz bassist; b. Pittsburgh, Pa., April 22, 1935; d. N.Y., Jan. 4, 1969. Dunbar studied baritone horn and tuba in his preteen years; at age 13, his family moved to Detroit and he took up the bass. In 1954 he did his first professional work on the road with Paul Quinichette, ending up in N.Y. In 1955 he joined Miles Davis's working groups, remaining with Davis through 1963. He appeared on many of Davis's classic recordings of this period. At the same time, he was virtually house bassist for the Prestige label, often working with pianist Red Garland on dozens of sessions. He also recorded as a member of Garland's trio from 1955 to 1959. After leaving Davis, Chambers formed a cooperative trio with Wynton Kelly and Jimmy Cobb. This group appeared frequently with Wes Montgomery in the mid-1960s and recorded with him as well as Kenny Burrell. He contracted tuberculosis in 1968, and sucumbed to the disease early the following year.

In November 1961 John Coltrane said, "A bassist of the stature of Paul Chambers is difficult to find in N.Y., because he creates a fusion: he listens to the piano and the drums, and all his work consists of improvising in relation to those instruments. His melodic line is a sort of result of the melodic lines of the two other musicians." In the process, Chambers did more than just keep a solid walking line; he created some original effects. This can be heard on his triplets behind Coltrane's last chorus on "Blue Train," his fills and ostinatos on "My Funny Valentine" (live with Davis, September 1958), his beautiful and distinctive work on "Invitation," and his pedal points on "So What." He was also known for his fleet bowed work. Coltrane named "Mr. P.C." for him. As an accompanist, his accurate and buoyant swing is often noted, but he also creatively broke up the beat on occasion.

DISC.: *Chambers' Music* (1955); *High Step* (1955); *Whims of Chambers* (1956); *Bass on Top* (1957); *East/West Controversy* (1957); *Paul Chambers Quintet* (1957); *Ease It* (1959); *Go* (1959); *Just Friends* (1959); *1st Bassman* (1960); *Paul Chambers Stars* (1960).

WRITINGS: *Paul Chambers Quintet* (1957).

BIBL.: J. Stinnett, *The Music of Paul Chambers* (1983).—**LP**

Chambonnières, Jacques Champion, Sieur de,

French harpsichordist, dancer, teacher, and composer; b. Paris, 1601 or 1602; d. there, April or May, 1672. His father was the keyboard player and composer Jacques Champion, known as La Chapelle (b. probably in Paris, before 1555; d. there, 1642), who served in the king's chamber as a gentilhomme ordinaire. By 1632 Chambonnières was associated with the court, where he became esteemed as both a harpsichordist and dancer. In 1641 he founded a series of private concerts known as the Assemblée des Honnestes Curieux, with which he was active as director and performer. In 1643 he succeeded his father as a gentilhomme ordinaire in the king's chamber. Chambonnières was an influential teacher, numbering among his pupils the Couperin brothers, D'Anglebert, Hardel, Lebégue, Cambert, and Nivers. In 1662 he retired from his court duties and was succeeded by D'Anglebert. Chambonnières was the founder of the French Classical school of harpsichord playing, and was one of the first to adapt the lute idiom to the composing of harpsichord music. He composed only works for solo harpsichord and publ. *Les Pièces de clavessin* (two vols., Paris, 1670). All of his works were ed. by P. Brunold and A. Tessier (Paris, 1925; new ed., 1961).

BIBL.: R. Neill, *Seventeenth Century French Clavier Style as Found in the Pièces de clavecin of J.C.d. C.* (diss., Univ. of Colo., 1965).—**NS/LK/DM**

Chaminade, Cécile (Louise Stéphanie),

French composer and pianist; b. Paris, Aug. 8, 1857; d. Monte Carlo, April 13, 1944. She was a pupil of Lecouppey, Savard, and Marsick; later studied composition with Godard. She became successful as a concert pianist, and also wrote a great number of agreeable piano pieces, in the salon style, which acquired enormous popularity in France, England, and America. She made her American debut playing the piano part of her *Concertstück* with the Philadelphia Orch. (Nov. 7, 1908). She also wrote a lyric sym., *Les Amazones* (Antwerp, April 18, 1888), two orch. suites, two piano trios, and more than 200 piano pieces in a Romantic style.

BIBL.: M. Citron, *C. C.: A Bio-Bibliography* (Westport, Conn., 1988).—**NS/LK/DM**

Champagne (actually, Desparois dit Champagne), Claude (Adonaï),

Canadian composer; b. Montreal, May 27, 1891; d. there, Dec. 21, 1965. He studied violin, piano, and composition in Montreal; then went to Paris, where he took courses in composition with Gédalge, Koechlin, and Laparra (1921–28). He then taught at McGill Univ. in Montreal (1932–41). From 1942 to 1962 he served as asst. director of the Conservatoire de Musique du Québec à Montreal. In his music, he followed the modern French tradition.

WORKS: *Hercule et Omphale*, symphonic poem (1918; Paris, March 31, 1926); *Prélude et Filigrane* for Piano (1918); *Suite canadienne* for Chorus and Orch. (Paris, Oct. 20, 1928); *Habanera* for Violin and Piano (1929); *Danse villageoise* for Violin and Piano (1929; also orchestrated); *Quadrilha brasileira* for Piano (1942); *Images du Canada français* for Chorus and Orch. (1943; Montreal, March 9, 1947); *Evocation* for Small Orch. (1943); *Gaspesia* for Orch. (1944; rev. as *Symphonie gaspesienne*, 1945); Piano Concerto (1948; Montreal, May 30, 1950); String Quartet (1951); *Paysanna* for Small Orch. (1953); *Suite miniature* for Flute, Cello, and Harpsichord (1958; rev. as *Concertino grosso* for String Orch., 1963); *Altitude* for Chorus, Orch., and Ondes Martenot (1959; Toronto, April 22, 1960); organ pieces; songs.
—**NS/LK/DM**

Champion de Chambonnières

See **Chambonnières, Jacques Champion**

Chance, Michael,

noted English countertenor; b. Penn, Buckinghamshire, March 7, 1955. He was a choral scholar at King's Coll., Cambridge (1974–77). He first made a name for himself as a concert artist via appearances with British ensembles, mainly as an exponent of early music. In 1983 he made his formal operatic debut at the Buxton Festival as Apollo in Cavalli's *Giasone*. His European operatic debut followed in 1985 in Lyons as Handel's Andronico. In 1987 he created the role of the military governor in Weir's *A Night at the Chinese Opera* in Cheltenham. He made his first appearance at the Paris Opéra in 1988 as Tolomeo in *Giulio Cesare*. In 1989 he sang Britten's Oberon at the Glyndebourne Festival, and in 1993 at the Australian Opera. He was engaged as the Voice of Apollo in *Death in Venice* for his debut at London's Covent Garden in 1992, and also appeared that year as Monteverdi's Anfinomo at the English National Opera in London and as Handel's Giulio Cesare at the Scottish Opera in Glasgow. In 1994 he appeared in the premiere of Birtwistle's *The Second Mrs. Kong* at the Glyndebourne Festival. After singing Dick in *The Fairy Queen* at the English National Opera in 1995, he returned there as Gluck's Orfeo in 1997. His engagements as a concert artist took him all over Europe and North America, and were greeted with critical accolades for his naturally cultivated vocal gifts.—NS/LK/DM

Chancy, François de, French lutenist and composer; b. place and date unknown; d. Aug. 1656. After serving Cardinal Richelieu (1631–35), he was a chamber musician to the king (from 1635), and also was in charge of the children in the royal household (from 1644). He was a skillful composer of chansons.

WORKS: *Tablature de mandore de la composition du Sieur Chancy* (Paris, 1629); *Livre d'aires de cour à quatre parties* (2 vols., Paris, 1635, 1644); *Les équivoques* (5 vols., Paris, 1640–55); also instrumental pieces in collections by Philidor and in treatises by Mersenne. See A. Souris, ed., *Oeuvres de Chancy, Bouvier, Belleville, Dubuisson, Chevalier* (Paris, 1967).—LK/DM

Chang, Sarah, gifted American violinist; b. Philadelphia, Dec. 10, 1980. She was born to Korean parents who saw to it that she received training in violin from the age of 4. At 5 she began to perform in public in Philadelphia. In 1987 she received the Starling Scholarship at the Juilliard School in N.Y., where she studied with Dorothy DeLay and Hyo Kang. She soon came to the attention of Zubin Mehta, who was so taken by her extraordinary musicianship that he invited her to make her N.Y. Phil debut under his direction in 1988 as soloist in Paganini's first Violin Concerto. In 1991 she was a soloist with Muti and the Philadelphia Orch. at its 90th anniversary gala concert. In 1992 she became the youngest participant of the "Concert for Planet Earth" at the Rio de Janeiro Earth Summit. By the time she was 15, she had appeared as a soloist with many of the most prestigious orchs. of the world, among them the Chicago Sym. Orch., the Los Angeles Phil., the Pittsburgh Sym. Orch., the San Francisco Sym., the London Sym. Orch., the Gewandhaus Orch. of Leipzig, and the Berlin Phil. She also performed at many principal festivals. On May 24, 1995, she was soloist in the Mendelssohn Violin Concerto with Kurt Masur and the N.Y. Phil., which appearance was telecast live to the nation by PBS. She was awarded the Avery Fisher Prize in 1999. —NS/LK/DM

Chanler, Theodore Ward, American composer; b. Newport, R.I., April 29, 1902; d. Boston, July 27, 1961.

He studied in Boston with Hans Ebell (piano) and with Arthur Shepherd (composition), then at the Cleveland Inst. of Music with Bloch. He later took courses at the Univ. of Oxford (1923–25), and also studied with Nadia Boulanger in Paris. He returned to America in 1933 and wrote music criticism. He taught at the Peabody Cons. of Music in Baltimore (1945–47) and then at the Longy School in Cambridge, Mass. In 1944 he held a Guggenheim fellowship. His music, mostly in smaller forms, is distinguished by a lyrical quality; his songs are particularly expressive; he employed the modern idiom of polytonal texture without overloading the harmonic possibilities; the melody is free, but usually within tonal bounds.

WORKS: *The Pot of Fat*, chamber opera (Cambridge, Mass., May 8, 1955); *Pas de Trois*, ballet (1942); Violin Sonata (1927); violin pieces; piano music, including *5 Short Colloquies* (1936), *Toccata* (1939), *The Second Joyful Mystery* for 2 Pianos (1942), and *A Child in the House* (1949); organ pieces; Mass for 2 Women's Voices and Organ (1930) and other choral works; about 50 songs.

BIBL.: E. Nordgren, *An Analytical Study of the Songs of T. C. (1902–1961)* (diss., N.Y.U., 1980).—NS/LK/DM

Chapin, Schuyler G(arrison), American music administrator; b. N.Y., Feb. 13, 1923. He received training from Boulanger at the Longy School of Music in Cambridge, Mass. (1940–41). After working for NBC (1941–51), Tex and Jinx McCary Enterprises (1951–53), and Columbia Artists Management (1953–59), he was head of the Masterworks Division of Columbia Records (1959–63). He later was associated with N.Y.'s Lincoln Center for the Performing Arts, and, from 1969 to 1971, was executive producer for Amberson Enterprises. He then was general manager of N.Y.'s Metropolitan Opera (1972–75). From 1976 to 1987 he served as dean of Columbia Univ.'s School of the Arts. He was vice-president of worldwide concert and artist activities for Steinway and Sons (1990–92). In 1994 he became chairman of cultural affairs for the city of N.Y. He publ. his memoirs as *Musical Chairs: A Life in the Arts* (1977). He also publ. *Leonard Bernstein: Notes From a Friend* (1992) and *Sopranos, Mezzos, Tenors, Bassos and Other Friends* (1995).—NS/LK/DM

Chapin, Thomas, American saxophonist b. Manchester, Conn., March 9, 1957, d. Providence, R.I., Feb. 13, 1998. Though leukemia tragically ended his life when he was only 40 years old, he spent nearly a decade working as a leader and left behind a legacy of many excellent albums and performances and a reputation as a versatile musician's musician who was unfailingly gentlemanly. He moved freely between the dual (and sometimes dueling) N.Y.C. factions of the avant-garde downtown scene and the mainstream scene and was respected in both. Though in his trio work he would sometimes play outside time, unlike some avant-gardists he often played metered music even in non-mainstream settings. His natural exuberance made him an expressive showman, yet there was never the slightest sense that he compromised his musicality in any context; he was able to communicate directly and unassumingly in even the most challenging sonic contexts.

He attended the Hartt School of Music at the Univ. of Hartford and later went to Rutgers Univ., studying with Jackie McLean, Paul Jeffrey, Ted Dunbar, and Kenny Barron. Starting in 1981 he spent six years as the musical director for Lionel Hampton's big band; he also worked in Chico Hamilton's group for a while. In the late 1980s he formed his own groups and soon made a name for himself. When the downtown N.Y.C. club The Knitting Factory started a record label, he was the first artist it signed. Bassist Mario Pavone was a frequent collaborator, and they worked closely in Chapin's trio and in Pavone's own bands. His versatility made him a popular addition to many groups, from obscure avant-garde big bands in which he was sometimes the most famous player (Walter Thompson Big Band, Joe Gallant's Illuminati) and improvisors on the fringes of jazz (John McCracken, Machine Gun) to such notables as John Zorn, Ned Rothenberg, and Anthony Braxton.

His final album was recorded in 1996 but delayed until he could work on its production during a period of remission from his illness. It came out the same week he died. The Chapin-penned poem in the CD booklet, called *Sky Piece*, captures its mood perfectly: "So much sky/in the space of desert/my soul/rises/from a mournful Earth/into a clarity/above Time./While Time is/it is best to be/in both worlds/Music/as the bridge.

Disc.: *Radius* (1990); *Knitting Factory Tours Europe* (1991); *Third Force* (1991); *Inversions* (1992); *Insomnia* (1992); *Anima* (1992); *I've Got Your Number* (1993); *Menagerie Dreams* (1994); *Song for (Septet)* (1994); *You Don't Know Me* (1995); *What Is Jazz? 1996* (1996); *Haywire* (1996); *Dancers Tales* (1997); *Seven Standards 1996* (1997); *Sky Piece* (1998).—**SH**

Chapi (y Lorente), Ruperto, Spanish composer; b. Villena, near Alicante, March 27, 1851; d. Madrid, March 25, 1909. He studied at the Cons. of Madrid, and received a stipend from the Spanish Academy for further study in Rome (1874). He wrote some operas (*La hija de Jefte, La hija de Garcilaso,* etc.), but discovered that his talent found more suitable expression in the lighter zarzuela, in which form his first success was won with *La Tempestad* (Tivoli, March 11, 1882). His work is noted for elegance, grace, and exquisite orchestration. Of one of his zarzuelas (*La revoltosa,* Apolo, Nov. 25, 1897), Saint-Saëns remarked that Bizet would have been proud to sign his name to the score. His last zarzuela, *Margarita la Tornera* (Madrid, Feb. 24, 1909), was produced shortly before his death. Chapi wrote 155 zarzuelas and 6 operas. In 1893 he founded the Sociedad de Autores, Compositores y Editores de Musica.

Bibl.: A. Salcedo, *R. C., Su vida y sus obras* (Madrid, 1929); J. Aguilar Gomez, *R. C. y su obra lirica* (Alicante, 1973). —**NS/LK/DM**

Chappell & Co., London music publishers, concert agents, and piano manufacturers, founded in 1810 by Samuel Chappell, J.B. Cramer (the pianist), and F.T. Latour. Cramer retired in 1819, Latour in 1826, and S. Chappell died in 1834, when his son William (1809–88) became the head of the firm. In 1840 he established the Musical Antiquarian Soc., for which he ed. Dowland's songs; he also ed. and publ. *A Collection of National English Airs* (two vols., 1838–39), later enl. as *Popular Music of the Olden Time* (two vols., 1855–59; rev. by H.E. Wooldridge and publ. in two vols., 1893); he left an unfinished *History of Music* (vol. I, London, 1874). His brothers, Thomas Patey (1819–1902) and S. Arthur (1834–1904), were respectively the founder and manager of the Monday and Saturday Popular Concerts. In 1897 the partnership became a limited company, and Thomas was succeeded by his son, T. Stanley (d. 1933), as board chairman; later, William Boosey became managing director. In 1929 the firm was acquired by Louis Dreyfus. The American branch, under the direction of Max Dreyfus, brother of Louis, publ. the songs and musical comedies of Richard Rodgers, Jerome Kern, Cole Porter, Harold Arlen, and other popular composers.—**NS/LK/DM**

Charlap, Bill, American pianist; b. N.Y., Oct. 15, 1966. Able to paint with a rich and melodic pallet, while possessing a pure and bell-like tone, he is a player who is actively looking for new ways to express himself and compliment any musical situation. His sophisticated harmonic knowledge and sense of drama make him one of the most stimulating pianists around. It should come as no surprise that he would pursue a career in music; his parents are Broadway composer Moose Charlap and vocalist Sandy Stewart. At the age of three, he began his piano studies, and his formal musical education included graduation from N.Y.'s H.S. of the Performing Arts.

Over the past several years, he has gained valuable experience through work with Gerry Mulligan, Benny Carter, Louis Bellson, Sheila Jordan, Bobby Short, Barry Manilow, and Tony Bennett, among many others. He has been a key member of the Phil Woods Quintet since 1995, a position that has found him appearing at many of the world's major jazz festivals, and even guesting on Marian McPartland's *Piano Jazz* radio show. He also leads his own piano trio and has recorded for the Chiaroscuro and Criss Cross labels. His talent is worthy of wider critical attention and public awareness.

Disc.: *Along with Me* (1994); *Souvenir* (1995); *Distant Star* (1997).—**CH**

Charles, Denis (also **Dennis**), jazz drummer, percussionist; b. St. Croix, Virgin Islands, Dec. 4, 1933; d. N.Y., March 26, 1998. His father played congas, guitar, and banjo. He played congas as child; the family moved to N.Y. in 1945 and he took up drumming (1954), teaching himself by listening to records by Art Blakey and Roy Haynes. Charles played at West Indian parties and dances with calypso and mambo bands in Harlem in late 1950s. He met Cecil Taylor at Connie's Inn and became one of the few drummers to play and record (1955–61) with him. He also recorded with Steve Lacy (1957, 1963–64, 1979, 1982). He was in the Jack Gelber play *The Connection.* Charles played with Gil Evans (1959), Jimmy Giuffre, Wilbur Ware, Archie Shepp (1967), and Don Cherry; he recorded West Indian folk tunes with his brother Frank and Sonny Rollins. He worked with Lacy again in the 1970s, and with Billy Bang (1981–82) and Lacy in the 1980s. He made his first recording as a leader of his own group in 1989. He died of a heart attack after returning from a European tour.

DISC.: *Queen Mary* (1989). C. Taylor: *Jazz Advance* (1955); *Looking Ahead!* (1958); *Cell Walk for Celeste* (1961). S. Lacy: *Soprano Sax* (1957). G. Evans: *Great Jazz Standards* (1959).—**LP**

Charles, Ray (originally, Robinson, Ray Charles),

legendary, genre-crossing singer/pianist; b. Albany, Ga., Sept. 23, 1930. Ray Charles grew up in Greenville, Fla., and was blinded by glaucoma at the age of seven. From 1937 to 1945 he attended the St. Augustine (Fla.) School for the Deaf and Blind, where he learned piano and, later, clarinet and alto saxophone, as well as composing and arranging. Orphaned at 15, Charles struck out on his own, performing in bands around Fla. In 1948 he moved to Seattle and formed the Maxim Trio (also known as the McSon Trio and the Maxine Trio), a group grounded in the style of Nat "King" Cole and Charles Brown. As the Maxine Trio, they scored a major R&B hit in 1949 with "Confession Blues" on the Downbeat label. Charles toured with blues artist Lowell Fulson in the early 1950s, scoring R&B hits with "Baby Let Me Hold Your Hand" and "Kiss Me Baby" on the small, Los Angeles–based Swingtime label.

In 1952 the N.Y.–based Atlantic label bought Ray Charles's recording contract and, shedding his Nat "King" Cole stylization and adapting gospel music techniques to blues lyrics, he soon hit with "It Should Have Been Me." In 1954 he arranged and played piano on Guitar Slim's top R&B hit "Things That I Used to Do" for Specialty and formed his own band. In early 1955 Charles hit in both the popular and R&B fields with his own composition, "I've Got a Woman." Using top-flight studio musicians such as saxophonist David "Fathead" Newman, Charles scored consistently on the R&B charts through the late 1950s with songs such as "A Fool for You," "Drown in My Own Tears," "Hallelujah I Love Her So," and "Lonely Avenue," the recording debut of his backup female vocal group, the Raeletts. He also became popular with jazz fans, recording two highly acclaimed records with Modern Jazz Quartet vibraphonist Milt Jackson and performing a startling set at the 1958 Newport Jazz Festival. Finally, in 1959, Charles established himself as a popular recording artist and pioneer of soul music with the release of his own top R&B/smash pop hit composition "What'd I Say." The song was later covered by a variety of artists, including Jerry Lee Lewis, Bobby Darin, and Elvis Presley.

Sensing that Atlantic was still basically an R&B organization, Ray Charles switched to ABC-Paramount Records in late 1959. Through 1961 he scored with the top pop hits "Georgia on My Mind" and "Hit the Road Jack" (a top R&B hit) and the major pop hits "Ruby" and "Unchain My Heart" (another top R&B hit). He also recorded *Genius + Soul = Jazz* for Impulse (ABC's jazz subsidiary label), with arrangements by Quincy Jones played by the Count Basie Band. Yielding a near-smash pop/top R&B hit with the instrumental "One Mint

Julep," this album and one recorded with Betty Carter for ABC-Paramount brought him an increasing measure of popularity with jazz fans, black and white.

In 1962 Ray Charles formed Ray Charles Enterprises, comprised of Tangerine Records, Tangerine Music, and Racer Music Company, opening studios and offices in Los Angeles in 1963. By then he was utilizing 40-piece orchestras and large vocal choruses for his recordings. With this full, commercial sound, his *Modern Sounds in Country and Western* became phenomenally popular, producing the crossover smash hits "I Can't Stop Loving You" backed with "Born to Lose," and "You Don't Know Me." Within a year, *Volume II* of country-and-western material was released with the crossover smash hits "You are My Sunshine" backed with "Your Cheating Heart," and "Take These Chains from My Heart." On ABC Charles scored major pop hits with "Busted," "That Lucky Old Sun," "Crying Time," and "Together Again." Major hits on ABC/Tangerine included "Let's Go Get Stoned" (a top R&B hit), "Here We Go Again," and The Beatles' "Yesterday" and "Eleanor Rigby."

During the 1960s Ray Charles also became involved with film work, appearing in the 1962 film *Swingin' Along* (a.k.a. *Double Trouble*) and the 1966 British film *Ballad in Blue* (a.k.a. *Blues for Lovers*), and recording the soundtracks for the films *Cincinnati Kid* (1965) and *In the Heat of the Night* (1967). By 1967 he had begun performing on the nightclub circuit, touring with his own package revue from 1969 into the 1970s.

In 1973 Ray Charles left ABC Records, retaining the rights to his ABC material and transferring his Tangerine operation to the new label Crossover. During 1976 he recorded *Porgy and Bess* with English songstress Cleo Laine for RCA Records. He returned to Atlantic in 1977, moving to Columbia in the 1980s and Warner Bros. in the 1990s. In 1978 Dial Press published Ray Charles's autobiography, written with David Ritz, and in 1980 Charles appeared in *The Blues Brothers* movie and scored a minor country hit for his duet with Clint Eastwood, "Beers to You," from the film *Any Which Way You Can*. Charles achieved a major country hit with "Born to Love Me" in 1982 and later recorded duets with country stars on *Friendship*. The album yielded five major country hits, including "We Didn't See a Thing" (with George Jones), "Seven Spanish Angels" (with Willie Nelson), and "Two Old Cats Like Us" (with Hank Williams Jr.). Charles also played a major role in the recording of USA for Africa's "We are the World" single in 1985.

Inducted into the Blues Foundation's Hall of Fame in 1982, Ray Charles was inducted into the Rock 'n' Roll Hall of Fame in its inaugural year (1986). In late 1989 Charles had his first major pop hit in over 20 years with the Quincy Jones recording "I'll Be Good to You," featuring himself and Chaka Khan. During the 1990s Ray Charles appeared in a series of stylish commercials for Pepsi and was the subject of a PBS documentary.

In the 1990s Ray Charles continued to work about eight months a year, touring with a large orchestra. He lived in Los Angeles, where he was involved with RPM International, a corporation that includes Crossover Records, the music publishing companies Tangerine and Racer Music, and RPM Studios, where he records. In 1990 Ray Charles began recording for Warner Bros. Records, recording 1993's *My World* with Eric Clapton, Billy Preston, Mavis Staples, and June Pointer.

A multitalented blind black musician, Ray Charles pioneered soul music, which became enormously popular among both black and white audiences beginning in the late 1950s. In secularizing certain aspects of gospel music (chord changes, song structures, call-and-response techniques, and vocal screams, wails, and moans) and adding blues-based lyrics, he essentially invented a new genre of popular music. Along with musicians such as Horace Silver, Charles was instrumental in leading many jazz musicians away from the abstracted and relatively inaccessible music of bebop as practiced by Charlie Parker, John Coltrane, Dizzy Gillespie and others, back to the roots of soul and funk musics.

Ray Charles's gospel-based vocal style influenced virtually all the soul singers of the 1960s, as well as many of the white English singers that emerged in the 1960s (Mick Jagger, Eric Burdon, Joe Cocker, Rod Stewart and others). In using the electric piano on his first major pop hit, "What'd I Say," Charles introduced the instrument to jazz and rock music. Moreover, the vocal work of his female back-up group, The Raeletts, set the standard for black vocal groups that was so successfully exploited by Motown Records in the 1960s. Additionally, in applying his gospel-oriented style to country-and-western material in the early 1960s, Ray Charles became the first black artist to score hits in the country field and the first male black singer to make a major impact on the white adult market.

With David Ritz, *Brother Ray: Ray Charles' Own Story* (N.Y., 1978).

DISC.: *The Great* (1957); *Hallelujah I Love Her So* (1957); *At Newport* (1958); *Yes Indeed!* (1958); *The Genius of* (1959); *What'd I Say* (1959); *The Genius Hits the Road* (1960); *In Person* (1960); *Dedicated to You* (1961); *Genius + Soul = Jazz* (1961); *The Genius after Hours* (1961); *The Genius Sings the Blues* (1961); *The Greatest Ray Charles/Do the Twist with Ray Charles!* (1961); *Modern Sounds in Country and Western, Vols. 1, 2* (1962); *Ingredients in a Recipe for Soul* (1963); *Have a Smile with Me* (1964); *Sweet and Sour Tears* (1964); *Live in Concert* (1965); *Meets Rhythm and Blues* (1965); *Together Again/Country and Western* (1965); *Crying Time* (1966); *Ray's Moods* (1966); *Invites You to Listen* (1967); *A Man and His Soul* (1967); *A Portrait of Ray* (1968); *Doing His Thing* (1969); *I'm All Yours, Baby* (1969); *Love Country Style* (1970); *Volcanic Action of My Soul* (1971); *A Message for the People* (1972); *Through the Eyes of Love* (1972); *Come Live with Me* (1974); *Renaissance* (1975); *True to Life* (1977); *Love and Peace* (1978); *Ain't It So* (1979); *Brother Ray is at It Again* (1980); *Wish You Were Here Tonight* (1983); *Do I Ever Cross Your Mind* (1984); *Friendship* (1984); *The Spirit of Christmas* (1985); *From the Pages of My Mind* (1986); *Just Between Us* (1988); *Seven Spanish Angels and Other Hits (1982–86)* (1989); *Would You Believe?* (1990); *The Birth of Soul—The Complete Atlantic Rhythm & Blues Recordings, 1952–59* (1991); *Birth of a Legend* (rec. 1949–52; rel. 1992); *My World* (1993); *Strong Love Affair* (1996). Milt Jackson: *Soul Meeting* (1952); *Soul Brothers* (1958). The Ray Charles Sextext (with David "Fathead" Newman): *Ray Charles Sextet* (1959). Betty Carter: *And Betty Carter* (1961). The Ray Charles Orch.: *My Kind of Jazz* (1970); *Jazz Number II* (1973); *My Kind of Jazz, Part 3* (1975). Cleo Laine:

Porgy and Bess (1976).

BIBL.: David Ritz, *Ray Charles: Voice of Soul* (N.Y., 1994). **—BH**

Charpentier, Gustave, famous French composer; b. Dieuze, Lorraine, June 25, 1860; d. Paris, Feb. 18, 1956. He studied at the Paris Cons. (1881–87), where he was a pupil of Massart (violin), Pessard (harmony), and Massenet (composition). He received the Grand Prix de Rome in 1887 with his cantata *Didon*. He evinced great interest in the social problems of the working classes, and in 1900 formed the society L'Oeuvre de Mimi Pinson, devoted to the welfare of the poor, which he reorganized during World War I as an auxiliary Red Cross society. His fame is owed to one amazingly successful opera, *Louise*, a "roman musical" to his own libretto (his mistress at the time was also named Louise, and like the heroine of his opera, was employed in a dressmaking shop), which was premiered at the Opéra-Comique in Paris on Feb. 2, 1900. The score is written in the spirit of naturalism and includes such realistic touches as the street cries of Paris vendors. Its success was immediate, and it entered the repertoire of opera houses all over the world. Encouraged, Charpentier wrote a sequel under the title *Julien* (Paris, June 4, 1913), but it failed to arouse comparable interest.

BIBL.: A. Homonet, *Louise* (Paris, 1922); M. Delmas, *G. C. et le lyrisme français* (Paris, 1931).**—NS/LK/DM**

Charpentier, Jacques, French composer and organist; b. Paris, Oct. 18, 1933. He studied piano with Maria Cerati-Boutillier, then lived in Calcutta (1953–54), where he made a study of Indian music. He prepared a valuable thesis, *Introduction à l'étude de la musique de l'Inde*. Upon his return to Paris, he studied composition with Aubin and analysis with Messiaen at the Cons. In 1954 he was appointed organist at the church of St.-Benoit-d'Issy. In 1966 he was named chief inspector of music of the French Ministry of Cultural Affairs, and in 1975 Inspector General of the Secretariat of State for Culture. In 1974 he was named official organist of the Church of St. Nicolas du Chardonnet in Paris. From 1979 to 1981 he was director of music, lyric art, and dance in the French Ministry of Culture. Several of his works are based on Hindu melorhythms.

WORKS: DRAMATIC: *La Femme et son ombre*, ballet (1967); *Béatrice de Planisoles*, opera (Aix en Provence, July 23, 1971). **ORCH.:** Violin Concerto (1953); 7 syms.: No. 1, *Symphonie breve*, for Strings (1958), No. 2, *Sinfonia sacra*, for Strings (1965), No. 3, *Shiva Nataraja* (Shiva—the King of the Dance; 1968; Paris, March 2, 1969), No. 4, *Brasil*, in homage to Villa-Lobos (1973), No. 5, *Et l'imaginaire se mit à danser* (1977), No. 6 for Orch. and Organ (1979), and No. 7, *Acropolis* (1985); Ondes Martenot Concerto (1959); *Alla francese*, concertino for Ondes Martenot, Strings, and Percussion (1959–60); Octuple Concerto for 8 Winds and Strings (1963); *Prélude pour la Genèse* for Strings (1967); *Récitatif* for Violin and Orch. (1968); 10 concertos: No. 1 for Organ and Strings (1969), No. 2 for Guitar and Strings (1970), No. 3 for Harpsichord and Strings (1971), No. 4 for Piano and Strings (1971), No. 5 for Saxophone and Strings (1975), No. 6 for Oboe and Strings (1975), No. 7 for Trumpet and Strings (1975), No. 8 for Horn and Strings (1976), No. 9 for Cello and Strings (1976), and No. 10 for Clarinet and Strings (1983);

Trumpet Concerto (1976). **CHÁMBER:** 2 string quartets (1955, 1956); Piano Quintet (1955); Ondes Martenot Quartet (1958); *Suite karnatique* for Ondes Martenot (1958); *Prelude and Allegro* for Bass Saxophone and Piano (1959); *Lalita* for Ondes Martenot and Percussion (1961); *Pour Diane* for Horn and Piano (1962); *Pour Syrinx* for Flute and Piano (1962); *Mouvement* for Flute, Cello, and Harp (1965); *Gavambodi 2* for Saxophone and Piano (1966); *Pour le Kama Soutra* for Percussion Ensemble (1969); *Pour une Apsara* for 2 Harps (1970); *Esquisses* for Flute and Piano (1972); *Tu dors mais mon coeur veille* for Violin (1974); *Et le jour vint...* for 13 Instruments (1977); *Vitrail pour un temps de guerre* for Winds (1982). **KEYBOARD: P i a n o :** *Toccata* (1954); *Études karnatiques* (4 cycles, 1957–61). **O r g a n :** *Messe* (1964); *Répons* (1968). **VOCAL:** *4 Psaumes de Toukaram* for Soprano and Orch. (1957); *Tantum ergo* for 4 Voices and Orch. (1962); *La Croisade des pastoureaux*, oratorio (1964); *Musique pour un Zodiaque*, oratorio (1971); *La Genèse*, oratorio (1973); *Une Voix pour une autre* for 2 Women's Voices, Flute, Clarinet, and Percussion (1974); *Te Deum* (1978); *Prélude pour une nuit étoilée* for Chorus and Orch. (1986); *Le Miroir de Marie- Madeleine* for Soprano, Women's Voices, and Orch. (1988).—**NS/LK/DM**

Charpentier, Marc-Antoine,

significant French composer; b. Paris, c. 1647; d. there, Feb. 24, 1704. He studied with Carissimi in Italy. After returning to Paris, he became active as a composer to Molière's acting troupe; he was also in the service of Marie de Lorraine, the Duchess of Guise, later serving as her haute-contre, and finally as her maître de musique until her death (1688); likewise he was in the service of the grand Dauphin. Louis XIV granted him a pension (1683), and he subsequently served as music teacher to Philippe, Duke of Chartres, was maître de musique to the Jesuit church of St. Louis, and finally held that post at Sainte-Chapelle (1698–1704). Charpentier was one of the leading French composers of his era, distinguishing himself in both sacred and secular works. He wrote some 30 works for the stage, including the tragédies lyriques *David et Jonathas* (1688) and *Médée* (1693), cantatas, overtures, ballet airs, pastorals, incidental pieces, airs sérieux, airs a boire, etc. H. Hitchcock has prepared *Les OEuvres de Marc-Antoine Charpentier: Catalogue raisonné* (Paris, 1982).

BIBL.: D. Loskant, *Untersuchungen über die Oratorien M.-A. C.s* (diss., Univ. of Mainz, 1957); A. Parmley, *The Secular Stage Works of M.-A. C.* (diss., Univ. of London, 1985); H. Hitchcock, *M.-A. C.* (Oxford, 1990); P. Ranum, ed., *Vers une chronologie des oeuvres de M.-A. C.* (Baltimore, 1994); C. Cessac, *M.-A. C.* (Portland, Ore., 1995).—**NS/LK/DM**

Charteris, Richard,

Australian musicologist; b. Chatham Islands, New Zealand, June 24, 1948. He was educated at Victoria Univ. in Wellington (B.A., 1970), the Univ. of Canterbury (M.A., Honors, 1972, and the Univ. of Canterbury in London (Ph.D., 1976, with the diss. *John Coprario (Cooper) c. 1575–1626: A Study and Complete Critical Edition of His Instrumental Music*). After serving as Rothmans Research Fellow in the music dept. at the Univ. of Sydney (1976–78) and Research Fellow in the music dept. at the Univ. of Queensland (1979–80), he joined the music dept. at the Univ. of Sydney, successively as Australian Research Grants Scheme Chief Investigator (1981–90), Australian Research Council Se-

nior Research Fellow (Reader, 1991–94), and Prof. in Historical Musicology and ARC Senior Research Fellow (from 1995). In 1990 he was elected a Fellow of the Australian Academy of the Humanities. His scholarly interests include European music of the 16th, 17th, and 18th centuries. He has publ. over 100 books and editions, in addition to many articles in professional journals.

WRITINGS: *John Coprario: A Thematic Catalog of His Music with a Biographical Introduction* (N.Y., 1977); *A Catalogue of the Printed Books on Music, Printed Music and Music Manuscripts in Archbishop Marsh's Library, Dublin* (Kilkenny, 1982); *Alfonso Ferrabosco the Elder (1543–1588): A Thematic Catalogue of His Music with a Biographical Calendar* (N.Y., 1984); ed. *Altro Polo: Essays on Italian Music in the Cinquecento* (Sydney, 1990); *Giovanni Gabrieli (ca. 1555–1612): A Thematic Catalogue of his Music with A Guide to the Source Materials, and Translations of his Vocal Texts* (N.Y., 1996); *Adam Gumpelzhaimer's Little-Known Score-Books in Berlin and Kraków* (Neuhausen-Stuttgart, 1996); *Newly Discovered Music Manuscripts from the Private Collection of Emil Bohn* (Holzgerlingen, 1999).—**NS/LK/DM**

Charton-Demeur, Anne,

prominent French mezzo-soprano; b. Saujon, Charente Maritime, March 5, 1824; d. Paris, Nov. 30, 1892. She studied in Bordeaux with Bizot, making her operatic debut there as Lucia di Lammermoor in 1842. After appearances in Toulouse and Brussels, she made her first appearance in London as Madeleine in *Le Postillon de Longjumeau* on July 18, 1846. In 1847 she married the Belgian flutist Jules-Antoine Demeur in London and took the professional name of Charton-Demeur. In 1849–50 she was the leading female member of Mitchell's F French troup in London, and in 1852 she sang at Her Majesty's Theatre; she also appeared in concert with the Phil. Soc. in 1850. After singing at the Paris Opéra-Comique, she appeared with notable success in St. Petersburg, Vienna, and America; she also became a great favorite at the Paris Théâtre-Italien. She was befriended by Berlioz and did much to promote his music. She created the roles of Béatrice in his *Béatrice et Bénédict* (Baden-Baden, Aug. 9, 1862) and Dido in his *Les Troyens à Carthage* (Paris, Nov. 4, 1863). From 1869 she pursued a concert career. —**NS/LK/DM**

Chasalow, Eric (David),

American composer and teacher; b. Newark, May 25, 1955. He received training in music and biology at Bates Coll. (B.A., 1977), attended the New England Cons. of Music in Boston (1975–76), and studied composition with Davidovsky, George Edwards, and Beeson and flute with Sollberger at Columbia Univ. (M.A., 1979; D.M.A., 1985). He served as executive director of the Guild of Composers (1980–85) and of the Music Alliance (1988–90) in N.Y. In 1983 he held an NEA composer's fellowship, in 1984, 1986, and 1998 Norlin/MacDowell fellowships, in 1986–87 the Charles Ives fellowship of the American Academy of Arts and Letters and a Guggenheim fellowship, and in 1989 and 1994 received prizes from the ISCM. In 1990 he joined the faculty of Brandeis Univ., where he became chairman of the music dept. in 1996.

WORKS: O R C H.: *Leaping to Conclusions* for Chamber Orch. (1987; Boston, April 10, 1988). **CHAMBER:** *Anti-Chambers* for Flute (N.Y., April 19, 1979); *Verses and Fragments* for Horn, Percussion, and Electronic Sounds (N.Y., April 13, 1979); *Reverses* for Improvisers and Electronic Sounds (N.Y., June 2, 1980); *Falling Forward* for Flute (N.Y., Feb. 10, 1980); *Two From Three* for Violin, Cello, and Piano (1980); *Returning to the Point* for Flute, Violin, Viola, and Cello (1981; N.Y., Jan. 31, 1982); *A Circumstance of Dancing* for Flute and 11 Instruments (1982–84); *Hanging in the Balance* for Cello and Electronic Sounds (1983); *Over the Edge* for Flute and Electronic Sounds (1986); *Fast Forward* for Percussion and Electronic Sounds (1988); String Quartet (1989–90); *Winding Up* for Horn (1990; Swiss Radio, Lausanne, Dec. 1991); *In the Works* for Flute, Clarinet, Violin, Cello, Percussion, and Piano (1993); *Out of Joint* for Trumpet and Electronic Sounds (1994); *To the Edge and Back* for Flute and Piano (1997); *'Scuse Me* for Electric Guitar and Computer-generated Sounds (1998); *Yes, I Really Did*, piano trio (1998); *Suspicious Motives* for Flute, Clarinet, Violin, Cello, and Computer-generated Sounds (Boston, Nov. 19, 1999). **KEYBOARD: P i a n o :** *Groundwork* (1986); *Little Word* (1991); *A Loose Translation* (1995–96). **VOCAL:** *Words* for Chorus (1980); *Triptych* for Soprano and Piano (N.Y., June 17, 1984); *The Furies* for Soprano and Electronic Sounds, after Anne Sexton (1984; WBAI Radio, N.Y., March 21, 1985); *The Shampoo* for Soprano and Piano (1989); *Pass it On* for Soprano and Piano (1995); *Five Simic Songs* for Soprano and String Quartet (Waltham, Mass., Nov. 14, 1998). **TAPE:** *This Way Out* (1991); *The Fury of Rainstorms* (1992); *And it flew upside-down* (1994); *Left to His Own Devices* (1996); *Portrait of the Artist* (1997; Boston, Feb. 6, 1998). **OTHER:** *The Pagan Book of A. Rimbaud*, sound design (1995); *Seven Variations on Three Spaces*, computer-generated sounds (1999).—**NS/LK/DM**

Chase, Allan (S.), jazz saxophonist, composer, educator, researcher; b. Willimatic, Conn., June 22, 1956. He grew up in Phoenix, Ariz., and received his bachelor's degree in music theory and composition from Ariz. State Univ. (1978), where he studied composition. While still a student, he performed in clubs, concerts, and festivals with local jazz musicians. In the summers of 1978 and 1979, he studied improvisation and composition with Roscoe Mitchell, George Lewis, Karl Berger, Anthony Braxton, and others at the Creative Music Studio in Woodstock, N.Y. Chase and jazz drummer Lewis Nash formed a duo (1979–80), performing locally. He moved to Boston in 1980 and completed a year of graduate study in jazz performance and arranging at New England Cons. From 1981 to 1990, he was a member of the faculty at Berklee Coll. of Music. In 1981 he joined Your Neighborhood Saxophone Quartet (YNSQ), which performed throughout New England; YNSQ recorded 13 of Chase's compositions and seven of his arrangements. During the 1980s, he also led small jazz groups and played as a sideperson in and around Boston with Mick Goodrick, Donald Brown, Alan Dawson, Teddy Kotick, D. Sharpe, Bob Moses, the Jazz Composers Orch., the Either/Orch., Julius Hemphill, Muhal Richard Abrams, and JoAnne Brackeen. In 1992 he completed an M.A. in ethnomusicology at Tufts Univ. He lived in N.Y. from 1990 to 1996, where he performed with John Zorn, Rashied Ali, William Parker, Andrew Cyrille, Fred Hersch, Harvie Swartz, the Microscopic Septet, and the Walter Thompson Orch., while continuing to tour and record with YNSQ. He has done studio recordings for feature films, popular music records, TV, and radio. Since 1996 he has been the chairperson of the Jazz Studies and Improvisation Department at the New England Cons. of Music (where he has taught since 1994). He has appeared on recordings led by Zorn, Gunther Schuller, Joe Mulholland, Victor Mendoza, and others.

DISC.: *Composers in Red Sneakers* (1984); *Dark Clouds with Silver Linings* (1995); *Phoenix* (1996). Your Neighborhood Saxophone Quartet: *Your Neighborhood Saxophone Quartet* (1985); *The Walkman* (1987); *What's Gone* (1988); *Boogie Stop Shuffle* (1990); *Plutonian Night* (1991); *Wolf Tone* (1994). D. Katz and Jazz Composers' Orch., featuring J. Hemphill: *Dreamland* (1989). D. Eade: *The Ruby and the Pearl, featuring Stanley Cowell* (1991). Prima Materia, featuring R. Ali: *Peace on Earth* (1995); *Bells* (1996); *Meditations* (1996). P. Johnston: *Normalology* (1997); *Music for Films* (1998).—**LP**

Chase, Gilbert, eminent American musicologist; b. Havana (of American parents), Sept. 4, 1906; d. Chapel Hill, N.C., Feb. 22, 1992. He studied at Columbia Univ. and the Univ. of N.C. at Chapel Hill. From 1929 to 1935 he lived in Paris and was active as a music correspondent for British and American music periodicals. In 1935 he returned to the U.S.; during 1940–43, he was consultant on Spanish and Latin American music at the Library of Congress in Washington, D.C. He simultaneously was active in an advisory capacity to musical radio programs. From 1951 to 1953 he was cultural attaché at the American Embassy in Lima, and from 1953 to 1955 served in the same capacity in Buenos Aires. He then was director of the School of Music at the Univ. of Okla. (1955–57), and from 1958 to 1960 cultural attaché in Belgium. From 1960 to 1966 he was a prof. of music and director of Latin American studies at Tulane Univ. in New Orleans. From 1961 to 1969 he was director of the Inter-American Inst. for Musical Research, serving as ed. of its yearbook (1964–76). In 1963 he organized the first Inter-American Conference on Musicology in Washington, D.C. In 1955 the Univ. of Miami bestowed upon him the title of Honorary Doctor of Letters. He also taught at the State Univ. of N.Y. in Buffalo (1973–74) and at the Univ. of Tex. in Austin from 1975 to 1979.

WRITINGS: *The Music of Spain* (N.Y., 1941; 2nd ed., 1959; in Spanish, Buenos Aires, 1943); *America's Music: From the Pilgrims to the Present* (N.Y., 1955; 3rd ed., rev., 1983; also tr. into German, French, Portuguese, and Spanish); *Introducción a la musica americana contemporánea* (Buenos Aires, 1958); *A Guide to the Music of Latin America* (Washington, D.C., 1962); *The American Composer Speaks: A Historical Anthology, 1770 to 1965* (Baton Rouge, 1966); *Two Lectures in the Form of a Pair: 1, Music, Culture and History; 2, Structuralism and Music* (Brooklyn, 1973); *Roger Reynolds: Profile of a Composer* (N.Y., 1982).—**NS/LK/DM**

Chasins, Abram, multitalented American pianist, teacher, writer on music, broadcaster, and composer; b. N.Y., Aug. 17, 1903; d. there, June 21, 1987. He was a student of Hutcheson (piano) and Goldmark (composition) at N.Y.'s Juilliard School of Music. He also was a protégé of Hofmann, and later studied analysis with Tovey in London (1931). From 1926 to 1936 he taught at the Curtis Inst. of Music in Philadelphia, and later privately. He also was active as a pianist and composer. His most popular work for piano was the *Three Chinese*

Pieces (1928; orchestrated 1929), which became a favorite encore piece with piano virtuosos. Chasins was soloist in the first performances of his two piano concertos (Philadelphia, Jan. 18, 1929 and March 3, 1933). From 1941 to 1965 he presented classical music braodcasts on WQXR in N.Y. In 1949 he married his pupil **Constance Keene**, with whom he subsequently appeared in duo recitals. In 1972 he became musician-in-residence at the Univ. of Southern Calif. in Los Angeles, where he also was director of its radio station, KUSC (1972–77).

WRITINGS (all publ. in N.Y.): *Speaking of Pianists* (1957; 3rd ed., rev., 1981); *The Van Cliburn Legend* (1959); *The Appreciation of Music* (1966); *Music at the Crossroads* (1972); *Leopold Stokowski: A Profile* (1979).—NS/LK/DM

Chatman, Stephen (George),

American composer and teacher; b. Fairbault, Minn., Feb. 28, 1950. He was a pupil of Aschaffenburg and Joseph Wood at the Oberlin (Ohio) Coll. Cons. of Music (B.M., 1972) and of Finney, Bassett, Bolcom, and Eugene Kurtz at the Univ. of Mich. (M.M., 1973; D.M.A., 1977). In 1974 he held a Fulbright grant, in 1975 he was awarded the Charles Ives Prize of the National Inst. of Arts and Letters, in 1977 he held an NEA fellowship, and in 1978 he was awarded a Martha Baird Rockefeller grant. In 1976 he joined the faculty of the Univ. of British Columbia in Vancouver as an asst. prof., and subsequently was made an assoc. prof. in 1982 and a prof. of composition in 1987. Chatman is an eclectic composer whose output has ventured beyond post-serialism. His orch. and vocal works have been widely performed in North America and abroad.

WORKS: ORCH.: *Occasions* (1975–77); *Grouse Mountain Lullaby* (1978; also for Symphonic Band, 1979); *They All Replied* for Symphonic Band (1978); *Crimson Dream* (1982–83); *Mountain Sojourn* for Symphonic Band (1984); *Mirage* (1987); *Variations on a Canadian Folk Song* for 2 Pianos and Orch. (1989); *Piano Concerto* (1990); *Dream Fantasy* (1992); *Walnut Grove Suite* for Symphonic Band (1997); *Prairie Dawn* for Clarinet and Orch. (1998; Vancouver, June 13, 1999); *Tara's Dream* (1999; Vancouver, Jan. 7, 2000); *Fanfare for the Millennium* (1999; Vancouver, Jan. 7, 2000). **CHAMBER:** *Music for Timpani, Alto Flute, Trombone, and Piano* (1971); *O lo velo* for Alto Saxophone and Percussion (1973); *On the Contrary* for Clarinet and 9 Players (1973–74); *Quiet Exchange* for Alto Saxophone or Clarinet and Percussion (1976); *Northern Drones* for Viola and Offstage Percussion (1976); *Outer Voices* for 8 Players (1978); *Variations on "Home on the Range"* for String Quartet or Saxophone Quartet (1979); *Nocturne* for Flute, Violin, Viola, and Cello (1980); *Screams and Whimpers* for Saxophone Quartet (1981); *Gossamer Leaves* for Clarinet and Piano (1981); *Douce bordure* for Bass Clarinet, Vibraphone, and Harp (1984); *Twenty Moods of Emily* for Flute, Oboe, Clarinet, and Horn (1985); *Cycles* for Chamber Ensemble (1988); *Clarinet Quintet* (1988); *Night Awakening* for Chamber Ensemble (1989); *Music for 2 Alto Saxophones* (1989); *Creatures of Earth and Sky* for Harp (1992); *Music for Cello and Piano* (1993). **KEYBOARD: Piano:** *4 Preludes* (1972); *Bittersweet Rag* (1979); *Black and White Fantasy* (1981); *Fantasies* (1993); *Escapades* (1996); *Bells and Blues* for Piano, 4-Hands (1997). **VOCAL:** *Whisper, Baby* for Chorus, Piano, and Percussion (1975); *Moonset* for Chorus, 5 Percussion, and Organ (1979); *Shadow River* for Soprano and 5 Instruments (1981); *An Elizabethan Spring* for Chorus (1983); *Love and Shapes High Fantastical* for Narrator, Chorus, English Horn, Piano, and Harp (1984);

There is Sweet Music Here for Chorus and Oboe (1984); *An Elizabethan Summer* for Chorus (1988); *Lo in a Manger* for Chorus and Piano (1989); *Blow, Blow, Thou Winter Wind* for Chorus (1991); *5 Songs* for Soprano and Piano (1993); *Greater Love* for Chorus and Oboe (1996); *Due West* for Chorus (1997); *Reconciliation* for Men's Chorus and Flugelhorn (1997); *In Flanders Fields* for Men's Chorus (1998); *Gloria* for Chorus (1998); *A Destiny in Song* for Chorus, Brass Quintet, and Organ (1999).
—NS/LK/DM

Chaumont, Lambert,

South Netherlands priest and composer; b. probably in Liège, c. 1630; d. Huy, April 23, 1712. He became a lay brother at the Carmelite monastery in Liège in 1649. After completing his novitiate at the Rheims monastery, he returned to the Carmelite monastery in Liège. In 1674 he became rector of the parish of St. Martin in Huy. From 1688 he was pater of the Carmelites in Huy and a priest in the parish of St. Germain. He publ. a fine vol. of *Pièces d'orgue sur les 8 tons* (Huy, 1695; ed. in Monuments leodiensium musicorum, series A, I, 1939, and in Le pupitre, XXV, 1970).—LK/DM

Chausson, (Amédée-) Ernest,

distinguished French composer; b. Paris, Jan. 20, 1855; d.in a bicycle accident in Limay, near Mantes, June 10, 1899. He studied with Massenet at the Paris Cons., then took private lessons with Franck, and began to compose. The influence of Wagner as well as that of Franck determined the harmonic and melodic elements in Chausson's music. Despite these derivations, however, he succeeded in establishing an individual style, tense in its chromaticism and somewhat flamboyant in its melodic expansion. The French character of his music is unmistakable in the elegance and clarity of its structural plan. He was active in musical society in Paris and was secretary of the Société Nationale de Musique from 1889 until his death. He composed relatively little music; possessing private means, he was not compelled to seek employment as a professional musician.

WORKS: DRAMATIC: Opera: *Les Caprices de Marianne* (1882–84); *Hélène* (1883–84); *Le Roi Arthus* (1886–95; Brussels, Nov. 30, 1903). **INCIDENTAL MUSIC:** To Shakespeare's *The Tempest* (Paris, Dec. 1888), Aristophanes's *The Birds* (1889), and Boucher's *La Légende de Sainte Cécile* (1891; Paris, Jan. 25, 1892). **ORCH.:** *Viviane*, symphonic poem (1882; rev. 1887); *Solitude dans les bois*, symphonic poem (1886; not extant); Sym. in B-flat major (1889–90; Paris, April 18, 1898); *Poème* for Violin and Orch. (1896; Paris, April 4, 1897); *Soir de fête*, symphonic poem (1897–98). **CHAMBER:** Piano Trio (1881); *Andante and Allegro* for Clarinet and Piano (1881); *Concert* for Piano, Violin, and String Quartet (1889–91); Piano Quartet (1897); *Pièce* for Cello or Viola and Piano (1897); String Quartet (1897–99; unfinished; completed by D'Indy); piano pieces. **VOCAL:** *Jeanne d'arc*, scene lyrique for Solo Voices, Women's Voices, and Piano (c. 1880); *Hymne à la nature* for 4 Voices and Orch. (1881); *L'arabe*, cantata for Tenor, Men's Voices, and Orch. (1881); *Hymne védique* for 4 Voices and Orch. (1886); *Poème de l'amour et de la mer* for Solo Voice and Orch. (1882–90; rev. 1893); *Ballata* for 4 Voices (1896–97); *Chanson perpétuelle* for Soprano and Orch. (1898); songs for Solo Voice and Piano; sacred works, including 8 motets (1883–88) and a *Tantum ergo* (1891).

BIBL.: H. Oulmont, *Musique de l'amour: E. C. et la "bande à Franck"* (Paris, 1935); J.-P. Barricelli and L. Weinstein, *E. C.* (Norman, Okla., 1955); J. Gallois, *E. C.: L'Homme et son oeuvre* (Paris, 1967; rev. ed., 1994); R. Grover, *E. C.: The Man and His Music* (London, 1980).—NS/LK/DM

Chávez (y Ramírez), Carlos (Antonio de Padua),

distinguished Mexican composer and conductor; b. Calzada de Tacube, near Mexico City, June 13, 1899; d. Mexico City, Aug. 2, 1978. He studied piano as a child with Pedro Luis Ogazón, then studied harmony with Juan B. Fuentes and Manuel Ponce. He began to compose very early in life. He wrote a Sym. at the age of 16, and made effective piano arrangements of popular Mexican songs and also wrote many piano pieces of his own. His first important work was a ballet on an Aztec subject, *El fuego nuevo* (1921), commissioned by the Secretariat of Public Education of Mexico. Historical and national Mexican subject matter remained the primary source of inspiration in many of his works, but he rarely resorted to literal quotations from authentic folk melodies; rather, he sublimated and distilled the melo-rhythmic Mexican elements, resulting in a sui generis style of composition. In 1922–23 he traveled in France, Austria, and Germany, and became acquainted with the modern developments in composition. The influence of this period on his evolution as a composer is reflected in the abstract titles of his piano works, such as *Aspectos, Energía,* and *Unidad.* Returning to Mexico, he organized and conducted a series of concerts of new music, giving first Mexican performances of works by Stravinsky, Schoenberg, Satie, Milhaud, and Varèse. From 1926 to 1928 he lived in N.Y. In 1928 he organized the Orquesta Sinfónica de Mexico, of which he remained the principal conductor until 1949. Works of modern music occupied an important part in the program of this orch., including 82 first performances of works by Mexican composers, many of them commissioned by Chávez; Silvestre Revueltas was among those encouraged by Chávez to compose. During his tenure as conductor, Chávez engaged a number of famous foreign musicians as guest conductors, as well as numerous soloists. In 1948 the orch. was renamed the Orquesta Sinfónica Nacional; it remains a permanent institution. Chávez served as director of the Conservatorio Nacional de Música from 1928 to 1933 and again in 1934; he was general director of the Instituto Nacional de Bellas Artes from 1946 to 1952. Beginning in 1936 Chávez conducted a great number of concerts with major American orchs., and also conducted concerts in Europe and South America. Culturally, he maintained a close connection with progressive artists and authors of Mexico, particularly the painter Diego Rivera; his *Sinfonía proletaria* for Chorus and Orch. reflects his political commitment. In 1958–59 he was the Charles Eliot Norton Prof. of Poetry at Harvard Univ.; these lectures were publ. as *Musical Thought* (Cambridge, Mass., 1960). Chávez also publ. a book of essays, *Toward a New Music* (N.Y., 1937).

WORKS: DRAMATIC: O p e r a : *Panfilo and Lauretta* (1953; in Eng., N.Y., May 9, 1957; rev. Spanish version as *El Amor propiciado,* Mexico City, Oct. 28, 1959; later retitled *The Visitors*). **B a l l e t :** *El fuego nuevo* (1921; Mexico City, Nov. 4, 1928); *Los cuatro soles* (1925; Mexico City, July 22, 1930); *Caballos de Vapor* (1926; 1st perf. in Eng. as *HP,* i.e., *Horsepower,* Philadelphia, March 31, 1932); *Antígona* (Mexico City, Sept. 20, 1940; 1st perf. as incidental music for Sophocles' *Antigone,* 1932); *La hija de Cólquide* (1943; 1st perf. as accompaniment to the Martha Graham Dance Company as *Dark Meadow,* N.Y., Jan. 23, 1946); *Pirámide* (1968). **ORCH.:** *Sinfonía* (1915); *Cantos de Méjico* for Mexican Orch. (1933); 7 syms.: No. 1, *Sinfonía de Antígona,* derived from his incidental music for *Antigone* (Mexico City, Dec. 15, 1933), No. 2, *Sinfonía India* (1935; broadcast, N.Y., Jan. 23, 1936), No. 3 (1951; Caracas, Dec. 11, 1954), No. 4, *Sinfonía romántica* (1952; Louisville, Feb. 11, 1953), No. 5 for Strings (Los Angeles, Dec. 1, 1953), No. 6 (1961; N.Y., May 7, 1964), and No. 7 (1960; unfinished); *Obertura republicana* (Mexico City, Oct. 18, 1935); Concerto for 4 Horns (Washington, D.C., April 11, 1937; rev. 1964); Piano Concerto (1938–40; N.Y. Phil., Jan. 1, 1942); *Cuatro nocturnos* for Soprano, Contralto, and Orch. (1939); Toccata (1947); Violin Concerto (1948; Mexico City, Feb. 29, 1952); *Soli No. 3* for Bassoon, Trumpet, Viola, Timpani, and Orch. (Baden-Baden, Nov. 24, 1965); *Resonancias* (Mexico City, Sept. 18, 1964); *Elatio* (Mexico City, July 15, 1967); *Discovery* (Aptos, Calif., Aug. 24, 1969); *Clio,* symphonic ode (Houston, March 23, 1970); *Initium* (1972; Akron, Ohio, Oct. 9, 1973); *Mañanas Mexicanas* (1974; orig. for Piano, 1967); *Sonante* for Strings (1974); Trombone Concerto (1975–76; Washington, D.C., May 9, 1978). **CHAMBER:** Piano and String Sextet (1919); 3 string quartets (1921, 1932, 1944); *3 Pieces* for Guitar (1923); Violin Sonatina (1924); Cello Sonatina (1924); *Energía* for 9 Instruments (1925; Paris, June 11, 1931); Sonata for 4 Horns (1929); 3 of 4 pieces under the generic title *Soli* (No. 1 for Oboe, Clarinet, Trumpet, and Bassoon, 1933; No. 2 for Wind Quintet, 1961; No. 4 for Brass Trio, 1966); *3 Espirales* for Violin and Piano (1934); *Xochipilli Macuilxochitl* for 4 Wind Instruments and 6 Percussionists (N.Y., May 16, 1940); *Toccata* for 6 Percussionists (1942; Mexico City, Oct. 31, 1947); 2 of 3 instrumental pieces, under the generic title *Invention* (No. 2 for String Trio, 1965; No. 3 for Harp, 1967), introducing an inductive method of thematic illation in which each musical phrase is the logical consequent of the one immediately preceding it; *Upingos* for Oboe (1957); *Fuga HAG,C* for Violin, Viola, Cello, and Double Bass (1964); *Tambuco* for 6 Percussionists (1964); *Variations* for Violin and Piano (1969). **KEYBOARD: P i a n o :** 6 sonatas (*Sonata fantasía,* 1917; 1919; 1928; 1941; 1960; 1961); *Berceuse* (1918); *7 Madrigals* (1921–22); *Polígonos* (1923); *Aspectos I* and *II* (1923); Sonatina (1924); *Blues* (1928); *Fox* (1928); *Paisaje* (1930); *Unidad* (1930); *10 Preludes* (1937); *Fugas* (1942); *4 Études* (1949); *Left Hand Inversions of 5 Chopin Études* (1950); *Invention* No. 1 (1958); *Estudio a Rubinstein,* in minor seconds (1974); *5 caprichos* (1975–76). **VOCAL: C h o r a l :** *Tierra mojada* for Chorus, Oboe, and English Horn (Mexico City, Sept. 6, 1932); *El Sol* for Chorus and Orch. (Mexico City, July 17, 1934); *Sinfonía proletaria (Llamadas)* for Chorus and Orch. (Mexico City, Sept. 29, 1934); *La paloma azul* for Chorus and Chamber Orch. (1940); *Prometheus Bound,* cantata (1956; Aptos, Calif., Aug. 27, 1972). **V o i c e and O r c h . :** *Cuatro nocturnos* for Soprano, Contralto, and Orch. (1939). **V o i c e and P i a n o :** *3 exágonos* (1923); *Inutil epigrama* (1923); *Otros 3 exágonos* (1924); *3 poemas* (1938); *La casada infiel* (1941).

BIBL.: R. Morillo, *C. C., vida y obra* (Buenos Aires, 1960); R. Halffter, compiler, *C. C., Catalogo completo de sus obras* (Mexico City, 1971); R. Parker, *C. C., Mexico's Modern-Orpheus* (Boston, 1983); G. Carmona, ed., *Epistolario selecto de C. C.* (Mexico City, 1989); J. Alcaraz, *C. C.: Un constante renacer* (Mexico City, 1996); R. Parker, *C. C.: A Guide to Research* (N.Y., 1998).—NS/LK/DM

Chaynes, Charles,

Chaynes, Charles, French composer and broadcasting administrator; b. Toulouse, July 11, 1925. He first studied with his parents, who taught at the Toulouse Cons., and then entered the Paris Cons., where he took courses in violin with Gabriel Bouillon, in chamber music with Joseph Calvet, in composition with Milhaud and Rivier, and in harmony and fugue with N. and J. Gallon (Premier Grand Prix de Rome, 1951, with the cantata *Et l'homme vit se rouvrir les portes*). After composing at the French Academy in Rome (1952–55), he returned to Paris and joined the ORTF as a radio producer in 1956. He then was director of its France-Musique channel (1965–75) before serving as its chief of the music service (1975–90). In 1960 he won the Concours Prince Rainier of Monaco, in 1965 the Grand Prix de la Ville de Paris, in 1979 the UNESCO composition prize, and in 1998 the Prix Cino del Duca de l'Institut de France. As a composer, Chaynes has pursued an independent course in which free atonality is enlivened by infusions of East Asian and African modes of expression.

WORKS: DRAMATIC: O p e r a : *Erzsebet* (1982; Paris, March 28, 1983); *Noces de sang*, after García Lorca (1986); *Jocaste* (1991–92); *Cecilia* (1998). **ORCH.:** *Divertissement* for Strings (1949); *Danses symphoniques* (1951); Concerto for Strings (1953); *Ode pour une mort tragique* (1953–54); Sym. (1955); 2 trumpet concertos (1956, 1995); 2 violin concertos (1958, 1993); *Deuxième Concerto* (1960; Monte Carlo, Nov. 25, 1962); *Quatre illustrations pour "La Flûte de jade"* for Flute and Orch. (Aix-en-Provence, July 23, 1960); Piano Concerto (1961; Paris, Feb. 17, 1966); *Expressions contrastées* (1965; Strasbourg, June 23, 1966); Organ Concerto (1966); *Irradiations* for Violin, Cello, Harpsichord, and Strings (1968; Bordeaux, June 9, 1969); *Transmutations* (1969; Besançon, Sept. 4, 1971); *Lieu de lumière* (1972); *Mazapan* (1973; Paris, June 7, 1974); *Peintures noires* (1974; Paris, April 27, 1975); *Visions concertantes* for Guitar and Strings (Besançon, Sept. 11, 1976); *Les Caractères illisibles* for Chamber Orch. (1978; Paris, Jan. 21, 1980); Clarinet Concerto (1978; Orléans, Dec. 2, 1979); *Visages Myceniens* (1983); *Litanies* (1988); 2 flute concertos (1991, 1994). **CHAMBER:** Violin Sonata (1952); *Serenade* for Wind Quintet (1954); *Lied, Scherzando et Final* for Double Bass and Piano (1957); *Variations sur Tanka* for Flute and Piano (1962); *Trois Études linéaires* for Chamber Group (1963); *Commentaires concertants* for Chamber Group (1964); *Concordances* for Bronte, Percussion, and Piano (1967); String Quartet (1970); *Séquences pour l'Apocalypse* for 6 Instruments (1971–72); *Tarquinia* for Ondes Martenot, Piano, and Percussion (1973); *Onze visages ou l'Antifugue* for 11 Strings (1979); *Valeurs transposées* for Chamber Group (1979); *Lorsque Cecile chantait* for 5 Instruments (1983); *Kermesse flamande* for 15 Wind Instruments (1987); *Comme un raga* for Violin (1988); *Pour caresser la silence* for Flute, Clarinet, Violin, Cello, Harp, Piano, and Percussion (1992); *Pour faire le portrait d'un oiseau* for 11 Strings (1994). **KEYBOARD: P i a n o :** *M'zab* (1971); *Et si c'etait une valse* for 2 Pianos (1977). **O r g a n :** *A la recherche du sacré* (1983); *Vers la lumière* (1990). **VOCAL:** *Et l'homme vit se rouvrir les portes*, cantata (1951); *Par ces Chemins du coeur*, 6 prayers for Soprano and Orch. or Piano (1953); *Joie aux âmes* for 4 Soloists and 5 Instruments (1962); *Quatres Poèmes de Sappho* for Soprano and String Trio (1968); *Pour un Monde Noir* for Soprano and Orch. (1976–78); *Oginoha* for Soprano, Flute, Celtic Harp, and Percussion (1986); *Au-delà de l'Espérance* for Mezzo-soprano and Piano (1989).

—NS/LK/DM

Cheap Trick,

Cheap Trick, the power pop band that wouldn't go away (f. 1973, Rockford, Ill.). **MEMBERSHIP:** Robin Zander, voc. (b. Loves Park, Ill., Jan. 23, 1953); Rick Neilson, gtr. (b. Rockford, Ill., Dec. 22, 1946); Tom Petersson, bs. (b. Rockford, Ill., May 9, 1950); Bun E. Carlos (real name, Brad Carlson), drm. (b. Rockford, Ill., June 12, 1951).

Rick Neilson's parents sang opera and choral music professionally. They also owned a music shop in Rockford, Ill. This gave Neilson access to a variety of instruments. He started playing the drums, but with the coming of the Beatles, he took up the guitar. Brad Carlson, the son of a roofer, was two grades behind Neilson in the same school. He bought his first drum set at Neilson's father's store. Tom Petersson started out on the guitar, but switched to bass because he wanted to play with Neilson.

The three wannabe stars played in myriad local bands through the 1960s, both together and separately. Neilson and Petersson recorded a single in 1967 as the Grim Reapers and an album for Epic in 1969. The record went nowhere. The Reapers relocated several times under several names, finally settling back in Rockford as Cheap Trick. They brought Carlos and Zander on board, rounding out the quartet in 1974. Between 1974 and 1977, they played 200 dates a year, opening shows for groups ranging from KISS to the Kinks.

Epic once again signed the group in 1976, releasing their debut in 1977. It didn't chart in the U.S., but went gold in Japan where the young girls couldn't get enough of Zander's good looks. They put out *In Color* in 1978, a softer, slicker album than their debut. Despite little radio play and no hit singles, the record crept to #73 on the album charts, and went gold in Japan. Later that year, they released *Heaven Tonight*. The song "Surrender" got some album rock play and even managed to garner enough pop radio play to hit #62. The album hit #48. In Japan it went platinum.

By 1978 Cheap Trick were superstars in Japan. They sold out the big Budokan Arena in two hours. They recorded the concert with thoughts of a Japanese live album. Surprisingly, the album started to sell well in the U.S. as an import. Epic tested the water with a nine-track EP serviced to rock radio. The live version of "I Want You to Want Me" started getting considerable play. It rose to #7 in the charts. Epic released the record in the U.S. and it rose to #4, selling platinum (and eventually over 4 million copies). The album went triple platinum in Japan. They followed the hit single with another live track, a cover of Fats Domino's "Ain't That a Shame," which hit #35.

By the time *Live at Budokan* came out in the U.S., Cheap Trick had finished their next studio album, the highly produced *Dream Police*. The album hit #6 in the U.S., with the title track rising to #26 on the singles chart. A 10" EP, *Found All the Part*, consisting of previously unreleased tracks from their first four albums, hit #39. In 1979 the band went into the studio with producer George Martin and recorded *All Shook Up*. Despite the absence of a Top 40 single, the record manages to reach #24 and sold gold.

By 1980 the band had been touring or recording nearly continuously for seven years. Feeling burned out from the constant road work, Petersson left the band. He relocated to N.Y. with his wife. They formed a band and released an album.

The group replaced Petersson with Jon Brant (b. Feb. 20, 1954) in time for him to get on the cover of *One on One*. With a polished studio sheen, the album went platinum, despite peaking at #39. 1983's rawer, more energetic *Next Position Please* topped out at #61, and their next two albums fared little better. These were not the kind of chart numbers Epic wanted from a multi-platinum band.

Before their 1988 album *Lap of Luxury*, several things happened. The band asked Petersson to rejoin the group. The record company brought in outside song-writers to provide the band with some power ballads, the musical flavor of the year. They recorded the material, although they were personally indifferent to it. One of the tunes, "The Flame," became the group's first chart-topping single. Their cover of Elvis Presley's "Don't Be Cruel" hit #4, the first Elvis tune to hit the Top Ten after the King passed on. The album hit #18 and went platinum.

The group tried to recreate this success with 1990's *Busted*, recording more power ballads and another Elvis cover. Their version of "Can't Stop Falling in Love" hit #12, but the album peaked out at #48. Zander cut a solo album in 1993 that didn't chart. The band left Epic and after a while signed on with Warner Bros. Their Warner debut, 1994's *Woke Up with a Monster*, debuted on the charts at #123 and dropped off two weeks later. That same year, Epic released *Budokan II*.

The band continued to tour for their core fans. Several influential bands such as the Smashing Pumpkins, who considered the band a major influence, asked them to open tours. They played the 1996 Lollapalooza tour. That same year, Epic released a boxed set of the band's hits, misses, and unreleased tracks.

The band signed with independent Red Ant records in 1997 and recorded the critically lauded *Cheap Trick*, but the album didn't sell well. They played a series of concerts that recapped their first four albums song for song. Several of these tracks found their way onto the live hits package *Music for Hangovers*. Despite this brief foray into nostalgia, the band promises to continue to create and rock until they drop, or their fans lose interest.

Disc.: *Cheap Trick* (1977); *In Color* (1977); *Heaven Tonight* (1978); *Dream Police* (1979); *Live at Budokan* (1979); *All Shook Up* (1980); *One on One* (1982); *Next Position Please* (1983); *Standing on the Edge* (1985); *The Doctor* (1986); *Lap of Luxury* (1988); *Busted* (1990); *I Want You to Want Me* (1992); *Voices* (1992); *Budokan II* (live; 1994); *Woke up with a Monster* (1994); *Cheap Trick* (1997); *Music for Hangovers* (live; 1999).—**HB**

Cheatham, Doc (actually, Adolphus Anthony),

famed, long-lived jazz trumpeter, saxophonist; b. Nashville, June 13, 1905; d. Washington, D.C., June 2, 1997. He gained his nickname through having several relatives in the medical profession. Cheatam was originally taught by "Professor" N. C. Davis in Nashville. He gained his first professional experience playing with Marion Hardy's Band for the "Sunshine Sammy" Show (he later claimed that he worked with Bessie Smith during this period, but this can't be substantiated), then toured with John "Bearcat" Williams' Synco Jazzers (c. 1924). After moving to Chicago, he played cornet, soprano and tenor saxophones in Albert Wynn's Band, then led his own band (1926). He first heard New Orleans–style music in Chicago. From King Oliver's valet, Cheatham acquired the brass and copper mute he used from then on. He recorded on soprano saxophone with Ma Rainey. He joined Bobby Lee in Philadelphia on trumpet, then worked there with Wilbur de Paris (1927–28). After a brief spell with Chick Webb, he joined Sam Wooding in N.Y. and sailed with him to Europe (1928–30). He returned to U.S. with Marion Hardy's Alabamians (1930–32), also playing for a spell in McKinney's Cotton Pickers (summer 1931–32). Cheatham worked with Cab Calloway (1933–39, including a 1934 trip to Europe), then joined the Teddy Wilson Big Band (October 1939). After a brief stint with Benny Carter (1940), he worked with Fletcher Henderson (1941), Teddy Hill, and the Eddie Heywood Sextet (September 1943–45). Then, reportedly suffering a nervous breakdown and quitting the stage, partly in response to the changes in jazz styles, Cheatham taught beginners regularly at his own N.Y. studio and worked in the post office. He also played with Claude Hopkins (1946) and then began working regularly in Marcelino Guerra's Band (1948–50). Throughout the 1950s and 1960s, he did a considerable amount of work with Latin American bands, including Perez Prado (1951–52) and Machito. He toured with Cab Calloway (summer 1951), then worked mainly in Boston (1952–55) with Vic Dickenson. During this time, he began a long friendship with George Wein when both played in the house band at Wein's Mahogany Hall Club; he also had a spell leading Wilbur de Paris's "second" ("New New Orleans") band; he was first brought in to second the leader's brother Sidney, but soon was given more solo responsibilities. He recorded and toured with Wilbur de Paris, including trips to Africa (1957) and Europe (1960); he also toured Europe with Sam Price (1958) and Africa with Herbie Mann's Latin-oriented group (1960). He led his own band at the International on Broadway for five years (1960–65). He worked regularly with Benny Goodman (1966–67, including trip to Belgium), and toured Europe with the "Top Brass" package (1967). He frequently visited Europe, often with his good friend Sammy Price; it was Price who, during a 1975 recording session in Paris, encouraged Cheatham to make his first recorded vocal, "What Can I Say Dear After I Say I'm Sorry?" Cheatham continued to freelance in many varied musical aggregations, including regular appearances as soloist with Ricardo Ray's Latin American Band and frequent playing trips to Puerto Rico. Throughout his career, he has taken part in freelance recording sessions with Count Basie, Max Kaminsky, Pee Wee Russell, John Handy, Leonard Gaskin, and Juanita Hall, among others. He played at President Jimmy Carter's White House Jazz Party (June 1978). From the early 1980s until his death, he appeared every Sunday at the afternoon brunch at Sweet Basil in N.Y. Until about 1990, he prided himself on his health and took long walks daily. Towards the end, he could hardly walk because of arthritis, but he avoided wheelchairs and hated a widely distributed picture of him in a rocking chair because he said it made him look old. He last performed on May 31, 1997, at the Blues Alley club in Washington, as part of a tour with Nicholas Payton. The next morning, as he prepared to depart from his hotel for N.Y., he suffered a stroke and died.

DISC.: *Adolphus D.C.* (1973); *Hey Doc!* (1975); *Doc and Sammy* (1976); *Good for What Ails Ya* (1977); *Black Beauty* (1979); *John, Doc and Herb* (1979); *It's a Good Life* (1982); *I've Got A Crush on You* (1982); *Too Marvelous For Words* (1982); *At the Bern Jazz Festival* (1983); *Fabulous* (1983); *Highlights in Jazz* (1985); *Tribute to Billie Holiday* (1987); *Tribute to Louis Armstrong* (1988); *Echoes of New Orleans* (1992); *You're a Sweetheart* (1992); *Legendary Pioneers of Jazz: The Eighty-Seven Years of D.C.* (1993); *Swinging Down in New Orleans* (1995); *D.C. and Nicholas Payton* (1994). **—JC/LP**

Cheek, John (Taylor), American bass-baritone; b. Greenville, S.C., Aug. 17, 1948. He received a B.Mus. degree from the N.C. School of the Arts, and then studied in Siena with Gino Bechi at the Accademia Musicale Chigiana, where he received the Diploma of Merit. He made his professional debut in 1975. On June 6, 1977, he made his first appearance with the Metropolitan Opera as Ferrando during the company's visit to the Wolf Trap Farm Park. He then made his formal debut with the company in N.Y. as the physician in *Pelléas et Mélisande* on Oct. 11, 1977; he later sang Pimen in *Boris Godunov*, Ferrando in *Il Trovatore*, Wurm in *Luisa Miller*, Klingsor in *Parsifal*, and also Panthée in *Les Troyens* at the opening-night celebration of the Metropolitan's centenary season in 1983–84. In 1987 he won the N.C. Arts Prize. In 1990 he sang Ramfis in Cincinnati, and in 1996 he returned there as Don Pasquale. On Aug. 28, 1999, he created the role of Lawyer Royall in Paulus's *Summer* in Pittsfield, Mass.**—NS/LK/DM**

Chemin-Petit, Hans (Helmuth), German composer and teacher; b. Potsdam, June 24, 1902; d. Berlin, April 12, 1981. His family was of remote French origin. Both his father and grandfather were professional musicians. He studied cello in Berlin with Hugo Becker and composition with Paul Juon. He subsequently was mostly active as a cello teacher, serving on the staff of the Berlin Hochschule für Musik and later at the Akademie der Künste; in 1968 he was appointed director of its music dept. As a composer, he followed the median line of neo-Classicism.

WORKS: CHAMBER Opera: *Der gefangene Vogel* (1927); *Lady Monika* (1930); *König Nicolo* (1962); *Die Komödiantin* (1968); *Die Rivalinnen* (1970). **ORCH.:** 2 syms. (1932, 1949); Cello Concerto (1932); *Concerto for Orchestra* (1944); Concerto for Organ, Strings, and Kettledrums (1963); *Musik* (1968). **OTHER:** 2 recorder sonatas (1958, 1960); Symphonic Cantata (1967); other cantatas; church music; piano pieces.

BIBL.: A Witte, *H. C.-P.* (Berlin, 1987).**—NS/LK/DM**

Chen Yi, Chinese composer and teacher; b. Guangzhou, April 4, 1953. She studied at the Beijing Central Cons. (1977–86), where her composition mentors were Wu Zu-qiang and guest composer Alexander Goehr. In 1986 she went to the U.S. and pursued training with Chou Wen-chung and Mario Davidovsky at Columbia Univ. (D.M.A., 1993). From 1993 to 1996 she served as composer-in-residence of the Women's Phil in San Francisco and of the Aptos Creative Arts Program. In 1996 she became a teacher of composition at the Peabody Cons. of Music in Baltimore, and in 1998 a prof. of composition at the Univ. of Mo.–Kansas City Cons. of Music. In 1999 she received the first $25,000.00 Eddie Medora King Award for Musical Composition of the Univ. of Tex. at Austin, the third largest composer's monetary award in the U.S. Her music interweaves traditional Chinese musical rituals and contemporary Western techniques.

WORKS: ORCH.: *Xian Shi*, viola concerto (1983); *Duo Ye No. 1* (1985) and *No. 2* (N.Y., Oct. 11, 1987); 2 syms.: No. 1 (Beijing, May 31, 1986) and No. 2 (1993; San Francisco, Jan. 29, 1994); *Sprout* for Strings (Beijing, May 31, 1986); *Two Sets* of Wind and Percussion Instruments (Beijing, May 31, 1986); Piano Concerto (1992; N.Y., Oct. 14, 1994); *Shuo* for Strings (1994; San Jose, Calif., Jan. 22, 1995); *The Linear* (1994; Oakland, Calif., June 3, 1995); *Ge Xu* (1994; Berkeley, Jan. 28, 1995); *Romance of Hsiao and Ch'in* for 2 Violins and String Orch. (1995; N.Y., Aug. 11, 1996); *Golden Flute* for Flute and Orch. (Duluth, Nov. 8, 1997); *Fiddle Suite* for Huqin and Strings (1997; Tokyo, April 19, 1998; also for Chinese Fiddles, Huqin, and String Quartet); *Romance and Dance* for Strings (1998); Percussion Concerto (1998; Singapore, March 8, 1999); *Eleanor's Gift*, cello concerto (San Francisco, Dec. 10, 1998; rev. version, N.Y., May 21, 1999); *Momentum* (1998; N.Y., May 2, 1999); *Dunhuang Fantasy*, concerto for Organ and Winds (1999); Violin Concerto (2000). **CHAMBER:** String Quartet (1982; Zagreb, July 5, 1985); Woodwind Quintet (Wellesley, Mass., Aug. 5, 1987); *Near Distance*, sextet (1988; Kraków, Jan. 8, 1989); *Sparkle*, octet (N.Y., Oct. 21, 1992); *Song in Winter* for Harpsichord, Di, and Zheng (1993; N.Y., March 23, 1994; also for Flute, Zheng, Piano, and Percussion, Boston, March 2, 1994); *Qi* for Flute, Cello, Piano, and Percussion (1996–97; San Francisco, March 17, 1997); *Fiddle Suite* for Chinese Fiddle, Huqin, and String Quartet (1997); *Feng* for Wind Quintet (1998); *Sound of the Five* for Cello and String Quartet (1998). **VOCAL:** *Three Poems from the Song Dynasty* for Chorus, after Li Qing-zhao, Xin Qi-ji, and Su Shi (1985); *As In A Dream* for Soprano, Violin, and Viola, after Li Qing-zhao (N.Y., Oct. 17, 1988); *A Set of Chinese Folk Songs* for Chorus (San Francisco, April 24, 1994); *Tang Poems*, cantata for Chorus and Chamber Orch. (Peoria, April 27, 1995; also for Chorus); *Singin' in the Dark* (Songs of the American Frontier) for Chorus and Orch. (San Francisco, July 22, 1995); *Chinese Myths*, cantata for Men's Chorus and Orch. (San Francisco, June 14, 1996); *Lament of the Twin Stars* for Men's Chorus, arranged from Cantonese music (1996); *Spring Dreams* for Chorus (Ithaca, N.Y., Nov. 15, 1997); *Feng* for Woodwind Quintet (1998; Berkeley, Jan. 13, 1999); *Sound Of The Five* for Cello and String Quartet (N.Y., Nov. 15, 1998); *Chinese Poems* for Children's Chorus (San Francisco, May 24, 1999). **OTHER:** Piano pieces, numerous works for solo instruments, and several works for orchestras and ensembles of Chinese instruments, including *The Tide* for Xun, Yangqin, Pipa, Zheng, Percussion, Gaohu, and Erhu (N.Y., Oct. 30, 1988), *Suite*, quintet for Pipa, Di, Yangqin, Sanxian, and Erhu (N.Y., Oct. 27, 1991), and *Pipa Rhyme* for Pipa and 14 Players (N.Y., June 25, 1993).**—LK/DM**

Cher (originally, **Sarkisian, Cherilyn**), pop culture triple-threat with award-winning records, films, and TV shows; b. El Centro, Calif., May 20, 1946. The first 17 years of Cher's life were tough. Her mother was a model and actress, her father a truck driver who left the family when Cher was a few months old (Cher's mother remarried him twice). When she was young, Cher was placed in a Catholic home until her mother could support her. In her teens, she ran away from home and met aspiring music mogul Sonny (real name, Salvatore) Bono (b. Detroit, Feb. 16, 1935) in a coffee shop in 1963.

Bono worked as a general assistant to wall-of-sound producer Phil Spector. Bono got Cher work as a backing vocalist on sessions for the Ronettes and the Crystals (both Sonny and Cher can be heard in the background on "Da Do Ron Ron"). By 1964 Cher and Bono had married. Spector produced her first record that year, "Ringo, I Love You," released under the nom de disc of "Bonnie Jo Mason." She and Bono then cut a couple of unsuccessful sides as Caesar & Cleo before opting for the more straightforward Sonny and Cher in 1965.

That year Cher was signed as a solo artist to Imperial as Cherilyn. Sonny put her into the studio, where they cut "Baby Don't Go." Spector offered Bono $500 for it, so Bono figured it was good and started shopping it. He and Cher landed at Atlantic's offshoot label, Atco. Their meteor started to take off with their single "I Got You Babe." It went gold and topped the charts for three weeks in August 1965, their only chart topper together. At the same time, Cher's cover of Dylan's "All I Really Want to Do" rose to #15 for Imperial. More hits followed over the next three months: "Laugh at Me" (Sonny, solo, #10), "Where Do You Go" (Cher, solo, #25), "Baby Don't Go" (#8), "Just You" (#20), and "But You're Mine" (#15). They were also featured in one of the infamous beach movies of the day, *Wild on the Beach*. With their proto-hippy clothes and image, they established a visual presence to go with their musical mien.

As summer turned to winter, Sonny and Cher's fortunes cooled off with the weather. Their next single, "What Now My Love" only reached #14. After eight months, "Little Man" only hit #21. Cher's solo career fared a little better, landing her first major solo hit with Sonny's "Bang Bang (My Baby Shot Me Down)" got as high as #2. Her version of "Alfie" stalled at 32. In January 1967 the duo landed one more major hit, "The Beat Goes On," which got as high as #7. Cher also hit with "You Better Sit Down Kids." The tune, dealing frankly with divorce, hit #9. After that, Sonny and Cher's pop careers started to ebb. They played themselves in William Friedkin's minor 1967 film *Good Times*. Sonny then tried his hand at filmmaking, hoping to launch Cher as a major movie star with *Chastity* in 1969. The film stiffed, costing the duo a good portion of their savings.

The duo put together a nightclub act and settled in Vegas. The act, featuring music and a wise-cracking Cher to Sonny's straight man, launched them into their next career as the stars of their own TV variety show. The show ran from 1971 to 1974 (although they divorced in 1973). In addition to elevating Sonny and Cher to

major celebrities, it revived their recording careers. "All I Ever Need is You" rose to #7 in the fall of 1971, topping the Adult Contemporary charts. At around the same time, Cher topped the charts with her gold single "Gypsies, Tramps and Thieves." Early in 1972, the duo's "A Cowboy's Work is Never Done" (#8) competed with Cher's solo version of "The Way of Love" (#7). She followed that with "Living in a House Divided" (#22), which was followed by the last Sonny and Cher hit, a rewrite of a Budweiser beer commercial "When You Say Love" (#32).

The show also elevated Cher as a fashion plate and sex symbol. Thanks to her love of often-outrageous costumes (many designed by Bob Mackie), she became a regular winner of the annual "Worst Dressed" awards given by various journalists and magazines. Nonetheless, the tackier (and more revealing) the outfit, the more her fans seemed to enjoy it.

After their marriage dissolved, Cher took the TV show solo for a year. In the meantime, she continued to have hit records. "Half Breed" topped the charts for a week in the summer of 1973, followed by another chart topper, "Dark Lady" in the winter of 1974. Both went gold. In the spring of 1974, she returned to the chart with "Train of Thought" which only rose to #27. In 1975 she started an on-again, off-again relationship with Allman Brothers' keyboard player Gregg Allman. Their first marriage lasted a grand total of nine days, after which they reconciled, divorcing in 1977. The marriage produced one album, *Two the Hard Way: Allman and Woman* and a son, Elijah Blue, who leads the band Deadsy.

Cher's solo TV show didn't work out as well as the solo recording career, so Sonny was brought back for the 1976–77 TV series, but the spark was out of the relationship and it showed. Sonny started dabbling in acting, appearing on celebrity driven television shows like *The Love Boat* and *Fantasy Island*, before trying his hand as a restauranteur and moving into politics.

Cher moved to N.Y. After a gold disco record, "Take Me Home" (#8, 1979) and singing background for Meatloaf's "Dead Ringer for Love," she decided to try her hand at acting, too. Eventually she landed a role in the off-Broadway play *Come Back to the Five and Dime, Jimmy Dean, Jimmy Dean* in 1981. When the play became a film a year later, Cher reprised her role. That led to a role in the movie *Silkwood* opposite Meryl Streep, which earned her an Oscar nomination. Her music career took a back seat to her burgeoning film career, which included lead roles in *Mask*, *The Witches of Eastwick*, *Suspect*, *Mermaids*, and an Oscar-winning turn in the 1987 romantic comedy *Moonstruck*.

Capitalizing on her fame from *Moonstruck* and her relationship with David Geffen, Cher started recording again in 1988, hitting #10 with "I Found Someone." This was followed by the #14 "We All Sleep Alone," produced by Jon Bon Jovi. The following year, she had three Top Ten hits, the gold-selling #6 duet with Peter Cetera "After All," the gold #3 "If I Could Turn Back Time," and the #8 "Just Like Jesse James." "If I Could Turn Back Time" also raised eyebrows thanks to Cher's live concert video, featuring one of her scantiest-ever costumes, filmed before a crowd of girl-crazy sailors.

Cher's career slowed following her late 1980s hits. She had but one hit in 1990, the #20 "Heart of Stone." Early in the following year, she hit #33 with a cover of "The Shoop Shoop Song (It's in His Kiss)" that was featured in *Mermaids*, followed at about six-month intervals by "Love and Understanding" (#17) and "Save Up All Your Tears" (#37). With her recording and film career experiencing a slowdown, Cher made exercise videos, which she pitched during a series of infomercials. She also became a spokesperson for various products and services, and did cameos in a couple of Robert Altman films.

By the mid-1990s, Cher's career seemed to have gone into a terminal tailspin. In 1996, Cher filmed *Faithless*, which got panned, directed and starred in an episode of HBO's abortion anthology, *If These Walls Could Talk*, and released her first recording in five years, *It's a Man's World*.

In 1998 Sonny (by then Sen. Salvatore Bono of Calif.) died in a skiing accident. Cher delivered a tearful eulogy, which some found to be in poor taste, and produced and hosted a special for CBS called "Sonny and Me: Cher Remembers." Then, like the proverbial phoenix, Cher scored an unexpected major success with her 1999 disco-revival album, *Believe*. The album went double platinum on the strength of the platinum title track, relaunching her career. She began a successful tour, with many lavish costume changes, that was broadcast live from Las Vegas over HBO.

Her 1999 success made Cher the first female singer to enjoy #1 pop hits in all four decades from the 1960s to the 1990s. One of the world's most beloved entertainers, Cher seems virtually unstoppable.

DISC.: *All I Really Want to Do* (1965); *Cher* (1966); *The Sonny Side of Cher* (1966); *Backstage* (1968); *With Love, Cher* (1968); *3614 Jackson Highway* (1969); *Cher* (1971); *Gypsys, Tramps & Thieves* (1971); *Cher Superpak, Vol. 2* (1972); *Foxy Lady* (1972); *Half-Breed* (1973); *Bittersweet White Light* (1974); *Dark Lady* (1974); *Stars* (1975): *I'd Rather Believe in You* (1976); *Cherished* (1977); *Two the Hard Way (Allman & Woman)* (1977); *This Is Cher* (1978); *Take Me Home* (1979); *Prisoner* (1980); *I Paralyze* (1982); *Cher* (1987); *Heart of Stone* (1989); *Outrageous* (1989); *Love Hurts* (1991); *All I Really Want to Do/The Sonny Side...* (1992); *It's a Man's World* (1996); *You Better Sit Down Kids Great Hits* (1996); *Believe* (1998).

WRITINGS: *The First Time* (N.Y., 1998).

BIBL.: Lawrence J. Quirk, *Totally Uninhibited: The Life and Wild Times of Cher* (N.Y., 1991).—**HB**

Chéreau, Patrice, prominent French theater, film, and opera producer; b. Lézigne, Maine-et-Loire, Nov. 2, 1944. He was a leading theater producer from 1964, serving as co-director of the Théâtre National Populaire (1979–81) and director of the Théâtre des Amandiers in Nanterre (from 1982). As an opera producer, he caused a major stir with his deconstructionist version of the centennial mounting of Wagner's *Ring* cycle at the Bayreuth Festival (1976–80); he also produced the premiere staging of the three-act version of Berg's *Lulu* in Paris (1979) and brought out *Wozzeck* there (1992). In

1994 he staged *Don Giovanni* at the Salzburg Festival. He publ. the book *Si tant que l'opéra soit du théâtre: Notes sur le mise en scène de la création mondiale de l'oeuvre integrale d'Alban Berg "Lulu"* (Toulouse, 1992).—**NS/LK/DM**

Cherkassky, Shura (Alexander Isaakovich), remarkable Russian- born American pianist; b. Odessa, Oct. 7, 1911. He began piano training with his mother. While still a child, he was taken by his family to the U.S., where he continued his studies with Josef Hofmann at the Curtis Inst. of Music in Philadelphia. After making his debut in Baltimore at the age of 11, he appeared as a soloist with Walter Damrosch and the N.Y. Sym. Orch. and performed at the White House in Washington, D.C. (1923); he made his first tour abroad in 1928 with visits to Australia and South Africa. Following a major tour of Europe in 1946, he pursued extensive tours to most of the major music centers in the world. In 1976 he went to Russia for a series of acclaimed concerts, and returned there in 1977 and 1987. He gave many recitals at N.Y.'s 92nd Street Y, which honored him in 1986 with the establishment of the Shura Cherkassky Recital Award to be given annually to a gifted young pianist. On Dec. 2, 1991, he celebrated his 80th year with a recital at N.Y.'s Carnegie Hall in a program of works by Schumann, Chopin, Bach- Busoni, Tchaikovsky-Pabst, Josef Hofmann, and well-received encores. As one of the last representatives of the hallowed Romantic school of piano virtuosity, Cherkassky regaled audiences with a bravura technique and singing tone in the grand Russian manner.

BIBL.: H. Fazzari, ed., *Per un omaggio a S. C.* (Milan, 1998). —**NS/LK/DM**

Cherney, Brian (Irwin), Canadian composer and teacher; b. Peterborough, Ontario, Sept. 4, 1942. He studied composition with Dolin in Toronto (1960–64) and also studied at the Univ. of Toronto (piano with Jacques Abram, 1961–62; Mus.Bac., 1964; composition with Weinzweig; Mus.M., 1967; Ph.D. in musicology, 1974, with the diss. *The Bekker-Pfitzner Controversy: Its Significance for German Music Criticism During the Weimar Republic*). He likewise attended the summer courses in new music given by Ligeti, Stockhausen, Kagel et al. in Darmstadt (1966, 1969). In 1971–72 he was a lecturer at the Univ. of Victoria. In 1972 he became an asst. prof., in 1976 an assoc. prof., and in 1986 a prof. at McGill Univ. He publ. the biography *Harry Somers* (Toronto, 1975). Cherney's String Trio (1976) tied for first place among the recommended works at the International Rostrum of Composers in Paris in 1979, and his *River of Fire* for Oboe d'amore and Harp (1983) won the Jules Léger Prize for Chamber Music in 1985. In his later works, he developed an individualistic style marked by harmonic coherency, poetry, lyricism, and color.

WORKS: ORCH.: 2 sets of *Variations* (1962, 1967); Violin Concerto (1964); *6 Miniatures* for Oboe and Strings (1968); *7 Images* for 22 Players (1971); *Adieux* (1980); *Into the Distant Stillness...* (1984); *Illuminations* for Strings (1987); Oboe Concerto (1989); *Transfiguration* (1990); *Et j'entends la nuit qui chante dans les cloches...* for Piano and Orch. (1990); *Et la solitude dérive au fil des fleuves...* (1995). **Concert Band:** *In the Stillness* *between...* (1982). **CHAMBER:** Violin Sonata (1961); Quintet for Alto Saxophone and String Quartet (1962); Wind Quintet (1965); 4 string quartets (1966, 1970, 1985, 1994); *Kontakion: Quiet Music for 11 Players* (1969); *Notturno* for Wind Quintet (1974); Chamber Concerto for Viola and 10 Players (1975); *Tangents I* for Cello and Tape (1975) and *II* for Oboe and Tape (1975–76); String Trio (1976); *Group Portrait—with Piano* for Wind Quintet (1978); *Trois petites pièces desséchées...en forme de sandwich* for Viola and Piano (1979); *Triolet* for Flute, Harp, and Bassoon (1980); *Playing for Time* for Oboe, Percussion, and Piano (1981); *Beyond the 7th Palace* for Viola and Percussion (1982); *Gan Eden* for Violin and Piano (1983); *River of Fire* for Oboe d'Amore and Harp (1983); *Accord* for Accordion, Oboe, and Cello (1985); *In Stillness Ascending* for Viola and Piano (1986); *In the Stillness of the Summer Wind* for Oboe and String Quartet (1987); *Shekhinah* for Viola (1988); *Dunkle Stimmen...am Rande der Nacht* for Viola, Cello, and Double Bass (1988); *Apparitions* for Cello and Chamber Ensemble (1991); *Doppelgänger* for 2 Flutes (1991); *In the Stillness of September 1942* for English Horn and 9 Strings (1992); *Like Ghosts from an Enchanter Fleeing* for Cello and Piano (1993); *Music for a Solitary Cellist* (1993); *Die klingende Zeit* for Flute and Chamber Ensemble (1993–94); *Echoes in the Memory* for Clarinet, Cello, and Piano (1997); *Jam for Frances* for Trombone (1997); *Entendre marcher un ange...* for Flute and Percussion (1998). **KEYBOARD: P i a n o :** *6 Miniatures* (1965); *Fantasy* (1966); Sonata (1966); *Jest* (1967); *Intervals, Shapes, Patterns* (1968); *Pieces for Young Pianists* (1968); *Elegy for a Misty Afternoon* (1971); *Dans le crépuscule du souvenir* (1977–80); *In the Stillness of the 7th Autumn* (1983); *Quelquefois, à l'ombre de la nuit...au lointain...* (1991–92); *Tombeau* (1996). **O r g a n :** *Gothic Scenes and Interludes* (1983–87). **VOCAL:** *2 Songs* for Soprano and Chamber Orch. (1963); *Mobile IV* for Soprano and Chamber Ensemble (1969); *Eclipse* for Soprano, Flute, and Piano (1972). —NS/LK/DM

Chernov, Vladimir, Russian baritone; b. Moscow, Sept. 22, 1953. He received training at the Moscow Cons. (graduated, 1981) and at the opera school at Milan's La Scala. He won prizes in the Tchaikovsky (Moscow, 1982), Bussetto (1983), and Helsinki (Tito Gobbi prize, 1984) competitions. In 1983 he became a member of the Kirov Theater in Leningrad, where he excelled in the baritone repertoire. In 1985 he made his first tour of England and Ireland as a soloist with the Moscow Radio Sym. Orch. His U.S. debut followed in 1988 when he sang Marcello with the Opera Co. of Boston. In 1990 he appeared as Figaro at London's Covent Garden. He sang Posa at the Metropolitan Opera in N.Y. in 1992. In 1995 he made his debut at Milan's La Scala as Stankar in *Stiffelio*. In 1996 he appeared as Don Carlo at the Metropolitan Opera, and returned there in 1997 as Eugene Onegin. His guest engagements also took him to many other leading opera houses in Europe and North America. In addition to the Russian repertoire, Chernov has won special praise for his roles in the Italian and French repertoire.—NS/LK/DM

Cherry, Don(ald Eugene), influential avant-garde jazz trumpeter, cornetist, leader, wooden flutes, percussion; b. Oklahoma City, Okla., Nov. 18, 1936; d. Malaga, Spain, Oct. 19, 1995. He moved to Los Angeles in 1940 and studied trumpet and harmony while attending high school. In 1951 he worked with Red Mitchell,

Wardell Gray, and Dexter Gordon. He also played piano in an R&B band with Billy Higgins. By 1957 he was playing with Ornette Coleman in L.A. and for a week in Vancouver; in 1958 he played on Coleman's first LP, performing on a small "pocket" trumpet. In 1958 he, Coleman, and Higgins worked at the Hillcrest Club in L.A., from which two LPs were later issued. He and Coleman went to the Lenox (Mass.) School of Jazz in the summer of 1959 and debuted at N.Y.'s Five Spot in November 1959. Their new style of playing was roundly dismissed by the critics, and many audience members reacted negatively to them. Cherry also recorded with John Coltrane in 1960 (although it was not issued at the time), played with Steve Lacy and Sonny Rollins, including dates in N.Y. (1962) and a European tour (early 1963). He was a co-founder of the N.Y. Contemporary Five (1963–64) with Archie Shepp and John Tchicai. After 1963, he toured extensively in Europe and Africa. Cherry worked in Europe with Albert Ayler, Gato Barbieri, and George Russell. He lived in Paris and then Sweden in the 1970s, playing with Coleman, Ed Blackwell, Charlie Haden, Frank Lowe, and others on his frequent visits to N.Y.

By the early 1970s, Cherry gradually became immersed in world music. He adopted flutes, bells, gamelon, and other instruments of other folk cultures in his performances. He earned respect by proving himself to be a very individual composer, not restricted to the Coleman mold. In 1976 he started working with a group of Coleman alumni that blossomed into Old and New Dreams. He received a 1982 grant from the NEA. He co-founded Codona in the late 1970s Codona's name derived from the opening letters of Colin Walcott, Don Cherry, and Nana Vasconcelos. The group performed and recorded together until 1984. Cherry worked with Jabbo Smith in 1986. In 1987 he performed on a "reunion" tour with Coleman, Charlie Haden, and Ed Blackwell; they reunited again for a tour in 1993. Cherry settled in San Francisco in the late 1980s, working with his own groups Nu and Multikulti through the 1990s. He was living in Spain at the time of his death.

Cherry's daughter Neneh Cherry is a well-respected pop singer who enjoyed one major hit in the early 1990s with the song "Buffalo Stance." His son is also a pop singer who performs under the name Eagle Eye Cherry.

DISC.: *Avant-Garde* (1960); *Complete Communion* (1965); *Live at the Montmartre, Vols. 1, 2* (1965); *Brooklyn is Now* (1966); *Symphony for Improvisers* (1966); *Where is Brooklyn* (1966); *Eternal Rhythm* (1968); *Human Music* (1969); *Mu, First Part and Second Part* (1969); *Orient* (1971); *Organic Music Society* (1972); *Relativity Suite* (1973); *Brown Rice* (1975); *Hear and Now* (1976); *Journey* (1977); *Old and New Dreams* (1978); *Don Cherry/Latif Khan* (1982); *El Corazon with Ed Blackwell* (1982); *Art Deco* (1988); *Multi Kulti* (1988); *Something Old, Something New* (1992). Codona: *Codona, Vol. 1* (1978); *Codona, Vol. 2* (1980); *Codona, Vol. 3* (1982); *Featuring Ornette Coleman and Steve Lacy* (1999). A. Ayler: *Vibrations* (1964).

BIBL.: M. Hames, *The Music of Don Cherry on Disc and Tape* (Ferndown, England, 1980).—LP

Cherubini, (Maria) Luigi (Carlo Zenobio Salvatore), famous Italian composer and teacher; b. Florence, Sept. 14, 1760; d. Paris, March 15, 1842. He first studied music with his father, the maestro al cembalo at the Teatro della Pergola in Florence, and then composition with Bartolomeo Felici and his son Alessandro and with Bizarri and Castrucci. In 1778 he received a grant from the Grand Duke Leopold of Tuscany, which enabled him to continue his studies with Sarti in Milan. By this time he had composed a number of works for the church and also several stage intermezzi. While studying with Sarti, he wrote arias for his teacher's operas as well as exercises in the early contrapuntal style. His first operatic success came with *Armida abbandonata* (Florence, Jan. 25, 1782). In the autumn of 1784 he set out for London, where he was commissioned to write an opera for the King's Theatre. *La finta principessa* was given there on April 2, 1785, followed by *Il Giulio Sabino* (March 30, 1786), which brought him public acceptance and the admiration of the Prince of Wales. He made his first visit to Paris in the summer of 1785, where he was introduced to Marie Antoinette by the court musician Giovanni Battista Viotti; in the spring of 1786 he made Paris his home. He made one last visit to Italy to oversee the production of his opera *Ifigenia in Aulide* (Turin, Jan. 12, 1788). His first opera for Paris, *Démophon* (Paris Opera, Dec. 2, 1788), was a failure, due largely to J.F. Marmontel's inept libretto and Cherubini's less than total command of French prosody. In 1789, Leonard, a member of the Queen's household, assisted by Viotti, obtained a license to establish an Italian opera company at the Tuileries (Théâtre de Monsieur); Cherubini became its music director and conductor. After the company moved to a new theater in the rue Feydeau, he produced his opera *Lodoïska* (July 18, 1791), with notable success; with this score, he effectively developed a new dramatic style, destined to have profound impact on the course of French opera. The increased breadth and force of its ensemble numbers, its novel and rich orchestral combinations, and its generally heightened dramatic effect inspired other composers to follow his lead, particularly Méhul and Le Sueur. With the French Revolution in full swing, the Italian Opera was disbanded (1792). Cherubini then went to Normandy, but returned to Paris in 1793 to become an inspector at the new Inst. National de Musique (later the Cons.). His opera *Médée* (March 13, 1797), noteworthy for its startling characterization of Medea and for the mastery of its orchestration, proved a major step in his development as a dramatic composer. With *Les Deux Journées, ou Le Porteur d'eau* (Jan. 16, 1800), he scored his greatest triumph with the public as a composer for the theater; the opera was soon performed throughout Europe to much acclaim.

In 1805 Cherubini received an invitation to visit Vienna, where he was honored at the court. He also met the foremost musicians of the day, including Haydn and Beethoven. He composed the opera *Faniska*, which was successfully premiered at the Kärnthnertortheater on Feb. 25, 1806. After Napoleon captured Vienna, Cherubini was extended royal favor by the French emperor, who expressed his desire that Cherubini return to Paris. When Cherubini's opera *Pimmalione* (Nov. 30, 1809) failed to please the Parisians, Cherubini retired to the château of the Prince of Chimay, occupying himself with botanizing and painting. At the request to compose

a Mass for the church of Chimay, he produced the celebrated three-part Mass in F major. He subsequently devoted much time to composing sacred music. In 1815 he was commissioned by the Phil. Soc. of London to compose a sym., a cantata, and an overture; he visited London that summer for their performances. In 1816 he was appointed co-superintendent (with Le Sueur) of the Royal Chapel, and in 1822 became director of the Paris Cons., a position he held until a month before his death. In 1814 he was made a member of the Inst. and a Chevalier of the Légion d'honneur, and in 1841 he was made a Commander of the Légion d'honneur, the first musician to be so honored. He was accorded a state funeral, during which ceremony his Requiem in D minor (1836) was performed.

Cherubini was an important figure in the transitional period from the Classical to the Romantic eras in music. His influence on the development of French opera was of great historical significance. Although his operas have not found a permanent place in the repertoire, several have been revived in modern times. He also played a predominant role in music education in France during his long directorship of the Paris Cons. His influence extended beyond the borders of his adoptive homeland through his valuable treatise *Cours de contrepoint et de fugue* (with Halévy; Paris, 1835; Eng. tr., 1837). As the all-powerful director of the Paris Cons., he established an authoritarian regimen; in most of his instruction of the faculty he pursued the Italian type of composition. He rejected any novel deviations from strict form, harmony, counterpoint, or orchestration, regarding Beethoven's Ninth Sym. as an aberration of a great composer's mind. He rejected descriptive music and demonstratively refused to attend rehearsals or performances of the *Symphonie fantastique* by Berlioz, who was then a student at the Paris Cons.

WORKS: A. Bottée de Toulmon prepared a *Notice des manuscrits autographes de la musique composée par feu M.-L.-C.-Z.-S. C.* (Paris, 1843); it contains the composer's own catalog of works. A modern catalog is included in A. Damerini, ed., *L. C. nel II centenario della nascita* (Florence, 1962). **DRAMATIC** (only wholly extant works listed): *Il giuocatore*, intermezzo (1775); untitled intermezzo (dei Serviti, Florence, Feb. 16, 1778); *Armida abbandonata*, opera (Teatro alla Pergola, Florence, Jan. 25, 1782); *Mesenzio re d'Eturia*, opera (Teatro alla Pergola, Florence, Sept. 6, 1782); *Il Quinto Fabio*, opera (Torre Argentina, Rome, Jan. 1783); *Lo sposo di tre e marito di nessuna*, opera (San Samuele, Venice, Nov. 1783); *Olimpiade*, opera (c. 1783); *Il Giulio Sabino*, opera (King's Theatre, London, March 30, 1786); *Ifigenia in Aulide*, opera (Teatro Regio, Turin, Jan. 12, 1788); *Démophon*, opera (Opéra, Paris, Dec. 2, 1788); *La Molinarella*, parody (Tuileries, Paris, Oct. 31, 1789); *Lodoïska*, heroic comedy (Feydeau, Paris, July 18, 1791); *Eliza, ou Le Voyage aux glaciers du Mont St.-Bernard*, opera (Feydeau, Paris, Feb. 23, 1794); *Médée*, opera (Feydeau, Paris, March 13, 1797); *L'Hôtellerie portugaise*, comic opera (Feydeau, Paris, July 25, 1798); *La Punition*, opera (Feydeau, Paris, Feb. 23, 1799); *La Prisonnière*, pasticcio (Montansier, Paris, Sept. 12, 1799; in collaboration with Boieldieu); *Les Deux Journées, ou Le Porteur d'eau*, opera (Feydeau, Paris, Jan. 16, 1800; in Eng. as *The Water Carrier* and in German as *Der Wasserträger*); *Epicure*, opera (Favart, Paris, March 14, 1800; in collaboration with Méhul); *Anacréon, ou L'Amour fugitif*, opéra-ballet (Opéra, Paris, Oct. 4, 1803); *Achille à Scyros*, ballet-pantomime (pasticcio, but most of the music by Cherubini; Opéra, Paris, Dec. 18, 1804); *Faniska*, opera (Kärnthnertorth-eater, Vienna, Feb. 25, 1806); *Pimmalione*, opera (Tuileries, Paris, Nov. 30, 1809); *Le Crescendo*, opera (Opéra-Comique, Paris, Sept. 30, 1810); *Les Abencérages, ou L'Étendard de Grenade*, opera (Opéra, Paris, April 6, 1813); *Bayard à Mézières*, comic pasticcio (Opéra-Comique, Paris, Feb. 12, 1814; in collaboration with with Boieldieu, Catel, and Nicolo); *Blanche de Provence, ou La Cour de fées*, pasticcio (Tuileries, Paris, May 1, 1821; in collaboration with Berton, Boieldieu, Kreutzer, and Paër); *La Marquise de Brinvilliers*, pasticcio (overture by Cherubini; Opéra-Comique, Paris, Oct. 31, 1831); *Ali-Baba, ou Les Quarante Voleurs*, opera (Opéra, Paris, July 22, 1833). **VOCAL:** 15 masses (4 not extant), including the Requiem Mass in C minor (1816; St. Denis, Jan. 21, 1817), Mass in A major (Rheims, May 29, 1825; for the coronation of Charles X), and Requiem Mass in D minor (1836; Paris, March 23, 1838; composed by Cherubini for his own funeral); 14 cantatas (4 not extant); motets, Kyries, Credos, Glorias, etc.; other vocal works and sets of solfeggi. **ORCH.:** Sym. in D major (1815); Overture in G major (1815); marches; dances. **CHAMBER:** 6 string quartets (1814, 1829, 1834, 1835, 1835, 1837); String Quintet in E minor (1837). **KEYBOARD:** 6 sonatas for Harpsichord (1780); Fantasia in C major for Piano (1810).

BIBL.: C. Place, *Essai sur la composition musicale: Biographie et analyse phrénologique de C.* (Paris, 1842); L. Picchianti, *Notizie sulla vita e sulle opere di L. C.* (Milan, 1843); B. Gamucci, *Intorno alla vita ed alle opere di L. C.* (Florence, 1869); E. Bellasis, *C.: Memorials Illustrative of His Life* (London, 1874; 3rd ed., rev., 1912); F. Crowest, *C.* (London, 1890); M. Wittmann, *C.* (Leipzig, 1895); R. Hohenemser, *L. C.: Sein Leben und seine Werke* (Leipzig, 1913); M. Quatrelles-L'Épine, *C. (1760–1842): Notes et documents inédits* (Lille, 1913); L. Schemann, *C.* (Stuttgart, 1925); P. Espil, *Les Voyages de C. ou l'enfance de Mozart* (Bayonne, 1946); G. Confalonieri, *Prigionia di un artista: Il romanzo di L. C.* (2 vols., Milan, 1948); M. Selden, *The French Operas of L. C.* (diss., Yale Univ., 1951); F. Schlitzer, *Ricerche su C.* (Siena, 1954); A. Damerini, ed., *L. C. nel II centenario della nascità* (Florence, 1962); C. Reynolds, *C.* (Ilfracombe, 1963); B. Deane, *C.* (London, 1965); G. Confalonieri, *C.* (Turin, 1978).—**NS/LK/DM**

Cheslock, Louis, English-born American composer, violinist, and teacher; b. London, Sept. 9, 1898; d. Baltimore, July 19, 1981. He was taken to the U.S. as a child and became a citizen through the naturalization of his father. He studied at the Peabody Cons. of Music in Baltimore, taking diplomas in violin (1917), harmony (1919), and composition (1921). After teaching violin there (1916–22), he remained on its faculty as a teacher of theory and composition (1922–76). He also was a violinist in the Baltimore Sym. Orch. (1916–37). His music was basically neo-Romantic, although in later years he experimented with modern elements ranging from jazz to dodecaphony. He publ. an *Introductory Study on Violin Vibrato* (Baltimore, 1931) and ed. *H.L. Mencken on Music* (N.Y., 1961).

WORKS: DRAMATIC: *The Jewel Merchants*, opera (1930; Baltimore, Feb. 26, 1940); *Cinderella*, ballet (Baltimore, May 11, 1946; rev. 1958). **ORCH.:** Violin Concerto (1921; Baltimore, Feb. 25, 1926); 3 tone poems: *Cathedral at Sundown*, *'Neath Washington Monument*, and *At the Railway Station* (1922; Chicago, April 29, 1923); Symphonic Prelude (1927); *Serenade for Strings* (1930); Sym. (1932); *Themes and Variations* for Horn and Orch. (1934); Horn Concerto (1936); *The Legend of Sleepy Hollow*

(1936; Baltimore, May 2, 1978); *Rhapsody in Red and White: An American Divertissement* (1941); *Set of 6* for Small Orch. (1946); Suite for Oboe and Strings (1953); *Homage a Mendelssohn* for Strings (1960). **CHAMBER:** Violin Sonata (1917); Piano Sonatina (1932); *Shite Ami I* for String Quartet and Harp (1932) and *II* for Violin, Cello, and Harp (1932); String Quartet (1941); Cello Sonatina (1943); Concertinetto for Brass, Piano, and Percussion (1954); *Descant* for Clarinet (1970). **VOCAL:** *Psalm CL* for Chorus (1931); *David*, oratorio for Chorus (1937); *3 Period Pieces* for Chorus (1940); *The Congo*, oratorio for Chorus (Akron, Ohio, Oct. 30, 1942); song cycles; solo songs; anthems; part songs.

BIBL.: E. Sprenkle, *The Life and Works of L. C.* (diss., Peabody Cons. of Music, 1979).—**NS/LK/DM**

Chestnut, Cyrus, pianist; b. Baltimore, Md., Jan. 17, 1963. A superb musician who credits a gospel influence in his music, Chestnut first attracted national notice while touring with Betty Carter (1987–89). His father was a church pianist who began teaching him when he was seven years old. He attended Peabody Prep. Inst. and then the Berklee Coll. of Music, graduating in jazz comp. and arranging in 1985. Besides working with Carter, he's also played with Jon Hendricks, Terence Blanchard–Donald Harrison, and Wynton Marsalis. In 1995–96, he toured with the Lincoln Center Jazz Orch. He also appeared in Robert Altman's film, *Kansas City*.

DISC.: *Revelation* (1994); *Dark Before the Dawn* (1995); *Earth Stories* (1996); *Blessed Quietness* (1996); *C.C.* (1998); *A Charlie Brown Christmas* (2000). **CYRUS CHESTNUT TRIO:** *Nut* (1992); *Another Direction* (1993).—**LP**

Chevillard, (Paul Alexandre) Camille, French conductor and composer, son of **Pierre (Alexandre François) Chevillard;** b. Paris, Oct. 14, 1859; d. Chatou, Seine-et-Oise, May 30, 1923. He studied piano with Georges Mathias and was chiefly self-taught in composition. In 1897 he became asst. conductor to Lamoureux at the Lamoureux Orch. in Paris, whose daughter he married. In 1899 he succeeded Lamoureux as its conductor. From 1914 he was conductor of the Paris Opéra. He wrote the orch. works *Ballade symphonique* (Paris, Feb. 23, 1890), *Le Chêne et le roseau* (Paris, March 8, 1891), and *Fantaisie symphonique* (Paris, Oct. 21, 1894), chamber music, piano pieces, and songs.—**LK/DM**

Chevillard, Pierre (Alexandre François), Belgian cellist, pedagogue, and composer, father of **(Paul Alexandre) Camille Chevillard;** b. Antwerp, Jan. 15, 1811; d. Paris, Dec. 18, 1877. He entered the Paris Cons. at age 8, graduating in 1827 with a premier prix in cello, and then studied theory with Fétis. He was solo cellist at the Théâtre Gymnase in Paris and also made successful tours as a concert artist. In 1831 he became solo cellist at the Théâtre-Italien in Paris. In 1835 he founded the Société des Derniers Quatuors de Beethoven, which presented public recitals from 1849 promoting Beethoven's late quartets; in 1855–56 it toured throughout France and Germany. In 1860 he became a prof. at the Paris Cons. He publ. a *Méthode complète de violoncelle* (Paris, c. 1850) and composed pieces for the cello. **NS/LK/DM**

Chevreuille, Raymond,

Belgian composer; b. Brussels, Nov. 17, 1901; d. Montignies-le-Tilleul, May 9, 1976. He took a course in harmony at the Brussels Cons., but was largely self-taught in composition. From 1936 to 1959 he was employed as a sound engineer at the Belgian Radio. His style of composition embodies distinct elements of French impressionism; his searing melodies and rich harmonies are often housed within a framework of emancipated tonality, often verging on polytonal syncretism.

WORKS: DRAMATIC: Opera: *Atta Troll* (1952). Ballet: *Jean et les Argayons* (1934); *Cendrillon* (1946); *La Bal chez la portière* (1954); *Spéléomagie*, miniature ballet for TV (1959). Symphonic Radio Plays: *D'un diable de briquet* (1950); *L'Élixir du révérend père Gaucher* (1951). ORCH.: 3 piano concertos (1937, 1952, 1968); *Mouvements symphoniques* (1938); 9 syms.: No. 1 (1939), No. 2, *Symphonie des souvenirs*, with Soloists and Optional Chorus (Brussels, Nov. 23, 1945), No. 3 (Brussels, June 25, 1952), No. 4, *Short Symphony* (1952), No. 5, *Symphonie printanière* (1954), No. 6 (1957), Sym. for Chamber Orch. (1958), No. 7 (1964), and No. 8 (1970); 2 cello concertos (1940, 1965); 3 violin concertos (1941, 1953, 1965); Concerto for Oboe, Clarinet, Bassoon, and Orch. (1943); Double Concerto for Piano, Saxophone or Viola, and Orch. (1946); *Concerto for Orchestra* (1947); *Divertissement* for Chamber Orch. (1948); *Barbe-Bleue* (1949); Horn Concerto (Brussels, July 12, 1950); Trumpet Concerto (1954); *Récréation de midi* for Strings (1955); *Mouvements*, suite for Brass (1956); *Carnaval à Ostende*, suite (1959); *Presto Giocoso* (1961); *Concerto Grosso* for 2 Trumpets and Orch. (1961); Concerto for Flute and Chamber Orch. (1961); *Bruegel, peintre des humbles*, suite (1963); Concerto for Clarinet, Strings, and Percussion (1968); *2 Airs* (1971). CHAMBER: 6 string quartets (1930, 1934, 1934, 1939, 1943, 1945); Piano Trio (1936); String Trio (1937); Piano Quartet (1938); Cello Sonata (1941); *Divertissement* for Wind Quintet (1942); *Musiques lilliputiennes* for 4 Flutes (1942); Quartet for 4 Cellos (1942); *Variations* for Violin and Piano (1946); *Récit et Air gai* for Clarinet and Piano (1950); 5 Bagatelles for String Quartet (1952); *Serenade* for Wind Quintet (1958); Wind Quartet (1964); Trio for Flute, Viola, and Double Bass or Piano (1961); Clarinet Quintet (1968). VOCAL: Cantatas: *Le Fléau* (1930); *Le Cantique de soleil* (1941); *L'Éléphant et le papillon* (1941); *La Dispute des orgues* (Brussels, Jan. 10, 1942); *Évasions* (1942); *Saisons* (1943); also *Prière pour les condamnés à mort* for Narrator and Orch. (Brussels, Oct. 14, 1945); *Assonances* for Narrator and Chamber Orch. (1962); *Rhapsody* for Woman's Voice and Chamber Orch. (1969).—NS/LK/DM

Chiara, Maria(-Rita),

Italian soprano; b. Oderzo, near Venice, Nov. 24, 1939. She studied with Antonio Cassinelli, who later became her husband, and with Maria Carbone. In 1965 she made her operatic debut in Venice as Desdemona. She subsequently appeared with the Bavarian State Opera in Munich and with the Vienna State Opera (1970); her debut at London's Covent Garden came in 1973 as Liù. In 1977 she made her U.S. debut as Manon Lescaut at the Chicago Lyric Opera; her Metropolitan Opera debut in N.Y. followed on Dec. 16, 1977, as Violetta. In 1985 she appeared as Aida at Milan's La Scala. She sang Amelia in *Un ballo in maschera* in Naples in 1989. In 1991 she appeared as Leonora in *Il Trovatore* in Turin. Among her most noted roles are Anna Bolena, Maria Stuarda, Amelia Boccanegra, Aida, and Elisabeth de Valois.—NS/LK/DM

Chic,

the most commercially successful black disco group of the late 1970s. MEMBERSHIP: Nile Rodgers, gtr. (b. N.Y., N.Y., Sept. 19, 1952); Bernard Edwards, kybd., bs., voc. (b. Greenville, N.C., Oct. 31, 1952); Tony Thompson, drm. (b. Queens, N.Y., Nov. 15, 1954). Vocalists included Norma Jean Wright and Luci Martin; Wright was replaced by Alfa Anderson in 1978.

Chic featured the lean, funky bass-playing of Bernard Edwards—perhaps the most imitated bassist since Larry Graham of Sly and the Family Stone—and the sophisticated lead guitar playing of Nile Rodgers. As the writers, arrangers, and producers, Edwards and Rodgers provided Chic with a playful, glistening sound flavored with strings and jazzy ornamentation. In addition, the rhythm track to Chic's "Good Times" served as the foundation to the early rap hit "Rapper's Delight" by the Sugarhill Gang. As a producer Rogers later created one of the most engaging and successful sounds of the 1980s, on albums by a wide range of performers, including Diana Ross's *Diana*, David Bowie's *Let's Dance*, and Madonna's *Like a Virgin*.

Bernard Edwards lived in N.Y. since age 10 and Nile Rodgers grew up in Greenwich Village and Hollywood. As a guitarist, Rodgers played a wide variety of styles, from folk to classical to jazz. Jimi Hendrix was a major influence. Rodgers was a member of the house band at the Apollo Theater in the early 1970s and a session and nightclub musician from 1971 to 1977. Rodgers was introduced to Edwards in 1970, and in 1972 the two formed the Big Apple Band with drummer Tony Thompson to back up the vocal group N.Y.C., who scored a major pop hit with "I'm Doin' Fine Now" in 1973. After years of studio and tour work, the three formed Chic in early 1977 with female vocalists Norma Jean Wright and Luci Martin. They soon hit with the silly "Dance, Dance, Dance (Yowsah, Yowsah, Yowsah)" on Budda, and switched to Atlantic in fall 1977.

Wright left in 1978, to be replaced by Alfa Anderson. Chic then scored a top R&B and pop hit with "Le Freak." Still dismissed as purveyors of superficial disco music, Rodgers and Edwards achieved a measure of recognition for their distinctive sound with the Chic hits "I Want Your Love" and "Good Times" (which served as the basis for several early rap songs) and their production of Sister Sledge's "We Are Family." Although subsequent recordings by Chic were far less successful commercially, Rodgers soon found great success as a producer, beginning with the recording of Diana Ross's 1980 *Diana*, the best-selling album of her career.

Chic broke up in 1983, and Nile Rodgers and Bernard Edwards each recorded solo albums. Rodgers successfully applied his production talents to David Bowie's comeback album *Let's Dance* (1983), Madonna's *Like a Virgin* (1984), and Mick Jagger's *She's the Boss*. In 1984 Rodgers joined Robert Plant, Jimmy Page, and Jeff Beck in the supergroup the Honeydrippers, hitting with a remake of Phil Phillips's 1959 smash "Sea of Love." In 1985, with Bernard Edwards as producer, Tony Thompson recorded with Robert Palmer and John and Andy Taylor (of Duran Duran) as the Power Station, scoring near-smashes with "Some Like It Hot" and "Get It On." Edwards produced and provided the bass for Robert

Palmer's top 1986 hit "Addicted to Love." In 1992 Edwards and Rodgers briefly regrouped as Chic with vocalists Sylvester Logan Sharp and Jenn Thomas on Warner Bros. Records.

Disc.: CHIC: *C.* (1977); *C'est C.* (1978); *Risqué* (1979); *Greatest Hits* (1979); *Real People* (1980); *Take It Off* (1982); *Tongue in C.* (1982); *Believer* (1983); *Dance, Dance, Dance—The Best of C.* (1991); *The Best of C., Vol. 2* (1992); *Everybody Dance* (1995); *Chicism* (1992). **NILE RODGERS:** *Adventures in the Land of the Good Groove* (1983); *B Movie Matinee* (1985). **THE HONEY-DRIPPERS:** *Volume 1* (1984). **THE POWER STATION:** *The Power Station* (1985).—**BH**

Chicago, long-lived pop-rock group featuring big-band instrumentation. **MEMBERSHIP:** Robert Lamm, kybd., voc. (b. Brooklyn, Oct. 13, 1944); Terry Kath, gtr., voc. (b. Chicago, Jan. 31, 1946; d. Woodland Hills, Calif., Jan. 23, 1978); Peter Cetera, bs., gtr., voc. (b. Chicago, Sept. 13, 1944); James Pankow, trmb. (b. Chicago, Aug. 20, 1947); Lee Loughnane, trpt., perc., voc. (b. Chicago, Oct. 21, 1946); Walt Parazaider, sax., clrt., flt. (b. Chicago, March 14, 1945); Danny Seraphine, drm. (b. Chicago, Aug. 28, 1948). Bill Champlin, kybd., gtr., voc. (Chicago, 1953) joined in 1982.

A big-band rock group that initially featured compelling jazz-style improvisation, Chicago launched their career by issuing three double-record sets in two years, saturating the market and perhaps overextending the group's creativity. Sustained by a series of hit singles (including the smash hits "25 or 6 to 4," "Saturday in the Park," and "Just You 'n' Me") and best-selling albums through the mid-1970s, Chicago became perhaps the second most successful American rock band of all time, excelled by only the Beach Boys. Degenerating into purveyors of melodic but inconsequential ballads and pop songs, Chicago suffered a lapse of popularity following the departure of mentor-producer James William Guercio in 1977. Rebounding under producer-writer David Foster beginning in 1982, Chicago continued to score major pop and easy-listening hits through the 1980s despite the departure of lead vocalist Peter Cetera for a solo career in 1985.

Self-taught guitarist Terry Kath and saxophonist-clarinetist Walt Parazaider were members of Jimmy and the Gentleman in 1966. While studying classical clarinet at Chicago's DePaul Univ., Parazaider met fellow music students James Pankow, Lee Loughnane, and Danny Seraphine. Parazaider, Kath, Pankow, and Seraphine subsequently decided to form their own band, the Missing Links, recruiting Loughnane and Robert Lamm. Lamm had moved to Chicago at the age of 15 and studied piano and composition at Roosevelt Univ. Renamed the Big Thing, the group began rehearsals in early 1967, making their concert debut in May. In August, Parazaider's friend James William Guercio spotted the group playing the Midwest bar and club circuit. They added bassist-vocalist Peter Cetera at the end of 1967, as Guercio relocated to Los Angeles, where he produced the Buckinghams' *Portraits* and Blood, Sweat and Tears' second album.

Moving to Los Angeles in 1968 at the behest of Guercio, who renamed the group Chicago Transit Au-

thority, the band recorded their debut album at the beginning of 1969. It featured two long and exciting jams on Lamm's "Beginnings" and Steve Winwood's "I'm a Man" and yielded a minor hit with "Questions 67 and 68." The album remained on the album charts for more than three years and eventually sold more than two million copies. Shortening their name to Chicago in July 1969, the group toured the U.S. during 1970, scoring smash hits with Pankow's "Make Me Smile" and Lamm's "25 or 6 to 4" from *Chicago II* and Lamm's "Does Anybody Really Know What Time It Is?" and "Beginnings" from their debut album. *Chicago III* included the hits "Free" and "Lowdown."

Chicago continued to record successfully under manager-producer James William Guercio through 1977, moving toward mainstream pop as the decade progressed. Their stint as the first rock group to play at N.Y.'s Carnegie Hall in April 1971 resulted in a live four-record set (their fourth multirecord set in a row). *Chicago V* yielded the smash hit "Saturday in the Park" and the major hit "Dialogue," while *Chicago VI* featured two smash hits, Cetera and Pankow's "Feelin' Stronger Every Day" and Pankow's "Just You 'n' Me." Touring the world in 1972, Chicago permanently added percussionist Laudir de Oliveira in 1974, when Lamm recorded the solo album *Skinny Boy*. The near-smash hits for Chicago continued with "(I've Been) Searchin' So Long," Loughnane's "Call on Me," and Cetera's "Wishing You Were Here" (a top easy-listening hit) from *Chicago VII*, and Lamm's "Harry Truman" and Pankow's "Old Days" from *Chicago VIII*. Touring with the Beach Boys in 1975, Chicago's subsequent hits included the top pop and easy-listening hit ""If You Leave Me Now" and the smash pop hit "Baby, What a Big Surprise," both written by Cetera.

Chicago's career momentum stalled after James William Guercio ceased managing and producing the group in 1977. On Jan. 23, 1978, Terry Kath died of an accidental self-inflicted gunshot wound in Woodland Hills, Calif. *Hot Streets*, coproduced by Phil Ramone and recorded with guitarist Donnie Dacus, yielded two major hits with "Alive Again" and "No Tell Lover," but the group would not score another major hit for more than three years. In 1995, virtually all Chicago albums originally released on Columbia were reissued on the group's own Chicago label.

Chicago eventually began a remarkable comeback on Full Moon Records in 1982 under producer David Foster. Joined by singer-songwriter-keyboardist Bill Champlin, the long-time leader of northern Calif.'s Sons of Champlin who had just released the solo album *Runaway*, Chicago scored a top pop and easy-listening hit with Cetera and Foster's "Hard to Say I'm Sorry." *Chicago 17* and *18* (the latter on Warner Bros. Records) each yielded four hits, most notably "Hard Habit to Break," "You're the Inspiration," and "Will You Still Love Me?" *Chicago 19*, produced by Ron Nevison for Reprise Records, contained five hits, including the top pop and easy-listening hit "Look Away," the smashes "I Don't Wanna Live without Your Love" and "What Kind of Man Would I Be?," and the near smash "You're Not Alone." However, Seraphine soon left the group and

Chicago never achieved another major hit. In 1995, with Champlin, Parazaider, Lamm, Loughnane, and Pankow as mainstays, they recorded their versions of big- band standards on *Night and Day* for Giant Records.

Peter Cetera recorded a solo album for Full Moon Records in 1982 and left Chicago for a solo career in early 1985 following *Chicago 17*. In 1986, *Solitude/Solitaire* yielded a top pop and easy-listening hits with "Glory of Love" (included in the movie *Karate Kid Part II*) and "The Next Time I Fall," recorded with Amy Grant. "One Good Woman" and "After All" (recorded with Cher) became top easy- listening and smash pop hits in 1988 and 1989, and "Restless Heart" was a top easy-listening and moderate pop hit in 1992. By the end of 1993, Cetera had switched to the Chicago-based independent label River North Records.

DISC.: *Chicago Transit Authority* (1969); *II* (1970); *III* (1971); *Live at Carnegie Hall* (1971); *V* (1972); *VI* (1973); *VII* (1974); *VIII* (1975); *Greatest Hits, Vol. 1* (1975); *X* (1976); *XI* (1977); *Hot Streets* (1978); *XIII* (1979); *XIV* (1980); *Greatest Hits, Vol. 2* (1981); *16* (1982); *17* (1984); *18* (1986); *19* (1988); *Twenty 1* (1991); *Night and Day* (1995). Bill Champlin: *Single* (1978); *Runaway* (1982). Peter Cetera: *Peter Cetera* (1982); *Solitude/Solitaire* (1986); *One More Story* (1988); *World Falling Down* (1992); *One Clear Voice* (1995). —BH

Chickering, Jonas,

American piano manufacturer; b. Mason, N.H., April 5, 1797; d. Boston, Dec. 8, 1853. He worked as an apprentice to John Gould, a New Ipswich, N.H., cabinetmaker before settling in Boston in 1818, where he worked as an apprentice to the cabinet-maker James Barker. In 1819 he was apprenticed to the piano maker John Osborne, with whom he worked until 1823 when he founded a partnership with the English piano maker James Stewart, who had been active with Osborne. The firm was organized as Stewart & Chickering, and continued until Stewart returned to England in 1826. John Mackay became active in the firm with Chickering in 1830. The firm became known as Jonas Chickering & Co. in 1837. After Mackay's son, William H. Mackay, joined the firm, the enterprise was known as Chickering and Mackays from 1839 until the death of the elder Mackay in 1841. In 1842 the firm became Chickering & Mackay, but that same year the younger Mackay sold his interest to Chickering. By 1840 the firm was the leading American manufacturer of grand pianos. In 1843 it introduced and patented the one-piece cast-iron frame for the grand piano. The Chickering factory was destroyed by fire in 1852, but Chickering commenced rebuilding. After his death the following year, his eldest son, Thomas E. Chickering (b. Boston, Oct. 22, 1824; d. there, Feb. 14, 1871), became president of the firm, a post he held until his death. His second son, Frank (Charles Francis) Chickering (b. Boston, Jan. 20, 1827; d. N.Y., March 23, 1891), settled in N.Y. in 1859 to oversee the firm's business interests there. His third son, George Harvey Chickering (b. Boston, April 18, 1830; d. Milton, Mass., Nov. 17, 1899), served as manager of the Boston factory. The firm received the gold medal of the Paris Universal Exhibition in 1867 and Frank Chickering was awarded the Imperial Cross of the Légion de'honneur. In 1878 P.J. Gildemeester became a member of the firm, and in 1886 he became a

partner. During the last years of the century, C.H.W. Foster and George L. Nichols joined the Chickering brothers in running the firm. It became a division of the American Piano Co. in 1908. In 1927 the factory was moved to East Rochester, N.Y. In 1932 the Aeolian American Corp. took control of the firm. In 1985 the Wurlitzer company took over the firm.

BIBL.: R. Parker, *A Tribute to the Life and Character of J. C. by one who Knew him Well* (Boston, 1854); *The Commemoration of the Founding of the House of C.* (Boston, 1904).—NS/LK/DM

Chihara, Paul (Seiko),

American composer, arranger, and teacher; b. Seattle, July 9, 1938. As an American of Japanese descent, he was relocated with his family to Minadkoka, Idaho, after the Japanese attack on Pearl Harbor in 1941. He received piano lessons as a child, and then studied English literature at the Univ. of Wash. (B.A., 1960) and at Cornell Univ. (M.A., 1961; D.M.A., 1965), where he also received instruction in composition from Robert Palmer. He also studied composition with Boulanger in Paris (1962–63), Pepping in Berlin (1965–66), and Schuller at the Berkshire Music Center at Tanglewood (summer 1966). From 1966 to 1974 he taught at the Univ. of Calif. at Los Angeles. After serving as the Andrew W. Mellon Prof. at the Calif. Inst. of Technology (1975), he taught at the Calif. Inst. of the Arts (1976). He was the first composer-in-residence of the Los Angeles Chamber Orch. under Neville Marriner (1971–74), and also composer-in-residence of the San Francisco Ballet (1979–87). In 1963 he won the Lili Boulanger Memorial Award. Chihara returned to the Univ. of Calif. at Los Angeles in 1998, becoming a prof. in 2000. In 2000 he directed the light projections for perf. with the Milwaukee Sym. Orch. under Andreas Delfs of Scriabin's *Prometheus*. Chihara has explored serial techniques, occasionally adopting aleatory procedures. An oriental influence is heard in a number of his scores, and in his choral works he follows the time-honored polyphonic methods of the Renaissance. In addition to his many concert scores and works for film and television, he has also worked on Broadway, arranging music for *Sophisticated Ladies* (1980) and composing music for *James Clavell's SHOGUN, the Musical* (1990).

WORKS: DRAMATIC: Ballet: *Shinju* (Lover's Suicide; 1975); *Mistletoe Bride* (1978); *The Infernal Machine* (1978–80; rev. as the musical *Oedipus Rag*); *The Tempest* (1980). **ORCH.:** 2 viola concertos (1963, 2000); *Forest Music* (1968; Los Angeles, May 2, 1971); *Windsong* for Cello and Orch. (1971); *Grass* for Double Bass and Orch. (1971; Oberlin, Ohio, April 14, 1972); *Ceremony III* for Flute and Orch. (1973), *IV* (1973), and *V, Symphony in Celebration* (1973–75; Houston, Sept. 8, 1975); Guitar Concerto (1974); Concerto for Saxophone and Orch. (1978; Boston, Jan. 30, 1981); Sym. No. 2, *Birds of Sorrow* (1979; Los Angeles, March 10, 1982); *Aubade* for Chamber Orch. (1989); Concerto for String Quartet and Orch., *Kisses Sweeter Than Wine* (1997–2000; Salt Lake City, March 15, 2001); *Love Music*, concerto for Violin, Clarinet, and Orch. (2000). **CHAMBER:** *Logs* for Double Bass (1966); *Branches* for 2 Bassoons and Percussion (1966); *Driftwood* for String Quartet (1967); *Redwood* for Viola and Percussion (1967); *Willow, Willow* for Bass Flute, Tuba, and Percussion (1968); *Logos XVI* for Amplified String Bass and Tape (1970); *Ceremony I* for Oboe, 2 Cellos, Double Bass, and Percussion (1971) and *II* for Amplified Flute, Amplified Flute, 2

Amplified Cellos, and Percussion (1972); *Elegy* for Piano Trio (1974); *The Beauty of the Rose is in its Passing* for Bassoon, 2 Horns, Harp, and Percussion (1976); 2 string quartets: No. 1, *Primavera* (1977) and No. 2, *Sequoia*, with Tape (1980); *Sinfonia Concertante* for 9 Instruments (1980); *Ellington Fantasy* for String Quartet (1981); *G. Schirmer*, piano trio (1982); String Trio (1984); *Shogun Trio* for Violin, Clarinet, and Piano (1987); *Forever Escher* for Double Quartet (String Quartet and Saxophone Quartet) (1995; Chautauqua, July 15, 1999); *Mambo Cane* ("A Dog's Mambo") for Concert Wind Ensemble (1996); *Minidoka* for Viola, Clarinet, Harp, Percussion, and Tape (N.Y., Nov. 20, 1996); Viola Sonata, *De Profundis* (1998; also as a Clarinet Sonata and as a Soprano Saxophone Sonata). **VOCAL:** *Magnificat* for 6 Women's Voices (1965); *Psalm XC* for Chorus (1965); *Nocturne* for 24 Solo Voices (1966); *Ave Maria—Scarborough Fair* for 6 Men's Voices (1971); *A Slumber Did My Spirit Seal* for Chorus (1972); *Lie Lightly Gentle Earth* for Chorus (1973); *Missa Carminum* ("Folk Song Mass") for 8 Voices (1975); *Midoka (Reveries of...)* for Chorus, Percussion, and Tape (San Francisco, Nov. 14, 1998); *Under the Greenwood Tree* for Chorus, after Shakespeare and Marlowe (1999); *Siren Songs* for Soprano, Clarinet, Viola, and Piano, after Jack Larson and Langston Hughes (1999). **OTHER:** Reorchestration of Chopin's Piano Concerto in E minor, op.11 (2000–01); more than 80 film and television scores. **—NS/LK/DM**

Chilcot, Thomas, English organist and composer; b. probably in Bath, c. 1700; d. there, Nov. 24, 1766. He became organist at the Bath abbey church in 1728, and was also active as a performer and director in local concerts. His *Six Suites of Lessons* for Harpsichord (London, 1734) reveal his talent as a composer of keyboard music. He also publ. two sets of 6 harpsichord concertos each (London, 1744, 1756).**—LK/DM**

Child, William, English organist and composer; b. Bristol, 1606 or 1607; d. Windsor, March 23, 1697. He most likely studied with Bevin at Bristol Cathedral, and later pursued his education at Oxford (B.Mus., 1631; D.Mus., 1663). In 1630 he entered the royal service at St. George's Chapel, Windsor, where he shortly afterward became organist. He lost his position during the Civil War, but resumed it at the Restoration in 1660. He also became organist at the Chapel Royal. He was the organist at the coronations of Charles II, James II, and William and Mary. Child's sacred music was highly regarded, especially his *First Set of Psalmes* (1639). Among his other sacred works were about 18 services, more than 60 anthems, a *Te Deum*, a *Jubilate*, mass sections, and motets. He also wrote a few secular vocal pieces and some instrumental works.**—NS/LK/DM**

Childs, Barney (Sanford), American composer and teacher; b. Spokane, Wash., Feb. 13, 1926; d. Redlands, Calif., Jan. 11, 2000. He studied intermittently with Ratner, Chávez, Copland, and Carter, and obtained a B.A. degree in English from the Univ. of Nev. (1949), an M.A. from the Univ. of Oxford as a Rhodes Scholar (1955), and a Ph.D. in literature from Stanford Univ. (1959). He taught English at the Univ. of Ariz. (1956–65), and then served as dean of Deep Springs Coll. in Calif. (1965–69). From 1969 to 1971 he taught theory and composition at Wisc. Coll.-Cons. in Milwaukee. In 1971

he joined the faculty at Johnston Coll. of the Univ. of Redlands in Calif., and then was a prof. there from 1973 to 1994. Not overly concerned with public tastes and current fashions of cosmopolitan styles, Childs cultivated indeterminate structures. He ed., with Elliott Schwarz, *Contemporary Composers on Contemporary Music* (N.Y., 1967; rev. 1998).

WORKS: 6 *Interbalances* for Various Groups (1941–64); 2 violin sonatas (1950, 1956); 5 wind quintets (1951–69); 8 string quartets (1951–74); 2 syms. (1954, 1956); *Concerto da camera* for Trumpet and Woodwinds (1951); Trio for Flute, Oboe, and Clarinet (1952); Quartet for Clarinet and Strings (1953); Bassoon Sonata (1953); Concerto for English Horn, Strings, Harp, and Percussion (1955); Quartet for Bassoons (1958); Oboe Sonata (1958); Brass Trio (1959); Flute Sonata (1960); Trombone Sonata (1961); Quartet for Flute, Oboe, Double Bass, and Percussion (1964); 6 *Events* for Band (1965); Music for Piano and Strings (1965); *The Golden Bubble* for Double Bass Sarrusophone and Percussion (1967); *Music* for 6 Tubas (1969); *Keet Seel* for Chorus (1970); Concerto for Clarinet and Orch. (1970); *Supposes: Imago Mundi* for Band (1970); *When Lilacs Last in the Dooryard Bloom'd...* for Soloists, Chorus, and Band (1971); Trio for Clarinet, Cello, and Piano (1972); *Of Place, as Altered* for 5 Clarinets (1972); *Of Place, as Particular* for Soprano and Tape (1973); *Concert Piece for Tuba and Band* (1973); Quintet for Winds, Harp, and Percussion (1974); *The Golden Shore* for Band (1974); *Lanterns and Candlelight* for Marimba and Soprano (1975); *A Question of Summer* for Tuba and Harp (1976); *4 Pieces for 6 Winds* for Wind Quintet and Saxophone (1977); *Quartet/Fantasy* for 4 Tubas (1977); *September with Band* for Band (1978); *Featuring:"Mighty" Joe Nowhere und die Greater Wairopi All*Stars*for 7 Equal Instruments (1978); *Overture to Measuring a Meridian* for Wind Sextet and Percussion (1978); *7 Quiet Studies* for Percussion (1978); *6 Gamut Studies* for Marimba (1978); *Mosaic on a Theme of Balakirev* for Alto Saxophone (1979); *A Continuance, in 7 Parts* for Band (1979); *Clay Music* for 4 Players on special handmade clay instruments (1980); *!BANANA FLANNEL-BOARD!—the Historic 1st Album* for 3 Readers and Tape Delay (1980); *Orrery* for Band (1980); *13 Classic Studies for the Contrabass* (1981); *The Edge of the World* for Bass Clarinet and Organ (1981); *Real Music* for 2 Clarinets (1981); *81 Licks for Trombone* (1983); *Pastorale* for Bass Clarinet and Tape (1983); *Sunshine Lunchh, & Like Matters* for Bass Clarinet, Baritone, Percussion, and Electronic Music Machine (1984; "Lunchh" is the emphatically designated rendering by the composer); Horn Octet (1984); *Instant Winners* for E-flat Clarinet (1986); *A Box of Views* for Wind Quintet and Piano (1988); Concerto for Timpani and Orch. (1989); *Fantasy Variations* for Violinist Who Also Reads (1991); *Quite a row of them sitting there* for Clarinet and Piano (1992); *Intrada: Be someone else* for Saxophone Quartet (1992). **—NS/LK/DM**

Chilesotti, Oscar, Italian writer on music; b. Bassano del Grappa, July 12, 1848; d. there, June 23, 1916. He took a law degree from the Univ. of Padua. He became a fine lutenist as well as an authority on the instrument. His writings on and eds. for the lute are of great value.

WRITINGS: *I nostri Maestri del passato* (Milan, 1882); *Biblioteca di rarità musicale* (9 vols., Milan, 1883); *Sulla lettera critica di B. Marcello contra A. Lotti* (Bassano del Grappa, 1885); *Di G.B. Besardo e del suo "Thesaurus Harmonicus"* (Milan, 1886); *Sulla melodia popolare del cinquecento* (Milan, 1889); *Lautenspieler des 16. Jahrhunderts* (Leipzig, 1891); *L'evoluzione nella musica, appunti sulla teoria di H. Spencer* (Turin, 1911).

BIBL.: *O. C.: Diletto e scienza agli albori della musicologia italiana: Studi e ricerche* (Florence, 1987).—NS/LK/DM

Chilingirian, Levon, Cypriot violinist; b. Nicosia, May 28, 1948. After studies in Nicosia, he pursued formal training at the Royal Coll. of Music in London and with M. Parikian. With the pianist Clifford Benson, he won first prize in the BBC Beethoven Competition in 1969 and in the Munich International Competition in 1971; they toured widely in recital from 1970. In 1971 he organized the Chilingirian String Quartet, which acquired a fine reputation.—NS/LK/DM

Chilton, John (James), jazz trumpeter, flugelhornist, composer, researcher, author; b. London, England, July 16, 1932. Although he was a member of the George Melly group for years, Chilton primarily made his mark as one of the outstanding researchers in jazz. His works combine interviews, newspaper research, and other sources to provide biographical information that is accurate and reliable. Besides the many editions of his jazz biographical encyclopedias, Chilton has worked as a swing-style trumpeter since the mid-1950s.

WRITINGS: *Who's Who of Jazz: From Storyville to Swing Street* (London, 1970; 4th ed. 1985); *Billie's Blues* (N.Y., 1975); *McKiney's Music: A Bio-discography of McKinney's Cotton Pickers* (London, 1978); *Jazz* (Sevenoaks, U.K., 1979); *Sidney Bechet: The Wizard of Jazz* (N.Y., 1987); *The Song of the Hawk: The Life and Recordings of Coleman Hawkins* (Ann Arbor, Mich., 1990); *Let the Good Times Roll: The Story of Louis Jordan and His Music* (Ann Arbor, Mich., 1997); *Who's Who of British Jazz* (London, 1997); *Ride, Red, Ride: The Life of Henry "Red" Allen* (N.Y., 1998). With Max Jones: *Louis: The Louis Armstrong Story* (N.Y., 1971).—JC-B/LP

Chin, Unsuk, Korean composer; b. Seoul, July 14, 1961. She studied piano at an early age, and then had composition training with Sukhi Kang at the National Univ. of Seoul (graduated, 1985). She received a Deutscher Akademischer Austauschdienst stipend and pursued further compositional studies with György Ligeti in Hamburg (1985–88). Chin then was active at the electronic music studio of the Technical Univ. in Berlin. Her compositions explore the acoustic properties of sound.

WORKS: ORCH.: *Santika Ekatala* (Sanskrit for "Harmony to Ward Off Evil Consequences") (Tokyo, Oct. 6, 1993); Piano Concerto (1996; Cardiff, June 6, 1997); *Miroirs des temps* (1999). **CHAMBER:** *Fantaisie mécanique* for 5 Instrumentalists (1994); *ParaMetaString* for String Quartet and Prerecorded String Sound on Tape (1996); *Xi* (Nucleus) for Ensemble and Tape (1998; Paris, Feb. 24, 1999). **VOCAL:** *Die Troerinnen* for Women Soloists, Chorus, and Orch. (1986; rev. version, Oslo, Sept. 23, 1990); *Akrostichon-Wortspiel* for Soprano and Ensemble (1991; rev. version, London, Sept. 8, 1993). **TAPE:** *Gradus ad Infinitum* (1989); *El Allento de la Sombra* (1992); *Allegro ma non Troppo* (1993–94).—LK/DM

Chiriac, Mircea, Romanian composer and teacher; b. Bucharest, May 19, 1919. He studied at the Bucharest Cons. (1936–45), where he later taught (1966–84).

WORKS (all 1st perf. in Bucharest unless otherwise given): **DRAMATIC:** *Iancu Jianu*, ballet (1959–63; Feb. 7, 1964); *Văpaia*, ballet (1973–74; Feb. 17, 1974); film music. **ORCH.:** *Nocturnă* (1945; Feb. 20, 1946); 2 rhapsodies: No. 1 (Oct. 12, 1951) and No. 2 (1955; Sibiu, May 6, 1956); *Poem* for Violin and Orch. (May 23, 1953); *Uvertură festivă* (1953; Aug. 14, 1954); *Bucureştii de altă dată* (Dec. 9, 1957); *Simfonieta* (1965; Feb. 27, 1966); 4 concertos for Strings: No. 1 (1966; March 21, 1968), No. 2 (1983), No. 3 (April 23, 1983), and No. 4 (1987); *Simfonia de cameră* (1969; March 3, 1970); Simphonic Triptych (1971; Jan. 14, 1972); *Divertisment* for Strings (Nov. 16, 1972); Symphonic Variations for Piano and Orch. (1979; May 10, 1980); *Thalassa*, symphonic poem (1982; Timişoara, April 23, 1983); Triple Concerto for Flute, English Horn, Harp, and Orch. (1984; Nov. 14, 1985). **CHAMBER:** 4 string quartets (1945, 1972, 1980, 1985); Trio for Piano, Violin, and Cello (1975); Clarinet Sonata (1981); Quintet for Flute, Oboe, Clarinet, Horn, and Bassoon (1982); Cello Sonata (1986); Violin Sonata (1987). **VOCAL:** Choral pieces; songs.—NS/LK/DM

Chisholm, Erik, Scottish composer and conductor; b. Glasgow, Jan. 4, 1904; d. Rondebosch, South Africa, June 7, 1965. He first studied music in Glasgow; then in London and in Edinburgh with Tovey (composition) and Puishnov (piano). He received his Mus.Bac. in 1931, and his Mus.Doc. in 1934 from the Univ. of Edinburgh. He was conductor of the Glasgow Grand Opera Soc. from 1930 to 1939. In 1940 he joined the Carl Rosa Opera Co. as conductor, and in 1945 he founded the Singapore Sym. Orch. In 1946 he was appointed prof. of music and director of the South African Coll. of Music at Cape Town Univ.; also conducted operas in South Africa. His book, *The Operas of Leos Janáček*, was publ. posth. (N.Y., 1971). Chisholm's style of composition was marked by considerable complexity; elements of oriental scale formations are notable.

WORKS: DRAMATIC: O p e r a : *The Feast of Samhain* (1941); *The Inland Woman* (Cape Town, Oct. 21, 1953); *Dark Sonnet*, after O'Neill (Cape Town, Oct. 20, 1952); *Simoon*, after Strindberg (1953); *Dark Sonnet* and *Simoon* were later combined with a 3rd short opera, *Black Roses*, with a libretto by the composer, to form a trilogy entitled *Murder in 3 Keys* (N.Y., July 6, 1954). **B a l l e t :** *The Pied Piper of Hamelin* (1937); *The Forsaken Mermaid* (1940); *The Earth Shapers* (1941); *The Hoodie* (1947). **ORCH.:** *Straloch Suite* (1933); 2 syms. (1938, 1939); *Piobaireachd Concerto* for Piano and Orch. (1940); *Pictures from Dante* (1948); *Hindustani Concerto* for Piano and Orch. (Cape Town, Nov. 22, 1949); Violin Concerto (Cape Town, March 18, 1952); *Concerto for Orchestra* (Cape Town, March 29, 1952). **CHAMBER:** Double Trio for Clarinet, Bassoon, Trumpet, Violin, Cello, and Double Bass; piano pieces. **VOCAL:** *The Adventures of Babar* for Narrator and Orch. (1940); choral works; songs.—NS/LK/DM

Chittison, Herman ("Ivory"), jazz pianist, b. Flemingsburg, Ky., Oct. 15, 1908; d. Cleveland, Ohio, March 8, 1967. Chittison began playing piano at the age of eight, and later studied at the Waldron Boys' School in Nashville, Tenn., with a brief spell at the Ky. State Coll. (1927). He left to play with the Kentucky Derbies at the Lexington State Fair. He worked with Zack Whyte from 1928–31, then toured as accompanist for comedian Stepin Fetchit. Later, he toured with Adelaide Hall and

Ethel Waters, and also did freelance recordings with Clarence Williams in 1930 and 1933. Chittison joined Willie Lewis in N.Y. (spring 1934) and then sailed to Europe with him. Working on and off with Lewis in Europe from 1934–38, he also toured with Louis Armstrong (1934), and led his own band and worked in Egypt early in 1935. He left Lewis late in 1938 and worked with several ex-Lewis sidemen (Bill Coleman, Joe Hayman, etc.) in Egypt as The Harlem Rhythmakers. Returning to N.Y. in spring 1940, he formed own trio, and toured again with Fetchit in the autumn of 1940. Throughout the 1940s and 1950s, Chittison led his own trio in N.Y. He also did regular weekly broadcasts for seven years under the name "Ernie the Blue Note Pianist" from 1942–51 in the CBS radio series *Casey—Crime Photographer* (of which tapes survive). He continued playing regularly in the early 1960s, with residencies in Boston, N.Y. etc., and recorded LPs in 1962 and 1964. He worked mainly in Cleveland (also Akron and Columbus) during the last two years of his life. He died of lung cancer.

DISC.: *Master of the Stride Piano* (1933); *The Melody Lingers On* (1944); *Piano Genius* (1944); *Herman Chittison with Thelma Carpenter* (1950); *P.S. with Love* (1964).—JC/LP

Chladni, Ernest (Florens Friedrich),

eminent German acoustician; b. Wittenberg, Nov. 30, 1756; d. Breslau, April 3, 1827. At first a student and prof. of law at Wittenberg and Leipzig, he turned to physics and made highly important researches in the domain of acoustics. He discovered the "Tonfiguren" (tone-figures; i.e., the regular patterns assumed by dry sand on a glass plate set in vibration by a bow), and also invented the Euphonium (glass-rod harmonica) and Clavicylinder (steel-rod keyboard harmonica). To introduce his ideas and inventions, he made long journeys and delivered many scientific lectures. His earlier publications, *Entdeckungen über die Theorie des Klanges* (1787), *Über die Longitudinal- schwingungen der Saiten und Stabe*, and a series of minor articles in various periodicals, were followed by the important works *Die Akustik* (1802; 2nd ed., 1830; Fr. tr., 1809), *Neue Beiträge zur Akustik* (1817), *Beiträge zur praktischen Akustik* (1821), and *Kurze Übersicht der Schall- und Klanglehre* (1827).

BIBL.: W. Bernhardt, *Dr. E. C., der Akustiker* (Wittenberg, 1856).—NS/LK/DM

Chlubna, Osvald,

Czech composer; b. Brünn, June 22, 1893; d. there (Brno), Oct. 30, 1971. Following attendance at the Czech Technical Coll. (1911–13) and the Commercial Academy (1913–14), he studied composition with Janáček at the Brno Organ School (1914–15); he later attended Janáček's master class in Brno (1923–24). Although Chlubna made his living as a bank clerk until 1953, he devoted much time to composing. He also taught at the Cons. (1919–35; 1953–59) and at the Janáček Academy of Music (1956–58) in Brno. His works followed along Romantic lines, being notable for their lyrical and rhapsodic elements. Chlubna orchestrated act three of Janáček's first opera, *Šárka*. With B. Bakala, he rev. and reorchestrated Janáček's last opera, *Z mrtvého domu* (From the House of the Dead), for its

posthumous premiere. He also completed Janáček's unfinished symphonic poem, *Dunaj* (The Danube). His multi-vol. study of Janáček's compositional style remains in MS.

WORKS: DRAMATIC: O p e r a : *Pomsta Catullova* (Catullus's Revenge; 1917; Brno, Nov. 30, 1921; rev. 1959); *Alladina a Palomid čili Síla touhy* (Alladina and Palomid, or The Power of Desire; 1921–22; Brno, Jan. 31, 1925); *Nura* (1928–30; Brno, May 20, 1932); *V den počátku* (In the Day of the Beginning; Brno, Jan. 24, 1936); *Freje pana z Heslova* (The Affairs of the Lord of Heslov; 1939; Brno, Jan. 28, 1949); *Jiří z Kunštátu a Poděbrad* (Jiří of Kunštát and Poděbrady; 1941); *Kolébka* (The Cradle; 1952); *Eupyros* (n.d.). **ORCH.:** *Distance and Dreams* (1916); Sinfonietta (1924); 3 syms.: No. 1, *Symphony of Life and Love* (1927), No. 2, *Brno Symphony* (1946), and No. 3 (1960); *From the Hillsides, Mountains, and Forests* (1934); Piano Concerto (1937); Cello Concerto (1938); *Nature and Man: From the Spring, Summer Serenade*, and *Autumn Carnival* (1949–53); Violin Concerto (1950); *This Is My Country: The Fountains of Brno, Macocha Ravine, Oh, Upwards, Boys, Upwards!, Pernštejn Castle*, and *My Land is Beautiful* (1955–57). **CHAMBER:** 5 string quartets (1925, 1928, 1933, 1963, 1969); Sonata for Violin and Cello (1925); Violin Sonata (1948); Cello Sonata (1948); piano pieces. **VOCAL:** Cantatas; choral cycles; song cycles.

BIBL.: M. Černohorská, *O. C.* (Brno, 1963).—NS/LK/DM

Chmura, Gabriel,

Polish-born Israeli conductor; b. Wroclaw, May 7, 1946. His family emigrated in 1955 to Israel, where he studied piano, theory, and composition at the Tel Aviv Academy of Music. He then studied conducting with Dervaux in Paris (1968), Ferrara in Siena (1969), and Swarowsky in Vienna (1969–71). He won the Gold Medal at the Cantelli Competition in Milan and first prize at the Karajan Competition in Berlin in 1971; he subsequently served as Karajan's assistant until 1973. He was Generalmusikdirektor in Aachen (1974–82) and of the Bochum Sym. Orch. (from 1982), and appeared throughout Europe as a guest conductor, making his North American debut with the N.Y. Phil. in 1980. From 1987 to 1990 he was principal conductor and music director of the National Arts Centre Orch. in Ottawa.—NS/LK/DM

Chollet, Jean Baptiste (Marie),

French baritone, later tenor; b. Paris, May 20, 1798; d. Nemours, Jan. 10, 1892. He received his training at the Paris Cons. He appeared as a baritone in Switzerland, in Le Havre (1823–25), at the Paris Opéra-Comique (1825), and in Brussels (1826). Returning to the Opéra-Comique, he turned to tenor roles and sang in the premiere of Hérold's *Marie* (Aug. 12, 1826). He then created the title roles in Auber's *Fra Diavolo* (Jan. 28, 1830) and Hérold's *Zampa* (May 3, 1831) there. After engagements in Brussels (1832–34) and The Hague (1834–35), he returned once more to the Opéra-Comique and created the role of Chapelou in Adam's *Le Postillon de Longjumeau* (Oct. 13, 1836). In 1844 his health declined and in 1847 he was compelled to leave the Opéra-Comique. After serving as director of theaters in Bordeaux (1847–48) and The Hague (1851), he resumed his career as a singer with appearances in Toulouse (1848), London (1850), and Paris (1852–54) before retiring from the operatic stage.

BIBL.: A. Laget, *C.* (Toulouse, 1880).—NS/LK/DM

Chomiński, Józef Michal, eminent Polish musicologist; b. Ostrów, near Przemyśl, Aug. 24, 1906. He took courses in musicology with Chybiński and in ethnography with Adam Fischer at the Univ. of Lwów (1926–31; M.A., 1931; Ph.D., 1936), then completed his Habilitation in 1949 at the Univ. of Poznań. He taught at the Poznań music school (1945–48) and the Univ. of Warsaw (1947–76), and also served as chairman of the music division in the art inst. of the Polish Academy of Sciences (1951–68). He ed. *Muzyka* (1956–71) and the Monumenta Musicae in Polonia series (1964–71).

WRITINGS: *Preludia Chopina* (Kraków, 1950); ed. with Z. Lissa, *Muzyka polskiego Odrodzenia* (Music of the Polish Renaissance; Warsaw, 1953; 4th ed., 1958); ed. with K. Wilkowska-Chomińska, *Formy muzyczne* (Kraków; vol. I, *Male formy instrumentalne* [Small Instrumental Forms], 1954; 2nd ed., aug., 1983; vol. II, *Wielkie formy instrumentalne* [Large Instrumental Forms], 1956; vol. III, *Piesn* [Song], 1974; vol. IV, *Opera i drama* [Opera and Drama], 1976; vol. V, *Wielkie formy wokalne* [Large Vocal Forms], 1984); ed. with Z. Lissa, *Kultura muzyczna Polski ludowej 1944–1955* (Musical Culture of the People's Republic of Poland 1944–1955; Kraków, 1957); ed., *Historia muzyki powszechnij* (A General History of Music; Kraków, 1957–64); *Historia harmonii i kontrapunktu* (3 vols., Kraków, 1958, 1962, 1988); *Sonaty Chopina* (Krakow, 1960); ed., *Z zycia i twórczości Karola Szymanowskiego* (Life and Works of Karol Szymanowski; Kraków, 1960); ed., *Slownik muzyków polskich* (A Dictionary of Polish Music; Kraków, 1964–67); *Muzyka Polski ludowej* (Music in the People's Republic of Poland; Warsaw, 1968); *Studia nad twórcościa Karola Szymanowskiego* (Krakow, 1969); *Chopin* (Krakow, 1978); with T. Turo, *Katalog dziel Fryderyka Chopina: A Catalog of the Works of Frederick Chopin* (Kraków, 1990).—NS/LK/DM

Chookasian, Lili, American contralto; b. Chicago, Aug. 1, 1921. She studied with Phillip Manuel, then made her concert debut as soloist in Mahler's Third Sym. with Bruno Walter and the Chicago Sym. Orch. (1957). Her operatic debut followed as Adalgisa at the Ark. Opera Theater in Little Rock (1959), and, after additional training with Rosa Ponselle, she made her Metropolitan Opera debut in N.Y. as La Cieca in *La Gioconda* (March 9, 1962). She remained on the Metropolitan roster until 1978, where she again was a member from 1979. She made her first European appearance at the Bayreuth Festival in 1963 and in subsequent years sang widely in both opera and concert performances, appearing often in contemporary works.—NS/LK/DM

Chopin, Frédéric (-François) (actually, **Fryderyk Franciszek**), greatly renowned Polish composer, incomparable genius of the piano who created a unique romantic style of keyboard music; b. Zelazowa Wola, near Warsaw, in all probability on March 1, 1810, the date given by Chopin himself in his letter of acceptance of membership in the Polish Literary Soc. in Paris in 1833 (but in his certificate of baptism the date of birth is given as Feb. 22, 1810); d. Paris, Oct. 17, 1849. His father, Nicolas Chopin, was a native of Marainville, France, who went to Warsaw as a teacher of French; his mother, Tekla Justyna Krzyzanowska, was Polish. Chopin's talent was manifested in early childhood; at the age of eight, he played in public a piano concerto by Gyrowetz, and he had already begun to compose

polonaises, mazurkas, and waltzes. He received his primary musical instruction from the Bohemian pianist Adalbert ywny, who resided in Warsaw at the time. A much more important teacher was Joseph Elsner, director of the Warsaw School of Music, who gave him a thorough instruction in music theory and form. Chopin was 15 years old when his Rondo for Piano was publ. in Warsaw as op.1. In the summer of 1829 he set out for Vienna, where he gave highly successful concerts on Aug. 11 and Aug. 18, 1829. While in Vienna, he made arrangements to have his variations on Mozart's aria *Là ci darem la mano*, for Piano and Orch., publ. by Haslinger as op.2. It was this work that attracted the attention of Schumann, who saluted Chopin in his famous article publ. in the *Allgemeine Musikalische Zeitung* of Dec. 7, 1831, in which Schumann's alter ego, Eusebius, is represented as exclaiming, "Hats off, gentlemen! A genius!" The common assumption in many biographies that Schumann "launched" Chopin on his career is deceptive; actually Schumann was some months younger than Chopin, and was referred to editorially merely as a student of Prof. Wieck. Returning to Warsaw, Chopin gave the first public performance of his Piano Concerto in F minor, op.21, on March 17, 1830. On Oct. 11, 1830, he was soloist in his Piano Concerto in E minor, op.11. A confusion resulted in the usual listing of the E-minor Concerto as first, and the F-minor Concerto as his second; chronologically, the composition of the F-minor Concerto preceded the E-minor. He spent the winter of 1830–31 in Vienna. The Polish rebellion against Russian domination, which ended in defeat, determined Chopin's further course of action, and he proceeded to Paris, visiting Linz, Salzburg, Dresden, and Stuttgart on the way. He arrived in Paris in Sept. 1831, and was introduced to Rossini, Cherubini, and Paër. He also met Bellini, Meyerbeer, Berlioz, Victor Hugo, and Heinrich Heine; he became particularly friendly with Liszt. Paris was then the center of Polish emigration, and Chopin maintained his contacts with the Polish circle there. He presented his first Paris concert on Feb. 26, 1832. He also taught the piano. The Paris critics found an apt Shakespearean epithet for him, calling him "the Ariel of the piano." In 1834 he went with Hiller to Germany, where he met Mendelssohn and Clara and Robert Schumann. In July 1837 he went with Pleyel to London. In 1836 he met the famous novelist Aurore Dupin (Mme. Dudevant), who publ. her works under the affected masculine English name George Sand. They became intimate, even though quite incompatible in character and interests. Sand was involved in social affairs and held radical views; Chopin was a poet confined within his inner world; it has been said that she was the masculine and he the feminine partner in their companionship. In the winter of 1838–39, Chopin accompanied Sand to the island of Majorca, where she attended to him with total devotion; yet she portrayed him in her novel *Lucrézia Floriani* as a weakling. Indeed, she was quite overt in her reference to him as a lover; in a personal letter dated 1838 she said that she had difficulty in inducing him to submit to a sensual embrace, and implied that she lived as an immaculate virgin most of the time they were together. They parted in 1847; by that time he was quite ill with tuberculosis; a daguerreotype taken of him represents a prematurely aged man with facial features showing sickness and exhaustion, with locks of black hair partly covering his forehead. Yet he continued his concert career. He undertook a tour as pianist in England and Scotland in 1848; he gave his last concert in Paris on Feb. 16, 1848. *La Revue et Gazette Musicale* of Feb. 20, 1848, gives a precious account of the occasion: "The finest flower of feminine aristocracy in the most elegant attire filled the Salle Pleyel," the paper reported, "to catch this musical sylph on the wing." Chopin played his last concert in London, a benefit for Polish émigrés, on Nov. 16, 1848. He died the following year; Mozart's Requiem was performed at Chopin's funeral at the Madeleine, with Habeneck conducting the orch. and chorus of the Paris Cons. and Pauline Viardot and Lablache singing the solo parts. He was buried at Père Lachaise between the graves of Cherubini and Bellini; however, at his own request, his heart was sent to Warsaw for entombment in his homeland.

Chopin represents the full liberation of the piano from traditional orch. and choral influences, the authoritative assumption of its role as a solo instrument. Not seeking "orchestral" sonorities, he may have paled as a virtuoso beside the titanic Liszt, but the poesy of his pianism, its fervor of expression, the pervading melancholy in his nocturnes and ballades, and the bounding exultation of his scherzos and études were never equaled. And, from a purely technical standpoint, Chopin's figurations and bold modulatory transitions seem to presage the elaborate transtonal developments of modern music.

WORKS: KEYBOARD: PIANO: *Albumleaf (Moderato)* in E major (1843); *Allegro de concert* in A major, op.46 (1832–41); *Andante spianato* in G major, op.22 (1834); *Andantino* in G minor (1838); 4 ballades: G minor, op.23 (1831–35); F major/A minor, op.38 (1836–39); A-flat major, op.47 (1840–41); F minor, op.52 (1842); *Barcarolle* in F-sharp major, op.60 (1845–46); *Berceuse* in D-flat major, op.57 (1843–44); *Introduction* in C major and *Bolero* in A minor/A major, op.19 (1833); *Canon* in F minor (1839?); *Cantabile* in B-flat major (1834); 3 *Écossaises*, in D major, G major, and D-flat major, op.72, no. 3 (1826); 24 études: 4, in F major, F minor, A-flat major, and E-flat major, op.10, nos. 8–11 (1829); 2, in G-flat major and E-flat minor, op.10, nos. 5–6 (1830); 2, in C major and A minor, op.10, nos. 1–2 (1830); C minor, op.10, no. 12 (1830); C major, op.10, no. 7 (1832); E major, op.10, no. 3 (1832); C-sharp minor, op.10, no. 4 (1832); 6, in A minor, E minor, G-sharp minor, D-flat major, G-flat major, and B minor, op.25, nos. 4–6 and 8–10 (1832–34); A minor, op.25, no. 11 (1834); F minor, op.25, no. 2 (1836); C-sharp minor, op.25, no. 7 (1836); 2, in F major and C minor, op.25, nos. 3 and 12 (1836); A-flat major, op.25, no. 1 (1836); *Fantaisie* in F minor/A-flat major, op.49 (1841); *Fantaisie-impromptu* in C-sharp minor, op.66 (1835); *Fugue* in A minor (1841–42); *Funeral March* in C minor, op.72, no. 2 (1827); 3 impromptus: A-flat major, op.29 (1837); F-sharp major, op.36 (1839); G-flat major, op.51 (1842); *Introduction and Variations on the German air Der Schweizerbub* in E major (1826); *Introduction* in C major and *Rondo* in E-flat major, op.16 (1832); *Introduction and Variations on Hérold's "Je vends des scapulaires" from Ludovic* in B-flat major, op.12 (1833); *Largo* in E-flat major (1837?); 56 mazurkas: D major (1820?; not extant); A-flat major (1825; earlier version of op.7, no. 4); A minor (1825; earlier version of op.17, no. 4); 2, in G major and B-flat major (1826); A minor, op.68, no. 2 (1827); F major, op.68, no. 3 (1829); C major,

op.68, no. 1 (1829); D major (1829); A minor (1829; earlier version of op.7, no. 2); 4, in F-sharp minor, C-sharp minor, E major, and E-flat minor, op.6 (1830); 5, in B-flat major, A minor, F minor, A-flat major, and C major, op.7 (1831); B-flat major (1832); 4, in B-flat major, E minor, A-flat major, and A minor, op.17 (1832–33); C major (1833); A-flat major (1834); 4, in G minor, C major, A-flat major, and B-flat minor, op.24 (1834–35); 2, in G major and C major, op.67, nos. 1 and 3 (1835); 4, in C minor, B minor, D-flat major, and C-sharp minor, op.30 (1836–37); 4, in G-sharp minor, D major, C major, and B minor, op.33 (1837–38); E minor, op.41, no. 2 (1838); 3, in C-sharp minor, B major, and A-flat major, op.41, nos. 1, 3, and 4 (1839–40); A minor (1840); A minor (1840); 3, in G major, A-flat major, and C-sharp minor, op.50 (1842); 3, in B major, C major, and C minor, op.56 (1843); 3, in A minor, A-flat major, and F-sharp minor, op.59 (1845); 3, in B major, F minor, and C-sharp minor, op.63 (1846); A minor, op.67, no. 4 (1846); G minor, op.67, no. 2 (1849); F minor, op.68, no. 4 (1849); *Military March* (1817; not extant); 21 nocturnes: E minor, op.72, no. 1 (1827); C-sharp minor (1830); 3, in B-flat minor, E-flat major, and B major, op.9 (1830–31); 2, in F major and F-sharp major, op.15, nos. 1–2 (1830–31); G minor, op.15, no. 3 (1833); C-sharp minor, op.27, no. 1 (1835); D-flat major, op.27, no. 2 (1835); 2, in B major and A-flat major, op.32 (1836–37); C minor (1837); G minor, op.37, no. 1 (1838); G major, op.37, no. 2 (1839); 2, in C minor and F-sharp minor, op.48 (1841); 2, in F minor and E-flat major, op.55 (1843); 2, in B major and E major, op.62 (1846); 15 polonaises: G minor (1817); B-flat major (1817); A-flat major (1821); G-sharp minor (1822); D minor, op.71, no. 1 (1825?); B-flat minor, *Adieu* (1826); B-flat major, op.71, no. 2 (1828); F minor, op.71, no. 3 (1828); G-flat major (1829); 2, in C-sharp minor and E-flat minor, op.26 (1834–35); A major, op.40, no. 1 (1838); C minor, op.40, no. 2 (1839); F-sharp minor, op.44 (1840–41); A-flat major, op.53 (1842); *Polonaise-fantaisie* in A-flat major, op.61 (1845–46); 26 preludes: A-flat major (1834); 24, op.28 (1836–39); C-sharp minor, op.45 (1841); rondos: C minor, op.1 (1825); F major, op.5, "à la Mazur" (1826); C major (1828; earlier version of the Rondo in C major for 2 Pianos, op.73); 4 scherzos: B minor, op.20 (1831–32); B-flat minor, op.31 (1837); C-sharp minor, op.39 (1839); E major, op.54 (1842); 3 sonatas: C minor, op.4 (1828); B-flat minor, op.35, *Funeral March* (1839; 3rd movement is a *Funeral March* in B-flat minor, composed in 1837; B minor, op.58 (1844); *Sostenuto* in E-flat major (1840); *Tarentelle* in A-flat major, op.43 (1841); 3 nouvelles études, for Moscheles's *Méthode* (1839); Variation No. 6, in E major, from the *Hexameron (Variations on the March from Bellini's I Puritani)* (1837; other variations by Liszt, Thalberg, Pixis, Herz, and Czerny); Variations in A major, *Souvenir de Paganini* (1829); 19 valses: A-flat major (1827); E-flat major (1827); B minor, op.69, no. 2 (1829); D-flat major, op.70, no. 3 (1829); E major (1829); E minor (1830); E-flat major, op.18 (1831); A minor, op.34, no. 2 (1831); G-flat major, op.70, no. 1 (1833); A-flat major, op.34, no. 1 (1835); A-flat major, op.69, no. 1, *L'Adieu* (1835); F major, op.34, no. 3 (1838); A-flat major, op.42 (1840); F minor, op.70, no. 2 (1841); A minor (1843?); 3, in D-flat major (*Minute*), C-sharp minor, and A-flat major, op.64 (1846–47); *Galopp* in A-flat major (1846); B major (1848). **4-HANDS:** *Introduction, Theme, and Variations* in D major (1826). **2 PIANOS:** Rondo in C major, op.73 (1828; later version of Rondo in C major for Solo Piano). **WITH ORCH.:** *Variations on Mozart's "Là ci darem la mano" from Don Giovanni* in B-flat major, op.2 (1827); *Fantasia on Polish Airs* in A major, op.13 (1828); *Krakowiak*, rondo in F major, op.14 (1828); Piano Concerto No. 2, in F minor, op.21 (1829–30; Warsaw, March 17, 1830, composer soloist; although listed as

"No. 2," it was his 1st concerto in order of composition); Piano Concerto No. 1, in E minor, op.11 (1830; Warsaw, Oct. 11, 1830, composer soloist; although listed as "No. 1," it was his 2nd concerto in order of composition); *Grand Polonaise* in E-flat major, op.22 (1830–31); Piano Concerto "No. 3" (n.d.; reconstruction by Alan Kogosowski, based on the *Allegro de Concert*, which Chopin had indicated was the 1st movement of a 3rd Piano Concerto; Detroit, Oct. 8, 1999). **CHAMBER:** Piano Trio in G minor, op.8 (1828–29); *Introduction and Polonaise* for Cello and Piano, in C major, op.3 (1829–30); *Grand Duo on Themes from Meyerbeer's "Robert le diable"* for Cello and Piano, in E major (1832); Cello Sonata in G minor, op.65 (1845–46). **VOCAL:** 17, op.74 (to Polish texts; 1829–47).

BIBL.: COLLECTED EDITIONS, SOURCE MATERIAL: A number of so-called complete eds. of Chopin's works have been issued since the 19th century. The complete ed. begun by Paderewski and publ. by the Chopin Inst. of Warsaw and Polskie Wydawnictwo Muzyczne of Kraków (26 vols., 1937–66) is extensively annotated but is unreliable in parts since the editors did not always have access to important sources. In 1967 a new "National Edition" was begun under the editorship of J. Ekier. Breitkopf & Härtel publ. a *Thematisches Verzeichniss der im Druck erschienenen Kompositionen von Friedrich C.* (Leipzig, 1852; 2nd ed., rev., 1888). Another thematic catalog was prepared by F. Listy and H. Opieński (Warsaw, 1937). The most valuable is M.J.E. Brown, *C.: An Index of His Works in Chronological Order* (London, 1960; 2nd ed., rev., 1972). Other sources include the following: B. Sydow, *Bibliografia F.F. C.a* (Warsaw, 1949; suppl., 1954); K. Michalowski, *Bibliografia chopinowska/A C. Bibliography 1849–1969* (Kraków, 1970); A. Hedley, *Catalogues des manuscrits de F. C.* (Kraków, 1971); K. Kobylańska, *F. C., Thematisch-bibliographisches Werkverzeichnis* (Munich, 1979); D. Pistone, ed., *Sur les traces de F. C.* (Paris, 1984); J. Chomiński and T. Turo, *Katalog dzieł Fryderyka C.a: A Catalogue of the Works of Frederick C.* (Kraków, 1990); J. Samson, ed., *The Cambridge Companion to C.* (Cambridge, 1992). **CORRESPONDENCE:** M. Karlowicz, ed., *Nie wydane dotychczas pamiatki po C.ie* (New Unpubl. Souvenirs of C.; Warsaw, 1904; French tr., 1904); B. Scharlitt, ed., *Friedrich C.s gesammelte Briefe* (Leipzig, 1911); H. Opieński, ed., *C.; Collected Letters* (tr. from the original Polish and French, with a preface and editorial notes by E. Voynich; N.Y., 1931); B. Sydow, ed., *Korespondencja Fryderyka C.a* (2 vols., Warsaw, 1955; French tr., 1953–60); A. Hedley, ed., *Selected Correspondence of Fryderyk C.* (London, 1962); J. Smoter, *Spór o "listy" C.a do Delfiny Potockiej* (The Controversy over C.'s "Letters" to Delfina Potocka; Kraków, 1967); M. Gliński, ed., *C.: Listy do Delfiny* (C.: Letters to Delfina; N.Y., 1972); K. Kobylańska, ed., *Korespondencja Fryderyka C.a z rodziny* (C.'s Correspondence with His Family; Warsaw, 1972). In addition to the writings listed below, consult *Rocznik chopinowski/Annales C.* and *C. Jahrbuch* for important articles on his life and works. **BIOGRAPHICAL:** G. Sand, *Un Hiver à Majorque* (Paris, 1842; 5th ed., 1929); idem, *Histoire de ma vie* (Paris, 1854; 7th ed., 1928); M. Karasowski, *Friedrich C.: Sein Leben, seine Werke und Briefe* (2 vols., Dresden, 1877; 4th ed., 1914; Eng. tr., London, 1879; 3rd ed., 1938); F. Niecks, *Frederick C. as a Man and Musician* (2 vols., London, 1888; Ger. tr., Leipzig, 1890; 3rd Eng. ed., 1902); C. Willeby, *F.F. C.: A Biography* (London, 1892); J. Huneker, *C.: The Man and His Music* (N.Y., 1900; new ed., 1925); J. Hadden, *C.* (London, 1903; 2nd ed., rev., 1935); F. Hoesick, *C.* (Warsaw, 1904; rev., enl. ed. as *C.: Zycie i twórczość* [C.: Life and Work], 3 vols., 1910–11; further rev., 4 vols., Kraków, 1962–68); H. Leichtentritt, *C.* (Berlin, 1905); E. Ganche, *F. C.: Sa vie et ses oeuvres* (Paris, 1909; Eng. tr., 1922; 7th Fr. ed., 1949); B. Scharlitt, *C.* (Leipzig, 1919); Z. Jachimecki,

Fryderyk C. (Kraków, 1926; Fr. tr., 1930; 2nd Polish ed., 1949); G. de Pourtalès, *C. ou Le Poète* (Paris, 1927; Eng. tr. as *Frederick C.: A Man of Solitude*, 1927; 2nd ed. as *Polonaise: The Life of C.*, 1933; 10th Fr. ed., 1963); E. Vuillermoz, *La Vie amoureuse de C.* (Paris, 1927; 2nd ed., rev., 1960); L. Binental, *C.* (Paris, 1934); W. Murdoch, *C. and His Life* (London, 1934); B. Ferra, *C. and George Sand in Majorca* (Palma de Mallorca, 1936); A. Hedley, *C.* (London, 1947; 3rd ed., rev., 1974); A.-E. Cherbuliez, *F. C., Leben und Werk* (Zürich, 1948); W. Rehberg, *C., Sein Leben und seine Werke* (Zürich, 1949); H. Weinstock, *C.: The Man and His Music* (N.Y., 1949; 2nd ed., 1959); K. Wierzyński, *The Life and Death of C.* (N.Y., 1949; in Polish, 1953; 2nd Eng. ed., 1972); R. Bory, *La Vie de F. C. par l'image* (Geneva, 1951); A. Coeuroy, *C.* (Paris, 1951); F. Zagiba, *C. und Wien* (Vienna, 1951); M. Idzikowski and B. Sydow, eds., *Portret Fryderyka C.a* (Kraków, 1952; Fr. tr., 1953; 2nd Polish ed., enl., 1963); J. Iwaszkiewicz, *C.* (Kraków, 1955; Ger. tr., 1958; 2nd ed., 1964; Fr. tr., 1966; 3rd Polish ed., 1965); K. Kobylańska, *C. w kraju: Dokumenty i pamiatki* (C. in His Homeland: Documents and Souvenirs; Kraków, 1955; Eng. tr., 1955); E. Long, *A History of the Therapy of Tuberculosis and the Case of F. C.* (Lawrence, Kans., 1956); C. Bourniquel, *C.* (Paris, 1957; Eng. tr., 1960); J. Rousselot, *La Vie passionnée de F. C.* (Paris, 1957); A. Czartkowski and Z. Jezewska, *Fryderyk C.* (Warsaw, 1958; 5th ed., 1975); M. Godeau, *Le Voyage à Majorque de George Sand et F. C.* (Paris, 1959); I. Boelza, *Fryderyk F. C.* (Moscow, 1960; Polish tr., 1969); A. Boucourechliev, *C.: Eine Bildbiographie* (Munich, 1962; Eng. tr., 1963); M. Gliński, *C. the Unknown* (Windsor, Ontario, 1963); J. Grenier, *C.* (Paris, 1964); V. Seroff, *Frederic C.* (N.Y., 1964); M. Mirska and W. Hordyński, *C. na obczyźnie: Dokumenty i pamiatki* (C. Abroad: Documents and Souvenirs; Kraków, 1965); A. Harasowski, *The Skein of Legends around C.* (Glasgow, 1967); A. Murgia, *The Life and Times of C.* (London, 1967); Smoter, *Spór o "listy" C.a do Delfiny Potockiej* (Warsaw, 1967); L. Ripoll, *The Majorcan Episode of C. and George Sand 1838–1839* (Palma de Mallorca, 1969); W. Duleba, *C.* (Kraków, 1975); A. Orga, *C.: His Life and Times* (Tunbridge Wells, 1976); A. Zamoyski, *C.: A New Biography* (Garden City, N.Y., 1979); J. Chomiński, *Fryderyk C.* (in Ger.; London, 1980); A. Orga, *C.* (Sydney, 1983); G. Belotti, *C.* (Turin, 1984); J. Bruzzone, *F. C., ou, Le Chant d'un exilé* (Gourdon, 1984); A. Karenberg, *F. C. (1810–1849) als Mensch, Patient und Künstler* (Bergisch Gladbach, 1986); W. Atwood, *Fryderyk C.: Pianist from Warsaw* (N.Y., 1987); G. Ladaique, *Les Ancêtres paternels de F.F. C.: 1676–1844* (2 vols., Paris, 1987); E. Burger, *F. C.: Eine Lebenschronik in Bildern und Dokumenten* (Munich, 1990); A. Neumayr, *Musik und Medizin: C., Smetana, Tschaikowsky, Mahler* (Vienna, 1991); R. Tames, *Frydryk C.* (N.Y., 1991); I. and P. Zaluski, *The Scottish Autumn of F. C.* (Edinburgh, 1993); J. Lotz, *F. C.* (Reinbek bei Hamburg, 1995); J. Samson, *C.* (Oxford, 1996); F. Bastet, *Helse liefde: Biografisch essay over Marie d'Agoult, F. C., Franz Liszt, George Sand* (Amsterdam, 1997); T. Szulc, *C. in Paris: The Life and Times of the Great Composer* (N.Y., 1998). **CRITICAL, ANALYTICAL:** F. Liszt, *F. C.* (Paris, 1845; Eng. tr., London, 1877; Ger. tr., Leipzig, 1880); J. Kleczyński, *C. w cenniejszych swoich utworach* (Warsaw, 1886; Eng. tr. as *C.'s Greatest Works: How They Should Be Understood*, London, 1896; 2nd ed., 1898); G. Jonson, *A Handbook to C.'s Works* (London, 1905; 2nd ed., rev., 1908); R. Koczalski, *C.-Zyklus: Vier Klavier-vorträge* (Leipzig, 1909); E. Kelley, *C. the Composer* (N.Y., 1913); J. Dunn, *Ornamentation in the Works of Frederick C.* (London, 1921; 2nd ed., 1930); H. Leichtentritt, *Analyse der C.schen Klavierwerke* (2 vols., Berlin, 1921 and 1922); E. Ganche, *Dans le souvenir de F. C.* (Paris, 1925); H. Windakiewiczowa, *Die Urtypen der C.'scher Melodik in der polnischen Volksmusik* (Kraków, 1926); S. Barbag, *Über die Lieder von F.*

C. (Lwow, 1927); E. Ganche, *Voyages avec F. C.* (Paris, 1934); J. Porte, *C.: The Composer and His Music: An Analytical Critique of Famous Traditions and Interpretations* (London, 1935); R. Koczalski, *F. C.: Betrachtungen, Skizzen, Analysen* (Cologne, 1936); M. Ottich, *Die Bedeutung des Ornaments im Schaffen Friedrich C.s* (Berlin, 1937); G. Abraham, *C.'s Musical Style* (London, 1939; 4th ed., rev., 1960); L. Bronarski, *Études sur C.* (2 vols., Lausanne, 1944 and 1946); idem, *C. et l'Italie* (Lausanne, 1946); A. Gide, *Notes sur C.* (Paris, 1948; Eng. tr., 1949); A. Cortot, *Aspects de C.* (Paris, 1949; Eng. tr. as *In Search of C.*, London, 1951); B. von Pozniak, *C.: Praktische Anweisungen für das Studium der C.-Werke* (Halle, 1949); J. Holcman, *The Legacy of C.* (N.Y., 1954); J. Chomiński, *Sonaty C.a* (C.'s Sonatas; Kraków, 1960); Z. Lissa, ed., *The Book of the First International Musicological Congress Devoted to the Works of F. C., Warsaw 16–22 February 1960* (Warsaw, 1963); A. Walker, ed., *F. C.: Profiles of the Man and the Musician* (London, 1966; 2nd ed. as *The C. Companion*, 1973); Z. Lissa, ed., *Studia nad twórczócia Fryderyka C.a* (Kraków, 1970); D. Branson, *John Field and C.* (London, 1972); D. Żebrowski, ed., *Studies in C.* (Warsaw, 1973); J. Samson, *The Music of C.* (Oxford, 1985; 2nd ed., 1994); S. Guignard, *F. C.s Walzer: Eine text- und stilkritische Studie* (Baden-Baden, 1986); J.-J. Eigeldinger, *C.: Pianist and Teacher as Seen by His Pupils* (Cambridge, 1987); J. Samson, ed., *C. Studies* (Cambridge, 1988); J. Parakilas, *Ballads without Words: C. and the Tradition of the Instrumental Ballade* (Portland, Ore., 1992); J. Samson, *C.: The Four Ballads* (Cambridge, 1992); M. Deschaussées, *F. C.: 24 études, verse une interprétation* (Fondettes, 1995); J. Kallberg, *C. at the Boundaries: Sex, History, and Musical Genre* (Cambridge, Mass., 1996); J. Rink, *C.: The Piano Concertos* (Cambridge, 1997); W. Smialek, *F. C.: A Guide to Research* (N.Y., 1999).—**NS/LK/DM**

Chordettes, The, beauty-shop quartet turned hit vocal group, formed 1946, Sheboygan, Wisc. **MEMBERSHIP:** Janet Ertel, Carol Buschman, Dorothy Schwartz, Jinny Lockard.

Between 1954 and 1961, the Chordettes put nine tunes into the Top 40, but none so successfully as their first hit, 1954's "Mr. Sandman." They came together in 1946 in Sheboygan, Wisc., with Dorothy Schwartz singing lead, Janet Ertel singing bass, Carol Buschman singing baritone, and Jinny Lockard singing tenor. Three years later, they won Arthur Godfrey's Talent Scouts, earning them a contract to continue as regulars on the show. They stayed with the show for five years.

When Godrey's music director Archie Bleyer formed Cadence Records, the group left Godfrey and Columbia Records (where they had only nominal success) and went along with Bleyer. They topped the charts for seven weeks with "Mr. Sandman" around the same time Ertel married Bleyer. They followed this with "Eddie" (#14, 1956), "Born to Be with You" (#5, 1956), "Lay Down Your Arms" (#16, 1956), and "Just Between You and Me" (#8, 1957). In 1958 they had their second most popular hit, "Lollipop," which spent two weeks at #2. They had three more Top 40 records between 1958 and 1961, but decided to call it a day in 1963, seeing the advent of the Beatles as the end of the vocal groups.

In the early 1990s, with families raised and several of the working Chordettes retired, they started playing again, albeit without Ertel, who died of cancer in 1988. At a showcase that year in N.Y.C., Julius Dixon, the author of "Lollipop" was in the house. He said that they sounded just like they did in 1958.

DISC.: *Best of Chordettes* (1989): *Golden Classics* (1997); *Greatest Hits* (1996).—**HB**

Chorley, Henry F(othergill), English writer on music; b. Blackley Hurst, Lancashire, Dec. 15, 1808; d. London, Feb. 16, 1872. He was at various times active as a dramatist, translator, art critic, poet, novelist, and journalist. From 1831 to 1868 he was music critic of the *London Athenaeum*. During his extensive travels he heard all the best music of the day and met many musical celebrities. A partisan of Mendelssohn and Spohr, he was intolerant toward new musical ideas and attacked Chopin, Schumann, and particularly Wagner, with extraordinary violence. In addition to his writings on music, he also publ. a novel, *A Prodigy: A Tale of Music* (three vols., 1866).

WRITINGS: *Music and Manners in France and Germany* (3 vols., London, 1841); *Modern German Music* (2 vols., 1854); *Thirty Years' Musical Recollections* (2 vols., 1862; abr. American ed., N.Y., 1926); *Autobiography, Memoirs and Letters* (2 vols., 1873; ed. by H.G. Hewlett); *National Music of the World* (1880; ed. by Hewlett; 3rd ed., 1911); *Handel Studies* (1859).

BIBL.: R. Bledsoe, *H.F. C.: Victorian Journalist* (Brookfield, Vt., 1998).—**NS/LK/DM**

Choron, Alexandre (Étienne), French music editor and theorist; b. Caen, Oct. 21, 1771; d. Paris, June 28, 1834. A student of languages, and passionately fond of music, he took interest in music theory and through it in mathematics, which he studied till the age of 25. Through several years' serious application to the Italian and German theorists, he acquired a thorough knowledge of the theory and practice of music. Becoming (1805) a partner in a music publishing firm, he devoted his entire fortune to editing and publishing classic and theoretical works and compositions, meanwhile contributing new works of his own. In 1811 he became a corresponding member of the Académie Française. He was entrusted with the reorganization of the maîtrises (training schools for church choirs), and was appointed conductor of religious festivals. In 1816, as director of the Académie Royale de Musique, he reopened the Cons. (closed in 1815) as the École Royale de Chant et de Déclamation. Losing his directorship (1817) because he favored new works by unknown composers, he established, with a very moderate subsidy, the Institution de Musique Classique et Religieuse, for which he labored indefatigably until the July Revolution (1830).

WRITINGS: *Principes d'accompagnement des écoles d'Italie* (1804); *Principes de composition des écoles d'Italie* (3 vols., 1808; 2nd ed., 6 vols., 1816); *Dictionnaire historique des musiciens* (2 vols., 1810–11; with Fayolle); *Méthode élémentaire de musique et de plainchant* (1811); rev. and enl. Francoeur's *Traité général des voix et des instruments d'orchestre* (1813); trs. of Albrechtsberger's *Gründliche Anweisung zur Komposition* and *Generalbassschule* (1814, 1815; new ed., 1830; Eng. tr. by A. Merrick, 1835) and of Azopardi's *Musico prattico* (1816); *Méthode concertante de musique à plusieurs parties* (written for his Cons., 1818; new ed., 1833); *Méthode de plainchant* (1818); *Manuel complet de musique vocale et instrumentale, ou Encyclopédie musicale* (1836–39; 6 vols. letterpress and 5 vols. plates; with La Fage)

BIBL.: L.E. Gautier, *Éloge de C.* (Caen, 1845); H. Réty, *Notice historique sur C. et son école* (Paris, 1873); J. Carlez, *C., Sa vie et ses travaux* (Caen, 1880); G. Vauthier, *C. sous l'Empire* (Poitiers, 1909).—NS/LK/DM

Chorzempa, Daniel (Walter), American-born Austrian keyboard player, conductor, musicologist, and composer; b. Minneapolis, Dec. 7, 1944. He received training in piano at the Cologne Hochschule für Musik (diploma, 1968) and studied musicology with Johannes Riedel at the Univ. of Minn. (Ph.D., 1971, with the diss. *Julius Reubke: Life and Works*). He also studied organ, harpsichord (with Gustav Leonhardt), composition (with Herbert Eimert), and conducting (with Volker Wangenheim), being awarded diplomas in both in 1979. In 1969 he gave piano recitals in Berlin and Hamburg, and also appeared as an organist in London. In 1971 he made his debut as a soloist with the New Philharmonia Orch. of London under John Pritchard's direction. He made his debut as a conductor in Wiesbaden in 1980. Thereafter, he pursued a varied career as a keyboard player and conductor. In 1995 he became a naturalized Austrian citizen. In addition to the piano, organ, and harpsichord, Chorzempa has explored the repertoire of the clavichord and fortepiano. As a conductor, his repertoire includes 18th and 19th century opera, 19th century symphonic music, and 20th century scores.—NS/LK/DM

Chou Wen-chung, remarkable Chinese-born American composer; b. Chefoo, June 29, 1923. He studied civil engineering at the National Univ. in Chungking (1941–45), then went to the U.S. on a scholarship to study architecture. Turning his attention to music, he studied composition with Slonimsky in Boston (1946–49), Luening at Columbia Univ. (M.A., 1954), and Varèse in N.Y. (1949–54). He then held two Guggenheim fellowships (1957, 1959). In 1958 he became a naturalized American citizen. He was composer-in-residence at the Univ. of Ill. in Urbana (1958), and on the faculties of Brooklyn Coll. (1961–62), Hunter Coll. (1963–64), and Columbia Univ. (from 1964). During his long tenure at Columbia Univ., he served as chair of the music division of the School of Arts (1969–89) and as the Fritz Reiner Prof. of Music Composition (1984–89). He also founded the Center for U.S.-China Arts Exchange there in 1978, and subsequently served as its director. From 1970 to 1975 he was president of Composers Recordings, Inc., and in 1971–72 he was composer-in-residence at the Berkshire Music Center in Tanglewood. In 1982 he was elected a member of the Inst. of the American Academy and Inst. of Arts and Letters. After Varèse's death in 1965, Chou became the musical executor of his estate. As such, he ed. and reconstructed a number of Varèse's scores. In 1998 Chou prepared two previously unheard Varèse works for performance: *Tuning Up* for Orch. and *Dance Burgess* for Chamber Orch. His own compositions combine Chinese elements of structure and scale formation with free dissonant counterpoint related to Varèse's theory of "organized sound."

WORKS: ORCH.: *Landscapes* (1949; San Francisco, Nov. 19, 1953); *All in the Spring Wind* (1952–53); *And the Fallen Petals* (1954; Louisville, Feb. 9, 1955); *In the Mode of Chang* for Chamber Orch. (1956; N.Y., Feb. 2, 1957); *Metaphors* for Winds (1960–61); *Riding the Wind* for Winds (1964); *Pien*, chamber concerto for Piano, Percussion, and Winds (1966); *Beijing in the Mist* (1985); Cello Concerto (N.Y., Jan. 10, 1993). **CHAMBER:** Suite for Harp and Wind Quintet (1950); *2 Miniatures from the T'ang Dynasty* for 10 Instruments (1957); *To a Wayfarer* for Clarinet, Harp, Percussion, and Strings (1958); *Soliloquy of a Bhiksuni* for Trumpet, Brass, and Percussion (1958); *The Dark and the Light* for Piano, Percussion, Violin, Viola, Cello, and Double Bass (1964); *Yü Ko* for 9 Instruments (1965); *Ceremonial* for 3 Trumpets and 3 Trombones (1968); *Yün* for 2 Pianos, 2 Percussion, and Wind Sextet (1969); *Echoes from the Gorge* for Chamber Group (N.Y., April 27, 1989); *Windswept Peaks* for Violin, Cello, Clarinet, and Piano (1990); *Clouds*, string quartet (1996). **VOCAL:** *7 Poems of the T'ang Dynasty* for Soprano or Tenor, 7 Winds, Piano, and Percussion (1951; N.Y., March 16, 1952); *Poems of White Stone* for Chorus and Instrumental Ensemble (1958–59). **OTHER:** Film scores.—NS/LK/DM

Christensen, Axel (Waldemar), American ragtime pianist, teacher, and composer; b. Chicago, March 23, 1881; d. Los Angeles, Aug. 17, 1955. He studied piano in his youth, and then pursued a career mainly as a ragtime pianist, becoming known as the "Czar of Ragtime" and later as the "King of Jazz Pianists." From 1903 he taught ragtime piano, eventually setting up schools all over the U.S. and even in Europe. He was the publ. and ed. of the periodical *Christensen's Ragtime and Popular Music Review* (1914–18), the composer of piano rags, and the author of pedagogical works on rags, jazz, and swing music.—LK/DM

Christian, Charlie (actually, Charles), seminal jazz guitarist; b. Dallas, Tex., July 29, 1916; d. Staten Island, N.Y., March 2, 1942. His father was Clarence James, mother was Willie Mae Jones. For some reason, his mother listed his birth (on his death cert.) as Jan, 6, 1917. All four of his brothers were musicians, two (at least) worked professionally: Edward (piano, bass; b. 1906) and Clarence (Jr.; b. 1911); their father, a blind musician, played guitar and sang. The family moved to Oklahoma City in 1921. Charlie started on trumpet, then concentrated on guitar from the age of 12; he also worked on string bass and piano during the 1930s. He played in the family band from his early teens, did local club work at 15 and there met Lester Young. He played in his brother's band, the Jolly Jugglers, during the early 1930s, and is also reported to have worked as a tap dancer, singer, baseball pitcher, and prize fighter. After playing in Anna Mae Winburn's Band, he led his own group, worked with trumpeter James Simpson in Oklahoma City, and toured (playing bass and guitar) with Alphonse Trent (c. 1938). He was with the Leslie Sheffield Band (1939), when his skill was noticed by Teddy Wilson, Norma Teagarden, and Mary Lou Williams. On the recommendation of John Hammond, he joined Benny Goodman in Los Angeles (August 1939), and subsequently made his N.Y. debut with Goodman in September 1939. He was featured mainly with the sextet, but also played a few numbers in front of the full band. His solos were of necessity short on the 78 discs of the day. Fortunately, he was also recorded while jamming in Harlem (at Minton's and Monroe's), so he can be heard "stretching out." While on a Middle West tour with Goodman, he was taken ill and later admitted to N.Y.'s Bellevue Hospital (June 1941), where tuberculosis was diagnosed. He was transferred to the Seaview Hospital (Sanitarium), Staten Island, and died there. He was buried in Oklahoma City on March. 4.

The electric guitar was being used for fairly flowing solos in Western swing groups as early as 1935, and in a choppy jazz style by Eddie Durham in 1938, but Christian's irresistible swing and long-flowing lines were a revelation that helped catapult the electric instrument into standard use. He probably knew the music of his predecessors on the instrument, as well as his colleague Lester Young, and he certainly knew the works of Reinhardt and Armstrong. His playing was deeply felt and intellectually stimulating, with his habit of varying and developing short phrases, and the long lines with which he "ate up the changes" on the modulations of a bridge (as on "Stompin' at the Savoy" from Minton's, 1941). Every early jazz electric player—Tiny Grimes, Al Casey (who switched from acoustic)—named him as an inspiration, as did Les Paul, T-Bone Walker, and B.B. King. As early as 1940, he had protégés as far away as Norway (Robert Normann) and Argentina (Oscar Aleman). He is featured on a video, *The Genius of Christian.*

DISC.: *Charlie Christian with Benny Goodman and the Sextet* (1939); *Solo Flight: The Genius of Chralie Christian* (1939); *Charlie Christian with the Benny Goodman Sextet and Orchestra* (1940); *Charlie Christian/Lester Young: Together 1940* (1940); *Solo Flight with the Benny Goodman Sextet* (1940); *Memorable Sessions* (1941); *Jazz Immortal* (1941); *Live Sessions at Minton's Playhouse* (1941); *Harlem Jazz Scene* (1941).

BIBL.: J. Evensmo, *The Guitars of Charlie Christian, Robert Normann, Oscar Aleman (in Europe)* (Hosle, Norway, 1976); S. Ayeroff, *Charlie Christian* (N.Y., 1979); D. Fox, *Charlie Christian, the Art of the Jazz Guitar* (N.Y., 1988); P. Broadbent, *Charlie Christian: The Story of the Seminal Electric Guitarist* (Newcastle-Ypon-Tyne, England, 1977).—JC/LP

Christian, Emile (Joseph; aka **"Boot-mouth"),** jazz trombonist, bassist, slide cornet, clarinet; b. New Orleans, La., April 20, 1895; d. there, Dec. 3, 1973. He came from a musical family; his brother Frank Joseph (b. New Orleans, Sept 3, 1897; d. there, Nov. 27, 1973) played cornet, and another brother, Charles, was also a musician. Emile began on cornet (taught by his brother, Frank) and by 1912 was playing in Ernest Giardina's Band. He played with brothers Charles and Frank in groups led by Papa Jack and Alfred Laine, and in Fischer's Brass Band (c. 1915), then again with Frank. He then worked with Merritt Brunies in 1916 in both New Orleans and Chicago. In 1916, he was offered the job as cornetist with Johnny Stein's Band for a residency in Chicago, but he declined and Nick LaRocca took the job. He went to Chicago the following year to join Bert Kelly's Band; later that year he re-joined Brunies, who was now leading the Original New Orleans Jazz Band in Chicago. He joined the Original Dixieland Jazz Band in N.Y. in 1918 (Eddie Edwards having joined the U.S. Army). He played in England with the O.D.J.B, 1919–21, returned to N.Y., did three weeks with Phil Napoleon in the Original Memphis Five, then returned to England

with the American (and Broadway) Sextets (1922–23). From 1924, he doubled on trombone and string bass with various bands in Europe: with Eric Borchard in Berlin (1924), with Tommy Waltham's Ad Libs, Al Wynn's Band in Berlin and Hanover (c. 1928), Leslie Sterling in Paris, etc. (c. 1928–30). He was mainly with Lud Gluskin's Band (1930–34), then in Switzerland with Benton Peyton's Jazz Kings (spring 1935). He was with Benny French in Paris (1936), then went to the Taj Mahal Hotel, Bombay, India, with Leon Abbey (November 1936). He was with Abbey in France, Denmark, etc. (1937–39), and returned to U.S. in October 1939. He played trombone and bass at Monte Carlo Club, N.Y., in 1940, then worked in a defense plant during WWII. He moved back to New Orleans in the 1940s and was active on string bass and trombone during the 1950s and 1960s with Armand Hug, George Girard, Leon Prima, Sharkey Bonano, etc., and toured with Louis Prima in 1957. He was featured at Disneyland Jazz Festival (1967), and the New Orleans Jazz Festivals in 1968 and 1969.

DISC.: *Emile Christian and his New Orleans Jazz Band* (1958). —JC/LP

Christie, William (Lincoln), outstanding American-born French conductor and harpsichordist; b. Buffalo, Dec. 19, 1944. He began his musical training with his mother. After studying harpsichord with Igor Kipnis at the Berkshire Music Center in Tanglewood, he took courses in music and art history at Harvard Univ. (B.A., 1966), and in harpsichord with Ralph Kirkpatrick, organ with Charles Krigbaum, and musicology with Claude Palisca and Nicholas Temperley at Yale Univ. (M.Mus., 1970). In 1971 he proceeded to Europe to complete his harpsichord studies with Kenneth Gilbert and David Fuller. In 1979 he founded Les Arts Florissants, a vocal and instrumental ensemble he developed into one of the foremost performing groups of French, Italian, and English music of the 17th and 18th centuries. From 1982 to 1995 he was a prof. of early music at the Paris Cons., the first American ever to serve on its faculty. In 1983 he conducted Monteverdi's *In ballo delle ingrate* at the Opéra du Rhin in Strasbourg, and returned there in 1985 with Rameau's *Anacréon* and Charpentier's *Actéon.* After conducting Rameau's *Hippolyte et Aricie* at the Opéra-Comique in Paris in 1985, he returned there in 1987 to great critical acclaim with Lully's *Atys.* In 1989 he conducted the latter work at the Brooklyn Academy of Music, and also conducted Purcell's *The Fairy Queen* at the Aix-en-Provence Festival. His subsequent engagements in Aix-en-Provence included Rameau's *Les Indes galantes* in 1990 and *Castor et Pollux* in 1991, and Mozart's *Die Zauberflöte* in 1994. In 1990 he led performances of *Actéon* and Purcell's *Dido and Aeneas* in London. After conducting the latter composer's *King Arthur* at London's Covent Garden in 1995, he was engaged as a conductor at the Glyndebourne Festival in 1996 for Handel's *Rodelinda.* He led Les Arts Florissants on tours to many leading music centers of the world, and also appeared as a guest conductor in Europe and abroad. In 1993 he was awarded the Légion d'honneur of France. In addition to his performances of the celebrated masters of the Baroque era, Christie has also championed the works of such lesser-known composers as Bouzignac, Lambert, Montéclair, Moulinié, and Rossi.—NS/LK/DM

Christoff, Boris (Kirilov),
celebrated Bulgarian bass; b. Plovdiv, May 18, 1914; d. Rome, June 28, 1993. He sang in the Gusla Choir in Sofia, where he was heard by King Boris, who made it possible for him to go to Rome to study with Stracciari; he later studied in Salzburg with Muratti. He made his debut in a concert in Rome in 1946; that same year he made his operatic debut there at the Teatro Argentina as Colline in *La Bohème*. He made his first appearance at La Scala in Milan in 1947, at Covent Garden in London in 1949, and his U.S. debut as Boris Godunov with the San Francisco Opera on Sept. 25, 1956. During his distinguished career, he appeared with many leading opera houses, singing most of the principal bass roles in the operas of Verdi, as well as such roles as Gurnemanz, Ivan Susanin, Hagen, Rocco, Konchak, and King Marke. He was most renowned for his dramatic portrayal of Boris Godunov, which recalled the interpretation of Chaliapin. His brother-in-law was **Tito Gobbi**.

BIBL.: F. Barker, *Voice of the Opera: B. C.* (London, 1951); G. Lauri-Volpi, *Voci parallele: B. C.* (Milan, 1955); O. Dejkova, *B. D.* (Sofia, 1965); A. Bozhkov, *B. Khristov* (Sofia, 1985); V. Pravchanska-Ivanova and N. Pravchanski, *Sreshti s B. Khristov* (Sofia, 1990); C. Curami and M. Modugno, *B. C.: La vita, la voce, l'arte* (Parma, 1996).—NS/LK/DM

Christoff, Dimiter,
Bulgarian composer and musicologist; b. Sofia, Oct. 2, 1933. He studied composition with Goleminov at the Bulgarian State Cons. in Sofia (1951–56) and completed his Habilitation in 1975. In 1970 he joined the faculty of the Bulgarian State Cons., where he beame a prof. in 1976. He served as vice president of the Bulgarian Composers Union from 1972 to 1985. From 1975 to 1979 he was general secretary of the International Music Council of UNESCO. He was ed.-in-chief of the musicological journal of the Bulgarian Academy of Sciences, and also publ. several books, including a study of the theoretical foundations of melody (three vols., 1973, 1982, 1989).

WORKS: DRAMATIC: O p e r a : *Game* (1978); *The Golden Fish Line*, chamber opera (1984). **ORCH.:** 3 piano concertos (1954, 1983, 1994); *Sinfonietta* for Strings (1956); 3 syms. (1958, 1964, 1969); *Symphonic Episodes* (1962); 3 violin concertos (1966, 1997, 1998); *Chamber Suite* for Flute, Piccolo, and Chamber Orch. (1966); Cello Concerto (1969); *Quasi una fantasia-gioco* (1981); *Game* for Cello and Orch. (1983); *Perpetui mobili in pianissimi* (1987); *Silent Adagio* (1989); *Cantilena sopra due toni* (1990); *Merry-go-round of the Suffering* (1991); *It Streams, It Runs Out* (1994); *Await Your Pizzicatti* for Strings (1994); *High Up, It Shines* (1999). **CHAMBER:** *Suite* for Wind Quintet (1953); *2 Dances* for Trumpet and Piano (1960); Sonata for Solo Cello (1965); Concerto for 3 Small Drums and 5 Instruments (1967); String Quartet (1970); Quartet for Flute, Viola, Harp, and Harpsichord (1973); *Ricercari* for Cello and Piano (1987); *Cortège presque sans chef d'orchestre* for 5 Instruments (1989); *Meditations of a Lonesome Violoncello* for Cello (1991); *Sad Silk Bows* for Violin and Viola (1996). **KEYBOARD: P i a n o :** 12 sonatas (1962–98); *Toccata on All Soul's Day* (1993). **VOCAL:** Choruses; songs.—NS/LK/DM

Christophers, Harry,
esteemed English conductor; b. Goudhurst, Kent, Dec. 26, 1953. He began his training at the Canterbury Cathedral Choir School (1963–66), where he was head chorister. Following further studies at the King's School, Canterbury (1966–72), he completed his education at Magdalen Coll., Oxford (1973–77; B.A. in music, 1977). In 1977 he founded The Sixteen, a choral group which he molded into one of the finest of its kind. In 1986 he also founded the Orch. of the Sixteen, which he renamed the Sym. of Harmony and Invention in 1997. He made his first appearance at London's South Bank in 1983. After making his debut at the Salzburg Festival in 1989, he conducted for the first time at the London Promenade Concerts in 1990. In 1994 he conducted Gluck's *Orfeo* at the Teatro São Paulo in Lisbon. He made his debut in Vienna in 1998 and in Amsterdam in 1999. In 2000 he was engaged to make his debut at the English National Opera in London. His highly successful tours with The Sixteen and the Sym. of Harmony and Invention have taken him throughout Europe, the U.S., Israel, Japan, Australia, and Brazil. In his numerous recordings, he has surveyed a vast repertoire ranging from Taverner, Byrd, Palestrina, Handel, and Bach to Stravinsky, Britten, and Messiaen. —NS/LK/DM

Christou, Jani,
remarkable Greek composer; b. Heliopolis, Egypt (of Greek parents), Jan. 8, 1926; d. in an automobile accident near Athens, Jan. 8, 1970. He studied at Victoria Coll. in Alexandria, then took courses in philosophy under Wittgenstein at King's Coll., Cambridge (M.A., 1948). He concurrently studied composition with Hans Redlich in Letchworth (1945–48), then enrolled in the summer courses of the Accademia Musicale Chigiana in Siena (1949–50); during the same period, he attended Karl Jung's lectures on psychology in Zürich. Christou returned to Alexandria in 1951, and then lived on his family estate on the island of Chios. He evolved a system of composition embracing the totality of human and metaphysical expression, forming a "philosophical structure" for which he designed a surrealistic graphic notation involving a "psychoid factor," symbolized by the Greek letter psi; aleatory practices are indicated by the drawing of a pair of dice; a sudden stop, by a dagger, etc. His score *Enantiodromia* (Opposed Pathways) for Orch. (1965; rev. 1968; Oakland, Calif., Feb. 18, 1969), in such a graphic notation, is reproduced in the avant-garde publication *Source*, 6 (1969). His notation also includes poetry, choreographic acting, special lighting, film, and projection meant to envelop the listener on all sides. At his death, he left sketches for a set of 130 multimedia compositions of a category he called *Anaparastasis* ("proto-performances, meant to revive primeval rituals as adapted to modern culture").

WORKS: *Phoenix Music* for Orch. (1948–49); 3 syms.: No. 1 (1950; London, April 29, 1951), No. 2 for Chorus and Orch. (1954–58), and No. 3 (1959–62); *Latin Mass* for Chorus, Brass, and Percussion (1953; Athens, Sept. 26, 1971); *David's Psalms* for Baritone, Chorus, and Orch. (1953); *6 Songs* for Voice and Piano, after T.S. Eliot (1955; orchestrated 1957); *Gilgamesh*, oratorio (1958); *Patterns and Permutations* for Orch. (1960; Athens, March 11, 1963); *Toccata* for Piano and Orch. (1962); *The 12 Keys* for Mezzo-soprano and Chamber Ensemble (1962); *The Breakdown*, opera (1964); *Tongues of Fire*, Pentecost oratorio (Oxford, June 27, 1964); *Enantiodromia* (Opposed Pathways) for Orch. (1965; rev. 1968; Oakland, Calif., Feb. 18, 1969); *Mysterion*, oratorio for Soli, 3 Choruses, Actors, Orch., and Tape, to ancient Egyptian myths (1965–66); *Praxis for 12* for 11 Strings and Pianist-Percussionist-Conductor (Athens, April 18, 1966; also as *Praxis for 44 Strings and Pianist-Percussionist- Conductor*); *Oresteia*, "super-opera," after Aeschylus (1967–70; unfinished). Performable works from the cycle *Anaparastasis* are: *The Strychnine Lady* for Female Violist, 2 groups of Massed Strings, Brass, Percussion, Tapes, Metal Sheet, Sound-producing Objects and Toys, Red Cloth, and 5 Actors (Athens, April 3, 1967); *Anaparastasis I (Astron)* for Baritone and Instrumental Ensemble (Munich, Nov. 12, 1968); *Anaparastasis III (The Pianist)* for Actor, Variable Instrumental Ensemble, and 3 Stereo Tapes (Munich, Nov. 13, 1969); *Epicycle* for Variable Instrumental Ensemble that may take a chiliad or a hebdomad, a nanosecond or a quindecillion of non-zero moments to perform (concise version, Athens, Dec. 15, 1968; extended version, Athens, Dec. 20, 1968); stage music for *The Persians* (1965), *The Frogs* (1966), and *Oedipus Rex* (1969).

BIBL.: J. Papaioannou, *J. C. and the Metaphysics of Music* (London, 1970).—NS/LK/DM

Chrysander, (Karl Franz) Friedrich, eminent German musicologist and editor; b. Lübtheen, Mecklenburg, July 8, 1826; d. Bergedorf, near Hamburg, Sept. 3, 1901. He began his career as a private tutor. In 1855 he received his Ph.D. from Rostock Univ. His major undertaking was a biography of Handel, but it remained incomplete, bringing the account only to 1740 (three vols., 1858–67; reprint, 1966). With Gottfried Gervinus, the literary historian, he organized the Deutsche Händelgesellschaft in 1856 for the purpose of publishing a complete ed. of Handel's works. After the first vol. was issued in 1858, disagreements among the members caused Chrysander and Gervinus to carry the task alone. King George of Hannover granted them, in 1860, an annual subvention of 1,000 thaler, which they continued to receive until the annexation of Hannover by Prussia in 1866; in 1870, Prussia renewed the subvention from Hannover; after the death of Gervinus in 1871, Chrysander continued the task alone. The resulting publication, *Georg Friedrich Händels Werke: Ausgabe der Drutschen Händelgesellschaft* (100 vols., Leipzig and Bergedorf bei Hamburg, 1858–94; 6 suppl. vols., 1888–1902), was a monumental achievement, but it was superseded by the new critical edition ed. by M. Schneider and R. Steglich (Kassel, 1955–). Chrysander also served as ed. of the *Allgemeine Musikalische Zeitung* (1868–71, 1875–82), to which he contributed many articles. He ed. an important collection of essays in the *Jahrbuch für Musikalische Wissenschaft* in 1863, and again in 1867. In 1885 he helped to found (with Philipp Spitta and Guido Adler) the *Vierteljahrsschrift für Musikwissenschaft*, and contributed to it until 1894. His other writings include *Über die Molltonart in den Volksgesangen* (Schwerin, 1853), *Über das Oratorium* (Schwerin, 1853), and *Handels biblische Oratorien in ge-schichtlicher Betrachtung* (Hamburg, 1897; 4th ed., 1922).

BIBL.: W. Schardig, *F. C.: Leben und Werk* (Hamburg, 1986).—NS/LK/DM

Chueca, Federico, Spanish composer; b. Madrid, May 5, 1846; d. there, June 20, 1908. He was a medical student. He organized a band at the Univ. of Madrid, also conducted theater orchs. He began to compose for the stage in collaboration with Valverde, who helped him to harmonize and orchestrate his melodies. Thanks to his prodigious facility, he wrote a great number of zarzuelas, of which *La gran via*, produced in Madrid (July 2, 1886), became his greatest success, obtaining nearly 1,000 performances in Madrid alone; it has also been performed many times in Latin America and the U.S. The march from his zarzuela *Cadiz* served for a time as the Spanish national anthem; dances from his *El año pasado por agua* and *Locuras madrileñas* also enjoyed great popularity. Chueca is regarded as one of the creators of the "género chico" (light genre) of Spanish stage music. —NS/LK/DM

Chung, Kyung-Wha, brilliant Korean violinist, sister of **Myung-Wha** and **Myung-Whun Chung;** b. Seoul, March 26, 1948. She began violin study as a small child, and made her orch. debut in Seoul at the age of nine, playing the Mendelssohn Concerto. In 1961 she went to the U.S., where she studied with Galamian at the Juilliard School of Music in N.Y. In 1967 she shared first prize with Zukerman in the Leventritt Competition. In 1968 she appeared as soloist with the N.Y. Phil., and she made her European debut in 1970 with the London Sym. Orch. She subsequently toured regularly throughout the world as a virtuoso of the first rank. She gave numerous trio concerts with her sister and brother, and also appeared as a soloist with her brother acting as conductor.—NS/LK/DM

Chung, Myung-Wha, gifted Korean-born American cellist, sister of **Kyung-Wha** and **Myung-Whun Chung;** b. Seoul, March 19, 1944. She studied cello in Seoul, and made her orch. debut there in 1957. In 1961 she went to the U.S., where she studied with Rose at the Juilliard School of Music in N.Y. (B.A., 1965). She then attended a master class given by Piatigorsky at the Univ. of Southern Calif. in Los Angeles. She made her U.S. debut in San Francisco (1967) and her European debut in Spoleto (1969). She won first prize in the Geneva Competition (1971), the same year she became a naturalized American citizen. She appeared as soloist with orchs. in Europe and America, and also played trio concerts with her sister and brother.—NS/LK/DM

Chung, Myung-Whun, talented Korean-born American conductor and pianist, brother of **Myung-Wha** and **Kyung-Wha Chung;** b. Seoul, Jan. 22, 1953. He played piano as a child, making his debut as soloist with the Seoul Phil. when he was seven. He then went to the U.S., where he studied with Nadia Reisenberg (piano) and Carl Bamberger (conducting) at the Mannes Coll. of Music in N.Y., and at the Juilliard School (diplomas in piano and conducting, 1974); he received additional tutelage in conducting there from Sixten Ehrling (1975–78). He made his conducting debut in Seoul (1971), subsequently winning second prize in piano at the Tchaikovsky Competition in Moscow (1974). He became a naturalized American citizen in 1973. He pursued a dual career as a pianist and conductor; he gave trio concerts with his sisters; was asst. conductor of the Los Angeles Phil. (1978–81), and chief conductor of the Saarland Radio Sym. Orch. in Saarbrücken (1984–90). On Feb. 21, 1986, he made his Metropolitan Opera debut in N.Y. conducting *Simon Boccanegra*. In 1989 he became music director-designate and in 1990 was confirmed in the position of music director of the new Opéra de la Bastille in Paris. While his tenure was initially successful, the election of a new French government led to a change in the administration of the Opéra. Although Cung's tenure as music director was to extend to the year 2000, the new administration in 1994 sought to end his tenure by 1997, freeze his salary, and deny him artistic control of the Opéra. His refusal to accept these altered terms led to an abrupt dismissal, although he conducted the opening performances of the season in Oct. 1994 with *Simon Boccanegra* before taking leave of the embattled company.—NS/LK/DM

Chusid, Martin, American musicologist; b. N.Y., Aug. 19, 1925. He studied at the Univ. of Calif. at Berkeley (B.A., 1950; M.A., 1955; Ph.D., 1961, with the diss. *The Chamber Music of Schubert*). Chusid taught at the Univ. of Southern Calif. in Los Angeles (1959–63) and at N.Y.U. (from 1963), where he also served as chairman of the music dept. (1967–70), assoc. dean of the graduate school of arts and sciences (1970–72), and director of the American Inst. for Verdi Studies (from 1976). He edited the Norton Critical Score edition of Schubert's *Unfinished Symphony* (N.Y., 1968; 2nd ed., 1971), and was a contributor to the new critical editions of the complete works of Schubert and of Verdi.

WRITINGS: *A Catalog of Verdi's Operas* (Hackensack, N.J., 1974); with W. Weaver, *The Verdi Companion* (N.Y., 1979; 2nd ed., rev., 1988); *Verdi's Middle Period* (Chicago, 1997); *A Companion to Schubert's "Schwanengesang"* (New Haven, 2000).—NS/LK/DM

Chybiński, Adolf (Eustachy), eminent Polish musicologist; b. Kraków, April 29, 1880; d. Poznań, Oct. 31, 1952. After attending the Univ. of Kraków, he pursued musicological studies with Sandberger and Kroyer at the Univ. of Munich (Ph.D., 1908, with the diss. *Beiträge zur Geschichte des Taktschlagens*; publ. in Kraków, 1912); he also studied composition privately with Thuille in Munich (1905–7) and completed his Habilitation at the Univ. of Lemberg in 1912 with his *Teoria mensuralna w polskiej literaturze muzycznej pierwszej polowy XVI wieku* (Mensural Theory in Polish Music Literature of the First Half of the 16th Century; publ. in Kraków, 1912). He joined the faculty of the Univ. of Lemberg (later Lwów) in 1912, and was prof. of theory at the Lemberg (later Lwów) Cons. from 1916. In 1945 he became director of the musicological inst. at the Univ. of Poznań, a position he retained until his death. Chybiński particularly distinguished himself as an authority on Polish music history. He ed. several Polish music journals and prepared a number of early Polish compositions for publication, including works by G.G. Gorczycki, Jan of Lublin, and M. Zielenski. His autobiography, *W czasach Straussa i Tetmajera* (In the Time of Strauss and Tetmajer), was publ. posth. (Kraków, 1959). On his 50th birthday, he was honored with a Festschrift (Kraków, 1930), and again on his 70th birthday (Kraków, 1950).

WRITINGS: "Tabulatura organowa Jana z Lublina" (The Organ Tablature of Jan of Lublin), Kwartalnik muzyczny, I (1911–13); "Przyczynki bio- i bibliograficzne do dawnej muzyki polskiej" (Bio- and Bibliographical Contributions to Early Polish Music), *Przegląd muzyczny*, II, nos. 1, 4, and 5 (1926) and V, nos. 2 and 11 (1929); "Z dziejow muzyki polskiej do 1800 roku" (The History of Polish Music to 1800), *Muzyka*, IV/7–9 (1927); *Grzegorz Gerwazy Gorczycki. Cz. I:Życie, dzialalność, dziela* (A Study of His Life and Music; Poznań, 1928); "Stosunki muzyczne Polski z Francją w XVI stuleciu" (Musical Relations between Poland and France in the 16th Century), *Przegląd muzyczny*, IV, nos. 3 and 4 (1928; also publ. separately, Poznań, 1928); *Mieczyslaw Karlowicz* (Warsaw, 1939; 2nd ed., aug., 1949); *Slownik muzykow dawnej Polski do roku 1800* (A Dictionary of Early Polish Musicians to 1800; Kraków, 1949).—NS/LK/DM

Ciamaga, Gustav, Canadian composer; b. London, Ontario, April 10, 1930. He studied theory with Weinzweig and Beckwith at the Univ. of Toronto (1953–56) and studied composition and musicology with Berger, Shapero, and Irving Fine at Brandeis Univ. In 1963 he was appointed to the music faculty at the Univ. of Toronto, where he was director of its electronic music studio. His electronic scores include *Ottawa 1967* (1966), *Curtain Raiser* (1969), *One-Part Invention* (1965), eight *Two-Part Inventions* (1965–70), and *Ragamuffin Nos. 1* and 2 (1967). He also wrote several scores of computer music, among them *Canon for Stravinsky* (1972), as well as *Solipsism while Dying* for Voice, Instruments, and Tape (1972).—NS/LK/DM

Ciampi, Vincenzo (Legrenzio), Italian composer; b. probably in Piacenza, c. 1719; d. Venice, March 30, 1762. He was a pupil of Leo and Durante in Naples, where he brought out six comic operas between 1737 and 1745. His comic opera *Bertoldo, Bertoldino e Cacasenno*, first performed in Venice on Dec. 26, 1748, proved notably successful and subsequently was influential in the development of the opéra-comique genre. After teaching at the Ospedale degli Incurabili there in 1748–49, he went to London as music director of the first Italian opera company, for which he composed *Il trionfo di Camilla* (March 31, 1750) and *Didone* (Jan. 5, 1754). About 1756 he returned to Venice, where he composed several more operas before his early demise. Among his other works were various instrumental scores, including concertos and sonatas, oratorios, motets, and other sacred music.

BIBL.: C. Anguissola, *V.L. C.: Musicista piacentino del Settecento* (Piacenza, 1934; 2nd ed., 1936).—LK/DM

Cibber, Susanne Maria, celebrated English actress and mezzo-soprano, sister of **Thomas Augustine Arne**; b. London, Feb. 17, 1714; d. there, Jan. 31, 1766. After vocal training from her brother, she made her debut at the Little Theatre in the Haymarket in 1732 in J.F. Lampe's *Amelia*. In 1734 she became a member of the Drury Lane Theatre. That same year she married Theophilus Cibber, the disreputable son of the actor and dramatist Colley Cibber who admired her talent and served as her mentor. Her first great success was as Polly in *The Beggar's Opera*, which made her one of the leading lights on the London stage. Her notoriety was further enhanced when her husband allowed one of her admirers, John Sloper, to become her intimate upon payment of a fee. The ensuing scandal prompted Susanna and her new mate to elope. All the same, Handel engaged her for his oratorio productions in Dublin in 1741. On April 13, 1742, she sang in the premiere of his *Messiah* there. Returning to London, she sang in other oratorios by Handel while pursuing her career as an actress. Handel chose her to create the roles of Micah in *Samson* (1743) and Lichas in *Hercules* (1745). From 1744 she was the leading lady at Drury Lane, where she was acclaimed as an actress in tragic roles.

BIBL.: *An Account of the Life of S.M. C.* (London, 1887); M. Nash, *The Provoked Wife: The Life and Times of S. C.* (London, 1977).—**NS/LK/DM**

Ciccimarra, Giuseppe, admired Italian tenor and teacher; b. Altamura, May 22, 1790; d. Venice, Dec. 5, 1836. He became a principal member of the Teatro San Carlo in Naples, where he gained notable distinction for his roles in Rossini's operas. He created Rossini's Iago (1816), Goffredo in *Arminda* (1817), Aronne in *Mosè* (1818), Ernesto in *Ricciardo e Zoraide* (1818), Pilade in *Erminione* (1819), and Condulmiero in *Maometto II* (1820). After his retirement in 1826, he went to Vienna as a teacher of voice and piano. Among his pupils were Clara Heinefetter, Sophie Loewe, Joseph Staudigl, and Joseph Tichatschek.—**NS/LK/DM**

Ciccolini, Aldo, distinguished Italian pianist and pedagogue; b. Naples, Aug. 15, 1925. He began piano lessons at a very early age, and at age nine he was granted entrance to the Naples Cons., where he studied piano with Paolo Denza, taking first prize in 1940. He also took first prize in composition there in 1943. In 1941 he made his debut as soloist in Chopin's F minor Concerto in Naples. In 1947 he became a prof. of piano at the Naples Cons. He was co-winner of the Grand Prize in the Long-Thibaud Competition in 1949. On Nov. 2, 1950, he made his U.S. debut as soloist in Tchaikovsky's First Piano Concerto with the N.Y. Phil., and subsequently pursued a notable international career. He was a prof. at the Paris Cons. (1971–88). Ciccolini maintains a comprehensive repertoire, which extends from Bach to contemporary composers. His virtuoso technique is enhanced by a particularly refined lyricism.—**NS/LK/DM**

Ciconia, Johannes, important Liégeois composer and music theorist; b. Liège, c. 1370; d. Padua, between June 10 and July 13, 1412. He was a choirboy in Liège by 1385. By 1390 he was in Rome, where he was active at Santa Maria in Trastevere. He was in Padua by 1401 and awarded a benefice. From 1403 he was custos and cantor at the Cathedral. Ciconia was one of the most influential composers of his era. He was a master of both the French and Italian styles of his time, being particularly notable for his adept handling of rhythmic, melodic, and harmonic elements. Among his extant works are five Glorias, two Gloria and Credo pairs, a Credo, four isorhythmic motets, four cantilena motets, four madrigals, eight ballate, two virelais, and a canon. He was also the author of three treatises, including *Nova musica* (ed. by O. Ellsworth, Lincoln, Nebr., 1993).

BIBL.: S. Clercx, *J. C. de Leodio* (Utrecht, 1952); idem, *J. C.: Un Musicien liégeois et son temps* (Brussels, 1960); A. Kreutziger-Herr, *J. C. (ca.1380–1412): Komponieren in einer Kultur des Wortes* (Hamburg, 1991).—**NS/LK/DM**

Ciesinski, Katherine, American mezzo-soprano, sister of **Kristine Ciesinski;** b. Newark, Del., Oct. 13, 1950. She studied at Temple Univ. (B.M., 1972; M.M., 1973) and at the Curtis Inst. of Music in Philadelphia (opera diploma, 1976); she won first prize in the Geneva International Competition (1976) and Grand Prize in the Paris International Competition (1977). She made her concert debut with the Philadelphia Orch. (1974) and her operatic debut as Leonora in *La Favorite* with the Opera Co. of Philadelphia (1975). She sang Erika in Barber's *Vanessa* at the Spoleto Festival U.S.A. (1978), then gained wide recognition as Countess Geschwitz in the first U.S. production of the three-act version of Berg's *Lulu* at the Santa Fe Opera (1979). In 1988 she sang in the premiere performance of Argento's *The Aspern Papers* in Dallas. She made her Metropolitan Opera debut in N.Y. as Nicklausse in *Les Contes d'Hoffmann* in 1988. In 1993 she was engaged as Handel's Xerxes at the Santa Fe Opera. As a concert artist, she appeared with leading orchs. in both North America and Europe; she also gave duo recitals with her sister. Among her prominent roles are Ottavia in *L'incoronazione di Poppea*, Laura in *La Gioconda*, Eboli in *Don Carlos*, Dalila in *Samson et Dalila*, Charlotte in *Werther*, Octavian in *Der Rosenkavalier*, and the Composer in *Ariadne auf Naxos*.—**NS/LK/DM**

Ciesinski, Kristine, American soprano, sister of **Katherine Ciesinski;** b. Wilmington, Del., July 5, 1952. She studied at Temple Univ. (1970–71), the Univ. of Del. (1971–72), and Boston Univ. (1973–74; B.A., 1974); in 1977 she won the Gold Medal in the Geneva International Competition and first prize in the Salzburg International Competition. She made her N.Y. concert debut as a soloist in Handel's Messiah (1977) and her European operatic debut as Baroness Freimann in Lortzing's *Der Wildschütz* at the Salzburg Landestheater (1979), remaining on its roster until 1981; was subsequently a member of the Bremen State Opera (1985–88). She made guest appearances with the Cleveland Opera (1985), Glasgow's Scottish National Opera (1985), Toronto's Canadian Opera Co. (1986), Leeds's Opera North (1986), the Augsburg Opera (1986), Cardiff's Welsh National Opera (1986), Munich's Bavarian State Opera (1989), London's English National Opera (1989–93), and Milan's La Scala (1992). In 1996 she appeared as Salome at the English National Opera. She also sang extensively in concerts, often appearing with her sister. Her finest roles include Iphigénie, Medea, Beethoven's Leonora, Cassandra, La Wally, Eva, Elisabeth in *Tannhäuser*, Chrysothemis, Ariadne, Salome, and Tosca. She married **Norman Bailey** in 1985.—**NS/LK/DM**

Cifra, Antonio, Italian composer; b. probably near Terracina, 1584; d. Loreto, Oct. 2, 1629. He was a choir boy at the church of S. Luigi dei Francesci (1594–96), where he studied with G.B. Nanino. He served as maestro di cappella at the Seminario Romano (1605–07) and the Collegio Germanico (1608–09) in Rome, at Santa Casa di Lorento (1609–22), at S. Giovanni in Laterano in Rome (1623–26), and again at Santa Casa di Lorento (from 1626). His finest works are the solo monodies included in his *Scherzi sacri* (two vols., 1616, 1618) and his secular scherzi (four vols., 1613, 1614, 1615, 1617). Among his other works are eight vols. of concertato motets (1609–15), other motets, Psalms, two vols. of masses (1619, 1621), and six vols. of madrigals (1605–23).—NS/LK/DM

Cigna, Gina (real name, **Ginetta Sens**), French soprano of Italian descent; b. Paris, March 6, 1900. She was a pupil of Calvé, Darclée, and Storchio. After making her operatic debut as Freia at Milan's La Scala in 1927, she was on its roster (1929–43); also appeared at London's Covent Garden (1933; 1936–37; 1939). On Feb. 6, 1937, she made her Metropolitan Opera debut in N.Y. as Aida, and sang there until 1938 in such roles as Leonora in *Il Trovatore*, Gioconda, Norma, Donna Elvira, and Santuzza. After World War II, she taught voice in Milan; also was on the faculty of the Royal Cons. of Music of Toronto (1953–57). —NS/LK/DM

Cikker, Jan, eminent Slovak composer and pedagogue; b. Banská Bystrica, July 29, 1911; d. Bratislava, Dec. 21, 1989. He was a student of Křička (composition), Dědeček (conducting), and Wiedermann (organ) at the Prague Cons. (1930–35), where he then attended Novák's master class in composition (1935–36). He concurrently studied musicology at the Univ. of Prague, and then pursued conducting studies with Weingartner in Vienna (1936–37). After settling in Bratislava, he was prof. of theory at the Cons. (1938–51) and prof. of composition at the Academy of Music and Dramatic Arts (1951–81). In 1955, 1963, and 1975 he was awarded state prizes. In 1966 he was named a National Artist by his homeland, and that same year was awarded the Herder Prize of the Univ. of Vienna. In 1979 he received the UNESCO Prize. In a number of his works, Cikker utilized Slovak melodies. In others, he moved toward expressionism and eventually embraced serial procedures. His works for the stage were particularly notable.

WORKS: DRAMATIC: O p e r a : *Juro Jánošík* (1953; Bratislava, Nov. 10, 1954; rev. version, Bratislava, May 7, 1956); *Beg Bajazid* (Bajazet Bey; 1956; Bratislava, Feb. 16, 1957); *Mr. Scrooge*, after Dickens (1957–59; 1st perf. as *Evening, Night, and Morning*, Kassel, Oct. 5, 1963); *Vzkriesenie* (Resurrection), after Tolstoy (1961; Prague, May 18, 1962); *Hra o láske a smrti* (A Play of Love and Death), after Romain Rolland (1968; Munich, Aug. 1, 1969); *Coriolanus* (1971; Prague, April 4, 1974); *Rozsudok: Zemetrasenie v Chile* (The Sentence: Earthquake in Chile; 1978; Bratislava, Oct. 8, 1979); *Obliehanie Bystrice* (The Siege of Bystrica; 1981; Bratislava, Oct. 8, 1983); *Zo života hmyzu* (From the Life of Insects; 1986; Bratislava, Feb. 21, 1987). **ORCH.:** 3 syms.: No. 1 (1930; arranged from the Piano Sonata, 1927), No.

2, *Jarná symfónia* (Spring Sym., 1937), and No. 3, *Symfónia 1945* (1974; Bratislava, May 22, 1975); *Epitaf*, symphonic poem (1931; rev. 1973); *Prologue symphonique* (1934); *Capriccio* (1936); *Symphonietta* (1939; arranged from the Piano Sonatine, 1933); *O živote* (About Life), cycle of 3 symphonic poems: *Leto* (Summer; 1941), *Vojak a matka: Boj* (Soldier and Mother: Battle; 1943), and *Ráno* (Morning; 1944–46); Piano Concertino (1942); *Slovenská suita* (1943); *Spomienky* (Recollections) for 5 Winds and Strings (1947); *Dramatická fantázia* (1957); *Meditácie na tému Heinricha Schütza* (Meditations on a Theme of Heinrich Schütz; 1964); *Orchestrálne štúdie k činohre* (Orchestral Studies on a Drama; 1965); *Hommage à Beethoven* (1970); *Variácie na slovenskú ľudovú pieseň* (Variations on a Slovak Folk Song; 1970); *Paleta* (Palette; 1980). **CHAMBER:** 1 unnumbered string quartet (1928); 2 numbered string quartets (1935, 1935); Suite for Violin and Viola (1935); *Domovina* (Homeland) for String Quartet (1986). **KEYBOARD: P i a n o :** Sonata (1927); Sonatine (1933); *Variácie* (Variations; 1935); *V samote* (Dance of Solitude; 1939); *Tatranské potoky* (The Tatra Streams), 3 études (1954); *Čo mi deti rozprávali* (What Children Told Me), 15 aquarelles (1957); *Variácie* (Variations), on a Slovak folk song (1973). **VOCAL:** *Vianočná kantata* (Christmas Cantata) for Chorus and Piano (1930); *Veľkonočná kantata* (Easter Cantata) for Chorus and Orch. (1931); *Cantus filiorum*, cantata for Bass, Chorus, and Orch. (1939); *O mamičke* (About Mother), song cycle for Voice and Piano (1940); *Óda na radosť* (Ode to Joy), oratorio for Soloists, Reciter, Chorus, and Orch. (1982).

BIBL.: J. Samko, *J. C.* (Bratislava, 1955).—NS/LK/DM

Cilèa, Francesco, Italian composer and pedagogue; b. Palmi, Calabria, July 23, 1866; d. Varazze, Nov. 20, 1950. He studied at the Naples Cons. (1881–89) with Cesi (piano) and Serrao (composition), where he later taught piano (1894–96). He then taught harmony at the Istituto Musicale in Florence (1896–1904). He was head of the Palermo Cons. (1913–16) and of the Cons. di San Pietro a Majella in Naples (1916–35). He was a member of the Reale Accademia Musicale in Florence (1898) and a knight of the Order of the Crown of Italy (1893).

WORKS: DRAMATIC: O p e r a : *Gina* (Naples, Feb. 9, 1889); *La Tilda* (Florence, April 7, 1892); *L'Arlesiana* (Milan, Nov. 27, 1897; rev. version, Milan, Oct. 22, 1898); *Adriana Lecouvreur* (Milan, Nov. 6, 1902); *Gloria* (Milan, April 15, 1907); *Il matrimonio selvaggio* (1909). **OTHER:** *Poema sinfonico* for Soloist, Chorus, and Orch. (Genoa, July 12, 1913); Piano Trio (1886); Cello Sonata (1888); *Variations* for Violin and Piano (1931); piano pieces; songs.

BIBL.: E. Moschino, *Sulle opere di F. C.* (Milan, 1932); C. Gaianus, *F. C. e la sua nuova ora* (Bologna, 1939); T. d'Amico, *F. C.* (Milan, 1960).—NS/LK/DM

Cillario, Carlo Felice, Argentine-born Italian conductor; b. San Rafael, Feb. 7, 1915. He studied at the Bologna Cons. and in Odessa. In 1946 he founded the Orch. da Camera in Bologna. In 1948 he organized the sym. orch. of the Univ. of Tucumán in Argentina, and was resident conductor of the Orquesta Sinfónica del Estado in Buenos Aires from 1949 to 1951. He later devoted himself mainly to conducting opera. In 1961 he made his British debut at the Glyndebourne Festival conducting *L'elisir d'amore*, and that same year he made his first appearance at the Lyric Opera in Chicago conducting *La forza del destino*. He made his debut at

London's Covent Garden in 1964 conducting *Tosca*. In 1970–71 he was music director of the Elizabethan Opera Trust in Sydney. On Oct. 17, 1972, he made his Metropolitan Opera debut in N.Y. conducting *La sonnambula*. He was principal guest conductor of the Australian Opera from 1987 to 1996, and then of Opera Australia from 1996 to 1999. His guest engagements also took him to opera houses in Buenos Aires, San Francisco, Venice, Florence, Milan, Paris, Berlin, Hamburg, Vienna, and Stockholm.—NS/LK/DM

Cima, Giovanni Paolo, Italian organist and composer; b. Milan, c. 1570; d. after 1622. By 1609 he was organist at S. Celso in Milan. Publications of his works, including *Concerti ecclesiastici* and motets, appeared between 1599 and 1626. His *Partito de Ricercari e Canzoni alla francese* (Milan, 1606) is a keyboard collection with an appendix containing rules for tuning keyboard instruments. The *canzoni alla francese* of this collection are specially written for keyboard, and the ricercari are highly developed in their use of imitation. —NS/LK/DM

Cimarosa, Domenico, famous Italian composer; b. Aversa, near Naples, Dec. 17, 1749; d. Venice, Jan. 11, 1801. He was the son of a stonemason. After his father's death, his mother placed him in the monastery school of the church of S. Severo dei Padri Conventuali in Naples, where he began his musical training with Father Polcano, the monastery organist. He then enrolled at the Cons. di S. Maria di Loreto (1761), where he studied voice, violin, and keyboard playing with Fenaroli, P.A. Gallo, and Carcais. Following his graduation in 1771, he studied voice with Giuseppe Aprile. His first opera, *Le stravaganze del conte*, was staged in Naples in 1772. From 1776 he composed operas at a prolific rate, producing about 65 works for the major Italian opera centers as well as those abroad. In 1779 he was named supernumerary organist of the Royal Chapel in Naples; in 1785 he became its second organist. He also served for a time as maestro of the Ospedaletto, a cons. for girls in Venice. In 1787 he was given the post of maestro di cappella to the court of Catherine the Great in St. Petersburg. During his Russian sojourn, he wrote three operas and various other works for the court and the nobility. However, the court cut back on its funding of music and Cimarosa's contract was allowed to lapse in 1791. He proceeded to Vienna, where Emperor Leopold II appointed him Kapellmeister. He then composed his masterpiece, *Il matrimonio segreto*, which was premiered with great acclaim at the Burgtheater on Feb. 7, 1792. The Emperor was so taken by the opera that he ordered that it be repeated that evening, undoubtedly the most elaborate encore in operatic annals. The opera's fame spread throughout Europe, and Cimarosa returned to Italy in 1793 as one of the most celebrated musicians of the age. In 1796 he was appointed first organist of the Royal Chapel in Naples. In 1799 he welcomed the republican movement in Naples by composing a patriotic hymn for the burning of the royal flag; however, the monarchy was restored later that year and Cimarosa's efforts miscarried. In consequence of this, he was arrested in Dec. 1799 and sent to prison for four months.

He was released only after the intervention of several prominent individuals. He then went to Venice, where he died while working on his opera Artemisia. It was rumored abroad that he had been poisoned by order of Queen Caroline of Naples; the rumor was so persistent, and popular feelings so pronounced, that the Pope's personal physician, Piccioli, was sent to Venice to make an examination; according to his sworn statement (April 5, 1801), Cimarosa died of a gangrenous abdominal tumor.

Cimarosa was an outstanding composer of Italian opera buffa in his day. His melodic inventiveness, command of form, superb vocal writing, and masterly orchestration were unexcelled until Rossini arrived upon the scene.

WORKS: DRAMATIC: Opera: *Le stravaganze del conte* (Naples, Carnival 1772); *La finta parigina* (Naples, Carnival 1773); *I sdegni per amore* (Naples, Jan. 1776); *I matrimoni in ballo* (Naples, Carnival 1776); *La Frascatana nobile* or *La finta frascatana* (Naples, 1776); *I tre amanti* (Rome, Carnival 1777); *Il Fanatico per gli antiche romani* (Naples, 1777); *L'armida immaginaria* (Naples, 1777); *Gli amanti comici, o sia La famiglia in scompiglio* (Naples, 1778?); *Il ritorno di Don Calandrino* (Rome, Carnival 1778); *Le stravaganze d'amore* (Naples, 1778); *Il matrimonio per raggiro* or *La Donna bizzarra* (Rome, 1778–79?); *L'Italiana in Londra* (Rome, Carnival 1779); *L'infedeltà fedele* (Naples, 1779); *Le Donne rivali* (Rome, Carnival 1780); *Cajo Mario* (Rome, Carnival 1780); *I finti nobili* (Naples, Carnival 1780); *Il Falegname* (Naples, 1780); *Il capriccio drammatico* (Turin, 1781?); *Il Pittor parigino* (Rome, Carnival 1781); *Alessandro nell'Indie* (Rome, Carnival 1781); *L'Amante combattuto dalle donne di Punto* (Naples, 1781); *Giunio Bruto* (Verona, 1781); *Giannina e Bernardone* (Venice, 1781); *Il convito* (Venice, Carnival 1782); *L'amor costante* (Rome, Carnival 1782); *L'Eroe cinese* (Naples, Aug. 13, 1782); *La Ballerina amante* (Naples, 1782); *La Circe* (Milan, Carnival 1783); *I due baroni di Rocca Azzurra* (Rome, Carnival 1783); *La Villana riconosciuta* (Naples, 1783); *Oreste* (Naples, Aug. 13, 1783); *Chi dell'altrui si veste presto si spoglia* (Naples, 1783); *I matrimoni impensati* or *La bella greca* (Rome, Carnival 1784); *L'apparenza inganna, o sia La villeggiatura* (Naples, 1784); *La vanità delusa* or *Il mercato di Malmantile* (Florence, 1784); *L'Olimpiade* (Vicenza, July 10, 1784); *I due supposti conti, ossia Lo sposo senza moglie* (Milan, 1784); *Artaserse* (Turin, Dec. 26, 1784); *Il Marito disperato* or *Il Marito geloso* (Naples, 1785); *La Donna sempre al suo peggior s'appiglia* (Naples, 1785); *Il Credulo* (Naples, Carnival 1786); *Le trame deluse* (Naples, 1786); *L'Impresario in angustie* (Naples, 1786); *Volodimiro* (Turin, Carnival 1787); *Il Fanatico burlato* (Naples, 1787); *La felicità inaspettata* (St. Petersburg, March 1788); *La Vergine del sole* (St. Petersburg, 1788?); *La Cleopatra* (St. Petersburg, Oct. 8, 1789); *Il matrimonio segreto* (Vienna, Feb. 7, 1792); *Amor rende sagace* (Vienna, April 1, 1793); *I traci amanti* (Naples, June 19, 1793); *Le astuzie femminili* (Naples, Aug. 26, 1794); *Penelope* (Naples, Carnival 1795); *Le nozze in garbuglio* (Messina, 1795); *L'impegno superato* (Naples, 1795); *La finta ammalata* (Lisbon, 1796); *I Nemici generosi* (Rome, Carnival 1796); *Gli Orazi ed i Curiazi* (Venice, Carnival 1797); *Achille all'assedio di Troja* (Rome, Carnival 1797); *L'imprudente fortunato* (Rome, Carnival 1797); *Artemisia regina di Caria* (Naples, 1797); *L'apprensivo raggirato* (Naples, 1798); *Il secreto* (Turin, 1798); *Artemisia* (Venice, Carnival 1801; left unfinished); some 30 other stage works have been attributed to Cimarosa, but many are doubtful. **ORATORIOS:** *Giuditta* (Venice, 1782?); *Absalom* (Venice, 1782); *Il sacrificio d'Abramo* (Naples, 1786); *Il trionfo delle fede* (Naples, May 1794); *Il martirio* (Naples, 1795); *S. Filippo Neri che risuscita Paolo*

649

Massimi (Rome, 1797). **OTHER**: Many masses and other sacred works; secular cantatas; a Harpsichord Concerto; a Concerto for 2 Flutes; chamber music; keyboard pieces.

BIBL.: M. Trevisan, *Nel primo centenario di D. C.* (Venice, 1900); R. Vitale, *D. C., La vita e le opere* (Aversa, 1929); G. Biamonti, *Il matrimonio segreto di D. C.* (Rome, 1930); F. Schlitzer, *Goethe e C.* (Siena, 1950); J. Johnson, *D. C. (1749–1801)* (diss., Univ. Coll., Cardiff, 1976); R. Iovino, *D. C.: Operista napoletano* (Milan, 1992); N. Rossi and T. Fauntleroy, *D. C.: His Life and His Operas* (Westport, Conn., 1999).—NS/LK/DM

Cirri, Giovanni Battista, Italian cellist and composer; b. Forlì, Oct. 1, 1724; d. there, June 11, 1808. He studied with his brother, Ignazio Cirri (1711–87), organist at Forlì Cathedral from 1759, and with Giovanni Balzani, organist at the church of the Madonna del Fuoco. After taking holy orders in 1739, he was a cellist and composer at the Basilica of S. Petronio in Bologna. In 1759 he was elected a member of the Accademia Filarmonica of Bologna. In 1764 he went to London as a chamber musician to the Duke of York and as director of music to the Duke of Gloucester, brother of King George III. He also was active as a concert artist. Returning to Forlì in 1780, he assisted his brother at the Cathedral. In 1782 he was made principal cellist at the Teatro dei Fiorentini in Naples. In 1787 he was named his brother's successor as maestro di cappella at Forlì Cathedral. He wrote much chamber music, demonstrating a special flare for the cello, and also composed sacred works.
—LK/DM

Ciuciura, Leoncjusz, Polish composer; b. Grodzisk Mazowiecki, July 22, 1930. He studied composition with Tadeusz Szeligowski at the State Higher School of Music in Warsaw (1954–60). He founded the music publishing firm Carmina Academica, with which he was active as an editor. In 1960 he received the Minister of Culture and Arts Award, in 1962 first prize in the International Competition for Composers in Prague, and in 1963 third prize in the Grzegorz Fitelberg Competition in Katowice. Virtually all of his works are essays in combinatorial permutation with optional instrumental or vocal additions, subtractions, multiplications, or divisions.

WORKS: *Suita warmińsko-mazurska* (Warmia and Mazury Suite) for Solo Voices and Chorus (1960); *Canti al fresco* for 9 Women's Voices and Instrumental Ensemble (1961); *Concertino da camera* for Chamber Orch. (1961); *Ornamenti* for Flute, Clarinet, Bassoon, and Strings (1963-); *Penetracje* (Penetrations) for 4 Orch. Groups, 4 Conductors, and Composer (1963-); *Emergenza* for 2 Choruses, Orch., 3 Conductors, and Composer (1963-); *Spirale I per uno* for Baritone and 36 Percussion Instruments (1964-) and *II* for Optional Instrumental Ensemble (2 versions, 1964-); *Creatoria I* and *II* for Various Performers (1964-); *In infinitum I* and *II* for Various Performers (1964-); *Incidenti I* for Various Performers (1964-); *Rencontre I* and *II* for Various Performers (1964-); *Intarsio I* and *II* for Various Performers (1969-); *Per 5* for Any Combination of Flute, Oboe, Horn, Bassoon, and Trumpet (1972); *Musica* for Solo Flute and 8 Instruments (1976).—NS/LK/DM

Clapisson, (Antoine-) Louis, French composer, curator, and pedagogue; b. Naples, Sept. 15, 1808; d. Paris, March 19, 1866. He received training in violin in Naples. In 1830 he entered the Paris Cons., where he studied violin with Habeneck (second prix, 1833), and also took lessons in counterpoint and fugue with Reicha. From 1832 to 1838 he was a violinist in the Paris Opéra orch., and then was notably successful as a composer of opéras-comiques. In 1847 he was named a Chevalier of the Légion d'honneur and in 1854 he was elected over Berlioz to replace Halévy at the Académie des Beaux-Arts. He acquired and restored a collection of early instruments, which he later oversaw as curator at the Paris Cons., where he also was a prof. of harmony from 1862. Clapisson's opéras-comiques were quite popular in his lifetime, but they failed to retain a place in the repertoire.

WORKS: DRAMATIC (all opéras-comiques and 1st perf. in Paris unless otherwise given): *La figurante, ou L'amour et la danse* (Aug. 24, 1838); *La symphonie, ou Maître Albert* (Oct. 12, 1839); *La perruche* (April 28, 1840); *Le pendu* (March 25, 1841); *Frère et mari* (July 7, 1841); *Le code noir* (June 9, 1842); *Les bergers trumeaux*, opéra bouffon (Feb. 10, 1845); *Gibby la cornemuse* (Nov. 19, 1846); *Don Quixotte et Sanche*, musical sketch (Dec. 11, 1847); *Jeanne la folle*, opera (Nov. 6, 1848); *La statue équestre* (1850; not perf.); *Les mystères d'Udolphe* (Nov. 4, 1852); *La promise* (March 17, 1854); *Dans les vignes* (Dec. 31, 1854); *Le coffret de Saint Domingue* (1855); *Les amoureux de Perrette* (Baden-Baden, 1855); *La fanchonnette* (March 1, 1856); *Le sylphe* (Baden-Baden, Aug. 18, 1856); *Margot* (Nov. 5, 1857); *Les trois Nicolas* (Dec. 16, 1858); *Madame Grégoire* (Feb. 8, 1861); *La poularde de Caux*, operetta (May 17, 1861; in collaboration with others). **OTHER**: Chamber music; over 200 songs.—LK/DM

Clappé, Arthur, Irish-American bandmaster and composer; b. Cork, July 22, 1850; d. Washington, D.C., Nov. 22, 1920. He was educated at the Royal Military School in London (graduated, 1873). He began his career as a bandmaster in the British Army in India. After serving as director of the Canadian Governor-General's Foot Guards in Ottawa (1877–84), he went to N.Y. as ed. of the journal *Metronome* (1884–91). From 1891 to 1895 he was director of the U.S. Military Academy Band at West Point. In 1893 he founded the journal *The Dominant*, which he owned and publ. from 1895 to 1910. In 1911 he organized the U.S. Army Music School at Fort Jay in N.Y. In 1918 he was commissioned a captain in the U.S. Army, and oversaw the founding of a training school for bandmasters. He publ. manuals and composed band pieces.—LK/DM

Clapton, Eric (originally, **Clapp, Eric Patrick**), rock music's first guitar hero and the world's most famous guitarist, was one of the finest lead guitarists to emerge during the 1960s; b. Ripley, Surrey, England, March 30, 1945. As a member of three of the most influential English blues groups of the 1960s (The Yardbirds, John Mayall's Bluesbreakers, and Cream), Clapton set the standard for the "clean" school of lead playing with his tasty, precise, yet fluid guitar work. Cream, rock music's first supergroup and first powerhouse vocal and instrumental trio, made virtuoso playing an art form within rock and sparked the late–1960s blues revival.

The short-lived Blind Faith continued the improvisatory tradition, as did Clapton's first group, Derek and the Dominos. Indeed, *Layla and Other Assorted Love Songs* was a remarkably focused and intense work, uniting two of rock's most revered guitarists, Clapton and Duane Allman. Clapton's subsequent solo work emphasized his modest songwriting and vocal talents. However, his hit recording of Bob Marley's "I Shot the Sheriff" introduced reggae to a wider audience, and "Lay Down Sally" and "Promises" expanded his audience into the country field. Recently he has scored astounding successes with his acoustic *Unplugged* album, taken from the MTV series, and his album of covers of blues standards, *From the Cradle*.

Eric Clapton took up guitar at 15, later playing in a number of bands such as The Roosters and Casey Jones and the Engineers before joining, in October 1963, the Metropolis Blues Quartet, which later changed its name to the Yardbirds. Clapton stayed on through March 1965, but he became increasingly disturbed by the growing pop direction of the group. Seeking to remain a blues purist, Clapton sought out musicians dedicated to the traditional sound of the blues, joining John Mayall's Bluesbreakers in April 1965. While with the Bluesbreakers, he received extensive adulation as England's premier lead guitarist.

Clapton left the Bluesbreakers in July 1966 to form Cream, rock's first supergroup, with bassist Jack Bruce and drummer Peter "Ginger" Baker. Cream revolutionized rock music with their patented improvisational jams and pioneered the power trio (guitar-bass-drums) format. With internal strains becoming increasingly apparent by mid-1968, Cream announced their intention to disband, performing their final concert at London's Royal Albert Hall in December. Almost immediately, Clapton helped form another supergroup, Blind Faith, with Cream alumni Ginger Baker, Traffic's Stevie Winwood, and Family's Rick Grech. Unable to live up to the overly enthusiastic expectations of the rock community, Blind Faith completed one English and one American tour and recorded one album before disbanding at the end of 1969. The interesting, if flawed, album featured Winwood's "Sea of Joy" and "Can't Find My Way Back Home" and Clapton's "In the Presence of the Lord."

Clapton next participated in a number of sessions for other artists before joining the Delaney and Bonnie and Friends tour of 1970. Their studio album produced a major hit with Dave Mason's "Only You Know and I Know." Many of these "friends" later assisted Clapton in recording his first solo album, *Clapton*. They included Delaney and Bonnie, Leon Russell, Rita Coolidge, Steve Stills, organist Bobby Whitlock, bassist Carl Radle, drummer Jim Gordon, saxophonist Bobby Keys, and trumpeter Jim Price. The album yielded a major hit with J. J. Cale's "After Midnight" and featured outstanding lead guitar work on "Blues Power" and "Let It Rain."

In May 1970 Eric Clapton formed Derek and the Dominos on the U.S. West Coast with Whitlock, Radle, Gordon, and the Allman Brothers' Duane Allman. Recorded between Aug. 26 and Oct. 2 at Miami's Criteria Studio, *Layla and Other Assorted Love Songs* was a stunning album of tortured love and traditional blues. The album contained excellent ensemble playing on

extended versions of the originals "Anyday," "Keep on Growing," and "Why Does Love Got to Be So Sad" (by Clapton and Whitlock), "Layla" (by Clapton and Gordon), Clapton's "Bell Bottom Blues," and the blues standards "Have You Ever Loved a Woman" and "Key to the Highway," plus Jimi Hendrix's "Little Wing." In 1971 Derek and the Dominoes toured without Allman; live recordings from the tour were issued in 1973. However, the group disbanded and Clapton, disillusioned by the death of Duane Allman and the failure of the "Layla" single (it became a near-smash hit when re-released in 1972), went into near-retirement; a growing addiction to heroin also contributed to his withdrawal from performance. Clapton performed only twice (at George Harrison's Concert for Bangladesh in August 1971 and at Leon Russell's Rainbow Theater engagement in December 1971) before finally being coaxed into reemerging by the Who's Pete Townshend at the Rainbow Theater in January 1973.

Clapton's first album of new material in several years, *461 Ocean Boulevard*, released in 1974, showcased his modest vocal talents, relegating his guitar playing to a support role. The album yielded one of Clapton's biggest hit singles with his cover of Bob Marley's "I Shot the Sheriff," plus the major hit remake of Johnny Otis's "Willy and the Hand Jive." That year he also began attempts to clear up his alcohol and heroin habits and moved in with George Harrison's ex-wife Patti (the object of "Layla"), whom he married in 1979.

Clapton toured the United States again in 1974 and 1975, and live recordings from the tour were issued as *E. C. Was Here*. He began concentrating on his songwriting, and 1976's *No Reason to Cry* produced a major hit with his own "Hello Old Friend." *Slowhand* included J. J. Cale's "Cocaine" and yielded a smash pop hit (and major country hit) with "Lay Down Sally," and a major hit with the love song "Wonderful Tonight." Subsequent major hits through 1985 included "Promises," "I Can't Stand It," "I've Got a Rock 'n' Roll Heart," and "Forever Man." During the 1980s Clapton toured regularly, usually accompanied by an outstanding second guitarist, such as Albert Lee, Tim Renwick, or Mark Knopfler.

Eric Clapton's relationship with Patti Harrison ended in 1986 and the couple divorced in 1988. He finally overcame his alcohol and heroin addictions in 1987 and has been in a recovery program ever since. Surrounded by tragedy most of his life, as evidenced by the deaths of Duane Allman, Yardbirds lead vocalist Keith Relf, and Domino Carl Radle (in 1971, 1976, and 1980, respectively), the murder of Cream producer Felix Pappalardi in 1983, and the institutionalization of Domino Jim Gordon in 1984, Clapton further suffered the loss of Stevie Ray Vaughan in a helicopter crash minutes after the two had performed together in August 1990. Then, on March 20, 1991, his son Conor (by Italian actress Lori Del Santo) fell to his death from the 53rd floor of the Galleria Condominium in N.Y. Grief-stricken, Clapton ultimately reemerged in early 1992 with the poignant smash hit "Tears in Heaven," written for his son, and an inspiring appearance on MTV's *Unplugged*. The album from the show later yielded a surprise hit with a slowed-down acoustic version of

"Layla," which amazingly sold more than seven million copies. Cream reunited in 1993 when the trio was inducted into the Rock and Roll Hall of Fame. In 1994 Clapton recorded the best-selling *From the Cradle*, an album of traditional blues that included covers of songs by Willie Dixon, Elmore James, and Muddy Waters, and conducted a blues-only tour of arenas and halls. In May 1995 Eric Clapton appeared in a 90-minute PBS television special that focused on the blues. Recorded at the Fillmore in San Francisco, the special was produced by filmmaker Martin Scorsese.

DISC.: ERIC CLAPTON WITH JOHN MAYALL'S BLUESBREAKERS: *Bluesbreakers* (1967). BLIND FAITH: *Blind Faith* (1969). ERIC CLAPTON WITH DELANEY AND BONNIE: *On Tour with E. C.* (1970). DEREK AND THE DOMINOS: *Layla and Other Assorted Love Songs* (1970); *The Layla Sessions* (1990); *In Concert* (1973); *Live at the Fillmore* (1994). THE RAINBOW CONCERT: *E. C.'s Rainbow Concert* (1973). ERIC CLAPTON: *E. C.* (1970); *History of E. C.* (1972); *E. C. at His Best* (1972); *Clapton* (1973); *461 Ocean Boulevard* (1974); *There's One in Every Crowd* (1975); *E.C. Was Here* (1975); *No Reason to Cry* (1976); *Slowhand* (1977); *Backless* (1978); *Just One Night* (1980); *Another Ticket* (1981); *Time Pieces/Best of E. C.* (1982); *Time Pieces/Live in the 1970s* (1988); *Crossroads* (1988); *The Cream of Clapton* (1995); *Money and Cigarettes* (1983); *Behind the Sun* (1985); *August* (1986); *Homeboy* (soundtrack; 1989); *Journeyman* (1989); *24 Nights* (1991); *Rush* (soundtrack; 1992); *Unplugged* (1992); *From the Cradle* (1994).

WRITINGS: *E.C.: In His Own Words* (N.Y., 1993).

BIBL.: Ray Coleman, *Clapton!: An Authorized Biography* (N.Y., 1986); John Pidgeon, *E.C.: A Biography* (London, rev.ed., 1985); Marc Roberty, *E.C. Scrapbook* (N.Y., 1994); Marc Roberty, *Slowhand: The Life and Music of E.C.* (N.Y., 1993); Christopher Sandford, *Clapton, Edge of Darkness* (N.Y., rev. ed., 1999); Michael Schumacher, *Crossroads: The Life and Music of E.C.* (N.Y., 1995); Harry Shapiro, *E.C.: Lost in the Blues* (N.Y., 1992); Steve Turner, *Conversations with E.C.* (London, 1976).—**BH**

Clarey, Cynthia, black American mezzo-soprano; b. Smithfield, Va., April 25, 1949. She studied at Howard Univ. in Washington, D.C. (B.Mus.) and at the Juilliard School of Music in N.Y. (postgraduate diploma). She began her career with the Tri-Cities Opera Co. in Binghamton, N.Y. In 1977 she appeared in Musgrave's *The Voice of Ariadne* at the N.Y.C. Opera, and then in the U.S. premiere of Tippett's *The Ice Break* in Boston in 1979. She made her British debut as Monteverdi's Octavia at the Glyndebourne Festival in 1984, returning there in 1986 as Gershwin's Serena. In 1984 she sang in the premiere of Tippett's *The Mask of Time* in Boston. After singing Polinesso in *Ariodante* at the Wexford Festival in 1985, she returned there in 1986 as Thomas's Mignon. In 1992 she appeared as Serena in the Covent Garden premiere of *Porgy and Bess* in London, and then sang Bess in Cape Town in 1996. She appeared with major orchs. in the U.S. and abroad. Among her other roles were Handel's Rinaldo, Zerlina, Carmen, Dalila, Preziosilla, Octavian, and Cio-Cio-San.—**NS/LK/DM**

Clari, Giovanni Carlo Maria, Italian composer; b. Pisa, Sept. 27, 1677; d. there, May 16, 1754. He studied with his father and with Francesco Alessi in Pisa, then under Colonna at Bologna, where his opera *Il Savio delirante* was produced in 1695. From 1703 to 1724 he was in Pistoia as maestro di cappella of the Cathedral; then went to Pisa. His best-known work is a collection of madrigals for two and three voices (1720; reprinted by Carli, Paris, 1825). He also wrote masses, Psalms, a Requiem, and other sacred music.

BIBL.: J. Grundy Fanelli, *The Oratorios of G.C.M. C.* (Bologna, 1998).—**NS/LK/DM**

Clark, Frederick Scotson, English organist, pedagogue, composer, and clergyman of Irish descent; b. London, Nov. 16, 1840; d. there, July 5, 1883. He studied piano and organ with his mother, with Sergent in Paris, and with E.J. Hopkins. After representing Great Britain at the Paris Exhibition in 1878, he continued his training with Sterndale Bennett and Goss at the Royal Academy of Music in London. He was active as an organist in London, where he organized an organ school which later became the London Organ School. In 1865 he became organist at Exeter Coll., Oxford. In 1867 he received his B.Mus. from Oxford and completed his studies for the priesthood. After serving the Lutheran church in Stuttgart, he settled in London in 1873. He wrote over 500 works, including piano, harmonium, and organ pieces. Among the latter were 48 effective voluntaries. He also publ. a *Method for the Harmonium* (London, 1858).—**NS/LK/DM**

Clark, Graham, English tenor; b. Littleborough, Nov. 10, 1941. He studied with Richard Bonynge, in London with Bruce Boyce, and in Bologna. In 1975 he became a member of the Scottish Opera in Glasgow. From 1976 to 1985 he also made regular appearances at the English National Opera in London. He made his Bayreuth Festival debut as David in *Die Meistersinger von Nürnberg* in 1981, and continued to sing there until 1992. On Oct. 17, 1985, he made his Metropolitan Opera debut in N.Y. as Števa in *Jenůfa*, where he remained on the roster until 1993. In 1991 he sang in the premiere of Corigliano's *The Ghosts of Versailles* there. In 1997 he appeared at the Salzburg Festival in Ligeti's *Le Grand Macabre*. As a guest artist, he sang in Berlin, Vienna, Munich, Rome, Chicago, San Francisco, and elsewhere. He also appeared as a soloist with many orchs. —**NS/LK/DM**

Clark, John (Trevor), jazz french hornist; b. Brooklyn, N.Y., Sept. 21, 1944. Clark grew up mostly in Rochester, N.Y., studied composition and arranging at New England Cons. with George Russell, Jaki Byard and Ran Blake, and was a member of the Scholarship Brass Quintet. He was a member of the Gil Evans Orch. (1974–88), recording six albums. He has also performed with a wide range of groups including Leroy Jenkins, Speculum Musicae, McCoy Tyner, Carla Bley, George Russell and Joe Lovano. In 1982, he was winner of the *Down Beat* Critics' Poll, and in 1986 received the NARAS Award for Most Valuable Player in the recording field. His compositions and arrangements have been performed and/or recorded by The Pugh-Taylor Project, The Aspen Wind Quintet, The Meridian Arts Ensemble, the McCoy Tyner Big Band, the Gil Evans Orch. and the Mohawk Trail Concerts (Mass.).

DISC.: *I Will* (1997).—LP

Clark, June (actually, Algeria Junius), jazz cornetist; b. Long Branch, N.J., March 24, 1900; d. N.Y., Feb. 23, 1963. His family moved to Philadelphia in 1908. Clark was taught piano by his mother, then played bugle before graduating to baritone horn and cornet. He worked as a Pullman porter before becoming a professional musician with S. H. Dudley's "Black Sensations." Clark and James P. Johnson left the show and worked together in Toledo, Ohio, where they met Jimmy Harrison. In late 1920, Clark returned to gig in Philadelphia, then joined the band accompanying Josephine Stevens for a year. He toured theaters with Willie "the Lion" Smith and with "Holiday in Dixie" show. When the show folded in Detroit, Clark worked in the Buick factory for a while, rejoined Harrison and played in Fess Williams' Band. He settled in N.Y., and led his own bands at various venues between 1924–30. He also took his band to Saratoga for summer of 1925 and worked for brief spells with various other leaders. He continued to work in N.Y., occasionally leading his own bands through 1933, then spent two years in Philadelphia. He was back in N.Y., working with other leaders through early 1937, when he quit regular playing due to failing health. He worked for a while as Louis Armstrong's road manager, then entered Otisville Sanitarium in August 1939, suffering from tuberculosis. He left Otisville in October 1941, worked as musical adviser to various bands, including that of Earl Hines (1944), then became road manager for the famous boxer Sugar Ray Robinson. He remained with Robinson until forced to quit through illness shortly before his death.—JC/LP

Clark, Petula (originally, Owen, Sally), English singer and actress; b. Epsom, Surrey, Nov. 15, 1932. Clark had a lengthy and varied career, beginning in radio and extending to TV, films, and recordings, all before she became an adult. A star in the U.K. in the 1940s and in Europe in the 1950s, she attained stardom in the U.S. in the 1960s with a series of pop-rock recordings, including "Downtown," "I Know a Place," "My Love," "I Couldn't Live without Your Love," "This is My Song," and "Don't Sleep in the Subway." In the 1980s and 1990s she starred in stage musicals.

Clark was encouraged by her parents to become a singer and was performing publicly by the age of seven. In 1941 she successfully auditioned at the BBC and became a radio performer, also frequently singing for the troops during World War II. Signed to a film contract, she appeared in at least 23 films between 1944 and 1957. From July to November 1946 she appeared on *Cabaret*, an early TV program. In 1949 EMI's Columbia label released her first single, "Put Your Shoes on Lucy," after which she signed to Polygon Records (later renamed Nixa, then Pye). From November 1950 to July 1953 she had her own TV series, *Pet's Parlour*, on the BBC.

Clark scored her first U.K. hit with "The Little Shoemaker" (music by Rudi Revil, French lyrics by

Avril Lamarque, English lyrics by Geoffrey Parsons and John Turner), which reached the charts in June 1954 and peaked in the Top Ten in July. In September she launched another TV series, *Pet's Parade*, which ran until February 1957. Her recording of "Suddenly There's a Valley" (music and lyrics by Chuck Meyer and Biff Jones) peaked in the Top Ten in January 1956.

In 1957, at age 24, Clark stopped using her father as her manager and moved away from home into her own apartment. "With All My Heart" (music by Pete De Angelis, lyrics by De Angelis and Bob Marcucci) peaked in the Top Ten in September, followed by "Alone" (music by Morton Craft, lyrics by Selma Craft) in December. In November 1958 she performed a concert in French in Paris at the behest of her French label, Vogue Records, and met Vogue promotion man Claude Wolff, who became her manager and whom she married on June 8, 1961.

Clark moved to France and began to focus more on the European market, although her recordings also continued to score in Great Britain. In February 1961 she topped the U.K. charts with "Sailor" (music by Werner Scharfenberger, German lyrics by Fini Busch, English lyrics by Alan Holt), an adaptation of a German song called "Seemann." "Romeo" (music by Robert Stolz, English lyrics by Jimmy Kennedy) peaked in the British Top Ten in August, followed by "My Friend the Sea" in December. In 1962 her European hits included "Monsieur," sung in German, and "Chariot" (music by J. W. Stole and Del Roma, lyrics by Jacques Plante), sung in French. (Given an English lyric by Norman Gimbel and Arthur Altman, "Chariot" became a U.S. hit for Little Peggy March in 1963 under the title "I Will Follow Him.")

Clark gave birth to her first child, a daughter named Barbara Michele, in 1962. In 1963 her European hits included "Casanova," sung in German, and "Ya Ya Twist" (an adaptation of "Ya Ya," music and lyrics by Lee Dorsey, Clarence Lewis, and Morgan Robinson). That year she gave birth to her second daughter, Catherine Natalie.

Clark renewed her ties to her native country in 1964, making appearances there and working with songwriter/producer Tony Hatch. Their first collaboration was "Downtown," which peaked in the U.K. Top Ten in December 1964. Warner Bros. Records picked up the record for American distribution and it topped the U.S. charts in January 1965, going gold and earning Clark Grammy nominations for Record of the Year, Best Vocal Performance, Female, and Best Rock & Roll Recording; she won in the last category. Warner Bros. released a *Downtown* LP that spent more than eight months in the charts and earned the singer another Grammy nomination for Best Vocal Performance, Female. It was the first of 14 U.S. chart albums through 1971.

Clark and Hatch returned with "I Know a Place," which peaked in the U.S. Top Ten in May and won her second Grammy for Best Contemporary (R&B) Vocal Performance, Female. She scored two more Top 40 hits before the end of the year, then returned to #1 with "My Love" (music and lyrics by Tony Hatch) in February

653

1966. Her U.K.-only single "You're the One," which she co-wrote with Hatch, was a Top 40 hit there; in the U.S. the Vogues took it into the Top Ten.

Clark toured the U.S. performing in such nightclubs as the Copacabana in N.Y. and at hotel/casinos in Las Vegas. In the U.K. in June and July 1966 she had another TV series, *This Is Petula Clark*. Her next major hit, "I Couldn't Live without Your Love," which Tony Hatch wrote with his wife, Jackie Trent, peaked in the British Top Ten in July and the American in August, also hitting #1 on the U.S. easy-listening charts. After a couple of Top 40 hits, Clark's recording of "This is My Song," Charles Chaplin's theme from his 1967 film *A Countess from Hong Kong*, topped the U.K. charts in February 1967 and peaked in the U.S. Top Ten in April. In July her final major U.S. hit, "Don't Sleep in the Subway" (music and lyrics by Tony Hatch and Jackie Trent) peaked in the Top Ten and topped the easy-listening charts; it earned her Grammy nominations for Best Contemporary Single, Best Vocal Performance, Female, and Best Contemporary Solo Vocal Performance, Female.

Clark continued to reach the U.S. Top 40 with her singles through mid-1968, meanwhile expanding her concerns to other areas of entertainment. On April 8, 1968, she starred in her first U.S. television special, *Petula*, and in October she co-starred with Fred Astaire in the film version of the Burton Lane–E. Y. Harburg musical *Finian's Rainbow*. Disappointed with her diminishing record sales, she split with Tony Hatch in January 1969, but her sales continued to decline. In April 1969 she starred in her second U.S. TV special, *Portrait of Petula*, and in August 1969 co-starred with Peter O'Toole in a musical remake of the film *Goodbye, Mr. Chips*.

Clark left Pye and Warner Bros. Records in 1971 to record for MGM Records; she continued to place songs in the charts regularly through 1974. On Sept. 7, 1972, she gave birth to a son, Patrick Philippe, after which she was less active, although she continued to make occasional recordings and television appearances. In 1980 she made her West End debut starring in a revival of *The Sound of Music* that ran 14 months. With this she became more active, appearing in a non-singing role in George Bernard Shaw's *Candida*; performing with the London Philharmonic Orch. at the Royal Albert Hall in February 1983 for a live album release; and returning to U.S. appearances in 1986. A dance remix of her recording of "Downtown" hit the U.K. Top Ten in the fall of 1988. In 1989 she was able to mount *Someone Like You* (Cambridge, England, Oct. 25, 1989), a musical about the American Civil War that she co-wrote, and it reached the West End briefly in March 1990.

Clark made her Broadway debut in Willy Russell's musical *Blood Brothers* on Aug. 16, 1993. In January 1996 she took over the starring role in Andrew Lloyd Webber's musical *Sunset Boulevard* in London, remaining with the show through 1997. In 1998 she began touring the U.S. in a road production of *Sunset Boulevard* scheduled to run through 2000, and she released a new album through Varèse Sarabande Records, *Here for You*.

BIBL.: A. Kon, *This Is My Song: A Biography of P. C.* (London, 1983).—**WR**

Clark, Spencer W., jazz bass saxophonist, cornetist, multi- instrumentalist; b. Baltimore, Md., March 15, 1908; d. Webster, N.C., May 27, 1998. His family moved to N.Y. in 1909. Clark played mandolin, marimba, and clarinet before doing his first gigs on C melody sax in New Rochelle, N.Y. (c. 1923). After hearing Adrian Rollini, Clark switched to bass sax and worked in a local movie-house orchestra from late 1924. He subbed for Rollini during 1925–26 and recorded with the California Ramblers at the Ramblers' Inn. In autumn 1926 he led "Little Ramblers" (Lenny Hayton, Carl Kress, etc.) at Ramblers' Inn. He was with various bands until sailing to Europe with George Carhart in July 1928, working with Carhart in France, and then joined Julian Fuhs in Berlin. He was with Lud Gluskin in Europe (on bass sax, trumpet, and guitar) from March 1929 until returning to the U.S. in January 1931. He was with Bert Lown in N.Y. for most of 1931, then with Fred Waring (1932). He played trumpet with Ozzie Nelson (late 1932–early 1933), sax with Irving Conn (1933–36) and with Dick Stabile (1936–38), and also worked on string bass during this period. He left full-time music, worked for a newspaper while gigging until August 1939, then entered aviation. He worked for commercial and private airlines until moving to Ill. in 1954. He became purchasing Agent for City of Highland Park, and later began playing bass sax again. He worked (and recorded an LP) with Freddie Wacker's Windy City Seven (1957), and continued to play occasional gigs in the 1960s. In 1971, he retired to N.C.—**JC/LP**

Clarke, George F., jazz tenor saxophonist; b. Memphis, Tenn., Aug. 28, 1911; d. Bronx, N.Y., Sept. 1985. Clarke became Jimmie Lunceford's pupil while attending Manassas H.S. in Memphis, became a member of Lunceford's first band, and remained with him until 1933. He settled in Buffalo and played for various leaders: Guy Jackson (1933–34), Stuff Smith, and Lil Armstrong (1935), among others. He worked again with Smith in 1939, then led his own band which played a long residency at the Anchor Bar, Buffalo, throughout the 1940s. Clarke moved to N.Y. in 1954, played regularly with Cootie Williams (including tour of Europe in early 1959); toured Africa with Cozy Cole in late 1962. He was occasionally active through the 1960s in N.Y. —**JC/LP**

Clarke, Henry Leland, American composer and teacher; b. Dover, N.H., March 9, 1907; d. March 30, 1992. He received training in piano, organ, and violin before pursuing his education at Harvard Univ. (M.A., 1929), where he studied composition with Holst (1931–32; Ph.D., 1947, with a diss. on John Blow). He also studied with Boulanger at the École Normale de Musique in Paris (1929–31) and with Weisse and Luening in Bennington, Vt., and N.Y. (1932–38). Clarke taught at Bennington (Vt.) Coll. (1936–38), Westminster Choir Coll. in Princeton, N.J. (1938–42), the Univ. of Calif. at Los Angeles (1947–58), and the Univ. of Wash. in Seattle (1958–77). He publ. the book *Sound and Unsound: Ideas on Music* (Seattle, 1973). In his compositions, he developed such innovations as "Intervalescent Counterpoint" (with interval values constanting changing one voice to another), "Lipophony" (with certain notes systematically omitted), "Word Tones" (whenever a word recurs, it is assigned to the same pitch), and "Rotating Triskaidecaphony" (a 12-tone series returning to note 1 for the 13th note, with the next row starting and ending on note 2, etc.).

WORKS: DRAMATIC: O p e r a : *The Loafer and the Loaf* (1951; Los Angeles, May 1, 1956); *Lysistrata* (1968–72; Marlboro, Vt., Nov. 9, 1984). **ORCH.:** *Lyric Sonata* for r Strings (1932; rev. 1960); *Monograph* (1952); *Saraband for the Golden Goose* (1957); *Points West* for Wind and Percussion (1960; also for Full Orch., 1970); *Encounter* for Viola and Orch. (1961); *Variegation* (1961). **CHAMBER:** 3 string quartets (1928, 1956, 1958); *Danza de la muerte* for Oboe and Piano (1937); *Nocturne* for Viola and Piano (1955); *A Game That 2 Can Play* for Flute and Clarinet (1959); *Concatenata (Quodlibet)* for Wind Quintet (1969); *Danza de la vida* for Oboe and Piano (1975); *3 From Foster, Fuguing Trio* for Flute, Violin, and Cello (1980–81); *Drastic Measures* for Trombone (1982); *Salute to Justin Morgan* for Flute, Violin, and Harpsichord (1982); much piano and organ music. **VOCAL: C h o r a l :** *No Man is an Island,* after Donne (1951); *The Young Dead Soldiers,* after MacLeish (1970); *These are the Times that Try Men's Souls,* after Paine (1976); *Choose Life,* after *Deuteronomy* 30: 19 (1983); *The Sun Shines Also Today,* after Emerson (1983); *We Believe,* after Von Odgen Vogt (1984); *The Earth Mourns,* after *Isaiah* 24 (1984). **O t h e r :** Many songs.

BIBL.: O. Daniel, *H.L. C.* (N.Y., 1970).—NS/LK/DM

Clarke, Hugh Archibald,

Scottish-American organist, pedagogue, and composer; b. near Toronto, Canada, Aug. 15, 1839; d. Philadelphia, Dec. 16, 1927. He was the son and pupil of the Scottish organist James Paton Clarke (b. 1808; d. Toronto, Aug. 27, 1877). In 1859 he settled in Philadelphia, where he was a church organist. He also served as prof. of music at the Univ. of Pa. (1875–1925). He publ. textbooks, including *A System of Harmony* (Philadelphia, 1898), and also publ. *Music and the Comrade Arts* (Boston, 1899) and *Highways and Byways of Music* (N.Y., 1901). Among his compositions were incidental music to Aristophanes's *Acharnians* (1886) and Euripides's *Iphigenia in Tauris*, the cantata *The Music of the Spheres* (1880), the oratorio *Jerusalem* (1890), three piano sonatinas (1874), and songs.—NS/LK/DM

Clarke, Jeremiah,

English organist and composer; b. probably in London, c. 1674; d. there (suicide), Dec. 1, 1707. He was a chorister in the Chapel Royal before serving as organist at Winchester Coll. (c. 1692–95). In 1699 he was made vicar-choral and organist at St. Paul's Cathedral in London, where he assumed the position of Master of the Choristers in 1703. In 1700 he became a Gentleman Extraordinary of the Chapel Royal, and in 1704 he was made joint organist there with Croft. Clarke shot himself over a hopeless love affair with one of his pupils of noble lineage. His most celebrated score is the *Trumpet Voluntary,* erroneously ascribed to Purcell for many years and included in a harpsichord anthology as *The Prince of Denmark's March* (1700). It also appeared in a suite for wind instruments. Among his other works were theater music, services, about 20 anthems, including one for the coronation of Queen Anne (1702), odes, and harpsichord pieces.

BIBL.: T. Taylor, *Thematic Catalog of the Works of J. C.* (Detroit, 1977).—NS/LK/DM

Clarke, Kenny

(actually, **Kenneth Spearman**; aka **"Klook"; "Klook-mop"; Salaam, Liaquat Ali**), influential bebop drummer, leader; b. Pittsburgh, Pa., Jan. 9, 1914; d. Paris, France, Jan. 26, 1985. His brother and father were musicians. While in school, he played piano, trombone, drums, and vibes. Clarke worked with Leroy Bradley's Band in the early 1930s, had a brief spell with Roy Eldridge, then worked in St. Louis with Jeter- Pillars Band. Towards the end of 1935, he relocated to N.Y. He joined Edgar Hayes in 1937, and toured Europe with in spring 1938. After briefly working with Claude Hopkins in late 1939, he was with Teddy Hill's Band (1940–41); Dizzy Gillespie was one of his bandmates. Hill gave him his nickname "Klook," complaining about his "klook-mop" sound. Clarke then became house-musician at Minton's Club in N.Y., along with pianist Thelonious Monk, and bassist Nick Fenton, where Hill was the manager. During famous afterhours sessions at Minton's, several N.Y.–based musicians developed a new musical style that would become known as bebop. Clarke worked briefly with Louis Armstrong and with Ella Fitzgerald in early 1941 before spending a year with Benny Carter 1941–42. He was with the Henry Allen Sextet in Chicago, then led his own band in N.Y. before serving in the U.S. Army (1943–46). He was with Gillespie 1946, and again in 1948; after a European tour he remained in France for some months. He joined Tadd Dameron in 1948, returning to Paris with him in 1949. He toured the U.S. with Billy Eckstine in 1951. Clarke was a founding member of the Milt Jackson Quartet in early 1952. That August, the group became the Modern Jazz Quartet. Clarke remained with them until 1955, then went on to extensive freelance work before moving to Paris in summer 1956. He played extensively with visiting American jazzmen, as well as leading his own octet and co-leading a big band with pianist François "Francy" Boland from 1960–73. Based in Cologne, Germany, the big band performed frequently and made many recordings. It received considerable critical acclaim, and included numerous musicians of many nationalities, notably Benny Bailey, Dusko Goykovich, Idrees Sulieman, Ake Persson, Nat Peck, Johnny Griffin, Ronnie Scott, Karl Drewo, and Sahib Shihab. After the big band folded, Clarke continued to work actively in Europe as a freelancer. He revisited the U.S. on occasion to play festivals in 1972, 1979, and 1984.

Clarke was probably the most important figure in the transition from swing to early bebop drumming. His most notable innovation was shifting the basic time-keeping role from the bass drum to the ride cymbal, and then using the bass and snare drums to interject accents ("bombs") against the beat. He was there "at the founding" of the style, and contributed to many historic recordings of Charlie Parker, Dizzy Gillespie, and other boppers. He also co-composed several early bop standards, including "Epistrophy" with Monk and the ever-popular "Salt Peanuts" with Gillespie.

DISC.: *Paris Bebop Sessions* (1950); *Telefunken Blues* (1954); *Kenny Clarke, Vol. 1* (1954); *Kenny Clarke All- Stars* (1954); *Trio*

(1955); *Septet* (1955); *Plenty for Kenny* (1955); *Kenny Clarke, Vol. 2* (1955); *Bohemia After Dark* (1955); *Klook's Clique* (1956); *Plays Andre Hodeir* (1957); *Kenny Clarke in Paris, Vol. 1* (1957); *Pieces of Time* (1983). Charlie Christian: *C.C.with Dizzy* (1941). Miles Davis: *M.D. Vol. 1* (1952); *Walkin'* (1954); *Ascenser Pour L'Echafaud* (1957). Clarke-Boland Big Band: *Jazz Is Universal* (1961); *Golden Eight* (1961); *Now Hear Our Meanin'* (1965); *Open Door* (1967); *Sax No End* (1967); *All Smiles* (1968); *Volcano* (1969); *Rue Chaptal* (1969); *At Her Majesty's Pleasure* (1969); *Live at Ronnie Scott's* (1969); *Off Limits* (1970); *Latin Kaleidoscope* (1973).

BIBL.: M. Hennessey, *Klook: The Kenny Clarke Story* (Pittsburgh, 1994).—JC/LP/DK

Clarke, Rebecca (Thacher),

English-born American composer and violist; b. Harrow, Aug. 27, 1886; d. N.Y., Oct. 13, 1979. She studied violin with Hans Wessely at the Royal Academy of Music (1902–04) and composition with Stanford at the Royal Coll. of Music (1904–10) in London. She then switched to the viola, taking a few private lessons from Tertis and becoming the first female member of Henry Wood's Queen Hall Orch. (1912). In 1928 she formed the English Ensemble, with which she played until 1929. She married **James Friskin** in 1944; she then lived in N.Y. Her music, comprising entirely chamber works, was quite advanced, being on the fringe of atonality in outline, but remaining firmly rooted in English Impressionism. For some of her compositions, she used the name Anthony Trent.

WORKS: Violin Sonata (1909); *Morpheus* for Viola and Piano (1917); Viola Sonata (1919); Piano Trio (1921); String Quartet (1924); *Epilogue* for Cello and Piano (1921); *Chinese Puzzle* for Violin and Piano (1921); *Rhapsody* for Cello and Piano (1923); *Midsummer Moon* for Violin and Piano (1924); *3 Old English Songs* for Voice and Piano (1924); *3 Irish Country Songs* for Voice and Violin (1926); *Prelude, Allegro, and Pastorale* for Clarinet and Viola (1941; Berkeley, Calif., Aug. 6, 1942); *Combined Carols* for String Quartet and Strings (1941); *Passacaglia on an Old English Tune* for Viola and Piano (1941); over 60 songs.
—NS/LK/DM

Clarke, Stanley (M.),

highly influential jazz-fusion bassist; b. Philadelphia, Pa., June 30, 1951. He began playing in rock bands in the 1960s before moving into jazz and fusion. A one-time violinist and cellist from Philadelphia, Clarke approached acoustic bass like a guitar, with dazzling, rapid patterns his specialty. He and his friend Lenny White dazzled a Carnegie Hall audience with Freddie Hubbard in June/July 1972. They both moved on to Chick Corea's Return to Forever (1972–76); Clarke played only electric bass in this group, and also launched a solo career during this time. His 1975 album *Journey to Love* produced the funky single "Silly Putty." He continued to make albums combining jazz and funk and helped to expose the bass as a versatile instrument capable of taking both lead and rhythm roles. Clarke achieved chart success in 1981 with the George Duke collaboration "Sweet Baby" and then with Jeff Beck and the New Barbarians. Since 1978, he has produced records for a variety of artists including Roy Ayers and Dee Dee Bridgewater and has contributed to sessions for McCoy Tyner, Aretha Franklin, and Donna Summer. In 1986, he embarked on a rare solo

tour. He partnered again with George Duke in 1989, and in the early 1990s worked with the group Animal Logic. He has also scored several films, including *Boyz in the Hood* and *Poetic Justice.*

Clarke introduced the funk "slap-'n'-pop" style of bass players like Larry Graham into the jazz world. His solos recall the work of rock guitarists like Jimi Hendrix, while his backing and melodic style owed much to Scott LaFaro. It was Clarke's desire to be a melody player that led him to develop the electric version of the piccolo bass. Clarke also uses a tenor bass (a regular bass, tuned one fourth higher, with lighter-gauge strings), and the Folyde acoustic bass guitar (looks like a guitar, but is tuned lower and has four strings).

DISC.: *Children of Forever* (1972); *Stanley Clarke* (1974); *Journey to Love* (1975); *Live* (1976); *School Days* (1976); *Modern Man* (1978); *Clarke/Duke Project, Vol. 1* (1981); *Clarke/Duke Project, Vol. 2* (1983); *If This Bass Could Only Talk* (1988); *Live at the Greek* (1993); *Live in Montreux* (1994); *Rite of Strings* (1995).
—MM/LP/PMac

Clash, The,

the first British punk band to capture the attention of American audiences. **MEMBERSHIP:** Joe (real name, John Mellor) Strummer, voc., rhythm gtr. (b. Ankara, Turkey, Aug. 21, 1952); Mick Jones, voc., lead gtr. (b. Brixton, London, England, June 26, 1953); Paul Simonon, bs. (b. London, England, Dec. 15, 1956). Early guitarist Keith Levene left after the group's first tour. The group's drummers were Tory "Terry" Chimes, Nicky "Topper" Headon (b. Bromley, England, May 30, 1955), and Pete Howard. Mick Jones left in 1983, to be replaced by guitarists Vince White and Nick Sheppard.

The Clash persevered with their assured, overtly political music while the Sex Pistols quickly self-destructed as a consequence of their defeatist nihilism. Along with Elvis Costello, the Clash were the prime innovators to emerge from punk and displayed a remarkable eclecticism (unlike their contemporaries), exploring reggae and rockabilly, as well as rock, from their very start. Ironically, while establishing themselves in Great Britain with disenfranchised working-class youth in the late 1970s, the Clash broke through in the United States to middle-class audiences with their 1982 hits "Should I Stay or Should I Go" and "Rock the Casbah." Hailed for both their debut album and *London Calling*, the Clash ultimately disintegrated in the mid-1980s.

Formed in May 1976 by musicians from the 101ers and London SS, the Clash toured Great Britain and the United States on the Sex Pistols' ill-fated Anarchy in the U.K. tour that December. Early guitarist Keith Levene, who later surfaced in Public Image Ltd. with former Sex Pistols vocalist Johnny "Rotten" Lydon, left the band after the first tour, when the band added drummer Terry Chimes. Signed to Columbia Records in February 1977, the Clash's debut album was judged too crude to be issued in the United States. It was eventually released, in altered form, on Epic in 1979. Hailed as the definitive punk album, *The Clash* included the rebellious "White Riot," "London's Burning," and "Hate and War," and featured musical attacks on unemployment ("Career Opportunities"), record companies ("Complete Control"), and cultural imperialism ("I'm So Bored with the U.S.A."), plus their signature song, "I Fought the Law."

With Nicky "Topper" Headon taking over on drums and Joe Strummer and Mick Jones acting as the group's primary songwriters, the Clash recorded their next album (and American debut), *Give 'Em Enough Rope*, with Blue Öyster Cult producer Sandy Pearlman. The album contained their first British hit single, "Tommy Gun," and included "All the Young Punks," "Guns on the Roof," "English Civil War," "Safe European Home," and "Stay Free." They debuted as headliners in the United States in February 1979 and subsequently recorded *London Calling*. The album featured explorations of reggae ("Revolution Rock" and "Wrong 'Em Boyo") and rockabilly ("Brand New Cadillac"), and included "London Calling," "Lost in the Supermarket," the ballad "Lover's Rock," and their first major American hit, "Train in Vain (Stand By Me)."

Established in America as the only extant British punk band, the Clash next recorded the sprawling 36-song *Sandinista* album. Their biggest hits came off their next album, 1982's *Combat Rock*: the moderate hit "Should I Stay or Should I Go" and the near-smash "Rock the Casbah," written by drummer Topper Headon. The Clash opened for the Who's Farewell tour in late 1982. Headon soon left the band due to ongoing problems with drug addiction; he was replaced by original drummer Chimes, and then in 1983 by Pete Howard. At the pinnacle of their popularity, Strummer and Simonon fired Mick Jones in late 1983. By 1984 only Strummer and Simonon remained from the original group; they managed to record one final album, *Cut the Crap*, before disbanding in 1986.

Joe Strummer turned to acting (*Straight to Hell*) and production, and later recorded *Earthquake Music* and toured with the Pogues, while Mick Jones formed Big Audio Dynamite with New Wave filmmaker-keyboardist Don Letts. The group broke up in 1989; Jones subsequently assembled Big Audio Dynamite II with entirely new members, scoring a moderate hit with "Rush" in 1991. By then Paul Simonon had formed Havana 3 A.M. with Sex Pistols' guitarist Steve Jones.

DISC.: THE CLASH: *The C.* (1979); *Give 'Em Enough Rope* (1979); *London Calling* (1980); *Black Market Clash* (1980); *Sandinista!* (1981); *Combat Rock* (1982); *Cut the Crap* (1988); *The Story of the Clash, Vol. 1* (1988); *Clash on Broadway* (1991). **JOE STRUMMER:** *Earthquake Weather* (1989). **JOE STRUMMER AND THE LATINO ROCKABILLY WAR:** *Permanent Record* (soundtrack; 1988). **BIG AUDIO DYNAMITE:** *This Is Big Audio Dynamite* (1985); *No. 10 Upping St.* (1986); *Tighten Up, Vol. '88* (1988); *Megatop Phoenix* (1989); *Planet Bad Greatest Hits* (1995); *Punk* (1995). **BIG AUDIO DYNAMITE II:** *The Globe* (1991). **HAVANA 3 A.M.:** *Havana 3 A.M.* (1991).

BIBL.: *The C.* (London, 1981).—BH

Claussen, Julia (née Ohlson), Swedish mezzo-soprano; b. Stockholm, June 11, 1879; d. there, May 1, 1941. She studied at the Royal Academy of Music in Stockholm (1897–1902); then in Berlin with Friedrich (1903–05). She made her operatic debut as Leonora in *La Favorite* at the Stockholm Opera (Jan. 19, 1903); was engaged there from 1903 until 1932; made her debut at Covent Garden in London in 1914; was a member of the Chicago Opera Co. (1912–14; 1915–17). She made her first appearance at the Metropolitan Opera in N.Y. as Dalila on Nov. 23, 1917, and remained on its roster until 1929; in 1934 she returned to Stockholm as a teacher at the Cons.—NS/LK/DM

Claxton, Rozelle, jazz pianist, organist, arranger; b. Memphis, Tenn., Feb. 5, 1913; d. Chicago, Ill., March 30, 1995. A member of a large musical family, Claxton's sister taught him to read music, and he played piano from the age of 11. From c. 1930, he played in trumpeter Clarence Davis' Rhythm Aces, and worked with this band when they toured with W. C. Handy (1932). He played and arranged for Harlan Leonard from c. 1934, and performed many solo residencies in Chicago during the late 1930s, and later worked with Emie Fields (1939), briefly subbed for Count Basie in summer 1939, and played with Eddie South. He played at Elmer's, in Chicago (1940), then with Walter Fuller from September 1940. From September 1946, he worked with George Dixon's quartet. A prolific freelance arranger, Claxton scored for Count Basie, Earl Hines, Red Norvo, Jimmie Lunceford, and Andy Kirk, and also worked as accompanist for various singers, including Pearl Bailey in 1958 and again from 1978–83. From 1959 through the late 1960s he worked on and off with saxophonist Franz Jackson. He also played solo gigs at various Chicago-area clubs through his retirement in the late 1980s. He sometimes was confused with another Chicago pianist, Rozelle I. Gayle.—JC/LP

Clay, Frederic (Emes), English composer; b. Paris (of English parents), Aug. 3, 1838; d. Great Marlow, near London, Nov. 24, 1889. He was a student of Molique in Paris and of Hauptmann in Leipzig. He began his career as a British civil servant. After composing incidental music to Tom Taylor's play *Court and Cottage* (London, 1862), he devoted himself mainly to composing for the theater. His collaboration with the librettist W.S. Gilbert on *Ages Ago* (London, Nov. 22, 1869) proved a fine success. Clay collaborated with others in composing *Babil and Bijou* (London, Aug. 29, 1872), for which he wrote the successful song *Nobody Knows as I Know*. With Gilbert again as librettist, he wrote *Princess Toto* (Nottingham, June 26, 1872), which was successfully heard abroad. With George Sims as librettist, he composed his most celebrated score in *The Merry Duchess* (London, April 23, 1883), which was also mounted successfully abroad. Their final collaboration, *The Golden Ring* (London, Dec. 3, 1883), likewise was received well. Soon after its premiere, Clay suffered a stroke, which ended his career.

WORKS: DRAMATIC: Musical Theater (all 1st perf. in London unless otherwise given): *Constance* (Jan. 23, 1865); *The Bold Recruit* (Canterbury, Aug. 4, 1868); *Ages Ago* (Nov. 22, 1869); *The Gentleman in Black* (May 26, 1870); *Happy Arcadia* (Oct. 28, 1872); *Babil and Bijou* (Aug. 29, 1872; in collaboration with Hervé, J. Rivière, and J.-J. de Billemont); *Ali Baba à la Mode* (Sept. 14, 1872; in collaboration with J. Mallandaine, G. Richardson, and G. Goldsmith); *The Black Crook* (Dec. 23, 1872; in collaboration with G. Jacobi); *Oriana* (Feb. 16, 1873); *Cattarina* (Manchester, Aug. 17, 1874); *Don Quixote* (Sept. 25, 1876); *Princess Toto* (Nottingham, June 26, 1876); *The Merry*

Duchess (April 23, 1883); *The Golden Ring* (Dec. 3, 1883); also incidental music to *Monsieur Jacques* (1876) and *The Squire* (1881). V O C A L : C a n t a t a s : *Lallah Rookh* (Brighton Festival, 1877; includes the well-known aria *I'll Sing Thee Songs of Araby*) and *Saradanapalus* (Leeds Festival, 1882). O t h e r : Many songs, including *She Wandered Down the Mountainside, The Sands of Dee,* and *Tis Better Not to Know.*—NS/LK/DM

Clay, Shirley, jazz trumpeter; b. Charleston, Mo., 1902; d. N.Y., Feb. 7, 1951. Clay worked with bands in and around St. Louis from 1920, toured with John "Bearcat" Williams' Synco Jazzers (c. 1923–24), then settled in Chicago. He played regularly with Detroit Shannon's Band (c. 1925–26), Carroll Dickerson (1927), briefly with Louis Armstrong's Stompers (1927), then with Clifford "Klarinet" King Big Band (1928), and also took part in many freelance recording sessions. He was with Earl Hines (1929–31), Marion Hardy (1931), then with Don Redman from late 1931–36. During this period, Clay also recorded with other leaders: Benny Goodman (1933), Putney Dandridge (October 1935), and with Ben Pollack (1933). He was with Claude Hopkins (1937–39), Earl Hines again in 1940, then played in Leon Abbey's Band. He was with Horace Henderson (autumn 1941), Cootie Williams' Big Band (1942); and from June 1943, did a six-month U.S.O. tour in a band led by Herbie Cowens. Clay led his own band at the Cinderella Club, N.Y. (1944), with George James' Band (June 1944), then rejoined Claude Hopkins (October 1944). Again he led his own band, played in Harry Dial's Quartet until spring of 1946. He led another band before working at Camp Unity, Wingdale, N.Y. He played in Manzie Johnson's Band (from September 1949). During the last years of his life often co-led bands with Edgar Battle.—JC/LP

Clay, Sonny (actually, **William Rogers Campbell**), early jazz drummer, multi-instrumentalist; b. Phoenix, Ariz., May 15, 1899; d. Los Angeles, April 1973. He did first gigs in Phoenix c. 1911, began doubling on sax., trpt., and trmb. After a season at Riverside Park, Ariz., moved to West Coast c. 1916. He played drums with Jelly Roll Morton and xylophone with Johnny Spikes, and also worked with George Morrison's Band. He played with Kid Ory during the early 1920s, then played piano, sax, and drum in his own Eccentric Harmony Six (late 1922). Clay led his own bands in Los Angeles area from then until the early 1940s, played for many theater shows, and did extensive touring including trip a to Australia (from January 1928). He retired from full-time music in the 1940s, doing occasional gigs and working as a piano tuner. —JC/LP

Clayton, Buck (actually, **Wilbur Dorsey**), famed swing-era trumpeter, arranger; b. Parsons, Kans., Nov. 12, 1911; d. N.Y., Dec. 8, 1991. His father played tuba and trpt. in local church orchestras. Buck began playing piano at the age of six, switched to trpt. in his early teens, and took lessons from his father. At 19 he went to Calif. for four months. After a succession of non-musical jobs he returned to Kans., completed high

school studies, then returned to the West Coast. After working with various bandleaders in Los Angeles, Buck was appointed leader of Earl Dancer's Band in 1934; this 14-piece unit was heard by Teddy Weatherford, who booked the full band for a residency at the Canidrome Ballroom, in Shanghai, China, during 1935. Weatherford occasionally played concerts with the band in Shanghai but was not a regular member of the group. Later Buck led a smaller band at the Casanova Club, Shanghai. He returned to Los Angeles in 1936 and again led his own big band, the 14 Gentlemen from Harlem; also gigged with various bandleaders including Charlie Echols. In autumn 1936, while on his way to N.Y. to join Willie Bryant's Band, Buck stopped off in Kansas City, where Count Basie persuaded him to take the trpt. place recently vacated by Hot Lips Page. He remained with Count Basie until his Army call-up in November 1943 (except for temporary absence in mid-1942 for a tonsillectomy), was stationed for most of the time at Camp Kilmer, N.J., and played regularly with all-star service bands. He had an honorable discharge early in 1946. During this period, he did arrangements for Count Basie, Benny Goodman, Harry James, etc. In October 1946 he took part in the first national Jazz at the Philharmonic tour and subsequently played on several of Norman Grant's tours. From 1947 he led his own sextet at Café Society (Downtown), N.Y. From September 1949–June 1950 he made his first European tour, leading his band in France. During the early 1950s, he had long spells with Joe Bushkin Quartet, worked with Tony Parenti, and led a band on tours with Jimmy Rushing. He returned to Europe in 1953, working mainly with Mezz Mezzrow. Throughout the 1950s he achieved considerable success with his own specially formed recording groups. He appeared with Benny Goodman in *The Benny Goodman Story,* and played with Goodman in N.Y. in 1957; went to Brussels in summer 1958 to work with Sidney Bechet at the World's Fair Concerts. He toured Europe early in 1959; joined Eddie Condon's Band; during the 1960s he played for Condon on several occasions, including a tour of the Far East in the spring of 1964. He toured with Jimmy Rushing in summer of 1962, and worked with Peanuts Hucko early in 1964. During the 1960s Buck made annual tours of Europe and was featured at major jazz festivals throughout the U.S. After appearing at the New Orleans Jazz Fest in June 1969, Buck was temporarily absent from music while he underwent lip surgery. He played dates in N.Y., Washington, and Cleveland (spring 1970), then had hernia operations that put him out of commission until late 1971. He made a State Department tour of the Middle East (1977) and toured France (spring 1978). He retired from trumpet playing during the1970s but continued to work as an arranger and lecturer in jazz up to his death.

DISC.: *Buck Clayton Jam Session* (1953); *How Hi the Fi* (1953); *Hucklebuck and Robbin's Nest* (1953); *Meet Buck Clayton* (1953); *Jumpin' at the Woodside* (1954); *Buck Meets Ruby* (1954); *Buck Clayton Jams Benny Goodman* (1954); *All the Cats Join In* (1956); *Big Band at the Savoy Ballroom* (1957); *Copenhagen Concert* (1959); *Kansas City Nights* (1960); *Olympia Concert* (1961); *Meets Joe Turner* (1965); *Le Vrai Buck Clayton, Vol. 2* (1966); *Baden, Switzerland 1966* (1966); *Jam Session* (1974); *Buck Clayton Jam Session*

(1975); *Jazz Spectacular* (1977); *Heart and Soul* (1987); *Swingin' Dream* (1988).

WRITINGS: With F. Hoffman and N. M. Elliott, *Buck Clayton's Jazz World* (N.Y., 1987).

BIBL.: B. Weir, *Buck Clayton: Discography* (Chigwell, England, 1989).—**JC/LP**

Clemencic, René, Austrian recorder player, harpsichordist, conductor, and composer; b. Vienna, Feb. 27, 1928. He took courses in philosophy and musicology at the Sorbonne in Paris, the Collège de France, and the Univ. of Vienna (Ph.D., 1956), and studied recorder, harpsichord, and theory with H. Staeps, harpsichord with E. Harich-Schneider, early music with J. Mertin, analysis with E. Ratz, and theory with J. Polnauer in Vienna. He also received recorder training from J. Collette in Nijmegen and from L. Hoffer v. Wintersfeld and W. Nitschke in Berlin. In 1958 he founded the Musica Antiqua in Vienna, which became the Ensemble Musica Antiqua in 1959; with this group, he gave performances of music from the Middle Ages to the Baroque, utilizing authentic instruments. In 1969 he founded the Clemencic Consort, and led it in a vast repertoire, extending from the medieval period to the avant-garde. He also taught at the Vienna Academy of Music and authored two books, *Old Musical Instruments* (London, 1968; also in German) and *Carmina Burana, Kommentar zur Gesamtausgabe der Melodien* (Munich, 1979).

WORKS: DRAMATIC: *Sesostris I,* monodrama for Speaker and 5 Players (1970); *Der Berg,* chamber opera for 4 Voices and Chamber Ensemble (1993). **ORCH.:** *Musik zum "Prinz von Homburg"* (1983); *Flauto II* for Recorder and Strings (1984); *Revolution* for 7 Drums and Orch. (1989). **CHAMBER:** *Fantasia Dodekafonica* for Recorder (1964); *Maraviglia I* for Recorder (1968), *II* for Recorder (1968), *III/Iter Exstaticum* for Speaker and Chamber Ensemble (1968), and *IV/Lucerna Eius* for Chamber Ensemble (1969); *Bicinia Nova* for 2 Recorders or Piccolo Flutes (1969); *Experience One* for Recorder, Harpsichord, and Tape (1971); *Nova Bicinia Nova* for 2 Recorders (1971); *Sesostris IV* for Recorder and Strings (1990); *Chronos I* for Recorder, Violin, and Tape (1971), *II* for 4 Recorders (1975), and *III* for 4 Instruments (1976); *Flauto Magico I* for Recorder (1978); *Sicut Navis* for Cello and Piano (1981); *Unus Mundus* for 10 Instruments and Tape (1986); *Estasi* for 6 Percussionists (1988); *Passatempo* for Brass and Wind Quintet (1989); *Musica Instrumentalis* for Chamber Ensemble (1989); *Musica Hermetica* for 2 Violins and Tape (1989); *Strukturen* for Saxophone Quartet (1989); *Opus* for Recorder and Strings (1991); *AES Fanfare* for Brass and Percussion (1992); *Jeruschalajim,* piano trio (1995); *Lux intelligentia* for Recorder, Violin, Cello, and Percussion (1995); *Emblamata* for Trombones and Percussion (1997). **VOCAL:** *Maraviglia V* for Voice and 4 Players (1972); *Sesostris II* for Speaker, 2 Loudspeakers, 4 Singers, and Chamber Ensemble (1976); *Realitäten* for Voice and Chamber Ensemble (1979); *Musik zum "Urfaust"* for Voice and Chamber Ensemble (1980); *Missa Mundi (Ossiacher Marienmesse)* for 5 Voices, Chorus, and Orch. (1981); *Musik zu "Tolldreiste Szenen"* for Voice and Chamber Ensemble (1981); *Stufen* for Countertenor and 5 Instruments (1981); *Requiem pro Vivis et Mortuis* for 5 Voices, Chorus, and Orch. (1986–87); *Drachenkampf* for Speaker and 7 Players (1987); *Kabbala,* oratorio for 5 Voices, Brass, and Percussion (1992);

Apokalypsis, oratorio for 5 Voices, Women's Chorus, Brass, Percussion, and Double Basses (1996); *Um Mitternacht* for Voice and 4 Instruments (1998); *Reise nach Niniveh* for 12 Voices (1999). —**NS/LK/DM**

Clemens non Papa (real name, **Jacob Clement**), eminent Franco-Flemish composer; b. probably in Ieper, c. 1510; d. Dixmuiden, near Ieper, 1555 or 1556. He was first called "non Papa" in 1545 when he entered into business transactions with the Antwerp publisher Susato. It was formerly believed that "non Papa" meant "not the Pope," to distinguish him from Pope Clement VII, but it was also suggested that it was intended to differentiate him from the poet Jacobus Papa, who also resided in Ieper. The real meaning of the designation has been lost. Nothing is known of his early years. His earliest extant work, the chanson "Le departir est sans department," was publ. in 1536. In the records of St. Donaas in Bruges, he is mentioned as presbyter in 1544; that same year he was nominated succentor "per modum probae." He served as succentor at Bruges Cathedral in 1544–45 and was active with the Marian Brotherhood in 's-Hertogenbosch in 1550. He was a prolific composer of sacred music, producing 15 masses (two mass fragments are also extant), over 230 motets, two Magnificat cycles, and 159 three-voice souterliedekens and lofzangen (the first polyphonic settings of the 150 Psalms in Dutch; publ. by Susato in Antwerp, 1556–57). His secular works include 89 chansons (ten are doubtful), eight Dutch songs, and several other pieces. K. Bernet Kempers ed. *Clemens non Papa: Opera omnia* in Corpus Mensurabilis Musicae, IV/1–21 (1951–76).

BIBL.: K. Bernet Kempers, *Jacobus C. n. P. und seine Motetten* (Augsburg, 1929).—**NS/LK/DM**

Clément, Edmond (Frédéric-Jean), esteemed French tenor; b. Paris, March 28, 1867; d. Nice, Feb. 24, 1928. He was a pupil of Warot at the Paris Cons. in 1887, taking first prize in 1889. His debut was at the Opéra-Comique, Nov. 29, 1889, as Vincent in Gounod's *Mireille.* His success was instantaneous, and he remained there until 1910 with frequent leave for extended tours; sang in the principal theaters of France, Belgium, Spain, Portugal, England, and Denmark. On Dec. 6, 1909, he made his debut at the Metropolitan Opera in N.Y. in one of his finest roles, Massenet's Des Grieux; from 1911 to 1913, sang with the Boston Opera Co. His voice was a light tenor of very agreeable quality, with a range of two octaves. He created the chief tenor parts in the following operas (all at the Opéra-Comique): Bruneau's *L'Attaque du Moulin* (1893), Saint-Saëns's *Phryné* (1893), Cui's *Le Flibustier* (1894), Godard's *La Vivandière* (1895), Dubois's *Xavière* (1895), Hahn's *L'Île du rêve* (1898), Erlanger's *Le Juif polonais* (1900), Saint-Saëns's *Hélène* (1904), Dupont's *La Cabrera* (1905), and Vidal's *La Reine Fiammette* (1908). —**NS/LK/DM**

Clement, Franz, Austrian violinist and composer; b. Vienna, Nov. 17, 1780; d. there, Nov. 3, 1842. He learned to play the violin as a child, and at the age of ten went to London, where he appeared as a soloist at

concerts directed by Salomon and Haydn. Returning to Vienna, he continued his successful career. He was conductor at the Theater an der Wien (1802–11), and made a tour in Germany and Russia (1813–18). He also participated in the concerts of the famous singer Angelica Catalani. Clement was greatly esteemed as a violinist and musician by his contemporaries. Beethoven wrote his Violin Concerto for him, and Clement gave its first performance in Vienna (Dec. 23, 1806). He wrote six concertos and 25 concertinos for violin, as well as numerous technical studies.
—NS/LK/DM

Clementi, Aldo, prominent Italian composer and pedagogue; b. Catania, May 25, 1925. He began training in piano at age 13 and in composition at age 16 in Catania. He pursued piano studies with Giovanna Ferro at the Conservatorio di Santa Cecilia in Rome (diploma, 1946), and then attended Scarpini's master class at the Accademia Musicale Chigiana in Siena (1947). From 1945 to 1952 he also studied composition with Alfred Sangiorgi in Catania and Bolzano, who introduced him to 12-tone writing. Following further composition studies with Petrassi at the Conservatorio di Santa Cecilia (1952–54; diploma, 1954), he attended the summer courses in new music at Darmstadt (1955–62) and was active at the Studio di Fonologia in Milan (1956–62). From 1971 to 1992 he taught theory at the Univ. of Bologna. Among his honors were first prize in the ISCM competition in 1963 for his *Sette scene* for Chamber Orch. and the Abbiati Prize in 1992 for his opera *Interludi: Musica per il Mitro di Eco e Narciso.* Clementi is one of the leading avant-garde composers of Europe. As such, he sees his main task as that of creating works which fulfill his vision of contemporary music as a vehicle for the dissolution of music as we know it.

WORKS: DRAMATIC: *College,* azione musicale (Rome, May 14, 1962); *Blitz,* azione musicale (Royan, April 18, 1973); *Collage 4,* azione mimo-visiva (1979; Florence, May 30, 1981); *Finale,* azione lirica (Rome, Oct. 13, 1984); *Interludi: Musica per il Mito di Eco e Narciso,* opera (Gibellina, July 23, 1992); *Carillon,* opera (1994; Milan, Oct. 16, 1998). ORCH.: *Tre studi* for Chamber Orch. (1956–57; Darmstadt, July 27, 1957); *Episodi* (1958; Brussels Radio, Jan. 13, 1959); *Sette scene* for Chamber Orch. (1961; Florence, May 20, 1964); *Informel* (1961–63; Palermo, Oct. 1, 1963); *Variante B* (1963; Venice, Sept. 12, 1964); *Sinfonia da camera* for Chamber Orch. (Milan, April 21, 1974); Concerto for Piano, 24 Instruments, and 12 Carillons (1975; Milan, Feb. 12, 1976); Concerto for Double Bass, Orch., and 12 Carillons (Royan, March 21, 1976); *Clessidra* for Chamber Orch. (Bergamo, May 22, 1976); Concerto for Violin, 40 Instruments, and 12 Carillons (Brescia, June 8, 1977); *Capriccio* for Viola and 24 Instruments (1979–80; RAI, Naples, April 4, 1980); *Halleluja* (RAI, Naples, Oct. 8, 1982); *Das Alte Jahr* for Chamber Orch. (Milan, April 27, 1985); *O du selige* (RAI, Naples, Dec. 6, 1985); *Berceuse* (1989); *Romanza* for Piano and Orch. (RAI, Rome, March 16, 1991). CHAMBER: Flute Sonatina (1950; Bergamo, June 6, 1983); Sonata for Trumpet, Guitar, and Piano (1955; Zürich, June 2, 1957); *Concertino in form di variazioni* for 9 Instruments (1956; London, May 27, 1957); *Ideogrammi 1* for 16 Instruments (1959; Palermo, May 13, 1960) and 2 for Flute and 17 Instruments (1959; Venice, Sept. 21, 1960); *Triplum* for Flute, Oboe, and Clarinet (1960; Darmstadt, Sept. 2, 1961); *Informel 1* for 11 Instrumentalists (1961; Venice, Sept. 6, 1970) and 2 for 15

Instruments (1962; Venice, April 16, 1963); *Reticolo: 11* for 11 Instruments (Venice, Sept. 6, 1966); 4 for String Quartet (1968; Warsaw, Sept. 28, 1969), and 12 for 12 Strings (1970; Como, Sept. 20, 1971); *Intermezzo* for 14 Instruments and Prepared Piano (Naples, June 17, 1977); *Sphinxs* for Violin, Viola, and Cello (Naples, June 15, 1978); String Quartet (1978; Venice, Oct. 1, 1979); *L'Orologio di arceua* for 13 Instrumentalists (Venice, Sept. 30, 1979); *Pastorale en Rondeau* for 2 Violins, Viola, Harpsichord, and Carillons (Perugia, June 21, 1981); Concerto for 16 Instruments (1981–82; Champigny, April 18, 1983); *Aeb* for 17 Instruments (RAI, Naples, May 13, 1983); *Adagio* for Quintet and Prepared Piano (Naples, Nov. 22, 1983); *Ouverture* for 12 Instruments (Chiusa di Chianciano, July 22, 1984); *Scherzo* for Flute, Clarinet, Violin, and Viola (1985; Zürich, Nov. 22, 1987); Concerto for Piano and 14 Instruments (1986; Genoa, Feb. 2, 1987); *Prélude: Hommage à Ravel* for 12 Instruments (Montpellier, July 21, 1987); *Fantasia* for 4 Guitars (Sermoneta, June 24, 1988); *Cantabile* for 12 Instrumentalists (Siena, Aug. 23, 1988); *Sei canoni* for Flute and Harpsichord (1990); *1492* for 16 Instruments (Latina, June 30, 1992); *Settimino* for 7 Instruments (Milan, April 22, 1993); *C.A.G.* for Flute, Violin, Vibraphone, and Guitar (Bologna, May 4, 1993); *...Im Himmelreich* for 9 Instruments (Amsterdam, May 16, 1994); *G.F.F....* for 5 Instruments (Rome, May 18, 1994); *Albumblatt* for Flute, Guitar, and Vibraphone (Rome, May 29, 1995); *"C.A.B.E."* for Flute and Violin (Sermoneta, June 9, 1995); piano pieces; organ music. VOCAL: *Due poesie* for Voice and Piano (1946); Cantata for Reciter, Soprano, Chorus, and Chamber Orch. (1954); *Variante A* for Chorus and Orch. (1964; Venice, Sept. 9, 1976); *Silben* for Woman's Voice, Clarinet, Violin, and 2 Pianos (1966; Rome, March 1, 1968); *Otto frammenti* for Soprano, Countertenor, Organ, Lute, and Viola da Gamba (Naples, June 17, 1978); *Im Frieden dein, O Herre mein* for 8 Voices (Bologna, Sept. 7, 1980); *Cent sopirs* for Chamber Chorus and Orch. (RAI, Rome, April 16, 1983); *Ach ich fühl's* for Voice and 15 Instruments (Milan, April 21, 1985); *Mottetto su re, mi...* for 18 Women's Voices (1989); *Cantilena* for Voice and Double Bass (1989–90); *The Plaint* for Woman's Voice and 13 Instruments (Melbourne, May 22, 1992); *Rapsodia* for Soprano, Contralto, and Orch. (Stuttgart, April 24, 1994); *Vocalizzo* for Voice and Instrumental Groups (Sermoneta, June 10, 1994). ELECTRONIC: *Collage 2* (1960; Venice, April 15, 1962) and 3: *Dies irae* (1966–67; RAI, Aug. 27, 1967); *Studio per una passacaglia* (Milan, May 3, 1993).

BIBL.: R. Cresti, *A. C.: Studio monografico e intervista* (Milan, 1990).—NS/LK/DM

Clementi, Muzio (baptized **Mutius Philippus Vincentius Franciscus Xaverius**), celebrated Italian pianist and composer; b. Rome, Jan. 23, 1752; d. Evesham, Worcestershire, England, March 10, 1832. He began to study music as a child with Antonio Buroni, and at the age of seven commenced studies with the organist Cordicelli. He later studied voice with Giuseppe Santarelli. By Jan. 1766 he was organist of the parish San Lorenzo in Damaso. About this time Peter Beckford, cousin of the English novelist William Beckford, visited Rome. He was struck by Clementi's youthful talent and, with the permission of Clementi's father, took the boy to England. For the next seven years Clementi lived, performed, and studied at his patron's estate of Stepleton Iwerne in Dorset. During the winter of 1774–75, Clementi settled in London, making his first appearance as a harpsichordist in a benefit concert on April 3, 1775. For the next several years he appears to have spent most of his time as harpsichordist at the King's Theatre, where he conducted operatic performances. In 1779 his six sonatas, op.2, were publ., which brought him his first public success, both in England and on the Continent. In 1780 he embarked on a tour of the Continent, giving a series of piano concerts in Paris; in 1781 he continued his tour with appearances in Strasbourg, Munich, and Vienna. It was during his stay in Vienna that the famous piano contest with Mozart took place at court before Emperor Joseph II on Dec. 24, 1781. In 1786 several of his syms. were performed in London, only to be eclipsed by the great syms. of Haydn. In 1790 he retired from public performances as a pianist, but he continued to conduct orch. concerts from the keyboard. After 1796 he appears to have withdrawn from all public performances, devoting himself to teaching, collecting large fees. He lost part of his fortune through the bankruptcy of Longman and Broderip in 1798; however, with John Longman, he formed a partnership on the ruins of the old company and became highly successful as a music publisher and piano manufacturer; his business acumen was keen, and he remained most successful with subsequent partners during the next three decades. From 1802 to 1810 he traveled extensively on the Continent, pursuing business interests, teaching, composing, and giving private concerts. While in Vienna in 1807, he met Beethoven and arranged to become his major English publisher. He returned to England in 1810, and in 1813 helped organize the Phil. Soc. of London, with which he appeared as a conductor. In 1816–17 he conducted his syms. in Paris, followed by engagements in Frankfurt am Main in 1817–18. He again visited Paris in 1821, and was in Munich in 1821–22. In Jan. 1822 he conducted his works with the Gewandhaus Orch. in Leipzig. Returning to England, he made several more conducting appearances with the Phil. Soc. until 1824; however, his syms. were soon dropped from the repertoire as Beethoven's masterpieces eclipsed his own efforts. In 1830 he retired from his mercantile ventures, and eventually made his home at Evesham, Worcestershire. As a teacher, Clementi had many distinguished pupils, including Johann Baptist Cramer, John Field, Karl Zeuner, Alexander Klengel, Friedrich Kalkbrenner, and Ludwig Berger.

WORKS: The Oeuvres complettes de M. C. was publ. by Breitkopf & Härtel (13 vols., Leipzig, 1803–19; facsimile reprint, 15 vols., N.Y., 1973); however, it is not complete. A. Tyson prepared a *Thematic Catalogue of the Works of M. C.* (Tutzing, 1967). Clementi composed a number of syms., but many of them have not survived. MSS are now housed at the Library of Congress in Washington, D.C., and the British Library in London. Autographs of 4 syms. survive, but they are not complete. Alfredo Casella reconstructed 2 of the syms., 1 in C major (listing it as No. 1) and 1 in D major (listing it as No. 2). He conducted his version of the C major in Turin on Dec. 13, 1935, and the D major in Rome on Jan. 5, 1936. He publ. them in Milan in 1938. Another D-major sym., now listed as No. 4, survives in the form of a 1st movement in autograph, and sketches for the remaining movements. There is also a G-major sym., known as the *Great National Symphony*, which survives in autograph movements and fragments. Two early syms., one in B-flat major and the other in D major, op.18 (1787), have been ed. by Renato Fasano (Milan, 1959–61). His other works include over 100 keyboard sonatas (about half with violin, cello, or flute), 6 duets for 4-Hands, 2 duos for 2 keyboard instruments, fugues, preludes, and exercises, etc. With the exception of the op.36 sonatinas and several of the sonatas, Clementi's works have been generally neglected; however, in recent years, the publication of new eds. of some of his works, as well as the issuing of recordings, has brought renewed interest in his output. Also of interest is the didactic *Introduction to the Art of Playing on the Pianoforte*, op.42 (London, 1801; reprint, N.Y., 1973), which includes 50 lessons for the beginner. His major didactic work, the *Gradus ad Parnassum* (3 vols., Leipzig, 1817–26), contains 100 compositions that attest to his greatness as a teacher of piano.

BIBL.: The Clementi-Archiv of the Netherlands issues the *Blätter aus dem C.-Archiv*. See also G. Froio, *M. C., La sua vita, le sue opere e sua influenza sul progresso dell'arte* (Milan, 1876); M. Unger, *M. C.s Leben* (Langensalza, 1914); G. Paribeni, *M. C. nella vita e nell'arte* (Milan, 1921); A. Stauch, *M. C.s Klavier-Sonaten im Verhältnis zu den Sonaten von Haydn, Mozart und Beethoven* (diss., Univ. of Cologne, 1930); E. di Laura, *L'estetica nell'arte didattica di M. C.* (Rome, 1934); J. Kohn, *The Manuscript Sonatas by M. C. at the Library of Congress: A Comparative Edition with Commentary* (diss., Univ. of Iowa, 1967); L. Plantinga, *C.: His Life and Music* (London, 1977); M. Stoelzel, *Die Anfänge vierhändiger Klaviermusik: Studien zur Satztypik in den Sonaten M. C.s* (Frankfurt am Main, 1984).—NS/LK/DM

Cleobury, Nicholas (Randall), English conductor, organist, pianist, and harpsichordist, brother of **Stephen (John) Cleobury;** b. Bromley, June 23, 1950. He was educated at Worcester Coll., Oxford (M.A.). After serving as asst. organist at Chichester Cathedral (1971–72) and Christ Church, Oxford (1972–76), he was chorus master at the Glyndebourne Festival and asst. director of the BBC Singers (1977–79). From 1981 to 1988 he was principal opera conductor at the Royal Academy of Music in London, and also artistic director of Aquarius from 1983 to 1992. He was principal guest conductor of the Gävle Sym. Orch. in Sweden from 1989 to 1991, and was artistic director of the Cambridge Sym. Soloists from 1990 to 1992 and of the Cambridge Festival in 1992. From 1990 to 1994 he was music director of Broomhill Arts. In 1992 he became director of the Britten Sinfonia. He also was a guest conductor of the Zürich Opera from 1993 and music director of the Oxford Bach Choir from 1997. As a guest conductor, he appeared widely with orchs. and operas houses in England and abroad.—NS/LK/DM

Cleobury, Stephen (John), English conductor and organist, brother of **Nicholas (Randall) Cleobury;** b. Bromley, Dec. 31, 1948. He was educated at St. John's Coll., Cambridge (M.A.; Mus. B). He was organist at St. Matthew's, Northampton (1971–74) and sub-organist at Westminster Abbey in London (1974–78) before serving as master of music at Westminster Cathedral (1979–82). In 1982 he became a fellow, director of music, and organist at King's Coll., Cambridge, in 1983 conductor of the Cambridge Univ. Musical Soc., in 1991 organist of the Univ. of Cambridge, and in 1995 chief conductor of the BBC Singers. He also served as president of the International Assn. of Organists (1985–87), the Cathedral Organists' Assn. of England (1988–90), and of the

Royal Coll. of Organists (1990–92). Cleobury has become well known through his many tours and recordings with the King's Coll. Choir, as well as through its annual live worldwide broadcast each Christmas Eve of the Festival of Nine Lessons and Carols.—NS/LK/DM

Clérambault, Louis Nicolas, French composer and organist; b. Paris, Dec. 19, 1676; d. there, Oct. 26, 1749. He studied with André Raison. He was organist at various Paris churches. He was a successful composer of theatrical pieces for the court: *Le Soleil vainqueur* (Paris, Oct. 21, 1721); *Le Départ du roi* (1745); etc. He also wrote a number of solo cantatas, in which genre he excelled. He also composed much organ music, some of which is republ. in Guilmant's *Archives des maîtres de l'orgue*. His son, César François Nicolas Clérambault (1700–1760), was also an organist and composer.

BIBL.: C. Cessac, *N. C.* (Paris, 1998).—NS/LK/DM

Clercx, Suzanne, Belgian musicologist; b. Houdeng-Aimeries, June 7, 1910; d. Liège, Sept. 27, 1985. She studied at the Univ. of Liège, and also took courses in musicology with Charles van den Borren, obtaining her Ph.D. in 1939 with the diss. *Essai sur l'évolution de la musique instrumentale dans les Pays-Bas au XVIII siècle.* She was then a librarian at the Royal Cons. in Brussels (1941–49). In 1945 she was appointed lecturer at the Univ. of Liège. She became a prof. in 1966, where she was active until 1975; in 1980 she was made prof. emeritus. In 1952 she was made a corresponding member of the American Musicological Soc.

WRITINGS: *Henri-Jacques de Croes* (Brussels, 1940); *Grétry, 1741–1813* (Brussels, 1944); *Le Baroque et la musique* (Brussels, 1948); *Pierre van Maldère* (Brussels, 1948); *Johannes Ciconia: Un Musicien liégeois et son temps* (Brussels, 1960).—NS/LK/DM

Clérice, Justin, French composer; b. Buenos Aires (of French parents), Oct. 16, 1863; d. Toulouse, Sept. 9, 1908. He went to Paris as a teenager, which was to be the center of his activities. After studies with Delibes and Pessard at the Cons. (1882), he devoted himself to composing for the theater. He had his first success with *O Moliero d'Alcala* (Lisbon, April 10, 1887). His efforts to obtain success in Paris came slowly, and he first attracted notice there with his songs. His first major stage score was *Le Troisième Hussards* (March 14, 1894), followed by the successful pantomime *Leda* (1896). His *La Petite Vénus* was first performed in London in an Eng. tr. as *The Royal Star* (Sept. 16, 1898). While such Parisian works as *Ordre de l'Empereur* (March 4, 1900) and *Les Filles Jackson et Cie* (Nov. 29, 1905) received only respectful attention at home, they were more warmly received abroad. Among his other works were *Minnie* (Paris, Feb. 6, 1905) and *Au temps jadis* (Monte Carlo, April 16, 1905). —NS/LK/DM

Cless, (George) Rod(erick), jazz clarinetist, saxophonist; b. Lenox, Iowa, May 20, 1907; d. N.Y., Dec. 8, 1944. He was a brother-in-law of Bud Freeman. He played in his first band while attending Drake Univ., later played in The Varsity Five at Iowa State Univ. He

left in 1925, moved to Des Moines, Iowa, and met Frank Teschemacher there. Two years later he moved to Chicago and played with "Tesch" in Charlie Pierce's Orch. and various other bands. In late 1928 he toured the South (including New Orleans). He returned to Chicago, played residency at the Wig-Wam Club, then joined the Louis Panico Band (1929). He was briefly with Jess Stacy's quartet, then did commercial work (mostly on sax.) at various clubs in Chicago, including long stay at the High Hat. He played in Frank Snyder's Rhythm Kings in 1936; the next three years he worked mainly at Silhouette Club and Winosa Gardens: he also taught clarinet. In April 1939 he joined Muggsy Spanier's Ragtimers in Chicago, remaining until they disbanded in N.Y. in December 1939. He was with Art Hodes (1940–41) and Marty Marsala (1941); also toured Canada with Ed Farley's Band in late 1941. He was with Art Hodes, Georg Brunis, and Bobby Hackett in 1942, briefly with "Wild Bill" Davison early in 1943, then again worked with Art Hodes. He worked in Canada (early 1944); from mid-1944 he played at the Pied Piper Club in N.Y. with Max Kaminsky. On December 1944, after leaving that club, he suffered grave injuries as a result of falling over apartment railings; he died four days later in St. Vincent's Hospital, N.Y.—JC/LP

Cleva, Fausto (Angelo), Italian-born American conductor; b. Trieste, May 17, 1902; d. while conducting at the odeum of Herodes Atticus in Athens, Aug. 6, 1971. He studied at the Trieste Cons. and the Milan Cons. After making his conducting debut with *La Traviata* at the Teatro Carcano in Milan in 1920, he emigrated to the U.S. and became a naturalized citizen in 1931. In 1921 he joined the staff of the Metropolitan Opera in N.Y., where he later was chorus master (1935–42). On Dec. 4, 1938, he made his first appearance there as a conductor in a Sunday evening concert. His formal debut with the company followed on Feb. 14, 1942, when he conducted *Il Barbiere di Siviglia*. He then conducted at the San Francisco Opera (1942–44; 1949–55) and was music director of the Cincinnati Summer Opera (1943–63). He also rejoined the roster of the Metropolitan Opera in 1950, where he conducted every season until his death.—NS/LK/DM

Cleve, Johannes de, German composer; b. Kleve, 1528 or 1529; d. Augsburg, July 14, 1582. He spent his early years in the Netherlands and then became a singer in the Vienna Hofkapelle of Emperor Ferdinand I in 1553. After the emperor's death in 1564, the chapel was dissolved and Cleve was made Kapellmeister to the emperor's son, Karl II of Styria, in Graz. In 1568 he resigned his position and went to Vienna. From 1579 he lived in Augsburg as a teacher. Cleve distinguished himself as a composer of sacred works, both Catholic (masses, 1559; motets, 1559, 1579–80) and Protestant (hymns, 1569–74).—LK/DM

Cliburn, Van (actually, Harvey Lavan Jr.), brilliant American pianist; b. Shreveport, La., July 12, 1934. His mother, Rildia Bee Cliburn, a pupil of Arthur Friedheim, was his only teacher until 1951, when he entered the Juilliard School of Music in N.Y. as a student of Rosina Lhévinne, graduating in 1954. He was four when he made his first public appearance in Shreveport; after winning the Tex. State Prize in 1947, he appeared as a soloist with the Houston Sym. Orch. In 1948 he won the National Music Festival Award, in 1952 the Dealy Award and the Kosciuszko Foundation Chopin prize, in 1953 the Juilliard School of Music concerto competition, and in 1954 the Roeder Award and the Leventritt competition in N.Y.; that same year he appeared as a soloist with the N.Y. Phil. In 1958 he captured first prize at the Tchaikovsky Competition in Moscow, the first American to achieve this feat; upon his return to N.Y., he received a hero's welcome in a ticker-tape parade. In subsequent years he toured extensively, appearing as a soloist with leading orchs. and as a recitalist. In 1978 he withdrew from public performances, but appeared again in 1987 as a recitalist in a concert for President Reagan and Soviet General Secretary Gorbachev at the White House in Washington, D.C. In 1989 he appeared as soloist in the Liszt and Tchaikovsky first piano concertos with the Philadelphia Orch.; that same year he accepted Gorbachev's invitation to perform in Moscow, and on Sept. 8 was the soloist with Eduardo Mata and the Dallas Sym. Orch. in the gala opening of the Morton H. Meyerson Sym. Center. In the summer of 1994 he toured the U.S. as soloist with the Moscow Phil. Van Cliburn's playing combines a superlative technique with a genuine Romantic sentiment, particularly effective in the music of Tchaikovsky and Rachmaninoff. The Van Cliburn International Piano Competition was organized in 1962 and is held quadrennially in Fort Worth, Tex., the home of the Van Cliburn Foundation.

BIBL.: A. Chasins, *The V. C. Legend* (N.Y., 1959); H. Reich, *V. C.* (Nashville, Tenn., 1993).—**NS/LK/DM**

Clicquot, family of French organ builders:

(1) Robert Clicquot; b. Rheims, c. 1645; d. Paris, July 21, 1719. He began his career working with his brother-in-law, the organ builder Etienne Enocq, in Rheims. He later worked with Enocq in Paris, where he became facteur d'orgues du Roy, a title retained by his family. Upon Enocq's death in 1682, he pursued his activities independently until joining in partnership with Alexandre Thierry. Upon the latter's death in 1699, Clicquot became the principal organ builder in Paris. Among his most important organs were those for Rouen Cathedral (1689), the collegiate church of St. Quentin (1703), and the great chapel of Versailles (1710–11). His two sons were also organ builders:

(2) Jean Baptiste Clicquot; b. Rheims, Nov. 3, 1678; d. Paris, March 16, 1746. He learned his profession from his father, and then was a partner of Alexandre Thierry.

(3) Louis-Alexandre Clicquot; b. Paris, c. 1684; d. there, Jan. 25, 1760. He served as facteur d'orgues du Roy, and was later joined by his son, **(4) François-Henri Clicquot.**

(4) François-Henri Clicquot, the most celebrated member of the family; b. Paris, 1732; d. there, May 24, 1790. He worked with his father from 1751, and was responsible for completing the outstanding organ at St. Roch in Paris. Upon his father's death in 1760, he took control of the family enterprise and gained a foremost reputation as a master organ builder and restorer. Among his notable achievements were the completion of the organ of St. Louis in Versailles and the construction of the organ at St. Sulpice in Paris. He wrote a treatise which was completed by his son, Claude François Clicquot (b. Paris, 1762; d. there, March 29, 1801), who also was an organ builder and restorer. The treatise was publ. in a facsimile ed. by J. Martinod as *Théorie pratique de la facture d'orgues* (Kassel, 1969).

BIBL.: N. Dufourcq, *Les. C.* (Paris, 1942); J. Villard, *F.-H. C., facteur d'orgues du roi* (Poitiers, 1975).—**NS/LK/DM**

Cliff, Jimmy (Chambers, James), established in the Caribbean, Latin America, and Europe as a reggae artist by the late 1960s, introduced reggae to a mainstream American audience with the 1973 film *The Harder They Come*; b. Somerton, Jamaica, April 1, 1948.

Cliff starred in the movie and provided the enduring songs "Sitting in Limbo" and "The Harder They Come" to the soundtrack. Along with Bob Marley and Peter Tosh, Cliff was a prime purveyor of reggae music, and although his albums have been criticized as pop-oriented, he did provide authentic reggae in concert.

Jimmy Cliff moved to Kingston, Jamaica, after his primary-school graduation. He recorded his first single in Jamaica in 1958, and scored his first local hit with "Hurricane Hattie" in 1961. Cliff toured the United States as part of a ska revue in 1964, and subsequently signed with Island Records and moved to England. Established in Europe, the Caribbean, and Latin America by 1965, he returned to Jamaica in 1968 and scored his first major American hit with "Wonderful World, Beautiful People" in 1970. Reggae finally broke big in the United States in 1973 with the release of the film *The Harder They Come*, starring Cliff. The soundtrack album included three Cliff originals, "You Can Get It If You Really Want," "Sitting in Limbo," and "The Harder They Come," Cliff's version of Bob Marley's "Many Rivers to Cross," plus the Melodians' "Rivers of Babylon," the Slickers' "Johnny Too Bad," and the Maytals' "Pressure Drop."

By the late 1970s Jimmy Cliff's recorded music was moving in a pop direction, but his tours provided authentic roots music. Recording for Columbia in the 1980s, he costarred with Robin Williams in the 1986 movie *Club Paradise* and toured with Stevie Winwood that year. Switching to JRS Records for 1992's *Breakout*, Jimmy Cliff tours six months per year, performing to his most enthusiastic audiences in Brazil and Africa.

DISC.: *Can't Get Enough of It* (1969); *Wonderful World, Beautiful People* (1970); *The Harder They Come* (soundtrack; 1973); *Struggling Man* (1974); *Unlimited* (1973); *Music Maker* (1974); *Follow My Mind* (1975); *In Concert: The Best of J. C.* (1976); *Give Thanx* (1978); *I Am the Living* (1980); *Give the People What They Want* (1981); *Special* (1982); *The Power and the Glory* (1983); *Cliff Hanger* (1985); *Club Paradise* (soundtrack; 1986); *Hanging Fire* (1988); *Breakout* (1992).—**BH**

Cliff Richards and The Shadows, first great British band of the rock 'n' roll era. **MEMBERSHIP:** Cliff Richard (real name, Harry Roger Webb), voc. (b. Locknow, India, Oct. 14, 1940); Hank Marvin, gtr., voc. (b. Newcastle, England, Oct. 28, 1941); Bruce Welch, gtr., voc. (b. Bognor Regis, England, Nov. 2, 1941); Jet Harris, bs. (b. July 6, 1939); Tony Meehan, drm. (b. London, England, March 2, 1942).

Cliff Richard and The Shadows have displayed tenacious longevity, with over five decades of hits in their native England, both collectively and for Richard alone. Richard is one of the few teen idols who has been able to remain a major star, albeit primarily in his home country.

Richard was born in India, then a colonial outpost for England; his family returned home when he was seven. He began playing guitar as a teenager, inspired by the skiffle movement, and eventually formed his own backup band, originally called The Planets, and then briefly The Drifters. Around this time, he came up with the stage name of Cliff Richard. By summer 1958, they were known as The Shadows and released their first hit record, "Move It," a #2 hit in Britain that launched their career.

While rock 'n' roll was popular in Britain in the mid- and late 1950s, British teens had no native stars to faun over as did their American counterparts. Richard filled the roll handily, and became a major draw in teen films and on TV as well as on tour. A major European star, between 1958–64, he scored dozens of vocal hits, but only two made it to the U.S. charts, 1959's "Living Doll" and 1964's "It's All in the Game," both in the lower reaches of the Top 40. The Shadows, meanwhile, had their own separate career as a Ventures-styled instrumental band, scoring many hits—most notably 1960's #1 U.K. hit, "Apache"—thanks to the "twangy" guitar of Hank Marvin.

In 1966, appearing alongside the famed preacher Billy Graham, Richard announced that he was a long-time believer; he followed this announcement with a series of gospel recordings. (In fact, his 1967 film Two a Penny was funded by Graham). He also began to speak out against the sex and drugs part of the rock 'n' roll equation, although he continued to record secular songs. In 1968, The Shadows went off on their own, although throughout the next two decades they would reunite with from time to time, mostly for live concerts. Throughout the 1970s, Richard pursued a singing and acting career. He hosted a series of variety shows on the BBC, one of which launched a young Australian singer named Olivia Newton-John. When one aspect of his career faded, another one could be counted on to pick up the slack.

Surprisingly, between the mid-1970s and the early 1980s, Richard staged a remarkable comeback, finally cracking the U.S. charts in a major way. In 1976, his single "Devil Woman" rose to #6 Stateside and went gold. He followed with more hits, including "We Don't Talk Anymore," a #1 U.K. song that charted #10 in the U.S. in 1979. In the fall of 1980, "Dreaming" rose to #10 on the U.S. charts, and his duet with Olivia Newton-John for the Xanadu soundtrack, "Suddenly," rose to #20. A few lesser hits followed in 1981 and 1982, and then Richard disappeared once again from the U.S. charts.

While this marked the end of his chart career in America, Richard continued to be a music-business force around the world, especially in England. He recorded duets with American stars old and new, working with Phil Everly in 1983 and Janet Jackson the year after. He appeared on the London stage through the mid-1980s in the smash hit play Time; during the mid-1990s he performed similar duty in the play Heathcliff. In the late 1980s and early 1990s, he enjoyed another period of Top Ten hit-making in the U.K., releasing several best-selling albums.

Through the 1980s and 1990s, Richard was also well-known for his annual gospel concert, a major charity event, and his Christmas singles. A number of these reached #1 status, includng his 1989 duet with rocker Van Morrison on "Whenever God Shines His Light" and his solo hit "Saviour's Day" from the following year. Entering his fifth decade as a recording artist, Richard generated a bit of controversy in fall 1999 by setting "The Lord's Prayer" to the tune of "Auld Lang Syne" and calling it "The Millennium Prayer." Although the BBC refused to play it, by Christmas 1999 it was the #1 record in England, remaining on top into the new year.

DISC.: CLIFF RICHARD AND THE SHADOWS: *Me & My Shadows* (1960); *In Spain with The Shadows* (1963); *Summer Holiday* (original soundtrack; 1963); *Cliff Richard & The Shadows* (1984). CLIFF RICHARD: *Cliff* (1959); *Cliff Sings* (1959); *Listen to Cliff* (1961); *The Young Ones* (1961); *21 Today* (1961); *32 Minutes &17 Seconds* (1962); *Wonderful to Be Young* (1963); *Wonderful Life* (1963); *Swingers Paradise* (1963); *It's All in the Game* (1964); *Aladdin & His Wonderful Lamp* (1964); *Cliff Richard in Spain* (1964); *Cliff Richard* (1965); *When in Rome* (1965); *Love Is Forever* (1965); *Kinda Latin* (1966); *Finders Keepers* (1966); *Cinderella* (1967); *Don't Stop Me Now* (1967); *Good News* (1967); *Cliff in Japan* (1968); *Two a Penny* (1968); *Sincerely* (1969); *About That Man* (1970); *Tracks & Grooves* (1970); *His Land* (1970); *Take Me High* (1973); *Help It Along* (1974); *The 31st of February Street* (1974); *Japan Tour 1974* (1975); *Live* (1976); *I'm Nearly Famous* (1976); *Every Face Tells a Story* (1977); *My Kind of Life* (1977); *Small Corners* (1977); *Green Light* (1978); *Rock 'n' Roll Juvenile* (1979); *Thank You Very Much* (1979); *We Don't Talk Anymore* (1979); *I'm No Hero* (1980); *Wired for Sound* (1981); *Love Songs* (1981); *Now You See Me Now You Don't* (1982); *When in Spain/When in Rome* (1983); *Silver* (1983); *Walking in the Light* (1984); *Hit List* (1995); *Songs from Heathcliff* (1995); *Real As I Wanna Be* (1999). THE SHADOWS: *The Shadows Door Knob* (1961); *Out of The Shadows* (1962); *Dance with The Shadows* (1964); *The Sound of The Shadows* (1965); *Shadow Music* (1966); *Hank Bruce Brian & John* (1967); *Out of The Shadows 2* (1967); *Jigsaw* (1967); *Established 1958* (1968); *Shades of Rock* (1970); *Rockin' with Curly Leads* (1974); *I Maesrti* (1974); *Specs Appeal* (1975); *Live at the Paris Olympia* (1970); *Tasty* (1977); *Surfing with The Shadows* (1980); *Change of Address* (1980); *Life in the Jungle/Live at Abbey Road* (1982); *XXV* (1983); *Guardian Angel* (1984); *Shadows (The Vocal)* (1984); *Images Castle* (1992); *Vocals* (1997); *Shadstrax* (1998); *Moonlight Shadows* (2000); *Shadows* (2000); *Dream Time* (2000).
—HB

Cline, Patsy (originally, **Hensley, Virginia Patterson**), one of country's best-known vocalists, still celebrated nearly 30 years after her death; b. Winchester, Va., Sept. 8, 1932; d., in a plane crash en route to

Nashville, Tenn., March 5, 1963. Cline was among the first country stars to make the crossover into mainstream pop, and undoubtedly if she had lived she would have become a middle-of-the-road chanteuse. Whether this would have been a step forward or backward for country music depends very much on one's attitude toward the increasing commercialization of Nashville's musical product in the1960s.

Growing up in Winchester, Va., Cline won an amateur talent contest as a tap dancer at the ripe old age of four; she began singing soon after. Trained on the piano, she performed in the local church choir as well as in school plays. Winning an audition with Wally Fowler of the Grand Ole Opry when she was 16, young Cline so impressed him that he invited her to Nashville; however, she was unable to obtain a recording contract, and eventually returned to her home town. She performed throughout her high school years, eventually signing with the local Four Star label in 1956. Her 1950s recordings were unexceptional, although she did score one hit in 1957 with "Walkin' after Midnight" after performing it on the *Arthur Godfrey Talent Scouts* TV program, leading to a contract with Decca Records.

Cline worked with producer Owen Bradley from 1957 to 1960, originally in a fairly standard country mold, gaining moderate success on the country charts. It wasn't until 1961's "Crazy" (written by Willie Nelson), followed by "I Fall to Pieces" (co-written by Harlan Howard and Hank Cochran) that her characteristic, sad-and-lonesome vocal sound fell into place. A brief two-year hit-making career followed, including "When I Get Through with You," "Leavin' on Your Mind," and the posthumously released "Sweet Dreams."

Cline's death in an airplane accident, along with stars Hawkshaw Hawkins and Cowboy Copas, helped solidify her place in the country music pantheon. She combined a lonesome country vocal sound with fairly smooth, popish delivery, thus bridging the gap between honky-tonk singer and pop chanteuse. Many country stars cite her as an influence, including Loretta Lynn, who was befriended by the older performer when she first came to Nashville, and, of course, new country star k.d. lang, who has ventured into the same big-throated pop style that made Cline famous. (Her original backup band, the re-clines, was named in homage to the earlier singer.) Cline's lasting impact was reinforced in 1986 by the release of the Hollywood film *Sweet Dreams*, starring Jessica Lange.

DISC.: *Her First Recordings, Vols. 1–3* (1950s-era recordings); *Live, Vol. 2* (radio transcripts made between 1956 and 1962); *Patsy Cline* (1957); *Patsy Cline Showcase* (1961); *Patsy Cline's Golden Hits* (1962); *Sentimentally Yours* (1962); *In Memoriam* (1963); *Encores* (1963); *A Legend* (1963); *Reflections* (1964); *A Portrait of Patsy Cline* (1964); *That's How a Heartache Begins* (1964); *Today, Tomorrow, Forever* (1964); *Gotta Lot of Rhythm in My Soul* (1965); *Stop The World and Let Me Off* (1966); *Greatest Hits* (1967); *The Last Sessions* (1980); *Try Again* (1982); *Sweet Dreams* (film soundtrack; 1985); *Live at the Opry* (1988); *Live—Vol. Two* (1989); *The Birth of a Star* (1996); *Live at the Cimarron Ballroom* (1997).

BIBL.: Jones, Margaret, *Patsy: The Life and Times of Patsy Cline* (N.Y., 1996).—**RC**

Clinton, George, leader The Parliaments, an R&B vocal group during the 1950s and 1960s; b. Plainfied, Ohio, July 22, 1940. The Parliaments lost the use of their name in the late 1960s. They regrouped as the rock-oriented Funkadelic, incorporating the innovations of Sly Stone and Jimi Hendrix. Funkadelic continued to record on a separate label once Clinton regained use of the Parliament name (now without the s). Augmented by bassist William "Bootsy" Collins and horn players Maceo Parker and Fred Wesley from James Brown's JBs, Parliament recorded a series of bizarre, oddly conceptual albums of so-called funk music, perhaps the last vestige of R&B music not overwhelmed by the rise of mindless disco music. Appealing primarily to African-American teenagers—and promoting humanitarian ideals such as equality and self-determination through an off-the- wall synthesis of ghetto jargon, science fiction fantasies, parodied psychedelia, and spiritual values— Parliament finally broke through to mainstream success with 1976's *Mothership Connection* album and tour.

George Clinton subsequently concentrated on the Funkadelic side of the group, achieving enormous success with 1978's *One Nation Under a Groove*. He also recorded various members of the Parliament-Funkadelic "family" such as Walter "Junie" Morrison, the Horny Horns, Parlet, and the Brides of Funkenstein; he formed his own label, Uncle Jam, for recordings by the Sweat Band and the P-Funk All-Stars. Former member William "Bootsy" Collins launched his own career with Bootsy's Rubber Band, as did Roger Troutman with his family band Zapp.

Recording sporadically on his own in the 1980s, George Clinton served as inspiration to the hip-hop movement, and saw many of his hit songs sampled by rap acts. He ultimately joined Prince's Paisley Park label for *The Cinderella Theory*, hailed as his comeback, and enjoyed renewed popularity as a result of his appearances with the Red Hot Chili Peppers at the Grammy Awards in 1993 and his participation in the Lollapalooza tour of 1994.

In 1955 George Clinton formed the Detroit R&B vocal group the Parliaments with Raymond Davis, Calvin Simon, Clarence "Fuzzy" Haskins, and Grady Thomas. They first recorded for ABC in 1956, and subsequently recorded for a number of different labels before signing with Motown in 1964. They eventually scored a major pop and smash R&B hit with "(I Wanna) Testify" on Revilot in 1967, but the company soon folded and Motown claimed the rights to the Parliament name. Nevertheless, they managed to record *Osmium* for Holland-Dozier-Holland's Invictus label before losing the rights to the name.

George Clinton, assuming the persona of Dr. Funkenstein, augmented Parliament with guitarists Eddie Hazel and Lucius Ross, keyboardist Bernie Worrell, drummer Ramon Fullwood, and vocalist Ray Davis, and the group took the name of Funkadelic. Signed to the Detroit-based Westbound label in 1969, Funkadelic recorded a series of albums that attempted to bridge the gap between 1960s rock and contemporary R&B styles. Through 1976 Funkadelic scored a series of minor-to-moderate R&B hits, highlighted by "I'll Bet You," "I Wanna Know if It's Good to You?," and "On the Verge of Getting It On," while recording modest-selling albums such as *Maggot Brain, America Eats Its Young, Cosmic Slop,* and *Tales of Kidd Funkadelic* for Westbound.

With Clinton regaining the use of the Parliament name by 1974, the group signed with Casablanca Records, recording bizarre yet entertaining albums backed by Funkadelic that included the near-smash R&B hit "Up for the Down Stroke." The astounding success of the classic "Tear the Roof Off the Sucker (Give Up the Funk)" single (a major pop and smash R&B hit) and best-selling *Mothership Connection* album finally brought the group mainstream success in 1976. By then the members of Parliament-Funkadelic included veteran guitarists Bernie Worrell, Eddie Hazel, and Ray Davis, horn players Maceo Parker and Fred Wesley, and bassist William "Bootsy" Collins, all former members of James Brown's band, plus former Ohio Players keyboardist Walter Morrison. A weird conceptual album blending brilliant if erratic music and Clinton's funk monologues regarding science fiction and psychedelic and spiritual fantasies, *Mothership Connection* was supported by a sell-out tour that incorporated odd costumes and massive stage props, including a spaceship dubbed the Mothership.

The success of *Mothership Connection* paved the way for subsequent best-selling albums by Parliament, including *Funkentelechy vs. The Placebo Syndrome,* which yielded a major pop and top R&B hit with "Flash Light." Subsequent R&B hits for Parliament through 1980 included the top hit "Aqua Boogie" and the near-smashes "Theme from the Black Hole" and "Agony of DeFeet." By 1977 Funkadelic had switched to Warner Bros. Records, where they scored a top R&B and major pop hit with the title song to the classic *One Nation Under a Groove* album. Toward the end of 1979 Funkadelic scored a top R&B hit with "(Not Just) Knee Deep—Part 1" from *Uncle Jam Wants You.*

The members of Parliament-Funkadelic began taking on solo projects in 1975. Junie Morrison recorded three albums for Westbound before switching to Columbia by 1980; he later recorded for Island. Bootsy's Rubber Band, headed by Bootsy Collins, began recording for Warner Bros. in 1976. The group produced a smash R&B hit with "The Pinocchio Theory" in 1977, and a top R&B hit with "Bootzilla" in 1978. An offshoot of Bootsy's Rubber Band, the Sweat Band (with Maceo Parker), recorded an album for Clinton's newly formed Uncle Jam label in 1980, the year Collins began recording on his own for Warner Bros. In 1982 he had a major R&B hit with "Body Slam!" He eventually switched to Columbia Records for 1988's *What's Bootsy Doin'?* and formed the New Rubber Band and Zillatron in the 1990s.

In 1977 Fred Wesley and the Horny Horns (again with Maceo Parker) recorded an album for Atlantic, and Eddie Hazel recorded one for Warner Bros. Also in 1977, three of the original Parliaments, Clarence Haskins, Calvin Simon, and Grady Thomas, left Parliament-Funkadelic to eventually record an album for LAX records as Funkadelic. In 1978 the vocal trio Parlet, with

Mahalia Franklin and Shirley Hayden, began recording for Casablanca, and the Brides of Funkenstein, with Lynn Mabry, Dawn Silva, Ran Banks, and Larry Demps, recorded the first of two albums for Atlantic, producing the smash R&B hit "Disco to Go." Bernie Worrell recorded an album for Arista in 1979, and in 1980 Roger Troutman formed Zapp with his brothers Lester, Tony, and Larry. Through 1983 they achieved R&B smashes with "More Bounce to the Ounce—Part 1," "Dance Floor (Part 1)," "Doo Wa Ditty (Blow That Thing)," and "I Can Make You Dance (Part 1)." Roger began recording on his own in 1981, scoring a top R&B hit with "I Heard It Through the Grapevine," which featured his use of the voice-box device. In 1986 Zapp hit the R&B charts with "Computer Love," and in 1987 Roger topped the R&B charts with "I Want to Be Your Man."

In 1980 George Clinton withdrew from his high profile in the popular-music world. He recorded on his own for Capitol Records during the 1980s, scoring a top R&B hit with "Atomic Dog" from *Computer Games* in 1983. Around 1982 he formed the P-Funk All-Stars, whose album *Urban Dancefloor Guerrillas* came to be regarded as a funk masterpiece. He also produced albums by Jimmy Giles and the Tac-Heads, the Brides of Motown, and the Red Hot Chili Peppers' second album. Bernie Worrell assisted in the recording of the Talking Heads' celebrated 1980 *Remain in Light* album, and joined the group's 1983 tour that produced the excellent concert film *Stop Making Sense.* By 1988 George Clinton had switched to Prince's Paisley Park label for *The Cinderella Theory,* lauded as his comeback. In 1989 he toured with a new edition of his P-Funk All-Stars.

During the 1990s Bernie Worrell returned to recording after a stint with the Talking Heads, and Fred Wesley and Maceo Parker established themselves as jazz artists. Roger Troutman returned with 1991's *Bridging the Gap* after a four-year absence, and George Clinton recorded *Hey Man, Smell My Finger* with veterans Bootsy Collins, Bernie Worrell, and Maceo Parker, plus Prince and rappers Ice Cube and Dr. Dre. Clinton's renewed career got a boost from his appearance with the Red Hot Chili Peppers at the Grammy Awards in 1993 and his successful performances with the P-Funk All-Stars on the Lollapalooza 1994 tour.

DISC.: PARLIAMENT: *Osmium* (1971); *Up for the Down Stroke* (1974); *Chocolate City* (1975); *Mothership Connection* (1976); *The Clones of Dr. Funkenstein* (1976); *P-Funk Earth Tour* (1977); *Funkentelechy vs. The Placebo Syndrome* (1977); *Motor Booty Affair* (1978); *Gloryhallastoopid (Pin the Tale on the Funky)* (1979); *Trombipulation* (1981); *Greatest Hits (The Bomb)* (1984); *The Best of Parliament: Give Up the Funk* (1995); *Tear the Roof Off (1974–1980)* (1993). **FUNKADELIC:** *Funkadelic* (1970); *Free Your Mind and Your Ass Will Follow* (1970); *Maggot Brain* (1971); *America Eats Its Young* (1972); *Cosmic Slop* (1973); *Standing on the Verge of Getting It On* (1974); *Greatest Hits* (1975); *Let's Take It to the Stage* (1975); *Tales of Kidd Funkadelic* (1976); *Best of the Early Years, Vol. 1* (1977); *Hardcore Jollies* (1976); *One Nation Under a Groove* (1978); *Uncle Jam Wants You* (1979); *The Electric Spanking of War Babies* (1981); *Who's a Funkadelic* (1992). **GEORGE CLINTON:** *The G. C. Band Arrives* (1974); *Computer Games* (1982); *You Shouldn't-Nuf Bit Fish* (1984); *Some of My Best Jokes Are Friends* (1985); *R&B Skeletons in the Closet* (1986); *The Best of G. C.* (1987); *G. C. Presents Our Gang Funky* (1989); *The Cinderella Theory* (1989); *Hey*

Man, Smell My Finger (1993). **BOOTSY'S RUBBER BAND:** *Stretchin' Out in Bootsy's Rubber Band* (1976); *Ahh ... The Name Is Bootsy, Baby!* (1977); *Bootsy? Player of the Year* (1978); *This Boot Is Made for Funkin'* (1979); *Jungle Bass* (1990). **THE SWEAT BAND:** *The Sweat Band* (1980). **WILLIAM "BOOTSY" COLLINS:** *Ultra Wave* (1980); *The One Giveth, the Count Taketh Away* (1982); *Back in the Day: The Best of Bootsy* (1994); *What's Bootsy Doin'?* (1988); *Keepin' Dah Funk Alive 4 1995* (1995). **BOOTSY'S NEW RUBBER BAND:** *Blasters of the Universe* (1994). **ZILLATRON:** *Lord of the Harvest* (1994). **WALTER "JUNIE" MORRISON:** *When We Do* (1975); *Freeze* (1976); *Suzie Super Groupie* (1976); *Bread Alone* (1980); *Junie 5* (1981); *Evacuate Your Seats* (1984). **FRED WESLEY AND THE HORNY HORNS:** *A Blow for Me, a Toot for You* (1977). **FRED WESLEY:** *New Friends* (1991); *Comme Ci Comme Ça* (1992); *Swing and Be Funky* (1993); *Amalgamation* (1995). **MACEO PARKER:** *Roots Revisited* (1990); *Mo' Roots* (1991); *Life on Planet Groove* (1992); *Southern Exposure* (1994). **EDDIE HAZEL:** *Gumes, Dames, and Other Thangs* (1977). **PARLET:** *Pleasure* (1978); *The Best of Parlet, Featuring Parliament* (1994). **BRIDES OF FUNKENSTEIN:** *Funk or Walk* (1978); *Never Buy Texas from a Cowboy* (1980). **BERNIE WORRELL:** *All the Woo in the World* (1979); *Funk of Ages* (1990); *Blacktronic Science* (1993). **ZAPP:** *Zapp* (1980); *Zapp II* (1982); *Zapp III* (1983); *The New Zapp IV U* (1985); *Zapp V* (1989). **ROGER TROUTMAN:** *The Many Facets of Roger* (1981); *The Saga Continues* (1984); *Unlimited* (1987); *Bridging the Gap* (1991). **ZAPP AND ROGER:** *All the Greatest Hits* (1993). **THE SWEAT BAND:** *The Sweat Band* (1980). **FUNKADELIC (FORMER MEMBERS):** *Connections and Disconnections* (1981). **P-FUNK ALL-STARS:** *Urban Dancefloor Guerrillas* (1984).—**BH**

Clinton, Larry, swing-era arranger, composer, leader, trumpeter; b. Brooklyn, N.Y., Aug. 17, 1909; d. Tucson, Ariz., May 2, 1985. A prolific freelance arranger from the early 1930s, he scored for Ferde Grofe, Isham Jones, Casa Loma, Claude Hopkins, Louis Armstrong, Bunny Berigan, and Tommy Dorsey, for whom he wrote many hits. Clinton is principally remembered for the big swing band that he led (1937–41). He used the Dorsey hit "The Dipsy Doodle" as his theme and made over 200 sides for RCA in less than four years, more than 30 of them big hits, mostly songs like "My Reverie" and "Deep Purple" (1938–39). He was known for "swinging the classics." He served in the Army Air Force (1942–46), including long posting in the Orient. Clinton temporarily reorganized his own band (1948–50), recording for U.S. Decca; he had a few more hits. In later years, he was active as an A&R man for N.Y. record companies and in music publishing.—**MM/LP**

Clive, Kitty (actually, **Catherine** née **Raftor**), famous English actress and soprano; b. London, 1711; d. Twickenham, Dec. 6, 1785. She studied with Henry Carey. As a protégé of Colley Cibber, she was engaged at the Drury Lane Theatre in 1728 and gained renown in ballad opera in his *Love in a Riddle or Damon and Phillida* (Jan. 1729). She continued to sing there with extraordinary success until 1743. After appearing at Covent Garden (1743–45), she returned to Drury Lane and remained a leading figure there until her retirement in 1769. Although she was most celebrated as a comic actress, she acquitted herself well as a singer of ballad farces and comic songs. She also sang Irish ballads, and even works by Handel, Purcell, and Arne. Handel wrote the role of Dalila in *Samson* for her, as well as the arioso *But lo, the Angel of the Lord* in *Messiah*. Clive herself wrote a comedy, *The Rehearsal or Bays in Petticoats* (London, March 15, 1750), for which Boyce composed the music.

BIBL.: P. Fitzgerald, *The Life of Mrs. C. C....together with her Correspondence* (London, 1888).—**NS/LK/DM**

Clooney, Rosemary, American singer; b. Maysville, Ky., May 23, 1928. Among the finest jazz-influenced popular singers of the post-World War II era, she is a masterful interpreter of the American songbook. Though she rose to popularity singing novelty tunes, she has always possessed a warm, husky voice and the gift, like all great singers, to emotionally inhabit her material. She broke into show business singing on the radio in Cincinnati with her sister Betty. Local gigs brought them to the attention of band leader Tony Pastor, and in 1947 the Clooney Sisters made their debut in Atlantic City. After two years on the road, Betty returned to Cincinnati and Rosemary went to N.Y., where she was quickly signed by Columbia Records. Beginning in the early 1950s, she scored a series of hits produced by Mitch Miller, starting with "Come on-a My House." Her fame increased when she moved to Hollywood, married actor Jose Ferrer, and began appearing in movies, including *Here Come the Girls, The Stars and Singing,* and *White Christmas,* which began her long association with Bing Crosby. She maintained her jazz credentials through her recordings with the Benny Goodman Sextet, Woody Herman and the Hi-Lo's, and her classic album with Duke Ellington and Billy Strayhorn, *Blue Rose.* Prescription drug abuse and emotional problems sidelined her in the late 1960s, but she began performing again in the mid-1970s and by the end of the decade had begun her remarkable series of albums for the Concord label. Working with tenor saxophonist Scott Hamilton, cornetist Warren Vache Jr., and other musicians from the Concord roster, she has recorded nearly two dozen albums, often focusing on the work of one composer, or lyricist, or song-writing team.

DISC.: *Blue Rose* (1956); *Love* (1963); *Everything's Coming up Rosie* (1977); *Rosie Sings Bing* (1978); *Sings the Music of Cole Porter* (1982); *Sings the Music of Harold Arlen* (1983); *Sings the Music of Irving Berlin* (1984); *Sings the Music of Jimmy Van Heusen* (1986); *Sings the Lyrics of Ira Gershwin* (1987); *Sings the Lyrics of Johnny Mercer* (1987); *Sings Rodgers, Hart, and Hammerstein* (1990); *For the Duration* (1991); *Marian McPartland's Piano Jazz with Guest Rosemary Clooney* (1992); *Girl Singer* (1992); *Do You Miss New York?* (1993); *Blue Rose; Still on the Road* (1994); *Dedicated to Nelson* (1996).—**AG**

Clovers, The, the most popular R&B vocal group of the first half of the 1950s. **MEMBERSHIP:** John "Buddy" Bailey, lead ten. (b. Washington, D.C. c. 1930); Matthew McQuater, second ten.; Harold "Hal" Lucas, bar. (b. c. 1923, d. Jan. 6, 1994); Harold Winley, bass voc.; Bill Harris, gtr. (b. Nashville, April 14, 1925; d. Dec. 10, 1988). Other members included Charles White (b. c. 1930, Washington, D.C.) and Billy Mitchell.

Formed in 1946 in Washington, D.C. by Harold "Hal" Lucas," the group called themselves the Four Clovers after John "Buddy" Bailey joined the group. When Bill Harris joined in 1949, they officially became the Clovers. Signed to Atlantic Records after one single for Rainbow, the Clovers scored a string of top and smash R&B hits beginning in 1951 with "Don't You Know I Love You." Featuring the occasional ballad and saxophone accompaniment on up-tempo blues-based songs, they scored smash R&B hits with "Fool, Fool, Fool," "One Mint Julep" (covered by Ray Charles in 1961) backed with "Middle of the Night," "Ting-a-Ling" backed with "Wonder Where My Baby's Gone," "Hey Miss Fannie" (considered by some to be the first rock 'n' roll record) backed with "I Played the Fool," and "Crawlin.'" In 1952 Charlie White became the new lead while Bailey served a stint in the Army. White was featured on the hits "Good Lovin,'" "Comin' On," and "Lovey Dovey" (covered by Buddy Knox in 1961) backed with "Little Mama."

In early 1954 the Clovers performed on Alan Freed's first rock 'n' roll show. By April, White had left, to be replaced by Billy Mitchell. When Bailey returned in the fall of 1954 the group began featuring twin lead tenors Bailey and Lucas. Subsequent R&B hits included ""I've Got My Eyes on You" backed with the classic "Your Cash Ain't Nothin' but Trash" (covered by Steve Miller in 1974), "Blue Velvet" (covered by Bobby Vinton in 1963), "Nip Sip," and "Devil or Angel" (covered by Bobby Vee in 1960) backed with "Hey, Baby Doll." The Clovers scored their first major pop hit in 1956 with "Love, Love, Love," but their Atlantic contract expired in July 1957. Subsequently recording for Poplar Records, they managed one final hit with "Love Potion No. 9" in late 1959 on United Artists. The group broke up in 1961, and Buddy Bailey and Harold Winley formed a new group of Clovers in 1961. Hal Lucas formed a second set of Clovers in 1962. Bill Harris died of pancreatic cancer on Dec. 10, 1988; Hal Lucas died of cancer on Jan. 6, 1994.

The Clovers were one of the first such groups to be acknowledged as rock 'n' roll artists, playing in Alan Freed's shows in 1954. Recording the classics "Blue Velvet," "Devil or Angel," and "Your Cash Ain't Nothin' but Trash," the Clovers featured the accompaniment of some of the finest saxophone players in N.Y. and utilized twin lead tenors beginning in 1954, years before the Temptations adopted the practice.

DISC.: *The Clovers* (1956); *In Clover* (1958); *Dance Party* (1959); *Love Potion Number Nine* (1959).—BH

Cluytens, André, noted Belgian-born French conductor; b. Antwerp, March 26, 1905; d. Neuilly, near Paris, June 3, 1967. He studied piano at the Antwerp Cons. His father, conductor at the Théâtre Royal in Antwerp, engaged him as his assistant (1921); later he conducted opera there (1927–32). He then settled in France, and became a naturalized French citizen in 1932. He served as music director at the Toulouse Opera (1932–35); in 1935 he was appointed opera conductor in Lyons. In 1944 he conducted at the Paris Opéra; in 1947 he was appointed music director of the Opéra- Comique

in Paris. In 1949 he was named conductor of the Société des Concerts du Conservatoire de Paris. In 1955 he became the first French conductor to appear at the Bayreuth Festival. On Nov. 4, 1956, he made his U.S. debut in Washington, D.C., as guest conductor of the Vienna Phil. during its first American tour. In 1960 he became chief conductor of the Orchestre National de Belgique in Brussels, a post he held until his death. Cluytens was highly regarded as an interpreter of French music.

BIBL.: B. Gavoty, *A. C.* (Geneva, 1955).—NS/LK/DM

Coasters, The, rock 'n' roll's first consistently successful comedy-vocal group. MEMBERSHIP: Carl Gardner, lead voc. (b. Tyler, Tex., April 29, 1928); Bobby Nunn, bass voc. (b. Birmingham, Ala., 1925; d. Los Angeles, Nov. 5, 1986); Leon Hughes, ten. (b. ca. 1938); Billy Guy, lead voc., bar. voc. (b. Attasca, Tex., June 20, 1936); Adolph Jacobs, gtr. Later members included Young Jessie; Cornelius "Cornell" Gunter (b. Los Angeles, Nov. 14, 1936; d. Las Vegas, Feb. 26, 1990); Will "Dub" Jones (b. Los Angeles, c. 1939); Earl "Speedo" Carroll (b. N.Y.C., Nov. 2, 1937); Ronnie Bright (b. Oct. 18, 1938).

The Coasters evolved out of the Robins, an R&B vocal group formed in Los Angeles in 1949. In early 1950 the group scored an R&B hit with "If It's So, Baby," with the Johnny Otis Band, and backed Esther Phillips on her top R&B hit "Double Crossing Blues." Songwriters Jerry Leiber and Mike Stoller began recording the group after they formed Spark Records in late 1953. The Robins enjoyed regional success with the classic "Riot in Cell Block Number 9" and had their first national hit with "Smokey Joe's Cafe," when reissued on Atco in late 1955.

In 1955 Leiber and Stoller signed what was likely the first independent production deal with the Atco subsidiary of the N.Y.–based Atlantic label. Atlantic acquired the Spark catalog and the producers attempted to coax the Robins into joining them at the new label. Not all were willing, so Leiber and Stoller convinced Bobby Nunn and Carl Gardner to form a new group, the Coasters, with Leon Hughes, Billy Guy, and Adolph Jacobs. Their first single, "Down in Mexico," became a major R&B hit and their third single, "Youngblood/ Searchin,'" became a smash pop/R&B hit for the group and their songwriter-producers.

In 1957 Young Jessie replaced Leon Hughes in the group. Moving to N.Y. with Leiber and Stoller by 1958, the group replaced Jessie with Cornelius Gunter and the retiring Bobby Nunn with Will "Dub" Jones of the Cadets ("Stranded in the Jungle"). Beginning with the smash hit "Yakety Yak," the Coasters were accompanied by the ribald saxophone playing of King Curtis. Through 1959 the group scored smash hits with "Charlie Brown," "Along Came Jones" (backed with "That is Rock 'n' Roll"), and "Poison Ivy" (backed by the lewd "I'm a Hog for You"). "Run Red Run/What about Us" and "Wake Me, Shake Me" proved only moderate successes, and the funky "Shoppin' for Clothes," featuring an unusually lewd saxophone break by King Curtis, fared even less well. The Coasters achieved their last major hit with "Little Egypt" in 1961, the year Earl "Speedo" Carroll of the Cadillacs ("Speedo") replaced Cornell Gunter. In 1963 Leiber and Stoller and the Coasters parted company, and by 1965 the group was comprised of Gardner, Guy, Carroll, and bass vocalist Ronnie Bright. They left Atco in 1966, subsequently recording for the Date subsidiary of Columbia.

The Coasters performed on various shows during the rock 'n' roll revival of the early 1970s. Several editions of the Coasters toured during the 1970s and 1980s. The various leaders were Cornelius Gunter, Bobby Nunn, Will Jones and Billy Guy, Leon Hughes, and Carl Gardner and Ronnie Bright. Bobby Nunn died on Nov. 5, 1986, of a heart attack in Los Angeles. Inducted into the Rock 'n' Roll Hall of Fame in 1987, the Coasters (Gardner, Guy, Jones, and Gunter, with Tom Palmer) performed at Atlantic Record's 40th Anniversary Birthday Concert in May 1988. Cornelius Gunter was found shot dead in his car in Las Vegas on Feb. 26, 1990, at the age of 53.

The Coasters provided a number of wry and satirical songs of adolescent pathos under the direction of the premier 1950s songwriting-production team, Jerry Leiber and Mike Stoller. One of the first R&B vocal groups to achieve widespread popularity with white youth, the Coasters later featured the lusty saxophone playing of King Curtis, who helped establish the instrument as the third most important in rock 'n' roll, behind guitar and piano.

DISC.: The Robins: *Rock 'n' Roll with the Robins* (1958); *Best* (1975). The Coasters: *The Coasters* (1958); *Greatest Hits* (1959); *One by One* (1960); *Coast Along with the Coasters* (1962); *That's Rock and Roll* (1964); *Greatest Recordings/The Early Years* (1971); *It Ain't Sanitary* (1972); *On Broadway* (1973); *Greatest Hits* (1978); *Greatest Hits* (1991); *50 Coastin' Hits* (1992); *Very Best* (1994). —BH

Coates, Albert, eminent English conductor; b. St. Petersburg, Russia (of an English father and a mother of Russian descent), April 23, 1882; d. Milnerton, near Cape Town, South Africa, Dec. 11, 1953. He went to England for his general education. He enrolled in science classes at the Univ. of Liverpool, and studied organ with an elder brother who was living there at the time. In 1902 he entered the Leipzig Cons., studying cello with Julius Klengel, piano with Teichmüller, and conducting with Nikisch; served his apprenticeship there and made his debut as conductor in Offenbach's *Les Contes d'Hoffmann* at the Leipzig Opera in 1904. In 1905 he was appointed (on Nikisch's recommendation) chief conductor of the opera house at Elberfeld. From 1907 to 1909 he was a joint conductor at the Dresden Court Opera (with Schuch), then at Mannheim (1909–10, with Bodanzky). In 1911 he received the appointment at the Imperial Opera of St. Petersburg, and conducted many Russian operas. From 1919 he conducted in England, specializing in Wagner and the Russian repertoire; was a proponent of Scriabin's music. Having made his first appearance at London's Covent Garden in 1914 with *Tristan und Isolde,* he conducted there regularly from 1919. From 1919 to 1921 he was

principal conductor of the London Sym. Orch. In 1920 he made his American debut as guest conductor of the N.Y. Sym. Orch.; during 1923–25, he led conducting classes at the Eastman School of Music in Rochester, N.Y., conducted the Rochester Phil., and appeared as guest conductor with other American orchs. Subsequent engagements included a season at the Berlin State Opera (1931) and concerts with the Vienna Phil. (1935). In 1938 he conducted for the last time at Covent Garden. In 1946 he settled in South Africa, where he conducted the Johannesburg Sym. Orch. and taught at the Univ. of South Africa at Cape Town. Coates was a prolific composer, but his works had few performances. He was, however, one of the most outstanding, if unheralded, conductors of his generation; he excelled in the Romantic operatic and symphonic repertoire, conducting particularly memorable performances of Russian music and Wagner's music dramas.—NS/LK/DM

Coates, Edith (Mary), English mezzo-soprano; b. Lincoln, May 31, 1908; d. Worthing, Jan. 7, 1983. She studied at Trinity Coll. of Music in London and with Carey and Borgioli. In 1924 she joined the Old Vic Theatre in London, where she sang major roles from 1931 to 1946. In 1937 she appeared at London's Covent Garden, where she was on the roster until 1939 and again from 1947 to 1963. She sang in the premieres of Britten's *Peter Grimes* (1945) and *Gloriana* (1953), and of Bliss's *The Olympians* (1949). Among her other roles were the Countess in *The Queen of Spades*, Carmen, Delila, Amneris, Ortrud, and Azucena. In 1977 she was made an Officer of the Order of the British Empire. —NS/LK/DM

Coates, Eric, English composer and violist; b. Hucknall, Nottinghamshire, Aug. 27, 1886; d. Chichester, Dec. 21, 1957. He took instruction at the Royal Academy of Music in London with Tertis (viola) and Corder (composition). He was a member of the Hambourg String Quartet, with which he made a tour of South Africa (1908); was first violist in the Queen's Hall Orch. in London (1912–19). In 1946 he visited the U.S., conducting radio performances of his works; in 1948 he toured in South America. A detailed account of his career appears in his autobiography *Suite in Four Movements* (London, 1953). As a composer, Coates specialized in semi-classical works for orch. His valse serenade *Sleepy Lagoon* (1930) attained enormous popularity all over the world, and was publ. in numerous arrangements. His *London Suite* (1933) was equally successful, its *Knightsbridge* movement becoming one of the most frequently played marches in England and elsewhere. He further wrote an orch. suite, *4 Centuries* (1941), tracing typical historical forms and styles in four sections (*Fugue, Pavane, Valse,* and *Jazz*); *3 Elizabeths* for Orch.; a great number of songs and instrumental pieces.

BIBL.: G. Self, *In Town Tonight: A Centenary Study of the Life and Music of E. C.* (London, 1986).—NS/LK/DM

Coates, Gloria, compelling American composer; b. Wausau, Wisc., Oct. 10, 1938. She was educated at La. State Univ. (B.Mus. in composition and voice; M.Mus. in composition and musicology), and pursued postgraduate studies at Columbia Univ. She also attended the Cooper Union Art School. Her principal mentors in composition were Otto Luening and Alexander Tcherepnin. In 1969 she went to Munich, and in 1971 she founded the German-American Contemporary Music Series in both Munich and Cologne, serving as its director until 1983. From 1975 to 1984 she taught music for the Univ. of Wisc. International Programs in Munich, and also in London in 1976. Coates gained wide recognition with the premiere of her *Music on Open Strings* (Sym. No. 1) at the Warsaw Autumn Festival on Sept. 20, 1978. While she has composed a number of distinguished scores in several genres, it is as a symphonist that she has made her most significant contribution to the late 20th century repertoire. Her syms. often display a remarkable originality, assured technique, dramatic sweep, and luminous expressivity. A number of CD recordings of her works have been adorned with her original paintings.

WORKS: ORCH.: 11 syms.: No. 1, *Music on Open Strings*, for String Orch. (1973–74; Warsaw, Sept. 20, 1978), No. 2, *Illuminato in Tenebris* or *Music in Abstract Lines* (1988; N.Y., Nov. 16, 1989; based on *Planets* for Chamber Orch., 1974; Hannover, Feb. 2, 1975), No. 3, *Symphony Nocturne*, for String Orch. (1976–77; Heidelberg, June 24, 1988), No. 4, *Chiaroscuro* (1984–90; Stuttgart, June 22, 1990), No. 5, *Three Mystical Songs*, for Chorus and Orch. (1985–86; Berlin, Nov. 7, 1990), No. 6, *Time Frozen* (1994–95; 1st perf. of 2nd movement as *Music in Microtones* for Chamber Orch., Boston, Nov. 6, 1987), No. 7 (1990–91; Munich, Feb. 21, 1997), No. 8, *Indian Sounds*, for Tenor or Soprano Solo Vocalise or Soprano and Alto Duet and Orch. (1991; Dresden, Feb. 27, 1992), No. 9, *Homage to Van Gogh* (1992–93; Dresden, March 25, 1995), No. 10, *Drones of Druids on Celtic Ruins* (1993–94; Erding, Oct. 8, 1995), and No. 11 (1998–99; Zell on the Pram, Austria, July 8, 1999); *Transitions* for Chamber Orch. (1984–85; Munich, June 12, 1985). **CHAMBER:** Trio for 3 Flutes (1966; N.Y., March 19, 1967); *Five Abstractions of Poems by Emily Dickinson* for Woodwind Quartet (1966–75; Geneva, Jan. 27, 1976); 5 string quartets: No. 1 (1966; Munich, Dec. 15, 1983), No. 2, *The Olympic* (1971–72; Munich, Sept. 19, 1972), No. 3 (1975; Munich, July 12, 1976), No. 4 (1977; Berlin, April 21, 1978), and No. 5 (1988; Munich, March 16, 1995); *Tones in Overtones* for Piano (1971–72; Munich, Oct. 2, 1973); *May the Morning Star Rise* for Viola and Organ (Starnberg, March 22, 1974); *Spring Morning in Grobholzes' Garden* for 3 Flutes and Tape (WDR, Cologne, Sept. 8, 1976); *Breaking Through* for Alto Recorder (1987; Heidelberg, June 26, 1988); *Breaking Through* for Flute (1987–88; Munich, Oct. 18, 1988); *Lunar Loops* for 2 Guitars (1987–88; Munich, June 8, 1989); *Floating Down the Mississippi* for 8 Guitars (1987–97; Munich, March 8, 1998); *Lichtsplitter* for Flute, Harp, and Viola (1988; Munich, June 14, 1989; also for Flute, Harp, Viola, and Percussionist, 1989, Munich, Nov. 18, 1990, and as *Transfer 482* for Harp, Flute, Viola, and 2 Percussionists, 1992); *In the Mt. Tremper Zen Monastery* for 2 Percussionists, Viola, and Harp or Piano (1988–92; Dresden, Oct. 8, 1992); *In the Glacier* for 10 Flutists and Percussion (Munich, Oct. 18, 1992); *Königshymne* (Royal Anthem) for 10 Flutists and Percussion (1992; Dresden, June 2, 1993); *Blue Flowers* for 10 Flutists (Munich, Oct. 18, 1992); *Blue Steel Bent* for 10 Flutists (Munich, Oct. 18, 1992); *Night Music* for Tenor Saxophone, Piano, and Gongs (1992; Erfurt, July 26, 1993); *Turning To* for 2 Flutists (Munich, Nov. 19, 1995); *Homage to Novalis* for Flute, Harp, and 2 Cellos or Cello, and Viola (1996; Passau, June 24,

1997); *Fairytale Suite* for Flute (Passau, June 24, 1997). **VOCAL:** *7 Songs with Poems by Emily Dickinson* for Voice and Chamber Orch. (1962–88; Munich, Dec. 14, 1989); *15 Songs on Poems by Emily Dickinson* for Voice and Piano (1965–97); *The Force for Peace in War* for Soprano and Chamber Orch. (1973–88; Bonn, May 29, 1989); *Fragment from Leonardo's Notebooks* for Soli and Orch., after Leonardo da Vinci (1976–84; Bayreuth, Aug. 25, 1984); *Fonte di Rimini (Sinfonia brevis)* for Chorus and Orch., after Leonardo da Vinci (1976–84; Bayreuth, Aug. 25, 1984); *The Beatitudes* for Chorus (1978; Munich, May 8, 1979); *The Swan*, dramatic scene for Soprano, Oboe or English Horn, Timpani, and 2 Percussionists, after Mallarmé (1988; Munich, May 11, 1989); *Cette Blanche Agonie* for Soprano and Chamber Orch., after Mallarmé (1988–91; Munich, Feb. 27, 1992); *Wir tönen allein* for Soprano and Chamber Orch., after Celan (1989–91; Dresden, Feb. 27, 1992); *Rainbow Across the Night Sky* for Women's Voices, Violin, Viola, Cello, and 2 Percussionists (1991; Bremerhaven, June 20, 1992).—**NS/LK/DM**

Coates, John, English tenor; b. Girlington, Yorkshire, June 29, 1865; d. Northwood, Middlesex, Aug. 16, 1941. He studied with his uncle, J.G. Walton, at Bradford. He sang as a small boy at a Bradford church. He began serious study in 1893, and took lessons with William Shakespeare in London. He sang baritone parts in Gilbert and Sullivan operettas, making his debut at the Savoy Theatre in London in *Utopia Limited* (1894); toured in the U.S. with a Gilbert and Sullivan company. He made his debut in grand opera as Faust at London's Covent Garden (1901); also sang Lohengrin in Cologne and other German cities with considerable success; later sang nearly all the Wagner roles in English with the Moody-Manners Co., the Carl Rosa Co., and with Beecham (1910); from 1911 to 1913 he toured with Quinlan's opera company in Australia and South Africa. He served in the British army during World War I; in 1919, he returned to London, devoting himself chiefly to teaching; he also gave recitals of songs by English composers. In 1926–27 he made a concert tour of the U.S.—**NS/LK/DM**

Coates, John (Francis Jr.), jazz pianist; b. Trenton, N.J., Feb. 17, 1938. He made his first recordings while in high school, playing with Kenny Clarke and Wendell Marshall. Coates joined Charlie Ventura's band (1956; recording 1957), after which he left to attend Rutgers Univ. A local legend in Trenton, his trio accompanied visiting stars Coleman Hawkins, Clark Terry, Joe Newman, and Zoot Sims (1965). Coates eventually wound up an editor, composer, and arranger for the Shawnee Press, Pa., and also played at the Deer Head Inn with such visiting musicians as Keith Jarrett, Al Cohn, Zoot Sims, and Phil Woods. He did much of his recording as a leader (1974–80), quitting Shawnee Press in 1977 to devote full attention to playing and writing. His solo piano explorations have reportedly influenced or at least been admired by Keith Jarrett.

DISC.: *Portrait* (1955); *Jazz Piano of John Coates Jr.* (1974); *Alone and Live at the Deer Head* (1977); *After the Before* (1978); *Tokyo Concert* (1979).—**LP**

Cobb, Junie (actually, **Junius C.**), early jazz clarinetist, alto and tenor saxophonist, pianist, banjo player, composer; b. Hot Springs, Ark., Dec. 31, 1896; d. Chicago, Ill., Jan. 1970. He was the brother of the late Jimmy Cobb (trumpet). He had his first piano lessons from his mother at the age of nine. During his teens he worked in small band with Johnny Dunn. He moved to New Orleans to study house building, and there bought his first clarinet. In the late teens, he moved to Chicago, gigged on piano, then formed his own band for residency at the Club Alvadere (1920–21). He worked on clarinet with Everett Robbins and his Jazz Screamers (1921), later played in Mae Brady's Orch. in Chicago and firmly established himself as a multi- instrumentalist. He was with King Oliver (mainly on banjo) from late 1924 until spring 1925; later rejoined King Oliver from late 1926–spring 1927. During this period, he made several recordings as a leader for the Vocalion label. He was with Jimmie Noone late 1928 to spring 1929, then led his own band in Chicago. He went to Europe in early 1930, played saxophone and fronted the band at Jose Alley's Royal Box Club in Paris, and returned to Chicago (c. August 1930). He led own band in Chicago during the early 1930s, but disbanded in the depression period and formed a double act with vocalist Annabelle Calhoun; they worked together until c. 1946, then Junie did long residencies as a solo pianist. He retired from full-time music in 1955, but continued to play regularly, usually on piano, sometimes on banjo and clarinet. During the 1960s he played with Jasper Taylor's Creole Jazz Band (1962), with Walbridge's Hot Four (on banjo, 1967), and did gigs with drummer Wayne Jones. A prolific composer, his works range from "Once or Twice" to the World War II song "Put the Axe to the Axis."

DISC.: *Junie C. Cobb and His New Hometown Band* (1961). Chicago: *The Living Legends* (1961).—JC/LP

Cobbett, Walter Willson, English patron of music; b. London, July 11, 1847; d. there, Jan. 22, 1937. He was a businessman and amateur violinist. An ardent enthusiast, he traveled widely in Europe and met contemporary composers. He was particularly active in promoting the cause of British chamber music, and arranged a series of Cobbett Competitions. He also commissioned special works and established a Cobbett Medal for services to chamber music. Early recipients included Thomas Dunhill (1924), Mrs. E.S. Coolidge (1925), and A.J. Clements (1926). Among composers who received the Cobbett commissions and awards were Frank Bridge, York Bowen, John Ireland, Vaughan Williams, and Herbert Howells. Cobbett ed. the extremely valuable *Cobbett's Cyclopedic Survey of Chamber Music* (two vols., London; vol. I, 1929; vol. II, 1930; a suppl. to vol. I. was publ. in London in 1957; to vol. II, in 1963).—NS/LK/DM

Cobb(s), Arnett(e Cleophus), jazz tenor saxophonist; b. Houston, Tex., Aug. 10, 1918; d. there, March 24, 1989. He played piano and violin before specializing on tenor sax. His first professional work was with drummer Frank Davis in 1933, subsequently with Chester Boone (1934–36) and Milton Larkin (1936–42). He replaced Illinois Jacquet in the Lionel Hampton band in

November 1942 until early 1947, then formed his own band. He was forced by illness to disband in 1948, resumed leading from 1951 until 1956, then was seriously injured in a car crash and spent the rest of his life on crutches. He resumed touring in 1957 and 1958, then returned to Houston and led his own big band there during the late 1950s. In 1960 Cobb managed the El Dorado Club in Houston and continued leading his own band, but long spells in the hospital eliminated touring. In 1973 he appeared at N.Y.'s Town Hall with fellow saxophonist Illinois Jacquet; this appearance was well-received and led to a renewed career in U.S. clubs and Europe, often with the group The Texas Tenors, which included Jacquet and Buddy Tate. He continued to record and tour right up to his death.

Cobb's big, fat, vivid tone is a jazz classic. His notes are filled with emotion whether he's blowing a muscular, up-tempo solo or slowly romancing a ballad. Along with Jacquet, Cobb's colorful, stomping style defined the early Houston, Tex. tenor sound, a swinging sound equally at home in jazz, soul/blues, or early R&B.

DISC.: *Very Saxy* (1959); *Smooth Sailing* (1959); *Party Time* (1959); *Go Power!* (1959); *Blow, Arnett, Blow* (1959); *Blue and Sentimental* (1960); *Jazz at Town Hall* (1973); *Again with Milt Buckner* (1973); *Live in Paris 1974* (1974); *Jumpin' at the Woodside* (1974); *Wild Man from Texas* (1976); *Live at Sandy's!, Vols. 1 & 2* (1978); *Arnett Cobb Is Back* (1978); *Live* (1982); *Showtime* (1987); *Tenor Tribute, Vol. 2* (1988); *Tenor Tribute, Vol. 1* (1988). L. Hampton: *Smooth Sailing.*

BIBL.: B. Demeusy, *Arnett Cobb, the Wild Man of the Tenor Sax* (Basel, Switzerland, 1962).—JC/LP/BJH

Cobelli, Giuseppina, Italian soprano; b. Maderno, Lake Garda, Aug. 1, 1898; d. Barbarano di Salò, Aug. 10, 1948. She studied in Bologna, Cologne, and Hamburg. In 1924 she made her operatic debut as Gioconda in Piacenza; after singing with the Italian Opera in the Netherlands, she joined Milan's La Scala in 1925, where she was one of its principal artists until deafness compelled her to leave the company in 1942. She was notably successful in such Wagnerian roles as Isolde, Sieglinde, and Kundry, as well as in the standard and modern Italian repertory.—NS/LK/DM

Cocchi, Gioacchino, Italian composer; b. probably in Naples, c. 1720; d. probably in Venice, after 1788. He may have studied with Giovanni Veneziano at the Conservatorio di S. Maria di Loreto in Naples. He began his career as a composer for the theater with the opera *Adelaide* (Rome, Carnival 1743), subsequently bringing out many operas for Rome and Naples, winning his most popular success with *La Maestra* (Naples, 1747). He was in Venice by 1750, where he served as choir director at the Ospedale degli Incurabili until 1757. He then went to London as composer and music director of the Haymarket Theatre until 1762. He returned to Venice c. 1772. He excelled in opera buffa; among such works, in addition to those given above, were *L'Elisa* (Naples, 1744), *L'Irene* (Naples, 1745), *I due fratelli beffati* (Naples, 1746), *La Serva bacchettona* (Naples, 1749), *La mascherata* (Venice, Dec. 27, 1750), *Il Tutore* (Rome, 1752), and *Il*

Pazzo glorioso (Venice, 1753). He also composed a significant number of other stage works, oratorios, serenatas, cantatas, vocal chamber pieces, and instrumental music.—NS/LK/DM

Coccia, Carlo, Italian composer; b. Naples, April 14, 1782; d. Novara, April 13, 1873. He was nine when he began musical training with Pietro Casella. He then studied singing with Saverio Valente and counterpoint with Fedele Fenaroli at the Conservatorio S. Maria di Loreto in Naples, and with Paisiello. He served as maestro accompagnatore al pianoforte in the private musical establishment of Joseph Bonaparte, King of Naples (1806–08). He also began his career as a composer, becoming best known for his operas semiseria and scoring his greatest success with *Clotilde* (Venice, June 8, 1815). In 1820 he went to Lisbon as maestro concertatore at the Teatro San Carlos, and in 1824 went to London as conductor at the King's Theatre; he also taught at the Royal Academy of Music. He returned to Italy in 1827 and scored a fine success with his opera *Caterina di Guise* (Milan, Feb. 14, 1833). He was made inspector of music and director of singing at the Accademia Filarmonica in Turin in 1836, and then settled in Novara as maestro di cappella at S. Gaudenzio (1840). He wrote 38 operas, which, in addition to those listed above, included *La verità nella bugia* (Venice, 1809), *Maria Stuart, regina di Scozia* (London, June 7, 1827, excerpts only), *Enrico di Monfort* (Milan, Nov. 12, 1831), and *Giovanna II regina di Napoli* (Milan, March 12, 1840). He also wrote various other secular vocal works, including cantatas and songs, and much sacred music.

BIBL.: G. Carotti, *Biografia di C. C.* (Turin, 1873). —NS/LK/DM

Cochereau, Pierre, eminent French organist, pedagogue, and composer; b. St. Mandé, near Paris, July, 9, 1924; d. Lyons, March 5, 1984. He studied piano with Marius-François Gaillard and Marguerite Long (1933–36), and then organ with Marie-Louise Girod (1938) and Paul Delafosse (1941); in 1944 he entered the Paris Cons., where he took lessons in organ with Dupré, in harmony with Henri Challon and Duruflé, in fugue with N. Gallon, in composition with Aubin, and in music history with Dufourcq, winning various prizes. From 1942 to 1954 he was organist at St. Roch in Paris. In 1955 he became organist at Notre Dame in Paris, which position he held with great distinction for the rest of his life. He also made numerous recital tours of Europe, North and South America, Japan, and Australia, winning critical acclaim for his mastery of improvisation. He also served as director of the conservatories in Le Mans (1950–56), Nice (1961–80), and Lyons (from 1980). Among his works were a Sym. (1957), two organ concertos, a Piano Quintet, and various solo organ pieces.—NS/LK/DM

Cochlaeus (real name, Johannes Dobnek), German music theorist; b. Wendelstein, near Nuremberg, Jan. 10, 1479; d. Breslau, Jan. 10, 1552. He studied philosophy at the Univ. of Cologne (B.A., 1505; M.A., 1507), becoming a prof. there in 1509. In 1510 he taught history and geography in Nuremberg. From 1515 he traveled in Italy. After obtaining the degree of doctor of theology in Ferrara (1517), he was ordained a priest in Rome. He subsequently held various ecclesiastical posts in Germany. During the last seven years of his life he was at the Breslau Cathedral. Cochlaeus opposed Luther at the councils of Worms and Augsburg. He publ. numerous theological papers, and was also the author of the treatise *Musica* (Cologne, 1507; enl. ed., under the title *Tetrachordum musices*, Nuremberg, 1511, and 6 later eds.; Eng. tr. by C. Miller in Musicological Studies and Documents, XXIII, 1970).

BIBL.: M. Spahn, *J. C.*(Berlin, 1898).—NS/LK/DM

Cochran, Eddie, rockabilly legend; b. Oklahoma City, Okla., Oct. 3, 1938; d. Chippenham, Wiltshire, England, April 17, 1960. With his family, Eddie Cochran moved to Albert Lea, Minn., as an infant, and then to Bell Gardens, Calif., in 1949. He began playing guitar at 12 and joined country singer Hank Cochran (no relation) as back-up guitarist in 1954. They toured and recorded as the Cochran Brothers until 1956. Switching to rock 'n' roll after seeing Elvis Presley in Dallas in late 1955, Eddie Cochran demonstrated his skill as a rockabilly guitarist on a number of sessions in Los Angeles. In the fall of 1956 he met songwriter Jerry Capehart, who secured him a contract with Liberty Records. His first Liberty single, the tame "Sittin' in the Balcony," became a major hit in early 1957. During the year, he appeared in two films, *The Girl Can't Help It*, with Gene Vincent and Little Richard, performing the classic "Twenty Flight Rock," and *Untamed Youth*, with Mamie Van Doren. However, his next hit didn't come until the summer of 1958, when the classic "Summertime Blues" became a near-smash. For the recording, Cochran overdubbed his voice (some say) or his voice and all instruments (according to others). He toured tirelessly, yet his next single, the raucous "C'mon Everybody," proved only a moderate hit.

In 1959 Eddie Cochran appeared in the film *Go, Johnny, Go* with Chuck Berry, Ritchie Valens, and Jackie Wilson. Like Gene Vincent, Cochran was far more popular in England, and in early 1960, he embarked on his only European tour. Upon completing the tour, while on his way to London airport, Eddie Cochran was killed in an auto crash near Chippenham, Wiltshire, on April 17, 1960. Seriously injured in the crash were his songwriting girlfriend Sharon Sheeley (author of Rick Nelson's "Poor Little Fool" and co-author of Cochran's "Somethin' Else") and Gene Vincent. Cochran continued to have posthumous hits in Great Britain (although not the U.S.) in the 1960s and exerted a strong influence on the development of British rock 'n' roll. Eddie Cochran was inducted into the Rock 'n' Roll Hall of Fame in 1987.

One of rock 'n' roll's first "legends" due to early accidental death, Eddie Cochran was an early performer of rockabilly music and one of its most exciting and dynamic guitar players. He wrote many of his songs and helped pioneer the studio technique of overdubbing, as evidenced by his oft-covered classic 1958 smash, "Summertime Blues." Although his popularity was short-lived in the U.S., he remained remarkably popular in Great Britain even after his death in 1960, and his sound influenced British groups such as the Who, the Sex Pistols, the Clash, and the Stray Cats.

DISC.: *Singin' to My Baby* (1957); *Summertime Blues* (1958); *Eddie Cochran Memorial Album* (1960); *Never to be Forgotten* (1963); *Eddie Cochran* (1969); *Legendary Masters, Vol. 4* (1971); *Very Best (15th Anniversary Album)* (1975); *Singles Album* (1979); *Best* (1987); *On the Air* (1987); *The Early Years* (1988); (1990).—**BH**

Cochran, William,

American tenor; b. Columbus, Ohio, June 23, 1943. He studied at Wesleyan Univ., with Singher at the Curtis Inst. of Music in Philadelphia, and with Melchior and Lehmann in Calif. In 1968 he sang Froh in *Das Rheingold* in San Francisco, and on Dec. 21 of that year he made his Metropolitan Opera debut in N.Y. as Vogelsang in *Die Meistersinger von Nürnberg*. After winning the Lauritz Melchior Heldentenor Foundation Award in 1969, he joined the Frankfurt am Main Opera in 1970. In 1974 he made his first appearance at London's Covent Garden as Laca in *Jenůfa*. He returned to San Francisco in 1977 to sing Tichon in *Kát'a Kabanová*. In 1985 he was engaged as Bacchus at the Metropolitan Opera. After appearing as Otello with the Welsh National Opera in Cardiff in 1990, he sang Siegfried in Paris in 1991. He sang Aegisthus in *Elektra* at the London Promenade Concerts in 1993. In 1997 he returned to San Francisco to portray Herod in *Salome*. —**NS/LK/DM**

Cochrane, Michael,

jazz pianist, composer, educator; b. Peekskill, N.Y., Sept. 4, 1948. He attended Boston Univ. (B.A., 1970). He has resided in the Tri-state area since 1974 and has performed or recorded with Sonny Fortune, Michael Brecker, Chico Freeman, Yoron Israel, Hannibal Peterson, the Spirit of Life Ensemble, and Eddie Gomez. He is a member of Lines of Reason, a co-operative band with Calvin Hill, David Gross, and Alan Nelson. He has been a part-time instructor at N.Y.U. since the fall of 1985. He has received two fellowship grants in jazz performance from the N.E.A. In 1999 he received a grant from the Puffin Foundation Ltd. to complete a project that combines a jazz piano trio with a string quartet

DISC.: *Elements* (1985); *Song of Change* (1992); *Impressions* (1995); *Cutting Edge* (1997); *Gesture of Faith* (1998); *Music of Wayne Shorter* (1998); *Lines of Reason* (1998).

WRITINGS: *Reunion* (N.Y., 1989); *Elements* (N.Y., 1989); *Solo Piano Arrangements from Elements* (N.Y., 1989); *The Melodic Line* (N.Y., 1993).—**LP**

Cockburn, Bruce,

a superstar north of the 45th parallel, with one hit record south of Canada; b. Ottawa, Canada, May 27, 1945. Although Cockburn is a quarter-of-a-century veteran of the rock wars, in the U.S. that tenure has garnered him but one hit single, 1979's "Wondering Where the Lions are," which reached #21. There have been several more underground hitlets, like the college-radio fueled "If I Had a Rocket Launcher," but Cockburn's reputation for political correctness, in some circles, overshadows his musical achievements. In his native Canada, however, Cockburn has 13 gold albums, three platinum albums, ten Juno awards, and was named to the Order of Canada.

Cockburn always risked an outspoken stand in his work, taking on issues and morality to the detriment of his popular appeal. No artist since Phil Ochs has taken such strong political stands. His first ten albums strongly reflected his Christian humanism. During this period, which roughly encompassed the 1970s, he rarely left Canada to perform. With the release of his 1981 album, *Dancing in the Dragon's Jaws*, Cockburn downplayed his devotion in favor of the politics of human relations and expanded his folky handle with elements of non-western music. The result was his only hit in the U.S., "Wondering Where the Lions Are."

Cockburn was unable to follow this up with another hit, and his American record company went out of business as his next album came out. He remained popular in Canada and a cult performer in the U.S. Sony Music decided to take a chance on Cockburn in 1991, releasing *Nothing but a Burning Light*. An extremely musical album, it featured players like Jim Keltner, Mark O'Conner, T-Bone Burnett (who also produced), Booker T. Jones, and Jackson Browne. Despite their best efforts, including an aggressive reissue program making all his work available in the U.S., some for the first time, Cockburn continued to sell indifferently in the U.S. His second Sony release, *Dart Through the Heart*, produced the hitlet "If I Had a Rocket Launcher," but failed to raise his profile appreciably.

Cockburn's 1997 release, *The Charity of the Night*, featured heavyweight players such as jazz vibes player Gary Burton, bassist Rob Wasserman, and the slide guitar of Bonnie Raitt, as well as appearances by Annie DiFranco, Bob Weir, Maria Muldaur, and others. Nonetheless, it too made little impact beyond Cockburn's circle of devoted listeners. His high-energy show is neatly captured on 1998's *You Pay Your Money and You Take Your Chance*. His 25th album, *Breakfast in New Orleans, Dinner in Timbuktu* prominently featured an array of female singers, including Lucinda Williams and fellow Canadian Margo Timmins from the Cowboy Junkies. It also delved into a renewed interest in non-western sounds spurred by a trip to Mali (captured in the film *River of Sand—Exploring Life on the Desert's Edge*), prominently using a traditional African harp called a *kora*.

Perhaps someday Cockburn will manage to shed some of the labels that hinder him—folk artist, Christian artist, leftist artist—and music fans will assess him merely as an artist. Until then, he seems content to play for his fans in Canada and his cult audience elsewhere.

DISC.: *Circles in the Stream* (1997); *Bruce Cockburn* (1971); *High Winds White Sky* (1971); *Sunwheel Dance* (1972); *Night Vision* (1973); *Salt Sun & Time* (1974); *Joy Will Find a Way* (1975); *In the Falling Dark* (1976); *Dancing in the Dragon's Jaws* (1979); *Humans* (1980); *Inner City Front* (1981); *Trouble with Normal* (1983); *Stealing Fire* (1984); *World of Wonders* (1986); *Big Circumstance* (1989); *Nothing but a Burning Light* (1991); *Christmas* (1993); *Dart to the Heart* (1994); *Charity of Night* (1997); *You Pay Your Money and You Take Your Chance* (1998); *Breakfast in New Orleans, Dinner in Timbuktu* (1999).—**HB**

Cocker, Joe (John),

gravelly voiced, British R&B/rock vocalist; b. Sheffield, Yorkshire, England, May 20, 1944. Joe Cocker joined his first band, the Cavaliers, in 1959, and by 1963 he was the lead vocalist of Vance Arnold and the Avengers. Forming the Grease Band with musical mentor Chris Stainton in 1966, Cocker scored a minor English hit with Stainton's "Marjorine" in 1968. The follow-up, a slow blues version of Lennon and McCartney's "With a Little Help from My Friends," became a top British and minor American hit. Cocker's debut album for A&M Records featured the playing of Jimmy Page and Stevie Winwood and included a driving version of Dave Mason's "Feelin' Alright."

In 1969 Cocker and Stainton regrouped the Grease Band for a successful U.S. tour that culminated in Cocker's much-heralded appearance at the Woodstock Music and Art Fair in August. During the tour, he met sessions keyboardist Leon Russell, who later produced and played on *Joe Cocker!*, which yielded a minor hit with Russell's "Delta Lady" and a moderate hit with Lennon and McCartney's "She Came in Through the Bathroom Window." Russell subsequently assembled a large revue for Cocker dubbed Mad Dogs and Englishmen, with a full horn section and vocal chorus (which included Rita Coolidge), for an enormously successful 1970 tour. The double-record set of recordings from the tour remained on the album charts for a year and eventually produced two near-smash hit singles with "The Letter" and "Cry Me a River." The tour launched the popular careers of Leon Russell and Rita Coolidge and marked the high point of Cocker's career.

Exhausted physically and financially by the tour, Joe Cocker abandoned England for Calif., and his subsequent success was limited to the U.S. *Joe Cocker*, recorded with Grease Band veterans Chris Stainton and Alan Spenner, yielded two major hits, "High Time We Went" and "Midnight Rider," and two minor hits, "Woman to Woman" and "Pardon Me Sir." However, Stainton quit the band in early 1973 and Cocker's 1974 tour was a virtual disaster due to his excessive drinking. He did not achieve another major success until 1975's "You are So Beautiful," co-written by Billy Preston, became a smash hit. Dumped by A&M, Cocker switched to Elektra/Asylum in 1978 and Island in 1982. On Island, he soon scored a top hit with Jennifer Warnes on the love theme from the film *An Officer and a Gentleman*, "Up Where We Belong." By 1984 he had moved to Capitol Records, where he eventually had a major hit with "When the Night Comes" in 1989. In 1994 Cocker switched to 550 Music for *Have a Little Faith*. The 1995 A&M anthology set *Long Voyage Home* featured Joe Cocker's recordings for A&M, Elektra, Island, and Capitol.

DISC.: *Joe Cocker!* (1969); *With a Little Help from My Friends* (1969); *Mad Dogs and Englishmen* (1970); *Joe Cocker* (1972); *I Can Stand a Little Rain* (1974); *Jamaica Say You Will* (1975); *Stingray* (1976); *Greatest Hits* (1977); *Luxury You Can Afford* (1978); *Sheffield Steel* (1982); *One More Time* (1983); *Civilized Man* (1984); *Cocker* (1986); *Unchain My Heart* (1987); *One Night of Sin* (1989); *Joe Cocker Live!* (1990); *Box Set* (1992); *Night Calls* (1992); *Best* (1993); *Have a Little Faith* (1994); *The Long Voyage Home* (1995); *Across from Midnight* (1998).

Coclico, Adrianus Petit,

Flemish composer and music theorist; b. in Flanders, 1499 or 1500; d. Copenhagen, after Sept. 1562. Although reared as a Catholic, he converted to Protestantism. After being imprisoned on account of his religious convictions, he went to Wittenberg in 1545 to teach music privately. He then lived in Frankfurt an der Oder and in Stettin before matriculating at the Univ. of Königsberg (1547). He subsequently entered the service of the Duke of Prussia. While living apart from his wife and seeking unsuccessfully for a dissolution of his marriage, he became intimate with his housekeeper, with whom he fathered a son in 1550. He deemed it best to go to Nuremberg, where he was active as a teacher. By 1555 he was in Schwerin, but soon went to Wismar as director of the choirboys at the ducal chapel of Mecklenburg. He eventually settled in Copenhagen, where he was a singer and musician at the court of King Christian II and later of Marcellus Amersfortius. His motet collection, *Consolationes piae: Musica reservata* (Nuremberg, 1552; ed. in Das Erbe Deutscher Musik, first series, XLII, 1958), is of historical interest for the use of "musica reservata" in the title. He also wrote the treatise *Compendium musices* (Nuremberg, 1552; facsimile ed. by M. Bukofzer, 1954; Eng. tr. by A. Seay, 1973).

BIBL.: M. van Crevel, *A.P. C.: Leben und Beziehungen eines nach Deutschland emigrierten Josquinschülers* (The Hague, 1940); E. Sholund, *The Compendium Musices by A.P. C.* (diss., Harvard Univ., 1952).—NS/LK/DM

Coelho, Rui,

Portuguese composer; b. Alcácer do Sal, March 3, 1891; d. Lisbon, May 5, 1986. He was a student of Colaço (piano) and of Ferreira and Borba (composition) at the Lisbon Cons., and then of Humperdinck, Bruch, and Schoenberg in Berlin (1910–13) and of Vidal at the Paris Cons. Upon his return to Lisbon, he devoted himself mainly to composition and music criticism; he also made appearances as a pianist and conductor. His compositions were predicated upon nationalist principles.

WORKS: DRAMATIC: Opera: *O serão da infanta* (1913); *Crisfal* (1919); *Auto do berço* (1920); *Rosas de todo o ano* (1921; Lisbon, May 30, 1940); *Belkiss* (1923; Lisbon, June 9, 1928); *Inês de Castro* (1925; Lisbon, Jan. 15, 1927), *Cavaleiro das mãos irresistíveis* (1926); *Freira de beja* (1927); *Entre giestas* (Lisbon, 1929); *Tá-mar* (Lisbon, 1936); *Dom João IV* (Lisbon, Dec. 1, 1940); *A feira* (1942); *A rosa de papel* (Lisbon, Dec. 18, 1947); *Auto da barca do inferno* (1949; Lisbon, Jan. 15, 1950); *Inês Pereira* (Lisbon, April 5, 1952); *O vestido de noiva* (1958; Lisbon, Jan. 4, 1959); *Auto da alma* (1960); *Orfeu em Lisboa* (1964–66); *Auto da barca da glória* (1970). **Ballet:** *Princesa dos sapatos de ferro* (1912); *O sonho da princesa na rosa* (1916); *A história de carochinha* (1916); *Bailado do encantamento* (1917); *O sonho da pobrezinha* (1921); *A feira* (1921); *Bailado africano* (1930); *Inêz de Castro* (1939); *Passatempo* (1940); *Dom Sebastião* (1943); *Festa na aldeia* (1966). **ORCH.:** 5 *Sinfonia camoneana* (1912, 1917, 1948, 1951, 1957); 4 symphonic poems: *Nun' Alvares* (1922), *Alcácer* (1925), *Rainha santa* (1926), and *O castelo de Lisboa* (1962); 4 *Suite portuguesa* (1925, 1927, 1928, 1956); 2 *Pequena sinfonia* (1929, 1932); *Cenas bíblicas* (1933); 2 *Rapsódia portuguesa* (1934, 1942); *Fantasia portuguesa* for Violin and Orch. (1935); 2 piano concertos (1939, 1948); 3 syms. (1939, 1955, 1956); *Egypcienne* for Violin and Orch. (1950); *Rapsódia de Lisboa* (1961); *Viagens na minha terra*, 4 suites (1964–67); *Sinfonia* *henriquina, prólogo* (1966); *Sinfonia de além mar* (1969). **CHAM-BER:** 2 violin sonatas (1910, 1923); *Largo* for 2 Violas, Cello, and Piano (1911); Piano Trio (1916); String Quartet (1942); piano pieces. **VOCAL:** *Fátima,* oratorio (1931); *Missa a Santa Terezinha* (1934); *Oratória de paz* (1967); songs.

BIBL.: *R. C.: Sua acção e sua obras de 1910 a 1967* (Lisbon, 1967).—**NS/LK/DM**

Coenen, Cornelis, Dutch violinist, conductor, teacher, and composer, brother of **Johannes (Meinardus) Coenen;** b. The Hague, March 19, 1838; d. Arnhem, March 15, 1913. He studied violin as a youth and made tours of Germany and France. He then was conductor of the Utrecht orch. (1860–92). In 1892 he went to Nijmegen, where he was active as a conductor and teacher. He wrote vocal works, chamber music, and piano pieces.—**LK/DM**

Coenen, Frans, Dutch violinist, pedagogue, and composer, brother of **Willem Coenen;** b. Rotterdam, Dec. 26, 1826; d. Leiden, Jan. 24, 1904. After making his public debut as a violinist in 1838, he studied with Molique in Stuttgart (1840–42) and Vieuxtemps in Brussels (1842–43). He then taught violin in Rotterdam. Following a major tour of the U.S. (1848–50), he toured Mexico, Venezuela, and the West Indies with Henri Herz. From 1851 to 1854 he toured South America with Ernst Lübeck. He then went to Amsterdam, where he founded his own string quartet in 1856; he also played in orchs. and in 1871 became director of the choral societies Amstel Mannenkoor and Vereeniging tot Beoefening van Oude Muziek. In 1877 he remained director of the latter until his retirement in 1895. He composed a Sym., chamber music, piano pieces, including popular mazurkas in a salon style, two oratorios, choral works, and songs.—**NS/LK/DM**

Coenen, Johannes (Meinardus), Dutch bassoonist, conductor, and composer, brother of **Cornelis Coenen;** b. The Hague, Jan. 28, 1825; d. Amsterdam, Jan. 9, 1899. He received training at the royal music school at The Hague. He was a bassoonist in the court orch. (1840–42), and also made tours as a recitalist. In 1851 he settled in Amsterdam as conductor of the Dutch theater of van Lier. He then was conductor of the Felix Meritis orch. (1857–65) and subsequently of the orch. of the Paleis voor Volksvlijt (1865–96). He composed two operas, about 50 ballets, a Sym. (1865), the overture *Floris V,* concerti, chamber music, piano pieces, and vocal works.—**NS/LK/DM**

Coenen, Willem, Dutch pianist, teacher, and composer, brother of **Frans Coenen;** b. Rotterdam, Nov. 17, 1837; d. Lugano, March 18, 1918. After traveling in South America and the West Indies, he was active in London (1862–1909). He wrote an oratorio, *Lazarus* (1878), masses, cantatas, songs, and piano pieces. —**NS/LK/DM**

Coerne, Louis (Adolphe), American conductor, teacher, and composer; b. Newark, N.J., Feb. 27, 1870; d.

Boston, Sept. 11, 1922. He studied violin with Kneisel in Boston and composition with Paine at Harvard Univ. (1888–90). After training in organ and composition with Rheinberger in Munich (1890–93), he became the first to obtain a Ph.D. in music at an American univ. with his diss. *The Evolution of Modern Orchestration* at Harvard Univ. in 1905 (publ. in N.Y., 1908). He served as music director in Troy, N.Y. (1907–09), director of the Olivet (Mich.) Coll. Cons. (1909–10), director of the Univ. of Wisc. School of Music (1910–15), and prof. at Conn. Coll. for Women in New London (1915–22). His works include the opera *Zenobia* (1902; Bremen, Dec. 1, 1905), the melodrama *Sakuntala,* incidental music, overtures, and symphonic poems, including *Hiawatha* (1893), a *Romantic Concerto* for Violin and Orch., a String Quartet, *Swedish Sonata* for Violin and Piano, piano pieces, songs, and partsongs.—**NS/LK/DM**

Coertse, Mimi, South African soprano; b. Durban, June 12, 1932. She studied in Johannesburg and Vienna. She made her debut with the Vienna State Opera on tour in Naples in 1955; then sang in Basel and at the Teatro San Carlo in Naples. In 1957 she became a member of the Vienna State Opera; she also appeared in London, Cologne, Rome, Brussels, and other major European music centers.—**NS/LK/DM**

Cohan, George M(ichael), unabashedly patriotic and theatrical American composer, playwright, and actor; b. Providence, R.I., probably July 4, 1878 (his birth certificate lists July 3, but biographer John McCabe makes a reasonable case that he was actually born on July 4, as he claimed); d. N.Y., Nov. 5, 1942. Among the 87 Broadway shows in which Cohan participated between 1901 and 1940, 23 were musicals that he composed and that in many cases he also produced, directed, and starred in. They featured such standards as "Give My Regards to Broadway" and "You're a Grand Old Flag," while his best-known song, "Over There," was written in response to the U.S. entry into World War I. His contribution to popular music and to theater was a brash, vernacular style that broke show music free from European- influenced operetta and forged a new theatrical form: the musical comedy.

Cohan was born into the theater. He was a second-generation descendant of Irish immigrants whose original family name was O'Caomhan, simplified to Keohane and then to Cohan when his grandparents arrived in the U.S. His father, Jeremiah Joseph (Jerry) Cohan, became a minstrel-show entertainer, dancing, playing harp and violin, and writing his own music. His mother, Helen Frances (Nellie) Costigan, joined his father in a vaudeville act after their marriage in 1874. He was brought out onstage for the first time when he was four months old. He showed early musical talent and took violin lessons briefly when he was seven. At that same age he and his eight-year-old sister Josephine (Josie) joined the family act, eventually dubbed "the Four Cohans."

Cohan had no formal education. At the age of ten he began writing songs. In 1891 he made his N.Y. debut with his family in the title role of *Peck's Bad Boy and His*

Pa. His first published song was "Why Did Nellie Leave Her Home?" (1893); another early effort, "Hot Tamale Alley" (1894), was introduced by vaudeville star May Irwin.

By 1896 the Four Cohans had become one of the top acts in vaudeville, and he began to write sketches as well as songs for them and for other performers. Ethel Levey (whose real name was Ethelia Fowler, 1881–1955) first popularized his song "I Guess I'll Have to Telegraph My Baby" (1898), which was then successfully recorded by Arthur Collins, Len Spencer, George J. Gaskin, and Silas Leachman. He married Levey in July 1899, and she appeared in several of his early shows. (Her performance of his song "I Was Born in Virginia" in *George Washington Jr.*, became so closely identified with her that it was popularly known as "Ethel Levey's Virginia Song.") Their daughter, Georgette, was born in 1900. They were divorced in February 1907, and he married dancer and singer Agnes Mary Nolan on June 29, 1907. They had three children: Mary, Helen, and George M. Jr.

Cohan's first full-length theatrical work, the "musical farce" *The Governor's Son*, was an expanded version of a Four Cohans vaudeville sketch that ran for only 32 performances in N.Y., although, like many Cohan shows, its relatively brief stay on Broadway was augmented by an extensive national tour. *Running for Office* was another vaudeville sketch padded out to full length. Cohan contributed several songs to *Mother Goose* (N.Y., Dec. 2, 1903), among them "Always Leave Them Laughing When You Say Goodbye," which became a hit recording for Billy Murray four years later. By then, Murray, whose chipper style matched the composer's, had become the preeminent interpreter of Cohan's songs on record. (The composer himself made only a handful of recordings.)

Cohan's breakthrough musical, and the show that helped to establish the musical comedy form in the theater, was *Little Johnny Jones*, in which he played the part of an American jockey in England. Although it had an initial run of only 52 performances in N.Y., he toured it around the country and brought it back to Broadway twice during 1905. From the score, Murray had his first major hit with a Cohan song early in that year with "Yankee Doodle Boy," a characteristic Cohan march song that drew upon "Yankee Doodle Dandy," "Dixie," and even "The Star-Spangled Banner" in its patriotic fervor. Murray also scored a major hit from the show with "Give My Regards to Broadway," which has become an anthem of the entertainment business. Cohan himself recorded a third song from the show, "Life's a Funny Proposition, After All," when he finally took up recording in 1911, and had one of his only record hits with it. *Little Johnny Jones* was made into film twice in the 1920s.

With *Forty-Five Minutes from Broadway*, Cohan proved he could write and direct a hit show without appearing in it. The musical, set in New Rochelle, N.Y., starred Fay Templeton and Victor Moore. Murray found another hit in its title song, and both Corrine Morgan and Ada Jones made a hit out of "So Long, Mary." Cohan returned to the stage with *George Washington, Jr.*

Seven months before it opened in N.Y., Murray had a major hit (reportedly the biggest selling disc Victor Records issued in the decade) with a song written for the show that was then called "The Grand Old Rag." Cohan had found inspiration for the patriotic march from an encounter with a Civil War veteran who used the phrase affectionately to describe the American flag. When the term "rag" was criticized, Cohan changed the lyric and the title to "You're a Grand Old Flag." It was the first song to sell a million copies of sheet music.

Following the massive success of three consecutive musicals in 15 months, Cohan expanded into other areas, forming a producing partnership with Sam H. Harris and starting to write straight plays. His first nonmusical effort, *Popularity*, was a failure. (He revised it successfully as a musical, *The Man Who Owns Broadway*.) But he could still do well with musicals: *The Talk of New York*, starring Moore, was a sequel to *Forty-Five Minutes from Broadway* and featured the songs "When We Are M-A-Double-R-I-E-D," a hit for the duo of Jones and Murray; "I Want You," a hit for Henry Burr; and "When a Fellow's on the Level with a Girl That's on the Square," which Murray scored with alone. Although he was clearly repeating himself, Cohan also succeeded with *Fifty Miles from Boston*, which featured the jaunty, Irish-flavored "Harrigan," another song in which a word with two r's is spelled out in the chorus. It was a tribute to the vaudeville comedian Ned Harrigan and became another big record seller for Murray, who recorded it well before the N.Y. opening. Cohan later had a hit record with "A Small Time Girl" (released as "The Small-Time Gal") from the show.

After 1908, Cohan began to spend most of his time producing and writing straight plays. He and Harris produced Winchell Smith's *The Fortune Hunter* (N.Y., Sept. 4, 1909), starring John Barrymore, which ran for 345 performances. Cohan's first significant success with a play from his own pen came with an adaptation of George Randolph Chester's Wallingford stories, *Get-Rich-Quick Wallingford*, starring Hale Hamilton and Edward Ellis, which ran for 424 performances. He returned to writing and starring in his own musicals with *The Little Millionaire*, which enjoyed a healthy run, but his biggest song hit of the period came with "That Haunting Melody," an interpolation into *Vera Violetta* (N.Y., Nov. 20, 1911), in which it was sung by emerging star Al Jolson. Jolson recorded the song at his first recording session for Victor on Dec. 22, 1911, and it became his first hit record.

Cohan's next big success came with his mystery play *Seven Keys to Baldpate*, which ran 320 performances in N.Y. In 1917 it was made into a silent film in which he starred (he also made silent versions of his plays *Broadway Jones* and *Hit-the-Trail Holliday* at the same time), and it was remade four times: in 1925, 1929, 1935, and 1947. He turned from book musicals to musical revues with *Hello, Broadway!* and *The Cohan Revues* of 1916 and 1918. His greatest musical success of the 1910s came with the one-off song "Over There," which he wrote the day after the U.S. entered World War I in April 1917. The stirring song was popularized by vaudeville star Nora Bayes, who recorded a popular version.

Cohan's biggest hit recording was performed by the American Quartet, and there were also hit versions by Murray, who was the quartet's leader, and by the Peerless Quartet in the fall of 1917. Prince's Orch. released successful records of both "You're a Grand Old Flag" and "Over There." Enrico Caruso's version of "Over There," sung partly in French, was a major hit just before the end of the war in November 1918. By then the song had sold over a million records and two million copies of sheet music. Cohan was awarded a medal of honor by Congress in 1936 for writing "You're a Grand Old Flag" and "Over There." His sequel to "Over There," "When You Come Back (and You Will Come Back)," was a hit for John McCormack and for the Orpheus Quartet in early 1919.

Cohan and Harris broke up their production company in the wake of the Actors Equity strike of 1919, which Cohan had opposed. (They later reconciled and returned to producing together in 1936.) On his own, Cohan produced such musical hits as Otto Harbach, Frank Mandel, and Louis Hirsch's *Mary* (N.Y., Oct. 18, 1920) and *The O'Brien Girl* (N.Y., Oct. 3, 1921). *Little Nellie Kelly*, the first musical Cohan had written in nearly four years, was another hit, featuring "Nellie Kelly, I Love You," successfully recorded by the American Quartet and by Prince's Orch., and "You Remind Me of My Mother," a hit for Burr. The show was made into a 1940 movie starring Judy Garland, with a score largely written by Roger Edens.

Cohan's greatest successes of the 1920s were his plays, most prominent among them the farce *The Tavern* and *The Song and Dance Man*. His last musical was *Billie*, a musicalized version of *Broadway Jones*. In the 1930s he began to work more frequently as an actor in other people's projects. He appeared in the film *The Phantom President* (1932), which had a score by Richard Rodgers and Lorenz Hart, although he got to sing "You're a Grand Old Flag," and in a movie version of his play *Gambling* (1934), in which he sang his song "My Little Girl." Onstage he starred in Eugene O'Neill's *Ah, Wilderness!* (N.Y., Oct. 2, 1933), and he portrayed Pres. Franklin Roosevelt in Rodgers and Hart's musical *I'd Rather Be Right* (N.Y. Nov. 2, 1937). His final Broadway appearance came with the brief run of his sequel to *The Tavern*, *The Return of the Vagabond*. At the time of his death he was working on a new musical, *The Musical Comedy Man*.

Shortly before he died, Cohan saw and approved his film biography, *Yankee Doodle Dandy* (1942), which starred James Cagney, who won the Academy Award for Best Actor. (Cagney reprised his Cohan portrayal in the Eddie Foy film biography *The Seven Little Foys* in 1955.) The success of the movie and the onset of World War II brought Cohan's music back into fashion, and in 1943 Fred Waring's Pennsylvanians had a hit version of "The Yankee Doodle Boy," while Bing Crosby revived "Mary's a Grand Old Name" from *Forty-Five Minutes from Broadway*. During the next several years, "Over There" and "Give My Regards to Broadway" turned up in half a dozen films.

Cohan's songs formed the basis for *Mr. Broadway*, a TV musical directed by Sidney Lumet and starring Mickey Rooney, which was broadcast May 11, 1957. *Forty-Five Minutes from Broadway* was revived on TV in 1959, the year that a statue of Cohan was erected in Duffy Square in the middle of the Broadway theater district. *George M!* (N.Y., April 10, 1968), a musical biography of Cohan starring Joel Grey, was a Broadway hit, running more than a year. Cohan's songs were also used in the Broadway revues *A Musical Jubilee* (N.Y., Nov. 13, 1975), *Dancin'* (N.Y., March 27, 1978), and *Tintypes* (N.Y., Oct. 23, 1980). A revival of *Little Johnny Jones* was mounted by the Goodspeed Opera House in 1980 with Tom Hulce in the title role. A touring version of the production featuring David Cassidy and then Donny Osmond arrived on Broadway on March 21, 1982, but played only one night.

Cohan's enormous importance to 20th-century American theater as an actor, director, and producer is beyond the scope of this consideration. In musical terms, he was critically important as a theater composer steeped in vaudeville who caught the exuberant mood of turn-of-the-century America and brought a powerful sense of entertainment to show music. His tunes were simple, catchy, and irresistible, and they influenced the course of Broadway musicals and popular music in general.

WORKS (dates are N.Y. openings unless otherwise noted): **MUSICALS/REVUES:** *The Governor's Son* (Feb. 25, 1901); *Running for Office* (April 27, 1903); *Little Johnny Jones* (Nov. 7, 1904); *Forty-Five Minutes from Broadway* (Jan. 1, 1906); *George Washington Jr.* (Feb. 12, 1906); *The Honeymooners* (a revised version of *Running for Office*; June 3, 1907); *The Talk of New York* (Dec. 3, 1907); *Fifty Miles from Boston* (Feb. 3, 1908); *The Yankee Prince* (April 20, 1908); with G. Evans, *The Cohan and Harris Minstrels* (Aug. 3, 1908); *The American Idea* (Oct. 5, 1908); *The Man Who Owns Broadway* (Oct. 11, 1909); *The Little Millionaire* (Sept. 25, 1911); *Hello, Broadway!* (Dec. 25, 1914); *The Cohan Revue of 1916* (Feb. 9, 1916); *The Cohan Revue of 1918* (Dec. 31, 1917); *The Voice of McConnell* (Dec. 25, 1918); *The Royal Vagabond* (Feb. 17, 1919); *Little Nellie Kelly* (Nov. 13, 1922); *The Rise of Rosie O'Reilly* (Dec. 25, 1923); *The Merry Malones* (Sept. 26, 1927); *Billie* (Oct. 1, 1928). **PLAYS:** *Popularity* (Oct. 1, 1906); *Get-Rich-Quick Wallingford* (Sept. 19, 1910); *Broadway Jones* (Sept. 23, 1912); *Seven Keys to Baldpate* (Sept. 22, 1913); *The Miracle Man* (Sept. 21, 1914); with M. Marcin, *The House of Glass* (Sept. 1, 1915); *Hit-the-Trail Holliday* (Sept. 13, 1915); *A Prince There Was* (Dec. 24, 1918); with R. Weiman, *The Acquittal* (Jan. 5, 1920); *The Tavern* (Sept. 27, 1920); *Madeleine and the Movies* (March 6, 1922); *The Song and Dance Man* (Dec. 31, 1923); *American Born* (Oct. 5, 1925); *The Home Towners* (Aug. 23, 1926); *The Baby Cyclone* (Sept. 12, 1927); *Whispering Friends* (Feb. 20, 1928); *Gambling* (Aug. 26, 1929); *Friendship* (Aug. 31, 1931); *Confidential Service* (Philadelphia, March 28, 1932); *Pigeons and People* (Jan. 16, 1933); *Dear Old Darling* (March 2, 1936); *Fulton of Oak Falls* (Feb. 10, 1937); *The Return of the Vagabond* (May 17, 1940).

WRITINGS: *Twenty Years on Broadway: And the Years It Took to Get There* (N.Y., 1925).

BIBL.: W. Morehouse, *G. M. C., Prince of the American Theater* (Philadelphia, 1943); J. McCabe, *G. M. C.: The Man Who Owned Broadway* (N.Y., 1973).—WR

Cohen, Arnaldo, Brazilian pianist; b. Rio de Janeiro, April 22, 1948. He received training in piano and violin at the Federal Univ. of Rio de Janeiro. In 1970 he took first prize in the Beethoven Competition, and then in the Busoni Competition in 1972. After making his London debut at the Royal Festival Hall in 1977, he appeared in various venues in the British capitol and also on the Continent. From 1988 to 1992 he played in the Amadeus Piano Trio. He made his U.S. debut as a soloist with the Lexington (Ky.) Phil. on Sept. 15, 1995. His N.Y. recital debut followed on Feb. 9, 1997, at the Frick Collection. Cohen displays a fine talent for the Romantic repertoire.—LK/DM

Cohen, Harriet,

distinguished English pianist; b. London, Dec. 2, 1895; d. there, Nov. 13, 1967. She studied piano with her parents, then took an advanced course in piano with Matthay. She made her first public appearance as a solo pianist at the age of 13. She then engaged in a successful career in England, both as a soloist with major orchs. and in chamber music concerts. She made a specialty of early keyboard music, but also played many contemporary compositions; Vaughan Williams, Arnold Bax, and other English composers wrote works for her. After damaging her right hand in 1948, she played works for the left-hand alone. In 1938 she was made a Commander of the Order of the British Empire. She publ. a book on piano playing, *Music's Handmaid* (London, 1936; 2nd ed., 1950). Her memoirs, *A Bundle of Time*, were publ. posthumously (London, 1969).—NS/LK/DM

Cohen, Isidore (Leonard),

American violinist and teacher; b. N.Y., Dec. 16, 1922. He studied violin with Galamian and chamber music with Salmond and Letz at the Juilliard School of Music in N.Y. (B.S., 1948). After playing in the Schneider (1952–55) and Juilliard (1958–66) quartets, he was a member of the Beaux Arts Trio (1968–93), with which he toured internationally; he also appeared as a soloist with orchs. and as a recitalist. He taught at the Marlboro (Vt.) Music School (from 1957), at the Juilliard School of Music (1957–65), and at the Mannes Coll. of Music in N.Y. (1970–88).

BIBL.: N. Delbanco, *The Beaux Arts Trio: A Portrait* (London, 1985).—NS/LK/DM

Cohen, Joel (Israel),

American lutenist and conductor; b. Providence, R.I., May 23, 1942. He took courses in composition and musicology at Brown Univ. (B.A., 1963) and Harvard Univ. (M.A., 1965), then studied theory and composition with Boulanger in Paris (1965–67). In 1968 he became conductor of the Boston Camerata, which he led in works from the medieval, Renaissance, and Baroque eras.—NS/LK/DM

Cohen, Leonard,

Canadian poet/singer/songwriter of dark-themed songs; b. Montreal, Canada, Sept. 21, 1934. Cohen studied English literature at McGill and Columbia Univs. and published his first book of poetry, *Let Us Compare Mythologies*, in 1956. During the 1960s, he published a number of books of poetry as well as two novels, *The Favorite Game* (1963) and *Beautiful Losers* (1966). The latter became standard college literary fare and sold more than 300,000 copies.

Taught the classics of music as a child, Leonard Cohen began playing guitar at age 13 and singing at 15, performing with a barn-dance group called the Buckskin Boys during his late teens. His first popular acclaim came when Judy Collins recorded one of his most romantic compositions, "Suzanne," for her 1966 *In My Life* album. Cohen launched his performing career through appearances at the Newport Folk Festival and N.Y.'s Central Park (with Collins) in 1967.

Signed to Columbia Records by John Hammond, Leonard Cohen's debut album included "Suzanne," the alienated "Stranger Song," the sorrowful "Hey, That's No Way to Say Goodbye," and the compassionate "Sisters of Mercy." The latter three songs had appeared on Collins's *Wildflower* album. In 1969 Cohen successfully toured North America and Europe and issued *Songs from a Room*, recorded in Nashville. It contained "The Story of Isaac," "Tonight Will Be Fine," and the oft-recorded classic "Bird on a Wire." Retiring from public performance at the end of 1970, he released *Songs of Love and Hate* the following year. It contained "Famous Blue Raincoat," "Joan of Arc," "Dress Rehearsal Rag," "Diamonds in the Mine," and "Love Calls You by Your Name." He also provided the songs for the soundtrack to the 1971 Robert Altman film *McCabe and Mrs. Miller*.

In 1972 Leonard Cohen published another volume of poetry, *The Energy of Slaves*, and toured the U.S. and Europe with Jennifer Warnes as one of his backup singers. *New Skin for the Old Ceremony*, with "There is a War" and "Chelsea Hotel," was issued in 1974 and Cohen toured again in 1975. He collaborated with songwriter-producer Phil Spector for the controversial *Death of a Ladies' Man* in 1977 and recorded *Recent Songs* for Columbia in 1979. In 1985 he toured again in support of *Various Positions*, but Columbia did not issue the album, instead leasing it to the small Passport label. The album was quickly deleted, despite the inclusion of "The Broken Hallelujah," "Dance Me to the End of Love," and "Heart with No Companion."

In 1986 longtime associate Jennifer Warnes recorded an entire album of Leonard Cohen songs, *Famous Blue Raincoat*, which became a commercial success and revived interest in his career. Already a well-respected figure in Europe, Cohen's 1988 *I'm Your Man* sold spectacularly there and further reawakened interest in his songs in North America. Hailed as a masterpiece, the album contained a number of haunting, compelling songs such as "First We Take Manhattan," "Ain't No Cure for Love," and "Take This Waltz." The less impressive follow-up, *The Future*, included "Democracy," "Light as a Breeze," and "Waiting for a Miracle." The 1993 book *Stranger Music: Selected Poems and Songs* assembled Cohen's poems, prose, and lyrics.

Contemporary alternative artists such as R.E.M., Nick Cave, and the Pixies paid tribute to Leonard Cohen with 1991's *I'm Your Fan*, while 1995's *Tower of Song* tribute featured mainstream artists such as Elton John, Willie Nelson, and Billy Joel. Cohen's son Adam moved to the U.S. from Europe in 1992 and began concentrating on his music in N.Y. the following year. In 1998, he made his recording debut on Columbia

Records and conducted his first national tour.

Cohen was one of the most powerful song poets to emerge in the 1960s. Despite the limited musical effectiveness of his gruff monotonic voice and sparse musical settings, his poetics more than compensate for any musical shortcomings. His lyrics, legitimately described as brooding and gloomy, even depressing, ultimately succeed through the underlying intensity of their humanity. One of the first artists to bring a spiritual and poetic sensibility to rock music, Cohen became an acclaimed musical figure in Europe, where he was sometimes compared to Jacques Brel. In the U.S., he endured years as a cult figure.

WRITINGS: *The Spice Box of Earth* (N.Y., 1961); *The Favorite Game, A Novel* (N.Y., 1963); *Flowers for Hitler* (Toronto, 1964); *Beautiful Losers* (N.Y., 1966); *Let Us Compare Mythologies* (Toronto, 1966); *Parasites of Heaven* (Toronto, 1966); *Selected Poems, 1956–68* (N.Y., 1968); *The Energy of Slaves* (N.Y., 1973); *Death of a Lady's Man* (Toronto, 1978); *Book of Mercy* (Toronto, 1984); *Stranger Music: Selected Poems and Songs* (N.Y., 1993).

DISC.: *Songs of Leonard Cohen* (1968); *Songs from a Room* (1969); *Songs of Love and Hate* (1971); *Live Songs* (1973); *New Skin for the Old Ceremony* (1974); *Best* (1976); *Death of a Ladies' Man* (1977); *Recent Songs* (1979); *Various Positions* (1985); *I'm Your Man* (1988); *The Future* (1992); *Cohen Live—Leonard Cohen in Concert* (1994). Jennifer Warnes: *Famous Blue Raincoat: The Songs of Leonard Cohen* (1986); *Private Music* (1991). Tribute albums (various artists): *I'm Your Fan—The Songs of Leonard Cohen* (1991); *Tower of Song: The Songs of Leonard Cohen* (1995).

BIBL.: Patricia A. Morley, *The Immoral Moralists* (Toronto, 1972); Michael Gnarowski, ed., *Leonard Cohen: The Artist and His Critics* (Toronto, 1976); Stephen Scobie, *Leonard Cohen* (Vancouver, 1978); L. S. Dorman and C. L. Rawlins, *Leonard Cohen: Prophet of the Heart* (London, 1990); Ken Norris and Michael Fournier, eds., *Take This Waltz: A Celebration of Leonard Cohen* (Ste-Anne-de-Bellevue, Quebec, 1994); Ira Bruce Nadel, *Various Positions: A Life of Leonard Cohen* (N.Y., 1996).—**BH**

Cohn, Arthur, versatile American composer, conductor, lexicographer, and publishing executive; b. Philadelphia, Nov. 6, 1910; d. N.Y., Feb. 15, 1998. He studied violin and later took a course in composition at the Juilliard School of Music in N.Y. with Rubin Goldmark. Returning to Philadelphia, he was director of the Edwin A. Fleisher Collection at the Free Library (1934–52). From 1942 to 1965 he conducted the Sym. Club of Philadelphia, and also the Germantown Sym. Orch. (1949–55), the Philadelphia Little Sym. (1952–56), and the Haddonfield (N.J.) Sym. Orch. (1958–91). From 1956 to 1966 he was head of symphonic and foreign music at Mills Music Co., and from 1966 to 1972 held a similar position with MCA Music. In 1972 he was appointed Director of Serious Music at Carl Fischer. He publ. *The Collector's Twentieth-Century Music in the Western Hemisphere* (N.Y., 1961), *Twentieth-Century Music in Western Europe* (N.Y., 1965), *Musical Quizzical* (N.Y., 1970), *Recorded Classical Music: A Critical Guide to Compositions and Performances* (N.Y., 1981), *The Encyclopedia of Chamber Music* (N.Y., 1990), and *The Literature of Chamber Music* (4 vols., Chapel Hill, 1997).

WORKS: 6 string quartets (1928–45); *5 Nature Studies* (1932); *Retrospections* for String Orch. (Philadelphia, April 3, 1935); *Music* for Brass Instruments (1935); Suite for Viola and Orch. (1937); *Machine Music* for 2 Pianos (1937); *4 Preludes* for String Orch. (N.Y., May 26, 1937); *4 Symphonic Documents* (1939); *Music for Ancient Instruments* (1939); Quintuple Concerto for 5 Ancient Instruments and Modern Orch. (1940); Flute Concerto (1941); *Variations* for Clarinet, Saxophone, and String Orch. (1945); *Music* for Bassoon (1947); *Quotations in Percussion* for 103 Instruments for 6 Players (1958); *Kaddish* for Orch. (1964); Percussion Concerto (1970).—**NS/LK/DM**

Cohn, James (Myron), American musicologist, inventor, and composer; b. Newark, N.J., Feb. 12, 1928. He studied with Barlow at the Eastman School of Music in Rochester, N.Y. (1940–41), Harris at Cornell Univ. (1941–43), and Wagenaar at the Juilliard School of Music in N.Y. (B.S., 1949; M.S., 1950), and later pursued postgraduate studies with Ruth Anderson at Hunter Coll. of the City Univ. of N.Y. (1973). He was a musicologist for ASCAP from 1954 to 1984. Cohn invented electronic devices that can be applied to keyboards or fingerboards to control pitch, intonation, loudness, vibrato, and tremolo.

WORKS: DRAMATIC: O p e r a : *The Fall of the City* (1952; Athens, Ohio, July 8, 1955). **ORCH.:** Sinfonietta (1946); Piano Concertino (1946); 8 syms.: No. 1 (1947), No. 2 (1949; Brussels, Dec. 11, 1953), No. 3 (1955; Detroit, Dec. 17, 1959), No. 4 (1956; Florence, Oct. 1, 1960), No. 5 (1959), No. 6 (1965), No. 7 (1967), and No. 8 (1978); *Homage*, overture (1959); *Variations on "The Wayfaring Stranger"* (1960; Detroit, Oct. 4, 1962); *Enchanted Journey* (1961); *Prometheus*, overture (1962); Concerto for Concertina and Strings (1966); *The Little Circus* (1974) (9) *Miniatures* (1975); *A Song of the Waters* (1976); *March-Caprice* for Bassoon and Strings (1982); 2 clarinet concertos: No. 1 (1986; Lubbock, Tex., July 10, 1997) and No. 2 (1996; Cali, Colombia, July 31, 1998); *Mt. Gretna Suite* for Chamber Ensemble (Mt. Gretna, Pa., July 14, 1991); Concerto for Trumpet and Strings (1996; Lexington Park, Md., April 26, 1998); *Caprice* (1998; Ostend, Belgium, July 6, 1999). **CHAMBER:** Septet for Winds and Strings (1947); Sextet for Winds and Piano (1948); 3 string quartets, including Nos. 2 (1950) and 3 (1961); *Sonata Romantica* for Double Bass or Cello and Piano (1952; also for Bassoon and Piano, 1978); Sonata for Solo Cello (1953); Sonata for Solo Violin (1959); Flute Sonata (1974); *Sonata Robusta* for Bassoon and Piano (1980); 2 wind quintets (1981, 1992); *Concerto da Camera* for 5 Instruments (1982); *The Goldfinch Variations* for 3 Treble Instruments (1984); Viola Sonata (1987); Oboe Sonata (1988); Trio for Piano, Violin, and Cello (1988); Horn Sonata (1988); *Serenade* for Flute, Violin, and Cello (1990); *Sonata Notturna* for 2 Flutes and Piano or Flute, Oboe, and Piano (1993); *Arkansas Reel* for Wind Quintet (1994); Suite for Clarinet and Guitar (1994); Piano Quartet (1995); Trio for Clarinet, Violin, and Piano (1995). **KEYBOARD: P i a n o :** *12 Variations on an Original Theme* (1944); 5 sonatas (1947, 1956, 1964, 1981, 1986). **VOCAL:** Choral pieces.—**NS/LK/DM**

Coker, Henry (L.), jazz trombonist; b. Dallas, Tex., Dec. 24, 1919; d. Los Angeles, Nov. 23, 1979. His big buttery sound was a part of Basie's band in the 1950s. Raised in Omaha, Nebr., Coker played piano from an early age; he studied music at Wiley Coll., Tex. Coker's first regular work was with trumpeter John White's Band (1935). He was with Nat Towles' Band from 1937–39 and then worked in Honolulu, Hawaii, with drummer Monk McFay and others until 1941. He was in

Pearl Harbor Hospital with a broken ankle in 1942 before being repatriated to U.S. Coker played with Benny Carter from c. 1944 until 1946 and also did studio work with Eddie Heywood (1946–47) and Benny Carter (1948). He played regularly with Illinois Jacquet in late 1940s and early 1950s and was with Count Basie from February 1952 until 1963, then did extensive studio work in N.Y. He played regularly with Ray Charles' Orch. from 1966 until 1971, then freelancing in Calif. until his death.—JC/LP

Colasse, Pascal, French composer; b. Rheims, Jan. 22, 1649; d. Versailles, July 17, 1709. He was a pupil of Lully, who entrusted him with writing out the parts of his operas from the figured bass and melody. Later Colasse was accused of appropriating scores thrown aside by his master as incomplete. In 1683 he was appointed Master of the Music, and in 1696 royal chamber musician. He was a favorite of Louis XIV, and obtained the privilege of producing operas at Lille, but the theater burned down. His opera *Polyxène et Pyrrhus* (1706) failed, and his mind became disordered. Of ten operas, *Les Noces de Thetys et Pelée* (1689) was his best. He also composed songs, sacred and secular. —**NS/LK/DM**

Colbran, Isabella (Isabel Angela), famous Spanish soprano; b. Madrid, Feb. 2, 1785; d. Bologna, Oct. 7, 1845. She studied with Pareja in Madrid, then with Marinelli and Crescentini in Naples. She made her debut in a concert in Paris in 1801. After her successful appearances in Bologna (1807) and La Scala in Milan (1808), the impresario Barbaja engaged her for Naples in 1811; she became his mistress, only to desert him for Rossini, whom she married on March 16, 1822 (they were legally separated in 1837). She created the leading soprano roles in several of Rossini's operas, beginning with *Elisabetta, Regina d'Inghilterra* (1815) and concluding with *Semiramide* (1823). With her voice in decline, she retired from the stage in 1824. During the early years of the 19th century she was acclaimed as the leading dramatic coloratura soprano.—**NS/LK/DM**

Colding-Jørgensen, Henrik, Danish organist, choirmaster, and composer; b. Riisskov, March 21, 1944. He studied composition with Holmboe in Copenhagen, and pursued training at the Royal Danish Cons. of Music there, where he graduated as an organist in 1966 and as an organ pedagogue in 1967. He then studied instrumentation, electroacoustics, and composition on his own. After teaching at the Musikhøjskole in Copenhagen (1967–70) and at the Funen Academy of Music in Odense (1969–75), he became organist and choirmaster at the Hundige and Kildebrønde churches near Copenhagen in 1975. From 1981 to 1991 he also was a member of the executive board of the Danish Composers' Soc. While his works have been influenced by Stravinsky, Berg, Webern, and Ligeti, he has developed an individual style in which strict structuralism is complemented by a liberating expressivity.

WORKS: ORCH.: Sym. No. 1 (1965); *At elske musikken* (To Love Music; 1975); *Ballade* for Tuba and Chamber Orch. (1979);

Nuup Kangerlua (1985); *Le Alpi nel Cuore* (1988); *Babylon* for Piano and Orch. (1991). **CHAMBER:** *Mourn* for Guitar (1969); *Suite à deux* for Flute and Clarinet (1971); *Cello* for Cello (1972); *Balancer* (Balances) for Violin and Percussion (1974); *Boast* for Tuba (1980); *Performances* for Brass Quintet (1981); *Recitativ og Fuga* for Piano and Cello (1983); *Toccata, Aria e Minuetto* for Oboe (1986); *Sjaelen og sommerfuglen* (The Soul and the butterfly) for Sopranino Recorder and Harpsichord (1990); *Som en rejsende* (As a traveller) for Cello and Percussion (1992); *Krystal: Metamorfose* for String Quartet (1993); *Diskurs Med Tiden* (Discourse with Time) for Chamber Ensemble (1996); *Sourires* (Smiles) for Tuba (1997). **KEYBOARD: Organ:** *Magnus* (1972); *To moendi i hvide klaeder: Duo viri in vestibus albis* (1999). **VOCAL:** *Lapidary Landscapes* for Mezzo-soprano, Bass-baritone, Oboe, English Horn, Viola, Cello, and Percussion (1965); *På din taerskel* (At your doorstep) for Contralto and Orch. (1966); *Barbare* for 6 Soloists, Chorus, and Orch. (1967); *Enfance III* for Contralto, Horn, and Harp (1967), *IV* for Contralto and Piano (1968), and *II* for Mezzo-soprano and Clarinet (1983); *Altid noget andet* (Always something else) for Tenor and Viola d'Amore (1973); *Ava Maria* for Contralto (1974); *Victoria Gennem Skoven* (Victoria Through the Forest) for Contralto and Orch. (1975); *An de Nachgeborenen I* (1980) and *II* (1984) for Soprano and Wind Quintet; *Det er mig der vaelter* (It is I who am Overturned) for Soprano, Mezzo-soprano, and Organ (1981); *Dein Schweigen* for Mezzo-soprano, Clarinet, and Piano (1982); *Du sollst nicht* for Mezzo-soprano, Clarinet, and Piano (1984); *Sic Enim* for Mezzo-soprano and Organ (1985); *2 Songs by Keats* for Soprano and Guitar (1988); *Nunc Est* for Mezzo-soprano, Clarinet, and Organ (1989); *4 British Songs* for Girl's Chorus (1997).—**NS/LK/DM**

Cole, Cozy (actually, **William Randolph**), noted jazz drummer; b. East Orange, N.J., Oct. 17, 1906; d. Columbus, Ohio, Jan. 29, 1981. The family moved to N.Y. in 1926 and Cole played drums from an early age, turning professional in 1928. He played with Wilbur Sweatman (c. 1928), and led his own band in late 1920s. Cole recorded with Jelly Roll Morton in 1930, and he worked with various leaders through the 1930s, including Blanche Calloway (1931–33), Benny Carter (late 1933–34), Willie Bryant (1935–36), and Stuff Smith (early 1936–38). In November 1938, he began his nearly four-year association with Cab Calloway, where he first attracted widespread acclaim. His solos were the highlights of several Calloway recordings of this period, including "Crescendo to Drums" and "Paradiddle." From 1942–45 Cole worked as a member of the CBS radio staff orch., while also leading his own trio, from time to time, at N.Y.'s Onyx club. His drumming was featured in the Broadway production of *Carmen Jones* in the "Beat Out Dat Rhythm on a Drum" number. He worked with Benny Goodman in the *Make Mine Music* film (June 1944), and also in Billy Rose's *Seven Lively Arts* theatrical production (1945–46).

During the 1940s, Cole did extensive studies at Juilliard, regular studio work 1946–48, and led own quintet in 1948, and septet in early 1949. He was with Louis Armstrong All Stars from spring of 1949 until October 1953, where his playing again was a major draw. He played regularly at the Metropole, N.Y., during the 1950s and also did freelance studio work; in 1954 Cole started a drum school in partnership with

Gene Krupa (which remained in business until Krupa's death in 1973). In autumn of 1957, he toured Europe with "All Stars" led by Jack Teagarden and Earl Hines. In 1958 Cozy gained a hit parade success with his single "Topsy" and subsequently led his own band on national tours. He led his own group at the Metropole during early 1960s, toured Africa with his own quintet (autumn 1962–early 1963), and was regularly featured on television shows. He was a member of the Jonah Jones Quintet (1969–76); then was artist-in-residence at Capital Univ. in Columbus, Ohio. He did freelance work through the 1970s, touring Europe in 1976 with Benny Carter's quartet as part of Barry Martyn's show "A Night in New Orleans." He appeared in several films including *Make Mine Music* and *The Glenn Miller Story*, and also did the soundtrack for *The Strip* in 1951.

DISC.: *Concerto for Cozy* (1944); *Cozy Cole* (1955); *Topsy* (1957); *Cozy Conception of Carmen* (1961); *Drum Beat Dancing Feet* (1962); *It's a Cozy World* (1964). L. Young: *Blue Lester* (1944). D. Gillespie: *Groovin' High* (1945).—**JC/LP**

Cole, Freddy, American singer, pianist; b. Chicago, Ill., Oct. 15, 1931. Although he sounds a lot like his famous brother, **Nat "King" Cole** (d. 1965), he has a style all his own. The youngest of the five children of Edward and Paulina Nancy Cole, Freddy was influenced by three older brothers, Eddie, Ike, and Nat. The family moved from Ala. to the South side of Chicago where he was born. He had started playing by age six; by his early he teens was playing professionally. Brother Eddie (d. 1970) was a bassist who led his own bands, Nat played piano, and brother Ike resides and works as a singer-pianist in Ariz. Cole has been recording since he was 21 years old, starting his career in 1952 with the single, "The Joke's on Me," for the obscure, Chicago-based Topper Records. Some moderate hit singles for various small labels followed and, in the 1980s, Cole formed his own label, First Shot.

In spite of his early talents, Cole was set to pursue a career in football until he injured his hand at age 16, and subsequent infection, operations, and intensive physical therapy kept him from realizing his gridiron dream. He began playing piano and singing in hometown clubs, pursued formal musical education at the Roosevelt Inst. in Chicago, and in 1951 was accepted into the Juilliard School of Music. In 1953 he spent several months on the road with Earl Bostic's band with Johnny Coles and Benny Golson. He studied further at Boston's New England Cons. of Music, earning a master's degree in 1956. In N.Y.C. he established his career, developing a vast repertoire of songs in Manhattan's posh bistros, performing commercial studio work as a pianist, and later, as vocalist. His recordings during the 1970s helped establish his international career and, able to sing a few songs in French, Portuguese, and Spanish, he continues to enjoy a big following in Brazil. Living in the shadow of older brother Nat, fame eluded him for years until his pivotal 1991 Sunnyside album, *I'm Not My Brother, I'm Me* (now out of print), and albums as leader for Sunnyside, Laserlight, and Muse. After signing with the Fantasy label in 1994 and making four albums, Cole has achieved the broader recognition he deserves. He tours widely with his trio throughout Europe, the Far East,

and Brazil, in addition to performing at major U.S. jazz festivals and in nightclubs.

DISC.: *A Circle of Love* (1993); *I Want a Smile for Christmas* (1995); *Always* (1995); *I'm in Love* (1996); *To the Ends of the Earth* (1997); *Love Makes the Changes* (1998).—**NAL**

Cole, June (Lawrence), early jazz bassist, tuba player, singer; b. Springfield, Ohio, 1903; d. N.Y., Oct. 10, 1960. In 1923 he played in the Synco Jazz Band in Springfield and thus became an original member of McKinney's Cotton Pickers. He left the band in late 1926 to join Fletcher Henderson and was with Henderson until late 1928, then Cole sailed to Europe to join Benton Peyton. He toured Europe with Peyton until late 1929, then joined Sam Wooding. He remained in Europe with Willie Lewis after Wooding disbanded in November 1931. From early 1936 Cole was forced by serious illness to quit playing for almost three years. He returned to performing with Willie Lewis in January 1939 and remained with the band until return to U.S., in Sept. 1941. Cole led his own small group during the 1940s, also played in Willie "The Lion" Smith's Quartet in 1947, and later ran own record shop on 116th Street in Harlem. However, he continued to gig in N.Y through the 1950s.—**JC/LP**

Cole, Nat "King" (originally, **Coles, Nathaniel Adams**), American singer, pianist, and actor; father of **Natalie Cole;** b. Montgomery, Ala., March 17, 1917; d. Santa Monica, Feb. 15, 1965. Beginning his career as a jazz pianist, Cole went on to become one of the most successful singers of the 1950s. His light, supple baritone was especially effective on ballads such as his biggest hits—"(I Love You) For Sentimental Reasons," "Nature Boy," and "Mona Lisa"—but he also handled novelties and rhythm songs effectively. Although he worked in radio, TV, and film, he achieved his greatest success through personal appearances and on records, charting 41 albums and 104 singles between the 1940s and the 1990s.

Cole was the son of the Rev. Edward James Coles and Perlina Adams Coles. His mother, who played keyboard and led the choir in his father's church, gave him his earliest musical instruction. The family moved to Chicago when he was a small child. At about the age of 11 he played organ in his father's church and sang in the choir; at 12 he began taking piano lessons. While attending high school, he studied music with N. Clark Smith and Walter Dyett. By his teens he was playing in local bands. He made his recording debut in July 1936 with the Solid Swingers, a band also featuring his brother Eddie on bass. The following year, he joined the orchestra of a touring company of the revue *Shuffle Along*; while on tour, he married dancer Nadine Robinson. They divorced in January 1948.

The tour ended in Los Angeles, where Cole remained, playing in clubs as a solo pianist and various combinations with other musicians, finally working as part of a trio with guitarist Oscar Moore and bass player Wesley Prince that came to be called the King Cole Trio. The group played jazz instrumentals as well as songs on which they sang together, and gradually Cole was featured as the sole singer. They recorded for various labels between 1939 and 1943, the most prominent being Decca Records, for which they did four sessions in 1940 and 1941. Although they performed primarily in L.A. and N.Y., they also appeared in other major cities. In August 1942 Prince was drafted and replaced by Johnny Miller. In November "That Ain't Right" (music and lyrics by Cole and Irving Mills), which the group had recorded for Decca more than a year earlier, entered the R&B charts, rising to #1 in January 1943. In August 1943 they were filmed performing "Straighten Up and Fly Right" (music and lyrics by Cole and Irving Mills) for the feature *Here Comes Elmer*, which was released in October, and they also were in *Pistol Packin' Mama*, released in December.

Capitol Records signed the trio and reissued their October 1942 recording of "All for You" (music and lyrics by Robert Scherman), originally released on the Excelsior label. It topped the R&B charts in November 1943 and became the their first pop chart entry in December. The King Cole Trio had done its first Capitol session in November 1943, and from it came a recording of "Straighten Up and Fly Right" that entered the R&B charts in April 1944, rising to #1 and becoming the biggest R&B hit of the year. In May it entered the country charts, hitting #1 in June. And in June it reached the pop charts, peaking in the Top Ten in July, but it was bested by a cover by the Andrews Sisters. The trio returned to #1 on the R&B charts in October with "Gee, Baby, Ain't I Good to You" (music by Don Redman, lyrics by Redman and Andy Razaf), which also reached the pop charts. Their success on records allowed them to launch a six-month national tour in September. They also performed in two films released during the year, *Stars on Parade* and *Swing in the Saddle*.

The King Cole Trio was back in Los Angeles in March 1945, the month their album, *The King Cole Trio*, hit #1. In May they appeared in the film *See My Lawyer*. Their next movie appearance came July 1946 in *Breakfast in Hollywood*. The same month, *King Cole Trio—Vol. 2* reached the album charts, hitting #1 in August. During the summer, they were in N.Y. hosting the *Kraft Music Hall* radio series during Bing Crosby's vacation. The stint was successful enough that the trio launched its own weekly 15-minute network radio series, *King Cole Trio Time*, in October; it ran until April 1948. This increased exposure, in turn, further stimulated record sales. The group's revival of the 1931 song "You Call It Madness (But I Call It Love)" (music and lyrics by Con Conrad, Gladys Du Bois, Russ Columbo, and Paul Gregory) made the pop Top Ten in September and "(I Love You) For Sentimental Reasons" (music by William Best, lyrics by Deek Watson) became their first pop #1 in December. That same month they peaked in the Top Ten with the million-seller "The Christmas Song (Merry Christmas to You)" (music by Mel Tormé, lyrics by Robert Wells), which became a perennial hit and is notable as the first instance in which Cole's vocal was backed by a string section as well as the trio. In 1974 the recording was inducted into the Grammy Hall of Fame.

The trio embarked on an extensive tour of the Northeast and Midwest in December 1946, continuing to do their radio series in remote broadcasts. They returned to Los Angeles in May 1947, remaining on the West Coast for the summer and then returning to the road. Oscar Moore left the group in October and was replaced by Irving Ashby. The trio hit the Top Ten of the album charts with *King Cole Trio—Vol. 3* in January 1948, and in April "King Cole," as he was billed, reached the charts with "Nature Boy" (music and lyrics by Eden Ahbez), on which he abandoned the piano and sang backed by an orchestra. The song hit #1 in May and sold a million copies. On March 28 Cole married singer Maria (Marie) Hawkins Ellington. They had three children and adopted two. Their first child, **Natalie Maria Cole** (b. Los Angeles, Feb. 6, 1950), became a successful singer. The trio continued to tour extensively during 1948; Johnny Miller left the group in August and was replaced by Joe Comfort.

Cole toured the Northeast with Woody Herman and His Thundering Herd in the late winter of 1949, adding a bongo player, Jack Costanzo, to his group, which came to be billed as Nat "King" Cole and His Trio. In April he appeared in the film *Make-Believe Ballroom*. The album *King Cole Trio—Vol. 4* reached the Top Ten in July. He toured the South in June and July, then hooked up with Herman again for a West Coast tour into August and back on the East Coast in the fall. As of 1950 his record releases were credited to Nat "King" Cole and often featured orchestras and choruses in addition to or in place of the trio. In June he scored his first major single hit in more than two years, "Mona Lisa" (music and lyrics by Jay Livingston and Ray Evans), which topped the charts in July and sold a million copies. In the fall he toured Europe for the first time. "Orange Colored Sky" (music and lyrics by Milton De Lugg and William Stein), on which Cole and trio were accompanied by Stan Kenton and His Orch., hit the Top Ten in November, and "Frosty the Snowman" (music and lyrics by Steve Nelson and Jack Rollins) hit in December.

Cole again topped the charts in June 1951 with the million-seller "Too Young" (music by Sid Lippman, lyrics by Sylvia Dee). That summer, Irving Ashby and Johnny Miller quit the group, and although Cole replaced them, he was billed as a solo artist thereafter; by 1955 he had disbanded the trio and toured with an orchestra. In November 1951 he reached the charts with "Unforgettable" (music and lyrics by Irving Gordon), one of his more impressive recordings. An *Unforgettable* album, released in November 1952, eventually sold a million copies. He hit the Top Ten with two songs in 1952: "Walkin' My Baby Back Home" (music and lyrics by Roy Turk and Fred Ahlert) in July and "Somewhere Along the Way" (music by Kurt Adams, lyrics by Sammy Gallop) in August. In October his album *Penthouse Serenade* made the Top Ten, and he had another Top Ten single with "Pretend" (music and lyrics by Lew Douglas, Cliff Parman, and Frank Levere) in March 1953. In April he played himself in the mystery film *The Blue Gardenia*, singing the title song. The following month he was in the musical *Small Town Girl*.

In January 1954 Cole released the album *Nat King Cole Sings for Two in Love*, which, like Frank Sinatra's concept albums of the time, was a collection of thematically chosen romantic ballads performed with an orchestra, which was conducted by Nelson Riddle. It was a Top Ten hit. Cole also reached the Top Ten in April with the single "Answer Me, My Love" (music by Gerhard Winkler and Fred Rauch, English lyrics by Carl Sigman), with the album *10th Anniversary* in July, and with the single "Smile" (music by Charlie Chaplin, lyrics by John Turner and Geoffrey Parsons) in October. Continuing to tour extensively, he had a three-week engagement at the Sands in Las Vegas in January, the start of a three-year contract with the hotel, and he toured Europe for a second time in March.

Cole had another three songs in the Top Ten in 1955: "Darling Je Vous Aime Beaucoup" (music and lyrics by Anna Sosenko) in April and both sides of the single "A Blossom Fell" (music and lyrics by Howard Barnes, Harold Cornelius [real name Fields], and Dominic John [real name Joe Roncoroni])/"If I May" (music and lyrics by Charles Singleton and Rose Marie McCoy) in May. He starred in a 20-minute film biography, *The Nat King Cole Story*, released during the summer. In April 1956 he appeared in his next feature film, *The Scarlet Hour*. Among his nine singles chart entries in 1956, the most successful was "Night Lights" (music by Chester Conn, lyrics by Sammy Gallop), which reached the Top 40 in October Continuing to make live appearances, he toured Australia in February and signed a new three-year deal with the Sands for $500,000. On Nov. 15, 1956, the premiere episode of *The Nat "King" Cole Show*, a weekly 15-minute music program, was broadcast on network television. The show ran on Monday nights through June 1957 and was expanded to a half-hour on Tuesday nights from July to December 1957.

Cole's TV exposure increased his record sales. The album *Love is the Thing*, another collection of romantic ballads, arranged by Gordon Jenkins, released in March 1957, hit #1 in May, selling a million copies. "Send for Me" (music and lyrics by Ollie Jones) became his first Top Ten single in two years in July, also topping the R&B charts. *Just One of Those Things*, released in November, hit the Top Ten in December. He also found time to act and sing in supporting roles in two films: *Istanbul* in January and *China Gate* in May. The following year he had his only starring role in the movies, playing the part of W. C. Handy in the film biography *St. Louis Blues*, released in April 1958. His single "Looking Back" (music and lyrics by Brook Benton, Belford Hendricks, and Clyde Otis) made the Top Ten in May and was nominated for a Grammy Award for Best Rhythm & Blues Performance.

Cole toured South America in 1959, promoting his Spanish-language album *Cole Español* and acted in the film *Night of the Quarter Moon*, released in March. His single "Midnight Flyer" (music and lyrics by Mayme Watts and Robert Mosely) reached the Top 40 in September; it earned a Grammy nomination for Best Rhythm & Blues Performance and won the Grammy Award for Best Performance by a "Top 40" Artist.

Cole toured Europe in 1960. His album *Wild Is Love*, released in September, reached the Top Ten and earned Grammy nominations for Album of the Year and Best Vocal Performance, Male. He re-recorded his better-known songs for the multidisc set *The Nat King Cole Story*, released in 1961, and it earned him a Grammy nomination for Album of the Year. In 1962 he toured Japan. For his U.S. performances he mounted an elaborate stage show, Sights and Sounds. He had his first Top Ten single in four years with the million-selling "Ramblin' Rose" (music and lyrics by Noel Sherman and Joe Sherman) in September 1962. It was nominated for a Grammy Award for Record of the Year, and a *Ramblin' Rose* LP reached the Top Ten, sold a million copies, and remained in the charts more than three years.

Cole's final Top Ten single came in June 1963 with "Those Lazy-Hazy-Crazy Days of Summer." He toured Great Britain that summer. His seasonal LP *The Christmas Song*, released in September, eventually went gold.

In the summer and fall of 1964, Cole shot his last film, the comic Western *Cat Ballou*, acting as a singing narrator; it was released in June 1965. He died of lung cancer in February 1965. In the wake of his death, his current album, *L-O-V-E*, released in January, hit the Top Ten in March. Capitol Records successfully repackaged his recordings for many years. *The Best of Nat King Cole*, released in August 1968, eventually went gold. The album *20 Golden Greats*, released in the U.K., hit #1 there in April 1978. In June 1991, Natalie Cole released *Unforgettable, with Love*, an album on which she performed songs associated with her father. On "Unforgettable," she overdubbed her voice onto her father's original recording. Released as a single, it reached the Top 40, sold a million copies, and won Grammy Awards for Record of the Year and Best Traditional Pop Performance. *Collectors Series*, another compilation of Cole's hits released simultaneously, went gold.

DISC.: *From the Very Beginning* (1941); *Anatomy of a Jam Session* (1945); *Big Band C.* (1950); *Jazz Encounters* (1950); *The Billy May Sessions* (1951); *Penthouse Serenade* (1952); *Unforgettable* (1952); *N. K. C. Sings for Two in Love (and More)* (1954); *In the Beginning* (1956); *The Piano Style of N. K. C.* (1956); *Love Is the Thing* (1957); *Just One of Those Things* (1957); *The Very Thought of You* (1958); *Wild Is Love* (1960); *The Magic of Christmas* (1960); *N. K. C. Sings/George Shearing Plays* (1961); *The N. K. C. Story* (1961); *Ramblin' Rose (and More)* (1962); *The Christmas Song* (1963); *The Best of N. K. C.* (1968); *Hit That Jive, Jack: The Earliest Recordings, 1940–41* (1990); *Greatest Country Hits* (1990); *The Jazz Collector Edition* (1991); *The Trio Recordings* (1991); *The Complete Capitol Recordings of the N. K. C. Trio* (1991); *The Trio Recordings, Vol. II* (1991); *The Trio Recordings, Vol. III* (1991); *The Trio Recordings, Vol. IV* (1991); *N. K. C.* (box set; 1992); *The Unforgettable N. K. C.* (1992); *The Best of the N. K. C. Trio: Instrumental Classics* (1992); *Early Years of the N. K. C. Trio* (1993); *N. K. C. & the K. C. Trio: Straighten up & Fly Right* (radio broadcasts, 1942–48; 1993); *The Greatest Hits* (1994); *The N. K. C. Trio: World War II Transcriptions* (1994); *Spotlight on N. K. C.* (1995); *The Jazzman* (1995); *To Whom It May Concern* (1995); *Swinging Easy down Memory Lane* (1995); *The Complete after Midnight Sessions* (1996); *Sweet Lorraine* (1938–41 transcriptions; 1996); *Best of: Vocal Classics 1947–50* (1996); *The Vocal Classics* (1996); *The N. K. C. TV Show* (1996); *The McGregor Years: 1941–45* (1996); *Love Is the Thing* (1997); *Revue Collection* (1997); *C., Christmas, and Kids* (1997); *A&E Biography: A Musical Anthology* (1998); *The Best of the N. K. C. Trio* (1998); *Christmas for Kids: From One to Ninety-Two* (2000).

BIBL.: M. Cole (his widow) with L. Robinson, *N. K. C.: An Intimate Biography* (N.Y., 1971); J. Haskins with K. Benson, *N. K.*

C.: A Personal and Professional Biography (N.Y., 1984; rev. ed. 1990); C. Garrod and B. Korst, N. "K." C.: His Voice and His Piano (Zephyrhills, Fla., 1987); L. Gourse, Unforgettable: The Life and Mystique of N. K. C. (N.Y., 1991); K. Teubig, "Straighten Up and Fly Right": A Chronology and Discography of N. "K." C. (Westport, Conn., 1994).—WR

Cole, Natalie, R&B diva with a checkered career, and daughter of pop crooner Nat "King" Cole; b. Los Angeles, Feb. 6, 1950. As a child, Natalie Maria; Cole had the opportunity to sing with Duke Ellington, Sarah Vaughn, and Ella Fitzgerald, or Uncle Duke, Aunt Sarah, and Aunt Ella as she called them, in her living room. Her mother, Marie Ellington Cole, had sung in Duke Ellington's band. Her father, **Nat "King" Cole,** was one of the most successful African-American performers of his generation. While this gave Natalie a head start, it also gave her a pretty tough act to follow.

After graduating with a degree in psychology from the Univ. of Mass., Natalie signed on with her father's old label, Capitol Records. Her first album, 1974's Inseparable produced the two chart-topping R&B hits, "This Will Be" (#6 pop) and the title track (#32 pop). The album went gold and Cole came home from the 1975 Grammy Awards with statuettes for Best New Artist and Best R&B Vocalist, Female. Natalie continued her streak of #1 R&B hits with "Sophisticated Lady (She's a Different Lady)" (#25 pop), which won her a 1977 Grammy for Best R&B Vocal Performance, Female. While the singles were straight ahead R&B with a dance beat and a strong sense of swing, Cole still managed to toss in the odd standard like "Good Morning Heartache" on her albums.

Natalie continued her streak of #1 R&B singles with the gold "I've Got Love on My Mind" (#5 pop) from the platinum Unpredictable in 1977. Almost exactly a year later, she scored another gold, chart-topping R&B hit with "Our Love" (#10 pop) from the platinum album Thankful.

The hits began to slow down in the 1980s. In 1980, she had hit #21 with "Someone That I Used to Love." By 1983 she had been dropped by two record companies and was in rehabilitation for drug abuse. Through the mid-1980s, Cole put out several commercially and artistically disappointing albums, finally coming back in 1987 with Everlasting. The album went gold, producing three hit singles: the #13 hits "Jump Start" and "I Live for Your Love" and a #5 cover of Bruce Springsteen's "Pink Cadillac." Her next album yielded the #7 single "Miss You Like Crazy" and the #34 "Wild Women Do," which was featured in the film Pretty Woman.

After 17 years as a recording artist in her own right, Cole finally felt she had earned the right to pay homage to her father without being accused of trying to ride his coattails to success. In 1991 she broached the idea with her record company, and when they weren't interested, she moved to Elektra Records. The album, Unforgettable, with Love, became a record business phenomenon. The title track, a digitally recreated duet with her father on his 1952 hit "Unforgettable," rose to #14 (two places shy of where her father's version peaked), but sold gold. The album went septuple platinum and started a re-evaluation of standards among the pop audience. The album won seven Grammy awards that year, of which she took home three: Album of the Year, Best Traditional Pop Performance, and Record of the Year.

Cole followed this with the gold Take a Look album in 1993. Another more traditional pop recording, it found Cole recording 18 lesser-known songs by artists such as Ella Fitzgerald and Aretha Franklin. It earned her another Grammy for Best Vocal Performance. She continued her exploration of standards with Stardust, which also went gold. After a three-year break, she started to move back to more contemporary pop with 1999's Snowfall on the Sahara collection. With 21 albums in a quarter of a century as a performer, Cole's career has covered rock, R&B, jazz and standards, proving her one of her generation's most versatile singers.

DISC.: Inseparable (1975); Natalie (1976); Thankful (1977); Unpredictable (1977); Natalie...Live! (1978); I Love You So (1979); Don't Look Back (1980); Happy Love (1981); Dangerous (1985); Everlasting (1987); Collection (1988); Good to Be Back (1989); Unforgettable, with Love (1991); I've Got Love on My Mind (1992); Take a Look (1993); Holly & Ivy (1994); Stardust (1996); Snowfall on the Sahara (1999).—HB

Cole, Paula, Grammy-winning singer who combines confessional lyrics with a slightly jazz-flavored delivery; b. Rockport, Mass., April 5, 1968. Paula Cole's somewhat bohemian parents didn't have a radio and rarely turned on the TV. Instead, her father, an entomologist who taught biology at Salem State Coll. and played bass in a polka band, and her mother, a visual artist, would sing and make music together.

Through high school, Cole was class president, a straight A student, and even prom queen. She enrolled in Berklee Coll. in Boston, studying voice. She also began writing songs at this time. When she graduated, she moved to San Francisco, holing up like a hermit and working on the songs that would become her debut album, Harbinger. She played a special showcase for Terry Ellis, president of Imago Records, who quickly signed her. She passed an advance copy of the record to a member of Peter Gabriel's band, and Gabriel asked her to tour with him. With this exposure, Harbinger was set up for great things. Unfortunately, just as Harbinger came out, Imago lost its distribution and eventually went out of business.

Cole signed with Warners Bros. They reissued Harbinger in 1995, but it received little attention. While working on her next album, she convinced the label to let her scrap $80,000 worth of work with a producer, and make the album herself. The record, This Fire, came out in 1996. The song "Where Have All the Cowboys Gone?" became a hit, becoming the first video to be heavily promoted on VH1's "inside track." The song reached #8 on the charts. Although Cole meant it to be bitingly sarcastic, many interpreted the song as a nostalgic anthem to the barefoot-and-pregnant housewife. The producers of the TV show Dawson's Creek chose her song "I Don't Want to Wait" as its theme song, making the song ubiquitous during the show's high-profile launch, and it rose to #11. This Fire topped out at #20 and went double platinum. Cole also performed as part of the first Lillith Fair tour, which helps promote female singer/songwriters.

Cole earned seven 1998 Grammy nominations, becoming the first woman to be nominated as best producer. Performing on the awards program, more notice got paid to the fact that she didn't shave her armpits than to her performance. She took home the Award for Best New Artist, ironic as she had released her major label debut recording four years before.

DISC.: *Harbinger* (1994); *This Fire* (1996).—**HB**

Cole, Rossetter Gleason, American composer, organist, and teacher; b. Clyde, Mich., Feb. 5, 1866; d. Lake Bluff, Ill., May 18, 1952. He studied music with C.B. Cady. In 1890 he went to Germany, where he studied composition with Max Bruch in Berlin, and organ with Middleschulte. Returning to America in 1892, he occupied various posts as a teacher and organist in Wisc., Iowa, and Ill.; lived mostly in Chicago.

WORKS: DRAMATIC: O p e r a : *The Maypole Lovers* (1931; suite, Chicago, Jan. 9, 1936). **ORCH.:** *Ballade* for Cello and Orch. (Minneapolis, 1909); *Symphonic Prelude* (Chicago, March 11, 1915); *Pioneer Overture* (composed for the centenary of the state of Ill.; Chicago, March 14, 1919); *Heroic Piece* for Organ and Orch. (Chicago, Feb. 11, 1924). **CHAMBER:** Violin Sonata; also various piano pieces, including *From a Lover's Notebook, In Springtime, Sunset in the Hills,* etc.; oran works. **VOCAL: C a n t a t a s :** *The Passing of Summer* (1902); *The Broken Troth* (1917); *The Rock of Liberty* (1920). **O t h e r :** *Hiawatha's Wooing* for Narrator and Orch. (1904); *King Robert of Sicily* for Narrator and Orch. (1906); songs.—**NS/LK/DM**

Cole, Vinson, black American tenor; b. Kansas City, Mo., Nov. 20, 1950. He studied at the Curtis Inst. of Music in Philadelphia, where he sang Werther while still a student in 1975; then was an apprentice at the Santa Fe Opera, and was chosen to create the role of Innis Brown in Ulysses Kay's *Jubilee* in Jackson, Miss., in 1976; that same year he made his European debut as Belmonte with the Welsh National Opera in Cardiff. From 1976 to 1980 he appeared at the Opera Theatre of St. Louis. He sang Nicolai's Fenton at the N.Y.C. Opera in 1981. In 1992 he was engaged as Donizetti's Edgardo in Detroit. After singing Nadir in *Les Pêcheurs de perles* in Seattle in 1994, he portrayed Jason in Cherubini's *Medea* in Athens in 1995. In 1996 he sang Renaud in Gluck's *Armide* at Milan's La Scala. He returned to Seattle as Werther in 1997, and then sang Idomeneo at the Lyric Opera in 1998. As a concert artist, he toured widely in the U.S. and abroad, appearing with major orchs. Among his admired operatic portrayals are Gluck's Orfeo, Percy in *Anna Bolena*, Des Grieux in *Manon*, Lensky, Gounod's Faust, and Bizet's Nadir.—**NS/LK/DM**

Coleman, Bill (actually, **William Johnson**), jazz trumpeter, flugelhornist, singer; b. Centerville, Ky., Aug. 4, 1904; d. Toulouse, France, Aug. 24, 1981. He moved with his family to Cincinnati in 1909. Coleman's early efforts were on clarinet and "C" melody sax, then he specialized on trumpet from about 1916, taking trumpet lessons from Wingie Carpenter. He made his

debut in an amateur band led by J. C. Higginbotham; also played in a roadhouse quintet with Edgar Hayes, and taught himself to read music. His first professional work was with Clarence Paige, then he joined a band led by Lloyd and Cecil Scott, moving with them to N.Y. in December 1927. He worked with the Scotts in N.Y. off and on through 1930 in various bands, and also played with Luis Russell on three different occasions (1929, 1931, 1932). Coleman spent the 1930s working with various leaders, including his first tour of Europe (with Lucky Millinder, June–October 1933). From late 1934–spring 1935, he was with Teddy Hill's orch; during this period, he also recorded with Fats Waller. In Sept. 1935, Coleman sailed to Europe to work with Freddy Taylor's band in Paris; he subsequently worked in Bombay, India (November 1936–April 1937) with Leon Abbey's Orch, returned to Paris for a stint with Willie Lewis (June 1937–December 1938), and then co-led the Harlem Rhythmakers Swing Stars in Cairo and Alexandria, Egypt. Finally, in March 1940 he returned to the U.S. Again, he worked with a number of leaders, staying on average four to six months with each band; highlights included stints with the Teddy Wilson Sextet (July 1940–May 1941), Andy Kirk (Sept. 1941–February 1942), Ellis Larkin's Trio (March–December 1943), and Mary Lou Williams's Trio (most of 1944). He then worked briefly in Los Angeles with John Kirby (early 1945) and Boston (June 1945), before undertaking USO tours for about a year, including concerts in the Philippines and Japan. After working with Sy Oliver (late 1946–47) and Billy Kyle's Sextet (late 1947–48), Coleman moved to France in December 1948. Other than vacations in the U.S. in 1954 and 1958, he lived in France for the remainder of his life. Coleman has led his own bands in France, Belgium, Switzerland, Holland, Sweden, Italy, Spain, and Germany and has made many appearances at European Jazz Festivals, including a guest spot with Count Basie at Antibes in 1961. He toured extensively in the decades up to his death, eventually limited to performing while seated because he was too weak to stand. Coleman died following cardiac and respiratory troubles in 1981.

DISC.: *Coleman Rarities* (1952); *Swingin' in Switzerland* (1957); *Great Parisian Session* (1960); *From Boogie to Funk* (1960); *Bill and the Boys* (1969); *Bill Coleman Meets Guy Lafitte* (1973); *Really I Do* (1980).

WRITINGS: *Trumpet Story: Souvenirs d'un Grand du Jazz.* Paris (Cana, 1981).

BIBL.: J. Chilton, *Bill Coleman on Record* (London, 1966); J. Evensmo, *Trumpets of Bill Coleman* (Olso, 1978).—**JC/LP**

Coleman, George (Edward), jazz/R&B tenor, alto and soprano saxophonist, leader, keyboardist; b. Memphis, Tenn., March 8, 1935. His background was in blues and R&B; he had two stints in B.B. King's band during the early and mid-1950s. He left Memphis for Chicago with Booker Little (1957), and the duo joined Max Roach's quintet (1958–59). Coleman then worked in several bands during the 1960s, most famously Miles Davis' quintet (1963–64), as well as groups led by Lionel Hampton, Lee Morgan, Elvin Jones, Shirley Scott, and Cedar Walton. He also worked with his wife, bassist/vocalist/organist Gloria Bell Coleman. He writes for groups of all sizes and plays many gigs at colleges. Coleman has been a leader since the late 1960s, heading quintets, quartets, and octets; his octet played at the Camden Jazz Festival (1981). His students include Ned Otter. During the 1990s, he has worked in a quartet that usually featured pianist Harold Mabern. He was part of a "Jazz Tenor Battle Royale" held at N.Y.'s Lincoln Center in the mid-1990s.

Disc.: *Revival* (1976); *Eastern Rebellion* (1976); *Meditation* (1977); *Big George* (1977); *Amsterdam After Dark* (1977); *Playing Changes* (1979); *At Yoshi's* (1987); *My Horns of Plenty* (1991); *Bongo Joe* (1992).

Bibl.: J. Alexander, *George Coleman's Transcribed Solos* (Houston, 1994).—MM/LP

Coleman, Ornette (Randolph Denard),

avant-garde jazz saxophonist, composer, trumpeter, violinist, and one of the major forces in the history of jazz; b. Fort Worth, Tex., March 9, 1930. His parents were Randolph and Rosa Coleman, both probably from Calvert, Tex. There was a piano in the house and his father loved to sing. His older sister, Truvenza "Trudy" (b. c. 1929), was a professional singer but has been retired since the late 1970s. Ornette was largely self-taught; he served his apprenticeship playing in carnival and R&B bands. He taught himself to play the alto saxophone and to read music in 1944, performing in school marching band. One year later, he formed his first band; a year after that, he switched to tenor, and played in numerous local R&B groups, including one led by Thomas "Red" Connors. Surrounded by racial segregation and poverty in Fort Worth, he took to the road by the age of 19 with a carnival band. He was dismissed from the tent show for playing bebop; he was stranded in New Orleans, then threatened by racist sheriffs in Miss. In Baton Rouge, a gang of roughnecks beat him up and threw his tenor off a hill, so he went back to the alto, which is still his principal horn. Coleman moved to Los Angeles with Pee Wee Crayton's blues band in 1950, and spent the better part of the 1950s there, working at various odd jobs, studying music theory, practicing and composing whenever he could. His approach to harmony was already unorthodox and led to his rejection by established musicians in Los Angeles. While working as an elevator operator, he studied harmony and played a Grafton plastic alto saxophone at obscure nightclubs. Until then, all jazz improvisation had been based on fixed harmonic patterns. In the "harmolodic theory" that Coleman developed in the 1950s, improvisers abandoned harmonic patterns ("chord changes") in order to improvise more extensively and directly upon melodic and expressive elements. Because the tonal centers of such music changed at the improviser's will, it became known as "free jazz."

Coleman continued to develop his own expression, and gradually a few musicians began to understand. He started playing with Ed Blackwell, Bobby Bradford, and later George Newman, Billy Higgins, Don Cherry, James Clay, and Charlie Haden. He worked his first gig as a leader with Cherry, Don Friedman, and Higgins at the Jazz Cellar in Vancouver for a week in 1957. Red Mitchell was instrumental in securing him his first recording date, *Something Else* (1958; rel. 1959). He played with Paul Bley at Los Angeles' Hillcrest Club later in 1958, and formed the nucleus of quartet with the other band members, Cherry, Higgins, and Charlie Haden. With the help of admirer John Lewis, he soon found himself recording for Atlantic and spending the summer of 1959 at the Lenox (Mass.) School of Jazz. The albums *The Shape of Jazz to Come* and *Change of the Century* shook the jazz world; his radical conception of structure and the urgent emotionality of his improvisations aroused widespread controversy. He made his first performance at N.Y.'s Five Spot on Nov. 17, 1959; the distinguished crowd included Leonard Bernstein, Gunther Schuller, Nesuhi and Ahmet Ertegun, John Hammond, and others. His recordings *Free Jazz* (1960), which used two simultaneously improvising jazz quartets, and *Beauty Is a Rare Thing*, in which he experimented with free meters and tempos, also proved influential.

There were periods of inactivity in the early 1960s as he decided to fight the establishment by charging more for his performances; he formed a trio in 1964 with David Izenzon and Charlie Moffett and toured Europe the next year. By then, he had switched to a Selmer metal saxophone. Coleman later traded his Grafton for a bassoon, which he only played once in concert. There were more accomplishments in the mid 1960s: new ensembles, pieces for classical chamber groups such as *Forms and Sounds* for Woodwind Quintet (1967), challenging film soundtracks, recordings with his son Denardo (from his marriage to poet Jayne Cortez; b. Los Angeles, Calif., April 19, 1956) from when he was 11 on, and solos on trumpet and violin, which he taught himself. In 1968 he added Dewey Redman, who joined him on two recordings with Elvin Jones and Jimmy Garrison and became a regular member of Coleman's group through 1972. He opened a loft, Artist House, in Manhattan's Soho area as center for exhibitions and concerts (1971). His classical ensemble writing continued to thrive into the 1970s; his orchestral masterpiece *Skies of America* was premiered at the Newport Jazz Festival (July 4, 1972) and he recorded it that year with the London Symphony Orch.

For much of the 1970s, Coleman performed irregularly, fed up with the music business, preferring instead to compose. Influenced by his experience of improvising with native musicians in the Rif Mountains of Morocco [The Master Musicians of Jajouka] in 1973, Coleman formed an electric band called Prime Time, whose music was a fusion of rock rhythms with harmonically free collective improvisations; this band remains his primary performance vehicle to this day. He added electric guitar, bass, and congas in 1975. Denardo is a member and also helps to manage his father's career. Ornette continued to write chamber music, such as *Sex Spy* (1977). In 1985 he recorded "Song X" and toured with Pat Metheny. In 1988 *Virgin Beauty* featured Grateful Dead guitarist Jerry Garcia, and Coleman also performed with the Dead that year. Younger converts to his method have included Ronald Shannon Jackson, James Blood Ulmer, and Jamaaldeen Tacuma.

Coleman's activities in the 1990s have included "Architecture in Motion" (1995), his first Harmolodic ballet, as well as work on the soundtracks for the films *Naked Lunch* (1991) and *Philadelphia*. He has won numerous honors and celebrations, including the Guggenheim (c. 1970), honorary degrees from the Univ. of Pa. (1989), Calif. Inst. of the Arts (1990), Boston Cons. of Music (1993), and the New School for Social Research; he also won the 1994 MacArthur Fellowship award and was elected to Amer. Acad. of Arts and Letters (1997). Ornette Coleman's multimedia show "Civilization" project, which completed its first leg on July 4, 1998 at the La Villette Jazz Festival in Paris, held its second half at the Lincoln Center Festival July 8–11, featuring performances of "Skies of America," "In All Languages," and the multimedia show, "Tone Dialing" with Lou Reed and Laurie Anderson. His goal is to complete a symphony, *The Oldest Language*, "conceived as a performance piece for ethnic players from around the world.

Coleman's playing and writing have inspired two generations of "avant-garde" players, and like John Cage, his ideas have had an even broader impact than his music. His writing, which has been derided as incoherent, is better perceived as poetry. For example, he wrote on the back of *This Is Our Music* that his life was pretty much the same as anybody's—"Born, work, sad and happy and etc." His personal speech is equally poetic, and all his acquaintances have their stories—for example, when he met the wife of his guitarist, Kenny Wessel, and she told him she didn't play an instrument but was an anthropologist, he said, "Well, then you play the world!" He told Juilliard students at a rehearsal with Joel Sachs in the late 1990s, "It's not an idea yet, so it doesn't have a tempo. If you hear a different note from the one that's written, play the one you hear and it will sound like it was written. You played that half step like a whole step. (Sachs says this means it lacked the tension of a half step.)" He told Henry Martin: "If you go up from C to D it's a whole step, but down again from D to C is not really a whole step." His ideas about musical relationships developed into what he calls Harmolodics: relationships between harmony and melodic ideas.

DISC.: *Music of Ornette Coleman: Something Else!!* (1958); *Twins* (1959); *Tomorrow Is the Question!* (1959); *Shape of Jazz to Come* (1959); *Change of the Century* (1959); *This Is Our Music* (1960); *Jazz Abstractions* (1960); *Free Jazz* (1960); *Ornette!* (1961); *Ornette on Tenor* (1961); *Town Hall Concert* (1962); *Who's Crazy* (1965); *At the "Golden Circle" in Stockholm, Vols. 1 & 2* (1965); *Empty Foxhole* (1966); *Saints and Soldiers* (1967); *Forms and Sounds* (1967); *N.Y. Is Now* (1968); *Love Call* (1968); *Ornette at 12* (1969); *Crisis* (1969); *Friends and Neighbors* (1970); *Science Fiction* (1971); *Broken Shadows* (1971); *Skies of America* (1972); *Dancing in Your Head* (1973); *Body Meta* (1976); *Soapsuds, Soapsuds* (1977); *Of Human Feelings* (1979); *Prime Design Time Design* (1985); *Opening the Caravan of Dreams* (1985); *In All Languages* (1985); *Virgin Beauty* (1988); *Jazzbuhne Berlin '88* (1988); *Languages* (1994); *Tone Dialing* (1995); *Colors* (1996); *Sound Museum "Hidden Man"* (1996); *Sound Museum "Three Women"* (1996).

WRITINGS: With J. Litweiler, *Ornette Coleman: A Harmolodic Life* (London, 1992).

BIBL.: D. Wild, M. Cuscuna, *Ornette Coleman 1958–1979: A Discography* (Ann Arbor, 1980); J. Y. LeBec, *Ornette Coleman* (Montpellier, 1990).—**LP**

Coleridge-Taylor, Samuel, important English composer, conductor, and teacher; b. London, Aug. 15, 1875; d. Croydon, Sept. 1, 1912. His father was a black Sierra Leone physician and his mother was English. After violin lessons with Joseph Beckwith in Croydon, he entered the Royal Coll. of Music in London in 1890 to continue his violin training; in 1892 he became a composition student of Stanford there, and in 1893 he won a composition scholarship; before completing his studies in 1897, he had several of his works premiered there. His first public success came with his Ballade in A minor for Orch., which was premiered at the Three Choirs Festival in Gloucester on Sept. 14, 1898. It was soon followed by what proved to be his most successful score, the cantata *Hiawatha's Wedding Feast*, which was first performed under Stanford's direction at the Royal Coll. of Music on Nov. 11, 1898. It was subsequently performed widely in Europe and the U.S. Although he continued to compose in earnest, he never duplicated this popular success. He also was active as a conductor, leading various orchestral and choral aggregations. He likewise was engaged in teaching, serving as prof. of composition at Trinity Coll. of Music (from 1903) and at the Guildhall School of Music (from 1910) in London. In 1904, 1906, and 1910 he visited the U.S. While greatly influenced by Dvořák, Coleridge-Taylor's works also reveal a fascination with black subjects and melodies.

WORKS: DRAMATIC: *Dream Lovers*, operatic romance (1898); *The Gitanos*, cantata-operetta (1898); *Thelma*, opera (1907–09). Incidental music to Stephen Phillips's *Herod* (1900), *Ulysses* (1901–02), *Nero* (1906), and *Faust* (1908); also to Noyes's *The Forest of Wild Thyme* (1910) and Shakespeare's *Othello* (1910–11). **ORCH.:** *Ballade* for Violin and Orch. (1895); Sym. (London, March 6, 1896); *Legende* for Violin and Orch. (1897); *4 Characteristic Waltzes* (1899); *Ballade* (Gloucester, Sept. 13, 1898); *Romance* for Violin and Orch. (c. 1899); *Solemn Prelude* (Worcester, Sept. 13, 1899); (4) *Scenes from an Everyday Romance*, suite (London, May 24, 1900); *Idyll* (Gloucester, Sept. 11, 1901); *Toussaint l'Ouverture* (London, Oct. 26, 1901); *Ethiopa Saluting the Colours*, march (1902); *4 Novelletten* for Strings, Tambourine, and Triangle (1903); *Symphonic Variations on an African Air* (London, June 14, 1906); *Fantasiestück* for Cello and Orch. (New Brighton, July 7, 1907); *A Lovely Little Dream* for Strings and Harmonium (c. 1909); *The Bamboula*, rhapsodic dance (Norfolk, Conn., June 1, 1910); *Petite suite de concert* (1910); Violin Concerto (Norfolk, Conn., June 1912); *From the Prairie*, rhapsody (1914). **CHAMBER:** (3) *Hiawathan Sketches* for Violin and Piano (1893); Piano Quintet (c. 1893); Clarinet Sonata (c. 1893); Nonet for Piano, Strings, and Woodwinds (1894); *Suite de* [4] *pièces* for Violin, Piano, and Organ (1894); (5) *Fantasiestücke* for String Quartet (1895); *2 Romantic Pieces* for Violin and Piano (c. 1895); Clarinet Quintet (1895); String Quartet (1896); *Gypsy Suite* for Violin and Piano (1897); *Valse Caprice* for Violin and Piano (1898); *Ballade* for Violin and Piano (1907); *Variations on an Original Theme* for Cello (1907); Violin Sonata (1912); *Variations* for Cello and Piano (publ. 1918); also many piano pieces, including *2 Moorish Tone-pictures* (1897); *African Suite* (1897); *3 Silhouettes* (1897); *24 Negro Melodies* (1905); (4) *Scènes de ballet* (1906); (5) *Forest Scenes* (1907); *Three-fours*, valse suite (1909). **VOCAL:** Scenes from *The Song of Hiawatha*, cantata (1: *Hiawatha's Wedding Feast* for

Tenor, Chorus, and Orch., London, Nov. 11, 1898; 2: *The Death of Minnehaha* for Soprano, Baritone, Chorus, and Orch., Hanley, Oct. 26, 1899; 3: Overture, Norwich, Oct. 6, 1899; 4: *Hiawatha's Departure* for Soprano, Tenor, Baritone, Chorus, and Orch., London, March 22, 1900); *The Soul's Expression*, 4 sonnets for Chorus and Orch. (Hereford, Sept. 13, 1900); *The Blind Girl of Castél*, cantata for Soprano, Baritone, Chorus, and Orch. (Leeds, Oct. 9, 1901); *Meg Blane*, rhapsody for Mezzo-soprano, Chorus, and Orch. (Sheffield, Oct. 3, 1902); *The Atonement*, sacred cantata for Soloists, Chorus, and Orch. (Hereford, Sept. 10, 1903); *5 Choral Ballads* for Baritone, Chorus, and Orch. (Norwich, Oct. 25, 1905); *Kubla Khan*, rhapsody for Mezzo-soprano, Chorus, and Orch. (1905); *Endymion's Dream*, cantata for Soprano, Tenor, Chorus, and Orch. (1909; Brighton, Feb. 4, 1910); *Bon-bon Suite*, cantata for Baritone, Chorus, and Orch. (1909); *A Tale of Old Japan*, cantata for Soloists, Chorus, and Orch. (London, Dec. 6, 1911); also works for Solo Voice, including *Zara's Ear-rings* for Voice and Orch. (1895) and songs, part songs, and choruses with piano accompaniment.

BIBL.: W. Berwick Sayers, *S. C.-T., Musician: His Life and Letters* (London, 1915; 2nd ed., rev., 1927); J. Coleridge-Taylor, *S. C.-T.: A Memory Sketch* (London, 1942); idem, *C.-T.: Genius and Musician* (London, 1943); W. Tortolano, *S. C.-T.: Anglo-Black Composer, 1875–1912* (Metuchen, N.J., 1977); A. Coleridge-Taylor, *The Heritage of S. C.-T.* (London, 1979); J. Thompson, *S. C.-T.: The Development of His Compositional Style* (Metuchen, N.J., 1994); G. Self, *The Hiawatha Man: S. C.-T.* (Brookfield, Vt., 1995). —NS/LK/DM

Coles, Johnny (actually, **John**), trumpeter, flugelhornist; b. Trenton N.J., July 3, 1926; d. Philadelphia, Pa., Dec. 21, 1997. He was mainly self-taught, although he had some training while playing in a military band in 1941. He was an important part of the Philadelphia scene, working there since at least 1946 with John Coltrane, Jimmy Heath, Ray Bryant and many others. He and Coltrane toured with Eddie Vinson (1948–49); Coles worked with Earl Bostic in the mid-1950s, as well as with James Moody (1956–58) and Oscar Pettiford (in Greenwich Village; 1958). He worked with arranger/composer Gil Evans's band from 1958–64, and then played on and off with Charles Mingus through most of the 1960s In the late 1960s–early 1970s, he worked with the Herbie Hancock Sextet (1968–69), briefly with the Ray Charles Orch. (1969–70), and then with Duke Ellington's Orch. (1970–74). He rejoined Charles for two more years after Ellington died, then played with Art Blakey (1976), and Dameronia and Mingus Dynasty through the early 1980s. He moved to Los Angeles in 1985 and worked for a year with Count Basie. However, his health had already begun to fail, and he moved back to Philadelphia in 1990. He was sporadically active until his death, although he suffered from long periods of illness in 1995 and shortly before his death.

DISC.: *Warm Sound* (1961); *Little Johnny C* (1963); *Katumbo* (1971); *New Morning* (1982).—LP

Coletti, Filippo, noted Italian baritone; b. Anagni, May 11, 1811; d. there, June 13, 1894. He studied with Alessandro Busti in Naples, making his debut there at the Teatro del Fondo in Rossini's *Il Turco in Italia* in 1834. He subsequently established himself as a distinguished interpreter of roles in operas by Bellini, Donizetti, and Verdi.—NS/LK/DM

Colgrass, Michael (Charles), American composer; b. Chicago, April 22, 1932. He received training in percussion and composition at the Univ. of Ill. (Mus.B., 1956), and also studied composition with Foss at the Berkshire Music Center in Tanglewood (summers, 1952, 1954) and Milhaud at the Aspen (Colo.) Music School (summer, 1953). He then took private composition lessons with Riegger (1958–59) and Ben Weber (1959–62) in N.Y. After working as a freelance solo percussionist in N.Y. (1956–67), he settled in Toronto, where he devoted himself fully to composition. In 1964 and 1968 he held Guggenheim fellowships, and in 1978 he was awarded the Pulitzer Prize in Music for his *Déjà vu*, a concerto for four Percussionists and Orch. In his output, he has utilized various styles and techniques, with percussion often playing a significant melorhythmic role.

WORKS: DRAMATIC: *Virgil's Dream*, music theater (1967); *Nightingale, Inc.*, comic opera (1971); *Something's Gonna Happen*, children's musical (1978). ORCH.: *Divertimento* for 8 Drums, Piano, and Strings (1960); *Rhapsodic Fantasy* for 15 Drums and Orch. (1965); *Sea Shadow* (1966); *As Quiet as...* (1966); *Auras* for Harp and Orch. (1973); *Concertmasters* for 3 Violins and Orch. (1975); *Letter from Mozart* (1976); *Déjà vu* for 4 Percussionists and Orch. (1977); *Delta* for Clarinet, Violin, and Percussion Orch. (1979); *Memento* for 2 Pianos and Orch. (1982); *Chaconne* for Viola and Orch. (Toronto, Sept. 27, 1984); *Demon* for Amplified Piano, Percussion, Tape, Radio, and Orch. (1984); *The Schubert Birds* (1989); *Snow Walker* for Organ and Orch. (1990); *Arctic Dreams* for Symphonic Band (1991). CHAMBER: *3 Brothers* for 9 Percussion (1951); *Percussion Music* for 4 Percussion (1953); *Chamber Music* for 4 Drums and String Quartet (1954); Percussion Quintet (1955); *Variations* for 4 Drums and Viola (1957); *Fantasy Variations* for Solo Percussion and 6 Percussion (1960); *Rhapsody* for Clarinet, Violin, and Piano (1962); *Light Spirit* for Flute, Viola, Guitar, and Percussion (1963); *Night of the Raccoon* for Harp, Flute, Keyboard, and Percussion (1978); *Flashbacks* for 5 Brass (1979); *Winds of Nagual—A Musical Fable* for Wind Ensemble (Boston, Feb. 14, 1985); *Strangers: Irreconcilable Variations* for Clarinet, Viola, and Piano (1986); String Quartet, *Folklines* (1987); piano pieces. VOCAL: *The Earth's a Baked Apple* for Chorus and Orch. (1969); *New People* for Mezzo-soprano, Viola, and Piano (1969); *Image of Man* for 4 Solo Voices, Chorus, and Orch. (1974); *Theatre of the Universe* for Solo Voices, Chorus, and Orch. (1975); *Best Wishes, U.S.A.* for 4 Solo Voices, Double Chorus, 2 Jazz Bands, Folk Instruments, and Orch. (1976).—NS/LK/DM

Colin, Pierre, French composer and organist who flourished in the mid-16th century. He was master of the choirboys (c. 1539–61) and organist (1562–65?) at St. Lazarus Cathedral in Autun. He was a fine composer of sacred works, including 36 particularly notable motets. Other works include 26 masses, ten Magnificats, and some chansons.—LK/DM

Colista, Lelio, significant Italian composer; b. Rome, Jan. 13, 1629; d. there, Oct. 13, 1680. His career was centered on his native city, where he served as maestro di cappella at S. Marcello in the 1660s, and as first lutenist for the Arciconfraternità del Ss. Crocifisso. In the 1670s he was active at S. Luigi dei Francesi and in 1675 was made a member of the Arciconfraternità delle Sacre Stimmate at S. Francesco. Colista was the foremost Italian composer of instrumental music of his era. He excelled in writing trio sonatas. Among his other works were six sinfonias for plucked instruments, church sonatas, oratorios, and cantatas.

BIBL.: H. Wessely-Kropik, *L. C., ein römischer Meister vor Corelli: Leben und Umwelt* (Vienna, 1961).—**LK/DM**

Colla, Giuseppe,

Italian composer; b. Parma, Aug. 4, 1731?; d. there, March 16, 1806. He was maestro di cappella at the court of Duke Ferdinand of Parma (from 1766), where he also engaged in teaching. In 1780 he married **Lucrezia Aguiari**, who sang in his operas in Italy, Paris, and London.

WORKS: DRAMATIC: O p e r a : *Adriano in Siria* (Milan, Dec. 31, 1762); *Tigrane* (Parma, 1766 or 1767); *Enea in Cartagine* (Turin, Dec. 26, 1769); *Vologeso* (Venice, May 24, 1770); *L'eroe cinese* (Genoa, Aug. 8, 1771); *Andromeda* (Turin, Dec. 26, 1771); *Didone* (Turin, Carnival 1773); *Tolomeo* (Milan, Dec. 26, 1773); *Sicotencal* (Pavia, 1776). **OTHER:** Sacred music. —**LK/DM**

Collard, Jean-Philippe,

French pianist; b. Mareuil-sur-Ay, Jan. 27, 1948. He began piano studies as a child; then studied at the Paris Cons. with Pierre Sancan, graduating at age 16 with a premier prix; subsequently won several honors, including third prize in the Long-Thibaud Competition in 1969. Collard appeared as soloist with leading European orchs. and in recitals. He made his American debut in 1973 with the San Francisco Sym.; then made a number of coast-to-coast tours of the U.S.—**NS/LK/DM**

Colles, H(enry) C(ope),

eminent English music scholar; b. Bridgnorth, Shropshire, April 20, 1879; d. London, March 4, 1943. He studied at the Royal Coll. of Music in London with Parry (music history), Walter Alcock (organ), and Davies (theory). Subsequently he received an organ scholarship to Worcester Coll., Oxford; then entered the Univ. of Oxford, obtaining his B.A. (1902), Mus.Bac. (1903), and M.A. (1907) degrees; later received an honorary Mus.Doc. (1932). In 1905 he became music critic of the Academy; from 1905 to 1911 he was asst. music critic and from 1911 to 1943 chief music critic of the *Times*; in 1919 he was appointed teacher of music history and criticism at the Royal Coll. of Music; was also music director of Cheltenham Ladies' Coll. He was the editor of the third and fourth eds. of *Grove's Dictionary of Music and Musicians* (1927–29 and 1939–40); also edited vol. VII of *The Oxford History of Music* (1934).

WRITINGS: *Brahms* (1908); *The Growth of Music: A Study in Music History for Schools* (3 vols., 1912–16; 3rd ed., 1956); *Voice and Verse, a Study in English Song* (1928); *The Chamber Music of Brahms* (1933); *English Church Music* (1933); *The Royal College of Music; A Jubilee Record, 1883–1933* (1933); *On Learning Music* (1940); *Walford Davies* (1942); *Essays and Lectures* (1945). —**NS/LK/DM**

Collette, Buddy,

American musician; b. Los Angeles, Calif., Aug. 6, 1921. A pillar of the Los Angeles jazz scene since the early 1940s, he is a fine improvisor on alto and tenor sax, clarinet and especially flute, an instrument on which he was an early innovator. Though best known for his long-time friendship and musical association with Charles Mingus, he also played an important role breaking down the color barrier in L.A. studios in the early 1950s. He took piano lessons as a youth before moving on to various wind instruments. He played with a number of bands, including Les Hite, in the early 1940s, and then led a dance band in the Navy. He founded the short-lived Stars of Swing with Lucky Thompson, Britt Woodman, and Mingus in 1946, then became a busy freelancer, working for such leading West Coast bandleaders as Benny Carter, Gerald Wilson, Johnny Otis, Louis Jordan, and Edgar Hayes. He became the first black musician to hold a staff position in a Los Angeles studio band, playing on Groucho Marx's TV and radio shows (1951–55), among others. He gained widespread exposure with the original edition of drummer Chico Hamilton's popular "cello" quintet (the group was featured in the 1958 film, *Jazz on a Summer's Day*, about the Newport Jazz Festival) and made a number of strong recordings of his own for Contemporary in the late 1950s. In 1964 he gained attention for organizing the band Mingus triumphed with at Monterey, and two years later he assembled a big band for Dizzy Gillespie's Monterey appearance. He continues to work and teach around L.A., and though he has never achieved national attention commensurate with his talents, a number of his students—including flutist James Newton, who can be heard with Collette on *Flute Talk* —have gone on to become major figures. In 1994 Issues Records released a two-CD "audio biography," a fascinating, episodic oral history covering his career and his relationships with Mingus, Eric Dolphy, Groucho, and the racial and Cold War politics of the 1950s.

DISC.: *Tanganyika* (1954); *Man of Many Parts* (1956); *Nice Day with Buddy Collette* (1957); *Jazz Loves Paris* (1958); *Flute Talk* (1988).—**AG**

Colley, Scott,

jazz bassist; b. Los Angeles, Nov. 24, 1963. From the age of 13, he played in jazz clubs around the Los Angeles area. In 1984 he received a full scholarship to Calif. Inst. for the Arts (B.M.), where he focused on composition and jazz studies. During his time, he studied simultaneously with Charlie Haden and Fred Tinsley (bassist with the Los Angeles Philharmonic). In 1986, after Colley graduated and moved to N.Y., he began touring and recording with Carmen McRae. He has performed and recorded with Dizzy Gillespie, Clifford Jordan, Roy Hargrove, and Art Farmer, touring Europe, Japan, and South America. He has also performed and recorded with John Scofield, James Newton, Fred Hersch, Joe Henderson, Billy Hart, Mike Stern, Thelonious Monk Jr., Phil Woods, and Jim Hall. In 1997 he toured with Joe Lovano, Jim Hall, and Yoron Israel; he also played Japan with Toots Thielemans and Bobby Hutcherson. Colley also did two European tours with Lost Tribe and worked in a trio with Ravi Coltrane and Al Foster and in a duo and trio with Jim Hall.

DISC.: *Portable Universe* (1997); *This Place* (1997).—**LP**

Collier, Marie, Australian soprano; b. Ballarat, April 16, 1926; d. in a fall from a window in London, Dec. 7, 1971. She studied with Wielaert and Gertrude Johnson in Melbourne, where she made her operatic debut as Santuzza. She then completed her training in Milan with Ugo Benvenuti Giusti (1955–56). In 1956 she made her first appearance at London's Covent Garden as Musetta, where she sang regularly until her death; she also appeared at the Sadler's Wells Opera in London. From 1965 to 1968 she sang at the San Francisco Opera. On March 17, 1967, she created the role of Christine Mannon in Levy's *Mourning Becomes Electra* at her Metropolitan Opera debut in N.Y.; she remained on its roster until 1968, and then returned for the 1969–70 season. Collier was highly regarded for her performances of contemporary operas, excelling in such roles as Kát'a Kabanová, Emilia Marty in *The Makropulos Affair*, Jenůfa, Marie in *Wozzeck*, Katerina Izmailova, Walton's Cressida, and Hecuba in Tippett's *King Priam*, which she created.—**NS/LK/DM**

Collier, Ron(ald William), Canadian composer, arranger, conductor, trombonist, and teacher; b. Coleman, near Lethridge, Alberta, July 3, 1930. He studied in Vancouver (1943–50), where he played trombone in the Kitsilano Boys' Band. Following composition training with Gordon Delamont in Toronto (1951–54), he became the first jazz composer to receive a Canada Council grant, which allowed him to pursue studies with George Russell and Hall Overton in N.Y. (1961–62). He played trombone in dance bands and orchs., and eventually led his own jazz groups and big band. In 1972 he became composer-in-residence at Humber Coll. in Toronto, where he taught composition and arranging from 1974. Collier was a principal figure in the Third Stream movement in Canada.

WORKS: Sonata for Piano and Jazz Quintet (c. 1955); *The City* for Narrator-Singer and Orch. (1960); *Requiem for JFK* for Big Band (1964); *Hear Me Talkin' to Ya* for Narrator-Singer and Octet (1964; in collaboration with Don Francks); *Aurora Borealis*, ballet (1966); *Carneval* for Narrator, Flugelhorn, and Orch. (1969); *Celebration* for Piano and Orch. (1972; in collaboration with Duke Ellington); *Humber Suite* for Big Band (1973); *Jupiter* for Big Band (1974); *Reflections on 3* for Wind Sym. (1980); *Never in Nevis* for Big Band (1983); *4 Kisses* for Big Band (1983); *To Prussia with Love and a Little Jive* for Jazz Ensemble (1988); also film and television scores; arrangements.—**NS/LK/DM**

Collin (Colin) de Blamont, François, prominent French composer; b. Versailles, Nov. 22, 1690; d. there, Feb. 14, 1760. He commenced his musical training with his father, Nicolas Colin, who served as ordinaire de la musique du roi, then entered the service of the Duchess of Maine when he was 17, becoming a pupil of Lalande. In 1719 he was made surintendant de la musique de la chambre, and, upon Lalande's death, was named his successor as a maître de musique de la chambre (1726). He received Letters of Nobility (1750) and was made Chevalier of the Order of St. Michel

(1751). With Fuzelier, he created the ballet héroïque with their *Festes grecques et romaines* (1723). He publ. the polemical book *Essaie sur les goûts anciens et modernes de la musique françoise relativement aux paroles d'opéra* (Paris, 1754), which was aimed primarily at Rousseau.

WORKS: DRAMATIC: *Les Festes grecques et romaines*, ballet héroïque (Paris, July 13, 1723; in collaboration with Fuzelier); *Le Retour des dieux sur la terre*, divertissement (for the marriage of Louis XV, 1725); *La Caprice d'Erato ou Les Caractères de la Musique*, divertissement (1730); *Endymion*, pastorale héroïque (Paris, May 17, 1731); *Les Caractères de l'amour*, ballet héroïque (1736); *Les Fêtes de Thétis*, ballet héroïque (Versailles, Jan. 14, 1750). **OTHER:** Several secular cantatas; numerous "airs sérieux et à boire"; a vol. of motets, which includes a *Te Deum* (Paris, 1732).

BIBL.: C. Massip, *F. C.d.B.: Musicien du roi* (diss., Paris Cons., 1971).—**NS/LK/DM**

Collingwood, Lawrance (Arthur), English conductor and composer; b. London, March 14, 1887; d. Killin, Perthshire, Dec. 19, 1982. He studied at the Guildhall School of Music in London and later at Exeter Coll., Oxford (1907–11). In 1912 he went to Russia and took courses at the St. Petersburg Cons. with Glazunov, Wihtol, Steinberg, and Tcherepnin; in 1918 he returned to England and became active as a conductor; was principal conductor (1931–41) and music director (1941–47) at Sadler's Wells in London. In 1948 he was made a Commander of the Order of the British Empire. His compositions include two operas, *Macbeth* (London, April 12, 1934) and *The Death of Tintagiles* (concert perf., London, April 16, 1950); Piano Concerto; Piano Quartet; 2 piano sonatas.—**NS/LK/DM**

Collins, Anthony (Vincent Benedictus), English conductor and composer; b. Hastings, Sept. 3, 1893; d. Los Angeles, Dec. 11, 1963. He studied violin at the Royal Coll. of Music in London, and composition there with Holst; was then a violist in the London Sym. Orch. and in the orch. of the Royal Opera House, Covent Garden; from 1936 he pursued a career as conductor, appearing with the Carl Rosa Opera Co., the Sadler's Wells Opera, and the London Sym. Orch. From 1939 to 1945 he conducted and composed for films in the U.S. After pursuing his career again in England (1945–53), he settled in the U.S. He wrote four operas, two syms., two violin concertos, chamber music, and various lighter pieces.—**NS/LK/DM**

Collins, Arthur (Francis), prominent American minstrel and novelty singer; b. Philadelphia, Feb. 7, 1864; d. Tice, Fla., Aug. 3, 1933. Collins was originally a vaudeville star who established himself in the infant record industry in his mid-30s. He recorded prolifically, frequently performing the same song for several different labels. His early hits included such comic fare as "When You Ain't Got No More Money, Well, You Needn't Come Around" (1899) and "Bill Bailey, Won't You Please Come Home" (1900).

In 1901, Collins teamed up with Byron Harlan, Joe Natus, and A. D. Madeira in the Big Four Quartet for the hit "Good-Bye, Dolly Gray." He and Harlan formed a more permanent association the same year, his baritone voice providing a humorous contrast to Harlan's high tenor. The pairing resulted in such successful recordings as "Alexander's Ragtime Band" (1911) and "When the Midnight Choo Choo Leaves for Alabam'" (1913), both written by Irving Berlin. From 1909 to 1918, Collins was a member of the Peerless Quartet; during his tenure with the group he sang on such hits as "Let Me Call You Sweetheart" (1911), "I Didn't Raise My Boy to Be a Soldier" (1915), and "Over There" (1917). But his biggest hit was the solo monologue "The Preacher and the Bear" (1905), about a minister who goes hunting on Sunday and ends up treed by his prey. The title sold two million copies and was the best-selling record in history until 1920. (Phil Harris charted with a remake in 1947.) All told, Collins appeared on more than 30 major record hits between 1899 and 1918, making him one of the most successful American recording artists of the first two decades of the 20th century.—WR

Collins, John (Elbert),

pop-jazz guitarist best remembered as a member of Nat "King" Cole's trio; b. Montgomery, Ala., Sept. 20, 1913. His mother was pianist-bandleader Georgia Gorham. He originally played clarinet, then switched to guitar, moved to Chicago and studied with Frank Langham. He worked (with his mother) in trumpeter Elbert B. Topp's Orch. at Radio Inn, Chicago, in 1932, then played regularly in his mother's band until early 1935. He was with Jimmy Bell and his Tampa Tunesters in spring 1935, then worked at Three Deuces, Chicago, with Art Tatum and Zutty Singleton before joining Roy Eldridge in Sept. 1936. He performed with Roy Eldridge in Chicago and N.Y. until 1940. In 1941–42 he worked for various leaders, including Lester Young (early 1941), Fletcher Henderson, and Benny Carter (1942). He served in the U.S. Army until 1946, then he joined the Slam Stewart Trio (spring 1946–48). Collins was in Paris in the Errol Garner Trio (May 1948), then worked mainly with pianist Billy Taylor until early 1951 (including brief spells with Coleman Hawkins, 1949, and Artie Shaw, late 1950). He was with Art Tatum Trio (May–August 1951), and then joined the Nat "King" Cole Trio on Sept. 5, 1951, and remained until that leader's death in 1965. During the late 1960s Collins continued playing regularly, including a long spell with vocalist Bobby Troup's Trio (1965–71). He worked with Cat Anderson in Calif. (spring 1971) and led his own quartet during the 1970s and 1980s, including a tour of France and Spain in 1983. He worked with Carmen McRae in 1988, and then gigged and taught private guitar lessons around Los Angeles in the early 1990s.—JC/LP

Collins, Judy,

folk-pop guitarist, pianist, and singer with a clear soprano voice; b. Seattle, Wash., May 1, 1939. Judy Collins moved as a child to Los Angeles, then Denver, Colo., with her family. She began classical piano lessons at the age of five, and studied for eight years under female symphony conductor Antonia Brico. Making her classical piano debut at 13, she took up guitar at 15 and began singing in Boulder, Colo., folk clubs at 19. At the beginning of the 1960s, Collins moved to Chicago, then N.Y., where she immersed herself in the burgeoning Greenwich Village folk music scene. Signed to Elektra Records in 1961, she recorded two albums of standard folk fare before recording protest songs such as Bob Dylan's "Masters of War" and Woody Guthrie's "Deportees." She subsequently began recording the songs by then-unknown songwriters. *Concert* contained Tom Paxton's "The Last Thing on My Mind," and her *5th Album* included Richard Farina's "Pack Up Your Sorrows," Eric Andersen's "Thirsty Boots," and Gordon Lightfoot's "Early Morning Rain," as well as three Bob Dylan songs.

With *In My Life*, Judy Collins broke away from the folk singer role and established herself as a performer of a wide range of contemporary material. The album contained Dylan's "Tom Thumb's Blues," Farina's "Hard Lovin' Loser" (her first albeit minor hit), Randy Newman's "I Think It's Gonna Rain Today," and two Leonard Cohen songs. The popularity of one of those songs, "Suzanne," effectively launched the musical career of poet and novelist Cohen. *Wildflowers*, the best-selling album of her career, included two of her own songs, plus two more Cohen songs and two songs by Joni Mitchell. One of these, "Both Sides Now," became Collins's first major hit and spurred the career of Mitchell. *Who Knows Where the Time Goes* continued the presentation of outstanding contemporary material with the inclusion of Cohen's "Bird on a Wire," Robin Williamson's "The First Boy (Girl) I Loved," Ian Tyson's "Someday Soon," and Sandy Denny's title song.

After *Whales and Nightingales*, which yielded her second major hit with the traditional gospel song "Amazing Grace," and two other albums, Judy Collins withdrew from music to produce and codirect a documentary film on the life of her former piano teacher, Antonia Brico. The film, entitled *Antonia: A Portrait of the Woman*, premiered in September 1974 and garnered an Academy Award in 1975.

Judy Collins moved fully into the pop field with her recording of Stephen Sondheim's "Send in the Clowns," a moderate hit in 1975 and a major hit upon re-release in 1977. She achieved a minor hit with "Hard Time for Lovers" in 1979, the year she debuted in the Nev. casino circuit.

She continued to perform six months a year, appearing with symphony orchestras and at concerts and supper clubs around the country. Following 1984's *Home Again*, Elektra Records dropped Collins from its roster and she subsequently recorded two albums for the small Gold Castle label, including *Trust Your Heart*, which also served as the title to her autobiography. In 1990 Collins switched to Columbia for *Fires of Eden*, moving to Geffen for 1993's *Judy Sings Dylan*. In 1995 Pocket Books published Judy Collins's first novel, *Shameless*, the title of her second album for yet another label, Mesa Records.

Along with Joan Baez, Collins set the standard for female folk artists in the early 1960s. Popular as a protest singer after her second album, Collins demonstrated impeccable taste in her selection of material during the middle and late 1960s, popularizing the songs of then-obscure songwriters such as Gordon Lightfoot, Joni Mitchell, Randy Newman, Leonard Cohen, and others. She was instrumental in launching the career of Cohen and Mitchell with her recordings of "Suzanne" and "Both Sides Now" in 1966 and 1967, respectively. She matured into a cabaret-pop singer of the first rank.

WRITINGS: *Trust Your Heart: An Autobiography* (Boston, 1987); *Shameless* (N.Y., 1995); *Singing Lessons: A Memoir of Love, Loss, Hope and Healing* (N.Y., 1998).

DISC.: *A Maid of Constant Sorrow* (1961); *Golden Apples of the Sun* (1962); *No. 3* (1963); *Concert* (1964); *5th Album* (1965); *In My Life* (1966); *False True Lovers* (1967); *Wildflowers* (1967); *Who Knows Where the Time Goes* (1968); *Recollections* (1969); *Whales and Nightingales* (1970); *Living* (1971); *Colors of the Day* (1972); *True Stories and Other Dreams* (1973); *Judith* (1975); *Bread and Roses* (1976); *So Early in the Spring: The First Fifteen Years* (1977); *Hard Time for Lovers* (1979); *Running for My Life* (1980); *Times of Our Lives* (1982); *Home Again* (1984); *Trust Your Heart* (1987); *Sanity and Grace* (1989); *Fires of Eden* (1990); *Judy Sings Dylan: Just Like a Woman* (1993); *Come Rejoice! A Judy Collins Christmas* (1994); *Shameless* (1995). Richard Stoltzman: *Innervoices* (1989).

BIBL.: Vivian Claire, *Judy Collins* (N.Y., 1977).—**BH**

Collins, Lee(ds),

New Orleans–style jazz trumpeter, singer; b. New Orleans, La., Oct. 17, 1901; d. Chicago, Ill., July 3, 1960. His father was a trumpeter; his uncle was a trombonist. He started on trumpet at 12, with lessons from his father and "Professor" Jim Humphrey. At 15 he did his first regular playing at the Zulu's Club, then with Pops Foster organized the Young Eagles. In 1917–18 Collins worked with the Columbia Band and the Young Tuxedo Orch., while he continued playing with the Young Eagles. He played with Bud Roussel's Band, Papa Celestin, Jessie Jackson's Golden Leaf Orch., and Zutty Singleton (1919–22); had a residency at the Cadillac Club, then toured Fla. with his own band (1923). In 1924 Collins moved to Chicago to join King Oliver, recorded with Jelly Roll Morton, and then returned to New Orleans. He played with several local leaders through the end of the decade, except for a brief tour with "Professor" Sherman Cook's Revue. Collins co-led band for Jones-Collins' "Astoria Hot Eight" recordings (1929). In 1930 he moved briefly to N.Y., worked with Luis Russell Band replacing Henry "Red" Allen who was vacationing in New Orleans. From 1931 through 1950, he mostly did club work in Chicago, working with many different New Orleans–style bands. In 1951 he toured Europe with Mezz Mezzrow, but had to leave the tour due to illness; he returned to Chicago and then played with Joe Sullivan's band in the summer of 1953 in San Francisco. He went again to Europe with Mezzrow in fall 1954, and was again sidetracked by illness. He returned to Chicago, then suffered a stroke. For the last years of his life Collins was musically inactive due to chronic emphysema.

DISC.: Jones-Collins: "Astoria Hot Eight" (1929).

BIBL.: L. Collins, M. Collins, F. J. Gillis, J. W. Miner, *Oh, Didn't He Ramble: The Life Story of Lee Collins* (Urbana, 1989).—**JC/LP**

Collins, Michael,

remarkable English clarinetist; b. London, Jan. 27, 1962. He commenced clarinet training when he was ten, and later pursued his studies with David Hamilton at the Royal Coll. of Music in London; later was a student of Thea King. While still a student, he attracted notice as winner of the BBC-TV Young Musician of the Year prize. In 1984 he made his debut at the London Promenade concerts as soloist in Thea Musgrave's Clarinet Concerto, and that same year he appeared for the first time at N.Y.'s Carnegie Hall. In 1985 he became the youngest prof. ever appointed to the faculty of the Royal Coll. of Music. In 1988 he became principal clarinetist of the Philharmonia Orch. in London. In addition to his appearances as a virtuoso soloist with orchs., he also played in many chamber music settings and appeared in duo recitals with Mikhail Pletnev. His extensive repertoire, ranging from the masters to contemporary composers, showcases a musician whose virtuosity is equalled by impeccable taste. —**NS/LK/DM**

Collins, Phil,

Genesis drummer who became a pop icon; b. London, Jan. 31, 1951. One of pop music's most unlikely stars, Phil Collins began his career as a child actor, largely thanks to his mother, a talent agent. In his early teens, he was one of the screaming extras in the Beatles' *A Hard Day's Night* and played the Artful Dodger in a London stage production of *Oliver*.

However, Collins's passion was for playing the drums. After a brief stint with the short-lived band Flaming Youth, he took the drummer's throne in the progressive rock group Genesis. Upon the sudden exit of lead vocalist Peter Gabriel, Collins sat through hundreds of auditions for a new vocalist, although he had already done the job on several songs, like "More Fool Me" from *Selling England by the Pound*. The band finally agreed that Collins should take over as singer. On stage, he was freed from his drumming chores by former Yes drummer Bill Bruford. As he long maintained that he was a drummer who sang, however, he kept his playing sharp during hiatuses from Genesis by working with the jazz-rock group Brand X.

With Collins on vocals, Genesis started to move away from progressive rock bombast to a more smooth pop sound. After building a following over the course of several albums, *And Then There Were Three...* finally broke the band in a big way on the U.S. pop market. The song "Follow You, Follow Me" reached #23 on the pop charts. Their next album, *Duke* furthered this with the AOR hit "Turn It On Again." "Misunderstanding" from the same album hit #14.

In 1980 Collins started working on a solo album featuring the Earth Wind and Fire horn section, among others. At the same time, Genesis started work on a new album and Collins brought the horn section with him. His album *Face Value* spawned the soulful "I Missed Again," featuring the horns, which climbed to #19, as did the gold follow-up, "In the Air Tonight." The album also went gold and hit #7, and eventually sold over five million copies. As the singles from *Face Value* started tapering off, Genesis' *ABACAB* hit.

Collins continued his solo career with *Hello, I Must Be Going* in 1982, led off by a cover of the Supremes' "You Can't Hurry Love." The song hit #2 in England

and went to #10 in the U.S. The follow- up single, "I Don't Care Anymore" reached #39. Collins also became active as a producer, working on the solo album *Something's Going On* by Frida from Abba and *Strip* by Adam and the Ants.

Collins's popularity rose to such an extent that filmmaker Taylor Hackford asked him to write the theme to his 1984 film *Against All Odds*. Taking an out-take from *Face Value* and slightly rewriting it, he came up with "Against All Odds (Take a Look at Me Now)." The song did better than the film, standing three weeks at the top of the charts and going gold, earning Collins an Academy Award nomination and a Best Pop Vocal Performance Grammy. Collins himself started acting again, taking a guest role on the TV show *Miami Vice*.

The next year, his affiliation with EWF continued, this time in the form of a duet with the group's vocalist Phillip Bailey. That tune, "Easy Lover," was the #2 song on the charts for a couple of weeks and went gold. Collin released *No Jacket Required* and the album and single "One More Night" both hit #1 on their respective charts the same week.

The single went gold, as did the following chart-topping single, "Sussudio." "Don't Lose My Number" followed that into the #4 slot. While the album had one more single in it, the #7 "Take Me Home," Collins also topped the charts again with "Separate Lives," a duet with Marilyn Martin cut for the film *White Nights*. *No Jacket Required* eventually earned Collins a diamond award (for sales in excess of ten million), as well as Album of the Year and Best Pop Vocal Performance, Male, Grammys. It represents the height of Collins's career as a recording artist, as well as a performer in clever video clips. ("Take Me Home" featured Collins singing the song from various locations around the world; "Easy Lover" showed Collins and Bailey clowning around on a soundstage.)

Over the next couple of years, Collins's solo career slowed down. His work with Genesis garnered a massive hit album, *Invisible Touch*, which generated five Top Ten singles and went quintuple platinum. Additionally, Collins took the lead role in the film *Buster*, playing the mastermind behind the Great Train Robbery. Two songs from the soundtrack album, "Groovy Kind of Love" and "Two Hearts," topped the charts, with the former earning a gold record. The film, however, failed to launch a second career for Collins as a leading man.

In 1989 Collins released his next solo album, *...But Seriously*. It led off with the gold single "Another Day in Paradise," a rather bleak meditation on homelessness that spent four weeks at the top of the charts. "I Wish It Would Rain," featuring Eric Clapton (with whom Collins had toured), went to #3, and the subsequent two singles—"Do You Remember" and "Something Happened on the Way to Heaven"—both rose to #4. The album went triple platinum that year, adding another million sales along the way, and topped the charts for three weeks. Collins took the album out on tour, releasing a recording of the show as *Serious Hits— Live!* The live album went to #14, eventually selling 4 million copies.

Collins turned his attention back to Genesis for a while, releasing the album *We Can't Dance*, and two live albums drawn from the following tour. The title track "I Can't Dance" was a hit, and was promoted by a clever video that satirized glitzy dance-oriented video artists like Michael Jackson and also TV advertisements for blue jeans. Despite this success, the band was on its last legs. Collins left the band officially in 1995.

Collins played every instrument on his next solo release, *Both Sides*. The album "only" went platinum, hitting #13 on the charts and yielding two singles: "Both Sides of the Story" hit #25 and "Everyday" got as high as #24. His next album, *Dance in the Light* went gold, but didn't generate any hits. This gave Collins license to try something different, and he took a big band on tour, recording an album conducted by Quincy Jones. While on the road with the big band, Atlantic released a greatest hits album, *...Hits*. Meanwhile, Collins worked on composing music and songs for the Disney animated movie *Tarzan*. The album went platinum and the single "You'll Be in My Heart" garnered Collins his first Academy Award in 2000.

DISC.: *Face Value* (1981); *Hello, I Must Be Going* (1982); *No Jacket Required* (1985); *12'ers* (1987); *But Seriously* (1989); *Serious Hits—Live!* (1990); *Both Sides* (1993); *Dance into the Light* (1996); *...Hits* (1998); *Hot Night in Paris* (1999) *Tarzan* (1999).—**HB**

Collins, Shad (actually, **Lester Rallingston**), jazz trumpeter; b. Elizabeth, N.J., June 27, 1910; d. N.Y., June 1978. A subtle stylist, he was evidently a favorite of Lester Young, who worked with him in Basie's band and then chose him for his own group after leaving Basie. Raised in Lockport, N.Y., his first professional work was in a band led by Charlie Dixon (fronted by vocalist Cora LaRedd), then, from late 1929 until 1930, Collins was in a band led by pianist Eddie White. He spent the 1930s working with a number of leading bands, including Chick Webb (1931), Benny Carter (1933), Tiny Bradshaw (1934), Teddy Hill (1936–37); had a short stay with Don Redman and then with Count Basie from December 1938 until January 1940. In February 1940 he joined Carter's Band, then from October worked in Freddy Moore's Band. Collins was with the Lester Young Sextet in N.Y. (February 1941), then worked with Buddy Johnson until replacing Dizzy Gillespie in Cab Calloway's Band in Sept. 1941. He was with Cab until June 1943 and again 1944–46. Collins worked with Buster Harding's Band (1948), Al Sears (1950), toured with Jimmy Rushing in the early 1950s, and then worked in N.Y. for various leaders, including a long spell with tenorist Sam "The Man" Taylor. He left full-time music but continued to gig in the 1960s.—**JC/LP**

Collum, Herbert, German organist, harpsichordist, conductor, and composer; b. Leipzig, July 18, 1914. He studied organ with Straube and Ramin at the Hochschule für Musik in Leipzig, and also piano with Adolf Martienssen and composition with J.N. David. In 1934 he became organist of the Kreuzkirche in Dresden. He founded the Collum Concerts (1935) and the Collum

Choir (1946) of Dresden. He was a distinguished interpreter of the music of Bach, both as organist and as harpsichordist; he also composed concertos for harpsichord and many vocal works.—NS/LK/DM

Colombo, Pierre, Swiss conductor; b. La Tour-de-Peilz, May 22, 1914. He received training in piano, voice, and flute, and also pursued studies in science at the Univ. of Lausanne. He studied conducting at the Basel Cons. (diploma, 1942), his principal mentors being Scherchen and H. Münch; he also studied with Krauss. He conducted choral groups and in 1950 founded the Geneva Chamber Orch. After conducting the Johannesburg (South Africa) Sym. Orch. (from 1953), he was an administrator with the Geneva Radio (from 1955). He also appeared as a guest conductor throughout Europe. —NS/LK/DM

Colonna, Giovanni Paolo, Italian organist, organ builder, and composer; b. Bologna, June 16, 1637; d. there, Nov. 28, 1695. He studied organ with Filipucci in Bologna. After training in composition with Abbatini, Benevoli, and Carissimi in Rome, he served as organist in S. Apollinare there before pursuing his career in Bologna. In 1659 he was made second organist and in 1661 organist at S. Petronio, and then served as its maestro di cappella from 1674 until his death. He also was maestro di cappella at the church of the Madonna della Galliera (1673–88) and at S. Giovanni in Monte (1689–90). In 1666 he helped to found the Accademia dei Filarmonici of Bologna, which he served as principe from 1672. Colonna was a distinguished composer of oratorios, six of which are extant. Among his other fine works were two vols. of motets (Bologna, 1681) and the *Messe e salmi concertati* (Bologna, 1691).—NS/LK/DM

Colonne, Édouard (actually, **Judas**), notable French conductor; b. Bordeaux, July 23, 1838; d. Paris, March 28, 1910. He studied violin with Girard and Sauzay and composition with Elwart and Thomas at the Paris Cons. After playing violin in the Pasdeloup Orch. and other Paris ensembles, he conducted at Niblo's Garden in N.Y. Upon his return to Paris, he founded the Concert du Grand Hôtel in 1871, and then the Concerts Nationaux in 1873. In 1874 he founded the Concerts du Châtelet, which became the famous Association Artistique des Concerts Colonne in 1878. He also conducted at the Paris Opéra (1891–93), and made tours as a guest conductor in Europe and the U.S. Colonne acquired a distinguished reputation for his willingness to conduct contemporary works, and he later became a leading champion of Berlioz.—NS/LK/DM

Coltellini, Celeste, Italian mezzo-soprano; b. Livorno, Nov. 26, 1760; d. Capodimonte, near Naples, July 28, 1828. She studied with G.B. Mancini and G. Manzuoli, then sang at La Scala in Milan (1780). In 1781 she became a member of the Teatro dei Fiorentini in Naples. She was well known for her interpretations of roles in operas by Mozart, Paisiello, and Cimarosa. —NS/LK/DM

Coltrane, Alice (MacLeod; aka Sagitananda Turiya), avant-garde jazz pianist, organist, harpist; wife of **John Coltrane** and mother of **Ravi**

Coltrane; b. Detroit, Mich., Aug. 27, 1937. She was the fifth of six children. Her mother, Anne Johnston, played piano and sang in a church choir. Alice began the piano at age seven, and her early idol was Terry Pollard. Alice's half-brother, Ernie Farrow, was an accomplished bassist who played with and encouraged the young Alice as she progressed. She played at churches in Detroit and studied classical music in N.Y. for a bit. She went to Europe (1959), and while in Paris she spent some time with Bud Powell, another major influence. She also played with Lucky Thompson and Oscar Pettiford. She married the singer Kenny "Pancho" Hagood overseas, and they had a daughter, Michelle (b. 1960). After that marriage broke up, Alice returned to Detroit with her daughter. Around 1962, she was performing around Detroit in a cooperatively led group with Farrow and George Goldsmith, George Bohannon, and Bennie Maupin, as well as freelancing on vibraphone and "organa" (probably a small portable organ), even adding background vocals as needed for hotel lounge acts. She worked and made her first recordings with the Terry Gibbs quartet (1963). She met John Coltrane when Gibbs shared the bill with him at N.Y.'s Birdland (July 1963). She began traveling with Coltrane and that fall they lived together. John W. Coltrane Jr., was born to them on Aug. 26, 1964; Ravi John Coltrane was born Aug. 6, 1965. They went to Mexico around Aug. 1966 and John obtained in one day a divorce from his wife Naima, and a marriage to Alice. Soon after, they moved to Long Island, N.Y., where Oranyan Olabisi Coltrane, was born on March 19, 1967. From the end of 1965, Alice replaced McCoy Tyner in the Coltrane quartet.

After John's death, Alice lived for a while in Englewood, N.J., and continued to perform and record. Her groups included Rashied Ali, Pharoah Sanders, Jimmy Garrison, and later Ben Riley, Vishnu Wood or Reggie Workman, and Frank Lowe. She supervised the release of John's unissued work, although she drew some criticism for overdubbing strings onto his tapes to produce *Cosmic Music*. She worked with Archie Shepp and Ornette Coleman, who was responsible for the transcription of music on *Universal Consciousness*. Wood claims to have introduced her to the Swami Satchidananda when he visited the U.S. around 1970. She became an advanced disciple, converted to Hinduism, and visited shrines in India and Sri Lanka. In the early 1970s, she continued to perform, sometimes with string ensembles including violinists Leroy Jenkins, John Blair, and cellist Calo Scott. She performed during the first John Coltrane festival in Los Angeles, which she began in 1987, but now she only helps direct the festival and rarely performs. She was known for a time as Turiya Aparna, and since she became a teacher herself she has been known as Sangitananda Turiya (also written as one word instead of two). Around 1975, she founded the Vedantic Center, a religious retreat just west of Los Angeles. In 1978 she authored a "spiritual autobiography" entitled *Monument Eternal*, and she produced a regular half-hour spiritual program for a local Los Angeles TV channel, on which she played piano and read poems and prayers. In 1982 Alice Coltrane attempted to close the Church of John Coltrane in San

Francisco, with which she was initially connected, with a $7.5 million lawsuit; she charged that John would not have approved of the way in which they use his image and that they unlawfully using his name for profit, but the case was dismissed. Although she has performed only sporadically since the mid-1980s, she has continued to appear with her sons in special circumstances. Around 1993 there was a BBC program *Rhythms of the World* which centered on a collaboration between Don Cherry, L. Shankar, his wife Caroline, and Alice Coltrane. In 1998 she played a duet with her son Ravi at Town Hall, N.Y.

DISC.: *Monastic Trio* (1968); *Huntington Ashram Monastery* (1969); *Ptah the El Daoud* (1970); *Journey in Satchidananda* (1970); *World Galaxy* (1971); *Universal Consciousness* (1971); *Lord of Lords* (1973); *Eternity* (1975); *Radha-Krsna Nama Sankirtana* (1976); *Transcendence* (1977); *Transfiguration* (1978).—LP

Coltrane, John (William Jr.), hugely influential jazz tenor and soprano saxophonist who reshaped the whole way jazz is perceived; husband of **Alice (McLeod) Coltrane;** father of **Ravi Coltrane;** b. Hamlet, N.C., Sept. 23, 1926; d. Huntington, N.Y., July 17, 1967. Both of his parents came from literate families in N.C. His mother was musical, singing and playing piano, and his father played violin, ukulele, and possibly clarinet for his own amusement. Probably beginning in the fall of 1939, Coltrane received his first instrumental training playing alto horn in a community band under Warren B. Steele; he soon switched to the clarinet. Probably in September 1940, he joined a band that had just started at his William Penn H.S. Around this time, he took up the alto saxophone, inspired by Lester Young. From 1938–40, his family was devastated by a series of unrelated deaths, including that of his father, and his mother moved the family to Atlantic City, N.J., probably during his senior year of high school, 1942–43. John lived alone with boarders in High Point until his graduation from high school in 1943. He then moved to Philadelphia; he took saxophone lessons and theory classes with Mike Guerra (1944) and played in the concert band at the Ornstein School of Music. There, he met Bill Barron, Vance Wilson, and Johnnie Splawn. In 1945 Coltrane began picking up professional engagements, beginning in a trio with a pianist and a guitarist. Early that year, he began practicing with Benny Golson. He went to see Dizzy Gillespie perform with Charlie Parker (1945); from that point, he emulated Parker. Coltrane was in the Navy (August 1945–August 1946); he was sent to Pearl Harbor, where he played saxophone and clarinet in a band known as the Melody Masters. He first recorded July 13, 1946, in an impromptu session, not for release, with a small group of musicians from the segregated white band including drummer Joe Theimer; the eight titles included a number of recent Parker tunes. After the Navy, Coltrane probably resumed saxophone lessons, but his primary focus beginning probably in the fall of 1946 and continuing until somewhere between 1950 and 1952 was studying music at the Granoff Studios, where his veteran's benefits paid his tuition. There he studied on and off, when he was in town, with Dennis Sandole. He also began picking up steady freelance work alongside Ray

Bryant, Golson, and others. He called his "first professional job" a tour he made with Joe Webb (1946) in Philadelphia, alongside Cal Massey, who remained a lifelong friend. He then joined the band of King Kolax (February–April 1947). While in Los Angeles with Kolax, he also first met Parker by attending his recording session on Wednesday, Feb. 19, 1947. From about May 1947 through the end of 1948, Coltrane freelanced around Philadelphia, often with Jimmy Heath's big band.

By 1948 Coltrane was drinking heavily, smoking perhaps as much as two packs a day, and using heroin. These habits caused him to be personally inconsistent and were probably a major factor in his obscurity over the next seven years. Although everyone recognized him as a fine musician, and took notice of his incessant practicing, no one could have predicted that he would become a major force in musical history. He first played tenor professionally while touring on one-nighters with Eddie Vinson (November 1948–April or May 1949), alongside Johnny Coles and Red Garland. His inspirations on tenor included Lester Young, Coleman Hawkins, Dexter Gordon, Wardell Gray, and Sonny Stitt. From Sept. 16, 1949, he played lead alto in Dizzy Gillespie's big band, but he kept his now preferred tenor around and used it on recordings with singer Billy Valentine. Gillespie formed a small group (c. August 1950) and retained Coltrane on tenor, who had apparently impressed the trumpeter. Five 20-minute radio broadcasts survive of the Gillespie group at Birdland (January–March 1951). He recorded with Gillespie and his solo on "We Love to Boogie" (1951) was his only work available to the general public until he joined Miles Davis late in 1955. With Gillespie, he learned about sophisticated harmonies, Latin music, and vamps. He began seeking out any and all method books, even the piano books of Hanon and Czerny. By early April 1951, he was back in Philadelphia, freelancing and playing in a group named the "Dizzy Gillespie Alumni." In January 1952, he recorded with the Gay Crosse group. He continued to study and practice relentlessly, saw Sandole for lessons on a regular basis, and got together with fellow musicians to exchange ideas, including the legendary pianist and theorist Hasaan Ibn Ali. Coltrane toured with Earl Bostic from 1952; Bostic was a virtuoso and Coltrane said "He showed me a lot of things on my horn." In late 1953 or March 1954, he joined the band of his early idol Johnny Hodges. Though he did not solo on Hodges's studio recordings, he was featured on a live recording of the band. He must have left Hodges around the beginning of September 1954, because he was gigging then in Philadelphia with Mop Dudley. He also played in several contexts with Bill Carney, a singer, percussionist, and impresario active since the late 1940s. In 1954 Carney put together a group called the Hi-Tones with Shirley Scott, Al "Tootie" Heath, and Coltrane. Coltrane worked with them and freelanced between engagements.

In September 1955, Coltrane was working at Spider Kelly's in Philadelphia with organist Jimmy Smith, when two major events changed his life: he was "discovered" by Miles Davis and he married for the first time. On Sept. 27, 1955 in Baltimore, he began his first engagement with Miles Davis. Perhaps bolstered by his new security, he was joined by his friend Naima and they married there on Oct. 3. Naima (her Muslim name; b. Juanita Austin, 1926; d. Oct. 1, 1996) was a single mother whose daughter, Syeeda (or Saeeda), was about five years old; the couple later divorced. Shortly after, he married Alice McLeod; they had three children. Coltrane's alcohol and drug addictions continued to interfere with his performance. When Davis fired him because of his unreliability after an engagement that ended on April 28, 1957, Coltrane finally rid himself of the heroin habit by quitting "cold turkey" during a week in May while he was leading a quartet in Philadelphia. He planned to continue leading his own group and did so for a few gigs, and cut his first record as a leader on May 31. During this period, he began his next significant association, with Thelonious Monk. He had first recorded with Monk on April 16 and now began visiting him and playing with him informally on an occasional basis. He began working on multiphonics, the playing of several notes at once; he said that Monk "just looked at my horn and 'felt' the mechanics of what had to be done to get this effect," but that he learned the specifics of it from John Glenn, a local Philadelphia player. Monk asked Coltrane to join his group at the Five Spot (July 18 or 19–New Year's Eve 1957). The engagement was critical for both of them; Coltrane's playing drew raves from most critics. In addition, his album *Blue Train* was recorded during this stint and released that December; it brought increased attention to his brilliance as a composer, in that all but one of the five tunes were his. Composing was a major preoccupation for Coltrane and something he took as seriously as his performing.

At the end of the Monk engagement, Davis rehired Coltrane (January 1958). Coltrane was then using the blinding flurries of notes that Ira Gitler had dubbed "sheets of sound" (the term is sometimes inappropriately applied to his work from other years). However, by 1959, he was using the sheets of sound more sparingly. During the spring of 1959, he recorded on Davis's *Kind of Blue* and his own *Giant Steps*, his first album as a leader for Atlantic. This time, all seven compositions were his own; the title piece represented the culmination of Coltrane's developing interest in third- related chord movement, also employed on a number of pieces during 1959–60, notably "Countdown," "Exotica," "Satellite" (a variation on "How High the Moon"), "26–2" (based on Parker's "Confirmation"), and his arrangements of "But Not for Me" and "Body and Soul." However, from 1960 onward, Coltrane consistently referred to his interest in third-relations as a passing phase. Through the influence of Davis and the *Kind of Blue* album, in his own groups, and in his composing, modal pieces would predominate. Coltrane had for some time wanted to lead his own group—he did so periodically between gigs with Davis—and in late July 1959 he quit Davis. When Jimmy Heath was unable to remain in his place and Adderley had announced his intention to leave in September, Coltrane was persuaded to return to Davis's group in mid-August, but left for good after Davis's tour of Europe (March–April 1960). On the first concert of the tour, at the Olympia

Theater in Paris, Coltrane found himself in the midst of controversy. A chorus of boos from the audience during one solo led to a heated debate in the French press over his approach. Elsewhere on the tour, he was received enthusiastically.

On April 16, 1960, Coltrane led a group at Town Hall, N.Y., on a bill with Gillespie and others; on May 3, he began a two-month engagement at the Jazz Gallery. Apparently he had wanted hire McCoy Tyner on piano, Art Davis on bass, and Elvin Jones on drums; but none of them were available, so he opened with Steve Kuhn on piano, Steve Davis on bass, and Pete Sims "LaRoca" on drums. Tyner joined in about a month, and Jones between Sept. 26 and Oct. 1, while the group was on tour in Denver. The bass chair changed around—Reggie Workman played for most of 1961, sometimes in tandem with Art Davis—and finally went to Jimmy Garrison at the end of 1961. Coltrane had purchased a soprano saxophone around Feb. 1, 1959 and tried it out that week on a gig at the Sutherland Hotel in Chicago. He began using it regularly in May 1960; his recording of "My Favorite Things" that October re-established the soprano, rarely used in modern jazz, as a favored jazz instrument. His arranging concept was equally brilliant as his playing; essentially, he took one chorus of the song and extending it vastly with long vamp sections. That same week he recorded all the material that would eventually become *Coltrane Plays the Blues* and *Coltrane's Sound*. He signed with the Impulse record label in April 1961. He was becoming increasingly popular; *Down Beat* honored him as "Jazzman of the Year" (1961); in both their International Critics Poll and Readers Poll that year, he won for best tenor saxophonist and for miscellaneous instrument (soprano saxophone); the critics also voted his the new star combo. But his detractors grew louder with the addition of Eric Dolphy to the group for most of 1961. A majority of English critics lambasted him on his first European tour that November. The Nov. 23 issue of *Down Beat* contained a scathing review from John Tynan, who spoke of "musical nonsense currently being peddled in the name of jazz—a horrifying demonstration of what appears to be a growing anti-jazz trend." Coltrane and Dolphy responded with an article in *Down Beat* published April 12, 1962. Coltrane also considered expanding his group to a sextet with the addition of guitarist Wes Montgomery. They performed together in Calif. in September 1961 and again in 1962. Neither Montgomery nor Dolphy stayed, and Coltrane's best known quartet—Tyner, Garrison, and Jones—remained intact from April 1962 through the fall of 1965. Just as "My Favorite Things" was a soprano feature, "Impressions" became his tenor theme song. This is based on the same AABA structure and D dorian mode (E-flat for the bridge) as "So What," but the A section (main) melody was derived from Morton Gould's "Pavanne" (*sic*) and the B section was taken from yet another pavane, Maurice Ravel's "Pavane pour une infante défunte" (or from the popular song that was based on it, "The Lamp Is Low"). Far from indicating any paucity of inspiration on Coltrane's part, this is a characteristic example of his remarkable breadth of interests and his ability to apply these diverse sources to jazz. He was among the first to play what is now called world music. He demonstrated how world music, classical music, and classical theory can all be incorporated into powerful blues-based jazz. For some years Coltrane had been exposed to the music of other cultures—India, parts of Africa, Latin America—through Dennis Sandole, Gillespie, Yusef Lateef, and others. He must have also learned about Middle Eastern music from Ahmed-Abdul Malik, the bassist during most of his Monk engagement, and John invited him to play the tamboura on "India" at the Village Vanguard (November 1961). He arranged to meet Ravi Shankar in N.Y. (December 1961), the first of a handful of informal lessons. He even named his second son Ravi. He based some of his pieces on the sources he found. His "Spiritual" is a melody for "Nobody Knows De Trouble I See" from James Weldon Johnson. "Olé" was based on a song known as "Venga Vallejo" or as "El Vito." The notes to *Africa/Brass* state that "He listened to many African records for rhythmic inspiration." "India" appears to be based on a recorded Vedic chant that was issued on a Folkways LP at the time. It wasn't only the sound of world music that attracted him; Coltrane was interested in all kinds of religion, and in all kinds of mysticism. He knew that in some folk cultures music was held to have mystical powers, and he hoped to get in touch with some of those capacities.

Coltrane's mystical, spiritual interests are explicit in *A Love Supreme*, his best-known and still best-selling album, recorded December 1964. Its four sections—"Acknowledgement," "Resolution," "Pursuance," and "Psalm"—suggest a kind of pilgrim's progress, in which the pilgrim acknowledges the divine, resolves to pursue it, searches, and eventually celebrates what has been attained in song. Virtually the whole piece is based on the little "A Love Supreme" motive chanted by Coltrane (overdubbed as two voices) at the end of Part One. Perhaps most striking is the way he incorporates his poem, which appears in the liner, into Part Four. His saxophone solo is a wordless "recitation" of the words of the poem, beginning with the title, "A Love Supreme." Eventually Coltrane accepted the diversity of human belief as representing different ways of recognizing one God. The titles of Coltrane's last compositions suggest a mixture of religious influences—only "The Father and the Son and the Holy Ghost" is specifically Christian; others such as "Dear Lord" and "Meditations" are more general, while "Om" suggests Eastern beliefs. He is quoted on the back of *Meditations* saying, "I believe in all religions." *A Love Supreme* was voted album of the year by both *Down Beat* and "Jazz" (1965), and *Down Beat* readers also named Coltrane as Jazzman of the Year, best tenor saxophonist, and elected him to the magazine's Hall of Fame.

But Coltrane continued to excite controversy; he was enamored of Ornette Coleman and the so-called avant garde. Coltrane talked quite a bit about music with Coleman, and they reportedly discussed putting a group together but never did, although Coltrane recorded an album with Coleman's band members in 1960 (released in 1966). He was also very interested in the music of Albert Ayler. He helped to arrange recording sessions at Impulse for Archie Shepp and others, and he was always generous about letting these younger play-

ers sit in with his group at performances. On June 28, 1965, he gathered ten musicians for the recording session that produced "Ascension." Besides his regular quartet, and bassist Art Davis, he used trumpeters Freddie Hubbard and Dewey Johnson, alto saxophonists Marion Brown and John Tchicai, and tenor saxophonists Pharoah Sanders and Archie Shepp. By September, Sanders was a regular member of the group. On Oct. 1, 1965, they recorded "Om," which opens with chanting of words from the *Bhagavad-Gita*. Coltrane is said to have been tripping on LSD, and this is likely, but his work, disturbing to some, revelatory to many more, continued to have profound musical substance and his own solos were as tightly argued as ever. The posthumous release *Interstellar Space* is the perfect place to hear this because it consists entirely of duets with drums. He also came upon a richer tone, with fuller vibrato, than he had ever used before. He was playing in free time, without the bass walking, and decided to try out two drummers on a regular basis. Beginning at the Village Gate in N.Y. in November 1965, he hired Rashied Ali as a second drummer. However, this prompted the departure of Tyner by the end of 1965. Jones left in early 1966. Jimmy Garrison stayed with Coltrane through the summer of 1966 (although he returned for recording sessions) along with Sanders, Rashied Ali, and pianist Alice McLeod Coltrane, his second wife.

In fall 1966, Coltrane began to cut back on touring and made plans to stay around N.Y., probably as much for family reasons as for health reasons; he was not yet aware of any serious illness. He had begun to take control of his own business affairs. He had arranged for his own label imprint, and was planning some self-produced concerts jointly with percussionist Olatunji; they already had reserved Jan. 14, 1968, at Lincoln Center's Philharmonic Hall (now known as Avery Fisher Hall). He spoke of opening a space in N.J. or in Greenwich Village where rehearsals and performances would be open informally to the public for a nominal charge. By the spring of 1967, he was reportedly planning on performing less often or even taking a break altogether, while he concentrated on producing younger artists and possibly doing some teaching. A third son, Oran, was born in March 1967. By the spring of 1967, his health was failing. On April 23 1967, he appeared in a benefit concert for and at the new Olatunji Center of African Culture on East 125th Street. His final performance was in Baltimore on May 7. He died in the hospital of liver cancer. The cause has never been definitively found, but it was apparently not related to the drugs and alcohol he ingested as a youth, though it might have been a long-term effect of a dirty needle causing hepatitis. A funeral service was held on July 21, 1967, at St. Peter's Church in Manhattan. A thousand people attended. Cal Massey read the poem "A Love Supreme." Reportedly to fulfill one of Coltrane's last requests, the quartets of Ornette Coleman and Albert Ayler each performed one number. After the ceremony, the family drove out to Pinelawn Memorial Park in Farmingdale, where Coltrane was interred. North 33rd Street, Philadelphia, is now the base of the John W. Coltrane Cultural Society; historical markers have been raised in Hamlet and High Point. A Christian church in

San Francisco (known as the Church of John Coltrane) centers its ritual around the album and poem *A Love Supreme*.

DISC.: *First Broadcasts, Vol. 2* (1951); *Coltrane 1951* (1951); *Traneing In* (1957); *John Coltrane/Ray Draper Quintet* (1957); *Cattin' with Coltrane and Quinichette* (1957); *Blue Train* (1957); *Trane's Reign* (1958); *Settin' the Pace* (1958); *Coltrane Time* (1958); *Giant Steps* (1959); *Coltrane Jazz* (1959); *My Favorite Things* (1960); *Coltrane's Sound* (1960); *Coltrane Plays the Blues* (1960); *Avant Garde* (1960); *Exotica* (1960); *Olé Coltrane* (1961); *Live in Stockholm* (1961); *Live at the Village Vanguard* (1961); *Impressions* (1961); *Complete Paris Concerts* (1961); *Africa/Brass* (1961); *Duke Ellington and John Coltrane* (1962); *Complete Graz Concert, Vol. 1, 2* (1962); *Complete 1962 Stockholm Concert* (1962); *Coltrane* (1962); *Bye Bye Blackbird* (1962); *Ballads* (1962); *Live at Birdland* (1963); *John Coltrane and Johnny Hartman* (1963); *Newport '63* (1963); *A Love Supreme* (1964); *Crescent* (1964); *Transition* (1965); *Sun Ship* (1965); *Om* (1965); *Meditations* (1965); *Live in Seattle* (1965); *Live in Paris* (1965); *Live in Antibes* (1965); *Kulu Sé Mama* (1965); *John Coltrane Quartet Plays* (1965); *Infinity* (1965); *First Meditations* (1965); *Ascension* (1965); *Live in Japan* (1966); *Live at the Village Vanguard Again* (1966); *Cosmic Music* (1966); *Stellar Regions* (1967); *Interstellar Space* (1967); *Expression* (1967).

BIBL.: T. Gelatt, *About John Coltrane* (N.Y., 1974); C. Simpkins, *A Biography* (N.Y., 1975); J. C. Thomas, *Chasin' the Trane* (N.Y., 1975); B. Cole, *J. C.* (N.Y., 1976); D. Wild, *Recordings of John Coltrane* (Ann Arbor, 1977); D. N. Baker, *Jazz Style of John Coltrane* (Hialeah, Fla., 1980); B. Priestley, *J. C.* (London, 1987); A. N. White, *The Music of John Coltrane* (Hal Leonard, 1991); L. Porter, *John Coltrane: His Life and Music* (Ann Arbor, 1998).—**LP**

Coltrane, Ravi (John), jazz tenor and soprano saxophonist, son of **John and Alice Coltrane;** b. Huntington, N.Y., Aug. 6, 1965. He started on clarinet, and began working on tenor saxophone in earnest while attending the Calif. Inst. of the Arts (1986). He was in a student band there that won a *Down Beat* award, and his piece "Dear Alice," a tribute to his mother, is on their CD. Since 1991, he has performed and recorded with such artists as Elvin Jones, Steve Coleman, Geri Allen, Jack DeJohnette, Joanne Brackeen, and Art Davis. His mother's association with Terry Gibbs has been continued in his close friendship and musical association with Terry's son, Gerry.

DISC.: *Moving Pictures* (1997). E. Jones: *Elvin Jones in Europe* (1991); *Going Home* (1992). R. Kisor: *Minor Mutiny* (1991). D. Murray: *MX* (1992). C. Moffett: *Evidence* (1993). S. Coleman: *Def Trance Beat* (1994); *Metrics* (1994); *The Sign and the Seal* (1996); *Genesis and the Opening of the Way* (1997). A. Davis: *A Time Remembered* (1995). B. Mseleku: *Beauty of Sunrise* (1995). G. Gibbs: *The Thrasher* (1995).—**LP**

Columbus, Chris(topher) (originally, **Morris, Joseph Christopher Columbus**), jazz drummer, leader, father of **Sonny Payne;** b. Greenville, N.C., June 17, 1902. He led his own band through the 1930s, 1940s, and 1950s; he played regularly with Louis Jordan in 1949. He founded the first jazz organ combo in late 1940s with Wild Bill Davis and Bell Jennings. He worked mainly in the Wild Bill Davis Trio in the late 1950s to early 1960s, then accompanied vocalist Damita Jo through the mid-1960s. He was briefly in Duke Ellington's Orch. (1967), then led his own group in the

1970s. He made a European tour with Davis in 1972. With wife Mary Lee, he fathered Sonny Payne in 1926; some musicians maintain that at Payne's death his father appeared and said that Columbus had raised Payne but was not his father. However, Columbus insisted that he was Payne's biological father.—**LP**

Colvig, William, American instrument maker and performer; b. Medford, Ore., March 13, 1917; d. Capitola, Calif., March 2, 2000. He was born into a musical family, and studied piano from the age of six. He played in bands and orchs. during his formal studies at the Univ. of Calif. at Berkeley and the Coll. of the Pacific in Stockton. In 1967 he initiated an association with the composer Lou Harrison, for whom he built many instruments, including psalteries, harps, flutes, monochords, and several complete gamelans. He performed on these instruments in many of Harrison's compositions, as well as on traditional instruments in concerts and lectures. His instruments have been used by the San Francisco Sym. and San Francisco Opera Co., among others; he built the gamelans housed at the Univ. of Calif. at Berkeley and at Mills Coll. in Oakland. —**NS/LK/DM**

Colyns, Jean-Baptiste, Belgian violinist, conductor, teacher, and composer; b. Brussels, Nov. 25, 1834; d. there, Oct. 31, 1902. He studied with L.J. Meerts at the Brussels Cons., where he won a premier prix for violin. He was solo violinist at the Théâtre Royal de la Monnaie in Brussels and also first violinist in the court string quartet. As a soloist, he toured with success in Belgium, England, France, Germany, and the Netherlands. In 1863 he became a teacher at the Brussels Cons., and in 1888 at the Antwerp Cons. He wrote two comic operas, *Sir William* (Brussels, April 1877) and *Capitaine Raymond* (Brussels, April 8, 1881), a *Scherzo symphonique*, a Violin Concerto, and chamber pieces.—**LK/DM**

Combarieu, Jules (-Léon-Jean), eminent French music historian; b. Cahors, Lot, Feb. 4, 1859; d. Paris, July 7, 1916. He studied at the Sorbonne, and later in Berlin with Spitta. He received the degree of docteur ès lettres, and was a prof. of music history at the Collège de France (1904–10).

WRITINGS: *Études de philologie musicale:* 1. *Théorie du rhythme dans la composition moderne d'après la doctrine antique* (1896), 2. *Essai sur l'archéologie musicale au XIXe siècle et le problème de l'origine des neumes* (1896), and 3. *Fragments de l'Enéide en musique d'après un manuscrit inédit* (1898); *Éléments de grammaire musicale historique* (1906); *La Musique: Ses lois, son évolution* (1907; Eng. tr, 1910); *Histoire de la musique des origines au début du XXe siècle* (3 vols., Paris, 1913–19; 9th ed. of vol. I, 1953; 6th ed. of vol. II, 1946; 3rd ed. of vol. III, 1947; rev. 1955). —**NS/LK/DM**

Combs, Sean "Puffy" (aka **"Puff Daddy"**), one of rap music's most successful artists and entrepreneurs; b. N.Y.C., Nov. 4, 1969. When he produces or does commerce for his Bad Boy Records and other businesses, he's Sean Combs, businessman. When he performs, he's Puff Daddy and he calls his posse the

Family. In both guises, he has proven one of the most successful music creators of the 1990s.

Sean Combs was born in Harlem. His mother taught school. His father died in a car accident when Combs was a toddler. At two years old, he was modeling for Baskin-Robbins ice cream, a luminary even then. He grew up in the Westchester suburb of Mount Vernon and went to Mount St. Michael's, an all-boys Catholic school. Through school, he maintained several paper routes. He started attending college at Howard Univ. During his junior year, he got an internship at Uptown Records through one of their artists, his Mount Vernon homeboy Heavy D. He proved so invaluable at Uptown that they hired him. He worked on projects with Mary J. Blige, Heavy D, Father MC Jodeci, and others.

Combs and Heavy D also promoted a benefit basketball game at City Coll. in 1991. The game featured some noted rap stars, coming together to shoot hoops to raise money for the fight against AIDS. More people turned out for the event than the venue could handle and nine people were trampled to death in the ensuing crush to enter the stadium. This did little to enhance rap's violent reputation.

Venturing out on his own, Combs formed Bad Boy Entertainment out of his apartment. Within a year, he had hits with Craig Mack and the Notorious BIG. When Mack's "Flava in Your Ear" went platinum and BIG's album, *Ready to Die* went double platinum he was on his way.

Combs signed BIG's wife Faith Evans and his backing group Total to the label, as well as 112, expanding Bad Boy's reach into R&B. He firmed up the label's grip on hip-hop signing Mase and the LOX. Additionally, he continued producing outside acts, including Mariah Carey, Boys II Men, and Aretha Franklin.

In 1997 BIG was shot to death outside of a party in Los Angeles. Three weeks later, his second album, *Life After Death*, came out, debuting at #1. Combs had been working on a solo project, but delayed it as he mourned his friend. He finally unleashed the debut project by Puff Daddy and the Family during the summer of 1997. The single "Can't Nobody Hold Me Down" spent nearly two months at the top of the charts. The second single, "I'll Be Missing You," a tribute to BIG that heavily sampled the Police's "Every Breath You Take," also zoomed to the top of the chart. The song earned Combs ASCAP Songwriter of the Year honors, took home the 1998 Grammy Award for Best Rap Performance, and sold triple platinum. When the album, *No Way Out*, hit the stands, it debuted at #1 as well, eventually selling octuple platinum. The album spawned the gold single "Victory" and the platinum "Been Around the World." It won the 1998 Grammy for Best Rap Album.

Diversifying even further, Combs invested his money in a restaurant and a line of clothing. He worked on a posthumous BIG release and continued producing. For the soundtrack to the movie *Godzilla*, he duetted with Jimmy Page on the platinum single "Come with Me." Bad Boy also reached into the realm of rock, signing another performer from the *Godzilla* soundtrack, the band Fuzzbubble. In 1998 *Forbes* magazine featured

him on the cover, extolling his business acumen. Combs also found himself in trouble with the law again, accused of beating a record company executive over a controversial image in a video.

His second album, 1999's *Forever*, featured a host of guest artists, ranging from Bad Boy signees such as Mase and Faith Evans to hip-hop stars such as Jay-Z, Busta Rhymes, and Li'l Kim to R&B stars such as R. Kelly. Beyond his success in music, Combs was hard at work in 1999 on a Puff Daddy and the Family cartoon, as well as various charitable pursuits. No matter which way the music business goes, Combs will continue to be an influential force.

DISC.: *No Way Out* (1997); *Forever* (1999).—HB

Comden, Betty (originally, Cohen, Basya), and Adolph Green,

clever American lyricists, librettists, and screenwriters. Comden (b. N.Y., May 3, 1915) and Green (b. N.Y., Dec. 2, 1915) maintained a remarkably durable partnership lasting more than 60 years, during which they wrote the lyrics for 14 Broadway musicals. In many cases they also wrote the books for the musicals, and they wrote screenplays and songs for movies. Their primary collaborators were Jule Styne, Leonard Bernstein, and Cy Coleman. Their efforts brought them six Tony Awards and a Grammy Award. Usually set in contemporary N.Y., their works were peopled by eccentric characters, and their stories and lyrics generally had a satiric tone. Though best known for their shows, which included *On the Town, Bells are Ringing*, and *The Will Rogers Follies*, they also scored several song hits, among them "Just in Time," "The Party's Over," and "Make Someone Happy."

Comden was the daughter of Leo Cohen, a lawyer, and Rebecca Sadvoransky Cohen. She studied drama at N.Y.U., graduating with a B.S. in 1938. Green, the son of Daniel and Helen Weiss Green, became a runner on Wall Street after graduating from high school. The two met as aspiring actors and formed a nightclub act, the Revuers, along with Judy Tuvim (later Holliday), Alvin Hammer, and John Frank, in 1938. They were sometimes accompanied by a friend of Green's, pianist Leonard Bernstein. Writing their own shows, the group performed successfully at the Village Vanguard in N.Y., then at the Rainbow Room in 1939. They also performed on radio and records. Green married Elizabeth Reitell on June 20, 1941. Comden married designer Siegfried Schutzman (later Steven Kyle) on Jan. 4, 1942. They had two children and remained married until Kyle's death in 1979.

The Revuers went to Hollywood, where they had small parts in the film *Greenwich Village*, released in September 1944. By that time the group had split up, and Comden and Green had their own nightclub act back in N.Y. They gave it up when they were approached by Bernstein, who was expanding his ballet, *Fancy Free*, into a Broadway musical. The result was the war-themed *On the Town*, about three sailors on leave in N.Y., with book and lyrics by Comden and Green, who were also members of the cast. Opening in December

1944, the show ran 462 performances. They then wrote book and lyrics for the 1945 musical *Billion Dollar Baby*, which had music by Morton Gould. It was less successful but still ran 220 performances.

Comden and Green signed to MGM in 1947, and although they never moved permanently to Hollywood, they worked primarily in film for the next several years. They wrote the screenplay and the lyrics to one new song with music by Roger Edens for an adaptation of the De Sylva, Brown, and Henderson musical *Good News*, which was released in December 1947. With Edens, they wrote four songs for the box-office hit *Take Me Out to the Ball Game*, released in March 1949; they wrote the screenplay for the final Fred Astaire-Ginger Rogers film, *The Barkleys of Broadway*, released in May 1949; and they wrote the screenplay and six new songs with Edens for the movie version of *On the Town*, released in December 1949.

Comden and Green returned to Broadway to write sketches and lyrics to Jule Styne's music for the revue *Two on the Aisle*, which opened in July 1951 and ran 281 performances. Back in Hollywood they wrote the screenplay and the lyrics to one song with Edens for the box-office hit *Singin' in the Rain*, released in March 1952. They scored their biggest Broadway hit yet in February 1953, writing lyrics to Leonard Bernstein's songs for *Wonderful Town*, based on the story and play *My Sister Eileen*, which ran 559 performances and won them a Tony Award for Best Musical. The cast album was a Top Ten hit. In July, MGM released a film version of the Arthur Schwartz Howard Dietz musical *The Band Wagon* starring Fred Astaire. Comden and Green's screenplay earned them an Academy Award nomination.

The pair wrote several songs with Jule Styne for a musical version of *Peter Pan* starring Mary Martin that opened on Broadway in October 1954. The film *It's Always Fair Weather*, released in September 1955, for which they wrote the songs with André Previn, brought them their second Academy Award nomination, for Best Screenplay. They released their own album of the songs written for the film, as well as an album of their own recordings of songs written for earlier shows and movies.

Comden and Green reunited with Judy Holliday, by now a successful singer and comic actress, who starred in the 1956 musical *Bells are Ringing*. They wrote the book and collaborated with Jule Styne on the songs. The show was their longest running yet, with 924 performances; two chart singles emerged from the score: "Just in Time," which reached the Top 40 for Tony Bennett, and "The Party's Over" for Doris Day; and the cast album reached the charts. Comden and Green's next musical was *Say, Darling*, for which they wrote the songs with Styne. Opening in April 1958, it ran 332 performances, and Perry Como scored a Top 40 hit with "Dance Only with Me" from the score. Comden and Green next wrote the screenplay for *Auntie Mame*, released in December, and they performed in their own revue, *A Party with Comden and Green*, opening in December and running 82 performances. Their cast album for the show earned them their first Grammy nomination for Best Comedy Performance, Musical.

On Jan. 23, 1960, Green married singer-actress Phyllis Newman; they had two children. Comden and Green adapted *Bells are Ringing* into a film starring Judy Holliday and Dean Martin, released in June 1960. The soundtrack album spent three months in the charts. They then wrote the lyrics to Jule Styne's music for the musical *Do Re Mi*, which opened in December. The show ran 400 performances, the cast album was in the charts for five months, and Perry Como scored a chart entry with "Make Someone Happy." A year later, Comden and Green wrote the book and lyrics for *Subways are for Sleeping*, another musical with Styne. It ran 205 performances and the cast album was in the charts for two and a half months.

Comden and Green's stage and film projects came less frequently after the early 1960s. Lena Horne reached the charts in November 1963 with "Now!," a civil rights song for which they provided lyrics with music adapted from "Hava Nagila" by Jule Styne. They wrote the screenplay and collaborated with Styne on the songs for the May 1964 box-office hit *What a Way to Go!* The same month, the musical *Fade Out—Fade In*, for which they had written the book and lyrics and Styne had written the music, opened on Broadway. It ran 271 performances and the cast album spent two months in the charts. They next wrote the lyrics to Styne's music for the musical *Hallelujah, Baby!*, which opened in April 1967, running 293 performances and winning them their second Tony Award, as Best Lyricists. Their third Tony Award came for *Applause* (N.Y., March 30, 1970), named Best Musical, for which they wrote the book only.

Comden and Green next collaborated with Jule Styne on a reworking of his show *Gentlemen Prefer Blondes*. Retitled *Lorelei* and featuring a revised score, the show opened in January 1974 and ran 320 performances. The lyricists first worked with composer Cy Coleman on songs for the Off-Broadway revue *Straws in the Wind* (N.Y., Feb. 21, 1975), directed by Phyllis Newman. They wrote the book for another Off-Broadway revue, *By Bernstein* (N.Y., Nov. 23, 1975), which featured little-known Leonard Bernstein songs cut from earlier works. They then revived their own revue, *A Party with Betty Comden and Adolph Green* (N.Y., Feb. 10, 1977), again recording it and performing it on television.

On the Twentieth Century, based on the 1934 film *Twentieth Century*, marked Comden and Green's return to writing both book and lyrics for a Broadway musical in 1978. The show, with music by Cy Coleman, ran 460 performances, winning Tony Awards for Best Book and Best Score. The lyricist/librettists collaborated with composer Larry Grossman on the unsuccessful *A Doll's Life* in 1982 and adapted their screenplay into a musical book for *Singin' in the Rain* (N.Y., July 2, 1985). But they capped their career by writing the book and lyrics to Coleman's music for *The Will Rogers Follies* in 1991. The show ran 963 performances and won the Tony Award for Best Score, while the cast recording won the Grammy Award for Best Musical Show album. Comden and Green's shows continue to be revived in regional productions and on Broadway, such as the Broadway revival of *On the Town* during the 1998–99 season.

WORKS (only works for which Comden and Green were primary, credited lyricists are listed): **MUSICALS/REVUES** (dates refer to N.Y. openings): *On the Town* (Dec. 28, 1944); *Billion Dollar Baby* (Dec. 21, 1945); *Two on the Aisle* (July 19, 1951); *Wonderful Town* (Feb. 25, 1953); *Bells Are Ringing* (Nov. 29, 1956); *Say, Darling* (April 3, 1958); *A Party with C. and G.* (Dec. 23, 1958); *Do Re Mi* (Dec. 26, 1960); *Subways Are for Sleeping* (Dec. 27, 1961); *Fade Out—Fade In* (May 26, 1964); *Hallelujah, Baby!* (April 26, 1967); *Lorelei* (Jan. 27, 1974); *On the Twentieth Century* (Feb. 19, 1978); *A Doll's Life* (Sept. 23, 1982); *The Will Rogers Follies* (May 1, 1991). **FILMS:** *Take Me Out to the Ball Game* (1949); *On the Town* (1949); *It's Always Fair Weather* (1955); *Bells are Ringing* (1960); *What a Way to Go!* (1964). **TELEVISION:** *I'm Getting Married* (March 16, 1967).

WRITINGS: B. C., *Off Stage* (N.Y., 1995); A. G., ed., *The New York Musicals of C. and G.: On the Town, Wonderful Town, Bells Are Ringing* (N.Y., 1996).

BIBL.: A. Robinson, *B. C. and A. G.: A Bio-Bibliography* (Westport, Conn., 1994).—**WR**

Comes, Juan Bautista,

Spanish composer; b. Valencia, 1582; d. there, Jan. 5, 1643. He was a choirboy at Valencia Cathedral (1594–96) and a pupil of Juan Peréz. After serving as maestro de capilla at Lérida Cathedral (1605–08), he returned to Valencia and was vice-maestro at the Patriarca (1608–13) and maestro de capilla at the Cathedral (1613–18). He was vice-maestro at the Royal Chapel in Madrid (1618–28) before returning to Valencia, where he was again vice-maestro at the Patriarca (1628–32) and maestro de capilla at the Cathedral (1632–38). About 200 of his works are extant, mainly sacred.

BIBL.: M. Palau, *La obra del músico Valencianoo J.B. C.* (Valencia, 1943); J. Climent, *J.B. C. y su tiempo* (Madrid, 1977). —**NS/LK/DM**

Comet, Catherine,

French conductor; b. Fontainebleau, Dec. 6, 1944. She studied at the Paris Cons. (1958–63), where she took a premier prix in piano; concurrently received private training in analysis, harmony, counterpoint, and fugue from Boulanger before pursuing conducting studies with Morel at the Juilliard School of Music N.Y. (1964–68), where she received B.A. and M.A. degrees. In 1966 she won first prize in the Besançon conducting competition, and in 1967 she made her professional conducting debut with the Lille Radio Sym. Orch. at the Besançon Festival. In 1970–71 she was an assistant to Boulez with the BBC Sym. Orch. in London. She was conductor of the Paris Opéra Ballet from 1972 to 1975; from 1979 to 1981 she was music director of the Univ. of Wisc. sym. and chamber orchs. in Madison. After serving as the Exxon-Arts Endowment Conductor of the St. Louis Sym. Orch. (1981–84), she was assoc. conductor of the Baltimore Sym. Orch. (1984–86). In 1986 she became music director of the Grand Rapids (Mich.) Sym. Orch. In 1988 she was named co-recipient of the Seaver/NEA Conductors Award. From 1990 to 1992 she was music director of the American Sym. Orch. in N.Y. Comet has appeared with fine success as a guest conductor with principal North American orchs., including those of Boston, Chicago, Cincinnati, Detroit, Minneapolis, Philadelphia, San Francisco, Toronto, and Washington, D.C.—**NS/LK/DM**

Comissiona, Sergiu,

prominent Romanian-born American conductor; b. Bucharest, June 16, 1928. He studied conducting with Silvestri and Lindenberg, making his conducting debut at the age of 17 in Sibiu in a performance of Gounod's *Faust*. He became a violinist in the Bucharest Radio Quartet (1946), and then in the Romanian State Ensemble (1947), where he was subsequently asst. conductor (1948–50) and music director (1950–55). From 1955 to 1959 he was principal conductor of the Romanian State Opera in Bucharest. Being Jewish, he was moved to emigrate to Israel, where he was music director of the Haifa Sym. Orch. (1960–66) and founder-director of the Ramat Gan Chamber Orch. (1960–67). In 1963 he appeared in North America as conductor of the Israel Chamber Orch., and, in 1965, as guest conductor of the Philadelphia Orch. He then was music director of the Göteborg Sym. Orch. (1966–77), music adviser of the Northern Ireland Orch. in Belfast (1967–68), and music director of the Baltimore Sym. Orch. (1969–84). On July 4, 1976, he became a naturalized American citizen. He was music director of the Chautauqua (N.Y.) Festival Orch. (1976–80), music advisor of the Temple Univ. Festival in Ambler (1977–80), and music advisor of the American Sym. Orch. in N.Y. (1977–82). He seserved as artistic director (1980–83), music director-designate (1983–84), and music director (1984–88) of the Houston Sym. Orch. From 1982 he was chief conductor of the Radio Phil. Orch. in Hilversum. In 1987–88 he was also music director of the N.Y.C. Opera, and then was chief conductor of the Helsinki Phil. from 1990 to 1993. In 1990–91 he was music director designate, and from 1991 until 2000, music director of the Vancouver (B.C.) Sym. Orch. He subsequently served as its conductor emeritus.—**NS/LK/DM**

Commodores, The,

R&B band with strong pop appeal and some of the biggest crossover hits of the 1970s and 1980s, formed, Tuskegee, Ala., 1967. **MEMBERSHIP:** Lionel Richie, voc., kybd., sax. (b. Tuskegee Ala., c. 1950); Milan Williams, kybd., trmb., gtr. (b. Miss., c. 1949); Ronald LaPread, bs., trpt. (b. Ala., c. 1950); Walter Orange, drm. (b. Fla., Dec. 9, 1946); William King Jr., horns (b. Ala., Jan. 29, 1949); Thomas McClary, gtr. (b. Fla., c. 1950).

The singing groups the Mighty Mystics and the Jays came together at the prestigious Tuskegee Inst. mostly for fun and to meet girls. They joined forces in 1967 and picked the name the Commodores out of a dictionary. They became local favorites, so much so that the school sent them to N.Y.C. to play a benefit concert at Town Hall. The publicist for the event was Benny Ashburn. When the band came back to N.Y. that summer, Ashburn set up some auditions for them and then became their manager. Using their business school acumen, they soon incorporated as Commodores Entertainment.

Ashburn booked the group on a cruise ship and around the south of France, mostly because he knew Ed Sullivan vacationed there. The band impressed Sullivan, but he was unable to use them on his family-oriented variety show. They also impressed Ahmet Ertegun, who signed them to Atlantic, but when their debut album failed to sell, they were dropped from the label.

A Motown executive caught their act and asked the group to audition as the opening act for one of their bands. The band turned out to be the Jackson 5. By passing the audition, they found themselves signed to Motown and off on the road for the next year and a half.

The Commodores finally released their Motown debut, *Machine Gun*, in 1974. The album only reached #138, though the title instrumental track climbed to #22. It was even more popular in Asia and Africa: Nigerian television and radio played the song after the national anthem when they signed off!

The band's second album, *Caught in the Act*, reached #26 on the charts, powered by the #19 pop hit (and R&B chart topper) "Slippery When Wet." The song's success led the Rolling Stones to invite them to open their 1975 concert tour. They also managed to release *Movin' On* later in the year, another chart success, propelled by the Lionel Richie ballad "Sweet Love."

Their next album, 1976's *Hot on the Tracks*, continued their winning streak with another Richie ballad, the R&B chart topping, #7 ballad "Just to Be Close to You." A year later, their fifth album, *Commodores*, rose to #3. It held two singles that represented the dual personality the group was developing. On the one hand, there was "Brick House," a slab of funk as sweaty as anything Detroit ever produced. Then there were the ballads, like "Easy," which hit #4 pop and topped the R&B charts. They followed that with another funky thang, "Too Hot to Trot," another R&B chart topper that only reached 24 pop. It was clear that their crossover success was based on Richie's gentler ballads.

After a live album, the band released *Natural High* in 1978, which sported another Richie ballad, the chart topping "Three Times a Lady." The hit helped the album go platinum. In addition to all the other pop and R&B accolades, the song earned Richie a Country Songwriter Award from ASCAP. The next year, *Midnight Magic*, the group's next original album (and, like the previous three, a #3 on the album chart), produced two more Richie ballads. "Sail On" hit #4, and before it could even slip out of the Top Ten, "Still" hit the charts. It reached #1.

In 1980 the band released the platinum *Heroes*. While the album only produced the #20 hit "Old-Fashion Love," the group still had momentum. Richie took advantage of this to further his burgeoning solo career. He wrote the song "Lady" for Kenny Rogers, and it topped the charts for six weeks. He duetted with Diana Ross on the title track to the movie *Endless Love*. The song topped the charts as well. The Commodore's momentum continued with 1981's platinum *In the Pocket*. Although the record only hit #13, it produced the upbeat #8 single "Lady (You Bring Me Up)" and the ballad "Oh No."

"Oh No" would prove to be Richie's last hit for the Commodores. He left the band to record his own album and embark on a hugely successful solo career. Around the same time, Ashburn died of a heart attack. Rudderless, the band released another greatest hits record while trying to map out a new direction. Their next original album, *Commodores 13*, proved to be extremely unlucky, topping out at #103 in 1983.

Desperate to make a change, the group took on their first new member since leaving Tuskegee: English vocalist J. D. Nicholas, who had had his share of hits with the band Heatwave. His first song with the band was Orange's tribute to recently deceased soul stars Marvin Gaye and Jackie Wilson. The tune, "Nightshift," hit #3, driving the album by the same name to #12, gold sales, and something the Commodores hadn't achieved, even with Richie: a Grammy award for Best R&B Performance, Duo or Group, with Vocal. However, this hit proved to be a flash in the pan. Although the group continues to perform, they have not achieved their earlier level of success.

DISC.: *Machine Gun* (1974); *Caught in the Act* (1975); *Movin' On* (1975); *Hot on the Tracks* (1976); *Commodores* (1977); *Live!* (Motown; 1977); *Zoom* (1977); *Natural High* (1978); *Midnight Magic* (1979); *Heroes* (1980); *In the Pocket* (1981); *Love Songs* (1981); *Commodores 13* (1983); *Machine Gun/Movin' On* (1983); *Nightshift* (1985); *There's a Song in My Heart* (1985); *United* (1986); *Hot on the Tracks/In the Pocket* (1987); *Rise Up* (1987); *Rock Solid* (1988); *Solitaire* (1988); *Natural High/Midnight Magic* (1991); *No Tricks* (1993); *3 Times a Lady* (1993); *Live* (Polygram; 1998).—HB

Como, Perry (actually, Pierino Ronald),

American singer with relaxed style; b. Canonsburg, Pa., May 18, 1912. Como was the most successful pop singer for the period 1945–60. He scored 52 Top Ten hits, 12 million-selling singles, and four gold albums, his biggest songs being "Till the End of Time," "If," and "Wanted." Heavily influenced by Bing Crosby, he sang in a casual, becalmed style suited to the light romantic ballads and novelty tunes he recorded. His comfortable manner also made him an ideal radio and television host, and he emceed musical variety shows from the early 1940s to the early 1960s.

Como was the son of Pietro and Lucia Como. His father was a mill worker, and he was put to work early to help feed his 12 brothers and sisters. At age 12 he was apprenticed to a barber, and at 14 he ran his own barbershop, turning to the work full-time after he graduated from high school in 1929. In spring 1933 he successfully auditioned for bandleader Freddie Carlone. After joining the band, he married Roselle Beline on July 31, 1933; they had one child and adopted two more.

Como joined the more prestigious orchestra of Ted Weems in 1935, making his recording debut with "You Can't Pull the Wool Over My Eyes" in spring 1936. Decca, Weems's label, hesitated to record Como because of his similarity to Bing Crosby, who also recorded for Decca. Based in Chicago, Weems and his band made many radio appearances, notably on the *Fibber McGee and Molly* comedy series in 1936–37 and on their own series, *Beat the Band*, in 1940–41. When Weems disbanded to join the merchant marines in December 1942, Como intended to return to his barbershop but was talked out of it by a booking agent who found him work as a solo performer in N.Y. nightclubs. This led to a radio series, *The Perry Como Show*, more prominent club bookings, such as an extended engagement at the Copacabana, and, on June 17, 1943, a recording contract with RCA Victor.

Como made his solo recording debut on June 20, 1943, with "Goodbye Sue" (music and lyrics by Jimmy

Rule, Lou Ricca, and Jules Loman), which reached the charts in October. His first Top Ten record was "Long Ago (and Far Away)" (music by Jerome Kern, lyrics by Ira Gershwin) in June 1944. He signed a contract with 20th Century–Fox and went to Hollywood, where he appeared in his first motion picture, *Something for the Boys*, in November 1944. Subsequently, he appeared in *Doll Face* (December, 1945) and *If I'm Lucky* (September 1946), but he then chose to end his contract. He made a final film cameo in the Richard Rodgers–Lorenz Hart movie biography *Words and Music* in December 1948.

Como's film career had fallen victim to his far more successful career on radio. On Dec. 11, 1944, he became the host of the 15-minute radio series *The Chesterfield Supper Club* on Mondays, Wednesdays, and Fridays each week, and remained with the show for nearly five years. The exposure buoyed his recording career, and he scored his first million-seller with a revival of the 1933 song "Temptation" (music by Nacio Herb Brown, lyrics by Arthur Freed) in June 1945. But his breakthrough hit was his second million-seller, "Till the End of Time" (music and lyrics by Buddy Kaye and Ted Mossman, adapted from "Polonaise in A-Flat Major," by Frederic Chopin), which went to #1 in September 1945. By the end of the year he released a third million-seller, the novelty tune "Dig You Later (A Hubba-Hubba- Hubba)" (music by Jimmy McHugh, lyrics by Harold Adamson), which he sang in *Doll Face*.

Como's fourth million-seller came with a revival of the 1931 song "Prisoner of Love" (music by Russ Columbo and Clarence Gaskill, lyrics by Leo Robin), which went to #1 in May 1946. He returned to #1 in August with "Surrender" (music and lyrics by Bennie Benjamin and George David Weiss). That September his first album, *Perry Como*, reached the Top Ten, followed two months later by a chart-topping seasonal album, *Merry Christmas Music*, which would return to the Top Ten in 1947, 1948, and 1949. His next #1 single was "Chi-Baba Chi-Baba (My Bambino Go to Sleep)" (music and lyrics by Mack David, Jerry Livingston, and Al Hoffman) in June 1947; the flip side, a revival of the 1898 song "When You Were Sweet Sixteen" (music and lyrics by James Thornton) was also a major hit, and the record sold a million copies.

Como's next 78, *A Sentimental Date with Perry Como*, hit #1 in February 1948. In March came his sixth million-seller, a revival of the 1902 song "Because" (music by Mrs. W. I. Rhodes under the pseudonym Guy d'Hardelot, lyrics by Edward Lockton under the pseudonym Edward Teschemaker).

Christmas Eve 1948, marked the initial television broadcast of *The Chesterfield Supper Club*, NBC's weekly half-hour program cohosted by Como and Peggy Lee. Keying off the program, Como's next album, *Supper Club Favorites*, became a Top Ten hit in March 1949. His next #1 single was "'A'—You're Adorable" (music and lyrics by Buddy Kaye, Fred Wise, and Sidney Lippman) in May, and he returned to the top of the charts in July with "Some Enchanted Evening" (music by Richard Rodgers, lyrics by Oscar Hammerstein II). With 15 chart records during the year, he was the top recording artist of 1949.

Como was back at #1 in June 1950 with "Hoop-Dee-Doo" (music by Milton De Lugg, lyrics by Frank Loesser). For the 1950–51 television season he moved to CBS for *The Perry Como Show*, which ran for 15 minutes three times a week. His revival of the 1934 song "If" (music by Tolchard Evans, lyrics by Robert Hargreaves and Stanley Damerell) hit #1 in March 1951. There were six more chart records that year, and another nine in 1952, but his next chart-topper and seventh million-seller did not come until January 1953 with the country-flavored "Don't Let the Stars Get In Your Eyes" (music and lyrics by Winston Moore under the pseudonym Slim Willet; Cactus Pryor; and Barbara Trammel).

Como returned to #1 with "No Other Love" (music by Richard Rodgers, lyrics by Oscar Hammerstein II) in Aug. and again ranked as the top recording artist of the year for 1953. He also returned to radio in 1953, with *The Perry Como Show*, which ran through 1955. He began 1954 with the religious album *I Believe*, which hit the Top Ten in February, followed by the million-selling single "Wanted" (music and lyrics by Jack Fulton and Lois Steele), which went to #1 in April. Taking advantage of the mambo craze, he scored his ninth million-seller in the fall with "Papa Loves Mambo" (music and lyrics by Al Hoffman, Dick Manning, and Bix Reichner).

Como won a 1954 Emmy Award as Best Male Singer on television. In September he moved back to NBC and launched a new version of *The Perry Como Show* as an hour-long Saturday evening musical variety series. The following month his album *So Smooth* reached the Top Ten. He won two 1955 Emmy Awards, for Best Male Singer and for Best MC or Program Host. In May 1956 he hit #1 with his tenth million-seller, "Hot Diggity (Dog Ziggity Boom)" (music and lyrics by Al Hoffman and Dick Manning, music adapted from "España, Rhapsody for Orchestra" by Alexis Charbrier).

Como's television show was among the ten most popular programs for the 1956–57 season, and he won his fourth Emmy, as Best Male Personality—Continuing Performance. He next topped the charts in April 1957 with his 11th million-seller, "Round and Round" (music and lyrics by Lou Stallman and Joe Shapiro) and returned to the Top Ten of the LP charts in September with *We Get Letters*, named after a popular segment of his TV show. In December a long-playing version of his *Merry Christmas Music* album reached the Top Ten, as it did again in 1958; in 1966 it was certified gold.

December 1957 also saw the release of the single "Catch a Falling Star" (music and lyrics by Paul Vance and Lee Pockriss), which hit #1 in March and became Como's twelfth million-seller, the first record actually certified as such by the Record Industry Association of America on March 14, 1958. (Its flip side, "Magic Moments" [music by Burt Bacharach, lyrics by Hal David], hit #1 in the U.K.) It also won him his only Grammy Award, for Best Vocal Performance, Male. Two days after that award was given out, he won his fifth Emmy Award, for Best Performance by an Actor (Continuing Character) in a Musical Variety Series for the 1958–59 season of *The Perry Como Show*.

For the 1959–60 television season the Como show was sponsored by Kraft, rechristened *The Kraft Music*

Hall, and moved to Wednesday nights. That fall, Como had a new Christmas album, *Seasons Greetings*, which was certified gold three years later and became a perennial seller.

Como ended his weekly appearances on television at the close of the 1962–63 season on June 12, 1963. For the next two years, however, he hosted occasional broadcasts of *The Kraft Music Hall* and after that did television specials, notably an annual Christmas show. Another seasonal LP, *The Perry Como Christmas Album*, released in Aug. 1968, was certified gold after 14 years.

In June 1970, Como performed live for the first time in more than 20 years with appearances in Las Vegas. Thereafter he toured regularly. He scored his first major hit in more than 12 years with "It's Impossible" (music by Armando Manzanero, English lyrics by Sid Wayne), which topped the easy-listening charts in December 1970 and reached the pop Top Ten in January 1971, earning a Grammy nomination for Best Pop Vocal Performance, Male. His last notable hit was "And I Love You So" (music and lyrics by Don McLean), which went to #1 on the easy-listening charts in May 1973 and earned another Grammy nomination, for Best Pop Vocal Performance, Male.

And I Love You So the album was released in May 1973; it was certified gold in the U.S. and topped the U.K. charts in January 1974. Como returned to #1 in Great Britain in November 1975 with the compilation album *40 Greatest Hits*. He continued to reach the charts until 1983, and he released his last new album on RCA, *Perry Como Today*, in 1987. He continued to perform concerts on occasion into the 1990s.

DISC.: *Supper Club Favorites* (1952); *Around the Christmas Tree* (1953); *A Sentimental Date with Perry Como* (1955); *Relaxing with Perry Como* (1955); *So Smooth* (1955); *Merry Christmas Music* (1957); *We Get Letters* (1957); *Dream Along with Me* (1957); *Saturday Night with Mr. C.* (1958); *When You Come to the End of the Day* (1958); *Como Swings* (1959); *Season's Greetings* (1959); *For the Young at Heart* (1961); *Sing to Me, Mr. C.* (1961); *By Request* (1962); *The Songs I Love* (1963); *Easy Listening* (1964); *Sentimental Date* (1964); *TV Favorites* (1964); *The Scene Changes* (1965); *Lightly Latin* (1966); *Perry Como in Italy* (1966); *The Christmas Album* (1968); *Seattle* (1969); *It's Impossible* (1970); *I Think of You* (1971); *And I Love You So* (1973); *Perry* (1974); *Just Out of Reach* (1975); *Perry Como* (1980); *I Wish It Could Be Christmas Forever* (1982); *Today* (1987).—**WR**

Compère, Loyset, French composer; b. Hainaut, c. 1445; d. St. Quentin, Aug. 16, 1518. He was a chorister in St. Quentin. He sang in the chapel of the Duke of Milan (1474–77), and then was a singer in the service of Charles VIII of France until at least 1498. After serving as dean of the church of St. Géry in Cambrai (1498–1500), he was provost of the collegiate church of St. Pierre in Douai until about 1504. From 1491 he also held a canonry at the collegiate church in St. Quentin. His extant works include Masses, mass sections, motetti, missales, a Magnificat, motets, motet-chansons, and frottolas. L. Finscher ed. his works in the Corpus Mensurabilis Musicae series (1958–72).

BIBL.: L. Finscher, *L. C. (c. 1450–1518): Life and Works* (Rome, 1964).—**NS/LK/DM**

Condon, Eddie (actually, **Albert Edwin**), early jazz banjo player, guitarist, singer, bandleader, club owner; b. Goodland, Ind., Nov. 16, 1905; d. N.Y., Aug. 4, 1973. He started on ukelele, then switched to banjo (and eventually guitar). He did local gigs with Bill Engleman's Band in Cedar Rapids (September 1921), later worked in Hollis Peavey's Jazz Bandits (1922). He played in Chicago and Syracuse with Bix Beiderbecke, then rejoined Peavey's Jazz Bandits. He returned to Chicago in 1924, gigged with the Austin High Gang, and did residencies and summer seasons with various groups. He co-led recording group with Red McKenzie in 1928. Condon moved to N.Y. in 1928, led his own recording group, and did freelance recording sessions with Louis Armstrong and Fats Waller. He fell in with several musicians with whom he maintained long associations, including Max Kaminsky, Jack Teagarden, Sid Catlett, Pee Wee Russell, and Bud Freeman. He toured with Red Nichols (1929), then worked in N.Y. and Fla. with Red McKenzie and the Mound City Blue Blowers (1930–31) and again in 1933. Condon played piano with George Carhart's Band on a cruise to South America and worked with Mike Reilly and Eddie Farley (1935), then with Red McKenzie in N.Y. Critically afflicted with pancreatitis in April 1936, he recoverd and then worked from summer of 1936 as co-leader of a band with Joe Marsala and played on liner cruise with Marsala (December 1936). He left early in 1937, worked regularly leading his own group at a N.Y. club, Nick's. In 1938 he helped to launch Milt Gabler's Commodore label with a series of small-band recordings. He was with Bobby Hackett from summer of 1938, Bud Freeman's Summa Cum Laude Band (1939–40) and regularly led his own recording band through the 1930s. Condon performed again with Bobby Hackett (1940), Joe Marsala (1941), and in 1942 organized the first televised jam session and began running his own jazz concerts at N.Y.'s Town Hall; some were broadcast to servicemen during World War II. Condon worked at Nick's with Brad Gowans (1943), with Joe Marsala Big Band, then with Miff Mole (1944). In December 1945 he opened his own club, Condon's, in N.Y., where he promoted integration of the bandstand — an idea to which he was fully committed. The club changed premises in February 1958 and finally closed in July 1967. From the 1950s, Condon only played occasionally at the club; he did brief tours and occasional residencies in Chicago, Calif., Canada, etc. He led a group for a tour of Britain (early 1957) and Japan, Australia, and New Zealand (spring 1964). Condon underwent serious operations in 1964 and 1965. Early in 1970 he worked with Roy Eldridge–Kai Winding group in N.Y., sharing guitar duties with Jim Hall. During the late 1960s and 1970s he appeared at many U.S. jazz festivals and led his own group in Raleigh, N.C., for part of 1970. He then toured with Barney Bigard, Wild Bill Davison, and Art Hodes (October 1971).

He was also the author of celebrated wisecracks. When French critic Hugues Panassie came to N.Y. to produce records, Condon quipped "Do I tell him how to jump on a grape?" On the subject of Bop, he said "We don't flatten our fifths, we drink 'em."

DISC.: "Jammin' at Commodore" (1938); "Dixieland All Stars" (1939); "Gershwin Program" (1941); *Night at Eddie Con-*

don's (1944); *Jam Sessions* (1944); *Town Hall Concerts, Vols. 1–9* (1945); *Eddie Condon Floor Show* (1949); *Dr. Jazz Series, Vol. 5* (1951); *Dr. Jazz Series, Vol. 1* (1952); *Jammin' at Condon's* (1954); *Condon Concert* (1956); *Dixieland Jam* (1957); *Chicago Jazz* (1961); *Midnight in Moscow* (1962); *In Japan* (1964); *Legend* (1965); *Jazz as It Should Be Played* (1968); *Eddie Condon Jam Session* (1970); *Spirit of Condon* (1971); *Jazz at the New School* (1972).

BIBL.: R. Gehman, ed., *E. C.'s Treasury of Jazz* (N.Y., 1956); H. O'Neal, *E. C. Scrapbook of Jazz* (N.Y., 1973); B. White, *The E. C. Town Hall Broadcasts 1944–45: A Discography* (Oakland, Calif., 1980); G. Lombardi, *Eddie Condon on Record, 1927* (Milan, 1987). **—JC/MM/LP**

Cone, Edward T(oner), American composer, pianist, teacher, and writer on music; b. Greensboro, N.C., May 4, 1917. He studied composition with Sessions at Princeton Univ. (B.A., 1939; M.F.A., 1942), and also took piano lessons with Jeffrey Stoll, Karl Ulrich Schnabel, and Eduard Steuermann. He joined the faculty of Princeton Univ. in 1946, being made an assoc. prof. in 1952 and a full prof. in 1960, retiring in 1985. He received a Guggenheim fellowship in 1947. In addition to composing and teaching, he gave piano recitals. He was also active as a writer, and ed. of the periodical *Perspectives of New Music* (1966–72).

WORKS: ORCH.: Sym. (1953); Elegy (1953); *Nocturne and Rondo* for Piano and Orch. (1955–57); Violin Concerto (1959); *Music* for Strings (1964); *Variations* (1967–68); *Cadenzas* for Violin, Oboe, and Strings (1979). **CHAMBER:** 2 string quartets (1939–49); 2 violin sonatas (1940, 1948); *Rhapsody* for Viola and Piano (1947); Piano Trio (1951); Piano Quintet (1960); *Funereal Stanzas* for Wind Quintet (1965); String Sextet (1966); *Capriccio* for String Quartet (1981); Piano Quartet (1983). **KEYBOARD: Piano:** *Fantasy* (1950); *Prelude, Passacaglia and Fugue* (1957); *Fantasy* for 2 Pianos (1965). **VOCAL:** *Scarabs* for Soprano and String Quartet (1948); Philomela for Soprano and Chamber Ensemble (1954–70); *Around the Year* for Madrigal Group and String Quartet (1956); songs.

WRITINGS: *Musical Form and Musical Performance* (N.Y., 1968); *The Composer's Voice* (Berkeley, 1974); co-ed. (with B. Boretz), *Perspectives on Schoenberg and Stravinsky* (Princeton, 1968), *Perspectives on American Composers* (N.Y., 1971), and *Perspectives on Notation and Performance* (N.Y., 1975); ed. *Roger Sessions on Music* (Princeton, 1979); P. Morgan, ed., *Music: AView from Delft: Selected Essays* (Chicago, 1989).**—NS/LK/DM**